A SHORT-TITLE CATALOGUE OF BOOKS PRINTED IN ENGLAND, SCOTLAND, & IRELAND

AND OF ENGLISH BOOKS PRINTED ABROAD

1475–1640

VOLUME 3

A PRINTERS' & PUBLISHERS' INDEX

OTHER INDEXES & APPENDICES

CUMULATIVE ADDENDA & CORRIGENDA

A SHORT-TITLE CATALOGUE OF BOOKS PRINTED IN ENGLAND, SCOTLAND, & IRELAND

AND OF ENGLISH BOOKS PRINTED ABROAD

1475—1640

FIRST COMPILED BY

A. W. POLLARD & G. R. REDGRAVE

VOLUME 3

A PRINTERS' & PUBLISHERS' INDEX

OTHER INDEXES & APPENDICES

CUMULATIVE ADDENDA & CORRIGENDA

BY

KATHARINE F. PANTZER

WITH A

CHRONOLOGICAL INDEX

BY

PHILIP R. RIDER

LONDON

THE BIBLIOGRAPHICAL SOCIETY

1991

Oxford University Press, Walton Street, Oxford OX2 6DP
Oxford New York Toronto
Delhi Bombay Calcutta Madras Karachi
Petaling Jaya Singapore Hong Kong Tokyo
Nairobi Dar es Salaam Cape Town
Melbourne Auckland
and associated companies in
Berlin Ibadan

British Library Cataloguing in Publication Data
Pollard, Alfred William, 1859–1944
A short-title catalogue of books printed in England, Scotland, & Ireland and of English books printed abroad 1475–1640.
Vol. 3, A printers' & publishers index, other indexes & appendices, cumulative agenda & corrigenda.
1. Books in English. Bibliographies
I. Title II. Redgrave, G. R. (Gilbert Richard)
III. Pantzer, Katharine F. (Katharine Ferriday), 1930–
IV. Rider, Philip R. V. Bibliographical society
011.221
ISBN 0-19-721791-5

Printed in Great Britain by
Courier International Ltd,
Tiptree, Essex

CONTENTS

Preface vii

Introduction viii

Reference Works xv

Symbols and Abbreviations xviii

Index 1: Printers and Publishers, A–Z 1
- Supplementary Lists 194
  - 1 'Authors'
  - 2 Patrons/Publishers
  - 3 Patentees
  - 4 Journeymen Printers
  - 5 Pseudonyms
- Appendices A–E: Lists of books relating to the English Stock
  - A Books of prayer, 1578 197
  - B Tottell's entries, 1583 198
  - C Titles yielded to the Company, 1584 198
  - D English Stock titles, 1620 200
  - E Books not present in Appendix D 202
- Appendix F: The Livery of the Company to 1644 202

Index 2: Places other than London 206
- A British Isles and Colonies 207
- B The Continent 215
- C Fictitious Places 225

Index 3: Selected London Indexes
- A Some genuine London printing 227
- B False London imprints 230
- C Some books imported to London 230
- D Signs 232
- E Addresses 241
  - Maps
    - Paul's Churchyard facing 243
    - London facing 247

Index 4: Anomalous Imprints 260

Cumulative Addenda and Corrigenda 261

Concordances: Bosanquet, Duff, Greg 319

———————

A Chronological Index 325

PREFACE

Ever since the inception of the revision of the *Short-Title Catalogue* it was the Bibliographical Society's intention to publish with it an index the scope of which would extend beyond that provided by Paul Morrison's *Index of Printers, Publishers and Booksellers* (1950), although that work had already proved its value as a supplement to the original edition. During the years that followed, which saw the process of revising the main text sadly interrupted by the death of its original editor, William A. Jackson, in 1964, and happily resumed under the editorship of Katharine F. Pantzer, the need for an index was never forgotten, and provision was made for it to be printed as a separate volume. Originally conceived as an imprint index, with concordances to the other main bibliographical compendia, its scope has now grown. When publication of the main text in two volumes was completed in 1986, Miss Pantzer was able to concentrate on the form and detail of the third volume.

The work now offered to members of the Bibliographical Society and other readers is a notable contribution to STC just as the revised main text, the work of many hands over many years, represented a significant advance both in quantity and quality over the first edition. The new volume provides valuable assistance to those consulting volumes 1 and 2. In addition to listing in alphabetical order all the members of the book trade and other individuals and groups appearing in STC imprints, Miss Pantzer has compiled several supplementary lists which amplify our knowledge of the nature and methods of printing and publishing. Furthermore, there is a series of appendices that cast revealing light on matters vital to the Stationers' Company. Her analyses of places of publication, especially the book-trade 'geography of London', will be a new and useful guide to the dissemination of books and other printed material in the period covered. The addenda and corrigenda bring the information given in volumes 1 and 2 right up to date. The concordances to Bosanquet, Duff, and Greg, and Dr. Philip Rider's chronological index complete the task.

How the project grew and developed in the process of compilation is described in the Introduction which follows. It remains for the Bibliographical Society only to record its profound gratitude to Dr. Rider for his work on the Chronological Index and to Miss Pantzer for her work, the merits of which will be disclosed in the new research it generates; it is a distinguished conclusion to the great task of revision to which she set her hand nearly thirty years ago.

INTRODUCTION

THE work of compiling an index volume to the revised *Short-Title Catalogue* began in 1984 and proceeded piece by piece as I felt my way toward the creation of indexes and the gathering of other information which I myself found useful and thought of potential value to others to have in easily available, compendious form. The main sections are treated individually below. The user of this volume should know, however, that more immediately relevant information is often given in headnotes to sections and subheadings, and he or she would do well always to consult them until they are known by heart.

PRINTERS' AND PUBLISHERS' INDEX

The first edition of STC had to wait twenty-four years—until 1950—for the *Index of Printers, Publishers and Booksellers* compiled by Paul G. Morrison and arranged by publisher, year, and STC number. Although Morrison's index was the model for the first index in the present volume, the new one includes several additional features. Following a publisher's name is a headnote giving the date-range of his total activity and usually a printers' dictionary or other work in which his name is listed. For a publisher on the continent this is normally all that appears unless he had a predecessor, successor, or close colleague (named in boldface) also included in the index.

For publishers in the British Isles and colonies I have included more. The date of their freedom in the Stationers' Company, if it differs from the earliest imprint or record of other activity, is given first in round brackets. Similarly, the date of death, if it follows a *known* retirement (e.g. Christopher Barker), is given last in round brackets. For most fifteenth and sixteenth century publishers nothing more is needed than a reference to Duff, *Century* or *Dict. 1* (for these and other reference works *see* pp. xv–xvii). For seventeenth century publishers—and earlier where relevant—a few sources are regularly cited: DFM (apprentices), *St. Giles* (parishioners, omitting a few; *see* the headnote to area I. on pp. 250–1), and two extracts from Stationers' Company records: *Loan Book* and *Poor Book*. Although I often consulted Arber, *Register B* (*Reg. B*), and *Court-Book C* (*C-B C*) in difficult (e.g. the Thomas Joneses and the William Lees) or obscure (e.g. Rice Jones) cases, I have made no attempt to integrate more than a little of the information in them into the headnotes in Index 1.

A number of times, however, the printers' dictionaries contained incomplete or confused or occasionally erroneous information and, in a few cases, inadvertently omitted a publisher entirely (e.g. Edward Wright). In order to correct palpable errors and omissions but without any intention of replacing the dictionaries—indeed, this index includes *only* individuals whose names appear or have been supplied in extant STC imprints or in an occasional entry in the Stationers' Register of a book surviving with another's imprint—I have provided more detailed information, largely drawn from the above sources and two others: William A. Jackson's interleaved and annotated copies of the printers' dictionaries (his *Century* includes transcriptions of additions which Duff made to his own copy now at Cambridge University Library) and much more precise information on publishers' places of business.

Although Jackson had always wished to include more details of addresses than appeared in the dictionaries and had recorded a number of them in his interleaved copies, the address information in the present index is based primarily on an examination of imprints found in the University Microfilms International series of STC items. The films were searched for one or more of a publisher's first and last imprints. If addresses in these differed, an attempt was made to discover when the move occurred. It was not possible nor, perhaps, even desirable, considering the time consumed in this process, to examine every imprint of every individual; consequently, scholars working exhaustively on a particular publisher may find that a move took place not during one year but in the course of that preceding. A different complication was added by publishers who rarely if ever used an address. I searched a fair number of imprints of such men, and if no address was found, the formula runs: 'No address noted.' instead of 'No address used.'

The addresses are given in modern spelling with care taken to note whether the term 'dwelling' (dw.) or 'shop' is used. The latter always means '*his* shop', and examples of 'her shop' and 'their shop' are so transcribed. These confirmed addresses (STC items in which they appear are given in round brackets following the date) were of great help in tentatively establishing the identity of publishers of the same name with overlapping dates and in properly allocating their imprints. For London publishers and those in Westminster after 1500 an address has a further annotation consisting of letter and number (e.g. C.1) referring to areas in Index 3E, London Addresses, where the publisher will be found listed along with his contemporaries in the same place. One minor caution concerns stationers at several signs in Paul's Churchyard: either imprints did not establish any specific location in the churchyard, or because of ambiguity, the position was liable to misinterpretation. Peter W. M. Blayney, in *The Bookshops in Paul's Cross Churchyard* (Occasional Papers of the Bibliographical Society, forthcoming), working from documentary evidence, has been able to place most of the signs exactly. Although the locations in the sections of London signs and addresses (Indexes 3D–E) have been rectified according to almost all Blayney's findings, Index 1 still gives the old locations in areas A and B. *See* the **WARNING** on pp. 232 and 243.

Groups, corporate bodies, and holders of royal patents or civic appointments are also to be found in the alphabetical sequence. For at least two of these (Cambridge University—Printers and Eliot's Court Press) the index attempts to rectify inconsistencies occurring in vols. 1 and 2. The headnotes for all these groups are especially worth consulting, and the major ones in addition to those just mentioned are Ballad Partners, several beginning King's Printer, Oxford University—Printers, Printer to the City of London, Stationers' Company, London, and Stationers's Society, Dublin.

As for the index portion itself, Morrison has been followed in supplying 'sold', 'f.', 'sumpt.', 'in aed.', and various other phrases appearing in imprints. I have devised a more rigorous method than his to reveal supplied imprints. When a name or a place (for the latter *see* Indexes 2–3) is supplied in STC in square brackets, the STC number in the index has been put in square brackets, with a query if necessary. Exceptions are a few publishers, like the Eliot's Court Press, whose imprints are always supplied, as indicated in their headnotes. Dates supplied are of four gradations: (d) date supplied, (d?) date queried, (c) circa date supplied, and (c?) circa date queried. Those who find the method cumbersome can go directly to the STC items in question, but those who are interested in overt imprints and hard dates will find some preliminary sifting done for them.

A further refinement is afforded by the tags (false), (forged), and (repeat); for definitions of these *see* the terms on p. xix, but (false) is the 'default' term, used when neither of the other terms has been deemed overriding. If the STC number preceding a tag is without brackets, the name or place being indexed is false, forged, or repeated; if the STC number is in square brackets, the name indexed is the genuine printer or place of printing of an item in which a false imprint appears. There are several forgeries of an imprint of John Wolfe, 1599, but a glance at the rest of the items indexed under his name shows that among surviving imprints he himself used false ones between 1584 and 1591. Publishers newly named or dates appearing *only* in the addenda are signified by (***A***3) if they are cited only in that section of the present volume, and by (***A***) if they appear in vol. 1 or 2 as well. Amendments to printers' shares in a book have not normally been signaled; consequently those interested in the product of a printer should consult the Addenda for all works credited to him and not just those marked ***A***. Publishers *deleted* in the Addenda from imprints erroneously supplied in vols. 1 and 2, do not have the rejected item indexed under their names.

Supplementary Lists

At the end of Index 1 are two small sections. The first contains a few supplementary lists derived from the index itself. The one for 'authors' includes editors, compilers, and translators as well as those who wrote texts of their own, provided that 'for the author' or 'for [the individual's name]' appears in the imprint. A few others have been included for whom prefatory statements to the same effect have been noted in STC. This is probably the most complete of these lists since it was planned almost from the beginning, yet even so, there are undoubted omissions; for example, I now recall John Dee, who must certainly have paid for the publication of the 100 (or 50) copies of STC 6459, though I must remind myself that information of this sort passes well beyond the recording of STC *imprints*, which is the main concern here.

The second supplementary list, of patrons/publishers, gathers those who paid for the publication of works not their own and had no known connection with the book trade. There may be a number of inadvertent omissions here because such statements as 'at the commandment of ...' when transcribed in the title portion of an STC entry, were not recorded on the imprint slips, and there may be other examples of such phraseology not noted in STC at all, perhaps most of all with publications of Caxton, whose way of acknowledging his patrons makes him difficult to deal with in modern imprint bibliography. The patentees are those who held royal letters patent, in some cases for classes of books and in others for a single book.

The germ for the list of journeymen printers can be found in the headnote for John Bill 1 and is allusively continued in that for the King's Printer. I may have overlooked a few of the journeymen whose names appear in imprints or, occasionally, in entries of rights in the Stationers' Registers of a book that survives with another's imprint, but the group even as it stands now should prove interesting. Of the pseudonyms, names designated '*pseud.*' in the index were easy to pick out. What may be missing here are genuine names that were falsely used or forged one or more times, though I have managed to retrieve a fair number. In spite of the fact that these lists are admittedly incomplete, I believe I have made a good beginning and hope that others will join in completing them and in drawing up other lists.

Appendices

Of the information in the appendices I am much more sure. The first five, A–E, have annotated lists of books relating to the English Stock, lists first written down, respectively, in 1578, 1583, 1584, and 1620, together with a few titles omitted from the 1620 list. To the compilers of these lists a familiar title (e.g. *Right godly rule*, A/6) or a simple reference (e.g. *Table to Hen. IV*, D/55) was sufficient to bring exactly to mind the book in question. Until now, however, the modern scholar at work on the Stationers' Company has had two problems: what *is* the book in question and where might he find it in STC if a copy survives. These problems are now solved.

My only regret is that the headnote in Appendix D dealing with the origins of the group of Latin school books (pp. 200–1) is so complex. The story itself is complicated and, indeed, murky. The information—as far as it goes—is, I believe, basically reliable; nevertheless, there may have been a renewal of Thomas Marsh's patent in 1584 or later. Even though working with the headnote for Latin school books will be painful, it has already been of some use to David McKitterick in helping to round out his analysis of relations between the Printers to the University, Cambridge, and the Stationers' Company in his forthcoming history of the press in Cambridge.

The last appendix, members of the Livery of the Company to 1644, gathers information somewhat scattered in Arber and, for the period 1606–44, not elsewhere available in print. Information in it has not normally been mentioned under the individuals in Index 1, but I have made a few exceptions for publishers with the same surname, for example the Lowneses and the Rothwells; in fact, it was puzzles such as they offered that suggested the usefulness of Appendix F.

A last word about Index 1: Morrison, indexing the work of others, said in his Introduction: 'In general, to index is not to revise.' I have felt free to ignore this precept and have included and indexed changes appearing only in the present addenda, when what appeared in vols. 1 and 2 turned out to be erroneous. Furthermore, I have sometimes felt it necessary to comment on the reliability of the dating or the assignment to some publishers of the items indexed under their names. Some examples that come readily to mind are Richard Bankes, both Coplands (but particularly William), Thomas Godfray, John Mychell, Heyndrik Peetersen van Middelburch, Thomas Raynald, and there are surely others who worked in that particularly mysterious period in English printing of the early sixteenth century. Here are printers ripe for further study, which can now be undertaken with an enlarged corpus of their publications to work upon, with the prospect of separating their true publications from those herein dubiously or incorrectly ascribed to them.

Index of Places other than London

Since the conventions used here are essentially the same as in Index 1, only two things need to be mentioned. First, the arrangement is primarily geographical, and within the two large groupings of the British Isles and colonies and of the Continent, the order is alphabetical by modern nations. The other point is that for the lists of publishers, the date or date-range cited is that of their STC imprints.

Selected London Indexes

These evolved toward the end of the project and were particularly challenging. For the first three, dealing with various types of imprints, the only index slips were those for which 'London' appeared or was supplied as the sole information available. Rectifying this situation required a rapid scanning of vols. 1 and 2. As their headnotes make clear, these indexes are almost certainly incomplete, and anyone who uses them should read and re-read the headnotes. I felt, however, that what they *attempted* to do was so interesting that it would be wrong not to share them with others.

The data for the two last indexes, of signs and addresses, had already been compiled in Index 1, and at first all I had to do was to collect them under the two headings. The signs proved the easier to deal with. Nevertheless, knowing that adjectives (particularly colours) were sometimes omitted from signs, I made my first sorting by the noun in the sign. The result revealed that 'White' and 'Black' were most subject to vagary but that the problem could be dealt with by cross-references, and the signs have been placed under adjective or noun, whichever seemed to be more commonly used for a sign at a particular location. For example, most often 'Bible' is without colour, but Michael Sparke's in Green Arbour was Blue, and Ralph Harford's in Paternoster Row was Gilt.

Deciding what to do with the addresses was more difficult. On pp. 323–35 of *Dict. 1* addresses are given alphabetically. I thought a geographical arrangement would be more revealing and made two specimens for publishers without Newgate (area D in Index 3E). This area ultimately proved to be the most difficult one outside Paul's Churchyard, which was, of course, put off till last. One specimen listed all the publishers without Newgate chronologically, with brief indications of more precise location. The other was organized first by location and then chronologically by publishers. The latter seemed to work better and was followed in the other areas.

The headnotes in Index 3E must really be consulted for full orientation, and only a few points need be mentioned here. First, working on a couple of difficult problems, I developed a theory that the less precise a location is, the closer it is to Paul's Churchyard, which was the center of the book trade in London. Indeed, the only sign without any location—the Black Boy or Morens in 1530—I have queried in the Churchyard at the little North door (A.1), where later uses of the sign place it. It may not belong there (if not, then perhaps at the West end (A.10), near the house of the Vicars Choral, though the sign appears in the colophon of a secular rather than religious music book, 22924), but I am quite convinced that it was somewhere in Paul's Churchyard. Lettou and de Machlinia's All Hallows' Church was one of eight in London in 1482, but I have queried the one at the corner of Bread and Watling streets (N.10) because it is the closest to the Churchyard. Unlocated signs in Fleet Street (W.2) may well have been near the eastern end, toward the Churchyard, but since the street was populated by bookshops throughout its length, I have refrained from inference here.

Next, concerning the two maps. The one of Paul's Churchyard is a version of that developed by Peter W. M. Blayney as fig. 1 in his *The Bookshops in Paul's Cross Churchyard* (Occasional Papers of the Bibliographical Society, forthcoming). He has generously provided it with Pardon Churchyard, parishes, wards, and numbered letters according to my locations. Although most of my work on the Churchyard preceded his, he rapidly overtook me. We exchanged information and urged one another on, sometimes sorrowfully.

The map of London was my concern. I thought originally of reproducing John Leake's survey after the Great Fire, engraved by Hollar in 1667, with the addition of a grid conforming as closely as possible to Ogilby's. I was brought to see that it would be better to have a map *based* on Leake's but voided of the buildings still standing after the fire so that names like Little Britain and Cow Lane could be added. In addition, Leake's lettered wards have been replaced by my lettered area locations. I am grateful to John Mitchell for carrying out my intentions so handsomely.

Anomalous Imprints

This section is very brief. It gathers imprints which make some kind of comment, whether jocular, ironic, or triumphant. I had thought we noted them all in the course of the STC revision until I came across several in imprints of John Bastwick which had not been transcribed in STC. It is possible that one or two more have escaped the list.

Cumulative Addenda and Corrigenda

Included here are the addenda and corrigenda already printed in vols. 1 and 2 as well as those that have come to my attention since. The system of 'bullets' preceding most of the numbers is explained in the headnote on p. 261. Let me say here only that I devised it for those who might wish to update their copies of vols. 1 and 2, in order to spare them the trouble of looking up numbers they had already dealt with.

Although some libraries have continued to report acquisitions to me, locations of copies have not been entered in the addenda unless only a single copy is recorded in vol. 1 or 2. Some day after STC is put online (though not by me), it may become possible to keep up with the movement of old copies and the emergence of new ones. I decided long ago, however, not to burden myself or the addenda with such a chore.

Abbreviations not available in the desktop system I used have been signified by an underlined letter; for example, a barred 'u' is given as u and the 'rum' sort as r; e can mean either a barred 'e' or the 'e' with a curl under it; a tilde substitutes for a bar over letters that allow it: ã, ñ, õ. Some abbreviations occur in imprints, which STC convention requires to be in italic, and some others cannot be meaningfully expanded. For examples of some of the problems *see* 11511.2, 14117, and 19048, all of which appear in the original addenda in vols. 1 and 2 as well as in vol. 3. I am not especially pleased with the solution, but it will at least alert the scholar to the fact that there is an accent or abbreviation of some kind in the original item.

Concordances

There are three of these: between Bosanquet's almanacks, Duff's incunabula, and Greg's drama and STC. In the course of making them I discovered that a very few citations were accidentally omitted from STC and have noted them in the addenda. Not repeated here is the concordance between STC numbers and the listings in Halkett and Laing, *A Dictionary of Anonymous and Pseudonymous Publications in the English Language, Third (revised and enlarged) Edition, 1475–1640*, ed. John Horden, Harlow, 1980, pp. 257–68. Scholars should be aware of that concordance and consult it for attributions of 'authorship' in the same broad sense used in Supplementary List 1 in the present volume.

Chronological Index

This was independently compiled by Philip R. Rider and uses conventions he developed for himself. To learn how to work with his index, the reader should go directly to Rider's introduction on pp. 327–9. It fell to me, however, to cull the addenda new to vol. 3 which concern dates and to incorporate them into his index. Any errors or omissions in this regard should be attributed to me.

Acknowledgements

My most sustained debt is to Janet Eagleson Critics, a former assistant of the STC revision, who returned to work part time in 1967 on the first two indexes in this volume. She selected about fifty items as specimens and explored whether the index could be compiled as a data base using a computer. The outcome was not encouraging, and we decided that she should create the index manually on four-slip pads of NCR paper. These she both wrote and sorted for most of the revision, the task being completed and the slips for vol. 1, following its publication, verified by John Lancaster, my former colleague at the Houghton Library and currently head of Special Collections at the Amherst College library. I owe them both enormous gratitude for their many hours of punctilious and dreary travail.

In 1984, when I started to think about the index in earnest, I knew that I wanted to proof all those STC numbers only once and learned that the best way to do so was to employ a personal computer in a word-processing mode. My instructor in these matters was Zack Deal, of Harvard's Office for Information Technology. We decided that I should use an IBM PC XT, entering the text and numbers with coding for final formating to be done on the main frame and using a draft-quality printer in my office for proofing the STC numbers. Its output *was* proofable though scarcely readable, but the first two indexes were constructed in this manner. With portions of Index 3—especially the signs and addresses—I turned to an uncoded, clear-text input because I did not know how I wanted them to look.

When in April 1989 I came to the addenda and applied to Dr. Deal for advice about coding for indentation, small caps, and superscripts, he appreciated my desire to switch eventually to a Macintosh and encouraged me to buy it then rather than after completion of vol. 3. I have never had cause to regret that decision. He helped me transfer files to my Macintosh SE/30 and suggested using the software Microsoft Word 3.02 together with a LaserWriter II NT. Next, I imitated the design of vols. 1 and 2 to the best of my ability. My original printouts were in the Times typeface that came with the LaserWriter. Late in 1989 I acquired the Monotype Imprint typeface, a version of that used in vols. 1 and 2. Final page make-up has been done with QuarkXPress 2.12. The result may now and then be unorthodox, for there were a few problems which reference to vols. 1 and 2 could not solve, but I trust the result will be found workable. Production of the volume from camera-ready copy has been arranged by the Oxford University Press. What the reader beholds is indeed the result of my own handiwork!

I have gone into this much detail, however, only to emphasize the changes the files have undergone since the original proofing. I have taken every care I could, but it seems to me unlikely that a few errors have not crept in. I can only apologize in advance and offer to correct them in a future collection of addenda and corrigenda.

Two others have contributed greatly to the indexes. Peter W. M. Blayney, in addition to his fine investigations of Paul's Churchyard, sent so many notices of amendment and addition in connection with his ongoing research into the London printing houses and their books, 1592–1610, that I finally had to signal 'no more!' When his work is completed and ultimately published, it will outmode the STC revision in printer attributions for the period in question. He also furnished me with the dates of freedom and masters' names of Drapers and Grocers engaged in the book trade. For her kind and generous sharing of information on John Bill 1, various Nortons, and the ballad-publishing Wrights, I am greatly obliged to Sheila Lambert. Finally, I owe a debt, undoubtedly greater than I know, to the President of the Bibliographical Society, Dr. R. C. Alston, and to other officers of the Society, past and present, for their help and advice at every stage.

Financial support for work on the present volume has continued from two stalwart sources: the Harvard College Library and the National Endowment for the Humanities. My debt, and that of all scholars of the English renaissance, needs repeated and renewed expression. To them, for their interest, patience, and moral support—as important to me as the financial aid—I return my thanks with this volume.

A final word for those who consult its various sections. I found most of the work on it deeply engrossing. Because I am so familiar with its contents, however, I know their limitations. For this reason I again urge: Remember to read the headnotes.

KATHARINE F. PANTZER
The Houghton Library

August 1990

REFERENCE WORKS

Listed below are primarily works cited in Index 1: Printers and Publishers, and in Index 3E: London Addresses. Although some of the most frequently used books duplicate reference works listed in vol. 1 of the STC revision, for others mentioned only rarely and for those cited in the Addenda, the reader should also consult the list in vol. 1.

Ames *Typographical Antiquities*, London, 1749; *see* also Herbert below.

Arber *A Transcript of the Registers of the Company of Stationers of London; 1554–1640*, ed. Edward Arber, 4 vols., London, 1875–77; vol. 5, Birmingham, 1894.

Benzing Josef Benzing, *Die Buchdrucker des 16. und 17. Jahrhunderts im Deutschen Sprachgebiet, 2. Auflage*, Wiesbaden, 1982.

Benzing, *Verleger* Josef Benzing, *Die Deutschen Verleger des 16. und 17. Jahrhunderts*, Frankfurt am Main, [1977]. (Also in *Archiv für Geschichte des Buchwesens* XVIII, Lieferung 5–6, 1977.)

Blagden Cyprian Blagden, *The Stationers' Company: a History, 1403–1959*, London, [1960].

Blayney, *Origins* Peter W. M. Blayney, *The Texts of 'King Lear' and their Origins*, vol. 1, Cambridge, [1982].

Blom J. M. Blom, *The Post-Tridentine English Primer*, Catholic Record Society, 1982.

BMC *Catalogue of Books printed in the XV*th *Century now in the British Museum*, ed. A. W. Pollard *et al.*, vols. 1–10, 12, London, 1908–85; vols. 1–8 also in lithographic reprint, 1963.

Borsa Gedeon Borsa, *Clavis Typographorum Librariorumque Italiae 1465–1600, Tomus I (secundum nomina)*, [Baden-Baden,] 1980.

Bremme Hans Joachim Bremme, *Buchdrucker und Buchhändler zur Zeit der Glaubenskämpfe ... 1565–1580*, Geneva, 1969.

Briels J. G. C. A. Briels, *Zuidnederlandse boekdrukkers en boekverkopers in de Republiek der Verenigde Nederlanden omstreeks 1570–1630*, Nieuwkoop, 1974

BS *Biographical Studies.*

Carlton *Bibliotheca Pepysiana: Part IV. Shorthand Books*, by William J. Carlton, London, 1940.

Carter, 'Laud' Harry Carter, 'Archbishop Laud and scandalous books from Holland,' *Studia Bibliographica in honorem Herman de la Fontaine Verwey*, Amsterdam, 1968: 43–55.

C-B C *Records of the Court of the Stationers' Company 1602 to 1640*, ed. William A. Jackson, London, 1957.

Chaix Paul Chaix, *Recherches sur l'imprimerie à Genève de 1550 à 1564*, Geneva, 1954.

Christianson C. Paul Christianson, *A Directory of London Stationers and Book Artisans 1300–1500*, New York, 1990.

Cook G. H. Cook, *Old S. Paul's Cathedral*, London, [1955].

DAB *Dictionary of American Biography.*

D&E Robert Dickson and John Philip Edmond, *Annals of Scottish Printing ... to the beginning of the Seventeenth Century*, Cambridge, 1890.

Denizations *Letters of Denization and Acts of Naturalization for Aliens in England, 1509–1603*, ed. W. Page, Huguenot Society Publications, VIII (1893).

Dict. 1 *A Dictionary of Printers and Booksellers in England, Scotland and Ireland 1557–1640*, ed. R. B. McKerrow, *et al.*, London, 1910.

Dict. 2 *A Dictionary of the Booksellers and Printers who were at work in England, Scotland and Ireland from 1641 to 1667*, ed. Henry R. Plomer, London, 1907.

Dict. 3 *A Dictionary of the Printers and Booksellers ... from 1668 to 1725*, ed. Henry R. Plomer, [London,] 1922.

DFM Donald F. McKenzie, *Stationers' Company Apprentices 1605–1640*, Charlottesville, 1961.

DFM II Donald F. McKenzie, *Stationers's Company Apprentices 1641–1700*, Oxford, 1974.

DNB *Dictionary of National Biography.*

Duff, *Century* E. Gordon Duff, *A Century of the English Book Trade ... to 1557*, London, 1905.

Duff, *Provincial* E. Gordon Duff, *The English Provincial Printers, Stationers and Bookbinders to 1557*, Cambridge, 1912.

EBST *Edinburgh Bibliographical Society Transactions.*

GJ *Gutenberg Jahrbuch.*

Globe Alexander Globe, *Peter Stent, London Printseller circa 1642–1665*, Vancouver, 1985.

Greg, *Companion* W. W. Greg, *A Companion to Arber*, Oxford, 1967.

Gruys J. A. Gruys and C. de Wolf, *Typographi & Bibliopolae Neerlandici usque ad annum MDCC Thesaurus*, Nieuwkoop, 1980.

Herbert William Herbert, *Typographical Antiquities ... Begun by the late Joseph Ames. Considerably augmented*, 3 vols., London, 1785.

Hind Arthur M. Hind, *Engraving in England in the sixteenth and seventeenth Centuries*, 3 vols., Cambridge, 1952–64; vol. 3 completed by Margery Corbett and Michael Norton.

Histoire du livre et de l'imprimerie en Belgique, 6 parts in 3 vols., Brussells, 1923–34.

HLB *Harvard Library Bulletin.*

Judge Cyril B. Judge, *Elizabethan Book-Pirates*, Cambridge, [Massachusetts,] 1934.

Leake John Leake, 'An exact surveigh ... of London, 1667', plates 20–1 in *A collection of early maps of London 1553–1667*, ed. John Fisher, Lympne Castle, Kent, 1981.

Lepreux Georges Lepreux, *Gallia Typographia ou Répertoire biographique et chronologique de tous les imprimeurs de France jusqu'à la revolution*, 4 vols. Paris, 1909–1913.

Loan Book W. Craig Ferguson, *The Loan Book of the Stationers' Company with a List of Transactions, 1592–1692*, London, 1989 (Occasional Papers of the Bibliographical Society, no. 4).

Lottin Auguste-Martin Lottin, *Catalogue chronologique des libraires et des libraires-imprimateurs de Paris depuis l'an 1470, jusqu'à présent*, Paris, 1789.

Madan Falconer Madan, *Oxford Books*, 3 vols., Oxford, 1895–1931.

Memorials C. Paul Christianson, *Memorials of the Book Trade in Medieval London*, Cambridge, 1987. (Information relevant to STC publishers is also given in *The Library* 11 (1989): 352–6.)

Morgan Paul Morgan, *Warwickshire Apprentices in the Stationers' Company of London, 1563–1700*, Leeds, 1978 (Dugdale Society Occasional Papers, no. 25).

Muller Jean Muller, *Dictionnaire abrégé des imprimeurs / éditeurs français du seizième siècle*, Baden-Baden, 1970.

NCBEL *The New Cambridge Bibliography of English Literature, vol. 1: 600–1660*, gen. ed. George Watson, Cambridge, 1974.

New Grove *The New Grove Dictionary of Music and Musicians*, ed. Stanley Sadie, 20 vols., [London, 1980].

OBS Proceedings *Oxford Bibliographical Society Proceedings*

Ogilby John Ogilby, *A large and accurate map of the city of London [1676]*, ed. Ralph Hyde, Lympne Castle, Kent, 1976.

Parisiens *Imprimeurs & Libraires Parisiens du XVIe siècle; ouvrage publié d'après les manuscrits de Philippe Renouard*, ed. Erwana Brin *et al.*, Paris, 1964–

PBSA *Papers of the Bibliographical Society of America*

Plomer, *Wills* Henry R. Plomer, *Abstracts from the Wills of English Printers and Stationers, from 1492 to 1630*, London, 1903.

Poor Book W. Craig Ferguson, 'The Stationers' Company Poor Book, 1608–1700', *The Library* 31 (1976): 37–51.

Reg. B *Records of the Court of the Stationers' Company 1576 to 1602—from Register B*, ed. W. W. Greg and E. Boswell, London, 1930.

*Répertoire 16e* *Répertoire bibliographique des livres imprimés en France au seizième siècle*, 30 livraisons, Baden-Baden, 1968–80

*Répertoire 17e* *Répertoire bibliographique des livres imprimés en France au XVIIe siècle*, 16 vols., Baden-Baden, 1978–89.

Renouard Philippe Renouard, *Répertoire des imprimeurs parisiens ... jusqu'à la fin de seizième siècle*, ed. J. Veyrin-Forrer and B. Moreau, Paris, 1965.

Returns *Returns of Aliens dwelling in London, Henry VIII to James I*, ed. R. E. G. Kirk and Ernest F. Kirk, 3 parts, Huguenot Society Publications, vol. X, 1900–08.

RH *Recusant History.*

Rhodes *Catalogue of Seventeenth Century Italian Books in the British Library*, ed. D. E. Rhodes, 3 vols., [London,] 1986 (especially vol. 3: Indexes).

Rostenberg Leona Rostenberg, *English Publishers in the Graphic Arts 1599–1700*, New York, 1963.

Rouzet — Anne Rouzet, *Dictionnaire des imprimeurs, libraires et éditeurs des XVe et XVIe siècles dans les limites gégraphique de la Belgique actuelle*, Nieuwkoop, 1975.

St. Giles — William E. Miller, 'Printers and Stationers in the Parish of St. Giles Cripplegate 1561–1640', *Studies in Bibliography* 19 (1966): 15–38.

SB — *Studies in Bibliography*.

Southern — A. C. Southern, *Elizabethan Recusant Prose 1559–1582*, London, [1950].

Stow — John Stow, *A survey of London, 1603*, ed. C. L. Kingsford, 2 vols., Oxford, 1908.

Taylor — E. G. R. Taylor, *The Mathematical Practitioners of Tudor & Stuart England*, Cambridge, 1954.

Thieme-Becker — *Allgemeines Lexicon der Bildenden Künstler von der Antike bis zur Gegenwart*, ed. Ulrich Thieme, Felix Becker, *et al.*, 37 vols., Leipzig, 1907–50.

TLS — *Times Literary Supplement*.

TBS — *Transactions of the Bibliographical Society*.

TCBS — *Transactions of the Cambridge Bibliographical Society*.

Vincent — Auguste Vincent, 'L'imprimerie à Louvain jusque 1800', *Le livre, l'estampe, l'édition en Brabant du XVe au XIXe siècle*, Gembloux, 1935.

Wing — Donald Wing, *Short-Title Catalogue of Books printed in England, ... and British America ... 1641–1700. Second edition*, 1972–88. (Citations of items found *only* in the revised ed. of vol. 1 are in the form: Wing, 2nd ed., B525; to the revised eds. of vols. 2 and 3, in the form: Wing^2 G 54.)

Wood, *Ath. Ox.* — Wood, Anthony a, *Athenæ Oxonienses*, ed. Philip Bliss, London, 1813–20.

Woodfield — Denis B. Woodfield, *Surreptitious Printing in England 1550–1640*, New York, 1973.

Worman — E. J. Worman, *Alien Members of the Book-Trade during the Tudor Period*, London, 1906.

SYMBOLS AND ABBREVIATIONS

The symbols and abbreviations below are primarily those used in Indexes 1–4. Three of the symbols (*, †, §) differ in meaning from those found in vols. 1 and 2 and in the Addenda, and for their significance in the latter section, the reader should consult vol. 1. For the symbols used in Philip Rider's Chronological Index, *see* his Introduction on pp. 327–9.

[ ]	surrounds a number: [541], for which the name or place being indexed is supplied in STC itself.
[?]	indicates the name or place supplied is queried.
‹ ›	surrounds words conjecturally restored in the title or imprint of books known only by a defective copy or copies.
—	repeats preceding information; used a) with STC numbers in series, e.g. Cambridge Act Verses (4474.1, —.2), Indulgences (14407c.1, —.2), and Newsbooks (18507.1, —.2) and b) with phrases in addresses, e.g. in Paul's Churchyard, — at the Rose, — at the great North door.
———	divides items issued during a publisher's lifetime from those imprints or assignments of copyrights occurring after his death
*	indicates various information; *see* the headnote of the publisher or place being indexed.
†, ?†	indicate year of death or conjectural year of death.
§	refers, in Indexes 3D and 3E, to Peter W. M. Blayney's forthcoming *The Bookshops in Paul's Cross Churchyard* (Occasional Papers of the Bibliographical Society).
•	indicates, in the Addenda, new information in the present volume.
◦	indicates, in the Addenda, information in the present volume outmoding that appearing in vol. 1 or 2.
$	means 'sign of' or 'sign of the', e.g. $ Rose.
A	indicates information found in the Addenda of vol. 1 or 2 as well as in the present volume.
***A*3**	indicates information found only in the Addenda in the present volume.
A.1, T.5, etc.	refer to places of business under such listings found in the London Addresses, Index 3E.
A/1, E/6, etc.	refer to items under such listings found in Appendices A–E of Index 1.

Although some of the most frequently used abbreviations duplicate those listed in vol. 1 of the STC revision, for others mentioned only rarely and for those found in the Addenda, the reader should also consult vol. 1.

1604/05	form of date indexed for two categories: a) Almanacks calculated for the latter year but printed before the end of the former year (mainly numbers between 385.3 and 532.11) or b) items printed before 25 Mar. of the latter year but dated the former year by old-style English reckoning (mainly official documents like statutes, proclamations, etc., and a few items proved to be of old-style reckoning)
a̲, r̲, etc.	underlining indicates an accented letter or abbreviation, e.g. 'am' and 'rum'; cf. some of the Indulgences in the Addenda (14407c.25G, etc.)
aed.	aedibus (house or shop)
ag	against
anom.	anomalous (imprint; *see* Index 4)
ap.	apud (at shop of)
ass'd	assigned (transferred copyrights)
ass'n(s)	assignee, assignees
ass't	assignment
b.	born
(c), (c?)	'circa' date or such date queried.
Ch	Church
Chyd	Churchyard
Co.	Company (i.e. Stationers')
Cx1, etc.	*See* Caxton headnote
(d), (d?)	supplied date or such date queried.
(d/error)	date printed is erroneous
(d/var)	date is a variant of an operative date (before death)
dr	door

dw.	dwelling
ent.	entered (in the Stationers' Register)
ex assig.	ex assignatione (by assignment)
exp.	expensis (at the expenses of)
ext.	extant (are for sale)
f.	for
(false)	imprint in book is false; *see* also (forged) and (repeat)
(forged)	imprint is a counterfeit of one in a previous edition, usually a genuine one; *see* also (false)
imp.	impensis (at the expense of)
n.d.	no date (imprint without date)
(note)	information is in a note to the STC entry
nr	near
off.	officina (printing house)
ov/ag	over against (opposite)
par	parish
per	printed by
Pr	printer
prælum	printing house
pro	printed for
prost.	prostant (are for sale)
(repeat)	original imprint repeated at a later date, usually for authenticity (e.g. statutes) or antiquarian interest (e.g. 22274e.3–.5); *see* also (false)
shop	*his* shop; the pronouns 'her' and 'their' are always transcribed
SR	Stationers' Register
Tr1, etc.	*See* Robert Wyer headnote
unident	unidentified (in London addresses)
unloc	unlocated (in London addresses)
sumt., sumpt.	sumptibus (at the expense of)
ven.	venales apud, venduntur, etc. (are sold by)
w/i	within
w/o	without

INDEX 1: PRINTERS AND PUBLISHERS

This is an alphabetical listing of all individuals and groups whose names appear in imprints or have been determined to have printed or published items in STC. In a few cases, e.g. Ballad Partners, King's (Queen's) Printer(s), Printers to the City of London, members of the group or holders of the title are cited, under whom all or most of the publications are indexed. In the address section of the headnotes of London printers and publishers, for example Francis Adams, references in the form (D.4), (T.6), (S.3) are to the areas so denoted in Index 3E: London Addresses.

A

A., C.
Publisher in London, 1596. May be a pseudonym for Anthony Copley, the author.
No address used.
1596: 5737.

Aberdeen 'Donatus', *Printer of. See* Printer of ...

Abrahamsz van der Marsce, Joris. *See* Marsce.

Adam, *anonymous. See* Anonymous, A.

Adam, Jean.
Bookseller, printer, and typefounder in Paris, 1516–1543. [Duff, *Century*; *Parisiens*.]
1516: 16197 per. **1521:** 16203 imp.

Adams, Elizabeth.
Bookseller in London, 1620–1625 (1638†). Widow of **Thomas Adams**. [*Dict. 1*.]
her shop in Paul's Churchyard (A.4), 1620 (3407)
at the Bell in Paul's Churchyard (A.4), 1620? [11824]
1620: 3407 f., [11824 sold] (d?), [11825 sold] (d?), 14982 f.
1625: 4510 ass'd, 13781 ass'd, 13794a.5 ass'd.

Adams, Francis (Frank).
Bookseller and bookbinder in London, (1568) 1577?–1594. One of the *assignees of* **R. Day**. [*Dict. 1*.]
dw. in the Green Arbour without Newgate (D.4), 1577? (26049.2)
dw. at the Black Raven in Thames Street, near London Bridge (T.6), 1578? (26049.3(*A*3))–1584 (26049.14)
dw. in Distaff Lane near Old Fish Street at the $ Aqua Vitae Still (S.3), 1594 (26049.16)
1577: [26049.2 f.] (d?). **1578:** 26049.3(*A*3) (d?). **1579:** 26049.4 (d?). **1580:** 26049.6 [f.]. **1581:** 26049.8–9.10 [f.]. **1583:** 26049.13 (*A*3) [f.]. **1584:** 26049.14 [f.]. **1594:** 26049.16.

Adams, John.
Bookbinder and bookseller in Oxford, 1604–1637. [*Dict. 1*.]
No address used.
1637: 21811 imp., 21812–2.7 pro.

Adams, Richard.
Stationer in London, 1559–1579. [*Dict. 1*.]
No address used.
1559: 3726 f. (d).

Adams, Thomas.
Bookseller in London, (1590) 1591–1620†. Husband of **Elizabeth Adams**. One of the *assignees of* **J. Battersby**. [*Dict. 1*.]
in Paul's Churchyard, 1593–1609, and until his death
dw. — against the great North door (A.2), 1593 (14801); also in 1602 (14803) and 1608 (14804), possibly as carry-overs from preceding eds.
dw. at the White Lion — (A.2), 1594 (20996.7)–1609 (5696)
dw. at the Blue Bell — (A.4), 1609 (5979); no later use noted
1591: 182 ent., 5633.3 ent., 12159 f., 14801(*A*3) ent., 20740 ent., 20996.7 ent., 21002a ent., 22418 ent.
1592: 20977 f.
1593: 12160 f., 12259 ent., 14801 f., 15015.3 imp.
1594: 20996.7 f.
1595: 7299 imp., 12161 f., 22418 ass'd (d?).
1596: 182 f., 12162 f., 14802 f.
1597: 13881 f., 13882 (forged).
1598: 13883 f., 14809 ent., 20740 f., 21161 ent.
1599: 12163 f.
1600: 19287.3 f. (c), [22419? f.] (d?).
1602: 12164 f., 14803 f., 14809 at charges.
1603: 7092.5 sold, 7096 f., [18292(*A*3)] sold, [18292.3(*A*3)] sold.
1604: 7097 ent., 11431 ent., 21161 f., 22420 f.
1605: 3996 f., 23337 f. (d).
1606: 1468 at charges, 3961 ent., 6268 f. (d), 20142 f., 20741 f., 20997 f.
1607: 20741 f.
1608: 5982 f., 12165 f., 14804 f.
1609: 5696 f., 5979 f., 14810 f., 18853 f., 20629 f., 20757 f., 24472 f.
1610: 2963 imp., 3066 f., 4509 ent., 7099 f., 7100 f., 20992 f.
1611: 48.5 imp., 50 imp., 50.5 ent., 4510 ent., 4913.5 ent., 11425 f., 11431 ent., 12166 f., 13792 imp., 14587(*A*3) ent., 14811 ent., 15052 ent., 16619 ent., 20029.5 ent., 20758 f., 22421 f., 25865 ent.
1612: 650 f., 4787 ex off., 20981 f., 21003 f.
1613: 45 ex off., 20994 f., 21162 f.
1614: 5762 ent., 13793 imp., 15237 f., 20742 f., 20756 f., 20986 f.
1615: 11938 f., 13779 f., 14805 f., 20987 f., 20987.5 f., 23338 imp.
1616: 54 ent., 7472 f., 13779 f. (d?), 13780 ent., 13895 f., 20988 f., 20991.7 f.
1617: 2917 f., 3418 f., 11431 f., 17872 sold, 21034a f., 25865 f.
1618: 15241 f., 22422 f.
1619: 13447.5 f., 14983 f., 14984 f., 14984.5 f.
1620: [11824 sold] (d?), [11825 sold] (d?), 13448.4 f., 13794 imp., 14811 f.

Adderton, William.
Bookseller in London, 1628–1671. His first book was published with and sold by **Robert Swaine 2**: at the Bull's Head in Paul's Churchyard (A.2). [*Dict. 2*; DFM 1110.]
shop in Bethlehem (Bethlem) without Bishopsgate (K.1), 1633 (21175)
their shops in Duck Lane (E.5), 1638 (20610, with T. Slater)–1639 (6044, 'his' shop); no shop sign used before 1641.
1629: 15593 f. **1633:** 21175 f., 21176 f. **1638:** 20610 f. **1639:** 6044 f., 21771 ent.

Aelst (Janssen), Andries Jansz van.
Printer at Zutphen, 1613–1630. [*Dict. 1*: 154–5; Gruys; Briels 333.]
1619: 11812 chez (d?). **1620:** 11812.5 chez (c?).

Aertssens, Henri.
Printer at Antwerp, 1613–1663†. [*Histoire du livre* IV.75–6.]
1630: 1431.30 ap.

Aggas, Edward.
Bookseller in London, (1573?) 1576–1625†. [*Dict. 1.*]
dw. at the Red Dragon in Paul's Churchyard (B), 1576 (18136)–1581 (13091.5)
shop at the West end of St. Paul's Church (A.10), 1588 (18144)–1594 (19448)
dw. near the West end of St. Paul's Church (A.10), 1595 (20106.5)
dw. in Long Lane at the Oaken Tree (E.9), 1603 (18252); sign varies: 'sub quercu viridis' (18251)
1576: 18136 f.
1577: 18137 f., 24172 f., 25346 f. (d).
1578: 11844 imp., 15230.5 f.
1580: 937 f. (d?), 10920–0.3 f.
1581: [3977 f.], 13091.5 f.
1585: 335 f., 5061 ent., [13108 f.], 13109 f. (d), 15137 f. (d), 17468 f. (d).
1586: 10512 f., 11373 f. (d?), 12508 f., 13111 f.
1587: 5160.5 ent., 12241 ent., 12293 f. (d), 12608 f. (d), 13100 ent., 15215 f., 18487 ent., [19078.6 f.], 23652 ent.
1588: 11093 ent., 11542.5 f., 13093 f. (d), 15215 f., 18103 f., 18144 f.
1589: 11261 ent., 13969 f., [26033.5 sold], [26034 sold], [26034.3 sold], [26034.7 sold].
1590: [11272 f.], 15701 ent., 19520 ent.
1591: 7365.5 f., 19498.5 [f.].
1592: 10268.2 f., 10919 f., 23869 f.
1594: 19448 f.
1595: 18041 ent., 20106.5 f.
1599: 26019a f.
1601: 26026 ent.
1603: 18251 pro, 18252 f.
1610: 14267 f.
1615: 18349 ent.

Albert, Philippe.
Printer in Geneva, 1609–1619 at least.
1619: 21805.9 (note).

Alberti, Giovanni.
Printer in Venice, 1585–1619. [Borsa.]
1606: 1431.19 ap.

Albyn (Albine), Samuel.
Stationer in London, (1610) 1611–1633 (*C-B C*: 424). [*Dict. 1*; DFM 2340.]
shop in Chancery Lane (W.10d), 1621 (3681, adds: near the Six Clerks' Office)–1630 (5666.5)
1611: 26014.3(*A*3) f. **1621:** 3681 f. **1630:** 5666.5 sold.

Alchorn, Thomas.
Bookseller in London, (1625) 1627–1642?†. [*Dict. 1*; DFM 1771; *Poor Book*, (& wife) 1639–42.]
shop at the Green Dragon in Paul's Churchyard (A.3), 1627 (20504)–1639 (12073)
1627: 20504 f.
1630: 6982 f., 11174 sold, 22849.1 sold.
1631: 4992 sold, 4993 sold, 14780 f., 22849.3 sold.
1632: 12083 f., 22834 f., 22845.3 sold, 22847 f.
1633: 23193.2 ven., 24539.7 sold.
1634: 6168.5 sold, 11052 f., 12080 f., 12084 f., 20161 f., 23403 f.
1635: 12075 f., 12076 f., 12078 f., 12081 f., 12086 f., 12088 f., 19110.5(*A*) sold, 19781 f., 23404 f.
1636: 5004 f. (d), 6168.7 f., 6757 sold, 12071 f., 12074 f., 12085 f., 17694.5 f., 23193.4 ven.
1637: 5410 f., 17218 sold, 21442 sold.
1638: 12072 f., 12087 f., 23193.6 ven., 23625 f., 24433 f., 25823 f.
1639: 721 f., 12071.5 f., 12073 f., 12079 f., 12082 f., 23193.8 ven.

Aldred, Robert.
Stationer in Southwark, 1620. [*Dict. 1*; DFM 596.]
dw. in Southwark near the Market Place, 1620 (20923)
1620: 20923 sold (d).

Alexandre, Jean.
Bookseller in Angers, 1484–1504. [Muller 3.]
1500: [15576.7(*A*3) f.] (c).

Alison (Allison), Robert.
Composer in London, fl. 1592–1606. [*New Grove.*]
his house in the Duke's place near Aldgate (L.2), 1599 (2497, in title)
1599: 2497 sold.

Allam, John.
Bookbinder and bookseller in Oxford, 1613?–1638. [*Dict. 1.*]
No address used.
1638: 91 f.

Allam, Thomas.
Bookseller in Oxford, 1636–1639. [*Dict. 1.*]
No address used.
1636: 4188 sold, 4679 imp. **1637:** 4680 f., 21812.5 ven., 21812.9 pro.
1638: 21813 pro. **1639:** 20364 imp., 20588.5 f.

Allde, Edward.
Printer in London, 1584–1627† (*C-B C*: 475). Son of **John** and **Margaret Allde**; husband of **Elizabeth**; stepfather? of **Richard Oulton**. Printed as the *assignee of* **Thomas Symcock** in 1620 and probably until 1623. [*Dict. 1*; *St. Giles*, 1588–96; *Library* 10 (1929): 121–62.]
in the Long Shop under (adjoining, etc.) St. Mildred's in the Poultry (O.1), 1584 (1245)–1588 (25089.5); 1607 (3490, colophon on $Q10^{v}$, possibly as landlord of the shop)
dw. in the Fore Street without Cripplegate at the Golden Cup (I.3), 1589 (17488.7)–1590 (21744, omits 'in ... Street', has 'Gilded' Cup) and probably until 1596
dw. in Aldersgate over against the pump (G.1), 1597 (3299, address from Haz. III.47)
dw. on Lambeth (Lombard, Lambert, etc.) Hill near Old Fish Street (S.7), 1604 (3489a)–1612 (18584)
(near) Christ Church (C.1), 1612? (21389)–1627 (23060); some variations:
dw. in Little St. Bartholomew's near — (E.8), 1614 (5741)
his house joining to —, 1616 (26060)
dw. in Pentecost Lane near Butchers' Hall at the east end of —, 1623 (8716.5, in advt.)
1584: 1245, 12798, 14522.7 (c).
1585: 19533, 20287.5 (c), 24062a.
1586: 1848.5 ent., 3313, 6563.5 (d), 13481, 20922.5 ent., 24920.5 ent.
1587: 11474, 15533, 21546, 24896.
1588: 5541, 7557 (d?), 12556.3, 12576, 13595.5 (d), 13694 (d), 13854, [17261.5?] (d?), 19433.7, 19521, 25089.5 (d).
1589: 542 ent., 543 ent., 5114 (d), [5530.5?] (d), 5841.5, [11485.5] (d), 14522.7 (c), 17488.7, 24286.
1590: [541] (d?), 5633.3 (d?), [7520.5] (d?), 13146, [16957.5 (*A*3)] (c), 17029, 21546.5, 21547, 21744, 21744a, [22714] (d?).
1591: [332] (d), [781], [5253], [5813], 5840 (d), 6818, [17143], 19172.3 (d), 19657, [19876], [19965] (d), [22663?], [22684?], [22706], [24652], 24897.
1592: [733], [1542(*A*3)] (d?), [3845(*A*3)], 10268.2, [10841a–42?] (d?), 10919, [12261] (d), 12296, 12563 ap., 15086 (d), [15353.7?], 18649, 19660, 22185, [22707], 22894 (d?).
1593: 13496, [23685a(*A*3)] (d?).
1594: 6160, 6243.4, 17423 (d?), [19448], 19531, 24898.
1595: [3125], 6546, [10922], 12562, 13465, 13658, 13674, [20106.5], 20288 (c), 22747.3 ass'd, [23401.5] (d), [25254] (d?).
1596: 2785 (note), 5803, [6392] (d), [6820] (d?), 7521, 11976, [12774(*A*3)] (d), [12783(*A*3)], 18007, 18650.
1597: 3299, 3487, 4115.5 (d), 5043.5 (d), 6395, [12906], [14678?], 15111, 17673 (d), [22322?].
1598: [3544] (d), 4307, 14959.5 ent., 16902, 18868, 20700.
1599: [1070], [3470], 11570.5, [11831], [12995], [18454], [18470], 18632, [20121.5], [20122], [20511?], [20861], [21301], [21309], 22895, 22895a, [24216].
1600: [772.3], [3796?] (c?), [5044], 6381, [6555.7?] (c), [6768.5] (c?), 10188.3, 14923, [16799], 17868, [19861], [20575], 20891 (d), [20922.5] (c), 24578.5 (d).
1601: 2759.5, [12294], 17547.
1602: 3022.7 (d?), [3714], 5446, 6520.7–[6521], 10597.5, [12197],

Allde, Edw. — *cont.*
[16754], [17876], [18454.5], [18471], [19839], [22425.5], 23679.
1603: [4303], [6518], 6558.5 ent., [6791], [8300?] (false), 11571, 13703 (d), 14354, [14422?], [18472], [18520], 19803.5, 19804, [20580], 20874.5 (d?), [23382.7], 24293.5 ent.
1603/04: [414.3?], 451.14, 466.7, 489, 501.4.
1604: 3489a, [3657], 3682, 6264, [6510], 6513, 7211, 7211.5, 7212, 7213, [11548.5] (false), [11936?], 21398, [25868].
1604/05: 451.15, 525.10.
1605: 3020.5 (c), 3489a, [3674], 7078, [10513], 11497, [11581], 11923.5, 14668 (d?), [15422], [17428], 18589, 18851, 18852, 20093, [21385.5], 21549, [21635], 25408, [25967].
1605/06: [434.18], [452.5], [501.6].
1606: 1598, 5194, 6396, 6522, 6552, [10665], 11576, [11924], 12302, 12568, 17350, 17428a, 18582, 20960, 20960.5, 22880.9, 22881, 22881.5, [23383], 23464.
1606/07: [452.7], [489.5], [501.7], [532.6].
1607: [1376.5?], 1429, 3218.5 (d?), [3218.7], 3490, 3707.4, [5933–3.3], 6537, 11548.7, 14531, [17334], 17350.5–51, [17890], 17892, [18021] (d), [18532], 20400, [21368], 21395, 22380, [22384], 23131, [24063–3a].
1607/08: [434.20], [532.7].
1608: 3647, [4181], 4865, [6416], [6481], [6482], 6646.7, 7690.7 ent., [10826], [12488.5], [13360], [13489], 13497, [18784], [18785], [21368.5] (d?), [21368.7], 21386, [22795–5.7] 23679.5, [24053], [24053.5], [24080].
1609: [2530.5(*A*3)], [6486], 6519, 6519.2, 6519.4, [6637.5], [12805] (d), [13018.3], [13361], 17805, [18105], [18108], [18265] (d), 21378, [21387], [22142], [23060.5], 23138, 24308, [25022], [25022.5], 25948, 25970.
1609/10: [420.3], [508].
1610: 1599.7, 3130, 3190, [3717.3] (d), 4307.5, 5208 (c?), 5208.5, 6016, 6393 (d), 10204.5, 10712.5, [11068] (d?), 13159, [15111.3], [15111.5], [15182] (d), 17617, [20401], [20755], 20768 per (d?), 21005, [21315.2], [21395.5], [23384], 24308a.
1610/11: [420.4], [483.9], [508.3], [531.1].
1611: 3707.7, 5120 (note), 6341 (d), [6890], 11374, [11564.5], [17702], 21388, [22330], [22992.7].
1611/12: [420.5], [483.10], [507.7], [517.14], [531.2].
1612: 3708, [4895.7] (d?), 7174 ?ent., [10358?], 13566, [16638], 16759, 16959.5, 17701, 17705, 18457, [18507.43(*A*3)], (d/error), 18584, [21027], 21389 (d?), 21550, [23385], 23760, 23760.5, 23791, [24083], 25915.
1613: 3292, 3709, 3908.2, [5193?], [5194.4], [13507], [13507.3], [17699.5] (d), [17700.5] (d), 18591, [21392] (d), [21392.3] (d?), [23763], [25602] (false), [25840], [26021].
1613/14: [420.7].
1614: 3491, 4539, 5740, 5741, [11796], 11830a, 17697.7, 18274, 19967, [20569] (d), 20756, [21381?].
1614/15: [435.4], [435.33], [527.4], [531.5].
1615: 563, [5610.5] (c), 10198.5, 10275.3, [14419.5], 16760, [16864a.1] (c), 16948, 17698, [18720], 21493.5, 21494, [21821.8], 23190, 23250, 23533, 23680, [23804] (false), 24091.5.
1616: 10275.7, [13567], [13567.5], [14418], [14420], 17335, [18585] (false, note), 18591a, 21494.5, 23061, 26060 [by and] f.
1617: 10945, 14523, 17335, 23060, 23062, 23680.3, [23748.5?], 24435.
1618: 7547, 10713, 12013, 12450, 19614, [23332], 23784.
1619: [3212.5?] (false), 7547, 12289.5, [12859?] (note), 17699 (d), 20746, [23063?] (d).
1620: 1329.5 (c), 1554.7 (c), 3300, 5948, [6773?], 6791.5 (c), 6792.3 (c), [6924] (c), 8615, [8646] (d), [8647] (d), [8648] (d), [10815], [10815.5], [11352] (false), [13541.5] (c), 14716 (c), 15112, 17620.5 (note), 17782.5, 19527 (c), 20747, 20923 (d), [21061], [21378.3] (c), 21451, 22133, 22137.5, [23063.3?] (d), 23387, 23680.5, 23757, [23788].
1620/21: [465.9], [489.23?], [522].
1621: [2024.7], 6266, [7447?], [8651] (d), [8652] (d), [8653] (d), [8654] (d), [8658], 10514, [11303] (false), [11303.5] (false), [11304] (false), [11353] (false), 11483, 13920, [16798] (false), [17125], [17672?] (false), 17895, [22083] (false), [22130], 22710, 23786, [23793] (d), 23795.7 (d), 23799, [23800], [23800.5], [24629].
1622: 794, 3492, 5765 (d), [6386?], [8685.5] (d), [8686.5] (d), 11360.5 (d?), 13573, [13598] (false), [14428], [17182?], [17831], [18507.36] (false), [—.37] (false), [—.42], [—.43(A3)?] (d), —.47, —.48, [—.55], [—.56], —.58, [—.65], —.67, —.71, —.76,

Allde, Edw. — *cont.*
[21829], [23063.5?] (d), 23680.7, 23728, [23742], [23742.5], [23762], 23812, 23812.3, [24915] (false).
1623: 794 (d?), 1409.5, 3906, 5025, [8716.5], [12357], 13541.7, 16913, [18507.97], [—.98], [—.99], [—.109], —.123, —.125, —.127, —.128, —.129, —.130, —.131, —.132, —.135, —.136, —.137, 20129, [23063.7?] (d), 23778, [23789–9.3], 23812.3, 23816, 24630, [24630.5], 24921.
1624: 735 ent., [1015], [5022.5?] (d), 5549.7 ent., [5636.8], 6272, 8721 (d), [10213.7], 10921 (d), 11040 ent., 11624, 12240 ent. 12268 ent., [12573.5] (d?), 13260, 16640 ent., 17260, 17632, 18507.138, —.139, —.140, —.142, —.143, [—.146?], —.147, —.147A, [—.151?], [—.155?], —.156, —.157, 18676, 19431 ent., 19499, 20334, [23064?] (d), 23787, [23787.5], 24900, 26061.
1624/25: [441], [457], [494.3], [515.8].
1625: [1433.5] (c), 3710.5, 4318, [5611.7] (c), 5677 (c), 10349, 11469, [13918.5] (c?), 18507.162, [—.166?], [—,170?], [—.176?], 18605, [18641.4?] (d?), [19254.5] (c), 21378.7 (c), [22918.5] (c), [23062.5?] (c), [23064.3?] (d), 23681, [23755] (forged), [23772] (d), 23772a (d).
1626: 1016, [1066], [4016.5] (d), [6272.5] (d), 7744, 10882, 12755, 14524.3, 18544, 18615, 20332, 21452, 21551.7, 22711, [23064.5?] (d).
1626/27: [429], [456.7], [464.10], [490.3], [515.10].
1627: [1052], [12456.5] (d), 14484.7, 16857.7, 16960, [21060.5(*A*3)] (d), 23060, [23060.3(*A*3)?] (d?), [23064.7?] (d), 23726, 23726a.

Allde, Elizabeth.
Printer in London, 1628–1636†. Widow of **Edward Allde**; mother (or stepmother) by a previous marriage of **Richard Oulton.** [*Dict. 1.*]
dw. near Christ Church (C.1), 1629 (20924)–1634 (5209).
1628: 5208.7, [5876.8] (c), [7746.4], [8881.7?] (d), [8897.5?] (d), 12974, [16864a.12] (c), [19272] (d), [21368.5] (d/error), 23059, [23064.9?] (d), [24973.5?].
1628/29: [490.5].
1629: 1184, 3301, 3711, 5911, 6117, 6313, 16640 ass'd, [9250], [20457], [20460], 20924, 21452.5, [21624], 24909.5.
1629/30: [448.15], [457.6], [460.5], [490.6], [495.5], [515.13].
1630: [1590.5] (c), 4279, [4500–0.5?], 4931, 6118.7, 6506, [6920.5?] (c), [10654?] (c), 12268, [12725?] (c?), 14708.1, 14708.5, [16758.3] (c), [17916.3], [20458], [20461], 22711.5, 23574, [23725], 23741.5 (c), 23761, [24974], 25821.
1630/31: [411], [448.16], [490.7], [495.6], [514], [515.14].
1631: 1920, 1921, 5850, 6589, [10264], 10276.3, 18631, 19194 (note), 19437, [20688], [21457] (d?), 22456.
1632: 900, 1920, 6061, 6571, 14625.5, 21379, 22711.7, 22808.
1632/33: [490.9], [495.8], [515.16], [522.13], [529.7].
1633: 735–5.3, 3493, 5850.5, 5941.5, 7444, 15458, 16915, 19432, 20464–4a, 22439.
1633/34: [529.8].
1634: 3302, 5209, 12240, 12334, 16915, [19254] (d), 21524, [23525.6?], [23525.7?].
1634/35: 490.11, [495.10], 496.2, 515.18, 522.15.
1635: [6317?] (c), 13736, 21380, 22109, 23017.5, [23525.8?].
1635/36: 442, 490.12, [495.11].
1636: 13505.3.

1637: 22808 ass'd.
1640: 21380 ass'd.

Allde, John.
Printer in London 1555–1584†. Husband of **Margaret Allde;** father of **Edward**. *See* also Appendix A/15. [Duff, *Century*.]
at the Long Shop next to (adjoining unto, etc.) St. Mildred's Church in the Poultry (O.1), 1561 (5950)–1582 (7689) and until his death
1560: [1752.7(*A*)] (d?), 13257 (d?).
1561: 5950 (d), 25258 (d?).
1562: 3725 (d), 7688.4, 11298, 11484 (d), 11485 (d), 11486 (d?), 13290 (d).
1563: 4829, 20189, 22139 (d).
1564: 16988.5 (d).
1565: 25017 (d?).
1565/66: 431.7.
1566: 1033, 14046.
1566/67: [401.3] (d).

Allde, J. — *cont.*
1567: 7688.6, 13912.
1568: 1990 ent., 6451 ent., 11473, 11473.5 (c?), 14522.7 ent., 21451 ent.
1569: 13302, 15033, 16853.
1570: 1244 (note), 14326 (d?), 14837a.5 (c), 15034 (d), 17410 (d?), 20287 (d?), 21351.5 (d?), 23688, 24933 (d?).
1571: 5772 (d), 15032 f., 15033.7 (d).
1572: 12107.
1573: [7582.5] (d?), 10993, 10993.4, 26075.
1574: 1209 (d), 7688.8.
1575: 4055.5 (d), 4803.4 (d?), 18577 (d?), 23239.5 (d?), [24886] (d?), [24887] (d?), 24888 (d?).
1576: [6140?], 18136, 18490.
1577: [1312.7], [11050?] (d), 18137, [18448] (d), 18656 (d?), 23188, 25710.5 (d).
1578: 3486.
1579: [10880(*A*3)] & sold (d), [11537.5] (d), 18276, 22185 ent., 24062.
1580: [937?] (d?), 4070 (d?), 5259, [10627?] (d?), [18281] sold (d), 19120.7 (d), 24557.5 (c).
1581: 13091.5, [14257.5?], 15031 (d), 16860 (d).
1582: 7689, [10608.5?] (d?), 19460 ent.
1584: 18259.7 (c), 24895.

1587: 7688.6 (d/error).

Allde, Margaret.
Bookseller in London, 1584?–1603. Widow of **John Allde;** mother of **Edward**. It is possible that management of the shop passed to **Henry Rocket** after 1601. [*Dict. 1.*]
at the Long Shop adjoining (under) St. Mildred's Church in the Poultry (O.1), (from 1584), 1590 (7690)–1603? (6791); variation: her shop under St. Mildred's, etc., 1601 (21224).
1590: 7690 f. **1601:** 21224 f. (d). **1602:** [10597.5(*A*3)?] sold. **1603:** 6791 f.

Allen, Benjamin.
Bookseller in London, 1631–1646†. He may well be the 'Bejamin Allam, Allan, or Alliam' who sought refuge in 1638 with **Willem Christiaens** in Leiden (Carter, 'Laud', p. 48). [*Dict. 2*; DFM 708.]
in Pope's Head Alley (O.11), 1631–1645 (Haz. I.147); variations:
— over against the Horseshoe, 1631 (22112.5)
dw. —, 1632 (22563)
at the Fleur-de-lis —, 1636 (3151)
1631: 6606.5 sold, 22112.5 sold. **1632:** 22563 sold. **1633:** 25216 sold. **1634:** 3174 sold, 17993 ven. **1636:** 3151 sold. **1637:** 5445.7 sold.

Allen, Elias.
Instrument maker and bookseller in London, fl. 1606–1654. [Taylor 198, where additional addresses are given.]
dw. without Temple Bar over against St. Clement's Church (X.2), 1623 (12521.3 sqq., in 2nd state of frontispiece)–1639 (18899b.5, has 'shop')
1632: 18899a f. **1639:** 18899b.5 f.

Allen, John.
Bookseller in Leicester, (1630?) 1639. [*Dict. 1*; DFM 1065?]
No address used.
1639: 11250.3 sold.

Allie, Pepper, *pseud.*
Printer? or place of printing? 1589. = J. Charlewood. It is not clear whether 'printed by Pepper Allie' means by a person or near to a place. Stow's *Survey* mentions a Pepper Alley in Southwark near St. Mary Overy's.
1589: 19457–7.7.

Allison. *See* Alison.

Allott, Mary.
Bookseller in London, 1635–1637. Widow of **Robert Allott.** [*Dict. 1.*]
at the Black Bear in Paul's Churchyard (B), 1636 (6033)
1635: 14739.5 ent.

Allott, Mary — *cont.*
1636: 1616.7(*A*) f., [5742.3(*A*3)?] ven., 6033 sold, [13282] sold, 19720 sold, [26113] sold.
1637: 1238 ass'd, 10427 ass'd, 11688 ass'd, 13737 ass'd, 21707 ass'd, 22274e.3 ass'd, 23684 ass'd, 26068 ass'd.

Allott, Robert.
Bookseller in London, 1625–1635†. Husband of **Mary Allott**; brother of **Thomas**. One of his apprentices, **Andrew Crooke 1**, stayed on at Allott's second shop and started publishing books there beginning in 1632. [*Dict. 1*; DFM 794.]
in Paul's Churchyard (B), 1626–1635
dw. at the Greyhound —, 1626 (1607)–1627 (1608)
shop at the Black Bear —, 1627 (1203)–1635 (14739.5); sometimes 'Black' is omitted, e.g. in 1629 (24965) and 1631 (14753.5, sub tp)
1626: 75 ent., 748 ent., 1241 ent., 1606.5 f., 1607 f., 1920 ent., 5395 f., 5537 ent., 5850 ent., 5910 f., 6589 ent., 6595 ent., 6746.5 sold, 6854.2 sold, 10679.3 sold, 12487 f., 12552 ent., 14625.5 ent., 16915 ent., 18969 f., 19803 f., 20791 f., 25911a f.
1627: 1203 f., 1607.5 f., 1608 f., 3926 imp., 5940.5 f., 12490 f., 15405 f., 18630.3 f., 20788 f., 21728 f., 24985 f.
1628: 1608.3 f., 3442 f., 4219 sold, 4221 ent., 5368.2 f., 5911 f., 7441 f., 11380.3 f., 15305.7 sold, 18916 f., 20615.5 ven., 23367 ent.
1629: 550 ven., 556.5 ap., 971 f., 1149 sold, 1608.7 f., 1608.9(*A*3) f., 1623.5 tros, 5911 f., 6198 f., 7442 f., 11689 f., 14441 f., 15405.5 f., 17642 f., 18630.7 f., 19718 sold, 20051 imp., 21846 f., 24965 f.
1630: 75 f., 290 f., 553 sumpt., 557 ap., 1609 f., 1609.2 f., 1624 tros, 4222 f., 4222.5 sold, 7443 f., 10719 f., 10722 f., 11688 f., 11690 f., 12612 f., 15406 f., 18917 f., 19788 f., 20687 f., 22966 sold, 23113 f., 24928 ent., 24928a f.
1631: 291 sold, 1609.4 f., 1609.6 f., 1920 f., 1921 f., 4911 sold, 5850 f., 6589 f., 13280 f., 14753.5 f., 18631 f., 20070 sold, 20688 f., 21178.7 f., 21848 ent.
1631/32: 24155–5a f., 24156 f.
1632: 554 sumpt., 608 sold, 1610 f., 1610.3 f., 1920 f., 3075 f., 12620 f., 14625.5 f., 17638 f., 17638.5 f., 18918 f., 19718.5 sold, 21706 sold, 21729 f., 22274–4a f., 22274e.3–e.5 (repeat), 22801 f., 22808 f., 25912 f., 26068 f.
1633: 291 f., 1237 f., 1610.5 f., 1611 f., 4223 f., 5850.5 f., 5941.5 f., 6646 f., 7444 f., 10704 imp., 10886 f., 12368 ent., 12369 f., 12369.5 f., 12888 f., 13281 f., 15407 f., 16915 sold, 18631.5 f., 19719 sold, 25912 f.
1634: 291 f., 291.5 f., 1238 f., 1241 f., 1612.5 f., 6443.5 f., 6595 f., 10720 f., 10723 f., 12370a f., 15407.3 f., 16915 sold, [19203] sold, 24794 imp., 25700a–a.7 sold, 25706 f., 25900 f.
1635: 1613 f., 1614 f., 3409 f., 4200.5 ven., 4998 f., 6033 ent., 12613 f., 13736 f., 14625.7 f., 14739.5 f., 14904 sold, 19719.7(*A*3) sold, 20689 f., 24984 f., 25900 f.

1636: [1618?] f., 14739.8 f. (d/var.).

Allott, Thomas.
Bookseller in Dublin and London, 1637–1643†. Brother of **Robert Allott**. [*Dict. 1*; DFM 562; *Library* 25 (1945): 140–61.]
Dublin, their shop near the Castle Bridge, 1637 (5465.3, with A. Crooke 1)
Dublin, at the Greyhound in Castle Street, 1637 (22800.5, with A. Crooke 1)
Dublin, near the Castle, 1638 (22454a, with E. Crooke)
London, at the Greyhound in Paul's Churchyard (B), 1639 (11064, with J. Crooke)
Dublin, at the Castle Gate, 1640 [22452?]
1637: 5465.3 f., 22800.5 sold. **1638:** 22454a sold. **1639:** 11064 f. **1640:** [22452?] sold.

Alsop, Bernard.
Printer in London, 1615–1652? In partnership with **Thomas Creede** in 1616 and possibly in early 1617 (4897); with **Thomas Fawcet** in 1625–1643. For these years of partnership, imprints supplied in square brackets in the STC entries can name one or both partners but should not be construed as definitive since the nature and extent of the partnership have not been studied. Alsop apparently printed as the *assignee of* **R. Hawkins** in 1618 (24136); and of **J. Man** and **G. Norton** in 1620 (11857sq.); with Fawcet as the *assignees of* **R. Barker** in 1625 (18760). [*Dict. 2*; DFM 505; *Loan Book*, 1633–36; *St. Giles*, 1636.]

Alsop, B. — *cont.*
dw. in Garter Place in Barbican (I.1), 1617 (13073)
his house next to St. Anne's Church near Aldersgate (G.2), 1618 (21405)–1620 (13932); variation: dw. by St. Anne's, etc., 1619 (12430)
dw. at the Dolphin in Distaff Lane near Old Fish Street (S.3), 1621 (21860)–1624 (18097)
dw. in Grub Street near the lower pump (I.6), 1625 (18760)–1640 (11167.5) and possibly later
1615: [13427.5] (false).
1616: 686, 4578, 5918, 6342, 12891, 13019, 13428, [14358 (*A*3)], 18522, 19159a, 19163, 22382, 23099, 24175.7, 24316.
1617: 687, 3664.5, 4897, 5536.5, [10641], 12247, 13073, 13074, 15329, 15381, 15538, 16682, 21087, 21603, 21603.3 (d?), 23094, 25159, 25180.
1618: 1803, 3637, 4319, 4320, 4328, 10945.3, 13039, 13931, 15329, 15538, 18011, 18413.3, 18413.5, 18413.7, 20328, 21405, 21773, 22527–7a, 24136.
1619: 1547, 3497, 5706, 11169a, 12430, 12572, 13823, 13823.5, 14358.5, 16689, 18170.
1620: 3407, 3580, 4281, 4316.5, 5700.5 (d?), 11857–7.3, 12011, 12756, 13050.5, 13932, 17278.1, 17804, 18226, 19080.5, 19824, 21603.7, [23583?], [24525(*A*3)], 24805a.
1621: [4208], 4329, 4692, 5710.3 (note), 5974, 6017, 6376, 10441.5, 11988, 12237, [12356], 13051, 14358.7(*A*3), 19174a, 20789, 20792, 21860, 23269, 23270, [25854].
1622: 1705, 1705.5, 1706, 4988, 5701.3, 5709, 7373, 7373.2, 12602, 12820, 12828, 12849, 16927, 17644, 17644a, 17713, [17728.7?] (false), [18461], [18462] (false), [18507.40], [—.44], —.51, —.54, —.60, —.66, [—.81?], —.82, —.91, 20166, [21828.5], 21857, 21861, 23538, 25306, 25309.7–10.
1623: 1001, 4803, 11062, [11062a], 11598, 12604, [15316.7(*A*3)], 15367, 17634, 19801, 19825, [20163.5], 21222, 23108.2, 25298.
1624: [3221], 5389, 6204, [7052], 11189, [13968?] (note), 14359, 17361, 17860, 18097, 18507.351 (d), [19934], [22614], 23657 (d).
1625: [904], 3722, [6045], [7743.5], 18507.351 (d/error), —.353, —.354, 18760, 19838.5, 20980, 20980.5, 21863.
1626: 7434.4, 11467, [13579–9.3], [13579.5], [13585.5], [14526] (false), 15370.5, [16753], [16845?], [18903], [19803], 21324, 23473, 24711.
1627: 1203, 1550, 5318, [5864], 14375, 18516, 20165, 20504 (note), 20946.9 (d), [20947], 23561, 23718, 24705, 26022.
1628: 1820 (note), [4157], [4157.5], [4471], 5370, [7749], [8893.3], [8893.5], 17862, 21496.3, 21708.5, 21709.
1629: [4136], [5911], [6017.7], [6019.5], [6983], [12997] (forged, d?), 13901, 17642, [18040] (false), 18200, [21718(*A*3)?] (false), [23507.5], 24965.
1630: 1021, 1688, 3372, 3733, [4500–0.5], [4581], [5714], 5805.5, 6492.5, 6980, 11174, 11346, [12687?], 14360, [18917], [19807.3] (d), [19966], 19968, [20164], [20164a], [20164a.5], 22444, [24258], [23725].
1631: 4, 194, 194.1, 383, 3565, 3565.5, 6529, 10189, 11202, [11288.5?], 13272, 13538.5, [16847.5], [17181.9(*A*3)] (d), 17645, 18329, 20168, [20865], 22387, [23340], 23682.
1632: 3538, 3538.5, 3663, 11346.3, 11346.5 (d/error), 11977, 13268, 13334, 13538.5, 14360.5, [17202] (d?), 18507.262, 20221.7, 21420, 21550.5, [23340], [23520], 23682.5.
1633: 5906, 6104, 7032, 7032a, 10687, 11167, 12537, 13505, 14269, [20684], 22436, 22462, 24712, [25375a.10] (d).
1634: 10276.7, 11170, 17333, 17670, [21164], 21604, 23447, [23682.7] (d?).
1635: 4998, [5714.8], [6273.3], 10199, 11221, 12417, 12418, 12584, [13372.5], [13736], 19825.5(*A*3) (c), 21604.
1636: [3536], [6453.5], 10199.5, 11175, 11346.5 (d), [12937], 15382, [17284], [20780], [21640], [22181], 22391.6.
1637: 3997.5–98, [4297] (d), [5490], [18691], [19131], 19160, [22232], 22391.3, [22391.5] (d?), 23119, 23119.5.
1638: 6042, 10187, 10200, 10666, 14069, 20384, 21551, 22391.4, 23444.
1639: 3712, 4986, 10201, 18098, [18507.297?], [—.304?], 19164, 21643.5, [22132].
1639/40: [18507.317?].
1640: 1554.5, 3712.3(*A*), 5716.5, 5874, 6043, 7334, [7750], 10188 (d), 11167.5, 11657.5, [12735], 12885, 14066, 14754 (note), 17328, [18507.325?], [—.328?], [—.329?], [—.332?], [—.335?], 20383, 21551, [22641], [22641.5], [23809.5].
1640/41: [10009], 25247.5 (note).

Alsop, Nicholas.
Bookseller in London, 1632–1640. Son of William, of Perwich, Derby; apprenticed to T. Pavier 10 Oct. 1624 and freed 28 Sept. 1631. [Omitted from *Dict. 2*; DFM 2122.]
at the Angel in Pope's Head Alley (O.11), 1632 (6099)–1640 (20552); variation: Pope's Head 'Palace', 1632 [13314(*A*3)]
1632: 6099 sold, 7235 f., [13314(*A*3)] sold, 24809 sold.
1634: 1540 f.
1636: 7236 sold, 7237 sold (engr. tp/repeat).
1637: 20537 f.
1639: 20543 ent., 20551.
1640: [4338(*A*3)] sold, [7239] sold, [13170?] sold, 20552 f.

Amazeur, Jean.
Printer in Paris, 1534–1556. [Duff, *Century*; *Parisiens.*]
1555: 16217. **1556:** 15844.

Anchoran, John.
Foreigner? schoolmaster? licentiate in divinity, and editor, fl. 1631.
No address used.
1631: 15078a sumpt./f.

Anderson, George.
Printer in Edinburgh and in Glasgow, 1636?–1647†. [*Dict. 2.*]
Edinburgh, in King James's College, 1637 (136)–1638 (72)
Glasgow [no address], 1638 (22047)–1640 (3446a)
Glasgow, in Hutchesons' Hospital in the Trongate, 1647 (Wing D 1398); since the first part of the Hospital did not open until late 1643 and final payment for its construction was made in 1650 (William H. Hill, *History of Hutchesons' Hospital*, Glasgow, 1881), Anderson probably did not move there until 1647.
1636: [20469] (d?).
1637: 136, 139.
1638: [69] (false), 72, 135, 6031.5, 7259.4, 12578, 20657, 21440.5, [21903], [21903.3], [21903.5], [21904], [21904.3], 22025.7(*A*3) (d), [22026] (d), [22026.2] (d), 22027, [22030], [22030.3], [22036?] (d), [22036.5?] (d), [22037], [22038], 22047, 22047.5, [22054], [22054.5] (d).
1639: 3446, 21441.3.
1640: [1205], 3446a.

Andrewe, Lawrence.
Printer and bookseller in London, 1527–1529. His types passed to **John Mychell**. [Duff, *Century.*]
at the Golden Cross in Fleet Street (W.2), 1527 (13435)
1427: 13436 (d/error). **1527:** 3274.5 (d), 13435, 24764 (d?). **1528:** 6445 (d?), 13436 (d?) **1529:** [13177.5 f.] (d), [13437?] (d?).

Andrewes, John.
Preacher, author, and bookseller in London, fl. 1602–1645. [*DNB.*]
No address used.
1614: 594 (note). **1621:** 592 (note). **1630:** 590.3 f.

Andrewes, Thomas.
Bookseller and bookbinder? in London, (1621) 1624? 1637–1639. The second address below is also associated with **Richard Badger**, who printed the item in question and to whom the shop possibly belonged. [*Dict. 1*: 8, 9 (two men); DFM 1334.]
in Smithfield (E.8), 1637 (13171)–1638 (22632, adds 'shop near the Hospital Gate')
?sold at the Little Shop in St. Dunstan's Churchyard turning up to Clifford's Inn (W.9), 1639 (13172)
1637: 13171 sold. **1638:** 22632 f. **1639:** 13172 f.

Angelin, Pierre.
Publisher in London, 1552, 1566. Perhaps the man who became a denizen on 20 Feb. 1562, from the dominion of the Duke of Savoy (*Denizations*: 6). [*Carl H. Pforzheimer Library*, New York, 1940, I.232–3.]
No address used.
1552: 6003.5 [f.], 16572.3(*A*3, note). **1566:** 199 à inst.

Angier, Michel.
Bookseller in Caen, 1508–1541. [Muller 10; *Répertoire 16e*, 22: 47–80.]
519: 16128.2.

Anoke, John, *pseud.*
Printer, no place specified, 1589. = T. Orwin.
1589: 17463–3.7 (d).

Anonymous, Adam, *pseud.*
Printer in 'Augsburg', 1545. = S. Mierdman, Antwerp. The pseudonym was used earlier by J. van Hoochstraten but only in books in Dutch.
1545: 10488.

Antoine-Velpius, Hubert 1, *widow of.*
Printer in Brussels, 1630–1635. [*Dict. 1*; *Histoire du livre* IV.36.]
1632: 19794. **1633:** 17663.

Antoine-Velpius, Hubert 2.
Printer in Brussels, 1633–1670 at least. [*Histoire du livre* IV.36.]
1637–38: 7072.4. **1639:** 23230.5.

Antonielli, Antoniello degli *heirs of, pseud.*
Printers in 'Palermo', 1584, 1587. = J. Wolfe (Woodfield nos. 34–7).
1584: 17159, 17159.5, 17167. **1587:** 17163 (d).

Antonius, Wilhelm.
Printer in Hanau, 1593–1611†. [Benzing 186.]
1594: [18100]. **1605:** [11741]. **1607:** 12685.3 (note).

Antony. *See* Antoine-Velpius.

Applow (Applay, Apple), Richard.
Stationer in London, 1557–1566? [Duff, *Century*.]
dw. in Paternoster Row hard by the Castle Tavern (C.7), 1563 (3076)
1563: 3076 f. (d).

Arbuthnet, Alexander.
Printer in Edinburgh, 1576–1585†. **King's Printer in Scotland** from 1579. [*Dict. 1.*]
dw. at the Kirk of the Field, 1579 (2125)
1579: 2125, [17328.7] (d?). **1580:** [321.5] (c). **1582:** 3991, 25239 ap.
1584: 21887 (d).

Archer, Thomas.
Bookseller in London, 1603–1631 (1633†). For corantos he may have published in 1621–1622 *see* **Broer Jansz**. [*Dict. 1*; *Poor Book*, 1630–33, widow thereafter.]
at the Little Shop by the [Royal] Exchange (O.10), 1603 (18472)
shop in Pope's Head Palace near the Royal Exchange (O.11), 1607 (6537)–1622 (23538), 1628 (23539, possibly a carry-over from previous eds.; variations: omits 'near ... Exchange', 1612 (13121.5); at least once 'Alley' is substituted for 'Palace', 1607 (18455)
in Pope's Head Palace over against the $ Horseshoe (O.11), 1622 (21828.5)–1625 (18507.353); variation: adds 'hard by the Royal Exchange', 1622 (21829)
1603: 18445.5 f., 18472 f., 18472a f., 24079 f.
1604: 12199 f.
1607: 1376.5 f., 6537 f., 18455 f., 21368 f.
1608: 3719 ent., 21368.5 f. (d?), 24080 f., 24315.5 sold.
1609: 773 f., 6519 f., 6519.2 f., 6519.4 f., 21386 ent., 24081 f., 24313 sold, 25948 f.
1610: 1794 f., 21395.5 f.
1611: 5920 f., 17908 f., 24082 f.
1611/12: 22182a.5.
1612: 5895 f., 6538 f., 13121.5 f., 18457 f., 22183 f., 24083 f., 25178 f.
1613: 385 f., 5921–1.2 f., 10511.7 f., 12600 f., 14676 f., 17476 f., 17476.5 f.
1614: 5896 f., 15710 sold, 17229 f.
1615: 5921.5 f., 21369.5 f. (c), 23533 f., 23534 f.
1616: 5922.2 f., 15711 f., 17477 f., 17878 f., 23535 f., 24084 f.
1617: 23058 f., 23536 f.
1618: 5923 ass'd.
1619: 20367(*A*3) ass'd, 22851 sold, 23537 f.
1620: 24085 f.
1621: [11353 f.?] (false), [18507.18–.25 f.?] (headnote: false?).
1622: 1898 f., 5766 f., 13573 f., 13575 f., [18507.45 f.?] (d), —.46 f.,

Archer, T. — *cont.*
—.47 f., —.48 f., —.51 f., —.52 f., —.55 f., —.56 f., —.57 f., —.58 f., —.59 f., —.61 f., —.62 f., —.64 f., —.65 f., —.66 f., —.67 f., —.69 f., —.70 f., —.71 f., —.73 f., —.74 f., —.76 f., —.80 f., —.85 f., —.87 f., —.90 f., 20864 f., 21828.5 f., 21829 f., 23538 f.
1623: 18507.96 f., —.98 f., —.100 f., —.102 f., —.104 f., —.105 f., —.107 f., —.109 f., —.113 f., —.114 f., —.116 f., —.117 f., —.124 f., —.129 f., —.130 f., 22992.9 f. (d).
1624: 3597.5 f. (d?), 4606.5 f. (d?), 10011.6 f. (d), 18507.142 f., —.346–7 f. (d), —.348 f., —.349 f., [—.350 f.] (d), —.351 f. (d), —.352 f.
1625: 17308 f., —.351 (d/error), —.353 f., —.354 f., 19838.5 sold, 20980 f., 20980.5 f., 23930 f.
1627: 24295 f.
1628: 18507.355 f., —.356 f., —.357 f., —.358 f., 21368.5 f. (d/error), 23539 f.
1631: 25179 ass'd.

Arnold, John.
Bookseller in London, 1568–1581. *See* also Appendix A/22. [*Dict. 1.*]
at the North door of St. Paul's Church (A.2), 1570 (1244 (note), 19974.2)
1569: 7679 ent. **1570:** 1244 (note, sold), 19974.2 f. (d).

Arundell (Arondell, Erondell), William.
Bookseller in London, (1613) 1614–1617. [*Dict. 1*; DFM 39.]
at the Angel in Paul's Churchyard (A.3), 1614 (132)–1617 (5621)
1614: 132 f., 7355 ent., 11830a f., 25157 ent.
1615: 133 f., 10840 f.
1616: 15141 f.
1617: 5621 f., 16835.5 f., 19779 f., 19812.5 ent., 25159 f.

Ascanius, *Master*. *See* Renialme, A. de.

Ascensius. *See* Badius.

Ash, Henry. *See* Esch.

Askell, Leonard.
Printer in London, (1556) 1562–1563. [*Dict. 1.*]
No address used.
1562: 6177. **1563:** 18879(*A*3) (d).

Aspley, William.
Bookseller in London, (1597) 1599–1640. [*Dict. 1.*]
in Paul's Churchyard, 1599–1640
dw. — at the Tiger's Head (A.2), 1599 (4556)–1600 (6517)
shop — [no sign (B)], 1604 (17479)
dw. — at the Parrot (A.3), 1608 (20085)–1640 (5055, omits 'dw.'); variation: has 'shop', 1619 (13447)
1599: 4555.5 f., 4556 f., 10799 f., 14478 f. (d?), 19833.5 f., 25089 f.
1600: 6517 f., 22288 f., 22288a f., 22304 f., 24207 ent.
1601: 19343 ent., 24207.3(*A*3) ass'd by.
1602: 6336 f.
1603: 1117 sold, 7448 sold, 7459 sold, 10800 f., 14365 f., 14365.5 f., 17510 sold.
1604: 94 f., 5650 sold, 6457 ent., 12062 f., 12062.3 f., 14429.5 f., 14430 f., 14430.5 f., 17479 f. (d), 17480 f. (d), 17481 f. (d).
1605: 1113(*A*) ent., 4970 f., 4971 f., 4972 f., 4973 f., 18626a.5 ent., 20085 ent.
1606: 3959 f., 4103 f. (d), 4103.3 f., 12407.5 f. (d?), 19886 ent.
1607: 4966 f.
1608: 38 f., 38.5 f., 4967 f., 5051 f. (d?), 12408 f. (d?), 12894 f., 20085 f.
1609: 3051 f., 3455 sold, 12894a f., 18626a.5 f., 22353 sold.
1610: 3456 sold, 3456.4 sold, 3456.7 sold, 3458 f., 3459 f., 3459.3 f., 4509 ent.
1611: 3458.3 f., 3460 f., 3460.2 f., 10806 f., 11580 ent., 13455.7 f., 13456 f., 13456.5 f., 22393 f.
1612: 3460.5 f., 3052 f., 4741 f., 10807 f.
1613: 206 f., 3460.6 f., 3462 f., 3464 f., 17854 f. (d), 17854a f.
1614: 3462.7 f., 19777 imp., 25661 f.
1615: 3458.5 f., 3459.7 f., 3460.7 f., 3462.3 f., 3463 f., 3463.3 f., 3465 f., 3465.4 f., 5052 f. (d?), 10802 f.
1616: 3460.3 f., 3460.8 f., 3463.7 f., 3465.7 f., 3466a f., 10804 f., 18626a.6 f.
1617: 3467 f., 25652 f., 25664 f.
1618: 4103.5 f., 12410 f. (d?).

Aspley, W. — *cont.*
1619: 13447 f.
1620: 5053 f. (d?), 13448 f.
1621: 13448.7 f.
1622: 3452 f.
1623: 18626a.7 f., 19621 f., 22273 at charges.
1629: 3453–4 f.
1630: 3453 f., 5054 f.
1632: 22274 f., 22274b f.
1633: 18626a.8 f.
1637: 4510.6 f.
1638: 3454 f.
1640: 5055 f.

Astile, John, *pseud.*
Printer, no place specified, 1589. = T. Orwin.
1589: 17463–3.7 (d).

Astley, Hugh.
Bookseller in London, 1588–1609?†. Freed as a Draper by **Abraham Veale** on 2 Oct. 1583; transferred to the Stat. Co. in 1600. His shop passed to **John Tapp**. [*Dict.1*; Morgan.]
at St. Magnus' corner (T.8), 1588 (19521)–1608 (23264); variations: has 'dw.', 1596 (18650), 1600 (3189) or 'shop', 1605 (21549), 1608 (23264)
1588: 19521 sold.
1592: 18649 f.
1596: 5803 f., 18650 f., 21548 ent. for.
1600: 3189 f., 3189.5 f., 5803 ent., 18629(*A*3) ent., 20580 ent., 21548 ent.
1603: 20580 f.
1605: 21549 f.
1608: 23264 f.

Aston, John.
Bookseller in London, 1637–1642. [*Dict. 2*; DFM 764.]
in Cateaton Street at the Bull's Head (H.3), 1637 (13367)–1638 (13312.5) and probably later
1637: 13312 f., 13367 f. **1638:** 13312.5 f.

Atfend, Abraham.
Bookseller in Norwich, 1639–1640. [*Dict. 1.*]
No address used.
1639: 11250 sold. **1640:** 11061a f.

Aubri, Daniel.
Printer in Hanau, c. 1602–1619, and largely in Frankfurt am Main, c. 1617–1627†. [Benzing 187–8, 189–90.]
1607: 2787.

Aurik, Jacob, *pseud.*
Printer in 'Emden', 1534. = G. van der Haghen, Antwerp.
1534: 14829.

Auroi (Ouroy), Pierre.
Printer in Douai, 1596–1631†. Brother-in-law of **Charles Boscard**. It is not clear whether the 1631 item below was printed by Auroi or his widow. [Muller 17; *Répertoire 17*[e], IV.6.]
1604: [14568.3].
1606: [632] (d), [632.7], [9504] (false, d).
1607: [25972.4] (false).
1608: [11025] (false), [25972.2] (false).
1609: [13454], [24730] (d).
1610: [11019], [20485].
1611: [1836], [14568.7].
1612: [16905], [16908.5].
1613: [11317], [17273].
1614: 11, [16095.5].
1615: [11018], [20450], [20450.5] (d?).
1616: [4960], [10403].
1617: [1837], [10414], [11320], [14910], [23212].
1618: [1340.5], [14569].
1621: [14911].
1623: [12], [12.5], [12.7(*A*)], [16098.3].
1624: 14570.
1631: 1922 (widow?).

1640: 14568.3 (note).

Author, *anonymous.*
Publisher in Amsterdam? 1635. Although the following volume of multilingual verses has engravings by Crispin van de Passe 2, it is unlikely that 'voor den autheur' refers to him.
1635: 17976.5(*A*3).

Auvray, Pierre.
Bookseller in Paris, 1614–c. 1646. [Lottin 2: 4.]
1624: [20390.5] (false).

Auzoult, Richard.
Printer in Rouen, c. 1495–c. 1506, successors to 1518. [Muller 98; *Répertoire 16*[e], 22: 13–33.]
1506: [16118(*A*3)?]. **1515:** [23147.2] (c).

Awdely (Sampson), John.
Printer in London, (1556) 1559–1575†. The items dated 1576 were presumably printed by his heirs. His printing material later passed to **John Charlewood**. It is uncertain what relationship, if any, he had with 'John Awdley prynter', buried in 1563 (*St. Giles*). [Duff, *Century*.]
dw. beyond Aldersgate by Great St. Bartholomew's (F.4), 1560 (23005)–1561 (5951)
dw. in Little Britain by Great St. Bartholomew's, 1562 (11002)–1563? (992)
dw. in Little Britain Street beyond Aldersgate, 1564/65 (10910)–1575 (994, has 'without' Aldersgate)
1559: 996 (d).
1560: 989 (c), 993 ent., 4053 ent., 7280 ent., 20034 ent., 23005, 25938.5 ent.
1561: [995.5] (c), 1881, 2980.4, 3499.5 ent., 5950 ent., 5951, 18662, 23006.
1562: 11002.
1563: 992 (d?), 2980.6, 2980.8, [6572.3] (d?).
1564: [24726].
1564/65: 10910.
1565: 993, 2981, [5633?] (c?), [19304] (c), 25149 (c).
1566: 12445, 12445a, 14119.7, 21307a.1, 24716, 24999.
1567: 23007, [13175.19c?] (c).
1568: 11003, 17194 (d).
1569: 990, 995 (d?), 2981.5, [6222] (d), 6699 (d?), 18492 (d), 22192a.3 ent.
1570: 991, 6700 (d?), 6700.3 (d?), 11449.5, 12131, 15030, 15030.5 (d), 18643.7, 19178 (d?), 22210.
1571: 3077, 11450, 17495 (d).
1572: 1783, [6679] (d), 6679.2, 6701.3 (d?), 6701.5 (d?), 6701.7 (d?), 11451, 25825.7.
1573: 1784, 6088.7, 6679.3, 6691 (d), 11003.5, 11421.7 (d?), 11554 (d?), 12446, 13307 (c), 25826.
1574: 2982, 3499.5, 3500, 3500.5, 6679.4, 6684.5, 6684.7, 6692, 11422, 11452, 14120, 21050, 21855, 25826.
1575: 994, 1286, 4053, 6092, 6679.5, [14326.3] (d?), [22161.5] (d?), 25827, 25827.5.

1576: [3368] (d), 4183, 6685.
1582: 1808 ass'd, 5633.3 ass'd, 6080 ?ass'd, 11003.5 ass'd, 11835 ass'd, 12447 ass'd, 13302 ass'd, 13304 ass'd, 13307 ass'd, 14040 ass'd, 20108(*A*3) ass'd.

Awen, William.
Bookseller in London, 1551–1554. [Duff, *Century*.]
in Paul's Churchyard (B), 1553 (3204)
dw. in Paternoster Row at the Cock (C.7), 1554 (24810a.5)
1551: 5179 f. **1553:** 3204 [f.] (d). **1554:** 24810a.5 f. (d).

B

B., I. or **J., 1.**
Publisher? or patron? in Paris? 1500. [Duff, *Century*.]
1500: 16174 [f.].

B., I. or **J., 2,** *pseud.*
Printer in 'Rotterdam', 1626. = Unidentified London? printer.
1626: 1043.

Bache, Ellis.
Stationer in London, 1610. [Not in *Dict. 1*; DFM 2260.]
shop in Paul's Churchyard near St. Austin's gate (A.7), 1610 (12770)
1610: 12770 sold.

Bache, John.
Bookseller in London, 1607–1614. [*Dict. 1*; DFM 2123.]
(near) the Royal Exchange, 1607–1614
shop in Pope's Head Palace, near — (O.11), 1607 (1429)–1608 (17398)
shop at the entering in of — (O.8), 1612 (21390.5)–1613 (21391)
shop on the backside of — (O.8), 1614 (3609)
1607: 1429 f., 14696 f.
1608: 12494 f., 17398–8a f., 17399 f., 19057 f., 25965 f.
1612: 21390.5 f.
1613: 21391 f.
1614: 3609 f.

Back, Goovaert (Godfray).
Printer in Antwerp, 1493–1511 (1517†). [Rouzet.]
1510: [18873.7] (c), 23153.9 (c), 25155 (c), [23164.1] (c).
1511: 13606.3 (c).

Badger, Richard 1.
Bookseller in London, (1610) 1614–1629, and printer, 1625–1626 (as partner of **George Miller**, where other possible Badger items may be listed) and independently, 1629–1641†. In at least 1640 he shared several imprints on royalist publications with **Robert Young,** though the nature of the relationship has not been established. Brother of Thomas (DFM 447); father of George, John, Richard 2 (DFM 24–6) and **Thomas Badger**. Beadle of the Stat. Co. from 29 Jan. 1618 (*C-B C*: 98); died before 30 Aug. 1641 when he was succeeded in the office by **Joseph Hunscott**. In at least the following R. Badger used the style: Printer to the Prince his Highness, 1639 (15298 sq.) and 1640 (9260). He had an office or shop in Stationers' Hall (Q.1) from 12 Nov. 1621 and a printing house in its outbuildings from 10 Mar. 1630 (*C-B C*: 139, 215). [*Dict. 2*; DFM 353; *Loan Book*, 1618–21, 1623–38; *Poor Book*, 1618–34 (as beadle, for warning pensioners); Morgan.]
No address used; addresses found in some of his imprints but not identified as 'his shop' are:
sold in Paul's Churchyard (B), 1636 (1232), 1637 (25379.5)
sold in St. Dunstan's Churchyard near the church door (W.9), 1636 (20160)
sold in St. Dunstan's Churchyard in Fleet Street at the (Little) Shop turning up to Clifford's Inn (W.9), 1636 (1232, 3919), 1637 (15326.5, 15327, 25379), 1638 (21178.3, *see* also 21178 (*A*3)), and 1639 (13172, for T. A[ndrewes]). Since a version of this address was used by George Badger in 1641 (Wing T 2047), perhaps he or someone else in the family tended the shop before then.
1621: 16786.4(*A*3) ent.
1623: 23785 f.
1625: 4111, 4220a.5, 10725, 25646.
1626: 6746.5, 10725, 12117, 15303 f., 23488, 23493.7.
1627: 17751 f., 17751.5 f.
1628: 6299–300 f., 15305–5.7 f.
1629: 602 pro, 606 f., 6399.
1630: 75, 3911, 6597.7, 7443, 10147, 12876, 21213.10, 23494, 23610.
1631: 607, 10331.5 (d), 13167, 13167.5, 17478a (note), 20231, 20232, 20255, 23610, 23611.
1632: 249, 607.5, 608, 2633, 3075, 4803.2, [6948?], 12083, 12502, [12620], 12854.5,[12855?], 12877, 18918, 19585, 20233, 21212, 22352, [23847], 24314.7, 25912.
1633: 108, 291, [3564], 4595, 10137.7 (d?), 10147.7, 10167 (d?), 10182.7 (d?),10280.3 (d), 10296.7 (d?), 10363.7 (d?), 12368–70, 20233a, 20262, 20263, [23847.5], 25912.
1634: 291, 291.5, 609, 1636, 10147.8, 10147.10 (d?), 10185.5 (d), 11052, 12084, [12370a], 13871, 19203, 19828, 20161, 20263–4, 20936, 23403, 23490, 25096, 25706.
1635: 609, 1637, 3408, 3409–9.5, 4596, 5930.6, 10147.8A (d?), 10217, 10265.5 (d?), 10297, 10332, 10336, 10350, 10364, 10370, 14739.5, 19781, 21212.7, 23404, 23495, 24349, 25383, 25384, 25384.5.

Badger, R. — *cont.*
1636: 60.3, 610, 1232, [1618?], 3919, 4597, 5942 (d/error), 10171, 10298, 10298.3, [10427?], 10742–2.5, 12040, 12897.5, 14739.8, 18945, 19910, 20160, 20387, 21707, 21710.3, 25385, 26113.
1637: [973], 10169.5 (d?), 10169.7 (d), 10266, 13171, 15306, 15307, 15326–6.5, 15326.7(*A*), 15327, 18945.5, 20075, 20076, 20250, 20265, 20265.5, 21707, 22634.5(*A*3) ?ent., 24075, 24175, 25379–9a, 26114.
1638: 3454, 10185, 10197, 10245, 10351 (d?), 14501, 18193, 18967, 20226, 20227, 21178(*A*3), 21213, 22498, 22498a, 26111.
1639: 60.7, 5930.8, 5942, 13172, 15298, 15299, 19437a, 20227, 20743, 23066, 23199.7, 25752.
1640: 1345, 2369, 5055, [5751.5], [5752], [5752.5], 6190, [7060], 7345, 9260, 9261, 10267, 11530 typis, 12661, 12661.5, 14347 typis, 20884, 21542, [23299], 23300, 23304, [23310], 23312.

Badger, Thomas.
Printer in London, (1633) 1635–1646. Son of **Richard Badger 1**. For other items possibly printed by him *see assignees of* **T. Purfoot 2**. [*Dict. 2*; DFM 27; *Loan Book*, 1638–41.]
No address noted.
1635: 3408 ent., 3409 ent.
1636: 1232 ent., 20160 ent.
1639: 60.7, 11763, [19882.5], 22491.
1640: 3240, 2696.5, 6181.4, 6181.5, 7431, 9172.5 (d), 10136, 10246, 10282, 13724, 13872, 15135, 17178, 19883, 19883.5, 22151, 22491.

Badius, Conrad.
Printer in Paris, 1546–1548, and in Geneva, 1550–1562. Son of **Jodocus Badius**. [Duff, *Century*; *Parisiens*; Chaix 143.]
1557: 2871, [15611.7], [15612], [15613].

Badius Ascensius, Jodocus.
Printer in Paris, 1503–1535. Father of **Conrad Badius.** [Duff, *Century*; *Parisiens*.]
1504: 23885.3 ven. **1510:** 21789.1 in aed., 21799.4 in aed., 21799.6 in calcog. **1511:** 21799.8 in calcog. **1531:** 24623.5 prelo.

Bagfet (Bagford, Barfet), Joseph.
Stationer in London, (1611) 1613 (1629?† or 1635?†). [*Dict. 1*; DFM 331; *St. Giles* (I.4), 1620–29.]
No address used.
1613: 22424 f.

Note: *Dict. 1* has details of various **John Baileys**. Their biographies and addresses have been tentatively allocated below.

Bailey, John 1.
Bookseller in London, 1600–1610. Apprenticed to and mentioned in 1589 in the will of **John Wight,** a Draper-bookseller in whose name he was freed on 20 Feb. 1594; transferred to the Stat. Co in 1600; was associated in 1607, 1610 with some publications of **William Barley**, also formerly a Draper.
shop near the little North door of Paul's Church (A.1), 1600 (18546)–1603 (18586); no later use noted
1600: 18546 f. **1603:** 18586 f. **1604:** 6202 ent. **1607:** 10011 f., 10011.2 f., 10011.4 f. **1610:** 3791 f., 20755 f.

Bailey, John 2.
Bookseller in London, (1600) 1601–1603. Apprenticed to Joseph Hunt in 1592 and freed by **John Newbery** in 1600. On 28 May 1602 John Bailey the younger entered 6373, and on 22 July 1603 he assigned his rights in this work to **Roger Jackson**. John 2 is queried as publisher of a 1602 work in Latin without address, not congruent with the other publications of either John, but its original publisher, Henry Hooper, also had a shop in Chancery Lane.
in Chancery Lane (W.10d), 1601–1603
shop at the door of the Office of the Six Clerks —, 1601 (3679.5)–1602 (3680, 25304)
shop — near to the Office of the Six Clerks, 1602 (6373)–1603 (13626)
1601: 3679.5 f. **1602:** 3680 f., 6373 f., 25304 f., 25954? imp. **1603:** 13626 f.

Bailey (Baily, Baley, Bayly), Thomas.
Bookseller in London, (1607) 1617–1642. [*Dict. 2*; DFM 830.]
the corner shop in the Middle Row in Holborn near adjoining unto Staple Inn (V.9), 1617 (26116)–1634 (21403); from 1619 (3574) onward all addresses noted substitute 'his' for 'the corner' and omit 'adjoining unto'
1617: 26116 sold.
1618: 6181.2 f., 13815 f., 24415a f.
1619: 3574 f., 13816 f., 18496 f.
1622: 13814 f., 22372.5 sold.
1623: 22373 sold.
1634: 21403 f., 26117 f.

Baio, Antonio, *pseud.*
Printer in 'Paris', 1585. = J. Charlewood (Woodfield no. 6).
1585: 3934, 3937.

Baker, George.
Bookseller in London, (1627) 1631–1632. [*Dict. 1*; DFM 2634.]
near Charing Cross at the White Lion (X.14), 1631 (22561)
1631: 17845 f., 22561 sold, 24905 f. **1631/32:** 24156 f.

Baker, Michael.
Bookseller in London, (1606) 1610–1613. [*Dict. 1*; DFM 2189.]
shop in Paul's Churchyard at the Greyhound (B), 1611 (13771)–1613 (7142)
1610: 24261 ent. **1611:** 13771 f. **1613:** 7142 f.

Balduinus. *See* Boudins.

Baldwin, William.
Author, editor, and translator, fl. 1547–1570. Printer in London, 1549–1550. Worked as press corrector for **Edward Whitchurch**, whose house at the time was in Fleet Street (W.5), and apparently used Whitchurch's printing material. [Duff, *Century*; *DNB*; *NCBEL.*]
No address used.
1549: 2768. **1550:** [1254?], [4407?], [4407.5?], [4408?].

Bale, John, *Bishop.*
Protestant reformer and author, b. 1495–1563†. Publisher in London, 1549, 1551. His 1549 book has the address of **Richard Foster**. Although no known bookseller had the following address, it is doubtful that it was Bale's. [Duff, *Century*; *DNB*; *NCBEL.*]
?sold within Paul's Chain at the $ St. John the Baptist (A.9), 1551 (1273.5, tp to pt. 2)
1549: 15445 [f.]. **1551:** 1273.5 f.

Bales, Peter.
Writing-master and teacher of shorthand, b. 1547–1610. [Carlton 9–11.]
[his] house in the upper end of the Old Bailey (D.7), 1590 (1312).
1590: 1312 sold (d).

Ball, Roger.
Bookseller in London, (1634) 1636. [*Dict. 1*; DFM 624.]
shop without Temple Bar at the Golden Anchor, next the Nag's Head Tavern (X.1),1636 (5484; 13553.5, omits 'shop')
shop at the Golden Anchor in the Strand near Temple Bar, 1636 (21620,21688)
1636: 5484 f., 12051 sold, 12052 sold (d), 13553.5 sold (d), 21620 f., 21688 sold.

Ballad Partners.
Private partnership of individual Stat. Co. members formed by 6 Nov. 1624 for pooling ownership in a large collection of ballad titles. [*C-B C*: xiii–xiv; *SB* 6 (1954): 161–80.]
As far as can be ascertained from the scanty remains, through at least 1640 and possibly until 1655 only a single partner's name appeared in the imprint of any one edition though other editions may bear the name of a different partner. These imprints are indexed under the relevant partner's name. Members before 1641 in order of longevity are:

Thomas Pavier, 1626†
John Grismand, 1638†

Ballad Partners — *cont.*
Cuthbert Wright, 1638†
Henry Gosson, 1641†
John Wright 1, 1646†
Edward Wright, 1656†
Francis Coles (succeeded Pavier by 1629), 1680†

The following index is restricted to entries in the *Stationers' Register* to the Ballad Partners of items which survive in STC editions, though not always with the imprint of one of the partners. For a comprehensive list of all ballad entries for the period 1557–1709 *see* Hyder E. Rollins, *An Analytical Index to the Ballad-entries in the Registers of the Company of Stationers of London*, Chapel Hill, 1924, which can occasionally help to identify ballads entered by a variant title or first line. A few of the items listed below may also be included under the name of the partner who made the entry; on the other hand, there may be some entries by a partner which are omitted here.

That the 1627 entries below to John Wright 1 were for the Ballad Partners is suggested by the phrase 'received of them' (Arber IV.176). The last large entry before 1641 to the partners as a group was on 16 July 1634 (Arber IV.323). The later ballads indexed below in square brackets were entered to individual partners without mention of others, perhaps through inadvertence.

A query preceding a number indicates uncertainty whether the title entered refers to the item indexed.
1624: 15.3, 22, 853.5, 1328, 1328.7, 1331, 1331.3, 1433.5, 3194.5, 3694.3, 3728, 3729, 3797, 4541.5, 5129.5, 5611.7, 5631.3(*A*3), 5639.5, 5772.5, 5876.8, 6317, 6557.4, 6557.8, 6558.5, 6922.7, 7384.5, 7505, 10413, 10610.3, 10611.7, 11745.3, 12384.5, 12542.5, 12573.5, 14032.5, 14498.5, 14543, 14544, 14553.3, 16751, 17262, 17915.5, 18644, 19165.5, 19460, 20509.7, 21776.7, 22406.3, 22463.5, 22654.5, 22919.9, 22920.1, 22920.7, 23435a.5, 23635, ?24092.3, 24094, 24293.5, 25108, 25611.
1625: ?5876.8.
1627: 12871.5, 20131.5.
1629: 1105.5, 1327, 1539.5, 4687, ?5417, 6809.2, 6907, 10654, 16856.3, 16864a.9, 17915.5, 19228, 19232, 19239, 19282, ?20186.3, ?22919.7, 23291, 25283, 25998.
1630: 1332, 5425, 6102, 18316.3.
1631: 5420.5, 12543.3, 12547.9, 16856.7, 16866, 21551.3, 22919.3.
1632: 5143, 5428.5, 5429.5, 12326, 12544, 15264, 20315, 20319, 20323, 20822.5, 21138.5, 23445.5, 25972.8.
1633: 150.5, 732, 6926, 12546, 16861, 16864a, 18580, 18699, 19252, 20313, ?21025, 22925, 23260, 24047.
1634: 1799, 5416, 5421, ?5422, 5428.5, 11152.5, 12545, ?16802.3, 19261, 20186, 25937, 25973.
1638: [11155], [16868], [16869], [19076], [19263].

Ballard, Henry.
Printer in London (1586) 1597–1609†. He seems to have run the press which **William Barley** set up in Little St. Helen's (J.3) for working the music patent, 1599–1601. In 1607 Ballard acquired the printing material of **Valentine Simmes**. *See* also Appendix B/36–7. [*Dict. 1*; *SB* 22 (1969): 216–7.]
dw. without Temple Bar over against St. Clement's Church at the Bear (X.2), 1597 (3394; 15392, omits 'over ... Church'); no later address or use of this one noted
1597: 3394, 15392.
1599: [1882], [10697], [13563], [18131] (d).
1600: [18115.5], [25219.5].
1601: [4649?], [10254?].
1607: 10257 (d), 25057.
1608: [23], 1233,[5434(*A*3)], 5694, 6054.2–4.4 (note), 6357, [7218], 7493, 11206, 13489, 13497, 15536, [15686.7?], 17888, 21241.
1609: 6499, 24577.

Ballard, Richard.
Bookseller in London, 1577?–1585†. Freed as a Draper by **Abraham Veale** on 16 Mar. 1578. [*Dict. 1*; *Library* 10 (1988): 6, n.13.]
shop at St. Magnus' corner (T.8), 1579 (18276)–1585 (18648, colophon)
1577: [4269?] f. (d?). **1579:** 18276 sold. **1580:** 10627 f. (d?).
1581: 18647 f. **1582:** 10608.5 sold (d?). **1584:** 4700.5 f., 18259.7 f. (c), 21545 f. **1585:** 18648 f.

Bamburg, Nicolaus, *pseud. See* Nicolaus, *Bamburgensis.*

Bamford, Henry.
Journeyman printer in London, (1571) 1577–1586. [*Dict. 1.*]
No address used.
1577: 1075 ent., 11471 ent., 11475 ent., 24713 (d).

Bankes, Richard.
Bookseller and printer? in London, 1523–1533? and 1538?–1547? He is described as a bookbinder for the lay subsidy of 1523 (*Library* 9 (1908): 258). Although Bankes appears to have had two periods of activity, it is not possible to define clearly either the extent of his role as a publisher or whether he actually did print, in spite of his self-proclaimed title of 'typographus', 1540 (9290.5) and the imprints as recorded in STC. Much further work needs to be done on the types, initials, and other decorative material in the items listed below. Of the two 1545 addresses that in the Old Bailey may have belonged only to **Richard Lant** and that in Paul's Churchyard only to Bankes. [Duff, *Century*.]
dw. in the Poultry at the Long Shop beside St. Mildred's Church door at the Stocks [Market] (O.1), 1523 (7260)–1528 (11550.6, omits all after 'Poultry')
dw. in Gracechurch (Gratious) Street beside the conduit (P.4), c. 1538? (3022)
?in Fleet Street at the White Hart (W.2), 1539 (10437, A. Clerke's address?)
in (ex) aedibus R. Taverni (W.2), 1539 [23711a]–1540 (4843)
?sold next to the White Hart in Fleet Street (W.2), 1542? (2968.3)–1543? (2967.5, R. Taverner's address?)
in the Old Bailey (D.7), 1545 (14126.5, with R. Lant)
in Paul's Churchyard (B), 1545 (3365.5, 20197.3; both with R. Lant)
1523: 7260.
1523/24: [470.8(*A*3)].
1525: 13175.1, 22153 [f.].
1526: 13175.2, 15946.5 sumpt., 22153a [f.] (d?), 24199 [f.] (d?).
1528: 7542.5 [f.] (d?), 11550.6 at costs.
1531: 864 (c).
1532: 5018 f.
1533: 13608.4 f. (d?).
1538: 3022 (c?).
1539: [2748?], 10437, [23709], [23711a], 23712.5, 23713 (repeat).
1540: 1473.5 f. (d?), 2967 (d?), 2968 (d?), 2969 (d?), 4241.5 f. (c), 4268.5 [f.] (d), 4843 per, 9290.5 per, 10445, 12206a.3 [f.] (d), 12206a.7 [f.] (d), 18052 [f.] (d?), 22880.2 (note), 22877.6 [f.] (d).
1542: 2967.3 (d?), 2968.3 (d?), 2970 (d?), 9291 [f.?], 9343.7 f. (d?), 12047 f. (d?), 12468 f. (d), 23713 [f.] (d?), 24601 f. (d).
1543: 2967.5 (d?), 2969.3 (d?), [3327].
1545: 439.5 f. (c), 2967.7 (d?), 2968.5 (d?), 2970.3 (d?), 3365.5, 9343.8 f. (forged? c?), 14126.5, 20197.3.
1546: 2969.5 (d?).
1547: 2968.7 (d?).

1574: 9295 (reissue).

Bankworth, Richard.
Bookseller in London, 1594–1614† (*TLS* 7 June 1923: 388). Freed as a Draper by **Abraham Kitson** on 15 Mar. 1589. Succeeded to the latter's shop in 1594, and it is uncertain which man was responsible for the items of that year and for which either name has been indiscriminately supplied in STC. Continued Kitson's work as London agent for books printed in Cambridge. Transferred to the Stat. Co. in 1600. His widow remarried **Edward Blount**. [*Dict. 1.*]
shop in Paul's Churchyard at the Sun (A.3), 1594 (19531)–1612 (11380, has 'dw.')
1594: [6227] sold, [6443?] sold, [12208–8.2] ext., [16678?] sold, 19531 f.
1595: [1566] sold, [5883–4] sold, [14121.5] sold, [19703] sold, [19760] sold, [19760.5] sold, 23361 (note).
1596: [6708] sold, 23362 (note to 23361), [24011] ext.
1600: [6709] sold.
1601: 14058 f.
1602: 10546 f.
1603: 1814 f., 1822 f., [6710] sold, 10545 f.
1604: 5062 ent.
1605: 10566.5 f., 25093 f. (d).
1606: 6716.5 (note), 24341 sold.
1607: 6641 f., 25678–8a sold, 25693 sold.

Bankworth, R. — *cont.*
1608: 20763.3 imp.
1610: 4509 ent., 21073 f.
1611: 6642 f., 15514.5 f.
1612: 11380 f., 11380.2 f., 24027 f.

1636: 4510.4 ass'd.

Bannatyne, Thomas.
Patron in Edinburgh, 'one of his Majesty's servants', 1634. [*EBST* 2 (1941): 96 (no. 66), 101.]
No address used.
1634: [12534.6?] at expenses.

Bapst, Valentin.
Printer in Leipzig, 1542–1556†. [Benzing 279; *Library* 4 (1950): 274–5.]
1548: [16459] (false).

Barbier, Jean.
Printer in London, 1496–1497, in Westminster, 1498, and possibly in Paris, 1502–1516†. In partnership with **Julian Notary**, 1496–1498. [Duff, *Century*; *Parisiens*.]
An action was brought in 1495 [*sic*] against a John Barbour, brewer, lately of Coventry, *alias* John Berbier, printer, lately of Coventry (*Library* 1 (1910): 295; the regnal year is definitely 10 [not 16] Hen. VII). This is surely not the Paris printer, who was a native of France; whether he is Notary's partner is uncertain.
London, near (apud) [the church of] St. Thomas the Apostle (S.6), 1496 [270]–1497 [15884]
Westminster, [no address], 1498 (16172)
1496: [270] (d). **1497:** [15884]. **1498:** 16172 per. **1504:** 13829.5 per.
1511: 3269.5 (c). **1511/12:** 23427a.3.

Barcker, Thomas, *pseud.*
Printer in 'London', 1588. = Unidentified Dutch printer(s).
1588: 9194.5, 9194.7, 9194.8.

Barker, Christopher.
Bookseller and printer (from 1577) in London, 1569–1587 (1599†). **Queen's Printer**, 1577–1587 (*see* King's Printer); from 15 Dec. 1579 (8116) he added 'most excellent' before 'Majesty' in his style as Queen's Printer. Freed as a Draper by John Petyt (possibly a son or other kin of **Thomas Petyt**) in 1559; transferred to the Stat. Co. on 4 June 1578 (Arber II.677). For titles he yielded to the Stat. Co. in 1584 *see* Appendix C/1–6. Father of **Robert Barker**. One of the *assignees of* **F. Flower**. *See* also *Deputies* and *Deputy of* **C. Barker**. [*Dict. 1.*]
in Paul's Churchyard, 1571 (according to T. Hill's report on Ii2^{v} of 13482)–1577
at the Grasshopper — (B), 1575 (11643, colophon)–1576 (2876, colophon)
dw. — at the Tiger's Head (A.2), 1576 (2878)–1577 (2879, colophon)
dw. in Paternoster Row at the Tiger's Head (C.7), 1577 (2119)–1579 (2126, colophon)
at Bacon House (G.3), 30 Apr. 1579 (8112)–1585 (9485, colophon to Pardon: has 'in B. H. near Foster Lane'); no later use noted
1569: 24477.5 ent.
1574: 24477.5 f.
1575: 2876, 2877 f., 11643 f., 11643a f., 24324 f., 24328 f. (d).
1576: 2117, 2118, 2876, 2878, 15231.
1577: 2119, 2120, 2879, 2879.2, 8093, 8094, 8095 (repeat), 8096, [10102.18] (d?), 10126 (d?), 11348, 14059, 15000, 15232, 16306.6 (d?), 19969.2 (d).
1578: [1417.5] (d), 2123, 2124 by ass't of, 2351.7 (d?), 2368.3 (note), 2879.4 [f.] (d?), [2879.6] (d?), 2879.8 (c), 2880, 4924 (d?), 4924.5 (d?), 8097.5, 8098 (repeat), 8098.5, 8099 (repeat), 8100, 8101, 8102, 8103 (repeat of lost ed.), 8105, 8105.3 (repeat), 9187.9–.10 (d?), 9477a, 9527.5 (d), 11236 ex off., 11248, 11620.7 ent., 14141 (d), 15001, 16306.7 (d?), 16479.5 (d?), 16480, [16707.3] (d), 20978, 20979 f., 22470 [f.].
1578/79: 8108, 8108.3 (repeat), 8109 (repeat of lost ed.), 8110, 8111 (repeat).
1579: 2126, 2127, 2128, 2880.3, 2880.5, 8112, 8113, 8114, 8115, 8116, 8117 (repeat), 8118, 9314 (and *A*3 note), 9528, 9528.5, 10034.7 (d?), 10041, 14060, 16306.9 (d?), 18158, 18159, 24782, 24917.

Barker, C. — *cont.*
1579/80: 8119.
1580: 2056 imp., 2129, 2129.5, 2130, 2881, 2881.3, 2881.5 (c), [3368.5-Miller] (c), 4925, 5005, 8047.10 (c?), 8120, 8123, 8124, 8125, 8126, [10102.20] (d?), 10126.5 (d?), 10155.7, 10174.5 (d?), 13228b (d), 13228b.1 (d), 16307, 16309, 16481 (d?), 16512(*A*3), 16513(*A*3), [16762] (c), 18160, 20203, 21507.5, [21947] (repeat).
1580/81: 8127–8.
1581: [153.7], 1219, 2057.5 imp., 2131, 2132, 2881a, 2881a.5, 5006, 5007, 8129, 8131, 8131.3 (repeat), 8132, 8134, 8134.3 (repeat), 9484, 9484.5, 9529, 10042, 10042.5, 13228b.2 (d), 14142, 15163 by ass't of, 16309.1, 16309.2 (d?), 16309.3 (d?), 16309.4, 18161, 18161.5, 18533, 18533.5 f.
1582: 2004, 2133, 2134, 2882, 2883, 4536, 4962, 8135, 8137, 8138, 8139 (repeat of lost ed.), 10157, 10787.2 (c), 13228b.3 (d), 13656, 13672 [f.], 15164 by ass't of, 15164a by ass't of, 16309.5 (d?), 16309.5c(*A*3) (d?), 17774, 18775a, 20372.
1583: 1220, 2005 (d?), 2136, 2136.5, 2137, 2885, [4901] (d), [4902], 4962, 8123.3 (d?), 8140, 8141, 8143, 8143.3 (repeat), 9315, 9315.5 (d?), 10104 (note), [10104.4] (d), 10126.7 by assent of (d), 10127 (d), 13228b.4 (d), 13228b.5 (d), 14060.5, 14596, 14597, 14597.5, 15145 ent., 16309.6 (d?), 16309.7 (d?), 18744, 18744.5.
1583/84: [4903], 8144–4.5.
1584: 1221, 2139, [2140] (d), 2141, 2142, 4583 in aed. (d), 8146, 8147 (repeat of lost ed.), 13657(*A*3), 16309.8 (d?), [24050], [24050.5], [24051], [24051.5].
1585: 2060.3 imp., 2143, 2144, 4089, 4089.5, [5010], 8152, 8153, 8154 (d), 9189, 9189.5, 9190, 9191, 9192, 9193, 9485, 9485.5, 9485.7, 9486, 13105, 13228b.6 (d), 14129.5 (d), 15002 by ass't of, 16310 (d?), [16310.5] (c?), 16311, 19342 (d), 19342a (d), 19342a.5 (d), 19617 in aed. (d), 19617.5 in aed. (d).
1585/86: 8155.
1586: 2145, 2145.5, 2886, 2887, 4587 (d), 4587.3 (d), 6052, 7288 (d), 7577, 8059 (d?), 8157, 8157.3 (repeat), 8159, 8160, 9530, 10043, 13228b.6B (d), 16311.3, 16311.4 (d?), 16311.5 (d?), 16311.6, 16517.
1586/87: 8161, 8162, 9194.
1587: 2146, 2147, 6053, 7938 (d?), 7939 (repeat), 8163, 9305.3 f., 9487, 9487.5, 16311.7, [16311.9?] (d?), 16518.

1588: 14061 ex assig.
1589: 9198.5 (false), 15232.5 f.
1593: 8226.5 by consent of.
1595: 14062 ex assig.
1599: 10017.5 (false), 14063 ex assig.
1603: 14064 ex assig. (error?).

Barker, Christopher, *Deputies of.*
Queen's Printers in London, 1587–1599 (*see* King's Printer). From 1587 the deputies were **George Bishop** and **Ralph Newbery**, joined in 1593 by Christopher's son, **Robert Barker**, under whose names may be found other items produced by the deputies. Printing very likely continued to be done at Bacon House near Foster Lane (G.3). [*Dict. 1.*]
No address noted.
1495: 2161 (d/error), 2162 (d/error).
1579: 15195 (d/error).
1587: 2887.3, 8164, 8164.3, 8165, 8166, 8167, [14143] (d), [14144] (d), 16312.
1587/88: 8168, 8168.5, 8169, 8170, 8170.5 (repeat).
1588: 2148, 2149, 2347, [2742], 8172, 8172.3, 8173, 8174, 8175, 8176, 8177, 8178, 9317, 13228b.7 (d), 16312.7(*A*3) (d?), 16313, 16519, 16520, 23011, [24632].
1588/89: 8178.7–79, 8181, 8182.
1589: 2150, 2151, 2152, 2152.5, 2887.5, 2888, 2888.5, 5682, 5683, 5683a, 8185, 8185.3 (repeat), 8186, 8187, 8188, 8189, 9196, 9197, 9198, 9487.7, 9487.9(*A*), 9488, 9488.5, [10104.7 f.] (d?), 10129 (d?), 12625, 13228b.8 (d), 13228b.9 (d), 13228b.10 (d), 16314, 16314.5 (d?), 16521.
1589/90: 8189.7, 8192, 8192.5 (repeat), 8193.
1590: [22.2(*A*)?] (d?), 2153, 2154, 8048 (c?), 8195, 8196 (repeat), 8197, 8198, 8199, 8199.5, 10044, [10377], 16314a, [16314a.5] (d?), [16315] (c), 16482 (d?), 16522, 16523, 16523.3, 16523.5 (d?), 16523.7 (d).
1590/91: 8199.3, 8200, 8201 (d), 8201.5.
1591: 2156, 2156.5, 2157, 2890, [5820], 8202, 8203, 8204, 8204.5 (repeat), 8206, 8207, 8208, [8209] (d), 8210, 8212, 8212.3 (repeat), 8213, 8214 (repeat), 9318, [10105 f.] (d?), 10130 (d), 16315.5.

Barker, C., *Deputies of* — *cont.*
1591/92: 8215, 8216, 8217, 8218, 8219 (repeat of lost ed.).
1592: [2061], 2157, 2158, 2158.5, [2794], 2891, 5823, 8220, 8221, 8222, 8223, 8224, 8225, 9199, 9531, 13228b.11 (d), 16316, [16316.5] (d?), 16317, 23450, [23455].
1592/93: 8226.
1593: 2159, 2160, 2892, 3063, 3065, 5821, 5822 (d), 8229, 8230, 8231, 8232, 8233, 8234, 8235, 9200, 9200.3, 9489, 9490, 9491, 10045, 10046, 16524 (d), [21747], 23468.
1593/94: 8236.
1594: 2160, 2161, 2162, 2163, 2164, 5366, 7927 (d), 8089 (d?), 8237, 8238 (repeat of lost ed.), 8238.5, 8240, 9201, 9319, 13228b.12 (d), 16318, [16318.5] (d?), 16525, 16525.3 (d), 16525.7, [21748].
1594/95: 8241.
1595: 2165, 2166, 2167, 8239, 8242, 8243, 8244, 8245, 8245.5, 8246, 8247, 8247.2, 8247.4, [9201.5], 9202, [10108] (d), 10131, 16320, 16320.3 (d?), 16320.5, 23451.
1595/96: 8247.8.
1596: 2162, 2167.5, 2169, 2894, 2894.5, 8248, 8249, 8250, 8251, 8253, 8253.3 (repeat), 8255, 8255.5, 9203, 9204, 9205, 9205.3 (false), 9206, 9207, 9208, 16321, 16321.5, 16321a, 16321a.5(*A*), 16322, 16466.5, 16526, 16527, 16527.5, 23463.
1596/97: 8256.
1597: 2168, 2169, [2170] (d), 2171, 2172, 2895, [4341], [4908] (d), 8257, 8258, 8259, 8260, 8261, 8261.5, 9208.2, 9208.3, 9208.4, 9208.5, 9208.6 (false), 10066, 10066.5, 13228b.13 (d), 15195 (d), 16322, [16322.1] (d?), 16322.2 (d?), 16528, 16528.5, 16528a, 16528a.5, [24122].
1597/98: 8262, 8263.
1598: 1460, 2171, 2172, 2896.5, [4491.5(*A*3)], [8261.7] (d?), [8264], 8265, 8266, 9321, 9492.7 (d), 9493.5 (d), 9494 (d), 9494.3 (d), 9494.5 (d), 9494.7 (d), 9494.11 (d), 9494.12 (d), 10066.5 (d?), 13228b.14 (d), 16322.3, [16322.5] (d?), [16322.6] (d?), 16322.7, 16529, [21588.3] (d?).
1598/99: 8267, 8268.
1599: 2173, 2174–80 (forged), 8269, 10017, 10067, 13228b.15 (d), [14131?] (d?), 14146, 16322.7, 16323, 16323.3, 16437, 16530.
1600: 2181 (post-dated?).

Barker, Christopher, *Deputy of (to).*
Individuals delegated to publish particular texts. Deputy 'to', 1588–1589 = G. Bishop; deputy 'of', 1589–1600 = T. Dawson.
No address used.
1588: 22908, 22909.
1589: 2887.7 'of', 22912 'to'.
1591: 2890 (note), 10787.3.
1595: 2893.
1596: 2894.3.
1597: 2895.3.
1598: 2896.
1600: 2897.

Barker, Robert.
Printer in London, (1589) 1593–1634 (1645†). One of the *Deputies of* **C. Barker**, who was his father. **Queen's** and from 1603 **King's Printer**, 1600–1617, and intermittently thereafter (*see* King's Printer). Father-in-law of **John Legat 2**. In 1634 his share in the office was mortgaged to M. Flesher, J. Haviland, and R. Young, and he himself went to debtors' prison although his name continues in imprints until 1645. The stationer of this name buried in 1629 (*St. Giles*) was possibly his son. *See* also *Deputies (etc.) of* **R. Barker**. [*Dict. 2*; *Poor Book*, 1645; *Library* 2 (1901): 353–75.]
Around the beginning of his tenure as Queen's Printer the establishment was moved to Northumberland House, St. Martin's Lane, almost by Aldersgate (G.8); c. 1625 it was moved again, to Hunsdon House, Blackfriars (Q.6); *see* the location information under King's Printer.
No address noted.
1593: 2061.5.
1594: 15238.
1595: 23451 ent.
1596: 690, 21783.
1597: 1445, 2062, 15195 ent.
1598: 1460 ent., 10066 ent., 12626.
1599: 12626, 12626a, 23265, 23449, 23457, 23460.
1599/1600: 8270, 8271, 8272.

Barker, R. — *cont.*
1600: 2182, 2899, 8273, 8274, 8275, 8276, 9208.7, 12626, 12626a (note), 13228b.16 (d), 14447, 14447.5 (false), 16323.5, 16324, 16324.3, 16324.4(***A***3), 16531.
1600/01: 8277, 8278, 8279, 8280, 8281, 8282, 8283, 8284, 8285.
1601: 1133, 2183, 2184, 2184.5 (note), 2900, [2900.3], [7578], 8286, 8287, 8288, 9495, 9496, 9496.5, 9497, 9497.5, 9497.7 (d?), 16324.4(***A***3), 16324.5, 16324.7, [19392] (d).
1601/02: 8289, 8290.
1602: 2185, 2186, [2187] (d), 2188, 2902, [2902.3] (d?), 8291, 8292, 8293, 8294, 8295, 8301 (false), 13228b.17, 22164.
1602/03: 8296, 8297, 8298, 8299.
1603: 43, 2189, 2190, 2192, 2193, 2903.5, 2991(***A***3) ent., [3400?], 8301 (false), 8302, 8303, 8304, 8305, [8306], 8307, 8308, 8309, 8310, 8311, 8312, 8313, 8314, 8315, 8316, 8317, 8318, 8319, 8320, 8321, 8322, 8323, 8323.5 (false), 8324, 8325, 8326, 8326.5, 8327, 8328, 8329, 8330, 8331, 8332, 8333, 8334, 8335, 8336, 8337, 8338, 8339, [8340], 8453.5 (d), 9209, 13228b.18, [14362.5] (d), 16324.9, 16325, [16325.3] (d), 16489, 16532, 17151, 17151a, [19056].
1603/04: 8341, 8342, 8343, 8344, [8345?] (d), 8346, 8347, [8348] (d), 8349, [9209.5], 16326, 16326.5.
1604: 597, 597.3, 597.7, 1459.5 (false), [7748.3] (d?), 8352, 8353, 8354, 8355, 8359, 8360, 8361, 8363, 8364, 8365, [8453.7] (d?), [9175i.3?] (d), 9500, 9500.2, 9500.4, 9500.6, 9500.8 (d?), 10069.3, 10070, 10070.3, 10070.5, 10070.7, 10071.5 (d/repeat), 12210 (note), 14363, 14390, 14390.3, 16327, 16328, 16328.5, 16328a, 16328a.5, 16483 (d), 16533, [19040] (d), 23461 (false).
1604/05: 8367, 8368, 8369, 8370, 10019, 10019.5.
1605: 1401, 2194, 2195, 2196, 8372, 8373, 8374, 8375, 8377, 8378, 8379, 8379.5, 8380, 8381, 8382, 8383, 8384, 8386, 9211, 10047, 10047.3 [f.], 13229, 14392, 14392.5, 14393, 16329, 16329a, 16329a.5, 16534, 16535 (d), 21456.
1605/06: 8387, 8389, 8390.
1606: 615, 1402, 2196, 2197, 2198, 2905, 2905.2(***A***), 4002.5 (d), 4003, 4895, 4895.5, [7748.5] (d?), 8391, 8392, 8392.5, 8393, 8394, 8395, 8396, 8397, 8398, 9212, 9502, 9502.5, 9503 (d), 10181, 11618, 11619, 11619a, 11619a.5, 13230, 13678, 14394, 16330, 16330.3, 16331, 16490, 16494 (d?), [16536] (d?), 16537, [19482], 20145, 21759 ent., 21961.
1607: 2199, 2200, 2201, 2201.5, [2905.3] (c), 2905.5, 3104, 3105, 8399, 8400, 8401, 8402, 8403, 8404, 8405, 8406, 8407, 8408, 8409, 8410, 9505, 13231, 14395 (d), 14400, 14403, 16332, 16332.2, 16332.4, 16332.5, 16467, 18814.
1607/08: 8411, 8412, 9214, 9214.3.
1608: 44 [f.], 2202, 2203, 2204, 2205, 2906, 7705, 7705.2, 8413, 8414, 8415, 8416, 8418.5, 9215, 9217, 10071.5 (d?), 13232, 16332.5, [16332.6] (d), 16332.8, 16333, 16333.3(***A***), 24515.
1608/09: 8427, 8428.
1609: 626, 626.5, 1127, 2206, 2906.5, 2907, 8431, 8432, 8433, 8434, 8434.5, 8435, 8436.5, 8437, 8438, 8439, 8439.5, 8440, 8441, 8442, 8443, [8454] (c?), 9216, 9341, 14396 (d), 14396.3 (d), 14396.7 (d), 14401, 14401.5, 14402, 16333.5, 16334.
1609/10: 7759, 8444, 8445, 8445.5.
1610: 596, 598 (d?), 598.5 (d?), 604, 612, 612.5, 616 (d?), 618, 619 (d?), 627, 628, 2208, 2210, 2211, 2212, 2213, 2214, 2908, 8446, 8447, 8450, 8451, 8452, [8458?] (d?), [9175i.8] (d), 16335.5, 9506, 9506.5, 16495 (d?), [19050] (d), 19204, [20754], 22629, 24516.
1610/11: 8461, 9221, 9221.5 (d), 9222, 9223.2.
1611: 613 (d?), 614 (d?), 620, 621, 2212, 2213, 2214, 2215, 2216, 2217, 2218, 2224, 2909, 2909.5, 4118, 4868.7 [f.] chez, 8376, 8465, 8466, 8467, 8468, 8469, 8470, 8471, 8474, 8475, [9175i.9?] (d), 9225, 13232.5, 16335.5, 16336, 16337, 16538, 24032, [25743.5] (d).
1611/12: 8476.
1612: 2218, 2219, 2220, 2221, 2222, 2223, 2225, 2228, 2910, 8477, 8478, 8479, 8480, 9233, 9234, 10048, 10072, 10072.5, 10072.7, [13248.2], 16337a.3, [16786.12] (d), [21588.5] (d?).
1612/13: 7760, 8481, 8482, 8483.
1613: 2223, 2224, 2225, 2226, 2227, 2228, 2229, 2230, 2231, 2232, 2233, 2911, 2911.5, 2912, 2912.3, 2912.5, [8455] (c?), 8484, 8485, 8486 (d), 8487, 8488, 8489, 8490, 8491, 8492, 8493, 8494, 8495, 8496, [9175i.11?] (d), 9235, 13000, 13233, 16337a.5, 16337a.7, 16338, 16338.3, 16339, 16539, [17330.5] (d), 17597.
1613/14: 8497, 8498, 8498.5, 14166.
1614: 622, 2230, 2231, 2232, 2233, 2234, 2235, 2236, 2237, 2238, 2247, 2912.3, 2912.5, 8500, 8500.7, 8501, 8502, 8503, 8504, 8505, 8506, 8507, 8508, 8509, 8510, 14167, 14167a, 16339, 16341, 16341.5, 16342.3, 16342.5, 16342.7.

Barker, R. — *cont.*
1614/15: 8511, 8512, 8513, 8514.
1615: 2234, 2236, 2239, 2240, 2241, 2242, 2243, 2408 (note), 2913, 2914, 2914.5, 8515, 8516, 8517, 8518, 8519, 8520, 8521, 8523, 8524, [8525], 8526, 8527, 8528, 8529, 8530, 8531, 8532, 8533, 8533.3, 13234, 16343, 16343.5, 16344, 16344.5, 16345, 16345.5, 16346, [23634.7] (c), [24844.7?] (d?).
1615/16: 8534, 8535.
1616: 2243, 2244, 2245, 2246, 2915, 2915.5, [3368.5-Paine] (d?), [4908.5] (d), [6996], [6998], 8538, 8539, 8539.5, 8540, 8543, 8544, 10049, 10073, 14344, 14345, 14397 (d), 14397.3 (d), 14397.7 (d), 16347, 16347a, 16348a, [16551(***A***3)] (c?).
1616/17: 8546, 8547, [8548], 8549, 8550, 8551, 8552–3.
1617: [1882.5] (d), 2247, 2248, 2249, 2916, 2918.3, [7492.5] (d), [7605.7] (d), [8456] (c?), 8554, 8555, 9238, 16349, [26093].
1618: 624.5 [f.], 2252.
1619: 8621, 8622, 16353.
1619/20: 8624, 8624.5, 8625–6, 8627, 8629, 8630, 8632.
1620: 611, 2258, 2261, 7754.4, 8633, 8634, 8636, 8637, 8638, 8639, 8640, 8641, 8642–2.5, [9503.3] (c?), 14345, 14346.5 ap., 14381.5, 14383 ap., 14412, 16353, 16354, [16354.5?] (d?), 16355, 16359, 16496, 21761, 25728.5.
1620/21: 8654.7–56, 8659, 8660.
1629: 8934.5(***A***), 8935, 8936, 9509, 16548.3, 16548.7.
1629/30: 8937, 8937.5, 8939, 8940, 8941, 9250.3 [f.].
1630: 2289.5, 2290, 2291, 2292, 2292.3, 2292.5, 2295.3, 2295.4, 2295.5, 2295.6, 2295.8, 2298.7, 2349, 2349.5, [2746], 2936.5, 2937, 8942, 8943, 8944, 8946, 8947, 8950, 8951, 8952, 8954, 8955, 8956–7, 8958, 8959, 8960, 8961, 8962, 8963–4, 8965, 8966, [8967], 8969, 8970, 9250.5, 9250.7, 9251, 9251.3, 9342, 9509, 16378, 16378.5, 16380.7, 16380.9, 16381, 16381.5, 16382, 16439, 16497.5, 16549.
1630/31: 8971, 9252, 9252.2, 9252.4, 14220.
1631: 2295.3, 2295.4, 2295.5, 2295.6, 2295.8, 2296, 2297, 2297.2, 2297.3, 2297.5, 2297.6, 2297.7, 2297.9, 2298, 2300, 2301, 2302, 2304, 2938, 2939, 2940, 7684, 8973, 8974, 8975, 8976, 8977, 8978, 8979, 8980, 8982, 8983, 8983.5, 9254, 10056, 12784 ap., 16383, 16384, 16384.7, 16385, 16472, 16485.7, 16497.7, 16549.5, 16550, 18023.5, 18024.
1631/32: 8984, 8985, 8986, 8987, 14128.7.
1632: 2297.9, 2298.5, 2298.7, 2300, 2301, 2302, 2302.3, 2302.5, 2303, 2304, 2304.5, 2305, 2941.5, 8988, 8989, 8990, 8991, 8992, 8993, 8994, 8994.5, [9254.3(***A***)] (d?), 10057 (forged), 16385.7, 16386, 16386.7, 16387, 16388, [16388a] (d), 16388a.5, 16389, 16390, 16391, 16550.3 (d).
1632/33: 8995, 8996, 8997, 8998.
1633: 2303, 2305, 2306, 2307, 2308, 2942, 2943, 7755, 8999, 9000, 9001, 9002, 9003–4, 9254.7, 9256, 10058, 10058.5 (forged), [10363], 16390, 16391, 16392, 16392.5, 16393, 16393.5, 16393.7, [16394.3], 16395, 16396, 16397, 16473, 16550.5, 16550.7, 18026, 21475 ap.
1633/34: 9005, 9006–7, 9008, 9009, 9010, 9011–2, 9256.5.
1634: 2306, 2312, 2313, 2313a, 2313b, 2313b.5, 2314, 2314.3, 2314.5, 2315, 2318, 9013, 9014, 9015, 9015.5, 9016, 9017, 9018, 9019, 9020, 9021, 9023, 9024, 9025–6, 9027–8, 9029, 9258, 16396, 16397, 16397.3, 16397.7, 16398, [16399], 16399.5, 16474, 16486, 16498, [21164].
1634/35: 9031, 9032, 9033.
1635: 2315, 2318, 2319, 2325, 2948, 7695, 9034, 9035, 9036, 9037, 9038, 9039, 9040, 9041, 9042, 9043, 9044, 9045, 9046, 9047, [9048], 9049, 9050, 9051, [9175m] (d), 16402, 16402.5, 16402.7, 16486.3, 16499, 16552.
1635/36: 9052, 9053, 9054, 9056, 9057.
1636: 2313b.5, 2322, 2322.3, 2322.5, 2324.5, 2951, 2951.5, 9058, 9059, 9060–1, 9062, 9063, 9064, 9065, 9066, 9067, 9068, 9069, 9070, 9071, 9072, 9073, 9074, 9075, 9076, 9077, [10365], 16403, [16403.5] (d?), 16404, 16404.3, 16404.4, 16404.5, 16404.7, 16475, 16486.7, 16500, 16553, 16553a, 16555, 16555.5, 16769, 16769.5, [23948].
1636/37: 7756, 9078, 9080–1, 9082, 9083.
1637: 2323, 2324, 2324.3, 2324.5, 2325, 2328.5 (forged), 2328.8 (forged), 2329, 2953.3(***A***), 7757, 7757.2, 9084, [9085], 9086, 9087, 9088, 9089, 9090, 9091, 9092, 9093, 9093.5 (false), 9094, 9095, 9096, 9097, 9098, 9099, 16404.9, 16405, 16408, 16408.5, 16486.7, [18527].
1637/38: 9100, 9101, 9102, 9103–5, 9106–7, 9108, 9109.
1638: 2323, 2325, 2329, 2329.2, 2329.4, 2329.6, 2329.8, 2330–0.9

Barker, R. — *cont.*
(forged), 2334.5, 2335, 2680.7 (forged), 2953.5, 2954 (forged), 2954.3, 9110, 9111, 9112, 9113, 9114, 9115, 9116–7, 9118, 9119–20, 9121, 9122, 9123, 9124, 9125, 9126–7, 9128, 9129, 10060, [11121], 16409, 16411, 16413, 16413.3, 16413.5, 16414, 16414.3, 16414.5, 16415, 16477, 16487, 16501.
1638/39: 9130, 9131, 9132, 9133, 9134,9134.5(*A*3), 9135, 9137, 9138, 9139.
1639: 2335, 2336, 2337, 2337.3, 2339, 2342, 9140, 9141, 9142, 9143, 9144, 9145, 9146, 9147, 9148, 9149, 9150, 9335, 9335.5, 16415, 16416, 16417, 16417.2, 16417.3, 16417.5, 16417.7, 16418, 16418a, 16418b, 16418c–c.5 (forged), 16419, 16419.5, 16478, 16556, 18196, 18196a, 18196a.5 (repeat), 22005.
1639/40: 9152, 9153.
1640: 2339, 2340, 2342, 2343, 2343.3, 2343.7, 2956, 2957, 4686, 9154, 9155, 9156, 9157, 9158, 9159, 9160, 9161, 9162, 9163, 9164, 9165, 9166, 9167, 9168, 9169, 9170, 9171, 9172, 9173, 9262, 9336, 9511, 9512.5, 10061, 10080, 16421, 16421.3, 16421.5, 16422, 16488, 16502, 16557, 16558, 16558.5, 16559, 26102.
1640/41: 9175.
1641: 2340.
1642: 2340.
1644: 2316.5 (forged).

1669: 2330.6 (forged).
1673: 2330.9 (forged).

Barker, Robert, *Deputies (etc.) of.*
Exceptional forms of imprint, 1600–1625. Those for 1608 and 1608/09 read 'Deputies of' with the deputies unidentified; those for 1617–1618 read 'Deputies and assignees of' = B. Norton and J. Bill. The items indexed for other years have miscellaneous wording as indicated.
1600: 2897 dep. of, [10110 by ass't of] (d?), 10133 by ass't of.
1603: [14064?] ex assig.
1605: 2904 dep. of/by ass'ns of.
1608: 7705.4, 8419, 8420, 8421, 8422, 8423, 8424, 9219.
1608/09: 8425, 8426, 8429, 8430.
1609: 14064.3 ex assig.
1613: 1222 by ass't of.
1617: 8557, 9238.3.
1617/18: 8558, 8562, 8563, 8564, 9238.5.
1618: 2250(*A*3), 2918.3, 2918.5, 8558, 8565, [16349.3(*A*3)?] (d?), 16349.7(*A*3), 16350, 16468.
1625: 18760 by ass'ns of.

Barker, Thomas. *See* Barcker.

Barley (Barlow), William.
Bookseller in London, 1591–1614†. Freed as a Draper by **Yareth James** on 30 Sept. 1587. Transferred to the Stat. Co. in 1606. Published music, 1598?–1602 as the *assignee of* **T. Morley**. *See* also *assignee(s) of* **W. Barley**. [*Dict. 1*; DFM 640; *Poor Book*, 1612; *SB* 22 (1969): 214–23; *Library* 11 (1989): 10–46.]
shop in Newgate Market (C.4), 1591 (11921)–1595 (19855); sometimes adds: near Christ Church door, 1594 (21009)
shop (in) Gracechurch (Gratious) Street (P.4), 1592 (22140; 5867 has 'dw.')–1609 (21127); variations:
at the upper end of —, 1592 (5867)
— over against Leaden Hall, 1593 (23356); next unto L.H. gate, 1595 (14068.5)
Little St. Helen's (J.3), 1599 (1882, as assignee of T. Morley)
shop over against Cree Church near Aldgate (L.1), 1612 (6568)–1613 (19792, has 'dw.')
dw. in Bishopsgate Street (J.2), 1614 (25409)
1591: 11921 f., 15704 f.
1592: 1030.5 f. (d), 5867 sold, 5867.3 (repeat), 5871.4 f., 12789 f., [12789.5 f.] (d), 21087.3 sold, 22140 f.
1593: 18378a sold, 19535 sold, 22666 sold, 23356 sold, 25122 f.
1594: 5871.5 f., 16679 sold, 20746 (note, f.), 21009 sold, 21321 sold, 23356 sold.
1595: 1343 sold, 3665 sold, 5000 sold, 5262.5 f., 12562 f., [12924.5] sold, 12925 f., 12960 sold, 14068.5 f., 14707 f., 14708.3 sold, 17748 sold, 19855 sold, 20002 sold, 21083 f. (d), 21088 sold, 25153(*A*3) f. (d?), 25782 sold.
1596: 1433 f., 4910 f., 5323a.8 f., 5865.5 f., 14708 f., 19464 f., 19799 f., 19974 sold.

Barley, W. — *cont.*
1597: [18504.5] sold.
1598: 2495 [f.] (d?), 3696 f., 10433 f., 16680 sold, 17764 f. (d).
1599: 1882 [f.], 2497 [f.], 10697 [f.], 13563 [f.], 18131 [f.] (d).
1600: 18115.5 [f.], 25219.5 [f.].
1601: 10254 [f.], 23606.5 sold.
1602: 6566 [f.].
1603: 14939.5 f., 19766.3 f.
1604: 11501.5 f. (d).
1606: 14691.3 f., 21085 sold.
1607: 5876 sold, 6508 f., 6567 f., 10011 f., 10011.2 f., 10011.4 f.
1607/08: 23224.5 [f.].
1608: 19307 f., 25202 [f.].
1609: 14934 f., 19936(*A*3) ent., 20759(*A*3) [f.], 21127 [f.].
1610: 3791 f., 5208.5 f., 13137 f., 20755(*A*3: i), 20755(*A*3: ii) (d).
1612: 6568 f.
1613: 11358 f., 11359 f., 19792 f.
1614: 6568 ass'd, 19307 ass'd, 25409 f.

Barley, William, *Assignee(s etc.) of.*
Various forms of imprint as indicated, which were used by those who published music with Barley's permission, primarily J. Windet, T. East, T. Snodham, M. Lownes, and John Browne 1.
1606: 356 ass'n, 5679 ass'n, 7461 ass'n, 18123 ass'n.
1607: 4244.5 ex assig., 11166 ass'n.
1608: 6040 ass'n, 25204 ass'n, 26105 ass'n.
1609: 14734 [f.] ass'ns.
1610: 4258 [f.] ass'n, 14736 ass'ns.
1611: 4255 ass'n, 18132 f. ass'n.
1612: 5769 ass'd by, 7098 by ass't of, 11826 ass'n.
1613: 15588 f. ass'ns, 19923 f. ass'ns.

Barlow, Timothy.
Bookseller in London, (1615) 1616–1625. [*Dict. 1*; DFM 769.]
shop in Paul's Churchyard at the Bull Head (A.2), 1616 (1442)–1620 (11658)
1616: 1442 f., 7342 f., 13410 f. **1617:** 13074 sold. **1618:** 1443 f., 1444 f. **1620:** 11519 sold, 11658 sold. **1622:** 5537 ent. **1625:** 5537 ass'd.

Barlow, William. *See* Barley.

Barnes, John.
Bookseller in London, 1601–1625. Son of **Joseph Barnes** of Oxford; it is not clear what role, if any, John played in occasional London forgeries of his father's imprint. The 1613 address at the Harrow was also that of **William Wright 1** though no imprints were shared; it is worth noting, however, that their names both first appeared in the *Poor Book* in 1608. [*Dict. 1*; *Loan Book*, 1605–08; *Poor Book* (& wife), intermittently 1608–25.]
dw. in Fleet Street at the Great Turk (W.7), 1602 (5347)–1603 (6333, has 'Turk's Head')
without Newgate (D.9), 1605–1615; variations:
dw. — by St. Sepulchre's Church at the $ Paris, 1605 (6334)
dw. near Holborn conduit, 1612 (24187)–1613 (20304)
dw. on Snow Hill at the Harrow, 1613 (20333)
shop under the $ Cardinal's Hat —, 1614 (19201)
shop over against St. Sepulchre's Church —, 1614 (5857)–1615 (6845)
dw. in Hosier Lane near Smithfield (E.7), 1616 (1013)–1617 (20329)
dw. in the Long Walk near Christ Church (E.8), 1619 (11107)
1601: 6520.7 ent., 14695 f.
1602: 1195 ent., 1556 f., 4098a sold, 4754 ent., 4755 ent., 4756 ent., 4759 ent., 4761 ent., 4764 ent., 4765 ent., 5347 f., 13884 sold, 19773 ent., 20148 sold, 20155 sold, 20155.5 sold (forged?), 20606 ent., 21031.5 ent., 21698 ent., 22807 sold, 23913.5 sold.
1603: 2023.7 f., 6333 sold, 13885 sold.
1605: 1560 imp., 6334 sold.
1611: 6335 sold, 6846 f.
1612: 6847 f., 7343 f., 13706 sold, 13707 sold, 13708 sold, 13711 sold, 13722 sold, 14459 sold, 20138 f., 24187 sold, 24947.3 sold, 24949 sold, 25592 sold.
1613: 1861 sold, 1871 sold, 3194 ven., 4092 f., 7306 sold, 11544 sold, 13623 sold, 14957 sold, 16831 f., 16831.5 f., 19022 ven., 19171a sold, 19297 f., 20138 f., 20304 sold, 20304.5 sold (forged?), 20333 f.
1614: 5857 f., 5858 f., 19201 f., 20300 sold, 25606 ent.

Barnes, John — *cont.*
1615: 6845 f., 7319 f.
1616: 1013 f., 1196 f. (forged?), 13567 f., 13567.5 f., 18585 f. (forged?), 19778 ent., 20330 f., 20609.5 sold.
1617: 20329 f., 21603 sold, 21603.3 sold (d?).
1619: 1196(*A*) ass'd, 4193 ass'd, 4199.5 ass'd, 5835 sold, 7325 ass'd, 11106 f., 11107 f., 11107.3 f., 12622 ass'd, 13014 ass'd, 13030 ass'd, 13512 ass'd, 13515.5 ass'd, 14975 ass'd, 14986 ass'd, 14987 ass'd, 16698 ass'd, 18497 f., 20346 ass'd, 20352 ass'd, 20619 ass'd, 21833 ass'd, 21841 ass'd, 21845 ass'd, 22372.3 sold, 22879 ass'd, 24596.5 sold.
1620: 6105 ass'd, 11545 ass'd, 17620.5 f.
1621: 2024.7 f., 21510 ass'd.

Barnes, Joseph.
Bookseller and printer in Oxford, 1573–1617 (1618†). Father of **John Barnes**. **Printer to the University** (*see* Oxford University) from 1584. For a complete listing of all items printed in Oxford during his tenure, including bookplates, *see* Index 2Ai. From documentary evidence he had a house at the West end of St. Mary's Church. [*Dict. 1.*]
No address used.
1585: 3071, 4759 ex off., 7286 ex aed., 7287 ex aed., 13960.5 ex off. (d?), 19340 ex off., 19340.5 typis, 19359.1–60.7 (note: most eds. may be forged), 20371, 20371.5, 23021.5 (d).
1586: 2762, 3552.3 ex off., 4837–8 ex off., 4999.7, 5002, 5789, [5789a] (false), 6167 ex off., 10215 (d), 14016 (d), 14017 (d), 14635 ex off., 17631, 18924, [19887] (d), 20184, 20368.5, 20621, 20621.5, 22405 (d), 22406 ex off., [24568] (false).
1587: 2025, 15387 typis, 19611, 20369, 20612 ex off., 22551 ex off., 22552, 23107 ex off. (d), 24532.
1588: 4755, 4761, 13030, 13031, 13966, 20368, 23937.
1589: 13099 ex off., 13206 ex off., 14015 (d), 21031.5, 22619, 24533.
1590: 1181 ex off., 11734, 14814, 24279 ex off.
1591: 1464.8, 12589, 13225 in off., 23019, 23642(*A*3), 24275 ex off., 24534.
1592: 1430, 2003, 3552.5 ex off., 3683, 3845 (note), 4763, 5237, 7600, 10215.5 (d), 11515, 11516, 17002, 19017.5 ex off., 21733 (d), 24042, 25841a.5.
1593: 751, 11500, 11732, 23024.
1594: 1653, 15109, 15556, 19336, 20157, 23023, 24277.
1595: 10139.7 (d?), 18061, 24277.5, 24535, [25260].
1596: 4758 ex off., 4760 ex off., 10943, 10944, 18114, 19772.5, [19945a] (d?), 20606 ap., 24520–0.5.
1597: 196 ex off., [3716.5] (d), 4196.5, 4765 ex off., 6575, 14976, 19945, 20207, 20612.2 ex off., 22555 ex off., 25722 ex off.
1598: 36 ex off., 958.5, 1997 ex off., 2362.3, 4197, 4764, 14086, 16698, 20158 ex off.
1599: 959, 4754, 4756 (d), 10304 (d), 13596, 14977, 21137, [24600.5].
1600: 4198, 13596.5, 14978, 19773, 21089, 23913, 24527.
1601: 10934, 13597, 18926, [19002.5] (d?), 24536.
1602: 1195, 4012, 4098a, 13442, 13442.5 (forged), 13884, 13886, 13886.5, 14641, [20146.5] (false), 20148, 20155, 20155.5 (forged), 21698, 22807, 23913.5.
1603: 3716, 4636, 6333, 10143, [11740.5] (d?), [11948] (d), 13885, 19010–0.5, 19011, 19012, 19012a (d), 19018, 19019, 20587 ap., 23295, 24947.7, 25759.
1604: 37, 5755a.5, 5756, 10307, 13899, 19013, 19172, 19296, 20144, 21734, 21736, 23947.
1605: 6334, 10305, 14023, 14035, 14449 ap., [14449.5] (d), 15006, [19016] (d), 19043, 19049.5 ap., 21735, 21737, 24036 (d?), 24947, 24952.
1606: 13887, 14974, [19002.7] (d), 19046, 20773, 24263, 24881, 24948.
1607: 4097, 5393, 5702, 6172, 14452, 14975, 14985, 20362, 24939, 24939.5.
1608: 5126, 5671, 12621, 12621a, 14445, 14986, 14987, [15266.5] (d?), 19016.1, 19171, 20296, 20298, 20301, 20612.3 ex off., 21743, 24405, 24936, 25589.
1609: 4192, 6172a, 7325, 7325.5, 13014, 20914, 21700.
1610: 1867, 4091, 7354, 10305.5, 13622, 14446, 20292, 20630, 22877.8, 22890.5, 25858.3.
1611: 1870, 6335, 14534 (forged), 20941.
1612: 5394 (forged), 6420, 6422, [7343], 13706, 13707, 13708, 13711, 13722, 14459, 18164–4.5, 19020, 19047, 19170, 19896.5, 20773a, 20941.3 ap., 21033, 21833, 21841, 21845, 22791, 22878,

Barnes, Joseph — *cont.*
24187, 24251, 24947.3, 24949, 25592.
1613: 1546, 1861, 1869, 1871, 2749, 3194, 4117, 4242, 5571, 7306, 11544, 11907, 13515, 13623, 13709, 14957, 19022, 19044, 19048, 19171a, 19814, 20133, 20172, 20291, 20299, 20304, 20304.5 (forged), 20612.5, 20612.7, 20613, 20619.
1614: 594, 1868, 6389, 6425, 11956, 12045, 13723, 14594, [19003] (d), [19016.2] (d), 19043.5, 20300, 20331, 20344, 20352, 20609, 20612.7, 20613.
1615: 698 (d), 1872, 5756.5, 6421, 6423, 6426, 10140, 10583–4, 12622, 16447, 18143, 20346, 21701, 22826, 24940.
1616: 1196 (forged), 11461, 11957, 11965, 13971.5, 18585 (forged), 19777.5, 19778–8.5, 20609.5, 21106.
1617: 7278, 22827.

Barnes, Richard.
Stationer in London, (1631) 1632. [*Dict. 1*; DFM 1235.]
No address used.
1632: 12027 f.

Barnes, Roger.
Bookseller in London, (1609) 1610–1627. He sold his first book in the shop of his former master, **John Smethwick**: in St. Dunstan's Churchyard under the dial (W.9). [*Dict. 1*; DFM 2390; *Poor Book*, 1627.]
shop in Chancery Lane over against the Rolls (W.10e), 1611 (1428)–1613 (23248)
shop in St. Dunstan's Churchyard in Fleet Street (W.9), 1615 (10783)
1610: 14816 sold. **1611:** 1428 f. **1612:** 4275 ent., 17439–9.5 f., 24136 ent. **1613:** 23248–8a f. **1615:** 10783 f., 23249 sold.

Barrenger (Barringer), William.
Bookseller in London, (1608) 1609–1631† (*C-B C*: 234). In partnership with **Bartholomew Sutton**, 1609–10. [*Dict. 1*; DFM 1772.]
at the great North door of St. Paul's Church (A.2), 1609 (14758, with B. Sutton)–1627 (23250.5, has 'dw.'); variation: 1611 (13325, has 'shop')
1069: 20999 f. (d/error).
1609: 6637.5 f., 13018.3 f., 14758 f., 15537.5 f., 20999 f. (d).
1610: 15537.5.
1611: 13325 f.
1612: 6184 f., 6638 f.
1613: 7433 sold.
1617: 15538 f.
1618: 15538 f.
1620: 11838 f.
1627: 23250.5 f.

Barrett, Hannah.
Bookseller in London, 1624–1626. Widow of **William Barrett**. Often published jointly with **Richard Whitaker**, whose address, if any, is given: at the King's Head in Paul's Churchyard (A.3). [*Dict. 1.*]
No separate address used.
1624: 12635 f. (note)
1625: 1115 f., 1147 f., 1148 f., 1174 f., 1174.5 f., 5030 f., 13552 f., 14625 f.
1626: 1116 f., 1149 ass'd.

Barrett, William.
Bookseller in London, (1605) 1608–1624†. Husband of **Hannah Barrett**. Often published jointly with others whose addresses, if any, are given, especially **Edward Blount**: at the Black Bear in Paul's Churchyard (B), in whose shop Barrett may have worked, e.g. in 1610 (24833(*A*3)). [*Dict. 1*; DFM 378.]
in Paul's Churchyard, 1608–1618
shop — at the Green Dragon (A.3), 1608 (17651)
dw. — at the Three Pigeons (A.3), 1614 (25390)–1618 (22772); no later use noted
1608: 1201 f. (d), 17651 f., 25394 f.
1609: 12686 f. (d?), 13541 f., 15460 f., 17417 f., 20772 f., 26055 f.
1610: 5659 f., 5808 ent., 10425 f., 13473 f., 19565 f., 24833 f., 25395 f.
1611: 11099 f.
1612: 4915 f., 25396 f.

Barrett, W. — *cont.*
1613: 12686.3 f. (d?), 13474 f., 17418 f., 18042 f., 25659.5 f.
1614: 4930–0.5 f., 5469 imp., 25390 f.
1615: 13475 f., 17527 f., 21726 f., 22771 f., 22962 f., 25392 f.
1616: 6996 ent., 6998 ent., 13475 f., 18903 ent., 21019 f., 25397 f.
1617: 11258 f., 13046 ent., 13476 f., 16834 f., 17064 f., 20154 ent., 22361 f., [22544a.3 f.?] (d?), [22544a.5 f.?] (d?), 25380 f.
1618: 18179 f., 22772 f.
1619: 18180 f.
1620: 7148 f. (d?), 15641 ass'd, 22965 f., 25372 f.
1621: 4528 ent., 14969–9.5 f., 18963.3 f., 21727 f.
1622: 1155 imp., 1159 f., 1160 f., 1185 f., 13046 f.
1623: 5031 f., 5032 f., 5033 f., 5470 imp., 11923 f., 18963.7 f.
1624: 12648c imp., 13455 f., 14624 f., 14624.5 f., 18038 f., 18039 f., 24508.7 ent., 24508.9(*A*3), 24509 f., 24925–5a f., 25389–9.5 f., 25389a f.

Barrevelt, Gerardus.
Stationer in London? 1494–1495. In partnership with **Frederick Egmont**. [Duff, *Century*.]
No address used.
1494: [15797 f.] (d), 15874 imp., 16167 imp.
1495: [15801 f.], [15801.5 f.] (d?).

Barrouwe, A. *See* Berghen.

Bars, John.
Stationer? or patron? in London? 1503. His only book was published jointly with **George Chastelayn**. [Duff, *Century*.]
No address used.
1503: 14079 at instance of (d).

Barthelet. *See* Berthelet.

Bartlet, John.
Bookseller in London, 1619–c. 1658. Most publications of his first two years bear the address of his former master, **Thomas Man 1**: at the Talbot in Paternoster Row (C.7). Bartlet was in trouble with the authorities in 1637–38, imprisoned, and forced to move his shop. [*Dict. 2*; DFM 1906; *Loan Book*, 1639–42.]
at the Gilded (Gilt) Cup in Cheapside (N.5), 1620 (24953)–1637 (4599, has 'shop'); sometimes adds: in Goldsmiths' Row, 1621 (23840), 1634 (23842, has 'Golden' Cup); one misprint gives the erroneous sign: Gilt 'Bible', 1635 (4596)
near St. Austin's gate (A.7), 1638–1640
shop in Paul's Churchyard —, 1638 (21341)
shop at the Gilt Cup —, 1639 (22488)–1640 (12826, omits 'shop')
1619: 23837 f.
1620: 22427 ent., 22427a f., 23830.7 f., 23831 f., 23838 f., 24953 f.
1621: 23840 f., 24553.5 f.
1622: 12831 f., 18507.56A f., 23843 f., 25233 f.
1623: 4681 f., 23841 f.
1624: 1413 f., 1415 f., 1415.5 f., 12832 f., 12839.5 f., 12839.7 f., 12840 f., 14485 f., 21479 pro, 23853 f., 23854–5 f., 24554 f.
1625: 12840a f., 20389 f., 23854–5 f.
1626: 12821 f., 12829 f., 12833 f., 12836 f., 12837 f., 12841 f., 12850 f., 22922 f.
1627: 12842 f., 12852.5 f., 19583 f., 19591 f.
1628: 12824 f., 12825 f., 12847 f., 12851.5 f., 12853 f., 14127 f., 19584 f., 23832 f., 23845 f.
1629: 12843 f., 19569a.5 f., 19573 sumpt., 19578 f., 19586 f., 19592 f., 23833 f., 23846 f.
1630: 12114 f., 12822 f., 12830 sold, 12838 f., 12851 sold, 12851.7 f., 12852 f., 12854 f., 14715 f., 23850 f.
1631: 12115 f., 12834 f., 12844 f., 19582 f., 19588 sumpt., 23850a f., 24554a f.
1632: 1635 ent., 1649 ent., 12854.5 f., 12855 f., 19585 f., 23519 f., 23834 f., 23847 f.
1633: 22492 ent., 23847.5 f., 23856 f.
1634: 12816 f., 12845 f., 23842 f., 25409.5 f., 25410 f.
1635: 4596 f., 12816 f., 19570 f., 23848 f., 23849 f.
1636: 4597 f., 4598 f., 23819.5 f. (d?), 25411 f.
1637: 4599 f.
1638: 21341 f., 21341.5 f.
1639: 22488 sold, 22492 sold.
1640: 4615.5 f., 12395 f., 12826 f., 12846 f., 24958 ent., 24959.5 f.

Bartlet, William.
Journeyman printer? and bookseller in London, 1574–1587. Undoubtedly the William Bartlay apprenticed for ten years to Alexander Lacy in 1564 (Arber I.230). [*Dict. 1*.]
in St. Sepulchre's parish, (D.8) 1574 (19936.5(*A*3)); no later address used.
1574: 19936.5(*A*3) [f.]. **1578:** 4322 [f.] (d?), 18438 [f.] (d). **1581:** 6095 ass'd. **1582:** 10608.5 f. (d?). **1583:** 10844.8 (note).

Bassandyne, Thomas.
Printer, bookseller, and bookbinder in Edinburgh, 1564–1577†. **King's Printer in Scotland**, 1572–1573. His widow, Catherine, may have been responsible for the 1578 item; she later remarried **Robert Smyth**. [*Dict. 1*.]
dw. at the Nether Bow, 1572/73 (21941)–1575 (16580); 1578 (16580.3, omits 'dw.')
1565: 2996.3(*A*) at expenses. **1571:** 185.5. **1572:** 21938 (d). **1572/73:** 21941. **1573:** 21942 (d), 21943 (d), 21943a (d). **1574:** 15660. **1575:** 16580, [21944.5] (d). **1576:** 2125.

1578: 16580.3 [widow?].

Basse (Baise), Robert.
Bookseller in London, (1614) 1615–1616. [*Dict. 1*; DFM 1350.]
shop under St. Botolph's Church (F.3), 1615 (6503)–1616 (6504, F, HN copies adding: without Aldersgate)
1615: 6503 f. **1616:** 6504 f.

Basson, Thomas.
Bookseller in Cologne, c. 1578–c.1583, and in Leiden (printer from 1594), c. 1584–1613?†. His 1586–87 imprints below, with the exception of 25340, were printed by or in the shop of **Andries Verschout**. Basson later acquired some of the printing material and unsold sheets of **Nikolaus Bohmberg**. [*Dict. 1*; Gruys; J. A. van Dorsten, *Thomas Basson*, Leiden, 1961; *Quaerendo* 15 (1985): 195–224.]
1586: 17847.8, 25340 [sold].
1587: 7285.5, 7287.5, [7288.5] (d), 7289.4, [7289.5] (d).
1599: 18468.5.
1609: 9211.2, 9211.3 (false), 9211.4 (false).

Bastiaensz, Matthijs, *Widow of.*
Printer in Rotterdam, 1628–1648. [Gruys.]
1639: 24869.5.

Bate, Humphrey.
Stationer in London, 1579–1600. The term 'clothworker' describing him in 1579 (Arber II.96) is apparently an erroneous repetition of the profession of his apprentice's father. [*Dict. 1*; *St. Giles*, 1600.]
shop in Paternoster Row at the Black Horse (C.7), 1587? (2779.5)
1587: 2779.5 f. (d?).

Bateman (Batman), Stephen.
Author and translator, fl. 1534–1584†. [*DNB*.]
No address used.
1580: 1584 f. (d?).

Battersby, John, *Assignees of.*
Partners in working the patent of Battersby as **King's (Queen's) Printer for Latin, Greek, and Hebrew**, 1597–1604, and again in 1613–1619, after Battersby's patent was upheld following a period during which **John 1** and **Bonham Norton** successfully contested it. In effect the partners contented themselves with publishing two lucrative titles: 'Lily's Grammar' and Camden's Greek grammar. In 1598 the assignees were: C. Burby, T. Dawson, W. Leake 1, and E. White 1 (Arber III.133); in 1619 after Battersby's death they were: T. Adams, Eliz. Bishop, E. Blount, J. Dawson 1, W. Leake 1, B. Norton, G. Swinhowe, and S. Waterson (*C-B C*: 117). [*Dict. 1*; *C-B C*: xii, 116–18.]
No address used.
1597: 15623 [f.].
1598: 4511.7 per assig.
1599: 15623.5 [f.], 15624 [f.].
1602: 15624.5 [f.].
1604: 4512 per assig.

Battersby, J., *Assignees of — cont.*
1613: 15626.5.
1615: 4513.7 per assig.
1617: 4514 per assig., 15626.7 per assig.
1619: 15626.8, 23279 typis.

Baudous, Robert de.
Engraver and printseller in Amsterdam, 1591–1644, and later in Leiden. [*Dict. 1*; Gruys; Thieme-Becker.]
1608: 11810 (note: A3, B2b) chez/to buy at.

Baudry, Guillaume.
Bookseller in Paris, 1628–1640 at least. [*Dict. 1*; Lottin 2: 8.]
1640: 10890.

Bayly, Baylie. *See* Bailey.

Beadle (Bedell, Bedle), Thomas.
Journeyman printer in London, (1590) 1602 (*Reg. B*: 84)–1618 (1635†). Apprenticed to R. Day in 1580, to G. Dewes in 1581; freed by T. Dawson in 1590 (Arber II.98, 105, 707). Signed the journeymen's petition in 1613 (*C-B C*: 437). Used materials of **John Bill** except for a ship cut belonging to **Edward Allde.** [Not in *Dict. 1*; *Loan Book* (as Bedell), 1602–10, 1623–26; *Poor Book*, 1626–35, widow thereafter.]
No address used.
1618: 16785.3 [f.].

Beale, John.
Printer in London, (1608) 1611–1643†. At various times he shared a printing house with others: in 1611-13 with **William Hall**, in 1613 with **John Pindley**, in 1629–30 with **Thomas Brudenell**, and in 1640 with **Stephen Bulkley;** the rare occasions during these years when two names appear in an imprint are indicated by an asterisk (*). Items without imprint before 1614 where Beale's name has been supplied may well have been printed by his partner at the relevant date. The 'Iohn Beale Printer' buried in 1625 (*St. Giles*) was possibly his son. [*Dict. 2*; DFM 2631.]
No address noted.
1115: 14666 (d/error).
1609: 9175q (note).
1611: [23039] (d), [23039d] (d?), [23039e] (d?), [23039e.2] (d?), 23045*.
1612: 363*, 1141, 4683*, 12814 ent., 17530–0.3(*A*3), 22395, [23039.2] (d?), [23039a] (d?), [23039e.3] (d?), 23055 ent.
1613: 1064.5, [1453], [3704.3], [3704.5], [6247], 7140, 7142*, 21754, 13822.5*, 13930*, 17531, 20611, 20915, 22125, [23039.2A(*A*)], [23039.3] (d?), [23039d.2] (d?), [22945.5] (d), 23067, 23067.2, 23067.4, 24314, 25281, [25840].
1614: 840.5, [841], 1065, 3578, 4032.3(*A*3), 4236, 6568 ent., 6935, 6935.5, 9175q ent., 10190.7, 12986, 13471, 14578(*A*3) ent., 14691.7 ent., [14845?] (d?), [15267], 19307 ent., 21401 ent., 22976, 23273, 23274, [23658], 23810, 25409 ent., [25605.5] (false), 26022.5, 26023.
1615: 73, [2551], 3588, 3927, 5700, [5859], [9175q: ii?] (c?), 12113, 12126, 12736, 13919, 14292, 14311, [14418.5?], [14419], [14419.7], 14665 ex off., 14666 (d), [14850] (c), 15267.3, 17342, [18590], 18621, [23039d.3] (d?), 23056, [24588], [24916.7?] (c?).
1616: [1686], 10709, 11522, 12122, 12126.5, 14054, 14054.5, 21714, 23031, [23039d.4] (d?), 23056.5, 23067.8, 23068, [23731.3?], 23811, [24589].
1617: [1143] (forged, c), [3322.5?], 3511, [9343.5(*A*3)] (c?), [11527], 12221, 13401, 18205, 19873.5, 20187, 20187a, 21098, [22984.7?], [23039.4] (d?), [23039d.5] (d?), [23100a?], [23731.5?], 26096, [26096a].
1618: 1626, [3062.2] (d?), 3568.5, 5809, 11597, 12747, 13411, 13412, 13423, [14844?] (d?), 15268.3, 20807, 21098.3, [23039a.2] (d?), [23039d.6] (d?), [23039f] (d?), 24024.
1619: 148 ent., [1670], 3511.5, 3782, 7409 ent., 7569, 8597 (d), 8597.5, [8611] (d), 8613 (d), 9240 (d), 10329.3, 11560, 11873, 11933, 12123, 12747, 13379–9a, 13412.5, 14388.3, 14513, 15364, 17770, 21244, 22636, [22933.5] (d?), [23039d.7] (d?).
1620: [1144] (forged, c), [6766.5?] (c?), [7615.7] (c), [10945.6], 13379a, 13402, 13413.5, 14388.5, [15365.7–66], [16838?], 17372, 18623, [19320?], 23032, [23039f.2] (c), 25890.
1620/21: [448.6?], [515.4?].

Beale, J. — *cont.*
1621: 11560.5, 11874, 12127, 13402.2, 14388.7, [15366] (d), [16840?], 22774.
1622: 3782.5, 3512, 13413a, 16640 ent., 22933.7, [23039d.8] (d?).
1623: 3512, 3840, 12127.5, 17065, 17343, 20808, 22934, [23039.5] (d?), 23046.3, [23046.7–47], 23488 ent.
1624: [1425?], [6269] (d), 6935.7, [7455], 7616, [8459] (c?), 12635–5b, 13381, 13397 ent., 14578, 18624.5, 19768.5 (note), 21245, [22067?] (false), [22084?] (false), [22084a?] (false), 22351.
1625: 5537 ent., 12635 (note, (*A*3) ent.), 13381, 13413a.3–a.5.
1626: 3783, 12109, 13403, 23065 ap., 23065.5 ap., 23069.5 ex off. (d?), 24617.
1627: 3513, 11395, 12109, 12109a, 12128.
1628: [5316], 12636–7.7, 13385 ent., 13413a.7, 25059 (d).
1629: 162*, 5852, 5911*, 7617, [10699], 11561, 16640 ent., 17743, 23489*, 25060.
1630: 4229, [4327], [4500], [12114], 13414, [20687?], 23725, 23774.
1631: 291, 1551.7, 1909.7 ex off., 4911–1.2, 6031, 7315, 7409, 10938–9, [11120], 11561.3, 12129, 12529, 12844, 13313, 14753.5, [15036–6a], 15463, 15557.5, 19588, 20271, 21211, [21371], 22117, [23340], 23732, [23745], [23745.5], 23811.7, [23824?].
1632: 1909.7 ex off., 1930, 3784, 4661, 5127.5, [11080], 12855, 13018.7, 13168, 13404, 13414a, [13458], 13913, 13988, 14442, [15463.5], 15534, 17443–3.5, 17638–8.5, 19390, 19496.5, [20641.5?], [20642?], [23340], [23517.5], [23518], 24143, 25845.
1633: 22.5, 1400, 3515, 5537, [6789?], [6929.5(*A*3)?], 7536.1, 11156, 11164, 11982, 12888, 13383.5–84, 13988, 16640, 16640.5, 17412, 17708, [17715], 18626a.8, 18881, 19580.5, 20003.5–04, 20235, 20275, 20276, [20433?], [22063], [22461], 23518.5, 23732.3, 23856, 24695.
1634: [1541], 1552, 3515, 7618, 12639–40, 13383.5–84, 13427 ent., [20249], [20273], [21416], [23842], [24956].
1635: 1552, [6934.3] (c?), 7394, 7397, 7409a, 10381.7, 10710, 12130, 13377.9 (d?), 13384, 13384.7 ent., 13405, 13415, 14593, 14691.7–.9, [16641] (c), [17719?], [17783], 18626, [20237], [20282], [20603], 23732.7, 23732.8(*A*3), [23849], 24116, [24145], 25292.3.
1636: [1981], [3368.5-Tonbridge] (d), 3515.3, 3515.4, 4145.5, [6572], [10172] (d?), 10409, [10865.5], 12130.5, 13416, [15464], 18626.5, [23889.8], 25991.
1637: 3785, 10147.11 (d?), 12110.5, 19307.5, 23573.
1638: 4310, 7536.4, 13405.5, 25823.
1639: 1151, 6107, 10410, 12110.5, 13416.5, 23733.
1640: 11561.5, 12983*, [16641.3?] (c?), 18626a, 20491*.
1642: [22084?] (false, d/error).

Bearkes (Barkes, Berke, Birks, Byrke), Randall.
Stationer in London, 1602–1619, 1633–1638, apparently spending the interim in Bermuda (*Poor Book*). [*Dict. 1*; *Poor Book*, (& wife) as 'Byrke' 1608, as 'Berke' 1611-19, 1633, 1638; *St. Giles* (I.4), 1606–12.]
at the White Unicorn in Pope's Head Alley (O.11), 1602 (3699)
1602: 3699 f., 13929 ent.

Beauchesne, Jean de. *See* De Beau Chesne.

Beckeneth, Balthasar, *pseud.*
Printer in 'Strassburg', 1531. = M. de Keyser, Antwerp.
1531: 2777.

Becket, James.
Bookseller in London, 1636–1641. Son of **Leonard Becket**; stepson of **Nicholas Vavasour.** [*Dict. 2*; DFM 701.]
shop in (at) the Inner Temple gate (W.11), 1636 (13311)–1640 (22377, adds: in Fleet Street); in one item there is apparently a misprint: at the 'Middle' Temple gate, 1638 (19517)
1636: 13311 sold.
1637: 13364 f.
1638: 6492 sold, 15014 sold, 15465 f., 19517 f., 19518 f., 22841.3 sold.
1639: 11273 sold.
1640: 17889 sold, 22377 f., 22447 sold, 23706 sold.

Becket, Leonard.
Bookseller in London, (1605) 1608–1632?†. Father of **James Becket.** His widow remarried **Nicholas Vavasour**, who had taken over the shop in 1633. [*Dict. 1*; DFM 1632; *Poor Book*, 1616 as 'Berkett'.]

Becket, L. — *cont.*
shop in the Temple near (to) the church (W.11), 1608 (23433.5)–1632 (1909.7); variations:
shop in the Inner Temple, 1615 (18514), 1618 (6234.3, omits 'Inner')
shop near the Temple church, 1624 (997.5)
1608: 23433.5 f.
1609: 22061.5 f.
1610: 6016 f.
1611: 6018 f., 24753 f.
1612: 19298 f.
1613: 1908.5 sumpt. (d), 4316 f.
1614: 22062 f.
1615: 4897 ent., 18514 f.
1616: 1909 sumpt., 14358 f.
1618: 6234.3 f., 24892 f.
1619: 1547 f.
1620: 1548 f., 13050.5 f., 13051.3 ent., 18515 f.
1621: 1549 f., 13051 f.
1622: 1909.3 sumpt., 5372 sold.
1623: 1000 f., 1549.5 f.
1624: 997.5 f., 998 f., 5374 sold.
1627: 1550 f., 5835.5 f.
1628: 1551 f.
1629: 1551.3 f.
1630: 1551.5 f., 13051.3 f.
1631: 1551.7 f., 1909.7 sumpt.
1632: 1909.7 sumpt.

Bedell (Bedle), Thomas. *See* Beadle.

Bee, Cornelius.
Bookseller in London, 1634–1672†. Not a member of the Stat. Co. Published jointly with **Laurence Sadler** in 1635 and 1639/40. [*Dict. 2.*]
at the King's Arms in Little Britain (F.4), 1634 (20099a)–1640 (19210, omits sign, with L. Sadler)
1634: 20099a f. **1635:** 21817.3 f. **1639/40:** 19210 sumpt.

Beeston (Beaston), Hugh.
Bookseller in London, (1631) 1633–1634. [*Dict. 1*; DFM 848.]
shop near (next) the Castle in Cornhill (O.7), 1633 (11156; 11164, has 'dw.')–1634 (11157)
1633: 11156 f., 11164 f. **1634:** 11157 f.

Bell, Henry.
Journeyman printer and bookseller in London, (1602) 1604–1641†. Apprenticed to A. Jeffes in 1594, turned over to R. Robinson in 1597; freed by R. Bradock in 1602 (Arber II.199, 217, 731). Father of **Moses Bell**, who became his partner in 1628. One item in 1607 (19541) has an address called 'his' shop which is actually that of his co-publisher, F. Faulkner: in New Fish Street near to Eastcheap (T.4). [*Dict. 1*; *Loan Book*, 1626–32; *Poor Book*, 1626–41, widow thereafter.]
on Holborn Hill (V.6), 1606–1610
dw. —, sold at his shop next the cross, 1606 (12337)
shop — near the $ Cross Keys, 1608 (24414)–1610 (22886)
(near) Bishopsgate, 1613–1619
shop within — (J.2), 1613 (12335.5, 17703)
shop without — (K.2), 1614 (12337.6)–1619 (3497)
shop at the Sun in Bethlehem (Bethlem (K.1)), 1620 (12333)–1621 (12248)
(at) the Hospital gate (near) Smithfield (E.8), 1622–1623
shop at the Lame —, 1622 (17440)
shop within — in —, 1622 (21382)
shop within St. Bartholomew's gate near —, 1623 (3498)
dw. in the Little Old Bailey in Eliot's Court (D.1), 1627 (19544)–1631 (3499, has 'his house'); no later use noted
1606: 12337 f.
1607: 19541 f.
1608: 24414 f., 24414.5 f.
1609: 12335.3 f.
1610: 22886 f.
1613: 12335.5 f., 12337.5 f., 17703 f.
1614: 12337.6 f.
1615: 5567 f., 12336 f., 14720 f., 23511.5 f., 25743 f.
1616: 11077 sold, 12327 f., 12333.5 f.
1617: 12236 f., 12247 f., 17440 ent.

Bell, H. — *cont.*
1618: 12328 f., 18413.3 sold, 18413.5 sold.
1619: 3497 f., 22886.5 f.
1620: 12329 f., 12333 f., 19080.5 f.
1621: 3504 f., 11545 f., 12237 f., 12248 f.
1622: 17440–0a f., 21382 f.
1623: 143 f., 3498 f.
1627: 19544 f.
1628: 12331 f., 12332 f., 12335 f.
1629: 12249 f.
1630: 19544.5 f. (c).
1631: 3499 f., 15718 f., 22887 f.
1634: 12331.5 f., 12332a f.
1637: 12238 f., 12250 f.

Bell, Moses.
Bookseller and printer (sometime after 1640) in London, (1624) 1628–1648?†. In partnership with his father, **Henry Bell**, from 1628, probably in Eliot's Court (D.1). [*Dict. 2*; DFM 703; *Loan Book*, 1632–35, 1645–48.]
No address noted before 1641.
1628: 12331 ent., 12332 ent., 12335 ent. **1632:** 15718 ent. **1634:** 12331.5 f., 12332a f. **1637:** 12238 f., 12250 f.

Bellamy, John.
Bookseller in London, 1620–1654†. The first two years his items were sold in the shop of his former master, **Nicholas Bourne**: at the South entrance of the Royal Exchange (O.8). In 1640 Bellamy took on **Ralph Smith** as partner. [*Dict. 2*; DFM 849.]
in Cornhill near the Royal Exchange (O.9), 1622–1640 at least
shop at the Two Greyhounds —, 1622 (17744)–1623 (25210)
shop at the Three Golden Lions —, 1624 (25855)–1640 (23303, with R. Smith, has 'their' shop); sometimes omits 'in Cornhill', 1624 (11274)
1620: 22837 f.
1621: 3589 f., 20283 f., 20284 f., 20286 f., 22111 f., 23861 f.
1622: 213 f., 217 ent., 218 f., 4023 f., 5727 f., 6149 f., 11134 ent., 17744 f., 20074 f., 20285 f., 20285.3(*A*3) f., 21012 ent., 22565.5 f.
1623: 11511.2(*A*) sold (d?), 22568 f., 25210 f., 25210a.5 f.
1624: 4236.2 f., 11274 f., 13381 sold (note), 22877.2 sold, 23598 f., 25848 f., 25855 f.
1625: 1434 f., 1657 f., 4236.9 ent., 11998 f., 11999 f., 17388 f.
1626: 219 f., 6370 sold, 21112a ent.
1627: 219 f., 1439.5 f., 3770b.2 f., 13431 pro, 18484 f., 21219 f., 25217 f.
1629: 21012 f.
1630: 5854 f., 5854.2 f., 14489 f., 18485 f., 20682 f., 25211 f.
1631: 11463 f., 17730 f., 19652.5 sold, 19653.5 sold, 19653b.5 sold, 22112 f., 25770 ent., 25770.5 f.
1632: 4236.3 f., 17730.2(*A*3) f., 22563 f., 25207.3 f., 25207.5 f., 25212 f., 25213a f., 25214 f., 25215 f., 25217.3 f.
1633: 4223 f., 5454 f., 21167 f., 21169 f., 25207 f., 25211.3 f., 25216 f.
1634: 5855 f., 23598.5 f., 25212.5 f., 25957 f.
1635: 17389 f., 19070.3 f., 21170 f., 21171 f., 21173 f., 25958 f.
1636: 21172 f., 21173 f., 25208 f., 25208.3 f., 25208.5 f., 25211.5 sold, 25213a.5 f., 25214.5 f., 25216.5 f., 25217.5 f., 25218 sold.
1637: 4236.6 f., 4237 f., 12039 ent., 24758 f., 25209 f.
1638: 21114 f., 22569 f., 24759 f., 24760 f.
1639: 220 f., 17390 f., 18981 f., 25959 sold.
1640: 232 ent., 4225 f., 21168 f., 21173 f., 23299 f., 23300 f., 23303 f., 23304 f., 23306 f., 23307–7.5 f., 23308 f., 23309 f., 23310 f., 23311 f., 23312 f., 23313 f., 24049 sold.

Bellerus (Bellère, Beelaert), Balthazar.
Printer and bookseller in Antwerp, 1589, and in Douai, 1590–1639†. Son-in-law of **Jean Bogard**. [*Dict. 1*; Rouzet.]
1626: 16769.9(*A*3) ex off. **1631:** [18066] (d?). **1632:** 1802.

Bellerus, Joannes, *pseud.*
Printer in 'Douai', 1575. = W. Carter, London. For the genuine Bellerus, active 1553–1595† *see* Rouzet.
1575: 274.

Bellet, François.
Printer in St. Omer, 1603–1609, and later in Ypres to 1624? [Lepreux I.100.]
1603: [19416]. **1604:** [19413], [19414], [19416]. **1606:** [19352]. **1607:** [19354.5], [19417]. **1609:** [6991.5] (false), [6991.7] (false), [22813].

Beltrano, Ottavio.
Printer in Naples, 1622–1647 at least. [Rhodes.]
1635: 17920.5 ap.

Benard. *See* Bernard.

Benneyman. *See* Bynneman.

Bense, Peter.
Frenchman, teacher of languages, and author in Oxford, 1637. [Wood, *Ath. Ox.* I.624.]
No address used.
1637: 1885 imp.

Benson, E.
Bookseller in London, 1636. The name occurs only on the engr. tp of one item and is undoubtedly an error for J. Benson.
No address used.
1636: 22968 sold.

Benson, John.
Bookseller in London, (1631) 1635–1667†. [*Dict. 2*; DFM 1875; *Loan Book*, 1634–40.]
shop in St. Dunstan's Churchyard in Fleet Street (W.9), 1635 (21470)–1640 (25177) at least
1635: 21470 f.
1636: 18383 sold, [22968(*A3*)?] sold.
1637: 10324 f., 11066 f., 11067 f. (forged), 17219 f., 23509 f.
1638: 17220 f., 17759–9.5 f.
1639: 6307 (note), 21056.4 f.
1640: 5549.7 f., 13798 f., 14771 f., 22344 sold, 25177–7a f.

Berghe, N. van den. *See* Hill.

Berghen (Barrouwe), Adriaen van.
Printer in Antwerp, c. 1500–1541 (1542†). [Duff, *Century*; Rouzet.]
1503: [782] (d?). **1510:** 13606 (d?).

Bernard (Benard), Guillaume.
Bookseller in Rouen, 1490–1517 at least. [Duff, *Century*; Muller 98.]
1506: 16182 imp. **1508:** 16182a imp. **1514:** 16194 exp. **1516:** [16103 f.] (d?), 16196 imp. **1517:** 16104 sumpt., 16222 imp.

Berthelet (Barthelet), Thomas.
Printer in London, 1524–1555†. **King's Printer,** 1530–1547. Probably the Thomas Bercula, printer, who was a servant to **John Rastell** in 1517 and later worked for **Richard Pynson**. Uncle of **Thomas Powell**, who may have assumed responsibility for the printing house c. 1548 and occasionally continued to use imprints 'in the house of T. B.' or 'in the house late T. B.'s' after Berthelet's death. Master of **Henry Wykes,** to whom the house ultimately passed. Berthelet's sales outlet, possibly next door to the printing house, passed to **Ralph Newbery.** Because of the quantity of Berthelet's undated and repeated-date items, the chronology of his publications is especially provisional. [Duff, *Century*; *TBS* 8 (1904–06): 187–220; *GJ* 1966: 177–81.]
in Fleet Street (W.5), 1524 (19816.5, adds: near the conduit at the $ Roman Lucrece)–1546 (24848.5); mention of the conduit and sign is usually omitted after 1535 though some later reprints occasionally carry over the wording, e.g. in 1548 (10999)
1524: 19816.5 in aed.
1526: 10474 in house (d?), 10477 in house (d?), 10892 in house (d?), 10892.4 in house (d?).
1527: 9562 in aed., 10478.7 in house (d?), 10892.7 in house (d?).
1528: 9642 in aed., 9648 in aed., 21596.
1529: 193 in house (d?), 862, 9932 in aed., 9933 in aed. (d?), 17034 in house (d?), 24856 in house (d?), 24856.5 in house (d?).
1530: 815, 5550 (d?), 7774 (d), 7775 (d), 7776 (d), 10948, 14286 in off., 15731 in aed., 20056.7 in house (d?), 21597, 23881.
1531: 4890.5 (d?), 5550.5 (d?), 7635 in aed., 9271 in aed., 9369.5 (d?), 10474.5 (d?), 10476.3 (d?), 10477.5 (d?), 12510 in aed. (d), 12510.5 in aed. (d), 14287 in house, 18393 in aed., 20052 (d?), 21563, 21563.5, 21564, 24857 in house (d?).

Berthelet, T. — *cont.*
1532: 863.5 in house (d?), 7778 (d), 9271 in aed., 9372 (d?), 9565 in aed., 10470.8 in house (d?), 11918 (d?), 11919 (d?), 11919.5, 12143, 16894 in aed. (d?), 20057 in house (d?), 21310 (d), 21587 in aed. (d?), 21587.3 in aed. (d?), 21587.5 in aed. (d?), 21587.7 in aed. (d?), 23665 in house (d?), 26069.
1533: 7668 in aed., 7672 in aed., 7672.5 in aed., 7712.2 in aed. (c), 7778.4 (d), 7779 (d), 9177 in aed., 9358.9 (d?), 9361.5 in aed. (d?), 9362.11 (d?), 9366.3 (d?), 9370 (d?), 9372.3 (d?), 9376 in aed. (d), 9376.3 in aed. (d?), 10449 in aed., 10471 in aed., 10475 in aed., 10995.5 in house (d?), 11006.5 in aed. (d?), 12511 in house (d?), 12511a in house (d?), 14024 in aed., 14278 in house (d?), 14871.5 in aed. (c), 15583.5 in aed. (c), 15982.5 (d?), 16939 in aed., 19902 in aed., 20898.5 in aed. (c), 21584 in aed., 24943 (d?).
1533/34: 23899 in aed.
1534: 2354 exp., 6157 in aed., 7779.2 (d), 7779.8 (d), 7780, 7782 (d), 7782.2 (d), 7782.3 (d), 7782.4 (d), 7782.6 (d), 7782.8 (d), 9178 in aed., 9372.5 (d?), 9381 in aed. (d?), 9386 (d?), 9389.7 (d), 10449 in aed., 10958 in aed., 10995.7 in house (d?), 11218 in aed., 14130.5 (*A3*), 14270, 14575 in aed., 16934, 21585 in aed., 23551.5 in aed., 24226 in aed. (d?).
1535: 1537 in aed. (d), 2055, 7696.5 in aed., 7783 (d), 7784 (d), 7785 (d), 9370.2 (c?), 9376.5 in aed. (d?), 9379 in aed. (d?), 9379.5 in aed. (d?), 9380 in aed. (d?), 9386.3 (d?), 9932.3 in aed., 9933.3 in aed. (d?), 10951 in aed., 10951.5 in aed., 11584 in aed., 12436 in aed., 12436.5 in aed., 14873 in aed. (c?), 15583.7 in aed. (d?), 16936 in aed., 16940 in aed., 17656 in house, 21598 in aed., 21681 in aed. (d?).
1536: 7713 in aed., 7762.7 (d?), 7776.5 (d?), 7778.8 (d?), 7787 (d), 7788 (d), 7788.1 (d), [7788.3] (d), 9366.5 in aed. (d?), 9372.7 (d?), 9391 (d?), 9391.3 (d?), 9393.7 (d?), 9394 (d?), 10033 in aed. (d), [10033.2 in aed.] (d), 10033.4 in aed. (d), 10033.6 in aed. (d), 10033.8 in aed. (d), 10084.7 (d), 12437 in aed., 13077 in aed., 13077.5 in aed., 14025 in aed., 15731.3(*A3*) in aed. (d), 18113.3 in aed., 18113.5 in aed., 18113.7 in aed., 19214 in aed., 23236 in aed. (d).
1537: 5163 in aed., 5164 in aed., 5165 in aed. (false?), 5166 in aed., 5167 in aed., 7636, [7642.5] (d?), [7682?] (c?), 7696.7 in aed., 10465.5 in aed., 10958.5 in aed., 12437 in aed., 13081.7 in aed., 13082 in aed. (false), 13090 in aed., 15286, 15287, 18109 in aed., 18109.5 in aed., 20899.5 in aed. (c?), 21447 in aed., 26071.
1538: 817 in aed., 7659 in aed., 7788.7 (note and *A3*, d?), 7790 (d), 7799 (d?), 9338 in aed., 9338.3 in aed., 9373 (d?), 9377 in aed., 9377.3–.9 in aed. (repeat), 9386.5 (d?), 9394.3 (d?), 9394.5 (c?), 10085 (d?), [10086] (d), 10087 (d?), 10505 in aed., 11219 in aed., 12438 in aed., 13080 in aed., 13080.3 in aed., 13080.5 in aed., 13080.7 in aed., 13081 in aed., 13081.3 in aed., 13081.5 in aed., 13082.3 in aed., 13090.3 in aed., 15761 in aed. (d), 16937 in aed., 20900.5 in aed. (c?), [21447.5], 23407 in aed., 23883 in aed., 23900 in aed., 24237 in aed., 24248 in aed.
1539: 2067 f., 2844 f., 2845 f. (d), 6156 in aed., 6158 in aed., 7630 in aed., 7642.7 in aed., 7643 in aed., 7791 in aed. (d), 7792 (d), 9397 in aed., 9397.5 in aed., 9397.7–98 (repeat), 11008 in aed., 11402 in aed., 12438 in aed., 14026 in aed., 14026.5 in aed., 14270.5 in aed., 14876 in aed., 15584.5 in aed., 16941 in aed., 18110 in aed., 18110.5 in aed., 18110.7 in aed., 18111 in aed., 18112 in aed., 18113 in aed., 19211 in aed., 21679 in aed., 24322 in aed., 24322a in aed., 24846.5 in aed.
1540: 201 in aed., 2069 f., 7657.5 in aed., 7664 in off., 7673 in aed., 7697.5 in aed., 7713.3 in aed., 9274 in aed., 9338.5 in aed., 9366.7 in aed. (d?), 9370.4 (d?), 9391.5 (d?), 9400.4 in aed., 9400.5 in aed., 9400.6–02 ex aed. (repeat), 9403.2, 9403.4 (d?), 9403.8 ex aed. (d?), 9403.9 ex aed. (d?), 10996 in house (c?), 11393 in aed., 11470 in aed., 14027 ex off., 15604 ex off., 15610.5 ex off., 15610.6 (note), 20521 in aed., 24847 in aed.
1541: 7644 in aed. (d), 7645 in aed., 7646 (repeat), 7664 in off., 7792.3 (d), 7792.5 (d), 7794, 7795, 7796 (d), 9274 in aed., 9403.6 ex aed. (d?), 10751 in off., 15732.5 in aed., 16935 ex aed., 21599 in aed., 24858 in aed., 24859 (repeat).
1542: 203 in aed., 7631 in aed., 7659.5 in off., 7660 (repeat), 7797 (d), 7798 (d), 9179 in off., 9179.3 in off., 9400.6 ex aed. (d?), 9404 ex off., 9404.5 ex off., 9404.7–05.5 (repeat), 12439 in off., 14639 in off., 15610.6 in off.
1543: 19.2 in off., 5168, 5168.7, 5169, 5170, 5170.3, 5170.5, 5170.7, 5171, 5173, 5174, 5176, 5879 in off., 7800 (d), 7800.3 (d), 7800.5 (d), 7800.6 (d), 7800.7 (d), 7801 (d), 7802 (d), 9301 in off., 9301.3 (repeat), 9303 (repeat), 9303.4 in aed., 9339 in aed., 9359 (d?),

Berthelet, T. — *cont.*
9361.6 (d?), 9363 (d?), 9374 (d?), 9382 in off. (d?), 9387 (d?), 9400.7 ex aed. (d?), 9404.7 ex off. (d?), 9406.7, 9406.8, 9407, 9408 (repeat), 9409.5, 9409.6, 9409.8 (d), 9409.9 (d), 10506 in off., 15584.9 in aed., 15610.7 in off., 15610.8 in off., 20902.3 in aed. (d?), 21313 in aed.
1544: 2994 in off., 2995 in off., 3001.7, 3002, 3002.3, 5178 ap., 5718 in aed., 7637 in aed., 7646 in aed. (d?), 7665 in off., 7697.9 in aed., 7713.5 in aed., 7802.7 (d), 7803 (d), 7803.7 (d), 7804 (d), 7804.5 (d), 7805 (d), 9334, 9410 in aed., 9410.3 in aed., 9410.7–11.5 (repeat), 10620, 10621, [10621.5 f.] (d), 10621.7 f., 10622 f., 10622.5 f., 10623.3 (d?), 10997.3 in aed., 14271 in aed., 14637 in off., 14877 in aed., 15610.8 in off., 16938 in aed., 23900.5 in aed., 24848 in aed., 26072 in aed.
1545: 202 in aed., 3002.5, 3002.7, 3003, 3003.5–04 in house (repeat), 3005 (repeat), 4818, 4818.5, 4819, 4891 (d?), 5177, 7631.5 in aed., 7632 (repeat), 7658 in aed., 7660, 7674, 9394.7 (d?), 10623.5 (d?), [15764.5], 22250 in off.
1546: 1801 in aed., 7638 in aed., 7805.3, 7805.5, 7805.7, 7806 (d), 7807 (d), 7808 (d), 7809 (d), 9378 in aed., 9392, 9397.7 in aed., 9398 (repeat), 9412, 9412.5 (repeat), 9414.7 in aed., 10625.3, 11011 in aed., 11591 (note), 12440 in aed., 12440.5 in house, 13291, 15610.9 in aed., 16700, 16932 in aed., 24848.5.
1547: 1801 in aed., 3003.5 in house (c?), 3004 in house (c?), 4822, 6920, 7646.5 in aed., 9370.6 (d?), 9408, 9414.9 in aed., 10476, 24859 in aed.
1548: 3005, 4822.5 in house (d?), 5719 in aed., 7661 in house, 9405 ex off. (c), 9410.7 in aed. (c?), 10999 in house.
1549: [1499 in house] (d), 7666 in house, 7666.2 in house, 7670 in house (c?), 10500 in house (d), 15217 in house, 24018 in house, 24023 in house.
1550: 868 in house (c), 4823 in house (c), 4824 in house (c), 5276, 7632 in aed. (d?), 7647 in house (d?), 9301.3 in off. (c?), 9401 ex aed. (c), 13292 in house, 13294.5 in house, 14279 in house (c), 24020 in house, 24849 in house, 26073 in house (d?).
1551: 9303.6 in aed., 9303.7 in aed., 9360 (d?), 9363.2 (d?), 9367 in aed. (d?), 9375 (d?), 9383 in off. (d?), 9388 (d?), 9395 (d?), 16612a.7 in house.
1552: [4391?], 7662 in aed., 9362, 9398 in aed. (d?), 9412.5 (c).
1553: 203.5 in aed. (d), 3006 in house (c?), 7639 in house, 9370.8 (d?), 9405.5 ex off. (c), 9545 in aed., 10476.7 in house, 12441 in house, 14637.5 in off., 25874 in house.
1554: 12144, 12558 in house, 12559 in house, 14860.5 in aed., 14861 in aed.
1555: [13296 in house].

1556: 9408.5 in house (c), 9411 in aed. (c?).
1557: 7649 in house late (d?), 10501 in house (d?).
1559: 7663 in aed. nuper, 12444 in late house.
1560: 4891.3 in house late (c), 13297 in house late, 15218 in house late, 22226 in house late, 22250.2 in off. nuper, 23901 in house late.
1561: 9396 (repeat, d?).
1562: 9368 in aed. (repeat), 9375.5 (repeat, d?), 9400 (repeat), 9406 (repeat, d?), 25876 in late house, 22250.4 in off. nuper.
1565: 5686 in aed. quondam.
1568: 5719 in aed. (d/error).
1569: 10500 in house (d/error), 10501 in house (d/error), 15217 in house (d/error).
1575: 9406.5 (repeat, d?).

Besongne (Besonge), Jacques, *pseud.*
Printer in 'Paris', 1621 = Birchley Hall Press? and in 'Rouen', 1626 = M. Flesher? and B. Alsop and T. Fawcet. For the genuine printer in Rouen, 1601–1632?† *see* Lepreux III/1: 70–2. [*Dict. 1.*]
1621: 5352. **1626:** 14536.

Best, Richard.
Bookseller in London, 1640–1653. [*Dict. 2*; DFM 2622.]
shop near Gray's Inn gate in Holborn (V.10), 1640 (23704)
1640: 3555 f. — or his assignees, 3555.4 f., 3590 f. — or his assignees, 3590a f., 23704 f.

Bienayse, Jean.
Exporter of books to London, 1503; bookseller, printer, and typefounder in Paris, 1506–1521 at least. [Duff, *Century*; *Parisiens.*]
1506: 15805.7 imp. **1510:** [15809]. **1511:** 16189 sumpt. **1515:** [15811.5]. **1516:** 16197 imp. **1521:** 16203 imp.

Bignon, Jean.
Bookseller and printer in Paris, 1509–1544 at least. [Duff, *Century*; *Parisiens.*]
1521: 15932 (d?).

Bilaine. *See* Billaine.

Bill, John 1.
Bookseller and printer in London, (1601) 1604–1630†. Agent for Sir Thomas Bodley, James I, and others in acquiring books printed abroad. Many of his trade publications from 1605 were issued jointly with **John Norton 1**, his former master, and with the latter's **Officina Nortoniana.** One of the **King's Printers** from 1616 (14344) or 1617 with occasional interruptions. For the reprints of Elizabethan proclamations made for Humphrey Dyson, not included below even though Bill's name is one of those supplied in STC, *see* King's Printers, where the positions of the King's Printing House during Bill's activity (G.8, Q.6) are also detailed. *See* also *assignees of* **John Bill**. [*Dict. 1*; *Library* 2 (1901): 353–75.]
Although Bill continued to publish independently copyrights of his own after he had become one of the King's Printers, it is unlikely that he was seriously involved in several publications for others having decorative material of the King's Printing House. It seems more likely that a few of the journeymen were allowed—or took—some latitude in using the material when not specifically engaged in official work. Items probably produced in this manner by printers are by T. Beadle, who remained a journeyman, 1618 (16785.3), and by two who became master printers: T. Harper, 1624 (861(*A*3), 23922, 26011, the last with Bill's name in the imprint but entered to Harper) and R. Badger, 1626 (15303), 1628 (15305–5.7). Booksellers for whom journeymen were apparently working are J. Hodgets, 1617 (10822), 1621 (6427.5), 1622 (4323) and T. Walkley, 1627 (24746). There are undoubtedly other items of a like nature yet to be identified.
in Paul's Churchyard (A.6), 1605 (21361, with J. Norton 1); no later address or use of this one noted
1604: 3070 f., 11029.5 f. (d), 13790 pro, 24262.
1605: 17043 excudi curavit, 17047 ent., 21361 sold.
1606: 10548 f., 11188 f., 14895 imp., 16897 f., 18855 [f.] (d/repeat?), 20008 imp., 21759 f., 24031 ent.
1607: 1939 f., 7176 f., 24951 f.
1608: 5830 ent., 18191 f., 18855 [f.] (d?), 24263.3 ap., 25394 f., 26121a.3 sumpt.
1609: 1940 f., [14525 f.].
1610: 4637 ent., 15049 f., 18183 f., 25395 f.
1611: 3067 imp., 7335(*A*3) ent., 17661 ent.
1612: 12496 ent., 19021 imp., 19021.5 imp., 19560 imp., 25396 f.
1613: 4566 ap., 4631 ap., 7178 f., 20563 ap., 22625 ap., 22977 f., 24551 ent.
1614: 1398 ap., 2812, 3612 ap., 3613 ap., 3618 f., 4002 ap., 4745 ap., 5604 f., 7335 ap., 14989.5 f., 14990 f.
1615: 988 f., 1387 imp., 3614 ap., 3614.5 ap., 4632, 4744 (false), 4744.5 (false), 4744.7 (false), 6580.4, 10259, 11306.5 (false), 14272 ap., 14367, 14367.5, 17527 f., 19561 imp., 20563.5 ap., 22574 f.
1616: 3908.8, 6580.7, 6597, [6597.4], 6996 ap., 6998 [f.], 7174 ap., 10549 f., 11941–2 ap., 11945 ap. [f.], 12610, 12972 f., 14344–5, 14368 ap., 16431, 17991 ap., 25397 f.
1617: 1128 ap., 1153 ap., 2918 f., 2918.3, 6994 ap., 7002 ap., 7003, 7004, 8557, 9238.3, [10822], 11328 ap. (d), 11328.1 ap. (d), 11431a f., 11462 ap., 17992 ap., 20564 ap., 21034.3 f., 24311 ap. (d).
1617/18: 8558, 8562, 8563, 8564, 9238.5.
1618: 46 ap., 148–8.5 ap., 623, 624, 1153a, 1154, 2250, 2251, 2255, 2918.3, 2918.5, 2918.7, [3368.5(*A*)-Clemetson?] (c?), [3368.5-Suckling?] (d?), [3368.5(*A*)-Tomson?] (c?), 3534 ap., 4005, [6847.5?] (d), [7004.5], 7005, 7179 by & f., 7758.3, [7758.7] (d), 8565, 8569, 8569.5, 8570, 8572, 8573, 8574, 8575, 8576, 8578, 8579, 8580, 9238.7, 9238.9, 9239, 9305.7, 11328.2 ap. (d), 11328.3 ap. (d), [16349.3] (d?), 16349.7, 16350, 16468, 16491, 16695 ap., [16785.3], 17183.5 ap., 19933, 20652.5, 20653, 23108, 23401, 24310.5 ap., [25601] (false).
1618/19: 8588, 8589, 8591, 8592, 8593, 8595, 8596, 8598, 8599, 8600, 8603–4, 14171.
1619: 47 ap., 148–8.5 ap., 1130, 1131, 1152, 2253, 2254, 2255, 2256, 2257, 2258, 2260, 2918.7, 2919, 2920, 3615 ap., 3615.5 ap., 7066, 7066.5, [8593.2] (d?), [8593.4] (d?), [8593.5] (d?), [8593.6] (c?),

Bill, John 1 — *cont.*
[8593.7] (c?), 8605, 8606, 8607, 8608, 8609, 8610, 8612, 8617, 8618, 8619–20, 8620.3, 8621, 8622, 9240.3, 9240.5, [10359], 11192, 11328.4 ap. (d), 11328.6 ap. (d), 11432 (note), 11685, 13235, 14346–6.5 ap., 14384, 14385 ap., 16351, 16352, 16352.5, 16353, [16783.5] (d), 17183.5 ap., 19562 ap., 20907 ap., 21760 ap., [23510] (d), 24073, [25599].
1619/20: 514.3, 8625–6, 8628, 8629, 8630, 8632.
1620: 611, 1109 ap. (note), 1132 (d), 1162–3 ap., 2258, 2259, 2260, 2261, 2262, 2348, 2920.7, [3208?], 6995.5 ap., 7119 ap., 7754.4, 8633, 8634, 8636, 8637, 8638, 8639, 8640, 8641, 8642–2.5, 8643, 8644, 8645, 8649, 8650, [9503.3] (c?), 10218.5, 10329.7, 11328.8 ap. (d), 11328.10 ap. (d), 13235, 13794a imp., [14050.5] (false), 14345, 14346.5 ap., 14381.5, 14382(*A3*), 14383 ap., 14412, 16353, 16354, [16354.5?] (d?), 16355, 16356, 16359, 16484 (d), 16496, 18178 ap., 21478, 21761, [21764], 23103 ap., [24259] (d), 25728, 25728.5.
1620/21: 8654.7–56, 8659, 8660.
1621: 1941 ass'd, 2262, 2263, 2921, 2922, 3434.5 ap., 6346 ap., [6427.5], 7154 ap., 8661, 8662–3, 8664, 8665, 8666, 8667, 8668, 8669, 8670, 8671, 8672, 8675, 8675.2, 8675.4, 8675.6, [9506.7] (d), 10133.9, [11329.4] (false), [11329.5] (false), 11942 ap. (d?), 13238, 14399, 16357, 16357.3, 16357.5, 16357.7, 16438, 19444 ap., 23512.
1621/22: 8676, 8676.5, 8677–8, 8679, 8680–1, 9241.
1622: 1132 (d/error), 2264, 2265, 2795 ap., 2924, 3619, [4323], [4718.5] (d), 6132, [7705.5] (d?), [8457?] (c?), [8682], 8683, 8684, 8685, 8686, 8687, 8688, 8689, 8691, 8692, 8693, 8694, 8695, 8696, 8697–8, 9242, 9242.5, 12991, 13238, 15300, 16358.5, 16359, 16360, 17175, 17594, 21648.5(*A3*), 23647, 25378, 25669.
1622/23: 8699, 8700–2, 8703, 8704, 8705.
1623: 2265, 2266, 2267, 2925, 2925.3, 7683, 8706, 8707, 8708, 8709, 8710, 8711, 8713, 8714, 8715, [8716], [8716.2], 8717, 8719, 9243, 12987.3 collected by, 12987.5 collected by, 12989, 12992, 13659, 13675, 16361, 16362, 16362.3, [16434], 16492, 16496.5, 25020, [25908], [25910], [25910.5], [25910.7], [25910a] (d), [25910a.3], [25910a.5?].
1623/24: 8722, 8723.
1624: 167 ap., [861(*A3*)], 1396.5 ex off. (false), 2268, 2269, 2270, 2925.5, [3368.5-Bill?] (d?), 3620 f., 4567 ap., 4750 ap., 4751, 4752, 7006 [f.], 7007 [f.], 7320 ap., 8724–5, 8726, 8727, [8728], [8729], 8730, 8731, 8732, 8733–4, 8736, 8738, 8739, 8740, 8741, 8742, 8744, 9507, 9507.3, 9507.5, 10050, 10050.3, 11511.3 per (c), 12524, 12990, 13003, 13628 [f.] (d?), 14128.5, 16363, 16363.5, 18421 [f.], 23699 [f.], [23922], 25389 f., 26011.
1624/25: 8746, 8747–9, 8750, 8751, 8752, 8753, 8754.
1625: 1458 [f.], 2270, 2271, 2272, 2273, 2273.5, 2926, 2926.5, 7180 [f.], 7345.5 ap., 7751.6 (false), 8754.5, 8755, 8756, 8757, 8758, 8759, 8760, 8761, 8762–2.5, 8763, 8764, 8765, [8766], 8767, 8768–9, 8770, 8770.5, 8771, 8772, [8773], 8774–5, 8776–7, 8778, 8779–80, 8781, 8782, 8783, 8785, 8786, 8787, 8788, 8789 f., 8790 f. [by], 8792 f., 8793 f. [by], [8794 f.], 8796 f., 8796.3 f. [by], 8798 f., 8798.3 f. [by], 8800 f., 8800.3 f. [by], 8800.7 f., 8801 f. [by], 8801.7 f., 8802 f. [by], 8804 f., 8804.3 f. [by], 8804.7 f., 8805 f. [by], 8806, 8807, 8808, 8809, 8810, 8811, 8812, 8813, 8815, 9244, 9244.3, 9245 [f.], 9245.2 [f.], 9245.4 [f.], 9508, [10205], 15302, 15304, 16364, 16365, 16497, 16540, 16541, 16542, [21712.5] (d), 21758, 25723 [f.], 25723a [f.], 25935 per.
1625/26: 8816, 8817–8, [8819], 8820, 8821.
1626: 2275, 2276, 2277, 2278, 2280.5, 2927, 4527 [f.], 7683.5, 7686, 8822, 8823, 8824–5.3, 8826–8, 8829–30, 8831–2, 8833–4, 8835, 8836, 8837, 8837.5, 8838, 8839, 8840, 8841, 8842, 8843–4, 8845, 8846, 8847, 8847.3, 8847.5, 9246, 9247 (d/repeat?), [15303], 16365.5, 16366, 16367, 16485, 16543, 16544, 21035.5 f., 21766 [f.], [22532.5] (d).
1626/27: 8848–9, 8850, 8851, 8852, 8853, 8854, [8855], 8856.
1627: 2279, 2280, 2280.5, 2928, 2929, 3770b f., 8857, 8858, 8859, 8860, 8861, 8862, 8863, 8864, 8865, 8866, 8867, 8868, 8868.3 (false), 8869–70, 8871–2, 8873, 8874, [10146], [10206], 10294, 11574, 16368, 16369.3, 16369.7, 16369.9(*A3*), 16370, 16370.5, 16371, 16469, 19562.5 ap., 22178 ent., [24746].
1627/28: 8875, 8876, 8877, 8878, 8879–81, 8882, 8883–4, 8885, 8886, 8887, 8888, 8888.5.
1628: 2281, 2282, 2283, 2283.5, 2930, 2931, 3616.5 ap., 3771.6 f., [5019?] (d), 7446.5 (d), 8889, 8892–3, 8894, 8895, 8896, 8897, 8898,8899, 8900, 8902, 8904, 8905–6, 8907, 8908, 8909, 8910, 8911,[9175j.3?] (d?), 9247 (d/note), 9510, 10051, 10074 [f.], 10074.3 (forged), 11331 prost., 11331.2 prost., 11946 ap., [15305–5.7], [16372] (d?), 16373, 16373a, 16373b, 16497.1 (c?), 16497.3 (c?), [16545] (d?), [16545.5] (d?), [16546] (d), [16546.5] (d), 16547.5, 16548, 21362, 25727 [f.], 25729.
1628/29: 8912, 8913–4, 8915, 8916, 8917, 8918, 8919–20, 9249, 16547(*A3*).
1629: 824 ap., 2284, 2286, 2287, 2288, 2936, 2936.3, [7492.7] (d), 8921, 8922, 8923, 8924, 8926, 8927, 8928, 8929, 8930, 8931, 8932, 8933, 8934, 8934.5(*A*), 8935, 8936, 9509, 10052, 10227.2, 10295, 10379.7, [10404.7(*A3*)?] (d?), [11944] (false), 12884, 16374, 16376, 16376.5, 16376.7, 16377, 16377.5, 16470, 16485.3, 16548.3, 16548.7, 21762.
1629/30: 8937, 8939, 8940, 8941, 9250.3 [f.].
1630: 2289, 2289.5, 2290, 2295.3, 2936.5, 3772 f., 8942, 8943, 8944, 9342, 9509, 10053–55.5 (forged), 16378, 16378.5, 16380.5, 16380.7.

1631: 2295.3.
1632: 3908.9 ass'd, 4425 ass'd, 6597.7 ass'd, 7175 ass'd, 7181.5 ass'd, 10076 ass'd, 13003 ass'd, 13660 ass'd, 13676 ass'd, 13796 ass'd, 23648 ass'd.

Bill, John 1, *Assignees of.*
Partners in the office of **King's Printer**, 1630–1660. John 1 bequeathed his share to his son, John 2, whose name does not appear in imprints before 1660. The other assignees were probably John 1's widow, Jane, and at least one of his executors, Martin Lucas, who subsequently married Jane. [*Dict. 2*; *TCBS* 2 (1957): 280.]
No address noted.
1629/30: 8937.5.
1630: 2291, 2292, 2292.3, 2292.5, 2295.4, 2295.5, 2295.6, 2295.8, 2298.7, 2349, 2349.5, 2937, 8952, 8954, 8955, 8956–7, 8958, 8959, 8960, 8961, 8962, 8963–4, 8965, 8966, [8967], 8969, 8970, 9250.5, 9250.7, 9251, 9251.3, 16380.9, 16381, 16381.5, 16382, 16439, 16497.5.
1630/31: 8971, 9252, 9252.2, 9252.4, 14220(*A3*).
1631: 2295.4, 2295.5, 2295.6, 2295.8, 2296, 2297, 2297.2, 2297.3, 2297.5, 2297.6, 2297.7, 2297.9, 2298, 2300, 2301, 2302, 2304, 2938, 2939, 2940, 7684, 8973, 8974, 8975, 8976, 8977, 8978, 8979, 8980, 8982, 8983, 8983.5, 9254, 10056, 12784 ap., 16383, 16384, 16384.7, 16385, 16472, 16485.7, 16497.7, 16549.5, 16550, 18023.5, 18024.
1631/32: 8984, 8985, 8986, 8987, 14128.7.
1632: 2297.9, 2298.5, 2298.7, 2300, 2301, 2302, 2302.3, 2302.5, 2303, 2304, 2304.5, 2305, 2941.5, 8988, 8989, 8990, 8991, 8992, 8993, 8994, 8994.5, [9254.3(*A*)] (d?), 10057 (forged), 16385.7, 16386, 16386.7, 16387, 16388, [16388a] (d), 16388a.5, 16389, 16390, 16391, 16550.3 (d).
1632/33: 8995, 8996, 8997, 8998.
1633: 2303, 2305, 2306, 2307, 2308, 2942, 2943, 7755, 8999, 9000, 9001, 9002, 9003–4, 9254.7, 9256, 10058, 10058.5 (forged), [10363], 16390, 16391, 16392, 16392.5, 16393, 16393.5, 16393.7, [16394.3], 16395, 16396, 16397, 16473, 16550.5, 16550.7, 18026, 21475 ap.
1633/34: 9005, 9006–7, 9008, 9009, 9010, 9011–2, 9256.5.
1634: 2306, 2312, 2313, 2313a, 2313b, 2313b.5, 2314, 2314.3, 2314.5, 2315, 2318, 9013, 9014, 9015, 9015.5, 9016, 9017, 9018, 9019, 9020, 9021, 9023, 9024, 9025–6, 9027–8, 9029, 9258, 16396, 16397, 16397.3, 16397.7, 16398, [16399], 16399.5, 16440, 16474, 16486, 16498.
1634/35: 9031, 9032, 9033.
1635: 2315, 2318, 2319, 2325, 2948, 7695, 9034, 9035, 9036, 9037, 9038, 9039, 9040, 9041, 9042, 9043, 9044, 9045, 9046, 9047, [9048], 9049, 9050, 9051, [9175m] (d), 16402, 16402.5, 16402.7, 16486.3, 16499, 16552.
1635/36: 9052, 9053, 9054, 9056, 9057.
1636: 2313b.5, 2322, 2322.3, 2322.5, 2324.5, 2951, 2951.5, 9058, 9059, 9060–1, 9062, 9063, 9064, 9065, 9066, 9067, 9068, 9069, 9070, 9071, 9072, 9073, 9074, 9075, 9076, 9077, [10365], 16403, [16403.5] (d?), 16404, 16404.3, 16404.4, 16404.5, 16404.7, 16475, 16486.7, 16500, 16553, 16553a, 16555, 16555.5, 16769, 16769.5, [23948].
1636/37: 7756, 9078, 9080–1, 9082, 9083.
1637: 2323, 2324, 2324.3, 2324.5, 2325, 2328.5 (forged), 2328.8 (forged), 2329, 2953.3(*A*), 7757, 7757.2, 9084, [9085], 9086, 9087,

Bill, J., *Assignees of — cont.*
9088, 9089, 9090, 9091, 9092, 9093, 9093.5 (false), 9094, 9095, 9096, 9097, 9098, 9099, 16404.9, 16405, 16408, 16408.5, 16486.7, [18527].
1637/38: 9100, 9101, 9102, 9103–5, 9106–7, 9108, 9109.
1638: 2323, 2325, 2329, 2329.2, 2329.4, 2329.6, 2329.8, 2330–0.9 (forged), 2334.5, 2335, 2680.7 (forged), 2953.5, 2954 (forged), 2954.3, 9110, 9111, 9112, 9113, 9114, 9115, 9116–7, 9118, 9119–20, 9121, 9122, 9123, 9124, 9125, 9126, 9127, 9128, 9129, 10060, [11121], 16409, 16411, 16413, 16413.3, 16413.5, 16414, 16414.3, 16414.5, 16415, 16477, 16487, 16501.
1638/39: 9130, 9131, 9132, 9133, 9134, 9134.5(*A*3), 9135, 9137, 9138, 9139.
1639: 2335, 2336, 2337, 2337.3, 2339, 2342, 9140, 9141, 9142, 9143, 9144, 9145, 9146, 9147, 9148, 9149, 9150, 9335, 9335.5, 16415, 16416, 16417, 16417.2, 16417.3, 16417.5, 16417.7, 16418, 16418a, 16418b, 16418c–c.5 (forged), 16419, 16419.5, 16478, 16556, 18196, 18196a, 18196a.5 (repeat), 22005.
1639/40: 9152, 9153.
1640: 2339, 2340, 2342, 2343, 2343.3, 2343.7, 2956, 2957, 4686, 9154, 9155, 9156, 9157, 9158, 9159, 9160, 9161, 9162, 9163, 9164, 9165, 9166, 9167, 9168, 9169, 9170, 9171, 9172, 9173, 9262, 9336, 9511, 9512.5, 10061, 10080, 16421, 16421.3, 16421.5, 16422, 16488, 16502, 16557, 16558, 16558.5, 16559, 26102.
1640/41: 9175.
1641–42: 2340.
1644: 2316.5 (forged).

1673: 2330.9 (forged).

Billaine (Bilaine), Pierre.
Bookseller in Paris, 1614–1638 at least. [Lottin 2: 12.]
1625: 12173.3 chez.

Bindoni, Francesco.
Printer in Venice, 1523–1553. [Borsa.]
1549: 6832.22.

Binet, Denis.
Bookseller and printer in Paris, 1589–1614. [Renouard.]
1611: [25596.5?] (false).

Bing, Isaac.
Stationer in London, (1572?) 1582–1604†. Married the widow of **Francis Coldock**; stepfather of **Simon Waterson**. [*Dict. 1.*]
No address used.
1594: 152 ent. **1595:** 11053 f. (d). **1598:** 16920 f., 18142 ent. **1600:** 18142 f.

Binneman. *See* Bynneman.

Birch, Philip.
Bookseller in London, 1618–1623. [*Dict. 1*; DFM 2127.]
shop at the Guildhall (H.5), 1618 (20655)
at the Bible near Guildhall gate, 1619 (23624.7)
1618: 7259.7(*A*3) f. (d?), 16862.5 f. (d?), 20655 f. (d).
1619: 21404 ent., 23624.7 sold.
1620: 14694.2(*A*3) f., 17362 ent.

Birchley Hall Press.
English secret press operated by recusants, 1615–1621. John Gee (STC 11701 sqq.) mentions one suppressed in Lancashire, c. 1621; it was probably at Birchley Hall, near Wigan. = A&R secret press no. 12. [*Library* 7 (1926): 137–83, 303–20.]
All items below have this press's imprint supplied in square brackets in STC, where the queries indicate uncertainty about the precise location of the press; the items indexed do form a true group.
1615: 26001.
1616: 12797.
1617: 3900, 4932.5.
1618: 3899, 5879.5 (c), 26000 (false).
1619: 17506, 21022, 23924.
1619/20: 3207.5(*A*).
1620: 3607 (false), 3608, 7072.3, 17276.2, 19409.5, 19410.
1621: 3607.5 (false), 5352 (false).

Birckman, Arnold 1, *Heirs of.*
Booksellers and printers in Cologne, 1541?–1585; also booksellers in Antwerp and London for most of that period. The items below were printed during the tenure of Arnold 2, the son of Arnold 1 and nephew of **Franz Birckman 1**. Arnold 2 apparently also had agents in London for the sale of books, but this is not recorded in any extant imprints. [Duff, *Century*; *Dict. 1*; Benzing 239; Rouzet.]
1561: 13433. **1562:** 24366. **1568:** 24367.

Birckman (Byrckman), Franz 1.
Citizen of Cologne and bookseller in London, Cologne, and Antwerp, 1504–1530?†. Brother of Arnold 1; uncle of Arnold 2; *see* also **Franz 2**. A few of Franz 1's books were: sold by the stationers in Paul's Churchyard (B), 1511 (15912), 1514–15 (15920), 1520 (15925). [Duff, *Century*; Benzing 239; Rouzet.]
sold by F. B. in Paul's Churchyard (A.6), 1516 (15921)–1528 (15864); variations: adds: near the new schools [i.e. Colet's?], 1518 (16129); has: sold by [him] or his servants, 1523 (16236)
1504: 16181 imp.
1510: 16188 imp.
1511: 15912 imp., 16188 imp.
1512: [15861.7 imp.].
1514: 15810 imp., 15916 imp., 15918 imp., 15920 imp., 16193 imp.
1515: 15920 imp., 16141.5 imp., 16195 imp.
1516: 15812 imp., [15813 f.] (d?), 15921 imp. & ven., 16258.7 exp., 16259 exp.
1518: 16129 imp. & ven., 16137 imp.
1519: 15790 imp., 15816 imp., 15923 imp. & ven., 15924 imp., 16200 imp., 16235 imp. & ven.
1520: 15790a imp., 15925 imp.
1521: 15930 imp. & ven., 15931 imp. & ven.
1522: 16260 exp., 16260.5 imp.
1523: 16146 ven., 16236 imp. & ven.
1524: 13828.2 imp. & ven. (d?), 15818 imp.
1525: 15819 imp., 15822 imp., 15939 imp. & ven., 16131 imp., 17111 ven.
1526: 15822 imp.
1527: 15953 imp. & ven., 15953.5 imp. & ven., 15956 imp. & ven., 16206 imp., 16207 ven.
1528: 15864 imp. & ven.

Birckman, Franz 2.
Bookseller in London, 1530. Undoubtedly related to the other Birckmans but how closely is unknown. Called 'junior' in 16240.5; it is not clear if 16240 should be attributed to him or to **Franz 1**. [Duff, *Century*.]
in [his] house in Paul's Churchyard (B), 1530 (16240.5)
1530: 16240 imp., 16240.5 imp. & ven.

Bird, Robert.
Bookseller in London, (1621) 1623–1641†. Shared many copyrights with **Edward Brewster** and sometimes published jointly with him. [*Dict. 1*; DFM 2124.]
shop at the Bible in Cheapside (N.1), 1623 (11666)–1631 (3324)
shop at the Bible in St. Lawrence Lane (H.6), 1631 (3789)–1640 (18626a); variation: has 'dw.', 1631 (21211)
1623: 7158.5 ent., 11666 f., 14520 f., 14694.3 f., 19862 f., 21404 ent.
1624: 5692.3 f., 5692.5 f., 13018.5 ent., 13203.5 f., [14483.5 f.] (d), 19774 f.
1625: 6181.3 sold, 10601.9 f., 15684 f., 23100 f., 24594 f., 25646 f.
1626: 382.5 ent., 1313.3 ent., 1315 ent., 3031 ent., 3324 ent., 3698.3 ent., 4290 ent., 4309 ent., 4910 ent., 6478 ent., 6554.5 ent., 6571 ent., 10601.3 f., 10602 f., 10714 ent., 10865.5 ent., 11561 ent., 12637.4 ent., 12734.5 ent., 15094 ent., 15534 ent., 16960 ent., 17783 ent., 19436.5 ent., 21213.9 ent., 21851 ent., 22138 f. (d?), 22673 ent., 23390 ent., 23616 ent., 25136 ent., 25435 ent., 25655 ent., 25990 ent.
1627: 1315 ent., 12637 ass'd, 16960 by ass'ns of, 18625 f., 19431 f.
1628: 1313.2(*A*) sold, 6553.5 f., 13018.5 f. (d?), 14694.5 f., 21210.3 f., 21370 f., 22673 f.
1629: 1315 f., 11561 f., 18625.5 f., 21213.9 f., 25435 f., 25645 f.
1630: 1313.3 sold, 3031 f., 4290 f., 4309 f., 6478 f., 21210.5 f., 21213.10 f., 22138.3 f. (c), 22337–8 f., 23616 f., 25136 f. (d?), 25990 f., 26037a sold.
1631: 1316 sold, 3324 f., 3789 f., 3790–0.5 f., 4143 f., 6479 f., 6554 f., 11561.3 f., 14684 sold, 16961 f., 19437 sold, 21211 f., 21371 f., 22674 f.

Bird, R. — *cont.*
1632: 1313.5 sold, 6571 f., 13018.7 f., 15534 f., 21212 f., 22675 f., 24400 f.
1633: 1317 sold, 3031.5(*A*) f., 4204 sold, 14694.7 f., 23717 f., 24401 f.
1634: 10714 ass'd, 21372 f., 23394 ass'd.
1635: 1318 sold, 3032 f., 3533.5 pro, 4144 f., 4922 f., 10601.7 f., 10602.5 f., 17783 f., 18626 f., 21212.7 f., 22138.5 f. (c), 23617 f.
1636: 1981 f., 4145 f., 4145.5 f., 6572 f., 17783.3 f., 6572 f., 10409 [f.], 10865.5 f., 18626.5 f., 24401.3 f., 25991 f.
1637: 1313.7 f., 1318.3 f., 6555 f., 22676 f., 24401.7 f., 25645.5 f.
1638: 3032.5 f. (d?), 4310 f., 10410 ass'd, 21213 f.
1639: 19437a f.
1640: 6555.3 f., 11561.5 f., 18626a f., [22138.7 f.?] (c).

Birkes. *See* Bearkes.

Bishop, Edward.
Bookseller in London, (1600: Arber II.727) 1604–1618?†. Husband of **Elizabeth Bishop**; kinsman of his former master, **George Bishop**. [*Dict. 1.*]
in Paul's Churchyard at the Brazen Serpent (A.3), 1606 (6628.5)–1617 (6631)
1604: 7526 f. **1605:** 18201(*A*3) ent., 24770 ent. **1606:** 6628.5 f. **1607:** 6629 f., 24770 f. **1609:** 6629.5 f., 24770.5 f. **1610:** 4509 ent., 6630 f. **1611:** 6630.3(*A*) f. **1612:** 6630.5 f., 24771 f. **1613:** 18201 f. **1615:** 24771.3 f. **1616:** 6630.7(*A*) f. **1617:** 6631 f.

Bishop, Elizabeth.
Bookseller in London, 1619–1620. Widow of **Edward Bishop**. One of the *assignees of* **J. Battersby**. [Not in *Dict. 1.*]
in Paul's Churchyard at the Brazen Serpent (A.3), 1619 (6631.5)–1620 (24771.7)
1619: 6631.5 f. **1620:** 4510.8 ass'd, 24771.7 f.

Bishop, George.
Bookseller in London, (1562) 1566–1611†. Husband of Mary Bishop, the daughter of **John Cawood**; kinsman of **Edward Bishop**. Usually published jointly with **Luke Harrison**, 1569–1577, and often with others. Was, with **Ralph Newbery** and later **Robert Barker**, one of the *Deputies of* **C. Barker**, 1587–1599, and as such had a share in the Queen's Printing House (*see* King's Printer). Bishop, Newbery, and R. Barker published both individually and jointly as well as under the 'Deputies' imprint; items with 'Deputies' *alone* in the imprint are not included below; items with Bishop's name *and* 'Deputies' are generally listed at both places. Bishop apparently acquired the shop of his former master, **Robert Toy**, and afterward bequeathed it to **Thomas Adams:** the (Blue) Bell in Paul's Churchyard (A.4). [*Dict. 1*; *Library* 14 (1959): 35–6.]
No address noted.
1569: 13061 f., 13062 f.
1570: 5263 f., 11271 f. (d), 24113 f. (d).
1571: 2036 imp., 4395 f., 15551.5 f.
1572: 4055 f., 4074 f.
1573: 7369 f., 19114 f.
1574: 3548 f., 4444 f., 4445 f., 4449 f., 13063 f., 15003 f., 17408 f.
1575: 13960 imp., 15552 f., 19115 f. (d?), 19832 f.
1576: 4096 f., 4426.4 imp., 5759.1 ent., 15004 f.
1577: 2036.5 imp., 4400 f., 4448 f., 5264 f., 13058.5 imp., 13063.5 f. (d?), 13568a f. (d), 18670 f. (d?), 19115.5 f. (d?).
1578: 3548.5 f., 3549 f., 4393 f., 4394 f., 11417 pro, 13568 ent., 21181 f. (d), 21181.5 f. (d), 21685 f., 23284 f. (d), 24995 f. (d).
1579: 2032 ent., 2056 ent., 3550 f., 4426.6 imp., 4441 f., 4446 f., 4453 f., 4697 f., 6037 ent., 6229.5 f., 11418 imp., 11433 f., 17003.3 ent., 18671 f., 21182 f., 23285 f.
1580: 2046 f., 2056.4 imp., 2359.2 imp., 3551.5 f., 4446 f., 4446a f., 4464 f., 5723 f., 11449 f., 11456 f., 15005 f., 16814.5 f., 19116 f., 19961 ent., 20624 imp., 22907 f., 24584 imp., 24919 f.
1581: 2058a imp., 4437 f., 4442 ent., 4455 f., 11421 f., 11448 f., 11455 f., 21682 f., 25956 f.
1582: 13961 imp., 13961.5 imp., 22906 f., 22910 imp., 23873 pro, 24632 ent., 25285 imp.
1583: 758 imp., 761 imp., 1983.5 imp., 4399 f., 4442 f., 11234 imp., 11430–0.5 f., 19962 pro, 20370 f., 22110 imp., 22114 imp., 22906.5 f., 22910 imp., 23873.5 pro.
1584: 2962 imp., 4447–7.5 f., 5759.1 imp., 11429 imp., 13569 ent., 13962 imp., 20626 imp.

Bishop, G. — *cont.*
1585: 1982.5 imp., 2059 imp., 4398 imp., 7262 imp., 13064 f. (d?).
1586: 3748 ent., 4027 f., 13843.5 f., 15233 f., 15694 imp., 15697(*A*3) imp.
1587: 1491 imp. (d?), 11237 imp., 13569–9.5 at expenses, 16608, 19826 imp.
1588: 1998–9, 2888 ent., 4024 imp., 7300 imp. (d), 10747 imp., 15516 ent., 20571 imp., 20627, 22908, 22909, 24632 imp.
1589: 2019 typis, 5759.1 (note), 9196 ent., 12625, 15102, 15234 imp., 15238 ent., 15244 imp., 16612 imp., 16882 imp., 18099 imp., 19955.5 imp., 20054.5 typis, 22912.
1590: 753.5 imp., 2352, 4505 imp., 4913.5, 6475, 10377 [f.], 14464, 14636, 15698–9 imp., 15700.7, 16619, 19955.5 imp., 20881, 21746(*A*: 2 eds.), 23471, 24689.5 imp., 25841–1a.
1591: 6575.3, 7301 imp. (d), 10748 imp., 13629, 19953 imp., 19956 imp., 20054.7 ?ent., 23458, 23471, 23472 [f.], 24822 (d).
1592: 3552 imp., 6575.5, 15694.3 imp., 19152.5 imp.
1593: 2061.5, 4785 imp., 15699, 21747 ent.
1594: 4506 imp., 15235 imp., 15238, 15240 ent., 18100 ap., 19957 imp.
1595: 3167, 19954 imp., 23451 ent., 23650 imp.
1596: 690, 21783.
1597: 1445, 2062, 15195 ent., 19959, 25862 ent.
1598: 1460 ent., 5077 imp., 10066 ent., 12626, 18044 imp., 20628 [f.], 25863 imp.
1599: 12626, 12626a, 20055 typis, 23265, 23449, 23457, 23460.
1600: 4507 imp., 12626, 12626a (note), 14447, 14447.5 (false), 14453 imp., 15481 imp.
1601: 51 imp., 2900.3 imp., 6439 imp., 6440 imp., 11543 imp., 11937 imp., 15240 imp., 20029.5 imp.
1602: 3610 imp., 3611 imp., 5081 imp., 14809 at charges, 14898(*A*3) ent., 15007 imp., 15051 ent., 15236 imp., 20063 ent., 20625 imp.
1603: 4786 imp., 20068a f.
1604: 12059 imp., 13951 ?ent., 14391 imp., 23461 (false), 23465 f., 24280 imp., 24280.5 imp.
1605: 737 imp. (d), 855 f., 15239 imp., 18173.5 imp., 18174 imp., 21322 imp., 23337 f. (d), 25864 imp.
1606: 48 imp., 1468 at charges, 3193 imp., 3961 ent., 5397 imp., 13790a imp., 14586 imp., 18175.5 imp.
1607: 49 imp., 4508 imp., 14611 imp., 23354 imp.
1608: 13791 imp., 19957.3 imp.
1609: 50.5 imp., 14810 f., 15491 imp., 18176 imp.
1610: 4509 imp., 18177 imp.
1611: 2917 ass'd, 2963 ass'd, 4510 ass'd, 4787 ass'd, 11431 ass'd, 13792 ass'd, 14587(*A*3) ass'd, 23338 ass'd.

Bishop, Richard.
Printer in London, (1634) 1636–1654. Brother-in-law of **Miles Flesher** (Arber III.701). Succeeded to the printing material of **William Stansby**. *Dict. 2* gives his address as St. Peter's, Paul's Wharf (R.8), but whether by inference from Stansby's or from an imprint is not clear. [*Dict. 2*; DFM 241.]
No address noted.
1636: 883, 3151, 5742.3, 7429, 11105, 14682.5 (d?), 22170.
1636/37: [4293].
1637: 1313.7, 1318.3–.5, 10635.7, 12987, [13267], [13267.5], 13877.7, [14007], 23029, 23029.5, 23029.7 (forged), 23054, 24646, 24647, 25645.5.
1637/38: 495.13, 496.5.
1638: 1789, 3151a–a.5, 4935, 7430, 10691, 13191, 13720 (note), 18645, 19598, 22521, 23625, 24647.
1638/39: 411.5, 479.5.
1639: 439.29 (d?), 1236, 1790, 1996 (d?), 4936 ent., 6105 ent., 11064, 11908, 11911, 12073, 12079, 12082, 12977, 12997a ent., 13720, 16777, 17254 (d?), 20933, 21063, 22214 ent., 23193.8 typis, [25025].
1639/40: 479.6.
1640: 1269 (c), 2695, 3555–5.4, 6879, 12363, 13638, 14683 (c), 14753, 17168, 17921, 19600 (d), [19997.5?] (d), [20884?], 21290a (c), 22168, [23551], [23746?].
1640/41: Wing A 1858.

Blacklock. *See* Blaiklock.

Blackman, William.
Bookseller in London, (1596) 1597–1598. [*Dict. 1.*]
dw. near the great North door of Paul's (A.2), 1597 (3184.4)
1597: 3184.4 f. **1598:** 12372 ent.

Blackmore (Blackamore), Edward.
Bookseller in London, (1615) 1618–1658†. [*Dict. 2*; DFM 1799; *Loan Book*, 1632–35, 1638–41.]
in Paul's Churchyard, 1618–1640 at least
shop — at the Blazing Star (B), 1618 (19347)–1621 (4692)
shop at the great South door of Paul's (A.8), 1623 (17634)–1628 (23033); at least once omits 'great', 1625 (23921)
— at the Angel (A.3), 1629 (1948.5)–1640 (1952); sometimes has 'shop', 1638 (17635)
1618: 19347 f.
1620: 17804 f.
1621: 4692 f.
1623: 17634 f., 19801 f.
1624: 17632 f., 20111 f.
1625: 23921 f.
1626: 1946 f., 1960 f., 25614 f.
1627: 1943 f., 1946.3 f., 1946.7 f., 1947 f., 21415.5 f.
1628: 1948 f., 19085 f., 23033 sold.
1629: 1926–6.5 f., 1944 f., 1948.5 f.
1630: 150.5 f. (c), 357.5 f., 1941.5 sold, 1945 f., 1949 f., 16755 sold, 25668 f. (c).
1631: 358 f., 1928 f., 6444 ent., 6516 f., 19259 f. (d?), 20320 f. (d), 22581 f. (d).
1632: 1433.3 f. (d?), 1950 f., 12213 f., 13843 f. (d?), 19086 f., 22790d f.
1633: [16755.5 f.] (d).
1634: 1950.5 f.
1635: 1951 f., 1959 sold, 20320.5 f. (c), 25822 sold.
1638: 17599 imp., 17633a f., 17635 f., 19084 f.
1640: 1952 f.

Blackwall, George.
Journeyman printer in London, (1623) 1626–1645†. Son of **William Blackwall.** [*Dict. 1*; DFM 310; *Poor Book*, 1628–45, widow thereafter; *St. Giles*, 1629.]
No imprints exist.
1626: 21710.7(*A*3) ass'd. **1636:** 21687 ent.

Blackwall (Blackwell), William.
Bookseller in London, (1586) 1591–1625. Father of **George Blackwall**. [*Dict. 1*; *Poor Book*, 1623–25.]
shop over against Guildhall gate (H.5), 1594 (6160)–1618 (20860.5)
1594: 6160 f.
1595: 3125 f., 18289 f. (d), 23401.5 f. (d), 25254 f. (d?).
1596: 6820 f. (d?), 12929 f.
1597: 3126 f.
1600: 1329 f. (c), 3796 f. (c?), 7565.4 f. (c?).
1606: 4658 f. (d).
1618: 20860.5 f.

Bladen, William.
Bookseller in London, (1610) 1612–1625. In 1612 he was in partnership with **John Royston**. Bladen possibly went to Dublin c. 1626 to help his former master, **Arthur Johnson**, in managing the affairs of the Irish Stock (*see* Stationers' Co.—Irish Stock) and became sole agent there by 1631. As his name has been only rarely supplied in Dublin imprints, for the full range of his potential activity there *see* Stationers' Society and also Index 2Aii. In 1639 he bought out the patent for **King's Printer for Ireland** and printed in Dublin under his own name, 1641–1663†. [*Dict. 2*; DFM 1726; *Loan Book*, 1613–25.]
their shop at the great North door of Paul's at the Bible (A.2), 1612 (5188, with J. Royston)–1625 (12870.5, has 'his' shop); sometimes omits 'at the great North door of Paul's', 1612 (1782), 1620 (11667); sometimes omits sign, 1623 (1068)
1612: 1782 f., 5188 f., 11794 f., 24578 f.
1613: 18213 f.
1614: [1125(*A*3)] sold, 1782.5 f., 12870.3 f., 24312–2.3 f.
1615: 3529 f.
1617: 25035 f.
1618: 245 f., 1642 f., 25036 f.
1619: 11670 sold, 11676 f.
1620: 244 ent., 3523 f., 11667 f., 11678 f., 11679 f., 24702 ent.
1621: 10874–4.5 f.
1622: 1642.5 f., 7143 f., 11651.5 f., 11677 f., 12119 f., 18483 sold, 25037 f.

Bladen, W. — *cont.*
1623: 1068 f., 11666a f., 11681 f., 21415 f., 25399.5 ent.
1624: 11653 f., 25855 f., 25856 f.
1625: 12870.5 f.
1626: 7144 ass'd, 11652 ass'd.
1632: [19474] (d?), [20520].
1638: 24552 ent.
1640: [11495.5?].

Blaeu, Willem Jansz (Johnson, William).
Geographer and printer in Amsterdam, 1608–1638†. [*Dict. 1*; Gruys.]
1612: 3110. **1622:** 3112. **1625:** 3113. **1632–33:** [551?]. **1635:** 3113.3.

Blageart, Françoise.
Printer in Paris, 1633–1658. Widow of **Jérôme Blageart**. [*Dict. 1*; Lottin 2: 12.]
1633: [4554] (false). **1636:** [922.5], [16162], 23992. **1637:** 11322, [25403.5]. **1638:** [911], [914], [6844.4], [16828]. **1639:** [1019] (false).

Blageart, Jérôme.
Printer in Paris, 1619–1633†. Husband of **Françoise Blageart**. [Lottin 2: 12.]
1621: [21138.3(*A*3)]. **1630:** [4551].

Blaiklock (Blacklock), Lawrence.
Bookseller in London, 1638–1654. For an analysis of some of his editorial transgressions *see SB* 40 (1987): 120–40. [*Dict. 2*; DFM 1157; *Loan Book* (as Blacklock), 1641–44.]
shop at the Sugarloaf next Temple Bar in Fleet Street (W.14), 1638 (20536.5)–1640 (18338) at least
1638: 20536.5 sold.
1639: 17922 f., 24969 sold.
1640: 1665 f., 4914 sold, 12503.5 f., 17921 f., 18338 f.

Blainchard (Blanchard), William.
Stationer in London, (1609) 1613–1631 (*C-B C*: 227). His only book was sold by its printer, **George Eld**: in Fleet Lane at the $ Printer's Press (D.2). [*Dict. 1*; DFM 2739.]
No separate address used.
1613: 11309 f.

Blanchier, Michel.
Printer in Geneva, 1557–1564. [Chaix 149–50; Bremme 117.]
1557: [2383.6], [16561.5?].

Bland, George, *Gentleman.*
Publisher in London, 1628? [STC.]
No address used.
1628: 3126.5 f. (d?).

Blond (Bloome, Le Blond), Nicholas.
French bookbinder in London, 1553–1585 at least. Grandfather of **Jacob Bloome**. Admitted as Brother of the Stat. Co. in 1559 (Arber I.125). Lived in the liberty of St. Martin le Grand, Aldersgate Ward (G.9). [Duff, *Century* 90; Worman.]
No address used.
1571: 23641 f.

Bloome (Blome), Jacob.
Stationer in London, 1618–1670. Grandson of **Nicholas Blond**; stepson of **George Edwards 1**. Former apprentice of **Ralph Mabb**, whose shop he took over. [*Dict. 2*; DFM 1886; *Loan Book*, 1628–34; *Poor Book*, 1667–70.]
in Paul's Churchyard at the Greyhound (B), 1618 (7408.5)–1621 (23057, has 'shop'); no later address used before 1641.
1618: 7408.5 f.
1619: 11828 f.
1621: 13773 ass'd, 23057 f.
1631: 12502 ent., 13168 ent.
1633: 108 f., 12368 f., 12369.5 f.
1634: 806 f., 13190.
1635: 1578 ent., 7614 ent.
1638: 12503 f., 13191 f.

Blore. *See* Blower.

Blount (Blunt), Edward.
Bookseller in London, (1588) 1594–1632†. In partnership with **William Barrett**, 1608–1613. Married the widow of **Richard Bankworth.** One of the *assignees of* **J. Battersby**. [*Dict. 1*; *Loan Book* (for Bankworth's orphans), ?1627, ?1630; ?*Poor Book*, 1633.]
in Paul's Churchyard, 1597–1622 at least
shop over against the great North door of Paul's Church (A.2), 1597 (23918)–1598 (11098)
shop — at the Black Bear (B), 1609 (17417)–1622 (17420); no later use noted but he did not often use an address
1594: 15216 f.
1597: 23918 [sold] chez.
1598: 11098 f., 17413 f.
1599: 22554 f.
1600: 5624 f., 11634 f., 18041 ent., 22213 ?ent.
1601: 5119 f.
1603: [6258 f.] (d), 6259 f. (d), 6260 f., 12551 imp., 18041 f., 24343 f.
1604: 94 f., 337 f., 343 f., 346 f., 350 f., 5782 f., 5782.5 f., 14756 f., 14782 ent., 18895 f.
1605: 6200(*A*3) f. (d/repeat), 6201 f., 6239 f., 17384.5 f., 21649 ent., 21649a.5 ent.
1606: 3958 f., 4103 f. (d), 4103.3 f., 12050 f., 17775.5 sold, 21665 ent.
1607: 344 f., 6263 f., 7274 f., 12028 f., 12555–5.5 imp.
1608: 1201 f. (d), 5051 f. (d?), 22334 ent., 25638.5 ent.
1609: 12686 f. (d?), 13541 f., 15460 f., 17417 f., 20772 f.
1610: 5659 f., 5808 ent., 10425 f., 13473 f., 19565 f., [24833(*A*3)] sold.
1611: 11099 f.
1612: 4915 f.
1613: 6197 f., 12686.3 f. (d?), 13474 f., 17418 f., 14973 by ass't of, 18042 f., 25659.5 f.
1614: 6678 f., [6683.3 f.] (d), 6731.5 f., 16884 f., 16919 f., 21652 ass'd.
1615: 4917 ent., 5052 f. (d?), 25660 f.
1616: 10426 f.
1617: 127, 5367 f., [7407(*A*3)] sold, 17419 f.
1618: [1635(*A*3)] sold, 1670 ent., 4103.5 f., [7610(*A*3)] sold, [11707(*A*3)] sold.
1619: [12390 f.]
1620: 3957 f., 4916 f. (d?), 4917 f., 5053 f. (d?).
1622: 288 f., 4919 f., 6643.5 f., 11546 ent., 18897 f., 17420 f.
1623: 288 f., 289 f., 19621a f., 22273.
1624: 17421 ass'd.
1628: 7439 f., 7440–0.2 f., 13551 f., 17088 ent.
1630: 5054 f., 6058 f.
1632: 6061 f., 10686 f., 14830.7 f., 17088–9 f.

1636: 4510.4 ass'd.
1640: 5055 f. (engr. tp/repeat).

Blower (Blore), Ralph.
Bookseller in London, (1594) 1595–1596; printer 1597–1619. In partnership with **George Shaw** in 1597. In 1612 **Valentine Simmes** and in 1615–16 **Lionel Snowdon** apparently worked in Blower's shop. Sometime in 1616 Blower sold his printing material to **William Jones 3**. In 1619 Blower printed in the house of **George Eld.** [*Dict. 1*; *SB* 21 (1968): 248–53.]
shop in Fleet Street near Middle Temple gate (W.13), 1595 (10922)
dw. on Lambeth (Lambert) Hill near Old Fish Street (S.7), 1613 (11076, 21851); no other use of this address noted
1595: 10922 f.
1596: 20869 f., 23606 f.
1597: 1311, 6554.2(*A*3) ent.
1598: 6054 ent.
1599: 3353 ent., 6554.2(*A*3).
1600: 17679 (d), 22425, 24145.7 (c), 25154 (d).
1601: 256.5, 23606.5.
1602: 20128 (d).
1603: 18248, 19766, [19766.3].
1604: 7292, [17294?] (d), 20339.
1605: 10158, 10289.7, [16681.5] (d?).
1606: 4658 (d), 6514, [10668], [21787].
1607: 5876, [10011], [10011.2], [10011.4], 10159, 10314.4, 11232, 23607.

Blower, R. — *cont.*
1607/08: [23224.5?].
1608: 10277.
1609: 10225, 10372.2.
1610: [7090.5] (d), [13137], [18596], [20755], [25654], [25989?].
1612: 693, 3353, [6569], 14691.5, 17844, 23608.
1613: 11076, [13855.8] (d), 15433, 21851.
1614: 840.5 ent., [20860.3(*A*3)] (d), [25968.5?] (d).
1615: [198.7?] (c), 1328.7 (c), [6921.5?] (c), 6924.5 (c), 17622, [21213.3(*A*3) in shop of], [21369] (c), [21369.5] (c), 21401, [23752], [25993(*A*3) in shop of].
1616: 11077, [14948(*A*3) in shop of], [21013(*A*3) in shop of], [21014(*A*3) in shop of], [21018?], 23609.
1619: 11040.
1626: 23610 ass'd.

Blunden, Humphrey.
Bookseller in London, (1635) 1636–1655. [*Dict. 2*; DFM 2460; *Loan Book*, 1636–39.]
shop near the Castle Tavern in Cornhill (O.7), 1637 (6410)–1640 (13182) at least; some variations: in Cornhill near the Royal Exchange, 1637 (22849.7); in Cornhill at the Castle near the Royal Exchange, 1638 (3946); at the Castle in Cornhill, 1640 (13182)
1637: 6410 f., 11785 pro, 14788 f., 22849.7 sold, 23120 f.
1638: 975 f., 3946 sold, 22849.7 sold, 24157 f.
1639: 1418 f., 5930.8 sold, 6315 f., 22149.3 sold.
1640: 13182 f., 22404.8 sold, 22404.9 f., 24606 f., 25870 f.

Blunt. *See* Blount.

Bocard, André.
Printer in Paris, 1491–1531. [Duff, *Century*; Renouard.]
1501: 17107.
1502: 16116, 23427.3 imp.

Bodington (Boddington), John.
Journeyman printer in London, (1633) 1640–1661? Apparently bought the copyright of **Thomas Purfoot 2,** his former master, for printing church briefs, about which there was some dispute (*C-B C*: 332). Probably the same man whose assignees issued such briefs in 1660–61 (Wing C 2933, C 3642, C 3647). [Not in *Dict. 2*; DFM 432; *Loan Book*, 1637–40.]
No address used.
1640: 9172.5 f. (d).

Bodleian Library. *See* Oxford University.

Boeidens. *See* Boudins.

Bogard (Bogardus), Jean.
Printer and bookseller in Louvain, c. 1562–c. 1597, and in Douai, c. 1572–1626. Father of **Martin Bogard;** father-in-law of **Balthazar Bellerus**. [*Dict. 1*; Rouzet; *Répertoire 17e*, IV.7.]
1564: 12758. **1566:** 17497. **1567:** 13889. **1576:** 17775 ap. (false).
1579: 4568.5 per (false, d?).

Bogard, Martin.
Printer in Douai, 1627–1636†. [*Dict. 1*; Lepreux I.22–4; *Répertoire 17e*, IV.8.]
1630: 6385. **1634:** 13468.5. **1635:** 3272, 11314.4, 24924. **1636:** 17618.5.

Bohmberg (van Bohmbergen), Nikolaus, *pseud.?*
Printer in Cologne? c. 1574–1580, of works of the Family of Love. His name, in none of the English translations listed below, does appear in a few editions in Dutch, but it is possible that the English items were printed somewhat later and possibly at a different place. Bohmberg's existence has not yet been documented, and it would be more accurate to consider the following items as produced by 'the Hendrik Niclas Press'. Some of its printing material and unsold sheets eventually passed to **Thomas Basson.** [Benzing 246; *Quaerendo* 6 (1976): 241–3; 15 (1985): 196–9.]
1574: [7573] (d?), [10843] (d?), [18550] (d?), [18551] (d?), [18554] (d?), [18555] (d?), [18557–7.5] (d?), [18560], [18562], [18564.5] (d), [21529].
1575: [1858], [10681.5] (d), [18548.5], [18549] (d), [18552] (d?), [18556] (d?), [18558] (d?), [18561] (d?), [18563] (d?), [18564] (d?).
1579: [77].

Boler, Anne.
Bookseller in London, 1635–1638†. Widow of **James Boler 1**, whose 1636 items were undoubtedly sold by her. Joined and later succeeded at the shop by **Francis Eglesfield**. [*Dict. 1*.]
dw. at the Marigold in Paul's Churchyard (B), 1635 (1791)–1638 (1231, omits 'dw.')
1635: 1791 f.
1636: 1223 sold, 4863 sold, 18531.7 f.
1637: 1223.5 sold, 1224 f., 14588 imp., 20274 f., 20961 sold, 22469.7 f.
1638: 1229 f., 1231 f., 20226 f.

1639: 20227 f. (engr. tp/repeat).
1935: 1791(*A*3) (d/error) f.

Boler (Bowler), James 1.
Bookseller in London, (1613) 1624–1635†. Husband of **Anne Boler**; father of **James 2** and **Thomas Boler**. The 1636 items below were undoubtedly sold by his widow. [*Dict. 1*; DFM 812; *Loan Book*, 1629–35.]
at the Marigold in Paul's Churchyard (B), 1627 (21346)–1635 (23815, has 'dw.')
1624: 11669 f.
1626: 11395 f., 14587 imp., 21163 sold, 24209.5 f.
1627: 10614.5 f., 11395 f., 15495 f., 21346 f., 22525.7–26 sold.
1628: 11691 f., 11933.5 f., 17528 f., 19579 f., 19983.7 sold, 24513a f.
1629: 1926 sold, 4019 sold, 5722 sold, 10699 f., 11691 f., 13394a ent., 19580 f., 19653a ent., 19698 ent., 20003.5 ent., 21752 f., 23814 f., 23893 sold.
1630: 12528 f., 13414 sold, 14954 f., 14956 f., 19984 sold, 20270 sold, 20270.5 sold, 20370.5 f. (c), 23725 f., 23774 f., 25738 f.
1631: 6031 f., 12529 f., 15557.5 ent., 17066 sold, 17863–3.1(*A*3) sold, 18531 f., 19652.5 sold, 19653.5 sold, 19653a (note), 19653b f., 19653b.5 sold, 20271–1a f., 23745–5.5 f., 23775.5 f., 23824 f.
1632: 1435 sold, 1435.5 f., 4661 f., 11080 f., 11085 f., 12393–3.5 f., 13458 f., 13988 sold (note), 14956.3 f., 15463.5 f., 16857.9(*A*) f., 18531.3 f., 19985 sold, 21010.7 f., 23518 sold.
1633: 1223 ent., 13988 f., 17529 ent., 17712 f., 18881 f., 19580.5 f., 20003.5–04 sold, 23518.5 f., 25685 sold.
1634: 1541 f., 11439 sold, 13383.5 ass'd, 13427 ass'd, 15643 f., 20273 f., 23776 f.
1635: 14954.3 f., 14956.7 f., 19570 f. (note), 19580.7 f., 19986 sold, 21223.3 sold, 23815 f.

1636: 12523 f. (post-dated?), 23776.5 f. (engr. tp/repeat).

Boler, James 2.
Bookseller? in London, 1640?–1649. Son of **James Boler 1**. Apprenticed in 1637 but apparently never freed. The 1640 item credited to him is probably the result of an unaltered engr. tp with his father's name; the shop at that date was in the possession of **Francis Eglesfield**. [*Dict. 1*; DFM 1301; *Poor Book*, 1646, 1647.]
?at the Marigold in Paul's Churchyard (B), 1640 (23777)
at the Marigold in Fleet Street, 1649 (Wing B 4341)
1638: 12394 ent. in trust, 19581 ent. in trust, 23777 ent. in trust.
1640: 23777 f. (engr. tp/repeat?).

Boler, Thomas.
Son of **James Boler 1**; not active as a bookseller.
No address known.
1638: 1225 ent. in trust, 1230 ent. in trust, 20226 ent. in trust.

Bollifant, *alias* **Carpenter, Edmund.**
Printer in London, (1583) 1585–1602†. One of the partners in the **Eliot's Court Press**, where items without imprint are listed even though Bollifant's name may be supplied in STC. Items indexed below are almost exclusively those in which his name appears. Imprints below in which Bollifant's name appears with another partner are indicated by an asterisk (*). [*Dict. 1*; *Poor Book* (widow), 1611–31.]
dw. in the Little Old Bailey in Eliot's Court (D.1), 1585 (187); no later use noted
1585: 187, 5266.4*, 5299*, 5309* ap., 5309.2* ap., 5309.3* ap., 20109* ap.
1586: 3072*, 4087, 15233, 19485 ent.
1587: 3166, 15454, 19486, 19826.
1588: 1347, 6656, 24579 ent., 25889 (d).

Bollifant, E. — *cont.*
1589: 16611.5–12a.5 per.
1590: 21698 ent., 24407.
1591: 19953 ent., 20083.5 per.
1594: 19365.
1595: 4511, 4848 (note), 6986, 21662.
1596: 5259.5 ent., 5445.5, 12919, 15176, 21662a, 22872.
1597: 11750, 12920.
1598: 14585 ent., 18044, 23643, 25862.
1599: 1312.3 ent., 5234, 19260, 19622, 19833.5, 24131.
1600: 4518, 10547, 11513 ent., 11634, 23453 ent., 23462.
1601: 3398, 3399, 4334 ent., 11940, 25083.

Bolton (Boulton), Richard.
Bookseller in London, (1612) 1615–1618. Son of **Robert Bolton.** [*Dict. 1*; DFM 832.]
(in) Chancery Lane (V.12), 1615–1618
shop in — near Holborn, 1615 (24304)
at — end in the new buildings, 1618 (12025)
1615: 20282.5 f., 24304 sold. **1618:** 12025 f.

Bolton, Robert.
Bookseller in London, (1584) 1604–1623. Father of **Richard Bolton**. [*Dict. 1*; *Loan Book*, 1599–1602, 1620–1623.]
shop at Chancery Lane end (V.12), 1604 (25760)–1605 (25762, adds 'near Holborn')
shop in Smithfield near Long Lane end (E.9), 1606 (20941.7)–1611 (14297a.3, has 'dw.')
1604: 25760 f., 25761 f. (d), 25761.5 f. **1605:** 25762 f. **1606:** 20941.7 sold. **1607:** 25763 f. **1608:** 7187.5 sold. **1609:** 7188 sold. **1610:** 14528 f. **1611:** 14297a.3 f.

Bonfons, Nicolas.
Bookseller in Paris, 1572–1623. [Renouard.]
1580: 6832.50 chez.

Bonham, William.
Bookseller in London, c. 1520–1557†. Father-in-law of **William Norton;** grandfather of **Bonham Norton**. In the 1520s he was twice a sub-tenant of **John Rastell** at the Mermaid in Cheapside (N.2). [Duff, *Century*.]
in Paul's Churchyard, 1542–1551 at least
dw. at the King's Arms — (A.6), 1542 (5069)–1546? (2755)
— at the Red Lion (B), 1550? (5071)–1551 (2086, has 'dw.')
1542: 5069 [f.], 10661 [f.] (d), 16021.3(*A*3) [f.] (d?), 16026 [f.].
1546: 2755 [f.] (d?).
1550: 5071 [f.] (d?), 19494.7 at costs.
1551: 2086 f.

Bonhomme, Y. *See* Kerver.

Bonian (Bunnian), Richard.
Bookseller in London, 1607–1612. In partnership with **Henry Walley**, 1609–1610. [*Dict. 1*; DFM 2673.]
in Paul's Churchyard (A.2), 1607–1612 .
dw. at the Spread Eagle right over against the great North door of Paul's, 1607 (5564)–1610 (11068, omits 'dw.', with H. Walley), variation: at the Spread-Eagle —, 1609 (14778)
shop — at the Fleur-de-lis and Crown, 1611 (15227)–1612 (23545, omits 'and Crown'); variation: 1611 (21839, has 'dw.')
?sold at the Red Lion upon London Bridge (T.7), 1609 (18347.5); although this item was printed for 'Bunnian', the shop is almost certainly not his, but it has not been associated with any other bookseller
1607: 5564 f.
1608: 5565 f., 17907 f. (d), 19078.8 f.
1609: 4976 f., 7371 f., 14436 f., 14757 ent., 14778 f., 18347.5 f., 20759 f., 22331–2 f.
1610: 11068 f. (d?), 13538 f., 18323 ent., 18323a f., 21028.5 f., 21847 f.
1611: 10535 f., 10536.5 f., 15227–7.5 f., 21838 ent., 21839 f.
1612: 23545 f.

Bonifante, Radulph, *pseud.*
Printer in 'Basel', 1542. = M. Crom, Antwerp. [Duff, *Century*.]
1542: 3047.

Booth, Thomas.
Printseller in London, c. 1635? [Globe 212; Hind III.89.]
at the Glove [*sic*, not 'Globe'] in Cornhill, c. 1635? (12561.8)
1635: 12561.8 sold (c?).

Bordeaux, Jean de.
Bookseller and printer in Paris, 1610–1636†. [Renouard, under Jean II; Lottin 2: 37.]
1610–11: 21648.5(*A*3) chez.

Boscard, Charles.
Printer in Douai, c. 1602–1610, and in St. Omer, 1610–1629†. Son of Jacques and husband of **Jeanne Boscard**. Brother-in-law of **Pierre Auroi**. [*Dict. 1*; *Répertoire 17e*, IV.8.]
1263: [13033.4] (d/error).
1603–10: [22126.7] (d), [22969.5] (d).
1604: [12574] (d?).
1605: [17270], [25972.5].
1606: [3268] (c).
1607: [4868.5] (d?), [11334] (d?).
1608: [11025] (false), [12349] (false).
1609: [4830], [17271].
1610: [20485].
1614: 11728.
1615: 24924.5.
1616: [16096.5].
1617: [11320a] (d/repeat), [16232.5].
1618: [632.3], [11314.2].
1619: [20486].
1620: [742.3], [4284], [4959], [17276], [24627a.4].
1621: [3895.5], [16098], [24731b].
1622: [1341], [1779], [4572], [10541.7], [11320a] (d), [13033], [13034], [13036], [18902], [22970].
1623: [3801.5], [3902], [13033.4] (d), [17276.3].
1624: [13], [934], [1837.3], [3606], [3895], [11113], [11617.6], [13033.6], [21693], [21697], [23990].
1625: [535.7], [3895.3], [3895.7], [4603], [6185], [17276.4], [21697.5], [23233].
1626: [1780], [4469], [16227].
1627: [12808.3].

Boscard, Jacques, *Widow of.*
Printer in Douai, c. 1578–1611. Mother of **Charles Boscard.** [Muller 16; *Répertoire 17e*, IV.8.]
1601: 26000.9.

Boscard (Burée), Jeanne.
Printer in St. Omer, 1629–1652. Widow of **Charles Boscard**. [*Dict. 1*, under husband; Lepreux I.101–2.]
1630: [742.7], [743], [17506.3], [18482], [21144], [24734], [25774].
1631: 985.5 (note), [13037], [16099], [16100], [24748.5].
1632: 986 (note), [16922a.3], [21147], [21150].
1633: [1844], [25071].
1634: [10676.5], [13033.8].
1635: [12144.5].
1638: [1841?], [1842?], [5645.5].
1639: [4572.5].

Bosco, Arrigo del, *pseud.*
Printer in 'Leida' [Leiden], 1588. = J. Wolfe (Woodfield no. 13).
1588: 15414.6.

Bosselarius, Henricus.
Printer? in Middelburg, 1631. [Gruys.]
1631: 1431.32.

Bostock, Robert.
Bookseller in London, (1625) 1626–1656†. [*Dict. 2*; DFM 1900; *Loan Book*, 1628–34.]
at the King's Head in Paul's Churchyard (A.3), 1626 (3573)–1640 (15567, has 'dw.') at least
1626: 3573 f.
1628: 11468 f.
1629: 15467 f., 17743 f.
1630: 3395 f., 3563 sold, 5133 f., 11691.5 ent.
1631: [3591?] sold, 20934 f., 20935 f., 25768.5(*A*3) f.
1632: 20927 f., 20935 f.

Bostock, R. — *cont.*
1633: 3564 sold, 3576 ven.
1634: 3553 sold, 20936 f., 24348 f.
1635: 3554 sold, 3569 f., 3581.7 f., 20928 f., 22553 f.
1636: 3554.5 sold, 3567.5 sold, 20932 f., 20932.5 f. (forged?).
1637: 20936.5–37 f.
1638: 3553 ent., 3554 ent., 3554.5 ent., 20929 ent., 20929a f., 20931 f., 20931.5 f. (forged?).
1639: 20930a f., 20933 f.
1640: 15567 f., 20938 f., 21253 ent.

Boswell, John.
Printseller in London, c. 1611. [Hind II.313–14.]
in Lombard Street (O.12), c. 1611 (6345.7)
1611: 6345.7 sold (c).

Boudins (Balduinus, Boeidens), John.
Bookseller in London, 1502–1503†. Lived in the parish of St. Clement's, Eastcheap (T.3). In 1502 (23427.3) he seems to have had an agent or colleague in Antwerp. [Duff, *Century* 15.]
No address used.
1502: 16116 imp., 23427.3 ven.

Boulenger, (Bullenger), Giles.
French refugee in London, c. 1573–1594†, and publisher, c. 1593. Son-in-law? of **Giles Godet;** father? of **Paul Boulenger**. Called a 'printer of storyes' in 1593 (*Returns* III.445). Lived in the parish of St. Anne's, Blackfriars (Q.5). [*Returns* II.253, 356 (both 'Bullinger'; III.445.]
No address used.
1593: 6445.3 [f.] (c).

Boulenger, Jean. *See* Le Boullenger.

Boulenger, Paul.
Printer? or printseller? in London, c. 1607–1616 at least. Son? of **Giles Boulenger**; grandson? of **Giles Godet**. [*Dict. 1.*]
in the Blackfriars (Q.6), 1615 (7627.5)
1607: [13851?]. **1615:** 7627.5 [f.]. **1616:** [13526.5?].

Boulton. *See* Bolton.

Bounel, Philip.
Journeyman printer? in London, 1545. Probably the Philip Bonnell mentioned in the subsidy rolls for 1544 as living in the parish of St. Leonard, Foster Lane, Aldersgate Ward (G.5) (*Returns* I.82) since his only item was printed for **John Walley**, who lived there also. Bounel seems to have worked in the shop of **Nicholas Hill** or borrowed some of his printing material.
No address used.
1545: 15732.9.

Bourman, Nicholas.
Bookseller and printer? (until 1542) in London, 1539–1566? The printing material in his books was used previously and also later by **John Herford,** and it is possible that the following items were printed by Herford for him. [Duff, *Century*; *Library* 16 (1936): 406, n.2.]
in Aldersgate Street (F.2), 1539 (14118)–1542 (21807)
1539: 14118, 23152.5.
1540: 7378 (d?), 16016, [16016.5?] (d?).
1540/41: 474.5.
1542: [16021–1.3(*A*3)?] (d?), 21807 (d).

Bourne, Nicholas.
Bookseller in London, 1608–1660† (Smyth's *Obituary*: 52, as 'Browne'). Master of **John Bellamy**, who apparently continued to work in Bourne's shop, 1620–21. Publisher of Newsbooks and news pamphlets, often with others, especially **Thomas Archer** in 1622 and **Nathaniel Butter** from 1622. In 1625–27 Bourne and Butter used the pseudonym **Mercurius,** *Britannicus*, and such imprints, *not* indexed below, are listed under that heading. One of the *assignees of* **C. Cotton**. [*Dict. 2*; DFM 129; *Loan Book*, 1608–11, 1620–27; *Library* 12 (1957): 23–33.]
(at) the Royal Exchange (O.8), 1608–1640 and undoubtedly later; some variations:
shop under —, 1608 (25965)
at —, 1610 (12769)–1620 (22759, has 'shop')

Bourne, N. — *cont.*
shop at the entering in of —, 1612 (712)
shop at the South entry of —, 1615 (12570)–1616 (23480)
shop at the South entrance of —, 1625 (13204)–1640 (6188)
1608: 22932 ent., 25965 f.
1609: 14680(*A*3) ent., 18455.7–56 f., 22710 ent., 22756 ent., 23492 ent.
1610: 12769 f.
1611: 20449–9.5 f., 23486 f.
1612: 712 f., 6617 f., 22756 f., 22932 f.
1613: 6618 f., 23492 f.
1614: 889.5 sold, 6365 f., 22757 f.
1615: 12570 f., 19202 f., 21486 f.
1616: 6597.4 f., 7079 ent., 13318 ent., 19208.5 f., 22933 f., 23480 f., 23493 f.
1617: 5620 f., 20187 sold, 22758 f., 22974 f., 23115.5 f., 23487 f., 25296 f.
1618: 5538 f., 7065 f., 23116 f., 23481 f.
1619: 15569 f., 22933.3 f., [22933.5 f.] (d?).
1620: 22759 f., [22837(*A*3)] sold, 24810 sold.
1621: [3589(*A*3)] sold, 12136 ent., 12137 f., [20283(*A*3)] sold, [20284(*A*3)] sold, [20286(*A*3)] sold.
1622: 5766 f., 5767 f., 13573 f., 13575 f., 15568 f., [18507.45? f.] (d), —.46 f., —.47 f., —.48 f., —.51 f., —.52 f., —.55 f., —.56 f., —.57 f., —.58 f., —.59 f., —.61 f., —.62 f., —.64 f., —.65 f., —.66 f., —.67 f., —.69 f., —.70 f., —.71 f., —.73 f., —.74 f., —.76 f., —.81 f., —.82 f., —.85 f., —.87 ent., —.88 f., —.89 f., —.91 f., 20864 ent., 22933.7 f., 23493.5 f.
1623: 898.5(*A*) f., 11366 f., 12092 f., 14623 sold, 17221 sold, 17985 f., 18507.92 f., —.93 f., —.94 f., —.95 f., —.96 ent., —.97 f., —.99 f., —.100 f., —.102 f., —.103 f., —.104 f., —.105 f., —.106 f., —.107 f., —.109 f., —.110 f., —.112 f., —.113 ent., —.115 f., —.119 f., —.121 f., —.122 f., —.124 ent., —.126 f., —.132 sold, —.135 f., —.136 f., —.137 f., 22934 f., 22992.9 f. (d), 23009 f.
1624: 219 ent., 1021.5 f., 6618.5 f., 7323 f., 14280 f., 18507.138 f., —.143 f., —.147 f., —.147A f., —.148 f., —.149 f., —.151 f., —.152 f., —.154 f., —.155 f., —.156 f., —.157 f., —.158 f., 20111 ent., 22711 ass'd, 25963 ent., 26005 f.
1625: 1336 ent., 1338.5 f., 5131 f., 10725 f., 12603 f., 13204 f., 14928 f., 14928.5 f., 23074 f., 23636.5 sold.
1626: 10725 f., 10726 f., 10739 f., 14497 f., 15248 f., 18544 f., 20392 f., 23473 f., 23488 f., 23493.7 f., 26003 f.
1627: 7450 ent., 16857.7 f., 18507.187 ent., 20392.5 f., 20779.5 ent., 24295 f., 25742 sold.
1628: 7161–1.3 f., 7449 f., 7744.5 ?ent., 7746.8 ?ent., 10726.5 f., 18545 f., 23072 f., 25964 ent.
1629: 5133 ent., 6313 sold, 9250 f., 10743 f., 11363 f., 11363.5 f., 12641 f., 13248.4 f., 16854 f., 17223 sold, 17298 f., 18507.200 f., —.201 f. (d), —.202 f., —.203 f., —.203A f., 19555 f., 20241 f., 20241.3 f., 20241.7 f., 20251 sold, 20252 f., 20253 f., 23489 f., 23898 sold, 25183 f.
1630: 5133.3 f., 6597.7 f., 7101 f., 7536.7 f., 7746.8 ?ent., 10727 f., 15333 f., 17916.5 f., 17916.7–.9 f., 18507.204 f., —.205 f., —.206 f., —.207 f., 20208 f., 20209 f., 20242 f., 20243 f., 20254 f., 20385 pro, 21487 f., 23494 f., 24258 f., 25219 f., 26090 f.
1631: 11288.5 f., 11299 f., 12532 f., 16847.5 f., 18329 pro, 18507.208 f., —.209 f., —.210 f., —.211 f., —.212 f., —.213 f., —.214 f., —.215 f., —.217 f., —.218 f., —.219 f., —.220 f., —.221 f., —.222 f., —.223 f., —.224 f., —.225 f., —.226 f. (d), —.227 f., —.228 f., —.229 f., —.230 f., —.231 f., —.232 f., —.233 f., —.234 f., —.235 f., 20209 f., 20210 f., 20231 sold, 20232 sold, 20244 f., 20255 f., 20256 f., 20865 f., 24524 f., 26087 f.
1632: 4600 f., 10741 f., 18507.236 f., —.237 f., —.238 f., —.239 f., —.240 f., —.241 f., —.242 f., —.243 f., —.244 f., —.245 f., —.246 f., —.247 f., —.248 f., —.249 f., —.250 f., —.251 f., —.252 f., —.253 f., —.254 f., —.255 f., —.256 f., —.257 f., —.258 f., —.259 f., —.260 f., —.261 f., —.262 f., —.263 f. (d), —.264 f., —.265 f., —.266 f., —.267 f., —.268 f., —.269 f., —.270 f., —.271 f., —.272 f., —.273 f., —.274 f., —.275 f., —.276 f., 20211 f., 20233 sold, 20257 f., 21820 f., 23507 f., 23519.5 f., 23520 f., 23521 f., 23522 f., 23523 f., 23524–4a f.
1633: 7121 f., 10728 f., 12534 (note), 12743.5 f., 13552.5 f., 18896 f., 18899b sold, 20233a sold, 20245 f., 20258 f., 20262 f., 20263 f., 21819 f., 23345 sold, 23345.5 (d/repeat), 23525 f., 23525.1 f., 23525.3–.4 f., 25866 f.
1634: 1636 f., 7122 f., 12640.5 f. (note), 19203.3 f., 20212 f., 20213 f., 20234 sold, 20246 f., 20258.5 f., 20259 f., 20263 f., 20264 f., 23523.5 f., 23525.2 f., 23525.5 f., 23525.6 f., 23525.7 f., 24930 f., 24956 f., 25183.5 f.
1635: 1637 f., 7162 f., 17224 f., 20260a f., 23272 ent., 23366 f., 23495 f., 23525.8 f., 23525.9 f., 25930.3 sold.
1636: 7149 f., 10730 f., 17224 f. & sold, 17224.5 sold, 20387 ent.
1636/37: 4293 f.
1637: 3597 f., 4293.2 f., 4293.4 f., 11364 f., 13125 ent., 20213 f., 20265–5.5 f.
1638: 4293.6 sold, 10740 f., 11673 f., 11674 f., 18193 ent., 18507.277 f., 20226 f., 20227 f., 22475 f., 22498 f., 22498a f.
1638/39: 18507.283 f., —.285 f.
1639: 4293.8 f., 7123 f., 12735 ent., 10729 f., 12735 ent., 13870.7 (note), 18507.278 f., —.279 f. (d), —.280 f. (d), —.281 f., —.282 f., —.284 f., —.286 [f.] (d), —.287 f., —.288 f., —.289 f., —.290 f. (d), —.291 f., —.292 f., —.293 f., —.294 f., —.295 f., —.296 f., —.297 f., —.298 f., —.299 f., —.300 f., —.301 f., —.302 f., —.303 f., —.304 f., —.305 f., —.306 f., —.307 f., [—.308 f.] (d), —.309 f., —.310 f., —.311 f., —.312 f., —.313 f., —.314 f., —.315 f., 20227 f. (note), 20247 f., 20863 f., 22132 f., 22475 f., 22491 f., 24048 f. (note), 25184 f., 25963 f., 26122 f., 26122.5 f.
1639/40: 18507.326 f.
1640: 6188 f., 7079 f., 7117 f., 7748 f., 13467 f., 13468 f., 13918 f., 22491 f., 23809 ent., 25960–1 f.
1641: 18507.345C(*A*3) ent., 20383 ent., 23345.5 f. (repeat, c?).

Bourne, Robert.
Printer in London, (1581: Arber II.684) 1586, 1591?–1593. In July 1586 he was recorded as having one press (Arber V.lii); on 30 Oct. the same year it or another press was seized in Middlesex (*Reg. B*: 21). In 1592 he was using printing material of **John Wolfe**, perhaps as foreman or manager for Wolfe and actual printer of most of the work indexed under Wolfe for 1591–93. [*Dict. 1.*]
No address noted.
1592: 287.5, 799 (d), 1030.5 (d), 5966 ent., 12296, 15696, 16767 (d), 19699.5, 19700(*A*3), [20977–7.5(*A*3)], 22140, 23869, 24899.
1593: [1?] (d), 19700.5(*A*3), 23867.5.

Bourne, Thomas.
Bookseller in London, (1623) 1628–1671†. Documentary evidence places him in or near Bethlehem Hospital (K.1) in 1628 and 1671. [*Dict. 1*; *Dict. 2*; DFM 1773.]
No address noted.
1628: 10182 f. (d). **1631:** 10182.5 f.

Boursette, Madeleine.
Printer in Paris, 1541–1556†. Widow of **François Regnault**. [Duff, *Century*; Renouard.]
1552: 6832.31 chez. **1554:** 15836 ap. **1555:** 15836–7 ap. **1556:** 15844 ap.

Bouvier (Bover, Bonner), Francis.
French refugee and publisher in London, 1583–1618 at least. Brother-in-law of **Ascanius de Renialme**. Although he lived in St. Anne's parish (Q.5), Blackfriars, his son James was buried at St. Giles Cripplegate. [*Dict. 1*; *St. Giles*, 1593.]
No address used.
1584: 14583 ap. **1589:** 24718 ap.

Bouwensz, Jan.
Printer in Leiden, 1571–1614. [Gruys.]
1585: 1431.8. **1586:** 25340.

Bowen, John.
Journeyman printer in London, (1586) 1588–1590. His daughter was buried in 1593 (*St. Giles*). [*Dict. 1.*]
dw. in St. John's Street (E.10), [Clerkenwell,] 1590 (12804, with J. Morris)
1588: 11542.5 f. **1590:** 12804 [f.], 13114 f.

Bowler. *See* Boler.

Bowman, Francis.
Bookseller in Oxford, 1634–1668. [*Dict. 2*; Madan II.540–1, III. 429–31.]
No address used.
1634: 3129 sold, 3129a sold. **1636:** 11105 sold. **1638:** 11570 f., 19042 f., 20694 f. **1639:** 12402a.2 ven., 12455 f. **1640:** 20695–5.5 f.

Bowring, James.
Journeyman printer in London, (1583) 1585–1589. Freed by W. Hoskins on 2 Sept. 1583 (Arber II.690). The only extant item in which he is named as one of the printers was produced in R. Robinson's house in Fetter Lane (V.7). [Not in *Dict. 1*; *St. Giles*, 1589.]
No separate address used.
1585: 1848.

Boyle, Richard.
Bookseller in London, (1584) 1587–1625?† In partnership with **William Jones 3** 1612–13. Although the last specific mention of him is 1620 (*C-B C*: 121), it is probable that he did not die until 1625, the year his widow, Ellen, turned over his copyrights. [*Dict. 1*; *Poor Book* (widow), 1629–41; *Loan Book*, 1616–19; *Library* 19 (1964): 59–60, 64.]
at the Rose in Paul's Churchyard (A.3), 1587 (24008)–1588 [3599 (*A*3)]; still there in July 1589 (17458, A3ᵛ)
dw. in Blackfriars (Q.6), 1603 (1338)–1613 (7537); this address also appears in 2751, currently dated c. 1590? but possibly published a decade or so later.
1587: 24008 ext. (d).
1588: [3599(*A*3)] sold.
1590: 2751 f. (c?).
1593: 1335 f. (d), 1336 f. (note).
1595: [15638 f.] (d), [20190? f.] (c).
1600: 1335.7 f. (d?).
1603: 1338 f.
1606: 13244 pro.
1607: 1334 f., 1337 f., 1339 f.
1608: 1069 f., 6027 ent.
1609: 4610 sumpt., 4611 sumpt., 13123 f., 20826.5 f.
1610: 1337.5 f.
1611: 5861 f., 5861.2 f.
1612: 5833 f., 24233 f., 24596 f.
1613: 7537 f., 13952 sumpt.
1623: [1336(*A*3)? f.].

1625: 1336 ass'd, 1338.5 ass'd.

Boys, Michael, *pseud. See* Wood, Michael, *pseud.*

Brachius, J. See Bray.

Bradock, Richard.
Printer and bookseller (from 1609) in London, (1577) 1581, 1598–1615. His items of 1581 were apparently printed in the house of **Richard Jones** or at least with material borrowed from Jones. By 1598 he had married the widow of **Robert Robinson** and succeeded to the latter's printing material. In Oct. 1608 he began negotiations to sell the business to **William Hall** and **Thomas Haviland** (*C-B C*: 36). [*Dict. 1.*]
dw. in Aldermanbury a little above the conduit (H.2), 1581 (25966); no later use of this address or any other noted.
1560: [25259.5] (d/error).
1581: 12531.3, 25966–6.5.
1598: 1559, 1823, 2402.5, [3092], 4032(*A*, note), 4172, 6819, 11482, 11558 (note), 12322, 12372, 12717, 12718.5, 16906.5, 17438, 18617.7, 21225, [22984.3(*A*3)], 23328, 23328.5, 24890.
1599: 4263, [5403.5], 7353.5, 12312–13, 12313.5–14, [12719], 12923.5, 13076, [19143.5(*A*3)], 20307, [22358a], [24766.7?].
1600: 25, 3666, [3677.5], [3678?], [12287.5(*A*3)], [18617.9(*A*3)] (d?), [18763], [22302], 24612, 25282.
1601: [1073?], 2403.3, [3648], [3649], [3672?], [3700.5], [17173.5?], [18269], [18271].
1602: [3081], [7298.5], [14781], [17473], [17474], [19144], [22359] (d?), 24613–3.5.
1603: [3685], [5333], [6627], 6788, [7120], [12311], [12988], [14365], [14599?], [17289?], [24079], [24599.5(*A*3)], 24769a.
1604: [1793.5?], 5650, 10650, 11558, [11558.3] (c), [11936?] (d), [18675?], [22254.7].
1605: [190], 737 (d), 3022.9, [6344] (d?), [10047.3], 11575, [17077(*A*3)], 20575.5 ex off., [25259.5] (d), [25259.7].
1605/06: [483.4], [489.3], [532.5?].
1606: [795], 2773, 3023, 3023.5, [3636], 3691.3, 5344, [6329], 7225.5 (d?), [11158], 12337, 13546, [17078(*A*3)], [18850], 19500, [23452–2a.5], [25085?], [25942].

Bradock, R. — *cont.*
1606/07: [408.2–.3], [434.19], [461.2], [480], [507.2].
1607: [5300.7], [5759.3], 11482.4, 11559, 12373, 19500.5, 22667.5, [24614].
1607/08: [467], [483.6].
1608: [27], 3024, 5334, [5759.4], [6411], 6958, 6959.5, 12734.5, [13453], [17879–9a], 19330, [21606], 22340, [25988].
1608/09: [408.5(*A*3)].
1609: 2784 f., 6960, 9175q ass'd, 18618.7 f.
1610: 18620 f.
1612: 4032.2 f., 11482.7 f., 18620.5 f.
1614: 4032.3(*A*3) f.
1615: 3306(*A*) ass'd, 11560 ass'd.

Bradshaw, Henry.
Grocer and publisher in London, 1559–1561. [*Dict. 1.*]
No address used.
1559: 10664.5 [f.]. **1561:** 5076.3 [f.].

Bradwood, Melchisidec.
Printer in London, (1584) 1602–1618† but primarily in Eton, 1610–1618. One of the partners in the **Eliot's Court Press.** Items listed below either have Bradwood's name in the imprint or a variant thereof, or in the SR entry, or they were printed at Eton. Other London items printed during Bradwood's period of activity without any name in the imprint, including those for which his name has been supplied in STC, are listed *only* under the Eliot's Court Press. [*Dict. 1*; *St. Giles* (I.4), 1589–1603, 1613; *Library* 2 (1922): 175–84; 3 (1923): 194–209.]
London, in the Little Old Bailey (D.1), 1604–1606
dw. — in Eliot's Court, 1604 (19901)
dw. — near to the King's Head, 1606 (10301); no later use noted
Eton, in Collegio regali, 1610 [14622]–1615 [12347]
1602: [13787a.5] (false, d), 13788 ap., 23459 ap.
1603: 4519, 15435, 18210.
1604: 3070, 12407, 19901, 24030, 24120.
1605: 1014.5, 5482, 24268.
1606: 4520, 6164, 10301, 19748, 23448.
1607: 6263, 7274, 10188.5, 12028, 13789 ap., 17996, 24719.
1608: 38, 38.5, 12408 (d?), 12648, 12648a, 12648a.5, 12699, 12894, 18191.
1609: 6629.5, 11538, 12894a, 13386, 15460, 18626a.5, 24770.5.
1610: 6630, [12346], [14622], [14629].
1611: [2353.5(*A*3)] (d), 6630.3(*A*), 11099, [14629.5].
1612: 5483, 6630.5, 7023, 12650, 13417, [14629], [14629.5], [14629a], 20432, 20910, 24771.
1613: 131, 206, 3460.6, 3807, [6899(*A*3)] (d?), 13391, 13418, [14629a], 18042, [26065].
1615: [12347].

Bramerau, Jacques.
Printer in Avignon, 1586–1606. [*Dict. 1*: 53; Muller 7.]
1601: 5141.5 ap.

Bramridge (Barmeridge), John.
Bookseller in London, (1621) 1623. [*Dict. 1*; DFM 2613.]
shop near Strand Bridge (X.4), 1623 (860)
1623: 860 f.

Bray (Brachius), John.
Bookseller in London, 1495–c. 1510 at least. Formerly keeper of Ludgate prison. [Duff, *Century*; *Library* 1 (1910): 295–6; Christianson 73.]
No address used.
1504: 23885.3 ven.

Bray, T. du. *See* Du Bray.

Brel. *See* Du Brel.

Bretton, William.
Grocer, Merchant of the Staple in Calais, and publisher in London, 1505–1510 (1526?†). [Duff, *Century*; *SB* 32 (1979): 49–50, abstract of will.]
No address used.
1505: 17109 imp. **1506:** 15903 imp., 16258 exp. **1507–08:** 15862 imp. **1510:** 4115 imp., 15909 imp., 23030.7 sumpt.

Breughel, Cornelis Gerrits van.
Printer in Amsterdam, 1631–1636. [*Dict. 1*; Gruys; Briels 187–8.]
1632: 2735.

Brewster (Bruster), Edward.
Bookseller in London, (1615) 1616–1647†. Shared many copyrights with **Robert Bird** and sometimes published jointly with him. Treasurer of the **English Stock** (*see* Stationers' Company) from 1610 (*C-B C*: 320) until his death (H.11, Q.1). His first shop was shared with **Robert Redmer** until 1619 though there are no joint imprints. Brewster's second shop in Paul's Churchyard was among those marked for removal c. 1632 (*Library* 3 (1902): 267–8); he was not one of those petitioning for relief in Jan. 1636 when the final order came (Greg, *Companion*: 337–8). [*Dict. 2*; DFM 2707.]
in Paul's Churchyard, 1616–1635
at the Star at the West end of Paul's Church (A.10), 1616 (13877.5)–1624 (21245); variation: at the great West door of Paul's [no sign], 1624 (4881)
shop at the Bible — (A.2), 1625 (5131)–1635 (1643); sometimes adds: near the great North door of Paul's, 1626 (12117), 1627 (21246, omits 'great')
shop at Fleet Bridge at the Bible (W.3), 1635 (1643.5)–1640 (21196, has 'on' Fleet Bridge) at least
1616: 13877.5 sold.
1617: 25142 f.
1619: 15557 f., 21244 f.
1620: 21201 f.
1621: 21194 f., 21244.5 f., 21250 f.
1622: 23862 f.
1623: 21199 f.
1624: 4881 f., 21245 f.
1625: 5131 f.
1626: 382.5 ent., 1313.3 ent., 1315 ent., 3031 ent., 3324 ent., 3698.3 ent., 4290 ent., 4309 ent., 4910 ent., 6478 ent., 6571 ent., 7144 ent., 10714 ent., 10865.5 ent., 11561 ent., 11652 ent., 12117 f., 12121 ent., 12734.5 ent., 15094 ent., 15534 ent., 16960 ent., 17783 ent., 19436.5 ent., 21213.9 ent., 21370 ent., 21851 ent., 22138 ent., 22673 ent., 23390 ent., 23616 ent., 25136 ent., 25399.5 ent., 25435 ent., 25655 ent., 25990 ent.
1627: 1315 ent., 6554.5 f., 18625 f., 19431 f., 21241.7 f., 21246 f.
1628: 1313.2(*A*) sold, 6553.5 f., 12637.4–.7 f., 15554 sold, 21210.3 f., 21242 f., 22673 f., 25038 f.
1629: 1315 f., 13461 f., 18625.5 f., 21247 f.
1630: 1313.3 sold, 3031 f., 3279 f., 25136 f. (d?).
1631: 1316 sold, 1319 f., 12116 f., 21243 f., 21247.5 f., 22674 f.
1632: 1313.5 sold, 1320 f., 12125 f., 13462 f., 21198 f., 21200 f., 21202 f., 21248 f., 22675 f., 25399.5 f.
1633: 1317 sold, 3031.5(*A*) f., 13459 f.
1634: 12121 f., 12639.7 f.
1635: 1318 sold, 1643–3.5 f., 3032 f., 13463 f., 21243.5 f., 25032 f.
1636: 12116.5 f., 12118 f., 13460 f.
1637: 1318.5 f., 1321 f., 11652 f., 21249 f., 22676 f., 25400 f.
1638: 3032.5 f. (d?).
1640: 1313 f., 11656 f., 21196 f.

Brewster, William.
English refugee printer in Leiden, 1617–1619. His principal workmen were John Reynolds (DFM 418) and Edward Winslowe (DFM 84). [J. R. Harris and S. K. Jones, *The Pilgrim Press. Partial reprint with new contributions*., ed. R. Breugelmans, Nieuwkoop, 1987.]
1617: [6973], [10849], [15647], [24186], [25333].
1618: [4709], [4929], [6469], [6876], [12862], [21115a].
1619: [4360], [6877], [10567].

Brière, Annet.
Printer in Paris, 1551–1566. [Renouard.]
1565: 1884.5 ap.

Bright, Timothy.
Physician, b. 1550?–1615†. Patentee for all works in shorthand and all works he should compile (Pat. Rolls 31 Eliz., part 9, 26 July 1589). His assignee in the items below = J. Windet. [*DNB*; Carlton 2–6.]
No address used.
1588: 3743 by ass'n of. **1589:** 11229 at ass't of.

Brinkley, Stephen. *See* 'Greenstreet House' Press; Fr. Parsons' Press.

Briscoe, Thomas.
Stationer in London, (1626) 1636–1638. His only imprint was shared with **John Williams**, with whom Briscoe seems briefly to have worked. [*Dict. 1*; DFM 814.]
at the Crane in Paul's Churchyard (A.3), 1636 (20078)
1636: 20078 sold.

Britannicus, Mercurius. *See* Mercurius, *Britannicus*.

Brome. *See* Broome.

Brooke, Thomas.
One of the **Printers to the University of Cambridge.** (*See* Cambridge University), 1608–1624? (1629†). The asterisk (*) indicates an imprint shared with another Printer to the University. [*Dict. 1.*]
No address used.
1608: 19722*.

Brooks (Brooke), William.
Bookseller in London, (1616) 1631?–1640. The following addresses probably all refer to the same shop. [*Dict. 1*; DFM 673.]
within the Turning Stile in Holborn (V.13), 1631 [6589(*A*3)?]
in Turnstile Alley near Lincoln's Inn Fields, 1637 (11321)
shop in Holborn in Turnstile Lane, 1639 (4549)
dw. at the upper end of Holborn in Turpin's rents, 1640 (11032)
1631: [6589(*A*3)?] sold. **1637:** 11321 f., 14628.5 f. **1639:** 4549 f.
1640: 11032 f.

Broome (Brome), Joan.
Bookseller in London, 1591–1601†. Widow of **William Broome**. From 1596 she was agent in London for the sale of books printed in Oxford. Succeeded by her former apprentice, **George Potter**. [*Dict. 1.*]
at the Bible in Paul's Churchyard (A.2), 1592 (17083)–1601 (1074); variation: dw. at the Bible near unto the North door of Paul's, 1600 (12287.5(*A*3))
1591: 5445 f., 17050 f., 22665 f.
1592: 12286 f., 17080 f., 17083 f., 18150 f., 25081 f.
1595: 12287 f.
1596: 4760 ven., [10943] sold, [10944] sold, 18604 f., [23670] sold, 25082 f.
1597: 4765 ven., 6575 ven., [14976] sold, 17049 ent., 17087 ent., 18150 ent., [19945] sold, [20207] sold, [22555] ven., [23670.5(*A*3)] sold, 25082a f., [25087] sold.
1598: 1559 f., 4172 f., 21225 f.
1599: [13076(*A*3)] sold, [14977] sold, [21137] sold.
1600: 12287.5(*A*3) f., [14978] sold, [19773] sold, [21089] sold, [23913] sold, [24527] sold.
1601: 1073 f., 1074 f., [13597(*A*3)] sold, [24536] sold.

Broome (Brome, Browne), William.
Bookseller in London, (1575?) 1577–1591†. Probably the William 'Browne' apprenticed to Arthur Pepwell for 9 years from 29 Sept. 1566 (Arber I.324). In 1584–88 often published jointly with **Thomas Man 1**. [*Dict. 1.*]
No address noted.
1577: 13923 [f.], 13924 f., 18448 [f.] (d).
1582: 25713 f., 25714 f.
1583: 4739 f., 24669 at costs.
1584: 6141 [f.], 10224 f. (d), 15251.7(*A*3) ent., 21864 [f.], 24489 f., 24501 f.
1585: 22217 ent., 25185a f., 25622 ent., 25888 f.
1586: 5964.5 f., 18325.7 f., 25625 f.
1587: 5964.5 f., 12498.5–99 f. (d?), 25622.7 f. (d).
1588: 23858.5–59.3, 24492 f. (d?).
1591: 17049 f., 17087 f.

Browne, Alice.
Bookseller in London, 1623–1625. Widow of **John Browne 1**. Briefly continued publishing music with her husband's partners, **Thomas Snodham** and **Matthew Lownes**. She then remarried out of the Stat. Co., but her new husband apparently died of the plague, and in 1625 her livery share in the English Stock was

Browne, Alice — *cont.*
turned over for a yeomanry share (*C-B C*: 166, 180; the effects of the original transaction duplicated, 177). [*Dict. 1*, under husband.]
No address used.
1623: 5780.7 ass'd, 19451.5 ass'd. **1624:** 7466 f., 19924 f.

Browne, Francis. *See* 'Greenstreet House' Press.

Browne, John 1.
Bookseller in London, (1594) 1598–1622†. Husband of **Alice** and father of **Samuel Browne**. One of the *assignees of* **W. Barley**. The only Browne to be elected to the livery (1611) before 1640. Not a bookbinder. One of his early books was published with **John Herbert** and sold at the latter's shop: in Chancery Lane at the Paper Book (14830.3). [*Dict. 1.*]
in Fleet Street, 1598–1621
shop — over against Whitefriars at the Sugarloaf (W.7), 1598 (24890)
at the Bible — (W.5), 1599 (24.5)–1600 (25)
shop in St. Dunstan's Churchyard — (W.9), 1603 (3646)–1621 (153)
1598: 6170 f., 14830.3 f., 16906.5 f., 24890 f.
1599: 24 f., 24.5 f., 7353.5 f.
1600: 25 f., 17395 sold, 18974 f.
1601: 3648 f., 3649 f., 3672 f.
1603: 3646 f., [6535] sold, [6535.3] sold (d?), [6535.5] sold (d?), 11214.8 f., 13589 f.
1604: 19451 f., 22426 f.
1605: 26 f., 3691.2 f., 6344 f. (d?), 17619 f.
1606: 1539 f., 3649 (*A*1, note), 3691.3 f., 5679 f.
1607: 3687 f., 4538 f., 11166 sold, 17879 ent., 20778 f. (d).
1608: 27 f., 24611 sold.
1609: 3688 f., 3691.5 f., 17620 f., 10827 f., 10828 f., 19451.5 f., 21333 f., 25619a f.
1610: 4542 f. (d), 5118 f., 5768 f., 5777 f., 14763 ent., 18120 ent.
1611: 4980 f., 17749 f., 18120 ent., 18132 f., 21533 ent.
1612: 4989 ent., 4994 f., 5769 f., 7098 f., 7226 f. (d), 14763 ass'd, 19507–8 f.
1613: 3691.7 f., 4546 f., 4546.5–47 f. (d?), 7227 f., 15588 f., 17355 f., 19923 f.
1614: 17356 f.
1615: 17356a f., 18299 f.
1617: 28 f., 12796 sold, 18300 f., 18301 ent.
1618: 1587 f., 7463 f., 7465 f., 20760 f.
1619: 7464 f., 17239 f., 17887 f., 18120 f., 24624 f.
1620: 14763–4 sold.
1621: 153 f.
1622: 24099 f.

Browne, John 2.
Bookbinder and bookseller in London, (1605) 1612–1634 (cf. DFM 920) at least. This is the man included by John Gee among the dispersers of popish books, e.g. on $T1^v$ of 11704. Almost certainly the man assessed in 1633 for Dr. Lamb (*C-B C*: 423). [*Dict. 1*; DFM 1667; ?*Loan Book*, 1629–36.]
in Little Britain (F.4), c. 1615–1625 at least; variations:
dw. — right over against St. Bartholomew's gate, c. 1615 (3908.3)
shop —, 1617 (17944); usually adding 'without Aldersgate', 1617–20 (19744a), 1625 (17945.5)
shop — near Duck Lane end, 1620 (3580)
1615: 3908.3 bound by (c). **1617:** 17944 sold, 17944a.1 [sold] (d). **1620:** 3580 f., 17944a.10 [sold] (d). **1625:** 17945.5 sold.

Browne, John 3.
Bookseller in London, (?1621) 1625. In 1624 the shop belonged to Nicholas Vavasour and by 1627 it had passed to Francis Constable. [Not in *Dict. 1*; ?DFM 770.]
shop in Paul's Churchyard at the Crane (A.3), 1625 (14440, 14488, omits 'shop')
1625: 14440 f., 14488 f.

Browne, Joseph.
Bookseller in London, 1611–1626 at least. Possibly a rolling-press printer (Globe 213). [*Dict. 1*; DFM 106; *Poor Book*, 1626.]
in Paul's Churchyard at the Bull Head (A.2), 1623 (16913, sub tp following p. 595); no earlier address used.
1611: 21016 ent. **1612:** 21016a f., 21017 f. **1616:** 12022.7 f. **1623:** 16913 sold, 16914 f.

Browne, Nathaniel.
Bookseller in London, 1617–1651†. [*Dict. 1*; DFM 2688; *Poor Book*, 1641–51, widow thereafter; Globe 213.]
at the great North door of Paul's Church (A.2), 1617? (3062)–1618 (4629; 11281, has 'next shop to' the great ...)
(in) the Long Walk (E.8), 1624–1625
shop at the upper end of — near Little St. Bartholomew's, 1624 (12030)
in — near Christ Church, 1625 (3722)
1617: 3062 sold (d?).
1618: 4629 f., 11281 f., 24333 f., 25747 sumpt., 25748 sumpt.
1624: 12030 f.
1625: 3722 sold.

Browne, Nicholas. *See* Bourne.

Browne (Broun), Samuel.
Bookseller in London, (1633) 1638–1642, c. 1662–1665†; bookseller and later printer in the Hague, c. 1644–1655, and in Heidelberg, 1655–1662. Son of **John Browne 1**. The second shop below was previously that of **Nicholas Fussell.** [*Dict. 2*; DFM 2255; Benzing 198; Gruys; *Library* 5 (1950): 14–25.]
in Paul's Churchyard, 1639–1640 at least
— at the $ Fountain (B), 1639 (11991)
shop at the White Lion and Ball — (A.2), 1640 (549.5; 5771, omits 'and Ball')
1638: 13220 imp.
1639: 11991 f., 13220 imp.
1640: 549.5 f., [4697.5(*A*3)] sold, 5771 f., [16943(*A*3)] sold.

Browne, William.
Bookseller in Dorchester, 1635. [Not in *Dict. 1.*]
No address used.
1635: 1235.2 sold.

Brudenell, Thomas.
Printer in London, (1618) 1629–1651 at least. In 1629–30 he was a partner of **John Beale** though the 1630 imprints are not shared; in 1631–41 he probably worked as a journeyman, having no further imprints until 1642. [*Dict. 2*; DFM 111.]
No pre-1641 address noted.
1629: 162, 5911, 23489.
1630: 1551.5, 12854, 13051.3, 21210.5.
1633: 6929.5 ent.
1635: 1400 ent.

Brugensis, Theophilus. *See* Theophilus.

Brumen (Brumeau), Thomas.
Bookseller in Paris, 1559–1588†. [*Dict. 1*; Renouard.]
1573: 24476 ap. **1580:** 12969. **1581:** [4124?], [12729], [22031]. **1582:** 16907.

Bruneau (Bruney), Robert.
Printer in Antwerp, 1602–1614, at least. [*Dict. 1.*]
1605: 21361.

Bruster. *See* Brewster.

Bry (Brij), Theodor (Dietrich, Dirk) de.
Engraver and publisher largely on the continent, c. 1570–1598†. Worked in England, 1586–1588, afterwards in Frankfurt am Main. [Rouzet; Hind I.124.]
1587: 15224 engr. by.
1590: 12786 sumpt.

Bryson, James.
Printer in Edinburgh, 1638–1642†. Succeeded to the printing house of the *heirs of* **A. Hart**, which may still have been on the north side of the High Street a little below the Cross. [*Dict. 2.*]
No pre-1641 address noted.
1638: 21441 f.

Bryson, J. — *cont.*
1639: 21904.5, 21904.7 (false), 21905, 21905a, 21905b, 21905b.5 (false), 21907, 21908 (forged), 21908.5 (false), 22048, [22048a] (d), 22050–1, 22051.5, 22057 (false), 22060.
1640: 2723, 2724, 4390.7, 13155, 16601, 21910, 21910.3, 21910.5, 21910.7, 21911, 21912, 21912.3, 21912.7, 21914, [21916].

Bryson, Robert.
Bookseller and printer in Edinburgh, 1637–1645†. Succeeded to the printing material of **Thomas Finlason** and the Edinburgh equipment of **Robert Young.** [*Dict. 2.*]
shop at the $ Jonah, 1639 (2722.5)–1640 (21919)
1639: 2722.5, [2954.7] (d?), 4849.8, 7352.5, 10478.5, 23193.9, 23431.7.
1640: 2957.3, 3980.5, 5303.8, 6784.3, 15708 (d), 15709, [18062], [21440.7?] (c), [21917?] (d), 21919, 21919.5 (forged), [21920], 21922, 21923, 21923.5 (forged), [21927.5], [21929], [24523].

Buck, George.
Stationer in London, (1560) 1562?–1567. [*Dict. 1.*]
No address used.
1562: 22228 f. (d?). **1563:** 3933 f. **1565:** 3933.5 f. (c).

Buck, John.
Printer and bookbinder in Cambridge, 1625–1668†. Brother of **Thomas Buck**. One of the **Printers to the University** (*see* Cambridge University), 1625–1635. [*Dict. 2.*]
Cambridge imprints of this period have been recorded in STC with considerable variability, and the present indexes represent an attempt to rectify the situation. Indexed below are *only* items in which John Buck's name appears on the title-page; imprints shared with another Printer to the University are indicated by an asterisk (*). For items having *only* 'Printers ...' or 'ex acad. ...' on the title-page (even though individual names may be supplied in STC) *see* Cambridge University. For a comprehensive list of all items printed or sold at Cambridge including those without any imprint at all *see* Index 2Ai.
No address used; for the various locations of the press *see* Cambridge University.
1626: 21767* ap.
1627: 6296* ap., 11081* ap., 11772*, 19770*, 26015*.
1629: 2285–5.5*, 2617.7*, 16375*.
1630: 2293*, 2294*, 2624*, 2624.5*, 6297* ap., 16380*, 16380.3*, 21767.5* ap.
1631: 2298.3*.
1633: 2310*.
1634: 755* ap., 6294* ap., 6301.5* ap.
1635: 12211* ap.

Buck, Thomas.
Printer and bookbinder in Cambridge, 1625–1670†. Brother of **John Buck**. One of the **Printers to the University** (*see* Cambridge University, 1625–1640, 1650–1653? [*Dict. 2.*]
Cambridge imprints of this period have been recorded in STC with considerable variability, and the present indexes represent an attempt to rectify the situation. Indexed below are *only* items in which Thomas Buck's name appears on the title-page; imprints shared with another Printer to the University are indicated by an asterisk (*). For items having *only* 'Printers ...' or 'ex acad. ...' on the title-page (even though individual names may be supplied in STC) *see* Cambridge University. For a comprehensive list of all items printed or sold at Cambridge including those without any imprint at all *see* Index 2Ai.
No address used; for the various locations of the press *see* Cambridge University.
1626: 21767* ap.
1627: 6296* ap., 11081* ap., 11772*, 19770*, 26015*.
1629: 2285–5.5*, 2617.7*, 16375*.
1630: 2293*, 2294*, 2624*, 2624.5*, 6297* ap., 16380*, 16380.3*, 21767.5* ap.
1631: 2298.3*, 6301 ap.
1632: 2796–7 ap., 6192, 11774, 17767 ap.
1633: 2310*, 4480*, 5272* (d?), 6900* ap., 13183*, 13184* (d), 13184.5–85*, 13518–8.5*, 23889.6* ap.
1634: 755* ap., 6294* ap., 6294.5(*A*)* ap. (d/error), 6301.5* ap., 11633*, 12964 ap., 13186*.
1635: 2285.5* (c), 2320*, 12211* ap., 13187*, 23516* (note).

Buck, T. — *cont.*
1636: 7236–7* (note).
1637: 2327*, 2327.5*, 2674*, 7365* ap., 10339* (d?), 15632.3*.
1638: 2327.5*, 2331–1.3*, 2682*, 2683*, 6903*, 10351.5*, 11778*, 13188*, 14274* ap., 14964* ap., 15632.3*, 16410*, 18977* ap.
1639: 2338*, 2346*, 2692*, 6294.5(*A*)* ap. (d?), 6295 ap., 6298 ap., 10320, 11464, 12531.
1639/40: 406.5, 436.12, 505.14, 517.8.
1640: 2346*, 11465* f., 11779* f., 11779.5* f. (note), 16420*.

Budge, John.
Bookseller in London, (1606) 1607–1625†. For a good part of his career he had two shops simultaneously. [*Dict. 1*; DFM 1774; *Loan Book*, 1608–11.]
in Paul's Churchyard, 1607–1625
shop at the great South door of Paul's (A.8), 1607 (15535)–1618 (5944, one variant); variation: great South 'gate', 1609 (17359)
shop — at the Green Dragon (A.3), 1618 (5944, other variant)–1625 (12777)
in Britain's Burse (X.10):
shop —, 1610 (11795)–1617 (5930)
at the $ Windmill —, 1625 (21141)
1607: 5926.5 f., 5933 f., 15535 f.
1608: 5937 f., 24315.7 sold.
1609: 953.5 f., 5919.5 f., 5937.3 f., 12032 f., 12203 f., 17359 f., 17894–4.5 f., 18472a.5 f., 23683.3 ass'd (& *A*3, note).
1610: 877 f., 3130 f., 5413 f., 5917 f., 5928.5 f., 11795 f., 11813 sold, 13140 f., 13147.5–.7 f., 13161 f., 17309 f., 18323 f., [20754 f.], 21028.5 f., [22629] sold, 24303.7 f.
1611: 5414 f., 5912 f., 5920 f., 5929 f., 6591 sold, 9226 f., 13142 f.
1612: 4974 f., 5929.2 f., 5936 f., 5938 f., 6383 ent., 9227–8 f., 10854 f., 12618 pro, 14618.3 f., 18014–4.5 [f.], 18019 f., 21024 sold.
1613: 384 f., 736 imp., 1046 f., 4545 f., 4974 f., 5848 f., 5913 f., 5919 f., 5921–1.2 f., 5926 f., 5934 f., 13157 f., 14308 sold, 18347 f., 18526.5 f., 23683.3 f., 24130 sold.
1614: 110 f., 5536 ent., 5857 ent., 5858 sold, [5914 f.], 5915 f., 5927 f., 11745 ent., 12068 f., 14315 sold, 18611 f.
1615: 73 f., 114 f., 878 sold, 5849 f., 5921.7(*A*3) f., 5928 f., 5938.5 f., 12775 f., 12775.5 f., 20586 f., 23128 f., 25433.3 sold.
1616: 109 f., 111 f., 1963.7 f., 3656 f., 5918 f., 5921.5–22 f., 5932 f., 5943 f., 15402 f.
1617: 5930 f., 15402.5 f., 19947 f., 22839.9(*A*3) sold.
1618: 5923 f. (note), 5939 f., 5944 f., 12776 f., 15403 f., 15403a f.
1619: 5923 f., 5931 f., 5945 f., 6588 f., 7252.5 f., 12485 f., 20346 ent., 20352 ent., 22850 f., 25156 f., 25618 f.
1620: 76 f., [1883–3.5 f.] (d), 6583 f., 6587 f., 12485 f., 18629 f., 25615 f.
1621: 879 sold, 1963 f., 3930.3 f., 6583.7–84.5 f., 15404 f., 20351 f., 25155 f.
1622: 74 f., 5537 ass'd, 7316 ent., 13914 f., 15404.3(*A*3) f., 19072.5 sold, 21708 f., 25911 f.
1623: 1240 f., 3930.5 f., 5909 f., 6590 f., 11511 f., 12486 f.
1624: 6590.5 f., 6594 sold, 7138.7(*A*3) f., 18630 f.
1625: 5849.5 f., [12481?] sold, 12777 f., 19566.5 f., 21141 f.

1626: 748 ass'd, 1920 ass'd, 5537 ass'd, 5910 ass'd, 5940.5 ass'd, 6595 ass'd, 12552 ass'd, 25911a ass'd.

Bulkley, Joseph.
Bookseller in Canterbury, 1609–1622 at least. Father of **Stephen Bulkley.** Although the imprint of Joseph's earlier item is silent on the place of sale: 'London, printed for Joseph Bulkley, 1609' (24966a-HN), the author is actually Thomas Wilson, *Divine*, of Canterbury (H&L[3] E 176). [*Dict. 1.*]
No address used.
1609: 24966a f. **1622:** 14302 f.

Bulkley (Buckley), Stephen.
Printer (1639) 1640–1680†; in London, 1640–41, and later in York, Newcastle upon Tyne, and Gateshead. Son of **Joseph Bulkley**. In London he was a partner of **John Beale**. [*Dict. 2*; DFM 270; W. K. Sessions, *Bulkley & Broad, White & Wayt*, York, 1985/6.]
No pre-1641 address used.
1640: 12983, 20491.

Bulmer, Robert.
Bookseller in London, 1623–1624 at least. Not a member of the Stat. Co. [*Dict. 1.*]
shop near the Tennis Court in the Middle Row in Holborn (V.9), 1623 (10584.5)
1623: 10584.5 f.

Bunnian. *See* Bonian.

Buray, Pierre.
Bookseller and printer in Paris, 1614. [Lottin 2: 19.]
1614: 4958.

Burby, Cuthbert.
Bookseller in London, 1592–1607†. Husband of **Elizabeth Burby**; father-in-law of **Thomas Snodham**. One of the *assignees of* **F. Flower**. He was living in the parish of St. Faith's at the time of his death, and he bequeathed the lease of his second shop to his former apprentice, **Nicholas Bourne**. [*Dict. 1*; Plomer, *Wills*: 41–3.]
the Middle Shop in the Poultry under St. Mildred's Church (O.1), 1592 (19974.6)–1594 (10715)
shop at (by, near, adjoining) the Royal Exchange (O.8), 1594 (23667)–1602 (23483, omits 'Royal')
in Paul's Churchyard at the Swan (A.5), 1602 [17307], 1603 (7085, has 'dw.')–1607 (24719, has 'White' Swan); variation: has 'shop', 1605 (12588)
1592: 12283 f., 12283.5 f., 12306 f., 13133 f., 15696 f., 17206 f., 19974.6 f., 22663 ent., 22697 f., 22718 f.
1593: 662 f., 22697.5 f.
1594: 796 f., 10715 f., 10715.3 f., 12265 f., 17084 f., 18380 f., 18381 f., 22698–8.5 f., 22699 f., 23667 sold, 25781 f.
1595: 542 f., 6225 f., 6403 f., 20366 f., 22710 ent., [22747.3 f.] (d?).
1596: 7501 f., 14677 f., 15028 f., 16677 sold, 20366a f., 21817 f., 23668 sold.
1597: 4115.5 f. (d), 5043.5 f. (d), 12906 ent., 14678 f., 17866 f.
1598: 1214 sold, 16902 f., 17085 f., 17834 f., 18868 f., 18869 f., 22294 f., 22747.5 f., 23277.5 ent.
1599: 1423 f., 6404 f., 7502 f., 12212 f., 12266 f., 18370 f., 18870 f., 22323 f., 22748 f., 22752(*A3*) ent.
1600: 378–80 f., 1424 f., 6518 ent., 7064 f., 14750 ent., 14766 ent., 17679 f. (d), 18376 ent., 21387 ent.
1601: 256.5 f., 13003.5 sold, 17556 f., 18417 f., 18871 f., 23475 sold, 23491 sold.
1602: 780 ent., 13003.7 sold, [17307] sold, 19724.7 ent., 22752 f., 23475.5 f., 23483 f., 25744a f.
1603: 6595.7 f., 6625.5 f., 6640 f., 6788 ent., 7085 f., 7120 f., 12984 f., 12988 f., 12995.5 ent., 15633.4 ent., 17153 ent., 19105.5 ent., 21032 ent.
1604: 3439–40 f., 7118 f., 7133 f., 13004 f., 13011 f., 13122 f., [14361 f.], 16784 f., 19722 ent., 19731 f., [19747.5] sold, [19747.7] sold, 19807.7 f., 22992.5 f., 23452 ent., 23476 f., 23484 f. (d?).
1605: 12317 f., 12588 f., 18184 f., 18184.5 f., 19853 f., 22753 f.
1606: [207] sold, 1468 at charges, 3961 ent., 6625.6 f., 12591 f., 19335 imp., 19683 ent., 19732 f., [19748] sold, 23448 f., 25360 f., 26004 f.
1607: 5141.7 f., 6103 ent., 6405 f., 12592 f., 13005 f., 13005a f., [17996] sold, 19724.9 f., 19732a f., [19735.4] sold, 21507 ent., 22324 ass'd, 22754 f., 23477 f., 23669 ass'd, 24719 f.

Burby, Elizabeth.
Bookseller in London, 1607–1609. Widow of **Cuthbert Burby**. She remarried out of the Stat. Co. in Oct. 1609 (*C-B C*: 38, 71–2). [*Dict. 1.*]
her shop in Paul's Churchyard at the Swan (A.5), 1607 (19854)–1609 (7135); variations: has 'White' Swan, 1609 (17741) or omits sign, 1609 (23478)
1607: 19854 f., 20367(*A3*) ent.
1608: 7134 f., 14679 f., 23485.5 f., 26009 f.
1609: 6104 ass'd, 6625.7 f., 7135 f., 12985 f., 13565 f., 17741 f., 18184(*A3*) ass'd, 18191(*A3*) ?ass'd, 22710 ass'd, 22755 f., 22756 ass'd, 23478 f., 19107.5 ass'd, 19649 f. (note), 23492 ass'd.

Burdon, John.
Bookseller in Edinburgh, 1622 at least. [*Dict. 1.*]
shop beside the Trone on the South side of the [High] Street, 1622 (3905)
1622: 3905 sold.

Burre, Walter.
Bookseller in London, (1596) 1597–1622†. [*Dict. 1.*]
in Paul's Churchyard, 1599–1621 at least
— at the Fleur-de-lis (A.2), 1599 (3064)–1600 (16883.5)
shop — at the Fleur-de-lis and Crown, 1601 (14773, 21802, omits 'shop')
at the Crane — (A.3), 1603 (5122)–1621 (6108, has 'shop')
1599: 3064 f.
1600: 16883.5 sold, 17415 sold, 18376 f., 20891 f. (d).
1601: 14766 f., 14773 f., 21802 f., 26039 f.
1603: 5122 sold, 7539 f., 20343 f.
1604: 5588 sold, 26040 f., 26043.3 sold.
1606: 7456 f., 22061 f.
1608: 5694 f., 17888 f., 24395 ent.
1609: 5694.5 f., 13894 f.
1610: 7048 f., 14783 ent., 23289 f., 24832–2a(*A3*) sold.
1611: 4705 sold, 6906 f., 7026 ent., 14759 f.
1612: 1501 ent., 14755 f., 14763 ent., [15324 f.], 17818 sold, 23350 f.
1613: 1674 f., 15323 f., 17870 f., 23111 f., [23780 f.?] (false).
1614: 16884 ent., 16885 f., 20637 f.
1615: 5695 f., 14894.7 sold, 14894.8 sold, 14894.9 sold, 21445 ent., 23612 sold, 24100 f., 24101 f.
1616: 11319 f., 18579 f., 20748 f.
1617: 17872a sold, 20638 f., 20638a f. (d/repeat).
1618: 19651 f. (note).
1621: 6108 f., 6108.3 f., 18529, 18530 f., 18530.5 f., 20638a f. (d), 20639 f., 25109 f.
1622: 20640 ass'd, 24811 f.

Burrel, James.
Bookseller in London, 1548? Since the HD copy of the following item was formerly bound with 2998.5, 4822.5, and 4828, Burrel's activity has been redated accordingly. [*Dict. 1.*]
dw. without the North gate of St. Paul's in the corner house of Paternoster Row opening into Cheapside (C.7), 1548? (20203.5)
1548: 20203.5 [f.] (d?).

Burton, Francis.
Bookseller in London, (1602) 1603–1617?† (*C-B C*: 92). Father of **Simon Burton**. His 1603 items were sold at the shop of his former master, **Thomas Adams:** in Paul's Churchyard at the White Lion (A.2). [*Dict. 1*; *Loan Book*, 1604–10.]
in Paul's Churchyard, 1606–1617
shop — at the Fleur-de-lis and Crown (A.2), 1606 (11094)–1607 (24063, has 'dw.')
dw. — at the Green Dragon (A.3), 1610 (24261)–1617 (25897, has 'shop')
1603: 18292 f., 18292.3 f.
1604: 26014 f., 26014.3(*A3*) ent.
1605: 3701 sold, 10930 f., 19822 ent., 25232–2.5 f., 26014.3(*A3*) ent.
1606: [10931 f.] (d?), 11094 f., 11160 f., 13868.7 f., 17775.5 sold, 19334 f., 21511 f.
1607: 22384 sold, 23131 f., 24063–3a f., 24634.5 f.
1608: 1919 ent., 12682 ent.
1610: 3198 ent., 24261 f.
1611: 605 f., 3198.5 sold.
1612: 605.5 f., 25915 ent., 25992 f.
1613: 11149–9.3 f., 13822.5 f., 25891 f., 25891.5 f., 25892 f., 25893 f. (forged), 25894 f.
1614: 1919a f., 13821 f., 25790 f., 25895 f.
1615: 25798 f., 25896 f.
1617: 13824 f., 25897 f.

Burton, John.
Bookseller in Wells, 1634. [*Dict. 1.*]
No address used.
1634: 3129.7 sold.

Burton, Simon.
Bookseller in London, (1636) 1637–1641. Son of **Francis Burton**. [*Dict. 1*; *Dict. 2*; DFM 597.]
shop next the Mitre Tavern within Aldgate (L.1), 1640 (20561)
1637: 21442 f. **1640:** 20561 f.

Burwell, Hugh.
Bookseller in Cambridge, 1593?–1601? He lived in the parish of Great St. Mary's. [*Dict. 1.*]

Burwell, H. — *cont.*
No address used.
1597: 19712 f. (note), 19724.5 f.

Busby, John 1.
Bookseller in London, (1585) 1590–1613†. Father of **John Busby 2.** [*Dict. 1*; *Poor Book*, 1612–13; *St. Giles*, 1613; *Library* 7 (1985): 1–15.]
at the West end of St. Paul's Church (A.10), 1590 (12253, colophon, with N. Ling)
at (near to) the West door of Paul's (A.10), 1591 (16657)–1594? (7214), both with N. Ling; variation: 1592 (16656) and 1593 (16662) both have Busby's name alone and 'his shop'
in St. Dunstan's Churchyard in Fleet Street at the Little Shop near Clifford's Inn (W.9), 1596 (16660)
in Paul's Churchyard at the Crane (A.3), 1598 (17485)–1599 (20307, has 'shop')
'his' house in Carter Lane, next the Paul's (Powle) Head [Tavern] (R.1), 1600 (22289, with T. Millington)
shop under St. Peter's Church in Cornhill (Cornwell (P.2)), 1604 (7293)–1609 (19936, with G. Loftus, omits 'shop')
1590: 12253 f., 16664 f., 22645 f. (d?), 23633a f. (d).
1591: 4800.3 f. (note), 16654 f. (d), 16657 f., 22656–6.5 f., 22657 f.
1592: 5578.2 f., 5654.5 sold, 5656 sold, 16656 f., 16665 f., 18372 f., 18373 f.
1593: 16662 f., 18374 f., 19539 f. (d).
1594: 7205 f., 7206 f., 7214 f. (d?), 11622 f., 26124 f.
1595: 7192 f. (d), [7214.5 f.?] (d?), 14631 ent., 22955 f., 22955.3 f. (d/repeat), 22955.5 f., 22971 f., 25941.5 ent.
1596: 16660 f., 22972 f. (d/repeat), 22973 f.
1597: 12225 f.
1598: 17485 sold.
1599: 13341 ent., 20307 f., 22955.3 f. (note, d?).
1600: 22289 f., 22972 f. (note, d?).
1602: 22299 ent.
1604: 7293 f., 7593 f. (d).
1606: 22384 ent.
1607: 21513.5 ent., 22292 ent., 22380 ent.
1608: 13360 f.
1609: 12805 f. (d), 13361 f., 19936 f., 25022 ent.
1610: 3717.3 f. (d), 15182 f. (d).
1612: 5878 ent.

Busby, John 2.
Bookseller in London, 1607–1631† (*C-B C*: 230). Son of **John Busby 1.** [*Dict. 1*; DFM 952.]
in Fleet Street (W.9), 1607–1616
at the Little Shop next Clifford's Inn gate —, 1607 (21605)–1608 (21606), both with J. Helme
shop — in St. Dunstan's Churchyard, 1608 (6485)–1616 (6488)
1607: 21605 f.
1608: 6485 f., 19330 ent., 21606 f.
1609: 1417 ent., 6486 f., 17805 f., 18629(*A*3) ent.
1610: 14763 ent., 17617 f., 18640–0b f.
1612: 6487 f., 7226 f. (d).
1613: 7227 f., 19332–2.5 f.
1615: 18628 f., 24593 f.
1616: 6488 f.

Bush, Edwin.
Journeyman printer and bookseller in London, (1611) 1633–1635 (?1661). His only items were published with **Francis Constable** and have the latter's address: at the Crane in Paul's Churchyard (A.3). [*Dict. 1*; DFM 50; ?*Poor Book*, 1656–61.]
No separate address used.
1634: 20783.5 f. **1635:** 20781 f.

Bushell, Thomas.
Bookseller in London, 1599–1618†. Beadle of the Stat. Co., 1612–1618 (Q.1), and the payments in the *Poor Book* for that period are undoubtedly for warning the pensioners. [*Dict. 1*; *Loan Book*, 1599–1602, 1614–17.]
shop at the great North door of Paul's (A.2), 1599 (25224)–1602 (12571, omits 'shop')
his house in the Petty Canons (A.2), 1605 (11575); no later use of this address or any other noted
1599: 17154 f., 25224 f.

Bushell, T. — *cont.*
1600: 3675 f., 3675.5 f., 11578 f., 20150 f.
1601: 3012.3 f., 3160 ent., 11578.5 f., 20053 f.
1602: 17.3 f., 3088.5 f., 12571 f., 12571.5 f., 19735.6 ent., 20151 f., 22107 f.
1603: 20151.5 f.
1604: 17429 f., 17874.3 f., 19975 ent.
1605: 11575 f.
1607: 12582.24 ent.
1610: 5862 f., 22107.5 ass'd.
1612: 19458.5–.7 f., 21027 f.
1613: 3704.3 f., 3704.5 f., 13572 f., 25949 ent.
1614: 3664 f.
1616: 21527 ent.
1618: 25387 f.

Butler, Charles.
Schoolmaster, clergyman, and author, b. 1579–1647†. [*DNB.*]
No address used.
1629: 4194.5 imp., 4200 imp. **1633:** 4190 f., 4195 imp. **1634:** 4191 f., 4194 f. **1635:** 4200.5 pro. **1636:** 4196 f.

Butler, John.
Bookseller in London, 1528?–1535 at least. [Duff, *Century*.]
in Fleet Street at the $ St. John the Evangelist (W.2), 1528? (23172)–1531? (12944)
1528: 11691a.3 [f.] (d?), 23172 [f.] (d?).
1529: 23160.7 [f.] (d?), 23174.3 f.
1530: 23150.3 f. (d?), 23182.8 [f.] (d?), 23429a.5 [f.] (d?).
1531: 11691a.5(*A*3) [f.] (d?), 12944 [f.] (d?).

Butler, Thomas.
Bookseller in Oxford, 1619?–1628. [*Dict. 1.*]
No address used.
1628: 24989 sold.

Note: *Dict. 1* has two stationers named **William Butler**, but their biographical details are conflated. They have been tentatively distinguished as follows.

Butler, William 1.
Bookseller in London, (1613) 1615–1617 (1619?†). [*Dict. 1*; DFM 2587; ?*Poor Book*, (widow Joan) 1620–62.]
dw. in the bulwark near the Tower (U.3), 1615 (23741)–1617 (21015, has 'shop', 'Tower of London')
1615: [18753(*A*3)?] f., 23741 f., [23752?] f.
1616: 21013 f., 21014 f., 21018 f.
1617: 21015 f.

Butler, William 2.
Bookseller in London, 1615–1625†. His widow Mary assigned his copyrights in 1626 to **William Stansby** (Arber IV.162). [*Dict. 1*; DFM 1890; ?*Loan Book*, 1615–18.]
shop in St. Dunstan's Churchyard in Fleet Street (W.9), 1616 (19059)–1621 (23050.5)
shop near Bishopsgate (J.2), 1623 (23051)
1615: 12654 f.
1616: 13406 f., 19059 f., 19569a f.
1617: 12707 f. (note), 13394 f., 13394a ent.
1618: 1438 f., [3212.5 f.] (false, d).
1620: 6326.5 sold, 12708 f. (note).
1621: 12014 f., 23050.5 f.
1623: 23051 f.
1625: 12635(*A*) ass'd.

1626: 13394a ass'd, 23051.5 ass'd.

Butter, Joan.
Bookseller in London, 1590–1594. Widow of **Thomas** and mother of **Nathaniel Butter**. Remarried **John Newbery** and following his death published in 1603 as **Joan Newbery 1**. [*Dict. 1*, under first husband.]
her shop under St. Austin's Church (N.7), 1594 (11214.7)
1590: 20889.7 f. **1594:** 11214.7 f. (d).

Butter, Nathaniel.
Bookseller in London, 1604–1664†. Son of **Thomas** and **Joan Butter**. Treasurer of the **English Stock** (*see* Stationers' Company), c. 1603–1606 (A.10) (*C-B C*: 21 (11 and 20 July)). Publisher of Newsbooks and news pamphlets, often with others, especially **Nicholas Bourne** from 1622. In 1625–27 Butter and Bourne used the pseudonym **Mercurius,** *Britannicus*, and such imprints, *not* included below, are listed under that heading.). [*Dict. 2*; *Loan Book* (for Joan Newbery 2), 1646–49, 1655–58; *Poor Book*, 1652–62; *Library* 12 (1957): 23–33.]
in Watling Street under St. Austin's Church (N.7), 1604 (1818.5); variation: shop near St. Austin's gate in the Old Change, 1604 (15682)
a) in Paul's Churchyard (A.7), *b*) near St. Austin's gate, *c*) at the Pied Bull, 1605–1640/41 at least
The full imprint with all 3 elements rarely appears, e.g. in 1608 (22292, has 'shop'), 1609 (6536, has 'dw.'), and 1640/41 (12675, no 'dw.' or 'shop').
More often only 2 elements appear, e.g. in 1605 (6071, has 'dw.', *a*, *b*; 13328, has 'shop', *a*, *b*; 22333, has *b*, *c*).
Sometimes there is only one, e.g. in 1607 (21513.5, has 'dw.', *a* = tp; colophon has all 3 elements), in 1627 (20779.5, has 'dw.', *b*). Many items have no address at all.
1604: 1818.5 f., 15682 sold.
1605: 1827 ent., 3057.7–58 f., 6071 f., 13328 f., 13527–7.5 f., 18288 f., 21417 f., 22333 f., 22869–9.3 f., 24072 f.
1606: 2773 f., 5344 f., 6329 f., 6522 f., 12568 f., 13329 f., 13336 f., 13336.5 f. (d), 13509 sold, 20905 f., 24071 f.
1607: 5492–2.2 f., 5492.4 f., 6532 f., 6541 f., 17659 f., 18532 f., 19567 f., 21513.5 f., 21514 f.
1608: 4580 f., 5334 f., 5342 f., 6480 f., 6480.5 f. (forged?), 6481 f., 6482 f., 6659.5 (note), 11262 f., 13330 f., [13360] sold, 18325–5.3 f., 18784 f., 18785–5.5 f., 22292 f., 22293 (forged?), 25638.5 f., 25885.5 sold.
1609: 6330 f., 6499 f., 6536 f., 11366.5 f., 12362 f., 13337 f., [13361] sold, 17155 f., 18594–5 f., 24132 ent., 25022 f., 25022.5 f.
1610: 13564 f. (d?), 7322 f., 18596 f., 22385 f., 25795 f. (note).
1611: 13134 f., 13503 ent., 13634 f. (d?), 21738 f., 22992.7 f., 24119 imp., 25795 f.
1612: 7312 f., 12056 f., 12064 imp., 13566 f., [15140] sold, 22395 f., 22397 f., [23791] sold, 24026 imp.
1613: 4116 imp., 6063.2 f., 6066 f., 11357 f., 13332 f., 13539–9a f., 18285(*A*3) ent., 18322 f., 21418 f., 21621 f., 22424 f., 24132 f.
1614: 4116.5 imp., 4580.5 f., 6063.3 f., 6067 f., 11091 f., 11745 f., 11796 f., 13361a f., 13636 f. (d?), 19777 imp., 23779 f., 23792 f.
1615: 4216 f., 5045 f., 5859 f., 6069 f., [7319] sold, 7626 f. (d), 7626.5 f. (d), 9237 f., 12654 f., 13540–0.5 f., 13637 f. (d?), 13841 f., 22386 f., 23806 f.
1616: 6483 f., 7371.5–72 f., 7401 f., 7627 f. (d?), 12108 f., 13503 f., 13624 f. (d?), 16833 f., 22399 f., 23806 f., 24560 f.
1617: 4217 f., 4234 f., 4909 f., 10805 f., 12705 f., 12707 f. (note), 21622 f.
1618: 4214 f., 6063.5 f., 6067.3 f., 6434 f., 10213.3 f., 11525 f., 12101 f., 12656 ent., 12656.5 f., 12710.7 ent., 12710.9–11 f.
1619: 6063.6 f., 12674 ent., 15352 f., 18801 f., 22293 (forged? d), 25265 f.
1620: 4164 f., 5796–6.3 f., 6105 ent., 6480.5 f. (forged? c), [10814 f.] (false, d?), 11162 f., 11700 f., 12029 imp., 12657 f., 12674a f., 12708 f. (note), 24070 pro, 24178 f.
1621: 731 f., 4704 f., 11895.5 f., 12356 f., 12708 f. (note), 18507.29 f., —.30 f., —.31 f., —.32 f., —.33 f., —.34 f., —.35 f., 21419 f., 22130 f.
1622: 1898 f., 4022 f., 6386 f., 12657a f., 12714.5 f., 12748 f., 14322 f., 17600.3 chez, 18507.49 f., —.50 f., —.51A f., —.54 f., —.60 f., —.68 f., —.72 f., —.75 f., —.77 f., —.78 f., —.79 f., —.80 f., —.81 f., —.82 f., —.83 f., —.84 f., —.85 f., —.86 f., —.88 f., —.89 f., —.90 f., —.91 f., 20769 f., 25716 f.
1623: 59 f., 533 f., 3416 f., 5025 f., 5461 f., 5636.2 f., 5636.4 f., 5636.6 f., 11306 f., 11366 f., 12092.2 f., 12357 f., 12646 f., 12658 ent., 12658.5 f., 12665 f., 13333 f., 13338 f., 13613 f., 18507.92 f., —.93 f., —.94 f., —.95 f., —.96 f., —.97 f., —.98 f., —.99 f., —.100 f., —.101 f., —.102 f., —.103 f., —.104 f., —.105 f., —.106 f., —.107 f., —.108 f., —.109 f., —.110 f., —.111 f., —.112 f., —.113 f., —.114 f., —.115 f., —.116 f., —.117 f., —.118 f., —.119 f., —.120 f., —.121 f., —.122 f., —.123 f., —.124 f., —.125 f. —.126 f., —.127 f., —.128 f., —.129 f., —.130 f., —.131 f., —.132 sold, —.133 f., —.134 f., —.135 f., —.136 f., —.137 f., 22992.9 f. (d), 23009 f., 24177 f.

Butter, N. — *cont.*
1624: 4747 f., 5636.8 f., 6272 f., 10213.7 f., 11189 f., 12635 f. (note), 12715 f., 13574 f., 17183 f., 18507.138 f., —.139 f., —.140 f., —.141 f., —.142 f., —.143 f., —.144 f., —.145 f., —.146 f., —.147 f., —.147A f., —.148 f., —.149 f., —.150 f., —.151 f., —.152 f., [—.153 f.] (d), —.154 f., —.155 f., —.156 f., —.157 f., —.158 f., 24900 f., 25160.7–61 f., 25719 f. (d), 26061 f.
1625: 4318 f., 5029 f., 6063.8 f., 6067.5 f., 12603 f., 12635 f. (note), 12635b f., 14711 imp., 14928 f., 14928.5 f.
1626: 4215 f., 5724.5 f., 10817 ent., 11467 f., 12659 f., 12713 f., 13615 f., 13616 f., 13619 f., 16845 ent.
1627: 4218 f., 10262 f., 18507.186(*A*3) ent., —.186A f., —.187 f., —.188 f., —.189 f., —.190 f., —.191 f., —.192 f., —.193 f., —.194 f., 20779.5 f., 21327 imp., 23718 imp., 25720 f., 25720.5 f. (d).
1628: 4219 f., 10263 f., 11293 f., 12636 f. (note), 12636.3 f., 12690 f., 12690.5 f., 12692 f., 15134 f., 16846 f., 18507.195 f., —.196 f., —.197 f., —.197A f., —.198 f., —.199 f., 21252 f., 22106 f.
1629: 4205 f., 5144 f., 12693 f., 12709–9.5 f., 12709a f., 13504 f., 15134 f., 25721 f.
1630: 342 f., 4581 f., 4931 f., 6506 f., 12677 f., 10206.5 f. (d?), 12687 f., 12691 f., 13362 f., 13504.5 f., 14443 f., 17916.3 f., 17916.5 f., 17916.7–.9 f., 18507.206 f., —.207 f., 23570 f., 23571 f., 23572 f., 23574 f., 24258 f., 24928 f.
1631: 383 f., 4180 f., 6063.9 f., 11120 f., 11288.5 f., 11299 f., 12532 f., 12688–8.5 f., 16847.5 f., 18329 pro, 18507.208 f., —.209 f., —.210 f., —.211 f., —.212 f., —.213 f., —.214 f., —.215 f., —.217 f., —.218 f., —.219 f., —.220 f., —.221 f., —.222 f., —.223 f., —.224 f., —.225 f., —.226 f. (d), —.227 f., —.228 f., —.229 f., —.230 f., —.231 f., —.232 f., —.233 f., —.234 f., —.235 f., 20865 f., 22387 f., 24524 f., 24544.5 sold.
1632: 6067.7 f., 12702 f., 13334 f., 14442 f., 18507.236 f., —.237 f., —.238 f., —.239 f., —.240 f., —.241 f., —.242 f., —.243 f., —.244 f., —.245 f., —.246 f., —.247 f., —.248 f., —.249 f., —.250 f., —.251 f., —.252 f., —.253 f., —.254 f., —.255 f., —.256 f., —.257 f., —.258 f., —.259 f., —.260 f., —.261 f., —.262 f., —.263 f. (d), —.264 f., —.265 f., —.266 f., —.267 f., —.268 f., —.269 f., —.270 f., —.271 f., —.272 f., —.273 f., —.274 f., —.275 f., —.276 f., 19496.5 f., 21420 f., 21820 f., 23519.5 f., 23520 f., 23521 f., 23522 f., 23523 f., 23524–4a f.
1633: 2767 imp., 12534 f. (note), 12646a.5 f., 12689 f., 12702 f., 12704 imp., 13263 f., 13339 f., 13505 f., 14713 f., 17600.7 chez, 21739 f., 23525 f., 23525.1 f., 23525.3–.4 f., 25617 f.
1634: 10211 f., 10265 f. (d), 12639.5 f., 12640.5–.7 f., 13624.5 f. (d?), 19203.3 f., 23523.5 f., 23525.2 f., 23525.5 f., 23525.6 f., 23525.7 f., 24956 f.
1635: 12645–5a imp., 12647 f., 14712 imp., 23366 f., 23525.8 f., 23525.9 f.
1636: 4212 f., 6427 f., 12691.5 f., 13505.3 f., 20555 f.
1636/37: 4293 f.
1637: 3597 f., 4212 f., 4293.2 f., 4293.4 f., 11364 f., 12710 f., 13125 f., 14064.7 prost., 24758 f.
1638: 4293.6 sold, 12710.3 f., 13363 f., 18507.277 f., 21844 f., 24759 f., 24760 f.
1638/39: 18507.283 f., —.285 f.
1639: 4293.8 f., 5335 f., 12646b f., 13335 f., 13505.5 f. (d?), 13870.7 (note), 18507.278 f., —.279 f. (d), —.280 f. (d), —.281 f., —.282 f., —.284 f., —.286 [f.] (d), —.287 f., —.288 f., —.289 f., —.290 f. (d), —.291 f., —.292 f., —.293 f., —.294 f., —.295 f., —.296 f., —.297 f., —.298 f., —.299 f., —.300 f., —.301 f., —.302 f., —.303 f., —.304 f., —.305 f., —.306 f., —.307 f., [—.308 f.] (d), —.309 f., —.310 f., —.311 f., —.312 f., —.313 f., —.314 f., —.315 f., —.315A f., 20863 f., 22132 f., 26122 f., 26122.5 f.
1639/40: 18507.317 f., —.319 f., —.326 f.
1640: 6105 sold, 11512 f., 12648b sold, 12661 f., 12661.5 f., 12735 f., 15114 f., 18507.316 f., —.318 f., —.318B(*A*3) f., —.320 f., —.321 f., —.322 f., —.323 f. (d), —.324 f., —.325 f., —.327 f., —.328 f., —.329 f., —.330 f., —.331 f., —.332 f., —.333 f., —.334 f., —.335 f., —.336 f., —.337 f., —.338 f., —.339 f., —.340 f., —.340N(*A*3) f., —.341 f., —.342 f., 21479.5 f., 23424.5 f., 23809 ent., 23809.5 f.
1640/41: 12675 f., 12676 f., 18507.343 f., [—.344 f.], —.345 f., —.345C(*A*3) f.

Butter, Thomas.
Bookseller in London, (1574?) 1576–1590†. Husband of **Joan** and father of **Nathaniel Butter**. One of the assignees of **R. Day**.

Butter, T. — *cont.*
[*Dict. 1.*]
(near) St. Austin's gate, 1576–1585 at least
dw. in Paul's Churchyard near to — at the $ Ship (A.7), 1576 (1356.4)
by — near Watling Street (N.7), 1580 [4123.5]
dw. at —, 1584 (23287)–1585 (6180, has 'shop near')
1576: 1356.4 f.
1580: [4123.5] sold (d), 5400 ent., 15047.
1581: 18534 f.
1584: 19817 f. (d), 19817.5 f., 23287 f.
1585: 6180 f.
1588: 14728 f.
1590: 84.5 f.

Byddell, *alias* **Salisbury, John.**
Bookseller and printer in London, 1533–1545?†. His second shop had previously belonged to his former master, **Wynkyn de Worde**, and it later passed to **Edward Whitchurch**. In 1538 Byddell had an agent in Salisbury. [Duff, *Century*.]
dw. at the $ Our Lady of Pity next to Fleet Bridge (W.3), 1533, 15 Nov. (10479)–1535? (10498)
dw. at the Sun in Fleet Street next to the conduit (W.5), 1535, 16 June (15988)–1544, 19 Nov. (10483)
1533: 10479 f.
1534: 1471, 5547 f., 5547.2, 10453.5 f., 10480 f., 10503 (d?), 14841.5 f. (d?), 15986 (d), 21789.3 (d), 23552 f., 25127.
1535: 5292 (d?), 10498 (d?), 14821, 14842, 15988, [16794.5(*A*3)] (d), [21798.5] (d?).
1535/36: 421.17.
1536: 1806, 2987, 2987.5 per, 14577.5 (d?), 15991.
1537: 15997.5 (d?), 16820, 16820.3.
1538: 5611 (d?), [9290] (d?), 10326 (d), 10480.5, [15610] (d?), 15671, 21752.5, 21753, 23152.3 (d?), 24358 ap.
1538/39: 471.9.
1539: 2067, 2747.5.
1540: 5279, 9985.5 (d), 10468.
1541: 6127.5 per, 10482.
1542: 9935.7(*A*) [in shop of] (d?), 9986 (d).
1544: 10483, 10484.

Bynneman (Benneyman, Binneman), Henry.
Bookseller and printer in London, 1566–1583†. At least twice in 1578 he used the style 'servant to the right hon. Sir Christopher Hatton' (1972, 5226). On many occasions he published jointly with other Stationers and used the form of imprint 'H. B. *and* X. Stationer', which should be interpreted 'by H. B. for himself and X. Stationer'. With **Ralph Newbery** he published one title (15164 sqq.) by the assignment of **R. Tottell** and **C. Barker**. Bynneman's printing material passed to the **Eliot's Court Press**, some of whose partners may have worked as journeymen for him in 1583 and following his death. For the full list of Bynneman's copyrights yielded to the Stat. Co. in 1584 *see* Appendix C.; *see* also headnote following Appendix D/60. [*Dict. 1*; *Library* 12 (1957): 81–92.]
in Paternoster Row (C.7), 1566–1567
— at the Black Boy, 1566, 14 Oct. (6076)
— at the Mermaid, 1567 (3180; 8000, omits sign; 16705.3, 13 Sept., has 'dw.' and sign)
dw. in Knightrider Street at the Mermaid (R.2), 1567/68, 3 Jan. (8000.7)–1575 (205) and probably later
shop at the Northwest door of Paul's Church (A.10), 1572 (13602)–1573 (12464); variation: adds 'at the Three Wells', 1572 (6901)
dw. in Thames Street near unto Baynard's Castle (R.6), 1580 (4699)–1583 (24807); 1584 (16952)
1566: 2995a ent., 6076 [f.].
1566/67: 415, 493.3 ent.
1567: 3180, 6089, 8000, 8000.3 (d), 10423, 10510.5, 12787.5 (note), 16705.3, 16754.5, 18739, 19124, 20072, 22990.
1567/68: 8000.7, 8001 (repeat).
1568: 297, 302 (d?), 4344, 5011, 6581 in aed., 8004 (repeat of lost ed.), 11476, 11710, 14327, 17244, 20097, 23950, [24774].
1568/69: 361.3.
1569: 3114, 3164.5, 5787, 6106.3 ent., 6893, 8008.7 (d), 8009 (repeat), 11269, 12419, 13061, 13062, 17573.5 (d), 18602, 18679.5, 18680, 18681, 18682, 21827(*A*3, note) ?ent., 23885.7(*A*3) ent., 24872 in aed.

Bynneman, H. — *cont.*
1570: 17.5 (d), 5037 (d), 5263, 5788, [5792.5?] (d), [5793?] (d), 6832, 7241.5 (d), 7624 (d?), 10352 (d), 11271 (d), 11927 (d), 15532 (d), [18600.5] (d?), 20906 per, 23002 ap., 24113 (d), 24788 ap.
1570/71: 449, 485.
1571: 2036, 3181, 3736 (d), 4845.5 ap., [4896?] (d?), 5113, 5295, 6858, 10451 per, 15551.5, 20057.5, 23555, 24634 (d?), 24726.5 (d).
1572: 545 (d?), 1048 (d), 3115, 4074, 5952, 6901, 11759, 13602, 13603 (d), 15320, 18926.3 in aed., 19136, 19137.5 (d?), 19139 in aed., 19196 (d), 19990.5, 22991, 24287 ap., 24788a ap., 25427, 25428.
1573: 3737, 4846.3(*A*, note), 5039 (d), 6135, 7622 ent., 7623, 10194.5 (d), 11635 (pt, d), 11985, 12464, [13845] (false), 13846 ex off., [13847] (false), 15336 ent., 15541, 19060, 20309 in aed., 22241, 23003 ap., 23885.7(*A*3) ass'd, 24171, [24778?], 25010, 25428, 25429.
1574: 3169, [3422] (d?), 3548, 4444, 4445, 4449, 6136, 10393, 13063, 13493, 15003, 17408, 23324 (d), 25004 ap., 25430, 25430.5, 25431.
1575: 205, [2110–13a.3] (pt), [3368.5-Thame] (d), 4911.3 ex off. (c), 6139, [6787.4] (c), 11266 (d), 11636 (d), 12188 ex off., 12433 (d?), 13960 typis, 15552, 18478–8a.5 ex off., 19115 (d?), 19832, 20801, 23325 (pt? d), [23928] (d), [24324], 24328 (d).
1576: 1532, 5201, 11645, 12420, 12465, [12629] (d?), 14092, 14093, 15004, 15336 (note), 18477 ex off., 22243, 23665.5 ent., [25974].
1577: [186.5?], 1651, 4783 ap., [5549], 5791, 10889, 11986, 12174, 12899 ex off., 12904–4.5 ex off., 12905 ex off., 13485, [13568–8b] (d), 14094, 18670 (d?), 18950, 19593 (d), 20801.3–1.7(*A*3), 23622 (d), 24287.3.
1578: 712.5–3.5, 1972, 2018.5, 3419.7, [4322] (d?), 5226 (d), [5239], 5647, 10823, 11627 (d), 11628 (d), 12469 ent., 12901 ex off., 12905 ex off., 13486, 14465, 16807 (d), 16987, 18309, [18445] (false), 20089 (d), 23284 (d), 23687.5, [25405], [25406].
1579: 714, 6137, 6843 ex off., 6848, 7602, 7602.5, 11629, 11755, 13228, 13494, 14724–4a, 16995, 16996, 18925 (d?), [20092], 20801.3, 21500, 23325.7 (pt? d).
1580: 4699, 5259 ent., 6761, 6838, 6841, 11987, [13766.5] (d?), 14094.5, [16512–3(*A*3, note)?] (pt), 16951, 16951.5, 17576(*A*) ent., 18772 ex assig., [23025], [23025.5], 23095, 23333 (d).
1581: [570?], 753, 828 ex off., 1582 ass'd by, 1982 ex off., 6037 ex off., 10327, 10552, 12461 ent., 12934, [13630–1?], 14632–2a, 15163, 15254 ap., 16950, 16954, 16954.5, 18533.5, 19961 ex off., 19990.7, 20054 ex off., 20395 ex off., 20761 ex off., 24688 ex off.
1582: 1983 ex off., 5400.5 ex off. (pt), [10796], 11128 ap., 14613.5, 14614, [15532.5], 15164, 15164a, 18772.5 ex assig., 18773 ex assig., 18773.3 ex assig., 18773.7 ex assig., 18774 ex assig., 20802, 20962, 21488 ex off. (d?), [25713].
1583: 2793 ent., [6168], [6650(*A*3)?], 11430–0.5, 12371 ex off., 12909.7, 12910, 12911–1.3, 12911.5 (d), 14603, 18101 in aed., [18277.5?] (d?), [21805?] (d?), [24785?], 24807.

1584: 5689 in aed., 6106.3 (note), 6848 (note), 10451 (note), 13495 (note), 15336(*A*3, note), 16952 [Deputies], 21827(*A*3, note).
1596: 7275 ?ass'd.

Byrckman, Byrchman. *See* Birckman.

Byrd, William, *Assignee of.*
Printer of music, 1588–1595? = T. East. An abstract of the 21-year patent granted on 22 Jan. 1575 to Byrd and Thomas Tallis is printed in 23666. For blank ruled music paper printed by East and possibly others *see* 7467.5. Items below all have 'assignee' except as noted.
1588: 4253, 4253.3, 4253.7, 26094, 26094.5.
1589: 4246, 4247 ex assig., 4256, 4256.5 (d/repeat).
1590: 25119, 25583.
1591: 4248 ex assig., 6220, 6221, 10698.
1592: 2482.
1593: 18121.
1594: 2488, 18284.
1595: 4256.5 (d?).

Bythner, Victorinus.
Hebrew grammarian and author, b. 1605?–1670?†. [*DNB*.]
No address used.
1637: 4261 imp. **1638:** 4259 imp.

C

C., Edm. *See* Bollifant.

Cadman, Thomas.
Bookseller in London, (1560) 1574–1589. [*Dict. 1.*]
dw. at (near unto) the great North door of St. Paul's at the Bible (A.2), 1585 (12299)–1588 (12285, omits 'great'); variation: has 'shop', 1585 (5415)
1574: 15206.5 f.
1584: 5255 f., 17047.5 f., 17048 f., 17048a f., 17086 f., 17086.5 f.
1585: 5415 f., 5448 f., 7596 f., 12299 f.
1586: 5228 f. (d), [16617(*A*3)] sold, 25079 f.
1587: 5261 f., 12293 f. (d), 13100 f., 15215 f., 18149 f., 18487 f. (d), 25349 f. (d).
1588: 723 f., 5444 f., 12285 f., 15215 f., 18836.5 f.
1589: 3145 f., 12309 f., 12310 f., [13098.4 f.], 13098.5 f., 15106 f., 17131 por, 17132 f., 25080 f.
1597: 17049 ass'd.

Caen. *See* Canin.

Caesar. *See* Keyser.

Caillard, Jean.
Bookseller in Rouen, 1515–1522. [Duff, *Century*; Muller 98.]
1515: 16141 imp. **1517:** 13833.5 imp., 16234 imp. **1518:** 16198 imp. **1520:** 16104.5 imp. **1521:** 16204.5 imp. **1522:** 16144 pro.

Caly, Robert.
Printer in Rouen, 1551, and in London, 1553–1558 (1566). Succeeded to the printing house of **Richard Grafton**. Most of the printing material eventually passed to **Richard Tottell**, but it is not clear if Tottell acquired some of it in 1553 or whether Caly printed for him or he for Caly before 1559. The London reissue of Caly's first book was: sold in Paul's Churchyard at the Bishop's Head (A.2), 1553? (11592, note), but it seems unlikely that the shop was his. [Duff, *Century*.]
within the precinct of the late dissolved house of the Greyfriars, now converted to an hospital called Christ's Hospital (C.2), 1553 (14642)–1556 (13557); variation: omits mention of Christ's Hospital, 1553 (3838)
within the precinct of Christ's Hospital (C.2), 1558, 10 Feb. (25112)–7 June (25114)
1551: [11592] (d).
1553: 3838, 11592 (note, d?), 14642, 25388 in aed.
1554: 3839, 3839.5, 10896 in aed., 13556, 13560.5, 13561, [16151], 17517 in aed., 20407, 20826(*A*3) in aed. (d?), 23207 in aed., 24754.
1555: 3281, 3442.8 in aed. (d), 4844.4 ex aed., 10744 in aed., 10745 in aed. (c), 11916.5, 13559, [15840], 16062 in aed., [16156], 20408, [22429?], 22817–7.5 in aed., 23208.
1556: 10897 in aed., 12795, 13557 in aed., 13558, 16073 in aed., [16073.5] (d?), 24755.
1557: 7482 in aed., [7605.5?], 13559.5.
1558: 3280.7 in aed. (d), 10117 in aed., 25112 in aed., 25112.5 in aed., 25113 in aed. (forged), 25114 in aed.

Cambier, Andreas.
Bookseller in Heidelberg, 1597–1620. [Benzing, *Verleger*.]
1614: 1431.24A imp.

Cambridge University—Printers.
Printers in Cambridge from 1583. Items in which individuals are named in the imprint, or with names supplied in square brackets in STC before 1625, are indexed *only* under the relevant name, and following is a list of those who held University appointments as printers, 1583–1640, and whose names appear in at least one imprint:

Thomas Thomas, 1583–1588
John Legat 1, 1588–1609 (1620)
John Porter, before 1593–1608
Cantrell Legge, 1606–1625
Thomas Brooke, before 1608–1624?
Leonard Greene, 1622–1630

Cambridge University—Printers — *cont.*
John Buck, 1625–1635
Thomas Buck, 1625–1639; 1650–1653?
Roger Daniel, 1632–1650

From documentary evidence the press was situated in University Street, c. 1583–c. 1609; next to the Rose Inn on the north side of Market Hill, c. 1609–c. 1625; at the Angel Inn across from the north side of Market Hill, c. 1625–c. 1630; and in the former refectory of the Austin Friars in Free School Lane, c. 1630–c. 1655. [David McKitterick, *Four Hundred Years of University Printing and Publishing in Cambridge, 1584–1984*, Cambridge, 1984, p. 13.]

For a comprehensive listing of all items printed or sold in Cambridge before 1641, including those for which [*Cambridge*] alone has been supplied as an imprint, *see* Index 2Ai.

Indexed below are items after 1624 in which the imprint states *only* 'by the printers to the University of Cambridge', 'ex typographia academiae Cantabrigiensis' or similar phrases, *without* the names of particular individuals even though they have occasionally been supplied in STC itself. Many of the items were Latin school books and other titles belonging to the Stationers' Company—English Stock, regarding which *see* the headnote following Appendix D/60 and D/61–93.

1624/25: 501.15, 505.
1625/26: 501.16, 516.
1626: 10315.5, 18722 ex acad.
1626/27: 436, 446, 478, 501.17, 505.2, 516.5, 524.
1627: 10242, 10338 (d?), 23857.5, 25058.
1627/28: 431, 517.
1628: 172.9 ex acad., 1786, 2608, 2609, 2610, 2610.3, 2610.5 (forged), 2610.7, 2932–3.3, 4696, 6673, 6673.2 (d).
1628/29: 431.1, 436.2, [501.19], 505.3.
1629: 15627.7.
1629/30: 501.20, 505.4.
1630: 5271 ex acad., 5271.2 ex acad., 10243 (d), 15627.7.
1630/31: 427.3, 430, 436.3, 469, 501.21, 505.5.
1631: 705 ex acad., 4775 ex acad., 5303 ex acad., 6301 ex acad., 14276.5 ex acad., 18206 ex acad., 18954 ex acad., 20761.7 ex acad., 22257 ex acad., 23661 ex acad.
1631/32: 427.4, 501.22.
1632: 6099, 11060, 11769, 20692–2a, 21823 ex acad., 22986 ex acad., 24793 ex acad.
1632/33: 430.2, 436.5, 469.2, 501.23, 505.7, 517.1, 518, 530, 4475.
1633: 173.7 ex acad., 2647, 4489.7, 4491 ex acad., 4776 ex acad., 5761 ex acad., 6106.5 ex acad., 10296, 10317, 11054 ex acad., 11082–2.5, 11199, 12936 ex acad., 14903, 18724(*A*: 2 eds.) ex acad., 21873, 24854 ex acad.
1633/34: 430.3, 436.6, 469.3, 501.24, 505.8, 517.2, 518.2, 530.3.
1634: 2654, 4485–5.3, 6009 ex acad., 7056, 7058, 11771 ex acad., 15521, 15630, 19052.4, 20693, 21460–0.3, 22987 ex acad.
1634/35: 430.4, 436.7, 469.4, 501.25, 505.9, 515.25, 517.3, 530.4.
1635: 174 ex acad., 706 ex acad., 5272.6 ex acad., 5303.4 ex acad., 6106 ex acad., 10244, 11775, 14904, 16401, 18930 ex acad., 20762 ex acad., 21824 ex acad., 22400, 22404.2 (d), 22988 ex acad., 23516, 23661.5 ex acad., 24854.5 ex acad.
1635/36: 419.5, 430.5, 436.8, 441.9, 469.5, 501.26, 517.4, 530.5(*A*), 4479 ex acad.
1636: 1880 ex acad. (d), 4329a, 4776.5 ex acad., 6194 ex acad., 7236, 13553–3.5, 15522, 17285 ex acad., 18725 ex acad., 21638 ex acad., 22571 ex acad., 23889.9 ex acad.
1636/37: 430.6, 436.9, 469.6, [501.27], 505.11, 518.4, 530.6(*A*).
1637: 2326, 2675, 4108 ex acad., 4492 ex acad., 10319, 16406, 18172 ex acad.
1637/38: 430.7, 436.10, 469.7, 469.11, 501.28, 505.12, 517.6, 518.5, 530.7.
1638: 16412.
1638/39: 436.11, 517.7, 518.6.
1639: 2692.5 (forged), 4330, 5273 ex acad., 18173 ex acad., 20762.4 ex acad.
1639/40: 501.30.
1640: 19770.5.

Campen, Peter Hendricksz van.
Printer in Leeuwarden, 1579–1586. [Gruys; Paul Valkema Blouw in *Quaerendo* (forthcoming).]
1579: [17450(*A*3)].

Campion, E.
Publisher? or bookseller? of anti-papist persuasion in Canterbury sometime between 1538 and 1547. [Duff, *Century*.]
No address used.
1538–47: 14006(*A*3) f.

Campo, R. del. *See* Field.

Candos, Guillaume.
Bookseller in Rouen, 1504–1509 at least. [Duff, *Century*; not in Muller.]
1506: 15904.5 pro (d?). **1509:** 16186 imp.

Canin, Abraham.
Printer at Dordrecht, 1595–1605. Brother of **Isaac Canin**. His widow remarried **Joris Waters**. [*Dict. 1*; Gruys; Briels 197, 208–12.]
1601: 16588.

Canin (Caen), Isaac Jansz.
Printer at Dordrecht, 1594–1621 (1637†). Brother of **Abraham Canin**. [*Dict. 1*; Gruys; Briels 197, 212–19.]
1597–98: 12498. **1599:** 11513. **1601:** 2184.5, 2702, 2901. **1603:** 2903.

Canne, John. *See* Richt Right Press.

Canter, Richard.
Bookseller in London, 1603. Not a member of the Stat. Co. His only imprint was published jointly with **George Potter**, but the address given is not Potter's. [*Dict. 1*.]
dw. in Pope's Head Alley near the [Royal] Exchange (O.11), 1603 (11726)
1603: 11726 f.

Car, Roger.
Printer in London, 1548. [Duff, *Century*.]
No address used.
1548: 2375, 18764.

Carmarden, Richard.
English? patron for whom an ed. of the Great Bible was printed in Rouen, 1566. [*Dict. 1*.]
No address used.
1566: 2098 at cost of.

Carpenter, E. *See* Bollifant.

Carre, Henry.
Bookseller in London, (1576?) 1578–1604. In 1589 he had two addresses, and such may also have been the case earlier. [*Dict. 1*.]
in Paul's Churchyard, 1580–1590
shop — next to the Holy Lamb (A.6), 1580, 17 Oct. (18277)
— [no sign] (B), 1583 (10845)
— over against the Blazing Star (B), 1584 (4461)
— at the Blazing Star (B), 1585 (23396)–1590 (14425.3); variation: 1589 (16947.5, colophon, has 'shop')
in the Old Change (N.8), 1581, 1589
dw. — at the Three Conies, 1581 (18268)
dw. — at the Cat and Fiddle, 1589 (16947.5, colophon)
1580: 18277 f.
1581: 18268 f., 26079 ?ent.
1583: 10844.8, 10845 f.
1584: 4461 f. (d), 16947 f., 16947.3(*A*3) f., 19427 f., 23399.2(*A*3) f.
1585: 3412.7 f. (d), [15002] sold, 23396 f. (d).
1586: 4270.5 ent., 19428 f., 21688.5 ?ent.
1587: 22267 f. (d).
1588: 5552 f. (d), 6910.7 ent., 12576 f., 15207 f., 24215 f.
1589: 16947.5, 21309 (note).
1590: 84.5 f., 14425.3 f., 22694.5 f.
1604: 5256 ?ent.

Carre, Thomas.
Bookseller in Norwich, 1631.
No address used.
1631: 3790.5 sold.

Carter, William.
Recusant printer in London, (1573?) 1575–1579? (1584†). Wood, *Ath. Ox.* II.69 indicates that a press of Carter's was seized at his house on Tower Hill (U.3) in 1578 after having printed 1250 copies of 17508. In the bookseller Thomas Thorpe's *A Catalogue of Ancient Manuscripts upon Vellum and Paper*, issued in 1838, item 104 documented an examination of Carter in 1583 about the same incident in which his house is said to have been on Holborn Bridge (V.2) and 1000 copies printed, of which all but a few went to one Cowper of Lancaster. [*Dict. 1*; Southern 350–3.]
No address used.
1575: [274] (false), [23443.5] (c?), [23967] (forged, c).
1576: [16645.3] (c), [17136] (false), [17775] (false).
1577: [18843] (c).
1578: [10899] (d?), [17508] (false).
1579: [4568.5] (false, d?), [14563.7] (false, d?), [16641.5] (d), [16646] (d).
1580: [16645.5] (c).

Cartwright, John.
Bookseller in Coventry, 1633–1635 at least.
No address used.
1633: 14692.5 sold. **1635:** 1235.3 sold.

Cartwright, Richard.
Bookseller in London, (1615) 1627–1647†. Brother of **Samuel Cartwright.** [*Dict. 2*; DFM 834; *Loan Book*, 1638–41, 1644–47.]
in Duck Lane near Smithfield (E.5), 1627 (3836)–1638 (12766, has 'shop')
1627: 3836 f., 6267 f. **1638:** 12766 f.

Cartwright, Samuel.
Bookseller in London, (1622) 1626–1650†. Brother of **Richard Cartwright.** [*Dict. 2*; DFM 979.]
dw. at the Hand and Bible in Duck Lane (E.5), 1628 (24513)–1640 (12363, omits 'Hand and') at least
1626: 22404 ent. **1628:** 24513 f. **1630:** 22404 f. **1633:** 22404.1 f., 23124 ent. **1634:** 13124.5 f. **1635:** 17824 f. **1639:** 22404.4 f., 22404.5 f. **1640:** 12363 f., 21542 f. **1641:** 22404.5 f.

Case, John.
Bookseller in London, 1548–1552? [Duff, *Century*.]
at the West side of Paul's under Peter College (A.10), 1548 (1774)
dw. in Peter College rents, 1549? (2760)–1551 (2761.5)
dw. at the Ball in Paul's Churchyard (A.10), 1552? (15113.5)
1548: 1774 sold. **1549:** 2760 (d?). **1551:** 2761.5 f. (d). **1552:** 15113.5 f. (d?).

Casson. *See* Causon.

Castellan. *See* Chastelain.

Castelvetro, Giacomo.
Editor and publisher in London, 1589–1591 at least. A brother of the Stat. Co.
No address used.
1589: [10511] (false). **1591:** 12414 a spese.

Castleton, Thomas.
Bookseller in London, 1610. [*Dict. 1*; DFM 1727.]
shop without Cripplegate (I.2), 1610 (22379)
1610: 22379 f.

Cathkin (Gathkin), James.
Bookseller in Edinburgh, 1601?–1631†. Both of his items were published jointly with **Richard Lawson**. [*Dict. 1*.]
No address used.
1607: 16589.5 f. **1610:** 2704 sold (c).

Causon (Casson), Edmund.
Bookseller in Norwich, 1615–1631 at least. Apprenticed in London to W. Ferbrand in 1600 but never made free of the Stat. Co. [*Dict. 1*: 62.]
in the Market Place at the Bible, 1623 (11598; 18481, has 'shop' and 'Market Stead')
1615: 18480.5 f. **1617:** 26096a f. **1623:** 11598 sold, 18481 f. **1631:** 15036a sold.

Cawood, Gabriel.
Bookseller in London, 1576–1602†. Son of **John Cawood**. [*Dict. 1*.]
dw. in Paul's Churchyard at the $ Holy Ghost (A.5), 1576 (11641); no later use of this or any other address noted.

Cawood, G. — *cont.*
1576: 11641 f.
1577: 5549 f., 10889 f.
1578: 17051 f. (d).
1579: 17052 f. (d), 17053 f.
1580: 16702 f. (d), 16708 f. (d), [16899.3 f.] (d?), 17053.5 f., 17054 f., 17068 f., 17069 f., 17070 f.
1581: 17055 f., 17055.5 f., 17071 f.
1582: 5549.5 f., 17072 f., 25118a f. (d).
1584: 17072.5 f.
1585: 17056 f., 17080 ent.
1586: 11642 f., 17073 f.
1587: 17057 f., 20090 f.
1588: 17074 f.
1590: 17058 f. (d?).
1591: 22950 f.
1592: 17074.5 f., 22950.5 f., 26062 f.
1593: 3201 ent., 17059 f. (d?).
1594: 152 ent., 22951 [f.].
1595: 1343 ent., 22956 f.
1596: [22951.5(***A***) f.] (d?).
1597: 16704 f., 17060 f. (d?), 17075 f., 22958 f.
1598: 2995a.3 ent.
1599: 22959 f.
1600: 10889.5 f.
1601: 17076 f.
1602: 22960a f.

Cawood, John.
Bookseller in London, 1541–1553, and **Queen's Printer** (*see* King's Printer), 1553–1572†, from 1559 sharing the title with **Richard Jugge**. Father of **Gabriel Cawood;** father-in-law of **George Bishop** and **Thomas Woodcock**. [Duff, *Century*.]
in Paul's Churchyard, 1553–1570 and until his death
— at the $ Holy Ghost (A.5), 1553 (923)–1558 (24318); latest use of the sign is on an item without Cawood's name, 1568/69 [466.9], but this address passed to his son and was probably the shop mentioned in 1565 as being next to Paul's gate (Plomer, *Wills*: 16)
— [no sign] (B), 1559 (10466)–1570 (3546); this was a printing house and need not have been in the same location as the shop
1546: 16701 (d/repeat).
1550: 2821 pro, 17562 (false, d/error).
1551: 16704.3(***A***3) (d/repeat).
1553: 923, 1462 (d), 6274.5, 7283 (d), 7848 in aed., 7849 in aed., 7850 in aed., 7851 in aed., 7852 in aed., 7853 in aed., 7854 in aed., 7855 in aed., 11722 in aed., 12556.7 (d), 12794 in aed.
1553/54: 9182 in aed., 9182.5 in aed.
1554: 3280.3 in aed. (d), 5207, 7753.6–.8 in aed., 7856 in aed., 7857 in aed., 7858 in aed., 7859 in aed., 7860 in aed., 7861 in aed., 7862 in aed., 7863 in aed., 9440.8 in aed., 9440.10 in aed., 9440.12–.16 (repeat), 9443 in aed., 9443.5 in aed., 9444–4.8 (repeat), 10248 in aed., 10491 in aed., 12753 in aed., 14077c.147 in aed. (d), 16701 (d), 16704.3(***A***3) (forgery of lost ed., d?), 17469 in aed., 19836 in aed. (d?), 24633.5, 25115, 25115.3, 25115.5.
1555: 548.7 (d), 3281.5 in aed. (d), 3282 in aed., 3283 in aed. (d), 3283.3 in aed. (d), 3283.5 in aed. (d), 3283.7 in aed. (d), 3285.1 (d), 3285.2–.4, 3285.5, 3285.6, 3285.7, 3285.8, 3285.9, 3285.10, 7864 in aed., 7865 in aed., [7866] (d), 7867 in aed., 7867.3 in aed., 7867.5 in aed., 7867.7 in aed., 7867.9 in aed., 9339.3(***A***) in aed. (d?), 9447.3 in aed., 9447.5 in aed., 9447.7 in aed., 9447.8 in aed., 9447.9–50 (repeat), 9450.3 in aed., 9450.5 in aed., 9450.7–54.5 (repeat), 9455–5.5 (d/error, repeat), 10249 [f.], 16787.2 (c), [16787.4?] (c), [16787.6] (c), 17562a (false), 19811 (d?), [23446] (c), 24855 (d?), 25291.5 in aed. (d).
1556: [3006.5?], 3201, 4184 (d), 5219 (d), 5990 in aed., 6005.5 (note), 7868 in aed., 7868.3(***A***) in aed., 7869 in aed., 7870 in aed., 7871 in aed., 7872 in aed., 9444 in aed. (d?), 9447.9 in aed. (d?), 9450.7 in aed. (d?), 14077c.147A in aed., 23966, 23967 (forged).
1556/57: 7873 in aed.
1557: 923.5, 1543.5, 7874 in aed., 7875 in aed., 7876 in aed., 9339.4(***A***3) in aed. (d?), [10455], 11708, [14009.3?] (d?), 18076 at costs of, 20088.5 in aed. (d).
1557/58: 7877 in aed.
1558: 7878 in aed. (d), 7879 in aed., 7880 in aed., 7881 in aed., 7882 in aed., 7883 in aed., 7884 in aed., 7885 in aed., 9448 in aed. (d?), 9450.9 in aed. (d?), 9457 in aed., 9457.2 in aed., 9457.4 in aed., 9457.6 in aed., 9457.8 (repeat), 11709 (d?), 24318.

Cawood, J. — *cont.*
1558/59: 7890, 7890.5 (repeat), 7891.
1559: 7892, 7893, 7894, 7895 (repeat), 7897, 7897.3 (repeat), 7898, 7899 (repeat), 7900 (repeat of lost ed.), 7902, 7902.3 (repeat), 7903, 7904, [7905], [7905.5], 7907, 9448.3 in aed. (c?), 9458.7, 9459, 9459.3, 9459.5, 9459.7–60 (repeat), 10099.5 (d), 10100 (d?), 10100.3 (d?), 10100.5 (d?), 10102 (d?), 10118, 10118.5 (d?), 10466 (d), 13648, 13648.5, 16292 in off., 16292a in off. (d/error?), 16293 in off., 16293.3 in off., 16293.5 in off. [f.].
1559/60: 7908, 7909, 7909.5 (repeat), 7910, 7910.7, 7911, 7911.5.
1560: 2094, 7913, 7914–5, 7916, 7916.5, 7917 (d), 7918 (d), 7920, 7921, 7921.5 (repeat), 7924, 7924.3 (repeat), 9183.5, 9184 (d), 9444.2 in aed. (c), 9451 in aed. (d?), [11309.7] (d), 13649, 13649.5, 16294 in off., 16294a.3 in off., 25286 (d?).
1560/61: 7928, 7929 (repeat).
1561: 2094, [7799.5] (d?), 7917 (note, d?), 7924.5 (d?), 7931, 7931.3 (repeat), 7932, 7933, 7934 (d), 7936, 7936.3 (repeat), 7936.7, 7940, 9339.5 (d), [10102.2] (d?), 10119 (d?), 13680.8 (d?), 16292a in off. (d?), 22943, 22944.
1561/62: 7941, 7942, 7943, 7944.
1562: 7924.6 (d?), 7946, 7947, 7948, 7949, 7950 (d), 7951 (d), 7951.3 (repeat), 7952 (d), 7953a, 7953a.5 (repeat), 7954 (repeat of lost ed.), 7954.5 (d?), 7954.7 (d?), 8046.5 (c?), 9187.3, [10102.3] (d?), 10120 (d?), [10657] (d), 13650, 13650.3, 13650.7, 16295 in off., 16504.3(***A***3) (d), 16704.6 (d), [16827?].
1562/63: 7956.
1563: 5548, 7957, 7957.3, 7957.7 (d), 7957.9, 7958, 7959, 7960, 7962, 7962.3 (repeat), 7962.5, 7963 (repeat), 7964–4.5, 7965 (repeat), 9462, 9462.5, 9463.5, 9464–5 (repeat), 10038.3 (d?), 10888 (d?), 13651, 13663, 13663.3, 13663.7, 13664, 13664.5, 13665, 13666, 13666.7, 13667 (d/repeat), 16505 (d), 16506 (d), 16506.3–.7 (d), 16506.9(***A***3) (d), 16507, 16507.5 (d).
1563/64: 7966, 7967, 7968 (repeat), 7969, 7970, 7972.
1564: [7777] (d?), 7920.5 (d?), 7947.3 (d?), 7955 (d?), 7973, 7974, 7974.5, 7975 (repeat), 7976, [7976.7] (d?), 7978, 7978.3 (repeat), 7981 (d), 7982 (d), 7983, 7984, 9342.4 (d?), 9342.5 (repeat), 9464 (d?), 9464.5 (d?), 10038.5 (d?), [10102.4] (d?), 10120.5 (d?), 16296 in off., 16296.3 in off.
1564/65: 7986, 7986.3 (repeat).
1565: 7987, 7988, 7988.5, [7988.7] (d?), 7989, 7990 (repeat), 7991, 7992, 7993, [9185] (c?), 9459.7 (c?), 9465 (d?), 16296.5 in off.
1565/66: 7994, 7995.
1566: 1427 in aed., 5059 (d), 7924.9 (d?), 7995.3, [7995.4] (d?), 7995.5, 7996, 7997, 7998, 7998.3 (d?), 8047 (c?), 9427.3 (note), 9432.5 (note), [10102.5] (d?), 10121 (d?), 16297, 16297.5, 16510 (d), 23967.5.
1566/67: 7999.5 (d), 9468.2, 9468.3.
1567: 7925 (d?), 7955.3 (d?), 9448.7 in aed. (d?), 9452 in aed. (d?), [10102.6] (d?), 13667, 16298.
1568: 2102, 8003, 8003.3 (repeat), 8005, 8006, 8007 (repeat), 8048.7 (d?), [10102.7] (d?), 10121.5 (d?), 16298.5 in off.
1568/69: [466.9] sold, 8008, 8008.3, 8010, 8011, 8012, 8013, 8013.5 (repeat), 8014–4.3, 8014.5 (repeat).
1569: 2102, 2102.5, 2103–4 (d?), [2873.7?] (d?), 8015, 8015.5 (repeat), 8016, 8017, 8018, 8018.5 (repeat), 8019, 8020, 8020.5 (repeat), 8021, [8022], 8049 (d?), 13652.
1569/70: 8023, 8023.5 (repeat), 8024 (d), 8025 (d), 8027, 8027.3 (repeat).
1570: [3419.5?] (d?), 3546 (d), [6836.5] (d?), 7926 (d?), 8028, 8029, 8030, 8031, 8032, 8033, 8034, 8034.5 (repeat), 8035, 8047.4 (c?), 9440.12 in aed. (d?), 9449 in aed. (d?), [10102.8] (c?), 10123 (c?), [12723a(***A***3 & TH8z in headnote)?] (c?), 13668, 13679.2 (d?), 13679.4 (d?), [13679.7] (d?), 13680 (d?), 13680.4 (d?), 13680.6 (d?), 16299 in off., 16300, [18482.5?] (d?), [25073] (d?).
1571: 7953a.3 (c?), [8036], [8036.3], 8037, 9471.4, 9471.6, 9471.8, 9472–3 (repeat), [10030], 10038.7, 10038.9, 10038.11, 10039, 10039.3, 13669, 16301.3 in off., 16301.5.
1571/72: 8039, 8040, 8041, 8042–3, 8044.
1572: 8047.6 (c?), 9460 (d), 9472 (d?).

Caxton, William.
Mercer and printer in Bruges, 1473?–1476, and in Westminster, 1476–1491 (1492?†). His printing material and premises passed to **Wynkyn de Worde**. The basic chronology of Caxton's publications is listed in Paul Needham's *The Printer & the Pardoner*,

Caxton, W. — *cont.*
Washington, 1986, pp. 83–91. Although addenda corrections in the index below repair most of the larger discrepancies between dates in STC and those in Needham's list, for ease of reference his enumeration, cited in the form 'Cx4', is given for all items below except two Images of Pity: 14077c.6, —.8, which he omits.
For an assessment of documents relating to Caxton's tenements in Westminster see *Library* 31 (1976): 305–26. [Duff, *Century*; Rouzet.]
in the Almonry at the Red Pale, 1477? [4890]
1473: [15375(***A*3**)] (d?) Cx4.
1474: [4920] (d) Cx5.
1476: [4851] (d) Cx12, [14077c.106] (d) Cx16, [15867(***A*3**)] (d) Cx11, [17009(***A*3**)] (d) Cx13, [17019(***A*3**)] (d) Cx14, [21458(***A*3**)] (d) Cx10.
1477: [3303] (d?) Cx29, [4850] (d) Cx22, [4890] (d?) Cx24, [5082] (d) Cx17, [5090] (d?) Cx28, [5091] (d) Cx27, 6826–7 Cx26, 6828–9 (repeat), [14551] (c) Cx20, [15383] Cx25, [16228] (d) Cx23, [17008] (d?) Cx19, [17018] (d?) Cx18, [17030] (d?) Cx15, [17032] (d?) Cx21.
1478: [3199] (d?) Cx31, 7273 Cx30, [24188.5–89(***A*3**)] (d) Cx32.
1479: [5758] Cx34, [15868(***A*3**)] (d?) Cx33.
1480: 6828 (d?) Cx38, 9991 Cx39, 13440a Cx40, [14077c.83G (***A*3**)] (d?) Cx44, [—.107] (d) Cx36, [—.107C(***A*3**)] (d) Cx42, [—.110] (d) Cx43, [15848] (d?) Cx37, [24190.3] (d?) Cx35, [24865] (d) Cx41.
1481: 5293 Cx45, 13175 Cx48, [14077c.112] (d) Cx50, [—.113] (d) Cx49, [16253(***A*3**)] (d) Cx47, [24762] (d) Cx46.
1482: 9992 Cx53, 13438 per (d) Cx52, [20919(***A*3**)] (d) Cx51.
1483: [4852] (d) Cx56, [4853] (d?) Cx68, [4921] (d) Cx57, [5057] (d) Cx58, [5083] (d) Cx55, 5087 (d) Cx59, [5094] (d) Cx60, 6473–4 Cx64, 12142 (d) Cx66, [17015(***A*3**)] (d) Cx61, 17023(***A*3**) (d) Cx63, [17024(***A*3**)] (d) Cx62, 17957 Cx54('book' ed. of pt. 2), Cx65 (pt. 1), 24873(***A*3**) Cx67, 24874(***A*3**) (repeat).
1484: 175 Cx70, [3259] (d) Cx75, [3356.7] (d) Cx71, [14554] (c) Cx74, [15296] Cx69, [15871(***A*3**)] (c) Cx77, [15872(***A*3**)] (c) also Cx77, 17720(***A*3**) (c) Cx76, 22588(***A*3**) per (d) Cx72, 24874(***A*3**) (c) also Cx67, [25853(***A*3**)] (d) Cx73.
1485: 801 Cx80, [5013] Cx81, [14077c.25G(***A*3**)] (d) Cx79, 19206 per Cx82, [21429(***A*3**)] (d) Cx83.
1487: [7013] (d) Cx78, [14077c.6] (c), [15394] Cx84, [15847.3 (***A*3**)] (c) Cx87, [15854(***A*3**)] (c) Cx86, 16164 imp. Cx110, 17957(***A*3**) (c, 'booc' ed. of pt. 2) Cx85.
1488: [16136 f.] Cx111.
1489: 6829 (d) Cx93, [7269] Cx90, [14077c.114] (d) Cx88, [—.115] (d) Cx89, 17722 (d) Cx91, [20920] (d) Cx92, 21431 (d) Cx94.
1490: [789] (d) Cx98, [1007] (d) Cx100, [3124] (d) Cx101, 3260 (d) Cx96, [12138] (d?) Cx99, [14077c.8] (c), 24763 (d) Cx95, [24796] (d) Cx97.
1491: [786] (d) Cx109, 3305 (d) Cx108, [9348] (d?) Cx102, 15872 (note) Cx106–7, 17959 (d) Cx103–4, 20195 (d) Cx105.

1493: 12142 (d/error), 24875 (repeat).
1495: 23153.4 in house (d).
1496: 7016 in domo (d?), 17103–3.5 in domo.
1497: 17011 in house (d?), 23163.7 in house (d?).
1499: 23153.5 in house (d).

Certain, William.
Stationer in London, (1635) 1638. His only item was published jointly with **Laurence Chapman** and sold at the latter's shop: at Chancery Lane end in Holborn (V.12). [*Dict. 1*; DFM 555.]
No separate address used.
1638: 17780 f.

Cervicornus, Eucharius.
Printer and bookseller in Cologne, 1516–1547; also in Marburg, 1535–1538. [Duff, *Century*; Benzing 232, 236, 323.]
1520: 6044a.5 in aed. **1535:** [2063–3.5?].

Chalwood. *See* Charlewood.

Chambers, Richard.
Stationer in London, 1618. His only imprint was published jointly with **Thomas Thorpe** and was sold by one of Chambers's former masters, **Edward Blount:** at the Black Bear in Paul's Churchyard (B). [*Dict. 1*; DFM 637; *Loan Book*, 1620–23.]

Chambers, R. — *cont.*
No separate address used.
1618: 11707 f.

Champaigne (Champion), Piers de.
Patron in London, 1509. Esquire for the Body to Henry VIII and searcher in the port of Southampton, dead before 27 Oct. 1511 (*L&P Hen. VIII*, I[1] p. 486, no. 969(8)).
No address used.
1509: 12512 imp.

Chapman, Laurence.
Bookseller in London, (1618) 1620–1655. [*Dict. 2*; DFM 698; *Loan Book*, 1638–41.]
shop in Holborn over against Staple Inn, hard by the bars (V.9), 1620 (4281)
shop at Chancery Lane end (V.12), 1627 (5318)–1640 (3956, adds 'in Holborn') at least; variation: at the upper end of Chancery Lane, 1629 (13901)
1620: 4281 f., 19824 f., 23583 f.
1627: 5318 f., 18516 f.
1629: 13901 f.
1631: 13902 f., 13903 f.
1633: 1357.5 sold, 6104 f., 22494 ent.
1634: 3587 sold, 13627 f., 19455 f.
1635: 4369 ent., 17979 sold.
1636: 3955 f., 22515 f., 22516 f.
1637: 17979.3 sold, 22494 f., 22495 f., 22517 f.
1638: 17780 f., 20691 ven., 22496 f., 22518 f.
1639: 12205 sold, 12457.5 sold, 22485 f.
1640: 3956 f., 20695.5 sold.

Chard (Chare, Chayre), Thomas.
Bookseller in London, (1575?) 1577–1624†. He took over the address of his former master, **Humphrey Toy**. *Dict. 1* cites an address in Bishopsgate Churchyard, for which Ames 396 (followed by Herbert II.1195) gives the year 1600, but no surviving Chard book of this date has any address. [*Dict. 1*; *Poor Book*, (& wife) 1612–24, widow thereafter; *Library* 4 (1923): 219–37.]
at the Helmet in Paul's Churchyard (A.2), 1578 (14608)–1585? (24891); no later use of this address or any other noted
1577: 24172 f.
1578: 14607.5 ent., 14608 imp., 26049.3(***A*3**) sold.
1580: 10920–0.3 f., 26049.6 sold.
1581: 18253 f., 25358 imp., 25359 imp., 26049.8 sold.
1582: 19200 f., 19768 f., 25713 f., 25714 f.
1583: 1081 f., 1095 f., 24173 f., 24669 at costs of, 25357 imp., 25362 imp.
1584: 1082 f., 5819.5–.7 f., 18439 f.
1585: 21713 f., 24891 f. (d?), 25364a f.
1586: 1096 f., 16436 at costs of, 24530 imp.
1587: 3734 f., 4473 imp., 11379.5 f.
1588: 1090 f., 10232 f., 14609 (d/error).
1589: 25432 f.
1590: 1083 f., 1097 f., [23419.5 f.] (d).
1591: 1094 f., 11056 f., 14584 imp., 15061 f.
1592: 1086 f., 15288 imp.
1593: 12463 f.
1595: 1089 f.
1596: 1084 f., 1087 f., 1091 f., 1098 f., 2959 ent.
1597: 1311 f., 18071–1.5 f.
1598: 18072 f.
1599: 16638 ent.
1600: 6234 f., 10180 f., 14592 f.
1602: 1085 f.
1604: 1088–8.5 f., 24035 f.
1606: 4769 f.
1607: 20028 imp.
1615: 1077 f., 1078 by ass't of.
1616: 21714 f.
1618: 1079 ass'd.
1622: 14593 ass'd, 16640 ass'd.

Charlewood, Alice.
Printer in London, 1593. Widow of **John Charlewood**; remarried **James Roberts**. [*Dict. 1*; *St. Giles* (under Roberts), 1593.]
dw. in Barbican at the Half-Eagle and Key (I.1), 1593 (6707)

Charlewood, Alice — *cont.*
1593: [5012], 6707, 10833–3a at [her] house, 12160, [12259], 18366 ent., [19382(*A3*, note: ed. ii)?] (d?), 19539 (d), 20846.
1594: 4826.7 ass'd, 6690 ass'd, 6710.5 ass'd, 6710.7 ass'd, 6712 ass'd, 25834 ass'd.

Charlewood, John.
Bookseller in London, 1557?–c.1574, and printer c. 1574–1593†. Freed as a Grocer by **Richard Grafton** in 1552 and transferred to the Stat. Co. c. 1574. Husband of **Alice Charlewood.** His first two imprints were shared with **John Tisdale**. He succeeded to most of the printing material of **William Williamson** and **John Awdely**, and the question of who printed the items indexed below before 1575 requires further study. In 1581 (18535) and 1583 (13858) he used the style: servant *or* printer 'to the right honourable Earl of Arundel', and he was said to have been printing a popish book in the Charterhouse (E.2) about Feb. 1587 (17453, p. 24; *see* also 1032, 22946, possibly printed in Arundel House (X.4) a little later). In 1583 (3341.7 sqq.) he printed one title as the *assignee of* **R. Tottell**. *See* also Appendix A/12–13. [Duff, *Century*; *St. Giles*, 1588.]
in Holborn near to the conduit at the Saracen's Head (D.9), 1557? (5229(*A3*); 17236(*A3*) has only: at Holborn conduit)
in Barbican (I(headnote), I.1), 1563–1589 and until his death
dw. — [no sign], 1563 (24190.7)–1564 (24191a)
dw. — at the Half-Eagle and Key, 1566 (24932)–1589 (11818)
1557: 5229(*A3*) (d?), 17236(*A3*) (d?).
1563: 24190.7 [f.], 24191 [f.], 24191a f.
1564: 24191a f., 24438.5, 24464.
1566: 24932, 24191a.5(*A3*) f.
1567: 6089 f., 24932a.
1568: [24192?].
1569: [17857.5].
1572: 24193 f., [24886.7?] (d?).
1573: [16624] (d?).
1574: [24193.5].
1575: [79] (c), 10306.5 (d), [17575?], [19181.3], 24194, 24816, [24887?] (d?).
1576: 1356.4, [2049] (d), [4347], [11640], [11644] (d?), [11920], [12156], [20739], 21239, 25976, [26110–0.3(*A3*)] (d?), [26110.5 (*A3*)] (d?).
1577: 1306, 6679.7, 6679.8, 6679.9, [18269.5(*A3*)] (d), [20665] (d?), 24061 (d?), 24195, 25975.
1578: [4432], [6685.5] (d?), 6688 (c?), 6702, 6922.7 ent., 7241 (d), 11423, 12355 (d?), [15190.5(*A3*)] (d?), [18438] (d), 19864 (d), 19896, [23629], 25295, [25347], 25828.
1579: [982], 1191 ent., 1376 (d), [2761], 3054 ent., [4042.7?] (d), [5455(*A3*)?] (d), [6319], [10566?] (d), 11453, [11620.7], [12157], 12606 (d), 13483 ent., 16955 (d), 18335.5 (d), 22221 (note), 23406 (d), [24196], 25828–9.
1579/80: [486.3].
1580: 692 (d), 4123.5 (d), [4304.5] (d?), 6689 (c?), 6703, 6710.5, 6710.7, [6794.5] (d?), [8121?] (d), [17321?] (d?), 17848, [18277], [18281] (d), 18283, [21090.3(*A3*)] (d?), 21818, [22416] (c), [24413], [24664] (d?).
1581: [980?], 3501, 3646.5, 6075, 6075.5, 6081, 6095 ent., 6680 (d?), 6689.2, 6689.4 (d), 6710.8, 6710.9, 13868.5 (d), 14121, [14921] (d), [17124–4a] (d), 17180 (d), 18259.3 (d), [18264], 18268, 18535–6a, 19161 ent., 22432, 24197, [25095], [26123].
1582: 886 ent., 1808 ent., 5633.3 ent., 5806 ent., 6080 ?ent., 6088.7 ent., 6711, 6711.5, 7544.5 ent., 11003.5 ent., [11835] (c?), [12158], 12447 ent., 12924, 13302 ent., 13304 ent., 13307 ent., 13751 ent., 14040 ent., [18261], 18262–2a, [18270], [18270.5], 18272, 18663.5 (d?), 18664, 18667 (d?), 18667a (d?), 18667b (d?), 20034 ent., 20108(*A3*) ent., 20797 ent., 20922.5 ?ent., 21050 ent., 21066 (d), 21121.7 ent., 23030 (d), [23414] (d), 23589 ?ent., 25345 (d), 25830.
1583: [982.5], 3341.7 (d), 3342 (d), 3342.3 (d), [3939] (d?), 6693, 6712, 6712.3, 6712.5, [11693], 13858, 13859 (repeat), [16738.5] (c?), 19523, 20844 (d?).
1584: [978], [3060] (d), [3935], [3936] (false), [3938] (false), [3940] (false), [4461] (d), 6697, 6704, 6713, [7170], [12276], 13480.7, 16947, 16947.3(*A3*), [18282], [18282a], 18943 (c), 19817 (d), 19817.5, [21483.5(*A3*)] (d?), [22928], 23287, [24167.5], 25831.
1585: [181.5] (d?), [3934] (false), [3937] (false), 5211, 5212, 5829 (d), [7289], [12158.5?], [12786.5?] (d), 13106, [14800.5] (d?), [17785], [19447?], [19796–6.5], 21292a, [22571.5], [22416.5] (c).

Charlewood, J. — *cont.*
1586: 586, 5212.3, 6091 (d), 6705, [8158?] (d), 11424, 24902 (d?), 25172.
1587: 3179, 6055, 6178 (d?), 6714, 10275 ent., [11238] (d?), [12262.5(*A3*)], 12343 (d), 13193 (d), 13194 (d), [13657], [13673], [16712?] (d?), 17786, [18149], 20699, 20995, 21801, 22895a.5–6.5, [22946?] (false, d?), 23674–4.5.
1588: 981, [1032?] (false, d?), 6084, 6715, 10209 ent., 11819.5, 12158.7(*A3*) (d), 13209 (d?), 17116, [17122.5?], 18260, 19157, [19935], 22697 ent., 23702.5, 23703, 23858.5–9.3, [24931] (d?), 25118.5, 25832.
1589: 4088, [5678], 6698, 6706, [10753], 11818, [12219], [16520.5] (d), 18064, 18364, 19364, [19456] (false), [19456.5] (false), [19457–7.7] (false), 19537, 20366 ent., 21080.
1590: 84.5, [979], 1662, 3658.5, 6715.4, 12307, 13215, 17786, 18273, 18365, [18424] (d), 19380, [19450] (false), 20845, 22645 (d?), [24197.3].
1591: [4911.7] (d), 5376–6.2, 5633.3 ent. (proviso to print), [7275?], [11625], 12159, 17050, 19381, [19429?], [20853], [22536], [22659], 22687, [22703?], [23359] (d), [24598], 26134–4.5.
1592: 7, 629, 3216 ent., [5231?], [5577–8.2], 5637, 5871.3, 6243.2, 6243.3, [11273.5] (d), [16909?], 17080, [18371], 19382(*A3*, note: ed. i), [19974.6], 22718, 23671, 23867.
1593: [5248 in shop of] (d), 17346, [22137], [22700.5], [22701.5], [22709], 23360, 25833.

Charlton. *See* Chorlton.

Charteris, Henry.
Bookseller and printer (from 1581) in Edinburgh, 1568–1599†. Father of **Robert Charteris**. Succeeded to the printing material of **John Ross.** *See* also *heirs of* **H. Charteris** and **King's Printer in Scotland**. [*Dict. 1*; *Library* 14 (1959): 44–5.]
shop (buith) on the North side of the [High] Street (gait) above the tron [= public beam for weighing merchandise], 1568 (15658)–1571 (15659); no later use noted
1568: 15658–8.5 at expenses.
1569: 185 at expenses, 15658.5 at expenses.
1570: 185 at expenses, 13149 at expenses.
1571: [1377.5? at expenses] (d?), 15659 at expenses.
1575: 16579.5 f.
1577: 21463 ap.
1578: 2996.7 f., 3971 ap., 21254 f.
1579: 3973 pro, [3974 f.], 6781 pro, 6783 pro, 7074 f., 22651 pro.
1580: [3975 f.], 5606 pro, 13956 f.
1581: 5962, 11183.
1582: 15662, 21885.
1588: 14376, 21887.5 (d).
1589: 14380, 21266.
1592: 15663.
1593: 13150, 13165.
1594: 13150, 15679, 16584.5.
1595: 16585.
1596: 7487.1, 16585–5.5, 21284, 22024.
1597: 15664, 15664.3.
1599: 7487.2, 21101 ap., 21271.

1603: 14349.5(*A3*) (false).

Charteris, Henry, *Heirs of.*
Booksellers in Edinburgh, 1601. Possibly a false imprint masking the activities in London of **Bonham** and **John Norton 1**. For an order of 30 June 1601 requiring the Stat. Co. to investigate the charges of **Robert Barker** that the two Nortons had connived with **Andro Hart** of Edinburgh to have English Bibles and metrical Psalms printed at Dordrecht *see Acts P.C., 1601–1604*, pp. 14–15. [*Dict. 1.*]
1601: (all 'at expenses') 2184.5, 2702, 2901, 16588.

Charteris, Robert.
Printer in Edinburgh, 1600–1610†. Son of **Henry Charteris**. **King's Printer in Scotland**, 1603–1610. His printing material passed to **Andro Hart**. [*Dict. 1.*]
on the North side of the [High] Street over against (fornent) the salt tron [= public beam for weighing merchandise], 1600–01 (13150.5)

Charteris, R. — *cont.*
shop (buith) on the North side of the Street (gait) at the West side of the old Provost's entry way (closehead), 1602 (15681)–1603 (19528, advt. at end, adds 'a little above the salt tron')
1600: 5587, 7487.3, 13150.5, 21465.5, 21555.5 (d).
1601: 7487.4, 13150.5, 21468, 21555.7 ap.
1602: 15681–2.
1603: 2703, 5969, 5971, 14846.5, 14962, 17811, 19528, 19888.
1604: 2765.5, 5588, 7487.5, 17812 (d?), 20103.
1605: 5460.4, 5460.7, 7487.6, 13857a, 15664.7, 18051, 21270.
1606: 3089, [14846] (d), 17813, 18051.3, 21281, [21960.5] (d), 21960.7, [21962] (d), 21964, 21965.
1607: 7487.7, 14847, 14849.
1608: 6580, 21555.12, [21963] (d).
1609: 14852, 14855, 14857, 21892.7, 21893.
1610: 14854, 18307, 20755.5, [22024.5?] (c).

Charteris, Robert, *Heirs of, pseud.*
Printers in 'Edinburgh', 1628. = Unidentified printer, probably in London. [*Dict. 1.*]
1628: 22640.3, 22640.7.

Chastelain (Castellan), George.
Bookseller in Oxford, 1502–1513†. [Duff, *Century.*]
dw. in the street of St. Mary the Virgin at the $ St. John the Evangelist, 1508? (16899)
1503: 14079 at instance (d). **1508:** 16899 exp. (d?).

Chaudière, Regnault.
Bookseller and printer (from 1516) in Paris, 1509–1554. [Duff, *Century*; Renouard.]
1550: [22819] (d?).

Chayre. *See* Chard.

Chepman, Walter.
Publisher in Edinburgh, 1508–1510 (1529?†). In partnership with **Andrew Myllar** in 1508. [Duff, *Century.*]
in the Southgait [modern Cowgate], 1508 (11984)
1508: [3307] (d?), 5060.5, [7347] (d), [7348] (d), [7349] (d), [7542] (d?), 11984, [13148] (d?), [13166] (d?), [13594] (d?), 17014.3.
1509–10: 15791 imp.

Chettle, Henry.
Printer in London, (1584) 1591, and author until 1607?†. In partnership with **John Danter** and **William Hoskins**, whose address in 1592 was in Fetter Lane (W.8). [*Dict. 1*; *DNB*, *NCBEL.*]
No address used.
1591: 16654 ent., 22656–6.5, 22664, [22665].

Chevallon, Claude.
Bookseller and printer in Paris, 1506–1537†. [Duff, *Century*; Renouard.]
1511–14: 3269.5 ven. **1531:** 15830 imp.

Chorlton (Charlton), Jeffrey (Geoffrey).
Bookseller in London, 1603–1614†. Freed as a Draper by **Thomas Wight** on 29 Sept. 1602; transferred to the Stat. Co. in 1603. [*Dict. 1*: 66; *Poor Book*, 1611–14, widow thereafter.]
shop at (adjoining to) the great North door of Paul's Church (A.2), 1603 (12061)–1609 (20985); no later used noted
1603: 12061 f.
1604: 10855 f., 17874.3 sold, 17875 f., 17875.5(*A*3) f., 19975 f., 21000–1 f.
1605: 3701 sold, 11600 f., 19001–2 f., 24148.7 f., 25232–2.5 f.
1606: 20983 f., 24916 f., 24916.3.
1607: 7261 f., 12582.24 ent., 12918 sold, 18495 f., 24346 f.
1608: 6122(*A*, note), 15536 f., 19511.5 f.
1609: 6582 f., 20985 f.
1610: 12582.24 f.
1613: 17757 f.
1614: 17758 f.

Christiaens van der Boxe, Willem.
Printer in Leiden, 1631–1658. In at least 1638 **Benjamin Allen** seems to have been working with him. [*Dict. 1*; Gruys 14; Briels 184–5; Carter, 'Laud', pp. 48, 52–5.]
1634: 12581.

Christiaens van der Boxe, W. — *cont.*
1637: [1568], [1572], [1573], [1574], [1575], [4788?], [11896], [16452].
1638: [1570], [13738], [16452.5], [22026.4?], [22031.5?].
1639: [552], [13738.5], [26126].
1640: [2344], [2344.5] (d/repeat), [21919.5] (forged), [21923.5] (forged), [21927.7].
1644: [2344.5] (d).

Chrouch. *See* Crouch.

Church, Francis.
Stationer in London, 1634–38 (1684?). His only imprints were issued in partnership with **John Jackson 2.** In Oct. 1638 he was assessed for the city charter (*C-B C*: 432), and he is probably the man of this name in the *Poor Book*, 1675–84. [*Dict. 1*; DFM 1902.]
at the King's Arms in Cheapside (N.1), 1634 (13357, 13585)
1634: 1577.5 sold, 13357 f., 13585 sold.

Claeszoon (Nicolai), Cornelis.
Printer and bookseller in Amsterdam, 1582–1609†. [*Dict. 1*; Gruys; Briels 238–9.]
1593: 1431.13 ven. **1598:** 1431.16 ven. **1602:** 14787, [14787.2] (d?), [14787.6] (d?). **1603:** [14787.4], [14787.8]. **1605:** 1431.18 ven.

Claeszoon van Dorp. *See* Dorp.

Clardue (Clerdewe), Timothy.
Stationer in London, (1629) 1631. [DFM 582.]
No address used.
1631: 4152.3(*A*3) f. (d).

Clarke. *See* also Clerke.

Clarke, Adrian, *pseud.*
Printer in 'the Hague', 1621. = Unidentified printer, probably in London.
1621: 18507.28.

Clarke, John 1.
Bookseller in London, 1619–1669†. Father of John 3, who was freed by patrimony in 1641 (DFM II.799). Of the other John Clarkes before 1641 three were never freed (DFM 1019, 2005, 2166); the one freed in 1608 (DFM 689) took an apprentice that year and was dead before 1636 (DFM 1008); and John 2, freed in 1628 (DFM 2004), was a hot-presser (*C-B C*: 431). [*Dict. 2*; DFM 786; *Loan Book*, 1640–47; ?*Poor Book*, 1664; Globe 213.]
under St. Peter's Church in Cornhill (P.2), 1619 (11040)–1639 (12977, has 'shop') at least; variation: 1637 (23029, has 'dw.')
1619: 1363 f., 11040 f.
1620: 12329 sold.
1621: 15193a f.
1622: 1187 f.
1623: 15194 f.
1624: 6111 ent., 17610 f.
1625: 14306 f., 14316 f., 17602 f.
1626: 17608 f., 17613 f.
1627: 14319 f., 17603—3.5 f., 17605 f., 17614 f., 24987—7.5 f.
1628: 14318 f., 14318.5 f., 17605a f.
1629: 11547 f., 14318 f., 20134 f.
1630: 5388 sold, 17604 f., 17606 f.
1631: 14312 f.
1632: 12976 f.
1633: 20135 ent., 20135.7 sold.
1634: 14313 f., 17611 f., 17612 f., 20136—6.3 f.
1635: 14309 f., 17609 f.
1636: 7088 f., 7089 f., 12937 f., 13536 f., 14310 f., 20780 f., 22181 f.
1637: 3997.5 f., 6111 f., 7090 f., 7551 f., 13267 f., 13267.5 f., 13533 f., 14007 f., 17179 f., 17768 f., 17768.5 f., 22232 f., 23029 f., 23029.5 f., 23029.7 (forged), 23119 f., 23119.5 f., 24691 f.
1638: 5138 sold, 5139 f., 17765 f., 17769 f.
1639: 12977 f., 14500 f., 19510 f.

Clarke (Clerke), Martin.
Bookseller in London, (1605) 1606–1611. Freed by redemption. The earliest address in one of his imprints is not his: sold in Paul's Churchyard at the new shop of the Stationers (ad novam

Clarke, M. — *cont.*
Librariorum officinam) (?A.10), 1606 (11924(*A3*)). [*Dict. 1*; DFM 1016.]
shop without Aldersgate (F.1), 1607 (24967); no later address used
1606: 11924(*A3*) imp., 19683 f., 22880.9, 22881 f. **1607:** 6103 f., 7116, 24967 f. **1609:** 3455 f. **1610:** 7322 f. **1611:** 1782 ent.

Clarke (Clerke), Robert.
Stationer in London, (1605) 1616. [*Dict. 1.*]
his house called the Lodge, in Chancery Lane over against Lincoln's Inn (V.12a), 1616 (22788)
1616: 22788–8.5 f.

Clarke, Sampson.
Stationer in London, 1583–1598. [*Dict. 1.*]
shop by the Guildhall (H.5), 1584 (16653)
behind (at the backside of) the Royal Exchange (O.8), 1589 (12272)–1591 (14644, has 'shop')
1584: 16653 f. **1589:** 12272 f. **1591:** 14644 f.

Clarke, Thomas.
Bookseller in London, (1600) 1604–1607. [*Dict. 1.*]
at the Angel in Paul's Churchyard (A.3), 1604 (17570)–1607 (17839)
1604: 17570 f., 21660 f. **1605:** 20600 f. **1607:** 921.5 f., 17838 f., 17839 f.

Class. *See* Dorp.

Clavell, John.
Reformed highwayman and poet in London, 1628. Dedicatory epistles before his release were written from the King's Bench prison. [*DNB.*]
1628: 5369.2 f. [his] use.

Clémence, Abel.
Printer in Rouen? 1561–1567. [Muller 98; *Répertoire 16ᵉ*, 8: 55–6, 22: 78–9; *Library* 20 (1939): 136–53.]
1566: [10388] (d).

Clerke. *See* also Clarke.

Clerke, Anthony.
Bookseller in London, 1539?–1561. All his imprints are in association with **Richard Bankes** and **Richard Taverner**, and it is not clear to whom the address below actually belonged. [Duff, *Century.*]
in Fleet Street at the White Hart (W.2), 1540? (2969)–1546? (2969.5)
1539: [2748? f.], [10437? f.].
1540: [2967] sold (d?), [2968] sold (d?), 2969 sold (d?).
1542: [2967.3] sold (d?).
1542: 2969.3 sold (d?).
1546: 2969.5 sold (d?).

Clifton, Fulke.
Bookseller in London, (1619) 1620–1650. [*Dict. 2*; DFM 1287.]
on New Fish Street hill (T.4), 1620–1640 (13726)
shop — under St. Margaret's Church, 1620 (11680)
dw. — at the Lamb, 1623 (11665)
shop — under St. Margaret's Church at the Holy Lamb, 1627 (11647)
1620: 11680 f.
1621: 3521 f., 26088 f.
1622: 3782.5 sold, 23546 f., 26085 f.
1623: 6163.5 f., 11659 f., 11665 f., 26086 f.
1624: 11654 f., 11660 f., 11662 f., 11669 f., 22152.5 f.
1626: 7434.4 f.
1627: 11647 f.
1629: 19877.5 f.
1630: 3733 f., 18486 f., 20682 ent., 20682a f., 25312 sold.
1631: 25770 f.
1632: 22563 f.
1635: 13736 (note), 25789 sold (c).
1637: 11652 (note), 11652a f., 13731 sold.
1640: 11656 f., 13726 f., 13732 sold.

Cloeting (Clouting), Andries Jansz.
Printer in Delft, 1629–1648. [*Dict. 1*; Gruys; Briels 243.]
1630: [12535]. **1631:** 12533, [22142.7?].

Cloppenburg, Evert.
Bookseller in Amsterdam, 1631–1644. [Gruys.]
1631: 1431.31 ap.

'Cloppenburg' Press.
Printers in Amsterdam? of books in English, 1640–1641. Occasionally used the device, or a version of it, of J. E. and **Evert Cloppenburg.** [*Dict. 1*; *Library* 13 (1958): 280–2.]
All items below have this press's imprint supplied in square brackets in STC.
1640: 4148, 4154, 6805.3? 7435.5, 10008? 10649, 13855, 13917, 20467, 21916.5, 21921, 21921.5, 21924 (false), 21926 (false), 21928.
1641: 10649.

Clotterbuck. *See* Clutterbuck.

Clouting. *See* Cloeting.

Cluen, Gerard.
Bookseller in London, 1504. His only imprint was shared with **Francis Birckman 1**. [Duff, *Century.*]
No address used.
1504: 16181 imp.

Clutterbuck (Clotterbuck), Richard.
Bookseller in London, (1632) 1633–1648†. [*Dict. 2*; DFM 1245.]
at the Ball in Little Britain (F.4), 1633 (1504)–1637 (25227, has 'shop', 'Golden Ball') at least
1633: 1504–4.5 f. **1634:** 12452 f. **1637:** 25226.5 sold, 25227 sold.

Coblencz (Confluentinus), Hanse de.
Bookseller in Paris, 1495–1517. [Renouard.]
1504: 17108 imp.

Coblencz (Cowelance), Philippe de.
Bookseller in Paris, 1515. [Duff, *Century*: 34; Renouard.]
1515: 7018.5 ven.

Coccius, Joannes.
Bookseller and printer in Antwerp, 1536–1541. Possibly identical with the John Cockes listed in Duff, *Century*, as being denizen and bookseller in London, 1541–1544, and living in Paul's Churchyard. [Rouzet.]
1539: 5543b.7 imp.
1541: 16133 imp.

Cock, James, *pseud.*
Printer in 'Flesh' [?for La Flèche], 1619. = Unidentified French printer.
1619: 15518.5.

Cock (Cowke), Simon.
Printer and bookseller in Ghent, 1513, and in Antwerp, 1521–1562. [Duff, *Century*; Rouzet.]
1524: 13828.2 per (d?).
1531: [1470?] (d?), [11386.5?] (d?), [12731.4] (d?), [24437] (d).
1535–36: 3014.

Cockes, John. *See* Coccius.

Cockyn, Henry.
Stationer in London, (1573?) 1576–1578. [*Dict. 1.*]
dw. in Fleet Street at the Elephant a little above the conduit (W.5), 1577 (3091)
1577: 3091 f. **1578:** 3091.5 f.

Coeffin (Coffin), Martin.
Norman bookseller and bookbinder in Exeter, c. 1505–c. 1540. He lived in the parish of St. Martin's from at least 1522. [Duff, *Century*; *Library* 10 (1988): 220–30 (the lost *Tractatus verborum defectivorum* was probably an edition of 23163.4).]
No address used.
1505: 18872 f. (d).

Coke. *See* Cooke.

Colby (Coleby), John.
Bookseller in London, 1637–1639. His first book was issued from the address of his former master, **Robert Milbourne**: at the Unicorn near to Fleet Bridge (W.3). [*Dict. 1*; DFM 1955.]
shop at the Holy Lamb on Ludgate Hill (Q.4), 1638 (1902)–1639 (1903)
shop under the King's Head Tavern at Chancery Lane end in Fleet Street (W.10b), 1639 (21063)
1637: 14492 f.
1638: 1902 f., 12453 sold, 17918.5 sold.
1639: 1903 f., 21063 f.

Coldock (Coldoke), Francis.
Bookseller in London, (1557) 1561–1603†. He married the mother of **Simon Waterson**; she later remarried **Isaac Bing.** Coldock was the father-in-law of **William Ponsonby**. [*Dict. 1*; *Library* 14 (1959): 35–6.]
dw. in Lombard Street over against the Cardinal's Hat (O.12), 1561 (1289, also has 'shop')
dw. in Paul's Churchyard at the Green Dragon (A.3), 1566 (22644)–1581 (25402, HD variant) at least; variation: 1574 (22241.5, subtp before bk. 4, has 'shop')
1561: 1289 f.
1566: 22644 f. (d).
1567: 23498 f. (d).
1569: 13041 f. (d?).
1572: 11759, 19990.5.
1573: 6135 f., 21498 f., 22241 f.
1574: 6136 f., 22241.5 f., 22242 f.
1575: 745.5 f. (c), 2112 [f.], 12188 pro.
1576: 826 imp. (d).
1577: 825 pro, 1651, 5791, 13042 f.
1578: 827 pro, 5647, 20089 (d), 25405 [f.], 25406 [f.].
1579: 6137 f.
1580: 18884.7 imp.
1581: 828 pro, 19990.7, 25402 f.
1582: 20962 pro.
1583: 14596 ent.
1584: 21809 pro.
1586: 6138 f., 24417 f.
1587: 13043 f.
1588: 6166 f.
1589–90: 829 pro.

Cole, George.
Stationer in London, 1602–1637. Professor of the civil law and proctor in the Court of Arches. Not active as a bookseller but an important member of the Stat. Co. [*Dict. 1.*]
1623: 3916 ass'd.
1628: 1160.5 ent., 6561 ent., 19984 ent., 20640 ent., 21654 ent., 22548 ent., 23085 ent., 23087.5 ent., 24539 ent.

Cole, Peter.
Bookseller and printer (from 1643) in London, 1637–1665†. [*Dict. 2*; DFM 711.]
in Cornhill near the Royal Exchange (O.10), 1637–1640 at least
at the Glove —, 1637 (13877.7)–1639 (19879)
at the Glove and Lion —, 1639 (22493)–1640 (25024, has 'shop'); variation: 1640 (25030, substitutes 'over against the conduit' for 'near ... Exchange')
1637: 5445.7 sold, 13877.7 sold, 22502 sold.
1638: 20266 sold, 22502 sold, 24518 f.
1639: 19878.5–79 f., 22493 f.
1640: 11657.5 pro, 25024 f., 25030 f.

Coleby. *See* Colby.

Coles (Coules, Cowles), Francis.
Bookseller in London, 1624–1680†. Became one of the **Ballad Partners** by 1629, under which SR ballad entries are listed). His pre-1641 imprints usually have the spelling 'Coules'. Addresses cited below are from dated imprints except for the 1624 example. [*Dict. 2*; DFM 2792; *SB* 6 (1954): 161–80.]
(in) the Old Bailey (D.7), 1624–1663; no shop sign noted before 1641 so that the two cited in *Dict. 2*: the Half-Bowl (cf. 1695 (*A*3)) and the Lamb, are undoubtedly post-1640; the Vine Street address post-dates the Great Fire.

Coles, F. — *cont.*
dw. at the upper end of —, 1624 (547)
at the upper end of — near Newgate, 1626 (23812.7), 1633 (5537, has 'shop')
dw. in —, 1629 (24909.5), 1638 (23778.5)
dw. in — near to Newgate, 1630 (12402a.6)
at the upper end of — near the Sessions House, 1635 (19266)
shop — near the Sessions House, 1640 (21710.7)
1624: 547 f. (d), 19224.7 f. (d), 20509.7 f. (d?).
1625: 439.25 f. (d?).
1626: 21377 ent., 21710.7(*A*3) ent., 21712 f. (d), 22918.3 f. (d?), 23812.7 f.
1627: 9978 f. (d?), [16802?] f., 19283 f. (c), 25229.7 f. (c).
1628: 6367 f. (d), 6934 f., 25146 f. (d?).
1629: 6771 f., 10586 ent., 14708.5 ent., 19219 f. (d?), 19232 f. (d), 19282 f. (d), 24909.5 f., 25283 f. (d).
1630: 1361.5 f. (c), 5104.5 f. (c), 5425 f. (d?), 5612 f. (c), 6906.5 f. (c), 6920.5 f. (c), 7172.5 f. (c?), 12402a.6 sold, 14708.1 f., 14998.3 sold, 16770 sold, 16855 f. (c), 17189.3 f. (c), 17234 f. (c), 18104 f. (c), 18416.7 f. (c), 19245 f. (c), 22364 sold, 22920.5 f. (c), 23580 f., 24829.5 f. (c), 25078 ent.
1631: 5667 f., 12547.9 f. (d?), 14684 sold, 19266 ent., 25610.5 f. (d?).
1632: 1812 sold, 5143 f. (d?), 5428.5 f. (d?), 12544 f. (d?), 15264 f. (d), 19453 sold (d?), 20323 f. (d), 23445.5 f. (d?).
1633: 5537 sold, 16861 f. (d?), 16865.3 f. (c), 18580 f. (d), 19228 f. (d), [22365 sold] (c?).
1634: 1799 f. (d?), 5416 f. (d?), 5421 f. (d?), 19261 f. (d).
1635: 592.3 f., 3839.7 f. (c), 5203 f. (c), 5422 f. (c), 5605a.5 f. (c?), [5608.5? f.] (c), 5640 f. (c), 6934.3 f. (c?), 14685 sold, 15264.5 f. (c), 17189.7 f. (c), 18009 f. (d?), 19221 f. (d), 19266 f., 24301 f. (c), 25078 f., 25108.5 f. (c), 25822 sold, 25973 f. (c).
1636: 16771 sold, 22366 sold.
1637: 12012 f.
1638: 11155 f. (d?), 23778.5 f., 24830 f. (d?).
1640: [1331 f.] (c), 5427 f. (c), 10413 f. (c), 11152.5 f. (c?), 11154 f. (c?), 12545 f. (c?), 12546 f. (c?), 13441 f. (c?), 13852 f. (c), 14553.3 f. (d?), 16864 f. (d?), 17230 f. (c), 18672 f. (c), [19266.5 f.] (c), 19554 f. (d?), 21710.7 f., 22920 f. (c), 24094 f. (c), 25611 f. (c), 25937 f. (c).
1650: 1965(*A*3) sold (c?).

Collins, Richard.
Bookseller in London, (1628) 1630–1636. Probably a different man from the publisher in 1648 (Wing D 572 'Collings'). [*Dict. 2*; DFM 2674; *Loan Book*, 1633–36.]
at the Three Kings in Paul's Churchyard (A.2), 1631 (13990)–1633 (11165, has 'shop')
shop under St. Martin's Church near Ludgate (Q.3), 1635 (6505)
1631: 13990 f., 15008 f. **1632:** 14831–1a f., 18609 f. **1633:** 11165 f.
1635: 6505 sold.

Colman, Nicholas.
Bookseller in Norwich, 1586. Possibly the man buried in London in Sept. 1603 (*St. Giles*). [*Dict. 1.*]
dw. in St. Andrew's Churchyard, 1586 (23259)
1586: 6564 f. (d), 23259 f. (d).

Colom (Columne), Jacob Aertsz.
Map and bookseller in Amsterdam, 1624–1667. [Gruys.]
1633: 5575.2. **1637:** 5575.3. **1639:** 5575.5. **1640:** 5575.5–.7.

Colomiès, Raimond.
Printer in Toulouse, 1590–1629 at least, with a temporary office in Venes, 1603. [Muller 112; *Répertoire 17*[e], VI.228–30.]
1603: 18415.

Colson, William.
Schoolmaster, recusant exile, and author, fl. c. 1585–1621. [*Leodium* 59 (1972): 17–42.]
1612: 5584 at expenses.

Columne. *See* Colom.

Colwell, Thomas.
Printer in London, 1560?–1575. Succeeded to the printing house of **Robert Wyer**, whose printing material Colwell continued to use at later addresses. The Wyer house passed to **Nicholas Wyer**. Colwell's widow remarried **Hugh Jackson**, who took over

Colwell, T. — *cont.*
the last address and the printing material. Because so many of Colwell's publications are undated, dates supplied below should be considered especially tentative, and it seems likely that the items indexed for 1560 below may actually be a year or two later. [*Dict. 1*; *Library* 19 (1964): 223–6.]
dw. in the house of R. Wyer at the $ St. John the Evangelist beside Charing Cross (X.14), 1560? (24206a)–1562, 12 Jan. (3381)
in St. Bride's Churchyard over against the North door of the church (W.4), 1562, 6 Nov. (1288)–1563, 28 Apr. (22225)
in Fleet Street beneath the conduit at the $ St. John the Evangelist (W.5), 1565, Oct. (6277)–1575 (23263)
1560: 868.6 (c), [11553] (d?), 20955 (d?), 24206a (d?).
1561: 17255(*A*3) ?ent., [18223.7?] (d?).
1562: 439.15 (d?), 1288, 3381 (d), 18876 ?ent., 20481.7 (d?), 23263 ent., 23435a.5 ent., 24725.7.
1563: 1875 (d), 11932 ent., 12048, 21688.5 ?ent., 22225.
1565: 1020.5 (c), 1876 (c), [3183?] (c), 3184.8 ent., 3358 (d), [4104], 6277, 6774 (d), 7565 (d), 13805.5 (d?), 14836.7, [17820] (d), 18971, 21850.3 ent., 24206a.5.
1566: [275] (d?), 5223 (d), 17802 (d), 18224 (d), 19865 (d?), 22222, 22224, [24934] (d).
1567: 22618 (d).
1568: 11632.5 ent., 12186 (d), 15336 ent.
1569: 1420 (d?), 7562 (d?), 7563 (d?), 7622 (d), 11380.7 ?ent., 20570 (d).
1570: 868.8 (c), 1421 (d?), 7553 (d), 7560 (d), 13876 (d?), 14085 (d?), 19421 (d), [21850.3] (c).
1571: 5532, 7556 (d), 23297 (d).
1572: 7552.5 (d), [15101] (d?).
1573: 18752 (d?).
1574: 3184.8.
1575: 3358a (d?), [13876.5?] (d?), 23263, 24207.

Combi, Giovanni Battista.
Printer in Venice, 1616–1637 at least. [Rhodes.]
1627: 1431.29 ap.

Comes, N. *See* Lecomte.

Confluentinus, J. *See* Coblencz.

Congeth, Peter, *pseud.*
Printer at 'Paris', 1535. = J. van Hoochstraten, Malmö?
1535: 14667.

Conincx, Arnout.
Bookseller and printer (from 1586) in Antwerp, 1579–1617†. [*Dict. 1*; Rouzet.]
1587: [370.5].
1588: [368?], [22590] (d).
1591: 4868.
1592: [19412.5].
1593: [22994].
1594/95: [19398] (false).
1599: [9?], 16094, [19415].
1601: 3893 (false), [18334.5?], [18858] (false), [19391.5] (d), [21359].
1602: [11016], [19392.5] (d), [19411], [19418].
1603: 19815, [24994.5].
1604: 16095.
1606: 18746.

Conington (Conyngton), Paul.
Stationer in London, (1572?) 1577–1589. [*Dict. 1*.]
shop in Chancery Lane at the Black Bear (W.10a), 1578 (25295)
1578: 25295 f.

Constable, Francis.
Bookseller in London, (1614) 1615–1647†. [*Dict. 2*; DFM 541; *Loan Book*, 1617–20, 1647–50.]
shop in Paul's Churchyard at the White Lion (A.2), 1615 (6257)–1624 (20993); variation: at the White Lion over against the great North door of Paul's Church, 1619 (1676)
shop at the Green Man in Leadenhall Street right over Billiter Lane (L.3), 1625 (19503, engr. tp in F copy)
shop in Paul's Churchyard at the Crane (A.3), 1627 (19503, letterpress tp)–1635 (18027); variation: 1630 (16825, has 'dw.')

Constable, F. — *cont.*
shop under St. Martin's Church near (at) Ludgate (Q.3), 1637 (22457)–1639 (6314)
shops in King Street at the Goat (X.16) and in Westminster Hall (X.17), 1640 (3818)
1615: 6257 f., 21493.5–94 f., 21869 f.
1616: 4682 f., 11176 f., 21342 f., 21494.5 f., 21869 f., 21870 f., 21871–1a f. (d/repeat), 21871a.7 f., 22074 f.
1617: 4683.5 f., 21328 imp., 21495 f.
1619: 1676 f., 21328 imp.
1620: 19515 f., 21325 f.
1621: 13227 f.
1622: 1678 f., 19502 f., 21325.5–26 f., 21871 f., 21871a f.
1624: 16828.5 f., 20993 f.
1625: 21872 f.
1627: 19503 f., 20946.10 f.
1630: 16825 f., 17877 f., 19462 f., 21331 f. (d), 24605 imp., 24619 f., 24623 f.
1631: 6347 ent., 22456 f.
1632: 6347.2 ven., 17646 f., 21423 f.
1634: 19504 f., 19509 sold, 19516 f., 20783.5 f.
1635: 18026.5–27 f., 20781 f.
1636: 18027a f.
1637: 14064.7 imp., 20785 f., 22457 f.
1638: 1109 (note), 3581 f., 18028 f., 20784 f., 20786 f.
1639: 6314 f., 18028.5 f.
1640: 3818 f., 3820 f., 11910 f., 11914 f., 21871a.3 f.

Constantius, Marcus Antonius, *pseud.*
Printer in 'Rome, by the Vatican Church', 1555. = E. van der Erve, Emden. [Duff, *Century*.]
1555: 24361.

Cooke, Francis.
Translator, maker and seller of scientific instruments in London, 1590–1596 at least. Possibly related to **Toby Cooke** though not his brother. Advertisements for instruments sold by him also appear in 1590 (13699) and 1596 (13701). [Taylor 189.]
[his] house in Mark Lane (U.2), 1590 (15250)–1591 (13070, adds: over against the Red Harrow)
1590: 15250 sold. **1591:** 13070 sold (d).

Cooke, Matthew.
Bookseller in London, (1605) 1606–1607†. Son of **Toby Cooke.** In partnership with **Samuel Macham**. His widow remarried **Laurence Lisle.** [*Dict. 1*; DFM 801; *Loan Book*, 1606–09.]
their shop in Paul's Churchyard at the Tiger's Head (A.2), 1606 (5101)–1607 (21461); both with S. Macham
1606: 3775 f., 5101 f., 12642 f., 12666 ent., 12666a f., 12667a f., 13399.5 f., 15561 f., 24508.5 f.
1607: 12643 ass'd, 12668 ass'd, 21461 f.

Cooke (Coke), Toby.
Bookseller in London, (1577) 1578–1599†. Father of **Matthew Cooke**; possibly related to **Francis Cooke.** Between at least 1586–1592 he was agent in London for the sale of books printed in Oxford. Chosen Beadle of the Stat. Co. (A.10) in 1598 but in 1599 appointed as his deputy his former apprentice, **John Hardy**, who seems to have succeeded to the shop below in 1594. [*Dict. 1*; *Loan Book*, 1597–99.]
dw. in Paul's Churchyard at the Tiger's Head (A.2), 1578 (21064.5, with P. Eede)–1593 (4166)
1578: 21064.5 f.
1579: 4457 f., 6768.3 f. (d), 15256 f.
1580: 25014 f.
1581: 937.5 f., 11845 f., 11845.5 f., 11857.5 f., 11862.5 f., 15061 ent.
1582: [11845.7 f.] (d?), 11846 f., 11849 f., 11858 f., 11860 f., 11860.5 f., 11863 f.
1583: 11846.5 f., 11849.3 f., 11861 f., 11863.5 f., 11863.7 f. (d).
1584: 11493.5 f., 11858.5 f., 11864 f.
1586: [4837] ven., 10824 f., 11848.3 f., 11861.5 f., [14016] sold (d), [14017] sold (d), [17631] sold, [20368.5] sold.
1587: [2025] sold, 5003 f., 11852 f., [19611] sold, [20369] sold, [24532] sold.
1588: [13030] sold, [13031] sold, [13966] sold, [20368] sold.
1589: 1708.5 f., 11853 f., [14015] sold (d), [21031.5] sold, [22619] sold, 22620 f., [24533] sold.

Cooke, T. — *cont.*
1590: 11862 f., 11869 f., 13139 f., 13697 f., 13699 f.
1591: 4167 f., 11862.3 f., 11868 f., 13070 ent., [24534] sold.
1592: [3683] sold, 4170 f., [24042] ven.
1593: 4166 f., 11850 f., 13284.5(***A***, note).
1594: 4168.5 f.
1596: 11866 f.
1597: 14290 f.
1598: 11859 f., 13632 ent.
1599: 4166 ass'd, 4167 ass'd, 4168.5 ass'd, 4174.5 ass'd.

Cooke, William.
Bookseller in London, (1630) 1632–1642. From 1637 he often published jointly with **Andrew Crooke 1**. [*Dict. 2*; DFM 1483; *Loan Book*, 1631–34, 1637–40; *Library* 25 (1945): 140–61.]
shop near (at) Furnival's Inn gate in Holborn (V.8), 1632 (22437)–1640 (12587)
1632: 19260 f., 22437 f.
1633: 1353 f., 22436 f., 22439 f., 22458.5 f., 22459 f., 22459a.5 f., 22459b f., 22462 f.
1634: 12583 f., 24812 f. (d?).
1635: 4369 f., 4369.5 f., 5489 f., 12584 f., 22458 f.
1636: 6453 f., 6453.5 f., 12584a f.
1637: 3997.5–98 f., 5490 f., 22442 f., 22443 f., 22446 f., 22448 f., 22463 f., 26089 f.
1638: 353 f., 11895 f., 22441 ent., 22441a–b f.
1639: 1353 f., 1691 f., 4995 f., 4996 f., 6454 f., 6454.5 f., 12585 f., 18947 f., 19973 f., 22449 ent., 22450–0a f.
1640: 11072 f., 12585 f., 12586 f., 12587 f., 22440 f., 22447 f., 22451 f.

Copland, Robert.
Translator, author, and printer in London, 1508–1548?†. Servant to **Wynkyn de Worde**, from whose house Copland issued his first imprint. His second address passed to **William Copland,** possibly a son and perhaps the printer of the items indexed below for 1548, which all share certain 94 mm. textura sorts and other characteristics, e.g. s^1, s^2, w^{5a}, w^{14} (with 1 vertical line in each curve), 'diamond' T, and catchwords. [Duff, *Century*; Frank C. Francis, *Robert Copland*, Glasgow, 1961.]
in Fleet Street, 1514?–47?
— at the Sun (W.5), 1514? (7706.5)
— at the Rose Garland (W.3), 1515 (14865)–1547? (3386); variation: 1532 (5018, has 'dw.', adds 'by Fleet Bridge')
1514: [6035–5.5?], 7706.5 (d?).
1515: 14865.
1521: 1386.
1522: 14552, 15206, 23148.3, 23707.
1523: [3123] (d?).
1524: 15050.
1525: [14077c.11A?] (c), [—.17A?] (c).
1528: 770, 11550.6, 25421.2.
1529: 6933, 14563, 20196, 22141.
1530: 25421.3.
1531: 15707, 17545.
1532: 5018.
1533: [14552.7] (d?).
1534: 5547, 10453.5, 13608, 14841.5 (d?).
1535: 13608.
1536: 5732 (d?).
1545: [5204.5] (d?), [22594] (d?), [22601] (d?), [22615] (d?).
1547: 3386 (d?), 13175.11 (d?), [23664.5(***A***3)?] (d?).
1548? [13175.12?], [18222.5?], [22160?], [24203.7? (main text: Walley portion)].

Copland, William.
Printer in London, 1545?–1568?†. Possibly the son of **Robert Copland**, whose printing house he took over. [Duff, *Century*.]
So many of William's publications are undated and his types of such a mixed character that all of the items indexed below would benefit from further scrutiny. In particular, there are two groups of items, each in a different 94 mm. textura, which have been very tentatively attributed in STC to William, largely because of his later use of a woodcut initial or two. One group has also been doubtfully attributed to Robert Copland, under whom it is described and listed above. The other group has s^2, w^3 (rarely), w^{5b}, w^{14} (with one vertical line in each curve), y^{11}, plain T with a long tail, 'sh' ligature often cast low on the body, and commas gradually supplanting virgules. The items in this second group, queried between 1545 and 1550, are distinguished below by an asterisk (*); two other items which seem to be in the same types are both datable to 1540 (12206a.7, 22880.2 (***A***3)).
in Fleet Street at the Rose Garland (W.3), 1548 (11220)–1558 (14276, pt. 2 colophon dated 1 Jan.); variation: 1554 (1011, has 'dw.')
in St. Martin's parish in the Vintry upon the Three-Crane Wharf (S.9), 1558, 7 Oct. (14653)–1562? (14837, omits 'in ... parish', adds 'in Thames Street')
in Lothbury over against St. Margaret's Church (H.9), c. 1563 (5731)–1567 (19972)
1525: 260 (d/error).
1545: [9343.8*?] (note, c?), [16017.5(***A***3)*?] (c?).
1547: [3310–0.3*?] (d?), 14106.
1548: [6802.5?] (d), 11220 (d), [17626?] (false, d?), 18056 (d?), [24203.7*? (prelims: Tab portion)] (d?), 24451 (d?).
1549: 2857, [12732] (d?), 21043 (d?), 24459, [26053.5?] (d?).
1550: [852.5?] (c), 2757, 2861, 2976, 10447–7.5 ex aed., 11013–3.3 (c), [13304*?] (c), [14040*?] (d?), [14109.3?] (c), [14643] (c), 14651.5 (d?), [19903] (c), [19903.5] (c), [21306?] (c), 23715–5.5 (d?), 24078 (d?).
1551: 2758, 12944.5, 20204.
1552: 1654 (d?), [11797.2] (d?), 13175.15–.15A (d?), 19495–5.7 (d?), [21308] (d?), 22160.3–.4(***A***3).
1553: 7073 (d?), 7508 (d), [12541.5] (c?), 14651.7 (d?), 15378, [24797].
1554: 1010–1.5, [22595–5.5] (d?), [22602–2.5] (d?), [22616–6.5] (d?).
1555: 3383 (d?), 7543 (c?), [10563.5] (d?), 11551 (d?), [12951–2], 21299 (c), 24571.7 (c).
1556: 3310.7–11 (d), 3312 (d?), [6005.5] (d), [13090.5?] (d), 13221 (d?), 14652 (c), 24223 (d?).
1556/57: [477.9(***A***)?].
1557: 804, [6451] (d?), 9989.5 (d), [10455.5], [12442], 14276, [21600], [26074].
1558: 3079 ent., 3312.3 (d?), [3496.5] (d?), 6452 (d?), 14276, 14653 (d), [25196.5] (d?).
1559: [2980.3(***A***3)], 3007, 3483, 4826 (d), 13175.18 (d?).
1560: [807–7.5] (d?), 1988.8 (d?), 3312.5 (d?), 6089.5 ent., 7572 (c?), 10564 (d?), [11362] (d?), 13301 (d?), 13691 (d?), [14653.3] (c), 15118.5 (c), [18223–3.3 (d?), 19496, 20524 (d?), 23112 (d?).
1561: 3363.3 (d), 3494 (d?), [4102.3] (d), [14113] (d?), 24303 (d?), 24453, 24461 (d?), [25938.5] (d?).
1562: 3385 (d?), 14837 (d?), [24829] (d?).
1563: 5728.5 ?ent., 5731 (c), 5954 (d?).
1565: 259 (c), 260 (d?), 261 (c), 1807 (c), 1989 (d?), 3312.7 (d?), 4382.5 ass'd, 5734 (c), 5954.2 (d?), 6472.5 (d?), [7544.5?] (c?), 10565.5 (d?), 12542 (c), [13691.3?] (c?), [14110] (d?), 14112 (d?), 14282 (d?), 14837a (d?), 17014 (c), 18504, [20439.7] (d?), 22653.9 (d?), 24303.3 (d), 24572 (c), 25149.5 (c).
1566: 13480.5 ent.
1567: 5730 (c?), 11553.3 (c?), [13498.5] (d), 19972.

Copley, Anthony.
Poet and religious controversialist, b. 1567–1606. Possibly the 'C. A.' in the imprint of Copley's work below. [*DNB.*]
1596: [5737?] f.

Coppens van Diest. *See* Diest.

Corne, Hugh.
Stationer in London, (1578) 1580–1583?†. [*Dict. 1.*]
No address traced.
1580: 1061 f.

Corro (Corranus), Antonio de.
Expatriate Spanish theologian, author, and translator, b. 1527–1591†. In England from 1568. [*DNB.*]
No address used.
1579: 2761 exp.

Corvinus, Christoph.
Printer in Herborn, 1585–1620†, with a second press in Siegen, 1595–1599. [Benzing 203, 417.]
1596: 25363.3(***A***3) typis.

Coryate, Thomas.
English traveller and author, b. 1577?–1617†. [*DNB.*]
No address used.
1611: [5808 f.].

Coste. *See* also La Coste.

Coste, Philippe.
Bookseller and parchment maker in Rouen, 1506–1520? at least. [Duff, *Century*; Muller 99.]
1506: 16182 imp. **1520:** 16143 ven. (d?).

Costerden, Matthew.
Stationer in London, (1599) 1635–1640. [*Dict. 1.*]
No address used.
1635: 19110 f. **1636:** 19111 f. **1640:** 19112 f.

Cotes, Richard.
Printer in London, (1621) 1627–1653†. Brother of **Thomas Cotes**, worked in the latter's house, and succeeded him. Richard's name does not appear in imprints between 1633–1640 with one probably erroneous exception, and the few items during this period where it has been supplied in STC are omitted below. [*Dict. 2*; DFM 140.]
No address noted.
1627: (all SR entries) 266.5, 630, 891, 899, 6063, 6690, 6723.5, 19389, 22274, 25789.
1628: 1811, 6947, 15134.
1629: 15134, 17366, 19189 ent., 19684.1, 21752, 25837.
1630: [1811.5?] (c), 6816.7, 13449, 13450, 13451, 16825, 19192, 19217.5 ent., 19462, 22337 ent., 24188, 24700, 24927, 25211.
1631: 900 ent., 6063, 21645 ent.
1632: 1812.
1633: (all SR entries) 1184.5, 12017, 17993, 19248, 19275, 22140.5, 23541.
1634: 14704 ent.
1635: 15251 ent., 19302 ent.
1636: 19846 ent.
1637: 22502 ent.
1638: 10693 ent., 10694 ent.
1639: 21068 ent., 22404.5 (d/error?).
1640: 4694 ent.
1641: 14704 (note), 22404.5.

Cotes, Thomas.
Printer in London, (1606) 1627–1641†. Brother of **Richard Cotes**, who worked with and succeeded him. Apprentice of **William Jaggard** and took over the printing material from William's son, **Isaac Jaggard**. Was in charge of the **Parish Clerks' Press** (S.10), 1636–1641. [*Dict. 2*; DFM 289; *St. Giles* (I.4), 1613–41.]
No address noted.
1627: 266.5 ent., 630 ent., 891 ent., 899 ent., [1608], 6063 ent., 6690 ent., 6723.5 ?ent., 19389 ent., [21728], 22274 ent., 25789 ent.
1628: 1811, [4140.4], [4147] (false), [4147.5], [4157], [4157.5], 4221, [5669–70.2], [5697], 6947, [11691], 15134, 18787.5, [20455], [20455a], [20649–9.1] (false), [20649.3–.5] (false), [20649.7?] (false), [21383], 22592, [23016], [23016.5], 24513–3a.
1629: [556.5], 3323, 4126–6.5, [4270], [7442], 11069, [11691], [14122?], 15134, 15344, 17146, 17366, 18997, 19684.1, [19684.2?], 21213.9, 21752, 21840, 22529 typis (d), [23016.5], [23016.7], [23017], 23814, 24926, 25435, 25645, 25837.
1630: [557], [603.5?], [1811.5?] (c), 3234.5, 6666.4, 6723.5, 6816.7, 11542, 13449, 13450, 13451, 16825, 17367, 18854(*A*3) (c), 19462, 20278–8.5, [23017], [23017.3], [23192], 24188, 24700, 24926a, 24927, 25211, [25670].
1631: 6063, 6724, 7020, 10866 per, 11203, 11463, 11700.5(*A*3), 13202, 17730, 19217.5, 20281, 21645, 22112–2.5, [23017.3], [23048.5], 24548, 24701, 25770–0.5, 26087.
1631/32: 407.15.
1632: 266.5, 900, 1812, [6544], 7235, [7453], 10273, 10323, 14048, 14702, 17730.2(*A*3)–0.3(*A*3), [19274.5] (d?), 19275 [by &] f. (d?), 20221.5–.7, 20222, 21719, 21720, 22274–4e, 22274e.3–.5 (repeat), 22563, [23049], 23519, 25207.3, 25207.5, 25212, 25213a, 25215, 25217.3.
1633: 891, 900.5, 3236, 4670, 4673, 5454, [6543] (d?), 10558.5, 14692–2.5, 15079–9.5, [17712], [18979], 19248, 19389, 20222, [20464–4a], [20765?], 21167, 21169, 22140.5, [22404.1], 23193.2 typis, 25207, 25211.3, 25216.

Cotes, T. — *cont.*
1634: [3082], 3174, 6252, 6724.5, [10318?], 11075, 12080, 12942, 14482, 14704, 17993–3b ex off., 19189, [20765?], 20783, 23124–4.5, 23541, 25212.5, [25409.5?], 25700a (note), 25838, [25871] (d?), 25957.
1635: 899, 2659.5, 2661, 3074, [3083], 6113, 6243.8, 10186 (d), [10214.5], 10323.3, 12075, 12076, 12078, 12081, 12086, 12088, 15283, 17369, 17824–4.5, 19070.3, 19301, 19570–0.5, [19781], 20099a.5, 20281a.3, 21170, 21171, 21173, [21315.8] (c?), 21646, 22339, 22531 typis, [23815], [23848], [24310], 24984, 25789 (c), 25839, 25958.
1635/36: 479.2, 494.12, 522.16, 527.26.
1636: 2659.5, 5004 (d), 6033, [10139] (d?), 10695 typis (d?), 12071, 12074, 12085, [13274], 13275, 15251, 15283.5, [16743] (d), [16745] (d), 17369.5, 19846, 21172, 21173, 21806, [22533a.3(*A*3)] (d?), 23193.4 typis, 25208, 25208.3, 25211.5, 25217.5, 25218, 26006, 26112.7.
1636/37: 407.20, 496.4.
1637: 267, 767 (d?), 2672.7, 5410, 6410, [9079?] (d), 10576, 11785 ap., 14788, 14832a, 15035, [17825], 18698, [18980], [19242?] (d), 20537, 21642, 21721, [21730], 21806, 22446, 22448, 22463, 22502, 22532 typis, 23542, 25209, 26089.
1637/38: 407.21.
1638: 353, [5905?], 7267, [10693], 10694, 11895, 12072, 12087, 12454, 12503, 13725, 13740, 15105, 16432 typis, 17370, 19222, 19273, 21722, 22454–4a, 22490, 22502, 22519, 23193.6 typis, 24157.
1638/39: 407.22.
1639: [1370], 1691, 4995, 4996, 5466, [5670.5], 5851, 6181, 6454, 6454.5, 10306, 12017, 12585, [17826], 18690, 18938, 18981, 19973, 20228, 20551, 21068, 22404.4, 22450–0a, 22488, 22492, 22493, 22520, [22529.5?] (d), [23774.5] (d), [25025], 26056.
1639/40: 407.23, 409.
1640: [1123], 1184.5 (c), 4694, 4826.7, 4889, 4946, 11072, 12582.1, 12585, 12586, 12587, 13316, 13730, 14959, 14963, 15048–8a, 15408, 17371, [18933?] (false, c), [18937] (c), 18939, 19249, 19302, 20543, 20552, [20649.9?], [20650], 21011, 22344, 22440, 22447, 22449, 22451–1a, [22452], [23017.6(*A*3)], [23125?], 23302, 23308–8.5, 23310, 25024 (note), [26084].
1640/41: Wing A 1242, A 1298.
1641: 14704 (note), 14959.

Cotton, Clement, *Assignees of.*
Publishers, 1630–1639, of John Downame's abridgment of Clement Cotton's concordance to the Bible. = N. Bourne and R. Young. [*Dict. 1*; *C-B C*: 271–2.]
No address used.
1630: 7125.5 [f.]. **1632:** 7128 [f.]. **1633:** 7128.5 [f.] (d?), 7128.7 [f.].
1635: 7129 [f.] (d?), 7130 [f.] (d?). **1639:** 7132 [f.].

Cotton, William.
Bookseller in London, 1602–1609†. Treasurer of the **English Stock** (*see* Stationers' Company and H.11), 1606–1609 (*C-B C*: 21, 31). [*Dict. 1.*]
?sold at London Bridge (T.7), 1603 (14365.5, with W. Aspley)
shop near (adjoining to) Ludgate (Q.3), 1604 (21853)–1606 (24422)
in Paternoster Row at the Golden Lion (C.7), 1607 (13472.4)–1609 (4396, has 'dw.')
1602: 3646 ent., 19677.5 ent., 21532 ent.
1603: 14365–5.5 f.
1604: 5672 f. (d?), 5672.5 f. (d?), 17874.7 f., 21853 f.
1605: 13044 f., 24421 f.
1606: 13045 f., 13472 f., 17483 f., [17488(*A*3)–8.3(*A*3)] sold, 23452–2a.5 f., 24422 f.
1607: 13472.4 f., 18517 sold, 20147.5 f., 20152 f., 24422.5 f.
1608: 11206 f., 13472.7 f., 24423 f.
1609: 4396 sold, 13472.7 f., 19677 ent., 22142 f., 23434 f.

1617: 13476 ass'd.

Coules. *See* Coles.

Courant (Fournières), Marie.
Printer in Rouen, 1631–1645? Widow of **Nicolas Courant**. [*Dict. 1*; Lepreux III/1: 113.]
1631: 985–5.5, [11112?]. **1632:** [3608.5]. **1633:** 579, [7238].

Courant, Nicolas.
Printer in Rouen, 1625–1631†. Husband of **Marie Courant**. [*Dict. 1*; Lepreux III/1: 112–13.]
1630: 7234 (d), 11109, 25779.3 (note). **1631:** 1017.

Courteneufve, Antoine de.
Printer? in Toulouse and Venes, 1603 at least. [*Répertoire 17e*, VI.228–30.]
1603: 18415.

Cousin, Jacques.
Bookseller in Rouen, 1503–1537. [Duff, *Century*; Muller 99.]
1515: 16195.5 imp.
1516: [16103 f.] (d?), 16142 imp.
1517: 16104 ven./sumpt., 16222 imp.
1518: 16129.3 ven.
1519: 16201–1.3 exp., [16201.7 f.].
1520: [13835 f.].
1521: 16204 imp.
1525: 15940 imp.
1526: 15946 in aed., 23148.7 imp., 23159a.12 sumpt. (d?).
1528: 15958 imp. (d).
1534: 15985a imp. (d?).
1537: 15994 imp., 16148.4 pro.

Cousturier (Le Cousturier), Jean.
Printer? or bookseller? in Rouen, 1627–1640. [*Dict. 1*; Blom 52–4.]
1627–28: [24733].
1630: [3605.5] (c?), [16876.5] (c), 17277.3 f.
1631: 984, 984.5 (repeat), [21145–6].
1632: [10615.5(*A*3)], [12957], [20001], 20001.5 ap.
1633: 2946, 7234.5, 12958, 14123.5, 15188.7, 16101.4, 16101.6, 23991.
1634: 3605.7, 4874, 17001.
1635: 2321, 10928.6 (c), 18571 (c).
1636: 24736.
1637: 17277.7.
1638: 3073.7, 4875, 16101.7(*A*3).
1639: 16162.7, 21628, [21628a].
1640: 4871.5.

Cousturier (Sutor), Raoul.
Printer in Paris, 1499–1511. [Duff, *Century*; Renouard.]
1511: 16189 diligentia.

Cowelance, Philippe. *See* Coblencz.

Cowke. *See* Cock.

Cowles. *See* Coles.

Cowper (Cooper), John.
Bookseller in London, (1629) 1630–1640. [Not in *Dict. 2*; DFM 963; *Loan Book*, 1637–40.]
at the Holy Lamb near (at) the East end of St. Paul's Church (A.6), 1637 (25129)–1639 (21501); no earlier address used.
1630: 6492.5 f.
1637: 25129 f.
1638: 3406 f., 4935 sold, 18286 sold, 20335 f., 21422 sold.
1639: 21501 sold.

Crafford (Crafoorth), Thomas.
English exile and publisher in Amsterdam, 1633–1644? [Gruys; Carter, 'Laud', pp. 151–4.]
1633: 2309 f. **1639:** 26126 f. **1644:** 2316.5 (note).

Cramoisy, Sébastien.
Bookseller and printer in Paris, 1602–1669†. [*Dict. 1*; Renouard; Lottin 2: 33.]
1635: 7361.

Cranepoel. *See* Kranepoel.

Crashaw, William.
Clergyman, poet, and religious controversialist, b. 1572–1626†. [*DNB*.]
1624: [6010] imp.

Creede, Thomas.
Printer in London, (1578) 1593–1617 (1619?†). Took **Bernard Alsop** into partnership in 1616 and turned the business over to him in 1617. [*Dict. 1*; *Loan Book*, 1597–99; *Poor Book* (& son), 1617–19; *St. Giles*, 1585–88.]
dw. in Thames Street at the Catherine Wheel, near the Old Swan (T.5), 1594 (12310a)–1595 (14057); variation: omits sign, 1595 (21086)–1596 (4997, also omits 'dw.')
shop in Watling Street over against the $ Cock, near Friday Street (N.9), 1600 (21081)
dw. in the Old Change at the Eagle and Child near Old Fish Street (S.2), 1600 (4887)–1610 (18053, colophon) at least
1593: 5202 ent., 12263, 12270.
1594: 52, [153.3] (d?), 6817, 12310a, 12751, 13072 ent., 16679, 19078.4, 21009, 26099.
1595: 1343, 3795 ent., 3796 ent., 14057, [14516.5] (d), 17162, 18375, 19855, 20002, 21086, 21088, 21528, [22535], 23077, 25782.
1596: 4997, 5060, 11438 ent., 12246, 15321, 15322, 15340, 15379, 16808, 19161, 19974, 24709, 24803.
1597: 90, 798, 1182, 1426.5, 3705, 4664, 5411.5, 7087, 11279, 11573, 12716, 14633, 18096, 18200.5, 19158, 19724.5(*A*3: ii), 19946, 21602, 23093.
1598: 1804, [2995a.3] (false), 5382, 11171, 11275, 11754, 12308, 13072, 16680, 16899.5 (d), 17085, 17954, 21082, 22315.
1599: [3258(*A*3)], 3706, 4207, 4667, 5450a, 6151, [11168] (d?), 11171.2, 12233, 17154, 17843, 18198–8.5, 18870, 19963–4, 22323, 23690, 24709.5.
1600: 1748 ent., 4887, 6991, 14058.3, 15026, 17188, 18974, 19154 per, 19154.3, 21081, 22289, 24804, 25144.
1601: [1884] (false), [3106] (false, d?), [5724] (false), [6626], [6626.5(*A*)], 7083, [7243].
1602: 17.3, 3669, 3680, [3684], [5594], 6036, 6147, [7434?], [12415], [12571], [12571.5], 16616, 16629(*A*3) ap., 16630, 16681, 17675, [18759], 22290, 22299, 22316, 23939, 24727, 25304.
1603: 3646, 4780, [5339], 5340, 5385, [6070–0.5], 6476, 6476.2, 6535, 6535.3 (d?), 6535.5 (d?), [6640], [7120], 11214.8, 12678, 13589, 14410, 14410.5(*A*3: 2 eds.), [14411(*A*3)], 15706, [16676], 17153, 17215, 18445.5, 18586, 18627, [19735.6], 21496.5, 21497, 23632.
1604: [1456], [1456.5(*A*3)], 6265, 6477, 6510, 6968, 11171.5, 11935, 12199, 12752, 13122, 13510, 16784, 17781, 17874.3, 17874.7, 17875, 17875.5(*A*3), [21000], 21001, 21853, 22992.5, 23614, 23909.
1604/05: 525.10.
1605: [1164], 1825(*A*), 1833, [3685.5] (d?), 3691.2, 3721, [6071], 6203 (d?), 7276, 11171.5, 17619, [18288(*A*3)], 18995, 19706.5, [19733(*A*3)], 20575.7, 22317, 22333, 22753, 24421.
1606: 364, 1827, 3707, 4983–4, 6498, [6498.2], 6628.5, 7081, 13898.5, [15425], 18995.5, 19707, 19733a, [24422?].
1607: 4663, [5141.7], 6508, 7082, 11169, [12373], 13392.3, 13398.5, 14426, 15380, 19707.5, 23135, 23432.3, 24317, 24805.
1608: 1980, 5966.5 (d?), 11172, 20338, 24263.7, 24315.5–.7, 24497, 25683–3a.
1609: 4888, 6624, 7469, 10537, [10616] (d?), 11172, [12032], 13393, 13399, 14087, 14934, [17620], 18053 ent., 19162, 19708, [20337–7.3], [22334(*A*3)], [22335(*A*3)], 23276, 23654, 25300.
1610: [1919], [5385.5], [5566], [6965], 13538, [15423.5], [15643.5], 18053, 18323–3a.
1611: [1919], 5392, 6938, [6966], 7115, 12318, [13771], [17955], 22182–2a, 22381, [24269].
1612: [5386], [6507], 7494, 11687, 12318, 15426, 18588–8.5, 21081a, 21265, 22318, [25941].
1613: 1976, [4275], 4613, 5699, 7433, 10538, 11358, 11359, 12857.6, 15423, 15423.7, 16830, 19792, 24710, [25893] (forged).
1614: 3664, 5387, 6148, 10539, 11841, 12289, 12870–0.3, [14008], 16924, [17196.3–.5], 18652, [18903.5], 18907, 22062, 24394–4a.
1615: 1667, 3529, 3710, 5693, 6961, 11173, 12562a, 15423.3, 18908, 19159, 19333, 19789, 19790, 22871–1a, 24175.3, [24312.7] (d?), [25240] (false), [25244], 25981.
1616: 686, 4578, 5918, 6342, 11523, 12891, 13019, [14358 (*A*3)], 18522, 19159a, 19163, [20337.5], 22382, 23099, 24175.7, 24316, 25151.
1617: 4897.

Crespin (Crispin), Jean.
Printer in Geneva, 1550–1572†. [Duff, Century; Dict. 1; Chaix 164–5; Bremme 145–6.]

Crespin, J. — *cont.*
1556: 4380, 16561, 16565. **1558:** 12020. **1560:** 15060. **1568–70:** 2106.

Crinitus, Joannes.
Printer in Antwerp, 1538–1547. [Rouzet.]
1540: 6832.3.

Cripps, Henry.
Bookseller in Oxford, 1620–1642. The bookseller of the same name in London, 1648–1662, was his son (DFM 2092). [*Dict. 2.*]
No address used.
1620: 7338 f., 11958–8.5 f.
1621: 4159 f. .yr 2 1623: 5832 f., 11959 f.
1623: 5832 f., 11959 f.
1624: 4160 f.
1625: 1792 f., 4676 f., 11960 f., 14460 f., 20356 pro.
1626: 12515 f.
1627: 12515 f., 21020 f.
1628: 4161 f., 11961 f., 23947.5 propter.
1631: 11962 f., 19194.7 imp., 20157.5 imp.
1632: 4162 f., 22231 imp.
1633: 11963 f.
1634: 1397 imp., 22652 imp.
1635: 4677 f.
1636: 20344.7(*A*3) sold.
1637: 3630 ven., 4119 imp., [23271?] f.
1638: 4163 f., 11964 f., 22653 pro.
1639: 11401 imp., 13972 f.

Crispin. *See* Crespin.

Crom, Matthias.
Printer in Antwerp, 1536?–1546. In partnership with his brother-in-law, **Steven Mierdman**, from 1543. [Duff, *Century*; Rouzet.]
1536: [2832?], [2833?], [2834?], [11390] (c?).
1537: [2066].
1538: 2836, [2836.5(*A*)], [2837(*A*)].
1539: 2842.
1540: [22880.7] (d).
1541: [4045] (d), [4070.5?] (d).
1542: [3047] (false), [10808] (d?).
1543: [2848?] (c?), [5014] (d).
1544: [4079.5?] (d?).

Crooke, Andrew 1.
Bookseller in London, (1629) 1632–1674† and in Dublin, 1637. Brother of **John** and **Edmond Crooke.** He worked in and eventually succeeded to the shop of one of his masters, **Robert Allott.** From 1637 he often published plays jointly with **William Cooke.** [*Dict. 2*; DFM 2188; *Library* 25 (1945): 140–61.]
London, in Paul's Churchyard, 1632–1641 at least
at the (Black) Bear — (B), 1632 (249)–1633 (20235), 1636 (3136, omits 'Black')–1639 (5851); 1640 [1622?]; variation: omits sign, 1636 (19846)
their shop at the Greyhound — (B), 1637 (22800, with J. Crooke and R. Sergier 2)
shop at the Green Dragon — (A.3), 1640 (4946)–1641 (14959) and later
Dublin, shop near the Castle Bridge, 1637 (5465.3, with T. Allott)
Dublin, at the Greyhound in Castle Street, 1637 (22800.5, with T. Allott)
1632: 249 imp.
1633: 12368 ent., 20235 f., 20275 f., 20276 f.
1634: 20249 f.
1635: 20237 f., 20277 f., 20282 f.
1636: 3136 f., 3136.3–.7 f., 13553 sold/f., 19846 sold.
1637: 767 f. (d?), 1238 ent., 1618a f., 3137 f., 4510.4 f., 5465.3 f., 10427 ent., 11688 ent., 12552 ent., 13728 f., 13733 f., 13739 f., 14753.5 ent., 15035 f., 17642 ent., 20250 f., 21667–7.5 f., 21707 ent., 21730 f., 21846 ent., 22274e.3 ent., 22442 f., 22443 f., 22446 f., 22448 f., 22463 f., 22800–0.5 f., 22801 ent., 22808 ent., 24660 sold, 25379a f., 26068 ent., [26114(*A*3)] sold.
1638: 1619 f., 1619.5 f., 1619.7 f. (false?), 1620 f. (false?), 1620.5 f., 3138 f., 7445 f., 10382 f. (d?), 13725 f., 13727 f., 13729 f., 13737 f., 13739 f., 13740 f., 14958 f., 18919 f., 22441 f., 22441b f., 22454 ent., 23684 f.

Crooke, Andrew 1 — *cont.*
1639: 1621 f., 1691 f., 4995 f., 4996 f., 5851 f., 10306 f., 13555 f., 18690 f.
1640: [1622?] sold, [1623?] sold, 4946 f., 11072 f., 13554 f. (note), 13554.5 sold, 13621a.5 f., 13730 f., 14753 sold, [14771 f.], 14777 ent., 14779 ent., 14782.5 ent., 14959 f., 15408 f., 21036b.3 f., 22440 f., 22449 f., 22451–1a f., 22452 f., 23307–7.5 f., 23310 f., 23313 f.
1641: 14959 f.

Crooke, Andrew 2.
Bookseller in Dublin, 1681–1731; King's Printer in Ireland from 1686. Son of **John Crooke**. In partnership with **Samuel Helsham**, 1685–1689. [*Dict. 3.*]
1685–89: 14264 (d). = Wing, 2nd. ed., C 4103B.

Crooke, Edmond.
Bookseller in Dublin, 1638†. Brother of **Andrew 1** and **John Crooke**. [*Dict. 1*; DFM 1303; *Library* 25 (1945): 140–61.]
Dublin, near the Castle, 1638 (22454a, with T. Allott)
1638: 22454a sold.

Crooke, John.
Bookseller in London, (1635) 1637–1669†; also in Dublin, 1640–1641 at least, and King's Printer in Ireland, 1660–1669. Brother of **Andrew 1** and **Edmond Crooke.** In partnership with **Richard Sergier 2.** [*Dict. 2*; DFM 2630; *Loan Book*, 1658–61; *Library* 25 (1945): 140–61.]
London, their shop at the Greyhound in Paul's Churchyard (B), 1637 (22800, with A. Crooke 1 and R. Sergier 2)–1639 (11064, with T. Allott)
Dublin, at the $ St. Austin in Castle Street, 1640 (14073; engr. tp has: next the Castle gate, 1641; both tpp with R. Sergier 2)
1637: [5465(*A*3)] sold, [13319] sold, 22800 f.
1638: [3234(*A*3)] sold, [3254(*A*3)] sold, 12310b f., 12454 f., 12455 ?ent., 22454 sold, 22490 f.
1639: 4627 f., 5466 sold, 11064 f., [21068] sold, 23307 ent.
1640: 14073 sold, 23307.5 f., 23310 f., 23313 f.

Crosley (Crossley), Elizabeth.
Bookseller in Oxford, 1613. Widow of **John Crosley**. Called 'wydowe Crosley of Oxon.' on 2 Jan. 1613 (*C-B C*: 57). [*Dict. 1*, under husband.]
No address used.
1613: 14308.5 f.

Crosley, John.
Bookseller in Oxford, 1597–1612†. Husband of **Elizabeth Crosley**. Although he was made free of the London Stat. Co in 1611, it seems unlikely that he ever had a shop there. In Oxford he lived in the High Street, 1607–1611 at least. [*Dict. 1*; DFM 2444.]
No address used.
1612: 7341 f., 12618a imp., 14618 f., 24852 ent.

Crouch (Chrouch), Humfrey.
Ballad-writer and pamphleteer, fl. 1635–1671. [*DNB.*]
No address used.
1640: 3920 f. (c).

Crouch (Crowch), John.
Journeyman printer and printer (from 1652) in London, 1635–1655 at least. His earliest book was sold at the address of one of his former masters, **Robert Raworth**: near the White Hart Tavern in Smithfield (E.1), 1636 (19501.5). [*Dict. 2*; DFM 93.]
No separate address used.
1635: 5157.5(*A*) ent., 13356 ent. **1636:** 13352 f., 19501–1.5 f. **1637:** [10667 f.]. **1640:** 13353 f., 13354 f. (false).

Crowley, Robert.
Author, publisher, and clergyman in London, b. 1517?–1588†. Rector of St. Giles, Cripplegate. Made free of the Stat. Co. by redemption in 1578. In spite of imprints naming him as printer, most—probably all—of his items were printed by others. [Duff, *Century*; *Publishing History* 14 (1983): 85–98.]
dw. in Ely rents in Holborn (V.5), 1549 (6094)–1551 (6090)
1549: 2725 [f.], 6087 [f.], 6094 [f.], 6095 [f.].

Crowley, R. — *cont.*
1550: 6088 [f.], 6088.3 [f.], 6095 [f.], 6096 [f.], 19897.3 [f.], 19906 [f.], 19907 [f.], [19907a [f.], 21612 [f.], 21613 [f.], 21614 [f.], 25588 [f.].
1551: 2761.5 (d), 2983, 6089.5 [f.], 6090 [f.], 21690.2 [f.].

Croy. *See* La Croy.

Crumpe (Crompe), James.
Bookseller and bookbinder in London, (1628) 1638–1666. [*Dict. 2*; DFM 1980.]
No pre-1641 address used.
1638: 26111 ent.

Ctematius, Gellius. *See* Erve.

Cupere, Pieter de. *See* Mathew, C.

Curteyne, Henry.
Bookseller in Oxford, 1625–1651†. [*Dict. 2.*]
No address used.
1625: 14460 f.
1626: 23915 f.
1627: 17950 imp.
1628: 3368.5-Curteyne [f.] (d?), 4532 sold, 21814 imp., 25376 f.
1629: 4109 f., 4937 f., 21674 imp.
1630: 4373 imp.
1631: 4106 imp., 11101 imp., 19194.5 imp., 20280.3–.7 f., 20934.5 sold, 21814.5 imp.
1633: 6153 imp., 11770 imp., 21675 imp.
1634: 20516 imp., 22652 imp.
1635: 4677 sold.
1636: 20344.7(*A3*) sold.
1637: 3630 ven., 4107 imp., 4119 imp., [23271?] f., 25328–8.3 imp.
1638: 11102.5 imp., 22653 pro.
1639: 21815 imp.
1640: 14480 f.

Curtigiane, *of Rome, pseud.*
Printer, 1556. = E. van der Erve, Emden; imprint repeated, possibly in London, by an unidentified printer.
1556: 15693, 15693.5(*A3*).

D

Dab, Dabbe. *See* Tab.

Dainty, Thomas.
Stationer in London, (1623) 1637–1652†. [*Dict. 2*; DFM 2258; Globe 213.]
at the Three [remainder cropt], 1637 (3061)
1637: 3061 sold.

Dalderne, John.
Bookseller in London, 1588–1589. [*Dict. 1*; *Loan Book*, 1641–44.]
in Canon Lane at the White Horse (A.2), 1589 (7538)
1588: 12803 f., 25733.5 imp. **1589:** 1579 f., 7538 f., 19898a.3 f.

Daniel, Roger.
Bookseller in London, 1620?–1629?, 1650–1666; one of the **Printers to the University of Cambridge** (*see* Cambridge University), 1632–1650. Not a member of the Stat. Co. His earliest activity in London was as a printseller. In 1628 he was agent in London for the sale of books printed in Cambridge. [*Dict. 2*; Globe 213.]
Cambridge imprints from 1625 have been recorded in STC with considerable variability, and the present indexes represent an attempt to rectify the situation. Indexed below are *only* items in which Roger Daniel's name appears on a title-page; imprints shared with another Printer to the University are indicated by an asterisk (*). For items having *only* 'Printers ...' or 'ex acad. ...' on the title-page (even though individual names may be supplied in STC) *see* Cambridge University. For a comprehensive list of all items printed or sold at Cambridge including those without any imprint at all *see* Index 2Ai.

Daniel, R. — *cont.*
London, in Lombard Street at the Angel (O.12), 1620? (6344.3)–1629? (4498(***A***), engr. frontispiece only); dated examples are: 1622 (794, letterpress tp: Haz. I.290)–1628 (2610.7)
Cambridge, no address used; for the various locations of the press *see* Cambridge University.
1620: 6344.3 sold (d?).
1622: 794 sold.
1623: 794–4.5 sold (engr. tp, d?), 4955.5 sold, 6345.5 sold (c).
1625: 653 sold (c), 17467 sold (d?), 22527a.5 sold (c).
1628: 1786 sold, 2609 sold, 2610 sold, 2610.3 sold, 2610.5 sold (forged), 2610.7 sold, 4696 sold.
1629: 2285.5 (d/repeat), 4498 (***A***, note) (d?).
1633: 4480*, 5272* (d?), 6900* ap., 13183*, 13184* (d), 13184.5–85*, 13518–8.5*, 23889.6* ap.
1634: 755* ap., 6294* ap., 6294.5(***A***)* ap. (d/error), 6301.5* ap., 10463, 11633*, 13186*, 15520.
1635: 2285.5* (c), 2320*, 12211* ap., 13187*, 23516* (note).
1636: 7236–7* (note).
1637: 2327*, 2327.5*, 2674*, 7365* ap., 10339* (d?), 15632.3*.
1638: 2327.5*, 2331–1.3*, 2682*, 2683*, 6903*, 10351.5*, 11778*, 13188*, 14274* ap., 14964* ap., 15632.3*, 16410*, 18977* ap., 22533a ex off. (d).
1639: 2338*, 2346*, 2692*, 2692.5 sold (forged), 4489.5, 6294.5(***A***)* ap. (d?), 7237, 7365.8–66.
1640: 1313, 2346*, 4008.5, 4338, 4495 ap., 6293 ex off., 7117, 7239, 10578 ex off., 10779–80, 11061–1a, 11465*, 11769.5, 11779*, 11779.5, 13040 ex off., 13554–4.5, 15245 ex off., 15633, 16420*, 18197 ex off., 18948–8.5, 19154.5, 20130 ex off., 20693a.
1640/41: Wing A 1591, A 2127.

Daniel, Samuel.
Poet, b. 1562–1619†. Patentee for publishing his own historical works, 1618 (6248, note). [*DNB*; *NCBEL.*]
No address used.
1612: [6246 f.]. **1618:** 6248 f. (d).

Danter, John.
Printer in London, (1589) 1591–1599†. Collaborated in pirating 'Lily's Grammar' somewhere in Middlesex as early as 1586 (*Reg. B*: 21). His earliest open printing was in partnership with **William Hoskins** and **Henry Chettle.** [*Dict. 1*; *St. Giles* (& family), 1598–1603; *SB* 23 (1970): 21–44.]
dw. in Fetter Lane (W.8), 1592 (12561, with W. Hoskins)
dw. in Duck Lane near Smithfield (E.5), 1592 (25785)
dw. in Hosier Lane near Holborn Conduit (E.7), 1592 (24863)–1594 (1487, has 'his house') and probably until 1597 (*Reg. B*: 56)
1591: [7675] (d?), 16654 (d), [22537], [22656], 22656.5, 22664, [22665].
1592: 5871.4, 6784.7, 12223, [12245], [12306], 12561, 12789–9.5, 13601, [18377], 18377a, [19974.6], 22678, [22717], 24863, 25785.
1593: [5123] (d?), 18377b–78a, 18960, 21082 ent., 22666, 23356, [25018.5], [25122].
1594: 1480, 1487, [5871.5], [10314] (d), 12265, 14708.5 ent., 16678, 18379, [19863.7] (d), 21321, 22328, 22991.5, 23356, 25781.
1595: 585a, [3388], 3665, 3696 ent., 5000, 5124, 10922.5, 12321, 14032 ent., [14707], 15115.5, 17748, 19545, 19775, [20014.3], [20014.5], [20366], [21105.5?] (d?), 21294, [22679] (d).
1596: [1433], [5323a.8], 5737 (note), 7503, [14567?], [14677], [14708], [19856.3], 18369, [19429.5?], [19464], 20366a.
1597: 17866, 17916, 22322.
1598: 14691.1.

1600: 7504 ass'd, 7505 ass'd.

Datier (Dature, Detter, Deyter, Dotier), Martin.
Bookbinder and bookseller in London, 1527?–1563†. From at least 1541 he lived in the parish of St. Mary Magdalen, Old Fish Street (S.1). [Duff, *Century*; Worman 16; *Library* 16 (1936): 410–11; *SB* 32 (1979): 50-1 (abstract of will).]
No address used.
1543: 16150(*A3*) [f.].

Daubman, Joannes (Hans).
Printer in Nürnberg, 1545–1553, and in Königsberg, 1554–1573†. [Benzing 260, 359.]
1548–49: 6832.19.

Davidson, Thomas.
Printer in Edinburgh, 1535?–1541 at least. **King's Printer in Scotland**, 1540?–1541. [Duff, *Century*.]
dw. over against (fornens) the Blackfriars' (Frere) Wynd, 1540? (3203)
dw. above the Nether Bow on the North side of the [High] Street (gait), 1541 (21878.5)
1535: [7072.8] (c), 14435 ap. (c?). **1540:** 3203 (d?). **1541:** 21878.5.

Davies (Davis), James.
Bookseller in London, 1616–1617 at least. There is no record of the binding or freeing of a Stationer of this name though a Samuel Davis was freed in 1616 in the name of the former printer R. Bradock (DFM 112) and had a son christened in 1619 (*St. Giles*). There is a James Davis in the *Poor Book*, 1623, followed by his widow. A second James Davis (*Dict. 1*) was a dealer in second-hand books in the Barbican (part of which is in the parish of St. Giles), 1628. It is not clear which James is the father of the son christened in 1623 (*St. Giles*) or the seller of the items below.
shop near Fleet conduit (W.5), 1616 (10709)–1617 (6343, has: at the Red Cross near Fleet Street conduit)
1616: 10709 sold. **1617:** 6343 sold.

Davies, John, *of Mallwyd.*
Doctor of Divinity, Welsh lexicographer, and translator, b. 1570–1644†. [*DNB*.]
No address used.
1632: 6347–7.2 imp., 19390 tros.

Davis (Davies), William.
Bookbinder and bookseller in Oxford, 1609–1651. [*Dict. 1*.]
No address used.
1622: 11568 f. **1624:** 11296 f. (d). **1629:** 19008 imp. **1631:** 11566 imp., 21703 imp. **1638:** 11569 f. **1640:** 21704 imp.

Dawlman (Dolman), Robert.
Bookseller in London, (1626) 1627–1659†. From 1635–1640 at least his shop and many of his imprints were shared with **Luke Fawne**. [*Dict. 2*; DFM 964.]
at the Bible in Fleet Street near the great conduit (W.5), 1627 (21705; 22855.5, sub tp of pt. 2 omits sign)
shop at the Brazen Serpent in Paul's Churchyard (A.3), 1628 (21709)–1640 (4129, omits 'shop') at least; variation: 1629 (22503, has 'dw.')
1627: 21705 f., 22230 f., 22855.5 sold.
1628: 21708.5–09 f., 22856 f.
1629: 18200 f., 20208 ass'd, 22503 f.
1630: 3514 sold, 22479 f., 26043 sold.
1631: 13009 sold, 22480 f., 22481 f., 23851 f.
1632: 13735 f., 13735.5 f., 21706 f., 22482 f.
1633: 4839 f., 22507 f., 23823 f.
1634: 3225 f., 22507–7.5 f.
1635: 13726.2 f., 13736 f., 21710 f., 22483 f., 22508 f., 22508.5 f., 23821 f., 23852 f.
1636: 7429 f., 12037 f., 12037.5 f., 12040 f., 12041 f., 12041.3 f., 12041.5 f., 13726.3 f., 21710.3 f., 22509 f., 22510 f.
1637: 12033 f. (note), 12033.5 f., 12043a f., 13726.6 f., 21707 f., 22504 f., 23584 f.
1638: 4127 f., 7430 f., 12034 f. (note), 12034.5 f., 12038 f., 12042 f., 12044 f., 12044.5 f., 13726.8 f., 13734 f., 22484 f., 22511 f., 22521 f., 22578 f., 23240 f., 23953 f.
1639: 4128 f.
1640: 3732 ent., 4129 f., 4130 ent., 7421 ent., 12031 ent., 22404.7 ent.

Dawson, Ephraim.
Bookseller in London, 1608–1616, 1620–1638 (*C-B C*: 428). In partnership with **Thomas Downes 1**, 1608–1616, 1620–1625. [*Dict. 1*; DFM 2331.]
(at) the Inner Temple gate in Fleet Street (W.11), 1608–1609, 1624–1636 at least; items dated 1616 and 1620 have no address; variations:
their shop at —, 1608 (17156.3, omits 'in Fleet Street')–1609 (10537)
at the Rainbow near —, 1624 (24545, with T. Downes)–1636 (24297)
1608: 17156.3 f.

Dawson, E. — *cont.*
1609: 10537 f., 20337–7.3 f.
1610: 12582.25 f.
1616: 11521–1.3 f., 20337.5 f.
1620: 7109 sold.
1624: 24545 f. (d).
1625: 24546 f.
1629: 24547 f.
1632: 6756 sold.
1633: 6938.5 ent.
1636: 24297 f.

Dawson, John 1.
Printer in London, (1609) 1613–1634?†. Nephew of **Thomas Dawson**, to whose business he succeeded. Husband of **Mary** and father of **John Dawson 2**. One of the *assignees of* **J. Battersby**. [*Dict. 1*; DFM 164; *Loan Book*, 1621–24.]
No address noted.
1613: 20982 ent.
1620: 24810 ent.
1621: 1788, [2574], 3521, 3589, 6370 ent., 12136, 17195, 19375, 20284, 22111, 23860, 23861, 24893, 26088.
1622: 1788.5, 4023, 5727, 5766, 6118.2, 6149, 10787.5, 12831, 12962, 13575, 15568, 16841, 17744, 18507.46, —.52, —.53, —.56A, —.57A, —.59, —.62, —.63, —.64, —.65, —.69, —.70, —.73, —.74, [18599.5] (d?), 18826, [20074], 20285, 20285.3(*A*3), 20669, 20675, 20864, 23493.5, 23546, 23843, 23934.7(*A*3), 25233, 26085.
1623: 1475, [2583.5], 6114, 6118.3, 6118.4, 7423, [11306], 14651, 17448, 17985, [18507.98], [—.99], [—.100], [—.102?], [—.103?], [—.104?], [—.109?], [—.112?], [—.118?], [—.124?], 18826a, 20752, 20752.5, [22070], [22568], [22789] (d), [22992.9?] (d), 23841, 23934.8, 23934.9, 25210, 25210a.5.
1624: 188, 1021.5, 1146, 1415, 1477, 1477.5, 1478.5, 4236.2, 4640, 6118.5, 7305, 7323, 7415, 11274, [11706], 12832, 12839.5, 12839.7, 13381, [18507.349?], 18826a.2(*A*3), 20111, [21479], [22103], 22760, 22790, 22877.2, 23598, 23934.9, 24554, 25848, 25855–6.
1625: [680], 1434, [2593.5], [3062.6] (c?), 3537, [3771.5] (d?), 4641, 5763, 6118.6, 6976, 13204, 14316, 17388, 18169, 22790a, 23074.
1626: 6110, 6370, 10788, 13928, [14494], 14497, 15248, 18156, 20392, 22790b, 23488, [26003].
1626/27: [450], [456.7], [457.3].
1627: 1439.5, [2601.5], 6665.5, 13431, 18830.8, [20392.5], 21219–9a, 22115.5, 22790c, [23035], [23036] (d/repeat), 23039g.7, 23041.8–42, [23660.5].
1628: 6976.5, [7449], [10788.3] (c), [21130], 21210.3, 22116, 23072, 25850, [25964].
1629: 5676, 18828, 20241, 20241.3, 20241.7, [21187], 23367.5, 24547.
1630: [3062.7] (c?), [10788.5?] (c), 20242, 20243, [20388], 22404, 22934.2, [25399].
1631: 3232, [9979], [14495], [18507.229?], [—.232?], [—.233?], 20244, 22790c.5, 22934.3, 23040, 23043, 23048.5, [24524?].
1632: 4236.3, 4236.9, 7450, 7450a, 10788.7, 11085, 12393–3.5, [18507.237?], [—.238?], [—.239?], [—.240?], [—.241?], [—.242?], [—.243?], [—.244?], [—.245?], [—.246?], [—.247?], [—.248?], [—.249?], [—.250?], [—.251?], [—.252?], [—.253?], [—.254?], [—.255?], [—.256?], —.257, –.258, —.259, —.260, —.261, —.263 (d), —.264, —.265, —.266, —.267, —.268, —.269, —.270, —.271, —.272, —.273, —.274, —.275, —.276, 21192, 21426, 21820, 22790d, [23036] (d?), 23049, [23519.5], 23520, [23521], [23522], [23523], [23524–4a], 25207.5, 25214.
1632/33: 435.22, 531.24.
1633: 6110.3, 6118, 6118.8, 6371, 18382, 18828.5, 18830.9, 20245, 21188, 21819, 22118, 23934.19(*A*3), 24142.
1633/34: 419.3, 435.23, 531.25.
1634: 3274, 6938.5, 10789, 18829, 20246, 22934.5, [23525.7], 23598.5, 24930.
1634/35: 435.24, 531.26, 532.9.

Dawson, John 2.
Printer in London, (1634) 1637–1648?†. Son of **John 1** and **Mary Dawson.** [*Dict. 2*; DFM 151.]
No address noted.
1637: 548 [by &] f., 548.3, [2672.3], 4231, [4293.2], 7357, 22120, 25436, [25725.6?].

Dawson, John 2 — *cont.*
1637/38: 435.27, 522.18, 531.29.
1638: 5904, 6913.5, 11201, 11550–0.4, 12454, 13048, 13544, 18343, 20266, 20281a.7, 20335, 21114, 21190, 22501, 22934.9, 23936, 24518, [24715], 25356, 25436 (note), 25436a.
1638/39: 490.15, 495.14, 496.6, 531.30.
1639: 3, [552], 1227, 17341, 17922, 18337, 18343a, 18384, 18830.2, 18946, 19878.5–79, 20247, 20542, 20660 [by &] f., 21056, 22477, 22493, 22935, 23513, 23515, 24048, [24715], 24969 [by &] f., 25025–5a, 25959.
1639/40: 496.7, 531.31.
1640: 1226.3–.7, 1228, 4620, 4914, 7545, 7746.6, [7746.7], [7746.9], [7746.13], 7747, 7747.3, 11466–6.3, 12875, 12875.3(*A*3), [13732], [14754], 21168, 21173, 21775, 22403, 22453, 23303, 23311–1.5, 23514, [23551], [23777?], [23815.3(*A*3)] (d?), 24048–9, 24049.3(*A*3), 24979.
1640/41: [6844], [7746.10]; Wing A 2112, A 2828.
1641: [14754].

Dawson, Mary.
Printer in London, 1635–1637. Widow of **John Dawson 1** and mother of **John 2**. [*Dict. 1.*]
No address noted.
1635: 6939, 18830, 19350–0.5, 22119, 22934.7.
1635/36: 435.25, 531.27, 532.10.
1636: [7021.5] (d), 7317, 10789.5, 17448.5–49, 23935.5(*A*3), [23985], 24297, 25208, 25208.5, 25213a.5, 25214.5, 25216.5.
1636/37: 435.26, 479.3, 522.17, 531.28, [4293].
1637: 5445.7, 18782, 18830.1, 20961, 21193, 22469.7, 22934.8(*A*3), 24563.

Dawson, Thomas.
Printer in London, (1568) 1576/77–1620†. Uncle of **John Dawson 1**. In partnership with **Thomas Gardiner**, 1577–1578. Printed 8° and 16° New Testaments in the Bishops' version as the *Deputy of* **C. Barker** and broadside almanacks with the assent or as assignee of **R. Watkins** and **J. Roberts**; *see* Appendix C/6, 14; *see* also Appendix A/20. Was one of the *assignees of* **J. Battersby**. [*Dict. 1.*]
The apparent drop in his productivity after 1585 may mask what was a specialized and highly perishable part of his later output, e.g. catechisms: Openshaw/Pagit by 1579 (18816) and Fenton by 1591 (10787.3); school texts: 'Lily's Grammar' beginning in 1585 (15621.7) and Camden by 1598 (4511.7); 8° New Testaments by 1589 (2887.7; no 16° editions of the Bishops' version have survived); broadside almanacks possibly by 1594/95 (424?). Standing type has been observed in at least the Fenton between 1591–1626 and in the Lily between 1596–1607 so Dawson may not have had much type to spare for ordinary trade publications. His unusual career deserves further study.
(nigh) the Three Cranes in the Vintry (S.9), 1576/77 (401.9)–1618 (18825, has 'at') at least; variations: 1577 (3356, has 'nigh unto'), 1617 (6099.7, has 'dw. near')
1544: [24166?] (d/repeat).
1576/77: 401.9.
1577: 3356, 3423, 3715 (d), 4066 (c), 4269 (d?), [4400], [4448], 5141 (d?), [5264], 10502, [11454], 11803a.7, 11804, 11804.5, [13063.5] (d?), [19115.5] (d?), 22467, 24172.
1578: 307, [3131], [3432], 4394, 7607 (d), 11096 (d), 11805–5.2, 11805.4–.6, [15230.5?], [19819.5] (d?), 21064.5, [21183] (d?), 21352, 21797, 24911.
1579: 3550, 4067, 4439, 4446, 4452–4, 4457, 4697, 10031, 10529, 11418 typis, 11808, 11902, 12093, [12097], [12097.5], 13066.5, 13975 ent., 14034, 15037.5, 15038, 15040, 15046, 15256, [16809(*A*3)], 17445–5.5, 18258 ent., 18671, 18816, [19809], 21121 (d), 21184 (d), 21353, 22180 (d?), 22468, 23285.
1580: 2 (d?), 2045, 2046, 4426.8, 4446–6a, 4460, 4464, 4882, 5001, 5723, 6039, 10920–0.3, 11240 in aed., 11241, 11255, 11805.8, [11872], 15047, 15074.8, 16814.5, [16985(*A*3)] (c), 17446, 17790, 18006–6.5, 18817, 18817.5, 19116, [21184.5] (d?), [23634.3?] (c), [24919], 25014.
1581: 937.5, 1591, [2050], [3099], [3977], 4437, 4455, 4456–6.5, 7629, 11421, 11455, 11457, 11845, [11845.5], [11857.5], [11862.5], 12411.5, [12422], 12746, [16812], 17771, 18534, 18574 ent., 18818, 22469, 25586, 25631, 25956.
1582: 1894, 3132, [4077], 10835, 11310, [11845.7] (d?), [11846], 11849, 11858, 12624, 16813, 16946, 18819, 19200, 19768, 20751,

Dawson, T. — *cont.*
20818.5, 20886, 22906, 22910, [24779], 24922, 25012, 25285, 25714.
1583: 1983.5 ex off., 4399, 4739, 5008, [6652?], [6729], 10607, [11846.5], 11848, 11849.3, [12269], [17450.3] (d), 18820, 21067, [21518], 22906.5, 22910, 23676, 23719, 24173, 24786.5.
1584: 2962, 4447–7.5, [5255], [6653], 10032, 10032.3, 10032.5, [15045], [17047.5], [17048], [17048a], 17086, 17086.5, 18821, 20623, 22469.3, 23286, 23399.2(*A*3).
1585: 3119 (d), 4398, 4784 ap., [10773.5] (d?), [12299], 13975.5 (note), [15002], [15621.7], 18574, [19358], [19358.5], [19820] (c), 23399.3, [24166?] (c).
1586: 6138, 6576 ap., 12094, [15621.7], [18830.2A] (d?), 18830.3, 20623.5, [21047?], [24417], [25625].
1587: 3420, 6839, [11237], [12098], 15316, 20888.
1588: 14061, 14728, 23689.
1589: [2887.7], 4803.8, [10104.7?] (d?), 15232.5, 16947.5, 18830.4, 19490, 24504.5.
1590: [4206], 19491.
1591: 2890 (note), 2904 (note), [10105?] (d?), [10787.3], 11056, 11185, 18830.4*(*A*3), 21121.3, 22533a.5, 25613.
1592: 3593, 13698, [15288?], 23283.
1593: 11105.5, 12590 ent.
1594: 13906 in aed., [20047], 20803.5.
1594/95: [424?].
1595: [2893], 6368.4, 6372, 10836, 14062, 17772.
1596: [2894.3], 5445.5 f., 14894.3(*A*3) ent., 14947, [15623], 20580 ent., 21548 ent.
1597: [2895.3], [15623].
1598: [2896], [4511.7], 17447, [18637] (d), 18822.2, 23277.5 ent.
1598/99: 425.
1599: 6368.7, 14063, 14894.3, [15623.5], [15624], 18830.4A, 20819, 23294 [f.].
1599/1600: [466.2?].
1600: [2897], 5803 ent., 18830.5.
1600/01: [525.6].
1602: 5260.5, [15624.5], 18830.6.
1603: 4303 ent., 14064, 15633.4, 18822.6.
1603/04: 466.6, 489 f., 532.3 f.
1604: [4512], [7133], 20887, 23328 (note), 23328.5 (note).
1605: 2904 (note).
1606: [15625].
1607: 6369, 6405, 22754.
1608: [14679?], 18258, 23934.2 ent.
1609: 14064.3, [17741], 18822.8, 22755.
1610: 2963.
1611: [48.5], [2537], [14534?] (forged).
1612: [650], [2541], [16785] (d?), [20981], [21003], 22756.
1613: 20982, [20994], [21162].
1614: 18823, [20986], 22757.
1615: 133, [2551.3], 10787.4, 10840, 23338.
1616: [2555], [2555.3], 12183.
1617: [2555.3], [2557.3], 6099.7, 18830.7, 22758.
1618: 15374.7, 18825, 23934.5.
1619: [2564.4], [2564.6], 6631.5, 18458, 21828, [23279], 23934.6.
1620: 1629, 18154, 22759, 22837, 24771.7, 24810.

1621: 10787.5 ass'd.
1679: 21184 (d/error).

Day, John 1.
Printer in London, 1546?–1584†. Father of **Richard Day**; possibly great-grandfather of **John Day 2**. Father-in-law of **George Pen**. Published jointly with **William Seres**, 1548–50 at least. Transferred from the Stringers' to the Stat. Co. in 1550 (*TBS* 6 (1900–02): 19). **Printer to the City of London** (*see* Printers …), possibly from 1557, definitely 1564–84. Patentee for printing the ABC and Catechism (20.4, 20.6), the Sternhold and Hopkins metrical Psalms (2427, 2429, etc.), and numerous other works. *See* also *assignees of* **J. Day** and of **R. Day**. For the full list of Day's copyrights yielded to the Stat. Co. in 1584 *see* Appendix C/15–49; *see* also Appendices A/1–2 and D/75, 94, 99, 103, 108, 113, 121, 123. [Duff, *Century*; C. L. Oastler, *John Day*, Oxford, 1975; *Library* 27 (1972): 220–32.]
Items by or attributed to Day's press before 1559 and his relationship to other printers and publishers during this period, particularly **Steven Mierdman**, still require further study. The

Day, John 1 — *cont.*
index below will undoubtedly be subject to revision following a more systematic investigation of Day's early publications.

presses:

dw. in Sepulchre's parish at the $ Resurrection a little above Holborn conduit (D.5), 1547, 21 Oct. (13213)–1549 (12887.3)

dw. at Aldersgate (G.1), 1549 (4463)

dw. over Aldersgate beneath St. Martin's (G.1), 1550 (15549)–1584 (2468); the latest 'beneath St. Martin's' has been noted is 1580 (5992); later and occasionally earlier this phrase is omitted, e.g. in 1574 (924)

shops:

the New Shop by the little conduit in Cheapside (N.3), 1549 (4463, 5109.5; 2077, omits 'new shop')

at the $ Resurrection by the little conduit in Cheapside (N.3), 1550, 6 Feb. (1721)–1553 (4812)

shop under the gate [Aldersgate] (G.1), 1560 (14612)–1580 (2454, colophon) at least

shop at the West door of Paul's (A.10), 1576 (11224)–1579 (5447) at least; variations: has 'Long Shop', 1578 (1359, colophon; 1728, colophon also has 'Northwest' door)

1160: 14020 (d/error).

1546: [10884?] (d), [25590?] (false), [25590.5?] (false).

1547: 96, [96.5], [1034.7–35?], [1035.5–36?], 1733.5 [f.] (d?), 3039 (d), 5717 [f.?], [6084.5?] (d?), [6088.9(*A*)?] (d?), [13089?] (d), 13213, [17313.7?], [17314] (false), [17314a] (false), 24457, [24470?] (d?), [24471?] (d?).

1548: 166.5 (d?), [683] (d?), 1544 (d), 2853, 3258.5 (d?), 3815, 3816, [4411?] (d?), 4412 (d?), [5605a] (d?), 6082 (d), 6083 [f.?] (d), [6086] (d), 6086.5 (d), 11391 (d?), 11842a [f.] (d?), [11884 f.] (d?), [13052] (d?), 13214 (d), 15178 (d), 15291 (d), 15292a (d), 15461, 15683 (d?), 16822 (d?), 17630 (d?), 18575 (d?), 19463 (d?), 23004 [f.], 23004.5 [f.], [24163(*A*3)] (d), 24359 [f.] (d), 24361.5 [f.] (d?), 24362 [f.] (d?), 24441a (d), 24784 [f.] (d?), [25591?] (d?), [25591a?] (d?).

1549: 1712 (d?), 2077 [f.], 2087.2, 2087.5, 2856 (note), 4436 (d), 4463 (d), [5058?] (d), 5109 (d), 5109.5 (d), [7507] (d), 12887.3 (d), 12887.7 (d?), [14554.5?] (d?), [15109.3–.7], 15270.5 (d), 15270.7 (d), 15272 (d), 15272.5 (d), 15274 [f.] (d), 15274.3 (d), 15274.7 (d), [16050.5?].

1549/50: 483.13(*A*), 507.15.

1550: 84, 1275 [f.] (d?), 1298 [f.] (c), 1709 (d), 1719.5 (c), 1721, 1721.5, [1725.7?] (c), 1733 (d?), 1751 (c), 2087.3, 2087.4, 2087.6 [f.], [2860 f.], 3603, 13757 (d), 13763 (d), 13764 (d?), 14019, 14824, 15289 (d), 15290 (d/repeat), 15293 (d), 15543, 15543.5, 15543a, 15547, 15548–8.5 (d), 15549, 22428 (d).

1551: 1720, [1720.3] (c), 1722 (d?), 2087, 2088, 2865 [f.] (d?), 3552.7 (d?), [11886] (d), 11887 (d?), 13757.5 (d?), 15544 (d), 15546 (d), 15546.3 (d), 18766 (d?), 18767 (d?), 22992 [f.] (d?).

1552: 1294 [f.] (d?), 5628 (d?), [10486–6.5?] (d?), [10990?] (d/repeat), 13758 (d?), [14932.5(*A*3)] (d).

1553: 20.4 (d?), 1752.5 (d?), 4812, [5160.3?] (false), [11583] (d), [11585] (false), [11586] (false), [11593] (false), 11885.5 (d?), 15290 (d?), [19970] (d?).

1554: [5157?] (false), [5630?] (false), [6934.5?] (false), [7279?], [10016?] (false), [10383?] (false), [15059?] (false), [15074.4?] (d), [16981?] (false), [17773?] (false), 24810a.5 (d).

1556: 2980.2 (d?), [4825?], 6849.5 (d?), [10990?], [16075?].

1557: [3286?] (d?), 7633–3.3, [16079], 24372 ent.

1557/58: 432.

1558: 1744, [3478.5?] (d?), 4039 (d), 4040 (d), 4797.3 ?ent., [7886?] (d), [7889?] (d), 13489.5 (d?), 14075 ap., 14075.5, 14795, [22596–6b] (d?), [22603–3b] (d?), [22617–7a.5] (d?), 24356 (note), 24850–0.3 (d?).

1558/59: 400.

1559: [1005–6] (false), [3479?] (d), 4041 (d), 6119 in off., 11800 (d), 18694, 21051.

1560: 785 (d?), 1710, 1726 (d?), 1754 (c), 1756.5 (c), [2427], 4450 (d), [4939] (d), 6046 (d?), 6047 (d?), 6418, 14018, 14020 (d), 14612 (d), [14613] (d?), 19848–8a, 20114 (d), [23187] (d?), [25387.5(*A*3)] (c?).

1561: 1720.5, 1746, 1757 (d), [2428], 2429, 2739, 2739.5(*A*), 4061, 4938.5, 5459 in off., [6774.5 f.], 10286 (d), 15261, 18412 (d), 18812, 19930.5 in off., 24662.5 in off., 26135 (d?).

1562: 2429.5, 2430, 12955a.5 (d?), 15276, [17565] (d).

1563: 1710, 1746.5, 1755 (d), 2430.5, 2431, 7956.3 (d), 11222, [11222a] (d), 11230 (d), 11230.5 (d?), 11249 (d?), 22600 (d?).

Day, John 1 — *cont.*

1564: 1710, 2432, 2433, 5886, 12377, 12378 per, 16705 (d), 24265, 24265.5, 24565, 24670.

1565: 374, 1747, 1757.5, 2434, 2435, 6419, 11801, 24777 (d).

1566: 159 (d?), 159.5 (d?), 1727, 1747.3, 2437, 2437.5, 2740, 2740.3(*A*), 11263 (d), 15262.

1567: 1747.5 (c), 2438, 2729 (d?), 11893.

1568: 1758 (d), 11894, 11996, 15142 ex off., 16705.7, [18601] (d), 18603 chez, 24672, 25708 (d?).

1568/69: 466.9.

1569: 1581, 1753, 2439.3(*A*3), 2439.5, 2439.7, 2440, 3817.4 (d?), 3817.7 (d?), 6428, 11997, 12000–0.5, [13869?] (d?), [13870] (d?), [18685.3] (d?), 18685.7 (d).

1570: 830 (d?), 832, 933 (c?), [1720.7?] (c?), 1747.7 (c), 1759, 2441, 2441.5 (c), 3817 (d?), 4397, 6694 (d?), 6694.5 (d?), 7171 (d?), 7171.5 (d?), 7172 (d?), 10560, 11223, 11242, 11242.3, 11242.6, 16997.5 (d), 18677 (d), 18677.5 (d), 18678 (d), 18678a (d), 18678a.5 (d), 18679 (d), 18685 (d), 18686 (d?), 18708, 18768 (d?), 24913a.5.

1571: 375, 834, 2441.7 (d?), 2961, 3967, [3968] (repeat), [3978] (d), [3981] (d), 4043 ap., 4782 ap., 4879 (d?), 4880 (d?), 6006 ex off., [9187.5] (d?), 10036 ap., [10037.5] (d), 10062.5–63 (d), 10063.5 (d), 10064 (d), 11036 (d), 11247 ap., [11504] (d), [11505] (d), [11505.5] (d), [11506] (d), 14943 (d?), 15277, 15278 (repeat), 18440 ap., 18441, 18709, [23296?] (d), 25584.

1572: 1760, 2442, 2442.5, 3368.5-Day, J. (c?), 4044, 7166 (d), 7168 ap., [9187.6] (d?), 11239, 13959 ap., 13959.5 ap., 15277, 16706, 16706.3 (d), 17520, 17521, 18730, 19292 in aed., 24436.

1573: 99–9.5 ap., 785.5 (d?), 835, 2442.7 (c), 2443, [2443.5] (d?), 4062, 5407 ap., 6462 ap., 8056 (d), 10030.5 (d?), [10037.7] (c?), 13963 ap., 14021, 16979, 18710, 18711 ap., 19299 ap., 23101.5 ap. (d), 24436.

1574: [863] (d), 924, 1761, 2444, 4345 in aed., 4348 in aed., 4349 in aed., 4451 (d), [7627.7] (d), 18704 ap., 18711a ap., 18712 in aed., 19292 in aed. (d), 19465.7, [20998] (d), 25005 in aed.

1575: 925, 2445, 2445a.5, 6695 (c?), 6696 (c?), 10037 ap., 10037.3 ap., 10352.5 (d?), 10567.5 ap., 11243 [f.], 15278 (d), 16706.7, 18710a, 18726 ap., [18730.3] (d?), 19466, 25712.

1576: 1761.5, 2446, 2447, [10037.9] (c?), 11224, 16707 (d), 17850 [f.], 18705 ap., 18710a, 18710a.5, 18713 in aed., 18730.7, 19467.

1577: 926, 1711, 1718, 1762, 2448, 2448.5, 2449, 2449.3, 2449.5, 6459, 11244, 12476, 12593 ex off., [16707.1] (d), 18710a.5, 18713.5 ap., 18727 ap., 18731, 19467.5 [f.].

1578: 1359, 1492 ap., 1728, 1748, 2449, 2449.7, 2450, 2450.5, 2451, 2451.5, 6119 (note), 6429, 15279, 16998, 18728 ap., 20850, 22215 [f.].

1579: 835.5, 1492 ap., 1762.3, 2452, 2452.5, 2452.7, 5447, 6219, 7432, 10194.7 (d), 11231, 11742, [14655], 18732, 21180, 25665.

1580: 1753.5 (c), 1762.4, 2453, 2454, 2456, 2456.2, 2456.4, 2456.6 (c), 5992, 6805.6 (c?), 12594, 14022, 16708.5 (c), [16762.5?] (c), 18706 ap., 24251.3.

1581: 2457, 2458, 2458.3, 2459, 2459.3(*A*3), 2459.5, 2459.7, 3128, 4409, 6430, 6734 [f.], 12594, 18714 ap., 19468, 22857 ent.

1582: 1762.5, 1762.7 f., 2460, 2460.5, 2461, 2461.3(*A*), 2461.5, 16709 (d).

1583: 2460, 2462, 2463, 2464 [f.], 2465, 2466 [f.], 2466.5, 2466.7, 2466.9(*A*), 11225, 18711.5 ap., 18733 [f.].

1584: 836 (note), 1728 (note), 1748 (note), 2466.5, 2467, 2467.3, 2468, 6119 (note), 6697 (note), 7168 (note), 10037 (note), 10062.5 (note), 14022 (note) 15280, 16710 (d), 17850 (note), 18711b ap., 18714.5 ap., 18714.7 ap. (forged?), 20998 (note), 24670 (note), 24672 (note).

1587: 21227 (note).

2570: 16997.5 (d/error).

Day, John 1, *Assignees of.*
Publishers of the ABC and Catechism, 1582?

1582: 20.6(*A*3) [f.] (d?).

Day, John 2.
Bookseller in London, 1629–1634. Probably the 'Joseph' Day, son of 'Edward', freed by patrimony in 1628 (DFM 1169), since a Joseph at this date is otherwise unknown and a John begins activity. Apparently the son (or, less likely, brother) of Joseph, freed in 1600 (Arber II.725), who bound his last apprentice in 1609 (DFM 1167); this Joseph was the son of Edward Day, who was

Day, John 2 — *cont.*
the son of **John Day 1** and active 1577–1602 (Arber II.82, 268). John 2 was granted permission to transfer from the Stat. Co. to the Brewers on 1 Dec. 1634 (*C-B C*: 261). He is possibly identical with the John Day designated a Fishmonger who on 27 Feb. 1636 was allowed by the Corporation of London (*TBS* 14 (1915): 234) to receive higher payment for printing weekly bills of prices and rates for commodities (cf. the similar but earlier items entered at 9175z.5 sqq.). [Not in *Dict. 2.*]
shop at Guildhall gate (H.5) 1629 (18068.5)
their shop in Little Britain (F.4), 1631 (24398, with D. Pakeman)
1629: 18068.5 f., 24397 sold. **1631:** 24398 sold.

Day, Richard.
Editor, bookseller, and printer in London, 1579–1584; clergyman thereafter (1607†: *C-B C*: 24). Son of **John Day 1**, with whom he was co-patentee in numerous copyrights. *See* also *assignees of* **R. Day**. [*Dict. 1*; *Poor Book*, (widow) 1608–15; C. L. Oastler, *John Day*, Oxford, 1975, pp. 65–9.]
dw. at Aldersgate (G.1), 1579 (25711)
at the Long Shop at the West end of Paul's (A.10), 1580 (19181.5); variation: in occident. Cœmeterio D. Pauli sub Arbore, 1580 (1489)
1575: 3368.5-Day, R. (d?). **1579:** 4409 ent., 11231, 25711. **1580:** 1489 ap., 4654 ent., 19181.5. **1584:** [18714.7?] (forged?).

Day, Richard, *Assignees of.*
Successors, 1584–1604, to the patents originally granted to **John Day 1** and later jointly to him and his son **Richard** for the ABC and Catechism, the metrical Psalms, and other works. The initial assignees were F. Adams, T. Butter, E. White, J. Wolfe, and W. Wright 1. For a list of many of the members in 1594 *see Reg. B*: 48. The rights were subsequently granted to the Stat. Co. and exercised by the English Stock (*see* Stationers' Co.). [*Dict. 1.*]
No address used.
1584: 2468.5, 18733.3 f.
1585: 927, 1764, 2469, 2470, 2470a, 2470a.3, 2470a.6, 11245.
1586: 928 f., 2471 f., 2472 f., 2472.5 f., 2473 f., 2473a f., 18715 pro.
1587: 1764.5, 2474 f.
1588: 2475 f., 2475.3 f.
1589: 2475.5 f., 2475.7 f., 2476 f., 11226 (note).
1590: 2476.5 f., 2477 f., 6431 f., 18715.5 pro.
1591: 1764.7 f., 2477.7 f., 2478 f., 2478.5 f., 2479 f., 2479.5 f.
1592: 2480 f., 2481 f., 2481.5 f.
1593: 2483 f., 2483.5 f., 2484 f., 2484.3 f., 2484.5 f., 2485 f., 18716 pro, 18733.5 f.
1594: 1765 f., 2486 f., 2487 f., 2487.3 f., 2487.6 f.
1595: 2489 f., 2490 f., 2490.2 f., 2490.3 f., 2490.4 f., 2490.5 f., 2492 f., 18706a, 18717 pro, 19468.5 f.
1596: 2490.6 f., 2490.7 f., 2490.8 f., 11226.
1597: 1766.3 f., 2491 f., 2492 f., 2492a f., 2492a.5 f., 11226a, 18733.7 f.
1598: 2493 f., 2494 f., 2494a f., 2494a.5 f., 18718 pro.
1599: 2497.3 f., 2497.5 f., 2497.7 f., 2498 f., 2498.5 f., 2500 f.
1600: 2500 f., 2500.3 f., 2500.5 f., 2500.7 f., 2501 f.
1601: 20.7 f., 2502 f., 2503 f., 2503.5 f., 2504 f., 2505 f., 19469 f.
1602: 2506 f., 2506.5 f., 2507 f.
1603: 2508 f., 2509 f., 2510 f., 2510.5 f., 2511 f., 2511.5 f.
1604: 2512 f.

Day (Daye), Steven.
Locksmith in Cambridge, England, 1618?–1638? and printer in Cambridge, New England, 1638?–1668†. Regarding the forgery of the 'Oath of a Freeman' *see Book Collector* 36 (1987): 449–70; 37 (1988): 9–28, especially 460–3, 469, 9–22. [*DAB*; G. P. Winship, *The Cambridge Press 1638–1692*, Philadelphia, 1945.]
No address used.
1640: [2738].

Deane, John.
Bookseller in London, 1601–1623. [*Dict. 1.*]
shop at (just under) Temple Bar (W.14), 1602 (15490)–1619 (21411); variation: 1616 (18591a, has 'dw.')
1601: 3648 f., 3649 f., 3672 f.
1602: 15490 [f.], 25304 f.
1603: 15189 f.

Deane, J. — *cont.*
1606: 3649(*A*, note), 21407 f. (d?).
1607: 21366 f.
1608: 772.7 f.
1609: 21367 f., 21413 f.
1613: 21410.5 [f.] (d?), 21414 f.
1616: 18591a sold.
1619: 21411 f.
1620: 21402 f.
1622: 2015 f.
1623: 2016 f.

De Beau Chesne, John.
Frenchman, schoolmaster, and author, fl. 1565–1618. [*Dict. 1*: 28.]
dw. in the Blackfriars (Q.6), 1597 (23626)
1597: 23626 [f.].

De la Coste. *See* La Coste.

De la Noue. *See* La Noue.

Denham, Henry.
Printer in London, (1560) 1563–1590? From 1578 he was the *assignee of* **W. Seres** for printing books of private prayer and other works belonging to the Seres patent. In 1584, along with **Ralph Newbery**, Denham took over many of the copyrights belonging to **Henry Bynneman**; others they yielded to the Stat. Co. (*see* Appendix C/50–63, 72–82). Denham's printing material passed to **Richard Yardley** and **Peter Short**. *See* also Appendix D/107, 109, 112, 114–18, 122. [*Dict. 1.*]
in White Cross Street (I.8), 1564 (21504)
dw. in Paternoster Row at the Star (C.7), 1565, 3 Sept. (4558)–1583 (4730)
dw. in Aldersgate Street at the Star (F.2), 1585 (23976)–1587 (2399.7 C^5 copy) at least
1563: [24190.7], [24191], 24191a.
1564: 724.5, 1209.7, 2017, 5540, 6811, 11529, 21504, 24191a.
1564/65: 462.5.
1565: 4368, 4558, 5723.5, 6812, 18740 ent., 19150.
1565/66: 493.
1566: 306, 1534, 3168 (d?), [6076], 6077, [6078?], 13207, [15075?], 15347 (d), 18358 (d), 19121, 19425 (d), 19438 (d), 20031 (d), 21453, 22221 (note), 22229 (d), 24191a.5(*A3*), [24508] (d?).
1567: 2960, 10374 (d), [11530.5], [12404] (d?), 12606 ent., 16435, 17296, 18939.5, 18940, 18940.5, 19893a.7 (d?), 21615, 23969, 24326, 25592 ent.
1568: 6179, 6725 (d), 10499 (d), [10588] (d?), 10590 (d), 13874, [17320.5] (d?), 19894, 23969.5, 23970, 23971 (repeat), 24076, 24076.3, 24076.7, 24230.
1569: 309, 1585, 6093, 10326.5, 12147, 11798 ent., [12890?], 18941.
1570: 1925 (d), 3053, 3601, 4559, 6578, 12366 (d?), 12889, 13480.5 ent., 15011, 18942 (d?), 19895, 20117, 23408, 23621.5 (d?), 24327, [24373?].
1570/71: 454.
1571: 6577 ap., [10250?] (d), [10375?], [13482], 23971 (d?), 24077, [24374?].
1572: 6701 (d?), [10797], [12404?], 17574 (d), 25013.
1573: 4560 (d?), 4560.5, 5684, 5684.2, [5687], 24077.5, [24375?].
1574: 1410 (d), 6797, 13484 (d?), 17303, 17304, 21865.
1575: [17575].
1576: [10155], 11798, 15353.3, 21866.
1577: 4779, 6364, [10155.3], 24077a.
1578: [310], 2396, [5688], [10376?] (d?), 19896 f., 21867.
1579: 2397 (d), 11037.3, [12582.2] (d), [12582.3], 13483 ass'd, 17790.5, 21235, 23603, 24144 ent.
1580: 1411, 2360, 2397.3, 3154, 3983.5 imp., 4086, 4086.5, 4474.71 ex off., —.115 ex off., 4733, 11037, 11038 (d), 11047 (d), 12582.4, 12582.21, 17321 [f.] (d?), 20064, 21677, 23973, 24380, 24409.
1581: 938, 944, 950, 2028.5, 2034, 2397.7, 4086.7, 4733.2, 11041, 14010, 15033.3, [25197.5].
1582: [20.6(*A3*)] (d?), 1892, 1893, [1894], 11048, 22136, 23974.
1583: 2399, 4730, 4730.5, 12582.6, 13975, 24144–4.5 f., 24669.
1584: 884, 4336 (note), 4606, 4733.4 f., 4779 (note), [5689], 5797, 5819.5, 6131 (note), 6761 ent., 9342.8, 15222 ent., 18101 ent., 18203.5, [21864], 23325.2 ent., 23325.8, 23334 ent., 23975, 24040.5 (d), 24678 (d), 24885, 24889, 25329.

Denham, H. — *cont.*
1585: [2399.5], 13569 (note), 13975.5 in house, 14860 f., [16516] (d), 18204, [20032], 20109 imp., 23976 in house, 24381 in house (d).
1586: 4733.7 f., 11042, 12582.7, 13569 (note), 24382 in house (d).
1587: [1764.5], [2399.7], 4731, [9305.3], [13569–9.5], 13976, 23326 (d), 23995 ent.
1588: 2475.2, 2475.3 in house, 5402 pro (d?), 13972.5.
1589: 13977, 14011, 23978, 26018 ent.
1590: [15222] (d).

Derwen. *See* Okes.

Dever (Dewer), John.
Journeyman printer and printer (from 1646) in London, (1626) 1630–1647? [*Dict. 2*; DFM 165.]
No address used before 1641.
1630: 11498 f.

Dewe, Thomas.
Bookseller in London, 1621–1625†. Freed by **Anne Helme**, whose shop he seems to have taken over or managed. [*Dict. 1*; DFM 1597.]
shop in St. Dunstan's Churchyard in Fleet Street (W.9), 1621 (7024)–1625 (6770)
1621: 7024 f., 11104 f. (d?), 18302 f.
1622: 5674 f., 7228 f., 7229–30 f., 7342.3(*A*3) f. (d?), 11520 f., 12304 sold, 14647 f., 17387.3 f., 17912 f., 21140 f., 24393.7 f.
1623: 7373.2 f., 7438 ex off., 14535 f., 24630 sold.
1624: 2782 f., 2783 f., 17995.5 f., 21609 f.
1625: 2776 f., 2783 f., 6770 f., 7025 f.

Dewes, Garrat.
Bookseller in London, (1560) 1562–1591†. One of the *assignees of* **F. Flower**. In 1584 he seems to have become a partner of **Henry Marsh.** [*Dict. 1.*]
dw. in Paul's Churchyard at the East end of the church (A.5), 1562 (6768)
dw. in Paul's Churchyard at the Swan (A.5), 1578 (6984)–1587 (694)
1562: 6768 f. (d), 23437 ap.
1566: 15262a, 23001 [f.].
1566/67: 422 f.
1567/68: 422.3 f.
1568: 2800 ap., 12787.5 (note).
1568/69: 422.4(*A*) f.
1575: 2113 [f.].
1578: 6984 sold, 7364 f. (d).
1581: 17589 f.
1584: 4940 [f.], 5298.8, 17406.5, 22254, 22983.5.
1587: 694 [f.]

Dexter, Gregory.
Journeyman printer and printer (from 1641) in London, 1637–1644, and colonist in New England, 1644?–1700?†. Although not freed in the name of Elizabeth Allde until 1639, he confessed in 1637 to disorderly printing in the house (near Christ Church (C.1)) of her successor, **Richard Oulton**, with another Allde apprentice, **William Taylor**. However, it is not certain that 20454.3 is the edition in question. [*Dict. 2*; DFM 13; B. F. Swan, *Gregory Dexter*, Rochester, N.Y., 1949.]
No address used before 1641.
1637: [20454.3?] (d).

Dexter, Robert.
Bookseller in London, (1589) 1590–1603†. [*Dict. 1.*]
In 1595 Dexter seems to have been appointed by the Stat. Co. to oversee printing of Latin school books which had apparently fallen under its administration. In 1597 Henry Stringer, one of Queen Elizabeth's footmen, received a patent for some of these titles and also entered them in the SR together with Dexter, who was possibly acting as Stringer's agent (Arber (II.16, III.87); for further details *see* the headnote following Appendix D/60. Whatever interest in them Dexter may have had, passed in 1603 to the **English Stock** (*see* Stationers' Company) along with his personal copyrights. All potential rights either reverting or first passing to the Company in 1603 are separately indexed under that year as follows:

Dexter, R. — *cont.*
Latin school books of which at least one Dexter edition survives are in *italic* within square brackets, and those included in Stringer's patent have '*-HS*' appended; two titles in English which also passed to the English Stock are given in roman type within square brackets with their numbers in Appendix D appended; the five titles mentioned by name in the 1603 entry have no brackets. These last did not pass into the English Stock, but the Company allowed rights to individual Stationers; *see* Appendix E/4–8.
dw. at the Brazen Serpent in Paul's Churchyard (A.3), 1590 (5471a)–1603 (24769a)
1590: 3363.9(*A*3, note), 4072 ent., 4858 ent., 5181 ent., 5471 f., 5471a f., 11807(*A*3) ent., 13699 f.
1591: 3363.9(*A*3, note), 17842.7 f., 21656 ap., 24274 f.
1592: 2988 f., 6125 f., 15241.3 f., 15419 f., 18245 f., 22775.3 f.
1593: 7527.9 ent., 22775.7 f., 25433.7 f.
1594: 2989 f., 22776 f., 22777 f., 24767.5 f., 24768 f.
1595: 5300.4 imp., 21821 imp., 24768.5 f.
1596: 362 f., [1510] sold, 4374, 5472 f., 5711 f., 13478 ent., 13701 f., 15420 f., 18197.3 ap., 18197.7 f., 18199 f., 18246 f., 22779 f.
1597: 7087 f., 7527.9 f., 7581.5 sold, 11127 imp., 12716 f., 18200.5 f., 21499 f., 23021 f., 23888 [f.], 24769 f.
1598: 3092 f., 4848.2(*A*) ap., 12322 f., 12717 f., 12718.5 f., 22780 f., 22930 ent., 22984.3 [f.].
1599: 5403.5 ap., 11834, 12312 f., 12314 f., 12719 f., 18198 f., 19143.5 ap., 19964 f., 22254.3 ap., 22752(*A*3) ass'd, 22761 ass'd, 22780.5 f.
1600: 2991 f., 12314.5 f., 24769.5 f.
1601: 172.2 ap., 1055 f., [1511] sold, 3363.9 f., 4771.7 ap., 5181 f., 6626 f., 6626.5 f., 7083 ent., 12315 f., 15633.4(*A*3) ?ent., 17173.5 f., 17239.5 ap., 21622.8 ap., 21821.2 ap., 22984.4 ap.
1602: 6626.7 f., 7298.5 f., 10462 imp., 12718 f., 19144 ap., 23410 f., 24791.3 ap.
1603: 5320 ap., 6125.3 f., 6622 ent., 6627 f., 17289 ap., 21215 f., 24769a f.
1603: (copyrights: *see* headnote) [*172.2-HS*], [3364-D/96], [*4771.7*], [*4848.2(A3)-HS*], [*5300.4-HS*], [*5320-HS*], [5711-D/97], 6627, 7528, [*10462*], 12317, [*17239.5*], [*17289*], [*19144*], 21215, [*21622.8*], [*21821.2*], [*22254.3*], [*22984.4*], [*23888-HS*], 24770, [*24791.3-HS*].

Dicæophile, Eusebius, *pseud.*
Printer in 'London', 1569. = J. de Foigny, Rheims.
in Fleet Street at the $ Justice Royal against the Black Bell (W.14), 1569 (15505)
1569: 15505.

Dickenson, William.
Journeyman printer? in London, (1565) 1578 (*Reg. B*: 7)–1585. His only extant imprint was shared with **Abel Jeffes:** in Sermon Lane near Paul's Chain (R.4). [*Dict. 1.*]
No separate address used.
1584: 17979.7.

Diest (Coppens van Diest), Ægidius (Gillis).
Printer and bookseller in Antwerp, 1533–1572†. [*Dict. 1*; Rouzet 45–6.]
1563: 24752 ex off., 25859 ex off.
1564: 20726.
1565: 10589, 12759.5 typis (d), [12763.5] (d), 13888, 15653, 18887, 20727, 20728.

Dietrich, Katharina.
Printer at Nürnberg, 1597–1605†. Widow of August Philipp Dietrich. [Benzing 362.]
1599: [2792.5(*A*)], [2792.6(*A*)].
1600: [2792.5(*A*)] (d), [2792.7(*A*)].

Dight, Edward.
Bookseller in Exeter, 1631–1635 at least. [*Dict. 1*, under John Dight.]
No address used.
1631: 1661.5 sold, 10939 f. **1635:** 1235.4 sold, 19522 sold.

Dight, Walter.
Bookseller and printer in London, (1589) 1590–1618† (cf. DFM 1185). His surviving publications consist largely of woodcut illustrations and diagrams. Although he possessed some kind of

Dight, W. — *cont.*
press for printing them, he is not among those listed as having a press in 1615 (*C-B C*: 75). In 1591 he was living in St. Bride's parish (W.4: *Library* 10 (1909): 104). The second address below has been queried for Dight since he is the only Stationer known to have worked in Shoe Lane, but the devotional character of the text separates it from Dight's known works. The last shop passed to Dight's former apprentice, **Richard Shorlayker**. [*Dict. 1*; *Loan Book*; 1600–03.]
(in) Shoe Lane, c. 1600?–1616
at the Harp in — (W.6), c. 1600? (10021.7)
?near — end in Holborn (V.3), 1608 [13545.5], sold by W. E. [*sic*]
in — at the Falcon (W.6), 1612 (19511)–1616 (11695)
1590: 15107 f. **1600:** 10021.7 (c?). **1602:** 18454.5 f. **1603:** 19766(*A*3) ent. **1608:** [13545.5?] sold. **1612:** 19511 (d). **1615–16:** 11695.

1627: 21826 ass'd.

Disle (Disley, Dizle), Henry.
Bookseller in London, 1574–1582 at least. Former apprentice of **William Jones 1** and apparently succeeded to his shop. [*Dict. 1.*]
?at the Corner Shop at the Southwest door of Paul's Church (A.10), 1574 [20998]
at the Southwest door of Paul's Church (A.10), 1574/75 (443.13, has 'occidentalis')–1578 (7517, has 'dw.')
dw. in Paternoster Row (C.7), 1580 (7518)
shop in Canon Lane near the great North door of Paul's Church (A.2), 1580 (7518)–1582 (19433.2(*A*))
1574: [20998?] sold. **1574/75:** 443.13 ap. **1576:** 7516 [f.?], 16620 f. (d). **1578:** 7517 [f.?]. **1580:** 1855 f., 7518 [f.]. **1582:** 7520 ass'd, 19433.2(*A*) f.

Dix, Henry.
Teacher of shorthand and author, 1633–1641 at least. [Carlton 46–8.]
shop at the Golden Anchor in Paternoster Row (C.7), 1633 (6929.5)
1633: 6929.5 f.

Doesborch (Duisbrowghe), Jan van.
Printer and bookseller in Antwerp, 1504–1530 at least, and in Utrecht, 1531–1532. In 1523 he had a shop or agent in London in the parish of St. Martin's in the Fields (X.13). [Duff, *Century*; Rouzet; Gruys.]
1505: 793.3 (d?).
1507: 13606.5 (d?).
1509: 23153.7 (d?).
1510: 18873.5 (c).
1512: [13689.5?] (c?).
1515: [19969.8] (d?), 23155.2 (c).
1515/16: [470.2?].
1518: 5405 (d?), 11361, 17557 (d?), 24828 (d?).
1519: [10563] (c?).
1520: [4593] (c), 7677 (d?), [14894.5] (c), [24591?] (c?).
1527: 13837.5 (d?).
1530: [6815?] (d?).

Dolman. *See* Dawlman.

Dooms, Jodocus (Joos).
Printer in Ghent, 1620–1636. [*Dict. 1.*]
1627: 13926 typis. **1628:** 15188.3. **1632:** 1860 (d), 17552.

Dorcaster, Nicholas, *pseud.*
Printer in 'Wittenburg', 1554. ? = J. Day 1.
1554: 5630, 6934.5, 15059.

Dorne. *See* Thorne.

Dorp, Jan Claeszoon (Class) van.
Printer in Leiden, 1595–1634. [*Dict. 1*; Gruys; Briels 262–3.]
1616: 3756.

Dowland, John.
Musician and author, b. 1563–1626†. [*DNB*; *New Grove.*]
his house in Fetter Lane near Fleet Street (W.8), 1604 (7097)
1604: 7097 sold (d).

Downes, Bartholomew.
Bookbinder and bookseller in London, 1609 (cf. DFM 1204)–1636. Brother of **Thomas Downes 1**. A brother of the Stat. Co., who completed his yeomanry share in the English Stock in 1616 and in 1636 asked that it be granted to his son, Thomas 2 (*C-B C*: 85, 289). References to 'Mr. Downes' in Stat. Co. records from 1616 are to Thomas 1. [*Dict. 1.*]
his house near Fleet Bridge (W.3), 1622 (18507.71A)
1621: 18507.35A f., —.35C f., 19843.5 ent.
1622: 1898 f., 18507.35B f., —.71A f., —.77 f., —.83 f., —.84 f., —.86 f., —.87 f., —.90 f.
1623: 18507.92 f., —.93 f., —.96 f., —.98 f.

Downes (Downe), Thomas 1.
Bookseller in London, (1606) 1608–1658†. Brother of **Bartholomew Downes**. In partnership with **Ephraim Dawson** 1608–1616, 1620–1625, with whom all imprints but one (12582.26) during these periods are shared. All of his publications from 1628 are published with or printed by **Robert Young.** Was active in the affairs of the **Irish Stock** (*see* Stationers' Co.) and apparently one of its agents in Dublin, 1618–1620. [*Dict. 2*; DFM 2832.]
(at) the Inner Temple gate in Fleet Street (W.11), 1608–1609, 1624–1625; variations:
their shop at —, 1608 (17156.3, omits 'in Fleet Street')–1609 (10537)
at the Rainbow near —, 1624 (24545)–1625 (24546)
?at the great North door of Paul's (A.2), 1628 (14261); no later use of this address or any other noted, and it may not be that of Downes.
1608: 17156.3 f.
1609: 10537 f., 20337–7.3 f.
1610: 12582.25 f.
1616: 11521–1.3 f., 12582.26 f., 20337.5 f.
1618: 7154.7.
1619: [17762].
1620: 7109 sold, 7154.3 (d?), 7154.5 (d).
1624: 24545 f. (d).
1625: 5029 ent., 24546 f.
1628: 1805(*A*) ent., 14261 f.
1629: 5844 ent., 14262 f.
1631: 5845–5.5 f., 24548 f.
1633: 22549 f.
1635: 5846 f.
1638: 5846.7 f., 22550 f.

Drawater, John.
Bookseller in London, (1593) 1595–1617†. [*Dict. 1*; *Poor Book*, 1608–17, widow thereafter.]
shop in Paternoster Row at the Swan (C.7), 1595 (15562, 15563)
shop in Canon Lane near Paul's (A.2), 1595 (15564)–1596 (15565, adds: at the Unicorn)
1595: 15562 f., 15563 f., 15564 f. **1596:** 15565 f.

Dring, Thomas.
Bookseller in London, (1648) 1649–1668†. For a label advertising the second shop below and inserted in copies of STC plays *see* Greg III.1155; the label also appears in the HD copy of 17646 and the Y copy of 4963. [*Dict. 2*; DFM 2283; Greg III.1508.]
in Fleet Street, 1655–1668 at least
at the George — near St. Dunstan's Church, 1655–1659 (Greg)
at the White Lion near Chancery Lane end — (W.10b), 1667–1668 (Greg)
1629: 18040.5 f. (d/error; = Wing M 2475 [1659]).

Driver, Andrew.
Bookseller in London, (1625) 1627–1635 (cf. DFM 1215). [Not in *Dict. 1*; DFM 2201; *Loan Book*, 1631.]
shop at Staple Inn gate in Holborn (V.9), 1627 (16823)
1627: 16823 sold.

Du Bois, Franciscus, *pseud.*
Printer in 'Mussipons' [= Pont à Mousson], 1609. = Eliot's Court Press. For the genuine Du Bois, active in various French places, 1605–29, see *Répertoire 17e*, X.160, 206, 214, 218, 250.
1609: 1408.3 ap.

Du Bois, M. *See* Wood, M.

Du Bray, Toussaint, *pseud.*
Bookseller in 'Paris', 1632. = T. Harper for R. Whitaker (Woodfield no. 29). For the genuine man, active in Paris, 1605–1641 at least, *see* Lottin 2: 55.
1632: 12455.5 chez.

Du Brel, Arnold, *pseud.*
Printer in 'Tholosa' [Toulouse], 1606. = Unidentified French printer, possibly in Bordeaux.
1606: 5725.

Dugrès, Gabriel.
Teacher of French and author, 1636–1643? [Wood, *Ath. Ox.* III. 184.]
No address used.
1636: 7294 imp.
1639: 7295 imp.

Duisbrowghe. *See* Doesborch.

Duncan, Charles.
Bookseller in London, (1636) 1640–1646. [*Dict. 2*; DFM 2749.]
over against St. Botolph's Church near Aldersgate (F.3), 1640 (1881.5)
1640: 1881.5 f.

Dunne, Thomas.
Journeyman printer in London, (1579) 1585–1586 at least. Freed by H. Middleton on 8 Oct. 1579 (Arber II.681). One of those accused in 1585 of pirating the ABC and Catechism and 'Lily's Grammar' (Arber II.790–3, 794–800) and found printing the latter text again in Middlesex, 1586 (*Reg. B*: 21). The only extant item in which he is named as one of the printers was produced in R. Robinson's house in Fetter Lane (V.7). [Not in *Dict. 1*.]
No separate address used.
1585: 1848.

Dunscomb (Duncomb), Robert.
Bookseller in London, (1626) 1637–1666. [*Dict. 2*; DFM 1465.]
in Lilypot Lane (G.6), 1638 (12039)
1638: 12039 f.

Dunstall, John.
Stationer in London, (1615) 1620. [*Dict. 1*; DFM 2769.]
No address known.
1620: 12516 ent.

Du Pré (De Pratis, Larcher), Jean.
Printer and bookseller in Paris, 1481–1504†. [Duff, *Century*; Renouard.]
1488: [15870?] (d?). **1499:** [15804]. **1500:** 16175 ab. **1504:** 16178 ab successoribus.

Durand, Zacharie.
Printer in Geneva, 1551–1571? (1578). [*Dict. 1*; Chaix 181–2; Bremme 154.]
1560: 16561a.5(*A*3). **1561:** 16563. **1566:** [16578]. **1571:** [16579–9.3?].

E

E., W.
Bookseller in London, 1608. Possibly a misprint for **Walter Dight**, who was the only Stationer of the time with a shop in Shoe Lane, but the devotional character of the text differs from Dight's usual items.
near Shoe Lane end in Holborn (V.3), 1608 (13545.5)
1608: 13545.5 sold.

East India Company.
Publisher in London, 1632.
No address used.
1632: 7450 f., 7450a f.

East, Lucretia.
Bookseller in London, 1609–1610 (1631?†: *C-B C*: 232–3). Widow of **Thomas East**. Published as the *assignee of* **W. Barley**. [*Dict. 1*, under husband.]
[her] house in Aldersgate Street near the gate (F.2), 1610 (4258)
1609: 21289 ass'd. **1610:** 4258 [f.].

East (Est, Este), Thomas.
Printer in London, (1565) 1567–1608†. Husband of **Lucretia East**. He shared printing material and most imprints with **Henry Middleton**, 1567–72. He succeeded to much of the printing material of **John Day 1**, c. 1585. For printing music he was successively the *assignee of* **W. Byrd**, 1588–94, of **T. Morley**, 1600–02, and of **W. Barley**, 1606–08. His printing material passed to his former apprentice, **Thomas Snodham**. [*Dict. 1*; *Library* 19 (1964): 1–10.]
in Fleet Street near to St. Dunstan's Church (W.9), 1567, 29 Mar. (11974, with H. Middleton)
?sold in Ivy Lane at the Black Horse (C.3), 1568 (4028, colophon, East for Middleton)
in Bread Street at the nether end (S.4), 1568, 6 Oct. (17250)
at London Wall (H.8), 1571–1575
dw. — by the $ Ship, 1571, 17 July (24722, with H. Middleton)
dw. — at the Black Horse, 1575 (11376)
(by) Paul's Wharf (R.8), 1577–1588
dw. between — and Baynard's Castle, 1577 (11758)
dw. by —, 1579 (17797)–1588 (4253)
in Aldersgate Street (F.2), 1589–1599? and until his death
dw. — at the Black Horse, 1589 (4256)–1594 (2488)
dw. — [no sign], 1597 (15010)
dw. — over against the George, 1599? (4254)
1565?–1608?: [7467.5?].
1567: 11974.
1568: 4028, 17250, 20956.
1569: 18949.
1570: 22415 (d?).
1571: 4395, 11445 per, 11477, 23641, 24722.
1572: 4055, 4655, 11445.5 per, 14724a.3, 14724a.7 (d).
1573: 7369, 19114, 21498.
1575: 745.5 (c), [2001(*A*)] (d?), 3376 (d), [6226?], [11287], 11376, [11386?] (c?), [11885] (d?), [12448], [16704.3(*A*3)] (d?), 24851.5 (c).
1576: [11641], 14484.3 (d), 19626–6.5, 21118 ent., 21360.
1577: 4367, 6787 per, [10251?], 11758–8.5, [13060?], 21756.
1578: 805 (d), [1416?], [3549?], 5158, 11844, [17051] (d), 18859 (d).
1579: 12469, 17053, 17797, 20182a.5, 24776.
1580: 1057 (d), 1301(*A*3) (c), 1584 (d?), [1968.3], 3086, 3425, 3551.5, [4404] (c), 7642, 10881, 11376.3 (c?), 13057.8, 16702 (d), 16708 (d), 17053.5, 17054, 17068, 17069, 17070, 18769, 18860 (d?), 21469, 24905.3.
1581: 3170, 4700, 13058, 17055, 17055.5, 17071, 17299, 23090, 23413–3.5.
1582: 439.17 ent., 719a–a.5, 805 ent., 808 (d), 1538, 3377 ent., 11860, [11863], 12538, 16806, 17072, 17251 (d?), 17301, 18808 ent., 18862 ent., 20956 ent., 23414 (d), 24723 ent.
1583: 4557, 14729, [15257?], 18866, 20173.
1584: 1261, 3425.5, 4700.5, 6131, 12262, 16653, 17072.5, [17300.5?] (d?), [24528?]
1585: 439.17 (c?), 1990 (c), 5415, 5448, 14654, 17056, 18648, 18862–2.5, [21084] (d).
1586: 11529a, 11531, 12423, 12447, 17073, 18864 (d?), 23091, 24723.
1587: 3377, 3426, [4058?], [13657], [13673], 17057, [18487?] (d), [20090], 21227 (note).
1588: 723, 4253, 4253.3, 4253.7, 4791, 7498 ap., 17074, 17122, 17166, 23895, 26094, 26094.5.
1589: 4246, 4247, 4256, 4256.5 (repeat), [4928?].
1590: 1083, 4336, [11272?], 17577, 25119, 25583.
1591: 1092 (d), 1263, 4248, 6220, 6221, 10698.
1592: 2482, 3427, [3845(*A*3)], 17578, 17579.5 (repeat).
1593: 566, [4250] (d?), 5248 ent., 18121.
1594: 2488, 3682.5 ent., [4249] (d?), 18127, 18284.
1595: 3683 ?ent., [4251] (d?), 4256.5 (d?), [8247.6?] (d), 18116, 18118, 18119, 21288.
1596: 1264, 1589 (d?), 3428, 4247 ent., 4248 ent., 4256 ent., 5286, 13199, 25119 ent., 26094 ent.
1597: 3632, 4032.5 (d), 15010, 23918 par, 23918.3(*A*) par, 25205, 26095.
1598: 439.18(*A*3) (c), 3378, 5260, 15265, 18129, 18865 (d?), 18867, 21133, 21134, 25203, 25619, 25619.3(*A*3) (repeat), 25619.5.
1599: 1093, 3682.5, 4254 (d?), 17579.5, 18861 (d?), 18863, 21288.3.
1600: 1265, [4249.5] (c), [4250.5] (c), 6234, 7095, [10180], 17997, 18117, 18128, 21288.3, 25206.
1601: 18130, 18130.5, [23037] (d?), 24637.

East, T. — *cont.*
1602: 3703, [6749.8?], 12571, 12571.5, 13013, 18122, 21288.5, 24638.
1603: [6967–7.5], [12988(*A*3)], 14939 sold, 15529, 21128, 21784 sold, [22024.3], 25205.
1604: 1586, 2514, 2515, 3069, [5882–2.5], 7460, 10157.5 (d?), 12324.5, 21433.5.
1605: 439.19 (c), 1265.5, 1590, 4243.5, 5287(*A*3) (c), [15107.7(*A*3)] (c), [15239], 19922, [21288.7] (c).
1605/06: [452.5?], [532.5?].
1606: 4644, 6268 (d), 6514 (note), 6622, 6750, 6954, 13587, 17685, 17690, 18123, 25318.
1606/07: [434.19], [532.6].
1607: [2522.3(*A*3)], 4244.5, 4701, 17686, 25319.
1607/08: [532.7].
1608: 772.7, 4168, [5937], 6040, [7145], [7467.5?] (c?), 11413–3.5, 23653, 25204, 25319.3, [25653.5], 26105.

1609: 7140.5–41 (post-dated?), 11413.7 (d/variant), 25619a alias Snodham.

Eastland, George.
Publisher of music in London, 1600. [*Library* 12 (1931): 365–80.]
his house near the Green Dragon and Sword in Fleet Street (W.2), 1600 (7095, in title)
1600: 7095.

Edderman, Francis.
Author? and publisher in Dublin, c. 1558?
No address known.
1558: 7481.7 [f.?] (c?).

Edgar, Eleazar.
Bookseller in London, (1597) 1600–1618. Many of his earliest imprints were sold: at the Swan in Paul's Churchyard (A.5), the shop of **Cuthbert Burby**, for whom Edgar may have been working. He often published jointly with others. [*Dict. 1*; *Loan Book*, 1598–1601.]
?at the Little Shop at the [Royal] Exchange (O.10), 1607 [14526.5?]
in Paul's Churchyard 1608–1612 at least
their shop — (A.2), 1608 (12662, with S. Macham, whose sign was the Bull Head)
their shops — (B), 1608 (12648a.5, with S. Macham)
shop — at the $ Windmill (B), 1609 (19053)–1611 (12663.4, with A. Garbrand); 1610 (53, has 'their shop')
— at the $ Jonas (B), 1612 (21016)
1603: 14365 ent., 14410 ent.
1604: 19747.5 f., 19747.7 f.
1605: 1900 ent., 6498 ent.
1606: 17488 ent., 19748 f.
1607: 1692 ent., [14526.5?] f., 17996 ent., 18592 ent., 19735.4 f.
1608: 12648 f., 12648a f., 12648a.5 f., 12661.7 f., 12662–2.5 f., 12663.2 f., 17888 ent.
1609: 7469 f., 7470 f., 12693.7 f., 12694 f., 12696 ent., 12697 f., 12712 f., 19053 f., 19649 (note), 23138 f., 23594 f., 24148 f., 24395 f.
1610: 53 f., 12649 ent., 12649a f., 13005a.5 f., 17942 f.
1611: 10221 f., 12663.4 f.
1612: 21016 f.
1613: 19650 (note), 24397 ass'd.
1616: 11292.5 f.
1618: 19651 (note).

Edmonds, Alexander, *pseud.*
Printer in 'Basel', 1554. ? = S. Mierdman and J. Gheylliaert, Emden.
1554: 19890 (d).

Edmonds, Godfrey. *See* Emerson.

Edmonds, Walter.
Bookseller in London, (1635) 1638–1641. [*Dict. 2*; DFM 2726.]
at the Crown near Ludgate (Q.3), 1638 (12453)–1639 (25955)
1638: 12453 sold. **1639:** 20509.3 f., 25955 f.

Note: There are three Stationers before 1641 named **George Edwards:** the two below whose identities were conflated in *Dict. 1* and are tentatively separated here, and the third freed by translation in 1634 (DFM 1244), of whom nothing further is definitely known. One of them is in the *Poor Book*, 1655–66.

Edwards, George 1.
Bookseller and bookbinder? in London, (1608) 1616–1640 at least. Married the widow of his former master, Manasses Blond/Bloome. Acquired the shop and several copyrights of **Ralph Mab**, which afterwards passed to George 1's stepson, **Jacob Bloome**. George 1 appears to have lost interest in publishing books after 1618, assigning one of his copyrights to John Beale in 1619 and others to George Hodges in 1621 (Arber III.649, IV.54). In the latter year he was chosen to the livery of the Stat. Co. and remained active in its affairs (*C-B C*: 135, etc.). After 1622 he is usually called 'Mr. Edwards' in Stat. Co. records. [DFM 797; *Loan Book*, 1618–21.]
shop in Paul's Churchyard at the Greyhound (B), 1617 (7615.5)–1618 (25166.3)
1616: 7408.5 ent.
1617: 7615.5 f., 18057–7a f., 25166 f.
1618: 13772.5 f., 25166.3 f.
1619: 7615.7 ass'd.
1621: 13773 ass'd.

Edwards, George 2.
Bookseller in London, (1622) 1624–1647† (E&R I.282–3). Transferred from the Haberdashers' to the Stat. Co. on 3 June 1622 (*C-B C*: 147, 154). In 1624 several works of Henry Smith were entered to George Edwards junior (Arber IV.118), and later editions of these and most of the other items below bear the address in Green Arbour. In Stat. Co. records George 2 is usually called 'Mr. Geo. Edwards' or 'George Edwards'.
in Green Arbour without Newgate (D.4), 1628 (25322), 1630 (25324)
his house in the [Little] Old Bailey in Green Arbour at the Angel (D.4), 1629 (22798)–1640 (25317)
1624: 22760 f.
1626: 22711 f.
1628: 25322 f., 25322.7 f.
1629: 22781 f., 22798 f.
1630: 7311 f., 7337 f., 22711.5 f., 25323–4 f.
1632: 22476 ent., 22500 ent., 22711.7 f., 22782 f.
1633: 4223 sold, 22799 f., 25167 sold.
1634: 17654 f., 17654a.5 f.
1636: 13319 ent.
1637: 7337.5 f., 22677.5 f., 22800–0.5 f., 22783 f., 25314 f., 25316 f.
1638: 22478 f., 22500–0.5 f., 22505 f., 25168 sold.
1639: 22476 f., 22500–0.5 f., 22506 f.
1640: 22712 f., 25317–7.3 f.

Eede, Philip.
Bookseller? in London, 1578. Not a member of the Stat. Co. His only imprint was issued jointly with **Toby Cooke** and sold at the latter's shop: at the Tiger's Head in Paul's Churchyard (A.2), 1578 (21064.5, colophon). [Not in *Dict. 1*.]
No separate address used.
1578: 21064.5 f.

Egenolff, Christian.
Printer in Strassburg, 1528–1530, and in Frankfurt am Main, 1530–1555† with a second press in Marburg, 1538–1543. [Benzing 120, 324, 442.]
1554: [16571] (d?).

Egenolff, Paul.
Printer in Marburg, 1586–1621 (1625†). [Benzing 324–5.]
1610: [22868] (d).

Eglesfield, Francis.
Bookseller in London, (1636) 1637–1688? His second address is that of his former masters, **James** and **Anne Boler**. [*Dict. 2*; DFM 815; *Loan Book*, 1659–62, 1671–74; Globe 213–14.]
?at the Marigold in Goldsmith's Row in Cheapside (N.5), 1637 [1224?]

Eglesfield, F. —*cont.*
at the Marigold in Paul's Churchyard (B), 1637 (21663a.5)–1640 (24870) at least
1637: [1224?] sold, 1231 ent., 21663a.5 f.
1638: 160.5 f., 1225 f., 11201 f., 12454 f., 13048 f., 13734 f., 20227 f., 22435 sold, 22501 f.
1639: 189 f., 1227 f., 19581 f., 20542 f., 22449 ent., 25025 sold.
1640: 1226 f., 1226.3–.7 f., 1228 f., 1230 f., 7545 f., 12394 f., 12875.3(*A3*) sold, 20130 ap., 22453 f., 24870–0.5 f., 25101 sold.

Egmont, Frederick.
Dutchman and bookseller in London, 1493–1511?†. Many of his publications were in partnership with **Gerardus Barrevelt**. An action at law noted by Duff in his own copy of *Century* now in Cambridge University Library, establishes that Egmont was born in the province of Holland, had a shop in Paul's Churchyard (B), and was dead before the end of Michaelmas Term (approx. 25 Nov.) 1511 (Common Pleas, roll 997.m.384a). The bookseller in Paris, 1517–1527, may have been a son. [Duff, *Century*.]
No address used.
1493: 15856 imp.
1494: [15797] (d), 15874 imp., 16167 imp., 16168 [f.].
1495: [15801 f.], [15801.5 f.].
1499: 20434 exp.

Eld (Ellde), George.
Printer in London, (1600) 1604–1624†. Married the widow of **Richard Read;** took **Miles Flesher** as partner in 1617 (*C-B C*: 98) though Eld's name continues to appear alone in many imprints and is usually the only one supplied in square brackets. In 1604 he printed as the *assignee of* **R. Lever and W. Elmhurst**. In 1619 **Ralph Blower** printed in Eld's shop. [*Dict. 1*; *Poor Book* (on behalf of Richard Reynolds), 1617.]
his house in Fleet Lane at the $ Printer's Press (D.2), 1607 (24149)–1615 (1078, has 'dw.')
dw. in Little Britain (F.4), 1621 (17525); no other use noted
1604: 343, 350, [414.7?], 5672 (d?), 5672.5 (d?), [5782], [5782.5], 7690.5, [12062], [14429.5], [14430], [14430.5], [14756], [18151], [18895(*A3*)], [21161?], 22420, 25760–1, 26014.
1605: 1900, 3996, 4521, [4963], [4970–1], [4972], [4973], [6200], [6201], 6239, 13951, 14782, 17384.5, [22543–3a], [23337] (d), 25633, 26002.
1606: 3775, 4103–3.3, 4339 (d?), 5101, 5693.5–.7, 6262, [11160], 12407.5 (d?), [13472?], 13868.7, 15453.7, 17685.5, 17775.5, 17832, 19309, 19310, 20142, 20342, 20444, 20941.7, 20997, [21085], 21511, [23030.3], [24422].
1607: [945.7?], 1014, 1466–6a, 3775.3, [4340], [5884.5], [6162], [6417], 6539, [10377.5], 12135, [12555–5.5?], [12995.5] (forged, c?), [14688], [14783], 17487, [17838], [17839], 19295, 21531, 22244, [22434] (d), 24104, 24149, [24996–6.5], [24996a], 25263, [25662].
1608: 1201 (d), [1812.7] (d?), 4026, 4968, [6161.5], [6485], 6613, 6613.5, 7183, 7185, 7187–7.5, [12165], 12374, [13882(*A3*)] (forged, d), [14761] (d), [17651], 17896–6a, [17907] (d), [18786(*A3*)], 19822, [23440], 24150, [25262] (d), [25634].
1609: 3050.3, 5696, [6647], 6971, [7186], 7188, 12375, [12686] (d?), 13838, 15485, 17430, 18153, [21424], 22331–2, 22353–3a, 23820, [25634a].
1610: 916, 3220–0.5, 4083 ent., 5868, 6524, 6614, [6619], [6945.2], [10424–5], [10857.7], 11526, [13529], 13839, [14528], [14689], 20290, 22171, 23289, 24603, [24832–2a].
1611: 1502, 1502a, 3050.5, 3198–8.5, [5810], 6614.5, [6619.5], [6648], [6945.4], [11425], [12166], 12569, 17431, [18296], 22245, [22277], 24119, [24649].
1612: 6368, [7373.6], 11207, 13158, 14030, 14672, [14691], [17660], 17661, 17747, [17818], 21526, [22655.5] (d), 23411, 25992.
1613: 3013.5, 4981 (d), 6339, 11200, 11309(*A3*) by & sold, [12686.3] (d?), [12857.2], [12857.4], [13539–9a], 13572, 14516, 14697, [18234?], [18287?], [18368], 19057.3, 19823, [20304.5] (forged), [23780] (false), 25181, 25891, 25891.5, 25892, 25893 (forged), 25894, 25949, 26092.
1614: [413], [809], [1125], 1594, 3830–0.3, [5056], [5452], [6616], [7160.5], [12630], [14068], [14068.3?], 17662, [18611], 18906, [19120], 21028, [21406?] (d?), [23813.3] (d?), 26121a.7.
1615: 1077–8, 7281, 7626 (d), 7626.5 (d), [10783], 12214 ent., [12547.7] (c?), 17622, 18254, [18598.5] (c), [18919.3] (d), [18921.7] (d), 20028.5 (c), 20584, 21096.5, [23741], 24005.5, 25660.

Eld, G. — *cont.*
1616: [1196] (forged), [1813], [3643], [3644], [3658?], 3792, 5977, 6475.5, 14997.3, 17381 (d?), 17897, 18314.5, [18920] (d?), 20330, [21087.7?] (d), 21527, [24059.5] (d), [24757] (d), [25598].
1617: 5528, 6343, 6615, [6620], [6993], 7495, 14997.7, [16864a.5] (c), 17064, [17911–1a], 18788, [21315.4] (c), 21510, [22406.5] (c), [23765] (d?), 24089 (c).
1618: 1079 ent., 1412, 3050.7, [3062.3] (d?), 3641, [4103.5], 4650, [5056.5], 5371.5, 5529, [6183], [6525], [8571?] (d), 10260, 10851–2, 11707, 13815, [17148–8.3], [18236?], [18319], [20860.5], 23736, 23737, 24415a, 25387.
1619: 146 ap., 3574, 3664.2, 4651, 5371.7, [11040(*A3*) in shop of], 11106, 11107, 11107.3, 13816, [14898.5] (d), 14899.1(*A3*) (d?), 16836, 17623, [18237?], 18496, 18801, [19057.7], 20494, 24997.5(*A3*).
1620: 917, [1328.3] (c), 1404 ap., 3207 (d?), 3989 ap., 4652, [4877.7] (c), 4953, [10816], 13525, [14537], 18515, 21402, [23751] (false), 23770.
1621: 1549, 5371.9, 5986, 6934 ent., 7155 (d), 10261, [10690], [11107.5] (d?), 14491, 15193a, 17525, 17886, [18237.5?], 22137.7, [23737.5?], 23796, 26098–8.3.
1622: 288, 1079, [1390], 1909.3 ex off., [3062.5] (c?), 3830.5, 4022, 4653, 5372, [5767], [7268.5] (d), 7611, 10330, 10689, 11546, 14998, 17401–2, 18507.72, [—.79?], [—.89?], 19072.5, 19321, 21444, [22565.5], 23738, 23738.5, 23771, 23813, 25104.
1623: 197.3 (c), 288–9, 537, [589], 1000, 1549.5, 3416, [5764.5] (c), 7681.3, 10315, [10601], [11090], 11180, [11366], 12092–2.2, 13025.4, [13333], [13338], [16865.7] (c), [18507.92?], [—.94?], [—.95?], [—.96?], [—.97], [—.98], [—.100], [—.106?], [—.110?], [—.114?], [—.115?], [—.133?], [19125.5] (d), 20961.5, [21124], 21806.5(*A*), [22568], [23009], [23495.5], 23789.7, 24091, 24648, 25103, [25210].
1624: 997.5, 998, [3718], 5374, [6272], [7007?], 10861, [13574?], [18507.141?], [—.145?], [—.148?], [—.149?], 22246–6.5, 23496, 24702.5.

Eliot's Court Press.
Syndicate of printers whose house was in Eliot's Court in the Little Old Bailey (D.1). They succeeded to the printing material of **Henry Bynneman**. The list below of partners before 1641 differs from that in *Library* 2: 179–81, 184, in omitting **George** and **Elizabeth Purslowe**, who had a separate establishment at the east end of Christ Church (C.1). Whether these two were partners or only shared in the printing of various unidentified items needs further study. [*Library* 2 (1922): 175–84, 3 (1923): 194–209.]

Ninian Newton, 1584–1586
John Jackson, 1584–1596
Edmund Bollifant, *alias* **Carpenter**, 1584–1602
Arnold Hatfield, 1584–1612
Melchisidec Bradwood, 1602–1618
Edward Griffin 1, 1613–1621
John Haviland, 1621–1638
Anne Griffin, (1621) 1633–1643
Edward Griffin 2, 1637–1652

STC items with any of these names appearing in the imprint are listed *only* under the relevant name, as are entries in the SR. Also under the name are items of which another variant bears the name. Finally, the publications of the press at Eton are listed *only* under Bradwood because he is considered to be the sole partner in charge there.
Listed below are items without any partner's name in the imprint. For most of these [*Eliot's Court Press*] has been supplied in STC. Items below distinguished by an asterisk (*) have had a partner's name supplied in STC but are indexed *only* here and not under the partner's name because such attributions during the course of revising STC were not made on any systematic basis.
1513: 1703 (d/error)
1584: 19427.
1585: 19357.5*? 20054.3? (c), 25364a? 25364b.
1586: 1192.5, 1193? 4430 (false), 4503, 13198.
1587: 4058? 4431 (false), 4504.
1588: 1199–200? 4024, 7300 (d), 20571.
1589: 12914(*A3*) (false, d), 15234, 15244, 18099, 19955.5.
1590: 534(*A3*)? (false, d), 4505, 15698, 15699, 19955.5, 23280? 24689–9.5.
1591: 7301? (d), 10748, 19953, 19956, 23472.

Eliot's Court Press — *cont.*
1592: 3552, 5577–8.2, 19957.7, 23334 (d).
1593: 4785, 18635, 19958, 21611.
1594: 4506, 15235, 19957, 21748.
1595: 18289 (d), 19954, 21441.7.
1596: 12779.5.
1598: 5259.5*? 20628.
1599: 20055?
1600: 4507, 15481.
1601: 51, 6439, 11543, 11937, 15240.
1602: 3610, 3611, 15236, 20625.
1604: 10068, 12059, 14355?
1605: 2518(*A*3), 16692, 17043, 17047, 18173.5, 18174–4a, 21322, 23337 (d).
1606: 48, 11188, 14586, 16897, 18855 (d/repeat?), 20008, 21759, 24031.
1607: 3222.5–.7, 4508, 4966, 5300.7, 6532? 6629*, 7176, 10192.5, 11620, 14414, 17595, 17659? 20152*, 23354, 24770.
1608: 4967, 5051 (d?), 5982, 14524.7, 18455.3, 18855 (d?).
1609: 50.5, 1408, 1408.3 (false), 4469.5, 14405, 14579, 15491, 23284.5, 25934*.
1610: 4509, 9220 (d), 18183, 24833.
1611: 4424, 4742, 13906a (note), 14580.
1612: 4740, 9229–30, 9232, 19021(*A*3)?
1613: 1703 (d), 1704, 2546, 10192.6, 13392*, 18347, 22977, 24551.
1614: 3618, 4745, 4964, 4977, 5604, 7335, 11699, 13583–3.5 (d), 14989.5, 14990, 18904*.
1615: 2554, 4216*, 5052 (d?), 7319, 10802? 11938, 12654, 14416, 14838*, 19076.5 (c), 19561, 22574.
1616: 161–1.5 (d), 8536 (d), 8537 (d), 8545 (d?), 10804? 11292.5, 11941, 12972, 21871a.7*, 25598, 25605 (false).
1617: 708, 3585* (false), 4804, 11431–1a, 17199, 17944(*A*3), 25166*.
1618: 140.5 (note), 624.5*, 6434*, 8577 (d), 16773*, 25166.3*.
1619: 5321.5, 10161–1.5, 10379, 14983, 14984, 14984.5, 19812.5 (d?).
1620: 2572*? 3957, 4917, 5053 (d?), 10293, 12029, 12599, 13374, 13375, 13375.5, 14050, 20286.3* (false), 21673.5.
1621: 1941, 2572*? 3584(*A*3) (d), 5712.5, 10162, 17732, 20286.7* (false), 25155.
1622: 288, 1390, 1898? 7376 (d?), 10240, 11329.7 (false), 11329.8 (false), 14322? 17440–0a, 18029* (d), 18507.80? —.83? —.85? —.86? —.87? —.90?, 18913(*A*3), 20769, 25716.
1623: 289, 533*, 3572* (note), 3787*, 5461–1.2, 5636.2, 5636.4, 5636.6, 11329.9 (false), 11330 (false), 12357, 13613, 15439, 18507.93? —.101? —.105? —.107? —.108? —.111, —.113? —.117? —.119, —.120, —.121? —.122? —.126? 20171.
1624: 6621, 10192.4, 11330.2 (false), 11330.3 (false), 11564.7, 13628 (d?), 15560 (note), 18507.348? 19768.5–9.3, 21479*, 23699, 24542, 24959, 25855–6.
1625: 1115*, 1174*, 1174.5*, 1458, 4325.5 (c), 7345.5, 9245, 9245.2, 9245.4, 10241, 11511.7 (c), 12870.5 (note), 13324, 15082.5 (c), 17308, 19553.5 (c), 25723, 25723a.
1626: 1116*, 1946?, 3185, 3573* (note), 3652, 3698.5, 4527, 4892.5, 10737*, 12244, 16854.3* [in shop of] (d?), 19328*, 20764*? 21766, 23390*, 23559, 23563, 23567, 23568, 23569, 24033*, 26083?
1627: 1947, 2604*, 4893, 16774, 18484*, 19431–1.5, 19562.5, 21186.7? 21835*, 23390.5*, 23563.
1628: 172.8, 2604*, 7746.2, 12824, 12853, 18674, 25322–2.3, 25322.7–2a.
1629: 2614*, 10924, 12198.5 (d), 13222, 23391*, 24058.
1629/30: 9250.3.
1630: 1813.5, 5133–3.3*? 5388, 6977*, 7233*? 12830*, 12851*, 12998, 14900(*A*3)? (c), 17711*, 19544.5 (c), 20270, 20270.5, 21220*, 23391.5*, 25312*, 25323–4.
1631: 588, 589.5*, 3651, 5289, 7676*, 14673, 6479, 6527, 11299? 22423, 22732*.
1632: 6978*, 13383.5, 23392.5*, 25684*.
1633: 22365* (c?), 24819, 25684*, 25687*.
1634: 184*, 7310*? 24059.
1635: 22553, 25822*?
1636: 3555.7* (c), 3653*.
1637: 5047*, 5048*, 5049.5*, 5050*, 5050.2*, 5050.5*, 5356*? 6453, 14065*, 22747*, 23245, 25724, 25725, 25725.2.
1638: 11121 (note), 21094?
1639: 552*, 22485.
1640: 10779 (note), 14861a.5, 22892.5*? (d), 25317.

Ellis, Thomas.
Bookbinder? and bookseller in London, (1615) 1617 (cf. DFM 1261)–1634. [*Dict. 1*; DFM 2265.]
at the Christopher in Paul's Churchyard (B), 1629 (6170.5)
his house in the Old Change (N.8), 1634 (25852.3)
1629: 6170.5 f. **1634:** 25852.3 sold.

Elmhurst, William. *See* Lever, R.

Elzevir, Bonaventura and Abraham.
Booksellers and printers (from 1625) in Leiden, 1620–1652†. [*Dict. 1*; Gruys; Briels, 267, 274–6.]
1633: [2798], [2798.5], [2813.3]. **1636:** [22175.3].

Emerson (Emondson, Edmonds), Godfrey.
Bookseller in London, (1613) 1622–1647. [*Dict. 2*; DFM 2343; *Loan Book*, 1634–37.]
their shop at the Crane in Paul's Churchyard (A.3), 1622 (14301, with N. Vavasour)
shop in Little Britain without Aldersgate (F.4), 1634 (12566)–1640 (20491, omits 'without Aldersgate') at least; variation: 1638 (17668, has 'near' Aldersgate)
1622: 14301 f.
1623: 14305 f.
1630: 6982 f., 21446 sumpt.
1631: 688 f., 4992–3 sold.
1632: 17666 f.
1634: 765.5 f., 12566 f., 12959 ent., 17293–3.5 f.
1636: 16892.7 imp.
1637: 1350 sold, 23857.7 sold, 23858 f.
1638: 17668 f., 21072a sumpt., 23943.9(*A*3) sumpt.
1639: [12402] ven., 12402a ven., 23944 sumpt.
1640: 20491 f., [21476?] ven.

Emery, Jasper.
Bookseller in London, 1629–1641. His first shop was among those marked for removal from the great North door of Paul's, c. 1632 (*Library* 3 (1902): 267–8). [*Dict. 2*; DFM 2324.]
in Paul's Churchyard, 1630–1631, 1635–1640 at least
shop — at the Fleur-de-lis (A.2), 1630 (25369)–1631 (7242, omits 'shop')
at the Eagle and Child — near (next) Watling Street (A.7), 1635 (21343)–1640 (13638, has 'shop'); variation: omits 'near … Street, 1636 (13352), 1639 (5942)
1630: [11691.5?] f., 25369 f. **1631:** 7242 f. **1635:** 21343 f. **1636:** 5942 (d/error?), 13352 sold. **1638:** 3583a f. **1639:** 5942 sold, 20000 f. **1640:** 13638 f., 20884 f.

Emilie, Dionis (Emsley, Dennis).
Stationer in London, (1564) 1566–1575. [*Dict. 1*.]
No address used.
1570: 7679 f. **1575:** 10306.5 f. (d).

Emlos, Theophyll, *pseud.*
Printer at 'Basel', 1540? The surname is that of the ostensible author, Thomas Solme, spelled backwards. = Catherine van Ruremund, Antwerp. [Duff, *Century*.]
1540: 22897 (d?).

Emondson. *See* Emerson.

Emperour. *See* Keyser.

Enderby, Samuel.
Bookseller in London, 1637–1645. Before his freedom in 1638 he began working in and succeeded to one of the shops of his former masters, **Joan 2** and **Nathaniel Newbery**. [*Dict. 2*; DFM 2025; *Loan Book*, 1639–40.]
at the Star in Pope's Head Alley (O.11), 1637 (1627)–1640 (20681) at least; called 'his shop' in 1639 (21639)
1637: 1627 sold, 1633 sold, 5852.5 sold, 5853 sold.
1639: 21639 f.
1640: 10636 f., 20681 f., 21190.5 f.

Endhoven, C. *See* Ruremund.

Endovianus, Melchior.
Printer? in Antwerp, 1557–1558. Probably related to **C. van Ruremund**, whose types appear in his only imprint. [Rouzet.]
1558: 16249.5 ap.

England (Ingland), Nicholas.
Stationer in London, 1557–1568. Used an address very infrequently; in 1566 (5059, colophon) a book is said to be: printed in Paul's Churchyard by N. England, but the tp gives this address to the actual printer, J. Cawood, and has no separate address for England. [Duff, *Century*.]
dw. in Paul's Churchyard (B), 1558 (293)
dw. in Paternoster Row (C.7), 1562 (296)
1558: 293 f., 6463.2 imp., 7599 f. (d), 15483.5 imp.
1560: 300 f., 17164 f., 19848–8a f.
1561: 4938.5 pro.
1562: 296 f., 305 f., 17164 f., 24800 f.
1563: 301 f.
1566: 5059 f. (d).
1567: 3180 f., 19124 f.

English (Englysshe), Michael.
Alderman of London between 1520–1531 (1539†.) and patron. [A. B. Beaven, *The Aldermen of London*, 1908–13, II.24.]
No address used.
1532, before: 864 at request of.

English Churches in the Netherlands. *See* Index 4A.

English College Press.
Roman Catholic press set up at the English College at St. Omer, 1608–1642, and after 1671. It was largely under the supervision of John Wilson, a secular priest. [*Library* 10 (1919): 179–90, 223–42; 7 (1927): 303–20.]
All items below have this press's imprint supplied in square brackets.
1511: 8448 (d/error).
1608: 3604.5–05, 19408, 24140.5–41, 25771.
1609: 15362, 15362.5, 19412, 25002.
1610: 1699, 14628, 16644, 19000, 24992.
1611: 8448 (d), 13122.5, 13840, 18999.
1612: 1700, 1702, 6383, 10914, 11111, 11538.5, 19409, 23938.
1613: 11021, 11022, 11114, 18334, 23987, 24993.
1614: 1699.5, 3941, 10912, 10916, 11023, 13996, 13996a, 13997, 13997a, 13997b, 15519, 24994, 26045.
1615: 16225, 18657, 25003.
1616: 6384, 20967, 22948, 22963, 25069, 25290.7, 26049.
1617: 269, 1650 (false), 11116, 18000, 23529, 23532.
1618: 715, 1838, 10675, 13998, 15517, 16877, 19938, 21676.
1619: 1707, 4955, 5475, 11490, 14527, 18657.5, 20483, 26046.
1620: 910, 983, 3134, 10809, 11110.7 (false), 11315, 19354.6, 22964, 23531, 23989.
1621: 741, 942.5, 1838.5, 5349.8 (d), 5350, 5350.4, 5350.7, 11020, 13576, 15518, 15524, 18327, 18658.5, 18659, 22812.
1622: 1839, 5350, 5476, 5742.7, 13577, 17658, 18443, 18658, 19354.7, 19937.5, 20968, 25773, 26046.5.
1623: 575, 1023.5, 1839, 16226, 7000, 10910.4, 10916.5, 11118, 14945.5, 16877.5, 18001, 18305, 18660, 24732, 26044, 26048.
1624: 7454, 14475, 14570.3, 16878, 17542.7, 18306, 18661, 20487, 23528, 23989.5, 25070.5, 25289 (false).
1625: 578, 6777.7, 10910.7–11, 10916.5, 11539, 17276.8, 22872.5.
1626: 4872 (false), 10911, 10916.5, 11033, 11540, 15117.3, 20585.5, 21316 (false).
1627: 4912 (false), 17533, 21148–9, 22811.
1628: 11540 (d?).
1629: 21023 (false).
1630: 14502, 16922a, 21023a (false), 22370.
1631: 4873 (false), 5576, 15117.7.
1632: 3073.3 (false), 4625, 4871 (false), 10677, 16161.5, 17181 (false), 20492 (false), 24140 (false).
1633: 577, 4264, 10676, 19354.9.
1634: 580, 6798.3, 13035, 16922a.7, 17093, 18333, 18984, 24735 (false), 25778.
1635: 4625.5, 18331, 21102.
1636: 4263.5.
1637: 4263.7, 13469, 25070.
1638: 11110, 25775, 25780.
1639: 11115, 11117, 15117, 16162.3.
1640: 576, 20200.7 (d?), 20308, 25772. 14050, 21673.5.

English Nation. *See* Index 4A.

English Secret Press.
Indexed below are only those items for which [*English secret press*] or a similar imprint has been supplied in STC in square brackets. Groups of items with typographic similarities mentioned only in notes, e.g. 10814, 24514(*A*3), are not included. Items for which a printer or place has been supplied, with or without a query, are indexed only under those names. Cross-references have been given to a few of the more prominent names.

—Recusant.
Any one of a number of secret recusant presses operating in England after 1557 not more specifically identified in STC. = secret presses 4–11, 13–14, and 'unassigned' in A&R, which should be consulted for better defined groups of works.
The other secret A&R presses have been indexed, or included in indexes, as follows:

1. **John Charlewood**, 1587?–1588?
2. **Fr. Garnet's first press**, 1592–1596?
3. **Fr. Garnet's second press**, 1596–1599?
12. **Birchley Hall Press**, 1615–1621

See also **William Carter**, **'Greenstreet House' Press**, **Rhiwledyn Press**, **Peter Smith**, **Thackwell**, and **Richard Verstegan**.
1595: 14627 (false), 17265 (c), 18326 (false), 22949.5.
1596: 17265.5 (d), 17265/7(*A*3) (d?), 17278.6 (c), 26038.8 (false).
1597: 14566.5 (c?).
1598: 17538 (false), 22126.3 (false).
1599: 3800 (false), 17266 (false), 19395 (false), 24627a.2.
1600: 6181.7 (false), 13470–0.3 (false), 21307.7 (d?), 22949.5 (d), 26038.4 (false), 26038.5 (false).
1601: 3893 (false), 6385.5? (d?), 19396 (false).
1602: 742 (false), 17505 (false, d?).
1603: 3519, 3897, 3897.5 (false), 4282 (d), 4291 (c), 17267.5 (d?), 22969.3 (d?).
1604: 1834 (false, d?), 3096, 3604, 4008 (d?), 4835 (false), 6777 (false), 10432.7 (false), 14432, 17267 (d), 19940.5 (false), 26038.6 (false, d?).
1605: 535.5 (c), 1835.5 (false), 3942.5, 4868.3 (false), 10915.5, 20602, 22947, 24627a.3 (false), 24714, 25972.6 (d?).
1606: 18188 (d).
1607: 3097, 20448.
1608: 3098, 17197.5.
1609: 18185a (d?).
1611: 4007 (d?).
1614: 4623.5, 17505.5 (d?).
1615: 4621, 4624, 23988.
1616: 1840 (false), 5827 (false), 17275.5, 26047.
1617: 16097.
1618: 5860 (false), 7072.5 (false).
1619: 7072.6 (false).
1623: 7072.7 (false), 13033.2, 18330 (false).
1626: 3073.5 (false).
1628: 660 (false).
1630: 5351, 17277 (false), 25779 (false).
1636: 918, 17548, 25777.
1640: 17506.7 (d?).

—Puritan.
In addition to the item indexed below *see* also: **John Day 1**, 1553–1554 (various pseudonyms), **John Stroud**, 1572–1574? (Cartwright press), **Robert Waldegrave**, 1587–1589 and **John Hodgkins**, 1589 (Marprelate press), and **William Jones 3**, 1604–1608.
1575: 25433?

—Other.
The following items printed in 75–77 mm. roman and italic are all works in defence of John Darrell, the exorcist. It seems more likely that they were printed somewhere in England rather than across the Channel, but the query indicates uncertainty about the location of this press.
1600: 6283? 6288? **1602:** 6284? 6285?

English Stock. *See* Stationers' Co.

Erondell. *See* Arundell.

Erve, Egidius (Gillis) van der (Gellius Ctematius).
Refugee in London, 1550–1551 at least, and printer in Emden, 1554–1566. In partnership in the latter city with **Nicholas Hill** until 1557 although Hill's name is often not supplied in STC imprints. [Duff, *Century*; Benzing 104; *Library* 12 (1932): 336–52.]
1554: [15069] (false), [16571] (d?), [16571a] (false), [17863.5] (false), [18309.5?] (false).
1555: [673] (c), [10024] (d?), [18797] (false), [21046], [21799.2] (d?), [21854] (d), [24356] (d?), [24361] (false), [26140] (false).
1556: [921?] (d?), [5999] (d?), [6152], [15693] (false), 16574, [17864] (d?), [18798] (false), [19892] (d?), [21047.3], [21047.7?], [25009] (false).
1563: [16572], [16572.1(*A*3)].
1566: [1040], [3964], [4065], [6079] (d), [10389] (d), [10390] (d), [10391] (d).

Esch (Ash), Hendrik van.
Printer in Dordrecht, 1632–1677. [*Dict. 1*; Gruys; Briels 280.]
1639: 19099.

Est, Este. *See* East.

Estienne (Stephanus), Antoine *pseud.*
Printer in 'Paris', 1625 = R. Young; 1634 = T. Harper. For the genuine Paris printer, 1614–1674†, two of whose imprints are reprinted below, *see* Lottin 2: 62.
1625: 4609. **1634:** 19203.3 (note).

Estienne, Paul.
Printer in Geneva, 1598?–1637? The version of the 'Noli altum sapere' device, McK. 351, appears in only the one STC item below, though other versions (McK. 310–11, 348–50) were in use in London. The item has been queried for Paul but may possibly belong to another Estienne press.
1615: [14272?].

Estienne, Robert 1, *pseud.*
Printer in 'Paris', 1549. = M. Bradwood, 1602. For the genuine printer, in Paris 1526–1550, and in Geneva 1550–1559† *see* Renouard; Chaix 184, n.3; Elizabeth Armstrong, *Robert Estienne*, 1986.
1549: 13787a.5 ex off.

Estienne, Robert 2.
Printer in Paris, 1555–1569; was in Geneva 1569–1570†. [Renouard; Bremme 159–60.]
1567–68: 22856.5 ex off.

Evans, Dorothy.
Patron of music in London, 1613?
No address used.
1613: 4251.5 f. (d?).

Ewen, Thomas.
Bookseller in Marlborough, 1634.
No address used.
1634: 3129.8(*A*3) sold.

F

Faber, Baptista, *pseud.*
Printer in 'Augusta' (Strassburg), 1620–1621. = J. Bill; also used by Eliot's Court Press.
1620: 14050.5 ap., 20286.3 ap.
1621: 20286.7 ap.

Faber, Theophilus, *pseud.*
Printer in 'Albionopolis', 1613–1614. = Ed. Allde; also used by J. Beale; also appears in a forged foreign item.
1613: 25602 ex off. **1614:** 25602.5 ex off., 25605.5 ap.

Fairbeard (Fayerbeard), George.
Book and printseller in London, (1617) 1618–1629, and apparently a rolling-press printer. Undoubtedly husband of **Sarah Fairbeard.** [*Dict. 1*; DFM 851; Globe 214.]

Fairbeard, G. — *cont.*
shop in Pope's Head Alley at the George near the Royal Exchange (O.11), 1618 (22527a)
shop at the North side (door) of the (Royal) Exchange (O.2), 1619 (16689)–1629 (6017.7); variation: has North 'entrance into', 1619 (16836)
1618: [4319?] sold, [4320?] sold, 22527 ent., 22527a f.
1619: 16689 f., 16836 f.
1620: 3417 f., 4953 f.
1621: 24871 ent.
1622: 3419 f., 3702.5 f.
1625: 6017.5 f.
1629: 6017.7 f., 6019.5 f.

Fairbeard, Sarah.
Bookseller in London, 1636. Undoubtedly widow of **George Fairbeard**. [*Dict. 2* (erroneous date).]
at the North door of the Royal Exchange (O.2), 1636 (26112.7)
1636: 26112.7 sold.

Fakes. *See* Faques.

Falconer, Falkner. *See* Faulkner.

Faques, M. *See* Fawkes.

Faques (Fakes, Fawkes, Fax), Richard.
Printer and bookseller in London, 1507?–1531. Succeeded to the printing material of **William Faques** and was probably related to him. Between 1523 and 1530 he had two shops. [Duff, *Century*.]
in Paul's Churchyard, 1509–1513? 1521?–1530 at least
— at the Maiden's Head (A.4), 1509 (12512)–1510? (9357.9 (Beale S111), has 'dw.')
dw. — [no sign] (B), 1512 (17973)–1513? (11088.5)
dw. — at the ABC (B), 1521? (15932)–1530 (17542, omits 'dw.')
dw. within the Austin Friars (J.1), c. 1515 (6933.5)
dw. in Durham rents (X.9), 1523 (22610)–1530 (17542, adds 'without Temple Bar')
1507: [14077c.44(*A*3)?] (d).
1509: [7762] (d), 12512.
1510: 9357.9 (d?), [14077c.41(*A*3)] (c), 19918(*A*3) (d?).
1511: 16189 sumpt.
1512: 17973 (c).
1513: 11088.5 (d?), [22593] (d).
1515: 6933.5 (c).
1518: [14077c.42] (d?), [—.92] (d).
1519: 14077c.93 per (d), —.94 per (d).
1520: 14077c.95 per (d).
1521: 15932 pro (d?).
1522: 19305.5 (d?).
1523: 14550 (c), 22610.
1524/25: 390.
1525: [321] (d?), 1696 (c).
1526: [14077c.80] (d).
1527: 14077c.79 per (d).
1528: [768] (c).
1530: 3273.3 (c), 14546.7 (d?), 17542.
1531: 14077c.34 per (d).

Faques, William.
Printer in London, 1504–1507? Was the first to style himself **King's Printer**, though the phrase seems at that date to have meant 'printer at the King's command' and appears in the Latin Psalter (16257) as well as the proclamation (7760.4) and statutes (9357). His printing material passed to **Richard Faques**, who was undoubtedly related to him. [Duff, *Century*.]
within St. Helen's (J.3), 1504 (7760.4, 9357)
in Abchurch Lane (O.13), c. 1505 (23907.3)
1504: 7760.4 (d), 9357 (d?), 16257, [23153.6] (d?).
1505: [7016.3] (c), [18846] (d?), [23154.7] (c), 23907.3 (c).
1507: [14077c.44(*A*3)?] (d).

Farmer, John.
Musician and author, b. 1570?–1601. [*New Grove*.]
[his] house in Broad Street near the Royal Exchange (O.3), 1591 (10698)
1591: 10698 sold.

Farnaby, Thomas.
Schoolmaster, classical scholar, and author, b. 1575?–1647†. [*DNB.*]
No address used.
1626: 10706.4 (note). **1640:** 10706 ex assig.

Faulkner (Falconer, Falkner), Francis.
Bookseller in London, 1605–1615 at least, and in Southwark, 1624–1648. [*Dict. 2*; DFM 2779.]
London, in New Fish Street (T.4)
'his' shop — near to Eastcheap, 1607 (19541, with H. Bell)
shop — under St. Margaret's Church, 1614 (22839)–1615 (13909)
Southwark, dw. near St. Margaret's Hill, 1624 (22848.7)–1636 (12292) at least
1607: 19541 f.
1614: 22839 sold.
1615: 13909 f.
1624: 22848.7 f., 22853 f.
1626: 3676 f., 7496 f.
1627: 17587 f., 19543 f.
1628: 22840.5 sold.
1629: 12290 f.
1631: 3719 f., 7497 f.
1632: 12291 f., 17618 f.
1635: 12291.5 f. (c), 14685 sold.
1636: 12292 f.

Favo, Jathrous, *Heirs of, pseud.*
Printer in 'Rhotomagi' (Rouen), 1585. = Rhiwledyn Press, Wales, 1587. The pseudonym may refer to a priest in a cave. [*BS* 2 (1953): 48.]
1585: 21077 ap.

Fawcet (Forcet), Thomas.
Printer in London, (1621) 1625–1655 (Wing P 2858) at least. In partnership with **Bernard Alsop** from 1625. Through 1640 Fawcet's name never appears alone in an imprint, and the last item indexed below does not belong in STC. An asterisk (*) has been used to indicate those imprints supplied in STC in square brackets from which Fawcet's name has been inadvertently omitted. [*Dict. 2*; DFM 4; *?Loan Book*, 1645–48; *Poor Book*, 1652–54; *St. Giles*, 1626–39.]
dw. in Grub Street near the lower pump (I.6), 1625 (18760)–1640 (11167.50); both with B. Alsop
1625: 3722, 18760.
1626: 7434.4, 11467, [13579–9.3], [13579.5], [13585.5], [14526] (false), 15370.5, [16753], [16845?], [18903*], [19803], 21324, 23473, 24711.
1627: 1203, 1550, 5318, [5864], 14375, 18516, 20165, 20504 (note), 20946.9 (d), [20947], 23561, 23718, 24705, 26022.
1628: 1820 (note), [4157], [4157.5], [4471], 5370, [7749], [8893.3], [8893.5], 17862, 21496.3, 21708.5, 21709.
1629: [4136], [5911], [6017.7], [6019.5], [6983], [12997] (forged, d?), 13901, 17642, [18040] (false), 18200, [21718(*A*3)?] (false), [23507.5], 24965.
1630: 1021, 1688, 3372, 3733, [4500–0.5], [4581], [5714], 5805.5, 6492.5, 6980, 11174, 11346, [12687*?], 14360, [18917], [19807.3] (d), [19966], 19968, [20164], [20164a], [20164a.5], 22444, [24258], [23725].
1631: 4, 194, 194.1, 383, 3565, 3565.5, 6529, 10189, 11202, [11288.5?], 13272, 13538.5, [16847.5], [17181.9(*A*3)] (d), 17645, 18329, 20168, [20865], 22387, [23340], 23682.
1632: 3538, 3538.5, 3663, 11346.3, 11346.5 (d/error), 11977, 13268, 13334, 13538.5, 14360.5, [17202] (d?), 18507.262, 20221.7, 21420, 21550.5, [23340], [23520], 23682.5.
1633: 5906, 6104, 7032, 7032a, 10687, 11167, 12537, 13505, 14269, [20684], 22436, 22462, 24712, [25375a.10] (d).
1634: 10276.7, 11170, 17333, 17670, [21164], 21604, 23447, [23682.7] (d?).
1635: 4998, [5714.8], [6273.3], 10199, 11221, 12417, 12418, 12584, [13372.5], [13736*], 19825.5(*A*3) (c), 21604.
1636: [3536], [6453.5], 10199.5, 11175, 11346.5 (d), [12937], 15382, [17284*], [20780], [21640], [22181], 22391.6.
1637: 3997.5–98, [4297] (d), [5490], [18691], [19131], 19160, [22232], 23119, 23119.5.
1638: 6042, 10200, 10666, 20384, 21551.

Fawcet, T. — *cont.*
1639: 3712, 4986, 10201, 18098, [18507.297*?], [—.304?], 19164, 21643.5, [22132].
1639/40: [18507.317?].
1640: 1554.5, 3712.3(*A*), 5716.5, 5874, 6043, 7334, [7750], 11167.5, 11657.5, [12735], 12885, 14066, 14754 (note), 17328, [18507.325?], [—.328?], [—.329?], [—.332?], [—.335?], 20383, 21551, [22641], [22641.5], [23809.5], [25247.5*] (note).
1640/41: [10009].
1642: 19968a (d?).

Fawkes, Michael.
Printer in London, 1534?–1535. In 1535 he was in partnership for one book with **Robert Copland** at the latter's house: at the Rose Garland in Fleet Street (W.3). [Duff, *Century*.]
No separate address used.
1534: [3275] (d?), 3276 (d?), [14077c.11B?] (d?).
1535: 13608.

Fawkes, R. *See* Faques.

Fawne, Luke.
Bookseller in London, (1629) 1631–1666†. His first shop was marked for removal, c. 1632, to make way for renovations to St. Paul's (*Library* 3 (1902): 267–8). In 1635 he became a partner of **Robert Dawlman**, and in 1639 was joined by **Samuel Gellibrand.** [*Dict. 2*; DFM 1956; *Loan Book* (as surety), 1659.]
shop at the great North door of Paul's (A.2), 1631 (6548.8)–1633 (6549, has 'dw.', omits 'great')
at the Brazen Serpent in Paul's Churchyard (A.3), 1635 (21710, with R. Dawlman)–1640 (7431, with S. Gellibrand)
1631: 6548.8 f., 13992 f., 15539 f., 23251 f.
1633: 6549 sold.
1635: 13726.2 f., 21710 f., 22483 f., 23821 f.
1636: 7429 f., 12037 f., 12037.5 f., 12040 f., 12041 f., 12041.3 f., 12041.5 f., 13726.3 f., 21707 f., 21710.3 f.
1637: 12043a f., 13726.6 f., 23584 f.
1638: 4127 f., 7430 f., 12038 f., 12042 f., 12044 f., 12044.5 f., 13726.8 f., 22484 f.
1639: 4128 f., 11763 f., 15082 sumpt., 23590–0.5 f.
1640: 4129 f., 7414 f., 7431 f., 22151 f.

Fax. *See* Faques.

Fayerbeard. *See* Fairbeard.

Featherstone. *See* Fetherstone.

Feild. *See* Field.

Feirabendius. *See* Feyerabend.

Fenricus, M. [i.e. Master?]
Probably a schoolmaster, 1627. A Nicholas Fenricus of the ward of Faringdon within is on the subsidy rolls for April 1625 (*Returns* III.293). [*Dict. 1.*]
[his] house next to the Greyhound Tavern in the Blackfriars (Q.6), 1627 (23897)
1627: 23897 sold.

Ferbrand (Firebrand, Forbrand), William.
Bookseller in London, (1597) 1598–1609†. [*Dict. 1.*]
Lothbury (H.9), 1598–1599
shop in — at the hither end of Coleman Street, 1598 (20700)
at the corner of Coleman Street near —, 1599 (20122)
shop at the Crown near Guildhall gate (H.5), 1600 (16799)–1601 (17547, has 'dw.'); variation: Crown over against the Maiden's Head near Guildhall, 1600 (775.5)
in Pope's Head Palace (Alley (O.11)), 1602–1609
shop — Alley over against the tavern door, near the Royal Exchange, 1602 (16754)–1607 (21395, omits 'near ... Exchange)
— Palace, near the Royal Exchange, 1607 (5933.3)
shop — Palace right over against the tavern door, 1608 (21386); mention of the tavern door is perhaps carried over from 21395, the source of some of the poems
shop — Palace, 1609 (21387)

Ferbrand, W. — *cont.*
1598: 20700 f.
1599: 20121.5 f., 20122 f.
1600: 772.3 f., 775.5 f., 5044 f., 6381 f., 16799 f., 21392.7 f., 21393 f., 21393.5 f.
1601: 14291 ent., 17547 f.
1602: 12197 f., 16754 f.
1603: 21364 f.
1603/04: 414.3 f., 414.7 f.
1604: 14291 f., 21398 f., 21399 f.
1605: 772.5 f., 11497 f., 13857 f., 13857.5 f., 18454.7 f. (d), 21394 f. (d?).
1606: 5916 f., 5926.5 ent., 6514 f., 6552 f., 6553 f.
1607: 3218.7 f., 3471 f., 5926.7 f., 5933 ent., 5933.3 f., 21395 f.
1608: 12488.5 f., 21386 f.
1609: 5919.5 f., 5920 ass'd, 5937.3 ass'd, 21378 f., 21386 ass'd, 21387 f.

Ferrand, David.
Printer in Rouen, 1615–1660. [Lepreux III/1: 173–6.]
1636: 6832.62.

Ferrebouc, Jacques.
Printer and bookseller in Paris, 1492–1530. [Duff, *Century*; Renouard.]
1509: 16160 pro. **1510:** [15809]. **1511:** 16189 sumpt. **1515:** [15811.5].

Fetherstone (Featherstone), Henry.
Bookseller in London, (1607) 1608–1647†. Although he essentially ceased publishing in 1626, when management of the shop possibly began to be shared with **Robert Martin** and/or **George Thomason**, both former apprentices of his, Fetherstone continued active in Stat. Co. affairs and was at least for a while an importer of books from Italy (10837). [*Dict. 2*; DFM 380.]
shop in Paul's Churchyard at the Rose (A.3), 1609 (10561)–1626 (20508).
[sold] in officina Fetherstoniana, 1628 (10837, in title)
1608: 7395 ent.
1609: 6625.7 f., 7373.5 f., 10561 f., 26055 f.
1610: [894] sold, 7528 f., 10562 f., 11526 f.
1611: 12739 f., 17840 f.
1612: 697 f., 7528.5 f., 13937 f.
1613: 20505 f., 25699 sold.
1614: 20506 f., 25699a sold.
1615: 1077 f., 4180.5 f., 7529 f., 7530 f., 11599 f., 12526 f., 17526–7 f., 18480 f.
1616: 1658 sold, 4099 f., 5811–2, 6625.8 f., 7395 f., 12683 f., 21843 f.
1617: 1024 f., 7396 f., 7531 f., 7531a f., 12705 ent., 12705a f., 12705b f., 12707 f., 20507 f., 23827 f.
1618: 1207 f., 11597 f., 12656 f., 12710.7 f., 13716 f., 21834 ent., 23828 f.
1619: 1208 ent., 20503 f., 20614 pro, 21834a f.
1620: 7532 f., 12657.5 f., 12674 f., 12708 f.
1621: 7533 f., 12684 f., 12708 f., 20509 ent., 26098–8.3 f.
1622: 755(*A*) ent., 1079 f., 10330 f., 19679 f.
1623: [10838? f.] (d), 12646 ent., 12646a [f.], 12657a ent., 12658 f., 12665 ent., 12665.3 f., 12714.5 ent., 13025.4 f., 20502 sold.
1624: 12635 ass'd.
1625: 7533.5 f., 20509 f.
1626: 20508–8.5 f., 21338 ass'd, 25985 ass'd.
1628: 10331 f., 10837 ven. (in title).

Feyerabend (Feirabend), Sigmund.
Bookseller in Frankfurt am Main, 1560–1590. [*Dict. 1*; Benzing, *Verleger*.]
1590: 12786 ven.

Fickaert (Ficardus), Frans.
Printer in Antwerp, 1610–1654.
1616: 1431.25 ap.

Field (Feild), Nathaniel.
Bookseller in London, (1611) 1624–1630 (cf. DFM 1318). [*Dict. 1*; DFM 2471.]
shop in the Blackfriars (Q.6), 1625 (10862)
1624: 10861.5 f. **1625:** 10862 f. **1628:** 10863 f., 13516.

Field (del Campo), Richard.
Printer in London, (1587) 1588–1624†. Married **Jacqueline Vautrollier**, the widow of **Thomas Vautrollier**. On Field's death the printing material passed to his former apprentice, **George Miller**. The items indexed below for 1625 are possibly post-dated. [*Dict. 1*; Morgan; *Library* 12 (1931): 1–39.]
dw. in the Blackfriars near Ludgate (Q.6), 1589 (20519.5)–1602 (6449); sometimes omits 'near Ludgate', 1602 (6743.5)
dw. in Wood Street (H.17), 1613 (6765)–1624 (19893a.3, has 'Great' Wood Street); his sign of the Splayed-Eagle is mentioned in his will but has not been noted in an imprint.
1588: 15412 f., 15413 f., 15413.5 f., [15414.2 f.], [15414.3 f.], [15414.4 f.], [21948.3–.7?] (repeat, d?).
1589: 2785 ent., 3056–6.5, [3057?], 3908.4, [7597], [7597.3], [7597.6], 10653, 11289, 11291, [11371.5], 11372, 13098.7, 13098.8, 13102.5, 13586.5, 14379 ent., 18100.5, 18134.7 ent., 18885, 18952, 20519–9.5.
1590: 1509, [3361.3?], 3850 (note), 5265, 5471a, 6290, 6291, 6762.5, 6849, 13114, 13248.8 ex off., 16890, 20803, [22680], 23633a.5 (c).
1591: 746, 1094, [3363.7] (d), 5315.3, 6741.5, [15061], 15510.5, 17752, 17842.7, 22660, [22681], 22685.5(*A*), 22686, 22705, 22716, 23256, 23652.3.
1592: 2988, 3985 ex off., 4170, [6125], 6448.5 (c), 6545.5, 10865, [12286], [13787–7a], 15241.3, 17176.2, 17648, 18245, 20054.7, 22775.3, [24479], 24653.
1593: [1034], [1352(*A*)], 4166, [4202], 5399.8, [6445.3] (c), 6742, [7574], 13588, 14938, 15015.3–16 in aed., 15230 ent., 16697, [18135] (d), 19498, 19977, [21508], 22354, 22719, 22775.7, [25018.5].
1594: 1054, 2810a.3–.5, 2989, 4990, 5266.9 ex off., 7373.4, [12220], 12459 ent., 13253, [13595], 15701, 17648.3, 18929, 19948, 22345, 22355, 22776, 22777, [24485] (d), 24767.5, 24768.
1595: [1335.3] (c), 4372.5 in aed., 4544 ex off., 14595, 17176.3, 17280, 17648.7, 19949 ex off., 20067–7.5, 20083.7, [22356?] (d?), [24484], [24768.5].
1596: 1510, 2959 en casa, [3057.3], 4374, 4391.5 en casa, 5309.6, 5472, 5481, 12771.5 (d), 12772, [12773.5] (d), [12773.7] (d), 12779, 12779.5, 13701, [15318], 19952, 20804, 22357, 22779 (false?), [23082], [23086], [24483], 24540.
1597: 4426 en casa, 6743, [7263], 7527.9, 16696, [19761], 20083.9, [23626], [24482], 24607 (note).
1598: [1381], [1500], 3928, 11847, 19557.7, [19838], 21670, [22541], 22780, [24627a.6].
1599: 1041.3, 2810a.7, [6054], [6351], 6355–5.2, 6355.4, 6763, 11834, 11849.5, [11866.5], 11867, 12459, 13120, 16970 ent., 17281, 19741 en casa, [22554], 22780.5, [24487], 24580 en casa.
1600: 34–4.5, 366, 1312.3, 2991, 5309.7, 15451, 17176.4, [18139], [22855], [23708], 24578.3 en casa, 24769.5.
1601: [1025.3?], 1055, 1511, 2787.7 ex off., [4771.7], [5119], 5181, 5309.8, 6382, [11412], 17226a, 17227, [21821.2(*A*3)], [22855], [22984.4(*A*3)], [23864], [25125].
1602: 4165a, 4178.5, 4543, [5557], [5736], [5795], 6356, 6449, 6468, 6743.5, [7102], 15449, 16970, 18835, 20071, 23410, [25123].
1603: [1338], [3667], [4786], [5320], [6125.3], 6547, 6595.7, [6911.7], 11851, [12988], [13239.5], 13243, 14353, 17225, 19960 ap., 20068–8b, [21432], [21659], [23866], [25672].
1604: 337, 346, 738, [1111], [1112], [4710], 5267.4 ex off., 6764, [7490–0.3, headnote: 1b, 2i,ii)], [12057], [12750], [13419], 14385.5, [14386], [14391], [16786.3(*A*3)] (d?), 17176.5, 19731, 19747.5, 19747.7, [21434], [21660], [23465], 24035, [25704].
1605: [855], 2704 (note), 12554, 13948.7–49, 13950, 19853, [20600], [21408], [24639] (d), [25864].
1606: [2521.3], [2521.6], [3958–9], [3961], [5397], 6014, [10137.3], [15229.7(*A*3)] (d?), [13790a–b], [18175.5], 18185, [23469], [23470], 24587.
1607: [49], 747, [2524], [2525], 4013, [4179.5], 6744, [10553], 10574, 20069 ent.
1608: [2527], [2527.7], 6596, [13791–1.5], 17281.3, [19957.3], [21317], 23290, [24263.3], [25394], [26009].
1609: [2530.3], [2531], [3103], 6745, 6751, [12644.5], 17176.6, [18176], [18181].
1610: 1512, [2535.5], [5474], [5659], 6450 (c), [7339], [13246], 15452 (false), [18177], 20069, [21751], [25395].
1611: [3067], 3361.7, [4868.7], [6039.5], 12550, [13218], [13634] (d?), [13792–2a], [21751], 23871, [25596] (false).
1612: [2542], [2544.2], [2544.3], [4787], 5309.9, 5310, [5833], 6752, 11847.5, 12055, 14889, [18058], [19810], 20069, 22374, 23028,

Field, R. — *cont.*
24026, [24229.5], [24596], [25076], [25396], [25597] (false).
1613: 35, [45], [2546.5(*A*)], [6197], 6765, [17239.7], [17281.5], [18059], [21686], [24791.7].
1614: [5469], 13636 (d?), [13793–3a], 15230, [15237], 15470 ent., 16683, 16916.7, 16919, 17176.7, 21825, [25390].
1615: 6548, 6753, 7529, 11197.5 ent., 13637 (d?), 13909, 14890, 16976, 17995, [21726], [22646], 25392.
1616: [2556], [2556.5], 5310.2, 6436, 6745.5, [8541.3] (d), [13624] (d?), 16973, 21618, 25397.
1617: 1513, [24792], [2558], [2558.3], [2559.5], 3925, 4236.1, [5064], [11132], 13476, 14467–7.5, 17238.5, [18952.4], [20763.7], 25380.
1618: [245], [2561], [2561.3], 5310.5, 5400 ent., 6974, 12460, 16883, [17282], [18179], 22391.
1619: 1649, [2565], 4236.8, 6607, 6754, [7411], [7412], 7620, 10575, 10716, 14088–8.5, 15528, 16879 ent., 21221.5.
1620: [2571], [3363.8?] (d), 4220, 6603.5, 6603.7, 6604, 7313, [7413], [7426], 7431.5, [13794–4a], [18952.5], 19443 ent., 22121, [22965], 23673, 24818, 25999.
1621: [3571], [3616], 5387.5, 6599, 17176.8, [21727], 22389, 24074.
1622: 1851.5, 3767, 4220.5, 5842, 6603, 6605, 6975, 7358, 16843, 25241.
1623: 5470, 6599.3 (d?), 6754.4, 7314, [7620.5], 7621, 15311, 16844, 21504.5, 22390.
1624: 1514, [2586], 4220a, 4502, [6269] (d), 17754, [17995.5], 19768.5 (note), 19893a.5.

1625: 6548.4, 12887a, 15684, 23599.

Finch, Robert.
Stationer in London, 1595–1603†. From at least 1598 he lived in the parish of St. Giles, Cripplegate (I.4). [*Dict. 1*; *St. Giles*, 1598–1603.]
No address survives.
1595: 17090 ent.

Finlason, Thomas.
Printer in Edinburgh, 1602–1628†. Acquired the printing material of **Robert Smyth** and **Robert Waldegrave**. In 1612 he became **King's Printer in Scotland**. He was succeeded by his heirs and then by the Edinburgh press of **Robert Young**. [*Dict. 1.*]
at Nidrie's Wynd head, 1604 (6512); no later use noted
1604: 5783, 6512, 13948.5, 14390.7.
1606: 21960.3.
1607: 22564, 25659.
1609: 5959, 11596, 12168, 22624, 22626, 24515.5.
1610: 7487.8, 15665, [15680].
1611: 14851, 21892, 21894, 21894.5.
1612: 7487.9, 13946, 13947, 14848, 21555.18, 21895, 21896.
1613: 7487.10.
1614: 7487.11, 14853, 14858, 14859, 21555.23 (d).
1617: 11713, 15368, 15369, 15371, 15373, 21555.28, —.30, 21897, [21898] (d).
1618: 140, 573, [21899] (d).
1619: 21965.5 (d).
1620: 698a, 16605, 21966 (d), 21967 (d), 21968 (d).
1621: 21900, 21901.
1622: 16842, 22567.
1623: 5742.8, 22567, 25243.
1624: 22567.
1625: [21901.2] (d), [21901.4] (d), 21969 (d).
1626: 21970.
1627: 3444, 21971 (d), 21972 (d), 21973 (d), 21974 (d).
1628: 21975 (d), 21975.5 (d), 21976 (d), 21977 (d), 21978 (d), 21979 (d), 21980 (d), 21981 (d), 21982 (d).

Finlason, Thomas, *Heirs of.*
Printers in Edinburgh, 1628–1631. Successors to Finlason's appointment as **King's Printer in Scotland**. [*Dict. 1.*]
No address noted.
1628: 21983 (d).
1629: 13955, 21984 (d), 21987 (d), 21987.5.
1630: 21901.6, [21901.8] (d), [21988] (d), [21988.5] (d).
1631: [21989] (d).

Firebrand. *See* Ferbrand.

Fisher, Benjamin.
Bookseller in London, 1622–1637. Apprentice of **Thomas Man 1**, whose shop Fisher seems to have managed until 1625 and with whose widow and sons he continued to work closely. [*Dict. 1*; DFM 1910; ?*Poor Book*, (widow) 1639.]
at the Talbot in Paternoster Row (C.7), 1622 (217)–1625 (4497)
at the Talbot in Aldersgate Street (F.2), 1626 (22784)–1636 (679, has 'shop'); variations: has 'dw.', 1631 (194); has 'without Aldersgate' for 'in ... Street', 1627 (20165), 1634 (13373)
1622: 213 f., 217 f.
1623: 3886 ent., 3890 ent., 11062 f., [11062a] sold, 17858 f., 17861 f., 20163 f., 20163.5 f., 20171 f., 21222 sold, 25298 f.
1624: 4220a f., 4236.2 f., 5389 f., 11998 ent., 12720 f., 17361 f., 17859 f., 17860 f., 18507.346 f. (d), —.347 f. (d), 22877.2 sold.
1625: 1025.7 sold, 4236.9 ent., 4497 f., 11989 f., 20205.5 f.
1626: 4500 ent., 4709 ent., 22784 f.
1627: [5864 f.], 14375 f., 20165 f., 20946.9 f. (d), 20947 f., 22785 f.
1628: 4236.3 ass'd, 4236.9 ass'd, 4471 f., 17862 f., 20947.3 f., 21496.3 f.
1629: 3771.7 ent., 5289 ent., 5764 ent., 6977 ent., 6983 f., 12822 ent., 12830 ent., 12851 ent., 20947.7 f., 21220 ent., 21223 ent., 22732 ent., 23656 ent., 24819 ent., 25312 ent., 25321 ent.
1630: 4500–0.5 f., 20164 f., 20164a f., 20164a.5 f.
1631: 194–4.1 f., 17341 ent., 17716 f., 20168 f., 20948 f.
1632: 156 f., 156.3 f., 156.7 f., 7031 f., 10530–1 f., 20641.5–42 f., 20642.5 f., 20950 f.
1633: 156a f., 1166 with permission, 6789 f., 7032 f., 7032a f., 11692.7 f., 17715 f., 20643–3.5 f., 20644 f., 20951 f., 22122 f.
1634: 12816 f., 13373 f., 17333 f., 25321 f.
1635: 4501 f., 6979 [f.], 12816 f., 13372.5 f., 17719 f., 17947 ent., 20162 f., 23656 ent., 25313 [f.].
1636: 156a.5 f., 679 f., 3536 f., 5764 f., 7344 f., 20162 f., 20646 f., 20652 f., 22786 f., 25238 [f.].
1637: 6625 [f.], 22734 [f.], 24498–8.5 [f.].

Fisher, Thomas.
Bookseller in London, 1600–1602. Freed as a Draper on 8 Nov. 1596 by Richard Smith; transferred to the Stat. Co. in 1600. His 1602 items were shared with **Matthew Lownes** and sold in the latter's shop: in St. Dunstan's Churchyard (W.9). [*Dict. 1.*]
shop at the White Hart in Fleet Street (W.2), 1600 (22302)
1600: 3678 f., 22302 f. **1602:** 17473 f., 17474 f.

Fisher, William.
Stationer in London, 1604–1622 at least. He took various apprentices between these dates (cf. DFM 1334–9). [*Dict. 1.*]
No address survives.
1622: 7376 ent.

Fitzer, William.
Freed by Thomas Man 1 in London, 1624; bookseller in Frankfurt am Main, 1625–1638, and in Heidelberg, 1649–1671. [DFM 1909; Benzing, *Verleger*; *Library* 24 (1944): 142–64.]
1628: 10933 f. **1629:** 20567.3 sumpt.

Fitzours, Edmund, *pseud.*
Printer in 'Roan' (Rouen), at the Three Lilies, 1632. = Society of Stationers, Dublin.
1632: 4326.5 (d).

Flasket, John.
Bookseller in London 1594–1616†. Freed as a Draper in the name of **John Wight** on 18 June 1593. Shared a shop and most imprints with **Paul Linley**, 1595–1599. Transferred to the Stat. Co. in 1600. [*Dict. 1*; *St. Giles*, 1616.]
at the great North door of St. Paul's (A.2), 1594 (13130a)
their shop in Paul's Churchyard at the Black Bear (B), 1595 (18428, with P. Linley)–1607 (25658, has 'his' shop; omits 'in P. C.')
1594: 13130a sold, 13138 sold (d).
1595: 18428 f.
1596: 23620 f.
1597: 6677 f., [6733.3 f.] (d), [17678] sold, [22993] sold, 23621 f.
1598: 16918 f.
1600: 3191 f., 3421 ent., 5457 ent., 13121 f., 16883.5 ent., 16919 ent., 17415 f., [18429] sold, 23895 ent., 24817 ent.
1601: 14071 f., 18417 f.

Flasket, J. — *cont.*
1602: 1695 f., 21455 f.
1603: 18017 f., 18018 f.
1604: 7215 f.
1606: 7225.5 f. (d?), 10655 f., 13001 sold, 17416 f., 22637 f.
1607: 312.5 ent., 7204 sold, 13002 f., 13201 ent., 17232.5 f., 25656 f., 25657 f., 25658 f., 25658.5 f., 25662 f.
1608: 5830 ass'd.

Flavius, Jean-Christophe.
Printer in Louvain, 1611–1617. Afterwards went to Cologne and by 1623 was in Coblenz, though if he printed in these cities it must have been as a journeyman. [Vincent 62; Ian Philip, *Dragon's Teeth: the Crown versus the Press in England in the XVII Century*, Honnold Library Society, Claremont, California, 1970.]
1615: [4744] (false).

Fleming, Richard.
Bookseller in London, (1616) 1617–1621? [*Dict. 1*; DFM 1775.]
shop at the great South door of Paul's on the right-hand side going up the steps (A.8), 1617 (22927)–1618 (22527)
shop at the Three Fleurs-de-lis in St. Paul's 'Alley' (i.e. Chain) near St. Gregory's Church (A.9), 1619 (18170, 25386); although the only two items with addresses this year both name Paul's Alley (north; A.1), this is undoubtedly an error for Paul's Chain (southwest; A.9)
1617: 22927 f. **1618:** 22527 f. **1619:** 10347 f., 14088 f., 18170 f., 25386 f. **1620:** 10276 f. **1621:** 10348 f. (d?).

Flesher (Fletcher), Miles.
Printer in London, (1611) 1617–1664†. Became a partner of **George Eld** until 1624, when Flesher succeeded to the printing house. Imprints supplied in square brackets in STC during the partnership may name one or the other or both partners but should not be regarded as definitive. Brother-in-law of **Richard Bishop** (Arber III.701). One of the *assignees of* **John More**. Acquired an interest in the office of **King's Printer** in 1634. [*Dict. 2*: 76; DFM 178.]
dw. in Little Britain (F.4), 1634 (12639.3); no other use noted
1618: 1079 ent.
1619: 146 ap., 4651, 17623 ent., 20494.
1620: 917, 1404 ent., 3989 ent., 4652.
1621: 5986, 6934 ent., 17525 ent., 23796 ent., 23813 ent.
1622: 1079, 5372, 19072.5 ent., 21444 ent.
1623: 3416, [19125.5] (d), 21806.5(*A*) ent., 24091, 25103.
1624: [4747], 4952.5 (d), 5374, 5961 ex off., 6161, [7007?], [7384.5] (d?), 10861.5, 12635–5b [by &] f., 15198 (d?), 15198.5, 22246, 22246.5, 23018 ?ent., 24702.5, [25160.7–1.5].
1625: [15.3] (c), [1182.7(*A*)] (c), [1487.5(*A*3)] (c), [4497], 4643.5, 5987 (d?), [6923] (c), [6927.5] (c), 10862, [12603], 12635–5b [by &] f., 12930, 13552, 14549 (c), [14711], [14928], [14928.5], [15470a.5] (c), 17373, 17729, [18294.5] (c), [18416(*A*3)], [18607], [18662.5] (c), [19969.6] (c), 20293, 21636, [22556] (c), [22919.1] (c), 23100, [23729], [23743], [23758?], 24909, [25051], 25182.5, [25940].
1626: 219, 1239, [3650], 4634–5, [6441], 6665, 7028, [10145.7] (d), 10349.5, [10368], [10734], 12659, 12713, [13499.5], 14526 (note), [16802.3] (d), [19328], [21850.7], 22138 (d?), [23497], [23813.5], [24609], 25026, [26083].
1627: 219, 3798, 4642, [6554.5], 7068, [10262], 12636–7.7, [12871.5] (c), 14319, 14933, 15110, [16802], 17603–3.5, 17605, [19223.5] (c), [19283] (c), 19850, [20567.7] (c), 21327, [21835], 22525.5–.7, 22526–6a, [23036.5] (d/error), [24295], 24987–7.5, 25027, 25031, 25033a.5, 25042.5, 25045.5, 25048.5, 25051.5, 25053.5, [25054.5] (d), [25056.5], [25217], [25229.7] (c).
1628: 1551, 1904 ent., 3354, 3690.7, [3691.9?], 5675 (d?), [6934], 11078, 11125, [11992], [11995], [12016?], 12636–7.7, [12640.3], 12692, [14297], 14318, 14318.5, [14510], [15037], 17605a, 18302.4(*A*3), [19267] (d), [21112a], [21252], [21757a], [22106], 24648 ent., 25031, [25763.5].
1629: [1107], 1551.3, [3219], [5144–4.3], [5911], 6122, 6198, 6771, [7070], [10138], [10731], [11079], [11547], 12693, 12709–9.5, [12709a], [13222], 14318, 15467, [15785], [16856.3] (c), 18302.4 (*A*3), [19219] (d?), [19235] (d?), 19452, [20134], [21012], 22503, [23588], [25102], 25183.
1630: [150.5] (c), [5104.5] (c), [5453?], [6056], [6209], [6906.5] (c), [12793], 14288 (c), [14476] (d), 14998.3, 15199, [15333], [15789], [17234] (c), [17604], [17606], [18104] (c), [18416.7] (c), [18485], [20186.3] (c), 20533, [20682–2a], 22138.3 (c), [22479], [22920.1] (c), [22920.5] (c), [23113], [23114], [25399], [25849], 26043.

Flesher, M. — *cont.*
1631: [5209.5], 5983, [6981], 10452 in aed., 12509 typis, [12547.9] (d?), [13320], 13548, 14312, 18043, 18302.5, 20549, [22480], 22481, 25166.7.
1632: [5143] (d?), [7417], 7427, [7437], 9329, [12326] (d), 12702, [12873], [12976], 13532, [13735], [13735.5], 15334, [17740], 18043, 18899c.5, 19453 (d?), [20321] (c), 20529, 20534, 22482, 24633, [25276].
1633: 561, 1372, [3692], 4839, 6122.4 (d), 7045, 7069, 7175, 10635.3, 10635.5, 11993, [12547] (d?), 12640.5, 12646a.5, 12689, 12702, 12704, [14902], 14998.7 (c), 15162.3 (d), 15200, 15786, 16461, 18182, 20530, 20534, 21151, 22507, [23525], [23525.1], 23823, 25167, 25866.
1634: 962, [1369], [3225], [3693], [4326?] (d), 6112, 10183, 11994, 12639–40, 12640.5–.7, 14313, [14689.3] (d?), [17611], [17612?], 17737, [19244] (d), [19247] (d), [19276] (d), 20136–6.7, 20535, 22507–7.5, [23525.6], [23525.7], 25182, 25183.5, [25869] (d?).
1635: 963, [3839.7] (c), [5608.5?] (c), [6122.5(*A*)] (d), [6210], 7046, 9330, [10967], 11107.7, [12092.8?] (d?), [12548] (c?), [12645–5a], 12647, [13726.2], [14040.3?] (c), 14309, [14721?], 17609, 17738, [18790.5] (c), 19453.3, 19570, 20830, 21710, 22138.5 (c), 22483, 22508, 22508.5, [23525.8], [23525.9], 23821, 23852, 24574, 24576.3, 25851–1.5.
1636: 1369.5, 1373, 4212, 6427, 6771.5, 7088, 7089, 9330, 10137.9, [10872], 12037, 12037.5, [12041?], [12041.3], [12041.5], [12937], 13536, [13726.3], 14310, 14999, [16615], [17637], 18034 per, 18427, 18900, [20206] (d), 20531, [20538], 20555, [20718], 20831, [20875] (d), 22509, 22510, 24576.5.
1637: 1080, [3694], 4212, 7090, 7551, 10184, 12033–3.5, 12043a, [13125], [13267], [13267.5], 13533, [13726.6], 17179, 17768, 17768.5, [19277] (d), 22504, 23584, 24691.
1638: 4127, [4163], 4806, 4945, [5139], 6122.7 (d), 6772, 12034–4.5, 12038, [12042], 12044, 12044.5, 12552, 13734, 17765, 17769, 18303, 20532, 20536–6.5, 20548, 22484, 22511, [22578], 23240, [23953], 25168, [25651].
1639: 4128, 7047, 10453 in aed., 12553 typis, 12646b, 13335 ent., 13505.5 (d?), 15082, 15787, [18507.315A?], 19210, 19250.7 (d), 19645, 20317 (d), 23590–0.5, 24575, 25184.
1640: [1371?], 2062.5 typis, 3476 typis, 4129, 4517.7 typis, 6064, 6068, 6074a.4 (d?), 6484, [7038], 9331, 9769.5 typis, 10511.5, 12031, 12648b, 15162.7, 18035–5a typis, 18036.5 typis, [22138.7] (c), [24576.7], 26084.
1640/41: 12675, [12676].
1646: [23036.5] (d?).

Flinton, George. *See* Fr. Parsons' Press.

Flower, Francis, *Assignees of.*
Partners in working Flower's patent as **Queen's Printer for Latin, Greek, and Hebrew** (*see* King's Printer for ...). The main work included in this patent was 'Lily's Grammar'. The assignees were C. Barker, G. Dewes, John Harrison 1, W. Norton, R. Watkins, and J. Wight. [*Dict. 1.*]
No address used.
1574: 15617, 16427 per assig.
1575: 15618 per assig.
1577: 15620.
1578: 15622.
1584: 15621.
1585: [15621.3], 15621.5 per assig., 15621.7.
1586: 15621.5 per assig., 15621.7.
1587–89: 15622.
1590: 15622.3, 23280.
1592: 15622.7 per assig.
1593: 15622.8(*A*3).
1594: 15622.7 per assig., 16428 per assig.
1596: 15623.

Foigny, Jean de.
Printer in Rheims, 1561–1587. [*Dict. 1*; Muller 94.]
1569: [15505] (false). **1580:** [14074] (d?). **1581:** [369?] (false), [888] (d?). **1582:** [369.5?], 2884, 17503. **1583:** 18537.

Foigny, Simon de.
Printer in Rheims, 1605–1642. [Lepreux II.264–5.]
1603: [14912]. **1608:** 14909.

Fonti-silvius, Guilielmus, *pseud.*
Printer in 'Cosmopolis' (i.e. London), 1615. = William Welwood, the author.
1615: 25240.

Forrest, Edward.
Bookseller in Oxford, 1625–1656 at least. His son, Edward 2, published his first imprint in 1646 (Madan II.538, 541). [*Dict. 2.*]
No address used.
1624: 716 f. (d/error).
1625: 19589 f., 24991 f.
1626: 4531–1.5 f., 24988 f.
1628: 7072 sold, 19576a sold.
1629: 19574 imp., 19577 f., 19590 f., 20618 f.
1630: 19571 f., 19941 f.
1631: 11101 imp., 11566 imp., 19942 f.
1632: 19587 f.
1633: 7152 f., 19575 pro.
1634: 716 f., 7158 sold, 10935 sold, 19943 f., 22652 imp.
1635: 717 f., 7153–3.3 f., 19570 f. (note), 19570.5 f.
1636: 10936 sold, 19944 f.
1637: 3630 ven., 4119 imp., 10937 f., 14268 sold, 21350 f., 25328.3–.5 imp.
1638: 17657 imp., 20667 f., 22653 pro, 25640 f., 25640.5 f.
1639: 1167 f., 12209 imp., 23993 f.
1640: 1167–7.5 f., 3627 imp., 10829 sold.

Fosbrooke, Nathaniel.
Bookseller in London, 1605–1629. Granted a pension by the Stat. Co. on 23 Feb. 1613 provided that he stay out of the city and not trouble it or the Co. (*C-B C*: 59). [*Dict. 1*; *Poor Book*, 1611–14, 1616.]
in Paul's Churchyard, 1605–1611
shop at the West door of Paul's (A.10), 1605 (18851)
shop — at the $ Helmet (A.2), 1606 (3636)–1607 (4340, with J. Wright 1)
at the Talbot at the West end of Paul's (A.10), 1610 (21315.2)
at the West end of Paul's near to the Bishop of London's gate (A.10), 1610 (13159)–1611 (13933a, has 'shop', West 'door', adds 'the Corner Shop')
shop at the upper end of the Old Bailey amongst the Sadlers (D.7), 1614 (15111.7)
shop in Pope's Head Alley near to Lombard Street (O.11), 1629 (11079)
1605: 8 f., 11923.5 imp., 13343 f., 18851 f., 18852 f., 25408 f.
1606: 889 ent., 3636 f., 4339 ent., 18850 f.
1607: 4340 f., 5884.5 f., 20028 ven.
1610: 12567 f., 13159 f., 13933 f., 15111.3 f., 15111.5 f., 21315.2 f., 21520.5 f.
1611: 13933a f.
1614: 11699 f., 15111.7 f.
1618: 7245 f.
1627: 16960 f.
1629: 11079 f.

Foster, Richard 1.
Bookseller in London, 1549. [Duff, *Century*.]
in Fleet Street at the Crown next unto the Whitefriars gate (W.7), 1549 (1290)
1549: 1290 f., [15445] sold.

Foster, Richard 2.
Bookseller in York, 1626.
near the Minster gate, 1626 (6441)
1626: 6441 sold.

Foüet, Jacques, *pseud.*
Printer in 'Rouen', 1619, 1623. = English secret press.
1619: 7072.6. **1623:** 7072.7.

Fowler, Francis, *pseud.*
Printer in 'Douai', 1600. = English secret press. For a genuine Francis Fowler, probably nephew to **John Fowler**, who may have inspired the pseudonym *see RH* 12 (1973): 70–8.
1600: 6181.7.

Fowler (Fouler), John.
English recusant printer in Louvain, 1565–1575, and in Antwerp, 1566, 1573–1579†. [*Dict. 1*; Rouzet.]
1565: [21694].
1566: 11333 ex off., 12760 ex off., 20082 ap., 20728.5 ex off., 20729 ex off., 21695 ap.
1567: 372 ap., 7063 ap., 12761 ap., 20725 ap., 21692 ap., 21696 ap., 23231 ap.
1568: 5035 ap., 12763 ap., 18889 ap., 21691 ap., [24625.5] (d).
1569: 20088 ap.
1570: 20130.5 ap.
1571: [15506] (false).
1572: [7601], [15503] (d).
1573: 18083 ap., [23617.5] (d).
1574: 3799 ap., 24626 ap.
1575: 14563.3 ap., 14563.5 ap., 14563.7 ap. (forged).
1576: 3800.5 pro, 11181 ap., 14563.5 ap.
1578: 17508 ap. (false).

Foxe, Francis, *pseud.*
Printer in 'Argentine' (Strassburg), 1530. = M. de Keyser, Antwerp.
1530: 2370, 13828.4.

Francis (François), Hercules.
Dutch refugee bookseller in Paris, 1554–1571, and in London, 1576?–1603†. Possibly identical with the bookseller in Rochelle, 1590–1597 (Muller 96). In London he lived in the parish of St. Benet Fink, Broad Street Ward (O.4). *See* also **Tres Viri**. [*Dict. 1*; Renouard; *Library* 14 (1959): 33–4.]
No address used.
1579: 17003.3 sumpt. **1580:** 2032.5 imp. **1603:** 19558 imp.

Franckton (Franke, Franton), John.
Printer in Dublin, 1600–1618 (1620† Royal Irish Academy, *Proceedings* 30-C (1912): 329 and pl. XXXVII). Obtained a patent as **King's Printer in Ireland** in 1604; in 1618 it was apparently voided and a new one granted to the **Stationers' Company**, London (*see* under their Irish Stock). [*Dict. 1*; *TBS* 8 (1907): 221–7; *Library* 2 (1922): 43–8; 7 (1927): 321–2.]
at the bridge foot, 1600 (14147)
dw. in St. Patrick's Street, 1603 (14151)
in Castle Street, 1617 (17836.3, colophon)
1600: 14147.
1601: 14147a.
1602: 2958, 14148, 21031.
1602/03: 14149, 14150.
1603: 14151.
1604/05: 14152, 14153, 14154.
1605: 14155.
1605/06: 14156.
1606: 4895.3, 14157, 14158.
1607: 14159, 14160.
1608: [7690.7] (d?), 14128.3, 14161, 16433, 18786(*A*3) (repeat of lost ed.).
1609: 14162 (d).
1611: 14163 (d).
1611/12: 443.5.
1612: 14164, 21487.5.
1613/14: 14165.
1615: 6361, 14133, 14260.
1617: 17836.3.
1618: 14168.

Franckton, John, *Deputies of.*
Printers in Dublin, 1619. = F. Kingston and possibly T. Downes. In 1618 Kingston went to Ireland on behalf of the Irish Stock of the **Stationers' Company** to set up the **Stationers' Society** in Dublin. [*C-B C*: xii–xiii.]
No address used.
1619: 17762 typis.

Frankenbergh (Vrankenbergh), Henry.
Bookseller in London, 1477–1486? at least. In 1482 he shared the lease of St. Mark's Alley, off St. Clement's Lane (O.14). [Duff, *Century*; *Book Collector* 4 (1955): 191–2.]
No address used.
1486: 26012 exp. (d?).

Freeman, Conrad, *pseud.*
Printer in 'Greenwich', 1554. = W. Rihel, Strassburg; subsequently also used by an English printer, possibly J. Day 1. [Duff, *Century*.]
1554: 16980, 16981.

Frellon, Jean.
Printer in Lyons, 1536–1568. [Duff, *Century*; Muller 35.]
1549: 3045.

French, Peter.
Stationer in London, 1555–1584†. [Duff, *Century*; *Dict. 1*.]
No address survives.
1580: 1591 ent.

Frere (Fryer), Daniel.
Bookseller in London, (1634) 1635–1649†. [*Dict. 2*; DFM 1332.]
shop without Aldersgate (F.1), 1635 (20277)
at the Red Bull in Little Britain (F.4), 1636 (22215.5)–1640 (20770); variations: 1636 (4941.5, has 'shop', omits 'Red'); 1637 (13269, has 'dw.')
1635: 15143 f., 15144 ent., 20237 sold, 20277 sold, 20282 sold, 21223.7 sold, 23122 f., 24145 f.
1636: 4941.5 f., 22215.5 f.
1637: 10838.5 sold, 13269 sold, 20647 f., 24145.3 f.
1638: 4945 f., 6316 sold, 7302 sold, 18845 ent.
1639: 4942 f.
1640: 4943 f., 6008 imp., 17328 f., 20770 f., 21011 f., 23302 f., 23305 imp., 23306 f., 23307–7.5 f., 23308.5 f., 23309 f., 23310 f., 23313 f.

Frethren, Thomas.
Bookseller in London, 1581. Not a member of the Stat. Co. [*Dict. 1*.]
on the Royal Exchange at the Half-Rose and Half-Sun, next to the North door (O.2), 1581 (26049.10)
1581: 26049.8 sold, 26049.10 sold.

Fries, Augustin.
Printer in Zurich, 1540–1549, and in Strassburg, 1550–1556. [Duff, *Century*; Benzing 447, 523.]
1547: 13741, 13745. **1549:** [13746] (d?).

Froschauer, Christoph 1.
Printer in Zurich, 1521–1564†. [Duff, *Century*; Benzing 522.]
1541: [5888] (d?). **1543:** [17793?]. **1550:** [361], 2079.8, 2090 (note), 2859.7. **1553:** 6832.32 ap.

Froschauer, Christoph 2.
Printer in Zurich, 1564–1585†.
1570: 6832.44 ap. **1574:** [19292a?]. **1579:** 6832.48 ap.

Fryer. *See* Frere.

Fuchs, Hero.
Printer in Cologne, 1520–1541. [Benzing 238.]
1525: [2823?] (d).

Fussell, Nicholas.
Bookseller in London, (1624) 1626–1665. His first shop was shared with **Humphrey Moseley** until 1634; this was the corner shop near the great North door of St. Paul's, one of those marked for removal, c. 1632, and ordered demolished in Jan. 1636 (*Library* 3 (1902): 267–8; Greg, *Companion*: 337–8). **Charles Greene** may have worked in his second shop, the White Lion, since several of Greene's books were sold there: 548–8.3, 18339, 18341, 18342, 18344; it is likely that Fussell's name ought to be supplied as shop owner. In 1640 the shop passed to **Samuel Browne**. [*Dict. 2*; DFM 967; *Loan Book*, 1662; *Poor Book*, 1652–65.]
in Paul's Churchyard (A.2), 1627–1640
at the Ball —, 1627 (15537, with H. Moseley)–1635 (24116); sometimes omits sign: 1634 (7056); variation: 1632 (15713, has 'their shops — at the Ball and the White Lion', with H. Moseley)
at the White Lion and Ball —, 1637 (23566.5)–1639 (12206a, has 'shop', adds 'at the great North door'); variation: 1638 (18343, omits 'and Ball')
1626: 21840 ent.

Fussell, N. — *cont.*
1627: 15537 f., 23564–4.5 f.
1629: 21840 f.
1630: 6747 sold, 17378 sold.
1631: 12888 ent., 17378 sold, 20829 f.
1632: 15713 sold.
1634: 7056 sold.
1635: 24116 f.
1637: 23566–6.5 sold, 25234.5 f.
1638: 12402 ent., [18339] sold, 18343 sold.
1639: 976 sold, 12206a sold, [18337] sold, [18340–0.5] sold, [18343a] sold, [18345–5a] sold, 25437 sold.

G

G., T., *pseud.*
Unidentified printer or publisher in London, 1595. Although the item was 'sold in Paul's Churchyard' (B), this statement is probably also intentionally misleading.
1595: 18758.

Gachet. *See* Gaschet.

Gailliart. *See* Gheylliaert.

Gale, Thomas.
Surgeon and author, b. 1507–1587. [*DNB*.]
No address used.
1563–64: 11529 f.

Gamonet, Estienne.
Printer in Geneva, 1605–1635 at least.
1629: 16826.5.

Garbrand, Ambrose.
Bookseller in London, 1610–1623†. Shared a shop his first two years with **Eleazar Edgar**. [*Dict. 1*; DFM 132; *Poor Book*, 1615, 1620–23, widow thereafter.]
their shop in Paul's Churchyard at the Windmill (B), 1610 (53, with E. Edgar)–1613 (23479, has 'his' shop)
1610: 53 f., 13005a.5 f., 23479 ent.
1611: 54 f., 10221 f., 12663.4 f.
1612: 4683 f., 10258 f.
1613: 10222 f., 23479 f.
1616: 23480 ass'd.

Garbrand (Harkes), Richard.
Bookseller in Oxford, 1573–1602†. [*Dict. 1*.]
No address used.
1600: 34 sold.

Gardiner, Thomas.
Printer in London, 1576–1578. In partnership with **Thomas Dawson**, whose name has often been the only one supplied in square brackets in STC for items produced during the partnership. [*Dict. 1*.]
nigh unto the Three Cranes in the Vintry (S.9), 1577 (3356)–1578 (11805)
1577: 3356, 3423, 3715 (d), 4066 (c), 4269 (d?), 5141 (d?), [5264], 10502, [11454], 11803a.7, 11804, 11804.5, 22467, 24172.
1578: 11805–5.2, 11805.4–.6.

Fr. Garnet's First Press.
Recusant press set up in or near London, 1592?–1595? by Henry Garnet, *S. J.*, primarily for publishing his own works or translations. = A&R English secret press no. 2. [*BS* 1 (1951): 11.]
All items below have this press's imprint supplied in square brackets.
1592: 14626.5 (d?).
1593: 11617.2 (d), 11617.8 (d), 17264.5 (c).
1594: 11617.4 (d?).
1595: 4571.5 (d?).

Fr. Garnet's Second Press.
Recusant press in or near London, 1596?–1599? = A&R English secret press no. 3.

Fr. Garnet's Second Press — *cont.*
All items below have this press's imprint supplied in square brackets.
1596: 3801 (d?), 11617.5 (d?), 16642 (d?), 24748 (d?).
1597: 3941.5, 15353, 16645.7 (d?), 17504 (false, c), 22968.5 (d?).
1599: 3941.1 (d?), 3941.2 (d?), 3941.3 (d?), 3941.4 (d?).

Garnich, Jacobus, *pseud.*
Printer at 'Mussipons' [= Pont à Mousson], 1609. = Eliot's Court Press. For the genuine Garnich, active at Pont à Musson and Nancy, 1608–31, see *Répertoire 17e*, X.112, 160.
1609: 1408.3 ap.

Garrett, Nicholas.
Only known activity in London, 1631. Either a relative of **William Garrett** or an error in the SR for that name since the item Nicholas entered was published by William. [Arber IV.252.]
1631: 1796 ent.

Garrett, William.
Bookbinder (*C-B C*: 176) in London, (1621) 1622–1674?†. [*Dict. 2*; DFM 2228; *Loan Book*, 1655; *St. Giles* (I.4), 1626–32.]
shop in Paul's Churchyard at the Bull's Head (A.2), 1625 (5660); no other pre-1641 use of any address noted.
1622: 13580 f., 16843 f.
1623: 3992.5 ent., 16844 f.
1624: 13260 f.
1625: 5660 f.
1626: 17522 ent.
1630: 603 f., 603.3 f., 603.5 f.
1631: 1796 f., 10144 f., 19925 ent.
1639: 12979 ent., 12980 ent.
1640: 12978 ent., 21779 f.

Gaschet (Gachet, Catchet), John.
French bookseller and bookbinder in York, 1509–1517, in Hereford, 1517, and again in York, 1526–1535. [Duff, *Century*.]
York, dw. beside the minster, 1516 (16221)
1509: 16160 pro.
1516: 16221 sumpt., 16250.5 imp. (d?).
1517: 13833.5 imp., 16135 imp.
1526: 15858 exp.
1530: 16161 imp. (d?), 16223 sumpt., 16251 imp.
1533: 15859 exp.

Gathkin. *See* Cathkin.

Gaultier, Thomas.
French printer and publisher in London, 1550–1553. **King's Printer in French for the Channel Islands**, 1553 (16430). [Duff, *Century*; *Bibliothèque d'Humanisme et Renaissance* 39 (1977): 143–8; 41 (1979): 353–8.]
dw. at Fleet Bridge in the new rents (W.3), 1552? (10532)
1550: 2821 in off., [13750.5?], 16051 (c), 19494–4.7, 20922.
1551: 2957.6–.8(*A*), 2977, 9525–6 in off.
1552: 4391 [f.?], [6003.5?], 10532 (d?), [16573(*A3*)?].
1553: [2957.9(*A*)], 16430 [f.].

Gaver, James.
Dutch bookseller in London, before 1535–1545†. Assistant to **Wynkyn de Worde** and one of the latter's executors along with **John Byddell**, in whose house he lived. [Duff, *Century*.]
dw. in [Fleet Street] at the Sun (W.5), 1539 (23152.7)
1539: 23152.7.

Geele, Thomas.
Printseller in London, 1630 at least. The set of portraits in 13581.7 appears in an earlier state in 1628 (17528, with C. Holland's imprint) and in a later one in 1638 (17529, with Geele's name removed); *see* Hind II.133–4 and p. 121, no. 1. [Globe 214.]
at the Dagger in Lombard Street (O.12), 1630 (13581.7)
1630: 12561.6 sold (c), 13581.7 sold.

Gellibrand, Samuel.
Bookseller in London, (1637) 1639–1675†. Shared a shop with **Robert Dawlman**, one of his former masters, and **Luke Fawne**, but imprints before 1641 link him only with the latter. [*Dict. 2*; DFM 1309; *Loan Book*, 1647–50.]

Gellibrand, S. — *cont.*
at the Brazen Serpent in Paul's Churchyard (A.3), 1639 (11763)–1640 (7431), both with L. Fawne
1637: 12033 ent. **1639:** 11763 f., 15082 sumpt., 23590.5 f. **1640:** 7414 f., 7431 f., 22151 f.

Gellibrand, Thomas.
Publisher (patron? or schoolmaster?) in London, 1597. [*Dict. 1.*]
in the street called St. Mary Axe (J.4), 1597 (23408.2)
1597: 23408.2 imp.

Geminus (Gemini), Thomas.
Engraver, publisher, and instrument maker in London, before 1545–c. 1563. His real name was Thomas Lambrit of Lexhe, a village near Liège. [Duff, *Century*; Hind I.39–58; Taylor 165–6.]
within the Blackfriars (Q.6), 1555 (435.35)–1562 (6850, has 'dw.')
1553: 11715.5–16 f.
1555: 435.35, 11713.5, 11718.7 per.
1556: [435.37], 435.39, 6849.5 f. (d?).
1559: 11718 [f.].
1561: 6849.8.
1562: 6850.

Gering, Ulrich.
Printer in Paris, 1470–1483 and 1494–1508 (1510†). [Renouard.]
1497: 16169. **1498:** [16138(*A3*)] (d).

Gessner, Andreas.
Printer in Zurich, 1553–1559†. [Benzing 524.]
1551: [16576] (d?). **1553:** 4811.

Gething, Richard.
Writing master and author, b. 1585?–1652?†. [*DNB.*]
his house in Fetter Lane at the Hand and Golden Pen (W.8), 1616 (11802.7)
1616: 11802.7 sold.

Ghelen (Ghelius), Jan 2 van.
Printer and bookseller in Antwerp, 1544?–1583†. [Rouzet.]
1569: 6832.40.

Gheylliaert (Galliart), Jan.
Printer in Emden, 1554–1558? In partnership with **Steven Mierdman**. [Benzing 104, under Mierdman.]
1554: [19890] (d).

Gibbs, George.
Bookseller in London, (1608) 1613–1662. During 1624–1626 most of his items were published jointly with **Henry Holland**. [*Dict. 1*; DFM 1090; *Loan Book* (with H. Holland), 1624–27; *Poor Book*, 1643–62.]
at the Fleur-de-lis, 1614–1632
shop in Paul's Churchyard — (A.2), 1614 (19129)–1617 (23807)
— in Pope's Head Alley (O.11), 1624 (6339.5, with H. Holland)–1631 (7020, has 'dw.'); variations: has 'Golden' Fleur-de-lis, 1625 (6340); has 'shop', 1628 (18998), 1630 (11346)
shop — by the little South door of St. Paul's (A.9), 1632 (11346.3)
1614: 19129 f.
1615: 3435.7 f., 14838 f.
1616: 10784 f., 21342 f.
1617: 10781 f., 23807 sold.
1624: 6339.5 f.
1625: 5535 f., 6340 f., 25663 f.
1626: 16753 f.
1627: 23228 f.
1628: 18998 f.
1630: 11346 f.
1631: 7020 f.
1632: 11346.3–.5 f., 15334 f.
1633: 11346.5 f. (d).

Gibson, Thomas.
Printer and bookseller in London, 1535–1539, 1552? **Printer to the City of London** in at least 1538 (*TBS* 6 (1900–02): 17). Practised medicine, 1557?–1562†. [Duff, *Century*.]

Gibson, T. — *cont.*
No address noted.
1535: 3046.
1536: 4593.5, [24945] (d?).
1537: [2351.5] (c), [6455].
1538: [2841], [15998] (d?), 21042 in house (d), 21307a.5 in house (d), [24650] (d?).
1539: 2372.6 in house, 13178 in aed., 21307a.7 [f.] (d?).
1552: 21308 [f.] (d?).

Giffart, René.
Printer in Paris, 1618–1625†. [Lottin 2: 70.]
1619: 20664.

Giglio (Lilius), Domenico.
Printer in Venice, 1538–1540 and 1550–1567. [Borsa.]
1550: 6832.26 ap. (c?).

Gilbert, Thomas.
Bookseller in London, 1588–1590. Apparently not a member of the Stat. Co. [*Dict. 1.*]
dw. in Fleet Street near to the $ Castle (W.5), 1588 (19625)
1588: 19625 f.
1590: 6842 ent.

Gilbertson, William.
Bookseller in London, (1647) 1649?–1664†. [*Dict. 2*; DFM 2799.]
1640: 14689.7 f. (d/error for 1649?) = Wing² J 809A.

Gilman, Anthony.
Stationer in London, 1601–1628† (*C-B C*: 202). Published only one item but was otherwise active in the affairs of the Stat. Co. [*Dict. 1*; *Poor Book*, (wife) 1628.]
No address used.
1620: 18509 f.

Giolito de Ferrari, Gabriel, *Heirs of, pseud.*
Printer in 'Piacenza', 1587. = J. Wolfe (Woodfield no. 33). For the genuine printer, active in Venice 1536–1578, *see* Borsa.
1587: 17161.

Girardone, Vincenzo.
Printer in Milan, 1562–1570. [Borsa.]
1567: [21076?]. **1568:** [5450.5?].

Godet (Godhed, Goddard), Giles.
Refugee wood engraver and printer in London, 1547–1568 at least. [Duff, *Century*; Worman 25.]
dw. in Blackfriars (Q.6), 1560? (10022)
1560: 10022 (d?).
1562: 564.6(*A*) ent.
1563: [7588] (d), 11930.6 (d?).
1564: 13851 ent.
1565: [11930.2?] (c?), [11930.4] (c?).
1566: 11930.8 (d).

1616: 13526.5 (note).

Godfray, Thomas.
Printer in London, 1531?–1536 at least. Only two of Godfray's imprints have dates, the Chaucer, 1532 (5068) and the *Subvention in Ypres*, 1535 (26119), and neither of them has an address. It is possible that the second address below is actually the earlier. Dates supplied for Godfray in STC must be regarded as more tentative than usual, and his work is in need of a new evaluation. His 94 mm. textura apparently came from **Richard Pynson**, and Godfray may have been working with it as early as 1530 (19166) for **John Hawkins**; this fount seems to have been afterwards acquired by **Richard Lant**. The woodcut initials of the *Boccus*, 1531? (3186), of which one 'L' (2nd D3ᵛ) appears in the Chaucer (5068, 3F5ʳ), and the *Boccus* 91 mm. textura apparently belonged to the Canterbury monk and patron, **Robert Saltwood**; they passed to **John Mychell**. [Duff, *Century*.]
at Temple Bar (W.14), 1531? (23963, colophon on y8ᵛ), 1534? (10634)
in the Old Bailey (D.7), 1534? (23163.2)
1531: 1915 (d?), 3186(*A3*) (d?), [3187(*A3*)?] (d?), 22600.5 (d?), 23963 (d?).
1532: 5068, 12731.6 (c), [20036.5] (c).

Godfray, T. — *cont.*
1533: 7377 (d?), 10488.7 (d?).
1534: 2371 (d?), 2752 (d?), 5641 (d), 10489 (d?), 10634 (d?), 11211 (d?), 17313.3 (d), 23163.2 (d?).
1535: 1915.5 (c), 4240 (d?), [4240.5] (d?), 4370 (d?), 5099.5 (c), 14027.5 (c), 15988a (d?), 16818 (c), 21558.5 (d?), 21588 (d?), 21789.4 (d?), [23185.5] (d?), 24236 (d?), [24238] (d), [24239] (d?), 26119.
1536: [198.3] (c), [2831?], [13089a] (d?), 22575 (d), 24462 (d?), 24463 (d?).

Godlif (Godly), Francis.
Bookbinder in London, 1562–1596. Apparently worked in Chester as a binder in 1566–67. [*Dict. 1.*]
dw. at the West end of Paul's (A.10), 1577 (11050); no earlier address used.
1562: 6177 f. **1577:** 11050 [f.] (d).

Godwin (Goodwine), Joseph.
Bookseller in Oxford, 1637–1667. [*Dict. 2.*]
No address used.
1637: 21812.3 ven., 21812.9 pro. **1638:** 4876 f., 21813 pro. **1639:** 4877 f. **1640:** 24882.3 imp.

Godwin, Paul.
Stationer in London, (1635) 1638. Son of bishop Francis Godwin. Probably the translator of the item he entered. [DFM 96.]
No address used.
1638: 13523 ent.

Goes, Hugh.
Printer in York, 1506?–1509, and in London, 1512–1513? In the latter city he worked in partnership with **Henry Watson**. [Duff, *Century*; *The Gardyners Passetaunce*, ed. F. B. Williams, Jr., London, 1985: 42–50, 54–6.]
York, in the Steengate, 1509 (16232.4, Herbert III.1437)
Beverly, in the Highgate, n.d. (Herbert III.1439)
London, at Charing Cross (X.14), 1513? (11562.7)
1506?–09: [13689.3] (d), [13829.7] (d).
1506: [14077c.63(*A3*)] (d).
1509: 16232.4 per.
1513: 11562.7 (d?).

Goinus, Antonius.
Printer in Antwerp, 1537–1544. It is not clear whether he or a successor printed the 1545 items. [Rouzet.]
1543: [1309] (false).
1544: [1276], [1291.5] (d?), [1291a] (d?).
1545: [1303] (false), [14823] (false).

Golding, Percival.
Patron in London, 1608. Probably related to the translator and author, Arthur Golding.
No address used.
1608: 11399 f.

Goodale, John.
Translator and publisher in London, 1550?
No address used.
1550: 17788 f. (d?).

Goodwin, Goodwine. *See* Godwin.

Gosse (Gos), Nathaniel.
Stationer and instrument-maker in London, 1611–1637 (cf. DFM 1425–6) at least. [DFM 73; Morgan.]
dw. at Ratcliff [in Stepney] (U.5), 1624 (12523, state 3 of frontispiece)–1625 (150) at least
1625: 150 f.

Gosson, Alice.
Bookseller in London, 1601–1622. Widow of **Thomas** and mother of **Henry Gosson**. She seems to have been active as a Stationer (cf. DFM 1429–32), and the first and third addresses listed under Henry were probably her own. [*Dict. 1.*]
at the widow Gosson's in Panyer Alley (C.6), 1622 (24090)
1622: 24090 sold.

Gosson, Henry.
Bookseller in London, (1601) 1603–1641† (*C-B C*: fol. 177^v, called 'lately deceased' on 30 Aug. 1641). Son of **Thomas** and **Alice Gosson.** Married a daughter of **Thomas Pavier** (*SB* 6 (1954): 165). One of the **Ballad Partners.** The first and third addresses below, never called 'his', probably belonged to Alice. [*Dict. 1*; *Loan Book*, 1627–30; *Poor Book*, (at least in part for son's scholarship) 1622–41.]
at the Sun in Paternoster Row (C.7), 1606 (10668)–1609 (22334)
shop at London Bridge (T.7), 1608 (11403, colophon)–1640 (20396, has 'dw. on'); variation: 1635 (23782 has 'shop on', adds 'near to the gate'); in 1613 (25840, C2^v) there is a description of damage done by wind to his house, placed in Catherine Wheel Alley (T.5) close to Thames Street near London Bridge.
in Panyer Alley (C.6), 1615 (24588), 1621 (6266), 1622 (23728, 23742)
1606: 4102.5 f. (d), 10668 f.
1607: 4102.7–.9 f. (d), 14690 f., 25639 f. (d).
1608: 23 f., 1968.7 f., 4181 f., 6646.7 f., 10826 f., 11403 f., 18786 ent., 24053–3.5 f.
1609: 6557.2 f. (d?), 22334 f., 22335 f.
1611: 23791 ent.
1612: 13157.5 f., 23760 ent., 23769 ent.
1613: 5193 f., 5194.4 f., 17699.5 f. (d), [17700.5 f.?] (d), 23763 f., 25840 ent.
1614: 12630 ?ent.
1615: 3720 f., 11332 f. (d?), 18590 f., 23619.5(*A3*) f., 24588 f.
1616: 19997 f. (d), 24589 f.
1617: 6993 f., 23748.5 f.
1618: 4932 f., 6183 f., 17148–8.3 f., 23736 f., 23737 f., 23784 ent.
1619: 20746 f.
1620: 1328.3 f. (c), 1848.5 f. (c), 4877.7 f. (c), 5433 f. (d?), 6924 f. (c), 15120 f. (c?), 17190 f. (d?), 20747 f., 23012 f. (d?), 23757 f., 23788 f., 23802 f., 25088 f. (c).
1621: 197.3 ent., 6266 f., 17125 f., 17895 f., 23786 f., [23793 f.] (d), 23795.7 f. (d), 23799 f., 23800 f., 23800.5 f., 23802.5 f., 23808a f.
1622: 11360.5 f. (d?), 23728 f., 23742 f., 23742.5 f., 23762 f., 23812 ent., 23812.3 f., 24090 f.
1623: 1409.5 f., 23789–9.3 f., 23789.7 ent., 23812.3 f., 23816 f., 24115 ent.
1624: 3194.5 f. (d?), 5022.5 f. (d), 7384.5 f. (d?), 17770.3 f. (d), 23787 f., 23787.5 f., 23801 f., 23808.5 f.
1625: [15.3 f.] (c), 22 f. (d), 546.5 f. (c), 1433.5 f. (c), 4541.5 f. (c?), 5559 f. (c), 5611.7 f. (c), 6444 f. (c), 6922.7 f. (c), 6923 f. (c), 6927.5 f. (c), 10610.3 f. (c), 12018 f. (c?), 12018.3 f. (c?), 12384.5 f. (c?), 13686.5 f. (c), 14426.3 f. (d), 14549 sold (c), 15470a.5 f. (c), 17235 f. (d?), 18294.5 f. (c), 18662.5 f. (c), 19231 f. (c), 19254.5 f. (c), 22556 f. (c), 22918.5 f. (c), 22919.2 f. (c), 23435a.5 f. (c), 23635 f. (d?), 23729 f., 23743 f., 23758 f., 23772–2a f. (d), 25353 f. (c).
1626: 23741.5 ?ent., 23812.7 ass'd, 23813.5 f.
1627: 9978 f. (d?), 12871.5 f. (c), 23726–6a f., 23753 f., 24746.3 f. (d).
1628: 7745.7 f., 14960.5 f. (c), 16864a.12 f. (c), 19272 f. (d), 23813.7 f.
1629: 1107 f., 5063 f., 6907 f. (d?), 14708.5 ent., 16856.3 f. (c).
1630: 4241 f. (c?), 4298 f. (d?), 5129.7 f. (c), 11380.7 f. (c), 12547.3 f. (c), 12725 f. (c?), 13440b.5 f. (c?), 14045.5 f. (c), 14708.1 f., 16758.7 f., 16765 f. (c), 16770 f., 16801.7 f. (d), 17915.5 f. (c), 18316.3 f. (d), 18699.7 f. (c), 19227 f. (d?), 20131.5 f. (c), 20132 f. (c), 22579 f. (c), 22898 f. (c), 22920.1 f. (c), 22920.9 f. (c), 23291 f. (d?), 23741.5 f. (c), 23761 f., 24098 f. (c).
1631: 5420.5 f. (d?), 12015.5 ent., 12543.3 f. (d?), 21457 f. (d?), 21551.3 f. (d?), 22919.3 f. (d?), 23745 f.
1632: 5429.5 f. (d?), 5872.5 f. (c), 12092.6 f. (c), 12326 f. (d), 13920a f. (c), 20315 f. (c), 20482 ent., 20822.5 f. (d), 21138.5 f. (d?), 23803 ent., 24412 ent., 25972.8 f. (d?).
1633: 3945.7 f. (d), 6926 f. (d?), 6927 f. (d?), 18699 f. (d?), 23260 f. (d), 24047 f. (d).
1634: 20186 f. (d), 23808(*A3*) ent.
1635: 1332 f. (c), 3728 f. (c), 5627 f. (c), 6921 f. (c), 6922 f. (c), 12545.5 f. (c), 13705 f., 14040.3 f. (c), 18700 f. (d?), 20185 f. (d?), [22901 f.] (c), 22904 f. (c), 23727 f., 23730 f., 23731 f., 23744 f., 23781 f., 23782–2.5 f., 23794 f., 23817 f., 25736 f. (c).
1636: 3717.5 f., 3717.7 f., 3719.5 f., 16771 f., 20824 f., 23735 f., 23756 f., 23764a f., 23805 ent.

Gosson, H. — *cont.*
1637: 13015 f. (d?), 23759 f., 24335.5 f.
1638: 10610.5 f. (d?), 12403.5 f., 16868 f. (d?), 16869 ent., 19076 f. (d), [19263 f.?] (d), 20482 f. (d?), 23739 f., 24087 f. (d?).
1639: 189 ent.
1640: 10534 f. (d?), 12724 f. (d?), 14032.5 f. (c?), 14543 f. (c), 16751 f. (d?), 16866 f. (c), 19258 f. (d?), 20396 f.

Gosson, Thomas.
Bookseller in London, (1577) 1579–1599?†. Husband of **Alice** and father of **Henry Gosson**. [*Dict. 1*.]
dw. in Paul's Churchyard next the gate, the corner shop to Cheapside, at the Goshawk in the Sun (A.5), 1580, 5 Jan. (Herbert III.1338)
in Paternoster Row (C.7), c. 1579?–1591 and probably until his death
dw. — next to the $ Castle, c. 1579? (4270.5)–1581 (1968.5)
dw. — at the Sun, 1582 (12095)–1591 (24598)
shop on London Bridge adjoining to the gate (T.7), 1591 (24598)–1595 (5124, has 'shop by London Bridge gate')
1579: 4270.5 [f.] (c?).
1580: 1968.3 f.
1581: 1968.5 f.
1582: 12095 f. (d).
1590: 4032 ent., 20580 ent.
1591: 24598 f.
1592: 10777 ent., 16909 f.
1594: 11819 f.
1595: 903 ent., 3388 f., 5124 f., 15115.5 f., 21294 f., 22679 f. (d).
1596: 16909.5 f., 17866 ent., 19856.3 f.
1598: 16920 ent.
1599: 1423 f.

Gough (Gowghe), John.
Bookseller in London, 1523–1543† at least. For the lay subsidy of 1523 Gough, listed as a bookseller in St. Bride's parish (W.4), had goods valued at £5 (*Library* 9 (1908): 260). He was still there in 1528, in Fleet Street. [Duff, *Century*.]
dw. at (next) Paul's Gate in Cheapside (N.2), 1532 (4350)–1536 (15992)
in Lombard Street against (near unto) the Stocks Market at the $ Mermaid (O.12), 1539 (15453, colophon)–1540 (25587.5)
dw. in Smart's Quay next Billingsgate (T.13), 1542 (18813)
1532: 4350 f. (d), 4351 f. (d), 21472 f. (d?).
1533: 656 f. (d).
1535: 5892 [f.] (d?), [20418.5 f.] (d?).
1536: 5098 f. (d?), 11470.5 f. (d), 15992 [f.].
1537: 15285 pro (d), 16999 f. (d), 18849 f., 18878 f., 20840.5 f.
1539: 15453 [f.].
1540: 1323.5 [f.], 25587.5 [f.].
1541: [1739 f.] (d?).
1542: [1713 f.] (d), 1714 f., 1715 f., 1717 f., 1734 f., 1735 f., 1740 f., 1742 f., 1749 f., 1775 f., 3378.5 f. (d), 4045.5 f., 14640 f., 18813 f. (d), 19187 f. (d?).
1543: 977.5 f. (d?), 1730.5 f., 1731 f., 1734.5 f., 1738 f., 1743 f., 1750 f., 1776 f., 4047 f., 4048 f. (repeat?), 10507 [f.] (d?). .rip
1546: 4048 f. (repeat? d?).

Goupil, Richard.
Printer in Rouen, 1510–1519 at least. In view of the dates printed in his books, the date of the item below should perhaps be revised to c. 1510. [Duff, *Century*; Muller 100.]
1506: 15904.5 in off. (d?).

Grafton, Richard.
Grocer, publisher, and printer (from 1539) in London, 1537–1553, 1559, (1573†). Father-in-law of **Richard Tottell**. Usually published jointly with **Edward Whitchurch**, 1537–1541. Used the style 'Printer to the Prince's grace', 1544? (16033.5), 1546 (16044). **King's Printer**, 1547–1553. The addresses below are all variations on the same establishment. [Duff, *Century*; *PBSA* 52 (1955): 262–82; J. A. Kingdon, *Incidents in the Lives of T. Poyntz and R. Grafton*, London, 1895, and *Richard Grafton*, London, 1901.]
within the house late the Greyfriars (= Christ's Hospital (C.2)), 1540 (16015, with Whitchurch)
dw. within the circuit of the late Greyfriars, 1544? (16033.5)

Grafton, R. — *cont.*
within the precinct of the late dissolved house of the Greyfriars, 1545 (10460)–1546 (16044), 1549 (16050, possibly carried over from previous editions)
in the parish of Christ Church within Newgate, 1547 (754, 11797); no later use noted
1537: [2066 f.].
1538: 2817 f.
1539: 2068, 2818.5 [f.], 2843 (d?), 19465.5.
1540: 2070, 2071, 2072, 2073, 2076, 2368, 2846 (d), 2847 in off., 2971, 2971.5, [4268.5] (d), [16014] (d?), 16015, [22877.6] (d), 22880.2 (note).
1541: 2072, 2073, 2075, 2076, 7793 (d).
1542: [5069–70], [9291?], 10443, [10661–2] (d), 11917 in off., [14123.7(*A*3)] (d?), [16026–7], 16027.5, 24334, 24894 (d).
1543: [2972.7] (d?), 5015 in off. (d), 12766.7 in off., 12767 ex off., 20062 in off.
1543/44: 393, 508.5 f., 523.
1544: [10621.5] (d), 10621.7, 10622, 10622.5, 15835 per, 16033.5 (d?), 20200 (d?).
1544/45: 420.15.
1545: 4853.5 ex off. (d), 10460, 16034, 16035, 16036, 16040, 16042 ex off.
1545/46: 447.5 ex off.
1546: 2848.5 in off., 2973.2, [2973.3] (d?), 3329 ex off. (d?), [14919?], 16042 ex off., [16042.5] (d?), 16043.5, 16044, 16047, 24654, 24655–6.
1547: 754, [5717?], 7809.7 (d), 7810 (d), 7811 in aed. (d), 7811.2 in aed. (d), 7811.5 in aed. (d), 7811.9 in aed. (d), 7812 in aed., 10087.5 (d), 10088, 10089, 10090, 10090.3, 10090.5, 10091, 10093.5, 10114 (d), 10115 (d?), 10115.5 (d?), 10116 (d?), 10116.5 (d?), 11797, 12857 in aed., 13638.5, 13638.7, 13639, 13639.5, 13640, 13640.5, 14918, 16048, 16048a, [26093.5] (d).
1547/48: 7813 in aed.
1548: [165.5] (d?), [165.7], 2375.5, 3196 in aed., 7814 in aed., 7815 in aed., 7816 in aed., 7818 in aed., 9181.3 in aed. (d), 9181.5, 9419 in aed., 9420 in aed., 9421–1.7 (repeat), 10093.7, 10148, 10148.5, 12431 in aed., 12721–2 in off., 12723a(*A*3, note), 13642, 16049.5 (d?), 16456.5, 16457, 16458.3, 16503 in aed., 19476.5, 21039 in aed., 22268 in aed., [23004?], [23004.5?].
1548/49: 7819 in aed. (d), 7819.2 in aed.
1549: [166], 2377, [2725], [6087], [6094], [6095], 7506, [7819.4] (d), 7819.6 in aed. (d), 7819.8 in aed. (d), 7819.10 in house (d), 7819.12 in aed., 7820 in aed., 7820.5 in aed., 7821 in aed., 7822 in aed., 7823 in aed., 7824 in aed., 7825 in aed., 7826 in aed., 7827 in aed., 7827.3 in aed., 7827.7 in aed., 7828, [7828.3(*A*3) f.] (d), 7829, 9421 in aed. (d), 9421.1 in aed. (d), 9422 in aed., 9422.5 in aed., 9423 in aed., 9427.3 in house (d), 13643 in aed., 16050 [f.], 16268 in off., 16269 in off., 16269.5 in off., 16274 in off., 16275 in off., 16462, 16462.5.
1549/50: 9428, 9429, 9429.3, 9429.7 (repeat).
1550: 3331 ex off. (d), 4853.7 ex off., [6088], [6088.3], [6095], 7830, 7831, 7832, 7833, [9342.2?] (c), 9421.2 in aed. (d), 11313, 12723, 12723a, [14999.5] (c), 16441, 17300, [19906], [19907], [19907a], 20792.5, [21612], [21613], [21614], [25588], [25824] (c).
1550/51: 7758, 7834.
1551: [2761.5] (d), [2983?], [6089.5], [6090], 7363 (d), 7835, 7836, 7837, 7838, 7839, 7840, 7841, 7842, 7843, 7844, 7844.2, 9429.7 (d?), 9432.3, 9432.5, 9432.7, 13646 in aed. (d?), 13647 in aed., [15545] (d), 16053 in aed., 16054, 16504 (d), [21690.2], 24657, 25809, 25816–7 in aed., [25852(*A*3)] (d?).
1551/52: 7844.4.
1552: 2380a.5, 4343, 7844.6, 7844.8, 7844.10, 9423.5, [9423.7] (d?), 9424–6.5 (repeat), 9433, 9433.3, 9433.5, 9433.7, 9435.5, 9436 [f.], 9437.3–.7 (repeat), 12595 ex off., 14992.5, 16057, 16284.5 in off., 16285–5.5 in off., 16285.7–5a in off., 16286 in off., 16286.2–.3 in off., 16286.5 in off., 16290 in aed., 21557, 25810.
1552/53: 7845.
1553: 2092, 3033.5 in aed., 4854 in off., [6159.3(*A*)], 7363.5, 7846 in aed., 7847 in aed., 9421.3 in aed. (d?), 9430, 9430.5–32 (repeat), 9439 in aed., 9439.5 in aed., 9440 in aed., 9440.2 (repeat), 10034–4.2, 16290 in aed., 19547, 25799, 25811.
1559: 9459 (note), 16291 in off.
1565: 12167 (note).

Graphaeus, Joannes.
Printer in Antwerp, 1527?–1569. [Duff, *Century*; Rouzet.]

Graphaeus, J. — *cont.*
1529: [10883?] (d?). **1533:** [24440?] (d?). **1534:** [5542.6?], [14893.5] (d).

Graphaeus, Richardus, *pseud.*
Printer in London, 1578–1579. = R. Schilders.
No address used.
1578: 10674 typis.
1579: 10673–3.5 typis, 10674.3 typis, 10674.7 typis.

Grave, Claes (Nicolas) de.
Printer in Antwerp, 1511?–1540? (1549†). [Duff, *Century*; Rouzet.]
1516/17: 470.3.

Greene, Charles.
Stationer in London, (1631) 1633–1648. Although when an address does appear in his items, it is in Paul's Churchyard, there are several books which have no address at all. The White Lion is never described as 'his' shop and is more likely to have belonged only or predominantly to **Nicholas Fussell,** 1637–39, whose name probably ought to be supplied instead of Greene's; in 1640 the shop passed to **Samuel Browne**. [*Dict. 2*; DFM 2689; *PBSA* 80 (1986): 369–74.]
?in Paul's Churchyard, 1637–1638
sold — [no sign] (B), 1637? (18203)
sold at the White Lion — (A.2), 1637 ([548], 548.3, 18341, 18342)–1638 (18339, 18344)
1633: 14744.5 f., 18202 ent.
1634: 7036 sold.
1637: [548] sold, 548.3 f., 974 sold, 18203 f. (d?), 18341 f., 18342 f., 25436 f.
1638: 630.5 sold, 975 sold, 18339 f., 18343 f., 18344 f., 25436 (note), 25436a f.
1639: 976 f.

Greene, Francis.
Bookseller in Cambridge, 1628–1635, and member of the Stat. Co., London. Undoubtedly the son of **Leonard** and **Joan Greene**. He lived in the parish of Great St. Mary's. [*Dict. 1*; DFM 1457.]
No address used.
1632: 11060 f. **1633:** 13184 sold (d), 13185 sold. **1634:** 13186 sold.

Greene, Joan.
Stationer in Cambridge, 1631–1634 (1637). Widow of **Leonard Greene** and undoubtedly mother of **Francis**. She lived in the parish of Great St. Mary's until 1632. [*Dict. 1*.]
No address used.
1631: 20271–1a f. **1634:** 20273 f.

Greene, Leonard.
Bookseller in Cambridge, 1606–1630† and member of the Stat. Co., London. Husband of **Joan Greene** and undoubtedly the father of **Francis**. One of the **Printers to the University of Cambridge** (*see* Cambridge University), 1622–1630, though as far as his imprints reveal his main activity remained publishing rather than printing. The single imprint during this time shared with another Printer to the University is indicated by an asterisk (*). His shop was on the south side of the steeple of Great St. Mary's. [*Dict. 1*; DFM 2182.]
No address used.
1606: 12680.5 ent., 24996 ent.
1607: 19677.5 f., 24996.5 f., 24996a f., 25678 f.
1608: 12670 ent., 12682 ent., 12685 ent., 19678 f., 19715 ent., 19755 f.
1609: 19649 (note), 19677 ent.
1610: 25689.3 f.
1611: 25690 f.
1612: 23825 f., 23830.3 f.
1613: 19650 (note).
1614: 25679 f.
1615: 25433.3 ent.
1618: 19651 (note), 23822 ent., 23822a.5 f., 23826 ent.
1620: 25691.5 f.
1622: 6195 imp., 23823.5 ent., 23830 ent., 25315 f., 25679 ent., 25680 ent., 25689 ent., 25689.7 ent.
1623: 5973 imp., 11062a f.
1626: 21767* ap.
1630: 20270 f., 20270.5 f.

Greensmith, John.
Stationer in London, (1635) 1636–1642. [*Dict. 2*; DFM 665; *St. Giles*, 1635–40 at least.]
at the White Hind without Cripplegate (I.2), 1636 (10646)
1636: 10646 sold.

'Greenstreet House' Press.
Recusant English secret press supervised by Stephen Brinkley, 1580–1581. Documentary evidence places it at the following successive sites: Greenstreet House, East Ham; house of Francis Browne; Stonor Park, near Henley-on-Thames. [*Dict. 1*, under Brinkley; Southern 353–8, 362–3; *Library* 6 (1951): 50–1.]
All items below have this press's imprint supplied in square brackets.
1580: 3802 (false), 13377 (false), 17278.4 (false, d?), 17278.5 (d?), 19394 (false).
1581: 4536.5 (d), 19393 (false), 19402 (d).

Grey, Richard, *3rd Earl of Kent.*
Patron in London, b. 1477?–1523†. [C., G. E., *The Complete Peerage*, vol. 7 (London, 1929): 168–9.]
No address used.
1518: 17242 at instance (d?). **1520:** 17242.5 at instance (d?).

Griffin, Anne.
Publisher in London, 1621–1643, and printer, 1633–1637. Widow of **Edward Griffin 1** and mother of **Edward 2.** One of the partners in the **Eliot's Court Press**, which was situated in the Little Old Bailey (D.1). [*Dict. 2*; *Loan Book* (via T. Harper), 1627–30.]
Indexed below are *only* items which she entered in the SR or in which her name appears in the imprint. In the items distinguished by an asterisk (*) her name is on one title-page and a partner's name on a different one. Items *without* imprint, including those for which her name has been supplied in square brackets in STC, are listed *only* under Eliot's Court Press.
No address noted.
1621: 11671 ent., 15176 ent., 15338 ent., 24006.5 ent.
1622: 6204a ent., 18483 ent.
1623: 1108 ent., 3916 ent., 15439 ent.
1624: 15325 ent.
1625: 3566.5 (d/error), 11951 ent., 12792.5 ent.
1626: 1177 ent.
1627: 14971 ent., 22794 ent.
1631: 17340 (d/error).
1633: 12878.
1634: 765.5, 3255*, 4425, 7321.5, 7322.5, 12583, 14966–7, 17293–3.5.
1635: 1235–5.7, 1791–1.3, 2656, 3566.5, 3567, 5365, 5871, 10637, 11878, 12497, 12879, 13781, 19522, 20522, 24396.5.
1636: 1223, 4863, 5483.7–84, 5764–4.2, 6667, 7181.5, 17365, 18954.5 typis, 19598.4, 20223, 21544, 21806 typis, 23017.7.
1637: 1223.5–24, 1432.5, 1627, 1633*, 1719, 2669, 5046, 7614, 10812.5, 10813* (note), 11404 typis, 11406, 11652*–2b.5*, 13319, 15080, 15331.7*, 17340 (d?), 17354, 21806 typis, 23740, 23749.
1638: 4863.5 ent., 19598 ent., 25231 ent.
1639: 18948 ent.
1640: 6906.5 ent., 12052.5 ent., 14577 ent., 19274 ent., 19600 ent., 22892.5 ent.

1935: 1791(*A*3) (d/error).

Griffin, Edward 1.
Printer in London, (1611) 1613–1621†. Husband of **Anne Griffin** and father of **Edward 2**. One of the partners in the **Eliot's Court Press,** which was situated in the Little Old Bailey (D.1). *Dict. 1* has mention of an earlier Edward, apprenticed to Henry Conway on 8 Oct. 1589 and freed by him (as 'Griffithe') on 29 Sept. 1596 (Arber II.164, 717), but this Edward's only apprentice (DFM 228) was freed by Mrs. Griffin in 1606 so that he was apparently dead by then. [*Dict. 1*; DFM 248.]
Indexed below are *only* items which he entered in the SR or in which his name appears in the imprint or in a variant thereof. Items *without* imprint, including those for which his name has been supplied in square brackets in STC, are listed *only* under Eliot's Court Press, with the exceptions of 6683.3, which STC

Griffin, Edward 1 — *cont.*
has severed from its proper preliminaries, 6678; an advertisement (17123.5) for a book he both entered and printed; and a false imprint (25604) fashioned upon his name.
No address noted.
1613: 3779, 4116, 14493, 18201, 19569, 25740.
1614: 538.9, 765.3, 1012, 3779, 4116.5, 5927, 6063.3, 6067, 6678, [6683.3], 6731.5, 7398, 11091, 17837, 18905, 19129, 21074, 23408.8, 23779, 25717 (d), 26027.
1615: 114, 539, [1387], 1388, 3435.7, 3458.5, 3459.7, 3460.7, 3462.3, 3635, 3704.7, 5859, 5928, 7399, 7530, 7612, 10818, 11191, 14418.5 (note), 23501, 23806, 25165, 25798.
1616: 1013, 1442, 3460.8, 3463.7, 3465.7, 4682, 7146, 7342, 7371.5, 7372, 7401, 7408, 7408.2, 7615, 7627 (d?), 10784, 11176, 12108, 13503, 16833, 18626a.6, 18909, 18910, 18911, 20776, 20835, 21843, 21870, 22074, 22372, 22399, 23317, 23806, 24393, 24560, [25604] ap. (false).
1617: 1024, 3467, 4217, 4234, 4683.5, 4909, 7531, 10781, 10805, 12705–5a, 12705b, 12707, 13247, 13394, 13410.5, 13530, 20297, 21328, 21495, 21622, 23807, 24315, 25652, 25664, 25962.
1618: 245, 1207, 1443–4, 1642, 4214, 6063.5, 6067.3, 6327, 6515, 6515.5, 7408.5, 10598, 11517, 11525, 12410 (d?), 12656–6.5, 12710.7–11, 13772.5, 16772, 18912, 21097, 25041, 25046.
1619: 766 typis, 1022, 1208, 3211.5, 4541, 6063.6, 6326, 6987, 11518, 11670, 11676, 11828, 11830a.5, 15338(*A*3) ent., 15352, 17123, [17123.5] (d), 17742, 17844 ent., 18497, 18799, 18805, 19316, 19568, 19843, 21328, 22372.3, 24006 ent., 25265, 25907.
1620: 1023, 1863, 3523, 3566, 5305 (d), 6098, 6326.5, [6769.5], 6769.7, 11519, 11655, 11658, 11678, 11679, 11680, 12657–7.5, 12708, 14982, 18012, 18508, 19791, 20286.3 ent., 21201, 21214, 22427–7a, 24643, 24970, 25441, 25902.
1621: 10874–4.5, 12708, 14320, 21013.5, 21244.5, 23057.

Griffin, Edward 2.
Printer in London, (1636) 1637–1652† Son of **Edward 1** and **Anne Griffin**. One of the partners in the **Eliot's Court Press,** which was situated in the Little Old Bailey (D.1). [*Dict. 2*; DFM 230; *Loan Book*, 1639–46.]
Indexed below are *only* items which he entered in the SR or in which his name appears in the imprint. In the items distinguished by an asterisk (*) his name is on one title-page and a partner's name on a different one. Items *without* imprint, including those for which his name has been supplied in square brackets in STC, are listed *only* under Eliot's Court Press.
No address noted.
1637: 1633*, 2418.7, 2672.3, 6669, 10813*, 21442, 22513.5.
1638: 160.5, 1109–10* typis, 1225, 1229, 1231, 1680, 1789, 1907, 2676, 2681.3, 4863.5, 12039, 15331.7*, 17375, 17397, 17668, 19118, 19598, 20787, 21072a typis, 22497–7.5, 22499, 23943.9(*A*3) typis, 24760.5, 24760.7, 24761, 25640, 25640.5.
1639: 1314, 1432, 1592 typis, 1673, 1685–5.5, 2685, 7422, 11161, 11440, 15081–1.5, 15339, 17643, 18947, 19564 typis, 19581, 19596.5, 20945–6, 21639, 23944 typis, 25231.
1640: 41, 1230, 1396, 1625, 2693, 2697.5(*A*), 3590–0a, 3908.9, 3956, 3988 ap., 5549.7, 11441, 11656, 12052.5, 12133–4, 12145, 12978 typis, 12978a, 14295, 14706 (d), 14970, 15081.5–.7, 16651, 16652, 16881 in off., 19223 (d), 19238, 19258.5 (d), 19274 (d), 20561, 20946, 21190.5, 22712, 26102.5–03.

Griffio. *See* Gryphius.

Griffith (Gryffyth), William.
Printer and bookseller in London, 1552?–1571. Although the ornamental material in his items of 1553 and 1556 belonged to other printers, Griffith's having two addresses from 1553 suggests that he may actually have printed from the beginning, occasionally borrowing from others. [Duff, *Century* 61.]
in Fleet Street, 1552?–1571
— a little above the conduit at the Griffin (W.5), 1552? (5246); 1553 (1655)–1556 (20091); both with 'shop'
— at the Falcon against St. Dunstan's Church (W.9), 1553 (1655)–1571 (17311.5, omits 'against ...')
shop in St. Dunstan's Churchyard (W.9), 1561 (3477, has 'the little shop')–1571 (17311.5); variation: after 'Churchyard' adds 'in the West', 1563 (11435, colophon)
1552: 5246 (d?).
1553: 1655 [f.] (d).

Griffith, W. — *cont.*
1556: 20091.
1561: 3477.
1563: 11435.
1564: 1422 (d), 7503 ent.
1565: 4800.3 ?ent., 17311.5(*A*) ent., 18684.
1566: 5230 (d), 10456.
1567: 12787, 12787.5, 19917.
1568: 18876.
1569: 2985.5, 11554.5, 12019.
1570: 1244, 1979, 3195, 5104, 5224, 5227, 7510, 20289.
1571: 11436, 17311.5(*A*).

Grismand (Grismond), John.
Bookseller and typefounder in London, (1616) 1618–1638†. Married a daughter of **Thomas Pavier** (*SB* 6 (1954): 165). One of the **Ballad Partners.** His first shop previously belonged to his former master's son, **Edward White 2**; his last shop passed to his former apprentice, **Philip Nevill.** [*Dict. 1*; DFM 2742.]
shop near unto the little North door of St. Paul's at the Gun (A.1), 1618 (120)–1619 (4308, has 'dw. at')
shop in Paul's Alley at the Gun (A.1), 1621 (25044)–1626 (880, omits 'shop')
dw. in Ivy Lane at the Gun (C.3), 1627 (12109a)–1636 (883, omits 'dw.'); variation: 1631 (17730.5, has 'shop')
1618: 120 f., 12450 f.
1619: 121 f., 4308 sold.
1621: 10514 f., 17624 f., 21666 f. (d), 25043 (note), 25044 f., 25044.5 f., 25047 f., 25049 f., 25049a f., 25925 ent., 26051 f. (d).
1622: 112 f., 7228 f., 7229–30 f., 10223 f., 23110(*A3*) ent., 25033a f., 25042 f., 25045 f., 25050 f., 25052 f., 25053 f., 25055–5.5 f., 25903–3b f.
1623: 106 f., 106.5 f., 115 f., 7021 f., 12127.5 sold, 15093 sold, 16913 sold, 17734 sold, 17739 sold, 17739.5 sold, 21302 sold, 25030.5 f., 25048 f., 25173 f.
1624: 115 f., 129 f., 17830 f., 21302a sold, 21826.2 sold, 25054 f., 25056 f.
1625: 13806 imp., 17729 f., 18416 f., 20293 f., 22919.9 f. (c), 25051 f.
1626: 115 f., 880 sold, 6441 f., 10368 f., 21035.7 f.
1627: 11548 f., 12109a f., 12360 f., 17731 f., 18104.5 f. (c), 25031 f., 25033a.5 f., 25042.5 f., 25045.5 f., 25048.5 f., 25051.5 f., 25053.5 f., 25054.5 f. (d), 25056.5 f.
1628: 3514 ent., [6531?] f., 7342.5 ent., 13403.3 sold, 18965 sold, 25031 f., 25899 sold.
1629: 104 f., 12172 ent., 13477.5 sold, 14708.5 ent., 19239 f. (d), 20668.5 sold.
1630: 104–5 f., 10654 f. (c), 13403.6 sold, 17735 f.
1631: 1218 sold, 16856.7 f. (c), 17730 f., 17730.5 f., 17731.3–.7 f., 19652.5 sold, 19653.5 sold, 19653b.5 sold.
1632: 6491 sold, 10369 f., 12172 f., 17730.3(*A3*) f., 20832–2.5 f.
1633: 14670.3 sold, 22831.3 ven., 24289 ex imp., 25685a sold, 25912.5 f., 25929 f.
1634: 10372.7 f. (d?), 12331.5 sold, 23656 sold, 25355 f., 25700a sold (note), 25700a.5 sold, 25900 ent., 25900a f.
1635: 5930.6 sold, 7327 f., 20030a sold, 21035.7 ent., 23110 f., 25032 f., 25900a f.
1636: 883 sold, 10371 f., 25032 f.

Grove, Francis.
Bookseller in London, (1623) 1624–1663† (*SB* 6 (1954): 164). [*Dict. 2*; DFM 1788.]
Grove's shop is described in various ways, of which those given below are selected, dated examples. Sometimes only a single element is mentioned, e.g. without Newgate, 1624 (11037.5); at the upper end of Snow Hill, 1627 (1183). The Saracen's Head is most commonly given, e.g. in 1624 (below) and 1640 (4889), but in three examples noted St. Sepulchre's Church is substituted, in 1629 (19452), and in 1630 and 1640 (both below). The only terms which might aid in dating the many undated items indexed are the sign of the Windmill, so far noted only in 1630 (below), and 'over against' which appears in 1624 (below) through 1629 (6122, 19452), but apparently thereafter is replaced by 'near unto' in 1630 (below) and then by 'near' in 1633 (18979, 15094)–1640 (4889, 22627.5).
shop over against the Saracen's Head without Newgate (D (headnote), D.9), 1624 (3718)

Grove, F. — *cont.*
on Snow Hill at the $ Windmill near unto St. Sepulchre's Church, 1630 (23686)
shop at the upper end of Snow Hill near the Saracen's Head without Newgate, 1634 (23541)
shop on Snow Hill near St. Sepulchre's Church, 1640 (22627.5)
1624: 595.4 sold, 3718 f., 11037.5 sold.
1625: [1182.7(*A*) f.] (c), 19252.5 f. (c), 19264 f. (c).
1626: 21452 sold.
1627: 1183 f., 20567.7 f. (c).
1628: 6798.7(*A3*) sold (d?), 12016 f., 19246 sold (d?), 23539 ent.
1629: 1184 f., 3301 sold, 3711 sold, 6122 sold, 19235 ent., 19255 f. (d?), 19280 f. (d), 19283.5 f. (d), 19452 sold, [22179 f.] (d?), 22849.1 ent.
1630: 1331.7 f. (c), 5424 ?ent., 12015 f. (c), 13693 f. (c), [14476 f.] (d), 16857.3 f. (c), 17235 ent., 19220 f. (d?), 19224 f. (d?), 19231.5 f. (c), 19243 f. (d), 20322.3 f. (c), 20602.5 ent., 23686 sold, 25333.5 f. (c).
1632: 6123 f., 18008 f. (d), 19250 f. (d), 19252 f. (d), 19253 f. (d), [19274.5 f.] (d?), 19275 sold (d?).
1633: 18979 f., 15094 f., 19225 f. (d), 19233 f. (d), 19248 f., 20576 ent.
1634: 12942 f., 19270 f. (d), 23541 sold.
1635: 1800 f. (c), 19236 f. (c), 19236.5 f. (c), 19240 f. (c), 19249.5 f. (c), 19253.5 f. (c).
1636: 5430 ?ent., 5451 f. (d).
1637: 18980 f., 19218 f. (d), 22917.5 sold, 23542 f.
1638: 6101 f. (d), 13544 sold, 19222 f., 19253 ?ent., 19273 f., 19881 f. (d?), 20183 f. (d?), 20326 ent., 21643 f., 25088 ?ent.
1639: 12017 sold, 16801.3 f. (d), 22406.7 f. (d?).
1640: 4889 f., 14066 f., 19249 sold, 22627 sold, 22627.5 sold.

Grove, John.
Bookseller in London, (1620) 1622 (cf. DFM 1483)–1669. Since no other John Grove is recorded as free of the Stat. Co. to 1700, though one bound an apprentice in 1655 (DFM II.1839), the man in the various sources is presumably the same person. [*Dict. 1*; *Dict. 2*; DFM 747; *Loan Book*, 1627–30, 1633–36; *Poor Book*, 1645–46, 1665–69.]
shop at Furnival's Inn gate in Holborn (V.8), 1629 (11541)–1631 (11203)
dw. in Swan Yard within Newgate (C.8), 1632 (17443)
shop near the Rolls in Chancery Lane, over against the Six Clerks' Office (W.10d), 1632 (7437)–1641 (Wing N 61, omits 'near the Rolls', has 'Subpoena' Office)
1629: 11541 f., 22460 f.
1630: 5125 ent., 6056 f., 6980 f., 11542 f., 22444 f.
1631: 11203 f.
1632: 7437 sold, 17443–3.5 f.
1633: 17708 f., 22461 f.

Growte (Groyat), John.
Norman bookseller and bookbinder in London, 1532–1549 at least. [Duff, *Century*.]
dw. within the Blackfriars next the church [St. Anne's] door (Q.5), 1533 (15979)–1534 (15985)
1532: 15978 imp. **1532–33:** 15979 at expenses. **1534:** 15985 at expenses. **1536:** 16106 pro.

Gryffyth. *See* Griffith.

Gryphius (Griffio, Grifi), Joannes.
Printer in Venice, 1544–1576. [Duff, *Century*; Borsa.]
1551: 20779.

Gryphius, Sébastien, *pseud.*
Printer in 'Lyons', 1572 = T. Vautrollier, and 1598 = T. Creede. For the genuine Gryphius, active in Lyons, 1524–1556, heirs to 1564, *see* Muller 36. In addition to forging his imprint, Vautrollier and Creede each made a copy of his device, McK. 246 and 339, respectively.
1572: 2995a.2. **1598:** 2995a.3.

Guarinus. *See* Guérin.

Gubbin (Gubbins), Thomas.
Bookseller and bookbinder in London, (1586) 1587–1629† and in York, 1603 at least. Son-in-law of **John Harrison 1**. Usually

Gubbin, T. — *cont.*
shared imprints, most often with **Thomas Newman**. W. A. Jackson has a note in his copy of *Dict. 1* that Gubbin bound a MS. armorial for the College of Arms, where his receipt, dated 1624, is still preserved. [*Dict. 1*; *Loan Book*, 1615–18, 1623–30; *Poor Book*, 1613–19, widow from 1630.]
in Paternoster Row (C.7), 1588
?sold — over against the Black Raven, 1588 (6558, with T. Orwin)
dw. — at the Griffin, 1588 (23859)
?sold at the West end of Paul's (A.10), 1592 (12234, probably N. Ling's shop)
shop near Holborn conduit (D.5), 1614 (3579)
1587: 3179 f., 6055 f., 25118.4 f., 25246 f.
1588: 847 f., 2051 f., 4088 ent., 4090 f. (d), 4090.5 f., 6558, 11338 ent., 11342 imp., 11343 ent., 11344–5 f., 11819.5 f., 14926 f., 19709 ?ent., 19721.5(*A*3) f., 23859 sold, 24490 f., 24507 f. (d), 25118.5 f.
1589: 6229 f., 15251.7 imp., 22217 imp., 24493 f., 25118.6 f.
1590: 16664 f., 19657 ent., 19752 f. (d?), 19752.3 f. (d?), 19752.5(*A*3) f. (d?), 23685 f., 24852.7 ent.
1591: 12241 f., 19753 f.
1592: 5654.5 f., 5656 f., 12234 f., 16665 f., 19710.5 f., 19753.5 f.
1594: 1480 f.
1596: 12782 f., 12783 f., 16666 f., 25118.8 f.
1598: 16667 f.
1614: 3579 f.
1615: 12235 f.

Gueffier, François.
Bookseller and bookbinder in Paris, 1579–1623†. [Renouard.]
1607: 20448 (note).

Guenther, Johann.
Printer in Nürnberg, 1541–1544. [Benzing 359.]
1541: 6832.9.

Guenther (Gunter), Wolfgang.
Printer in Leipzig, 1549–1554 (1557†). [Benzing 280.]
1551: 16423 in off.

Guérin, Pierre.
Bookseller in Rouen, c. 1505–1547. [Duff, *Century*; Muller 100.]
1505: [15902] (d?). **1510:** 15911 pour (d?).

Guérin (Guarinus), Thomas.
Printer in Lyons, 1553–1555, and in Basel, 1561–1592†. [Muller 37; Benzing 41; *Library* 2 (1947): 286, top.]
1573: [13844] (false). **1577:** [4715]. **1579:** [15211?] (false).

Guillermo, Juan.
A Spanish adaptation of the name of W. Jones 3, used by him in 1623.
1623: 16925.

Guyot, Christoffel.
Printer in Leiden, 1598–1605†. [*Dict. 1*; Gruys; Briels 293, 300–3.]
1603: 14786.

Gwillim, John.
Stationer in London, (1614) 1615–1618. [*Dict. 1*; DFM 1818; *Loan Book*, 1615–18.]
shop in Britain's Burse (X.10), 1615 (3635)
1615: 3635 f.

Gybkyn, John.
Dutch bookseller in London, (1541) 1547–1557? [Duff, *Century*.]
in Paul's Churchyard at the Spread-Eagle (A.6), 1551 (24365, colophon)
1551: 19783 per, 24365 sold.

Gymnich (Gymnicus), Johann 1.
Bookseller and printer (from 1520) in Cologne, 1516–1544. [Benzing 238.]
1544: 24350.5.

H

H., G.
Publisher? or patron? in Paris? 1500. [Duff, *Century*.]
1500: 16174 [f.].

H., I. or J., 1496–97. *See* Huvin.

H., I. or J.
Patron? in Cambridge? or London? 1635.
1635: 22404.2 f.

H., I. or J., *pseud.*
Printer in 'Amsterdam', 1604. = W. Jones 3.
1604: 3526.

H., M., *pseud.*
Printer in 'Altmore', 1621. = Unidentified London printer.
1621: 18507.26, —.27.

H., W.
Recusant patron? or bookseller? in Rouen? or England? 1627–28.
1627–28: 24733 f.

Hacket, Thomas.
Bookseller in London, before 1557–1590†. [Duff, *Century*.]
shop in Cannon (Cannynge) Street over against the Three Cranes (T.1), 1560 (18970)
shop in Lombard Street (O.12), 1562 (3184.6)–1566 (13207)
shop in Paul's Churchyard at the Key (B), 1568 (23950)
shop in the Royal Exchange at the Green Dragon (O.8), 1572? (545)–1574 (3169)
shop in Lombard Street under the $ Pope's Head (O.11), 1584 (18282)–1590 (17786)
1557: 20.5 (c?).
1560: 18970 [f.] (d).
1561: 492.7 ent., 13251, 11725.
1562: 3184.6 (d), 13742, 13752, 24686 f.
1563: 20970 f. (d).
1566: [1367 f.] (d?), 3168 f. (d?), 13207 f., 15347 f. (d), 18358 f. (d), 19425 f. (d), 19438 f. (d), 20031 f. (d), [24508 f.?] (d?).
1567: 545 ent., 16754.5 f.
1568: 20097 f., 23950 f.
1570: 14653.7 (c).
1572: 545 f. (d?).
1574: 3169 f., 3422 [f.] (d?), 12609 [f.].
1577: 3170 ass'd.
1584: 978 f., 3060 f. (d), 18260 ent., 18282 f., 18282a f., 22928 f., 24167.5 f.
1585: 17785 f., 19447 f., 20032 f., 22571.5 f.
1587: 12343 f. (d), 17786 f., 20033 f., 20699 f., 22895a.5–96.5 f.
1588: 981 f., 23702.5 f., 23703 f.
1589: 18364 f., 21080 f.
1590: 979 f., 17786 f., 18365 f.

Haeghen (Dumaeus), Govaert van der.
Bookbinder, bookseller, and printer (from 1533) in Antwerp, 1518–1535†. [Duff, *Century*; Rouzet.]
1527: [5542 f.]. **1528:** 16131.5 imp. **1529:** [5542.2 f.] **1534:** [2830 f.], [14829] (false). **1535:** [2830 f.].

Haestens (Hastenius, Hastings), Hendrik Lodowijcxsoon van.
Printer in Leiden, 1596–1621, and in Louvain, 1622–1629†. [*Dict. 1*: 121, 131; Gruys; Briels 305–9.]
1610: 14336, [14337]. **1627–28:** 13926a ex off.

Haghe, Inghelbert.
Bookseller from Rouen active in London, 1505 (*Library* 1 (1910): 296–7), and in Hereford, 1510. [Duff, *Century*.]
No address used.
1505: 15793 imp.

Hall, Arthur.
Translator, member of parliament, and author, fl. 1563–1604. [*DNB*.]
No address used.
1576: [12629 f.] (d?).

Hall, Henry.
Printer in Oxford, 1642–1680. One of the Printers to the University from 1644. [*Dict. 2.*]
1662: [16703.5] (repeat, c); possibly = part of Wing W 654.

Hall, Rowland.
Printer in Geneva, 1559–1560, and in London, 1561–1563†. Freed as a Draper in 1547. His printing material apparently passed to **Richard Serle**. [Duff, *Century*; Chaix 193–4.]
No Geneva address used.
dw. in Golden (Golding) Lane at the Three Arrows (I.5), 1561 (18507)
dw. in Gutter Lane at the Half-Eagle and Key (G.4), 1562 (11725)–1563 (23433)
1559: 2384.
1560: 2093.
1561: 4372 (d), 4438–8.5, 4467 (d), 5306, 18507, 22017.
1562: 296, 304.5–05, [724?] (d?), 1209.5, 3484, 4375, 4458, 4470, 6214, 11725, 12191, 13299.5 (d?), 16849, 16849.3, 16849.7, 24800.
1562/63: 490.18, 490.20.
1563: 301, 2006.7, 3933, 4381, 5553, 11408 (d), 11529, 12191a, 12633, 15542, 17174, 19849, 20970 (d), 23433.
1563/64: 432.5.

Hall, William.
Printer in London, (1584) 1609–1613. Succeeded to the printing material of **Richard Bradock** in 1609, taking **Thomas Haviland** as partner until 1611, but their names do not appear together in any imprint. In partnership with **John Beale** from 1611, but their names only rarely appear together in imprints, e.g. in 1611 (23045). [*Dict. 1.*]
No address noted.
1608: 24288.5(*A*3) ent.
1609: 1417, 2784, 3510, 5694.5, 6625.7, 6944.7, 9175q ent., [10137.3c(*A*3)], [12740], 12985, 13123, [14525], 16875 (note), [17079?], 17755, 20629, 24472.
1610: 1934, [3066], [4258], 4961, [6029], 6937.5, 6944.4, 6945, 12500–1, 12817, [15049], 18620, [20806], [21821.6], [22768], 25795.
1611: [50], [7026] (d), 7115, 7182, 10600, 12501, 12171, 12818, 13424, 13456, 20775, 23041, 23045, [23331], 25266, 25795.
1611/12: 22182a.5.
1612: 363, 1141 ent., 1601.5, 4032.2, 4683, 5127, 5128 (d), [5878], 5895, 6959, [7312], 11482.7, 11692, 12814, [13121.5], [15140], 17530 ent., 17924.5, 18620.5, [19560], 21241.5, 22183, 22375, [22397], 23041, [23769?] (d), 25293.
1613: 7142, 11149–9.3, 13822.5, 13952, 23041.2(*A*3) (d?), 23055, 23500.

Halley, Edmund.
Bookseller in London, (1560) 1562–1565. [*Dict. 1.*]
in Lombard Street at the Eagle near unto the Stocks Market (O.12), 1562 (11298)
1562: 3725 f. (d), 11298 f.

Hamillon, Cardin 2.
Printer in Rouen, 1566–1615. [*Dict. 1*; Muller 100.]
1566: 2098. **1609:** 10928–8.3. **1613:** 16647, 17274, 22128. **1614:** 11318, 17275.

Hamillon, Richard.
Printer in Rouen, 1541–1559. [Duff, *Century*; Muller 100.]
1554: [16155], 16215 ex off., 16216 ex off.
1555: [16155a], 16216 ex off., 16248.
1557: 16249.

Hamilton, John.
Archbishop of St. Andrews, b. 1511?–1571†. [*DNB.*]
1552: 12731 at command.

Hamman, Johann. *See* Hertzog de Landoia.

Hamman (Hamon), John. *See* Hammond.

The Hammermen [i.e. Company of Metalworkers].
Publishers in Glasgow, 1638.
1638: 22025.7(*A*3) f. (d).

Hammond, Henry.
Bookseller in Salisbury, 1633–1637 at least. Probably son or grandson of a Stationer of the same name freed in 1556 (Arber I.36) and from at least 1571 resident in Salisbury (*Dict. 1*); probably brother of **Walter Hammond**.
No address noted.
1633: 7393.5 sold. **1635:** 1235 sold, 19350.5 sold. **1637:** 7164.3 sold, 7165.3 sold.

Hammond (Hamon, Hamman), John.
Stationer, maker of Writing Tables, and printer (surreptitiously from 1625) in London, (1612) 1614–1651. Had apprentices between 1615–1641 (DFM 1501–6). Master of **Richard Hammond** but not old enough to be his father. Illegal presses of his were seized in the following locations: Southwark, 1625; Lambeth Hill (S.7), 1628; Petticoat Lane (M.4), Mar. 1632; Shoreditch (K.3), Sept. 1632 (*C-B C*: 174, 201, 240, 243). In testimony of 4 Jan. 1630 he stated that he was 42 years old and living in the parish of St. Thomas Apostle (S.6; annotation in W. A. Jackson's copy of *Dict. 1*; cf. *C-B C*: xx n.2, xxi n.6). [*Dict. 1*; *Dict. 2*; DFM 2584; *St. Giles*, 1638.]
dw. in Angel Alley in Aldersgate Street (F.2), 1617 (24991.5)
1614: 23810 f.
1616: 23731.3 f., 23811 f.
1617: 23731.5 f., 24991.5 sold.
1618: 26050.14 made by (title).
1627: 23731.7 f., 23811.3 f.
1628: [18671.3?] f. (c).
1630: [18671.7?] f. (c).

Hammond (Hamon), Richard.
Stationer in London, 1626–1635 (cf. DFM 1508). Freed by **John Hammond** but not young enough to be his son. It is likely that the widow Judith who bound an apprentice in 1637 (DFM 1507) was Richard's wife and that in 1639 she freed his second apprentice (DFM 1509) in Richard's name. She may also be the widow in the *Poor Book*, 1646. [DFM 1502.]
shop at the upper end of Fleet Lane (D.2), 1630 (10586)
1630: 10586 f.

Hammond (Hamman), Walter.
Stationer in London, (1628) 1632–1641. Described when he was apprenticed in 1620 as the son of Henry, of Salisbury, bookseller, deceased; probably brother of **Henry Hammond.** [*Dict. 1*; DFM 28.]
No address used.
1633: 7393.5 f., 7393.6(*A*3) f.
1634: 25096–7 f., 19350 ent.
1635: 25097.5 f., 25098 f.
1636: 25099 f.
1637: 7164 f., 7165 f., 25100 f.
1638: 20447–7.5 pro.
1639: 25100.5 f.
1640: 25101 f.

Hancock, Ralph.
Stationer in London, (1580) 1581–1595. [*Dict. 1*; *St. Giles*, 1583–93.]
the shop over against St. Giles's Church without Cripplegate (I.4), 1595 (19545, colophon, with J. Hardy)
1595: 19545 sold.

Hanson, John.
Author and publisher? in London, 1604.
No separate address used.
1604: [12750?] f.

Harber. *See* Herbert.

Hardesty, John.
Bookseller in London, (1634) 1639–1658†. His only STC imprint was shared with **Michael Spark 1** and sold at the latter's shop: at the Blue Bible in Green Arbour (D.4). [*Dict. 2*; DFM 1147; *Poor Book* (child, under Atley), 1659.]
No separate address used.
1640: 14295 f.

Hardouyn, Germain.
Bookseller and printer in Paris, 1500–1541. [Duff, *Century*; Renouard.]
1528: 15959 per (d?). **1530:** 15965 in aed. **1533:** 15982 in aed. (d?).

Hardy, Eustache.
Printer in Rouen, 1517–1522? [Duff, *Century*; Muller 100; *Répertoire* 16e, 8: 32–3.]
1517: 13833.5. **1518:** 16198. **1522:** [16144(*A3*)?].

Hardy, John.
Bookseller in London, 1594–1612†. He seems to have taken over the shop of his former master, **Toby Cooke**, and then succeeded him as Beadle of the Stat. Co. (A.10, H.11, Q.1) in 1600 (*Reg. B*: 75). [*Dict. 1*; *Loan Book*, 1602–11; *Poor Book* (& wife/widow), 1608–12, as Beadle.]
dw. in Paul's Churchyard at the Tiger's Head (A.2), 1594 (4169; 11870, has 'his shop')–1596 (4171)
dw. on St. Peter's Hill (R.9), 1606 (7019)
1594: 4169 f., 11870 f., 15489 ent.
1595: 19545 sold, [24535(*A3*)] sold.
1596: 4171 f., 4174.5 f.
1599: 4166 ass'd, 4167 ass'd, 4168.5 ass'd, 4174.5 ass'd.
1606: 7019 f., 13001 f.
1607: 21507 f.
1609: 25934 ent.

Harford (Hartford), Ralph.
Bookseller and bookbinder (*C-B C*: fol 199^{r}) in London, (1627) 1629–1659 (Wing E 3532). Many of his pre-1641 imprints were shared with **Nicholas Bourne**. [*Dict. 2*; DFM 1201; *Loan Book*, 1634–37.]
in Paternoster Row, in Queen's Head Alley at the Gilt Bible (C.7), 1631 (20231)–1640 (22149.5; variation, 1638 (25607, has 'shop')
1631: 20231 sold, 20232 sold.
1632: 20233 sold.
1633: 20233a sold.
1634: 3255 f., 20234 sold.
1638: 20226 f., 20227 f., 22475 f., 22478 ent., 22478a f., 22498 f., 22498a f., 25023.5 f., 25607 f., 25608 f., 25609 f.
1639: 20227 (note), 22149–9.3 f., 22475 f., 22491 f.
1640: 22149.5 f., 22491 f.

Harford, W. *See* Herford.

Harison. *See* Harrison.

Harnisch, Wilhelm, *Heirs of.*
Printers in Neustadt an der Haardt, 1597–1604. [Benzing 347.]
1603: 26121a sumpt.

Harper, Richard.
Bookseller in London, 1633–1652. [*Dict. 2*; DFM 2588.]
in Smithfield (E.8), 1633?–1640 at least
—, 1633? (20821)
shop — at the Hospital gate, 1634 (21525.5)–1637 (4274)
— at the Bible and Harp, 1639 (21643.5)–1640 (13855.2); variation: 1640 (21644, adds 'near to the Hospital gate')
1633: 6367 ent., 20821 f. (d?).
1634: 6171 f. (d?), 19269 f. (d), 21512.5 f., 21525.5 f.
1635: 6073 f. (d?), 6169 f. (c?), 17989 f. (d?), 19234 f. (c), 21513 f.
1637: 4273 f. (d), 4274 f., 6074 f., 6074a f. (d?).
1638: 17745 f. (d).
1639: 11346.7 f., 11347.5 f. (d), 19072.7 f., 21643.5 f.
1640: 5423 f. (c), 6074a.4 f. (d?), 13855.2 f., [14963?] f., 17232 f. (c), 17990 f. (d?), 18501.5 f., [19526 f.?] (d?), 21644 f., 22007.5 f., 23424.7 f. (d), 25998 f. (c).

Harper, Thomas.
Bookseller and printer (from 1628) in London, (1611) 1614–1656†. Brother of **William Harper**. Three items of 1624 were printed in the King's Printing House, and it seems possible Harper may have been working as a journeyman there or that **John Bill** allowed him the use of the material. In 1628 Harper acquired the printing material that had passed from **Thomas Snodham** to **George Wood.** Harper was apparently one of the *assignees of* **Joan Man**, 1635–37. At the time of his death he was living in Little Britain (F.4). [*Dict. 2*; DFM 121; *Loan Book* (for A. Griffin), 1627–30; Globe 214.]
their shop in Paul's Churchyard (B), 1614 (17697.7, with W. Harper); no later use of this or any other address noted
1536: 10887 (d/error)
1614: 1012 f., 17697.7 f., 25605.5 ent.
1615: 21017 f.
1624: 861(*A3*) [f.], 23922 [f.], 26011 ent.
1625: 13324 f.
1626: 14479 f., 18615 f., 20332 f.
1628: [4187], 5363, [10074], 10863, 11468, [11946], 13516, 13551, 14905, 15374.9, [25727].
1629: 104, [2612], 4498, [4514.7], 4979, 5911, 12348 typis, [14441?], 14483, 17098, 19877.5, 20051 typis, 20952, 21474 typis, 21846, 23819.
1630: 104–5, [603], [2612], [2619?], 4239, [4515], 6175 [by &] f., 6176, 6303, 6982, 7210, 11326, 11688, 11690, [11691.5?], 17891, 17893, 20686, 20686.5, 20828, 21446 typis, 22301, 22383, 23772a.5.
1631: 688, [3790–0.5?], 4992–3, 5463, 5780.7–81, 14780, 14791, 14930, 17716, 18898 ap., 19092, 20808.5, [20829], 21117, [23775.5], 25223, 25768.5(*A3*).
1632: 861.3, 2734, 5464, 5780.7–81, 6154 ap., 6456.8 ap., 7031, [10369], 10530–1, 10686, 11767, [11786], [12455.5] (false), [12993], 13822, 14792, 14830–31a, 17636, 19522.5, 20809, 21329, 22834, 22847.
1633: 352, 1357–7.5, 1361, 1426, 2648, 2767 ap., 6937, 10189.5 (d?), 11692.7, 12539, 13273, 13517, 14713, 14793, 15196, 15267.7, 15268.7, 17345, 17384, 17588, 19182.5, 21425, 21739, 22122, [23525.3–.4], 24323, 24618, [25067–7a], 25617, 25929.
1634: [31], 1577–7.5, 3587, 6874 ap., 6949–9.3, 10211, 10216, [10265?] (d), [10271] (d?), 10918.5, 13038, 13373, 13511, 13542.5, [13624.5] (d?), 13627, [15466], 15555, 16892.3 ap., 17694, [17978.5] (d), 19203.3 (note), 19455, 21323 ap., [21512.5?], 21525.5, 23525.5, 23525.6, 23525.7, 24432, 25852.3, 24956, 25932–2.5.
1635: [31.5], 1099, 1100, 1506, 1578, 3239, 3569, 4501, [6979], 10190 (d?), 12959 ap., 13169, 13543, 14712 ap., 17004 ap., 17513.5 (note), 17979, 18003, 20162, [21513], 22553, 23123, 23366, [23525.8], [23525.9], [23550], 25234, [25313].
1636: 32–2.5, 679, 2736, 3955, 4525, 4899, [4941.5?], [6176.5], 6427, 6668, 7511, [9058.7?] (d), 10887 (d), 12893, 13274, [13275], 16892.3–.7 ap., [16997], [17694.5], [18003.1], 20162, 20652, 20810, 21619.5–20, 21806 typis, 22515, 22516, 22786, [25238].
1637: 347, 1102, 2670 (note), [2736.5] (d?), 2736a, 4293.4, 4526, [4900], [6074], [6625], 7511.2, 10838.5, 12710, [13267], 13796 ap., 13796.5 (forged), [14832a], 17979.3, 19089, 21806 typis, 22494, 22495, 22517, 22734, 23857.7–58, [24498–8.5], 24910, 25234.5.
1638: 861.6, 905, 1333, 1554, [3273.9(*A*)] (d?), 3474.5, 3772.2–.4, [3904], 4293.6, 5680, [7467], 7512, 10207, [12710.3], 13220, [13312.5], 17745 (d), 17780, [18507.277?], 20610, 20691 ap., 20963 ap., [20964] (d?), [20965] (d?), 21093, [21094], 22496, 22518, 22533 (d), [22550], 24760.
1639: 721, 4293.8, 4549–50, 5335, 6044, 6306, 7266, [7511.5], 11071, 11346.7, 11347.5 (d), 11369, 11369.5, 12205–6a, 12457–7.5, 13220, 16873, 17514 typis, 17667, 17717, [18507.284?], [—.292?], [—.305?], [—.313?], 19072.7, [20863], 22485, 24978.
1639/40: [18507.319?], [—.326?].
1640: 157, 3133, [3931], 6007–8 typis, 6105, 7240, 10139.3 (d), 10213, 10218, [10876], 11369a, 15114, 17511.5 chez, 17515 typis, [18501.5], [18507.316?], [—.331?], [—.333?], [—.334?], [—.337?], [—.338?], [—.339?], [—.340?], [—.341?], [19215], 19379, 21479.5, [21644], 21775, [22007.5], 23059.5 (d?), [23424.5].
1640/41: [21589.7], 25248.5 (note), 25248.7 (note).
1641: 14754a.

Harper, William.
Stationer in London, (1612) 1613–1616. Brother of **Thomas Harper**. [*Dict. 1*; DFM 97; *Poor Book*, 1616.]
their shop in Paul's Churchyard (B), 1614 (17697.7, with T. Harper)
1613: 17045 sumpt. **1614:** 1012 f., 17697.7 f., 25605.5 ent.

Harrigat, John.
Stationer in London, (1622) 1624–1640 (*C-B C*: 330) at least. [*Dict. 1*; DFM 1539.]
at the Holy Lamb in Paternoster Row (C.7), 1624 (14490)–1630 (6561)
1624: 14490 f. **1630:** 6561 sold, 20828 f. **1634:** 6949.3 sold. **1635:** 5627 ?ent.

Harrington, John.
Bookseller? or patron and translator? in London, 1549–1550. In the first item below the address of its printer, **Thomas Raynald**, is given: in Paul's Churchyard at the Star (B). [Duff, *Century*.]
It is very likely that this man is John Harington of Stepney, father of Sir John Harington. Objections to this identification are based on a notice in Herbert (III.1309) of the 'widow of John Harrington', but Herbert did not see the volume in question since he gives no format. It must have contained at least two items: the first a Sternhold Psalms (cf. 2420, 2422) and the last 2727 below, with one line (given here in italics) of the colophon omitted: ... | by the wydowe of Jhon | *Herforde, for Jhon* | Harrington the | yeare of our | lorde. | M.D. and L. |
No separate address used.
1549: 2726 [f.]. **1550:** 2727 f.

Harris, Andrew.
Stationer in London, (1595) 1598–1625†. [*Dict. 1*; *Poor Book*, 1608–25, widow thereafter.]
shop under the $ Pope's Head next to the Royal Exchange (O.11), 1598 (19807)
1598: 19807 f.

Harris, William.
Bookseller in London, 1636/37–1641 (Wing G 1168). One of this name (DFM 1533) was apprenticed in 1628 but apparently never made free; he or another was thought to own an illegal press seized in the Minories (M.3) in 1632 (*C-B C*: 243). [*Dict. 1.*]
in Coleman Street (H.4), 1636/37 (419.6)–1640 (10658, adds: at the White Hind)
1636/37: 419.6 sold.
1638/39: 436.11 sold, 517.7 sold.
1639/40: 406.5 sold, 501.30 sold, 505.14 sold.
1640: 10658 sold.

Note: The identities of the four Stationers below named **John Harrison** are clearly set out through 1640 in Duff, *Century* and *Dict. 1*. Allocation of their respective imprints during years of overlapping activity is based primarily on rights recorded in the SR, on addresses in imprints, and on epithets like 'elder', 'younger', 'Master', etc., in the SR or occasionally in imprints, though it must be remembered that over time the younger became the elder. In the absence of such information, allocation has been based largely on partnerships or printers; for example, John 1 often published jointly with G. Bishop and W. Norton and used H. Middleton as printer while John 2 sometimes shared rights with T. Man 1 and used other printers. Three doubtful items below are preceded by a query but have been placed under the John most likely to have been involved: under John 2, 1580 (24891), 1615 (12562a), and under John 4, 1618 (19347).

Harrison (Harison), John 1.
Bookseller in London, (1556) 1558–1617†. Possibly the son of **Richard Harrison**; son-in-law of **Reyner Wolfe**. Half-brother of **John Harrison 2**; father of **John 3** and **Joseph Harrison**. Father-in-law of **Thomas Gubbin**. One of the *assignees of* **F. Flower**. *See* also **Tres Viri**. [Duff, *Century*.]
On 21 Sept. 1612 John 1 assigned a number of his school texts to the **English Stock** (*see* Stationers' Company). Assignments of items that year indexed in square brackets indicate that the assignment is not mentioned in STC itself. For further information about this group of books *see* the headnote following Appendix D/60.
at the White Greyhound in Paul's Churchyard (B), 1582 (6649.7)–1594 (22345); sometimes omits 'White', e.g. in 1588 (23689, colophon)
dw. in Paternoster Row at the Greyhound (C.7), 1596 (20804)–1613 (6661); sometimes 'White' is added to the sign, e.g. in 1605 (17584)

Harrison, John 1 — *cont.*
1570: 14326 f. (d?).
1573: 18543 f., 22630 [f.].
1574: 20813 [f.].
1575: 2111.5 [f.], 17406 (note), 18577 f. (d?), 20801, 24677 f.
1576: 5759.1 ent.
1577: 2044 imp., 4400 f., 12201 f. (d), 13568 f. (d), 20801.3, 20801.7(***A*3**), 23659.3 ent.
1578: 3294.3 f., 4393 f., 10470 imp., 13029 f., 13785 imp., 19287 ent.
1579: 2056 ent., 3294.5 f., 4042.7 f. (d), 4452 f., 6037 ent., 11683 f., 13785 imp., 17003.3 ent., 17302 f., 20762.5 pro, 20801.7.
1580: 2033, 2056.2 imp., 2359 imp., 17176 ent., 18884 ent., 18884.3 imp., 19961 ent., 24789 imp.
1581: 2057 imp., 3294.7 f., 4442 ent., 4456.5 f., 17287.7 pro, 22109.5 imp.
1582: 1982 ?ent., 6649.7 f., 20802, 23659.3(***A***) ent., 23873 pro.
1583: 4399 f., 4443 f., 6650 f., 6651 f., 6652 f., 6652.5 f., 15257 f., 19962 pro, 22110.5 imp., 22114 ent., 22114.5 imp., 23873.5 pro, 24790 imp.
1584: 5759.1 imp., 6653 f., 19064 pro, 24790.3 imp.
1585: 2060.5 imp., 6654 f., 13786.5 imp., 18926.7 imp., 23659.3 ent., 25185 f.
1586: 6655 f., 12201.5 f., 20802.5 f.
1587: 5309.5 imp., 6655.5 f., 13569–9.5 at expenses, 15470a f.
1588: 6656 f., 20762.7 pro, 23659.3 ent., 23689 f.
1589: 5759.1 (note), 6657 f., 16612a.3 imp., 18885 imp., 18952 imp., 20054.7 ent.
1590: 6658 f., 16890 f., 20803 f., 24689 imp.
1591: 5315.3 imp., 17581 sold, 23256 f.
1592: 10865 f., 13787 imp., 20054.7 imp., 24653 imp.
1593: [22354] sold.
1594: 2810a.3 imp., 6360 ent., 18929 imp., 19287 f., 20803.5 f., 22345 f., [22355] sold.
1595: 6658.2 f., 17280 imp., 20763 pro, 21622.8 ent., [22356 f.?] (d?).
1596: 17582 sold, 20804 f., 22357 f.
1598: 6658.4 f., 19557.7 imp., 22346 f.
1599: 2810a.7 imp., 5315.5 imp., 6658.5 f., 17281 imp.
1600: 6658.6 f., [17583(***A*3**)] sold, 20804.3 f., 22347 f., 22348(***A*3**) (repeat), [24581] sold.
1601: 11925.5 ent., 18952.1 imp.
1602: 6658.8 f., 18926.9 imp., 18929.3 imp., 20814 f., 22348(***A*3**) (d), 24475–5.5 f.
1603: 19558 imp., 20341.
1605: 2810b imp., 17584(***A*3**) f., 20804.7(***A*3**) [f.].
1606: 6659 f., 19558.7 imp., 24852.7(***A*3**) ent.
1607: 6659.5 f., 20805 f., 22349 f.
1608: 17281.3 f., 20763.4 imp.
1609: 17585 f., 19559 imp.
1610: 17585 f., 20806 f.
1611: 6660 f., 6660.5 f.
1612: (*see* John 1 headnote): 2812 ass'd, [5315.8 ass'd], [cf. 5689 ass'd], [cf. 15244.3 ass'd], 17281.5 ass'd, 18927.5 ass'd, 18929.5 ass'd, 18952.3 ass'd, 18976.8 ass'd, [20055.5 ass'd], 20763.7 ass'd, 23659.7(***A*3**) ass'd, 24852.7 imp. (d?) & (***A*3**) ass'd.
1613: 6661 f.

Harrison, John 2.
Bookseller in London, (1569) 1579–1618†. Possibly the son of **Richard Harrison.** Half-brother of **John Harrison 1**; father of **John 4**, **Josias**, and **Philip Harrison**. *See* also Appendix A/21. [*Dict. 1.*]
dw. in Paternoster Row at the Anchor (Anker, Anger (C.7)), 1580 (3086)–1617 (23094, has 'shop'); the sign is usually plain 'Anchor' through 1603 (11086); in 1606 (11087) it is 'Blue Anchor', and in at least 1586 (2790) and 1615 (25244)–1617 (23094) it is 'Golden Anchor'.
1580: 3086 f., 4404 f. (c), 4404.5 f. (c), 4460 f., [22044 f.] (d), 24251.5 f., ?24891 ent.
1581: 13774 f., 23090 f.
1582: 19054 f. (d), 19915 f.
1583: 10764–4.3 f., 13775 f.
1584: 3602 f., 19863.3 f. (d), 24528 f.
1585: 22247 f.
1586: 2790 f., 23091 f., 23283 ent.
1587: 18134.7 f. (d?).

Harrison, John 2 — *cont.*
1589: 14376.5 ent., 23277 f., 23277.5 pro (d/error).
1591: 23092 f.
1592: 23283 pro.
1597: 23093 f.
1598: 23277.5 pro (d), 23278 pro.
1599: 19766.5 ent.
1601: 5329 f., 10846 f.
1603: 11086 f., 14376.5 f. (d), 14377, 24041 f.
1606: [356] sold, 11087 f.
1610: 4314 f.
1614: 23257 ent.
1615: ?12562a f., 25244 f.
1616: 13019 f., 14948 f.
1617: 23094 f.

Harrison, John 3.
Printer in London, (1599) 1600–1604†. Son of **John Harrison 1**. Acquired the printing material of **Thomas Judson**; this later passed to **George** and **Lionel Snowdon**, though John 1 may well have owned it. [*Dict. 1*; ?*St. Giles*, 1600; *SB* 7 (1955): 127–8, etc.; Blayney, *Origins*: 14, etc.]
John 3's address is the same as his father's, and it is difficult to tell them apart. For the purposes of this index, John 3 has been deemed responsible for printing and John 1 for bookselling. The least ambiguous imprint—in a work entered to John 3—is:
printed by John Harrison at the Greyhound in Paternoster Row (C.7), 1601 (4941)
1600: 14, 367, [1335.7?] (d?), 6658.6, 17583(*A*3), 20804.3, 22347, 22348(*A*3) (repeat), 24581.
1601: 4941, [6626.5(*A*)], 11925.5, 16910.5, 18952.1, 19100, 21622.8 typis, 25331.
1602: 6658.8, 10462, 12718, [13929], 18926.9, 18929.3, 20814, 22348(*A*3) (d), [23454], 24475–5.5.
1603: 1814, 6625.5, [6967], 6967.5, [12988], 19558, 21433.
1604: 23329.

Harrison, John 4.
Bookseller in London, (1600) 1602–1641 at least. Son of **John Harrison 2.** He had a son, John 5, freed in 1627 (DFM 1551), of whom no definite signs of activity before 1641 have been noted. John 5 may be the man whose nameless daughter was buried in 1632 (*St. Giles*) and/or the one in the *Poor Book*, 1639–41, 1644–76, since the next John (DFM II.1990) was not freed until 1647. [*Dict. 1*; ?*Loan Book*, 1608–11, 1613–16.]
in Paternoster Row (C.7), 1602–1641 at least
dw. — at the Golden Unicorn and Bible, 1602 (13929)–1603 (25643, omits 'Golden')
— at the Golden Unicorn, 1614 (4032.3(*A*))–1641 (Wing M 666); variation: has 'shop', omits 'Golden', 1636 (20810), 1640 (20811)
1602: 13929 f.
1603: 25643 f.
1609: 16685 f.
1614: 4032.3(*A*) sold, 25244 ent.
1617: 23100a(*A*3) f.
1618: ?19347 f., 25094 sold.
1619: 23257 f.
1620: 17804 ent., 19289 f., 23258 f., 25902 f.
1624: 17632 f.
1630: 1021 ent., 3323 ent., 11767 ent., 6666 f., 11934 ent., 12893 ent., 21850.7 ent.
1631: 15331.3 f., 17339 f., 17340 f. (d/repeat), 17344 f., 17353 f., 17364 f., 17374 f., 17396 f., 20808.5 f.
1632: 4803.2 f., 6948 f., 11767 f., 20809 f., 22352 f.
1633: 1426 f., 6937 f., 15267.7 f., 15268.7 f., 17345 f., 17384 f., 17396.5 f. (d?), 17588 f., 24618 f.
1634: 6949–9.3 f., 15555 f.
1636: 6667 f., 6668 f., 12893 f., 17365 f., 20810 f.
1637: 15331.7 f., 6669 f., 17340 f. (d?), 17354 f.
1638: 6670 f., 15331.7 f., 17375 f., 17397 f., 17633 f.
1639: 19290 f.
1640: 20811 f.

Harrison, Joseph.
Bookseller in London, (1604) 1606–1608. Son of John Harrison 1. Although Joseph is the nominal printer of the first item, the work was probably done by the Snowdons. His address is that of his father. [*Dict. 1.*]
dw. at the Greyhound in Paternoster Row (C.7), 1608 (17874)
1606: 5776–6.3. **1608:** 17874 f.

Harrison, Josias.
Bookseller in London, (1605) 1611 (cf. DFM 1560)–1619. Son of **John Harrison 2.** The address in his imprints is that of his father, and 'dw.' or 'his shop' is never used. [*Dict. 1.*]
sold at the Golden Anchor in Paternoster Row (C.7), 1615 (22871)–1616 (24175.7)
1615: 1667 f., 12358 f., 22871–1a f., 24175.3 f. **1616:** 24175.7 f.

Harrison, Luke (Lucas).
Bookseller in London, (1556) 1558–1578†. From 1570 most of his imprints were shared with **George Bishop**. [Duff, *Century*; *Library* 14 (1959): 28, 35–6.]
dw. in Paul's Churchyard (A.3), 1558/59 (492)–1576 (568) at least; adds 'at the Crane', 1563 (3811)–1569 (12961)
1558/59: 492 f.
1560: 13012 ent.
1561: 6776 (d?).
1562: 435.39 ent., 6850 ent., 16851 (d).
1563: 3811.
1564: 2017 f., 6811 f.
1565: 4368 f., 5723.5 f., 6812 f.
1566: 1534 f.
1568: 5011 f., 23554 f. (d?).
1568/69: 361.3 f.
1569: 11269 f., 11286 f., 12961 f., 13061 f., 13062 f., 18679.5 f., 18680 f., 18681 f., 18682 f., [18685.7] sold.
1570: 5037 f. (d), 5263 f., 6832 f., 11271 f. (d), 17410 f. (d?), 21351.5 f. (d?), 24113 f. (d).
1571: 4395 f., 23555 f.
1573: 7369 f., 19114 f.
1574: 4444 f., 4445 f., 4449 f., 13063 f., 15003 f., 17408 f.
1575: 2111 [f.], 19115 f. (d?), 19832 f.
1576: 568 f., 4096 f., 6726 [f.], 15004 f.
1577: 4448 f., 5264 f., 6727 [f.], 11454 f., 13063.5 f. (d?), 13568.5 f. (d), 15042, 19115.5 f. (d?).
1578: 4441 ass'd, 4442 ass'd, 4446 ass'd, 4449 ass'd, 6737 ass'd, 13064 ass'd, 13569 ass'd, 15043, 21352 ass'd.

Harrison, Philip.
Bookseller in London, 1603–1620. Son of **John Harrison 2**. [*Dict. 1*; *Poor Book*, 1617–20.]
(at) the [Royal] Exchange (O.10), 1608–1609
at the Little Shop at — over against the conduit, 1608 (18455.3)
shop in Cornhill over against —, 1609 (25934)
1608: [18258(*A*3)] sold, 18455.3 f. **1609:** 25934 f.

Harrison, Richard.
Printer in London, before 1557–1563†. Possibly the father of **John Harrison 1** and **2**. [Duff, *Century*.]
in White Cross Street (I.8), 1562 (4416)
1561: 4415. **1562:** 2096, 4416, 7663 ent., 25612, 25612.5.

Harrison, Stephen.
Architect, designer, and author, fl. 1603. [*DNB*; Hind II.17–29.]
[his] house in Lime Street at the $ Snail (P.6), 1604 (12863)
1604: 12863 sold.

Hart, Andro.
Bookseller, bookbinder, and printer (from 1607) in Edinburgh, 1587–1621†. Succeeded to the printing material of **Robert Charteris** in 1610. Husband of **Jonet** and father of **John Hart**, who most often printed as the *heirs of* **A. Hart.** Regarding the 1601 items indexed below *see heirs of* **H. Charteris**. [*Dict. 1.*]
shop (buith) on the North side of the [High] Street (gate) a little below the cross, 1610 (2209) and until his death, though no later use has been noted
1601: 2184.5 at expenses, 2702 at expenses, 2901 at expenses, 16588 at expenses.
1602: 14787 [f.], 14787.2 at expenses (d?), 14787.6 sumpt. (d?).
1603: 14786 sumpt., 14787.4 at expenses, 14787.8 sumpt.
1607: 16589.5.

Hart, A. — *cont.*
1608: 7147.5, 10554.
1610: 2209, 2704 (c), 21555.14, —.15, [22024.5?] (c).
1611: 3986, 4389, 13151–1a, 14853.5, 16590, 16591, 18356, 21555.16, —.17 (d).
1612: 339, 18976.8, 19889, 21555.19, 24794.5.
1613: 340, 1771, [6267.5] (c), 7257, 11357.5, 13160, 21555.20, —.21, 21610, 23601, 25188.
1614: 338, [572.5] (d?), 1145, 1406, 2705, 5848.5, [7253–4] (d?), 7258–9, 12202.5, 15666, 18349–9a ex off., 21555.22.
1615: 1403, 2706, 2708, 3990–0.5 ex off., 7487.12, 13031.3, 13031.4, 16592, 17841.9, 18294, 21555.24, 23104, 23601.
1616: [71.32] (d), 1378, 2708.5, 3482, 3793, [7252.3] (d), 7255–6, 7487.13, 7546, 20988.5 (d?), 21272, 21283, 21555.27, 23067.6, 23105, 23106, 23601.
1617: 6781.4, 6997, 6999, 7252, 7487, 7487.14, 12483, 12970, 13953, 14916, 15372, 15667, 16593, 17842, 18357, 21553, 21555.29, 25191.
1618: 140.5 (note), 142, 1405, 4898, 5301.6, 5759.5, 7487.15, 13024, 13152, 15715, 16593.5, 21438, 21555.31, —.32.
1618/19: 435.61.
1619: 1407, 2920.3, 7487.16, 14284, 14708.7, 15667.5, 18350, [21056.2?], 21277, 21856, 23431.3, 23889.
1620: 71.5, 137, 1379, 4849, 7487.17, 10478.3, 13153, 17616, 17814, 21256, 24853.
1621: [186] (d), 2998, 3980, 3987, 6781.5, 7487.18, 13258, 13954.3, 13983.5, 16594, 23660.

1622: 16594 (post-dated?).
1634: 5303.2 [heirs], 15670 [heirs].

Hart, Andro, *Heirs of.*
Printers in Edinburgh, 1622–1639. Principally Hart's widow, **Jonet**, and his sons Samuel and **John**. They were succeeded by **James Bryson**. [*Dict. 1.*]
No address noted.
1622: 7487.19, 17120.
1623: [7247–9], 7487.20.
1625: 2710, 7487.22.
1625/26: 435.63.
1626: 13766.
1627: 138, 6782 sumpt., 7246, 7487.24, 14906.
1628: 2935, 3446a.5, 13025.7, [22998.5(*A*3)] (d?), 23367, 23370.
1629: 3445a (note), 3447, 7487.26, 13954.7, 16595.5, 23368.5.
1630: 2715, 2715.5, 7250, 15669, 16596.5.
1631: 6780 sumpt., 21257, 21439.
1632: 2717, 2718, 5760, 5941, 6784, 7487.30, 21555.43, 23369.
1633: 2720, 2721, [7076] (d), 7486, [13952.5] (d?), 19172.7, 19173, 20656.
1634: 5303.2 [heirs], 15670 [heirs], 15680.5, 16598, 21212.3, 21273, 21555.44.
1635: 574.5, 16599, [21257.3] (c), [21257.7] (c), 21555.46.
1636: 1617.5, 18290.
1637: 11777, 15244.7.
1638: [665] (d).
1639: 22049.

Hart, John.
Printer in Edinburgh, 1630–1639? Son of **Andro** and **Jonet Hart**. *See* also *heirs of* **A. Hart**. [*Dict. 1.*]
No address noted.
1630: 1609.3, 7251. **1631:** 1609.5, 2941.3, 11772.5.

Hart, Jonet.
Printer in Edinburgh, 1622?–1639 (1643†). Second wife and widow of **Andro** and mother of **John Hart**. *See* also *heirs of* **A. Hart**. [*Dict. 1*, under husband and Heirs.]
No address noted.
1631: 7487.28.

Hart, Michael.
Stationer in London, (1592) 1593, and bookseller in Exeter, 1596?–1601 at least. His first item was shared with **Toby Cooke** and sold at the latter's address: in Paul's Churchyard at the Tiger's Head (A.2). [*Dict. 1.*]
No separate London address or address in Exeter used.
1593: 11850 f. **1601:** 17173.5 sold.

Harvey, John.
Bookseller in London, 1539. [Duff, *Century*.]
in Lombard Street at the Holy Lamb (O.12), 1539 (23711a)
1539: 23711a sold.

Harvey, Richard.
Bookseller in London, before 1557–1566? [Duff, *Century*.]
dw. in Foster Lane (G.3), 1552? (7555.5)
1552: 7555.5 [f.] (d?). **1557:** 24318 ent.

Haslop (Hassellup), Henry.
Journeyman printer and publisher in London, 1586–1591. One or both of the items indexed below may actually have been printed by Haslop working in the shops of his former masters, **Roger Ward**, possibly still near Holborn conduit (D.5: 16617), and **William How**, possibly still at Temple Bar in Fleet Street (W.14: 12926). [*Dict. 1*; ?*Poor Book* (widow Alice), 1608–18.]
No address used.
1586: 16617 [f.] **1587:** 12926 f., 22267 ent., 24931 ent.

Hastenius, Hastings. *See* Haestens.

Hatfield, Arnold.
Printer in London, (1581) 1584–1612†. One of the partners in the **Eliot's Court Press**. [*Dict. 1*; *Library* 2 (1922): 175–84; 3 (1923): 194–209.]
Indexed below are *only* items which Hatfield entered in the SR or in which his name appears in the imprint. In the items distinguished by an asterisk (*) the imprint is shared with another partner. Items *without* imprint, including those for which his name has been supplied in square brackets in STC, are listed *only* under Eliot's Court Press.
in the Little Old Bailey, in Eliot's Court (D.1), 1587 (12200)
1584: 4094*, 19355*.
1585: 376.3*, 4332* ap., 13786* ap., 19356.5*.
1586: 6655*, 13843.5, 19485.
1587: 6655.5, 7285, 7285.2, 12200, 15454 ent.
1588: 14630.5, 24579 en casa.
1589: 829 in off., 6657, 17131 en casa.
1590: 829 in off., 4333, 21698 ent., 24481.
1594: 5242.
1595: 5245.
1596: 5238, 5249, 5254, 5602.
1597: 764, 13881, 19366.
1598: 11098, 13174, 13883, 16649, 19951, 23644.
1599: 1312.3 ent., 4423, 5315.5, 11749 ex off., 14585, 19260 ent.
1600: 4518 ent., 5624, 11513 ent., 14453, 18626a.4, 20084, 23453, 23462 ent., 23698.
1601: 4334, 5603, 11940 ent.
1602: 23454.
1603: 14366, 18018, 19899, 20063, 20132.5.
1604: 10801, 11029.5 (d), 13248, 19546.5, 23645.
1605: 13971, 20149, 23645.
1606: 10548, 15561.
1607: 765, 1939, 6103, 19854, 24951.
1608: 12662–2.5, 12663.2, 20085.
1609: 1940, 3776.5, 20772.
1611: 12703, 22393.
1612: 12496, 12703a, 13937, 20910 ent., 23646.

Haukyns. *See* Hawkins.

Haultin (Hawlton), Jérôme.
French typefounder in London, 1574–1586, and printer in La Rochelle, 1587–1600†. While in London he lived in St. Anne's parish, Blackfriars (Q.5). [*Dict. 1*: 133; Muller 96.]
1590: [3443.5?] (c).

Haveland. *See* Haviland.

Haviland, John.
Printer in London, (1613) 1621–1638† (*C-B C*: 316). Nephew of **Thomas Haviland**. One of the partners in the **Eliot's Court Press**; one of the *assignees of* **J. More, esq.** In 1634 Haviland acquired an interest in the office of **King's Printer**. [*Dict. 1*; DFM 261; *Loan Book*, 1632–37 (for E. Purslowe), 1636–37 (for John Phillips); *Library* 2 (1922): 175–84; 3 (1923): 194–209.]

Haviland, J. — *cont.*
Below are two categories of Haviland publications. First, items beginning in 1629 which belong to More's patent for law books and which have Haviland's name in the imprint or supplied in STC in square brackets are included below, though the full range of 'More' publications is listed only under that name. Second, for the ordinary Eliot's Court Press publications *only* those items are included which Haviland entered in the SR or in which his name appears in the imprint or a variant thereof. In the items distinguished by an asterisk (*) a partner's name appears on another title-page. Eliot's Court items *without* imprint, including those for which Haviland's name has been supplied in square brackets in STC, are listed *only* under Eliot's Court Press.
his house in the Little Old Bailey in Eliot's Court (D.1), 1627 (17947)
in the Old Bailey over against the Sessions House (D.7), 1634 (11955)
1621: 11671 ent., 11675, 15176 ent., 15338 ent., 24006.5 ent.
1622: 213, 217–8, 1155, 1642.5, 3452, 3786, 4110, 6386, 7318, 10325, 11651.5, 11677, 12119, 12657a, 12714.5, 12748, 12791 typis, 13513, 14301–2, 18483, 18507.51A, —.68, 18897, 19052.8, 23862, 25037, 25315.
1623: 59, 143, 160, 1068, 1108 in off., 1156 in off., 3498, 4193, 5031–2, 5033, 6015, 6204a, 6831, 11659, 11665, 11666–6a, 11681–1.3, 11768, 11923, 12646–6a, 12658–8.5, 12665–5.3, 12792, 12891.5, 13514, 14305, 15184, 15330, 15439 ent., 17382, 18626a.7, 19621–1b.5, 20767, 21199, 21415, 23288, 23785, 25325, 26064.
1624: 1108 in off., 3992.5 in off., 4073, 4881, 6108.5?, 6204a.5, 7006.5, 11653, 11654, 11660, 11662, 11669, 12330, 12635–5b by & f., 12715, 12840, 14458 ex off., 14485, 14624, 14624.5, 15325, 15338, 18610, 22152.5, 22790, 23853, 23854–5, 24508.7, 24508.9(*A3*), 24509–9a, 25620.
1625: 1147–8, 3047.5, 3916, 5030, 5535, 5660, 6063.8, 6067.5, 11951, 12635–5b by & f., 12792.5, 12840a, 14625, 17945, 21663, 22790a, 23854–5.
1626: 219, 1168, 1177 in off., 11648, 11952, 13515.5, 14968, 15331, 17946, 22790b.
1627: 219, 1169, 5436.7, 7049, 11548, 11647, 11663, 11671, 12636–7.7, 14971, 17731, 17751, 17751.5, 17947, 18156a, 19436.5, 19583, 22790c, 22794, 23228, 23564–4.5, 23731.7, 23753, 23811.3, 24576, 24956.5.
1628: 1160.5–.7, 1170, 1864, 3992.9 in off., 7342.5, 11953, 12331, 12332, 12335, 12636.7, 13403.3, 14965, 18998, 19584, 21370, 24703 typis.
1629: 1124, 1149, 1161, 1170 (note), 1862, 1865, 1866, 4200, 6198, 6649.3, 7281.5, 10192.7E, 11204, 11689, 12249, 13477–7.5, [15785], 16880 in off., 17522 typis, 19600.8, 21831 ent., 22781, 25721.
1630: 3395, 3404, 3514, 3563, 3772, 5437, [6209], 12822, 12838, 13403.6, 13618, 14489, [15789], [21583], 21836, 22364, 22796, 22966, 25738.
1630/31: 6542.
1631: 1171, 3499, 11954, 13047–7.5, 15718, 16961, 17066, 17730, 17730.5, 17731.3–.7, 19653a–b.5, 21339, 22787, 22790c.5, 22887.
1632: 1150, 1435–5.5, 5438, 9329, 12400, 17666, 21832, 22675, 22782, 22790d, 23507, 23803.
1633: 12639–40, 15162.3 (d), 15786, 18845, 18845a, 25685–5a.5.
1634: 188.5, 3255*, 10587, 11439, 11955, 12639–40, 12816, 15643, 19516, [20839] (d), 20944, 22968, 25700a–a.7.
1635: 1172, 1951, 4200.5, 5439, [6210], 9330, 12816, 13802, 17513–3.5 typis, 18026.5–27, 20781, 20944.
1636: 4196, 5440, 6168.7, 6757, 6779, 7282, 9330, 13802, 17067, 18027a, [20718], 22366, 22968, 23565, 24510.
1637: 5465–5.3, 5770, 10212, 10324, 11652–2b.5*, 13733, 13739, 14064.7 in off., 14718, 16923, 17218, 17219, 22457, 22676, 22783, 23566–6.5, 23586.
1638: 1109–10*, 1151 ent., 1158, 2677, [3556] & ent., 3586, 5354.3, 6048, 6304, 11650, 12238 ent., 12250 ent., 13477 ent., 13618 ent., 13727, 13739, 13803, 13804, 15176 ent., 15643 ent., 15339 ent., 17220, 17759–9.5, 17918–8.5, 18028, 18086 typis, 18919, 19084, 19653a ent., 20784, 20786, 21339 ent., 21837, 22968 ent., 23420, 23684, 24006.5, 24433, 24553.

1639: (all post-dated?) 1173, 2686.8, 6049, 15787.

Haviland (Haveland), Thomas.
Printer, bookbinder, and bookseller in London, (1582) 1585–1619†. Uncle of **John Haviland**. In 1585 he shared in printing an item in the house of **Robert Robinson**: in Fetter Lane (V.7). In 1609–1611 he shared a printing house with **William Hall**, but their names do not appear together in any imprint nor has their address been noted. Although Haviland's name has occasionally been supplied below in square brackets, many other anonymous imprints from their house are listed under Hall, who was connected with the press longer; however, the actual extent of each partner's contribution has not been established. [*Dict. 1.*]
shop in Giltspur Street without Newgate (D.3), 1613 (3807)
1585: 1848.
1609: 1446, 1446.5, 3051, 6963, 9175q ent., 14694, 16685, 16916.3, 18618.7, 24288.5.
1610: [4258], 5413, 6971.3, 10159.2 (d?), 10198, 12582.25, [15049?], 21520.5, 23315–5.5, [24831.3] (d), 24831.7.
1611: 5414, 13456.5, 20018, 21738, 21785, [23331], [24833.2].
1613: 3807 f.

Haw. *See* How.

Hawkins (Haukyns), John.
Grocer and publisher? in London, 1530. Third husband of Margaret Pynson, the daughter of **Richard Pynson** (Stanley H. Johnston, Jr., Ph.D. dissertation, University of Western Ontario, 1977: *A Study of the Career and Literary Publications of Richard Pynson*, pp. 3, 530.) He may have supervised publication of the item below in Fleet Street at the George (W.9) following Pynson's death or possibly employed **Thomas Godfray**, to whom some of Pynson's 94 mm. textura types eventually passed. [Duff, *Century*.]
No address used.
1530: 19166 imprinting finished by.

Hawkins, Richard.
Bookseller in London, (1611) 1612–1637?†. In 1618 (24136) **Bernard Alsop** printed as his assignee. [*Dict. 1*; DFM 912.]
in Chancery Lane (W.10c), 1613–1634 at least
shop — near (unto) Serjeants' Inn, 1613 (4613; 4275, has 'dw.'), 1630 (22306)
shop — adjoining to Serjeants' Inn gate, 1628 (1683), 1634 (1684)
dw. — near the Rolls, 1633 (10558.5), 1634 (14482, has 'shop')
1613: 24136 ent., 4275 f., 4613 f., 17360 f.
1614: 14739.2 f.
1616: 5778 f., 5780 f.
1617: 5780 f., 17360a f.
1618: 6358 f., 24136 by ass'n of, 25145 f.
1619: 4276 f., 4278 f., 6358 f., 9240 sold (d).
1622: 6359 f.
1623: 4861 f., 25867.5 imp.
1624: 4862 f.
1625: 25867 f.
1627: 12636 (note).
1628: 1683 f., 4277 f., 12690 f., 12690.5 f.
1629: 17217 f., 17421 f.
1630: 1679 f., 12691 f., 22306 f.
1631: 1672 f., 16928 f., 18124.
1632: 6544 f., 17202 f. (d?), 22274 f., 22274c f.
1633: 10558.5 f.
1634: 1684 f., 12639 (note), 14482 f.
1636: 12691.5 f.

Haydock, Richard.
Translator in Oxford, 1598, and physician, fl. 1605. [*DNB.*]
No address used.
1598: 16698 f.

Hayes, Lawrence.
Stationer in London, (1614) 1617–1637. Son of **Thomas Hayes**. [*Dict. 1*; DFM 1584.]
shop near Fleet Bridge over against St. Bride's Lane (W.4), 1617 (18257)
shop on Fleet Bridge (W.3), 1637 (22298)
1617: 18257 f. **1619:** 22298 ent. **1637:** 22298 f.

Hayes (Haies, Heyes), Thomas.
Stationer in London, (1584) 1600–1604?†. Father of **Lawrence Hayes.** [*Dict. 1.*]

Hayes, T. — *cont.*
in Paul's Churchyard at the Green Dragon (A.3), 1600 (22296)–1601 (16901)
1600: 378–80 f., 7434.7 f., 22296 f. **1601:** 16901 f. **1602:** 14978 ent., 24537 ent.

Hearne (Herne, Heron), Richard.
Printer in London, (1632) 1635–1646. After Sept. 1639 he succeeded to the printing material of his former master, **Adam Islip**. [*Dict. 2*; DFM 272; *Loan Book* (as Herne), 1642–45.]
No pre-1641 address noted; *Dict. 2* gives: near Smithfield, apparently from some later item.
1637: 13358 f.
1640: 949, 3515.5(*A*3) (d?), 3931, 5874, 11562, 13219, [14541?], 20938, 23445, [25317], 25641.
1649: 3515.5(*A*3) (d/error).

Hebb, Andrew.
Bookseller in London, (1621) 1625–1648†. He succeeded to the shop and to some old stock of his former masters, **Thomas** and **Elizabeth Adams**. [*Dict. 2*; DFM 542.]
at the Bell in Paul's Churchyard (A.4), 1625 (21230)–1640 (18968) at least
1625: 183 ent., 651 f. (d?), 4510 ent., 11939 f. (d?), 13794a.5 ent., 14587(*A*3) ent., 14812 ent., 20743 ent., 21230 sold, 22423 ent., 23340 ent., 23466 f. (d?).
1626: 15481.5 f. (c), 15492 f. (c?), 21163 f.
1627: 3770 f.
1628: 183 f.
1629: 602 pro.
1630: 13794a.5 imp.
1631: 16857.9(*A*) ent., 19116.5 f., 23340 ent.
1632: 14812 f.
1633: 19117 f.
1634: 184 f., 188.5 f., 21164 f., 22628 f.
1635: [3193.5(*A*3)] sold (c), 13781 f., [25234] sold.
1636: 5764.2 f., [21724 sold].
1637: 4510 f., 21725 f., [21817.7 sold].
1638: 18967 f., 19118 f., 21725 f.
1639: 20743 f.
1640: 12978a f., 14813–3a f., 18968 f., [19997.5 f.] (d).

Heerstraten, Aegidius van der.
Printer in Louvain, 1485–1488. [Duff, *Century*; Rouzet.]
1486: 19767.7 (d).

Heigham, John (Roger).
English recusant bookseller and publisher in Douai, c. 1603–1613, and in St. Omer, 1614–1631. Corrections in the Addenda indicate that from 1614 Heigham's activity was in St. Omer even though many of the items continued to be printed in Douai. [*Dict. 1*; *RH* 4 (1958): 226–42.]
1604: [14568.3 f.].
1611: 14568.7 [f.].
1612: 16905 [f.], 16908.5 [f.].
1613: 11316.5 [f.], 11317 [f.], 17273 [f.].
1614: 16095.5 [f.].
1615: 11019.5 [f.], 17275.3 f., 20450 [f.].
1616: 4960 [f.], 10403 [f.], 16096.5 [f.].
1617: 1837 [f.], 11320 [f.], 11320a (repeat), 16232.5 [f.], 23212 [f.].
1618: 632.3 [f.], 7072.5 (false), 11314.2 [f.], 14569 [f.].
1620: 4959 f., 17276 [f.]. .yr 1621: 16098 [f.].
1622: [1341 f.], 1779 f., 4572 f., 10541.7 f., 11320a [f.] (d), 13036 [f.], 22970 [f.].
1623: 1023.5 f., 3801.5 f., 3902 f., 16098.3 f., 17276.3 f., 26048 f.
1624: 632.5 f., 934 f., 1837.3 [f.], 3606 f., 11617.6 f., 14570 f., 21693 f., 21697 f., 23990 [f.].
1625: 535.7 f., 4603 f., 6185 f., 14626 f., 16906 f., 17276.4 f., 17276.6 f., 21697.5 f., 22872.5 f., 23233 f.
1626: 1780 f., 4469 f.
1627: 12808.3 f.
1630: 17506.3 f.
1631: 1922 f., 13037 [f.], 16099–100 [f.], 24748.5 f.

Heinszoon. *See* Heyns.

Hellen (Hellenius), Hans (Johannes) van der.
Printer in Zierikzee, 1615–1616, and in Middelburg, 1618–1661. [*Dict. 1*; Gruys.]
1620: 25844. **1621:** 18460.3 (false).

Helme, Anne.
Bookseller in London, 1617–1627. Widow of **John Helme**. In 1621 she apparently became a silent partner of her former apprentice, **Thomas Dewe**. [*Dict. 1.*]
her shop in St. Dunstan's Churchyard in Fleet Street (W.9), 1617 (18301)–1621 (26042); variation: has 'under St. Dunstan's Church' for 'in … Churchyard, 1618 (13423)
1617: 18301 f., 21608 f., 24600 f.
1618: 13423 f.
1620: 18105.7 f., 26041 f.
1621: 17362 f., 18302 ent., 26042 f.
1627: 2776 ass'd, 2783 ass'd, 5675 ass'd, 26043 ass'd.

Helme (Helmes), John.
Bookseller in London, 1607–1616†. Husband of **Anne Helme**. [*Dict. 1*; DFM 1855.]
in Fleet Street (W.9), 1607–1616
at the Little Shop next Clifford's Inn gate —, 1607 (21605)–1608 (21606, both with J. Busby 2); also in 1609 (21607, alone, possibly carried over from the previous edition)
shop in St. Dunstan's Churchyard —, 1608 (6411)–1616 (23623); variation: has 'under the dial' for 'in Fleet Street', 1615 (19512)
1607: 21605 f.
1608: 6411 f., 17879–9a f., 19330 sold, 21606 f.
1609: 1417 sold, 14631 f., 17156.7 sold, 17755 f., 21607 f.
1610: 22171 f., 22174 procur.
1611: 14646 f., 19615 f.
1612: 7226 f. (d), 21607.3(*A*3) f., 24600 ent.
1613: 4989 sold, 7227 f., 19513–3.5 f.
1614: 12627 f., 21520 f., 22177 f.
1615: 19512 f., 19514 f.
1616: 23623 f.

Helsham, Samuel.
Printer and bookseller in Dublin, 1681–1689. In partnership with **Andrew Crooke 2**, 1685–1689, as King's Printer in Ireland. [*Dict. 3.*]
1685–89: 14264 (d). = Wing, 2nd ed., C 4103B.

Hendricksz (Henry, Henrickszoon), Aelbrecht.
Printer in Delft, 1573–1591, and in the Hague, 1590–1605. [Gruys; Briels 312–15.]
1595: 7581. **1597:** 9208.6 chez.

Henricius (Heyndrickx, Henricsz), Henricus.
Printer and bookseller in Antwerp, 1572–1588, and also in Louvain, 1575–1576. [Rouzet.]
1576: 1431.4 chez. **1579:** 1431.5 ap. **1583:** 1431.6 ap.

Henricius, Jacobus.
Printer and bookseller in Antwerp, 1572?–1581, and in Malines, 1581–1582. [Rouzet.]
1578: 3972 ap.

Henry VII.
King of England, b. 1457–1509† and patron, 1504. [*DNB.*]
1504: 16179 mandato & imp., 16257 ex mandato (in title).

Henry, A. *See* Hendricksz.

Henson, Francis.
Stationer and bookbinder in London, (1580) 1581–1604. Freed by W. Norton on 7 Oct. 1580 (Arber II.683). [*Dict. 1.*]
dw. in the Blackfriars (Q.6), 1601 (23864)
1601: 23864 f.

Herbert (Harber), John.
Stationer in London, (1597) 1598–1607 (*C-B C*: 29). Possibly the man of this name in the *Poor Book*, 1620. [*Dict. 1.*]
at the $ Paper Book in Chancery Lane (W.10a), 1598 (14830.3, with John Browne 1 but not Browne's address)
1598: 14830.3 f.

Herford (Hereford, Hertford), John.
Foreigner working as printer in St. Albans, 1534–1539? and in London, 1542?–1548?†. He may also have printed the items produced during the interim listed under **Nicholas Bourman**. Husband of **Katherine** and probably father of **William Herford**. [Duff, *Century*: 70; *Library* 16 (1936): 403–8.]

Herford, J. — *cont.*
in Aldersgate Street (F.2), 1542 (21794)–1548? (17115)
1534: [256].
1535: [15793.5] (c).
1536: [12557].
1537: [14117.7(*A3*)].
1539: [6456.5] (d?).
1542: 21794 (d?).
1544: [14562] (c?), 15440 ap.
1544/45: 477.
1545: 2973 (c), 5106.5, 5408, 11714 in off., 25000, 26054 (d?).
1545/46: 477.5.
1546: [7380] (d?), 11588, 11589, 11591, 11591.3, 11718.9 (d?), 13910, 14119, [14828.5], 19785.5 (d?), 21678 in aed., 22815, 22820–0a.
1547: 5409, 19195 ex off., [20423] (d?).
1547/48: 507.13.
1548: [1472?] (d), 2853.5 ex off., 3041.5 (d?), 17115 (d?), [20203.5] (d?), [20424] (d?), 21680 in aed.

Herford, Katherine.
Printer in London, 1549?–1550. Widow of **John** and probably mother of **William Herford**. [Duff, *Century*: 71.]
in Aldersgate Street (F.2), 1549? (13761)–1550 (2727)
1549: 13761 (d?).
1550: 920, 2727, [2756.5(*A*)?] (d?), 10450 (d?).

Herford (Harford), William.
Printer in London, 1555?–1559. Probably the son of **John** and **Katherine Herford**. [Duff, *Century*: 71.]
in Aldersgate Street (F.2), 1555? (634)–1559 (19969.4)
1555: 634 (d?). **1559:** 19969.4.

Herlock. *See* Hurlock.

Herne, Heron. *See* Hearne.

Herstraten. *See* Heerstraten.

Hertzog de Landoia (Hamman, Hamann), Joannes.
Printer in Venice, 1482–1509. [Duff, *Century*; Borsa 178; *Essays in Honour of Victor Scholderer*, Mainz, 1970: 349–68.]
1493: 15856.
1494: [15797] (d), [15800] (d), 15874, 16167, 16168.
1495: 15801, [15801.5] (d?).

Herwijck, Abraham van.
Printer in Utrecht, 1614–1635. [Gruys.]
1624: [22105–5.5] (d).

Hester, Andrew.
Bookseller in London, (1538) 1539–1557†. [Duff, *Century*.]
in Paul's Churchyard at the White Horse (A.6), 1539 (16010)–1551 (24368, has 'dw.', adds 'next to Paul's School')
1539: 2966.7 sold (d), 16010 sold, 16011 sold (d?). **1550:** 2080 f.
1551: 24368 f.

Hester, John.
Distiller, translator, and publisher, fl. 1575 (cf. 19181.3)–1593†. His address was given primarily for the sale of his distillations. [*DNB*.]
at Paul's Wharf (R.8), 1582–1591 at least
— at the $ Furnace, 1582 (10879, advt. on R8^{r})
dw. — at the $ Stillatory, 1591 (7275, colophon on R2^{v})
1582: 10879 f. **1591:** 7275 sold.

Heyberghs (Heybergius), Jacob.
Printer in Louvain, c. 1567–1596. [Rouzet.]
1578: [3972?].

Heyes. *See* Hayes.

Heyndrickx. See Henricius.

Heyns, Zacharias.
Bookseller and printer in Amsterdam, 1592–1605, and at Zwolle, 1607–1629 at least. [*Dict. 1*; Gruys; Briels 317–19.]
1605: 3867.5.

Higgenbotham, Richard 2.
Bookseller in London, 1615–1636† (cf. DFM 1612). His father, Richard 1 (Arber II.85, 696), is the one in *St. Giles*, 1591. Richard 2 was apparently in Dublin on behalf of the **Irish Stock** (*see* Stationers' Company) in 1619 (*C-B C*: 112). [*Dict. 1*; DFM 1864; *Loan Book*, 1615–18, 1634–37.]
shop at the Cardinal's Hat without Newgate (D.9), 1615 (14292), 1616 (17387), 1617 (25180, has 'near St. Sepulchre's Church' for 'without Newgate')
in Paul's Churchyard, 1619–1630
at the Angel — (A.3), 1619 (1677)–1624 (5837, has 'shop')
?at the Greyhound — (B), 1625 (5838)
— at the White Lion (A.2), 1630 (7404)
shop in the bulwark near the Tower at the Unicorn (U.3), 1635 (19780)
1615: 3704.7 f., 14292 sold, 18919.3 f. (d), 18919.7 f. (d).
1616: 17387 f., 19159a f.
1617: 134 ent., 3641 ent., 3664.5 f., 25180 f.
1619: 1676 ent., 1677 f., 11830a.5 f.
1621: 134 f.
1624: 5836.5–37 f.
1625: [4934.3?] sold, 5838 f., [13318?] sold.
1630: 7404 sold.
1635: 3704.9 f., 19780 f.

Higgins (Higins), John.
Patron, 1590. More probably the controversialist in STC than the poet, if he is either.
No address used.
1590: 15316.5 imp.

Higman, Jean.
Printer in Paris, 1484–1500†. [Duff, *Century*; Renouard.]
1500: 16174 per.

Higman, Nicolas.
Printer in Paris, 1495–1537? [Duff, *Century*; Renouard.]
1512: 15913.5 (d). **1519:** 15816, 15924, 16200. **1520:** 15926 (d?).

Hill, Anthony.
Journeyman printer in London, (1573?) 1586–1588. The press he was listed as having in July 1586 (Arber V.lii) was ordered taken away on 12 Oct. the same year (*Reg. B*: 20). [*Dict. 1*.]
No address survives.
1586: 13854 ?ent. **1588:** 20961 ent.

Hill, John.
Bookseller in London, (1586) 1588–1590. [*Dict. 1*.]
in Paternoster Row (C.7), 1588–1590
dw. — at the Three Pigeons, 1588 (Herbert II.1242, lost sermon by Adam Hill)
dw. — at the Golden Eagle and the Child, 1590 (4206)
1590: 4206 f.

Hill (Hyll, van den Berghe, Montanus), Nicholas (Niko-laos).
Dutch printer in London, 1542?–1553, and in Emden, 1554–1557†. In England from about 1519, Hill did not take out letters of denization until 1544, and that same year he was living in St. John's Street. His name does not appear in a dated imprint until 1546, but earlier items have been attributed to him on the basis of three series of metal initials which appear consistently in his work and in 1553 passed to **John Kingston.** Most of Hill's putative early publications were Yearbooks of law reports, the earliest with the imprint of **John Byddell** and the later ones published by **Henry Smith**, who may have employed Hill to work a press until late 1545 or 1546, when syndicate publishing begins and the first false imprint may appear. Others who possibly worked in Hill's shop or borrowed some of his printing material are **Philip Bounel** and **Cutbere Mathew**, both of whom printed for **John Walley**. In Emden, Hill sometimes used a pseudonym fashioned upon his name: **Collinus Volckwinner**, and worked in partnership with **Egidius van der Erve**, under whom most Emden items are to be found. [Duff, *Century*; *Library* 12 (1932): 336–52.]
in St. John's Street (E.10), 1546 (19786)–1553 (11716, has 'dw.')
1542: [9935.7(*A*)?] (d?).
1543: [9906.3(*A3*)], [9913.5(*A3*)], [9929.3], [10507?] (d?).

Hill, N. — *cont.*
1544: [9619] (d?), [9627] (d?), [9643] (d?), [9649] (d?), [9660] (d?), [9930.3] (d?), [9931.3] (d?), [9934.3] (d?), [9946.9(*A*)] (d?), [9954.7] (d?), [9961.7] (d?).
1545: [7687?], [9633] (d?), [9638] (d?), [9653] (d?), [9665] (d?), [9932.5] (d?), [9933.5] (d?), [9946.3(*A*)] (d?), [10953] (d?), [14117], 15587.5 (d?), [18221–1a] (d?), [18397].
1546: [851?] (false), [2755] (d?), [3328–8.5], [7379] (d?), [7380] (d?), [7699–703] (d), 7717.4 per, [7717.7–20], [7732], 7732.5 in aed., [7733–4], [9293.6?] (d?), [14117], 14879 in aed., [14879.5–9b], [15586], 15586.5, [15586a–87], 19786 (d), [20903], [24203.3] (d?), [24468?] (false, d?).
1546/47: 507.11.
1547: [95] (false, d?), [851?] (false), 12403.9 (d?), [21305?] (d?), [21616].
1548: [3287] (d), [4409.5] (d?), [5195], 5992.5, 5993, [5994], [20560.7(*A*3)] (d?), [21305.3?] (d?).
1549: [1725.3] (d?), 2379.5 (note, c), [2419] (d?), [16050?], [16270a], [18770–1].
1550: 3368.4 (c), [5071–4] (d?), [6832.23(*A*3)?] (c), 7688–8.2, 9301.3 (note), 9343.10 (d?), [11393.5–.7] (d), [13749], [13750], [13754] (d?), 14638, [15029(*A*3)] (d?), [19903a?] (d?), [23916], [24666].
1550/51: [464].
1551: 2083–6.5.
1551/52: 507.17(*A*3).
1552: 1281–3 (d?), 2089, 2738.7, 4049–52.7, [9436], [10440–0.2], [10989a], [10999.5–11000] (d?), 15113.5 (d?), 15260.7, [20191?] (c).
1552/53: 462.
1553: [2091], [2092], [2728], [2749.5], [2984], 2985, [3019] (d?), 3022.5, 4844–4.2, 11715.5–16, 15260.5, [16430], 19493, 21754–5a.5.
1554: [16571a] (false), [17863.5] (false).

Hill, Thomas.
Translator, editor, and author, b. 1528?–1574?†. In 1571 he was possibly working with **Christopher Barker**, in whose shop in Paul's Churchyard (B) he said he could be found (Ii2^v–3^r of 13482). [*DNB*; *Huntington Library Quarterly* 7 (1943): 329–51.]
No address used.
1558: 13489.5 f. (d?).

Hill (Hyll), William.
Bookbinder and printer in London, 1547?–1586. Collaborated with **Thomas Raynald** in a few items, but the nature of the relationship is not clear. [Duff, *Century*.]
in Paul's Churchyard at the $ Hill (A.10), 1547? (2974)–1549 (1741); variations: has 'at the $ Green Hill', 1549? (22238); 'at the $ Hill at the West door of Paul's, 1549? (24442)
1148: 18576 (d/error).
1547: 2974 (d?), [4071] (d?).
1548: [846?] (d?), [852] (d?), 919, [1280.5?] (d?), 1473 (d), 1774, 2975 (d?), 3040, [4048.5?] (d?), [4312] (d?), [4410] (d?), 5100 (d?), [5189.7] (d?), 10494.5 (d?), 11211.2 (d?), [11385.5] (d?), [11802], [14942] (d?), 18576 (d), 18842 (d?), [19882] (d?), 20499, [20661] (d?), [21309.7(*A*3)?] (d?), [24363] (d), [24448] (d), 24450 (d?), 24458 (d).
1549: 1741 sold, 2078, [16458.5] (d?), 20500, 20500.5, 22238 (d?), 24442 (d?).

Hillenius Hoochstratanus (Hillen), Michael.
Printer and bookseller in Antwerp, 1506–1546 (1558†). [Duff, *Century*; Rouzet.]
1520: 16128.3 per (c). **1531:** 7481.4. **1533:** 5542.4 ap. **1535:** [2829?] (c?).

Hills, William.
Bookseller in London, 1636–1640. Apparently never formally made free of the Stat. Co. Both his publications were in association with **Daniel Pakeman**. [*Dict. 1*; DFM 1248.]
in Little Britain at the White Horse (F.4), 1636 (17160)
1636: 17160 f. **1640:** 17168 f.

Hilten, Jan van.
Bookseller in Amsterdam, 1626–1652. [Gruys.]
1633: [18507.359 f.], [—.360 f.] (d), [—.361 f.] (d).

Hinde, John 1.
Stationer in London, (1560) 1561–1583. [*Dict. 1*.]
dw. in Paul's Churchyard at the Golden Hind (B), 1583 (19523)
1583: 19523 f.

Hinde, John 2.
Printseller in London, 1620?–1641. Undoubtedly related to **Thomas Hinde**. [Globe 214–15.]
at the Black Bull in Cornhill near the Royal Exchange (O.9), 1620? (18921.5)–1635 (197.7)
1620: 18921.5 sold (d?). **1635:** 197.7 sold (d).

Hinde, Thomas.
Printseller in London, 1637–1652 at least. Undoubtedly related to **John Hinde 2**. [Globe 215.]
at the Black Bull in Cornhill near the Royal Exchange (O.9), 1637 (6798.5, W. A. Jackson's transcription)–1652 (Wing D 1761)
1637: 6798.5 sold. **1640:** 19518.7 sold.

Hippon, John.
Bookseller in London, (1602) 1603. [*Dict. 1*.]
shop in Watling Street adjoining to the Red Lion gate (N.10), 1603 (17215)
1603: 17215 f., 23632 f.

Hitprick, Hans, *pseud.*
Used or copied by various printers: in 'Winchester', 1545 = L. von der Muelen, Bonn; no place, 1547? = unidentified London printer, possibly related to A. Scoloker; 1548? = W. Copland?
1545: 24355. **1547:** 17627 (d?). **1548:** 17626 (d?).

Hodges, George.
Bookseller in London, 1621–1632. [*Dict. 1*; DFM 2677; *Loan Book*, 1623–29.]
shop at the Greyhound in Paul's Churchyard (B), 1622 (5841)–1624 (887)
shop at the Maiden Head in Cornhill (O.6), 1625 (25182.5)
1622: 5841 f. **1623:** 13773 f., 25166.5 f. **1624:** 887 f. **1625:** 25182.5 f. **1628:** 7148.5 sold (c?).

Hodges, Richard.
Schoolmaster, accountant, and author, in Southwark, fl. 1631.
[his] house within the close near St. Mary Overy's Church, 1631–1634 (13548 and MS. alteration of date)
1631: 13548 sold.

Hodgets, John.
Bookseller in London, (1593) 1596–1625†. Husband of **Margaret Hodgets**. [*Dict. 1*; *Loan Book*, 1596–1605, 1607–10.]
shop at the Fleur-de-lis in Fleet Street near (to) Fetter Lane end (W.8), 1601 (12294)–1602 (18972)
in Paul's Churchyard, 1604 (6501, has 'shop')–1616 at least; variations:
dw. — a little beneath Paul's School (A.6), 1605 (1486)
his house — (A.6), 1608 (6496)
at the King's Arms — (A.3), 1616 (24028); no later use noted
1601: 12294 f.
1602: 18972 f.
1604: 6501 f., 6501.5 sold.
1605: 1486 sold, 1900 sold, 6502 sold, 13971 f., 17475 f., 18589 sold, 20753a sold (d).
1606: 5693.5–.7 f., 6412–3 sold, 6498 sold, 7081 sold, 20342 sold.
1607: 1692 sold, 1693 sold, 6540 sold, 7082 sold, 13371 sold, 18592–3 sold.
1608: 6496 sold.
1611: 20775 f.
1612: 1601.5 f., 11692 f.
1613: 1602 f., 24397 ent.
1614: 538.9 f., 1602.2(*A*) f., 24964 f.
1615: 539 f., 1602.3 f.
1616: 1602.5 f., 1602.7 f., 3435.5 f., 20835 imp., 23626.5 f., 24028 f.
1617: 1602.8 f., [4804 f.?], 10822 f., 23585 f.
1619: 1603 f., 13823–3.5 f.
1620: 1604 f., 18226 f.
1621: 1604.5 f., 6427.5 f., 20789 f., 20792 f.
1622: 4323 f.

Hodgets, J. — *cont.*
1623: 1605 f.
1624: 1606 f., 20334 f., 20790 f.
1625: 11469 f.

Hodgets, Margaret.
Bookseller? in London, 1625. Widow of **John Hodgets**. [*Dict. 1*, under husband.]
No address survives.
1625: 14625.5 ent., 21728 ent.

Hodgkins (Hoskins), John.
Surreptitious printer of two Marprelate tracts in Wolston? 1589. *See* also English Secret Press—Puritan. [*Dict. 1*.]
1589: [17457] (false, d), [17458] (d).

Hodgkinson, Richard.
Printer in London, (1616) 1624–1675† (*Loan Book*). Operated the **Parish Clerks' Press** in their Hall in Broad Lane in the Vintry (S.10), 1629–1633. Starting in 1637 he seems to have acquired printing material from various sources. He may have worked for **Thomas Purfoot 2** and continued as one of Purfoot's assignees and/or possibly shared a printing house with **Thomas Badger**, to whom some of the imprints supplied below may belong. He also may have obtained in 1640 some material from the widow of **Marmaduke Parsons**. [*Dict. 2*; DFM 1634; *Loan Book*, 1623–26, 1656–59, 1670–73.]
No pre-1641 address noted.
1624: 24435.5 ent.
1629: 16742 (d).
1630–33: [16743] (headnote, d).
1635: 21619.5 ent.
1637: [5902], [12250], 13269, [14628.5?], 20647, [24145.3].
1638: 6316, 7302, 10321.5, 12874, 18845 ent.
1638/39: [18507.283?], [—.285?].
1639: 4942, [5753–5] (forged), 7266, [9136.5] (d), 10271.5, 12402–2a.2 per, 13216, 14500–0.5, 17718–8a, [18507.288?], [—.291?], [—.293?], [—.294?], [—.296?], [—.299?], [—.302?], [—.307?], [—.310?], [—.315?], 24331–1.5.
1640: 1665, 4615.5, 4943, 6007–8 typis, 7032a (note), 10272, 12983 (note), 13662, 13662.5 (forged), 15176.5 (d?), 18338, 19210, 21476 ap., 21849(*A*3), 23302, 23305 typis, 23309, 24959.5, 25870.

Hoff, Ubright, *pseud.*
Printer in 'Lipse' (Leipzig), 1541. = Catherine Ruremund, Antwerp.
1541: 17798 (d).

Hoffmann, Wolfgang.
Printer in Frankfurt am Main, 1624–1647? [Benzing 134.]
1635: 21537.3.

Hogard, Miles, *pseud.*
Publisher of protestant propaganda in 'London', 1555. ? = H. Singleton, Wesel. For the genuine Roman Catholic author of the time *see* STC and *DNB*.
1555: 9981 at request of (d).

Hokerus, J. *See* Vowell.

Holder, Robert.
Stationer and bookbinder? in London, before 1544–1566. In at least 1549 he was living in St. Faith's parish (Paul's Churchyard (A.4)). [Duff, *Century*.]
No address used.
1554: 26098.7 ap. (d?).

Hole, William.
Engraver in London, 1607–1624†. [Hind II.316.]
No address used.
1613: 18697 intagliate (d).

Holland, Compton.
Printseller in London, 1616?–1622? Possibly related to **Henry Holland**. [Globe 215–16.]
at the Globe over against the [Royal] Exchange (O.9), 1617 (20892)–1622 [24602, adding 'in Cornhill']

Holland, C. — *cont.*
1616: 656.3, 18921.3 (d?), 18994.5(*A*3) (d). **1617:** 20892 sold. **1618:** 13581 sold. **1620:** 7289.7 (c). **1621:** [12561.4] sold (d?), 23737.5 f. **1622:** [24602] sold.

Holland, Henry.
Stationer in London, (1608) 1609–1650. Possibly related to **Compton Holland.** Only one book has been noted with a firm address. Most of the other items were either sold by or issued jointly with others and bear their addresses if any is stated at all. [*Dict. 1*; DFM 392; *Loan Book* (with G. Gibbs), 1624–27; *Poor Book*, 1647–50; Morgan.]
shop in Ivy Lane at the Holy Bush (C.3), 1612 (17660)
1609: 7186 f.
1610: 5112(*A*3) f.
1612: 17660 f.
1614: 13583 f. (d), 13583.5 imp. (d).
1615: 14838 f.
1617: 20892 f.
1618: 13581 f.
1620: [13582 f.] (d), 24602 ent.
1624: 6339.5 f.
1625: 5535 f., 6340 f., 25663 f.
1626: 13579–9.5 imp., 13585.5 f., 16753 f.
1630: 6175 f.
1632: 26068 f.
1633: 13584 ent.
1636: 6176.5 f.

Hollins (Hollens), Richard.
Stationer in London, (1580) 1581–1596?† (Arber II.213). [*Dict. 1*; *Poor Book* (widow Margery), 1608–31.]
shop over against the $ Bell within Aldgate (L.1), 1581 (12531.3)
1581: 12531.3 f.

Note: There is some confusion in Arber and in *Dict. 1* about various men named **William Holme(s)**. Their biographical details have been tentatively allocated below.

Holme (Holmes), William 1.
Apprenticed to J. Hinde 1 in 1564 (Arber I.227). Nothing more is definitely known of him, and it is possible he was never freed.

Holme (Holmes, Hulme), William 2.
Apprenticed to John Harrison 1 in 1569 and freed by him in 1580 (Arber I.396, II.683). William 2 took William 3 as an apprentice in Jan. 1582 (Arber II.110, 853). Later the same year William 2 was involved in binding pirated copies of the ABC and Catechism, at which time he was living in the parish of St. Michael le Querne (Arber II.753–67). He seems still to have been in London in 1590, and possibly again in 1599, when William 3 is called 'junior' (Arber II.553, 233). If a London stationer of this name moved to Chester in 1591, William 2 seems a possible candidate. In terms of relative ages, William 2 was probably the father of John Holme, freed by patrimony in 1607 (DFM 1641).

Holme (Holmes, Hulme), William 3.
Bookseller in London, (1589) 1590–1607† (*SB* 38 (1985): 209, n.14). Apprenticed to William 2 in 1582 and freed by John Harrison 1 in 1589 (Arber II.110, 705). His first entry, as William 'junior' was a work of Edward Vaughan in 1590 (24597, Arber II.553). The only other occasion when 'junior' is used in the SR is in 1599 at the taking of an apprentice (Arber II.233). None of the imprints below or the remaining SR records make any distinction between elder or younger, suggesting that there was only one William present in London between 1591–98 and 1600-07 or only one sufficiently active to be recorded. Linking William 3 to the active man are the publications of Vaughan, in 1590, 1598 (19153), and 1603 (24599.5). This man was called to the livery of the Stat. Co. in 1604 (Arber II.875) and left a legacy of 60 pounds to his children (two daughters and a son, Thomas), to be held in trust by the Stat. Co. (*C-B C*: 41, 160). The widow Holmes in the *Poor Book*, 1609–11, is possibly the widow of Edward Holme (Arber II.138, 712), also in the *Poor Book*.
shop near the great North door of Paul's (A.2), 1592 (5231, 5578)

Holme, William 3 — *cont.*
Ludgate Hill (Q.4), 1594–1598
at the Golden Angel near unto the Belle Savage [Inn], 1594 (Hazlitt IV.387–8)–1595 (21441.7)
on — at the Holy Lamb, 1597 (19338)–1598 (19153, has 'dw,', omits 'Holy')
in Fleet Street, 1600–1606
shop at Serjeants' Inn gate — (W.7), 1600 (14767)
dw. at the Spread-Eagle over against Serjeants' Inn —, c. 1600 (24145.7)
at the Peahen, over against Serjeants' Inn —, 1603 (24599.5)
shop in St. Dunstan's Churchyard — (W.9), 1606 (4983)
1590: 24597 f.
1591: 5840 f. (d).
1592: 5231 f., 5578 f.
1594: 5242 f.
1595: 5245 f., 21441.7 f.
1596: 5238 f., 5249 f., 5254 f.
1597: 19338 f.
1598: 19153 f.
1599: 11171.2 sold.
1600: 14767 f., 14768 f., 24145.7 f. (c).
1603: 24599.5 f.
1606: 4983–4 f.

1612: 24600 ass'd.

Holmes (Houlmes), William 4.
Bookseller in London, 1614–1615. Freed by T. Pavier in 1614. [DFM 2128.]
shop in Pope's Head Palace (O.11), 1614 (3541)–1615 (18590)
1614: 3541 f. **1615:** 18590 f.

Holost, Hu., *pseud.*
Printer in 'Bruges', 1576. = W. Carter and J. Lion.
1576: 17136.

Hondius, Henricus 1.
Engraver and bookseller in the Hague, 1602–1650†. Not related to **Henricus 2** and **Jodocus Hondius.** [Gruys; Briels 321–3; Thieme-Becker.]
1633: 13263 sold. **1637:** 13265 sold, 13685 (note).

Hondius, Henricus 2.
Engraver and bookseller in Amsterdam, 1616–1651†. Son of **Jodocus Hondius 1**. [*Dict. 1*; Gruys; Briels 324, 326; Thieme-Becker.]
1630: 20202 f. **1636:** 17827. **1638:** 17828.

Hondius, Jodocus 1.
Engraver in London, 1584?–1593? and in Amsterdam, 1593?–1612†. Bookseller? or printer? in the latter city, 1605–1611. Father of **Henricus Hondius 2**. [*Dict. 1*; Gruys; Briels 322–5; Thieme-Becker; Hind I.154.]
1605: 24931.5. **1608:** [13395?]. **1609:** [20605]. **1611:** 3754.

Hoochstraten (Hillenius Hoochstratanus), Joannes.
Printer in Antwerp, 1525–c. 1530, in Lübeck, 1531–1532, in Malmö, 1533–1535, and again in Antwerp, 1535?–1543†. [Duff, *Century* 74; Rouzet 93–4.]
1528: [24446] (false), [24454] (false).
1529: [1462.3] (d?), [10493] (false), [11394] (false).
1530: [1462.5] (false), [2350] (false), [3021] (false), [24045] (d), [24465] (false).
1533: 19525.
1533/34: [471.7].
1535: [14667] (false), 24167 (note).
1538: 20193 (note).

Hood, Henry.
Bookseller in London, 1635–1654. He succeeded to the shop of his former master's widow, **Anne Moore**. [*Dict. 2*; DFM 1970.]
in St. Dunstan's Churchyard in Fleet Street (W.9), 1635 (1135, with A. Moore)–1639 (14510.3(*A*3)); called 'his shop' beginning in 1637 (24676)
1635–36: 1135 sold. **1637:** 24646–7 f. **1638:** 18645 f., 24647 f. **1639:** 14510.3(*A*3) f.

Hood, Thomas.
Mathematician and author, fl. 1577–1598. His books were sold where he lectured: in the Staplers' Chapel within Leadenhall (P.5), 1590 (15250). [*DNB*; Taylor 179.]
1590: 15250 f.

Hooke, Henry.
Bookbinder (*Reg. B*: 8, 79) in London, (1583) 1590–1605?†. [*Dict. 1.*]
No address used.
1590: 13702 f. **1603:** 14379.3.

Hooker. *See* Vowell.

Hooper, Humphrey.
Stationer in London, (1572?) 1590–1613. One of the *assignees of* **J. Roberts** in publishing Almanacks in 1603/04. His 1613 imprint was shared with **Samuel Man** and sold at the latter's shop: in Paul's Churchyard at the Ball (A.2). [*Dict. 1.*]
at the Black Bear in Chancery Lane (W.10a), 1597 (1137)–1600 (15566, has 'shop', omits 'Black')
1596: 25953 imp. **1597:** 1137 f., 1137.5 f. **1598:** 1138 f. **1600:** 15566 f. **1603:** 19881.5 ent. **1603/04:** 489 f., 532.3 f. **1613:** 17847 f.

Hope, William.
Bookseller in London, (1630) 1634–1665? [*Dict. 2*; DFM 855.]
at the Glove, over against the conduit in Cornhill near the Royal Exchange (O.10), 1634 (20258.5)–1636 (20387, simplified to: shop at the Glove in Cornhill)
at the Unicorn near to the Royal Exchange (O.9), 1637 (20265.5)–1648 (Wing B 1158) at least
1634: 3174 sold, 17993a ven., 20258.5 sold.
1635: 21646 sold.
1636: 20387 f., 23075 f., 26006 f.
1637: 20265.5 sold.
1638: 1333 f., 3151a sold, 7267 f., 10693 f.
1639: 3085.5 sold.
1640: 6345 ent., 11769.5 sold.

Hopyl, Wolfgang.
Printer in Paris, 1489–1522†. [Duff, *Century*; Renouard.]
1494: 11608a.7 per.
1495: 17964 per.
1500: 16174 per.
1503: [15901?] (c).
1504: 16181 diligentia, 17108 arte & imp.
1505: [15805.4] (c), 17109 diligentia.
1506: 15903 per, [16258].
1507–08: 15862 opera.
1510: 4115 opera, 16188 opera, 23030.7 per.
1511: 16188 opera.
1512: [15861.7].
1514: [15918?], [15920?], 16193 opera.
1515: [15920?], [16141.5], 16195 a, [17543] (c).
1516: [15812], [15921?].
1518: 16137 per.
1519: 15790 per, 16235 per.
1520: 15790a per.

Horseman, Richard.
Bookseller in London, c. 1629–1659 at least. Apprenticed to J. Budge in 1621. Never formally freed, but in 1659 at the apprenticeship of his son Thomas (DFM II.220, also not freed) Richard is described as stationer, St. Martin's in the Fields. [*Dict. 1*; DFM 930.]
shop in the Strand near unto York House (X.12), 1639 (4986)
1639: 4986 sold.

Hoskins, William.
Printer in London, (1571) 1575–before 1604†. His career is puzzling since his imprints are divided into two brief periods. He was an apprentice of **Richard Tottell**, two of whose large criblé initials appear in early Hoskins imprints. He gave up copyrights in 1577 and 1580 (Arber II.309, 369; *see* also Appendix A/18) and is not among those recorded as having a press in 1583 and 1586 (Arber I.218, V.lii). However, from about 1576 he had two apprentices not formally bound, James Luffman (Arber II.703,

Hoskins, W. — *cont.*
853) and **James Bowring** (II.690, 856), the latter definitely a journeyman printer, and Hoskins was considered a master printer in taking on **Henry Chettle** and **John Danter** as partners in 1591 (*Reg. B*: 38). It seems possible that he continued working as foreman of the Tottell printing house, only occasionally venturing to print on his own account. [*Dict. 1*; *Poor Book* (widow Helen/Ellen), 1608–21.]
in Fleet Street at the Temple gate (W.13), 1575 (11475)
shop joining to the Middle Temple gate, within Temple Bar (W.13), 1576 (11471)
dw. in Fetter Lane (W.8), 1592 (12561, with J. Danter but apparently Hoskins's own address)
1575: 11475.
1576: 11471.
1578: 4303.5 [f.], 11039 ent.
1591: 16654 (d), 22656–6.5, 22664, [22665].
1592: 12561.
1596: 18133 ent.

Hostingue, Laurent.
Printer in Rouen, 1499–1516? and in Caen, 1508–1526 (1537). [Duff, *Century*; Muller 10, 100.]
1505: 18872 in off. (d).

Houduoyn, René.
Printer in Paris, 1541–1545, and in Geneva, 1555–1556. [Renouard; Chaix 195.]
1556: 11884.5.

Houic, Antoine.
Bookseller in Paris, 1566–1585 (1597). [Renouard.]
1569: 6832.42.

Houlmes. *See* Holme.

Hovius (Hoyoux), Guillaume.
Bookseller and printer at Liège, 1611–1623. [*Dict. 1*; Rouzet, under Henricus Hovius.]
1623: 7001.

Hovius, Henricus.
Printer and bookseller in Liège, 1567?–1611. [Rouzet.]
1589: 1431.10 ap. **1591:** 1431.11 ap. **1595:** 1431.14 ap. **1597:** 1431.15 ap. **1600:** 1431.17 ap. **1604:** 1431.17B ap. **1610:** 1431.20 ap.

How (Howe, Haw), William.
Printer in London, (1556) 1565–1591? (1603). In 1578 **Roger Ward** and **Richard Mundee** were possibly working in his house and in 1587 **Henry Haslop** may have done the same. Most of How's printing material passed to **Valentine Simmes**, who also printed one book as his assignee. *See* also Appendix A/8–9. [Duff, *Century*.]
in Fleet Street (W.14), 1568 (18512)–1574 at least; variations:
— dw. over Temple Bar, 1572 (2010)
— dw. at Temple Bar, 1574 (24408)
1565: 3933.5 (c).
1566: 25968 (d).
1568: 171.5, 12192 ent., 18512 (d).
1569: 97.5, 4376.5, 10441, 10821 (d), 13897, 18600 (d), 20523 (d), 21745 (d), 24935 (d).
1570: 1326 (d), [3291.5?] (c), [6325] (d), 7555 (d), 7679, 11493 (d), 13012 (d?), 15015 (d), 18687.5 (d), 19071 (d?), 19863 (d?), 19870 (d), 19974.2 (d).
1571: 719, 3010, 5652, 15032, 24583, 25943.
1572: 2010, 2037, 4377, 5652.3.
1573: [4684], 4685, 6150 (d), 6748, 12192 (d), 24801.
1574: 2038, 12193a, 24408 (d).
1575: 1059, 3367 (d), 4078, 4378, [5652.5] (c?), 6129, 12605 (d), [21104.5?] (c), 21601 (d), 24336.
1576: 709 ent., 5592 (d), 10487.
1577: 2039, [3654].
1578: 2040, 11975 (d), [13067–8] (d), 14920, [20402].
1579: [4283], [11471a–72], [15589], [20397(*A*3)] (d).
1580: [3358a.5(*A*3)?], [13203] (d), 21593.
1581: [13875?], [26123].

How, W. — *cont.*
1582: 6749, 6749.2 (d?), 6749.4 (d?), [23414] (d).
1584: 24802.
1585: 3011.
1586: [15590].
1587: 12926, 22267 (d).
1588: 11343–5, 12803 f., 16782 (c?).
1590: 4379 (d?), 5721, 17058 (d?).
1591: [11625?].
1594: 3011.5 ass'n.

Howell (Mathews), Ralph.
Bookseller in London, (1598) 1600–1603. [*Dict. 1.*]
shop near the great North door of Paul's at the White Horse (A.2), 1600 (15190)–1602 (13934, has 'dw.')
1600: 15190 f. **1602:** 13934 f., 13935 f.

Howes, Robert.
Stationer in London, (1618) 1620–1648 (cf. DFM II.2246) at least.
No address survives.
1620: 6344.3 ent.

Hudsebaut, Denis (Dionysius).
Printer in Douai, 1638–1640. [*Répertoire 17ᵉ*, IV.9.]
1638: 17542.3.

Hudson, Richard.
Stationer in London, (1557) 1566–1600 (cf. DFM 1680) at least. [*Dict. 1.*]
dw. in Hosier Lane at the $ Woolsack (E.7), 1588 (12556)
1588: 12556 [f.] (d).

Huenefeld, Andreas.
Printer in Gdansk (Danzig), 1609–1652 (1666†). [Benzing 78.]
1639: [12478.5].

Huggins, Thomas.
Bookseller in Oxford, 1623 (Madan I.277)–1636. He lived in St. Mary's parish. [*Dict. 1.*]
No address used.
1625: 13277 sold.
1626: 1600 imp., 24988 f.
1627: 13278 f., 17950 imp.
1628: 21814 imp.
1629: 13279 f.
1630: 3622 f.
1631: 3623 f., 17951 imp., 19194 imp., 24882 pro.
1632: 3624 sold.
1633: 1166 f., 10597 sold, 11514 f., 14439 ven., 18087 imp.
1634: 1391 imp.
1636: 17953 f.

Huguelin. *See* Kerbriant.

Hulsius (van Hulsen), Maria.
Bookseller in Frankfurt am Main, 1606?–1610, in Oppenheim, 1610–1619, and again in Frankfurt from 1619. Widow of Levinus van Hulsen. [Benzing, *Verleger.*]
1619: 4869 (note & *A*3).

Humble, George.
Book and printseller in London, c. 1603–1640†. Member of the Leathersellers' Co. Nephew of **John Sudbury**, whose partner he was c. 1603–1618 though Sudbury's name remains unerased in a few later issues of engraved material. [*Dict. 1*; Globe 216.]
in Pope's Head Alley (O.11), c. 1603? (7579.5)–1634 and until his death; in 1615 (23041.2, text to accompany most maps) 'Palace' is substituted for 'Alley'
— against the [Royal] Exchange, 1610 (many maps in 23041, e.g. Sussex, Surrey)
at the White Horse —, 1604? (775.7, possibly should be dated later), 1611 (23045), 1634 (19052.4)
1603: 7579.5 sold (c?), 13087.5 sold (d?).
1604: 775.7 sold (d?).

Humble, G. — *cont.*
1609: [23434.5?] f.
1611: 23041 sold, 23045 sold.
1612: 7058.5 sold (d), 23041 sold.
1613: 12863a sold (c).
1614: 23041.4 sold, 23046 sold.
1615: 3715.5 sold (d), 23041.2 f.
1616: 23044 sold.
1617: 10690.5 sold (d).
1618: 3062.2 sold (d?), 3062.3 sold (d?).
1619: 656.6 sold (d), 11803 sold.
1620: 11088.3 sold (c?), 23034.5 sold (c).
1622: 3062.5 sold (c?), [4484.5] sold, [4485.5] ven., [19052.2] sold, [19052.6] sold.
1623: 23041.8 sold, 23046.3 f., 23046.7–47 sold.
1625: 3062.6 sold (c?), 6271.5 sold (d), 6273.2 sold (c).
1627: 23035 sold, 23036–6.5 (repeat), 23039g.7 f., 23042 sold, 23043 sold, 23048 sold.
1630: 3062.7 sold (c?).
1631: 23040 f., 23048.5 f.
1632: 23036 sold (d?), 23049 f.
1634: 4485.3 sold, 19052.4 sold.
1635: 3062.8 sold (c?), 3305.5 sold (d?).

Humble, Thomas.
Stationer in London, (1563) 1566–1581. His 1581 item was published with E. Aggas and bears the latter's address: at the Red Dragon in Paul's Churchyard (B). [*Dict. 1.*]
dw. at the George in Lombard Street (O.12), 1566 (11028)
1566: 11028 f. **1581:** 13091.5 f.

Humfrey, John.
Patron? in London, 1633.
No address used.
1633: 551 ap.

Hunne, John.
Publisher in London, 1577. Member of the Haberdashers' Co. Son-in-law of **Reyner Wolfe** and one of the beneficiaries of Wolfe's widow, Joan. [Plomer, *Wills*: 19–22.]
No address used.
1577: 13568b (d).

Hunscott, Joseph.
Bookseller in London, (1612) 1624–1660†. His first two books were sold by others. In 1632 he was granted the reversion of the office of Beadle in the Stat. Co., and on 30 Aug. 1641 he succeeded following the death of **Richard Badger 1** (*C-B C*: 244 and fol. 177ᵛ). [*Dict. 2*; *Loan Book*, 1619–26, 1633–36, 1643–46; *Poor Book*, 1646–59, widow thereafter.]
his house in Crane Court in the Old Change (N.8), 1639 (3127.5)
1624: 5389 f. **1637:** 23245 f. **1639:** 3127.5 f.

Hunt, Christopher.
Bookseller in London, (1592) 1593, in Exeter, 1594, and again in London, 1606. Probably related to **Thomas Hunt 2.** [*Dict. 1*; *Poor Book* (wife), 1608–13.]
London, in Paternoster Row (C.7), 1606
dw. in Lovell's Inn — (5441)
dw. — near the King's Head (5441.2)
1593: 5152 f. **1594:** 13892 f., 23697 f. **1606:** 5441–1.2 f., [11620.5? f.] (d?).

Hunt, Joseph.
Bookseller in London, (1587) 1599–1613. Before 1611 his books were sold at the shops of others. [*Dict. 1.*]
shop in Bethlehem (Bedlam) near Moorfield gate (K.1), 1611 (4900.5)–1613 (6528); variation: has 'his house', 1612 (18588)
1599: 20121.5 f.
1605: 18589 ent.
1608: 3719 ent.
1609: 21424(*A*3) f., 23421 ent.
1611: 4900.5 f. (d).

Hunt, J. — *cont.*
1612: 10785 f., 18588–8.5 f.
1613: 6528 f., 23763 f., 25840 f., 25950 f.

Hunt, Matthew.
Bookseller in Oxford, 1639–1640. [*Dict. 1.*]
No address used.
1639: 11567 sold. **1640:** 4672 f., 4675 f., 10013 imp.

Hunt, Thomas 1.
Bookseller and printer (from 1483) in Oxford, 1473–1486 at least. Printed in partnership with **Theodoric Rood**. [Duff, *Century*.]
No address used.
1483: [695] (d), [696] (d), [922] (d?), [23904] (d).
1485: [315] (d?), 19827.
1486: [17958].

Hunt, Thomas 2.
Bookseller in Exeter, 1631–1648. Probably related to **Christopher Hunt**. [*Dict. 2.*]
in St. Peter's Churchyard, 1640 (14706)
1631: 17863 sold. **1640:** 14706 sold (d).

Hunter, John.
Bookseller in London, 1576–1582. Freed as a Draper by **Abraham Veale** in 1571. [*Dict. 1.*]
on London Bridge (T.7), 1576–c. 1580
dw. — at the Black Lion, 1576 (5592)
dw. — nigh unto the drawbridge, c. 1580 (24557.5)
1576: 5592 f. (d). **1580:** 24557.5 [f.] (c).

Hurlock (Herlock), George.
Bookseller in London, (1624) 1632–1669† (cf. DFM II.2308). Brother of **Joseph Hurlock** and succeeded to the shop. [*Dict. 2*; DFM 2678.]
shop at St. Magnus corner (T.8), 1636 (21640, letterpress tp)–1640 (21551) at least
1632: 861.3 sold.
1634: 3712 ent., 19968a ent., 21551 ent.
1636: 21640 f.
1637: 18691 f.
1638: 861.6 sold, 21551 f.
1639: 3712 f., 21092 sold.
1640: 3712.3(*A*) f., 21551 f.
1642: 19968a f. (d?).

Hurlock, Joseph.
Bookseller in London, (1626) 1631–1634?†. Apparently married the widow of **John Tapp** and succeeded to the latter's shop, which afterward passed to his brother, **George Hurlock**. [*Dict. 1*; DFM 2714.]
shop at St. Magnus corner (T.8), 1632 (23682.5)
1631: 3712 ent., 19668a ent., 26022 ent.
1632: 861.3 sold, 21550.5 f., 23682.5 f.
1634: [23682.7? f.] (d?).

Hury, Pierre.
Bookseller and printer in Paris, 1585–1595. [*Dict. 1*; Renouard.]
1588: 4568.

Hutton, George.
Bookseller in London, (1635) 1636–1648 (Wing N 977). [*Dict. 2*; DFM 2435.]
at (within) the turn (turning) stile in Holborn (V.13), 1636 (1558, has only noted use of a sign: the Sun)–1640 (11913, has 'shop'); variation: has 'dw.', 1639 (11912)
1636: 1558 sold.
1637: 21721 sold.
1638: 3586 f., 11550.2 sold.
1639: 11251 sold, 11912 f., 19998 sold.
1640: 11913 f., 15081.7(*A*3) sumpt./f.

Hutton, Richard.
Patentee? in London, 1583.
No address used.
1583: 18101 per assig.

Huvin (Huuyn), Jean.
Bookseller and bookbinder in Rouen, 1501–1525. Possibly also the I. H. who was in partnership with **Julian Notary** and **Jean Barbier** in London, 1496–1497. [Duff, *Century*; Muller 100.]
1496: [270] (d). **1497:** [15884?]. **1501:** 15805.1 exp., 16176 imp. **1506:** 16182 imp. **1508:** 16182a imp., 16185 imp. **1515:** 16195.5 imp.

Hyll. *See* Hill.

Hyperphragmus. *See* Zuttere.

I

I. or J., A.
If a printer, he might be A. Islip. However, the initials are more likely repeated from a previous French edition and signify **A. Janon**.
1607: 11548.7 (date altered by pen to 1604).

I., G., *Publisher at 'Geneva'*, 1545. *See* Joye, George.

I., Joh. *See* Jackson, John 1.

Ingland, N. *See* England, N.

Ireland, Richard.
Bookseller in Cambridge, 1632–1652. He lived in the parish of Great St. Mary's. [*Dict. 2.*]
No address used.
1632: 20692a sold. **1634:** 20693 sold. **1640:** 20693a sold.

Ireland, Roger.
Stationer in London, before 1557–1576? His only surviving imprint was apparently sold in J. Cawood's house: at the $ Holy Ghost in Paul's Churchyard (A.5). [Duff, *Century*.]
No separate address used.
1568: 1244 ent. **1568/69:** 466.9 f.

Irish Franciscans' Press.
Printers in Louvain, c. 1614–1618
1614: [18791] (c), [18792] (c). **1614–18:** [11314.9]. **1616:** [6778]. **1618:** [17157].

Irish Stock. *See* Stationers' Company.

Isaac, Godfrey.
Bookbinder? in London, before 1579–1594 at least. Freed as a Draper in 1573. In 1579 an apprentice bound to C. Barker was allowed to serve with Isaac and in 1584 was turned over to E. White 1 (Arber II.94, 122). In 1594 Isaac was listed as one of the *assignees of* **R. Day** (*Reg. B*: 48). His only imprint was shared with **Thomas Butter**. [*Dict. 1.*]
No address used.
1581: 18534 f.

Isam, John.
Journeyman printer? in London, (1615) 1619–1622†. In 1608 he took as his first wife Elizabeth Roberts, probably the daughter of his master, **James Roberts**, and lived in the parish of St. Giles, Cripplegate (I.4). [*Dict. 1*; DFM 461; *Poor Book*, 1622, widow thereafter; *St. Giles*, 1608–22.]
No address survives.
1619: 12011 ent.

Islip, Adam.
Printer in London, (1585) 1591–1639†. In 1594 he acquired much of the printing material of **John Wolfe**. After Islip's death his printing material passed to **Richard Hearne**. [*Dict. 1.*]
In 1605 Islip took over the printing material and received permission to print law books which the **English Stock** (*see* Stationers' Co. and Appendix D/1–60) had bought from **Thomas Wight** (*C-B C*: 16). Because of the continuity of printing material, Islip's name has often been erroneously supplied or implied in STC as the printer of Wight's publications and once in the case of Wight's predecessor, Jane Yetsweirt, i.e. in:

3345	5496	11414	15753	20045
3346	5499	11415	15754	20732
4719	5499.2	11415a	17291	21560
5493	5502	11906	19368.5	21576
5493.4	5502.3	13200	19369	21577
5493.7	9283	14901	19641	25270
5495	11410	15022		

Islip's name or 'f.' should be deleted from these items, and they are all omitted from the index below. In 1629 the law patent passed to the *assignees of* **J. More, esq.** Between 1605 and 1629 inclusive, items below *not* in the law patent are distinguished by an asterisk (*).
No address noted.
1594: 542.5 ent., 543 ent., 4168.5, 5077 ent., 5411, [12267], 12448.5, 13488, 13890–2, 18838, 19540 ent., 19618, 22951, 24599.
1595: [542], 4176.2, 5262.5, [5324(*A*3)] (false), 12449, 14000, [19662], [19667], [19702a], 22797.
1596: 3355, 4182, 4910, 12412, 13478, 13893, 16655, 16677, 18839, 24491, 26035.
1597: 1659, [12301a.9(*A*3)], 12451, 12531.5, 18839.5, 23281 ex typ.
1597/98: 403.9.
1598: 542.5, 760, 3947, 5077–9, 10433, 15228–8.5, 17413, 19054.5, 21365.
1599: 4691, 14946, 15229, 18146, 19540, 23931.
1600: 1596.5, [11367], [14767], 16613 (& *A*3 note: faked), [17573?], 21548.
1601: 13048.5, 17092, 17569, 20029, [23932], [25124–4.5] (false).
1602: 3160, 3397, 5080, 11743, 17092.5, 18839a, [19830], 23932.5.
1603: 15051, 23456 per.
1604: 1599.3, 1818, 3439, 4883, 7113, 7118, 7526, 13704, 13894, [26040].
1605: [5504], [9297], [25271].
1606: 1468*, 3193–3.5*, [5505], [5525], [7723.3], [9547], [9602], [10982], [15157], 19732*, 21032*, [25279].
1607: [3346.5], [5505], [5509], [5509.5], [9298], [15023], [15171], [18592–3?]*, [19724.9]*, 19732a*, [20038], [20713], [21054?], [21578], [23218], [23224].
1608: [5511], [5511.2], [9284], [9548], 11744*, 12374*, [15755], [15755.3], [15779], 17747* ent.
1609: [840], [5494], 6332*, [7387], [7540], [7540.5], [9616], [10964.5], 12375*, 17311*, [19642], [20495], [20714].
1610: [5497], [5500], [5503], 15052*, [15158], [15172], [20047.5], [20496], [25272].
1611: [3347], [5513], [5513.2], 5830*, 17661* ent., [9298.5], [9324], [25279.3].
1612: 1660*, [5507], [7723.5], [9549], [15158.5], [15755.7], [15756], [15780], 17747*, 18147*.
1613: [5515], [10870], [15024], 17676*, 17710*, [20046], [21580].
1614: [5488], [5518], [9928], [15159], [15173], [19643].
1615: 988*, [5516], [5521], [7723.7], [9325], [17292], [19062.5 (*A*3)]* (d?), [20497], [20715], [25273].
1616: [3347.5], [3403]*, [5522], 10549*, [10965], [11197], 13895*, [15781], [16786]*, [25605]* (false).
1617: 127*, [2917–8]*, [9299], [9550], [10983], [15756.5], [15757], 21034–4a*.
1618: [5498], [5503.4], [5519], [6205], [8568?]* (d), [9285], [9328], [11416], [20715a], 21437* by ass't of, [25279.5], [25648].
1619: 4017*, [5494.3], [5501], [5523], [6206], [9554], [9904], [15160].
1620: [9904], [11411], 15053*, 17677*, [25649].
1621: [3348], 4528–9*, [5510], [7390.5], [9327], 15053*, [15758], [15782], [19644], [19644.5].
1622: [6207], [7393], 17222*, [18029]* (d), [25275].
1623: 4018*, [6212], [15025], [20498], 25382*.
1624: [5508], 10261.5*, 13326*, [15161], [20716].
1625: 4529.5–30*, 7180*, [7724], [9300].
1626: [5514], [6208], [15161.5], 21035–5.7*.
1627: [5517], [10871], 12376*, [15783], [21219?]*, [25279.7].
1628: [6213], [6362], 13048.5* ass'd, [15784], 21383* ass'd, [25650].
1629: 4019*, 4524*, [5512], [5520], 11126*, 13984*, 15053* ent., 17223*, [20717], 22798*, 23898–8a*.
1630: [5322], 11947, [16768.14] (c), [17283.5].
1631: 1661–1.5, 11228, 15054.

Islip, A. — *cont.*
1632: 5831, 11228, 11228.3.
1633: 11751, 13620, 21036a.
1634: 20030.
1635: 3193.5(*A*3) (c.), 13327, 20030a.
1636: 4020, 11752, 17224–4.5.
1638: 15055.

J

J. For initials I. or J. *see* I.

Jackman, John.
Stationer in London, (1628) 1631. [*Dict. 1*; DFM 1793.]
No address survives.
1631: 6533 ent., 21416 ent.

Jackson, Hugh.
Printer and bookseller in London, (1572?) 1576–1616†. Married the widow of **Thomas Colwell** and succeeded to the business. From about 1580 Jackson seems to have done less and less actual printing although credited with one press in 1583 and in 1586 (Arber I.248, V.lii); however, not all items have been examined to establish whether Jackson was the printer or not. His copyrights but not his shop passed to **Roger Jackson**, who was perhaps a relative. *See* also Appendix A/16. [*Dict. 1.*]
in Fleet Street beneath the conduit at the $ St. John the Evangelist (W.5), 1576 (25018)–1597 (6216, omits sign); most imprints have 'dw.'; some omit the sign, 1594 (12220); a few omit the sign and 'beneath the conduit', 1593 (19498), 1596 (5582); last use of sign noted, 1595 (6546); in 1590 (3118) one L variant has misprint: 'dw. at Fleet Bridge', corrected in the other L copy.
shop under Temple Bar gate (W.14), 1596 (5582)
1576: 3382, 25018, 25978 (d).
1577: 1356.5, 5644 ent., 6278, 10929, 13923–4, 19497, [19870.5] (d?), 20958.
1578: 11632.5, 24663.
1580: 869 (c), 869.5 (c), 3358a.5(*A*3) [f.] (c), 14521 (d?), 18225 (d).
1581: 572, 13875 [f.?].
1583: 21805 [f.] (d?).
1584: [3495.7] (c?), 12217 f., [19874.5] (d), 19875.
1585: 7383, 11932, 14009.7 (c?), 21850.3(*A*3, note) [f.] (c).
1587: 4076 imp. (d).
1588: 19872, 19875.5.
1589: 12219 [f.].
1590: 3118, 19873, 19875.3.
1592: 6545.5 sold.
1593: 19498 f.
1594: 12220 [f.].
1595: 6546 sold.
1596: 172, 5582 [f.].
1597: 6216 [f.].
1598: 542.5 sold.
1603: 6547 sold.
1606: 7558.
1616: 1021 ass'd, 3322.5 ass'd, 7558 ass'd, 11527 ass'd, 21850.7 ass'd.

Jackson, John 1.
Printer in London, 1584–1596. Freed as a Grocer by **John Charlewood** in 1570. One of the partners in the **Eliot's Court Press**, which was situated in the Little Old Bailey (D.1). [*Dict. 1*; *Library* 2 (1922): 175–84; 3 (1923): 194–209.]
Indexed below are *only* items which Jackson entered in the SR or in which his name appears in the imprint. In the items distinguished by an asterisk (*) the imprint is shared with another partner. For other items in which he may have been involved *see* Eliot's Court Press.
No address noted.
1585: 5266.4*, 5299*, 5309* ap., 5309.2* ap., 5309.3* ap., 7262 ap.
1586: 3072*, 19485 ent.
1587: 165 ap., 5210, 12200 ent.
1588: 1346, 12908, 20762.7 ex off., 24579 ent.
1589: 17132.
1590: 6658, 21698 ent.

Jackson, John 1 — *cont.*
1591: 19619.
1592: 26062.
1593: 21516.
1594: 16428–9.
1595: 11053 (d), 20763 ex off., 21658.
1596: 17003.7, 19365.5, 21658.5.

Jackson, John 2.
Bookseller in London, (1633) 1634–1643 (Wing J 1240). Son of **Roger Jackson**. Began in partnership with **Francis Church**. [*Dict. 2*; DFM 1394.]
at the King's Arms in Cheapside (N.1), 1634 (13357, with F. Church)
in the Strand (X.1), 1638 (631); variation has: shop — at the $ P[remainder cropt], dated c. 1635 but may be later
dw. without Temple Bar (X.1), 1640 (21774)
1634: 1577.5 sold, 10135 f., 13357 f., 13585 sold. **1635:** 6612 f. (c).
1638: 631 sold. **1640:** 21774 f.

Jackson (Jacson), Ralph 1.
Bookseller in London, 1588–1601†. Many of his imprints to 1594 are shared with **William Young** and from 1596 with **Robert Dexter**. His shop passed to **Cuthbert Burby**. [*Dict. 1.*]
in Paul's Churchyard at the Swan (A.5), 1589 (6625.3, with W. Young)–1601 (12316, has 'shop'); often used no address
1589: 6625.3 f., [21556 f.] (d).
1590: 13702 sold, 18247 f.
1591: 20588 f.
1594: 6625.4 f.
1595: 4098 f., 4101 f., 4102 f.
1596: 5711 f., 10638.5 f., 13478 f., 18199 f., 19702a.5 f.
1597: 11127 imp., 16609 f., 18200.5 f., 19712 (note), 19724.5 f.
1598: 12323 ?ent., 12927 f., 12927.5 f.
1599: 7304 f., 12313 f., 12313.5 f., 18198 ent., 18198.5 f., 19963 f.
1600: 12314.5 ent., 12314.7 f., 12315 ent., 12928 f., 19646 (note).
1601: 12316 f., 18810 f.

1602: 12317 ass'd, 19647 (note).

Jackson, Ralph 2. = misprint in 1615 (5378) for Roger Jackson.

Jackson, Richard.
Stationer in London, (1565) 1566–1569. [*Dict. 1.*]
in Gutter Lane at the Red Lion (G.4), 1569 (10326.5)
1569: 10326.5 f.

Jackson, Robert 1.
Bookseller in London, 1607. He apparently managed or worked in the shop of his former master, **Cuthbert Burby**. [*Dict. 1*; DFM 133.]
at the shop under the Royal Exchange (O.8), 1607 (21507)
1607: 1692 ent., 21507 sold.

Jackson, Robert 2. = misprint in 1615 (5378.1) for Roger Jackson.

Jackson, Roger.
Bookseller in London, (1599) 1601–1625†. Father of **John Jackson 2.** Possibly related to **Hugh Jackson**, whose copyrights he took over. The second address is that of his former master, **Ralph Newbery**, for whom Roger managed it until he succeeded to it in 1604. [*Dict. 1*; *Loan Book*, 1604–06.]
in Fleet Street, 1601–25
— at the White Hart (W.2), 1601 (13499)
— a little above (near) the conduit (W.5), 1602 (12243, with J. North)–1625 (17395.5); has 'his shop' from 1604 (10650)
1601: 13499 sold.
1602: 12243 f.
1603: 6374 ent., 13589 f.
1604: 1793.5 f., 3650 ent., 10650 sold, 12752 f., 18675 f., 20339 f.
1605: 25633 f.
1606: 11926.5 f., 25942 f.
1607: 4131 f., 20340 f., 23019.5 f., 23020 f., 24614 f.
1608: 55 f., 744 f., 6374 f., 6959.5 f., 10651 f., 13453 f., 25634 f.
1609: 744.5 f., 6944.7 f., 6960 f., 10652 f., 20305 f., 25634a f.
1610: 6945 f., 6945.2 f., 6965 f., 20290 f.
1611: 745 f., 6375 f., 6945.4 f., 6966 f., 11764 f., 12318 (note), 21264 f., 24614.5 f.

Jackson, Roger — *cont.*
1612: 24615 f.
1613: 1077 ent., 5381 f., 6611 f., 14516 f., 20294 f., 20295 f.
1614: 6661.5 f., 6935 f., 6935.5 f., 6945.6 f., 7160.5 imp., 11767.5 f., 14296 f., 14305a f., 14512–2.3 f., 15267 f., 17336 f., 17586 ent., 21772 f.
1615: 3927 f., 5378–8.2 f., 6662 f., 6961 f., 11765 f., 15267.3 f., 17342 f., 20806.5 f., 21096.5 f.
1616: 686 f., 1021 ent., 6662.3 f., 7558 ent., 11522 f., 11523 f., 12891 f., 17337 f., 17381.5 f., 21850.7 ent., 22350 f., 25151 f.
1617: 687 f., 3322.5 f., 11527 f., 12221 f., 15329 f., 19873.5 f., 21098 f., 24616 f., 25035 f.
1618: 14294 f., 15268.3 f., 15329 f., 20807 f., 21773 f., 25036 f.
1619: 1196(*A*) ent., 4193 f., 11933 f., 12622 ent., 13512 (note), 13515.5 ent., 14512.7 f., 14513 f., 16698 ent., 17586 f., 20282.3 f., 20619 ent.
1620: 6611.5 f., 6662.7 f., 6945.8 f., 12756 f., 13512 f., 14512.7 f., 17372 f., 17586 f.
1621: 6376 f., 6663 f., 6946 f., 11766 f.
1622: 6664 f., 15254.5 f., 25037 f., 25150a.5 f.
1623: 4193 f., 11126.5 f. (c), 11768 f., 12891.5 f., 15330 f., 17338 f., 17343 f., 17382 f., 17395.3 f., 20808 f.
1624: 1425 f., 6935.7 f., 22351 f.
1625: 11780 f., 17363 f., 17373 f., 17395.5–.7 f., 21636 f.

1626: 6936(*A*) ass'd, 6947 ass'd, 13499.5 ass'd, 25150a.5 ass'd.

Jackson, Simon.
Bookseller in Oxford, 1618. [*Dict. 1.*]
No address used.
1618: 22828 propter.

Jacobi. *See* also Wouw.

Jacobi, Henry.
Bookseller and bookbinder in London, 1505–1512? and in Oxford, 1512–1514†. Between 1505–08 his items were usually issued jointly with **Joyce Pelgrim**. Four items of 1510–11 issued with **Jean Petit 1** have no address, and it is possible Jacobi was in Paris, where they were printed, rather than in London. [Duff, *Century*.]
London, in Paul's Churchyard (A.6), 1505–1512? variations:
— at the $ Holy Trinity, 1505 [17109], 1506? (12351), 1510 [4115, has Holy 'and Indivisible' Trinity]
dw. near the new school and St. Paul's Church, 1509 (13830.3, colophon)
dw. — at the new schools, 1512 (15861.7)
Oxford, at the $ Holy Trinity, 1513? (22580)
1505: [17109] ven.
1506: 12351 ven. (d?), [15903(*A3*)] ven., [16258].
1507: 11605.5 imp., 11614.5 imp., [15862] ven.
1508: 696.4 imp., [15862] ven., 23940a imp.
1509: 13830.3 ven.
1510: [4115] ven., 21789.1 ven., 21799.4 ven., 21799.6 ven., [23030.7] ven.
1511: 21799.8 ven.
1512: 15861.7 imp.
1513: 22580 ven. (d?).

Jacobi, Isaac, *pseud.*
Printer in 'Lutetia Britannorum', 1609. = F. Bellet, St. Omer.
1609: 6991.5–.7 ap.

Jacobs, Abraham, *pseud.*
Printer in 'Delft', 1633?–c. 1635? = Unidentified Dutch? printer.
1633: 1612 (d?). **1635:** 1616 (c?), 1616.5 (c?).

Jacobson, Oliver, *pseud.*
Printer in 'Zurich', 1543. = A. Goinus, Antwerp.
1543: 1309.

Jacobsz van Wouw, H. *See* Wouw.

Jacobszoon, J. P. *See* Paets.

Jacson. *See* Jackson.

Jaggard, Dorothy.
Printer in London, 1627. Widow of **Isaac Jaggard** and undoubtedly continued in Aldersgate Street (F.2). [*Dict. 1*, under husband.]
No address survives.
1627: [630], 22274 ass'd, 25789 ass'd.

Jaggard, Elizabeth.
Bookseller in London, 1623–1626. Widow of **John Jaggard**. [*Dict. 1.*]
at the Hand and Star near the Middle Temple gate (W.13), 1623 (20752.5)–1624 (1146)
1623: 20752.5 f. **1624:** 1146 f. **1626:** 1149 ass'd, 3404 ass'd.

Jaggard, Isaac.
Printer in London, (1613) 1616–1627†. Son of **William** and husband of **Dorothy Jaggard.** His name occasionally appears in imprints before he succeeded in 1623 to his father's business, which in 1627 apparently passed briefly to his wife before being acquired by **Thomas Cotes**. **Printer to the City of London**, 1623–1627. [*Dict. 1*; DFM 290.]
dw. in Aldersgate Street (F.2), 1627 (25793); no other use noted.
1616: 18304.
1617: 13372(*A3*), 19191.
1620: 3172.
1623: 16728.9 (d?), 22273.
1624: [3788?], 4630 (note), 5692.3–.5, 6690, 13203.5, 19774.
1625: [62?] (c), 1657, 3173, 6722, [11960], [14460], 16729.1, 16729.2, [16729.3] (d), [16729.4?] (c).
1626: 266, [1606.5], [1607], [4633–3.5], 5462, [13927].
1627: 630 f., 4137.3 (note), 6723, [10614–4.5], 18915, [23015.7], [23071?] (d), 25793.

Jaggard (Jagger), John.
Bookseller in London, (1593) 1594–1623†. Brother of **William Jaggard**; husband of **Elizabeth.** He succeeded to the shop of his former master, **Richard Tottell**. [*Dict. 1*; *Loan Book*, 1622–25 (transferred to John jun. in 1623).]
within (near) Temple Bar at the Hand and Star (W.13), 1594 (12190)–1622; variations: has 'shop', 1598 (1485); adds 'dw. in Fleet Street' and omits sign, 1609 (24526); for 'within ... Bar' substitutes 'near the Temple gate', 1622 (12962)
1594: 12190 f.
1598: 1485 f.
1599: 18974 ent.
1600: 22425 f., 23698 f.
1601: 3398 f., 3399 f.
1602: 3397 f., 4615 f.
1603: 3400 f.
1605: 21635 f.
1606: 1139 f.
1608: 3401 f., 21625 f.
1609: 21625 f., 24526 f.
1611: 3402 f.
1612: 1139.5 f., 1141.5 f., 6348 f., 15393 f.
1613: 1142 f., 1143–4 f. (forged), 6349 f.
1616: 3403 f.
1622: 12962 f.

Jaggard, William.
Journeyman printer, bookseller, and printer (from 1600?) in London, (1591) 1594–1623†. Brother of **John** and father of **Isaac Jaggard**. He was printing in a small way by 1600 (cf. 22425) and had rights to playbills by 1602 (*C-B C*: 1–2). By 1605 he was working in the same street as **James Roberts** and succeeded to the latter's printing materials before the end of 1606. **Printer to the City of London**, 1610–1623. [*Dict. 1.*]
shop in Fleet Street in St. Dunstan's Churchyard (W.9), 1594 (7086)–1595 (13973, has: at East end of Church)
dw. in Barbican (I(headnote), I.1), 1605 (7606)–1623 (10717)
1594: 7086 f. (d), 7086.5 f. (d?).
1595: 263, 13973 f.
1598: 24627a.6 f.
1599: 264 f., 13502 f., [22341.5? f.] (d?), 22342 f.
1600: 22425 (note).
1601: 14343(*A3*) [by? &] f.
1603: [5871.7?], 12465.5 f.

Jaggard, W. — *cont.*
1604: 12466, [23357].
1605: 1486, [3794], 7606, [10930(*A*3)], [13044], [15085], 18279 (d), 21786, [22869–9.3], [23405], [23615], [24148.7].
1606: 889, [1139], [11094], [13045], [19334], 20741, [21407] (d?), 23558, 24293, [24422].
1607: [797], 4102.7–.9 (d), 6337, [6396.5], [6540], 6641, [7261], 10209.3(*A*), 13371, 13967, [14690?], [15282], [17334], 18495, [19295?], 20741, [21366], [21513.5], [21605], 22915 (d), 22915.5 (d), 22916 (d), [23982.3], [24057], 24123, [25635], 25639 (d).
1608: 1824, 1832, [3401], [6496], [11045], 11922 typis, 12467, [17927?], 19385.5, 20493, [21625], 24124, [24423], [25280].
1609: 898, [2528], [2530.5(*A*3)], 5979, [7470], [11246], 13366, [17925.5] (d?), [17933?] (d?), [21413], [21625], [23421] (d), [24125].
1609/10: [434.22].
1610: 894–4.5, 1810, [7657], [10378?], 11691a, [12663.4], [16724 (*A*3)] (d?), 16764 (c), 16764.3 (c), [17309], 17926, [17934], 19386, [20992], [22008], [24126], [25132].
1611: [3402], 4093–3.5, 6718, 16724.5 (d), 16911.5, 18263, 18267, 18267.5.
1612: 890, [1139.5], [1141.5], [6348], 10209.5(*A*) (d), [10854], [11380], [15393], [16725] (d), [17439–9.5], [17935] (d?), [20393?] (d), 22343, [22975] (d?), 25786.
1613: [1142], [6247], [6349], 10237 (d), 10290 (d), 10314.7 (d), 13483, 16725.3 (d), [17925?] (d?), [17930?] (d?), 17936.
1614: 889.5, 6682.3, 6719, [20742], 25791.
1615: 107, 1810 ent., 6062, 6690 ent., 10147.4 (d?), 10159.5 (d?), 12570, [13637] (d?), 14418.5 (note), [14419.5], 16725.7 (d), [19202], 19387, 21486.
1616: 5811–2, 6062.2, 10147.5 (d), [13624] (d?), 18304 ent., 19191 ent., 20782, 23493, 25787.
1617: 265, 4886, 6720, 16727, 16727.1, 16727.3, [17931?] (d?), 20638a (d/error), 21015, 24991.5, 25296, 25835, 25836.
1618: 893, 6062.4, 10291 (d), 14341, [26050.14?].
1619: 3213, 3832, [14529], 17936.5, [18796] (d/false), 19388, [22291] (d/false), [22293] (false, d), [22297] (false, d), [22300] (false), [22303] (false, d), [22341], [26101].
1620: 3172 ent., 6721, [12967.5] (d?), 13859, 16727.7, 16727.9, 19443, [20397.3(*A*3)] (d?), 25792, 25796.
1620/21: 407.4.
1621: 6108, 6108.3, [12391], 16728, 16728.3 (d), [19087.7] (d), 20638a (d), 20639, [23918.5] (d), 25109.
1622: [1119.5–20] (false, c?), [4179] (d), [13859.5], 16728.5, 16728.7 (d), [24393.7], 24756, 25788.
1623: 898.5(*A*), [1336], 6721.5, [8704.5(*A*3)] (d), 10717, [16768.32] (d), 22273 at charges of.

1624: 4630 (post-dated?).

Jagger. *See* Jaggard.

James, Jacob (Jacques), *pseud.*
Printer in 'Edinburgh', 1574, etc. = B. Jobin, Strassburg, and other unidentified continental printers. [*Dict. 1.*]
1574: 1463 ex typ., 1464 ex typ., 1464.2 ex typ., 1464.3 ex typ.
1575: 1464.4, 1464.5.
1593: 1464.7.

James, Yareth.
Bookseller in London, 1581–1602 at least. Although no Draper of his name was freed, an 'Edward' James was freed by **Anthony Kitson** in 1575; Yarath James freed the Draper **William Barley** on 30 Aug. 1587. [*Dict. 1*; *St. Giles*, 1606.]
dw. in Newgate Market over against Christ Church (C.4), 1581 (7557.7)–1585 (376.3, colophon)
shop without Cripplegate (I.2), 1602 (18547)
1581: 7557.7 f. (d). **1582:** 20404 ent. **1584:** 12798 f., 21483 f. (d).
1585: 376.3 f. **1586:** 15108 ent., 21456.5 ent. **1602:** 18547 sold.

Janon, A.
King's notary? and printer? in the province of Dauphiné, France, 1604. His name may only have appeared as the authorizing official on the original document from which the following reprint was made. *See* also I., A.
1604: 11548.5.

Janss, Ashuerus, *pseud.*
Printer in 'Goricum' [Gorinchem], 1624. Originally used by N. Okes, then copied by W. Jones 3.
1624: 22103, 22103.3, 22103.7, 22104.

Janssen van Aelst. *See* Aelst.

Jansson (Janssonius, Jansz), Jan 1.
Printer? print and bookseller in Arnhem, 1597–1634. [*Dict. 1*; Gruys 52.]
1620: 13582 [by? &] imp. (d).

Jansson (Johnson), Jan 2.
Printer and bookseller in Amsterdam, 1608–1665; also in Stockholm, 1649, 1656, and in Uppsala, 1654. [*Dict. 1*; Gruys 50–1.]
1620: 3111. **1625:** 3112.5. **1634:** 551.5, 1571.5 ap. **1636:** 17827.
1638: 17451.

Jansz (Janson, Johnson), Broer.
Printer in Amsterdam, 1604–1652†. It is not clear whether the following are genuine imprints or London forgeries possibly made for T. Archer. [Gruys.]
1621: [18507.18?], [—.19?], —.20, —.21, —.22, —.23, —.24 (d), —.25.

Jansz (Johnson, Vennecool), Cornelis.
Dutch refugee and Brother of the Stat. Co. in London, 1567–1571 at least; printer in Dordrecht, 1578, and in Delft, 1581–1590 (1623†). Possibly the same man as **Cornelis Woltrop**. [Gruys; Briels 497–8; Worman 34.]
1582: 16572.2(*A*3).

Jascuy, Samuel, *pseud.*
Publisher in 'Paris', 1558. ? = J. Petit 2, Rouen.
1558: 15673 expenses, 15674–4.5 expenses.

Jaye (Jaey), Henry.
English recusant bookseller and printer in Brussels, 1607–1610, and in Malines, 1610–1643†. [*Dict. 1*: 152; *BS* 1 (1951): 86–111.]
1611: 23948.5(*A*3) [f.?].
1613: 4125.
1615: 16096.
1616: 14296.5, 23988.5.
1618: 16854.5.
1619: 18316.7.
1620: 6099.5, [19461], 26000.3.
1621: [7072.2], 17998.
1623: [7435] (false), 7435.2, 17999, [18327.5].
1635: 1837.7.

Jeffes, Abel.
Printer in London, (1580) 1583–1599. In 1584 he had a journeyman printer working with him, **William Dickenson**. [*Dict. 1*; *St. Giles*, 1585–87.]
dw. in Sermon Lane near Paul's Chain (R.4), 1583 (2368.3)–1584 (17979.7)
dw. in the Fore Street without Cripplegate near Grub Street at the $ Bell (I.3), 1586 (15336)–1587 (11638, omits sign)
dw. in Philip Lane at the $ Bell (H.14), 1589 (836)
dw. in the Old Bailey at the Golden Cup (D.7), 1591 (22696.5)
dw. in Paul's Churchyard at the great North door of Paul's (A.2), 1591 (22696)–1592 (6146)
dw. in the Blackfriars near Puddle Wharf (Q.6), 1596 (15337)
1561: 22696.5 (d/error).
1583: 2368.3 (d).
1584: 2368.3 (note), 17979.7.
1585: 4584 in aed. (d?).
1586: 3351 ent., 15336, 23926.
1587: 3182, 11638–9, 12403, 13100, 16953, 24077a.5, 24330.
1589: 836, 839, 5802, 17566.7 (d).
1590: [10877.5], 10878, [21078], 22695, 22695.5, 24569–9.5.
1591: 6859, 11921, [15704], 22696, 22696.5 (d), [22714.5?], [22715?], [22715.5?].
1592: [1086], 5077 ent., 5551, [5577–8.2], 5654.5, 5656, 6146, 10611, 10711 (note), 12234, 15086 ent., 16656, 16665, 17074.5, 18372, 18373, 21087.3, 22708–8.5.
1593: 8226.5 (d), 18374, 19535.
1594: 10413 ent., 10715, 10715.3, 15087.

Jeffes, A. — *cont.*
1595: 5324(*A*3) (forged), 5324.3–.5, 5324.7, [7214.5] (d?), 12924.5–25, 12960, [14068.5(*A*3)], 14708.3, 19797 ?ent., 21083 (d), 25153(*A*3) (d?).
1596: 10711 ass'd, 15337, [16660], [16666], [19799(*A*3)].

Jehannot, Étienne.
Printer in Paris, 1495–1499? [Renouard.]
1495: [15881] (d?), [15881.3] (d?), [15881.5] (c).

Jehannot, Jean.
Printer in Paris, 1497–1521†. [Duff, *Century*; Renouard.]
1498: 15888 per, [15890] (d). **1500:** [15895.5] (d?).

Jenner, Thomas.
Grocer, engraver, print and bookseller in London, 1621–1673†. [*Dict. 2*; Globe 216–17.]
in Cornhill at the White Bear (O.6), 1621 (Hind II.291, no. 10); this address also appears in 1625? (12360.7), possibly left unaltered from an earlier state before the plate was dated 1625
at the Royal Exchange (O.8), 1624–1673; variations:
at the Exchange, 1624 (10404.5, 23499), 1625 (4643.5, has 'Royal' Exchange), 1637 (19615.5)
at the South entrance (entry) of the Royal Exchange, 1626 (14494), 1630 (24697.3), 1631 (14495)
1623: 18003.7.
1624: 10404.5 sold (d), 11511.3 sold (c), 23499 sold (d).
1625: 4643.5 sold, 12360.7 sold (d?).
1626: 14494 sold.
1630: 1497.5 sold (c), 24697.3 sold (d).
1631: 14495 sold.
1637: 19615.5 sold (d), 24697.5 sold (d).
1640: 10671.5 sold (c?), 17469.6 sold (c), 24697.7 sold (d).

Jennings, Miles.
Bookseller in London, 1577–1585. Freed as a Draper in 1576. [*Dict. 1.*]
dw. in Paul's Churchyard at the Bible (A.2), 1577 (20452)–1581 (23413) at least
1577: 15416a f., 20452 f. **1578:** 17203 f. **1579:** 25343 f. (d). **1580:** 20453 f. **1581:** 23413–3.5 f. **1582:** 23414 imp. (d).

Jhones. *See* Jones.

Jobin, Bernhard.
Printer in Strassburg, 1570–1594?†. [Benzing 449.]
1575: [1464.4?] (false), [1464.5?] (false).

John, *Archbishop of Canterbury. See* Morton, J.

John, *Archbishop of St. Andrews. See* Hamilton, J.

Johnes. *See* Jones.

Johnson (Jonson), Arthur.
Bookseller in London, (1601) 1602–1624? and in Dublin, 1624?–1631†, as agent there until 1628 for the **Irish Stock** (*see* Stationers' Company). For other Dublin imprints he may have been involved with *see* Stationers' Society. [*Dict. 1*; *Loan Book*, 1610–13, 1616–19.]
London, in Paul's Churchyard (A.2), 1602–1621 at least
shop — at the Fleur-de-Lis and Crown, 1602 (22299)–1603 (11851)
at the White Horse over against (near) the great North door of Paul's, 1604 (1818)–1621 (5387.5, omits sign); sometimes has 'shop', 1606 (13898.5) or 'dw.', 1608 (7493)
1602: 4025 f., 5434 ent., 18759 f., 21523 f., 22299 f.
1603: 11851 sold.
1604: 1818 f., 23909 f.
1605: 1819 f., 3676 ent., 4405 f., 21408 f.
1606: 13898.5 f., 15425 f., 17913 f., 22384 ent.
1607: 7103 sold, 14531 sold, 16631 sold, 17890 f., 17892 f., 22380 sold, 23131 f.
1608: 1819.5 f., 3013 f., 4026 f., 5434 f., 7493 f.
1609: 12682 f., 15424 f.
1610: 1919 sold, 3717.3 sold (d), 5566 f., 15423.5 f., 17376.5 sold.
1611: 1919 sold, 5435 f., 14979 sold, 15197 f., 17955 imp., 21651 sold, 22381 sold, 24269 f., 24537 sold.
1612: 3907 f., 5386 sold, 7494 f., 12868–8a sold, 13158 f., 15426 f., 21265 f., 24270 f., 25915 f., 25941 f.

Johnson, A. — *cont.*
1613: 5699 f., 10538 f., 12857.2 f., 12857.4 f., 12857.6 f., 15423 f., 15423.7 f., 26092 f.
1614: 5387 sold, 5436 f., 10539 f., 11841 f., 12706–6a f., 12870 f., 16924 f., [21381] sold.
1615: 12706a f., 12707 ass'd, 15423.3 f., 19789 f., 19790 f., 19983 sold.
1616: 22382 sold, 23317 f., 26082–2.5 sold.
1617: 7495 f., 17064 sold, 19983.3 sold, 24538 sold.
1618: 5436.3 f., 12460 sold.
1619: 19756 sold, 22300 f. (false?).
1620: 1647 ent., 11857.3 sold, 12184 sold, 19791 f.
1621: 5387.5 sold, 24074 f.
1626: [18914].

Johnson, Broer. *See* Jansz.

Johnson, John. *See* Jansson, Jan 2.

Johnson, Thomas, *Printseller.*
Bookbinder? and printseller in London, (1611) 1612 (cf. DFM 1734)–1633. [*Dict. 1*; DFM 2770; *Loan Book*, 1630–33; *Poor Book* (widow), 1636–54; Globe 217.]
in Britain's Burse (X.10), 1630 (654)
1630: 654 sold, 11807.7 sold (c), 18051.5 sold (c), 22527a.7 sold (d?).

Johnson, Thomas, *Printer.*
Printer in London, (1656) 1658?–1677. [*Dict. 2*; DFM II.1506.]
1661: [13354] (forged, d?) = Wing² H 1786A.

Johnson, William. *See* Blaeu.

Jones, Rice.
Stationer in London, (1577) 1578–1592 at least, and possibly until 1629. Conflated in Arber's index with Richard Jones, to whom references are usually in the form 'Richard' or 'Ric'. The only clear mentions of 'Rice' or 'Ryce' are: apprenticed to O. Rogers from 25 Mar. 1566 and freed by W. Norton 22 Apr. 1577 (Arber I.289, II.674); took at least five apprentices, in 1578, 1583, 1587, 1590, and 1592 (II.88, 120, 149, 167, 179), none of whom was ever freed though the first was rebound and the last had been previously bound to others (II.98, 171). Not all imprints of Richard have been re-examined to see if one or more belongs to Rice. [?*Poor Book*, 1629, and daughter, 1636.]
shop without Aldgate over against the church [St. Botolph's] (M.1), 1590 (3658.5)
1578: 18277 ent. **1590:** 3658.5 f.

Jones (Jhones, Johnes), Richard.
Bookseller and, intermittently, printer in London, 1564–1613. Father of **Thomas Jones 1**; possibly related to **William Jones 1**. In 1577 (22463.6(*A*3)) he once used the humorous style: by authority of the Duke of Shoreditch's privilege. In 1581 he allowed **Richard Bradock** either to print in his house or to borrow printing material. It is possible that some of the items below listed as printed '[f.]' Richard Jones were actually printed *by* him and vice versa. [*Dict. 1*; *Loan Book*, 1604–06; *Poor Book*, 1608–13.]
in Paul's Churchyard (A.10), 1565–1576; variations:
shop — at (joining to) the Southwest door of Paul's Church, 1565 (4104)–1575 (3695)
?at the Little Shop adjoining to the Northwest [*sic*, misprint for 'Southwest'?] door of Paul's Church, 1566 (1033)
shop under the Lottery House, 1568 (18512)–1569 (24935)
shop at the West end of Paul's Church between the brazen pillar and Lollards' Tower, 1576 (11881)
dw. in the upper end of Fleet Lane at the Spread-Eagle (D.2), 1567? (25439)–1574 (4295, omits 'dw.'); sometimes simply: in Fleet Lane, 1571 (7514, also omits sign)
over against St. Sepulchre's Church without Newgate (D.8), 1576 (24411)–1580 (21593, has 'shop')
near Holborn Bridge (V.2), 1581–1594; variations:
dw. without Newgate —, 1581 (14921)
dw. over against the Falcon —, 1581 (7564), 1582 (3655), 1589 (19534)
dw. at the Rose and Crown —, 1583 (24412)–1594 (15027, tp); in 1588 (20698.5) there is the misprint Holborn 'conduit'
at the Rose and Crown over against the Falcon, 1589 (19534)

Jones, Richard — *cont.*
at the Rose and Crown near to (next above) St. Andrew's Church in Holborn (V.4), 1594 (22884, has 'dw.'; 15027, colophon)–1602 (3673, omits sign); variation: at the Rose and Crown nigh unto Saffron Hill in Holborn, 1595 (15695, colophon; tp as in 22884)
1565: 4104 [f.], 21104.5 ent.
1566: 1033, 6794 (d?), 24517.
1567: 1059 ent., 6794.3 (d?), 7514 ent., 22134.5 (note), 25439 (d?).
1568: 18512 f. (d).
1569: 97.5 f., 10821 f. (d), 13897 f., 21745 f. (d), 24935 f. (d).
1570: 7555 f. (d), 15015 f. (d), 18687.5 f. (d), 19071 f. (d?), 19421 (d), 19863 f. (d?), 19868 (d), 19870 f. (d), 22890 (d).
1571: 3413, 3414, 7514(***A****3*), 11836 (d?), 19869(***A****3*), 24583 f., 25943 f.
1572: 3901, 6235, 13028, 21090, 23589.
1573: 13578, 16636 (d), 19425.5, 22870(***A****3*), [25440] (d).
1574: 4295, 17865 (d), [19936.5(***A****3*)].
1575: 79 [f.] (c), 1059 f., 3695, 12605 f. (d), [21104.5 f.] (c).
1576: 4347 [f.], [7516?], 11640 [f.], 11644 [f.] (d?), 11881 f., 11920 [f.], 24411.
1577: 3410.5 (d?), 3654 [f.], 20665 ?ent., 21134.5, 22463.6(***A****3*) (d),
1578: 1075, [7517?], 12605.5 (d), 13067 [f.] (d), 13068 [f.] (d), 20402 [f.], 22406.3 ent., 23629 [f.], 25347 [f.].
1579: 333 (d?), 982 [f.], 1076, 3054 ent., 4283 [f.], 10566 [f.] (d), 11471a–72 [f.], 12606 (d), 13483 ent., 15589–9.5 [f.], 20397 [f.] (d), 20666 ?ent., 22221 ent.
1580: 6794.5 [f.] (d?), 13203 f. (d), 21090.3(***A****3*) [f.] (d?), 21593 f., 24413 [f.].
1581: 7564, [12531.3 in house of?], 14921 (d), 25095 [f.], [25966(***A****3*) in house of?], 26123 [f.].
1582: 3655, 7515, 12924, 21135, 25337.
1583: 800, [1062?] (d), 10844.8 (note), 11694, 11880 (d), 23376–6.5 [f.], 23377 [f.], 24412, 25344.
1584: 5615, 7559, 17155.5 (d), 19426, 21105, 23377.5, 23588.5, 25341.
1585: [3655.5] (c), 13092.5, 18634, 20127, 23378, 25339, 25342.
1586: 6401 sold, 6557.6 (d), 7594.5 (d?), 10252, 15590 [f.], 22137 ent., 25341.5.
1587: 11409, 14925, [20852] (d), 21778, 23228.7, 25334–4a.
1588: 6910.7 ent., 7582 (d?), 10746, 14067 f., 20698.5 sold, 22920.7 ent., 25229–9.3 [f.].
1589: 644, 3411, 16674 [f.], 19534 [f.].
1590: 3363.9(***A****3*, note), 6363, 16674.5 [f.], 17425, 19546, 22163 [f.], 22883 [f.], 25783.
1591: 3363.9(***A****3*, note), 3633, 7199 [f.], [14685.5?] (d), 16632–2.5, 19429 [f.], 19498.5, 20853 [f.], 21136, 23381.
1592: 6402 [f.], 12542.5(***A****3*) ent., 18371 [f.], 23382 [f.].
1593: [1 f.] (d), 17426 [f.], 22137 [f.], 25338 [f.].
1594: 3298, [12578.5] (d), 15027 [f.], 15694.7 [f.], 20854 [f.], 22884 [f.].
1595: 1060, 4999, 5738, 6403, 6820.5 in aed., 12096, 15694.7–95 [f.], 19337, [20587.5] (d), [21105.5 f.] (d?), 21535, 21536, 21537, 22885(***A****3*), 23379(***A****3*), 24296.
1596: 5737, 5739, 12096.5, 17844 ent., 19429.5 [f.], 21512, 21534, 21817.
1597: 3631, 3634, 17427, 17833, 24607 ap., 25108 ent.
1598: 19880 f.
1599: 4263 imp., 12916 f., 12923.5 f.
1600: 3677 ent., 20575 f.
1601: 24079 ent.
1602: 3673 f.

Note: In *Dict. 1* there are at least two stationers named **Thomas Jones** conflated under one notice. Their identities have been tentatively allocated below.

Jones, Thomas 1.
Stationer in London, (1596) 1599–1605 (Arber II.840) and possibly until 1612. Son of **Richard Jones**. He bound an apprentice in 1599 and probably others in 1604, 1610, 1612 (Arber II.239, 274; DFM 1748, 1743, none of whom was freed). [*Loan Book*, 1597–1603.]
Another Thomas Jones was freed in 1601 (Arber II.252, 728), but since he had been bound in the country and served his time there, it seems probable he had no activity in London.

Jones, Thomas 1 — *cont.*
dw. near Holborn conduit (D.5), 1600 (3677)
1600: 3677 f., 3677.5 f.

Jones, Thomas 2.
Bookseller in London, 1614–1637. Freed by Richard Moore in 1614 but never formally bound. In partnership 1614–1617 with **Richard Meighen**, who was freed by redemption in 1614. [DFM 1971.]
their shop without Temple Bar under (near, at) St. Clement's Church (X.2), 1614 (312.5)–1617 (4897, omits 'their shop'), both with R. Meighen
shop in Chancery Lane over against the Rolls (W.10e), 1619 (5706)–1622 (17713)
in Westminster Hall (X.17), 1621 (4329)–1622 (17713)
shop in the Strand at the Black Raven near unto St. Clement's Church (X.2), 1622 (7051)–1627 (7035, omits 'near ... Church')
shop in St. Dunstan's Churchyard (W.9), 1629 (23857)–1633 (17714, adds 'in Fleet Street'); variation: at the East end of St. Dunstan's Church, 1630 (25091)
shop in the Strand (X.12), 1634 (25092)–1637 (4900, adds 'near York House')
1614: 312.5 f.
1615: 312.5 f., 18523 f., 19333 f., 25981 f.
1616: 10639.3 f., 18524 f.
1617: 1687 ent., 4897 f.
1619: 1668 ent., 5706 sold, 14358.5 f.
1620: 10945.6 f., 16838 ent., 23583 f.
1621: 4329 f., 14358.7(***A****3*) f.
1622: 7051 f., 7053–3.5 f., 7054 f., 17644–4a f., 17713 f.
1623: 7039 f., 7057 f.
1624: 7033–3a f., 7034 f., 7052 f., 7057.5 f., 14359 f., 18430 f., 25090a sold, 25090a.3(***A****3*) sold.
1625: 1687 sold, 7040 f., 7042 f., 14897 f.
1626: 3783 sold (note), 7035 f., 7041 f., 7050 f., 14897 f., 19328 f.
1627: 7035–5a f., 16887 f.
1629: 23857 f.
1630: 1668 f., 1688 f., 14360 f., 25091 sold.
1631: 16888 f., 17645 f.
1632: 14360.5 f.
1633: 17714–4a f., 18431 f.
1634: 25092 sold.
1635: 16889 f. (note).
1636: 4899 f.
1637: 4900 f., 19131 f.

Jones, William 1.
Bookseller in London, (1558) 1559–1574†. Possibly related to **Richard Jones**. His last address apparently passed to his former apprentice, **Henry Disle**. [*Dict. 1.*]
dw. in Creed Lane (Q.2), 1565/66 (433)
in Paul's Churchyard (A.10), 1565/66–74
the Long Shop at the West end of Paul's Church, 1566 (19121, colophon)–1572; variations: omits 'Long', 1565/66 (433, has 'his shop'); has 'the new' or 'his new' Long Shop, 1571 (11426, 17849); has West 'door', 1572 (14724a.7)
his new Long Shop near to the bishop's palace, 1573 (11427)
dw. — at the Southwest door of Paul's Church, 1573 (11427)–1574 (11537.3)
1565/66: 433 f.
1566: 19121 f.
1571: 11426–6.2 f., 11445 imp., 17849 f.
1572: 11426.7 [f.] (d?), 11445.5 imp., 14724a.3 f., 14724a.7 f. (d).
1573: 11427 [f.], 16624 [f.] (d?).
1574: 11428 [f.], 11537.3 [f.], 14724a.9 [f.], 14725 [f.].

Jones, William 2.
Bookseller in London, (1587) 1589–1618† (between 8 Jan. and 17 Sept.: *C-B C*: 98; Arber III.632). His last SR entry was on 11 Feb. 1614 (III.541) with the possible exception of one on 17 Mar. 1617 (III.605). [*Dict. 1.*]
near Holborn conduit (D.5), 1591–1615
shop —, 1591 (3508)
dw. — at the Gun, 1594 (17437)–1615 (18235); occasionally has 'shop', e.g. in 1612 (24519.5)

Jones, William 2 — *cont.*
1591: 3508 f.
1594: 17437 f., 18379 f.
1595: 10922.5 f., 12321 f., 12325 f.
1596: 18073 f.
1597: 17090 f., 17916 sold, 19797 f.
1598: 4965 f., 6819 f., 17438 f., 18230 f.
1599: 10684 f.
1600: 7147 f., 11491 f.
1601: 17680 f., 23932 f.
1602: 19798 f., 21532 f.
1603: 18513.5 f.
1604: 5650 f.
1605: 3659 f., 3661 f., 24519 f.
1606: 795 f., 18231 f., 19500 f.
1607: 2024 f., 19500.5 f.
1608: 2024.3 f.
1609: 5106 f., 10923 f.
1610: 18232 f.
1611: 18233 f., 21533 ass'd.
1612: 24519.5 f.
1613: 18234 f.
1614: 1594 f.
1615: 18235 f.
1618: 18236 ass'd.

Jones, William 3.
Bookseller and printer in London, (1596) 1601–1643†. Father of **William Jones 4.** Operated a secret puritan press, 1604–1608, the location of which is uncertain. Succeeded to the printing material of **Ralph Blower** in 1616. Took **Thomas Paine** as partner in 1635 and was forced to cede the business to him in 1637 (Greg, *Companion*: 343–4, where he describes himself in 1636 as an 'aged man'). [*Dict. 1*; *Loan Book*, 1619–26; *Poor Book*, primarily 1639–43, widow thereafter; *St. Giles*, 1599–1639; *Library* 19 (1964): 38–66, where, however, he is said to have died in 1626.]
dw. in Red Cross Street in Ship Alley (I.7), 1601 (17227)–1604 (13248, has 'at $ Ship')
shop at the end of White [*sic*, not a misprint] Cross Street by (near) the church [St. Giles, Cripplegate] (I.8), 1613 (18059, 21686)
dw. in Red Cross Street (I.7), 1617 (5662)–1639 (14721.5) at least; occasionally adds: near St. Giles's Church without Cripplegate, 1618 (7139)
1601: 17227 f.
1603: 13239.5 [f.], 13243 imp.
1604: [3509?] (d?), [3526] (false), [3527], 13248 f.
1605: [3516], [3524], [3525], [3530], [6814], [15646], [16779.12?] (d?).
1606: [3522], [7736], [14329], [25332].
1607: [11460], [13395], [22236].
1608: [13395], [14084].
1610: 13246 f.
1612: 5833 f., 13248.2 [f.], 18058 f., 24229.5 f., 24596 f.
1613: 7537 f., 13952 sumpt., 18059 f., 21686 f.
1616: 6887 (d), [8585] (d?), 14321.
1617: 5662, 5834, 6286, 6884, [7186a] (d?), 14935, 21365.5, 23254, 23487, 26116.
1618: 4629, [6181.2], 7065, 7139, [8559] (d), 8559.5, [8586?] (d?), [8586.5] (d?), [8587] (d?), 11281, 11496–6.3, 14656, 15553, 18318, [18800], 19909, [20655(*A*3)] (d), 21060, 21186, 21437, [21776.3?] (c), 22124, 22919.5 (d?), 23364, 24333, 25744a.6 sold, 25989.5.
1618/19: [531.10].
1619: 5835, 6065, [8594] (d), [8614] (d), [12858], 15515, 15569, [18802?] (d), 20101 per, 20282.7, 22186, 24596.5.
1620: [382.5] (c), [3205?], [3206?], [3210?] (false), [3214?], [3215?] (false), 3370 per, 3430, 4288.5, 6098 ent., 6100.5 (c), [6558.5?] (c), [8583] (d?), 10559, [10810?], 10814 (note), [11349?], [11350?], [11351?] (false), [11351.3?] (false), [11356?] (false), [11376.5] (c), 11667, 12180, 12184, 12516, [13541.3] (c), [15401?] (c), [17469.8] (c), [20327] (c), 20398, 21062, 21185, 22555.5 (c), 22792.
1621: [244], [5663], 5663.2, 5764.7 (d), 11982.5 imp., 12499.7, [12802] (d), [16776.4] (d), [16776.6] (d), 17042, 23388, [24283] (d), 24642, 24694, 25749.
1622: 1034.3, 3702.5, 4111.5, 5663a, 5664, 5664.2, 6109 (d?), 6195 per, [8522] (d), [8690] (d), 10713.5, 10832, 12181, 14717.5, 18507.49, —.50, —.55, —.56, —.57, 22565.5, 22793, 23314, 23526, 23527, 24908, 25750.
1623: 6570, 7158.5, [8712] (d), [10533.5] (d), [11537.7?] (c), 12517, 12519, 12521–1.9, 14520, 14694.3, [15113?], 16925, 17221, [18505] (c), [18507.99], 19676.5, 19862, 22568, 23389, 23389.3, 24694.3.
1624: 3739, 4289, [6191.5] (d), 6193 per, 6196 per, [6618.5?], [8720] (d), [10220] (d), 12402a.4 (d?), 12522–2.5, 14280, 15553.5, [17770.3] (d), 18507.352, [20946.4] (false), [22104] (false), 23389.7, [24935b.5] (d), 26005, [26076.5] (d?).
1625: 1338.5, 5131, 5658, 10601.9, [11728.4] (d?), [12343.5] (d?), 13240, 14747, 17144, [17697.3] (d?), 21522, 22398, 23636.5, [25654.5] (c), [25655].
1626: 3354 ent., 3837, 4153, 4153.3, 10601.3, 10602, 20102 per, 20471, 21347, 21347.3, 21630, 23610 ent., 24209.5, 24694.5.
1627: 1571, 4137, 4137.3, 6267, 20472, [20473], 21631.
1628: 4155, 4646 per, 5665, 7137 ass'd, 13018.5 (d?), 14694.5, 15554, 23108.4, 23638, 23639 (d?), 24820, [25076.5?].
1629: [1926–6.5], 4646.5–47, 12641, [13248.4], 17217, 19488, [20241.3], [20241.7], 20251, 20252, 20253, 23073 (d).
1630: 5666–6.5, 5854–4.4, 7101, [8893.7] (c?), [10533.7] (d), 11898, 12402a.6, 12522.5 (c?), [14045.5] (c), 14715, [17120.5?] (d), [17916.7–.9], [18416.3] (c), [18507.207], [19267.5] (c?), 20208, 20209, [20242], [20243], 20254, 20385, 23850, 25399, 26090.
1631: 3431, 5667, 8981, 12115 (note), 12834, 14741, [18507.213?], [—.214?], 18692, 20209, 20210, [20231], [20244], 20256, 21342.5, 23505, 23850a, 23851, [24402].
1632: 250, 4600, 12456, 15249, 20211, 23226, 23365.
1633: 246, 251 ex off. (d), [1222.5?] (d?), 3535 ent., 14722, 14744.5, 14748, 20464–4a.
1634: 1684, 5855, 11494, 16824, 18693, 21403, 22396, [23598.5], 26117.
1635: [1932?], [3062.8?] (c?), [3540?], 4260.5 typis, 4260.7 typis, 10644–5, 11495, 11712, 11712.5, 14723, 15249.3, 17389, 19110, 19110.5(*A*), 21343, [21776.7?] (c), 21817.3, 21817.5 typis, 22396.5, 24864.
1636: 4648, 12406, 12523, 14749, [15249.7], 19111, 19111.5, 24314.3.
1637: 14742, 18022, 21817.7, 24695a, 25400.
1639: 14721.5 f.

Jones, William 4.
Journeyman printer? in London, (1621–1627†). Son of **William Jones 3**, christened 23 Dec. 1599. Following his burial at St. Giles's on 13 Mar. 1627 the daughter of a William was christened on 24 June of the same year but none thereafter, so it is probable that the deceased was William 4. Had he still been alive in 1636, it is unlikely that he would have termed himself 'aged'. [*Dict. 1*, with William 3; DFM 303; ?*Poor Book* (widow Ellen), 1626–39; *St. Giles*, 1599, 1623–27.]

Jonson. *See* Johnson.

Jouve (Jove), Michel.
Bookseller in Lyon, 1556–1580. [Muller 38.]
1558: 6832.34. **1573:** 6832.46.

Joye, George.
Author and protestant controversialist, fl. 1527–1553†. [*DNB.*]
1545: 14823. **1549:** 14822 [f.] (d?).

Judson, John.
Stationer in London, 1542?–1589† at least. Father of **Thomas Judson**. *See* also Appenidx A/4–5. [Duff, *Century.*]
in Newgate Market (C.4), 1542? (9986.5); no later use noted
1542: 9986.5 [f.] (d?). **1558:** 5871.9(*A*) ?ent. **1570:** 23621.5 f. (d?). **1575:** 2111.7 [f.]. **1577:** 23640 ent. **1580:** 1585: 20579.5 ent. **1590:** 4032 ass'd.

Judson, Thomas.
Printer in London, (1581) 1584, 1598–1600. Son of **John Judson**. In 1584 he was in partnership with **John Windet**, under whom are listed other items Judson may have helped to print. In early 1600 he sold his business to **John Harrison 3**. [*Dict. 1*; *SB* 7 (1955): 126–7; Blayney, *Origins*: 13–14, etc.]
No address used.
1584: 11503, 11503.3, 11858.5, 12217, 18958, 21545, 24503.
1589: 23277.5 (d/error).

Judson, T. — *cont.*
1598: 11859, 14830.3, 23277.5 (d), 23278.
1599: 24, 24.5, [3834–4.5(*A*3)] (d), [6658.5(*A*)?], [12995], 13502, [18370], [19217(*A*3)], [22342].

Jugge, Joan.
Printer? in London, 1577–1588†. Widow of **Richard** and mother of **John Jugge**. During her widowhood the presses were under the nominal control of her son in 1583 and of her son-in-law, **Richard Watkins**, in 1586 (Arber I.248, V.lii). [*Dict. 1.*]
dw. near unto Christ Church (C.1), 1579 (14798.5, colophon)
1575: 14798.5–99a (d/repeat). **1579:** 5800, 14798.5–99a. **1584:** 5801.
1585: [21159?] (d?).

Jugge, John.
Stationer in London, (before 1574) 1576–1588. Son of **Richard** and **Joan Jugge**. No record of his freedom survives, but he was admitted to the Livery 1573–74 (Arber I.467) and was still alive when his mother's will was proved in 1588. Listed as having two presses in 1583 (Arber I.248), but seems not to have been active as a printer. [*Dict. 1*, with mother.]
dw. at the North door of Paul's (A.2), 1580? (24664)
1577: 17203 ent., 25710.5 (d). **1580:** 24664 [f.] (d?).

Jugge, Richard.
Bookseller and printer (from 1558) in London, (1541) 1545?–1577†. Husband of **Joan** and father of **John Jugge**. Father-in-law of **Richard Watkins**. Became **Queen's Printer** (*see* King's Printer) by 20 Nov. 1558 (Arber I.564, payment for delivering 7886 on that date); joined in that office by **John Cawood** by 7 Feb. 1559 (7890). [Duff, *Century*.]
in Paul's Churchyard, 1547–1573; variations:
at the North door of Paul's (A.2), 1547 (17313.7), 1547/48 (470, has 'dw.')
— at the North door, at the Bible, 1548 (20843)
— at the Bible, 1555 (645)
dw. at the North door of Paul's at the Bible, 1558 (14795)
— [no sign or location] (B), 1558/59, 22 Mar. (7891)–1573, 11 June (8063)
by Newgate Market next unto Christ Church (C.1), 1573, 28 Sept. (8064)–1575, 15 July (8070), and until his death, though no later use has been noted
1545: 18221.3 f. (d?).
1547: 17313.7 sold.
1547/48: 470 [f.], 470.1 [f.].
1548: 1297 [f.] (d?), 2852 [f.], 11383 [f.], 16503.5 in aed., 17795 [f.] (d?), 17796 [f.] (d?), 20843 sold, 24450 sold (d?).
1549: 3963 [f.] (d).
1549/50: 517.15(*A*) [f.].
1550: 2757.5 (c), 13750 [f.], 6832.23(*A*3) [f.] (c), 13750.5 [f.], 23916 [f.].
1551: 19293 (d?).
1552: 2867 [f.] (d), 2868 [f.] (d), 10999.5 [f.] (d?), 19495 f. (d?), 20191 [f.] (c).
1553: 2090 [f.], 2869 [f.] (d), 2870 [f.] (d), 7509 (d).
1555: 645 [f.].
1557: 2999.5 ?ent., 25876 ent.
1558: 7886 [f.?] (d), 7887 (repeat), 7888 (repeat of lost ed.), 7889 [f.?], 7889.5 (repeat), 14075 f., 14075.5 f., 14795 f., 24799 f.
1558/59: 7890, 7890.5 (repeat), 7891.
1559: 7892, 7893, 7894, 7895 (repeat), 7897, 7897.3 (repeat), 7898, 7899 (repeat), 7900 (repeat of lost ed.), 7902, 7902.3 (repeat), 7903, 7904, [7905], [7905.5], 7907, 9458.7, 9459, 9459.3, 9459.5, 9459.7–60 (repeat), 9460.5–1.5 (d/repeat), 10099.5 (d), 10100 (d?), 10100.3 (d?), 10100.5 (d?), 10102 (d?), 10118, 10118.5 (d?), 11901 (d?), 13648, 13648.5, 16292 in off., 16292a in off. (d/error?), 16293 in off., 16293.3 in off., 16293.5 in off. [f.], 16454.
1559/60: 7908, 7909, 7909.5 (repeat), 7910, 7910.7, 7911, 7911.5.
1560: 7913, 7914–5, 7916, 7916.5, 7917 (d), 7918 (d), 7920, 7921, 7921.5 (repeat), 7924, 7924.3 (repeat), 9183.5, 9184 (d), [11309.7] (d), 13649, 13649.5, 16294 in off., 16294a.3 in off., [21156?], 25286 (d?).
1560/61: 7928, 7929 (repeat).
1561: 2028 ent., 2872 (d?), [5010.5] (d?), 5798, [7799.5] (d?), 7917 (note, d?), 7924.5 (d?), 7931, 7931.3 (repeat), 7932, 7933, 7934 (d),7936, 7936.3 (repeat), 7936.7, 7940, 9186 (d) 9339.5 (d),

Jugge, R. — *cont.*
10034.4 (c?), [10102.2] (d?), 10119 (d?), 13680.8 (d?), 14796, 16292a in off. (d?).
1561/62: 7941, 7942, 7943, 7944.
1562: 2027 (d?), [2872a] (c?), 2872b (c?), [2872c] (c?), [2872c.3] (c?), [2872c.5] (c?), 7924.6 (d?), 7946, 7947, 7948, 7949, 7950 (d), 7951 (d), 7951.3 (repeat), 7952 (d), 7953a, 7953a.5 (repeat), 7954 (repeat of lost ed.), 7954.5 (d?), 7954.7 (d?), 8046.5 (c?), 9187.3, [10102.3] (d?), 10120 (d?), 13650, 13650.3, 13650.7, 16295 in off., 16504.3(*A*3) (d).
1562/63: 7956.
1563: 7957, 7957.3, 7957.7 (d), 7957.9, 7958, 7959, 7960, 7962, 7962.3 (repeat), 7962.5, 7963 (repeat), 7964–4.5, 7965 (repeat), 9462, 9462.5, 9463.5, 9464–5 (repeat), 9466–7.5 (d/repeat), 10038.3 (d?), 13651, 13663, 13663.3, 13663.7, 13664, 13664.5, 13665, 13666, 13666.4, 13666.7, 13667 (d/repeat), 16505 (d), 16506 (d), 16506.3–.7 (d), 16506.9(*A*3) (d), 16507, 16507.5 (d).
1563/64: 7966, 7967, 7968 (repeat), 7969, 7970, 7972, 16704.9.
1564: [7777] (d?), 7920.5 (d?), 7947.3 (d?), 7955 (d?), 7973, 7974, 7974.5, 7975 (repeat), 7976, [7976.7] (d?), 7978, 7978.3 (repeat), 7981 (d), 7982 (d), 7983, 7984, 9342.4 (d?), 9342.5 (repeat), 9464 (d?), 9464.5 (d?), 10038.5 (d?), [10102.4] (d?), 10120.5 (d?), 16296 in off., 16296.3 in off.
1564/65: 7986, 7986.3 (repeat).
1565: [2872c.7] (c?), 7987, 7988, 7988.5, [7988.7] (d?), 7989, 7990 (repeat), 7991, 7992, 7993, [9185] (c?), 9459.7 (c?), 9465 (d?), 10034.5 (c?), 16296.5 in off., [21157], [21157.5], 21158 (d/repeat).
1565/66: 7994, 7995.
1566: 2873 (d?), 7924.9 (d?), 7995.3, [7995.4] (d?), 7995.5, 7996, 7997, 7998, 7998.3 (d?), 8047 (c?), 9427.3 (note), 9432.5 (note), [10102.5] (d?), 10121 (d?), 10387 (d), 16297, 16297.5, 16510 (d).
1566/67: 7999.5 (d), 9468.2, 9468.3, 9468.4, 9468.6–9.5 (d/repeat), 9471.2.
1567: 7925 (d?), 7955.3 (d?), [10102.6] (d?), 13667, 14797, 16298, 17518 f. (d?), 17519 (d?), [17652].
1568: 2099 (d), 2099.2 (d), [2873.3] (d?), 8003, 8003.3 (repeat), 8005, 8006, 8007 (repeat), 8048.7 (d?), 9468.6 (d?), [10102.7] (d?), 10121.5 (d?), 16298.5 in off.
1568/69: 8008, 8008.3, 8010, 8011, 8012, 8013, 8013.5 (repeat), 8014–4.3, 8014.5 (repeat).
1569: 2105, 8015, 8015.5 (repeat), 8016, 8017, 8018, 8018.5 (repeat), 8019, 8020, 8020.5 (repeat), 8021, [8022], 8049 (d?), 13652, 13653.
1569/70: 8023, 8023.5 (repeat), 8024 (d), 8025 (d), 8027, 8027.3 (repeat).
1570: 2873.5 (c?), 7926 (d?), 8028, 8029, 8030, 8031, 8032, 8033, 8034, 8034.5 (repeat), 8035, 8047.4 (c?), 9468.8 (d?), [10102.8] (c?), 10123 (c?), 10391.5 (d?), 13668, 13679.2 (d?), 13679.4 (d?), [13679.7] (d?), 13680 (d?), 13680.4 (d?), 13680.6 (d?), 16299 in off., 16300, 16777.1A(*A*3) (d?), [20188.7] (c).
1571: 7953a.3 (c?), [8036], [8036.3], 8037, 9471.4, 9471.6, 9471.8, 9472–3 (repeat), 9474 (d/repeat), [10030], 10038.7, 10038.9, 10038.11, 10039, 10039.3, 10194.3 (d?), 13669, 16301.3 in off., 16301.5.
1571/72: 8039, 8040, 8041, 8042–3, 8044.
1572: 2107, 5799, 8047.6 (c?), 8050 (d?), 8050.5 (d), 8052, 8052.3 (repeat), 8053, 8054(*A*3, repeat), [9440.14?] (d?), [9444.4?] (d?), 9460 (d), 9472 (d?), 9477a.5, 9478–9 (repeat), [10102.10] (d?), 10123.5 (d?), 16301.7, 16302, 16302.5, 16511 (d), 21158 (d?).
1573: 2108, 7937 (d?), 8057 (d), 8062, 8063, 8064, 8065, [9449.6] (d?), [9454] (d?), [9457.8] (d?), 9466 (d?), 9473 (d?), 10040, [10102.12] (d?), 10124 (d?), 16303, 16303.5, [18419] (d?).
1574: 2109, 2875 (d?), [8047.8] (c?), 8066, 8067 (repeat of lost ed.), [9455?] (d?), 9460.5 (d?), 9469 (d?), 9474 (d?), 9478 (d?), 9478.3 (d?), 9478.5 (d?), [10102.14] (d?), 10124.5 (d?), 13654, 13670, 16304.5, 16304.6.
1575: 2110–3a.3, 2114, 2875a (c), [2875a.5?] (c), 4582 (d?), [8068.3?] (d?), 8070, 8070.3 (repeat), 8071, 8072 (repeat), 8073, 8075, 8075.3, 8075.5 (repeat), [9444.6?] (d?), [9450?] (d?), [9455.5] (d?), 10040.5 (c?), 14798, 16304.7 in off., 16305 in off., 16305a, 16466 (d?), [16761.5] (c), [19476] (d), 23659 (d?).
1575/76: 9480.7, 9481, 9482.
1576: 2115, 5799.5, 8076 (repeat of lost ed.), 8077, 8079, 8079.3 (repeat), 8080 (repeat of lost ed.), 8082, 8083 (repeat), 8084, 8085 (repeat), 8086, 8087 (repeat), 8088, 9461 (d), 9467 (d?), 9479 (d), [10102.16] (d?), 10125 (d?), 13655, 13655.5, 14140.5 (d), 16306, 16479 (d).

Jugge, R. — *cont.*
1576/77: 8091.
1577: 649, 2121, 2122, 8058 (d?), 9314(*A*3, note), [9440.16?] (d?), [9444.8] (d?), [9446.7?] (d?), [9454.5?] (d?), 9461.5 (d), 9467.5 (d?), 9469.5 (d), 13671, 16306.2, 16306.3, 16306.5.

Junius. *See* Young.

K

Kaetz, Peter.
Bookseller in London, 1522?–1525, and in Antwerp, 1525–1526. Although Duff indicates his shop was in Paul's Churchyard, that address appears only on a Francis Birckman variant (16146) of a book also sold by Kaetz. [Duff, *Century*; Rouzet.]
No London address used.
1523: [15935 f.] (d?), 16145 ven., 16236.3 imp. & ven.
1524: 15818.5 [f.], 15938 imp., 15938.5 ven., 16130 ven, 16261 ven.
1525: 16236.7 imp. & ven.

Katsaïtes, Jeremias.
Greek cleric and patron, 1625.
No address used.
1625: 3047.5 [at costs].

Kearney (Carney, Kerny), William.
Printer in Dublin, 1571? and 1593?–1597? and bookseller in London, 1590–1592. Documentary evidence indicates that in 1593?–1595 Kearney's press was in Trinity College Dublin. [*Dict. 1*; *Proceedings of the Royal Irish Academy* 28-C (1910): 157–61.]
London, dw. within Cripplegate (H.1), 1590 (22680)–1592 (3845); variation: dw. in Addle (Addling) Street, 1591 (19183)
Dublin, in the Cathedral Church of the Blessed Trinity [modern Christ Church], 1595 (14145)
1571: [22.3?], [19844.5].
1590: 3361.3 [f.], 22680 [f.].
1591: 3363.7 [f.] (d), 19183(*A*3) [f.], 22663 [f.], 22681 [f.], 22684 [f.].
1592: 3845(*A*3) [f.].
1595: 14145, 14145a.
1596: 2958 (d?).

Keerberghen, Jan van.
Printer and bookseller in Antwerp, 1586–c. 1624. [*Dict. 1*; Rouzet.]
1600: 17546.

Keerberghen, Peeter van.
Printer and bookseller in Antwerp, 1552–1570. [*Dict. 1*; Rouzet.]
1563: 17847.4. **1567:** 25195.5.

Keere (Keerius), Pieter van der.
Engraver in England, 1585?–1593, and in Amsterdam, 1593?–1646? In partnership in the latter city with **Joris Veseler** in publishing newsbooks in English, 1620–1621. [Briels 337, 340–2; *Library* 4 (1949): 166–70; 5 (1950): 130–2.]
No English address used.
1620: 18507.1 sold, —.2 sold.
1621: 18507.3 sold, —.4 sold, —.5 sold, —.6 sold, [—.7 sold] (d), [—.10 sold] (d), [—.11 sold] (d), [—.12 sold] (d), [—.14 sold], [—.15 sold], [—.16 sold], [—.17 sold].

Kele, Richard.
Bookseller in London, 1540–1552† at least. [Duff, *Century*.]
in Lombard Street near unto the Stocks [Market] (O.12), 1540 (12206a.7)
dw. at the Long Shop in the Poultry under St. Mildred's Church (O.1), 1543? (16030)–1545 (7687)
dw. in Lombard Street at the Eagle (O.12), 1547 (14106)–1552 (10440, adds 'near unto the Stocks Market')
1540: 12206a.7 sold (d).
1543: 16030 (d?).
1544: 14562 [f.] (c?).
1545: 5204.5 [f.] (d?), 7687 [f.], 18221a [f.] (d?), 22594 [f.] (d?), 22601 [f.] (d?), 22615 [f.] (d?).

Kele, R. — *cont.*
1546: 7700 [f.] (d), 7717.7 [f.], 7732 in aed., 14879.5 in aed., 15586 per [f.].
1546/47: 507.11.
1547: 14106 [f.], 20423 [f.] (d?).
1548: 3041.5 f. (d?), [16049.3?] (c), 20424 [f.] (d?).
1549: 21043 f. (d?).
1550: 5072 [f.] (d?), 10447.5 f., 11013 f. (c), 15029 (d?), 19494.3 at costs, 23715 f. (d?), 25824 [f.] (c), 26143 [f.].
1551: 2086.3 f., 9525.5 [f.], 20204 f.
1551/52: 410.4 [f.], 507.17(*A*3).
1552: 1282 f. (d?), 4051 f., 10440 [f.], 10989a [f.], 10999.7 [f.] (d?), 13175.15A f. (d?), 21740 f. (d?), 22160.3 f.

Kellam, Laurence 1.
English recusant printer in Louvain, 1597–1600, in Valenciennes, 1601–1603? and in Douai, 1603–1612?†. Succeeded by his widow, **Marguerite**, and by his sons **Thomas** and **Laurence 2**. [*Dict. 1*; Rouzet; *Répertoire 17e*, IV.9.]
1598: 19354.3.
1599: 16922.
1600: 12730.
1603: 5554, 14912.
1604: 1835, 10541.4, 16157.5–58, 17268, 19940, 25068 (false).
1605: 1835.5 (false), [11335], [11337], 14913, 22809.
1606: [11016.5], 11017, 14560.5, 22809a.
1607: [14107.5], [25972.4] (false).
1608: [26000.8?] (d).
1609: 2207, [15363].
1610: 2207, 3271, 16159.
1611: [11026].

Kellam, Laurence 2.
Printer in Douai, 1621–1639, 1652–1661. Son of **Laurence 1**. [*Répertoire 17e*, IV.9.]
1621: 933.5.
1622: 26000.2, 26000.4–.6.
1623: 21446.3.
1625: [14077c.23C] (d?).
1626: 22889.
1633: 1923, 24285.5.
1634: [14107.7?], 17185.
1635: 15351.3.
1639: 17128, 17129.

Kellam, Marguerite.
Printer in Douai, 1613–1620. Widow of **Laurence 1**. [*Dict. 1*, under husband; *Répertoire 17e*, IV.9.]
1613: 17197. **1614:** 24731.5, [25290]. **1615:** 24731a, 25290.3. **1616:** [24675.5] (d). **1618:** 19203.7.

Kellam, Thomas.
Printer in Douai, 1618–1620. Son of **Laurence 1**. [*Dict. 1*; *Répertoire 17e*, IV.9.]
1618: 19203.7, 26000 (false).

Kembe, Andrew.
Bookseller in Southwark, (1631) 1632–1665 (Wing C 4602). [*Dict. 2*; DFM 1759; ?*Poor Book* (widow Cemb), 1670–71.]
dw. by the Sessions House in long Southwark, 1635 (11495)
dw. at (by) St. Margaret's Hill in Southwark, 1635 (19453.3)–1639 (22520, has 'shop') at least; variation: has 'long Southwark', 1636 (12406)
1632: 266.5 sold.
1635: 11495 f., 15249.3 f., 19453.3 sold, 22396.5 f.
1636: 12406 f., 21251 f.
1637: 267 sold, 24075 f., 25848.5 f.
1638: 22519 sold.
1639: 4802.5 f., 22520 f., 23757.5 f.

Kempe de Bouchout, Adriaen.
Bookseller and printer? in Antwerp, 1535–1547? [Duff, *Century*; Rouzet.]
1535: [3014(*A*3) f.]. **1536:** 2833 (note), [3014(*A*3) f.].

Kerbriant (Huguelin), Jean.
Printer in Paris, 1516–1550. [Duff, *Century*; Renouard.]
1516: 16197 per. **1525:** [15822a] (c?). **1528:** 15823 opera. **1530:** 15827.5(*A*3) in aed. **1531:** [13828.6?].

Kerver, Thielman.
Printer in Paris, 1497–1522†. Succeeded by his widow, **Yolande Kerver**. [Duff, *Century*; Renouard.]
1497: [15885 f.]. **1503:** 16177 per. **1506:** 15805.5 per. **1510:** 15909 per. **1511:** [15912]. **1514:** 15810 per. **1515:** [15811] (d?). **1518:** [16129]. **1521:** [15931].

1524: 15818. **1532–33:** 15979 in house. **1534:** 15985 in house.

Kerver (Bonhomme), Yolande.
Printer in Paris, 1522–1557†. Widow of **Thielman Kerver**. [Duff, *Century* 16; Renouard 45, 244.]
1524: [15818]. **1525:** 15819. **1526:** [15821a] (c?). **1527:** 15956. **1528:** 15957. **1530:** 15828, 15829. **1532:** 15978, [15979]. **1533:** [15979]. **1534:** 15985.

Keyser (Le Rouge), Françoise de.
Printer in Antwerp, 1536–1541. Widow of **Merten de Keyser.** [Rouzet.]
1537: 5543b.4 ap. **1539:** 5543b.7.

Keyser (Caesar, Lempereur), Merten de.
Printer and punchcutter in Paris, before 1525, and in Antwerp, 1525–1536†. Husband of **Françoise de Keyser.** [Duff, *Century*: 21; Rouzet.]
1529: [5542.2?].
1530: [2370] (false), [13828.4] (false).
1531: [845] (d?), [2777] (false), [2788] (d?), [20036] (d?), [24443].
1532: [61] (false).
1533: 21318.
1534: [2351], 2372, [2778], 2826, [2830], [5542.8(*A*)] (d?), 23153.2 ap.
1535: [564] (d?), [2830], [2830.3] (c), [2830.5?] (c), 5543a ap. (d).
1536: 5543b ap.

Kid (Kyd), John.
Journeyman printer? in London, (1584) 1591–1593?†. [*Dict. 1.*]
No address survives; the place of sale cropt from 1030.7 may have been his but more probably belonged to another.
1591: 1030.7 f. (d?). **1592:** 1030.5 ent., 15095 f., 15353.7 ent.

King (Kyng), John.
Printer in London, 1554–1561 at least. [Duff, *Century*.]
in Creed Lane (Q.2), 1554? (22599, with T. Marsh)–1557 (21287)
in Paul's Churchyard at the Swan (A.5), 1559 (9973)–1561 (13179)
1554: 3366(*A*3) (d?), [9970.5] (d), 10989a.5–.6(*A*3) (d?), 22599 (d?).
1555: 9971 (d), 13175.16–.17 (d?), 16067, 21742 (c).
1556: 6808 (d?), 10448 (d?), 16074, [23716] (d?).
1557: 1807 ent., 3291 ent., 12103 (d?), [14111a?] (d), 17788 ent., 20954 ent., 21287.
1558: 10990.3 (d?).
1559: 9973 (d).
1560: [258.5] (d), 1384a.5 (c), 6472, 9975 (d), 12105, 14112.5 (d), [15187.5] (d), 16933, 18067, 19971, 23112 ent., 24237.5, 25016, 25149 ent., 25938.
1561: 19.4 (d?), 13175.19 (d), 13179, 25825.3 (d?).

King's (Queen's) Printer(s).
The chronological survey of imprints below is based primarily on original printers of statutes and proclamations since these are the earliest texts to be recognized as privileged. However, the terms 'King's Printer' and 'Printer to the King's Grace', even when they do appear in early years, may mean only 'printed at the King's command'. Pynson styled himself 'impressor nobilissime Regis gratie' under Henry VII as early as 6 Jan. 1506 [o.s.?] (16117.5) but did not get the printing of statutes firmly within his grasp until 3 May 1510 (9357.8, note) under Henry VIII. His successor, Berthelet, reprinted earlier statutes of others, but from his retirement as King's Printer in 1547 until C. Barker's 1587 edition of the statutes at large (9305.3), reprints of statutes were made by individual King's Printers and the successors to their private businesses. Only with C. Barker was it finally established that the right to reprint resides in the office rather than in the man. For a more detailed account of statutes *see* the headnote preceding 9346 in vol. 1 of STC.

King's Printer — *cont.*
The men whose names below are in italic were never styled King's Printer, but they certainly performed the function. On the other hand, in 1634 R. Barker's share in the office of King's Printer was mortgaged to **Miles Flesher**, **John Haviland**, and **Robert Young;** however, their names do not appear in official imprints, the printing material in the King's Printing House undergoes no alteration, and they are not included in the survey of imprints. The deputy for the King's Printers in Newcastle upon Tyne in 1639 was **John Legat 2**.

Months and days cited are dates of issue printed in official publications—primarily proclamations—or, when in square brackets, are based on documentary evidence, as indicated, or in TRP or SRP. [Cr. I.xxxiv–xxxvi; *Library* 2 (1901): 353–75; 11 (1989): 1–9.]

William de Machlinia, 1484 (9347)
William Caxton, 1491 (9348)
Wynkyn de Worde, 1492 (9351a.7)–1497? (cf. 9355.5)
William Faques, 1504 (9357)
Wynkyn de Worde, 1505 (7761)–1509 (7761.3)
Richard Faques, 1509 (7762)–1510? (9357.9, possibly the first edition)
Richard Pynson, 1510 [after 3 May] (9357.8, note)–1529 [before 6 Mar.] (7772)
John Rastell, 1529 [17 Dec. (end of session) or later] (7773)–1530? (9363.6)
Thomas Berthelet, 1530 [after 2 Feb. (*TBS* 8 (1904–06): 187)]–1546, 8 July (7809)
Richard Grafton, 1547 [24 May] (7809.7)–1553, 19 July (7847)
John Cawood, 1553 [28 July] (7848)–1558 [July?] (7885)
Richard Jugge, 1558 [20 Nov.] (7886)–27 Dec. (7889)
Richard Jugge and John Cawood, 1559, 7 Feb. (7890)–1572, 1 Mar. (8044)
Richard Jugge, 1572, 16 Sept. (8052)–1577, 16 Feb. (8091)
Christopher Barker, 1577, 16 Sept. (8093)–1587, 23 May (8163)
Deputies of **Christopher Barker**, 1587, 12 Oct. (8164)–1599, 2 Aug. (8269)
Robert Barker, 1600, 14 Jan. (8270)–1608, 2 June (8415)
Deputies of **Robert Barker**, 1608, 5 July (8419)–1609, 18 Feb. (8430)
Robert Barker, 1609, 7 Apr. (8431)–1617, 12 Aug. (8555); toward the end of this period James I's *Workes* has on the engr. tp and in the colophon: *Robert Barker and John Bill, printers to the King's Maiestie*, 1616 (14344), an unexplained anomaly
Bonham Norton and John Bill, *deputies and assignees of* **Robert Barker**, 1617, 23 Dec. (8557)–1618, 26 Apr. (8565)
Bonham Norton and John Bill, *deputy printers*, 1618, 24 May (9238.9)–10 Nov. (8580)
Bonham Norton and John Bill, 1618, 11 Dec. (9239)–1619, 14 Nov. (8619)
Robert Barker and John Bill, 1619, 9 Dec. (8621)–30 Dec. (8622)
Robert Barker, 1620, 7 Feb. (8623)–25 Feb. (8627)
Robert Barker and John Bill, 1620, 29 Feb. (8629)–28 July (8642)
Bonham Norton and John Bill, 1620, 4 Aug. (8643)–6 Nov. (8644)
John Bill, 1620, 24 Dec. (8649)–28 Dec. (8650)
Robert Barker and John Bill, 1621, 30 Jan. (8655)–8 Mar. (8660)
Bonham Norton and John Bill, 1621, 30 Mar. (8661)–1629, 11 Oct. (8934)
Robert Barker and John Bill, 1629, 27 Dec. (8963)–1630, 23 Apr. (8944)
Robert Barker, 1630, 7 May (8946)–27 May (8950)
Robert Barker and *assignees of* **John Bill**, 1630, 13 June (8952)–1641, 8 Mar. (9175) and later

Until the retirement of Christopher Barker in 1587 each King's or Queen's Printer possessed his own printing house privately, and the addresses before that date are to be found under the individuals' names. However, just as Christopher established his right to reprint all the statutes at large, his acquisition of Bacon House in 1579 as his place of printing led ultimately to the concept of a royal printing house under joint ownership and to the omission of

King's Printer — *cont.*
its location from imprints. The following addresses are based on inference and other evidence as follows:

Bacon House, Foster Lane (actually in the lane's continuation, Noble Street (G.3)), 1587–c. 1600; inference that Christopher's deputies continued printing in the same place he had.

Northumberland House, St. Martin's Lane, almost by Aldersgate (G.8), c. 1600–c. 1625; the move here took place between 1598 and 1603 (Stow's *Survey*, 1598 (23341): 246–7, where it is called Queen Jane's Wardrobe, and 1603 (23343): 311, where it is described as 'now a printing house'). In a copy of the 1598 edition at McGill University is the MS. annotation, c. 1613: about the year 1600 it was purchased by Mr. Robert Barker and by him converted into the King's Printing House.

Hunsdon House, Blackfriars (Q.6), c. 1625–1640+; Plomer's article (*Library* 2 (1901): 364, 374) cites evidence of this location by 1629 and suggests the move was instigated by Bonham Norton. If Plomer is correct, it seems possible that the move did not occur until sometime after the beginning of the comparatively stable series of Norton and Bill imprints in 1621, and c. 1625 has been chosen to represent a midpoint.

Employment provided at the King's Printing House was all that saved journeymen printers from being 'utterly impoverished' according to their petition of 1613 (*C-B C*: 436–7). For a note of at least some probable activities of journeymen at a slightly later date *see* John Bill 1 and also Supplementary List 4.

Below are indexed two kinds of items: 1) those with dates in which a version of the term 'Regius Typographus/Regia Typographia' appears without the name of a printer (all of which have also been indexed under the pertinent name or names at that date); 2) those without imprint or date indexed under the years 1618 and 1619. The item queried for 1619 might have been produced under any one of a number of imprints around that date and has [*King's Printing Office*] supplied in STC.

In the 1618 group are the reprints of Elizabethan proclamations made for Humphrey Dyson, which repeat the Elizabethan imprint, if any. Although for these STC has uniformly supplied the imprint: [*B. Norton a. J. Bill*, c. 1618.] on the analogy of the imprint in Dyson's preliminaries (7758.3, actually has the 'Deputy Printers' version), it is by no means certain that the reprints were all made at one time. An event which may well have stirred Dyson either to begin collecting originals or to have those already in hand reprinted for others to peruse was the publication in 1610 of James I's collected proclamations (7759). That Dyson's Elizabethan efforts probably continued after 1618 is indicated by at least two printed items (7912, 8081) together with others transcribed in MS. which are not included in his table. More concentrated studies would undoubtedly cast further light on Dyson's noble but bibliographically confusing work and require adjustments in the dating and even the identifying of the reprints made for him. [*HLB* 1 (1947): 76–89.]

These '1618' items have *not* been included under B. Norton or J. Bill. For this group *only*, the following convention applies to each item listed: 7887 = [*King's Printing House*, c. 1610?–c. 1618?]. Items with an asterisk (*) repeat an Elizabethan imprint for which no original copy survives; it should be noted, however, that 7954 omits 'at London in Paul's Churchyard' and may represent an imprint inexpertly supplied by Dyson for something seen only in MS. Items with a double asterisk (**), in addition to having no printed original, have no imprint at all.

1592: 2061–2, 2794, 23455.
1593: 21747.
1594: 21748.
1618: (*see* headnote) 7887, 7888, 7889.5, 7890.5, 7895, 7897.3, 7899, 7900*, 7902.3, 7909.5, 7912**, 7921.5, 7924.3, 7929, 7931.3, 7936.3, 7939, 7951.3, 7953a.5, 7954*, 7962.3, 7963, 7965, 7968, 7975, 7978.3, 7986.3, 7990, 8001, 8003.3, 8004, 8007, 8009, 8013.5, 8014.5, 8015.5, 8018.5, 8020.5, 8023.5, 8027.3, 8034.5, 8052.3, 8054(*A*3), 8067*, 8070.3, 8072, 8075.5, 8076*, 8079.3, 8080*, 8081**, 8083, 8085, 8087, 8095, 8098, 8099, 8103*, 8105.3, 8108.3, 8109*, 8111, 8117, 8131.3, 8134.3, 8139*, 8143.3, 8145**, 8147*, 8148**, 8157.3, 8170.5, 8185.3, 8192.5, 8196, 8204.5, 8212.3, 8214, 8219, 8238*, 8253.3, 9342.5, 16727.5.

King's Printer — *cont.*
1619: [884.5] (d?).
1636: 23948 e typog.
1637: 18527 ex typog.
1638: 11121 ex typog.

King's Printer for Wales and the Marches.
John Oswen, 1549 (Duff, *Century*), 1551 (13756)–1553 (9440.4)

King's Printer in French for the Channel Islands.
Thomas Gaultier, 1553 (16430)

King's (Queen's) Printer in Latin, Greek, and Hebrew.
Except for John Norton 1, the following patentees did not usually use their style. Except for him and Reyner Wolfe, exercise of the patent was limited to 'Lily's Grammar' and other school texts related to it.

Reyner Wolfe, 1547 (Duff, *Century*), 1548 (22269)–1553 (4809); 1558 (15613.3)–1573 (18707)
assignees of **Francis Flower**, 1574 (15617)–1596 (15623)
assignees of **John Battersby**, 1597 (15623)–1604 (4512); 1613 (15626.5)–1619 (23279)
John Norton 1, 1603 (12059.5)–1612 (9232); 1613 (14629a, engr. tp)
Bonham Norton and assignees, 1613 (4513.4); 1621 (15627)–1634 (23279.5)
Roger Norton and assignees, 1636 (15631)–1640 (4517.7) at least.

In 1624 (*C-B C:* 164–5) the following titles were in stock, preceded by their quantities and followed by identifications, a few of them revised:

3625—Cambdens	W. Camden, *Institutio Graecae grammatices*, 1617 (4514)
693—Stockwoods	J. Stockwood, *Disputatiuncularum grammaticalium libellus*, 1619 (23279)
4000—gramers	'Lily's Grammar', *Brevissima institutio*, 1621 (in 15627)
3000—Lillies	*Lilies rules construed*, ed. W. Hayne, 1603 (15633.4)
3000—Accedences	'Lily's Grammar', *Short introduction of grammar*, 1621 (in 15627)
866—Grangers	T. Granger, *Syntagma grammaticum, or an easie explanation of Lillies Grammar*, 1616 (12183)
1054—Cawdries	T. Caudry, *Examination of the Accidence*, 1606 (4867)
961—Stockewoods fig:	J. Stockwood, *Treatise of the figures*, 1609 (23284.5)
313—Barnards	Unidentified but possibly a lost work or an edited version of another's work by Samuel Bernard, master of Magdalen School, Oxford, 1617–1625
2578—Cleonard[9]	N. Clenardus, *Graecae linguae institutiones*, 1612 (5404)

For works dealing with 'Lily's Grammar' but not in the above list *see* especially J. Danes, *A light to Lilie*, 1637 (6232), R. K., *Lillies light*, 1599 (14894.3), J. Leech, *Book of grammar questions*, 1618 (15374.7), and two other Stockwood titles: 1590 (23280) and 1592 (23283) but also 3770b.5, 4863.5, 15374.2, 21060.5(*A*3), and 21061.

King's (Queen's) Printer in Ireland.
No imprints survive before 1641 with this style. The names in boldface held patents; those in italic performed the function by printing official publications. At times when there was no printer in Dublin or on other special occasions, printing was done in London by the King's (Queen's) Printer.

Humphrey Powell, 1550 (Duff, *Century*), 1561 (14138)–1564 (14139)
William Kearney, 1595 (14145)
John Franckton, 1600 (14147)–1618 (14168)
deputies of **John Franckton**, 1619 (17762)
Stationers' Company, London (*see* their Irish Stock), 1618–1639; imprints under this patent name:
Felix Kingston, the incumbent agent, 1618 (14169)–1619 (14172)
Stationers' Society, Dublin, 1620 (14173)–1640 (14253)
William Bladen, 1639–1663; not named in Dublin imprints until 1641.

King's Printer in (for) Scotland.
Below are listed those who printed official publications—largely statutes and proclamations—in Scotland. Names in boldface have one or more imprints bearing the style of King's Printer(s); those in italic, although performing the work, never used the style.

Thomas Davidson, 1540? (3203)–1541 (21878.5)
Robert Lekpreuik, 1565 (21880)–1573 (21882); 1582 [21886?]
Thomas Bassandyne, 1572 (21938)–1573 (21942)
John Ros, 1575 (21883, 21943a.5); 1580 (21884, 21946.5)
Henry Charteris, 1582 (21885); 1588 (21887.5)
Alexander Arbuthnet, 1584 (21887)
Thomas Vautrollier, 1585 (21948)
Robert Waldegrave, 1590 (*Dict. 1*), 1592 (21949.7(*A*)–1603 (21958); apparently briefly succeeded by his widow, *Mary Waldegrave*, 1604 (21959)
Robert Charteris, 1603–1610 (*Dict. 1*); 1606 (21964)–1609 (21893)
Thomas Finlason, 1611 (21894)–1628 (21982)
heirs of Thomas Finlason, 1628 (21983–1631 [21989]
Robert Young, 1632 (*Dict. 2*), 1633 (21902)–1640 (12053) and to 1642 although in 1639–40 the office was exercised in London

The items listed below have imprints with the style of King's Printer, but either have no name (or only initials) or were printed elsewhere than in Edinburgh.

1633: 2311–1a, 2721.3 (false?), 2944.5(*A*3), 2945, 2945.5, 16394, 16394.3, 17142.
1634: 2311a, 2316, 2316.5 (false), 16399, 16399.7–400.
1638: 65, 66, 70.
1639: 21906(*A*3), 22001–1.5(*A*3), 22002(*A*3), 22003(*A*3), 22004 (*A*3).
1640: 9260(*A*3, note), 12053, 21915(*A*3, note).

Kingston (Kyngston), Anthony.
Bookseller in London, 1548–1551. Possibly related to **John Kingston**. [Not in Duff, *Century*.]
in Saint Andrew's parish in the Wardrobe (Wardrop (R.6)), 1548 (20749, with T. Raynald)
at the West door of Paul's (A.10), 1551 (15545)
1548: 20748.5, 20749. **1551:** 15545 sold (d).

Kingston, Felix.
Printer in London, 1597–1652, and in Dublin, 1618–1619 as agent for the **Irish Stock** (*see* Stationers' Company). Son of **John Kingston** and **Joan Orwin**. Freed as a Grocer by patrimony in 1595; transferred to the Stat. Co. in 1597. Operated the **Parish Clerks' Press**, 1626–1629. Items below printed in Dublin are distinguished by an asterisk (*). [*Dict. 2*; *Loan Book*, 1610–13.]
London, in Paternoster Row (C.7), 1599–1644 at least; variations:
dw. — over against the $ Chequer, 1599 (6851.2), 1605 (6852)
his house — at the Golden Cock, 1623 (25375a.8, mentioned in text as a place where collections can be turned in), 1644 (Wing B 2035)
dw. — [no sign], 1627 (10680), 1633 (10681)
Dublin, [no address] 1618 (14169)–1619 (14172)
1161: 12060a (d/error).
1560: [3866] (d/error).
1597: 10133.7, 11871, 14290, 16609, 19712, 19955, [22538] (d?), 22722, 24791.
1598: 726.3, 3921, 4176.5, 4387a.5, [4614], 5267.2 ex typ., 5383, 7374, 11847, 11854, 12927, 12927.5, 13289, 14959.5–60, 17414, [19367(*A*3)], 20740, 21131, 21348, 22882 ex typ., 24096, 25106–6a.
1599: [3841], [3864], 6851.2, 7303 ex off., 7304, 10799, 11849.5, [11866.5], 11867, 12312–3, 12313.5–14, 15342–2.5, 18249(*A*, note), [19766.5–.7], 19818, 22723, 23652.7, 23659.5, 24496, 25703, 26124.5.
1600: 1596, 3189–9.5, 3505, [3865], [3866] (d), [5330], 5384, 11487, 12314.5–.7, [12392] (c?), 12928, 13342, [15190], [17415], [18546], [23335] (d), 24904, 25698–8.3.
1601: [1188], [5735], [6440], 11814, 12315–6, 12922, 17695, 18348, [18417], 18810, [21030], 22724, [23336] (d), [25126].
1602: [1555], [1695], 4025, 4165a, 6910.4 (d), [7102], 11692.3, 11815, [12196], 12866, [12984.5], 13935, 17259, [17846], 18075, 21269–9.5, 21446.7, 22401, [23409], 24134.

Kingston, F. — *cont.*
1603: [6967.5], 11851, 14350, 14351, 16743.9 (nos. 8–10), [16778.12?] (d?), 20141, 20141.3(*A*), 20141.5(*A*), 21215, 21282, 21286, 23929 ent., [25672], 25694, 25698.5.
1604: [3439–40], [5882–2.5], 7133, [7215], 13011, [14361], [17851], 22667, 22725, 22737, [24280], [24280.5], 25610, [25692].
1604/05: 435.59.
1605: [726.5] (c), 4405, [4772], 6852, 12317, 12588, 12867, [15156 (*A*3)], 18184, 18184.5, 20156, 20444 ent., 22877.1, 23337 (d), 23592, 23870.
1606: 3437, [5267.6], 6625.6, [9213] (d), 12591, 12867, 13001, [17416], 19335 ex typ. Kingstoniano, [19683], 19724, 19724.3, 22402, 23593, 25085, 25360, 26004.
1607: 1334, 1337, 1339, 3776, [3908.7], [4848.3], 6957–7.5, 6970, 7116, 7204, 12592, 13002, 13392.7, 17040, 17232.5, 18517, 19370, 19735.4, 19898a.7, 20017, [20028], 20146, 20147.5, 22249–9.3, 22726, 22738, 25656, 25657, 25658, 25658.5.
1608: 1069, 1927, 6951, 6955, 7125, 7134, 7140.5, 7145, [7691] (d), 13472.7, 23274.5, 24963, 25686.
1609: 3455, 4396, 4610, 7124, 7135, 7141, 7204.5, 12204, 13446, 13472.7, 13541, 13565, 13768, [13770], 15692, 17041, 19372, 19649 (note), 19677–7.3, 22668, 22727, 22938, 25162.
1610: 377, [726.7] (c), 1337.5, [3364], 3456, 3456.4, 3456.7, 3458, 3459, 3459.3, [4848.5], 5391, 5697.5, 6941, [6950], 6952, 7528, [7691.2] (d?), [7691.4] (d), 12063, 13446, 13473, 17687, 17691, 20096, 21217, 23275, [24919.5] (d?), [25164], 25301, 26020.
1611: 3228, 3458.3, 3460, 3460.2, 4707.5, [5267.8], 6964, 7138, 10314.6 (d), 10806, 12060, 12060a (d), 12063.5, 13455.7, [17700], [22255], 22393, 22669, 22728, [22939], [23888.5].
1612: [2540], [2540.5], 3052, 3229, 3460.5, 4741, [5404], 6624.4, 6956, 6971.5, 7136, 7528.5, [7691.6–.8] (d?), 10807, 11847.5, 12864, 12868–8a, 14700, [15136], 19373, 21203, [23440.3], 24111, 24233, 24833.4, [25901].
1612/13: 25705, 25707 typis.
1613: 1663–4 (d), 3462, 3464, [4513.4], 4576, [7140], 7184, 7474, 7537, 10872.7, [17854–4a], 19650 (note), 22218, [22984.6], [24148.3], [24151], 24833.6, 25143, 25354, [25603], 25699.
1614: [172.3], 810–0.5, 3230, [3462.7], 4982 (d?), [5268], [5321?], 6406, 6853, 6944, 6971.7, 10328, 12818.5, 17869.5(*A*3) ent., 18493, [19130], 19777, [20862], 25661, 25699a.
1615: 3463–3.3, 3465–5.4, [5315.8], 5378–8.2, [7693] (c?), 13396, 13772, 15700, 17492, 18437–7.5, 19374, 21204, 24833.8.
1616: [1602.5], 1935–5.5, 1963.7, 1964.3, 3460.3, 3466a, 4577, 4707.7, [5268.3], 5847, [10701.3], 12022.7–23, 13397, 13877.3–.5, 15202, [18075.5], 20306, 21218, [23440.7], 23672, 26058, 26082 (note).
1617: 726.9, [1314.3(*A*)], 1645, 1645.5, 1955, [4514], 5618, 5621, 5622, 6624.7, 7531a, 11292, 11305, 12796, 12819, 12869, 14893, 16835.5, 20390, [22256], 22671, 23432.5.
1618: 1436, 1437, 1628, 1648, [2560], [2560a], [2561.5], 3230.5, 4226, 6943, 6953, 7154.7* (d), [10340?], [12025], 12848, 14169*, 14170*, 15700.3, 19312, 19651 (note), 20654a.5(*A*3)*, 21221, 22730, 25308, 25952.
1619: 1439, [1603], 1641, [2564.2], 7142 (note), [11328.7], 12827–7.3, 12827.5, 13447–7.5, 14172*, [17762*], 18420, 18459, 18804, [18929.4(*A*3)?], 19601, 20654a.5(*A*3)*, 21165, 23837, 25297, 25305–5a, 25309–9.3, 25320.
1620: 76, [1604], 4466, 7104, 7109–9.3, 7532, 7613, 10227, [11328.9], 11838, 12708, 13448–8.4, 18761, [20055.7], 20544, [22362], 23412.5, 23830.7–31, 23838, [24841] (d), [24841.2–.4], 24841.6–.8, [24842] (d), 24953, 25372.
1621: [172.6], 1942, 3930.3, [5268.4(*A*)], [6908], 7533, 12708, 13448.7, 14969–9.5, 15301, 17923.5, 18037, 18316, 18507.35A, —.35C, 19843.5, 20351, [20546], 20942, [23441], 23840, 24553.5.
1622: 74, 1185, 1905, [2575a], 5726, 5726.5, 7143, 7342.3(*A*3) (d?), 12021, 12499.5, 13046, 14378, 18227, 18507.35B, [—.71A], [18688.5] (d), 20943.3, [22647?], 22672, 22731, [24843] (d), 24844, 25306, 25373, 25375–5a, [25375a.2–.7] (d).
1623: 1240, [1605], 1956, 1956.3, 1956.7, [2581], 4681, [4849.2], [5268.5], 5909, 7316, 19026, 21035.5 ent., [23352], 25299, 25374, [25375a.8] (d).
1624: [1606], 1787, 1957, [2585], [2585.5], [7694] (d?), [8743] (d), 12022, 12714, 19079, 20550, [23889.2], 24844.3, 25299.
1625: 1045–5.5, 3231, 3250, [5301.8], 5851.5 (c), [5975], 6854, 7105, [7694.3] (d?), 10341, 10703, 17598, 19878, 25996.
1626: 727, 1960–1, 3251, [5268.7], 5910, 6854.2, 7106, 10679–9.3, [18996], 20545, 21035(*A*3, note), [23039d.10] (d?), [23039e.6] (d?), [23039f.4] (d?), 25171.

Kingston, F. — *cont.*
1627: 1943, [2602], [2603.5], 3769–70b.2, 5306.5, 7106.5, 10680, [10706.7] (d?), [11330.8] (false), [20056], [22985], [23039.6] (d?), [23442], [23889.3], 25170.5.
1628: 1393, 1962, 1964.7, 3771.6, [4849.4], 10758, 12974, 23033, [23039a.3] (d?), [23039d.11] (d?), [23039e.7] (d?), 22731.5, 24641, 24645, 25311.
1629: [173], 602, 971, 1394, 1623.5, 1694, 1944, [5045.3] (d), [5270], 5722, [6307], 7144, 10701, 10703.5, 10758, [11163–3.3], [12026], 17099, [23889.4], 23896.
1630: 553, [599?], 728, 1624, 1941.5, 1945, [1949?], [2623], 3252, 5354.7, 5467, 6666, 6855, 10719, 10722, 10733, [12114?], 13794a.5–95, [17756], 19788, 21010, [23039.7] (d?), [23039b] (d?), [23039d.12] (d?), [23039e.8] (d?), 23570, 24928–8a.
1631: 1928–8.5, [2630.5], 3238, 3591, 4238, [5271.4], [7694.5] (c?), 10707, 11228, 20683, 20934–4.5, 20935, [21010.3], 21178.7, [23039d.13] (d?), [23039e.9], 23889.4c(*A*3), 24007a.
1632: [2637.8], [2638], 3575, 11228, 11228.3, 20927, 20935, [21010.7], 22801, [23039a.4] (d?), [23039e.10], [23039f.5] (d?).
1633: 108, [2645.7], 3564, 3576, 7121, 10342, 10681, 10704, 13620, 21036a, [23039d.14] (d?), [23039e.11], 23889.5], 24289.
1634: 729, 948.5, 1129, [2652], [2653], 3553, 6856, 7122, 10702, [10720], [10723], 12865, 22220, [23039.8] (d?), [23039e.12], [23039f.6] (d?), 24794.
1635: 948.5, [1614], 1959, 2659, [2661.5], [2662], 3554, 3581.7, [5272.4], 7107, 14625.7, [18929.7], 19155, [20056.5], 20277, 20928, 21036a.3 ent., [22649], [23039e.13], [23443], [23889.7].
1636: [706.5], 3554.5, 3567.5, [4140.8?], [4141?], 7149, 10343, [14137?] (repeat), [18952.9], 20932, [23039d.15] (d?), [23039e.14].
1636/37: 494.13, 515.20, 527.27.
1637: 730, 4510–0.8, [6097], 6857, 10192.8, 10343.5, 11066, 11067 (forged), [20762.3], 20936.5–37, [23039d.16] (d?), [23039e.15].
1637/38: 419.7, 479.4, 527.28.
1638: [5272.8], 5361, 10708, 20929–9a, 20931, [21094], [23039d.17], [23039e.16], [23039f.7] (d?), [23039f.8].
1638/39: 419.8, 527.29.
1639: 5360, 13620.5, [23039f.9].
1639/40: 419.9, 527.30.
1640: 13620.7–21a.5, 13621a.7(*A*3), 14297a, 15567, 21036a.3–b.7, [22650], [23039e.17], [23551], 24289.5.
1640/41: Wing A 1328, A 2707.
1640, after: [1965(*A*3)] (d).

Kingston, John.
Printer (from 1553) in London, 1551–1584?†. Freed as a Grocer in 1542 by **Richard Grafton**, in whose house Kingston's first item was printed. Possibly related to **Anthony Kingston.** Succeeded to the printing material of **Nicholas Hill** and was in partnership 1553–1557 with **Henry Sutton**. Kingston's widow successively remarried **George Robinson** and **Thomas Orwin** and printed herself as **Joan Robinson** and **Joan Orwin**. The printing material ultimately passed to John and Joan's son, **Felix Kingston**. *See* also the headnote following Appendix D/60 and also Appendix E/1. [Duff, *Century*; *Dict. 1*.]
dw. in Paul's Churchyard (B), 1553 (11971, with H. Sutton)
at the West door of Paul's (A.10), 1557 (20820)–1564 (10444, has 'shop'); no later address or use of this one noted; since in both examples cited the shop is for the *selling* of books, the printing house may have been elsewhere.
1551: 15545 [f.] (d).
1553: [1655] (d), 2425, 2426, 11971, [12526.5] (d), [20373].
1553/54: 481.
1554: 16152, [16153], [16154], [16244], [18054] (d), [19547] (d?), 23010.7.
1554/55: [447.7].
1555: [2979] (c?), 3197, [9447.7], [10249], 15839, 16134, 16218, [16245], 16252, 16266.
1556: 15842, [16075.5?] (d?), 16108, 25875.
1557: 7605.5 (note), 16081, [16109] (d?), [16109.5?] (d?), [16219], [19784], 20820 by & sold by.
1558: 293, 7599 (d), 24799, [25113] (forged).
1559: 3726 (d), 9459 (note), 9459.5 (note), 10663–4.5, 10831, [11718], 13648 (note), [16293.5].
1560: 300, 4380.5, [12723a] (d?), 17164, 25800.
1561: 5075–6.3, [20733].
1562: 4033 (d), 4035, [4845], [7280] (d?), 11621 (d), 17164, 25801.
1563: 20736, 20925a.5 (d), 25802, 25812.

Kingston, J. — *cont.*
1564: [4036] (d), 4036.5, 10444, 18059.5, 20736–6a.
1565: 4376, 12167 (d), 18060, 20736a.
1566: 199, [1736], [10028] (d?), 11028, 17625.5 (d), [19121].
1566/67: 422, 484.
1567: 4382.5, [11530.5], 17518 (d?), 25803, 25813, 25814 (d/repeat).
1567/68: 422.3, 493.7.
1568: 1210, 4382.7, 15486.
1568/69: 422.4(*A*), 463.
1569: [977] (false, d), 4383, 10472, [15486.5(*A*3)] (d?), 22980.
1569/70: 484.5.
1570: [12366?] (d?), 18926.1.
1571: 4770.4, 11426–6.2, 17849, 18663, 18664.5.
1572: 15551, 22981, 23431.
1573: 4037, 5265.7, 5290, [16624?] (d?), 17286 ap., 21810.3, [23101.5] (d).
1574: 5265.8 ap., 5314.5, 5323.5, 12416.5, [13784], 15487, 20761.2, [20813], 20973 (c).
1574/75: 443.13.
1575: 5307, [11243], [19781.5(*A*3)] (c?).
1576: [17850], [19467], 23439, 24667 ex typ., 24788a.5 ex typ.
1577: 4384.5, [4857.7], 5315 ex typ., [12201] (d), [14927], [15416–6a], [18005–5a], [19467.5], 20452, [21118?] (d), 21810.7 ex typ., [24920.5] (d).
1578: 4038, 4342, [5251], [6231], 7364 (d), [13197], [13785], [15417], [17203], [22215].
1579: 4034 ent., [4304], 4771 ass'd, [5115] (d), [5235–5.2] (d), [5243] (d), [5244] (d?), [13020], [13785], 20974, [21634] (d), [23267] (d), 23439.5(*A*) ent., [25343] (d).
1580: 298, 303 (d), [3495], 4385, 4385.5 (c), 4404 (c), 4404.5 (c), [4433], 5240, [5247] (d), 5250, 13531, [15005], 20453, 22272, [24901], 25804, 25815.
1581: [6075], [6734], 13480.5, [16978], 18647, [19468], [20996], [21002], 25623, [26123].
1582: 4386, 5266.1(*A*), [6649.5], 10879, [17576], 19433.2(*A*), [21004], [23414].
1583: [3939] (d?), [4626.5] (d?), [4626.7] (d?), [4800.3?], [10104] (d), 10126.7 (d), [10324.5] (d?), 13775, 17450.3 (d), [18733], [20996.3], [23376–6.5], [23377], [24786].
1584: [4305] (d?), [4858], [5681] (d), [5794], [8145.5] (d), [10224] (d), 12276, 20560, [21002a], 25805, 25814 (d?).

1593: 23439.5 ass'd.

Kirkham, Henry.
Bookseller in London, 1568 (Arber I.374)–1593†. Father of **William Kirkham**. [*Dict. 1*.]
dw. at the Black Boy at the middle North door of Paul's (A.1), 1570 (12187)–1571 (19549); variation: omits sign, has 'shop', 1570 (1326)
at the little North door of Paul's at the Black Boy (A.1), 1572 (15551, colophon)–1593 (11208, has 'shop'); variation, has 'dw.', 1592 (23683); the change from 'middle' to 'little' North door undoubtedly represents a change in terminology rather than a shift in location.
1570: 1326 f. (d), 11843 f. (d), 12187 f. (d?), 22890 f. (d).
1571: 3077 f., 19549 f. (d), 19550 f. (d), 19551 f. (d).
1572: 15551 f.
1573: 4684 [f.], 4685 f., 21485.
1575: 20973 f. (c), 22805 [f.].
1577: 20665 sold (d?), 21118 f. (d).
1579: 20974 f.
1580: 3495 f., 22272 f., 24901 f.
1581: 3371 (d), 20975 f.
1582: 20158.5 f. (d?), 25401.
1586: 24902 f. (d?).
1589: 7060.5, 20976 f.
1590: 21037 f. (d?), [22919?] (c).
1591: 11821 sold.
1592: 23683 f. (d).
1593: 11208 f.

Kirkham, William.
Bookseller in London, 1593–1616? Son of **Henry Kirkham**. [*Dict. 1*; ?*Poor Book*, 1616.]
at the little North door of Paul's Church at the Black Boy (A.1), 1593 (7721.5)–1599 (24344, has 'dw.') at least
1593: 7721.5. **1595:** 24345 f. (d?). **1598:** 23634.5 f. **1599:** 24344 f.

Kirkman, Francis.
Scrivener and bookseller in London, 1653–1682 (Wing P 2885, K 634). [*Dict. 2.*]
1661: [13354 f.] (forged, d?) = Wing² H 1786A.

Kirton, Joshua.
Bookseller in London, (1636) 1638–1667†. In partnership with **Thomas Warren**, 1638–1641. [*Dict. 2*, under Joseph as well as Joshua; DFM 100; *Loan Book* (as surety for John Orme), 1658.]
their shop in Paul's Churchyard at the White Horse (A.2), 1639 (12124)–1640 (18036) at least
1638: 1459 sold, 11943 f., 11943.5 sold.
1639: 12124 f., 12979 prost., 12980 prost., 17554 f., 21063.7 sold, 22392 sold.
1640: 18035a ven., 18036–6.5 ven., 24046 sumpt.

Kitson, Abraham.
Bookseller in London, 1579–1594. Son of **Anthony Kitson**. Freed as a Draper by patrimony on 12 Oct. 1579. From 1589 he was the agent in London for selling books printed in Cambridge. His shop passed to **Richard Bankworth**, who may actually have sold some of the items below dated 1594 and vice versa. [*Dict. 1.*]
dw. in Paul's Churchyard at the Sun (A.3), 1579/80 (486.3)–1594 (24010)
1579/80: 486.3 f.
1581: 13480.5 f.
1584: 13480.7 f.
1589: [1564] sold, [2020] sold (d?), 24008.5 ext., 24474 sold (d).
1591: 1565 sold (d?), 5376 f., 19655a ext. (d?), 19658 sold (d?).
1592: [15516] sold, 19656–6.5 ext., 24009 ext.
1593: [1830] sold, [18074] sold, 19688 sold, [19758] sold, 23360 f., 24009.5 ext.
1594: [6443?] sold, [16678?] sold, [18074.5] sold, 24010 ext.

Kitson, Anthony.
Bookseller in London, c. 1553–1578†. Freed as a Draper by **Thomas Petyt** on 24 Nov. 1550. Father of **Abraham Kitson**. [Duff, *Century*.]
dw. in Paul's Churchyard at the Sun (A.3), 1555 (20192.9(*A*3)–1572/73 (486) and until his death
1553: 12631.7 [f.] (c).
1555: 10450.4 in aed., 16264 [f.] (d), 20192.9(*A*3) [f.], 23014a [f.] (d?).
1556: 4825 [f.] (d).
1557: 10455 [f.], 14009.3 [f.] (d?).
1558: 22596 [f.] (d?), 22603 [f.] (d?), 22617 [f.] (d?).
1560: 13306 [f.] (c).
1564: 24726 f.
1565: 19304 f. (c).
1567: 13175.19c f. (c).
1571: 24634 sold (d?).
1572: 770.3 f., 1048 f. (d), 22868.5 (note).
1572/73: 486.
1573: 11554 f. (d?).
1575: 14326.3 f. (d?), 22161.5 f. (d?).
1576: 3368 f. (d).

Knight, Clement.
Bookseller in London, 1594–1630. Freed as a Draper by **Abraham Veale** on 7 Sept. 1590; transferred to the Stat. Co. in 1600. Father of **Thomas Knight**. [*Dict. 1.*]
shop at the little North door of Paul's Church (A.1), 1595 (16658)–1596 (17127)
dw. in Paul's Churchyard at the Holy Lamb (A.6), 1602 (6749.8)–1630 (23192); variation: has 'shop', 1604 (5882.5)
1595: 16658 f.
1596: 17126.5 f., 17127 f., 17867 f.
1600: 23190 ent., 24804 ent.
1602: 6468.5 f., 6749.8 f.
1603: 3068 f., 5881 f., 13592 f., 14422 f., 15355 pro, 21433 f., 24918 f.
1604: 3069 f., 5882–2.5 f., 6872 f., 10255 f., 21433.5 f.
1605: 10256 f., 13506 f., 17684–4.5 f., 17688 f.
1606: 4644 f., 5880 f., 6750 f., 17685 f., 17685.5 f., 17690 f., 21435 f., 25818 f.
1607: 10209.3(*A*) f., 17278.1 ?ent., 17686 f., 23624.3 imp.
1608: 11206 f., 12488 f., 20493 f.
1609: 4300 f., 5919.5 ent., 5937.3 ent., 6388 f., 6751 f., 12488.3 f., 14298 f., 14303 f., 16685 f., 18115 f., 23683.3 ent., 24064 f.

Knight, C. — *cont.*
1610: 10226 f., 17687 f., 17691 f., 24424 f.
1611: 4645 f.
1612: 117 f., 6752 f., 10358 f., 14304 f., 24416 f.
1613: 122 f., 18981.5 f., 24424.7 f.
1614: 118 f., 10238 f., 17692 f., 17697.7 ent., 24425 f., 25819 f.
1615: 124 f., 6168.5 ent., 6753 f., 17698 f., 23190 imp.
1616: 119 f., 125 f., 24426 f.
1617: 21603.3 by ass'ns of (d?), 24427 f.
1619: 6754 f., 17693 f., 24428 f.
1620: 17278.1 f., 24805a by ass't of.
1621: 24429 f.
1623: 6754.4 f., 25820 f.
1624: 23191 sumpt.
1625: 24429.5 f.
1627: 23191.3 sumpt.
1628: 6754.7 f.
1629: 23191.7 sumpt.
1630: 23192 sumpt.

Knight, Philip.
Bookseller in London, 1615–1617. [*Dict. 1*; DFM 1599.]
shop in Chancery Lane over against the Rolls (W.10e), 1615 (23250)–1616 (7244)
1615: 12247 ent., 23250 f., 25145 ent. **1616:** 7244 f.

Knight, Thomas.
Stationer in London, (1627) 1629–1660. Son of **Clement Knight**. His books were often sold by others. [*Dict. 2*; DFM 651.]
shop in Paul's Churchyard at the Holy Lamb (A.6), 1630 (25821)–1633 (352); no later use noted
1629: 6168.5 ent., 23193.2 ent.
1630: 24431 f., 25821 f.
1631: 351 f., 6755 f.
1632: 6756 f.
1633: 352 f., 23193.2 imp.
1634: 6168.5 f., 17694 f., 24432 f.
1635: 25822 f.
1636: 6757 f.
1637: 17218 f.
1640: 24434 f.

Köpfel, Wolfgang.
Printer in Strassburg, 1522–1554†. [Benzing 441; *Library* 4 (1950): 274.]
1542: [3759.5] (false, d?). **1544:** [292] (d?).

Köpfel, Wolfgang, *Heirs of.*
Printers in Strassburg, 1554–1557, and in Worms, 1557–1565? [Benzing 448, 512; *Library* 4 (1950): 275–6.]
1555: [10023.7?] (d?), [20175?].
1556: [17200], [20175a?], [20178].

Kranepoel, Herman Theunisz.
Printer in Wesel, 1612, and in Haarlem, 1618–1629 at least. [Benzing 482; Gruys; Briels 345.]
1629: 22941.5.

Kyd, Kyng, Kyngston. *See* Kid, King, Kingston.

Kyrfoth, Charles.
Printer in Oxford, 1519. [Duff, *Century*.]
dw. in St. John the Baptist Street, 1519 (5613)
1519: 5613 per.

L

L., T.
Publisher in Amsterdam, 1637–1638. Possibly the same person as **Thomas Lappadge** in Rotterdam, 1640.
at his chamber in Flowingburrow near unto the English Church, 1638 (13728.5)
1637: 13726.4 f. **1638:** 13728.5 f., 20221.3 f. (c).

La Coste, Jean de.
Bookseller and printer in Paris, 1630–1671† at least. [Lottin 2: 41.]
1638: 20487.5 chez.

La Coste, Nicolas de.
Printer in Paris, 1628–1638 at least. [Lottin 2: 41.]
1631: 943. **1638:** 20487.5 chez.

La Coste, Philippe. *See* Coste.

La Croy, Johannes de, *pseud.*
Printer in 'Leiden', 1589. = J. Wolfe.
1589: 11735.

Lacy, Alexander.
Printer? in London, (1556) 1557 (Arber I.42)–1571. Some of the woodcut initials he used belonged to R. Jugge and J. Cawood, the Queen's Printers, and it is not clear what Lacy's relationship to them was. [Duff, *Century*.]
in Aldersgate Street, dw. beside the well (F.2), 1563 (18491, 25350)
without Aldersgate in Little Britain Street (F.4), 1563? (16504.5)–1566 (25766, omits 'Street'); variation: omits 'without Aldersgate', 1566 (11626)
at St. Katherine's beside the Tower of London over against the Bear Dance (U.4), 1570 (19974.1)–1571 (19551, omits all after 'Katherine's')
1560: [1332.5?] (c).
1562: 3078(*A*3) (d), 6095 ent., 6768 (d).
1563: 3076 (d), 11631 ?ent., 16504.5 (d?), 18491, 25350 (d?).
1565: 3080 (d), 7550(*A*3) (c).
1566: 4555 (d), 5236 (d), 11626 (d), 13028 ?ent., 17803 (d), 19969, 22644 (d), 25766.
1568: 22890 ent., 23631 (d).
1570: 1058 (d?), 11843 (d), 12187 (d?), 19974.1 (d).
1571: 19549 (d), 19550 (d), 19551 (d).

Laet (Latius), Hans (Jan) de.
Printer and bookseller in Antwerp, 1545–1566†. [*Dict. 1*; Rouzet.]
1556: 11092a en casa.
1564: 7062, 17496.
1565: 371, 1778, 7061, 12762, 18888, 23230, 23232.
1566: 23234.

Lambert, Thomas.
Bookseller in London, 1633–1669†? (*Loan Book*). [*Dict. 2*; DFM 2803; *Loan Book*, 1664–67.]
in Smithfield (E.8), 1633–1640 at least
— near the Hospital gate, 1633 (20684)
at the Horseshoe —, 1634 (4326)–1640 [19230]; variation: adds 'near the Hospital gate', 1636 (13369), 1638 (18229)
1633: 5417 ?ent., 5429 f. (d?), 6924 ent., 12547 f. (d?), 19186 f. (d), 20324 f. (d), 20684 f.
1634: 197 f. (d), 3140.5 f. (d?), 3704.9 ent., 4326 f. (d), 6924 ent., 19242.5 f. (d), 19244 f. (d), 19245.5 f. (d), 19246.5 f. (d), 19247 f. (d), 19251.7 f. (d), 19256 f. (d), 19257 f. (d), 19265 f. (d), 19276 f. (d), 25869 f. (d?), 25871 ent., 25984 f. (d).
1635: 3730 f. (d?), 11107.7 f., 12092.8 f. (d?), 19226 f. (d?), 19251.5 f. (d?), 19285 f. (d?), 22431 sold (d).
1636: 3141 f. (d?), 13369 f., 15407.5 f., 17707 ?ent., 19250.5 f. (d), 19251.3 f. (d).
1637: 5428 f. (d?), 19242 f. (d), 19277 f. (d), 22917.5 sold.
1638: 6191 ?ent., 15706.5 f. (d), 18229 f., 22919.5 ent., 23795.3 f.
1639: 19250.7 f. (d), 20317 f. (d).
1640: [12052.5] sold, [19223] sold, [19230] sold (d), [19238] sold, [19258.5] sold (d), 19262 f. (d?), [19274] sold (d), 19281 f. (d?), 20316 f. (d?), 21503 f. (d?).

Lambrecht, Joos.
Printer and punchcutter in Ghent, 1536–1553, and in Wesel, 1553–1556†. The printing in English queried for him the first two years below seems largely to have been done for **Hugh Singleton**, who then apparently branched out on his own. In 1556 Lambrecht's printing material passed to **Pieter Anastasius de Zuttere**. The group of books listed below was originally linked to Lambrecht in F. S. Ferguson's collations for the STC revision. [Rouzet; Benzing 481.]
1553: [1307?] (false), [4392?] (false), [11587?] (false).
1554: [1716?] (false), [1730?] (false), [13457?] (false), [15059.5?] (false), [21683?] (false).
1556: [3504.5?] (d?), [5996?] (d?), [7376.5?], [10432?].

Lancelot, Johann.
Printer in Heidelberg, 1597–1619†; also in Speyer, 1597–1600. [Benzing 197, 425.]
1614: 1431.24A.

Lange, Paul.
Printer in Hamburg, 1603–1630. [Benzing 182.]
1620: 16688.

Langford, Bernard.
Bookseller in London, (1637) 1638–1639. [*Dict. 1*; DFM 2436.]
at the (Blue) Bible at (on) Holborn Bridge (V.2), 1638 (11550, 24399)–1639 (5989)
1638: 11550 sold, 20447 ven., 24399 sold.
1639: 5989 f., 19897 f., 24331.5 sold.

Langham, Edward.
Stationer in London, (1621), and bookseller in Banbury, 1628–1642 at least. [*Dict. 1*; DFM 1975.]
No address used.
1628: 25322.3 f., 25322a f. **1630:** 25323 sold. **1634:** 17654a f., 17655 sold. **1638:** 22478b f., 22505.5 f. **1640:** 25317.5 f.

Langley, Thomas.
Bookseller in London, (1614) 1615–1646†. His first address is that of his former master, **Thomas Pavier**. [*Dict. 1*; DFM 2130; *Poor Book*, 1635–46, widow thereafter.]
in Ivy Lane (C.3), 1615 (12214, 26091)
their shop over against the Saracen's Head without Newgate (D.9), 1615 (15091, with J. White)–1623 (15093a); has 'his' shop from 1616 (17897); variation, substitutes: dw. on Snow Hill, 1622 (24693)
1614: 21056.8 f. (d?).
1615: 12214–5 sold, 15091 sold, 15091a f., 26091 f.
1616: 11925.7 f., 17381 f. (d?), 17897 f., 21087.7 sold (d).
1617: 14997.7 sold.
1618: 6020 sold, 13430 f., 14045.7 f. (d), 15092 f.
1619: 3951 ent., 14975 ent., 14986 ent., 14987 ent., 22879 ent., 24006 f.
1620: 13541.5 f. (c), 14498.5 f. (c), 14674 f., 20327 f. (c).
1621: 14056 f., 17362 f.
1622: 24693 f.
1623: 11537.7 f. (c), 15093a sold.
1625: 22919.1 f. (c), [22919.7?] f. (c).
1629: 1331.7 ent.
1635: 22431 f. (d).

Langton, Richard.
Bookseller? or patron? in London, 1581. [*Dict. 1.*]
dw. in Swithun's Lane (T.2), 1581 (16812)
1581: 16812 f.

La Nouë, Guillaume de.
Bookseller in Paris, 1572–1601†. [Renouard.]
1599: [4894] (d).

Lant, Richard.
Printer in London, (1537) 1539?–1561. He succeeded to most of the types of **Thomas Godfray**. His career, with its meager output, problematic dating, and frequent change of premises, is not very clear. The Paul's Churchyard address may have belonged only to **Richard Bankes** and that in the Old Bailey only to Lant, though some items name both at each address. Lant may be, or be related to, the man of this name buried in 1589 (*St. Giles*). [Duff, *Century*.]
in the Old Bailey (D.7), 1542 (18813, adds: in St. Sepulchre's (Pulcher's) parish)–1545 (14126.5, with R. Bankes; also 19.6, 24216a, both undated and alone); 1546 (17764.5)
in Paul's Churchyard (B), 1545 (3365.5, 20197.3, both with R. Bankes)
in Aldersgate Street (F.2), 1552? (5225.5)–1553? (11186)
in Paternoster Row (C.7), 1553? (10615, 23292)
in Smithfield (E.8), 1559 (17559; 7561, adds: in the parish of St. Bartholomew's Hospital)
1539: [21307a.7] (d?).
1540: [1323.5] (d), [12206a.3] (d), [22880.4] (d).
1542: 692.5 (d?), 18813 (d), 19187 (d?), 19465.3 (d?), 21808 (d), 22249.5 (d?).

Lant, R. — *cont.*
1543/44: 508.5, 523 f.
1544/45: [476.5?].
1545: 19.6 (c), 3365.5, 14126.5, 20197.3, 22598 (d?), 24216a (d?).
1546: 17764.5 (d), 20394 (d).
1547: 24203.5.
1552: [1656] (d?), 4999.5 (d?), 5225.5 (d?), 5252 (d?), 5258 (d?), 23251.5 (d?).
1553: 10615 (d?), 11186 (d?), 23292 (d?).
1554: [26098.7?] (d?).
1558: 19.6 ent.
1559: 7561, 17559 (d).
1561: 1419 (d).

Lappadge, Thomas.
Publisher in Rotterdam, 1640. Probably an English merchant or dissenter. Possibly the same person as **T. L.** in Amsterdam, 1637–38. [*Dict. 1.*]
sold at his shop in the Wine Street by the Old Head, or at his house on the Iron Bridge, 1640 (4129.5; 3732 is sold only at his house)
1640: 3732 f., 4129.5 f.

Laquehay, Jean.
Printer and bookseller in Paris, 1610–1634 at least. [Lottin 2: 101.]
1611: 4570.

Lash, William.
Stationer in London, (1628) 1634. [*Dict. 1.*]
No address used.
1634: 15466 f.

Latham (Lathum, Lautham), George.
Bookseller in London, 1620–1658†. Son-in-law of **Matthew Lownes**, his former master. [*Dict. 2*; DFM 1865; *Loan Book*, 1622–28.]
in Paul's Churchyard, 1621–1640 at least
shop — at the Brazen Serpent (A.3), 1621 (17195)–1626 (4235, omits 'shop')
at the Bishop's Head — (A.2), 1627 (906)–1640 (11882); variation: has 'dw.', 1630 (4327)
1620: 18200 ent., 24772 ent.
1621: 17195 f., 17196 f.
1622: 6632 f., 14090 f., 20640 ent., 25169 f.
1623: 4211 f., 19621b f.
1624: 18610 f.
1625: 6125.6 f., 6632.5 f., 13413a.5 sold.
1626: 4235 f., 24772 f.
1627: 906 f., 13508 sold, 20894 f., 22240.5 f.
1628: 1160.5 ent., 6561 ent., 19984 ent., 20640 f., 21654 ent., 22548 ent., 23085 ent., 23087.5 sold (d?), 24539 ent.
1629: 6633 f., 12806 f. (d).
1630: 1561.5 f., 4327 f., 6639 dros.
1631: 6634 f., 13718 sold (d), 14471 sold, 18124, 19652.5 sold, 19653.5 sold, 19653b.5 sold.
1632: 1435 sold, 1435.5 f., 3140 f., 13718 sold (d), 15115 sold.
1633: 6634.5 f., 24539.5 sold, 24772.5 f.
1634: 14472 sold, 15270 f., 19828 f., 20641 f.
1635: 907 f., 6635 f., 13719 sold (d), 24773 f.
1636: 4212 f., 13719 sold (d), 24773 (note).
1637: 1161.5 f., 4212 f., 4510.8 f., 6636 f.
1638: 3139 f., 7467 f., 26111 f.
1639: 13720 sold (d), 15409 sold, 21850 f. (d), 26112–2.3 f.
1640: 6637 f., 11882 f.

Lathum, Roger.
Printer? in London, 1539? [Duff, *Century*.]
in the Old Bailey (D.7), 1539? (23175)
1539: 23175 (d?).

Latin Stock. *See* Stationers' Company.

Latius. *See* Laet.

Latomus, Sigmund.
Printer in Frankfurt am Main, 1599–1625?†. [Benzing 130.]
1620: [11329] (d).

Laughton. *See* Lawton.

Laurensz (Laurenson, Laurentius), Hendrick.
Printer and bookseller in Amsterdam, 1607–1648. [*Dict. 1*; Gruys.]
1608: 11811 (A3 in note to 11810) ven. **1611:** 3754. **1612:** 11212. **1622:** 1431.27 ex off. **1623:** 1431.28 ex off. **1624:** 1431.28A ex off. **1628:** 5028.

Lautham. *See* Latham.

Law (Lawe), Matthew.
Bookseller in London, 1595–1629†. Freed as a Draper by **Abraham Veale** on 26 June 1579; transferred to the Stat. Co. in 1600. Father of **Thomas Law 2.** His daughter, Alice, successively married **John Norton 2** and **Thomas Warren.** [*Dict. 1*; *Poor Book*, 1619–20 (scholarship for son Matthew, cf. *C-B C*: 111), ?1620–22 (John, a poor scholar).]
shop in Paul's Churchyard near unto St. Austin's gate at the Fox (A.7), 1601 (26076)–1629 (22320, has 'dw.'); sometimes omits 'near ... gate', 1604 (22282), 1612 (17924.5) or omits sign, 1609 (16916.3); other variations:
in Paul's Churchyard, 1601 (1449), 1616 (20019, has 'shop')
dw. in Paul's Churchyard near Watling Street, 1601 (1454)
1595: 4268 f.
1596: 21296 f.
1600: 21591.5 ven.
1601: 1449 sold, 1454 f., 18249 imp., 26076 f.
1602: 5594 f., 11761.7 sold, 12196 f., 17092.5 f., 18891 f., 18892 f.
1603: 5121 (note), 12577 f., 15529 f., 19803.5 f., 19804 f., 19806 f., 20017 ent., 22310 ent.
1604: 1456 f., 1456.5 f., 17781 sold, 22282 f.
1605: 1457 f., 5595 f., 16916.2(*A*3) f., 22317 sold.
1606: 1451 f., 1455 f., 1455.5 f., 4960.5 f.
1607: 1447 f., 1452 f., 1452.5 f., 17917 f., 20017 f.
1608: 5596 f., 22283 f., 22310–1 f.
1609: 1446 f., 1446.5 f., 1450 f., 4014 f., 14694 f., 16916.3 f., 20302 f., 25300 f., 25300.5 f.
1610: 4961 f., 25301 f.
1611: 20018 f.
1612: 17924 f., 17924.5 f., 22318 sold.
1613: 14950.5 sold, 22284 f., 23500 f., 25281 f.
1614: 5597 f., 13583 f. (d), 14951 sold, 14954.6(*A*3) sold, 16683 f., 16916.7 f., 18209 sold.
1615: 4692a sold, 7173 f., 22312 f., 23501 f.
1616: 14952 sold, 19344 f., 19349 f., 20019 f., 22839.5 sold, 23502 f., 25302 f., 25995 f.
1617: 14954.7 sold, 20003 f., 20012 sold.
1618: 4693 sold, 14953 sold, 14955 sold, 22848 sold.
1619: 22848 sold.
1621: 5598 f.
1622: 22285 sold, 22319 sold.
1623: 1001 f., 11598 f., 20003 f.
1624: 5433.5 f., 12530 f., 13260 sold [his] shop.
1625: 26037 f.
1626: 16886 sold.
1627: 12741 f.
1629: 22320 sold.

Law, Thomas 1.
Stationer in London, 1584–1589. Addresses in his imprints, if there are any at all, are those of his partners in particular books, Y. James: in Newgate Market (C.4: 21483) and T. Nelson: at the West door of Paul's (A.10: 21483.5). [*Dict. 1.*]
No separate address used.
1584: 21483 f. (d), 21483.5(*A*3) f. (d?).
1585: 20889.5 f., 21084 [f.] (d).
1589: 5114 ent.

Law, Thomas 2.
Stationer in London, (1619) 1622–1633 (cf. DFM 1806) at least. Son of **Matthew Law**. His only imprint was shared with **William Garrett**, a former apprentice of his father's. [DFM 1802.]
No address used.
1622: 13580 f.

Lawson, Richard.
Bookseller in Edinburgh, 1607–1622†. [*Dict. 1.*]
No address used.
1607: 16589.5 f. **1608:** 10554. **1610:** 2704 sold (c), 15680 f. **1615:** 4803.5(*A*) [f.].

Lawton (Laughton), Augustine.
Stationer in London, (1564) 1567–1590. [*Dict. 1*: 168–9.]
shop in Paul's Churchyard at the Grasshopper (B), 1571 (11477)
dw. in Maiden Lane near Wood Street (G.7), 1590 (13113)
1571: 11477 f. **1590:** 13113 f.

Laybourne, *Master* (i.e. Roger?).
Barber-surgeon in London and bookseller, 1602.
dw. upon St. Mary [at] Hill near Billingsgate (T.12), 1602 (5446)
1602: 5446 sold.

Lea. *See* Lee.

Leake, William 1.
Bookseller in London, (1584) 1586–1619 (1633†). Father of **William Leake 2.** One of the *assignees of* **J. Battersby**. Treasurer for the *assignees of* **R. Day** and of **W. Seres**, 1599–1601 at least (*Reg. B*: 69, 83) with an office in or near Stationers' Hall (A.10). Although William 1 retired to Herefordshire in 1619, he retained a few copyrights, and three apprentices were freed in his name (DFM 1816, 1817, 1820). [*Dict. 1*; *PBSA* 73 (1979): 86–9.]
in Paul's Churchyard, 1593–1613 at least
shop — at the Crane (A.3), 1593 (22700.5)–1595 (19859)
shop — at the Greyhound (B), 1596 (19861.5)–1601 (15639); variation: 1599 (22342, has 'dw.')
dw. — at the $ Holy Ghost (A.5), 1602 (11438)–1613 (17063); variation: 1608 (23996.5, has 'shop')
1560: 25259.5 f. (d/error).
1593: 22700.5 f., 22701.5 f.
1594: 16644.5 f., 22701 f., 22701.3 f., 22702 f., 22702.3 f.
1595: 19165 ent., 19859 f., 19861.3 f., [22747.3 f.] (d?), 24716.5 f.
1596: 19861.5 f., 22358 ent.
1597: 19857 f., 19859a f., 19861.7 f.
1598: 257 f., [19856.7 f.?] (d?), 22747.5 f., 23277.5 ent., 23996 sold.
1599: 22342 sold, 22358 f., 22358a f., 22748 f., 22761 ent.
1600: 18763 f.
1601: 3700.5 f., 6832.65 ent., 15639 f., 18269 f., 18271 f., 26033 ent.
1602: 2995a.3 ent., 6832.65(*A*3, note), 10889.5 ent., 11438 f., 17061 ent., 17077 ent., 18163 f., 19165 f., [22359 f.] (d?), 22360–0b f. (forged), 22761 f., 22765 f., 22952 f., 22961 ent.
1603: 12311 f., 14599 f., 15633.4 ent.
1605: 190 f., 17077 f., 22766 f., 25259.5 f. (d), 25259.7 f.
1606: 17061 f., 17078 f.
1607: 6038 f., 15640 f., 17062 f., 22360 f. (forged, d?).
1608: 19990 f., 22360a (false, d?), 22767 f., 23996.5 sold, 26033 f.
1609: 17079 f., 22953 f., 22961 f. (d?), 25162 f.
1610: 15640.5 f., 15643.5 f., 22360b f. (false, d?), 22768 f., 25164 f.
1611: 17700 f.
1612: 15136 f., 22769 f.
1613: 17063 f., 22769 f.
1614: 5762 ent.
1617: 21034.7 f.
1618: 16879 ent.
1626: 21035.3 f.
1627: 3769 f.

Leake, William 2.
Bookseller in London, (1623) 1631 (*C-B C*: 227)–1673†. Son of **William Leake 1**. [*Dict. 2*; DFM 1820; *PBSA* 73 (1979): 86–9 (abstract of will).]
shop in Chancery Lane (W.10e), 1636 (19598.4)–1640 at least
— near (unto) the Rolls, 1637 (22445)–1640 (12133, has 'joining to'); variations: in 1639 one issue (1685) has: near 'the Six Clerks' Office', the other (1685.5) is as above, and another item (11440) has 'betwixt the Rolls and Serjeants' Inn'
1635: 11440 ent.
1636: 19598.4 f.
1637: 17422 f., 22445 f., 22461 ent.
1638: 3772.4 f.
1639: 1673 f., 1685–5.5 f., 11440 f., 15339 f.
1640: 11441 f., 12133–4 f., 12398 sold, 26102.5 ent., 26103 f.

Le Blanc, Jean.
Printer in Paris, 1556–1579? [Duff, *Century*; Renouard.]
1556–57: 15847 ex typ./typis.

Le Blond, N. *See* Blond.

Le Boullenger (Boulenger), Jean.
Printer in Rouen, 1618?–1680. [*Dict. 1*: 43; Lepreux III/1: 234–6; Blom 63–4.]
1630: 16098.7, [25779.3], 25779.5.

Le Bret, Guillaume, *Widow of.*
Bookseller in Paris, 1550–1554. [Renouard.]
1552: 6832.30 chez.

Le Chandelier, Pierre, *pseud.*
Printer in 'Caen', 1598. = Unidentified continental printer for English recusants. For the genuine man, active in Caen, 1562–1591, *see* Muller 11.
1598: 19785.

Le Comte (Comes), Nicholas.
French bookseller in London, 1494–1498. [Duff, *Century*; Renouard.]
in Paul's Churchyard at the $ St. Nicholas (B), 1494 (11608a.7)
1494: 11608a.7 imp. **1495:** 17964 imp. **1498:** 15888 pro.

Lee (Lea, Leigh), Richard.
Bookseller in London, 1615–1616. [*Dict. 1*; DFM 943.]
shop at (on) the North entry of the Royal Exchange (O.2), 1615 (18254)–1616 (10536)
1615: 12022.7 ent., 18254 f.
1616: 3792 f., 10536 sold, 12023 sold.

Note: There are three Stationers named **William Lee** mentioned in one entry in *Dict. 2*. Their identities, addresses, and publications have been tentatively allocated below.

Lee, William 1.
Stationer in London, (1613) 1626?–1640 at least. Apprenticed to **Edward Venge** and possibly stayed on with Venge's widow from 1606. Called to the Livery on 18 Dec. 1626. This is apparently the Lee who attempted to become a master printer in partnership with **George Wood** c. 1626 (*C-B C*: xvi; cf. *Bevis of Hampton* (1993), which has no address but, in terms of text and appearance, is unlike any book connected with William 2.) When that venture failed, William 1 apparently tried bookselling, but the few occurrences of his name in imprints are in books to which others held the copyright. He was still alive in 1640, since William 2 continues to be called 'Master Lee junior' (*C-B C*: 333, 489); however, because of William 1's relative inactivity in publishing and Stat. Co. affairs, it is likely that most citations in Arber and *Court-Book C* relate to William 2 whether qualified by 'junior' or not. Only two apprentices (DFM 1831–2) can definitely be ascribed to William 1, neither of them formally bound (for the first, G. Wilne, see *C-B C*: 485). [DFM 495.]
at the Crown in Lothbury (H.9), 1628 (22849)–1629 (25060, has 'Hand and Crown')
1626: 1993 f. (d?). **1628:** 13413a.7 sold, 22849 sold. **1629:** 25060 sold.

Lee, William 2.
Bookseller in London, 1620–1671 at least. Apprenticed to **Thomas Downes 1**; a few of his early publications were news pamphlets published jointly with **Bartholomew Downes**. Was a successful publisher of a variety of texts. Two authors, Horace (13800 sqq.) and John Reynolds (20942 sqq.), provide the connection between his two shops in Fleet Street. Called to the Livery on 4 June 1629. Most of the references in Arber and *Court-Book C* are probably to William 2 whether they are qualified by 'junior' or not. At least two apprentices (DFM 1827, son of Bartholomew Downes, and 1828, from William 2's home town) listed under William 'senior' probably belong to William 2 in addition to those under William 'junior' (DFM 2833–6). [DFM 1208; Globe 217 (Wm. II).]
in Fleet Street (W.7), 1620–1671 at least
shop — at the Golden Buck near Serjeants' Inn, 1620 (21098.5)–1625 (13800)
at the Great Turk's Head next to the Mitre Tavern —, 1626 (1168, engr. tp)–1640 (6879); he was apparently still there in 1671 (Gibson, *Bacon*, no. 229); variation: omits 'Great' and has 'next to the Mitre and Phoenix', 1627 (7190)
1620: 21098.5 sold.
1621: 208 f., 18507.35a f., —.35c ent., 18890 f., 19843.5 f., 20942 f.,

Lee, William 2 — *cont.*
21098.7 f., 23270 f.
1622: 7367 f., 18507.35B f., 20186.7 f., 20943.3 f.
1623: 20943.5 f., 21862 f., 24962.5 ent.
1624: 20943.7 f.
1625: 13800 f. (d).
1626: 1168 f.
1627: 1168 f., 1169 f., 7190 f.
1628: 1170 f., 21757a f., 23696 f.
1629: 1170 f., 3219 f., 20943 f.
1631: 1171 f., 7191 f., 13801 f. (d).
1633: 25685a.3 sold.
1634: 20944 f.
1635: 1172 f., 13802 f., 20944 f.
1636: 13802 f.
1638: 1158 f., 6048 f., 13803 f.
1639: 1173 f., 6049 f., 20945 f., 20946 f.
1640: 6879 f., 12145 f., 20946 f.

Lee (Ley), William 3.
Bookseller in London, (1637) 1638–1657. Apprenticed to **George Latham**. Can usually be distinguished from other William Lees by his preference for the spelling 'Ley' (but note the exceptions 'Lee' in 1639 (14552.3, but 'Ley' in Arber IV.450) and 1641 (Greg no. 602)). [DFM 1795; Globe 217 (Wm. I).]
shop in Paul's Churchyard near Paul's Chain (A.9), 1639 (23766)–1640 (23746, omits 'in ... Churchyard'); still in that vicinity in 1656 (Greg no. 761)
1639: 14552.3 f., 23766 f. **1640:** 13798 f., 23746 f.

Leeu, Geraaert.
Printer in Gouda, 1477–1484, and in Antwerp, 1484–1493†. [Duff, *Century*; Rouzet.]
1486: 23907. **1488:** 17721. **1492:** 15384, [15873] (d?), 19207, 22905 (d). **1493:** 9994.

Legat (Legate, Legatt), John 1.
Printer in London, (1586), in Cambridge, 1588–1610, and again in London, 1611–1620†. Married the stepdaughter of **Thomas Thomas**. Father of **John Legat 2**, who may actually have printed some of the items below dated 1620. One of the **Printers to the University of Cambridge** (*see* Cambridge University), 1588–1620. [*Dict. 1*; *TCBS* 3 (1959): 96–103.]
Cambridge, no address used; for the location of the press *see* Cambridge University
London, his house in Trinity Lane (S.5), 1612 (19664, 19650 vol. 1); no later address or use of this one noted
1061: [19713] (d/error).
1589: 89 ex off. (d?), 1564, 2020 (d?), 5291 ex off., 23887 ex off., 24008.5 ex off., [25365.3] (d?), [25365.5] (d?).
1590: 2477.5, 2889 (d?), 12338, 13590, 19655 ex off., 24695a.5 ex off. (c), 25365, 25675 ex off.
1591: 1565 (d?), 2155, 19655a ex off. (d?), 19658 (d?).
1592: 15244.3 ex off., 15516, 15702 ex off., 19656–6.5 ex off., 19661.5, 19735 ex off., 19735.2 ex off., 22891, 23659.3 ex off., 24009 ex off., 25695 ex off. (d?), 26119.5.
1593: 1830, [5898], [11055] (d), 17121, 18074, 19688, 19758, 21684, 24009.5 ex off.
1594: 6227, 6443, 12208–8.2 ex off., 12938 ex off., 18074.5, 24010 ex off., 25363.
1595: 1566, 5883–4, 6575.7 (d?), 17003, 19662 [f.], 19667 [f.], 19702a f., 19703, 19711 f., 19742(*A*), 19754 f., 19754.3 f., 19760, 19760.5, 20058, 20599 ex off., 22891.5 f.
1596: 2990, 11492 [f.], 19685, 19696, 19704, 19742.5, 22913 ex off., 22913a, 24011 ex off.
1597: 80 ex off., 19083 ex off., 19663 [f.], 19705, 19735.8, 19743, 19761 [f.].
1598: 3087, 3088, 5117, 10235, 11062a.5, 14364 ent., 19682, 19736(*A*), 19749 ex off., 23316, 23890 ex off., 25621.
1599: 6883, 20086, 25368 ex off., 26120.
1600: [10314.1] (d), 19646, 19689.5(*A*), 19743.3(*A*), 19754.7 f., 19761.1, 21781, 24012 ex off., 25367, 25370 ex off.
1601: 7446, 10235.5, 13479, [19713] (d), 19728, 19757, 19757.5, 19763.5, 19764.
1602: 1955.5, 4877.4, 5301 ex off., 6881 ex off., [10314.2], 19105.5, 19647, 19750, 25673.

Legat, John 1 — *cont.*
1603: 4493 ex off., 6889, 6892 ex off., 7598, 13266, 14357, 19647, 19690, 19724.7, 19728.5, 19743.5, 19751.5, 20010, 20025, 22371 ex off., 22376, 22874, 25676.
1604: 3438, 10236, 11817, 17257, 18809 ex off., 19668, 19680, 19699, [19713.5], 19734 ex off., 19737, 25704.
1605: 1831, 5899 ex off., 6885, 6891 ex off., 7737 ex off., 10314.3, 15363.3, 19106 (c), 19648, 20027, 25682.
1606: 6882 ex off., 6888, 10683 f., 13429, 19669, 24013 ex off.
1607: 1936, 5900, 10236.5, 13398, 13426, 15703.5 ex off., 19681, 19683 ent., 19735.4 ent., 19751, 21228, 23891 ex off.
1608: 13422, 19649, 19670, 19715.
1609: 1937 f., 1952.5, 12696 f., 19649.
1610: 24014 ex off.
1611: 6242–3, 6642, 19106.5, 19671, 19686.5, 19691, 19705.4, 19725, 19729, 19738, 19745, 19761.3, 20011.
1611/12: [461.7].
1612: 1953, 17615, 18987 ex off., 19650, 19664.
1613: 13378, 19107, 19650.
1614: 1567, 4522, 13378, 19671.5, 23892 ex off., 25677.
1615: [6257], 8533.7, [14805(*A*3)], 19107.5 ent., 19687, 19692, 19715a, 19726, 19730, 19746, 19761.5, [20987], [20987.5], 21869, 24015 ex off., 24771.3, 25753 per.
1616: 666, 667 per, 4083, 6630.7(*A*), 7468, 10329, [19146], 19651, 19705.7, 19715a.5, [20988], [20991.7], 21342, 21869, 25754.
1617: [3418], 6631, 17704, 19651, 19681, 19716, 20012, [25865].
1618: [15241], 19717.
1619: 10926, 13379, 19672, 19739, 19756, 19761.7, 24016 ex off.
1620: 13379, [14811–1a], 24017 ex off.

Legat, John 2.
Printer in London, (1619) 1620–1658†. Son of John Legat 1 and may have printed some of the items listed there under 1620. Son-in-law of **Robert Barker** and acted as the latter's deputy as **King's Printer** in Newcastle upon Tyne, 1639. Although John 2 was appointed Printer to the University of Cambridge in 1650, he does not appear to have been active in that place. [*Dict. 1*; *Dict. 2*; DFM 334; *Library* 11 (1989): 1–9.]
dw. in Little Wood Street (H.7), 1621 (19664.5), 1623 (11063); still there at the time of his death.
1616: 21871–1a (d/error).
1621: 1937 ent., 4084, [5974], 13227, 13379 ent., 13398 ent., 13422 ent., 13426 ent., 13429 ent., 17196, 19652 ent., 19653 ent., 19664.5, 19673 ent., 19687.5, 19693, 19696 ent., 19706 ent., 19717.5 ent., 19726.5, 19730.3, 19740 ent., 19746.3, 19750 ent., 19751.5 ent., 19756 ent., 19761.9, 20012 ent., 21229, 23893 ent.
1622: [1003–3.5], [3419], 5978 ex off., 10209.7(*A*), 14090, 17226, 17986, 17987, [19502], 21325.5–26, [21871], [21871a].
1623: 4890.3, 6113.5, 6115, 6163.5, 6579, 11063, 11128.3, [13773?], 16686, 19107.5, 19652, 21842, 21873.5, [25909.5?], 26086.
1624: 5836.5–37, 6115.5, 6594–4.5, 11657, 11983, 13381, 16828.5, 20672, 22150, 24052.
1625: 57, 4112, 4232, 5838, 6116, 10202, 13318, 13555.3, 18359–9.5, 19687.7, 19693.5, 19726.7, [19730.5] (d), 19746.7, 19762.5, 21230–0a, 21872, 22150a, 24594, 25769.
1626: 15481.4 (c), 19652, 20791.
1627: 1414, 19108, 19108.5, 19108.7, 19717.5, [20788].
1628: [183], [1631], 3442 (note), 4221 ent., 5911, [10263], 10837 typis, [18916], 19109, 19673.
1629: 1954–4.5, 18630.7, 19718, 21231, 23893.
1630: [1609?], 4222, 4222.5, 10192.3 (d?), 19109.2 (c).
1631: [1609.4?], [1609.6?], 18832 typis, 19116.5, 19652.5, 19653–3.5, 19706, 24017.5 ex off., 24554a.
1632: 554, [1610?], [1610.3?], 14812–2a, 17150, 19109.3, 19674, 19694, 19718.5, 19747, 19763, [23524], 23524a, 26068.
1633: [1610.5?], [1611?], 2640, 4223, 6057, 10886, 14444, 14892, 18631.5, 19117, 19719, 20003.5–04, 21232, 23525, 23525.1.
1633/34: 407.17.
1634: 1238, 1241, 2651a, 3253, 6443.5, 6595, 10720, 10723, 13383.5–84, 19109.4 (d?), [19504], [19509], 19740, 20783.5, 22628, [23523.5], 24821, 24826 per, 24826.5 per, 25700a (note).
1634/35: 407.18.
1635: 972, 1323, 19654, 19675, 19719.7(*A*3).
1635/36: 407.19.
1636: 2663, 2666.2, 3136, 3136.3–.7, 3233, 4224, 11706.6, 19676, 19720.
1636/37: 407.20.

Legat, John 2 — *cont.*
1637: 60.5, 973, 1238 ent., [1618a?], 3137, 3233a, 4510–0.8, 4789 typis, 5851 ent., 10427 ent., 11688 ent., 11706.6, 12552 ent., 13728, 13737 ent., 14753.5 ent., 17642 ent., 18919 ent., 20250, 21707 ent., 21725, 21730 ent., 21846 ent., 22274e.3 ent., 22801 ent., 22808 ent., 23245, 23684 ent., 25129, 26068 ent.
1637/38: 407.21.
1638: 1177.5, 1178, 1178.5, 3138, 3234, 3254, 4753, 6233 typis, 7445, 13729, 19687a (c), 19694.5 (c), 19721, 19727 (c), 19730.7 (c), 19747.3 (c), 19763.3 (c), 21725, 23936, 24827 typis.
1638/39: 407.22.
1639: 1505, 2689, 6233 typis, 9143(*A*3, note), 9335.5(*A*3, note), 18196a.5 (note), 19998, 21233, (22003(*A*3, note), 25029 typis, [25963?].
1639/40: 407.23, 409.
1640: 1179, 1622, 1623, 2696.5, 2698, 2699, 4225, 10706 typis, 11882, 12397–8, 12898, 14813–3a, 18986, 19109.4D(*A*3) (c), 22918, 22936, 23551, 23648, 25024 (note), 25971–1a, 25972.
1640/41: Wing A 1298.

Legge (Legg), Cantrell.
Printer in Cambridge, (1599) 1607–1625?†. A member of the Stat. Co., London. One of the **Printers to the University of Cambridge** (*see* Cambridge University), 1606–1625. [*Dict. 1*; Greg, *Companion*: 178–92.]
No address used; for the location of the press *see* Cambridge University.
1607: 25678–8a, 25693.
1608: 3441, 3441.5, 10314.5, [10533.3?] (d?), 14950, 19697, 19722, 24971.
1609: 13427, 19649, 20026.
1610: 668, 10195, 11058–9, 18983, 18983.5, 19698, 20005, 25689–9.3, [25698.7].
1611: 10289.9, 19723, 25689.7–90.
1612: 4474.33 typis, 4481–2 ex off., 5563, 18473 ex off., 20005a, 20174, 23825–5a, 23830–0.5.
1613: 6786, 10196, 13378 (note), 14950.5, 19650, 21069, 25434 f.
1614: 14951, 14954.6(*A*3), 18209, 25679–9.5, 25680.
1615: 1314.2, 4692a, 13877, [14417], [14419a], 17800, 26081.
1616: 5180, 10688, 12100, 14369, [14420.7], 14484, 14952, 26082–2.5.
1617: 1314.3(*A*), 5561, 13394a, 14954.7.
1618: 4693, 14953, 14955, 19651, 23822–2a.5.
1619: 635 (false), 636 ex off. (false), 4489 ex off., [7686.2], [7686.4], [7686.6], 10292, 12527, 13379 (note), 14370, 14371, 23595, 23823.5, 23826.
1620: 25691–1.5.
1621: 15627.2, 15627.3, 20006.
1622: 4484.5, 4485.5 per, 18982 ex off., 19052.2, 19052.6, 23830 ent., 25679 ent., 25680 ent., 25689 ent., 25689.7 ent.
1623: 2584, 2584.5, 4487–8 ex off., [5973], 13181 ex off.
1624: 5129, 13381 (note).
1624/25: 405.
1625: 4477–8, 4484.

1629: 13394a ass'd, 14954 ass'd, 14956 ass'd, 19698 ass'd, 20003.5 ass'd, 23824 ass'd.
1634: 13383.5 ass'd.

Lekpreuik, Robert.
Printer and bookbinder in Edinburgh, 1561–1571, in Stirling, 1571, in St. Andrews, 1572–1573, and again in Edinburgh, 1573–1582? Appointed **King's Printer in Scotland** in 1568. [*Dict. 1.*]
Edinburgh, his house at the Nether Bow, 1563 (12968), 1581 (11213)
No address used in Stirling or St. Andrews.
1561: 2026, 18688, 22018.
1562: 2000, 16564.
1563: 6320, 10819, 12968, 15074.
1564: 145, 16577.
1565: 4604, 5970, 11684, 16577a, 19458, 21879.
1566: 21875–6a, 22041, 24623a.
1567: 16604, 21930 (d), 21931, 21932, 22192, [22194] (d), 22196, 22197, 22199.
1568: 21880, 21933 (d), 21934, 22626.5.
1569: 185, [13870.3] (d?), 15074.2, [15315] (d?).

Lekpreuik, R. — *cont.*
1570: 185, 13149, 14915 (d?), [15315.5] (d?), 16579, 21935, 21936, 21937, [22046] (d), 22187, [22187a], 22187a.5, [22189] (d), 22191, 22192a.3, 22192a.5, 22193, 22195, [22200(*A*3)] (d), 22201, [22201.5] (d), 22204, 22205–6, [22208], 22209, 22211.
1571: *Edinburgh*: [1377.5] (d?), 12968.5; *Stirling*: [3966.5] (d), 3967 according to Lekpreuik's copy, 3968 (false), 3968.5, 15076, 22188, 22194.5.
1572: 3982, 5487, 6909.5, 10820, 15062, 21940, 22011, 22028, 22200.5, 22202, 22203, 22204.5.
1573: *St. Andrews*: 6321, 20105, 21882; *Edinburgh*: [147?] (d), 7485, 8055, 22207.
1574: [6323] (d), 22043.
1580/81: 22019, 22019.5 (repeat).
1581: 144, 11213, 22190 (d).
1582: [21886?]

Le Mareschal (Marescalus, Marshall), Henri.
Bookseller in Rouen, 1539? 1566? 1578–1605. It is not clear whether the first two items indexed below belong under the later Le Mareschal or under one or more different Henris. The date in the first, a Sarum Primer, was supplied by Hoskins and may be erroneous; in the second, a reissue of a Geneva-printed Form of Prayers and Psalms, Rouen has been supplied in default of finding an H. le Mareschal elsewhere. [Duff, *Century* 99; Muller 101.]
Rothomagi, commorans in via magna Horologii, 1539? (16012)
1539: 16012 ven. (d?). **1566:** 16578 pour. **1580:** 14564 ap., 24626.3 ap.

Le Moyne de Morgues (Le Moine, Morgan), Jacques.
French artist in London, 1582–1588†. Lived in St. Anne's parish, Blackfriars (Q.5). [*Dict. 1*; Thieme-Becker.]
No address used.
1586: 15459 pour (d).

Lempereur. *See* Keyser.

Le Noir, Phillipe.
Printer in Paris, 1522–1544. [Renouard.]
1525: [23894(*A*3)?] (c?).

Le Prest (Prest), Jean.
Printer in Rouen, 1542–1561. [Duff, *Century*; Muller 101.]
1554: 16058. **1555:** 2978.5, 16068, [16070?], [16072].

Le Preux, Esaïe.
Printer in Geneva, 1613 at least.
1613: [12619], [17045].

Le Preux, Jean.
Printer and bookseller in Paris 1561–1563, in Geneva 1563–1571, in Lausanne 1571–1579, in Morges 1580–1585, and again in Geneva, 1585–1609†. [Renouard; Bremme 195–7.]
1584: [4904.5?] (false).

Le Roux (Rowse), Jean.
French printer? in London, before 1536–1549. Lived in Shoe Lane (W.6). [Duff, *Century*.]
No address used.
1543: 14106.2.

Le Roux (Rufus), Nicolas.
Printer in Rouen, 1530–1557. In the first item below either the date, derived from the first year in the almanack, is wrong, or the item was printed by a predecessor of Le Roux. [Duff, *Century*; Muller 101.]
1528: [15958] (d).
1530: [16161?] (d?), [16223?], [16251?].
1534: 15985a per (d?).
1536: [15992.5] (c), [15993?], 16106 per, [21789.6?].
1537: 15994 per, [15995?].
1538: [2965], [2965.2], [2965.4], 16001 per, 16002.5 per, 16004, [16006], [16007], [16008.3–.5], 21790.5 (d), [21791].
1543: 16150 typis.
1550: [2081].
1551: 16055 per.

Le Tailleur, Guillaume.
Printer in Rouen, 1487–1491? [Duff, *Century*; BMC VIII.lxxxi, 389–92.]
1490: 15721 per (d), [23238] (d).

Le Tellier, Pasquier.
Printer in Paris, 1543–1553. [Renouard.]
1546: 6832.11. **1548:** 6832.15.

Lettou, John.
Printer in London, 1480–1483? In partnership with **William de Machlinia** from 1481? [Duff, *Century*; *Library* 18 (1937): 21–2, 335–7.]
next to the church of All Saints (All Hallows (?N.10)), 1482 (15719)
1480: 581 per, [14077c.108] (d), [—.109] (d).
1481: [9513] (d?), [14077c.111(*A*3)] (d), 19627 per.
1482: [4594?] (c?), [9742] (d?), [9749] (d?), [13922] (d?), 15719 per (d).
1483: [9731] (d?).

Lever, Richard, and Elmhurst, William.
Clerks of the Customs House in London, 1604–1608 at least, and charged with overseeing the Book of Rates, the printing of which they assigned to G. Eld. [*C-B C*: 33–4.]
sold by them at the Customs House in London (U.1), 1604 (7690.5)
1604: 7690.5 ass'n.

Levet, Pierre.
Printer in Paris, 1485–1503. [Duff, *Century*; Renouard.]
1494: 15799 per. **1497:** 16169 imp.

Le Villain, Claude.
Bookseller in Rouen, 1599–1625 at least. [Muller 101.]
1611: 6832.58. **1625:** 6832.60.

Lewes, William.
Stationer in London, 1559–1566. [*Dict. 1*.]
dw. in Cow Lane above Holborn conduit over against the $ Plough (C.4), 1566 (17803)
1566: 17803 f. (d).

Ley. *See* Lee.

Libius, Joannes, *pseud.*
Printer in 'Augusta', 1618. = J. Bill.
1618: 25601 ap.

Lichfield, John.
Printer in Oxford, 1617–1635, and one of the **Printers to the University** (*see* Oxford University), during that time. Father of **Leonard Lichfield**. In partnership with **James Short**, 1618–24, and with **William Turner** 1624–27 and occasionally thereafter. [*Dict. 1*.]
No address used.
1617: 638, 639, 12628, 14314, 17152, 19023, 23912.
1618: 640, 641 (forged), [642] (d), 4199, 10710.5, 19169, 21702, 22828.
1619: 1781, 1938, 2362.7, 5976, 10308, 11031, 17245, 19024, 20777.
1620: 37.3(*A*3), 6424, 7338, 11958–8.5, 11979–9.5, 14450, 20619 (note), 24406.
1621: 3806, 4159, 6586, 13276, 21782, 24038.
1622: 33, 4678, 5432, 11568, [13880(*A*3)] (d), [14037.5] (d), 14573, 19014, 19025.
1623: [643.5?] (d?), 5832, 11295, 11959, 19027.
1624: 716 (d/error), 4160, 10372.5, 11031.5, 11296–7, 12973, 19028, 19029, 20358.5, 20685.
1625: 1792, 4201, 4676, 7751.6 (false), 8789, 8790 (repeat), 8792, 8793 (repeat), [8794] (d), 8796, 8796.3 (repeat), 8798, 8798.3 (repeat), 8800, 8800.3 (repeat), 8800.7, 8801 (repeat), 8801.7, 8802 (repeat), 8804, 8804.3 (repeat), 8804.7, 8805 (repeat), 10372.6, 11509, 13277, 14437, 14454, 14972, 14992, 15494, 18474, 19030, 19031, 19589, 20356, 20359, 20361, 20774, 23754, 23755 (forged), 23914, 24991, 25326.
1626: 1474, 1600, 4531, 4531.5, 10140.5, 12615, 20347, 20357, 20358, 20911, 23915, 24988.
1627: 10754, 12611, 13278, [19016.9] (d), 19445, [21020], 21036, 24941, 24986.

Lichfield, J. — *cont.*
1628: 4161, [4736?], 6822, 7072, 10309, [11961], 12514, 19576a, [21435.7–36], 23026–7, 23947.5, 24989, 25376.
1629: 1071, 1791.7, 4109, 4757.5, 4800, 10214, 10310, 19008, [19009] (d), 19574, 19577, 19590, 20363, 20618, 23027, 24294, 26131a.
1630: 1025, 1601, 2365, 3622, 4373 typis, 4737, 7228 (note), [12998?], 19032, 19571, 19942, 20157.5, [25593] (d?), [25594].
1631: 92.3–.7 typis, [93], 3623, 4106, 10141, 10210, 11566, 11809.5 (d), 11962, 19032.5, 19096–6a, 19194–4.7, 20382 ap., 21703, [24884], [25593], [25595].
1632: 3624, 4162, 6435, 10311, 18966, 19587, 22231.
1633: 1166, 5398, 6153 ap., 6273.3 (note), 7152, 10597, 11514, 11770 ap., 11963, 12344, 14439, 18087, 19033, 19034–4a, 19035–5a.5, 19345, 19575 ap., 21675, 24158, 24473, 24473.3 (forged).
1634: 716, 1391, 1397, 3912–2.5, 5825, 10935, 17596, 19004, 19005, 19943, 22652, 26128.
1635: 717, 4677, 5097–7.3, 7153–3.3, 10142, 10312, 10724, 14448, 14451, 15328.

Lichfield, Leonard.
Printer in Oxford, 1635–1657† and one of the **Printers to the University** (*see* Oxford University) during that time. When his printing house burned down in 1644, it was in Butcher Row (modern Queen Street). Son of **John Lichfield**. [*Dict. 2*.]
No address used.
1634: 17829a (d/error).
1635: 7110–1, 15410, 18033, 19016.17 (d), [23508], 24942.
1636: 4187.5–88, 4679, 5026, 7112, 10038, 10595, 10936, 17953, 19036, 19351, 19944, 20344.7(*A*3), 20345, 24942.5, 26132.
1637: 4119, 4680, 10937, 14268, 14307, 19037 (d), 20345, 21350, 23271, 23916.5, 23917–7.5, 25328–8.5, 26017–7a.
1638: [4163], 4876, 5138–8.2, 10142.5, 10313, 10373 (d?), 11569, 11570, 11964, 14317, 17657, 19038, 19042, 20694, 23724, 24571.
1639: 1167, 3085–5.5, 4877, 7295, 11250–1, 11567, 12209–9.5, 12399–9.3, 12455, 13972, 16448, 17750, 20364, 20588.5, 23993, 24159, 25261.
1640: 1167–7.5, [3905.5] (c), 4672, 4675, 10013, 10636, 10829, 11065, 11073, [17469.2] (d), 19039–9.5, 20695, 21179, 21704, 22888, 24161.5, 24404, 24473.7, 26129.
1643: 17829a (d) = Wing M 1761.

Lightfoot, Benjamin.
Bookseller in London, (1612) 1613–1614. [*Dict. 1*; DFM 652.]
shop at the upper end of Gray's Inn Lane in Holborn (V.10), 1613 (13365)–1614 (1065, has 'the Corner Shop')
1613: 1064.5 f., 13365 sold, 13930 sold.
1614: 1065 f., 22842 sold.

Lilius. *See* Giglio.

Lin. *See* Lynne.

Ling (Lyng), Nicholas.
Bookseller in London, (1579) 1580–1585, in Norwich, 1585–1590? (*SB*: 206), and again in London, 1590–1607†. Often published jointly with others, especially with **John Busby 1**, 1590–1594. [*Dict. 1*; *St. Giles*, 1598; *SB* 38 (1985): 203–14.]
in Paul's Churchyard (A.10), 1580–1584, 1590–1601; it is not clear whether the variations below refer to more than one shop or house.
at the West door of Paul's Church, 1580 (5259), 1584 (4402), 1591 (16657), 1595 (18375, has 'shop' and 'Northwest' door), 1598 (12504, has 'little' West door), 1600 (17868, has 'shop')
at the West end of Paul's Church, 1590 (12253, with J. Busby 1), 1596 (22973, has 'shop'), 1599 (18370)
dw. — at the Mermaid, 1582 (18272)
dw. — [no sign], 1590 (18273)
shop —, 1600 (7196, no sign in HD; F variant has 'at the Crane' (A.3)), 1601 (22736)
in Fleet Street (W.9), 1602–1607
shop — near (under) St. Dunstan's Church, 1602 (7197)–1604 (22276)
shop in St. Dunstan's Churchyard —, 1606 (10457)–1607 (23669)
1580: 5259.
1582: 18272 f.

Ling, N. — *cont.*
1584: 4402 f., 11503 f., 11503.3 f., 24489 f., 24501 f., 24503 f.
1585: 10208 f., 10268 f. (d).
1590: 12253 f., 16664 ent., 18273 f., 23633a f. (d).
1591: 16657 f., 22656–6.5 f., 22657 f., 22664 f.
1592: 16656 ent.
1594: 7203 f., 7205–6 f., 7214 f. (d?), 11622 f., 17412 ent., 26124 f.
1595: 10418 f., 11622a f., 18375 f., 22971 sold [his] shop.
1596: 4032 f., 6360 f., 7232 f., 16666 f., 22972 (d/repeat), 22973 sold [his] shop.
1597: 3651 ent., 3713 f., 7193 f., 11573 sold, 15685 f.
1598: 6785 ent., 7193.2 f., 7194 f., 12504 f., 15685.5 f., 15686 f., 15686.3 f., 16667 f.
1599: 381–2 f., 7195 f., 11579 f., 12253.7(*A3*) f., 12273 f., 17994 f., 18370 f., 22735 f.
1600: 378–80 f., 1891.5 f., 3702 f., 7196 f., 12254 f., 14769 f., 14923 f., 17868 f., 22972 sold [his] shop (d?).
1601: 12226 f., 22736 f., 25220 f.
1602: 3088.5 f., 7197 f., 12254.5 f., 26026 f.
1603: [6535] sold, [6535.3] sold (d?), [6535.5] sold (d?), 7189 f., 16676 f., 19735.6 f., 22275 f., 25221 f.
1604: 7211 f., 7211.5 f., 7212 f., 7213 f., 15686.5(*A3*) f., 16668 f., 19546.5 sold, 22276 f., 22737 f.
1605: 7216 f., 12227 f., 12273.5 f., 22276a f.
1606: 4165a.5 f., 7225.5 f. (d?), 10457–8 f., 11576 f., 22881.5 f., 25222 f.
1607: 6785 f., 12228 ass'd, 12255 f., 12255.5 ass'd, 12274 ass'd, 12373 f., 19735.6 ass'd, 22277 ass'd, 22294 ent., 22324 ass'd, 22738 f., 22862 ass'd, 23669 f.

Linley, Paul.
Bookseller in London, (1586) 1595–1600†. Shared a shop and most imprints with **John Flasket**. [*Dict. 1*; *Loan Book* (as Lynlay), 1597.]
their shop in Paul's Churchyard at the (Black) Bear (B), 1595 (18428, with J. Flasket)–1599 (10204, has 'dw.')
1595: 18428 f.
1596: 3421 ent., 5457 ent., 23620 f., 23895 ent., 24817 ent.
1597: 6677 f., [6733.3 f.] (d), [17678] sold, [22993] sold, 23621 f.
1598: 16918 f., 17414 f., 18468 f. (d).
1599: 10204 f. (d).
1600: 5457 ass'd, 16883.5 ass'd.

Lion (Lyon), John.
Journeyman printer in London, (1564) 1569–1576, and bookseller in Louvain, 1579 at least; apparently in Douai, 1580–1601. Apprenticed to J. Cawood in 1556 and freed by him in 1564 (Arber I.42, 278). Contributed in December 1569 to the Stat. Co. assessment to provide and arm eight soldiers for the Queen (*Liber A*, fol. 14^{v}). Surreptitious printer in 1576 with **William Carter**, another Cawood apprentice (*Library*). Beginning in 1580 his name was forged in several books by the **'Greenstreet House' Press**. [*Dict. 1*: 182; Rouzet; Southern 344–6; *Library* 6 (1951): 49–50.]
1576: [17136] (false).
1579: 13376 f.
1580: 3802 (false), 13377 (false), 19394 (false).
1581: 19393 (false).

Lipsius, Rufus, *pseud.*
Printer in 'Albionopolis', 1616. = A. Islip.
1616: 25605 ap.

Lisle (L'isle, Lyle), Laurence.
Bookseller in London, (1607) 1608–1626. Married the widow of **Matthew Cooke** and succeeded to the latter's shop. In 1619 Lisle's former apprentice, **Henry Seile**, took over effective management of the shop. [*Dict. 1*; DFM 1341; *Loan Book* (as Lysle), 1610–13; Globe 217.]
at the Tiger's Head in Paul's Churchyard (A.2), 1608 (5757)–1618 (18912, has 'shop'); variation: 1614 (24394, has 'dw.')
1608: [4968] sold, 5757 f., 6519 ent., [14761] sold (d), [25262] sold (d).
1609: 12644 f., 12644.5 f., 12670 f., 12682 f.
1610: [13136] sold.
1614: 3830–0.3 f., 4539 f., 4964 f., 4977 f., [11370] sold, 12706–6a f., 12991 ?ent., 14008 f., 18903.5 f., 18904 f., 18905 f., 18906 f., 18907 f., 24394–4a f.

Lisle, L. — *cont.*
1615: 12706a f., 18908 f.
1616: 161–1.5 f. (d), 162 ent., 10688.5 f., 12683 ass'd, 12707 ass'd, 18903 ent., 18909 f., 18910 f., 18911 f., 18921.3 ent., 24393 f.
1617: 24435 f., 25962 f.
1618: 6515 f., 6515.5 f., 18912 f.
1622: 18913 f.

Lisle, William.
Anglo-Saxon scholar, translator, and poet, b. 1569?–1637†. [*DNB.*]
No address used.
1631: 13047–7.5 at charges of.

Lithgow, William.
Scottish traveller, author, and poet, b. 1582–1645?†. [*DNB.*]
No address used.
1618: 15715 at expenses of. **1640:** 15709 at expenses of.

Lobley (Loblee), Michael.
Bookseller in London, before 1531–1567†. Probably related to **William Lobley**. [Duff, *Century*.]
in Paul's Churchyard, 1539–1563
— at the $ St. Michael (B), 1539 (16010)–1558 (21796, has 'dw.')
dw. — [no sign] (B), 1560 (5225)
— at the Corner Shop on the right hand as you come out of Cheap[side] (A.5), 1563 (11408)
1539: 2966.7 sold (d), 16010 sold, 16011 sold (d?).
1558: 11211.2 ent., 21796 f. (d).
1560: 5225 f., 19137 at costs.
1563: 11408 f. (d), 20189 f.

Lobley (Loble), William.
Bookbinder in London, (1557) 1562–1583. Probably related to **Michael Lobley**. [*Dict. 1.*]
No address used on the tp, but the item is imperfect at the end.
1562: 12732 ent., 25825.7 ent. **1566:** 18307.5 f. (d?).

Lodge, Thomas.
Author, b. 1558?–1625†. [*DNB.*]
1589: 16674 ent.

Loe, Hendrik van der.
Bookseller and printer in Antwerp, 1566–1581. [*Dict. 1*; Rouzet.]
1578: 6984.

Loftus (Loftis), George.
Bookseller in London, 1601–1615. Not a member of the Stat. Co. [*Dict. 1.*]
in Pope's Head Alley (O.11), 1601 (13048.5, has 'shop')–1605
at the Golden Ball —, 1602 (21409)–1604 (584)
— near the [Royal] Exchange, 1605 (21385)
under St. Peter's Church in Cornhill (P.2), 1609 (19936, with J. Busby 1)
shop under St. Sepulchre's Church (D.8), 1612 (21390)
in Bishopsgate Street near the Angel (J.2), 1615 (21401)
1601: 13048.5 f.
1602: 21409 sold.
1603: 21364 f.
1604: 584 sold, 21398 f., 21399 sold.
1605: 21385 sold.
1609: 19936 f.
1612: 21390 sold.
1614: 21381 f.
1615: 21401 sold, 21401.5 f.

Long, John.
Bookseller in Dorchester, 1634. [*Dict. 1.*]
No address used.
1634: 3129.5 sold.

Lopes, Simão.
Bookseller and printer in Lisbon, 1583–1598 at least.
1597: [19087.5?] (d?).

Lorraine, Jean de.
Printer in Rouen, 1500–1501. [Duff, *Century*; Muller 102.]
1500: 16139.

Loven, Hermes van, *pseud.*
Printer in 'Schotland buyten Danswijck' [Scotland, outside of Danzig?], 1609–1610. = Unidentified Dutch printer.
1609: 17845.3(*A*3). **1610:** 17845.7(*A*3).

Lowe, George.
Merchant Taylor, printer and seller of engraved items in London, 1613?–c. 1615? [*Dict. 1*; Globe 217.]
in Lothbury (H.9), 1613? (4251.5)–c. 1615 (4252, adds 'his house')
1613: 4251.5 sold (d?). **1614:** 22788 (note). **1615:** 4252 (c).

Lowndes (Lownds), Richard.
Bookseller in London, (1639) 1640–1675. [*Dict. 2*; DFM 2325; *Loan Book*, 1647–50.]
shop near adjoining without Ludgate (Q.4), 1640 (601, 23126)
1640: 601 f., 2814 ven., 23126 sold.

Lownes, Humphrey 1.
Bookseller and printer (from 1604) in London, (1587) 1590–1630†. Brother of **Matthew** and father of **Humphrey Lownes 2**; probably related to **William Lownes**. His first wife was a daughter of **Thomas Man 1**; he remarried **Emma Short** and succeeded to her printing house. His former apprentice **Robert Young** started printing in Lownes's shop in 1624 and became a partner toward the end of 1627, though many imprints continue to have either Lownes's or Young's name alone and in others one or the other name or both have been supplied in square brackets on no firm principle. Lownes was called to the Livery on 1 July 1598 (Arber II.873); in 17th century Stat. Co. records he is usually called 'Mr. Lownes' or 'Mr. Lownes senior'. [*Dict. 1*; *Loan Book* (payment for John Ashton), 1618.]
at the West door of Paul's (A.10), 1590 (13114)–1605 (19446); sometimes has 'shop', 1592 (14686)
dw. on Bread Street Hill at the Star (S.8), 1604 (13980, colophon)–1629 (19300, colophon, with R. Young, omits 'dw.')
1590: 13114 sold.
1592: 14685.7–86 f., 23398 f.
1595: 1483 f., 1484 f., 3314 f.
1596: 7208 f. (d).
1597: 6559 ent., 16857 f.
1598: 14960 f., 21348 f., 25106–6a f.
1599: 15342 ent., 15342.5 f., 19766.5 f., 19818 f.
1600: 13342 f., [22855.5] (d/repeat).
1602: 7102 f., 7189 ass'd, 12984.5 f., [22360a] (d/repeat).
1603: 7231 f., 7231.3 f.
1604: 945.3, 1088–8.5, 1768, 5882, [6510], [6513], 6872, 7209, 12169, 13004, 13767.5, 13980, 14979 ent., 16768.2 ent., 16777.10 ent., 16779.2 ent., 19807.7, 21216, 24537 ent.
1605: [1113–4], [2516(*A*3)], 3701, 6968.5, 12582.15, 12679–9.5, [12685] (d?), 13343, 17684–4.5, 19446, 19979.5, 21216a, [21417], 21649–9a, [22543–3a], [23982].
1606: 6954.5, 6969, 7093, 10357, [10683], 10857, 11087, 12642, 12667–7a, 12680, 12680.3, 12680.5, 12680.7, [17061], 18140, 18880, 19156, [19884], 21435, [21649a.5], [23422–4], 24508.5, 25818.
1607: 189.5, 921.5, [1769], 3434, 5564, 6038, 7103, 10367, 12643, 12668–9, 12671, 12681, 13472.4, 15363.7, 15640, [17062], 18141, 18155, 18986 ex off., 19677.5, [19977.3] (c), 21665, 23109, 23624.3 ex off., 24422.5.
1608: 3775.5, 5565, 6027, [6432], 6990, 7125, 12264, 12488, 12582.16, 12661.7, 12700, 13389, 13406.3, 18134, 18141.5, 19078.8, 19678, 19980, 19990, 21650, 21671 ent., [22360a] (d?), 23996.5, 24396, 24635, 26033.
1609: 1886, 1963.3, 3157, 3775.7, 4976, 6028, [6245], 7373.5, 7490.5–91 (Prelims A6, Aii, 1c, 1d in headnote), 12488.3, 12693.7, 12701, 12712, [13633] (d?), 13981, 14810, 18115, 19981, 22961 (d?), 23083, [23982.5], 26008.
1610: [1769.5], 4244, 4245, 6990.5, [11227], 11227.3, 11564, 13406.5, 13521, 15640.5, [19470], 20916 typis, 23399.
1611: [703], 4645, 4732, [4773], 5961.5, 6041, 12582.17, 13406.7, 14462, 14979, 19982, 21651, 23077.3, 23083.3–84, [23086.3] (d), 23093.5, 23129, 23130, 24537.
1612: [946], [2539], [3768], [3770b.5], 3774, 4859, 5938, 6638, [7226] (d), 7340–1, 13407, 14463, 14618–8.3, 22769, 23083.7, 23087, 23127, 23576, [23577] (d).
1613: 3774.3, 4859.5, 5913, 5926, [6247], 7094, 7227, 13344,

Lownes, Humphrey 1 — *cont.*
13407.5, [17063], [17757], 17869.5(A3) ent., 21652, 22544–4a, 22769, 23083.7, 23087, 23577.5–78, 24282.5, 24424.7, 24527.5, 25237, 25931.
1614: [2407.5], 3921.5–22, 5762, 6942, 12652, 12706–6a, 12815, 13409, [17758], 22670, 22729, [23581], [24425].
1615: [587], [2408], 3510.5, 3752, [3771], 3780, 5938.5, 6972, 12582.18, [12582.22?], 12654, 12706–6a, 13392.5, 13409.5, 13427.5 (false), 13982, [14013.7], 14466, 19983, [21623], 23084 (d?), [23582], 25039, 25896.
1616: [704], 5288, 12683, 13406, 13410, 14466.5, 19569a, 22742, 22788–8.5, [23582a] (d?), 23997, 25040, 25302.
1617: 187.5, 3773, 13031.5, 16835, 19983.3, 22927, 23077.7, 23085, [23086.7] (d), 23983, 24538, 25897.
1618: 1638, [2412], 3771.3, 5939, 11216, 13249, 13983, 14981, 18963, 25731, 25747 per, 25748 per.
1619: 1646, [1771.5], [4774], 4918, 6559, 11217, 12383, 13345, [14467.7(*A*)] (d?), 17693, [19471], [22743].
1620: 1647, [3368.5-Ashall] (c?), 11253, 14811–1a, 21653.
1621: [947.5], 3771.4, 7331, [12616], 13799, 14468, 17039 typis, 17600, [18720.5], 21194, [21250], 21653.
1622: [1390], 1476, 3774.5, 4860, 5011.5, 6632, [7228], [12617], 22394, 22545.5–46, 25169.
1623: 4211, [5981], 14468.5, 17852, 17861, 22546a, 24990.
1624: 39–9.7, 4588, [5436.5], 6398, 7451, 7452, 10738–8.3, 11701, 11702–2.3, 11703, 11704, 12573.3, 14089, 14693, 19983.5, [21479], 23504.
1625: [172.7], [4497], 6632.5, [10360] (d), [11998], 17470, [18030], 18030.5, 18031, [18721], 20391, [22429.5], [24543].
1626: 1478, 4235, 6560, 7309–9a, [10718], 12833, 13346, [13927], 14469 in off., [14587], [20679], [21163], 24772.
1627: 906, 5843, [11395], 12842, 13508, 14470 in off., 15495, 20894, 21129 in off., [21186.5], [21346], 21654 ent., [22230], 22855.5, 23085 ent., 24539 ent.
1628: 1160.5–.7, [2605?], [2605.5?], 14127, [17528], 19579, 19983.7, 20640 [by &] f., 22547, [22856], 23087.5 (d?), [23832], [23845], 23998, 23999, [24823].
1629: [948], 4205, [4669], 6633, 12806 (d), [13461], [17494], 19300, 19580, 19592, 20668–8.5, 20680 [by &] f., 21191, 22548–8a, [23833], [23846], [23984], 23999.
1630: 6561, [7125.5], [7126], [12114], 12528, 12851.7, 12852, 14954, 14956, 19984, [12115], 20668, 20673.

Lownes, Humphrey 2.
Journeyman printer? in London, 1612–1625† (*C-B C*: 179). Son of **Humphrey Lownes 1**. In the only confirmed Stat. Co. records relating to him he is called 'Humphrey Lownes junior' (Arber III.495, 505, 683; *C-B C*: 60, 179); other records almost certainly belong to his uncle, **Matthew Lownes**. [*Dict. 1*; DFM 360.]
No address found; possibly worked in his father's house.
1612: 23576 ent.

Lownes, Matthew.
Bookseller in London, (1591) 1595–1625†. Brother of **Humphrey 1** and father of **Thomas Lownes 4;** probably related to **William Lownes**. Father-in-law of **George Latham**. One of the *assignees of* **W. Barley**. Called to the Livery on 3 July 1602 (Arber II.874); in 17th century Stat. Co. records he is usually called 'Mr. Matt. Lownes' or 'Mr. Lownes junior'. Most of the records in *C-B C* and several of those in Arber indexed under Humphrey Lownes junior actually belong to Matthew. [*Dict. 1*.]
shop in St. Dunstan's Churchyard [in Fleet Street] (W.9), 1596 (7207)–1602 (1555) at least
in Paul's Churchyard (A.2), 1605–1621 at least
shop — [no sign], 1605 (1114), 1608 (12264), 1621 (7331, has 'dw.')
dw. — at the Bishop's Head, 1610 (7462), 1611 (11374.5, omits 'dw.'), 1619 (11217, has 'shop')
1595: 7656 sold.
1596: 7207 f., 12367 f., 17386 f. (d).
1597: 22538 f. (d?).
1598: 4614 f., 5259.5 f., 23363 f., 24096 f., 25067 ent.
1600: 23698 f.
1601: 18348 f.
1602: 1555 f., 3081 f., 7189 ass'd, 14781 f., 17473 f., [17474] sold, 17846 f.
1603: 15435 f.

Lownes, M. — *cont.*
1604: 7490.3 f., 17851 f., 23083 ent.
1605: 1113–4 f., 15448 f., 17135 f., 22543a f.
1606: 6014 imp., 18140 f., 19156 f., 19884 f., 23422–4 f., 23558 ent.
1607: 189.5 f., 3434 f., 4179.5 f., 15540 f., 18053 ent., 18141 f., 18155 f.
1608: 6027 ent., 6054.4 f., 7125 sold & f., 6990 f., 11413.3–.5 f., 12264 f., 18141.5 f., 24396 f.
1609: 3202 f., 6028 f., 7124 f., 7490.5 f., 7491 f., 11413.7 f., 13123 ent., 22938 f., 23083 f.
1610: 6990.5 f., 7462 sold, 11564 f., 18120 ent., [18983] sold.
1611: 5120 f., 6041 f., 11374 f., 11374.5 f., 11564.5 f., 13714 sold, 14462 f., 22939 f., 23077.3 f., 23083.3–84 f., [23086.3 f.] (d), 23093.5 f., 23130 f., 24525 ent.
1612: 5769 f., 7098 f., 7226 f. (d), 14463 f., 15140(*A*3) ent., 20174 sold, 23083.7 f., 23087 f.
1613: 4546.5–47 f. (d?), 7227 f., 12614 f., 15588 f., 19923 f., 22544a f., 23083.7 f., 23087 f.
1614: 2766 prost., 12815 f.
1615: 988 f., 1559.5 f., 1561 f., 14466 imp., 21152 imp., 23084 f. (d?), 24176 f.
1616: 14466.5 imp.
1617: 3143 sold, 13716 sold, 14467–7.5 imp., 23077.7 f., 23085 f., [23086.7 f.] (d).
1618: 1587 f., 7463 f., 7465 f., 11216 f., 20760 f., 21060 sold, 25731 f.
1619: 3144 sold, 4918 f., 7464 f., 11217 f., [14467.7(*A*) f.] (d?), 18120 f., 22544a.7 ent., 24624 f.
1620: 13859 sold.
1621: 7331 f., 12616 f., 14468 imp., 15301 f., 18037 f., 18963.3 ent.
1622: 1155 imp., 1159 f., 1160 f., 12617 f., 20640 ent., 22545.5 f., 22546 f., 24099 f.
1623: 1156 imp., 14468.5 imp., 17852 f., 19621b.5 f., 20767 f., 22546a f., 24990 f.
1624: 4588 f., 7466 f., 11564.7 f., 13455 f., 14693 f., 18038 f., 18039 f., 19924 f., 25389a sold.
1625: 1045.5 sold, 3173 f., 17470 f., 18030 f., 18030.5 f., 18031 f.

Lownes, Robert.
Stationer in London, (1611) 1615–1633 (*C-B C*: 424) at least. Not related to any of the other Lowneses. (The Robert who obtained the reversion of an annuity in 1620 (*C-B C*: 131) was the son of Matthew Lownes and his wife Alice, née Halwood, and was not a Stationer.) [*Dict. 1*; DFM 1105.]
shop at the little North door of Paul's (A.1), 1615 (16)
1615: 16 f.

Note: *Dict. 1* distinguishes four possible Stationers named **Thomas Lownes**. Although only the last had any imprints, it seems worthwhile to sort them out a little less tentatively below.

Lownes, Thomas 1 and 3.
Stationer in London, (1598) 1603 (Arber II.272)–1609†. Son of Roger Lownes and cousin of **Humphrey 1** and **Matthew Lownes**. Apprenticed to **William Lownes**, probably also a relative. This must be the Thomas fined on 4 Oct. 1604, probably for non-appearance on the quarter day (Arber II.840). When he made his will on 31 Aug. 1609, he was living in St. Sepulchre's parish (D.8). The Thomas who witnessed the will and owed him money must be Thomas 2 since Thomas 4 was still a minor. [*Dict. 1*; *Poor Book*, 1608–09; ?widow Joan, 1610.]

Lownes, Thomas 2.
Stationer in London, (1605–1609). Son of **William Lownes** and freed by patrimony on 22 Jan. 1605 (Arber II.738). Witnessed the will of Thomas 1 and 3 and owed him money. [*Dict. 1*; *Poor Book*, 1609.]

Lownes, Thomas 4.
Stationer in London, (1621) 1622–1627† (*C-B C*: 198). Son of **Matthew Lownes**. [*Dict. 1*; DFM 1866.]
shop in Paul's Churchyard at the Golden Ball (A.2), 1623 (5981)
1622: 5011.5 f.
1623: 5981 f.
1627: 1149 ent., 1160.5 ass'd, 18965 ent., 20640 ent., 22547 ent., 23085 ent.

Lownes, William.
Stationer and bookbinder? in London, (1579) 1590–before 1605†. Probably uncle or older brother of **Humphrey 1** and **Matthew Lownes**. Father of **Thomas Lownes 2**. [*Dict. 1*; *Poor Book* (widow Elizabeth, cf. DFM 1858), 1608–34.]
No address survives.
1590: [23419.5 f.].

Loys (Louis), Jamet.
Printer in Rouen, 1499–1515. [Duff, *Century*; Muller 102.]
1505: 18872 in off. (d). **1508:** 16185.

Loyselet (L'Oiselet), George.
Printer in Rouen, 1557–1604. For other items produced 1582–1585 using some of his material but apparently on a separate press *see* Fr. Parsons' Press. [*Dict. 1*; Muller 102; Southern 359–62; *Library* 6 (1951): 50–1.]
1580: [14564], [24626.3].
1583: [24627].
1584: [15507], 16908, [19354].
1585: [23968].
1586: 16903.
1589: [17264].
1590: [24627a].
1599: 16904 (forged).

Luetzenkirchen, Wilhelm.
Printer in Cologne, 1586–1634. [Benzing 247.]
1610: 1431.21.

Luft, Hans, *pseud.*
Printer in 'Malborough' or 'Marborch' (Marburg), 1528–1537 = J. Hoochstraten and others; in 'Wittenberg', 1547 = J. Day. For the genuine Lufft active in Wittenberg, 1523–1584†, *see* Benzing 499. [Duff, *Century*; *TBS* 11 (1909–11): 197–214; *Library* 9 (1928): 153–9.]
1528: 24446, 24454, 24455.5(*A*3) (forged).
1529: 10493, 11394.
1530: 1462.5, 2350, 3021.
1535: 24447.
1537: 24447.3.
1547: 17314, 17314a.

Lugger (Luggard), William.
Bookseller in London, (1597) 1599–1658†. [*Dict. 2*; *Loan Book*, 1610–13.]
at the Blind Knight over against St. Andrew's Church in Holborn (V.4), 1603 (15706)–1604 (17294, has 'shop', omits sign)
shop upon Holborn Bridge (V.2), 1606 (10665)
shop in Bethlehem (Bedlam) near Moorfields (K.1), 1619 (12383)
at the postern gate at (on) Tower Hill (U.3), 1628 (Greg, *Companion*: 241, as 'Huyger'), 1633 (19182)–1640 (3113.7)
1603: 15706 f., 18627 f. **1604:** 17294 f. (d). **1606:** 10665 f. **1619:** 12383 f. **1633:** 19182 f. **1634:** 1541 f., 3274 f. **1638:** 10666 f. **1640:** 3113.7 sold.

Lycosthenes, Ptolomé and Nicephore, *pseud.*
Booksellers in 'London', 1569. = Unidentified English importers of recusant books.
'in Paul's Churchyard at the signs of Time and Truth by the Brazen Serpent' (A.3), 1569 (15505, colophon)
1569: 15505 sold.

Lynde, *Sir* **Humphrey.**
Puritan controversialist and patron, b. 1579–1636†. [*DNB*.]
1624: 14458 (note).

Lyng. *See* Ling.

Lynne (Lin), Walter (Gualter, Wouter van).
Bookseller in London, c. 1540–c. 1570† and possibly earlier in Antwerp, 1533–c. 1546. [Duff, *Century*; Rouzet 130.]
dw. upon Somer's Quay by Billingsgate (T.11), 1548 (20843)–1550 (4626, colophon)
sold in Paul's Churchyard next the great school at the $ Spread-Eagle (A.6), 1550 (4626)
1548: 822 [f.], 3287 f. (d), 5992.5, 5993 f., 5994 f., 16964 f., 16982 f., 17115 at costs (d?), 20843 f., 20849 [f.], [21826.6 f.] (d?).
1549: 4079 f., 17119 f., 18770 f., 18771 f.
1550: 920 f., 4626 f., 17117 f., 20177 f., 24223.5 f., 24666 f., 25255 f.

Lyon. *See* Lion.

M

M., I. C.
Patron in London, 1589.
1589: 11735.7 exp.

Mab (Mabbe), Ralph.
Bookseller in London, 1610–1642. After 1616 he seems not to have been actively involved with the sale of his books. His second shop was probably by the end of that year in the hands of **George Edwards 1** and by the end of 1618 had passed to **Jacob Bloome**, Mab's former apprentice and Edwards's stepson. Many of Mab's later books were sold by others. [*Dict. 2*; DFM 1821; *Loan Book*, 1619–30, 1638–41; ?*Poor Book* (widow), 1659–64.]
in Paul's Churchyard, 1611–1616 at least
at the Angel — (A.3), 1611 (22182a)–1613 (11830)
— at the Greyhound (B), 1614 (110.5)–1616 (7146, has 'shop'); no later address noted
1610: 12500 sold, 12501 f.
1611: 12501 f., 22182a f., 24119 imp.
1612: 712(*A*3) sold, 23830.5 sold, 25158 f., 25163 f.
1613: 131 f., 131a f., 7355 f., 11829 f., 11830 f., 25157 f.
1614: 109 ent., 110–0.5 f., 7398 f., 17837 f.
1615: 114 f., 3435.7 f., 7399 f., 7400 f., 7612 f., 10818 f., 11191 f., 25165 f.
1616: 7146 f., 7401 f., 7408 f., 7408.2 f., 7615 f., 11837 f., 13772.5 ass'd, 20776 f., 25166 ass'd, 25294 sold.
1617: 7615.5 f., 7615.7 ass'd.
1618: 7613 ass'd.
1619: 7142 (note), 7145 (note).
1622: 23830 ent.
1623: 26064 f. .yr 1624: 23225 f.
1624: 23225 f.
1626: 12112 f.
1627: 5151 f., 11978 f., 25377 f.
1629: 162 f., 4126–6.5 f., 6313 sold, 23367.5–68 f.
1631: 163 f., 4911.2 sold, 13167 f., 13167.5 f.
1632: 12502 f., 13168 f., 13913 f.
1634: 1577–7.5 f., 13542.5 f.
1635: 972 f., 1099 f., 1100 f., 1506 f., 1578 f., 12503 ass'd, 13169 f., 13543 f.
1636: 13169 f.
1637: 973 ass'd, 974 f., 7614 f.
1638: 630.5–31 f., 975 f., 4349.5 f., 13544 f., 19273 f., 21094 f., 22501 ent.
1639: 976–6.5 f., 1505 f., 1507 f., 20660 f., 22477 f., 24048 f., 24138 f.
1640: 4914 f., 13170 f., 14922 ent., 21095 f., 22512 f., 24048–9 f., 24049.3(*A*3) f.

Macé, Richard.
Bookseller and bookbinder in Rouen, 1502–1525. [Duff, *Century*; Muller 102.]
1506/07: [504]. **1515:** 15811.5 imp. **1520:** [16202.5 f.] (c).

Machabeus (Nachabeus), *Dr., pseud.*
Patron in 'Copmanhouin' (Copenhagen), 1554, 1559.
1554: 15672 at expenses (d). **1559:** 15675 at expenses (d).

Macham, Joyce.
Bookseller in London, 1615–1628, 1634? Widow of **Samuel Macham 1** and mother of **Samuel 2**. The second address below may not be hers. Her name on a subtitle dated 1634 is almost certainly erroneously carried over from previous editions. [*Dict. 1*.]
in Paul's Churchyard, 1615–1616 at least
— at the Bull Head (A.2), 1615 (3780)–1616 (25040)
?sold — at the $ Time (A.10), 1618 (25041); no later address noted
1615: 3780 f.
1616: 25040 f.
1617: 3511 f., 13401 f., 13410.5 f.
1618: 13411 f., 13412 f., 25041 f.
1619: 3511.5 f., 3782 f., 13379 (note), 13412.5 f.
1620: 13402 f., 13413.5 f.
1621: 13402.2 f.
1622: 3512 f., 3782.5 f., 13413a f.

Macham, Joyce — *cont.*
1623: 3512 f.
1624: 13381 (note).
1625: 13381 (note), 13413a.3 f.
1628: 13403.3 ass'd.
1634: 13383.5 (note).

Macham, Samuel 1.
Bookseller in London, (1605) 1606–1615†. Husband of **Joyce Macham** and father of **Samuel 2**. Shared a shop with **Matthew Cooke**, 1606–1607, and with **Eleazar Edgar** for part of 1608 (12662). [*Dict. 1*; DFM 2679; *Loan Book*, 1608–11.]
in Paul's Churchyard (A.2), 1606–1615
their shop — at the Tiger's Head, 1606 (5101)–1607 (21461), both with M. Cooke
shop — at the Bull Head, 1607 (12668)–1615 (25039)
1606: 3775 f., 5101 f., 12642 f., 12666 ent., 12666a f., 12667a f., 13399.5 f., 15561 f., 24508.5 f.
1607: 3775.3 f., 3776 f., 12643 f., 12668 f., 12671 f., 15363.7 f., 21461 f.
1608: 3775.5 f., 12648 f., 12648a f., 12648a.5 f., 12661.7 f., 12662–2.5 f., 12663.2 f., 12699 f., 12700 f., 13389 f., 13406.3 f., 24635 f.
1609: 3510 f., 3775.7 f., 3776.5 f., 12644 f., 12644.5 f., 12670 f., 12672 f., 12682 f., 12693.7 f., 12694a f., 12696 ent., 12697a f., 12701 f., 12712 f., 13245a f., 13386 f., 13427 sold, 13633 f. (d?), 14699–9.5 f., 20026 sold, 24508.3 f. (d), 26008 f.
1610: 7339 f., 12649 f., 12663.4 ent., 13406.5 f., 23408.4 ex off.
1611: 3777 f., 7022 f., 12663.6 f., 12703 imp., 13406.7 f., 13424 f., 24393.3 f.
1612: 7023 f., 7340 f., 12650 f., 12703a imp., 13407 f., 13417 f., 20432 f.
1613: 3779 f., 12673 f., 13378 (note), 13391 f., 13392 f., 13407.5 f., 13418 f., 14493 f., 19569 f.
1614: 3779 f., 12652 f., 12706–6a f., 13409 f.
1615: 3510.5 f., 12683 ass'd, 12706 f., 12707 ass'd, 13392.5 f., 13409.5 f., 13427.5 (false?), 25039 f.

Macham, Samuel 2.
Stationer in London, 1631–1636. Son of **Samuel 1** and **Joyce Macham**. Although he was freed by J. Grismand in 1631, Samuel 2 seems not to have had a shop, and his career is obscure. [*Dict. 1*; DFM 1477.]
No address noted.
1628: 3514 ent. in trust for.
1632: 3784 f., 13404 f., 13424 ent.
1633: 3515 f., 20433 f.
1634: 3515 f., 13383.5 (note), 13415 ent.
1636: 3515.3 f.

Machlinia, William de.
Printer in London, 1481?–1486? In partnership with **John Lettou** through 1482. [Duff, *Century*; *Library* 18 (1937): 21–2, 335–7.]
near the church of All Saints (All Hallows (?N.10)), 1482 (15719, with J. Lettou)
near Fleet Bridge (W.3), 1483? (15720)
in Holborn (V.2), 1484? (9737)
1481: [9513] (d?).
1482: [4594?] (c?), [9742] (d?), [9749] (d?), [13922] (d?), 15719 (d).
1483: 258 per (c), [273] (d?), [7014.5] (c?), [9176] (d), [9731] (d?), 15720 per (d?), [20917] (d), [23905] (d?).
1484: [9347] (d?), 9737 per (d?), [9755] (d?).
1485: [4589] (c), [4590] (c), [4591] (c), [9264] (d?), [15869] (d).
1486: [9993] (d?), [14096] (d), [23906] (d?), 26012 per (d?).

Machuel, Jean.
Bookseller in Rouen, 1603–1658. [Lepreux III/1: 294, n.3.]
1609: 13452.

Madeley, Roger.
Printer? in London, 1553. [Duff, *Century*.]
in Paul's Churchyard at the Star (B), 1553 (25105)
1553: 25105 (d).

Maes (Masius), Jean.
Printer and bookseller in Louvain, 1567–1616. [Rouzet 143–4.]
1579: 13376. **1589:** [4000].

Maheu, Didier (Desiderius).
Printer and bookseller in Paris, 1510–1543 (1546†). [Duff, *Century*; Renouard.]
1526: 16147.

Maire, Dirk (Theodorus).
Printer in Leiden, 1636, and in the Hague, 1637–1645. [Gruys.]
1636: 22175.7 ap.

Maire, Jean.
Printer and bookseller in Leiden, 1601–1657. [Gruys; Briels 352–3.]
1617: 24893.5 ap. **1618:** 19595.7 ap., 24893.7 ap. **1636:** 22175.7 ap.
1639: 12399.3 [f.].

Malassis, Adam.
Bookseller? in Rouen, 1600–1636. [Lepreux III/1: 307.]
1600: 6832.56.

Mammarello, Benedetto.
Printer in Ferrara, 1587–1600. [Borsa.]
1591: 13218 (note).

Man, Joan, *Assignees of.*
Publishers in London, 1635–1637. Joan was the widow of **Paul Man** (*C-B C*: 257–8). The SR entries for 1635 listed below were made to her personally along with her partner **Benjamin Fisher**. It seems likely that **Thomas Harper** was one of the assignees, at least for printing the items. [*Dict. 1.*]
No address used.
1635: 6979 [f.], 11692.7 ent., 22122 ent., 23656 ent., 25313 [f.].
1636: 5764 f., 25238 [f.].
1637: 6625 [f.], 22734 [f.], 24498–8.5 [f.].

Man, Jonas (Jonah).
Bookseller in London, 1607–1634† (*C-B C*: 257). Son of **Thomas Man 1** and brother of **Thomas 2** and **Paul Man.** Although in 1626–27 (22784–5) he shared an imprint with **Benjamin Fisher**, the address: at the Talbot in Aldersgate Street (F.2), is probably Fisher's alone, but the bulk of Jonas's copyrights eventually passed to Fisher. *See* also *assignees of* **Jonas Man.** [*Dict. 1*; DFM 1911; *Loan Book*, 1608–11; *Poor Book*, 1631–34.]
at the Star at the West door of Paul's Church (A.10), 1608 (6951)
dw. in Paternoster Row at the Talbot (C.7), 1608 (4168, with T. Man 1)–1622 (25310, omits 'dw.', with P. Man)
1607: 23109(*A*3) ent.
1608: 4168 f., 6951 f., 6963 ent., 24963 ent.
1609: 1963.3 f., 6940 ent., 23315 ent., 23820 ent., 24966 ent.
1610: 4707.5 ent., 5391 ent., 12817 ent., 20096(*A*3) ent.
1611: 5961.5 f., 11580 ent., 12171 f., 21203 ent.
1612: 18494 f., 21241.5 f., 25237 ent.
1613: 20611 f., 21204 ent.
1614: 5390 ent., 13471 f.
1615: 3752 ent., 22024.7 f. (c).
1616: 5288 ent., 26058 f.
1617: 187.5 ent., 3925 f., 4236.1 f., 11132 f., 17238.5(*A*3) f.
1618: 12848 ent., 21221 ent., 25308(*A*3) ent.
1619: 4236.8 f., 12827 ent., 24818 ent., 25305 ent.
1620: 22121 ent., 22427 f.
1621: 6908 f., 25306 ent.
1622: 4220.5 f., 25310 f.
1624: (all SR entries): 188(*A*), 3769, 3771.5, 5289, 5388, 5763, 6976, 12821, 12829, 12850, 19653a, 19724.3, 21219, 21223, 22877.2, 23656, 24819, 25620(*A*3), 25684, 25687, 25700a.
1626–27: 22784–5 f.
1629: 5289 ass'd, 5764 ass'd, 6977 ass'd.
1634: 4177 f.

Man, Jonas, *Assignees of.*
Publishers in London, 1620, 1627–1634. *See* also *assignees of* **T. Man 1**, where imprints 2) and 4) almost certainly include Jonas. Imprints below which have 'by assignment of' instead of the usual term are so indicated.
No address used.
1620: 11857–7.3.
1627: 21219–9a by ass't of.
1628: 6976.5 f., 22731.5 by ass't of.
1631: 22732 [f.].

Man, Jonas, *Assignees of — cont.*
1632: 6978 [f.], 25684 f.
1633: 24819 [f.], 25684 f., 25687 f.
1634: 23656, 25700a (note).

Man, Paul.
Stationer in London, (1621) 1622–1630?† (*C-B C*: 217). Son of **Thomas Man 1**, brother of **Thomas 2** and **Jonas**, and husband of **Joan Man**. Transferred from the Haberdashers' to the Stat. Co. in 1621 (*C-B C*: 136). *See* also *assignees of* **Paul Man**. [*Dict. 1*; DFM 1898.]
shop in Chancery Lane at the Bowl (W.10a), 1622 (20166)
in Paternoster Row at the Talbot (C.7), 1622 (25310, with Jonas Man)
1622: 20166 f., 25310 f.
1624: (all SR entries): 188(*A*), 3769, 3771.5, 5289, 5388, 5763, 6976, 12821, 12829, 12850, 19653a, 19724.3, 21219, 21223, 22877.2, 23656, 24819, 25620(*A*3), 25684, 25687, 25700a.

Man, Paul, *Assignees of.*
Publishers in London, 1627–1634. *See* also *assignees of* **T. Man 1**, where imprints 2) and 4) almost certainly include Paul. Imprints below which have 'by assignment of' instead of the usual term are so indicated.
No address used.
1627: 21219–9a by ass't of.
1628: 22731.5 by ass't of.
1631: 22732 [f.].
1632: 6978 [f.], 25684 f.
1633: 24819 [f.], 25684 f., 25687 f.
1634: 23656, 25700a (note).

Man, Samuel.
Bookseller in London, (1612) 1613–1674†. Not related to any of the other Mans. He was in Ivy Lane (C.3) at the time of his death. [*Dict. 2*; DFM 2711.]
in Paul's Churchyard, 1613–1640 at least
shop — at the Ball (A.2), 1613 (15428)–1616 (21075)
dw. — at the Swan (A.5), 1618 (19319)–1640 (19303.3, omits 'dw.')
1613: 15428 f., 17847–7.2 f., 24314 f.
1614: 376.7 f., 19314 f., 21074 f., 24693.5 f.
1615: 19315 f.
1616: 7468 f., 12185 f., 21075 f., 23056.5 f.
1618: 4226 f., 19312 f., 19319 f.
1619: 19316 f., 19568 f., 21165 f.
1620: 19320 f., 21214 f.
1621: 24694 f.
1622: 4110 f., 4227 f., 5134 ent., 5135 f., 19321 f., 20050 f.
1623: 3410 f., 5132 f., 6831 f., 24694.3 f.
1624: 5130 f., 25236 ent.
1625: 15103 f., 15354 f., 19316.3 f. (c).
1626: 22466 f., 24694.5 f.
1627: 3798 f., 4695 f., 14484.7 f.
1630: 1929 f., 6427.7 sold, 25236 f.
1632: 1930 f., 19311 f., 21166 f.
1633: 19311.5 f., 19317 f., 24695 f.
1634: 1931 f.
1635: 1932 f., 25292.3 f.
1636: 19313 f., 19318 f., 24314.3 f.
1637: 24695a f.
1640: 1933 f., 19303.3 sold.

Man, Thomas 1.
Bookseller in London, (1575?) 1578–1625†. Father of **Thomas 2**, **Paul**, and **Jonas Man**. Father-in-law of **Humphrey Lownes 1**. In 1622 his former apprentice, **Benjamin Fisher**, seems largely to have taken over active management of the shop. *See* also *assignees of* **T. Man 1**. [*Dict. 1.*]
dw. in Paternoster Row at the Talbot (C.7), 1583 (5963)–1623 (4803)
1578: 4303.5 [f.], 11844 imp.
1579: 1376 (d), 4303.7 [f.], 4439 f., 4457 f., 15256 f.
1580: 3750 f., 3751 f., 4460 f., 11434 f. (d?), 11434.5 f. (d?), 15450 f. (d), 16812 ent., 20558 f., [22044 f.] (d), 23872 imp., 24251.5 f.
1581: 1039 ent., 2051 ent., 10844 f. (d), 10844.3 f. (d?), 11897–7.5 f., 13774 f., 18807 f., 23874 pro, 25623 f., 25631 f.

Man, Thomas 1 — *cont.*
1582: 3744 imp. (d), 16813 f., 18807.3 f., 19915 f., 20559 f.
1583: 585 f., 3746 imp., 5963 f., 10764–4.3 f., 13775 f., 15068 f. (d), 19102 f., 19109.5 f., 19109.7 f. (d?).
1584: 5964 f., 6141 [f.], 15251.7(*A3*) ent., 20560 f., 24489 f., 24501 f., 25624.5 f. (d?).
1585: 24503.7 f. (c), 25185 ent., 25185a f., 25622 f., 25888 f.
1586: 5964.5 f., 18325.7 f., 19105 f., 25625 f.
1587: 5964.5 f., 12498.5 f. (d?), 12499 f. (d?), 24504 f. (d?), 25620.5 f., 25622.5 f. (d).
1588: 2051 f., 4090.5 f., 14573.5 f. (d?), 24490 f., 24492 f. (d?), 24502 f., 24507 f. (d).
1589: 1358 f., 1708.5 f., 5965 f., 7159 f., 15251.7 imp., 19916 f., 19916.3 f., 22217 imp., 22658 f., 22930 f., 24493 f., 24504.5 f., 25624 f., 25627 f. (d).
1590: 13144 pour (d), 13145 f., [14815 f.] (d?), 22712.5 imp., 23652 f.
1591: 15510.5 f., 19916.7 f., 22659 f., 22660 f., 22680 ent., 22684 ent., 22685 f., 22685.5(*A*) f., 22686 f., 22687 f., 22703 f., 22703.5 f., 22705 f., 22716 f., 23652.3 f., 25626 f.
1592: 799 f. (d), 15511 f., 16767 f. (d), 19665 f., 19665.5 f., 22662 ent., 22678 imp., 22688 ent., 22690 ent., 22704 f., 22717 f., 22718 f., 24899 f., 25696 f.
1593: 13588 f., 22719 f., 23397 f., 24494 f., 25018.5 f., 25019 f., 25701 f.
1594: 4174 f., 7373.4 f., 13891 f., 22720 f., 22720.5 f., 23697a f. (d), 25697 f.
1595: 585a f., 3436 f., 4176 f., 4176.2 f., 13898 f., 15489 f., 18207 f., 18539.5 f., 22677 f., 22721 f., 24495 f., 25629 f.
1596: 11866 f., 18540 f., 22400.5 f., 22679 ent., 24491 f., 25702 f.
1597: 5966 f., 11848.5 f., 11871 f., 16609 f., 18614 f., 19712 (note), 22722 f., 23408.2 ent., 23652.5 f., 25630 f.
1598: 3928 f., 4176.5 f., 5382 f., 5383 f., 7374 f., 11754 f., 11854 f., 18142 ent., [21131(*A3*)] sold, 21670 f.
1599: 4166 ent., 4167 ent., 4168.5 ent., 4174.5 ent., 11866.5 f., 13120 f., 15342–2.5 f., 18146 f., 19766.7 f., 22723 f., 23652.7 f., 24496 f., 25703 f.
1600: 14 f., 366 f., 367 f., 1596 f., 1596.5 f., 3505 f., 5384 f., 11855 f., 18142 f., 19646 (note), 24909 f., 25698–8.3, 26097.5 sold.
1601: 6439 ent., 6440 ent., 19100 f., 21030 f., 22724 f.
1602: 4165a f., 4178.5 f., 6468 f., 11692.3 imp., 14898(*A3*) ent., 22401 f.
1603: [367.5 f.?], 5385 f., 6911.7 f., 6967–7.5 f., 7231 f., 7231.3 f., 13589 ass'd, 18210 f., 21215 f., 21432 f., 21433 f., 22024.3 f., 25672 f., 25694 f., 25698.3 f. (d), 25698.5 f.
1604: 4710 imp., 4883 f., 6968 f., 7113 f., 7209 ent., 12057 imp., 12324.5 f., 13767 f., 13767.5 f., 20889 f., 21032 ent., 21216 f., 21433.5 f., 21434 f., 22725 f., 25610 f., 25692 f.
1605: 1590 f., 4617(*A3*) ent., 6968.5 f., 20147 imp., 21216a f., 22877.1 f., 23870 f., 25682 ent.
1606: 3437 f., 3961 ent., 6622 f., 6954 f., 6954.5 f., 6957 ent., 6969 f., 13587 f., 19724 f., 19724.3 f., 22402 f., 25318 f.
1607: 6957.5 f., 6970 f., 13392.3 f., 13392.7 f., 13398.5 f., 22726 f., 23109 f., 23432.3 f., 25319 f.
1608: 4168 f., 5966.5 f. (d?), 6951 ent., 6955 f., 6958 f., 20763.2(*A3*) imp., 20763.5 imp., 23653 f., 24497 f., 24963 f., 25319.3 f., 25683 f., 25686 f.
1609: 1963.3 f., 6624 f., 6940 f., 6963 f., 6971 f., 13393 f., 13399 f., 13768 f., 19649 (note), 22727 f., 23315 ent., 23654 f., 23820 f., 24966 f., 25300 f., 25300.5 f., 25319.5 f.
1610: 377 f., 4314 f., 5385.5 f., 5391 f., 6941 f., 6952 f., 6971.3 f., 12817 f., 20096 f., 21217 f., 23315.5 f., 25301 f.
1611: 4707.5 f., 5961.5 f., 6964 f., 11577 f., 11580 f., 11582 f., 12818 f., 22728 f.
1612: 3768 f., 3770b.5 f., 3774 f., 4859 f., 5386 f., 6624.4 f., 6956 f., 6959 f., 6971.5 f., 21203 f.
1612/13: 25705 f., 25707 imp.
1613: 2002 f., 3774.3 f., 4859.5 f., 13378 (note), 19650 (note), 23055 f., 25237 f., 25699 f.
1614: 3921.5–22 f., 4236 ent., 5387 f., 5390 f., 5762 f., 6942 f., 6971.7 f., 12818.5 f., 22729 f., 25699a f.
1615: 3752 f., 3771 f., 5378–8.2 f., 6972 f., 21204 f., 23655 f., 26058 f.
1616: 4707.7 f., 5288 f., 9550 ent., 20306 f., 21218 f., 23672 f., 25302 f.
1617: 187.5 f., 3773 f., 3925 f., 6624.7 f., 10769 ent., 11132 f., 12819 f., 17238.5 f., 21034 f., 23432.5 f.

Man, Thomas 1 — *cont.*
1618: 3771.3 f., 6943 f., 6953 f., 6974 f., 12848 f., 18963 f., 19651 (note), 21221 f., 22730 f., 23822 ent., 23822a f., 23826 ent., 25308 f.
1619: 12827 f., 12827.5 f., 13379 (note), 21221.5 f., [23837] sold, 25297 f., 25305 f., 25309 f., 25320 f.
1620: 22121 f., 23673 f., [23830.7] sold, 23831 f., [23838] sold, 24818 f.
1621: 3771.4 f., 5387.5 f.
1622: 3767 f., 3774.5 f., 4860 f., 6975 f., 12499.5 f., 12820 f., 12828 f., 12849 f., 22731 f., 23110(*A3*) ass'd, 25306 f., 25309.7 f., 25689 ent.
1623: 4803 f., 21222 f., 25299 f.
1624: 188 f., 5289 ass'd, 5388 ass'd, 12829 ent., 12850 ent., 13381 (note), 21223 ent., 22122 ent., 22877.2 f., 25298 ent., 25299 f., 25310 ass'd, 25620(*A3*) ass'd, 25687 ass'd.
1625: 5763 f., 6976 f.

Man, Thomas 1, *Assignees of.*
Publishers in London, 1628–1635. On 3 May 1624 Thomas 1 assigned most of his copyrights to his surviving sons, **Paul** and **Jonas Man.** Apparently at a previous date he had granted publication rights to **Thomas Pavier** and **John Bellamy** in return for a fee (*C-B C*: 181). The imprints indexed below are as follows:
1) 1628: *assignees of T. and Jonas Man*
2) 1629–1631 (5289, 19653a sub tp), 1632 (13383.5 sub tp): *assignees of T. Man, etc.*
3) 1631 (22732)–1634: *assignees of T., P., and Jonas Man*
4) 1635: as in 2)
Sometime in 1635 the imprint associated with the copyrights becomes: *assignees of* **Joan Man** and **B. Fisher**.
No address used.
1628: 6976.5 f.
1629: 21223.
1630: 3771.7, 5388 [f.], 6977 [f.], 12830 [f.], 12851 [f.], 21220 [f.], 25312 [f.].
1631: 5289 [f.], 19653a (note), 22732 [f.].
1632: 6978 [f.], 13383.5 (note), 25684 f.
1633: 24819 [f.], 25684 f., 25687 f.
1634: 23656, 25700a (note).
1635: 13383.5 (note), 21223.3–.7.

Man, Thomas 2.
Bookseller in London, 1604–1610. Son of **Thomas Man 1** and brother of **Jonas** and **Paul Man**. The widow of Thomas 2 died in 1618 (*C-B C*: 103), and there seem to have been no surviving children. [*Dict. 1.*]
Listed below are only items with 'junior' in the imprint or in the SR entry, including the following ambiguous case: in 1608 Thomas 2 entered an item (19511.5) with J. Chorlton, and although both names are given in the imprint, Thomas 2 is not described as 'junior'; however, the place of sale was Chorlton's address: the great North door of Paul's (A.2). The bulk of Thomas 2's SR entries were made together with his father. With the sole exception of the destroyed copy of 23315, none of the imprints so far known specifies 'junior', and he is recorded, therefore, only as entering them.
dw. in Paternoster Row at the Talbot (C.7), 1605 (20149)
at the Fleur-de-lis and Crown in Paul's Churchyard (A.2), 1610 (23315, annotation in W. A. Jackson's copy of *Dict. 1*)
1604: 6501 ent., 6510 f., 6513 f., 7209 sold, 22426 ent., 25610 ent.
1605: 4617(*A3*) ent., 20149 f., 22877.1 ent., 25318 ent.
1608: 5804 ent., 6506 ent., 19511.5(*A3*) f.
1609: 3190 ent., 18629(*A3*) ent., 18640 ent., 18652 ent., 20581 ent.
1610: 20096(*A3*) ent., 23315 f.

Mang, Christoph.
Printer in Augsburg, 1603–1617†. [Benzing 21.]
1614: 1843.

Manilius, Gislenus.
Printer in Ghent, 1558–1573. [Rouzet.]
1565: [17213.5], [17696].

Mannenby, Leigh, *pseud.*
Printer in 'Edinburgh', 1578. = H. Bynneman. [*Dict. 1.*]
1578: 18445.

Mansell. *See* Maunsell.

Mansion, Colard.
Calligrapher, bookseller, and printer in Bruges, 1454–1484. Apparently collaborated with **William Caxton,** but in what capacity is subject to dispute. [Duff, *Century*; Rouzet.]
1473: [15375(*A*3)] (d?). **1474:** [4920] (d).

Mantell, Walter.
Stationer in London, (1583) 1585–1588. [*Dict. 1.*]
No address used.
1585: 7289 [f.], 21084 [f.] (d).

Mapes, Gualtherus, *pseud.*
Printer in 'Oxford', 1626? = Unidentified Dutch printer.
1626: 902 ap.

Marcant, Marcantius. *See* Marchant.

Marchant, Edward.
Bookbinder and bookseller in London, (1585) 1604 (Arber II.281)–1638†. [*Dict. 1*; *Poor Book*, 1608–37, widow thereafter; *St. Giles*, 1638.]
shop in Paul's Churchyard over against (at, near) the Cross [Paul's Cross] (A.6), 1612 (18588.5)–1616 (24316, has 'dw.'); variation: omits mention of the Cross, 1615 (23741)
1612: 5878 f., 6507 sold, 18588.5 sold, 19200.3(*A*3) sold.
1612/13: 25901 f.
1613: 13355 f., 23722 sold, 25261.5 f., 25872 f.
1615: 12235 sold, 18254 sold, 18437–7.5 f., 18445.7 f., 18446a f., 18747 sold, 23741 sold.
1616: 11292.5 sold, 24316–6a f.

Marchant, Jean.
Bookseller in Rouen, 1536–1538 at least. In 1537–38 his name is supplied on the basis of a device or cuts with his initials. It is not clear whether he is related to **John Marchant**. [Duff, *Century*.]
1536: 16106 pro. **1537:** [15994 imp.]. **1538:** [16006].

Marchant (Marcantius), John.
Bookseller in York, 1579. Possibly related to **Jean Marchant**. Probably not the same man as the one who, with five others, made submission to the Stat. Co. in London on 27 Jan. 1578 (*Reg. B*: 3) and bound and freed apprentices, 1584–1586 (Arber II.124, 142, 695). [*Dict. 1*: 185.]
No address used.
1579: 4866(*A*3) ap. [f.].

Marchant, Mathurin, *pseud.*
Printer in 'Verdun', 1588. = J. Wolfe. Repeats the imprint of a continental edition, of which there are several (Woodfield no. 31 and his Appendix B8–11). For a genuine printer in Verdun, 1572–87, named Martin Marchant *see* Muller 117.
1588: 15212.5.

Marchant (Marcant), Nicolas.
Printer? or bookseller? in Paris? 1500. [Duff, *Century*.]
1500: 23163.9 (d).

Marchant, R.
A misprint for Edward Marchant.
1615: 12235 sold.

Marche. *See* Marsh.

Marcus, Jacob.
Bookseller in Leiden, 1611–1648. [Gruys.]
1610: [14337 f.?].

Mareschal, H. *See* Le Mareschal.

Mareschal, Pierre.
Printer in Lyons, 1492–1529†. [Muller 41.]
1525: 24868.3 (c).

Margaret [Beaufort], *Countess of Richmond and Derby.*
Mother of Henry VII, translator, and patron, b. 1443–1509†. Toward the end of her life she appointed **Wynkyn de Worde** as her printer. [*DNB*, under Beaufort.]
1504: 23954.7 (title to bk. 4) at command of (d).
1505: [15793 at expenses].
1507: 15806a imp.

Marius, Adrian.
Bookseller in London, 1600?–1614 at least. [*Dict. 1.*]
dw. in the Blackfriars (Q.6), 1614 (11699)
1614: 11699 sold.

Marprelate, Margery, *pseud.*
Printer in 'England', 1640. = The 'Cloppenburg' Press, Amsterdam?
1640: 21924, 21926.

Marprelate, Martin, *pseud.*
'Author' and 'publisher' in England, 1588–1589. The author = Job Throkmorton; the printer = R. Waldegrave at various locations. Below are listed only items with Marprelate's name in the imprint.
1588: 17453 at cost of (d). **1589:** 17459 pub'd by (d).

Marprelate, Martin, junior, *Assignees of, pseud.*
Printer in England, 1589. = J. Hodgkins, Wolston.
1589: 17457 (d).

Marriot, John.
Bookseller in London, (1613) 1616–1660 (Wing M 913). Father of **Richard Marriot**. [*Dict. 2*; DFM 1633.]
in Fleet Street, 1616–1640 at least
shop at the White Fleur-de-lis near Fetter Lane end — (W.8), 1616 (6342)–1619 (20990)
shop in St. Dunstan's Churchyard — (W.9), 1620 (29)–1640 (24576.7, engr. tp)
1616: 6342 f.
1617: 20989 f., 20989.3 f.
1618: 16772 sumpt., 16773 f., 20989.7 f., 21097 f., 25046 f.
1619: 17742 f., 20990 f.
1620: 29 f., 3689 f., 17620.3 f. (d), 18105.3–.7 f.
1621: 17624(*A*3) ent., 17732 f., 25043 (note), 25044 f., 25044.5 f., 25047 f., 25049 f., 25049a f., 25925 ent., 25926 f., 25926.5 f., 25927 f., 25928–8.3 f., 25928.5 f., 25928.7 f., 25970.5 f., 26051 f. (d).
1622: 7228 f., 7229–30 f., 17733 f., 17831 f., 20991 f., 25033a f., 25042 f., 25045 f., 25050 f., 25052 f., 25053 f., 25055 f., 25055.5 f., 25903 ent.
1623: 5780.7 ent., 6059 ent., 15056 f., 17357 ent., 17734 f., 17739 f., 17739.5 f., 18302.5 ent., 19451.5 ent., 19509 ent., 23495.5 f., 25030.5 f., 25048 f.
1624: 30 f., 5374 sold, 7471 f., 18608 f., 23496 f., 25054 f., 25056 f.
1625: 5661 f., 6060 f., 13806 imp., 18607 f., 25051 f.
1626: 14968 f., 23497 f., 25031 ass'd.
1627: 16774 f., 16887 f., 24576 f.
1628: 3690.7 f., 3691.9 f., 11992 f., 11995 f., 18302.4(*A*3) f.
1629: 18302.4(*A*3) f., 20526 f.
1630: 3691 f., 20526.5 f., 20533 f., 20686 f., 20686.5 f.
1631: 5780.7 f., 16614 f., 18302.5 f., 20549 f., 24576.3 ent.
1632: 5780.7–81 f., 16775 f., 17740 f., 20527 f., 20527.5 f., 20529 f., 20534 f.
1633: 3692 f., 7045 f., 11993 f., 20530 f., 20534 f.
1634: 3693 f., 7029 f., 11994 f., 17737 f., 19509 f., 20535 f.
1635: 7030 f., 7046 f., 17738 f., 20528 f. (c), 20528.5 f. (c), 20528a f. (c), 20528a.5 f. (c), 20540 sold [his] shop, 20540.5 sold [his] shop, 24574 f., 24576.3 f.
1636: 16615 f., 17637 f., 20531 f., 20538 f., 24576.5 f.
1637: 3694 f.
1638: 18303 f., 20532 f., 20536–6.5 f., 20548 f.
1639: 7047 f., 16776 f., 17740.5 f., 24575 f.
1640: 24576.7 f.

Marriot, Richard.
Bookseller in London, (1639) 1640–1680 (Wing L 2572). Son of **John Marriot**, with whom he began his career. [*Dict. 2*; DFM 1923; *Loan Book*, 1647–53; Globe 217.]
in St. Dunstan's Churchyard in Fleet Street (W.9), 1640 (7038)
1640: 7038 f.

Marsce (Maersche), Joris Abrahamsz van der.
Printer in Leiden, 1613–1652. [Gruys; Briels 351.]
1614: [21115(*A*3)].

Marsh, Edward.
Stationer in London, 1591. Son of **Thomas** and brother of **Henry Marsh.** [*Dict. 1.*]

Marsh, E. — *cont.*
No address known.
1591: (all SR assignments) 435.55, 726, 1018, 1304, 1360, 2801(***A***), 3810, 4608, 5159, 5233, 6215, 6851, 7655, 11192.5, 13289, 13308, 13496, 13498, 19475, 21826.8, 22161, 22254.3, 23133, 23884a.5, 23952.3, 24687, 25118.2.

Marsh, Henry.
Printer in London, 1584–1589. Son of **Thomas** and brother of **Edward Marsh**. In 1584 he seems to have been a partner of **Garrat Dewes**, and he apparently worked in his father's printing house. [*Dict. 1.*]
in Fleet Street (W.9), 1587 (13445)
1584: 5298.8, 17406.5, 19530, 22254, 22983.5.
1585: [6909], 14944.5, 25118.2.
1587: 13445, 22465.5.
1589: 839 by consent of.

Marsh (Marshe, Marche), Thomas.
Printer in London, 1554–1587 at least. Father of **Edward** and **Henry Marsh**. His earliest? books were published jointly with **John King**, with whom he may briefly have worked. Granted a patent in 1572 (Arber II.15) for Latin school books (excluding 'Lily's Grammar'). After Marsh ceased printing, the patent (or at least these titles) seems to have fallen under the administration of the **Stationers' Company**. For further details *see* the headnote following Appendix D/60. [Duff, *Century*: 100.]
in Creed Lane (Q.2), 1554? (3366(***A***3), 10989a.5(***A***3), 22599), all with J. King
in Fleet Street, 1554–1587
dw. — at the Prince's Arms (W.11), 1554 (18054)–1555 (3332, omits 'dw.'); variation: adds 'at the hither Temple gate', 1554? (22602.5). The item mentioned by Herbert II.848 as having 'King's' Arms in the sign, 1554/55 (410.7) actually has 'Prince's'.
— near to St. Dunstan's Church (W.9), 1556 (15768.5)–1587 (13288, colophon, has 'near unto'); the change from 'near' to 'near unto' as the favored term seems to have taken place in 1567/68 (511), 1568 (12345.5)
1157: 17228 (d/error).
1540: [9403] (d/repeat).
1554: 3366(***A***3) (d?), 10989a.5(***A***3) (d?), 18054 [f.], 22599 (d?), 22602.5 [f.] (d?).
1554/55: 410.7, 483.14.
1555: 3332, 3332.4, 5580, 9293a.3, 10908, 14104, [16246?], 16264–5 (d), 23014–4a (d?).
1555/56: [410.9?], [410.10?], 410.11, [410.11A(***A***)].
1556: 443.9 in aed., 9277 in aed., 9293a.5, 9972 (d), 15768, 15768.5, 23211.
1556/57: 410.12.
1557: [7640], [12427], 12443, 16817, 17112.5, 17228 (d?), 23318.7 (d).
1557/58: [482?].
1558: 443.11 in aed., 1988.8 ent., 10878.5 (d), 10878.7 (d?), 13497.5 ent., 21299 ent., 21796 (d), [25113?] (forged).
1558/59: 520.
1559: 1247 in aed. (d), 15217.5 in aed.
1559/60: 458, 521.
1560: 1243, 10990.5 (c), 11001 (d?), 11013.6 (c).
1560/61: [488?], 521.5.
1561: 5317 (d), 5720, 7651 (d?), 9976 (d), 24019.
1562: 360.7, 3966 (d), [9384.5] (d/repeat), 10990.7, 12207 (d), 21446.7 ent., 24687 (d?).
1562/63: [482.5?].
1563: 1248 (d), [11396.7] (forged, c), [11397a] (forged, c), 13490 (d), 13964 (d), 22250.5(***A***) in aed., 22464, [24650.5] (d?).
1563/64: 482.7.
1564: 435.41 (d), 10579 (d), 24290.
1565: 5602 ?ent., 7167 in aed., 7641 in aed., 10991 (c?), 12632, 15192, 17214, 23319 in aed.
1565/66: 510.5.
1566: 1736, 6850.3, 13805, 20926 ent., 22143 in aed., 23319.5 (d), 23325.4 (d).
1566/67: 510.7.
1567: 435.43, 1356.1, 1737, 4009 ex off., 13797, 23325.5 (d).
1567/68: 511.
1568: 3020, 12345.5, 12428, 13491, 13941 ent., 14105, 22250.6 in aed., 22608 (d), 23901.3.

Marsh, T. — *cont.*
1568/69: 482.9, [482.10?], 511.3, 515.27.
1569: 5294 (d), 5314 (d), 6215, 11746 (d?), 12939, 19122, 19138.5 ex off., 21622.2 ex off.
1570: 6850.5, [9377.9?] (repeat, c?), 10878.9 (c?), 10991.5 (c?), 17404, 17405 ent., 17406 ent., 17466 (d), 17653–3a.3 ex off., 22250.8 ap., 23322 (d), 24291.
1570/71: 511.7.
1571: 838, 1249, 13497.5, 20926.
1572: 7652, 13492, 13941 in aed., 18242, 18977a (d), 22251 ap., 23901.7, 24631 (d).
1573: 2801, 4607, 4770.6 ap., 6871 ap., 15525.3, 17653a.7 ex off., 22982 ap., 23323.5 (d), 23325.6 (d), 23885.7(***A***3, note).
1574: 435.45, 1250, 1304, 4770.7 ap., 4846.3(***A***, note), 5296 ap., 13065, 13443, 18243, 19140 ap., 22252 ap.
1575: 700.3, 1251, 1360, 5159 ex off., 5232, 5318.3 ap., [9360.7] (d?), [9362.2] (d?), [9363.4] (d?), [9368.5] (d?), [9371.5] (d?), [9375.7] (d?), [9378.5] (d?), [9384.5] (d?), [9389.5] (d?), [9393.5] (repeat, d?), [9396.5] (d?), [9400.3] (d?), [9403] (d?), [9406.5] (repeat, d?), [9409.3] (d?), [9411.5] (repeat, d?), [9414.5] (d?), 13444, 17406, 19123, 19141 ap., 23885.7 ex off., 23902.
1576: 435.47, 4608, 4686 ex off., 4770.9 ap., 7652.5, 13066, 13287, 13498, 15456, 15527, 17980, 18243.5, 18886, 19475, 22982.3 ap.
1577: 1583, 4771 ap., 4846.5 ap., 5274, 5297.3 ap., [9303.2], [10993.7?] (d?), 13287, 22253 ap., 22982.5 ap.
1578: 435.49, 725, 1018, 1252–2.5, 1852, 5233, 6850.6, 11192.5, 13974, 18977b, 21357, 24292.
1579: 1356.3, 4034, 5297.5 ap., 10993.9 (d?), 19142 ap., 23885.9 (***A***3).
1580: 700.7, 4771.3 ap., 5318.7 ap., 7653, 18510, 18978, 19125 (d?), [22253.3] (d?), [22253.5] (d?), 22982.7 ap.
1581: 11183.5, 11213 ent., 12745, 12745.5, 13224 ent., 15457, 17295, 17823 ent., 22221, 21826.8, 23133–3.5, 23133a, 23134, 23903, 23952.3.
1582: 3810, 5400.5 ex off./ex assig., 15209 ent., 22253.7 ap., 22983 ex off.
1583: 435.51, 701 ex off., 17405, 23884a.2, 23886 ex off.
1584: 435.51, [4940], 5298.8 ex assig., 13224, 17239.3, 22254 ex assig., 22465, 22983.5 ex assig.
1585: 435.53, 6850.7, 23886.5 ex off. (d?), 25118.2 ex assig.
1587: [694], 7655, 13288, 13445 ass'n.

Marshall, H. *See* Le Mareschal.

Marshall, William.
Translator and publisher in London, 1534–1538? [Duff, *Century*; *PBSA* 58 (1964): 219–31.]
No address used.
1534: [5641 f.] (d), [10504 f.] (d), [10504a f.] (d), 15986 f. (d), 21789.3 f. (d), [25127 f.].
1535: 10498 f. (d?), 15988 f., 17817 f., [21798.5 f.] (d?), 24238 f. (d), 24239 f. (d?).
1536: 16983.5 [f.] (d?).
1538: [15998 f.] (d?).

Martens (Martinus), Thierry.
Printer and bookseller in Alost 1473–1474, 1486–1492, in Antwerp 1493–1497, in Louvain 1498–1501, again in Antwerp 1502–1512, and again in Louvain 1512–1529. [Duff, *Century*; Rouzet 140.]
1499: 15805. **1507:** [11605.5], [11614.5]. **1508:** 696.4 per, [23940a].

Martin, junior. *See* Marprelate, Martin, junior.

Martin, Edme.
Bookseller and printer in Paris, 1601–1645†. [Lottin 2: 120.]
1629: 12641 (note).

Martin, Edward.
Bookseller in Norwich, 1632–1646 at least. [*Dict. 2.*]
No address used before 1641.
1632: 20832–2.5 sold.

Martin, Robert.
Importer of books and bookseller in London, (1622) 1633–1650 (Wing[2] M 849A) at least. Never formally bound but served with **Henry Fetherstone;** transferred to the Stat. Co. in 1622. Al-

Martin, R. — *cont.*
though the following addresses appear in the titles of his catalogues rather than in the imprints, it is sensible to include them here. In STC the imprints of all should be continued: [*f. R. Martin,*]. [*Dict. 2*; DFM 1311.]
in Paul's Churchyard (?A.3), 1633 (17512)–1635 (17513), probably at the Rose, Fetherstone's address
in the Old Bailey at the $ Venice (D.7), 1639 (17514, adds: not far from the pump)–1641 (Hazlitt II.669)
1633: [17512 f.]. **1635:** [17513 f.]. **1639:** [17514 f.]. **1640:** [17511.5 f.], [17515 f.].

Martin (Martyne), William.
Bookseller in London, 1552–1563. [Duff, *Century*.]
shop joining to the middle North door of Paul's at the $ Black Boy (A.1), 1561? (3494)
1561: 3494 f. (d?).

Martinus. *See* Martens.

Martyne. *See* Martin.

Masius. *See* Maes.

Masse, Jan, *pseud.*
Printer in 'Lydden' (Leiden?), 1625? = Unidentified printer, possibly in London. [*Dict. 1.*]
1625: 17884 (d?).

Masselin, Robert.
Printer in Paris 1548–1553, in Rouen 1554, and in Thiers, 1556–1557. [Duff, *Century*; Renouard.]
1553: 24623.7 ex off.

Mather, John.
Journeyman printer? in London, 1575†. In partnership with **David Moptid**. [*Dict. 1.*]
dw. in Red Cross Street next adjoining to St. Giles's Church without Cripplegate (I.7), 1575? (11885)
1575: 2001(*A*) [f.] (d?), 11885 [f.] (d?).

Mathew, Cutbere.
Journeyman printer? in London, c. 1549. Worked for **John Walley**. Possibly the Pieter de Cupere from Ypres who was servant to **Nicholas Hill** in 1550 (Worman 12, 30), since the item has types used by Hill.
in Whitechapel parish at the $ Friar (M.2), c. 1549 (2379.5)
1549: 2379.5 (c).

Mathewes (Mathusius), Augustine.
Printer in London, (1615) 1619–1638, and journeyman printer? until 1653 at least. Printed briefly in 1619 with **John White**, under whom are listed some 1620 items which Mathewes probably printed, and succeeded to the White printing material. Had **John Norton 2** as a partner 1624–1626. In 1637 he was deprived of his press, and the printing material passed to **Marmaduke Parsons**, for whom Mathewes may have continued to work. One of the *assignees of* **H. Ogden**. [*Dict. 1*; DFM 236; *Loan Book*, 1631–34; *St. Giles*, 1616–17; *Library* 16 (1936): 425–32.]
dw. in St. Bride's Lane in Fleet Street, in the Parsonage House (W.4), 1620 (6489)–1623 (23723)
dw. in the Parsonage Court near St. Bride's (W.4), 1632 (18899)
1619: 3951 ap., 13512 (note), 14512.7, 20282.3, 21375, 25616.
1620: 1527.7 (c), 3417, 4087.7 (c), 5433 (d?), 6489, [6611.5], [11278], [11796.5?] (c), 13512, 14512.7, 14618.5 (c), 14674, 14694.2(*A3*), [17372], 18105.3 (note), [20440] (d?), 26041.
1621: 6583.7–4.5, 6601, 7024, 11545, [12014], [14056?], 17362, 17624, [18302], 24702 typis, [25044.5], 25047, 25049, 25049a, 25090, [25925–5.5], [25926.5], [25928–8.3], [25928.5], [25928.7], [25970.5?], 26042, [26051?] (d).
1622: 112, [5674], 6359, 6601.5, 7051, 7054 (note), [7228], 7229–30, 7367, [10223], 10860, 13814, 14647, 14896 (d), 17332, 17733, 17912, 18598 (c), 19068, 20186.7, 20991, [23797] (false), 25033a, 25042, [25045], 25050, 25052, 25053, 25055, 25055.5, [25903–3b].
1623: 106, 106.5, 115, 595.9, 843, 860, 4861, 7021, 7039, 7057 (note), 7336, 14535, 14668.5–69, 15093–3a, 17734, 17739, 17739.5, [18481], 19068, 20943.5, 21302, 21376, [21862], 23723, 24962.5, 25030.5, 25048, 25173, [25899.5] (d?).

Mathewes, A. — *cont.*
1624: [30], 40, 115, 129, [853.5?] (d?), 1498, 3442.2, 3442.4, 3662, 5433.5, 6059, 7033–3a, 7034, 7057.5 (note), 7619, 7742, 10192.7, 11037.5, 11705, 12530, 12720, 17830, [18421], 18430, 18507.144, 18608, 20832a, 20943.7, 21302a, 21609, 24347, 25054, 25056, 25090a, 25090a.3(*A3*).
1625: 115, 130, 1025.7, [1182.7(*A*)] (c), [1328] (d?), [1687], [4541.5?] (c?), 5379, 6072, [6270] (d), [6791.7] (c?), [6792.7] (c?), [6901.5] (d?), 7040, 7619, 12481, 13800 (d), 14440, 14488, 14897, [16864a.7] (c), 17331, [19264] (c), 20405, 21141, 23108.3, 24512, [24562], 26037.
1626: 115, [1168], 3676, [4514.3], 5876.5, [7035], [7050], 7496, [11395], 12515, 14897, 16886, [17391–1.5], [19529], [19529.5] (d), 21091, 21129.5, [21490].
1627: [1169], [3222], [4137.3], [7035–5a], [7190], [9978?] (d?), [12360–0.3], 12515, [16887], [17392], [20462], [20463], 21377, 21412, 24268.7, [24739.5–40], [24741], [24742], 24743, 24744, 24745.
1628: [1170], 1683, [7745], [7745.5], [7745.7], [7746], [12690.5], 13989, 16691.5, [17201] (d), [17403], 18673, [19229.5] (d), 23539, 23696, [23813.7], [24824].
1629: 104, [1105.5?], 5533, [7425], 7478, 7480, [10173], 11541, [13248.6], [14703] (d), 17298, 17421, [17857.7(*A*)] (c?), [19232] (d), [20457], [20459.7] (d?), 20943, 21831, 23108.5, 23857, 25637.
1630: 104, [1361.5] (c), [1668], 1679, [4241] (c?), 4643, 5359, 5380, [5425] (d?), 6302, 7476 [by &] ven., 7505 (c), 7534, 10586, [11380.7] (c), [12015] (c), 12965, 15186.5 (c), 16755, [16855] (c), 17095, 17100, 17641, 17735, [19165.7(*A3*)] (c), 19168, [19271.5] (c), 19772, 21331 (d), 22306, [24115?], 24929–9a, 25091, [25769.5], [26118] (c).
1631: 358, 1672, 3468, [3643.5?], 4113, 4114, 6516, 7191, 7242, 7329, 7535, 7536, 11879.2, 11980–1, 12933, 13205, 13801 (d), 13902, 13903, 13990, 13992, 14684, 15510, 16888, 17845, 19388a, [21551.3] (d?), 22561, [22919.3] (d?), 23340, 24905, 25688.
1631/32: 527.21, 24155–5a, 24156.
1632: 595.10, 3638, [3644.5?], 3819, 5355, 6491, 7330, 10174, 11879.4, 11879.6, 11879.8, 11879.9, 12027, [12092.6] (c), 12172, [12544] (d?), 12771, 12935, 12967, [13843] (d?), 13920a (c), 14479.3, 17096, 17100a, 18899, 20832–2.5, 21706, 23340, 23374 typis, 24108, 25930.
1632/33: 527.23.
1633: 2947, 5354, [6414], 7041 ent., 7394.5, 10227.5 (d), 11327, 11432, 12416, 13180 per, 13259, 14670.3–.5, 15094, 16889 ent., 17400, 17442, [17471], 17472, 17512 typis, 17714–4a, 17715, 18020, 18431, [18699] (d?), 18711c, 18737, 18899b, 18899c, 18901, 18991 ex off., 19182, [20275], [20464–4a], 21421, 23108.6, 23132–2a, [23436(*A3*)?] (c?), 25582–2a, 26010–0.5 typis.
1633/34: 496, 527.24.
1634: [3082], [5357], 5371, [5416] (d?), 6602, 6902, [7029], 7036, 7321, 11070, [13991], 17141, [18901a] (d?), 18992 ex off., [20513], 20944, [21731], 25092, [25355], 25900–0d.
1634/35: 527.25.
1635: 1669, 1689, [3083], [5358], 5870, [6308], [6921?] (c), [7030], 7418, 7428, [12141], [13223], [13705], 14685, 16889, [17357–8], [18190], [19236] (c), [19236.5] (c), [19240] (c), 20944, [23110], [23727], [23730], [23731?], [23744], [23781], [23782–2.5], [23794], [23817], [24293.7] (c), [25032], 25900–0d.
1636: [6305], [6309], [10194], [10371], [12202?], [12956], [13270], [13270.5], [18646(*A3*)], 23764–4a, 23805, 24559, [25032].
1637: 4236.4–.6, [5901], [13015] (d?), [13271], [15108] (c), [17937], 21303, 21667–7.5, 25027.5–28 imp.
1638: 7037.

Mattes, Edmund.
Bookseller in London, (1590) 1597–1613. Brother of **William Mattes**. [*Dict. 1.*]
at the Hand and Plough in Fleet Street (W.2), 1597 (17231)–1606 (5776) at least
1597: 17231 f. **1598:** 17482 f. **1599:** 5642 f. **1600:** 5775 f., 24135 f. **1601:** 5774 f., 5775 f. **1606:** 4622 f. (d), 5776–6.3 f. **1612:** 4275 ass'd.

Mattes, William.
Bookseller in London, (1592) 1594–1597†. Brother of **Edmund Mattes**. [*Dict. 1.*]
dw. in Fleet Street at the Hand and Plough (W.2), 1594 (25118)–1597 (90, has 'shop')
1594: 18755 f., 25118 f. **1595:** 4274.5 f., 21789 f. **1596:** 3117 f. (d), 16655 f. **1597:** 90 f., 17231 ent.

Mauditier, Jean.
Printer in Rouen, 1499–1508. [Duff, *Century*; Muller 102.]
1502: 16163. **1505:** [15793].

Maunsell (Mansell), Andrew 1.
Bookseller in London, 1576–1604 at least. Freed as a Draper by **John Wight** on 6 Dec. 1574. Father of **Andrew Maunsell 2**. Although he is called 'Stationer' in 1604 at the time of his son's binding (Arber II.285), he never formally transferred to the Stat. Co. In 1590 many of his copyrights were entered to **Robert Dexter** without Maunsell's name being mentioned (Arber II. 566). [*Dict. 1*.]
in Paul's Churchyard, 1576–1589
dw. — at the Parrot (A.3), 1576 (21239)–1581 (4072, omits 'dw.')
shop at the West end of Paul's Church (A.10), 1582 (16814)–1583 (21067)
dw. — at the Brazen Serpent (A.3), 1584 (4858)–1589 (11807)
shop in the Royal Exchange (O.8), 1592 (12561)
in Lothbury (H.9), 1594 (12896)–1595 (17669, has 'dw.')
1576: 14484.3 f. (d), 21239 f.
1577: 3363.9(*A*3) ent., 4857.7 f., 11803a.7 f., 11804 f., 11804.5 f., 15416 f., 20452 ent.
1578: 4342 f., 5251 f. (d), 6231 f., 7241 f. (d), 11805–5.2 f., 11805.4–.6 f., 15417 f.
1579: 5243 f. (d), 13066.5 f., [17445.5] sold, [17797] sold.
1580: 11805.8 f., [17446] sold.
1581: 4072 f., 13059 f., 21233.3–.7 f.
1582: 11806 f., 16814 f., 21066 f. (d).
1583: 11806.5 f., 21067 f., 24669 at costs of.
1584: 4858 f., 24775 f.
1585: 5181 ent., 21226 f., 21226.5 f.
1586: 6438 f., 10825 f., 21067.3 f.
1587: 21227 f.
1588: 15418 f., [17489] sold.
1589: 11807 f., 17491 f., 21237 f.
1592: 4440 sold, 12561 f., 23995 sold [his] shop.
1594: 12895 imp., 12896 sold.
1595: 17669 f.
1596: 13680.9 f., 13681–1.3 f.

Maunsell, Andrew 2.
Stationer in London, (1613) 1614. Son of **Andrew Maunsell 1**. [*Dict. 1*; DFM 2691.]
No address known.
1614: 21381 ent.

Mayer, Johann.
Printer in Heidelberg, 1562–1577, and in Neustadt an der Hardt, 1578†. [Benzing 195, 346.]
1565: 16575.

Maylard (Maylerd), Leonard.
Bookseller in London, (1564) 1567–1568. [*Dict. 1*.]
in Paul's Churchyard at the Cock (B), 1567 (10423, 20072)
1567: 10423 f., 20072 f. **1568:** 11476 f., 17244 f.

Mayler, John.
Grocer and printer in London, 1539–1545. Succeeded to the printing material of the first press of **John Wayland**. [Duff, *Century*; *Library* 11 (1930): 319–41.]
in Botolph Lane at the White Bear (T.10), 1539 (16010)–1543 (1738)
1538/39: [392.3?].
1539: 2966.7 (d), 16010, 16011 (d?), 16795 (note).
1540: 2799, [5871.9(*A*)?] (c), 16018–8.5 (d?), [25587.5], [25823.3?] (d?).
1541: [1739] (d?), 16022 (d).
1542: [1713] (d), 1714, 1715, 1717, 1734, 1735, 1740, 1742, 1749, 1775, 4045.5, [9175b.10?] (d?), 14640.
1543: 977.5 (d?), 1730.5, 1731, 1734.5, 1738, 1743, 1750, 1776, 4047, 4048 (d/repeat), 5175.
1543/44: [394], 488.9.
1545: 15441.7, 15445.5.
1546: 4048 in house (d?).

Maynard, John.
Bookseller in London, (1635) 1638–1642. [*Dict. 2*; DFM 1067.]

Maynard, J. — *cont.*
shop in Fleet Street at the George near St. Dunstan's Church (W.9), 1638 (20929)–1640 (25641, omits 'shop') at least
1638: 20929 f. **1639:** 20930 f. **1640:** 25641 f.

Maynyal, Guillaume.
Printer in Paris, 1480, 1487–1490. [Duff, *Century*; Renouard; BMC VIII. xxix.]
1487: 16164. **1488:** 16136.

Mead, Robert.
Stationer in London, 1608–1656. Although he began binding apprentices in 1608 (DFM 1935), was called to the Livery in 1616 (*C-B C*: 89), and later was active in Stat. Co. affairs, he seems never to have published anything. [*Dict. 2*; DFM 2452.]
No address known.
1638: 1680 ent., 6545 ent., 17202 ent.

Mede, Joseph.
Biblical scholar and author in Cambridge, b. 1586–1638†. [*DNB*, under Mead.]
No address used.
1627: 17766 imp.

Meietti, Paolo.
Printer in Venice 1569–1596, and in Padua 1571–1598; also bookseller in Vicenza 1591–1594. [Borsa.]
1592: 1431.12 ap.

Meighen, Richard.
Bookseller in London, 1614–1642?†. Freed by redemption in 1614 and shared a shop and most imprints with **Thomas Jones 2** until 1617. Between 1618 and 1630 Meighen often had two shops simultaneously. [*Dict. 2*; DFM 1947.]
shop without Temple Bar under (near, at) St. Clement's Church (X.2), 1614 (312.5, with T. Jones 2, has 'their' shop)–1622 (3150); variation: adds 'over against Essex House', 1618 (24025)
shop at Westminster Hall (X.17), 1618 (24025)–1620 (21538)
shop without Temple Bar at the $ Leg over against the Chequer Tavern betwixt Arundel House and Strand Bridge (X.4), 1623 (4494)–1628; variations:
at the Leg in the Strand, 1625 (25940)
at the Leg near Arundel House in the Strand, 1628 (5370)
in St. Dunstan's Churchyard in Fleet Street (W.9), 1625 (25940)–1630 (13618); in 1629 (11069) this is the only address
shop next to the Middle Temple gate (W.13), 1630 (13618)–1639 (15119, omits 'gate', adds 'in Fleet Street'); variation: has 'shop', adds 'near Temple Bar', 1633 (11982)
1614: 312.5 f.
1615: 312.5 f., 18523 f., 19333 f., 24043 f., 25981 f.
1616: 10639–9.3 f., 14752 sold, 18524 f.
1617: 4897 f., 10641 f., 19812.5 ent.
1618: 20328 f., 24025 f., 24025.5(*A*3) f. (d?).
1619: 18606 f.
1620: 21538 f., 23544 f.
1621: 3150 sold, 22634 f.
1622: 3150 sold.
1623: 4494 f., 7438 ex off.
1624: 22731.5 ent.
1625: 12635.5 f., 25940 f.
1627: 3770a f., 21219a f.
1628: 1393 f., 5369 f., 5370 f., 11706.6 ent., 22731.5 f., 23052 sold.
1629: 1394 f., 11069 f.
1630: 13618 f., 17891 f., 17893 f., 22301 f., 22383 f.
1631: 11980–1 f., 23340 imp.
1632: 11977 f., 22274 f., 22274d f., 23340 imp.
1633: 11982 f., 13517 sold, 17442 f.
1634: 5371 f., 11070 f.
1635: 1593 f., 6308 f., 22175 pro.
1636: 6305 f., 6309 f., 11706.6 f., 22175.3 (repeat), 22176 (repeat).
1637: 973 f., 11706.6 f.
1638: 6042 f., 10187 f., 23444 f.
1639: 15119 f.
1640: 10188 f. (d), 14754 f.

Melagrano, Giovanni Andrea, *pseud.*
Printer without place specified, 1589. = J. Wolfe (Woodfield no. 48).
1589: 19913.

Melvill, David.
Bookseller in Aberdeen, 1622–1643†. [*Dict. 2.*]
No address used.
1622: 7349.5 f., 24067 imp.
1622/23: 404.5 f.
1623: 5960 f., 6779.5 imp., 6783.5 imp., 13025 imp., 22007 f., 24846 imp.
1623/24: 445.19 f.
1624: 6781.7 imp., 12492 f., 22185.5 f.
1624/25: 405.3 f.
1625: 16594.5 f.
1625/26: 405.5.
1626: 2711 f., 2712 f., 2713 f., 2713.5 f.
1628: 4390 f., 15668 f.
1629: 2714 f., 16595 f., 16596 f., 24795 imp.
1630: 1995 f., 5302 imp., 13154 f., 16596 f., 18953 imp.
1631: 5957 f., 23193 imp., 24881.5 imp.
1632: 2719 f.
1633: 2721.5 f., 16597 f.

Mense, Conradus, *pseud.*
Printer in 'Basel', 1560. = Unidentified printer, probably in a German-language area. [*Dict. 1.*]
1560: 14794.

Menyman, William.
Priest, editor, and patron in London, 1505? Fellow of Whittington College, College Hill, upper Thames Street, on the site formerly and later the parish church of St. Michael Paternoster Royal (**18** 10:12 (#51)).
1505: 18846 ad rogatum (d?).

Merchant. *See* Marchant.

Mercurius, *Britannicus, pseud.*
Publisher of newsbooks and news pamphlets in London, 1625–1627. = N. Butter and N. Bourne. The items indexed below are *not* listed under Butter or Bourne.
No address used.
1625: 3595 f., 15571 f., 18507.159 f., —.160 f., —.161 f., —.162 f., —.162A f., —.163 f., [—.164 f.], —.165 f., —.166 f., —.167 f., —.168 f., —.169 f., —.170 f., —.171 f., —.172 f., —.173 f., —.174 f., —.175 f., —.176 f.
1626: 6877.5 f., 10419 f., 10817 f., 16845 f., 16845.5 f., 18507.177 f., [—.178 f.?] (d), —.179 f., —.180 f., —.181 f., —.182 f. (d), —.183 f., —.184 f.
1627: [18507.185] f. (d), —.186 f.

Meredith, Christopher.
Bookseller in London, (1624) 1625–1653†. Shared a shop and copyrights with **Philemon Stephens** through 1640 at least. [*Dict. 2*; DFM 2174.]
their shop at the Golden Lion in Paul's Churchyard (B), 1625 (13825)–1640 (1179, omits 'their shop') at least; variation: 1627 (4228.5, has 'dw.')
1625: 57 f., 4220a.5 sold, 13825 f., 18359 f.
1626: 56 f., 4233–3.3 f., 11648 f., 11952 sold, 13820 f.
1627: 4228–8.5 f., 5362 f., 7049 f., 7527 f.
1628: 1160.5–.7 sold, 4205 ent., 4221 sold, 4236.3 ent., 4236.9 ent., 5144 ent., 7137 ent., 11953 sold, 12637 f., 21436 sold.
1629: 1161 sold, 7144 f., 12348 imp.
1630: 3911 f., 4222 sold, 4229 f., 4239 f., 12876 f., 21125 f., 23610 f., 24007 f., 25849 f.
1631: 4238 f., 23610–1 f., 24017.5 ven.
1632: 4236.9 sold, 6154 imp., 12771 f., 12873 f., 12877 f., 13822 f.
1633: 4223 f., 6057 f., 7137 f., 12878 f., 14892 imp., 17493 imp., 21151 f.
1634: 4230 f., 7137 f., 12640 f., 22220 imp., 26078 f.
1635: 1887 f., 12879 f., 25718 f.
1636: 60.3 f., 12897.5 f., 19910 f., 21544 f., 25718 f.
1637: 60.5 f., 4231 f., 4236.4 f., 11652 (note), 11652b f., 21126 f., 21543 imp., [23245] sold, 24498.5 f.
1638: 59.5 f., 1177.5 f., 1178 f., 1178.5 f., 1680 ent., 3772.2 f., 6181.4 ent., 6233 imp., 6545 ent., 12874 f., 14501 f., 17202 ent., 21816 imp.
1639: 58 f., 60 f., 60.7 f., 6233 imp., 12871 f., 13908 f., 14500.5 f., 21816 imp., 21816.5 ven., 23066 imp., 23199.7 f., 25029 imp., 25752 f., 25971 ent.

Meredith, C. — *cont.*
1640: 59.7 f., 1179 f., 2369 imp., 4225 f., 10706 imp., 11530 sumpt., 12898 f., 13724 f.

Merlin, Guillaume.
Bookseller in Paris, 1538–1574. [Duff, *Century*; Renouard.]
1555: 16217 ap. **1556:** 15844 ap./pro, 15847 ap./pro. **1557:** 15847 ap./pro.

Mesens (Mesius), Jacob 1.
Printer and bookseller in Antwerp, c. 1592–1625†. [Rouzet.]
1611: 18791.5 ap.

Mesens, Jacob 2.
Printer in Antwerp, 1631–1639 at least.
1639: 12808.7.

Meslier, Hugo.
Editor? or proof-corrector? working in 1508? with **Richard Pynson**: at the George near St. Dunstan's Church in Fleet Street (W.9). [Duff, *Century*.]
No separate address used.
1508: 16899 cum cura ac diligentia (d?).

Mestais, Jean.
Printer and bookseller in Paris, 1618–1640 at least. [Lottin 2: 124.]
1640: 21454.

Metaxas, Nikodemos.
Greek editor and printer in London, 1623?–1627. He worked with **William Stansby**, **William Jones 3**, and **John Haviland**; it was with the last, at the **Eliot's Court Press**, that the item below was printed. Toward the end of 1627, using some of the decorative printing material he had acquired from these men, Metaxas briefly established the first Greek press in Constantinople. [*Library* 22 (1967): 13–43; *HLB* 15 (1967): 140–68.]
1626: [16854.3] (d?).

Meteren (Demetrius), Emanuel van.
Dutch merchant and author in London, 1552–1612†. [*Dict. 1*; Worman.]
No address used.
1609: 17845.3 voor. **1610:** 17845.7(*A*3) voor.

Mettayer, Jean, *dit* **Jamet.**
Printer in Paris 1573–1589, in Blois and Tours 1589–1593, and again in Paris 1593–1605. [Renouard.]
1579: 24718 (note).

Mettayer, Pierre, *dit* **Jamet.**
Printer and bookseller in Paris 1589, in Tours 1591, and again in Paris, 1595–1639†.
1634: 19203.3 (note).

Meurer, Ignatius.
Printer in Stockholm, 1612–1660 at least.
1626: 17658.5.

Meuris, Aert, *pseud.*
Printer in 'the Hague', 1621. = Edward Allde. For the genuine printer of this name, active in the Hague 1602–1644 at least, *see* Gruys; Briels 361–2.
1621: 11353, 17672, 22083.

Michel, Marin.
Printer in Rouen, 1614–1680†. [Lepreux III/1: 325–6.]
1614: 5161.5, 19072.3. **1615:** 20451 in house.

Michell, John. *See* Mychell.

Michell, Roger.
Bookseller in London, 1627–1631† (G1ʳ of STC 5569). [*Dict. 1*; DFM 1912.]
dw. in Paul's Churchyard at the Bull's Head (A.2), 1628 (12974; 5670, omits 'dw.')
dw. in Charterhouse Lane (E.2), 1631 (21010.3)
1627: 5669 ent.
1628: 1904 f., 5670–0.2 f., 12974 f., 13900 f., 13900.5 f.
1630: 21010 f.
1631: 15463 f., 21010.3 f.

Middleton, Henry.

Printer in London, 1567–1587†. Son of **William** and husband of **Jane Middleton**. In 1567–1572 he shared printing material and most imprints with **Thomas East;** afterwards he moved into premises formerly owned by **William Griffith**. Middleton's printing material passed after his death to **Robert Robinson**, and his sales shop was acquired by **Thomas Newman**. *See* also Appendices A/10–11 and E/9–10. [*Dict. 1*; *SB* 32 (1979): 53–4 (abstract of will).]

in Fleet Street near to St. Dunstan's Church (W.9), 1567 (11974, with T. East)

?sold in Ivy Lane at the Black Horse (C.3), 1568 (4028, colophon, East for Middleton)

dw. at London Wall by the $ Ship (H.8), 1571 (24722, with T. East)

dw. in Fleet Street at the Falcon (W.9), 1573 (12788, colophon)–1587 (11557.5)

shop in St. Dunstan's Churchyard (W.9), 1573 (12788, colophon)–1577 (793.7, colophon) and undoubtedly later

1567: 11974.
1568: 4028 f.
1569: [10289?] (d), 18949.
1570: 4029.
1571: 4395, 11445 per, 11477, [20738?], 23641, 24722.
1572: 700 ap., 4055, 4655, 4846 in aed., 11445.5 per, 14724a.7 (d).
1573: 540 (d?), 3542 ap., 10473 ap., [11635?] (d), [12155] (d?), 12788, 13570, 21622.4 ap., 21622.6 ap., [22630], 25710.
1574: 567 (d), 4029.5, [4826.6?] (d?), [10229?], 10793a, 11555, 12432, 15206.5, 22241.5, 22242, 23438.7 in aed., 24477.5.
1575: 5691 (d), [10550?] (false), 10794, 11643–3a, 24677.
1576: [164], [826] (d), 4029.7 (d?), [4738], [6726], [11049], 11556 (d?), 11881, 15175–5.5, [19151], [25348].
1577: 793.7, 825 ex typ., [3091], [4056], [6727], [10795], [12426], [12434], 13042, [18413?], 22265, 22266.
1578: 827 in off., [2879.4?] (d?), [3091.5], [3294.3], 4030 (d?), 4393, [6274], [6728], 10470 typis, 11417 per, 11478, [12425], 13029, [13905], [19138], 20979, [21181] (d), [21181.5] (d), [22470?], 24995 (d).
1579: 2056–6.8, [4441], 6229.5, 11433, 11683, [11832], 17302, 20762.5 ex off., 21182.
1580: 2033, 2056–6.8, 2359–9.4, 3750, 3751, 5103, [5684.5], 11434 (d?), 11434.5 (d?), 11456, 13743, 15450 (d), 18884–4.7, 20558, 20624, [22044?] (d), 22907, 23872, [24251.5?], 24584, 24789.
1581: 569, 2057–8a.5, [3294.7], 11039, 11448, 11557, 11833, 11897–7.5, 13059, 18807, 21233.3–.7, 21682, 22109.5, [23874], [24242.5?].
1582: 3744 (d), 4421, 11479, 11806, [13656], [13672], 13961, 13961.5, 18807.3, 23873, 24780, 25997.
1583: 758, 1081, 1095, 1846, 3746, 4442–3.5, 5322.8–23, 6199 (d?), 11806.5, [12269.5] (d?), 15145, [19179.5] (d?), 19962, 22110–0.5, 22857, 23873.5, 24144–4.5, [24669], 24790, 25362.
1584: 1082, 4031, [4057], 5478, 11429, 11493.5, [12435], 13962, 15147, 16747, 19064, 22858, 24790.3.
1585: 1982.5, 2059–60.5, 18926.7, 21713, 24891 (d?).
1586: 1096, 6438, 11480, 12201.5, 20802.5, 24530, 25404.
1587: 1491 (d?), [4058?], 4076 (d), 4422, [9305.3?], 11557.5, [13043], 15148, 21236, 21541, 23977.

Middleton, Jane.

Publisher in London, 1588? Widow of **Henry Middleton** and abortively attempted to succeed him as a printer (*Reg. B*: 26, erroneously identified as 'Eliz.'). [*Dict. 1*, under husband.]

No address used.

1588: 5402 pro (d?).

Middleton (Myddylton), William.

Printer in London, 1541–1547†. Father of **Henry Middleton.** William succeeded to the house and printing material of **Robert Redman** as well as to Redman's trade as principal printer of law books. These passed in turn to **William Powell,** who married Middleton's widow. [Duff, *Century*.]

in Fleet Street at the George next to St. Dunstan's Church (W.9), 1541 (25420)–1547 (9293.8)

1541: 19631 in aed., 25420.
1542: 9287 (d?), 9524, 9538 (d?), 9544 (d?), 9544.5 (d?), 9751 (d?), 9765 (d?), 9821 (d?), 11396.5 (d?), 11396.7 (forged), 12102 (d?), 23884 (c).
1543: [7716.5], 9292, 9987.5 (d), 10952, 10972, 10997 (d?), 11009 (d?), 14878 in aed. (d?), 15585, 20902 per, 21570.

Middleton, W. — *cont.*

1543/44: [394.5?].
1544: 3378.7 (d), 7698 (d?), 7717 per, 7731 per, 9293, 9670 (d?), 9722 (d?), 9727 (d?), 9756.5 (d?), 9773 (d?), 9988 (d), 13300 (d?), [13305.5] (d?), 14878.3 in aed. (d?), 15763, 18407, 22156, 24203.
1545: 3327.9, 9293.3, 9676 (d?), 9785 (d?), 10954 (note: 3), 10987, 14109.7 (c), 14522.5 (c), 15585.5, 15733, 17660.5 (c), 18220 (d?), 18396 (d?), 20902.5, 23965 (d?), 24112 (c).
1546: 3326.5 (d?), 13175.10, 14117(*A*, note), 17501, 22821.
1547: 3373.5, [5205?] (d?), 7720.4 per, 7734a per, 9293.8, 9620 (d?), 9626, 9644 (d?), 9659 (d?), 9687 (d?), 9791 (d?), 9890 (d?), 9929.5, 9930.5 (d?), 9931.5 (d?), 9934.5 (d?), 9947 (d?), 9955 (d?), 9962 (d?), 10446 ex aed., 10997.7 (c?), 11012 (d?), 17502, 22216, 22821, 23714 (d?).

1564: 3378.7 (d/error).

Mierdman (Mierdmans, Nuyts), Steven.

Printer in Antwerp 1543–c. 1548, in London c. 1548–1553, and in Emden 1554–1559†. Brother-in-law of **Matthias Crom**. While in London Mierdman did much printing for **Richard Jugge**, **Walter Lynne** and others and lived in the parish of St. Mary at Hill, Billingsgate Ward (T.12). In Emden he was in partnership with **Jan Gheylliaert.** [Duff, *Century*; Rouzet; Benzing 104; *Library* 18 (1963): 275–87.]

The year of Mierdman's arrival in London is uncertain, and it is possible that items dated 1547 and 1548 for which [*Antwerp*] has sometimes been supplied in STC were actually printed in London. Mierdman's characteristic 78 mm. 'Dutch' textura occurs in some publications of **John Day** dated 1547, e.g. 11884, 13213, but it is not clear whether Day had his own casting or if Mierdman was perhaps involved.

No address used.

1544: [14828], [24354] (false, d?).
1545: [1296.5?] (d?), [3765] (false), [10488] (false), [4797.3] (false), [5889] (false).
1546: [1270] (false), [1462.9?] (false), [11382].
1547: [17789] (false).
1547/48: [470?], [470.1?].
1548: [822], [1274a] (c), [1297?] (d?), [2852], [6083?] (d), [11235?], [11383], [11884] (d?), [16964], [16982], [17795] (d?), [17796] (d?), [18877], [20843], [20849], [21826.6] (d?), [24359] (d), [24784] (d?).
1549: [1290], [2077], [2725], 2856 (note), [3963] (d), [6085] (d?), [7828.3(*A*3)?] (d), [11235.5?], [13753], [13760], [14822] (d?), [15274] (d), [15445], [16050.3] (c), [17119].
1549/50: [517.15(*A*)].
1550: [1275] (d?), [1298] (c), [2080?], [2087.6?], [2860], [2864] (d?), [4626], [6096], [12723], [17117], 17330, 18311, [18599?] (c), [20177], [21305.7?] (c), [24223.5], [25255].
1551: [1273], [1273.5], [2865] (d?), 4042.4, [5179], 11233, 15260, 15263 in off., 16566, [18094], [19783], [22992?] (d?), 24365, [24368].
1552: [1294] (d?), [2867] (d), [2868] (d), [9980?] (d?), [9980.5?] (d?), [11903], [13940], [14119.3], 15259 per, 17863.3.
1553: 2090 (note), [2091], [2869] (d), [2870] (d), [3204(*A*3)?] (d), [3496] (d), [4813] (d), [13208] (d?), [14941?] (d?), [17791] (d), [18244], [20188(*A*3)?], 21307.3.
1554: [19890?] (false, d).

Milanges, Simon, *pseud.*

Printer in 'Bordeaux', 1589. = T. Orwin. For the genuine man of this name, active 1572–1623, who undoubtedly printed the French original of the following English translation, *see* Muller 9. [*Dict. 1.*]

1589: 13098.2.

Milbourne (Milburne, Mylbourne), Robert.

Bookseller in London, 1617–1643?†. His first two years all but one of his books (7410, which has no address) were sold at the shop of **Edward Blount:** at the (Black) Bear in Paul's Churchyard (B), where Milbourne may have been working. [*Dict. 2*; DFM 621, 2712.]

in Paul's Churchyard, 1619–1635

shop at the great South door of Paul's (A.8), 1619 (7411)–1627 (24705, omits 'shop')

shop — at the Greyhound (B), 1628 (7424)–1635 (3083, omits 'shop')

Milbourne, R. — *cont.*
at the Unicorn near Fleet Bridge (W.3), 1636 (12202)–1639 (5360); variation: adds 'in Fleet Street', 1638 (17101)
at the Holy Lamb in Little Britain (F.4), 1640, (26084) and probably later
1617: 7407 f.
1618: 1635 f., 7410 f., 7610 f.
1619: 1649 f., 7411 f., 7412 f., 7620 f., 14088 ent., 14088.5 f., 15528 f.
1620: 1647 f., 7413 f., 7426 f., 7431.5 f., 10816 f., 14091 f., 25999 f.
1621: 6601 f., [10690 f.], 14491 f., 22389 imp., 25845 ent., 25846 ent.
1622: 3830.5 f., 6601.5 f., 6603 f., 7611 f., 10689 f., 14717.5 f., 21123 f., 25104 f.
1623: 7336 f., 7620.5 f., 7621 f., 11180 f., 11510 f., 14651 f., 15311 f., 21124 sold, 22390 imp., 23920 pro, 23923 f., 25103 f.
1624: 39–9.7 f., 40 f., 4640 f., 7415 f., 7619 f., 10738–8.3 f., 11701 f., 11702–2.3 f., 11703 f., 11704 f., 11705 f., 11706 f., 14488 ent., 20832a f., 23504 f., [24347] sold, 24925–5a f., 26013.5 sold.
1625: 1045 sold, 1960 ent., 4641 f., 5379 f., 7619 f., 10885 ent., 12887a f., 25769 f.
1626: 1239 f., 1961 f., 4634–5 f., 6598 f. (d), 7067 imp., 7415.5 f., 10718 f., 10734 imp., 10735–6 f., 10737 f., 11395 f., 18186 f. (d?), 18996 f., 25026 imp., 26083 f.
1627: 4642 f., 6607.5 ent., 6608 f., 6608.3 f., 6608.5 f., 7068 imp., 11395 f., 12963 f. (d), 14933 f., 18973 f., 24705 f., 25027 imp.
1628: 5363 imp., 7416 f. (d?), 7424 f., [11078(*A*3)?] sold, 17097 f., 18187 f., 24703 imp.
1629: 7070 f., 7416.5 f., 7425 f., 10731 f., 14483 f., 17098 f., 17099 f., 25102 f., 25769.3 f.
1630: 1928 ent., 4643 f., 5354.7 imp., 5359 f., 5380 f., 10733 f., 10885 f., 12965 imp., 17095 f., 17100 f., 25769.5 f.
1631: 1928.5 f., 4113 f., 4114 f., 5845.3 sold, 5983 f., 7419 f., 11879.2 f., 18189 f., 12966 imp., 19524 imp., 19652.5 sold, 19653.5 sold, 19653b.5 sold, 22787 sold, 25688 f.
1632: 1635 ent., 1649 ent., 5355 imp., 7417 f., 7420 f., 7427 f., 10227.3 f., 11879.4 f., 11879.6 f., 11879.8 f., 11879.9 sumpt., 12964.5 imp. (d), 12967 imp., 17096 f., 17100a f., 25845 f.
1633: 5354 sumpt., 7069 imp., 7394.5 f., 14670.3(*A*3) sold, 14670.5 sold, 16461 f., 18182 f., 23132 f.
1634: 3082 f., 5357 f., 5984 f., 6602 f., 12964 ven., 16440 [sold], 20513 f., 23132a.5 f., 25700a (note), 25700a.7 f., 25900 ent.
1635: 3083 f., 5358 f., 7418 f., 7428 f., 12141 f., 18190 f., 25900b f.
1636: 5984.5 f., 10194 f., 12202 f., 13270 f., 13270.5 f., 18646 f., [21666.5?] f.
1637: 5356 imp., 5985–5.7 f., 11728.6 pro (d), 13271 f., [14492(*A*3) sold], 14492.3(*A*3) f., 20238 ent.
1638: [2747 f.], 5354.3 sumpt., 5361 f., 17101 f., 17918 f.
1639: 5360 f., 10284 f., 10511.3 f.
1640: 10511.5 f., 12582.1 f., 14297a f., 26084 f.

Millard, William.
Bookseller in Shrewsbury, 1635.
No address used.
1635: 23915.5 f.

Miller, George.
Printer in London, (1611) 1618–1646†. In 1625 he succeeded to the printing material of his former master, **Richard Field,** and that year and part of the next took **Richard Badger** as partner. [*Dict. 2*; DFM 200; *Loan Book*, 1628–31.]
dw. in Blackfriars (Q.6), 1626 (12543)–1641 (Wing B 5729) and until his death
1618: 6599 ent.
1619: 6603.5 ent., 6607 ent.
1625: 4111, 4220a.5, 6746, 10725, [11330.4] (false), 12887a (note), [13825], [17283], [23829], 25646.
1626: [56], 748 ent., 999, 1515 ent., 4233–3.3, 6548.6 ent., 6598 (d), 6746.5, 6766 ent., 7479 ap., 10576 ent., 10725, 10726, 10739, 12111–2, 12117, 12487, 12543, 13820, 14461, 16974 ent., 16977 ent., 17176.9 ent., 18186 (d?), 20070 ent., 23488, 23493.7, 25614.
1627: 1946.3, [1947], [5362], 5940.5, 6607.5–08, 6608.3–8.7, 7527, 12892, 15537, [21138.7], 21241.7, 21246, 21415.5, 21830, 23897, 24985.
1628: [1948], [2606], [6299–300], [7161–1.3], 10726.5, 13987, [15177?] (false), 17097, [17283.3], 18187, [19085], 19419, 21242, 22673, 25038–8.5.

Miller, G. — *cont.*
1629: 606, [1948.5], 3453, 13461, 15593, 21247.
1630: 357.5, 1889 (d?), 3279, 3453, 5054, 6747, 7311, 7337, 22633, [25136] (d?).
1631: 3740, [3789], 4143, 6548.6, 6606–6.5, 12116, 15078–8a, 15542a.5, 20070, 21243, 21247.5, 22674.
1632: 1320, 1950, 2636, [2636.3(*A*)], 2637.3, 3242, 6600, 12125, 13462, 19086, 21198, [21200], 21202, 21248, [21729], 24400, 25399.5.
1633: 748, 1237, 2642, 2645.3, 3243, 6549, 6766, 7393.5, 7393.6 (*A*3), 10556, 10728, 13459, 15411, 22799.
1634: 748, 1515, 1950.5, 2650, 2650.5, 2651, 4230, 12121, 17649, 17654–4a, 17654a.5–55, 20540 (note), [21139], 21189, 25096, 25097, 26078.
1635: 1887, 2657, 2660, 3244, 3256, 4144, 10557, 13463, 16974, 20540, 20540.5, 25097.5, 25098, 25718.
1636: 1890, 2665, 2665.5, 2666, 4145, 5310.7, 10576, 12116.5, 12118, 24401.3, 25099, 25718.
1637: 2670, 2671, 2671.5, 3249, 7164–4.3, 7165–5.3, 10145, 16977, 17176.9, 22677.5, 22800–0.5, 24401.7, 25100, 25314, 25316.
1638: 2678, 2678.2, 2678.4, 2680, 2680.1–.6 (forged), 3226, 10740, 20447–7.5, 21384, 22500–0.5, 22505–5.5, 25023.5, 25607, 25608, 25609.
1639: 1516, 2686, 2686.2, 2686.3, 2686.4, 2686.6, 2688, 2688.5, 3245, 3257, 6549.7–50, 10558, 12124, 14721.5, 17709, 19379 ent., 21384, 22149–9.3, 22152, 22391.8–92, 22475, 22476, 22500–0.5, 22506, 25100.5.
1640: 1622, 1623, 1952, 2696, 2696.3, 2697, 3227, 10145.3, 11197.5, 21196, 22149.5, 22149.7, 22649.5, 25101, 25317–7.5.

Millington, Joan.
Bookseller in London, 1604. Widow of **Thomas Millington**. [*Dict. 1.*]
her shop under St. Peter's Church in Cornhill (P.2), 1604 (7592)
1604: 7592 f.

Millington, Thomas.
Bookseller in London, (1591) 1594–1603†. Husband of **Joan Millington**. [*Dict. 1*; *Loan Book*, 1601–04.]
at the little North door of Paul's at the Gun (A.1), 1594 (22328, = E. White 1's shop)
shop under St. Peter's Church in Cornhill (Cornwall (P.2)), 1594 (26099)–1603 (5121)
1594: 17412 ent., 18654 f., 22328 sold, 26099 f.
1595: 5066 f., 13119 f., 18644 ent., 18895.5 sold (d), 21006 f.
1596: 10611.7 ent.
1597: 6559 ent., 19793 f.
1598: 13852 ent., 14032 f., 24093 f. (d).
1600: 5631.3 f. (c), 21006a f., 22289 f., 26100 f.
1602: 6569 ass'd, 22330 ass'd.
1603: 5121 f. (d), 5122 f., 17153 f.

Minsheu, Edward.
Son of **John Minsheu** and beneficiary of the Stat. Co., c. 1626–1639 at least. *See* also *children of* **John Minsheu**. The imprints below both state 'for the benefit of'.
1637: 5985.7, 21667.5.

Minsheu, John.
Linguist, editor, and publisher in London, fl. 1611–1625?†. Father of **Edward Minsheu** and other children. [*DNB*; *Joseph Quincy Adams Memorial Studies*, ed. J. G. McManaway and others, Washington, 1948, pp. 755–73.]
1617: 17944 at charges of. **1625:** 17945 at charges of.

Minsheu, John, *Children of.*
Beneficiaries of the Stat. Co., c. 1626–1639 at least. *See* also **Edward Minsheu**. The imprints below all state 'for the benefit of'.
1626: 15481.5 (c). **1633:** 23132a. **1634:** 5984, 23132a.5. **1636:** 5984.5. **1637:** 5985.5. **1639:** 7123.

Mogar, John, *pseud.*
Printer in 'Douai', 1604. = Unidentified recusant English secret press.
'at the Compass', 1604 (4835)
1604: 4835.

Molaeus (Du Moulin), Jacobus, *pseud.*
Printer in 'Rouen', 1601. = T. Creede. [Lepreux III/1: 157.]
'at the Phoenix', 1601 (3102, 3106)
1601: 3102 ap., 3106 per.

Mommaert (Mommart), Jan.
Printer in Brussels, 1587–1631†. Husband of **Martine Mommaert**. [*Dict. 1*; Rouzet.]
1608: 11093–3.5 chez. **1611:** [4868.7]. **1614:** [4623] (d).

Mommaert, Martine.
Printer in Brussels, 1631–1635? Widow of **Jan Mommaert**. [Rouzet, under husband.]
1634: 1528.

Montanus, Guilielmus.
Printer and bookseller in Antwerp, 1538–1542. [Rouzet.]
1538: [2840].

Montanus, N. *See* Hill.

Moore, Anne.
Bookseller in London, 1635–1636. Widow of **Richard Moore**. She shared the shop with her husband's former apprentice, **Henry Hood.**
her shop in St. Dunstan's Churchyard (W.9), 1635 (1235.5)–1636 (1135, with H. Hood, omits 'shop', adds: 'in Fleet Street')
1635: 1135 sold, 1235.5 f. **1636:** 1135 sold.

Moore (More), Richard.
Bookseller in London, (1607) 1608–1633?†. Husband of **Anne Moore**. [*Dict. 1.*]
shop in St. Dunstan's Churchyard in Fleet Street (W.9), 1608 (6416)–1631 (13202) and until his death
1608: 1233 f., 6054.2 f., 6416 f., 11413 f.
1609: 1886 f.
1610: 7333 f., 11123 f.
1611: 7027 f., 13778 (note).
1612: 1234 f., 4923 f., 5742 f., 25084 sold.
1613: 3831 f., 19156.3(*A*3) f.
1614: 3192 f., 13201 f.
1616: 20153 f.
1618: 6024 f.
1619: 1969 f.
1620: 17677 sold, 20544 f., 24643 f.
1621: 13799 f., 18316 f., 20546 f., 24642 f.
1622: 19052.8 f., 24643.5–44 f.
1623: 14669 sold, 20154 f.
1624: 25389a sold.
1625: 12635a f.
1626: 999 f., 7028 f., 20545 f.
1627: 15110 f., 21129 sumpt.
1628: 12636.5 f., 13987 f., 14297 f., 14510 f., 24641 f., 24645 f., 25311 f.
1629: 6307 f., 15785 sold, 22548a sold.
1631: 11700.5(*A*3) f., 13202 f., 20808.5 sold.
1633: 24539.3 sold.

Moptid, David.
Journeyman printer? in London, (1573?) 1575?–1587†. Related by marriage to his former master, **Thomas East**. His only imprints are shared with **John Mather.** [*Dict. 1.*]
dw. in Red Cross Street next adjoining to St. Giles's Church without Cripplegate (I.7), 1575? (11885, colophon)
1575: 2001(*A*) [f.] (d?), 11885 [f.] (d?).

Morberius, Gualterus, *pseud.*
Printer at 'Liège', 1571. = J. Fowler, Louvain. For the genuine Morberius, printer and bookseller in Antwerp, 1553–1555, and in Liège, 1555–1595 *see* Rouzet. [*Dict. 1.*]
1571: 15506.

More. *See* also Moore.

More, John, esq., *Assignees of.*
Publishers in London, 1629–1641, 1665, under the patent for law books originally granted to John More on 19 Jan. 1618. = M. Flesher, J. Haviland, and R. Young, whose names have not always been supplied in imprints in STC. For a list of the titles *see* Appendices D/1–60 and E/2–3. No effort has been made to determine whether the printing material in the items below belonged to any of the partners, or if it was acquired from the previous law printer, **Adam Islip**. For a broadside against revival of the patent following the Restoration *see* Wing C 1017. [*Dict. 2.*]
All imprints below have 'by assignees of' except as specified.
No address used.
1629: 15785.
1630: 1134 [f.], 6209, [15789], 21583 [f.].
1631: 3349, 5524, 5524.3 (repeat), 5526.5, 6981 [f.], 15162 (d).
1632: 7437 [f.], 9329, 25276 [f.].
1633: 14902 per assig., 15162.3 (d), 15786.
1634: 20839 per assig. (d).
1635: 1135 [f.], 5498.5 per assig., 5501.5, 5503.7 per assig., 6210, 9330, 10967 [f.].
1636: 1135 [f.], 3350, 5494.8 per assig., 5510.5, 9330, 10872 [f.], 14887.3 f., 20718.
1637: 6051, 7725.6, [14887.5 f.].
1638: 9804, 14888, 21582, 21582.5, 25651.
1639: 1136 [f.], 15759, 15787, 19645.
1640: 3476 assig., 3804 [f.], 5527 per assig., 9331, 9769.5 assignat.

Morel, Claude.
Printer in Paris, 1598–1626. [*Dict. 1*; Renouard.]
1614: 3094.

Morgan, Ellis.
Bookseller in London, 1638–1641? (?Wing E 582). Not a member of the Stat. Co.
shop in Little Britain (F.4), 1638 (21093).
1638: 21093 sold.

Morgan, John.
One of the agents in London for the province of Maryland, 1635. *See* also **William Peasley**.
[his] house in High Holborn over against the Dolphin (V.11), 1635 (17571)
1635: 17571 [sold].

Morin, Martin.
Printer in Rouen, 1490–1523. [Duff, *Century*; Muller 102.]
1492: 15795.5 per (d?), 16166 imp. & arte.
1494: [15877?] (d?).
1496: 15802 industria.
1497: [16170] (d?), 16171 opera.
1499: 17966 per.
1501: [16176].
1506: 16182 per.
1508: 16183 arte, 16184 per, 16233 per.
1510: 16187 arte, 16188.5 per.
1511: 16188.5 per.
1514: 16194(*A*3) [f.].
1515: 16141 in off., 16195.5.
1517: 16234 per.
1519: [16199].

Morin, Michael.
Bookseller in Paris? 1497, and in London, 1504–1506. The imprints below were all shared with **Wynkyn de Worde.** [Duff, *Century*; Renouard; *British Library Journal* 2 (1976): 161–5.]
No address used.
1497: 16169(*A*3) imp. **1504:** 23885.3 ven. **1506:** 15805.5 imp.

Moring, William.
Journeyman printer? in London, (1591) 1594. He seems to have been a partner of or worked for **Adam Islip**. (Arber III.702, no. 1). [*Dict. 1.*]
No address known.
1594: 542 ent.

Moris. *See* Morris.

Morley, Thomas.
Musician, b. 1557?–1602†. Publisher of music under the patent granted 28 Sept. 1598. *See* also *assignee of* **T. Morley**. [*DNB*; *New Grove.*]
dw. in Little St. Helen's (J.3), 1601 (4649)
1601: 4649 [f.].

Morley, Thomas, *Assignee (with assent, etc.) of.*
Publisher of music under Morley's patent. = W. Barley, 1598?–1600, 1602; T. East, 1600–1602; P. Short, 1600–1603. The patent was later exercised by the *assignees of* **W. Barley**. The imprints below all state 'by the assignee of' except as indicated.
For addresses *see* the individuals named.
1598: 2495 (d?).
1599: 1882, 2497, 10697, 13563, 18131 (d).
1600: 7092, 7095, 14732 with assent, 18115.5, 18117, 18128, 25206.
1601: 14733 by assent, 18130, 18130.5, 21332 with assent.
1602: 6566, 18122.
1603: 7096 by ass't of a patent granted to.

Morrant, John.
Bookseller? in London, 1609. Unless 'John' is an error for Edward Morrant, freed by R. Barker in 1608 (DFM 58), he was not a member of the Stat. Co. [*Dict. 1.*]
No address known.
1609: 10561 ent.

Morrett, John.
Stationer in London, (1617) 1620 (cf. DFM 1980)–1651. [DFM 1228; *Poor Book*, 1641, 1643, 1645–51.]
at the Two Tuns in Little Britain (F.4), 1634 (21164)
1634: 21164 sold.

Morris, John.
Journeyman printer in London, (1580) 1587–1590. [*Dict. 1.*]
dw. in St. John's Street, [Clerkenwell,] (E.10) 1590 (12804, with J. Bowen)
1587: 15511a ent. **1590:** 12804 [f.].

Morris (Moris), Thomas.
Journeyman printer in London, (1583) 1585. Freed by Joan Jugge 10 Apr. 1583 (Arber II.688). The only extant item in which he is named as one of the printers was produced in the house of **Robert Robinson:** in Fetter Lane (V.7). [Not in *Dict. 1.*]
No separate address used.
1585: 1848.

Morton, John, *Archbishop of Canterbury.*
Canon lawyer, member of the Privy Council, and cardinal, b. 1420?–1500†. [*DNB.*]
1500: 16173 imp.

Moseley, Humphrey.
Bookseller in London, 1627–1661†. In partnership at the first address with **Nicholas Fussell,** 1627–1634. All his shops were near the great North door of St. Paul's, the second in process of being demolished in Jan. 1636 (Greg, *Companion*: 337–8), and the third described as being 'over against Paul's greater North door' in 1646 (*OBS*: 63, engr. tp of Wing T 2089). [*Dict. 2*; DFM 1868; *OBS Proceedings* 2 (1929): 59–142.]
in Paul's Churchyard (A.2), 1627–1659 and probably until his death
— at the Ball, 1627 (15537)–1634 (7056, has 'their shop'); variation: 1632 (15713, has 'their shops — at the Ball and the White Lion'); all with N. Fussell
shop at the Three Kings —, 1634 (13991)–1636 (20831)
at the Prince's Arms —, 1637 (14832a)–1659 (Greg no. 423b)
1627: 15537 f., 23564 f.
1629: 21840 f.
1630: 6747 sold, 17378 sold.
1631: 12888 ent., 17378 sold, 20829 f.
1632: 15713 sold.
1634: 7056 sold, 13991 f., 14832 f.
1635: 3074 f.
1636: 20831 f.
1637: 14832a f., [25436] sold.
1638: 1157 f., 1158 f., 15105 f., 18086 prost., 22521 sold, [25436a] sold.
1639: 778 f., 19882.5 f., 21765 f., 26133 f.
1640: 13872 f., 15135 f., 17178 f., 19883 f., 19883.5 f.

Moseley, Samuel.
Stationer in London, (1607) 1608. Bound to Thomas Dawson, junior, on 6 Oct. 1600 and freed by him on 7 Dec. 1607 (Arber II.249, III.683; Stat. Co., *Register of Freemen*, fol. 4^v); dead before 1623 when his son (DFM 767) was apprenticed. [Not in *Dict. 1*; not in DFM.]

Moseley, S. — *cont.*
shop in Pope's Head Alley near to the Royal Exchange (O.11), 1608 (5341a, C^2 copy)
1608: 5341a sold.

Moulert, Geraert (Gerrit).
Printer in Middelburg, 1637, 1643. Probably the son of **Symon Moulert** and also printed as one of the latter's heirs. [Gruys.]
1637: 11596.5.

Moulert, Symon, *Widow and Heirs of.*
Printers in Middelburg, 1623–1642. Probably included **Geraert Moulert**. [Gruys.]
1631: 1431.32 ap.

Moungwell. *See* Mungwell.

Mountford, Thomas.
Bookseller? in London and Clerk of the Stat. Co., 1614–1631†. (*C-B C*: 221–2). He undoubtedly had an office in Stationers' Hall (Q.1). [*Dict. 1*; DFM 1967.]
No address survives.
1614: 11370 ent.

Moxon, James.
Printer in Delft 1637, in Rotterdam 1638–1643, and in London 1646–1655, possibly until 1663. Father of Joseph Moxon and grandfather of James 2, who began working as an engraver in 1673 and collaborating with Joseph in 1677 (Moxon xxxix, xliv). [*Dict. 2*; Gruys; Joseph Moxon, *Mechanick Exercises on ... Printing*, ed. H. Davis and H. Carter, London, 1958, xix–xxi, xxxvi, n.1.]
1637: 13265.

Muelen (Mylius), Laurenz von der.
Printer in Cologne 1539–42, in Bonn 1542?–1550, and again in Cologne, 1553. [Benzing 56–7, 241; *Library* 4 (1949): 276.]
1542: [3764] (false, d?). **1543:** [24353] (false). **1545:** [24355] (false).

Muller, Pieter.
Printer in Leiden, 1622–1625. [Gruys.]
1622: 1431.27.

Mullot, Nicolas.
Bookseller in Rouen, 1509–1521. [Muller 102.]
1520: [16202.5 f.?] (c).

Mundee (Munday), Richard.
Journeyman printer in London, (1577) 1578. His only imprint was shared with **Roger Ward**; since its sole woodcut initial belonged to **William How**, whose address is also that listed below, Mundee and Ward were possibly How's employees. [*Dict. 1.*]
dw. at Temple Bar (W.14), 1578 (16949)
1578: 16949.

Mungwell (Moungwell), John.
Bookseller in Exeter, 1620–1635 at least.
No address used.
1620: 10940.3 f. **1635:** 19522 sold.

Muschio, Andrea, *pseud.*
Printer in 'Vinegia', 1587. = J. Wolfe. For the genuine Muschio, who printed in Venice 1565–1623, including the edition which Wolfe imitated, *see* Borsa. (Woodfield no. 28 and his Appendix B4–6.)
1587: 12004.

Mutton, Edmund.
Stationer in London, (1598) 1603. [*Dict. 1.*]
dw. in Paternoster Row at the Huntsman (C.7), 1603 (7605.3)
1603: 2772 f., 7605.3 f.

Mychell (Michell), John.
Printer in London 1530–32? in Canterbury 1533–47? again in London 1548? and again in Canterbury 1549–1556?†. [Duff, *Century*; *Library* 32 (1977): 155–6; 33 (1978): 172; *Book Auction Records* 14 (1916): iii.]

Mychell, J. — *cont.*

Most of Mychell's books are undated, the earliest date being 1549 (2380). Many are without imprint, and some are mere fragments. The following entries reflect numerous amendments found only in the Addenda and Corrigenda in the present volume, based in part on the fact that printing of heretical books was discovered in Canterbury in 1536 (*Library* 1977) and in part upon a more co-ordinated examination of the items listed below with their texts, printing characteristics (virgules, catch-titles, etc.), types, and woodcut initials. A fairly coherent pattern can be seen, but whether it is correct is not yet clear.

Mychell's earliest types were apparently acquired from **Laurence Andrewe**. If Maunsell (STC 17669, pt. 1, p. 6: cited in Herbert III.1454 and *Book Auction Records*) is correct, Mychell's press in Canterbury may first have been set up in St. Augustine's Abbey, where Mychell's early patron and possible owner of some of Mychell's types and initials, **Robert Saltwood**, was keeper of the chapel of the Virgin Mary. One or more of the heretical books of 1535–36 (Frith and Tyndale) may have been printed in London (24455.5 has Berthelet's tp border, McK. & F. 16), but at present all are queried for Canterbury in order to keep down the number of times the woodcut initials and, apparently, the types would have had to travel between there and London. No address has been found for his conjectured second period of activity in London, in 1548, but Mychell printed at least two books (16983, 20847) for **Hugh Singleton** and part of another (12723a) for **Richard Grafton**, using in the last some of Grafton's special initials, so it seems reasonable to suppose Mychell was in London at the time.

London, in the Poultry at the Stocks [Market] at the Long Shop by St. Mildred's Church (O.1), 1530–32? (17327(*A*3)); 12353(*A*3) specifies London without address
London? 1548? (Mychell not mentioned in imprints)
Canterbury, in St. Paul's parish, 1534? (17013(*A*3))–1547? (10459(*A*3)), and 1549 (2380)–1553 (9970); in 1533–34? (15192.5(*A*3)) and 1556 (10149) Canterbury is specified without address

1530–32? [11691a.5(*A*3)], [15187(*A*3)], 17327(*A*3).
1532? 12353(*A*3).
1533–34? 15192.5(*A*3), 21647(*A*3).
1534? 17013(*A*3).
1535? [909.5(*A*3)], 23153(*A*3).
1535–36? [11385(*A*3)], [11387(*A*3)], [24447.7(*A*3)], [24455.5 (*A*3)].
1537? [16820.5(*A*3)], [16821(*A*3)].
1538? [7788.7(*A*3)].
1538–47? 10459(*A*3), 14006(*A*3), 17651.5(*A*3), 21040–1(*A*3).
1548? [12723a(*A*3)], [16983(3)], [20847(*A*3)], [23553(*A*3)].
1549: 2380, 16052(*A*3) (d?).
1550: 2380a, 15181 (d?).
1552: 9968 (d), 9969 (d).
1553: 9970.
1556: [2996] (d?), [4820] (d?), 10149 (d), [17776(*A*3)] (d?).

Myddleton, Myddylton. *See* Middleton.

Mylbourne. *See* Milbourne.

Mylius. *See* Muelen.

Myllar, Andrew.
Bookseller in Edinburgh, 1503, possibly in Rouen, 1505–1506, and printer again in Edinburgh, 1508. Printed in partnership with **Walter Chepman**. [Duff, *Century*; Muller 102.]
in the Southgait [modern Cowgate], 1508 (11984)
1505: 11604.5 imprimi suppetebat.
1506: [16118 f.].
1508: [3307] (d?), 5060.5, [7347] (d), [7348] (d), [7349] (d), [7542] (d?), 11984, [13148] (d?), [13166] (d?), [13594] (d?), 17014.3.

Mylner, Ursyn.
Bookbinder and printer in York, 1511–1519 at least. His printing material passed to **John Warwyke**. [Duff, *Century*.]
dw. in St. Peter's Churchyard, 1514? (15861.3(*A*3))
dw. in St. Helen's parish, in Blake Street, 1516 (25542)
1513: 15861 (d?).
1514: 15861.3(*A*3) (d?).
1516: [15609.3] (d?), 25542.
1517: [17979.5] (d?).
1519: [14077c.48?] (d?), [—.84A] (d).

Mynne (Myn), Richard.
Bookseller in London, (1623) 1624 (cf. DFM 1995)–1650. [*Dict. 2*; DFM 503.]
shop in Little Britain at the $ St. Paul (F.4), 1627 (22526a)–1639 (12553) and undoubtedly later
1627: 22525.5 f., 22526–6a f.
1630: 20686 sold, 20686.5 sold.
1634: 962 f., 17670 f., 24059 f.
1635: 963 f.
1639: 12553 prost.

N

Nachabeus. *See* Machabeus.

Nafield, Jean, *pseud.*
Printer in 'Edinburgh', 1587–1589. = Unidentified printer in Paris.
1587: 3107 chez. **1588:** 3108 chez. **1589:** 3109 chez.

Nautonier, Guillaume de.
Author and patron in Venes, France, 1603.
1603: 18415 aux frais.

Nealand (Nayland), Samuel.
Stationer in London, (1613) 1618–1640†. His earliest imprint was shared with **Nathaniel Browne** and sold at the latter's address: at the great North door of Paul's (A.2). [*Dict. 1*; DFM 2693; *Poor Book*, 1636.]
shop at the Crown in Duck Lane (E.5), 1631 (4)
1618: 24333 f. **1631:** 4 f. **1632:** 3538–8.5 f.

Nelson, Thomas.
Bookseller in London, (1580) 1583–1592. [*Dict. 1.*]
at the West door (end) of Paul's (A.10), 1584? (21483.5, with T. Law 1)–1585 (997, has 'dw.')
shop upon London Bridge (T.7), 1586 (18425)
shop at the great South door of Paul's (A.8), 1591 (11727)
dw. in Silver Street near to the $ Red Cross (H.15), 1592 (12223)
1583: 5431 ?ent.
1584: 5681 f. (d), 21483.5(*A*3) f. (d?).
1585: 997 f. (d), 6280 f., 18211 f., 21949.5 f.
1586: 14544 ent., 18425 f. (d).
1590: 335.5 ent., 336 ent., 10004 f., 12307 ent., 13141.7 f., 19197 f., 20582.5 f., 21293 f., 22713.5 f.
1591: [334] sold, 11727 f., 11795.5 f., 12271 f., [12279 f.], 12279.4 f., 12279.7 f., 13142.5 f. (d), 14657.5 f., 19965 f. (d), 24652 f.
1592: 5871.3 f., 10842 f. (d?), 11273.5 f. (d), 12223 f., 12280 f., 19799 ent.

Nering, Abraham.
Printer in Rotterdam, 1630–1634. [Gruys.]
1631: 19798.3.

Neuss, Melchior von.
Printer in Cologne, 1525–1551. [Benzing 238.]
1526: [16778].

Nevill, Philip.
Bookseller in London, (1637) 1638–1643. He took over the shop of his former master, **John Grismand**. [*Dict. 2*; DFM 1478.]
at the Gun in Ivy Lane (C.7), 1638 (17983)–1643 (Wing T 1057A)
1638: 17983 f., 21668 f.
1639: 976 (note), 976.5 sold, 15409 sold, 17341 sold, [22001?] sold, 24048 sold.
1640: 2737 ent., 4517.7 ven., 13621a.7(*A*3) f., 13730 f., 21036b.7 f., 21637 f., 24048 sold, 24289.5 ex imp.

Newbery, Joan 1.
Bookseller in London, 1603–1617 (cf. DFM 2022) at least. Successively widow of **Thomas Butter** and of **John Newbery.** (*C-B C*: 13) and published 1590–1594 as **Joan Butter**. Mother of **Nathaniel Butter**. [*Dict. 1*, under husbands.]
her shop in Paul's Churchyard at the Ball (A.2), 1603 (5340)
1603: 5340 f. **1604:** 20152(*A*3) ent.

Newbery, Joan 2.
Bookseller in London, 1637–1638 (1658†?). Widow of **Nathaniel Newbery**. Her shop was soon shared with and passed to **Samuel Enderby**, her husband's former apprentice. [*Loan Book* (via N. Butter), 1646–49, 1655–58; *Poor Book* (son's scholarship), 1636–43.]
at the Star in Pope's Head Alley (O.11), 1637 (21193)
1637: 1627 f., 1633 f., 5852.5 f., 5853 f., 21193 f., 24563 f.
1638: 21190 f.

Newbery, John.
Stationer in London, (1591) 1594–1603†. Cousin of **Ralph Newbery** and husband of **Joan 1**. [*Dict. 1.*]
dw. in Paul's Churchyard at the Ball (A.2), 1602 (24613.5)–1603 (6070); variation: 1602 (17259, has 'shop', omits sign)
1594: 10796 ent., 12435 ent., 14605(*A3*) ent., 15150 ent., 15168 ent., 23335 ent.
1600: 4579.5(*A3*) f., 24852.7(*A3*) ent., 25118.8 ent.
1602: 6910.4 sold (d), 17259 sold, 23337 ent., 24613.5 sold.
1603: 5333 f., 5339 f., 6070–0.5 f., 19735.6 f.

Newbery, Nathaniel.
Bookseller in London, 1614–1636†. Transferred from the Haberdashers' to the Stat. Co. in 1615 (*C-B C*: 76, 457). Husband of **Joan Newbery 2**. One of his former apprentices, **William Sheffard**, apparently continued to work for Newbery in 1621 and published occasionally with him later. Between 1617 (1645) and 1625 (3204.5) Newbery had two shops simultaneously. The first passed to **Samuel Ward** and the second eventually to **Samuel Enderby**, both apprentices of Newbery. [*Dict. 1*; DFM 2026; *Loan Book*, 1625–28, 1636–39; *Poor Book* (son's scholarship), 1630–36.]
shop under (at, near) St. Peter's Church in Cornhill (P.2), 1616 (5977)–1625 (3204.5, omits 'shop'); this was given the $ Star by 1619 (1439) though it is sometimes omitted, e.g. in 1622 (1476)
in Pope's Head Alley (O.11), 1617 (1645)–1636 (7317); from at least 1623 (7423) this also has the $ Star, which is usually mentioned; variations:
— over against the White Horse, 1618 (1436)
at the Star —, 1625 (3204.5, substitutes 'Palace' for 'Alley')
1614: 13546.5 sold.
1616: 1964.3 sold, 5847 f., 5977 sold.
1617: 1645 f., 1645.5 f., 5618 f., 5622 f., 5851.5 ent., 11292 f., 11305 f., 14893 f., 16835 f., 20390 f.
1618: 1436 f., 1437 f., 1626 f., 1628 f., 1638 f., 1648 f., 7065 f., 14283 f.
1619: 1439 f., 1440 f., 1641 f., 1646 f., 11284 f., 13611 f., 15364 f., 17555 f., 18420 f., 18458 f., 18459 f., 18803–4 f., 19601 f., 20115 f., 21828 f.
1620: 1629 f., 4466 f., 7307–8 f., 7313 f., 7336.5 f., 15558 f., 18154 f.
1621: [1788(*A3*)] sold, 5364 f., 7331 ent., 11300 ent., [11675(*A3*)] sold, 16859 f., 17600 f., 23656.5(*A3*) ent., [23860(*A3*)] sold, [24893(*A3*)] sold, 24912 f.
1622: 1476 f., 3512 sold, 4710.5 f., 5842 f., 5843 ent., 16841 f., 18507.53 f., —.57A f., —.63 f., 20669 f., 20675 f.
1623: 1475 f., 3512 sold, 7314 f., 7316 f., 7332 f., 7423 f., 20678 f.
1624: 1477 f., 1477.5 f., 1478.5 f., 7305 f., 7328 f., 7451 f., 7452 f., 7616 sold, 18507.151 f., 19768.5–9.3 f., 23115 f.
1625: 680 f., 3204.5 f., 4575.7 f., 5851.5 f. (c), [7021.3 f.] (d), 16858 f., 20391 f., 23599 f., 23656.5 f.
1626: 1478 f., 7021.7 f., 7309 f., 18156 f., 20679 f.
1627: 5843 f., 11301 f., 18156a f., 21186.5 f., 21186.7 f.
1629: 5852 f., 20668 f., 20680 f., 21187 f., 21191 f.
1630: 20668 f., 20673 ent.
1631: 5844 f., 7315 f., 20683 f.
1632: 1435 f., 7453 f., 21187.5 f., 21192 f.
1633: 21188 f.
1634: 21189 f.
1635: 5365 f., 7310 f.
1636: 7021.5 f. (d), 7317 f.

Newbery (Nuberie), Ralph.
Bookseller in London, 1560–1604† (*C-B C*: 340). Cousin of **John Newbery**. Succeeded to the sales outlet of **Thomas Berthelet**. Often published with **Henry Bynneman** from 1578; in 1581–82 they collaborated as the *assignees of* **R. Tottell** and **C. Barker**. In

Newbery, R. — *cont.*
1584, along with **Henry Denham**, Newbery took over many of Bynneman's copyrights; others they yielded to the Stat. Co. (*see* Appendix C/50–71). From 1586 he often published with **George Bishop** and with him in 1587 became the *Deputies of* **C. Barker**, where other items are listed. His shop was managed in 1602 by two former apprentices, **John North** and **Roger Jackson**, and passed to the latter in 1604. *See* also Appendix A/19. [*Dict. 1.*]
in Fleet Street (W.5), 1560–1602 and until his death
dw. — a little above the conduit, 1560 (19148, colophon has 'shop'), 1563 (12048, tp adds 'in the late shop of T. Berthelet'), 1577? (24061), 1602 [12243(*A3*)]
dw. —, 1565 (19150), 1571 (10228.5, omits 'dw.'), 1573 (5684)
1560: 4325 f., 19148 f.
1561: 19149 f.
1563: 12048 f.
1565: 19150 f.
1570: 15532 ent.
1571: 10228.5 [f.].
1573: 5684 f., 5684.2 f., 25010 f.
1574: 567 f. (d), 10229 [f.], 10793a f., 12432 f.
1575: 5691 f. (d), 10794 f., 11266 f. (d), 12433 f. (d?).
1576: 4738 f., 11049 f., 15175–5.5 f., 19151 [f.].
1577: 4056 [f.], 9526.7 ent., 10230 [f.], 10795 f., 12426 f., 12434 f., 24061 f. (d?).
1578: 713–3.5, 2018.5, 5239 [f.], 6274 f., 12425 f., 12469 ent., 13905 [f.].
1579: 13228 [f.], 14724a, 16995, 16996, 18925 (d?), 20092 [f.].
1580: 5684.5 f., 5685, 10230.5 [f.] (d), 18772 [f.], 23025 [f.], 23025.5 [f.], 23333 [f.] (d).
1581: 570 [f.], 1582, 13630–1 [f.], 14632–2a, 15163.
1582: 10796 [f.], 14613.5, 14614, 15164, 15164a, 18772.5 ap., 18773 ap., 18773.3 ap., 18773.7 ap., 18774 ap.
1583: 14603, 15145, 15164a.5 f.
1584: 4057 [f.], 4606, 5689 ent., 6761 ent., 10353 [f.], 12435 [f.], 13569 ent., 14604, 15147, 15175 (note), 16747, 18101 ent., 23325.2 ent., 23325.8, 23334 ent., 24678 (d).
1585: 14860 f., 16516 [f.] (d), 18204 ent., 19342 ent., 20109 imp.
1586: 4503 per, 5486 [f.], 13843.5 f., 15233 f.
1587: 4058 [f.], 4076 imp. (d), 4504 per, 13569–9.5 at expenses, 15148, 23326 (d).
1588: 1998–9, 2888 ent., 15165–6.
1589: 5682 ent., 9196 ent., 12625, 15102, 15238 ent.
1590: 6475, 14464, 14636, 16619, 20881, 21746(*A*: 2 eds.), 23325.2, 23471, 25841–1a.
1591: 15149, 15166, 23458, 23471, 24822 (d).
1592: 15167, 23334 (d).
1593: 2061.5.
1594: 10796 ass'd, 14605 f., 15150 f., 15168, 15238, 23335 ass'd.
1595: 23451 ent.
1596: 690, 21783.
1597: 1445, 2062, 15195 ent.
1598: 1460 ent., 10066 ent., 12626.
1599: 12626–6a, 23265, 23449, 23457, 23460.
1600: 12626–6a, 14447, 14447.5 (forged), 23335 [f.] (d).
1601: 23336 [f.] (d).
1602: [12243(*A3*)] sold, 23337 ass'd.
1604: 2917 ass'd, 11431 ass'd, 23461 (forged).

Newman, E.
Publisher in London, 1594. Widow of **Thomas Newman**. She possibly continued in St. Dunstan's Churchyard (W.9).
No address used.
1594: 709–9.5 f., 1480 f.

Newman, Thomas.
Bookseller in London, 1586–1593?†. Husband of **E. Newman**. Usually published jointly with others, especially **Thomas Gubbin**. In 1587 or 1588 Newman bought the shop and sales stock of **Henry Middleton** (*Library* 10 (1909): 103–4) although that address has so far been noted in only one imprint. [*Dict. 1.*]
shop in Fleet Street in St. Dunstan's Churchyard (W.9), 1592 (12261)
1587: 3179 f., 6055 f., 25118.4 f.
1588: 847 f., 4088 ent., 11338 ent., 11342 imp., 11343 ent., 11344–5 f., 25118.5 f.
1589: 1579.5 f., 12224 f., 20059 f., 25118.6 f., 25407.

Newman, T. — *cont.*
1590: 6842 (d), 12251 f., 19657 ent., 23685 f.
1591: 7675 f. (d?), 12241 f., 22536 f., 22537 f.
1592: 5759.2 imp., 12261 f. (d).
1593: 25018.5 ent.

Newton, Ninian.
Printer in London, (1579) 1584–1586. One of the partners in the **Eliot's Court Press**, situated in the Little Old Bailey (D.1). [*Dict. 1*; *Library* 2 (1922): 175–84; 3 (1923): 194–209.]
Indexed below are *only* items which Newton entered in the SR or in which his name appears in the imprint. In the items distinguished by an asterisk (*) the imprint is shared with another partner. Items *without* imprint, including those for which his name has been supplied in square brackets in STC, are listed *only* under Eliot's Court Press.
No address noted.
1584: 4094*, 19355*.
1585: 376.3*, 4332* ap., 13786* ap., 13786.5 ap., 19356.5*, 19357.
1586: 6655*, 6985, 19485 ent.

Newton, Thomas.
Stationer and bookbinder? in London, (1577) 1579–1613 (cf. DFM 2029). [*Dict. 1*; *St. Giles* (I.4), 1583–93.]
No address used.
1579: 5455(*A3*) [f.] (d).

Nicholes (Nicholls), Thomas.
Bookseller in London, (1636) 1637–1641†. His earliest imprint was shared with one of his former masters, **Nicholas Alsop** and sold at the latter's shop: at the Angel in Pope's Head Alley, 1637 (20537). [*Dict. 2*; DFM 1411.]
at the Bible in Pope's Head Alley (O.11), 1637 (20265)–1640 (15048a, omits sign)
1637: 7357 f., 10813 f., 20265 sold, 20537 f.
1638: 1907(*A*) ent., 3151a.5 sold, 13737.5 f., 23240 sold.
1639: 22152 f.
1640: 15048a sold.

Nicholson (Nicolson), Henry, *pseud.*
Printer in 'Wesel', 1546. = S. Mierdman, Antwerp. [Duff, *Century*.]
1546: 1462.9.

Nicholson (Nicolson, Nicolai, Nycolson), James.
Printer in Southwark, 1535–1538. A man of this name described as a glazier from the dominion of the emperor became a denizen on 26 Feb. 1535 (*Denizations*: 180) and may possibly be the printer. *Returns of Aliens* has at least three other James Nicholsons between 1564 and 1571, none of whom seems likely to be the printer. [Duff, *Century*.]
in St. Thomas's Hospital, 1537 (2065)
1535: [2063.3], [20418.5] (d?).
1536: [2063.5], [4021?] (d), [5015.5(*A*)] (d), [5098] (d?), 11470.5 (d), 24455 [by &] f.
1537: 1873 (d?), 2064 [by &] f. (d), 2065 (d), 2752.5, 6832.1–.2, 15285 (d), 16999 (d), 17262.5, 18849, 18878, 20840, 20840.5, 24219.5, [24443.5] (d?).
1538: [1724.5], 2816 (d), 2816.5–.7 (d), [2838] (d?), [2838.3] (d?), [2838.7] (d?), [2839] (d?), 4054, 16979.7, 17000–0a (d), 20841, 24444 (d).
1538/39: [392.3?].

Nicholson, John.
Stationer in London, (1635) 1640–1642. [*Dict. 2*; DFM 2119.]
shop under St. Martin's Church near Ludgate (Q.3), 1640 (6174)
1640: 6174 sold.

Nicholson (Nicolson), R., *Gent.*
Patron in London? 1594.
No address used.
1594: 18638.5 imp. (d).

Nicolai, C. *See* Claeszoon.

Nicolai, James. *See* Nicholson.

Nicolaus, *Bamburgensis, pseud.*
Printer, no place specified, 1548? = D. van der Straten, Wesel.
1548: 1287 per (d?).

Nicolaus, Gerardus.
Printer in Antwerp, 1521–1526. [Rouzet.]
1524: 13828.2 per (d?).

Nicolini, Domenico.
Printer in Venice, 1557–1605. [Borsa; Rhodes.]
1563: 6832.36 ap.

Nicolson. *See* Nicholson.

Nolck (Nolick), Marten Abrahamsz van der.
Printer in Flushing, 1607–1623. [*Dict. 1*; Gruys; Briels 378.]
1613: 1431.23 ap. **1621:** 25842, 25846. **1622:** 25843. **1623:** 25847.

North, John.
Stationer in London, (1601) 1602. His only imprint was shared with **Roger Jackson**, also a former apprentice of **Ralph Newbery**, and sold at the latter's shop: in Fleet Street a little above the conduit (W.5). [*Dict. 1*; *Loan Book*, 1601–03.]
No separate address used.
1602: 12243 f.

Northon, John.
Publisher in London, 1612. Almost certainly a misprint for John Norton 1.
No address used.
1612: 4757 ap.

Norton, Bonham.
Stationer in London, 1594–1635†. Son of **William Norton**, grandson of **William Bonham**, and cousin of **John Norton 1** with whom he was apparently a partner in the **Officina Nortoniana**. Father of **Roger Norton**; another son, John, was not a Stationer but a lawyer (*Library* 6 (1951): 94). In partnership with **Thomas Wight** in the law-book patent, 1597–99 (*see* Appendix D/1–60), which had its own press; items below distinguished by an asterisk (*) should have A. Islip's name as printer and/or '[f.]' deleted from the imprint. Concerning Norton's involvement from 1613 with the grammar patent *see* **B. Norton and assignees**.
For most of the period between 1617 and 1629 Norton was one of the **King's Printers**. For the reprints of Elizabethan proclamations made for Humphrey Dyson, not included below even though Norton's name is one of those supplied in STC, *see* King's Printers, where the positions of the King's Printing House during Norton's activity are also detailed. [*Dict. 1*; *Library* 2 (1901): 353–75; indexes to *Reg. B* and *C-B C*.]
No address noted.
1513: 1703 f. (d/error).
1594: 2810a.5 imp., 4372.5 ent., 19948 imp.
1595: 13465 f., 20067 f.
1596: 5481 f., 18007 ass'n, 19952 ent., 20797 ass'd by.
1597: 11750 f., 19955 ent., 25277.
1598: 5078 at charges of, 9321, 10964 in aed., 15022* in aed., 17291*, 20710, 21576*, 23643 f., 23644 f., 25269.
1599: 4423 f., 9769 in aed., 11196, 12357.7 in aed., 15152, 15169, 15753* in aed., 20045* in aed.
1600: 10547 f.
1601: 2184.5 (note).
1602: 19558 ent.
1613: 1703 f. (d), 1704 [f.], 7178 f., 24551 [f.].
1614: 2812, 13793a imp.
1617: 8557, 9238.3, [10822].
1617/18: 8558, 8562, 8563, 8564, 9238.5.
1618: 2250, 2251, 2255, 2918.3, 2918.5, 2918.7, [6847.5?] (d), 7758.3, [7758.7] (d), 8565, 8569, 8569.5, 8570, 8572, 8573, 8574, 8575, 8576, 8578, 8579, 8580, 9238.7, 9238.9, 9239, 9305.7, [16349.3] (d?), 16349.7, 16350, 16468, 16491, 20652.5, 20653, 23401.
1618/19: 8588, 8589, 8591, 8592, 8593, 8595, 8596, 8598, 8599, 8600, 8603–4, 14171.
1619: 2253, 2254, 2255, 2256, 2257, 2258, 2260, 2918.7, 2919, 2920, [8593.2] (d?), [8593.4] (d?), [8593.5] (d?), [8593.6] (c?), [8593.7] (c?), 8605, 8606, 8607, 8608, 8609, 8610, 8612, 8617, 8618, 8619–20, 8620.3, 9240.3, 9240.5, [10359], 13235, 14346–6.5 ap., 14384, 14385 ap., 16351, 16352, 16352.5, [23510] (d).
1619/20: 8628.

Norton, B. — *cont.*
1620: 1162 ap., 2258, 2259, 2260, 2262, 2348, 2920.7, 8643, 8644, 8645, 13235, 16356, 16484 (d), [21764].
1621: 2262, 2263, 2921, 2922, 8661, 8662–3, 8664, 8665, 8666, 8667, 8668, 8669, 8670, 8671, 8672, 8675, 8675.2, 8675.4, 8675.6, [9506.7] (d), 13238, 14399, 16357, 16357.3, 16357.5, 16357.7, 16438.
1621/22: 8676, 8676.5, 8677–8, 8679, 8680–1, 9241.
1622: 2264, 2265, 2924, [4718.5] (d), [7705.5] (d?), [8457?] (c?), [8682], 8683, 8684, 8685, 8686, 8687, 8688, 8689, 8691, 8692, 8693, 8694, 8695, 8696, 8697–8, 9242, 9242.5, 13238, 15300, 16358.5, 16359, 16360, 25378.
1622/23: 8699, 8700–2, 8703, 8704, 8705.
1623: 2265, 2266, 2267, 2925, 2925.3, 7683, 8706, 8707, 8708, 8709, 8710, 8711, 8713, 8714, 8715, [8716], [8716.2], 8717, 8719, 9243, 16361, 16362, 16362.3, [16434], 16492, 16496.5, 25020.
1623/24: 8722, 8723.
1624: 2268, 2269, 2270, 2925.5, 4750 ap., 4751, 4752, 8724–5, 8726, 8727, [8728], [8729], 8730, 8731, 8732, 8733–4, 8736, 8738, 8739, 8740, 8741, 8742, 8744, 9507, 9507.3, 9507.5, 10050, 10050.3, 12524, 14128.5, 16363, 16363.5.
1624/25: 8746, 8747–9, 8750, 8751, 8752, 8753, 8754.
1625: 2270, 2271, 2272, 2273, 2273.5, 2926, 2926.5, 7751.6 (false), 8754.5, 8755, 8756, 8757, 8758, 8759, 8760, 8761, 8762–2.5, 8763, 8764, 8765, [8766], 8767, 8768–9, 8770, 8770.5, 8771, 8772, [8773], 8774–5, 8776–7, 8778, 8779–80, 8781, 8782, 8783, 8785, 8786, 8787, 8788, 8789 f., 8790 f. [by], 8792 f., 8793 f. [by], [8794 f.], 8796 f., 8796.3 f. [by], 8798 f., 8798.3 f. [by], 8800 f., 8800.3 f. [by], 8800.7 f., 8801 f. [by], 8801.7 f., 8802 f. [by], 8804 f., 8804.3 f. [by], 8804.7 f., 8805 f. [by], 8806, 8807, 8808, 8809, 8810, 8811, 8812, 8813, 8815, 9244, 9244.3, 9508, [10205], 15302, 15304, 16364, 16365, 16497, 16540, 16541, 16542, [21712.5] (d).
1625/26: 8816, 8817–8, [8819], 8820, 8821.
1626: 2275, 2276, 2277, 2278, 2280.5, 2927, 7683.5, 7686, 8822, 8823, 8824–5.3, 8826–8, 8829–30, 8831–2, 8833–4, 8835, 8836, 8837, 8837.5, 8838, 8839, 8840, 8841, 8842, 8843–4, 8845, 8846, 8847, 8847.3, 8847.5, 9246, 9247 (d/repeat?), [15303], 16365.5, 16366, 16367, 16485, 16543, 16544, [22532.5] (d).
1626/27: 8848–9, 8850, 8851, 8852, 8853, 8854, [8855], 8856.
1627: 2279, 2280, 2280.5, 2928, 2929, 8857, 8858, 8859, 8860, 8861, 8862, 8863, 8864, 8865, 8866, 8867, 8868, 8868.3 (false), 8869–70, 8871–2, 8873, 8874, [10146], [10206], 16368, 16369.3, 16369.7, 16369.9(*A3*), 16370, 16370.5, 16371, 16469.
1627/28: 8875, 8876, 8877, 8878, 8879–81, 8882, 8883–4, 8885, 8886, 8887, 8888, 8888.5.
1628: 2281, 2282, 2283, 2283.5, 2930, 2931, [5019?] (d), 7446.5 (d), 8889, 8892–3, 8894, 8895, 8896, 8897, 8898, 8899, 8900, 8902, 8904, 8905–6, 8907, 8908, 8909, 8910, 8911, [9175j.3?] (d?), 9247 (d/note), 9510, 10051, 10074 [f.], 10074.3 (forged), [15305–5.7], [16372] (d?), 16373, 16373a, 16373b, 16497.1 (c?), 16497.3 (c?), [16545] (d?), [16545.5] (d?), [16546] (d), [16546.5] (d), 16547.5, 16548.
1628/29: 8912, 8913–4, 8915, 8916, 8917, 8918, 8919–20, 9249, 16547(*A3*).
1629: 2284, 2286, 2287, 2288, 2936, 2936.3, [7492.7] (d), 8921, 8922, 8923, 8924, 8926, 8927, 8928, 8929, 8930, 8931, 8932, 8933, 8934, 10052, [10404.7(*A3*)?] (d?), 16374, 16376, 16376.5, 16376.7, 16377, 16377.5, 16470, 16485.3, 21762.
1630: 2289, 2289.5, 10053–5.5 (forged), 13795 imp., 16378, 16380.5.
1632: 6597.7 ass'd, 13796 ass'd, 21758 ass'd, 21763 ass'd.
1633: 2813.

Norton, Bonham, and Assignees.
Publishers of grammars in London, 1613, 1619?–1634. On 6 Jan. 1613, following the death of John Norton 1, Bonham Norton received a grant for 30 years as **King's Printer in Latin, Greek and Hebrew** (*Cal.S.P.D., 1611–1618*: 166), under which he attempted to contest the right of the *assignees of* **J. Battersby** to print Latin and Greek grammars. By 1615 (*C-B C*: 74) Norton had himself become one of Battersby's assignees, and following Battersby's death in 1619 he successfully asserted his own rights, which eventually passed to **R. Norton and assignees**.

Imprints may name Norton or his assignees; the latter are so indicated below. Surviving editions are extremely rare: in 1624 Norton had in stock at least ten different texts in quantities up to 4,000 (*C-B C*: 165; *see* also King's Printer in Latin, ...). As a

Norton, B. and Assignees — *cont.*
result, it is impossible to tell from what is extant whether 'assignees' was used periodically or in a precise sense, or whether in some cases phrasing may have been carried over from a previous tp imprint or colophon.

No address used.
1613: 4513.4 typis, 15626.4.
1621: 15627 ass'ns.
1626: 4514.3.
1627: 4514.5, 15627.5 ass'ns.
1628: 15627.6.
1629: 4514.7.
1630: 4515, 15627.9, 15628.
1631: 15628, 15628.3.
1632: 4516, 15628.3, 15628.5, 15628.7 ass'ns.
1633: 15628.7 ass'ns, 15633.6 (d?).
1634: 4517.3, 15629, 23279.5 per assig.

Norton, Felix.
Bookseller in London, 1600–1604?†. Grandson of **John Cawood**. He had two brothers: John, bound 3 Apr. 1598 (Arber II.225) but never freed, and Luke (DFM 185, 400), a journeyman printer. Not related to other Nortons in this index. [*Dict. 1.*]
dw. in Paul's Churchyard at the Parrot (A.3), 1600 (20084)–1604 (1111, omits 'dw.')
1600: 7243 ent., 17323 ent., 18626a.4 f., 20084 f.
1601: 19343 f.
1603: 1117 f., 14381 f.
1604: 1111 f., 1112 f., [10801 f.], 12407 f.

1605: 20085 ass'd.

Norton, George.
Bookseller in London, (1609) 1610–1624. Not related to other Nortons in this index, but the Elinor who requested on 13 June 1622 that her share in the English Stock go to **Edward Blackmore** may have been his wife (*C-B C*: 147; cf. STC 17634). Norton's books 1622–24 were sold at the address of their printer, **Bernard Alsop**: at the Dolphin in Distaff Lane (S.3). [*Dict. 1*; DFM 1913.]
near Temple Bar (W.14), 1610–1618
shop in Fleet Street under the Black Bell —, 1610 (5385.5)
shop — [no sign], 1611 (24622.5)–1615 (17509)
at the Red Bull —, 1616 (25918)–1618 (18011, has 'shop')
1610: 5385.5 f., 24950 f.
1611: 21838 f., 24622–2.5 f.
1612: 4708 sold, 6338 f., 11856 f., 24111 f.
1613: 376.7 ent., 1663–4 f. (d), 1964 f., 3914 f. (d), 4981 f. (d), 7184 f., 21174 f., 24307 f., 26130 f.
1614: 3583 f., 3917 f., 4982 f. (d?), 25916 f.
1615: 17509–9.5 f., 25917 f., 25917.5 f., 25920 f., 25921 f., 25922 f.
1616: 3915 f. (d?), 3915.5 f., 25918 f.
1617: 19174 f., 25906 f.
1618: 18011 f.
1619: 21840 ass'd.
1620: 11857 ass'n.
1622: 1705 f., 1705.5 f., 1706 f.
1623: 17634 ent.
1624: 13968 f.

Norton, Jocosa. *See* Norton, Joyce.

Norton, John 1.
Bookseller in London, (1586), in Edinburgh, 1587–1592? and again in London, 1590, 1593–1612†. Nephew of **William**, cousin of **Bonham**, and husband of **Joyce Norton**. Probably uncle of **John Norton 2**. Appointed **King's Printer in Latin, Greek and Hebrew** in 1603 and used that style in imprints, e.g. in 1603? (12059.5) and in the Greek books printed for him at Eton, 1610–13; the patent also included Latin and Greek grammars. Apparently associated with Bonham Norton in the **Officina Nortoniana**, which usually published jointly with **John Bill**. *See* also **Tres Viri**. [*Dict. 1.*]
in Paul's Churchyard (A.6), 1594 (18355, has 'dw.', adds 'near Paul's School')–1605 (21361, with J. Bill); no later use noted, but he was still living in St. Faith's parish at the time of his death (Plomer, *Wills*: 45)
1590: 2048 imp.

Norton, John 1 — *cont.*
1593: 14938 f.
1594: 16428.5 typis, 18355 f., 19948 ent.
1595: 19949 ent.
1596: 5602 f.
1597: 11750 f.
1598: 13174 f., 16649 imp., 23643 f., 23644 f.
1599: 11749 imp.
1600: 14453 imp.
1601: 2184.5 (note), 5603 f., 18857 [f.] (d?).
1602: 13788 imp., 14898(*A*3) ent., 15051 ent.
1603: 6595.7 ent., 12059.5 typis (d?), 12059.7, 14350 f., 14351 f., 14353 f., 19558 imp., 20068b f.
1604: 5824, 10068 [f.], 13790 pro, 14355 [f.], 14385.5 imp., 14386 [f.], 16429 typis, 23645 f., 24120 f.
1605: 2810b imp., 5482 f., 15374.5, 16692 [f.], 18173.5 imp., 18174a, 21361 sold, 23645 f., 25682 ent.
1606: 3961 ent., 4867, 10548 f., 13790b, 15625–6 [f.], 18175 [f.], 18175.5 imp., 18855 [f.] (d/repeat?), 19558.3 ex off., 23469 f., 23470 f.
1607: 747 f., 3908.7 [f.], 4508 imp., 7176 f., 10553 f., 11620 [f.], 13789 imp., 14414 [f.], 15626, 17595 f., 23278.7 typis, 23354 imp.
1608: 4513 typis, 6596 f., 13791.5 imp., 14404 [f.], 15626.1, 18855 [f.] (d?), 21317 [f.], 25683a f., 25686 f.
1609: 3103 [f.], 14405 [f.], 14406 [f.], 14408 chez (false), 14579–80 [f.], 15049 ent., 18176 imp., 19559.5 imp., 23284.5 [f.].
1610: 2811.5 [f.], 4509 imp., 4637 imp., 5474 chez, 12346 [f.], 14622 [f.], 14629 [f.], 15626.2, 18177 imp.
1611: 2353.5(*A*3) [f.] (d), 4424 f., 4742 [f.], 13792a imp., 14580 [f.], 14580.5, 14629.5 [f.], 15626.3, 18356a f., 20631.
1612: 2812 ent., 4740 [f.], 4740.3(*A*)–.5(*A*) (false), 4757? ap., 4859 ent., 4869 chez, 5404 typis, 5483 f., 9229–30 chez, 9231 chez (false), 9232 typis, 14629–9a [f.], 19560 imp., 23646 f.

1613: 14629a (engr. tp/post-dated?).
1615: 14272 ap. haeredes.

Norton, John 2.
Printer in London, (1616) 1621–1640†. Probably nephew of **John Norton 1**; son-in-law of **Matthew Law**. This may be the man whose imprint appears on two books by Salomon de Caus: 'Institution harmonique' and 'Les raisons de forces mouvantes', both having: *a Francfort en la boutique de Jan Norton*, 1615. Norton began printing in partnership with **Augustine Mathewes**, 1624–27, apparently near St. Bride's Church (W.4); he moved on to an irregular partnership with **Nicholas Okes**, 1628–35, in Foster Lane (G.3), though they shared imprints only in 1628–29, and continued there when the Okes printing house moved elsewhere. Norton's widow, Alice (Law) Norton, kept up his printing house and in 1642 remarried **Thomas Warren**, who took over its management. [*Dict. 2*; DFM 278; *Loan Book*, 1634–37; *SB* 7 (1955): 131–4; Blayney, *Origins*: 304–12.]
?sold at the Golden Key near the Middle Temple (W.13), 1635 [5988]; this was entered to and printed by Norton though the imprint does not name him. It seems unlikely to have been a shop of his own.
1621: 24629 [f.].
1623: 24630 f.
1624: 40, 1498, 7619, 7742, 11705, 18430, 24347, 25090a, 25090a.3 (*A*3).
1625: 115, 130, 1025.7, 5379, 6072, 7619, 14440, 14488, 14897, 17331, 24512, 26037.
1626: 4264.5, [5876.5 f.], 12932, 14897, 16886, [18507.183?], 21091, 21129.5.
1627: 12741.
1628: 6021.5, 6493, [21362], 22840.5, 22849.
1629: 595, 22320.
1630: 4290, 5599, 12007, 14776, 17640–0.5, 22337–8, 23587, 23616, 25990, 26037a.
1631: 912, 1399, 1796, 4151–2, 4152.3(*A*3) (d), 5125, 5897, 10144, 10362.5, 11083, 17478, 19925, 24086, 25179.
1632: 3929, 17646, [18048] (d), 19311, 21166, 22286.
1633: 1353, 4204, 10076, 10077 (d/repeat), 10078–8.9 (forged), 10380, 13584, 13660, 13660.5 (d/repeat), 13676, 13676a, 14694.7, 16917, 19311.5, 19317, 20003.5–04, 21175, 21176, 22458.5, 22459, 22459a.5, 22459b, 23503, 23717, 24401.

Norton, John 2 — *cont.*
1634: 595.1, 1931, 3129–9.7, 3129.8(*A*3), 3129a, [3368.5-Hutton, G.?] (d?), 5600, 12566, 13585, 16945, 21363, 21372, 22313, 22321.
1634/35: 464.7.
1635: [3533.5], 3621, 4922, [5988], 13660.5 (d), 13661, 13676a, 17357–8, [22458], 23617.
1636: 1349, 1503, [10074.3?] (false, d?), 10380.5, [12051–2], [12994], 21687, 21688, 26038.
1637: 174.3(*A*), 1350, 3994.5 in off., 4237, [5217], 20274, 22442, 22443, 22486, 22513, 23015, 25638.
1638: 1459, 3758–9, 5218, 10382 (d?), 11791, 11943–3.5, 12453, 13547, 14958, 18738, 19303, 22441–1b, [22499?], 22514, 24715 ex typ.
1638/39: 442.5, 505.19.
1639: 1797, 3930, 4627, 6390, 10217.5 (d?), 10366, 12979 typis, 12980 typis, 17390, 17393, 18725.5, 19303, 20509.3, 20930–0a, 21063.3–.7, 22287, 24715 ex typ., 25955.
1639/40: 442.7, 495.15.
1640: 1933, 10077 (c?), 10381, 10658, 13662, 13662.5 (forged), [16945.5] (c), 19303.3, [20938(*A*3)], 21779, 23704, 24046, 25641.
1640/41: Wing A 2099, A 2409, A 2670, A 2791.

Norton, Joyce (Jocosa).
Publisher in London, 1632–1638. Widow of **John Norton 1**. All her imprints were shared with **Richard Whitaker**, whose address was in Paul's Churchyard at the King's Arms (A.6); it seems probable that she was not herself engaged in the sale of books. [*Dict. 1.*]
No separate address noted.
1632: 3059.6 f., 3617 ent., 3908.9 ent., 4567 ent., 5483.7 ent., 6597.7 ent., 7175 ent., 7320 ent., 11946 ent., 12990 ent., 12993 ent., 13003 ent., 13628 ent., 13660 ent., 17596 ent., 19563 ap., 20908 ent., 21036b ent., 21758 ent., 21763 ent., 22178 ent., 23648 ent.
1633: 10076 f., 10077 (repeat), 10078–8.9 (forged), 11751, 13660 f., 13660.5 (d/repeat), 13676 f., 13676a f.
1634: 1129 imp., 4425 f., 21363 f.
1635: 3621 f., 5871 f., 11878 f., 12497 f., 13660.5 f. (d), 13661 f., 13676a f.
1636: 7181.5 f., 11752, 18954.5 sumpt., 21806 imp.
1637: 4510.2 f., 5046 f., 11404 sumpt., 11406 f., 13796 imp., 13796.5 (forged), 21806 imp.
1638: 765.7 f., 1109–10 prost., 20787 f.

Norton, Roger, and Assignees.
Publishers of grammars in London, 1636–1640 and later, in succession to **B. Norton and assignees** under the patent for **King's Printer in Latin, Greek, and Hebrew**. Roger was the son of **Bonham Norton**; he married in 1626 (*Library*: 364), was called 'Master' by 1633 (*C-B C*: 250), but was not freed—by patrimony—until 1635, the year of his father's death. Called to the Livery in December 1635, he died in 1662, at which time he was living in Blackfriars (Q.3). [*Dict. 2*; DFM 387; *Library* 2 (1901): 353–75.]
Since the only imprints which survive before 1641 may mention Norton himself or his assignees on different title pages of the same book, the latter form may be carried over from much earlier imprints. In at least 1636 (15631) the printing material seems to have belonged to **Robert Young**.
No address noted.
1636: 15631 ass'ns.
1637: 6232 f., 15631, 15632.7.
1638: 15633.8.
1639: 2813.7 pro, 15632.7 ass'ns.
1640: 4517.7 per assig., 15633.2 ass'ns/typis.

Norton, Thomas.
Bookseller in London, (1616) 1617–1618. Not related to other Nortons in this index. The Anne who in 1621, with her husband **Richard Whitaker**, was administering Thomas's estate, may have been his widow (*Cal.S.P.D., 1619–1623*: 306). In any case, the shop passed to Whitaker. [*Dict. 1*; DFM 1869.]
shop in Paul's Churchyard at the King's Head (A.3), 1617 (708)–1618 (11517)
1617: 708 f., 13530 f. **1618:** 11517 f.

Norton, William.
Bookseller in London, before 1557–1593†. Son-in-law of **William Bonham**, father of **Bonham Norton**, and uncle of **John**

Norton, W. — *cont.*
Norton 1. One of the *assignees of* **F. Flower**. He only rarely used an address. *See* also Appendix A/3. [Duff, *Century*.]
in Paul's Churchyard (A.6), 1577 (18005a)–1589 (3908.4, has 'dw. — at the Queen's Arms'); the earliest use of the sign noted is 1580 (18006); Norton was still in St. Faith's parish when he died (Plomer, *Wills*: 30)
1562: 23431 ent., 19972.5 ?ent.
1570: 1925 f. (d), 12366 f. (d?), 21021 f. (d).
1571: 24726.5 f. (d).
1572: 4655 f., 5952 f., 19136 f., 19137.5 f. (d?).
1573: 17286 sumpt., 17286.5 imp.
1574: 13784 ap.
1575: 2110 [f.], 12448 f.
1576: 19626 f.
1577: 5485 ent., 5485.3 f., 12201 f. (d), 13058.7 imp., 18005–5a [f.], 20796 ent., 23659.3 ent.
1578: 4418 f., 10470 imp., 13785 imp., 19138 f.
1579: 2056 ent., 6037 ent., 11832 f., 12458 f., 13785 imp., 17003.3 ent.
1580: 1584 f. (d?), 2056.6 imp., 2359.4 imp., 4426.8 f., 18006–6a f., 18884 imp.
1581: 2058 imp., 11833 f., [17287 f.], 17287.3 pro.
1582: 4421 f.
1584: 5478 f.
1585: 2060 imp., 13786.5 imp.
1586: 12201.5 f.
1587: 4422 f., 5309.4 imp., 10502.5 imp. (d?), 15470.5 f.
1588: 5479 f., 16969 f.
1589: 3908.4 f., 5480 f.
1590: 3908.5 ass'ns, 3908.5A ass'ns.
1591: 3908.6 ass'ns.
1592: 13787a imp.
1593: 2061 imp., 15016 imp.

Nortoniana, Officina.
Publishers in London, 1605–1621? usually in association with **John Bill**. The precise meaning of this imprint is unclear. It undoubtedly has some connection with the patent of **John Norton 1** as **King's Printer in Latin, Greek, and Hebrew** but generally appears on scholarly works, some of them imported from abroad, rather than on the grammars to which John 1 also laid claim. It seems likely that **Bonham Norton** may have been a partner from the beginning and taken over following John 1's death in 1612. From 1616 the Officina Nortoniana overlapped with the **Latin Stock** (*see* Stationers' Company) and in 1621 apparently became amalgamated with that Stock.
No address noted.
1605: 17047 ex, 24031 ex, 14898 ex.
1608: 24263.3 ex, 26121a.3 sumpt.
1610: 22868 ex (d).
1611: 13906a in.
1613: 4566 ex, 4631 in, 12619 in.
1614: 1398 ex, 4002 ex, 4745 ex, 7335 ex.
1616: 11941–2 ex, 11945 ex [f.], 14368 ex.
1617: 6994 ex, 7002 ex, 11328 ex (d), 11328.1 ex (d), 24311 ex (d).
1618: 46 ex, 3534 ex, 11328.2 ex (d), 11328.3 ex (d).
1619: 47 ex, 11328.4 ex (d), 11328.6 ex (d).
1620: 6995.5 ex, 7119 ex, 11328.10 ex (d), 23103 ex.
1621: 11942 ex (d?).

Notary, Julian.
Printer, bookseller, and bookbinder in London, 1496–1497, in Westminster, 1498–1500, and again in London 1503?–1523 (*Library* 9 (1908): 259, placing him in St. Faith's parish, Paul's Churchyard at the last date (A.4)) at least. A native of Vannes in Brittany (*Library* 11 (1956): 278). [Duff, *Century*.]
London, near St. Thomas Apostle (S.6), 1496 [270]–1497 [15884]
Westminster, 1498, 20 Dec. (16172)–1500, 2 Apr. (15895, adds 'dw. in King Street')
London, (near, in, at) Temple Bar in St. Clement's parish (X.1), 1503?–1510
dw. at —, 1503/04, 16 Feb. (24877, letterpress in device at end)–1504, Aug. (9998)
in —, dw. at the Three Kings, 1505, 1 June (252)–1510, 22 June (13226, has 'juxta limina', near the porch of St. Clement's); from 1507 (9351) it is usually 'without' Temple Bar

Notary, J. — *cont.*
London, in Paul's Churchyard (A.10), 1510, 1515–1520; variations:
[sales] shop — at the Three Kings, 1510, 22 June (13226, has 'cellula'), 1510, 2 Oct. (16122, has 'in atrio Sancti Pauli')
[printing house] — at the West door of Paul's beside [the Bishop] of London's palace , 1515 (10000)
dw. near St. Paul's Church at the $ St. Mark, 1516, 27 Aug. (25498)
— at the Three Kings, 1518 (1375, adds 'at the West door ... palace' as in 1515 above)–1520 (10435)
1496: [270] (d).
1497: [15884].
1498: 16172 per.
1499: 17968 per.
1500: 5089 for [sic:ecit.] (d?), 15895.
1503: [14077c.115A] (d), 15900 (d?).
1503/04: 24877.
1504: 9998.
1505: 252 per, 16117, 23940.3 per.
1506: 17970 (d?).
1507: 9351, 14043, 18565.
1508: 12473 per, [13829.9?] (d?), 20435 per.
1509: 12513 per/imp.
1510: [1009.5] (c), [1988.2] (c), 13226 in aed., 16122 ven./per, 24115.5 (c).
1515: [1988.4] (c), 10000, [13960] (c?), [13998.5] (c), [14077c.125] (d), [—.125A] (c).
1516: 18091 (d?), 25459.6 per, 25498 per, 25511 per.
1518: 1375, [22410] (d?).
1519: 10629.
1520: 10435, [14077c.90] (d?), [—.90A] (d?), 19305.3(*A*3), 23102 (d?).

Novimago, Rainaldus de.
Printer in Venice, 1477–1496. [Duff, *Century*; Borsa.]
1483: 15795 per.

Nuberie. *See* Newbery.

Nycolas the Grave. *See* Grave.

Nycolson. *See* Nicholson.

O

O., P., *pseud.*
Printer in place unspecified, 1569. = J. Kingston.
1569: 977 (d).

Oakes. *See* Okes.

Ockould, Henry.
Stationer in London, (1632) 1639–1640. Son of **Richard Ockould**. [*Dict. 1*; DFM 1995.]
No address used. *Dict. 1* gives: the Swan in Little Britain, but on what authority has not been traced.
1640: 12983 f.

Ockould, Richard.
Stationer in London, (1593) 1596–1634† (*C-B C*: 261). Father of **Henry Ockould**. His first book was sold at the shop of **Joan Broome**: at the Bible in Paul's Churchyard (A.2). [*Dict. 1.*]
No separate address used.
1596: 23670 f. **1597:** 23670.5 f. **1605:** 1164 ent. **1606:** 3405 f., 25768 ent. **1607:** 12981–1.5 f. **1629:** 1165 ass'd.

Officina Nortoniana. *See* Nortoniana, Officina.

Ogden, Hester, *Assignees of.*
Publishers in London, 1633. Mrs. Ogden was a daughter of the religious controversialist, William Fulke, and obtained a patent to publish his annotated edition of the Rheims version of the New Testament. **Augustine Mathewes** printed as one of her assignees. [Greg, *Companion*: 57–9.]
No address used.
1633: 2947, 11432.

Okes (Oakes), John.
Printer in London, 1627–1643†. Son of **Nicholas Okes,** became a partner in the printing house sometime in 1635, possibly after the move to Little St. Bartholomew's, and exercised essential control of it from 1638 onwards. Imprints supplied in square brackets may name him or his father or both on no fixed principle. [*Dict. 2*: 141; DFM 417; *SB* 7 (1955): 134–6; Blayney, *Origins*: 311–3, etc.]
in Little St. Bartholomew's (E.8), 1635–1640 and until his death; variations:
dw. in the Wellyard — near unto the Lame Hospital gate, 1635 (12009)
dw. —, 1637 (13349), 1640 (5570)
dw. — in the Wellyard, 1639 (593)
1627: [5864], [5864.2], 16823, 17904.7.
1630: (all SR entries): 592, 5473, 6022, 12495, 13322, 13340, 13365, 22835, 22838, 22840.7, 22845.3, 22849.1, 22854.5, 24102.
1633: [17216].
1635: 595.2 ent., [1328.5?] (d), 3997, [4369], [4369.5], 7359, 7360, 7362, 12009, 12010, 12010.3, 12010.5, 21470, 23122.
1635/36: 494.12, 532.10.
1636: 1553, 1558, [5215?], [5216?], [13365.5], 13369 ent., 17379–9.5, 18806, [18976], [18976.2], 20219, [22215.5], 22631.
1636/37: 442.3, 494.13.
1637: 1557, [1901.5], 3237, [5217], [11321], 11347, 13349, 13364, 13367, 15717, 17444, 18165, 18922, 20220, 21091.5, 22445, 22845.7, 22849.7, 22917.5, 23509, 24660, 25226.5 ent., 25371.
1638: 592.7, 1157, [1901.5], 1902, 3583a, 3758, 3946, 4349.5, 4671, [5218], 11792, 12310b(*A*3, note), 12766, 13359, 13368, [15706.5?] (d), 15014, 17444a, 18286, 18320, 20221, 20221.1, 20585, 21422, 21643, 22435, 22487, [22497], 22632, 22841.3, 22849.7 (note), 22849.9, 23778.5, [23790] (d), 23795.3, 23798, 24392.
1639: 174.5, 593, 595.2, 778, 1354, 1903, 6315–5a, 7108, 7587, 10283, 10853, 11273, 11991, 13350, 14552.3, 19113, 19290, 20000, 20512, 21056.4, 21092, 21765, 23747, 23757.5, 23766, 23774.5 ent., 23783 (d), 26133.
1639/40: 479.6.
1640: 549.5, 1881.5, 2694, 3818, 3820, 4697,5, 5570, 5771, 6174, 11909, 11910, 11914, 11934, 13798, 14771, 15714, 16943, [17889], 19112, 19306, [19554] (d?), 20225, 20770, 20811, 21771–1.5, 22377, 22627, 22627.5, 22846, 23125–6, 23706.
1642: 22846 (note).

Okes, (Derwen, de Quercubus), Nicholas.
Printer in London, (1603) 1606–1645† (Blayney 313). Father of **John Okes**. Succeeded to the printing material of **George Snowdon**. In 1624 he married as a second or third wife the widow of **Christopher Purset**. He took **John Norton 2** into an irregular partnership, 1628–36, though they shared imprints only in 1628–29. He began sharing imprints with his son in 1635 and yielded him effective control of the business about 1638; imprints supplied in square brackets for the period may name either or both on no fixed principle. [*Dict. 1*; *Loan Book*, 1623–26; *SB* 7 (1955): 129–35; Blayney, *Origins*: 20–30, 292–313, etc.]
dw. near Holborn Bridge (V.2), 1607 (16623a)–1613 (13310.3, adding 'at the Hand'); the sign is used by 1609 (24313.3)
dw. in Foster Lane (G.3), 1618 (18278)–1626 (17898) and probably until 1635
dw. in the Wellyard in Little St. Bartholomew's near unto the Lame Hospital gate (E.8), 1635 (12009)–1639 (593, omits 'near ... gate') and until his death
1069: 20999 (d/error).
1607: 2024, 4131, [5491–2.2], [5492.4], 6541, [6659.5], 12555–5.5 ex off., 16623a–a.5, [16874], 19541, 19567, [20340], [20805], 21757, 22349, 23019.5, 23020, [23982.3].
1607/08: [467].
1608: 55, 744, 2024.3 f., [4026], 4580, 5342, 6374, [6480], [6481], 12488.5, 13545.5, 17398–9, 17874, [17888], 19057, 20763.2–.5, 20825, [22292], 23433.5, [24414.5], 25965.
1608/09: [408.5].
1609: 744.5, 773, 1816, 3116, 4611, 5106, [6500], [6536], [6944.7], 12335.3, [14757], [14758], 14778, 15424, 15537.5, [16875], 17359, 17585, 17904.3, [19559–9.5], 20826.5, 20999 (d), 22061.5, 24064, 24309, 24313–3.5.
1609/10: [434.22], [461.5], [508].
1610: 1794, [3791], 6809.5, [6945], [6950], [7077], 10857.7, 13136, 13776, 14267, 15537.5, 17376–6.5, 17585, 22886, [24388] (d), 25150, 25222.5, [25797].
1611: 605, 1364, [1428], [4900.5] (d), [5304], [6018], 6660, 6660.5, 7027, 10535, 10536.5, [11187], [11374.5], [13325], 13778 (note), 13783, [15197], [17908], 18068, [20449–9.5], 23101, [23331], [23625.5], [24082], 24209, 24753, 25150a, 26014.3(*A*3).
1612: 605.5, [1501] (false), 1782, 4708, 5584, [6184], 6246, 6530, [6538], 10785, [11794], 13309, [13778], 13938, 18952.3, 18988–8.5 ex off., [19298], 24578, 24852.7 (d?), 25178.
1613: [385], 968, 1222, [1674], 1908.5 ex off. (d), 4316, 5105, [6528], 6661, [10511.7], 12335.5, 12337.5, 13310–0.3, [13323], [13355], 13365, [13930], 14676, [15323], 17352, 17703, 17903, 17904, 21045–5.5, [21355], [22424], [23204], [23204.3], [23204.5–.7], [23206.4] (d), [23206.6] (d), [23722–2.5], [23750] (false), 24151, 25174.
1614: 969, [1782.5], 2766, [3541], 3579, 3583, [3609], 3917, [5673], 5896, 10314.8, [10857.5] (d?), [11370], [11745], [11841], 12336 ent., 12337.6, 13546.5, 13939, 15710, [16884–5a], [17229], 17625, [17662], 19314, 22839, 22841.7–42, [23205], [23206.8?] (d), 23721, 24312–2.3, 24636, 24693.5.
1615: 5695, 6503, 7173, 10594, [13321], 13779, 13936, 14720, 14894.7, 14894.8, 14894.9, [15222.5], 17377, 17509–9.5, 18235, [18445.7], 18514, 20282.5, [23206], 23249, [23511.5], 23612, 24100, 24101, 24105 (c), 24304, 25905.
1616: [3915] (d?), 6504, [6649], 10536, 11319, 12185, 13545, 13779 (d?), [13780], 15711, 17477, 17878, 18351, 18579, 19088–8.3, 19091, 19344, 19349, 20019, 20159, 21075, 22839.3–.5, 22842.5, [23206.2], 23502, 24084, 25995, 26024.
1617: 5701, 6397, 6550.5, 17872–2a.5, 17899, 18357 ent., 19174, 21044, 21122, 22839.7–.9(*A*3), 22840, 22847.7, 23058, 23543, 24106, 25906.
1618: 543, 6020, 6248 (d), [12025?], 14283, 18278, [18352], 18989 ex off., 19347, 21096, 21594, 22848, 23136–6a, [23332], 25094.
1619: 544, [1676–7], 5710, 7370, 12749, [14028], 17871, 17873, 17902, 21096, 22848, 22851, 23257, 23767, 24006, 24298, 25914.
1620: 970, 1548, [1681–1.5], 5698, 6497, [17904.5], 18975, 19289, 19515, 20584.5, 21098.5, 21325, 22836, 22838, 22843, 22852, 23120.5, 23258, 23802, 24085, 24525.
1620/21: [421.6].
1621: 590, 592, 3504, 3681, 5473, [5710.3], 6249–50, [11074], 12248, 12495, 14693.5, 18255, 18256, 20283, 20286, [20638a–39], 21098.7, 23117, 23802.5, 24074, [25926], [25927].
1622: [1682], [5701.3], 6021, 6643–3.5, [10599], 11205, [13599], 17900, 18990 ex off., 22305, 22848.3, [23773], 23795, 24107, [24693], 24811.
1623: [255.5] (d?), 3410, 4523, 6238, 12009.5, 13873, 14623, 15712, 17377a, 17901, [20163.5], 22844, 22848.3, 23720, 25176.
1624: 595.4, 1413, 3913, 5130, 14300, 15559, 16856, 20790, [22076?], [22078?] (d), [22078.5], [22103] (false), [22103.3] (false), [22103.7] (false), 22848.7, 22853, 23768, 25175, 25284.
1625: 4969, [13591], [14905.5] (c), 17939, 19316.3 (c), 22835, 22845, [23930], 24299, 25767.
1626: [4633–3.5], [4634–5], [6251], [13927], 17898, 20585 ass'd, [22784].
1627: 595.3, [17904.7], [22785].
1628: [1904], [3913.5] (d?), 6021.5, 6493, [6531], [6644], [7424], [7746.3], [10018.5], [11079.5], [13900], [13900.5], 22840.5, 22849.
1629: 595, [1165], [6509] (d), 6671, [22460(*A*3)], [24397].
1630: 589.5 ass'd, [590.3?], 592 ass'd, 595.5 ass'd, [4500], 5473 ass'd, 6639, 12495 ass'd, 13365 ass'd, 17378, [17916.5], [19088.7], 22835 ass'd, 22838 ass'd, 22849.1, 24007, [24605], 24619.
1631: [3324], 6645, 13351, 15008, 15331.3, 17339, 17344, 17353, 17364, 17374, 17378, 17396, [19851], 20948, 22840.7, 22849.3.
1632: [3059.6], 13322, 13340–0.5, 13347, 15712.5–13, 16944, 20950, 22845.3.
1633: 750–0.5, 6022, 6646–6.2, 10582, 11165, 13315 ent., 13348, 17216, [17396.5] (d?), 20098, 20951, 22845.4(*A*3), 22849.5.
1634: 1977, 10318 [f.?], 12452, 13357, 20099–9a, 22854.5, 23137, 24102, 24103 (repeat).
1634/35: 479.
1635: 1675, 1675a (forged), 3997, 6505, 7359, 7360, 7362, [11095], 12009, 12010, 12010.3, 12010.5, 14760, 14760.5, 21470, 22841, 23122, 24310 [f.].
1635/36: 494.12, 532.10.
1636: 1553, 1558, 3994.3 in off., [7344], [13369], 16942, 17379–9.5, 18383, 18806, [18976], [18976.2], 19111, 19313, 20219, [22215.5], 22631, [23735?].

Okes, N. — *cont.*
1636/37: 442.3, 494.13, [4293].
1637: 1557, 3412.3, 4944, [11321], 13364, 17422, 17444, 18922, 20220, 22845.7, 23509, 24660, 25226.5, 25227, 25371, [25726].
1638: 592.7, 3583a, 17444a, 18229, 19517, 22849.7 (note).
1639: 593, 595.2.
1640: 24103 (c).
1642: 22846 (note).
1700: 23795 (d/error?).

Oliffe (Olive), Richard.
Bookseller in London, (1588) 1590–1603†. [*Dict. 1*; *Poor Book* (widow), 1608–17.]
shop in Paul's Churchyard at the Crane (A.3), 1590 (13131)–1592? (1542(*A*3), omits 'shop')
dw. in Long Lane (E.9), 1596 (12246)–1601 (7243)
1590: 10763 f., 13131 f.
1591: 3059.2 f.
1592: 1542(*A*3) f. (d?), 1777 imp.
1596: 12246 f., 12412 sold.
1597: 1182 f.
1598: 11171 f., 20595.5 f. (d).
1599: 6151 f., 11171.2 sold.
1600: 6358 (note, c?), 6991 f., 17188 f., 25144 f.
1601: 7243 f.

1613: 21520 ass'd.

Oliver, Mary.
Printseller in London, '1609'. (This is almost certainly a case of an altered imprint in an engraving with the date left unchanged, but no later book or printseller of this name has been traced.) [Hind I.254–5.]
in Westminster Hall (X.17), 1609 (20917.5)
1609: 20917.5 sold (d).

Oliver, Reginald.
Bookseller and bookbinder in Ipswich, 1534–before 1556†. [Duff, *Century*; *TLS* 21, 28 Apr. 1927: 280, 299.]
in the Fishmarket, 1534 (14893.5)
1534: 15893.5 ven. (d).

Olivier, Pierre.
Printer in Rouen, 1500–1530. [Duff, *Century*; Muller 102; *Répertoire 16ᵉ*, 22: 34–71.]
1500: 16139 opera.
1502: 16163 opera.
1505: [15793].
1509: 16140.3 opera.
1510: [16140.7].
1514: [16194(*A*3)?].
1516: 16142 in off., 16196 opera, 16221 opera, 16250.5 opera (d?).
1517: 16135 in off., 16222 opera.
1519: 16201–1.3 opera.
1520: 13835 per, 16143 in off. (d?).
1521: 16204–4.5 opera.
1525: [15820], [15821].

Olney, Henry.
Bookseller in London, 1595–1596. Possibly the Henry Ovie/Onie bound to and freed in 1594 by John Harrison 1 (Arber II.129, 713). [*Dict. 1.*]
shop in Paul's Churchyard at the George near to Cheap gate (A.5), 1595 (22534)
shop in Fleet Street near the Middle Temple gate (W.13), 1596 (17091)
1595: 22534 f. **1596:** 17091 f.

Orphinstrange, John.
Stationer in London, (1595) 1606–1641?†. [*Dict. 1*; *Poor Book*, 1640–41.]
shop near Holborn Bridge (V.2), 1607 (16874)–1609 (16875, adds 'by the Cock and Catherine Wheel')
1607: 16874 f. **1609:** 16875 f. **1630:** 18854(*A*3) f. (c).

Orwin, Joan.
Printer in London, 1593–1597. Successively widow of **John Kingston**, **George Robinson**, and **Thomas Orwin**; mother of **Felix Kingston**. For her earliest imprint *see* **Joan Robinson**. *See* also the headnote following Appendix D/60. [*Dict. 1.*]
No address noted, but the printing house evidently continued in Paternoster Row over against the $ Chequer (C.7)
1593: 24494, 24790.7, 25019.
1594: 701.5, 4174, 4387, [6227], 17441, [22720], [22720.5], 25697, 26124.
1595: 762, 3436, 4176, [4268], 5267 ex typ., [5883–4], [6403], 7656, 13898, 15489, [16658], 18207–8, 18539.5, [19711], 19754, 19754.3, [20014], [21789], 22677, 22721, [22891.5], 25629.
1596: [182], 435.57, 702, 5711, 6749.6, [11866], 12367, 13586, 17127, [17867], 18540, [18604], 19702a.5, 20015, 20020, 21296, 22400.5, [23088], 23670, 25082, 25702.
1597: 11127, 11848.5, 18614, [19663], 19712, 23670.5, 25082a, 25630.

Orwin, Thomas.
Printer in London, (1581) 1587–1593†. His widow, who had previously been married to **John Kingston** and **George Robinson**, succeeded to the business as **Joan Orwin**. *See* also the headnote following Appendix D/60. [*Dict. 1.*]
?sold in Paternoster Row over against the Black Raven (C.7), 1588 (6558, with T. Gubbin)
dw. in Paternoster Row over against the $ Chequer (C.7), 1590 (11816)–1593 (10678)
1587: [3734], [5103.5], [10502.5] (d?), [11852], [12293?] (d), [12608] (d), 15215, [19078.6?], [24060], [25349] (d).
1588: 847, 1090, 4090 (d), 4665, 4668 (d), [5257], 5444, 5479, 6558, 6910.7, 10232, 11338 (d), 11342, 11542.5, 12285, 12803, 13093 (d), 14573.5 (d?), 14926, 15215, 18103, 18836.5, 19625, 19721.5(*A*3), 20519 ent., 24502, 25733.5.
1589: 644, 1358, 1708.5, [3944], 5480, 5965, 6229, 6625.3, [6790], 7060.5, 7159–9.3, [8183?] (d), [10252.5], 11820, 12272, [13098], [13098.2] (repeat), [15106], 15251.7 ex aed., 15447 ap., [16674], [17452], [17462?] (d?), [17463–3.3] (false, d), [17463.7] (false, d), [17464?] (d?), [17465] (d), 17491, [18653], 18776 ex off., 19477 ap., 20976, [22620], 22658, 22930, 24493, 24817, 25080, 25128, 25432, 25627 (d).
1590: 633, 1097, 1312 (d), 1968, [3421] (d?), 3908.5, 3908.5A, [3945], 4032 ent., [5061] (d?), 5266.6 ex typ., [6731], [7284], [10763], 11816, [11862], 12253, 13113 (d), 13131, [13139], 13144 (d), 13145, 13702, 15316.5, 16664, [16674.5], 18247, 19709, [20579.5] (d?), [22163], [22712.5], [22883], [23078], 23633a (d), 23652, 24597, 25732, 25732.5, 25733.
1591: 1018 ent., [1030.7(*A*3)] (d?), 1304 ent., 1360 ent., 2801(*A*) ent., [3059.2], 3810 ent., 3908.6, 4608 ent., 5159 ent., 5233 ent., 5445, 5457, 5590–0.5, 6215 ent., [7199], 7655 ent., 10233 (d), 10878.5 ent., [11097], 11192.5 ent., 11338.5–39, 11340, 11821, 11868, 13289 ent., 13308 ent., 13496 ent., 13498 ent., 14105 ent., [14644], 15190 ent., 15457 ent., 15644, [16657], 17049, 17087, 17112.5 ent., 17295 ent., 17653 ent., 17980 ent., 18243.5 ent., 18510 ent., 18886 ent., 18977a ent., 19120.3 ap., 19123 ent., 19125 ent., 19475 ent., 19710, 19753, 19916.7, 20588, 21057, 21446.7 ent., 21826.8 ent., 22161 ent., 22254.3 ent., 22685, 22687, [22703.5], [23078], [23079], 23133 ent., 23884a.2 ent., 23952.3 ent., 24687 ent., [24913], 25118.2 ent., 25626.
1592: 435.55, 726, [6402], 6851, 10711, [11341], 12923, 14685.7–86, [15095?], 19665, 19753.5, 20966, 22718, [23382], [24913a], 25081, 25696.
1593: [1335?] (d), 4387 ent., 5152, 5266.8 ex typ., 6737, [7202], 7721.5, 10678, [11208], 11469.5(*A*3) ent., 17914, 20820 ent., [22719], 22942, 23439.5 ent., 24288, 24790.7(*A*3) ent., [25338], 25433.7, [25652.5], 25815 ent.

Oswen, John.
Printer in Ipswich, 1548, and in Worcester, 1549–1553, with a shop or agent in Shrewsbury for the sale of books, 1549–1551. Appointed **King's Printer for Wales and the Marches** in 1549, he seems to have used that style in imprints at least twice, in 1551 (13756) and 1553 (9440.4). [Duff, *Century*; Janet Ing Freeman in *TCBS* (forthcoming).]
Ipswich [no address], 1548 (4435)
Worcester, 1549, 30 Jan. (12564)–1553 (9440.4); variation: adds 'in the High Street', 1551, 3 Apr. (4068)
Shrewsbury [no address], 1549 (13645)–1551 (4068)

Oswen, J. — *cont.*
1548: 3362 (d), 4435–5.7, 13021, 14126 (d?), 17315–6, 18055 (d), 18056.5 (d), 20192.7 (d), 20663.
1549: 2378, 12564, 13022, 13645, 16271 in off., 16276 in off.
1550: 2862, 2862.5 (d?), 12365, 24682, 26141.
1550/51: 464.3.
1551: 4068, 4069, 13756, [15546.7] (d?).
1552: 16287 in off.
1553: 9440.4, 13759 (d).

Oulton, Richard.
Printer in London, (1632) 1633–1643. Son or stepson of **Elizabeth Allde** by a previous marriage. He succeeded to the establishment in 1636. [*Dict. 2*; DFM 10; Bradford F. Swan, *Gregory Dexter*, Rochester, N.Y., 1949, pp. 15–17.]
dw. near Christ Church (C.1), 1636 (5209.3)–1637 (19433); no later use noted.
1633: 12334 ent.
1636: 3717.5, 3717.7, 5209.3.
1636/37: 442.3, 490.13, 495.12.
1637: 974, 10667, 13358, 18341, 18342, 19433, 21543 ap.
1637/38: 490.14, 515.21.
1638: 630.5–31, 975, 18339, 18344, 21094.
1638/39: 435.28, 515.22.
1639: 189, 976–6.5, 1507, 18035a.7(*A*3) typis, 18340–0.5, 18345–5a, [18507.278?], [—.280?] (d), [—.286?] (d), [—.303?], [—.306?], [—.309?], 24138.
1639/40: 435.29, 515.23.
1640: 601, 3302 ent., [12648b?], 13855.4, 14922, 18036 typis, [18507.318?], —.318B(*A*3, note), [—.320?], [—.336?], 20322.7 (c), 20925–5a, 21095, 21380 ent., [22824.3?], 24299.5 (c).
1640/41: Wing A 1541, A 1957, A 2398.
1641: [10078?] (forged, c?).

Ounkel. *See* Unckel.

Ouroy. *See* Auroi.

Oursel, Louis.
Printer in Rouen, 1639–1645 at least. [Lepreux III/1: 342.]
1639: 12173.5 chez.

Overton, Henry.
Bookseller in London, 1629–1648. He married the widow of his former master, **William Sheffard**, and succeeded to the shop. [*Dict. 2*; DFM 2355.]
shop at the entering in of (into) Pope's Head Alley out of Lombard Street (O.11), 1629 (6117)–1640 (12031) and undoubtedly later; variation: has 'entrance into', 1629 (5676), 1640 (41)
1629: 5676 f., 6117 f., 21187 f.
1630: 4236.3 ent., 4236.9 ent., 6118.7 f., 11675 ent., 22934.2 f.
1631: 5845.5 sold, 15557.5 f., 22117 f., 22934.3 f.
1632: 21187.5 f., 24143 f.
1633: 3535 sold, 4223 f., 6110.3 f., 6118 f., 6118.8 f., 6937 sold, 21188 f., 22118 f., 24142 f.
1634: 21189 f., 22934.5 f.
1635: 899 sold, 22119 f., 22934.7 f.
1637: 4236.5 f., 11652 (note), 22120 f., 22504 f., 22934.8(*A*3) f.
1638: 1907 f., 3758–9 sold, 11792 sold, 21190 f., 22497.5 sold, 22934.9 f., 25023.5 sold, 25356 f.
1639: 1314 f., 14496 f., 17390 f., 17393 f., 22935 f.
1640: 41 f., 4225 f., 7421 f., 7747 f., 7747.3 f., 12031 f., 21190.5 f., 22936 f., 23299 f., 23300 f., 23304 f., 23306 f., 23307–7.5 f., 23310 f., 23311.5 f., 23312 f., 23313 f., 25971a sold.

Overton, John.
Bookseller? or patron? in Ipswich, 1548. [Duff, *Century*.]
No address used.
1548: 1295 [f.].

Owen. *See* also Awen.

Owen, William.
Bookseller? in London, 1562.
at the Little Shop at the North door of Paul's Church (A.2), 1562 (3078(*A*3))
1562: 3078(*A*3) f. (d).

Oxenbridge, John.
Bookseller in London, (1589) 1591–1600†. [*Dict. 1*.]
dw. in Paul's Churchyard at the Parrot (A.3), 1595 (20083.7)–1599 (13341) at least
1591: 18633 ent.
1592: 15015.3 ent., 20977 ent., 20977.5 f.
1593: 12259 ent., 15015.7 imp., [23867.5 f.].
1594: 18626a.1 f.
1595: 1041.3 ent., 20083.7 f.
1596: 15340 f., 18633 f., 18748 f.
1597: 6170.7 f., 17323 f., 18626a.1C(*A*3) f., 20083.9 f.
1598: 12099 f. (d), 18626a.3 f., 20991.3 f., 22735 ent.
1599: 1041.3 f., 13341 f., 18626a.2 f.
1600: 13342 f.

Oxford University—Bodleian Library.
Publisher in 1620.
1620: 14450 imp.

Oxford University—Printers.
Printers in Oxford from 1584. Items in which individuals are named in the imprint or with names supplied in square brackets in STC are indexed *only* under the relevant name, and following is a list of those who held appointments before 1641:

Joseph Barnes, 1584–1616
William Wrench, 1617
John Lichfield, 1617–1635
James Short, 1618–1624
William Turner, 1624–1640
Leonard Lichfield, 1635–1657

For a comprehensive listing of all items printed or sold in Oxford before 1641, including those for which [*Oxford*] alone has been supplied as an imprint, *see* Index 2Ai.
Indexed below are items in which the imprint states *only* 'by the printers to the University' *without* the names of particular individuals.
1633: 20135–5.7.

P

P., M.
Publisher in London, 1625. Possibly = M. Partrich.
1625: 1687 f.

P., R.
Printer in Middelburg, 1584. = R. Schilders (Painter).
1584: 19356.

Paets (Paedts, Pates) Jacobszoon, Jan.
Printer in Leiden, 1578–1622†. [*Dict. 1*; Gruys; Briels 380–4.]
1582: 24806. **1585:** 1431.8. **1586:** 25340. **1593:** 1431.13 ex off.

Pafraet (Pafroed), Richard.
Printer in Deventer, 1477–1511. [Duff, *Century*; Gruys.]
1489: 696.1 per.

Page, William.
Puritan 'disperser' of John Stubbs's *Gaping gulf*, 1579. [Camden's *Annales/Historie*, under year 1581.]
1579: [23400 f.].

Paine (Payne), Thomas.
Bookseller and printer (from 1635) in London, (1628) 1630–1653. Became a partner of **William Jones 3** beginning in 1635 though they shared relatively few imprints; in 1637 Jones was forced out of the partnership. Paine took **Matthew Simmons** as a partner in 1640. [*Dict. 2*: 146; DFM 153; *St. Giles*, 1635–36; *Loan Book*, 1639–42; *Poor Book*, 1652 ('Printer, Payne'), 1652–53.]
in Trinity Lane at the Horseshoe (S.5), 1632 (12456)
'his' shop near Moorgate (H.12), 1634 (4177, with M. Simmons and probably his shop)
dw. in Red Cross Street (I.7), 1636 (4648, with W. Jones 3); no other address or use of this one noted
1630: 20388 f.
1632: 12456 f.
1634: 4177 sold.
1635: 4260.7 ent., 6113 f., 10645, 17389, 19110, 21343.

Paine, T. — *cont.*
1635/36: 479.2.
1636: 4648, 10646, 13242, 17160.
1636/37: 479.3.
1637: 2670.5, 21663a.5, 25848.5.
1638: 59.5, 2679, 10344, 21816 typis, 22569.
1639: 58, 60, 4260 typis, 10345, 11912, 21501, 21816–6.5 typis, 22257.5 ex typ.
1639/40: 435.29.
1640: 59.7, 1226, 4130, 7414–4.5, 7421, 10346, 11913, 12394, 13170, 13182, 13918, [15462], 19616 (d), 20240.3, [21774], [22165], 22404.7–.9, 22512, 24137–7.5, 24606, 24870–0.5, 25870.
1640/41: Wing A 1541, A 2791.

Painter. *See* Schilders.

Pakeman, Daniel.
Bookseller in London, (1628) 1631–1664†. [*Dict. 2*; DFM 1209.]
their shop in Little Britain (F.4), 1631 (24398, with J. Day 2)
at the Rainbow near the Inner Temple gate in Fleet Street (W.11), 1634 (6938.5)–1640 (17168, omits 'in ... Street') at least
1631: 24398 sold.
1634: 6938.5 f.
1635: 6939 f., 24297 ent.
1636: 17160 f.
1639: 11908 f., 11911 f., 23513 sold, 23515 sold.
1640: 15176.5 f. (d?), 17168 sold.

Papst. *See* Bapst.

Parent (Parant), Jean.
Bookseller in Paris, 1573–1593. [Renouard.]
1579: 17003.3(*A3*, note).

Parish Clerks' Press.
Press established in London, in the Parish Clerks' Hall in Broad Lane, Vintry (S.10), to print bills of mortality, 1626–1640 and later. [James Christie, *Some Account of Parish Clerks*, 1893, pp. 177, 187–8.]
Following are the printers appointed before 1641:

Felix Kingston, 1626–1629
Ralph Hodgkinson, 1629–1633
Thomas Cotes, 1636–1641

1630–36: [16743]. **1635:** [16744.5]. **1636:** [16745]. **1638:** [16745.3]. **1638–39:** [16745.5]. **1640–41:** [16745.7].

Parke, Francis.
Bookseller? in London, 1619. Not a member of the Stat. Co. [*Dict. 1.*]
shop in Lincoln's Inn gate in Chancery Lane (V.12a), 1619 (19454)
1619: 19454 sold.

Parker, John.
Bookseller in London, 1617–1648†. Although he seems to have lost interest in bookselling between 1628–1632 and after 1634, he remained active in the affairs of the Stat. Co. [*Dict. 2*; DFM 1312; Morgan.]
in Paul's Churchyard, 1618–1634 at least
dw. — at the Ball (A.2), 1618 (23934.5)–1619 (21834, has 'shop')
— at the Three Pigeons (A.3), 1620 (1863)–1625 (15642, has 'shop')
shop — at the Holy Lamb (A.6), 1634 (25932)
1617: 25985 f.
1618: 11597 f., 13617 f., 23136a f., 23934.5 sold, 25986 f.
1619: 1207 ent., 1208 f., 18805 f., 21338 f., 21833 ent., 21834 f., 21841 ent., 21845 ent., 23934.6 sold.
1620: 1863 f., 5583 sold, 10940 f., 13377.5 sold (d?), 15641 f., 17065 ent., 18783 sold, 21859 sold, 22362 f.
1621: 22774 f.
1622: 1079 sold, 10941 f., 10942 f., 19679 f., 21340–0a f., 23934.7(*A3*) sold.
1623: 17065 f., 21344 f., 23934.8 sold, 23934.9 sold.
1624: 5436.5 f., 6398 f., 13477 ent., 14089 f., 21345 f., 22966 ent., 23934.9 sold.
1625: 15642 f., 22775 f., 25996 f.

Parker, J. — *cont.*
1626: 1149 ent., 11597 ent., [18903 f.], 21338 ent., 23559 f., 23563 f., 23567 f., 23568 f., 23569 f., 24510(*A3*) ent., 25985 ent.
1627: 354 f., 21835 f., 23561 f., 23563 f., 23564 f.
1628: 14905 f.
1629: 22781 ass'd.
1633: 25685a.5 sold.
1634: 748 f., 18003 ?ent., 25932 sold.
1638: 1151 ass'd, 5440 ass'd, 24552 ent., 24553 f.

Parnell, Josias.
Stationer in London, (1584) 1595–1625†. The first three references to Josias in the index to *C-B C* are actually to William Parnell, who was called to the Livery 29 June 1616. [*Dict. 1.*]
No address used.
1595: 19855(*A*) ent. **1598:** 16899.5 f.

Parsons, Marmaduke.
Printer in London, (1608) 1637–1639†. Took over the establishment of **Augustine Mathewes** when the latter was evicted as master printer in 1637, though Mathewes may have continued to work as a journeyman for Parsons. The printing material was dispersed by Parsons's widow in late 1639 or early 1640 (*C-B C*: 329), a portion of it apparently going to **Richard Hodgkinson** (cf. 21849(*A3*)), even though the widow seems to have kept an apprentice until 1641 (DFM 427). Items below indexed for 1640 and later should be scrutinized for error in either date or printer supplied. [*Dict. 1*; DFM 474; *St. Giles* (I.4), 1611–19; *Library* 16 (1936): 425–32.]
No address noted.
1637: 3597, 11728.6 (d), 13264, 19218 (d), [21126], 22298, 24758.
1638: [2747?], 3638.5, 6101 (d), 6492, [10170] (d?), 10610.5 (d?), 11155 (d?), 12403.5, [12997a] (d?), 13370, 13739.5–.7, 14031, 14698, 15465, 17101, 18729, 19518, 20183 (d?), 20238, 20482 (d?), [21178(*A3*)], 21178.3, 23739, 24087 (d?), 24559a, 24759, 24830 (d?).
1638/39: 527.29.
1639: 220, 1690, 5610.7 (d?), 10018–8.2, [10284], 10511.3, 13739.5, 15119, [16801.3] (d), 17919, 20224, [22406.7] (d?).
1639/40: 527.30.

1640: [3920] (c), [10193], 12724 (d?), [12735], 17920 (d/var), [25024].
1641: [10078?] (forged, c?).

Fr. Parsons' Press.
English recusant press in Rouen, 1582–1585. Although at least some of the printing material belonged to **George Loyselet**, the items below were apparently produced at a separate press by George Flinton, later joined by Stephen Brinkley, both of whom were aides to Robert Parsons, *S. J.* [Southern 359–63; *Library* 6 (1951): 50–1.]
1582: [19353], [19401], [19406] (d).
1583: [17263], [24626.7].
1584: [373] (d), [10541], [16641.7].
1585: [19354.1].

Partrich (Patrich, Partridge), Miles.
Bookseller in London, (1613) 1615–1625? [*Dict. 1*; DFM 953.]
in Fleet Street, 1615–1618
shop — near unto Chancery Lane (W.10b), 1615 (1355)
shop near St. Dunstan's Church — (W.9), 1615 (1356)–1618 (13249); variation: adds 'at the George', 1616 (1686)
1615: 1355 f., 1356 f. **1616:** 1686 f. **1617:** 1687 ass'd, 10945 f. **1618:** 10945.3 f., 13249 f. **1625:** 1687? f.

Partridge, John.
Bookseller in London, (1622) 1624–1649†. His shop was apparently shared from 1632 with **John Rothwell 2,** his former apprentice, but their names do not appear together in any imprint. [*Dict. 2*; DFM 2694; Globe 219.]
in Paul's Churchyard at the Sun (A.3), 1628 (14965)–1638? (12998(*A3*, note), letterpress tp) at least
1624: 3992.5 sumpt.
1625: 4530 sold.
1628: 3992.9 sumpt., 14965 sold, 19419 f.
1629: 16880 sumpt., 17522 imp.
1630: 3404 sold, 12998 f.

Partridge, J. — *cont.*
1631: 912 f., 19566 f.
1632: 3993 sumpt.
1633: 14444 f.
1636: 12999 f.
1638: 12998(*A*3, note) (d?).
1640: 16881 sumpt.

Parvus. *See* Petit.

Pasini, Maffeo.
Printer in Venice, 1524–1551. [Borsa.]
1549: 6832.22.

Passe (Paas), Crispin 1 van de.
Engraver in Antwerp, Cologne, and Utrecht, c. 1585–1637† and also publisher in Utrecht. [Hind I.281; II.39, 145–6, 245.]
1620: 13582 imp. (d).

Passe, Crispin 2 van de.
Engraver and publisher in Cologne, Utrecht, Paris, and Denmark, c. 1610–1647?†. *See* also Author, *anonymous*. [Hind II.245–6.]
1615: 19459 f.

Pates. *See* Paets.

Patté, Gérard.
Printer? in Douai, 1613–1614, and bookseller there, 1622–1653. [*Répertoire 17ᵉ*, IV.9.]
1613: [11316.5]. **1614:** [13032].

Pavier, Thomas.
Bookseller in London, 1600–1625†. Freed as a Draper by **William Barley** on 9 Apr. 1600; transferred to the Stat. Co. the same year. Daughters of his married **Henry Gosson, John Grismand**, and **Cuthbert Wright** (*SB* 6 (1954): 165). One of the **Ballad Partners**, where SR entries of ballads after 1623 are listed. [*Dict. 1*.]
shop at the Cat and Parrots near the (Royal) Exchange (O.9), 1600 (18795)–1612 (17701, has 'dw. ... Cats and Parrot'); variations:
his house in Cornhill at the Cat and Two Parrots, 1601 (14343)
shop at the entrance (entering) into the [Royal] Exchange [no sign], 1603 (5871.7), 1604 (23357), 1605 (3794), 1610 (25132), 1611 (22669)
shop on [*sic*] Cornhill near to the Exchange [no sign], 1608 (22340)
shop in Ivy Lane (C.3), 1614 (3026.5)–1625 (21210, has 'dw.').
No sign noted so far but consider: *f. R. Pott, sold at the Cat and Parrot in Ivy Lane*, 1624 [25644(*A*3)], probably by Pavier.
1600: 3696.7 ent., 6554.5 ent., 6919 f. (c?), 11502 f., 12925(*A*3) ent., 18795 f., 18796 (d/false), 22289 ent., 22667 ent., 23357 ent., 23405 ent., 23677 ent., 23683.3 ent., 25154 f. (d).
1601: 4286 f., 11502.5 f., 12504.5 f., 14343 f., 18892.3 f., [18892.7 f.], 18893 f., 18894 f., 20890 f., 22577 f.
1602: 3022.7 f. (d?), 4287 f., 6553.5 ent., 6569 ent., 15089 f., 16681 f., 17675 f., 18454.5 sold, 18471 f., 19839 f., 20128 f. (d), 21006a ent., 22290 f., 22330 ent., 22425.5 f., 24651–1a f., 24651b f., 25132 ent., [25652.7 f.?] (c), 26101 ent.
1603: 5871.7 f., 6476 sold, 6476.2 sold, 7589 f. (d?), 7594 f., 10798 f., 14421 f., 14671 f., 15089a f., 20192.5 f. (c), 22045 f., 25987 f.
1604: 3022.8 f., 4287.5 f., 6477 sold, 22667 f., 23357 f.
1605: 3022.9 f., 3794 f., 10158 f., 15085 f., 23405 f., 23615 f., 25653 f. (d).
1606: 3023 f., 3023.5 f.
1607: 797 f., 11232 sold, 11559 sold, 22434 f. (d), 22667.5 f.
1608: 1980 f., 3024 f., 3050.3 (note), 12734.5 f., 13330a f., 21368.7 f., 22291 (d/false), 22340 f., 25653.5 f., 25988 f.
1609: 774 f., 3025 f., 21204.5 f., 21204.7 f., 21205 f., 22668 f., 24628 f.
1610: 3025.5 f. (d?), 4288 f., 13331 f., 15090 f., 21206 f., 25132 f., 25654 f., 25989 f.
1611: 3026 f., 15090 f., 19484 ent., 22669 f.
1612: 4946.9 f., 6569 f., 10025 f., 12324 f., 12864 sold, 17701 f., 21207 f., 21213.1 f., 22406.5 ent., 24350 ?ent., 25992 f.
1613: 4947 f., 18587 sold, 21207.3 f., 21213.2 f., 23677 f., 25061 f., 25134 f.
1614: 3026.5 f., 22670 f., 25994 f.
1615: 4032.3(*A*3) ent., 4948 sold, 5692 f., 11560 ent., 12547.7 f. (c?), 18621 f., 21213.3 f., 21369 f. (c), 21491.3 f., 21851 ass'd, 22900 f. (c), 25062 f., 25135 f., 25993 f.
1616: 3027 f., 11925.7 f., 12175 f., 12176 f., 12177 f., 12179 f., 12182 f., 21207.5 f., 24371 sold.
1617: 7259.7 ?ent., 21213.4 f., 21365.5 f., 21491.7 f., 22671 f.
1618: 21186 f., 21437 f., 25989.5 f.
1619: 3028 f., 7325 ent., 11560 f., 18796 f. (d), 21207.7 f., 21213.5 f., 22291 f. (d), [22297 f.] (false, d), [22300 f.] (false), [22303 f.] (false, d), 22341 f., 26101 f.
1620: 382.5 f. (c), 4288.5 f., 4308 ent., 11796.5 f. (c), 12303 (note), 16960 ent., 17782.5 ent., 18623 f., 19436.5 ent., 21208 f., 21213.6 f., 23387 f., 25135.5 f. (d?).
1621: 1941 f., 3029 f., 11560.5 f., 12178 f., 14320 f., 21013.5 f., 22137.7 f., 23388 f., 23678 f.
1622: 3786 f., 7318 f., 10713.5 f., 12791 prost., 13513 f., 21209 f., 21213.7 f., 22672 f., 25315 f.
1623: 3787 f., 6570 f., 7318 f., 12792 imp., 13514 f., 19676.5 f., [19862] sold, 23389 f., 23389.3 f.
1624: 188 sold, 853.5 f. (d?), 1314.7 f., 3788 f., 4073 f., 4289 f., 5534 f., 7326–6.5 f., 12635 f., 13381 (note), 18624.5 f., 23389.7 f., [25644(*A*3)?] sold.
1625: 3030.5 f., 5763 sold, 6976 sold, 12635 f., 21210 f., 21213.8 f., 25108 f. (d?), [25654.5 f.] (c), 25655 f.

1626: (all SR assignments): 1313.3, 1315, 3324, 4910, 6478, 10714, 12637.4, 12734.5, 19436.5, 21210.3, 21213.9, 21370, 21851, 22138, 23390, 23616, 25435, 25655.
1905: 25653 f. (d/error).

Paxton (Packston), Edmund.
Stationer in London, (1630) 1636–1655. [*Dict. 2*; DFM 1889 as 'Edward'.]
dw. at Paul's Chain near Doctors' Commons (R.3), 1636 (19501)
1636: 19501 sold.

Paxton (Packston), Peter.
Stationer in London, (1618) 1619–1627. [*Dict. 1*; DFM 2229; ?*Poor Book* ('Packson'), 1622.]
at the $ Cross in Paul's Churchyard (B), 1619 (14529)
shop at the Angel in Paul's Churchyard (A.3), 1627 (1414)
1619: 14529 f. **1627:** 1414 f.

Payne. *See* Paine.

Peake, Robert 1.
Painter, seller of prints and books in London, fl. 1611–c. 1630?†. Father of **Robert 2** and **William Peake**. [*DNB*; Rostenberg 20–1.]
shop near Holborn conduit next to the Sun Tavern (D.9), 1611 (22235)
1611: 22235 f.

Peake, *Sir* Robert 2.
Painter and printseller in London, 1634–1645 at least (1667†). Son of **Robert 1** and brother of **William Peake.** [Globe 219; Rostenberg 21–4; *TCBS* 8 (1982): 173–85.]
near (over against) Holborn conduit (D.9), 1634–c. 1640; variations:
[his] house over against —, 1634 (4485)
their house —, 1635 (3163, with W. Peake)
his shop —, 1637? (19518.5, engr. of St. Matthew), c. 1640? (10007.5, tp)
1634: 4485 sold. **1635:** 3163 f. **1637:** 19518.5 sold (d?). **1640:** 10007.5 sold (c?).

Peake, William.
Printseller in London, c. 1630–1643 at least. Son of **Robert 1** and brother of **Robert Peake 2**. [Globe 219; Rostenberg 21–4.]
near Holborn conduit (D.9), c. 1630–1635 at least; variations:
his shop — next the Sun Tavern, c. 1630 (Hind II.168, no. 10, state III)
their house —, 1635 (3163, with R. Peake 2)
1635: 3163 f., 11921.1 sold (c), 11921.2 sold (c), 11921.6 sold (c).

Peasley, William, *esq.*
One of the agents in London for the province of Maryland, 1635. *See* also **John Morgan**.
[his] house on the back side of Drury Lane near the Cockpit playhouse (X.5), 1635 (17571)
1635: 17571 [sold].

Peele (Pele), Stephen.
Stationer in London, (1570) 1577–1593 at least. [*Dict. 1*; ?*Poor Book* (widow), 1608–12.]
shop in Rood Lane (P.7), 1577 (1306)
1577: 1306 f. **1579:** 18258 ent.

Peerse, Elias.
Bookseller and bookbinder in Oxford, 1614–1639. [*Dict. 1*.]
shop in St. Mary's Churchyard, 1635 (10724)
1625: 20774 f. **1629:** 20363 ven. **1635:** 10724 sold. **1639:** 20364 imp.

Peetersen van Middelburch, Heyndrik.
Printer, bookseller, and bookbinder in Antwerp, 1520–1549?†. [Rouzet.]
Five of the items below (11381, 20193, 24167, 24447, 24447.3) have been tentatively attributed to his press on the basis of a woodcut border or of initials found in some of his signed works: C. Cellarius, *Oratio*, 1531; *Bibel*, 1535; *Missale Traiectense*, 1540 (Nijhoff and Kronenberg 548, 407, 1531 respectively). For example, the tp border of 24447 is found in the Cellarius; four similar 'G' blocks found on A2^r and E2^v of 24447 and 24447.3 also appear with two more among the Psalms on A4^v–6^r of the Bible. On the other hand, three of the items below (2828, 2828a, and 13970) have none of this group of initials and on re-examination seem more likely to have come from a different, unidentified press or presses.
1533: [11381?] (false).
1535: [2828?] (d?), [2828a?] (d?), [24167?], [24447?] (false).
1537: [13970?] (d?), [24447.3?] (false).
1538: [20193?] (false).
1540: 6832.5 (d?).

Pelgrim, Joyce (Jodocus).
Bookseller in London, 1496 (*Library* 1 (1910): 297)–1514 at least. In partnership with **Henry Jacobi**, 1505–1508. [Duff, *Century*.]
dw. near St. Paul's Church (B), 1504 (13829.5)
in Paul's Churchyard at the $ St. Anne (B), 1505 [17109]–1508 (23940a, omits sign)
1504: 13829.5 per [f.].
1505: [17109] ven.
1506: [15903(*A*3)] ven., [16258].
1507: 11605.5 imp., 11614.5 imp., [15862] ven.
1508: 696.4 imp., [15862] ven., 23940a imp.

Pemell (Pennell, Parnell), Stephen.
Bookseller in London, (1630) 1632–1635. [*Dict. 1*; DFM 1031.]
on London Bridge (T.7), 1632 (6123)–1635; variations:
at the Black Bull —, 1633 (735.3)
— near the gate, 1635 (22109)
1632: 6123 sold. **1633:** 735.3 sold, 19251 sold. **1635:** 22109 f.

Pen (Pennie), George.
Bookseller in London, (1571?) 1582, and in Ipswich, 1584. Son-in-law of **John Day 1** (Percy Simpson, *Proof-reading*, London, 1935, p. 138). [*Dict. 1*.]
No address used.
1582: 10879 f. **1584:** 11720(*A*3) f. (d).

Penkethman, John.
Scrivener, practical mathematician, and author, fl. 1624–1638.
at the scrivener's shop in Clifford's Inn Lane (W.9), 1624 [19600.2]–1626 [21805.5(*A*3)?]
[his] shop against the Rolls in Chancery Lane (W.10e), 1629 (19600.8)
[his] chamber in Symond's Inn in Chancery Lane (W.10e), 1638 (19598, engr. tp)
1624: [19600.2] sold (d). **1625:** [19598.2] sold (d?), [19600.4] sold.
1626: [12805.5(*A*)?] sold. **1629:** 19600.8 sold. **1638:** 19598 (note).

Penny, John.
Stationer in London, (1588) 1591–before 1598†. [*Dict. 1*.]
dw. in Paternoster Row at the Greyhound (C.7), 1591 (6328)
1591: 6328 f.

Pepermans, Jean.
Printer in Brussels, 1620–1635. [*Histoire du livre* IV.36.]
1624: 11314.6, 22936.5(*A*3). **1628:** 19167. **1630:** [11314.8].

Pepwell, Arthur.
Stationer in London, 1556?–1568?†. Possibly the son of **Henry Pepwell**. Son-in-law of **Robert Toy**. [Duff, *Century*.]
dw. in Paul's Churchyard at the King's Head (A.3), 1566 (5236)
1566: 5236 f. (d).

Pepwell, Henry.
Printer (to 1525?) and bookseller in London, 1518–1541?†. Possibly the father of **Arthur Pepwell**. [Duff, *Century*.]
in Paul's Churchyard (A.6), 1518–1539 (15609); adds 'at the $ Trinity', 1518 (18476)–1531 (7481.4)
1518: 18476.
1519: 23154.3.
1520: 170.3 (d?), 10450.3 per.
1521: 6834, 7271, 7709 (d?), [14077c.11c?] (d?), 20972.
1523: 6835 (d?), 25502.5 in aed.
1525: 10632 (d?).
1531: 7481.4 imp.
1539: [5543b.8 f.] (d?), 15603, 15609.

Percival, George.
Bookseller in London, (1625) 1628. [*Dict. 1*; DFM 2132.]
shop at the Bible in Fleet Street near the conduit (W.5), 1628 (17201)
1628: 17201 f. (d).

Perez, Francisco.
Printer in Seville, 1590–1608 at least.
1604: [25068?] (false).

Pernetto, Giovanni Vincenzo del, *pseud.*
Printer in 'Turin', 1589. = J. Wolfe (Woodfield no. 25).
1589: 10752.7.

Perrin (Perin), John.
Bookseller in London, 1580–1592?†. His widow briefly continued the business. [*Dict. 1*.]
dw. in Paul's Churchyard at the Angel (A.3), 1580 (5247)–1592 (21750, omits 'dw.')
1580: 5103 f., 5247 [f.] (d), 11872 f., 14257.5 ent.
1582: 13745.5 f. (d?).
1583: 24785 f., 24786 f., 24786.5 f.
1585: 2029 f. (d?), 6905 f., 19796–6.5 f., 22237 f.
1586: [6992 f.?] (d), 24707 f.
1587: 2031 f., 5103.5 f., 24708 f.
1588: 4090 f. (d), 5541 f.
1590: 17029 f.
1591: 17143 f., 19172.3 f. (d), 21749 sold, 22706 f.
1592: 16909 f., 17313 f. (c), 21750 sold, 22707 f.

Perrin, John, *Widow of.*
Bookseller in London, 1593. [*Dict. 1*, under husband.]
her shop in Paul's Churchyard at the Angel (A.3), 1593 (22709)
1593: 22709 f.

Perry, Hugh.
Book and printseller in London, 1626–1645. His first shop was acquired by **William Sheares**. [*Dict. 2*; DFM 931; Globe 219–20.]
shop in Britain's Burse at the Harrow (X.10), 1626 (12932)–1631 (25179), 1633 (25582, omits sign, has 'their' shop, with W. Sheares)
at the New Exchange [= Britain's Burse] (X.10), 1637 (1102)
shop next to Ivy Bridge in the Strand (X.8), 1639 (22287)
1626: 12932 sold, 23493.7 sold.
1627: 17392 f.
1628: 1864 sold, 5368 f., 5562 f., 10408.7 sold, 13581.3 f., 15305.5 sold.
1629: 1862 sold, 1865 sold, 1866 sold, 13222 f., 13248.6 f.
1630: 5599 sold.
1631: 3719 ent., 5125 f., 5897 f., 17478–8a f., 24086 f., 25179 f.
1633: 25582 f.
1636: 12051–2 f.
1637: 1102 f.
1639: 17390 f., 17393 f., 22287 sold.

Persons. *See* Parsons.

Peterson. *See* also Peetersen.

Peterson, Jan, *pseud.*
Printer in 'Amsterdam', 1547? = N. Hill. For the genuine Jan Peterssoon (Pietersz), active in Amsterdam, 1547?–1566 *see* Gruys.
1547: 95 (d?).

Petit (Parvus), Jean, *of Paris.*
Bookseller in Paris, 1492–1530. [Renouard.]
1502: 23427.3 ven.
1510: 21789.1 ven., 21799.4 ven., 21799.6 ven.
1511: 21799.8 ven., 23427a.3 (note).
1516: 16197 imp.
1521: 16203 imp.
1527: 16205.5 imp.
1528: 15823 imp.
1530: 15827.5(*A*3) imp., [15829].

Petit, Jean, *of Rouen.*
Printer in Rouen, 1555–1588. [Muller 102.]
1558: [15673?] (false), [15674–4.5?] (false).

Petyt, Thomas.
Printer (to about 1547), and bookseller in London, 1536–1556? (1565†). Freed as a Draper by John Hutton in 1518. At least some of his printing material seems to have passed to **Thomas Raynald** and **William Hill** by 1548. Dates supplied below for undated items are of undetermined reliability, and Petyt deserves further study. [Duff, *Century*; *SB* 32 (1979): 54–5 (abstract of will).]
in Paul's Churchyard at the Maiden's Head (A.4), 1536 (11550.8)–1554 (16059, has 'dw.', omits sign); the latest use of the sign noted is 1550 (7688.2); his house was beside that of R. Toy, in St. Faith's parish (Plomer, *Wills*: 12)
1536: 11550.8.
1537: 6127.
1538: 19 (d), 7789.3 (d), 7789.7 (d), 16796 (d), 16821.5.
1539: 2844, 2845 (d), 15603.5, 24201.
1540: 2069, 11691a.7 (c?), 16017 (d), 21793 (c), 24202.
1541: 10971, 12104.5, 13175.8, 15762 (d?), 16019 per, 16020.
1542: 6128, 9276, 9523, 16028.
1543: 9987 (d), [10986], 16028.5–29.
1544: 10623, 16032 per, 16033, 18406.
1545: 1908 (c), 2967.7 sold (d?), 10624, 10997.5 (c?), 16041 per, 18221.5 f. (d?), 18225.4 (d?), 20953 (d?), 23175.5 (c).
1546: 10625.7, [17764.5(*A*3)?] (d), 24203.3 f. (d?).
1547: 22818.
1548: [2851?].
1550: 2855 (note), 5073 [f.] (d?), 7688.2 f., 11393.5 [f.] (d), 18408 [f.] (d?).
1551: 2084 f.
1554: 1010 f., 16059.
1556: 2980.2 f. (d?).
1561: 12104.5 (d/error), 16019 per (d/error).

Phigrus, Ruardus, *pseud.*
Printer in 'Albionopolis', 1616. = E. Griffin 1.
1616: 25604 ap.

Philippe (Philippus), Jean.
Printer in Paris, 1494–1519. [Duff, *Century*; Renouard 344–5.]
1497: [15885]. **1501:** 15805.1 industria.

Philoponos, Joannes, *pseud.*
Printer in 'Malborow' [Marburg], 1538. ? = H. Peetersen van Middelburch, Antwerp.
1538: 20193 per.

Pickering, Elizabeth. *See* Redman, E.

Pickering, William.
Bookseller in London, before 1557–1571. [Duff, *Century*.]
dw. upon London Bridge (T.7), 1557 (23318.3)
dw. at St. Magnus' corner (T.8), 1558, 8 Mar. (10917)–1570 (11493, has 'shop'); variation: dw. under St. Magnus' Church, 1564 (3079)

Pickering, W. — *cont.*
1557: 23318.3 [f.] (d).
1558: 5229 ent., 10917 f.
1561: 13251.
1564: 3079 (d), [14545 f.] (d), 22902 f. (d?).
1564/65: 462.5 f.
1565: 12419 ent.
1566: 15676 [f.], 17237 f., 19869.5 f., 24920.5 ent., 25968 f. (d).
1567: 10510.5 f.
1567/68: 462.7 f.
1568/69: 463 f.
1569: 6325 ent., 7279 ent.
1570: 11493 f. (d), 13012 f. (d?).
1571: 15032 f.

Pigouchet, Philippe.
Printer in Paris, 1488–1515 (1518†). The last item below must be by a successor or a different press. [Duff, *Century*; Renouard.]
1494: [15879?]. **1495:** [15880?], [15883]. **1498:** 15887 per, [15889] (d). **1501:** 15896 per. **1502:** 15897 per. **1507:** [15905] (d?). **1519:** [15923?].

Pilgrim Press. *See* Brewster, W.

Pinchon (Pinson), Gérard.
Printer at Douai, 1609–1636. [*Dict. 1*; *Répertoire 17*ᵉ, IV.10.]
1629: 14914, 20594. **1630:** 4833, 11323. **1632:** 11316. **1634:** 22937. **1635:** [17130], [19910.5]. **1636:** [7373.8].

Pindley, John.
Printer in London, (1607) 1612–1613†. Shared a printing house with **John Beale**, but their names only rarely appear together in imprints. [*Dict. 1*; DFM 516.]
No address noted.
1612: (all SR entries): 4946.9, 11368.5(*A*), 12216, 12252, 12297, 13006, 17418, 23344, 23479, 23492, 26027, 26036.
1613: 6063.2, 6066, 12673, 13822.5, 13930, 15428, 17847–7.2, 23480 ass'd.

Pinson, G. *See* Pinchon.

Pinson, R. *See* Pynson.

Piper (Pyper), John.
Bookseller in London, (1613) c. 1615–1625†. [*Dict. 1*; DFM 2681; *St. Giles* (I.4), 1625.]
shop at Paul's gate next (un)to Cheapside at the Cross Keys (A.5), c. 1615 (13567a(*A*3))–1619 (3213, omits sign)
in Paul's Churchyard at the Cross Keys, 1620 (7338); no later use noted
1615: 13567a(*A*3) f. (c).
1617: 6550.5 f.
1618: 14283 f.
1619: 3213 f.
1620: 4316.5 sold, 7338 sold, 11958.5 sold, 14891 imp., 24525 f.
1621: 11988 f., 14693.5 sold, 14891 imp., 18255 f., 18256 f., 23117 f.
1622: 13879 f.
1624: 3913 sold.

Pistus, Hieronomus, *pseud.*
Printer in 'Basel', 1612. = N. Okes.
1612: 1501 ap.

Plantin, Christopher.
Printer, bookseller, and bookbinder in Antwerp, 1548–1589† with a shop in Paris, 1566–77. He spent part of 1582–85 setting up in Leiden the **Officina Plantiniana**, which in 1586 was turned over to his son-in-law, **Franciscus Raphelengius**. [*Dict. 1*; Rouzet; Briels 385–92.]
1576: 19595.3 ap. **1585:** 689 (false), 689.3 (false). **1586:** 25438 in house.

Plantiniana, Officina.
Printing house in Leiden managed in 1586–1597 by **Franciscus Raphelengius**, son-in-law of **Christopher Plantin**.
1592: 15703 ex off. **1597:** 24893.3 ex off.

Plateanus. *See* Straten.

Plater, Richard.
Printer in Amsterdam, 1625–1629. One of the *successors of* **G. Thorp**, where other items are listed which Plater may have helped to print. [*Dict. 1*; Gruys; *Library* 5 (1950): 230–42.]
1618: [230] (d/error). **1625:** 1106. **1626:** 11130. **1628:** [230] (d), [231], 231.5. **1629:** 1106.5.

Plomier, Alard.
Merchant and patron in Paris, 1528, and possibly later in London. [Duff, *Century*.]
1528: 15957 exp.

Poitevin (Poytevin), Jean.
Bookseller in Paris, 1498–1518. The ascription to Poitevin of the first item below is based on a leaf with his device found in one of the two copies known. It may not belong, or the date supplied may be erroneous. [Duff, *Century*; Renouard 352.]
1495: [15881.5 f.?] (c). **1498:** 15890 pro (d).

Ponsonby, William.
Bookseller in London, (1571) 1577–1604†. Son-in-law of **Francis Coldock**. He only rarely used an address. [*Dict. 1*.]
in Paul's Churchyard (A.2), 1591–1598 at least; variations:
dw. — at the Bishop's Head, 1591 (11340); a copy of a book of 1598 (11275) without Ponsonby's name in the imprint but with inscription of purchase from him giving the Bishop's Head sign, was sold at Christie's 24 July 1970, lot 59.
dw. — near unto the great North door, 1593 (22540)
shop —, 1598 (3544)
1577: 4066 f. (c).
1579: 4067 f., 20182a.5 f.
1582: 4077 f., 5116, 11310 f., 25012 f.
1583: 1846 pro, 5322.8–23 pro, [12269.5 f.] (d?), 17590, 21518 f.
1584: 12262 f.
1585: 24109 f. (d).
1586: 24110 f.
1587: 12262.5 f.
1589: 3056 ent.
1590: 2020 ?ent., 12915 f., 22539–9a f., 23078 f., 23080–1a f.
1591: 11338.5–39 f., 11340 f., 20651 f., 23078 f., 23079 f.
1592: 13466 f., 18138 f., 25117 imp.
1593: 12263 f., 12270 f., 22540 f.
1594: 4990 f., 15701 f., [19618?] f., 19991.5 sold.
1595: 11623 f., 12462 f., 15565 ent., 17162 f., 19988 f., 22534.5 f., 22535 f., 23076 f., 23077 f.
1596: 3057.3 f., 15318 f., 23082 f., 23086 f., 23088 f.
1597: 7263 f., 15565 ent., 22244 ent.
1598: 1381 f., 1500 f., 3544 f. (d), 18142 ent., 19838 f., 22538 ent., 22541 f.
1599: 6054 f.
1600: 18139 f., 18142 f., 20063 ent., 22244 ent., 22855 f., 22855.5 (repeat), 23708 f.
1601: 22855 f., 11412 f.
1603: 1382 f.
1604: 7490 f.

Porter, John.
Bookseller in London, (1576?), and in Cambridge, 1587?–1608†. Most of his imprints were shared with **Thomas Gubbin** and other London booksellers, who probably arranged for printing and distribution in that city while Porter may have provided the manuscripts—at least those of William Perkins—and managed the Cambridge end of the business. In Cambridge he lived in the parish of Great St. Mary's from 1589. [*Dict. 1*, where he is listed as two men, one in each city.]
No address or place used except in 1607 (24996.5 sq.), where 'of Cambridge' may especially refer to Leonard Greene, Porter's former apprentice.
1061: 19713 f. (d/error).
1587: 19721.3 ent.
1588: 14926 f., 19721.5(*A*3) f.
1589: 6229 f.
1590: 19709 f., 19752 f. (d?), 19752.3 f. (d?), 19752.5 f. (d?).
1591: 19710 f., 19753 f.
1592: 19665 f., 19665.5 f., 19700(*A*3) [f.], 19710.5 f., 19753.5 f.
1593: 19700.5(*A*3) [f.].
1595: 3436 f., 18207 ent., 18208 f., 19711 f., 19754 f., 19754.3 f.
1596: 19702a.5 f.

Porter, J. — *cont.*
1597: 16609 f., 19712 f.
1598: 22882 imp.
1600: 19646 (note), 19754.7 f.
1601: 19713 f. (d).
1602: 19647 (note).
1603: 18210 ent.
1604: 19713.5 f.
1605: 12679 f., 12679.5 f., 12685 ent.
1606: 3437 f., 12666 f., 12667 f., 12680 f., 12680.3 f., 12680.5 f., 12680.7 f., 19670 (note), 19714 f.
1607: 12669 f., 12681 f., 24996.5 f., 24996a f.

Post Pascha, Peter.
Bookseller? or patron? in London, 1499. His only imprint is shared with **Frederick Egmont**. [Duff, *Century*.]
No address used.
1499: 20434 exp.

Pott (Potts), Roger.
Bookseller in London, 1621–1624. [*Dict. 1*; DFM 1903.]
dw. at the Fleur-de-lis in Paul's Churchyard (A.2), 1621 (11379)–1624 (6594.5, omits 'dw.')
?sold at the Cat and Parrot in Ivy Lane (C.7), 1624 (25644, more likely the address of T. Pavier)
1621: 11379 f. **1624:** 6594.5 f., 25644 f.

Potter, George.
Bookseller in London, (1598) 1599–1627†. Succeeded to the shop of his former master, **Joan Broome**; by 1611 the shop had passed to **John Royston**. [*Dict. 1*; *Loan Book*, 1619–22.]
shop at (near unto) the great North door of Paul's at the Bible (A.2), 1602 (4173)–1609 (12288.5, has 'dw.')
1599: 24131 f.
1600: 13076(*A*3) ent.
1601: 5415 ent., 12288 ent., 18151 ent.
1602: 1074.5 f., 4173 f., 25083 f.
1603: 4616 f., 11726 f.
1604: [12750?] sold, 18151 f., 18162 ent.
1605: 4617 f.
1606: 18162 f., 25085 f.
1607: 12288 f.
1609: 12288.5 f., 18455.7–56 f., 24577 f.
1612: 25084 f.
1614: 12289 f.
1619: 12289.5 f.

Poullain (Poulain), Jacques.
Printer in Paris? 1551? and in Geneva, 1555–1558. [Duff, *Century*; *Dict. 1*; Renouard; Chaix 215.]
1556: 11884.5. **1558:** [15063?], 15067, [15070], 16561a.

Pounder (Puntar), Christopher.
Bookseller in Norwich, 1616–1621.
shop at the Angel, 1616 (23106)
1616: 23106 f. **1621:** 26098.3 sold.

Powell, Humphrey.
Printer in London, 1548–1550? and in Dublin, 1550–1566. In the latter city he served as **King's Printer in Ireland.** Probably related to **William Powell**. [Duff, *Century*; *Library* 6 (1915): 228–34.]
London, dw. above Holborn conduit (D.5), 1548 (4059)–1550? (21690.6); variation: has 'a little above', 1549 (2376)
Dublin, in the great tower by the crane, 1551 (16277)
Dublin, in St. Nicholas Street, 1566 (14259)
1548: 1384a (d?), 4059, 4956, 6793.6 (d?), 18787 (d?), 24676, 24679.
1549: 2376.
1550: 21690.6 (d?), 21690.8 (d?).
1551: 16277 in off.
1558: [7481.7?] (c?).
1561: 14138 (d).
1564: 14139.
1566: 14259.

Powell, John.
Bookseller in Taunton, 1629.
No address used.
1629: 1954.5 sold.

Powell, Thomas.
Printer in London, 1556–1563. Nephew of **Thomas Berthelet**, succeeded to the latter's printing house in 1556, and may have managed it from about 1548. Complete listings of imprints in the form 'in the house of' Berthelet, some of which are indexed below, will be found only under Berthelet. The establishment ultimately passed to **Henry Wykes.** [Duff, *Century*; *TBS* 8 (1904–06): 187–220.]
in Fleet Street, 1556 (13293)–1563 (24850.7)
1556: [9408.5] (c), 13293, 13295, 13308.
1557: [7649?], 9392.5, 9413, [10501] (d?), 12560, 13290.7 (d), 24860.
1558: [9377.3] (c?).
1560: 7650 (d?), [15218], [23901].
1561: [9396] (d?).
1562: 5277, [9368], [9375.5] (d?), [9377.7] (c), [9384], 9389 (d?), 9393, 9393.5 (repeat), [9400], [9402] (d?), [9406] (d?), [9409], 9414 (d?), 13285, 14615–6, 22228 (d?), 24021, [25876].
1563: 9303.9, 9360.5 (d?), 9362.1 (d?), [9363.3] (d?), 9371 (d?), 24850.7.

Powell, William.
Printer in London, (c. 1540) 1547–1570. Probably related to **Humphrey Powell**. Married the widow of **William Middleton** and succeeded to the latter's printing house. Continued printing law books until 1553, when **Richard Tottell** obtained a patent. [Duff, *Century*; *Library* 6 (1915): 228–34.]
in Fleet Street (W.9), 1547–1569/70 (511.5); adds: at the George next (near) to St. Dunstan's Church, 1547 (10973)–1566 (21052, has'dw.')
1547: 20 (c?), 821 in aed., 2819, 3380 (d), 10973.
1547/48: 410.
1548: 2819, 3330 (d?), 9615a (d?), 9838.5 (d?), 9839.5 (d?), 9936, 10485, 15765, 17792, 22157, [23877.3] (d?).
1549: 2820, [2975.5] (d?), [4079?], [9988.3] (d), 10987.5, 10999.3 (d?), 20406.
1549/50: 410.1(*A*).
1550: 857a.5, 859.5, 955, 3310.5 (c), 3330.5 (d?), [4824a?] (c), 9653a in aed. (d?), 9840.5 (d?), 9862 (d?), 9906.5 (d?), 9932.7 (d?), 9933.7 (d?), 9947.4 (d?), 9955.3 (d?), [9962.5] (d?), 9988.5, 10439, 13175.13, 14880 in aed., 21065 (d?).
1550/51: [410.2], [410.3?].
1551: 179, 5654 (d?), 9293a, 9526 [f.], 10974, 15765.5, 18397.5, 24204.
1551/52: 410.4.
1552: 857a (d), 1849 in aed., 3374, 7704, 7721, 9802.5, 9989, 10988.5, 20904 in aed. (d?), 25668.5 (d?).
1552/53: 410.5.
1553: 15736, 18408.5.
1553/54: 410.6.
1554: 3196.5 (d), 12090 in aed.
1554/55: 410.8.
1555: 179.5 (c), 645–8, 2980 (c?), [25196] (d?).
1556: 7667, 20091 (note), 22412.
1557: 3374.5–75 (d).
1559: 22413.
1560: [3291] (d?), 3306(*A*) ?ent., 20922 ent.
1562: 4028 ent., 22161.
1562/63: 492.9 (note).
1563: [24293.3] (c).
1564: 3481 (c), 3481.5 (c).
1565: 4028 ent., 10617 (c), 23628.5 (c?).
1566: 17237, 19869.5, 21052, 21052.5.
1567: 3380 (d/error).
1569/70: 511.5.

Pratum, Theophilus, *pseud.*
Printer in 'Cosmopolis', 1611–1612. = R. Field; also forged, apparently by D. Binet, Paris.
1611: 25596 ap., 25596.5 ap. **1612:** 25597 ap.

Pré. *See* Du Pré.

Prest. *See* Le Prest.

Preston, John.
Bookseller in London, 1582–1584. His only imprint was shared with **Henry Carre**. Not a member of the Stat. Co. and possibly the man freed as a Draper in 1553. In 1582 he signed a petition against Stat. Co. regulations and other restraints of trade. He or another Draper of this name freed in 1596 had the services of one of the apprentices of **Thomas Dawson** in 1600. [Arber II.245–6, 777–8.]
No address used.
1584: 16947.3(*A*3).

Prével, Jean.
Printer in Rouen, 1510–1513, and in Paris, 1517–1528. [Renouard; Muller 103.]
1526: 15946.5 arte.

Prévost, Claude.
Printer in Paris, 1627–1639 at least. [Lottin 2: 143.]
1634: 19203.3 (note).

Prévost, Nicolas.
Printer in Paris, 1525–1532. [Duff, *Century*; Renouard.]
1527: 15863 in off., 15953 in off., 15953.5 in off., 16206 opera.
1528: 15864 in off.
1530: 16240 ex off., 16240.5 ex off.
1532: 15865 in off.

Prévosteau, Estienne (Stephanus).
Bookseller and printer in Paris, 1579–1610. [*Dict. 1*; Renouard.]
1602: 5589. **1604:** 11336.

Primrose, James.
Clerk of the Scottish Privy Council, 1599–1641, and patentee in Scotland for the publication of *God and the King*. [*DNB*.]
1616: 14420 for the only use of.

Printer of the Aberdeen 'Donatus'.
Printer in Scotland? c. 1507? Possibly the same press as that following next. [Isaac I, fig. 91.]
No address known.
1507: [7018] (c?).

Printer of 'The Tua mariit wemen and the wedo'.
Printer in Scotland? 1507? Possibly the same press as that immediately above. [Isaac I, fig. 90.]
No address known.
1507: [7350] (d?).

Printer to the City of London.
Printer of official Corporation orders, etc. and other items required for use in London. Dates in square brackets below are from documentary evidence, most of it cited in *TBS* 14 (1915–17): 188–95. Regarding T. Gibson see *TBS* 6 (1900–02): 17. For more on J. Wolfe and on J. Windet's appointment *see Library* 14 (1933): 266–72.

Richard Pynson, [1517–1528]
Thomas Gibson, [1538]
John Day 1, [1557: Arber I.74, 77], 1564 (16705)–1584 (16710)
Hugh Singleton, [1584, 4 Aug.] 1586? (19070.5)–1593 (16713.5)
John Wolfe, [1593] 1595 (16715)–1599 (9494.9) [1601]
John Windet, [1601] 1602 (9499)–1608 (16723) [1610]
William Jaggard, [1610, 17 Dec.] 1610? (16724(*A*3))–1622 (16728.7) [1623]
Isaac Jaggard, [1623, 4 Nov.] 1623? (16728.9)–1625 (16729.2) [1627]
Robert Young, [1627, 20 Mar.] 1628 (16729.5)–1640 (16737.7) [1642]

Proctor, John.
Bookseller in London, 1589–1590. He was serving an apprenticeship in 1585 (Arber II.137), but there is no record of his freedom. [*Dict. 1*.]
shop on Holborn Bridge (V.2), 1589 (21121.5)–1590 (21078, o copy)
1589: 21121.5 f. **1590:** 21078 f., 21482 f., 22693 f., 22694 f.

Pulleyn (Pullen), Octavian.
Bookseller in London, (1629) 1635–1667. In partnership with **George Thomason** until 1645. [*Dict. 2*; DFM 1904.]
at the Rose in Paul's Churchyard (A.3), 1637 [4789, in title]–1639 (15496), both with Thomason
1635: 21537.3 imp.

Pulleyn, O. — *cont.*
1637: [4789] ven.
1638: 4753 ent.
1639: 15496–7 f., 17553 ent., 20488 pour, 20489 pour, 22058 f.

Puntar. *See* Pounder.

Purfoot, Thomas 1.
Bookseller and printer (from 1566) in London, 1546–1605? (1615†). Father of **Thomas Purfoot 2**. From at least 1583 he printed *A treatise of limning* (24254) as the assignee of R. Tottell; *see* Appendix B/38. In 1587 he acquired the right to print briefs for collections (Arber II.463; cf. 8151 and some of the cross-references in STC vol. 1, p. 347). In 1605 he was granted the right to print one sheet of the 'primers' (*C-B C*: 15; cf. 20.7 sq., 16090 sqq., 20377.3 sqq.). [Duff, *Century*.]

Although normally in this index a son is considered to have succeeded his father only upon the latter's death, Thomas 1 was aged 97 or thereabouts in 1615. Between 30 Mar. 1591 (Arber II.577; cf. 4323.2) and 25 June 1603 (III.239 = 14299) entries in the SR were made jointly to Thomas 1 and 2 with the following exceptions: to Thomas 1 alone on 12 May 1592, 30 Mar. 1598, and 5 Feb. 1599 (II.612, III.109, 137); to Thomas 2 alone on 2 June 1596 (with R. Blower) and 2 June 1601 (III.65 = 20869, 186 = 18432). On 12 Aug. 1605 one entry was made to Thomas 1 (III.298 = 18454.7). Beginning with 17 Feb. 1606 (III.314) entries were solely to Thomas 2, and in this index it is assumed that he took over effective management of the establishment that year. More intensive study of the publications 1591–1615 might yield more subtle criteria for distinguishing between the father and the son.

dw. in Paul's Churchyard at the $ Lucrece (B), 1550? (13754)–1577 (21533.7); sometimes only the sign is given, e.g. in 1573 (11442)
dw. in Newgate Market, within the new rents at the $ Lucrece (C.4), 1579 (4271)–1596; the last use noted of the sign in imprints is 1580 (14275) except for the 1594 shop address below, though it continues to appear in devices (McK. 151, 161, 173); variations:
dw. in Newgate Market, 1582 (6804)
dw. in the new rents, 1588 (17591), 1596 (17592)
dw. within the new rents in Newgate Market, 1591 (1213)
shop without Newgate over against St. Sepulchre's Church (D.8), 1581 (936)–1587 (22162, omits 'over ... Church'); variations: omits 'without Newgate', 1581 (4401), 1582 (6804); 1585 (22108, has 'right over against')
shop at the $ Lucrece at the little North door of Paul's Church (A.1), 1594 (25882)
dw. in St. Nicholas Shambles within the new rents (C.5), 1598 (14077, colophon)–1605 (17593)

1546: [17764.5?(*A*3)] f. (d).
1550: 13754 [f.] (d?).
1561: 19.4 ?ent.
1563: [7576.7] (d), 18879(*A*3) f. (d).
1564: 21742 ent., 25877 ent.
1565: 21299.3(*A*) ent.
1566: 401 (d?), 6769 (d), 13017, 15676, 19424.
1566/67: 417, 506.5(*A*).
1567: 7369.5 ent., 24271.
1568: 11721 ent., 21008 ent., 25878.5.
1569: 3184, 10593 (d), 11286, 12961, 19548 (d).
1570: 7554 (d), 10591 (d), 18004 (d?), 19595 praelum, 20377.3 (c), [20377.5?] (c), 21021 (d).
1571: 10830 (d?), 19595 praelum.
1573: 11442 praelum, 11443.
1574: 935, 1210a, 5784, 25879.
1575: 5786, 6758, [8068] (d?), 14076, 15677.
1576: 568, [1210a.5], 4096, 17209, 20870, 21299.3(*A*), 25977, 25979.
1577: 21533.7.
1578: 10289.3.
1579: 4271, 10203, 25879.5.
1580: 1211, 1855, [7369.5] (c?), 11399 ent., 13625 ex off., 14275.
1581: 936 (d?), 4401, 4403 (d), 14609.5 (d?), 15678, 17589, 25880, 25934.5 ex off.
1582: 4301 (d?), 5116, 6804, 19308 ap.
1583: 1103 (d?), 1104 (d?), 1212, 5431 ?ent., 6275 (d?), 10251.5, 11234, 17210, 17590, 20871, 24254.

Purfoot, Thomas 1 — *cont.*
1584: 13904, 25086 (d), 25880.5.
1585: [335?], [689?] (false), [689.3?] (false), 22108.
1586: 8151, 10179 (d), 11377 (d), 14610, 17210.3, 18426.5 (d), 19208 ent., 20872, 21769, 24573 ent., 24920.5 ent., 25881.
1587: 8068 (note), 19293a (d), 22162 (d).
1588: 8171 (d), 17210.7, 17591, 20873, 24255.
1589: 1031, 13103, 13112, 13112.5.
1590: [1209.3?] (c), [8191?] (d), 21319.3 par, 21319.7.
1591: 1213, 4323.2 ent., [8203.5?] (d), 11290 (d), 12461, 13856 (d).
1593: 18432 ent.
1594: 17211, 20874, 25882.
1595: [4323.2].
1596: 3117 (d), 3171.5, 17592, [23606], 24256.
1597: 6759, [3115.7] (d?), 16869.5, 19338, 25087.
1598: 1214, [2368.5] (d), 6181.2 ent., 6223(*A*3) ?ent., 6276, 14077, 18869, 19807, 24093 (d).
1599: 11711, 19808, 25883.
1600: 1424.
1601: 20.7, 13999.
1602: 1215, 19595.5(*A*3) ent., 21299.5, [21299.7] (c), [24651–1a], [24651b], 25884.
1603: 10356.5, 14299.
1604: [1088], 1118–8.5, [6903.5] (d?), 8358 (d), 8362 (d), 18745, [19975].
1605: [20.8], [1164], 1819, [1825(*A*)], [13328], 14481, 17475, 17593, 18454.7 (d), 19595.5 praelum.

Purfoot, Thomas 2.
Printer in London, (1590) 1591–1638 (1640?†). Son of **Thomas Purfoot 1**, under whom are listed items which Thomas 2 may have helped to print 1591–1605. In 1591 he was granted the reversion of his father's place as a master printer (*Reg. B*: 39). Although Thomas 2 has been credited with printing items in 1596 and 1601 which were entered in those years to him alone, for purposes of indexing it has been assumed that he took over effective management of the whole establishment in 1606. *See* also *assignees of* **T. Purfoot 2**. [*Dict. 1*.]

dw. within the new rents in St. Nicholas Shambles (C.5), 1607 (1215.5); no later use noted.

1591: 4323.2 ent., 11290 ent., 12461 ent.
1593: 18432 ent.
1596: 20869, 23606 f.
1597: 16869.5 ent.
1598: 6181.2 ent., 6223(*A*3) ?ent., 6759 ent., 11711 ent., 19808 ent., 24093 ent.
1601: 18432, 18432.5.
1602: 19595.5(*A*3) ent.
1603: 14299 ent.
1606: 3405, [5693.5], [6553], 7456, [11368], 11572, [13329], [13336], 17483, 17913, 25740 ent.
1607: 1215.5, [8400.5] (d), [8400.7] (d), [12288], 12981–1.5, 16618, 16623, 16631–1.5, [17890], [25768].
1608: 1819.5, 3013, 5757, 6760, 11262, [13330–0a], 11399, 18325–5.3, 25638.5, 25885–5.5.
1609: 4300, 6582, 10207.5, 12644, 12670, 12672, 12682, [13337], [19936].
1610: 4323.3, 11813, [13147.5–.7], [13331], [13826.5?], [22379], [22385], 24005, 24261.
1611: [5435?], [5653], 8472 (d), 11400, 13134, 16870, 18961.7(*A*3), 21711, [24005.3(*A*3)] (d?), 24269, 24325–5.5, 24329.
1612: 1216, 3907, 5188, 8480.5 (d), 16870, 18962, 24270, 25941.
1613: 384, 5848, 8483.3 (d), [13332], [21418], 23677, 25061.
1614: 132, [2548], [5436?], 5581.5, 8510.3 (d), [13361a], 15104, [24389].
1615: 1217 ent., [2550], [2551.5], 4301 ent., 4323.4(*A*3) ent., 5849, 8541 ent., [10268.3] (c?), 11443 ent., 13999 ent., 14077a, 16871 ent., 21300 ent., [22312], 24573 ent.
1616: 125, [2555.5], [6483], 7346 ex typ., 8541, 8542 (d), 11925.7, 12582.26, 22847.3, [24426], 25886.
1617: 1217, [2557.5?], 10137, [10268.5] (d?), [24427].
1618: [2560.5], [2560a.5], [5436.3], [8567?] (d), 10239, 14387.
1619: [2564.8], [5323a.2] (d), 6821, 8590 (d), 8601 (d), 8602 (d), [8602.3] (d?), 8602.5 (d), [8610.5] (d), 8616.5 (d), 8620.7 (d), 8621.5 (d), 14388, [24428].
1620: [2570], [2570.5], [3138.5] (c), 6945.8, 8631 (d), 8635 (d), 10219.5, 10268.7, [24390].

Purfoot, Thomas 2 — *cont.*
1621: [2572.3], [2745], [5323a.6] (d), [5598], 6946, [21419], 23678, [24429].
1622: 8686.3 (d), 13580, 22285, 22319.
1623: 8708.7 (d), [22562], 25820.
1624: 6268.5, [23191].
1625: [2590.5?], 6181.3, 8785.7 (d), 10269, [24429.5].
1626: 5668, 10270, [11528], [12456.3] (d), [12456.7] (d), 19874, [12222].
1627: [2599.5], 4698, 6936, 17587, [23191.3].
1628: 6754.7, 10182 (d), 11933.5.
1629: [2614.5], 4323.4, 12290, [23191.7].
1630: [2620.5], 3031, [4500], 8960.5 (d), 10727, 11498? 21445, [24391], [24431].
1631: 351, 1218, 3719? 6755, 7497, 8981 (note), 10270.5, 10759, 24697.
1632: 2635, 6756, 12291, 17618.
1633: 2641, [3368.5-Audley] (d?), 3535, 4323.6, 14077b, 21300.
1634: 6168.5, 9021.5 (d), 9022 (d), 11157, 12845, 16871, 23842, 25887.
1635: 2656.5, [3368.5-Ashmole(i)] (d?), 4323.8, 12291.5 (c).
1636: 5715, 9055 (d), 9058.5 (d), 15099, 23819.5 (d?).
1637: [21.3], [3368.5-Ashmole(ii)] (c?), [5716], 24573.
1638: [5716], 6670.

Purfoot, Thomas 2, *Assignee(s) of.*
Printer(s) in London, 1638–1639. On 29 Feb. 1640 **Thomas Badger** petitioned Archbishop Laud to be admitted a master printer in the place of the deceased **Thomas Purfoot 2**, indicating that he had worked with permission as Purfoot's assignee for the two previous years (*Cal.S.P.D., 1639–1640*, p. 499). Although Purfoot printing material appears in T. Badger's publications, it also appears in items printed by **Richard Hodgkinson**, and the relationship between the latter and Badger during these years is not clear. It is possible that **John Bodington**, a former Purfoot apprentice, also had access to the material. Items indexed here and under all of the men require further study. The imprint is in the plural form except as noted.
1638: 9120.5 (d), 13737–7.5.
1639: 12871 ass'n, 13908 ass'n, 19510, 19882.5 ass'n.
1640: [23310].

Purset, Christopher.
Bookseller in London, (1597) 1604–1616 (cf. DFM 2201) at least. His widow remarried **Nicholas Okes** in 1624 (Blayney, *Origins*: 301). The first item in which Purset's name appears was sold in the shop of its printer, **Humphrey Lownes**: at the West door of Paul's Church (A.10). [*Dict. 1.*]
at the $ Mary Magdalen's Head in Holborn, near to Staple Inn (V.9), 1605 (3999.5)–1611 (6039.5, has 'dw.')
1604: 12169 f.
1605: 3660 f., 3999.5 f.
1606: 11158 f.
1607: 5491 f., 20340 f., 22249 sold, 22249.3 f.
1611: 3568 f., 6039.5 f.

Purslowe, Elizabeth.
Printer in London, 1632–1646. Widow of **George Purslowe**. Possibly a member of the **Eliot's Court Press**, though the same reservations apply that are cited under her husband. [*Dict. 2*; *Loan Book* (via J. Haviland), 1632–37.]
dw. at the East end of Christ Church (C.1), 1635 (12305)–1636 (13010)
dw. near Christ Church (C.1), 1639 (6556)
1632: 6123, 20257, [25972.8?] (d?).
1633: [600], 7043, 7044, 10760, 12015.5 (d?), 12361, [12743.5?], 13552.5, 17639, 18896, 19251, [20236], 20258, 23345, 24699.
1634: 3255, 4294, 10760, 12331.5, 12332a, 16848, [18240], [19261?] (d), 20234, 20258.5, 20259, 20348, 20349, 24348.
1635: 3396, 3700, [5145], 5657, [5714.8], 7162, 10761, [11153] (c), 12305, [12543.7?] (c?), 15144, 20260a, 20350, [20689], 22215a, 23272, [24301?] (c), 24044, 25930.3, [25973] (c), [26053], [26104] (c).
1636: [1392.5], 2662.5, [5146], [5715], 5907, 10761, [12292], 13010, [13274], [13275], 23075, [23662], 23756.
1637: 3723, 4293.2, [5146.3], [5716], 5852.5, 5853, 5908, [10178], 11364, [12012], 23759, 24335.5, 26036.5.

Purslowe, Elizabeth — *cont.*
1638: [1839.5], 4575.3, [5716], 10299, 10299.5, 11159, 11673, 11674, 14784, 17240, 20226, 22475, 22478–8b, 22498, 22498a, 22989 ex typ., 24399.
1639: 6107.3, 6314, 6556, 7123, 14496, 18035a.7(*A*3) typis, 19505, 19897, 20490, 22491, 25963.
1640: 601, [1122], [1331(*A*3)] (c), 7079, [10406?], [11152.5] (c?), [11154] (c?), 11796.7 (c), 12386 (c), [13016?] (c), 13467, 13468, [13852] (c), 14739 (d?), [16869?] (c), 18036 typis, 18507.318B(*A*3, note), [19216], [19216.5?], 20396, 21710.7, 22491, 23809, 23986, 24434, 25030, [25937] (c), 25960–1.
1640/41: [21589–9.3], [21589.5], 25248 (note), 25248.3 (note), Wing A 1957, A 2112.

Purslowe, George.
Bookseller and printer (from 1615) in London, (1609) 1613–1632†. Husband of **Elizabeth Purslowe**. Acquired the printing material of **Simon Stafford**. Usually considered a partner in the **Eliot's Court Press** but was a master printer on his own with a separate establishment nearby. It is not clear whether he ever actually worked in the Old Bailey, or whether he may have borrowed a few ornaments from the Eliot's Court Press, or only contracted with the partners to share in printing some of their publications. [*Dict. 1*; DFM 118; *Loan Book*, 1631–34 (renewed in 1632 for E. Purslowe); *Library* 2 (1922): 175–84; 3 (1923): 194–209.]
dw. at the East end of Christ Church (C.1), 1616 (12252) and until his death, though no later use has been noted.
1613: (all SR entries): 543, 11368.5(*A*), 12216, 17419, 23344, 23480, 23492.
1614: 26027 f.
1615: 16, 124, 4948, 5567, 5921.5, 5921.7(*A*3), [11926], 12297, 12336, [12775], [12775.5], 18275, [18445.7], 20586, 21017, 22638, 23096, 23128, 23534, 25743, 26036.
1616: 109, 111, 1909 ex off., 3656, 5778, [5779], 5836, 5921.5–22.2, 5932, 10426, 11837, 12252, 12327, 12333.5, 13006, 15717.5, 18266, 19624, 21519–9a, 23480, 26028.
1617: 3503, 4100, 5367, 5930, 12216, [12236], 13824, [15402.5], 15493, 17198, 17360a, 17419, 18152, [18257], 19947, [20329], [20989], [20989.3], 23585.
1618: 120, 1634, 4100.5, 4213, 5944, 6358, 7410, 12328, 12776, 13006.5, [15403(*A*3)], 19319, [20989.7], 23344, [23386], 23481, 25145, 25741.
1619: 121, 1363, 3211, 4209.5, 4213.5, 4219.5, 4232.5, 4233.5, 4235.5, [4276], 4278, 4308, 4638, 5931, 5945, 6358, 6588, 7252.5, [10347], 11524, [12390], 12485, 15656, 20566, [20990], 22850, 25156, 25386, 25618, [26077].
1620: 698.5 (c), [4793?] (c?), 4948.5, [5796–6.3], [5980], [10276], 12303, 12329, 12333, 12485, 13007, [16879], 17909–10, 18509, 19320, [20564.5?] (d?), [21404] (d?), 22463.5 (c), [22579.5] (c), [23765.5], [25292], 25615.
1621: [208], 353.5 (d), 591, 3696.7, [10348] (d?), [11279.5], 11379, [11766], [18890], [21666] (d), [23050.5], [23808a], [25044], 26029.
1622: [1002], [1004], 1187, [1678], 3697, 3699.4, 4085, [4849.1], [4919], 5134–5, [5604.5] (d), [5604.6] (d), [5604.7] (d), 11368.5, 12304, 15254.5, 17387.3, 17420, 21123, [21140], [21382], 21708, [24090], [25063] (d?), 25150a.5.
1623: 3698, 3930.5, 4949, 5132, 6590, 10379.5, [10755] (d?), 11126.5 (c), [11510–1], 12486, 13008, 15194, [15330], 18321, [19594], [20163], [25867.5].
1624: 1415.5, [4747], [4862], [6010], 7326–6.5, 7471, 12030, [14490], 17610, [17859], [19268] (d), 19600.2 (d), [23225], 23801, 24825, [24853.3].
1625: [150], [196.5] (c), 1392, [3698.3] (d?), [4497], [4687] (c), 5661, 5849.5, [6102.5] (c), 6023, [6038.5] (d?), [6060], [6520], [6520.4], [12384.5] (c?), [14050a] (c), 14306, 17363, 17602, [19252.5] (c), [19278] (c), 19566.5, 19598.2 (d?), 19600.4, [19600.6] (d?), 20565, [22919.2] (c), [23435a.5] (c).
1626: 12805.5, 12821, 12829, 12850, 17608, 17613, [18238], 19599.
1627: 1183, 3836, [5151], [5713], 7475 chez, [10172.5], [11978], [12852.5], [13537] (d?), 16864a.3 (c), 17614, [18507.186?], 19543, [25377], 25742.
1628: [4277], [6809.2] (d?), 7477 chez, [10756], [19224.3] (c), [19684], [20319.5] (c), [24853.7], [25146] (d?), [25745], [25751].
1629: [11363], [11363.5], 12843, [18068.5], [18238.5] (d?), [18507.203A], [19555], [20241.3], [20241.7], 22798.
1630: [3699.7?] (c), [4298] (d?), [4327], [5714], 6100 (c), [6427.7], [6478], 10206.5 (d?), [12547.3?] (c), [14040.2] (c), [14524.5] (c),

Purslowe, G. — *cont.*
16862.7 (c), [18507.205?], 19376.5, [20208], [20209], [20242], [20243], [21125], [23580], [23683.7] (c), 23686, [25369], [26103.5] (c).
1631: [11120?], 12298, [12532], 13009, 15332, 16928, [18239], [18507.209?], [—.210?], [—.211?], [—.212?], [20209], [20210], [20244], 22871a.5, [24398].
1632: [5428.5?] (d?), 7453, 10741, 12213, 18609, 19260, 19311, [20211], [20939] (d), 21423, 22437, [25746].

1633: 19311.5 (d/var).

Pynson (Pinson), Richard.
Printer, bookseller, and bookbinder in London, 1490?–1529?†. Although he styled himself **King's Printer** at least twice under Henry VII, in 1506, 6 Jan. (16117.5) and in 1508, 3 id. Sept. (9266) and received royal patronage as early as 1504, 23 Dec. (16179), his earliest surviving official printing is the statute of Henry VIII's first parliament, 1510 (9357.8). He was also **Printer to the City of London**, 1517–1528 at least (*TBS* 6 (1900–02): 17). He was dead or incapacitated by 17 Dec. 1529 since **John Rastell** printed the statute of that session (7773, 9363.6). His daughter's third husband, **John Hawkins**, finished one book (19166) following Pynson's death, and then his rival, **Robert Redman**, took over the printing house and material. Regarding the Pynson-Redman rivalry in so far as it concerns the Yearbooks *see* the headnote preceding 9551. [Duff, *Century*; Stanley H. Johnston, Jr., *A study of the career ... of Richard Pynson*, Ph.D. thesis, University of Western Ontario, 1977, copies available at L, O, F, HD(STC office).]
in the parish of St. Clement Danes without New (Middle) Temple Bar (X.1), 1492 (316)–1500; variations:
dw. without Middle Temple Bar, 1495 (23885)
without Temple Bar, 1500 (3297, pt. 1)
dw. within New Temple Bar (W.9), 1501 (17727)
dw. in the parish of St. Dunstan's at the George (W.9), 1502, 10 July (17969)–1529; variations:
dw. in Fleet Street at the George, 1503, 9 Mar. (11604), 1523 (23196a.4)
in Fleet Street, 1523, 28 Jan. (11396), 1527, 21 Feb. (3176), 1529? (22899)
1490: 9770 per (d?), 9771 per (d?), 9825 per (d?), 15721 ad instantiam (d), 23238 per [f.] (d).
1491: [14077c.51] (d).
1492: 316 per, [5084] (d?), 7014 (d), 9332 (d?), [12477] (d).
1493: 15851 per (d?), [15873.5] (d?), 17010 (d), [17325] (d), 17960 (d), 17961 (d), 19212, [21297] (d).
1494: 3175, 3262 (d), [13808] (d?), 15395, 18385 (d), [20921] (d), 23425 per, 23877.7 (d?), 23885 (note).
1495: 790 (d?), [15850] (d?), [15882] (d), 19812 (d?), 23885.
1496: [9355] (d?), [9784] (d?), [9790] (d?), [9796] (d?), [9806] (d?), [9812] (d?), [9819] (d?), 11601, 11609 per, [14477] (d), [15722] (d), 15855 per (d), [16111] (d), [16253.5] (c), 17246 (d), 23163.14 (d), 23878 per (d), 24867(*A3*) per (d?), [25001] (d?).
1497: 176 (d?), 280 (d?), [14099] (d), 15574.5 per, 15852 per (d), 15886 per (d), 16112 per, 17724 ad imprimendum dedit, [23163.8] (d?), [23242.5] (d?), 23885 (note), [23939.5] (d?).
1498: [277] (d), 317, [385.7] (d?), [7566] (d?), [12470] (d), [14077c.134] (d), [—.135] (d), [—.136] (d), [—.137] (d), [15572] (d?), [15891] (d), [16113], 17725 ad imprimendum dedit, 23426 per.
1499: [494.8], 9514 per, 9515 (d/repeat), [14077c.138] (d), [—.139] (d), [—.140] (d), [—.140A] (d), [—.141] (d), [—.142] (d), [—.142C(*A3*)] (d), [—.143] (d), 14078 (d?), [15576.6] (d?), 17105 (d), 17106 per (d), 17966.5, 20434 per.
1500: 177 (d?), [177.3] (d?), [317.5] (d?), 3297, [4814] (d), [7017] (d), 9265 (d?), [9650] (d?), [9691] (d?), [9836] (d?), 11611 per, 12471 per, [12540] (d?), [13688] (d?), [14077c.100] (d), 15396 (d), [15893] (d), [15894] (d), 16173 per, 18386 (d).
1501: [494.9] (d), [7705.7] (d?), 12351.5 (d?), [15575.5] (d?), 16232.6 per, 17727 ad imprimendum dedit.
1502: 168 per, [494.10], [772] (c), [9603] (d?), [9784.4] (d?), [9790.4] (d?), [9796.5] (d?), [9806.4] (d?), [9812.5] (d?), [9819.5] (d?), 11612 per, [14077c.144] (d), [—.145] (d), [15573] (d?), [15722.5] (d?), [16116a.5], 16232.8 per, 17969 per.
1503: 1988 (d?), 9515 per (d?), [9691.5] (d?), 11604, 14079 (d), [14556.5(*A3*)] (c), 17033.3 (d), 17728 per, [20921.5] (c?), [23243] (d?), [23940] (d?), 23954.7–55, [24301.5] (d?).

Pynson, R. — *cont.*
1504: [11721] (d?), [14077c.27] (d?), 16179 per, [18362] (d?), 23954.7 (d), 23955 (d?).
1505: 319.3, 696.3 per, [1186.3] (c), [1967.3?] (d?), 3296 (c), [3945.5] (d?), [4813.6] (d?), [7705.8] (d?), [9337] (d?), [9837] (d?), 12380 (d?), [13432] (d?), [14077c.28] (d?), [—.62] (d), [—.88(*A3*)] (c), [—.89(*A3*)] (c), [—.153] (c), 14862 (d?), 15579.3 per (d?), 17007.5 (c), 17109.3 per (c), 17181.5, 23139.5 per (d?), 23155.4 (c), 23155.6 (c), [23163.17] (d?), 23427a per, [24133] (d?).
1506: 3263 (d), 4602 (d/error), 6894.5 (d?), [14077c.29] (d), 16117.5 per, 16140, 18387 (d?), 22408.
1506/07: [504].
1507: 9889 (d?), 15806a arte, 21430a [f.] (d), 24878.5 [f.].
1508: 9266 cura, 9357.7 (d?), [9928.5] (d?), 11606, 12474 per, [14077c.103B] (d). [—.104–.105C] (d), [15807] (d), 16899 per (d?), 17728.5, 19917.5, [23940.7] (d?), [25071.5] (d).
1509: 3359 per (d?), 3545, 11615 per, [12413] (d), 13830–0.3 per, 16121a per, 17558 (d), [21800] (d), 23155.8 (d?).
1510: [7680.5] (d?), [9357.8] (d?), 9631 ere & imp., [9732] (d?), [9744] (d?), [9771.5] (d?), 9779 ere & imp. (d?), 9999, 10905, 13605 (d?), [14077c.18] (c), [—.23] (c), [—.38?] (d), [—.49] (c), [—.116] (c), [—.117] (c), 14116 in off., [14505.5] (c), [15723] (d?), [15910.5] (d?), [16102] (d?), 17853 (d?), [17970.5(*A3*)] (c), [20107.5?] (c), [21071.5?] (d?), 22409.3 (c), [22653.7] (c), 23143 (d?), [23143.5] (c), 23156 (d?).
1511: 7762.5(*A*) (d?), 9586 per (d?), 9588 per (d?), 9611 per (d?), [9613] (d?), 9710 (d?), 9716 (d?), 12549, 14077c.30 per (d), [—.36?] (c), [—.37?] (c), [—.55G(*A3*)] (d), [—.129] (d), [—.130] (d), 16123 per, 17017.
1512: 735.7 industria, [5545] (d?), 11562.5 (d?), [14077c.24] (d), [—.60(*A3*)] (d), [—.117A] (c), [—.117B] (c), [—.118] (c), [—.119] (c), [—.120] (c), [—.121] (c), [—.121A] (c), 16190 per, 25479.2 (d?), 25585 opera & imp., [25947.7] (d).
1513: 319.5, 5579, [7763] (d), 9333, 9358 (d?), [9358.3] (d?), [9361] (d), [9361.4] (d), 14517 (d?), 14789 per, 15601.3 per, [15915] (d?), 20060 in aed., 23179, 25443.8 per (d?).
1514: 9267 per, [9362.3A] (d), 11607, 15917 per, 23179.5.
1515: 3270 (c), [7766] (d), [7767] (d), 9351a.4 (d?), [9362.3] (d), 9362.4 (d), 10604 (c), [12973.5] (c), [14077c.35] (c), [—.52?] (d), [—.56] (d?), [—.57] (d?), [—.60A] (c), [—.61] (c?), [—.82] (c), [—.124] (c), [—.127] (d), 16127 per, [17568.5(*A3*)] (c?), 18571.5 per (c), [22992.1] (d?), 23166.5 per (d?), [23879] (c), 24787 [by &] ven. (c), 25479.3 (d?), 25496.5 per (d?), 25509.7 per, [25525.5].
1516: 320, 4602, [7767.5] (d?), 9362.6 (d?), 9913 (d?), 10659, 12512.5 exp., [14077c.25], [—.60*(*A3*)] (d), [—.102] (d?), 15724 per, 18874.5 per, 20894.4, 23428a.5 per.
1517: 1859 (d), 7768 (d), 9358.5 (d?), 9590 per (d?), 9591 per (d?), 9592 per (d?), 9593 per (d?), 9594 per, 9597 per (d?), 9624 per (d?), [14077c.1?] (d), [—.5] (c), [—.58] (d?), [—.101] (d), [—.126] (d), [—.131] (d?), [—.132] (d?), [22409.7] (d?), 23957–8.
1518: [1833.5] (d?), 9553 in aed., 9596 per, 9651 per (d?), 9983.3 (d?), 14077c.31 per (d), [—.91] (d), [—.103?] (c), —.103A (c), [—.133] (d), 17242 (d?), 18388 per (d?), 19081a per, 24320 per, 25527.8 per (d?), 25545.5 per.
1519: 9268 cura, 9598 per, 13811 per, [18362.5] (d?), [20824.5(*A3*)] (d), 23181, 25461.5 per.
1519/20: [406.7], 470.5, 470.6.
1520: 699 per (d?), [1375.5?] (c), 5639 ex off., 7707 per (d?), [7769.2] (d), 9362.5 (c), 9362.7 (c), 9576 ex off. Pynsoniana, 9595 in aed., 10630 (d?), 13256 (d?), [14077c.26] (c), [—.67A] (d), [—.68A] (c), [—.72] (c), [—.73] (c), [—.84] (d?), —.96 per (d), —.97 per (d), —.98 per (c), [—.99] (d), [—.149] (c), [—.150] (c), [—.154?] (c), 14323.5 (c), 14807, 16202 per, 16224.5 (c), 17035 (d?), [17241] (d?), 17242.5 (d?), 18088 in aed. Pynsonis, [19816(*A3*)] (c?), [21310.5] (c), 23147.8 (d?), [23196a.2] (c), [23879.5] (c), 23954 (c), 25446.5 per (c), 25479.15 ex off., 25529 per, 25570 ex chalcog.
1521: 1384b (d?), 3506, 5311 opera & sumpt., 6279 per, 9358.7 (d?), 9516 per, 9518.7 per, 9883 per (d?), 13078 in aed. Pynsonianis, 13083 in aed. Pynsonianis, 13807 in aed. Pynsonianis, 14077c.32 per (d), [—.65] (d), [—.66] (d), [—.67] (d), 14867, 15580 per (d?), 15606 in aed. Pynsonianis, [25547.3] (d).
1522: [7769.4] (c), [9361.3] (d?), 11531.5 in aed. Pynsonianis (d?), 11532 in aed. Pynsonianis, 11534 in aed. Pynsonianis (d?), 13079 in aed. Pynsonianis, 14077c.33 per (d), [15118] (d?), 15606.7 (d), 15725.5 per, 15933 per, 20398.3 per (d?), 21626(*A3*) (d?), 24319 in aed., 25502 in aed., 25517 in aed., 25561 in aed. Pynsonianis.

Pynson, R. — *cont.*
1523: 7726 per (d?), 9362.9 (d?), [9806.7] (d?), [9820] (d?), 10994 (d?), 11005, 11396, 11533 in aed., 14077c.39 per (d), —.40 per (d), [18088.5–89], 20140 in aed. Pynsonianis, 20896 (d?), 23148.4 (d?), 23159a.5 (d?), 23196a.4, 24728 in aed. Pynsonianis, 24729 in aed. Pynsonianis (d), 25450 in aed., 25465 per, 25485 in aed., 25517 in aed., 25532 in aed., 25549 in aed., [25561.5] (d?).
1524: 9784.7 (d?), 9790.7 (d?), [9797] (d?), 9813 (d?), 11535 in aed. Pynsonianis, [14077c.2] (d), 15634 ap., 16262 per, [19166] (c), 23168.3 (d?), 23181.9 in aed. Pynsonianis, [25562.7] (d?).
1525: [177.7?] (d?), 538.5 (c), 812 in aed. (d?), 1967 (d?), 3507 (c), 9362.10 (d?), 9658 per (d?), 9669 per (d?), 9692 per (d?), 9826 (d?), 11397, 11397a (forged), 15636 in aed. Pynsonianis (d?), 15637 in aed. Pynsonianis (c), 15726 in aed., 18389 in aed., 21627 (d?), 23880 in aed., 25451 in aed., 25468.5 per, 25486.7 in aed., 25552.5 in aed., [25947.3] (d?).
1526: 3277, 4186 (d?), 5086, 5088 (d?), 5096 (d?), 7769.6 per (d), 9738 per (d?), 9750 per (d?), 9756 per (d?), 9764 per (d?), 9833 per (d?), 9839 (d?), 10946 in aed., 11006, 13084 in aed. Pynsonianis, 13084.5 in aed. Pynsonianis, [14077c.101A] (d), [—.101B] (d?), [19082] (d?), 23182.3 in aed. Pynsonianis, 25577.5 ex chalcog.
1527: 3176, [5542.1] (d?), 7769.8 per (d), 9269.5 in aed., 9561 per (d?), 9617 per (d?), 9637.5 per (d?), 9681 per (d?), 9698 per (d?), 9851 per (d?), 9856 per (d?), 9876 per (d?), 10604.5 (d?), 13085 in aed. Pynsonianis, 13086 (d?), [14077c.121C] (d), [—.146] (c), 16790 per (d?), [16791] (d?), [16793?] (d?), 16793.5 per (d?), [16797?] (d?), 25471 per, 25489.3 in aed., 25505.5 in aed.
1528: [3361] (d?), 5631 (d?), 7770 per (d), 7771 per (d), 9518.7 per, 9611a per (d?), 9631a (d?), 9704 per (d?), 9840.3 per (d?), 9845 (d?), 9856 per (d?), 9865 per (d?), 9871 per (d?), 9889.5 per (d?), 9896 per (d?), 9930 (d?), 9931 per (d?), 9945 per (d?), [12382] (d?), 13086.5 (d?), 13087 (d?), 14077c.54 (d), —.55 (d), [—.76] (d), 15728 in aed., 18390 in aed., 20058.5 (d), 22609 (d).
1529: [7772] (d), [14077c.122] (d), 22899 (d?), [24323.5] (d).

Pyper. *See* Piper.

Q

Quentel, Heinrich.
Printer in Cologne, 1478–1501†. [Duff, *Century*; Benzing 233.]
1492: [696.2]. **1496:** [16110] (d).

Quentel, Peter.
Printer in Cologne, 1520–1546†. [Duff, *Century*; Benzing 237–8.]
1525: [15578.5] (d).

Quercubus, N. de. *See* Okes.

Quinqué, Adrien.
Printer in Tournai, 1623–1645 at least. [*Dict. 1.*]
1623: 19480, 19481.

R

R., *Mr.*
Author? publisher? or patron? of a ballad in London, c. 1625.
No address used.
1625: 6102.5 f. (c).

R., I., *pseud.*
Printer in 'Douai', 1580? = 'Greenstreet House' Press, London.
1580: 17278.4 (d?).

Raban, Edward.
Printer in Edinburgh 1620, in St. Andrews 1620–1622, and in Aberdeen 1622–1650 (1658†). In the last two cities he was printer to the universities and in Aberdeen also printer to the city. [*Dict. 1*; *Dict. 2*.]
Edinburgh, dw. at the Cowgate Port at the $ A.B.C., 1620 (22565)
St. Andrews, his printing house in the South Street of the city at the $ A.B.C., 1620 (17856)
St. Andrews, dw. in the Kirk Wynd at the $ A.B.C., 1622 (15370)
Aberdeen, dw. upon the Marketplace at the town's arms, 1624 (16694)–1636 (22055, has 'at the arms of the city') at least

Raban, E. — *cont.*
1620: *Edinburgh*: [17810], 22565; *St. Andrews*: 17856, 24069.
1621: 1496, 21555.33, 22566, 22567.5, 22570, [24368.5] (d?).
1622: *St. Andrews*: 3905, 15370, 15683.5, 20113, [20597] (d); *Aberdeen*: 21.9 (d), 71.6, 7349.5, 10442, 12482, 24067.
1622/23: 404.5.
1623: 71.7, 71.30, 71.33, 5960, 6779.5, 6783.5, 13025, 18790, 22007, 24846.
1623/24: 445.19.
1624: 71.8, 6781.7, 12492, 16694, 22185.5.
1624/25: 405.3.
1625: 71.9, 71.34, 11595, 12070, 16594.5, 25187.
1625/26: 405.5.
1626: 71.10, 71.35, 2711, 2712, 2713, 2713.5, [3368.5-Anderson, G.] (d?), 12489.
1627: 71.11, 71.12, 71.13, 71.14, 71.15, 71.36, 11147, 12479, 12971, 24430.
1628: 4390, 14709, 15668.
1629: 71.16, 2714, 11139–40, 16595, 16596, 20658, 24795.
1630: 71.37, 1995, 5302, 12484, 13154, 16596, 18953, 24431a.
1631: 71.17, 71.38, 1493, 2941, [3368.5-Hervie] (d), 5957, 11138, 16930, 23193, 23347, 24881.5.
1631/32: 405.7.
1632: 2719, 11144, 14710, 14714, 25192.
1633: 71.18, 1495, 2721.5, 12480, 16597, 20659, 21099, 25190 (d/error?), 25194.
1634: 71.19, 71.19A, 71.39, 17857, 25189.
1635: 71.20, 71.31, [3368.5-Aberdeen] (d), 6824, 11151, 12065, 25190 (d?).
1636: 71.21, 11141, 22055, 23935.
1637: 71.22 (d), 71.23, [71.24] (d), 71.40, 2366, 6124, 11776, 12491, 13027, 25193.
1638: 64, 68, 69 (forged), 71, 71.25 (d), 71.41 (d), 11142, 11781, 20596 printed by the author, [21997] (d), 21999.5.
1638/39: 446.3.
1639: 12478, 12493, 22059, 24854.7(*A*3).

Rade, Gilles van den.
Printer and bookseller in Ghent 1569–1571, in Antwerp 1571–1586, and in Franeker, 1586–1615†. [Rouzet; Briels 393–9.]
1576: 1431.4. **1579:** 1431.5. **1583:** 1431.6.

Radeus, Jacobus, *pseud.*
Printer in 'Hanau', 1602. = Joseph Barnes, Oxford.
1602: 20146.5.

Rammazeyn, Pieter.
Printer in Gouda, 1626–1651†. [Gruys; Briels 402–5.]
1626: 25234–4.5 (note).

Rand, Samuel.
Bookseller in London, 1609–1651. [*Dict. 2*; DFM 305; *Poor Book*, 1646–51.]
dw. at (near, on) Holborn Bridge (V.2), 1609 (24313.5)–1650 (Wing W 1037); many imprints have 'shop', e.g. 1610 (6809.5)
1609: 24313.5 sold.
1610: 6809.5 f.
1611: 24209 f.
1612: 13938 f., 21027 sold.
1613: 13310 f., 23722–2.5 f.
1614: 3578 f., 13939 f., 21372.5 f.
1615: 22638 f., 23096 f.
1616: 5836 f., 21373 f.
1618: 3637 f., 21374 f.
1619: 21375 f.
1622: 4085 f.
1623: 21376 f., 23108.2 f.
1624: 3662 f., 22614 f.
1625: 23108.3 f.
1627: 21377 f.
1628: 23108.4 f.
1629: 23108.5 f.
1632: 3638 f., 3663 f.
1633: 23108.6 f.
1634: 674 f.
1636: 23108.7 f.
1638: 3638.5 f.
1639: 20318 f. (d).

Raphelengius, Franciscus.
Editor, bookseller, and printer in Antwerp, 1575–1585, and in Leiden, 1585–1597†. Son-in-law of **Christopher Plantin** and managed his Antwerp printing house from 1583 before taking charge of the **Officina Plantiniana** in Leiden. [*Dict. 1*; Rouzet; Briels 406–13.]
1586: 25438. **1592:** 15703 ap. **1593:** 17523. **1597:** 24893.3 ap.

Rastell, John.
Barrister and printer in London, 1509?–1533 (1536†). Father of **William Rastell.** He seems to have had printing relationships with **Richard Bankes** and **Peter Treveris**, but their nature has been largely unexplored, and how much he was involved in later items using his types and even his devices is unclear. Following his death the house in Cheapside passed to **Lewis Sutton.** [Duff, *Century*; *Library* 24 (1944): 66–73, Nash fragments now = L; 1 (1979): 34–42.]
Items whose numbers are indexed in round brackets below have one of Rastell's devices: McK. 37 with his name or McK. 40 but no name in the imprint, if there is any.
dw. at the Fleet Bridge at the Abbot of Winchcomb's place (W.3), 1510? (19897.7)
on the South side of Paul's (A.9), 1512 (15635)–1515; variations:
dw. on the South side of Paul's Church beside Paul's Chain, 1512? (17778)
before the South door of Paul's, 1515? (7018.7, 12798.5)
in Cheapside next to Paul's gate (N.2), c. 1520 (23954.3)–1529 (18084, adds 'at the Mermaid) and still one of his properties at his death; the earliest use of the sign noted in imprints is 1525 (22869.7); he started paying rent on the property in 1519 (*Memorials* 52)
1509: [9895] (d?), [23153.8(*A*3)] (d?).
1510: 19897.7 (d?)
1512: 15635 (d), 17778 (d?), 18361 (note).
1514: (9599) (d?).
1515: 7018.7 per (c), 12798.5 per (d?).
1516: [10954].
1517: 10955 imp. & industria, 12798.7 per (d?).
1518: [14077c.55A] (d?).
1519: 9515.5, [14077c.50] (d).
1520: [14077c.45] (d?), [20722] (d?), (23954.3) (c).
1523: (20701) (c), (23879.7) (c).
1524: (15759.5) (d?).
1525: [5091.5] (d?), (20700.3) (c), (20702) (c), 20721 me imprimi fecit (c), 20723 me fieri fecit (c), [22153], (22869.7), (23880.3) (c).
1526: [7695.5] (d?), [7712] (d?), (7727) (d?), [14871] (d?), [15581.2] (d?), [20897] (d?), [22153a] (d?), (23664), [24199] (d?).
1527: 9518 per, [20703], [22611] (d?), [23148.8] (d?).
1528: [7542.5?] (d?), 9520 imprimi me fecit, 21559 per, [22604] (d?).
1529: [7773 f.] (d), (15760) (d?), (18084).
1530: [3356.3] (c), [9363.6] (d?), [9363.8] (d?), [9533.2] (d?), 16895 [f.] (d?), [17324.5?] (c), (20703.3) (c), 20719, 20719.5–20, [20724] (d?), [22607 f.] (d?), (23663(**A**3) (c).
1532: [6800.3] (c).
1532/33: 517.12 [f.].
1535: [5892 in shop of] (d?).

1540/41: [392.11(*A*) successor of].

Rastell, William.
Printer in London, 1529–1534, and later barrister, editor, and judge (1565†). Son of **John Rastell**. [Duff, *Century*.]
in Fleet Street against the conduit (W.5), 1531, 28 July (1461; 20836, colophon to pt. 2 has his 'house', omits 'against the conduit')
in Fleet Street in St. Bride's Churchyard (W.4), 1533 (18081)–1534 (9536.5)
1529: [18092] (d), [18093] (d).
1530: [3288.5] (d?), [4337] (d), [5275] (d?), [18085], [17779] (d?), [20765.5] (d?).
1531: 1461, [9521] (d?), [9533.8] (d?), 20836–6.5 ap./by & sold.
1532: 10909, 15976, 18079.
1533: 9536, 10660, 11966, 13298, 13299, 13305, 18078, 18080, 18081, 18090, 18414, 18793.5.
1534: [7781?] (d), 9536.5, 11594, 13303, 18077, 18394, 18394.5.

Raven, Richard.
Journeyman printer in London, (1619) 1624 (*C-B C*: 163), apparently in Amsterdam, 1631, and again in London, 1633†. [DFM 186; *St. Giles*, 1633.]
No address used.
1631: 23050.

Ravynell, James.
Printer? in Rouen, 1495, and/or bookseller in London in the 1490s. A London stationer of this name brought an action sometime between 1493 and 1500 in a matter in which Joyce Pelgrim and Frederick Egmont were also concerned (Christianson 151). It seems likely that the following item was printed by an unidentified Rouen printer for Ravynell in London. It is just possible that the initials in the device at the end of both parts should be read as 'I R' rather than 'P R', with the 'I' having a loose, curling extension around which the cord is looped. [Duff, *Century*; BMC VIII. lxxxiii, 400.]
1495: 17963–3.5.

Raworth, John.
Printer in London, (1632) 1638–1645†. Son of **Robert Raworth**. At the time of his death he was living in the parish of St. Benet, Paul's Wharf. His widow remarried Thomas Newcomb. [*Dict. 2*; DFM 459; *Loan Book*, 1637–43.]
No address noted.
1538: 3617 ap. (d/error).
1638: 765.7, 2676, 3406, 3617 ap. (d), 3772.2–.4, 10302 (d?), 13363, 13523, 17633–3a, 17635, 21844.
1639: 3127.5, 10227.7, 13335, 15496–7, 17554, 20488, 20489, 22058, 26122, 26122.5.
1639/40: 495.15.
1640: 11032, 11512, 12503.5, [12735], 13353, 13354 (forged), 14073, 15464.5(*A*3), 20811, 21763, 22438, 22455, 23307–7.5, 23313, 25177–7a.
1640/41: Wing A 2099, A 2707.

Raworth, Robert.
Printer in London, 1606–1608 and 1633–1636 (1653). Father of **John Raworth.** Both periods of his overt activity were terminated by the seizure of his press (Arber III.703–4; *C-B C*: 264, 272). In 1621 he was employed at Stepney (U.6) by **George Wood** in pirating almanacs and primers (*C-B C*: 375–7). [*Dict. 2*; DFM 11; *Poor Book*, 1636–53; *Library* 3 (1922): 227–47; Blayney, *Origins*, pp. 24–5, 308–9, etc.]
dw. in Old Fish Street near St. Mary Magdalen's Church (S.1), 1633 (13315)
his house near the White Hart Tavern in Smithfield (E.1), 1635 (13356)–1636 (19501.5(*A*3), omits 'his house')
1606: 11215.
1607: 1692–3, 3471, 3671–1.5, [5491–2.2], [5492.4], [14526.5 (*A*3)], [14696(*A*3)], [22360] (forged, d?).
1608: 1968.7, [11403], 12494, [22767], 24414.
1633: 1504–4.5, 13315.
1634: 4177, 10135, 19203.3, [22530].
1635: 3668, 5157.5(*A*3), 12421, 13348a, 13356, 20501.
1636: 156a.5, 6533, 13311, 13352, 19501, 19501.5(*A*3) by & sold, 20646, 24954.

Raynald, Thomas.
Physician and printer in London, 1539?–1552. In early 1540 Raynald was living near Hallywell (I.10), i.e. near the old Manor of Finsbury (*TBS* 6 (1900–02): 20–22). Some of his printing material belonged earlier to **Peter Treveris.** It is likely that the printer of reformation tracts and literature beginning in 1548, sometimes in association with **Anthony Kingston** or **William Hill**, was a different man: the Thomas 'Reynolds' freed as a Draper by **Thomas Petyt** in 1547, since Petyt printing material is present in these items. A more extensive analysis of the items below would undoubtedly clarify the situation. [Duff, *Century*.]
in St. Andrew's parish in the Wardrobe (Waredropt (R.6)), 1548 (11802)–1549 (20750); variation: has 'beside Baynard's Castle' for 'in the Wardrobe', 1548? (18842, with W. Hill)
in Paul's Churchyard at the Star (B), 1549 (2726, with J. Harrington)–1551 (20827, omits sign)
1539: [5543b.8?] (d?).
1540: [564.2?] (c?), 21153.
1545: 21154.

Raynald, T. — *cont.*
1548: [846] (d?), 1271, 1724.7(*A*) (d?), [3363?] (d), [5189.7] (d?), 10494.5 (d?), 11802, 17317 (d), 17318 (d?), 17319 (d?), 18842 (d?), 20662, 20748.5, 20749, 22823, 24450 (d?).
1548/49: 398.5.
1549: [1741], 2078, [2379] (d), 2726, [16458.5] (d?), 20750, 24266 (d?).
1550: 1374 (c), 2975.7, 5611.4 (c), 12631, 12631.3 (d?), [12631.5] (c?), 13755, 13762, 14825, 26142–3.
1551: 2759, 5870.5, 20827.
1552: [5241] (c), 21155, [23925] (d?).

Raynes. *See* Reynes.

Read, Richard.
Printer in London, (1580) 1601–1603†. He married **Frances Simson**, the widow of **Gabriel Simson**, and succeeded to their printing material. She afterwards remarried **George Eld**, who took over the establishment. [*Dict. 1.*]
dw. in Fleet Lane (D.2), 1601 (4662)–1602 (3415)
1601: [1074], [1454], 4662, [5775], [5867.3?] (d?), [10846], [14773], [17680?], 21523 ent., [21802], [26076].
1602: [1074.5], 3415, [4173?], [12164], [13934], [14803?], [18471], [18892], [21532].
1603: [1117], [4616], [6260], [7120], [7448], [7459], [7594?], [10798?], 10800, [11086], 12061, [12551], [12984], [12988(*A*3)], [14377(*A*3)], [14421(*A*3)], [17510], 18292, 18292.3, 24041, [24343], [25643].

Reave. *See* Reeve.

Reboul (Rebul), Antoine.
Printer in Geneva, 1558–1561. [*Dict. 1*, under J. Poullain; Chaix 216.]
1558: [15063?], 15067, [15070], 16561a.

Redborne, Robert.
Bookseller in London, before 1556–1566 at least, and in Oxfordshire, 1571. [Duff, *Century*; *Dict. 1.*]
in Paul's Churchyard at the Cock (B), 1560? (807)
1560: 807 [f.] (d?).

Reddell. *See* Riddell.

Redman (Pickering), Elizabeth.
Printer in London, 1540–1541. Widow of **Robert Redman** and occasionally mentioned her maiden name in imprints. In 1541 she remarried out of the Stat. Co., and the printing house passed to **William Middleton**. [Duff, *Century*: 121.]
in Fleet Street dw. at the George next to St. Dunstan's Church (W.9), 1540? (9535)–1541 (9543)
1540: 9535 (d?), 10970, 23210 ex aed.
1541: 7716 (d?), 9275 (d?), [9542.3?] (d?), 9543 (d), 10970, 10985 (d?), 13175.7 (d?), 18219 (d?), [15584.7(*A*3)?], 20901 (note), 22155 (d?).

Redman, John.
Printer in London, (1530), in Southwark, 1534?–1536? and again in London, 1536–1541, during the last period paying rents in Paternoster Row (*Memorials* 52). The earliest book from which a date can be inferred is 5313, in which the translator, Robert Whittinton, refers on $\mathrm{A3}^{v}$ to another translation (5278, printed by de Worde and dated 30 Sept. 1534) as soon to be published. The other Southwark items are indexed as 1534–36? below. [Duff, *Century*.]
London, in Paternoster Row (C.7), 1539/40 (392.7)–1540 (22880.6, 473, both adding: at the $ Our Lady of Pity)
1534: 5313 (d?).
1534–36? 2792(*A*3), 14548(*A*3), 17030.9(*A*3).
1539/40: 392.7(*A*3).
1540: 1473.5 (d?), 2972–2.2 (d?), 4241.5 (c), 5543b.9 per (c), 22880.6 (d).
1540/41: [392.9?], [392.10(*A*)?], 473.

Redman, Robert.
Printer in London, 1524 (*Library* 9 (1908): 261)–1540†. Husband of **Elizabeth Redman**. Herbert's view that Redman had three successive establishments with the sign of the George seems to be correct. Before the end of 1530 (7713.9, 15582) Redman had access to at least one former device of **Richard Pynson** (McK. 3), and there are two undated Yearbooks, 1531? (9733, 9929) with alternate sections in Redman's early types and in those formerly belonging to Pynson. Redman probably did not begin his final move until after 18 July 1530, the date on which the Palsgrave (19166) was published by **John Hawkins**, and he had not entirely vacated his previous premises by 28 Sept. 1531 (cf. 20836). Regarding the Pynson-Redman rivalry in so far as it concerns the Yearbooks *see* the headnote preceding 9551. [Duff, *Century*; Herbert I.385.]
in St. Clement's parish at the George (X.1), 1525, 9 id. May (9269)–1527, 15 Mar. (15581.5); variation: adds 'without Temple Bar', 1525? (9827)
in St. Dunstan's parish, 1527, 18 Apr. (*Hundred Court*, Herbert I.387)–1540 (9946, adds 'at the George'); variations: dw. in Fleet Street at the George, 1527, 14 Oct. (9632), 1531 (25421.5, omits 'dw.'); in Fleet Street [no sign], 1530 (7713.9), 1534 (17113), 1538 (15584); there are, however, two different localizations which are occasionally cited:
within Temple Bar (W.14), 1527 (9866); near Temple Bar, 1530? (14870); [sold at his] house at Temple Bar, 1531 (20836; a variant without Redman's name is dated 28 Sept.)
next to the (St. Dunstan's) Church (W.9), 1531, 1 June (21567, pt. 2 colophon), 1531, 1 Nov. (17025), 1534 (9272), 1538, 29 Dec. (10969), 1540 (2753)
1517: 9517.5 (d/error).
1523: 10949 (d/error).
1525: 9269 cura, [9772] (d?), [9780] (d?), 9827 (d?).
1526: 9618 (d?), 9625 per (d?), 9637 (d?), 9682 (d?), 9699 (d?), 9705 (d?), 9838.7 (d?), 9852 (d?), 9877 (d?), 9930.7 (d?).
1527: 9517.5 per (d), 9632 ere & imp., 9686 (d?), 9840 (d?), 9846 (d?), 9856a (d?), 9866 (d?), 9872, 9944.5 per (d?), 14869(*A*3), 15581.5(*A*3) per.
1528: 814 ap., 9519, 9569 (d?), 9935 per (d?), 10947 in aed., 12800 [f.], 15727 in aed., [18390.5(*A*3)] (d?), 19629 in aed., 23880.5 in aed.
1529: 9273, 9675 per (d?), 18391(*A*3) in aed.
1530: [7681.8] (d?), [7695.7] (d?), 7713.9 per, [7728] (d?), 9884 per (d?), 14870 (d?), 15730 (c), 15582 per, 17007a [f.] (c?), 17326 (d?), 18402.5 (d?), 25421.8 (d?).
1531: 4185 (d), [9533.4] (d?), 9733 per (d?), 9760 (d?), [9833.3] (d?), 9861 per (d?), 9906 per (d?), 9929 per (d?), 9934 (d?), 16892, 17025, 20836 sold, 21567, 22559.5, [23964] (d?), [23964.3] (d?), 25412 (d?), 25421.5, 25422.5.
1532: 5947, 7483, [9364] (d?), 9534.5 (d?), 9717 (d?), 9838 (d?), 10949 per (d?), [14077c.57A] (c), 15865 ven., 16790(*A*: note), 16791.5, [16792?] (d?), 18403, 19630 in aed., 20898, 21568, 21586 (d?), 23882, 25421.
1533: 3803 (d?), 6894 (d?), 7696 (d?), 7712.4 per, 9286 (d?), 9521a.5 (d?), 9533.9 (d?), 9664 (d?), 9711 (d?), 9935.3 (d?), 10950 per, 14872 (d?), 15583 per, 20899 (d?), 25423.5(*A*3).
1534: 5313 f. (d?), 9272, 9536.7 (d?), 9579 (d?), 9587 par, 9721 (d?), 9726 (d?), 10504 (d), 10504a (d), 12731.8 (d?), 14553, 14561 (d), 17113, 18395.5 (d?), [25413.7(*A*3)] (d?).
1534–36? 2792(*A*3) f., 14548(*A*3) f.
1535: [3036a] (d?), 5317.5 per (d?), 5947.5 (c?), 9538.7 (d?), 9570 (d?), 9573 (d?), [11396.5] (c), 15225 (d?), 15986.3 (d), 17027.5 (c), 18404, 20193.5 (d?), 20200.3 (d?), [23964.7] (d?), 25413(*A*3) (d?).
1536: 908, 3037 (d?), 9534 (d?), 9745 (d?), 10492 (d?), 10509 (d?), [15179] (d), [24441] (d?), [24441.3] (d?).
1537: 2964.5 (d?), [9533.6] (d?), 9534.7 (d?), 9539 (d?), 10473.5 (d?), 14561a (d), [15997] (d?), 20900, 21789.7 (d?), 24250 (d?), [24441.7] (d?), 25425.
1538: 2815, 2966.5 (d), 7697 (d?), 7714 per (d?), 7729 per, 9522 (d?), 9537 (d?), 9539.7 (c?), 9540 (c?), 9589 (d?), [9797.5] (d?), [9807] (d?), 9935.5 (d?), 10968, 10969, 10984 (d?), 14875 in aed. (d?), 15584 per, 15584.3 per, 15761.2 (d?), [16008], [16794?] (d), [16821.3?] (c), [17500?] (d?), 20900 (d?), 25415 (d?).
1539: 818 in aed., 909 (d?), 7730 per, 9273, 9542 (d?), 11007 in aed. (d?), 13175.5 (d?), 15731.5, 15761.4 (d?), 16821.7, 21792, 24200.
1540: 2069, 2753, 7697.7 (d?), [9365] (d?), [9780.5] (d?), 9814 (d?), 9946 per, 15732 (c), 15761.8 (d?), 18216 (d?), 18405, 21038 (d), 21038.5 (d), 22154 (d?), 22880.2 (note), 23209 in aed., 24202.5.

1541: 15584.7(*A*3) per (d/error?), 20901 (d/error?).

Redmer, Richard.
Bookseller in London, 1610–1632?†. From 1616 his shop was shared with **Edward Brewster** though there are no shared imprints. Redmer possibly went to Dublin in 1620 (*C-B C*: xiii) in connection with the **Irish Stock** (*see* Stationers' Company). His imprints 1623–1632 are all shared with others and bear their addresses. [*Dict. 1*; DFM 1871.]
at the Star at the great West door of Paul's (A.10), 1610 (13521; 4245 has 'Golden Star in Paul's Churchyard')–1619 (5710, omits sign); variations: shop .... West 'end', 1611 (22107.5) or West 'gate', 1611 (6341, engr. tp)
1115: 14666 (d/error).
1610: 4244 imp., 4245 imp., 13521 f.
1611: 6341 f. (d), 22107.5 f., 24146 f.
1612: 1895 f., 5895 f., 11687 f., 12814 imp., 13121.5 ent., 17530.3(*A*3) f., 24147 f., 25293 f.
1613: 17531 f., 18525 f., 25931 f.
1614: 23658 f.
1615: 587 f., 3588 f., 5693 f., 14666 imp. (d), 21519 ent.
1618: 3568.5 f., 12747 f.
1619: 5710 f., 12572 f., 12747 f., 13014 ent., 25616 f.
1622: 1475 ent.
1623: 20678 f.
1624: 20672 f.
1626: 20679 f.
1630: 20673(*A*3) ass'd.
1632: 7031 f.

Reeve (Rive), Edmund.
Schoolmaster and translator in London, and divine, fl. 1614?–1660†. [*DNB.*]
by Christ Church greater South door (C.1), 1623 [20129]; he was at this address, 1618 (21060, a4^{v})–1627 (21060.5(*A*3), A1^{r}) at least.
1623: [20129] sold.

Reeve (Reave), James.
Copperplate printer in London, 1626?–1639 at least.
No address used.
1626: 22790 (note, found in 22790b and later issues). **1630:** 22796 (note). **1639:** 5137.

Regnault, François.
French bookseller in London, c. 1496, where he apparently continued to maintain a shop or agent until about 1536, and printer in Paris, 1501–1540?†. Succeeded by his widow, who printed under her maiden name as **Madeleine Boursette**. [Duff, *Century*; Renouard.]
1519: 15816 imp., 15924 imp., 16199 imp., 16200 imp.
1525: 15820 imp., 15821 imp.
1526: 15858 in aed., 15943 in aed., 15944 per & ven., 15945 in aed. & ven., 16205 imp., 16205.3(*A*3) per.
1527: 15949 in aed., 15950–2 per & ven., 15954 per, imp. & ven., 15955 in aed., 16205.3(*A*3) per, 16208 per.
1528: 15824 per, 15826 in aed., [15961] (d?).
1529: [15961.3], 15961.5 per, 16148–8.2 per, 16210 per.
1530: 15963 in aed. & ven., 15964 per, 15968 per & ven., 16148.2 per, 16239 in aed.
1531: 15830 ere & imp., 15831 per, 15970 per, 15971 in aed. & ven., 15973 per, 15974 per (d), [15975] (d?), 16211 imp.
1532: 15831 ven., 15865 imp. & ven., 15977 per, 15980 in aed. & ven., 16212 imp., 16212.5 in aed. (c).
1533: 15832 per & ven., 15859 exp., 15981 per, [15981a] (d?), 16213(*A*3) sumpt., 16224 sumpt.
1534: 2354 per, 15984 per & ven. (d), 15985a.5 imp., 16214 in aed.
1535: 15833 per, 15840 (repeat), 15985a.5 imp., [15986.7 f.], 15987 ven.
1536: 15987 per, [15992.5 f.] (c).
1537: 15995 pro, 16148.6 per.
1538: 2817, [2965 f.?], 16001 imp., 16002 per, 16003, 16004 f., [16008.3–.5 f.?], [21790 f.?], [21791 f.?].
1539: [2068], [2818.5].
1540: [2070?].

Regnault, Pierre.
Bookseller in Rouen, 1489–1519, and also in Caen from 1492. [Renouard; Muller 10, 103.]
1507: 16119.5 imp.

Rembolt, Berthold.
Printer in Paris, 1494–1518. [Duff, *Century*; Renouard.]
1497: 16169 per. **1498:** [16138(*A*3)] (d). **1513:** 16191 per.

Remembrancers General.
Patentees for the Office of General Remembrance of Matters of Record, London, 1617. = John Ferrour, John Friend, and Henry Miles, esquires. The following item was sold by **Robert Wilson**, but the Office's address is as follows:
in Cursitor's Court, right over against Lincoln's Inn in Chancery Lane (V.12a), 1617 (18788, title)
1617: 18788 f.

Remey. *See* Rime.

Renialme, Ascanius de.
Born in Venice. Became a bookseller and importer of books in London, 1578–1600†. Admitted a Brother of the Stat. Co. in 1580. Stepfather of **James Rime** and brother-in-law of **Francis Bouvier**. *See* also *heirs of* **A. de Renialme.** He lived in the parish of St. Anne's, Blackfriars (Q.5). [*Dict. 1*; *Library* 14 (1959): 34–43.]
1597: 25862 ent.

Renialme (Rinialme), Ascanius de, *Heirs of*, *pseud.?*
Booksellers in Frankfurt am Main, 1605? and 1607? Since this imprint occurs only in editions of Joseph Hall's pseudonymously published *Mundus alter et idem*, it may also be a pseudonym or at least humourously intended; however, it might possibly refer to **James Rime**, the stepson of Ascanius, who reissued in 1605 a few editions of H. Zanchius printed in Germany.
1605: 12685 ap. [sold] (d?). **1607:** 12685.3 ap. [sold] (d?).

Renis. *See* Reynes.

Respeawe, Derick van, *pseud.?*
Printer in Middelburg, 1584. Since apparently only one book is known with this imprint, it may well be false. [*Dict. 1*; Gruys.]
1584: 19063.

Resslin. *See* Roesslin.

Reston. *See* Royston.

Reynes (Raynes, Renis), John.
Dutch immigrant to London by 1510; bookbinder and bookseller from at least 1523–1544†, during which time he lived in St. Faith's parish (Worman 54–5). [Duff, *Century*.]
at the $ St. George in Paul's Churchyard (A.5), 1527 (13440)–1542 (5070, has 'dw.')
1527: 13440 at expenses, 15863 imp. **1530:** 16263a ven. **1537:** 6832.1 f. **1540:** 7378 f. (d?). **1542:** 5070 [f.], 10662 [f.] (d). **1544:** 16242 imp.

Reyns, Jan.
Bookseller in Brussels, 1598–1609. [*Dict. 1*, under Mommart; Rouzet.]
1608: 11093 chez.

Reyston. *See* Royston.

Rhiwledyn Press.
Recusant press near Rhiwledyn, Caernarvanshire, 1587. *See* also **Roger Thackwell**. [*BS* 2 (1953): 37–54.]
1587: [21077] (false, d).

Rhodes, Matthew.
Journeyman printer in London, (1619) 1622–1642 at least. [*Dict. 1*; *Dict. 2*; DFM 187.]
shop at the upper end of the Old Bailey near Newgate (D.7), 1622 (17401)
1622: 17401–2 f. **1625:** 3722 f. **1629:** 4628 f.

Richard, *Earl of Kent*. *See* Grey.

Richard, Jean.
Bookseller in Rouen, 1490–1517. [Duff, *Century*; Muller 103.]
1494: 15879 pro.
1496: 15802 ere & imp.
1497: 15885 pro, 16171 imp.
1499: 17966 imp.

Richard. J. — *cont.*
1500: 16139 imp.
1502: 16163 imp.
1506: 16182 imp.
1508: 16183 imp., 16184 imp., 16233 imp.
1509: 16140.3 imp.
1510: 16187 imp.
1511: 16188.5 imp.

Richard (Rychard), Thomas.
Monk and printer or patron of a press in the exempt monastery, Tavistock, Devon, 1525, 1534? [Duff, *Century* 142.]
1525: 3200. **1534:** [6795.6?] (d).

'Richt Right' Press.
Printers in Amsterdam, 1637–1642. During that time the press was apparently supervised by John Canne, pastor of the exiled English Church. The press is named for the device with motto 'Richt Right' which appears in some of its publications, e.g. in 1638 (15309). Much of the other printing material came from the *successors of* **G. Thorp**. [*Library* 5 (1951): 231; Carter, 'Laud', pp. 48–9, 51, 53.]
1637: [13726.4], [20474].
1638: [1570.5], [15309], [15591], [15599], [20221.3] (c), [22013] (d), [22026.6], [22026.8], [22032] (d), [22032.5] (d), [22496.5], [24957], [25587], [26125].
1639: [4575], [7367.5], [7372.5], [12035], [15596], [15598], [20889.3], [21110], [21904.7] (false), [21908] (forged), [21908.5] (false), [22057] (false), [24844a.3], [24958], [25229.5], [26126.5].
1640: [222.5], [232], [1206], [11324], [12341], [26127].

Riddell (Reddell, Ryddell), William.
Bookseller in London, 1548–1565 at least. Mentioned in the latter year in the will of **Thomas Petyt**. [Duff, *Century*; *Dict. 1*.]
dw. at the George in Paul's Churchyard (A.5), 1548 (18764)–1552 (11903, omits 'dw.')
in Lombard Street at the Eagle (O.12), 1554 (17561)–1556 (6005.5)
1548: 18764 f. **1552:** 11903 [f.], 13940 ex off. **1554:** 13290.3 [f.?] (d), 17561 (d). **1556:** 6005.5 [f.] (d).

Riddiard (Ridiard), William.
Printseller in London, c. 1625?–1636 at least. Probably related to John Ruddiard (*Dict. 2*), who in 1662 was at the same address. [Globe 220.]
at the Unicorn in Cornhill near the [Royal] Exchange (O.9), c. 1625? (11227.5)–1636 (5363.5)
1625: 11227.5 sold (c?). **1634:** 25179.5 sold (d?). **1636:** 5363.5 sold.

Rider, Robert.
Bookbinder? in London, (1601) 1604–1646. Except for the single item below, translated by his son Henry, he appears only in documentary records. [*Dict. 1*; *Poor Book*, 1615, 1618–46.]
No address used.
1638: 13804 f.

Rider, Timothy.
Stationer in London, (1571) 1577?–1588†. Beadle of the Stat. Co. 1578–1587, during which time he had a dwelling in Stationers' Hall (A.10). [*Dict. 1*; *Reg. B*: xxxvi–xxxvii.]
No address used.
1577: 20665 f. (d?). **1579:** 20666 f. (d). **1582:** 7520 ent. **1584:** 19433.3 ent.

Ridge, Oliver.
Maker and seller of writing tables, 1628. Not a member of the Stat. Co.
at the Angel in Lombard Street (O.12), 1628 (26050.18, from W. A. Jackson's correspondence, August 1951)
1628: 26050.18 made & sold (in title).

Rihel, Wendelin.
Bookseller and printer (from 1535) in Strassburg, 1531–1555†. Succeeded by his heirs until 1557, probably his sons Josias and Theodosius before each set up business on his own. [Benzing 445; *Library* 4 (1950): 275.]
1554: [16980] (false). **1555:** [17562–3] (false), [24673.5].

1556: [21048 heirs] (d). **1557:** [658? heirs] (d).

Rime (Rymer, Rymey, Remey?), James.
Bookseller in London, 1599–1609 at least. Stepson of **Ascanius de Renialme**. *See* also the latter's *heirs*. [*Dict. 1*; H.M.C, 6th report, Appendix pp. 228a, 229a.]
No address used.
1602: 3368.5-Remey? **1605:** 26121, 26121.3, 26121.7, 26121a.

Rinialme. *See* Renialme.

Rither. *See* Ryther.

Ritherdon, Ambrose.
Bookseller in London, (1627) 1630–1633†. His shop was near the great North door of Paul's and was among those marked for demolition, c. 1632 (*Library* 3 (1902): 267–8). [*Dict. 1*; DFM 2175; *Loan Book* (as Retherden), 1631.]
at the Bull Head in Paul's Churchyard (A.2), 1630 (24929a)–1632 (5781)
1630: 24929–9a f. **1631:** 3591 sold, 5780.7 sold. **1632:** 5780.7–81 sold, 19522.5 f. **1633:** 23934.19(*A3*) sold.

Rive. *See* Reeve.

Roberts (Robards), Henry.
There are two Stationers of this name. Arber assigns to Henry 1 all activity except the freedom of Henry 2 by patrimony in 1595 (II.716). *Dict. 1* attributes all activity from 1595 to Henry 2.
There is no record of the apprenticeship or freedom of Henry 1, and he may have joined the Stat. Co. by translation or redemption during July 1571–June 1577 when the relevant records are missing. He freed an apprentice in 1580 (II.683). The next apprentice bound to a Henry—in 1604 (II.274), at which time the apprentice's father was living in the same parish as the address given below—was freed in 1611 (DFM 2243). Henry 1 may well have been the author of occasional STC publications between 1585 (21084) and 1616 (21087.7) and the man of this name in the *Poor Book*, 1608–16, with widow to 1633. None of the records or publications distinguishes between 'elder' and 'younger', and it seems that Arber's interpretation of this fact may be correct.
shop near to St. Botolph's Church without Aldgate (M.1), 1612 (16756.5); no earlier or later address used.
1606: 21085 f. **1612:** 16756.5 f. **1613:** 4576 f., 18587 f.

Roberts (Robarts), James.
Bookseller and printer (from 1593) in London, (1564) 1569/70–1606 (1618?†). In partnership with **Richard Watkins** in the Almanack patent 1571–1599/1600, which was then carried on into 1605/06 by the *assignee(s) of* **J. Roberts.** He married **Alice Charlewood** in 1593 and took over her printing materials; in late 1606 they passed to **William Jaggard**. [*Dict. 1*; *Poor Book*, 1608–18; *St. Giles*, 1593–1603.]
his house in Barbican (I.1), 1603 (5326)–1605 (12882); no earlier use noted
1569/70: 486.5 f.
1571/72: [459], 459.5.
1572/73: 459.7(*A*), 511.9.
1573/74: [459.9(*A*)], [482.12], [512].
1574/75: [401.7] (d?).
1575/76: 401.8, [401.8A(*A*)?], [488.3], 512.3, 512.4.
1577/78: 512.6.
1578/79: 488.5, [491], 512.7, [518.8].
1579/80: 512.9, [26049.6].
1580/81: 418, 454.5, 488.7, [491.5], 512.11, [26049.8–.10].
1581/82: 422.7, 480.3.
1582/83: 518.9(*A3*), [26049.13(*A3*)].
1583/84: 402.5, 423, 455, [517.9], [26049.14].
1584/85: 444, 455.3, 480.5, [501.32], 518.10.
1586/87: 443, [444.1], [444.2].
1587/88: 444.3, 451.
1588/89: 423.3, 434, 444.4, 444.5, 451.2, 455.7.
1589/90: 423.4, 423.5, 444.6.
1590/91: [423.6], 433.5–.7, 434.2, 444.7, 444.8, 451.4.
1591/92: 434.3, 444.9.
1592/93: [423.8], 428, 444.10, 451.6.
1593: [14801], [16662], 17059 (d?), 18366, [19382(*A3*: ed. ii)?] (d?), 25834 (d/error?).
1593/94: [403.7] (d?), 434.5, 444.11, 526, [26049.16].
1594: 1808 ent., 3054 ent., 4826.7 ent., 5633.3 ent., 5638 (d?), 6243.4, 6690 ent., 6710.5 ent., 6710.7 ent., 6712 ent., 7203, 7205,

Roberts, J. — *cont.*
7214 (d?), 10209, 10234, 11004 ent., 11622, 11870, [12392.5] (d), 13483(*A*) ent., 13859 ent., [18367], 18668 ent., 19161(*A*3) ent., 19383, 19858, [20572], 20797 ent., [20854], 22698 ent., 24197.5 (*A*3) ent.
1594/95: 424.3, 424.4, 434.6, 445, 451.8, 525, 526.5.
1595: 1089, 4306, 4985, [5638.3?] (d?), 6243.5, 6244 (note), 6715.7, 6840, 7192 (d), 14121.5, 16958–8.5, 17347, 17385, 17669, 19434, [22534], 22956, [24345] (d?).
1595/96: 424.5, 445.1.
1596: 1084, 1087, 6360, 6708, 7207–8, 7232, [11492], 15533.3, 16872, 16909.5, [17091], 17347.5, 17386 (d), [22951.5(*A*)] (d?).
1596/97: 445.2.
1597: 1336.5, 3184.4, 3713, 6677, [6681], [6683] (d), 6716, [6733.3] (d), 7193, 15533.3, 15685, 15685.5, [16704?], 16857, 17060 (d?), 17075, 18071–1.5, 19793, 20016, 20021, 22958.
1597/98: 424.7, 434.9, 445.3, 445.4, 451.11, 466, 525.2, 26050.
1598: 7193.2, 11004, 12504, 15685.5, 15686, 15686.3, 16918, 16920, 17482, 17485, 18072, 18468 (d), 19384, 20595.5 (d), 22296 ent.
1598/99: 434.10, 445.5, 525.3.
1599: 381–2, 734, 7195, 10553 ent., 12253.7(*A*3), [12260], 17349, 17486, 17486.5(*A*3) (forged), [17928] (d), 19384.5, 19435, 22735, 22959, [24344], 25834.
1599/1600: 434.11, 525.4, 525.5.
1600: 1891.5, 3191, 6681.5, 6709, 7196, [7523], 10889.5, 12254, 14592, 16754 ent., 18668, 19430, 22296, 22297 (forged), 22303 (forged), 22329, [23382.3], 24002, 24135.
1601: 14058, 15639, 16901, 16959, 17076, 19385, 22861, 24197.5, 26050.2.
1602: [780], 1085, 7197, 10546, 16911, 18163, 19165, [19449], 22275 ent., 22761, 22765, 22952, 22960a.
1603: [1382], [4321], 5326, 6710, 6716.5, 6717, 7189, 7231, 7231.3(*A*3), 10545, 12880, 16743.2 (d), 16743.3 (d), 22331 ent., 25834.5, [26050.4(*A*3)] (d?).
1604: 4884, 5062, 5327, [7085.5?], 7293, 10855, 12881, 15686.5(*A*3), 16668, 17570, 17932, 22276.
1604/05: 489.2.
1605: 1808, [1809] (c), [3432.3] (c?), [6628], 6682, 10566.5, [10930 (*A*3)?], 11600, 12227, 12273.5, 12882, 16916.2(*A*3), 19001–2, 19733(*A*3), 22276a, 25093 (d).
1606: 4102.5 (d), 4622 (d), [5441–1.2], 6682, 6716.5 (note), 10655, [10931] (d?), 13244, [18597] (d), 18669, 22637, 23591.
1615: 24991.5 ass'd.

Roberts, James, *Assignee(s, with assent) of.*
Publishers of Almanacks under the Watkins and Roberts patent. After Watkins yielded rights in the broadside variety to the Stat. Co. on 8 Jan. 1584 (Arber II.787; Appendix C/14; *see* also Appendix D/101–2), T. Dawson was apparently allowed to print them; cf. 425, 466.6. Following Watkins's death in 1599 E. White 1 was primary assignee for Almanacks in other formats. In 1603/04 they began to be published by the **English Stock**; *see* Stationers' Company.
Imprints below name 'assignee' except as specified.
1594/95: [424 with assent].
1598/99: 425 with assent.
1599/1600: 434.12 f., [466.2 with assent?].
1600/01: 501 [f.], 525.6 f.
1601/02: 434.14 f., 466.4 f., 483 f., 501.2 f., 525.7 f., 532 f.
1602/03: 452 f. ass'ns/ass'n, [457.8 f.], 501.3 f., [532.2(*A*) f.].
1603/04: 434.16 f. ass'ns, 452.3 f. ass'ns, 466.6 with assent, 483.2 by ass'ns, 525.9 f. ass'ns, 532.3 f. ass'ns.
1605/06: 532.5 f.

Robinson, George.
Printer in London, 1585–1587†. Freed as a Grocer by **John Kingston** in 1573; transferred to the Stat. Co. in 1585. Married Kingston's widow and succeeded to his printing material. His own widow printed one book as **Joan Robinson** before remarrying **Thomas Orwin**. *See* also the headnote following Appendix D/60. [*Dict. 1.*]
No address noted.
1585: [1064], [1786.5] (d), [2029] (d?), 5266.5(*A*3), [6394], [6905?], [10208], [11900–0.5], [12299], [12354.5], [13108], [13109] (d), [15137] (d?), [21949?] (false), [22416.5] (c), [24337] (d), 25806.
1586: 4386.5, 5228 (d), [6230], [6992] (d), [10512], [11373] (d?), [12508], [13111], [16776.10] (d), [16956], [16956.3(*A*3)] (d),

Robinson, G. — *cont.*
18425–5.5 (d), [18513], [19433.5] (d?), 23439.5, 24287.7, 25079.
1587: 2031, 5261, 18149, 24708.

———

1593: 23439.5 ass'd.

Robinson, Humphrey.
Bookseller in London, (1623) 1624–1670†. The first two editions of his earliest publication were sold at the shop of his partner in the copyright, **Robert Milbourne**: at the great South door of Paul's (A.8). [*Dict. 2*; DFM 1313.]
at the Three Pigeons in Paul's Churchyard (A.3), 1627 (4642, letterpress tp, with R. Milbourne)–1640 (24137.5) and until his death
1624: 4640 f.
1625: 4641 f.
1626: 7534 ent.
1627: 4642 f.
1628: 18673 f.
1629: 1124 f., 20567.3 sumpt.
1630: 4643 f., 7534 f.
1631: 3468 f., 7329 f., 7535 f., 7536 f., 13205 f., 15510 f.
1632: 551 ap., 7330 f., 12935 f., 14048 ent.
1633: 7536.1 f., 14269 f., 26010 ent., 26010.5 sumpt.
1636: 1698 chez, 10227.6 f., 12956 [f.].
1637: 17937 f., 23573 f.
1638: 7536.4 f., 20384 pro.
1640: 24137–7.5 sold.

Robinson, Joan.
Printer in London, 1587. Widow of **George Robinson**. She also printed later as **Joan Orwin**, widow of her next husband. *See* also the headnote following Appendix D/60.
No address used.
1587: 5266.5(*A*3) ex typ.

Robinson, John.
Stationer in London, (1613) 1615–1653†. He began in partnership with **William Tymme,** his former master. [*Dict. 1*; *Dict. 2*; DFM 2602; *Poor Book*, 1619, 1620–53, widow thereafter; *Loan Book*, 1637–40.]
their shop in Paternoster Row (C.7), 1615 (13936, with W. Tymme)
1615: 13936 f.

Robinson, Robert.
Printer in London, (1580) 1585–1597†. Freed by the widow of **William Seres 1** on 27 June 1580 (Arber II.682). He began printing while still a journeyman, including piracies of works in the patent of **John 1** and **Richard Day**. In 1587 he acquired the printing material and patents (the latter possibly licences to sell wine (cf. 9175n) and recognizances for alehouse keepers (cf. 9175q)) of **Henry Middleton**. In 1590 he became the primary printer of Latin school books (*see* the headnote following Appendix D/60). Robinson's widow remarried **Richard Bradock**, who succeeded to the business. *See* also Appendix E/9–11. [*Dict. 1*; Judge: 61–89.]
dw. in Fetter (Feter, Fewter) Lane near Holborn (V.7), 1585 (1848)–1588 (1853); he was still in St. Andrew's parish in 1591 (*Library* 10 (1909): 103)
1585: 1848.
1586: 1729 ent., 6074a.7 (d), 6564 (d), 14095, 23259 (d).
1587: 1262, 1356.9, 1970, 13868.
1587/88: 13921.
1588: 1853, 4032 ent., 4090.5, 11481 ent., 11558 ent., [12785], 19152, 20698, 20698.5.
1589: 1579–9.5, 5759.1 (note), 12224, 13050, [18617], 19916, 19916.3, 20059, 22217, 25118.6, 25407.
1590: 4579, 4771.4, 5299.8, 5402.5, 6842 (d), 19752 (d?), 19752.3 (d?), 19752.5(*A*3) (d?), 22984, 23641.5 (c), [23685], 25120, 25121.
1591: 171a, 3508, 5300, [7275?], [14584], 17288, 20593, [23642(*A*3)], [24750], 25764 sold.
1592: 171a.3(*A*), 2400.5, 4771.5, 4848, [12900.5], 18150, 18617.3, 19143, 19665.5, [22704], [22718], 25764a sold.
1593: 11481, [17426], 18617.5(*A*3), [22719], 22984.1, 25259, 25701.
1594: 5403, 6625.4, [17437].
1595: 4098, 4274.5, 5300.4, 18617.6(*A*), 21821, 22984.2(*A*3),

Robinson, R. — *cont.*
24768.5, 25941.5.
1596: 362, 1091, 1098, 4032, 4848 (note), 6216 ?ent., 10638.5, 11748 ex off., [12782?], 15420, 18013, [18197.3], 18197.7, [18199], 18246, 20634, 20635, 20636, 25118.8.
1597: 4511.4, 5966, 9175n ent., 12225, 18617.6c(*A*3), [19900], 21499, 23021, 23652.5, 23888 ex off., 24769, [25195].

Robinson, Thomas.
Bookseller in Oxford, 1639–1663. [*Dict. 2.*]
No address used.
1639: 4717 f. **1640:** 4718 f., 20518 imp.

Robothum. *See* Rowbotham.

Rocket, Henry.
Bookseller in London, 1602–1611†. Although from 1602 Rocket's is the bookseller's name most often found with the following address, **Thomas Archer** is once associated with it in 1604 (12199). It is possible that Rocket may only have managed the shop for **Edward** and **Margaret Allde** until some time in 1607. [*Dict. 1*; *Loan Book*, 1605–08.]
at the Long Shop under St. Mildred's Church in the Poultry (O.1), 1602 (17876)–1611; variations: adds 'under the dial', 1606 (12582), 1608 (17896a); has 'his shop', 1607 (17350.5), 1611 (25150a)
1602: [10597.5(*A*3)?] sold, 17876 f.
1603: 6518 f., [6791(*A*3)?] sold.
1604: [12199(*A*3)?] sold.
1605: 6540 ent., 7078 f., 12582 f., 21385.5 f.
1606: 7081 f., 12582 f.
1607: [3490(*A*3)?] sold, 6396.5 f., 7082 f., 13317 f., 17350.5–51 sold.
1608: 17896a sold, 22932 ent.
1609: 18108 f., 24125 f., 24308 sold.
1610: 4777 f., 12769 f., 24126 f., 24308a sold, 25150 f.
1611: 4319 ent., 4320 ent., 25150a f.

1616: 22933 ass'd.

Rocolet, Peter, *pseud.*
Printer at 'Paris', 1621. = Edward Allde. For the genuine Pierre Rocolet, who was active in Paris 1610–1662 and who may have printed the French original of the following item, *see* Lottin 2: 150.
1621: 16798.

Rodway, Rodwell. *See* Rothwell.

Roedius, Sibertus (Sebryght van Roye).
Dutch bookseller in London, 1549–1564 at least. A brother of the Stat. Co. In 1549 he lived in the parish of St. Botolph's, Billingsgate Ward (T.9), and in 1564 in the parish of St. Leonard's, Foster Lane, Aldersgate Ward (G.5) [Duff, *Century* 138, 139; Worman 56.]
No address used.
1556: 10450.5 [f.], 10471.7 [f.].

Roesslin (Resslin, Rosslin), Johann Weyrich 1.
Printer in Stuttgart, 1610–1644†. [*Dict. 1*: 226; Benzing 457.]
1616: 25186. **1619:** 25185a.5.

Rogers (ap-Rogers), Owen.
Bookseller and printer (1559–1562?) in London, 1555–1566. [Duff, *Century*; *Journal of the Welsh Bibliographical Society* 8 (1955): 58–63.]
in Smithfield by the Hospital in Little St. Bartholomew's (E.8), 1559 (17028); variation: dw. in Smithfield, 1559, 28 Apr. (17312)
dw. betwixt both St. Bartholomews at the Spread-Eagle (E.6), 1559/60 (506)–1561 (19908, colophon to pt. 2); variation: has 'near unto Great St. Bartholomew's gate' for betwixt ... Bartholomews, 1561, 21 Feb. (19908, tp to pt. 1)
dw. at St. Sepulchre's Church door (D.8), 1565 (6774)
1558: [3478.5 f.?].
1559: [3479 f.?] (d), 3726 (note), 13911 (d?), 17028 (d), 17312.
1559/60: 506.
1560: 5225, 5886 ent., [7922] (d), 18499 (d), 20087 (d).
1560/61: [506.3?].
1561: 10592 (d), [13294?], 19908.
1562: [24372.5?] (d).
1565: 6774 f. (d).

Roman, Aegidius.
Printer in Utrecht, 1636–1643. [Gruys.]
1638: 7076.5.

Roman (Rooman), Gillis.
Printer in Haarlem, 1585–1609. [*Dict. 1*; Gruys.]
1597: 19489.

Rood, Theodoric.
Printer in Oxford, 1478–1486. In partnership with **Thomas Hunt 1** from sometime in 1483. [Duff, *Century*.]
No address used.
1468: [21443] (d/error).
1478: [21443] (d).
1479: [158], [752].
1481: 314.
1482: [15297], [23163.13] (d?).
1483: [695] (d), [696] (d), [922] (d?), [5312] (d), [16693] (d?), [17102] (d), [21261] (d), [23904] (d).
1485: [315] (d?), 19827.
1486: [17958].

Roper, Abel.
Bookseller in London, (1637) 1638–1680†. [*Dict. 2*; DFM 2327; *Loan Book*, 1643–46; Globe 220.]
shop at the Black Spread-Eagle in Fleet Street over against St. Dunstan's Church (W.9), 1638 (1789)–1640 (21771.5) at least
1638: 1789 f. **1639:** 1790 f., 4550 f. **1640:** 21771–1.5 f.

Ross, Alexander.
Divine and miscellaneous writer, b. 1591–1654†. [*DNB*.]
No address used.
1632: 21329 sumpt.

Ross (Ros), John.
Printer and bookbinder in Edinburgh, 1574–1580†. He printed some Scottish statutes and proclamations and functioned as **King's Printer in Scotland** but apparently had no formal appointment. His printing material passed to **Henry Charteris.** [*Dict. 1.*]
No address used.
1575: 16579.5, 21258, 21881, 21883, 21943a.5 (d), 21944 (d), 21945 (d).
1576: [10551–1.5] (false)
1578: 2996.7, [16580.7?] (d?), 21254.
1579: 3973 ap., [3974], 6781 ap., 6783 ap., 7074, 22651 ap.
1579/80: 21884.
1580: [3975], 4847 ap., 5606 ap., [6767], 10478 ap., 13956, [15661] (d?), [21946.5] (d), 21947 (repeat), [23000] (d?).

1581: 3977 ad exemplar.

Note: The identities and activities of the two men named **John Rothwell** have been somewhat obscure and confused. Details are tentatively allocated below.

Rothwell (Rodwell, Rodway), John 1.
Bookbinder in London, 1600–1649†. Father of **John Rothwell 2**. Apprenticed to **Thomas Stirrop** on 2 Oct. 1592 and freed by the latter's widow on 7 Apr. 1600 (Arber II.183, 725). He apparently petitioned the Stat. Co. in 1600 to obtain a copyright of his late master (*Reg. B*: 77), but the 1601 edition (18249) has M. Law's name as publisher. Although John 1 bound and freed apprentices, was elected to the Livery on 6 July 1611, and was otherwise active in the affairs of the Stat. Co., the only clear evidence of his involvement in publishing is in 1628 when he registered a one-sixteenth share in L. Andrewes's *Sermons* (606(*A*3), Arber IV. 203). He had a large bookbinder's shop near the great North door of Paul's (A.2) which was marked for removal, c. 1632 (*Library* 3 (1902): 267–8), and he was one of the petitioners for relief on 22 Jan. 1636 (Greg, *Companion*: 337–8). It is not known where he moved thereafter. All forms of his name should be searched in Stat. Co. records. [*Dict. 2*; Arber; *C-B C*.]

Rothwell, John 2.
Bookseller in London, (1631) 1632–1660. Son of **John Rothwell 1.** He apparently acquired a share in the shop of his former master, **John Partridge**, although their names do not appear together

Rothwell, John 2 — *cont.*
in imprints. It was probably due to John 2's influence that the spelling 'Rothwell' superseded others. Book entries in the SR to 'John Rothwell' between 1633 and Mar. 1638 are to John 2, who was elected to the Livery on 29 Mar. 1638 and thereafter is usually called 'Master Rothwell junior' though it seems likely that John 2 is meant in all the joint entries of John Stoughton's works (Arber IV.475–80) whether his name is qualified by 'junior' or not. As a result, all surviving imprints have been listed under John 2. [*Dict. 2*; DFM 2116; *Loan Book*, 1635–38.]
in Paul's Churchyard at the Sun (A.3), 1632 (13261)–1640 (7414.5) at least; variation: 1635 (4260.5, has 'in bibliopolio Joannis Rothwell', i.e. in his shop)
1632: 13261 f.
1633: 24539 sold.
1634: 16945 f., 22854.5 sold.
1635: 4260.5 ven.
1636: 3994.3 sumpt., 5215 f., 5216 f.
1637: 3994.5 sumpt., 5217 f., 12033–3.5 f., 15717 f., 22486 f., 22513 f., 22513.5 f.
1638: 3758–9 f., 5218 f., 11791 f., 11792 sold, 12034 f., 22487 f., 22497–7.5 f., 22499 f., 22514 f., 24760.5 f., 24760.7 f., 24761 f.
1639: 7422 f., 23302 ?ent.
1640: 223 ent., 1625 f., 3515.5 f. (d?), 7414 (note), 7414.5 sold, 10779 f., 10780 f., 12978 prost., 16945.5 f. (c), 16651 f., 16652 f., 23299 f., 23300 f., 23304 f., 23306 f., 23307–7.5 f., 23310 f., 23311.5 f., 23312 f., 23313 f.
1649: 3515.5 f. (d/error).

Rounthwait, Ralph.
Bookseller in London, 1617–1628. Sometime in 1625 his second shop passed to **Philemon Stephens** and **Christopher Meredith**, who sold or were associated with all Rounthwait's later publications. [*Dict. 1*; DFM 971.]
in Paul's Churchyard, 1618–1625
shop — at the Fleur-de-lis and Crown (A.2), 1618 (1634)–1619 (4638)
shop — at the Golden Lion (B), 1619 (15656)–1625 (4232)
1617: 4100 f.
1618: 1634 f., 4100.5 f., 4213 f.
1619: 3211 f., 3211.5 f., 4209.5 f., 4213.5 f., 4219.5 f., 4232.5 f., 4233.5 f., 4235.5 f., 4638 f., 10782 f., 11524 f., 15656 f., 18799 f., 21840 ent., 26077 f.
1620: 2741.5 per, 4220 f., 21673.5 f., 25441 f.
1621: 11279.5 f., 15657 f.
1622: 4220.5 f.
1623: 21873.5 f.
1624: 4220a f., 5396 f., 10701.3 ent., 18359 ent.
1625: 4220a.5 f., 4232 f., 10706.4 imp., 15657.5 f., 18359.5 f.
1626: 4233–3.3 f.
1628: 4221 f.

Rowbotham (Robothum), James.
Bookseller in London, 1559–1580. Freed as a Draper by **John Wight** in 1557. *See* also Appendix A/14. [*Dict. 1.*]
shop in Cheapside under Bow Church at the Rose and Pomegranate (N.6), 1562 (1209.5)–1564 (724.5, omits sign)
shop in Paternoster Row (C.7), 1568 (15486), 1574 (15487, omits 'shop', adds 'at the Lute')
dw. at St. Magnus Corner (T.8), 1577 (24920.5)
1562: 724 [f.] (d?), 1209.5 f., 6214 f., 13299.5 f. (d?).
1562/63: 490.18 f., 490.20 f.
1563: 15542 f., 15542a [f.] (d?).
1564: 724.5 f., 1209.7 f., 20439.7 ent.
1568: 1210 f., 15486 f.
1569: [15486.5(*A*3) f.] (d?).
1574: 15487 f.
1577: 24920.5 f. (d).

Rowlands. *See* Verstegan.

Rowse. *See* Le Roux.

Roy, Salomon de.
Printer in Utrecht, 1590–1637. [*Dict. 1*; Gruys.]
1615: 19459.

Royal Printing Office. *See* King's (Queen's) Printer(s).

Royden, Roger.
Bookseller in Bristol, 1634. Possibly the man of this name who was apprenticed to Elizabeth Bankworth in 1614 but never freed (DFM 636).
No address used.
1634: 20513 sold.

Roye, Sebryght van. *See* Roedius.

Royston, John.
Bookseller in London, 1611–1613. Shared a shop with **William Bladen** from 1612. [*Dict. 1*; DFM 639.]
their shop at the great North door of Paul's at the Bible (A.2), 1612 (5188, with W. Bladen)–1613 (24282.5, alone, has 'his shop')
1612: 5188 f., 11794 f., 24578 f. **1613:** 24282.5 f., 24527.5 sold.

Royston (Reston, Reyston, Roystore), Richard.
Bookseller in London, 1627–1686. [*Dict. 2*; DFM 1479.]
in Ivy Lane (C.3), 1630–1640 at least
—, 1630 (6666.4), 1636 (1373, has 'dw.'), 1638 (7037)
shop — next the Exchequer Office, 1630 (1368), 1631 (11954), 1635 (14721)
— at the Angel, 1635 (19570.5), 1640 (13316); variation, 1639 (1370, has 'shop')
1627: 12360.3 f.
1629: 22.7 f., 10586 ent., 22529 ?ent.
1630: 1368 f., 6666.4 sold, 17367 sold, 17383.5 sold, 25670 sold.
1631: 1383 sold, 11954 sold, 13320 f., 18043 f.
1632: [1368.5 f.?] (d?), 11769 (note), 12400 f., 18043 f.
1633: 1372 f., 10635.3 f., 10635.5 f., 17384 sold.
1634: 1369 f., 17835 sold, 25900 ent.
1635: 5157.5(*A*3), 14721 f., 19301 sold, 19570 (note), 19570.5 sold, 25900c f.
1636: 1369.5 f., 1373 f., 17836 f.
1637: 10635.7 f.
1638: 7037 sold.
1639: 1370 f.
1640: 1371 f., 7038 f., 10636 f., 11061 f., 13316 f., 21063 ent., 23306 f.

Rudiard. *See* Riddiard.

Rudstone, *Sir* **John.**
Alderman of London between 1521–1531† and patron; Lord Mayor 1528–29. [A. B. Beaven, *The Aldermen of London*, 1908–13, II.24, 169.]
No address used.
1532, before: 864 at request of.

Ruelle, Jean.
Bookseller and printer (from 1554) in Paris, 1538–1571†. [Duff, *Century*; Renouard.]
1548: 6832.13 chez.

Rufus. *See* Le Roux.

Ruremund (Endoviensis), Catherine van.
Printer in Antwerp, 1532–1546. Widow of **Christoffel van Ruremund**. [Duff, *Century*; Rouzet 194.]
1532: 16132 in off., [16241].
1533: 16132 in off.
1534: 2825.
1535: [2372.4], 2827, [14820(*A*3)].
1536: [2832?], [2833?], [2834?], [15992], [21789.5] (d), [21799] (d).
1536/37: [513?].
1540: [22897] (false, d?).
1541: 16133 in off., [17798] (false, d), [21804] (false), [24217] (false).
1542: [13612], 16149 in off., 16241.5 in off.
1543: [1280] (d?), [4046?] (d), [14556?] (false), [14826] (false), [14830], 16149 in off., [21629] (d), [26138] (false).
1544: [1291] (d?), 16242 in off., [24165].
1545: 16243 in off.

Ruremund (Ruremond, Endoviensis, Endhoven), Christoffel van.
Printer and bookseller in Antwerp, 1523–1531†. He died in prison in Westminster. Husband of **Catherine van Ruremund**. Probably related to **Melchior Endovianus**, who used his types in 1558. [Duff, *Century*; Rouzet.]
1523: [15935] (d?), 16145–6 arte, 16236 per, 16236.3 per.
1524: [15818.5], [15937], 15938 opera, [15938.5], 16130 arte, 16261 opera.
1525: 15822 labore, 15939 per, 16131 per, 16236.7 per, 17111 diligentia.
1526: 15822 labore.
1527: [5542?], 16207 ascribendum est.
1528: 16131.5 per, 16209 opera & imp., [16237].
1529/30: 471.
1530: 15962 per, 15966 per, [16238] (d?), [16263a], [24868.7] (c).
1531: 15966 per, 15969 ex off.

1558: 16249.5 typis.

Russell, Edward.
Bookseller? or patron? in London, 1566. Not a member of the Stat. Co. His only surviving item was printed in Fleet Street by an unidentified printer. [*Dict. 1*.]
No address used.
1566: 5221 f. (d).

Russell, William 1.
Bookseller in Exeter, 1589. Probably the father of **William Russell 2** and dead before 1605 (Arber II.289). Possibly the man of this name who was apprenticed to John Harrison 1 in 1570 for 11 years (Arber I.397) though there is no record of his freedom.
No address used.
1589: 7159.3 f.

Russell, William 2.
Bookseller in Plymouth, 1631–1641 (Wing J 542) at least. Possibly the man freed by W. Dight in 1614 (DFM 1190) since there appears to be no further indication of his activity in London; if so, he is the son of **William Russell 1**.
No address used.
1631: 18531 sold. **1632:** 12393.5 sold. **1635:** 1791.3 f. **1640:** 24870.5 sold.

Rychard, Ryddell, Ryder. *See* Richard, Riddell, Rider.

Ryther (Rither), Augustine.
Engraver and copperplate printer in London, c. 1576–1595. [Hind I.138–49.]
shop a little from Leadenhall next to the $ Tower (P.5), 1590 (24481)
1590: 24481 sold.

S

S., M., *pseud.*
Printer in 'Rotterdam', 1626. = Unidentified printer, possibly in London.
1626: 1042.

Sadler, Laurence.
Bookseller in London, 1631–1664†. Although apprenticed in 1614, he was never freed and was not a member of the Stat. Co. Sometimes published jointly with **Cornelius Bee**. [*Dict. 2*; DFM 2309.]
in Little Britain at the Golden Lion (F.4)
1631: 25223 sold. **1635:** 21817.3 f. **1639:** 19210 sumpt. **1640:** 6007 imp., 19210 sumpt.

Saint Denys, Jean.
Bookseller in Paris, 1521–1531†. [Duff, *Century*: 143; Renouard.]
1525: 24827.5(*A3*) pour (c).

Salisbury, John. *See* Byddell.

Salisbury (Salesbury), Thomas.
Bookseller and bookbinder? in London, (1588) 1589–1622. If he is the bookbinder noted in *Dict. 1*, his house was in Paul's Churchyard (B) in 1596. [*Dict. 1*; *Poor Book*, 1608–22; *Journal of the National Library of Wales* 1 (1939): 52–3.]
No address used.
1589: 4803.8 f. **1593:** 21611 [f.]. **1597:** 23408.6 sold. **1603:** 2743 dros, 2744 a. **1604:** 12872 f., 14356 f. **1614:** 23408.8 sold.

Salisbury (Salesbury), William.
Lexicographer and translator, b. 1520?–1600?†. [*DNB*.]
dw. in Ely rents in Holborn (V.5), 1551 (2983, colophon)
1551: 2983 f.

Salter, John.
Bookseller in Exeter? 1640. Not a member of the Stat. Co. Because the term 'bookseller' is used in his only imprint, it seems likely that he lived outside of London. The imprint, which is defective, is conjecturally restored as follows: '[L]ondon, | [Printed by Richard Oulto]n, for Iohn Salter Booke-seller | [and are to be had] at his shop in S. Martins | [Lane? in ?Exe]ter. 1640 |
1640: 20925a(*A3*) f.

Saltwood, Robert.
Monk of St. Augustine's Abbey, Canterbury, fl. c. 1530?–1539. The types and woodcut initials in the London-printed items indexed below were apparently owned by Saltwood since they reappear in a work of Saltwood's authorship (21647) printed by **John Mychell** without place of printing and in an anti-Lutheran poem printed by Mychell at Canterbury (15192.5). [*DNB*.]
No address used.
1531: 3186(*A3*) at cost of (d?), [3187(*A3*) f.?] (d?).

Sampson. *See* Awdely.

Sanderson (Saunderson), Henry.
Bookseller in London, 1560–1571. Apparently not a member of the Stat. Co. [*Dict. 1*.]
dw. in Paul's Churchyard at the Red Ball (Baule (?A.2)), 1560 (4380.5)
shop near to the little North door of Paul's (A.1), 1567 (484, colophon)–1570 (484.5, reissue but address presumable still valid)
in the Burse [Royal Exchange] at the Three Crowns Imperial (O.8), 1571 (485)
1560: 4380.5 f. **1565:** 20188.3 f. (d). **1567:** 484 f. **1570:** 484.5 f. **1571:** 485 f.

Sanderson, William.
Merchant and patron in London, fl. 1571–1603 at least. [Hind I.168–73.]
No address used.
1592: 18003.3 sumpt., [18003.4(*A3*) f.]. **1603:** 18003.5(*A3*) sumpt.

Saunders, Thomas.
Bookseller in London, 1612–1614 (cf. DFM 2309). [*Dict. 1*; DFM 2021.]
shop in Holborn at the $ Mermaid (V.1), 1613 (17352)
1612: 23127 sold. **1613:** 17352 f.

Scarlet, Peter.
Bookseller in Cambridge, 1590–1640. He lived in the parish of Great St. Mary's. [*Dict. 1*.]
No address used.
1640: 15245 ven.

Scarlet, Philip, *pseud.?*
'Bookseller' in London? or Cambridge? 1597. Possibly = **Cuthbert Burby**, to whom the following item, on the Harvey side of the Harvey-Nash controversy, was entered. On the other hand, there were several Cambridge booksellers named Scarlet; although no Philip is known to have been active at this date, he may be a genuine person (if so, possibly the man following below), or the name may have been chosen to emphasize the Cambridge connection of the text. [*Dict. 1*.]
1597: 12906(*A3*) f.

Scarlet, Philip.
Bookseller in Cambridge, 1605–1634. Son? of an earlier Philip Scarlet in Cambridge who issued no imprints. He lived in the parish of Great St. Mary's. *See* also the pseudonymous Philip Scarlet immediately above. [*Dict. 1.*]
No address used.
1634: 21460 sold.

Scarlet, Thomas.
Printer in London, (1586) 1590–1596†. If the widow mentioned in the SR margin (Arber II.603) is his rather than Robert Bourne's, Scarlet was dead by 27 Aug. 1596. [*Dict. 1.*]
dw. at the Green Dragon in Addle (Adling) Street (H.1), 1590 (11268); no later address or use of this one noted.
1590: 355, 3361.3 ?ent., 10004, 11267.5 chez, 11268 (d), [12804 (*A*3)], [13126?], 19183 ent.
1590/91: 11209, 11210.
1591: 334, 3907.5, 3907.7, 5349, 11282.5 (d), [11727], 12241, 12271, 13142.5 (d), [13828], 18286.5, [18422.5(*A*3)], [19183(*A*3)], [19532] (d), [22657], 22662, 22662.5, 22688, 22689, 22690, 22691, [25735 (*A*3)], 25764.
1592: [10842.3] (d?), 12280, 12283, 12283.5, [13133], 15511, 17083, [17206?], 22692, 22697, [22717], [22718?], 22783.7, 25764a.
1593: [662], 1182 ent., [1352(*A*)], 5891, [11371], [13588], 22697.5.
1594: [796], 17084, 18380, 18381, [21788], 22698–8.5, 22699.
1595: [5197], [6225], 15562, 15563, [15564], [20190?] (c), [21788].
1596: 195, 6350 (note), [7501], [15028], [15565], [16662a–b], [18604], 19161(*A*3) ass'd, 20585.7, [22779?] (false?).

Schellem, John, *pseud.*
Printer in 'Utrecht', 1626. = Unidentified printer, probably in London. [*Dict. 1*; Gruys.]
1626: 22085.

Schenck, Johannes, *pseud.*
Printer in 'Edinburgh', 1596. = Unidentified printer, probably in Germany. [*Dict. 1.*]
1596: 13555.7.

Schilders, Abraham, *pseud.*
Printer in 'Middelburg', 1620. = Unidentified printer in London, probably either W. Jones 3 or W. Stansby. Other items possibly from the same press are noted at STC 10814. [Gruys.]
1620: 11351, 11351.3, 11356.

Schilders (Grapheus, Painter), Richard.
Low-Country refugee, journeyman printer in London, 1568–1579, and printer in Middelburg, 1580–1618 (1634†). In 1571 he lived in the parish of St. Michael's Bassishaw (H.10) and in 1576 in the parish of St. Martin's Ludgate, Farringdon Without (Q.4). In 1575 he was working in the house of **Thomas Vautrollier** in the Blackfriars. [*Dict. 1*; Gruys; Briels 435–8; *TBS* 11 (1909–11): 65–134.]
No London address used.
1575: 20051.5(*A*3).
1578: 10674 typis.
1579: 10673–3.5 typis, 10674.3 typis, 10674.7 typis, 17445 (note).
1581: [11888?].
1582: 3910–0.3.
1583: [12861], [12862.5].
1584: [10765.5], [10766], [10766.3], [10766.5], 19356.
1586: [10772], 16568.
1587: [2018(*A*3)] (d?), 2769, 5377, [7584] (d), [10771], 16569.
1588: 331 (d?), [7585], [10767] (d), [10768] (d?), 10768.5 (d?), 10778, [24183].
1589: [10872.5] (d).
1590: [4803.3(*A*)?], [6676] (d?), [6680.5], [6680.7] (d?), [6682.5] (d?), [6730], [6730.5] (d), [6732] (d), [6733] (false), 10776–7, [18106] (d?).
1592: [1521(*A*3)] (d).
1593: [10400] (d?).
1594: 2770, 16584, [24055(*A*3)], [24055.5(*A*3)].
1596: 2701, [4706].
1597: [3845.5] (d?), 3862, 3862a, 4387a, [17819].
1598: [149], [14340].
1599: 2499.9, [6282], [6287], [10872.5] (d/error), [13721], 14335, 16587, [20616], [24273].
1600: [14333], [18070], [18070.5], 20617.

Schilders, R. — *cont.*
1601: [20557], 25330.
1602: 2507.5, 10765, 16570, 16589, [18542], [18542.5], 18891.
1603: [3855].
1604: [3528], [3843], [3856], [3892], [3892.5], [5343], [14052], [14338], [23318].
1605: [3531], [4585], [5338], [6572.5].
1606: [63], [14037], [16450].
1607: [19294], [22877.3].
1608: [22876].
1609: [3858], [3872?], [3889.3] (d?), [14339], [19607?], [22875], [22877].
1610: [3877.3?] (d?), [3884], 11134, [11915], 13031.2, [16451].
1611: [3847] (d?), [3882].
1612: [14332].
1613: [14328].
1614: 11146, 11150.
1615: [4803.5(*A*)].
1616: 11131, 11136.

Schinckel, Bruyn Harmansz.
Printer in Delft, 1588–1625†. [Gruys; Briels 441–2.]
1598: 1431.16 ex off. **1605:** 1431.18 ex off. **1613:** 1431.22 ex off.

Schirat, Michael.
Printer in Frankfurt am Main, 1559–1561, and in Heidelberg, 1563–1578. [Benzing 123, 195; *Library* 2 (1948): 284–6.]
1574: [24184], [25442]. **1575:** [4714], [25443].

Schoeffer, Peter 2.
Printer in Mainz c. 1512–c. 1520, in Worms 1518–1529, in Strassburg 1529–1539, and in Venice 1541–1542 (1547†). [Duff, *Century*; Benzing 315, 443, 510; Borsa.]
1526: [2824?] (d?), [24438] (d).

Schoolmaster-Printer.
Printer in St. Albans, 1479–1486. Nameless, he is described as 'one sometime schoolmaster of St. Albans' in the colophon of de Worde's 1497 reprint of the *St. Albans Chronicle* (9996). Only the town is occasionally given in his own colophons. [Duff, *Provincial*: 34–42.]
1479: [6289] (d). **1480:** [268], [24190]. **1481:** [2993], [14621]. **1483:** [582] (d). **1485:** [9995] (d). **1486:** [3308] (d).

Schott, Johann.
Printer in Strassburg, 1500–1548†. [Duff, *Century*; Benzing 439.]
1527: [24223.3] (d). **1528:** [1462.7] (d).

Schramm, Nikolaus.
Printer in Neustadt an der Haardt, 1603–1609† and also in Mannheim, 1608–1609. [Benzing 321, 347.]
1603: 26121a typis. **1608:** 26121a.3 typis.

Scolar, John.
Printer in Oxford, 1517–1518, and in Abingdon, 1528. [Duff, *Century.*]
Oxford, dw. in St. John the Baptist's lane (viculo), 1518, 7 June (4123)
Abingdon, in the [Benedictine] Abbey (monasterio), 1528, 12 Sept. (15792)
1517: [4122], [18833] (d?).
1517/18: [470.4].
1518: 4123 per, 5607 per, 6458 per, [23196.4] (d?), 25460 per.
1528: 15792 per.

Scoloker, Anthony.
Printer in Ipswich, 1548, and in London, 1548–c. 1550. During his London period he often published jointly with **William Seres 1**. *See* also *successor of* **A. Scoloker**. [Duff, *Century.*]
Following are six items which have no imprint except that the first is dated 1548; the others are queried for 1547: 3766(*A*3), 10430, 17627, 20795, 20972.7(*A*3), 24514. They share a common typeface, noted at 24514, not known to be one of Scoloker's, but four of them have woodcut initials which he did use later. For a forceful argument, though based solely on circumstantial evidence, that they were printed by Scoloker at Ipswich *see* Janet Ing Freeman in *TCBS* (forthcoming).
Ipswich, dw. in St. Nicholas's parish, 1548 (5199.7)

Scoloker, A. — *cont.*
London, dw. in St. Botolph's parish without Aldersgate (F.3), 1548 (13211); variation: omits 'in ... parish' (11384, with W. Seres)
London, dw. without Temple Bar in the Savoy rents (X.7), 1548 (24466)–c. 1550 (4626.3), both with W. Seres
1548: *Ipswich*: [3034.7(*A*)] (d?), 5199.7, 13210, 16992, 18765, 21537.5, 26136; *London*: 1278 (d?), [1292] (d?), [3760] (false, d?), [3761] (false, d?), 5200, 6806 (d), [7071?] (d?), 11384, 13211 (d?), 13212(*A*3) (d), 21537.7, 24466, 24781 (d).
1549: 3017 (d?), 3017.5 (d?), 18841 (d), 19905(*A*3) (d?), 20182 (d?), 24467 (d?), 24566 (d?).
1550: 4626.3 (c).

Scoloker, Anthony, *Successor of?*
Printer in London, 1554? The following item has no woodcut initials, but the type most closely resembles Scoloker's 81 mm. textura (Isaac II, fig. 94b).
1554: [7279.5?] (d?).

Scot, John, *of London. See* Skot.

Scot, John 1.
Printer in St. Andrews and in Edinburgh. Documentary evidence places him in Edinburgh in 1539, but it is not clear whether he was in the book trade at that time. Many of his items have no date and/or place of printing; those which have both are cited below; those without one or both may have them erroneously supplied. [Duff, *Century* 149.]
St. Andrews, 1552 [12731], 1555 (5458)
Edinburgh, 1562 [25860, 25861], 1567 (16578.5), 1568–69 (15658–8.5), 1571 (15659)
1552: [12731].
1554: [15672] (false, d).
1555: 5458.
1556: [15314].
1558: [14932], [17566.5?] (d).
1559: [12731.2] (d), [15675] (false, d).
1561: 22016.
1562: [25860], [25861].
1565: [2996.3(*A*)?].
1567: [2996.5] (d), 16578.5.
1568–69: 15658–8.5.
1571: 15659.

Scot, John 2.
Antiquarian in Cambridge, fl. 1622–1634.
his house near Great St. Mary's Church, 1633 (4489.7)
1622: 4484.5 f., 4485.5 pro, 19052.2 f., 19052.6 pro.
1633: 4489.7 f. & sold.
1634: 4485 f., 4485.3 f., 19052.4 f.

Scotto (Scotus), Giovanni Maria, *pseud.*
Printer in 'Naples, 1563'. = J. Wolfe, 1591. For the genuine Scotto, active in Rome 1552, and in Naples 1558–1566 *see* Borsa. Wolfe forged one of Scotto's publications of the latter city.
1563: 20118a ap.

Scribonius. *See* Wreittoun.

Seale. *See* Seile.

Searl. *See* Serle.

Secret Press. *See* English Secret Press.

Seely. *See* Seile.

Seile (Seale, Seely, Seyle), Henry.
Bookseller in London, (1617) 1619–1661†. He worked in and succeeded to the shop of his former master, **Laurence Lisle**. This shop was near the great North door of Paul's and was marked for removal, c. 1632 (*Library* 3 (1902): 267–8), but Seile was not one of those petitioning for relief in Jan. 1636 (Greg, *Companion*: 337–8). [*Dict. 2*; DFM 1087.]
at the Tiger's Head in Paul's Churchyard (A.2), 1619 (19843)–1636 (5907, has 'shop'); variation: 1623 (160, has 'dw.')

Seile, H. — *cont.*
at the Tiger's Head in Fleet Street, 1637 (5146.3)–1640 (1396)
— between the bridge and the conduit (W.4), 1637 (5908)
— over against St. Dunstan's Church (W.9), 1638 (11159), 1640 (23125)
1619: 19843 f.
1621: 25749 sold.
1622: 18913 sold, 25750 sold.
1623: 160 f., 5025 f., 10755 f. (d?), 19594 f., 25744a.8 f.
1624: 7305 ent.
1625: 1392 f.
1627: 10245.3 f.
1628: 1393 f., 10756 f., 10758 f., 25745 f., 25746 (note), 25746.7 (note), 25751 f.
1629: 971 f., 1394 f., 1694 f., 10758 f., 11163–3.3, 24058 f., 24294 sold.
1630: 599 f., 5467 f.
1631: 6529 f., 10759 f., 13272 f., 24697 f.
1632: 6456.8 imp., 13268 f., 20939 f. (d), 25746 f.
1633: 600 f., 5906 f., 7043 f., 7044 f., 10760 f., 12361 f., 13273 f., 13584 sold, 14269 f., 17639 f., 24699 f.
1634: 4294 f., 10760 f., 16848 f., 20348 f., 20349 f., 23447 f.
1635: 3396 f., 5145 imp., 5657 f., 10761 f., 15144 f., 20350 f., 22215a f., 24044 f., 24396.5 f., 26053 f.
1636: 1392.5 f., 5146 imp., 5907 f., 10761 f., 13274 f., 13275 f., 22391.6 sold.
1637: 5146.3 imp., 5908 f., 6097 f., 10178 f.
1638: 1839.5 f., 4575.3 f., 5904 f., 5905 imp., 10299 f., 10299.5 f., 11159 f., 14069 f., 14784 f., 18036 ent., 25746.5 f.
1639: 10147.2 f., 18035a.7(*A*3) prost., 19505 f., 25746.7 f.
1640: 601 f., 1396 f., 23125 f.
1641: 21589 ent.

Selden, John.
Jurist and polymath, b. 1584–1654†. [*DNB*.]
No address used.
1610: 22174 imp.

Seldenslach, Jacob.
Printer? in Antwerp, 1621, 1630. Possibly the man of this name working in Breda, 1630 (Gruys). [*Dict. 1*.]
1621: 2923.
1630: 2937.5.

Selman, Matthew.
Stationer in London, (1594) 1600–1627. [*Dict. 1*.]
in Fleet Street, 1600–1612
— next (at) the Inner Temple gate (W.11), 1600 (6381, with W. Ferbrand)–1601 (14733, omits 'in ... Street')
dw. — near Chancery Lane (W.10b), 1612 (19810)
1600: 6381 f. **1601:** 14733 f. **1612:** 19810 f.

Serafini, Francesco.
Printer in Loreto, 1634–1663. [Rhodes.]
1635: 23884a.4, 23884a.6, 23884a.8.

Seres, William 1.
Bookseller and printer? (from 1560?) in London, 1546?–1579?†. He died between 9 Dec. 1578 (Arber I.484) and 18 Jan. 1580 (*Reg. B*: 9–10). Except for one item in 1551 (21435.5) his imprints before 1553 are shared with others, especially **John Day 1** and **Anthony Scoloker**, though his address is separate from theirs; where imprints are lacking there is no clear evidence of Seres's involvement, and his name may sometimes be erroneously supplied in square brackets as partner. Although he may later have owned a printing house, the material in his Elizabethan books is not of a distinctive nature and, indeed, occasionally seems to belong to other printers, notably **Henry Denham**, who eventually became his principal assignee.
Seres was patentee for prose Psalters (*see* 2b in the headnote preceding 2370), Primers (16089, 16090, 20373, 20378), and books of private prayer in general. In some of the last he allowed others to have a life interest; *see* Appendix A below. The patent passed to his son, William 2, but beginning in 1578 it was always worked by the *assignee(s) of* **W. Seres**. His last shop was acquired or at least managed by **Gregory Seton** in 1578. [Duff, *Century*.]

Seres, William 1 — *cont.*
dw. in Ely rents in Holborn (V.5), 1548 (24781, with A. Scoloker)
dw. in Peter College [in Paul's Churchyard] (A.10), 1548 (15291)–1550, 28 June (14019); variation: adds 'toward Ludgate', 1549 (2077); all with J. Day 1.
dw. at the West side (end) of Paul's toward Ludgate at the Hedgehog (A.10), 1551 (20827)–1576 (5111, colophon, omits 'toward Ludgate')
1501: 20380(*A*3, note) (d/error).
1546: [10884?] (d).
1547: [13089?] (d).
1548: 1278 (d?), [1292] (d?), 1544 (d), 2853, 3258.5 (d?), [3760] (false, d?), [3761] (false, d?), 3815, 3816, [4411?] (d?), 4412 (d?), 5200 f., 6082 (d), 6083 [f.?] (d), 6806 (d), 11384, [13052] (d?), 13212(*A*3) (d), 13214 (d), 15178 (d), 15291 (d), 15292a (d), 15461, 15683 (d?), 16822 (d?), 17630 (d?), 18575 (d?), 19463 (d?), 20499, 21537.7, 23004 [f.], 23004.5 [f.], [24163(*A*3)] (d), 24359 [f.] (d), 24361.5 [f.] (d?), 24362 [f.] (d?), 24441a (d), 24466, 24781 (d), 24784 [f.] (d?).
1549: 1712 (d?), 2077 [f.], 2087.2, 2087.5, 2760 f. (d?), 4436 (d), 4463 (d), [5058?] (d), 5109 (d), 5109.5 (d), 12887.3 (d), 12887.7 (d?), [14554.5?] (d?), [15109.3–.7], 15270.5 (d), 15270.7 (d), 15272 (d), 15272.5 (d), 15274 [f.] (d), 15274.3 (d), 15274.7 (d), 20500, 20500.5, 24467 (d?).
1549/50: 483.13(*A*), 507.15.
1550: 84, 1298 [f.] (c), 1709 (d), 1721, 1721.5, 1733 (d?), 2087.3, 2087.4, 2087.6 [f.], 3603, 4626.3 (c), 13763 (d), 13764 (d?), 14019, 14824, 15543, 15543.5, 15543a, 15547, 15549, 26143 [f.].
1551: 9525 [f.], 18767 (d?), 20827 f., 21435.5 (d).
1553: 2728 [f.], 2983.8 (d?), 2984–5 f., 19493 f., 20373 ex off., [20373.5] (d?), 20374 ex off. (d).
1555: 634 f. (d?), 646 [f.], 25196 [f.] (d?).
1556: 7667 [f.].
1557: 22135.
1558: 25196.5 [f.] (d?).
1559: 3007 f., 4826 f. (d), 15217.5, 16087, 16293 (note), [16454.5?] (d).
1560: 4462 (d?), 10133.5, 16089 ex off., [16090?] (c?), 19926–6.7, 20375 ex off.
1561: 3158 (d?), 4778, [4844.7?], 12132, 17863.7(*A*3), 19930, 20063.5.
1562: 2384.5 in off., [4813.4?] (d), 5042 (d), 6795.8, 12507, [16852], 19175, 19176, 19927.
1563: 2384.5 in off., 18815, 19931.
1563/64: 16704.7 (d).
1564: 13031.5 ent., 20378.
1565: 2384.7, 3152, 4335, 12598 (d?), 12897 in typ., [16091] (c), 16508 (d), 16509, 18955, 20377.3(*A*3, note).
1566: 3152, 4063, 6130 (d?), 10867 ent., 14726, 16092, 20376 (d?).
1567: 2386 in off. (d?), 2386.2 in off., 2386.4, 2386.6, 3493.5 (d), 4434 [f.?], 12596 ap., 12596.7 ap., 13520 ap., 18956.
1568: 1924 ap., 2386.6, 5036 (d), 20377 ex off., 20379, 24360.
1569: 2386.8, 5110, 12049, 12890 [f.], 21690, 22234, 24671.
1570: 262 (d?), 2386.8, 3153 (c), 4346 per, 11488 (d), 20377.3 ass'd by (c), [20377.5 ass'd by] (c).
1571: 2387.3, 2387.7, 10250 [f.?] (d), 10375 [f.?], 13482 [f.].
1572: 85a (c), 10267.5 [f.?] (d?), 10797 [f.], 10867 (d?).
1573: 20380–1.
1574: [2390.5], 3161 (d), 20381, 23640, 25197.
1575: 14799 [f.] (d/repeat), 16092, 18957, 22378 (d).
1576: 2394, 4561, 5111, 10155 [f.], 12597 ap.
1577: 10155.3 [f.], 10251 [f.].
1578: 2351.7 (note), 10376 [f.?] (d?).
1579: 14799 [f.].

Seres, William, *Assignee(s) of.*
Partners, 1578–1603, in the patent of **William Seres 1** and his son, William 2, for printing the prose Psalter, Primers, and books of private prayer. At first William 1 apparently contracted with **Henry Denham** to work the patent, and printing generally stayed with Denham and his successors. The rights eventually passed to the **English Stock** *see* Stationers' Company; *see* also Appendix D/98, 100, 106, 111–12, 119–20, and E/9–10.
Imprints below state 'assignee' except as noted.
1578: 2396.
1579: 2397 (d), 11037.3, 17790.5, 21235.
1580: 1411, 2360, 2397.3, 3154, 12582.4, [20377.7] (c?), 21677,

Seres, W., *Assignee(s) of* — *cont.*
23973, 24380, 24409.
1581: 944, 2397.7, 11041, 25197.5.
1582: 1893, 1894 f. ass'ns, 11048, 22136.
1583: 2399 ass'ns
1585: 2399.5 ass'ns.
1587: 2399.7.
1589: 14011 f. ass'ns.
1590: 2035 f. ass'ns, 24383 f. ass'ns (d).
1591: 4562 f. ass'ns.
1592: 2400.5 by ass'ns, 12597.5 propter assignatos, 13977.5 f. ass'ns, 23979 f. ass'ns.
1593: 4562 (note), 14012 f. ass'ns.
1596: 24409.5 by ass'ns.
1598: 2402.5.
1599: 2402.5 by ass'ns.
1601: 2403.3 f. ass'ns, 2505 f. ass'ns, 4562.3 by ass'ns, 14013.3 f. ass'ns.
1602: 13979.5 f. ass'ns, 24410.
1603: 2403.7 f. (d?), 2511–1.5 f. ass'ns.

Sergeant, F.
Bookseller in London, 1594, 1601. Not a member of the Stat. Co. but probably belonged to one of the crafts concerned with archery since both items he sold name the marks in Finsbury Field.
at the Swan in Grub Street (I.6), 1594 (Hazlitt, *Handbook*: 343, no. 16).
at the Friar in Grub Street (I.6), 1601 (1025.3)
1601: 1025.3 sold.

Sergier, Richard 1.
Stationer in London, (1578) 1579–1627†. Father of **Richard Sergier 2.** [*Dict. 1.*]
No address noted.
1579: 14034 f., 15037.5 f., 15038 f., 15040 f., 15046 f.
1580: 11240 imp., 11241 f.
1582: 6649.5 f., 24780 f.
1594: 22996 f., 22997 f.
1606: 23464 f.
1607: 22249 sold, 22249.3 f.
1608: 17781 ent., 20825 f., 24611 sold.
1609: [6500?] f.

Sergier, Richard 2.
Bookseller in London, 1637–1639, and in Dublin, 1640–1641. In partnership with **John Crooke**. [*Dict. 1*; DFM 2696; *Library* 25 (1945): 152–8.]
London, their shop at the Greyhound in Paul's Churchyard (B), 1637 (22800, with J. and A. Crooke 1)–1639 (4627, with J. Crooke)
Dublin, at the $ St. Austin in Castle Street, 1640 (14073; engr. tp has: next to the Castle gate, 1641; both tpp with J. Crooke)
1637: [5465(*A*3)] sold, [13319] sold, 22800 f.
1638: [3234(*A*3)] sold, [3254(*A*3)] sold, 12310b f., 12454 f., 12455 ?ent., 22454 sold, 22490 f.
1639: 4627 f., 5466 sold, 11064 ent., [21068] sold.
1640: 14073 sold, 14777 ent., 14779 ent., 14782.5 ent., 23299 f., 23307–7.5 f., 23310 f., 23313 f.

Serle (Searl), Richard.
Printer in London, 1563–1566. Freed as a Grocer by **Richard Grafton** in 1555. He acquired some of the printing material of **Rowland Hall**. [*Dict. 1.*]
dw. in Fleet Lane at the Half-Eagle and the Key (D.2), 1564 (192)–1566? (2009)
1563: 432.5 ent., 15676 ent., 20523 ent.
1564: 192(*A*3), 4376 ent.
1565: 2007 (d?), 2008 (d?), 20188.3 (d).
1565/66: 433.
1566: 2009 (d?), 18307.5 (d?).

Sermartelli, Bartolomeo, *pseud.*
Printer in 'Florence', 1600. = J. Windet. For the genuine Sermartelli, active in Florence 1563–1591 and apparently again 1601–1617 *see* Borsa and Rhodes. [*Dict. 1.*]
1600: 4954.

Sessa, Melchiorre.
Printer in Venice, 1505–1555, followed by his heirs to 1602. [Borsa.]
1541: 6832.7. **1548:** 6832.17.

1568: 6832.38 heirs. **1582:** 6832.52 ap. heirs.

Seton, Gregory.
Bookseller in London, (1574?) 1577–1612†. His earliest imprint was shared with **Thomas Woodcock** and sold at the latter's address: at the Black Bear in Paul's Churchyard (B). Seton's first shop had belonged to **William Seres**, and he may only have been manager of it until Seres's death. His second shop was apparently acquired from **John Day 1**. In 1590 (12914) Seton used the frivolous imprint: in Broad Street at the $ Packstaff, in combination with his device, McK. 261. His last imprint was shared with **Simon Waterson** and sold at the latter's address: in Paul's Churchyard at the Crown (A.5). [*Dict. 1.*]
at the Hedgehog at the West end of Paul's (A.10), 1578 (16987)–1581 (1591, substitutes 'in Paul's Churchyard' for 'at ... Paul's')
shop under Aldersgate (G.1), 1583 (6168)–1605 (24268)
1577: 13060 [f.].
1578: 16987 f.
1579: 21064.
1581: 1591 [f.], 21066 ass'd.
1582: 25997 f.
1583: 6168 f., 22857 f.
1584: 22858 f.
1586: 10179 f. (d), 25336 f.
1587: 7285 f., 7285.2 f.
1588: 1346 f., 1347 f.
1589: [3127 sold], [12914(*A*3) f.] (false, d), 22859 f.
1591: 21658 ent.
1594: 22860 f.
1595: 21658 f.
1596: 21658.5 f.
1600: 25282 f.
1601: 22861 f.
1603: 12061 ent.
1604: 19901 ent.
1605: 24268 f.
1608: 25280 f.

Seutin, George.
Printer in St. Omer, 1622–1635. [Lepreux I.130–1.]
1624: [632.5?].
1625: [14626?], [16906?].
1630: [21142], [21149.5] (d?), [24734?], 25779.3 (note), 25779.5 (note).
1631: [15523?], [21150.5].
1633: [17506.5?].

Sevestre, Pierre 2.
Printer in Paris, 1584–1616. [Renouard.]
1602: 7628 (d).

Sharlacker, Sharlakes. *See* Shorleyker.

Sharpe, Henry.
Bookbinder and bookseller in London, (1579), Northampton, c. 1589 (Marprelate tracts), and in Banbury, 1619. All his extant imprints and SR entries were of works shared with **Thomas Man 1**. His 1607 item has no address or place, and he may have been in London at that time. He assigned his rights to Man in 1620 (*C-B C*: 130–1). [*Dict. 1*, listed as two men.]
dw. in Banbury, 1619 (25305a)
1607: 6957 f.
1608: 6951 ent., 6963 ent.
1609: 6940 ent.
1610: 4707.5 ent.
1618: 12848 ent., 25308(*A*3) ent.
1619: 12827.3 f., 25305 ent., 25305a f., 25309.3 f.

Shaw, George.
Bookseller and journeyman printer in London, (1586) 1595–1598 (1610†). In 1597 (1311) he printed one item in partnership with **Ralph Blower**, and at least some of the factotums subsequently passed to Blower. [*Dict. 1*; *Loan Book*, 1601–04; *Poor Book*, 1608–10, widow thereafter.]
No address noted.
1595: 18289 f. (d).
1597: 1311, 3126, [21489(*A*3)].
1598: 1485, 19153, 24620 ap.

Shaw, James.
Bookseller in London, 1601–1603. [*Dict. 1.*]
shop near (nigh) Ludgate (Q.3), 1603 (13848, 18856, 23866)
1602: 5795 f., 6457 ent., 23865 [f.].
1603: 3667 f., 13848 f., 18856 f., 21659 f., 23866 f.

Shaw, John.
Inventor of improvements to the soil and author, fl. 1636–1638. It is not clear whether the London address below was temporarily Shaw's or only that of his agent. Shaw lived in Kent, at the first house in Butt Lane near to the upper style in Bromfield at lower Deptford, 1638 (22391.4, note).
at the Three Fleurs-de-lis in Fleet Street over against St. Bride's Lane end (W.4), 1637 (22391.3)
1637: [22391.3?] sold.

Sheares, William.
Bookseller in London, (1623) 1625–1662†. In 1632 and 1634–35 he had two shops simultaneously. [*Dict. 2*; DFM 593; *Loan Book*, 1630–33.]
shop at the Buck in the New Exchange [= Britain's Burse] (X.10), 1625 (24909, PN^2 copy)
shop at the Buck near Gray's Inn (V.10) 1627 (19850)
at the South door of Paul's (A.8), 1630 (23587)–1632 (22286, has 'shop' and 'great' South)
in Chancery Lane near Serjeants' Inn (W.10c), 1632 (22286)–1633 (17400, has 'shop')
at the Harrow in Britain's Burse (X.10), 1633 (6414; 25582 has 'their shop', with H. Perry)–1636 (32); sometimes omits the sign, e.g. in 1636 (16997, has 'shop')
shop near York House (X.12), 1634 (7321)–1635 (17357, bk. 2 tp adds 'in the Strand')
shop in Bedford Street over against (near) the New Exchange [= Britain's Burse] (X.11), 1638 (7512)–1639 (3930, after 'Street' adds 'in Covent Garden')
1625: 19850 ent., 24909 f.
1627: 19850 f.
1629: 23507.5 f., 23588 f.
1630: 11326 pro, 23587 f.
1631: 11083 f., 19851 f.
1632: 3929 f., 22286 sold.
1633: 6414 f., 11327 pro, 12416 f., 16917 sold, 17400 f., 17471–2 f., 21421 f., 25582–2a f.
1634: 31 f., 7029 sold, 7321 sold, 17141 sold, 21480 f., 21731–2 f.
1635: 31.5 f., 7030 sold, 15100 f., 16889 sold, 17357 f., 19852 f., 21330 imp.
1636: 32 sold, 32.5 f., 16997 f., 18003.1 f., 24510 sold, 24511 f. (d).
1637: 5901 f., 5902 f., 7511.2 sold, 23586 f.
1638: 7512 sold.
1639: 3930 f., 7511.5 f., 10018–8.2 f., 12457 sold, 12997a.5 f., 18098 sold.
1640: 15462 f., 15462.3 f.

Shefelde. *See* Sheffield.

Sheffard, William.
Bookseller in London, (1619) 1621–1629?†. His 1621 items were sold in the shops of his former master, **Nathaniel Newbery**: at the Star under St. Peter's Church in Cornhill and in Pope's Head Alley. Sheffard began in business near the latter. His shop ultimately passed to **Henry Overton**, a former apprentice who married Sheffard's widow. [*Dict. 1*; DFM 2027.]
Pope's Head Alley (O.11), 1622–1628
shop —, 1622 (5664)
shop at the entering (entrance) in of — out of Lombard Street, 1622 (17226)–1628 (1631)
shop — going into Lombard Street, 1626 (17391.5)
1621: 1788 f., 11675 f., 23860 f., 24893 f.
1622: 1788.5 f., 3782.5 sold, 4023 ent., 5664 sold, 5727 f., 6118.2 f., 11134 ent., 17226 f., 18507.49 f., —.50 f., —.53 f., —.57A f., —.63

Sheffard, W. — *cont.*
f., —.71A sold, —.77 f., —.78 f., —.79 f., —.84 f., —.88 f., —.89 f., —.91 f., —.94 f., —.95 f., 20669 f., 20675 f.
1623: 4890.3 f., 6113.5 f., 6114 f., 6115 f., 6118.3 f., 6118.4 f., 6579 f., 11128.3 f., 11306 f., 16686 f., 18507.97 f., —.99 f., —.101 f., —.103 f., —.108 f., —.110 f., —.111 f., —.112 f., —.117 ent., —.118 f., —.119 ent., —.120 f., —.123 f., —.125 f., —.127 f., —.128 f., —.131 f., 23009 f., 23288 f.
1624: 4236.2 f., 6115.5 f., 6118.5 f., 11657 f., 11983 f., 12573.3 f., 18507.139 f., —.140 f., —.144 f., —.151 f., 20672 f., 22150 f., 22877.2 sold, 23598 f., 24052 f.
1625: 4111 f., 4112 f., 4236.9 ent., 6116 f., 6118.6 f., 21230a sold, 22150a f., 23829 f.
1626: 794.5 ent. & note, 4264.5 f., 4734 f., 6110 f., 13928 f., 17391–1.5 f., 21129.5 sold.
1627: 4735 f., 6665.5 f., 6936 f., 12892 f., 21186.5 f., 21186.7 f., 22115.5 f., 22934.2 ent., 24956.5 f.
1628: 1631 f., 6947 f., 22116 f., 25038.5 f.

1630: 4236.3 ass'd, 4236.9 ass'd.

Sheffield (Shefelde), John.
Bookseller in London, 1550, 1561? Possibly the father of the John Sheffield indexed in Arber as bound to N. Bourman in 1556 and freed in 1567 (I.39, 345) and grandfather of the Nicholas Sheffield freed 16 Jan. 1604 (II.375). Maunsell (17669, pt. 1, p. 2) lists an issue? of St. Ambrose, 1561 (cf. 549), as printed for John Shefeld. [Duff, *Century*.]
dw. in Paul's Churchyard (B), 1550 (14638)
1550: 14638 f.

Sheldrake, John.
Journeyman printer? in London, (1584) 1590–1594. [*Dict. 1*.]
No address used.
1590: 7277 f., 24590 f. **1591:** 25613 ent. **1594:** 20851 ent.

Shelton, Thomas.
Stenographer and author in London, b. 1601–1650?†. [Carlton 29–46.]
[his] house in Cheapside over against Bow Church (N.6), 1630 (22404)–1635 (22404.2)
1630: 22404 sold. **1635:** 22404.2 sold (d).

Shepherd (Sheppard), Henry.
Bookseller in London, (1634) 1635–1658 (Wing R 377). [*Dict. 2*; DFM 1581.]
in Chancery Lane at the Bible (W.10b), 1635 (3567)–1640 (7334) at least; variation: adds 'between Serjeants' Inn and Fleet Street, near the King's Head Tavern', 1639 (11161)
1635: 3567 sold. **1636:** 13169 sold. **1637:** 17444 sold. **1638:** 1680 f., 13370 f., 17444a sold. **1639:** 11161 f., 25231 sold. **1640:** 7334 f.

Shepperd, John.
Bookseller in London, (1574) 1576–1580?†. He succeeded to the house of his former master, **Reyner Wolfe**. [*Dict. 1*.]
in Paul's Churchyard at the Brazen Serpent (A.3), 1576 (25979)–1577 (14927)
1576: 1532 f., 5201 f., 25974 [f.], 25979 f. **1577:** 14927 [f.].

Shorleyker (Sharlacker, Sharlakes), Richard.
Bookseller and printer in London, (1619) 1623–1633 (*C-B C*: 425). He succeeded to the shop of his former master, **Walter Dight**, and continued to print items which consisted mainly of woodcut illustrations or diagrams. The shop was in his widow's hands by sometime after Oct. 1636 (Greg, *Companion*: 259–60, in the italic additions). [*Dict. 1*; DFM 1191.]
in Shoe Lane at the Golden Falcon (W.6), 1623 (11211.5)–1632 (21821.4(*A3*), omits 'Golden')
1623: 11211.5. **1624:** [20113.5] (d?), 21826–6.2. **1630:** 776. **1632:** 21826.4(*A3*).

Short, Emma.
Printer in London, 1603–1604? Widow of **Peter Short**. Remarried **Humphrey Lownes 1**, to whom the establishment passed. [*Dict. 1*.]
dw. on Bread Street Hill near to the end of Old Fish Street at the Star (S.8), 1603 (6460.5, colophon; 23929, omits 'near ... Street')
1603: 2403.7 (d?), 2511.5, [5122?], 6460.5–61, 7092.5, 23929.
1604: 6461 (d?), 23484 (d?).

Short, James.
Printer in Oxford, 1618–1624. In partnership during that time with **John Lichfield** as one of the **Printers to the University** (*see* Oxford University). [*Dict. 1*.]
No address used.
1618: 640, 641 (forged), [642] (d), 4199, 10710.5, 19169, 21702, 22828.
1619: 1781, 1938, 2362.7, 5976, 10308, 11031, 17245, 19024, 20777.
1620: 37.3(*A3*), 6424, 7338, 11958–8.5, 11979–9.5, 14450, 20619 (note), 24406.
1621: 3806, 4159, 6586, 13276, 21782, 24038.
1622: 33, 4678, 5432, 11568, [13880(*A3*)] (d), [14037.5] (d), 14573, 19014, 19025.
1623: [643.5?] (d?), 5832, 11295, 11959, 19027.
1624: 4160, 10372.5, 11031.5, 11296–7, 12973, 19028, 19029.

Short, Peter.
Printer in London, (1589) 1590–1603†. Husband of **Elizabeth Short**. He succeeded to the printing material of **Henry Denham** and worked in partnership with **Richard Yardley** until 1593. [*Dict. 1*.]
dw. on Bread Street Hill at the Star (S.8), 1590 (6431, colophon, with R. Yardley)–1603 (19995); variations: after 'Hill' adds 'near the end of Old Fish Street', 1592 (24418); has 'dw. at the nether end of Bread Street at the Star' 1592 (23995, colophon, with R. Yardley)
1590: 2035, 6431, [24383] (d).
1591: 939, 951, 4562, 6328, 12582.8, 24419 ent.
1592: [1086], 1777 ap., 12597.5 per, 13977.5, 21672, 23979, 23995, 24418, [25117].
1593: 3155, 4562 (note), 12463, 12582.9, 14012, 16659, 24384 (d).
1594: 1765, 7086 (d), 11214.7 (d), 13130a, 15216, [15694.7], 16644.5, 18654, 18755, 19287, 19991–1.5, 19992, [22701], [22701.3], [22702], [22702.3], 22720, 22720.5, [22884], 22996, 22997, 23579 (d), 23667, 24582 en casa, 25118.
1595: 152, 312, 5066, 6244–4.3, 11623, [12462], 13119, 13973, [15694.7–95], 18428, 18895.5 (d), 19468.5, [19859], [19861.3], 19988, 21006, [22747.3] (d?), 23076, 24495, [24716.5].
1596: 11226, 12582.10, [19861.5], 19996, 23620, 23668, 23980, 24409.5.
1597: 944.5, 1766.3, 3156, 4731.5, 7091, 11226a, 13562, 13978, 17516, 17678, 18125, 18126, 18133, [19857], [19859a], [19861.7], [22314], [22993], 23621, 24385.
1598: 257, 4878, 6243.6, 7194, 10700, 11043, 14013, 14809 ent., 17834, [19856.7] (d?), 20601–1.5, 21661–1.5, [22279a] (d), 22280, 22346, 22747.5, 23363, 23996, 24419.
1599: 1423, 2402.5, 3064, 4555.5–56, 6261, 6404, 6460, 11579, 11799, 14478 (d?), 16910, 21661.5 (note), [22358], 22748, 24281, 24385.5.
1600: 945, 2403, 3702, 7092, 7488, 11883, 12582.11, 12582.12–.13, 13979, 14732, [14768], 16883.5, 17415, 17671–1a, 18429, 19977.7 (d?), 19993, 19993.5–.7, [23335(*A3*)] (d), 23980.5, 24281a.
1601: 2505, 4562.3, 14013.3, 14014, 14733, 19469, 19994, 19994.5, 21332, [23336(*A3*)] (d), [24636.3] (d?).
1602: 5353, 11044, 12002, [12243?], 12582.12, 12582.14, 13979.5, 14809, 14978 ent., 17305, 17306, 17307, 19978, 23981, 24282, 24410, 24537 ent.
1603: 2511, 5881, 7096, 12582.13–.14, [12988], 19978.5, 19995.

Shorter, Samuel.
Bookseller in London, 1594–1598. Not a member of the Stat. Co. Probably the Samuel 'Shorte' to whom the Draper, **John Wight**, bequeathed 40*s*. in unbound books in 1589 (Plomer, *Wills*: 29); he or another of his name was freed as a Draper in 1598. [*Dict. 1*.]
at the great North door of Paul's (A.2), 1594 (13118)–1598 (13695)
1594: 13118 sold. **1598:** 13695 sold (d).

Siberch (Lair von Siegburg), John.
German bookseller from c. 1514 and printer in Cambridge, 1520–1523? (1554†). His establishment was between the High Street (now Trinity Street) and the gatehouse of Gonville and Caius College at the King's Arms (Treptow, 22–3). [Duff, *Century*; Otto Treptow, *John Siberch*, tr. and abridged by Trevor Jones, ed. John Morris and Trevor Jones, Cambridge, 1970.]
No address used.
1520: 6044a.5 exp.

Siberch, J. — *cont.*
1521: [1242], 4082 per, 10496 per, 11536 per, [15601.5] (d?), 16896 per, 18324.5 per.
1521/22: 10898 per.
1522: 11719 per, [14077c.151] (d?), [—.152] (c).
1522/23: 389.7.
1523: [1383.5] (d?), [14077c.74] (c).

Silvius (Sylvius), Willem.
Printer and bookseller in Antwerp, 1558–1579, and in Leiden, 1579–1580†. [*Dict. 1*: 261; Rouzet; Briels 445–52.]
1565: 12759. **1566:** 13250.

Simmes (Sims, Symmes), Valentine.
Printer and bookseller in London, (1585) 1594–1623?†. In 1589 he helped to print some Marprelate tracts in Wolston, Warks. In 1594 he acquired the printing material of **William How** and printed one book (3011.5) as How's assignee. In 1598 **Simon Stafford** worked for him or borrowed material from him. After 1607 Simmes may have worked only as a journeyman, and in 1612 he was working for **Ralph Blower**. [*Dict. 1*; *Poor Book*, 1608, 1617, 1618–23; W. Craig Ferguson, *Valentine Simmes*, Charlottesville, 1968.]
dw. in Addle (Addling) Hill at the White Swan near Baynard's Castle (R.6), 1595 (4042, has erroneous 'Street' for 'Hill')–1605 (6457); variations: adds 'at the foot of' Addle Hill, 1600 (6523); omits 'near ... Castle', 1603? (20197.7(*A3*))
dw. in the Whitefriars near the Mulberry tree (W.7), 1610 (25765.5); it is not clear whether the Mulberry tree is a sign or an actual tree
1594: 709–9.5, 3011.5, 7086.5 (d?), 7206, [14605], 20996.7, 22860.
1595: 3012, 3314, 4042, 4101, 4102, [4946.8(*A3*)], [7299], [10418], 12161, [12287], [15638] (d), 22418 (d?), 22955, 22955.3 (d/repeat?), 22955.5, 22971, 23361, [25969] (c).
1596: 720, 1053, 1828, 1829, [4171], 4174.5, [5582], 7275 ?ent., 12162, [12774.7(*A3*)] (d), 14802, 15281, 17126.5, [17579], 19180, 19181.7, 20797, 22972 (d/repeat?), 22973, 23362, [26043.5] (false).
1597: 749, [3942], [6170.7], [6216], 10356, 15379, 17323, 17906, 18504.5, 22307, 22314, [22722], [22969] (d?), 23408.2 ex off., 23408.6, 24097.
1598: [1047] (d?), 3216, [3696 in shop of], 10253, 12099 (d), [16667], 18626a.3, 21311 (d), 22308, 22309, 23633a.7 (d), 24477.
1599: 4987, 12273, [16904?] (false), 17994, [18370], 22955.3 (note, d?), [23294], 24003, 25089, 25224, 26019.
1600: 3675, 3675.5, 3679, 4579.5(*A3*), 6523, 6798, 11578, 17885.5, 18249.5 (d), 18795, 20150, 21466, 21466.3, 22288–8a, 22304, [22419] (d?), 22972 (note, d?), 24152, 25225, 26100.
1601: 3012.3, 3679.5, 5336.5, [6236], 11578.5, [12226], 15379 ?ent., 18892.3–93, 18894, 19343, 20053, 20167, 22736, 24207.3(*A3*), 25220, 25226, 25765, 26039.
1602: 1556, 2771, [3088.5(*A3*)], 5347, [6237], [6336], 6373, [6467.5], 6468.5, [12254.5], 17621, 20151, [20155.5] (false), [22107(*A3*)], 24004, 26026.
1603: 2023.7, 2772, 3068, 5121 (d), [6258] (d), 6259 (d), 7085, 7539, 7605.3, 13592, 13848, 14376.5 (d), [14381(*A3*: ed. ii)], 15355, [16676], 18041, 20170, 20197.7(*A3*) (d?), 21466.5, 21466.7, 21467, 21467.5, [22275], 24905.7(*A3*), 25221.
1604: 94, 343, 3022.8, 3735, [5349.5] (d?), 6501, 6501.5, 12062.3, [14429.5], 14756, [17269], 17429, 17479 (d), 17480 (d), 17481 (d), 20889, 22282, 26040, [26043.3].
1605: [702.5], 1457, [1560], 1597 per (d?), 3057.7–58, [5595], 6071, 6457, 6502, [7216], [11575], 12582, 13857, 13857.5, 15448, 17135, 18288(*A3*), [20753] (d), 20753a (d), 21717, [22766], [24004.5](*A3*)] (c).
1606: [1455.5], 3012.7, 4165a.5, 4978, 5348, [6514], [10457–8], 12582, 13509, 14774, [20983], 25222.
1607: 344, 710, [4768], 5926.5–.7, 6785, 6930, 11842, [12255], [13317], 15535, 15540, 21461, 23669.
1610: 6524 ass'd, 24005 f., 25765.5.
1611: 5653 f., 14646, 15227–7.5, [24005.3(*A3*) f.] (d?), 25222.5 ass'd.
1612: 17844.
1619: 15338(*A3*) ass'd, 17844 ass'd, 24006 ass'd.

Simmons (Symmons), Matthew.
Bookseller and printer (from 1640) in London, (1632) 1634–1654†. Most items below were published with **Thomas Paine,** and Simmons became a partner in Paine's printing house in 1640. [*Dict. 2*; DFM 156; *St. Giles*, 1639–41; Morgan.]
his shop near Moorgate (H.12), 1634 (4177, with T. Paine)
shop at the Golden (Gilded) Lion in Duck Lane (E.5) 1635 (10645)–1636 (13242, omits 'shop')
[his] house in Barbican near the Red Cross (I.1), 1637 (13264)
in Goldsmiths' Alley in Red Cross Street (I.7), 1640 (6913.7, 22404.7)
1634: 4177 sold.
1635: 10420 sold, 10645 sold.
1636: 10421 sold, 13242 sold, 17449 sold.
1637: 13264 f.
1639: 13182 ent.
1640: 4130, 6913.7 f., 7421, 22404.7–.8 f.

Simon, Guillaume (William).
Bookseller in Antwerp, 1555–c. 1579. [Rouzet.]
1558: 16250 ap.

Simson, Frances.
Printer in London, 1601. Widow of **Gabriel Simson**. She successively remarried **Richard Read** and **George Eld**, to whom the printing material passed along with the house in Fleet Lane (D.2). [*Dict. 1*, under first husband.]
No address used.
1601: [5329], 22577.

Simson, Gabriel.
Bookseller and printer in London, (1583) 1585–1600†. Husband of **Frances Simson**. In partnership 1588–1596 with **William White**, another apprentice of **Richard** and **Joan Jugge**, to whose printing material—which had in the meantime apparently passed to **Richard Watkins**—the two partners succeeded, nominally by 1595 but possibly as early as 1588. After the partnership broke up, Simson retained the Jugge printing material. [*Dict. 1*.]
their house in Fleet Lane (D.2), 1591 (3888, with W. White)–1600 (14040.7, has 'dw. in'); variation: adds 'over against Seacoal Lane', 1597 (3.5)
1588: 3850 f. (d?), 3873 ent.
1590: [3851?] (d?), 3869 f., 5866 f.
1591: 3888 f., 3890–0.5 f.
1592: 5867 f., 5867.3 f. (forged).
1594: [3885?] (d).
1595: [3859] (d?), 3874.5, 12325.
1596: [2785], 5865–5.5, 5869, 14029 (d), 18073.
1597: 3.5, 2786, [17090(*A3*)], 19797.
1598: [4965(*A3*)], [18230(*A3*)], [19821.5(*A3*)] (d?), [21160(*A3*)], 23634.5.
1599: 3050.2, 10684, 12163.
1600: [3677?], 7147, [11491], 14040.7.

Singleton (Syngleton), Hugh.
Bookseller and intermittently printer? (from 1555?) in London 1547?–1553, in Wesel? 1553–1556? and again in London 1561–1593?†. His earliest Wesel books were apparently printed for him by **Joos Lambrecht**, under whom other items are listed which do not have Singleton's device. By 1555 he may have found a different printer or started printing for himself, in either case using a unique Schwabacher type which seems not to have been used by any German printer (letter from A. F. Johnson to W. A. Jackson 26 Aug. 1964) but which is found later in London; *see* especially the notes to 9981, 25258.3. Singleton was **Printer to the City of London**, 1584–1593. *See* also Appendices A/23, E/11. [Duff, *Century*.]
in Paul's Churchyard at the $ St. Augustine (B), 1548 (1472)–1550? (9980.5(*A3*))
in Thames Street at the Double Hood over against the Steelyard (Stiliard (S.11)), 1551/52 (427.7)–1553, 1 Aug. (20188)
'Rome, before the castle of Sant Angelo, at the $ St. Peter', 1553, Nov. [11587]–1554, July [15059.5]
'Strassburg', 1554, Aug. (13457)
dw. in Creed Lane at the Golden (Gilden) Tun (Q.2), 1574 (25250)–1585 (11239.5); sometimes adds 'near to Ludgate', 1579 (25258.5)
dw. in Smithfield at the Golden Tun (E.1), 1586? (19070.7)–1587? (16712)

Singleton, H. — *cont.*
shop at the North door in Christ's Hospital next unto the cloister, going to Smithfield (C.2), 1588 (18794, colophon)
1548: 1472 [f.] (d), 4312 [f.] (d?), 11235 per [f.], 16983(*A*3) [f.] (d?), 18787 sold (d?), 20847(*A*3) [f.] (d?), 21309.7(*A*3) [f.] (d?), [23553(*A*3) f.?] (d?).
1549: 11235.5 per [f.].
1550: 9980(*A*3) [f.] (d?), 9980.5(*A*3) [f.] (d?), 21690.6 sold (d?), 21690.8 sold (d?).
1551/52: 427.7.
1553: *Thames Street*: 2787.4 (d?), 13208 [f.] (d?), 14941 [f.] (d?), 20188 [f.]; '*Rome*': [1307 f.] (false), [4392 f.?] (false), [11587 f.] (false).
1554: '*Rome*': [15059.5 f.] (false); '*Strassburg*': [13457 f.] (false).
1555: [3480.5?] (d?), [9981?] (false, d), [17821?] (d?), [17822?] (d?), [18312–3?], [23619?], [24219?] (d?), [25249?] (d?), [25251–2?] (d?), [25256?] (d?).
1556: [2426.8?] (d?), [15066?] (d), [15074.6?] (d?), [18310?] (d?), [21777?].
1561: 674 ent., 25253 ent., 25258 f. (d?).
1566: 4863.5(*A*, note).
1574: 25250, 25253 (d?), 25258.3 (d?).
1576: 4798, 16620 (d).
1577: 16979.3, [26049.2] (d?).
1578: 2022, 5644, 25109.5(*A*).
1579: 2023, 2023.5, [4303.7], [16663?] (d), [19179] (d?), 20848, 23089, [23400], 25250.5, 25258.5 (d).
1581: 25110.
1582: 4799, 4962? f.
1583: 4962? f.
1584: 18616.
1585: 11239.5.
1586: 19070.5–.7 (d?).
1587: 11238 [f.] (d?), 16712 [f.] (d?), 16713 (d).
1588: 13209 f. (d?), 18794 f.
1589: 18617 f.
1590: 16763 (d?).
1592: 15454.5 (d), 18617.3 ass'n.
1593: 16713.5 (d), 16727.5 (repeat).

Skelton, Henry.
Stationer in London, (1620) 1623–1634. [*Dict. 1*; DFM 646; ?*Poor Book* (widow Ellen), 1637–38.]
shop a little within Aldgate (L.1), 1623 (15184)
in Little Britain (F.4), 1634 (6112)
1623: 15184 f. **1624:** 6111 ent. **1634:** 6112 f.

Skot, John, *of Scotland. See* Scot.

Skot, John.
Printer in London, 1521–1537 at least. So many of Skot's publications are undated or without his name in the colophon or survive only in fragments that dates supplied or queried below are especially doubtful. Some points noted in a limited review of selected items are: no 'sh' ligature into 1525? (7709.7); narrow 'sh' ligature with pointed bowl in 'h' (possibly three or more varieties, one of them cast low on the body), 1528 (12799)–1531 [23162]; fat 'sh' ligature with rounded bowl in 'h', 1535? (14553.7)–1537 (17545.5). The virgule is nearly vertical, 1521 (7270)–1535? (14553.7); it is angled about 45° and there are commas mixed in, 1536? (15707.5)–1537 (17545.5). [Duff, *Century*.]
without Newgate in St. Sepulchre's (Pulker's) parish (D.8), 1521, 17 May (7270)–1522, 29 Mar. (6896)
without Newgate in St. Sepulchre's parish, dw. in the Old Bailey (D.7), 1525? or after 1529? (7681, has narrow 'sh' ligature)
in Paul's Churchyard (B), 1525? (7709.7)–1529, 6 Apr. (18569)
without Bishopsgate in St. Botolph's parish, dw. at George Alley gate (K.2), 1530? (23150.5)
dw. in Foster Lane within St. Leonard's parish (G.3), 1535? (14553.7)–1537 (17545.5)
1521: [3288] (d?), 7270, 14866, 15580.5 per (d), [24242] (d?).
1522: [6895], 6896, 14324 (d?).
1525: 7681 (c?), 7709.7 (d?), 7713.7 (d?), 7726.7 (d?), [14077c.68] (c), [20896.5(*A*3)] (c?).
1528: 10606 (d?), [11691a.3] (d?), 12799, [12800], [23172] (d?).
1529: 18569, 23149 (d?), [23160.7] (d?), 23199 (d?).
1530: [6807] (d?), [14280.5] (c), [14324.5] (c), [17007a] (c?), 23150.5

Skot, J., *of London* — *cont.*
(d?), [23182.8] (d?).
1531: [12944] (d?), [23162].
1532: [10421.5] (d?).
1535: [10606.5] (d?), 14553.7 (d?).
1536: 198 (d?), 15707.5 (d?).
1537: [11489] (d?), 13175.4 (c?), 17545.5, 18570a (d?).

Slater (Slaughter), Thomas.
Bookseller in London, (1629) 1630–1653?†. His first book was sold at the shop of his former master, **Michael Sparke 1**: at the Blue Bible in Green Arbour (D.4). [*Dict. 2*; DFM 2439; *Loan Book*, 1641–44.]
shop in Blackfriars (Q.5), 1631 (4152; 15078 adds 'near the Church' [= St. Anne's])
dw. at the White Swan in Duck Lane (E.5), 1633 (15079.5, English tp)–1639 (20660, omits 'dw.' and 'White') at least
1630: 22796 f.
1631: 4152 f., 11202 ent., 15078 sumpt./f., 21645 sold.
1633: 3535 f., 15079.5 sumpt./f.
1634: 23124 f.
1635: 19350 f.
1636: 15077.3 sold, 20206? f. (d).
1637: 13358 sold, 20879 f.
1638: 905 f., 12766 ent., 13523 sold, 15077.5 sold, 20610 f., 20691 ven.
1639: 13216 f., 18384 sold, 20660 sold, 22477 sold.
1640: 15077.7 ent.

Smethwick, Francis.
Stationer in London, (1633) 1634–1642. Son of **John Smethwick**, in whose shop he worked. [*Dict. 2*; DFM 2395.]
'his' shop in St. Dunstan's Churchyard in Fleet Street under the dial (W.9), 1634 (16673.5, a variant of one of his father's imprints)
1634: 16673.5 f.

Smethwick (Smithick, Smythicke), John.
Bookseller in London, 1597–1641†. Father of **Francis Smethwick**. [*Dict. 1*; *Loan Book* (as Smythicke), 1603–06.]
shop in Fleet Street near the Temple gate (W.13), 1599 (23690)
shop within Temple Bar (W.13), 1600 (3679)
in St. Dunstan's Churchyard (W.9), 1602–1640 (22867) and until his death
shop — in Fleet Street, 1602 (3669), 1604 (23614), 1626 (7309a)
shop — under the dial, 1605 (25967), 1608 (7218), 1639 (6550)
1599: 23690 sold.
1600: 3666 ?ent., 3679 f., [6787.7 f.?] (d?).
1602: 3669 f., 3684 f., 23939 f.
1603: 3685 f., [6535] sold, [6535.3] sold (d?), [6535.5] sold (d?), 21496.5 f., 21497 f.
1604: 6788 (note), 12863 (note), 23614 f.
1605: 3691.2 f., 21635 ent., 25967 f.
1606: 3691.3 f.
1607: 3651 ent., 3687 f., 12255.5 ent., 19735.6 ent., 22295 ent., 22327 ent., 23669 ent.
1608: 7218 f., 15686.7 f.
1609: 3688 f., 3691.5 f., 12228 f., 16669 f., 22324 f., 22739 f., 22862 f.
1610: 7220 f., 12274 f., 15687(*A*3) f. (d?), 25222.5 f.
1611: 12229 f., 12255.5 f., 18296 f., 22277 f., 22740 f.
1612: 16670 f., 22863 f.
1613: 3691.7 f., 7080 f., 7221 f., 15687.3 f. (d?), 22741 f.
1615: 4792 sold, 15687.7 f. (c).
1616: 7221.5 f. (d?), 12230 f., 12256 f., 12275 f., 22742 f.
1618: 24698 f.
1619: 7222–3 f., 18993 f., 22743 f.
1620: 3689 f., 7223 f., 15688 f. (d?).
1621: 3670 f., 22864 f.
1622: 22325–5a f. (d).
1623: 16672 f., 22273 at charges of.
1624: 4139 f., 10458a f., 19886 f., 22744 [f.].
1625: 22278 f. (c), 24525.3(*A*3) sold (d?), 24558 f.
1626: 1149 ent., 3404 ent., 7309a f., 15689 f. (d?).
1628: 12231 f., 12974 (note), 15689.5 f. (d?), 22745 f.
1630: 7224 f., 11947.5 sold, 15690 f. (d?), 17756 f.
1631: 12258 f., [13047.5?] sold, 22169 prost., 22295 f., 22327 f.

Smethwick, J. — *cont.*
1632: 22274 f., 22274e f., 22746 f.
1633: 22865 f.
1634: 16673 f.
1635: 22866 f.
1636: 17379.5 f.
1637: 7225 f., 22279 f., 22326 f., 22747 f.
1639: 6550 sold, 12232 f.
1640: 15690.3 f. (c), 22867 f.

Smith (Smyth), Anthony.
Stationer in London, at least 1548–1560†. [Duff, *Century*.]
dw. in Paul's Churchyard (B), 1548 (2375)
1548: 2375 f. **1558:** 2375 ent., 25258 ent.

Smith, Francis.
Bookseller in London, (1632) 1633–1637?† (*C-B C*: 301). His first address, although called 'his' shop, is that of his former master, **Francis Grove**. His second shop was apparently acquired from **John Wright 2.** [*Dict. 1*; DFM 1480.]
shop on Snow Hill over against the Saracen's Head (D.9), 1634 (21524)
shop near Holborn conduit at the Sun (D.9), 1636 (18976.2)
1634: 21524 f. **1636:** 4941.5 ent., 18976 f., 18976.2 f.

Smith (Smythe), Henry.
Bookseller? or printer? in London, 1540–1546 (1550†). Son-in-law of **Robert Redman**. All but one (11193) of Smith's books appear to have been printed by **Nicholas Hill,** but it is not clear whether Hill had his own establishment before 1546 or whether he was only a manager for Smith. [Duff, *Century*.]
shop in Fleet Street between the two Temples (W.12), 1543? (10507)
dw. without Temple Bar in St. Clement's parish at the $ Trinity (X.1), 1543 (9929.3)–1546 (14117); sometimes omits sign, 1545 (19632, colophon) or omits 'in ... parish', 1545 (15732.7, colophon)
1543: 9906.3(*A*3) per [f.], 9913.5(*A*3) per [f.], 9929.3 [f.], 10507 sold (d?), 11193 ven. (d?).
1544: 9619 in aed. (d?), 9627 in aed. (d?), 9643 in aed. (d?), 9649 in aed. (d?), 9660 in aed. (d?), 9930.3 [f.] (d?), 9931.3 [f.] (d?), 9934.3 [f.] (d?), 9946.9(*A*) [f.] (d?), 9954.7 [f.] (d?), 9961.7 [f.] (d?).
1545: 820, 9633 in aed. (d?), 9638 in aed. (d?), 9653 in aed. (d?), 9665 in aed. (d?), 9932.5 in aed. (d?), 9933.5 in aed. (d?), 9946.3 (*A*) [f.] (d?), [10953 f.?] (d?), 14117 [f.], 15732.7, 18397 [f.], 19632 in aed.
1546: 3328 [f.], 7379 [f.] (d?), 7699 [f.] (d), 7718 [f.], 7733.3 in aed., 9293.6 [f.] (d?), 14117 [f.], 15586a per [f.].

Note: Stationers named **John Smith** are particularly subject to confusion. In addition to the two tentatively listed below, there were four others freed before 1641: in 1618 (DFM 644), 1620 (DFM 2428: son of William, the liveryman, and probably of Alice (cf. DFM 2401)), 1635 (DFM 1464), and 1640 (DFM 1182) besides one bound in 1640 and never freed (DFM 2204). It is not clear which of the earlier men is the one in the *Loan Book*, 1619–22, or the *Poor Book*, 1623–41 (widow Susan thereafter).

Smith, John 1.
Bookseller in London, (1597) 1604. He apparently died in 1609, when his only certain apprentice, **Robert Wilson** (DFM 837), was freed by **Robert Bolton**. [*Dict. 1*; *Poor Book*, 1608–09.]
shop at Paul's Chain near the Doctors' Commons (R.3), 1604 (98)
1604: 98 f.

Smith, John 2.
Bookseller in London, (1609?) 1613–1616? Probably the John Smith freed in 1609 by the widow of **Francis Coldock** and the one who bound apprentices in 1613 and 1616 (DFM 2413, 2406). The address below seems genuinely to be his, but since the first use is found only in MS. and the second is in an imprint forged at least in part, his activity is unusually perplexing. [DFM 1035?]
shop adjoining unto (under) St. Mildred's Church in the Poultry (O.1), 1613? (15111.5(*A*3 note), MS. alteration in L copy)–1615 (13427.5)
1613: 15111.5(*A*3, note) f. & sold. **1615:** 13427.5 f. (false?).

Smith, Peter.
Recusant printer in London, 1620–1624. First worked illegally under **William Stansby**. In 1623 a press of his was seized near Bunhill (I.9), where he was printing part of the item below. [*Dict. 1*; *C-B C*: 122, 137, 161, 169.]
1623: [10910.4].

Smith, Ralph.
Bookseller in London, (1639) 1640–1660. He started work in partnership with **John Bellamy**. [*Dict. 2*; DFM 883; *Loan Book*, 1645–48.]
their shop at the Three Golden Lions in Cornhill near the Royal Exchange (O.9), 1640 (23303)
1640: 232 ent., 21168 f., 21173 f., 23299 f., 23300 f., 23303 f., 23304 f., 23306 f., 23307–7.5 f., 23308 f., 23309 f., 23310 f., 23311 f., 23312 f., 23313 f., 24049 sold.

Smith (Smyth), Richard.
Bookseller in London, 1567–1597. Bound as a Draper in 1552 to John Petyt, probably the son or other kin of **Thomas Petyt**; freed in 1559 by another Draper, **John Wight**. Apparently still alive in 1611 (*C-B C*: 49). [*Dict. 1*; *Library* 3 (1948): 186–92; 12 (1957): 88.]
at the Corner Shop at the Northwest door of Paul's Church (A.10), 1571 (3181)–1575 (11637, omits 'at ... shop')
shop at the West door of Paul's Church (A.10), 1592 (629)–1597 (17348); sometimes omits 'shop', e.g. in 1596 (16909.5)
1567: 3180 f.
1571: 3181 f.
1573: 11635 f. (d).
1575: 3181.5 (c), 11636–7 f. (d).
1576: 11645 f.
1577: 186.5 [f.].
1587: [3182(*A*3) f.], [11638–9(*A*3) f.], [12403(*A*3) f.].
1592: 7 f., 629 f., 5637 f., 23867 f.
1593: 17346 f.
1594: 5638 f. (d?).
1595: 4985 f., [5638.3 f.?] (d?), 17347 f., 17385 f.
1596: 16909.5 f., 17347.5 f.
1597: 17348 f.

Smith, Robert. *See* Smyth.

Smith, Toby.
Bookseller in London, 1580–1583. [*Dict. 1*.]
dw. in Paul's Churchyard at the Crane (A.3), 1582 (24779)–1583 (24180.7)
1581: 18149 ent., 10844 f. (d), 10844.3 f. (d?), 11457 f., 18807 f., 25586 f.
1582: 18807.3 f., 24779 f.
1583: 5008, 17450.3 f. (d), 24180.7 f. (d), 24181 f.

Smithick. *See* Smethwick.

Smyth. *See* also Smith.

Smyth, Robert.
Bookseller and printer (from 1592) in Edinburgh, at least 1583–1602†. He was perhaps the man bound to H. Singleton in 1565 (Arber I.256). His first wife was the widow of **Thomas Bassandyne.** His printing material passed to **Thomas Finlason**. [*Dict. 1*; *Library* 14 (1959): 43–4.]
dw. at the Nether Bow, 1592 (21255, tp)–1602 (16586, pt. 2 tp); variation: in 1595 (21255, colophon, has 'his buith [shop]')
1592: 21255. **1595:** 21255. **1599:** 16586. **1600:** 2997. **1602:** 16586.

Snodham, G. or **L.** *See* Snowdon.

Snodham, *alias* **East, Thomas.**
Printer in London (bound in 1595 and freed as T. 'Susden' in 1602: Arber II.205, 732), 1603, 1609–1625†. Son-in-law of **Cuthbert Burby**. He printed in 1603 as a journeyman in the shop of his former master, **Thomas East**, and succeeded to the business toward the end of 1608 (*C-B C*: 36). Snodham occasionally printed music as one of the *assignees of* **W. Barley**. After his death the printing material passed briefly to **George Wood** and then to

Snodham, T. — *cont.*

Thomas Harper. *Dict. 1* gives the address as St. Botolph's [parish] without Aldersgate (F.3), apparently from Snodham's will, and he may have acquired the house of **Lucretia East**. [*Dict. 1.*]

No address noted.

1603: 14939, 15529, 21784.

1609: 439.21 (d?), 3025, 4702 ent., 4884.5, 5919.5, 5937.3, 10827, 10828, 11376.3(*A*3) ent., 14730 (d), 17156.7, [18853], [20757], 21204.5, 21333, [22953], 24966, 25300.5, 25319.5, 25619a.

1610: 439.23 (d?), 1266, 1958, [1992?] (c?), 3025.5 (d?), 4542 (d), [4777], 5928.5, [7099], [7100], 7462, 21289, 22174 typis, [23252] (c), 24303.7, 24424, [25619.3(*A*3) (d?).

1611: [2538.5], 3026, 3429, 4255, 5861, 5861.2, 5912, 5920, 5929, 7115, 11764, 12739, 17749, 18120 ent., 18132, 21264, 21838–9, 22107.5, [22235(*A*3], 23486, 23548, 23934.2, [24146], 24614.5, [24622–2.5].

1612: [697], [712], 1234, 1895–6, [4946.9], 4974, [5769], 5929.2, 5936, 6338, [6487], [6617], 7098 [by &] f., 7312, 10025, 11826, 12056, 12064, [12318], 12324, 14680 ent., 14755, 17251.5, [18494], 19484, 21207, 21213.1, 21390, [21390.5], 21471, [22932], [24147], 24416, [24578], 24615, 25158.

1613: 131a, 1046, [1602], [1964], 3691.7, 3831, [3914] (d), [4275], [4546], 4546.5 (d?), 4547 (d?), 4885, [4947], 4974, 4989, 5381, 5921–1.2, [6611], [6618], 7355, [11357], 11829, 11830, [12600], 12614, 13157, [13539–9a], 15588 f., 17355, [17360], 17476, [18285(*A*3)] (false, d), [18322], 18525, [18526.5], [18981.5], [19332–2.5], 19513–3.5, 19923 f., 20294, 20295, [20333], 21174, 21207.3, 21213.2, [21391], 21533, 21621, 23492, [23683.3], 25023, 25134, [26130].

1614: 110–0.5, 118, 376.7, 1919a, 3026.5, [3192], [4539], [4580.5], 5390, [5712], [5857], [5858], [5914] (d?), 5915, [6365], 6661.5, 6945.6, [10238], 11767.5, [11796], [12627], 13201, 13821, 14305a, [14512–2.3], 17336, 17356, [17692], [19201], [21520], [21772], [23659.7], [23792?], [24964], [25409], [25790], 25895, [25916], [25994].

1615: 1559.5, 1561, 4216, 4702 (d?), 5536, [5692], 6662, 7400, 11765, 14418.5 (note), 17356a, 17761, [18299], 19315, 20806.5, 21152, 21723, [22386], 23041.2, 23655, 24593, 25135, 25917, 25917.5, 25920, 25921.

1616: 3027, 3435.5, [3915] (d?), 3915.5, [4587.7] (d), 4766, 4767, [5780], 5943, 6625.8, 6662.3, 7395, 12175, 12176, 12177, 12179, 12182, [14420.3?], 14680, 17337, 17381.5, [19208.5], 20153, [20761.3], 22350, 22933, 23041.4, 23044, [23535], 23626.5, 24028, [24834] (d), 25918.

1617: [28], [2410.5], [2557], 4548 (d?), [5780], 7401.5, 7407, 7615.5, 18057–7a, [18300], [18301], 21213.4, 21491.7, [22974], 23115.5, [23536], 24600, 24616, [24839] (d?), 25035, 25142.

1618: 544 ent., 1587, 1635, 3950, 5538, 5923, 6024, 6104 ent., 7136 ent., 7463, 7465, 12755 ent., 12987 ent., 12997 ent., 13394a ent., 13397 ent., 13877.7 ent., 14294, 14891 ent., 17252, 17493 ent., 17601, 18641, 19107.5 ent., 20581, 20760, 22219 ent., 23116, 25036.

1619: 1314.5, 1440, 1969, 3028, 3949, 5923, 7138.5, 7464, 11284, 13379 [f.], 13611, 15557, 15600, 15601, [17239], 17555, 17586, 18120, 18803, 19453.7–54, 20115, 20367, 21207.7, 21213.5, 22933.3, [23537], 24624.

1620: [29], 1267 (c), 1267.3 (c), 1267.5 (c), 2741.5, 6583, 6587, 6662.7, 7307–8, 7336.5, 7402 (d?), 11122 (d), 14891, 15558, 17586, [18629], 19553, 21208, 21213.6, 21289.5 (c), [21822], [23659.9] (c), 24841.2–.4, 42841.6–.8, [25135.5] (d?).

1621: [134], 153, [2575], [2575.3], 3029, 5364, 6406.5, 6663, 12178, 14891, 16691, [16786.16] (d), 16859, [24842a] (d), 24912, 25923.

1622: 901, 4227, 4710.5, 5841, 6271, 6664, 7402.3 (d?), 11122.5, 13879, 13914, [16841], [18507.88?], 21209, 21213.7, 24099 [by &] f., 24643.5–44, 25911.

1623: 759 typis, 5909, 7318, 7332, 11124, 17338, 18280, 20003, 20154, 20678, 23920, 23923, 24177.

1624: 1314.7, 3221, 5534, [7006], 7138.7(*A*3), 7328, 7402.7 (d?), 7466, 11027, 18038, 18630, 19768.5 (note), 19924, 22123, 22219, [23039d.9] (d?), [23039e.4] (d), [24912.5], 25644, [25719] (d).

1625: [439.25] (d?), [1671], 3030.5, 3204.5, [3581.4?] (d?), 4575.7, [4849.3], 5029, 6407, [7021.3] (d), 11706.4, 12582.19, 12777, 15103, 15354, 15642, 16858, 17253, 21210, 21213.8, [23039e.5] (d), 23921.

1626: 5925 ass'd, 7137 ass'd, 19107.5 ass'd.

Snowdon (Snodham), George 1.

Printer in London, (1597) 1605–1606 and probably continued as a journeyman until 1630?†. A relative of **Lionel Snowdon**. He succeeded to the printing material of **John Harrison 3**, worked briefly in partnership with Lionel, and then turned the business over to **Nicholas Okes** in 1607. (George 2, freed in 1628 (DFM 1972) and probably also a relative, is very likely the man in the *Loan Book*, 1631–34, whose loan was repaid in 1632 following his death and whose widow ('Snodham') is in the *Poor Book*, 1633.) [*Dict. 1*; ?*Poor Book* (widow Mary 'Snodham', 1630); Blayney, *Origins*: 15–20.]

No address used.

1605: [2810b], 4617, 10256, [17584(*A*3)], 17688, [19706.7] (d), [20804.7(*A*3)], [21716].

1606: 3961, [5776–6.3], 5880, [6659], 11926.5, [19558.3], 19558.7, [23422–3].

1606/07: [483.5].

Snowdon (Snodham), Lionel.

Printer in London, (1604) 1605–1606, 1614–1616†. In the first period he was in partnership with his relative, **George Snowdon**; in the second, with **Ralph Blower** or at least working in the latter's establishment. [*Dict. 1*, also p. 250 'Snodham'; *Poor Book* (widow Anne), 1616–20; Blayney, *Origins*: 15–20.]

No address used.

1605: [2810b], [17584(*A*3)], 17688, [20804.7(*A*3)], [21716].

1606: 3961, [5776–6.3], 18162, 24071.

1606/07: [483.5].

1614: 840.5 ent.

1615: 21213.3, 25993.

1616: 14948, 21013, 21014.

Solempne, Anthony de.

Refugee from Antwerp and printer in Norwich, 1568–1572/73 (1584 at least). [Not in Duff, *Century*; *Library* 3 (1981): 15–32.]

in the parish of St. Andrew, 1570 (3835)–1572/73 [16510.5(*A*3), in MS.]

1566: 5600.5 (note). **1568:** 2741, 23557. **1569:** [5792]. **1570:** 401.6 ten huyse, 3835. **1572/73:** [16510.5(*A*3)].

Solme. *See* Emlos.

Soter, Johannes.

Printer in Cologne, 1518–1543†; also owner of a paper mill and possibly a printing house in Solingen, 1537–1543. Apparently collaborated with **Eucharius Cervicornus** in producing the Coverdale Bible. [Benzing 237, 420; *Library* 16 (1935): 280–9.]

1535: [2063?].

Soughton. *See* Stoughton.

Sparke (Sparkes, Wreichionen), Michael 1.

Bookseller in London, (1610) 1617–1653†. Father of **Michael Sparke 2**. Michael 1 was admitted to the Livery on 18 Dec. 1626, and since all entries in the SR after that date are to 'Mr. Sparke(s)', they have been credited to him. [*Dict. 2*; DFM 1204; Globe 220.]

dw. at the Blue Bible in Green Arbour [off the Little Old Bailey] (D.4), 1627 (10614)–1640 (14295, omits 'dw.') and until his death; sometimes omits sign, e.g. in 1638 (11550.4)

1617: 23583.5 (d).

1618: 6769.5 ent.

1619: 13030 ent.

1620: 6769.5 f., 17923.5 ent.

1621: 12391 f.

1622: 4160 ent., 7338 ent., 11959 ent.

1623: 23015.7 ent.

1624: 22790 f., 11509 ent.

1625: 62 f. (c), 20875 ent., 22790a f.

1626: 4633.5 f., 4635 f., 20102 pro, 22790b f., 24209.5 f.

1627: 630 f., 4137 f., 4137.3 f., 10614 f., 20473 f., 21412 sold, 22064 (note), 22790c f., 23015.7 f., [23018 f.?] (d), 24210 f.

1628: 652 f., 4140.4 f., [4147 f.] (false), [4147.5 f.], 4157 f., 4157.5 f., 5669 f., 5697 f., 7403 sold, 13048.5 ent., 13954 f., 17383 f., 18787.5 f., 21130 f., 21383 f., 23016 f., 23016.5 f., 24211 f.

1629: 3323 f., 4136 f., 4156 f., 4669 f., 6671 f., 7072.1 f., 15344 f., 17146 f., 17366 f., 18997 f., [20457 f.], 21231 sold, [21718(*A*3) f.], (false), 23016.5 f., 23016.7 f., 23017 f., 24212 f., 24926 f.

Sparke, Michael 1 — *cont.*
1630: 1021 f., 3234.5 ent., 4279 f., 6176 sold, 6666.4 f., 13449 f., 13450 f., 13451 f., 17367 f., 17383.5 f., 19192 sold, 19266 ent., 20278–8.5 f., [20458 f.], [20465 f.], [22796] sold, 23017 f., 23017.3 f., 24188 f., 24213 f., 24700 f., 24926a f., 24927 f.
1631: 1661–1.5 f., 3235 f., 3565–5.5 f., 4151 f., 6031 f., 6063 sold, 6344.5 f., 6666.7 f., 10635 f., 10866 imp., 10938 f., 14930 f., 15036–6a f., 15078 sumpt., 15078.5 f., 17368 f., 20272 f., 20280.3–.7 sold, 20281 f., 22790c.5 f., 23017.3 f., 24214 f., 24701 f., 24968 sold (d?).
1632: 900 sold, 3538–8.5 f., 14048 ent., 20221.5 f., 20221.7 f., 20222 f., 21719 f., 21720 f., 23517.5–18 f.
1633: 891 sold, 900.5 sold, 3236 f., 4673 f., 14692–2.5 f., 14793 sold, 15079 sumpt./f., 15458 f., 20222 f., 20236 f., 20464–4a f.
1634: 12334 sold, 20783 sold, 25096–7 sold.
1635: 1235.6 f., 6113 sold, [11221 f.], 12198 ent., 14723 f., 17369 f., 17824–4.5 f., 20281a.3 f., 21641 ent., 23017.5 f., 25097.5 sold, 25098 sold.
1636: 6345 f., 10576 f., 15251 sold, 18945 f., 20223 f., 21642(*A*3) ent., 24214.5 f., 25099 sold.
1637: 1432.5 f., 3237 f., 7165 sold, 10576 f., 15080 sumpt./f., 17825 f., 18945.5 f., 21721 f., 25100 sold.
1638: 1432(*A*3) ent., 10694(*A*3) ent., 11550.4 f., 18938(*A*3) ent., 20228(*A*3) ent., 20281a.7 f., 21722 f., 24969 ass'd, 25640 f., 25640.5 f.
1639: 1236 f., 15081–1.5 sumpt./f., 17826 f., 21384 (note), 25100.5 sold.
1640: 14295 f., 15048(*A*3) ent., 15081.5 sumpt.

Sparke, Michael 2.
Bookseller in London, 1631, 1636–1645†. Son of **Michael Sparke 1**. Not a member of the Stat. Co. Although he published and sold items at his father's address, Michael 2 owned no copyrights. Only imprints specifying 'junior' or the like are indexed below. [*Dict. 2*.]
at the Blue Bible in Green Arbour (D.4), 1631 (11202)–1640 (24049.3(*A*3))
1631: 11202 f.
1636: 13365.5 sold, 17369.5 f., 20875 f. (d), 23017.7 f.
1637: 21642 f.
1638: 6913.5 f., 10694 f., 17370 f., 21384 f.
1639: 1432 f., 5670.5 f., 18938 f., 18946 sold, 20228 f.
1640: 4008.5 sold, 15048–8a f., 17371 f., 18939 f., 18948 sold, 23017.6(*A*3) f., 24049.3(*A*3) sold.

Speed, Daniel.
Bookseller in London, (1614) 1616–1620. Son? or grandson? of **John Speed**. Although at the time of Daniel's binding in 1603 his father, John, is described as deceased (Arber II.272), in 1618 John, also called father, was present to give assurances concerning Daniel (*C-B C*: 100–1). [*Dict. 1*; DFM 546.]
shop in Paul's Churchyard at the Blazing Star (B), 1616 (23031)
shop under St. Mildred's Church in the Poultry (O.1), 1619 (21096)
1616: 23031 f. **1617:** 25836 sold. **1618–19:** 21096 f. **1620:** 13525 f.

Speed, John.
Merchant Taylor, cartographer, historian, and genealogist, b. 1552?–1629†. Father? or grandfather? of **Daniel Speed**. In 1603? he seems to have had access to a rolling press. [*DNB*; Hind I.322, II.163, 209.]
No address used.
1603: 23039g.3 (d?).

Speidell, John.
Mathematician and teacher, fl. 1600–1640? [*Dict. 1*; Taylor 195.]
[his] house in Coleman Street (H.4), 1609 (23060.5)
[his] house in the Fields [beyond Lincoln's Inn] between Prince's Street and the cockpit (X.5), 1616 (23061)–1617 (23062)
his dw. house in the Fields on the backside of Drury Lane, between Prince's Street and the new playhouse (X.5), 1619 (23063)–1625 (23064.3); both in title
in Queen's Street (X.5b), 1627 (23060)–1640? (23059.5); both in title
1609: 23060.5 sold. **1616–17:** 23061–2 sold. **1619–20:** 23063–3.3 sold. **1622–28:** 23063.5–4.9 sold.

Spencer, John.
Stationer in London, 1624–1680†. Brother of **Thomas Spencer**. Sub-librarian at Sion College, 1630–33 and Librarian, 1633–35 and 1640–80. Three early items were published jointly with **John Bartlet** and one of them (1415) sold at the latter's shop: at the Gilded Cup in Cheapside (N.5). [*Dict. 1*; DFM 947; Ernest H. Pearce, *Sion College and Library*, Cambridge, 1913: 232–7.]
shop on London Bridge (T.7), 1624 (16856)
beside the gate of Sion College [at this date opposite London Wall near Philip Lane] (H.16), 1635 (12417, A6ʳ preface)
1624: 1413 f., 1415 f., 1415.5 f., 16856 f.
1629: 24397 f.
1630: 11321 ent., 17889 ent., 21445 imp., 21446 sumpt., 25670 f.
1631: 24398 f.
1635: 1675? f., 1675a (forged), 3668? f., 12417–8 imp., 14760 f., 14760.5 f.
1638: 24399 f.
1639: 24331–1.5 f.
1640: 17889 f.

Spencer, Thomas.
Stationer in London, (1633) 1635–1648. Brother of **John Spencer**. [*Dict. 1*; DFM 2165; *Poor Book*, 1644–46, 1648.]
No address used.
1635: 12421 f. **1636:** 15099 f.

Spire (Spier), William 2.
Bookseller and bookbinder in Oxford, 1607–1636†. Son of William Spire 1, who produced no imprints; lived in St. Mary's parish. Obtained his freedom of the Stat. Co. in London by patrimony in 1616. [*Dict. 1*; DFM 2445, 2683.]
No address used.
1619: 1938 f.

Spooner, Hugh.
Stationer and bookbinder in London, (1573?) 1578–1586. [*Dict. 1*.]
dw. in Lombard Street at the Cradle (O.12), 1579 (16955)
1579: 16955 f. (d).

Spruyt, Franck van der.
Printer? in the Hague, 1640–1642. [Gruys.]
1640: 13264.7.

Stafford, Edward, *Duke of Buckingham.*
Patron in London, b. 1478–1521†. [*DNB*.]
1520: 13256 by commandment of (d?).

Stafford, John.
Printseller in London, c. 1631, and bookseller 1634–1664. Became a member of the Stat. Co. by redemption in 1637. [*Dict. 2*; DFM 2448; *Loan Book*, 1655–58.].
in Black Horse Alley (W.3), 1631–1640
— near Fleet Bridge, 1631 (23774, note)
dw. — near Fleet Street, 1634 (10723)–1640 (17920); variation: 1638 (20238, has 'his house')
in Chancery Lane over against the Rolls (W.10e), 1640 (20240.3)
1631: 5209.5 f., 23774 (note), 25907.5(*A*3) sold (c).
1634: 6443.5 sold, 6595 sold, 10720 sold, 10723 sold, 25706 sold.
1636: 10427 sold.
1637: 5209.5 ent., 24660 ent.
1638: 13739.5–.7 f., 20238 f.
1639: 13739.5–.7 f., 17919 f., 20224 f., 20239.5 f., 20318 ent.
1640: 11934 f., 17920 f., 20225 f., 20240 f., 20240.3 f.

Stafford, Simon.
Journeyman printer in Cambridge, c. 1591 (*TCBS* 3 (1959): 96–103) and active in London, 1596–1633?†, being a master printer 1599–1613. Freed as a Draper on 29 Aug. 1586 by **Christopher Barker**; transferred to the Stat. Co. in 1599. He testified that in January 1598 he had a printing house in Black Raven Alley (?L.3 or ?T.6), and from mid-March to at least the end of June that year he was living in Gracechurch Street ((R.6): Judge 123–4, 176–7); his one extant imprint of 1598 was produced in the house of **Valentine Simmes** or at least with material borrowed from Simmes. His printing material passed to **George Purslowe** in 1614. [*Dict. 1*; *Loan Book*, 1607–09; *Poor Book*, 1614–33, child thereafter; Judge 112–40, 160–81.]

Stafford, S. — *cont.*
dw. on Addle (Addling) Hill (R.1), 1599 (3502)–1601; adds 'near Carter Lane', 1600 (6134), 1601 (11879)
dw. in Hosier Lane near Smithfield (E.7), 1602 (20959.5)–1605 (12200.5)
dw. in the Cloth Fair (E.3), 1606–1609; variations: adds 'at the Three Crowns', 1606 (6988) or adds 'near the Red Lion', 1607 (14435.5), 1609 (17149)
dw. in Warwick Lane at the Bell (C.9), 1611 (1729.5); no later address or use of this one noted
1598: 3696.
1599: 3502, 3727, 7502, 12212, 12266, 22281.
1600: [5775], 6134, 6517, 6988 ent., [7064?], 10634.6 (d), 11119, [13121], [14750], 15437 per, 17395, 18376, 18642, 18944, [21291], 21591.5, 24610, 26097–7.5.
1601: 3054–4.5, [5774], 11879, 13499, [14071], [14766], [17082], 17556, [18417], [18871].
1602: 3699, 4317, 4615, 5593, 6749.8, [11438], 13049 ent., [13929], 15717.5 ent., 18548, 18583, [18972], 20959, 20959.5, [21455], 22752, 23865.
1603: 2743, 2744, 3115.3, 6165 ex off., 10626.5, 10648 ex off., 13626, 14379.3, 14675, 17770.7, [18017], 20169.
1604: 98, 584, 3115.5, 4132, 5222, 6202, 7592–3, 10175, 12872, 13388, 14356, 16627, [19451?].
1605: [772.5(*A*)], [1825(*A*)], 10176, 12200.5, 13527–7.5, 15343, 24072, 25232–2.5, 25238.5.
1606: [6514], [6522], 6988, 12940, [20112.5] (d), [21079].
1607: 1729, 14435.5, 16622, 18336, [18455], [18639].
1608: 3162, 13049, 23264, 24611.
1609: 6574, 12203, 17149, 18347.5, [18472a.5], [21607], [23434–4.5].
1610: 21847.
1611: 1729.5, 22235, 22336.
1612: 18014, 18014a, [24350?].
1613: 685.
1616: 15717.5 f.
1624: 26013.5 f.
1630: 23610 ass'd.

Stafford, Thomas.
Englishman and publisher in Amsterdam, 1640–1644 at least. [*Dict. 1.*]
sold at his house at the $ Flight of Brabant, upon the Milk Market over against the Deventer Wood Market, 1640 (2344)
1640: 2344 [f.], 2344.5 (repeat). **1644:** 2344.5 [f.] (d).

Stallenge, William.
Holder of a licence, granted 5 Jan. 1607, for publishing his own book on growing mulberry trees and silkworms (23138), he seems to have extended its application to another work on the same subject. [Greg, *Companion*: 153.]
No address used.
1607: 22249 with ass't of.

Stam, Jan Fredericksz.
Printer in Amsterdam, 1628–1664 (1667†). Married the *widow of* **Joris Veseler**. [*Dict. 1*; Gruys; *Library* 9 (1954): 185–93.]
1629: [2274] (false, c?), 2415–5.2, [15429] (d?).
1630: 16699, 20202.
1632: [3473].
1633: [903.5?], [904.5?], [2177] (false, d), 2309, [2499.4] (d), [18507.360?] (d), [—.361] (d).
1635: [1973.5], 1974, [3450], [4137.7] (d?), 18780, 18781, 19097, 22079.5(*A3*).
1636: [4134], [4137.9], [4140.7], [4142], [20456], [20476].
1637: [1569], 18202, [20454], [20475].
after 1637: [2328.5?] (false).
1639: [2179] (false, c), [2499.6] (c), 13031.8.
after 1640? [2328.7?] (false), [2174] (false), [2175] (false), [2176] (false), [2178] (false), [2499], [2499.2], [2499.3], [2499.5], [2692.5?] (false), 16414.3 (note).
1644: 2316.5 (note).
after 1645? [2328.8?] (false).
after 1650? [2330?] (false), [2680.1?] (false).

Standish, John 1.
Stationer in London, (1587) 1599–1613?† (cf. DFM 2449). [*Dict. 1.*]
No address used.
1599: 6351 f., 6355–5.2 f., 6355.4 f. **1602:** 6356 f. **1608:** 6357 f.

Standish, John 2.
Editor in London of metrical psalms, fl. 1631 (*C-B C*: 231–2)–1633.
dw. in Long Alley near to Christ Church (E.8), 1633 (2734, note)
1633: 2734 (note).

Stansby, William.
Printer and bookseller in London, 1597–1638† (*C-B C*: 315). Apprenticed to **John Windet** and probably worked for him as a journeyman until he acquired a share in the establishment in 1609; though in the latter year their imprints are separate, Stansby may have printed some of the items indexed under Windet with the name supplied in square brackets. Stansby succeeded to the establishment in 1610. In 1636 it passed to **Richard Bishop**. Mention of an address is exceptional. [*Dict. 1.*]
at Paul's Wharf at the Cross Keys (R.8), 1597 (24335, = Windet's house)
dw. in Thames Street by Paul's Wharf next to St. Peter's Church (R.8), 1620 (22214, colophon); no later address or use of this one noted
1597: 24335 f.
1609: 6777.4, 10561, 11366.5, 12288.5, 12694–4a, 24508.3 (d).
1610: [53], 877, [4637], [5118], 5768, [6945.2], [6965], 7048, [7220], 7322, 7333, 10562, [11123], [11795], [12274], [12567], [12649–9a], [13005a.5], [13161], [13933], [14736], 15687(*A3*) (d?), [17942], [18183], 18640, [24833], [24950].
1611: 54, 745, 1845, 3143 ent., 3568, 3777, [4705], [4980], 5807, 5808, 6375, 6585, 6591, 6906, [6945.4], [6966], [7022], [8470.5] (d), [8470.7] (d), [9226], [10221], 11099, 12229, [12255.5], 12663.4–.6, [13142], 13714, [13933a], [14759?], 15514.5, 16650.5, 16740 ent., 16743.7 ent., 17840, 20758, [22740?], 23200.5, 23201, 23201.5, [23548?], 24622–2.5, 25758 ent.
1612: 932.5, 4915, 4923, [4994], 5742, [9227–8], 10207.3, [10258], 11207, 11856, 12618, [15324], [16670], 17924, [18014], [18019], 19083a ap., [19458.5(*A3*)–.7], 19507, 20138, 21016–6a, 21024, [22397], 22863, 23203, [23350], [23545], [24027], [24852–2.3], [25084], 25163.
1613: 736 typis, 960 ap., 3149, 3749, [4545], [4566], 5107, 5583 (note), 5919, 5934, 7080, [7178], 7221, 10190.5, [10222], [11308], 13474, 14308–8.5, 14817, 15687.3 (d?), 17418, 17870, 20138, 20505, [20563], 22213, [22741], [22825], 23111, 24130, 24132, 24307, 25157, [25261.5], [25434?], 25659.5, [25872].
1614: 312.5, [3612], [3613], 4930–0.5, [12068], 14315, [14739.2], 15434, 18521, 18612, 20506, 20637, [20912], 22177, 22213.
1615: 312.5, 878, 1355, 1356, 3435, [3614], [3614.5], 4180.5, 4496 typis, 4792, 5045, 5805, 6069, 6845, 9237, 11599, 12358, 12526, 13475, 13540–0.5, 13841, 15687.7 (c), 17526–7, 18480, 18523, 18628, [18753], 19512, 19514, 22771, 22962, [24043], 24176, 25433.3.
1616: 345, 1657.5–58, 4099, [6488], 7221.5 (d?), 7244, [7472], 10639–9.3, [11254], [11941], 12230, 12256, 12275, 13475, 13716, 14751–2, 19059, 20748, [20914a], 21019, 23623, 24371, 25294, 25294.5 (d?).
1617: 3143, 5585, 5614, 7396, [10176.5], [11258], 12707, 13716, [16834], [17944], 17682, 19779, 20507, 20638, 21608, 22167, [22361], [22544a.3] (d?), [22544a.5] (d?), 23602 typis (d), 23827, 25985.
1618: 1438, [7245], [7410], 7610, [8581] (d), 13617, 13716, 22772, 23828, 24025, 24698, 25986.
1619: [635] (forged), [636] (forged), 3144, [3615.5], 7222–3, 10204.7, 11103 (d), 13384.3, [14708.8?] (false), [17887], [18180], 18606, 18782.5–83, 18993, 20503, 20614 imp., 21338, 21834–4a, 21858, 21858.5.
1620: [641] (forged, d?), [3205?], [3210?] (false), [3214?], [3215?] (false), 3689, 4164, [4916] (d?), 5583, [6480.5] (forged, c), 7148 (d?), 7223, [9175q: iii] (c), [10810?], [10814] (false, d?), 10940–0.3, 11162, [11349?], [11350?], [11351?] (false), [11351.3?] (false), [11356?] (false), 11700, 12518, 12674–4a, 13377.5 (d?), 13384.3, [14049], [14714.5], 14763–4, 15641, 15688 (d?), 17046 typis, 17681, 18783, [21538], 21859, 22214, 23412, [23544], 24070 typis, 24178.
1621: 731, 879, [1963], 2774, [3134.5] (d?), 3150, [3670], 4199.5 ap., [4704], [4749], [7353.8] (d), [8673] (d), [8673.5–74] (d), [9263.7] (d), 10585, 11104 (d?), 11895.5, 12684, 12708, 14760 ent., [15438], 15657, [16768.8] (d), [16777.6] (d?), [16778.2] (d), [20638a–39], 22634, 22830–0.5, 22864, [24034] (d), 24871 chez

Stansby, W. — *cont.*
(d), [25951.5] (d).
1622: 1159, 1160, 3150, [3833], 4484.5 ent., 4936, 7053–4, 7143, 10941, 10942, 13542, 13717, [13859.5], [14713.5] (false, d), [14714.5] (d?), [17600.3], 19052.2 ent., 19679, 21340–0a, [21717.5?] (forged, d?), [22325–5a] (d).
1623: 4494, 4936, 7438–8.2 typis & imp., 7527.5, [16695.5] (d?), 20502, 21344.
1623/24: [531.15?].
1624: [167], 341, [637], [887], 2782–3, 4139, [4567], 5396, [10738–8.3], 12648c per, 13455, 18039, 19886, [20795.5] (d), 21345, 22744, 23115, 24925–5a.
1625: 341a, 1000.5, [2590], 2776, 2783, 4934–4.3, [6017.5], 6770, 7025, 7148.3 (c?), 7533.5, 10570 per, 14038, 15083 ex off., [15657.5], 16740 (d), 16740.5 (d), 16741, 16741.7, [16743.8] (d), 16744, 20509, 22278 (c), 22775, 23353, 24525.3(***A***3, note), 24558, 24604, 25663, 25867.
1626: 439.27 ent., 806 ent., 880, [1067], 1993 ent., [2594], 4215, 4703 (d?), [5395], 5925 ent., 6104 ent., 6408 ent., 7137 ent., 10137.4(***A***), [11330.7] (false), 12755 ent., 12987 ent., 12997a ent., 13394 ent., 13394a ent., 13406 ent., 13615, 13616, 13619, 13877.7 ent., 14682 (d), 14730.5 (d?), 15689 (d?), 17253.5 ent., 17493 ent., 17835 ent., 18124 ent., 18964, 19107.5 ent., 19455 ent., 20508–8.5, [20521.2] (d), [20521.4] (d), 20521.6, 21290 ent., 21477, 22220 ent., 22466, 23051.5 (d?), [24609], 25850.5.
1626/27: [503.4?].
1627: [354], 4199.7 ap., 4218, 4228–8.5, 4496.5, 4695, [18507.193], [18973], 20392.5, [20779.5], 22547, 22831 per.
1628: 823 typis & imp., 1313.2(***A***), 4219, [5369–9.2], 7148.5 (c?), 7403, 7439–40, 7440.2, 7441, [8903], [11293], 12231, 12636 (note), 12690, [12690.5], [12692], 13377.7 (d?), 13384.5, 13954, 15134, 15689.5 (d?), [18545], 20521.8, 20615–5.5, 22547, [22648], 22745, 23052.
1629: [824], 1315, [4628], 10137.4c(***A***3), 10869, [12709.5], [12709a], [13504?], 15134.
1630: [342], 439.27 (c), 881, 1313.3, 1929, 1994 (c), [2620], [6058], 7224, 7404, [8949?] (d), [8953] (d), [8968] (d), 10137.5, 10885, 11947–7.5, 12677, [12691], [13362], 14443, 14731 (c), [18723], 19552, 21290 (c), [23570], 23571, 23572, [24623], 25236.
1631: 1316, [1319], [2625], 2626, 2630, 4180, 5925, 6063.9, 7419, 12258, 12688–8.5, 12966, 13718, 18124, 18189, [18929.5], 19524, 22169 typis, 22178, 22295, 22327.
1631/32: 419.1, 435.21, 522.12, 527.21, 531.23.
1632: 882, 1313.5, 2634, 3993 in off., 4165, 5569 (d?), 5925, 6067.7, 7420, 13718, 17088–9, 17253.5, 20124.5, 22746.
1632/33: 407.16, 527.23.
1633: 1317, 2641.5, 2644, 7137, 7405, 22831.3, 22865.
1633/34: 407.17, 527.24.
1634: 806, 2649, 7137, 7406, 10177, 13190–0.3, 13384.7, 17835.
1634/35: 407.18, 464.7, 479, 527.25.
1635: 1268 (c), 1318, 1593, 2418.5 (note), [3704.9], 6211, 6408 (d), 13377.9 (d?), 13719, 19780, 22175, 22866, 23053, 23550, 25758.
1635/36: 407.19.
1636: 13719, 14682.5 (d?), [17836], 22175.3 juxta exemplar, 22176 juxta exemplar.
1638: 7467 f.

1639: 1269 ass'd, 4936 ass'd, 6105 ass'd, 22214 ass'd.

Stationers' Company, London.
Company of booksellers, bookbinders, printers, and others connected with the stationers' crafts, granted a charter by Mary I in 1557 though a guild of stationers had been in existence from at least 1403. Became a liveried London company in 1560. Before 1603 mention in imprints of the Company (or Society) of Stationers is rare and usually anomalous.

In 1584 a number of copyrights were yielded to the Company, though many seem not to have attained a subsequent edition; *see* below and also Appendix C. Other rights which had lapsed also fell to the Company. Unfortunately, the record below of these last items is highly imperfect because the imprints give only the individual printer's name, and the usual form of citation in the SR (and occasionally in STC entries): 'Ent. to [X printer] to print one impression', did not often engender index slips under 'Stationers' Company'. Nevertheless, those few items that did receive slips have been indicated as 'allowed ent.', i.e. the Company granted permission to print a single edition.

Stationers' Company — *cont.*
From 1604 onward the overwhelming majority of imprints: *for the Company of Stationers, ex typographia Societatis Stationarum*, etc. have with relative certainty been assigned to one of the three stock ventures of the Company: the **English Stock** (not distinguished as 'English' until the Latin Stock was formed), the **Latin Stock,** and the **Irish Stock**. However, since the Master, Wardens, and Court of Assistants were responsible for all three stocks, a few item numbers below have a query (?) *after* them and appear under both the Company and the most likely stock or, in the case of the Irish law reports of 1628 (6362), under both the English and the Irish Stocks. [*Dict. 1*: 256–7; Blagden; *Reg. B*: v–lxxvi.]

in Paul's Churchyard, on part of the site of Peter College, near Ludgate (A.10), 1554–1606 (Blagden, 206–8); possibly also the general location of the following:
sold in Paul's Churchyard at the new shop of the Stationers (ad novam Librariorum officinam, (?A.10)), 1606 (11924 (***A***3), a Latin poem on the Gunpowder Plot); perhaps primarily an outlet for English Stock items.
in Milk Street (H.11; *see* headnote there), 1606–11
in Abergavenny House, between the wall of London, Amen Corner, and Ave Maria Lane (Q.1), 1611–1666; present Hall still on the same site (Blagden 212–22)

1565: 12167 (note).
1576: 15353.3 f. certain of the Co.
1584 (SR records): (Titles yielded to the Stat. Co. on 8 Jan. 1584 (Arber II.786–9). Item numbers in square brackets do *not* have the Arber reference cited in STC or Addenda. Those *preceded* by a query (?) or 'cf.' indicate uncertainty whether the STC item is a particular title yielded, and the reference following them is keyed to the list in Appendix C, which has STC identifications in Arber order, i.e. by donor and title.) [205], [?361.3] (C/49), [375], 402.5, [830], 836, 1261, 1356.9, [1710], [?1720.7] (C/22), 1728, [1733], 1748, [1753.5], [1755], [?1771.7] (C/22), [cf. 2854 and c in headnote preceding 2964.5] (C/3), [2887.7], [2995a], [3420], [4057], [4062], 4336, [cf. 4379 and 4386] (C/30), [4397], [4451], [4738], 4779, [4880], 5285, [5684], [5886], 6106.3, 6119, 6131, 6145, [6274], [?6430] (C/22), [6577 or 6577], 6697, 6848, 7168, 9305.3, 10037, [10043], 10062.5, [10104.7], [10129], 10451, [11049], [11249], [11632], [11894], [12048], [12426], [12955a.5], 13495, 13657(***A***3), [13673], 13867, [13963], 14022, [15142], 15175, 15336 (***A***3), [16625], 17850, [18309], 18943, 18958, 20998, 21827(***A***3), 21867, 22137, ?22221 (note), 23325.8, [24077a.5], [24287.7], [24436], [24467], 24670, 24672, [24788a], ?24852.7(***A***3) (C/58), [25197.5], 25808.
1592: 5077 allowed ent.
1594: 5077 allowed ent., 5266.9 allowed ent., 5309.6 allowed ent.
1596: 6749.6 f.
1599: 11711 f.
1602: 23329 allowed ent.
1603: 14354 f. others of the Stat. Co.
1604: 18162 allowed ent.
1606: 11232 allowed ent., 11924(***A***3) ven. ad novam Librariorum officinam.
1607: 23433.5 allowed ent.
1624: 25919 f. the Honest Stationers (d).
1625: 5975? (or Latin Stock?) ex typ., 17196.7? (or Latin Stock?) prost. ap. Soc. Londinensem.
1633: 15196? (or Eng. Stock?) with permission of.
1635: 15283? (or Eng. Stock?) f.
1636: 9064 (note), 15283.5? (or Eng. Stock?) f.
1637: 1719? (or Eng. Stock?) f.
1638: 4806? (or Eng. Stock?) f., 12394 ent. in trust., 19598 sold at the Stationers' shops.
1640: 6190? (or Eng. Stock?) f.

—English Stock.
Partnership in a group of titles acquired by the Stationers' Company by patents of 1603 and later and by private negotiation with previous patentees. The titles included Almanacks (from **R. Watkins** and **J. Roberts**), the A.B.C. and catechism and the Sternhold and Hopkins metrical Psalms (both **R. Day**), books of private prayer (**W. Seres**), and other lucrative texts. [Blagden 75–7, 92–106; *C-B C*: viii–xi.]
A limited number of Stationers had shares in the stock. Although new stockkeepers were elected annually, the treasurer was

Stationers' Company — English Stock — *cont.*
generally re-elected for longer periods. Treasurers from the later period of the Day and Seres patents through 1641 were:

Richard Watkins, at least 1591–99
William Leake 1, 1599–1601 at least
Nathaniel Butter, c. 1603–06
William Cotton, 1606–09
Edmund Weaver, 1610–38
Edward Brewster, 1639–47

The primary criterion for inclusion here of imprints after 1616 is the list of titles mentioned in the group of SR entries under 1620 below and also in Appendix D. Rights to print law books were taken over by the *assignees of* **J. More, esq.** beginning in 1629.

1603 (SR entries): (On 28 Nov. 1603 (Arber III.248, but *see* also III.87) Robert Dexter's copies passed to the Company. Only five were mentioned by title, and they were before long rejected from the English Stock; for further details *see* Appendix E/4–8. Items unmentioned in the list and given here in square brackets, are of two kinds: two titles in English originally owned by Dexter which entered the Stock (Appendix D numbers are appended); and several Latin school books in which Dexter may have had an interest. For further details of these last *see* the headnote following Appendix D/60.) [172.2], [3364-D/96], [4771.7], [4848.2(*A*3)], [5300.4], [5320], [5711-D/97], 6628, 7528, [10462], 12317, [17239.5], [17289], [19144], 21215, [21622.8], [21821.2], [22254.3], [22984.4], [23888.5], 24770, [24791.3].
1603/04: 451.14 f., 466.7 f., 489 f.
1604: 945.3 f., 1768 f., 2512a f., 2513 f., 2514 f., 2514.5 f., 2515 f., 22254.7 ex typ., 24387 f. (d), 26050.6 f.
1604/05: 434.17 f., 451.15 f., 483.3 f., 489.2 f., 501.5 f., 525.10 f.
1605: 20.8 f., 702.5 imp., 2516 f., 2517 f., 2518 f., 2518.7(*A*) f., 2704 (note), 4772 ex typ., 5504 f., 6628 f., 9297 f., 12582.15 f., 15156 f., 23982 f., 25271 f.
1605/06: 408 f., 434.18 f., 452.5 f., 461 f., 483.4 f., 489.3 f., 501.6 f., [507 f.].
1606: 2406 f., 2519 f., 2519.5 f., 2520 f., 2521 f., 2521.3 f., 2521.6 f., 5267.6 ex typ., 5505 f., 5525 f., 7723.3 f., 9547 f., 9602 ex typ., 10982 f., 14036 f., 15157 f., 19469.5 f., 22984.5 pro, 25279 f.
1606/07: 408.2–.3 f., 420 f., 434.19 f., 452.7 f., 461.2 f., 480 f., 483.5 f., 489.4 f., 489.5 f., 501.7 f., 507.2 f., 532.6 f.
1607: 945.7 f., 1769 f., 2522 f., 2522.3 f., [2522.5 f.] (d?), 2523 f., 2523.3 f., 2523.5 f., 2524 f., 2524.5 f., 2524.7 f., 2525 f., 3346.5 f., 4848.3 ex typ., 5300.7 ex typ., 5505 f., 5509 f., 5509.5 f., 5759.3 ex typ., 9298 f., 15023 f., 15171 f., 15282 f., 20038 f., 21054 f., 21578 f., 21821.4 ex typ., 23218 f., 23224 ex typ., 23330 f. (d), 23548 ent., 23982.3 f.
1607/08: 408.4 f., 434.20 f., 439 f., 461.3 f., 467 f., 483.6 f., 489.6 f., 501.8 f., 532.7 f.
1608: 2525.5 f., 2526 f., 2526.3 f., 2526.6 f., 2527 f., 2527.5 f., 2527.7 f., 5511 f., 5511.2 f., 5759.4 ex typ., 6432 f., 9284 f., 9323 f., 9548 f., 10462.5 ex typ., 11045 f., 12582.16 f., 15755 f., 15755.3 f., 15779 f., 18718.5 imp., 23440 ex typ.
1608/09: 408.5 f., 420.2 f., 434.21 f., 457.14 f., 467.5 f., 483.7 f., 489.7 f., 489.8 f., [501.9 f.], 507.4 f.
1609: 840 f., 2526.3 f., 2528 f., 2528.5 f., 2529 f., 2529.3 f., 2529.5 f., 2530 f., 2530.3 f., 2530.5 f., 2531 f., 2532 f., 3157 f., 4731.7 f., 5494 f., 7387 f., 7540 f., 7540.5 f., 9616 f., 10964.5 f., 11246 f., 18734 f., 19642 f., 20495 f., 20714 f., 23982.5 f., 26050.8 f.
1609/10: 408.6 f., 420.3 f., 434.22 f., 461.5 f., 483.8 f., 489.9 f., [501.10 f.], 507.5 f., 508 f., 531 f.
1610: 1769.5 f., 1815 f., 2533 f., 2533.3 f., 2533.5 f., 2534 f., 2534.5 f., 2535 f., 2535.5 f., 2536 f., 3364 f., 4562.5 f. (c), 4848.5 ex typ., 5497 f., 5500 f., 5503 f., 7657 f., 11227 f., 15158 f., 15172 f., 18719 imp., 19470 f., 20047.5 f., 20496 f., 21751 ex typ., 21821.6 ex typ., 24388 f. (d), 25272 f.
1610/11: 420.4 f., 434.23 f., 461.6 f., 465 f., 483.9 f., 489.10 f., [501.11 f.], 507.6 f., 508.3 f., 531.1 f.
1611: 703 imp., 2536.5 f., 2537 f., 2537.5 f., 2538 f., 2538.5 f., 2538.7(*A*) f., 3347 f., 4732 f., 4773 ex typ., 5267.8 ex typ., 5304 f., 5513 f., 5513.2 f., 5513.6 (repeat?), 9298.5 f., 9324 f., 12582.17 f., 21751 ex typ., 22255 ex typ., 23331 f., 23548 f., 23888.5 ex typ., 25279.3 f., 26050.10 f.
1611/12: 408.8 f., 420.5 f., 434.24 f., 461.7 f., 465.1 f., 468 f., 483.10 f., 489.10A f., 489.11 f., [501.12 f.], 507.7 f., 517.14 f., 531.2 f.
1612 (imprints): 946 f., 2539 f., 2540, 2540.5 f., 2541 f., 2541.5 f., 2542 f., 2544 f., 2544.2 f., 2544.3 f., 5507 f., 7723.5 f., 9549 f., 13778 f., 15158.5 f., 15755.7 f., 15756 f., 15780 f., 23440.3 ex typ.
1612 (SR entries): (Titles ass'd by John Harrison 1 on 21 Sept. 1612 (Arber III.497). Item numbers in square brackets do *not* have the Arber reference cited in STC or Addenda.) [5315.8], [?5689], [15244.3], 17281.5, 18927.5, 18929.5, 18952.3, 18976.8, [20055.5], 20763.7, 23659.7(*A*3), 24852.7(*A*3).
1612/13: 420.6 f., 426 f., 434.25 f., 440 f., [461.8 f.], 465.2 f., 468.2 f., 483.11 f., 489.12 f., 507.8 f., 527 f., 531.3 f.
1613: 2544.5 f., [2544.7 f.] (d?), 2545 f., 2546 f., 2546.5(*A*1) f., 2549.5 f., 5515 f., 6247 f., 10870 f., 15024 f., 17281.5 ex typ., 17239.7 ex typ., 20046 f., 21580 f., 22984.6 ex typ., 24791.7 ex typ.
1613/14: 413 f., 420.7 f., 426.2 f., 434.26 f., 435.31 f., 443.7 f., 445.9 f., [461.9 f.], 465.3 f., 468.3 f., 483.12 f., 489.13 f., 519 f., 527.3 f., 531.4 f.
1614: 172.3 pro, 841 by ass't of, 2407.5 f., 2547 f., 2548 f., 2548.5 f., 2548.7 f., 2549 f., 2549.3 f., 2549.4 f., 2549.5 f., 2549.7 f., 2549.9 f., 5268 ex typ., 5321 ex typ., 5488 f., 5518 f., 5712 f., 9928 f., 15159 f., 15173 f., 18735 f., 18927.5 ex typ., 19470.5 f., 19643 f., 20055.5 ex typ., 22646 ent., 23659.7 ex typ., 23982.7(*A*3) f., 24389 f.
1614/15: [420.8 f.], 421 f., 435.4 f., 435.33 f., 445.10 f., 465.4 f., 468.4 f., 489.14 f., 489.15 f., 502 f., 506.7 f., 519.2 f., 527.4 f., 531.5 f.
1615: 2408 f., 2409 f., 2550 f., 2551 f., 2551.3 f., 2551.5 f., 2552 f., 2552.3 f., 2554 f., 2554.5 f., 4032.3(*A*3 & note), 5315.8 ex typ., 5516 f., 5521 f., 7723.7 f., 9325 f., 11560 (note & *A*3), 12582.18 f., 12582.22 f., 13982 f., 14013.7 f., 15222.5 f., 17292 f., 18621(*A*3, note), 18720 imp., 20497 f., 20715 f., 21623 ex off., 21723 by ass't of, 21821.8 ex typ., 22646 ex typ., 25273 f., 26050.12 f.
1615/16: [420.9 f.], 421.1 f., 426.4 f., 435.5 f., 445.11 f., 448 f., 465.5 f., 468.5 f., 489.16 f., 502.2 f., 506.8 f., 519.3 f., 527.5 f., 531.6 f.
1616: 704 imp., 947 f., 2555 f., 2555.3 f., 2555.5 f., 2556 f., 2556.2 f., 2556.5 f., 2556.7 f., 3347.5 f., 5268.3 ex typ., 5522 f., 9550 ent., 10965 f., 11197 f., 13780 f., 15781 f., 19146 ex off., 20761.3 ex typ., 23440.7 ex typ., 24792 ex typ.
1616/17: 407 f., [420.10 f.], 421.2 f., 426.5 f., 435.6 f., 445.12 f., 448.2 f., 465.6 f., 468.6 f., 489.17 f., 502.3 f., 506.9 f., 519.4 f., 527.6 f., 531.7 f.
1617: 2410.5 f., 2555.3 f., 2557 f., 2557.3 f., 2557.5 f., 2558 f., 2558.3 f., 2559 f., 2559.5 f., 2562.6 f., 9299 f., 9550 f., 10983 f., 15756.5 f., 15757 f., 18952.4 ex typ., 20763.7 ex off., 22256 ex typ., 22984.7 ex typ., 23983 f.
1617/18: 407.1 f., [420.11 f.], 421.3 f., 426.6 f., 435.7 f., 445.13 f., 448.3 f., 465.7 f., 489.18 f., 489.19 f., 502.4 f., 506.10 f., 515 f., 519.5 f., 527.7 f., 531.8 f.
1618: 172.4 pro, 2412 f., 2560 f., 2560.5 f., 2560a f., 2560a.5 f., 2560a.7 f., 2561 f., 2561.3 f., 2561.5 f., 2562 f., 2562.2 f., 2562.4 f., 2562.8 f., 2562.6 f., 5498 f., 5503.4 f., 5519 f., 5526 f., 6205 f. & ent., 9285 f., 9328 f., 11416 f., 13983 f., 17282 f., 20715a f., 23332 f., 25279.5 f., 25648 f. & ent., 26050.14 f.
1618/19: [407.2 f.], 420.12 f., 421.4 f., 426.7 f., 435.8 f., 437 f., 445.14 f., 448.4 f., 489.20 f., 502.5 f., 506.11 f., 515.2 f., 519.6 f., 527.8 f., 531.9 f., 531.10 f.
1619: 172.5 pro, 1771.5 f., 2563 f., 2564 f., 2564.2 f., 2564.4 f., 2564.6 f., 2564.8 f., 2565 f., 2566 f., 2567 f., 2567.3 f., 2567.6 f., 2568 f., 2569 f., 4774 ex typ., 5321.5 ex typ., 5494.3 f., 5501 f., 5523 f., 6206 f., 9554 f., 9904 f., 15160 f., 15174 f., 18711b.5 sumpt., 18929.4(*A*3) ex typ., 19471 f.
1619/20: [407.3 f.], 420.13 f., 421.5 f., 426.8 f., 435.9 f., 437.5 f., 438 f., 445.15 f., 448.5 f., 489.21 f., 502.6 f., 506.12 f., 515.3 f., 527.9 f., 531.11 f.
1620 (imprints): 2569.7 f., 2570 f., 2570.5 f., 2571 f., 2571.3 f., 2571.5 f., 2571.7 f., 2572 f., 2575a (note), 9904 f., 11411 f., 18952.5 ex typ., 20055.7 ex typ., 21822 ex typ., 23659.9 pro (c), 24390 f., 25649 f.
1620 (SR entries): (Titles entered to the English Stock on 5 Mar. 1620 (Arber III.668–71). Item numbers in square brackets do *not* have the Arber reference cited in STC or Addenda. For identifications in Arber order, i.e. largely by category of text and title, *see* Appendix D.) 20.9, 21.4, 172.6, [407.4 and other Almanacks listed under 1620/21], 704.5, 840(*A*), 840.5(*A*), 947.5, 1748(*A*3), 1771.7, 2413.5, 2569.7, 3157, 3348, 3365, 3476, 3804, 3826, [3829], 4562.5, [4719], 4732, 4774, 4849.1, 5268.5, [5300.7], 5301.8, 5316, 5321.5, 5488, 5494.3, 5498, 5501, 5503.4, 5508, 5510, 5512, 5514, 5517, 5520, 5523, [5526], 5712.5, 5759.7, 6051,

Stationers' Company — English Stock — *cont.*
6106.5, 6247(*A*), 6432, 7387, 7390.5, [7393], 7724, 9285, 9300, 9327, [9328], [9552], [9554], [9585], [9602], [9610], [9616], [9697], [9769.5], [9804], [9904], [9928], 10462.5, 10870, [10957], 10965, 10983, 11045, 11197, 11227, 11411, 11416, 11906(*A*), 12357.7(*A*), 12582.19, 12582.22, 13983, 14013.7, [14902], 15025, 15160, 15174, 15223, 15758, 15782, [16087 and 16090], 17240, 17282, [17289], 17292, [18363], [18706a], [18710a.5], 18711c, 18720.5, 18729, 18736, 18927.5, 18929.5, 18952.5, 19147, 19471 (*A*3), 19644, 20038, 20046, 20047.5, 20055.7, [20373], [20498], 20716, 20764, 20839, 21054, 21581, 21623, 21822, 22256, 22647, 22984.9, [23224], 23332, 23441, 23550, 23660.5, 23889.2, 23984, 24390, 24410, 24792.5, 24853.3, 26050.16.

1620/21: 407.4 f., 421.6 f., 426.9 f., 438.2 f., 445.16 f., 448.6 f., 453 f., 465.9 f., 489.22 f., 489.23 f., 502.7 f., 515.4 f., 522 f., 527.10 f., 531.12 f.

1621: 172.6 pro, 947.5 f., 2572 f., 2572.3 f., 2572.6 f., 2573.5 f., 2574 f., 2574.3 f., 2574.5 f., 2575 f., 2575.3 f., 3348 f., 3365 f., 4849.1 ex typ., 5268.4(*A*) ex typ., 5510 f., 5712.5 f., 7390.5 f., 9327 f., 15758 f., 15782 f., 18720.5 f., 19644 f., 19644.5 f., 23441 ex typ.

1621/22: 407.5 f., 413.5 f., 421.7 f., 435.11 f., 438.3 f., 445.17 f., 448.7 f., 465.10 f., 489.24 f., 494 f., 502.8 f., 514.5 f., 515.5 f., 522.2 f., 527.11 f., 531.13 f.

1622: 2413.5 f., 2575a f., 2576 f., 2576.5 f., 2576.7 f., 2577 f., 2578 f., 2578.5 f., 2579 f., 6207 f., 7393 f., 20128.3 in off. & ent., 22647 ex typ., 22984.9 ex typ., 24792.5 ex typ., 25275 f.

1622/23: 407.6 f., 421.8 f., 435.12 f., 438.4 f., 445.18 f., 448.8 f., 464.5 f., 465.11 f., 489.25 f., 502.9 f., 515.6 f., 522.3 f., 527.12 f., 531.14 f.

1623: 704.5 imp., 2580 f., 2581 f., 2582 f., 2583 f., 2583.3 f., 2583.5 f., 2583.7 f., 2588.3 f., 4849.2 ex typ., 5268.5 ex typ., 6212 f., 15025 f., 15223 f., 20498 f., 21581 f., 23352 f. & ent.

1623/24: 407.7 f., 414 f., 421.9 f., 435.13 f., 438.5 f., 448.9 f., 456 f., 465.12 f., 489.26 f., 503 f., 506.15 f., 515.7 f., 522.4 f., 527.13 f., 531.15 f.

1624: 2414 f., 2585 f., 2585.5 f., 2586 f., 2587 f., [2587.3 f.] (d?), 2587.5 f., 2588 f., 2588.5 f., 5508 f., 5712a f., 5759.7 ex typ., 15161 f., 20716 f., 23889.2 ex typ., 24853.3 pro.

1624/25: 407.8 f., 421.10 f., 435.14 f., 438.6 f., 441 f., 448.10 f., 456.3 f., 457 f., 469.9 f., 480.7 f., 489.27 f., 494.3 f., 495 f., 503.2 f., 506.16 f., 514.7 f., 515.8 f., 522.5 f., 527.14 f., 529 f., 531.16 f.

1625: 172.7 pro, 2589 f., 2590 f., 2590.5 f., 2591 f., 2592 f., 2592.5 f., 2593 f., 2593.5 f., 3826 f., 4849.3 ex typ., 5301.8 ex typ., 7724 f., 9300 f., 12582.19 f., 17283 ex typ., 18721 imp., 18736 f., 21822.5 ex typ.

1625/26: 407.9 f., 421.11 f., 435.15 f., 438.7 f., 448.11 f., 464.9 f., 490 f., 494.4 f., 495.1 f., 503.3 f., 506.17 f., 515.9 f., 522.6 f., 527.15 f., 529.3 f., 531.17 f.

1626: 2594 f., 2595 f., 2596 f., 2597 f., 2597.2 f., 2598 f., 5268.7 ex typ., 5514 f., 6208 f., 15161.5 f., 20764 ex off., [26050.16 f.] (c?).

1626/27: 407.10 f., 421.12 f., 429 f., 435.16 f., 450 f., 456.7 f., 457.3 f., 464.10 f., 490.3 f., 495.2 f., 503.4 f., 506.18 f., 515.10 f., 522.7 f., 527.16 f., 531.18 f.

1627: [20.9 f.] (c), 2597.2 f., 2599 f., 2599.5 f., 2600 f., 2600.5 f., 2601 f., 2601.5 f., 2602 f., 2603 f., 2603.5 f., 2604 f., 5517 f., 5713 f., 10871 f., 15783 f., 20056 ex typ., 22985 ex typ., 23442 ex typ., 23660.5 pro, 23889.3 ex typ., 25279.7 f.

1627/28: 407.11 f., 421.13 f., 429.3 f., 435.17 f., 450.3 f., 457.4 f., 490.4 f., 494.6 f., 495.3 f., 503.5 f., 505.17 f., 506.19 f., 515.11 f., 522.8 f., 527.17 f., 531.19 f.

1628: 172.8 pro, 2604 f., 2604.5 f., 2605 f., 2605.5 f., 2606 f., 2607 f., 2607.5 f., 4849.4 ex typ., 5316 ex typ., 6213 f., 6362? (or Irish Stock?) f., 15784 f., 17283.3 ex typ., 18952.6 ex typ., 19471.5 f., 20761.5 ex typ., 22648 ex typ., 24853.7 pro, 25650 f., 26050.18 f.

1628/29: 407.12 f., 419.10 f., 421.14 f., 427 f., 435.18 f., 441.5 f., 448.14 f., 457.5 f., 460 f., 490.5 f., 495.4 f., 503.6 f., 515.12 f., 522.9 f., 527.18 f., 531.20 f.

1629: 173 pro, 948 f., 1771.7 f., 2612 f., 2612.5 f., 2614 f., 2614.5 f., 2615 f., 2615.5 f., 2615.7 f., 2616 f., 2616.5 f., 2617 f., 2617.5 f., 5270 ex typ., 5512 f., 5520 f., 13984 f., 20717 f., 23889.4 f., 23984 f.

1629/30: 407.13 f., 419.11 f., 421.15 f., 427.2 f., 435.19 f., 441.6 f., 448.15 f., 457.6 f., 460.5 f., 490.6 f., 495.5 f., 497 f., 503.7 f., 515.13 f., 522.10 f., 527.19 f., 531.21 f.

1630: 173.3 pro, 2612 f., 2618 f., 2619 f., 2620 f., 2620.5 f., 2621 f., 2622 f., 2622.5 f., 2623 f., 2623.5 f., 5322 ex typ., 5714 f., 17283.5 ex typ., 18723 imp., 18952.7 ex typ., 20128.5 in off., 24391 f.

1630/31: 407.14 f., 411 f., 412 f., 419 f., 421.16 f., 429.7 f., 435.20 f., 441.7 f., 448.16 f., 490.7 f., 495.6 f., 503.8 f., 514 f., 515.14 f., 522.11 f., 527.20 f., 531.22 f.

1631: 1772 f., 2796 ent., 2813 ent., 2625 f., 2626 f., 2627 f., 2629 f., 2630 f., 2630.5 f., 2631 f., 5271.4 ex typ., 17004 ent., 18929.5 ex typ., 20761.9 ex typ, 23889.4c(*A*3) ex typ.

1631/32: 407.15 f., 419.1 f., 435.21 f., 448.17 f., 490.8 f., 495.7 f., 515.15 f., 522.12 f., 527.21 f., 531.23 f.

1632: 1773 f., 2631 f., 2633 f., 2634 f., 2635 f., 2636 f., 2636.3(*A*) f., 2637 f., 2637.2 f., 2637.3 f., 2637.4 f., 2637.6 f., 2637.8 f., 2638 f., 2646 f., 2734 with permission of.

1632/33: 407.16 f., [419.2 f.], 435.22 f., 490.9 f., 495.8 f., 515.16 f., 522.13 f., 527.23 f., 529.7 f., 531.24 f.

1633: 21 f., 2639 f., 2640 f., 2641 f., 2641.5 f., 2641.7 f., 2642 f., 2644 f., 2645 f., 2645.3 f., 2645.7 f., 2646 f., 2648 f., 2653.5 f., 15196? (or Stat. Co.?) with permission of, 18711c pro, 18737 f., 18952.8 ex typ., 19472 f., 20765 ex off., 23889.5 ex typ.

1633/34: 407.17 f., 419.3 f., 435.23 f., 490.10 f., 495.9 f., 496 f., 515.17 f., 522.14 f., 527.24 f., 529.8 f., 531.25 f.

1634: 948.5 f., 2416 f., 2649 f., 2650 f., 2650.5 f., 2651 f., 2651a f., 2652 f., 2653 f., 2653.5 f., 4849.6 ex typ., 20765 ex off.

1634/35: 407.18 f., 435.24 f., 464.7 f., 479 f., 490.11 f., 495.10 f., 496.2 f., 515.18 f., 522.15 f., 527.25 f., 531.26 f., 532.9 f.

1635: 948.5 f., 2417 f., 2417.3 f., 2655 f., 2656 f., 2656.5 f., 2657 f., 2658.5(*A*3) f., 2659 f., 2659.5 f., 2660 f., 2661 f., 2661.5 f., 2662 f., 2662.3 f., 5272.4 ex typ., 5714.8 f., 6211 f., 15283? (or Stat. Co.?) f., 17004 pro, 18737.5 f. (c), 18929.7 ex typ., 20056.5 ex typ., 20128.7 in off., 22649 imp., 23443 ex typ., 23550 f., 23889.7 ex typ.

1635/36: 407.19 f., 435.25 f., 442 f., 479.2 f., 490.12 f., 494.12 f., 495.11 f., 522.16 f., 527.26 f., 531.27 f., 532.10 f.

1636: [21.2 f.], 706.5 ex typ., 2418.5 f., 2659.5 f., 2662.5 f., 2663 f., 2664 f., 2665 f., 2665.5 f., 2666 f., 2666.2 f., 2666.5 f., 2667 f., 2667.2 f., 2667.4 f., 5316.5 ex typ., 5715 f., 13984.5 f., 15283.5? (or Stat. Co.?) f., 17284 pro, 18952.9 ex typ., 23662 imp., 23889.8 ex typ., 23985 f.

1636/37: 407.20 f., 435.26 f., 442.3 f., 479.3 f., 490.13 f., 494.13 f., 495.12 f., 496.4 f., 515.20 f., 522.17 f., 527.27 f., 531.28 f.

1637: 21.3 f., 174.3(*A*) pro, 1719? (or Stat. Co.?) f., 2418.7 f., 2668 f., 2669 f., 2670 f., 2670.5 f., 2671 f., 2671.5 f., 2672 f., 2672.3 f., 2672.7 f., 2673 f., 2673.3 f., 2673.5 f., 2681.7 f., 5303.6 ex imp., 5716 f., 20762.3 ex typ.

1637/38: 407.21 f., 419.7 f., 435.27 f., 479.4 f., 490.14 f., 495.13 f., 496.5 f., 515.21 f., 522.18 f., 527.28 f., 531.29 f.

1638: 2676 f., 2677 f., 2678 f., 2678.2 f., 2678.4 f., 2679 f., 2680 f., 2680.1–.6 (forged), 2681 f., 2681.3 f., 2681.7 f., 2691 f., 4806? (or Stat. Co.?) f., 5272.8 ex typ., 5716 f., 17240 imp., 18729 pro, 18738 f., 19473 f., 22989 imp., 24392 f.

1638/39: 407.22 f., 411.5 f., 419.8 f., 435.28 f., 442.5 f., 447 f., 479.5 f., 490.15 f., 495.14 f., 496.6 f., 505.19 f., 515.22 f., 527.29 f., 531.30 f.

1639: 174.5 pro, 2684 f., 2685 f., 2686 f., 2686.2 f., 2686.3 f., 2686.4 f., 2686.6 f., 2686.8 f., 2688 f., 2688.5 f., 2689 f., 2690 f., 2691 f., 6107 pro, 6107.3 pro, 18725.5 pro, 19147 ex off., 22257.5 pro.

1639/40: 407.23 f., 409 f., 419.9 f., 435.29 f., 442.7 f., 447.3 f., 479.6 f., 490.16 f., 495.15 f., 496.7 f., 515.23 f., 527.30 f., 531.31 f.

1640: 949 f., 2693 f., 2694 f., 2695 f., 2696 f., 2696.3 f., 2696.5 f., 2697 f., 2697.5(*A*) f., 2698 f., 2699 f., 2700 f., 5716.5 f., 6190? (or Stat. Co.?) f., 22649.5 pro, 22650 imp., 23551 f., 23986 f.

1640/41: Wing A 1242 f., A 1298 f., A 1328 f., A 1541 f., A 1858 f., A 1957 f., A 2099 f., A 2112 f., A 2398 f., A 2409 f., A 2670 f., A 2707 f., A 2791 f., A 2828 f.

after 1640? 5513.6 f. (forged?).

—Irish Stock.
A joint venture under the aegis of the Stationers' Company, which obtained in 1618 a patent for the office of **King's Printer in Ireland.** Among the partners who went to Dublin to set up and supervise the press or to settle accounts were:

F. Kingston, 1618–19?
T. Downes, 1618–20?
T. Snodham? and/or **R. Higgenbotham**? 1619
R. Young, 1623–24, 1628
A. Johnson, 1624?–28
W. Bladen, c. 1626?–39

In 1639 Bladen bought out the partners and the patent though he did not print in Dublin under his own name until after 1640. [*C-*

Stationers' Company — Irish Stock — *cont.*
B C: xii–xiii, and its index under 'Irish Stock'; *Library* 8 (1907): 295–7.]

Following are listed *only* items related to the partners' activity in London: with 'Irish Stock' present or implied in the imprint or stated in the SR entry. It is possible that some SR entries to individuals (e.g. 24545) and some imprints in the relatively obscure form of 24553 have been overlooked. For items published by the partners in Dublin *see* **Stationers' Society** and Index 2Aii.

1620: 14130.
1625: 24543 f.
1628: 6362? (or Eng. Stock?) f.
1629: 1805(*A1*) ent., 4669 ent., 14261 ent., 14263 f., 24542 ent.
1631: 24544 f., 24544.5 f., 24549 f., 24555 f.
1633: 4670 f.
1634: 23490 f.
1638: 4671 f., 24552 ent., [24553] f.
1639: 5753 ent.

—Latin Stock.
A joint venture begun in 1616 by members of the Stationers' Company for the purpose of importing—and occasionally exporting—Latin works other than schoolbooks. Its business was apparently intended to supersede the publications of **Bonham Norton** and his **Officina Nortoniana** and the cross-Channel activities of **John Bill**, from both of whom the partners acquired their original inventory of books (*Library* 10: 105). Norton seems to have quit the field fairly soon, but Bill apparently remained in at least partial competition. In 1627 the Stock ceased to operate, but debts lingered until at least 1639. [*C-B C*: xi–xii, and its index under 'Latin Stock'; *Library* 8 (1907): 286–97; 10 (1909): 105–6.]

The items indexed below were, with the exception of 11329 and 21805.9, printed in London with sale at home and abroad in mind. Other titles selected for printing are given in the list transferred to the English Stock in 1631 (Arber IV.255) but found unprofitable (*C-B C*: 301). Imported books, undoubtedly forming the lion's share of the operation, are primarily to be found in the London versions of the Frankfurt Fair catalogues, 1617–28 (11328 sqq.) since virtually no effort was made to provide them with Latin Stock imprints. However, for a limited and highly imperfect list of books printed abroad with London publishers' names *see* Index 3C.

1616: 22167 [f.] & ent.
1617: 1501.3(*A3*) prost., 5064 ex off.
1618: (all SR entries): 2795, 2812.5, 16879, 17004, 20764, 21805.9.
1619: 11328.7 ex off., 16879 ent., 21805.9 ap.
1620: 11328.9 ex off., 11329 pro (d), 16879 ex off., 19443 ent.
1621: 3616 ex off., 4749 ex off. & ent., 11329.4 (note).
1622: 1390 pro & ent., 2812.5 ex off., 18029 pro (d).
1625: 5975? (or Stat. Co.?) ex typ., 17196.7? (or Stat. Co.?) prost. ap Soc. Londinensem.
1626: 21317.5 ap.
1627: 11331 (note).

Stationers' Society, Dublin.
Agents, 1618–1640, of the **Stationers' Company—Irish Stock** for printing under the patent of **King's Printer in Ireland** and for the exportation and importation of books to and from London. For items of 1618–19 and occasionally later printed in Dublin but not naming the Society or completely without imprint *see* Index 2Aii. [*Dict. 1*: 257.]

No address used.

1620: 12738, 12739.5, 14173, 24541.7 (c).
1620/21: 14174.
1621: 14130, 14175, 14399.5, 16358, 22545.
1621/22: 14175.5.
1622: 7179.5 f. (c), 12737.5, 14134, 14176, 14177, 14178, 14179, 14180, 14181, 22522.
1623: 4311, 14182, 14183, 14265.3, 15501, 22523.
1623/24: 14184, 14185, 14186, 14187, 14188, 14189.
1624: 1805, 14190, 14191, 14511, [21138], 24542, [24953.3].
1625: 583, 8814, 14131.5, 14190.5, 14191a, 14192, 14193, 14196, 14197, 14198, 14199, 14200, 14201, 14202, 14203, 14511.5, 15502, 17836.7, 21020.5, 22524.
1625/26: 14204.
1626: 14205, 14206, 14207, 14265.5, 18914, 25064.
1627: 4668.5, 14209, 14210, 18811.5, 22525–5.3.

Stationers' Society, Dublin — *cont.*
1627/28: 14211.
1628: 14212, 14213, 14214, 25065.
1629: 8925, 9249.5, 14208, 14215, 14216, 14265.1.
1629/30: 14217.
1630: 7265 ex off., 14218, 14219, 18811.
1630/31: [14221].
1631: 22.1, 5406, 7114, 14058.7, 14222, 14223, 24550 ex typ.
1631/32: 14224, 14225.
1632: [4326.5] (false, d), [12809], 14134.3, 14226, 14227, 20520, 23604, 24557 ex off.
1633: [12808], [12810], 14228, [14229], 14230, 14231, 14232, [23596], 25067–7a.
1633/34: 14233, 14234.
1634: 7725.3, 10059, [12812], 14135, 14135.3, 14135.7, 14208a, 14235, 14236, [14237], 23597, 25650.5.
1635: [12811], 14136, 14136.3, 14136.7, [14237.3(*A3*)] (d), 14265, 20690 (d?).
1635/36: 517.16 f.
1636: 14137 [f.?], 14208b.
1637: 1530, 6825, 14238, 14239, 14240, 14241, 14242, 14243, 14244, 15308, 15499, 16407.
1637/38: 14245, 14246, 14247.
1638: 3223, 14132, 14132.5, 14134.7, 14248, 14249, 14250, 14265.9, 24552.
1638/39: 14251.
1639: 1531, 3223.5, 5753–5 (false), 5755a, 14265.7, 15498 ex off., 15500, 24548a ex off., 25066.
1640: [5751], 9174, 9260.5, 9262.5, 13600 ex off., 14252, 14253, 14266.

Steelsius, Joannes.
Bookseller and printer? in Antwerp, c. 1533–1562†. [Duff, *Century*; Rouzet.]
1556: 11092 en casa.

Stell, Jan (Hans).
Bookseller in Antwerp, 1559–1566, and in London, 1568–1585. [*Dict. 1*; Briels 461–2.]
dw. at the Duke's Place by [St. Katherine] Cree Church (L.1), 1579 (17445); not used later, but he was still there in 1581 (Worman 65)
1579: 17445–5.5 f. **1580:** 17446 f. **1583:** 11694? **1585:** 18574 (note).

Stempe, John.
Stationer in London, (1627) 1628–1665†. [*Dict. 1*; DFM 915; *Poor Book*, 1644–65, widow thereafter.]
shop at the East end of St. Dunstan's Churchyard in Fleet Street (W.9), 1628 (6299)
1628: 6299 sold.

Stephanus. *See* Estienne.

Stephens, Philemon.
Bookseller in London, (1620) 1622–1665?†. His first two imprints were shared with **Robert Milbourne**, the first having the latter's address: at the great South door of Paul's (A.8). Between 1625 and 1641 he was in partnership with **Christopher Meredith**. The Philemon Stephens of Chancery Lane who died in 1670 was probably the son freed in 1659 (DFM II.4316). [*Dict. 2*; DFM 2022; *Loan Book*, 1626–32.]
their shop at the Golden Lion in Paul's Churchyard (B), 1625 (13825)–1640 (1179, omits 'their shop') at least; variation: 1627 (4228.5, has 'dw.')
1622: 3911 ent., 21123 f.
1623: 21124 sold.
1624: 14458 sumpt.
1625: 57 f., 4220a.5 sold, 13825 f., 18359 f.
1626: 56 f., 4233–3.3 f., 11648 f., 11952 sold, 13820 f.
1627: 4228–8.5 f., 5362 f., 7049 f., 7527 f., 25742 sold.
1628: 1160.5–.7 sold, 4205 ent., 4221 sold, 4236.3 ent., 4236.9 ent., 5144 ent., 7137 ent., 11953 sold, 12637 f., 21436 sold.
1629: 1161 sold, 5144.3 f., 7144 f., 12348 imp.
1630: 3911 f., 4222 sold, 4229 f., 4239 f., 12876 f., 21125 f., 23610 f., 24007 f., 25849 f.
1631: 4238 f., 23610–1 f., 24017.5 ven., 24544.5 sold.
1632: 4236.9 sold, 6154 imp., 12771 f., 12873 f., 12877 f., 13822 f.

Stephens, P. — *cont.*
1633: 4223 f., 6057 f., 7137 f., 12878 f., 14892 imp., 17493 imp., 21151 f.
1634: 4230 f., 7137 f., 12640 f., 22220 imp., 26078 f.
1635: 1887 f., 12879 f., 25718 f.
1636: 60.3 f., 12897.5 f., 19910 f., 21544 f., 25718 f.
1637: 60.5 f., 4231 f., 4236.4 f., 11652 (note), 11652b f., 21126 f., 21543 imp., [23245] sold, 24498.5 f.
1638: 59.5 f., 1177.5 f., 1178 f., 1178.5 f., 3772.2 f., 6181.4 ent., 6233 imp., 12874 f., 14501 f., 21816 imp.
1639: 58 f., 60 f., 60.7 f., 6233 imp., 12871 f., 13908 f., 14500.5 f., 21816 imp., 21816.5 ven., 23066 imp., 23199.7 f., 25029 imp., 25752 f., 25971 ent.
1640: 59.7 f., 1179 f., 2369 imp., 4225 f., 10706 imp., 11530 sumpt., 12898 f., 13724 f.

Stepneth (Stepney), John.
Bookseller in London, (1602: Arber II.732, as 'Stroney') 1609–1612. His first item was sold in the shop of **Walter Burre**: at the Crane in Paul's Churchyard (A.3). [*Dict. 1.*]
shop at the $ St. Paul at the West end of Paul's Church (A.10), 1611 (7182)–1612 (1896, omits sign)
1610: 24832–2a f. **1611:** 7182 f., 24146 f. **1612:** 1896 f., 14755 sold, 24147 f.

Sterne, Thomas.
Globemaker and mapseller in London, fl. 1619–1631. [Taylor 206.]
in Paul's Churchyard (B), 1619 (1186.7)
1619: 1186.7 sold.

Stevenage, Robert.
Abbot of St. Albans, and patron of a press there, 1534–1539. For other extant items during this period which he also probably subsidized *see* Index 2Ai: St. Albans. Stevenage's device, McK. 84, appears in both of the following items. [Duff, *Provincial*: 101–3.]
No address survives.
1536: [12557 f.]. **1537:** [14117.7(*A*3) f.].

Stevenson, Richard.
Stationer in London, (1633) 1640. [*Dict. 1*; DFM 860.]
shop in Prince's Street near Lincoln's Inn Fields (X.5a), 1640 (157)
1640: 157 f.

Stirrop (Sturruppe), Thomas.
Stationer in London, (1561) 1576–1600?†. [*Dict. 1*:.]
dw. in Paul's Churchyard at the George (A.5), 1576 (25976)–1597 (12531.5)
1576: 25976 f. **1577:** 25975 f. **1597:** 12531.5 f., 15623(*A*3) ent., 17673 f. (d), 21591.5 ent. **1599:** 18249(*A*) ent.

Stoer, Jacob.
Printers in Geneva, 1568–1670 at least. The eldest of this name died in 1610 (Chaix 223–4; Bremme 231–3). One or more namesakes evidently succeeded him.
1602: 1431.17A (d/error?). **1604:** 13790 ex off. **1608:** 1431.17A (d?), 1431.19A. **1621:** 22830.5 ap. **1622:** 1431.26. **1634:** 1431.34.

Stoltzenberger, Johann Nikolaus.
Printer in Frankfurt am Main, 1618–1636? [*Dict. 1*; Benzing 133.]
1628: 10933.

Stone, Thomas, *pseud.*
Printer in 'Lion' [Lyons], 1630. The following item may actually have been printed in Bordeaux.
in the street of the Hammer (Hamber) at the $ Heart, c. 1630? (4285)
1630: 4285 (c?).

Stonor Park Press. *See* 'Greenstreet House' Press.

Story, John.
Printer in Edinburgh, c. 1520. [Duff, *Century*.]
No address used.
1520: 15791.5 per (c).

Stoughton, Robert.
Printer and bookseller in London, 1548–1551. Possibly the man of this name who died in 1553. [Duff, *Century*.]
dw. within Ludgate at the Bishop's Mitre (Q.3), 1548 (12887)–1551/52 (427.6)
1548: 4080, 12887, 14835 (d?), 20842(*A*3) [f.], 24162, 24229(*A*3) (d?), 24445 (d?).
1550: 3018 (d?), 10450 f. (d?), 24078 sold (d?), 24665 (d).
1551: 21690.2 f., 25852(*A*3) [f.] (d?).
1551/52: 427.6.

Strand (Strond) Inn, Company of.
Patron in London, 1494? An Inn of Chancery belonging to the Middle Temple. Its building was among those demolished c. 1548 to make way for Somerset House.
1494: 23877.7 at instance of (d?).

Straten, Derick van der (Theodoricus Plateanus).
Printer in Wesel, 1546–c. 1565. [Duff, *Century*: 122; Benzing 480–1; *TBS* 11 (1909–11): 232–6; *Library* 16 (1936): 452–4.]
1546: [848] (false), [14717] (d), [16984(*A*3)] (d?).
1547: [850] (false), [1279] (d?), [1305] (d?).
1548: [1287] (false, d?), [1295], [15180] (d?), [17320].
1549: 1296 per.

Stroud, John.
Puritan minister, fl. 1568–1582?† and printer? or editor? in Hemel Hempstead, 1572–1573. [A. F. Scott Pearson, *Thomas Cartwright*, Cambridge, 1925, pp. 110-13.]
1572: [4713?] (d), [10392?] (d), [10847?] (d), [10848?] (d), [10850?] (d).
1573: [4711?] (d), [4712?] (d).

Stule, Charles (Karolus).
Patron in Edinburgh, c. 1520. Possibly the monk of the Abbey of Kiwinning who was incorporated in the University of Glasgow in 1519. [D&E I.101.]
No address used.
1520: 15791.5 mandato (c).

Sudbury, John.
Printseller in London, 1600?–1618? Possibly the John Sutbury apprenticed in 1568 (Arber I.371) of whom there is nothing further in Stat. Co. records. In partnership with his nephew, **George Humble**, c. 1603?–1618? It seems probable that his name was not immediately erased from the imprints of all plates when he died or retired around 1618. [*Dict. 1*; Globe 216.]
in Pope's Head Alley (O.11), 1600? (3171.8)–1618? (3062.5, BO copy; 3062.6, ILL copy); in 1615 (23041.2, text to accompany most maps) 'Palace' is substituted for 'Alley'
— against the [Royal] Exchange, 1610 (many maps in 23041, e.g. Sussex, Surrey)
at the White Horse —, 1604? (775.7, possibly should be dated later), 1611 (23045)
1600: 3171.8 sold (d?).
1603: 7579.5 sold (c?), 13087.5 sold (d?).
1604: 775.7 sold (d?).
1611: 23041 sold, 23045 sold.
1612: 7058.5 sold (d), 23041 sold.
1613: 12863a sold (c).
1614: 23041.4 sold, 23046 sold.
1615: 3715.5 sold (d), 23041.2 f.
1616: 23044 sold.
1617: 10690.5 sold (d).
1618: 3062.2 sold (d?), 3062.3 sold (d?).

1622: 3062.5 sold (c?).
1623: 23041.6 sold (d?).
1625: 3062.6 (c?).

Suethon. *See* Sutton.

Sultaceterus, Baocius, *pseud.*
'Printer' in 'Pesclavium', 1589. Anagram for Jacobus Castelvetrus, the editor. The actual printer was J. Wolfe.
1589: 10511 ap.

Superiors, *Ecclesiastical.*
Although recusant books often state on the title-page 'permissu superiorum', the following imprints are all satirical and appear in London-printed books attacking the jesuits.
1609: 14525 by permission of.
1613: 13539 by authority of, 21621 with authority of.

Sutor, Raoul. *See* Cousturier.

Sutton, Bartholomew.
Bookseller in London, (1608) 1609–1611† (*Loan Book*). In partnership with **William Barrenger**, who continued at the same address. [*Dict. 1*; DFM 2744; *Loan Book*, 1608–10.]
dw. in Paul's Churchyard near (at) the great North door of Paul's Church (A.2), 1609 (14757, alone; 14758, omits 'dw.', with W. Barrenger)
1069: 20999 (d/error).
1609: 6637.5 f., 13018.3 f., 14757–8 f., 15537.5 f., 20999 f. (d).
1610: 15537.5 f.

Sutton, Edward.
Bookseller and bookbinder in London, at least 1553–1570†. [Duff, *Century*.]
in Lombard Street at the Cradle (O.12), 1553 (18244, omits sign)–1563 (5553, has 'dw.'); the earliest use of the sign is 1555 (647, colophon)
1553: 18244 [f.].
1555: 647 [f.].
1562: 5034 f. (d), 11312 f. (d), 16849 f., 16849.3 f., 16849.7 f., 16850 f. (d), 21506 f.
1563: 5553 f.
1566: 5468 ent.

Sutton, Henry.
Bookseller and printer in London, c. 1550–1563 at least; died between 1577–78 and 11 Dec. 1581 (Arber I.478, II.685). In partnership 1553–1557 with **John Kingston**, under whom are listed other items during this period which Sutton may have helped to print. [Duff, *Century*.]
dw. in Paul's Churchyard at the Black Moryan (?A.1), c. 1550 (18848(*A3*))–1553 (11971, omits sign, with J. Kingston); in 1552? (4527.2, has Black 'Boy')
dw. in Paternoster Row at the Black Moryan (C.7), 1559 (295)–1561, 8 Jan. (15418, has Black 'Boy')
1550: 18848(*A3*) f. (c).
1552: 4527.2 (d?), 4527.4 (d?), 4527.6 (d?), 4527.8 (d?), [7555.5?] (d?), 18969.5 (d?).
1553: 2425, 2426, 11971, [12526.5] (d).
1553/54: 481.
1554: 16152, [16153–4], [16244], [19547] (d?), 23010.7.
1554/55: [447.7].
1555: [2979] (c?), 3197, [10249], 15839, 16134, 16218, [16245], 16252, 16266.
1556: 15842, 16108.
1557: 7605.5 (note), 10461 ex off., [14326.5] (d), 16081, [16109] (d?), [16109.5?] (d?), [16219], 24650.5 ent.
1558: 6463–3.2, 15483–3.5.
1558/59: 492.
1559: 295, 19893, 19893a.
1559/60: 482.3.
1560: 4325, 4770 ex off., 11419 ex off., 11420, 17864.5 (d?), 19137.
1561: 15415, 22223.
1561/62: 492.7 (note).
1562: 5034 (d), 11312 (d), 16850 (d), 21506, 24686.

Sutton (Suethon), Lewis.
Bookseller in London, before 1526–1541?†. He followed **John Rastell** at the Mermaid in Cheapside (N.2), 1536–41 (*Memorials* 52). [Duff, *Century* 153, 154.]
No address used.
1527: 15863 imp.

Sutton, William, *the younger.*
Clergyman, fl. 1628–1638; editor and publisher of his deceased father's work in Oxford. [Wood, *Ath. Ox.*, ed. Bliss, II.546.]
No address used.
1635: 23508 f.

Note: *Dict. 1* and *Dict. 2* each have an entry under **Robert Swaine**, but the end of the two men's careers were mistakenly transposed.

Swaine (Swayne), Robert 1.
Stationer in London, (1617) 1621–1641 at least. His last SR entry was made on 9 May 1632 (24633: Arber IV.276). [*Dict. 1*/*Dict. 2*; DFM 308.]
at the Bible in Britain's Burse (X.10), 1622 (21861)–1632 (24633)
1622: 21861 sold. **1625:** 19850 ent. **1627:** 18915 f. **1630:** 19772 f.
1632: 24633 f.

Swaine, Robert 2.
Bookseller in London, (1628) 1629–1630?†. Possibly dead or incapacitated by 23 Nov. 1630, when an apprentice from Dorset (DFM 2486), this Swaine's native county, was turned over to **Thomas Jones 2**. Swaine's widow, Martha, assigned her rights in 10634.7–10635.3 to **Richard Royston** on 6 Feb. 1632 (Arber IV.271). [*Dict. 2*/*Dict. 1*; DFM 1306.]
at the Bull's Head in Paul's Churchyard (A.2), 1629 (10634.7; 23368, has 'shop')
1629: 10634.7 f., 15593(*A3*) f. & sold, 23368 sold.
1632: 10635.3 ass'd.

Swartz, Giovanni, *pseud.*
Printer in 'Monaco', 1586. = J. Wolfe (Woodfield no. 42).
1586: 19769.7.

Sweeting, John.
Bookseller in London, 1639–1661†. [*Dict. 2*; DFM 560.]
shop in Cornhill near Pope's Head Alley at the Crown (O.11), 1639 (23747; 4330, omits 'shop' and sign)
1639: 4330 sold, 18173 ven., 23747 f.

Swingen (Swingenius), Hendrik.
Printer in Antwerp, 1587–1608 (1615†). [Rouzet.]
1601: 18857 typis (d?). **1608:** 24627a.8–.10 typis.

Swinhowe, George.
Stationer in London, (1589) 1602 (called to the Livery: Arber II.874)–1638 (*C-B C*: 428). Although active in the affairs of the Stat. Co., he seems not to have engaged in retail trade. His only entry in the SR is on behalf of the Latin Stock. One of the *assignees of* **J. Battersby**. [*Dict. 1*.]
No address known.
1620: 19443 ent.

Sylvius. *See* Silvius.

Symcock, Thomas.
Patentee for the printing of paper and parchment on one side only, 1619–1630? His partner 1619–26? was **Roger Wood**, and during this period **Edward Allde** seems to have done the actual printing for them. In 1628 Symcock set up his own press. [*Dict. 1*; *C-B C*: xvi–xxii; Greg, *Companion*: 164–75.]
No address used.
1620: 8615 ass'n, 8646 [f.], 8647 [f.], 8648 [f.].
1621: 8651 [f.], 8652 [f.], 8653 [f.], 8654 [f.], 8658 [f.].
1622: 8685.5 [f.], 8686.5 [f.].
1623: 8716.5 [f.].
1628: 8897.5 [f.] ass'ns, 8903 [f.].
1628–29: (all undated ballads having 'assignees' imprints): 15.5, 1327, 1331.3, 3694.7, 3729, 4541.7, 5773, 5877, 6102, 6191, 6809, 6922.4, 7565.6, 14544, 14577, 14961, 15186, 17187, 16758, 16862.1, 16862.9, 16863, 16864.5, 16864a.9, 16864a.11(*A3*), 16865, 17777.7, 18295, 19224.5, 19246, 19271, 20602.5, 21689, 22655, 22918.7, 23435a.7, 24092.7, 24369, 25230.
1630: [20314.7(*A3*) ass'ns?].

Symmes, Symmons. *See* Simmes, Simmons.

Symson, Andrew.
Printer and bookseller in Edinburgh, 1699–1706. [*Dict. 3*.]
1606: 14465.5 (d/error). **1706:** 14465.5 (d).

Syngleton. *See* Singleton.

T

Tab (Dabbe), Henry.
Bookseller in London, at least 1523 (when he was in St. Faith's parish (A.4): *Library* 9 (1908): 259)–1548†. It is possible that from 1547 he was also a printer. [Duff, *Century*.]
in Paul's Churchyard at the $ Judith (A.4), 1542 (12468)–1545? (22598, has 'dw.'); in 1547? (3310) omits sign
1542: 12468 f. (d). **1545:** 22598 f. (d?). **1547:** 3310 [f.] (d?). **1548:** 24203.7 [f.] (d?).

Taberniel. *See* Tavernier.

Tailer, W.
Publisher in London, 1596–1597. Possibly the William Taylor freed as a Draper in 1595 by **Abraham Veale**. [*Dict. 1*.]
No address used.
1596–97: 12919–20 imp.

Tailleur. *See* Le Tailleur.

Tanton. *See* Taunton.

Tapp (Tap), John.
Bookseller in London, 1600–1631†. Freed as a Draper on 31 Jan. 1597 by **Hugh Astley**; transferred to the Stat. Co. in 1600. His second shop came from Astley. Tapp's widow apparently remarried **Joseph Hurlock**, to whom the shop passed. [*Dict. 1*; Taylor 193.]
shop on Tower Hill near the bulwark gate (U.3), 1602 (3714)–1609 (6886)
shop at St. Magnus' corner (T.8), 1610 (3190)–1631 (23682)
1602: 3714 f., 23679 f.
1604: 3682 f.
1605: 20093 f.
1607: 3707.4 f.
1608: 3647 f., 22795–5.7 f., 23679.5 f.
1609: 5804 f., 6886 f., 22142 f.
1610: 3190 f.
1611: 3707.7 f., 6890 f.
1612: 3708 f., 21550 f.
1613: 3709 f., 21392 f. (d), [21392.3 f.] (d?), 26021 f.
1614: 12289 sold, 18652 f., 19967 f.
1615: 3710 f., 5805 f., 23680 f.
1617: 23680.3 f.
1619: 12289.5 sold.
1620: 5948 f., 12518 sold, 23680.5 f.
1621: 11483 f.
1622: 23680.7 f.
1623: 12521 (note), 12521.3–.5 sold, 24921 sold.
1624: 10921 f. (d), 18676 f.
1625: 23681 f.
1627: 26022 f.
1628: 18674 f.
1630: [1590.5 f.?] (c), 5805.5 f., 19966 f., 19968 f.
1631: 23682 f., 26022 ass'd.

Tathyll. *See* Tottell.

Taunton (Tanton), Henry.
Bookseller in London, (1631) 1632–1638†. Husband of **Sarah Taunton**. [*Dict. 1*; DFM 1924.]
shop in St. Dunstan's Churchyard in Fleet Street (W.9), 1632 (4140, omits 'in ... Street')–1638 (20221)
1632: 4140 f.
1633: 12370 f., 22849.5 sold.
1634: 12370a f., 25900 ent.
1635: 13223 f., 17358 f., 25900d f.
1636: 18427 f., 20219 f.
1637: 20220 f., 20221.1 (note).
1638: 20221 f.

Taunton, Sarah.
Bookseller in London, 1638. Widow of **Henry Taunton**.
her shop in St. Dunstan's Churchyard in Fleet Street (W.9), 1638 (20221.1)
1638: 20221.1 f.

Taverner, Richard.
Religious reformer, editor, and translator, b. 1505?–1575†. [*DNB*; *Library* 19 (1964): 212–14.]
He subsidized publication of his own works, which were issued largely in association with **Richard Bankes** and **Anthony Clerke**. Taverner's own 'in (ex) aedibus' imprints below have no address, but in other works of his the two following addresses appear, and both premises may have been owned by Taverner.
at the White Hart in Fleet Street (W.2), 1539 (10437)–1546? (2969.5), ? = A. Clerke
next (to) the White Hart in Fleet Street (W.2), 1542? (2968.3)–1543? (2967.5), ? = R. Bankes
1539: 23711a in aed.
1540: 4843 ex aed., 9290.5 ex aed., 10445 ex aed.

Tavernier (Taberniel), Artus.
Printer in Antwerp, 1580, and in Salamanca, 1603–c. 1615 at least. [Rouzet.]
1603: [21595] (d).

Tavernier (Tavernor), Melchior.
Engraver and printseller in Paris, c. 1614–1641†. [Thieme-Becker.]
1628: 23716.5.

Taylor, Henry.
Journeyman printer in Edinburgh 1599, in Louvain 1615–1616 at least, and in Douai 1624. Apprenticed to **William Hoskins** for seven and a quarter years in 1593 and freed by the latter's widow in 1604 (Arber II.187, 735). By Taylor's own testimony in 1616 he had helped print two books: in 1599 (14348) and in 1615 (4744); *see* Ian Philip, *Dragon's Teeth*, Honnold Library Society, Claremont, Calif., 1970, pp. 18–19, citing State Papers Foreign (Flemish): SP 77/12 (55). [*Dict. 1*; *Répertoire 17e*, IV.10.]
1624: 16922a.9(*A*3), 24738.

Taylor, John.
Member of the Watermen's Company, author, and traveller in London and elsewhere, b. 1580–1653†. [*DNB*.]
No address used.
1618: 23784 at charges of. **1623:** 23778 f.

Taylor, W. *See* Tailer.

Taylor, William.
Journeyman printer in London, 1637. Apprenticed to and freed in the name of **Elizabeth Allde**. Another Allde apprentice, **Gregory Dexter**, confessed to printing with Taylor a pamphlet of William Prynne's in the Allde establishment (near Christ Church (C.1)), though it is unlikely that 20454.3 is the edition in question. [DFM 16.]
1637: [20454.3?] (d).

Teage (Teague, Tege), John.
Bookseller in London, (1619) 1620–1623. [*Dict. 1*; DFM 2684; *Loan Book*, 1622–25.]
shop in Paul's Churchyard at the Golden Ball (A.2), 1620 (5980)–1622 (1002, omits 'Golden')
1620: 5980 f.
1621: 5974 f., 16691 f.
1622: 1002 f., 1003–3.5 f., 1004 f., 5134 f., 5978 imp.

Telotson (Tylotson), William.
Bookseller in London, 1543–1545. [Duff, *Century*.]
at the West door of Paul's (A.10) 1543 (3327, colophon)–1545, 10 Aug. (10438, colophon)
1543: 3327 sold (d), 11966.5 sold (d?), 15835 ven., 23712 sold (d?).
1543/44: 393 sold, 508.5 sold.
1544: 15835 sold, 20116 sold (d), 20200 sold (d?).
1545: 10438 sold.

Télu, Pierre.
Printer in Douai, 1618–1619. [*Dict. 1*; *Répertoire 17e*, IV.10.]
1618: 19073.

Thackwell, Roger.
Printer using a secret recusant press in Wales? c. 1585? *See* also **Rhiwledyn Press**. [*Dict. 1*; *BS* 2 (1953): 37–54.]
1585: [21077.5?] (c?).

Theophilus, *Brugensis, pseud.*
Printer 'outside London', 1554. ? = E. van der Erve, Emden.
1554: 18309.5.

Theunisz, Jan.
Printer in Leiden, 1600–1604, and in Amsterdam, 1605–1626. [Gruys; Briels 464.]
1605: [3849–9.5(***A***)?], [3863(***A***)?], [3881(***A***)?].
1606: [2780(***A***)?], 3867.7, [3891(***A***)?].

Thibout, Guillaume.
Printer and typefounder in Paris, 1544–1558. [Renouard.]
1552: 6832.29 chez.

Thomas, John.
Stationer in London, (1633) 1637 (Arber IV.389)–1644 at least. He is apparently the third John who was a Stationer, the two earlier ones (in *Dict. 1*: one died in 1587? and one was freed the same year) having bound apprentices but owned no copyrights. The present John, to whom the apprentices DFM 2532, 2538 should be attributed and who may be among those of this name receiving payment in the *Poor Book*, was probably the father of the next John, freed in 1656 (DFM II.4447). [*Dict. 2*; DFM 2562; *Loan Book*, 1634–37.]
No address used.
1640: 26016 f.

Thomas, Oliver.
Welsh author and clergyman, fl. 1630–1631.
1631: [24007a] f.

Thomas, Thomas 1.
Printer in Cambridge, 1583–1588†. One of the **Printers to the University** (*see* Cambridge University). His stepdaughter married **John Legat 1**. [*Dict. 1*; *TCBS* 4 (1967): 276–90, 339–62.]
No address used; for the position of the press *see* Cambridge University
1583: 20028.9(***A***3).
1584: 3745 ex off., 15243 ex off., 15255 ex off., 17524 ex off., 18951 ex off., 21354.
1585: 4474.1 ex off., 4474.79 ex off., 4476.5 ex off., 15253, 19929, 19929.5, 24529 ex off., 25364, 25674 ex off.
1586: [3059.4], 5009, 5155.
1587: 4660 ex off., 19974.8 ex off., 24008 ex off. (d), 24531 ex off.
1588: 25366.

Thomas, Thomas 2.
Bookseller in Bristol, 1639.
No address known.
1639: 11250 (note).

Thomason (Thompson, Tompson), George.
Bookseller in London, (1626) 1627–1666†. Apparently worked in and possibly by 1637 had succeeded to the shop of his former master, **Henry Fetherstone**. In partnership with **Octavian Pulleyn**, 1635–1645. [*Dict. 2*; DFM 1315; *Library* 13 (1958): 102–18; 14 (1959): 11–17.]
dw. at the Rose in Paul's Churchyard (A.3), 1637 [4789, in title], 1638 (17553)–1639 (15496, omits 'dw.', with O. Pulleyn) and until 1645
1628: 17528 f.
1635: 21537.3 imp.
1637: [4789] ven. (in title).
1638: 4753 ent., 17553.
1639: 15496–7 f., 20488 pour, 20489 pour, 22058 f.

Thompson, J. *See* Tomson.

Thorne (Dorne), John.
Bookseller in Oxford, before 1520–1528 at least. He lived in St. Mary's parish. [Duff, *Century* 41.]
No address used.
1526: 18833a ven. (c). **1527:** 15574 ven.

Thorp, Giles.
Printer in Amsterdam, 1604–1622?†. Worked primarily for the exiled (separatist) English Church there. The printing material passed to his *successors*. [*Dict. 1*; *Library* 5 (1951): 219–30.]
1604: [239], [1527] (d?), [3856.5?].

Thorp, G. — *cont.*
1605: [3848?].
1606: [1524] (d?), 3891 (note), [14662?].
1607: 228, [18435].
1608: [234], [3878?], [14660], 18553.
1609: 235, [3879.5], [14659?], [20605].
1610: [220.5], [3868], [3883], 5450, [21109].
1611: [221], [3876], [7751?], [7751.2?], [19608.5].
1612: 2407, [5449], [15351.7].
1613: 209, 12857.8, [20620].
1614: [20620].
1615: [229], [240], [21111].
1616: [210], [5556], [14330] (d).
1617: [212], [2411].
1618: [214], [2411].
1619: [215], [216], 12858 (false), [23235], [25647].
1620: [236], [2731?], [4354], [4355], [4365].
1621: [211], [563.7(***A***)?], [1640], [4352], [4361.5], [20410], [20411], [22015].
1622: [559], [21874].

Thorp, Giles, *Successors of.*
Printers in Amsterdam, 1623–1636. They augmented Thorp's printing stock with material formerly belonging to **William Brewster**. During at least part of 1625–1628 the press was apparently in the hands of **Richard Plater**, under whom are listed other items. In 1637 part of the printing material passed to the **Richt Right Press**. [*Library* 5 (1951): 230–42.]
1623: [226], [560], [2775].
1624: [222], [4356], [4357], [4358], [10404] (d?), [13531.5], [15431], [15432], [18837], [21107a].
1625: [1580] (c), [14425] (d), [15431.5], [21108], [21112], [21492], [24305].
1628: [20577] (false).
1629: [4153.7], [15428.5] (d).
1630: [227], [722], [4748], [19798.5].
1631: [11128.5] (d), [20484], [23605], [24402], [24403] (d?).
1632: [2734.5], [4574.5], [12531.7?] (d), [13071].
1633: [555].
1634: [4574], [7678], [14555?].
1635: [3753], [5846.4], [11129], [21107.5].
1636: [21107.7].

Thorpe (Thorp), Thomas.
Stationer in London, (1594) 1603–1625. Although he owned or shared many copyrights, he seems not to have been active in the retail trade. [*Dict. 1*; *Poor Book*, 1623–25.]
No address noted.
1603: 7448 f., 7459 f., 17510 f.
1604: 17479 ent., 26040 f., 26043.3 f.
1605: 4963 f., 4970 ent., 14782 f.
1606: 4978 f., 14774 f.
1607: 14783 f., 17487 f., 24996 f.
1608: 4968 f., 14761 f. (d), 25262 f. (d).
1609: 12686 ent., 22353–3a f.
1610: 10424 f., 13529 f.
1611: 1222 ent., 4705 f., 5810 f.
1612: 7373.6 f., 10782.5 f., 17818 f., 21526(***A***3) ent.
1613: 14973 f., 18368 f., 21355 f., 22528 f., 23750 ent.
1614: 5056 f., 6616 f., 16885a f.
1615: 24997 f.
1616: 5779 f.
1618: 5056.5 f., 11707 f., 18800 f.
1621: 591 f.
1622: 10860 f., 11546 f.
1623: 10782.7 f.
1624: 10861 f., 17421 ass'd.
1625: 4969 f.

Thrale, Richard.
Bookseller in London, (1623) 1625–1667. His shop was shared with or owned by **George Vincent 2**, 1625–1627. [*Dict. 2*; DFM 1069.]
at the Cross Keys at Paul's gate (A.5), 1625 (6746)–1640 (22918, has 'shop') at least; variations:
dw. in Paul's Churchyard at the Cross Keys, 1628 (14905), 1633 (13259, omits 'dw.')

Thrale, R. — *cont.*
shop at Paul's gate next to Cheapside [no sign], 1629 (25637)
1625: 6746 sold.
1628: 3913.5 f. (d?), 14905 sold.
1629: 6399 f., 7617 sold, 21831 f., 25637 f.
1630: 21220 f., 21836 sold, 24929 f.
1631: 12933 sold.
1632: 21832 sold, 23374 imp.
1633: 13259 f.
1634: 24826 pro, 24826.5 pro.
1635: 1323 f.
1636: 23935.5(*A*3) sold.
1637: 3537 ent., 3723 f., 6399 ent., 7512 ent., 23015 f., 25638 f.
1638: 10170 f. (d?), 23936 f., 24827 sumpt.
1639: 6390 pro, 20490 f., 21233 sold.
1640: 22918 f.

Timme. *See* Tymme.

Tisdale (Tysdale), John.
Printer in London, (1554) 1557?–1563 (before 1578†: Arber II. 676). His first two imprints were shared with **John Charlewood**. [Duff, *Century*.]
in Holborn near to the conduit at the Saracen's Head (D.9), 1557? (5229; 17236 has only 'at Holborn conduit'); both with J. Charlewood
in Smithfield at the Mitre (E.1), 1558, 5 Mar. (10917)
dw. in Knightrider Street near to the Queen's Wardrobe (Waredrop (R.2)), 1560 (4857)–1561 (12742, omits 'near ... Wardrobe')
shop in the upper end of Lombard Street in All Hallows' Churchyard near unto Grace Church (P.1), 1561 (24683)–1563 (17118, adds: at the $ Eagle's Foot); sometimes omits 'in All Hallows' ... Church', 1562 (19492)
1557: 5229(*A*3) (d?), 17236(*A*3) (d?).
1558: 10917.
1560: 1274, 1988.8 ent., 3020 ent., 4857, 10470.3 (d), [13306] (c), 13765 (d?), [18970] (d), 19148, 23884a (d?), 24658 (c).
1561: 1289, 12742, 17147(*A*3) ?ent., 19149, 24680 (d), 24681 (d), 24683, 24684 (d), 24685.
1562: 2028 (d?), 7280 ent., 9344, 13742, 13752, 19492, 21056.6 ent., 23949 (d?).
1563: 17118.

Tobie, George.
Putative bookseller in London, 1594. The imprint in which his name appears is in pen facsimile and very likely faked. [*Dict. 1.*]
1594: 13595 (note).

Toëus, Toius. *See* Toy.

Tomes, Henry.
Bookseller in London, (1597) 1598–1607. Undoubtedly the Henry 'Thomas' bound to Thomas Hodgkinson in 1590 and freed by the latter's widow in 1597 (Arber II.171, 720). [*Dict. 1.*]
shop near St. Sepulchre's Church at the White Bear (D.8), 1598 (Hazlitt H.147, from lost earlier ed. of 6181.2)
in Holborn (V.10), 1604–1607
shop by Gray's Inn new gate —, 1604 (18745)
shop at (over against) Gray's Inn gate —, 1605 (1164)–1607 (25768)
n.d.: 1119.5–20 (forged). **1604:** 1118–8.5 f., 18745 f. **1605:** 1164 f., 14481 f. **1606:** 3405 f. **1607:** 25768 f.

Tompson, G. *See* Thomason.

Tomson (Thompson), John.
Instrument maker and bookseller in London, fl. 1609–1648. [Taylor 200.]
his house in Hosier Lane (E.7), 1623 (12521.7)–c. 1630 (12522.5, frontispiece 4)
1632: 12521.7 sold.

Torriano, Giovanni.
Italian schoolmaster and author in London, fl. 1639–1688? (Wing T 1923).
his lodging in Abchurch Lane adjoining to Lombard Street (O.13), 1639 (24138)
1639: 24138 sold. **1640:** 24137.5 f.

Tottell (Tathyll, Tothill, Tottyl), Richard.
Printer and bookseller in London, (1547) c. 1550–1593†. Son-in-law of **Richard Grafton** and eventually succeeded to his printing material. Since the material was also used by **Robert Caly**, 1553–1558, it is not clear whether it was divided between them during that period or whether one printed for the other. Further study is indicated.
From 1553 Tottell was patentee for the printing of law books, superseding **William Powell** in that function. One of his apprentices, **William Hoskins**, freed in 1571, may have acted as Tottell's foreman for much of the time thereafter. The date of some of Tottell's editions is often repeated in subsequent ones or is entirely erroneous. Although an attempt to establish the true dates has been made with the Yearbooks (STC numbers between 9551 and 9967), multiple editions of the same date under other headings have not been re-examined. Following Tottell's death the law-book patent was exercised by **Charles** and **Jane Yetsweirt**. *See* also Appendices B, C/7–13, and D/1–60. [Duff, *Century*; *Library* 8 (1927): 199–232.]
in Fleet Street, 1552–1593.
— between the two Temple gates (W.12), 1552 (Herbert II.807, lost ed. of 24961)
dw. — between the two Temple gates at the Hand and Star (W.12), 1553, 26 Jan (9607), 11 Sept. (9693)
dw. — at the Hand and Star, within Temple Bar (W.13), 1553 (6142.5)–1593 (21575, omits 'dw.')
1550: [17770.5] (c), [18408?] (d?).
1553: 6141.5–42, 6142.5, 9607, 9670.5 (d?), 9677 per (d?), 9693, 9712 (d?), 9936.5 (d?), 9946.5 (d?), 9947.7 (d?), 10954 (note), 10959 in aed., 10960 (d/repeat), 18082 in aed., 20837 ap., 24595.
1554: 2426.5, 3177 in aed., 10975, 11905 in aed. (d?), 15737, 21570.5 in aed., 21571–1.5 (d/repeat), 22816 (d), 24747.
1555: 987 in aed., 1255.5 in aed. (c), 9277.5 (note), 9582 in aed., 9604 (d/repeat), 9605, 9666 (d?), 9682.5 (d?), 9688 (d?), 9896.5, 9906.7 (d?), 9914 (d?), 9922, 9923–3.5 (d/repeat), 11000.4 (d?), 12951 [f.], 19633 in aed., 22429 in aed.
1556: 3312 f. (d?), 5281, 9277.5 in aed., 9278 (d/repeat), 9582 in aed., 9621, 9628, 9634 (d?), 9639, 9694, 9700 (d?), 9706 (d?), 9718, 9723, 9728, 9734, 9735 (d/repeat), 9739, 9740 (d/repeat), 9746, 9747 (d/repeat), 9761, 9774, 9775–6 (d/repeat), 9808 (d/error), 9815, 9822, 9823–4 (d/repeat), 9828, 9829 (d/error), 9848, 9853, 9853.5 (d/repeat), 9857–8 (d/error), 9868, 9874, 9874.5–5.5 (d/repeat), 9878, 9880 (d/repeat), 9885 (d?), 9892, 9892.5 (d/repeat), 9937 (d/error), 9948 (d/error), 9955.7, 9956–7 (d/repeat), 9963, 9963.4–.7 (d/repeat), 14881, 15766–6.5, 15767, [18095–5.5], 21571 in aed. (d?).
1557: 1257 in aed., 9306 in aed., [9424] (d?), 9752, 9757 (d?), 9766, 9799, 9809 (d/repeat), 9810, 9859, 9863, 9863.5 (d/repeat), 13860 ap., 13861 ap., 13862 ap., 15738 ap., 15738.3 ap., 15738.7 ap., 18076 at costs of, 18398 in aed., 18398.5 in aed., 18408.7, 18409, 23219 in aed., 24372, 24798 ap.
1558: 5281.8, 5282 (d/repeat), 9781, 9786, 9791.5, 9792 (d/repeat), 9794 (d/repeat), 9833.5 (d?), 9897–7.5 (d/error), 20063.5 ent.
1559: 3332.7, 3333, 3334 (d/repeat), 7589.5 (d), 7590 (d), 9307 in aed., 9307.5 in aed., 9645, 9841.5, 9898 (d/repeat), 9899, 9908 (d?), 9915 (d?), 9923 (d?), 9957.5, 9963.4 (d?), 13863 ap., 13863.5–.7 ap., 14882, 14883, 22227, 22227a.
1560: 9278 in aed. (c?), 9293a.7 (c?), [9430.5] (d?), [9437.3] (d?), 9937.5, 9938 (d/repeat), 9948.4 (d?), 10960 in aed., 10976, 19634 ap. (d?), 23220 in aed.
1561: 3334, 6143 in aed., [9556] (d?), [9559] (d?), 9563, 9571, 9574, 9577, 9580, 9600 in aed., 9661, 18363 in aed.
1562: 1356.7 in aed., 3335, 9551, 9608, 9654, 9671, 9678, 9713, 12148 in aed., 15388, 24372.5 in aed. (d).
1563: 5282 (d?), 9608, 9614 in aed., 9615 (d/repeat), 9923.5 (d?), 9938 (d?), 9948.7 (d?), 9956 (d?), 9963.7 (d?), 12148–9 in aed., 20703.5 in aed.
1564: 1258, 9892.5 (d?), 9898 (d?), 9908.5 (d?), 9915.5 (d?), 12150 in aed.
1565: 9308 in aed., [9421.4] (c?), [9425] (d?), 9583 in aed., 9604 (c?), 9775 (d), 9777, 9848.5 (d?), 9853.5 (d?), 9868.5 (d?), 9874.5 (d?), 9881 (d?), 10956 in aed., 10956.5 in aed., 11631 in aed., 13864 ap., 19634.5 ap. (d?), 21571.5 in aed. (d?).
1566: 3336, 9308.5 in aed., 9729, 9735 (d?), 9740 (d?), 9747 (d?), 9762, 9782, 9787, 9788 (d/repeat), 9792 (d?), 9800, 9801 (d/repeat), 9809 (d?), 9823 (d?), 9829 (d?), 9834, 9835 (d/repeat), 9842, 9857 (d?), 9863.5 (d?), 9886, 9887 (d/repeat), 9939, 9949,

Tottell, R. — *cont.*
9958, 9964, 10977, 18399 in aed., 19121 f., 20730 in aed.
1567: 1259, 1356.8, 9293b, 9566, 9667, 9683 (d?), 9688.5, 9689 (d/repeat), 9701, 9707, 9714, 9719, 9724, 9753, 9758, 9767, 9816, 9817 (d/repeat), 9924, 9924.5 (d/repeat), 9940 (d/error), 9950 (d/error), 9959 (d/error), 10961 in aed., 10961.4–.7 (d/repeat), 11194, 13865 ap., 15739, 18399 in aed., 19635 ap., 19635.5 ap., 20704 in aed., 23213, 23221 in aed.
1568: 3336.5, 5283, 9309 in aed., 9635, 9640, 9900, 9900.5 (d/repeat), 9909, 9916, 11632 in aed., 12428, 15389, 15769.3, 23214.
1569: 3337, 3475 ap., 9941, 9951, 9960, 9966, 9966.3 (d/repeat), 12147 f., 14884, 15740, 21572 in aed.
1570: 6144 in aed., 9294, [9421.5] (c?), [9421.6] (c?), [9426] (c), [9431] (c), [9437.5] (c), [9440.2] (c), 9546 in aed. (d), 9615 in aed., 9622, 9629, 9646, 9655, 9662, 9695, 10223.5, 10992, 12151 in aed., 24373 in aed.
1571: 1259.5, 6144 in aed., 9776 (d?), 12153 in aed., 20040 in aed., 24374 in aed.
1571/72: 9345 in aed.
1572: 3338 in aed., 3393 in aed., 9311 in aed., 9783, 9788 (d?), 9794 (d?), 9811, 9824 (d?), 9830, 9843, 9849, 9854, 9864, 9869, 9875 (d?), 9880 (d?), 9893, 12152 in aed., 12154 in aed., 14129, 15741, 15742 (d/repeat), 15769.7, 18400 in aed., 20705 in aed., 25807 in aed.
1573: 3827 in aed., 9801 (d?), 9817 (d?), 9835 (d?), 9858 (d?), 9887 (d?), 9897.5 (d?), 9900.5 (d?), 9924.5 (d?), 11195, 23215, 24252, 24375 [f.?], 24376, 24377, 25671 ex bibliotheca Tottellina.
1574: [3368.5-Bacon, N.?] (d?), 5284, 9312 in aed., 9672, 9679, 9910, 9918, 9940 (d?), 9950 (d?), 9959 (d?), 9966.3 (d?), 13866 ap., 14885, 15742, 15770, 20731 in aed., 23222 in aed., 24378.
1575: 1260, 3339 in aed., 5284, 9609, 9702, 9708, 9715, 9720, 9725, 9736, 9741, 9748, 9754, 9759, 9763, 9768, [9927.5] (c?), 20706 in aed., 21573 in aed., 23325 (d).
1576: 3340 in aed., [3820.5?], 3828 in aed., 9280, 9281, [9432] (d?), [9437.7] (d?), 9584 in aed., 9609, 9730, 10961.4–.7 in aed., 15390, 15770.5, 18411, 19636 ap., 24378.5.
1577: 9526.7 in aed., 10957 in aed., 15743, 23216, 24379.
1577/78: 9527 in aed.
1578: 3341 in aed., 3821 in aed., 3821.5 in aed., [4303.5?], 9709, 9894, 20041 in aed., 20403 in aed.
1579: 1260a, 3341.3 in aed., 9897 (d), 9901, 9942, 9952, 9961, 9966.5, 11034 in aed., 14886, 15744, 20046.3 in aed., 20706.5 in aed., 20707 in aed., 23325.7 (d), 23934 in aed.
1580: 5285 (note), 9295.4, 9601 in aed., 9925 in aed., 14886–7, 15017 in aed., 18401 in aed., 18411.5 (d?), 21574 in aed., 21574.5 in aed.
1581: 3341.5 in aed., 9911, 9919, 10962 in aed., 15018 in aed., 15163 by ass't of, 15745, 15771, 19637 ap., 24253.
1582: 9636, 9641, 9668, 9684 (d?), 9689 (d?), 9778, 9824.5, 9831, 9844, 9850, 9855, 9870, 9875.5 (d?), 9882, 12429, 15164 by ass't of, 15164a by ass't of.
1583 (imprints): 3341.7 ass'ns (d), 3342 ass'ns (d), 3342.3 ass'ns (d), 5285, 9789, 9795, 9808 (d?), 9860, 9864.5, 9926 in aed., 9937 (d?), 9948 (d?), 9957 (d?), 9967, 10978 (d), 12357.3, 15746, 15772, 23223 in aed., 24254 ass'n.
1583 (SR entries): [Titles entered to Tottell on 18 Feb. 1583 (Arber II.419) except as noted. Item numbers in square brackets do *not* have the Arber reference cited in STC or Addenda. For identifications in Arber order *see* Appendix B.] 1261, 1356.9, 3341.7 (28 Jan., II.418), 3393, 3475, 3823, 3829, 6144, 9282, 9295.4, [9551], [9557], [9560], [9564], [9567], [9572], [9575], [9578], [9581], [9584], [?9601 and/or 9604], [9609], [9615.4], [9623], [9630], [9636], [9641], [9647], [9657], [9663], [9668], [9673], [9680], [9684], [9689], [9696], [9702], [9709], [9715], [9720], [9725], [9730], [9736.5], [9741.5], [9748.5], [9754], [9759], [9763], [9768], [9778], [9783.5], [9789], [9795], [9802], [9803], [9808], [9818], [9824.5], [9831], [9835.5], [9844], [9850], [9855], [9860], [9864.5], [9870], [9875.5], [9882], [9887.5], [9894.5], [Edw. V inadvertently omitted: 9902], [9912], [9919.5], [9926], [9927.5], [9943], 10957, 10963, 10978 (17 Feb., II.418), [10993.9], 11195, [11632], 13866, [14886], [15019], 15391, 15746, [15772], 18363, 18402, [18411.5], 19638, 20044, 20046.7, 20708, 20731, 20837, 21575, 23217, 23223, 23934, 24254, 25807.
1584: 3343 in aed., 3344 (d/repeat), 6145 in aed., [9557] (d?), [9560] (d?), 9564, 9623, 9630, 9647, 9783.5, 9802, 9818, 9835.5, 9887.5, 10979, 13867 (note), 18402 in aed., 20046.7 in aed., 25808 (note).
1585: 7388 in aed., 9567, 9572, 9575, 9578, 9581, [9657] (d?), 9902, 9926 in aed., 15019 in aed., 15747.
1586: 3344 in aed., 3829 in aed., [9421.7] (d?), [9426.5] (d?), [9673] (d?), [9680] (d?), [9696] (d?), [9736.5] (d?), [9741.5] (d?), [9748.5] (d?), 9894.5, 15773, 15773.5 ass'ns f., 19638 ap.
1587: 3823 in aed., 9282, 9615.4 in aed., 9663, 9803, [9912] (d?), 9919.5, 10980 (d), 15020 in aed.
1588: 3344.5 (d), 7391 in aed. (d), 10963 in aed., 15748, 20044 in aed., 24255 ass'n.
1590: 23217, 25267.
1591: 7389 in aed., 9943 in aed., 15391, 15749, [15750].
1592: 7389 in aed., 15021 in aed., 15774, 20708 in aed., 25267.5–.7, 25267a.
1593: 10981 (d), 15774, 19639 ap., 21575, [25276.3] (d).

Tottell, Richard, *Successor of.*
Printer with Tottell's material in London, 1594.
1594: [12190(*A*3)].

Tournes, Jean de.
Printer in Lyons, 1540–1564. [Duff, *Century*; Muller 48.]
1553: 3043.

Towreolde, William.
Stationer in London, (1578) c. 1580–1584. [*Dict. 1.*]
shop adjoining to the little conduit in Cheap[side] (N.3), c. 1580 (3050, colophon)
1580: 3050 f.

Toy, Elizabeth.
Bookseller in London, 1556–1558 (1565†). Second wife and widow of **Robert Toy** and continued at his address: at the Bell in Paul's Churchyard (A.4). The shop passed at some time after her death to **George Bishop**. [Duff, *Century*.]
No address survives.
1557: 1342 ent., 5229 ent., 7680 ent.

Toy (Toius), Humphrey.
Bookseller in London, (1558) 1560–1577†. Son of **Robert Toy**. His last publication was evidently post-dated. His shop passed to his former apprentice, **Thomas Chard**. [*Dict. 1*; *Library* 14 (1959): 28–9, 35–6.]
dw. in Paul's Churchyard at the Helmet (A.2), 1562 (4470)–1574 (25430, colophon) at least; this was apparently near the great North door (*L&P Hen VIII*, V: 102 (no. 218)).
1560: 11419 imp.
1562: 4470 f., 10657 [f.] (d), 16827(*A*3) ent.
1564: 24565 f.
1567: 2960 at costs, 10374 f. (d), 16435 at costs, 21615 f.
1568: 6725 f. (d).
1569: 6893 f., 12147 f.
1571: 3736 f. (d), 24726.5 f. (d).
1572: 19196 f. (d), 25427 f., 25428 f.
1573: 3737 f., 10194.5 f. (d), 20309 imp., 24171 f., 25428 f., 25429 f.
1574: 10393 f., 25430 f., 25430.5 f., 25431 f.
1575: 6139 f.
1576: 22243 f., 25978 f. (d).
1577: 6787 pro.

1578: 4419 f.

Toy, John.
Bookseller in London, 1531–1535†. [Duff, *Century*.]
in Paul's Churchyard at the $ St. Nicholas (B), 1531 (23162)–1534 (23153.2)
1531: 23162 [f.]. **1534:** 23153.2 ven.

Toy (Toëus), Robert.
Bookseller in London, (before 1534) 1542–1556†. Father of **Humphrey Toy**; **Elizabeth Toy** was his second wife. His daughter married **Arthur Pepwell**. [Duff, *Century*.]
in Paul's Churchyard (A.4), 1542? (16021)–1556 (3310.7, colophon on E4r); adds: at the Bell, 1545 (5106.5, has 'dw.')–1555 (648); this was in St. Faith's parish (Plomer, *Wills*: 12)
1542: 16021 [f.] (d?), 16027 [f.], 21794 f. (d?).
1545: 5106.5 at costs, 14124 (c), 18221 [f.] (d?), 25000 at costs, 26054 f. (d?).
1546: 7703 [f.] (d), 7719 [f.], 7733 in aed., 11588 at costs, 11589 at costs, 11591 at costs, 11591.3 at costs, 14879a in aed., 15586b per

Toy, R. — *cont.*
[f.], 19785.5 at costs (d?), 19786 at costs (d), 22815 at costs.
1547: 5409 f.
1550: 5074 [f.] (d?), 7688 f., 16051 at costs (c), 19494 at costs.
1551: 2083 f., 11233 imp., 12944.5 f.
1552: 4052 f., 5241 [f.] (c), 10486.5 [f.] (d?).
1553: 4844 f., 21755a f.
1554: 1011.5 f., 22595.5 [f.] (d?), 22616 [f.] (d?).
1555: 648 [f.], 16061 in aed., 16107 in aed.
1556: 3310.7 f. (d).

Trauth, Thomas, *pseud.*
Printer in 'Jericho, in the Land of Promise', 1542. = L. van der Meulen, Bonn.
1542: 3764 (d).

Tres Viri.
Booksellers? or patrons? in London, 1594. It seems just possible that the three men were the ones who published the 1603 edition of the same work (19558): **John Harrison 1, John Norton 1**, and **Hercules Francis**. The item was printed abroad, possibly in Frankfurt am Main.
1594: 19557.3 sumpt.

Treveris, Peter.
Printer in Southwark, 1525–1532. He occasionally collaborated with or printed for **John Rastell**. Some of his printing material passed to **Thomas Raynald**. [Duff, *Century*.]
dw. in the $ Woodhouses (Wodows, i.e. Wild People), 1526, 27 July (13176); no later use noted
1525: [783] (d?), 13434, [15609.5?] (d?).
1526: 13176, [18833a] (c), [23664].
1527: 13440, [14836–6.3] (d?), [15574], [23148.8] (d?), 23182.5 (d?), 25455.5 per (d?), 25471.5 per (d?), 25489.7 per (d).
1528: [5204.3] (d?), 7542.5 (note), [15607] (d?), [25564.8] (d?), [25578.5] (d?).
1528/29: 470.9 per.
1529: 967 (d?), 5542.3 per, [7773] (d), 13177–7.5, 23149.5 (d?), 25456.3 per (d?), 25474 per (d?), 25522 in off. (d?), 25555 per (d?).
1530: [1384] (c), 5743 (d?), [10633] (d?), 10995 (d?), [14039.5] (d?), [14077c.64] (c), [—.69] (d?), [14280.7] (c), 14520.5 (d?), [14520.7(*A*3)?] (c?), [16895?] (d?), 17994.5 (c), 21565, [22607] (d?), 23150.7 (d?), 23182.9 (d?), 23198.3 (d?), [23429a.5] (d?), 25491.7 per (d?), 25506.3 per (d?), [25566.3] (d?).
1531: 170.7 (d?), [4841.7] (d?), 10633.5 (d?), 15346 (note), 21566, 23162.5 (d?), 23174.6 (d?), [23961] (d?), 25422.3 (d?), 25457 per (d?), 25475 per (d?), 25492 per (d?), 25507 per (d?), [25536.5] (d?), 25556.5 per (d?), [25566.7] (d?).
1532: 10909 sold, [14077c.123] (d), 23151.3 (d?).
1532/33: [517.12].

Triplet, Robert.
Bookbinder and maker of writing tables (tablets) in London, 1603–1615 (1631). Transferred to the Brewers' from the Stat. Co. in July 1631 (*C-B C*: 407). In the items below his name as maker of the tables appears in the title rather than the imprint. [*Dict. 1*; *Loan Book*, 1604–07.]
dw. in Distaff Lane at the $ Aqua Vitae Still, near Old Fish Street (S.3), 1603? (26050.4, colophon); no later address used
1603: 26050.4(*A*3) (d?). **1604:** 26050.6. **1609:** 26050.8. **1611:** 26050.10. **1615:** 26050.12.

Trognesius, Joachim.
Bookseller and printer in Antwerp, 1583–c. 1620 (1624†). [*Dict. 1*; Rouzet.]
1586: 1431.9 ap. **1587:** 370. **1589:** [1038]. **1592:** [10005?]. **1593:** 20633. **1596:** 26038.8 (false), 26043.5 (false).

Troost, Jan, *pseud.*
Printer in 'Auryk' [Aurich], 1541. = Catherine van Ruremund, Antwerp.
1541: 21804.

Troyens, Jasper.
Printer in Antwerp, 1577–1584, and in Dordrecht, 1589–1627 at least. [Rouzet; Gruys; Briels 476–9.]
1582: 16572.2(*A*3).

Trundle, John.
Bookseller in London, (1597) 1603–1626†. Husband of **Margery Trundle**. Beginning in 1614 several of Trundle's publications were sold by **Edward Wright**: at Christ Church gate. [*Dict. 1*; *St. Giles*, 1595–1600; *SB* 39 (1986): 177–99.]
in Barbican (I.1), 1603–1623 (*SB* 181); in 1607 (18495.5) has 'dw.'
shop — near Long Lane end, 1603 (16743.2)
shop — at the $ Nobody, 1606 (18597)–1620 (25292)
shop in Smithfield near the Hospital gate (E.8), 1624 (17308.5, omits 'in Smithfield')–1626 (19529); variation: omits 'near ... gate' 1624 (19268)
1603: 16743.2 f. (d), 16743.3 f. (d), 22275 f.
1605: 6498 ent., 18589 ent., 20753 ent., 22869 ent.
1606: 6412 f., 18597 f. (d), 22384 ent.
1607: 6496 ent., 6532 ent., 14526.5 ent., 18495 ent., 18495.5 f.
1608: 17781 ent.
1612: 5878 ent., 6507 f.
1613: 13355 ent., 13507 f., 13507.3 f., 18287 f., 25261.5 ent., 25872 ent.
1614: 5673 f., 11796 (note), 14068 f., 14068.3 f., 19120 f., 21315.4 ent., 20569 [f.] (d).
1615: 6475.5 ent., 7505 ent., 7627.5(*A*) ?ent., 11089 f. (d), 11332.5 f. (d), 16864a.1 f. (c), 17386.5 f. (d), 18747 ent., 24341.5 f. (d), 26091 ?ent.
1616: 20744 f. (d?), 22920.3 f. (d?), 24757 f. (d).
1617: 17911–1a f., 23098 f. (c), [23765 f.?] (d?).
1618: 17148 ent.
1619: 14898.5 f. (d), 14899 f., 14899.1(*A*3) f. (d?), 23624.7 f.
1620: 4793 f. (c?), 11376.5 f. (c), 12599 f., 13374 f., 13375 f., 13375.5 f., 14056 ass'd, [14899.3 f.] (c), [14899.7 f.?] (c), 15401 f. (c), 17909 ent., 22579.5 f. (c), 23765.5? f., 25292 f.
1621: 5674 ass'd, 6266 ent., 23800 f., 23800.5 f., 23808a f.
1622: 23771 f., 24090 f., 25063 f. (d?).
1623: 5764.5 f. (c), 6161 ass'd, 11090? f., 16865.7 f. (c), 18505 f. (c), 23789.7 ent., 24830.2 f. (d).
1624: 5022.5 f. (d), 17308.5 f., 19268 f. (d), 23239 f. (d), 24435.5 f. (d).
1625: 196.5 f. (c), 4687 f. (c), 6038.5 f. (d?), 6520 f., 6520.4 f., 10412 f. (c), 14426.3 f. (d), 19278 f. (c), 20823 f.
1626: 16802.3 f. (d), 19529 f., [19529.5 f.] (d).

Trundle, Margery (Margaret).
Bookseller in London, 1626–1629†. Widow of **John Trundle**. [*Dict. 1*, under husband; *SB* 39 (1986): 179–80.]
her shop in Smithfield (E.8), 1628 (1811, 19684)
1628: 1811 sold, 6366 f. (d), 6809.2 f. (d?), 19229.5 f. (d), 19684 f., 20319.5 f. (c).
1629: 4687 ass'd, 17915.5 ass'd, 19684.1 f., 23291 ass'd, 23771 ass'd, 25283 ass'd.

Truthal, Christopher, *pseud.*
Printer in 'Southwark', 1556. = E. van der Erve, Emden. [Duff, *Century*.]
1556: 18798, 25009.

'The tua mariit wemen and the wedo', *Printer of*. *See* Printer of ...

Turke, John.
Bookseller in London, 1533–1561 (Arber I.159). [Duff, *Century*.]
in Paternoster Row at the Rose (C.7), 1540 (12206a.3)–1548/49 (522.20, has 'dw.'); sometimes omits the sign, e.g. in 1547 (13089); he rented this property 1533–54 (*Memorials* 53)
dw. in Paul's Churchyard at the Cock (B), 1553 (2749.5)
1540: [4268.5] sold (d), 12206a.3 sold (d), [22877.6] sold (d).
1547: 13089 [f.] (d).
1548: 21739.5 [f.] (d?).
1548/49: 398.5 f., 522.20 f.
1550: 15188 [f.] (d?).
1550/51: 464 [f.].
1552/53: 462 f.
1553: 2749.5 [f.].
1558: 3007 ent., 4826 ent.

Turner, D., *Heirs of, pseud.*
Printers in 'Frankfurt', 1601. = T. Creede.
1601: 1884.

Turner, Thomas.
Stationer in London, (1572?) 1577–1592. [*Dict. 1.*]
shop at Guildhall gate (H.5), 1580 (11038; 11047, colophon)
1580: 11038 f. (d), 11047 f. (d).

Turner, William.
Bookseller and printer in Oxford, 1610–1643†, and one of the **Printers to the University** (*see* Oxford University), 1624–1640. In partnership with **John Lichfield** 1624–27 and occasionally thereafter. Although Turner was made free of the Stat. Co. in 1622, his master was **John Crosley** of Oxford, and it is unlikely that Turner had any activity in London except for registering copyrights. [*Dict. 2*; DFM 1136; Madan II.511, 520–4.]
No address used.
1624: 4630 f., 20358.5, 20685.
1625: 1792, 4201, 4676, 7751.6 (false), 8789, 8790 (repeat), 8792, 8793 (repeat), [8794] (d), 8796, 8796.3 (repeat), 8798, 8798.3 (repeat), 8800, 8800.3 (repeat), 8800.7, 8801 (repeat), 8801.7, 8802 (repeat), 8804, 8804.3 (repeat), 8804.7, 8805 (repeat), 10372.6, 11509, 13277, 14437, 14454, 14972, 14992, 15494, 18474, 19030, 19031, 19589, 20356, 20359, 20361, 20774, 23754, 23755 (forged), 23914, 24991, 25326.
1626: 1474, 1600, 4531–1.5, 4633 f., 4634 f., 10140.5, 12615, 13927 sold, 20347, 20357, 20358, 20911, 23915, 24988.
1627: 10754, 12611, 13278, 13619.5, 14457, [17950], [19016.9] (d), 19445, 21036, 24986, 24704.
1628: 241, 3628, 4532, 10858, 19322, 19323, 21814, 24161, 24882.7–83, 25326.5, 25327.
1629: 550–0.5, 4194.5, 4937, 13026, 13279, [21631.5 f.], 21674.
1630: 290, 12612, 13683 imp., [17383.5], [19016.12] (d), [19289.5] (c), 19941, 24037.
1631: 2732, 3235, 3629, 6666.7, 10316, 10635, 11101, 13279.5–80, 17368, 17951, 19346, [20272?], 20280.3–.7 f., 21814.5, 23351, 24749, 24882 pro, 24968 (d?).
1632: 7156.
1633: 242, 1535, 1535.5 ap., 4190, 4195, 5591, 7157, 12198, 12623 f., 13281 [by &] f., 13614, 19033, 19034–4a, 19035–5a.5, 19487 sumpt., 20908 ap., 21848.
1634: 4191, 4194, 7158, 16893, 19005, [19016.15] (d), [19016.16] (d), 20516, 20517, 21055–5.5, 21641, 22831.7–32 by & imp., 22879 [by &] f., 24160, 24161.3.
1635: 10134 (d?), 10859, 12613, 19006.
1636: 1389, 12401, 13282, 15632, 16788, 17952, 26013.
1636/37: 419.6, 431.3, 532.11.
1637: 243, 1441a, 1885, 3630, 4107, 4261, 15077, 19347.5–48, 21811, 21812–2.9, 24674.
1638: 91, [4163], 4259, 6044a, 11102–2.5, [16789], 19007 typis, 20667, 20909 ap., 21813, 22653.
1639: 4717, 11401, 12399 (note), 13283–4, 13684, 14589, [21056], 21623.5, 21815, 22833 by & imp.
1640: 3627, 4120, 4718, 12757, 14480, 20515, 20518, [24473.3] (forged, c?), 24882.3.
1939: 13284 (d/error).

Turona, Franciscus de, *pseud.*
Printer in 'Savoy', 1542? = W. Köpfel, Strassburg.
1542: 3759.5 per (d?).

Tuthill, Hendrik.
Bookseller in Rotterdam, 1638. [*Dict. 1.*]
1638: 2737 f.

Twonson, Niclas, *pseud.*
Printer in 'Nürnberg', 1533. Used in 1546? by N. Hill in what may be a reprint of an earlier lost edition. [Duff, *Century*.]
1533: 24468.

Twyford, Henry.
Bookseller in London, 1640–1675. [*Dict. 2*; DFM 1836.]
at the Bear over against the Middle Temple gate in Fleet Street (W.13), 1640 (1226.7)
1640: 1226.7 sold.

Tyler, Evan.
Printer in London (1639) 1640? in Edinburgh 1640?–1651, in Leith 1651–1652, again in London 1652–1682†; also in Edinburgh 1660–1672. While in Edinburgh he worked as King's

Tyler, E. — *cont.*
Printer for Scotland. [*Dict. 2*; *Dict. 3*; DFM 525.]
No pre-1641 address used.
1633: 21902.5 (d/error). **1640:** 5206.5? (d?). **after 1640:** 21902.5 (d).

Tylle (Tylly), William.
Printer in London, 1548–1550. [Duff, *Century*.]
within Aldersgate (Aldrichgate) in the parish of St. Anne and Agnes (G.2), 1548–49 (2855)
1548–49: 2855. **1550:** [24056].

Tylotson. *See* Telotson.

Tymme (Timme), William.
Stationer in London, (1596) 1601–1615. In 1615 he had his former apprentice, **John Robinson**, as partner. [*Dict. 1*; *Poor Book*, 1609, 1611.]
in Paternoster Row (C.7), 1601–1615
at the Fleur-de-lis and Crown —, 1601 (17226a)–1606 (18582, has 'dw.', adds 'near Cheapside')
their shop —, 1615 (13936, with J. Robinson)
1601: 17226a f. **1605:** 26002 f. **1606:** 18582 f. **1607:** 26009 ent. **1615:** 13936 f.

Tysdale. *See* Tisdale.

U

Udall, Nicholas.
Dramatist and scholar, b. 1505–1556†. [*DNB*.]
No address used.
1550: 24665 f. (d).

Ulhart (Ulhard), Philipp.
Printer in Augsburg, 1522–1567. [Benzing 17.]
1550: 6832.24 (c?).

Unckel (Ounkel), Johann Karl.
Bookseller in Frankfurt am Main, 1615–1634. [*Dict. 1*; Benzing, *Verleger*.]
1619: 18045 cura & imp., 18046 by charges of, 18046.5 a cuestas, 18046.7 es frais, 18047 in Verlag.
1623: 11745.7.

Uphill, Anthony.
Stationer in London, (1620) 1625–1641 at least. [*Dict. 2*; DFM 1730.]
at the White Lion in Paul's Churchyard (A.2), 1625 (24512)–1626 (21324)
1625: 24512 f. **1626:** 21324 f.

Upton, James.
Stationer in London, (1629) 1630. [*Dict. 1*; DFM 1804.]
shop in Paul's Churchyard at the Fox (A.7), 1630 (12007)
1630: 12007 sold.

Ussher, John.
Alderman and patron in Dublin, 1571. [*Dict. 1.*]
above the bridge, 1571 (19844.5)
1571: 22.3 [at expense], 19844.5 [at expense].

Utenhove, Jan.
Dutch reformer and translator; refugee in England, 1548–1553, 1559?–1565†. [*DNB*.]
No address used.
1561: 2739 voor, 2739.5(*A*) voor.

V

Valentin, Florent.
Bookseller in Rouen, 1556–1561. In partnership with his father, **Robert Valentin**. [Duff, *Century*; Muller 103.]
1556: 15846 ap., 16078 in aed. **1557:** 16081.5 ap. (d?).

Valentin, Robert.
Bookseller in Rouen, 1524–1557. In 1556 he took his son, **Florent Valentin** into partnership. [Duff, *Century*; Muller 103.]
1551: 16055 pro, 16056 ap.
1554: 16058 pro, 16155 ven., 16215 ven., 16216 ven.
1555: 2978.5 in off. & f., 16068 imp., 16069 per & ven., 16070 imp., 16071 in aed., 16071.5 in aed., 16072 ven., 16155a ven., 16216 ven., 16248 imp.
1556: 15846 ap., 16076 imp., 16077 imp.
1557: 16249 imp. & ven.

Vallemand, Pieter, *pseud.*
Printer in 'Basel', 1573. = W. Williamson. At least one continental printer also printed an edition of the same text, with spelling 'Vuallemand'.
1573: 13847.5.

Vautrollier, Jacqueline.
Printer in London, 1588. Widow of **Thomas Vautrollier 1** and mother of **Thomas 2.** She remarried **Richard Field**, who succeeded to the printing house. [*Dict. 1.*]
dw. within the Blackfriars by Ludgate (Q.6), 1588 (16968, begun by Thomas 1 and finished by Jacqueline)
1588: 15412, 15413, 15413.5, [15414.2–.3], [15414.4], [16968–9].

Vautrollier, Thomas 1.
French refugee bookseller, bookbinder, and printer (from 1570) in London, 1562–1587†, with a bookshop in Edinburgh, 1580–1583, and a printing house there, 1584–1586. Husband of **Jacqueline Vautrollier**, who apparently supervised the London business during her husband's absences, and father of **Thomas 2**. In 1575 **Richard Schilders** printed a Dutch book in Vautrollier's house or with his material. Vautrollier was patentee for printing various texts, especially Latin classics used as school books (*see* the headnote following Appendix D/60). His last book was postdated and completed by his widow. [*Dict. 1*; *Library* 14 (1959): 31–3, 44; 22 (1967): 1–12; *GJ* 1960: 223–8.]
London, dw. in the Blackfriars (Q.6), 1570 (6445.5)–1587 (5400)
Edinburgh, no address used.
1566: 6738 (d/error).
1570: 6445.5, 15266.
1571: 361.5 in aed., [1024.5(*A*)] (d), 6446.
1572: [2995a.2] (forged).
1573: 479.8 ex off., 2355.5 ex off., 17278.8 ex off.
1574: 2802, 2803, 2803.5(*A*), 3363.5 (d), [4417], 15241.7, 15246, 16427, 17409, 18947.5, 18976.4.
1575: 2006, 2356, 2877, 5297, [11310.5] (false), [11311], 12902.5, 15469, 16965, [20051.5(*A3*) in house of], 23666.
1576: 2804, 4414, 4426.4 imp., 6738 (d), [7169] (d?), 10572, 13057.5, 13091 (d), 15242, 17175.7, 18926.5, 22248.
1577: 2036.5, 2044, 2047, 2805, 3969, 5485–5.3, 10572, 11458–9, 11757, 13056.5 ap., 13058.3–.7 ap., 13059.7 ap., 15490.5, 15512, 16966, 16975, 16975.5, [21463].
1578: 3970–1, 4418–9, 6739, [11108] (d), 11444–4.5, 14607.5–09, 15512.5, 15513, 15513.5, 16989, 16993, 18156a.5, 21685, 23927 (d).
1579: 2806, 4426.6, 4938, 5266, 5298, 5308, 5308.3, 5323.7, 6739.4, 12458–8a, 16990, 17278.9 ex off., 18157, 20065–6, 24180.
1580: 2032, 2032.5 typis, 2056–6.8, 2806.5(*A*), 3983–3.5, 5308.5, 6736, 6736.5, 6762, 11449, 13057 ap., 13059.4, 15514, 16967, 16991, 17176, 19556.
1581: 1854, 2006.5, 2057–8a.5, 2361, 4072, 5298.5, 5785, 6446.4, 6739.7, 6740, 11730, 14582, 15247, 16994, 17176.1, 17279 ex off., 17287–7.7, 17823–3.5, 18253–3a, 18976.6, 22212, 25358, 25359.
1582: 2809, 5399.9, 16814, 18250, 18951.5, 19308.5.
1583: 1508, 3984, 4427, 6741, 6735, 6823, 11757.5, 18927, 18928, 18928a, 20370, 22114–4.5, 24180.3, 24181, 24668, 25357.
1584: *London*: 4428, 4762, 4904, 4904.5 (false), [4906] (d), 5266.2, 5319, 15514.3, 18581, 21809, 24775; *Edinburgh*: 1340, 1763, 14373, 18314, 21671.
1585: *Edinburgh*: 4429 (repeat?), 14374, 21948, 21948.3–.7 (repeat), 21949 by ass't of; *London*: 1596.7, [3363.6] (c), 6446.7, 10573, 11737, 15251.3, 17279.5 ex off., 19101, 19557, [25118.10] (d?).
1586: 1851, 3747, 4429 (d?), 10568 ex off., [15459] (d).
1587: 2793, 2810, 5160.5, 5309.4–.5, 5400, [15071] (d), 15470–0a, 15511a, 16582, 16583.

1588: 14609 (d/error), 16968–9.

Vautrollier, Thomas 2.
Bookseller in London, (1604) 1605–1608†. Son of **Thomas 1** and **Jacqueline Vautrollier**. He lived in the parish of St. Giles, Cripplegate (I.4). [*Dict. 1*; *St. Giles*, 1605–08.]
No address used.
1605: 11741 ap. [sold].

Vavasour, Nicholas.
Bookseller in London, 1622–1643. In 1622–23 he was in partnership with **Godfrey Emerson**. He married the widow of **Leonard Becket**, whose shop he had taken over in 1633. Stepfather of **James Becket**. [*Dict. 2*; DFM 955; *Loan Book*, 1639–42.]
their shop at the Crane in Paul's Churchyard (A.3), 1622 (14301, with G. Emerson)–1624 (6108.5, has 'his shop')
dw. at the little South door of Paul's (A.9), 1632 (3819)
shop in the Inner Temple near the church (W.11), 1633 (17412)–1640 (17780.5); variations: omits 'Inner', 1634 (21416); has church 'door', 1636 (6533), 1638 (5680)
1622: 14301 f.
1623: 14305 f.
1624: 6108.5 f.
1632: 3819 sold.
1633: 17412 f., 22063 f.
1634: 1552 f., 21416 f.
1635: 1552 f., 20603 f.
1636: 1553 f., 4899 ent., 6533 f., 15249.7 f.
1637: 20075 (note).
1638: 1554 f., 5680 f.
1639: 12206 sold, 17667 sold.
1640: 1554.5 f., 12885 f., 17780.5 sold.

Veale (Vele), Abraham.
Bookseller, 1550?–1595. Freed as a Draper in 1542. Became a brother of the Stat. Co. by 1576 (Arber II.65). [Duff, *Century*.]
The spelling 'Vele' seems to be an early preference through 1557 (12442) and perhaps beyond. 'Veale' occurs in two books of 1552 (2089, 10486), again in 1560 (19848), and in all later books from 1569 (18600). Dates queried below for 1558 and 1560 are especially uncertain.
dw. in Paul's Churchyard at the Lamb (A.6), 1550? (25148, omits 'dw.')–1586 (21047)
1550: 25148 [f.] (d?).
1551: 1273 [f.], 2084.5 f., 18094 [f.].
1552: 1281 f. (d?), 2089 f., 4050 f., 10440.2 [f.], 10486 [f.] (d?), 22160.4(*A3*).
1553: 19493 f., 21755a.5 f.
1555: 2979 [f.] (c?), 13175.17 f. (d?), 24961 (c).
1556: 2980.2 f. (d?), 3311 [f.] (d), 18095–5.5 [f.], 25875 f.
1557: 6451 [f.] (d?), 10455.5 [f.], 12442 [f.], 21600 [f.], 26074 [f.].
1558: 22596a [f.] (d?), 22603a [f.] (d?), 22617a [f.] (d?), 24850.3 f. (d?).
1560: 3291 [f.] (d?), 11362 [f.] (d?), 18223.3 [f.] (d?), 19848 f., 20954 (d?), 23187 [f.] (d?), 23884.5 f. (c).
1569: 18600 f. (d).
1570: 19.5 f. (c), 3291.5 f. (c).
1571: 719 f.
1572: 2037 f.
1573: 6150 f. (d), 6748 f., 24778 [f.], 24801 f.
1574: 2038 f., 12193a f.
1575: 3367 f. (d), 4078 f., 6129 f., 21601 f. (d), 24336 f., 24851.5 f. (c).
1576: 10487 f., 19626.5 f.
1577: 1312.7 [f.], 2039 f.
1578: 2040 f., 6739 (note), 11975 f. (d), 14920 f.
1581: 12448 ent., 16978 f.
1582: 719a–a.5 f., 6749 f., 6749.2 f. (d?), 6749.4 f. (d?).
1584: 24802 f.
1586: 2040.5 f., 6230 f., 21047 f.

Veen, Otto van.
Dutch painter and engraver, b. 1556–1629†. Worked in Antwerp, 1592–c. 1612. [Thieme-Becker.]
1608: 24627a.8–.9 ven.

Velpius. *See* Antoine-Velpius.

Venge, Edward.
Bookseller and surreptitious printer in London, (1588) 1589–1606† (*C-B C*: 22). Between at least Oct. 1591 and Jan. 1598 he was living in the parish of St. Giles, Cripplegate, in the latter year in Golden Lane ((I.5): Judge: 133, n.3). In 1596 an illegal press of his was seized near Bishop's Hall (in the manor of Stepney (U.6)). [*Dict. 1*; *Poor Book* (widow Judith), 1615–24; *St. Giles*, 1591–98.]
shop without Bishopsgate (K.2), 1589 (17566.7)
in Fleet Street at the Vine (W.2), 1590 (23375)
dw. at the Black Bull near to the three cranes in the Vintry (S.9), 1599 (3727)
1589: 17566.7 f. (d). **1590:** 23375 f. (d). **1599:** 3727 sold. **1603:** 15355 ent.

Venge, Walter.
Bookseller and surreptitious printer in London, 1584–1598†. Freed as a Grocer in 1581 by **John Charlewood** and remained a member until 1585, when he attempted to transfer to the Stat. Co. (Judge: 139). He lived in the parish of St. Giles, Cripplegate (I.4), at least 1587–98 and in the latter year was named along with **John Danter** as pirating the *Accidence* (Judge: 118, n.2). [*Dict. 1*; *St. Giles*, 1587–98.]
dw. in Fleet Lane over against the Maiden Head (D.2), 1585 (3119)
1585: 3119 f. (d).

Vérard, Antoine.
Publisher and bookseller in Paris, 1485–1513?†. [Duff, *Century*; Renouard.]
1503: [791 f.] (d), [12379] (c), 15901 pro (c), [22407].
1504: 16180 imp.
1505: 16139.5 imp. (c).
1506: 15904.
1508: [14557 f.?] (d?), [16182a].

Verdussen, Hieronymus.
Printer and bookseller in Antwerp, 1579–1635. [Rouzet.]
1608: 24627a.10(*A*) ap.

Vernon, Richard.
Bookseller in London, (1580) 1581. [*Dict. 1*.]
in Paul's Churchyard at the Brazen Serpent (A.3), 1581 (12746)
1581: 12746.

Verschout, Andries.
Printer in Leiden, 1577–1587; printer and bookseller in Woerden, 1589–1599 (1624?†). In Leiden he sometimes worked with or for **Thomas Basson**. [Gruys; Briels 508–13.]
1586: 7287.7.

Verstegan (Rowlands), Richard.
Recusant printer in London, 1578?–1582, and editor, author (in STC under Rowlands), and propagandist in Paris and Rome, 1582–1586, and mainly in Antwerp, 1587–1640†. In 1582 his secret press was in Smithfield ((E.1): Southern 358, 378). [*Dict. 1*; *RH* 7 (1963): 82–103; 18 (1986): 128–42.]
1582: [4537] (d). **1583:** [17507 f.], [20632 f.?]. **1603:** 3897.5 (false).

Vervliet, Daniel.
Printer and bookseller in Antwerp, 1564–1610. [*Dict. 1*; Rouzet.]
1600: 2898.

Verwithagen. *See* Withagius.

Veseler (Veselde), Joris (George).
Printer in Amsterdam, 1618–1626†. Succeeded by his *widow*. In some Newsbooks of 1621 his name was apparently forged by a London printer. [*Dict. 1*; Gruys; Briels 513–16.]
1618: 19098.
1619: [4364].
1620: 18507.1, —.2.
1621: 16839, 18507.3, —.4, —.5, —.6, —.7 (d), —.8 (forged?), —.9 (forged?), —.10 (d), —.11 (d), —.12 (d), —.13 (forged?), —.14, —.15, —.16, —.17, [20408.5], 20409, 22131.

Veseler, Joris, *Widow of.*
Printer in Amsterdam, 1626–1628. Remarried **Jan Fredericksz Stam**, who succeeded to the printing material. [Gruys; *Library* 9 (1954): 185.]
1626: 13031.7. **1627:** [24903(*A3*)].

Vicars, Samuel.
Stationer in London, (1619) 1624–1625?†. [*Dict. 1*; DFM 916.]
No address known.
1624: 17421 ent.

Villain. *See* Le Villain.

Vincent, Anne.
Publisher in London, 1633–1637. Widow of **George Vincent 2**.
No address used.
1633: 23934.19(*A3*) f. **1636:** 23935.5(*A3*) f. **1637:** 3537 ass'd, 6399 ass'd, 23936 ass'd, 25638 ass'd.

Vincent, George 1.
Bookseller in London, (1590) 1595–1617?†. Husband of **Katherine Vincent** and father of **George 2**. [*Dict. 1*.]
in (Great) Wood Street (H.17), 1602–1617; variations:
at the $ Hand-in-Hand — over against St. Michael's Church, 1602 (5593), 1603 (24121, has 'dw. ... Great Wood', omits 'over ... Church')
dw. —, 1602 (13013), 1607 (25635), 1611 (25636), 1617 (6397); the last three have 'shop'
in — near the $ Castle, 1611 (23934.2, has 'Great')
1602: 5593 f., 13013 f. **1603:** 24121 f. **1606:** 4658 f. (d). **1607:** 6396.5 f., 25635 f. **1611:** 23934.2 f., 25636 f. **1617:** 6397 f.

Vincent, George 2.
Bookseller in London, (1624) 1625–1629. Son of **George 1** and husband of **Anne Vincent**. His shop was either shared with or managed by **Richard Thrale**, who apparently took over completely in 1628. [*Dict. 1*, merged with father; DFM 2106.]
at Paul's gate at the Cross Keys (A.5), 1625 (3537)–1627 (21830); variation: shop in Paul's Churchyard at the Cross Keys, 1627 (21835); no later address used
1625: 3537 f. **1627:** 21830 f., 21835 sold. **1629:** 25637 f.

Vincent, Katherine.
Publisher in London, 1618† (*C-B C*: 103, 105). Widow of **George Vincent 1**.
No address used.
1618: 23934.5 f.

Vincentsz (Spierinxhouck), Niclaes.
Printer in Dordrecht, 1612–1635. [*Dict. 1*; Gruys 85; Briels 457–9.]
1623: 25939.

Violette, Pierre.
Printer in Rouen, (1489) 1503–1517. [Duff, *Century*; Muller 103; Renouard.]
1505: [11604.5], [23140] (c).
1506: 15805.7 cura.
1507: [15857] (c), 16119–9.5 per.
1509: [16140.5] (c), 16186 in off., 16220 imp. (d?).

Visscher, Claes (Niclaes) Jansz 2.
Copperplate printer and publisher in Amsterdam, 1611–1647. [Gruys; Thieme-Becker.]
1625: 18936 (c).

Voegelin, Gotthard.
Printer in Heidelberg, 1598–1622 (1634†) and intermittently in Ladenburg, 1605–1607. [Benzing 197, 271.]
1611: [13906a].

Volckwinner, Collinus, *pseud.*
Printer 'outside London', 1554. = Nicholas Hill, of whose name it is an obscure translation: Volkwinner (Niko-laos) Collinus. At the time he was in partnership with E. van der Erve, Emden. [Duff, *Century*.]
1554: 16571a, 17863.5.

Volmar, Anne Marie.
Printer in Wurzburg, 1628. Widow of Johann Volmar. [*Dict. 1*; Benzing 515, under husband.]
1628: 1202.

Vorsterman, Willem.
Printer, bookseller, and bookbinder in Antwerp, c. 1504–1543†. [Duff, *Century*; Rouzet.]
1525: [17544] (c). **1530:** 24227.5 sold (c?).

Vostre, Simon.
Bookseller in Paris, 1486–1521†. He or an agent of his in London may have used the spelling **Symon Voter**. [Duff, *Century*; Renouard.]
1498: 15887 pro, 15889 pro (d). **1501:** 15896 pro. **1502:** 15897 pro. **1507:** 15905 pro (d?). **1512:** 15913 exp. (d), 15913.5 imp. (d). **1520:** 15926 imp. (d?).

Voter, Symon.
'Printer' or bookseller? in London, c. 1515. The name may represent **Simon Vostre** or an agent of his. [Duff, *Century*, under Vostre.]
in Fleet Alley (W.1), c. 1515 (17543)
1515: 17543 (c).

Vowell (Hooker), John.
Antiquary, author (in STC under Vowell), and chamberlain of Exeter, b. 1526?–1601†. [*DNB*, under Hooker.]
1587: 24886.3 opera & imp. (d).

Vrankenbergh. *See* Frankenbergh.

Vuolfius. *See* Wolfe.

W

Waelpot (Walpote), Jan Pietersz.
Printer in Delft, 1621–1656 (1667†). [*Dict. 1*; Gruys; Briels 524–8.]
1631: 1431.33 ex off. **1633:** [12680?], 13263. **1634:** [21009.5]. **1637:** 13264. **1638:** 13264.2, [13264.4].

Waesberghe, Isaac van.
Printer and bookseller in Rotterdam, 1618–1648†. [*Dict. 1*; Gruys.]
1635: 6312. **1636:** 6310.

Waesberghe, Jan 1 van.
Printer and bookseller in Antwerp, 1555–1589 (1590†). [Rouzet.]
1563: 17847.6.

Waesberghe, Pieter van.
Printer and bookseller in Rotterdam, 1622–1661†. [*Dict. 1*; Gruys; Briels 529, 538–41.]
1627: 4863.7. **1631:** 2632 f. **1639:** 24869.

Walbancke, Matthew.
Bookseller in London, (1617) 1618–1667. [*Dict. 2*; DFM 2777.]
his shops at the new and old gate of Gray's Inn (V.10), 1618 (18319)
shop at Gray's Inn gate (V.10), 1619 (14028)–1639 (10853) at least; variation: in 1619 (23767) has 'dw.'
1618: 10851–2 f., 18319 f.
1619: 14028 f., 23767 f.
1620: 20584.5 f.
1624: 14300 f., 23768 f.
1626: 20585 ent.
1630: 21583 f.
1636: 24954 f.
1638: 18320 f., 20585 f.
1639: 1353 ent., 1354 f., 10853 f.

Waldegrave, Mary.
Printer in Edinburgh, 1604. Widow of **Robert Waldegrave**. She sold the Edinburgh printing material to **Thomas Finlason** and returned to London, where she turned over one apprentice and freed another in 1604 (Arber II.282, 738). [*Dict. 1*, under husband; *Poor Book*, 1608–09.]
No address used.
1604: 9295.8, 21959, 21960.

Waldegrave (Walgrave), Robert.
Printer and bookseller in London (1576?) 1578–1589, in La Rochelle 1589, and in Edinburgh 1589–1603, returning to London not long before his death, 1603†. Husband of **Mary Waldegrave**. In 1588–89 he was the major printer of the Marprelate tracts: at East Molesey, at Fawsley, Northants., at Coventry, and at Wolston. In Edinburgh he was **King's Printer in Scotland**. He appears to have been in London in 1601? since Andrew Willet, in his preface to STC 25672 (∗1[r]), speaks of having sent a copy of STC 25698 (dated 1600) to James VI 'by your Maiesties Printer'; printing material acquired during that trip appears in at least 1602 (25235) as well as the 1603 items discussed in *Library* 13 (1958): 225–33. *See* also Appendix A/17. [*Dict. 1*; Judge: 90–111.]
without Temple Bar (X.6), 1580–1586; variations:
dw. — near unto Somerset House, 1580 (26057.7), 1583 (6433, 11756), 1585 (2012)
dw. — in the Strand near unto Somerset House, 1582? (2014), 1585? (849)
dw. —, 1584 (11839), 1586 (6409)
dw. in Foster Lane over against Goldsmiths' Hall (G.3), 1583 (1891; 13255, one variant adding: at the George); this apparently represents a brief interruption of the previous address
?sold at the White Horse in Canon Lane (A.2), 1585 [25364 (*A*)?]–1586 (571); not called 'his shop'
shop in Paul's Churchyard at the Crane (A.3), 1587 (6400)–1588 (12170)
Edinburgh, no address used.
1495: 7351 (d/error).
1578: 24911 f.
1580: 4315 ent., 18841.3, 26057.7.
1580/81 [[22019.5(*A3*)] (repeat), 22020, 22022.
1581: 1039, 3472 (d), 4439.5, 10844 (d), 10844.3 (d?), 11696.4 (d?), 11990 (d), 13774, 15059.5 ent., 16992 ent., 19877, 20975.
1582: 2014 (d?), 11696.7, 19915, 20559.
1583: 585, 1891 (d?), 6433 (d), [10394] (d), 10844.8, 10845, 11756, 11863.7 (d), 12912 ex off., 13255 (d), 13255.3 (d), 13756.5, 15068 (d), [17450.7] (false), 19109.7 (d?), 24114 ex off., [24180.7] (d).
1584: 4926, 4926.5, 5964, 6801, 10395, 10770 (d), 11697, 11838.5 (d?), 11839, 11840.5, [18714.7?], 19065, [19103–4] (d?), 19847, [19863.3] (d), [20201] (d?), 24217.5 (d?), 25624.5 (d?).
1585: 849 (d?), 2012, [2021] (c), 2779.5 ?ent., 3100, 4315 (d?), 7520, [7739] (d), [10396.5] (d?), 13826 (d?), 15252, 16567 (d?), 17145.7, 17411, 18777, 19433.3, 19721.7 (d?), 20585.3 (c), 24109 (d), 24218.5, 24503.7 (c), 24783, 24862, 25364(*A*, note), [25622], 25888.
1586: 571 (d), 1192.5 ent., 4927, 5964.5, 6401, 6409 (d?), 12744 (d?), 13495, 15319, [16711?] (d), 18325.7, 24110.
1587: 4305.5 (d?), 5964.5, 6400, 6402 ent., 6437 (d?), 12498.5–99 (d?), 18770 ent., 18959, 19871, 20589 (d), 20589.5 (d), 21227, 21315.6, [24504] (d?), 25620.5, 25622.5–.7 (d).
1588: 2051, 6173 (d), 11698 (d?), 12170, 13751 (d?), [17453] (false, d), [17454] (false, d), [19604] (d), [19605] (d), [19605.5–06], 24490, 24492 (d?), [24499] (d), [24505] (d), [24506] (d), [24506a] (d), 24507 (d), [25229].
1589: 4928 f., [6805] (d), [12342] (d), [17455] (d), [17456] (false, d), [17459(*A3*)?] (false, d), 17816 (d/error), [19602], [19613] (d).
1590: 1857, 6217, [6228] (d?), 6322, [7754], 14785, 17809, [19603] (d), [19612], 21278, 21459, 22023, 25242.
1591: 1562, 2053, 3923, 3924 (d?), 5192, 13023, 14379, 21280, 22783.3 (d?).
1592: 10769, 14293, 19661, 19666, 21949.7(*A*) (d), 22783.5.
1593: 14937 (d), 14940 (forged), 18354, 19689 (d?), 19701, 21267, 21888.
1594: 2053.5, [11214.2] (d), 11214.4 (d?), 11214.6 (d), 13941.5, 13943, 13944, [13948] (d), 17807, 18016 (d?), 18102–2a, [18355], 21268, 21275, 21889.
1595: 763, [2054], 3979.5 (d?), 5067, 5345.7, 6324, 7351, 7352, 7485.5, 12319, 21555.1.
1596: [4105] (d?), 5332, 5345.4, 5345.9, 21950, 21951, 21951a, [21952], [21953], 22779 (note), 23189.
1597: 7353, 11214 (d), 12323, 14364, 17815.5, 18049, 18049.5, 21285, 21555.2, 21877, 21891.
1598: 14409, 17816 (d), 18466, 21279, 21954, 21955, 24208 (note), [25245].
1599: 6350 (note), 13942, 14348, 16899.7, 19834, [19881.5] (d?), 20100, 20104, 21555.3, 21877.5, 21892.3, 22369, 22542, 24386.
1600: 348, 348.5 (forged), 1766.7, 3122, 13878, 16921, 18618.3, 20567, 21274, 21276, 21555.4, 21555.6, 21657, 21892.5, 21957, 22960 (d?).
1601: [4105.5] (d).

Waldegrave, R. — *cont.*
1602: 4716, 6324.5, 13945, 21555.8, 21555.9, 25235.
1603: 349, 2730, 5968, 7481, 8300 (forged?), [11726.2] (d), [13948.3?] (d), 14349, [14362] (d), 14366 f., 14411(*A3*) [f.], 14426.7 (d), 17511, 17841.7 (forged), 21555.10, 21555.11, 21958.

Waldkirch, Konrad von.
Printer in Basel, 1583–1616, with a brief period in Schaffhausen, 1592. [*Dict. 1*; Benzing 44, 405.]
1597: 3846. **1598:** 3860. **1599:** 3862a.3 ap.

Waldnelius. *See* Woutneel.

Waley. *See* Walley.

Walfe. *See* Wolfe.

Walkcliffe, Thomas.
Bookseller? in London, 1624. Possibly an error for **Thomas Walkley**.
No address used.
1624: 25161.5 f.

Walker, James, *Heirs of, pseud.*
Printers in 'Rouen', 1601. = T. Creede.
1601: 5724.

Walker, Robert.
Stationer in London, 1597–1599. He entered the 1597 item in the SR, and the address is probably his. 21131 was sold in the shop of his former master, **Thomas Man 1**: in Paternoster Row at the Talbot (C.7). [*Dict. 1.*]
?near the Golden Lion in the Old Bailey (D.7), 1597 [21489]
1597: [21489] sold. **1598:** 11859 f., 21131 f.

Walkley, Thomas.
Bookseller in London, 1618–1658. Possibly **Thomas Walkcliffe** is a misprint for this name. [*Dict. 2*; DFM 614.]
shop at the Eagle and Child in Britain's Burse (X.10), 1618 (10598)–1632 (24975); variation: omits sign, 1628 (16691.5)
shop near Whitehall (X.15), 1633 (12537)–1635 (24977)
at the Flying Horse near York House (X.12), 1636 (6779, engr. tp)–1639 (24978, has 'shop')
shop at the Flying Horse between Britain's Burse and York House (X.12), 1640 (4620), 1640/41 (7746.10); variation: has only 'near the New Exchange' [= Britain's Burse], 1640 (19616)
1618: 10598 f.
1619: 1670 f., 24298 sold, 25907 f.
1620: 1681–1.5 f., 25890 f.
1621: 11074 f.
1622: 1682 f., 4988 f., [10599 f.], 16927 f., 22305 f.
1623: 3221 f.
1624: 3221 f., 11027 f., 25161.5? f.
1625: 1671 f., [7743.5], 11706.4 f.
1626: 1016 f., 7744 f., 21490 f., 24299 sold.
1627: 21590.5 f., 24268.7 f., 24739.5–40 f., 24741 f., 24742 f., 24743 f., 24744 f., 24745 f., 24746 f.
1628: 7745 f., 7746 f., 7746.2 f., 7746.3 f., 7746.4 f., 10021.4 f., 11079.5 f., 16691.5 f., 23716.5 sold, 24823 f., 24824 f., [24973.5 f.].
1629: 12026? f., 13248.6 f., 17494 f., 21624 sold.
1630: 14776 f., 17640–0.5 f., 24974 f.
1631: 1399 f., 14762 f. (d).
1632: 24975 f.
1633: 1400 f., 12537 f.
1634: 4618 f., 14719 f., 24976 f.
1635: 11095 f., 17719 f., 24977 f.
1636: 6779 f., 19615.5(*A3*) ?ent.
1637: 5770 f., 14718 f., 16923 f.
1638: 6304 f., 23420 f.
1639: 6306 f., 13870.7 f., 17717 f., 17718–8a f., 24978 f.
1640: 4620 f., 7746.6 f., 7746.7 f., 7746.9 f., 7746.13 f., 9336 ent., [14754 f.], 19230 ent., 19616 f. (d), 21775 f., 24979 f.
1640/41: 6844 f., 7746.10 f., 7746.11 f.
1641: [14754 f.].

Walley, Henry.
Stationer in London, (1608) 1609–1655. Grandson of **John** and son of **Robert Walley**. His only imprints were shared with **Richard Bonian** at what was probably the latter's shop. In 1631 Walley was elected Clerk of the Stat. Co. and had a house beside the garden of Stationers' Hall ((Q.1): *C-B C*: 221–2, 232). [*Dict. 2*; DFM 2638; *Loan Book*, 1626–38.]
?at the Spread-Eagle in Paul's Churchyard over against the great North door (A.2), 1609 (22331)–1610? (11068; both with R. Bonian)
1609: 4976 f., 7371 f., 14436 f., 14757 ent., 14778 f., 20759 f., 22331–2 f.
1610: 11068 f. (d?), 13538 f., 18323a f., 21847 f.

Walley (Waley), John.
Bookseller in London, at least 1542–1586†. Father of **Robert** and grandfather of **Henry Walley**. Although he sometimes called himself 'typographus', e.g. in 1558 (20732.5), 1579 (20739.3), it is not certain that he ever owned a press; however, other printers have not been identified for all his books, and several of those dated 1548 and 1557 are potential candidates for a press of his. Two foreigners, **Philip Bounel** and **Cutbere Mathew**, printed single items for him in the 1540s with printing material of **Nicholas Hill**, but it is uncertain what Walley's relations with any of these men were. [Duff, *Century*.]
in Foster Lane (G.3), 1547 (21616)–1557 (14111a, has 'dw.') and until his death (Plomer, *Wills*: 26); variation:
— at the Hart's Horn, c. 1549 (2379.5), 1550? (7542.7), 1553 (4844.2)
1542/43: 475.
1545: 15587.5 f. (d?), 15732.9 f., 18221.7 f. (d?).
1546: 3328.5 [f.], 7380 [f.] (d?), 7701 [f.] (d), 7720 [f.], 7734 in aed., 14879b in aed., 15587 per [f.].
1547: 3310.3 [f.] (d?), 21616 [f.].
1548: 5195 [f.], 13175.12 [f.] (d?), 18222.5 [f.] (d?), 22160 [f.] (d?), 23877.3 [f.] (d?), 24203.7 [f.] (d?).
1549: 1725.3 [f.] (d?), 2379.5 f. (c).
1550: 2861 f., 7542.7 [f.] (d?), 11393.7 [f.], 13304 [f.] (c), 14040 [f.] (d?), 14125 [f.] (c), 14643 [f.] (c).
1551: 2086.5 f., 2977 f.
1552: 4052.5 f., 11000 [f.] (d?), 14119.3 [f.], 19495.3 f. (d?).
1553: 2978, 3019 [f.] (d?), 4844.2 f., 21755 f.
1554: 1011 f., 10469, 10469.5.
1555: 4813.8 (d?), [10469.7] (c), 12952 [f.], 13175.16 f. (d?), 16067 f., 24571.7 f. (c).
1556: 9972 (note), 25875 f.
1557: 19.4 ?ent., 1342 [f.] (d?), 7633.3 [f.], 7605.5 ent., 7680 (d?), 9989.5 ent., 10752, 11551.5 (d), 14110 ent., 14111a [f.] (d), 14522.5 ent., 18076 at costs of, 19784 [f.], 22160.5 [f.] (d?), 23431(*A3*) ?ent.
1558: 5229 ent., 20732.5 ex off., 22596b [f.] (d?), 22603b [f.] (d?), 22617a.5 [f.] (d?).
1559: 3007 f., 4826 f. (d), 22413 f.
1560: 181 ent., 18223 [f.] (d?), 19137 at costs of, 19285.6 (c).
1561: 20733 [f.], 20734.
1561/62: 509, 510, 510.3.
1562: 4845 [f.], 20734–5.
1563: 492.9 ent., 20735, 20735.5–36.
1564: 20736–6a.
1565: [14110 f.?] (d?), 16508.3 (d), 16508.7 (d), 20736a f.
1567: 20737.
1567/68: 493.7 f.
1569: 10289 [f.] (d).
1570: 181 f. (c), 15532 f. (d), 20906 pro, 22415 f. (d?).
1571: 20738 [f.].
1573: 10993.4 f., 12155 [f.] (d?).
1575: 2113a [f.], 14799a (d/repeat).
1576: 12156 [f.], 20739–9.7 [f.].
1579: 5633.3 ent., 12157 [f.], 14799a [f.], 20739.3 ex off.
1580: 22416 [f.] (c).
1582: 12158 [f.].
1583: [3341.7 f.] (d), [3342 f.] (d), [3342.3 f.] (d), 20739.7 ex off.
1585: 181.5 [f.] (d?), 12158.5 [f.], 14800.5 [f.] (d?), 22416.5 [f.] (c).

Walley (Waley), Robert.
Bookseller in London, (1568: freed as 'John [*sic*] Whallay', Arber I.391) 1571–1595 (*Reg. B*: 50). Son of **John** and father of **Henry Walley**. Already in Paul's Churchyard (B) by 1571 according to T. Hill's report on Ii2^{v} of STC 13482. [*Dict. 1.*]

Walley, R. — *cont.*
dw. in Paul's Churchyard (B), 1581 (21002)–1584 (21002a); no earlier or later use noted
1576: 25348 f.
1577: 9526.7 ent.
1578: 1416 [f.].
1579: 13020 [f.].
1581: 10275 ent., 20996 [f.], 21002 [f.].
1582: 21004 [f.].
1583: 4800.3 [f.], 20996.3 [f.].
1584: 21002a f.
1585: 1064 f.
1586: 25172 f.
1587: 13193 pro (d), 13194 pro (d), 20995 f.
1588: 12158.7(*A*3) f. (d).
1591: (all ent. & ass'd): 5633.3, 10752, 12159, 14801(*A*3), 20739.7, 20996.7, 22418.

Walpote. *See* Waelpot.

Waltem, Thomas, *pseud.*
Printer in 'Edinburgh', 1572. = Unidentified printer, probably in France.
1572: 3979.

Waltenell. *See* Woutneel.

Walter, Richard.
Stationer in London, (1605) 1607–1620 (cf. DFM 2643). [*Dict. 1.*]
No address known.
1607: 14696 ent.

Walters, G. *See* Waters.

Walton, Robert.
Printer, seller of prints and maps in London, 1647–1686 (1688†). Member of the Merchant Taylors' Co. The item below is included because it is issued with unaltered plates dated 1637. [*Dict. 2*; Globe 221.]
after 1668: [3061].

Wandsforth (Freez, Vreez), Gerard.
Dutch bookseller in York, 1507–1510†. Duff indicates he lived in the liberties of the cathedral. [Duff, *Century*.]
No address used.
1507: 16119 imp.

Ward, Roger.
Printer in London, (1575?) 1577–1596 (1597?†). In addition to the addresses below, secret presses of his were located in Lothbury (H.9) and Southwark Hospital, 1587 (Arber I.526, erroneously dated 1588); near his own house in the Little Old Bailey (D.6), early 1590; by the bankside, Southwark, later 1590 and removed to Hammersmith (X.18), 1591; and in the Temple (W.11), 1596 (*Reg. B*: 34, 36–7, 53), as well as others of unknown location. Between at least 1582 (Judge: 49) and 1585 (*Library*) he also had a bookshop in Shrewsbury. [*Dict. 1*; *St. Giles* (widow Helen), 1599; *Poor Book* (widow Ellen), 1608–25; *Library* 13 (1958): 247–68; Judge: 44–60.]
dw. at Temple Bar (W.14), 1578 (16949, with R. Mundee; possibly W. How's address)
dw. by (a little above, near) Holborn conduit at the Talbot (D.5), 1580? (4656, colophon)–1585 (21132.7); variation: 1585 (21131.5, omits sign)
dw. on Lambeth (Lambert, Lambard) Hill near Old Fish Street (S.7), 1589 (2013, 3057)
dw. at the $ Purse in the Little Old Bailey (D.6), 1590 (10877.5)–1591 (11625)
dw. in Holborn at the $ Castle (V.5), 1593 (5248; 14487 adds: over against Ely House)
dw. in Fleet Street over against the conduit at the $ Castle (W.5), 1594 (9976.5)
dw. in Salisbury Court at the $ Castle (W.5), 1596 (9977)
1578: 16949.
1580: 4656 (d?).
1582: 1762.7, 4654, 4657, 17800.5.
1583: 6650 (note), 6784.5, 11861, 11863.5, 15146 (d?), 15146.5 (d), 17800.5–01, 19109.5, 23380–0.5, 25980.
1584: 2399.3, 6145 in aed., 12278, 15690.7, 16634, 18733.3, 25784, 25808.
1585: [11492.5] (d?), 14945, 17156, [18211?], 21131.5–32, 21132.1, 21132.3, 21132.5, 21132.7, 21132.9.
1586: [16617], [25079].
1589: 2013, 3057 [f.], 3145, 12309, 12310, [13098.4], [13098.5], 18778, 21121.5, 25624.
1590: 1662 f., [4178(*A*3)?] (d), 5412, 7277, 10877.5 [f.], 10878 f., 14486, 16621 f., 17322.5, 21482, 22693, 22694, 22694.5, 22695 f., [23375?] (d), 24569 f., 24590.
1591: 6658 (note), 11625 f.
1593: 5248 (d), 14487.
1594: 9976.5 (d).
1596: 9977 (d).

Ward, Samuel.
Stationer in London, (1625) 1627–1632 (cf. DFM 2660). He succeeded to one of the shops of his former master, **Nathaniel Newbery**. [*Dict. 1*; DFM 2028.]
shop under St. Peter's Church in Cornhill at the Star (P.2), 1627 (3513)–1631 (12129, omits 'shop')
1627: 3513 sold. **1631:** 12129 sold.

Ward, William.
Publisher in London, 1628. Not a member of the Stat. Co. nor a citizen of London. He is the 'stranger' for whom **Nicholas Okes** printed the item below (*C-B C*: 475). [*Dict. 1.*]
dw. on Lambeth Hill near Old Fish Street (S.7), 1628 (10018.5)
1628: 10018.5 f.

Warren, Thomas.
Bookseller and printer (from 1642) in London, 1638–1661†. In partnership with **Joshua Kirton**, 1638–1641. In 1642 he married Alice (Law) Norton, the widow of **John Norton 2** and took over her printing house in Foster Lane. [*Dict. 2*; DFM 1781; *Library* 15 (1935): 499–500.]
their shop in Paul's Churchyard at the White Horse (A.2), 1639 (12124)–1640 (18036) at least
1638: 1459 sold, 11943 f., 11943.5 sold.
1639: 12124 f., 12979 prost., 12980 prost., 17554 f., 21063.7 sold, 22392 sold.
1640: 18035a ven., 18036–6.5 ven., 24046 sumpt.

Warwyke, John.
Printer in York, (1529) 1532. Succeeded to the printing material of **Ursyn Mylner**. [Duff, *Century*.]
at the $ Cardinal's Hat, 1532 (23151)
1532: 23151.

Washington, William.
Bookseller in London, 1627–1629. Succeeded to the shop of his former master's widow, **Anne Helme**. [*Dict. 1*; DFM 1598.]
shop in St. Dunstan's Churchyard (W.9), 1629 (1165)
1627: (all SR entries): 2776, 2783, 5675, 6771, 26043.
1629: 1165 f.

Waterhouse, Philip.
Bookseller in London, (1628) 1629–1632. Although his last book was printed in Cambridge, there seems to be no evidence that he himself moved there, and the item was sold in London by **Nicholas Alsop**: at the Angel in Pope's Head Palace (O.11). [*Dict. 1*; DFM 1013.]
shop at the $ St. Paul's Head in Cannon (Canning) Street near London Stone (T.1), 1629 (23898a)–1631 (13313, omits 'in ... Street')
1629: 23896 f., 23898a f.
1630: 5453 f., 20388 sold, 23114 f.
1631: 7409 sold, 13313 f., 25166.7 sold.
1632: 13314(*A*3) f.

Waters (Walters), Joris (George).
Printer and bookseller in Dordrecht, 1608–1623 at least. Apprenticed in London to A. Islip on 19 Jan. 1596 for 8 years (Arber II.208) but not freed. Married the widow of **Abraham Canin** and succeeded to the Dordrecht establishment. [*Dict. 1*; Gruys; Briels 543–4.]

Waters, J. — *cont.*
1609: [20607].
1610: 20608.
1611: 20095.
1612: 551.7.
1614: 3532.
1615: [11929], 12066, 12067.
1616: [11928] (false, d?), [11930] (d?).
1619: 3212 (d), 3212.5 (forged, d), 10811 (d), 11360.3, 12859.
1623: 25939 pour.

Waterson, John.
Bookseller in London, (1620) 1623–1656†. Son of **Simon Waterson**, in whose shop he worked before succeeding to it in 1635. [*Dict. 2*; DFM 2685; *Loan Book*, 1630–36, 1650–53.]
at the Crown in Paul's Churchyard (A.5), 1623 (25176)–1640 (14813a), also 1635 (19675); beginning in 1635 (23123) until 1639 (17643) 'his shop' seems to be used consistently whenever an address is given at all
1623: 13873 f., 25176 f.
1626: 14753.5(*A*3) ent., 24033 imp.
1630: 6302 f., 6303 f., 7210 f., 17641 f.
1632: 17636 f., 17638 ent., 20939 ent.
1634: 11075 f., 17640 ent.
1635: 6243.8 f., 14813a ent., 19675 sold, 20099a.5 f., 21036a.7 ent., 23123 f.
1636: 4525 f., 19676 sold.
1637: 4526 f., 11066 f., 11067 (forged), 18698(*A*3) f., 24910 f.
1638: 3474.5 f., 22550 f.
1639: 11071 f., 17643 f.
1640: 13621 f., 14813a f., 19109.4D(*A*3) sold (c), 19379 sold, 21036a.7 f., 25177a f.

Waterson, Simon.
Bookseller in London, (1583) 1584–1635† (*C-B C*: 266). His mother successively remarried **Francis Coldock** and **Isaac Bing**. The earliest address associated with Waterson's name is Coldock's: at the Green Dragon in Paul's Churchyard ((A.3): in an undated MS. note of purchase in the NY(Clawson) copy of STC 11049, which is itself dated 1576). One of the *assignees of* **J. Battersby**. Agent for sale in London of books printed at Cambridge, 1601–10, and at Oxford, 1603–06. Father of **John Waterson**, who worked in and succeeded to the shop below. [*Dict. 1*.]
in Paul's Churchyard at the Crown (A.5), 1589 (18064, accidentally omits 'Paul's')–1634 (6252, has 'dw.'; variation: in Paul's Churchyard at Cheap gate [no sign], 1591 (19381), 1592 (5577, has 'shop')
1585: 11900–0.5 f., 24337 f. (d).
1589: 18064 f.
1590: 5061 f. (d?), 19380 [f.].
1591: 5376.2 f., 19381 f.
1592: 5577 f., 6243.2 f., 6243.3 f., 19382 f.
1593: 6467 f.
1594: 6243.4 f., 19383 f.
1595: 4511 pro, 6243.5 f., 6244–4.3 f.
1596: 4032 f.
1597: 4511.4 imp., 24338 f.
1598: 6243.6 f., 14809 ent., 19384 f., 26120 ent.
1599: 6261 f., 19384.5 f.
1600: 25642 f.
1601: 6236 f., 12922 f., 13479 sold, 18810 f., 19385 f., 19728 sold, 19757.5 sold, 19764 sold.
1602: 1955.5 sold, 4877.4 sold, [5301] ven., 6237 f., 6467.5 f., 7434 f., 12415 f., 14809 at charges of, 19105.5 sold, 19750 sold, 25673 sold.
1603: 6640 f., 6889 sold, 12678 f., 12988 f., 13266 sold, 14357 sold, 19011 sold, 19012 sold, 19690 sold, 19724.7 sold, 19728.5 sold, 19743.5 sold, 19751.5 sold, 20010 sold, 20025 sold, 20132.5 f., 21128 f., 22376 sold, 22874 sold, 24947.7 sold, 25676 sold, 25759 sold.
1604: 37 sold, 3438 sold, 5755a.5 sold, 5756 sold, 6265 f., 7490.3 ent., 11817 sold, 12264 ent., 13419 f., 13704 f., 13899 sold, 17257 sold, 19013 sold, 19172 sold, 19296 sold, 19668 sold, 19699 sold, 19734 sold, 19737 sold, 20144 sold, 21734 sold, 23083 ent., 23705 f., 24030 imp., 25704 sold.
1605: [1831] sold, 4521 f., 5899 ext., 6239 f., 13420 f., 14023 sold, 14035 sold, 14738 sold, 15006 prost., 19106 sold (c), [19648] sold,

Waterson, S. — *cont.*
20027 sold, 21716 f., 21717 f., 21717.5 (forged), 21735 sold, 21737 sold, 22543 f., 24036 sold (d?), 24947 sold, 24952 sold.
1606: 6262 f., 10857 f., 10857.5 (repeat), 13429 sold, 13887 ven., 15453.7 f., 17832 f., 18984.5 sumpt., 18984.7 sumpt., 19669 sold, 20773 sold, [24013] ext., 24948 sold.
1607: 747 f., 6240 f., 6641 f., 13398 sold, 18986 sumpt., 19681 ent., 19751 sold, 23135 f., 24104 f.
1608: 13422 sold, 19385.5 f., 19649 sold, 19670 sold, 25280 f.
1609: 1952.5 sold, 3116 f., 6245 [f.], [14734] sold, 14735 sold, 14810 f., 19649 sold.
1610: 7077 f., 10857.7 f., 13776 f., 19386 f., [24014] ext., 25797 f.
1611: 6242–3 f., 6642 f., 11187 f., 13783 f., 19106.5 sold, 19671 sold, 19686.5 sold, 19691 sold, 19705.4 sold, 19725 sold, 19729 sold, 19738 sold, 19745 sold, 19761.3 sold, 20011 sold, [23101] sold.
1612: 1953 sold, 6246 ent., 17615 sold, 18987 sumpt., 18988–8.5 sumpt.
1613: 13378 (note), 19107 sold, 22544 f.
1614: 4522 f., 10857.5 f. (d?), 19671.5 sold.
1615: 4496 imp., 19387 f., 24105 f. (c).
1616: 19088–8.3 f., 19091 f., 22839.3 sold.
1617: 17872a.5 sold, 21122 (note), 22839.7(*A*3) sold, 24106 f.
1618: 18352 f., 18989 sumpt., 23136 f.
1619: 13379 (note), 19388 f.
1620: 14811a f.
1621: 4749 ent., 6250 f.
1622: 6643 f., 17986 f., 17987 f., 18990 sumpt., 22545.5–.7 f., 24107 f.
1623: 4523 f., 6238 f.
1624: 13381 (note).
1625: 13591 f.
1626: 6251 f., 21035(*A*3, note).
1627: 4496.5 imp., 19108 sold, 19108.5 sold, 19108.7 sold, 22547 f.
1628: 1962 sold, 1964.7 sold, 6644 f., 19109 sold, 19673 sold, 22547 f.
1629: 1954 sold, 4524 f., 22548 sold.
1630: 19088.7 f., [19109.2 sold] (c).
1631: 6645 f., 19388a f., 19706 sold.
1632: 14812a f., 19109.3 sold, 19674 sold, 24108 f.
1633: 6646.2 f., [17216] sold, 18991 sumpt., 19389 f., 20098 f., 22549 f.
1634: 6252 f., 13383.5 (note), 18992 sumpt., 19109.4 sold (d?), 20099 f., 23137 f.

Watkins, Richard.
Bookseller and printer? in London, (1557) 1561–1599†. Son-in-law of **Richard** and **Joan Jugge**; brother-in-law of **John Jugge**. One of the *assignees of* **F. Flower**. Partner with **James Roberts** in the Almanack patent, 1571–1599/1600 and yielded his rights in the broadside Almanack to the Stat. Co. on 8 Jan. 1584 (Arber II.787 and Appendix C/14; *see* also Appendix D/101–2). Treasurer for the *assignees of* **R. Day** and of **W. Seres**, at least 1591–1599 (*Reg. B*: 39, 70) with a room in Stationers' Hall (A.10). *See* also *assignees (etc.) of* **R. Watkins**. [Duff, *Century*.]
His printing material came from the Jugges and remained at least nominally under their control until 1583 when John was listed as having two presses (Arber I.248). The presses were listed under Watkins in July 1586 (Arber V.lii), but possibly by c. 1588 (3850) any actual printing may have been done by **Gabriel Simson**, who definitely had the material at a later date, and his partner at the time, **William White**, both former Jugge apprentices. Items below after 1587 with Watkins's name supplied in square brackets as printer have the Jugge printing material, but the question of how closely Watkins was involved requires further study. For the greater part of his career—except, possibly, for Almanacks—his books were printed by others.
in Paul's Churchyard (B), 1561 (549)–1587 (23674) at least; variations: adds 'at the $ Love and Death', 1570 (7625); has 'dw.', 1579 (3048)
1561: 549 (d).
1569/70: 486.5.
1570: 7625, 15011 f., 20444.5 (c).
1570/71: 422.5.
1571/72: [459], 459.5.
1572: 15320 f.
1572/73: 459.7(*A*), 511.9.

Watkins, R. — *cont.*
1573/74: [459.9(*A*)], [482.12], [512].
1574: 3738 (d), 17303, 17304.
1574/75: [401.7] (d?).
1575: 2113a.3 [f.], 2874 (d?), 6226 [f.].
1575/76: 401.8, [401.8A(*A*)?], 488.3, 512.3, 512.4.
1576: 19819 (d), 26110–0.3(*A*3) [f.] (d?), 26110.5(*A*3) [f.] (d?).
1577: 3715 ent., 13196.
1577/78: 512.6.
1578: 19819.5 [f.] (d?).
1578/79: 488.5, [491], 512.7, [518.8].
1579: 3048, 3049, 16809(*A*3) [f.], 19809 [f.].
1579/80: 512.9, [26049.6].
1580: [14894] (d).
1580/81: 418, 454.5, 488.7, [491.5], 512.11, [26049.8–.10].
1581: 12422 [f.].
1581/82: 422.7, 480.3.
1582: 518.10 ent., 20886 pro.
1582/83: 518.9(*A*3), [26049.13(*A*3)].
1583: 12907.
1583/84: 402.5, 423, 455, [517.9], [26049.14].
1584/85: 444, 455.3, 480.5, [501.32], 518.10.
1585: 19820 [f.] (c).
1586/87: 443, [444.1], [444.2].
1587: 1970 f., 19721.3 f., 23674–4.5 sold.
1587/88: 444.3, 451.
1588: [3850] (d?), 12908 f., 21160 ent.
1588/89: 423.3, 434, 444.4, 444.5, 451.2, 455.7.
1589: 5802 f., 16612a imp.
1589/90: 423.4, 423.5, 444.6.
1590: [3869], [5866], [13699], 19821 (c), [21159.5(*A*3)] (c), 23280 ent., 24407 pro.
1590/91: [423.6], 433.5–.7, 434.2, 444.7, 444.8, 451.4.
1591: [3888], [3890–0.5], 19619 f.
1591/92: 434.3, 444.9.
1592: 287.5 f., 3593 pro, [3845(*A*3)], 5551 f., [5867], 20556 pro.
1592/93: [423.8], 428, 444.10, 451.6.
1593: 10833 f.
1593/94: [403.7] (d?), 434.5, 444.11, 526, [26049.16].
1594: [3861] (d?), [3887?] (d?), 13890–0.5 f., 15139.
1594/95: 424.3, 424.4, 434.6, 445, 451.8, 525, 526.5.
1595: 21662 f.
1595/96: 424.5, 445.1.
1596: 21662a f.
1596/97: 445.2.
1597/98: 424.7, 434.9, 445.3, 445.4, 451.11, 466, 525.2.
1598: 19821.5(*A*3) [f.] (d?), 21160(*A*3) [f.].
1598/99: 434.10, 445.5, 525.3.
1599/1600: 434.11, 525.4, 525.5.

Watkins, Richard, *Assignees (with assent, etc.) of.*
Publishers of items, 1580–1603/04, to which Watkins held rights or which impinged on his patent for Almanacks. Imprints are in the form 'with assent of' except as specified.
1580: 3050 by assent (c).
1583: 12909.7, 12910, 12911–1.3, 12911.5 (d), 13255 by ass't (d), 13255.3 by assent (d), 23676 at ass't.
1594/95: [424].
1596: 5803 by ass'ns.
1597/98: 450.7.
1598/99: 425.
1599: 3050.2 by assent.
1599/1600: [466.2].
1603/04: 466.6.

Watleer, Jacob, *pseud.*
Printer in 'Amsterdam', 1585? = Unidentified printer and place.
1585: 693.3 (d?).

Watson, Henry.
Translator and journeyman printer in London, fl. 1509–1518. In at least 1509 he worked for **Wynkyn de Worde**: in Fleet Street at the Sun (W.5) but had a shop of his own in partnership with **Hugh Goes** in 1513? [Duff, *Century*; *The Gardyners Passetaunce*, ed. F. B. Williams, Jr., London, 1985, pp. 42–50, 54–6.]
at Charing Cross (X.14), 1513? (11562.7)
1513: 11562.7 (d?).

Wayght. *See* Wight.

Wayland, John.
Scrivener by 1534 and printer in London, 1537–1539 and 1554–1557 (1572?†). Patentee for printing primers under Mary I. His first set of printing material passed to **John Mayler**. His second house was acquired from **Edward Whitchurch**. *See* also *assignees of* **J. Wayland**. [Duff, *Century*; *Library* 11 (1930): 312–50; 16 (1936): 413–14.]
within Temple Bar at the Blue Garland (W.14), 1537 (10495)–1539, 15 July (16009, adds: in Fleet Street in St. Dunstan's parish)
dw. in Fleet Street at the Sun over against the conduit (W.5), 1554, 1 June (12950)–1556 (24205, tp has 'great' conduit)
in Fleet Street near to Temple Bar (W.14), 1557, Dec. (12427); this may indicate a return to his first shop or at least to its vicinity
1537: 10495, 25413.5, 25414, 25425.5.
1538: [3038.3] (d?), [3038.5] (d?), 26063.
1539: 2966.7 f. (d), 16009–9.5, 16010 f., 16011 f. (d?).
1554: 1246 in aed. (d?), 3177.5–78 in aed. (d?), 12950.
1555: 7552 (d), 16060, 16063, 16064–5, 16066, [16247?], [17629?] (d?), [17629.5?] (d?), [24204.5] (d?).
1556: 1256 (d), 3055 (d?), 3055.5 (d?), 4564–5 (d?), 5468 (d), [11000.7?] (d?), 24205.
1557: 12427 [f.].

Wayland, John, *Assignees of.*
Publishers of primers in London, 1557–1559, under the continuation of Wayland's patent.
1557: 16079 [f.], 16080.
1558: 16082, 16083, 16084, 16084.5 (d?), 16085, 16086.
1559: 16087 [f.].

Weaver (Wever), Edmund.
Bookseller in London, 1600–1638†. Freed as a Draper by **Thomas Wight** on 22 Nov. 1598; transferred to the Stat. Co. in 1600. Father of **Thomas Weaver**. Treasurer of the **English Stock** (*see* Stationers' Company), 1610–1638 (*C-B C*: 42, 305) with an office in the Hall (H.11, Q.1). His house and shop by the great North door of St. Paul's were among those marked for removal c. 1632 (*Library* 3 (1902): 267–8); Weaver was not one of the petitioners for relief in Jan. 1636 when the final order came (Greg, *Companion*: 337–8). His last three books were sold by **John Crooke** and **Richard Sergier 2**: at the Greyhound in Paul's Churchyard (B). [*Dict. 1.*]
shop at the great North door of Paul's Church (A.2), 1603 (20141.3)–1637 (3233a, a date variant with the address probably no longer relevant); variations: has 'dw.', 1616 (14321); omits 'shop' and has 'great South [*sic*, misprint] door', 1616 (4766)
1602: 21269 imp.
1603: 14299 sold, 18539 sold, 20141 f., 20141.3(*A*) f., 20141.5(*A*) f.
1604: 4884 f., 14427 f.
1605: 312.5 ent., 3429 ent., 10543 ent., 13201 ent., 18184 f., 18184.5 f., 18539 ent., 20156 f., 23548 ent., 23592 f.
1606: 18185 f., 19335 imp., 23464 f., 23591 f., 23593 f., 25360 f.
1607: 3429 ent., 18517(*A*3) ent., 19370 f., 19898a.7 sold.
1608: 6027 f., 18191 f., 23274.5 f.
1609: 4884.5 f., 18181 f., 19372 f., 19677 sold, 23276 f.
1610: 1958 f., 23275 f.
1611: 3228 f., 3429 f.
1612: 3229 f., 19373 f.
1613: 1077 ent., 3908.2 f., 4885 f.
1614: 3230 f., 18493 f., 23273.5 f.
1615: 19374 f.
1616: 1935 f., 4766 f., 4767 f., 6887 sold (d), 14321 sold, 15202 f.
1617: 1955 ent., 4886 f., 5834 sold, 13247 ent.
1618: 1079 ass'd, 3230.5 f., 23364 sold.
1619: 6065 f., 22186 f.
1620: 3430 f.
1621: 19375 f., 25925 ent.
1622: 7143 f.
1623: 1956 sold, 1956.3 sold, 1956.7 sold, 5461.2 f., 12519 sold, 12521 (note), 12521.9 sold, 23352 ent.
1624: 1957 sold, 4139 f., 12522–2.5 sold.
1625: 3231 f., 3250 f.

Weaver, E. — *cont.*
1626: 3251 f., 5462 f.
1629: 7144 ass'd.
1630: 3238 ent., 3252 f., 12522.5 sold (c?).
1631: 22169 prost.
1634: 3253 f.
1636: 3233 f.
1637: 3233a f., 5465(*A*3) f.
1638: 3234(*A*3) f., 3254(*A*3) f., 5466 ass'd.

Weaver, John.
Probably an error in the SR for **John Dever,** who was the publisher of the book in question.
1630: 11498 ent.

Weaver, Thomas.
Bookseller in London, (1627) 1630–1640. Son of **Edmund Weaver**. In 1628 he apparently went to Dublin with **Robert Young** in connection with the **Irish Stock** (*C-B C*: 202–3; *see* also Stationers' Company). His London address is that of his father. [*Dict. 1*; DFM 2699.]
his shop at the great North door of Paul's Church (A.2), 1630 (19376.5)–1632 (5464); no later address used.
1630: 19376.5 f.
1631: 3232 f., 3238 f., 3431 f., 5463 f.
1632: 5464 f., 23365 sold.
1635: 3239 f.
1638: 3234 ent., 3254 ent., 3431 ent., 19379 ent.
1639: 5466 f.
1640: 3240 f.

Webb, William 1.
Bookseller and bookbinder in Oxford, 1616–1652. [*Dict. 1*; *Dict. 2*.]
No address used.
1628: 4736 imp., 12514 sold, 23026–7 f., 24882.7–83 imp.
1629: 1071 f., 4498 sold, 20618 f., 23027 f.
1631: 92.3–.7 imp., 93 sumpt., 20382 pro, 24749 imp., 24884 imp.
1633: 19345 f., 20135 f., 24473 f., 24473.3 (forged).
1634: 3912.5 sold, 4499 f., 20136 sold, 20136.7 f.
1635: 7110–11 f., 15410 f., 19006 imp.
1636: 1389 imp., 7112 f., 10595 sold, 12401 imp., 16788 imp., 19351 f., 26013 imp.
1637: 19347.5–48, 23916.5 imp., 23917–7.5 imp., 26017–7a imp.
1638: 16789 imp., 19007 pro, 20667 f.
1639: 12399 imp., 14589 imp.

Webb, William 2.
Printseller in London, c. 1635–1645. [Globe 221.]
shop at the Globe in Cornhill over against the Royal Exchange (O.9), c. 1635 (5022)
1635: 5022 sold (c), 11921.8 sold (c), 11921.9 sold (c).

Webster (Webber), Richard.
Stationer in London, (1572?) 1578–1595?†. He began as a journeyman printer, and his sole imprint has printing material of **Thomas Dawson**, for whom Webster was probably working at the time: near the three cranes in the Vintry (S.9). He apparently turned his efforts elsewhere since he bound several apprentices from 1585 and was called to the Livery in 1594 (Arber II.872). [*Dict. 1*.]
No address used.
1578: 3131 [f.].

Wechel, Johann.
Printer in Frankfurt am Main, 1581–1593†. [*Dict. 1*; Benzing 127–8.]
1590: 12786 typis.

Wekes. *See* Wykes.

Welby, William.
Bookseller in London, (1604) 1605–1618†. [*Dict. 1*]
in Paul's Churchyard, 1605–1616 at least
shop — at the Greyhound (B), 1605 (1825)–1609 (12204)
shop — at the Swan (A.5), 1610 (6937.5)–1616 (18522); variations: has 'White' Swan, 1610 (5697.5); has 'dw.', 1613 (24833.6)

Welby, W. — *cont.*
1605: 1825 f., 1833 f., 18995 f., 19706.5 f., [19706.7 f.] (d), 19733 f., 20575.7 f.
1606: 1826 imp., 1827 f., 18995.5 f., 19683 f., 19707 f., 19733a f., 21079 f., 21787 f., 23452a–a.5 f.
1607: 14426 f., 18021 f. (d), 19707.5 f., 21757 f.
1608: 7140.5 f., 7145 f., 13049 sold, 19065 ent., 19721.3 ent., 20763.2 imp., 22795–5.7 sold, 23274.5 f., 24263.7 f.
1609: 1816 f., 6104 ent., 6406 ent., 6625.7 ent., 7124 f., 7140.5–41 f., 7204.5 f., 12204 f., 12986 ent., 13770 f., 18184(*A*3) ent., 18191 (*A*3) ?ent., 19107.5 ent., 19649 (note), 19708 f., 20367(*A*3) ent., 20826.5 f., 21387 ent., 23276 f., 23478 ent., 23594 f., 25744a.5 ent.
1610: 1934 f., 1958 f., 5697.5 f., 6029 f., 6937.5 f., 6944.4 f., 6950 f., 7142 ass'd, 13005a.5 ass'd, 13771 ass'd, 17376 sold, 23275 f., 23479 ass'd, 24831.7 f.
1611: 3456 ent., 5392 f., 6938 f., 7115 ent., 10600 imp., 12318 f., 22182 f., [24830.6 f.] (d?), 24833.2 f., 25266 f.
1612: 363 f., 5128 f. (d), 7136 f., 12318 f., 14700 f., 14889 imp., 24833.4 f.
1612/13: 25705 f.
1613: 7138.5 ent., 7140 f., 7474 f., 12754 f., 13323 f., 14817 f., 19650 (note), 22125 f., 22218 imp., 24148.3 f., 24151 f., [24830.7 f.] (d?), 24833.6 f., 25143 f., 25174 f., 25354 f., 25901 ent.
1614: 810–0.5 f., 6406 f., 6944 f., 12986 f., 18493 f., 19130 f., 20862 f., 23273.5 f., 26022.5–23 f.
1615: 1314.2 sold, 5700 f., 12736 f., 13396 f., 13877 sold, 13919 f., 14890 imp., 17492 imp., 18446 f., 24833.8 f.
1616: 4577 f., 4578 f., 13397 f., 13877.3–.5 f., 18075.5 f., 18522 f., 23068 sold, 24316(*A*3) ?ent.
1617: 1314.3(*A*) f./sold, 13394a ent., 25142 f., 25744a.6 ass'd.
1618: 544 ass'd, 12997 ass'd, 13394a ass'd, 19107.5 ass'd, 19651 (note).

Wells, John.
Stationer in London, (1617) 1620. It is not clear whether he had two shops or if the second one mentioned below means 'also sold ...' [*Dict. 1*; DFM 1915.]
sold by J. Wels at his shop in Fetter Lane (W.8) and in the Temple (W.11), 1620 (970, 18975)
1620: 970 sold, 18975 sold.

Welwood, William.
Scottish mathematician, lawyer, and author, fl. 1578–1622. By 1613 he was in London, where he published the following item under a pseudonym, **Gulielmus Fonti-silvius**. [*DNB*.]
'Cosmopolis', 1615 (25240)
1615: [25240 f.] (false).

Wendelen, Merten, *pseud.*
Printer 'outside London', 1566–1567. = Unidentified printer across the English Channel, possibly in Emden?
1566–67: 2740.5.

Wenssler, Michael.
Printer in Basel, 1472–1491, and later briefly in Lyons, Cluny, and Mâcon. [Duff, *Century*; *Library* 3 (1912): 283–321.]
1489: [16165] (d).

Westall, John.
Bookseller and bookbinder in Oxford, 1609–1643†. [*Dict. 1*.]
No address used.
1637: 21812.7 ven., 21812.9 pro. **1638:** 11102 imp., 21813 pro. **1640:** 20515 imp.

Wethered, William.
Stationer in London, (1637) 1638–1646. Transferred to the Stat. Co. in 1637, but even earlier, in 1634, he had been granted the reversion of the Clerkship of the Co. (*C-B C*: 256). His only STC imprint was published with **Lawrence Blaiklock** and has the latter's address: at the Sugarloaf next Temple Bar in Fleet Street (W.14). [*Dict. 1*; DFM 2722; *Loan Book*, 1638–41.]
No separate address used.
1638: 13725 ent., 13727 ent., 13739 ent., 13740 ent.
1640: 1665 f.

Wever. *See* Weaver.

Whaley, Peter.
Bookseller in Northampton, 1630–1635 at least. [*Dict 1.*]
No address used.
1630: 3234.5 f. **1635:** 1235.7 f.

Whitaker, Richard.
Bookseller in London, 1619–1648†. Married the widow of **Thomas Norton** and succeeded to the latter's shop. Most of his imprints in 1625–26 were shared with **Hannah Barrett** and in 1632–38 with **Joyce Norton**, but the address when one is given at all is always Whitaker's. [*Dict. 2*; DFM 1822; *Loan Book*, 1622–29.]
in Paul's Churchyard, 1619–1640 at least
shop — at the King's Head (A.3), 1619 (11518)–1626 (1116, with H. Barrett)
at the King's Arms — (A.6), 1631 (22178)–1640 (21763)
1538: 3617 (d/error).
1619: 11518 f.
1620: 3566 f., 18508 f., 24970 f.
1621: 3571–2 f.
1622: 10240 [f.].
1623: 3572 f., 6015 f., 11923 f., 17377a sold.
1624: 7006.5 f., 15559–60 f., 17260 f., 18610 f., 24508.7 f., 24509a f.
1625: 1115 f., 1147 f., 1174 f., 1174.5 f., 25767 f.
1626: 1116 f.
1631: 7181 f., 22178 f.
1632: 3059.6 f., 3617 ent., 3908.9 ent., 4567 ent., 5483.7 ent., 6597.7 ent., 7320 ent., 11946 ent., [12455.5 f.?] (forged), 12990 ent., 12993 [f.], 13003 ent., 13628 ent., 17596 ent., 19563 ap., 20908 ent., 21036b ent., 21758 ent., 21763 ent., 23648 ent.
1633: 2798 ap. [f.], 2798.5 ap. [f.], 2813.3 ap. [f.], 7175 imp., 10076 f., 10077 (repeat), 10078–8.9 (forged), 11751, 13660 f., 13660.5 (d/repeat), 13676 f., 13676a f.
1634: 1129 imp., 4425 f., 21363 f.
1635: 3621 f., 5871 f., 11878 f., 12497 f., 13660.5 f. (d), 13661 f., 13676a f.
1636: 7181.5 f., [10074.3 f.?] (false, d?), 11752, 12994 [f.], 18954.5 sumpt., 21806 imp.
1637: 4510.2 f., 5046 f., 5048 sumpt., 5050 f., 5050.2 f., 5050.5 ent., 10812.5 ent., 11404 sumpt., 11406 f., 13796 imp., 13796.5 (forged), 21806 imp., 25371 sold.
1638: 765.7 f., 1109–10 prost., 3617 pro (d), 3772.3 f., 16432 pro, 18193 imp., 20787 f.
1639: 1592 sumpt., 10227.7 f., 19564 sumpt., 19596.5 f.
1640: 3908.9 f., 10077 (c?), 10193 f., 13621a f., 13662 f., 13662.5 (forged), 21036b f., 21763 f., 22438 f., 22455 f., 23648 f.

Whitchurch (Whytchurch), Edward.
Haberdasher, publisher, and printer (from 1540) in London, 1537–1553, 1560 (1562†). In partnership with **Richard Grafton**, 1537–41, in the publication of Bibles and some liturgies and apparently worked with him: in the house late the Greyfriars (C.2), 1540–41; the nature of their collaboration then and afterward requires further study. The earliest address noted in Herbert I. 539, following Ames, is undated and seems to be based on documentary evidence: the Well and Two Buckets, St. Martin's. Around 1549–50 **William Baldwin** was working in Whitchurch's house as a corrector and may have printed a few items. The last address below passed to **John Wayland** [Duff, *Century*; *Library* 6 (1915): 228–34; *HLB* 16 (1968): 139–55.]
?sold in Paul's Churchyard at the Bible (?A.2), 1540 (16015, colophon); almost certainly not Grafton's shop but probably not Whitchurch's either
on the South side of Aldermary Church (N.11), 1544 (11967)
in the Old Jewry (H.13), 1544 (20116)–c. 1545 (2754); this is possibly earlier than the previous address
in Fleet Street at the Sun over against the conduit (W.5), 1545, 19 June (16037)–1553? (2424.6); no later address used
1537: [2066 f.].
1538: 2817 f., 21041(*A*3) f. (c?).
1539: 2068, 2818.5 [f.], 2843 (d?), 19465.5.
1540: 2070, 2072, 2073, 2076, 2846 (d), 2971.5, [16014?] (d?), 16015.
1541: 2072, 2073, 2074, 2075, 2076, 7793 (d), 15833.5–34 per.
1542: [9986.5] (d?), [23713] (d?).
1543: 3327 in aed. (d), 11193 typis (d?), 11966.5 (d?), 15835 in aed., 23712 (d?), [24164] (d?), 24720.

Whitchurch, E. — *cont.*
1544: 2374 (d?), 3327.3 (d?), 3327.6, 11967, 15835 per, 20116 (d).
1545: 837 in aed., 2753.5 (d?), 2754 (c), 10438, 15204 (d?), 16037, 16038, 16039.
1546: 2849 ex off., [2973.5?] (d?), 11899, 11969, 16043, 16045, 16046, [20310].
1547: 1253, 2756 (d?), 2850, 2999, 4827, 13641, 13641.3, 13641.5, 13641.7, 13641.9, 15205 (d), 21041(*A*3) f. (c?).
1548: 358.5, 359, 2854, 2854.2, 2854.3, 2854.4, 2854.5, 2998.5, 4828, 16049, 17799, [24361.5] (d?), [24362] (d?), 25823.7 (c).
1549: 2079, 2376 f., 2376.5, 2419 [f.] (d?), 2419.5 (d?), 2420, [2760] (d?), 2768 servant with, 2854.6–.7, 13644, 13753 [f.], 13760 [f.], 16049.7, 16267 in off., 16270–0a in off., 16272 in off., 16273 in off.
1550: 360, 361 (note), 1254 [in house of?], 2081 [f.], 2999.5 (d?), 3000, 4407–7.5 [in house of?], 4408 [in house of?], 11970, [14125(*A*3)?] (c), [15188?] (d?), [16051.5] (c), 16560, [16704.1?] (c), [24665] (d), 24721.
1551: 20.2, 20.3, 360, 360.3, 2422, [2423] (d), 2424, 2866, 2957.8(*A*) de l'imprimerie.
1552: 1254.5 (d?), 2424.1(*A*), 2866, 16279–80.5 in off., 16281 in off., 16281.5 in off., 16282.3 in off., 16282.7 in off., 16288 in off. (d?).
1553: 1255 (d?), 2091, 2424.2, 2424.4 (d?), 2424.6 (d?), [2424.8] (d?), 16288a in off. (d?), [16290.5].
1559: 9459 (note).
1560: 11972 [f.].

1567: 2999 (d/error).

White (Whitte), Andrew.
Bookseller in London, (1584) 1589–1593. Brother of **Edward White 1**, who sold the last book below: at the Gun at the little North door of Paul's (A.1). [*Dict 1.*]
shop at (by) the Royal Exchange over against the conduit in Cornhill (O.10), 1589 (5530.5)–1591 (781)
1589: 5530.5 f. (d). **1590:** 335.5 [f.], 336 f. **1591:** 781 f., 4911.7 ent., 25734 sold. **1593:** 13117 f.

White, Edward 1.
Bookseller in London, (1572?) 1577–1613?†. Brother of **Andrew White**; husband of **Sara** and father of **Edward White 2**, who succeeded to the shop. One of the *assignees of* **J. Battersby** and of **R. Day**. Published Almanacks between 1599/1600 and 1605/06, usually as the *assignee of* **J. Roberts**. Imprints 1605–12 have been construed as belonging to Edward 1 unless they are entered to Edward 2 or specify 'the younger'. [*Dict 1.*]
dw. at (near) the little North door of Paul's at the Gun (A.1), 1578 (4432)–1612 (17705); variations: omits 'dw.', 1579 (4304); has 'shop', 1584 (12276)
1578: 4432 f., 19866 f. (d).
1579: 4303.5 ent., 4303.7 [f.], 4304 f., 5115 f. (d), 5235–5.2 [f.] (d), 5244 [f.] (d?), 7557.4 f. (d), 11620.7 f., 21634 f. (d), 23267 f. (d).
1580: 4304.5 [f.] (d?), 4433 [f.].
1581: 980 f., 1030.3 f. (d?), 4439.5 f., 11039 f., 17124–4a f. (d), 18259.3 (d), 18536–6a sold, 22432 [f.].
1582: 11041 (note), 15532.5 f., 17212 f., 18262 ent., 18262a f., 18270 f., 18270.5 f., 23030 [f.] (d).
1583: 982.5 f.
1584: 4305 f. (d?), 12276 f.
1585: 6394 f., 7520 f., 19433.3 f.
1586: 1328.7 ent., 3351 f. (d?), 3598 sold, 6170.5 ent., 6922.7 ent., 11093 ent., 16956 f., 16956.3(*A*3) f. (d), 18425.5 f. (d), 18426.5 f. (d), 18513 f., [19433.5 f.] (d?), 22900 ent.
1587: 4305.5 f. (d?), 6391 f., 12239 f., 12277 f., 12926 sold, 15533 f., 21778 f., [23228.7] sold.
1588: 4665 sold, 6557 f., 6565 f., 6910.7 sold, 7505 ent., 10746, 12003 f., 12295 f., 12556.3 f., 18260 f., 19433.7 f., 20180.3–.7 f.
1589: 5841.5 f., 13143–3.3, 24286 f.
1590: 633 sold, [7520.5 f.] (d?), 10834 f., 11287.5 sold, 12260 ent., [13146] sold, 13692 f. (c?), 16957.5 f. (c), 17572 sold.
1591: 332 f. (d), 4864 sold [his] shop, 5253 f., 5813 f., 12279 ent., 13116.5 f. (d), 19657 sold, 19876 f., 24765.3 [f.], 24766.7 f., 25613 f.
1592: 733 f., 10711 sold, 12296 f., 13130 (d), 15086 f. (d), 15095 sold, 15353.7 f., 19660 sold, 19699.5 sold, 22894 f. (d?).
1593: 10833a f., [13117(*A*3)] sold, 23685a(*A*3) f. (d?).
1594: 12267 f., 12448.5 f., 15087 sold, 15343 ent., 17423 f. (d?),

White, Edward 1 — *cont.*
19540 ent., 22328 sold.
1595: 4306 f., 6840 f., 12449 f., 16958–8.5 f., 19434 f.
1596: 3355 f., 6392 f. (d), 6553.5 ent., 7521 f., 10711 ent., 15533.3 f., 16662a–b f., 26035 sold.
1597: 6395 f., 12301a.9(*A3*) sold, 12451 f., 15533.3 f.
1597/98: 26050 f.
1598: 403.9 f., 4307 f., 11004 f., 23277.5 ent.
1599: 734 f., 1070 f., 11570.5 f., 12260 f., 14946 f., 19435 f., 22895–5a f., 24216 f., 24766.7 f.
1599/1600: 434.12 f.
1600: 7523 f., 11367 sold, 17573 sold, 19430 f., 19861 f., 22329 f., 23382.3 f., 24002 f.
1600/01: 501 [f.], [525.6] f., 26050.2 f.
1601: 13999 sold, 16959 f., 17569 f., 22137.5 ent.
1601/02: 434.14 f., 466.4 f., 483 f., 501.2 f., 525.7 f., 532 f.
1602: 4296 f., 6520.7–21 f., 16911 f.
1602/03: 452 f., 501.3 f., [532.2(*A*) f.].
1603: 4303 f., 11571 f., 14354 f., 14422 f., 14423 [f.] (d), 15633.4 ent., 16676 f., 16948 ent., 18520 f., 20874.5 f. (d?), 23382.7 f., [26050.4(*A3*) f.] (d?).
1604: 3657 f., 7211 f., 7211.5 f., 7212 f., 7213 f., 11936 f. (d), 25868 f.
1605: 3674 f., 6392.5 f. (d), 10513 f., 11576 ent., 11581 f., 15422 f., 17428 f., 19288 f. (d?).
1605/06: 532.5 f.
1606: 1598 f., 6396 f., 7524 f., 11368 f., 12302 f., 17350 f., 17428a f., 20960 f., 20960.5 f., 23383 f.
1607: 16638 ent., 17334 f., 17387.5 f., [17387.7 f.] (d), 20146 f.
1608: 876 sold, 4865 f., 10712 f., 15533.7 f., 19430.5 f., 23383.5 f.
1609: 5549.7 ent., 12740 f., 18105 f., 25970 f.
1610: 1599.7 f., 4307.5 f., 6393 f. (d), 10712.5 f., 13826.5 f., 23384 f.
1611: 5393.3 f., 5653 sold, 16911.5 f., 17702 f., 22330 f.
1612: 16638 f., 16959.5 f., 17705 f., 23385 f.

White, Edward 2.
Bookseller in London, (1604) 1605–1624†. Son of **Edward 1** and **Sara White** and succeeded to their shop. Before 1613 only items which Edward 2 entered or with 'the younger' in the imprint have been credited to him. Sometime in 1618 the shop passed to **John Grismand**. [*Dict 1*.]
at the Gun at the little North door of Paul's (A.1), 1607 (22915, 22916; both omit 'little')–1618 (10713, has 'shop')
1607: 21507 ent., 22915 f. & ent., 22915.5 f. (d), 22916 f. (d).
1611: 1845 f.
1613: 22406.5 ?ent.
1616–17: 17335 f.
1618: 10713 f., 16639 f., 23386 f.
1619: 4308 f., 10713.5 (note).
1620: 10514 ass'd, 12303 (note), 17782.5 f., 22137.5 f.
1624: 11040 ass'd, 16640 ass'd.

White (Whyte), John, *fl. 1549*.
Almost certainly an error for **John Wight**.
No address used.
1549: 2379 [f.].

White, John.
Bookseller and printer (1618–19?) in London, 1613–1633 (cf. DFM 504) (1651†). Son of **William White.** Freed by patrimony 16 Aug. 1613; *Dict 1* mistakenly cites the freedom of another John White (DFM 1251, *C-B C*: 454) of whom nothing further is definitely known. The present John succeeded in 1618 to his father's printing material, which by sometime in 1619 had apparently passed to **Augustine Mathewes**, to whom the 1620 items below printed 'by' John White should probably be assigned. [*Dict 1*; DFM 508; *Poor Book*, 1639–51, widow thereafter.]
their shop over against the Saracen's Head without Newgate (D.9), 1615 (15019, with T. Langley)
at the Holy Lamb in Little Britain near Aldersgate Street (F.4), 1622 (4179)–1625 (6023, has 'shop)
1614: 4087.7 ?ent., 17763 f. (d), 21406 f. (d?).
1615: 3720 f., 12215 sold, 15091 sold, 15091a f., 16761.3 f. (c), 17192.3 f. (c), 18921.7? f. (d).
1616: 595.6 ent., 21087.7 f. (d).
1617: 17192.7 f. (c).
1618: 595.7, [4932], [7259.7(*A3*)] (c), 11179.5 (d?), 13430, [14045.7] (d), 15092, [16862.5?] (d?), [21374].

White, J. — *cont.*
1619: 3951.5 ap., 14512.7, 21411, 23624.7.
1620: 595.8, 14512.7, 17189 (c), 20440 f. (d?).
1622: 4179 f. (d).
1623: 11037.5 ass'd, 18321 f.
1625: 6023 f.

White, Sara.
Bookseller in London, 1613–1615† (*C-B C*: 80). Widow of **Edward 1** and mother of **Edward White 2.** [*Dict 1*, under husband.]
at the little North door of St. Paul's at the Gun (A.1), 1613 (3292)–1615 (16948, has 'her shop')
1613: 3292 f., 19165.5 ent. **1614:** 198.7(*A3*)? f. (d?). **1615:** 16948 f.

White, William.
Bookseller and printer in London, (1583) 1588–1617?†. Father of **John White.** In partnership with **Gabriel Simson**, 1588–1596. Although their earliest imprints specify 'for' them, they may already have taken over the printing material which **Richard Watkins** possessed. When White set up a house for himself in 1598, he acquired the printing material of **Richard Jones**. [*Dict 1*; *St. Giles*, 1590; *Loan Book*, 1605–08; *Poor Book*, 1611.]
their house in Fleet Lane (D.2), 1591 (3888)–1592 (5867); both with G. Simson
dw. in Cow Lane (E.4), 1598 (20166.5)–1617 (12242); variations: adds 'near Holborn conduit', 1598 (12734); adds: 'near Smithfield', 1604 (20574); since Smithfield is at the other end of Cow Lane from Holborn, the second variation may represent a move
1588: 3850 f. (d?), 3873 ent.
1590: [3851?] (d?), 3869 f., 5866 f.
1591: 3888 f., 3890–0.5 f.
1592: 5867 f., 5867.3 f. (forged).
1594: [3885?] (d).
1595: [3859] (d?), 3874.5, 12325.
1596: 5865, 5869, 14029 (d).
1598: 6170, 12734, 17140, 19880, 20166.5, 22294.
1599: [3834(*A3*)–4.5] (d), 7268, 12916, 12923.5, 14684 ent., 15088, 19536, [19933.5] (d), [26019].
1600: 775.5, 7434.7, 7505 ent., 11502, 16751 ent., 21006a, 21392.7, 21393, 21393.5, 25642.
1601: 4286, [6236], 11502.5, [12504.5], 20890.
1602: [3673], 4287, [4296], 5346.5, [6237], 15089, 18547, [19798], 21409, [24651a–b], [25744a].
1603: 376.5 (note), 994.5, 2772 ent., 3728 ent., 5639.5 ent., 6922.4 ent., 11314, [11726], 14423 ?ent., [14671], 15089a, [15189], 18472a, [18513.5], 18961, [21364], [22045], 22463.5 ent., 24121, 24918.
1603/04: [532.3].
1604: 4287.5, 5958, [10255], [11501.5] (d), 13767, [14291], 20574, 21399, 22426, 23705, [25761.5].
1604/05: [451.15].
1605: [26], [772.5(*A*)], 3659, 3661, [3849.7], 13506, 19094, 21385, [22869(*A3*)–9.3], [24519], [25762].
1605/06: [408], [461].
1606: [5916], 5956, [11620.5?] (d?), 12580, [14691.3], [18231], 22061.
1606/07: [507.2].
1607: [6567], 14684 ent., 16626, [16874], 21533.3, [23020].
1607/08: [434.20].
1608: 5341, 5341a, 17156.3, 22310–11.
1609: [774(*A3*)], 3874.7, [3880], 4731.7, 5336, 10923, 17149.5, [21204.7], [21205], [21367?], [22334(*A3*)], [22335(*A3*)], [24628].
1609/10: [461.5].
1610: 1331.5 (c), [1815], [3795?] (c?), 4288, [4314(*A3*)], 7200 (note), [10610?] (c?), [12769], 12770, 15090, 16633 (note), 16675 (note), [18232], [21206].
1610/11: [434.23].
1611: [5650.3], 6846, 11577, 11580, 11582, 14297a.3, 15090, [18233], 21396, [25636].
1611/12: [434.24].
1612: 117, [3851.5?] (c), 3867.9 (d?), 3870, 3874, 3889 (c), [5394] (forged), 6847, 11745.5, 14304, 16756.5, 20851, [24519.5].
1613: 122, 3218, 3886, 4092 (note), 7504, 11037.5 ent., [16831(*A3*)], [18587], 21397, 21410.5 (d?), 21414, 22284, [22528?].
1613/14: [435.31].
1614: [5597], [10857.5] (d?), 12975, [17763] (d), [21056.8] (d?),

White, W. — *cont.*
[21372.5], 25819.
1614/15: [435.4].
1615: [5650.5], [11089] (d), 12214–5, [12235], 15091–1a, [16761.3] (c), [17192.3] (c), 18747, 19831, 21491.3, 22900 (c), 25062, [25244], 25922, 26091.
1616: 119, 11521–1.3, 12931, [20744] (d?), 21207.5, [21373], [22920.3] (d?), 24267.5.
1617: 595.6, 12242, [17192.7] (c), [23098] (c), 25744a.5.

Whitte. *See* White.

Whytchurch. *See* Whitchurch.

Whyte. *See* White.

Widdowes, Giles.
Divine and author in Oxford, b. 1588?–1645†. [*DNB.*]
No address used.
1630: 20465 f. (false), 25593 f. (d?), 25594 f.
1631: 25593 f., 25595 f.

Wight (Wyght, Wayght, Whyte?), John.
Bookseller in London, 1549?–1589†. Freed as a Draper by **Thomas Petyt** in 1540. Father of **Thomas Wight.** One of the *assignees of* **F. Flower**. [Duff, *Century*.]
in Paul's Churchyard, 1551–1589
dw. — at the Rose (A.3), 1551 (2085)–1554? (22602)
dw. — [no sign] (A.3), 1559 (10831)–1561 (5075)
dw. — at the great North door of Paul's (A.2), 1578 (13197)–1589 (19364, omits 'dw. ... Churchyard'); variation: omits 'great', 1578 (310)
1549: 2379? f. (d).
1551: 2085 f.
1552: 1283 f. (d?), 4052.7 f., 10990 [f.], 13175.15 f. (d?), 19495.7 f. (d?).
1553: 3496 [f.] (d), 17791 [f.] (d).
1554: 22595 [f.] (d?), 22602 [f.] (d?), 22616.5 [f.] (d?), 23010.7 f.
1555: 3368.2 [f.] (c).
1556: 10990 [f.], 16108 f.
1557: 16109 f. (d?).
1558: 6452 f. (d?).
1559: 10831 f.
1561: 5075–6 f.
1562: 7280 f. (d?).
1566: 306 f.
1568: 297 f., 302 f. (d?).
1569: 17573.5 f. (d).
1572: 17574 f. (d).
1573: 17165 f.
1574: 3499.5, 3500, 3500.5, 4790 f.
1575: 17575 f.
1577: 3170 ent., 3423 f.
1578: 307 f., 310 f., 13197 f.
1579: 20065 ent., 20066 [f.].
1580: 298 f., 303 f. (d), 3425 f.
1581: 3170 f., 3501.
1582: 17576 f.
1584: 3425.5 f., 4094 f., 19355 f.
1585: 19356.5 f., 19357 f., 19357.5 f.
1586: 13198 f.
1587: 3426 f.
1588: 4791 f., 17166 f.
1589: 19364 f.

Wight, Thomas.
Bookseller and printer (from 1597) in London, 1590–1605 (1608?†). Freed as a Draper by patrimony on 1 Oct. 1589 in the name of his late father, **John Wight**. Patentee for law books, 1597–1605 in succession to **Charles** and **Jane Yetsweirt** and partner in the patent with **Bonham Norton**, 1597–99 (*see* Appendix D/1–60). Wight acquired the Yetsweirt printing material and press; items below distinguished by an asterisk (*) should have A. Islip's name as printer and/or '[f.]' deleted from the imprint: Islip obtained the material only in 1605. [*Dict 1.*]
shop at the great North door of Paul's (A.2), 1592 (12923)–1597 (19366) at least
1590: 17577 f.
1592: 3427 f., 12923 f., 17578 f., 17579.5 f.

Wight, T. — *cont.*
1594: 19365 f.
1595: 152 f., 312 f., 20067.5 f.
1596: 3428 f., 13199 f., 19365.5 f.
1597: 19366 f., 25277.
1598: 5079 at charges of, 9321, 10964 in aed., 15022* in aed., 17291*, 20710, 21576*, 25269.
1599: 9769 in aed., 11196, 12357.7 in aed., 15152, 15169, 15753* in aed., 17579.5 f., 19368.5*, 20045* in aed.
1600: 3345*, 5493* in aed., 7392 in aed., 9532, 9585 in aed., 11410*, 13200*, 15777.
1601: 1479, 3428.5, 4719* in aed., 5493.4* in aed. (d?), 5493.7* in aed., 7390 in aed., 9295.6, 9697 in aed., 11415*, 13200*, 15153, 19641* in aed., 25278.
1602: 5495* in aed., 5499* in aed., 5499.2* in aed., 7386 in aed., 9283* in aed., 11414*, 11415a*, 14901* in aed., 15154, 15170, 18538, 19369*, 20711.
1603: 7722, 9322, 18539, 20068 f., 25270*.
1604: 3346*, 3825 in aed., 5496* in aed. (d?), 5502* in aed., 5502.3* in aed., 9296, 11906* in aed., 15155, 15754* in aed., 15778, 21560* in aed., 21577*.
1605: 312.5 ass'd, 7723, 9610 in aed.

Wilcock, William.
Draper and bookseller? or patron? in London, 1480–1481. [Duff, *Century*; *Library* 18 (1937): 17.]
No address used.
1480: 581 exp. **1481:** 19627 exp.

Wilkes, Oliver.
Bookbinder in London, (1564) 1575–1588†. [*Dict 1.*]
No address used.
1575: 5307 f. **1577:** 4857.7 ent.

Wilkins, Timothy.
Publisher in Oxford, 1640–1641. Undoubtedly the younger brother of Bp. John Wilkins, one of whose works he published in 1641 (Wing[2] W 2202), and later a brewer in Oxford and superior bedell in the faculty of Theology, dying in 1671 (Wood, Anthony, *Life and Times*, ed. A. Clark, 1891–1900, II.231–2). [*Dict. 2.*]
No address used.
1640: 24473.7 sold.

Willems, Conrad, *pseud.*
Printer in 'Munster', 1533. ? = H. Peetersen van Middelburch, Antwerp.
1533: 11381.

Williams, Francis.
Book and printseller in London, (1625) 1626–1630. [*Dict 1*; DFM 586.]
shop at the Globe over against the Royal Exchange (O.9), 1626 (24609); variations: omits 'shop', adds 'in Cornhill' (12222); has only 'near the Royal Exchange' (3185)
1626: 3185 f., 3323 ent., 3650 f., 6665 f., 6936(*A*) ent., 6947 ent., 11528 f., 11767 ent., 11933.5 ent., 12222 f., 12244 f., 12892 ent., 13499.5 f., 13515.5 f., 15267.7 ent., 15331 f., 17383 ent., 19874 f., 20808.5 ent., 21774 ent., 21850.7 f., 22352 ent., 24609 f., 24617 f., 25150a.5 ent.
1627: 17587 f.
1628: 7744.5 ?ent., 7746.8 ?ent.
1630: 6344.5 ass'd, 6937 ass'd, 7746.8 ass'd.

Williams, Jacob, *pseud.*
Printer in 'Amsterdam' and 'Edinburgh', c. 1635? = Unidentified Dutch? printer.
1635: 1614.5 (c?), 1615 (c?).

Williams, John.
Bookseller in London, (1634) 1635–1678 (*Loan Book*). Son of **William Williams.** [*Dict. 2*; DFM 822; *Loan Book*, 1640–43.]
at the Crane in Paul's Churchyard (A.3), 1636 (20078, with T. Briscoe)–1640 (11466.3) at least
1635: 1172 sold.
1636: 20078 sold.
1637: 18782 f.
1639: 3 f., 7366 sold, 11464 (note), 22449 ent.
1640: 11465 sold, 11466–6.3 f., 11779 (note), 20542 ent., 22453 f., 23514 f.

Williams, William.
Bookbinder and bookseller in Cambridge, 1607–1635. Father of **John Williams**. He lived in Great St. Mary's parish and had a shop at the West end of the church, 1607–17 at least. [*Dict. 1.*]
No address used.
1633: 13518.5 ven.

Williamson, William.
Journeyman printer and printer (from 1572) in London, 1571–1575? His printing material passed to **John Charlewood**. [*Dict 1.*]
dw. in Paul's Churchyard at the White Horse (A.2), 1571 (18663, 18664.5)
dw. in Distaff Lane (S.3), 1572 (6674)
shop joining unto St. Peter's Church in Cornhill (P.2), 1573 (18665)
in Paul's Churchyard (B), 1573 (886)–1575? (18666)
1571: 18663 f., 18664.5 f.
1572: 770.3, 6674 (d), 24193.
1573: 486, 886, 7368, [13847.5] (false), 17165, 18543, 18665, 25011.
1574: 4790, 5182–2.2 (d?), 5411.7, [11537.3], [12609], [14724a.9–25], 21121.7 (d).
1575: 18666 (d?).

Willis, Robert.
Stationer in London, 1617–1622†. Transferred from the Innholders' to the Stat. Co. in 1617 (*C-B C*: 94, 460). Son of John Willis, whose books on stenography he sold. In 1617 Robert taught and lodged: at the house of M. Davies without Ludgate (Q.4) (25744a.5, D2^v). [*Dict 1*; DFM 2762; Carlton 21.]
sold by R. Willis, who lodgeth at the house of Ms. Stubbes, dw. in the alley adjoining to Ludgate on the outside of the gate (Q.4), 1622 (25750, H4^r)
1617: 25748 ent., 25749 ent. **1618:** 25744a.6 f., 25747 sumpt. **1622:** 25750 f.

Wilmot (Willimot), John.
Bookseller in Oxford, 1637–1665. Apprenticed to and freed in 1634 by **William Turner**. [*Dict 1*; DFM 494.]
No address used.
1637: 3630 ven., 4119 imp. **1638:** 22653 pro.

Wilne, George.
Stationer in London, (1637) 1638–1640. [*Dict 1*; DFM 1831.]
at the $ Spur under St. Mildred's Church in the Poultry (O.1), 1638 (13547)
1638: 13547 f., 19303 f. **1639:** 19303 f. **1640:** 19303.3 f.

Wilson, Anne.
Bookseller in London, 1640. Widow of **Robert Wilson.** [*Dict 1*, under husband.]
her shop at Gray's Inn gate in Holborn (V.10), 1640 (11909)
1640: 11909 f.

Wilson, John 1, *S.J. See* English College Press.

Wilson, John 2.
Although there was a journeyman printer, 1622–1625 (DFM 284; *St. Giles*, 1615–19; *Poor Book*, 1625 (?widow Dorothy thereafter), it is probable that the SR entry below is an error for **Robert Wilson**, publisher of the book in question but not related to John 2. [*Dict 1.*]
1616: 23099 ent.

Wilson, John 3.
Bookseller in Glasgow, 1634–1635. [*Dict 1.*]
No address used.
1634: 6825.5 f. **1635:** 4533 f.

Wilson, Robert.
Bookseller in London, (1609) 1610–1639?†. Husband of **Anne Wilson.** [*Dict 1*; DFM 837.]
shop in Holborn at the (new) gate of Gray's Inn (V.10), 1611 (1502)–1639 (1690); variations: omits 'in Holborn', 1614 (17625); has 'within' the new gate, 1617 (18788)
1610: 17400 ent.
1611: 1502 f., 1502a f.
1612: 14030 f.
1613: 14697 f., 19057.3 f.

Wilson, R. — *cont.*
1614: 969 sold, 1125 f., 5452 f., 17625 f.
1615: 20584 f.
1616: 23099 f.
1617: 5528 had at [his] shop, 18788 had of.
1618: 12025 f.
1619: 19057.7 f.
1623: 1000 f.
1628: 12590 f., 25763.5 f.
1636: 1503 f.
1638: 14031 f., 14698 f., 24559a sold.
1639: 1690 f.

Wilson, William.
Journeyman printer in London, (1626) 1628?–1665. [*Dict. 2*; DFM 174; *Loan Book*, 1634–37, 1654–57.]
No address used before 1641.
1628: 6798.7(*A3*) f. (d?).

Winde, Lodewijk de.
Printer in Douai, 1564–1576†. Briefly succeeded by his widow, who may have remained in Douai but possibly moved to Antwerp. [Muller 16; Rouzet, under widow.]
1576: 3800.5.

Winder (Windsor), George.
Bookseller in London, 1622–1628. [*Dict. 1*; DFM 1973.]
shop in St. Dunstan's Churchyard (W.9), 1622 (19068, sub tp on F3^r)–1624 (20550, adds 'in Fleet Street')
1622: 19068 f.
1623: 19068 f., 24648 f.
1624: 1787 f., 12022 f., 12635 (note), 12714 f., 19079 f., 20550 f.
1628: 15374.9(*A3*)? f.

Windet, John.
Printer in London, (1579) 1584–1610†. For at least part of 1584 he was in partnership with **Thomas Judson**. Succeeded to some of the printing material of **John Wolfe** in 1593 and followed him as **Printer to the City of London**, 1601–10. In 1609 Windet apparently sold a share in his house to his former apprentice, **William Stansby**, who may have printed some of the items below that year for which Windet's name has been supplied in square brackets. The whole establishment passed to Stansby in 1610. [*Dict. 1*; *SB* 38 (1985): 214–16 (abstract of will).]
dw. at the White Bear nigh (near) Baynard's Castle (R.6), 1585 (929)–1588 (18794); also 1593 (930.3, erroneously repeated from earlier ed.); variation: adds 'in Addle (Addling) Street' (misprint for 'Addle Hill'), 1587 (11761.5)
dw. at Paul's Wharf at the Cross Keys (R.8), 1588 (3599)–1604 (12607) and until his death
1584: [4402], 4733.4, 5819.5 (note), 11503, 11503.3, 11858.5, 12217, 18958, 21545, [24489?], [24501?], 24503.
1585: 929, 4913, 6654, 10231, 10268 (d), 13867, 17468 (d), [19359], 21226, 21226.5, 22237, 22247, [23022], 25185–5a.
1586: 691, 3748, 4733.7, [5486], 10542, 10824–5, 11642, 11761.3, 11848.3, 11861.5, 12752.5, 16436, 18613, [19363], 21067.3, 24707, 25336.
1587: 930, 2779.5 (d?), 3734, 4473 ex off., 5003, 11379.5, 11761.5, 15096, 17566.3 (d), 25246.
1588: 3599, 3743, 5401–2 (d?), [15097], 15418, 17489, 18794, 23641.5(*A3*, note).
1589: 7538, 11229, 11807, 11853, 12579.5, [19534], 19898a.3, 21237, 22859, 24474 (d).
1590: 5471, 7690, 11869, 12915, 13697, 15250, 17490, 21240, 22539–9a, 23547.
1591: 2479, 2479.5, 4167, 7275 (note), 11862.3, 13070 (d), [20651], [21656?], 23092, 23547, 23547.3(*A3*), 24274, 24339.
1592: 870, 2480, 2481, 2481.5, 4440, [13466], 15419, [18138], 20556 ex typ., 24339.5–40.
1593: 930.3, 930.7, [1344], [1344.5], 2483, 2483.5, 2484, 2484.3, 2484.5, 2485, [5202], [5262], 6467, 11850, 13712 (d), 14917, 18716 ex off., 18733.5, [22540], [25018.5].
1594: 2486, 2487, 2487.3, 2487.6, 3146, [4087.4?] (d?), 11819, 12895, 12896, 13118, 13138 (d), [18451.5], 18626a.1, [20885], 23697–7a, 25755.
1595: 871, 1467, 2489, 2490, 2490.2, 2490.3, 2490.4, 2490.5, 2492, 6244 (note), [7525?], 11276, [16715], [16716], [16717], [16718.3]

Windet, J. — *cont.*
(c), [16763.3(*A*)?] (c), 17669, [17943], 18717 ex off., [19912] (false, c), [22955.7], [22957], [23650].
1596: 2490.6, 2490.7, 2490.8, 6551, 7160, [7160.8] (d), [12774.5] (d), [12780], [12781], 13680.9, 13681–1.3, [13817], [16703], [17582], 17683, 18633, [18638], 18748, 24127, [24208], [25953].
1597: 872, 1137, 1137.5, 2491, 2492, 2492a, 2492a.5, 3147, 13712.5, [16805], 17231, 17348, 18452, 18626a.1c(*A*3), 18733.7, [21312], 24118, 24128, 24335.
1597/98: [450.7].
1598: 1138, 2493, 2494, 2494a, 2494a.5, [11747], [13239], 13632, 13635, 13695 (d), [15193?], [15691], [18433], [18465], [18467], 18718 ex off., [23341].
1599: 873, 2497.3, 2497.5, 2497.7, 2498, 2498.5, 2500, 3142, [3469], 5642, [9494.9], 10327.5, [12883], [13120.5], 13341, [17323.5] (d), [17324], [18452.7(*A*3)], [18453], 18626a.2, [23008], [23010], [23342].
1600: 874, 931, 2500, 2500.3, 2500.5, 2500.7, 2501, [4954] (false), [6832.65(*A*3)], 11855, 15566, 16628 (d?), [16718.5] (c), 18142, [21591], [23474].
1601: 875, 953.5 ent., [1449], 2502, 2503, 2503.5, 2504, [13003.5], 14695, 18249, [23475], 23491, 24129.
1602: 2506, 2506.5, 2507, [6467.5], [6832.65(*A*3)], 9499, 11761 (note), 11761.7, 13003.7, 13048.7, [13442.5] (forged), [18541?], [23454], 23475.5, 23483, [24636.7] (d).
1603: 1822, 2508, 2509, 2510, 2510.5, 12577, 14381(*A*3: ed. i), 14790, 16718.6 (d), 16739.5 (d), 16739.7 (d), 16743.1 (d), 16743.4 ent., 16743.9 (d), 17683a, 17683a.5, 19806, 20343, 22931, 23343.
1604: 1456, 1456.5, 2512, [2512a], 2513, 7097 (d), 12210, 12607, 12863, 12917, 13713, 14427, 16718.7, 16719 (d), 16743.10 (d), 16743.11 (d), 23476.
1605: 932, [2516], [2517], 3148, 6392.5 (d), 8366 (d), 10321, 13958, 14738, 16763.5 (c), 20147 ex typ., 25756.
1606: 207, 356, 1451, 1455, 1539, [2519], [2520], 3148, 4666, 4960.5, 5679, 6514 (note), [7019], 7461, [7524], [11924], 12050, 12666–6a, 14036, 16721 (d), 16722, 17488–8.3, 18984.5 ap., 18984.7 ap., 20905, 24341, [24916], [24916.3(*A*3)].
1607: 1447, 1452(*A*3), 1452.5, [2522], [2522.3(*A*3)], [2523], [2523.3], [2523.5], 3687, 4538, 6240, 11166, 12918, 13005, 13005a, 13957, 14456 (c), 14737, 17917, 20778 (d), [21507], [21513.5], [21514], [21821.4?], [23330] (d), 23477, 24346, 24967.
1608: 876, [2526], 2526.3, [5596], 10543, 10712, 15533.7, 16723, 16723.5 (d?), 19430.5, 19511.5, [22283], [23383.5], 23845.5(*A*3), [25202].
1609: 953.5, [1450], 2526.3, [2528], [2529], [2529.3], [2529.5], 3202, 3688, [3691.5], [4014], [5804], 6330, [6388], [6886], 6940, [7371], [12228], [12362], [12696–7a], [22862], 13245–5a, 14298, 14303, [14631], [14699–9.5], 14734–5, [16669], 17155, 17894–4.5, [18455.7–56], [18594], [19053(*A*3)], [19451.5], [20302], [20305], [20759], 20985, [21127], 22142, [22324], [22739], [23139], 23478, 23594, [24148], 24395, [24526], 24831, 25757, [26055].
1610: [2533.5], [5112], 5777, [5862], 5917, [8449] (d), 12582.24, [12996] (forged, d?), 13018, [13140?], [13564] (d?), 14816, 18640b, [19436.3] (c), [19565], [21028.5(*A*3)], 21073.

1611: 3749 ass'd.

Winnington, John.
Bookseller in London, (1586) 1587–1595†. [*Dict. 1.*]
(near) St. Dunstan's Church in Fleet Street (W.9), 1588–1595
at the Golden Tun near to —, 1588 (14630.5)–1589 (13050)
shop at the West end of —, 1595 (25941.5)
1587: 25246 f. **1588:** 14630.5 f. **1589:** 12224 f., 13050 f. **1591:** 7675 f. (d?). **1592:** 13601 f. **1593:** 25018.5 f., 25019 f. **1595:** 25941.5 f.

Wion *See* Wyon.

Wise (Wythes), Andrew.
Bookseller in London, (1589) 1593–1603. [*Dict. 1.*]
shop in Paul's Churchyard at the Angel (A.3), 1593 (18366)–1602 (22316, has 'dw.')
1593: 18366 sold.
1594: 18367 f.
1595: 20014 f., 20014.3 f., 20014.5 f.
1596: 20015 f., 20020 f.
1597: 20016 f., 20021 f., 22307 f., 22314 f.
1598: 20601–1.5 f., [22279a f.] (d), 22280 f., 22308 f., 22309 f., 22315 f.

Wise, A. — *cont.*
1599: 22281 f.
1600: 17671a f., 19154 pro, 19154.3 f., 22288–8a f., 22304 f.
1601: 16916.3 ent.
1602: 4543 f., 22316 f.

Withagius (Verwithagen), Joannes.
Printer in Antwerp, 1549–1587†. [Rouzet 236.]
1584: 1431.7 ap.

Wither, George, and Assignees.
Poet and pamphleteer, b. 1588–1667†. Patentee for his *Hymnes and songs of the church* with music by Orlando Gibbons, editions of which were to be bound with all Bibles. In 1623 the place for sale of these was: at the Blue Anchor in Paul's Churchyard, over against St. Gregory's Church ((A.9): 8704.5, advt.), not the address of any known bookseller. Only 25908 is 'for' Wither; the other editions are all 'by the assignees of'. [*DNB*; *SB* 19 (1966): 210–15.]
1623: 25908 f., 25909.5, 25910, 25910.5, 25910.7, 25910a (d), 25910a.3, 25910a.5, 25910a.7.

Witherings, Thomas.
A deputy postmaster for foreign parts by 1632 (8992), he held the patent himself by 1635 (9041, 25930.3). He was suspended from office in 1640 (9165).
No address used.
1635: 25930.3 at instance of.

Withernam, *Bailiff of, pseud.*
Purported publisher of one of the anti-Marprelate tracts, 1589.
1589: 17463–3.7 f. (d).

Wolf (Wolphius), Johannes.
Printer in Zurich, 1590–1626 (1627†). [Benzing 525–6.]
1595: 6832.54 ap.

Wolfe, Alice.
Publisher? in London, 1602–1612 (1618?†). Widow of **John Wolfe.** [*Dict. 1*, under husband; *Poor Book*, 1608–18.]
No address survives.
1602: 11761 (note).
1612: (all SR assignments): 4946.9, 13006, 23479, 23492, 26027, 26036.

Wolfe, Joan.
Bookseller in London, 1574. Widow of **Reyner Wolfe.** She continued at the Brazen Serpent in Paul's Churchyard ((A.3): Plomer, *Wills*: 20). [Duff, *Century*, under husband.]
No address used.
1574: 4417 [f.].

Wolfe (Woolfe), John.
Bookseller and printer in London, 1579–1601†. Husband of **Alice Wolfe.** Apprenticed to **John Day 1** in 1562 for a term of 10 years (Arber I.172) and served with him for 7 years (*Library*: 256); spent some time on the continent. In 1579 (92) he used the style 'servant to Sir Philip Sidney'. Operated secret presses at undisclosed places around London, 1581–84. Transferred from the Fishmongers' to the Stat. Co. in 1583. In 1587 he entered rights to the hornbook A.B.C. (cf. 21.4, Appendix D/95, and *C-B C*: 13). Beadle of the Stat. Co., 1587–98 with an office in the Hall (A.10). One of the *assignees of* **R. Day. Printer to the City of London**, 1593–1601. He was living in the parish of St. Benet's, Paul's Wharf (R.7), at the time of his death (*Library*: 267). [*Dict. 1*; *Library* 14 (1933): 241–88; Judge 32–44; Clifford C. Huffman, *Elizabethan Impressions: John Wolfe and His Press*, New York, 1988.]
Wolfe may have ceased to print in 1591, following the removal of his press from Stationers' Hall. The printing material apparently passed to **Robert Bourne**, perhaps as foreman or manager for Wolfe, and actual printer of most of the 1591–93 items below credited to Wolfe's press. Sometime in 1593 the printing material was dispersed, most of it being split between **Adam Islip** and **John Windet**; the latter printed the majority of Wolfe's publications from then on.
dw. in Distaff Lane over against (near) the $ Castle (S.3), 1582 (15441)–1588 (23266)
dw. in the Stationers' Hall (A.10), 1588 (12354); he moved his

Wolfe, J. — *cont.*
press from there after 1 Feb. 1591 (*Reg. B*: 36)
shop (right) over against the great South door of Paul's (A.8), 1590 (5400.3)–1592 (11260, has 'at the Little Shop'); variations: 1591 (26032, has 'broad' South door); 1592 (11270, omits 'great')
shop at Paul's Chain (A.9), 1592 (12300.5)
(in) Pope's Head Alley (O.11), 1598–1599
shop within — in Lombard Street, 1598 (23341), 1599 (19217)
shop in — near the [Royal] Exchange, 1599 (12995, 17324)
1560: 3866 (d/error).
1579: 92(*A*) [f.] (d?), 2761 per [f.].
1581: 3371 (d), 5137.5, 11762, 22929, 24486.
1582: 10275 (d), 11736 ap., 11860.5, 15441, 17212, 19054 (d), [19491.3 (*A*3)] (d), 20158.5 (d?), 23358, 25118a (d), 25401, 26079–80.
1583: 800 f., [2464], [2466], 3481.7(*A*3), 4946.5, 5431 (d?), 5963, 10764–4.3, 11693 [f.], 11739, 19102, 20626, [24180.7] (d), 25344.
1584: 3602, [4057], 4907, 4946.6, 5819.7 (note), [11720] (d), 11731 ap., 11739, 11864, [17159–9.5] (false), [17167] (false), [19911.5] (false), 23700, 23701 ap., 23702 ap.
1585: [927], [1764], [2469], [2470], [2470a], 5828, 6180, 11729 ap., 11740, [13064] (d?), 13092, 19914, 23246 ap., [23246.5] (false), 23649 nella stamperia.
1586: 928, 1365, 2471, 2472, 2472.5, 2473, 2473a, 2790, 3598.5, 4027, 5586 ap., 7605, [11728.8] (false), 13487, 16625, 18715 ap., [19769.7] (false), 20126 chez (d), 23091, [24906] (d?).
1587: 21.4 ent., 964, 2474, 2779, 5154 (d), 6391, 11733, 11738, [12004] (false), 12239, 12277, 13129, 15595, [17161] (false), [17163] (false, d), [17163.5], 17572 ent., 17580, 18134.7 (d?), 19721.3, [20033], 23077 ent., 24765.3 ent., 25118.4.
1588: [2475], 4781, 5552 (d), 6166, 6557, 6565, 11259, 11734.3, 11760 (d?), 12003, 12216 ent., 12295, 12354, [13100.5], [14003], [14003.7], [14004], 14067, 14285, 15097 [f.], [15414.6] (false), 15207, [15212.5] (false), [17158] (false), 17489.5, 18144, [19911], 19911.5 ent., 19935 [f.], 20180.3, 20126.7 ?ent., 20180.7. 22999, 23266, 24215, 24420, [24480] (false).
1588/89: 11734.7.
1589: 1041.7, 1599, 1979.5, 3127, 2475.5, 2475.7, 2476, 3410.3(*A*), 4952.3, 5043, 5636.1, [5638.7] (false), 5678 [f.], [10511] (false), [10752.7] (false), 10753, 11256, 11261, [11735] (false), 11735.3 ap., 11735.7 ap., 12506, 13096, 13101, 13102, 13143–3.3, 13969, 15213, [15213.5] (false, d), 15214, 15701 ent., 17784, 17943 ent., 18145, 18834, [19913] (false), 21309 ent., 21320, 21673, 23277, 24276, 25007.3, 26025, 26031, [26033.5], [26034], [26034.3], [26034.7].
1590: [335.5], 336, 684(*A*3), 684.5, [1069.5], [1312.5], [1708.3], 1855.5, 2476.5, 2477, 5045.5, 5400.3, [5638.9] (false), 5744 (d), 5790, 10834, 11265, 11287.5, 12251, 13113.5, 13128, 13130a.5, 13141.4, 13141.7, 14001a, 14002, [14425.3?], 15107, 15645, 15700.7 ent., 15701 ent., 17238, 17572, 18498, 18715.5 ex off., [19197], 19520, [20582.5(*A*3)], [20889.7], 21238, [21293?], 21669 ent., [22713?], [22713.5?], [23080–1a], 23628, 24481 ent., 24481a ent., 24570, [25151.5], [25151.7(*A*)], [25152], 25195 ent., 26030.
1591: 7 ent., 403.3, 664, 1026, 2477.7, 2478, 2478.5, 3355 ent., 3802.5, 4864, 4952, [5814?], 6878, 6910, 7365.5, 7583, 10433 ent., 10638, 11283, 11367 ent., [11795.5], [12279], 12279.4, 12279.7, 12281, 12359, 12414 per, 13116, [13116.5?] (d), 13156, 14106.5, [14657.5], 16810, 17581, 18328.5, 18450, 18451, 18654.3, 18655, 19154.7, 20118 ap., [20118a] (false, d), 21749, 22950, 23359 (d), [23633.5(*A*3)] (d), 24487.5–88, 24765.3, 24767, 25734, 26032.
1592: 287.5 f., 542 ent., 1027, 3947 ent., 5966 ent., 7575, 11260, 11270, 11277.5, 11285, [12245], 12282, 12296 ent., 12300–0.5, 12300.7, 12301a, 12301a.3, 12301a.5, 12301a.7, 12899.5–900, 12900.5, 13130 (d), 13133 ent., 13147, [13889.5] (d?), 14005, 14106.8, [17313] (c), 18464.5, 19054.5 ent., 19217 ent., 19957.7 imp., 21750, 22683, 22719 ent., 22783.7, 22950.5, 23241, 23435a.5 ent., 24418 ent.
1593: 1034 [f.], 1344 [f.], 1344.5 [f.], 1352(*A*), [1469] (d), 4102 ent., 4202 [f.], 5012 [f.], [5123] (d?), 5202 [f.], 5220, 5262, 6553.5 ent., 7574 [f.], 11088, 11288, 11371, 12448.5 ent., 12902, 12903, 12913, 13117, 15317, 16739.5(*A*) ent., 16743.4(*A*) ent., 16743.9(*A*) ent., 16883.5 ent., 17413 ent., 18380 ent., 19958 imp., 21508 [f.], 23931 ent., 24208 ent.
1594: 4087.4 [f.] (d?), 10137.2 [f.], 12392.5 [f.] (d), 18451.5 [f.], 20885 [f.], 21788 [f.], 23650 ent.
1595: 4946.8 [f.], 5197 [f.], 7525 [f.], 16715 [f.], [16716 f.?] (d), 16717 [f.], 16763.3(*A*) [f.] (c), 17943 [f.], [19912 f.] (false, c),

Wolfe, J. — *cont.*
21788 [f.], 22955.7 [f.], 22957 [f.].
1596: 13817 [f.], 16703 [f.], 16703.5 (repeat), 17582 [f.], 24208 [f.].
1597: 12301a.9(*A*3) [f.], 16805 [f.], 19900 [f.], 21312 [f.], 22992.3 [f.], 25195 [f.].
1597/98: 450.7 [f.].
1598: 4017 ent., 6832.65(*A*3) ent., 11747 [f.], 13239 [f.], 15193 [f.], 15691 [f.], 18433 [f.], 18465 [f.], 18467 [f.], 22969 ent., 23341 [f.], 24628 ent.
1599: 3258 [f.], 3469 [f.], 3470 [f.], 3841 [f.], 3864 [f.], 9494.9 [f.], 11831 [f.], 12883 [f.], 12995 [f.], 12995.5–97a (forged), 13048.5 ent., 13120.5 [f.], 16751.5 ?ent., 17323.5 [f.] (d), 17324 [f.], 18452.7(*A*3) [f.], 18453 [f.], 18454 [f.], 18470 [f.], 19217 [f.], 20511 [f.], 20861 [f.], 21301 [f.], 21309 [f.], 22931 ent., 23008 [f.], 23010 [f.], 23342 [f.], 24208 ent.
1600: 1361.5 ent., 3865 [f.], 3866 [f.] (d), 5330 [f.], 6832.65(*A*3) [f.], 11367 [f.], 14750 [f.], 17573 [f.], 21291 f., 21591 [f.], 23474 [f.], 24578.5 f. (d).
1601: 1449 [f.], 13003.5 [f.], 23475 [f.], 23491 ent.

1602: 11761 (post-dated? or d/error?).

Wolfe, Reyner (Reginald).
German bookseller and printer (from 1542) in London, c. 1530–1573†. Husband of **Joan Wolfe**; father-in-law of **John Harrison 1**. Specially admitted a freeman of the Stat. Co. in 1536. **King's (Queen's) Printer in Latin, Greek, and Hebrew**, 1547–53, 1559–73. [Duff, *Century*; *TBS* 13 (1913–15): 171–92.]
in Paul's Churchyard at the Brazen Serpent (A.3), 1543 (15443)–1573 (20800.8)
1542: [15446].
1543: 14634 ap., 15443 ap., 20797.5.
1544: [15440], [15442.5], 22270.
1545: 14630 in off., [15444–4.5].
1546: 15442 ap.
1547: 20816, 22822, 22824.
1548: [15610.10], 20817, [20842(*A*3)?], [21739.5] (d?), 22269 per.
1549: 2858, 10285, 15611 ap., 20176, 20797.7, [24673] (d).
1550: 2859, 5806, 6000, 6001, 6002, 10247.
1551: 5108 in off., 5990.5 (d?), 5991, 20798 (d?), 20812.
1552: 10555 ap., 20799.3, 26066 (d?).
1553: 4807–8 ap., 4809 ap., 4810 ap., 5539, [6004], [15611.3], 19904, 22258 ex off., 24810a ap.
1555: 12596.3 ap.
1556: 6186 ap., 20796.
1558: 15613.3 ap., 20799.5.
1560: 9183 ap. (d), 10151, 11309.5 ap., [11972?], 15613.5, 16424–4a (d), 19285.2, [19285.4?] (c), 24321.
1561: 4415, [6774.5], 20800.
1562: 9187 ap., 14581 ap., 14590, 18308.
1563: 10035 ap., 10152, 18308, 19285.8.
1564: 14591, 15613.7.
1565: 10026 (d?), 10027 (d?), 18847, 20794 (c?), 25403 ap.
1566: 10028 [f.] (d?), 15614 ap., 20800.2, 25403 ap.
1567: 10029 (d?), 10287–8, 15614 ap., 15614.2 ap., 15614.4 ap., 20818, 26067.
1568: 6464 ap., 15614.6.
1569: 10029.5 (d?), [15614.8], 16429.5 ap.
1570: 15614.9 ap., 18701 in off., 18701a in off., 19209–9a ap., 20800.4, 23229 ap.
1571: 10030 [f.], 16426 ap., 18702 in off., 18702.5 in off., 19209–9a ap., 19286, 20800.6.
1572: 15616 ap., 16426 ap., 18703 in off.
1573: 10153, 15616 ap., 18707 ap., 20800.8.

Wolphius. *See* Wolf *and* Wolfe.

Woltrop, Cornelis.
Bookseller? in London, c. 1570. Probably a Dutch refugee, but nothing seems to be known of him unless he is the Cornelius Johnson (**Cornelis Jansz**) cited by Worman as having become a brother of the Stat. Co. in 1571 (Arber I.446) and as living in the parish of St. Peter, Wood Street, Cripplegate Ward (N.4), the same year.
dw. at St. Anthony's [?Hospital (O.5) or ?St. Antholin's parish (N.12)], c. 1570 (24066)
1570: 24066 (c).

Wood, *Master.*
Patron? in London, 1566. Although he entered in the SR a sermon of John Knox, he was not a member of the Stat. Co. [*Dict. 1*: 299.]
1566: 15075 ent.

Wood, George.
Journeyman printer in London, (1613) 1619–1629. Patentee from 1619 for printing on linen cloth (8614). Secret presses of his were seized in Stepney (U.6) Dec. 1621 (*C-B C*: 142), at his house in Grub Street (I.6) Sept. 1622 (p. 377), near the Spital (K.4) July 1624 (p. 168), near Bethlehem (Bedlam (K.1)) Sept. 1624 (p. 169), near London Bridge (T.7) Sept. 1624 (pp. 169–70, in connection with 25919), and at Borley, Essex, near Sudbury, Suff. May 1626 (p. 187). He acquired the printing material of **Thomas Snodham** in 1626 but never became a master printer, and by sometime in 1628 the material had passed to **Thomas Harper**. [*Dict. 1*; DFM 175; *C-B C*: xiv–xvi; *St. Giles*, 1616; *Poor Book* (& wife), 1622, 1629.]
No address used.
1624: [25919] (d).
1626: 1993 (d?).
1627: 3926, 18630.3, [19503], [25217].
1628: 15374.9(*A3*)? f.

Wood, John.
Bookseller in Edinburgh, 1629–1633. [*Dict. 1*.]
shop on the South side of the High Street a little above the Cross, 1629 (13955)–1633 (23371)
1629: 13955 f. **1632:** 5967.3 f. **1633:** 18015 f., 23371 f.

Wood (Boys), Michael, *pseud.*
Printer at 'Geneva', 1545 (= A. Goinus, Antwerp), 1548? (= A. Scoloker and W. Seres), 1560? (= unidentified printer, London?); in 'Roane' [Rouen], 1553–54 (= J. Day 1, London?). For a genuine Michel Dubois, active in Geneva c. 1538–41, in Lyons 1553–57, and again in Geneva 1557–61†, *see* Chaix 176; Muller 33. [Duff, *Century*; *Library* 27 (1972): 220–32.]
1545: 1303.
1548: 3760 (d?), 3761 (d?).
1553: 11583 (note), 11585, 11586, 11593.
1554: 10016, 10383, 17773.
1560: 3763 (d?).

Wood, Roger.
Co-patentee with **Thomas Symcock** for the printing of paper and parchment on one side, 1619–1626? During this time **Edward Allde** seems to have done the actual printing for them. [*Dict. 1*; *C-B C*: xvi–xix; Greg, *Companion*:164–75.]
No address used.
1620: 8615 ass'n, 8646 [f.], 8647 [f.], 8648 [f.].
1621: 8651 [f.], 8652 [f.], 8653 [f.], 8654 [f.], 8658 [f.].
1622: 8685.5 [f.], 8686.5 [f.].
1623: 8716.5 [f.].

Wood, William.
Bookseller in London, 1598–1615 (*Loan Book*). Freed in 1598 by **Francis Coldock** (Arber II.722). [*Dict. 1; Loan Book*, 1599–1602, 1606–09.]
at the West end of Paul's (A.10), 1598–1601
shop —, 1598 (21661.5, sub tp $E1^r$)
— at the $ Time, 1599 (4207)–1601 (17082, has 'dw.')
1598: 4986 ent., 5638.3 ent., 12403 ent., 17349 ent., 21661.5 f.
1599: 4207 f., 5234 f., 5259.5 ?ent., 16910 f., 21661.5 f.
1601: 16910.5 f., 17082 f., 25226 f.

Woodcock, John.
Publisher in London, 1617. Not a member of the Stat. Co.; probably a scholar rather than a schoolmaster and possibly one of the Cambridge University graduates of this name.
[his] house near (juxta) Puddle Wharf (R.5), 1617 (23602)
1617: 23602 ven. (d).

Woodcock, Thomas.
Bookseller in London, (1570) 1575–1594†. Son-in-law of **John Cawood**. [*Dict. 1*.]
dw. in Paul's Churchyard at the Black Bear (B), 1575 (24816)–1594 (17441, has 'shop'); sometimes omits sign, e.g. 1594 (52, has 'dw.')

Woodcock, T. — *cont.*
1575: 9342.7 f. (c?), 24816 f.
1576: 164 f., 2049 f. (d).
1577: 13060 [f.], 18413 f.
1578: 568 ent., 2018 ent., 3432 f., 4442 ent., 4448 ent., 4449 ent., 6728 f., 6737 ent., 11096 f. (d), 11454 ent., 13064 ent., 13569 ent., 17408 ent., 19832 ent., 21352 f.
1579: 4441 f., 4446 f., 4454 f., 12097 [f.], 12097.5 f., 15044 f., 21353 f.
1580: 2045 f., 4446–6a f., 15005 f., 16985(*A3*) f. (c), 19116 f.
1581: 2050 f., 3099 [f.], 4456 f., 11696.4 sold (d?), 12411.5 f.
1582: 3132 f., 11696.7 sold, 12624 f., 13751 ent., 16946 f., 18775a ent., 20751 f.
1583: 4443.5 f., 6729 f., 12269 f., 23719 f.
1584: 4447 f./imp., 11697 sold, 15045 f., 19847 imp.
1585: 3100 f., 13064 f. (d?), 17411 f.
1586: 20125 imp.
1587: 3182 sold, 3420 f., 12098 f., 13569–9.5 at expenses of.
1588: [6084] sold, 11698 sold (d?), 13751–1.5 f. (d?), 17489.5 f., 23895 f., 25889 f. (d).
1589: 3944 imp., 6790 f., 13098 f., 18653 imp., 24817 f., 25128 f.
1590: 3421 f. (d?), 3945 imp., 6731–1.3 f.
1591: 5457 f., 5590–0.5 f., 11097 f., 15644 f., 24913 f.
1592: 11341 f., 24913a f.
1593: 6737 f., 7202 f., 22942 f., 25652.5 f.
1594: 52 f., 6817 f., 17441 f.

1596: 5457 ass'd, 23895 ass'd, 24817 ass'd.

Woodroffe, Richard.
Bookseller in London, 1614–1623† (*Loan Book*). [*Dict. 1*; DFM 1780; *Loan Book*, 1621–24; ?*Poor Book* (widow), 1638.]
shop in Paul's Churchyard at the Golden Key near the great North door (A.2), 1615 (3435)–1617 (5536.5); variation: omits 'in ... Churchyard' and has 'Gilded' Key, 1616 (21519)
1614: 5378 ent.
1615: 3435 f., 5536 f., [13427.5 f.] (forged).
1616: 13428 f., 21519–9a f., 22847.3 f.
1617: 5536.5 f.
1622: 5537 ass'd.

Woolfe. *See* Wolfe.

Worde, Wynkyn de.
Printer in Westminster, 1492–1500, and in London, 1501–1535†. Assistant to **William Caxton**, probably from the beginning of the latter's career in printing, and his successor in Westminster. In 1509 de Worde used the style 'Printer to the Lady Margaret, the King's [Hen. VII] mother' (18566, 23 Mar; 19305) and '... the King's [Hen. VIII] grandmother' (10900, after 10 May; 23164). Following de Worde's death his London establishment passed to **John Byddell**. [Duff, *Century*; *Library* 2 (1980): 73–6; 10 (1988): 107–21.]
Westminster, 1492 (3304)–1500 (13829, has 'near the Abbey called Westminster'); variation: adds 'in Caxton's house', 1496, 31 May (17103; 17539); 1497? (17011)
London, in Fleet Street at the Sun (W.5), 1501, 27 May (281)–1535 (5729)
London, [shop] in Paul's Churchyard at the $ Our Lady of Pity (B), 1509, 11 cal. Jan. = 22 Dec. 1508 (15808)–1509, 4 id. Feb. = 10 Feb. (16160, has 'image' for 'sign')
1417: 22558 (d/error).
1492: [3304] (d), [24766] (d?).
1493: [5065] (d), [17962], [24234] (d), [24875].
1494: 3261, [14042], [14097] (d), [15875] (d), [15876] (d), [15878] (d), [17962].
1495: [1536] (d), 11024 (d?), 13439, [13809] (d), [14098–8.5] (d), 14507, [17020] (c), [17032a] (d?), 17723 per, 23153.4 (d), [23154.5(*A3*)] (d?).
1496: 278, 1916, 1917 (repeat), 3309, 5572 (d?), [5759] (d?), [7016] (d?), 9349 (d?), 9351a.7 (d?), [9353] (d?), [9354] (d), 13608.7 (d?), 17103–3.5 per, 17539 (d), [17965], 19213, [21334] (d), [23163.6] (d?).
1497: 279, 284 (d?), 285 (c), 286 (d?), 287 (c), 787 (d), 9996, [12541] (d?), 13609 (d?), [14077c.85] (d), 15884 pro, 16169 imp., 17011 (d?), [17031] (d?), 23163.7 (d?), 24866 (d).
1497/98: [385.3].
1498: [283] (d?), 802, 5085, 6931 (d), 13440b, [14077c.86–7] (d),

Worde, W. de — *cont.*
15397 (d), 16172 imp., [17005] (d), 24876.
1499: [282] (d?), 1917 (d?), 5573 (d), 5643, 11602, [13810] (d), [14077c.148] (c), [14508] (d?), 16114 per, 16254 per, [17021] (d?), 17104 per, 17247, [17726] (d), [17840.7(*A*3)] (d?), [17967], 20412 (d), 21335 (d), 22597 (d?), 23153.5 (d), [23163.16] (d?), 23427 per.
1500: [1978] (d), [1987] (d), [1987.5] (c), [7541] (d), [9352] (d?), 11610 per, 13610 (d?), 13829 per, [14077c.14] (c), [14081] (d?), 14546 (d?), 16114 (note), [17006] (c), [17007] (d?), [17022] (d), [17033] (d?), [20878] (d), [24224] (d), 24766.3 (d?).
1501: 281, 9355.5 (d?), 14924 (d), [17037.5(*A*3)] (d?), 21070(*A*3) (d?), 21798(*A*3) per (d?), [23163.11] (d?), [24880.5(*A*3)] (d?).
1502: 285.5 (d?), 5198, 9997, 11603 per, 11613 per, 12472 per, 15376, 15898 per, 16116a per, [20439.3] (d?), 21286.2(*A*) (d?).
1503: 169 per, 319 per, 7016.2 per (d?), 15377, 15899 per, [15901.5] (c), 16255 per, 17249.
1504: [7760.6] (d?), [12945] (d?), 16256 per, 17728.3, 23885.3 ven.
1505: 792, [1008] (c), [1805.7] (c), 3295 (d?), 5728 (d?), [7761] (d), 11605 per, 11614 per, [13603.7] (d?), [14077c.14A] (c), [—.15?] (c), [—.81?] (d), 15579.4 per (d?), [18779] (d?), [19207a] (c), [19208] (c), [22653.5] (c), [23177.5] (c).
1506: 788, 1380.5, 5199, 6033.5, 9357.4, [11721.5] (d?), 12139 (d?), [12351] (d?), 12381, [12412.5] (d), 13689 (d?), 14863, 15805.5 imp., 17033.7 (d?), 21259, 21298 (d?), [22270.5] (d?).
1507: [3263.5] (d?), [3543] (d?), 6034, [13685.5] (d), [15257.5] (c), 15398, 15579.5 per (d?), 15806 exp., 21430–0a (d), 23140.5 (d?), 23164.2 (d?), 24878.3–.5.
1508: 253 per, 387, 3289, 4839.4 per, 7016.4 per (d?), 7016.5 per (d?), [7502.5] (d?), 7706 (d?), 9351a, 10902, 13604 (d), [15908] (d?), 16120 per, 16182a.5 imp., 17109.7 per, 17971, 18873.3, 20875.5, 22409 (d/error), 23163.4 per (d?), 23164.4 (d?), [25007] (d?).
1509: 954.5(*A*) per (d?), 3547, 4592 (d?), [7761.3] (d), [7761.7] (d), [7762.3] (d?), 10891 (d), 10900, 10901 (d?), 10903, 10903a–04 (repeat), 12475 per, 12943, [12943.5] (d?), [12946] (d?), 12948, 12953 (d), [13075] (d), [13075.5] (d), 13830.7 per, 14546.3, 15258, 15808 ven., 16121 per, 16160 per (false?), 17537 (d?), 18566, 19305, [20107] (d?), 21007, [23155.9] (d?), 23164, 23195.5 (d?), 23427.7 per, 23941 per/imp., 24541.3 per (d?).
1510: 254 per, 268.3 per, 270.5 per (c?), 696.5, 708.5, 922.2 (c), 1497 per (d?), [3297.5] (c), [9612] (d?), [9613a] (d?), [9615.7] (d?), [9912.5] (d?), 11606.5 per, 11615.5 per, 12091 (c), 14323 (d?), 14323.3(*A*) (d?), 14518 (d?), [14648] (d), 14864, 15345 (d?), 15576 per, 15576.8 per, 15579.6 per (c), 15908.5, 17012 (d?), 17016, 17026 (d), 17030.5 (d?), [17249.5] (d?), [17806] (d?), 17841(*A*3), 19596, [20034] (d), 20436(*A*3) per, [20881.3] (c), 21286.3 (c), 22597.5 (c), 23142 (d?), [23164.6] (d?), 23178, 23178.3, 23876, [23885.5] (c), [23907.7] (c), [24133.5] (d?), 24240 (d?), [24571.3] (c).
1511: [1966 f.?], 3273 per, 4592.5 (d?), 5574, 6573, 13831 per, 14522 (d?), 14806 (d?), 16189 sumpt., 17971.5, 18567, 20108, 21336, 22409.5, 23164.8 (d?), [23178.7] (d?), 23427a.3 ven./sumpt., [23878.5(*A*3)] (d?), 25443.4 per (d?), 25479 (d?).
1512: 4839.7 per, 6470 (d?), 7571, [12381.4] (d?), 15577 per, 16123a per, 16124 per, 18567a, 18874, 19767.3 per, 20437 per, 23427a.3 ven. (d), 24813, 24879, 25443.6 per (d?), 25509.3 per (d?), 25541 per.
1513: 254.3 per, 3290, 4840 cura, [7764] (d), 15914, 18934 in aed., 22580 per (d?), 23153.10, 23165.5 (d?), 25459.2 per (d?), 25459.3 per (d?), 25509.5 per.
1514: [169.5] (d?), 4841 per, 6035–5.5 [f.], 10903a (d?), 11608 per, 11616 per, 13832 per, [14077c.70], [—.71], 15919 per, 16125 per, 17540, 20079 per (d?), 22557, 23166 (d?), 23427a.7 per (d?), 24814 per, 25459.4 per (d?), 25496.3 per (d?).
1515: 268.7 per, 271 per (d?), [319.7] (d?), 320.5 per, [4841.3] (c), 10000.5, 10954 (note), 12352, 12942.5 (d), 14039 (d?), 14082, [14649] (c), 14864.5, 15579.8 per (c), [16102.5] (c), 16126 per, 17972, 20080 per (d?), [20881.7] (c), [21286.5] (c), [23013] (c), 23168.5 (d/error), 23180.3(*A*) (d?), 23196, 23428 per, 23943 imp., 25459.5 per (d?), [25525.3], 25526(*A*3) per (d?), [25707.5] (c).
1516: 170 per, 4601 in domo, 6915 (d?), [7016.7] (d?), [9558] (d?), 10627.5 (d?), [10954], 13833 per, 17498 per, 20081 per (d?), 20438 per, 22409 (d), 23428a per, 25444 per (d?), 25459.8 per (d?), 25479.5 (d?), 25496.7 per (d?), 25510 per, 25541.5 per.
1517: [696.7] (c), 3264, 3547a, 5095, 7016.9 per (d?), [9555] (d?), [9832] (d?), [11361a] (d?), 11608a per, 11616a per, 12475.5 per,

Worde, W. de — *cont.*
12949, 16128 per, [16259.3?] (c), 17110 per, 21071 (d?), 22558 (d), 23147.4 (d?), 23157 (d?), 23180.5 (d?), 23196.2 (d?), 25444.5 per (d?), 25445 per, 25459.9 per (d?), 25479.6 per (d?), 25479.8 per (d?), 25498.3 per (d?), 25511.5 per, [25525.7], 25526.5 per, 25527 per (d?), 25527.2 per (d?), 25527.3 per (d?), 25543 per.
1518: 1385 (d?), 3309.3 (d?), 5456 (d?), 5728.5 (d?), [5953] (d?), [10628] (d?), 11608a.3 per, 11617 per, [11721.7] (d?), 13834 per, [14077c.43] (d), [—.83] (c), 15578 per (d?), 18568, 18808, 18875, 20878.5 (d?), 23154 (d?), 23159.5 (d?), 23167.3 (d?), 23429 per, 23956 (d?), 25459.11 per (d?), 25479.9 per (d?), 25479.11 per (d?), 25498.7 per (d?), 25527.5 per (d?), 25545 per, 25545.3 per.
1519: 4815, [5456.3] (d?), 5609 (d?), 5609.5 (d?), 10450.6 ap., 10904 (d?), 14043.5, [14077c.53] (d), 15084 (d?), 15922, 17973.5, 20876, 20894.7, 21260 (d?), 23147.6, 23159a (d?), 23167.5 (d?), 23196.6 (d?), 23196.8, 23956 (d?), 25446 per, 25461 per, 25499 per, 25512 per, 25514 per, 25528 per, 25540.5 per, 25546 per.
1520: 6833, 10001, 10450.2 per (c), 10450.7 in aed., 10631 (d?), 12046 (d?), [14077c.59] (c), [14547.5] (c), 16259.5 per (c?), [16259.7] (c), 17027 (d?), [17030.7] (c), 17038 (d?), 17568 (d?), [19303.7] (c), 19795 (d?), [23111.5] (d?), 23148 (d?), 23148.2, 23159a.1 (d?), 23159a.2 (d?), 23167.7, 23181.2 (d?), [23181.3] (c), [23181.4] (c), 23196a (d?), 23429.5 in aed., 24241 (d?), 25462 ap., 25479.14 per, 25547 in aed., 25569.3 ap., 25569.5 ap., 25569.7 in aed.
1521: 965, 3288 [f.] (d?), 3600 (d?), 5204, 7725.9 per (d?), 10631.5 (d?), 10894 (d?), 14558, [18292.7] (c), [22611.5] (d?), 23159a.3 (d?), 23168, 23181.5, 23877, [24242 f.] (d?), [24242.3] (d?), 24879.5, 25443.2 in aed., 25448 per, 25464 ap., 25480.3 ex typis, 25480.7 ex typis, 25481 ex typis, 25482 ex typis, 25500 in aed., 25515 in aed., 25515a in aed., 25530 in aed., 25547.5 in aed., 25548 in aed., 25558 in aed., 25558.5 in aed., 25559 in aed., 25572 in aed.
1522: 389 (d), [5732.5] (c), 6895 [f.], [7571.5] (c), 10894.5 (d?), [14077c.59G(*A*3)] (d?), [15606.5(*A*3)] (d), [15932.5] (c?), [23159a.4] (d?), 24814.5 in aed., 25464.5 in aed., 25479.17 in aed., 25483.5 ex typis, 25484 ex typis, 25484.5 ex typis, 25501 in aed., 25501.5(*A*3) in aed., 25531 in aed., 25560 in aed., 25560.3 in aed., 25560.7 in aed., 25572.5 in aed., 25982.
1522/23: 389.3.
1523: 7709.5 (d?), [13686] (d?), [15581] (d?), 15934 per, 17499, [20453.5] (d?), 22978 per, 23181.7, 25449 in aed., 25450.3 in aed., 25466 in aed., 25503 in aed., 25533 in aed., 25573 in aed.
1524: [14077c.75] (d), 14083, 15576.4, 23159a.7 (d?), 23196a.5 (d?), 23429a in aed., 25450.7 in aed., 25466.5 in aed., 25467 in aed., 25486 ex typis, 25486.3 ex typis, 25518 in aed., 25550 in aed., 25551 in aed., 25562 in aed., 25562.3 in aed., 25574 in aed.
1524/25: [470.8B(*A*)?].
1525: 254.7 in aed., 670 (d?), 922.3, 1918, 3184.5 (c), 3266, [4841.5] (c?), 6780.5 in aed., [10608] (d?), 10906, 14044, [14077c.17] (d?), [14109] (d?), [15578.3] (d?), 15936(*A*3) per (c?), [15941?] (d?), 18528 (d?), [18528.5] (d?), 19898 (c), 20439.5 (c), [20876.5] (c), [20921a] (c), [21286.7] (c), 21471.5, 23148.5, 23159a.8 (d?), 23163.5 per (c), 23168.5 (d?), 23182, 23196a.6 (d?), [24827.5(*A*3) f.] (c), 25452 in aed., 25453 in aed., 25468 in aed., 25487 ex typis, 25504 in aed., 25534 in aed., 25552 in aed., 25563 in aed., 25576 in aed.
1526: 5575, 6897–7.5, [14077c.121B] (d), 15399 (d?), 15948 per, 17111.5 ap., 17532, 22979 per, 23159a.9 (d), 23159a.10 ap., 23168.7, 23169, [23169.5] (c), [23182.2] (d?), 23196a.7 (d?), 25469 ap. prelum, 25488 ex typis, 25488.5 ex typis, 25489 ex typis, 25520 in aed., 25564 in aed., 25577 in aed.
1527: 922.4, 966, 5733 (c), 6836, 10838.7 (d?), 10895 (d?), [14649.5] (d?), 15863 imp., 16128.5 per, 23159a.13 ap., 23160 ap., 23160.3 ap., 23197 (d?), 24880, 25454 in aed., 25470 ap. prelum, 25505 in aed., 25535 in aed., 25553.5 in aed., 25554 in aed., 25564.2 in aed., 25578 in aed.
1528: 6830, 10002, 10471.4, 13836 per, [14109.5] (c), [14125.5] (d?), 14519, 16891, 17974, 20439 per, 21008, 22411, 23148.10 (d), 23173, 23960 (d?), 24944 ap. (d?), 25490 ex typis, 25521 in aed., 25521.5 in aed., 25564.6 in aed.
1529: 803, 5136 (d?), 10907, 17112 ap., 17499.5, 17841.3, 18293, 23148.12 (d?), 23148a (d), 23174, [23174.3?], 23182.6, 23198 (d?), 23908, 24815 in aed., 25456 in aed., 25472 ap. prelum, 25491 ex typis, 25491.3 ex typis, 25506 in aed., 25536 in aed., 25556 in aed., 25565 in aed.
1530: 1912, 3267, 3313.3 (d?), 5092, 9983.7, 10685, [12139.5] (d?),

Worde, W. de — *cont.*
12947, 13812 per, [14111] (c), [14650] (d?), 15578.7 per, 16128.7 per, 17541, 18475 (d?), 19119 (c), 20413, 21337, 22559, 23150 (d?), [23150.3?] (d?), 23161, 23174.5, [24302] (c), [24946] (d?), 25422, 25565.5 in aed.
1531: 1913 (d?), 3278, 15601.7, 17014.7 (d?), 23183, 23244 per, 25456.7 in aed., 25474.3 per, 25474.7 in aed., 25506.7 in aed.
1532: 3183.5, 3273.5, 4350 (d), 4351 (d), 4842 per, 5610, 6035a (d?), 6126 per, 6932, 10467, 10839 (d?), 13837 per, 14559, 17975, 18570, 21472 (d?), 21810 ap., 22560, 23163, 24225, 25421.6.
1533: 78 (d?), 656 (d), [1988.6] (d?), 3313.5 (d?), 7377 (note), 7500, 10479, 14045, 15602, 15608 ap., 21827 ap., 25008 (d?), 25423, 25458 sub prelo, 25477 per, 25493.3 ex typis, 25493.7 ex typis, 25507.5 in aed., 25508 in aed., 25537 in aed., 25557 in aed., 25567 in aed., 25567.5 in aed., 25579 in aed.
1534: [391?] (d?), 5278, 5543 in aed., 5543b.9(*A3* note), 10467.5, 10480, 14546.5 (d?), 20882 (d?), 23151.7, 23152, 23174.7, 23184.5, [23198.7] (d?), 23552, 25494 ex typis.
1535: 171 ap., 5729.

Woutneel (Waldnelius, Waltenell), Hans (John).
Dutch book and printseller in London, 1576–1603 at least. Admitted a brother of the Stat. Co. in 1580. He was living in the parish of St. Anne's, Blackfriars (Q.5), 1576; in the parish of St. Dionis Backchurch (P.3), 1582–91; in the parish of St. Faith's = Paul's Churchyard (A.4), 1599. One of this name—but a denizen, which Woutneel apparently was not—was living in Cripplegate Ward in 1582–83 (Worman 69–70). Succeeded by his *widow*. [*Dict. 1*: 281–2; Globe 221; *Library* 14 (1959): 29–30.]
his house in Paul's Churchyard (A.4), 1601 (3161.5)
1601: 3161.5 f. **1602:** 22871a.3 (d?). **1603:** 10005.5 at charges of.

Woutneel, Hans, *Widow of.*
Bookseller in London, 1608.
her house in Paul's Churchyard (A.4), 1608 (3162)
1608: 3162 f.

Wouw (Jacobi, Jacobson), Hillebrant Jacobsz van.
Printer in the Hague, 1602–1622; succeeded by his widow and heirs to 1661. [*Dict. 1*; Gruys; Briels 552.]
1613: 1431.24 ex off. **1622:** 17728.7 (false), 18462 (false).

1630: 18469 (d?) widow & heirs. **1631:** 18463 widow & heirs.

Wreichionen. *See* Sparke.

Wreittoun (Scribonius), John.
Printer in Edinburgh, 1624–1639? (1640†). [*Dict. 1*; *EBST* 2² (1941): 91–104.]
his buith (shop) at the Nether Bow, 1624 (13993)–1625 (4366)
shop a little beneath the Salt Trone, 1626 (14929)–1635 (16600) at least
1624: 7487.21, 13993, 25736.3 ex off.
1625: 4366, 12069, [14940?] (repeat, c), 18654.7, 20386, 25736.5.
1626: 7487.23, 10692, 12726, 14929.
1627: 5460, 6032, 7075, 21555.34, 22363.
1628: 3445, 7487.25, 10696, 15592, 20385.5, 21555.35, 21555.36, [23070] (d?).
1629: 88, 3445a, 3448, 3449, 14931, 15312, 16610, 18063, 21555.37, 21555.38, 23540.
1630: 7487.27, 17207, 17208, 18360, 18572, 21555.39.
1631: 4390.4, [4391.3?] (c?), 7487.29, 14708.9, 18166 (d?), 18167, 18573, 20110, 20229, 21555.40, 21555.41.
1631/32: 527.22, [17206.5] (false).
1632: 5930.4, 5967–7.3, 13955.5, 16611, [17154.5] (d), 20215, 21555.42, 25737.
1633: [3445a.5?] (d?), 3447.5, 5023, 11151.5, 12532.5, 15716 (d), 17145, [17828.5], 18015–5.5, 18168, 20230, 21440.
1634: 5194.7, 6825.5, 7484, 12534.6, 17139, [17815], 19472.5, 19695, 20216, 20645, 22967.
1635: 14715.5, [14819?], 16600, 21555.45, 25737.5, [25737.7?] (c).
1636: 4803.6, 18050.
1638: [68.5?], [3904], [21903.7], [22039?].
1639: [17144.5] (d?).

Wrench, William.
Printer in Oxford, 1617. One of the **Printers to the University** (*see* Oxford University). [*Dict. 1.*]

Wrench, W. — *cont.*
No address used.
1617: 638, 639, 12628, 14314, 17152, 19023, 23912.

Wright, Benjamin.
Engraver, primarily of maps, in London, c. 1596–c. 1607, with an excursion to Amsterdam c. 1599; also in Italy c. 1607–1613. In 1596 he was also a rolling-press printer, though it is not entirely clear whether the address below was his own. [Hind I.212–20.]
?at the Hart's Horn in Paternoster Row (C.7), 1596 (26018(*A3*))
1596: 26018(*A3*).

Wright, Cuthbert.
Bookseller in London, (1610) 1613–1638† (will proved 17 Dec. 1638: Archdiocese of London). Brother of **John 1** and **Edward Wright.** Married a daughter of **Thomas Pavier**. One of the **Ballad Partners**, where SR entries of ballads after 1623 are listed. [*Dict. 1*; DFM 329; *SB* 6 (1954): 165, 179.]
in St. Bartholomew's near to the entrance into the Hospital (E.8), 1626 (6560)
shop in Little St. Bartholomew's, close to the Lame Hospital (E.8), c. 1635? (6792)
1616: 21527 sold.
1622: 6109 ent.
1623: 6109 ent., 7681.3 ent.
1624: 6161 f.
1625: 6791.7 f. (c?), 6792.7 f. (c?), 22654.5 f. (c).
1626: 6560 sold.
1629: 19235 f. (d?).
1630: 14708.5 f., 19267.5 f. (c?), 24065 f. (c).
1633: 732 f. (d?), 6562 sold.
1635: 6792 f. (c?), 6793 f. (c?).
1637: 6563 sold.

Wright, Edward.
Bookseller in London, (1611) 1612–1648? (1656†; will proved 20 May 1656: PCC 183 Berkeley). Brother of **John 1** and **Cuthbert Wright.** One of the **Ballad Partners**, where SR entries of ballads after 1623 are listed. His address is the first shop of John 1, whom he succeeded during 1614, possibly only as manager at first; items distinguished below by an asterisk (*) were tentatively attributed to him because of the address and should now have the question mark deleted from STC. [Omitted from *Dict. 2*; DFM 2806; *SB* 6 (1954): 165–6, 179; 39 (1986): 188–9.]
at (near) Christ Church gate (C.1), 1614 [14068(*A3*)]; 1615 (18753)–1640 (23809, has 'dw.') at least; variation: has 'shop', 1616 (14997.3), 1633 (15200)
1612: 932.5 f.
1614: 809 f., [14068(*A3*)] sold, [14068.3(*A3*)] sold, [19120(*A3*)] sold.
1615: 18598.5 f. (c), 18753 sold, 21851 ent., 23752 sold.
1616: 6662.3 (note), 14997.3 sold.
1617: 16864a.5 f. (c), [17911–1a] sold, 21315.4 f. (c).
1618: 3306(*A*) f., 18413.7 sold, [19614(*A3*)] sold.
1620: [12599(*A3*)] sold, [13374(*A3*)] sold, [13375(*A3*)] sold, [13375.5 (*A3*)] sold, 13541.3 f. (c), 17909 sold, [17910] sold, [23765.5(*A3*)] sold, [23770*] sold, [23788*] sold, 23802 sold.
1621: 591 sold, 21059 f., 23786 sold, 23795.7 sold (d), 23799 sold, 23802.5 sold.
1623: [23789–9.3*] sold.
1624: 15198 f. (d?), 15198.5 f., 23801 sold [his] shop.
1625: 1328 f. (d?), 17191 f. (d?), 17229.5 f. (d?), [23729*] sold, [23743*] sold, 24092.3 f. (c).
1626: [23813.5] sold.
1628: 5876.8 f. (c), [23813.7] sold.
1630: 1539.5 f. (c), 14708.5 f., 15199 f., 16801.7 sold (d).
1633: 15200 f.
1635: 6557.8 f. (c), 10612 f. (c?), 11153 f. (c), 21776.7 f. (c).
1637: 15108 f. (c).
1638: 20482 sold (d?).
1639: 5610.7 f. (d?).
1640: 16869 f. (c), 17262 f. (d?), 23809 f.

Wright, Francis.
Publisher in London? 1642–1643. Not a member of the Stat. Co. [*Dict. 2.*]
No address used.
1640: 11495.7 f. (d/error for 1642 = Wing G 42).

Note: The two Stationers below named **John Wright** were imperfectly identified in *Dict. 2*. Although they can now be distinguished, it has been impossible to recheck all imprints between 1634 and 1640 and all undated ballads. The emphasis on 'Giltspur Street' in John 1's imprints beginning in 1634 undoubtedly reflects the fact that his cousin, John 2, set up shop that year not very far away. From a brief survey of imprints, however, it seems likely that John 2 regularly stated 'the younger' in his imprints. Similarly, John 1's ballads without an address should probably be attributed to sometime before 1634, and those with one, e.g. 22925, currently dated 1633? on the basis of the SR entry but having the address 'dw. in Giltspur Street near Newgate', should be given a somewhat later date. A third John Wright, freed in 1605 (DFM 515), is undoubtedly the one who signed the journeymen's petition (*C-B C*: 437) and probably the one in *St. Giles*, 1609, and *Poor Book*, 1611.

Wright, John 1.
Bookseller in London, (1602) 1605–1646† (will proved 21 Mar. 1646: PCC 35 Twisse). Son of Thomas Wright of Buckbrook, Northants., yeoman; apprenticed to **Edward White 1** and freed by him although the SR erroneously specifies 'per patrimonium' (Arber II.194, 732). Brother of **Cuthbert** and **Edward Wright**, the latter succeeding to the first address below. Cousin of **John Wright 2**. One of the **Ballad Partners,** where SR entries of ballads after 1623 are listed. [*SB* 6 (1954): 165–6, 179.]

shop at Christ Church door (C.1), 1605 (15343, adds 'next Newgate Market')–1613 (25949); variations:
shop in Newgate Market near C. C. gate, 1610 (6524)
dw. at C. C. gate, 1612 (6530)
without Newgate (D.3), 1614–1640 at least
— at the Bible, 1614 (12630)–1633 (23393, has 'shop'); sometimes omits sign, 1624 (17435), 1631 (6527)
in Pye Corner [no sign], 1620 (5698, has 'dw.'), 1626 (22711, has 'shop'), c. 1633? (23436(*A3*), has 'near' for 'in'); it is unclear whether the southern entrance to Smithfield is meant (Ogilby map) or the small block further south between Giltspur street and St. Sepulchre's Church (Leake map); it may well represent a second address, where John 1 lived, rather than an alternate description of the shop at the Bible
shop at the Bible in Giltspur Street —, 1634 (18240)–1639 (18241) at least; sometimes all but 'in Giltspur Street' is omitted, c. 1635? (10869.5, has 'shop'), c. 1640 (1910, has 'dw.')

1605: 15343 f.
1606: 4339 f. (d?), 6553 f., 19309 f., 19310 f., 23030.3 f., [25264 f.] (d).
1607: 1466–6a f., 3671–1.5 sold, 4340 f., 4768 f., 5884.5 f., 6417 f., 14688 f., 25263 f.
1608: [1812.7 f.?] (d?), 6613 f., 6613.5 f., 7183 sold, 7187 f., 7187.5 sold, 18786(*A3*) f.
1609: 6647 f., 6777.4 f., 7186 sold, 7188 sold, 13838 f., 17430 f., [21424(*A3*)] sold, 22353a sold.
1610: [5112(*A3*)] sold, 5862 sold, 5868 sold, 6524 f., 6614 f., 6619 f., 13839 f., 14689 f., 21005 sold.
1611: 4093.5 sold, 6614.5 f., 6619.5 f., 6648 f., 6648.5 f., 17431 f., 24649 f.
1612: 6530 sold, 14672 f., 14691 f., [22655.5 f.] (d), 23760–0.5 f., 24350? f. (d?).
1613: 6339 f., 23763 sold, 25840 sold, 25949 f., 25950 sold.
1614: 3652 ent., 3664 ent., 6616 ent., 12630 f.
1615: 3306(*A*) ent., 5610.5 f. (c), 7281 f., 11926 f., 13321 f., 18921.7? f. (d), 24005.5 f.
1616: 1813 f., 3643 f., 3644 f., 6649 f., 17432 f., 24757 sold (d).
1617: 903 f. (d?), 3694.3 f. (c), 3698.5 ent., 6615 f., 6620 f., 22406.5 f. (c).
1618: 3641 f., 4932 sold, 6525 f., 10924 ent., 17148–8.3 sold, 18236 f.
1619: 3664.2 f., 17433 f., 18237 f., 24997.5(*A3*) f.
1620: 4308 ent., 5698 f., 12303 (note), 16960 ent., 17434 f., 17782.5 ent., 19436.5 ent., 23387 f.
1621: 18237.5 f., 21510 ent., 22137.7 f., 23388 f.
1622: 10713.5 f., 24998 f.
1623: 589 f., 10601 f., [11090?] sold, 13541.7 f., 14900 ent., 20583 ent., 23389 f., 23389.3 f., 23789.7 f.
1624: 5772.5 f. (c), 6161 f., 6526 f., 6621 f., 12573.5 f. (d?), 17175.3 f. (d), 17435 f., 23389.7 f.
1625: 1487.5? f., 5677 f. (c), 14050a? f. (c), 14423.3 f. (d), 17144

Wright, John 1 — *cont.*
sold, 17186.5? f. (c?), 19969.6 f. (c).
1626: 3652 f., 3698.5 f., 18238 f., 22364 ent., 22711 sold, 23390 f.
1627: 16960 by ass'ns, 19431.5 f., 19436.5 f., 23390.5 f., 24746.5 f. (d).
1628: 17435.5 f., 19267 f. (d).
1629: 6649.3 f., 7281.5 f., 10924 f., 13477 sold, 14708.5 ent., [18238.5 f.] (d?), 19684.2 f., 21223 sold, 23391 f., 23771 ent.
1630: 590.3 ent., 595.3 ent., 595.5 ent., 1433.7 f. (c), 1813.5 f., 3412 f. (c?), 5639.5 f. (c), 6977 sold, [14900 f.] (c), 15225.5 f. (c), 16758.3 f. (c), 19165.5 f. (c), 19165.7(*A3*) f. (c), 20186.3 f. (c), 20583 f. (d?), 22920.7 f. (c), 23391.5 f., 24115 f., 24293.5 f. (c), 26103.5 f. (c).
1631: 588 f., 588.5 ent., 589.5 f., 3643.5 f., 3651 f., 6527 f., 7676 f., 14673 f., 17436 f., 18239 f., 22423 f., 23392 f.
1632: 595.10 sold, 3644.5 f., 20319 f. (d), 20321 f. (c), 23392.5 f.
1633: [10581.5 f.] (d), 12015.5 f. (d?), 16864a f. (d?), [20313 f.] (d), 21025 f. (d?), 22925 f. (d?), 23393 f., 23436(*A3*) f. (c?).
1634: 10714 ent., [14689.3 f.] (d?), 18240 f., 22138.5 ass'd, 23394 ent.
1635: 1030 f. (c), 6317 f. (c), 10869.5 f. (c?), 12385 f. (c?), 12548 f. (c?), 16862.3 f. (c), 18644 f. (c), 18644.3 f. (c), 18644.5 f. (c), 22921 f. (c), 23394.5 f., 23732.7(*A3*) sold, 24088 f. (c), 24293.7 f. (c), 26104 f. (c).
1636: 588.3 f., 595.5 f., 3653 f., 7282 f., 10714 f.
1637: 588.5 f., 19684.7 f., 23395 f.
1638: (all SR entries): 1109, 1151, 5440, 12238, 12250, 13477, 13618, 15176, 15339, 15643, 17067, 21339, 21837, 22366, 22968, 23566, 24006.5.
1639: 18241 f.
1640: 1910 f. (c), 11796.7 f. (c), 12386 f. (c), 12542.5 f. (c), 13016 f. (c), 13855.4 ent., 15226 f. (c).

Wright, John 2.
Bookseller in London, 1634–1658† (will proved 3 June 1658: PCC 298 Wootton). Son of Richard Wright of East Haddon, Northants., husbandman; apprenticed to **Francis Coles** and freed 30 June 1634. Cousin of **John Wright 1**. In 1635 he sold an item (23732.8(*A3*)) of which John 1 sold another edition the same year; in 1637 (20321) he may have entered a ballad earlier published by John 1; and in 1640 (13855.4) he published an item entered to John 1. John 2 was apparently not a member of the **Ballad Partners** until sometime after 1640. [DFM 1047; ?*Poor Book*, 1650–52; *SB* 6 (1954): 161–8, 179.]

Undated ballads queried for 1635 in STC but bearing the second address below are indexed here as: after 1635.

dw. at the Sun at the lower end of Snow Hill (D.9), 1634 (19237, has 'on' for 'at ... end of'; 19254, adds 'near unto Holborn conduit')–1635 (10710, 14691.9; both omit 'dw.')
in the Old Bailey (D.7), 1635–1640 at least; the *dated* imprints all have 'shop' or no designation. The following analysis is based solely on terminology; although imprints with 'dw.' have been placed last in each group, it is uncertain whether the term has chronological significance.
at the upper end of the Old Bailey
shop — near (unto) Newgate, **1635** (23732.8(*A3*)), **1637** (21303)
shop —, n.d. (5420, 20326)
—, n.d. (5426)
dw. —, n.d. (5417, 5418, 5430, 6925, 14739, 17707, 19284, 20311, 20312, 20322, 20325, 20822)
in the Old Bailey
shop —, **1640** (13855.4, 20925), n.d. (24299.5)
—, **1640** (19306)
dw. —, n.d. (5424, 20314, 20322.7)

1634: 19237 f. (d), 19254 f. (d), [22576 f.?] (d?).
1635: 10710 sold, 14691.9 sold, 23732.8(*A3*) f.
after 1635: 5417 f., 5418 f., 5424 f., 6925 f., 17707 f., 19284 f., 20322 f., 20325 f., 20326 f., 20822 f.
1636: 5420 f. (d?), 5430 f. (d?), 20311 f. (d), 20312 f. (d).
1637: 20321 ?ent., 21303 f.
1638: 5426 f. (d?).
1639: 19231.5 ent., 19258 ent.
1640: 13855.4 f., 14739 f. (d?), 19306 sold, 20314 f. (d?), 20322.7 f. (c), 20925 f., 24299.5 f. (c).

Wright, Richard.
Publisher in Oxford, 1591, with patent for issuing Tacitus. [*Dict. 1*.]
No address used.
1591: 23642 f.

Wright, Thomas.
Typefounder and bookseller in London, 1627 (cf. DFM 2814)–1646 (Wing R 1149) at least. [*Dict. 1*; DFM 539.]
No address used.
1636: 26038.2(*A*3) sold (d?).

Wright, William 1.
Bookseller in London, (1574?) 1579–1613 (1624?†). In spite of the long pause in activity, the 1613 imprints have been construed as belonging to William 1 rather than William 2. The kind of text is congruent with William 1's earlier publications, and the shop seems to have been shared with **John Barnes;** though there are no joint imprints, Barnes's and William 1's names both first appear in the *Poor Book* in 1608. One of the *assignees of* **R. Day**. His earliest imprints were sold by **John Allde:** at the Long Shop in the Poultry adjoining to St. Mildred's Church (O.1), 1579–80 (10880(*A*3), 18281). [*Dict. 1*; *Poor Book*, 1608–24.]
shop in the Poultry, the Middle Shop in the row, adjoining to St. Mildred's Church (O.1), 1581 (23399.7)–1589 (19537, omits 'the Middle ... row')
dw. in Paul's Churchyard near to the French School (A.6), 1591 (3907.7; 12281, has 'shop')
shop near unto Paul's [*sic*, misprint?] School (A.6), 1591 (13828)
shop on Snow Hill at the Harrow (D.9), 1613 (1976; 16830, adds 'near Holborn conduit'); variation: adds 'near St. Sepulchre's (Pulcher's) Church' (11358, 11359)
1579: 10880 f. (d).
1580: 3705 ent., 18281 f. (d), 21818 f.
1581: 18264 f., 23399.7 f. (d).
1582: 18261 f.
1583: [5431] sold (d?), 23380–0.5 f.
1588: 19157 f.
1589: 19537 sold.
1590: 355 f., 1069.5 f., 1312.5 f., 10004 ent., 11265 sold, 11268 sold (d), 12307 f., 13113.5 f., 13126 f., 13128 sold, 13135 ent., 15107 sold, 15645 f., 18424 f. (d), 21293 sold, 22713 f., 22714 f. (d?), 25151.5 f., 25151.7(*A*) f., 25152 f.
1591: 1026 sold, 3907.5 sold, 3907.7 sold, 5813 f., 5814 f., 6191 ?ent., 11282.5 f. (d), 12281 f., 13827.5 f., 13828 f., 18422.5 f., 19532 f. (d), 22662.5 sold, 22689 sold, 22690 sold, 22691 sold, 25735 f., 26134–4.5 sold.
1592: 1027 f., 10841a f. (d?), 10842.3 f. (d?), 11273.5 sold (d), 11285 sold, 12245 f., 12282 f., 18464.5 sold, 22683 sold, 22718 ass'd, 22783.7 sold/f.
1593: 5123 f. (d?).
1594: 20572 f.
1596: 19158 ass'd, 19161(*A*3) ass'd.
1613: 1976 f., 11358 sold, 11359 f., 16830 f.

Wright, William 2.
Stationer in London, (1614–1619?†). Because he was not freed until 14 Oct. 1614, items and SR entries dated 1613 are now attributed to **William Wright 1** and William 2 has no known activity. The widow Alice in the *Poor Book*, 1619–56, 1660, may have been the widow of William 2. [*Dict. 1*; DFM 2190.]

Wyat, John.
Bookseller in London, 1691–1720? [*Dict. 3*.]
at the Rose in Paul's Churchyard, '1617' (24342)
1617: 24342 (d/error for 1717?).

Wyer, John.
Printer in London, 1550–1552† (H. R. Plomer, *Robert Wyer*, London, 1897: 1–2). Apparently not—or only distantly—related to the other Wyers. [Duff, *Century*.]
in Fleet Street, dw. a little above the conduit (W.5), 1550 (1299, colophons to pts. 1 and 3)
1550: 1299, 2985.3(*A*) (d), [16050.7(*A*3)] (c), [25148] (d?).

Wyer, Nicholas.
Bookseller in London, 1562–1577 (Arber I.111) at least. Not a member of the Stat. Co. Succeeded to the first address of **Thomas Colwell**; since these premises had originally belonged to **Robert Wyer**, Nicholas was probably Robert's son. He was undoubtedly the Nicholas listed in the parish records of St. Martin's in the Fields as being married on 13 July 1563 (*Register of Baptisms ... 1550–1619*, ed. Thomas Mason, Harleian Society: Registers, vol. 25, London, 1898: 61) and paying towards new pews between Jan. and Mar. 1569 (*Accounts of the Churchwardens ... 1525–1603*, ed. J. V. Kitto, London, 1901: 253). The Richard (*Accounts*: 237) or Nicholas (*Register*: 114) buried on 7 May 1568 may have been the Richard baptised on 7 Sept. 1565 (*Register*: 7), with 'Nicholas' a confusion with his father's name. Not in Duff, *Century*; H. R. Plomer, *Robert Wyer*, London, 1897: 2–3, 10–11.]
dw. at the $ St. John the Evangelist in St. Martin's parish beside Charing Cross (X.14), c. 1565 (3183)–1566 (5223)
1562: 3188a ent. **1565:** 3183 [f.] (c). **1566:** 5223 f. (d).

Wyer, Richard.
Bookseller and printer? in London, 1548–1550. Possibly a relative of **Robert Wyer**, whose types and initials appear in the items below and who may well have printed them for Richard. The items are mainly protestant tracts. [Duff, *Century*.]
shop in Paul's Churchyard (B), 1550 (5530); no earlier address used.
1543: 26138.5 (d/repeat).
1548: 5190 (d?), 5190.3 (d?), 26138.5 (d?), 26139.
1549: 13211.5 (d?), 24364a (d?).
1550: 5530 [f.] (d).

Wyer (Wyre), Robert.
Bookseller and printer (from 1529/30) in London, 1524 (*Library* 9 (1908): 262)–1556 at least and probably until 1560. Not a member of the Stat. Co. About 1561 his printing material passed to **Thomas Colwell,** who continued briefly in Wyer's house before moving elsewhere. The house then passed to **Nicholas Wyer**, probably Robert's son. For other items dated 1548–50 in which Robert's types and decorative initials appear *see* **Richard Wyer**, possibly a relative. [Duff, *Century*; H. R. Plomer, *Robert Wyer*, London, 1897; *Library* 5 (1914): 349–64.]
at the $ St. John the Evangelist in St. Martin's parish beside Charing Cross (X.14), 1529/30 [470.10]–1555/56 (406.3, has 'dw.', omits 'in St. ... parish'); sometimes omits sign, e.g. in 1555/56 (399.7). There are occasionally two alternate additions: 'in (the Bishop of) Norwich rents, 1531 (1914)–1536 or 'in the Duke of Suffolk's rents', 1536–1555/56 (399.7).
Since the large majority of Robert Wyer's work is undated, dates supplied in STC are of varying reliability. The most recent survey of his publications is by Mrs. P. B. Tracy in *Library* 2 (1980): 293–303 and offers a tentative chronology. Where her implied dates differ grossly from those supplied in STC, addenda corrections have been made, but it has not seemed wise to attempt wholesale addenda corrections at present. Instead, Tracy numbers in the form: Tr1–Tr145 have been added to most of the item numbers below to indicate her more systematic though still tentative view, one which intentionally *excluded* items only sold by Robert, most fragments, and the items listed above under Richard Wyer. Following are the Tracy numbers for Robert's dated or datable works, which in turn provide her relative ranking for the undated ones:

Tr1	1529/30	Tr37	1535, July	Tr82	1548
Tr5	1529/30	Tr41	1538/39	Tr83	1550, 11 Feb.
Tr9	1531	Tr42	1539	Tr100	1550?
Tr21	1532, 20 Jan.	Tr53	1542	Tr112	1552
Tr24	1532, 14 Oct.	Tr54	1542	Tr135	1555/56
Tr26	1533	Tr71	1543	Tr138	1555/56
Tr34	1534				

Some numbers in vol. 1 of STC were altered or added after Mrs. Tracy consulted the Printers' Index slips; her numbers are cited below at the STC numbers corresponding to the copies she saw. Numbers in vol. 2 of STC which she found to include two editions or issues have been individually indexed with the suffix (i) or (ii) and one location added to the STC number.
1528: [768] sold (c), [3361] sold (d?), [6445?] sold (d?).
1529: [22899] sold (d?).
1529/30: [390.5], [470.10] Tr5, [517.10?] Tr1.
1530: 1967.5 (d?) Tr13, 9611b (d?) Tr4, 14041 (d?) Tr3, [16816?] (c), 18214a (d?) Tr2, 20480 (d?) Tr6, 21561 (d?) Tr7.

Wyer, Robert — *cont.*
1531: 1914 Tr9, 5608 (d?) Tr25, 9270.5 (d?) Tr8, 15399.5 (c?) Tr12, 21562 (d) Tr23, 23961 (d?) Tr17, 23962 (d?) Tr18.
1532: [788.5] (d?) Tr14, 3357 Tr21, 6928 (d?) Tr19, [6928.5] (d?), 9984 (d?) Tr11, 11499 (d?) Tr16, 11549 Tr24, 18447.5 (d?) Tr22.
1533: 3034.5 (d?) Tr27, 10508 (d?) Tr29, 11210.5 (d?), 13608.4 (d?) Tr28, 15983 (d?) Tr26, [17542.5] (d?), 18214a.3 (c) Tr10, [18214a.5 (***A***)] (c) Tr15, 18214a.7 (c) Tr35, 23968.5 (d?), [24868?] (c).
1534: 3360 (d?) Tr20, 6928a(***A*3**) (d?) Tr36, 10493.5 (d?) Tr30–1, 10494 (d?) Tr32–3, 16962 (d) Tr34.
1534/35: [471.8(***A***)?].
1535: 675.3 (d?) Tr43, 675.7 (d?) Tr46, 14505 (d?) Tr49, 16988 (d?) Tr44, 17817 Tr37.
1536: [16983.5] (d?) Tr39.
1537: [5165?].
1538: 23186 (c) Tr38.
1538/39: 392.2(***A***) Tr41.
1539: 9984.5(***A*3**) (d?) Tr40, [15453] Tr42.
1540: 439.3 (d?) Tr51, 777 (c) Tr47, 1697 (c) Tr50, 10954 (note), 13175.6 (d?) Tr52, 17192 (d?) Tr70, [18052] (d?) Tr45, 18225.2 (d?) Tr55, 18841.7 (c), 22153b(i = L) (d?) Tr58.
1541: 1465 (d?) Tr48.
1542: 675a (d?) Tr59, 3378.5 (d) Tr69, 9343.7 (d?) Tr56, 12047 (d?) Tr53, 12468 (d) Tr54, 17297(i = F) (d?) Tr62, 24228 (d?) Tr60, 24601 (d) Tr57.
1543: 546 (d?) Tr71, 13175.8c (d?) Tr65.
1544: 866 (d?) Tr64.
1545: 439.5 (c) Tr68, 1179.5 (c) Tr66, 5160 (d?) Tr88, 9343.8 (forged, c?), 13521.7 (c) Tr63, 20196.5 (c).
1546: 867 (d?) Tr95.
1547: 769 (c) Tr76, [1733.5] (d?) Tr77, 10490 (d?) Tr79, [17789.5] (false), 18225.6(***A***: i = WIS) (d?) Tr67.
1548: 675a.3 (d?) Tr85, 3319.5 (d?) Tr61, [11842a] (d?) Tr80, [13051.7?] (d?) Tr72, [17137?] (d) Tr82, 20851.5 (d?) Tr73.
1549: 7272 (d?) Tr90, 18225.6(***A***: ii = G^2) (d?) Tr78, 20060.5 (d?) Tr86, [20196.9(***A*3**)?].
1550: 97 (c) Tr75, 439.7 (c) Tr94, 777.5 (c) Tr93, 1180 (c) Tr125, 1874 (d?) Tr110, 3188 (c) Tr129, 3188a (c) Tr89, 3325 (d?) Tr91, 3373 (d?) Tr96, 3382.5 (c) Tr101, [5530] (d), 6816 (d?) Tr136, [7542.7] (d?), 13560 (d?) Tr92, 14547 (d?) Tr87, 17297(ii = L) (c) Tr119, 17788 (d?) Tr81, 20398.7 Tr83, 20399 (***A***: i = NLM) (d?) Tr100, 20481 (d?) Tr107, 22153b(ii = NLM) (d?) Tr102, 24725 (d?) Tr130.
1551: 20480a(***A*3**) (d?) Tr114.
1552: 439.9 (c) Tr103, 675a.7 (d?) Tr97, [9983] (c) Tr108, [10228] (d) Tr112, 10634.3 (c) Tr116, 11930.10 (d?) Tr109, 13175.13c (c) Tr106, 20481.3 (d?) Tr141, 21740 (d?) Tr74, 24725.3 (d?) Tr99.
1553: 868.2 (d?) Tr98, 1874.5 (d?) Tr131, 20061.7(***A*3**) (c?) Tr123, 20399(***A*3**: ii = L) (d?) Tr120.
1554: 439.11 (d?) Tr127, 676 (d?) Tr113, 769.5 (c) Tr118, 769.7 (c) Tr105, 3380.5 (c?) Tr111, 7678.5 (d?) Tr84, 11930.12 (d?) Tr117, 12006 (d?) Tr115, 13522 (d?) Tr137, 23010.5 (d?) Tr132.
1555: 439.13 (d?) Tr128, 770.7 (d?) Tr134, 868.4 (d?) Tr104, 3319.7 (d?) Tr144, 10613 (d?) Tr140, 14834 (d?) Tr126, 18225.8 (d?) Tr124, 20061 (c) Tr121, 24725.5 (d?) Tr143.
1555/56: 399.7 Tr135, 406.3 Tr138.
1556: 634.5 (d?), 678 (d?) Tr145, 3320 (d?) Tr142, 6235.5 (d?) Tr122, 11931 (d?) Tr139, 18078.5(***A*3**) (d?) Tr133.

All the following items were printed 'in the house of' Wyer by T. Colwell. Those indexed under 1560 should probably be attributed to late 1561 or early 1562.
1560: 868.6 (c), 20955 (d?), 24206a (d?).
1562: 439.15 (d?), 3381(***A*3**) (d).

Wyght. *See* Wight.

Wykes (Wekes), Henry.
Printer in London, 1562–1572? Apprenticed to **Thomas Berthelet** sometime before the latter's death in Sept. 1555; although not formally made free until 15 Aug. 1565, he may have been out of his time earlier (Arber I.41, 317). Possibly worked at first with **Thomas Powell** and succeeded him by 1564. [*Dict. 1.*]
in Fleet Street (W.5), 1562 (3008)–1571; variations:
in the house formerly Berthelet's, 1565, 16 Mar. (5686)
— at the Black Elephant (Oliphant), 1565 (14606), 1566, 20 Jan. (14607)

Wykes, H. — *cont.*
— at the Elephant, 1566 (18742), 1571, 16 Sept. (14602)
1551: 9301.7 (d/repeat).
1557: 24861 (d/repeat?).
1562: 3008.
1564: 7634, 9301.7 (d), 9303, 21827(***A*3**, note).
1565: 745.3 ent., 5686 per, 14606, 14606.5, 18740, 18741.
1566: 718, 13286, 13797 ?ent., 13818, 14607, 18742, 25877.
1567: [4434], [11014?], 14600, 14600.5, 23498 (d), 23665.5, 24022 in aed., 24861 (d?).
1567/68: 462.7.
1568: 2995a ex off., 3009, 16777.1(***A*3**), 21356, 23554 (d?), 25878.
1569: 204, 3009.5 (d?), 4870, 5651 (d?), 13041 (d?).
1570: 181 (c), 14601, 23438 in aed.
1571: 14602, [17849], 23438.3 (note).
1572: 23438.3 in aed.

Wyon, Marc.
Printer in Douai, 1609–1630†. Succeeded by his *widow*. [*Dict. 1*; *Répertoire 17*^{e}, IV.10.]
1623: [3902]. **1625:** 3095. **1629:** 15348.

Wyon, Marc, *Widow of.*
Printer in Douai, 1630–1661. Succeeded her husband. [*Dict. 1*; *Répertoire 17*^{e}, IV.10–11.]
1630: 6929, 22809a.5.
1631: 4911.5, 22810, [24522.5?] (d).
1632: 1056 ap., 3898, 4552, 4553, 15347.5, 15349, 23630 ap.
1633: 3894.
1635: 15351.
1638: [12350–0.5].
1639: [1020], [1589.5], [12350.5].
1640: 15350, 17567.

Wyre. *See* Wyer.

Wythes. *See* Wise.

Y

Yardley, Richard.
Bookseller? and printer in London, (1575?) 1584? 1589–1593?†. In partnership with **Peter Short**. [*Dict. 1.*]
dw. on Bread Street Hill at the Star (S.8), 1590 (6431)–1593 (12582.9, omits 'dw.'); both with P. Short
1584: 17300.5 (note).
1590: 2035, 6431, 21669, [24383] (d).
1591: 939, 951, 4562, 6328, 12582.8, 24419 ent.
1592: 1777 ap., 12597.5 per, 13977.5, 21672, 23398, 23979, 23995.
1593: 3155, 4562 (note), 12582.9, 14012, 16659, 24384 (d).

Yetsweirt, Charles.
Patentee for the printing of law books for 30 years beginning in 1594, following the death of **Richard Tottell**. Succeeded in 1595 by his widow, **Jane Yetsweirt**. *See* also Appendix D/1–60. [*Dict. 1.*]
in Fleet Street, at his house within Temple Bar near to the Middle Temple gate (W.13), 1594 (25276.7)
1594: 779–9.5, 6050 in aed., 7603, 7603.5, 7580, 15151, 15488, 15751 in aed., 15775, [19624.5(***A*3**)] (false, d), 20047 in aed., 25268, 25276.5–.7.
1595: 7581 (repeat), 9320, 20709 ass'n.

Yetsweirt, Jane.
Successor to the law patent, 1595–1597. Widow of **Charles Yetsweirt**. The patent and printing material were apparently bought by **Bonham Norton** and **Thomas Wight** in 1597 though new letters patent were not issued until 1599 (*Reg. B*: 70). *See* also Appendix D/1–60. [*Dict. 1*, under husband; *Printing History* 9 (1987): 5–12.]
The item below distinguished by an asterisk (*) should have '[A. Islip? f.]' deleted from the imprint.
No address used.
1595: 15752 in aed. (d?), 20838 in aed. (d).
1596: 9531.5, 9552 in aed. (d), 20732* in aed. (d).
1597: 3824 in aed., 9903 in aed., 11035 in aed., 15776, 19640 in aed., 20037(***A*3**) in aed. (d?), 25268.5.

Yong. *See* Young.

Young, Michael.
Bookseller in London, 1639–1664. Apparently not a member of the Stat. Co. though he is possibly the man bound to William Sheares in 1631 and never freed (DFM 2359). [*Dict. 2.*]
shop in Bedford Street in Covent Garden near the New Exchange [= Britain's Burse] (X.11), 1640 (5874)
1639: 16873 f. **1640:** 5874 f.

Young (Younge), Richard.
Writer of Calvinist tracts, fl. 1636–1670. [*DNB*, under Younge.]
No address used.
1636: 26112.7 f.

Young (Junius), Robert.
Printer in London, (1612) 1624–1643†. Former apprentice of **Humphrey Lownes** and began printing in 1624 in the latter's house, becoming a full partner, 1627 (5843)–1630 (6561), though many imprints are not shared. The nature of the partnership is uncertain, and one or the other or both names have been supplied in STC on no firm principle. Young succeeded to the premises in 1630. Agent in Dublin for the **Irish Stock** (*see* Stationers' Company), 1623–24, 1628. **Printer to the City of London**, 1628–40 at least. **King's Printer for Scotland**, 1632–42, but it seems likely that many of the Edinburgh imprints were supervised by an agent (*Library* 7 (1985): 318–20, 325–6). In 1634 Young acquired an interest in the office of **King's Printer**; in 1640 he was associated with **Richard Badger** in several royalist publications. One of the *assignees of* **C. Cotton** and of **J. More, esq.** [*Dict. 2*; DFM 365; *Loan Book*, 1626–32.]
London, at the Star on Bread Street Hill (S.8), 1629 (19300, colophon, with H. Lownes)–1641? (ed. of 13624.1 at BR, has 'his house')
Edinburgh: no address used
1624: 24545 (d).
1625: [4609] (repeat), 22429.5 f., 24546.
1626: 4734, 7067, 12836, 12837, 12841, 22922.
1627: 4735, 5815.5, 5816–6.2, 5816.4, 5843, 10192.7C, 11301 (note), 15110, 17528 ent., 19591, 21654 ent., 21705, 23085 ent., 24539 ent.
1628: 1160.5, 1805(*A*) ent., 10361, 10331, [12825], [12847], 14261, 16729.5, 16729.7, 16729.9, 16764.5 (d?), 18965, 19983.7, 20640 f., 22547, 23998, 23999.
1629: [948], 1161, [4156], 4205, [4669], 12806 (d), [14262], 15134, [15785], 16730–0.5, 19189 ent., 19300, 19573, 19578, 19586, 20680 [by &] f., 21191, 22548–8a, [23984], 23999.
1630: [1134], [6209], 6561, [7125.5], [7126], [12114], 12528, 15690 (d?), [15789], 16731, 16731.3, 16731.5, 16731.7 (c), 19192, 19984, [20270], [20270.5], 20641 ent., 20673, 21654 ent., 23085 ent., 24539 ent.
1631: 1383, [1772?], 1986, 5844–5.5 [by &] f., 6634, [7127], 10182.5, 11228, 14471 in off., [16614], 16732, 16733, 18531, 19566, 19582, [20865], 22635 (d), 24544–4.5, 24549, 24555.
1632: 961 in aed., 1435–5.5, 3140, [4140], 6347–7.2 in aed., [7128], 9329, 11228, 11228.3, 13261, 15115, 19985, 21654, [23834].
1632/33: [16733.3] (d?).
1633: [2311–1a], 2641.7, [2645], [2721.3], [2944.5(*A3*)], [2945], 2945.3, [2945.5], 3031.5(*A*), 3443, 6562, 6634.5, [7128.5] (d?), [7128.7], 11916, 13394a ent., 15162.3 (d), 15786, [16394], [16394.3], [17142], 17493, 17529 ent., [19472], 21654, 21902, [21990], [21991], [21992], [21993], [21994], [21995], 22549 [by &] f., 23371, [24142], 24539–9.7, 24772.5, 25137.
1633/34: 16733.7, 16734, 16735(*A3*).
1634: [2311a], [2316], [2654.5], 12816, 14472 in aed., 15270, [16399], [16399.7], 16400, 16764.7 (d?), 19189, 20212, 20213, 20641 [by &] f., [20839] (d), 22430, [23279.5?].
1635: 907, [1135], 1643–3.5, 2722, 2949, 3032, [4163] (d?), 4533, 5818, 5846 [by &] f., [6210], 6635, [7129] (d?), [7130] (d?), 9330, 12816, 14954.3, [14956.7], 16736.5 (c), 17224, 19580.7, 19986, 21243.5, 23849, 24773.
1636: [21:2], [1135], 2328, 2666.2, 2952, 2953, 4212, 4598, 9330, 10076 (note), 10730, 12999, 13460, 13984.5, [14137] (repeat?), 15077.3, 16606–7, 18034 per, 18531.7, 19987, 20077, 20078, [20083.3(*A*)] (false, c?), [20206] (d?), [20718], [20875] (d).
1637: 1321, 2328, 2328.3, 2328.5–.9 (false), 2673.5, 2681.7, 2776.5, 3772.2 ent., 4212, 4510–0.8, 4599, 6232, 6563, 6625 ent., 6636, [7225], 10245.7 (d?), 10245.8 (d?), 13312, 13731, 14588, 16606, 16737, 18203(*A3*, note), 20213, 20785, 20879, 21249, 22279, 22326, 23120, 25138 (d?).
1638: 64.5, [65], 66, 70, 1619, 1619.5–20 (false), 2333, 2681.7, 2691, 2954.5, 2954.6(*A*), 3032.5 (d?), 3139, 3581, 5819, 5846.7 [by &] f., 12210.5 ex typ., 12728, 13264.4 f., 15077.5, 17529 by & f. himself & others, 17983–3.5, 19473, 21341–1.5, [21668], [21996], 21998, 21998.5, 21999, 22000, 22550 [by &] f.
1638/39: 447.
1639: [1136], 1167 f., 2691, 2813.7, 3772.6, 3772.8, 5819, [7132], 10729, 12232, 13264.1, 13264.6, 15409, 15787, [16737.3?] (d?), 17341 f., [18241], 19645, 21850 (d), 21906(*A3*), 22001–1.5(*A3*), 22002(*A3*), 22003(*A3*), 22004(*A3*), 24696 ap., 25963.
1639/40: 447.3.
1640: 1167–7.5 f., 1345, 2062.5 typis, 2367 ap., 2700, 2814, 3476 typis, [3804], 4517.7 typis, [5751.5], [5752], [5752.5], 6188, 6190, 6637, 7345, 9260(*A3*), 9261, 9331, 9769.5 typis, 12053, 12395, 12826, 12846, 13726 [by &] f., 13732, 14753 (note), 15077.7, 15162.7, 15690.3 (c), 16737.7, 18035–5a typis, 18036.5 typis, 19987.5, 20681 [by &] f., 21637, 21763, 21915(*A3*, note), 22867, 24000, 25139 (d?).

Young (Yong), William.
Bookseller in London, 1589–1612 (*C-B C*: 52). Freed as a Draper by **John Wight** on 14 Dec. 1584; transferred to the Stat. Co. in 1600. His imprints through 1594 were shared with **Ralph Jackson 1** and sold at the latter's address: in Paul's Churchyard at the Swan (A.5). [*Dict. 1*; *Loan Book*, 1606–11.]
dw. near the great North door of Paul's (A.2), 1596 (2785; 13586, has 'shop', adds 'in Canon Lane at the White Horse')
1589: 6625.3 f., [21556 f.] (d).
1590: 18247 f.
1591: 20588 f.
1594: 6625.4 f.
1596: 2785 f., 13586 f.
1603: 6625.5 ent., 7528 ent.
1606: 6625.6 f., 7395 ent.
1608: 20337 ent.

Z

Zetzner, Eberhard.
Bookseller in Strassburg, 1619–1658. [Benzing, *Verleger*.]
1629: 14472.3 sumpt. **1630:** 14472.5(*A3*) sumpt.

Zuttere (Hyperphragmus, Overdhaeghe), Pieter Anastasius de.
Protestant reformer and occasional printer: in Wesel, where he succeeded **Joos Lambrecht**, 1556–1558, in Emden 1570–1573, and in Ghent 1581 (1596?†). [Rouzet; Benzing 105; *Theologische Arbeiten*, N.F. 13 (1912): 117, n.1.]
1557: [19078?] (d), [24168–8.5?], [24170?].
1558: [24167.7?], [24169?], [24170?], [24174?].

SUPPLEMENTARY LISTS

The following lists are extracts of names in Index 1 grouped under certain topics. The date or date range of the imprints in which they appear has been given, with place if other than London, but for further details *see* Index 1 itself.

1. 'AUTHORS'

Included here are not only true authors but also translators, editors, and occasional corporate bodies who prepared texts for publication, *if their names appear in imprints*. Specific imprints may state 'for the author' or something similar, or they may give the name of the 'author'.

Alison, Robert, 1599
Anchoran, John, 1631
Andrewes, John, 1614–30
Author, *Anonymous*, Amsterdam, 1635

Baldwin, William, 1549–50
Bale, John, 1549–51
Bales, Peter, 1590
Bateman, Stephen, 1580?
Bense, Peter, Oxford, 1637
Bland, George, *Gentleman*, 1628
Bright, Timothy (patentee), 1588-89
Butler, Charles, mainly Oxford, 1629–36
Bythner, Victorinus, Oxford, 1637–38

Castelvetro, Giacomo, 1589–91
Clavell, John, 1628
Colson, William, 1612
Cooke, Francis, 1590–91,
?Copley, Anthony 1596
Corro, Antonio de, 1579
Coryate, Thomas, 1611
Cotton, Clement (patentee), 1630-39
Crashaw, William, 1624
Crouch, Humfrey, c. 1640
Crowley, Robert, 1549–51

Daniel, Samuel (also patentee), 1612–18
Davies, John, *of Mallwyd*, 1632
De Beauchesne, Jean, 1597
Dix, Henry, 1633
Dowland, John, 1604
Dugrès, Gabriel, 1636–39

East India Company, 1632
?Edderman, Francis, Dublin, c. 1558

Farmer, John, 1591
Farnaby, Thomas, 1626–40

Gale, Thomas, 1563–64
Gething, Richard, 1616
Godwin, Paul, 1638 (SR entry only)
Goodale, John, c. 1550

Hall, Arthur, 1576?
Hanson, John? 1604
?Harrington, John, 1549–50
Harrison, Stephen, 1604
Haydock, Richard, 1598
Hester, John, 1582–91
Hill, Thomas, *Londoner*, 1558
Hodges, Richard, 1631
Holland, Henry, 1620 [13582]
Hood, Thomas, 1590

Joye, George, 1545–49

Lisle, William, 1631
Lithgow, William, 1618–40
Lodge, Thomas, 1589 (SR entry only)

Margaret [Beaufort], *Countess of Richmond and Derby*, 1504
Marshall, William, 1534–38?
Mede, Joseph, 1627
?Meslier, Hugo, 1508?
Meteren, Emanuel van, 1609–10
Minsheu, John, 1617–25

Nautonier, Guillaume de, Venes, 1603

Oxford Univ.—Bodleian Library, 1620

Penkethman, John, 1624–38

Raban, Edward, St. Andrews, 1638 (20596)
Reeve, Edmund, 1618–27
Remembrancers General, 1617
Ross, Alexander, 1632

Salisbury, William, 1551
Scot, John 2, 1622–34
Selden, John, 1640
Shaw, John, 1637
Shelton, Thomas, 1630–35
Speed, John, 1603
Speidell, John, 1609–40?
Standish, John 2, 1633
Sutton, William, *the younger*, 1635

Taverner, Richard, 1539–46?
Taylor, John, *the Water Poet*, 1618–23

'Authors' — *cont.*

Thomas, Oliver, 1631
Torriano, Giovanni, 1639–40

Udall, Nicholas, 1550
Utenhove, Jan, 1561

Veen, Otto van, Amsterdam, 1608
Vowell (Hooker), John, 1587

Welwood, William, 1615
Widdowes, Giles, Oxford, 1630–31
Wither, George (also patentee), 1623
Witherings, Thomas (patentee), 1635

Young, Richard, 1636

2. PUBLISHERS / PATRONS

These are individuals not ostensibly connected with the book trade who nonetheless are named in imprints of works which they did not compose, compile, edit, or translate. A query before a name or initials indicates uncertainty about the identity or role of the individuals, including a few schoolmasters who published the occasional, useful text not of their own devising.

?Angelin, Pierre, 1552, 1566

?B., I., 1500
Bannatyne, Thomas, Edinburgh, 1634
?Bars, John, 1503
?Boulenger, Giles, 1593
Bouvier, Francis, 1584–89
Bradshaw, Henry, 1559–61
Bretton, William, 1505–10

?Campion, E., Canterbury, 1538–47?
Carmarden, Richard, Rouen, 1566
Champaigne, Piers de, 1509
Crafford, Thomas, Amsterdam, 1633–44?

Eastland, George, 1600
?Edderman, Francis, Dublin, c. 1558?
English, Michael, bef. 1532
Evans, Dorothy, 1613?

?Fenricus, M., 1627

?Gellibrand, Thomas, 1597
Golding, Percival, 1608
Grey, Richard, *3rd Earl of Kent*, 1518–20

?H., G., 1500
?H., I., 1635
?H., W., 1627–28
Hamilton, John, *Abp. of St. Andrews*, 1552
The Hammermen, Glasgow, 1638
?Harrington, John, 1549–50
Hawkins, John, 1530

Henry VII, *King of England*, 1504
Hester, John, 1582–91
Higgins, John, 1590
Humfrey, John, 1633
Hunne, John, 1577

Katsaïtes, Jeremias, 1625

?L., T., Amsterdam, 1638
?Langton, Richard, 1581
Lappadge, Thomas, Rotterdam, 1640
Laybourn, *Master*, 1602
Lynde, *Sir* Humphrey, 1624

M., I. C., 1589
Margaret [Beaufort], *Countess of Richmond and Derby*, 1504–07
Menyman, William, 1505
Morgan, John, 1635
Morton, John, *Cardinal, Abp. of Canterbury*, 1500

Nicholson, R., *gent.*, 1594

?Overton, John, Ipswich, 1548

Page, William, 1579
Peasley, William, *esq.*, 1635
Plomier, Alard, Paris, 1528
?Post Pascha, Peter, 1499

?R., *Mr.*, 1625
Richard, Thomas, Tavistock, 1525–34
Rudstone, John, bef. 1532
?Russell, Edward, 1566

Saltwood, Robert, Canterbury, 1531

Publishers / Patrons — *cont.*
Sanderson, William, 1592–1603
Stafford, Edward, *Duke of Buckingham*, 1520
Stafford, Thomas, Amsterdam, 1640–44
Stevenage, Robert, St. Albans, 1536–37
Strand Inn, *Company of*, 1494?
Stule, Charles, Edinburgh, c. 1520
?Tailer, W., 1596–97
?Tres Viri, 1594

Ussher, John, Dublin, 1571

Ward, William, 1628
?Wilcock, William, 1480–81
Wilkins, Timothy, 1640
?Wood, *Master*, 1566
Woodcock, John, 1617

3. PATENTEES

Following are those who held patents for printing, whether for a single text or for classes of publications. Regarding some of the most conspicuous patents *see* in Index 1 the headings beginning **King's (Queen's) Printer** and **Stationers' Company** and also **Appendices A–E.**

Arbuthnet, A. (King's Pr in Scotland), 1579–84

Barker, C. & deputies (Queen's Pr), 1577–1601
Barker, R. & deputies (Queen's/King's Pr), 1601–1640+
Barley, W., ass'ns (music), 1606–13
Bassandyne, T. (King's Pr in Scotland), 1572–73
Battersby, J., ass'ns (Queen's/King's Pr in Latin, etc.), 1597–1604, 1613–19
Berthelet, T. (King's Pr), 1530–47
Bill, J. & ass'ns (King's Pr), 1604–40+
Bladen, W. (King's Pr for Ireland), 1639–40+
Bright, T. (author), 1588–89
Byrd, W., ass'n (music), 1588–95

Cawood, J. (Queen's Pr), 1553–72
Charteris, R. (King's Pr in Scotland), 1603–10
Cotton, C., ass'ns (author), 1630–39

Daniel, S. (author), 1612–18
Davidson, T. (King's Pr in Scotland), 1540?–41
Day, J. 1 & ass'ns (metrical psalms, etc.), 1559–84
Day, R., ass'ns (—), 1584–1604
Faques, W. (King' Pr), 1504
Finlason, T. & heirs (King's Pr in Scotland), 1612–28
Flower, F., ass'ns (Queen's Pr in Latin, etc.), 1574–96
Franckton, J., & deputies (King's Pr in Ireland), 1604/05–19

Gaultier, T. (King's Pr in French for the Channel Islands), 1553
Grafton, R. (King's Pr), 1547–53

?Hutton, R., 1583

Jugge, R. (Queen's Pr), 1558–77

Lekpreuik, R. (King's Pr in Scotland), 1568
Lever, R. & Elmhurst, W. (bk of custom rates), 1604

Marsh, T. (Latin school bks), 1572–84
More, J., esq., ass'ns (law bks), 1629–40+
Morley, T. & ass'ns (music), 1598–1603

Norton, B. & ass'ns (law bks), 1597–99; (King's Pr in Latin, etc.), 1613, 1619?–34; (King's Pr), 1617–29
Norton, J. 1 (King's Pr in Latin, etc.), 1603–12
Norton, R. & ass'ns (—), 1636–40+

Ogden, Hester, ass'ns (W. Fulke's *New Testament*), 1633
Oswen, J. (King's Pr for Wales and the Marches), 1549–53

Primrose, J. (*God and the King*), 1616
Pynson, R. (King's Pr), 1510–29

Roberts, J. & ass'ns (almanacks), 1571–1605/06

Seres, W. 1 & ass'ns (bks of prayer, etc.), 1546–53, 1558–1603
Stallenge, W. (bk on silkworms), 1607

Patentees — *cont.*
Stationers's Company (almanacks, etc.), 1603–40+
Symcock, T. & ass'ns (all things printed on 1 side), 1619–30?

Tottell, R. (law bks), 1553–93

Vautrollier, T. (Latin school bks), 1573–84

Waldegrave, R. (King's Pr in Scotland), 1589–1603
Watkins, R. & ass'ns (almanacks), 1571–1603/04
Wayland, J. & ass'ns (primers), 1554–59
Wight, T. (law bks), 1597–1605
Wither, G. & ass'ns (author), 1623
Witherings, T. (postmaster for foreign parts), 1635
Wolfe, R. (King's/Queen's Pr in Latin, etc.), 1547–53, 1559–73
Wood, G. (printing on linen cloth), 1619–29
Wood, R. (all things printed on one side), 1619–26?
Wright, R. (Tacitus), 1591

Yetsweirt, C. & J. (law bks), 1594–97
Young, R. (King's Pr for Scotland), 1632–42

4. JOURNEYMEN PRINTERS

Listed below are primarily journeymen whose names appear in imprints *before* they became master printers, or *after* they had sold their printing house to another, or who never attained the status of master printer at all. Although some of the imprints indicate the item was printed 'for' the individual, it seems reasonable to expect that the journeyman did the printing in the house of whichever master printer owned the types and other material used. Also included, but in *italic*, are journeymen whose names appear not in imprints but only in an entry in the Stationers's Register, if that book is recorded in STC.

Badger, R., 1626–28
Badger, T., 1635–39
Ballard, H., 1597
Bamford, H., 1577
?Bartlet, W., 1574–83
Beadle, T., 1618
Bell, H. & M., 1606–37
Blackwall, G., 1626–36
Blower, R., 1595–96, 1616–19
Bodington, J., 1640
Bounel, P., 1545
?Bourne, R., 1591–93
Bowen, J., 1588–90
Bowring, J., 1585
Bradock, R., 1581
Brudenell, T., 1633–35
Bush, E., 1634–35

Crouch, J., 1635–40

Dever, J., 1630
?Dickenson, W., 1584
Dunne, T., 1585

Hammond, J., 1614–30
Harper, T., 1614–24
Haslop, H., 1586–87
Haviland, T., 1585
Hearne, R., 1637
Hodgkinson, R., 1624, 1635–40
Hoskins, W., 1575–78, 1596

Isam, J., 1619

Jaggard, I., 1616–20
Jaggard, W., 1594–1605
Jones, W. 3, 1601–13

Kid, J., 1591–92
Kingston, J., 1551

?Lacy, A., 1557–71
Lee, W. 1, 1626
Lownes, H. 2, 1612

Mather, J., 1575
?Mathew, C., c. 1549
Moptid, D, 1575
Moring, W., 1594
Morris, J., 1588–90
Morris, T., 1585
Mundee, R., 1578

Okes, J., 1627–37
Oulton, R., 1633

Paine, T., 1630–35
Purfoot, T. 2, 1591–1603

Raven, R., Amsterdam, 1631
Raworth, R., 1606–08, 1633–36
Rhodes, M., 1622–29
Robinson, R., 1585–86

Schilders, R., 1575–79
Shaw, G., 1595–98
Sheldrake, J., 1590–94
Simmes, V., 1610–12
Simmons, M., 1634–39
Simson, G., 1588–94?
Snodham, T., 1603
Snowdon, L. 1615–16
Stafford, S., 1598, 1616–24
Stansby, W., 1597

Taylor, H., Douai, 1624
?Tyler, E., 1640?

Venge, E., 1589–1603
Venge, W., 1585

Ward, R., 1578
Webster, R., 1578

Journeymen Printers — *cont.*
White, W., 1588–94?
Williamson, W., 1571
Wilson, W., 1628
Wood, G., 1626–27
Young, R., 1624–26

5. PSEUDONYMS

Following are pseudonyms used by printers and publishers of STC items. Names in *italic* are those of genuine people whose imprints were forged in one or more of the items indexed under their names or occasionally reprinted from works first printed across the Channel. Omitted are imprints deemed 'repeats', that is, English imprints in official documents like proclamations and statutes repeated by London printers for the sake of authenticity.

?A., C., 1596
Adams, T., 1597
Allie, Pepper, 1589
Anoke, John, 1589
Anonymous, Adam, 1545
Antonielli, Antoniello degli, *heirs of*, 1584–87
Astile, John, 1589
Aurik, Jacob, 1534

B., I., 1626
Baio, Antonio, 1585
Bankes, R., 1545?
Barcker, Thomas, 1588
Barker, C. & deputies, 1589, 1596,–97, 1599
Barker, R., 1600, 1602/03–04, 1632–33, 1637–39, 1644, 1669, 1673
Barnes, Jos., 1585, 1602, 1611–13, 1616
Beckeneth, Balthasar, 1531
Bellerus, Joannes, 1575
Benson, J., 1637
Berthelet, T., 1537
Besongne, Jacques, 1621–26
Bill, J. 1 & ass'ns, 1615, 1624–25, 1627–28, 1630, 1632–33, 1637–39, 1644, 1673
Bishop, G., 1600, 1604
Bishop, R., 1637
?Bohmberg, Nikolaus, c. 1574–80
Bostock, R., 1636, 1638
Bonifante, Radulph, 1542
Bosco, Arrigo del, 1588
Boys, Michael. *See* Wood.
Burton, F., 1613
?Butter, N., 1608

Caly, R., 1558
Cambridge University—Prs, 1639
Cawood, J., 1554?–56
Clarke, J., 1637
?Charteris, Henry, *heirs of*, 1601
Charteris, Robert, *heirs of*, 1628
Clarke, Adrian, 1621
Cock, James, 1619
Congeth, Peter, 1535
Constantius, Marcus Antonius, 1555
Crouch, J., 1640
Curtigiane, *of Rome*, 1556

Daniel, R., 1639
Day, J. 1, 1584
Dicæophile, Eusebius, 1569
Dorcaster, Nicholas, 1554
Du Bois, Franciscus, 1609
Du Bray, Toussaint, 1632
Du Brel, Arnold, 1606

Edmonds, Alexander, 1554
Eld, G., 1613
Emlos, Theophyll, 1540?
Estienne, Antoine, 1625–34
Estienne, Robert 1, 1549

Faber, Baptista, 1620–21
Faber, Theophilus, 1613–14
Favo, Jathrous, *heirs of*, 1585
Field, R., 1596, 1610
Fitzours, Edmund, 1632
Fonti-silvius, Guilielmus, 1615
Foüet, Jacques, 1619–23
Fowler, Francis, 1600
Fowler, John, 1578
Foxe, Francis, 1530
Freeman, Conrad, 1554

?G., T., 1595
Garnich, Jacobus, 1609
Giolito de Ferrari, Gabriel, *heirs of*, 1587
Graphaeus, Richardus, 1578–79
Gryphius, Sébastien, 1572–98
?Guillermo, Juan, 1623

H., I., 1604
H., M., 1621
Harper, T., 1637
Hitprick, Hans, 1545–48?
?Hodgkinson, R., 1640
Hoff, Ubright, 1541

Pseudonyms — *cont.*
Hogard, Miles, 1555
Holost, Hu., 1576

Jacobi, Isaac, 1609
Jacobs, Abraham, 1633?–35?
Jacobson, Oliver, 1543
Jaggard, J., 1613
James, Jacob (Jacques), 1574–93
?Janon, A., 1604
Janss, Ashuerus, 1624
?Jansz, Broer, 1621–22
Jascuy, Samuel, 1558
?Johnson, A., 1619

Kingston, F., 1637

La Croy, Johannes de, 1589
Le Chandelier, Pierre, 1598
Leake, W. 1, 1602
Legge, C., 1619
Libius, Joannes, 1618
Lichfield, J., 1618, 1625
Lion, John, 1580–81
Lipsius, Rufus, 1616
Loven, Hermes van, 1609–10
Lownes, H. 1, 1615
Luft, Hans, 1528–37
Lycosthenes, Ptolomé & Nicephore, 1569

Machabeus, *Dr.*, 1554–59
Mannenby, Leigh, 1578
Mapes, Gualtherus, 1626?
Marchant, Mathurin, 1588
Marprelate, Margery, 1640
Marprelate, Martin, 1588–89
Marprelate, Martin, *junior, ass'ns of*, 1589
Masse, Jan, 1625?
Melagrano, Giovanni Andrea, 1589
Mense, Conradus, 1560
Mercurius, *Britannicus*, 1625–27
Meuris, Aert, 1621
Middleton, W., 1542?
Milanges, Simon, 1589
Miller, G., 1638
Mogar, John, 1604
Molaeus, Jacobus, 1601
Morberius, Gualterus, 1571
Muschio, Andrea, 1587

Nafield, Jean, 1587–89
Newbery, R., 1600, 1604
Nicholson, Henry, 1546
Nicolaus, *Bamburgensis*, 1548?
Norton, B., 1625, 1627–28, 1630
Norton, John 1, 1609, 1612
Norton, John 2, 1633, 1640
Norton, Joyce, 1633, 1637

O., P., 1569
Okes, N., 1635
Pavier, T., 1600, 1608
Pernetto, Giovanni Vincenzo del, 1589
Peterson, Jan, 1547?
Phigrus, Ruardus, 1616
Philoponons, Joannes, 1538
Pistus, Hieronomus, 1612
Pratum, Theophilus, 1611–12
Pynson, R., 1525

R., I., 1580?
Radeus, Jacobus, 1602
Raworth, J., 1640
?Renialme, Ascanius de, *heirs of*, 1605?–07?
?Respeawe, Derick van, 1584
Roberts, J., 1599, 1600
Rocolet, Peter, 1621

S., M., 1626
?Scarlet, Philip, 1597
Schellem, John, 1626
Schenck, Johannes, 1596
Schilders, Abraham, 1620
Scotto, Giovanni Maria, 1563
Sermartelli, Bartolomeo, 1600
Short, J., 1618
?Smith, John 2, 1615
?Spencer, J., 1635
Stationers' Co.—English Stock, 1611, 1638
Stone, Thomas, 1630
Sultaceterus, Baocius, 1589
Swartz, Giovanni, 1586

Theophilus, *Brugensis*, 1554
Tomes, H., n.d.
Trauth, Thomas, 1542
Troost, Jan, 1541
Truthal, Christopher, 1556
Turner, D., *heirs of*, 1601
Turner, W., 1625
Turona, Franciscus de, 1542?
Twonson, Niclas, 1533

Vallemand, Pieter, 1573
Vautrollier, T. 1, 1584
Volckwinner, Collinus, 1554

Walker, James, *heirs of*, 1601
Waltem, Thomas, 1572
Waterson, J., 1637
Waterson, S., 1605
Watleer, Jacob, 1585?
Wendelen, Merten, 1566–67
Whitaker, R., 1633, 1637, 1640
Widdowes, Giles, 1630
Willems, Conrad, 1533
Williams, Jacob, c. 1635?
Withernam, *Bailiff of*, 1589
Wolfe, John, 1599
Wood (Boys), Michael, 1545–60
Wouw, H. J. van, 1622
Wyer, Robert, 1545?

Young, R., 1637

APPENDICES

The first five Appendices are all concerned with the formation and contents of the **Stationers' Company—English Stock**. The titles are listed in modernized form, and references between items appearing in more than one of the lists are given as **A/1**, etc. The final Appendix is a list of the Livery of the Company through 1644.

APPENDIX A: Books of Prayer, 1578

Following is a list of books of private prayer to which William Seres 1 laid claim and which had been first published by others with the exception of items 5 and possibly 15. By an agreement of 20 October 1578 except for items 13, 18, 22, and 23—all declared not to be prayer books—the individuals listed below were allowed a life interest in their respective titles, which were to pass into the Seres patent at their deaths. For each new edition they were to pay Seres one shilling. The agreement is in *Liber A*, fol. 36, and is printed in *Library* 10 (1955): 181–3. Items no longer extant are cited when possible from Maunsell's catalogue, STC 17669, part 1, by page and column number, from Herbert's Ames, and from SR entries. There are *no* references to this list in STC or the Addenda.

John Day 1 and Richard Day

1. *Flower of godly prayers* in all formats. (T. Becon, 1719.5 sqq.; latest ed. c. 1570? Maunsell 85[a], undated ed. Possibly included in **C/22**)
2. Last new book of prayers dedic. to the Queen, in 4°. (6429 sqq. Day eds. between 1578 and 1590; published by the English Stock in 1608; **D/113**; possibly included in **C/22**)

William Norton

3. A book of *Divine meditations*. (Maunsell 85[a]: *Divine meditations for the mild Christian*, 16°, for William Norton, 1574)

John Judson

4. *A Manuall of godly prayers*. (Arber I.95: *A compendious treatise or manual of prayers*, entered 1558–59; ass'd to T. Orwin 1 June 1590 and by Orwin to T. Gosson 26 June 1590)
5. *A tablet for gentlewomen*. (23640, Seres, 1574; ass'd by Seres to Judson 26 Mar. 1577)

Thomas Marsh

6. *Right godly rule*. (21446.7, F. Kingston, 1602; entered by Marsh in 1562–63 (Arber I.214))
7. *A defence for the soul*. (Herbert II.868: C., R. *A defence of the soul against the strongest assaults of Satan*, 16°, T. Marsh, 1578; ass'd to T. Orwin 23 June 1591 (Arber II.587))

William How

8. *The King's Psalms*. (3001.7 sqq. How eds. of 1571 and 1585 survive)
9. Sir John Conway's prayers. (5651 sqq. How eds. of 1571, 1572, and c. 1575?)

Henry Middleton

10. *Christian prayers*. (H. Bull, 4028 sqq. Middleton eds. between 1568 and 1584; **E/9**)
11. *The godly garden*. (11554.5 sqq. Middleton eds. between 1574 and 1587; **E/10**)

John Charlewood

12. *Prayers for householders*. (E. Dering, 6684.5 sqq. Charlewood eds. between 1578? and 1581)
13. *Treasure of gladness*; declared not a prayer book. (24190.7 sqq.; Charlewood eds. between 1563 and 1590)

James Rowbotham

14. *The pathway to salvation*. (James R., 20579.5 sqq. No Rowbotham imprint survives, but by 29 Oct. 1580 he had sold his rights to J. Judson (Arber II.380))

John Allde

15. Bradford's *Meditations*. (3486; Allde eds. between 1578 and 1633, but cf. a different Seres version, 3493.5, dated 1567)

Hugh Jackson

16. *The pathway to paradise*. (J. Phillips, 19872 sqq.; Jackson eds. between 1588 and 1617)

Robert Waldegrave

17. *The castle of the soul*. (24911, dated 1578)

William Hoskins

18. *The footpath leading the high way to heaven*; declared not a prayer book; ass'd by Hoskins to E. White 1 in 1580. (A. Fleming, 11039; for E. White, 1581)

Ralph Newbery

19. Marlorat's *Prayers upon the Psalms*. (Maunsell 86[a]: tr. by R. Warcop, 16°, W. How, 1571)

Thomas Dawson

20. *Heavenly recreations*. (Unidentified, but possibly something by W. Hunnis; cf. 13972.5 and 13975)

John Harrison 2

21. Calvin's *Prayers*. (Possibly an early version of Maunsell 84[b]: tr. by J. Field, 16°, for Harrison and H. Carre, 1583; entered to Harrison 12 Apr. 1583 as 'prayers used at the end of his [Calvin's] readings upon Hosea ... translated with other necessary godly prayers by J. Field.' If so, 10846 is a still later version omitting Calvin's prayers)

John Arnold

22. *An instruction for Christians*; declared not a prayer book. (Herbert II.1096: *Instructions for Christians, containing a fruitful and godly exercise as well in wholesome and fruitful prayers as in reverent discerning of God's holy commandments and sacraments*, by Richard Jones, schoolmaster of Cardiff, translated by Dorothy Martin, 8°, J. Charlewood, 1581. Not seen by Herbert; Jones may have written an epistle or preface but was not the author and was not mentioned when Arnold's rights were entered to Charlewood 24 Jan. 1581, with the following differences in the title: *The A.B.C. or instruction for ... sacraments, newly translated out of French by D. M.* (Arber II.387))

Hugh Singleton

23. *The precious pearl*; declared not a prayer book. (O. Werdmuller, 25255 sqq.; Singleton eds. between 1555 and 1579)

APPENDIX B: Tottell's entries, 1583

In 1583 Richard Tottell entered a number of titles he had previously printed. Most of them were law books falling under the terms of his patent and not normally requiring entrance. Since printing monopolies were under attack at the time by under-employed Stationers and others, perhaps Tottell wished to safeguard his interests. The first two items were entered individually, on 28 January and 17 February respectively (Arber II.418) and the remainder in a great list on 18 February (II.419). The items are identified below with information on author or heading where relevant, date of nearest edition, and STC number. STC numbers in square brackets do *not* have the Arber reference cited in STC or Addenda. For a list of these works in STC order *see* **Tottell** under 1583.

1. *Book of precedents*: 1583 (3341.7); **D/49**
2. *L'Office des justices de peace*: Sir A. Fitzherbert, 1583 (10978); **D/12**
3. Yearbooks, Hen. III, Edw. I and II: no printed Yearbooks known though a few cases from Edw. I onward are included in 9604; cf. B/16
4. Yearbooks, Edw. III: 1562 [9551]; 1584–85 [9557], [9560], [9564], [9567], [9572], [9575], [9578], [9581]; 1576 [9584]; **D/20**
5. Yearbooks, Ric. II: no proper Yearbook known but cf. Bellewe, 1585 (1848), not printed by Tottell—though it is clearly a law book—but by five journeymen printers, only two of whom (R. Robinson and T. Haviland) eventually became master printers; cf. B/36
6. Yearbooks, Hen. IV: 1576 [9609], and Hen. V: 1587 [9615.4]; **D/33**
7. Yearbooks, Hen. VI, part 1: 1582–87 [9623], [9630], [9636], [9641], [9647], [9657], [9663], [9668], [9673], [9680], [9684], [9689], [9696]; and part 2: 1575–86: [9702], 9709], 9715], [9720], [9725], [9730], [9736.5], [9741.5], [9748.5], [9754], [9759], [9763], [9768]; **D/34**
8. Yearbooks, Edw. IV: 1582–87 [9778], [9783.5], [9789], [9795], 9802], [9803], [9808], [9818], [9824.5], [9831], 9835.5], [9844], [9850], [9855], [9860], [9864.5], [9870], [9875.5], [9882], [9887.5], [9894.5]; **D/21**
9. [Yearbooks, Edw. V (inadvertently omitted): 1585 [9902]; **D/35**]
10. Yearbooks, Ric. III: 1587 [9912], [9919.5]; Hen. VII: 1583–85 [9926]; Hen. VIII: 1591 [9943]; **D/35**
11. Plowden's *Commentaries*, parts 1: 1588 (20044) and 2: 1584 (20046.7); **D/43**
12. Fitzherbert's *Abridgement*: 1577 (10957); **D/23**
13. Brook's *Abridgement*: 1586 (3829); **D/7**
14. Bracton, *De legibus Angliae*: 1569; **D/9**
15. *Book of Entries*: W. Rastell, 1574 (20731)
16. *Book of assizes*: Yearbooks, either 1580 [9601] or c. 1565 [9604]; cf. B/3 and **D/1**
17. *Register of writs*: 1553 (20837); **D/52**
18. Stanford, *Pleas of the crown*: 1583 (23223); **D/47**
19. —*King's prerogative*: 1590 (23217); **E/2**
20. Brook's *New cases*: 1587 (3823); **D/6**
21. *Court baron* and *Retorna brevium*: Kitchen, 1585 [15019]; **D/37**; cf. B/30
22. Littleton's *Tenures*: in Law French, 1583 (15746) and in English, 1583 [15772]; **D/40**
23. Fitzherbert's *Natura brevium*: 1588 (10963); **D/22**
24. The old *Natura brevium*: in Law French, 1584 (18402) and in English, 1580? [18411.5], respectively the last eds. extant
25. *Magna charta*: Statutes, 1587 (9282); **D/41**
26. *The digest of writs*: S. Theloall, 1579 (23934)
27. J. Perkins, *Profitable book*: 1586 (19638); **D/50**
28. *Doctor and student*: C. Saint German, 1593 (21575); **D/17**
29. T*he terms of the laws*: J. Rastell, 1592 (20708); **D/53**
30. The old *Justices of Peace*: 1580 [14886]; 'with others &c.' probably indicates the group of texts Tottell had last printed with it in 1574 [14885], i.e. reprints of 7704, 7721, 7734a, 15585.5, and 20904; the last of these, *Retorna*, had actually begun to appear in B/21.
31. Fortescue, *Commendation of the laws of England*: 1573 (11194); **D/27**
32. *A table to Henry VII's years*: Yearbooks, c. 1575? [9927.5]; **D/36**
33. *Novae narrationes*: 1561 (18363); **D/42**
34. *Institutions and principal grounds of the law*: Statutes, 1580 (9295.4); **D/30**
35. *Office of sheriffs, bailiffs, and constables*: Sir A. Fitzherbert, 1579? [10993.9], printed by T. Marsh

[Miscellaneous English Texts]

36. T*he accidence of armory*: G. Legh, 1591 (15391); not yielded in **C**, but this and the next were printed in 1597 by a former apprentice of Tottell's, H. Ballard, who had access to the extensive series of woodcut coats of arms; cf. B/5
37. *The concords of armory*: J. Bossewell, 1572 (3393)
38. T*he art of limning*: Treatise, 1583 (24254); not yielded in **C** since Tottell had already permitted T. Purfoot to print this edition as his assignee
39. *Moral philosophy*: W. Baldwin, 1584 (1261); **C/8**
40. *Songs and sonnets*: H. Howard, 1574 (13866); **C/13**
41. Cicero's *Offices* in Latin/English, 1583 (5285); **C/7**
42. Quintus Curtius in English: 1570–71 (6144); **C/10**
43. *English lovers*: B. Garter, 1568 [11632]; **C/12**
44. *Romeo and Juliet*: M. Bandello, 1587 (1356.9); **C/9**
45. Dr. [T.] Wilson, *Usury*: 1572 (25807); **C/11**

Not included in the list but of special interest:

46. Tusser, *Husbandry*: 1577 (24379); by 1580 (24380) Tottell had apparently sold the rights to H. Denham, who probably had printed editions 1570–73 for Tottell. Although it is not a prayer book, Denham seems to have grouped it with the books in the Seres patent. It ultimately came to the English Stock; **D/109**

APPENDIX C: Titles yielded to the Company, 1584

On 8 January 1584 several of the most prominent Stationers (most of them holders of patents) yielded rights to some of their titles to the Company for the use of the poor, i.e. a printer could obtain the Company's permission to print one edition by paying sixpence in the pound for the use of the poor of the Company. The list of titles is printed in **Arber II.786–9**. Following are the titles yielded, with information on author where relevant, date of nearest edition, and STC number. Titles numbered in **boldface** are those which attained an edition in 1584 or later by someone other than the copyright holder. STC numbers in square brackets do *not* have the Arber reference cited in STC or Addenda. For a list of these works in STC order *see* **Stationers' Company** under 1584.

II.786

Christopher Barker

With proviso that nothing yielded be prejudicial to his or his sucessors' patent as Queen's printer.

1. *Homilies*, vol. 1: 1587 (13657(A3)) and vol. 2: 1587 [13673], both J. Charlewood and T. East

2. *Statutes at large*: 1587 (9305.3), H. Denham and H. Middleton

II.787

3. Erasmus, *Paraphrases* upon the liturgical Epistles and Gospels; apparently never printed but it would have been a selec-

C: Titles yielded to the Company, 1584 — *cont.*

tion from 2866, dated 1552, in accordance with the texts represented in 2982, dated 1574, i.e. version (d) in the headnote preceding 2964.5

4. *Articles of Religion, 1562* [*o.s.*]: 1586 [10043]
5. *The Queen's Injunctions*: 1589? [10104.7] but cf. also 10104, J. Kingston; *and Articles*: 1589? [10129] but cf. also 10126.7, J. Kingston
6. Sir John Cheke's *New Testament* (the Bishops' translation) *in 8º with notes*: 1589 [2887.7], T. Dawson; *in 16º without notes*: none survives. (Barker yielded the 'profit and benefit' only and retained the printing, but it appears that he changed his mind and leased his rights in these two items to T. Dawson; cf. 2904)

Richard Tottell

7. Cicero's *Offices* in English/Latin: 1583 (5285); cf. 1596 [5286], T. East; **B/41**
8. *Moral philosophy*: W. Baldwin, 1584 (1261), T. East; **B/39**
9. *Romeo and Juliet*: M. Bandello, 1587 (1356.9), R. Robinson; **B/44**
10. Quintus Curtius in English: 1584 (6145), R. Ward; **B/42**
11. Dr. [T.] Wilson, *Upon Usury*: 1584 (25808), R. Ward; **B/45**
12. *Two English Lovers*: B. Garter, 1568 [11632]; **B/43**
13. *Songs and Sonnets* of the Earl of Surrey: H. Howard, 1585 (13876), J. Windet; **B/40**

Richard Watkins

14. The broadside Almanack: 1583/84 (402.5), R. Watkins & J. Roberts. (*See* also Buckminster 423.8, 424, 425 and T. Johnson 466.2, 466.6; T. Dawson possibly obtained the printing rights); **D/101**

John Day 1

15. Calvin upon *Daniel*: 1570 [4397]
16. *Pilgrimage of princes*: L. Lloyd, 1586 [16625], J. Wolfe. (Although no Day ed. is known, the fact that the 1586 and 1607 eds. were by unrelated printers without SR entries supports the identification)
17. *The jewel of joy*: T. Becon, 1550? [1733]
18. Becon, *Principles of religion*: c. 1580 [1753.5]
19. Dering's *Sermons in the Tower*: 1584 (6697), J. Charlewood
20. *Practise of prelates*: W. Tyndale, 1549? [24467]
21. *Cosmographical glass*: W. Cunningham, 1559 (6119)
22. All the prayer books which H. Denham had from Day: uncertain; possibly **A/1**, **2** and/or **D/113**, **121**, **123** are among the ones meant
23. Peter Martyr [Vermigli] *On the Judges*: 1564 (24670)
24. —*On the Romans*: 1568 (24672)
25. *The poor man's library*: W. Alley, 1571 [375]
26. Tyndale's, Frith's, and Barnes's *Works*: 1573 [24436]
27. Becon's whole *Works*: 1560–64 [1710]
28. Bullinger *Upon the Apocalypse*: 1573 [4062]
29. *Letters of the martyrs*: ed. M. Coverdale, 1564 [5886]
30. Calvin's *Catechism* in 16º: no London 16º eds. known. (W. How held the 8º Latin rights (4379), and J. Kingston and his successors had the 8º English rights (4386))

II.788

31. *Image of God*: R. Hutchinson, 1580 (14022)
32. *Image of nature and grace*: R. Cavendish, 1571? [4880]
33. *Relics of Rome*: T. Becon, 1563 [1755]
34. Haw[k]es's *Examinations*: 1562? [12955a.5]
35. Calvin's *Sermons upon Hezekiah*: 1574 [4451]
36. *Pomander of prayers* in 8º: T. Becon, c. 1567 [1747.5]. (The latest surviving ed. is 16º: 1578 (1748))
37. *Governance of virtue* in 8º: Becon, 1566 [1727] and in 16º: 1578 (1728); the next surviving ed. is in 12º: 1607 [1729], S. Stafford
38. Ascham's *Schoolmaster*: 1589 (836), A. Jeffes
39. —*Affairs of Germany*: 1570? [830]
40. *Saxon laws*: W. Lambard, 1568 [15142]
41. *Canons* in English: 1570? (10062.5)
42. *Vita et mors Juelli*: L. Humphrey, 1573 [13963]
43. *Articuli religionis*: 1575 (10037)
44. *Epistola Gildae*: 1568 [11894]
45. *Syllogisticon*: J. Foxe, 1563? [11249]

C: Titles yielded to the Company, 1584 — *cont.*

46. Drant *In Ecclesiasten*: 1572 (7168)
47. *A forest of histories*: P. Mexia, 1576 (17850), J. Kingston for Day
48. *A dialogue of Mercury and the English soldier*: B. Rich, 1574 (20998)
49. *Astronomer's game*: uncertain, but cf. N. Allen, 1568 [361.3], H. Bynneman for L. Harrison

Henry Bynneman

Deceased; yielded on his behalf by his assignees, R. Newbery and H. Denham.

in 16º:

50. *The brief chronicle*: with any additions to be in the same brief form and any controversies to be submitted to the judgment of the Court of Assistants: J. Stow, 1584 (23325.8); cf. 1598 [23328], R. Bradock; **D/105**

in 4º:

51. Musculus, *Commonplaces*: 1578 [18309]
52. Cornel. Agrippa *Of the vanity of sciences*: 1575 [205]
53. Digges's *Stratioticos*: 1579 (6848); cf. 1590 [6849], R. Field
54. *Art of shooting in great ordnance*: W. Bourne, 1587 [3420], T. Dawson for T. Woodcock

in 8º:

55. *The Spaniard's life*: Lazarillo, de Tormes, 1586 (15336(*A*3)), A. Jeffes
56. *Book of gardening*: T. Hill, 1586 (13495), R. Waldegrave
57. Erasmus, *Colloquia*: 1571 (10451); cf. **D/68**
58. *Exercitatio linguae Latinae*: L. Vives; no 16th century ed. known but cf. 24852.7(*A*3), N. Okes for J. Harrison 1, 1612? **D/93**
59. *Confabulationes Hessij*: H. Schottenius; no late 16th century ed. known but cf. 21827(*A*3), W. de Worde, 1533

II.789

60. Justinus, *Historia*: Trogus Pompeius, 1586 [24287.7], G. Robinson
61. Virgilius, *Opera*: 1572 [24788a]; the rights in this text, or versions of it, are not clear since both J. Kingston (8º) and John Harrison 1 (16º) had published eds. before Bynneman's rights were yielded; **D/92**
62. *Sententiae pueriles*: L. Culmann, c. 1600? (6106.3), printer unknown; **D/81**
63. *Psalmi Roffensis*: ed. Saint J. Fisher, 1568 [2995a], H. Wykes

Ralph Newbery

64. Bullinger's *Decades*: 1584 [4057], H. Middleton and J. Wolfe
65. Cooper's *Postill*: 1573, [5684]
66. *Panoply of epistles*: A. Fleming, 1576 [11049]
67. *Chronicle of ten emperors of Greece* [error for *Rome*]: A. Guevara, 1577 [12426]
68. *Galateo, Of good manners*: G. della Casa, 1576 [4738]
69. *Life of servingmen*: W. Darell, 1576 [6274]
70. Googe's *Songs and Sonnets*: 1563 [12048]
71. *Perambulation of Kent*: W. Lambard, 1576 (15175); cf. 1596 (15176), E. Bollifant

Henry Denham

72. *Pasquin in a trance*: C. S. Curio, 1584 (6131), T. East
73. *The hop garden*: R. Scot, 1578 (21867)
74. Ovid's *Metamorphoses*: 1584 (18958), J. Windet and T. Judson
75. *The courtier*: B. Castiglione, 1577 (4779); cf. 1603 [4780], T. Creede
76. Caesar's *Commentaries* in English: 1590 (4336), T. East
77. Ovid's *Epistles*: c. 1584 (18943), J. Charlewood
78. *Image of idleness*: W. Wedlock, 1581 [25197.5], Denham, the assignee of Seres
79. *Flower of friendship*: E. Tilney, 1587 [24077a.5], A. Jeffes
80. *School of virtue*: F. Seagar, 1593 (22137), J. Charlewood for R. Jones
81. Demosthenes, *Orations*: Latin, 1571 [6577] and English, 1570 [6578]
82. Two or three of Seneca's tragedies: no Denham or related ed. known, but he entered the *Hippolytus* and *Hercules Oetaeus* in the SR in 1566–67 (22221, note)

APPENDIX D: English Stock titles, 1620

On 5 March 1620 the partners in the English Stock entered a large number of titles, many of which had accrued under the patents originally granted to the Company in 1603 and enlarged in 1616 covering the classes of items previously in the patents of R. Watkins & J. Roberts, J. Day 1, and W. Seres (most of D/94–123 below). However, omitted from the Company patents were two large classes of books: law books (D/1–60) and Latin school books (D/61–93). The list is printed in **Arber III.668–71**, and is given below with information on author or main heading, where relevant, and STC number of the nearest edition. STC numbers in square brackets do *not* have the Arber reference cited in STC or Addenda. For a list of these works in STC order except for nos. 24, 80 *see* **Stationers' Company—English Stock** under 1620.

III.668: Law Books

Not included in the Company's perpetual patents. In 1605 the Company bought out the remaining term of T. Wight's patent extending to 1629. In 1618, however, J. More, esq., obtained a patent in succession to Wight's. The relevant imprints run: Tottell, 1553–93; Yetsweirt, 1594–97; (B. Norton &) T. Wight, 1597–1605; Stat. Co., 1605–29; assignees of J. More esq., 1629–40+

1. *Assize of Edw. III*: Yearbooks, 1606 [9602]; cf. **B/16**
2. Ash's *Table to the whole law*: 1614 (840.5(***A***))
3. ——*to Lord Coke*: 1618 [5526]
4. ——*to Lord Dyer*: 1622 [7393]
5. ——*Epieikeia*: 1609 (840(***A***))
6. Brook's *Cases*: 1625 (3826); **B/20**
7. —*Abridgement*: 1586 [3829]; **B/13**
8. Britton: 1640 (3804)
9. Bracton: 1640 (3476); **B/14**
10. Coke's *Reports*, parts 1: 1619 (5494.3), 2: 1618 (5498), 3: 1619 (5501), 4: 1618 (5503.4), 5: 1624 (5508), 6: 1621 (5510), 7: 1629 (5512), 8: 1626 (5514), 9: 1627 (5517), 10: 1629: (5520), 11: 1619 (5523)
11. [J.] Croke's *Reports*: R. Keilwey, 1633 [14902]
12. Crompton's *Justice of the peace*: Sir A. Fitzherbert, 1617 (10983); **B/2**
13. —*Instruction of courts*: 1637 (6051)
14. *Court leet*: Local Courts, 1625 (7724)
15. Dyer's *Reports*: 1621 (7390.5)
16. —*Abridgement*: 1609 (7387)
17. *Doctor and student*: C. Saint German, 1623: (21581); **B/28**
18. *Duties of constables*: W. Lambard, 1619 (15160)
19. *Entries 1614*: Sir E. Coke, 1614 (5488)
20. Edw. III (Yearbooks), parts 1: 1596 [9552], 2: 1619 [9554], 3 ('Quadragesimus'): 1600 [9585]; **B/4**
21. Edw. IV: Yearbooks, 1640 [9769.5]; **B/8**
22. Fitzherbert's *Natura brevium*: 1616 (10965); **B/23**
23. —*Abridgement*: 1577 [10957]; **B/12**
24. *Fleta*: 1647 [Wing F 1290]
25. Finch's book: *Nomotechnia*, 1613 (10870); the rights were apparently later construed as applying to the translation, 10871
26. *Forest laws*: J. Manwood, 1615 (17292)
27. Fortescue: 1616 (11197); **B/31**
28. *Fruits of pleading*: R. Cary, 1601 [4719]
29. Fulbecke's *Parallels*: 1618 (11416)
30. *Grounds of the law*: Statutes/Institutions, 1625 (9300); **B/34**
31. Gregory's *Abridgement*: 1599 (12357.7(***A***))
32. Glanville: 1604 (11906(***A***))
33. Hen. IV and V: Yearbooks, 1605 [9610]; **B/6**
34. Hen. VI (Yearbooks), parts 1: 1609 [9616], 2: 1601 [9697]; **B/7**
35. Hen. VII (also Edw. V, Ric. III, and Hen. VIII): Yearbooks, 1620 [9904]; **B/9**, 10
36. —*Abridgement*: Yearbooks, 1614 [9928]; **B/32**

III.669

37. Kitchen, *Court leet*: 1623 (15025); **B/21**
38. Lambard's *Justice of the peace*: 1619 (15174)
39. *Long quint* of Edw. IV: Yearbooks, 1638 [9804]; in **B/8**
40. Littleton: Law French, 1621 (15758) and English, 1621 (15782); **B/22**
41. *Magna Charta*: Statutes, 1618 (9285); **B/25**
42. *Novae narrationes*: 1561 [18363]; **B/33**
43. Plowden's *Reports*, parts 1: 1613 (20046), 2: 1610 (20047.5); **B/11**
44. —*Abridgement*: 1607 (20038)
45. Pulton's *Abridgement*: Statutes, 1618 [9328]
46. —*De pace regis*: 1623 [20498]
47. *Pleas of the crown*: Sir W. Stanford, 1607 [23224]; **B/18**; cf. **B/19**, **E/2**
48. *Preparative to the law*: W. Fulbecke, 1620 (11411)
49. *Precedents*: Book, 1621 (3348); **B/1**
50. [J.] Perkins: 1621 (19644); **B/27**
51. [W.] Rastell's *Abridgement*: Statutes, 1621 (9327)
52. *Register of writs*: 1634 (20839); **B/17**
53. *Terms of the law*: J. Rastell, 1624 (20716); **B/29**
54. *Table to Edw. IV*: Yearbooks [in 9769.5]
55. —*to Hen. IV [and V]*: [in 9610]
56. —*to Hen. VI*, both parts: [in 9616, 9697]
57. —*to Hen. VII* [etc.]: [in 9904]
58. —*to Quadragesimus to Edw. III*: [in 9585]
59. *View of the civil law*: Sir T. Ridley, 1607 (21054)
60. *Wills and testaments*: H. Swinburne, 1620 (23550)

Latin School Books

The rights to this group are particularly varied and obscure, and it seems probable that they were the earliest to fall under at least partial administration of the Company. The data of ownership follow immediately in a loose chronological fashion and are summarized in the list of titles. In both places the initials of *patentees* are given in italic except for titles with surviving SC (Stationers's Company) imprints.

HB Henry Bynneman entered in 1569–70 rights to four titles (67, 81, 90, 92; Arber I.407, 418); two of these plus another (81, 92, 93) were yielded in his name to the Stat. Co. in 1584. He also printed early eds. of 63, 70, 76, 79.

JK John Kingston from at least 1569 began printing or establishing rights to nine titles (62, 65, 68, 69, 73, 76, 85, 89, 92).

TM Thomas Marsh received in 1572 a patent for ten of the titles (61, 63, 64, 65, 67, 68, 69, 73, 79, 90; *Cal. Patent Rolls, 1569–1572*: 333, no. 2445). Two of these (67, 90; Arber I.272, 359, 418) had been acquired from Bynneman; three others (65, 68, 69; *Reg. B*: 9) were apparently obtained or otherwise appropriated from Kingston, as was a fourth (73). Marsh also had rights to three titles not in his patent (74, 82, 83).

TV Thomas Vautrollier received two patents in 1573–74 covering eight of the titles (62, 63, 64, 71, 76, 77, 78, 89; Arber II.886). Two of these (63—cf. *Reg. B*: 11—and 64) were also in Marsh's patent, and to three others Kingston apparently had some rights (62, 76, 89).

Bynneman died in 1583, and toward the end of 1584 the Marsh and Vautrollier patents expired. The latest dated Marsh imprint on any of his school books is 1584, and in 1585 Vautrollier printed at least one of his own (71). Between 1586 and 1589 inclusive, there are only three relevant surviving imprints: two by Kingston's successors:

G&JR George and Joan Robinson, 1586 (85) and 1587 (62)

and one title in Marsh's patent which was ultimately diverted to the grammar patent (*see* p. 98[2] above): Clenardus, 1588? (5401 sq.) printed by J. Windet. Beginning in 1590 imprints of most of these titles run:

RR Robert Robinson, 1590–94 (63, 65, 67, 69, 72, 73, 79).

RD Robert Dexter, 1595–1603 (RR's titles plus 64, 68, 74, 82, 83, 90, 91, 92).

SC for the Company of Stationers, 1604–40+ (all titles except 72, 80).

D: English Stock titles, 1620 — *cont.*

It is, therefore, difficult to escape the conclusion that the Company or its Court had basic control over these school books beginning from the mid to late 1580s, that R. Robinson became the principal printer of them by 1590 (his successor as a master printer, Richard Bradock, still had a considerable interest in them in 1601; cf. *Reg. B*: 32, 84), and that Dexter later became chief agent for the Company. Exceptional imprints and Company records furnish some evidence in support of this view, though it requires that 'entered' in the Stationers's Register be glossed as 'the Company allowed entry'.

T&JO Thomas Orwin, a later successor to Kingston, in 1593 entered five titles (62, 80, 84, 85, 92; Arber II.630). One of these (80) was so thoroughly used that no pre-1641 ed. survives; of another (84) the earliest extant is of 1625; a third (62) had been in Vautrollier's patent but with 8° rights apparently held by Kingston, who had also previously had rights to a fourth (85); the last (92) had been Bynneman's with Kingston also exercising 8° rights. Orwin's widow Joan printed at least two eds. of one of Marsh's patented titles (61).

JH1 John Harrison 1 owned (or shared with his colleagues George Bishop and William Norton) rights in the 1570s to at least four titles (66, 72, 87, 88) Only two of these (87, 88) were among the relevant nine titles Harrison yielded to the Company in 1612 (Arber III.497; designated by an asterisk (*) following his initials in the list below). Of the other seven, five had been in Vautrollier's patent (71, 76, 77, 78, 89, of which 71 and 89 were entered by Harrison in the 1590s). The other two (70, 93) had Bynneman provenance and were entered to Harrison in 1589 and 1606 respectively. The 1612 titles were printed through that year (e.g. 76) under Harrison's imprint, and his interest in these seems to have had more force than other SR entries allowed to himself and other individuals, perhaps because of a transaction similar to that concerning other copies of R. Dexter (**E/4–8**) or to T. Pavier's purchase (**E/9–11**). Titles belonging to Harrison *not* in the 1612 assignment (66, 72, and 82, the last—a non-patented Marsh title—being entered to him in 1595) had, as far as can be determined, remained under the Company's administration: the first has a Company imprint as early as 1607; the second survives in R. Robinson and Dexter eds. and the third in a Dexter ed.

Unfortunately for the Company, an outsider obtained a patent for several of the most popular and lucrative texts. Upon its expiration the Company received a similar patent, but three years before their patent expired, another interloper obtained its reversion, with the addition of a few more titles.

HS Henry Stringer, one of Queen Elizabeth's footmen, 1597–1611 (62, 63, 64, 66, 67, 69, 76, 77, 78, 80, 81, 89, 90, 92; cf. Arber II.16). Four of these (76, 77, 78, 89) were titles Harrison assigned to the Company in 1612. Stringer seems to have appointed Dexter as his agent or partner (Arber III.87).

SC Stationers' Company, 1613–34 (HS's titles). These titles were, therefore, in possession of the Company when the present list of 1620 was recorded.

RW Rudolph Weckherlin, a minor official under Charles I, 1634–55 (HS's titles plus 73, 84, 93). *See* Greg, *Companion*, 266–8, which apparently recapitulates the Stringer and Company patents.

Neither Stringer's nor Weckherlin's name appears in any imprint, but they presumably received either a royalty on each edition or an agreed annual payment. A further irritant to the English Stock's well-being came from Cambridge, where from at least 1626 competing eds. of most of the school books were published—from 1631 under an agreement with the Stock which attempted to control the number of copies printed there and their wholesale price; *see TCBS* 5 (1971): 155–66.

CUP Printers to the University of Cambridge, 1626–40+ (all titles except 63, 64, 67, 72, 74, 79, 80, 82, 85, 86, 88, 89)

The final two titles in the list below reached the English Stock by other means. One (75) was a Latin version of one of the books in Day's patent (cf. 108), and the other (86) was entered directly to the Stock on 21 Nov. 1614.

Titles associated with a particular individual *only* by mention in Stationers' records have the initials and date within square brackets.

61. Aphthonius: 1623 (704.5); *TM* 1575–83, T&JO 1594–96; SC 1605–36; also CUP 1631–35
62. Cicero, *Offices*: 1623 (5268.5); JK, G&JR 1573–87 (8° eds.), *TV* 1579–84 (16°), T&JO 1590–95 (8°), *HS*, SC 1606–38, *RW*; also CUP 1630–39
63. —*Epistolae*: 1607 [5300.7]; HB 1571, *TM* 1574–84, *TV* 1575–81, RR 1590–91, RD 1595, *HS*, SC 1607, *RW*
64. —*Sententiae*: 1619 (5321.5); *TM* 1575–80 (8°); *TV* 1584 (16°), RD 1603, *HS*, SC 1614–30, *RW*
65. Castalio's *Dialogi*: 1619 (4774); JK 1571, *TM* 1573–80, RR 1590–92, RD 1601, SC 1605–31; also CUP 1631–36
66. Cordier's *Colloquia*: 1624 (5759.7); JH1 [1576] 1584, [RR 1589], *HS*, SC 1607–24, *RW*; also CUP 1634
67. Cato: 1621 (4849.1); HB 1571, *TM* 1574–77, RR 1592, RD 1598, *HS*, SC 1607–34, *RW*
68. *Epitome Colloquiarum*: Erasmus, 1608 (10462.5); [JK 1573], [*TM* 1579], RD 1602, SC 1608; also CUP 1634; cf. **C/57**
69. Aesop's *Fabulae*: 1621 (172.6); [JK 1573], [*TM* 1579], RR 1591–92, RD 1601, *HS*, SC 1614–39, *RW*; also CUP 1628–35
70. *Isocrates ad Demonicum* in Greek: in Plutarch, 1620 (20055.7); HB 1581, JH1* 1589–99, SC 1614–35; also CUP 1638
71. [A.] Manutius, *Phrases*: 1618 (17282); *TV* 1573–85, JH1* 1595–1608, SC 1613–36; also CUP 1636
72. [P.] Manutius, *Epistolae*: 1603 [17289]; JH1 1573–81, RR 1591, RD 1603
73. Mantuan: B. Spagnuoli, 1622 (22984.9); JK 1569–72, *TM* 1573–84, RR 1590–93, RD 1598–1601, SC 1606–38, *RW*; also CUP 1632–35
74. Mancinus, *De quatuor virtutibus*: 1638 (17240); TM 1584, RD 1601, SC 1613–38

III.670

75. Nowell's *Catechismus* in Latin: *Larger*, 1595 [18706a] R. Wolfe/Day; *Shorter*, 1619 (18711c); *Middle*, 1621 (18720.5) and 1638 (18729, Latin/Greek); all Day; SC 1608–39; also CUP 1626–36: *Middle* (18722)
76. Ovid's *Metamorphoses*: 1620 (18952.5); JK 1570 (8°), HB 1572 (8°), *TV* 1576 (8°) 1582 (16°), JH1* 1585–1612, *HS*, SC 1617–36, *RW*; also CUP 1584, 1631
77. —*Epistolae cum epistolis A. Sabini*: 1631 (18929.5); *TV* 1583, JH1* 1594–1602, *HS*, SC 1631–35, *RW*; also CUP 1635
78. —*Fasti, de Tristibus, et de Ponto*: 1614 (18927.5); *TV* 1574–83, JH1* 1594–1602, *HS*, SC 1614, *RW*; the separate *De tristibus* (cf. 18976.8), also in the JH1 assignment, seems not to have been printed in London but it was by the CUP in 1638
79. Palingenius: 1639 (19147); *TM* 1569–79, HB 1572, RR 1592, RD 1599–1602, SC 1616–39
80. *Pueriles confabulatiunculae*: E. Gallus: [T&JO 1593], *HS*, *SC*, *RW*; no pre-1641 ed. survives but cf. 3773 and Wing G 182 sqq.
81. *Pueriles sententiae*: L. Culmann, 1633 (6106.5); [HB 1569–70]. *HS*, SC 1639, *RW*; also CUP 1633; **C/62**
82. Sallustius: 1615 (21623); TM 1569, [JH1 1595], RD 1601, SC 1615
83. Seton, *Logica* [error for *Dialectica*]: 1617 (22256); TM 1563–84, [T&JO 1591], RD 1599, SC 1604–39; also CUP 1631
84. Sturmius, *Epistolae*: Cicero, 1625 (5301.8); [T&JO 1593], SC 1625–37, *RW*; also CUP 1631–35
85. Susenbrotus, *Figurae*: 1621 (23441); JK, G&JR, 1576–86, [T&JO 1593], SC 1608–35
86. Smetius, *Prosodia*: 1622 (22647); SC 1615–40
87. Talaeus, *Rhetorica*: 1627 (23660.5); [JH1* 1577–88], SC 1614–36; also CUP 1592, 1631–35
88. Textoris, *Epitheta*: Ravisius, 1626 (20764); JH1* 1579–1608, SC 1616–34; cf. **E/1**
89. *Tusculanae Quaestiones*: Cicero, 1628 (5316); JK 1574–77, *TV*, JH1* 1591–99, *HS*, SC 1615–36, *RW*
90. Terentius: 1624 (23889.2); [HB 1569–70], *TM* 1575–85? RD 1597, *HS*, SC 1611–36, *RW*; also CUP 1589, 1633–36

D: English Stock titles, 1620 — *cont.*

91. *Terentius Christianus*: Schonaeus, 1620 (21822); RD 1595–1601, SC 1607–25; also CUP 1632–35
92. Virgilius: 1622 (24792.5); HB 1570–72. JK 1576 (8°), JH1 1580–84 (16°), T&JO 1593 (8°), RD 1602, *HS*, SC 1613–22, *RW*; also CUP 1632; cf. **C/61**
93. Vives, *De lingua Latina*: 1624 (24853.3); [HB 1584], JH1* 1612? SC 1624–28, *RW*; also CUP 1633–35; cf. **C/58**

[Miscellaneous English Texts]

Following the STC number is the name of the original copyright owner or patentee.

94. *A.B.C. with the catechism*: c. 1627 (20.9), Day
95. *The horn[book] A.B.C.*: c. 1620 (21.4), J. Wolfe
96. *Spelling A.B.C.*: Book, 1621 (3365), R. Dexter
97. *English Schoolmaster*: E. Coote, 1621 (5712.5), R. Dexter
98. *Primers*: 1553, etc., English: [16087, 16090 sqq., 20373 sqq.], Seres
99. [*Metrical*] *Psalms* (Sternhold and Hopkins): 1620 (2569.7), Day
100. [*Prose*] *Psalters* (Gt. Bible version, preceded by selections from the Book of Common Prayer): 1622 (2413.5), Seres; *see* also 2b in the headnote preceding 2370
101. *Almanacks*: *see* 2b in the headnote preceding 385.3, R. Watkins & J. Roberts; no individual almanacks have the English Stock SR entry noted, but *see* 407.4 and the others indexed under the English Stock for 1620/21; **C/14**
102. *Kalenders for Table Books*: Writing Tables, after 1625 (26050.16), Watkins & Roberts

III.671

103. *Acts and Monuments*: J. Foxe, 1610 (11227), Day
104. [S.] Daniel's *Chronicle* in 4°: 1613 (6247(*A*)), S. Waterson; the author also had a patent, and only one ed. was printed for the Stat. Co.
105. Howes's *Chronicle*: J. Stow, 1618 (23332), T. Marsh/Bynneman (cf. note to 23324); **C/50**
106. Blundeville's *Horsemanship*: 1609 (3157), Seres
107. [W.] Cary's *Farewell to physick*: 1611 (4732), Denham
108. Nowell's *Catechism* in English: *Larger*, 1577 [18710a.5] and *Middle*, 1625 (18736), both Day
109. Tusser's *Husbandry*: 1620 (24390), Tottell/Denham; **B/46**
110. *Testament of the twelve patriarchs*: Patriarchs, 1619 [19471], Day

Prayer Books belonging to the English Stock

These are items primarily in the Seres patent (*see* also Appendix A), which was worked after 1578 by his assignee, H. Denham. In at least one instance (D/112) Denham seems to have had a prior right before the book passed into the patent, and he added several others to it.

111. St. Augustine's *Prayers*: 1621 (947.5), Seres; Day also had a collection, of which the latest surviving ed. is 1586 (928)
112. *Alphabet of prayers*: J. Cancellar, c. 1610 (4562.5), Denham/Seres
113. *Christian prayers* in 4°: R. Day, 1608 (6432), Day; **A/2**; cf. **C/22**
114. *Diamond of devotion*: A. Fleming, 1608 (11045), Denham
115. *David's sling*: E. Hutchins, 1615 (14013.7), Denham
116. *Daily exercise*: T. Lant, 1623 (15223), Denham
117. *Enemy to security*: J. Habermann, 1625 (12582.19), Denham
118. *Enemy to atheism*: J. Habermann, 1615 (12582.22), Denham
119. *Garland of flowers*: T. Twyne, 1602 (24410), W. How/Seres
120. *Imitation of Christ*: Thomas, à Kempis, 1629 (23984), Seres
121. *Pomander of prayer*: T. Becon, 1578 (1748), Day; cf. **C/22**
122. *Seven sobs*: W. Hunnis, 1618 (13983), Denham
123. *Sick man's salve*: T. Becon, 1629 (1771.7), Day; **C/36**; cf. **C/22**

APPENDIX E: Books not present in Appendix D

The following three titles, one a Latin school book and the other two law books, were probably omitted from the list in Appendix D through inadvertence since their imprints satisfy all the criteria for inclusion.

1. J. Ravisius, *Epistolae*: 1628 [20761.5]; JK 1574; also CUP; cf. **D/88**
2. Sir W. Stanford, *King's prerogative*: 1607 [23218]; **B/19**; cf. **D/47**
3. W. West, *Symbolaeographia*, parts 1: 1622 [25275] and 2: 1627 [25279.7]

The following titles passed from R. Dexter to the Stat. Co. in Nov. 1603 (Arber III.248), and the Company granted individuals permission to publish as indicated, citing the last Dexter edition.

4. A. Dent, *Plain man's pathway*: 1603 (6672); one Stat. Co. edition in 1605; title acquired the same year by Edw. Bishop in return for a silver-gilt saltcellar; rights passed to his widow and then to G. Latham.
5. S. Egerton, *Brief method of catechising*: 1597 (7527.9); allowed in 1603 for life to W. Young, who turned it over with Company permission in 1608 to H. Fetherstone; rights then passed to H. Robinson
6. R. Greenham, *Works*: 1601 (12315); C. Burby allowed to print one edition, 1605; W. Welby ditto, 1611–12
7. Richard Rogers, *Seven treatises*: 1603 (21215); T. Man 1 had a half share in the rights; subsequent editions published by him and his assignees
8. M. Virel, *Learned treatise*: 1603 (24769a); allowed to Edw. Bishop in 1605 with later rights passing as in E/4

The following prayer books were acquired in 1615 by T. Pavier with permission of the English Stock, though he did not pay for them until 1619 (*C-B C*: 73, 109). The first two never passed into the Seres patent or officially into the English Stock, but were entered in the SR by R. Robinson, H. Middleton's successor, on 9 December 1588 (Arber II.510). The third item was allowed to Robinson for taking over H. Singleton's debt to the Company on 25 June 1593 (II.632). In 1615 Pavier also obtained the consent of Robinson's successor, R. Bradock, and entered all three items in the SR (III.564).

9. H. Bull, *Christian prayers*, 1614 (4032.3(*A*3)), H. Middleton/R. Robinson; **A/10**
10. *The godly garden*: 1619 (11560), W. Griffith/H. Middleton; **A/11**
11. J. Norden, *Pensive man's practise*, part 1: 1615 (18621), H. Singleton/R. Robinson

APPENDIX F: The Livery of the Company to 1644

In 1560 the Stationers' Company became one of the liveried companies of London. Following is a list of members of the Livery with the dates of their election. References in the form II.873 are to Arber, and in the form 9 are to the page number in the manuscript Call of the Livery on reel 41 in the microfilm series of Stationers' records produced by Chadwyck-Healey. *Names* in italic are members of the Court of Assistants before there was a Livery and are taken from Blagden 295–9; dates in the form *? to 1564?* indicate membership in the Court beginning sometime previous to 1557, with the date or presumed date of death or retirement. Although for most of the 16th century the term 'Master' in Company records was evidently reserved for members of the Court of Assistants (*see Library* 18 (1935): 235–60), toward the end of that period it apparently began to be extended, though somewhat erratically, to mem-

F: Livery of the Company to 1644 — *cont.*

bers of the Livery; e.g. Humphrey Lownes 1, elected on 1 July 1598, was named Master on 10 Oct. 1599 (Arber III.149), and his brother Matthew, elected on 3 July 1602, was named Master on 5 Nov. 1604 (III.274). John Bateman, Robert Bolton, Melchisidec Bradwood, Richard Sergier 1, and George Vincent, all elected on 1 July 1609, were named Master on 16 Oct. 1609 (*C-B C*: 38).

Adams, Richard	1629, 4 June	9
Adams, Thomas	1598, 1 July	II.873
Agborough, William	1619, 3 July	7
Alchorn, Thomas	1631, 2 July	10
Allde, Edward	1611, 6 July	4
Allen, George	1582, 6 May	II.865
Allott, Robert	1626, 1 July	8
Askew, James	1591, 3 July	II.871
Aspley, William	1611, 6 July	4
Badger, Richard	1631, 2 July	10
Badger, Thomas	1638, 29 Mar.	13
Baker, Michael	1611, 6 July	5
Bankworth, Richard	1602, 3 July	II.874
Barker, Christopher	1578, 25 June	II.865
Barker, Robert	1592, 1 July	II.871
Barrenger, William	1616, 29 June	6
Barrett, William	1610, 8 Feb.	3
Bartlett, John	1631, 2 July	10
Bateman, John	1609, 1 July	2
Beale, John	1616, 29 June	6
Bellamy, John	1629, 4 June	9
Bill, John	1606, 27 June	1
Bing, Isaac	1582, 6 May	II.865
Bird, Robert	1629, 4 June	9
Bishop, Edward	1606, 27 June	1
Bishop, George	1568, ?4 July	I.367
Bishop, Richard	1638, 29 Mar.	13
Bladen, William	1639, 2 Sept.	13
Bloome, Jacob	1629, 4 June	9
Blount, Edward	1611, 10 May	3
Boler, James 1	1622, 22 July	7
Bolton, Robert	1609, 1 July	2
Bonham, William	*? to 1557*	
Bourne, Nicholas	1616, 29 June	6
Boyle, Richard	1611, 6 July	4
Bradley, George	1636, 7 Nov.	12
Bradock, Richard	1598, 1 July	II.872
Bradwood, Melchisidec	1609, 1 July	2
Brewster, Edward	1629, 4 June	9
Browne, John 1	1611, 6 July	4
Browne, Samuel	1640, 1 June	14
Buck, George	1566, ?30 June	I.319
Budge, John	1616, 29 June	6
Burby, Cuthbert	1598, 1 July	II.873
Burre, Walter	1616, 29 June	5
Burton, Francis	1616, 29 June	5
Busby, John 2	1616, 29 June	5
Butter, Nathaniel	1616, 29 June	5
Bynneman, Henry	1578, 30 June	II.865
Camp, William	1592, 1 July	II.871
Cartwright, Samuel	1633, 7 Oct.	11
Cawood, John	*1557*	
Cawood, Gabriel	1578, 30 June	II.865
Chappell, John	1629, 4 June	9
Clark, Sampson	1598, 1 July	II.873
Clarke, John	1638, 29 Mar.	13
Coldock, Francis	1570, 29 June	I.421
Cole, George	1603, 2 July	II.874
Collins, Richard	1590, 3 Aug.	II.871
Combes, John	1616, 29 June	6
Connington, Paul	1589, 2 June	II.866
Constable, Francis	1618, 4 July	6
Constable, Robert	1631, 2 July	10
Conway, Henry	1570, 29 June	I.421
Conway, Peter	1578, 30 June	II.865
Cooke, Henry 1	*1557*	
Cooke, Henry 2	1607, 7 Dec.	1

F: Livery of the Company to 1644 — *cont.*

Cooke, William 1	1561, ?6 July	I.161
Cooley, Thomas	1604, 30 June	II.875
Coston, Simon	*? to 1564?*	
Cotes, Richard	1633, 7 Oct.	11
Cotes, Thomas	1628, 13 June	9
Cotton, William	1607, 7 Dec.	1
Crawley, William	1633, 7 Oct.	11
Crooke, Andrew 1	1638, 5 Mar.	12
Cro(o)ke, William	1573, ?5 July	I.463
Dainty, Thomas	1634, 30 June	11
Dawlman, Robert	1631, 2 July	10
Dawson, Ephraim	1625, 4 July	8
Dawson, John 1	1624, 3 July	7
Dawson, John 2	1638, 29 Mar.	13
Dawson, Thomas	1585, 6 May	II.866
Day, John 1	1561, ?6 July	I.161
Day, Richard	1578, 30 June	II.865
Denham, Henry	1573, ?5 July	I.463
Derbyshire, Thomas	1609, 1 July	2
Dewe, Thomas	1624, 3 July	7
Dewes, Garrat	1569, ?3 July	I.391
Dexter, Robert	1598, 1 July	II.873
Dight, Walter	1604, 30 June	II.875
Dockwray, Thomas	*? to 1558*	
Downes, Thomas 1	1616, 29 June	6
Downes, Thomas 2	1640, 1 June	14
Duxwell, Thomas	*1557*	
East, Thomas	1594, 1 July	II.872
Edwards, George 1	1621, 22 June	7
Edwards, John	1616, 29 June	5
Eld, George	1611, 6 July	4
Emery, Jasper	1635, 22 June	12
Exoll, Emanuel	1616, 29 June	5
Fawne, Luke	1638, 29 Mar.	13
Fetherstone, Henry	1611, 6 July	5
Field, Richard	1598, 1 July	II.873
Filken, John	1570, 29 June	I.420
Flesher, Miles	1626, 1 July	8
Foxe, John	1565, ?1 July	I.280
Fussell, Nicholas	1631, 2 July	10
Garford, Richard	1624, 3 July	7
Gilman, Anthony	1603, 2 July	II.874
Gonneld, James	*1565*	
Gould, Thomas	1638, 29 Mar.	13
Greene, Charles	1644, 26 Mar.	14
Greene, Richard	1571, ?1 July	I.448
Griffin, Edward 1	1616, 29 June	6
Griffin, Edward 2	1638, 29 Mar.	13
Grismand, John	1629, 4 June	9
Hacket, Thomas	1569, ?3 July	I.391
Harford, Ralph	1638, 29 Mar.	13
Harper, Thomas	1625, 4 July	8
Harrigate, John	1631, 2 July	10
Harrison, John 1	1564, ?2 July	I.241
Harrison, John 2	1585, 6 May	II.866
Harrison, John 4	1611, 6 July	4
Harrison, Luke	1568, ?4 July	I.367
Harrison, Philip 1	1616, 29 June	5
Harrison, Richard	*1563*	
Hatfield, Arnold	1611, 6 July	4
Haviland, John	1626, 1 July	8
Hawkins, Richard	1623, 7 Apr.	7
Hayes, Thomas	1602, 3 July	II.874
Herne, Richard	1641, 26 Mar.	14
Higgenbotham, Richard	1618, 4 July	6
Hill, Robert	1590, 4 July	II.871
Hodgkinson, Richard	1638, 29 Mar.	13
Holder, Robert	*1558*	
Holme, William 3	1604, 30 June	II.875
Holyland, James	*? to 1558*	
Hook, Henry	1598, 1 July	II.873

F: Livery of the Company to 1644 — *cont.*

Hooper, Humphrey	1592, 1 July	II.871
Hope, William	1638, 29 Mar.	13
Hoth, John	1619, 8 Oct.	7
How, William	1574, ?4 July	I.467
Hughes, Piers	1591, 3 July	II.871
Hunscott, Joseph	1638, 5 Feb.	12
Ireland, Roger	*1560*	
Islip, Adam	1607, 7 Dec.	1
Jackson, Ralph	1598, 1 July	II.873
Jackson, Roger	1611, 6 July	4
Jaggard, Isaac	1625, 4 July	8
Jaggard, John	1602, 3 July	II.874
Jaggard, William	1611, 6 July	4
Jaques, John	*1557*	
Johnson, Arthur	1611, 6 July	4
Jones, William 2	1604, 30 June	II.875
Judson, John	*1557*	
Jugge, John	1574, ?4 July	I.467
Jugge, Richard	*1557*	
Kemp, Leonard	1609, 1 July	2
Kevall, Stephen	*? to 1569*	
Keyle, John	1598, 1 July	II.872
Kingston, Felix	1607, 7 Dec.	1
Knight, Clement	1604, 30 June	II.875
Latham, George	1624, 3 July	7
Law, Matthew	1607, 7 Dec.	1
Leake, William 1	1598, 1 July	II.873
Leake, William 2	1638, 29 Mar.	13
Lee, William 1	1626, 18 Dec.	9
Lee, William 2	1629, 4 June	9
Legat, John 2	1629, 4 June	9
Ling, Nicholas	1598, 1 July	II.872
Lobley, Michael	*1557*	
Lothbury, Arnold	1564, ?2 July	I.241
Lownes, Humphrey 1	1598, 1 July	II.873
Lownes, Matthew	1602, 3 July	II.874
Man, Samuel	1618, 4 July	6
Man, Thomas 1	1586, 4 July	II.866
Marriott, John	1633, 7 Oct.	11
Marsh, Thomas	1562, ?5 July	I.188
Mathewes, Augustine	1630, 6 May	10
Meade, Robert	1616, 29 June	6
Meighen, Richard	1626, 1 July	8
Meredith, Christopher	1631, 2 July	10
Middleton, Henry	1577, 1 July	II.865
Milbourne, Robert	1629, 4 June	9
Miller, George	1629, 4 June	9
Moore, Richard	1616, 29 June	6
Morrett, John	1633, 7 Oct.	11
Moseley, Humphrey	1633, 7 Oct.	11
Mountford, Thomas	1616, 29 June	6
Newbery, Ralph	1570, 29 June	I.421
Newton, William	1599, 30 June	II.874
Nichols, Thomas	1638, 29 Mar.	13
Norton, Bonham	1594, 1 July	II.872
Norton, John 1	1598, 1 July	II.873
Norton, John 2	1625, 6 Dec.	8
Norton, Roger	1635, 22 June	12
Norton, William	1561, ?6 July	I.161
Ockould, Richard	1598, 1 July	II.873
Okes, John	1640, 1 June	14
Orryan, Allan	1602, 3 July	II.874
Orwin, Thomas	1592, 1 July	II.871
Oulton, Richard	1638, 29 Mar.	13
Overton, Henry	1633, 7 Oct.	11
Pakeman, Daniel	1638, 29 Mar.	13
Parker, John	1621, 5 Mar.	7
Parnell, William	1616, 29 June	5

F: Livery of the Company to 1644 — *cont.*

Partridge, John	1631, 2 July	10
Pavier, Thomas	1604, 30 June	II.875
Pepwell, Arthur	1562, ?5 July	I.188
Petty, Samuel	1635, 22 June	12
Pickering, William	1616, 29 June	5
Piper, John	1620, 7 Feb.	7
Ponsonby, William	1588, 6 May	II.866
Pullen, Octavian	1635, 22 June	12
Purfoot, Thomas 1	*1559 to 1563*	
Purfoot, Thomas 2	1611, 6 July	4
Riddell, William	*1557*	
Robbins, John	1619, 3 July	7
Roberts, James	1596, 25 June	II.872
Robinson, Humphrey	1631, 2 July	10
Robinson, Robert	1596, 25 June	II.872
Rogers, John	1598, 1 July	II.873
Rothwell, John 1	1611, 6 July	4
Rothwell, John 2	1638, 29 Mar.	13
Rothwell, William	1641, 29 Oct.	14
Rounthwait, Ralph	1644, 13 Nov.	14
Seile, Henry	1629, 4 June	9
Selman, Matthew	1611, 6 July	4
Seres, William 1	*1557*	
Seres, William 2	1578, 30 June	II.865
Sergier, Richard 1	1609, 1 July	2
Seton, Gregory	1590, 4 July	II.871
Sheffard, William	1626, 1 July	8
Sheriff, William	1629, 4 June	9
Short, Peter	1598, 1 July	II.873
Slater, Thomas	1638, 29 Mar.	13
Smethwick, John	1611, 6 July	4
Smith, Anthony	*1557*	
Smith, William	1604, 30 June	II.875
Snodham, Thomas	1616, 29 June	5
Sparke, Michael 1	1626, 18 Dec.	9
Standish, John	1598, 1 July	II.873
Stansby, William	1623, 8 Feb.	7
Stephens, Philemon	1631, 2 July	10
Stirrop, Thomas	1582, 6 May	II.865
Sutton, Edward	1561, ?6 July	I.161
Swinhowe, George	1602, 3 July	II.874
Thomas, John	1585, 6 May	II.866
Thomason, George	1635, 22 June	12
Thrale, Richard	1631, 2 July	10
Tom(b)es, Richard	1611, 6 July	4
Tottell, Richard	*1561*	
Toy, Humphrey	1561, ?6 July	I.161
Triplet, Ralph	1635, 22 June	12
Triplet, Robert	1618, 4 July	6
Turke, John	*1557*	
Tyler, Evan	1644, 6 May	14
Vavasour, Nicholas	1638, 29 Mar.	13
Vincent, George 1	1609, 1 July	2
Walbanck, Matthew	1633, 7 Oct.	11
Wall, Henry	1594, 1 July	II.872
Walley, Henry	1629, 4 June	9
Walley, John	*1557*	
Walley, Robert	1585, 6 May	II.866
Waterson, John	1627, 21 Feb.	9
Waterson, Simon	1592, 1 July	II.871
Watkins, Richard	1570, 29 June	I.420
Waye, Richard	*? to 1577*	
Weaver, Edmund	1607, 7 Dec.	1
Weaver, Thomas	1633, 7 Oct.	11
Webb(st)er, Richard	1594, 1 July	II.872
Welby, William	1611, 6 July	4
Wellins, Jonas	1625, 12 June	8
Whapland, Dunstan	1571, ?1 July	I.448
Whitaker, Richard	1624, 3 July	7
Whitaker, Thomas	1641, 29 Oct.	14
White, Edward 1	1588, 6 May	II.866

F: Livery of the Company to 1644 — *cont.*

White, John	1619, 3 July	7
Whitney, John	1561, ?6 July	I.161
Wilkes, Oliver	1582, 6 May	II.865
Williams, Francis	1626, 1 July	8
Williams, Rice	1625, 4 July	8
Windet, John	1586, 4 July	II.866
Wolfe, John	1598, 1 July	II.872
Wolfe, Reyner	*? to 1573*	
Woodcock, Thomas	1582, 6 May	II.865
Wright, Thomas	1636, 2 July	12
Yardley, Thomas	1616, 29 June	5
Young, James	1644, 26 Mar.	14
Young, Robert	1628, 13 June	9

INDEX 2: PLACES OTHER THAN LONDON

Places are listed under their respective countries in three categories:

A(i–v)	British Isles and Colonies
B(i–xiii)	The Continent
C	Fictitious Places

Under each place are listed chronologically the printers and publishers active there, with the first and last dates of their local STC imprints.

Cross-Index of Places

Aberdeen Aiii
Abingdon Ai
Alençon Biv
Albionopolis C
Altmore C
Andreapolis = Saint Andrews
Antipodes C
Amsterdam Bviii
Angers Biv
Antwerp (Anvers, Anwarpe) Bi
Argentina = Strassburg
Arnhem Bviii
Augsburg (Augusta, Augusta Vindelicorum, Ausborch) Bv
Augusta Trinobantum = London
Aurich (Auryk) Bv
Ausborch = Augsburg
Avignon (Avenio) Biv

Banbury Ai
Basel Bxiii
Belgium Bi
Bellositi Dobunorum = Oxford
Bengodi C
Bonn Bv
Bordeaux Biv
Bristol Ai
Bruges Bi
Brussels Bi

Caen (Cadomum) Biv
Calais (Calice) Biv
Cambridge Ai
Cambridge, New England Av
Canterbury Ai
Catuapolis = Douai
Cljath = Dublin
Cologne Bv
Copenhagen Biii
Cosmopolis C
Coventry Ai
Cracow = Kraków
Czecholovakia Bii

Danzig, Danswijck = Gdansk
Dauphiné Biv
Delft Bviii
Denmark Biii
Deventer Bviii
Dorchester Ai
Dordrecht (Dort) Bviii
Douai (Duacum, Catuapolis) Biv
Dublin (Cljath) Aii

East Ham Ai
East Molesey Ai
Eboracum = York
Edinburgh (Edinopolis) Aiii
Elysium C
Emden Bv
England Ai
Eton Ai
Exeter Ai

Fawsley Ai
Ferrara Bvi
La Flèche (Flesh) Biv
Florence Bvi
Flushing (Vlissingen) Bviii
France Biv
Frankfurt am Main Bv

Gdansk (Danzig, Danswijck) Bix
Geneva Bxiii
Germany Bv
Ghent (Gand) Bi
Gippeswicum = Ipswich
Glasgow Aiii
Gorinchem (Goricum) Bviii
Gouda Bviii
's Gravenhage = the Hague
Greenwich Ai
Groningen (Grunning) Bviii

Haarlem Bviii
The Hague (Haga Comitis, 's Gravenhage) Bviii
Hamburg Bv
Hanau (Hanovia) Bv
Heidelberg Bv
Helicon C
Hemel Hempstead Ai
Henley-on-Thames Ai
Hereford Ai
Holmia = Stockholm

Ipswich (Gippeswicum) Ai
Ireland Aii
Italy Bvi

Jericho C

Kalykow C
Kraków (Cracow) Bix

Lancashire Ai
Leicester Ai

Cross-Index of Places — *cont.*
Leiden (Leida, Lugdunum Batavorum, Lydden?) Bviii
Leipzig (Lipse) Bv
León Bxi
Liège (Leodium) Bi
Lincoln *See* Index 4A
Lipse = Leipzig
Lisbon Bx
London (Augusta Trinobantum, Llundain) *See* Index 3
Loreto Bvi
Louvain Bi
Lüneberg Bv
Lutetia = Paris
Lutetia Britannorum C
Lugdunum = Lyons
Lugdunum Batavorum = Leiden
Lydden ? = Leiden
Lyons (Lion, Lugdunum) Biv

Malines (Mechlin, Makline) Bi
Malmö Bxii
Marburg (Marborch, Malborow) Bv
Marlborough Ai
Mechlin = Malines
Middelburg Bviii
Milan (Ymlen) Bvi
Monaco Bvii
Mons (Mounts) Bi
Münster Bv
Mussipons = Pont-à-Mousson

N C
Naples Bvi
The Netherlands Bviii
Neustadt an der Hardt Bv
Newcastle upon Tyne Ai
Norwich Ai
Nova Belgia C
Nürnberg (Noriberga) Bv

Oenozythopolis C
Oxford (Bellositi Dobunorum, Rhydychen) Ai

Padua (Patavium) Bvi
Palermo Bvi
Pancridge C
Paradise C
Paris (Lutetia, Parigi) Biv
Patavium = Padua
Pesclavium C
Piacenza Bvi
Plymouth Ai
Poland Bix
Pomadie C
Pont-à-Mousson (Mussipons) Biv
Portugal Bx
Prague Bii

Raków (Racovia) Bix
Rheims (Reims) Biv
Rhydychen = Oxford
Roan = Rouen
La Rochelle Biv
Rome Bvi
Rotterdam Bviii
Rouen, (Roan, Rothomagum, Rowen) Biv

S. A. C
St. Albans Ai
St. Andrews (Andreapolis) Aiii
St. Omer (Audomarum) Biv
Salamanca Bxi
Salisbury Ai
Savoy Ai
Scotland Aiii
Seville Bxi
Shrewsbury Ai
Siegen (Sigena Nassoviorum) Bv
Southwark Ai
Spain Bxi
Stockholm (Holmia) Bxii
Stonor Park Ai
Strassburg (Argentina) Biv
Stuttgart Bv
Sweden Bxii
Switzerland Bxiii

Taunton Ai
Tavistock Ai
Tigurum = Zurich
Toulouse (Tholosa) Biv
Tournai Bi
Turin Bvi

Utopia C
Utrecht (Ultraiectum, Utrick) Bviii

Venice (Venetia) Bvi
Venes Biv
Verdun Biv
Vinegia C
Vlissingen = Flushing

Wales Aiv
Warrington Ai
Waterford Aii
Wells Ai
Wesel (Wesalia) Bv
Westminster Ai
Winchester Ai
Wirtsburgh = Wurzburg
Wittenberg Bv
Wolston Ai
Worcester Ai
Worms Bv
Wurzburg (Wirtsburgh) Bv

Ymlen = Milan
York (Eboracum) Ai

Zurich (Tigurum) Bxiii
Zutphen Bviii

A. BRITISH ISLES AND COLONIES

GREAT BRITAIN *See* Index 4A.

Ai. ENGLAND

Items below have *only* England as the place of printing. *See* also Index 1: English Secret Presses, and also Index 4A.

1480–90: [14077c.8A] (c).
1490: [14077c.7] (c), [—.9] (c), [—.10] (c), [—.11] (c), [—.12] (c), [—.19?] (c), [—.19A] (c), [—.20] (c), [—.21] (c).
1495: [14077c.23B] (c).
1500: [386] (c), [14077c.13] (c), [—.16] (c), [—.22] (c).
1520: [388] (c?).
1640: 21924 (false).

Abingdon.
John Scolar, 1528
1528: 15792.

Banbury.
Henry Sharp, 1619
Edward Langham, 1628–1640
1619: 12827.3, 25305a, 25309.3. **1628:** 25322.3, 25322a. **1630:** 25323. **1634:** 17654a, 17655. **1638:** 22478b, 22505.5. **1640:** 25317.5.

Bellositi Dobunorum. *See* Oxford.

Bristol.
Roger Roydon, 1634
Thomas Thomas 2, 1639
1634: 20513. **1639:** 11250 (note).

Cambridge.
Cambridge is only rarely given as a place name in the STC imprints of that city. Other forms of the name, however, as in 'Printers to the University of Cambridge', are frequently used, and all these have been construed below as overtly identifying Cambridge as the place of printing. On the other hand, Cambridge publishers, when they had a book printed in London or had at least a share in a London book (such items are distinguished below with an asterisk (*)) almost never identified themselves in the imprint as being of Cambridge, and STC itself sometimes fails to supply Cambridge as their residence, particularly in the case of John Porter but occasionally with others. Such inadvertent omissions are silently corrected in the index below. *See* also Index 1: Cambridge University—Printers.

John Siberch, 1520–1523/24
Thomas Thomas 1, 1583–1588
John Porter, 1588–1607
John Legat 1, 1589–1610; later items printed in London
Hugh Burwell, 1597
Cantrell Legge, 1607–1625
Leonard Greene, 1607–1630; one of the Printers to the University from 1622 but remained primarily a publisher
Thomas Brooke, 1608
John Buck, 1626–1635
Thomas Buck, 1626–1640
Joan Greene, 1631–1634
Francis Greene, 1632–1634
Richard Ireland, 1632–1640
William Williams, 1633
Roger Daniel, 1633–1640/41
Philip Scarlet, 1634
Peter Scarlet, 1640

The following London booksellers named *in imprints* acted as agents there for the sale of books printed in Cambridge:

R. Boyle, 1587
Abr. Kitson, 1589–94
R. Bankworth, 1594–96, 1607
S. Waterson, 1601–10
S. Macham 1, 1609
M. Lownes, 1610, 1612
R. Mab, 1612
M. Law, 1613–18
W. Welby, 1615, 1617
A. Johnson, 1616
R. Daniel, 1628
N. Alsop, 1632, 1636, 1640
N. Fussell & H. Moseley, 1634
R. Milbourne, 1634
R. Allott, 1635
R. Ball, 1636
J. Sweeting, 1639
W. Harris, 1639–40
J. Williams, 1639–40
W. Hope, 1640
M. Sparke 2, 1640

Ai: England — Cambridge — *cont.*
1520: [6044a.5*].
1521: 1242, 4082, 10496, 11536, [15601.5] (d?), 16896, 18324.5.
1521/22: 10898.
1522: [14077c.151] (d?), [—.152] (c).
1523: [1383.5] (d?), [14077c.74] (c).
1523/24: 389.7.
1583: [3368.5-Walsingham] (d), 20028.9(*A*3).
1584: 3745, [4474.61] (d?), [—.105] (d?), [—.110] (d?), 15243, 15255, 17524, 18951, 21354.
1585: 4474.1, —.79, 4476.5, 15253, 19929, 19929.5, 24529, 25364, 25674.
1585–90? [4474.7], [—.14], [—.17], [—.22], [—.30], [—.31], [—.56], [—.72], [—.82], [—.90], [—.101], [—.102], [—.111], [—.124], [—.125], [—.127], [—.133].
1586: [3059.4], [3368.5-Wickham] (d?), 4474.21, —.32, —.43, —.64, —.96, —.107, —.108, 5009, 5155.
1587: [3368.5-Nowell, -Wightman] (d?), 4660, 19974.8, 24008 (d), 24531.
1588: [14926*], [19721.5(*A*3)*], 25366.
1589: 89 (d?), 1564, 2020 (d?), [6229*], [20834.3?] (d?), 23887, 24008.5, [25365.3] (d?), [25365.5] (d?).
1590: 2477.5, 2889 (d?), [3368.5-Perne] (c?), 12338, 13590, 19655, [19709*], [19752*] (d?), [19752.3–.5*] (d?), 24695a.5 (c), 25365, 25675.
1590–1600? [4474.4], [—.15], [—.20], [—.24], [—.34], [—.57], [—.62], [—.67], [—.69], [—.74], [—.77], [—.94], [—.106], [—.113], [—.117], [—.131], [—.135].
1591: 1565 (d?), 2155, [3368.5-Banister?] (d?), 19655a (d?), 19658 (d?), [19710*], [19753*].
1592: [3368.5-Barker, -Bendlowes, -Howgrave, -Sheafe, -Sherard] (c?), 15244.3, 15516, 15702, 19656–6.5, 19661.5, [19665*], [19665.5*], [19700(*A*3)*], [19710.5*], 19735, 19735.2, [19753.5*], 22891, 23659.3, 24009, 25695 (d?), 26119.5.
1593: 1830, [4474.84] (d?), 5898, [11055] (d), 17121, 18074, 19688, [19700.5(*A*3)*], 19758, 21684, 24009.5.
1594: 6227, 6443, 12208–8.2, 12938, 18074.5, 24010, 25363.
1595: 1566, [3368.5-Rant(*A*)? -Tomlinson?] (c?), [3436*], [5883–4], [17003], [18208*], 19662*, [19667*], [19702a*], 19703, [19711*], 19742, [19754*], [19754.3*], 19760, 19760.5, 20058, 20599, [22891.5*].
1596: 2990, 11492*, 19685, 19696, [19702a.5*], 19704, 19742.5, 22913, 22913a, 24011.
1597: 80, [4474.35] (d), [—.88] (d), [12906(*A*3)*?], [16609*], 19083, 19663*, 19705, [19712*], [19724.5*], 19735.8, 19743, 19761*.
1598: 3087, 3088, 5117, 10235, 11062a.5, 19682, 19736, 19749, [22882*], 23316, 23890, 25621.
1599: [3368.5-Swift] (c?), 6883, 20086, 25368, 26120.
1600: [10314.1], 19646, 19689.5(*A*), 19743.3(*A*), [19754.7*], 19761.1, 21781, 24012, 25367, 25370.
c. 1600? [3368.5-Hart?], [4474.18], [—.37], [—.48], [—.98].
1600–07? [4474.9], [—.25], [—.38], [—.41], [—.44], [—.50], [—.52], [—.58], [—.60], [—.68], [—.70], [—.78], [—.81], [—.83], [—.85], [—.87], [—.92], [—.93], [—.95], [—.100], [—.101R(*A*3)], [—.103], [—.109], [—.112], [—.118], [—.121], [—.122], [—.128].
1601: [4474.53] (d), [—.76] (d), 7446, 10235.5, 13479, [19713] (d), 19728, 19757, 19757.5, 19763.5, 19764.
1602: 1955.5, [4474.120] (d), [—.132] (d), 4877.4, 5301, 6881, [10314.2], 19105.5, 19750, 25673.
1603: [3368.5-Johnson, W.] (d?), [4474.5] (d), [—.11] (d), [—.29] (d), [—.45] (d), [—.86] (d), [—.129] (d), 4493, 6889, 6892, 7598, 13266, 14357, 19690, 19724.7, 19728.5, 19743.5, 19751.5, 20010, 20025, 22371, 22376, 22874, 25676.
1604: [3368.5-Cursson, -Gouge] (d?), 3438, [4474.8] (d), [—.26] (d), [—.27] (d), [—.40] (d), 10236, 11817, 17257, 18809, 19668, 19680, 19699, [19713.5], 19734, 19737, 25704.
1605: 1831, 5899, 6885, 6891, 7737, 10314.3, [12679*], [12679.5*], 15363.3, 19106 (c), 19648, 20027, 25682.
1606: [3437*], 6882, 6888, 10683*, [12666*], [12667*], [12680*], [12680.3*], [12680.5*], [12680.7*], 13429, 19669, [19670*] (note), [19714*], 24013.
1607: 1936, [3368.5-Jenour] (d?), [4474.12] (d), [—.19] (d), [—.46] (d), [—.73] (d), [—.104] (d), [—.119] (d), 5900, 10236.5, [12669*], [12681*], 13398, 13426, 15703.5, [19677.5*], 19751, 21228, 23891, 24996.5*, 24996a*, 25678–8a, 25693.
1607–09? [4474.3], [—.6], [—.51].
1608: 3441, 3441.5, [4474.89] (d), [—.116] (d), 10314.5, [10533.3]

Ai: England — Cambridge — *cont.*
(d?), 13422, 14950, 19649, 19670, [19678*], 19697, 19715, 19722, [19755*], 24971.
1609: 1937, 1952.5, [4474.13] (d), [—.49] (d), [—.114] (d), [—.130] (d), 13427, 19649, 20026.
1610: 668, [3368.5-Cecil, W. (i)? -Henshaw? -Lumley?] (c?), 10195, 11058–9, 18983, 18983.5, 19698, 20005, 24014, 25689–9.3, [25698.7].
1611: [3368.5-Chace, -Garway? -Tredway] (c?), 10289.9, 19723, 25689.7–90.
1612: [3368.5-Garsett?] (d?), 4474.33, 4481–2, 5563, 18473, 20005a, 20174, 23825–5a, 23830–0.5.
1613: [3368.5-Rodeknight? -Willmer?] (c?), 6786, 10196, [13379*] (note), 14950.5, 19650, 21069, [25434*].
1614: 14951, 14954.6(*A*3), 18209, 25679–9.5, 25680.
1615: [1314.2], [3368.5-Nevile (i, ii)] (c?), [4692a], [13877], 14417, 14419a, [17800], 26081.
1616: [4493.5] (d?), 5180, [10688], 12100, 14369, 14420.7, 14484, 14952, 26082–2.5.
1617: 1314.3(*A*), [3368.5-Anguish? -Bennett] (c?), [4471.5(*A*)?] (d?), 5561, [8551.3(*A*)?] (d?), [8851.5(*A*)?] (d?), 13394a, 14954.7.
1618: [4493.7] (d?), [4693], 14953, 14955, 19651, 23822–2a.5.
1619: 635 (forged), 636 (forged), 4489, [7686.2], [7686.4], [7686.6] (d), 10292, 12527, [13379*] (note), 14370, 14371, 23595, 23823.5, 23826.
1620: 25691–1.5.
1621: [3368.5-Mountague] (d?), 15627.2, 15627.3, 20006.
1622: [4484.5], [4485.5], 6195*, 18982, [19052.2], [19052.6], [25315*].
1623: 2584, 2584.5, 4487–8, 5973, [11062a*], 13181.
1624: 5129, [10278] (d?), [10337] (d?), [13381*] (note).
1624/25: 405, 501.15, 505.
1625: [3368.5-Richardson, -Shawe(*A*3)?] (d?), [4474.66] (d?), [4476] (d), 4477–8, 4484, [4490] (d?), [4491.7] (d).
1625/26: 501.16, 516.
1626: [3368.5-Catcher(*A*3)? -Rayment(*A*3)?] (d?), 10315.5, 13579–9.5 (false), 18722, 21767.
1626/27: 436, 446, 478, 501.17, 505.2, 516.5, 524.
1627: [3368.5-Alvey] (c?), 6296, 10242, 10338 (d?), 11081, 11772, 17766, 19770, 23857.5, 25058, 26015.
1627/28: 431, 517.
1628: 172.9, 1786, 2608, 2609, 2610, 2610.3, 2610.5 (forged), 2610.7, 2932–3.3, 3442, [4491.3] (d), 4696, 6673–3.2.
1628/29: 431.1, 436.2, [501.19], 505.3.
1629: 2285–5.5, 2617.7, [3368.5-Dunster (i)] (d?), 15627.7, 16375.
1629/30: 501.20, 505.4.
1630: 2293, 2294, 2624, 2624.5, [3368.5-Bendish?] (c?), 5271, 5271.2, 6297, 10243 (d), [10279?] (d), 15627.7, 16380, 16380.3, [17228.5?] (c), 20270*, 20270.5*, 21767.5, 21768.
c. 1630? [4474.23], [—.47], [—.72R(*A*3)], [—.59], [—.91], [—.123].
1630/31: 427.3, 430, 436.3, 469, 501.21, 505.5.
1631: 705, 2298.3, [3368.5-Benlowes, -Carey, -Garbut] (c?), 4486, 4775, 5303, 6301, 11773, [13047.5*], 13519, 14276.5, 18206, 18954, [20271–1a*], 20761.7, 22257, 23661.
1631/32: 427.4, 501.22.
1632: 2796–7, [4474.66R(*A*3)] (c?), [—.103M(*A*3)] (c?), [—.120A] (c?), 6099, 6192, [10280?], 10323.7 (d?), 11060, [11769], 11774, 13314, 17767, 20692–2a, 21823, 22986, 24793, [24809].
1632/33: 430.2, 436.5, 469.2, 501.23, 505.7, 517.1, 518, 530, 4475.
1633: 173.7, 2310, 2647, [3368.5-Dunster (ii)] (d?), 4480, 4489.7, 4491, 4776, 5272 (d?), 5761, 6106.5, 6900, 10296, 10317, 11054, 11082–2.5, 11199, 12936, 13183–4, 13184.5–85, 13518–8.5, 14903, [18171.5] (d/error), 18724(*A*: 2 eds.), [20573] (d?), 21873, 23889.6, 24854.
1633/34: 430.3, 436.6, 469.3, 501.24, 505.8, 517.2, 518.2, 530.3.
1634: 755, 2654, [3368.6-Dunster (iii), -Holdsworth] (c?), 4485–5.3, 6009, 6294, 6294.5(*A*) (d/repeat), 6301.5, 7056, 7058, 10463, 11633, 11771, 12964, 13186, 15520, 15521, 15630, [16448.3] (d?), 19052.4, [20273(*A*3)*], 20693, 21460–0.3, 22987.
1634/35: 430.4, 436.7, 469.4, 501.25, 505.9, 515.25, 517.3, 530.4.
1635: 174, 706, 2285.5 (c), 2320, [3368.5-Dixon, -Dolben, -Kaye, T., -Land, -Pocklington, -Swale, -White] (c?), [4472] (c), [4474.10] (d?), [—.39] (d?), [—.55] (d?), 5272.6, 5303.4, 6106, 10244, 11775, 12211, 13187, 14904, 16401, 18930, 20762, 21824, 22400, 22988, 23516, 23661.5, 24854.5.
1635/36: 419.5, 430.5, 436.8, 441.9, 469.5, 501.26, 517.4, 530.5 (*A*), 4479.

Ai: England — Cambridge — *cont.*
1636: 1880 (d), [3368.5-Perrot, -Stanhope?] (d?), 4329a, [4476.3] (d), 4776.5, 6194, 7236, 7237(note), 7294, 13553–3.5, 14887.3, 15522, 17285, 18725, 21638, 22571, 23889.9.
1636/37: 430.6, 436.9, 469.6, [501.27], 505.11, 518.4, 530.6(*A*).
1637: 2326, 2327, 2327.5, 2674, 2675, [3368.5-Loftus, -Whalley] (d?), 4108, [4474.16] (d), [—.36] (d), [—.65] (d), [—.75] (d), [—.99] (d), [4490.5(*A*)?] (d), [4490.7(*A*)] (d?), [4491.6] (c), 4492, 7365, [10281] (d?), 10319, 10339 (d?), [14887.5], 15632.3, 16406, 18172.
1637/38: 430.7, 436.10, 469.7, 469.11, 501.28, 505.12, 517.6, 518.5, 530.7.
1638: 2327.5, 2331–1.3, 2682, 2683, [4472.3] (d), [4472.5] (d), [4474.134] (d?), 6903, [10300] (d), 10351.5, 11778, 13188, 14274, 14964, 15632.3, 16410, 16412, 18977, 22533a (d).
1638/39: 436.11, 517.7, 518.6.
1639: 2338, 2346, 2692, 2692.5 (forged), 4330, [4474.2] (d), [—.28] (d), [—.63] (d), [—.80] (d), 4489.5, 5273, 6294.5(*A*) (d?), 6295, 6298, 7237, 7365.8–66, 10320, 11464, 12531, [13555], 18173, 20762.4.
1639/40: 406.5, 436.12, 501.30, 505.14, 517.8.
1640: 1313, 2346, [3368.5-Cecil, W. (ii)? -Gilbert, -Mickelthwait] (c?), 4008.5, 4338, 4495, 6293, 7117, 7239, 10578, 10779, 10780, 11061–1a, 11465, 11769.5, 11779–9.5, 13040, 13554–4.5, 15245, 15633, 16420, 18197, 18948–8.5, 19154.5, 19770.5, 20130, 20693a.
1640/41: Wing A 1591, A 2127.
1663: [18171.5] (d) = Wing² M 2826A.

Canterbury.
John Saltwood, patron, 1531? and probably later proprietor of the press
John Mychell, 1533?–1547? 1549–1556
Joseph Bulkley, 1609–1622
1531? 3186(*A*3), [3187(*A*3)?].
1533–34? 15192.5(*A*3), [21647(*A*3)?],
1534? 17013(*A*3).
1535? [909.5(*A*3)], 23153(*A*3).
1535–36? [11385(*A*3)?], [11387(*A*3)?], [24447.7(*A*3)?], [24455.5 (*A*3)?].
1537? [16820.5(*A*3)?], [16821(*A*3)?].
1538? [7788.7(*A*3)?].
1538–47? 10459(*A*3), 14006(*A*3), 17651.5(*A*3), 21040–1(*A*3).
1549: 2380, 16052(*A*3) (d?).
1550: 2380a, 15181 (d?).
1552: 9968 (d), 9969 (d).
1553: 9970.
1556: [2996] (d?), [4820] (d?), 10149 (d), [17776(*A*3)] (d?).
1609: [24966a(*A*3)].
1622: 14302.

Coventry.
Robert Waldegrave (Marprelate press), 1589.
John Cartwright, 1633–1635
1589: [17455] (d), [17456] (d), [19613] (d). **1633:** 14692.5. **1635:** 1235.3.

Dorchester.
John Long, 1634
William Browne, 1635
1634: 3129.5. **1635:** 1235.2.

East Ham, Essex.
'Greenstreet House' Press (recusant press), 1580
1580: [3802] (false), [13377] (false), [17278.4] (false, d?), [17278.5] (d?), [19394] (false).

East Molesey, Surrey.
Robert Waldegrave (Marprelate press), 1588
1588: [17453] (d), [19604] (d), [19605.5–06(*A*3)], [24499] (d).

Eton.
Melchisidec Bradwood, 1610–1615
John Norton 1, 1610–1612
1610: 12346, 14622, 14629. **1611:** 2353.5 (d), 14629–9.5. **1612:** 14629–9a. **1613:** 6899 (d?), 14629a, 26065. **1615:** 12347.

Ai: England — *cont.*
Exeter.
Martin Coffin, 1505
William Russell 1, 1589
Christopher Hunt, 1594
Michael Hart, 1601
John Mungwell, 1620–1635
Edward Dight, 1631–1635
Thomas Hunt 2, 1631–1640
?John Salter, 1640
1505: 18872 (d). **1589:** 7159.3. **1594:** 13892, 23697. **1601:** 17173.5. **1620:** [10940.3]. **1631:** 1661.5, 10939, 17863. **1635:** 1235.4, 19522. **1640:** 14706 (d), [20925a(***A***3)?].

Fawsley, Northants.
Robert Waldegrave (Marprelate press), 1588
1588: [17454].

Greenwich.
Conrad Freeman, *pseud.*, 1554
1554: 16980–1 (false).

Hemel Hempstead, Herts.
John Stroud (Cartwright press), 1572–1573
1572: [4713?] (d), [10392?] (d), [10847?] (d), [10848?] (d), [10850?] (d).
1573: [4711?] (d), [4712?] (d).

Henley-on-Thames. *See* Stonor Park.

Hereford.
John Gaschet, 1517
1517: 13833.5.

Ipswich.
The gift-plates indexed below for 1613–1630 are all (***A***) items except as noted, all queried for Ipswich, and all assumed to have been done with a limited assortment of types clamped in a binder's pallet; for reproductions of most of them *see* John Blatchly, *The Town Library of Ipswich*, Woodbridge, Suffolk, [1989], pp. 182–5, where the date of their printing is given as between 1613 and 1617.
Reginald Oliver, 1534
John Overton, 1548
Anthony Scoloker, 1548
John Oswen, 1548
George Pen, 1584
1534: 14893.5 (d).
1548: 1295, [3034.7(***A***)?] (d?), 3362 (d), 4435–5.7, 5199.7, 13021, 14126 (d?), 16992, 17315–6, 18055 (d), 18056.5 (d), 18765, 20192.7 (d), 20663, 21537.5, 26136.
1584: 11720 (d).
1613? [3368.5(***A***)-Bloise, -Buckenham, -Burlingham, -Cole, P. (i), -Cole, R., -Day, E.?].
c. 1615? [3368.5(***A***)-Bacon, E., -Brewster(***A***3), -Bruning, -Cole, P. (ii), -Coppin, -Eldred, -Fisher, -Walter, -Ward, -Withepole?].
c. 1615–1620? [3368.5(***A***)-Blosse, -Brownrig, -Cage, -Cock, -Cutler, -Goodere, -Johnson, T., -Martin, R.?].
c. 1620? [3368.5(***A***)-Algate, -Barber, -Cole, W., -Hayles, -Knapp, -Osmond, -Randes?].
c. 1625? [3368.5(***A***)-Acton?].
c. 1630? [3368.5(***A***)-Dod?].
1636: 20469 (false, d?), 20469.3–70 (false).

Lancashire.
Birchley Hall Press, near Wigan (recusant press), 1615–1621
All items below have the imprint supplied in square brackets in STC.
1615: 26001.
1616: 12797.
1617: 3900, 4932.5.
1618: 3899, 5879.5 (c), 26000 (false).
1619: 17506, 21022, 23924.
1619/20: 3207.5(***A***).
1620: 3607 (false), 3608, 7072.3, 17276.2, 19409.5, 19410.
1621: 3607.5 (false), 5352 (false).

Ai: England — *cont.*
Leicester.
John Allen, 1639
1639: 11250.3.

Lincoln. *See* Index 4A.

London. *See* Index 3.

Marlborough.
Thomas Ewen, 1634
1634: 3129.8(***A***3).

Newcastle upon Tyne.
[J. Legat 2 f.] R. Barker and assignees of J. Bill, 1639
1639: 9143, 9335(***A***3) (repeat), 9335.5, 18196a(***A***3) (repeat), 18196a.5, 22005.

Northampton.
Peter Whaley, 1630–1635
1630: 3234.5. **1635:** 1235.7.

Norwich.
Anthony de Solempne, 1568–1573
Nicholas Colman, 1586
Edmund Causon, 1615–1631
Christopher Pounder, 1616–1621
Thomas Carre, 1631
Edward Martin, 1632
Abraham Atfend, 1639–1640
1566: [5600.5?]. **1568:** 2741, 23557. **1569:** [5792].**1570:** 401.6, 3835. **1573:** [16510.5] (d). **1578:** 151 (false). **1579:** 17450 (false). **1586:** 6564 (d), 23259 (d). **1615:** [18480.5]. **1616:** 23106. **1617:** [26096a]. **1621:** 26098.3. **1623:** 11598, 18481. **1631:** 3790.5, 15036a. **1632:** 20832–2.5. **1639:** 11250. **1640:** 11061a.

Oxford.
Two alternate place names appear for Oxford: its Welsh form, Rhydychen, 1595 (25260), and an antiquarian term coined from an ancient tribe, Bellositi Dobunorum, 1628 (24882.7–83). Items below distinguished by an asterisk (*) were printed elsewhere for an Oxford publisher. *See* also Index 1: Oxford University—Printers.
Theodoric Rood, 1478–1486
Thomas Hunt 1, 1483–1486
George Chastelain, 1503–1508?
Henry Jacobi, 1513?
John Scolar, 1517–1518
Charles Kyrfoth, 1519
John Thorne, c. 1526–1527
Joseph Barnes, 1585–1617
Richard Garbrand, 1600
John Crosley, 1612
Elizabeth Crosley, 1613
William Wrench, 1617
John Lichfield, 1617–1635
James Short, 1618–1624
William Spire, 1619
Henry Cripps, 1620–1639
William Davis, 1622–1640
William Turner, 1624–1640
Thomas Huggins, 1625–1636
Elias Peerse, 1625–1639
Henry Curteyne, 1625–1640
Edward Forrest, 1625–1640
Thomas Butler, 1628
William Webb 1, 1628–1639
Francis Bowman, 1634–1640
Leonard Lichfield, 1635–1640
Thomas Allam, 1636–1639
John Adams, 1637
John Wilmot, 1637–1638
Joseph Godwin, 1637–1640
John Westall, 1637–1640
John Allam, 1638
Matthew Hunt, 1639–1640
Thomas Robinson, 1639–1640
?Timothy Wilkins, 1640

Ai: England — Oxford — *cont.*

The following London booksellers named *in imprints* acted as agents there for the sale of books printed in Oxford:

T. Cooke, 1586–92, 1595
Joan Broome, 1596–1601
John Barnes, 1602–03, 1605, 1611–16
S. Waterson, 1603–06
J. Piper, 1620
P. Stephens & C. Meredith, 1628
R. Allott, 1629
H. Seile, 1629
M. Sparke 1, 1631
J. Clarke 1, 1633, 1638
W. Harris, 1637
G. Hutton, 1639

1468: 21443 (d/error).
1478: 21443 (d).
1479: 158, 752.
1481: 314.
1482: [15297], [23163.13] (d?).
1483: [695] (d), [696] (d), [922] (d?), [5312] (d), [16693] (d?), [17102] (d), [21261] (d), [23904] (d).
1485: [315] (d?), 19827.
1486: [17958].
1503: [14079*] (d).
1508: 16899* (d?).
1513: 22580* (d?).
1517: 4122, [18833] (d?).
1517/18: 470.4.
1518: 4123, 5607, 6458, [23196.4] (d?), 25460.
1519: 5613.
1526: [18833a*] (c).
1527: [15574*].
1576–81? [3368.5-Reade, of St. John's].
1585: 3071, [3368.5-Clarkson, -Gilpin, -Grindal, -Kirkby? -Martin, T. (i, ii)? -Meredith? -Robinson, B.] (c?), 4759, 7286, 7287, 13960.5 (d?), 19340, 19340.5, 19359.1–60.7 (note: most eds. may be forged), 20371, 20371.5, 23021.5 (d).
1586: 2762, 3552.3, 4837–8, 4999.7, 5002, 5789, [5789a] (false), 6167, 10215 (d), 14016 (d), 14017 (d), 14635, 17631, 18924, [19887] (d), 20184, 20368.5, 20621, 20621.5, 22405 (d), 22406, [24568] (false).
1587: 2025, 15387, 19611, 20369, 20612, 22551, 22552, 23107 (d), 24532.
1588: [3368.5-Warren] (d?), 4755, 4761, 13030, 13031, 13966, 20368, 23937.
1589: [3368.5-Robinson, H. (i)] (c?), 13099, 13206, 14015 (d), 21031.5, 22619, 24533.
1590: 1181, [3368.5-Garbrand, -Manfield] (c?), 11734, 14814, 24279.
1591: 1464.8, [3368.5-Malet] (d?), 12589, 13225, 23019, 23642(*A*3), 24275, 24534.
1592: 1430, 2003, [3368.5-Barne? -Hill, E., -Hutchins] (d?), 3552.5, 3683, 3845 (note), 4763, 5237, 7600, 10215.5 (d), 11515, 11516, [17002], 19017.5, 21733 (d), 24042, 25841a.5.
1593: 751, [3368.5-Bettes, -Bracegirdle] (d?), 11500, 11732, 23024.
1594: 1653, 15109, 15556, 19336, 20157, 23023, 24277.
1595: [3368.5-Bonde, -Cogan] (c?), 10139.7 (d?), 18061, 24277.5, 24535, [25260].
1596: [3368.5-Foster, -M., T.?] (c?), 4758, 4760, 10943, 10944, 18114, 19772.5, [19945a] (d?), 20606, 24520–0.5.
1597: 196, [3368.5-Cuffe (i), -Rainolds (i), -Robinson, H. (ii), -Williams] (d?), [3716.5] (d), 4196.5, 4765, 6575, 14976, 19945, 20207, 20612.2, 22555, 25722.
1598: 36, 958.5, 1997, 2362.3, [3368.5-Scott] (d?), 4197, 4764, 14086, 16698, 20158.
1599: 959, 4754, 4756 (d), 10304 (d), 13596, 14977, 21137, [24600.5].
1600: [34*], [3368.5-Braine? -Cholmondley? -Cuffe (ii), -Oxford, *Corpus*, -Temple?] (c?), 4198, 13596.5, 14978, 19773, 21089, 23913, 24527.
1601: [3368.5-Butler] (d?), 10934, 13597, 18926, [19002.5] (d?), 24536.
1602: 1195, [3368.5-Grosvenor, -Remey, -Singleton, -Vaughan] (d?), 4012, 4098a, 13442, 13442.5 (forged), 13884, 13886, 13886.5, 14641, [20146.5] (false), 20148, 20155, 20155.5 (forged), 21698, 22807, 23913.5.
1603: [3368.5-Ducket, -Walrond] (c?), 3716, 4636, 6333, 10143, [11740.5] (d?), [11948] (d), [13880.5?] (d), 13885, 19010–0.5, 19011, 19012, 19012a (d), 19018, 19019, 20587, 23295, 24947.7, 25759.
1604: 37, 5755a.5, 5756, 10307, 13899, 19013, 19172, 19296, 20144, 21734, 21736, 23947.
1605: [3368.5-Sheppard(*A*)?] (d?), [3757?] (d?), 6334, 10305, 14023, 14035, 14449, [14449.5] (d), 15006, [19016] (d), 19043, 19049.5, 21735, 21737, 24036 (d?), 24947, 24952.
1606: [3368.5-Percivall (ii)] (d?), 13887, 14974, [19002.7] (d), 19046, 20773, 24263, 24881, 24948.
1607: 4097, 5393, 5702, 6172, 14452, 14975, 14985, 20362, 24939, 24939.5.
1608: [3368.5-Broome?] (c?), 5126, 5671, 12621, 12621a, 14445, 14986, 14987, [15266.5] (d?), 19016.1, 19171, 20296, 20298, 20301, 20612.3, 21743, 24405, 24936, 25589.
1609: 4192, 6172a, 7325, 7325.5, 13014, 20914, 21700.
1610: 1867, 4091, 7354, 10305.5, 13622, 14446, 20292, 20630, 22877.8, 22890.5, 25858.3.
1611: 1870, 6335, 14534 (forged), 20941.
1612: [3368.5-Denton, -Mason] (c?), 5394 (forged), 6420, 6422, [7341(*A*3)*], 7343, [12618a(*A*3)*], 13706, 13707, 13708, 13711, 13722, 14459, [14618(*A*3)*], 18164–4.5, 19020, 19047, 19170, 19896.5, 20773a, 20941.3, 21033, 21833, 21841, 21845, 22791, 22878, 24187, 24251, 24947.3, 24949, 25592.
1613: 1546, 1861, 1869, 1871, 2749, 3194, 4092 (false), 4117, 4242, 5571, 7306, 11544, 11907, 13515, 13623, 13709, [14308.5(*A*3)*], 14957, 19022, 19044, 19048, 19171a, 19297 (false), 19814, 20133, 20172, 20291, 20299, 20304, 20304.5 (forged), 20612.5, 20612.7, 20613, 20619.
1614: 594, 1868, [3368.5-Bisse (i), -Chaloner, -Crossing, -Harris, -Mitton, -Rainolds (ii), -Waune] (d?), 6389, 6425, 11956, 12045, 13723, 14594, [19003] (d), [19016.2] (d), 19043.5, 20300, 20331, 20344, 20352, 20609, 20612.7, 20613.
1615: 698 (d), 1872, [3368.5-Bisse (ii)] (c?), 5756.5, 6421, 6423, 6426, 10140, 10583–4, 12622, 16447, 18143, 20346, 21701, 22826, 24940.
1616: 1196 (forged), [3368.5-Parr] (d?), 11461, 11957, 11965, 13971.5, 18585 (forged), 19777.5, 19778–8.5, 20609.5, 21106.
1617: 638, 639, [3368.5-Ritch] (d?), 7278, 12628, 14314, 17152, [19016.3] (d), 19023, 22827, 23912.
1618: 640, 641 (forged), [642] (d), [643?] (d?), [3368.5-Chapman, -Harington? -Hill, W., -Hoby, P.] (c?), 4199, 10710.5, [19016.4] (d), 19169, 21702, 22828.
1619: 1781, 1938, 2362.7, 5976, 10308, 11031, 17245, [19016.5] (d), 19024, 20777.
1620: 37.3(*A*3), [3368.5-Dison, -Popham, -Willoughby] (d?), 6424, 7338, 11958–8.5, 11979–9.5, 14450, 20619 (note), 24406.
1621: [3368.5-Bullock, -Parkhurst, -Vicars (i)] (c?), 3806, 4159, 6586, 13276, [19016.6] (d), 21782, 24038.
1622: 33, 4678, 5432, 11568, [13880(*A*3)] (d), [14037.5] (d), 14573, 19014, [19016.7] (d), 19025.
1623: [643.5] (d?), [3368.5-Reade, of Brasenose] (d?), 5832, 11295, 11959, 19027.
1624: 716 (d/error), [3368.5-Sanderson] (d?), 4160, 4630*, 10372.5, 11031.5, 11296–7, 12973, [19016.8] (d), 19028, 19029, [20343.7] (d), 20358.5, 20685.
1625: 1792, 4201, 4676, 7751.6 (false), 8789, 8790 (repeat), 8792, 8793 (repeat), [8794] (d), 8796, 8796.3 (repeat), 8798, 8798.3 (repeat), 8800, 8800.3 (repeat), 8800.7, 8801 (repeat), 8801.7, 8802 (repeat), 8804, 8804.3 (repeat), 8804.7, 8805 (repeat), 10372.6, 11509, 11960*, 13277, 14437, 14454, [14455?] (d?), 14460*, 14972, 14992, 15494, [18032] (d?), 18474, 19030, 19031, 19589, 20356, 20359, 20361, 20774, 23754, 23755 (forged), 23914, 24991, 25326.
1626: 902 (false, d?), 1474, 1600, [3368.5-Nevill] (c?), 4531–1.5, [4633*], [4634*], 10140.5, 12515*, 12615, 13927*, 20347, 20357, 20358, 20911, 23915, 24988.
1627: 10754, 12515*, 12611, 13278, 13619.5, 14457, 17950, [19016.9] (d), 19445, 21020, 21036, 24704, 24941, 24986.
1628: 241, [3368.5-Capper, -Cokayne (i, ii), -Curteyne, -Gyles] (c?), 3628, 4161, 4532, 4736, 6822, 7072, 10309, 10858, 11961, 12514, [19016.10] (d), 19322, 19323, 19576a, [21435.7] (d), 21436, 21814, 23026–7, 23947.5, 24161, [24882.7–83], 24989, 25326.5, 25327, 25376.
1629: 550–0.5, 1071, 1791.7, [3368.5-Washington] (d?), 4109, 4194.5, 4498*, 4757.5, 4800, 4937, 10214, 10310, 13026, 13279, 19008, [19009] (d), [19016.11] (d), 19574, 19577, 19590, 20363, 20618, [21631.5], 21674, 23027, 24294, 26131a.
1630: 290, 1025, 1601, 2365, [3368.5-Finch, H., -Gil? -Halton? -Heylyn, -Middleton, -Stuart, -Vicars (ii)] (c?), 3622, 4373, 4737,

Ai: England — Oxford — *cont.*
7228 (note), 12612, [12998?], 13683, [17383.5], [19016.12] (d), 19032, [19289.5] (c), 19571, 19941, 23228.3, 24037, 25593 (d?), 25594.
1631: 92.3–93, 2732, 3235, [3368.5-Fowke, -Frampton?] (d?), 3623, 3629, 4106, 6666.7, 10141, 10210, 10316, 10635, 11101, 11566, 11809.5 (d), 11962, [13047.5*], 13279.5, 13280, 17368, 17951, 19032.5, 19096–6a, 19194–4.7, 19346, 19942, 20157.5, 20272 (note), 20280.3–.7, 20382, [20934.5*], 21703, 21814.5, 23351, 24749, 24882, 24884, 24968 (d?), 25595.
1632: [3368.5-Bancroft?] (d?), 3624, 4162, 6435, 7156, 10311, 18966, [19016.13] (d), 19587, 22231.
1633: 242, 1166, 1535, 1535.5, [3368.5-Anderson, F., -Earnshaw, -Gildredge, -Glemham, -Nash? -Stone, -Underhill?] (d?), 4190, 4195, 5398, 5591, 6153, 6273.3 (note), 7152, 7157, 10597, 11514, 11770, 11963, [12198], 12344, 12623, 13281, 13614, 14439, 18087, [19016.14] (d), 19033, 19034–4a, 19035–5a.5, 19345, 19487, 19575, 20135–5.7, 20908, 21675, 21848, 24158, 24473, 24473.3 (repeat).
1634: 716, 1391, 1397, 3129*, 3129a*, 3912–2.5, 4191, 4194, 4499*, 5825, 7158, 10935, 16893, 17596, 17829a (d/error), 19004, 19005, [19016.15] (d), [19016.16] (d), 19943, [20136*], 20136.7(*A*3)*, 20516, 20517, 21055–5.5, 21641, 22652, 22831.7–32, 22879, 24160, 24161.3, 26128.
1635: [3368.5-Hanson?, -Leigh] (c?), 4677, 5097–7.3, 7110–1, 7153.3, 10134 (d?), 10142, 10312, 10724, 10859, 12613, 14448, 14451, 15328, 15410, 18033, 19006, [19016.17] (d), 19570* (note), [19570.5*], [23508], 24942.
1636: 1389, 4187.5–88, 4679, 5026, 7112, 10038, 10595, 10936, 11105*, 12401, 13282, 15632, 16788, 17952, 17953, 19036, 19351, 19944, 20344.7(*A*3), 20345, 24942.5, 26013, 26132.
1636/37: 419.6, 431.3, 532.11.
1637: 243, 1441a, 1885, 3630, 4107, 4119, 4261, 4680, 10937, 14268, 14307, 15077, 19037 (d), 19347.5–48, 20345, 21350, 21811, 21812–2.9, 23271, 23916.5, 23917–7.5, 24674, 25328–8.5, 26017–7a.
1638: 91, 4163, 4259, 4876, 5138–8.2, 6044a, 10142.5, 10313, 10373 (d?), 11102–2.5, 11569, 11570, 11964, 14317, 16789, 17657, [19007], 19038, 19042, 20667, 20694, 20909, 21813, 22653, 23724, 24571, [25640*], [25640.5*].
1639: 1167, 3085–5.5, 4717, 4877, 7295, 11250–1, 11401, 11567, 12209–9.5, 12399–9.3, 12402a.2*, 12455, 13283–4, 13684, 13972, 14589, 16448, 17750, [19016.18] (d), 20364, 20588.5, [21056], 21623.5, 21815, 22833, 23993, 24159, 25261.
1640: 1167–7.5, [3368.5-Mason, -Radcliffe] (c?), 3627, [3905.5] (c), 4120, 4672, 4675, 4718, 10013, 10636, 10829, 11065, 11073, 12757, 14480, [17469.2] (d), [19014.5] (d?), [19016.19] (d), 19039–9.5, 20515, 20518, 20695–5.5, 21179, 21704, 22888, 24161.5, 24404, 24473.3 (c?), 24473.7, 24882.3, 26129.
1643: 17829a (d) = Wing M 1761.
1662: [16703.5] (repeat, c) ? = pt. of Wing W 654.
1720: [5690?] (faked, c).
1939: 13284 (d/error).

Plymouth.
William Russell 2, 1631–1640
1631: 18531. **1632:** 12393.5. **1635:** 1791.3. **1640:** 24870.5.

Rhydychen. *See* Oxford.

Saint Albans.
Schoolmaster-Printer, 1479–1486
John Herford, 1534–1539, whose patron was Abbot Robert Stevenage
1479: 6289 (d). **1480:** 268, 24190. **1481:** 2993, 14621. **1483:** [582] (d). **1485:** 9995 (d). **1486:** 3308(*A*3) (d). **1534:** [256].**1535:** [15793.5] (c). **1536:** [12557]. **1537:** [14117.7(*A*3)].**1539:** 6456.5 (d?).

Salisbury.
Unknown agent for J. Byddell, at the [cathedral] close gate, 1538
Henry Hammond, 1633–1637
1538: 10326 (d). **1633:** 7393.5. **1635:** 1235, 19350.5. **1637:** 7164.3, 7165.3.

Shrewsbury.
Unknown agent for J. Oswen, 1549–1551
Unknown agent for R. Ward, 1582–1585; no imprints survive

Ai: England — Shrewsbury — *cont.*
but *see Library* 13 (1958): 247–68 for an inventory of the books there
William Millard, 1635
1549: 13645, 16271. **1550:** 2862.5 (d?), 12365, 24682. **1550/51:** 464.3. **1551:** 4068. **1635:** 23915.5.

Southwark.
Peter Treveris, 1525–1532/33
John Redman, 1534?–1539?
James Nicholson, 1535–1538
Christopher Truthal, *pseud.*, 1556
Robert Aldred, 1620
Francis Faulkner, 1624–1636
Richard Hodges, author, 1631
Andrew Kembe, 1635–1639
1525: [783] (d?), 13434, [15609.5?] (d?).
1526: 13176, [18833a] (c), [23664].
1527: 13440, [14836–6.3] (d?), [15574], [23148.8] (d?), 23182.5 (d?), [25455.5] (d?), [25471.5] (d?), [25489.7] (d).
1528: [5204.3] (d?), 7542.5 (note), [15607] (d?), [25564.8] (d?), [25578.5] (d?).
1528/29: 470.9.
1529: 967 (d?), [5542.3], [7773(*A*3)] (d), 13177–7.5, 23149.5 (d?), [25456.3] (d?), [25474] (d?), [25522] (d?), [25555] (d?).
1530: [1384] (c), 5743 (d?), [10633] (d?), 10995 (d?), [14039.5] (d?), [14077c.64] (c), [—.69] (d?), [14280.7] (c), 14520.5 (d?), [14520.7 (*A*3)?] (c?), [16895?] (d?), 17994.5 (c), 21565, [22607] (d?), 23150.7 (d?), 23182.9 (d?), 23198.3 (d?), [23429a.5] (d?), 25491.7 (d?), [25506.3] (d?), [25566.3] (d?).
1531: [170.7] (d?), [4841.7] (d?), [10633.5] (d?), 15346 (note), 21566, 23162.5 (d?), 23174.6 (d?), [23961] (d?), 25422.3 (d?), [25457] (d?), [25475] (d?), 25492 (d?), [25507] (d?), [25536.5] (d?), [25556.5] (d?), [25566.7] (d?).
1532: 10909, [14077c.123] (d), 23151.3 (d?).
1532/33: 517.12.
1534: 5313 (d?).
1534–39? 2792, 14548, 17030.9.
1535: [2063.3], [20418.5] (d?).
1536: [2063.5], [4021?] (d), [5015.5(*A*)] (d), [5098] (d?), 11470.5 (d), 24455.
1537: 1873 (d?), 2064, 2065, 2752.5, 6832.1–.2, 15285 (d), 16999 (d), 17262.5, 18849, 18878, 20840, 20840.5, 24219.5, [24443.5] (d?).
1538: [1724.5], 2816, 2816.5–.7, [2838] (d?), [2838.3] (d?), [2838.7] (d?), [2839] (d?), 4054, 16979.7, 17000–0a, 20841, 24444 (d).
1556: 18798 (false), 25009 (false).
1620: 20923(*A*3) (d).
1624: 22848.7, 22853.
1626: 3676, 7496.
1627: 17587(*A*3), 19543.
1628: 22840.5.
1629: 12290.
1631: 3719, 7497, 13548.
1632: 12291, 17618.
1635: 11495, 12291.5 (c), [14685], 15249.3, 19453.3, 22396.5.
1636: 12292, 12406, [21251].
1637: 24075, 25848.5.
1638: 22519.
1639: 4802.5, 22520, 23757.5.
2000: 17000a (d/error).

Stonor Park, near Henley-on-Thames.
'Greenstreet House' Press, 1581
1581: [4536.5] (d), [19402] (d).

Taunton.
John Powell, 1629.
1629: 1954.5.

Tavistock.
Thomas Richard, 1525, 1534.
1525: 3200. **1534:** 6795.6 (d).

Warrington.
Unknown printer of xylographic text, 1525.
1525: [14077c.82G(*A*3)] (d).

Ai: England — *cont.*

Wells.

John Burton, 1634.

1634: 3129.7.

Westminster.

Westminster has been considered as a place separate from London only through 1500. For a few of the items included below under 1500, Westminster has inadvertently not been supplied or queried in STC itself. Items distinguished by an asterisk (*) were printed elsewhere for a Westminster publisher.

William Caxton 1476–1491
Wynkyn de Worde, 1492–1500
Jean Barbier, 1498
Julian Notary, 1498–1500

1476: [4851] (d), [14077c.106] (d), [15867(*A*3)] (d), [17009(*A*3)] (d), [17019(*A*3)] (d), [21458(*A*3)] (d).

1477: [3303] (d?), [4850] (d), [4890] (d?), [5082] (d), [5090] (d?), [5091] (d), 6826–7, 6828–9 (repeat), [14551] (c), [15383], [16228] (d), [17008] (d?), [17018] (d?), [17030] (d?), [17032] (d?).

1478: [3199] (d?), 7273, [24188.5–89(*A*3)] (d).

1479: [5758], [15868(*A*3)] (d?).

1480: 6828 (d?), 9991, [13440a], [14077c.83G(*A*3)] (d?), [—.107] (d), [—.107C(*A*3)] (d), [—.110] (d), [15848] (d?), [24190.3] (d?), 24865 (d).

1481: [5293], 13175, [14077c.112] (d), [—.113] (d), [16253(*A*3)] (d), [24762] (d).

1482: 9992, [13438] (d), [20919(*A*3)] (d).

1483: [4852] (d), [4853] (d?), [4921] (d), [5057] (d), [5083] (d), [5087] (d), [5094] (d), 6473–4, 12142 (d), [17015(*A*3)] (d), [17023 (*A*3)] (d), [17024(*A*3)] (d), 17957 (pt. 1, 'book' ed. of pt. 2), 24873 (*A*3), 24874(*A*3) (repeat).

1484: 175, [3259] (d), [3356.7] (d), [14554] (c), 15296, [15871(*A*3)] (c), [15872(*A*3)] (c), 17720(*A*3) (c), 22588(*A*3) (d), 24874(*A*3) (c), [25853(*A*3)] (d).

1485: 801, [5013], [14077c.25G(*A*3)] (d), 19206, [21429(*A*3)] (d).

1487: [7013] (d), [14077c.6] (c), [15394], [15847.3(*A*3)] (c), [15854 (*A*3)] (c), [16164*], 17957(*A*3) ('booc' ed. of pt. 2, c).

1488: [16136*].

1489: 6829 (d), [7269], [14077c.114] (d), [—.115] (d), 17722 (d), [20920] (d), [21431] (d).

1490: [789] (d), [1007] (d), [3124] (d), [3260] (d), [12138] (d?), [14077c.8] (c), [24763] (d), [24796] (d).

1491: [786] (d), 3305 (d), [9348] (d?), 15872 (note), [17959] (d), [20195] (d).

1492: 3304 (d), [24766] (d?).

1493: [5065] (d), 12142 (d/error), 17962, [24234] (d), 24875.

1494: 3261, [14042], [14097] (d), [15875] (d), [15876] (d), [15878] (d), 17962.

1495: [1536] (d), 11024 (d?), 13439, [13809] (d), [14098–8.5] (d), 14507, [17020] (c), [17032a] (d?), 17723, 23153.4 (d), [23154.5 (*A*3)] (d?).

1496: 278, 1916, 1917 (repeat), 3309, 5572 (d?), 5759 (d?), 7016 (d?), 9349 (d?), 9351a.7 (d?), [9353] (d?), [9354] (d), 13608.7 (d?), 17103–3.5, 17539 (d), 17965, 19213, [21334] (d), [23163.6] (d?).

1497: 279, 284 (d?), 285 (c), 286 (d?), 287 (c), 787 (d), 9996, [12541(*A*3)] (d?), 13609 (d?), [14077c.85] (d), [15884*], [16169 (*A*3)*], 17011 (d?), [17031] (d?), 23163.7 (d?), 24866 (d).

1497/98: [385.3].

1498: [283] (d?), 802, 5085, 6931 (d), 13440b, [14077c.86–7] (d), 15397 (d), 16172, [17005] (d), 24876.

1499: [282] (d?), 1917 (d?), 5573 (d), 5643, 11602, [13810] (d), [14077c.148] (c), [14508] (d?), 16114, 16254, [17021] (d?), 17104, 17247, [17726] (d), [17840.7(*A*3)] (d?), 17967, 17968, 20412 (d), 21335 (d), 22597 (d?), 23153.5 (d), [23163.16] (d?), 23427.

1500: [1978] (d), [1987] (d), [1987.5?] (c), 5089 (d?), [7541] (d), [9352] (d?), 11610, 13610 (d?), 13829, [14077c.14?] (c), [14081?] (d?), 14546 (d?), 15895, 16114 (note), [17006?] (c), [17007?] (d?), [17022] (d), [17033?] (d?), [20878] (d), [24224] (d), 24766.3 (d?).

Winchester.

Hans Hitprick, *pseud.*, 1545

1545: 24355 (false).

Wolston, Warks. (Marprelate press).

John Hodgkins, 1589
Robert Waldegrave, 1589

1589: [17457] (d), [17458?] (d), [17459(*A*3)?] (d).

Ai: England — *cont.*

Worcester.

John Oswen, 1549–1553

1549: 2378, 12564, 13022, 13645, 16271, 16276.

1550: 2862, 2862.5 (d?), 12365, 24682, 26141.

1550/51: 464.3.

1551: 4068, 4069, 13756, [15546.7] (d?).

1552: 16287.

1553: 9440.4, 13759 (d).

York.

Items below distinguished by an asterisk (*) were printed elsewhere for a York publisher.

Hugh Goes, 1506–1509
Gerard Wandsforth, 1507
John Gaschet, 1509–1517, 1526–1533
Ursyn Mylner, 1513?–1519
John Warwyke, 1532
John Marchant, 1579
Richard Foster 2, 1626

1506: [13689.3] (c?), [13829.7] (c?), [14077c.63(*A*3)] (d).

1507: 16119*.

1509: [16160*], 16232.4.

1513: 15861 (d?), [15861.3(*A*3)] (d?).

1516: [15609.3] (d?), [16221*], 16250.5* (d?), 25542.

1517: [16135*], [17979.5] (d?).

1519: [14077c.48] (d?), [—.84A] (d).

1526: 15858*.

1530: 16161* (d?), [16223*], 16251*.

1532: 23151.

1533: 15859*.

1579: 4866(*A*3)*.

1626: 6441*.

Aii. IRELAND

Dublin.

Items below distinguished by an asterisk (*) were printed elsewhere for a Dublin publisher. For a list of books available in 1620? *see* 7154.3. *See* also in Index 1: King's Printer in Ireland, Stationers' Company—Irish Stock, and Stationers' Society.

Humphrey Powell, 1551–1566
Francis Edderman, c. 1558?
John Ussher, 1571
William Kearney, 1571? 1595–1596?
John Franckton, 1600–1618
Felix Kingston, 1618–1619
Thomas Downes, 1618–1620
Stationers' Society, 1620–1640
Andrew Crooke 1, 1637
Thomas Allott, 1637–1638
Edmond Crooke, 1638
John Crooke, 1640
Richard Sergier 2, 1640

1551: 16277.

1558: 7481.7 (c?).

1561: 14138 (d).

1564: 14139.

1566: 14259.

1571: [22.3], [19844.5].

1595: 14145, 14145a.

1596: [2958] (d?).

1600: 14147.

1601: 14147a.

1602: [2958], 14148, 21031.

1602/03: 14149, 14150.

1603: 14151.

1604/05: 14152, 14153, 14154.

1605: 14155.

1605/06: 14156.

1606: 4895.3, 14157, 14158.

1607: 14159, 14160.

1608: [7690.7] (d?), 14128.3, 14161, 16433, 18786(*A*3) (repeat of lost ed.).

1609: 14162 (d).

Aii: Ireland — Dublin — *cont.*
1611: 14163 (d).
1611/12: 443.5.
1612: 14164, 21487.5.
1613/14: 14165.
1615: 6361, 14133, 14260.
1617: 17836.3.
1618: [7154.7] (d), 14168, 14169, 14170, 20654a.5(*A*3).
1619: 14172, 17762, 20654a.5(*A*3).
1620: [7154.3] (d?), [7154.5] (d), 12738, 12739.5, 14130, 14173, 24541.7 (c).
1620/21: 14174.
1621: 14130, 14175, 14399.5, 16358, [22544a.7] (d), 22545.
1621/22: 14175.5.
1622: 7179.5 (c), [7264.5] (d), 12737.5, 14134, 14176, 14177, 14178, 14179, 14180, 14181, 22522.
1623: 4311, 14182, 14183, 14265.3, 15501, 22523.
1623/24: 14184, 14185, 14186, 14187, 14188, 14189.
1624: 1805, 14190, 14191, 14511, [21138], 24542, [24953.3].
1625: 583, 8814, 14131.5, 14190.5, 14191a, 14192, 14193, 14196, 14197, 14198, 14199, 14200, 14201, 14202, 14203, 14511.5, 15502, 17836.7, 21020.5, 22524.
1625/26: 14204.
1626: 14205, 14206, 14207, 14265.5, 18228.3 (d), 18914, 25064.
1627: 4668.5, 14209, 14210, 18811.5, 22525–5.3.
1627/28: 14211.
1628: 14212, 14213, 14214, 25065.
1629: 8925, 9249.5, 14208, 14215, 14216, 14265.1.
1629/30: 14217.
1630: 7265, 14218, 14219, 18811.
1630/31: [14221].
1631: 22.1, 5406, 7114, 14058.7, 14222, 14223, 24550.
1631/32: 14224, 14225, 17206.5 (false).
1632: [4326.5] (false, d), [12809], 14134.3, 14226, 14227, [19474] (d?), 20520, 23604, 24557.
1633: [12808], [12810], 14228, [14229], 14230, 14231, 14232, [23596], 25067–7a.
1633/34: 14233, 14234.
1634: 7725.3, 10059, [12812], 14135, 14135.3, 14135.7, 14208a, 14235, 14236, [14237], 23597, 25650.5.
1635: [12811], 14136, 14136.3, 14136.7, [14237.3(*A*3)] (d), 14265, 20690 (d?).
1635/36: 517.16.
1636: 14137 (false?), 14208b.
1637: 1530, 5465.3*, 6825, 14238, 14239, 14240, 14241, 14242, 14243, 14244, 15308, 15499, 16407, 22800.5*, [23029.7] (forged).
1637/38: 14245, 14246, 14247.
1638: 3223, 14132, 14132.5, 14134.7, 14248, 14249, 14250, 14265.9, 22454a*, 24552.
1638/39: 14251.
1639: 1531, 3223.5, 5753–5 (false), 5755a, 14265.7, 15498, 15500, 24548a, 25066.
1640: [5751], 9174, 9260.5, 9262.5, 11495.5, 13600, 14073*, 14252, 14253, 14266, 15462.7, 22452*.
1685–89: 14264 (d). = Wing, 2nd ed., C 4103B.

Waterford.
1555: 18797 (false).

Aiii. SCOTLAND

1507: [7018?] (c?), [7350?] (d?). **1582:** [24251.6(*A*3)?] (c). **1609–10:** 17845.3–.7 (false). **1616:** 14418 pro regione Scotiae, 14420 for the kingdom of Scotland. **1639:** [3368.5-Abercrombie] (d?). **1640:** [13952.7?] (c). **1660:** [21464?] (c), [21465?] (c).

Aberdeen.
David Melvill, 1622–1633
Edward Raban, 1622–1639
1622: 21.9 (d), 71.6, 7349.5, 10442, 12482, 24067.
1622/23: 404.5.
1623: 71.7, 71.30, 71.33, 5960, 6779.5, 6783.5, 13025, 18790, 22007, 24846.
1623/24: 445.19.

Aiii: Scotland — Aberdeen — *cont.*
1624: 71.8, 6781.7, 12492, 16694, 22185.5.
1624/25: 405.3.
1625: 71.9, 71.34, 11595, 12070, 16594.5, 25187.
1625/26: 405.5.
1626: 71.10, 71.35, 2711, 2712, 2713, 2713.5, [3368.5-Anderson, G.] (d?), 12489.
1627: 71.11, 71.12, 71.13, 71.14, 71.15, 71.36, 11147, 12479, 12971, 24430.
1628: 4390, 14709, 15668.
1629: 71.16, 2714, 11139–40, 16595, 16596, 20658, 24795.
1630: 71.37, 1995, 5302, 12484, 13154, 16596, 18953, 24431a.
1631: 71.17, 71.38, 1493, 2941, [3368.5-Hervie] (d), 5957, 11138, 16930, 23193, 23347, 24881.5.
1631/32: 405.7.
1632: 2719, 11144, 14710, 14714, 25192.
1633: 71.18, 1495, 2721.5, 12480, 16597, 20659, 21099, 25190 (d/error?), 25194.
1634: 71.19, 71.19A, 71.39, 17857, 25189.
1635: 71.20, 71.31, [3368.5-Aberdeen] (d), 6824, 11151, 12065, 25190 (d?).
1636: 71.21, 11141, 22055, 23935.
1637: 71.22 (d), 71.23, [71.24] (d), 71.40, 2366, 6124, 11776, 12491, 13027, 25193.
1638: 64, 68, 69 (forged), 71, 71.25 (d), 71.41 (d), 11142, 11781, 20596, [21997] (d), 21999.5.
1638/39: 446.3.
1639: 12478, 12493, 22059, 24854.7(*A*3).

Edinburgh.
Items distinguished by an asterisk (*) were printed elsewhere for an Edinburgh publisher.
Andrew Myllar, 1505–1508
Walter Chepman, 1508–1510
John Story, c. 1520
Thomas Davidson, c. 1535–1541
John Scot 1, c. 1556–1571
Robert Lekpreuik, 1561–1571, 1573–1582?
Thomas Bassandyne, 1565–1578
Henry Charteris, 1568–1599; *heirs, pseud.*? 1601
John Ross, 1575–1580
Alexander Arbuthnet, 1579–1584
Thomas Vautrollier, 1584–1585
Robert Waldegrave, 1590–1603
Robert Smyth, 1592–1602
Robert Charteris, 1600–1610; *heirs, pseud.*? 1628
Andro Hart, 1601–1622; *heirs*, 1622–1639
Mary Waldegrave, 1604
Thomas Finlason, 1604–1628; *heirs*, 1628–1631
James Cathkin, 1607–1610
Richard Lawson, 1607–1615
Edward Raban, 1620
John Burdon, 1622
John Wreittoun, 1624–1639?
John Wood, 1629–1633
Jonet Hart, 1630
John Hart, 1630–1631
Robert Young, 1633–1638
George Anderson, 1637–1638
James Bryson, 1638–1640
Robert Bryson, 1639–1640
1495: 7351 (d/error).
1505: [11604.5*].
1506: [16118*].
1508: [3307] (d?), 5060.5, [7347] (d), [7348] (d), [7349] (d), [7542] (d?), 11984, [13148] (d?), [13166] (d?), [13594] (d?), 17014.3.
1509–10: 15791.
1520: 15791.5 (c).
1535: [3368.5-Reid?] (c?), [7072.8] (c), 14435 (c?).
1540: 3203 (d?).
1541: 21878.5.
1554: [15672(*A*3)?] (false, d).
1556: [15314].
1558: [14932], [17566.5] (d).
1559: [12731.2] (d), [15675] (false, d).
1561: 2026, 18688, [22016], 22018.

Aiii: Scotland — Edinburgh — *cont.*
1562: 2000, 16564, 25860, 25861.
1563: 6320, 10819, 12968, 15074.
1564: 145, 16577.
1565: [2996.3(*A*1)?], 4604, 5970, 11684, 16577a, 19458, 21879.
1566: 21875–6a, 22041, 24623a.
1567: [2996.5] (d), 16578.5, 16604, 21930, 21931, 21932, 22192, [22194] (d), 22196, 22197, 22199.
1568: 15658–8.5, 21880, 21933, 21934, 22626.5.
1569: 185, [13870.3] (d?), 15074.2, [15315] (d?), 15658.5.
1570: 185, 13149, 14915 (d?), [15315.5] (d?), 16579, 21935, 21936, 21937, [22046] (d), 22187, [22187a], 22187a.5, [22189] (d), 22191, 22192a.3, 22192a.5, 22193, 22195, [22200(*A*3)] (d), 22201, [22201.5] (d), 22204, 22205–6, [22208], 22209, 22211.
1571: 185.5, [1377.5] (d?), 12968.5, 15659.
1572: 3979 (false), 21938.
1572/73: 21941.
1573: [147?] (d), 7485, 8055, 13844–5 (false), 21942, 21943, 21943a, 22207.
1574: 1463–4.3 (false), [6323] (d), 15660, 22043.
1574/75: 21943a.5, 21944, [21944.5], 21945.
1575: 1464.4–.5 (false), 16579.5, 16580, 21258, 21881, 21883.
1576: 2125, [10551–1.5] (false).
1577: 21463*.
1578: 2996.7, 3971*, 16580.3, [16580.7] (d?), 18445 (false), 21254.
1579: 2125, 3973–4, 6781, 6783, 7074, 15211 (false), [17328.7] (d?), 22651.
1579/80: 21884.
1580: [321.5] (c), [3975], 4847, 5606, [6767], 10478, 13956, 15661 (d?), [21946.5], 21947 (repeat), [23000] (d?).
1580/81: 22019, 22019.5 (repeat).
1581: 144, 3977 (repeat), 5962, 11183, 11213, 22190 (d).
1582: 3991, 11787 (false), 15662, 21885, [21886], 25239.
1584: 1340, 1763, 14373, 18314, 21671, 21887 (d).
1585: 4429 (false), 14374, 21948, 21948.3–.7 (repeat), 21949 (false).
1586: 4430 (false).
1587: 3107 (false), 4431 (false).
1588: 3108 (false), 14376, 21887.5 (d).
1589: 3109 (false), 14380, 17816 (d/error), 21266.
1590: 1857, 6217, [6228] (d?), 6322, [7754], 14785, 17809, [19603] (d), [19612], 21278, 21459, 22023, 25242.
1591: 1562, 2053, 3923, 3924 (d?), 5192, 13023, 14379, 21280, 22783.3 (d?).
1591/92: 21949.7(*A*).
1592: 10769, 14293, 15663, 19661, 19666, 21255, 22783.5.
1593: 1464.7 (false), 13150, 13165, 14937 (d), 14940 (forged, n.d.), 18354, 19689 (d?), 19701, 21267, 21888.
1594: 2053.5, [11214.2] (d), [11214.4] (d?), [11214.6] (d), 13150, 13941.5, 13943, 13944, [13948] (d), 15679, 16584.5, 17807, 18016 (d?), 18102–2a, [18355], 21268, [21275], 21889.
1595: 763, [2054], 3979.5 (d?), 5067, 5345.7, 6324, 7351, 7352, 7485.5, 12319, 16585, 21255, 21555.1.
1595/96: [21950], [21951], [21951a].
1596: [4105] (d?), [5332], 5345.4, 5345.9, 7487.1, 13555.7 (false), 16585, 16585.5, 21284, [21952], [21953], 22024, 23189.
1597: 7353, [11214] (d), 12323, 14364, 15664, 15664.3, 17815.5, 18049, 18049.5, 21285, 21555.2, 21877, 21891.
1598: 14409, 17816 (d), 18466, 21279, 21954, [21955], [25245].
1599: 6350 (note), [7487.2], 13942, 14348, 16586, 16899.7, 19834, [19881.5] (d?), 20100, 20104, 21101, 21271, 21555.3, 21877.5, 21892.3, 22369, 22542, 24386.
1600: [348], 348.5 (forged), 1766.7, 2997, 3122, 5587, 7487.3, 13150.5, 13878, 16921, 18618.3, 20567, 21274, 21276, 21465.5, 21555.4, —.5 (d), —.6, 21657, [21892.5] (d), 21957, 22960 (d?).
1601: 2184.5*, 2702*, 2901*, [4105.5] (d), 7487.4, 13150.5, [16588*], 21468, 21555.7.
1602: 4716, 6324.5, 13945, 14787*, [14787.2*] (d?), 14787.6* (d?), 15681–82, 16586, [21555.8], —.9, 25235.
1603: 349, 2703, [2730], [5968], 5969, [5971], [7481], 8300 (forged?), [11726.2] (d), [13948.3] (d), 14349, 14349.5(*A*3) (false), [14362] (d), 14410–0.5 (repeat), [14426.7] (d), 14786*, 14787.4*, 14787.8*, 14846.5, 14962, 17511, 17811, 19528, 19888, [21555.10], [—.11], 21958.
1604: 2765.5, 5588, 5783, 6512, 7487.5, 9295.8, 13948.5, 14390.7, 15682, 17812 (d?), 20103, [21959], 21960.
1605: 5460.4, 5460.7, 7487.6, 13857a, [15664.7], 18051, 21270.
1606: 3089, 14465.5 (d/error), [14846] (d), 17813, 18051.3, 21281,

Aiii: Scotland — Edinburgh — *cont.*
21960.3, 21960.5–.7, [21962], 21964, 21965.
1607: 7487.7, 14847, 14849, 16589.5, 22564, 25659.
1608: [3368.5(*A*3)-Nicolson (i)?] (d?), 6580, 7147.5, 10554, 21555.12, [—.13] (d?), [21963] (d).
1609: 5959, 11596, 12168, 14852, 14855, 14857, 21892.7, 21893, 22624, 22626, 24515.5.
1610: 2209, 2704 (c), [3368.5(*A*3)-Nicolson (ii, iii)?] (d?), 7487.8, 14854, 15665, 15680, 18307, 20755.5, [21555.14], —.15, [22024.5] (c).
1611: 3986, 4389, 13151–1a, 14851, 14853.5, 16590, 16591, 18356–6a, 21555.16, —.17, 21892, 21894, 21894.5.
1612: 339, 7487.9, 13946, 13947, 14848, 18976.8, 19889, 21555.18, —.19, 21895, 21896, 24794.5.
1613: 340, 1771, [6267.5] (c), 7257, 7487.10, 11357.5, 13160, 21555.20, [—.21], 21610, 23601, 25188.
1614: [338], [572.5] (d?), 1145, 1406, 2705, 5848.5, [7253–4] (d?), 7258–9, 7487.11, [12202.5], 14853, 14858, 14859, 15666, 18349–9a, 21555.22, —.23.
1615: 1403, 2706, 2708, 3990–0.5, 4803.5(*A*)*, 7487.12, 13031.3, 13031.4, 16592, 17841.9, 18294, 21555.24, [—.25] (c), [—.26] (c), 23104.
1616: [71.32] (d), 1378, 2708.5, [3368.5-Balcanquhall(*A*)?] (d?), 3482, 3793, [7252.3] (d), 7255–6, 7487.13, 7546, 16593, 20988.5 (d?), 21272, 21283, 21555.27, 23067.6, 23105, 23106.
1617: 6781.4, 6997, 6999, 7252, 7487, 7487.14, 11713, 12483, 12970, 13953, 14916, 15368, 15369, 15371, 15372, 15373, 15667, 17842, 18357, 21553, 21555.28, —.29, —.30, 21897, [21898] (d), 25191.
1618: 140–1, 142, 573, 1405, 4898, 5301.6, 5759.5, 7487.15, 13024, 13152, 15715, 16593.5, 21438, 21555.31, —.32, [21899].
1618/19: 435.61.
1619: 1407, 2920.3, 7487.16, 14284, 14708.7, 15667.5, 18350, [21056.2], 21277, 21856, 21965.5, 23431.3, 23889.
1620: 71.5, 137, 698a, 1379, 4849, 7487.17, 10478.3, 13153, 16605, 17616, [17810], 17814, 21256, 21966, [21967], 21968, 22565, 24853.
1621: 186 (d), 2998, [3368.5-Hope?] (d?), 3980, 3987, 6781.5, 7487.18, 13258, 13954.3, 13983.5, 16594, 21900, 21901, 23660.
1622: 3905*, 7487.19, [14115?] (d), 16594, 16842, 17120, 22567.
1623: 5742.8, [7247–9], 7487.20, 22567, 25243.
1624: 3171–1.3 (false), 7487.21, 13993, 22567, 25736.3.
1625: 2710, [3368.5-Raith] (d?), 4366, 5646 (false), 7487.22, 12069, 14940 (forged, c), 18654.7, 20386, [21901.2], [21901.4], 21969, 25736.5.
1625/26: 435.63.
1626: 7487.23, 10692, 12726, 13766, 14929, 21970.
1627: 138, 3444, 5460, 6032, 6782, 7075, 7246, 7487.24, 14906, 21555.34, 21971, 21972, 21973, 21974, 22363.
1628: 2935, 3445, 3446a.5, 7487.25, 10696, 13025.7, 15592, 20385.5, 21555.35, —.36, 21975, 21975.5, 21976, 21977, 21978, 21979, 21980, 21981, 21982, 21983, 22640.3–.7 (false), [22998.5 (*A*3)] (d?), [23070] (d?), 23367, 23370.
1629: 88, 3445a, 3447, 3448, 3449, 7487.26, 13954.7, 13955, 14931, 15312, 16595.5, 16610, 18040 (false), 18063, 21555.37, —.38, 21984, 21987, 21987.5, 23368.5, 23540.
1630: 1609.3, 2715, 2715.5, 7250–1, 7487.27, 15669, 16596.5, 17207, 17208, 18360, 18572, 21555.39, 21901.6, [21901.8], [21988], [21988.5].
1631: 1609.5, 2941.3, 4390.4, [4391.3] (c?), 6780, 7487.28, 7487.29, 11772.5, 14708.9, 18166 (d?), 18167, 18573, 20110, 20229, 21257, 21439, 21555.40, —.41, [21989].
1631/32: 527.22.
1632: 2717, 2718, 5760, 5930.4, 5941, 5967–7.3, 6784, 7487.30, 13955.5, 16611, [17154.5] (d), [17206.5] (false), 20215, 21555.42, —.43, 23369, 25737.
1633: 2311-1a, 2641.7 (note), 2720, 2721, 2721.3 (false?), 2944.5 (*A*3), 2945–5.3, 2945.5, 3443, [3445a.5] (d?), 3447.5, 5023, [7076] (d), 7486, 11151.5, 11916, 12532.5, [13952.5] (d?), 15716 (d), 16394–4.3, 17142, 17145, [17828.5], 18015–5.5, 18168, 19172.7, 19173, 20230, 20656, 21440, 21902, 21902.5 (d/repeat), [21990], [21991], [21992], [21993], [21994], [21995], 23371.
1634: 2311a (PH² copy), 2316, 2316.5 (forged), 2650 (note), 2654.5, 5194.7, 5303.2, [6825.5], 7484, 12534.6, 15670, 15680.5, 16399, 16399.7–400, 16598, 17139, [17815], 19472.5, 19695, 20216, 20645, 21212.3, 21273, 21555.44, 22967.
1635: 574.5, 1615 (false, c?), 2722, 2949, [4163] (d?), 4533, 14715.5,

Aiii: Scotland — Edinburgh — *cont.*
[14819?], 16599, 16600, [21257.3] (c), [21257.7] (c), 21555.45, —.46, 25737.5, [25737.7] (c).
1636: 1617.5, 2328, 2952, 2953, 4803.6, 16606, 16607, 18050, 18290, [20469] (false, d?).
1637: 136, 139, 2328, 2328.3, 2328.5–.9 (forged), 2776.5, [3368.5-Blythe?] (c?), 11777, 15244.7, 16606.
1638: 64.5, [68.5?], [69] (forged), 72, 135, [665] (d), [665.5?] (d), 2333, 2954.5, 2954.6, [3904], 6031.5, 7259.4, [11143?], 12578, 12728, 20657, 21440.5, 21441, [21903], [21903.3], [21903.5], [21903.7], [21904–4.3], [21996], 21998, 21998.5, 21999, 22000, [22025], [22025.5], [22026], [22026.2], 22027, [22030], [22030.3], [22036] (d), [22036.5] (d), [22037], [22038], [22039], [22054], [22054.5] (d), [25062.5] (d).
1639: 2722.5, [2954.7] (d?), 4849.8, 7352.5, 10478.5, [15313.5?] (d), [17144.5] (d?), [17842.3?], 21904.5, 21904.7 (repeat of lost orig.), 21905–5b, 21905b.5 (repeat), 21907, 21908–8.5 (repeat), 22048–8a, 22049, 22050–1, 22051.5, 22057 (repeat of lost orig.), 22060, 23193.9, 23431.7.
1640: 2723, 2724, 2957.3, 3980.5, 4390.7, [5206.5?] (d?), 5303.8, 6784.3, 13155, 15708 (d), 15709, 16601, [18062], [21440.7] (c), 21910, 21910.3, 21910.5, 21910.7, 21911, 21912, 21912.3, 21912.7, 21914, [21916], [21917] (d), 21919, 21919.5 (repeat), [21920], 21922, 21923, 21923.5 (repeat), [21927.5], [21929], [24523].
post-1640: 21902.5 (d).
1706: 14465.5 (d).

Glasgow.
John Wilson 3, 1634–1635
The Hammermen, 1638
George Anderson, 1638–1640
1634: 6825.5. **1635:** 4533. **1638:** 22025.7(*A*3) (d), 22047–7.5. **1639:** 3446, 21441.3. **1640:** [1205], 3446a.

Saint Andrews.
John Scot 1, 1552–1555
Robert Lekpreuik, 1572–1573
Edward Raban, 1620–1622
1552: 12731.
1554: 15672(*A*3)?] (false, d).
1555: 5458.
1572: 3982, 5487, 6909.5, 10820, 15062, 21940, 22011, 22028, 22200.5, 22202, 22203, 22204.5.
1573: 6321, 20105, 21882.
1620: 17856, 24069.
1621: 1496, 21555.33, 22566, 22567.5, 22570, [24368.5] (d?).
1622: 3905, 15370, 15683.5, 20113, [20597] (d).

Stirling.
Robert Lekpreuik, 1571
1571: [3966.5] (d), 3967–8 (repeat), 3968.5, 15076, 22188, 22194.5.
1573: 13847 (false).

Aiv. WALES

Both items below are recusant publications made on secret presses at obscure locations.

Roger Thackwell? c. 1585?
Rhiwledyn Press, 1587
1585: [21077.5?] (c?). **1587:** [21077] (false, d).

Av. NORTH AMERICA

Cambridge, New England.
Regarding the forgery of the 'Oath of a Freeman' *see Book Collector* 36 (1987): 449–70; 37 (1988): 9–28, especially 460–3, 469, 9–22.
Steven Day, 1640
1640: [2738].

B. THE CONTINENT

The following items all have 'printed abroad' supplied in square brackets in STC.

1536: 2835.4 (d?).
1555: 14944 (c).
1557: 3965 (d?).
1561: 16562?
1566: 2740.5? (false), 5600.5?
1567: 2740.5? (false).
1568: 2800?
1574: 1463–64.3 (false).
1578: 151 (false).
1579: 92(*A*) (d?).
1584: 14583 (note).
1589: 23875.
1593: 1464.7 (false), 19608? (d?), 19610? (d).
1598: 19785(*A*3) (false).
1599: 3862a.5.
1600: 14447.5 (false).
1603: 14349.5(*A*3) (false).
1605: 10431.5 (d?).
1606: 18175.
1608: 617 (false).
1610: 2811.5?
1615: 4744.5–.7 (false), 14942.5(*A*3) (c?).
1616: 24792.
1617: 3781?
1621: 18460.7 (d).
1624: 1396.5 (false).
1629: 15083.5 (false), 19069, 19072.
1630: 10432.3.
1632: 536? (d?), 19622b.5?
1635: 739.5? 22034?
1637: 23818 (d?).
1638: 1619.5, 1619.7?, 1620.
1640: 21307a.3.
after 1640: 2330.8–.9? (false), 2610.5? (false), 2680.7? (false), 16418c? (false).

Note: Continental printers and publishers are listed chronologically and in abbreviated form under their respective places, with the first and last dates of their STC activity.

Bi. BELGIUM

1475: [15794?] (c?). **1546:** 23435.5 (note).

Antwerp (Anvers).
G. Leeu, 1486–93
J. Boudins? 1502
A. van Berghen, 1503–10
J. van Doesborch, 1505–30?
T. Martens, 1507–08
G. Back, c. 1510–11
C. de Grave, 1516/17
M. Hillenius, c. 1520–25?
Chr. van Ruremund, 1523–31
G. Nicolaus, 1524?
S. Cock, 1524?–36
W. Vorsterman, c. 1525–30?
G. van der Haeghen, 1527–35
J. Hoochstraten, 1528–33
J. Graphaeus, 1529?–34
M. de Keyser, 1529–36
Cath. van Ruremund, 1532–45
H. Peetersen van Middelburch, 1533–40?
M. Crom, 1536–44?
F. de Keyser, 1537–39
G. Montanus, 1538
J. Coccius, 1539–41
J. Crinitus, 1540
A. Goinus, 1543–45
S. Mierdman, 1544–48?
J. Steelsius, 1556
H. de Laet, 1556–65
M. Endovianus, 1558
G. Simon, 1558
J. van Waesberghe 1, 1563
Æ. Diest, 1563–65
P. van Keerberghen, 1563–67
W. Silvius, 1565–66
J. Fowler, 1566, 1573–76
J. van Ghelen 2, 1569
H. Henricus, 1576–83
G. van den Rade, 1576–83
C. Plantin, 1576–86
J. Henricus, 1578
H. van der Loe, 1578
J. Troyens, 1582
J. Withagius, 1584
J. Trognesius, 1586–93
A. Conincx, 1587–1606
J. van Keerberghen, 1600
D. Vervliet, 1600

Bi: Belgium — Antwerp — *cont.*

H. Swingen, 1601–08
R. Verstegan, *pseud.*, 1603
R. Bruneau, 1605
J. Mesens 1, 1611
F. Fickaert, 1616
J. Seldenslach, 1621–30
H. Aertssens, 1630
J. Mesens 2, 1639

1486: 23907.
1488: 17721.
1491: [15873] (d?).
1492: 19207, 22905 (d).
1493: 9994.
1502: 23427.3.
1503: [782] (d?).
1505: 793.3 (d?), [5952.5?] (c?).
1507: 11605.5, 11614.5, [13606.5] (d?).
1508: 696.4, [23940a].
1509: [23153.7] (d?).
1510: 13606 (d?), 18873.5 (c), [18873.7] (c), 23153.9 (c), 25155 (c), [23164.1] (c).
1511: 13606.3 (c).
1512: [13689.5?] (c?).
1515: [19969.8] (d?), [23155.2] (c).
1515/16: [470.2].
1516/17: [470.3].
1518: 5405 (d?), 11361, 17557 (d?), 24828 (d?).
1519: [10563] (c?).
1520: [4593] (c), [7677] (d?), [14894.5] (c), 16128.3 (c), [24591] (c?).
1523: [15935] (d?), 16145–6, 16236, 16236.3.
1524: 13828.2 (d?), [15818.5], [15937], 15938, [15938.5], 16130, 16261.
1525: 15822, 15939, 16131, 16236.7, 17111, [17544] (c).
1526: 15822.
1527: [5542], 13837.5 (d?), 16207.
1528: 16131.5, [16209], [16237], [24446] (false), [24454] (false).
1529: [1462.3] (d?), [3036], [5542.2], [10493] (false), [10883?] (d?), [11394] (false).
1529/30: 471.
1530: [1462.5] (false), [2350] (false), [2370] (false), [3021] (false), [6815] (d?), [13828.4] (false), 15962, 15966, [16238] (d?), [16263a], [24045] (d), 24227.5 (c?), [24465] (false), [24868.7] (c).
1531: [845] (d?), [1470] (d?), [2777] (false), [2788] (d?), 7481.4, [11386.5] (d?), [12731.4] (d?), 15966, [15969], [20036] (d?), [24437] (d), [24443].
1532: [61] (false), 16132, [16241].
1532/33: [471.5?].
1533: 5542.4, [11381] (false), 16132, 21318, [24440] (d?), [24468?] (false).
1534: [2351], [2372], [2778], 2825, 2826, [2830], [5542.6], [5542.8 (*A*)] (d?), [14829] (false), [14893.5] (d), 23153.2.
1535: [564] (d?), [2372.4], [2827], [2828–8a] (d?), [2829] (c?), [2830], [2830.3] (c), [2830.5] (c), 3014, 5543a (d), [14820(*A*3)], [24167], [24447] (false).
1536: [2832], [2833], [2834], 2856 (note), 3014, 5543b, [11390] (c?), [15992], [21789.5] (c), [21799] (d).
1536/37: [513].
1537: [2066], 5543b.4, [13970] (d?), [24447.3] (false).
1538: 2836, [2836.5(A)], [2837(A)], [2840], [20193] (false).
1539: 2842, 5543b.7, [16013] (d?).
1540: 6832.3, [6832.5] (d?), [22880.7] (d), [22897] (false, d?).
1541: [4045] (d), [4070.5] (d), 16133, [17798] (false, d), [21804] (false), [24217] (false).
1542: [3047] (false), [10808] (d?), [13612], [16023], 16149, [16241.5].
1543: [1280] (d?), [1309] (false), [2848] (d?), [4046] (d), [5014] (d), [14556?] (false), [14826] (false), [14830], 16149, [21629] (d), [26138] (false).
1544: [1276], [1291] (d?), [1291.5] (d?), [1291a] (d?), [4079.5] (d?), [14828], [16242], [24165], [24354] (false, d?).
1545: [1296.5] (d?), [1303] (false), [3765] (false), [4797.3] (false), [5889] (false), [10488] (false), [14823] (false), [16243].
1546: [1270] (false), [1462.9] (false), [11382].
1547: [17789] (false).
1548: [1274a?] (c), [1297?] (d?), [2852?], [18877?].
1556: [10450.5?], [10471.7?], 11092–2a.
1558: 16249.5, 16250.
1558/59: 492.3 (false).
1563: 17847.4, 17847.6, 24752, 25859.
1564: 7062, 17496, 20726.

Bi: Belgium — Antwerp — *cont.*
1565: 371, 1778, 7061, 10589, 12759, 12759.5 (d), 12762, [12763.5] (d), 13888, 15653, 18887, 18888, 20727, 20728, 23230, 23232.
1566: 11333, 12760, 13250, 20728.5, 20729, [23001?], 23234.
1567: 25195.5.
1568: 21315 (false), 6832.40.
1573: 18083, [23617.5] (d).
1574: 3799, 24626.
1575: 14563.3, 14563.5, 14563.7 (false).
1576: 1431.4, 3800.5, 11181, 14563.5, 19595.3.
1578: 3972, 6984.
1579: 1431.5, [4866?].
1582: 16572.2(*A*3).
1583: 1431.6, 17450.7 (false).
1584: 1431.7.
1586: 1431.9.
1587: 370, [370.5].
1588: [368], [22590] (d), 24480 (false).
1589: [1038].
1591: 4868.
1592: [10005], [19412.5], [19885].
1593: 20633, [22994].
1595: 14627 (false), [19398] (false, d).
1596: 26038.8 (false), 26043.5 (false).
1598: 17538 (false), 22126.3 (false).
1599: [9], 3800 (false), 16094, [19415].
1600: 2898, 13470–0.3 (false), 17546, 26038.4–.6 (false).
1601: 3893 (false), [18334.5], [18857] (d?), [18858] (false), [19391.5] (d), [21359].
1602: [11016], [19392.5] (d), [19411], [19418].
1603: 3897.5 (false), [18856], 19815, [21805.05(*A*3)?] (d), [24994.5].
1604: 16095.
1605: 21361.
1606: 18746.
1608: 24627a.8–.10.
1611: 18791.5, 23948.5(*A*3).
1616: 1431.25, 2923.
1623: [42?].
1630: 1431.30, 2937.5.
1632: 16101.
1639: 12808.7.

Bruges.
W. Caxton, 1473?–74
C. Mansion, 1473?–74
H. Holost, *pseud.*, 1576

1473: [15375(*A*3)] (d?). **1474:** [4920] (d). **1576:** 17136 (false). **1624:** 25289 (false).

Brussels.
J. Mommaert, 1608–14
J. Pepermans, 1624–30
widow of H. Antoine-Velpius 1, 1632–33
M. Mommaert, 1634
H. Antoine-Velpius 2, 1637–39

1608: 11093–3.5. **1611:** [4868.7]. **1614:** [4623] (d). **1624:** 11314.6, 22936.5(*A*3). **1628:** 19167. **1630:** [11314.8]. **1632:** 19794. **1633:** 17663. **1634:** 1528. **1637–38:** 7072.4. **1639:** 23230.5.

Ghent.
G. Manilius, 1565
J. Dooms, 1627–32

1565: 17213.5, 17696. **1627:** [13926]. **1628:** 15188.3. **1632:** 1860 (d), 17552.

Liège.
G. Morberius, *pseud.*, 1571
H. Hovius, 1589–1610
G. Hovius, 1623

1571: 15506 (false). **1589:** 1431.10. **1591:** 1431.11. **1595:** 1431.14. **1597:** 1431.15. **1600:** 1431.17. **1604:** 1431.17B. **1610:** 1431.20. **1623:** 7001.

Louvain.
Æ. van der Heerstraten, 1486
T. Martens, 1499
J. Bogard, 1564–67
J. Fowler, 1565–72
J. Heyberghs? 1578
J. Maes, 1579–89
J. Lion, 1579
L. Kellam 1, 1598–1600
Irish Franciscans' Press, c. 1614–18
J.-C. Flavius, 1615
H. L. van Haestens, 1627–28

1486: [19767.7] (d).
1499: 15805.

Bi: Belgium — Louvain — *cont.*

1564: 12758.
1565: 21694.
1566: 17497, 20082, 21695.
1567: 372, 7063, 12761, 13889, 20725, 21692, 21696, 23231.
1568: 5035, 12763, 18889, 21691, [24625.5] (d).
1569: 20088.
1570: 20130.5.
1571: [15506] (false).
1572: [7601], [15503] (d).
1578: [3972?].
1579: 13376.
1580: 3802 (false), 13377 (false).
1589: 4000.
1598: 19354.3.
1599: 16922.
1600: 12730.
1604: 25068 (false).
1614: [18791] (c), [18792] (c).
1614–18: [11314.9].
1615: [4744] (false).
1616: 6778.
1618: [17157].
1627–28: 13926a.

Malines (Mechlin).
H. Jaye, 1611?–35

1611: [23948.5(*A*3)?]. **1613:** 4125. **1615:** 16096. **1616:** 14296.5, 23988.5. **1618:** 16854.5. **1619:** 18316.7. **1620:** 6099.5, [19461], 26000.3. **1621:** [7072.2], 17998. **1623:** [7435] (false), 7435.2, 17999, [18327.5]. **1635:** 1837.7.

Mons (Mounts).
1581: 369 (false).

Tournai.
A. Quinqué, 1623
1623: 19480–1.

Bii. CZECHOSLOVAKIA

Prague.
1620: 11352 (false).

Biii. DENMARK

Copenhagen.
1554: 15672 (false, d). **1559:** 15675 (false, d).

Biv. FRANCE

The following items have France supplied and sometimes queried in square brackets in STC. The imprints that do appear are false.

1532: 16105? (d?). **1536:** 2835? 2835.2? 2835.3? **1537:** 15996(*A*3)? **1567:** 10634.5? (d?). **1572:** 3979? (false). **1587:** 5160.5 (note). **1603:** 22030.7 (false). **1604:** 1459.5? (false). **1610:** 15452 (false). **1612:** 9231? (false). **1615:** 11306.5 (false). **1619:** 15518.5(*A*3)? (false). **1624:** 20946.1(*A*3)? (false). **1650:** 984.5? (false, c).

Alençon.
1575: 11310.5 (false).

Angers.
J. Alexandre, c. 1500
1500: [15576.7(*A*3)] (c).

Avignon.
J. Bramerau, 1601
1601: 5141.5.

Bordeaux.
S. Milanges, *pseud.*, 1589
1589: 13098.2 (false). **1606:** [5725?] (false). **1630:** [4285?] (false, c?)

Biv: France — *cont.*

Caen.
P. Regnault, 1507
R. Macé? 1515
M. Angier, 1519
P. Le Chandelier, *pseud.*, 1598

1507: 16119.5. **1515:** 15811.5 (note). **1519:** 16128.2. **1590:** 5638.9 (false). **1598:** 19785 (false).

Calais.
1599: 17266 (false).

Dauphiné.
A. Janon, *pseud.*? 1604
1604: 11548.5 (false).

Douai.
J. Bellerus, *pseud.*, 1575
L. de Winde, 1576
J. Bogard, *pseud.*, 1576–79?
J. Fowler, *pseud.*, 1578
I. R., *pseud.*, 1580?
J. Lion, *pseud.*, 1580–81
F. Fowler, *pseud.*, 1600
widow of Jac. Boscard, 1601
C. Boscard, 1603–10
L. Kellam 1, 1603–11
J. Mogar, *pseud.*, 1604
P. Auroi, 1604–31
J. Heigham, 1604–13
G. Patté., 1613–14
M. Kellam, 1613–18
T. Kellam, 1618
P. Télu, 1618
L. Kellam 2, 1621–39
M. Wyon, 1623–29
H. Taylor, 1624
B. Bellerus, 1626–32
G. Pinchon, 1629–36
M. Bogard, 1630–36
widow of M. Wyon, 1630–40
D. Hudsebaut, 1638

1575: 274 (false).
1576: [3800.5(*A*3)], 17775 (false).
1578: 17508 (false).
1579: 4568.5 (false, d?).
1580: 17278.4 (false, d?), 19394 (false).
1581: 19393 (false).
1582: 19406 (false, d).
1595: 18326 (false).
1599: 19395 (false).
1600: 6181.7 (false).
1601: 19396 (false), 26000.9.
1603: 5554, 14912.
1603–10: [22126.7], [22969.5].
1604: 1835, 4835 (false), 10541.4, [12574] (d?), [14568.3], 16157.5–58, 17268, 19940.
1605: 1835.5 (false), [11335], [11337], 14913, [17270], 22809, [25972.5].
1606: [632] (d), [632.7], [3268] (c), [9504] (false, d), [11016.5], 11017, 14560.5, 22809a.
1607: [4868.5] (d?), [11334] (d?), [14107.5], [25972.4] (false).
1608: [11025] (false), [12349] (false), [25972.2] (false), [26000.8] (d).
1609: 2207, [4830], [13454], [15363], [17271], [24730] (d).
1610: 2207, 3271, [11019], 16159, [20485].
1611: 1836, [11026], 14568.7.
1612: 16905, 16908.5.
1613: [11316.5], [11317], 17197, 17273.
1614: 11, 13032, 16095.5, 24731.5, 25290.
1615: [11018], 11019.5, 17275.3, 20450, [20450.5] (d?), 24731a, 25290.3.
1616: 1840 (false), 4960, 5827 (false), 10403, [24675.5] (d).
1617: 1837, [10414], [11320], [14910], 23212.
1618: 1340.5, 5860 (false), 7072.5 (false), 14569, 19073, 19203.7, 26000 (false).
1621: 933.5, [14911].
1622: 26000.2, 26000.4–.6.
1623: [12–12.5], [12.7(*A*)], 3902, 16098.3, 18330 (false), 19776, 21446.3.
1624: 14570, 16922a.9(*A*3), 24738.
1625: 3095, [14077c.23c] (d?).
1626: 19769.9(*A*3), 22889.
1627: [17213?].
1628: 660 (false).
1629: 14914, 15348, 20594.
1630: 4833, 6385, 6929, 11323, 22809a.5.
1631: 1922, 4911.5, [18066] (d?), 22810, [24522.5] (d).
1632: [1056], 1802, 3898, 4552, 4553, 11316, 15347.5, 15349, 20124, 23630.
1633: 1923, 3894, 24285.5.
1634: 13468.5, [14107.7], 17185, 22937.

Biv: France — Douai — *cont.*
1635: 3272, 11314.4, 15351, 15351.3, [17130], [19910.5], 24924.
1636: [7373.8], 17618.5, 17746.
1638: [12350–0.5], 17542.3.
1639: 1020, [1589.5], [12350.5], 17128, 17129.
1640: 15350, 17567.

La Flèche.
J. Cock, *pseud.*, 1619
1629: 15518.5 (false).

Lyons.
P. Mareschal, c. 1525
J. Frellon, 1549
J. de Tournes, 1553
M. Jouve, 1558–73
S. Gryphius, *pseud.*, 1572–98
T. Stone, *pseud.*, c. 1630?
1525: 24868.3 (c). **1549:** 3045. **1553:** 3043. **1558:** 6832.34. **1572:** 2995a.2 (false). **1573:** 6832.46. **1585:** 23246.5 (false). **1598:** 2995a.3 (false). **1630:** 4285 (false, c?).

Paris (Lutetia, Parigi).
G. Maynyal, 1487–88
J. Du Pré, 1488?–1504
W. Hopyl, 1494–1520
P. Levet, 1494–97
P. Pigouchet, 1494–1519
E. Jehannot, 1495?
J. Poitevin, 1495?–98
Mich. Morin? 1497
U. Gering, 1497–98
J. Philippe, 1497–1501
B. Rembolt, 1497–1513
T. Kerver, 1497–1521
J. Jehannot, 1498–1500?
S. Vostre, 1498–1520
I. B.? 1500
G. H.? 1500
J. Higman, 1500
N. Marchant? 1500
A. Bocard, 1501–02
J. Petit, 1502–30
A. Vérard, 1503–08
H. de Coblencz, 1504
J. Barbier, 1504–12
J. Badius, 1504–31
J. Bienayse, 1506–21
J. Ferrebouc, 1509–15
R. Cousturier, 1511
C. Chevallon, c. 1511–31
N. Higman, 1512–20
P. de Coblencz, 1515
J. Adam, 1516–21
J. Kerbriant, 1516–31?
F. Regnault, 1519–40
J. Bignon, 1521?
Y. Kerver, 1524–34
P. Le Noir, c. 1525?
J. St. Denis, c. 1525
D. Maheu, 1526
J. Prével, 1526
N. Prévost, 1527–32
A. Plomier? 1528
G. Hardouyn, 1528–33
P. Congeth, *pseud.*, 1535
P. Le Tellier, 1546–48
J. Ruelle, 1548
R. Estienne 1, *pseud.*, 1549
R. Chaudière, 1550?
G. Thibout, 1552
widow of G. Le Bret, 1552
M. Boursette, 1552–56
R. Masselin, 1553
J. Amazeur, 1555–56
G. Merlin, 1555–57
J. Le Blanc, 1556–57
A. Brière, 1565
R. Estienne 2, 1567–68
A. Houic, 1569
T. Brumen, 1573–82
J. Mettayer, 1579
J. Parant, 1579
N. Bonfans, 1580
A. Baio, *pseud.*, 1585
P. Hury, 1588
G. de La Noue, 1599
P. Sevestre, 1602
E. Prévosteau, 1602–04
F. Gueffier, 1607
J. de Bordeaux, 1610–11
D. Binet? 1611
J. Laquehay, 1611
P. Buray, 1614
C. Morel, 1614
R. Giffart, 1619
J. Besongne, *pseud.*, 1621
P. Rocolet, *pseud.*, 1621
J. Blageart, 1621–30
P. Auvray, 1624
A. Estienne, *pseud.*, 1625–34
P. Billaine, 1628
M. Tavernier, 1628
E. Martin, 1629
N. de La Coste, 1631–38
T. Du Bray, *pseud.*, 1632
F. Blageart, 1633–39
P. Mettayer, 1634
C. Prévost, 1634
S. Cramoisy, 1635
J. de La Coste, 1638
G. Baudry, 1640
J. Mestais, 1640
1487: 16164.
1488: [15870] (d?), 16136.
1494: 11608a.7, 15799, [15879].
1495: [15880], [15881] (d?), [15881.5] (d?), [15881.5] (c), [15883] (d), 17964.
1497: [15885], 16169.
1498: 15887, 15888, 15889 (d), 15890 (d), [16138] (d).
1499: 15804, [15892] (d).
1500: [15895.5] (d?), 16174, [16175], [23163.9] (d).
1501: 15805.1, 15896, 17107.
1502: 15897, 16116, 23427.3.
1503: 791 (d), [12379] (c), [15901] (c), 16177, 22407.

Biv: France — Paris — *cont.*
1504: 13829.5, 16178, 16180, 16181, 17108, 23885.3.
1505: [15805.4] (c), 16139.5 (c), 17109.
1506: 15805.5, [15805.7], 15903, 15904, 16258.
1507: 15806, 15862, 15905 (d?).
1508: [14557?] (d?), 15862, [16182a].
1509: [15808], [16160].
1510: 4115, 15809, 15909, 16188, 21789.1, 21799.4, 21799.6, 23030.7.
1511: [1966?], 3269.5 (c), 15912, 16188, 16189, 21799.8.
1511/12: 23427a.3.
1512: 15861.7, 15913 (d), 15913.5 (d).
1513: 16191.
1514: 15810, 15916, 15918, 15920, 16193.
1515: 7018.5, [15811] (d?), 15811.5, 15920, 16141.5, 16195, [17543] (c).
1516: 15812, [15813] (d?), 15921, 16197, 16258.7, 16259.
1518: 15814, [15815] (d?), 16129, 16137.
1519: 15790, 15816, 15923, 15924, 16199, 16200, 16235.
1520: 15790a, [15817?] (d?), 15925, 15926 (d?), [15926.5?] (d?), [15929] (d?).
1521: 15930, 15931, 15932 (d?), 16203.
1522: 16260, 16260.5.
1524: 15818.
1525: [15819], 15820, 15821, [15822a] (c?), [23894(*A*3)] (c?), 24827.5(*A*3) (c).
1526: [15821a] (c?), 15858, 15943, 15944, 15945, 15946.5, 16147, 16205, 16205.3(*A*3).
1527: 15863, 15949, 15950–2, 15953, 15953.5, 15954, 15955, 15956, 16205.3(*A*3), 16205.5, 16206, 16208.
1528: 15823, 15824, 15826, 15864, 15957, 15959 (d?), [15961] (d?).
1529: 15961.3, 15961.5, 16148–8.2, 16210, [16263?] (d?).
1530: 15827.5(*A*3), 15828, [15829], 15963, 15964, 15965, 15968, 16148.2, 16239, 16240, 16240.5.
1531: 13828.6, 15830, 15831, 15970, 15971, 15973, 15974 (d), [15975] (d?), 16211, [24623.5].
1532: 15831, 15865, 15977, 15978–9, 15980, 16212, 16212.5 (c).
1533: 15832, 15859, 15979, 15981, [15981a] (d?), 15982 (d?), 16213, 16224.
1534: 2354, 15984 (d), 15985, 15985a.5, 16214.
1535: 14667 (false), 15833, 15840 (repeat), 15985a.5, 15986.7, 15987.
1536: 15987, [15992.5] (c).
1537: [15995], 16148.4, 16148.6.
1538: 2817, 2965, 16001, 16003, [16004], 16008.3–.5, 21790, 21791.
1539: [2068], [2818.5].
1540: [2070?].
1546: 6832.11.
1548: 6832.13, 6832.15.
1549: 13787a.5 (false).
1550: [22009] (c), 22819 (d?).
1552: 6832.28–.31.
1553: 24623.7.
1554: 15836.
1555: 15836–7, 16217.
1556: 15844, 15847.
1557: 15847.
1558: 15673–4.5 (false).
1565: 1884.5.
1567: 22856.5.
1568: [21315?] (false), 22856.5.
1569: 6832.42, [15504?].
1573: 24476.
1576: 10551.5 (false).
1579: [14255?], 17003.3(*A*3, note), 24718 (note).
1580: 6832.50, 12969.
1581: 4124, 12729, [22031].
1582: 16907.
1583: [17507(*A*3)], 20632.
1584: 3940 (false), [5742.9].
1585: 3934 (false), 3937 (false).
1586: 5789a (false), 24568 (false).
1587: [3107] (false), 22946 (false, d?).
1588: [3108] (false), 4568.
1589: [3109] (false), 5638.7 (false), 15213.5 (false, d).
1599: [4894] (d).
1600: [5638.5?] (false).
1602: 5589, 7628 (d), [8301] (false).

Biv: France — Paris — *cont.*
1603: [8301] (false).
1604: 11336.
1605: [5633.5?].
1607: 20448 (note).
1608: 12349 (false), [13217?].
1609: 4569, [14408(*A*3)?].
1610: 21648.5(*A*3).
1611: 4570, 21648.5(*A*3), [25596.5?] (false).
1612: [4740.3–.5(*A*)?] (false).
1612–23: [3098.5?].
1614: 3094, 4958.
1615: 3170a.
1619: 14708.8 (false), 20664.
1620: [10808.5?].
1621: 5352 (false), 16798 (false), 21138.3.
1623: [15316.7(*A*3)?].
1624: [20390.5] (false).
1625: 4609 (false), 12173.3.
1626: 4872 (false), 21316 (false).
1627: 4912 (false).
1628: 17664–5 (false), 23716.5.
1629: 12641 (note), 21023 (false).
1630: [4551], 17277 (false), 21023a (false).
1631: 943, 4873 (false), [11109.5?].
1632: 3073.3 (false), 4871 (false), 12455.5 (false), 17181 (false), 20492 (false), 24140 (false).
1633: [4554] (false).
1634: 19203.3 (note), 24735 (false).
1635: 7361.
1636: 922.5, 16162, 23992.
1637: 11322, 25403.5.
1638: 911, 914, 1543, 6844.4, 16828, 20487.5, 24737 (false).
1639: [1019] (false), [20179?].
1640: 10890, 17278, 21253, 21454.

Pont à Mousson (Mussipons).
F. Du Bois, *pseud.*, 1609
J. Garnisch, *pseud.*, 1609
1609: 1408.3 (false).

Rheims (Reims).
J. Foigny, 1569–83
S. Foigny, 1603–08
1569: [15505] (false). **1580:** [14074] (d?). **1581:** [369] (false), [888] (d?). **1582:** [369.5], 2884, 17503. **1583:** 18537. **1601:** 25124–4.5 (false). **1603:** [14912]. **1608:** 14909.

La Rochelle.
R. Waldegrave, 1589
J. Haultin? c. 1590
1589: [6805] (d), [12342] (d), [19602]. **1590:** [3443.5?] (c). **1621:** 11303–3.5 (false), 11304 (false). **1628:** 4147 (false).

Rouen (Roan, Rothomagum).
G. Le Tailleur, 1490
M. Morin, 1492–1519
J. Richard, 1494–1511
J. Ravynell? 1495
J. de Lorraine, 1500
P. Olivier, 1500–25
J. Huvin, 1501–15
J. Mauditier, 1502–05
P. Violette, 1505–09
P. Guérin, 1505?–10
L. Hostingue, 1505
J. Loys, 1505–08
R. Goupil, 1506?
G. Candos, 1506?–09
R. Auzoult, 1506?–15
G. Bernard, 1506–17
P. Coste, 1506–20?
R. Macé, 1506–20?
J. Caillard, 1515–22
J. Cousin, 1515–37
E. Hardy, 1517–22
N. Mullot, c. 1520
N. Le Roux, 1528?–51
J. Marchant, 1536–38
H. Le Mareschal, 1539? 1566? 1580
R. Caly, 1551
R. Valentin, 1551–57
J. Le Prest, 1554–55
R. Hamillon, 1554–57
F. Valentin, 1556–57?
J. Petit? 1558
A. Clémence? 1566
C. Hamillon, 1566–1614
G. Loyselet, 1580–90
Fr. Parsons' Press, 1582–85
A. Malasis, 1600
J. Molaeus, *pseud.*, 1601
heirs of J. Walker, *pseud.*, 1601
J. Machuel, 1609
C. Le Villain, 1611–25
M. Michel, 1614–15
J. Foüet, *pseud.*, 1619–23
J. Besongne, *pseud.*, 1626
J. Cousturier, 1627–40

Biv: France — Rouen — *cont.*
J. Le Boullenger, 1630
N. Courant, 1630–31
M. Courant, 1631–33
E. Fitzours, *pseud.*, 1632
D. Ferrand, 1636
L. Oursel, 1639
1490: 15721 (d), [23238] (d).
1492: 15795.5 (d?), [16166].
1494: [15877] (d?), 15879.
1495: 17963–3.5.
1496: 15802.
1497: 15885, [16170] (d?), 16171.
1499: 17966.
1500: [15576.7(*A*3)?] (c), 16139.
1501: [15805.1], [16176].
1502: 16163.
1505: [11604.5], 15793, [15902] (d?), 18872 (d), [23140] (c).
1506: 15805.7, [15805.9(*A*3)?] (c), 15904.5 (d?), [16118(*A*3)], 16182.
1506/07: [504] (d).
1507: [15857] (c), 16119–9.5.
1508: [16182a], 16183, 16184, 16185, 16233.
1509: 16140.3, [16140.5] (c), 16186, 16220 (d?).
1510: [15911] (d?), [16101.8?] (c), 16140.7, 16187, 16188.5.
1511: [15809.5(*A*3)?], 16188.5.
1514: 16194.
1515: 15811.5 (note), 16141, 16195.5, [23147.2] (c).
1516: [16103] (d?), 16142, 16196, 16221, 16250.5 (d?).
1517: 13833.5, 16104, 16135, 16222, 16234.
1518: 16129.3, 16198.
1519: [16199], [16201–1.3], [16201.7].
1520: [13835], [15928] (d?), 16104.5, 16143 (d?), [16202.5] (c).
1521: 16204–4.5.
1522: 16144.
1525: 15820, 15821, 15940, [16236.5?] (c), [16236.6?] (c).
1526: 15946, 23148.7, 23159a.12 (d?).
1528: 15958 (d).
1530: [16161] (d?), [16223], [16251].
1534: 15985a (d?).
1536: [15992.5] (c), 15993, 16106, 21789.6.
1537: 15994, 15995, 16148.4.
1538: [2965], [2965.2], [2965.4], [2966?], 2966.3, 16001–2, 16002.5, 16002a, 16004, 16006, [16007], [16008.3–.5], [21790.5] (d), [21791].
1539: 16012 (d?).
1542: [2972.5?], 16024.
1543: 16150.
1550: [2081].
1551: [11592], 16055, 16056.
1553: 5160.3 (false), 11585 (false), 11586 (false), 11593 (false).
1554: 5157 (false), 10016 (false), 10383 (false), 16058, 16155, 16215, 16216, 17773 (false).
1555: 2978.5, [15860] (d?), 16068, 16069, 16070, 16071, 16071.5, 16072, 16155a, 16216, 16248.
1556: 15846, 16076, 16077, 16078.
1557: 16081.5 (d?), 16249.
1558: [15673?] (false), [15674–4.5?] (false).
1566: 2098, [10388?] (d), [16578?].
1578: 17504 (false).
1580: 14564, 24626.3.
1582: [19353], [19401], [19406] (false, d).
1583: [17263], [24626.7], [24627].
1584: [373] (d), [10541], [15507], [16641.7], 16908, 19354.
1585: [19354.1], 21077 (false), [23968].
1586: 16903.
1588: 1032 (false, d?).
1589: [17264].
1590: [24627a].
1599: 16904 (false), 24627a.3 (false), 6832.56.
1601: 3102 (false), 3106 (false, d?), 5724 (false).
1602: 742 (false), 17505 (false, d?).
1604: 1834 (false, d?), 6777 (false), 10432.7 (false), 19940.5 (false).
1605: 4868.3 (false), 24627a.3 (false).
1607: 25972.4 (false).
1608: 11025 (false), 25972.2 (false).
1609: 10928–8.3, 13452.
1611: 6832.58.
1613: 16647, 17274, 22128.
1614: 5161.5, 11318, 17275, 19072.3.

Biv: France — Rouen — *cont.*
1615: 20451.
1617–18: [17275.7?].
1619: 7072.6 (false).
1623: 7072.7 (false).
1625: 6832.60.
1626: 3073.5 (false), 14526 (false).
1627–28: [24733].
1630: [3605.5] (c?), 7234 (d), 11109, 16098.7, [16876.5] (d), 17277.3, 25779 (false), 25779.3–.5.
1631: 984–5.5, 1017, [11112], 21145–6.
1632: [3608.5], 4326.5 (false, d), [4535?], [10615.5(*A*3)], [12957], 16101.2 (false), [20001–1.5].
1633: 579, [2946], 4554 (false), [7234.5], [7238], [12958], [14123.5], 15188.7, [16101.4], [16101.6], [23991].
1634: [3605.7], [4874], [17001].
1635: 2321, 10928.6 (c), [18571] (c).
1636: 6832.62, [24736].
1637: [17277.7].
1638: [3073.7], [4875], [16101.7(*A*3)].
1639: 12173.5, [16162.7], [21628–8a].
1640: [4871.5].
1650: 984.5 (c).

Saint Omer.
F. Bellet, 1603–09
English College Press, 1608–40
C. Boscard, 1614–27
J. Heigham, 1614–31
G. Seutin, 1624–33?
Jeanne Boscard, 1630–39
1263: [13033.4] (d/error).
1511: [8448] (d/error).
1603: [19416].
1604: [19413], [19414], [19416].
1606: [19352].
1607: [19354.5], [19417].
1608: [3604.5–05], [19408], [24140.5–41], [25771].
1609: [6991.5–.7] (false), [15362], [15362.5], [19412], [22813], [25002].
1610: [1699], [14628], [16644], [19000], [24992].
1611: [8448] (d), [13122.5], [13840], [18999].
1612: [1700], [1702], [6383], [10914], [11111], [11538.5], [19409], [23938].
1613: [11021], [11022], [11114], [18334], [23987], [24993].
1614: [1699.5], [3941], [10912], [10916], [11023], 11728, [13996], [13996a], [13997], [13997a], [13997b], [15519], [16095.5(*A*3)], [24994], [26045].
1615: [11019.5(*A*3)], [16225], [17275.3(*A*3)], [18657], [20450 (*A*3)], 24924.5, [25003].
1616: [4960(*A*3)], [6384], [10403](*A*3)], 16096.5, [20967], [22948], [22963], [25069], [25290.7], [26049].
1617: [269], [1650] (false), [1837(*A*3)], [11116], [11320(*A*3)], 16232.5, [18000], [23212(*A*3)], [23529], [23532].
1618: 632.3, [715], [1838], [10675], 11314.2, [13998], [14569 (*A*3)], [15517], [16877], [19938], [21676].
1619: [1707], [4955], [5475], [11490], [14527], [18657.5], [20483], 20486, [26046].
1620: [910], [983], [3134], [4284], 4959, [10809], [11110.7] (false), [11315], 17276, [19354.6], [22964], [23531], [23989], 24627a.4.
1621: [741], [942.5], [1838.5], [3895.5], [5349.8] (d), [5350], [5350.4], [5350.7], [11020], [13576], [15518], [15524], 16098, [18327], [18658.5], [18659], [22812], [24731b].
1622: 1341, 1779, [1839], 4572, [5350], [5476], [5742.7], 10541.7, [11320a] (d), 13033, 13034, 13036, [13577], [17658], [18443], [18658(*A*: 2 eds.)], 18902, [19354.7], [19937.5], [20968], 22970, [25773], [26046.5].
1623: [575], 1023.5, [1839], [3801.5], [3902], [7000], [10910.4], [10916.5], [11118], [13033.4] (d), [14945.5], [16098.3(*A*3)], [16226], [16877.5], [17276.3], [18001], [18305], [18660], [24732], [26044], 26048.
1624: [13], 632.5, 934, 1837.3, 3606, [3895], [7454], [11113], 11617.6, [13033.6], [14475], 14570, [14570.3], [16878], [17542.7], [18306], [18661], [20487], 21693, 21697, [23528], [23989.5], [23990], [25070.5], [25289] (false).
1625: 535.7, [578], [3895.3], [3895.7], 4603, [6777.7], [10910.7–11], [10916.5], [11539], 14626, 16906, 17276.4, 17276.6, [17276.8], 21697.5, 22872.5, 23233.
1626: 1780, 4469, [4872] (false), [10911], [10916.5], [11033], [11540], [15117.3], [16227], [20585.5], [21316] (false).

Biv: France — Saint Omer — *cont.*
1627: [4912] (false), 12808.3, [17533], [21148–9], [22811].
1628: [11540] (d?).
1629: [21023] (false).
1630: [742.7], [743], [14502], 16922a, 17506.3, [18482], [21023a] (false), [21142], [21144], [21149.5] (d?), [22370], [24734], [25774], 25779.3 (note), 25779.5 (note).
1631: 985.5 (note), [1922(*A*3)], [4873] (false), [5576], 13037, [15117.7], [15523], 16099–100, [21150.5], 24748.5.
1632: [986], [3073.3] (false), [4625], [4871] (false), [10677], [16101.2?] (false), [16161.5], [16922a.3], [17181] (false), [20492] (false), [21147], [21150], [24140] (false).
1633: [577], [1844], [4264], [10676], [17506.5], [19354.9], [25071].
1634: [580], [6798.3], [10676.5], [13033.8], [13035], [16922a.7], [17093], [18333], [18984], [24735] (false), [25778].
1635: [4625.5], [12144.5], [18331], [21102].
1636: [4263.5].
1637: [4263.7], [13469], [25070].
1638: [1841], [1842], [5645.5], [11110], [24737?] (false), [25775], [25780].
1639: [4572.5], [11115], [11117], [15117], [16162.3].
1640: [576], [20200.7] (d?), [20308], [25772].

Savoy.
F. de Turona, *pseud.*, 1542?
M. Boys, *pseud.*, 1548? 1560?
1542: 3759.5 (false, d?). **1548:** 3760–1 (false, d?). **1560:** 3763 (false, d?).

Strassburg (Argentina).
J. Schott, 1527–28
F. Foxe, *pseud.*, 1530.
B. Beckeneth, *pseud.*, 1531
W. Köpfel, 1542?–44?
W. Rihel & heirs, 1554–57
heirs of W. Köpfel, 1555?–56
B. Jobin? 1575
E. Zetzner, 1629–30
1527: [24223.3] (d).
1528: [1462.7] (d).
1530: 2370 (false), 13828.4 (false).
1531: 2777 (false).
1542: [3759.5] (false, d?).
1544: [292] (d?).
1554: 1716 (false), 1730 (false), 13457 (false), [16980] (false), 21683 (false).
1555: [10023.7?] (d?), [17562–2a] (false), [17563], [20175], [24673.5] (d).
1556: [17200], [20175a], [20178], [21048] (d).
1557: [658] (d).
1559: 1005–6 (false).
1575: [1464.4] (false), [1464.5] (false).
1628: 20577 (false).
1629: 14472.3.
1630: 14472.5.

Toulouse (Tholosa).
R. Colomiès, 1603
A. de Courteneufve, 1603
A. Du Brel, *pseud.*, 1606
1603: 18415. **1606:** 5725 (false).

Venes.
R. Colomiès, 1603
A. de Courteneufve, 1603
1603: 18415.

Verdun.
M. Marchant, *pseud.*, 1588
1588: 15212.5 (false).

Bv. GERMANY

All items below have Germany supplied or queried in square brackets in STC. The imprints that do appear are false.

1531: 15346 (d). **1537:** 13082? (false, d?). **1557:** 10014? **1558:** 10015–5.5? (d). **1589:** 9198.5 (false). **1596:** 13555.7? (false). **1616:** 11945? **1622:** 13189.5. **1625:** 5646? (false). **1631:** 17181.7(*A*3)?

Bv: Germany — *cont.*

Augsburg (Augusta, Augusta Vindelicorum).

A. Anonymous, *pseud.*, 1545
P. Ulhard, c. 1550
C. Mang, 1614
J. Libius, *pseud.*, 1618
B. Faber, *pseud.*, 1620–21

1545: 10488 (false). **1550:** 6832.24 (c?). **1614:** 1843. **1617:** 1650 (false). **1618:** 25601 (false). **1620:** 14050.5 (false), 20286.3 (false). **1621:** 20286.7 (false).

Aurich (Auryk).

J. Troost, *pseud.*, 1541

1541: 21804 (false).

Bonn.

L. von der Muelen, 1542–45

1542: [3764] (false, d). **1543:** [24353] (false). **1545:** [24355] (false).

Cologne.

H. Quentell, 1492–96
E. Cervicornus, 1520–35
H. Fuchs? 1525
P. Quentell, 1525
M. von Neuss, 1526
J. Soter? 1535
J. Gymnicus, 1544
heirs of A. Birckman 1, 1561–68
N. Bohmberg, *pseud.*? 1574–79
W. Lützenkirchen, 1610

1492: [696.2].
1496: [16110] (d).
1520: 6044a.5.
1525: [2823] (d), [15578.5] (d).
1526: [16778] (d).
1535: [2063?].
1544: 24350.5.
1561: 13433.
1562: 24366.
1568: 24367.
1574: [7573] (d?), [10843] (d?), [18550] (d?), [18551] (d?), [18554] (d?), [18555] (d?), [18557–7.5] (d?), [18560], [18562], [18564.5] (d), [21529].
1575: [1858], [10681.5] (d), [18548.5], [18549] (d), [18552] (d?), [18556] (d?), [18558] (d?), [18561] (d?), [18563] (d?), [18564] (d?).
1579: [77].
1600: 5638.5 (false).
1610: 1431.21.
1620: 3607 (false), 11110.7 (false).
1621: 3607.5 (false).
1623: 7435 (false).
1639: 1019 (false).

Emden.

J. Aurik, *pseud.*, 1534
J. Gheylliaert, 1554
S. Mierdman, 1554
N. Hill, 1554–56
E. van der Erve, 1554–66

1534: 14829 (false).
1554: [15069] (false), [16571] (d?), [16571a], [17863.5] (false), [18309.5?] (false), [19890] (false, d).
1555: [673] (c), [10024] (d?), [18797] (false), [21046], [21799.2] (d?), [21854] (d), [24356] (d?), [24361] (false), [26140] (false).
1556: [921] (d?), [5999] (d?), [6152], [15693] (false), [16574], [17864] (d?), [18798] (false), [19892] (d?), [21047.3], [21047.7], [25009] (false).
1560: [16571a.5(*A*3)?].
1563: [16572], [16572.1(*A*3)].
1566: [1040], 3964, [4065], [6079] (d), [10389] (d), [10390] (d), [10391] (d).

Frankfurt am Main.

C. Egenolff, 1554?
T. de Bry, 1590
S. Feyerabend, 1590
J. Wechel, 1590
heirs of D. Turner, *pseud.*, 1601
heirs of A. de Renialme, *pseud.*? 1605?–07?
M. Hulsius, 1619?
J. K. Unckel, 1619—23
S. Latomus, 1620
J. N. Stoltzenberger, 1628
W. Fitzer, 1628—29
W. Hoffman, 1635

1554: [16571] (d?).
1590: 12786.
1594: [19557.3?].
1601: 1884 (false).
1605: 12685 (d?).

Bv: Germany — *cont.*

1607: 12685.3 (d?).
1608: [44?].
1613: [4631].
1614: [25602.5?] (false).
1617: 1501.3(*A*3), [24311?] (d).
1618: 24310.5.
1619: 4869 (note & *A*3), 18045–7.
1620: [11329] (d).
1621: 11329.4–.5 (false).
1622: 11329.7–.8 (false).
1623: 11329.9–30 (false), 11745.7.
1624: 11330.2–.3 (false).
1625: 11330.4 (false).
1626: 7548 (false), 11330.7 (false).
1627: 11330.8 (false).
1628: 10933.
1629: 20567.3.
1635: 21537.3.

Hamburg.

P. Lang, 1620

1620: 16688, [16690] (d). **1628:** 20649 (false). **1632:** 14555 (false?). **1639:** [12807?]. **1640:** 24260.

Hanau (Hanovia).

W. Antonius, 1594–1607?
J. Radaeus, *pseud.*, 1602
D. Aubri, 1607

1594: [18100]. **1602:** 20146.5 (false). **1604:** [23461]. **1605:** [11741]. **1607:** 2787, [12685.3] (d?). **1610:** [1708] (false).

Heidelberg.

J. Mayer, 1565
M. Schirat, 1574–75
G. Voegelin, 1611
J. Lancelot, 1614
A. Cambier, 1614

1565: 16575. **1574:** [24184], [25442]. **1575:** [4714], 10550 (false), [25443]. **1611:** [13906a]. **1614:** 1431.24A. **1620:** 14713.5 (false). **1622:** 24915 (false).

Leipzig (Lipsia, Lipse).

U. Hoff, *pseud.*, 1541
V. Bapst, 1548
W. Günter, 1551

1541: 17798 (false, d). **1548:** [16459] (false).**1551:** 16423.

Lüneberg.

1532: 61 (false).

Marburg (Marborch, Malborow).

H. Luft, *pseud.*, 1528–37
J. Philoponos, *pseud.*, 1538
P. Egenolff, 1610

1528: 24446 (false), 24454 (false), 24455.5 (false).
1529: 10493 (false), 11394 (false).
1530: 1462.5 (false), 2350 (false), 3021 (false), 24465 (false).
1535: 24447 (false).
1537: 24447.3 (false).
1538: 20193 (false).
1546: 848 (false), 851 (false).
1547: 850 (false), 851 (false).
1610: [22868] (d).

Münster.

C. Willems, *pseud.*, 1533

1533: 11381 (false).

Neustadt an der Haardt (Neostadium Palatinorum).

heirs of W. Harnisch, 1603
N. Schramm, 1603–08

1600: 26121.3 (note), 26121.7 (note). **1603:** 26121a. **1608:** 26121a.3.

Nürnberg (Noriberga).

N. Twonson, *pseud.*, 1533
J. Günther, 1541
J. Daubman, 1548–49
K. Dietrich, 1599–1600

1533: 24468 (false). **1541:** 6832.9. **1545:** 3765 (false), 5889 (false). **1546:** 25590–0.5 (false). **1548:** 6832.19. **1549:** 6832.20. **1599:** 2792.5, 2792.6. **1600:** 2792.5, 2792.7.

Bv: Germany — *cont.*
Siegen (Sigena Nassoviorum).
C. Corvinus, 1596
1596: 25363.3(*A*3).

Stuttgart.
J. W. Roesslin 1, 1616–19
1616: 25186. **1619:** 25185a.5.

Wesel (Wesalia).
H. Nicolson, *pseud.*, 1546
D. van der Straten, 1546–49
J. Lambrecht? 1553–56
H. Singleton? 1555–56
P. A. de Zuttere? 1557–58
1543: 14826 (false).
1545: 4797.3 (false).
1546: [848] (false), 1270 (false), 1462.9 (false), [14717] (d), [16984 (*A*3)] (d?).
1547: [850] (false), [1305] (d?), 17789–9.5 (false).
1548: [1287] (false, d?), [1295], [15180] (d?), [17320].
1549: 1296.
1553: [1307?] (false), [4392?] (false), [11587?] (false).
1554: [1716?] (false), [1730?] (false), [13457?] (false), [15059.5?], [21683?] (false).
1555: [3480.5?] (d?), [9981?] (false, d), [17821?] (d?), [17822?] (d?), [18312–3?], [23619?], [24219?] (d?), [25249?] (d?), [25251?] (d?), [25252?] (d?), [25256?] (d?).
1556: [2426.8?] (d?), [3504.5?] (d?), [5996?] (d?), [7376.5?], [10432?], [15066?] (d), [15074.6?] (d?), [18310?] (d?), [21777?].
1557: [19078?] (d), [24168–8.5?], [24170?].
1558: [24167.7?], [24169?], [24170?], [24174?].

Wittenberg.
H. Luft, *pseud.*, 1547
N. Dorcaster, *pseud.*, 1554
1547: 17314–4a (false).
1554: 5630 (false), 6934.5 (false), 15059 (false).

Worms.
P. Schoeffer, 1526
1526: [2824] (d?), [24438] (d).

Würzburg.
A. M. Volmar, 1628
1628: 1202.

HOLLAND *See* The Netherlands

Bvi. ITALY

Ferrara.
B. Mammarello, 1591
1591: 13218 (note).

Florence.
B. Sermartelli, *pseud.*, 1600
1600: 4954 (false).

Loreto.
F. Serafini, 1635
1635: 23884a.4, 23884a.6, 23884a.8.

Milan.
V. Girardoni? 1567–68
1567: [21076]. **1568:** 5450.5. **1584–94:** [21076.5?].

Naples.
G. M. Scotto, *pseud.*, 1563
O. Beltrano, 1635
1563: 20118a (false). **1635:** 17920.5.

Padua.
P. Meietti, 1592
1592: 1431.12.

Palermo.
(heirs of) A. Antonielli, *pseud.*, 1584–87
1584: 17159–9.5 (false), 17167 (false). **1587:** 17163 (false, d).

Piacenza.
heirs of G. Giolito, *pseud.*, 1587
1587: 17161 (false).

Bvi: Italy — *cont.*
Rome.
M. A. Constantius, *pseud.*, 1555
Curtigiane, *pseud.*, 1556
1553: 1307 (false), 4392 (false), 11587 (false). **1554:** 15059.5 (false). **1555:** 24361 (false). **1556:** 15693–3.5 (false). **1588:** 17158 (false). **1617:** 1897 (false).

Turin.
G. V. del Pernetto, *pseud.*, 1589
1589: 10752.7 (false).

Venice.
R. de Novimago, 1483
J. Herzog de Landoia, 1493–95
M. Sessa & heirs, 1541–82
F. Bindoni, 1549
M. Pasini, 1549
D. Giglio, c. 1550?
J. Gryphius, 1551
D. Nicolini, 1563
G. Alberti, 1606
1483: 15795. **1493:** 15856. **1494:** [15797] (d), [15800] (d), 15874, 16167, 16168. **1495:** 15801, [15801.5] (d?). **1541:** 6832.7. **1548:** 6832.17. **1549:** 6832.22. **1550:** 6832.26 (c?). **1551:** 20779. **1563:** 6832.36. **1568:** 6832.38. **1582:** 6832.52. **1584:** 3936 (false), 3938 (false). **1606:** 1431.19. **1627:** 1431.29.

Bvii. MONACO

Monaco.
G. Swartz, *pseud.*, 1586
1586: 19769.7 (false).

Bviii. THE NETHERLANDS

Most of the following have only The Netherlands or Holland supplied, often with a query, in square brackets in STC. Four items (2735, 11930, 13738, 13738.5) actually have The Netherlands in the imprint.

1563: [5742.10?] (d?).
1570: [15615?] (c).
1578: [6080?] (d).
1579: [14258(*A*3)?] (false), [14258.3(*A*3)?] (false).
1581: [12000.5?], [14258.5] (false).
1583: [3910.5?] (d?).
1588: [9194.5] (false), [9194.7] (false), [9194.8] (false).
1595: [14663.5?] (d),
1596: [9205.3] (false).
1599: [10017.5] (false).
1603: [8323.5] (false).
1609: [3844.5?] (d), [3844.7?] (d?), [3877.7?] (d?), [3889.7?] (c?), [17845.3(*A*3)] (false).
1610: [17845.7(*A*3)] (false).
1613: [22877.4?] (d?).
1615: [13054?].
1616: 11930 (d?).
1618: [2180?] (false, c?), [2499.7?] (d?), [13684.5?], [24251.7?].
1620: [17810(*A*)?], [20866?], [22101] (d/repeat).
1621: [4830.5?] (d?), [14650.5(*A*3)?], [22086.5?] (d), [24268.3] (d).
1622: [18507.39?], [22069] (false), [22069a–a.5] (false), [22080] (false).
1623: [10003?] (d), [13264.8] (false), [13385?], [22075] (d), [22079] (false), [22081] (false).
1624: [22089] (d), [22097a(*A*3)?] (d?), [22101] (d), [22102] (d).
1625: [7751.6] (false).
1626: [902] (false, d?), [7548?] (false), [25228.5?].
1627: [8868.3] (false).
1628: [3474?], [4359?].
1630: [23868?] (d?).
1631: [16804?].
1632: 2735.
1636: [4363?], [4363.5?].
1637: [9093.5?] (false).
1638: [664.7] (c), [4362.5?], 13738, [15591.5], [15648?].
1639: 13738.5, [21905b.5] (false).
1640: [223.5?] (false), [3517], [6120].
after 1640? [2316.5?] (false), [2330.2–.6?] (false), [2680.2–.6] (false), [2954?].

Bviii: The Netherlands — *cont.*

Amsterdam.

Names below in italic were Englishmen who occasionally published items in Amsterdam but were not printers or members of the book trade.

J. Peterson, *pseud.*, 1547?
J. Watleer, *pseud.*, 1585?
C. Claeszoon, 1593–1605
I. H., *pseud.*, 1604
G. Thorp, 1604–22
Z. Heyns, 1605
J. Theunisz, 1605–06
J. Hondius, 1605–11
R. de Baudous, 1608
H. Laurensz, 1608–28
W. J. Blaeu, 1612–35
J. Veseler & widow, 1618–27
P. van der Keere, 1620–21
J. Jansson 2, 1620–38
B. Jansz, *pseud.*? 1621
successors of G. Thorp, 1623–36
C. J. Visscher 2, c. 1625
R. Plater, 1625–29
J. F. Stam, 1629–c. 1650?
H. Hondius 2, 1630–38
E. Cloppenburg, 1631
R. Raven? 1631
C. G. van Breughel, 1632
J. van Hilten, 1633
J. A. Colom, 1633–40
T. Crafford, 1633–44
J. Williams? *pseud.*, c. 1635
T. L., 1637–38
'Richt Right' Press, 1637–40
T. Stafford, 1640–44
'Cloppenburg' Press, 1640–41

1547: 95 (false, d?).
1585: 693.3 (false, d?).
1589: [1526.5].
1593: 1431.13.
1596: [18433.7?].
1597: 5331, [5346?].
1598: 1431.16, 5345, [6281?].
1599: [5337?], [6280.5?] (d?).
1600: [14658?].
1602: [7298], 14787, 14787.2 (d?), 14787.6 (d?).
1603: [12340?] (d), 14664, 14787.4, 14787.8.
1604: [238?], [239], [1527] (d?), 3526 (false), [3856.5?].
1605: 1431.18, [3844?], [3848?], [3849–9.5(*A*)], [3863(*A*)], 3867.5, [3879?], [3881(*A*)], [24931.5].
1606: [1524] (d?), [2780(*A*)], 3867.7, [3891?], [14662].
1607: 228, [18435].
1608: [234], [2781?], 3875, [3878?], 11811 (A3 and B2b in note to 11810), [13395?], [14660], 18553, [20560.3?] (c?).
1609: 235, [3879.5], [14659?], [20605].
1610: [220.5], [3868], [3877?] (d?), [3883], 5450, [21109].
1611: [221], 3754, [3876], [3887.5?] (d?), [7751?], [7751.2?], [13053?], [13053.5?], [13055?], [14662.5(*A*3)?] (d), [14663?], [19608.5].
1612: 2407, 3110, [5449], 11212, [13056?], [15351.7].
1613: 209, [3867?] (d?), 12857.8, [20620].
1614: 4189, [20620].
1615: [229], [240], [556?], [1527.3?] (d?), 3755, [21111].
1616: [210], [5556], [14330] (d).
1617: [212], [2411], [14661(*A*3)?].
1618: [214], [230] (d/error), [2411], 19098.
1619: [215], [216], [4364], 12858 (false), [23235], [25647].
1620: [236], [2731], 3111, 3215 (false), [4354], [4355], [4365], 18507.1, —.2.
1621: [211], [563.7(*A*)?], 1037 (false), [1640], [4352], [4361.5], 16839, 18507.3, —.4, —.5, —.6, —.7 (d), —.8–.9 (false?), —.10 (d), —.11 (d), —.12 (d), —.13 (false?), —.14, —.15, —.16, —.17, —.18–.25 (false?), [20408.5], 20409, [20410], [20411], [22015], 22131, 25043.
1622: [559], 1431.27, 3112, 13598 (false), [21874].
1623: [226], [560], 1431.28, [2775].
1624: [222], 1431.28A, [4356], [4357], [4358], [10404] (d?), [13531.5], [15431], [15432], [18837], [21107a].
1625: 1106, [1580] (c), 3112.5, 3113, [14425] (d), [15431.5], 18936 (c), [21108], [21112], [21492], [24305].
1626: [4892?], 11130, 13031.7.
1627: [24903].
1628: [230–1], 231.5, 5028, 15177 (false), [20577] (false), 20766 (false).
1629: 1106.5, [2274] (false, c?), 2415–5.2, [4153.7], [15428.5] (d), [15429] (d?).
1630: [227], [722], [4748], 16699, [19798.5], 20202.
1631: 1431.31, [11128.5] (d), [20484], 23050, [23605], [24402], [24403] (d?).
1632: [551?], [2734.5], [2735?], [3473], 4574.5, [12531.7?] (d), [12534.2?] (d), [13071], [18789(*A*3)?] (d).
1633: [551?], [555], 903.5, 904.5, [2177] (false, d), 2309, [2499.4] (d), 5575.2, [16394.7?], 18507.359, [—.360] (d), [—.361] (d).

Bviii: The Netherlands — Amsterdam — *cont.*

1634: 551.5, [739?], [1101], 1571.5, [4574], [6311?], [7678], [14555?] (false?), [21116?].
1635: 1614.5 (false? c?), [1615?] (false, c?), 1973.5–74, 3113.3, [3450], [3753], [4137.7] (d?), [5846.4], [11129], [17976.5(*A*3)?], 18780, 18781, 19097, [21107.5], 22079.5(*A*3).
1636: [4134], [4137.9], [4140.7], [4142], 17827, [20456], [20476], [21107.7], [22176?], [24306?].
1637: [1569], 5575.3, 13726.4, 18202, [20454], [20474], [20475].
1638: [1570.5], [2328.5?] (false, c?), 13728.5, [15309], [15591], [15599], 17451, 17828, 20221.3 (c), [22013] (d), [22026.6], [22026.8], [22032] (d), [22032.5] (d), 22496.5, 24957, [25587], 26125.
1639: [2179] (false, c), [2499.6] (c), [4575], 5575.5, [7367.5], [7372.5], 12035, 13031.8, [15596], [15598], [20889.3], [21110], [21904.7] (false), [21908] (false), [21908.5] (false), [22057] (false), [24844a.3], 24958, [25229.5], [26126?], 26126.5.
1640: [222.5], [223.5], 232, [1206], 2344, 2344.5 (d/repeat), 3113.7, [3533?], [4148], [4154], 5575.5–.7, [6805.3], [7435.5], [10008], [10649], [11324], [12341], [13855], [13917], [18436?], [20467], [21916.5], [21921], [21921.5], [21924] (false), [21926] (false), [21928], 26127.
after 1640? [2174–6] (false), [2178] (false), [2328.7?] (false), [2499–9.3], [2499.5], [2692.5?] (false), 16414.3 (note).
1641: [10649].
1644 and later: [2316.5?] (false), [2328.8–.9?] (false), [2330?] (false), 2344.5, [2680.1?] (false), 16613(*A*3, note).

Arnhem.

J. Jansson 1, 1620

1620: [13582] (d).

Delft.

C. Jansz, 1582
B. H. Schinckel, 1598–1613
A. J. Cloeting, 1630–31
J. P. Waelpot, 1631–38
A. Jacobs, *pseud.*, 1633?–35?
James Moxon, 1637

1581: 15207.5, 15208 (d), 15209 (false).
1582: 16572.2(*A*3).
1598: 1431.16.
1605: 1431.18.
1613: 1431.22.
1630: [12535], 13262.
1631: 1431.33, 12533, 22142.7.
1632: 11133, 11135, 12534.4.
1633: 1612 (false, d?), 12860, 13263.
1634: [21009.5].
1635: 1616–6.5 (false, c?).
1637: 13264, 13265.
1638: 13264.2, [13264.4].

Deventer.

R. Pafraet, 1489

1489: 696.1.

Dordrecht (Dort).

I. J. Canin, 1597–1603
A. Canin, 1601
J. Waters, 1609–23
N. Vincentsz, 1623
H. van Esch, 1639

1589: [1526].
1590: [1518?], [1518.5?], [12339?].
1591: [1517?] (d?), [1523?].
1596: [1519?] (c?).
1597–98: 12498.
1599: 11513.
1601: 2184.5, 2702, 2901, 16588.
1603: 2903.
1609: [20607].
1610: [20608].
1611: 20095.
1612: 551.7.
1614: 3532.
1615: [11929], 12066, 12067.
1616: [11928] (false, d?), [11930] (d?).
1619: 3212 (d), 3212.5 (false, d), 10811 (d), 11360.3, 12859.
1620: 3210 (false), 23751 (false).
1622: 23797 (false).

Bviii: The Netherlands — Dordrecht — *cont.*
1623: 25939.
1624: 22072 (false).
1639: 19099.

Flushing (Vlissingen).
M. A. van der Nolck, 1613–23
1613: 1431.23. **1620:** 10812 (false). **1621:** 25842, 25846. **1622:** 25843. **1623:** 25847.

Gorinchem (Goricum).
A. Janss, *pseud.*, 1624
1624: 22103–4 (false).

Gouda.
P. Rammazeyn, 1626
1626: 25234 (note).

Groningen (Grunning).
1541: 24217 (false).

Haarlem.
G. Roman, 1597
H. T. Kranepoel, 1629
1597: 19489. **1629:** 22941.5.

The Hague (Haga Comitis, 's Gravenhage).
A. Hendricksz, 1595–97
H. J. van Wouw, & widow & heirs, 1613–31
A. Meuris, *pseud.*, 1621
A. Clarke, *pseud.*, 1621
H. Hondius 1, 1633–37
F. van der Spruyt, 1640
1595: 7581.
1597: 9208.6.
1607: 11810.
1608: 11810, 11811.
1613: 1431.24.
1620: [7550.5?] (d?), 10814 (false, d?).
1621: 11353 (false), 17670.5 (false), 17672 (false), [18459.5?] (d), 18507.28 (false), 22083 (false).
1622: 17728.7 (false), 18462 (false), 18507.36–.37 (false).
1629: 21718(*A*3) (false).
1630: 15313, 18469 (d?).
1631: 18463.
1633: 13263.
1637: 13265, 13685 (note).
1640: 13264.7.

Leeuwarden.
P. H. van Campen, 1579
1579: [17450(*A*3)].

Leiden (Leida, Lugdunum Batavorum, Lydden?).
J. Paets Jacobszoon, 1582–93
J. Bouwensz, 1585–86
C. Plantin, 1585–86
A. Verschout, 1586
F. Raphelengius, 1586–97
T. Basson, 1586–1609
A. del Bosco, *pseud.*, 1588
J. de La Croy, *pseud.*, 1589
Officina Plantiniana, 1592–97
C. Guyot, 1603
J. Marcus, 1610
H. L. van Haestens, 1610–28
J. A. van der Marsce, 1614
J. C. van Dorp, 1616
W. Brewster, 1617–19
J. Maire, 1617–39
P. Muller, 1622
J. Masse? *pseud.*, 1625?
B. & A. Elzevir, 1633–36
W. Christiaens van der Boxe, 1634–44
T. Maire, 1636
1582: 24806.
1585: 689–9.3 (false), 1431.8.
1586: 7287.7, 11728.8 (false), 17847.8, 25340, 25438.
1587: 7285.5, 7287.5, [7288.5] (d), 7289.4, [7289.5] (d), [15569.5] (d).
1588: 15414.6 (false).
1589: 11735 (false).
1592: 15703.
1593: 1431.13, 17523.
1597: 24893.3.
1599: 18468.5.
1603: 14786.
1609: 9211.2, 9211.3–.4 (repeat).
1610: 14336, [14337].
1614: [21115(*A*3)].
1616: 3756.

Bviii: The Netherlands — Leiden — *cont.*
1617: [6973], [10849], [15647], [24186], 24893.5, [25333].
1618: [4709], [4929], [6469], [6876], [12862], 19595.7, [21115a], 24893.7.
1619: [4360], [6877], [10567].
1622: 1431.27.
1625: 17884(*A*3) (false, d?).
1633: [2798], [2798.5], [2813.3].
1634: 12581.
1636: [1576?], [22175.3], 22175.7.
1637: [1568], [1572], [1573], [1574], [1575], [4788?], [11896], [16452].
1638: [1570], [13738], [16452.5], [22026.4?] (d), [22031.5?] (d).
1639: [552], 12399.3, [13738.5], [26126].
1640: [2344], [2344.5] (d/repeat), 16560.5 (c), [21919.5] (false), [21923.5] (false), [21927.7].
1644: [2344.5] (d).

Middelburg.
R. Schilders, 1581?–1616
D. van Respeawe, *pseud.*? 1584
A. Schilders, *pseud.*, 1620
H. van der Hellen, 1620–21
H. Bosselarius, 1631
widow & heirs of S. Moulert, 1631
G. Moulert, 1637
1581: [11888?].
1582: 3910–0.3.
1583: [12861], [12862.5].
1584: [10765.5], [10766], [10766.3], [10766.5], 19063 (false?), 19356.
1586: [10772], 16568.
1587: [2018(*A*3)] (d?), 2769, 5377, [7584] (d), [10771], 16569.
1588: 331 (d?), [7585], [10767] (d), [10768] (d?), 10768.5 (d?), 10778, [24183].
1589: [10872.5] (d).
1590: [4803.3(*A*)?], [6676] (d?), [6680.5], [6680.7] (d?), [6682.5] (d?), [6730], [6730.5] (d), [6732] (d), [6733] (false), 10776–7, [18106] (d?).
1592: [1521(*A*3)] (d).
1593: [10400] (d?).
1594: 2770, 16584, [24055(*A*3)], [24055.5(*A*3)].
1596: 2701, [4706].
1597: [3845.5] (d?), 3862, 3862a, 4387a, [17819].
1598: [149], [14340].
1599: 2499.9, [6282], [6287], 6350–0.5 (false, c?), [10872.5] (d/error), [13721], 14335, 16587, [20616], [24273].
1600: [14333], [18070], [18070.5], 20617.
1601: [20557], 25330.
1602: 2507.5, 10765, 16570, 16589, [18542], [18542.5], 18891.
1603: [3855], 18931–1a (false, c?).
1604: [3528], [3843], [3856], [3892], [3892.5], [5343], [14052], [14338], [23318].
1605: [3531], [4585], [5338], [6572.5].
1606: [63], [14037], [16450].
1607: [19294], [22877.3].
1608: [22876].
1609: [3858], [3872?], [3889.3] (d?), [14339], [19607?], [22875], [22877].
1610: [3877.3?] (d?), [3884], 11134, [11915], 13031.2, [16451].
1611: [3847] (d?), [3848.5?], [3857–7.5?], [3882].
1612: [14332].
1613: [14328].
1614: 11146, 11150.
1615: [4803.5(*A*)].
1616: 11131, 11136.
1620: 11351–1.3 (false), 11356 (false), 25844.
1621: 18460.3 (false).
1628: 20649.1–.7 (false).
1630: 18932 (false, c).
1631: 1431.32.
1637: 11596.5.
1640: 18933 (false, c).

Rotterdam.
The name in italic below was an Englishman who published two books but was neither a printer nor a member of the book trade.
M. S., *pseud.*, 1626
J. B., *pseud.*, 1626
P. van Waesberghe, 1627–39
A. Nering, 1631
I. van Waesberghe, 1635–36
H. Tutill, 1638
widow of M. Bastiaensz, 1639
T. Lappadge, 1640

Bviii: The Netherlands — Rotterdam — *cont.*
1613: 18285(*A*3) (false, d). **1615:** 23804 (false). **1626:** 1042–3 (false). **1627:** 4863.7. **1631:** 2632, 19798.3. **1635:** 6312. **1636:** 6310. **1638:** 2737. **1639:** 24869, 24869.5. **1640:** 3732, 4129.5.

Utrecht (Utrick).
S. de Roy, 1615
C. de Passe 2, 1615
A. van Herwijck, 1624
J. Schellem, *pseud.*, 1626
Æ. Roman, 1638
1615: 19459. **1620:** [6345.2?] (d?). **1624:** 20946.1–.3 (false), 22064, 22065–8 (false), [22105–5.5] (d). **1626:** 22085 (false). **1638:** 7076.5.

Zutphen.
A. J. van Aelst, 1619?–20?
1619: 11812 (d?). **1620:** 11812.5 (c?).

Bix. POLAND

Gdansk (Danzig, Danswijck).
H. van Loven, *pseud.*, 1609–10
A. Huenefeld, 1639
1609: 17845.3 (false). **1610:** 17845.7 (false). **1639:** [12478.5].

Kraków (Cracow).
1576: 10551 (false).

Raków (Racovia).
Site of the 17th-century university and printing facilities of the Socinians, northeast of Kraków, roughly halfway between Chmielnik and Sandomierz.
1609: 20083.3(*A*) (false).

Bx. PORTUGAL

Lisbon.
S. Lopes? 1597?
1597: [19087.5] (d?).

Bxi. SPAIN

León.
1594: 19624.5 (false, d).

Salamanca.
A. Tavernier, 1603
1603: [21595] (d).

Seville.
F. Perez? 1604
1604: [25068] (false).

Bxii. SWEDEN

Malmö.
J. Hoochstraten, 1533–35?
1533: 19525. **1533/34:** [471.7]. **1535:** [14667?] (false).

Stockholm.
I. Meurer, 1626
1626: 17658.5.

Bxiii. SWITZERLAND

Basel (Basle).
M. Wenssler, 1489
T. Emlos, *pseud.*, 1540?
R. Bonifante, *pseud.*, 1542
A. Edmonds, *pseud.*, 1554
C. Mense, *pseud.*, 1560
P. Vallemond, *pseud.*, 1573
T. Guérin, 1573–79
K. von Waldkirch, 1597–99
H. Pistus, *pseud.*, 1612
1489: [16165] (d). **1540:** 22897 (false, d?). **1542:** 3047 (false). **1543:** 24353–4 (false). **1554:** 19890 (false). **1560:** 14794 (false). **1573:** [13844] (false), 13847.5 (false). **1577:** [4715]. **1579:** [15211] (false). **1582:** [11787?] (false). **1597:** 3846. **1598:** 3860. **1599:** 3862a.3. **1612:** 1501 (false).

Bxiii: Switzerland — *cont.*
Geneva.
M. Wood (Boys), *pseud.*, 1545–60?
R. Houdouyn, 1556
J. Poullain, 1556–58
J. Crespin, 1556–70
C. Badius, 1557
M. Blanchier, 1557
A. Reboul, 1558
R. Hall, 1559–60
Z. Durand, 1560–71?
J. Stoer, 1602–34
E. Le Preux, 1613
P. Estienne? 1615
P. Albert, 1619
E. Gamonet, 1629
1545: 1303 (false), 14823 (false).
1548: 3760–1 (false, d?).
1555: 26140 (false).
1556: [4380], [11884.5], 16561, 16565.
1557: [2383.6], 2871, [15611.7], [15612], [15613], [16561.5].
1558: 12020, 15063, 15067, [15070], 16561a.
1559: 2384, 15064.
1560: 2093, 2871.5, 3763 (false, d?), [15060], [16561a.5(*A*3)].
1561: 2095, 16563.
1562: 2095.
1566: [16578].
1568–70: 2106.
1571: [16579–9.3].
1580: 24185.
1584: [16581?], [4904.5?] (false).
1602: 1431.17A (d/error?).
1604: [13790].
1608: 1431.17A (d?), [1431.19A].
1613: [12619], [17045].
1615: [14272].
1619: 21805.9 (note).
1621: 22830.5.
1622: [1431.26].
1629: 16826.5.
1634: 1431.34.

Zurich (Tigurum).
C. Froschauer 1, 1541?–53
O. Jacobson, *pseud.*, 1543
A. Fries, 1547–49?
A. Gessner, 1551?–53
C. Froschauer 2, 1570–79
J. Wolf, 1595
1541: [5888] (d?). **1543:** 1309 (false), 14556 (false), [17793?], 26138–8.5 (false). **1547:** 13741, 13745. **1548:** 26139 (false). **1549:** [13746] (d?). **1550:** [361], 2079.8, 2090 (note), 2859.7. **1551:** [16576] (d?). **1553:** 4811, 6832.32. **1570:** 6832.44. **1574:** [19292a]. **1579:** 6832.48. **1595:** 6832.54.

C. FICTITIOUS PLACES

All the places below are fictitious, and the printers' names are pseudonyms when any are given at all.

Albionopolis.
Theophilus Faber, 1613–14
Ruardus Phigrus, 1616
Rufus Lipsius, 1616
1613: 25602. **1614:** 25602.5, 25605.5. **1616:** 25604, 25605.

Altmore.
M. H., 1621
1621: 18507.26, —.27.

Antipodes.
1616: 11928 (d?).

Bengodi.
1584: 19911.5, 19912.

Cosmopolis.
Theophilus Pratum, 1611–12
Gulielmus Fonti-silvius, 1615
1611: 25596, —.5. **1612:** 25597. **1615:** 25240.

Elysium.
1624: 20946.4, —.5, —.6, —.7, —.8.

C: Fictitious Places — *cont.*

Helicon.
1622: 22080.

Jericho.
Thomas Trauth, 1542
1542: 3764 (d).

Kalykow.
1554: 15069.

Lutetia Britannorum.
Isaac Jacobi, 1609
1609: 6991.5–.7.

N.
1594: 19398. **1601:** 18858.

Nova Belgia.
1640: 223.5, 224.

Oenozythopolis.
1617: 3585.

C: Fictitious Places — *cont.*

Pancridge.
1613: 23750.

Paradise.
1624: 22084, 22084a. **1642:** 22084 (d/error).

Pesclavium.
Baocius Sultaceterus, 1589
1589: 10511.

Pomadie.
1639: 17923 (d).

S. A.
1565: 17564.

Utopia.
1613: 23780 sold in. **1629:** 11944.

Vinegia.
Andrea Muschio, 1587
1587: 12004.

INDEX 3: SELECTED LONDON INDEXES

Although alternate forms for 'London' are transcribed in STC occasionally (the Welsh *Llundain*, e.g. 2745) or more regularly (the Latin *Augusta Trinobantum*, e.g. 3222.5–.5, 15083.5 (false), 15370.5, 16434, 21764), this name has not normally been recorded or supplied as a place of printing or sale since it is reasonably estimated that 80 to 85 per cent of STC items were published there. Items with a London printer's or publisher's name appearing or supplied in STC ordinarily appear *only* in Index 1 under the appropriate name. A few exceptions considered to be potentially useful to scholars are included in sections A and B below. However, since the exact nature of these indexes had not been established at the time the original slips for the printers' and publishers' index were made, it is likely that there are some inadvertent omissions.

A. SOME GENUINE LONDON PRINTING

Included below are three kinds of items in STC: 1) those having 'London' as the *only* word appearing or supplied in the imprint or occasionally in a note; 2) those having 'London' supplied *and queried* in the imprint whether or not a printer's name has also been supplied; and 3) those with false or anomalous imprints, listed here under the date they actually were printed in London. In the last category 'anom.' distinguishes anomalous imprints, a full list of which is in Index 4. An item identified as 'false' gives somewhere other than London as the purported place of printing; the term 'forged' has been arbitrarily reserved for items reproducing or simulating an earlier London imprint. (A complementary index of these 'forged' items under their purported dates is included in Index 3B below.) Items in categories 2 and 3 for which printers have been identified or queried are distinguished by an asterisk (*). Following are samples of imprints in STC and their listing in the index:

1a)	*London*, 1622	10308.5
1b)	[*London*, c. 1620?]	[13528.5] (c?)
2a)	[*London*? 1547?]	[10430?] (d?)
2b)	[*London*? *Fr. Garnet's second press*, 1596–97]	[11617.5?*] (d?): sub 1596
3a)	*Printed for the yeare of better hope* [i.e. *London*? 1611]	[1525?](anom., d?)
3b)	*Flushing* [i.e. *London*,] 1620	[10812] (false)
3c)	*Pomadie* [i.e. *London*? 1639]	[17923(*A*3)?] (false, d)
3d)	*Edimburgi* [i.e. *London*, *H. Bynneman*,] 1573	[13845*] (false)
3e)	*J. Wolfe*, 1599 [i.e. *J. Windet*, 1610?]	[12996*] (forged, d?)

Not included among the listings below are several kinds of items to be found directly or indirectly in Index 1. For official publications of the City of London *see* **Printer to the City of London** and the 'London' heading in STC itself. *See* also **Parish Clerks' Press**. For items whose presses were at unidentified places possibly including London *see* **English Secret Press** and **William Jones 3**. Also *not* included here are two kinds of 'repeat' London imprints: the reprints of Elizabethan proclamations made c. 1610–1618 for Humphrey Dyson, which are gathered together under **King's Printer(s)**, and the reprints of dated editions of single parliamentary sessions from 24 Hen. VIII to 4 & 5 Ph. & M. (cf. 9377.3, 9457.8, and similar items between these two), since the purpose of these 'repeat' imprints has been judged to be authenticity rather than fradulence. For a similar reason simple misprints of dates have also been ignored below.

1482: [4594?*] (c?).
1485: [18361(*A*3)?] (c?).
1500: [16172.5?] (c?), [17037?] (d?).
1505: [15805.2?] (c).
1518: [14077c.3–.4] (d).
1520: [14077c.11*(*A*3)?] (c?), [—.23A] (c).
1530: 22924.
1535: 17.7 (c), [6470.5] (c?), [7786] (d), [16795.5] (d).
1536: [16795] (d).
1537: [2788.5?] (c?).
1539: [392.5?] (d?).
1540: [10454?] (c?), [11366.3] (c?), [15525] (c), [22880.2(*A*3)] (d).
1540/41: [474].
1541: [9175b.5] (d), [16021.5] (c).
1542/43: [474.7].
1543: [9175b.15] (d).
1543/44: [475.5], [476].
1544: [9175b.20] (d).
1544/45: [416.5].
1545: [564.4] (c?), [9175b.25] (d), [—.30] (d), [9343.8] (forged? c), [12345] (c?), [24165.5?] (d?).
1545/46: [395], [396].
1546: [23435.5?] (d), [24468?*] (false, d?), [25590*] (false), [—.5*] (false).
1547: [95*] (false, d?), [851*] (false, d?), [10430?] (d?), [17314*] (false), [17314a*] (false), [17627?] (false, d?), [17789.5*] (false), [20795?] (d), [20972.7(*A*3)?] (d?), [24469] (d?), [24514(*A*3)?] (d?).
1548: [3760*] (false, d?), [3761*] (false, d?), [3766(*A*3)?], [4877.2 (*A*)] (d?), [11593.5] (d?), 11718.4, [11884?] (d?), [12723a(*A*3)?*] (d?), [16983(*A*3)?*] (d?), [17626*] (false, d?), [20847(*A*3)?*] (d?), [23553(*A*3)?*] (d?), [26138.5–39*] (false).
1548/49: [398.3].
1549: [1725] (d?), [2376.3(*A*3)] (d?), [2856?] (note), [6795] (d), [25351.5] (d?).
1550: [14008.5] (c?), [14009] (c?), [14109.2(*A*)] (c), [22134.5] (c).
1550/51: [398.7].
1552: [16572.3], [—.7] (d).
1553: [5160.3?*] (false), [11583?*] (d), [11585?*] (false), [11586?*] (false), [11593?*] (false).
1554: [5157?*] (false), [5629?] (d?), [5630?*] (false), [6934.5?*] (false), [7279?*] (d?), [10016?*] (false), [10383?*] (false), [15059?*] (false), [15074.4?*] (d), [16453?] (d), [16981?*] (false), [17773?*] (false).
1555: [16067.5] (c), [16067.7(*A*3)] (c), [16224.7] (d?).
1556: [15693.5(*A*3)?] (false), [15767.5].
1558: [16453.5] (d), [—.7] (d), [24356?*] (note), [25113*] (forged).
1558/59: [400.3], [492.2], [492.3?] (false).
1559: [564.6] (c), [1005–6*] (false, d), [21690.4] (d?).

A: Some genuine printing — *cont.*

1559/60: [400.4(***A***)].

1560: [853] (c?), [3763?] (false, d?), [14281] (c), [17147(***A***3: 2 eds.)] (d?).

1560/61: [400.5].

1561: [693.6] (d), [4826.5].

1561/62: [400.7(***A***)], [492.7], [506.4(***A***)].

1562: 16455, [17145.3] (d), [17255(***A***3)] (d?).

1562/63: [492.9], [492.10].

1563: [11396.7*] (forged, c), [11397a*] (forged, c), [21056.6] (d?).

1563/64: [492.11], [492.13(***A***3)].

1564: [14656.5?] (d), [—.7?] (d?).

1565: [3368.5-Bickner? -Searle?] (c?), [15219–20], [24357] (c).

1566: [2098.5] (c?), [7754.8] (d).

1566/67: [493.3].

1567: [10931.4] (d?), [—.7] (d?).

1567/68: [401.4], [401.5].

1568: [7754.6] (d), [8001.5(***A***3)] (d).

1569: [977*] (false, d), [13869.5] (d?).

1570: [664.5] (c), [745.3] (c), [1324] (d?), [7754.9] (c?), [13104] (d), [19185?] (c), [19972.5] (c), [20957] (c), [22653.3] (c), [26098.5(***A***)] (c).

1571: [3968*] (false).

1572: [2995a.2*] (false), [22868.5] (d).

1573: [13845*] (false), [13847] (false), [—.5*] (false).

1574: [3368.5-Strange?] (c?).

1575: [274*] (false), [2759.7] (c), [10550*] (false), [11310.5*] (false), [16704.3(***A***3)*] (forged, d?), [18051.7] (d), [19002.3] (d), [23267.5 (***A***3)] (c?), [23967*] (forged, c).

1576: [6389.5] (d), [17136*] (false), [17775*] (false).

1577: [2879.1(***A***3)?] (c?), [4474.42] (c?), [—.54] (c?), [—.97] (d?), [20855?].

1578: [17508*] (false), [18445*] (false).

1579: [4568.5*] (false, d?), [14563.7?*] (false, d?), [20092.5] (d), [21805.1] (d).

1580: [1325] (d?), [3368.5-Dowriche?] (c?), [4605?] (c?), [5592a] (c?), [6223] (c?), [21805.2] (d?), [21947*] (false).

1580/81: [22019.5(***A***3)*] (false).

1581: [3368.5-Rokeby?] (c?), [3977*] (false), [19867] (d).

1582: [4474.126] (c?).

1583: [9175n] (c?), [17450.7*] (false), [19491.5] (d), [21805.7] (d).

1584: [3936*] (false), [3938*] (false), [3940*] (false), [15208] (note: false), [15209] (false, d), [17159–9.5*] (false), [17167*] (false), [18714.7*] (forged?), [19911.5*] (false).

1585: [689*] (false), [689.3*] (false), [691.5] (d), [3368.5-Holland? -Tresame?] (d?), 3909 (d?), [3934*] (false), [3937*] (false), 11469.5, 13127, [13254] (d?), [15191(***A***3)] (c), [16515], [16756] (c), [18821.5(***A***3)] (forged? c), [18836] (d), [19359.1–60.7?] (note: most eds. may be false), [20404] (d?), [21805.3] (c), [21949*] (false), [23246.5*] (false).

1586: [4429] (false, d?), [4430*] (false), [11728.8*] (false), [12092.4] (d), [12194?] (d?), [19769.7*] (false).

1587: [1191–2], [4431*] (false), [12004*] (false), [17161*] (false), [17163*] (false, d), [22946*] (false, d?).

1588: [194.3] (d?), [1032*] (false, d?), [15212.5*] (false), [15414.6*] (false), [17158*] (false), [19903a.5(***A***3)?] (anom., d?), [20126.7] (d?), [21948.3–.7*] (false, d?), [24480*] (false).

1589: [3171.6?] (d?), [5638.7*] (false), [10511*] (false), [10752.7*] (false), [11735*] (false), [12914*] (anom., d), [13098.2*] (false), [15213.5*] (false, d), [17461?] (d), [—.5?] (d?), [17462*?] (anom., d?), [17463–3.7*] (anom., d), [17464?] (d?), [19456–6.5*] (anom.), [19457–7.7*] (anom.), [19913*] (false), [21319.9(***A***3)] (d?), 23662.5 (d?).

1590: [534(***A***3)*] (anom., d), [1328.2(***A***)] (c?), [3368.5-Hoby, T.?] (c?), [5638.9*] (false), [7384.7] (c?), [13135] (d), [13855.6] (d), [15374.2] (c?), [—.3] (c?), [16802.7?] (c), 18423, [19450*] (anom.), [21805.5] (d?), [23633] (c), [24481a] (d), [25107] (c).

1591: [403], [3171.9] (d), [20118a*] (false, d), [19624.5(***A***3)*] (false, d).

1592: [1522a(***A***3)?] (d?), [3873] (d), [4495.5] (d), [12734.7] (d), [13696.5] (d?), [14626.5?*] (d?), [17290] (d?), [22923], [23432], 23634 (d).

1593: [11617.2?*] (d), [—.8?*] (d), [13284.5] (d?), [16768.20] (d), 16783, [17264.5?*] (c).

1594: [11617.4?*] (d?), [19624.5(***A***3)*] (false, d).

1595: [1072.5], [2742.5] (c), [3368.5-Nordan? -Pilkington(***A***3)?] (c?), [3859.5] (d?), [4571.5?*] (d?), [5324(***A***3)*] (forged), [6350?] (note: false), [7385] (c?), [14657?] (d?), [18641.2] (d), [18689] (d), [19912*] (false, c), [24956.3] (c).

1596: [195.5] (c), [3120], [3801?*] (d?), [8254] (d), [11617.5?*] (d?), [16642?*] (d?), [21057.5?] (d), [22779*] (forged?), [23594.5] (d?), [24748?*] (d?), [26043.5*] (false).

1597: [3941.5?*], [15353?*], [16645.7?*] (d?), [17504?*] (false, c), [18643.3] (d), [19724.5***A***3: i)], [22968.5?*] (d?).

1598: [2995a.3*] (false), [22272.5?] (d).

1599: 564.8, [3171.7] (d), [3941.1?*] (d?), [—.2?*] (d?), [—.3?*] (d?), [—.4?*] (d?), [6350.5?] (false, c?), [16904*] (false).

1600: [348.5] (false), [1334.5], [3368.6-Cecil, R.? -Lee? -Palmer?] (c?), [4954*] (false), [6106.3?] (c?), [6787.7?*] (d?), [9175q(i)] (c?), [11029] (d), [12384] (c), [17486.5(***A***3)] (forged, d?), [17773.5] (c), [18604.5] (d), [19287.7] (c), [19937(***A***3)?] (c), [21456.5] (c?), [21493?] (d?), [23432.7] (c), [24821.5?] (c).

1601: [1884*] (false), [3102] (false), [3106*] (false), [3518], [—.3], [—.5], [5724*] (false), [9175d.51] (d?), [9175f] (d?), [9175n] (c?), 18643, [25124–4.5*] (false).

1602: [9175d.52] (d?), [13442.5*] (false), [13787a.5*] (false, d), [18754(***A***3)?], [20155.5*] (false), [20562?] (d).

1603: [8300?*] (false), [—.5?] (d?), [9175g.10(***A***)] (d), [9342.9] (d?), [9343] (c?), [—.3] (c?), [18931] (false, c?), [18931a] (false, c?), [23517?].

1604: [3368.5-Austen] (d?), [3526*] (false), [5256] (d?), [6465] (d?), [6466] (d?), [8351.3] (d), [9501] (d), [11548.5*] (false), [20792.7(***A***3)] (d?).

1605: [3368.5-Banastre?] (c?), [9175e(***A***3)] (d), [16768.2] (c), 18759.5, [24765.7?] (c).

1606: [5328], [6256] (d), 6498.2, [8394.3] (d), [18807.7?] (d?), [24043.5] (d).

1607: [3368.5-Braythwait(***A***), -M., I.?] (d?), [12995.5*] (forged, c?), [22360*] (forged, d?).

1608: [3368.5-Church? -Pindar?] (d?), [5568?] (d), [9175z.5] (d?), 10322, 18786(***A***3) (includes repeat*), [22360a*] (forged, d?), [24830.4] (d), [25852.7].

1609: [1408.3*] (false), 5590.5, [7490.7], [13882(***A***3)*] (forged, d), [16743.4–.5] (d), [24830.9] (d?).

1610: [17] (c), [3368.5-Draper? -Treswell] (c?), 3810.5, [6163?] (d?), 7200, [9175z.15] (d?), 12054, [12996*] (forged, d?), [14479.7] (c), 16633, 16675, [16743.6] (d), [16778.6] (c), [20792.7(***A***3)] (c?), [22360b] (forged, d?), [23039c] (d?), [24830.5] (d).

1611: [1525?] (anom., d), [12055.5] (d?), [14534?*] (false), [16776.12] (d?), [16777.16] (d), [16778.7(***A***3)] (d?), [17947.5] (d?), [20126.3] (d), [25596*] (false).

1612: [1501*] (false), [5394*] (false), [25597*] (false), [26009.5] (d).

1613: [3368.5-Browne(***A***)?] (d?), [4092*] (false), [5207.7(***A***)] (d), [10020.5] (d), [16743.6E(***A***3)] (d), [18285*] (false), [19297*] (note: false), [20304.5*] (false), [23750*] (false, d), [23780*] (anom./false), [25602*] (false), [25893*] (forged).

1614: [3368.5-Harewood?] (d?), [4975] (d), [10413.5] (d?), [16786.2] (d?), 20913, [23952.7] (d?), [25605.5*] (false), [25606].

1615: [3908.3] (c), [4797.5?] (c?), [9175g.20] (c), [9175z.10] (c?), 10372.3, [13427.5*] (forged), 14415, [16787.9] (c), [18676.5] (d?), [22824.7] (c), [23253] (c), [23775] (d), [23804*] (anom./false), [25240*] (false).

1616: [1196*] (false), 5870.3, [6455.5], [8584] (d?), [16778.8–.10] (d), [17869.5(***A***3)] (d), 18228.5, [18421.5?] (d), [18585*] (false), [20834.7] (d?), [24962?], [25604*] (false), [25605*] (false).

1617: [1143*] (forged, c), [3585*] (false), [3741?] (d?), [10314.9] (d), [14379.7?], [14775].

1618: [643?] (d?), [6345.4] (d?), [8556] (d), [8582?] (d), [10301.5] (d?), [21053.7] (d), [22172], [—.3], [—.5], [—.7], [25601*] (false), [25929.5] (d).

1619: [635*] (false), [636*] (false), [3212.5*] (false, d), [4991], [9175g.25] (c?), [9175t(***A***-Rec. Gen.)] (d?), [11351?], [12858*] (false), [14708.8*] (false), 16768.6, [18796*] (forged, d), 19813, [20443] (d?), [22291*] (forged, d), [22293*] (forged, d), [22297*] (forged, d), [22300*] (forged?), [22303] (forged, d).

1620: [21.4–.5?] (c), [563.5], [641*] (false, d?), [1144*] (forged, c), [2180?] (note: false, issue (2), c?), [3210?*] (false), [3214?*], [3215?*] (false), [3368.5-Bassano?] (c?), [4994.5] (d?), [6030] (d), [6480.5*] (forged, c), [7682.5] (c?), 10314.10, [10812] (false), [10814*] (false, d?), [11351*] (false), [—.3*] (false), [11352*] (false), [11356*] (false), [11492.7] (c?), [11823] (d?), [12743?] (c?), [13528.5] (c?), [13970.5] (c?), [14050.5*] (false), [16539.5] (c), [16776.2] (c), [17777.5] (c?), [18831], [19483] (d?), [20286.3*]

A: Some genuine printing — *cont.*
(false), [22098?], [—.5?], [22100?], [—.2], [—.4], [—.6–.8], [22126?], 23575–5.5, [23683.5] (c), [23751*] (false), [25933], [26078.5] (c).
1620/21: [18003.9(***A***3)].
1621: [1037?] (false), [1545.5] (d), [1901?], [3217.5] (d), [3432.5] (d), [—.7] (d), [5323a.4] (d), [6044a.7] (d), [6191.3] (d), [7527.3], [10406.5] (d), [—.6] (d), [10885.5] (d?), [11264], [11300–0.3], [11303*] (false), [—.5*] (false), [11304*] (false), [11329.4*] (false), [—.5*] (false), [11353*] (false), [11395.3] (d), [—.5] (d), [12862.7] (d), [14777], [14961.5] (d?), [15203(***A***: 2 eds.)], [16743.7] (d), [16768.12] (d), [—.16] (d), [—.22] (d?), [—.24] (d?), [—.26] (d?), [—.30] (d?), [16777.2] (d), [—.4] (d), [—.8] (d?), [—.14] (d), [16778.4] (d), [16779.8] (d), [—.10] (d), [16785.7] (d), [16786.6] (d), [—.8–.10] (d), [16787] (d), [—.8] (d?), [—.10] (d), [—.12] (d), [—.14] (d), [16798*] (false), [17257.5] (d), [17670.5?] (false), [17672*] (false), [17748.5] (d), [18102a.2] (d), [—.3] (d), [18114.5] (d), [—.6] (d), [18307.3(***A***3)] (d), [18460], [—.3] (false), [18507.8?] (note: false?), [—.9?] (note: false?), [—.13?] (note: false?), [—.18–.25?*] (headnote: false?), [—.26] (false), [—.27] (false), [—.28] (false), [19519] (d?), [20181], [20286.7*] (false), [21420.5] (d), [21588.7?], [21781.5] (d?), [22083*] (false), [22087], [22270.7] (d?), [22463.7] (d), [23228.5] (d?), [23910] (d), [24044a.5] (d), [24690] (d), [25759.5] (d), [25856.5] (d), [25857] (d), [25858.7] (d?), [25954.5] (d?), [—.6(***A***3)] (d?).
1622: [1119.5–20*] (forged, c?), [3368.5-Burie?] (d?), [7457], [7458], [8690.5] (d), [9175t-Cr. Aud.] (d?), 10308.5, [10682], [11329.7*] (false), [—.8*] (false), [11375?], [13598*] (false), [14379.5] (d), [14713.5*] (false, d), [17258], [17697] (d), [17728.7?*] (false), [18297?] (d), [18462*] (false), [18507.36*] (false), [—.37*] (false), [—.37A], [—.38?], [21717.5*] (forged, d?), [23797*] (false), [24915*] (false).
1623: [3101], [3368.5-Bull(***A***3)? -Wynne(***A***)?] (d?), 5024.5, [6273] (d?), [6456] (d?), [9175t(***A***3-Cr. Aud.)?] (d?), [10732], [—.3], [11329.9*] (false), [11330*] (false), [14782.5] (d), [21177?], 21354.5(***A***3), [22077], [—.3], [—.5], [—.7].
1623/24: [25170].
1624: [1365.5] (d?), [1415.7] (d), [3171] (false), [—.3] (false), [6273.7] (d), [6674.5] (d), [8458.5] (c?), [9243.5] (d), [10147.9] (d?), [11330.2*] (false), [—.3*] (false), [14779] (d), [14961.7] (d), [15453.3] (d), [16768.4] (d?), [—.10] (d), [—.18] (d), [—.28] (d?), [16779.4] (d?), [18102a.5] (d?), [18643.5] (d), [18756?], [18901a.5] (d), [19126?], [20795.3] (d), [20946.2] (false), [—.3] (false), [—.4*] (false), [—.5] (false), [—.6] (false), [—.7] (false), [—.8] (false), [21176.5] (d), [22065] (false), [22066] (false), [22067*] (false), [22068] (false), [22071], [22072] (false), [22073], [—.2], [—.4], [—.6], [—.8], [22084*] (false), [22084a*] (false), [22086], [22088], [22103*] (false), [—.3*] (false), [—.7*] (false), [22104*] (false & forged), [22379.5] (d), [23254.5] (d), [24000.7] (d), [24179] (d), [24960], [—.5], [25919*] (anom., d), [26057.5] (d).
1625: [21.6?] (c), [4609*] (false), [5129.5] (c), [6918], [8737] (d), [8790] (repeat), [8793] (repeat), [8796.3] (repeat), [8798.3] (repeat), [8800.3] (repeat), [8801] (repeat), [8802] (repeat), [8804.3] (repeat), [8805] (repeat), [9175j.1] (d), [10611.7] (c?), [11330.4*] (false), [11745.3] (c), [12561.2] (d), [13920.5] (d?), [14413.5] (d), [14423.7] (d), [14772] (d), [15107.3] (d), [15341?], [16741.3] (d), [17882] (d), [17883] (d?), [17884(***A***3)?] (false, d?), [17885?], [18935?] (c), [—.3?] (c), [—.5?] (c), [—.7?] (c), [18935a?] (c), [19049?] (d), [19460] (d?), [20112] (c), [20835.5], [21688.5] (c), [23424.3] (c), [23755*] (false), [24953.5].
1626: [1042–3?] (false), [3368.5-Paynton?] (d?), [6798.6] (d), [11330.7*] (false), [—.8*] (false), [13579–9.5*] (false), [14526*] (false), [19855.5] (d), [21460.7] (d), [22085?] (false).
1627: 4237.5, [5864.4], [5875] (d), [13899.5] (d), [16776.14] (d), [24903.5], [26057.3] (d).
1628: [1342.5] (d), [4147*] (false), [5863], [—.2], [7450a.5(***A***3)] (d?), [7579] (c), [7744.5] (d), [10762] (d), [11904] (d), [15177*] (false), [16876] (d?), [17664?] (false), [17665?] (false), [18023.3(***A***3)] (d), 20477, —.5, [20649–9.1*] (false), [—.3–.5*] (false), [—.7*] (false), [20766] (false), [20835.3(***A***3)] (d), [22640], [22640.3?] (false), [—.7?] (false), [23235.5] (d?), [23748] (anom., d?), [24739] (d), [24953.7].
1628/29: [22645.5].

A: Some genuine printing — *cont.*
1629: [1126], [3902.5] (d), [11944*] (false), [12997*] (forged, d?), [13179.5] (d), [18040*] (false), 18069, [20459.3?] (d?), [21718 (***A***3)*] (false), [23467], [24000.5?] (d).
1630: [21.7?] (c), [81.5] (c), [3368.5-Dering, -Moundeford?] (c?), [6318] (c?), [8948] (d), [9175t(***A***3-Exchequer)] (d?), [16751.5] (c), [16776.8] (d), [16777.10–.12] (c), [16800(***A***3)] (anom.), [18932] (false, c), [19598.6] (c), [19856] (c?), [20465(***A***3)?*] (anom.), [20482.5?] (c).
1631: [1798] (d?), [3368.5-Lodington?] (d?), 16811, [18699.3] (d?), [23636] (d).
1632: [12455.5*] (false), [16986].
1633: [194.5] (d?), [2721.3?*] (false?), [3368.5-Kaye, J.? -Vernon?] (d?), [9000.3] (d?), [12534], [13534], [—.5], [16776.16] (c?), [21347.7], [21591.3] (d?).
1634: [3368.5-Bankes, -Childe(***A***)? -Downes, -Finch, J., -Fulwood, -Littleton, -Osbaldeston, -Plat, -Wyndham?] (d?), [4371], [6911.5?], [19846.5] (d), [23235.3(***A***3)] (d?), 23808, [24167.3?].
1635: [3368.5-Bacon, F., -Bacon, F. & N., -Barrow, -Clopton, -Dewhurst, -Eure, -Godebold, -Gregory, -Henden, -Hutton, R., -Moseley, -Phesaunt, -Rumsey, -Whistler] (d?), [3797] (c), [6071.5] (c?), [6557.4] (c?), [9050.3] (d), [10023.5] (c?), [12938.5?] (c?), [13535], [15193.5] (c), 15467.5, [19802.5] (d), [22406.3] (c), [22634.5] (c), [22636.5] (c).
1636: [3368.5-Armyne, -Brickenden] (d?), [3451?], [4135], [10074.3*] (forged, d?), [13870.5] (d), [14137?*] (false), 15464, [16786.18] (d?), [20083.3(***A***)] (false, c?), [20466?], [20469.3?] (false), [—.7?] (false), [20470?] (false), [20476.5?] (note), [21505?] (d), [24178.5?].
1637: [3368.5-Bladen] (d?), [3793.5(***A***)?] (d?), [13685?] (d?), 14065, [16768.34(***A***3)] (d), [19615.5] (d), [20454.5?] (d), [25725.4], [—.8].
1638: [3368.5-Lake?] (d?), [4362?], [12997a*] (forged, d?), [19489.5] (d), [19564.5] (d?).
1639: [5753–5*] (false), [6218] (d?), [9335(***A***3)] (repeat), [17923 (***A***3)?] (false, d), [18196a(***A***3)] (repeat).
1640: [223], [1812.3] (c), [3090], [3273.7] (c), [3368.5-Godman? -Paulett?] (d?), [3797.5] (c), [6045.5] (d), [7746.8] (d), [8483.5] (c?), [10408.5?] (d?), [10877] (d?), [11198], [12292.5] (c), [12364] (d?), [13599.5] (d), [13917.5], [15133?] (d?), [15597?] (d), [16448.7] (c), [16761] (c), [16779.2] (d?), [16786.4] (d), —.14 (c), [16823.5] (c), [17816.5] (c), [17915.7] (c), [18022.5(***A***3)] (d?), [18487.5(***A***3)] (c), [18700.5?] (d?), [18933*] (false, c), [19974.4] (c), [—.5] (d), [20557.5] (d?), [21448?] (c), [21468.5?] (d), [21636.5] (d?), [22013.5?] (d), [—.7?] (d?), [22142.3] (d?), [—.5] (d?), [22166], [22406.4] (c), [22639] (d), [23346] (d?), [23416], [24904.5] (c), [25930.5] (d).
1640/41: [15310–0.1], [—.3], [—.4], [—.6], [—.8], [25247], [—.5*], [25248*], [—.3*], [—.5*], [—.7*], [25632].

Note: With the exception of the four items in square brackets identified as belonging in Wing, all the following items have 'forged' London imprints before 1641 and are listed below under the date of actual printing as best can be estimated at present. Although their probable place of printing has been given or inferred here as London, it is entirely possible that some were printed in other British places. The few late, anomalous title-pages and the replacements for castrated leaves have been termed 'faked' in order to distinguish them from true forgeries of complete items.

after 1640: 5513.6, 10078, 16418c.5, 22274e.3–e.5 (faked), 23345.5 (faked).
c. 1650: 10078.3, 13662.5, 13796.5, 20931.5, 20932.5.
c. 1660: 10078.5–.9, [16776.16] (bulk entry of which some may belong in Wing).
after 1660: 10053, 10055.5, 10057, 10058.5.
c. 1661–63: 1675a, 10054–5, 11067, 13354.
1680: 5689(***A***) (note: faked), [22173] (forged, d).
c. 1685: [1617?] (belongs in Wing).
c. 1687: [25951] (belongs in Wing).
c. 1690: [224?] (false, belongs in Wing?).
c. 1705–28: 5689 (note: faked), 13569 (note: faked).

B. FALSE LONDON IMPRINTS

With two exceptions all the items below have false London imprints. Those without further qualification were printed elsewhere than London, the majority of them on the continent. A few specify 'buyten [outside] Londen', but since London is the operative word, they find their place here as well as in STC itself. Those characterized as 'forged' were printed in London at a different date or by a different printer from that recorded in the imprint. The two exceptions, in 1618 (22173) and in 1624 (22104) are listed in square brackets since the former gives no place or printer and the latter has a false continental imprint, but they are indeed forgeries of works the first editions of which were surreptitiously printed in London.

Items are listed according to the date in the false imprint. Where none is present, the item is listed under the date or presumed date of the genuine edition and 'n.d.' is included in round brackets. An asterisk (*) signifies that the identity of the real printer is known for at least one forged edition. Like Index 3A, the present index omits 'repeat' London imprints among the proclamations and statutes and uses 'faked' to signal title-pages printed at a considerable remove in time from the original, perhaps to repair imperfections in one copy or at most a few. The rare false imprints with dates after 1640 come from Bible volumes in which at least one of the other imprints falls before 1641.

For illustrations of original and forged woodblock material in several early 17th-century forgeries *see Library* 3 (1922): 227–47 and 15 (1934): 364–76.

1525: 11397a* (forged).
1537: 13082.
1542: 9343.8 (forged? n.d.), 11396.7* (forged, n.d.).
1548: 16459*.
1550: 17562* (d/error).
1554: 16571a* buyten (d?), 16704.3(*A*3)* (forgery of lost ed., n.d.), 17863.5* buyten, 18309.5* buyten.
1555: 9981* (d), 17562a*.
1556: 23967* (forged).
1558: 25113* (forged).
1566-67: 2740.5 buyten.
1569: 15505*.
1578: 3972*.
1579: 14255, 14258–8.3(*A*3).
1581: 14258.5.
1584: 4904.5*, 5689 (note & *A*: faked), 18714.7* (forged?).
1587: 5690* (faked).
1588: 9194.5–.8.
1589: 9198.5.
1590: 6733*.
1595: 5324(*A*3)* (forged).
1596: 9205.3, 16703.5*, 22779 (forged?).
1597: 9208.6*, 13882(*A*3)* (forged).
1599: 2174–80*, 10017.5, 12995.5–97a (forged), 17486.5(*A*3) (forged).
1600: 14447.5, 16613(*A*3, note: faked), 18796* (forged), 22297* (forged), 22303* (forged).
1602: 22360–0b* (forged).
1602/03: 8301.
1603: 8323.5, 22030.7.
1604: 1459.5, 1119.5–20 (forged, n.d.), 23461.
1605: 21717.5* (forged).
1606: 9504* (d).
1608: 617, 6480.5* (forged), 22291* (forged), 22293* (forged).
1609: 14408(*A*3).
1610: 1708, 15452.
1611: 5513.6 (forged).
1612: 4740.3–.5(*A*), 9231.
1613: 1143–4* (forged), 25893* (forged).
1615: 4744–4.7*, 11306.5, 13427.5* (forged).
1618: [22173] (forged).
1619: 22300 (forged?).
1622: 22069–9a.5.
1623: 13264.8, 22079, 22081.
1624: 1396.5, 20390.5*, [22104*] (false & forged).
1625: 7751.6.
1627: 8868.3.
1628: 10074.3* (forged).
1629: 15083.5.
1630: 10053–55.5 (forged).
1632: 10057 (forged), 22274e.3–.5 (faked).
1633: 10058.5 (forged), 10078–8.9* (forged), 23345.5 (faked).
1635: 1675a (forged).
1636: 20932.5 (forged), 22176.
1637: 2328.5*, 2328.8*, 9093.5, 11067 (forged), 13796.5 (forged), 23029.7.
1638: 1619.5–20 (forged?), 2330–0.9, 2680.1–.7, 2954, 16414.3* (note), 20931.5 (forged).
1639: 2692.5*, 16418c, 16418c.5 (forged).
1640: 5206.5 (false? d?), 13354* (forged), 13662.5 (forged).
1644: 2316.5.
1646: 2328.9.
1669: 2330.6.
1673: 2330.9.

C. SOME BOOKS IMPORTED TO LONDON

The following index is both limited and highly imperfect but may possibly be suggestive to others of an area for further investigation. All STC items printed abroad (in Index 2B) were intended for a British audience albeit some readers were exiles. What is attempted below is a listing of certain imported items naming London publishers in the imprint, usually on cancel title-pages though occasionally part of a continental edition may have been contracted for before the title-page was printed. Consciously omitted are all Liturgies. Many eligible STC items have undoubtedly also been omitted since the slips that exist were made as I was scanning STC for Indexes 3A and 3B (with 'London' in mind) and were essentially whatever happened to catch my eye as worth noting privately. However, it seemed that the information, though admittedly incomplete, might be of more general use, particularly in relation to the **Latin Stock** imprints (*see* Index 1: Stationers' Company). Just as the Frankfurt Fair catalogues give a better idea of what John Bill 1 and the Latin Stock imported between 1617–28 (11328 sqq.), so the catalogues of **Henry Fetherstone** in 1628 (10837) and his former apprentice, **Robert Martin**, in 1633–40 (17511.5 sqq.) reveal specific imported stock in trade of two individual publishers. *See* also Graham Pollard and Albert Ehrman, *The Distribution of Books by Catalogue*, Cambridge, 1965, pp. 85–94.

Items distinguished by an asterisk (*) mention **John Norton 1**, his **Officina Nortoniana**, or **John Bill 1**. The rare items with an English or Latin Stock imprint are so identified. Unique items consisting of London preliminaries or cancels combined with continental sheets of a decade or more earlier—obviously not commercial ventures—are designated 'presentation copy'.

1566: 23001.
1568: 2800.
1579: 92(*A*) (d?), 17003.3(*A*3).
1584: 14583.
1587: 5160.5.
1589: 24718.
1594: 18100, 19557.3(*A*3*).
1601: 18857* (d?).
1602: 18891.

C: Some imported books — *cont.*
1603: 18856.
1604: 13790*.
1605: 11741, 21361*, 26121, —.3, —.7, 26121a.
1606: 18175*.
1608: 44, 26121a.3*.
1610: 2811.5*, 22868* (d).
1611: 4868.7, 13218 (presentation copy), 13906a*.
1612: 4869*.
1613: 4631*, 12619*, 17045.
1616: 11945*, 24792 (English Stock).

C: Some imported books — *cont.*
1617: 24311* (d).
1618: 24310.5.
1619: 21805.9 (Latin Stock).
1620: 11329 (Latin Stock).
1622: 21648.5(*A*3)* (presentation copy).
1624: 1396.5*.
1629: 20567.3.
1633: 2798, 2798.5, 2813.3.
1635: 21537.3.
1637: 18203 (d?).

INDEX 3D: SIGNS

Included below are the signs in London and in the area between the city proper and Westminster as well as those for Westminster from 1501. For Westminster signs before 1501 and for all those in Southwark *see* the printers and publishers under those places in Index 2Ai. Tenure at one of the signs below has usually been confirmed only to 1640; the form of date: 1635–40+? indicates that activity may have continued there for an unspecified period. The dates cited are the minimum dates for which the sign appears in imprints with the following exceptions: publishers' names enclosed in square brackets indicate that no imprint noted has the sign but that there is documentary evidence (e.g. wills) or a close family or partnership succession. Names in round brackets indicate an individual associated with a sign probably not his own, either in shared imprints or publications of a journeyman who may have continued to work for a while in the shop of his former master.

References in the form (B), (C.7) are to the addresses in Index 3E, and 'unloc' indicates a sign without specific location within a large area like Paul's Churchyard or Fleet Street. Signs clearly not belonging to a publisher but named for ready identification are glossed as (next to $, over against $), i.e. next to or over against the relevant sign. At the end is appended a list of shops which usually had no signs but had distinctive features: Corner Shop, Little Shop, etc.

WARNING: After this list had been compiled, Peter W. M. Blayney investigated documentary evidence in leases and surveys which located more specifically several of the signs in Paul's Churchyard. When appropriate, the old locations below drawn from Index 1 are given in *italic*, and the new, under which the shopkeepers are listed in Index 3E, are signaled by a section mark (§); for an example *see* Black Bear. Blayney's full analysis will be set out in *The Bookshops in Paul's Cross Churchyard* (Occasional Papers of the Bibliographical Society, forthcoming).

A.B.C., Paul's Churchyard (unloc; B): R. Faques, 1521?–30

Anchor, Paternoster Row (C.7):
  Jn. Harrison 2, 1580–1617 (sometimes Blue or Golden —)
  Josias Harrison, 1615–16 (Golden —)
  H. Dix, (author), 1633 (Golden —)
—*See* also Blue, Golden —.

Angel, Bishopsgate Street (J.2): G. Loftus, 1615 (near $)
—Ivy Lane (C.3): R. Royston, 1635–40+?
—Green Arbour, [Little] Old Bailey (D.4): G. Edwards 2, 1629–40+?
—Lombard Street (possibly same as Pope's Head Alley below; O.12):
  R. Daniel (sometimes printseller), 1620?–29?
  O. Ridge, 1628
—Paul's Churchyard (northeast; A.3):
  J. Perrin & widow, 1580–93
  A. Wise, 1593–1602
  T. Clarke, 1604–07
  R. Mab, 1611–13
  W. Arundell, 1614–17
  R. Higgenbotham, 1619–24
  P. Paxton, 1627
  E. Blackmore, 1629–40+?
—Pope's Head Alley (possibly same as Lombard Street above; O.11):
  N. Alsop, 1632–40+?
  (P. Waterhouse, 1632)
  (T. Nicholes, 1637)
—*See* also Golden —.

Anne, *St.*, Paul's Churchyard (unloc; B): J. Pelgrim, 1505–06

Aqua Vitae Still, Distaff Lane, near Old Fish Street (S.3):
  F. Adams, 1594
  R. Triplet, 1603?

Arms. *See* King's, Prince's —.

Arrows. *See* Three —.

Augustine, *St.*, Paul's Churchyard (unloc; B):
  Unidentified agent for Antwerp printer, 1530–31 (15966, 15969)
  H. Singleton, 1548–50?

Ball, Little Britain (F.4): R. Clutterbuck, 1633–37
—Paul's Churchyard (possibly all shops and almost certainly those from 1613 were near the great North door of Paul's, the corner shop on the left as one approached the door; shop demolished in 1636; A.2):
  John Newbery, 1602–03
  Joan Newbery 1, 1603
  S. Man, 1613–16
  (H. Hooper, 1613)
  J. Parker, 1618–19
  J. Teage, 1620–22 (sometimes Golden —)
  T. Lownes 4, 1623 (Golden —)
  H. Moseley, 1627–34
  N. Fussell, 1627–35
——in Peter College rents (west; A.10): J. Case, 1548–52?
—*See* also Golden, Red —; White Lion and —.

Bear, Fleet Street, over against Middle Temple Gate (W.13): H. Twyford, 1640
—without Temple Bar, over against St. Clement's Church (X.2): H. Ballard, 1597
—*See* also Black, White —.

Bell, within Aldgate (L.1): R. Hollins, 1581 (over against $)
—Fore Street, without Cripplegate, near Grub Street (I.3): A. Jeffes, 1586–87
—Paul's Churchyard (St. Faith's parish; A.4):
  R. Toy, 1545–55
  [Eliz. Toy, 1556–65]
  [G. Bishop, ?–1611]
  T. Adams, 1609–20 (Blue — in only example noted)
  Eliz. Adams, 1620?
  A. Hebb, 1625–40+?
—Philip Lane (H.14): A. Jeffes, 1589

Bible, Britain's Burse (X.10): R. Swaine 1, 1622–32
—Chancery Lane, between Serjeants' Inn and Fleet Street, near the King's Head Tavern (W.10b): H. Shepherd, 1635–40+?
—Cheapside (N.1): R. Bird, 1623–31
—Duck Lane (E.5): S. Cartwright, 1628–40+? (sometimes Hand and —)
—Fleet Bridge (W.3): E. Brewster, 1635–40+?
—Fleet Street, near the great conduit (W.5):
  Jn. Browne 1, 1599–1600
  R. Dawlman, 1627
  G. Percival, 1628
—Giltspur Street (D.3): J. Wright 1, 1614–40+? (usually only 'without Newgate' until 1634)
—Guildhall gate (H.5): P. Birch, 1619
—Holborn Bridge (V.2): B. Langford, 1638–39 (sometimes Blue —)
—*St.* Lawrence Lane (H.6): R. Bird, 1631–40+?
—without Newgate. *See* Giltspur Street above.
—Paul's Churchyard (from 1548 and possibly before, this was near the great North door of Paul's; shop demolished in 1636; A.2):
  Unidentified agent for R. Grafton and E. Whitchurch, 1540 (16015)
  R. Jugge, 1548–58
  M. Jennings, 1577–81
  T. Cadman, 1585–88
  Joan Broome, 1592–1601
  (R. Ockould, 1596)
  G. Potter, 1602–09
  J. Royston, 1612–13
  W. Bladen, 1612–25
  E. Brewster, 1625–35

Bible — *cont.*
—Pope's Head Alley (O.11): T. Nicholes, 1637
—*See* also Blue, Gilt —; Hand and —.

Bible and Harp, Smithfield, near the Hospital gate (E.8): R. Harper, 1639–40+?

Bishop's Head, Paul's Churchyard (north; A.2):
Unidentified agent for R. Caly, 1553? (11592, note)
W. Ponsonby, 1591–98
M. Lownes, 1605–21
G. Latham, 1627–40+?

Bishop's Mitre, within Ludgate (Q.3): R. Stoughton, 1548–51

Black Bear, Chancery Lane (unloc; W.10a):
P. Conington, 1578
H. Hooper, 1597–1600 (sometimes omits 'Black')
—Paul's Churchyard (*unloc; B;* § = northeast; A.3):
T. Woodcock, 1575–94
(G. Seton, 1577)
P. Linley, 1595–99 (sometimes omits 'Black')
J. Flasket, 1595–1607
E. Blount, 1609–22
(R. Milbourne, 1617–18)
(R. Chambers, 1618)
R. Allott, 1627–35 (sometimes omits 'Black')
A. Crooke 1, 1632–39 (sometimes omits 'Black')
Mary Allott, 1636

Black Bell, within Temple Bar, in Fleet Street (W.14):
G. Norton, 1610 (under $)
E. Dicæophile, *pseud.*, 1569 (against $)

Black Boy (Morens, Moryens):
—Unlocated but probably in Paul's Churchyard (?A.1 or B): unidentified printer of music, 1530 (22924)
—Paternoster Row (C.7):
H. Sutton, 1559–61
H. Bynneman, 1566
—Paul's Churchyard (at 'middle' North door, 1561–71, and 'little' North door from 1572; A.1):
?H. Sutton, c. 1550–52?
W. Martin, 1561?
H. Kirkham, 1570–93
W. Kirkham, 1593–99
—*See* also Unlocated above.

Black Bull, in Cornhill, near the Royal Exchange (O.9):
J. Hinde 2, 1620?–35
T. Hinde, 1637–52
—London Bridge (T.7): S. Pemell, 1633
—Vintry, near the three cranes (S.9): E. Venge, 1599

Black Horse, Aldersgate Street (F.2): T. East, 1589–94
—Ivy Lane (C.3): (?T. East &) H. Middleton, 1568
—London Wall (H.8): T. East, 1575
—Paternoster Row (C.7): H. Bate, 1587?

Black Lion, London Bridge (T.7): J. Hunter, 1576

Black Morens (Moryens). *See* Black Boy.

Black Oliphaunt. *See* Elephant.

Black Raven, Paternoster Row (C.7): T. Gubbin & T. Orwin, 1588 (over against $)
—Strand, near St. Clement's Church (X.2): T. Jones 2, 1622–27
—Thames Street, near London Bridge (T.6): F. Adams, 1578?–84

Black Spread-Eagle, Fleet Street, over against St. Dunstan's Church (W.9): A. Roper, 1638–40+?

Blazing Star, Paul's Churchyard (unloc; B):
H. Carre, 1584 (over against $), 1585–90 (at $)
D. Speed, 1616
E. Blackmore, 1618–21

Blind Knight, Holborn, over against St. Andrew's Church (V.4): W. Lugger, 1603

Blue Anchor, Paul's Churchyard, over against St. Gregory's Church (A.9): unidentified agent for the assignees of G. Wither, 1623 (8704.5, note)
—*See* also Anchor.

Blue Bell, Paul's Churchyard. *See* Bell.

Blue Bible, Green Arbour, Little Old Bailey (D.4):
M. Sparke 1, 1627–53
(T. Slater, 1630)
M. Sparke 2, 1631–40+?
(J. Hardesty, 1640)
—*See* also Bible.

Blue Garland, within Temple Bar, St. Dunstan's parish (W.14): J. Wayland, 1537–39

Book. *See* Paper Book.

Bowl, Chancery Lane (unloc; W.10a): P. Man, 1622

Brazen Serpent, Paul's Churchyard (northeast; A.3):
R. Wolfe, 1542–73
P. & N. Lycosthenes, *pseud.*, 1569 (by $)
[Joan Wolfe, 1574]
J. Shepperd, 1576–77
R. Vernon, 1581
A. Maunsell, 1584–89
R. Dexter, 1590–1603
Edw. Bishop, 1606–17
Eliz. Bishop, 1619–20
G. Latham, 1621–26
R. Dawlman, 1628–40+?
L. Fawne, 1635–40+?
S. Gellibrand, 1639–40+?

Buck, New Exchange (= Britain's Burse; X.10): W. Sheares, 1625
—Gray's Inn (V.10): W. Sheares, 1627
—*See* also Golden —.

Bull, Little Britain (F.4): D. Frere, 1636–40+? (sometimes Red —)
—*See* also Black, Pied, Red —.

Bull('s) Head, Cateaton Street (H.3): J. Aston, 1637–38
—Paul's Churchyard (near the great North door of Paul's; shop demolished in 1636 or before; A.2):
S. Macham 1, 1607–15
E. Edgar, 1608
Joyce Macham, 1615–16
T. Barlow, 1616–20
Jos. Browne, 1623
W. Garrett, 1625
R. Michell, 1628
W. Adderton, 1629
R. Swaine 2, 1629
A. Ritherdon, 1630–32

Bush. *See* Holy Bush.

Cardinal's Hat, without Newgate (D.9):
John Barnes, 1614 (under $)
R. Higgenbotham, 1615–17
—Lombard Street (O.12): F. Coldock, 1561 (over against $)

Castle, Cornhill, near the Royal Exchange (O.7):
H. Beeston, 1633–34 (near $)
H. Blunden, 1637–40 (near — Tavern; sometimes at $)
—Distaff Lane (S.3): J. Wolfe, 1582–88 (over against $)
—Fleet Street, over against the conduit (W.5):
T. Gilbert, 1588 (near $)
R. Ward, 1594 (at $)
—(Great) Wood Street (H.17): G. Vincent 1, 1611 (near $)
—Holborn, over against Ely House (V.5): R. Ward, 1593

Castle — *cont.*
—Paternoster Row (C.7):
R. Applow, 1563 (by — Tavern)
T. Gosson, c. 1579?–81 (next to $)
—Salisbury Court (W.5): R. Ward, 1596

Cat and Fiddle, Old Change (N.8): H. Carre, 1589

Cat(s) and Parrot(s), Cornhill, near the Royal Exchange (O.9): T. Pavier, 1600–12
—Ivy Lane (C.3):
[T. Pavier, 1614–25]
(R. Pott, 1624)

Catherine Wheel, Thames Street, near the Old Swan (T.5): T. Creede, 1594–95
—Holborn Bridge (V.2): J. Orphinstrange, 1607–09 (by $)

Chequer, Paternoster Row (C.7):
T. Orwin, 1590–93 (over against $)
[Joan Orwin, 1593–97]
F. Kingston, 1599–1605 (—)
—without Temple Bar (X.4): R. Meighen, 1623–28 (over against the — Tavern)

Christopher, *St.*, in Paul's Churchyard (unloc; B): T. Ellis, 1629

Cock, Holborn Bridge (V.2): J. Orphinstrange, 1609 (by $)
—Paternoster Row (C.7): W. Awen, 1554
—Paul's Churchyard (unloc; B):
J. Turke, 1553
R. Redborne, 1560?
L. Maylard, 1567
—Watling Street, near Friday Street (N.9): T. Creede, 1600 (over against $)
—*See* also Golden —

Conies. *See* Three —.

Cradle, Lombard Street (O.12):
E. Sutton, 1555–63
H. Spooner, 1579

Crane, Paul's Churchyard (northeast; A.3):
L. Harrison, 1563–69
T. Smith, 1582–83
R. Waldegrave, 1587–88
R. Oliffe, 1590–92?
W. Leake 1, 1593–95
J. Busby 1, 1598–99
?N. Ling, 1600 (one variant)
W. Burre, 1603–21
(J. Stepneth, 1610)
G. Emerson, 1622
N. Vavasour, 1622–24
Jn. Browne 3, 1625
F. Constable, 1627–35
(E. Bush, 1634–35)
J. Williams, 1636–40+?
(T. Briscoe, 1636)

Cranes. *See* Three —.

Cross, Paul's Churchyard (apparently distinct from Paul's Cross, unloc; B): P. Paxton, 1619 (at $)
—*See* also Red, Golden —.

Cross Keys, Holborn Hill (V.6): H. Bell, 1608–10 (near $)
—Paul's Churchyard, at Paul's gate, next Cheapside (A.5):
J. Piper, c. 1615–20
G. Vincent 2, 1625–27
R. Thrale, 1625–40+?
—Paul's Wharf (R.8):
J. Windet, 1588–1604
(W. Stansby, 1597)

Crown, Cornhill, near Pope's Head Alley (O.11): J. Sweeting, 1639
—Duck Lane (E.5): S. Nealand, 1631
—Fleet Street, next to Whitefriars gate (W.7): R. Foster 1, 1549
—Guildhall gate, over against the Maiden's Head (H.5): W. Ferbrand, 1600–01
—Ludgate (Q.3): W. Edmonds, 1638–39
—Lothbury (H.9): W. Lee 1, 1628–29 (sometimes Hand and —)
—Paul's Churchyard, at Cheap gate (A.5):
S. Waterson, 1589–34
(G. Seton, 1608)
J. Waterson, 1623–40+?
—*See* also Fleur-de-lis and —, Rose and —.

Crowns. *See* Three —.

Cup. *See* Gilt, Golden —.

Dagger, Lombard Street (O.12): T. Geele (printseller), 1630

Dolphin, Distaff Lane, near Old Fish Street (S.3):
B. Alsop, 1621–24
(G. Norton, 1622–24)
—High Holborn (V.11): J. Morgan (agent of prov. of Maryland), 1635 (over against $)

Double Hood, Thames Street, over against the Steelyard (S.11): H. Singleton, 1551–53

Dragon. *See* Green, Red —.

Eagle, Lombard Street, near the Stocks Market (O.12):
R. Kele, 1547–52
W. Riddell, 1554–56
E. Halley, 1562
—*See* also Black Spread-Eagle, Half-Eagle, Spread-Eagle.

Eagle and Child, Britain's Burse (X.10): T. Walkley, 1618–32
—Old Change, near Old Fish Street (S.2): T. Creede, 1600–10
—Paul's Churchyard, near Watling Street (A.7): J. Emery, 1635–40+?
—*See* also Golden —.

Eagle's Foot, Lombard Street, upper end (P.1): J. Tisdale, 1561–63

Elephant (Oliphaunt), Fleet Street, a little above the conduit (W.5):
H. Wykes, 1565–71 (sometimes Black —)
H. Cockyn, 1577

Falcon, Fleet Street, against St. Dunstan's Church (W.9):
W. Griffith, 1553–71
H. Middleton, 1573–87
[Jane Middleton, 1588?]
—Holborn Bridge (V.2): Rich. Jones, 1581–89 (over against $)
—Shoe Lane (W.6):
W. Dight, 1612–16
R. Shorleyker, 1623–32 (sometimes Golden —)

Fiddle. *See* Cat and —.

Fleur-de-lis (Flower de luce), Fleet Street, near Fetter Lane end (W.8):
J. Hodgets, 1601–02
J. Marriot, 1616–19 (has White —)
—Paul's Churchyard (adds 'and Crown' as noted; almost certainly a single shop, by the great North door of Paul's; demolished in 1636 or before; A.2):
W. Burre, 1599–1601 (sometimes — and Crown)
A. Johnson, 1602–03 (has — and Crown)
F. Burton, 1606–07 (has — and Crown)
T. Man 2, 1610 (has — and Crown)
R. Bonian, 1611–12 (sometimes — and Crown)
G. Gibbs, 1614–17
R. Rounthwait, 1618–19 (has — and Crown)
R. Pott, 1621–24
J. Emery, 1630–31

Fleur-de-lis — Paul's Churchyard — *cont.*
— —by the little South door of Paul's (A.9): G. Gibbs, 1632
—Pope's Head Alley (O.11):
G. Gibbs, 1624–31 (sometimes Golden —)
B. Allen, 1636

Fleur-de-lis and Crown, Paternoster Row, near Cheapside (C.7): W. Tymme, 1601–06
—Paul's Churchyard. *See* Fleur-de-lis.

Fleurs-de-lis. *See* Three —.

Flower de luce. *See* Fleur-de-lis.

Flying Horse, between York House and Britain's Burse (X.12): T. Walkley, 1636–40

Fountain, Paul's Churchyard (unloc; B): S. Browne, 1639

Fox, Paul's Churchyard, near St. Austin's gate (A.7):
M. Law, 1601–29
J. Upton, 1630

Friar, Grub Street (I.6): F. Sergeant, 1601
—Whitechapel parish (M.2): M. Cutbere, c. 1549

Furnace, Paul's Wharf (R.8): J. Hester (distiller, translator), 1582

Garland. *See* Blue, Rose —.

George, Aldersgate Street (F.2): T. East, 1599? (over against $)
—Fleet Street, next to St. Dunstan's Church (W.9):
R. Pynson, 1502–29
(H. Meslier, 1508?)
(?J. Hawkins (patron), 1530)
R. Redman, 1531–40
Eliz. Redman, 1540–41
W. Middleton, 1541–47
W. Powell, 1547–66
M. Partrich, 1616
J. Maynard, 1638–40+?
—*See* also Temple Bar below.
—Foster Lane, over against Goldsmiths' Hall (G.3): R. Waldegrave, 1583
—Lombard Street (O.12): T. Humble, 1566
—Paul's Churchyard (near Cheap gate; A.5):
J. Reynes, 1523–44
W. Riddell, 1548–52
T. Stirrop, 1576–97
H. Olney, 1595
—Pope's Head Alley, near the Royal Exchange (O.11): G. Fairbeard, 1618
—within, at Temple Bar (W.14): R. Redman, 1527–31
—without Temple Bar, in St. Clement's parish (X.1): R. Redman, 1525–27

Gilded. *See* Gilt, Golden.

Gilt Bible, Cheapside. Misprint for Gilt Cup.
—Paternoster Row, in Queen's Head Alley (C.7): R. Harford, 1631–40+?

Gilt Cup, Cheapside (N.5):
J. Bartlett, 1620–37 (sometimes Gilded, Golden Cup)
(J. Spencer, 1624)
—Paul's Churchyard, near St. Austin's gate (A.7): J. Bartlet, 1639–40
—*See* also Golden Cup.

Globe, Cornhill, over against the Royal Exchange (O.9):
C. Holland, 1617–22
F. Williams, 1626
W. Webb 2, c. 1635

Glove, Cornhill, near the Royal Exchange, over against the conduit (O.10):
T. Booth (printseller), c. 1635?
W. Hope, 1634–36
P. Cole, 1637–40+? (sometimes — and Lion)

Goat, King Street (X.16): F. Constable: 1640+?

Golden. *See* also Gilt.

Golden Anchor, Strand, without Temple Bar (X.1): R. Ball, 1636
—*See* also Anchor.

Golden Angel, Ludgate Hill, near the Belle Savage (O.4): W. Holme 3, 1594–95

Golden Ball, Pope's Head Alley (O.11): G. Loftus, 1602–04
—*See* also Ball.

Golden Buck, Fleet Street, near Serjeants' Inn (W.7): W. Lee 2, 1620–25

Golden Cock, Paternoster Row (C.7): F. Kingston, 1623

Golden Cross, Fleet Street (unloc; W.2): L. Andrewe, 1527

Golden Cup, Old Bailey (D.7): A. Jeffes, 1591
—Fore Street, without Cripplegate (I.3): Edw. Allde, 1589–90 (sometimes Gilded Cup)
—*See* also Gilt Cup.

Golden Eagle and Child, Paternoster Row (C.7): J. Hill, 1590

Golden Falcon. *See* Falcon.

Golden Fleur-de-lis. *See* Fleur-de-lis.

Golden Hind, Paul's Churchyard (unloc; B): J. Hinde 1, 1583

Golden Key, Middle Temple (W.13): Unidentified agent for J. Norton 2, 1635 (5988)
—Paul's Churchyard, near the great North door (A.2): R. Woodroffe, 1615–17

Golden Lion, Duck Lane (E.5): M. Simmons, 1635–36
—Little Britain (F.4): L. Sadler, 1631–40+?
—Old Bailey (D.7): ?R. Walker, 1597 (near $)
—Paternoster Row (C.7): W. Cotton, 1607–09
—Paul's Churchyard (*unloc; B;* = northeast; A.5):
R. Rounthwait, 1619–25
P. Stephens & C. Meredith, 1625–40+?

Golden Star. *See* Star.

Golden Tun, Creed Lane, near Ludgate (Q.2): H. Singleton, 1574–85
—Fleet Street, near St. Dunstan's Church (W.9): J. Winnington, 1588–89
—Smithfield (unloc; E.1): H. Singleton, 1586?–87?

Golden Unicorn. *See* Unicorn.

Goshawk in the Sun, Paul's Churchyard, near Cheapside (A.5): T. Gosson, 1580

Grasshopper, Paul's Churchyard (unloc; B):
A. Lawton, 1571
C. Barker, 1575–76

Great Turk. *See* Turk's Head.

Green Dragon, Addle Street (H.1): T. Scarlet, 1590
—Paul's Churchyard (northeast; A.3):
F. Coldock 1566–81+
[S. Waterson, c. 1585?]
T. Hayes, 1600–01
W. Barrett, 1608
F. Burton, 1610–17
J. Budge, 1618–25
T. Alchorn, 1627–39
A. Crooke 1, 1640+
—Royal Exchange (O.8): T. Hackett, 1572?–74

Green Dragon and Sword, Fleet Street (unloc; W.2): G. Eastland (music publisher), 1600

Green Hill. *See* Hill

Green Man, Leadenhall Street, right over Billiter Lane (L.3): F. Constable, 1625

Green Oak. *See* Oak Tree.

Greyhound, Blackfriars (Q.6): M. Fenricus (schoolmaster?), 1627 (next to — Tavern)
—Paternoster Row (C.7):
J. Penny, 1591
Jn. Harrison 1, 1596–1613 (sometimes White —)
Jn. Harrison 3, 1601
Joseph Harrison, 1608
—Paul's Churchyard (*unloc; B;* § = northeast; A.3):
Jn. Harrison 1, 1582–94 (sometimes White —)
W. Leake 1, 1596–1601
W. Welby, 1605–09
M. Baker, 1611–13
R. Mab, 1614–16
G. Edwards 1, 1617–18
J. Bloome, 1618–21
G. Hodges, 1622–24
?R. Higgenbotham or unidentified agent of J. Legat 2, 1625 (5838)
R. Allott, 1626–27
R. Milbourne, 1628–35
A. Crooke 1, 1637
J. Crooke & R. Sergier 2, 1637–39
(E. Weaver, 1637–38)
T. Allott, 1639
—*See* also Two Greyhounds.

Griffin, Fleet Street, a little above the conduit (W.5): W. Griffith, 1552?–56
—Paternoster Row (C.7): T. Gubbin, 1588

Gun, Holborn, near the conduit (D.5): W. Jones 2, 1594–1615
—Ivy Lane (C.3):
J. Grismand, 1627–36
P. Nevill, 1638–43
—Paul's Alley (A.1): J. Grismand, 1621–26
—Paul's Churchyard, near the little North door (sometimes omits 'little'; A.1):
E. White 1, 1578–1612
(A. White, 1593)
(T. Millington, 1594)
E. White 2, 1607–18
Sara White, 1613–15
J. Grismand, 1618–19

Half-Eagle and Key, Barbican (I.1):
J. Charlewood, 1566–89
Alice Charlewood, 1593
—Fleet Lane (D.2): R. Serle, 1564–66?
—Gutter Lane (G.4): R. Hall, 1562–63

Half-Rose and Half-Sun, Royal Exchange (O.2): T. Frethren, 1581

Hand, Holborn Bridge (V.2): N. Okes, 1609–13

Hand and Bible. *See* Bible.

Hand and Crown. *See* Crown.

Hand and Golden Pen, Fetter Lane (W.8): R. Gething (author), 1616

Hand and Plough, Fleet Street (unloc; W.2):
W. Mattes, 1594–97
E. Mattes, 1597–1606

Hand and Star, Fleet Street, between the two Temples (W.12):
R. Tottell, 1553
——near Middle Temple gate (W.13):
R. Tottell, 1553–93
J. Jaggard, 1594–1622
Eliz. Jaggard, 1623–24

Hand-in-Hand, Wood Street (H.17): G. Vincent 1, 1602–03

Harp, Shoe Lane (W.6): W. Dight, c. 1600?

Harrow, Britain's Burse (X.10):
H. Perry, 1626–31
W. Sheares, 1633–36
—Snow Hill (D.9):
Jn. Barnes, 1613
W. Wright 1, 1613

Hart's Horn, Foster Lane (G.3): J. Walley, c. 1549–53
—Paternoster Row (C.7): B. Wright or his unidentified agent, c. 1596

Head. *See* Bishop's, King's, Maiden's, Mary Magdalen's, Paul's, Pope's, Saracen's, Tiger's, Turk's —.

Hedgehog, Paul's Churchyard (west; A.10):
W. Seres 1, 1551–76
G. Seton, 1578–81

Helmet, Paul's Churchyard (north; A.2):
H. Toy, 1562–74
T. Chard, 1578–85?
N. Fosbrooke, 1606–07

Hill, Paul's Churchyard (west; A.10): W. Hill, 1547?–49 (sometimes Green —)

Hind. *See* Golden, White —.

Holy Bush, Ivy Lane (C.3): H. Holland, 1612

Holy Ghost, Paul's Churchyard (northeast; *A.5;* § = A.3):
J. Cawood, 1553–68
(Rog. Ireland, 1568)
G. Cawood, 1576
W. Leake 1, 1602–13

Holy Lamb, Little Britain, near Aldersgate Street (F.4):
J. White, 1622–25
R. Milbourne, 1640+?
—Lombard Street (O.12): J. Harvey, 1539
—Ludgate Hill (Q.4):
W. Holme 3, 1597–98 (sometimes omits 'Holy')
J. Colby, 1638–39
—New Fish Street Hill (T.4): F. Clifton, 1623–27 (sometimes omits 'Holy')
—Paternoster Row (C.7): J. Harrigat, 1624–30
—Paul's Churchyard (east; A.6):
A. Veale, 1550?–86 (omits 'Holy')
H. Carre, 1580 (next to $)
C. Knight, 1602–30
T. Knight, 1630–33
J. Parker, 1634
J. Cowper, 1637–39

Holy Trinity. *See* Trinity.

Hood. *See* Double Hood.

Horse. *See* Black, Flying, White —.

Horseshoe, Pope's Head Alley (O.11):
T. Archer, 1622–25 (over against $)
B. Allen, 1631 (—)
—Smithfield (E.8): T. Lambert, 1634–40+?
—Trinity Lane (S.5): T. Paine, 1632

Huntsman, Paternoster Row (C.7): E. Mutton, 1603

John the Baptist, *St.*, within Paul's Chain (A.9): unidentified agent for J. Bale, 1551

John the Evangelist, *St.*, Charing Cross (X.14):
Robt. Wyer, 1529–55
T. Colwell, 1560?–62
N. Wyer, c. 1565–66
—Fleet Street (unloc; W.2): J. Butler, 1528?–31?
——beneath the conduit (W.5):
T. Colwell, 1565–75
H. Jackson, 1576–95

Jonas, Paul's Churchyard (unloc; B): E. Edgar, 1612

Judith, Paul's Churchyard (*St. Faith's parish; A.4;* § = northeast; A.3): H. Tab, 1542–45?

Justice Royal, Fleet Street, against the Black Bell (W.14): E. Dicæophile, *pseud.*, 1569

Katherine, *St.*, Paul's Churchyard (unloc; B): unidentified agent for Paris publisher, 1515 (7018.5)

Key, Paul's Churchyard (unloc; B): T. Hacket, 1568
—*See* also Golden —, Half-Eagle and —.

Keys. *See* Cross —.

King's (Queen's) Arms, Cheapside (unloc; N.1): F. Church & J. Jackson 2, 1634
—Little Britain (F.4): C. Bee, 1634
—Paul's Churchyard (*east; A.6;* § = northeast; A.3):
W. Bonham, 1542–46?
W. Norton, 1580–89
J. Hodgets, 1616
R. Whitaker, 1631–40+?
(Joyce Norton, 1632–38)

King's Head, Chancery Lane (W.10b):
H. Shepherd, 1639 (near — Tavern)
J. Colby, 1639 (under — Tavern)
—Little Old Bailey, in Eliot's Court (D.1): M. Bradwood, 1606 (near $)
—Paternoster Row (C.7): C. Hunt (nr $), 1606
—Paul's Churchyard (northeast; A.3):
A. Pepwell, 1566
T. Norton, 1617–18
R. Whitaker, 1619–26
(Hannah Barrett, 1624–26)
R. Bostock, 1626–40+?

Kings. *See* Three —.

Knight. *See* Blind —.

Lamb. *See* Holy —.

Leg, Strand (X.4): R. Meighen, 1623–28

Lion. *See* Black, Golden, Red, White —; also Glove and —.

Lions. *See* Three Golden —.

Love and Death, Paul's Churchyard (unloc; B): R. Watkins, 1570

Lucrece, Fleet Street (W.5): T. Berthelet, 1524–35 (sometimes Roman —)
—Newgate Market (C.4): T. Purfoot 1, 1579–80
—Paul's Churchyard (unloc; B): T. Purfoot 1 (printing house), 1550?–77
——at little North door (A.1): T. Purfoot 1 (shop), 1594

Lute, Paternoster Row (C.7): J. Rowbotham, 1574

Maiden('s) Head, Cornhill (unloc; O.6): G. Hodges, 1625
—Fleet Lane (D.2): W. Venge, 1585 (over against $)
—Guildhall gate (H.5): W. Ferbrand, 1600 (over against $)
—Paul's Churchyard (St. Faith's parish; A.4):
R. Faques, 1509–10?
T. Petyt, 1536–50

Man. *See* Green —.

Marigold, Cheapside, in Goldsmiths' Row (N.5): ?F. Eglesfield, 1637
—Paul's Churchyard (unloc; B):
J. Boler 1, 1627–35
Anne Boler, 1635–38
F. Eglesfield, 1637–40+?
?J. Boler 2, 1640

Mark, *St.*, Paul's Churchyard (west; A.10): J. Notary, 1516

Mary Magdalen's Head, Holborn, near Staple Inn (V.9): C. Purset, 1605–11

Mermaid, Cheapside, next Paul's gate (N.2):
J. Rastell, 1519–36
[W. Bonham, c. 1525]
[L. Sutton, 1536–41]
—Holborn (unloc; V.1): T. Saunders, 1613
—Knightrider Street (R.2): H. Bynneman, 1568–75
—Lombard Street, against Stocks Market (O.12): J. Gough, 1539–40
—Paternoster Row (C.7): H. Bynneman, 1567
—Paul's Churchyard (west; A.10): N. Ling, 1582

Michael, *St.*, Paul's Churchyard (unloc; B): M. Lobley, 1539–58

Mitre, within Aldgate (L.1): S. Burton, 1640 (next — Tavern)
—Fleet Street (W.7): W. Lee 2, 1626–71 (next — Tavern)
—Smithfield (unloc; E.1): J. Tisdale, 1558
—*See* also Bishop's —.

Mulberry Tree, Whitefriars (W.7): V. Simmes, 1610 (near $ or perhaps a real tree)

Nicholas, *St.*, Paul's Churchyard (unloc; B):
N. Le Comte, 1494
J. Toy, 1531–34

Nobody, Barbican, near Long Lane end (I.1): J. Trundle, 1606–20

Oak Tree, Long Lane (E.9): E. Aggas, 1603 (once Green —)

Old Swan, Thames Street (T.5): T. Creede, 1594–96 (near $)

Oliphaunt. *See* Elephant.

Our Lady of Pity, Fleet Bridge (W.3): J. Byddell, 1533–35?
—Paternoster Row (C.7): J. Redman, 1540
—Paul's Churchyard (unloc; B): W. de Worde, 1508–09

P[ ], Strand (all but first letter of $ missing; X.1): J. Jackson 2, c. 1635?

Paper Book, Chancery Lane (unloc; W.10a): J. Herbert, 1598

Paris, without Newgate/Snow Hill (D(headnote), D.9): Jn. Barnes, 1605

Parrot, Paul's Churchyard (northeast; A.3):
A. Maunsell, 1576–81
J. Oxenbridge, 1595–99
F. Norton, 1600–04
W. Aspley, 1608–40
—*See* also Cat(s) and Parrot(s).

Paul, *St.*, Little Britain (F.4): R. Mynne, 1627–39+?
—Paul's Churchyard (west; A.10): J. Stepneth, 1611

Paul's Head, Cannon Street (T.1): P. Waterhouse, 1629–31
—Carter Lane (R.1): J. Busby 1, 1600 (next to $)

Peahen, Fleet Street (W.7): W. Holme 3, 1603

Pen. *See* Hand and Golden —.

Pied Bull, Paul's Churchyard, near St. Austin's gate (southeast; A.7): N. Butter, 1605–41+?

Pigeons. *See* Three —.

Plough, Cow Lane (E.4): W. Lewes, 1566
—*See* also Hand and —.

Pomegranate. *See* Rose and —.

Pope's Head, Lombard Street/Royal Exchange = Pope's Head Alley (O.11):
T. Hackett, 1584–90 (under $)
A. Harris, 1598 (—)
—Paul's Churchyard (unloc; B): unidentified agent for W. Jones 3, 1633 (251)

Prince's Arms, Fleet Street (W.11), T. Marsh, 1554–55
—Paul's Churchyard (north; A.2): H. Moseley, 1637–59

Printer's Press, Fleet Lane (D.2):
G. Eld, 1607–15
(W. Blainchard, 1613)

Purse, Little Old Bailey (D.6): R. Ward, 1590–91

Queen's Arms. *See* King's Arms.

Rainbow, Fleet Street, near Inner Temple gate (W.11):
T. Downes 1, 1624–25
E. Dawson, 1624–36
D. Pakeman, 1634–40+?

Raven. *See* Black —.

Red Ball, Paul's Churchyard (?north; A.2): H. Sanderson, 1560

Red Bull, within Temple Bar (W.14): G. Norton, 1616–18
—*See* also Bull.

Red Cross, Barbican (I.1): M. Simmons, 1637 (near $)
—Fleet Street conduit (W.5): James Davies, 1617
—Silver Street (H.15): T. Nelson, 1592 (near $)

Red Dragon, Paul's Churchyard (unloc; B):
E. Aggas, 1576–81
(T. Humble, 1581)

Red Harrow, Mark Lane (U.2): F. Cooke, 1591 (over against $)

Red Lion, Cloth Fair (E.3): S. Stafford, 1607–09 (near $)
—Gutter Lane (G.4): Rich. Jackson, 1569
—London Bridge (T.7): unidentified agent for R. Bonian, 1609 (18347.5)
—Paul's Churchyard (unloc; B): W. Bonham, 1550?–51
—Watling Street (N.4): J. Hippon, 1603 (adjoining — gate)

Resurrection, Cheapside, by little conduit (N.3): J. Day 1, 1550–53
—Holborn conduit (D.5): J. Day 1, 1547–49

Roman Lucrece. *See* Lucrece.

Rose, Paternoster Row (C.7): J. Turke, 1533–54
—Paul's Churchyard (northeast; A.3):
J. Wight, 1551–54?
R. Boyle, 1587–89
H. Fetherstone, 1609–26
?R. Martin (no $), 1633–35
G. Thomason & O. Pulleyn, 1637–45
—*See* also Half-Rose and Half-Sun.

Rose and Crown, near Holborn Bridge (V.2): Rich. Jones, 1583–94
—Holborn, next St. Andrew's Church (V.4): Rich. Jones, 1594–1602

Rose and Pomegranate, Cheapside (N.6): J. Rowbotham, 1562–63?

Rose Garland, Fleet Street (W.3):
R. Copland, 1515–47?
W. Copland, 1548–58

Saracen's Head, near Holborn conduit/ Snow Hill (D(headnote), D.9):
J. Charlewood & J. Tisdale, 1557?
J. White, 1615 (over against $)
T. Langley, 1615–23 (—)
F. Grove, 1624–40+? (—)
(F. Smith, 1634)

Ship, London Wall (H.8): T. East & H. Middleton, 1571 (by $)
—Paul's Churchyard, near St. Austin's gate (A.7): T. Butter, 1576
—Red Cross Street (I.7): W. Jones 3, 1601–04

Snail, Lime Street (P.6): S. Harrison (author), 1604

Splayed-Eagle. *See* Spread-Eagle.

Spread-Eagle, Fleet Lane (D.2): Rich. Jones, 1567?–74
—Fleet Street (W.7): W. Holme 3, c. 1600
—near Great St. Bartholomew's (E.6): O. Rogers, 1559–61
—Paul's Churchyard, next the great school (east; A.6):
W. Lynne, 1550
J. Gybkyn, 1551
——near great North door of Paul's (A.2):
R. Bonian, 1607–10
(H. Walley, 1609–10?)
—Wood Street (H.16): [R. Field, 1613–24]
—*See* also Black —.

Spur, Poultry (O.1): G. Wilne, 1638

Star, Aldersgate Street (F.2): H. Denham, 1585–87
—Bread Street Hill (S.8):
R. Yardley, 1590–93
P. Short, 1590–1603
Emma Short, 1603
H. Lownes 1, 1604–29
R. Young, 1629–41
—Cornhill (P.2):
N. Newbery, 1619–25
S. Ward, 1627–31
—Paternoster Row (C.7): H. Denham, 1565–83
—Paul's Churchyard (unloc; B):
T. Raynald, 1549
(John Harrington (patron?), 1549)
R. Madeley, 1553
——West door/end (A.10):
Jonas Man, 1608
R. Redmer, 1610–19 (once Golden —)
E. Brewster, 1616–24
—Pope's Head Alley (O.11):
N. Newbery, 1623–36
Joan Newbery 2, 1637
S. Enderby, 1637–40+?
—*See* also Blazing —, Hand and —.

Stillatory, Paul's Wharf (R.8): J. Hester (distiller), 1591

Sugarloaf, Fleet Street, near Whitefriars (W.7): Jn. Browne 1, 1598
——next Temple Bar (W.14):
L. Blaiklock, 1638–40+?
(W. Wethered, 1640)

Sun, Bethlehem (Bedlam; K.1): H. Bell, 1620–21
—Fleet Street, near the conduit (W.5):
W. de Worde, 1501–35
(H. Watson, 1509)
(R. Copland, 1514?)
J. Byddell, 1535–44
(J. Gaver, 1539)
E. Whitchurch, 1545–53?
(W. Baldwin, 1549–50)
J. Wayland, 1554–56

Sun — *cont.*
—Holborn, near the conduit/Snow Hill (D(headnote), D.9):
R. Peake 1, 1611 (next — Tavern)
W. Peake, c. 1630–35 (—)
[R. Peale 2, 1634–c. 1640]
J. Wright 2, 1634–35
F. Smith, 1636
— —within the turnstile (V.13): G. Hutton, 1636
—Paternoster Row (C.7):
T. Gosson, 1582–91
?Alice or H. Gosson, 1606–09
—Paul's Churchyard (northeast; A.3):
Ant. Kitson, 1555–78
Abr. Kitson, 1579–94
R. Bankworth, 1594–1612
J. Partridge, 1628–38?
J. Rothwell 2, 1632–40+?
—*See* also Half-Rose and Half-Sun.

Swan, Duck Lane (E.5): T. Slater, 1633–39 (sometimes White —)
—Grub Street (I.6): F. Sergeant (bowyer?), 1594
—Paternoster Row (C.7): J. Drawater, 1595
—Paul's Churchyard (*east; A.6;* § = northeast; A.5):
J. King, 1559–61
G. Dewes, 1578–87
Ralph Jackson 1, 1589–1601
(W. Young, 1589–94)
C. Burby, 1602–07 (sometimes White —)
(E. Edgar, 1604–07)
Eliz. Burby, 1607–09 (sometimes White —)
W. Welby, 1610–16 (sometimes White —)
S. Man, 1618–40+?
—*See* also Old —, White —.

Talbot, Aldersgate Street (F.2): B. Fisher, 1626–36
—Holborn conduit (D.5): R. Ward, 1580?–85
—Paternoster Row (C.7):
T. Man 1, 1583–1623
(R. Walker, 1598)
T. Man 2, 1605
Jonas Man, 1608–22
(J. Bartlet, 1619–20)
P. Man, 1622
B. Fisher, 1622–25
—Paul's Churchyard (west; A.10): N. Fosbrooke, 1610

Three [ ], (remainder of sign and address missing): T. Dainty, 1637

Three Arrows, Golden (Golding) Lane (I.5): R. Hall, 1561

Three Conies, Old Change (N.8): H. Carre, 1581

Three Cranes, Cannon Street (T.1): T. Hacket, 1560 (over against $)
—Vintry. *See* Addresses: S.9.

Three Crowns, Cloth Fair (E.3): S. Stafford, 1606

Three Crowns Imperial, Burse (Royal Exchange; O.8): H. Sanderson, 1571

Three Fleurs-de-lis, Fleet Street (W.4): ?J. Shaw (inventor) or his agent, 1637
—Paul's 'Alley' = Chain, near St. Gregory's Church (south; A.9): R. Fleming, 1619

Three Golden Lions, Cornhill (O.9):
J. Bellamy, 1624–40+?
Ralph Smith, 1640

Three Kings, Paul's Churchyard (west; A.10): J. Notary, 1510, 1518–20
— —(near the great North door of Paul's; shop demolished in 1636; A.2):
R. Collins, 1631–33
H. Moseley, 1634–36

Three Pigeons, Paternoster Row (C.7): J. Hill, 1588
—Paul's Churchyard (northeast; A.3):
W. Barrett, 1614–18
J. Parker, 1620–25
H. Robinson, 1627–70

Three Wells, Paul's Churchyard (west; A.10): H. Bynneman, 1572

Tiger's Head, Fleet Street, between Fleet Bridge and the conduit (W.4): H. Seile, 1637
— —over against St. Dunstan's Church (W.9): H. Seile, 1638–40+?
—Paternoster Row (C.7): C. Barker, 1577–79
—Paul's Churchyard (near the great North door of Paul's; shop demolished in 1636; A.2):
C. Barker, 1576–77
T. Cooke, 1578–93
(P. Eede, 1578)
(M. Hart, 1593)
J. Hardy, 1594–96
W. Aspley, 1599–1600
M. Cooke & S. Macham 1, 1606–07
L. Lisle, 1608–18
H. Seile, 1619–36

Time, Paul's Churchyard (west; A.10):
W. Wood, 1599–1601
Joyce Macham or her unidentified agent, 1618

Tower, near Leadenhall (P.5): A. Ryther (engraver; next $): 1590

Tree, Paul's Churchyard (west; A.10): R. Day, 1580 (under $ or perhaps a real tree)
—*See* also Mulberry, Oak —.

Trinity, Paul's Churchyard, near the new school(s) (east; A.6):
H. Jacobi, 1505–12? (Holy —)
Unidentified agent for Parisian publishers, 1512?–15 (3269.5, 7018.5)
H. Pepwell, 1518–31
—without Temple Bar (X.1): H. Smith, 1543–46

Tun. *See* Golden —, Two Tuns.

Turk's Head, Fleet Street (W.7):
Jn. Barnes, 1602–03 (sometimes Great Turk)
W. Lee 2, 1626–71 (—)

Two Greyhounds, Cornhill (O.9): J. Bellamy, 1622–23

Two Tuns, Little Britain (F.4): J. Morrett, 1634

Unicorn, Canon Lane (A.2): J. Drawater, 1596
—Cornhill (O.9):
W. Riddiard, c. 1625?–36
W. Hope, 1637–48
—Fleet Bridge (W.3):
R. Milbourne, 1636–39
(J. Colby, 1637)
—Paternoster Row (C.7): Jn. Harrison 4, 1602–41+? (sometimes Golden — or — and Bible)
—near Tower of London (U.3): R. Higgenbotham, 1635
—*See* also White —.

Unicorn and Bible. *See* Unicorn.

Venice, Old Bailey (D.7): R. Martin, 1639–41

Vine, Fleet Street (unloc; W.2): E. Venge, 1590

White Bear, near Baynard's Castle (R.6): J. Windet, 1585–88
—Botolph Lane (T.10): J. Mayler, 1539–43
—Cornhill (unloc; O.6): T. Jenner, 1621
—near St. Sepulchre's Church (D.8): H. Tomes, 1598

White Fleur-de-lis. *See* Fleur-de-lis.

White Greyhound. *See* Greyhound.

White Hart, Fleet Street (unloc; W.2):
?R. Bankes, 1539–43? (at, next to $)
?R. Taverner, 1539–46? (—)
A. Clerke, 1540?–46? (at $)
T. Fisher, 1600
Roger Jackson, 1601
—Smithfield (unloc; E.1):
R. Raworth, 1635–36 (near — Tavern)
(J. Crouch, 1636)

White Hind, Coleman Street (H.4): W. Harris, 1639–40
—without Cripplegate (I.2): J. Greensmith, 1636

White Horse, Canon Lane. *See* Paul's Churchyard below.
—Little Britain (F.4): W. Hills, 1636
—Paul's Churchyard, next Paul's School (east; A.6): A. Hester, 1539–51
——Canon Lane, near great North door of Paul's (variations on the address are indicated below by PC, CL, gNd; north; A.2):
W. Williamson, 1571 (PC)
?R. Waldegrave or his unidentified agent, 1585–86 (CL)
J. Dalderne, 1589 (CL)
W. Young, 1596 (gNd, CL)
R. Howell, 1600–02 (gNd)
A. Johnson, 1604–21 (gNd)
J. Kirton & T. Warren, 1639–40+? (PC)
—Pope's Head Alley (O.11):
J. Sudbury, 1611–18?
G. Humble, 1611–34
N. Newbery, 1618 (over against $)

White Lion, Chancery Lane (W.10b): T. Dring, 1667–68
—near Charing Cross (X.14): G. Baker, 1631
—Paul's Churchyard (north; A.2):
T. Adams, 1594–1609
(F. Burton, 1603)
F. Constable, 1615–24
A. Uphill, 1625–26
R. Higgenbotham, 1630
?H. Moseley, 1632
N. Fussell, ?1632, 1637–39 (sometimes — and Ball)
(C. Greene, 1637?–38)
S. Browne, 1640 (sometimes — and Ball)

White Swan, Addle Hill (R.6): V. Simmes, 1595–1605
—*See* also Swan.

White Unicorn, Pope's Head Alley (O.11): R. Bearkes, 1602

Windmill, Britain's Burse (X.10): J. Budge, 1625
—Paul's Churchyard (unloc; B):
E. Edgar, 1609–11
A. Garbrand, 1610–13
—Snow Hill (D.9): F. Grove, 1630

Woolsack, Hosier Lane (E.7): R. Hudson, 1588

Corner Shop, Holborn, Gray's Inn Lane (V.10): B. Lightfoot, 1613–14
——Middle Row (V.9): T. Bailey, 1617–18
—Paul's Churchyard, Southwest door (A.10): ?H. Disle, 1574
——Northwest door (A.10):
Rich. Smith, 1571–75
N. Fosbrooke, 1610–11
——Paul's gate (A.5):
M. Lobley, 1563 (on right hand as you come from Cheapside)
T. Gosson, 1580 (corner shop to Cheapside)

Little Shop, near Clifford's Inn (W.9):
J. Busby 1, 1596 (near CI)
J. Helme & J. Busby 2, 1607–08 (next CI gate)
Unidentified agent for R. Badger, 1636–38 (in St. Dunstan's Churchyard, turning up to CI)
?T. Andrewes, 1639 (—)
—Paul's Churchyard, great South door (A.8): J. Wolfe, 1592 (over against door)
——?Southwest door (A.10): Rich. Jones, 1566 (misprinted 'Northwest' door)
——North door (A.2): W. Owen, 1562
—Royal Exchange; near conduit in Cornhill, (O.10):
T. Archer, 1603
?E. Edgar, 1607
P. Harrison, 1608

Long Shop, Paul's Churchyard, West end (A.10):
W. Jones 1, 1566, 1571–72 (called 'new', 1571)
J. Day 1, 1578–79
R. Day, 1580 ('sub Arbore', under tree or arbour?)
——Northwest door (A.10): W. Jones 1, 1573 (called 'new'; near Bishop's palace)
—Poultry, under St. Mildred's Church (O.1):
R. Bankes, 1523–28
J. Mychell, 1530–32?
R. Kele, 1543?–45
J. Allde, 1561–84
Edw. Allde, 1584–88, 1607
Margaret Allde, 1590–1603
H. Rocket, 1602–11

Middle Shop, Poultry, under St. Mildred's Church (O.1):
W. Wright 1, 1581–89
C. Burby, 1592–94

New Shop, Cheapside, by little conduit (N.3): J. Day 1, 1549
—Paul's Churchyard (southwest; A.10): Stationers' Co., 1606
—*See* also Long Shop, Paul's Churchyard.

INDEX 3E: ADDRESSES

This index is a departure from that found in *Dict. 1*: 321–35, which lists streets and other locations alphabetically and refers back to signs all those who had them. Instead, the present index provides a record of all stationers and other publishers appearing in STC imprints and with known addresses, whether they had signs or not, in a context showing who were their colleagues nearby. The addresses have been grouped geographically in twenty-four small areas labeled A–X, organized in five major districts:

Paul's Churchyard (A–B)
Along the Wall from Newgate to Aldgate (C–M)
East of St. Paul's to Leadenhall (N–P)
The Thames from Fleet Ditch to the Tower (Q–U)
West of Fleet Ditch (V–X)

The list of streets, lanes, churches, etc. below leads to the relevant area and to the location within it. Rare examples of an alley or other subaddress occasionally have the year it was used appended, e.g. Petty Canons A.2-1605. Saints are listed under their Christian names except for those characterized by 'Little' or 'Great', which are under those words. Abbreviations used are:

ag	against	unident	unidentified
Ch	Church	unloc	unlocated
Chyd	Churchyard	w/i	within
dr	door	w/o	without
nr	near	—	same name *or* location as preceding
ov/ag	over against		
par	parish		

Abchurch Lane O.13
Abergavenny House Q.1
Addle Hill R.1,6
Addle Street H.1
Aldermanbury H.2
Aldermary Ch N.11
Aldersgate (w/i) G
—(w/o) F
Aldersgate Street F.2
Aldgate (w/i) L
—(w/o) M
All Hallows' Ch, unloc, but ?Bread and Watling streets N.10
—Lombard Street P.1
Amen Corner Q.1
St. Andrew's Ch, Holborn V.4
—Wardrobe R.6
Angel Alley F.2-1617
St. Anne's Ch, Aldersgate G.2
—Blackfriars Q.5
St. Anthony's, unident, but ?St. Antholin's Ch (N.12) or ?St. Anthony's Hospital (O.5)
Arundel House X.4
St. Austin's Ch N.7
St. Austin's gate, w/i Paul's Chyd A.7
—w/o Paul's Chyd N.7
Austin Friars J.1

Bacon House G.3
Barbican I(headnote), I.1
St. Bartholomew's Hospital E.8
Baynard's Castle R.6
Bear Dance U.4
Bedford Street X.11
Bedlam K.1
Belle Savage Q.4
St. Benet's Ch, Paul's Wharf R.7
St. Benet Fink Ch O.4
Bethlehem K.1
Billingsgate T.9–13
Billiter Lane L.3
Bishopsgate J.2
Bishopsgate Street (w/i) J.2
—(w/o) K.2
Black Horse Alley W.3-1631
Black Raven Alley, ?Leadenhall Street L.3
—Thames Street T.6
Blackfriars Q.6
St. Botolph's Ch w/o Aldersgate F.3
—w/o Aldgate M.1
—Billingsgate T.9
—w/o Bishopsgate K.2
Botolph Lane T.10
Bow Ch N.6
Bread Street, nr Cheapside N.5
—nr Old Fish Street S.4
—nr Watling Street N.10
Bread Street Hill S.8
St. Bride's Ch W.4
Bride Lane W.4
Britain's Burse X.10–11, X.12-1639
Broad Lane, Vintry S.10
Broad Street O.3
Bunhill I.9
Burse O.8-1571

Cannon Street T.1
Canon Lane A.2
Carter Lane R.1
Cateaton Street H.3
Catherine Wheel Alley T.5
Chancery Lane end, Fleet Street W.10–10e
—Holborn V.12–12a
Charterhouse E.2
Charing Cross X.14
Cheap gate A.5, C.7-1548, N.2
Cheapside N.1–6
Christ Church C.1
Christ's Hospital C.2
St. Clement's Ch, Eastcheap T.3
St. Clement Danes Ch, Strand X.1–2
St. Clement's Lane O.14
Clifford's Inn W.9-1596, 1607, 1624, 1636, 1639
Cloth Fair E.3
Cockpit playhouse X.5
Coleman Street H.4
Conduits:
Aldermanbury H.2
Cheapside N.3
Cornhill O.10
Fleet Street W.5
Gracechurch Street P.4
Holborn D(headnote), D.5
Cornhill, nr Royal Exchange O.6–10
—nr St. Peter's Ch P.2
Covent Garden X.11
Cow Lane E.4
Crane Court N.8
Cree Church L.1–2
Creed Lane Q.2
Cripplegate (w/i) H
—(w/o) I
Customs House U.1

St. Dionis Backchurch P.3
Distaff Lane S.3
Doctors' Commons R.3
Drury Lane X.5–5b
Duck Lane E.5, F.4
Duke's Place L.2
St. Dunstan's Ch in the West W.9
Durham House X.9

Eastcheap T.4-1607
Eliot's Court D.1
Ely House V.5
Essex House X.2
Exchanges:
Royal Exchange, 1571–1640+ O.2–12
New Exchange, 1609–40+ X.10

St. Faith's Ch A.4
Fetter Lane end, Holborn V.7
—Fleet Street W.8
Finsbury I.10
Fleet Alley, unloc, but probably somewhere along Fleet Street W.1
Fleet Bridge W.3
Fleet Lane D.2
Fleet Street W
—Conduit W.5
Fore Street I.3
Foster Lane G.3
Friday Street N.9
Furnival's Inn V.8

Garter Place I.1-1617
George Alley K.2
St. Giles's Ch, Cripplegate I.4
Giltspur Street D.3
Golden (Golding) Lane I.5
Goldsmiths' Alley I.7-1640
Goldsmiths' Hall G.3-1583
Goldsmiths' Row, Cheapside N.5
Grace Ch P.1
Gracechurch (Gratious) Street P.4
Gray's Inn V.10
Great St. Bartholomew's Ch E.6, F.4
Great Wood Street H.17
Green Arbour D.4
St. Gregory's Ch A.9
Greyfriars C.2
Grub Street I.6
Guildhall H.5
Gutter Lane G.4

'Hallywell' I.10
Hammersmith X.18
St. Helen's J.3
High Holborn V.11
Holborn V
—Middle Row V.9
Holborn Bridge V.2
Holborn Conduit D(headnote), D.5, 9, E.4, 7
Holborn Hill V.6
Hosier Lane E.7
Hospitals:
St. Anthony's O.5
St. Bartholomew's E.8
Christ's C.2
St. Katherine's U.4
Spital K.4
Hunsdon House Q.6-1625

Inner Temple W.11
Ivy Bridge X.8
Ivy Lane C.3

St. John's Street E.10

St. Katherine's Hospital beside the Tower of London U.4
St. Katherine Cree Ch L.1–2
King Street X.16
King's (Queen's) Printing House: Bacon House, 1579–c. 1600 G.3
Northumberland House, c. 1600–25 G.8
Hunsdon House, c. 1625–40+ Q.6
King's (Queen's) Wardrobe R.2
Knightrider Street R.2

Lambeth (Lambard, Lambert) Hill S.7
St. Lawrence Lane H.6
Leadenhall P.5
Leadenhall Street L.3
St. Leonard's Ch, Foster Lane G.3, 5
Lilypot Lane G.6
Lime Street P.6
Lincoln's Inn V.12a
Lincoln's Inn Fields X.5a
Little St. Bartholomew's Ch E.7

Headnote — *cont.*
Little Britain F.4
Little St. Helen's J.3
Little Old Bailey D.1, 4, 6
Little Wood Street H.7
Lombard (Lumbard) Street, nr Royal Exchange O.12–13
—upper end, nr Grace Ch P.1
London Bridge T.7
London Stone T.1
London Wall H.8
Long Alley E(headnote), E.6-1633
Long Lane E.9, I.1-1603
Long Walk E(headnote), E.6-1619, 1624
Lothbury H.9
Lovell's Inn C.7-1606
Ludgate Q.3,4, Q.6-1588
Ludgate Hill Q.4
Lumbard Street O.12, P.1

St. Magnus' Ch T.8
Maiden Lane G.7
St. Margaret's Ch, Lothbury H.9
—New Fish Street T.4
St. Mark's Alley O.14
Mark Lane U.2
St. Martin le Grand, liberty of G.9
St. Martin's Ch in the Fields X.13–14
St. Martin's Ch, Ludgate Q.3
St. Martin's Lane, Aldersgate G.8
St. Mary Aldermary Ch N.11
St. Mary at Hill T.12
St. Mary Axe J.4
St. Mary le Bow Ch N.6
St. Mary's Ch, Whitechapel M.2
St. Mary Magdalen's Ch, Old Fish Street S.1
St. Michael's Ch, Bassishaw H.10
St. Michael's Ch, (Great) Wood Street H.17
Middle Row, Holborn V.9
Middle Temple W.13
St. Mildred's Ch, Poultry O.1
Milk Street H.11
Minories M.3
Moorgate (w/i) H
—(w/o) I.9–10

New Exchange X.10–11, X.12-1639
New Fish Street T.4
Newgate (w/i) C
—(w/o) D
Newgate Market C(headnote), C.4
St. Nicholas Shambles C(headnote), C.5
Northumberland House G.8
Norwich rents X.14-1529

Old Bailey D.7
Old Change, nr Thames Street S.2
—nr Watling Street N.8
Old Fish Street S.1–3, 7–8
Old Jewry H.13
Old Swan Lane T.5

Panyer Alley C.6
Parish Clerks' Hall S.10
Paternoster Row C.7
Paul's Alley A.1
Paul's Chain, w/i Paul's Chyd A.9
—nr Doctors' Commons R.3
Paul's Churchyard A–B
Paul's Cross A.6
Paul's gate A.5, C.7-1548, N.2
Paul's Head Tavern R.1
Paul's School A.6
Paul's Wharf R.8
Pentecost Lane C.1-1616
St. Peter's Ch, Cornhill P.2
—Paul's Wharf R.8-1620
—Wood Street N.4
Peter College A.10
St. Peter's Hill R.9
Petty Canons A.2-1605
Petticoat Lane M.4
Philip Lane H.14
Pie Corner D.3
Pope's Head Alley O.11
Poultry O.1
Prince's Street X.5-1616, X5a
Puddle Wharf (Dock) R.5
Pye Corner D.3
St. Pulchre (Pulker)'s Ch D.8

Queen's Head Alley C.7-1631
Queen's Street X.5b
Queen's Wardrobe R.2

Ratcliffe U.5
Red Cross Street I.7
Red Lion gate N.10
Rolls W.10e
Rood Lane P.7
Royal Exchange O(headnote), O.2–12

Saffron Hill V.4
Salisbury Court W.5-1596
Savoy X.7
Sea-coal Lane D.2-1591
St. Sepulchre's Ch D.8
Serjeants' Inn, Chancery Lane W.10c
—Fleet Street W.7
Sermon Lane R.4
Sessions House D.7-1624, 1634
Ship Alley I.7-1601
Shoe Lane end, Fleet Street W.6
—Holborn V.3
Shoreditch K.3
Silver Street H.15
Sion College H.16
Six Clerks' Office W.10d
Smart's Quay T.13
Smithfield E
Snow Hill D(headnote), D.9
Somer's Quay T.11
Somerset House X.6
Spital K.4
Staple Inn V.9
Stationers' Hall:
  Peter College, 1554–1606 A.10
  Milk Street, 1606–11 H.11
  Amen Corner, 1611 to present Q.1
Steelyard (Stillyard) S.11
Stepney U.6
Stocks (Market) O.1,12
Strand X.1–12
Strand Bridge X.4

Headnote — *cont.*
Suffolk rents X.14-1536
Swan Yard C.8
St. Swithun's Lane T.2
Symond's Inn W.10e-1629

Temple Bar (w/i) W.13-1553, W.14
—(w/o) X.1
Temple Ch W.11
Temple(s) W.11–13
Thames Street:
  Puddle Wharf to Paul's Wharf R.5–9
  Lambeth Hill to Steelyard S.7–11
  Old Swan Lane to Billingsgate T.5–13
  Customs House to the Tower U.1-5
St. Thomas Apostle Ch S.6
Threadneedle Street O.2
Three-Crane Wharf S.9
Tower of London U.3
Tower Hill U.3
Trinity Lane S.5
Turnstile Lane (Alley) V.13

Vintry S.9–10

Warwick Lane C.9
Watling Street N.7–12
Westminster Hall X.17
White Cross Street I.8
Whitechapel Ch M.2
Whitefriars W.7
Whitehall X.15
Wood Street H.17

York House X.12

The topographical approach has necessitated constant consultation of maps. Those found most useful are available in facsimiles published by Harry Margary, Lympne Castle, Kent, in association with Guildhall Library, London. The map in largest scale, which also has a separate though occasionally unreliable index volume available, is John Ogilby's *A large and accurate map of the city of London* [*1676*], ed. Ralph Hyde. It is in twenty sections (**1–20**) with a grid, and it lists a number of alleys and other small passages and courts not given in other early maps. Its major drawback is that considerable rebuilding after the Great Fire of 1666 had already taken place by the time Ogilby's survey was made, particularly in the area within Newgate. Facsimiles of earlier maps provide a corrective as well as views of the Strand and Westminster: *A collection of early maps of London 1553–1667*, ed. John Fisher. This work has twenty-one plates: *1–2*: Copperplate map, c. 1553–59; *3*: Braun and Hogenberg, 1572; *4–10*: 'Agas', c. 1562; *11–18*: Faithorne and Newcourt, 1658; *19*: Hollar's map of west central London, c. 1658; *20–21*: Leake's survey of London after the Great Fire, 1667. A plan largely based on the last faces p. 247 of the present volume. It has been supplied with a grid keyed as much as possible to the grid in Ogilby so that the same co-ordinates generally serve both maps. The Margary facsimiles are most useful, and anyone working with a range of London stationers in the seventeenth century and earlier would do well to acquire both sets for himself.

Map references are cited as follows:

13	number of section in the Ogilby map
8:9	grid co-ordinate, vertical before horizontal, taken from Ogilby but useful for the Leake adaptation facing p. 247
(B79)	house, church or other structure, or (i35) alley or court so identified in Ogilby
(#96)	church or company hall so numbered in Leake
19	number of plate in *A collection of early maps*

Listings of addresses in areas where there is no strong directional trend (primarily in the second and third districts) are alphabetical. Listings along Thames Street, Holborn, Fleet Street, the Strand and similar lengthy thoroughfares generally move in a direction away from St. Paul's and are signaled in the area headnote.

Three other volumes are of special use. The first two are: A. Prockter and R. Taylor, eds., *The A–Z of Elizabethan London*, London, 1979, which reproduces the 'Agas' map with overprinted grid, numerous further identifications, and indexes; and H. A. Harben, *A Dictionary of London*, London, 1918, which includes all but a very few addresses found in STC imprints. More readily available than the latter though less comprehensive is B. Weinreb and C. Hibbert, eds., *The London Encyclopedia*, London, 1983.

Following are the addresses of stationers and other publishers in London and its environs except for Westminster before 1501 and Southwark, both of which appear in Index 2Ai. Addresses have ordinarily been confirmed only to 1640, and the form of date: 1635–

PAUL'S CHURCHYARD & ENVIRONS

by Peter W. M. Blayney 1990

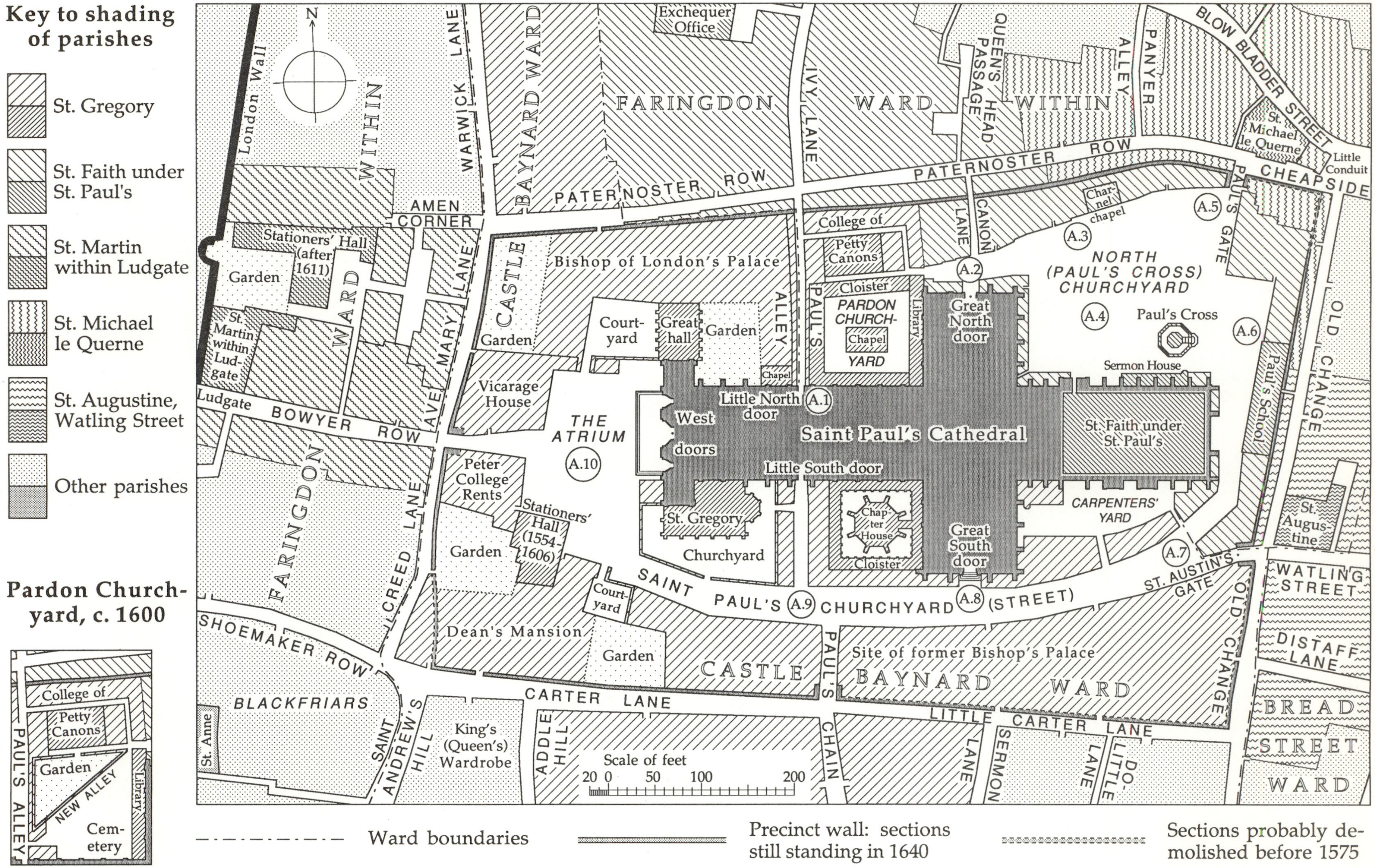
Key to shading of parishes
St. Gregory
St. Faith under St. Paul's
St. Martin within Ludgate
St. Michael le Querne
St. Augustine, Watling Street
Other parishes
Pardon Churchyard, c. 1600
College of
Petty Canons
Garden
NEW ALLEY
Library
Cemetery
PAUL'S ALLEY
London Wall
N
WITHIN
WARWICK LANE
BAYNARD WARD
FARINGDON
WARD
WITHIN
Exchequer Office
IVY LANE
QUEEN'S HEAD PASSAGE
ALLEY
PANYER
BLOW BLADDER STREET
St. Michael le Querne
Little Conduit
CHEAPSIDE
PATERNOSTER ROW
AMEN CORNER
Stationers' Hall (after 1611)
Garden
WARD
St. Martin within Ludgate
AVE MARY LANE
CASTLE
Garden
Bishop of London's Palace
Court-yard
Great hall
Garden
Chapel
ALLEY
PAUL'S
College of
Petty Canons
Cloister
PARDON CHURCHYARD
Chapel
Library
CANON LANE
Char-nel chapel
A.2
A.3
A.4
A.5
A.6
NORTH (PAUL'S CROSS) CHURCHYARD
Paul's Cross
Sermon House
PAUL'S GATE
Paul's School
OLD CHANGE
Great North door
Vicarage House
Ludgate
BOWYER ROW
THE ATRIUM
A.10
West doors
Little North door
A.1
Saint Paul's Cathedral
Little South door
St. Faith under St. Paul's
Peter College Rents
Stationers' Hall (1554-1606)
Garden
St. Gregory
Churchyard
Chapter House
Cloister
Great South door
CARPENTERS' YARD
A.7
St. Augustine
WATLING STREET
CREED LANE
FARINGDON
SAINT PAUL'S
A.9
CHURCHYARD
A.8
(STREET)
ST. AUSTIN'S GATE
Court-yard
Dean's Mansion
Garden
CASTLE
Site of former Bishop's Palace
BAYNARD WARD
OLD CHANGE
DISTAFF LANE
BREAD STREET WARD
SHOEMAKER ROW
BLACKFRIARS
St. Anne
SAINT ANDREW'S HILL
King's (Queen's) Wardrobe
CARTER LANE
ADDLE HILL
Scale of feet
20 0 50 100 200
PAUL'S CHAIN
LITTLE CARTER LANE
SERMON LANE
DO-LITTLE LANE
Ward boundaries
Precinct wall: sections still standing in 1640
Sections probably demolished before 1575

Headnote — *cont.*
40+? indicates that activity may have continued there for an unspecified period. Dates cited are the minimum dates for which the address appears in imprints with the following exceptions: stationers' names enclosed in square brackets indicate that no imprint noted has the address but that there is documentary evidence (e.g. wills) or a close family or partnership succession. Names in round brackets indicate a stationer associated with an address probably not his own, either in shared imprints or publications of a journeyman who may have continued to work for a while in the shop of his former master. A query preceding a stationer's name indicates uncertainty whether the sign used (given in round brackets) is in the same location as later shops with the sign, or whether an unknown agent rather than the publisher had the shop.

The terminology in the addresses is approximate, 'nr' being normally substituted for 'adjoining unto', 'beside', etc. Exact terminology and a sample of variations noted appear only in Index 1 under the relevant publisher.

PAUL'S CHURCHYARD

Signs have been regularly noted only in this district because, unless there is a gap of several decades, a single shop in the same location was surely intended, and sometimes only the sign is used. Signs enclosed in square brackets indicate shops whose location is based on documentary evidence rather than on imprints. Stationers not known to use a sign (no $) are so indicated.

WARNING: After this district had received its nearly final form in late 1989, research by Peter W. M. Blayney into leases and surveys of shops primarily in the northeastern sector of Paul's Churchyard uncovered material giving more specific locations to several of the signs. His evidence will be detailed in *The Bookshops in Paul's Cross Churchyard* (Occasional Papers of the Bibliographical Society, forthcoming), and the map of the Churchyard in the present volume is his version of one he prepared for use in that publication and has generously shared with STC. Signs *in a new location* based on his work are prefaced below by a section mark (§), and the shopkeepers at the signs have also been moved, e.g. in A.3. Signs *at an old location* have been left there, because the old location is what appears with the addresses in Index 1, but are given in *italic*, with the new location specified in the form: § = A.3; cf. area B below; owners of the sign have been deleted from these old locations. The narrative descriptions of the Churchyard and its smaller segments have been left essentially as they were in late 1989 even though Blayney's publication will render a number of details obsolete.

A. PAUL'S CHURCHYARD: Specific Locations

The accounts below and at the various stations in the churchyard are largely based on John Stow, *A survey of London*, 1598, 1603, 1618, 1633 (STC 23341–5, cited for convenience and for its superior index from the reprint of the 1603 edition by C. L. Kingsford, 2 vols. Oxford, 1908, and on G. H. Cook, *Old S. Paul's Cathedral*, London, [1955]. Stow is the quintessential source for knowledge of the pre-Fire churchyard and, of course, for a great deal of London besides. Cook reproduces many views of the exterior of the cathedral and includes a plan of the Bishop of London's palace (**A.10**) based on one drawn up by R. H. C. Finch. In spite of these aids, what the churchyard looked like at any particular time is difficult to establish. There are many gaps in our current knowledge that statements of location in imprints and the documentary evidence so far canvassed are unable to fill. It is hoped, however, that what follows will provide a few rough bearings.

From the mid-fourteenth century the churchyard was an enclosure through which there were six public entries: Paul's Alley (**A.1**), Canon Lane (**A.2**), Paul's or Cheap gate (**A.5**), St. Austin's gate (**A.7**), Paul's Chain (**A.9**), and the main entry leading from Ludgate (**A.10**). By Stow's time (I.326) and probably long before, most of the wall in the northeast was hidden by houses built on both sides. In 1670 as this area was under reconstruction following the

Paul's Churchyard — Specific Locations — *cont.*
Great Fire, the Dean and Chapter demised to the Corporation of London land in the northeast on which some of the wall had stood: a width of four feet from Paul's gate west to Paul's Alley (except the Canon Lane opening) and a width of two feet from Paul's gate south to St. Austin's gate (except for three houses which may already have been erected on the former wall's ground) in order to allow enlargement of the houses being rebuilt fronting on Paternoster Row and Old Change (Historical Manuscripts Commission, Ninth Report, part 1, pp. 58–9, no. 3021). On the other hand, in the western end by 1548 the grounds of Peter College extended from the churchyard all the way to Creede Lane (*Cal. Pat. Rolls, Edw. VI*: I.362).

Within the churchyard there were two major open spaces—indeed, almost two separate churchyards: in the northeast, where the Paul's Cross sermons took place as well as other proclamations and pronouncements of interest to the general public, and in the west, sometimes called the 'atrium', where other activities such as review of the armour belonging to the City companies and lotteries occurred. These two areas correspond fairly well with the portions of the two parishes, St. Faith's and St. Gregory's respectively, which fell within the churchyard.

The first change in the churchyard which affects us was in 1509 when John Colet's new school (**A.6**) began to be built. It is the earliest specific reference to position in the churchyard to appear in an imprint, followed in 1510 by mention of the 'atrium' (**A.10**). The next series of alterations in the churchyard began c. 1540 thanks to the enterprise of Reyner Wolfe. He began acquiring land in the northeastern sector (**A.3**), by 1542 was printing there, and in 1549 had caused to be carried away over 1,000 cartloads of bones from the charnel house (Stow I.293). On 10 April 1549 began the demolition ordered by the Lord Protector, the Duke of Somerset, of Pardon Churchyard (Pardon Church Haugh) between Paul's Alley and the north transept, along with its cloister containing paintings of the Dance of Death (Stow I.328). This action may have opened up ground close to the little North door of Paul's (**A.1**) for the first time. In 1554 the guild of Stationers acquired some part of the site of Peter College (**A.10**) in the western end of the churchyard as their new Hall prior to obtaining a royal charter of incorporation. The Bishop of London's palace (**A.10**), which was attached to the northwest side of the cathedral, apparently blocked easy passage between the northeastern and the western sectors of the churchyard until the late 1630s or later still, though one could—and often did—go through the cathedral itself.

From before the beginning of the STC period there were undoubtedly shops of various kinds within the churchyard, and the secularization of many areas in it must have speeded the process. Stow (II.19) was especially affronted by the masses of tall houses on the south side of the nave between St. Gregory's Church and the great South door (**A.9**), but there were virtually no booksellers there. Not until the reign of Charles I, and particularly the appointment of Laud as Bishop of London in 1628, was any serious attempt made to clear away the clutter of shops and houses along the cathedral's flanks. Notice in 1632 of a specific effort in this direction concerns booksellers and other tradesmen at the great North door (**A.2**) and along the eastern side of the north transept. By 1637 the last of these shops had finally been uprooted. During the same period Inigo Jones added a classical portico to the cathedral's western end. It is impossible to tell how many more booksellers the portico and other efforts toward repair and beautification displaced, but that some were cannot be doubted. Both the Leake and Ogilby maps show the space around Paul's cleared, but this was probably not the case until some time after 1640.

The circuit around the churchyard begins at the north side of the cathedral and proceeds in a clockwise direction. Stationers whose location within the churchyard is unknown are listed in area B.

A.1 North: Little North door/ Paul's Alley 12 8:8

Until 1549 the little North door was bordered on the west by the garden wall of the Bishop's palace and on the east by the western walk of the cloister surrounding Pardon Churchyard (Cook 65–7), and main access was from Paternoster Row and the cathedral itself. Further north on either side of Paul's Alley was other property be-

Paul's Churchyard — Specific Locations — Little North Door — *cont.*

longing to the Bishop and to the Petty Canons respectively, through which a few small passages may have led. In 1549 the Duke of Somerset had the cloister torn down (Stow I.328) except for the eastern walk, above which was the library, where Stow found very few books in 1598. Although some of the remaining ground went to the Petty Canons as a garden, probably enough space was left clear for both shops and means of approach from the east. The first tenant below has been queried here because of his sign, but he may have been elsewhere or not even in the churchyard. Sutton, with the same sign, gives no location except for the churchyard, and he too may have been elsewhere. The earliest specific reference is to the 'middle' North door. Between 1567 and 1571 'little' begins to supplant it, and by 1572 that is the predominant term.

Signs

Black Boy (Morens) | Gun | Lucrece

?Unident music printer (Black Boy, but no 'Paul's Chyd'), 1530 (22924)
?H. Sutton ('Paul's Chyd' but unloc), c. 1550–52
W. Martin (nr middle N dr), 1561?
H. Sanderson (nr little N dr), 1567–70
H. Kirkham, 1570–93 (at middle N dr, 1570–71; little N dr from 1572)
E. White 1 (at little N dr), 1578–1612
(A. White, 1593)
W. Kirkham (—), 1593–99
T. Purfoot 1 (—), 1594
(T. Millington, 1594)
C. Knight (—), 1595–96
J. Bailey 1 (—), 1600–03
E. White 2 (—), 1607–18
Sara White (—), 1613–15
Robt. Lownes (—), 1615
J. Grismand (—), 1618–19; (Paul's Alley), 1621–26

A.2 North: (Great) North door/ Canon Lane/ Petty Canons **12** 8:8, **13** 8:9

The first tenant below gives no location within the churchyard and is queried here because of his sign; the next bookseller at the Bible, Jugge in 1548, specified simply the cathedral's 'North' door, and so the description remained until about 1578, when the epithet 'great' began to come into use. Property owned by the Petty Canons stretched from the eastern side of Canon Lane westwards to Paul's Alley. Both sides of Canon Lane were in St. Faith's Parish (**A.4**), but the remainder apparently belonged in St. Gregory's parish (cf. **A.9**) or at least St. Gregory's was the church appointed for the Petty Canons' worship. In any case, the single mention of 'Petty Canons' as a place, in 1605, has been put here. Placement here of the Bishop's Head is based on Ponsonby's tenure; of the Helmet on a tenement acquired by H. Toy (*L&P Hen VIII*, V: 102 (no. 218)). Stationers marked with an asterisk (*) were warned to remove their shops (signs also with an asterisk) from the area of the great North door in 1632, when they flanked the door itself, clung to the eastern side of the north transept, and extended to the door into St. Faith's; the final order for removal came in 1636 (*Library* 3 (1902): 267–8; Greg, *Companion*, pp. 337–8).

Signs

*Ball
*Bible
[Bishop's Head]
*Bull('s) Head
*Fleur-de-lis (and Crown)
Golden Key
[Helmet]
Prince's Arms
Spread-Eagle
*Three Kings
*Tiger's Head
Unicorn
White Horse
White Lion

?Unident agent for E. Whitchurch & R. Grafton (Bible), 1540 (16015)
R. Jugge, 1547–58
Unident agent for R. Caly (Bishop's Head), 1553? (11592, note)
?H. Sanderson (Red Ball), 1560
W. Owen (no $), 1562
H. Toy, 1562–74
J. Arnold (no $), 1570
W. Williamson, 1571
C. Barker, 1576–77
M. Jennings, 1577–81
T. Chard, 1578–85?
J. Wight (no $), 1578–89
T. Cooke, 1578–93
(P. Eede, 1578)
John Jugge (no $), 1580?
H. Disle (Canon Lane, no $), 1580–82
R. Waldegrave or his unident agent (White Horse, Canon Lane), 1585–86
T. Cadman, 1585–88
J. Dalderne (Canon Lane), 1589
A. Jeffes (no $), 1591–92
W. Ponsonby, 1591–98
W. Holme 3 (no $), 1592
T. Wight (no $), 1592–96
Joan Broome, 1592–1601
(M. Hart, 1593)

Paul's Churchyard — Specific Locations — Great North Door — *cont.*

T. Adams, 1593–1609
J. Flasket (no $), 1594
J. Hardy, 1594–96
S. Shorter (no $), 1594–98
J. Drawater (Canon Lane), 1595–96
W. Young (Canon Lane), 1596
(R. Ockould, 1596)
W. Blackman (no $), 1597
E. Blount (no $), 1597–98
W. Aspley, 1599–1600
W. Burre, 1599–1601
T. Bushell (no $), 1599–1602
R. Howell, 1600–02
John Newbery, 1602–03
G. Potter, 1602–09
A. Johnson, 1602–21
F. Burton, 1603, 1606–07
Joan Newbery 1, 1603
J. Chorlton (no $), 1603–09
*E. Weaver (no $), 1603–37
T. Bushell (Petty Canons, no $), 1605
M. Lownes, 1605–21
M. Cooke, 1606–07
N. Fosbrooke, 1606–07
S. Macham 1, 1606–15
R. Bonian, 1607–12
E. Edgar, 1608
L. Lisle, 1608–18
B. Sutton (no $), 1609
(H. Walley, 1609–10?)
W. Barrenger (no $), 1609–27
T. Man 2, 1610
J. Royston, 1612–13
W. Bladen, 1612–25
S. Man, 1613–16
(H. Hooper, 1613)
G. Gibbs, 1614–17
Joyce Macham, 1615–16
R. Woodroffe, 1615–17
F. Constable, 1615–24
[*J. Rothwell 1, c. 1615?–36]
T. Barlow, 1616–20
N. Browne (no $), 1617?–18
(S. Nealand, 1618)
J. Parker, 1618–19
R. Rounthwait, 1618–19
*H. Seile, 1619–36
J. Teage, 1620–22
R. Pott, 1621–24
T. Lownes 4, 1623
Jos. Browne, 1623
W. Garrett, 1625
A. Uphill, 1625–26
*E. Brewster, 1625–35
*N. Fussell, 1627–35, 1637–39
G. Latham, 1627–40+?
*H. Moseley, 1627–34, 1634–59
T. Downes 1 or his unident agent (no $), 1628 (14261)
R. Michell, 1628
R. Swaine 2, 1629
(W. Adderton, 1629)
R. Higgenbotham, 1630
T. Weaver (no $), 1630–32
*J. Emery, 1630–31
*A. Ritherdon, 1630–32
R. Collins, 1631–33
*L. Fawne (no $), 1631–33
(C. Greene, 1637–38)
J. Kirton & T. Warren, 1639–40+?
S. Browne, 1640

A.3 Northeast: Brazen Serpent/ former chapel, its charnel house, and tenements **13** 8:9

To the east of Canon Lane lay the site of the former charnel house, chapel, and other tenements acquired by Reyner Wolfe beginning c. 1540. According to his will of 1573 (Plomer, *Wills*: 19) Wolfe owned three houses purchased as 'the Chappell' from the king (?Henry VIII or Edward VI) and had leases of other property from the Dean and Chapter of St. Paul's. Stow's account (I.330) may reasonably be understood as meaning that first the chapel was converted into dwelling houses; starting in 1549 the charnel house extending below it and perhaps much of the remainder of the property—when finally emptied of bones—was turned into warehouses for books, and in the space around the chapel—after the tombs had been razed—shops for stationers were erected. In any case, Wolfe's earliest imprint at the Brazen Serpent is 1542.

None of the signs below appears with a specific location in the churchyard in any imprint so far examined, but they or one of their owners are all found in documents mentioning the chapel or charnel house. The will of Wolfe's widow Joan mentions three (Brazen Serpent, Crane, Green Dragon), and a transfer of messuages in 1638 mentions three more (Angel, King's Head, Parrot; Plomer, *Wills*: 22, and 23, following n.8). Three more (Rose, Sun, Three Pigeons) are placed here in a document of 1656 reported in *Dict. 2*: 155–6 (under H. Robinson). The last five, distinguished below by a section mark (§), are placed here by Blayney's research. It is possible that a few more of the stationers in St. Faith's parish (**A.4**) and those in the churchyard without known location (**B**) had their shops or houses here.

Signs

[Angel]	[§Greyhound]	[Parrot]
[§Black Bear]	[§Holy Ghost]	[Rose]
[Brazen Serpent]	[§Judith]	[Sun]
[Crane]	[§King's (Queen's) Arms]	[Three Pigeons]
[Green Dragon]	[King's Head]	

Paul's Churchyard — Specific Locations —
Northeast — *cont.*

H. Tab, 1542–45?
W. Bonham, 1542–46?
R. Wolfe, 1542–73
J. Wight, 1551–61
J. Cawood, 1553–68
Ant. Kitson, 1555–78
L. Harrison, 1558–76
A. Pepwell, 1566
F. Coldock, 1566–81+
(Rog. Ireland, 1568)
P. & N. Lycosthenes, *pseud.* (by Brazen Serpent), 1569
[Joan Wolfe, 1574]
T. Woodcock, 1575–94
G. Cawood, 1576
J. Shepperd, 1576–77
A. Maunsell, 1576–81, 1584–89
(G. Seton, 1577)
Abr. Kitson, 1579–94
J. Perrin & widow, 1580–93
R. Vernon, 1581
T. Smith, 1582–83
Jn. Harrison 1, 1582–94
[S. Waterson (Green Dragon), c. 1585?]
R. Waldegrave, 1587–88
R. Boyle 1587–89
W. Norton, 1589
R. Oliffe, 1590–92?
R. Dexter, 1590–1603
W. Leake 1, 1593–1613
A. Wise, 1593–1602
R. Bankworth, 1594–1612
P. Linley, 1595–99
J. Oxenbridge, 1595–99
J. Flasket, 1595–1607
J. Busby 1, 1598–99
?N. Ling (Crane = one variant), 1600
T. Hayes, 1600–01
F. Norton, 1600–04
W. Burre, 1603–21
T. Clarke, 1604–07
W. Welby, 1605–09
Edw. Bishop, 1606–17
W. Barrett, 1608, 1614–18
W. Aspley, 1608–40
E. Blount, 1609–22
H. Fetherstone, 1609–26
(J. Stepneth, 1610)
F. Burton, 1610–17
M. Baker, 1611–13
R. Mab, 1611–16
W. Arundell, 1614–17
J. Hodgets, 1616
G. Edwards 1, 1617–18
T. Norton, 1617–18
R. Milbourne, 1617–18, 1628–35
(R. Chambers, 1618)
J. Bloome, 1618–21
J. Budge, 1618–25
Eliz. Bishop, 1619–20
R. Higgenbotham, 1619–24
R. Whitaker, 1619–26
J. Parker, 1620–25
G. Latham, 1621–26
G. Emerson, 1622
G. Hodges, 1622–24
N. Vavasour, 1622–24
(Hannah Barrett, 1624–36)
Jn. Browne 3, 1625
?R. Higgenbotham or unident agent of J. Legat 2, 1625 (5838)
R. Allott, 1626–35
R. Bostock, 1626–40+?
P. Paxton, 1627
F. Constable, 1627–35
T. Alchorn, 1627–39
R. Dawlman, 1628–40+?
H. Robinson, 1627–70
J. Partridge, 1628–38?
E. Blackmore, 1629–40+?
R. Whitaker, 1631–40+?
(Joyce Norton, 1632–38)
A. Crook 1, 1632–40+?
J. Rothwell 2, 1632–40+?
?R. Martin (no $, but ?Rose), 1633–35
(E. Bush, 1634–35)
L. Fawne, 1635–40+?
Mary Allott, 1636
(T. Briscoe, 1636)
(E. Weaver, 1637–38)
J. Crooke & R. Sergier 2, 1637–39
J. Williams, 1636–40+?
G. Thomason & O. Pulleyn, 1637–45
T. Allott, 1639
S. Gellibrand, 1639–40+?

A.4 St. Faith's parish: North and East 12 8:8, 13 8:9

The entrance from the churchyard into St. Faith's Church, situated in the cathedral crypt underneath the choir, was in the north side of the choir close to the north transept. Although the parish extended to parts of Paternoster Row and beyond, within the churchyard the boundaries seem to have run from a line extended north from the western end of the north transept (i.e. including both sides of Canon Lane, though by 1676 this lane was in St. Gregory's parish according to Ogilby) clockwise around to the north side of St. Austin's gate, i.e. part of **A.2**, all of **A.3–6**, and probably most of **A.7**. Parishioners *not otherwise located*—not only those with imprints specifying the churchyard but also those known solely by parish (par), even though they may have lived in Paternoster Row or elsewhere—have been arbitrarily placed here. At present there are three stationers known primarily by parish: Notary, who had earlier been at the west end of the churchyard (**A.10**, in St. Gregory's parish); Tab, who was later in the northeast sector (**A.3**); and Holder.

The signs listed below give the owner's name at the time St. Faith's was specified, with a brief reference to the sources with page numbers. These are three: Plomer, *Wills* (cited in the form P12); Duff's investigation of some early 16th-century lay subsidies in *Library* 8 (1909): 257–66 (D259); and Worman (W31). Further research among the subsidies would undoubtedly shift a number of the signs and names in the unlocated area (**B**) to St. Faith's parish.

Paul's Churchyard — Specific Locations —
St. Faith's Parish — *cont.*

Signs

[Bell (R. Toy) P12]
[*Judith* (Tab); § = A.3]
[Maidenhead (Petyt; beside Bell) P12]

R. Faques, 1509–10? (Maidenhead)
[J. Notary, 1523 (par, D259)]
[H. Tab, 1523 (par, D259)]
T. Petyt, 1536–54 (Maidenhead)
R. Toy, 1542?–56 (Bell)
[R. Holder, 1549 (par, W31)]
[Eliz. Toy, 1556–65 (Bell, P15)]
[G. Bishop, ?–1611 (—)]
H. Woutneel & widow, 1599–1608 (no $; W70, under Waltenell)
T. Adams, 1609–20 (Bell)
Eliz. Adams, 1620 (—)
A. Hebb, 1625–40+ (—)

A.5 Northeast: Cheap (Paul's) gate area 13 8:9

For shops outside the gate *see* C.7-1548, N.2

The George has been assumed to be a single house, placed here by Olney, even though he overlaps with Stirrop; possibly Olney had a shop within, before, or beside Stirrop's house. The sign of the Holy Ghost had been placed here under the assumption that it was the shop of J. Cawood mentioned by Eliz. Toy as being next to Paul's gate (Plomer, *Wills*: 16); however, Blayney shows it to be a little further west. Cawood's printing house may have been elsewhere in the churchyard.

Signs

Cross Keys
Crown
George
[§Golden Lion]
Goshawk in the Sun
[*Holy Ghost*; § = A.3]
[§Swan]

J. Reynes, 1523–44
W. Riddell, 1548–52
J. King, 1559–61
M. Lobley (Corner Shop on the right hand as you come from Cheapside, no $),1563
T. Stirrop, 1576–97
G. Dewes, 1578–87
T. Gosson (corner shop to Cheapside, next to the gate), 1580
Ralph Jackson 1, 1589–1601
(W. Young, 1589–94)
S. Waterson (at Cheap gate), 1589–1634
H. Olney (nr Cheap gate), 1595
C. Burby, 1602–07
(E. Edgar, 1604–07)
Eliz. Burby, 1607–09
(G. Seton, 1608)
W. Welby, 1610–16
J. Piper (at Paul's gate next Cheapside), c. 1615–20
S. Man, 1618–40+?
R. Rounthwait, 1619–25
J. Waterson, 1623–40+?
G. Vincent 2 (at Paul's gate), 1625–27
P. Stephens & C. Meredith, 1625–40+?
R. Thrale (—), 1625–40+?

A.6 East: Paul's School/ Paul's Cross 13 8:9

The King's Arms was in St. Faith's parish (Plomer, *Wills*: 30 (W. Norton); it had been placed here because of Hodgets's location in 1605 (he was freed by W. Norton); however, he seems to have moved to the sign sometime between 1608 and 1616. The Swan was also in St. Faith's parish (Plomer, *Wills*: 41 (C. Burby); it had been placed here because G. Dewes has the only imprint, in 1562, to give a position, but without the sign. Either Dewes moved to the sign before 1578, or his use of 'east' is too imprecise to bear the weight that must be placed upon it here.

Signs

Holy Lamb
[*King's (Queen's) Arms*; § = A.3]
Spread-Eagle
Swan; § = A.5
Trinity
White Horse

H. Jacobi, 1505–12 (nr new school(s) from 1509)
Unident agent for Parisian publishers (Trinity), 1512?–15 (3269.5, 7018.5)
F. Birckman 1 (nr new school, no $), 1516–28
H. Pepwell, 1518–39
A. Hester (next Paul's School), 1539–51
W. Lynne (next the great school), 1550
A. Veale, 1550?–86
J. Gybkyn, 1551
G. Dewes (East end of Ch, no $), 1562

Paul's Churchyard — Specific Locations — East — *cont.*

H. Carre (next $ Holy Lamb), 1580
W. Wright 1 (nr Paul's/French School, no $), 1591
J. Norton 1 (nr Paul's School, no $), 1594–1612
C. Knight, 1602–30
J. Bill (with J. Norton 1, no $), 1605
J. Hodgets (a little below Paul's School, no $), 1605–08
E. Marchant (ov/ag Paul's Cross, no $), 1612–16
T. Knight, 1630–33
J. Parker, 1634
J. Cowper (at East end of Ch), 1637–39

A.7 Southeast: St. Austin's gate/ Watling Street 13 8:9

For shops outside the gate *see* N.7

Signs

Eagle and Child, Gilt Cup, Ship, Fox, Pied Bull

T. Butter (nr gate), 1576
M. Law (nr gate and street), 1601–29
N. Butter (nr gate), 1605–41+?
E. Bache (—, no $), 1610
J. Upton, 1630
J. Emery (nr street), 1635–40+?
J. Bartlet (nr gate), 1638–40

A.8 South: (Great) South door 17 9:8, **18** 9:9

No signs

J. Wolfe (ov/ag), 1590–92
T. Nelson (at), 1591
J. Budge (at), 1607–18
R. Fleming (at, on right side going up the steps), 1617–18
R. Milbourne (at), 1619–27
(P. Stephens, 1622)
E. Blackmore (at), 1623–28
(H. Robinson, 1624–25)
W. Sheares, 1630–32

A.9 Southwest: Little South door/ Paul's Chain/ St. Gregory's Church 12 8:8, **17** 8:9 (Ch = #2)

For shops in Paul's Chain south of Carter Lane *see* R.3

Within the churchyard St. Gregory's parish extended from the southern side of St. Austin's gate clockwise around to a line reaching north from the western end of the north transept; both sides of Canon Lane were at this time in St. Faith's parish (**A.4**). Stow (II.19) says only that the church was appointed to the Petty Canons, probably because his descriptions are oriented to wards and the Canons' properties were in Faringdon within, whereas the remainder of St. Gregory's parish was in Castle Baynard ward. Outside the churchyard the parish boundary dipped south of Carter Lane and north of the western end of Paternoster Row. There seems to be virtually no documentary evidence about its parishioners. Blagden (293–4) cites payment of subsidy money for Stationers' Hall in 1582 to the collectors for St. Gregory's parish. Stow found no noteworthy monuments in the church.

Signs

Blue Anchor, St. John the Baptist, Three Fleurs-de-lis, Fleur-de-lis

J. Rastell (beside Chain, no $), 1512?–15?
Unident agent for J. Bale (within Chain), 1551 (1273.5)
J. Wolfe (at Chain, no $), 1592
R. Fleming (in Paul's 'Alley' = Chain, nr Ch), 1619
Unident agent for ass'ns of G. Wither (ov/ag Ch), 1623 (8704.5)
G. Gibbs (by little S door), 1632
N. Vavasour (—, no $), 1632
W. Lee 3 (nr Chain, no $), 1639–40+?

A.10 West: West end (door)/ Southwest door: Lollards' Tower & Lottery House/ Northwest door: Bishop of London's palace/ toward Ludgate: Peter College & Stationers' Hall 12 8:7–8, **17** 9:7–8

Between the west front of the cathedral and the main gateway to the churchyard leading from Ludgate, there was a large free area for public gatherings, originally known as the 'atrium' (Cook 71) though the only use of that term so far noted in an imprint is Notary's. The west end of the cathedral had three doors: the central one with a brazen pillar in its middle (Stow II.18), and two flanking it on either side. Although both the lateral doors also faced west, one

Paul's Churchyard —Specific Locations — West — *cont.*

is sometimes called 'Southwest' (by Lollard's Tower, which was partly surrounded by St. Gregory's church and near which temporary lottery houses were erected as occasion demanded) and the other 'Northwest' (by the bishop of London's Tower, which was surrounded by his palace). The palace and its outbuildings seem to have effectively enclosed the whole northwest corner of the churchyard and rebuffed encroachment (at least by most booksellers). Although Cook 65 indicates it ceased to be the bishop's London residence in 1556, Bonner and his successors must have continued to use it for many years during great occasions in the cathedral; in 1620 a banquet for James I was given in the palace hall (Cook 81). The bishop's 'gate' specified by Fosbrooke in 1610–11 may have referred either to the Northwest door of the cathedral or, more probably, to the gatehouse into the courtyard of the palace. It seems likely that the addition c. 1635 of Inigo Jones's classical portico to the west end of the cathedral required at least some dismantlement of shops and of portions of the palace.

In 1554 the Stationers' Company acquired a portion of the Peter College site and renovated it for their Hall. The College and its outbuildings or 'rents' lay north of the Dean's house and garden, stretching west to Creed Lane and east to the churchyard itself. At that date they abutted the southern edge of the highway to Ludgate. Stationers's Hall was in the southeastern sector of the site, and its position has been established by Peter W. M. Blayney.

Either the terminology of imprints is unusually imprecise in this western area or stationers sometimes made minor moves, perhaps as ecclesiastical tenements were increasingly leased to or acquired by secular owners or as formerly open land was built upon. The normal terminology and occasional variations are briefly noted below.

Signs

Ball, Mermaid, Three Kings, Hedgehog, St. Paul, Three Wells, Hill, Star, Time, St. Mark, Talbot

J. Notary ('in atrio'), 1510; (W door, beside palace), 1515–20
W. Telotson (W door, no $), 1543–45
W. Hill (W door), 1547?–49
J. Case (under College, in College rents,), 1548–52?
W. Seres (in College, no $), 1548–50; (W side/end, toward Ludgate), 1551–76
A. Kingston (W door, no $), 1551
[Stationers' Hall, 1554–1606; long-term officers with rooms in the Hall (Blagden 51–2; '+' indicates continuance in office in the Milk Street Hall, H.11):
Beadle:
J. Fayreberne (Fairbeard), bef. 1557–78 (Arber I.54; also acted as clerk to 1571)
T. Rider, 1578–87 (Arber I.478)
J. Wolfe, 1587–98 (also shops as cited below and at A.8–9)
T. Cooke, 1598–99
J. Hardy, 1600–06+
Clerk (*Reg. B*: xiii):
G. Wapull, 1571–75
R. Collins, 1575–1606+
Treasurer for the partners in the Day and Seres patents:
R. Watkins, at least 1591–99
W. Leake 1, 1599–1601 at least
N. Butter, c. 1603–06]
J. Kingston (W door, no $), 1557–64
Rich. Jones (Sw door, no $) 1565–76; (Little Shop at 'Nw' door, misprint? or an unident agent? 1566; under Lottery House, 1568–69; W end, between the Brazen Pillar and Lollard's Tower, 1576)
W. Jones 1 (no $), 1566–74; (Long Shop, W end, 1566–73 (called 'new', 1571); new Long Shop nr palace, 1573; Sw door, 1573–74)
Rich. Smith (Corner Shop, Nw door, no $), 1571–75; (W door, no $), 1592–97
H. Bynneman (Nw door), 1572–73
H. Disle (no $), ?1574–78; (?Corner Shop, Sw door, 1574; 'ad Occidentalem portam', 1575; Sw door, 1576–78)
J. Day 1 (Long Shop, W door, no $), 1576–79; ('Nw' door, 1578)
F. Godlif (W end, no $), 1577

LONDON
in December 1666

Based on John Leake's 'An exact surveigh contained within the ruines of the city of London . . . in December A^{o}. 1666' engraved by Wenceslaus Hollar in 1667, plates 20–1 in *A collection of early maps of London 1553–1667*, ed. John Fisher; with a grid adapted from John Ogilby's *A large and accurate map of the city of London*, 1676, ed. Ralph Hyde; both sets of facsimiles published by Harry Margary, Lympne Castle, Kent, in association with the Guildhall Library, London, the former in 1981 and the latter in 1976.

Conceived by Katharine F. Pantzer

Executed by John Mitchell

1990

London, The Bibliographical Society, 1991

Paul's Churchyard — Specific Locations — West — *cont.*

G. Seton (W end), 1578–81
R. Day (Long Shop, W end, no $ unless 'sub Arbore'), 1580
N. Ling (W door, usually no $), 1580–84; (W end/door, no $), 1590–1601; ('Nw' door, 1595; 'little' W door, 1598)
A. Maunsell (W end, no $), 1582–83
T. Nelson (W door/end, no $), 1584?–85
(T. Law 1 (—), 1584?)
J. Wolfe (in Stationers' Hall), 1588–91; also served as beadle
E. Aggas (W end, no $), 1588–95
J. Busby 1 (nr W door, no $), 1590–94?
H. Lownes 1 (W door, no $), 1590–1605
?T. Gubbin (W end, no $), 1592
W. Wood (W end), 1598–1601
(C. Purset, 1604)
N. Fosbrooke (W door, no $), 1605; (W end/door, Corner Shop nr Bishop's gate, usually no $), 1610–11
?Stationers' Co. (new shop), 1606
Jonas Man (W door), 1608
R. Redmer (W end/gate/door), 1610–19
J. Stepneth (W end), 1611–12
E. Brewster (W end), 1616–24; ('great' W door, 1624)
Joyce Macham or her unident agent ([W end], $ Time), 1618

B. PAUL'S CHURCHYARD: Unlocated Signs and Stationers

Below are signs whose location in the churchyard is unknown, followed by a chronological list of stationers at the signs together with stationers who gave no sign (no $) but stated simply 'in Paul's Churchyard'. Documentary evidence not yet noted may eventually place a number of them in St. Faith's parish (**A.4**) or at a more specific location within the parish.

Signs

A.B.C.	Golden Hind	Marigold
St. Anne	*Golden Lion*; § = A.5	St. Michael
St. Augustine	Grasshopper	St. Nicholas
Black Bear; § = A.3	*Greyhound*; § = A.3	Our Lady of Pity
Blazing Star	Jonas	Red Dragon
Christopher	St. Katherine	Red Lion
Cock	Key	Star
Cross	Love and Death	Windmill
Fountain	Lucrece	

N. Lecomte, 1494
J. Pelgrim, 1504–08
W. de Worde, 1508–09
[F. Egmont, c. 1510?]
Unident agents for F. Birckman 1 (no $), 1511–20 (15912, 15920, 15925)
R. Faques, 1512–13, 1521?–30
Unident agent for Paris publishers (St. Katherine), 1515 (7018.5)
J. Skot (no $), 1525?–29
F. Birckman 2 (no $), 1530
Unident agent for Antwerp printer (St Augustine), 1530–31 (15966, 15969)
J. Toy, 1531–34
M. Lobley, 1539–60
R. Bankes & R. Lant (no $), 1545
A. Smith (no $), 1548
H. Singleton, 1548–50?
T. Raynald, 1549–51
(J. Harrington (patron?), 1549)
J. Sheffield (no $), 1550
Rich. Wyer (no $), 1550
W. Bonham, 1550?–51
T. Purfoot 1, 1550?–77
W. Awen (no $), 1553
J. Kingston & H. Sutton (no $), 1553
R. Madeley, 1553
J. Turke, 1553
N. England (no $), 1558
J. Cawood (no $), 1559–70
R. Jugge (no $), 1559–73
R. Redborne, 1560?
R. Watkins (usually no $), 1561–87
L. Maylard, 1567
T. Hacket, 1568
[T. Hill (author), 1571]
A. Lawton, 1571
[J. Walley, 1571]
C. Barker, 1571–76
W. Williamson, 1573–75?
E. Aggas, 1576–81
(T. Humble, 1581)
R. Walley (no $), 1581–84
J. Hinde 1, 1583
H. Carre, 1583–90
?T. G., *pseud.*, or his agent (no $), 1595
[T. Salisbury, 1596]
W. Aspley, 1604
E. Edgar, 1609–12
A. Garbrand, 1610–13
T. & W. Harper (no $), 1614

Paul's Churchyard — Unlocated Signs and Stationers — *cont.*

D. Speed, 1616
E. Blackmore, 1618–21
P. Paxton, 1619
T. Sterne (mapseller, no $), 1619
J. Boler 1, 1627–35
T. Ellis, 1629
R. Martin, 1633–35 (or ?A.3)
Anne Boler, 1635–38
Unident agent for R. Badger (no $), 1636–37
C. Greene or his unident agent (no $), 1637 (18203)
F. Eglesfield, 1637–40+?
G. Thomason & O. Pulleyn, 1637–39+?
S. Browne, 1639
?J. Boler 2, 1640

ALONG THE WALL FROM NEWGATE TO ALDGATE

C. NEWGATE (within), including Paternoster Row 12 6-8:7–8, 13 7–8:9

Ogilby's map shows much post-Fire construction; Leake's is more relevant to the STC period.

C.1 Christ Church 12 7:8 (#4)
See also C.4, E.8-1614, 1619, 1633

R. Jugge (next, by Newgate Market), 1573–77
Joan Jugge (nr), 1579
J. Wright 1 (at door/gate, next Newgate Market), 1605–13
Edw. Allde (nr), 1612?–27; (in Little St. Bartholomew's = E.8, 1614: East end of C. C., 1616–27; Pentecost Lane = Pincock Lane (g78), 1623 at least)
E. Wright (at gate), 1614–40
G. Purslowe (East end), 1616–32
E. Reeve (author; by greater South door), 1618–27
Eliz. Allde (nr), 1628–36
Eliz. Purslowe (East end), 1632–39+?
R. Oulton (nr), 1636–37+?
[G. Dexter & W. Taylor (—), 1637]

C.2 Christ's Hospital (formerly Greyfriars) 12 7:8

R. Grafton, 1540–49?
(?E. Whitchurch, 1540–41)
R. Caly, 1553–58
H. Singleton (North door, next the cloister (#162), going to Smithfield), 1588

C.3 Ivy Lane 12 7:8

(?T East &) H. Middleton, 1568
H. Holland, 1612
T. Pavier, 1614–25
(T. Langley, 1615)
(R. Pott, 1624)
J. Grismand, 1627–36
R. Royston (next to Exchequer Office), 1630–40
P. Nevill, 1638–43

Long Walk (Alley). *See* E(headnote), E.8-1619, 1624, 1633

Lovell's Inn. *See* C.7-1606

C.4 Newgate Market 12 7:7
In the western end of Newgate 'Street' in Ogilby.

J. Judson, 1542?
T. Purfoot 1 (new rents), 1579–96; *see* also C.5
Y. James (ov/ag Christ Ch gate), 1581–85
(T. Law 1, 1584)
W. Barley (nr Christ Ch door), 1591–95

C.5 St. Nicholas Shambles 12 7:8
In the eastern half of Newgate 'Street' in Ogilby; called 'Middle Row' in Leake.

T. Purfoot 1 (new rents), 1598–1605; possibly here from 1579, but more likely indicates a move from Newgate Market (C.4)
T. Purfoot 2, 1607

Newgate (within) — *cont.*

C.6 Panyer Alley 13 7:9: ?H. Gosson or, more probably, Alice Gosson, 1615–22

C.7 Paternoster Row 12 8:8, **13** 7:9

For shops near its eastern end *see* also A.5, N.2. At the latter location is listed a single shop, the Mermaid, which *Memorials* 52 indicates is in Paternoster Row and Peter W. M. Blayney's *The Bookshops in Paul's Cross Churchyard* (Occasional Papers of the Bibliogrtaphical Society, forthcoming) places at the eastern end, opening into Cheapside. The four men listed there should be transferred here.

J. Turke, 1533–54
J. Redman, 1536–41
J. Burrel (corner house, w/o Paul's Chyd, opening into Cheapside), 1548?
R. Lant, 1553?
W. Awen, 1554
H. Sutton, 1559–61
N. England, 1562
R. Applow (by Castle Tavern, unloc), 1563
H. Denham, 1565–83
H. Bynneman (Mermaid (?i33)), 1566–67
J. Rowbotham, 1568–74
C. Barker, 1577–79
T. Gosson, 1579?–91 (next to $ Castle to 1581)
H. Disle, 1580
Jn. Harrison 2, 1580–1617
T. Man 1, 1583–1623
H. Bate, 1587?
T. Gubbin, 1588
J. Hill, 1588–90
T. Orwin, 1588–93
J. Penny, 1591
[Joan Orwin, 1593–97]
J. Drawater, 1595
?B. Wright or his agent, c. 1596
Jn. Harrison 1, 1596–1613
(R. Walker, 1598)
F. Kingston, 1599–1644+?
Jn. Harrison 3, 1601
W. Tymme, 1601–15 (nr Cheapside, 1601–06)
Jn. Harrison 4, 1602–41+?
E. Mutton, 1603
T. Man 2, 1605
C. Hunt (Lovell's Inn), 1606
?H. or Alice Gosson, 1606–09
W. Cotton, 1607–09
Joseph Harrison, 1608
Jonas Man, 1608–22
J. Robinson, 1615
Josias Harrison, 1615–16
(J. Bartlet, 1619–20)
P. Man, 1622
B. Fisher, 1622–25
J. Harrigat, 1624–30
R. Harford (Queen's Head Alley), 1631–40+?
H. Dix (author), 1633

Pentecost Lane. *See* C.1-1612?

Queen's Head Alley. *See* C.7-1631

C.8 Swan Yard 12 7:7 (g72): J. Grove, 1632.

C.9 Warwick Lane 12 7:7: S. Stafford, 1611

D. NEWGATE (without) 12 6–7:5–6

Names have been listed under the most specific form of the address, e.g. J. Wright 1 from 1614 usually gave 'without Newgate at the Bible' but is listed only under Giltspur Street, which he began to name in 1634. Addresses at any place below which include the following signs (all of them apparently taverns): Cardinal's Hat, Saracen's Head, both near St. Sepulchre's Ch, and the Sun, near Holborn conduit, have been gathered under Snow Hill (D.9).

D.1 Eliot's (Ellis, Elliott's) Court, Little Old Bailey **12** 7:6

See also D.4, 6

[N. Newton, 1584–86]
[J. Jackson 1, 1584–96]
E. Bollifant, 1584–1602
A. Hatfield, 1584–1612
M. Bradwood, 1602–18
[E. Griffin 1, 1613–21]
J. Haviland, 1621–38 (possibly from 1634 simply Old Bailey (D.7))
[A. Griffin, 1621–38]
[N. Metaxas, 1626?]
H. Bell, 1627–31
[?M. Bell, 1628–31?]
[E. Griffin 2, 1637–52]

D.2 Fleet Lane 12 7:6

See also W.1.

R. Serle, 1564–66?
Rich. Jones (upper end), 1567?–74
W. Venge, 1585
W. White, 1591–92
G. Simson (ov/ag Seacoal Lane), 1591–1600
[Frances Simson, 1601]
R. Read, 1601–03
G. Eld, 1604–15
(W. Blainchard, 1613)
R. Hammond (upper end), 1630

Newgate (without) — *cont.*

D.3 Giltspur Street 12 6:7

T. Haviland, 1613
J. Wright 1, 1614–40+? (to 1634 usually only: w/o Newgate; from 1620 occasionally: Pye Corner)

D.4 Green Arbour, Little Old Bailey **12** 7:6

See also D.1, 6

F. Adams, 1577?
M. Sparke 1, 1627–53
G. Edwards 2, 1628–40+?
(T. Slater, 1630)
M. Sparke 2, 1631–40+?
(J. Hardesty, 1640)

Holborn Bridge. *See* V.2

D.5 Holborn Conduit 12 6:6

See also D(headnote), D.9, E.4, 7

J. Day 1 (above), 1547–49
H. Powell (—), 1548–50?
R. Ward (—), 1580?–85
(?H. Haslop, 1586)
W. Jones 2 (nr), 1591–1615
T. Jones 1 (—), 1600
T. Gubbin (—), 1614

D.6 Little Old Bailey 12 7:6: R. Ward, 1590–91

See also D.1, 4

D.7 Old Bailey 12 7-8:6

J. Skot, 1525? or after 1529?
T. Godfray, 1534?
R. Lathum, 1539?
R. Lant, 1542–46
(R. Bankes, 1545)
P. Bales (author; upper end), 1590
A. Jeffes, 1591
?R. Walker, 1597
N. Fosbrooke (upper end), 1614
M. Rhodes (—), 1622
F. Coles (upper end; nr Sessions House), 1624–63
J. Haviland (ov/ag Sessions House, cf. D.1-1621), 1634
J. Wright 2 (upper end), 1635–40+?
R. Martin, 1639–41

Pye Corner. *See* D.3

D.8 St. Sepulchre's (Pulchre's) Church 12 6:6 (#96)

J. Skot (par), 1521–22
O. Rogers (at Ch door), 1565
W. Bartlet (par), 1574
Rich. Jones (ov/ag Ch), 1576–80
T. Purfoot 1 (—), 1581–87
H. Tomes (nr Ch), 1598
[T. Lownes 1 (par), 1609]
G. Loftus (under Ch), 1612

D.9 Snow Hill 12 6:6

References to CardHt, HC and SarHd below are to the Cardinal's Hat, Holborn conduit, and the Saracen's Head. *See* also D(headnote), D.5.

J. Charlewood & J. Tisdale (nr HC, $ SarHd), 1557?
R. Peake 1 (nr HC, next Sun Tavern), 1611
W. Wright 1 (nr Ch), 1613
Jn. Barnes (various), 1605–15
J. White (ov/ag $ SarHd), 1615
R. Higgenbotham ($ CardHt, nr Ch), 1615–17
T. Langley (ov/ag $ SarHd), 1615–23
F. Grove (upper end, nr Ch, ov/ag $ SarHd), 1624–40+?
W. Peake (nr HC, next Sun Tavern), c. 1630–35
J. Wright 2 (lower end, nr HC, $ Sun), 1634–35
R. Peake 2 (ov/ag HC), 1634–c. 1640
F. Smith (ov/ag $ SarHd, 1634); (nr HC, $ Sun), 1636

E. SMITHFIELD 5 4–5:6–7, 12 6:6–7

An early named approach was via Holborn conduit, without Newgate. In the 17th century the more popular (or at least populated) approach, the Long Walk or Alley, ran directly from within Newgate west of Christ Church cloister (#162, cf. C.2-1588), through the postern in the wall of London into the parish of Little St. Bartholomew's (E.8).

E.1 No specific location

J. Tisdale, 1558
[R. Verstegan (secret press), 1582]

Smithfield — no specific location — *cont.*
H. Singleton, 1586?–87?
R. Raworth (nr White Hart Tavern, unloc), 1635–36
(J. Crouch (—), 1635)

St. Bartholomew's Hospital. *See* E.8

E.2 Charterhouse 7 4:7
[J. Charlewood (secret press), 1587]
R. Michell (in — Lane), 1631

E.3 Cloth Fair 7 5:7: S. Stafford, 1606–09

E.4 Cow Lane 7 5:6, **12** 6:6
See also D.5
W. Lewes (above Holborn conduit), 1566
W. White, 1598–1617; (nr Holborn conduit, 1598; in Smithfield, 1604)

E.5 Duck Lane 7 5:7
See also F.4-1560, 1615
J. Danter, 1592
R. Cartwright, 1627–38
S. Cartwright, 1628–40+?
S. Nealand, 1631
T. Slater, 1633–39
M. Simmons, 1635–36
W. Adderton, 1638–39

E.6 Great St. Bartholomew's Church 7 5:7 (#98): O. Rogers (nr gate), 1558–61
See also F.4-1560, 1615

E.7 Hosier Lane 12 6:6
See also D.5
R. Hudson, 1588
J. Danter (nr Holborn conduit), 1592–94
S. Stafford, 1602–05
Jn. Barnes, 1616–17
J. Tomson (instrument maker), 1623–c. 1630

E.8 Little St. Bartholomew's Church (#97) **and St. Bartholomew's Hospital 12** 6:7
Regarding the Long Walk *see* E(headnote).
O. Rogers (nr Hospital), 1559
R. Lant (par), 1559
E. Allde (in Little St. B's, nr Christ Ch), 1614
The following are, except as noted, near the Hospital, usually at or by its gate:
Jn. Barnes (Long Walk, nr Christ Ch), 1619
H. Bell, 1622–23
N. Browne (upper end of Long Walk nr Little St. B's), 1624–25
J. Trundle, 1624–26
Margaret Trundle, 1628
C. Wright, 1626–c. 1635?
J. Standish 2 (author; Long Alley nr Christ Ch), 1633
T. Lambert, 1633–40+?
R. Harper, 1633?–40+?
N. & J. Okes (in the Wellyard, nr Hospital gate), 1635–40+
T. Andrewes, 1637–38

E.9 Long Lane 7 4:7
See also I.1
R. Oliffe, 1596–1601
E. Aggas, 1603
R. Bolton, 1606–11

Long Walk (Alley). *See* E(headnote), E.8-1619, 1624, 1633

Pye Corner. *See* D.3

beyond Smithfield

E.10 St. John's Street, Clerkenwell **2** 1–2:5, **7** 3:6
N. Hill, 1544–53
J. Bowen & J. Morris, 1590

F. ALDERSGATE (without) 7 3–5:8, **8** 5:9, **12** 5–6:8, **13** 6:9

F.1 No specific location
M. Clarke, 1607
D. Frere, 1635

F.2 Aldersgate Street 7 3:8, **8** 5:9, **13** 6:9
See also I(headnote), I.1
N. Bourman, 1539–42
J. Herford, 1542?–48?
Kath. Herford, 1549?–50
R. Lant, 1552?–53?
W. Herford, 1555?–59
A. Lacy (beside the well), 1563
H. Denham, 1585–87
T. East, 1589–1608
Lucretia East (nr gate), 1610
J. Hammond (in Angel Alley (e6)), 1617
B. Fisher, 1626–36
I. Jaggard, 1627
[Dorothy Jaggard, 1627]

Angel Alley. *See* F.2-1617

F.3 St. Botolph's Church 13 6:9 (#99)
A. Scoloker (par), 1548
R. Basse (under Ch), 1615–16
[T. Snodham (par), 1625]
C. Duncan (ov/ag Ch), 1640

F.4 Little Britain 12 6:8, **13** 6:9
See also E.5–6
J. Awdely, 1560–75 (by Great St. Bartholomew's Ch (#98), 1560–63; probably, like Jn. Browne 2 below, nr Duck Lane end)
A. Lacy, 1563?–66
Jn. Browne 2 (ov/ag [Great] St. Bartholomew's, nr Duck Lane end), c. 1615–25
G. Eld, 1621–24
M. Flesher, 1621–34+?
J. White (nr Aldersgate St), 1622–25
R. Mynne, 1627–39+?
J. Day 2 & D. Pakeman, 1631
L. Sadler, 1631–40+?
R. Clutterbuck, 1633–37
J. Morrett, 1634
H. Skelton, 1634
C. Bee, 1634–40+?
G. Emerson, 1634–40+?
D. Frere, 1636–40+?
W. Hills, 1636–40+?
E. Morgan, 1638
R. Milbourne, 1640
[T. Harper, ?before 1641–56]

G. ALDERSGATE (within) 13 6–7:9–10

G.1 Aldersgate 13 6:9
J. Day 1 (at, over gate), 1549–84 (also under gate, 1560–80)
R. Day (at gate), 1579
G. Seton (under gate), 1583–1605
E. Allde (in Aldersgate, ov/ag the pump), 1597

G.2 St. Anne's Church, Aldersgate 13 6:9 (#17)
W. Tylle (par), 1548–49
B. Alsop (next to Ch), 1618–20

Bacon House. *See* G.3-1579

G.3 Foster Lane 13 7:9
See also G.5
J. Skot (in St. Leonard's par), 1535?–37
J. Walley, 1547–86
R. Harvey, 1552?
Bacon House, nr Foster Lane (i.e. in Noble Street; later Scriveners' Hall (B2, #116): Queen's Printing House:
C. Barker, 1579–87
[deputies of C. Barker, 1587–c. 1600]
R. Waldegrave (ov/ag Goldsmiths' Hall (#117)), 1583
N. Okes, 1618–26
[J. Norton 2, 1628–41]

Goldsmiths' Hall. *See* G.3-1583

G.4 Gutter Lane 13 7:9–10
R. Hall, 1562–63
Rich. Jackson, 1569

G.5 St. Leonard's Church, Foster Lane 13 7:9 (#15)
See also G.3-1535?
[?P. Bounel (par), 1544]
[S. Roedius (par), 1564]

Aldersgate (within) — *cont.*

G.6 Lilypot Lane 13 6:9: R. Dunscomb, 1638

G.7 Maiden Lane 13 6:10: A. Lawton (nr [Great] Wood Street), 1590

G.8 St. Martin's Lane 13 6-7:9

[Northumberland House, almost by Aldersgate: Queen's/King's Printing House:]
[R. Barker, c. 1600–1621]
[J. Bill, 1616–c. 1625]
[B. Norton, 1617–c. 1625]

G.9 St. Martin le Grand, Liberty of 13 7:9: [N. Blond, 1553–85] Clearly marked in Leake's map.

Northumberland House. *See* G.8

H. CRIPPLEGATE and MOORGATE (within)
8 5:10–12, **9** 5:13, **13** 6–7: 10–12, **14** 6–7:13

H.1 Addle Street 13 6:10
For Addle 'Street' nr. Baynard's Castle *see* R.6
T. Scarlet, 1590
W. Kearney, 1590–92

H.2 Aldermanbury 13 6:11: R. Bradock (above conduit), 1581

H.3 Cateaton Street 13 7:11: J. Aston, 1637–38

H.4 Coleman Street 13 6:12
See also H.9-1598
J. Speidell (author), 1609
W. Harris, 1636–40+?

Great Wood Street. *See* H.17

H.5 Guildhall 13 6-7:11

T. Turner (at gate), 1580
S. Clarke (by), 1584
W. Blackwall (ov/ag gate), 1594–1618
W. Ferbrand (nr gate), 1600–01
P. Birch (—), 1618–19
J. Day 2 (at gate), 1629

H.6 St. Lawrence Lane 13 7:11: R. Bird, 1631–40+?

H.7 Little Wood Street 13 5:10: J. Legat 2, 1621–58

H.8 London Wall 8 5:11–12, **9** 5:13

Although the road termed 'London Wall' stretched from Cripplegate eastward to Broad Street and although Ogilby's map places the name south of Moorfields, it is very likely that the present address was near Cripplegate. Ogilby's Ship Yard, **8** 5:10 (e14) leading into Hart Street west of Cripplegate, may well have provided the sign for the first address below, and the later one, if the same or nearly so, is close to the one given by East's former apprentice, D. Moptid, probably also in 1575: without Cripplegate in Red Cross Street (I.7).

T. East & H. Middleton (by $ Ship), 1571
T. East, 1575

H.9 Lothbury 13 7:11–12, **14** 7:13
See also H.4
W. Copland (ov/ag St. Margaret's Ch (#72)), c. 1563–67
[R. Ward (secret press), 1587]
A. Maunsell, 1594–95
W. Ferbrand (corner of Coleman Street), 1598–99
G. Lowe (printseller), 1613?–c. 1615
W. Lee 1, 1628–29

St. Margaret's Church, Lothbury. *See* H.9

H.10 St. Michael's Church, Bassishaw 13 6:11 (#23): [R. Schilders (par), 1571]

Cripplegate and Moorgate (within) — *cont.*
St. Michael's Church, Wood Street. *See* H.17

H.11 Milk Street 13 7:10

Although Blagden 293–4 considers Company property in Milk Street to be a myth or else faintly pointing to a hall before 1555, close analysis of *Court-Book C* and of other documents by Peter W. M. Blayney in 'The four site saga: the early locations of Stationers' Hall', *Library* (forthcoming) indicates the Hall was here during 1606–11. Following are long-term officers with rooms in the Hall ('+' before and/or after the date indicates continuance in office from the earlier Hall in Peter College (A.10) or in the later Hall in Amen Corner (Q.1), respectively):

[Stationers' Hall, 1606–11
Beadle: J. Hardy, +1606–11+
Clerk: R. Collins, +1606–11+
Treasurer of the English Stock:
W. Cotton, 1606–09
E. Weaver, 1610–11+]

H.12 Moorgate 8 5:12
M. Simmons (nr gate), 1634
(T. Paine, 1634)

H.13 Old Jewry 13 7:12: E. Whitchurch, 1544

H.14 Philip Lane 8 5:10: A. Jeffes, 1589

H.15 Silver Street 8 5:10: T. Nelson, 1592

H.16 Sion College 8 5:11 (A61, #163): J. Spencer (beside gate), 1635

H.17 Wood (Great Wood) Street 13 6:10

G. Vincent 1 (ov/ag St. Michael's Ch (#25); nr $ Castle [Inn] (B10)), 1602–17
R. Field, 1613–24

I. CRIPPLEGATE (without) 8 3–5:9–12 and MOORGATE (beyond)

For this area records of stationers living in the parish of St. Giles have been culled to 1640. For the full range of names and dates *see* *SB* 19 (1966): 15–38. Included below are only those individuals who appear in Index 1 and who also occur in the St. Giles registers *more than once*, since a single wedding, christening, or burial—even of the stationer himself—seems insufficient to prove residence. St. Giles dates are given in square brackets: under the appropriate street, where such is known, or under St. Giles itself when no specific address has been found.

This additional information casts an oblique light on information based solely on imprints. For example, for at least a year Melchisidec Bradwood was a parishioner of St. Giles even though the printing house in which he was a partner lay a good distance away, in Eliot's Court without Newgate (D.1). Did this experience prepare him for work even further afield, in Eton, beginning in 1610? On a different scale, except for the burial of a servant in 1588, John Charlewood is not mentioned in the St. Giles registers. Was the Charlewood printing house in the western end of Barbican, which lies in the parish of St. Botolph without Aldersgate? Did his successor, James Roberts, bring it into the eastern or St. Giles end? Did William Jaggard move it back to the Aldersgate end of Barbican, perhaps to the corner of Aldersgate Street (F.2), where Isaac Jaggard's one noted address places him? Did Thomas Cotes, their successor and also parish clerk of St. Giles from 1627 to his death in 1641, return the printing house to his parish? No noted Cotes imprint carries an address. Printing houses were usually characterized as 'dwelling' houses, so it is natural to think that the printer, his family, and apprentices lived above or beside the printing shop. Occasionally this was obviously not the case, though Bradwood was only one of several partners. On the other hand, did printers sometimes make minor shifts in location not readily apparent from their imprints? Or

Cripplegate (within) and Moorgate (beyond) — *cont.*
are the parish records treacherous as evidence because individuals had a certain amount of licence to worship where they pleased? Perhaps subsidy rolls are the only class of records to have reliable information on where people resided.

I.1 Barbican 8 3:9

J. Charlewood, 1563–93
Alice Charlewood, 1593
J. Roberts, [1593–1603]; 1603–1605
J. Trundle, [1595–1600]; (nr Long Lane end, i.e. nr Aldersgate Street (F.2)), 1603–23
W. Jaggard, 1605–23
B. Alsop (Garter Place (b67, nr Red Cross Street)), 1617
M. Simmons (nr $ Red Cross), 1637

I.2 Cripplegate 8 5:10

Y. James, 1602 [1606]
T. Castleton, 1610
J. Greensmith, 1636 [1635–41]

I.3 Fore Street 8 5:11

A. Jeffes (nr Grub Street), [1585–86] 1586–87
E. Allde, 1589–90 [1588–96]

Garter Place. *See* I.1-1617

I.4 St. Giles's Church 8 4:10 (#100)

[T. Newton, 1583–93]
R. Hancock (ov/ag Ch), [1584–93]; 1595
[T. Creede, 1585–88]
[W. Venge, 1587–98]
[J. Bowring, 1589]
[M. Bradwood, 1589–1603, 1613]
[R. Finch, 1598–1603]
[J. Danter, 1598–99, family to 1603]
[T. Vautrollier 2, 1605–08]
[R. Bearkes, 1606–12]
[J. Isam, 1608–22]
[M. Parsons, 1611–19]
[T. Cotes, 1613–41]
[J. Flasket, 1616]
[A. Mathewes, 1616–17]
[J. Bagfet, 1620–29]
[J. Piper, 1625]
[G. Blackwall, 1629]
[W. Garrett, 1626–32]

I.5 Golden (Golding) Lane 8 3:9

R. Hall, 1561
[E. Venge (par), 1591–98; (document = GL), 1598]

Goldsmiths' Alley. *See* I.7-1640.

I.6 Grub Street 8 4:11

F. Sergeant (bowyer?), 1594–1601
[G. Wood (par), 1616; (secret press = GS), 1622]
B. Alsop [1636] & T. Fawcet [1626–39] (nr lower pump), 1625–40+?

I.7 Red Cross Street 8 4:10

J. Mather & D. Moptid (beside Ch), 1575?
W. Jones 3 (Ship Alley (c87)), 1601–04; (nr Ch), 1617–39 [1599–1639]
T. Paine, 1636 [1635–36]
M. Simmons (Goldsmiths' Alley (c78)), 1640 [1639–41]

Ship Alley. *See* I.7-1601.

I.8 White Cross Street 8 4:10

R. Harrison, 1562
H. Denham, 1564
W. Jones 3 (nr Ch), 1613

beyond Moorgate

I.9 Bunhill 4 1:13; also *13*: [P. Smith (secret press), 1623]

I.10 Finsbury *1*, *7*: [T. Raynald ('Hallywell' in old Manor of Finsbury), 1540]

J. BISHOPSGATE (within) 9 5:15–16, 14 6–7:15–16

J.1 Austin Friars, near Dutch Church 14 6:14 (#74): R. Faques, c. 1515

J.2 Bishopsgate and Bishopsgate Street 9 5:16, 14 6:15

H. Bell (w/i gate), 1613
W. Barley (in street, unloc), 1614
G. Loftus (in street, nr $ Angel [Court] (f84)), 1615
W. Butler 2 (nr gate), 1623

St. Helen's. *See* J.3

J.3 Little St. Helen's 14 6:16 (Great St. Helen's Ch = #77)

W. Faques (in St. Helen's), 1504
W. Barley, 1599
[H. Ballard, 1599–1601]
T. Morley (composer and patentee), 1601

London Wall. *See* H.8

J.4 St. Mary Axe 14 6-7:16: T. Gellibrand (schoolmaster?), 1597

K. BISHOPSGATE (without and beyond) 5 2–18, 9 3–5:15–16

K.1 Bethlehem (Bedlam) 9 5:15; also *13*

J. Hunt (nr Moorfield gate), 1611-13
W. Lugger (nr Moorfields), 1619
H. Bell, 1620–21
[G. Wood (secret press), 1624]
[T. Bourne, 1628–71]
W. Adderton, 1633

K.2 Bishopsgate (without) 9 3–5:16

J. Skot (at George Alley gate (c6), in St. Botolph's par; Ch=#101), 1530?
E. Venge, 1589
H. Bell, 1614–19

beyond Bishopsgate

K.3 Shoreditch *1*, *9*: [J. Hammond (secret press), 1632]

K.4 Spital *1*, *9*: [G. Wood (secret press), 1624]

L. ALDGATE (within) 15 7:17–18

L.1 Aldgate 15 7:18

R. Hollins (w/i, ov/ag $ Bell, unloc), 1581
W. Barley (nr, ov/ag Cree Ch (B68, #78)), 1612–13
H. Skelton (a little w/i), 1623
S. Burton (w/i, next the Mitre Tavern [between Cree Ch and Aldgate]), 1640

Black Raven Alley. *See* L.3

L.2 Duke's Place 15 7:17

J. Stell (by St. Katherine Cree Ch (B68, #78)), 1579–81
R. Alison (composer), 1599

St. Katherine Cree Church. *See* L.1–2

L.3 Leadenhall Street 15 7:17

[?S. Stafford (secret press, Black Raven Alley (h58)), 1598]; but *see* also T.6
F. Constable (right over Billiter Lane), 1625

M. ALDGATE (without) **10** 4:17, **15** 6–7:17–18

M.1 Aldgate 15 7:8

Rice Jones (ov/ag St. Botolph's Ch = #102), 1590
H. Roberts (nr St. B's Ch), 1604–12

St. Botolph's Church. *See* M.1

M.2 St. Mary's Church, Whitechapel *15* (no. 122): C. Mathew (par), c. 1549

M.3 Minories 15 8:19: [W. Harris (secret press), 1632]

M.4 Petticoat Lane 10 4:17: [J. Hammond (secret press), 1632]

EAST OF ST. PAUL'S TO LEADENHALL

N. CHEAPSIDE and WATLING STREET

The arrangement is by the two major thoroughfares: Cheapside and Watling Street, working west to east as best can be ascertained.

Cheapside **13** 8:9–11

N.1 No specific location

R. Bird (Bible), 1623–31
F. Church & J. Jackson 2 (King's Arms), 1634

N.2 at, next to Paul's gate 13 8:9

For nearby shops *see* also A.5, C.7-1548. Although both Rastell and Gough specify Cheapside, documentary evidence places the shop, the Mermaid, where all four men below lived, at the eastern end of Paternoster Row, and they should be transferred to C.7.

J. Rastell, 1519–36
[W. Bonham, c. 1525]
J. Gough, 1532–36
[L. Sutton, 1536–41]

N.3 near the Little Conduit 13 8:9

J. Day 1, 1549–53
W. Towreold, 1580

N.4 St. Peter's Church, Wood Street 13 7–8:10 (#26): [?C. Woltrop (par), 1571]

N.5 in Goldsmiths' Row 13 7:10

A section of the south side of Cheapside between the Cross (opposite Wood Street) and Bread Street

J. Bartlet, 1620–37
(J. Spencer, 1624)
?F. Eglesfield, 1637

N.6 near [St. Mary le] Bow Church 13 8:11 (#29)

J. Rowbotham (under Ch), 1562–64
T. Shelton (author; ov/ag Ch), 1630–35

Watling Street **13** 8:9–10, **18** 9:11

N.7 near, at St. Austin's gate 13 8:9

For shops within the gate *see* A.7

T. Butter, 1580–85
Joan Butter (under Ch (#12)), 1594
N. Butter (under Ch; nr St. A's gate in Old Change), 1604

N.8 Old Change 13 8:9

See also S.2

H. Carre, 1581, 1589
T. Ellis, 16341639
J. Hunscott (in Crane Court (i43)), 1639

N.9 near Friday Street 13 8:10: T. Creede, 1600

Watling Street — *cont.*

N.10 All Hallows' Church, Bread/ Watling streets 18 9:11 (#37).

See also S.4

The first address below names All Hallows' without giving its location. It has been assumed that the one closest to Paul's Churchyard is intended. The other seven all lay much further east except for the one in Honey Lane near Cheapside (**13** 7:11 (#28); approximately where Ogilby shows Honey Lane Market), but this was a very small parish and the church's location would almost certainly have been mentioned. Compare the similar surmise in Index 3D under the sign Black Boy, 1530.

?J. Lettou & W. de Machlinia (nr Ch), 1482
?J. Hippon (in WS, next Red Lion gate, probably k96, running into WS east of the Ch), 1603

N.11 St. Mary Aldermary Church 18 9:11 (#38): E. Whitchurch (on South side of Ch), 1544

N.12 St. Antholin/ Anthony's Church 18 9:11 (#42).: ?C. Woltrop (at St. Anthony's), c. 1570; but *see* also O.5

O. ROYAL EXCHANGE and environs **13** 7–8:12, **14** 7–8:13–14 (#166)

There are five major locations in the area surrounding the Royal Exchange (#166): farthest west is the Poultry running east to the Stocks Market (#165); from there three roads branch out: north of the RE (Threadneedle and Broad streets), south of the RE (Cornhill), and further south, Lombard Street, with Pope's Head Alley forming the major stationers' link between Cornhill and Lombard Street. The order, except for Pope's Head Alley, is west to east as best can be discerned. Signs are occasionally given in round brackets since they are sometimes used without specific locations.

Poultry

O.1 under St. Mildred's Church 13 8:12 (#47)

R. Bankes (at the Stocks (#165)), 1523–28
J. Mychell (at the Stocks, Long Shop), 1530?–32?
R. Kele (Long Shop), 1543?–45
J. Allde (—), 1561–84
W. Wright 1 (Middle Shop), 1581–89
Edw. Allde (Long Shop), 1584–88, ?1607
Margaret Allde (—), 1590–1603
C. Burby (Middle Shop), 1592–94
H. Rocket (Long Shop), 1602–11
J. Smith 2, 1613?–15
D. Speed, 1619
G. Wilne (Spur), 1638

North of the Royal Exchange

O.2 at the North (Threadneedle Street) side of RE 14 7:13

T. Frethren (next North door), 1581
R. Lee (North entry), 1615–16
G. Fairbeard (North side, door), 1619–29
Sarah Fairbeard (—), 1636

O.3 Broad Street 14 7:14: J. Farmer (musician; nr RE), 1591

O.4 St. Benet Fink Church 14 7:14 (#69): [H. Francis (par), 1576–99]

O.5 St. Anthony's Hospital, near French Church 14 7:14 (Ch = B62, #70): ?C. Woltrop (at St. Anthony's), c. 1570; but *see* also N.12

Although the Hospital had decayed by 1550 and its chapel had become the French Ch, its tenements were possibly still referred to as St. Anthony's.

Royal Exchange and environs — *cont.*

Cornhill

O.6 No specific location 14 8:13–14

T. Jenner (printseller; White Bear), 1621
G. Hodges (Maidenhead), 1625

O.7 near the Castle Tavern (Alley) 14 8:13 (i63)

H. Beeston, 1633–34
H. Blunden, 1637–40+?

O.8 in, at South entrance ('backside') of RE 14 8:13

L. Sanderson (in the Burse, 3 Crowns Imperial), 1571
T. Hacket (in RE, Green Dragon), 1572?–74
S. Clarke (at backside), 1589–91
A. Maunsell (in RE), 1592
C. Burby (at RE), 1594–1602
Robt. Jackson 1 (under RE), 1607
N. Bourne (at, under RE; South entrance from 1615), 1608–40+?
J. Bache (entering in, backside of RE), 1612–14
(J. Bellamy (South entrance), 1620–21)
T. Jenner (printseller; at RE, South entrance), 1624–73

O.9 near, over against RE 14 8:13–14

T. Pavier (nr, Cat and Parrots), 1600–12
C. Holland (ov/ag, Globe), 1617–22
J. Hinde 2 (printseller; nr, Black Bull), 1620?–35
J. Bellamy (nr, various signs), 1622–40+?
W. Riddiard (printseller; nr, Unicorn), c. 1625?–36
F. Williams (often also printseller; ov/ag, Globe), 1626
W. Webb 2 (printseller; ov/ag, Globe), c. 1635
W. Hope (nr, Unicorn), 1637–48
T. Hinde (printseller; nr, Black Bull), 1637–52
Ralph Smith (nr, 3 Golden Lions), 1640

O.10 over against the conduit 14 8:13–14

A. White, 1589–91
T. Archer (Little Shop), 1603
?E. Edgar (—), 1607
P. Harrison (—), 1608–09
W. Hope (Glove), 1634–36
T. Booth (printseller; Glove), c. 1635?
P. Cole (Glove (and Lion)), 1637–40+?

St. Peter's Church. *See* P.2

O.11 Pope's Head Alley 14 8:13

Locations toward the Cornhill/Royal Exchange (RE) side and to the Lombard Street (LS) side are given when known. It seems possible that the variation 'Palace' which occasionally predominates, refers to a shop or shops abutting the 'place' or yard of the tavern that gave its sign and name to the alley.

T. Hacket (in LS, under $ Pope's Head), 1584–90
A. Harris (next to RE, under $ Pope's Head), 1598
J. Wolfe, 1598–99 (in PHA in LS, 1598; nr RE, 1599)
J. Sudbury (printseller), 1600?–18? (ag RE, 1610; White Horse from 1611)
G. Loftus (Golden Ball, nr RE), 1601–05
R. Bearkes (White Unicorn), 1602
W. Ferbrand (in PHA, ov/ag Tavern door), 1602–07; (in 'Palace'), 1607–09
R. Canter, 1603
G. Humble (printseller), c. 1603–40 (ag RE, 1610; White Horse from 1611)
J. Bache (in 'Palace', nr RE), 1607–08
T. Archer (in 'Palace'), 1607–28 (nr RE, 1607–22, ?1628; ov/ag Horseshoe, 1622–25)
S. Moseley (nr RE), 1608
W. Holmes 4 (in 'Palace'), 1614–15
N. Newbery, 1617–36 (ov/ag White Horse, 1618; at Star from 1623)
G. Fairbeard (nr RE, George), 1618
W. Sheffard (at entrance out of LS), 1622–28
G. Gibbs ((Golden) Fleur-de-lis), 1624–31

Royal Exchange and environs — Pope's Head Alley — *cont.*

N. Fosbrooke (nr LS), 1629
H. Overton (at entrance out of LS), 1629–40+?
B. Allen, 1631–45 (ov/ag Horseshoe, 1631; at Fleur-de-lis, 1636)
N. Alsop (Angel), 1632–40+?
(P. Waterhouse (Angel), 1632)
Joan Newbery 2, 1637
S. Enderby (Star), 1637–40+?
T. Nicholes, 1637–40+?
J. Sweeting (in Cornhill, nr PHA, Crown), 1639

O.12 Lombard Street 14 8:13–14

The earliest addresses which give a location are near the Stocks Market (#165) at the western end of Lombard Street, and possibly all shops were there through 1579. By 1584 Pope's Head Alley began to attract booksellers, and it is possible that later addresses were in that vicinity even if unspecified. For the eastern end of the street *see* P.1.

J. Harvey (Holy Lamb), 1539
J. Gough (ag the Stocks, Mermaid), 1539–40
R. Kele (nr Stocks), 1540; (nr Stocks, Eagle), 1547–52
E. Sutton, 1553–63 (Cradle from 1555)
W. Riddell (Eagle), 1554–56
F. Coldock (ov/ag Cardinal's Hat, unloc), 1561
E. Halley (nr Stocks, Eagle), 1562
T. Hacket, 1562–66
T. Humble (George), 1566
H. Spooner (Cradle), 1579
J. Boswell (printseller), c. 1611
R. Daniel (sometimes also printseller; Angel), 1620?–29?
O. Ridge (Angel), 1628
T. Geele (printseller; Dagger), 1630

O.13 Abchurch Lane 19 9:13

W. Faques, c. 1505
G. Torriano (author; nr Lombard Street), 1639

O.14 St. Clement's Lane 19 9:14: [H. Frankenbergh, in St. Mark's Alley, unloc, 1482]

P. LEADENHALL and environs 14 7–8:15–16, 19 9:15–16

P.1 All Hallows' Church, Lombard Street 14 8:15 (#66): J. Tisdale (in Chyd, in upper end of Lombard Street nr Grace Ch (#81)), 1561–63

P.2 Cornhill (eastern end) 14 7–8:15

All addresses are under St. Peter's Ch (#68). *See* also O.6–10

W. Williamson, 1573
T. Millington, 1594–1603
Joan Millington, 1604
J. Busby 1, 1604–09
G. Loftus, 1609
N. Newbery, 1616–25
J. Clarke 1, 1619–39
S. Ward, 1627–31

P.3 St. Dionis Backchurch 19 9:15 (C56, #80): [H. Woutneel (printseller; par), 1582–91]

P.4 Gracechurch (Gratious) Street 14 8:15, **19** 9:15. *See* also P.1

R. Bankes (beside conduit), c. 1538?
W. Barley (upper end, ov/ag Leadenhall), 1592–1609
[S. Stafford, 1598]

P.5 Leadenhall 14 8:15 (#168)

T. Hood (author; in Staplers' Chapel), 1590
A. Ryther (engraver and printseller; a little from, next $ Tower, unloc), 1590

P.6 Lime Street 14 8:15–16: S. Harrison (author), 1604

Lombard Street, upper end. *See* P.1

St. Peter's Church. *See* P.2

P.7 Rood Lane 19 9:16: S. Peele, 1577

THE THAMES FROM FLEET DITCH TO THE TOWER

For stationers in Southwark on the southern bank of the Thames *see* Index 2Ai.

Q. LUDGATE and BLACKFRIARS **12** 8:6–7, **17** 9–10:6–7

Ludgate

Q.1 Amen Corner 12 8:7

[Stationers Hall (Abergavenny House, #104), 1611–66; present Hall on same site; long-term officers with rooms in the Hall ('+' indicates continuance in office from the earlier Hall in Milk Street, H.11):
Beadle:
J. Hardy, +1611–12
T. Bushell, 1612–18
R. Badger, 1618–41
Clerk:
R. Collins, +1611–13
T. Mountford, 1614–30
H. Walley, 1630–52
Treasurer of the English Stock:
E. Weaver, +1611–38
E. Brewster, 1639–47]

Q.2 Creed Lane 17 9:7

T. Marsh, 1554?
J. King, 1554?–57
W. Jones 1, 1565
H. Singleton (nr Ludgate), 1574–85

Q.3 Ludgate (within) 12 8:7

The term 'near' Ludgate has been interpreted as being within the gate.

R. Stoughton (w/i), 1548–51
Ja. Shaw (nr), 1603
W. Cotton (nr), 1604–06
R. Collins (under St. Martin's Ch (#3)), 1635
F. Constable (—), 1637–39
W. Edmonds (nr), 1638–39
J. Nicholson (under Ch), 1640

Q.4 Ludgate (without) and Ludgate Hill 12 8:6–7

[R. Schilders (St. Martin's par (Ch = #3), Farringdon w/o), 1575–76]
W. Holme 3 (LH, nr Belle Savage Inn (B77)), 1594–98
R. Willis (w/o), 1617–22
J. Colby (LH), 1638–39
R. Lowndes (w/o), 1640

Blackfriars **17** 9–10:6–7

Q.5 St. Anne's Church 17 9:7 (#5)

J. Growte (next Ch door), 1533–34
[J. Haultin (typefounder; par), 1574–86]
[H. Woutneel (par), 1576]
[A. de Renialme (par), 1578–1600]
[J. Le Moyne (artist; par), 1582–88]
[G. Boulenger (par), 1582–92]
[F. Bouvier (par), 1583–1618]
T. Slater (nr Ch), 1631

Q.6 in Blackfriars

T. Geminus, 1555–62
G. Godet, 1560?–67
T. Vautrollier 1, 1570–87
Jacqueline Vautrollier (by Ludgate), 1588
R. Field (—), 1589–1602

Blackfriars — *cont.*
A. Jeffes (nr Puddle Wharf), 1596
J. De Beau Chesne (calligrapher), 1597
F. Henson, 1601
R. Boyle, 1603–13
A. Marius, 1614
P. Boulenger, 1615
N. Field, 1625
[Hunsdon House (southeast of Apothecaries' Hall, #105): King's Printing House:]
[B. Norton, c. 1625–29]
[J. Bill 1 & assignees, c. 1625–40+]
[R. Barker, 1629–40+]
G. Miller, 1626–46
M. Fenricus (schoolmaster; next Greyhound Tavern, unloc), 1627

R. THAMES STREET 1: Puddle Dock to St. Peter's Hill **17** 9–10:9–8, **18** 9–10:9

This section is divided into an Upper Level, consisting of the area immediately south of Paul's Churchyard, and of a Lower Level, on both sides of Thames Street proper. The basic movement in each is from west to east.

Upper Level

Addle Hill. *See* R.1, 6

R.1 Carter Lane 17 9:8, **18** 9:9

S. Stafford (Addle Hill, nr CL), 1599–1601
J. Busby 1 (in CL, next Paul's Head [Tavern, in Paul's Chain opposite Paul's Bakehouse, k82]), 1600

Doctors' Commons. *See* R.3

R.2 Knightrider Street 17 9:8, **18** 9:9

J. Tisdale (nr King's/Queen's Wardrobe), 1560–61
H. Bynneman (Mermaid, unloc), 1568–75

R.3 Paul's Chain 17 9:8

Appears in Leake as the top portion of St. Benet's Hill. *See* also A.9, R.4

J. Smith 1 (nr Doctors' Commons), 1604
E. Paxton (—), 1636

R.4 Sermon Lane 17 9:8

A. Jeffes (nr Paul's Chain), 1583–84
(W. Dickenson, 1584)

Lower Level

R.5 Puddle Dock (Wharf) 17 10:7: J. Woodcock (Hebrew scholar; nr), 1617
See also Q.6-1596

St. Andrew's Church by the Wardrobe. *See* R.6

Addle Hill. *See* R.1, 6

R.6 near Baynard's Castle 17 10:8 (#160)

T. Raynald (in St. Andrew's par (Ch = #6), beside BC), 1548–49
(A. Kingston (par), 1548)
H. Bynneman (in Thames Street, nr BC), 1580–83
J. Windet (Addle Hill nr BC), 1585–88
V. Simmes (at foot of Addle Hill, nr BC), 1595–1605
(S. Stafford, 1598)

R.7 St. Benet's Church, Paul's Wharf (#7): [J. Wolfe (par), 1601]

Thames Street — Puddle Dock to St. Peter's Hill — *cont.*

R.8 at, by Paul's Wharf 17 10:8

T. East, 1577–88 (between PW and Baynard's Castle, 1577; by PW, 1579–88)
J. Hester (distiller; at), 1582–91
J. Windet (at), 1588–1610
(W. Stansby, 1597)
W. Stansby (in Thames Street by PW, next St. Peter's Ch (#8)), 1620

St. Peter's Church. *See* R.8-1620

R.9 St. Peter's Hill 18 10:9: J. Hardy, 1606

S. THAMES STREET 2: Lambeth Hill to the Steelyard 18 10–11:9–12

There are two levels: an Upper Level, consisting of Old Fish Street and its continuations in Trinity Lane and St. Thomas Apostle Street, and a Lower Level running along Thames Street. The basic movement is west to east.

Upper Level

Old Fish Street 18 9:9–10
See also S.7, 8

S.1 —St. Mary Magdalen's Church 18 9:9 (#11)

[M. Datier (par), 1541–63]
R. Raworth (nr Ch), 1633

S.2 —Old Change 18 9:9: T. Creede (nr Old Fish Street), 1600–10
See also N.8

S.3 —Distaff Lane 18 9:9
Includes the branch running south named Little Distaff Lane in the maps. The two earliest stationers specify no location in the lane, but the other four all have: near Old Fish Street.

W. Williamson, 1572
J. Wolfe (ov/ag $ Castle, unloc), 1582–88
F. Adams, 1594
R. Triplet, 1603?
B. Alsop, 1621–24
(G. Norton, 1622–24)

S.4 Bread Street 13 8:10, **18** 9:10: T. East (nether end), 1568
See also N.10, S.8

S.5 Trinity Lane 18 9:10-11

J. Legat 1, 1612
T. Paine, 1632

S.6 St. Thomas the Apostle Church 18 9:11 (#41)

J. Notary & J. Barbier (nr Ch), 1496–97
[J. Hammond (par), 1630]

Lower Level

S.7 Lambeth (Lambert, Lombard) Hill 18 9–10:9
See also S.1–3

R. Ward (nr Old Fish Street), 1589
Ed. Allde (—), 1604–12
R. Blower (—), 1613
W. Ward (not a Londoner; —), 1628
[J. Hammond (secret press), 1628]

S.8 Bread Street Hill 18 10:10
See also S.1–4

R. Yardley, 1590–93
P. Short (nr end of Old Fish Street), 1590–1603
Emma Short (—), 1603
H. Lownes 1, 1604–29
R. Young, 1624–41

Thames Street — Lambeth Hill to the Steelyard — *cont.*

S.9 Three-Crane Wharf, Vintry 18 11:11
Obliterated in Ogilby by the end of New Queen Street.

W. Copland (in Thames Street, upon the 3-CW), 1558–62
T. Gardiner (nr), 1577–78
T. Dawson (nr), 1576–1618
(?R. Webster, 1578)
E. Venge (nr), 1599

S.10 Parish Clerks' Hall, Broad Lane, Vintry 18 11:11 (#138)
Obliterated in Ogilby by New Queen Street. The following all operated the press kept in the Hall for printing mortality bills.

[F. Kingston, 1626–29]
[R. Hodgkinson, 1629–33]
[T. Cotes, 1636–41]

S.11 Steelyard (Stiliard) 18 11:12: H. Singleton (in Thames Street, ov/ag the Steelyard), 1551–53

T. THAMES STREET 3: Catherine Wheel Alley to Billingsgate 19 9–11:13–16

There are two levels: an Upper Level, running along Cannon Street and East Cheap, and a Lower Level along Thames Street. Cross streets which run between them have been placed in the Lower Level unless there is positive evidence otherwise.

Upper Level

T.1 Cannon Street 19 9:13

T. Hackett (ov/ag Three Cranes—almost certainly not the Three-Crane wharf, but such a sign is unlocated in Cannon Street), 1560
P. Waterhouse (nr London Stone, at west end of St. Swithun's Ch = #60), 1629–31

T.2 St. Swithun's Lane 19 9:13: R. Langton (patron?), 1581

St. Clement's Lane. *See* O.14

T.3 St. Clement's Church in the East 19 9:14 (#58): [J. Boudins (par), 1503]

T.4 New Fish Street (Fish Street Hill) 19 10:14
Both addresses are under St. Margaret's Ch (#83); in Ogilby the Ch is replaced by the pillar where the Great Fire began.

F. Faulkner, 1607–15 (nr Eastcheap, 1607; under Ch, 1614–15)
F. Clifton (under Ch), 1620–40

Lower Level

T.5 Catherine Wheel Alley 19 11:13
Shown in Leake but not Ogilby; between Old Swan Alley/Lane and Ebbgate Lane.

T. Creede (in Thames Street nr the Old Swan, at $ Catherine Wheel), 1594–96
[H. Gosson (house in Alley), 1613]

T.6 Black Raven Alley 19 11:13
Shown in Leake; n22 in Ogilby.

F. Adams (in Thames Street nr London Bridge, at $ Black Raven), 1578?–84
[?S. Stafford (secret press), 1598]; but *see* also L.3

T.7 London Bridge 19 11:14

W. Pickering (upon), 1557
J. Hunter (on, nr drawbridge), 1576–80
T. Nelson (upon), 1586
T. Gosson (on, nr gate), 1591–95

Thames Street — London Bridge — *cont.*
?W. Cotton or unident bookseller (at), 1603 (14365.5)
H. Gosson (at, on, nr gate), 1608–40
Unident agent for R. Bonian (upon; $ Red Lion), 1609 (18347.5)
J. Spencer (on), 1624
[G. Wood (secret press; nr), 1624]
S. Pemell (on, nr gate), 1632–35

T.8 St. Magnus' Corner 19 11:14 (Ch = #84)

W. Pickering (under Ch), 1558–70
J. Rowbotham, 1577
R. Ballard, 1579–85
H. Astley, 1588–1608
J. Tapp, 1610–31
J. Hurlock, 1632
G. Hurlock, 1636–40+?

near Billingsgate

T.9 St. Botolph's Church 19 11:15 (#85): [S. Roedius (par), 1549]

T.10 Botolph Lane 19 10:15: J. Mayler, 1539–43

T.11 Somer's Quay 19 11:15 (n32): W. Lynne, 1548–50

T.12 St. Mary at Hill 19 10:15 (Ch = #87)

[S. Mierdman (par), c. 1548–53]
Master Laybourne (barber-surgeon), 1602

T.13 Smart's Quay 19 11:16 (n34): J. Gough, 1542

U. THAMES STREET 4:
Customs House to the Tower and beyond
20 9–11: 17–20

U.1 Customs House 20 11:17 (#169): R. Lever & W. Elmhurst (patentees), 1604

U.2 Mark Lane 20 9-10:17: F. Cooke (instrument maker; ov/ag $ Red Harrow, unloc), 1590–91
Runs south into Tower Street opposite Water Lane.

U.3 near the Tower 20 9–11:18–20

[W. Carter (secret press), 1578]
J. Tapp (on Tower Hill, nr bulwark gate), 1602–09
W. Butler 1 (nr the Tower, in the bulwark), 1615–17
W. Lugger (on Tower Hill, at the postern gate), 1628–40
R. Higgenbotham (nr the Tower, in the bulwark), 1635

U.4 St. Katherine's Hospital beside (east of) the Tower 20 11:20: A. Lacy (ov/ag the Bear Dance), 1570–71

beyond the Tower

U.5 Ratcliffe *15*: N. Gosse (instrument maker), 1624–25

U.6 Stepney *15*

[E. Venge (secret press; nr Bishop's Hall), 1596]
[G. Wood & R. Raworth (secret press), 1621]

WEST OF FLEET DITCH

V. HOLBORN 11 6:1–4, 12 6:5

For the purpose of the present index the Holborn area begins with Holborn Bridge in the east and moves west as best can be ascertained.

Holborn Conduit. *See* D(headnote), D.5, 9, E.4, 7

V.1 No specific location

W. de Machlinia, 1484?
T. Saunders (Mermaid, unloc), 1613

Holborn — *cont.*

V.2 Holborn Bridge 12 6:5

[W. Carter (secret press), 1578]
Rich. Jones (nr Bridge, ov/ag $ Falcon), 1581–94
J. Proctor (on), 1589–90
W. Lugger (upon), 1606
J. Orphinstrange (nr, by $ Cock and Catherine Wheel, unloc), 1607–09
N. Okes (nr), 1607–13
S. Rand (at, nr, on), 1609–50
B. Langford (at, on), 1638–39

V.3 Shoe Lane end 11 6-7:4: ?W. Dight or unident bookseller, W. E. (nr), 1608
See also W.6

V.4 St. Andrew's Church 11 6:4 (#95)

Rich. Jones (next Ch, nr Saffron Hill (runs south into Holborn east of Ch), 1594–1602
W. Lugger (ov/ag Ch), 1603–04

V.5 Ely House 11 6:4

W. Seres (in rents), 1548
R. Crowley (author; in rents), 1549–51
W. Salisbury (author; in rents), 1551
R. Ward (ov/ag House), 1593

V.6 Holborn Hill 11 6:4: H. Bell (nr the $ Cross Keys, possibly A85, Cross Keys Inn), 1606–10

V.7 Fetter Lane end 11 6–7:3
See also W.8

R. Robinson (nr Holborn), 1585–91+?
(J. Bowring, T. Dunne, T. Haviland, T. Morris, 1585)

V.8 Furnival's Inn 11 6:3

J. Grove (at gate), 1629–31
W. Cooke (nr gate), 1632–40

V.9 Middle Row/Staple Inn 11 6:2

C. Purset (nr Inn), 1605–11
T. Bailey (in Row, nr Inn, Corner Shop), 1617–34
L. Chapman (ov/ag Inn, hard by the bars), 1620
R. Bulmer (in Row, nr the tennis court), 1623
A. Driver (at Inn gate), 1627

V.10 Gray's Inn 11 6:1

H. Tomes (by, ov/ag (new) gate), 1604–07
R. Wilson (at (new) gate), 1611–39
B. Lightfoot (upper end of GI Lane, Corner Shop), 1613–14
M. Walbancke (at new and old gates of Inn), 1618; (at gate), 1619–39
W. Sheares (nr Inn), 1627
Anne Wilson (at gate), 1640
R. Best (nr gate), 1640

V.11 High Holborn 11 6:1: J. Morgan (agent of prov. of Maryland; ov/ag $ Dolphin, unloc), 1635

V.12 Chancery Lane end 11 6:1
See also W.10–10e

Robt. Bolton, 1604–05
Rich. Bolton, 1615–18 (in the new buildings, 1618)
L. Chapman, 1627–40+?
(W. Certain, 1638)

V.12a —Lincoln's Inn 11 7:1-2

R. Clarke (ov/ag Inn, in house called the Lodge), 1616
Remembrancers General (patentees; ov/ag Inn, in Cursitor's Court), 1617
F. Parke (non-stationer; in Inn gate), 1619

V.13 Turnstile *19*
Runs north into Holborn east of Lincoln's Inn Fields.

W. Brooks (within the turnstile, in Turnstile Alley nr Lincoln's Inn Fields, in Turpin's rents), 1631?–40
G. Hutton (at, within the turnstile), 1636–40

W. FLEET STREET 12 8:5–6, 16 9–10:2–4, 17 9-10:5–6

Unlocated addresses are given first, followed by Fleet Bridge and Fleet Street, moving from east to west.

W.1 Fleet Alley, unlocated: S. Voter, c. 1515

Possibly an early term for Fleet Lane (D.2) but placed here under the assumption that it more probably relates to Fleet Street.

W.2 Fleet Street, unspecified

L. Andrew (Golden Cross), 1527
J. Butler (St. John the Evangelist), 1528?–31; possibly same location as T. Colwell's: beneath the Conduit, but Colwell apparently carried the sign with him from Charing Cross and need not have taken over an old sign.
W. Mattes (Hand and Plough), 1594–97
E. Mattes (—), 1597–1606
G. Eastland (music publisher; nr Green Dragon and Sword), 1600
?R. Bankes (at, next to White Hart), 1539–43?
?R. Taverner (at —), 1539–46?
A. Clerke (at —), 1540?–46?
E. Venge (Vine; possibly Vine Court **12** 8:5 (i12), which, though it exits into Shoe Lane, may have had a sign in Fleet Street), 1590
T. Fisher (at White Hart), 1600
Rog. Jackson (—), 1601

W.3 Fleet Bridge 12 8:6

W. de Machlinia (nr), 1483?
J. Rastell (at), 1510?
R. Copland (by, Rose Garland), 1515–47?
J. Byddell (next to), 1533–35?
(M. Fawkes, 1535)
W. Copland ([by], Rose Garland), 1548–58
T. Gaultier (at; in new rents), 1552?
B. Downes (nr), 1622
J. Stafford (nr, in Black Horse Alley (i17)), 1631–40
E. Brewster (at), 1635–40+?
R. Milbourne (nr), 1636–39
(J. Colby (—), 1637)
L. Hayes (on Bridge), 1637

W.4 St. Bride's Church/ Bride Lane 12 8:5, 17 9:5 (Ch = #94)

J. Gough (par), 1523–28
W. Rastell (in Chyd), 1533–34
T. Colwell (ov/ag North door of Ch), 1562–63
[W. Dight (par), 1591]
L. Hayes (nr Fleet Bridge, ov/ag Bride Lane), 1617
A. Mathewes (in Bride Lane, in parsonage house or court), 1620–32
(J. Norton 2 (—), 1624–27)
?Jn. Shaw (inventor) or his agent (ov/ag Bride Lane end), 1637
H. Seile (between Fleet Bridge and conduit), 1637

W.5 Conduit/ Salisbury Court area 12 8:5, 16 9:4, 17 9:5 (Court = #159)

The point of reference is the conduit unless otherwise specified; it was apparently a little *east* of the entrance to Shoe Lane. *See* also W.2-1528

W. de Worde ([next to], Sun), 1501–35
(H. Watson, 1509)
(R. Copland (—), 1514?)
T. Berthelet (nr), 1524–55
W. Rastell (ag), 1531
J. Byddell (next to, Sun), 1535–44
(J. Gaver (—), 1539)
E. Whitchurch (ov/ag), 1545–53?
(W. Baldwin, 1549–50)
J. Wyer (a little above), 1550
W. Griffith (—), 1552?–56
J. Wayland (ov/ag), 1554–56
T. Powell [nr], 1556–63
R. Newbery (a little above), 1560–1604
H. Wykes [nr], 1562–71
T. Colwell (beneath), 1565–75
H. Jackson (—), 1576–97
H. Cockyn (a little above), 1577
T. Gilbert (in FS, nr $ Castle), 1588
R. Ward (in FS, ov/ag conduit, at $ Castle), 1594; (in Salisbury Court at $ Castle), 1596
Jn. Browne 1 ([nr], Bible), 1599–1600
Rog. Jackson (a little above), 1602–25
(J. North (—), 1602)
Ja. Davies (nr), 1616–17
R. Dawlman (nr, Bible), 1627
G. Percival (nr), 1628

Fleet Street — *cont.*

W.6 Shoe Lane 12 9:5

See also V.3

[J. Le Roux, 1541–49]
W. Dight, c. 1600?–16
R. Shorleyker, 1623–32

W.7 Serjeants' Inn/ Whitefriars 16 9:4

For the Inn in Chancery Lane *see* W.10c

R. Foster 1 (next to Whitefriars gate), 1549
Jn. Browne 1 (ov/ag Whitefriars), 1598
W. Holme 3 (at SI gate, ov/ag Inn), 1600–03
Jn. Barnes ([nr SI], (Great) Turk's Head), 1602–03
V. Simmes (in Whitefriars), 1610
W. Lee 2 (nr SI, Turk's Head, next to Mitre Tavern, probably Mitre Court (k34)), 1620–71

W.8 Fetter Lane 16 9:13

See also V.7

W. Hoskins, J. Danter, H. Chettle, 1592
J. Hodgets (in FS, nr FL end), 1601–02
J. Dowland (composer; in FL, nr FS), 1604
R. Gething (calligrapher), 1616
J. Marriot (in FS, nr FL end), 1616–19
J. Wells, 1620

W.9 St. Dunstan's Church/ Clifford's Inn 16 9:3 (Ch = #93)

R. Pynson ([next Ch], George), 1501–29
(H. Meslier, 1508?)
(?J. Hawkins (patron), 1530)
R. Redman (next Ch, George), 1531–40
Eliz. Redman (—), 1540?–41
W. Middleton (—), 1541–47
W. Powell (—), 1547–69
W. Griffith (ag Ch, Falcon), 1553–71 (also shop in Chyd, 1561–71)
T. Marsh (nr Ch), 1556–87
T. East & H. Middleton (—), 1567
H. Middleton ([ag Ch], Falcon), 1573–87 (also shop in Chyd, 1573–77)
H. Marsh [nr Ch], 1587
[Jane Middleton, 1588?]
J. Winnington, 1588–95 (nr Ch, 1588–89; at West end of Ch, 1595)

Addresses below are all simply 'in St. D's Chyd' except as noted.

T. Newman, 1592
(?E. Newman, 1594)
W. Jaggard (East end of Ch), 1594–95
J. Busby 1 (in Chyd, Little Shop nr CI), 1596
M. Lownes, 1596–1602
(T. Fisher, 1602)
N. Ling (nr Ch), 1602–04; (in Chyd), 1606–07
J. Smethwick (in Chyd), 1602–40 (under dial, 1605–39)
Jn. Browne 1, 1603–21
W. Holme 3, 1606
J. Busby 2 & J. Helme (Little Shop next CI gate), 1607–08
J. Busby 2 (in Chyd), 1608–16
J. Helme, 1608–16 (under dial, 1615)
R. Moore, 1608–33
Rog. Barnes, 1610, 1615
M. Partrich (nr Ch), 1615–18
W. Butler 2 (in Chyd), 1616–21
Anne Helme, 1617–21
J. Marriot, 1620–40+?
T. Dewe, 1621–25
G. Winder, 1622–24
J. Penkethman (scrivener; CI Lane), 1624
R. Meighen, 1625–30
J. Stempe (East end), 1628
W. Washington, 1629
T. Jones 2 (East end), 1629–33
H. Taunton, 1632–38
(F. Smethwick, 1634)
Anne Moore, 1635–36
H. Hood, 1635–39
J. Benson, 1635–40+?
Unident agent for R. Badger, 1636–38 (nr Ch door, 1636; Little Shop in Chyd turning to CI, 1636–38)
Sarah Taunton (in Chyd), 1638
J. Maynard (nr Ch), 1638–40+?
H. Seile (ov/ag Ch), 1638–40+?
A. Roper (—), 1638–40+?
?T. Andrewes (Little Shop in Chyd turning to CI), 1639
R. Marriot (in Chyd), 1640

W.10 Chancery Lane 11 8:2, 16 9:3

Included here are unspecified locations as well as those mentioning Fleet Street. *See* also V.12–12a

W.10a—No location specified

P. Conington (Black Bear), 1578
H. Hooper ((Black) Bear), 1597–1600
J. Herbert (Paper Book), 1598
P. Man (Bowl), 1622

Fleet Street — Chancery Lane — *cont.*

W.10b—Chancery Lane end **16** 9:3

M. Selman (in Fleet Street nr CL), 1612
M. Partrich (—), 1615
H. Shepherd (between Serjeants' Inn and Fleet Street), 1635–40
J. Colby, 1639
T. Dring, 1667–68

W.10c—near Serjeants' Inn **16** 9:3 (B97)

For the Inn in Fleet Street near Whitefriars *see* W.7

R. Hawkins (nr gate), 1613–34
W. Sheares (nr Inn), 1632–33

W.10d—near the Six Clerks' Office **11** 8:2 (B72)

J. Bailey 2, 1601–03
J. Grove (ov/ag), 1632–41
S. Albyn, 1621–30

W.10e—near the Rolls **11** 8:3

Rog. Barnes (ov/ag), 1611–13
P. Knight (—), 1615–16
T. Jones 2 (—), 1619–22
J. Penkethman (scrivener and author; ag), 1629; (chamber in Symond's Inn (B71)), 1638
W. Leake 2 (nr), 1636–40
J. Stafford (ov/ag), 1640

W.11 Inner Temple/ Temple Church **16** 9-10:3 (Inner Temple Lane = k38, Ch = #158)

'In the Temple' without adjective is interpreted as Inner Temple.

T. Marsh (at 'hither' Temple gate), 1554–55
[R. Ward (secret press), 1596]
M. Selman (next IT gate), 1600–01
L. Becket (nr Ch), 1608–32
E. Dawson & T. Downes 1 (at IT gate), 1608–09, 1624–36 (Downes only to 1625)
?J. Wells (in the Temple), 1620
N. Vavasour (nr Ch door), 1633–40+?
D. Pakeman (nr IT gate), 1634–40+?
J. Becket (in, at IT gate), 1636–40

W.12 between the Temples **16** 9:3

H. Smith, 1543?
R. Tottell, 1552–53 (possibly the same as his 'w/i Temple Bar' = Middle Temple gate address, but for that *see* W.13)

W.13 Middle Temple **16** 9:3

'Temple gate' without an adjective is interpreted as Middle Temple gate.

R. Tottell (nr, w/i Temple Bar; Hand and Star), 1553–93
W. Hoskins (at gate), 1575–76
C. Yetsweirt (nr gate), 1594
J. Jaggard (nr gate, Hand and Star), 1594–1622
R. Blower (nr gate), 1595
H. Olney (—), 1596
J. Smethwick (—), 1599–1600
Eliz. Jaggard (—), 1623–24
R. Meighen (next gate), 1630–39
Unident agent for J. Norton 2 (nr MT, Golden Key), 1635
H. Twyford (ov/ag gate), 1640

W.14 at, within Temple Bar **16** 9:2

See also W.13-1552

R. Redman (nr, at), 1527–31
T. Godfray (at), 1531? 1534?
J. Wayland (w/i), 1537–39; (nr), 1557
W. How (over, at), 1568–74
E. Dicaeophile, *pseud.* (ag Black Bell), 1569
R. Ward & R. Mundee (at), 1578
(?H. Haslop, 1587)
H. Jackson (under TB gate), 1596
J. Deane (at), 1602–19
G. Norton (nr, w/i), 1610–18
L. Blaiklock (next), 1638–40+?
(W. Wethered (—), 1640)

X. THE STRAND, DRURY LANE, WESTMINSTER and beyond **16** 9–10:1–2; also *4, 11, 12, 19*

The addresses begin without Temple Bar and move southwest, with one excursion northwards. Stow (II.91–7) places X.1–4 and X.6–8 in the liberties of the Duchy of Lancaster; X.5–5b and X.9–17 are in the city of Westminster (II.97–124).

X.1 Temple Bar (without), St. Clement's parish **16** 9–10:2

R. Pynson (par), 1492–1500
J. Notary (—), 1503–10
R. Redman (—), 1525–27
H. Smith (—), 1543–46
R. Ball (nr TB, next Nag's Head Tavern, unloc), 1636
J. Jackson 2 (in the Strand), c. 1635?–40+?

X.2 St. Clement Danes Church/ Essex House **16** 10:1–2 (EH = #157)

H. Ballard (ov/ag Ch), 1597
T. Jones 2 (nr Ch), 1614–17, 1622–27
R. Meighen (nr Ch, ov/ag EH), 1614–22
E. Allen (instrument maker; ov/ag Ch), 1623–39

X.3 Not used.

X.4 Arundel House/ Strand Bridge **16** 10:1–2; also *12, 19*

[J. Charlewood (secret press, in AH), 1587?–88?]
J. Bramridge (nr SB), 1623
R. Meighen (between AH & SB, ov/ag Chequer Tavern, unloc), 1623–28

X.5 Drury Lane vicinity *11, 19*

J. Speidell (author; house in the Fields between Prince's Street and the cockpit (from 1619 the 'new playhouse'), 1616–25
W. Peasley (agent for prov. of Maryland; backside of DL, nr Cockpit playhouse), 1635

X.5a —Prince's Street *11*: R. Stevenson (nr Lincoln's Inn Fields), 1640

X.5b —Queen's Street *11*: J. Speidell (author), 1627–40?

X.6 Somerset House **16** 11:1; also *12, 19*: R. Waldegrave (nr, in the Strand), 1580–86

X.7 Savoy *12, 19*: A. Scoloker (in rents), 1548–c. 1550

X.8 Ivy Bridge, west of Salisbury House *12*: H. Perry (next IB), 1639

Westminster

For stationers in Westminster before 1501 *see* Index 2Ai.

X.9 Durham House *12*: R. Faques (in rents), 1523–30

X.10 Britain's Burse (New Exchange) *12*

A new mercantile exchange erected in the western grounds of Durham House and fronting on the Strand; opened in 1609.

J. Budge, 1610–17, 1625
J. Gwillim, 1615
T. Walkley, 1618–32
R. Swaine 1, 1622–32
W. Sheares, 1625, 1633–36
H. Perry, 1626–37
T. Johnson (printseller), 1630

X.11 Bedford Street, over against Britain's Burse *12, 19*

W. Sheares (nr Covent Garden), 1638–39
M. Young (non-stationer; —), 1640

Westminster — *cont.*

X.12 York House *12*
W. Sheares (nr), 1634–35
T. Jones 2 (nr), 1634–37
T. Walkley (nr, between YH & Britain's Burse), 1636–41
R. Horseman (nr), 1639

X.13 St. Martin's Church in the Fields *12*: [Unident agent for J. Doesborch (par), 1523]
See also X.14

X.14 Charing Cross *12*

H. Goes & H. Watson (at), 1513?
Robt. Wyer (beside; in St. M's parish), 1524–56+? (in rents fronting on the Strand owned by the Bp. of Norwich until 1536, by the Duke of Suffolk 1536–56, and belonging to York House thereafter)
T. Colwell (beside), 1560?–62
N. Wyer (—, in St. M's par), c. 1565–66
G. Baker (nr), 1631

X.15 Whitehall *12*: T. Walkley (nr), 1633–35

Westminster — *cont.*

X.16 King Street *4b, 12*: F. Constable, 1640
Runs south toward Westminster Hall. (There is a second King Street extending from the northwestern side of Covent Garden southwest to Bedford Street, but it is almost certainly not the one meant since there is no mention of Covent Garden and the bookseller had another shop in Westminster Hall.)

X.17 Westminster Hall *4b, 12*

Mary Oliver (printseller; in), 1609 (This is almost certainly a case of an altered imprint in an engraving with the date left unchanged, but no later Mary Oliver has been traced.)
R. Meighen (at), 1618–20
T. Jones 2 (in), 1621–22
F. Constable (in), 1640

beyond Westminster

X.18 Hammersmith: [R. Ward (secret press), 1591]

INDEX 4: ANOMALOUS IMPRINTS

All the following imprints are given in modernized spelling. Most of them are transcribed at least in part in STC itself. A few in John Bastwick's books of 1637 were omitted in STC but subsequently retrieved for Index 4B. It may be that some others have been inadvertently overlooked.

A. 'FOR THE BENEFIT OF'

The following few imprints mention groups to be benefited by the publication.

1616: pro regione Scotiae/for the kingdom of Scotland (14418, 14420)

c. 1626–39: for the benefit of the children of John Minsheu (15481.5, etc. *See* Index 1)

1628: for Great Britain (25899)

c. 1633–35? for the good of Great Britain (1612, 1614.5–16.5)

1637: for the Diocese of Lincoln (25724–6)

1637: for the benefit of our English nation (13726.4)

1637: for the benefit of Edward Minsheu (5985.7, 21667.5)

1638–39: for the (use and) benefit of the English Churches in the Netherlands (12035, 13738, 13738.5)

B. OTHER

Included below are imprints which make some kind of statement or comment, usually instead of giving place and printer. Most of them are unauthorized and illegal texts; a few simulate imprints of opponents; and some are lighthearted and humorous, intended to amuse rather than to deceive.

1555: Imprinted at London at the earnest request of M. Hog-herd (i.e. Hogard), [Wesel?] (9981, actually an attack on Hogard)

1572: Imprinted we know where and when, judge you the place and you can, [Hemel Hempstead?] (10850)

1577: Printed by authority of the said duke's [Duke of Shoreditch] special privilege, (London, 22463.6(***A***3))

1588: Printed oversea in Europe within two furlongs of a bouncing priest, at the cost and charges of M. Marprelate gentleman, [East Molesey] (17453)

1588: Printed on the other hand of some of the priests, [Fawsley] (17454)

1588? Printed either of this side or of that side of some of the priests, [London?] (19903a.5***A***3))

1589: Printed in Europe not far from some of the bouncing priests, [Coventry] (17456)

1589: Printed by the assignees of Martin junior without any privilege of the catercaps, [Wolston] (17457)

1589: Printed between the sky and the ground within a mile of an oak and not many fields off from the unprivileged press of the assignees of Martin junior, [London] (19456)

1589: Published by the worthy gentleman D Martin Marprelate D. in all the faculties, primate and metropolitan, [Wolston?] (17459 (***A***3))

1589: Printed with authority, [London] (17462)

1589: If my breath be so hot that I burn my mouth, suppose I was printed by Pepper Alley, [London] (19457)

1589: Imprinted by John Anoke and John Astile for the bailiff of Withernam, cum privilegio perennitatis, and are to be sold at the sign of the Crab Tree Cudgel in Thwackcoat Lane, [London] (17463)

1589: Printed in Broad Street at the sign of the Pack Staff, [London] (12914(***A***3))

1590: Imprinted at a place not far from a place by the assignees of Signior Somebody, and are to be sold at his shop in Trouble-Knave Street at the sign of the Standish, [London] (534(***A***3))

1590: Printed where I was and where I will be ready, by the help of God and my muse, to send you the May game of Martinism for an intermedium between the first and second part of the Apology, [London] (19450)

1609: London, printed by permission of the superiors (14525, an attack on jesuits)

1611: Printed for the year of better hope, [London?] (1525)

1613: London, by authority of the superiors, 1613 (13539; 21621, has 'with' authority; both are attacks on jesuits)

1613: Printed for merry recreation, and are to be sold at the Salutation in Utopia, [London] (23780)

1615: Rotterdam, printed at the sign of the Blue Bitch in Dog Lane, and are to be sold almost anywhere. And transported oversea in a cod's belly and cast up at Cuckolds' Haven the last spring tide, [London] (23804)

1616? Imprinted amongst the Antipodes, and are to be sold where they are to be bought, [Dordrecht] (11928)

1616? Imprinted in the Low Countries for all such gentlewomen as are not altogether idle nor yet well occupied, [Dordrecht] (11930)

1624: Imprinted for the honest Stationers, [London] (25919, meaning there are none)

1628? Printed by I per se I for O per se O and & per se &, and are to be sold at the sign of the Æ diphthong, [London] (23748)

1629: Printed the year & month wherein Rochelle was lost, [Amsterdam] (15428.5, referring to Oct. 1628, but actually printed early the following year)

1630: Printed at the Cat and Fiddle for a dancing mouse, [London] (16800(***A***3), an attack on jesuits)

1630: Imprinted for Giles Widdowes, [London] (20465, actually an attack on Widdowes)

1637: Printed by the special procurement and for the especial use of our English prelates, in the year of remembrance, [Leiden] (1572)

1637: Printed in the year of remembrance, [Leiden] (1573, 1574)

1637: Printed in the year of the English prelates' malice and cruelty, against and upon God's faithful people, [Leiden] (1575)

1638: Printed in the second year of remembrance, [Amsterdam] (25587)

1638: Printed in the year the beast was wounded, [Amsterdam] (15599)

1638: Printed in the year that the bishops had their downfall in Scotland, [Leiden, etc.] (22031.5–32.5)

1639: Printed in the year of hope, [Amsterdam] (15596)

1640: Printed in the year that sea-coal was exceeding dear, [London] (14861a.5, 22166) Although these are the earliest observations on the price of coal noted in an imprint, John Taylor uses the same expression in a quasi-colophon in 1628? (23748, note); regarding the patent of 1624 for inspection of coal *see* 8750, 22379.5.

1640: Reprinted in the time of Parliament, [Amsterdam] (6805.3; 10649, has 'Printed')

1640: Seen, allowed, and printed by us, &c., [Amsterdam] (13855)

ADDENDA AND CORRIGENDA

This section is a cumulation of addenda and corrigenda appearing in vols. 1 and 2 of the STC revision and of those which have become known since the earlier volumes were published. New items and information in the present section have been signaled in the margin by a bullet (•) and revisions to the previous addenda and corrigenda by a hollow bullet (◦).

•p. xlix^{2} *Amend location*: Buxton: Collection dispersed; some items now = O.

•p. l^{2} *Amend location*: Graham: Collection dispersed.

•p. li^{1} Kenyon, Lord. *For* a sale *read*: sales *After* 1975 *read*: and 6 Dec. 1989.

•p. li^{2} *Amend location*: L^{29} Baptist Union Library Partly deposited at O^{28}; the rest dispersed.

•p. li^{2} *Add location at bottom of column*: M(deposit) Now = E(deposit).

•p. lii^{2} *Amend location*: PFOR Now = TEX

•p. liii^{1} *Amend location*: Sparrow: Collection dispersed.

•11 *Add note*: A&R 14.

Add new entry:
12.7 —[Anr. issue, w. cancel tp:] By M. C. Read and perused by O. A. [*Douai, P. Auroi*,] 1623. Paris, Collège des Irlandais.

20.4 *Add note*: *See* also 4812.

•20.6 *Amend date*: 1582? *Begin note*: O(8° Z 189 Art.BS) has an 8° leaf w. lace orns. on verso and colophon on recto: [*H. Denham f.*] *the assignes of J. Daie, sold* [*by H. Denham*,] 1582 (dated above device McK. 211); it may belong to the present ed.

Add new entry:
◦22.2 —[Dutch—Hornbooks.] A B C [etc.] Dat Vader Onse. s.sh.8°. [*Deputies of C. Barker*? c. 1590?] Phillip Pirages, bookseller, McMinnville, Oregon.

Add new entry:
•37.3 —[Anr. issue, w. cancel tp, w. imprint:] *Oxford, J. L*[*ichfield*] *a. J. S*[*hort*,] 1620. N.J. Barker, London (tp only, imp., on same halfsheet as cancel tp for 24406).

56 *Add after date*: Ent. 23 no. 1625.

84.5 *Continue title*: Which sometime was the delight of Fraunces [Russell, 2nd] earle of Bedforde, deceassed. *Continue note*: Reprinted, omitting the dedic., in 4899.

92 *At beginning of imprint* add: [*Printed abroad f.*]

104 *Add after dates*: Meditations on the creed ent. 27 au. 1629.

151 *Add note*: A parody of Adrians' anti-protestant views; for further details *see Library* 3 (1981): 28–9.

Add new entry:
171a.3 —[Anr. ed.] 8°. *R. Robinsonus*, 1592. L(tp only, C.60.h. 16, fol. 55).

Add new entry:
174.3 —[Anr. ed.] 8°. *J. Nortonus pro Soc. Bibliopolarum*, 1637. L(tp only, Cup.652.ee.8, fol. 21).

188 *Add after date*: Ass'd to P. a. Jonas Man 3 my.

•192 *In imprint* delete: [*R. Hall f.*]

194.1 *Continue note*: Copies vary; 'To the Unknowne Patron' is missigned A2 or corrected to A3; L^{22}, Taussig have copies of both. The L^{22} copy of the former has the tp date altered by pen to 1634.

194.3 *Add location*: L^{11}(MPEE 25, formerly LRRO 1/575, imp.). *Continue note*: L^{11} has had the cartouches w. letterpress text cut out and replaced by much later reprints, e.g. 1st column of prose in lower left ends: 'hundred' whereas L^{8} and C^{6} have 'good'.

p. 9^{2} **Aggas, E.** *Add to 'tr.' cross-references*: 12508, 13091.5, 13092, ... 13100.

•198.7 *Correct end of imprint to*: *S. W*[*hite*? 1614?]

199 *Continue note*: For a trans. *see* 15184.

•207 *Add note*: There are 2 impressions, partly reset and reimposed: with (O) or without (F) orn. at head of A3^{r}.

256 *Add note*: There are 2 settings; B2^{v} last stanza begins: 'The said Albon' (L, O) or 'The sayd Albon' (R, frags. of B1, 2 only).

274 *After* A&R 3 *substitute*: Pt. 1 is answered by 23019. Pt. 2, sometimes erroneously attrib. to E. Rishton, is a version of Cardinal W. Allen's 'Articles' (cf. 3799), which is answered by 6084, 11458.

292 *Add after title*: [*Tr.* E. Allen.]

•319.7 *Continue note*: L^{2}(Frag. no. 18) has 4 imp. leaves paginary with G1,2,7,8 but in a different setting; G1^{r} line 3 of the small type begins: 'curro' (O) or '.i. curro' (L^{2}).

p. 14^{2} *Add new heading*:
Allègre, Antoine, *tr. See* 12431.

361.3 *Correct title*: ... game, or a game for three whetstones. That is to say, three almanacks and prognostications for 1569 by Buckmaster, Securis Low. Composed & set together by N. Allen.

378 *Add note*: *See* also 12407.

Add new entry:
392.2 —Almanacke for .xiiij. yeres. [1539–52.] 8°. (*R. wyer*,) [1539.] F.

•392.7 *Amend date to*: [1540.] *Continue note*: The new and full moons correspond with those for 1540 given in 392.2. References to Flanders, Holland, and Zeeland at the end suggest this was tr. from Dutch.

Add new entries:
392.10 —[A prognostication for 1541.] 4°. [*J. Redman*? 1541.] O (2 imp. leaves).
Heading towards bottom of one verso: 'What operatyon ... Eclypse of the Moone.' In 95 mm. textura with 'T' with long tail

392.11 —[Anr. ed.] 4°. [*Successor to J. Rastell's types*, 1541.] O (2 imp. leaves).
Heading towards bottom of one verso: 'what operacion ... Eclipse of the moone.' In 93 mm. textura with diamond 'T'.

Add new entry:
400.4 —[An almanack for 1560.] s.sh.fol. [*London*, 1560.] Taussig(frag. with Aug., in bdg. of STC 3332.7).
Column width is 52 mm.

Add new entry:
400.7 —[An almanack and prognostication for 1562.] 16° in 8's. [*London*, 1562.] P(frags., in bdg. of Pet. B.1.20).
Portions of the kalendar for Aug., Sept., Dec., w. 2 pp. of text on the eclipse of the moon on 16 July 1562.

Add new entry:
401.8A —[An almanack for 1576.] 16° in 8's. [*R. Watkins a. J. Roberts?* 1576.] P(2 leaves, in Pet. F.3.36).
The cuts for the months have xylographic text giving the hours of sunrise and sunset.

408.4 *Add note*: Title: 'Alleyns almanacke, or, a double diarie & prognostication.'

◦408.5 *In imprint* for *W. Hall*] read: *R. Bradock*] *Add note*: Title in this and the next is worded: An almanacke, or a double diary and prognostication.

408.8 *Add note*: Title: 'Allens almanack, or a diary and prognostication.'

Add new entry:
410.1 —1550. 8°. (*W. Powell.*) Earl of Iddesleigh(imp.). Taussig (4 imp. leaves).
See Library 2 (1980): 205–8. There are 2 settings; last full line above colophon has: 'snowe vpon' (Taussig) or 'snowe, vppon'.

Add new entry:
410.11A —[Anr. ed.] 1556. 2 pts.? 16° in 8's. [*T. Marsh.*] HD(frags. of prog. only, in Beale T 149).

Add new entry:
422.4 —1569. s.sh.fol. *J. Kyngston f. G. Dewes*. Ent. 1568–69. STU(frag., in Typ.NAn.B67SP).
Buckminster's name is lacking, but Dewes pub'd only his almanacks. Regarding a probable 8° ed. of this year *see* 361.3.

Add new entry:
•439.18 —[Anr. ed.] 8°. *T. Este*, [c. 1598.] F.
B8^r last paragraph names Queen Elizabeth.

•439.19 *Continue note*: B8^r last paragraph names King James.

458 *Continue note*: Title: 'A necessary almanack ... for 1560 ... seruing wel for these thre next yeares.'

Add new entries:
459.7 —1573. 8°. (*R. Watkins a. J. Roberts.*) L(prog. tp only, Cup.652.ee.8, fol. 41).
459.9 —1574. 8°. [*R. Watkins a. J. Roberts.*] L(tp only, Cup. 652.ee.8, fol. 42).

467 *Continue note*: HN has quire A largely in the same setting as its copies of 439 and 532.7.

•470.7 *Substitute cross-reference*: = 470.8.

•470.8 *Move colophon of* 470.7 *here*. *Revise locations*: L(imp., 1608/641, plus 2 leaves at Harl.5936/26). Bos. xi, xiii. *Substitute this note*: (Formerly 470.7, 15126, 20418)

Add new entry:
470.8B —[Prognostication in Latin for 1525.] 4°. [*W. de Worde?* 1525.] DE(frags., in bdg. of Downside 47969).
Compiler's name does not survive, but this closely resembles 470.9.

Add new entry:
471.8 —1535. s.sh.fol. [*R. Wyer?*] BO(top left quarter of sheet, in XfH.90.6).

Add new entry:
477.9 —1557. 8°. [*W. Copland?*] Arthur Houghton 269(A1,8 only, imp., in bdg. of STC 13862).

478 *Continue note*: Title: 'The countreymans kalender: with a plain prognostication.'

Add new entry:
483.13 **Moerbeke, Peter van.** A pronosticacion for . . . M. CCCCC.L. calculed vpon the meridiane of Anwarpe, by Peter of Moorbecke. Wherunto is added the iudgmẽt of C. Schute, of Bruges vpon the condicion of certaine prynces, contreys, and regions. *Tr.* out of Duch. By W. Harrys. 8°. (*J. Daye a. W. Seres,*) [1550.] Earl of Iddesleigh(imp.).
See Library 2 (1980): 205–8.

Add new entry:
•492.13 —1564. 2 pts.? [*London.*] F(b^8 only = end of prog., in 'STC 26145 no. 1a').
Differs slightly from 492.11, most notably in miscalling the Auster the north wind (e.g. b5^v) whereas 492.11 has correctly the south wind (B7^v).

501.8 *Add locations*: Warwick County Record Office(Newdigate papers).; HN(1, plus prog. only). *Add note*: The progs. at HN, which have no tp, are partly in 2 settings; e.g. C2^r line 8 from bottom ends: 'be-' or 'bee-'.

505.4 *Add location*: C^2(frags. of quire A, in Typog. Frags. Box 3). *Add note*: In title: 'The fift time amplified.'

Add new entries:
506.4 —1562. 16° in 8's. [*London.*] L^{16}(leaves 2,3,6,7 of prog., imp.).
Compiler's name does not survive, but this closely resembles other Rochefort progs.
506.5 —1567. 8°. (*T. Purfoote.*) Ent. 1566–67. HD(A1,2,3,6,7 of prog. only).
The prog. tp specifies no place for which it was calculated.

Add new entry:
•507.17 —1552. s.sh.fol. *N. Hyll f. R. Kele*. HER(2 imp. copies, in bdg. of D.8.VIII).

Add new entry:
Thongerloo or **Tongherloo, Cornelis van.**
517.15 —1550. s.sh.fol. [*S. Mierdman f.*] *R. Jugge*. Stevens Cox (frag., in bdg. of STC 19907).
Column width is 42 mm.

Add new entry:
•518.9 —1583. 8°. *R. Watkins a. J. Robertes*. BR(prog. only).
This and 518.10 were calculated for Oxford. The SR entry at 518.10 belongs here.

•518.10 *Amend location*: L(prog. only).

•530 *Begin note*: This was calculated for Cambridge; the following ...

Add new entries:
530.5 —1636. 8°. [*Cambridge,*] (*prs. to the University.*) L(sub tp only, Ames II.1310).
Title: 'The latter part of this almanack.'
530.6 —1637. 8°. *prs. to the Univ. of Cambridge*. L(imp.).

Add new entry:
532.2 —1603. 16° in 8's. [*f. E. White, the assign of J. Roberts.*] O^{13}(frags. of quire E).

532.7 *Add location*: ; HN. *Add note*: *See* also 467(*A*).

•534 *Amend date to*: 1590.]

538.5 *Add note*: A modernized version of Chaucer's Man of Law's tale.

546 *Continue note*: For other translations *see* 778, 6758.

p. 31[1] *Add new heading*:
Amazon, *River*. Breefe notes of the river. [1626.] *See* 12456.3.

552 *Continue note*: *See* also 13638.

555 *Continue note*: Answered in 4574. *See* also Greg, *Companion*, pp. 290–1.

556.5 *Continue note*: *See* also 11650.

Add new entry:
563.7 —[A revised version.] 8°. [*Amsterdam? G. Thorp?*] 1621. BO.
While this seems to be basically the same text as 563.5, in some portions checked it differs considerably.

564.6 *Add after date*: Ent. to G. Godet 1562–63.

591 *Add note*: This is by John Andrewes, vicar of Clerkenwell, who is a different man from the author of the other Andrewes items.

•602 *Correct SR entry to*: Ent. to A. Hebb by consent of R. Badger 21 my.

604 *Continue note*: Defended in 4116, 5561; *see* also 1782.

•606 *Correct SR entry to*: Ent. to Badger 10 se. 1628; a half share ass'd to 10 stationers 9 oc. 1628; Buckeridge's sermon ent. 2 jn. 1629.

609 *Add after dates*: Table ent. 16 ap. 1634.

626 *Continue note*: ... 4117, 4118, 5563.

p. 34[1] **Andrewes, L.** *Add to 'See also' references at bottom of column*: Bookplates, 5338, 5821.

651 *Add note*: Tp set in duplicate; line 4 has: 'Acts' or 'Actes'; both at HD.

666 *Add note*: Answered by 5832.

•684 *Continue note*: This ed. is later than 684.5.

•712 *Continue imprint*: *sould* [*by him a. R. Mab,*]

714 *Add note*: *See* also 7557.4.

755 *Add after date*: Ent to H. Fetherstone 31 oc. 1622.

p. 39[1] **Aristotle.** [*Ethica.*] *Add cross-references at end*: *See* also 4106, 6458.
—[*Organon.*] *Add cross-reference*: *See* also 4122.
—[*Physica.*] *Add cross-reference*: *See* also 12938.

772.5 *At beginning of imprint* add: [*W. White a. S. Stafford*]

•773 *Add reference after locations*: Greg 285.

•774 *At beginning of imprint* add: [*W. White*]

778 *Add note*: For other translations *see* 546, 6758.

•793.7 *Continue note*: O(in bdg. of Vet. A1e.141 = STC 11625) has frags. of E2,3,6,7 in a different setting from PN; e.g. E3r line 6 has: 'wind &' and E6v has catchword: 'seeth' whereas PN has: 'wind and' and 'pering' respectively.

794.5 *Continue 1st paragraph of note*: This set of plates is app. advertised in 5669. *Continue 2nd paragraph of note*: These same plates are also used in 6903.

798 *Add at end of title*: By H(en.) A(rth.)

810 *Add note*: Spaulding's dedic. specifies he took 'speciall care for the correction of such errors as were committed in the first edition', presumably 810.5.

826 *Continue note*: *See* also 11049.

840 *Add after date*: Ent. to the English Stock 5 mr. 1620.

840.5 *Continue SR entry*: ... 1614; the whole ent. to the English Stock 5 mr. 1620.

•861 *Begin imprint*: [*J. Bill f.*]

864 *Add at beginning of note*: Pr. in the same types as 3022.

888 *Continue note*: By R. Parsons.

Add new entry:
898.5 —The principles of Chrisitian [*sic*] religion. 8°. *W. Jaggard f. N. Bourne*, 1623. E[4].
Expanded from the 2nd pt. of 889.

900 *Continue SR entry*: 3rd pt. ent. to Sparke 12 no. 1631.

•909.5 *Correct format*: 8° in 4's. *Correct date*: [1535?]

921.5 *Add after date*: Ent. 22 jn.

Add new entry:
954.5 —Speculum peccatorum. [Anon.] 8°. (*per me w. de worde,*) [1509?] Private owner.
For a trans. *see* 929; *see* also 953.5.

1024 *Add note*: (Formerly also 4802) A version of the Heidelberg catechism; cf. 13028 sqq.

Add new entry:
1024.5 —[Heading A1r:] Rules made by E. B. for his children to learne to write bye. [In verse, w. woodcut.] fol. [*T. Vautrollier*, 1571.] L(MS.Egerton 2642, ff. 417–18).
In the same 1-column typesetting as 6446 but imposed so that the text is in 2 and a half pp. rather than 6. The verse is also pr. in 3361.3, 3363.5.

•1030.7 *Begin imprint*: [*T. Orwin*]

1038 *Continue note*: Not a trans.; written by R. Rowlands/ Verstegan and others.

1045 *Add after title*: [By Sir J. Bennet.]

1072.5 *Continue note*: Maps copied in 10420.

1113 *Add after date*: Ass'd to W. Aspley 28 ja., to M. Lownes 5 ap.

•1125 *In imprint* for *G. Potter?*] read: *W. Bladen,*]

1152 *Continue note*: A[6] is in 2 settings; translator's surname misprinted: 'GEORGE' (O) or corrected to 'GORGES' (2 L, HD, LC, PML); all copies of the latter have 'François' in line 10, and it appears that the 'Francais' reproduced in R. W. Gibson's Bacon bibliography, no. 45, is from a doctored photograph.

Add new entry:
1182.7 —[The famous history of Friar Bacon.] 4°. [*M. Flesher a. A. Mathewes f. F. Grove*, c. 1625.] Ent. to F. Grove 12 ja. 1624. HD(lacks tp).
D1r line 2 ends: 'the'; in 1183 sqq. this line ends: 'Fry-'. Flesher app. pr. at least A[4] and Mathewes at least G[4].

1196 *Add after date*: Ass'd from John Barnes to R. Jackson 26 fb. 1619.

1209 *In title, after* magistrale. *add*: First published by the commaundement of the king of Spain. Also the third book of Galen of curing of wounds of sinowes. [etc.] *Add note*: The inventor of the oil is called 'Aparice', i.e. Aparicio de Zubia. The trans. of Galen and some of the other sections are reprinted in 12469.

1219 *Add note*: The Confession is actually tr. by Hooper from J. Garnier; for other translations *see* 11620.7 sq.

1248 *Add note*: With additions by T. Sackville, etc.

•1273.5 *In imprint, before date* add: *solde wythin Paules chayne, at the sygne of S. John Baptist,*

•1301 *Amend date*: [c. 1580.]

Add new entry:
1313.2 —A short catechisme [without exposition]. Contayning the principles of religion. The twelfth impression. [Anon.] 8°. *W. Stansby, sold by E. Brewster a. R. Bird*, 1628. E[4].

1314.3 *Add note*: 1 F copy retains 2nd A1 (sub tp): A short catechisme, with an exposition. The second impression. [*Cambridge,*] *C. L*[*egge,*] *sold by W. Welbie*, [*London,*] 1617. Kingston app. pr. only 1st A[8].

Add new entry:
1328.2 —‹An ex›cellent newe ballet, made in the praise of ‹the› most noble and famous game of arche‹ry.› *Ballad.* s.sh.fol. [*London*, c. 1590?] O(imp.).

1331 *Begin imprint*: [*E. Purslowe* ...

1331.3 *Continue note*: Also erroneously entered as Wing N 559.

•1336 *In imprint* for *Ellen* read: *R.*

1336.5 *For* [Anon.] *read* [Init. Th. M. I. B.]

1341 *Continue note*: This ed. adds: The flowers of deuotion, w. sub tp on T7ʳ and preface by Heigham.

1352 *Add note*: T. Scarlet app. pr. R–V, 2O–2R; T. Creede (w. inits. borrowed from R. Field) 2K–2N, 3C–3E, 3I–3K; Wolfe the rest.

•1359 *In imprint* delete: (*sold ... Day*,])

1408 *Continue note*: Answered by 13840.

1408.3 *After* A&R 70 *add*: 1st quire differs: signed ¶ as in 1408, w. the imprint a press alteration (DE, Madrid NL) or signed πA (L); the latter is reset except for the tp, which is reimposed.

•1413 *Add note*: Tp differs: (i) orig., as above (C, HD) or (ii) a cancel, omitting '1621.' from line 5 of title (HN).

p. 64[1] *Continue last paragraph of headnote*: *See* also R. C. Alston, *A Bibliography of the English Language*, II (1967) and Supplement (1973), nos. 25–61 and 68 (really dated 1592). Further continental locations for some of the editions may be found in J. Peeters-Fontainas, *Bibliographie des Impressions Espagnoles des Pays-Bas Méridionaux*, 1965, I, nos. 329–30, 332–3, 336–47; in *De Gulden Passer*, 49 (1971): 197–221; and in *Annali*, Istituto Orientale di Napoli, Sezione Romanza, 17 (1975): 63–78.

1431.6 *Add note*: Antwerp, Archivum Capucinorum Belgii app. has another issue, w. beginning of title and imprint in French instead of Latin.

1431.33 *Add note*: Except for the tp, which is letterpress, this is the same setting as 1431.31, which has an engr. tp.

•1432 *In line 3 read*: Ent. to M. Sparke, sen., ...

1439.5 *Add after date*: Ent. 10 ja.

•1452 *Continue note*: This ed. is later than 1452.5.

•1456.5 *Continue note*: Creede pr. quires D, P; a 3rd printer quires I–L.

∘1462.3 *Add location*: Blickling(bd. w. 24045). *In note, before* W. Roy *add*: Jerome Barlow and

1462.7 *Continue note*: Also attrib. to Jerome Barlow and W. Roy.

1465 *Continue note*: For another answer *see* 4241.5.

•1487.5 *In imprint* for [*G. Eld*] read: [*M. Flesher*]

Add new entry:
•1501.3 —[Anr. issue, w. cancel tp, w. imprint:] *prostant Francofurti ap. Soc. bibliopolarum Londinensium*, 1617. L. Dresden, Sächsische Landesbibliothek. Kassel, Landesbibliothek. Kiel U. Munich, Bayrische Staatsbibliothek.

•1506 *In note read*: ... 23 lines of errata ... 17-line errata ...

•1521 *In line 4 read*: Anon. Now attrib. to J. Throkmorton.] *In imprint* read: *Schilders*, 1592.] *Continue note*: Answered by 23450.

•1522a *Amend imprint*: [*London*? 1592?]

1523 *Add at beginning of note*: Part of Greenwood's text, which answers 11862, is reprinted in 12340.

∘1542 *Amend date*: [1592?] *Begin note*: Quires H–L differ; (a) H1ʳ catchword: 'And'; postscript on K4ᵛ–L2ʳ (O) or (b) H1ʳ catchword: 'kindes'; L2ʳ has author's note and errata (L, HN, a revised version). According ... note in (b) this ...

p. 70[1] **Batt, A.** *Among 'tr.' cross-references delete*: 10890(*A*),

Add new entry:
1602.2 —The fourth edition. 12°. *f. J. Hodgets*, 1614. NLW.
A–Xx[12], pp. 1031; A7ʳ line 3: 'sixt time'. Because of the collation, the tp of this (also of 1602.3) may be more accurate than the edition statement in the dedic.

Add new entry:
•1608.9 —The 24. edition. 12°. *f. R. Allott*, 1629. WN[2](imp.).
A–Mm[12], pp. 814; A6ʳ line 5: '23. time'.

•1609.4 *Add location*: L.;

Add new entry:
1616.7 —The 36. edition. 12°. *f. M. Allot*, 1636. NLW.
A–Gg[12], pp. 701; A4ᵛ line 6: '36. *time*'.

1623.5 *Add note*: 500 copies were pr.; regarding a dispute between Allot and Vaughan over their delivery to Wales *see Dict 1*: 7.

•1635 *Continue imprint*: *sold* [*by E. Blount*,]

1655 *Add note*: The 1st psalm has music in 4 parts.

1656 *Continue note*: Answers 4527.8.

1659 *Add at beginning of note*: Tr. from J. Chassanion's Histoires memorables, 1586.

Add new entry:
1724.7 —[Anr. ed.] Newely corrected. 8°. (*T. Raynalde*,) [1548?] L.
22 lines; foliated. Tp border McK. & F. 33 has inits. 'T. R.' in the sill.

1735 *Add note*: Reprinted in 1775 sq.

•1748 *In line 2 read*: 1600; ent. to the English Stock 5 mr. 1620.

Add new entry:
1752.7 —[Anr. ed.] 8°. [*J. Allde*, 1560?] C(imp.).
(Formerly listed at 1751) Collates A–L[8]; A3ʳ catchword: 'Ther-'.

1775 *Add note*: A reprint, w. additions, of 1735.

1776 *In title, after* peace, *add*: called before the Pollecye of warre, lately recognised

•1791 *Add note*: HN has an early state w. imprint misdated: '1935.'

•1788 *Continue imprint*: *sold* [*in the shops of N. Newbery*,]

1805 *Add after date*: Ent. to T. Downes a. R. Young 18 mr. 1628; to the Irish Stock 20 de. 1629.

•p. 77[1] **Bell, F.** *Add to 'tr.' cross-references*: 22936.5(*A*3).

∘1825 *Correct beginning of imprint*: *T. C*[*reede, S. Stafford, a. T. Purfoot*] ... *In SR entry read*: 11 'my.' [i.e. ap.]. *Continue note*: In bk. 2 Stafford pr. A–F; Purfoot G–I.

•1837 *Continue imprint*: [*St. Omer*,]

p. 78[1] **Bellarmino, R.** *Continue anti-Bellarmino cross-references following STC 1845*: 3104, 4002, 4101, 5638.7, 6586, 6881, 6882, 6891, 6892, 7120, 7121, 7302, 12054, 12055, 12481, 12696, 13879, 18178, 20607, 23449, 23457, 24261, 24262, 25366, 25596, 25598, 26081.

1907 *Add after tp date*: Ent. to T. Nichols 26 my.

•1922 *Continue imprint*: [*St. Omer*,]

•1965 *Amend date*: [c. 1650?] *Add note*: From the shop sign used, this item undoubtedly belongs in Wing.

2000 *In title for* fourth *read*: [twenty-]fourth

2001 *At beginning of imprint* add: [*T. East f.*] *Add at beginning of note*: Possibly issued w. 11885.

2002 *Add note*: Pp. 110. The 2nd pt. (formerly also 11891) reprints 11884.5.

2006 *Add note*: B1 is a cancel in some copies; orig. B1^r last line ends: 'Suntq' and the cancel (pr. as A8) ends: 'æternus,'; both in C^2 copy.

•2018 *Correct date from* 1578?] *to*: 1587?]

2024.3 *Correct beginning of entry*: [A variant, w. imprint:]

2050 *Add note*: (11889 is pt. of this)

•2113a.3 *Add note*: *See* also 2874.

•2132 *Add*: L. *Delete*: PEN. *Add note*: For a metrical Psalms without tp issued with this *see* 2459.3(*A*3).

2216 *Add at beginning of last line of note*: Some copies (e.g. Arthur Houghton 40) have a letterpress gen. tp in border McK. & F. 231 as in 2217.

•2250 *In imprint,* after *deputies* add: *a. assignes*

2285 *Continue note*: Regarding 2 impositions of the text and 7 varieties of paper stock *see Transactions of the Cambridge Bibliographical Society* 8 (1984): 381–97.

2327.5 *Continue note*: 1 O has N.T. tp dated 1635.

2351.7 *Continue note*: *See* also *Acts P.C., 1577–1578*, pp. 188–9.

◦2353.5 *Begin title*: Δαβιδ του προφητοανακτος ευχη. *In imprint* after *Etonæ* add: [*M. Bradwood f.*] *Add note*: Prelim. epistle by I. Casaubon dated 16 kal. Feb. 1611.

•2354 Lord Kenyon's copy now = L^2.

•p. 96^2 *In paragraph* a. *at bottom of column, line 3 should end*: follow-

Add new entry:
•2376.3 —[Anr. ed.] 8°. [*London*, 1549?] L^2(Frag. no. 53, 2 imp. copies of sheet B (Ps. i–ix) and 2 leaves from another (Ps. xviii)).
23 lines; verso/recto headlines: The Psalter/of David; no marginal notes.

•2384.7 *Continue note*: Warsaw, Biblioteka Archidieczjalna (C.18.18^a) has E^8(imp.) of pt. 2 of an ed. paginary w. NY but a different, prob. earlier, setting; both have 29 lines of text to a page, but Warsaw has headlines and Latin psalm headings in black letter (same size as the text) whereas NY has them in roman type. E1^r last line (in Ps. xxxviii.41) begins: 'and imagined deceit al' (Warsaw) or 'and imagined deceipt all' (NY). A comparable BCP Psalter (16293.5) has 28 lines of text, headlines and headings in roman, and E1^r last line beginning: 'nesse, & imagined deceipt all'.

•p. 100 *Extend* Heth. 107 *to include*: 1569 | 2439.3(*A*3)

•p. 101 *Extend series* 8/50 *to include*: 1635 | 2658.5(*A*3)

•p. 101 *Delete series* 8/51. (2637.2 actually belongs to series 8/50).

•p. 102 *Add new series to begin 8°, 2 cols., rom*: 8/60* | 1581 | 2459.3(*A*3) | A–G^8 (no tp) | yes | E3^v, col. 1, p. 62 | G6^v, p 89.

•p. 102 *In series* 16/46, *in last 2 cols. read*: [Psalm ci:] *Aa3*^{r}, f. 150^r | [last numbered leaf:] *Ll 1*^{r}, f. 228.

•p. 103 *In series* 16/60 *for date* 1631 *add STC number*: 2630

Add new entry:
2424.1 —[Anr. ed.] All suche psalmes of Dauid [etc.] 8°. (*E. Whitchurche*, 1552 (13 my.)) CANT.
1 col., B.L., A–G^8 H^4; series 8/31. Readings are identical to 2424.2 but tp has border McK. & F. 56.

Add new entry:
•2439.3 —[Anr. ed.] 4° in 8's. *J. Daye, cum priuilegio per decennium*, 1569. F.
1 col., B.L., A^4 πB^2 B–Y^8 Aa–Ff^8 Gg^4; Heth. 107.

•2441.5 *Correct location to*: L.

2443.5 *Continue note*: This is the only ed. of this series w. 'C' of sig. C1 under 'd' of 'and'.

•2459 *Delete*: PEN.

Add new entry:
•2459.3 —[Anr. ed.] 8°. (*J. Daye*, 1581.) L.L^{14}.
2 cols., rom., A–G^8; series 8/60*(*A*3). Intended only for binding w. a Bible (2132) and has no tp, but above beginning of text on A1^r is the heading: *The whole booke of Psalmes with the Note.*

Add new entry:
2461.3 —[Anr. ed.] 16° in 8's. (*J. Daye*, 1582.) O(imp.).
1 col., rom., A–Y^8; series 16/57.

2466.5 *Continue note*: STU has a copy w. tp and colophon dated 1583, which is at least partly from a different setting; e.g. 'i' of sig. E1 is under 'r' of 'embrace' while in the other copies it is under the first 'e' of the same word.

Add new entry:
2466.9 —[Anr. ed.] 16° in 8's. *J. Daye*, (1583.) L.
1 col., B.L., *A–*Y^8 *Aa–*Mm^8; series 16/47.

•2475.3 Baron copy now = Carleton U, Ottawa.

2483 *Continue note*: Pluscarden Abbey, Elgin, Scotland, has a copy lacking tp and all after G5, which is a different setting from other eds. of this series; e.g. 'A' of sig. A2 is under 'd' of 'woundes'; it may belong to this ed.

•2500 *Delete* F *here and add at* 2500.3. *Add*: HN(imp., mixed sheets).

•2500.3 *Amend heading*: [A variant, w. colophon dated:] (1600.) *Add*: F. *and delete*: HN. *Amend*: Steele 190(Britwell copy, lacked F^8, untraced). *In note delete Heth. series.*

•2516 *In imprint* for [*A. Islip* read: [*H. Lownes*

•2518 *In imprint* for [*J. Windet*] read: [*Eliot's Court Press*]

Add new entry:
2518.7 The whole booke of psalmes, collected [etc.] 24° in 12's. *f. the Co. of Statrs.*, 1605. L.
1 col., rom., A–O^{12}; series 24/40.

•2522.3 *Begin imprint*: [*J. Windet a. T. East*] *Continue note*: Windet pr. A–F; East the rest.

•2527.7 The Nicholas copy now = C^2.

•2530.5 *Begin imprint*: [*W. Jaggard a. E. Allde*] *Continue note*: Jaggard pr. A–M; Allde the rest.

Add new entry:
2538.7 The whole booke of psalmes: collected. 24° in 12's. *f. the Co. of Statrs.*, 1611. AMVU.
1 col., rom., A–O^{12}; series 24/40.

Add new entry:
2546.5 The whole booke of psalmes: collected. 24° in 12's. [*R. Field*] *f. the Co. of Statrs.*, 1613. L(imp.).
1 col., rom., A–O^{12}; series 24/40.

•2571.7 *Add location*: YK(Cup. XVI).

2575a *For* —[Anr. ed.] *read*: The whole booke of psalmes. Collected [etc.]

•2600.5 *Add location*: ; Agecroft Hall, Richmond, Virginia.

Add new entry:
2636.3 —[A variant, w. imprint:] *f. the Co. of Statrs.*, 1632. NLW.
Identical in setting to 2636 except for omitting G. Miller's initials. NLW has: 'tooke rest' on F5^r, col. 2, verse 8.

•2637.2 *In note, for series* 8/51 *read*: 8/50.

Add new entry:
•2658.5 —[Anr. ed.] 8°. *f. the Co. of Statrs.*, 1635. L(imp.).
1 col., B.L., A–Aa^8; series 8/50.

Add new entry:
2697.5 —[Anr. ed.] 16° in 8's. *E. G*[*riffin*] *f. the Co. of Statrs.*, 1640. HD(lacks Mm8).
1 col., B.L., A–Y^8 Aa–Mm^8; series 16/48.

°2734 *Add location*: O. *Begin note*: Includes 3 psalms (xl, xli, xlii) derived in part from a trans. by Sir Philip Sidney. *Add at end of note*: *See* also *Court-Book C*, pp. 231–2.

2739 *For* L. *read*: L(bd. w. STC 15261).

Add new entry:

2739.5 —[Anr. ed., adding:] (De kleyne cathechismus.) 2 pts. 16° in 8's. (*London, J. Daye, voor den voorseyden ouersetter*, 1561 (31 au.)) HAGUE(tp to pt. 1 in facs.). Ghent U. Groningen U(imp.).

2740 *Add locations*: HAGUE. Amsterdam U. Ghent U.+ *Continue note*: Pt. 1 of this and 2740.3 includes the Formulier Kerckendienstes.

Add new entry:

2740.3 —[Anr. ed.] 8°. 2 pts. *Londen, J. Daye*, 1566 (12 se.) HAGUE. Utrecht U.
Text of Psalms in B.L. Pt. 2 also issued sep. as 15262.

2741.5 *Add after date*: Ent. as tr. by M. A. de Dominis 12 ap.

•2753.5 Sotheby's copy now = L.

Add new entry:

2756.5 [Selections from Proverbs, Ecclesiastes, Wisdom, etc. In verse.] fol(2?). [*K. Herford*? 1550?] C7(sheet 2 only, imp., Muniments XXXIX 116, w. blank verso used for college accounts of 1551).
3 columns of 6-line stanzas rhyming aabccb, to be read in triplets across the sheet. The triplets are numbered 11–22, and the 1st begins: 'Use not at borde/ To rayle in worde/ ...'

2780 *Correct imprint*: [*Amsterdam, J. Theunisz*?]

2785 *In 2nd paragraph of note after* O14, *add*: LINC, *After* A1–4 *add*: (2 bifolia) *After* Allde.] *add*: For a specimen leaf w. text and different commentary *see* the 3rd paragraph of the note to 3850.

•2792 *Amend date*: [1534–36?]

2792.5 *Add at beginning of note*: Gen. tp differs: letterpress or engraved, each w. title and imprint as above; examples of both at GOT.

2792.5–.7 After *Noribergae* add: [*widow of A. P. Dietrich*,]

2801 *Add after date*: Ass'd by E. Marsh to T. Orwin 23 jn. 1591.

Add new entry:

2803.5 —[Anr. ed.] 16° in 8's. *T. Vautrollerus*, 1574. L(tp only, Cup.652.ee.8, fol. 9).

Add new entry:

2806.5 —[Anr. ed.] 16°in 8's. *T. Vautrollerius*, 1580. William H. Allen, bkseller, Philadelphia (copy sold, cannot be traced).

2828 *Continue note*: The prelims. (table and prologue to Romans) were prob. added later and possibly pr. in London.

2836.5–37 *At beginning of imprint* add: [*Antwerp, M. Crom*,]

•2848.5 Private copy now = L.

•2874 *In note for* 2112.5 *read*: 2113a.3.

Add new entry:

•2879.1 —[Anr. ed. Geneva: Tomson.] 8°. [*London*? c. 1577] David John Veryard, Northampton, England(frags.).
35 lines to a full page. The only known 8° ed. of this version with text in B.L. and with pagination. Headlines and contents at beginning of chapters (usually only 1st half of normal Geneva-Tomson content-summary) in roman; divided into verses, but without marginal notes or commentary.
The portions extant, with occasional signatures and pagination, run from Y3r, p. 325 (Acts vi.15) to Cc8v, p. 400 (Romans ii.3). The main text app. began on B1r, p. 1 and ran approximately to Vv8v, p. 672; Acts would have begun on X1 or 2, pp. 305–8. Because of the uncharacteristic nature of this ed. it is possibly a piracy.

2881.5 *Continue note*: NY6 has an imp. copy lacking tp and all after Bb2 (Acts i.21) which is app. another and later ed.; it has D2v line 4 (Matt. xiv.32) ending 'in-'; NLW(lacking all before A2 and after Fff8, Rev. xii.8) has 'into'; O lacks all before Ii3. NY6 also has verse numberings in the text in a larger fount than in the chapter contents while in O and NLW both numberings are generally in the smaller fount.

Add new entry:

2905.2 The new testament of our lord Jesus Christ. [Geneva: Tomson.] 24° in 12's. *R. Barker*, 1606. L.

•2905.5 The Nicholas copy now = C2.

Add new entry:

•2944.5 —[Anr. ed.] 8°. *Edinburgh, prs. to the kings majestie*, 1633. L.
Ends Ee8 like 2948 sq.

2952 *Begin line 5 of note*: issue; regarding these illustrated copies *see Transactions of the Cambridge Bibliographical Society* 8 (1982): 173–85.

Add new entry:

2953.3 —[Anr. ed. Roy.] 24° in 12's. *R. Barker a. assignes of J. Bill*, 1637. L.

Add new entry:

2954.6 —[Anr. ed. Roy.] 24° in 12's. *Edinburgh, R. Young*, 1638. O6.

Add new heading and entries:

French

2957.6 Le nouueau testament, c'est a dire, la nouuelle alliance de nostre seigneur Jesus Christ, *tr.* de Grec en Francoys. Reueu par J. Caluin. 8°. *Londres, de l'imprimerie de T. Gaultier*, 1551. HART.
Regarding this and the following French versions *see Bibliothèque d'Humanisme et Renaissance* 39 (1977): 143–8; 41 (1979): 353–8.

2957.7 —[A variant, without imprint.] [*London, T. Gaultier*,] 1551. L(C.106.a.2, imp.). Paris, Bibliothèque de la Société de l'Histoire du Protestantisme Français.; BO6.

2957.8 —[A variant, w. imprint:] *Londres*, [*T. Gaultier f.*] *de l'imprimerie de E. Whytechurch*, 1551. Caen PL.

2957.9 —[Anr. ed.] *Tr.* & reueu de Grec en François. 8°. *Londres*, [*T. Gaultier*,] 1553. Paris, Bibliothèque de la Société de l'Histoire du Protestantisme Français.
Pr. in the same types and w. title in the same border (McK. & F. 135) as 6003.5, q.v.

2967.3 *Add locations*: C5. C12(lacks π4).

2967.7 *Add locations*: C3(imp.).LINC.STU.

2968 *Add locations*: C5(lacks π1).C12(w. π4 of 2968.3).

2968.3 *Amend to*: L(2, 1 = 3227.aa.4, destroyed; 1 = C.135.g.14, A–S4 only, w. π4 of 2968.5). *Add*: C12(π4 only, w. 2968).

2968.5 *Amend to*: L(... plus π4 only, w. 2968.3). *Add*: C3.LINC.

2968.7 *Add location*: STU. *In line 10 of note read*: ... time; STU has quire E w. side-notes in roman; *In line 11 of note for* well *read*: also

2969 *Add locations*: C5.C12.

2969.3 *Amend to*: L(2, 1 = ...; 1 = C.135.g.14). *Add*: C3(imp.). LINC(imp., w. at least S4 of 2969.5).

2969.5 *Add locations*: LINC(S4, w. 2969.3).STU.

2970.3 *Add locations*: C3.STU.

Add new entry:

•2980.3 —The epistles | and gospels, of euery | Sondaye, and holy day | through out the whole | yeare. After the vse | of the Churche | of England. 8°. [*W. Copland*,] 1559. CANT(H/L-4-12, imp.).
Variety (d); A–N8 + ?

•2980.4 *Begin entry*: —[Anr. ed.]

Add new entry:

2985.3 Christen prayers & godly meditacions vpon the epistles [*sic*] to the Romains, newly *tr.* out of Italian [by T. Becon.] 16° in 8's. *John Wyer*, [1550.] L(tp and 5 pp. of outer forme only of 1st quire, imp., in bdg. of C.131.aa.3 = STC 11383).
The preface was undoubtedly signed and dated by Becon as in 2985.5. On the other forme are pr. 3 pp. of an 8° primer in English: 16050.7(***A***3).

•2991 *Add after date*: Ass'd to R. Barker 7 fb. 1603.

Add new entry:

2996.3 Heir follouis, ane compendeous buke, of godlye psalmes and spirituall sangis newly translatit out of Latine into Inglis, gadderit out of diuers scripturis. [Attrib. to John, James, and Robert Wedderburn.] 8°. [*Edinburgh? J. Scot?*] *at the command and expensis of T. Bassandyne*, 1565. GOT.

3009 *Continue note*: ... 4826 and includes the Litany, on F5^r–G4^r in this and the next 2. O has a frag. w. most of the Litany in a quire signed O, in which the typesetting of the text is the same as the present ed., but the borders have type ornaments as in 3009.5 sq.; it app. belongs to a kindred but unidentified work.

3020.5 *Continue note*: There are 2 issues, w. prelims., O4, and S1 in different settings; e.g. ¶2^r ends: 'Farewell.' (L) or 'Farewel.' (F); L omits 1 Thess. on O4^v whereas it is present in F (a cancel).

•3031 *Add location*: O(lacks T1).

Add new entry:

3031.5 —[Anr. ed.] 12°. *R. Young f. E. Brewster a. R. Bird*, 1633. C^{16}.
Collates A–S^{12} like 3032 sq.

Add new entry:

◦3034.7 Notable textes of the scriptures which declare of what vertue, strength and holiness the pixed or boxed God is: with also, what fayth, is to be put in him. 8° in 4. [*Ipswich? A. Scoloker*, 1548?] NLW(lacks 3rd leaf).
For an earlier ed. *see* 10430. For a different text by L. Sheperd attacking holy wafers, originally in the same tract vol., *see* 4877.2(***A***3).

•3078 *Amend imprint date to*: [1562.]

•3088.5 *Begin imprint*: [*V. Simmes*]

3090 *Add note*: Also erroneously intered as Wing L 2833.

3113 *Add note*: *See* also 5575.2.

3117 *Add before locations*: Ent. to the Purfoots, sen. a. jun., 30 oc. 1596.

Add new entry:

•3129.8 —[A variant, w. imprint:] *J. Norton, sold by T. Ewen in Malborough*, 1634. Sotheby's, 24 July 1987, lot 421.

3175 *In note, after* M *add*: and Kraus.

•3182 *In imprint* before *sold* add: [*f. R. Smith*,]

3184.4 *In title, after* Guerin *add*: [i.e. Guercin du Crest]

•3186 *Correct date to*: [1530?]

•3187 After *Godfray*? read: *f. R. Saltwood*? 1530?]

•3193.5 *In imprint* for [*by G. Bishop*,] (1606.) read: [*by A. Hebb*, c. 1635.] *Begin note*: Retains Islip's colophon dated 1606.

•3204 *In imprint* for [*R. Jugge f.*] read: [*S. Mierdman? f.*]

3205, 3206 *Continue or add note*: Answers 3207.5(***A***).

Add new entry:

3207.5 —Informatio fundamentalis super discursu quodam circa modernum regni Bohemiae statum facto. Cui adjectus est tenor bullæ aureæ Caroli quarti. [By A. Schmid von Schmiedebach.] 4°. [*Lancs.? Birchley Hall Press*?] 1619 [o.s.] O.OS.
Answered by 3205, 3206.

•3234 *Continue imprint*: *sold* [*by J. Crooke a. R. Sergier*,]

•3254 *Continue imprint*: *sold* [*by J. Crooke a. R. Sergier*,]

•3255 *Continue note*: Some copies (1 HD, U) are without ¶^{4} (Table and errata for pt. 2) and may represent an early issue.

•3258 *In imprint* for [*J. Windet* read: [*T. Creede*

•3270 Camarillo copy now = L.

3273.7 *Add note*: A general bond to pay *x* the sum of *y* on *z* day; pr. in civilité w. a few roman and italic sorts mixed in. For other varieties of blank bonds and contracts *see* 9175m sqq.

Add new entry:

3273.9 —Noverint universi per præsentes me [ ] ... obligari in viginti libris bonæ monetæ ... The condition of this obligation [etc. Bond not to buy or sell the king's venison, pheasant, etc. for a year.] 1/2 sh.fol. [*T. Harper*, 1638?] C^{26}(V.C. Ct.III.34(179)).

3299 *Continue note*: L copy on Univ. Microfilms reel 197 is actually 6395.

•3304 *Delete*: L(1 leaf). (This frag. is really 24868 and listed there.)

3305.5 *Continue note*: Also erroneously entered as Wing S 2496.

Substitute revised entry:

3306 —[Heading A1^r:] The booke of fortune [xylographic, white on black] ... made in Italian, by L. Spirit [L. Spiriti's Libro di sorti], and *tr.* [by W. Lily? Partly in verse, w. woodcuts.] fol. (*f. E. Wright*, 1618.) ?Ent. to W. Powell 6 fb. 1560; ass'd by R. Bradock to J. a. E. Wright 9 jy. 1615. L(L^4 copy).

◦3308 *Correct imprint*: (*Sanctus albanus*,) [1486.] *Continue note*: 1 L is marked as printer's copy for 3309.

3325 *Add note*: Tr. from Le traicte de la vraye noblesse, which is a trans. of J. Clichtoveus, De vera nobilitate opusculum.

•3358a.5 *Begin imprint*: [*W. How? f.*]

3363.5 *In line 3 of note, after* specimens *add*: (2 of which also appear in 5400) *At end of note add*: *See* also 1024.5(***A***1).

•3363.9 *Add note*: Collates A–C^4 D^2. This text is app. derived from two others which were the subject of a dispute between Dexter and R. Jones on 3 my. 1591 (Greg, *Register B*, p. 37). Dexter's copy was in 5 sheets and attrib. in *Reg. B* to the authorship of Thomas Johnson; it is app. the text entered to A. Maunsell 11 fb. 1577, to Dexter 2 no. 1590, and to R. Jones 16 no. 1590 but crossed out by the order in *Reg. B*. Jones's copy was in 2 sheets, was entered to him on 3 my. 1591 (Arber II.581), and app. crossed out on 15 my. 1605 by the order noted at *Reg. B*, p. 37.

3368.5 **Bookplates.**

Note: None of the following entries has been heralded in the Bookplates section itself although cross-references have been added under most of the owners' or donors' names in the main run of headings in vol. 1 of the STC revision. Those gift-plates for which Ipswich is queried as the place of printing are assumed to have been done with a limited assortment of types clamped in a binder's pallet; for reproductions of most of them *see* John Blatchly, *The Town Library of Ipswich*, Woodbridge, Suffolk, [1989], pp. 182–5, where the date of their printing is given as between 1613 and 1617.

Add new entries:

p. 145^2 **Acton, George.** [Gift-plate.] The gift of G. Acton, one of the Common Counsell of Ipswich. [*Ipswich?* c. 1625?] Ipswich School.

Algate, Christopher. [Gift-plate.] The gift of C. Algate, one of the Common Counsell of Ipswich. [*Ipswich?* c. 1620?] Ipswich School.

p. 146^1 **Bacon, Edward,** *esq.* [Gift-plate.] The gift of master E. Bacon, esquier. [*Ipswich?* c. 1615?] Ipswich School.

3368.5 **Bookplates** — *cont. Add new entries*:

p. 146[1] **Balcanquhall, Walter,** *the elder*. [Gift-plate.] Vir sanctissimus magister W. Balcanquel, hunc librum, collegii Sancti Leonardi bibliothecæ legavit. CIC. DC. XVI. [*Edinburgh*? 1616?] STU(2).

• **Banastre, R.** *Add location*: L(in 222.a.28 = STC 18083).

Barber, Jeremy. [Gift-plate.] The gift of J. Barber, one of the Common Counsell of Ipwich [*sic*]. [*Ipswich*? c. 1620?] Ipswich School.

Barnes, A. *For* Goyder *read*: O(in Vet.A1d.38 = STC 23643).

p. 146[2] **Bloise, William.** [Gift-plate.] The gift of W. Bloise portman of Ipsewich. [*Ipswich*? 1613?] Ipswich School.

Blosse, Tobias. [Gift-plate.] The gift of master T. Blosse, portman of Ipswich. [*Ipswich*? c. 1615–20?] Ipswich School.

Braythwait, Thomas. [Gift-plate.] This booke was given by legacie from T. Braythwait of Ambleside gent. who died in ... 1607. unto George Preston of Houlker gent. [*London*, c. 1607?] Christie's, 8 Dec. 1982 (in lot 88A = STC 2199).

Brewster, Francis. [Gift-plate.] The gift of master F. Brewster, esquier. [*Ipswich*? 1615?] Ipswich School.
• —[Gift-plate.] The gift of F. Brewster esquire. [*Ipswich*? 1615?] Ipswich School.

p. 147[1] **Browne, Nathaniel.** [Gift-plate.] Liber Collegij D. Petri ex dono N. Broune, Londinensis mense Ianuarij. Anno 1613. [*London*? 1613?] C[19](on the cover of MS. 118).

Brownrig, Matthew. [Gift-plate.] The gift of master M. Brownrig, portman of Ipswich. [*Ipswich*? c. 1615–20?] Ipswich School.

Bruning, John. [Gift-plate.] The gift of J. Bruning, ship-carpenter of Ipswich. [*Ipswich*? c. 1615?] Ipswich School.

Buckenham, Henry. [Gift-plate.] Feb. 1613. The gift of H. Buckenham mercer, and one of the Common Counsell of Ipswich. [*Ipswich*? 1613?] Ipswich School.

• **Bull, William,** *esq.* [Gift-plate.] Ex dono W. Bull armigeri. 1623. [*London*? 1623?] Wells C(in Vicars Choral MS. 1).

Burlingham, Richard. [Gift-plate.] Feb. 1613. The gift of R. Burlingham mariner, and a free burgis of Ipswich. [*Ipswich*? 1613?] Ipswich School.

Cage, William. [Gift-plate.] The gift of W. Cage, portman of Ipswich. [*Ipswich*? c. 1615–20?] Ipswich School.

• **Catcher, Richard.** [Gift-plate.] Collegium Divi Petri in Academia Cantabrigiensi. Ex dono D. Richardi Catcher, Medicinae Professoris. MDCXXVI. [*Cambridge*? 1626?] C[19](3, e.g. in D.4.1).
Partly in same setting as the Rayment (*A*3) gift-plate.

Childe, Anne. [Gift-plate.] The gift of A. Childe, deceased 1634 the wife of Ralph Childe of this citie. [*London*? 1634?] BHP(B.A., 6 copies under horn on covers of St. Augustine, *Opera*, Paris, 1613–14).

Clemetson, Mabel. [Gift-plate.] The gift of M. Clemetson late deceased, executrix of the said James Tomson. [*J. Bill*? c. 1618?] Ipswich School(2, completing Tomson's gift).
In same woodcut border as the Suckling and Tomson (***A***) gift-plates.

Cock, Richard. [Gift-plate.] The gift of R. Cock, portman of Ipswich. [*Ipswich*? c. 1615–20?] Ipswich School.

3368.5 **Bookplates** — *cont. Add new entries*:

p. 147[2] **Cole, Peter.** [Gift-plate.] Feb. 1613. The gift of P. Cole grocer, and a free burgis of Ipswich. [*Ipswich*? 1613?] Ipswich School.
—[Gift-plate.] The gift of P. Cole, free-burgesse in Ipswich. [*Ipswich*? c. 1615?] Ipswich School.

Cole, Robert. [Gift-plate.] August. 1613. The gift of R. Cole tanner, late one of the Common Counsell of Ipswich. [*Ipswich*? 1613?] Ipswich School.

Cole, William. [Gift-plate.] The gift of W. Cole, free-burgesse in Ipswich. [*Ipswich*? c. 1620?] Ipswich School.

Coppin, George. [Gift-plate.] The gift of G. Coppin, free burgesse of Ipswich. [*Ipswich*? c. 1615?] Ipswich School.

Cutler, Robert. [Gift-plate.] The gift of master R. Cutler, portman of Ipswich. [*Ipswich*? c. 1615–20?] Ipswich School.

D., E. [Book-stamp.] E D [c. 1592?] L(Ames I.530, above tp border of STC 15167).
The last name is completed in MS. as Dingley.

Day, Edmond. [Gift-plate.] Febr. 1613. The gift of E. Day dier, and one of the Common Councell of Ipswich. [*Ipswich*? 1613?] Ipswich School.

Dod, Catherine. [Gift-plate.] The gift of mistris C. Dod widowe. [*Ipswich*? c. 1630?] Ipswich School.

p. 148[1] **Eldred, Thomas.** [Gift-plate.] The gift of T. Eldred, one of the Common Counsell of Ipswich. [*Ipswich*? c. 1615?] Ipswich School.

Fisher, Richard. [Gift-plate.] The gift of R. Fisher, free burgesse of Ipswich. [*Ipswich*? c. 1615?] Ipswich School.

p. 148[2] **Goodeere, Michael.** [Gift-plate.] The gift of master M. Goodeere, portman of Ipswich. [*Ipswich*? c. 1615–20?] Ipswich School.

• **Harborne.** *Add location*: ; F(on tp verso of STC 22541, copy 3).

p. 149[1] **Hayles, Thomas.** [Gift-plate.] The gift of T. Hayles, one of the Common Counsell of Ipswich. [*Ipswich*? c. 1620?] Ipswich School.

p. 149[2] **Jewel, John,** *Bp.* [Book-stamp.] Johan. Jewel. Episcop. Sarisb. + 1571 + [1571?] O[12](23).
A circular stamp, w. the above words around the rim and 'BEL AMI' across the center; *see Bodleian Library Record* 9 (1977): 256–7.

Johnson, Thomas, *of Ipswich*. [Gift-plate.] The gift of master T. Johnson, portman of Ipswich. [*Ipswich*? c. 1615–20?] Ipswich School.

Knapp, Robert. [Gift-plate.] The gift of R. Knapp, free-burgesse of Ipswich. [*Ipswich*? c. 1620?] Ipswich School(offset of a label that has been lost).

• **Layther, Thomas.** [Book-stamp.] Thomas Layther huius libri est possessor. [c. 1550?] USHAW(twice, in Gregory the Great, *Opera*, Paris, 1518).

p. 150[1] **Martin, Richard,** *of Ipswich*. [Gift-plate.] The gift of master R. Martin, portman of Ipswich. [*Ipswich*? c. 1615–20?] Ipswich School.

Add cross-reference:

p. 150[2] **Mosse, John.** *See* Bookplates (M., I.).

• **Nicolson.** *In all three imprints* for [*Aberdeen, E. Raban*? read: [*Edinburgh*?

Osmond, Benjamin. [Gift-plate.] The gift of B. Osmond, one of the Common Counsell of Ipswich. [*Ipswich*? c. 1620?] Ipswich School.

p. 151[1] • **Pilkington, John.** Sum Iohannis Pilkingtoni Dunelmensis. [*London*? c. 1595?] DUR(N.VI.29).

3368.5 **Bookplates** — *cont. Add new entries*:

p. 151^{2} **Randes, John.** [Gift-plate.] The gift of J. Randes, one of the Common Counsell of Ipswich. [*Ipswich*? c. 1620?] Ipswich School.

Rant, William. [Gift-plate.] Ex dono G. Rant socij huius collegij. [*Cambridge*? c. 1595.] C^{9}(3, under horn, e.g. on bdg. of D.6.1).

• **Raworth, Margaret.** Margaret Raworth. August XIIII. An. Dom. 1604. [*London*, 1604.] HN(on tp verso of STC 2506.5).
In a border similar to McK. & F. 191, but with the apostles 'SIMO[N]' and 'AND[REW]' at sides.

• **Rayment, Thomas.** [Gift-plate.] Collegium Divi Petri in Academia Cantabrigiensi. Ex dono D. Thomae Rayment Sacrae Theologiae Professoris, quondam Socii hujus Collegii. 1626. [*Cambridge*? 1626?] C^{19}(6, e.g. in D.9.3–6).
Partly in same setting as the Catcher (***A*3**) gift-plate.

p. 152^{1} • **Shawe, William.** [Gift-plate.] Collegium Divj Petrj in Academia Cantabr. Ex dono D. Guil. Shawe Sacræ Theologiæ Profess. 1625. [*Cambridge*? 1625?] C^{19}(8, in H.9.1–8).

Sheppard, Thomas. [Gift-plate.] Ex dono Thomæ Sheppard commensalis. [*Oxford*? 1605?] O^{13}(4).

• **Spenser.** Broxbourne copy now = R.A. Linenthal, London.

Starkey, John. [Record of baptism and death. 1634?] *See* 23235.3(***A*3**).

p. 152^{2} **Suckling,** *Sir* **J.** *Continue note*: For other gift-plates in the same woodcut border *see* Clemetson and Tomson (both in ***A***).

Tomson, James. [Gift-plate.] The gift of J. Tomson, late of Ipswich, glover. [*J. Bill*? c. 1618?] Ipswich School (4, in vols. 1–4 of St. Jerome, *Opera*, Basle, 1524–26).
Vols. 5, 6 have the label of his executrix, M. Clemetson (***A***). Both labels are in the same woodcut border as Suckling.

Tresame. *Amend to*: L(1 pasted at end of dedic. in 9087.k.6; 2 in ...

p. 153^{1} **Walter, Elizabeth.** [Gift-plate.] The gift of mistresse Walter, widdow. [*Ipswich*? c. 1615?] Ipswich School.

Ward, Samuel, *of Ipswich*. [Gift-plate.] The gift of master S. Warde, town-preacher in Ipswich. [*Ipswich*? c. 1615?] Ipswich School.

• **Whitaker, William.** Gulielmus Whitacherus. [*London*, c. 1563?] C^{9}(at least 2, e.g. in F.20.14).
• —Ιλερμος Ουιταχηρος. [*London*, c. 1563?] C^{9}(at least 3, e.g. in F.20.8).

p. 153^{2} **Withepole,** *Sir* **Edmond.** [Gift-plate.] The gift of sir E. Withepole, knight. [*Ipswich*? c. 1615?] Ipswich School.

Wynne, William, *the elder*. Ex dono Guliel. Wynn, Ar. fil. tert. Jo. Wynn de Guydder, in Com. Carnarvon, Mil. & Baronetti. 1623. [*London*? 1623?] L^{13}(several).

x**Wynne, William.** *Add to heading*: *the younger*.

•3381 *Continue imprint*: *in the house of R. Wyer*,

3388 *At end of title add*: (A new ... astrologie, inuented by maister Harlequin, calculated for the Leaguers merydian.) *Add note*: The 1st tp is on a sep. folding leaf. B1 is blank, and the 2nd pt., w. 'Astrologie' heading as above, begins on B2^{r}.

Add new heading:

•p. 155^{1} **Boules, George.** A spiritual directory. 1626. *See* 19769.9(***A*3**).

Add new entry:

3410.3 **Bourbon, François de,** *Duc de Montpensier*. [Heading A2^{r}:] La copie d'vne lettre cõtenant le progres des choses aduenues au voyage de ... le duc de Montpensier ... auec le discours des deux deffaictes des Gautiers rebelles. (Declaration faite par le duc de Montpencier, pour la reunion de ceux du clergé, & de la noblesse en l'obeissance de sa maiesté.) 8°. (*J. Wolfe*, 1589.) Caen, Musée des Beaux Arts(Mancel 804/1–2, lacks A1).
A^{8} B^{4} C^{2}, w. sub tp on B3^{r}. A trans. is included in 11256.

3440 *In note read*: ... blank), pr. by [*F. Kingston*].

◦3447 *Begin note*: In vol. 1 prelims. at least 1 O, 1 HN have an extra bifolium, *^{2}, w. Latin verse by Boyd to King Charles, etc.; not present in 4 F, 1 HN, HD, LC copies.

Add new entry:

•3481.7 —[Anr. ed.] 16° in 8's. *J. Wolf*, 1583. L^{2}.

•3490 *Continue imprint*: *sold* [*by H. Rocket*?]

•3515.5 *In imprint* for *R. H.* read: *R. H*[*earne*]

•3526 *In note before* 14023 *add*: 7081,

3568.5 *Add after date*: Ent. 30 my.

•3584 *In imprint* for [*J. Norton*, read: [*Eliot's Court Press*,

•3589 *At end of imprint* add: *sold* [*in the shop of N. Bourne*,]

•3599 *In imprint* for *J. Wight* read: *R. Boyle*. Maunsell (17669), pt. 1, p. 24^{b} (under Brownists) gives a variant or interpretive imprint with Boyle's name.

3604 *Continue note*: For evidence that 'Brereley' is actually James rather than Lawrence Anderton and for further details of the authorship of this and the following works *see Recusant History*, 16 (1982): 17–41.

3605.5 *Continue note*: Not by Brereley/Anderton; *see* note to 3604(***A***).

3608.5 *Continue note*: Not by Brereley/Anderton; *see* note to 3604(***A***).

3649 *Add note*: App. a later, enlarged ed.: Breton's longing: whereunto is added a definition of love, *J. B*[*rowne*] *a. J. D*[*eane*,] 1606, was in the Hessisches Landes- und Hochschulbibliothek, Darmstadt, but was destroyed during World War II; *see Notes and Queries*, April, 1978, p. 129.

Add new entry:

3712.3 —[Anr. ed.] 4°. *B. Alsop a. T. Fawcet f. G. Hurlock*, 1640. LINC.

3738 *Continue note*: Includes a refutation of the account of Pinder's possession given in 19936.5(***A*3**).

•3766 For [*A. Scoloker a. W. Seres*,] read: [*London*?] *Add note*: In the same types as 24514.

3770b.5 *Add note*: *See* also 4859.

3774 *Add note*: For the Latin text *see* 6106.3 sqq.

Add new entry:

3793.5 **Bristol.** The oath of a burgesse. You shall be good and true unto ... king Charles. 1/2 sh.fol. [*London*? 1637?] M^{2} (Halliwell's procs., etc. no. 729).
In the left margin is pr. 'Civitas Bristoll.', and the verso has a MS. endorsement dated 28 July 1637.

3799 *Continue note*: Based on a version of Cardinal W. Allen's 'Articles'; for another printed version *see* pt. 2 of 274(***A***); for answers to various versions *see* the notes at 274(***A***), 3800.5; *see* also 15037.5. For a concise account of the controversy and the books involved *see* Peter J. Milward, *Religious Controversies of the Elizabethan Age*, 1977, pp. 39–45.

•3800.5 *Amend imprint*: ... *Winde*, [*Douai*,]

3802 *Continue note*: Regarding Allen's 'Articles' *see* 3799(***A***); answered by 11448.

•3834–4.5 For [*J. Windet* read: [*W. White a. T. Judson* *Add note*: Judson pr. B–I; White the rest.

•3845 *Begin imprint*: [*T. East, R. Watkins, a. E. Allde f.*]

3849–9.5 *Correct imprint*: [*Amsterdam, J. Theunisz?*]

3850 *Continue 1st paragraph of note*: For a related work *see* 12981.

3863 *Correct imprint*: [*Amsterdam, J. Theunisz?*]

•3867.5 *Substitute this Hebrew*: משפחת דוד

3881 *Correct imprint*: [*Amsterdam, J. Theunisz?*]

3891 *In line 5 of note read*: ... 3849; possibly pr. by [*J. Theunisz.*]

•3897 *Correct STC number misprinted as* 3867 *to*: 3897.

3910 *Continue note*: Browne's books were suppressed by proclamation; *see* 8141.

3947 *Continue note*: For another trans. *see* 21634.

4028 *Correct last line of note*: 3483, 3484, 10617, 17776(*A*3); for extracts *see* 6428.

•4031 *Add location*: ; HD.

4032 *Continue note*: Regarding an ed. of which R. Bradock had 1200 copies in stock on 7 Aug. 1598 *see* Greg, *Register B*, p. 63.

Add new entry:
◦4032.3 —[Anr. ed.] 16° in 8's. *J. Beale f. R. Bradocke, sold by J. Harison* [*4*,] 1614. Ent. to T. Pavier w. Bradock's consent 3 mr. 1615. York U.
Pavier also acquired rights from the English Stock; *see* Appendix E/9.

Add new heading:
•p. 178[2] **Bull, William,** *esq. See* Bookplates(*A*3).

•4102.7 *Continue note*: This is later than 4102.9. F has B2 only (in 'STC 26145 no. 1a') in a different setting; B2ʳ line 2 of text ends 'away:' and line 3 has 'Horses'; HD and F, BO copies of 4102.9 have 'away: / horses' and F-4102.5 has 'awaie:'.

4115.5 *Add note*: Also intended to be issued as pt. 2 of 5043.5.

•4135 *In note, for* 'thtone' *read*: 'throne'

Add new entry:
•4152.3 —[A variant, w. imprint:] *J. N*[*orton*] *f. T. Clardue*, [1631.] YK.

•4178 *In imprint* for [*R. Waldegrave*, read: [*R. Ward*?

4254 *Add after date*: Ent. 6 de. 1596.

4296 *Add note*: This is a version of R. Greenham's catechism in 12312, and the author's inits. on the tp may be a misprint for R. G.

•4301 *Continue note*: The Dialogue is the same trans. as 6809.5.

•4314 *Begin imprint*: [*W. White*]

•4317 *In SR entry read*: 28 [i.e. 20] se.

•4323.4 *Add after date*: Ass'd to Purfoot, jun., 6 no. 1615.

•4338 *In imprint* for [*by him*] read: [*by N. Alsop*,]

4436 *In lines 3–4 read within brackets*: [in chap. 17 of the Institutio, 1539; later revised as bk. 3, ... Institutio, 1559.]

4469.5 *Continue note*: For Eng. translations *see* bk. 2 of 11346, 2nd pt. of 14525, and 14528.

4471 *Add after title*: [A defence of the office.] *Add a 2nd paragraph to note*: Includes a petition to the king from the Goldsmiths. For related publications *see* 8860.

Add new entry:
4471.5 **Cambridge.** [*Orders and regulations.*] Memorandum that [ ] being taken begging, vagrant, in the parish of [ ] in Cambridge [etc. Order to convey the vagrant parish by parish to an assigned town. *obl.*slip. [*Cambridge*? 1617?] C[26](V.C. Ct. III.23(132, pr. on both sides in same setting)).

Add new entry:
•4474.66R —Malum non est positivum.—Omnis peccans est ignorans. 1/2 sh.fol. [*Cambridge*, c. 1632?] O[3](in bdg. of W.N.4.7).

Add new entry:
•4474.72R —Monarchia est optimus reipublicæ status.—Habitus intellectuales non sunt species impressæ. 1/2 sh.fol. [*Cambridge*, c. 1630?] C[2](in bdg. of II.12.161).

Add new entry:
•4474.101R —Propter confessionem sub spe impunitatis legitimè promissa factam, condemnari quis non debet.—Index non tenetur officium suum interponere non petitum. 1/2 sh.fol. [*Cambridge*, 1600–07?] L(Add. MS. 69931, misc. outsize documents).

Add new entry:
•4474.103M —Pura elementa non sunt alimenta.—Habitus morales non sunt naturales. 1/2 sh.fol. [*Cambridge*, c. 1632?] O[3](in bdg. of W.N.4.7).

Add new entries:
4490.5 —Part of his majesties orders to the vicechancellour and heads of houses, for the better government of the universitie of Cambridge [etc. Against rowdy and raucous behaviour, etc.] 1/2 sh.fol. [*Cambridge*? 1637.] C[26](V.C. Ct. III.35(70)).

4490.7 —Pateat universis per præsentes, quòd ego [ ] in omnibus negotiis, litibus, [etc. Blank form for *w*'s appointment of *x* as proctor to act for him in the university courts, certified by *y* official on *z* date.] Dat. Cantab. 1/2 sh.*obl.*fol. [*Cambridge*, 1637?] C[26] (several, e.g. V.C. Ct. III.34(205), III.35(26)).

•4491.5 *In imprint* for *R. Barker* read: *Deputies of C. Barker*

4498 *Continue note*: The engr. frontispiece of Elizabeth's tomb (formerly also 7604) has imprint: *sould by R. Daniell*, [*London*,]

4543 *Add note*: Answered in 6259.

•4545 *Correct Greg number to*: 318–19.

4564 *Add note*: This is the later issue since the LINC tp is clearly a cancel.

Add new entry:
•4579.5 —[Anr. ed.] 4°. *V. S*[*immes*] *f. John Newberie*, 1600. Ent. 12 jn. Gdansk, Biblioteka Gdanska, PAN(Di 3552 (8°)/8).

•4580 *Delete SR entry.*

4587 *Continue note*: Homilies abridged from 13663.

•4617 *In SR entry read*: Man, sen. and jun.

4621 *Continue note*: Answered by 12610.

4623 *Continue note*: Answered by 12610.

•4627 *Correct Greg number to*: 551–2.

4648 *Add note*: Sermon reprinted from 11897.

4676 *Add note*: For details of printing and costs *see Bodleian Library Record* 10 (1978): 68–73.

•4697.5 *In imprint* for [*by C. Greene*,] read: [*by S. Browne*,]

4707.7 *Continue note*: Cartwright's short catechism at the end is also pr. anonymously in 4803 and 6968 sqq.

•4713 *After* [Anon. *read*: Not by Cartwright; attrib. to J. Throkmorton.]

Add new heading:
•p. 213[1] **Catcher, Richard.** *See* Bookplates(*A*3).

4738 *Continue note*: *See* also 11522.

Add new entries:

4740.3 —[Anr. ed.] 4°. *Londini, J. Norton* [really *Paris*?] 1612. PARIS.; ILL.
Pp. 38. This and the next omit Casaubon's dedic. to Sir T. Edmondes.

4740.5 —[Anr. ed.] 8° in 4's. *Londini, J. Norton* [really *Paris*?] 1612. C^{3}.GOT.PARIS(2).; LC.
Pp. 53.

4744 *Continue note*: *See* also Greg, *Companion*, pp. 257–8.

4755 *Add note*: 1 O copy has an extra leaf w. Latin presentation epistle to Sir Christopher Hatton, dated 1 Dec. 1588 and having Case's last name in full.

•p. 212^{2} **Castalio.** *Add cross-reference at end*:
—*See* also 14638(*A3*).

4798 *Continue note*: For a different version or trans. *see* 4962.

4800 *Continue note*: This is by John Geree; a slightly revised version is pr. under his name in Wing G 588.

4803 *Continue note*: By T. Cartwright and also pr. in 4707.7.

Add new entry:

4803.3 —A short catachisme. Brieflie contayning the whole summe of christian religion. 8°. [*Middelburg*? *R. Schilders*?] 1590. F(bd. w. 6676, collection (*a*)).
¶^{8}; 1: Wherefore hath God placed us in this world?

Add new entry:

4803.5 —Ane short catechisme conteyning the principall grounds of christian religion, quhilk quho neither will nor can learne, are not to be admitted to the Lords supper. 8°. [*Middelburg, R. Schilders f.*] *Edinburgh, R. Lawson*, 1615. E(lacks B4).
An earlier ed. of 4803.6, q.v., w. the same questions.

•4814 *Add location*: LONGLEAT(inner bifolium completing O, in bdg. of STC 3297). *After 1st sentence of note substitute this*: For a discussion and transcription of the frags., which represent two related though prob. separate items, *see Library* 12 (1990): 89–109.

Add new entry:

4846.3 —[Anr. ed. of 4845.5.] 8°. *ap. T. Marsh*, 1574. L(imp.).
A–G^{8}. Marsh acquired Bynneman's rights in exchange for Hill (13493) on 31 Mar. 1573; *see* Arber I.359, 418.

Add new entry:

∘4848.2 —[Anr. ed., w. omissions.] 8°. *ap. R. Dexter*, 1598. Dexter's copies ent. to the Stat. Co. 28 no. 1603. Ralph Hanna III, Dept. of English, Univ. of California, Riverside.
A–D^{8} E^{4}; although the tp calls for 1–6, 5 is omitted in the text.

4848.3 *In heading omit*: , w. omissions. *Continue note*: The tp no longer mentions 5.

4863.5 *In line 4 of note read*: … composition; however, it should be noted that in 1566–67 H. Singleton entered: 'thre commandmentes and lessons of olde Cato as he lay vpon his Death bedd &c.' (Arber I.330).

•4866 *Amend imprint*: [*Antwerp*? *f.*] *ap. J. Marcantium, Eboraci* [*York*,] 1579.

•4869 *Continue note*: *Hulsius*, [1619 or later.]

Add new entry:

∘4877.2 **Cautels.** [Cautels preservatory concerning the preservation of the gods which are kept in the pyx. By L. Shepherd?] 8°. [*London*, 1548?] NLW(lacks tp).
The title is modernized from Maunsell (17669), pt. 1, C4^{v}. Text begins on A2^{r}: 'Forasmuche as I se that most me̲ in theyr sience … ' and contains satiric instructions to keep holy wafers from mould, etc. Attrib. to Shepherd in John Bale, *Index*, ed. R. L. Poole, Oxford, 1902, p. 283. For a different text attacking the wafers orig. in the same tract vol. *see* 3034.7(*A3*).

4890.5 *Continue note*: For anr. trans. *see* 10424.

•4923 *In line 6 of note read*: … omitted following that phrase in line 21 of the cancel.

∘4941 *Continue note*: HD is app. an early issue without QQ^{4} QQQ^{1} (present in HN, NY) containing a 2nd chapter XX. Answered by 13266.

•4946.8 *In imprint* for [*J. Orwin*? read: [*V. Simmes*

•4960 *Continue imprint*: [*St. Omer*,]

4962 *Continue note*: The catechism is a different version or trans. of that pub'd by Singleton in 4798.

•4965 *In imprint* for [*J. Roberts*] read: [*G. Simson*]

5005 *Continue note*: For another trans. of the 'Conference' *see* 11346.

Add new entry:

5015.5 —The message of the emperoure and of the bisshoppe of Rome, sent (in 1533.) vnto Jhon, duke of Saxon. Concernynge a generall councell. The articles presented to the duke. [And 2 answers by the duke.] Newly *tr.* out of h‹igh› Almayne by M. Couerdale. 1536. 8°. [*Southwark, J. Nicolson*, 1536.] L(gen. tp only, C.60.h.16, fol. 28).P(6 imp. leaves of quire A, including 'Message' sub tp, in bdg. of Pet. D.9.8).

•5046 *Begin 2nd sentence of note*: At least

∘5096 *In locations for* C^{4}. *read*: L^{2}. *and delete*: + *Add note*: Issued w. 5086.

•5112 *Continue imprint*: *sold* [*by J. Wright 1*,]

•p. 231^{1} **Christian.** *Add cross-reference after* 5151:
—The christians directorie. 1635. *See* 5157.5(*A3*).

Add new entry:

∘5157.5 —The christians directorie, or, rules of christian pietie and wisedome. Written by a reverend divine deceased: and now revised and published [by] (R. R[oyston.]) Whereunto are annexed, Short points of christian religion [a catechism]. small 8°. *R. Raworth, sold by R. Royston*, 1635. Ent. to J. Crouch 26 my.; ass'd to Royston 6 jn. CB. Marvin Anderson, St. Paul, Minnesota(tp cropt, lacks engr. tp).

5159 *Add after date*: Ass'd by E. Marsh to T. Orwin 23 jn. 1591.

5190 *Add note*: By J. Frith; a MS. of it is answered by 18090; defended in 11381.

•p. 233^{2} **Christians.** *Add cross-reference following* 5195:
—The christians directorie. 1635. *See* 5157.5(*A3*).

Add new 1st entry:

5207.7 **Christ's Hospital.** By the maior. Unto the wardmote inquest…. From Christs hospitall this [ ] of December. [Endorsing a request for alms. In verse.] s.sh.4°. [*London*, 1613.] L^{8}(MS.3018/1, fol. 91).
Filled out in MS. for the parish of St. Dunstan's in the West, 28 Dec. 1613.

5208 *Continue note*: The music of this and the next 3 is by J. Farrant. For more details of these items *see* Royal Musical Association, *Proceedings* 88 (1961–62): 45–60, w. facs. of 5208.5; and N. M. Plumley, *The Organs and Music Masters of Christ's Hospital*, Christ's Hospital Papers 1 (1981), w. facs. of 5209.3.

5208.5 *Continue note*: , i.e. T. Stint?

Add new entry:

5209.3 —A psalme of thanksgiving, to be sung … on Tuesday in the Easter holy-dayes, … 1636. [With music by H. Semper? and the verses init. T. S.] 1/2 sh.fol. *R. Oulton*, 1636. Christ's Hospital Office, London.
Chorus begins: 'Orphans rejoyce …' Since this is a Tuesday psalm, there are no reports of charities.

•5229 *Amend date*: [1557?]

Add new entry:

5266.1 —(De officiis … libri tres.) 8°. (*J. Kyngstonus*, 1582.) C(imp.).
Reprints 5265.8 and collates like it except that C lacks the 1st quire.

•5266.5 *Continue note*: ILL has both tpp w. the 1587 imprint; at least quires A and Aa are the same setting as SAL and B, E–F, R are a different setting, e.g. B1ʳ line 2 of 'Ex Præfatione' ends: 'commu-' (SAL) or 'com-' (ILL). SAL prob. represents a late copy of a complete 1585 setting in which a few exhausted sheets were supplied in the 1587 setting.

•5266.8 *Add after date*: Ent. 7 my.

Add new entry:
5268.4 —[Anr. ed.] 8°. [*F. Kingston,*] *ex typ. Soc. Stat.*, 1621. NLW.
A–R⁸.

•5287 *Amend date*: [c. 1605.]

•5324 *Correct imprint*: *J*[*effes*, really *A. Islip,*] *Add a 2nd paragraph to the note*: The order of eds. is: 5324.7, 5324.3, 5324.5 (reissue, w. B inner forme reprinted by Islip), 5324 (with B inner forme reimposed). Islip app. salvaged some type pages when Jeffes's press was seized but had a new woodcut made and used his own woodcut 'sphinxes' factotum on B3ᵛ.

•5324.5 *In line 3 of note for* from *read*: in

•5354 *Substitute this note*: Pt. 1 is in 3 sections, the 2nd of which, Secunda praxis dialogica, reprints J. Leech's Dialogues in pt. 2 of 15374.7(*A*3). Pts. 2 and 3 tr. the 1st 2 sections of pt. 1.

5363.5 *Continue note*: For a sheet w. an early state of the engr. title and coats of arms *see* L(Harl.5944/219), which has Clarke's arms and engr. inscription: *Tr.* and inlarged by T C 1619. The P&D 1636 state of title and arms is cut up and mounted at top and sides of the posture plates and has no engr. inscription.

5364 *Add after date*: Ent. 16 ja.

•5406 *Correct misprinted STC number from* 5402 *to* 5406.

•5434 *In imprint* for [*F. Kingston*] read: [*H. Ballard*]

•5455 *Begin imprint*: [*J. Charlewood*? *f.*] *Put date in square brackets. Begin note*: End of text dated 1579; on 3 Aug. the same year R. Jones ...

•5465 *Continue imprint*: *sold* [*by J. Crooke a. R. Sergier,*]

5504 *In line 4 of note after* Reports). *add*: L²², F collate as described; in Taussig A⁸ precedes the Reports proper, and there is an extra set of prelims., π⁴, at the beginning of the vol. before De jure, w. π1 lacking (blank?), π2ʳ tp in same setting as A2ʳ, π3ʳ–4ᵛ prefaces in Latin and English in parallel columns but having the same contents as A3ʳ–4ᵛ (Latin) and A5ʳ–7ʳ (English). These extra prelims. may represent a provisional set, superseded and intended to be cancelled by the A⁸ prelims. w. table for both pts.

Add new entry:
5542.8 —[Anr. ed.] 8°. [*Antwerp, M. de Keyser*, 1534?] Stevens Cox(frags.).
App. collates like 5542.4. Methodus ends on verso (of A4?) line 16: '*studijs illustr‹ate.›*' The Aeditio has on recto (of E7?) lines 25–6: 'GVILLELMI LILII ANGLI | RVDIMENTA.'; and last page of Carmen de moribus, on verso (of F7?) line 1 begins: '*Clamor, rixa*'. The types in the Aeditio are 72 and 96 mm. bastarda and 80 mm. italic.

•5543b.9 *Continue note*: HN has A1,4 (imp.). of a 4° ed. like J. Redman's, w. colophon: *per me W. de Worde*, [1534?]

•5591 *Delete*: AMVU. (Error for 5991.)

5600.5 *Continue note*: *See* also *Library* 3 (1981): 17–32, especially p. 26.

5602 *Add note*: For a continuation *see* 6234.

5624 *Amend main heading to*: **Conestaggio, Girolamo Franchi di.**

•5631.3 *Add after date*: Ent. to the ballad ptnrs. 14 de. 1624.

5643 *Add note*: A Scottish MS. version of the verse is attrib. to William Touris.

5645.5 *Add note*: The Contract is *tr.* from Á. Arias de Armenta; it is also pr. in 11539, and it and the Testament are both pr. in 12144.5.

Add new heading:
•p. 254¹ **Contzen, Adam.** *See* 16800(*A*3).

•5680 *Continue note*: U has the orig. tp, w. misprint 'Dispaied,' in line 4.

5689 *Continue note*: C¹¹ has a different faked tp, also dated 1584 but having the anchor device, McK. 195, and having on the verso the address 'Cooperus Lectori', which appears there in 5688 but not in 5689 or the other faked tpp; it was app. pr. [*London*? c. 1680?]; the sheets are 5688, w. readings 'Annales,' and 'Ter.'

•5723.5 *In location delete*: (missing)

•5742.3 *In imprint* read: [*ap. M. Allot*?]

5742.7 *Add after title*: [By R. Rowlands/Verstegan.]

•p. 262² **Cottesford, Thomas.** *Begin 'tr.' cross-references*: 17863.7 (*A*3), 17864(*A*3),

Add new entry:
5871.9 —A spirituall counsayle, very necessarye for euery persone to haue. [Paternoster, creed, prayers, etc.] 32° in 8's. [*J. Mayler*? c. 1540.] ?Ent. to J. Judson 1558–59 (Arber I.95). L(C.106.a.24, lacks K8).
In part based on Hilsey's Primer, 16009.

Add new entry:
•5921.7 —[A variant, w. imprint on gen. tp:] *G. Purslowe f. J. Budge*, 1615. O.

•5944 *In line 2 of note for* green *read*: greene

6052 *In line 4 insert after bracket*: Concerning the execution of Mary, Queen of Scots.

6075 *Continue note*: Kingston pr. quires B–C.

Add new entry:
6088.9 —[The opening of the words of Joel, etc. In verse.] 8°. [*J. Day*? 1547?] L²(Frag no. 11, 2 imp. copies of sheet D).; HD(*63-1463F, fol. 58, 8 imp. leaves, B2,3,6,7; E1,4,7,10, the last blank).
The L² frags. have most of the text lacking in 6089.

6122 *Continue note*: App. an earlier ed., w. author's inits. 'W. J.' and imprint: *J. Chorlton*, 1608, was in the Hessisches Landes- und Hochschulbibliothek, Darmstadt, but was destroyed during World War II; *see Notes and Queries*, April, 1978, p. 129.

Add new entry:
6122.5 —[Anr. ed.] 4°. [*M. Flesher*, 1635.] L(imp.).
Letters redated 1635.

6153 *Add note*: For a trans. *see* 6159.3(*A*).

6157 *In line 1 of note add*: 6159.3(*A*),

Add new entry:
6159.3 —Two sermones very godlie and fruictful, made by sainct Ciprian, the one of patience, the other of mortalitie *tr.* into Englishe [by J. Brende.] 8°. [*R. Grafton,*] 1553. L⁴¹(tp only, 21700, fol. 42).; Sydney U(lacks prelims.).
Prelims. + A–G⁸ (G6–8 blank?). Translator and printer supplied from Maunsell (17669), pt. 1, p. 34.

6161.5 *Add before title*: [i.e. David Drummond.]

6166 *Add before format*: [By Gilbert Gifford?]

6168.7 Evans copy now = HD.

•6172a *Add note*: (Formerly also 7356)

•6200 *Continue note*: This ed. is later than 6201, possibly by several years.

•6223 *Add after date*: ?Ent. to T. Purfoot, sen. and jun., 5 ja. 1598.

•6226 *In line 3 read*: *tr.* [by T. Twyne.]

•6236 Buxton's copy now = O (2nd copy).

•6243.4 *Continue note*: Includes Greg 132.

6247 *Add after date*: Ent. to the English Stock 5 mr. 1620.

6294 *Add after 1st word of title*: [49] *Add at beginning of note*: ¶² (tp and index) A–Gg⁴.

Add new entry:
6294.5 —[Anr. ed.] fol. *Cantabrigiæ, ap. T. Buck & R. Daniel*, 1634 [1639?] L(tp only, Harl.5929/403).GOT.
¶² A–Hh⁴ Ii⁶ χ¹, w. ¶² in a unique setting w. device McK. 240 on the tp. Hh1–Ii6 adds the text of the 50th determinatio; χ¹ reprints the index on ¶2 but includes the 50th determinatio, w. a printer's note that it reached the printer after the 1st ed. had been pub'd and has been added to the present ed.

6295 *Add heading*: [Anr. issue, w. new prelims.] *Add note*: ¶⁴ (¶1 blank, ¶2ʳ tp, ¶3ʳ To Reader in Latin, ¶4 index in same setting as χ¹ of 6294.5) A–Hh⁴ Ii⁶.

•6342 *Add note*: In Overbury's name in the title there is a speck between 'E' and 'S' which may or may not be an apostrophe.

•6381 *Continue note*: *See* also 19413, 23453.

6430 *Continue note*: The HN copy on Univ. Microfilms reel 214 had mixed sheets as noted; it was later sold and replaced by an unmixed copy.

6445.3 *Add note*: F has bd. w. 3361.7 the 'M' and 'O' blocks of the italic examples belonging to the present work but pr. within lace borders whereas in the N copy the blocks have architectural borders.

6445.5 *After title delete*: [Based ... 1550.] (No French ed. of this date can be traced; the error app. arose from misreading the date of the Lyons, 1580 ed.)

6446 *Continue note*: This ed. adds Rules by E. B., pr. in 1 column in 6 pp. The type is reimposed in folio format in 1024.5(***A***). Later settings of the Rules in 6446.6 sqq., 3361.3 sqq., and 3363.5 sqq. are all in 2 columns.

•6448.7 *Replace entry with*: = 6449.

•6449 *Begin heading*: —[Anr. ed.] obl.4°. *Amend locations*: O.; F (imp., tp tampered with).

•6461 *Continue note*: Copies vary; title as above (HN) or w. round brackets and 'Aug. 9.' not pr. but added in MS. (F).

6545 *Amend date*: [c. 1655.] *In line 1 of note after* 1637. *add*: The tp gives Leake's address as 'the Crowne in Fleetestreete ...'; since his earliest recorded activity there is 1652, the present item really belongs in Wing.

Add new entry:
•6554.2 —The gentle craft. A discourse containing many matters of delight. [Init. T. D.] 4°. *R. Blower*, 1599. Ent 19 oc. 1597. Gdansk, Biblioteka Gdanska PAN(Di 3552(8°)/7).

•6554.5 *For* The gentle ... D.] *read*: [Anr. ed.] *In SR entry delete*: to R. ... ent.

•6564 *Delete*: R. *Amend note*: ... the N copy (formerly R) was at one time undivided.

•6589 *In imprint* read: *sold* [*by W. Brooks*?] ...

6626.5 For [*N. Okes*] read: [*J. Harrison 3 a. T. Creede*]

Add new entry:
6630.3 —The thirteenth impression. 8°. *M. Bradwood f. E. Bishop*, 1611. O.

Add new entry:
6630.7 —The fifteenth impression. 8°. *J. Legatt f. E. Bishop*, 1616. CANT.

•6650 *In imprint* for [*Eliot's Court Press*] read: [*H. Bynneman*?]

6658.5 For [*J. Harrison 3*?] read: [*T. Judson*?]

6682.5 *Continue note*: 5th letter reprinted from 13774.

6738 *Continue note*: ... French; its authorship is attrib. to Antoine Estienne, a Franciscan, by Brunet V.991; for a trans. *see* 24242.5.

6777 *For* 'by' M. de Comalada *read*: 'usually erroneously attrib. to'

•6791 *Continue imprint*: *sold* [*by her*? or *H. Rocket*?]

6794.5 *Add note*: Possibly a reissue of 11640 was intended.

6798.5 *Continue note*: Quaritch has a post-1657 state w. imprint: *sold by Ro: Walton* but retaining S. Baker's imprimatur dated 20 Nov. 1637; it is pr. on 2 sheets pasted together before printing.

•6798.7 *Amend date*: [1628?]

•6809.5 *Substitute this note*: The trans. and side-notes are identical to those in 4301, omitting A. Fleming's dedic. and prayer but having a preface by Golding which indicates that the Latin copy he worked from lacked the tp. The Latin, by J. Wittewronghelus, is at 25934.5.

Add new entry:
•6832.23 —[Anr. ed.] 8°. [*N. Hill? f.*] *R. Jugge*, [c. 1550.] CASHEL.
Contents like 6832.1.

•6832.24 *Continue note*: Contents like 6832.7.

•6832.65 *Begin SR entry*: Ent. 5 mr. 1598; ass'd to ... *Add note*: Quires A–B are of the 1600 printing; quires ¶ and ²A (1st leaf signed A8) app. represent additions pr. by Windet for a reissue by Leake? in 1602?

6858 *Add note*: T2ᵛ differs; has diagram of octohedron where dodecahedron should be (Y); corrected by a cancel slip (2 L) or in press (HD).

•6899 *In imprint* after *Etonæ* add: [*M. Bradwood*,

•6928a *Amend date*: [1534?]

•6929.5 *Begin imprint*: [*J. Beale*?] *f.* ...

6936 *Add after date*: Ass'd from R. Jackson to F. Williams 16 ja. 1626.

6968 *Continue note*: ... catechism, which is actually by T. Cartwright and is also pr. at the end of 4707.7.

•6977 *Delete*: AMVU.

6996 *Continue note*: Answered by 11116.

7022 *Continue note*: Sir Geoffrey's copies, some of which are listed here and below as GK, now all = C.

7040 *Continue note*: Also issued as pt. 4 of 7042, 7041.

•7079 *Add note*: Unsold sheets reissued w. added tp: Atheism defined and confuted, *W.H. f. N. Bourne*, 1656 (copy at HD).

•7085 *Continue note*: There are 2 impressions; e.g. D2ᵛ line 7 has 'speake' (HD, Blayney) or 'speak' (F).

•7094 Tenbury copy now = O.

Add new entry:
•7138.7 —[Anr. issue, w. cancel tp:] A treatise, tending to perswade all christians to the contempt of the world. *T. S*[*nodham*] *f. J. Budge*, 1624. HD(tp def.).

•p. 321² *Add cross-reference after* 7151:
—A treatise, tending to perswade. 1624. *See* 7138.7(***A***3).

•7238 *Add note*: A&R 285.

•7259.7 *Amend imprint*: [*J. White*] ... [1618?]

•p. 326^{1} **Du Bellay.** *Add cross-reference*:
—[La vielle courtisanne.] *See* 17359(*A*3).

•7335 *Add after date*: Ent. to J. Bill 27 no. 1611.

7337.5 *Add note*: Omits many of the old prayers and adds new ones.

•7341 *In imprint* after *Crosley*, add: [*in Oxford,*]

Add new entry:
•7342.3 —[Anr. ed., w. dedics. and title beginning as in 7342.5.] The fourth edition. 12°. *F. Kingston f. T. Dewe*, 162‹2?› Gervase Duffield, Abingdon, Oxford(imp.).

7353.8 *Continue note*: Concerning the patent *see* 8855.

•7393.5 *In title for* duty; *read*: duty, [w. comma]

Add new entry:
•7393.6 —[A variant, w. imprint:] *G. M*[*iller*] *f. W. Hammond*, 1633. CANT.

•7407 *Continue imprint*: *sold* [*by E. Blount,*]

7433 *Add note*: This is the Heidelberg catechism, largely taken verbatim out of the trans. of the Bastingius version in 1562 sqq., w. added prayers and graces.

Add new entry:
•7450a.5 —To the honorable the House of Commons ... The humble petition of the Company of Merchants of London trading to the East Indies. [Requesting either suppression of the Company or a public declaration of support, with a list of eleven benefits wrought by the Company.] s.sh.fol. [*London*, 1628?] L(Add. MS. 69932, misc. outsize documents).
Probably the petition read on 7 May 1628 and referred to the Committee for Trade; *see JHC* I.893a.

7457 *Add note*: This and 7458 are answered by 13598.

•7514 *In imprint delete*: [*W. Williamson f.*]

7529 *Continue note*: ... W. L., prob. the W. Lyndsell mentioned in Egerton's preface on A3^{r}. Anon. extracts including the verses are reprinted in 12402a.4.

•7550 *Amend date*: [c. 1565.]

7588 *Add note*: The portrait occurs w. other verse in the M copy of 10022.

7601 *In note, before* 23617.5 *add*: 8064,

7605 *Begin line 4*: K[yd? or T. Knell?]

•7610 *Continue imprint*: *sold* [*by E. Blount,*]

7620.5 Evans copy now = HD.

7627.5 *Add after date*: ?Ent. to J. Trundle 19 de.

•p. 347^{1} COLLEGE OF ARMS. *Amend line 1*: ... publications authorizing heralds or issued by them or from ... *Add new 1st cross-reference*:
—1568. *See* 8001.5(*A*3).

Add cross-reference:
•p. 350^{1} —[*Heraldic visitations.*] [Letter authorizing R. Cook to conduct them. 1568.] *See* 8001.5(*A*3).

•p. 350^{1} *Add cross-reference*:
—[*Oxford University.*] [Letter of Charles I dated 3 June 1636 confirming Laudian statutes. c. 1708?] *See* note to 19005(*A*3).

Add new heading:
•p. 353^{1} East India Company. To ... Commons. Petition [for a public declaration of support. 1628?] *See* 7450a.5(*A*3).

Add new heading:
•p. 354^{1} Monson, *Sir* Thomas. The attorneys of Yorke pl^{ts}. [Monson's case in a dispute over a patent. 1628.] *See* 18023.3(*A*3).

Add new entry:
7762.5 —[Proclamation enforcing a statute on apparel?] 4°. (*R. Pynson,*) [1511–12.] L(last leaf only, at end of C.24.a.13 = STC 11615).
Has Pynson's device McK. 9b in a state prob. earlier than 16190. Possibly the proclamation noted at Cr. 57 as mentioned in a letter (*Cal.S.P.Ven.*, II, no. 138, 14 Nov. 1511), but that cites enforcement beginning after Christmas, whereas the present item stipulates Candelmas (2 Feb.). All subjects are 'to vse & were [wear] accordynge to the tenoure Effecte & purporte of the sayde acte'. The text of the act (1 Hen. VIII, c. 14?) was prob. also pr. w. the proclamation.

•7773 *Begin imprint*: [*Southwark,*

•7788.7 *Correct imprint*: [*Canterbury? J. Mychell,*

Add new entry:
•7828.3 —[Anr. ed.] fol(3?). [*S. Mierdman? f. R. Grafton*, 1549.] Henry N. Ess III, New York City(1st sheet only).
In title: 'conteynyng'.

•7854 DNPK copy now = L.

7864 *Add note*: *See* also 9339.3(*A*3).

7865 *In line 3 read*: ... books, including Halle's Chronicle (12721 sqq.); suppressing ...

Add new entry:
7868.3 —[Anr. ed.] fol(2). *in æd. J. Cawodi*, 1556. L.
In line 1 of text: 'Henrye Dudley,'.

•7976.7 *Add location*: C^{2}(frag. of 1st sheet, in MS. R.9.17).

7995.4 *Add at beginning of imprint*: [

8000 *Add following line 4 of note*: F has the cuts pasted together in one large sheet following the proclamation.

Add new entry::
•8001.5 —Elizabeth by the grace of God ... For asmuch as God of his great clemencie [etc. Letter authorizing R. Cook, Clarenceux King of Arms, to make heraldic visitations south of the Trent as deemed necessary and to appoint deputies. 24 Mar. 1568.] s.sh.fol. [*London*, 1568.] L^{2}.

•8054 *Replace date with*: [i.e. *B. Norton a. J. Bill*, c. 1618.]

8065 *Add note*: *See* also 10030.5.

•8435 *Add location*: L^{2}.

•8448 *In note, after* A&R 265. *substitute*: The usual attribution to J. Cresswell is erroneous; *see Recusant History* 11 (1985): 348– 57. (The attribution to M. Walpole proved untenable upon further investigation.)

•8538 *Continue note*: For a liturgical form related to the ceremony of touching *see* 16551.

Add new entries:
8551.3 —Be it knowne ... that his maiesties farthing tokens are to be had at the signe of the Goat in Lumber streete ... according to [the] proclamation [cf. 8550.] *obl.*slip. [*Cambridge*? 1617?] C^{26}(V.C. Ct. III.23(133–4)).
There are 2 settings; line 15 begins: 'tion' or 'on'.
8551.5 —Be it knowne ... that his maiesties farthing tokens are to be had [ ] according to [the] proclamation. *obl.*slip. [*Cambridge*? 1617?] C^{26}(V.C. Ct. III.23 (135)).

8585 *Add after imprint*: Ent. to W. Jones w. 'other thinges of that nature' on 14 ap. 1617.

8620.7 *In line 1 for* repair *read*: complete *Add after imprint*: An earlier brief ent. 4 de. 1617.

•8704.5 *In imprint* for [*J. Beale*? read: [*W. Jaggard,*

Add new entry:
8934.5 —[Anr. ed.] fol(2). *R. Barker a. J. Bill*, 1629. L^{5}.; F.
Sheet 2, line 1 ends: 'finde ... a-'.

•8937 *Delete*: GOT., which has only 8937.5.

•p. 402[1] *In cross-reference following 9004, for* 9257 *read*: 9254.7.

•9126 *For* GCT. *read*: GOT.

Add new entry:

•9134.5 —[A proclamation for the careful custody and well ordering of the New River. Forbidding the unauthorized diversion of its contents, the corruption of its water, and the destruction of its banks, bridges, etc. 24 Feb. 1639.] fol(2). *R. Barker a. assignes of J. Bill*, 1638 [o.s.] Taussig(sheet 2 only).

This relates to a bill for a proclamation of the above date discussed by the Privy Council on 14 Feb.; *see P.C. Registers ... in facsimile, V, 4 Jan.–10 Apr. 1639*, p. 159. Later, slightly expanded versions of the proclamation were issued 23 June 1669 (Cr. 3528, Wing C 3460), 5 Mar. 1686 (Cr. 3827, Wing J 352), 26 Sept. 1689 (Cr. 4023, Wing W 2606), and 15 Feb. 1704 (Cr. 4368).

For an indenture of the New River Company and other references to supplying water to London *see* 18487.5(*A*3).

•9143 *Add note*: John Legat 2 was in charge of the press; *see Library* 11 (1989): 1–9.

•p. 409[1] *Under 'Tenths and subsidies' add new heading and entry immediately following* 9175d.52:

James I

•9175e REcepi de [·] pro decimis inde Domino Regi debitis ad festum natalis Domini. Anno ... [Receipt for the tenth.] *obl.*slip. [*London*, 1605.] Bedfordshire Record Office(2 settings: OR 1743/2 and /3, dated in letterpress 1605 and 1606 respectively, filled out in MS. for Podington Rectory).

Add new entry:

9175g.10 Debet super computum suum determinatum pro vno anno integro finito ad festum sancti Michaelis Archangeli anno [ ] Quos liberauit [ ] Receptori generali Domini Regis ... [Acquittance of obligations by the receiver general.] s.sh.*obl.*fol. [*London?* after 24 Mar. 1603.] Richard Hatchwell, Bkseller.

There are different settings; e.g. line 1 ends: 'vno anno' or 'inte-', the former dated in MS. 1603, the latter 1609.

9175i.8 *Continue note*: For the warrant of 5 May 1610 to pay Barker for pr. this and for other services *see Cal.S.P.D., 1603–1610*, p. 607.

Under Crown Auditor add new entry:

•9175t(*ii*) —In the Kings Maiesties name, I will and require you to appeare before me at [ ] in the Countie of [ ] [etc. Summons to bring accounts, money due, acquittances, etc.] *obl.*slip. [*London?* 1623?] Bedfordshire Record Office(OR 1748/3, form sent out on 2 July 1623 for an audit on 13 Oct. at Higham Ferrers, Northants., addressed to the farmer of Higham and Dichforde Mylles).

Add new entry:

9175t(*iii*) [Receiver-General. Southt'.] After hearty Commendations. These are to will and require you, ... That you, ... do personally appeare before me his Maiesties generall Receiver of the said Countie, at [ ] the [ ] day of October [etc. Summons to bring money due.] s.sh.4°. [*London*, 1619?] Private owner(Kingsmill papers item 1340, sent out 1 Aug. 1619 for a meeting at Andover on 19 Oct., addressed in MS. on the verso to Sir Henry Kingsmill as tenant of the manor of Sidmonton).

Add new entry:

9254.3 —His majesties speciall command is, that these articles following be observed by all. [Against three kinds of disruptive and indecorous behaviour in churches.] 1/2 sh.fol. [*R. Barker a. assignes of J. Bill*, 1632?] L[11](SP 16/229: 116).

p. 416[1] *Add cross-reference before* 9260:

—[Page 1 begins:] Carolus Dei gratia Angliæ ... rex ... Cum ob multiplicem ... statutorum varietatem [etc. Letter confirming the Laudian statutes of Oxford University. 3 June 1636.][*Oxford*, c. 1708?] *See* note to 19005(*A*3).

•9260 *Continue note*: The imprint includes Young's style as King's Printer for Scotland and Badger's as Printer to Prince Charles.

•9278 *In note for* 14a *read*: 24a.

•9286 *Amend locations*: Graham copy now = Taussig and belongs among British locations. *In line 16 of note for* Graham *read*: Taussig.

9314 *Continue note*: The reference to Arber I.115 noted at 9526.7 more likely pertains to the present text; *see* also *Acts P.C., 1577–1578*, pp. 188–9.

9332 *Continue note*: L[11] has identified another group of frags.: E 163/22/3/23, w. duplicates of b3,4, c1,2,5,6, including the rest of the colophon.

•9335 *Correct beginning of imprint*: *Newcastle* [i.e. *London*,] *Begin note*: This ed. is later than 9335.5, repeating its imprint; *see Library* 11 (1989): 1–9.

•9335.5 *Add note*: John Legat 2 was in charge of the Newcastle press.

Add new entries:

◦9339.3 —The kinge and the quenes moost excellent maiesties,... [have caused] to be abbridged the effecte of sundrye lawes, and statutes, [to be] put in execution accordynge as they haue by their former letters, commaunded their justices of peace, [etc.] fol. (*in æd. J. Cawodi*,) [1555?] L(Dept. of MSS., Althorp A1).

B6[v] last line of text: 'yarde.' 14 topics, as in 9339.5 except that the latter adds one more: against slanderous tales and news. App. related to 7864.

•9339.4 —[Anr. ed.] fol. *in æd. J. Cawodi*, [1557?] YK(XXXIV. D.7(8)).

In title: 'king'; B6[v] last line of text: 'Churcheyard.'

•9343.5 *Amend imprint*: [*J. Beale*, c. 1617?]

9343.8 *Continue note*: For earlier items in the same types *see* 12206a.7 (also has same init. 'E'), 22880.2.

•9354 *For* HD(lost) *read*: HD(imp.).

•9361.6 *In locations read*: Taussig(2, 1 mixed). *In line 2 of note after* HD. *add*: The mixed Taussig copy has at least sheets B3,4, C1,6, C3,4 of 9361.5 and A1,6 from a unique setting, w. cut below yr. 3 title having a face w. winged mustache (Beale cut 16) but w. line 5 ending: 'Ireland,' instead of 'Irelande,'.

•9366.5 *In title delete full stop before* VIII. *In note delete full stop after* ANNO *Add location*: Taussig.

•9410 *Delete*: O[14].

•9440.8 *Continue 1st paragraph of note*: At least some pages are in 2 settings; e.g. A5[r] has catchword: 'florisshing' (YK) or 'florysshinge' (HD).

•9447.7 *Add location*: YK.; *Amend note*: Ff. xxxiiii; [Last numeral is 'i' not 'j'.]

Add new entry:

9487.9 —[Anr. ed.] Anno xxxj. fol. *Deputies of C. Barker*, 1589. L[25]. Taussig(w. 9305.3).

Collates like 9487.7. Tp line 7: 'Ladie'; C1[v] line 6 from bottom has: 'foresayd'. In Subs-T Cc4[v] last line begins: (iii) 'to bee' and line 1 has 'Towns'.

9526.7 *In line 4 of note, after* 9527.5 sqq. *add*: (or more likely 9314 sqq.)

9791 *Continue note*: Has inits. 'W. S.' at end, app. those of the editor.

Add new entry:
•9906.3 —[Anr. ed.] Incipit annus primus Richardi tercii. (Nouiter emendatus.) fol. [*N. Hill f.*] *per me H. Smythe*, 1543. WOR.
Collates like 9906.

Add new entry:
•9913.5 —[Anr. ed.] Incipit annus secundus Richardi tercii. (Nouiter emendatus.) fol. [*N. Hill f.*] *per me H. Smythe*, 1543. WOR. Grantham Church.
A^8 B^4 C^6 D^4; ff. xxii.

9929.3 *Add note*: Collates like 9929.5.

•9929.5 *Add location*: WOR. *Add it also at*: 9930.3, 9931.3, 9932.7, 9933.5, 9934.3, 9936, 9947.4, 9955.3.

9935.7 *Add at beginning of imprint*: [*N. Hill? in the shop of*] *Continue note*: The criblé init. 'V' on $A1^r$ is the earliest known appearance of any of the distinctive sets of inits. associated w. N. Hill and used in 9929.3 and other Yearbooks pr. for H. Smith.

Add new entry:
◦9946.3 —[Anr. ed.] Incipit annus quartusdecimus Henrici viii. nouiter castigatus. fol. [*N. Hill f.*] (*H. Smyth*,) [1545?] SLC.WOR.
Collates like 9946.5, but the latter's title begins like 9946.

Add new entry:
9946.9 [18, 19 Hen. VIII.] De termino Michaelis [etc.] fol. [*N. Hill f.*] (*H. Smyth*,) [1544?] SLC.
Collates like 9947.

Add new entry:
◦9954.7 [26 Hen. VIII.] De termino Pasche [etc.] fol. [*N. Hill f.*] (*H. Smyth*,) [1544?] SLC.
Collates like 9955. This has at end: 'Explicit annus ... nouiter impressum [*sic*].' in same setting as 9961.7(***A***); 9955 has the same ending but has correctly: '... nouiter impressus.' in same setting as 9962.

Add new entry:
9961.7 [27 Hen. VIII.] De termino Pasche [etc.] fol. [*N. Hill f.*] (*H. Smyth*,) [1544?] SLC.
Collates like 9962. $A1^r$ catchword: 'le parson'. Except for the regnal year this and 9962 have explicit in the same settings, respectively, as 9954.7(***A***3) and 9955.

•9962.5 *Add location*: WOR(lacks I4).

•9980–0.5 *Correct date*: [1550?]

•9984.5 *Amend date*: [1539?]

10017 *Continue note*: ... 9 and pt. 2 of 11016.

10035 *Continue note*: For a verse paraphrase *see* 11907.

•10038.7 Williamson copy now = WIS.

•10080 *Continue note*: At least 1 HD has quire B in a different setting, w. $B1^v$ line 1 having '*fidelitie*' whereas 3 HD and most other copies have '*fidelity*'.

Add new entries:
•10137.3C —[James Mountague.] 4°. [*W. Hall*,] 1609. Somerset Record Office(D/D/Vm S/2340).
10137.4 —[Ordinary. By authority of George Abbot, Abp. of Canterbury, *sede vacante*.] 4°. *W. Stansby*, 1626. L.
•10137.4C —[Leonard Mawe.] 4°. *W. Stanby* [sic], 1629. Somerset Record Office(D/P/Fiv. 23/5(i)).

Add new entries:
10209.3 **Gloucester.** [Henry Parry.] 4°. *W.* [*Jag*]*gard f. C. Knight*, 1607. Glos. Record Office(GDR 102).
The 1st 3 letters of Jaggard's last name have not pr.
10209.5 —1612. [Metropolitical. George Abbot, Abp. of Canterbury.] 4°. *W. Jaggard*, [1612.] Glos. Record Office (GDR 115).
10209.7 —[Ordinary. Miles Smith.] 4°. *J. Legatt*, 1622. Glos. Record Office(GDR 146).

•10382 *Add location*: O(Fairfax deposit).

◦10392 *Before format add*: [Attrib. to J. Throkmorton.] *Continue note*: Often bd. w. 4713; reprinted in 10849.

•10394 *Add after title*: [By W. Stoughton.]

•10400 *In line 2 of note after* at C. *add*: Some copies (2 L) lack χ^4 (χ4 blank), w. heading on 1^r: 'A briefe aunswere to the principall pointes in the Archbishops Articles.... Wrirten [*sic*] about 1583.', usually found at the end of pt. 1 (1 L, HN, 2 HD, U).

•10403 *Continue imprint*: [*St. Omer*,]

•10404.7 *Amend date*: 1629?

•10430 *Continue note*: For a later ed. *see* 3034.7(***A***3).

•10450.3 *Add location*: St. Albans Abbey(A1 and last leaf only).

10455 *Continue note*: For a different English adaptation of the colloquy *see* 22886.

•10459 *Amend date*: [1538–47?]

10482 *Add note*: In the L colophon the last part of the date: 'xlj.' is sometimes misread as xij, producing the erroneous complete date of 1512.

•10597.5 *Continue imprint*: *sold* [*by M. Allde*? or *H. Rocket*?]

Exercise. *Add new first entry*:
•10615.5 —An exercise angelicall. For every day in the weeke. Whereby to styr up our selves to the love of the B. virgin. Composed by a Father of the Society of Jesus [i.e. *tr.* from P. Giustinelli, *S. J.*] 24° in 8's. [*Rouen, J. Cousturier*,] 1632. O.

•10694 *In line 3 read*: to Sparke, sen., ...

10738 *Add after date*: Ent. 20 ja.

10769 *Add after date*: Ent. to T. Man 21 ja. 1617.

10814 *In line 1 of note for* 1622–23 *read*: 1621? *In line 2 read*: ... 209–11; the documents are undated and possibly miscalendared in *Cal.S.P.D.* since the punishments seem to have occurred in early 1621; the proclamation referred to by Stansby may be 8649.

p. 482[2] **Ferrar, N.** *In line 10 of note read*: 311–32; George Henderson, 'Bible Illustration in the Age of Laud', *TCBS* 8 (1982): 185–216.

•10850 *In line 3 after* [Anon.; *read*: attrib. to J. Throkmorton.]

•10880 *Continue imprint*: *solde* [*by J. Allde*,]

•10930 *Begin imprint*: [*W. Jaggard a. J. Roberts*?] *Add note*: Jaggard pr. quires A, D–F; Roberts possibly the rest.

Add new entries:
•10989a.5 —[Anr. ed.] 8°. (*J. King a. T. Marshe*,) [1554?] LC.
•10989a.6 —[A variant, w. colophon:] (*J. King*,) [1554?] O(tp and col. only, Douce Add. 142/291).; HD.
(Formerly 10990.3).

•10990.3 *Replace entry with*: Now = 10989a.6(***A***3).

•10997.5 *Before* F. *add*: L.;

•11019.5 *Continue imprint*: [*St. Omer*,]

•11040 *Amend imprint*: *R. B*[*lower, in the shop of G. Eld*]

•11076 *Delete*: Sydney U.

•11078 *In imprint* read: *sold* [*by R. Milbourne*?]

•11158 *In locations for* E.+; *read*: CHATS.; *Delete*: Sydney U.

11256 *Add note*: 2nd and 3rd pts. tr. from 3410.3(***A***).

•11309 *Continue imprint*: *solde* [*by G. Eld*,]

•11320 *Continue imprint*: [*St. Omer,*]

11363 *Continue note*: For anr. trans. of the 20 articles *see* 13262.

11363.5 *Continue note*: For anr. trans. *see* 13262.

11368.5 *Add after date*: Ass'd to J. Pindley 22 jn. 1612; to Purslowe 2 no. 1613.

•11376.3 *Add after date*: Ent. to T. Snodham 17 jn. 1609.

•11385 *Amend imprint*: [*Canterbury? J. Mychell*, 1535–36?]

•11387 *Amend imprint*: [*Canterbury? J. Mychell*, 1535–36?]

•11412 *In line 1 of note after* dedic. *add*: in English *Continue note*: ... A2^{v} (HN, HD); at least F has on $*3$ a Latin trans. of the dedic., w. Fulbeck's name on $*3^{v}$ and $*4$ missing (blank?). Y has both dedics. but may be made up.

•11469.5 *Add after date*: Ent. to T. Orwin 7 my. 1593.

11476 *Add note*: Largely tr. from Le stile et manière de composer, ... toute sorte d'epistres.

Add new entry:
◦11511.2 —A mappe of the man of sin: wherin is ... delineated ... Antichrist. [Completely engraved, w. Biblical scenes and texts above and verses below.] s.sh.*obl.*fol. *sould by J. Bellamie at ye 2 Grey houds in Cornehill neer thexchang*, [1623?] PN.

•11560 *Continue note*: The title should have gone to the Seres patent for prayerbooks following H. Middleton's death; *see* Appendix A/11.

11617 *Add note*: Tp has woodcut w. scholar (Hodnett 927, GOT); L lacks tp and has substituted the tp of 11616a w. cut of schoolmaster and 3 pupils (Hodnett 920).

•11638–9 *Add before date*: [*f. R. Smith,*]

•11655 *Substitute this Hebrew*: משכיל לדוד

•11675 *Continue imprint*: *sold* [*in the shops of N. Newbery,*]

•11691a.5 *Amend beginning of imprint*: [*London, J. Mychell f.*] *Amend date*: [1530–32?]

Gee, John. *Add new first entry*:
•11700.5 —The christian store-house. A booke of prayers and meditations for every day in the weeke morning and evening. 24° in 12's. *T. Cotes f. R. More*, 1631. Ent. 29 ap. O.

•11707 *Continue imprint*: *sold* [*in the shop of E. Blount,*]

•11720 *In imprint* for *Wolfe f.*] read: *Wolfe*] *f.*

11741 *Add note*: With dedic. to King James by Gentilis's son Robert. Taussig has anr. issue w. A^{4} in a different setting, w. same dedic. but signed by Gentilis himself and imprint: *Hanoviæ, ap Guilielmum Antonium*, 1605.

•11807 *Add after date*: Ent. to R. Dexter 2 no. 1590.

11830a *Add after date*: Ass'd 13 ap.

11830a.5 *Add after date*: Ass'd 26 jn. 1617.

Add new heading:
•p. 525[1] **Giustinelli, Pietro,** *S. J.* An exercise angelicall. 1632. *See* 10615.5(*A*3).

11906 *Add after date*: Ent. to the English Stock 5 mr. 1620.

•11924 *Continue imprint*: *venundatur autem in cœmeterio Sancti Pauli ad novam Librariorum* [i.e. *Stationers'*] *officinam*,

11974 *Add note*: (L[16] copy formerly 3294)

12065 *Add note*: This belongs with the other theses for King's College, Aberdeen, following 71.19A.

Add new entry:
•12158.7 —[Anr ed., anon., w. title:] A briefe treatise ... Perused, corrected and augmented by W. W. Newly set forth 1588. 8°. *J. C*[*harlewood*] *f. R. Walley*, [1588.] F (imp.).

•12159 *Begin entry*: —[Anr. ed.] 8°.

12166 *Add note*: For a dispute between Adams and the Stat. Co. *see* notes to 13778, 13780.

•12190 For [*G. Shaw*] read: [*successor of R. Tottell*]

•12199 *Continue imprint*: *sold* [*by H. Rocket?*]

•12243 *Continue imprint*: *sold in* [*the shop of R. Newbery,*]

Add new entry:
•12253.7 —[Anr. ed. on continuous signatures.] 4°. *J. Roberts f. N. Ling*, 1599. Gdansk, Biblioteka Gdanska PAN(Di 3552 (8°)/2).
This and the following omit the prelims. of the 2nd pt.

•12254 *Substitute this heading*: [A variant, w. imprint:] *Omit the note.*

•12262.5 *In imprint* for [*J. Roberts*] read: [*J. Charlewood*]

Add new entry:
•12287.5 —[Anr. ed.] 4°. [*R. Bradock*] *f. J. B*[*roome,*] 1600. Gdansk, Biblioteka Gdanska PAN(Di 3552(8°)/5).

•12292.5 *For 2nd sentence of note substitute this*: Unlike earlier eds. both copies have medial 'v', e.g. 'have', but quires C–G are in different settings. F has B4^{r} line 15: 'heavy' and G1^{r} line 6: 'look'. Wolfson lacks A^{4}, has B^{4} as in F, but also has a different setting of B4 w. line 15 of recto having: 'heavie' and w. headlines as in quires C–G in his copy, where G1^{r} line 6 has: 'looke'.

Add new entry:
•12301a.9 —[Anr. ed.] 4°. [*A. Islip f.*] *J. Wolfe, sold by E. White*, 1597. Gdansk, Biblioteka Gdanska PAN(Di 3552 (8°)/ 1).
A–F^{4}; D3^{r} has catchword: 'the' and last line begins: 'woorthy'.

•12302 *Continue note*: and last line begins: 'worthie'.

◦12310b *In line 1 of note for* N. Okes *read*: J. Okes

12312 *Continue note*: Anr. version of the catechism beginning on Dd1 was pub'd sep. as 4296.

•12353 *Amend date*: [1532?]

12357.7 *Add after date*: Ent as 'Gregoryes abridgment' to the English Stock 5 mr. 1620.

•12361 *Continue note*: Includes Greg 489.

•12403 *Before date in line 4* add: [*f. R. Smith,*]

•12416 Buxton's copy now = O (2nd copy).

12469 *Begin note*: Baker's translations of Galen's bk. 3, etc. are reprinted from 1209, and his preface indicates that W. Clowes ...

•12493 *Delete*: L.

12503 *Add note*: A former HN copy (on Univ. Microfilms reel 990) lacked (a)^{4}, w. commendatory verses and To reader, and might represent an early issue; this quire varies: 1st page is signed (a) or missigned (a)2; both at TORONTO[2].

•12541 *Begin imprint*: [*Westminster*, ...

•12542.5 *Begin SR entry*: Ent. to R. Jones 5 ja. 1592; to the ...

•12599 *Continue imprint*: *sold* [*by E. Wright,*]

•12618a *In imprint* after *Crosley*, add: [*in Oxford,*]

12635 *Add before locations*: Contemplations vol. 3 ass'd from N. Butter and W. Butler, jun., to J. Beale 8 mr. 1625.

12706 *In line 6 before* Imprese *add*: 'No peace' ent. to Macham 9 de. 1611;

°p. 557[2] **Halle, Edward.** *Substitute the following for the 1st 4 paragraphs of the headnote and the A reference*:

Note: This is an exceptionally difficult work to grasp because of perplexities in the order of its printing, in the intentions of its publisher, and in the imperfect and/or sophisticated state of many surviving copies. Much more intensive study needs to be done. The following account, however, is based on further inspection of copies at L and C and considerable reflection upon the problematic career of the printer John Mychell.

The order of printing the earliest segment of text (*1a* and *1b*) should be reversed. The '1547' sheets (*1a*) were so designated in Graham Pollard's article in the *Bulletin of the Institute of Historical Research* 10 (1932): 12–17. His reason for giving them so early a date was based on the state of an initial 'A' also used in at least 2 eds. of Edward VI's *Injunctions* of 31 July 1547; the L copies he examined were C.25.h.11 (= STC 10090.5) and C.25.h.6(2) (= STC 10091); *see* p. 14, n.1 in his article. These are now considered to be among the latest eds. of the *Injunctions* though their actual date of printing has not been reliably ascertained. On the other hand, Grafton printed Ii2–5 and quires Kk–Rr in both *1a* and *1b*, and the state of some of the woodcut initials (e.g. the 'E' on Qq1^r and the 'W' on Qq6^r) seems more damaged in the *1a* setting.

In 1548? Grafton began to print, producing quires A–Rr (Hen. IV–Edw. IV) as distinguished in *1b* in the headnote. At this point he apparently decided to enlarge the edition size, printing larger quantities of the remaining text (*2ab*) This combination of text sheets (*1b*/*2ab*) was the first to be issued, without tables, in 1548 (12721 sq.). For some reason, probably connected with the pressure of his duties as King's Printer, Grafton farmed out to another printer, undoubtedly John Mychell, a large portion of the reprint of the first section (quires A–Hh and sheet Ii1,6). It is uncertain whether Mychell was in Canterbury or London at the time, but probably in the latter place since he was able to borrow some of Grafton's large woodcut initials. The *1a* sheets appear to have been put aside until the stock of *1b* should be used up.

In 1550 Grafton seems to have decided to print tables to accompany the remaining sheets, which included all or most of *1a*. He printed at least a table to Hen. VIII (*TH8c*) and possibly a new preface (*Pc*), both referring to line numbers in the text. However, the unsold sheets had no line numbers, and Grafton clearly determined to go forward with a whole new edition with line numbers and tables (the *d* printings), the work being shared with S. Mierdman and published in 1550 (12723). The significance of a second setting with line numbers of quires A–B (*1x*) is not yet clear: possibly a trial setting or a later replacement of damaged sheets.

Finally, when sheets of the improved edition were exhausted, most of the tables were reprinted (*Te*) and the remaining sheets of the first edition (largely *1a*/*2ab*) reissued with new—or partly new—preliminaries (*Pe:c*) by J. Kingston about 1560 (12723a). At an unknown date J. Cawood or his partner from 1557, R. Jugge, or one of the successors to their ornaments and initials into the 17th century reprinted the table to Hen. VIII (*TH8z*). Either early or late some copies began to be cannibalized in order to make up imperfections in others or to insert additional variants; many L copies exemplify this tendency.

Further amendments to the headnote:

1x *End distinction*: ETON, GOT, C(R.3.30) copies of 12723a.

TH8z *For 2nd sentence read*: In 82 mm. textura with normal rounded 'H', with a woodcut 'A' used by J. Cawood in at least 1554 (B1^r of 5207) and 1557 (H7^r of 11708) though the table may have been printed at a much later date; only known so far in L(G.6004 = 12723a), which has sheet B4,5 in the genuine Grafton (*Td*) setting.

•12723a *In heading read*: [Anr. issue of 12721, ... *Amend imprint in square brackets*: [*London*? *J. Mychell*, 1548; *J. Kingston*, 1560? *a. J. Cawood*? c. 1570?] *In line 6 of note read*: 175) and GOT (both of which, however, have *1x*) and O[10].

•12725 *In date for* c. *read*: [c.

•12774 For [*J. Windet*, read: [*E. Allde a. another*,

•12774.7 For [*J. Windet*, read: [*V. Simmes*,

•12783 For [*J. Windet*] read: [*E. Allde*]

•12804 For [*W. Kearney*? read: [*T. Scarlet* ...

12805.5 *Add before date*: [*by J. Penkethman*?]

•12875 *Add location*: L[4]. *Delete*: YK.+

Add new entry:
•12875.3 —[Anr. issue, w. cancel tp, w. imprint:] *J. Dawson, sold by F. Eglesfield*, 1640. YK.

•12906 *Amend imprint*: ... *Scarlet* [*pseud.*? *in London*? or *Cambridge*?]

•12914 *Amend date*: [1589.]

•12988 *In imprint* for *Eliot's Court Press* read: *R. Read*; for *Snodham* read: *East*. *Begin note*: Read pr. πA, V, *In line 2 of note for* Snodham *read*: East; *for* Q–V *read*: Q–T.

•12998 *In lines 2–3 of note read*: imprint but is possibly sophisticated; 1 L, 1 HN have ... lack prelims., and they may represent a reissue by Partridge [1638?] to accompany 12997a. *In line 5 of note before* DUR[5] *add*: L,

•13076 *In imprint* for *G. Potter* read: *J. Broome*

•13117 *Continue imprint*: solde [*in the shop of E. White*,]

•13133 *In imprint delete*: *solde* ... *Wright*,] (The address is Burby's at this date.)

•13212 *Amend date*: [1548.]

13232 *Add note*: There are 2 eds.; tp lines 4–5: '*contayning* ... Hebrue,' or '*containing* ... Hebrew,'; E3^r, heading of 2nd table has line 4 ending: 'Old and' or 'Olde and'; both at HN.

°13272 *Continue note*: ... letterpress tp in most copies; GOT has an early state of the letterpress tp w. imprint: *B. A. and T. F. for H. Seile*, 1631.

13284.5 *In line 3 of note read*: ... Reading; this may be the 'murther of Robert hayton' provisionally allowed to T. Cooke on 5 Feb. 1593; *see* Greg, *Register B*, p. 45.

•13314 *In imprint* for *R. Daniel*? read: *N. Alsop*,

13319 *In imprint* for *A. Crooke*? read: *J. Crooke a. R. Sergier*,

•13358 *Add note*: Includes Greg 528–30.

•13372 *In imprint delete*: [*W. Jaggard f.*]

•13374–75.5 *Continue imprint*: sold [*by E. Wright*,]

•13376 *Add note*: A&R 394.

13483 *In line 4 read*: ... 1579; to J. Roberts 31 my. 1594.

•13499 *Add pressmark*: (C.122.c.37).

•13499.5 *Add pressmark*: (C.122.c.38).

•13567a *At beginning of imprint* add: *f. Amend date*: [c. 1615.]

•13569 *In 2nd paragraph of note, last 3 lines, delete*: , and perhaps ... 1328–31 *and after* p. 697. *add*: For a discussion of cancellations and of the 1590 incident *see Huntington Library Quarterly* 50 (1987): 229–48.

•13581 *In line 6 of note read*: 1913; Levis's whole collection is at HN.

•13597 *In imprint* for *G. Potter*? read: *J. Broome*,

Add new entry:
•13621a.7 —[A variant, w. imprint:] *F. Kingston f. P. Nevill*, 1640. LK.

•13657 *In note read*: yielded ... on 8 Jan. 1584; *see* Arber II.786; *see* also Greg ...

•13662 *Continue note*: Regarding an attempt in Aug. 1639 by a Warden of the Stat. Co. and partner in the King's Printing House (app. H. Fetherstone) to stop the printing of this ed. *see Cal.S.P.D., 1639*, p. 458.

13799 *Add after date*: Ent. 26 mr.

Add new entry:
13829.9 —[Anr. ed.] 4°. [*J. Notary*? 1508?] O^{5}(1 imp. leaf, W.P.iii.41).
56? or 54? lines per column in 64 mm. textura; in the same types as Notary's parallel Promptorium, 20435. Column 1 of recto begins: 'Recubitus ...' whereas the 4° de Worde eds. and 13833.5 have this text on BB4^{r} (13831) or FF4^{r} (the others), column 2, line 17.

•13863.7 Sotheby's copy now = L.

•13880 *In imprint* for *J. Barnes* read: *J. Lichfield a. J. Short*

•13882 *In imprint delete*: [*G. Simson*] *Add after date*: [really *G. Eld*, 1609.]

13928 *Continue note*: There is another setting of the cancel for D2,3; D2^{r} catchword: c) 'ties' (O^{6}).

•14006 *Amend date*: [1538–47?]

•14042 *Add after locations*: Duff 203.

Although most of the addenda and corrigenda printed in vol. 1 of the STC revision continue to be valid, the following are superseded in the present volume, and the user of STC may wish to delete them from vol. 1:

22.2	2734	4877.2	9954.7
408.5	3034.7	4941	10392
1462.3	3308	5096	11511.2
1542	3447	5157.5	p. 557^{2} Halle, E.
1825	4032.3	9339.3	13272
2353.5	4848.2	9946.3	

•14049 *Add at beginning of note*: (Formerly also 10408)

•p. 1^{1} **I., G.** *Add cross-reference*:
—*tr. See* 21510.

•14058.7 *Add after title*: [By Stephen Jerome.]

•14068 *Continue imprint*: *sold* [*by E. Wright*,]

•14068.3 *Amend end of imprint*: ... *Trundle*, (*sold* [*by E. Wright*,] 1614.)

◦14068.5 *In imprint* for [*V. Simmes*?] read: [*A. Jeffes*] *Add after date*: Ent. to A. Jeffes 30 jy. Freeman copy now = F.

•p. 2^{1} **I., W.** *Add cross-reference*:
—Cupids messenger. 1608. *See* 6122(***A***).

Add new heading:
•p. 2^{1} **Ilderton, William.** *See* Elderton, W.

Add new entry:
•14077c.11* [Another copy of .10 with same text.] s.sh.16°. [*London*? c. 1510?] Ulster U, Coleraine(in 1R4 = R. de S. Victore, *Opuscula*, 1494, stamped on verso of tp in smudged impression).
The text is either in 95 mm. textura or in a xylographic imitation of it. The cut measures approx. 85 × 56 mm. whereas .10 and .11 measure 84 × 62 and 91 × 62 respectively.

Add new entry:
•.25G Arundel, Sussex, *Dominican Priory*. [I]N xpõ sibi dilectis [ ] Frater Joh'es Arundell prior ordinis fratr predicatoru Arundell ... [Letter of confraternity, dated 1485.] 1/2 sh.*obl*.fol. [*Westminster, W. Caxton*, 1485.] Warwick County Record Office (CR 895/ Bundle 13 (part 1)).

•.41 *For* 1522 *read*: c. 1510.

•.44 *In imprint* read: [*W.*? or *R.*? *Faques*, 1507.]

London, *Hospital of St. Thomas*. *Add new 1st entry*:
•.55G JOhãnes yonge Magister dom⁹ scti Thome martyris Cãtuariens dicte de Acoñ ... [Letter of confraternity, dated 28 Apr. 1512.] s.sh.*obl*.4°. [*R. Pynson*, 1512.] L^{8}.
Indulgences .56 is the same text w. a few minor changes.

Add new entry:
•.59G London, *St. Paul's Cathedral, Chapel of Jesus in the Crowds—Confraternity of the Name of Jesus*. These graces folowynge be graunted to all ye bredren & systers of Jesus fraternyte in ye crowdes vnder Poules. [Letter of confraternity.] s.sh.8°. [*W. de Worde*, 1522?] L(in Huth 54).
This is bd. at the end of an almanack (STC 389); bd. at the beginning is a woodcut of Jesus (Hodnett 546) which may be separate or may belong w. this rather than the almanack.

•14077c.60 *For* c. 1510 *read*: 1512.

London, *Savoy Hospital*. *Add new entry*:
•.60* Leo ep'us seruus seruorum dei [xylographic] ad f( )am rei memoriam ... [Reissue by Leo X, dated 4 kal. Mar. 1516, of the bull of Julius II, here dated 3 non. Sept. 1512, granting privileges as in Indulgences .60.] s.sh.*obl*.fol. [*R. Pynson*, 1516.] O(imp.).

•.63 For *Goes*,] 1506. read: *Goes*, 1506.]

Add new entry:
•.82G Warrington, Lancashire, *Augustinian Priory*. FRater Ricardus Prior localis ordinis Fratru heremitar Scti augustini Cõuentus Weringtonie dilectis sibi in xpo ... Data in conuetu ... Millmo Quigentissimo .xxv. [Letter of confraternity, entirely xylographic.] 1/2 sh.*obl*.fol. [*Warrington*, 1525.] Cheshire Record Office (DVE Acc.2401. S: L: 104).

Add new entry:
•.83G Westminster, *Hospital of St. Mary Rounceval near Charing Cross*. EDwardus ponyngis Cappellan⁹ dñi regis, Magister siue custos, hospitalis bte et gl'iose virgis Marie de Roucideuall iuxta charingcrosse. [Letter of confraternity.] 1/2 sh.*obl*.fol. [*Westminster, W. Caxton*, 1480.] LC(frags. of at least 4 copies).
See Paul Needham, *The Printer & the Pardoner*, Washington, 1986, especially pp. 42, 62–4.

•.87 *Add after locations*: Duff 213(variant).

•.88–9 For *W. de Worde* read: *R. Pynson*

•.107 *Add note*: In type 2*; line 6 begins: 'ecclesiã'.

Add new entry:
•.107C —[Anr. ed.] s.sh.*obl*.4°. [*Westminster, W. Caxton*, 1480.] L(2 frags., IA.55030a).O^{8}(frags., in O.1.25).O^{9}(frags., in SR 58g.1).
In type 4; line 6? begins: 'ex tue deuotionis'.

•.110 *In heading for* to line 7? *read*: line 9 begins: *Add location*: L(frags., IA.55030). *Continue note*: The L frags. supply most of the text missing in C^{2}.

•.111 *Amend date*: 1481.

Add new entry:
•.142C —[Anr. ed.] s.sh.*obl*.4°. [*R. Pynson*, 1499.] L^{11}(Indulgence E 135, 6/64).
18 lines. Line 2: 'dñi nostri pape cõmiarius [*sic*]. Vobis.'

Informatio. *Add cross-reference*:
•p. 9^{2} —Informatio fundamentalis super discursu circa Bohemiae statum facto. 1619. *See* 3207.5(***A***).

•14092 *After* Anon. *add*:]

14104 *Add note*: This is by Humfrey Braham. Copies vary: with (P) or without (L, O) his name at end of dedic.

Instruction. *Add cross-reference*:
•p. 10^{1} —[A brief and plain instruction for to learn the tablature, to the gittern. 1569?] *See* 15846.5(***A3***).

Add new entry:
14109.2 —[Enterlude of detraction, light judgment, verity, and justice.] 4°. [*London*, c. 1550.] HN(frags., consisting of most of E1 and E3).
Unique in having a fairly consistent rhyme scheme of abbacc.

•14109.3 *Add after title*: [*Tr*. from La vérité cachée.] *Add note*: *See PBSA* 71 (1977): 259–69.

•14109.5 *Add note*: (Formerly 6799)

14117 *Add note*: One C copy has cancel slips on tp and in colophon, w. imprint: *W. Middiltoñ* and colophon dated 1 May 1546.

Introduction. *Add new 1st ed.*:
•14117.7 —[An introduction for to learn ... 1536.] 8°. [*St. Albans, J. Herford f. R. Stevenage*,] (1537.) L(last leaf only, imp., Harl.5919/176).
With Stevenage's device, McK. 84; the text surviving on the other side agrees with the transcription in Herbert III.1436.

•14118 *Begin entry*: —[Anr. ed., revised.] *Continue title*: ... pen, or with the counters ... newly corrected. And certayne notable rules of false posytions thereunto added not before sene in Englyshe.

•14123.5 *Add note*: Includes a trans. of P. Canisius's Parvus Catechismus; cf. 4568.5.

•14123.7 *Amend imprint*: [*R. Grafton*, 1542?]

•14125 *In imprint* for [*R. Grafton* read: [*E. Whitchurch*?

Add new entry:
•14130.5 —[Ordinances for the government of Ireland. A2^{r} begins:] First it is ordeyned, that the kinges deputie make no warre ne peace with any Irishe man [etc.] fol. (*T. Berthelet*, 1534.) L^{11}(SP 63:2, ff. 64–71, lacks A1).
Collates A–B^{6}.

After 14161 *add cross-reference*:
•p. 12^{1} —By the Lord Deputie. [Announcing O'Dogherty's death and demanding the surrender of his allies. 7 July 1608.] Cr. 195(only in MS.). *See* 18786(***A3***).

•14220 *Continue imprint*: *a. assignes of J. Bill*

Add new entry:
•14237.3 —By the Lord Deputy and Councell. A proclamation concerning gun-powder and munition. [10 Apr. 1635.] s.sh.fol. [*Dublin, Soc. of Statrs.*, 1635.] L(Add. MS. 69932, misc. outsize documents). Cr. 309(MS. only).

•14255 *Correct format*: 4° in 2. *Add location*: HAGUE(Knuttel 399). *Add note*: A trans. of 14258.

•14258 *Add before title*: [Heading A1^{r}:] *Correct format*: 4° in 2. *Correct place of printing*: [i.e. *the Netherlands*?] *Add location*: HAGUE(Knuttel 401). *Add note*: For a trans. *see* 14255.

Add new entry:
•14258.3 —[Anr. ed.] 4° in 2. (*London* [i.e. *the Netherlands*?] 1579.) HAGUE(Knuttel 400).
In heading: 'Irelandt'.

•14259 *Add note*: For eds. intended for the Church of England *see* 10034.4 sqq.

•14290 *In imprint* read: *F. Kingston f.*

•14308.5 *In imprint* after *Crossley*, add: [*in Oxford*,]

•14318 *Continue note*: *See* also 4153.7, 4155.

Add new entry:
14323.3 —[Anr. ed.] Thystorye of Jacob and his twelue sones. 4° $^{6.8}$. (*W. de Worde*,) [1510?] C.

•14326 *Before* HN. *add*: ETON(frag.).;

•14328 *Add note*: Includes answers to 3065, 7115.

•p. 18^{2} **Jacobus,** *de Gruitroede*. *Add to cross-references*: 3295, 3586, 14548.

•14343 *In imprint* for [*E. Bollifant*?] read: [*W. Jaggard*?]

Add new entry:
•14349.5 —[Anr. ed.] 8°. *Edenburgh, H. Charteris*, [really *printed abroad*,] 1603. E.

•14358 *Begin imprint*: [*T. Creede a.*

Add new entry:
•14358.7 —Fourth edition. 12°. *B. Alsop f. T. Jones*, 1621. L.

•14363 *In locations delete*: G^{2}.

•14367 *Continue note*: Answers the original of 6384.

14371 *Continue note*: P may have the orig. tp as endpapers in D.5.15, w. misprint: '*indepencie*'.

•14377 For *V. Simmes* read: *R. Read*

•14379.5 *Continue note*: *See* also 13880.

•14381 *Add note*: There are 2 eds.; (i) pr. by [*J. Windet*] w. A4^{r} line 4 of heading ending: 'Written' (HD) and (ii) pr. by [*V. Simmes*] w. 'by' (2 F).

•14382 *In imprint* for *R. Barker* read: *J. Bill*

•14387 *Delete*: Y.

•14388.3 *Delete* (lacks tp) *from* Y.

•14388.5 *Amend locations*: Clarabut copy now = L. *Also add*: E.

•14392 *Continue title*: With a discourse of this late intended treason.

•14401 *In line 2 of note after* verso. *add*: Copies called in by proclamation; *see* 8431. *In last line of note before* 15362 *add*: 6991.7, 7306, 7322, 7335,

•14405 *In note before* 24119 *add*: 7119.

•14408 *Add after title*: [*Tr*. by J. Loiseau de Tourval.] *Amend imprint*: *Londres, chez J. Norton* [i.e. *Paris*?]

•14410 *Delete*: L.

•14410.5 *Continue note*: There are 2 eds.; A4^{r} line 4 has: (i) 'bee' (1 L, 2 F) or (ii) 'be' (1 L, O, E, YK, 2 F, HD). Quires B–C in the latter were app. pr. by [*J. Roberts*]. For further details *see Poetica* 23 (1986): 74–80.

•14411 *Amend imprint*: *London*, [*T. Creede f.*] *R. Walde-grave*,

•14421 For [*W. White*?] read: [*R. Read*]

14425.3 *In SR entry delete*: or 6

•p. 22^{2} **James, W.** *In 'See also' reference for* 10192.6 *read*: 10192.5 sq.

Add new heading:
•p. 22^{2} **Jansenius, Cornelius.** *See* pt. 2 of 13478.

Add new entry:
14467.7 —[Anr. ed. of 14466.] Janua linguarum, sive modus maxime accommodatus. [Editio tertia?] *Lat. a. Eng.* 4°. [*H. Lownes f. M. Lownes*, 1619?] C(tp def.).
Unique in having the Prooemium begin on ¶1^{r}.

•14472.3 *Add locations*: Berlin NL. Munich U. Wolfenbüttel, Herzog August Bibliothek.

•14472.5 *For* [Anr. ed.] *read*: [Anr. issue.] *Add locations*: GOT. Bonn U. Freiburg U. Munich, Bayerische Staatsbibliothek.+ *Add note*: In the O copy the prelims. and at least quires A–B, X–Y, Cc–Dd, Gg–Hh are partly or wholly reset; e.g. B1^{r}, no. 77 has in the English: '*vvelmeth*' whereas the C, HD copies of 14472.3 have '*vvhelmeth*'; other copies may differ.

•14477 *In line 3 for* [Henry VII's] *read*: [the Duke's]

•p.23[1] **Jegon.** *Add cross-reference*:
—Visitation Articles. *See* 10289.9.

•14492 *Add before date*: [*sold at the shop of R. Milbourne*,] *Add note*: With mortality totals in Newcastle and Garthside, most on a weekly basis, for 7 May–31 Dec. 1636.

Add new entry:
•14492.3 —[A variant, w. imprint:] *f. R. Milbourne*, 1637. Newcastle upon Tyne, Society of Antiquaries.

•p. 23[2] **Jenison.** *In 'See also' references delete*: 11114.

Add new heading:
•p. 23[2] **Jenour, Kenelm.** *See* Bookplates.

•14507 *In line 1 read*: patrum [xylographic, white on black]. *In line 3 read*: hermytes, ... wryten and also *tr.* out of Greke in to Latyn, by saynt Jerome & other solytarye relygyouse persons.—*Tr*.

•p. 24[1] **Jerome, Stephen.** *Add cross-references*:
—The arraignement of the whole creature. 1631. *See* 13538.5.
—The diversion. 1639. *See* 14510.3(*A*3).

Add new entry:
•14510.3 —[Anr. issue, w. cancel tp:] The diversion of Gods judgments: or, the penitents practice. In five sermons. *f. H. Hood*, 1639. YK.

•14513 *Substitute this note*: *See* 13538.5.

•14516 *In line 2 of note for* 15412.7 *read*: 14512.7. *Add below note*: —*See* also 14058.7(*A*3).

•14520.5 *Add pressmark*: (C.161.f.2(97)).

Add new entry:
•14520.7 —[A merry jest of a shrewd and cursed wife. By J. Bramis. In verse.] 4°. [*Southwark? P. Treveris?* c. 1530?] SH (frag.).
C1[r] line 1: 'The moder was ryght glade of this syght'.

•14521 *Add after dash*: [Anr. ed.] *Delete*: SH. *Add note*: B4[v] line 1: 'The mother was right glad of this sight,'.

•14525 *Add note*: For other translations of the 2nd pt. *see* 14528 and bk. 2 of 11346; for a Latin version *see* 4469.5.

•14526.5 *In imprint* for [*A. Islip*?] read: [*R. Raworth*]

•14528 *Add note*: The original is attrib. to J. Cambillon; for a Latin version *see* 4469.5; for other Eng. translations *see* bk. 2 of 11346 and the 2nd pt. of 14525.

•p. 25[1] *After* 14535 *add cross-reference*:
—Looke about you. 1630. *See* 16800(*A*3).

•14546.5 Hofmann & Freeman copy now = Robert Taylor.

•14548 *Amend date*: [1534–36?] *Add note*: Tr. from Colloquium peccatoris et crucifixi Jesu Christi, attrib. to Jacobus, de Gruitroede. For other translations *see* 3295, 3586.

•14553 Lord Kenyon's copy now = M. *Begin note*: Tr. from the Speculum passionis domini nostri Jesu Christi of Ulrich Pinder.

Add new entry:
•14556.5 —[The passion of Christ. In verse.] 4°. [*R. Pynson*, c. 1503.] HN(2 frags., totalling 10 lines).MEL(Foxcroft 17, 2 frags., totalling 25 lines).
In Pynson's 95 mm. textura with w[6].

•14560.5 *Add after title*: [By R. Southwell.]

•14569 *Continue imprint*: [*St. Omer*,]

•p. 26[1] *After* 14573 *add cross-reference*:
—The spirituall matrimonye bytwene Chryste and the soule. [1550?] *See* 17651.5(*A*3).

•14578 *Add after date*: Ent. 4 mr. 1614.

•14587 *Substitute this SR entry*: Ass'd from G. Bishop to T. Adams 14 mr. 1611; to A. Hebb 6 my. 1625.

•14590 *Begin line 3 of note*: This or 14591 answered ...

•14600 *Continue note*: Answers 12762; answered by 12763.

•14601 *In line 2 after* booke *add*: [12763]

•14605 *Add after date*: Ass'd to John Newbery 30 se.

•p. 27[1] **Jewel, J.** *After* 14614 *add cross-reference*:
—*See* also Bookplates(*A*).

•14618 *In imprint* after *Crosley*, add: [*in Oxford*,]

•p. 27[2] **Joannes,** *Campensis*. *Substitute these 'tr.' references*:
—*tr. See* 2354, 2368.3, 2368.5, 2372.4.

Add new heading:
•p. 27[2] **Joannes,** *de Hildesheim*. *See* 5572.

14628 *Continue note*: The title identifies the translator as 'Philip [Howard] late Earl of Arundell'.

14634 *Add note*: At least 1 C copy has paper w. horizontal chainlines.

•14638 *Amend title*: Theophilus [*pseud*., i.e. S. Castalio], and ...

After 14647 *add new heading*:
•p. 28[2] **John IV,** *King of Portugal*. The first manifest of the new king of Portugall. 1640 [o.s.] *See* 18507.345C(*A*3).

•14650.5 *In line 3 read*: ... Capistranus. Woodcut w. letterpress text.] *Amend imprint*: [*the Netherlands*?]

14651 *Add note*: At least P has the misprint: 'Mylborne' instead of 'Mylbourne' in the imprint.

•p. 29[1] **John Casimir.** *Add cross-reference*:
—*See* also 11348.

Add new heading:
•p. 29[1] **John Francis,** *Friar*. *See* 6091.

•14661 *Substitute this imprint*: [*Amsterdam*?]

Add new entry:
•14662.5 —[Heading (*⁎*)1[r]:] A note of some things ... controverted in the exiled English church at Amsterdam. [Anon.] 4° in 2. [*Amsterdam*? 1611.] BO.
BO is bd. w. and possibly issued w. 14663, but the present item does not appear in at least the L copy of the latter. Reprinted on M4[r]–N1[v] of 5449; authorship attrib. to Johnson on A3[r] of 209.

•p. 29[1] **Johnson, Francis.** *Add to 'See also' references*: 5449, 7298,

•14670.3 *Correct title*: arithmatick ... The secund *In imprint* after *Grismond* add: [*a.*] (*R. Milborne*,) *Add location*: HN.

•14670.5 *In heading read*: imprint on engr. tp altered:] *In line 2* for *Milborne* read: *Mylborne*

•14676 *Add note*: Plagiarized from 25341.

•14680 *Begin SR entry*: Ass'd to N. Bourne 16 oc. 1609; to Snodham ...

14691 *Continue note*: One O copy is an intermediate state, w. tp correctly dated 1612 but w. only the author's inits. on A3[r] and A4[v].

Add new heading:
•p. 30[1] **Johnson, Robert,** *Alderman of London*. *See* 14699, 14700 (both *A*3).

Add new entry:
•14694.2 —Dives and Lazarus, or rather, divellish Dives. Delivered in a sermon by R. I. 8°. *A. M*[*athewes*] *f. P. Byrch*, 1620. Ent. as by Robert Johnson 10 jn. 1619. L.

•14694.3 *Add before title*: [Anr. ed.] *For* Ent. *read*: Ass'd

•14696 For [*A. Islip*] read: [*R. Raworth*]

•14699 *Continue note*: This and 14700 are by Robert Johnson, *Alderman of London*, probably a different man from Robert Johnson, *Gent*.

•14700 *Add note*: *See* 14699(*A*3).

Add new heading:
•p. 30[2] **Johnson, Thomas,** *of Ipswich*. *See* Bookplates(*A*).

Add new heading:
•p.30[2] **Johnson, William,** *of Cambridge*. *See* Bookplates.

•14708.7 *Add note*: Attacks 7547.

•14717.5 *Add after title*: [Anon.] *Amend SR entry*: Ent. as by Anthonie Jones 4 ap. *Continue note*: O has inserted after the tp a bifolium, the 1st leaf of which is signed '1', w. epistle To loving friends. This bifolium is not present in L.

•p. 31[1] **Jones, I.** *Begin references*: 6306,

•14724a.3 Amend *location*: L(lacks tp and folding tables; has 1st table sep. in Tab.583.f.45, fol. 5).

•14729 *Add note*: On A3[r] Jones indicates he only 'set downe under euerie assertion of this short catechisme ... the proofe & place of scripture'; the questions and answers are from Pagit's catechism (18816(*A*). The proofs are different expansions of the biblical citations from those Openshaw supplies (18830.2A sqq.).

Add new heading:
•p. 31[2] **Jones, Thomas,** *Common Serjeant of London, ed. See* 5488.

•14751 *Begin note*: Regarding states of the engr. tp *see Library* 8 (1986): 152–6. *Add at end of note*: Includes Greg 304, 339–49.

•14753.5 *Amend SR entry*: The staple of news ent. to J. Waterson 14 ap. 1626; ass'd to Allott 7 se. 1631. *Delete*: HN. *After locations add*: Greg 455–7.

•14756 *Continue note*: There are 2 impressions of both pts.; in pt. 1 C3[r] line 1 has: 'shee' (O[9], 2 F) or 'she' (L[6], O, 1 F). In pt. 2 A2[r] line 8 has '*wondring*' (O, O[9]) or '*wondering*' (L[6], 1 F), but its sheets are mixed among themselves and found with either impression of pt. 1. *See* also 12863.

•14757 *Delete*: E.

•p. 33[1] **Jonson, B.** *Begin 'See also' references*: 4970,

Add new heading:
•p. 33[1] **Joope, John,** *ed. See* 5337.

•14794 *In imprint* after *Mense* add: [false imprint]

•14801 *Add after date*: Ent. to R. Walley 7 mr. 1591; ass'd to T. Adams 12 oc. 1591.

•14805 *In imprint* for [*T. Creede*] read: [*J. Legat*]

•p. 33[2] **Joseph,** *the Patriarch*. *Add cross-reference*:
—The historie of Joseph, sonne of Jacob. [Series of woodcuts. c. 1565?] *See* 11930.4.

•14809 *In SR entry delete*: to R. Walley ... 12 oc. 1591; ent.

•p. 34[1] **Josseline.** *Add cross-reference*:
—*See* also 19292a(*A*3).

•14820 *Amend imprint*: [*Antwerp, widow of C. Ruremond,*] *Add note*: End of text dated 27 Feb. The woodcut 'A' on A2[r] is identical to that on i7[r] of 16149, and the 95 mm. textura is an early state, without capital 'W' or 'sh' ligature, of the fount in 17798, 21804, and 24217; *see* Isaac, vol. 2, fig 62.

•14826 *Add note*: Answered by 11588.

•p. 34[2] **Joye, G.** *Add to 'See also' references*: 24468(*A*3).

•14836.3 *For* TEX. *read*: TEX[2].

•p. 34[2] **Juliers.** *Add cross-reference*:
—*See* also 5413.

Turn entry into a cross-reference:
•14868 — = 14869.

•14869 *Amend imprint*: (*R. Redman*, 1527.) *Amend locations*: O(tp and colophon only, Douce Add. 142/487, 490).; Henry N. Ess III, New York City. *Substitute this note*: (Formerly also 14868) Collates a–i[8] k[4]; tp + ii–lxxi + [5].

•14871.5 *In the note for* 7712.6 *read*: 7712.2.

•14886 *In the note for* L4–8 *read*: L3–8.

•14894.3 *Add after date*: Ent. 30 jn. 1596. *Amend location*: L(tpp only, ... and C.60.h.16, fol. 37).

Add new heading:
•p.37[1] **Kaye, John.** *See* Bookplates.

Add new heading:
•p. 37[1] **Kaye, Thomas.** *See* Bookplates.

•14897 *In the SR entry for* 22 mr. *read*: 25 mr.

•14898 *Add after date*: Ent. to G. Bishop, T. Man, a. J. Norton [*sic*, not 'Unton'] on 1 de. 1602.

Add new heading:
•p. 37[2] **Keeling, Edward.** *See* 6902.

Add new entry:
•14899.1 —[Anr. ed.] 8°. *G. E[ld] f. J. Trundle*, ‹1619?› O(cropt).
The tops of the figures in the date are barely visible.

•14900 *Begin imprint*: [*Eliot's Court Press?* ...

•14932 *Add note*: Answered by 6320.

•p. 38[2] **Kennedy, Q.** *Add cross-reference at end*:
—*See* also 12968.

Substitute this entry:
•14932.5 **Kenner,** *Mrs*. **John.** [Prose text begins:] Thou shalte vnderstande (chrysten reader) that the thyrde daye of August Anno. M.CCCCC.Lii. ... in Myddleton stonye ... the good wyfe was deliuered of thys double chylde, begotten of her late housbande John Kenner. [Woodcuts w. letterpress text, including verses in Lat. a. Eng.] fol(2). [*J. Day*, 1552.] L (Dept. of P&D: English Woodcuts—Anon., 16th and 17th centuries; cut up in 3 pieces and mounted).

•14937 *In locations delete*: Maxwell copy *and add it at*: 14940.

Add new entry:
•14942.5 —[Psalm civ. In verse.] s.sh.fol. [*Printed abroad*, c. 1615?] HD(*63-1463F, fol. 38, lower left portion only, stanzas 3–6).
This trans. is used in the Sternhold (cf. 2430) and in the Scottish (cf. 2701, 16577) psalms. The 'w' and the 'sh' ligature seem too small for the rest of the fount.

•14948 *Amend imprint*: *L. Snowdon* [*in the shop of R. Blower*] ...

Add new entry:
•14954.6 —Hallelu-iah: praise yee [etc. as in 14954.7] a loaden conscience. 8°. *C. Legge, pr. to the Univ. of Cambridge, sold* [*in London*] *by M. Law*, 1614. YK.

•14954.7 *Add after dash*: [Anr. ed.] *In title for* leaden *read*: loaden

•14963 *Delete*: L.

•15003 *At end of title add*: Whereunto is annexed a godly aduise touching mariage. *Add note*: An altered version of the 'aduise' is included in 20397.

p. 40² *Add new heading*:
Kirkby, John. *See* Bookplates.

•15017 *Continue note*: There are 2 eds.: end of preface on ¶5r dated 10 Oct. 1580 (1 Taussig, HD) or 10 Nov. 1581 (1 Taussig, HN); the latter is the ed. reissued in 15018 w. tp date altered in press to 1581.

•15027 *Add note*: Sometimes attrib. to R. Greene.

•p. 41¹ *Add new heading*:
Knapp, Robert. *See* Bookplates(*A*).

•15029 *Begin imprint*: [*N. Hill f.*] *In the note for* 9512.8 *read*: 7819.4.

•p. 41¹ **Knell, T.** *After* 15034 *add*:
—*See* also 7605(*A*3).

•15037.5 *Continue note*: Answers a version of the Motives in 3799.

•15048 *In line 3 read*: Ent. to M. Sparke, sen., ...

•p. 42² *Add new heading*:
Kolb, Conrad. *See* 5678.

•15077.3 For *Tr.* read: Much corrected and enlarged by *Delete*: L. and E.

•15079 *Continue note*: *See* also 12198.

•15081.7 *Substitute this entry*:
—[Anr. issue, w. cancel tpp:] Quint. editio. *E. Griffin, sumpt. G. Hutton* (*E. Griffin f. G. Hutton*,) 1640. Brent Gration-Maxfield, London(lacks Lat. tp).; CU.
Both tpp dated 1640; the sub tp on Q4r still has imprint: *f. M. Sparks* as in 15081 sq. The Lat. a. Eng. tpp both name Comenius rather than Anchoran as the editor, although the dedic., etc. signed by Anchoran are also retained.

•p. 43¹ *Add new heading*:
Kromer, Marcin, *Bp.* *See* Cromer, M.

•p. 45¹ **L., I.** or **J.** *In 'ed.' references following* 15107 *add*: 10871,

•15107.7 **L., M.** *Add new 1st entry*:
—[Heading on A3r:] Enuies scourge, and Vertues honour. [In praise of virtue. In verse.] 8°. [*T. East*, c. 1605?] Robert Taylor.
A2 has dedic. to Thos. Paget, esq., of the Middle Temple by M. L., his 'poore kinseman'.

•p. 45² **L., R.** *Add cross-reference at end*:
—*ed.* *See* 10758.

•15111 *Continue note*: *See* also G4r-v of 6607.5.

•15111.5 *Continue note*: Tp in red and black. L has Fosbrooke's imprint struck through and replaced by pen with that of John Smith 2, together w. other MS. alterations to the title as if providing copy for a cancel tp. O, SHEF lack A2,3 (To reader); present in L, SAL and in 15111.3 and 15111.7.

•15111.7 *Begin entry*: —[Anr. issue, w. cancel tp all in black, w. title:] A prophesie lyen hid [etc.] *f. N. Fosbrooke*, 1614.

•15115 *Add after title*: [By W. Loe, the elder.]

•p. 46¹ **L., W.** *Add cross-reference at end*:
—*See* also 4930.5, 7529.

•p. 46¹ **Labyrinthus.** *In cross-reference for* 12596 *read*: 12956.

•15118.5 *Continue note*: The verse is followed by various recipes for cooking buck and other dishes.

•p. 46² *Add new heading*:
La Fontaine, Robert de, *Professor of French, ed.* *See* 6749.8.

p. 46² *Add new heading*:
Lake, Anne. *See* Bookplates.

•15137 *Continue note*: *See* also 5638.7.

•15140 *Add after date*: Ent. to M. Lownes 11 fb.

•15156 *In imprint* for [*A. Islip*?] read: [*F. Kingston*]

•15177 *Add note*: Line 8 of title has 'Ignominious'; there is a 19th-century type facsimile which sometimes has the imprint: *J. Barker* cut from the bottom of its tp, but its title has 'Ignominiovs'.

•15184 *Add note*: This is a trans of 199.

•15187 *Amend imprint*: [*London, J. Mychell*, 1530–32?] *Continue note*: In the same types as 17327.

•15188.3 *In heading for* **Michael** *read*: **Nicolaus** [i.e. Mikolaj Lanczycki.]

•p. 47² *Add new heading*:
Land, John. *See* Bookplates.

•15190.5 *Amend imprint*: [*J. Charlewood*, 1578?] *Continue note*: Actually by W. Patten; *see English Literary Renaissance* 7 (1977): 297–306, and *TCBS* 7 (1977): 28–45. In spite of the speculations in *Library* 7 (1985): 115–25, the woodcut 'A' in the present ed. shows steady deterioration in the outer border in uses dated 1575–77, with its state here the worst of all; furthermore, the *Library* article offers no evidence that the cast factotum in 15191 was indeed used in English printing before 1580.

•15191 *Amend date*: c. 1585.

15192 *Continue note*: Some copies (O, 2 P) have a slip pasted on the cut on the tp verso or inserted after the tp w. 8 lines of verse beginning: 'In effigiem ... ' Quaritch catalogue 829 (1962), back cover, describes a copy w. tp verso blank and other indications of early issue.

•15192.5 *Before* In verse. *add*: Anon. *Correct format*: 4° in 6? *Amend date*: [1533–34?] *Correct location*: O(frags. of 1st and last leaves, Arch.Ae.114). *Add note*: Printed in the same types as 3186, 21647. For the complete text *see* F. J. Furnivall, ed., *Ballads from Manuscripts*, Ballad Society, 1868, I¹ 281–90; regarding the author *see* L. I. Guiney, *Recusant Poets*, London, 1939, pp. 24–30.

•15193.5 *Add note*: *See* Hind III.271. There is a later state at HD, Y also *without imprint*, but having, below the snake's head on the title-plate, a greyish irregular splotch approx. 22 × 12 mm. at its widest (cf. Wing¹ A 761 and Wing² J 661A). In addition HD has a post-1675 state w. imprint on title-plate: *sold by J. Garrett*, which has all 9 plates pr. on the recto of a single large sheet.

•p. 48¹ **Langeren.** *In 'See also' references before* 22634.5 *add*: 10420.

◦15203 *Add note*: There are 2 eds.; B2v line 2 has: (i) 'beganne' (2 C) or (ii) 'began' (L, O, 2 F, HD).

•p. 48² *Add new heading*:
Lanier, Emilia. *See* 15227.

15217 *Add note*: The colophon date is correct. C has the tp date corrected in MS. to 'M.D.XLIX.'

•15229.7 **La Perrière.** *Add new 1st entry*:
—[The theatre of fine devices. *Tr.* T. Combe.] 8°. [*R. Field*, 1606?] G²(imp.).
Emblem I, line 4 from bottom ends: 'their race,' whereas 15230 has: 'this race,'. Collates like 15230; the woodcut 'T' on A5r is in a state later than A6r of 19853, dated 1605, and probably earlier than E4r of 10553, dated 1607. The SR entry at 15230 belongs here.

•15230 *Begin entry*: —[Anr. ed.] *Delete*: G².

•15251.7 *Add after date*: Ent. to Man a. W. Broome 5 jn. 1584.

◦15259 *Add note*: (4406 is pt. of this) The dedic. is reprinted and tr. in 555.

•15261 *For* L. *read*: L(bd. w. 2739). *Add note*: For a 16° ed. dated 31 Aug. 1561 *see* pt. 2 of 2739.5(*A*).

•15262 *Begin note*: Text in B.L.; also issued as pt. 2 of 2740.3 (***A***); for anr. ed. w. text in roman *see* 2740(***A***).

•p. 51² **Latin Grammar.** *Add cross-reference*:
—De nominibus heteroclitis. [c. 1540.] *See* 5543b.9.

•p. 51² **Latomus.** *In cross-reference for* 5266.5 *read*: 5265.8.

•15296 *In imprint read*: ... *Caxton*, 1 Rich. III = 1484.]

15309 *Add note*: The heading on A1ʳ varies: '... *Observations upon a speech* ...' (F, HD) or corrected to 'OB | SERVATIONS *Upon the Arch-Bishops Epistle Dedicatory* | ...' (O).

Add new heading:
•p. 52¹ **Laude, John.** *See* Bookplates (Land).

•15311 *Add note*: A revised version of 20113, w. a new preface.

Add new heading:
•p. 52² **Laune, Pierre de,** *tr. See* 16431.

Add new entry:
•15316.7 **Lauze, François de.** Apologie de la danse et la parfaicte methode de l'enseigner tant aux cavaliers qu'aux dames. 4°. [*Paris? and London, B. Alsop,*] 1623. L.PARIS.
The main text and prob. the engr. tp were possibly pr. in Paris. The 1st 4 letterpress leaves in L, w. dedic. to the Duke of Buckingham and commendatory verses, were pr. in London. PARIS lacks one of these 4 leaves: w. verse 'A l'autheur.'

•15324 *Continue note*: Repudiated by Fowler and others in 11212.

Add new entry:
15326.7 —[Anr. ed.] 4°. *R. Badger*, 1637. C.C².
Tp line 5: 'MAIESTIE'. This ed. is the same setting as 15327, the latter having a variant tp w. 'Second edition' and different imprint. The present item is a different setting throughout from 15326 sq., which have 'MAIESTY' in line 5 of the tp.

15334 *Continue note*: C has the date unaltered and variant tp w. commas after 'Sermon' and '*Funerall*'.

Add new heading:
•p. 53¹ **Layther, Thomas.** *See* Bookplates(***A***3).

•15336 *Continue note*: Bynneman's rights yielded to the Stat. Co. 8 Jan. 1584; *see* Appendix C/55.

•15338 *Begin SR entry*: Ass'd by V. Simmes to E. Griffin 19 de. 1619; ent. to Mrs. [A.] Griffin a. ...

Add new heading:
•p. 53² **Lecherpière, Samuel de,** *tr. See* 6266.

•15351.7 *In title for* Mʳ. *read*: Mr. *Add full stop after* book *Add before format*: [Anon.] *Add note*: L³¹ has the author's name added in MS.

Add new heading:
•p. 54¹ **Ledley, John.** *See* Lidley, J.

Add new heading:
p. 54¹ **Lee, Robert.** *See* Bookplates.

•15374.2 *In title read*: ... Accidence [cf. 15610.5 sqq. Anon.]

•15374.5 *In title read*: ... Accidence [cf. 15610.5 sqq.]

•15374.7 *Delete the subtitle and continue the main title*: Hereunto are annexed foure little colloquies or dialogues in latine, every one of them verbally *tr. Continue note*: Dialogues reprinted in 5354(***A***3) w. a different English trans.

•15374.9 *Amend imprint*: ... *W*[*inder*? or *G. Wood*?]

•15375 *Amend date*: 1473?

•15379 *In SR entry delete*: to T. ... 1591; *and for* Ent. *read*: ?Ent. to V. ...

•15403 *In imprint* for [*S. Stafford*] read: [*G. Purslowe*]

Add new entry:
•15404.3 —The eighth edition. 12°. *f. J. Budge*, 1622. L(imp.).

•15407.3 *Add location*: L.;

Add new heading:
p. 55¹ **Leigh, Edmund.** *See* Bookplates.

•15423.5 *Add after date*: Ent. 26 jn.

•15425 *Amend beginning of SR entry*: Erroneously ent. following an entry for 1 jy. 1602; ...

Add new heading:
•p. 56¹ **Leigh, Wolley.** *See* Bookplates.

•15428.5–29 *In note for* Leaf 5 *read*: Last recto of Epistle to Parliament

•15433 *In line 3 of note delete*: by John Milton, father of the poet. (The epistle is by Leighton; Milton contributed music to 15434.)

•15434 Tenbury copy now = O.

Add new heading:
•p. 56² **Leipzig,** *Conference of Reformed Churches*. Colloquii ... de conciliandiis dissidiis. Anno MDCXXXI. consignatio. 1637. *See* 11785.

•15450 *Add note*: Regarding a contemporary trans. into Latin *see* 4882.

•p. 57¹ **Le Maçon.** *Add cross-references* (*currently under 'Massonius'*) *at end*:
—*ed. See* 24664, 24667, 24668.

•15463 *Add location*: F.

•15464.5 *Amend heading*: [Anr. ed., w. different title and prelims.] *Add format*: 12°. *Substitute this note*: F is reset throughout from 15463-F.

•p. 57² **Leo X.** *Add at beginning of 'See also' references*: 13083.

15485 *Add note*: The engr. tp exists in different states, including a variation in the portion transcribed: 'discription' (P, HD) or 'description' (2 O, C).

•p. 58¹ **Le Petit.** *Add to 'See also' references*: 12374.

Add new entry:
•15486.5 —[A brief and plain instruction for to learn the tablature, to conduct and dispose the hand unto the gittern. Anon.? *Tr.*] *obl.*4°. [*J. Kingston f. J. Robotham*, 1569?] Ent. to J. Rowbotham 1568–69. Peter Duckers, Copthorne, Salop(ff. 14–15).; PEN (fol. 13 and another).
The title is adapted from Maunsell (17669), pt. 2, p. 18. Headlines: 'An instruction to the Gitterne.' The musical directions are in French, e.g. 'Plus fredonnes.' The tablature types are the same as in 15486, 15487. The frags. are misimposed since versos do not follow on from rectos.

•p. 58² **Lesley, R.** *In cross-reference for* 9253.5 *read*: 9175m.

•p. 59¹ **L'Espine.** *Add to the 'See also' references*: 7186.

•15518.5 *For* [imprint false] *read*: [i.e. *France*?] *Continue note*: 'Flesh' may be intended to suggest La Flèche, on the Loire.

•15520 *For* TEX. *read*: TEX².

•p. 60² **Lever, T.** *Add cross-reference after* 15552:
—*ed. See* 3493.5.

•15574.5 *Continue note*: On this point and other sources of this and 15576.6 *see Vivarium* 17 (1979): 134–58.

•15576.6 *For the last sentence of the note substitute this*: This has many, though not all, of the subjects treated in 15574.5, q.v., but the order and most of the texts display considerable differences.

Add new entry:
•15576.7 —[Anr. ed.] Libellus sophistarum. 4° mostly in 8's. [*Rouen? f. J. Alexandre, Angers*, c. 1500.] E²(in Inc. 33).
With Alexandre's device, Silvestre 284, below the title. The colophon mentions: 'ad vsum Oxoniensium'; *see The Innes Review* 30 (1979): 77–9.

•15581.5 *Add location*: ; Henry N. Ess III, New York City. *Add note*: Collates A–E⁸; tp + ii–xxxviii + [2].

•15584.7 *Add note*: Since Redman died in 1540, either the date is wrong or this was pr. by his widow.

•p. 62¹ **Lidd.** *For* 7986.5 *read*: 7988.5, 7995.4.

•p. 62¹ **Lidley.** *Add to cross-references*: 17776(*A*3).

Add new heading:
p. 62¹ **Lightfoot, Edward.** *See* Bookplates.

•15593 *In imprint* for *Michell* read: *Swain*

•15601 *Correct SR entry to*: 9 mr.

•15603.5 *Add location*: A. Veryard, Northampton, Eng.(frags.).

•15606.5 *Amend date*: 1522.]

•p. 62² **Lily, W.** *Following* 15610, *add to 'See also' references*: 3306(*A*).

•15610.6 *Correct collation*: A–H⁴ I⁶.

Add new entry:
◦15622.8 —[Anr. ed.] 4° in 8's. *assignes of F. Flowar*, 1593. L¹³ (duplicates of 4 leaves, in bdg. of P.2.36).

•15623 *Add before locations*: Ent. to T. Dawson and T. Stirrop 18 ja. 1597.

•15633.4 *Begin SR entry*: ?Ent. to R. Dexter 30 de. 1591; ent. to Dawson ... *Add note*: *See* also 21060.5(*A*3).

•p. 64² *Following* 15633.8, *add to 'See also' references for 'Lily's Grammar'*: 3770b.5, 4863.5, 4867, 6232, 12183, 15374.2, 15374.5, 21060.5(*A*3), 23277.5.

•15635 *Correct format*: 4° in 6's.

Add new heading and cross-reference:
•p. 64² **Linche, Richard.** The fountaine of ancient fiction. [*Tr.*] R. Linche. 1599. *See* 4691.
—*See* also Lynche, R.

•p. 65¹ **Lincoln,** *Diocese*. *Add cross-reference*:
—A briefe homily, ... To be vsed throughout the diocesse of Lincolne. 1580. *See* 5684.5.

•15672 *Begin imprint*: [*Edinburgh?* or *St. Andrews?*

•15685.5 *Correct location*: O(A1, Q8, X2, Mm4–8 only, ...

•15686, 15686.3, 15686.7, 15687.3, 15688, 15689.5: Juel-Jensen copies now = O.

Add new entry:
•15686.5 —[Anr. ed., w. 'Third edition' on A3ʳ.] 8°. *J. R*[*oberts*] *f. N. Ling*, 1604. O(imp.).

•15687 *For* [1608?] *read*: [1610?]

•15693.5 *In the supplied imprint delete all 3 names; it should read only*: [i.e. *London?*] 1556.

•15697 *Begin imprint*: *imp. G. ...*

Add new heading:
p. 67¹ **Little, Clement.** *See* Bookplates.

Add new heading:
p. 67¹ **Littleton,** *Sir* **Edward.** *See* Bookplates.

Add new entry:
•15731.3 —[Anr. ed.] 8°. (*in æd. T. Bertheleti*,) [1536?] HD.
A–U⁸ X⁴; ff. 164. The HD tp has had the false date: 'M. D. XIX.' hand-stamped below the title.

•15731.5 *Add location*: Taussig. *Add note*: (Formerly also 15761.6)

•15750 *Delete*: F.

•15758 *Continue note*: This and the next have a table by I. L.

•15761.6 *Cancel entry*; = 15731.5. (The Sotheby's copy had been Herbert's and clearly lacked the colophon; it was bd. w. the Redman, 1532 ed. of Old Tenures (23882)).

•15793 *Delete*: [Pars estivalis.] *For* [Pp3ʳ:] *read*: 2 vols. *Correct date*: 1505 ([P.H.:] 1 non. jy.; [P.E.:] 2 non. au.)) *Add location*: WOR(lacks last 2 leaves of P.E.).

•15805.9 *Amend imprint*: [*Rouen?* c. 1506.]

Add new entry:
•15809.5 [Anr. ed.] 2 vols. 8°. [*Rouen?*] (1511 [P.H.:] (7 kl'. oc.); [P.E.:] (15 kl'. se.)) Lord Kenyon(imp.).

•15814 Private P.H. copy now = L.

•15819 Lord Kenyon's copy now = L².

15826 *Add note*: The Psalter collates a–q⁸, 40 lines to a column. C has substituted the Psalter from a different ed., collating a–q⁸, 38 lines to a column, like 15810, 15811.5, and 15815. It is a different setting from those three and is unique in having g8ᵛ, col. 1, last line beginning: 'Adesto ...'

Add new entry:
•15827.5 Portiforiu̲ seu breuiariu̲ ad vsum ecclesie Sarisburie̲sis. [Pars estivalis.] 8°. (*Parisijs, in ed. J. kaerbriand, eiusdem necnõ J. petit impensis*,) 1530 (fb.) EX.

15836 *Add note*: Only the P.H. tp is dated 1554; both colophons and the P.E. tp are dated 1555.

•15847.3 *Amend date*: c. 1487. *Add location*: HER(12 leaves, in bdg. of I.1.10). *Continue note*: *See Library* 4 (1982): 411, no. 2.

•15854 *Amend date*: [c. 1487.]

•15861 For *Officium Novum*. read: *Officia Nova*.

Add new entry:
•15861.3 [Another supplement to the Sanctorale. Ends:] Feliciter finiunt Festum visitationis beate Marie virginis secundum usum Ebor ... 8°. [*York*,] (*per U. Mylner, commemorantem* [sic] *in Cimiterio Ministerii Sancti Petri*, [1514?] HER(deposit, 2 imp. copies of halfsheet B).
See The Book Collector 30 (1981): 216–24.

•15867 *Amend date*: 1476.

•15868 *Amend date*: 1479?

•15871 *Amend date*: c. 1484.

•15872 *Amend date*: c. 1484.

•15903 *In imprint* read: *venales ... ap.* [*H. Jacobi a. J. Pelgrim*,]

•15932.5 *Correct holdings*: (6 sheets and 2 halfsheets, all imp.). *Continue note*: These come from at least 3 and possibly more eds., e.g. E8ᵛ of 2 of the sheets end respectively in the 3rd and the 9th Hours of the Cross; F1ʳ of another sheet begins in the Salve Regina, followed on F2ʳ by the 15 Oes of St. Bridget. Of the remaining sheets one has no sig. surviving, and the others are signed N, o; the halfsheets are S2,3,6,7 and T1,4,5,8.

•15936 *Amend date*: [1525?] *Continue note*: From the state of some of the cuts this is a little later than 15941, which shares other cuts (e.g. Hodnett 551, 562) with 15934, dated 1523. L(C.161.f.2(98)) has quire D only of an ed. paginary with 15936 but with cuts in a still later state than 15948, dated 1526; it has 'D' of sig. D1 under 'an' of 'euangelistã'. The order and dates should prob. be: 15934: 1523, 15941: [1524?], 15936: [1525?], 15948: 1526, unique quire D: [1528?]

•15941 *Amend date*: 1524? *Continue note*: ... 15936 and (*A*3).

•15951 *In* LC *delete*: 2, 1 (LC has only a single imp. copy.)

•15963 *Delete*: L^4. (which is actually 15968)

•15994 Lord Kenyon's copy now = L^2.

•15996 *In imprint* for [*R. Faques?*] read: [*France?*]

16002a *Add note*: The Inglis copy was sold at Sotheby's, 11 June 1900, lot 601, bought by Ellis, untraced. The tp was lacking and prob. supplied from a facs. of 16001 sq. The text sheets prob. belonged to 15971.

•16009 *Continue note*: *See* also 5871.9(***A***).

•16017.5 *Amend imprint*: [*W. Copland?* c. 1545?] *Continue note*: *See* also 16030(***A***3).

•16021 *Delete*: C^2 *and* 155 *in the Hoskins reference.*

Add new entry:

•16021.3 —[A variant, w. colophon to pt. 2:] (*W. Bonham*,) [1542?] C^2(frag. of pt. 1 and all of pt. 2, Sinker 95). Hoskins 155.

•16030 *Continue note*: This has 17 lines per page. C(in Syn. 2.50.1) also has C^8 only of another 17-line ed.; in both, the Hours begin on $C1^r$ but 16030 has the last line on this page beginning: 'shall be.' while the frag. has: 'vnto me'. App. the only other 17-line ed. is 16017.5(***A***3 note), but in it the Hours begin on $E7^v$.

•16038 *Substitute this note*: Collates a^8 $*^8$ A–T^8.

•16039 *Amend location*: LINC(K^8 only, w. colophon). *Substitute this note*: LINC is bd. w. the sheets of anr. ed. or eds., lacking tp and collating: a^8 A^8 b–h^8 I^8. The text beginning on $K1^r$ duplicates that on $I6^v$ ff.

•16043.5 Private copy now = L.

Add new entry:

•16050.7 [The primer in English.] 8°. [*John Wyer*, c. 1550.] L (3 pp. of Laudes, in bdg. of C.131.aa.3 = STC 11383).
19 lines. On the other side are pr. the tp and 5 other pp. of A outer forme of 2985.3(***A***).

•16052 *Amend date*: [1549?]

•16055 *Delete*: L(2). (Originally an error for O(2).)

•16067.5 *Continue note*: ... 16061 and 16067.7(***A***3).

Add new entry:

•16067.7 —[Anr. ed.] *Latin*. 8°. [*London*, c. 1555.] Lord Kenyon (imp.). Hoskins 206.
Collates A–I^8 K^4; the canticle: 'Ego dixi ...' begins on $I4^r$ line 18, like 16061, but line 1 begins: 'tasti' whereas 16061 begins: 'sti'; cf. also 16067.5 and other eds. noted there.

•16095.5 *Continue imprint*: [*St. Omer*,]

•16098.3 *Continue imprint*: [*St. Omer*,]

Add new entry:

•16101.7 The primer or offi‹ce› ... in ‹English.› 12°. [*Rouen*,] *J. Cousturier*, 1638. Crundale Rectorial Library(tp def., deposited at Wye College, Wye, near Ashford, Kent).

•16102.5 *Correct holdings*: (2 imp. sheets). *Add note*: 21 lines, no headlines; quire E retains its signature, followed by the catch title: 'Ebor.'

•16118 *In imprint* for *P. Violette* read: *R. Auzoult?*

•16138 *In imprint* after [*Paris*, add: *U. Gering a.*

•16144 *At beginning of imprint* add: [*Rouen? E. Hardy?*]

•16148 Lord Kenyon's copy now = L^2.

•16150 *Amend imprint*: ... *le Roux f.*] *M. Datier*, [*London*,] 1543.

•16165 *In Duff reference for* 323 *read*: 321.

•16169 *In imprint* after *de worde* add: [*in Westminster*]; after *morin* delete: [*both in London*]; after *leueti* read: [*both in Paris*]

•16176 *Add location*: L^2(frags.).

•16194 *In imprint* after (*Rothomagi*,) add: [*P. Olivier? f.*]

•16196 *Add location*: BTU.

Add new entry:

•16205.3 Missale ad vsum insiginis [*sic*] ac preclare ecclesie Sar. 4° in 8's. *in alma Parisiorum acad.*, (*per F. Regnault*,) 1526 (1527 (27 jy.)) A^2.YK(XI.L.16).
Reissued in 16208 with app. a cancel sheet for +1,2,7,8.

•16208 *Add note*: A reissue of 16205.3(***A***3).

•16213 *In imprint* for *imp*. read: *suptib⁹*

•16228 *In line 4 add*: Duff 336.

•16253 *Amend date*: [1481.]

•16259.3 *Continue note*: London, College of Arms has an imp. sheet of a similar, possibly earlier ed. in which $M1^v$ line 9 ends: 'brachiu' while YK has 'brachiuȝ'.

16259.7 *Continue note*: C has an imp. 20-line ed. (Rit.e.451.2) similar to HD, but C has lower-case signatures so that the 1st Canticle is on s7. It was also prob. pr. by de Worde and is possibly later than HD.

•p. 89 *Add new series*: 8/9.5 | 1600/1 | 16324.4(***A***3) | A–Z^8 Aa–Nn^8 | $E2^r$ | $Aa1^r$ (sub tp) | $Z7^v$; $Nn8^v$

•p. 89 *In series* 8/10 *correct Psalter*: $Aa1^r$ (sub tp); *correct Godly Prayers*: $\&3^r$; $Nn8^v$

p. 90 *Extend series 16/7 to include*: 1596 16321a.5(***A***)

•p. 90 *In series* 16/13 *correct collation*: $*^8$ B–Y^8

°p. 90 *Extend series 24/3 to include*: [1614] 16342.7(***A***3)

•p. 90 *Begin series 24/4 with*: 1615 16346

•16272 *Delete*: CB. (It belongs at 16273.)

•16285a *Add location*: $CANT^2$. *In note after* Act 5 *delete*: ? (present in $CANT^2$) *Continue note*: $CANT^2$ has C2 in the same setting as 16285 sq., with 'C' under 'ak' of 'awake'.

16291 *Continue note*: The C copy mentioned above also has, inserted after πA11, quires $ππA^2$ $πB^8$ as in 16292a (copy 4), w. Almanack beginning 1561 on $πB1^v$.

•16293 *In locations for* Bernard *read*: Barnet

•16302.5 Goyder copy now = L.

•16303.5 Harmsworth-Sotheby's copy now = ILL(Baldwin 4989, lacks all before A8 in pt. 1).

•16306.2 Seven Gables copy now = COR.

Add new entry:

•16309.5C —[Anr. ed.] 4° in 8's. *C. Barker*, [1582?] L(Davis P853)†.
1 col., B.L., ending Kk4; Heth 12, prob. between 12.3 (16309.2) and 12.5 (16309.6). 'C' of sig. C1 is under 'll' of 'shall'.

•16311 L(destroyed) copy now replaced: L(imp., bd. w. 2466.9 (***A***)).

Add new entry:

•16312.7 —[Anr. ed.] 4° in 8's. *Deputies of C. Barker*, [1588?] L(imp.)†.
1 col., B.L., ending Kk4; Heth 16. 'C' of sig. C1 is under 'ar' of 'roare'. Date suggested by the state of tp border McK. & F. 165. It is possible that the lost Harmsworth copy at 16314.5 belongs to this ed.

Add new entry:

16321a.5 —[Anr. ed.] 16° in 8's. (*Deputies of C. Barker*, 1596.) O^3(imp.).
1 col., B.L., ending Ss8; series 16/7. The Catechism begins $Y8^r$ and has as line 3 of the heading: 'of euerie childe, before hee'; in the C^2 copy of 16315, the only other extant copy of this series yet known, the comparable line is: 'euery childe, before hee he [*sic*, for 'be']'.

•16324.4 *Add new entry*:
—[Anr. ed.] 8°. *R. Barker*, 1600 (1601.) CANT.
1 col., B.L., ending Nn8; series 8/9.5(*A*3).

•16325.3 *Add location*: O(lacks πA^{4} A^{8})*.

◦16333.3 *Add new entry*:
—[Anr. ed.] 24° in 12's. *R. Barker*, 1608. C^{2}.
1 col., rom., ending P12; series 24/3.

•16337a.5 *Add location*: E(Psalter only).;

•16342.7 *Substitute this entry*:
—[Anr. ed.] 24° in 12's. [*R. Barker*, 1614.] L(lacks tp, bd. w. 2546.5(*A*)).
1 col., rom., ending P12; series 24/3. The imprint is supplied from the misdescribed Sotheby's copy, which cannot be traced. The L ed. is bd. w. 1613 Psalms and cannot be earlier than that year because of the State Prayers. The next series, 24/4, begins in 1615 (16346).

•16349.3 *In imprint* read: *Bill, deputies a. assignes*

•16349.7 *In imprint* read: *Bill, deputies a. assignees*

16353 *Continue note*: The Psalter sub tp varies: imprint names *R. Barker and J. Bill* or *R. Barker* alone; both at HN.

•16369.9 *Add new entry*:
—[Anr. ed.] 8°. *B. Norton a. J. Bill*, 1627. Agecroft Hall, Richmond, Virginia.
1 col., B.L., ending Z8; series 8/11.

•16432 *Correct format*: 8° in 4's.

•16439 *Substitute this note*: Printed as pt. of the Bible 2349 sq. though many copies, e.g. HD, have been detached from Bibles and are bd. only w. the Psalms, 2746.

•p. 102^{1} LITANY. *Add to references in headnote*: 20.2, 3009 sqq., 10617,

•16481 *Delete*: LINC.

•16504.3 *Add new entry*:
A prayer for the present estate, to be vsed in churches at the end of the letanye, on Sundayes, Wednesdayes, and Frydayes, through the whole realme. 8° in 4. (*R. Jugge a. J. Cawood*,) [1562.] HER(4 imp. copies, in bdg. of N.1.iii).
Tp in border McK. & F. 103. Pr. 2 copies per sheet by halfsheet imposition. For the complete text *see* W. K. Clay, *Liturgical Services*, Parker Society, 1847, pp. 458–9, 476–7.

•16506.9 *Add new entry*:
—[Anr. ed.] 8°. (*R. Jugge a. J. Cawood*,) [1563.] C^{3} (D–F^{8} = 'Homylye' only).
Homily not divided.

•16510.5 *Correct format*: s.sh.fol. *Amend date*: [1573.] *Amend location*: C^{8}(bd. in 1st section of B.3.29). *Add note*: Solempne's imprint and the date 1572 [o.s.] are given in MS. at the bottom.

•16512 *For last sentence of note substitute this*: C, HN have added E–F^{4}, app. pr. by H. Bynneman, w. 'A godlie Admonition' beginning on E2^{r} and w. F3^{v}–4^{v} blank. HN has orig. sub tp on E1^{r}: A discourse containing many wonderfull examples of Gods indignation, *C. Barker*, 1580, and report of earthquake on E1^{v}; C has only the stub of E1. The admonition and report are reprinted from 11987 without mention of Golding's authorship.

•16513 *For last sentence of note substitute this*: C^{3}, SAL(P.7.10(h)), F have added E–F^{4} partly reset and reimposed, w. E1^{r} blank, report on E1^{v}, admonition beginning on E2^{r}, and H. Bynneman's device, McK. 119, on F3^{v}. In at least C^{3} copy E1 is a cancel; SAL lacks E1,4.

16524 *Add note*: Tp varies: with (HN) or without (C) 'and commended … &c.' in the title.

•16526 *In title for* hir *read*: her *Correct format*: 1/2 sh.fol. *For* L^{5}. *read*: L. *Add note*: There are 2 settings; line 1 of text ends: 'vn-' (O, COL) or 'vnto' (L).

•16540 *Continue note*: *See* also 8787.

•16542 *Continue note*: *See* also 8812.

•16543 *Continue note*: *See* also 8833.

•16547 *Amend date*: 1628 [o.s.] *Continue note*: F4^{v} has a collect for the 1st day in Lent [18 Feb.]; observance of this is required in 8915.

•16547.5 *Continue note*: F4^{r-v} has a collect for 'our Armies … at Sea and Land'; this is the earlier version of the text, observance of which is required in 8889.

•16551 *Amend date*: c. 1616? *Add note*: L^{5} has H. Dyson's note: 'Tempore Jacobi regis'; this is possibly connected w. 8538 but might have been pr. at any time during James I's reign.

•16553 *Continue note*: *See* also 9075.

•16559 *Continue note*: *See* also 9170.

•16560 *Add note*: *See* also 16573(*A*3). *Also add cross-reference immediately below the note*:
Catecismo. (La forma de las oraciones. Con la manera de administrar los sacramentos.) 1596. *See* 4391.5.

•16561a.5 *Add new entry*:
—[Anr. ed.] 8°. [*Geneva*,] (*Z. Durant*, 1560.) O^{21}(imp.).
Collates a–z^{8} Aa–Nn^{8}. O^{21} lacks a1 (Form of prayers tp), g6 (Psalms tp) and Nn8; the imprint is from the Catechism tp on Bb3^{r}. Contents as in 16563; To Reader on g2^{r}–5^{r} is dated Geneva, 6 Mar. 1560 and specifies 'this fourth edition'.

•16571a *Add locations*: Amsterdam U. Ghent U.

•16571a.5 *Add new entry*:
—[Anr. ed.] 16° in 8's. [*Emden*?] 1560. AMVU. Brussels RL. Groningen U. Utrecht U(stolen).
For further details of this and the following *see Kerkhistorische Studiën* 7 (1956): 4–6.

•16572 *Add location*: Middelburg Provincial Lib. *Add note*: Tp date in roman numerals.

Add new entries:

•16572.1 —[Anr. ed.] 8°. [*Emden, E. van der Erve*,] 1563. L. Berlin NL. Ghent U. Utrecht U.
Tp date in arabic numerals.

•16572.2 —[Anr. ed.] 8°. *Antwerpen, J. Troyens* [*a.*] (*Delft, C. Jansz*,) 1582. Amsterdam U.

•16572.3 *Add note*: The types and title-page border (McK. & F. 135) are the same as in 6003.5, and P. Angelin may have been involved in the present publication also.

•16573 *Correct bracketed information*: [Derived from Calvin's liturgy (cf. 16560) as adapted by V. Poullain for Strassburg.] *Amend imprint*: *Londres*, [*T. Gaultier*?] *Add note*: Has an initial 'Q' as in 4391, and one of its types (73 mm. roman) is also used in 4391. It has, in addition, 54 mm. roman and italic types.

•16575 *Add location*: Utrecht U.

•16578.5 *Amend location*: … 2996.5; deposited at E).

•16587 *In note for* 2499.5 *read*: 2499.9.

•16594 *Add note*: (11724 is pt. of this)

•16613 *Add note*: A copy belonging to Dr. Saul B. Gilson, New York City, has the orig. tp with Islip's large device, McK. 324, replaced by one with the same imprint but with an ornament with winged torsos, prob. pr. [*Amsterdam*? after 1660.]

•p. 107^{2} *Add new heading*:
Livonia. A true and lamentable reporte of Livonia, (commonly called Lyffelande). 1603. *See* 19766(*A*3).

•16617 *Continue imprint*: *sold* [*by T. Cadman*,]

•16629 *For* [Anr. ed.] 12°. *read*: [Anr. issue, w. cancel tp, w. imprint:]

•p. 108^{2} *Add new heading*:
Lo., Ro., *ed. See* 12635.

•16663 *Add note*: Answered by 12095.

•16670 *Add format*: 4°.

•16673 Lord Latymer's copy now = John Wolfson, New York City.

•p. 109^{2} **Loe, W.,** *the Elder. Add cross-reference at end*:
—*See* also 15115(*A*3).

p. 109^{2} *Add new heading*:
Lodington, William. *See* Bookplates.

•p. 109^{2} *Add new heading*:
Loftus, John. *See* Bookplates.

•16693 *Add note*: Derived in part from P. Nicolettus (Paul of Venice) and J. Buridanus's Summulae of Aristotle's Organon; *see Medioevo* 4 (1978): 93–9.

•p. 109^{2} **Loiseau de Tourval.** *Add cross-references*:
—*ed. See* 13142.
—*tr. Add*: 10840, 14408, 21024.
—*See* also 11374.

16699 *Add note*: This is an anon. report of Loncq's expedition. It also includes a letter by D. van Waerdenburgh, of which a different trans. is pr. in 25219.

•16704.3 *At end of title add*: M. D. LI. *In imprint for* 1551 *read*: [1554? really *T. East*, 1575?] *Continue note*: Cawood is styled printer to the Queen's Majesty as in 16701 and undoubtedly did print a Marian ed. of an Edwardian text, both of which are now lost. The present item is considerably later and has the same woodcut 'F' as 16708.

•p. 110^{2} *After* 16718.3 *add cross-reference*:
—Certaine articles concerning reliefe of the poor, to be executed in London. 1599. *See* 9494.9.

•p. 110^{2} *After* 16718.5 *add cross-reference*:
—The effect of the act (for reliefe of the poore). For execution [in London.] 1602. *See* 9499.

•p. 110^{2} *After* 16719 *add cross-reference*:
—Orders and articles ... appointing what kinds of bread are to be made [etc. 31 Jan. 1604 (o.s.)] [1605.] *See* 8366.

•16724 *Amend imprint date*: 1610?] *Amend note*: Although Cambell ... 1608–09, Jaggard was not appointed Printer to the City until 17 Dec. 1610 (*TBS* 14 (1915–17): 193), and the proclamation app. represents a reprint of a lost original.

•p. 111^{1} *After* 16725.3 *add cross-reference*:
—By the maior. Unto the wardmote inquest. [Endorsing a request for alms for Christ's Hospital. In verse. 1613.] *See* 5207.7(*A*).

•16733.7 *Continue note*: For related price lists *see* 9009.

•16735 *Correct imprint*: *R. Young*, [1634.]

16739.5 *After* Ent. *add*: to J. Wolfe 14 jy. 1593; to Windet ...

•16743.2 *Continue title*: With a relation of many visitations by the plague. *Before location add*: 'Relation' ent. 27 jy. *Add note*: A later version of the text is printed in 20823 sq.

16743.4 *After* Ent. *add*: to J. Wolfe 14 jy. 1593;

Add new entry:
•16743.6E —From the [ ] to the [ ] 1613. s.sh.4°. [*London*, 1613.] C^{2}(2, bd. after F3 of STC 12158.5, one filled out in MS. for 16–23 Sept., the other for 14–21 Apr. w. the year altered by pen to 1614).

16743.9 *After* Ent. *add*: to J. Wolfe 14 jy. 1593; to Windet ...

•p. 113^{2} **London**—BILLS OF MORTALITY. *In the last sentence of cross-references at the end, before* 18248 *add*: 14492(*A*3).

•p. 113^{2} *After* 16748 *add cross-reference*:
—The city of London, as it was before the burning of St. Pauls steeple. [c. 1565?] *See* 11930.2.

16753 *After title add*: [*Ed.* H. Holland.]

•p. 113^{2} *After* 16754 *add cross-reference*:
—Civitas Londinum. [Woodcut map. 1633?] *See* 194.5.

Add new entry:
16763.3 —[Anr. ed.] The othe of euerie free man, of the cittie of London. s.sh.4°. [*J. Windet? f.*] *J. Wolfe*, [c. 1595.] HN.

•p. 114^{2} *After* 16768 *add cross-reference*:
—A very wonderful and strange myracle shewed in London. 1574. *See* 19936.5(*A*3).

•16768.32 *Add note*: *See* 8709.

London, *College of Heralds. Add new entry and cross-references*:
•16768.34 —You are to returne a certificate to the Office of Armes, neere Pauls chaine in London; of the time of the death, marriage, issue, ... of [ ] ... before the day of [ ] next or a montion [*sic*, for 'monition'] will be awarded against you in the Earle Marshals Court. Dated [ ]. *obl.*slip (6.6 × 14.4 cm.) [*London*, 1637.] L(Harl.MS. 2180, fol. 143^{v}).
With explanatory MS. 'the forme of the Tickett or proces out of the Earle marshalls Court 1637'. For a regulation requiring this kind of information *see* 8581.
—[Announcement by the Norroy King of Arms. 1578.] *See* 11108.
—[Direction to the Clarenceux King of Arms. 1568.] *See* 8001.5(*A*3).
—To all the [ ] of the hundred of [ ] [Summons to a heraldic visitation. 1634.] *See* 19846.5.

•16769 *Continue note*: Ordered enforced in 9063.

•16773 *For* TEX. *read*: TEX^{2}.

•16775 *For* L^{39} *read*: L^{39}(W).

•16776 *For* L^{39} *read*: L^{39}(W). *For* TEX. *read*: TEX^{2}.

•p. 115^{2} **London,** *Diocese of. Add cross-references*:
—An admonition to be redde in the churches. [1564.] *See* 16704.7.
Add at end:
—*See* also 3280.3, 9175b.5 sqq., 9182.

p. 115^{2} *Add new heading*:
London, *Doctors' Commons. See* Bookplates.

Add new entries:
•16777.1 **London,** *Dutch Church.* Theses seu articuli è sacrę scripturę fontibus desumpti, ex quibus ... diutini in ecclesia Christi Belgio-germanica Loninensi dissidij causa perspici. Sett-artikelen wt grondt der heyliger schrifft genomen: [etc.] *Lat. a. Dutch.* 8°. *ghedruckt to London by H. Wykes*, 1568. L(tp only, Harl.5919/241).

•16777.1A —[Anr. ed., in *Lat. a. Eng.*] Theses seu articuli ... Propositions or articles drawen out of the very fountaynes of holy scripture, wherby ... the cause of continuall variaunce in the dutche congregation ... in London may appeare. 8° in 4's. (*R. Jugge*,) [1570?] L^{13}.; NY^{5}.
Collates K–N^{4}, and other copies sometimes occur as an appendix to 10391.5, q.v. The L^{13} tp has a cropt MS. inscription: 'Jugge. 13 Noueb 15‹70?› Preface by the ministers of the Dutch Church is dated 18 Sept. 1568. The text is a letter from the ministers of Geneva containing 32 propositions, dated 25 June 1568 and signed by T. de Bèze and 18 others.

•16777.14 *Add location*: L^{5}(Lemon 594). *Continue note*: Also erroneously entered as Wing A 3296.

•p. 116^{1} **London,** *Goldsmiths. Add cross-reference*:
—[Petition to Charles I.] 1628. *See* 4471(*A*).

Add new heading:
•p. 116[1] **London,** *Gold-Wire-Drawers*. A true declaration of the state of the manufacture of gold and silver threed. [Appeal to the Privy Council.] [1623?] *See* 6456.
—*See* also 8711.

Amend heading and add new 1st entry:
•16778.7 **London,** *Merchant Taylors*.This indenture witnesseth ... [Apprenticeship indenture.] 1/2 sh.*obl*.fol. [*London*, 1611?] L(C.106.cc.3).
Pr. in civilité; in last line 'James' is xylographic.

•16778.8–.10 *Correct format*: 1/2 sh.*obl*.fol.

•16779.12 *Continue note*: Regarding petitions to parliament rather than the king *see* 11460, 20792.7.

Add new heading:
•p. 116[2] **London,** *Price Currents*. [Blank forms for listing commodity prices. 1608, etc.] *See* 9175z.5 sqq.

Add new entry:
•16786.3 —The humble petition of the stationers, printers and booke-sellers of London. [Requesting 'your Honors fauourable furtherance' of a bill to reform abuses in printing by limiting the number of master printers, etc.] 1/2 sh.fol. [*R. Field*, 1604?] L[5](Lemon 312).
Erroneously dated 1641? by Lemon and followed by Wing H 3580. Refers to the Star Chamber decree (23 June 1586) as 'aboue 17. yeares past' and ineffective and is prob. related to 'an Act for the good of the Company' which R. Field and others were appointed to pursue on 27 Mar. 1604; *see Court-Book C*, p. 6. The 'Honors' addressed may have been the Corporation of London.

•16786.4 *Add after date*: Ent. to R. Badger 4 oc. 1621.

•16786.8 *In last line of note for* 152–3 *read*: 52–3.

•16786.18 *Continue note*: *See* also 9082, 9097.

16790 *Continue note*: While both sections of 16790 have Pynson's colophon and sigs. w. arabic numerals, the prelims. (A[4]) have sigs. w. roman numerals and tp border McK. & F. 19 and may have been pr. by [*R. Redman*? 1532?]

•16794.5 *In imprint* for [*T. Berthelet*, read: [*J. Byddell*,

•16800 *Continue title*: ... Learne from a devill. [An attack on jesuits, *tr*. from one of their order: A. Contzen, Politicorum libri decem, bk. 2, chaps. 18–19.]

•16809 *Begin imprint*: [*T. Dawson f.*]

•16811 *In heading after* issue *add*: w. prelims. and G2 cancelled,

•16820.5–21 *Amend imprints*: [*Canterbury, J. Mychell*,

•16827 *Add after date*: Ent. to H. Toy 1562–63 (Arber I.200, where the 'title' given is from the dedic. heading).

Add new heading:
•p. 119[1] **Loss, Lucas.** *See* 24040.5(*A*3).

•p. 119[1] **Louis XIII.** The apologies. *In cross-reference for* 13124 *read*: 13122.5.

Turn entry into a cross-reference:
•16829.5 —Articles made [Sept. 1603] ... touching jesuits. 1612. Now = 13121.5.

•16831 *Begin imprint*: [*W. White*]

•p. 119[2] *After* 16844 *add cross-reference*:
—The [French] kings prohibition to use any traffique with Spaine. 1625. *See* 5029.

•p. 119[2] **Louis I,** *Prince*. *Add cross-reference at end*:
—*See* also 5042.

Add new entry:
16857.9 —Index postillanum [*sic*]. A briefe and plaine direction for the use of postils. 12°. *f. J. Boler*, 1632. Ent. to A. Hebb 14 no. 1631. C[5].

•p. 120[1] **Lover.** *In cross-reference following* 16862.9:
—A lovers complaint being ... *read*: [c. 1615.] *See* 5610.5.

•16864a.11 *In imprint only the date should be in square brackets. Amend* M[3] *location*: (imp.).

•16913 *In imprint* for *Allde*, read: *All-de*, *Add note*: Engr. tp only, w. angel w. cross at top left.

•16914 *Add note*: The cancel tp is engr., a copy in reverse of that in 16913, w. angel w. cross at top right.

•16915 *Add letterpress title*: Of prayer and meditation. *In imprint* for *E(liz.)* read: *Eliz*. *Substitute this note*: Has added engr. tp, an altered state of that in 16913: Granada's meditations. The 7th impression. *E. All-de, solde by R. Allot*, 1634.

Add new entry:
•16916.2 —A paradice of prayers: containing the purity of devotion, and meditation. 12°. *J. R[oberts] f. M. Law*, 1605. L.
See 16916.3 for the SR entry.

Add new entry:
•16922a.9 —[An extract.] A spiritual doctrine. Of prayers and meditations. Taken out of Lewes de Granado, for the daily use of the meanest capacitie. 24° in 8's. *Dowaie, H. Taylor*, 1624. Douai PL(X 1624/20).

Add new heading:
•p. 122[2] **Luján, Pedro de.** *See* 24076(*A*3).

Add new heading:
•p. 122[2] **Lumley,** *Sir* **Martin.** *See* Bookplates.

•16943 *In imprint* for [*by P. Nevill*,] read: [*by S. Browne*,]

Add new entry:
•16947.3 —[Anr. ed.] 8°. (*J. C[harlewood] f. H. Car a. J. Preston*, 1584.) NLW(imp.).

Add new entry:
•16956.3 —[A variant, w. imprint:] [*G. Robinson*] *f. E. White*, [1586.] C[5](lacks table, Gg–Hh[4] Ii[2]).
Text begins on B1[r] like 16956. Film of C[5] copy on Univ. Microfilms reel 1799 ('16957.5').

•16957.5 For [*J. Charlewood*?] read: [*E. Allde*] *Delete*: C[5]. *Continue note*: Text begins on A4[v]; cf. 16956.3(*A*3).

•16979.7 *After* Hollybush *delete*: [*pseud*. ... Coverdale.]

•16983 *At beginning of imprint add*: [*London? J. Mychell f.*]

•16983.5 *Substitute this note*: Loosely derived and enlarged from Luther's Wider den falsch gennanten geystlichen stand des Bapst, 1522.

•16984 *Amend end of imprint*: ... *Straten*, 1546?] *Add note*: Although the end of the text is dated 1543, this may be a misprint or possibly the date of the trans.

•16985 *For* W[ilkinson] *read*: W[atkinson]. *Amend date*: [c. 1580.]

•p. 124[1] **Luther.** *Following* 17000a *add to 'See also' references*: 11313,

•17003.3 *Amend imprint*: [*Paris*,] *sumpt. H. François, Londini*, 1579. *Add note*: In place of the London imprint, copies at C[2], CU, have: *Parisiis, ap. J. Parant*.

Add new heading:
•p. 124[2] **Lydd, Kent.** *See* 7988.5, 7995.4.

•17009 *Amend date*: 1476.]

•17013 *Amend date*: [1534?]

•17015 *Amend date*: 1483.]

•17019 *Amend date*: 1476.]

•17023–4 *Amend dates*: 1483.]

•17030.9 *Amend date*: [1534–36?]

•17031 *Add note*: Reprinted in 5075.

•17037.5 *Amend date*: 1501?]

•125^2 **Lydgate.** *Following* 17038 *add to 'See also' references*: 12138.

•17060 Lord Latymer's copy now = John Wolfson, New York City.

•17062 *For* [Anr. ... *Lownes*] *read*: [A variant, w. imprint:]

•17077 For [*E. Allde*?] read: [*R. Bradock*] Lord Latymer's copy now = John Wolfson, New York City.

•17078 *Begin entry*: —[A variant, w. imprint:] [*R. Bradock*] *f.* ...

•17090 For [*J. Roberts*] read: [*G. Simson*]

•17097 *In the note after* 11112, *add*: 13037,

Add new heading:
•p. 127^2 **Lyndsell, William.** *See* 7529(*A*).

Add new heading:
•p. 127^2 **Lynolde, Edmund.** *See* 4930.5.

•17121 *Add note*: For an earlier ed. of the Greek text *see* 6577.7.

•17122 *Delete*: D^2. *and replace it with*: Kent U(lacks colophon).

p. 129^1 **M., A.** *Add cross-references*:
•—A breefe discourse of the taking of E. Campion. 1581. *See* 18264.
—Chruso-thriambos. 1611. *See* 18267.

•p. 129^1 **M., E.** *Add cross-reference*:
—*tr. See* 12108.

•p. 129^2 **M., H.** *Add cross-reference*:
—*tr. See* 7263.

•p. 129^2 **M., I.** or **J.** *Add cross-reference*:
—[Bookplate.] *See* Bookplates.

•17141 *Substitute this note*: By J. Monlas; this is a reissue of 18020 w. A1–B1 cancelled and replaced by A^4.

•17147 *Add after date*: ?Ent. to J. Tisdale 1561–62 as A new ballett after the tune of kynge Salomon. *Add note*: There are 2 eds.; last line begins: (i) 'Longe lyfe' (L^5) or (ii) 'Longe life' (L).

•p. 130^1 **M., R.** *Add cross-reference*:
—*See* also 12108.

Turn entry into a cross-reference:
•17148.7 **M., R.,** *Minister of Gods Word.* Three treatises religiously handled. 1603. = 17683a.5.

Add new heading:
•p. 130^1 **M., R. G. S. D.** The defence of contraries. 1593. *See* 6467.

17154 *Continue note*: Ordered burned 1 June 1599; *see* Arber III.677–8.

Add new headings:
p. 130^2 •**M., Th.** A short catechisme. 1597. *See* 1336.5.

M., Thomas. *See* Bookplates.

•17155.5 *Amend location*: E(deposit).

•17156.3 *Add location*: E(lacks tp).;

•17163.5 *In title for* setti *read*: sette

•17172 *Amend date and cross-reference*: [1552?] Now = 13175.13C.

•17173 *Amend date and cross-reference*: [1543?] Now = 13175.8C.

•p. 131^2 **Macropedius.** *Add cross-reference at end*:
—*See* also 3542.

•17181.5 *Add note*: For a trans. *see* 6842.

Add new entries:
•17181.7 **Magdeburg.** [Heading A1^r:] A briefe, and true relation of the taking in of Magdenburch, by the emperours, and the catholique leagues commandours, 10. Maye 1631. old stile. 4°. [*Germany*? 1631.] C^5 (Gg.6.32^4, bd. w. STC 12534.4).

•17181.9 —The faire city of Magdenburg, with fortifications. [As] it was besiedged by count Tilly. [Bird's-eye view, engr. by J. Droeshout, w. letterpress caption and key.] s.sh.fol. [*B. Alsop a. T. Fawcet*, 1631.] L(2, 1 in Dept. of P&D; 1 in C.133.c.1 = STC 23523, following p. 116 of pt. 1).; HN(in STC 13248.4).
See Hind II.350.

Add new heading:
•p. 131^2 **Mahon, Edward.** *See* 11943, 11944.

•17197.5 *Continue note*: Answered in 10857.7.

Add new heading:
p. 132^2 **Malet, John.** *See* Bookplates.

•17231 *In the note transpose locations.* (O has dedic. signed 'A. M.' and L the other.)

•17236 *Amend date*: [1557?]

•p. 133^2 **Man.** *After* 17238 *add cross-reference*:
—The young mans kinde reply. [c. 1630.] *See* pt. 2 of 5612.

•17238.5 *Continue imprint*: *a. Jonas Man*, *Add location*: O.

•p. 133^2 **Manchester.** The description. *In cross-reference for* 6772.5 *read*: 6768.3.

•17239.5 Dougan copy now = HN.

Add new heading:
p. 134^1 **Manfield, Thomas.** *See* Bookplates.

•17255 *Correct format*: s.sh.fol. *Amend imprint and add SR entry*: [*London*, 1562?] ?Ent. to T. Colwell 1561–62 as 'Thus goeyth the worlde now in these our Dayes &c.'

•17263 *In line 1 of note read*: ... 14566; 4816 is E1–F7 of this)

Add new entry:
•17265.7 —[Anr. ed.] 16° in 8's. [*English secret press*, 1596?] David Rogers(imp.).
+2^r has almanack for 1596–1606; Jesus Psalter sub tp is on 1st B1^r.

•17275.3 *Continue imprint*: [*St. Omer*,]

Add new heading:
•p. 135^2 **Maraffi, Bartolomeo,** *tr. See* 6758.

Add new entry:
17311.5 **Marckant, John.** [A notable instruction for all men to beware the abuses] of dice, wyne and women. [In verse.] s.sh.fol. *W. Griffith*, 1571. Ent. 1565–66. O^8 (title torn).
Beginning of title supplied from Griffith's 1st entry in SR; *see* Arber I.293, 296.

•17327 *At beginning of imprint add*: [*London*,] *Amend date*: [1530–32?]

•17359 *Add note*: Derived from Du Bellay's La vielle courtisanne.

•17387.3 *Add location*: L.;

•17395.3 O^3(E) copy now = L.

•p. 139^{1} **Marlorat.** *In 'See also' references at end delete*: 2957.7 *and add*: 10747.

•17445 *Delete*: L. (It belongs with the next.)

◦17445.5 *Add note*: The cancel tp is in 2 settings; in imprint: '*soulde*' (L, P) or '*solde*' (C).

•17450 *In imprint* for [*A. de Solempne*,] read: [really *Leeuwarden, P. H. van Campen*, *Begin note*: The imprint is false, and the former attribution to Solempne is erroneous; for a discussion of the real printer *see* Paul Valkema Blouw in *Quaerendo* (forthcoming).

•17453 After *pseud.* add: [i.e. J. Throkmorton.] *Continue note*: Answered in 5682. For an ineffective attempt to stifle the Marprelate faction *see* 8182.
Regarding the identification of 17453–17459 and other works as by Job Throkmorton *see* Leland H. Carlson, *Martin Marprelate Gentleman*, San Marino, [1981.]

•17459 *In imprint* for [*Haseley*? read: [*Wolston*?

•17460 *Move this cross-reference immediately after* 17459 *since it ushers in the Martinist tracts rather than attacks them.*

Add new heading:
•p. 140^{2} **Marraffi, Bartholomew.** *See* Maraffi, B. (*A*3).

•p. 140^{2} **Marshall, W.,** *ed. In 'tr.' references at end for* 10503.5, *read*: 10504,

•17486.5 *Add after date*: [a forgery; really *London*, 1600?]

•17488–8.3 *Continue imprints*: *sold* [*by W. Cotton*,]

•p. 141^{2} **Marston.** *Add to 'See also' references*: 4970.

17492 *Add note*: Tp varies: with 'epigrammatωn' as transcribed (O, HD) or 'epigrammaton' (C).

•17505 *In line 1 of note before* 13388 *add*: 11147,

•17507 *In date delete*: [c. 1597.] (1597 was a confusion with the date of the reprint of the 'Epistles' in 17504.)

Add new heading:
•p. 142^{1} **Martin, Richard,** *of Ipswich. See* Bookplates (*A*).

•17523 *Substitute this Hebrew*: מַפְתֵּחַ לְשׁוֹן הַקֹּדֶשׁ

•17526 *For* M. *read*: M^{2}. *Add note*: *See* also 3832.

Add new entry:
•17530.3 —[A variant, w. imprint:] *J. Beale f. R. Redmer*, 1612. SAL(imp.).

•p. 143^{1} *In cross-reference following* 17534, *for* 15847.5 *read*: 15791.5.

•17545 *Transfer here the note at* 17545.5.

•17558 *Add location*: HER(B1,2,5,6 only, in bdg. of B.IV.13). *Add note*: *See Library* 4 (1982): 411–13, but the cut is Hodnett 1506, not 156.

•17566.5 *Add note*: *See Library* 12 (1932): 420–8.

Add new entry:
•17568.5 —[Homily on Mary Magdalen. A2^{r} begins:] In this present solemnite or fest, when we had ordeyned & porposed, good deuout people, to speke vnto the audience of your charyte, [etc.] 4° in 8's. [*R. Pynson*, c. 1515?] LINC (A2–8, B1 only).

17576 *Add after date*: 'The seconde Edicon' ent. to H. Bynneman 3 no. 1580.

•17583 *Amend imprint*: *J. Harison* [*3*,] *sold* [*by J. Harrison 1*,]

•17584 *Begin imprint*: [*G. a. L. Snowdon*] (*f.*)

•17587 *In imprint* after *Falkner*, add: *Southwarke*,

•17597 *In note after* 4960, *add*: 11022.

•17601 *Add note*: Dido's song is reprinted in 6074.

•17622 *Continue note*: Regarding the suppression of an enlarged ed. in 1632 *see Court-Book C*, pp. 236–8.

•17624 *Add after date*: Ent. to Grismand a. J. Marriott 31 my.

◦17627 *Add note*: This has the same types as 24514(*A*3) and is prob. earlier than 17628.

•17640.5 *Continue note*: ... reset, w. headlines in smaller type than in quires H and K. One L copy has quire I in the orig. setting but wrongly perfected.

•p. 146^{1} **Massonius.** *The cross-references should be moved to Le Maçon, R.*

Add new entry:
•17651.5 **Matrimony.** The spirituall matrimonye bytwene Chryste and the soule. 16° in 8. (*Canterbury, J. Mychell*,) [1538–47?] L(5 imp. leaves: C.60.h.16, ff. 23, 26^{v}).

17653a *Before last sentence of note add*: Some copies omit the beginning of the errata on **3^{v}; both at C.

•17654a.5 *Add*: MIN. *here and delete it from* 17655.

•17669 *Continue note*: *See* Greg, *Register B*, p. 54.

•17671 *Add note*: For a related ballad *see* 11029.

Add new heading:
•p. 147^{2} **Mawe, Leonard,** *Bp. See* 10137.4C(*A*3).

17687 *For 1st sentence of note substitute this*: The title as transcribed is a cancel. HN now has 2 copies w. the cancel, 1 of which also has the orig. tp omitting 'Together with the Agony of Christ', i.e. not calling for the reissue of 17691 as pt. 2.

•17697 *Add location*: L.

•p. 148^{1} **Maxwell.** *At end delete 'See also* 17141*' reference*. (The work is by J. Monlas.)

•17720 *Amend date*: c. 1484.]

•17727 Lord Kenyon's copy was resold at Sotheby's, 27 Sept. 1988, lot 99, bought by Kraus.

•17730 *Delete*: L. *Add*: L^{2}.

Add new entries:
•17730.2 —[Anr. issue of pt. 1 w. cancel gen. tp:] A commentarie upon the whole New Testament. In three volumnes. The third, containing the seaven catholique epistles, and the Revelation. *T. Cotes f. J. Bellamie*, 1632. L(lacks gen. tp)*.LICH.
The 3rd vol., issued only in 4° as 17731.3 sq., is not present.

•17730.3 —[Anr. issue, w. cancel gen. tp, w. imprint:] *T. Cotes f. J. Grismond*, 1632. CHES.EX.

•17730.5 *Add locations*: CHES.EX.

•p. 149^{1} **Mayerne Turquet, T. de.** *Add cross-reference*: —*See* also 12581.

Add new heading:
•p. 149^{2} **Mayneriis, Maynus de.** *See* 6815.

•17758 *Delete*: CAL. (which actually has 17768).

17764 *Add note*: The end of the Mecare news is dated 26 Jan. 1597, and the compiler's name is given as James Drucateen.

•17764.5 *Correct format*: 1/2 sh.fol. *In imprint* read: ‹*Purfoot*? or *Petyt*?› *Add note*: In the 2nd Ashburnham sale at Sotheby, Wilkinson & Hodge, 10 Dec. 1897, lot 2549 (untraced frags. different from those at O), the publisher's name is given as 'Porefut', i.e. Purfoot; however, it is possible that Petyt is the Thomas in question since the news sheet is app. 4 years earlier than the first imprint with Purfoot's name clearly visible.

17770.7 *Add note*: Prob. pr. on 1 sheet together w. 10626.5.

•17776 *Substitute this imprint*: [*Canterbury, J. Mychell*, 1556?] *Add note*: With a prayer mentioning Queen Mary on F7v. The name of John Ledley (Lidley) appears at the end of prayers on D5v, and a version of some of the prayers in the present item is printed in the 2nd section of 4028.

•p. 151[1] **Melanchthon.** *Among 'ed.' references at end for* 5266.5 *read*: 5265.8 *and add*: 13612. *Among 'See also' references add*: 13213.

17810 *Add note*: This is more prob. pr. in the Netherlands, in which case it does not belong in STC. The Palinodia is tr. from 149.

17823 *Continue note*: In both HD copies of this and most copies of 17823.5 G3 is cancelled. It is present in the C copy of 17823.5 and contains T. Norton's 'reporte unto the Reader' w. a MS. note: 'An approbation ... unapprowed'.

Merlin. *Add new 1st entry*:

•17840.7 —[Treatise of Merlin.] 4° in 8's. [*Westminster, W. de Worde*, 1499?] O5(B2,7 only).; LC(B1,2,7,8 only, in bdg. of 5643).

31 lines to a page, in Duff's de Worde type 4. *See Library* 2 (1980): 73–6.

•17841 *Add*: —[Anr. ed.] *Delete*: O5, LC. *Add note*: 33 lines (quire A) or 32 lines (B–G) to a page.

•17841.3 *Correct format*: 4° 8.4. *Add location*: LINC(G1,2,7,8 only, imp., plus complete duplicates of G1,8).

•17845.3 *Amend imprint*: ... *Loven* [i.e. *the Netherlands*,] (*Londen*, ... *Add locations*: CB.NY.

•17845.7 *Amend imprint as in* 17845.3. *Add locations*: GOT. PARIS.; N.NY. *Substitute this note*: In the NY copies of this and the preceding, the prelims., 1st A–T, and 4A–5E are in different settings. In the Appendix at the end, E4 of 17845.3 is cancelled and reprinted w. additions on E6 F8 of 17845.7.

•p. 152[2] **Meteren.** *Add cross-reference at end*:
—*See* also 12374.

•17848 *For* N[ewton?] *read*: N[icholas?]

Add new heading:

•p. 153[1] **Micanzio, Fulgentio.** *See* 14529.

Add new heading:

•p. 153[1] **Michell,** *Sir* **Francis,** *ed.* The view of Fraunce. 1604. *See* 6202.
—*See* also 7155.

Add new entry:

17857.7 **Michell,** *Sir* **John.** [Heading 1v:] Sir Anthonie Strelley. had issue [etc. In support of claims by Michell to the manors of Bilborough and Strelley.] 4° in 2. [*A. Mathewes*, c. 1629?] L11(SP 14/203:29).

Docketed: 'Sr John Michells case to bee communicated with My lord Keeper.' On 28 Jan. 1629 Michell petitioned the House of Commons, expressing a grievance against Bp. J. Williams, Lord Keeper from July 1621 to Oct. 1625; *see JHC* I.923. Though the present item may derive from that earlier period, it more likely accompanied or followed Michell's approach to Parliament.

Add new heading:

•p. 153[1] **Micklethwait, Paul.** *See* Bookplates.

Add new entry:

•17863.1 —[A variant, w. imprint:] *f. J. Boler*, 1631. F.

•p. 153[2] **Micron.** *Cross-reference*: —De kleyne ... *should be moved as indicated below.*

•17863.3 *Add location*: Leiden U.

Add new entry:

•17863.7 —‹Differences between the true Christ of holy scrip›ture and their counterfeated christ made by the fyue wordes of the massemongers. ... Set out in Latin by M. Micron, and *tr.* by T. Cottesford. 6. Julii. 1555. s.sh.fol. *W. Seres*, 1561. Scheide(beginning of title cropt, pasted on last leaf of STC 2066).

27 numbered articles, in a version essentially corresponding to nos. 1–13, 15, 17, 69–75 of Micron's Dutch 'Antitheses' included in *Waerachteghe historie*, 1556? For full details *see PBSA* 83 (1989): 337–52.

•p. 153[2] *Move*: —De kleyne ... *cross-reference here.*

•17864 *Delete*: [A trans.] *In line 3 read*: T. C[ranmer? or T. Cottesford?] *Add note*: This and the next are actually tr. from an earlier ed. of 18812 rather than 17863.3.

•17869.5 *Add SR entries*: Ent. to H. Lownes 1 de. 1613; crossed out and ent. to F. Kingston 6 jn. 1614. *Continue note*: There is app. an earlier ed. at Warwick Castle (MSS. Bl. 2763); last indented line to right of initial 'T' begins (i) 'hereof' (Warwick Castle) or (ii) '[ ] of lawful mony' (O). In the Warwick copy the printed regnal year is erased and 'thirteene' added by pen, making the full MS. date: 27 Mar. 1615. *See* also 4087.4, 18487.5(*A*3).

•17875 *Substitute these locations*: O.; F.Y. *Continue note*: B1v line 5 of text ends: 'Companyes'.

Add new entry:

•17875.5 —[Anr. ed.] 4°. *T. C[reede] f. J. Chorlton*, 1604. L.O. O8.; HN(w. A2,3 of 17875).HD.NY.

B1v line 5 of text ends: 'Companies'; quire A and parts of E and F are reimposed from 17875.

•17884 *In imprint* after *Masse* read: [i.e. *London*? 1625?]

•17886 *Add note*: Includes Greg 369–78.

•p. 154[2] **Middleton and Dekker.** *Add cross-reference following* 17908:
—The honest whore. 1604, etc. *See* 6501 sqq.

Add new heading at end of column:

p. 154[2] **Middleton,** *Sir* **Thomas.** *See* Bookplates.

Add new heading:

•p. 155[1] **Miélot, Jean,** *tr. See* 5758.

•17923 *In imprint* after *Pomadie* read: [i.e. *London*? 1639.]

Add new heading:

p. 155[2] **Miller, James.** *See* Bookplates.

•17926 *In line 2 of note before* 22824.7. *add*: 3832,

•17944 *In imprint* for *M. Bradwood* read: *Eliot's Court Press*

•17944a *In line 4 of note after* Allde. *add*: Beginning with 4 the names are continued on the verso, the last name on the recto being Mr. Trotman, w. the instruction 'Verte folium' below it; in at least one copy (Sotheby's, 3 Apr. 1979, in lot 240) the verso was accidentally left blank. *Add to the list in the note*:

4A Sir H. Berkley. Sussex U.

•17957 *In line 3 of note after* HN) *add*: the latter pr. c. 1487.

•17970 *Add note*: There are 2 eds.; a2r, col. 1, line 1: (i) 'The helpe and grace of' (P) or (ii) 'The helpe & grace of almy' (L, O, PLUME(w. colophon)).

•17970.5 *Amend date*: [c. 1510.] *Add location*: HART2(imp.). *For last sentence of note substitute this*: Some of the cuts are in a later state than 24878.3 sq.; *see PBSA* 76 (1982): 221–2.

•17975 *Delete*: HART2.

•p. 157[1] **Mirk.** *Following* 17975 *add cross-reference*:
—*See* also 3288.

Miroir. *Add new entry*:
•17976.5 —Le miroir des plus belles courtisannes de ce temps. Spiegel ... Spieghel ... The mirour of the most faire, famous and moderne curtizanes ... newly published. [Engrs. by C. van de Passe, the younger, w. letterpress verses.] *Fr., Dutch, Ger. a. Eng. obl.4°. [Amsterdam?] voor den autheur*, 1635. Rijksprentenkabinet, Rijksmuseum, Amsterdam.
The above title is in letterpress, and the English verses are pr. on the rectos below the engrs. while the French, Dutch, and German verses are pr. on the versos. There is also an engr. frontispiece w. intitulation in French, Dutch, and English, the last being worded: The loocking glass of the fairest Courtiers of these tymes. Other eds. of 1635 and earlier are known but without letterpress in English.

Add new heading:
p. 157[2] **Mitton, Thomas.** *See* Bookplates.

Add new heading:
p. 157[2] **Moerbeke, Peter van.** Almanack. 1550. *See* 483.13(*A*).

•18003.3 *Begin note*: The imprint actually appears as part of the dedication.

•18003.4 *Correct imprint*: [*f. W. Sanderson*,]

•18003.5 *Amend description*: [A revised state, w. imprint:] *sumptibus G. Sandersoni*, 1603.

•18003.9 *In title after* 1620 *add*: [o.s.] *In imprint for* 1620 *read*: 1621.

•18020 *Add note*: Reissued w. cancel prelims. and 1st leaf of text as 17141.

Add new entry:
•18022.5 **Monson, *Sir* John.** A note of the contents of the surrounded grounds in the level of Ancolne, undertaken to be drained by sir J. Monson. s.sh.fol. [*London*, 1640?] Y.
(Formerly Wing[1] M 2462A) Apparently intended for submission to the Privy Council, this mentions Robert Pye's petition against Monson; *see Cal.S.P.D., 1639–40*, pp. 403, 408.

Add new entry:
•18023.3 **Monson, *Sir* Thomas.** The attorneys of Yorke pl[ts] Sir Thomas Mounson defendant. [Rehearsal and defence of grants to Monson and his predecessors of the writing of all bills, process, and declarations as part of the office of Secretary to the King's Council in York.] s.sh.fol. [*London*, 1628.] L(Add. MS. 69932, misc. outsize documents).
The grant was voted a grievance on 30 May 1628; *see JHC* I.907a.

•18030 *In line 2 of note add*: 1239, 4153, ... 10737,

Add new entry:
•18035a.7 —Originum ecclesiasticarum, tomi prioris, pars posterior. fol. *typis R. O[ulton] & E. P[urslowe,] prostant ap. H. Seile*, 1639. YK.

•18036 *Begin entry*: —[Anr. issue, w. cancel tp:]

18044 *Add note*: This also includes the Second part tr. from Alonso Perez and Enamoured Diana tr. from G. Gil Polo. *See* also 153.3.

•18048 *Add note*: The husband is the same man as T. Moundeford, *Minister*, q.v.

Add new heading:
•p. 160[1] **Montmartin,** *Seigneur de*. *See* 7305.

•18056.5 *Add location*: C(1 leaf, in Syn.2.50.1).

Add new heading:
•p. 160[1] **Moorbecke, Peter of.** Almanack. 1550. *See* 483.13(*A*).

•18057 *In imprint delete*: *sold* [*by R. Mabb*,] (The shop was almost certainly in Edwards's hands by 1617.)

•p. 161[1] **More, J.,** *Preacher. Following* 18074.5 *add cross-reference*:
—*See* also 6679, 6717.

Add new heading:
•p. 161[1] **More, Thomas,** *S.J., tr. See* 11110.7.

•18077 *Begin note*: Actually pr. before Christmas 1533; *see The Complete Works of St. Thomas More*, Yale University Press, vol. 11, pp. lxxxvii, 222/17–8 and commentary.

•18078.5 *Amend date*: [1556?]

•18090 *Begin note*: Apparently pr. towards the end of 1532 but not released to the public until December 1533 along with 18077; *see Complete Works*, vol. 9, p. 125/8 and commentary. *In note before* 11381 *add*: 5190,

•18092 *Delete*: DNPK. and LIV. *Add*: M.

•18093 *Delete*: M. *Add*: LIV.

•18095 *Delete the* O *copies, which belong at* 18095.5.

Add new heading:
•p. 162[1] **Morgan, William,** *Bp., tr. See* 2347, 2742.

•18106 *Add note*: Answered in 5821.

•18115 *Add after date*: Ent. 22 mr.

•18120 *In 2nd SR entry for* 11 se. *read*: 3 se.

•18121 Tenbury copy now = O.

•18122 *Add location*: L(altus).

Turn entry into a cross-reference:
•18134.3 **Mornay.** A briefe refutation of a certaine calumnious relation. 1600. = 3rd pt. of 23453.

•18134.7 *For* [i.e. Pellison] *read*: [i.e. Pellisson?] For *Harrison* read: *Hatrison* [sic] Broxbourne copy now = L.

•18156a *Add after date*: Ent. 3 ja.

•18158 *Continue note*: A part of this (mainly chap. 11) is attacked in 4960.

•18162 *Delete last 2 lines of note*. (L headlines are cropt, but the quire is otherwise identical to F.)

•p. 164[1] **Mornay.** *Add to 'See also' references at end*: 13134.

•18176 *Continue note*: Answered by 10414.

18180 *Continue note*: C has another state of this halfsheet, signed Ss.

•18184 *Continue SR entry*: ... Weaver; Burby's share ass'd to W. Welby 16 oc. 1609.

•18188 *Continue note*: There are 2 eds.; (i) title as above (P, HN, HD) or (ii) with 'seditious' instead of 'slaunderous' (O). Quires O, P and parts of M, N are in the same setting.

•18191 *Add after date*: ?E. Burby's share ass'd to W. Welby 16 oc. 1609.

•18196 *Add note*: The order of this and the following should be: 18196a.5, 18196a, 18196; *see Library* 11 (1989): 1–9.

•18196a *Correct imprint*: ... *Tyne* [i.e. *London*,]

•18201 *Add after date*: Ent. 14 mr. 1605.

•18202 *Continue note*: Regarding an earlier suppressed ed. *see PBSA* 80 (1986): 369–74.

•18203 *Continue note*: The tp was pr. by [*R. Young*].

•18206 *Substitute this Hebrew*: הלכות תשובה

Add new heading:
p. 165[2] **Moseley, *Sir* Edward.** *See* Bookplates.

Add new heading:
•p. 165² **Mosse, John.** *See* Bookplates (M., I.).

Add new entry:
18214a.5 —[Anr. ed.] 8° in 4's. [*R. Wyer*, bef. 1536.] L(imp.).
121 chapters in the Table. On d4ᵛ 'by egall porcyon.' is the 2nd line while in 18214a.3 it is the 1st line.

18225.6 *Continue note*: a⁴ is in 2 settings; tp line 2 has: (i) 'Helthe,' (WIS) or (ii) 'helth.' (G²), the latter prob. pr. [1549?] In 18225.8 tp line 2 has: 'Helthe:'.

•18226 *Continue note*: *See* also 18048(*A*3).

Add new heading:
•p. 166¹ **Mounson,** *Sir* **Thomas.** *See* 18023.3(*A*3).

•p. 166¹ **Mountague, J.,** *Bp*. *Add cross-reference at end*:
—*See* also 10137.3C(*A*3) and Bookplates.

Add new heading:
•p. 166¹ **Mowet, Charles.** A direction to the husbandman. 1634. *See* 6902.

•18230 *Begin imprint*: [*G. Simson*]

•18242 *Continue note*: *See* also 6046.

18249 *Add after date*: Ent. to T. Stirrop 6 no. 1599. *Continue note*: The St. Paul's School copy, which lacks A1,2, is a different ed. from O and was pr. by [*F. Kingston*]. It has a 3-line ornamental init. on A6ʳ while O has a 2-line type init. Both eds. have the dedic. dated 17 Nov. 1599, and the St. Paul's School copy may represent an ed. of that year.

•18258 *In imprint* for *T. Archer* read: *P. Harrison*

•18263 *Add after date*: Ent. 27 jn.

•18264 *Add after title*: [Init. A. M.]

18267 *Add after title*: [Init. A. M.]

Add new entry:
•18269.5 —[Verso/ recto headline:] The defence/ of Pouertie. [A dialogue in verse between Irus and Poliphisius.] 8°. [*J. Charlewood*, 1577.] Ent. to Charlewood as by Munday 18 no. 1577. O(Vet.A1e.137(2), C2 only).
The SR entry continues the title: 'againste the Desire of worldlie riches Dialogue wise.' A 2nd leaf, prob. also from the same book (C7?), is headed on the recto: '***Prostors*** [sic, for 'Proctors'] Precepts' and has all but the last 3 lines of the poem reprinted on K4ʳ of 20402, but each of the long lines of the latter is pr. here as 2 lines.

•18277 *In SR entry for* R. Jones *read*: Rice Jones.

•p. 167² **Munday.** *Following* 18283 *add to 'tr.' references*: 11831.

•18285 *Correct date*: [1613.] *and add SR entry*: Ent. to N. Butter 27 ja. 1613.

•18288 *In imprint* read: *S*[*immes a. T. Creede*] *Continue note*: Creede pr. C–D.

•18292–2.3 *At end of imprints* add: *sold* [*in the shop of T. Adams*,]

•18297 *Add after title*: [By Abp. J. Williams.]

•p. 168² **Murray, John,** *Minister*. *Before* 22236 *add*: 4355,

Add new entry:
•18302.4 —Murrels two bookes of cookerie and carving. The third time printed, with new additions. 8°. *M. F*[*lesher*] *f. J. Marriot*, 1629 (1628.) David Segal (imp.).
The SR entry and note at 18302.5 belong here.

•18302.5 *Begin entry*: —[Anr. ed.]

Add new entry:
•18307.3 **Muscovia Company.** Reasons for the suppressing of the monopolizing patent granted to the Muscovia companie. s.sh.fol. [*London*, 1621.] L⁸(GL 4915).
Petition presented 24 Apr. 1621; *see* Notestein IV.254.

•18327–7.5 *Add after titles*: [By R. Rowlands/Verstegan.] *Add note*: *See Recusant History* 18 (1986): 128–42.

•18328.5 *Add location*: O.

•p. 171² **N., N.** *At end, following 'tr.' references, add*:
—*See* also 7152.

•18335.5 *Add after title*: [By T. Nicholas?]

•p. 171² **N., T.** *In 'ed.' references after* 1356.5 *add*: 3475.

•18348 *Add note*: In most copies C1,2 are a cancel bifolium w. chapter heading on C1ʳ: 'The aduise and counsell ...' whereas the orig. has: 'To bring a secret enterprise ...'; both at F.

•18355 *Add note*: Tp varies; '*Newlie Imprinted*' appears as the last line of the title or as the 1st line of the imprint; both at L.

•18357 *Continue note*: *See* also 6267.

•p. 172² **Napier.** *Add to 'See also' references at end*: and Bookplates.

•18361 *Amend date*: c. 1485?]

Add new heading:
•p. 173² **Nathanael,** *a Converted Jew*. *See* 11248.

Add new entry:
•18390.5 —[Anr. ed.] Wyth new addicions trewly correctyd. 16° in 8's. [*R. Redman*, 1528?] AMVU(imp., bd. w. 10947).
Title over Beale cut 12 (crowned rose in border which is double except on the right). Herbert I.386–7 notes Redman eds. of 16 Oct. 1525 and 16 Dec. 1528; this is prob. the latter.

•18391 *In date delete*: [1530]. (Redman seems always to have begun his year on 1 Jan.) *Add note*: Title as in 18389.

•18394 *In note for* 7714 *read*: 7705.7; *for* 7726 *read*: 7727.

Add new heading:
•p. 174¹ **Navarre,** *Casuist*. *See* 12696.

•18416 For [*Eliot's Court Press*] read: [*M. Flesher*]

18421 *Continue note*: This is a trans. of 7006.

•18422.5 For [*R. Robinson?*] read: [*T. Scarlet*]

•18425.5 *Add location*: L².

•18426 *Delete*: L². *and substitute*: A ghost derived in large part from J. P. Collier's *A Book of Roxburghe Ballads*, 1847, pp. 189–96. The only extract in broadside ballad format is 18426.5.

Add new heading:
•p. 174² **Nepenthiacus, Eucapnus,** *pseud*. *See* 3585.

•18439 *Add location*: HAGUE(Knuttel Supplement 703a).

•18443 *Continue note*: The Dutch orig., 'Anatomie van Calviniste calumnien', is by R. Rowlands/Verstegan, and the trans. is by him or possibly Joseph Cresswell; *see Recusant History* 18 (1986): 128–42.

Add new entry:
•18452.7 —Orders established by the lords the generall states, touching the mustring of the companies. Renewed the fourth of Februarie 1599. *Tr.* out of the Dutch coppy. 4°. [*J. Windet f.*] *J. Wolfe*, 1599. HAGUE (Knuttel Supplement 1096a).

•18455.7 *Add SR entry*: Ent. to N. Bourne 10 ap.

•18459 *Add after date*: Ent. 6 jy.

•18463 *Add location*: Leiden U(Bibl. Thysiana).

Add new heading:
p. 176² **Nevill, Charles.** *See* Bookplates.

•18486 *In title for* proposition *read*: proportion

Add new entry:

•18487.5 **New River Company.** [Indenture for a lease of supply of water by pipe.] s.sh.fol. [*London*, c. 1640.] C(frag., Sayle 7060).
Pr. in civilité. The extant portions mention 'Gouernor and Company'. MS. portions name Hugh and Sarah Standish and specify a payment of 20*s*. For earlier forms of the same nature *see* 4087.4, 17869.5; for a proclamation on behalf of the Company *see* 9134.5(*A*3); concerning lotteries to support a different water supply for London *see* 9050.3, 9136.5.

•18507.6 The Harl.MS. pressmark belongs with no. 18.

•.7 *Restore missing item number*: 7.

•.18 The pressmark for this is given in error at no. 6.

•.29 *Continue note*: Most of the Newsbooks below through 3 July 1624 (no. 149) were app. compiled by T. Gainsford; *see PBSA* 73 (1978): 80–1.

•.41 *In imprint for* [n.p. *read*: [*London*?

•.43 *In imprint for* [n.p.] *read*: [*E. Allde*?]

•.152 *Subsititute this note*: Advertises a map of the siege of Breda which has app. not survived. For similar maps pub'd by T. Archer *see* 3597.5, 4606.5.

•.186 *Add after date*: Ent. to N. Butter ?19 jn. [really 1 au.?] (Arber IV.182, last item).

•.203A *Substitute this note*: 11363 and 11363.5 are both called for and present in the Dahl copy.

•pp. 183[1–2] *Add*: L(Add. MS. 69930) *at the following numbers*: .231, .234, .235, .246.

•pp. 183[1]–4[1] *Add*: E(deposit) *at the following numbers*: .228, .229, .240, .241, .252, .258, .271, .272.

•.251 *In line 1 for* May 21. *read*: May 12.

Add new entry:

•.318B —Num. 89. A relation of certain differences, hapned betwixt the French ambassadour at Rome, and cardinall Barbarini, with the cause thereof. *Tr*., and with the French originall published. *Fr. a. Eng.* 4°. *f. N. Butter*, 1640 (20 fb.) G²(lacks 4X4, pp. 259–60).
4X–4Z⁴ (4Z4 blank), pp. 254–74. The 3rd quire was app. pr by [*R. Oulton* or *E. Purslowe*], the first 2 possibly by someone else.

Add new entry:

•.340N —Cent. 3. Numb. 44. The principall passages of Germany, Italy, France, and the Low Countries, continued for certaine weekes past to this present. 4° in 2's. *f. N. Butter*, 1640 (23 no.) BR(Metcalf Collection, vol. 1044).
[4T]⁴ 4V–4Y², pp. [2], 363–76.

•.344 *Delete angle brackets from title. Add location*: L(Add. MS. 69930).;

Add new entry:

•.345C —[Cent. 4. No. 3?] The first manifest of the new king of Portugall, declaring his right and title to the kingdome. 4°. *f. N. Butter*, 1640 [o.s.] Ent. to Butter a. N. Bourne 24 fb. 1641 (E&R I.14). BR(Metcalf Collection, vol. 1044).
[E]⁴ F⁴; pp. [3], 32–46. Prob. an extraordinary number in this series.

•.346 *Continue note*: For maps possibly intended to supplement this series *see* 3597.5, 4606.5.

•.349 *Add note*: At the end is an advt. for 10011.6.

•18510 *For* L³⁹. *read*: L³⁹(W, imp.).

•18517 *Add after date*: Ent. to F. Kingston, W. Cotton, a. E. Weaver 24 oc.

•p. 186² **Nicholas, T.,** *tr. Amend heading*: **Nicholas** or **Nicols,**
Add cross-references:
—*See* also 4557, 18335.5.

•18544 *Add after title*: [*Ed.*] Sʳ F. Drake baronet (his nephew). *In SR entry for* 32 oc. *read*: 23 oc.

Add new heading:

•p. 187² **Nicolaus,** *Pergamenus*. *See* 6815.

Add new headings:

•p. 187² **Nicolettus, Paulus.** *See* 16693.

Nicoll, Basil, *ed. See* 7104.

•p. 187² **Nicols, T.** A pleasant ... *Continue reference*: (This is the same man as T. Nicholas, q.v.)

•p. 188¹ **Niger.** *Add to 'See' reference*: 11899,

•18583 *Add note*: Plagiarized from 12049.

18597 *Correct format*: 4° w. perp. chainlines.

Add new headings:

•p. 188² **Nolano.** *See* Bruno, G.

Nomina. De nominibus heteroclitis. [c. 1540.] *See* 5543b.9.

Add new heading:

•p. 188² **Nordan, William.** *See* Bookplates.

◦18617.5 *Correct imprint*: *R. Robinson*, 1593. *Add location*: L.; *Begin note*: D3ʳ last line ends: 'diuers waies indaun-/'; ...

Add new entries:

18617.6 —[Anr. ed.] 12°. *R. Robinson*, 1595. LAMPORT.
D3ʳ last line ends: 'to thy diuine care and/'.

•18617.6C —[Anr. ed.] 12°. *R. Robinson*, 1597. WN².

Add new entry:

•18617.9 —[Anr. ed.] 12°. [*R. Bradock*, 1600?] F('STC 18618.2', imp.).
A8ʳ has Almanack for 1596–1605 but A5ʳ does not mention James I's coronation on 25 July 1603.

•18621 *Continue note*: *See* also Appendix E/6.

Add new entry:

•18626a.1C —The thirde time corrected and augmented. 12°. *J. W*[*indet*] *f. J. Oxenbridge*, 1597. WN².

•18626a.4 *Delete*: F. (It is actually 18617.9(*A*3)).

•18629 *Substitute these SR entries*: Ent. to H. Astley 3 no. 1600; ent. to T. Man, jun., a. ass'd to J. Busby, jun., 16 jn. 1609; ass'd to Budge 25 au. 1619.

•18631 *In imprint* for *Eliz.* read: *E*[*liz.*] *Add location*: CANT.

•18633 *In line 3 of note for* 2 Jan. *read*: 21 Jan.

18641.2 *Add note*: *See* Hind I.229–30.

•18646 *In imprint* for [*R. Badger*] read: [*A. Mathewes*] *Add note*: Answered by 3451.

18658 *Continue note*: Pt. 2 is in 2 settings, ending (i) p. '207' [i.e. 307] (OS, HD, U) or (ii) p. 247 (O, F).

Add new heading:

•p. 190² **North, Roger.** [Prospectus, etc. for the Guiana Company. 1626–27.] *See* 12456.3 sqq.

•18676 *In title for* 6858 *read*: 6859

•p. 191² **Norton, T.** *Following* 18687 *add to 'See also' references*: 4901,

•p. 191² **Norwich,** *City of*. *Add cross-reference*:
—Nordovicum Angliæ civitas. [Woodcut view of Norwich. 1578.] *See* the note to 6119.

•18698 For *W*[*illiams*,] read: *W*[*aterson*,]

•p. 192^{1} **Note.** *Add cross-reference*:
—A note of some things controverted at Amsterdam. [1611.] *See* 14662.5(***A*3**).

•18700.5 Private copy now = E(deposit).

18724 *Add note*: There are 2 eds.; A5^{r} is signed: (i) 'NOVVELLUS' (O^{4}, O^{17}, 1 C) or (ii) 'NOWELLUS' (1 C).

•18737 *Add location*: E^{4}.

Add new heading:
p. 193^{1} **Nowell, Robert.** *See* Bookplates.

•18753 *In imprint* for *B*[*arrett*?] read: *B*[*utler 1*?]

•18754 For [*V. Simmes*?] read: [*London*?]

•p. 195^{1} **O., H.** *Add cross-reference*:
—*ed. See* 5776.

•18755 *In title for* old *read*: olde *Amend locations*: *Delete* LAMPORT. (It became the HN copy long ago.) L^{4} was sold at Sotheby's 13 June 1977, lot 44; bought by John Fleming, *bkseller*, untraced. Arthur Houghton's copy now = Y.

Add new heading:
•p. 195^{1} **Obenheim, Christoph.** *See* 10747.

•18772.5 *Delete*: LINC. (It has only an imp. copy of 18773.3.)

•18786 *Continue title*: (By the Lord Deputie. [Demanding the surrender of the late O'Dogherty's allies. 7 July 1608.]) *Revise imprint*: *London*, [*G. Eld*] *f. J. Wright*; (*Dublin*, *J. Franckton*,) 1608. *Add note*: Last section reprints an Irish proclamation (Cr.-Ireland, no. 195, only in MS.; cf. 14161) repeating Franckton's orig. imprint.

•18789 *Amend date*: [1632.] *Add note*: Refers on p. 10 to 3599 as written '44. yeeres since.'

•18800 *In note for* Holderus *read*: Houlderus *Continue note*: A^{4} is in 2 settings: (i) as above (3 O, O^{2}, O^{3}, O^{18}, HN, HD) or (ii) title begins: 'BARNEVELTS' and end of dedic. has 'Houlders' (LINC).

•p. 197^{1} **Oliver, T.** *Following* 18810 *add cross-reference*:
—*See* also 24009(***A*3**).

•p. 197^{1} **Olney.** *For* 5780.7 *read*: 5775.

•18812 *Add location*: Ghent U. *Add note*: For an English trans. *see* 17864(***A*3**).

◦18816 *Amend location*: O(imp.).P(A2–5 only, bd. w. 11503.3). *Add note*: The author is actually Eusebius Pagit; Maunsell (17669), pt. 1, C4^{r}, lists a 1591 ed. of 'Paget his Catechisme' and a 1582 ed. of the enlarged version, 18830.2A sqq., as Openshaw's 'setting downe the testimonies ... quoted in Pagets Catechisme.' 19101 is a trans. of the orig. Pagit text. For an expansion of Pagit's questions and answers with an independent set of proofs earlier than Openshaw's *see* 14729.

•18818 *Add location*: Dundee PL(lacks tp).

Add new entry:
•18821.5 —[Anr. ed.] 8°. [*London*, c. 1585.] NLW(lacks A^{8}).
This is app. a pirated ed. w. all Bible citations in roman type whereas all genuine Dawson eds. have them in italic.

•18826 *Add after date*: Ass'd 20 mr. 1621.

Add new entry:
•18826a.2 —[Anr. ed.] 8°. *J. Dawson*, 1624. E^{4}.

Following 18830.4 *add new entry*:
•18830.4* —[Anr. ed.] 8°. *T. Dawson*, 1591. L.

•p. 198^{1} **Order.** *Preceding* 18841 *add cross-reference*:
—[Heading A1^{r}:] The order of housholde. [1584, etc.] *See* pt. 2 of 10765.5 sqq.

18845a *Substitute this note*: Although the text of the dedic. is the same setting in all copies, the dedicatees vary: Earl of Craven (L), Sir T. Middleton, kt. and bt. (F), Sir H. Berkeley, kt. and bt. (AAS), S. Marow (HD).

•18848 *Amend date*: [c. 1550.]

•18854 *Amend date*: [c. 1630.]

Add new heading:
•p. 199^{1} **Osbaldeston, Richard.** *See* Bookplates.

•18879 *Correct date in imprint*: [1563.]

Add new heading:
•p. 199^{2} **Osmond, Benjamin.** *See* Bookplates(***A***).

•p. 199^{2} **Osorio.** *Following* 18889 *add cross-reference*:
—*See* also 11234.

•18895 For [*V. Simmes*] read: [*G. Eld*]

•18895.5 *Add note*: The main report is signed: V. Duncalfe.

•p. 200^{1} **Overall.** *In 'See also' reference for* 8578.5 *read*: 8556.

•18903 *In 2nd SR entry for* 13 ap. *read*: 3 ap.

•18913 For [*A. Griffin*] read: [*Eliot's Court Press*]

18920 *Add note*: This adds reprints of 11332.5 and 23619.5 (***A*3**).

•18929.3 *Correct format*: 16° in 8's. *Add location*: O.

Add new entry:
•18929.4 —[Anr. ed.] 8°. [*F. Kingston*?] *ex typ. Soc. Stat.*, 1619. WN.

•18929.7 Quaritch copy now = HN.

•18938 *In line 3 read*: Ent. to M. Sparke, sen., ...

•18952.1 *Add location*: L.

•18961 *Add after date*: Ent. to W. White 3 mr. 1600.

Add new entry:
•18961.7 —[Anr. ed.] 4° in 8's. *T. Purfoot*, 1611. F. Edwards catalogue 951 (1971), item 408 (cannot be traced).

•18962 *For* [Anr. ... 8's. *read*: [A variant, w. imprint:]

•p. 202^{2} **Ovid.** [*Metamorphoses—Extracts*.] *Preceding* 18969 *add cross-reference*:
—[*Ceyx and Alcyone*.] *See* 13897.

•18972 *Correct format*: 4°.

•18976.8 *In line 4 read*: 21 se. 1612; also ent. to the Stock 5 mr. 1620.

•18987 *Delete*: WN. *and substitute*: NEP.

18990 *Add note*: Imprint varies: 'sumptibus' (O^{14}, C, F) or 'sumtibus' (O).

18991 *Add note*: Imprint varies: 'sumptibus' or 'sumtibus'; both at C.

Owen, John. *Immediately following* 18994 *add new entry*:
•18994.5 —[6-line poem in Latin, signed Joha: Ow: underneath engr. portrait by S. van de Passe of T. Egerton, Vct. Brackley, dated 1616.] s.sh.fol. *C. Holland*, [1616.] L(Dept. of P&D).O.O^{42}.PARIS.WIN.+; LC.
See Hind II.252–3.

•19000 *Continue note*: Coton's Letter declaratorie, which forms the bulk of the text, is answered by 5861, 5862; the latter includes a different trans. from the one here.

Add new heading following 19002:
•p. 203^{2} **Oxford,** *Diocese of*. To the minister ... of [ ] in the diocese of Oxon. [1622.] *See* 13880.

•19005 *Continue note*: This is the early version of the Laudian statutes; Charles I's letter of 3 June 1636 confirming them as revised was not pr. until c. 1708? (copies at O(5), CANT (W/P-8-42(2)).

19016.3 *Add location*: Daniel H. Woodward, Huntington Library, San Marino, Calif.(left half). *Add note*: *See The Book Collector* 16 (1967): 81–2.

•19021 For [*E. Griffin*?] read: [*Eliot's Court Press*?]

•19043.5 *Continue note*: For other verses on this occasion *see* 4930.5.

•p. 205[2] **Oxford U**—*Corpus*. *Immediately following* 19043.5 *add cross-reference*:
—*See* also Bookplates.

19048 *Add note*: C2[r] line 3 has 'quærat' (all Oxford copies, P, HN, HD). C has a frag. of leaves C2,3 only, in a different setting w. 'quęrat'.

•p. 205[2] **Oxford U**—APPENDIX. *Add cross-reference at beginning*:
—Assertio antiquitatis Oxoniensis academiæ. 1568. *See* 4344.

•19053 For [*W. Jaggard*] read: [*J. Windet*]

•19054.5 *Add location*: L(frags.).

•19057 *In line 3 read*: Ent. as by W. G. ...

•19062.5 *Amend imprint*: [*A. Islip*, 1615?] *Add SR entry*: Ent. as by Capt. Panton to Islip 29 ja. 1615. *Substitute this note*: Edward Panton was the 2nd commander of the Hon. Company of the Artillery Garden.

p. 207[1] **P., E.** *Add cross-reference*:
—*ed. See* 240.

Add new heading:
•p. 208[1] **P., J.,** *Public Writer*. Onomatophylacium. 1626. *See* 19599.

Add new heading:
•p. 208[1] **P., I. W.** Adtimchiol an chreidimh [etc. c. 1631?] *See* 4391.3.

19078.6 *Correct title, etc.*: ... to a friend of his at Rome: [on] the late treaty betweene the queene mother ... Nauarre. *Tr.* out of French. 8° in 4's. *Add note*: Tp has Aggas's device, McK. 199.

•19085 *Add after date*: Ent. 3 my. 1627.

19096a *Add note*: The cancel tp has a press variant in the portion transcribed: 'Command' (HD) or 'Commande' (C).

Add new heading:
•p. 209[1] **Paget, Charles.** *See* 7628.

19101 *Add note*: The orig. English, erroneously attrib. to R. Openshaw, is listed at 18816(*A*3).

Add new entry:
•19109.4D —[Anr. ed.] 12°. *J. L*[*egat*,] *sold by John Waterson*, [c. 1640.] NY.
F1[r] line 10: 'Aailon [*sic*]'; imprint clearly undated; title as in 19109.4. This is the only 12° STC ed. with initial 'u', e.g. 'unto'.

Add new entry:
19110.5 ——[A publisher's prospectus for 19110, w. heading:] A description of the multitude of Christians in the world. s.sh.fol. *W. J*[*ones*,] *sold by T. Alchorne*, 1635. HD (formerly in bdg. of 19111).
Imposed in 1 long and 4 short columns and prob. intended to accompany a map like 19111.5.

•19115.5 *Add location*: ; F(imp.).

Add new heading:
p. 210[1] **Paine, Hugh.** *See* Bookplates.

•19120 *Continue imprint*: *sold* [*by E. Wright*,] *Amend SR entry*: Ent. as tr. from French ...

•19120.3–.7 *Add notes*: The attrib. to Painter is erroneous; the author is W. Patten; *see TCBS* 7 (1977): 27–45.

•19126 *Continue note*: Tr. from Briefve information des affaires du Palatinat, 1624 (Knuttel 3504).

Add new heading:
•p. 210[2] **Paleotti, Dionisio.** *See* 5350.7.

•19137 *Amend location*: C(imp.). *Add note*: The C tp, which is all that remains of quire A, may be a cancel; L(C.60.h. 16, fol. 68) is a tp only, beginning: 'An exhortation to the knowledge and loue of God ...', which is the title it has in the SR entry and in Maunsell (17669), pt. 1, p. 78.

•19137.5 *In the note for* a reprint of 22268. *read*: 'An exhortation sent from a straunger, to Edward Duke of Somerset for the establishing of peace in the church of England', which is a different text from 22268.

•19143.5 *Begin imprint*: [*R. Bradock*,]

•19153 *Add note*: There are 2 issues; epistle dated 20 (C) or 23 (F) Jan. 1597.

Add new heading:
p. 210[2] **Palladius Rutilius Taurus Æmilianus.** *See* 25007(*A*).

Add new heading:
p. 211[1] **Palmer, Thomas,** *Book owner*. *See* Bookplates.

Add new entry:
•19156.3 —[Anr. issue, w. cancel tp:] A tutor for travailers: teaching how to demeane themselves abroad. *f. R. Moore*, 1613. P.D.G. Skegg, Dunedin, N.Z.
Tp pr. by [*W. Stansby*.] The orig. dedic. (A2–3) to Henry, Prince of Wales, is retained, but A4 (preface dated 1606) is lacking, possibly cancelled.

•19161 *In SR entry read*: ... 1581; ass'd to J. Roberts 31 my. 1594; W. Wright's and T. Scarlet's rights ass'd to T. Creede ...

•19165.5 *Add note*: Line 1 of title ends: 'loue.'

Add new entry:
•19165.7 —[Anr. ed.] 2 pts. s.sh.fol. [*A. Mathewes*] *f. J. W*[*right*, c. 1630.] L(Rox. I.436–7).
Line 1 of title ends: 'their'. Also erroneously listed as Wing[2] M 2882A.

Add new heading:
•p. 211[2] **Panton, Edward,** *Captain*. *See* 19062.5(*A*3).

•19174 *Add note*: *See* also 6023.

•19175 *Continue note*: C1 is in 2 settings: C1[r] last line has 'præclare' (HD) or 'præclarè' (L).

•19178 *Amend format*: A cropt *obl.* slip w. horizontal chainlines, measuring 67 × 87 mm. *Substitute this note*: Possibly part of a broadside or the last leaf of a 4° publication.

•19180 *Amend heading*: [Anr. ed., w. additions.] *Add note*: Includes reprint of antidotary from 7277.

•19183 *Begin imprint*: [*T. Scarlet f.*]

Add new heading:
•p. 212[1] **Paradise.** A paradise for the soule. 1574. *See* 5411.7.

Add new entry immediately following 19200:
•19200.3 —A decree of the court [of] Parliament of Paris. For the university, against the jesuits. [20 Aug. 1610. Forbidding jesuits to make public lectures.] Together, with an almanack, sent to the pope, this year 1612. concerning the imprisonment of the abbot of Bois. 4°. *sold by E. Marchant*, 1612. L.

•19201 *Add after date*: Ent. 2 jy.

•p. 212^{2} **Paris** [*Parlement*]. *Following* 19203.3 *add cross-references*:
—Other proceedings by date and STC number: 1590 (13113.5, 13145), 1594 (13118), 1611 (13121.5), 1618 (11281), 1621 (11279.5).

•p. 212^{2} **Paris University.** *Add to 'See also' references at end*: 5861, 6124,

19209a *Add note*: F is a further variant, w. the colophon leaf (5Y8) blank.

•19217 For [*J. Danter*? read: [*T. Judson*

•19217.5 Arthur Houghton's copy now = L.

19223 *Add note*: Also listed as Wing B 4811.

19226 *Add note*: Also erroneously listed as Wing D 1143.

•19245.5 Private copy now = E(deposit).

•19285 *In title for* on *read*: or

•19292a *In lines 2–3 read*: Englished [by J. Stubbs? from the Latin MS. vita attrib. to J. Josseline, w. hostile annotations and an attack on 19292], and to be added to the 69.

Add new heading:
•p. 215^{2} **Parker, Roger.** *See* Bookplates.

Add new heading:
•p. 215^{2} **Parkhurst,** *Sir* **Robert.** *See* Bookplates.

Add new entry:
•19305.3 —[Anr. ed.] 4°. (*J. Notary*, 1520.) Guildford Muniment Room(imp., at end of Loseley MS. 1327/2).
Title xylographic. *See* also *Library* 2 (1980): 199–202.

•19311 *Add after date*: Additions ent. 30 no. 1631.

•p. 216^{2} **Parry, H.,** *Bp. Add cross-reference at end*:
—*See* also 10209.3(***A***).

Add new heading:
•p. 216^{2} **Parry, Richard,** *Bp., ed. See* 2348.

•19340 *Add note*: For different verses on the same topic *see* 4837, 4838.

•19352 *Continue note*: Dedic. attacked in 5671.

•19364 *Add note*: Intended to be issued w. 4088.

•19367 *In imprint* for [*P. Short*?] read: [*F. Kingston*]

•19382 *Amend U. S. locations*: F(2).N.U. *Add note*: There are 2 eds.; in imprint (i) 'Charle- | wood' collating ¶^{6} *^{12} A–Y^{12} (L tp, 1 F, U) or (ii) 'Charl- | wood' collating A–Y^{12} (O, C, 1 F, N); the latter was app. pr. in 1593 by Charlewood's widow or J. Roberts.

•19408 *In the note after* 1446, *add*: 11189,

19409 *Continue note*: 1 P copy has errata for the preface on (q)2^{v}.

•19411 *In the note after* 4321 *add*: 5736.

•19413 *In the note delete*: 18134.3, *and continue*: ... attacks; *see* also 6381, 6385.5.

•19417 *In line 1 of note before* 18191 *add*: 11189,

•p. 219^{1} **Parsons.** *Add to 'See also' references at end*: 888,

•19419 *Continue title*: Newly gathered, and amended by James Partridge. *Add note*: For an earlier ed. *see* 1025.3.

Add new entry:
19433.2 —The widowes treasure, plentifully furnished with secretes in phisicke: & chirurgery. Hereunto adioyned, sundrie prety practises of cookerie. [Anon.] 8°. [*J. Kingston*] *f. H. Dizle*, 1582. Devon Record Office, Exeter(2309B/Z 8/1).
It was Disle's copy that Rider entered; *see* 19433.3.

•19458 *Add note*: Selected from Pasquillorum tomi duo, ed. C. S. Curio, [Basel,] 1554, supplemented by 7 other pasquils by George Buchanan.

•19458.5–.7 *In imprints* for [*T. Creede*?] read: [*W. Stansby*]

•p. 220^{2} **Passe, C.** *Add cross-reference*:
—Le miroir des plus belles courtisannes. 1635. *See* 17976.5(***A***3).

•19471 *Add after date*: Ent. to the English Stock 5 mr. 1620.

•19476 *Continue note*: For other elegies and verse now attrib. to Patten *see* ***A***3 at 2368.3, 2368.5, 19120.3, 19120.7. He is also the author of 15190.5; *see* the articles cited in ***A***3 under that number.

•p. 221^{2} **Paul V.** *Add to 'See also' references at end*: 3215,

•p. 221^{2} *Add new headings*:
Paul, *of Venice. See* 16693.
Paul, *Saint and Apostle*. The historie of S. Paule. [Series of woodcuts. 1563?] *See* 11930.6.

Add new entry:
•19491.3 —[The terrar, i.e. survey of lands, boundaries, tenants, etc. belonging to a manor.] fol(2 or more). [*J. Wolfe*, 1582.] C^{9}(1 sheet only).
The left-hand column has addresses 'To the Lordes and Owner', 'To the Reader', and 'To the Surueyor'. The right-hand column lists the contents from '1 The description of the Plat [map, to be hand-coloured]' to '51 Fiue and twentie Deuices ... which the Authour offereth to teach'. These devices are mentioned in 19491.5 as being previously listed in his Terrar, 1582. The C^{9} sheet is anon. but presumably Payne's name appeared on the map or on further sheets of text, if any.

•19495 *For* (lacks tp) *read*: (tp misbd. after A7)

Add new heading:
p. 222^{1} **Paynton, Dorothy.** *See* Bookplates.

•19500.5 *Amend heading*: [A variant, w. imprint:] *In imprint* for *Bradock* read: *Braddock*

•19501.5 *Continue imprint*: *sold* [*by R. Raworth*,]

•19503 *Continue note*: At least Y has added ¶^{2} w. dedic. to the Duke of Buckingham and his coat of arms.

•19508 *Delete*: L^{4}.

•19511.5 *In imprint* read: *T. Man* [*jun*.]

•19518.5 *Continue note*: and *TCBS* 8 (1982): 173–85.

•19529.5 *In the note for* A–E^{4} *read*: A–D^{4}.

•19543 *Add before date*: *Southwarke*,

19546 *Add note*: For a record that Jones paid the fee for this but the transaction was not entered in the SR *see* Arber II.36.

Add new heading:
•p. 223^{2} **Pegaso,** *pseud. See* 22463.6(***A***3).

•19558.3 *Delete* (imp.) *from* E^{2}. *Add location*: Leighton Library (frag.).

•p. 224^{1} **Pellison, P.** *Amend name*: **Pellisson**

•19570 *In 2nd paragraph of note for* HD, U *read*: C^{2}, CHI; *for* C^{2} *read*: HD; HD, U copies of 19570.5.

•19572 *In Wing reference for* P 1115 *read*: P 1114.

•19595.5 *Add after date*: ?Ent. w. title in English to the Purfoots, sen. and jun., 10 jn. 1602.

19596 *Add note*: This is tr. from St. Francis of Assisi.

Add new heading:
p. 225^{1} **Penketh, Thomas,** *ed. See* 581.

19596.5 *Add note*: For an earlier ed. *see* 3059.6.

•19599 *Continue title*: By J. P. publike writer.

•19598.4 *Amend heading*: … verse, also anon.] *Amend SR entry*: Ent. as by Penkethman to …

•19605.5–06 For [*Aldermanbury*? read: [*East Molesey*,

•19614 *Continue imprint*: *sold* [*by E. Wright*,]

Add new heading:
p. 226[1] **Percivall, Geoffrey.** *See* Bookplates.

•19615.5 *Add SR entry*: ?Ent. to T. Walkley 26 ap. 1636.

Add new heading:
p. 226[1] **Perez, Alonso.** *See* 18044(***A***).

•19624.5 *In imprint* for *R. Field* read: *C. Yetsweirt*

•19627 *Add note*: The explicit varies: 'sup̲ psalteriu̲ hucusqȝ expõnes.' (L, O, C, C^5) or 'super psalterium exposiciones.' (O^2).

Add new entry:
19689.5 —[Anr. ed.] 12°. *J. Legate, pr. to the Univ. of Cambridge*, 1600. NLW.

•19695 *Delete*: Anon.

•19700–0.5 *In imprints delete*: [*J. Wolfe f.*] After *Porter*, add: [*Cambridge*,]

•19703 *Add note*: For an answer to part of this *see* 13442.

•19709 *Delete the SR entry, which prob. refers to* 19721.5(***A***3).

Add new entry:
•19719.7 —[Anr. ed.] 8°. *J. Legatt, sold by R. Allott*, 1635. E^4.

Add new entry:
•19721.5 —[Anr. ed.? w. omissions and additions.] Foure treatises, necessarie to be considered of all christians. The first sheweth, how farre a wicked man may goe in christianitie. The second, of the conflicts of Sathan with the christian. The third that a papist cannot go beyond a reprobate. The fourth how the elect may goe beyond all reprobates. 8°. *T. Orwin f. J. Porter* [*of Cambridge*] *a. T. Gubbin*, 1588. ?Ent. as 'Three treatises' 21 au. C^9(frag. of quire A only).
Dedic. dated 28 Aug. 1588. Reprints treatises 2, 3 (and possibly 4) from 19721.3; a rearranged version is included as items 1, 5, 4, 2 of 19752.

•p. 229[1] *Following* 19721.7 *add cross-reference*:
—Foure treatises. 1588. *See* 19721.5(***A***3).

•19724.5 *Add note*: There are 2 eds.: (i) A–C^8, main text begins on A2^r (O); (ii) A–C^8 D^4, main text begins on A4^r (F). In addition to lacking the tp, O has no dedic., which is present in F and later eds., and may be the earlier ed. O is by an unidentified [*London*] printer.

•19733 *In imprint* read: *R*[*oberts a. T. Creede*] *Continue note*: Creede pr. 2nd B–I; Roberts the rest.

•19735.6 *In the 1st SR entry for* 23 no. *read*: 25 no.

19736 *Add note*: There are 2 eds.; A1^r line 2 of text ends: (i) 'descrip-' (P, HN) or (ii) 'discrip-' (2 C).

19742 *Add note*: There are 2 eds.; in title: (i) 'man, … manner' (HN) or (ii) 'man: … maner' (C).

Add new entry:
19743.3 —[Anr. ed. of 19742.5.] 12°. *J. Legate, pr. to the Univ. of Cambridge*, 1600. NLW.

•19752 *In last line of note for* 21204.5 *read*: 21204.7. *Continue note*: Partly reprinted from 19721.5(***A***3), and the SR entry app. belongs to that title.

•19752.5 *In heading for* issue … reset.] *read*: ed.] 8°.

19760 *Add note*: 19760–61.1 are called 'second edition'; 19761.3 sqq. have no ed. number except for 19761.5.

•p. 230[2] **Perkins.** *Add to 'See also' references at end*: 5194.7, 7186,

Add new heading:
p. 230[2] **Perne, Andrew.** *See* Bookplates.

•19766 *In lines 2–3 read*: … Pernaw, a cittie in Lifflande. Wherein is conteyned a prophesie of the famine, in 1602. And also of the great victorie lately atchived by the great Sophy, who overthrew the Turkish emperour. *Tr.* … Dutch. (A true … reporte of the miserable state of Livonia, (commonly called Lyffelande.)) *Add SR entry*: Ent. to W. Dight 23 no. 1602. *Add note*: Although both copies of this and the next collate ¶^{4} (Pernaw, ¶1 blank except for leaf orn.) B^4 (Sophy), A^4 (Livonia, A4 blank), the faulty order may be due to a misbound Dutch original; the gen. tp indicates previous printing at Nijmegen, the sub tpp at Hamburg.

Add new heading:
p. 230[2] **Perot, William.** *See* Bookplates.

•19769.3 Sparrow copy now = L.

Perrot, G. *Revise main heading and add new entry*:
•19769.9 **Perrot** or **Porret, George,** *alias* George Boules. A spirituall directory unitinge à devoute soule unto hir lord Jesus Christe. [Dedic. signed George Boules.] 12°. *Duaci, ex off. B. Belleri*, 1626. Swaffham Parish Church.
—*tr. See* 4469.

•p. 231[1] **Perrot, R.** *Add cross-reference*:
—*See* also Bookplates.

19776 *Continue note*: This is a trans. deriving ultimately from the MS. relation in Spanish by M. Garayzabal, in religion Prosper a Spiritu Sancto.

•19777.5 *Add*: L. *and delete it from* 19778.

•19781.5 *Amend imprint*: [*J. Kingston*, c. 1575?]

•19785 *Add before date*: [false imprint but *printed abroad*,]

•19799 For [*V. Simmes*?] read: [*A. Jeffes a. others*,]

•p. 232[2] **Petowe.** *Following* 19808 *delete 'See also …' cross-reference.*

•19816 *Amend date*: [c. 1520?]

•19819.5 Arthur Houghton's copy now = L.

Add new entry:
•19821.5 —[Anr. ed.] 4°. [*G. Simson f.*] *R. Watkins*, [1598?] Gdansk, Bibliotheka Gdanska PAN(Di 3552(8°)/9).
Collates A–Z^4 &^{4} like 19822.

•19825.5 *Amend date*: [c. 1635.]

Add new heading:
p. 233[1] **Phesaunt, Peter.** *See* Bookplates.

19830 *Continue note*: ¶ outer forme is in 2 settings; ¶4^v line 21: 'Arch' or 'Arche'; both at P.

•19837.5 *Amend imprint*: [*La Rochelle*? *J. Haultin*?] *Substitute this note*: Not an STC book. Usually attrib. to A. Pérez or J. Teixeira.

19838.5 *Continue note*: The dedic. mentioned is init. 'M. V.' and altered by pen to 'M. W.' in both the copies cited. O^{10} also has the dedic.

Turn entry into a cross-reference:
•19840 —The severall proclamations lately published by the king. 1604. Now = 22992.5. (*sic*, in vol. 2, *not* ***A***3)

19855 *Add after date*: Ent. to J. Parnell 25 fb.

Add new heading:
•p. 234[2] **Phillippes, W.** A caueat to England. 1573. *See* 4684.

19861.3 Phillipps copy now = L.

•19869 *In imprint delete*: [*W. Williamson f.*]

Add new heading:
•p. 235^{2} **Philomathes,** *pseud. See* 5347.

•19893–3a *In line 1 of notes for* B1^{r} *read*: B2^{r}.

•19897.7 *In title for* Mirãdula *read*: Myrãdula

•p. 236^{2} **Pie, Thomas.** *Add cross-reference*:
—*See* also 10568.

•19903a.5 *For* [1589?] *read*: [i.e. *London*? 1588?]

•19905 *Amend date*: [1549?]

•19912 *In line 3 of note for* Yy^{8} *read*: Xx^{8} Yy^{6}.

Add new heading:
•p. 237^{1} **Pilgrim,** *Poor, pseud. See* 4557.

•19918 *Amend date*: [1510?]

•19929 *Continue note*: Prelims. in 2 settings; in title: '*PILKINGTON*' or '*PILKINTON*'; both at C.

19930 *Add note*: The report is not by Pilkington, but it includes an account of his sermon of 8 June.

•p. 237^{2} **Pilkington, James.** *Add cross-reference at end*:
—*See* also 10390.

Add new heading:
•p. 237^{2} **Pilkington, John.** *See* Bookplates(***A*** 3).

•19936 *Add after date*: Ent. to Busby, sen., 15 ap.; ass'd to W. Barley 3 my.

Add new entry:
•19936.5 **Pinder, Rachel.** A very wonderful and strange myracle of God shewed in London at Gally Key, vpon a young mayde (R. Pinder): aboute xi. yeares olde: possessed with v. legions of deuylls. 8° in 4's? [*R. Jones f.*] *W. Bartlet*, 1574. O(Gough gen. top. 364 (549–553), frags. of 1st 4 leaves).
This account is refuted in 3738.

Add new heading:
•p. 237^{2} **Pinder, Ulrich.** *See* 14553(***A*** 3).

•19937 For [*V. Simmes*, read: [*London*?

•19967 *Correct 1st word of title*: Trigonometry ['y' not 'ie']

•p. 239^{1} **Pius II.** *Add cross-reference at end*:
—*See* also 12512.

•19974.4 *Amend description*: [Woodcut w. letterpress heading and verses.] s.sh.*obl*.fol. *Amend location*: C^{6}(2973/442).

Add new heading:
•p. 239^{1} **Plaix, César de.** Anti-Coton. 1611. *See* 5861.

•p. 239^{1} **Planudes.** *Add to references*: 4846.

•19990.5 *Add note*: Partly adapted in verse in 25440.

Add new heading:
p. 239^{1} **Plat, John.** *See* Bookplates.

•20025 *Delete*: L^{4}.

Plinius. *Add new 1st entry*:
•20028.9 —C. Plinii secundi Naturalis historiae liber II. In vsum philosophicæ lecturæ auditorum. 8° in 4's. *Cantabrigiae, T. Thomas*, 1583. C^{16}(2 sets of 1st halfsheet, in bdg. of I.12.5).

•20037 *Amend date*: [1597?]

•20046.3 *Continue note*: MEL has a 3rd variant or ed. with 'Henry Bridge' (w. final 'e').

Turn entry into a cross-reference:
•20048 —Les quæres del mounsieur Plowden. *f. W. Lee a. D. Pakeman*, [1645?] = Wing^{2} P 2610A.

Plutarch. *Add new 1st entry*:
•20051.5 —[*Conjugalia praecepta*.] Den spieghel des houwelicks, waer in ... gheleert wordt, hoe dat man ende wyf hen teghen elckanderen dragende, een vreetsaem, leuen met elckanderen sullen leyden. Wt den Grieckschen auteur Plutarchus ouergheset. 8°. [*London*,] *R. Schilders*, [*in the house of T. Vautrollier*,] 1575. Amsterdam U. Ghent U.

•20061.7 *Amend date*: [1553?]

•20070 *In imprint* for *Allot* read: *Allott*

•p. 242^{1} *Following* 20073 *add 'See also' reference*: 6893.

•p. 242^{2} **Pocklington.** *Add cross-reference at end*:
—*See* also Bookplates.

20083.3 *Add location*: F. *Substitute this for the beginning of the note*: '279' [i.e. 261] pp. On re-examination this ed. appears to be later: [*London*, *R. Young*, after 1635.] O has another ed. w. '350' [i.e. 250] pp., which may be English printed, prob. after 1640. There are ...

•p. 243^{1} **Politianus.** *After* 761 *add*: 13220 sq.

•20096 *In SR entry read*: Ent. to T. Man 1 and 2 and Jonas Man ...

•p. 243^{2} *Add new headings*:
Pontanus, Joannes. *See* 11027.

Pontanus, Joannes Isaacus, *ed. See* 13908.

•20108 *Add after date*: Ass'd from J. Awdely to J. Charlewood 15 ja. 1582.

•20113 *Add note*: Includes a trans. of 4604. For a slightly revised reprint *see* 15311.

Add new heading:
p. 244^{1} **Popham, John.** *See* Bookplates.

Add new heading:
•p. 244^{1} **Porret, George.** *See* 19769.9(***A*** 3).

•p. 244^{2} **Portugal.** *Add cross-reference*:
—The first manifest of the new king of Portugall. 1640 [o.s.] *See* 18507.345C(***A*** 3).

Add new heading:
•p. 244^{2} **Portugal Pearl.** *See* 7679, 12598, 18887.

•p. 244^{2} **Posy.** *Add cross-reference*:
—The posye of flowred prayers. [1570? etc.] *See* 5651 sqq.

•20134 *Add after date*: Ent. 20 mr.

20135.7 *Add note*: The HN tp is conjugate; the L tp may be a cancel.

•20136.7 *In imprint delete brackets around 'Oxford'*.

•p. 245^{1} **Poullain,** *ed.* For 16573 *read*: 16573(***A*** 3).

Add new heading:
•p. 245^{1} **Pounde, Thomas.** *See* 6075.

20141 *Continue note*: Although much of the type of this and the next two appears in only 1 setting and at most 2, there appear to be 3 distinct issues. In the present issue C4^{v} line 12 ends: '& abrode.'; D3^{r} line 5 has: 'Consequence' (L, 1 C, 1 E, and prob. all the copies listed at this number).

20141.3 *Add note*: C4^{v} line 12 ends: 'and abroade.'; D3^{r} line 5 has: 'Consequence' (1 O, 2 C, HD, and some of the other copies listed at this number).

Add new entry:
20141.5 —[Anr. issue.] *F. Kyngston f. E. Weaver*, 1603. O.E.P. C4^{v} line 12 ends: 'and abroade.'; D3^{r} line 5 has: 'consequence' (1 O, 1 E, P, and some of the other copies listed at 20141.3).

•20152 *Begin SR entry*: Ent. to Joan Newbery 9 mr. 1604; ass'd to Cotton ...

◦20163 *Add after date*: Ent. 26 mr. *Continue note*: At least L, O, F copies also have extra leaves w. dedics. to Sir James Ley, Sir Henry Hobart, and Sir Thomas Coventry, which are not reprinted in the following eds.

Add new heading:
•p. 246^{1} **Pownde, Thomas.** An aunswer to six reasons, that T. Pownde, required. 1581. *See* 6075.

•p. 246$^{1-2}$ **Poynet.** *Amend and add cross-references*:
—Diallacticon. 1557. *Continue note*: For a trans. *see* 21456.
—A warning for England. [1555.] *See* 10023.9.

•20186.7 *Delete*: [Anon.] (Prat's name is on A2^{v}.)

•20188 *In imprint* for [*R. Jugge f.*] read: [*S. Mierdman? f.*]

•p. 247^{1} **Prayer.** *Add cross-references*:
—A prayer made by a lady of honor ... 1574. *See* 4803.4.
—A prayer wherin may be seen whose praiers are receiued of God. [1575?] *See* 4803.4.

•20192.7 *Continue note*: For a different book of prayers pr. by Oswen *see* 3362.

Add new entry and cross-reference:
•20192.9 —[Another book of prayers?] 16°. [*f.*] (*Ant. Kitson*, 1555.) L(last leaf only, Harl.5927/338).
Last phrase of prayer (app. for Queen Mary): 'And finallye after thys lyfe, that shee maye attayne euerlastyng ioy and felicitye: Amen. Finis.'
•—A boke of prayers called ye ordynary fasshyon of good lyuynge. [1546?] *See* 3326.5.

Add new entry:
•20196.9 —Godly and necessarye prayers. 32° in 8's. [*R. Wyer*,] 1549. PML.

•20197.7 *Amend date*: [1603?]

•20200.3 *Correct format*: 8°. *Amend location*: CH(lacks pts. 5, 6).

•20203.5 *Continue note*: Reprinted in 12366.

20221.5 *Continue note*: Tp varies; init. 'J. P.' (L) or 'John Preston' (HN).

•20221.7 *Continue note*: Sub tpp vary: w. Preston's inits. (1 HD-Remedy; 2 HD-Doctrine) or w. his name in full (O, 1 HD-Remedy; O-Doctrine).

•20228 *In line 3 read*: Ent. to M. Sparke, sen., ...

•20271–1a *Continue imprints*: [*Cambridge*,]

•20273 *Continue imprint*: [*Cambridge*,]

•p. 250^{1} **Preston, J.,** *of East Ogwell. Following* 20282.7 *add cross-reference*:
—*See* also 13037.

•20283–4 *Continue imprints*: *sold* [*in the shop of N. Bourne*,]

Add new entry:
20285.3 —[Anr. issue, w. cancel tp:] The godly mans inquisition, wherein is laide forth the miserable estate of all men. *J. D*[*awson*] *f. J. Bellamie*, 1622. YK.

•20286 *Continue imprint*: *sold* [*in the shop of N. Bourne*,]

Add new entry:
•20314.7 —Good ale for my money. The good-fellowes resolution of strong ale. Ballad. 2 pts. s.sh.fol. *London*, [*assigns of T. Symcock*? 1630?] L(Rox I.138–9).
Has the Symcock shepherd cut as in 16863 but showing some damage to the right border.

•20339 *Add after date*: Ent. 27 jn.

Add new entry:
•20344.7 —Two decads of sermons. The first heretofore scatteringly set forth. The second now first added. 4°. *Oxford, L. Lichfield, sold by H. Crypps a. H. Curteyne*, 1636. WOR (lacks last sermon).
Prelims. collate §^{4} §§^{2} (§1 blank?); §2^{r} gen. tp, §3^{r}–§§1^{v} dedic. to E. Denny, Earl of Norwich, §§2^{r-v} contents list of 1st 10 sermons. Following Y1 (end of 10th sermon) is χ^2 w. sub tp and contests list for 2nd decade.

•20345 *Begin entry*: —[Anr. issue, w. §^{4} §§^{2} and χ^2 cancelled, w. cancel gen. tp:]

•20348 *In title after* English *add*: [by P. Heylyn.] *Add SR entry*: Ent. 24 ja.

•p. 252^{1} *Following* 20364 *add cross-reference*:
—Two decads of sermons. 1636. *See* 20344.7(*A*3).

•20367 *Substitute these SR entries*: Pts. 1, 2 ass'd to W. Welby 16 oc. 1609, to Snodham 2 mr. 1618. Pt. 3 ent. to E. Burby 6 oc. 1607, ass'd from T. Archer to Snodham 20 ap. 1619.

Add new heading:
•p. 252^{1} **Prime, Henry,** *ed. See* 25768.5(***A***3).

•20377.3 *In line 1 of note, before* Catechism *add*: 16 lines of text per page. *Add 2nd paragraph to note*: L^{2}(Frag. no. 52) has frags. of K1, 4–8 of a 16° ed. w. 15 lines of text per page containing the end of Evening prayer, the Blessing, and the beginning of the Seven Psalms. K2, 3 evidently had 3 set prayers as at the end of Evening prayer for Sunday in 20374 sq., 20377, whereas 20377.3 sqq. have 4 set prayers and 3 other collects. The frag. is possibly [*W. Seres*, c. 1565.]

•20380 *Add note*: A copy at HER(Kington deposit) has an early state of the title w. date misprinted '1501'.

•20384 *For* TEX. *read*: TEX^{2}.

•20393 *Amend location*: L(C.127.c.23). *Continue note*: Copies vary: heading in 5 lines as above (L, NY^{9}) or in 3 lines, omitting 'who deceased' (LINC); LINC also varies in some textual readings.

◦20397 *Add before format*: (The glasse of godly loue.) *In imprint* for [*J. Charlewood* ... read: [*W. How* ... *Add after date*: Ent. 20 ja. 1579. *Add note*: The Discourse is an altered excerpt from 15003, and the Glasse reprints 13208.

Add new entry:
•20397.3 **Prize.** A generall prize, for all those that desire to approve their skill, either with musket or long bow. 1/2 sh.fol. [*W. Jaggard*, 1620?] L(1889.e.5, vol. 4 (237)).DUL(Alleyn Papers II, fol. 87).
Notice of a contest to be held 'Monday next, being the xxj. day of August; in Saint Georges Fieldes' w. a list of prizes and entry fees, the latter to be paid in advance to '*Euan Floyd* gentleman, dwelling in Winchester house near S. *Mary Oueries* in *Southwarke*'.

◦20399 *Continue note*: There are 2 eds.; 1st line of title: (i) 'The Descripcion of the' (NLM, [1550?]) or (ii) 'The Descripci-' (L, L^{2}, C^{6}, [c. 1553]).

Add new heading:
•p. 253^{2} **Prodigal Son.** [The history of the prodigal son. Series of woodcuts. 1566.] *See* 11930.8.

•20418 *In supplied title for* 1523 *read*: 1524. *For* = 470.7 *read*: 470.8(*A*3).

•20435 *In last line of note for* 13828.8 sqq. *read*: 13829.9(***A***) and 13830 sqq.

•20436 *In date delete*: [1511] *Add location*: ; ILL(imp.).

•20444.5 *Add after title*: [In verse.]

•20447 *Continue note*: Davenant's text is reprinted in 6293.

•20448 *Continue note*: Answered in 10857.7.

•20449 *Add after date*: Ent. under the 20449.5 title as tr. by Thomas Wood 24 au.

•20450 *Continue imprint*: [*St. Omer*,]

Add new heading:
•p. 255[1] **Prurit-anus.** Prurit-anus. 1609. *See* 6991.5.

20458 *Continue note*: ¶2 is a cancel in some copies; orig. ¶2[r] line 1 of text ends: 'the'; the cancel has: 'pro-'; both at C.

•20464a *Add note*: 1 HD has both orig. Xxxx2,3 and the cancel bifolium.

•20465 *In imprint after* rather *add*: *London*?

20474 *Add note*: 1 C has 2 leaves of errata inserted after Yy3.

•20480a *Amend date*: [1551?] *Continue note*: This ed. should follow 20481.

•20488 *Add note*: A2 is in 2 settings; A2[r] has catchword: 'de' or 'tir', the latter having expanded text; both at O.

20506 *Add note*: The tp and at least 4 other leaves are in 2 settings. In title: 'Second edition, much enlarged.' or 'Second edition, of the first part (of fower intended). Much enlarged.'; both at F.

•20509 *In imprint* read: (*W. Stansby*) *f*. ...

Add new heading:
•p. 257[2] **Pye, William.** *See* 12794.

Add cross-reference:
•p. 257[2] **Pynder, Rachel.** *See* 3738, 19936.5(*A*3).

Add new heading:
•p. 259[2] **Quarles, William.** *See* Bookplates.

•20560.7 *Amend format and imprint*: fol(2). [*N. Hill*, 1548?]

20565 *Add after title*: *Lat., Eng., Fr., a. Ital.*

Add new heading:
•p. 260[2] **Quir, Ferdinand de.** *See* 10822.

•p. 261[1] **R., B.** *Add cross-reference*:
—*tr. See* 13224.

•p. 261[1] **R., H.** *Add cross-reference*:
—A concordance of letters to reade all the languages in Europe. [1628.] *See* 20835.3(*A*3).

•p. 261[2] **R., I.** or **J.** *Add to 'ed.' cross-references*: 4849, 4849.8, 11004.

•20582.5 For [*A. Islip*] read: [*J. Wolfe*]

Add new heading:
•p. 262[2] **Rabelais, François.** *See* 12974.

Add new heading:
p. 262[2] **Radcliffe, Samuel.** *See* Bookplates.

Add new heading:
•p. 262[2] **Rainalds, Paul.** *See* 4285.

•20611 *Add note*: End of text dated 4 July 1577. There are 2 eds.: (i) 12°, A[12] (O, C) or (ii) 4°, A[4] (O[17], LINC).

20612.5 *Continue note*: The Oratio in laudem artis poeticae is a different version of the text of 6787.4.

•20628a *Replace entry with*: —[A ghost.] (WN, YK = 20628; L = 20629.)

•p. 263[2] *Following* 20631 *add to 'See also' references*: 13887,

•20633 *Continue note*: Answered by 13945.

Add new heading:
p. 263[2] **Raith, James.** *See* Bookplates.

•20634 *Add after date*: Ent. 15 mr. *Continue note*: The true order of eds. is 20636, 20634, 20635.

•20649.9 *In note for* 'no ne' *read*: 'none'

•p. 264[2] **Raleigh.** *Following* 20652, *in 'Wine licences' reference for* 9187.8 *read*: 9175n.

Add new entry:
•20654a.5 —[Anr. ed.] A declartion [*sic*] of the demeanor [etc.] 4°. *Dublin, F. Kyngston*, 1618 (1619.) GOT.

•20655 For [*R. Blower*] read: [*W. Jones*]

Add new heading:
•p. 264[2] **Ralph,** *de Bourne, Abbot. See* 3419.5.

•20664 *In note, before* 7224 *add*: 7148 sqq. and

Add new heading:
•p. 265[1] **Ramusio, Giovanni Battista,** *tr. See* 4699.

•20673 *Continue SR entry*: Redmer's pt. ass'd to R. Young 12 my.

Add new heading:
•p. 265[1] **Randes, John.** *See* Bookplates(*A*).

•20694 *Correct Greg number*: 547–8.

Add new heading:
•p. 265[2] **Rant, William.** *See* Bookplates(*A*).

•20708 *Substitute this note*: In this and the following eds. the terms of the Old Tenures are integrated into the main alphabetical sequence.

•p. 266[2] **Rastell, J.,** *Barrister. Add to references at end*:
—*ed. See* 9599.
Add to 'tr.' references: 9515.5,

•p. 267[1] **Rastell, W.** *Add to 'ed.' references at end*: 9521,

•20752 *Add note*: Answered by 11113.

•20753a *Add after date*: Ent. to Hodgets 31 my. 1605.

•20755 *Continue note*: There are 2 eds.; (i) A–B[4] C[2] without colophon (L, F, HD) or (ii) A–B[4] with colophon on B4[v]: *f. W. Barly*, [n.d.] (LINC, B[4] only). 20755.5 is a further reduction to A[4].

20757 *Add note*: Copies vary: with (L, LC) or without (O) inits. 'T. R.' on A3[v].

•20759 *Correct 1st line of imprint*: [*J. Windet f.*] *W. Barley f.*

Add new heading:
•p. 267[2] **Ravensperger, Hermann.** *See* 12401.

•20763.2 *Add note*: Imprints on the sub tp (Dd2[r]) of this and the following vary; e.g. O has: *imp. T. Man*; the LK copy of 20763.5 has: *ex off. N. Okes*.

Add new heading:
•p. 268[1] **Raworth, Margaret.** *See* Bookplates(*A*3).

•p. 268[1] **Ray, J.,** *ed. Add to references*: 4849, 4849.8,

Add new heading:
•p. 268[1] **Rayment, Thomas.** *See* Bookplates(*A*3).

Add new heading:
•p. 268[1] **Re., Pere.,** *ed. See* 5343.

Add new headings:
p. 268[2] **Reade, John,** *of Brasenose. See* Bookplates.
Reade, John, *of St. John's, Oxford. See* Bookplates.

•20787 *In imprint* for *J.* read: *Joyce*

•20791 *Correct format*: 4°.

•20792.7 *Amend date*: 1604? *or* c. 1610?] *Add note*: Possibly related to 11460; for a comparable petition to the king *see* 16779.12.

•20801.7 *In heading read*: ... imprint on tp:] *Add location*: ; PN (colophon as in 20801.3).

•20804.7 *Begin imprint*: [*G. a. L. Snowdon f.*]

•20823 *In note after* sheet. *add*: For an earlier version *see* 16743.2 (*A*3).

Add new entry:

•20824.5 **Rede, *Sir* Robert.** [Begins:] Orate specialiter pro animabus dñi R. Reed militis: nuper capitalis iusticiarii de cõi bãco. Et Margarete consortis sue: [etc. Woodcut coat of arms w. letterpress text below, giving Sir Robert's death date: 8 Jan. 1518 (o.s.)] 1/2 sh.fol. [*R. Pynson*, 1519.] O(in Auct. 1Q1.8 = STC 16202).C(in B*.1.11).
The copy of 16202 in which the O copy is inserted also has cancel M3, w. another setting of the request for prayers imposed below the crucifixion cut on the verso but omitting the date of death.

20825 *Add note*: This is tr. from A. de Soto; for anr. trans. *see* 22937.

•20826 *Amend date*: [1554?] *Add note*: *See British Library Journal* 13 (1987): 33–57, especially no. 86 on pp. 44, 52.

•20832a *Add after date*: Ent. 17 de. 1623.

Add new heading:

•p. 270[1] **Refuges, Denis de.** *See* 7367.

Reginald, Henry. *Add new 1st entry preceding* 20835.5:

•20835.3 —A concordance of letters to reade all the learned, vulgar or forraign languages in Europe: with a most useful Radiographie [cf. 20834.7] of late invention. 1628. [Init. H. R. Engr.] s.sh.fol. [*London*, 1628.] L(MS. Sloane 4377, fol. 39).
This is a later state, w. heading pasted above and w. 2 extra lines of characters, of the folding plate in STC 24121.

•20842 *Begin imprint*: [*R. Wolfe f.*?]

•20847 *Begin imprint*: [*London*? *J. Mychell f.*]

Add new heading:

•p. 270[2] **Reid, Robert,** *Bp. See* Bookplates.

Add new entry and cross-reference to the man formerly known only as 'tr.':

•20860.3 **Reid, Thomas.** Memoriae sacr. castissimis manibus Honoriae, ... Londini, xvij kalend. Septemb. MDCXIV. extinctæ sylva funebris: Jacobo baroni Hayo, conjugi exhibita. [In verse.] 4°. [*R. Blower*, 1614.] A(BK Dor).
Following 'tr.' reference add:
—*See* also 1404.

Add new heading:

p. 271[2] **Remey, James.** *See* Bookplates.

•20892 *In title before* Langar-shore *delete*: the

Add new entry:

•20896.5 —[Anr. ed.] Returna brm. 4° 8.4. [*J. Skot*, c. 1525?] L (lacks B4).
Tp has cut w. garter arms surrounded by 4 border panels; 20894.4 tp has cut w. rose, and 20894.7 tp has different garter arms w. no border panels.

•20905 *Add note*: *See* also 6514 and *Court-Book C*, p. 17.

20917.5 *Add note*: *See* Hind I.254–5.

•20919 *Amend imprint*: ... *Caxton*, 1482.] *Continue note*: The trans was finished on 6 June 1481.

•20938 *Amend imprint*: *H*[*earne a. J. Norton*] *f*. ... *Add note*: Quires Aaa–Kkk were pr. by Norton, the rest by Hearne.

•20941.7 Arthur Houghton's copy now = L.

•20946.1 *In imprint* for [i.e. *London*,] read: [i.e. *France*?] *Continue note*: This has no 'sh' ligature in the roman or italic type, and only the verso of the last leaf in each quire has a catchword.

•20946.9 *Add note*: *See* also 8860.

•20946.10 *Add location*: L(1139.c.20, imp.)*. *Add note*: (L copy formerly 9248)

Add new heading:

•p. 274[2] **Rhaedus, Thomas.** Memoriae sacr. ... manibus Honoriae, sylva. [1614.] *See* 20860.3(*A*3).

•20961.5 *Add note*: *See* also 3101.

Rice, R. *Add new 1st entry*:

•20972.7 —An inuectyue agaynste vices take for vertue, gathered out of the scriptures. 8°. [*London*? 1547?] O(imp.).
In the same types as 24514(*A*3), w. the same woodcut 'W'.

•20973 *Begin entry*: —[Anr. ed., w. added preface by R. Crowley.]

•20976 *Add location*: L.

•20977 *In imprint* for [*T. Orwin*] read: [*R. Bourne*]

Add new heading:

•p. 276[2] **Rich, Penelope,** *Baroness. See* 6787.7.

Add new heading:

•p. 276[1] **Rich, Richard,** *1st Baron Rich. See* 9181.3.

•21013 *Amend imprint*: *L. Snowdon* [*in the shop of R. Blower*] ...

•21014 *Amend imprint*: *L. Snowdon* [*in the shop of R. Blower*] ...

Add new heading:

•p. 277[1] **Richardson, John,** *of Cambridge. See* Bookplates.

•21024 *In line 2 read*: [Init. D, i.e. J. Loiseau de Tourval.]

Add new heading:

•p. 277[1] **Ricques, Robert,** *called de La Fontaine, ed. See* 6749.8.

•21028.5 For [*E. Allde*] read: [*J. Windet*] *For 2nd sentence of note substitute this*: ¶[2] is app. a cancel for A1.

•21031 *Add note*: Answered by 11025.

•21035 *Add location*: O. *Add note*: The sub tpp of this and the following app. always give F. Kyngston as the pr., w. varying publishers; the new O copy of 21035 has: *F. Kyngston pro S. Waterson*.

•21040–1 *Amend dates*: [1538–47?]

•21051 *Add note*: Reprinted in 5886.

21053.7 *Add note*: The order is issued by Ridley as Vicar General to the Abp. of Canterbury.

Add new heading:

•p. 278[2] **Rime, James.** *See* Bookplates-Remey.

Add new heading:

•p. 278[2] **Rinaldi, Orazio.** *See* 1804, 12307.

Add new heading:

p. 278[2] **Ritch, Peter.** *See* Bookplates.

•21060 *Add locations*: ; HN(like C but has only 5 prelim. leaves). ILL(same contents as O(Opp.)).

Add new entry:

•21060.5 —[Heading A1r lines 25–6:] The rules of the Latine grammar construed, which were omitted in the booke called Lilies rules and the syntaxis construed [15633.4 sqq.] 4°. [*E. Allde*, 1627.] Ent. to E. Allde 5 my. 1627. L.O.
A1r begins w. advt. to the reader dated 20 Apr. 1627 and signed Edmund Reeve. The text sheets (A–L4) are known *only* in the reissue w. cancel tp dated 1657 (Wing R 669; Univ. Microfilms Thomason Tracts series, reel 135).

•21070 *Begin imprint*: (*in fletestrete* ... *Amend date*: [1501?]

•21074 *Add note*: 1 HN has 4 Latin presentation epistles: to the mayor of King's Lynn, Sir Nicholas Bacon, Sir J. Peyton, jun., and Sir H. Spelman, inserted following E5, H5, M2, and O4 respectively.

21079 *Add note*: Tp varies in the portion transcribed: '*Christian* the fourth, famous' (HD) or '*Christian*, the fourth famous' (C).

•21090 *Add note*: A⁴ B–E⁸ F⁴.

Add new entry:
•21090.3 —[Anr. ed.] 8°. [*J. Charlewood f.*] (*R. Jhones*,) [1580?] O(lacks tp).
A–D⁸. Maunsell (17669), pt. 1, C6ᵛ lists an ed. of 1580, and this may be it.

Add new heading:
•p. 279² **Roberts, James,** *ed. See* 11004.

Add new heading:
p. 280¹ **Robinson, Bernard.** *See* Bookplates.

Add new heading:
p. 280¹ **Robinson, Henry.** *See* Bookplates.

•21115 *In line 3 of title for* 13055 *read*: 13056 *Amend imprint*: [*Leiden, J. A. van der Marsce*,]

•21116 *Add note*: Answered by 4575.

•21131 *Continue imprint*: sold [*in the shop of T. Man*,]

21134.5 *Add note*: Tp varies: as transcribed (HD) or omitting the 1st line: 'A ... gift' (L).

•21138.3 *Amend imprint*: *Paris*, [*J. Blageart*,]

Add new heading:
p. 281² **Rodeknight, John.** *See* Bookplates.

•**21158** *In line 2 of note for* one has the *read*: (i) with *In line 4 for* the ... has *read*: (ii) with

•21159 *Continue note*: L³⁹(W) has a copy w. outer sheets I and R of 21158 (ed. ii) and A⁴ and K inner sheet in app. unique settings; e.g. A2ᵛ has catchword 'hard' and A1ʳ has tp border McK. & F. 141 w. royal arms at top as in 21159, but line 2 of title begins 'Of' whereas 21159 has 'of'.

Add new entry:
•21159.5 —[Anr. ed.] 4° in 8's. [*R. Watkins*, c. 1590.] L³⁹(W, lacks tp and last leaf).
Collates ¶⁴ B–F⁴ G⁸⁺² (G2 + χ^2) H–O⁸ w. the anatomical figures on G2ʳ–3ʳ and χ^2, and the birth figures on G3ᵛ–5ʳ, whereas all the following eds. collate A⁴ B–O⁸ w. anatomical figures on G2ʳ–4ʳ and birth figures on H6ʳ–7ᵛ.

•21160 *Begin imprint*: [*G. Simson f.*] *For* TEX. *read*: TEX².

•21178 *Amend imprint*: *R. Badger* [*a. M. Parsons*,] *Add note*: Badger app. pr. only the 1st quire.

Add new heading:
•p. 283¹ **Rogers, Mathew.** *See* 3478.5 sq.

•21204.5 *Begin note*: The added Perkins ... *and move it to* 21204.7. *At* 21204.5 *substitute this note*: *See* also 12324.

•21213.1 *Add note*: *See* also 12324.

•21213.3 *Amend imprint*: *L. S*[*nowdon in the shop of R. Blower*] ...

21215 *Add note*: *See* also 5694.

Add new heading:
•p. 284¹ **Rogers, Thomas,** *Book owner. See* Bookplates.

Add new heading:
•p. 285¹ **Rokeby, Ralph.** *See* Bookplates.

21256 *Add note*: For further details of this and the following eds. *see The Bibliotheck* 5 (1967): 67–72.

•21272 *Add after title*: [*Ed.*] (H. C[harteris and] W. A[rthur.])

Add new entry:
21286.2 —[Gesta Romanorum.] *Eng.* 4° in 8's. (*w. de worde*,) [1502?] BTU(lacks tp).
G1ʳ line 2: 'emperour named Andromyke'. The 16th story begins on D4ᵛ, 25 lines from the bottom: 'Somtyme there dwelled ... Pompey'. This ed. has no woodcuts.

•p. 286¹ **Rome.** *Following* 21292a *add cross-reference*:
—Newes from Rome concerning the blasphemous masse. [1550?] *See* 14006.

Add new entry:
21299.3 —[Anr. ed.] The history of the seuen wise maisters of Rome, now newly corrected with a pleasant stile, & purged from all old and rude wordes and phrases. [*Ed.*] (T. Greene.) 8°. *T. Purfoote*, 1576. L.
Collates A–Q⁸ R⁴; B1ᵛ last line is: 'or not.' Purfoot's SR entry for 1565–66 should be transferred from 21299.5 to the present entry.

•21307.3 *Add location*: Amsterdam U.

•21307.5 *Amend imprint*: [*printed abroad*, c. 1560?] *Add note*: Not an STC book.

Add new entry:
•21309.7 —A treatise wherin is moost plainlye expressed howe the bysshops of Rome with their good will, haue giuen vs gere to play withal, to kepe vs blynde styll. [In verse.] 4°. [*W. Hill? f.*] *H. Syngelton*, [1548?] L(cropt).
See British Library Journal 11 (1985): 93–4.

•p. 287¹ **Romeo.** *Add cross-reference*:
—The tragicall historie of Romeus and Juliet. 1587. *See* 1356.9.

Add new heading:
•p. 287² **Rosa, Johannes.** *See* 11916.

•21319.3 *Complete the author's Christian name*: **Laurentio.**

Add new entry:
•21319.9 —Laurentij Roscij ... echo. Et alij versus nonnulli. Ad Gualterum Mildmaium. [In verse.] s.sh.fol. [*London*, 1589?] L(C.38.l.6(4)).

•p. 287² **Rosdell.** *Add cross-reference*:
—*ed. See* 13745.5.

21324 *Continue note*: Pt. 1 reprints 21325.

Add new heading:
•p. 288¹ **Rosselli, Giovanne de.** *See* 10433.

Add new heading:
•p. 288¹ **Rotherham, Thomas.** *See* Bookplates.

Add new entry:
•21354.5 **Rousseel, Nicasius.** De grotesco. Perutilis atq3 omnibus quibus pertinebit valde necessari⁹ liber. ... J. Barra sculp. [Engr. tp and 9? plates of grotesque ornaments.] 8°? *Londinij*, 1623. Rijksprentenkabinet, Rijksmuseum, Amsterdam(imp.).
See Hind III.100.

Add new heading:
•p. 288² **Rowland, Hector,** *tr. See* 13092.5.

•21359 *Continue note*: Partly reprinted in 12407.

21360 *Add note*: C, HN lack *–**⁴, w. the 1st tp, Almanack, and Kalendar of saints' days, and may be a separate issue or at least a purchaser's option rather than imperfect.

•p. 289¹ **Rowlands** or **Verstegan.** *Add to 'See also' references*: 5742.7(*A*), 13576, 18327–7.5(*A*3), 18443(*A*3) and *Recusant History* 18 (1986): 128–42.

21386 *Add note*: This is largely composed of selections from 21385.5 and 21395.

•21408 *Add note*: BTU has a bifolium w. dedic. to Tobie Wood esquire on 1^{r} and the other 3 pp. blank; not present in F.

•p. 290^{1} **Rowlands, S.** *Following* 21414 *add cross-reference*:
—*ed. See* 14030.

•21424 *Continue imprint*: *sold* [*by J. Wright 1*,]

•21429 *Amend date*: 1485.

•21430a Lord Kenyon's copy was resold at Sotheby's, 27 Sept. 1988, lot 144.

•21431 *In colophon* for *fecii* [sic] read: *fecit Continue note*: … masse.', intended solely for priests and omitted from the main text at chap. 64. Roye was actually the dedicatee, and the author is anon.

•21438 *Continue note*: *See* also 4660.

Add new heading:
p. 291^{2} **Rumsey, Walter.** *See* Bookplates.

Add new heading:
•p. 291^{2} **Ruscovius, Valentinus.** *See* 5646.

•p. 291^{2} **Rusdorf.** *Amend heading*: **Rusdorff, Johann Joachim von.**

•21456 *Add note*: This is a trans. of J. Poynet's Diallacticon, [*Strassburg*,] 1557.

•p. 291^{2} **Russell, F.,** *2nd Earl. Following* 21456.5 *add cross-reference*:
—*See* also 84.5, 4899.

•21458 *In imprint delete*: '*Bruges* or' *and delete queries*.

•21480 *Add after title*: [By A. Symmer?]

Add new heading:
•p. 293^{1} **S., A.,** *Shorthand Writer. See* 7538.

•21483.5 *Begin imprint*: [*J. Charlewood*] *In imprint* for *&* read: *and*

•21489 For *G. S*[*imson*,] read: *G. S*[*haw*,]

•21491.3 *In the SR entry for* 29, i.e. 19, *read*: 10

•p. 293^{2} **S., G.** *Following* 21492 *add cross-reference*:
—*ed. See* 4806.

•21498 *Add note*: Attrib. to J. Sutton.

21500 *Add after date*: Ent. 16 my.

•21504 *Add note*: Now attrib. to J. Sutton.

•21506 *Add note*: Now attrib. to J. Sutton.

•p. 294^{1} **S., L.** *Following* 21508 *add cross-reference*:
—*ed. See* 5216.

•p. 294^{2} **S., R.** *Following* 21517 *add to 'tr.' references*: 7238,

•p. 294^{2} **S., R.,** *Gentleman, tr. Add cross-reference*: 7240,

•p. 295^{1} **S., T.** *Following* 21521 *add cross-reference*:
—A psalme of thanksgiving. 1636. *See* 5209.3(***A***).
In 'ed.' references at end after 997.5, *add*: 4777,

•21526 *Add after date*: Ent. to T. Thorp 13 fb.

•p. 295^{2} **S., W.** *In 'ed.' references at end before* 22761 *add*: 6637.5, 9292, 9791(***A***), 15733,

•p. 295^{2} **Sackville.** *In 'See also' references for* 1247 *read*: 1248

•21551.7 *Add after date*: Ent. 19 de. 1625.

Add new heading:
•p. 296^{1} **Sainliens, Claude de.** *See* Desainliens, C.

21555.10 *Add note*: O^{6}, which is imp., has the imprint corrected to: 'Walde-graue'.

•21574 *In imprint* for *Tottelli*,) 1580. read: *Tottelli*, 1580.) *Delete* (destroyed) *from* L. (Copy now replaced.)

•21574.5 *Correct imprint as in* 21574 *above*.

•21583 *Delete* (destroyed) *from* L.

Add new heading:
•p. 298^{2} **Saint Mary of Rounceval's Hospital,** *Westminster. See* Indulgences 83G(***A***3).

•p. 298^{2} **Saint Paul's Cathedral.** *Add cross-reference at end*:
—*Chapel of Jesus in the Crowds. See* Indulgences 59G (***A***3).

Add new heading:
•p. 298^{2} **Salad.** A salade for the simple. 1595. *See* 12960.

Add new entry:
•21607.3 —The fifth impression. 8°. *f. J. Helme*, 1612. Iowa U (Health Sciences Library).

•21626 *Amend date*: [1522?]

•21634 *Add note*: Tr. from G. M. Bruto's La institutione di una fanciulla; *see Library* 5 (1983): 53–7. For another trans. *see* 3947.

•21640 *Add after date*: Ent. 26 ja.

•21642 *In line 4 read*: Ent. to M. Sparke, sen., …

•21647 *Amend imprint*: [*Canterbury?*] (*J. Mychel*,) [1533–34?]
In the note after 3186 *add*: 15192.5.

Saluste du Bartas. *Add new 1st entry*:
•21648.5 —Les œuvres de G. de Saluste S^{r}. du Bartas. Derniere edition. (Suite des oeuvres.) 2 pts. fol. *Paris, chez J. de Bordeaux*, 1611 (1610) [*a*.] (*Londres, J. Bill*, 1622.) HD(in bdg. w. arms of James I).
In pt. 2, Bb5, Gg1, Ll 3, and Oo2 of the Paris ed. are cancelled, the contents rearranged to put the sections of days 3 and 4 of week 2 in their textual order, and 6 leaves pr. by Bill to accommodate this reshuffling, of which 4 are sub tpp w. his imprint as above.

•21653 *Add SR entry*: Some additions ent. 29 ja. 1620.

•21672 *Amend description of* L: (imp., in C.39.d.32, bd. between STC 23579 and 21669).

•p. 301^{2} *Following* 21673, *in 'See also' references before* 19540, *add*: 5667,

Add new heading:
•p. 301^{2} **Saluthius, Bartholomew.** *See* 4469.

•p. 301^{2} **Salvart, Jean-François.** *See* 5155.

•21687 *Add location*: ; Y.

Add new heading:
•p. 302^{1} **Sancto Vinculo, Claudius a.** *See* Desainliens, C.

•21694 *In line 2 of note before* 18739. *add*: 11448,

•21710.7 *Add after date*: Ass'd from G. Blackwall to Coles 21 ap. 1626.

21714 *Add note*: The tp is a cancel in O, C, P, HD (all?) copies.

•21716 *Continue note*: This ed. is later than 21717.

•21718 *Amend imprint within square brackets*: [i.e. *London, B. Alsop a. T. Fawcet? f. M. Sparke*,]

Add new heading:
•p. 304^{1} **Santa Cruz de Dueñas, Melchor de.** *See* 5738.

21746 *Continue note*: There are 2 eds.; A3^{r} line 1 of text ends: (i) 'e-' (O^{3}, O^{5}, O^{6}, P) or (ii) 'E-' (O, O^{6}, O^{7}, O^{8}, C, HD).

•21752 *In the note for* McK. *read*: McK. & F.

•21754 *In the note for* McK. *read*: McK. & F.

•p. 305[1] **Satan.** *Add cross-reference*:
—A commyssion sent to the bloudy butcher byshop of London, by Sathanas. [1557?] *See* 3286.

•p.305[2] **Savonarola.** *In the cross-reference following* 21789.3 *for* 32° in 8's. *read*: 8°.

•21796 *Add note*: This ed. is the only one to include Savonarola's meditation on ps. lxxx. The L copy may lack the prelims. as it has no tp but only a heading on A1^{r}.

•21798 *Amend imprint*: *worde, in Flete strete,*) [1501?]

•p.306[1] *In cross-reference following* 21798 *for* psalm *read*: psalme *For* 32° in 8's. read: 8°.

Add new entry immediately following 21805:
•21805.05 **Saxo-Bosco, D. de.** The rare vertue of a most excellent pil, beeing an antidotum against the plague. Newly invented and composed, by ... D. de Saxo-Bosco. *Tr.* out of the high Almain. And imprinted at Antwerp according to the copy imprinted at Coolen, by H. W. [Quack medicine advt.] 1/2 sh. fol. [*Antwerp*? 1603.] CANT(H/KK-15-1300(2)).
Has notice at end, pr. in civilité, that the pill can be had 'at the hows of [ ]', filled out in MS.: 'frauncis Wall barber chirurgeon dwellinge in tower streete.'

Add new heading:
•p. 306[2] **Scaliger, Joseph Justus,** *ed. See* 4849, 4849.8.

Add new entry:
21806.5 **Scarbrough, Gervase.** The summe of all godly and profitable catechismes, reduced into one. 12°. *G. Eld*, 1623. Ent. to Eld a. M. Flesher 30 my. L.

•21816.5 *Add note*: On a3^{r}–4^{r} is an extra dedic. to Abp. Laud by N. H[omes].

Add new heading:
•p. 307[2] **Schmid von Schmiedebach, Augustin.** *See* 3207.5 (***A***).

•21821.2 *Begin imprint*: [*R. Field*]

Add new heading:
•p. 307[2] **Schoock, Marten.** *See* 7076.5.

•21826.4 *In imprint delete*: [*widow of*]

•21827 *Continue title*: ... præceptis, per colloquia mutua. Authore H. Schottennio Hesso. *Add note*: This text, or a version of it, is app. the Confabulationes which H. Wykes was fined on 7 Aug. 1564 (Arber I.274) for printing and the Confabulationes Hesse which H. Bynneman entered in 1569–70 and yielded to the Co. in 1584 (Arber I.418, II.788); *see* Appendix C/59. *Following the note add cross-reference*:
—*See* also 13207.

Add new heading:
•p. 308[1] **Schuute, Cornelis.** Prognostications. 1544, etc. *See* 483.13(***A***), 508.5.

•21835 *For* O. *read*: O^{8}.

•21838 *Delete* (destroyed) *from* L. (Copy now replaced.)

21844 *Add note*: Tp varies; the author's and editor's names are spelled 'Slater' (HD) or corrected to 'Sclater' (C, F).

•21849 *In imprint delete*: [*A. Mathewes f.*]

•21850.3 *Continue note*: ... page; main text in 95 mm. textura. C^{2} has a frag. of the bottom of leaf E2 of an ed. [*f. H. Jackson*, c. 1585] w. main text in 83 mm. textura; it contains portions of 'How Skogin greased a fat sowe at the Arse. Tale .xl.' and tale xli; this text appears on D2^{r} of 21850.7 but with the tales unnumbered.

•21850.7 *In 2nd SR entry for* 1625 *read*: 1626.

Add new heading:
•p. 309[1] **Scogli.** Scogli de christiano naufragio. 1618. *See* 7004.5.

21869 *Add note*: This Scot may also be the author of 22064 sqq.

•21873 *Amend heading*: **Scot, Thomas,** *of Ipswich, d. 1640. Add note*: For other men of this name *see* 21869, 22064, 22107, 22108.

•21906 *Amend imprint*: *London, R. Young, his majesties printer for Scotland,*

•21915 *Begin imprint*: *London, Continue note*: This does *not* identify Young as King's Printer for Scotland.

Add new entry:
21949.7 —[Heading 1^{r}:] Ane act and proclamatioun for cunzie. [Reforming the coinage of Scotland. 13 Jan. 1591 (o.s.)] 8° in 4. (*Edinburgh, R. Walde-graue,*) [1592.] E. Cr.726 (MS. only).
Printed, like STC 1562, in 81 mm. Lettersnijder, which Waldegrave had previously used in Marprelate tracts, e.g. 17453.

•21968 *In line 2 for* June *read*: July

•21987.5 *Add location*: L(Add. MS. 69931).

•22001–2 *In imprints* after *Young*, add: *his majesties printer for Scotland,*

•22003–4 *Amend imprints*: [*London,*] *R. Young, his majesties printer for Scotland,*

•22005 *Add note*: John Legat 2 was in charge of the press; *see Library* 11 (1989): 1–9.

•22019 *Begin line 3 of note*: 5155, 5962; ...

•22019.5 *In imprint* after *Lekprewik* read: [i.e. *London, R. Waldegrave,*

Add new entry:
•22025.7 —[Anr. ed.] s.sh.fol. *Glasgow, G. Anderson f. the Hammermen,* [i.e. *Company of Metal-workers*, 1638.] Glasgow City Archives.

•22034 *Delete*: [By J. Spotiswood.] *Continue note*: An exposé of the episcopal party, including a memorandum drawn up by Bp. J. Spotiswood.

•22048 *In line 2 for* pt. 1 of 64.5 *read*: 12728

22058 *Continue note*: The 'deliberations' setting varies: with or without 'VII.' in the margin of B3^{v}. Quire A also has press variants; tp line 11 is misdated '1628' or corrected to '1638'; A4^{r} line 19 ends: 'Law-' and is with or without 'III' in the margin or ends: 'law-'; copies of all varieties at M.

22060 *Add note*: At least quire D is in 2 settings; D1^{r} catchword: 'Com-' (HN) or 'Commissi-' (HD).

Add new heading:
•p. 316[2] **Scott, Cuthbert.** Two notable sermones. 1545. *See* 5106.5.

◦22064 *Amend main heading*: **Scott, Thomas,** *B.D., d. 1626. In line 3 of note for* 5864.4 *read*: 5864. *Add a 3rd paragraph to the note*: This Scott is the son of the author of 22108. For other Scot/Scotts *see* 21869, 21873, 22107.

•22065 *In line 5 read*: ... Dutch [from Nieuwe, ongehoorde ... artijckelen, 1623 (Knuttel 3391.)]

•22072 *In the note for* D3– *read*: E1– *for* C3– *read*: D1–

22074 *Continue note*: This is by the eldest Scott, the author of 22108.

22076 *Add note*: Reprinted in 10009.

Add new entry:
•22079.5 —Josephs flight out of Ægypt. Delivered in a sermon upon Mat. 2. 15. Published after [Scott's] death, according to his owne manuscript, by T. All. 4°. *Amsterdam, J. F. Stam*, 1635. HD.

22083 *Add note*: This is not by Scott; it is a trans. from the Dutch 'Den Compaignon vanden verre-sienden Waerschouwer' (Knuttel 3204), pr. by A. Meuris.

•22086 *Continue note*: Tr. from W. Baudart's Progrez des conquestes, 1623 (Knuttel 3399).

•22097a *Amend date*: [1624?]

•22099 *In locations and in line 3 of note* O^{3} (former Evelyn copy) now = L.

•22101 *For* L. *read*: L(*^{4} only, w. 22100). *In lines 4 and 6 of note* O^{3} copy now = L.

•22103 *Add location*: MIN(see note). *In line 6 of note before* and CU *add*: MIN,

•22103.3 *In line 4 of note read*: HD, MIN, and ...

•22103.7 *Delete*: MIN.

•22105 *Continue note*: This is the later issue, w. I^{4} K1 of 22105.5 cancelled and replaced by I^{4}.

•22105.5 *In line 1 delete*: enlarged *Continue note*: This is the earlier issue.

•22107 *In imprint* for [*H. Ballard*] read: [*V. Simmes*]

◦22108 *Add note*: This Scott, who is also the author of 22074, actually preached only once at the Rolls Chapel. He was rector of Northwold and of Oxburgh in Norfolk, the father of the author of 22064 sqq., and died in 1616.

Add new heading:
p. 319^{1} **Scott, William,** *of Queen's College, Oxford. See* Bookplates.

Add new heading:
•p. 319^{1} **Scribanius, Carolus.** *See* 6016.

•22111 *Continue imprint*: *sold* [*in the shop of N. Bourne*,]

•p. 319^{1} **Scrougie.** *Add cross-reference*:
—*See* also 12065.

•p. 319^{2} **Scute.** *Add cross-reference*:
—*See* also 483.13.

•22133 *For* L^{39}. *read*: L^{39}(W).

Add new heading:
•p.320^{1} **Searle, Frances** or **Francis.** *See* Bookplates.

•22160 *Add note*: There are 2 eds.: (i) tp has no border (L^{19}, HD) or (ii) tp has border similar to, but not the same as, McK. & F. 28 (L). The L copy lacks the last 2 leaves and, though app. pr. by one of the Coplands, its date is uncertain and its colophon unknown.

•22160.3 *Delete*: NLM.

Add new entry:
•22160.4 —[A variant, w. colophon:] (*W. Copland f. A. Vele*, 1552 (12 au.)) NLM.

Add new heading:
p. 320^{2} **Segar, Thomas.** *See* Bookplates.

•p. 321^{2} **Selden.** *In 'ed.' references before* 7438, *add*: 7226,

Add new heading:
•p. 321^{2} **Semper, Humphrey.** *See* 5209.3.

•22199 *In pressmark for* fol. 17 *read*: fol. 26

•22200 *In line 1 read*: [Anon. On the murder of regent Moray.] *Amend date*: 1570.]

•22221 *In line 4 of note read*: Studley (Greg 79–81).

•22235 *Substitute this note*: The woodblocks for tpp borders and illustrations were first used in the Antwerp ed. of 1553; *see* McK. & F. 253–5. They were later used in the 1606 ed. in Dutch pr. in Amsterdam by C. Claeszoon, who also pr. them on sheets otherwise blank and shipped them to Basel, where letterpress in German was overprinted in 1608, and to London for the present ed. Snodham pr. only the bifolium following the 1st tp. Some copies have Peake's name—but not the address—in the imprint inked out (F, all tpp but bk. 3, which has no imprint; 1 HD, bk. 5 tp only).

22241.5 *Continue note*: The prelims. (a–b^{4}) are in the same setting in this and 22242. The gen. tp varies: with (O, F) or without (C) 'With an addition of the murther ...', which refers to Bk. 10; that portion is present in all 3 copies.

•22249 Juel-Jensen copies now = O.

Add new entry:
22250.5 —[Anr. ed., w. the same contents as 22250.6.] Petri Carteri Cantabrigiensis in J. Setoni Dialecticam annatationes [*sic*]. 8°. *in æd. T. Marshi*, 1563. Ent. 1562–63. L(tp only, Ames I.225).PLUME.

•22255 *Delete*: Y.

•22268 *In note for* Reprinted in *read*: *See* also

•22270 *For* Not written by Seymour *read*: By W. Patten?

•p. 324^{2} **Seyssel.** *In 'tr.' reference before* 24056 *add*: 6893,

•22273 *Continue note*: Includes Greg 309–406.

•22334 *In imprint read*: [*W. White a. T. Creede*] ... *Continue note*: Creede pr. quires B, F–I.

•22335 *Amend imprint as in* 22334. *Continue note*: Creede pr. quires E–I.

•22341.5 *In imprint delete*: *T. Judson?*

•22348 *Amend date*: 1600 [i.e. 1602.]

Add new heading:
•p. 327^{2} **Shakleton, Francis.** *See* Shakelton, F.

•p. 327^{2} **Sharp, J.** *Following* 22368 *add cross-reference*:
—Theses theologicæ ... J. Scharpio moderante. 1631. *See* 7487.29.

•22370 *In heading for* **John** *read*: **James.**

•22379.5 *Continue note*: *See* also 8750.

Add new heading:
•p. 328^{1} **Shawe, William.** *See* Bookplates(*A*3).

•p. 328^{1} **Shaxton.** *Add cross-reference*:
—*See* also 6083.

•22393 *For last sentence of note substitute this*: Pt. 3 also issued sep. as 13455.7.

Add new heading:
p. 329^{1} **Shepheard, Richard.** *See* Bookplates.

•22406.4 *Add location*: L(Rox I.504–5). *Add note*: Later eds. are not divided into stanzas.

Add new headings:
•p. 329^{2} **Shepley, Hugh.** The sorrowful soules solace. 1611. *See* 26014.3(*A*3).
• **Sheppard, Thomas.** *See* Bookplates(*A*).
Sherard, Roland. *See* Bookplates.

•22428 *Following title correct the Erasmus text*: [De pueris ad virtutem ... instituendis.]

•22443 *Add note*: K2^{v} varies; most copies (F, 2 HD, 1 BO) have line 1 beginning: 'As when ...'; 1 BO is an early state omitting this line and beginning: '*Wi.* I am ...'

•22451 *In title for* opportunity *read*: opportunitie

•22460 *In imprint* for [*J. Okes*] read: [*N. Okes*]

Add new entry:

•22463.6 **Shoreditch,** *Duke of*. The merry reioycing hystorie, of the notable feates of archerie, of Wylliam duke of Shordiche, of the Marchaunt Taylors ... the xij. daye of August. 1577. Published by his noble heralde Pegaso. 8°. *printed by authoritie of the sayd dukes speciall priuiledge, by R. Jhones*, [1577.] Ent. 23 au. 1577. London, Merchant Taylors' Hall(tp only).

Sictor, J. *Add new entry immediately following* 22533a:

•22533a.3 —Prophylacticum urbis Londinensis adversus pestem. [In verse.] s.sh.*obl*.fol. [*T. Cotes*, 1636?] PN.

•22534 *Add 2nd paragraph to note*: For the collation of Sidney's STC works with a census of known copies *see Sir Philip Sidney: An Anthology of Modern Criticism*, ed. Dennis Kay, Oxford, 1987, pp. 289–314. For the Psalms to French tunes mentioned on p. 310, of which xl, xli, xlii are in part derived from Sidney's trans., *see* 2734.

•22539 *Add location*: HD. *Continue note*: A4^{v} differs, either being blank (HN, HD; NY-22539a) or having an editor's note (PFOR; most copies of 22539a; this A4 is also inserted in HN-22539).

•22540 *Add note*: *See* also 7076.5.

•22541 *Add note*: Includes Greg 152.

•22546a *In note for* John Buxton *read*: 1 O

•p. 334^{1} **Sidney.** *Following 'tr.' references, add cross-reference*:
—*See* also 2734(*A*3), 6789.

Add new heading:

•p. 334^{2} **Silva, Juan de,** *Conde de Portalegre. See* 5624.

•p. 334^{2} **Simler.** *In 'tr.' references before* 4078 *add*: 4055.5, 4075,

•p. 334^{2} **Simson, A.,** *Minister. Following* 22563 *add cross-reference*:
—*ed. See* 6112.

Add new heading:

p. 335^{1} **Singleton, Thomas.** *See* Bookplates.

•22588 *Amend date*: [1484.]

•22590 *Continue note*: Suppressed by proclamation; *see* 8172.

•22624 *In note for* 11905 *read*: 11906.

Add new heading:

•p. 336^{2} **Skene, Robert,** *ed. See* 5957.

•22627 *Delete*: L^{16}. (It is a 19th century reprint.)

Add new heading:

•p. 336^{2} **Skinner, John,** *Factor of the East India Company. See* 7451.

•22634.5 *Add after date*: ?Ent. to R. Badger 24 ja. 1637. *Add locations*: L(3: in C.72.e.6; 1486.cc.5; and Davis P464). L^{14}(bd. w. DMH 645).O(Vet.A2f.49).

22660 *Continue note*: Also issued as pt. 3 of 22685.5(*A*).

Add new entry:

22685.5 —[Anr. ed.] 3 pts. *R. Field f. T. Man*, 1591. L(pt. 1 only, completed by 22686).; HD(imp.).
Collates A^{4} B–F^{8} G^{4} (Preparative); A–F^{8} G^{4} (Lords supper, also issued sep. as 22705); A–C^{8} D^{4} (Usury, also issued sep. as 22660).

22697 *Delete*: First serm. ... 1588.

22705 *Continue note*: Also issued as pt. 2 of 22685.5(*A*).

•22752 *Add after date*: Jonah serms. ass'd by R. Dexter to Burby 3 se. 1599.

22783.7 *Add after title*: 3 pts. *Add location*: L(2). *Continue note*: C^{4} collates: A^{4} (b)^{8} B^{8} (Pride); A–E^{8} F^{4} (Fall and Restitution, w. sub tp on C6^{r}); A–C^{8} (Wedding garment); w. all tpp dated 1592. In 1 L copy the Wedding garment is a reissue of 22714; in the other it is lacking.

•22790 *Continue note*: Bk. 6 is recommended for reading in 13450.

•p. 342^{2} **Smith, Miles,** *Bp. Add cross-reference at end*:
See also 10209.7(*A*).

•p. 343^{1} **Smith, Richard,** *Bp. Following* 22814 *add to 'See also' references*: 5576, ... 13600,

•p. 343^{1} **Smith, Richard,** *Dean. Following* 22824 *add cross-reference*:
—*See* also 4654.

•p. 343^{1} **Smith, Richard,** *Printer and Publisher*. Delete: *Printer and Add cross-reference*:
—*ed. See* 12403.

Add new heading:

•p. 343^{1} **Smith, Robert.** *See* 3478.5 sq.

•22837 *Continue imprint*: *sold* [*in the shop of N. Bourne*,]

Add new entries:

•22839.7 —Third edition. 8°. *N. Okes, sold by S. Waterson*, 1617. MEL(imp.). Peter W. M. Blayney, Silver Spring, Maryland(imp.).

•22839.8 —[A variant, w. imprint:] *N. Okes*, 1617. C^{4}(lacks folding table).

•22839.9 —[A variant, w. imprint:] *N. Okes, sold by J. Budge*, 1617. David C. Lachman, *bookseller*, Wyncote, Pennsylvania (list of Spring 1988, item 178, lacks C1).

•22840 *Delete*: C^{4}.

Add new entry:

•22845.4 —Tenth edition. 8°. *N. Okes*, 1633. O(no engr. tp).

22868.5 *Continue note*: Reprinted in 1048.

•22869 For [*J. Roberts* ... read: [*W. White* ... *In last line of note for* Roberts *read*: White

•22869.3 *Amend imprint as in* 22869.

•22870 *In imprint delete*: [*W. Williamson? f.*]

•22872 *Add after date*: Ent. 5 oc.

•22875 *Continue note*: ... 5450, 12567.

•22880.2 *Substitute this imprint*: [*London*, 1540.] *Continue 2nd paragraph of note*: The other item in the controversy in the same types as the present work is 12206a.7; a later item is 9343.8, q.v.

•22885 *In imprint delete names in square brackets. Substitute this note*: Jones himself pr. the prelims.

•22886 *Add after title*: [Partly derived from Erasmus's colloquy: Conjugium.]

Add new heading:

•p. 346^{1} **Socinus, Faustus Paulus.** *See* 12401.

22891 *Correct end of title to*: *Tr.* (N. G.)

22906 *Continue note*: Tp imprint varies: 'Bish.' (L, C^{2}) or 'Bishop.' (P).

Add new entry:

•22934.8 —The twentiethree [*sic*] edition. 12°. *M. D*[*awson*] *f. H. Onerton* [sic, for *Ouerton*], 1637. L(imp.).

Soto, A. de. *Add new 1st entry*:

•22936.5 —A brief instruction howe we ought to heare the mass, and with what dispostion, and præparation. With a summarie declaration of the misteries and ceremonies therof. *Tr.* out of Spanish by Br. Fracis Bell freer minor English. 12°. *Bruxelles, J. Pepermans*, 1624. Swaffham Parish Church.

•p. 348^{1} **Southampton.** *For* 7957.5 *read*: 7976.7.

22949.5 *Continue note*: Although written by the end of 1591, the text as pr. is dated 14 Dec. 1595 at the end. It was not pr. until shortly before 17 Dec. 1600; *see Cal.S.P.D., 1598–1600*, p. 499.

Add new entry:

22951.5 —[Anr. ed.] 8°. [*J. Roberts f. G. Cawood*, 1596?] USHAW (lacks tp).
Collates A–L^{8}; it is the only ed. to have a woodcut orn. w. 'IHS' on A8^{r}.

•p. 348^{2} *Following* 22955.5 *add cross-reference*:
—A poeme declaring the real presence. 1606. *See* 14560.5.

•22955.7 *Continue note*: *See* also 12407.

22956 *Add note*: Pr. later than 22957.

•22968 *In imprint read*: *E.* [i.e. *J.*?] *Benson*,

Add new entry:

•22984.2 —[Anr. ed.] 8°. *R. Robinsonus*, 1595. ETON.

•22984.3 *In imprint* for *Robinson* read: *Bradock*

•22984.4 *Begin imprint*: [*R. Field*,] *Add after date*: Dexter's copies ent. to the Stat. Co. 28 no. 1603.

Add new entry:

•22998.5 —[Heading:] The spyte of Spaine, or a thankfull remembrance of Gods mercie in Britanes dileuerie [*sic*] from the Spanish armado. 1588. [In verse.] 8°. [*Edinburgh, heirs of A. Hart*, 1628?] Edinburgh Bibliographical Society(2 imp. leaves, the 2nd and ?7th, deposited at E).
For a larger fragment of this text w. tp, possibly the same edition, *see* Hazlitt II.571.

•23010.5 *In note for* 6832.7 *read*: 6832.1.

Add new entry:

•23017.6 —The 28. edition. 24° in 12's. [*T. Cotes*] *f. M. Sparke junior*, (1640.) Lord Rothschild.
The 3 illustrations in this ed. are woodcuts, w. text pr. on the verso.

•p. 351^{2} **Speculum.** *Immediately preceding* 23030.7 *add cross-reference*:
—Speculum peccatorum. [1509?] *See* 954.5(***A***).

•p. 351^{2} **Speech.** The speech which ... *For* 13119.5 *read*: 13120.5.

23031 *Add note*: C has an early state of some sheets, including blank tp verso; P, HD have errata on tp verso.

•p. 352^{2} **Speed,** *Genealogies headnote*. *After* IIIc *add distinction*:
cc *euermore, Amen.* [i.e. both words in italic]

Add new entry:

23039.2A —[Anr. issue.] [*J. Beale*, 1613?] L(L.9.c.3, Fry 6).O^{16} (Fry 6).; HN(Fry 6 and Fry 22). Fry 6, 22.
Ib, <IIIf.>

•23039.5 *In distinctions for* IIIc *read*: IIIcc(***A***3).

•23039e.3 *In note, following distinctions add*: Another L(C.143.b.10) has IVb6, Va.

•23041.2 *In line 3 of note read*: (O, defective, also missing last 2 digits in date, which may have read 1613)

•23044 *In line 3 of note after* 1621.' *add*: GOT, PARIS(Dép. de la Géogr.) have similar but undated labels; at least GOT also has a cancel Latin dedic., B1, by Hondius to the United Provinces.

•23046.3 *In line 1 of note for* 11 *read*: 1

Add new entry:

•23060.3 —[Heading π1^{r}:] By John Speidell ... A table of interest upon interest for yeares, whereby with addition onely may be cast up what any summe with the interest will amount unto after 8. per cent. 4°. [*E. Allde*? 1627?] L(bd. w. pt. 1 of 23060, 23064.7, 23061).

•23063.3 *For 1st sentence of note substitute this*: This and the following have 4 added quires [N–Q]^{4}, w. logarithms of whole numbers 1–1000; in the L^{30} copies listed here and below sigs. have been added in MS.

•23064.7 *Substitute these locations*: L.NEP. *Add note*: Both copies have the long addition.

•p. 355^{2} **Speidell.** *Add cross-reference at end*:
—A table of interest. *See* 23060.3(***A***3).

•23080 *Continue note*: For extracts in phonetic spelling *see* 11873.

Add new heading:

•p. 357^{2} **Spenser, Thomas.** *See* Bookplates and ***A***3.

•23100a *In imprint* for *Harrison* [*2*] read: *Harrison* [*4*] (Since John 1 died before 11 Feb. 1617, John 4 was 'junior' at the time of entry, and the imprint has his address at the Unicorn.)

•23109 *In SR entry read*: Ent. to T. Man 1 and Jonas Man

•23110 *Add after date*: Ass'd 8 oc. 1622.

•p. 359^{1} **Stanbridge.** *In 'Accidence' headnote continue last paragraph*: For a kindred text with 14 leaves *see* 7018.5.

•23153 *Amend date*: [1535?]

Add new entry:

•23153.8 —[Anr. ed.] 4° in 6's? [*J. Rastell*, 1509?] M(b3,4 only, in 9765 = STC 7016.4).
b3^{r} last line: 'as louynge louande and his latin endeth in ans or in'.

•23153.9 The Robinson copy was sold at Sotheby's, 23 June 1988, lot 99.

•23154.3 *Amend location*: BIRM(Selbourne deposit, only C1 and its conjugate). *Continue note*: The BIRM copy is app. not the one Duff saw since it is in the binding of Martial, *Epigrammaton libri*, Paris, S. Colin, 1539.

•23154.5 *Begin imprint*: [*Westminster*,] *Amend date*: [1495?]

•23163.11 *Correct and continue end of note*: on A6^{r}; the film of C on Univ. Microfilms reel 1326 ('19441') omits A3 opening.

•23166 Quaritch copy now = L(C.135.e.11).

Add new entry:

23180.3 —[Anr. ed.] Uocabula magistri stãbrigi pri/mu̲ iam edita sua saltem editiõe. 4° $^{6.4}$. (*by Wynkyn de worde*,) [1515?] HN(69538).
The title is in a riband without a border, over Hodnett 920; at the end is the device McK. 19. Quires B–C are the same setting as 23180.5.

•23207 *Continue main heading*: *Archdeacon of Colchester.*

•p. 364^{1} *In 'ed.' reference following* 23211 *for the dash read*: **Standish, John,** *fl. 1632.*

•23212 *Continue imprint*: [*St. Omer*,]

23225 *Add note*: The extra leaf among the prelims.: 'Ad Lectorem.' is in 2 settings; line 5 of verse has: '*Causa*' (P) or '*causa*' (HN, HD).

Add new heading:

•p. 364^{2} **Stanhope, Philip,** *1st Earl. See* Bookplates.

•p. 365^{1} **Stapleton, Thomas.** *Following* 23234, *in 'See also' reference, before* 25363 *add*: 11418, 11429,

Add new entry:
•23235.3 **Starkey, John.** John Starkey was baptised in the parish church of Putney, the 10 day of October 1567. And died the eighth day of Decemher [*sic*] 1634. [etc.] s.sh.4°. [*London*, 1634?] CHI(in STC 2141, pasted on verso of N.T. tp).

•23235.5 *Add location*: L(1st sheet only, Cotton MS. Titus B.III, ff. 61–2).

•23259 *Add location*: C⁹. *Delete*: R. *Amend*: WOR(2). *Begin note*: N copy (formerly R) was at one time on undivided ...

Add new entry:
•23267.5 **Stile, *Sir* John.** Com. N. Parcell. Terrarum & possessionum Johannis Stile militis. [Specimen rental of a manor, intended as a guide for bailiffs or stewards, using fictitious names and recording various kinds of tenements and manorial profits.] s.sh.fol. [*London*, c. 1575?] O(J).
Possibly originally drafted in the 1560s when he was a manorial steward by Edmund Anderson, later Chief Justice of the Court of Common Pleas. His is the only name that appears in full besides that of 'Stile' and one of the rentals is a 21-year lease dated 11 May 1546, up for renewal in 1567.

•p. 366² **Stint.** *Following* 23270 *add cross-reference*:
—*See* also 5208.5.

•23283 *Add location*: NMU.

•p. 367¹ **Stockwood.** *Add to 'ed.' references at end*: 4882,

Add new heading:
p. 367¹ **Stone, Richard.** *See* Bookplates.

•23289 *Add after date*: Ent. 4 ja.

Add new heading:
•p. 367² **Storre, Benjamin.** *See* 4930.5.

23310 *Continue note*: The tp, a separate leaf, was set in duplicate; 1st line of imprint ends: '*H.*' or '*Bellamie*,'; both at C.

•23311.5 *Delete*: L. (It is actually 23311.)

•p. 368¹ **Stoughton, W.** *Add to 'See also' references at end*: 10770, 10772.

Add new heading:
•p. 368¹ **Stow, Elizabeth.** *See* Bookplates.

•p. 368² **Stow, J.** *At end of 'Chronicles' headnote add:* Concerning a difference of views with Richard Grafton *see* 12148, 12167.

•23322 *In title for* England, *read*: Englande,

•23335–6 *In imprints* for [*Eliot's Court Press* read: [*P. Short* *In* 23335 *line 1 of note replace* Eliot's Court Press *with* Short

•p. 369² **Strang, J.** *Add cross-reference at end*:
—*See* also 11916.

Add new heading:
•p. 369² **Strange, Thomas.** *See* Bookplates and *A*3.

•p. 370¹ **Stuart, H.** *Delete cross-reference*: —The kingis complaint ...

Add new heading:
p. 370¹ **Stuart, Frances,** *Duchess of Lennox and Richmond. See* Bookplates.

•p. 370² **Stuart, J.** *Add cross-reference*:
—The kingis complaint. [1570.] *See* 22200(*A*3).

•23379 *Delete*: [*J. Danter f.*] (Jones printed this himself.)

Add new entry:
•23399.2 —The theater [etc. as in 23399.3.] 8°. *T. dawson f. H. Carre*, 1584. L(dates on tp and in colophon largely erased).
Dedic. to Philip Howard, Earl of Arundel, and his brothers Thomas and William.

Amend entry:
•23399.3 —[Anr. issue, w. new prelims., w. imprint:] *T. Dawson*, 1585. HD(imp.).
Dedic. to Robert Rich, later 1st Earl of Warwick. The text of the dedic. is slightly revised from 23399.2.

•23422 *In line 2 of note delete*: , indexes,

•23423 *For* C². *read*: C⁹.

◦23428 *Add note*: For other items called 'Stans puer ad mensam' but w. texts in English *see* 17030 and 20953. *See* also 3303, 24866.

•23431 *Correct 1st SR entry*: ?Ent. to J. Walley 1557–58 (Arber I.75);

•23433 *Add note*: For another trans. *see* 11684.

•23434 *Add note*: The L copy has the Cavendish dedic.; O has one to Sir John Brett; both are signed by the publisher, W. C[otton].

Add new heading:
•p. 373¹ **Sursinus, J.** *See* 4511.4.

•p. 373¹ **Survey.** *Add cross-reference*:
—[A survey of lands, etc. belonging to a manor. 1582.] *See* 19491.3(*A*3).

•23436 *Begin imprint*: [*A. Mathewes?*] *Amend date*: [c. 1633?]

23439.5 *Add after date*: Ent. to J. Kingston 3 se. 1579.

•p. 373² **Suso.** *Following* 23443.5 *add cross-reference*:
—*See* also 3305.

•23451 *Continue note*: Selected remarks are answered by 4706.

•23453 *Begin note*: (18134.3 is pt. of this) *Conclude note*: *See* also 6381, 6385.5.

•23454 *In note read*: ... Windet pr. quire A; another pr. O–P; Harrison the rest.

•23485.5 *Begin imprint*: *J. Windet* *Add location*: O.

•23498 *Add note*: 21498, 21504, and 21506 are now considered to be by the same author.

•p. 375¹ **Swale.** *Add cross-reference*:
—*See* also Bookplates.

•23518.5 *For the last sentence of the note substitute this*: Both copies are bd. w. 13458.

•p. 376² **Sweet, J.** *Add cross-reference at end*:
—*See* also 10910.4, 10916.5.

•23547 *Delete last sentence of note.*

Add new entry:
•23547.3 —[A variant, w. tp imprint:] *J. Windet*, 1591. Taussig (without the errata leaf).

•23553 *Amend imprint*: [*London? J. Mychell f. H. Singleton?*

Add new heading:
•p. 377² **Sylburgius, Fridericus,** *ed. See* 5401.

•23578 *Begin note*: (13162 is pt. of this)

•23579 *In title delete*: —The ... Salustius. *Amend locations*: L(bd. w. 21672).; HN.

•23583.5 *Add after date*: Ent. 21 ja. 1617.

•p. 378[1] **Sylvester.** *Add cross-reference at end*:
—*See* also 13475.

•p. 378[1] **Symcocke.** *Add to references*: 8903.

•23586 *Add location*: L. *Add note*: This is a reprint of 23587, including the Hanbury dedic.

•23587 *Add note*: Dedic. differs: to Sir John Hanbury (L) or to George Symmer of Balzordy (L[3], same text but reset and prob. a cancel).

•p. 378[1] **Symmer.** *Following* 23588 *add cross-reference*:
—*See* also 21480(*A*3).

Add new heading:
•p. 378[2] **Symmes, Zachariah,** *ed. See* 13724.

Add new heading:
•p. 381[2] **T., H.,** *Minister, tr. See* 4769.

Add new entry:
◦23619.5 —A funerall elegie, upon the untimely death, of the honorable knight, sir T. Overburie. [In verse.] s.sh. fol. *f. H. Gosson*, 1615. LAMPORT(imp.).
Reprinted in 18920.

•23620 *Add after title*: [*Tr.* from Dutch by] (J. T[urner.]) *Add after date*: Ent. to Linley as tr. by John Turner 11 se.

•p. 381[2] **T., I.** or **J.** *In 'ed.' references following* 23622, *after* 3225 *add*: 9277,

Add new heading:
•p. 382[1] **T., P.** *See* Bookplates (Spenser).

•23626 *Continue note*: ... Tymme, but this is more likely by T. Talbot, author of 23662.5.

•p. 382[1] **T., T.** *Following* 23629 *add cross-reference*:
—*tr. See* 7241.

•23632 *For* 8°. *read*: 4°.

•23633.5 *Amend imprint*: [*J. Wolfe*, 1591.]

•p. 382[2] **Table.** *Add cross-references*:
—A most exact and accurat table of the first ten persecutions. [c. 1625?] *See* 11227.5.
—A table instructiue. [1546?] *See* 11718.9.
—A table of the X. first persecutions. 1610, etc. *See* 11227.3, 11228.3.

•23641.5 *Add note*: This may belong to 5402.5 or 5403, though no copy so far checked has it; an earlier ed. w. imprint: *typis J. Windet*, [1588?] is in the PH copy of 5401. Similar folding tables are found in 5404, q.v.

•23642 *In imprint for* [really ... *read*: [*and* *Begin note*: Robinson app. pr. only the dedic. on 1st ¶2[r-v].

•23656.5 *Add after date*: Ent. 13 no. 1621.

23659.3 *Toward end of SR entry before* 6 de. 1588. *add*: 5 de. 1582 and

•23659.7 *Add after date*: Ass'd by J. Harrison 1 to the English Stock 21 se. 1612.

•23660.5 *In SR entry for* 20 mr. *read*: 5 mr.

•p. 383[2] **Talbot, T.,** *Antiquary. Following* 23662.5 *add cross-reference*:
—*See* also 23626(*A*3).

•23663 *Amend date*: [c. 1530.] *Substitute this note*: Collates A–F[4]. There are 2 settings of at least D2,3; D3[r] line 15 from bottom has: 'questyõ' (L: Huth 31) or 'questiõ' (L: Nash frag. and Harl.5995/190). The device w. Rastell's name, McK. 37, is in a very late state in the Huth ed., and both settings are undoubtedly later than 23664.

•23664 *Substitute this note*; Collates A[4] B–E[6]. Has Rastell's name in device McK. 37. This ed. is earlier than 23663.

•23664.5 *Amend date*: 1547?]

•23670.5 *Continue imprint*: *sold* [*by J. Broome*,]

•23683.3 *Continue note*: An ed. dated 1609 w. Budge's imprint was in the Hessische Landes- und Hochschulbibliothek, Darmstadt but was destroyed during World War II; *see Notes and Queries*, April 1978, p. 129.

•23685a *Amend date*: [1593?]

•23698 *In title for* in *read*: into

•23704 *Add note*: Includes Greg 600.

•p. 385[1] **Taverner, R.** *In 'ed.' references at end after* 4845, *add*: 9290.5,

•23732 *Add location*: Stevens Cox(quire B of pt. 2 only, unfolded). *Delete note.*

•23732.7 *In imprint* for [*jun.*] read: [*sen.*] *Delete*: O[6].; *Add note*: Headlines in roman.

Add new entry:
•23732.8 —[Anr. ed.] 8°. *J. B*[*eale,*] *sold by J. Wright junior*, 1635. O[6].
Headlines in italic.

•23747 *Add location*: L(imp.).

•23757.5 *Amend title*: (The [first] second part ... bagge.) *Put imprint in round brackets.*

•23761 *Add note*: *See* also 4298.

•23765.5 *Continue imprint*: *sold* [*by E. Wright*,]

•23772a.5 Private copy now = E(deposit).

•23777 *Add after date*: Ent. in trust for J. Boler 2 on 7 se. 1638.

•23800 *Delete*: LINC. *and add it at* 23800.5.

•23808 *Add after date*: Ent. to H. Gosson 14 oc.

•23812.7 Private copy now = E(deposit).

Add new entry:
•23815.3 —[Anr. ed.] 8°. [*J. Dawson*, 1640?] L(lacks tp).
E8[v] lists contents of Taylor's Workes (23725) like 23815, but col. 2 last line has: 'eater' whereas 23815 has: 'Eater'.

•23822 *Correct beginning of SR entry*: ?Ent. as 'Cooke on the temptacons of Christ' to ...

•23827 *In title for* happiness: *read*: happinesse:

23845 *Continue note*: Tp in 2 settings; line 2 has: 'PRACTISE' (O) or 'PRACTICE' (C).

•23860 *Continue imprint*: *sold* [*in the shops of N. Newbery*,]

Add new heading:
p. 390[1] **Temple, Alexander.** *See* Bookplates.

23873 *Add note*: This and the next are usually bd. w. 19962.

•23878.5 For [*J. Rastell*, read: [*W. de Worde*,

•23884a.8 *In title for* lady *read*: ledy [*sic*]

•23885.7 *Add after date*: Ent. to H. Bynneman 1569–70. *Add note*: Marsh acquired Bynneman's rights in exchange for Stow (23324) on 31 Mar. 1573; *see* Arber I.272, 418.

Add new entry:
•23885.9 —[Anr. ed.] 8°. *T. Marshus*, 1579. L(tp only, Cup.652. ee.8, fol. 33).

•23888 *For* M[4]. *read*: F. S. Ferguson(untraced).

Add new entry:
•23889.4C —[Anr. ed.] 8°. [*F. Kingston*] *ex typ. Soc. Stat.*, 1631. O.

•23897 *Add note*: Includes Greg 415–16.

•p. 391² **Terentius.** *Add cross-reference at end*:
—*See* also 5318.3.

Add new heading:
•p. 391² **Terrar.** [The terrar, i.e. land survey. 1582.] *See* 19491.3 (***A***3).

•23916 *Add locations*: Gervase Duffield, Appleford, Abingdon, Oxon.(E² only, in bdg of STC 13750).; Sydney U. *Continue note*: The last bifolium is in at least 3 settings: E1ʳ line 5 from bottom begins: 'religyon:' (O) or 'religion:' (Duffield) or line 6 from bottom ends: 'relygion:' (Sydney U).

23918 *After title correct to*: 4 ptbks. *Add note*: The ptbks. have dedic. to Lady Penelope Rich on the recto of the 2nd leaf and 2 commendatory poems on the verso.

Add new entry:
23918.3 —[Anr. issue, w. imprint:] *par T. Este*, 1597. PARIS.
The dedic. to Lady Rich is omitted in all ptbks. and the 1st commendatory poem 'Alla louange' is moved from the verso of the 2nd leaf to the recto. The ptbks. collate: superius, contratenor, bassus: π² B–E⁴ F²; tenor: A–E⁴ F², w. the 2 quintus songs pr. on A4ᵛ and B1ᵛ.

Add new heading:
•p. 392² **Textor, Benoist.** *See* 12498.5.

Add new entries:
•23934.7 —The twelfth time imprinted. 12°. *J. Dawson, sold by J. Parker*, 1622. L(imp.).
•23934.19 —The twentie and third time imprinted. 12°. *J. Dawson f. A. V[incent,] sold by A. Ritherdon*, 1633. WN².
•23935.5 —The twentie and seventh time imprinted. 12°. *M. Dawson f. A. V[incent,] sold by R. Thrale*, 1636. L(imp.).

Theognis. *Add new 1st entry*:
•23943.9 —Θεογνιδος του Μεγαρεως γνωμαι. Theognidis Megarensis sententiæ. Ad usum juventutis excusæ. *Lat. a. Gr.* 8°. *typis E. G[riffin,] sumpt. G. Emersoni*, 1638. L(tp only, C.60.h.16, fol. 36).
The tp is in a different setting from 23944, and the latter is not a cancel. The SR entry at 23944 belongs here.

•p. 393¹ **Theophilus, J.,** *pseud., tr. After* 11786 *add*: 14638.

•23948.5 *Amend imprint*: *Antwerp*, [*f.?*] *H. Jaye*, [*Malines?*]

Add new heading:
•p. 393¹ **Theses.** Theses seu articuli è sacræ scripturæ fontibus desumpti. [1568? etc.] *See* 16777.1(***A***3).

Add new entry:
•23982.7 —[Anr. ed.] 12°. *f. the Co. of Statrs.*, 1614. L(imp.).

Amend description of L *copies*:
•23996 L(IX.Eng.80(2), imp.: B–K only, w. A⁶ of 23998).
•23998 L(IX.Eng.97(2): B–L only, w. A⁶ of 23999; also A⁶ bd. w. 23996).
•23999 L(A⁶ only, bd. w. 23998).

•24000.5 *Add note*: *See* also 7686.2 sqq.

Amend and add entries:
•24004 *Add note*: O(8° B 69 Th) has 'Sims' on the tp and 'Simmes' in the colophon.
•24004.5 —[Anr. ed.] 8°. [*V. Simmes*, c. 1605.] O(8° T 98(5) Th, imp.).
The only ed. w. A3ʳ last line: 'diuell, *Matthew* 4.' and P1ʳ catchword: '*Iura-*'.
•24005 *Add note*: B4ᵛ has 'Deus' factotum, line 2 from bottom has 'waye'.
•24005.3 —[Anr. ed.] 8°. [*T. Purfoot f. V. Simmes*, 1611?] O(8° S 232 Th, imp.).
B4ᵛ has 'Deus' factotum, line 2 from bottom has 'waie'.

•24006 *Add location*: O(Vet.A1f.166(2)).

•24009 *Add note*: The Tractatus is attrib. to T. Oliver.

Add new entry:
•24025.5 —[Anr. issue, w. cancel tp:] The pope arraigned, and by an inquest of learned and orthodoxe divines found to bee Antichrist. With the triall of guides. *f. R. M[eighen*, 1618?] SAL.
Retains sub tp w. imprint as in 24025; SAL also has a colophon on Aa4ʳ w. 24025 imprint whereas in at least the O, F copies of 24025 Aa4ʳ is blank. In the 1st pt. the 1st and 3rd sections prob. represent the sermon as preached, but the present title emphasizes the extensive 2nd section of what is actually a treatise.

Add new heading:
•p. 396¹ **Thongerloo, Cornelis Van.** [Almanack. 1550.] *See* 517.15(***A***).

•24040.5 *Add note*: Maunsell (17669), pt. 1, p. 37 gives the title: Confutation of Follie, containing certaine selected questions, pithie answeres, & sillogisticall obiections, touching places of holy scripture. Taken out of Lucas Lossius questions, by Henry Thorne, pr. by Denham in 1584.

Amend and add entries:
•24048 *For* YK. *read*: NLW(St. Asaph).
•24049 *For* [Anr. issue ... *read:* [A variant ...
•24049.3 —[A variant, w. imprint on gen. tp:] *J. Dawson, f. R. M[abb,] sold by M. Sparke junior*, 1640. YK(XV. C.24).

•24055–5.5 *In imprints* for [*London*, read: [*Middelburg, R. Schilders*,

•p. 397¹ **Throkmorton.** *Add to 'See also' references at end*: 1521, 4713, 6801, 6805, 10392, 10850, 17453–9, 24505. (These are all registered in ***A***3 and are based on attributions in Leland H. Carlson, *Martin Marprelate, Gentleman*, [1981.])

Add new heading:
•p. 397¹ **Tignonville, Guillaume de,** *tr. See* 6826.

•24076 *Continue title*: ... mariage. Largely adapted from the Coloquios matrimoniales of Pedro de Luján, who appears as one of Tilney's speakers.] *Continue note*: For reproductions of D2ʳ of 24076 and 24076.7 *see Library* 26 (1945): 175–81. The Gration-Maxfield copy sold at Sotheby's, 15 Dec. 1982, lot 19, and resold at Christie's, 27 Mar. 1985, lot 354, was sophisticated, with the tp in facsimile based on HN-24076.3 and most of the text sheets of 24077, which has D2ʳ line 3 from bottom ending 'drewe nere,' as in 24076.7 but in line 8 from bottom has 'our' whereas 24076.7 has 'oure'.

Add new heading:
p. 398² **Tomlinson, Robert.** *See* Bookplates.

Add new heading:
•p. 398² **Tomson, James.** *See* Bookplates(***A***).

Add new headings:
•p. 398² **Tonbridge School.** *See* Bookplates.
•**Tongherloo, Cornelis van.** [Almanack. 1550.] *See* 517.15(***A***).

24115.5 *Add note*: For a later ed. *see* 10608.

Add new heading:
•p. 398² **Tonstall, Anthony.** *See* 13540.5.

•24121 *Add note*: For a later state of the folding engr. of characterical letters *see* 20835.3(***A***3).

Add new headings:
•p. 399² **Touris, William.** *See* 5643(***A***).
•**Tournament.** The turnament of Tottenham. 1631. *See* 19925.

Add new heading:
•p. 400¹ **Townshend, Roger.** *See* 9771.5, 9779.

°24163 *Substitute this imprint*: [*J. Day a. W. Seres*, 1548.] *For* O *copy delete*: (frag.) *and add*: F(2). *Add note*: Collates π⁴; intended as a preface to 3816 (to which the colophon formerly cited belongs) and at least D, P, and 1 F copies are so bound.

•24178 *Add note*: For an attack on Traske's earlier views, of which the present item is a recantation, *see* 10675.

•24178.5 *Add location*: ; HN.

•p. 401[1] **Traske.** *Add cross-reference at end*:
—*See* also 13019.

•p. 401[1] **Travels.** *Add cross-reference at beginning*:
—The travailes of the three English brothers. 1607. *See* 6417.

•24188.5–89 *Amend dates*: 1478.]

Add new entry:
•24191a.5 —[Anr. ed.] And first imprinted 1563. 8°. (*H. Denham f. J. Charlewood*, 1566 (26 ap.)) L.

•24197.5 *Add after date*: Ass'd 31 my. 1594.

•24203.7 *Begin imprint*: [*R.* or *W. Copland*? ...

Add new entry:
•24207.3 —[Anr. ed.] The treasure of poore men. Containing sundry approoued remedies. Newly corrected and amended. 8°. *V. S[immes,] assigned by W. Aspley*, 1601. HN.
The SR entry at 24207 belongs here.

•24208 *For* by *M. de Comalada*, *read*: erroneously attrib. to

•24209 *Add note*: Both copies lack B6,7.

•p. 402[2] **Treatise.** *Add cross-reference*:
—A lytell treatyse confoundyng the great eresyes. [1538?] *See* 15192.5.

•24227.5 *Add location*: PARIS². *Add note*: *See* Nijhoff and Kronenberg 3979.

24228 *Add note*: For the 4th pt. of the Prick of Conscience *see* 3360.

•24229 *Amend date*: [1548?]

•24233 *Add note*: Imprint varies; with or without mention of Boyle's 'shop in the Black Friers'; both at L.

24242 *Continue note*: P has frags. of a later ed. w. tp, but pr. in de Worde's types.

•24242.5 *Add after title*: [By A. Estienne. *Tr.* from French.] *Add note*: The orig. French is included in 6738 sqq.

•p. 403[2] **Treatise** *Add cross-reference*:
—A treatise wherin is moost plainlye expressed howe the bysshops of Rome [etc. 1548?] *See* 21309.7(*A*3).

Add new entry:
•24251.6 —[Anr. ed., without dedic. or prayer for the Queen.] The holy exercise [etc.] 16° in 8's. [*Scotland*? c. 1582.] Lord Kenyon(bd. w. 16581).

Add new heading:
p. 404[1] **Tredway, Robert** and **Edmund.** *See* Bookplates.

24265 *Continue note*: This is a trans. of Pia et necessaria admonitio, Frankfurt, 1563, attrib. to M. Flacius.

•24273 *Add note*: The attrib. to Bradshaw is dubious; possibly by J. Balmford.

Add new heading:
•p. 405[1] **Tricorones.** Tricorones, sive soles gemini in Britannia. 1607. *See* 3222.5.

•24277 *Delete*: (imp.) *from* O *copy*.

•24288.5 *Add after date*: Ent. to W. Hall to print 1 ed. on 28 no. 1608.

•24316 *Add after date*: ?Ent. to W. Welby 7 mr.

24319 *Add note*: Tp verso is blank or has errata. Quires C and Z are in 3 settings; C1ʳ has no catchword, or has catchword: 'Quęstio' or 'Verum,' (the last at O, HN, HD); Z1ʳ line 12 has: 'communis' and line 21 has: 'additę' or 'cōmunis / additę'or 'communis / additæ'. Copies of all are at C except as noted.

•p. 406[2] **Tunstall.** *Preceding 'See also' cross-references at end add*:
—*ed. See* 2072.

•24330 *Delete*: (missing) *from* E² *copy*.

Add new heading:
•p. 407[2] **Turner, John,** *tr. See* 23620(*A*3).

•24333 *Add after date*: Ent. to Nealand 28 mr.

•24357 *Continue note*: ... Knox, but it actually is the same text as the 1st epistle in 10390; a slightly different version signed by A. G[ilby] is pr. in 11888.

Add new heading:
•p. 408[2] **Turrecremata, Joannes de,** *Cardinal. See* 12512.

•24371 *Add after date*: Ent. to Stansby 12 my.

•24401 *Add location*: E⁴.

•24406 *Add note*: Tp pr. on same halfsheet as cancel tp for 37.3 (*A*3).

•p. 409[2] **Twyne, T.** *In 'tr.' references at end add*: 6226,

•24443.5 *In line 2 for* L. Ridley *read*: H. Bullinger *Continue note*: L. Ridley may have tr. the Bullinger expositions and edited all 3 sections.

•24446 *Continue note*: Prohibited by proclamation; *see* 7775.

•24447.7 *Amend imprint*: [*Canterbury? J. Mychell*, 1535–36?]

•24454 *Add note*: Prohibited by proclamation; *see* 7775.

•24455.5 *Amend imprint*: [*Canterbury? J. Mychell*, 1535–36?]

•24468 *Begin note*: Also attrib. to G. Joye.

•24473 *Continue note*: The text sheets reappear under astonishing circumstances in 6273.3, w. new prelims. by A. Darcie intimating his own authorship.

•24487.5 *Add location*: LINC(tp def.).

•24488 *Delete*: LINC. *and add*: M.

•24503 *Add location*: P(imp., w. tp to 19796).

•24503.3 *Cancel entry and substitute this*: A ghost, based on imp. P copy of 24503.

•24505 *After* Anon. *add*: Prob. not by Udall but by J. Throkmorton.

Add new entry:
•24508.9 —[A variant, w. Udall dedic. and imprint:] *J. Haviland f. W. Barret*, 1624. E.

•24510 *In SR entry after* 3 ap. *add*: 1626.

Add new heading:
•p. 414[1] **Ulloa, Alfonso de,** *tr. See* 11488.

•24514 *In note add cross-references*: 3766(*A*3), 10430, 20972.7 (*A*3).

•24516 *Continue note*: *See* also 8465.

•24518 *In note delete*: HN ... facsimile; (HN-Halsey copy has genuine map.)

Add new heading:
p. 414[1] **Underhill, William.** *See* Bookplates.

•24525 *In imprint and in note* for *T. Creede* read: *B. Alsop*

Add new entry:
•24525.3 —[Anr. issue, also anon., w. A^4 cancelled and replaced by π^2 (tp and contents.)] The historie of Astrea. Containing many remarkable and delightfull stories, [etc.] *sold by J. Smithwicke*, [1625?] HD(imp.).
New prelims. pr by [*W. Stansby*.]

•24526 *For* [By I. Gentillet] *read*: [*Tr.* from Speculum Jesuiticum, attrib. to Joachim Beringer.]

•24535 *In imprint* for *T. Cooke*, read: *J. Hardy*,

•24557 *At end of 1st paragraph of note add*: All copies should have 2 paragraphs of errata on $Xx4^r$.

•p. 416^2 **Utie.** *Add cross-reference*:
—*ed. See* 10805.

Add new heading:
•p. 417^1 **Vair, William.** *See* Du Vair, G.

•24577 *Add after title*: [Anon.]

•24578 *Continue note*: The latter variety is anon.; both varieties have verses on $A2^v$, signed: 'P. C. Chiriatros' in the anon. variety and 'P. C. Chiratros [*sic*]' in the one w. Valentinus's name.

•24599.5 *Begin imprint*: [*R. Bradock*]

Add new heading:
°p. 419^1 **Vaughan, Walter.** *See* Bookplates.

Turn entry into a cross-reference:
•24623.3 [Rudimenta. *Edinburgh*, 1507.] = 7018.

•24623.5 *Delete*: [Anr. ed.] (This is a different text from that represented in 7018.)

Add new heading:
•p. 420^1 **Vedel, Anders Sørensen,** *tr. See* 13067.

24627a.10 *Add note*: There are copies at O, HN, HD w. tp imprint: *Antuerpiæ, venalia ap. auctorem, prostant ap. H. Verdussen*, 1608, but they have French verses substituted for the English and so do not qualify for STC. The imprint and text of the BRISTOL could not be checked.

•24632 *Add note*: The present Velcurio is Johannes Bernhardi; he is also the editor of 10471.7.

•p. 420^2 **Venice.** *Add cross-reference*:
—The popes bull gelded or an edict published by the duke and state of Venice. 1606. *See* 7019.

Add new heading:
•p. 421^1 **Vergara, Franciscus.** *See* 5402.5.

24667 *Add note*: Tp varies; line 5 ends: 'col-' (P) or 'volumen' (C).

Add new heading:
p. 422^1 **Vernon, Henry.** *See* Bookplates.

Add new heading:
•p. 423^2 **Vida, Marcus Hieronymus.** *See* 6216.

•p. 423^2 **Vignay.** *Add cross-reference*: 4920,

•24733 *In note after* A&R 856 *add*: At least STU has the date on the S. Patricke sub tp altered, app. by hand-stamping an extra 'I', to produce: M. DC. XXVIII.

•24790.7 *Add after date*: Ent. to T. Orwin 7 my.

•24791 *In line 2 of title read*: ... Fabricij obseruationes.

•24817 *Continue note*: Georgiks sub tp varies: w. Fleming's and Orwin's initials as on the gen. tp (1 O, HN, HD) or w. their names in full (1 O).

•24826 *Continue note*: *See* also 4604.

Add new entry:
°24827.5 —Les faictz merueilleux de virgille. 8° in 4's. (*Paris, pour J. sainct Denis*) [*a. for W. de Worde, London*, c. 1525.] O.
With de Worde's device, McK. 24, on $D4^v$; Brunet II.1167 describes a copy with McK. 11.

•24832–2a *Continue imprints*: *sold* [*by W. Burre*,]

•24833 *Continue imprint*: *sold* [*by E. Blount*,]

•24852 *In SR entry after* Crosley *add*: of Oxford

•24852.7 *Continue SR entry*: ... 1590; to John Newbery 12 jn. 1600; to J. Harrison 1 on 16 se. 1606; ass'd by Harrison to the English Stock 21 se. 1612. *Continue note*: This or an earlier version of the text was yielded by H. Bynneman to the Stat. Co. on 8 Jan. 1584; *see* Arber II.788.

Add new entry:
•24854.7 —[Anr. ed.] Colloquia, sive exercitationes Latinæ linguæ. 8°. *Aberdoniæ, E. Rabanus*, 1639. E.

•p. 429^2 **Vives.** *Add to 'See also' references at end*: 3483 (this portion reprinted in 4028, 6428), 3542.

•24867 *Amend date*: [1496?]

•24870.5 *Add location*: HN.

•24873 *Amend imprint*: ... *Caxton*, 1483 (20 no.)) *In line 1 of note for* de Worde *read*: Caxton

•24874 *Amend imprint*: ... *Caxton*, 1483 (20 no.)) [c. 1484.] *In lines 2–3 of note for* de Worde *read*: Caxton

•24880.5 *Amend date*: 1501?]

24883 *Add note*: The C and P copies have (∗)2 'Typographus lectori S.' removed; it is present in the C copy of 24882.7.

•24893 *Continue imprint*: *sold* [*in the shops of N. Newbery*,]

Add new heading:
•p. 431^1 **Vulcan.** A mery dema‹nd ...› betwene Vu‹lcan and Venus.› [1563?] *See* 6572.3.

•24895 *For* L(tp ... *read*: L(1 lacking A2, plus tp ...

•24903 *In imprint* for *J. F. Stam* read: *widow of J. Veseler*

Add new heading:
•p. 433^1 **W., F.** The miseries of a jaile. 1619. *See* 10782.

•24904 *For* TEX. *read*: TEX^2.

•p. 433^2 **W., H.,** *tr. For* 13119.5 *read*: 13120.5.

•p. 433^2 **W., I.** or **J.** *Preceding* 24907 *add cross-references*:
—Desiderius. Or a most godly, dialogue. 1625. *See* 6777.7.
—The devotion of bondage. 1634. *See* 6798.3.

•24908 *Add note*: The copies listed all have dedic. to G. Ridgeway. In 1977 E. P. Goldschmidt & Co. had a copy w. dedic. (not a cancel) to William Halliday/Holliday.

•24911 *Add location*: L^2(imp.).

•24912.5 *Begin note*: The prelims. are the 'cancelled' leaves of 5364, q.v.; C^{17} ...

•24916.3 *Begin entry*: —[Anr. impression, w. additions.]

•p. 435^2 **Wake,** *Sir* **I.** *Add cross-reference at end*:
—*See* also 3194.

•24956.5 *Add location*: L(C.119.dd.17).

•24966 *Begin note*: Not by Walkington but by Thomas Wilson, *Divine*, who was a minister in Canterbury at the time.

•24966a *Continue imprint*: [*Canterbury*,]

•p. 437^2 **Walpole, M.** *Add cross-reference at end*:
—*See* also 8448(*A*3).

Add new heading:
p. 437[2] **Walrond, John.** *See* Bookplates.

Add new entry:
•24997.5 —[Anr. ed.] 8°. *G. Eld f. J. Wright*, 1619. L.

•25002 *Continue note*: Answered in 7077.

25007 *Continue note*: Includes a few precepts on planting trees and vines derived partly from Palladius and partly from a text similar to 5952.5.

Add new heading:
•p. 438[1] **Walter, Elizabeth.** *See* Bookplates(***A***).

•p. 438[1] **Walther, R.** *Add cross-reference at end*:
—*See* also 10847.

Add new heading:
•p. 438[1] **Walton, Izaak.** *See* 7038.

Add new heading:
•p. 438[1] **Walton, Thomas.** *See* 5431.

•25022 *Add note*: *See* also 1417, 6184.

•p. 439[2] **Ward, S.,** *of Ipswich. Add to 'See also' references*: Bookplates(***A***).

•25073 *In note for* 6832.22 *read*: 6836.5.

•25089 *Add note*: For a pamphlet on the murder *see* 11985.

•25089.5 The privately owned copy now = E(deposit).

•25090a *Delete*: YK.

Add new entry:
•25090a.3 —[Anr. issue, omitting edition statement.] *A. Matthewes a. J. Norton, sold by T. Jones*, 1624. YK.
The tp is completely reset but does not appear to be a cancel. Its wording and quotations (Deut. xvi.18–20) are more like 25091, while 25090a resembles 25090 (John v.39 and Acts xvii.11).

Add new heading:
p. 441[1] **Warren, Richard.** *See* Bookplates.

Add new heading:
•p. 441[1] **Warrington, Lancashire,** *Augustinian Priory. See* Indulgences 82G(***A***3).

Add new heading:
p. 441[1] **Washington,** *Sir* **Laurence.** *See* Bookplates.

Add new heading:
•p. 441[2] **Waterhouse, Nathanael.** *See* 6902.

•p. 441[2] **Waterman, W.** *Add cross-references*:
—*See* also 5225, 25668.5(***A***3).

•p. 441[2] **Watkinson.** *Add to 'tr.' references*: 16985,

Add new entry:
25109.5 **Watson, Christopher.** Briefe principles of religion, collected for the exercise of youth. [Init. Chr. Wats. De., i.e. deacon.] 1/2 sh.fol. *H. Singleton*, 1578. C[4].
The 1581 ed., 25110, has Watson's name in full.

•25112 *Add locations*: L.; HD. *Continue note*: HD has Aa8 present and blank except for 5 repetitions of the word 'tyrant' at bottom of verso, intended for use as slip cancels, e.g. on A2^r last line, over 'triant'.

•25118 L[4] copy now = L.

Add new heading:
p. 442[2] **Waune, George.** *See* Bookplates.

•25136 *Add note*: The address in the imprint varies: 'the Bible in Pauls Church-yard' (Brewster) or 'the Bible in Cheapeside' (Bird); both at L.

Add new entry:
25151.7 —[Anr. ed.] Newly enlarged. 4°. [*J. Wolfe*] *f. W. Wright*, 1590. O[6].
B1^r catchword: 'Noble'; C2^r catchword: 'I haue'; 25151.5 has C2^r catchword: 'When'. The present item is largely reimposed, w. additions, from the standing type of 25151.5. These additions but no new ones appear in 25152, which in turn is partly reimposed from the present item. 25153 sq. are completely reset and reprint the unaugmented text of 25151.5.

•25153 *Amend date*: [1595?]

•25196 *Add*: LINC. *and delete it from* 25196.5.

•25206 *Add after date*: Ent. 15 oc. 1603 (Arber III.246).

25219 *Add note*: For a different trans. of the 1st pt. *see* 16699.

•25220 Arthur Houghton's copy now = L.

25226.5 *Add note*: Tp varies; in line 7: 'any. Aged' or 'any, aged'; both at HN.

•25244 *In the note correct Creede's portion*: Y to end of main text.

•25249 *Continue note*: Not by Werdmueller; tr. from a German version of part of Bullinger's commentary on St. Matthew's Gospel.

•p. 449[1] **West, W.** *Add to 'ed.' reference at end*: 10978,

•p. 449[1] **Westminster.** *Add cross-reference at end*:
—[Regulations for Westminster regarding the plague. 1564.] *See* 16704.9.

Add new heading:
•p. 449[1] **Westminster,** *Hospital of St. Mary Rounceval. See* Indulgences 83G(***A***3).

Add new heading:
•p. 449[2] **Weyer, Johann.** *See* 12498.5.

Add new heading:
•p. 449[2] **Whalley, Thomas.** *See* Bookplates.

•25308 *Add after date*: Ent. to T. Man, sen., Jonas Man, a. H. Sharpe 1 mr.

•25322 *In note for* 9248.5 *read*: 8897.5.

•25341 *Add note*: Partly plagiarized in 14676.

Add new heading:
•p. 451[1] **Whippey, George.** *See* Bookplates.

Add new heading:
p. 451[1] **Whistler, John.** *See* Bookplates.

Add new entry:
•25363.3 —[Anr. issue, w. cancel tp, w. imprint:] *Sigenae Nassoviorum, typis C. Corvini*, 1596. East Berlin, Deutsche Staatsbibliothek.; F.

25364 *Substitute this note*: The address is possibly that of R. Waldegrave since 571 is pr. by him and sold there in [1586]. By 1589 the shop belonged to J. Dalderne (cf. 7538, 19898a.3).
The 'Answer to Master Rainolds Preface' on 1st B–D[8] is not present in one of 3 C copies, and its absence prob. indicates an early issue. In the piracy, 25364b, the 'Answer' is on additional quires A[8] (1st 3 leaves signed A11, A13, A15) a[4], intended to be inserted after orig. A5. The additional quires are present in the C and HD copies of 25364b but not in the P copy.

25366 *Add note*: C has copies w. quires A, B, Mm, and Nn reimposed w. some correction and resetting; e.g. tp line 11 has 'magistro' or 'Magistro'; Nn2^r has grotesque mask or block of type orns.

•p. 452[1] **Whitaker, W.** *Following 'tr.' references add*:
—*See* also Bookplates(***A***3).

•25382 *Add after date*: Ent. 14 ap.

Add new entry to name formerly known only as 'tr.':
•25387.5 **White, James.** [Heading 1r:] Ad Elizabetham reginam Angliæ, ... de iustificatione elegiaca pauca. [In verse.] 4° in 2. [*J. Day*, c. 1560?] L(1213.m.10(3)).

•p. 453[1] **White, John,** *D.D. In 'See also' reference at end add*: 13476,

•p. 453[1] **White, John,** *of Dorchester. Add cross-reference*: —*See* also 13507.

•25399.5 *In SR entry delete*: R. Bird and

Add new heading:
•p. 453[1] **White, Robert.** *See* Bookplates.

•25407 *Add location*: L[4](YY.9.6, imp.).

•25408 *Add note*: Answered by 14662.

•25413 *Amend date*: [1535?] *Add location*: Hamill & Barker catalogue 7 (Nov. 1983), item 53. *For 1st sentence of note substitute this*: For pt. 2 *see* 25413.7(*A*3), 25415; for pt. 3 *see* 25423.5(*A*3), 25425.

Add new entry:
◦25413.7 —A dayly exercice and experience of dethe, gadred, [etc.] 8°. [*R. Redman*, 1534?] LINC(imp.).; Hamill & Barker (imp., bd. as pt. 2 of 25413).
This is a different ed. from 25415, which has in the title: 'deathe, gathered, ...' Both copies have D6–8 cancelled; on D5v begins a discussion of the witch Elizabeth Barton, executed in 1534; the conclusion of the text in 25414 sq. is revised, mentioning no names.

•25422.3 *Amend imprint*: (*Southwarke, P.* ...

Add new entry:
•25423.5 —[Anr. ed.] 8°. (*R. Redman*, 1533 (14 oc.)) Hamill & Barker catalogue 7, item 53 (bd. as pt. 3 of 25413).

•25440 *Continue note*: The 1st pt. is adapted from 19990.5.

•25442 *Add note*: Also attrib. to T. Wood.

•25444 *In* HN *for* (59564) *read*: (59565)

•25456.3 L[4] copy now = L. *Amend also the following* L[4] *locations to* L.: 25474, 25491.7, 25506.3, 25522, 25536.5, 25555, 25566.3, 25578.5.

•25479.6 *In* HN *for* (59563) *read*: (59564)

•25498.3 *In* HN *for* (59562) *read*: (59563)

Add new entry:
•25501.5 —[Anr. ed.] 4° 4.6. (*in edibus VVinandi de VVorde*, 1522 (Idibus Octobribus [*sic*].)) O(lacks tp).

•25515 *In* O *delete*: , lacks 2nd B2,5 (Univ. Microfilms reel 160 omits B2 opening in the O copy.)

•25525.7 *In* HN *for* (59565) *read*: (59567, pt. 2)

Restore original entry:
•25526 —[Pt. 1.] Roberti whitintoni lichfeldiensis, grãma-/tices magistri & prothouatis Anglie in floren-/tissima Oxoniensi achademia Laureati lucu-/brationes. De synoni-/mis. 4° 8.4. (*per wynan/dum de worde,*) [1515?] L(former untraced Quaritch copy).C[4](N.23.1, w. quires C–D of 25527.5).
(C[4] copy formerly 25527.6)

•25526.5 *For* [Pt. 1.] *read*: [Anr. ed.]

•25527.5 *Add location*: C[4](N.23.1, w. quires A–B of 25526(*A*3)).

Turn entry into cross-reference:
•25527.6 — = mixed C[4] copy of 25526(*A*3)/25527.5. (The Broxbourne(E) copy is actually 25528.)

•25528 *Add location*: L. (This is the former Broxbourne(E) copy erroneously listed at 25527.6.)

•25603 *Continue note*: Answered by 11023.

Add new heading:
•p. 461[2] **Wier, Johann.** *See* 12498.5.

•25619 *For 2nd sentence of note substitute this*: The order of eds. is: 25619.5, 25619, 25619.3. In the present ed. only tenor and sextus should have an unsigned leaf conjugate w. tp, w. dedic. and table; in the dedic., line 1 of text has '*renoumed*' and line 9 has '*whome*' (F). Dedics. found in other ptbks. of this and the next are sophistications and may be taken from one of the other eds.

•25619.3 *Amend imprint*: ... 1598 [i.e. *T. Snodham*, 1610?] *For 2nd sentence of note substitute this*: Like 25619, only tenor and sextus should have a dedic., here having in line 1 of text '*renowmed*' (HD).

•25619.5 *For 2nd sentence of note substitute this*: All ptbks. should have a dedic. conjugate w. tp; in the dedic., line 1 of text has '*renoumed*' and line 9 has '*whom*' (F).

•25619a *Add after date*: Ent. 27 fb.

•25620 *Add after date*: Ass'd by T. Man 1 to P. and Jonas Man 3 my.

•25633 *Add after date*: Ent. 22 fb.

•25638.5 *Delete SR entry*. (It belongs only to 22334.)

•25641 *Add before imprint*: 8°.

•25650.5 For *f. the Co. of Statrs.* read: *by the Soc. of Statrs.*

•25644 *Continue imprint*: *sold* [*by T. Pavier*?]

•25657 *Add after date*: Ent. 15 ja.

25665 *Continue note*: Copies vary; Y4v is blank or has errata; both at P.

•p. 463[2] **Wilkinson, W.** *At end delete the whole 'tr.' reference.*

•25668.5 *Continue note*: The attrib. to Baldwin is dubious; possibly by W. Waterman.

25703 *Continue note*: A4v varies; dedic. dated 'this present December. 1598.' (C) or 'this first of Ianuarie. 1599.' (P).

Add new heading:
•p. 465[1] **William,** *Duke of Shoreditch. See* 22463.6(*A*3).

Add new heading:
•p. 465[1] **William IV,** *Landgrave of Hesse Cassel. See* 11348.

•25720 *List only these locations*: L.O.; F. *Add note*: Other copies of this and 25720.5 may be at A, G[2], NLW.

•25720.5 *In title for* candlesticks *read*: candlestickes *Add locations*: C[3].BURY.; U.

•25721 *Add after date*: Ent. 2 au. 1626.

•25724 *In last line of note for* 25726?). *read*: 11321).

•p. 466[1] **Williams, J.,** *Abp. Add to 'See also' references at end*: 6273.7, ... 18297(*A*3).

Add new heading:
p. 466[1] **Williams, Richard.** *See* Bookplates.

•25735 For [*W. Kearney*?] *read*: [*T. Scarlet*]

•25738 *Distinguish main heading*: ... **Thomas,** *D.D., 1593–1639. Move the 'tr.' reference following* 25740 *to follow* 25738.

•25739 *Delete em dash.*

•25740 *Delete dash and add new heading*:
Williamson, Thomas, *Gent., b. 1543. Add note*: (Formerly also 25739) Includes woodcuts of popish practises w. letterpress verses below.

Add new heading:
p. 467[1] **Willmer, William.** *See* Bookplates.

Add new heading:
p. 467[1] **Willoughby, William.** *See* Bookplates.

Wilson, John, *Preacher. Add new 1st entry*:
•25768.5 —The application of redemption. A sermon. Since [Wilson's] death published by H. Pr(ime.) 8°. *T. Harper f. R. Bostocke*, 1631. Ent. 11 oc. Moscow, State Public Historical Society.
See Library 8 (1986): 397.

•p. 467[2] **Wilson, John,** *Priest. Add to 'ed.' references at end*: 11539,

•25779 *Continue note*: *See* also 4911.5.

Add new heading:
•p. 468[1] **Wilson, Nicholas.** *See* 10898.

•p. 468[2] **Wilson, T.,** *Divine. Following* 25794 *add cross-reference*:
—An exposition. [By T. Wilson.] 1609, etc. *See* 24966 (***A***3).

•p. 469[1] **Wilson, T.,** *Secretary. Add cross-reference at end*:
—*ed. See* 12595.

Add new heading:
•p. 469[2] **Windebank,** ***Sir* Francis.** *See* 9260.

25846 *Add note*: At least O, C, F (all?) copies have the misprint: 'preachcd' in the portion of the title transcribed.

•p. 469[2] **Wing, J.** *Add cross-references at end*:
—*tr. See* 7451.
—*See* also 5556.

•25852 *Begin imprint*: [*R. Grafton f.*]

•25853 *Amend date*: 1484.]

Add new heading:
•p. 470[1] **Winston, John,** *ed. See* 6937.5, 6944, 6944.7, 6950, 6951.

•p. 470[1] **Winterton, R.** *Add to 'ed.' reference at end*: 6900,

•25859 *Continue note*: Partly answered by 11684.

•p. 470[2] **Winzet, N.** *Add to 'tr.' references at end*: 10819,

•p. 470[2] **Wiseman,** ***Sir* W.** *Delete 'pseud.' in heading*. (10926 is indeed by him.)

•25874 Arthur Houghton's copy now = L.

Add new heading:
•p. 471[1] **Withepole,** ***Sir* Edmond.** *See* Bookplates(***A***).

25899 *In the note for* and ... 1645 *read*: inserted from a later (c. 1675?) unidentified ed.

•25899.5 *In lines 1–2 of note delete*: but 1 *and*: (Song ... vineyard)

•25907.5 *Amend date*: [c. 1631.]

•25908 *Continue note*: This is app. the last ed. printed.

•25910a *Continue note*: ... ed. and presumably the first.

•25930.3 *In note before* 9041 *add*: 8992,

•25934.5 *In note after* 4301, *add*: 6809.5.

•25954.5 *Delete*: L[8].

Add new entry:
•25954.6 —[A variant, w. heading:] To ... the Lords. [*London*, 1621?] L[8](GL 6448).

Add new heading:
•p. 474[2] **Wood, Thomas,** *Marian exile*. A brieff discours off the troubles at Franckford. 1574. *See* 25442(***A***3).

•p. 474[2] **Wood, Thomas,** *tr. In cross-references after* 19459 *add*: 20449(***A***3).

•25963 *Continue note*: The engr. portrait of Charles I also appears in 12205 sqq.

•25966 *Add note*: Printed in the house of R. Jones or at least w. material borrowed from him.

Add new headings:
•p. 475[2] **Worcester,** *Diocese of. See* 4585.
•**Worcester, William,** *tr. See* 5293.

•25993 *Amend imprint*: *L. S[nowdon in the shop of R. Blower]* ...

•26000.6 *Add location*: ; HD(imp.). *In line 1 of note for* This *read*: A[2]. *Continue note*: The HD vol. lacks all before p. 33 of pt. 1 and after p. 126 of pt. 3; it is otherwise like A[2] except that the tp and prelims. of pts. 3–4 (cf. 26000.4), instead of preceding the text of pt. 2 (as in 26000.5), are currently bd. at the beginning of the vol.

•26002 *Delete the note here and move it to* 26009.

•26013 *Add note*: *See* also 4736.

•26014 *Add location*: L(imp.).

Wrednot. *Add new entry*:
•26014.3 —The sorrowful soules solace.... Containing prayers, meditations, [etc.] The third edition. [Anon.] Enlarged with a preservative against temptation, and consolations for the sicke. By H. Shepley. 12°. *N. Okes f. S. Albyn*, 1611. 1st pt. ent. as by W. Wrednot to F. Burton 4 jn. 1604; 2nd pt. ent. as by Shepley to Burton 11 my. 1605. O(imp.).
Includes Burton's orig. dedic. to S. Smalman, signed F. B.

•26018 *Begin imprint*: *B. Wright sculpsit et excudebat*; ...

26024 *Add note*: Tp varies in the portion transcribed: with (HD) or without (C) a comma after 'TRVTH'.

•26037 *Amend main heading*: ... **Robert,** *Rector of St. Catherine Coleman. Put the 'ed.' and 'See also' references under the following heading*:
Wright, Robert, *Bp.*

•26038.2 *Correct format*: 1/2 sh.*obl*.fol. *Amend location*: O(Wood 416(2)).

•26039 *Add note*: L(Cup.652.ee.8, fol. 39) has a severely cropt trial? tp w. Wright's name in full and imprint: *Val. S[immes] f. Walter Burre*, 1601; it is the frag. cited as the 1st use of the device, McK. 333.

•26047 *In note before* 13998. *add*: 4572.5,

Add new entry:
•26049.3 —[Anr. ed.] 16° in 8's, gathered at the top. (*made by F. Adams, sold [by him] or else at* [sic] *T. Chayre*,) [1578?] L(C.124.b.28, B5–12, C[8] D[4] only).
B5[r] is the sixth coin illustration (cf. C4[v] of 26049.4 sqq.); text ends on D4[v] with last date: 9 Aug. 1577. The text is in B.L. types but is in a different setting from 26049.4 sqq. and represents a somewhat different arrangement with a few modifications in the text.

Add new entry:
•26049.13 —[Anr. ed., revised.] 16° in 8's, gathered at the top. [*R. Watkins a. J. Roberts f.*] *F. Adams*, 1583. CU.
This is the Benger copy noted at 26049.14 w. added E[8], w. Godly exercises of prayer.

•26049.14 *For* [Anr. ed., revised.] *read*: [Anr. issue.] *Substitute this note*: At least the tp, B5[r], C1[v], D7[v] are the same setting as 26049.13(***A***3); at least a1[v], a2[r] are reset.

•26050.2 *Add location*: L(lacks tp).

•26050.4 *Amend date*: [1603?]

•26050.6 *In title for* kalendar *read*: kalender.

Add new heading:
p. 479[2] **Wyndham, George.** *See* Bookplates.

•p. 479[2] **Wynne.** [Bookplate.] *Continue reference*: and Bookplates(***A***).

•26078.5 *Continue note*: *See* also 11061.

•26087 *Correct SR entry to*: Ent. 15 ja. 1630 and 27 ap. 1631.

Add new entry:
26098.5 —Yule in Yorke. [Two carols in verse, w. explanatory notes.] s.sh.fol. [*London*, c. 1570.] O.
Apparently pr. in defence of the ceremony of 'Yule riding' celebrated on 21 Dec.; the ceremony was suppressed in 1572.

•26110–0.5 *Begin imprints*: [*J. Charlewood f.*]

•p. 484[2] **Young, P.,** *ed. After* 5398, *add*: 11121.

•26114 *In imprint* for *M. Allot* read: *A. Crooke*

•p. 487[1] **Zanchius.** *In 'See also' references at end add*: 13479,

---

•p. 489[1] **Addenda.** *In the list of numbers at the top of the column delete*: 16633.3. (Error for 16333.3, which is now outmoded by ***A***3.)

Although most of the addenda and corrigenda printed in vol. 2 of the STC revision continue to be valid, the following are superseded in the present volume, and the user of STC may wish to delete them from vol. 2:

14068.5	17445.5	20397	23619.5
15203	17627	20399	24163
15259	18617.5	22064	p. 419[2] Vaughn
15622.8	18816	22108	24827.5
p. 90, series 24/3	20163	23428	25413.7
16333.3			

CONCORDANCES

Bosanquet — STC

Following is a concordance of numbers between those in Eustace F. Bosanquet, *English Printed Almanacks and Prognostications: A Bibliographical History to the year 1600*, London, 1917, with two supplements published in *The Library*, and those in the revised STC. For a chronological listing of all surviving Almanacks including those newly added in the Addenda above in this volume, *see* the Almanacks headings in the Chronological Index in the next section of this volume.

Bos	STC
i	386
ii	388
iii	403
iv	385.7
v	385.3
vi	494.8
vii	494.9
viii	470.2
ix	470.3
xa	470.5
xb	470.6
xi	470.8(*A*3)
xii	389.3
xiii	470.8(*A*3)
xiv	470.9
xv	470.10
xvi	517.10
vii	390.5
xviii	517.12
xix	471.5
xx	471.7
xxi	392.5
xxii	392.7
xxiii	473
xxiv	392.9
xxv	474
xxvi	474.5
xxvii	475
xxviii	394.5
xxix	475.5
xxx	488.9
xxxi	508.5
xxxii	476
xxxiii	420.15
xxxiv	416.5
xxxv	477
xxxvi	447.5
xxxvii	477.5
xxxviii	410
xxxix	507.13
xl	507.15
xli	410.5
xlii	"
xliii	481
xliv	483.14
xlv	"
xlvi	399.7
xlvii	443.9
xlviii	492
xlix	492.3
l	520
li	"
lii	506
liii	"
liv	488
lv	506.3
lvi	510
lvii	510.3
lviii	482.5
lix	490.20
lx	432.5
lxi	482.7
lxii	398.7
lxiii	433
lxiv	493
lxv	431.7
lxvi	510.5
lxvii	415
lxviii	511
lxix	463
lxx	482.9
lxxi	511.3
lxxii	511.5
lxxiii	454
lxxiv	422.5
lxxv	459.5
lxxvi	511.9
lxxvii	482.12
lxxviii	512
lxxix	443.13
lxxx	401.7
lxxxia	488.5
lxxxib	"
lxxxii	512.7
lxxxiii	454.5
lxxxiv	488.7
lxxxv	491.5
lxxxvi	422.7
lxxxvii	423
lxxxviii	455
lxxxix	443
xc	444.1
xci	444.3
xcii	451
xciii	423.3
xciv	434
xcv	444.4
xcvi	451.2
xcvii	455.7
xcviii	444.5
xcix	444.6
c	401.8
ci	433.5
cii	444.7
ciii	434.2
civ	423.6
cv	444.8
cvi	434.3
cvii	444.9
cviii	444.10
cix	451.6
cx	526
cx*	403.7
cxia	424.3
cxib	424.4
cxii	434.6
cxiii	445
cxiv	451.8
cxv	525
cxvi	526.5
cxvii	445.1
cxviii	445.2
cxix	445.3
cxx	525.2
cxxi	434.10
cxxii	445.5
cxxiii	525.3
cxxiv	434.11
cxxv	525.4
cxxvi	434.12
cxxvii	—
cxxviii	not STC
cxxix	470.4
cxxx	not STC
cxxxi	471
cxxxii	513
cxxxiii	474.7
cxxxiv	523
cxxxv	394
cxxxvi	395
cxxxvii	396
cxxxviii	507.11
cxxxix	470
cxl	464
cxli	462
cxlii	410.7
cxliii	447.7
cxliv	410.9
cxlv	482
cxlvi	400
cxlvii	521
cxlviii	509
cxlix	in 484
cl	459
cli	400.3
clii	402.5
cliii	424
cliv	425
clv	504
clvi	387
clvii	389
clviii	390
clix	391
clx	439.3
clxi	421.17
clxii	439.9
clxiii	439.13
clxiv	393
clxv	18054
clxvi	435.35
clxvii	435.39
clxviii	406.3
clxix	443.11
clxx	458
clxxi	435.41
clxxii	439.15
clxxiii	401
clxxiv	435.43
clxxv	484
clxxvi	417
clxxvii	485
clxxviii	479.8
clxxix	486
clxxx	435.47
clxxxi	435.49
clxxxii	418
clxxxiii	435.53
clxxxiv	435.55
clxxxv	435.57
clxxxvi	403.9
clxxxvii	439.17
clxxxviii	12153
clxxxix	12154
cxc	12155
cxci	12156
cxcii	12157
cxciii	26049.10
cxciv	12158
cxcv	12159
cxcvi	12160
cxcvii	12161
cxcviii	12162
cxcix	26050
cc	—

Library 8 (1928): 466–77

A.i	410.3
A.ii	410.12
A.iii	492.7
A.iv	493.3

Bos	STC
A.v	486.5
A.vi	449
A.vii	428
A.viiia	5324.5(*A*3)
A.viiib	5324(*A*3)
A.ix	447.7
A.x	439.7
A.xi	439.5
A.xii	484.5
A.xiii	435.51
A.xiv	403.3
A.xv	26049.14
A.xvi	26049.16
A.xvii	12163
Library 18 (1937): 55–66	
Aa.i	406.7
Aa.ii	392.3
Aa.iii	490.18
Aa.iv	401.5
Aa.v	512.3
Aa.vi	512.11
Aa.vii	480.3
Aa.viii	501.32
Aa.ix	423.4
Aa.x	445.4
Aa.xi	424.7
Aa.xii	466
Aa.xiii	434.9
Aa.xiv	451.11
Aa.xv	410.10
Aa.xvi	518.8
Aa.xvii	486.3
Aa.xviii	26049.6

Duff — STC

Following is a concordance of numbers between those in E. Gordon Duff, *Fifteenth Century English Books*, [London,] 1917 and those in the revised STC.

Duff	STC
1	13609
2	13610
3	158
4	175
5	176
6	177
7	268
8	270
9	258
10	273
11	277
12	278
13	279
14	280
15	282
16	283
17	284
18	285
19	286
20	287
21	314
22	315
23	316
24	317
25	not STC
26	581
27	582
28	695
29	696
30	696.1
31	696.2
32	752
33	786
34	787
35	789
36	790
37	9603
38	922
39	not STC
40	1536
41	1916
42	1917
43	1978
44	1987
45	3124
46	3175
47	3199
48	3259
49	3260
50	3261
51	3262
52	3297
53	3303
54	3304(*A*3)
55	3305
56	3308(*A*3)
57	3309
58	3356.7
59	15856
60	15794
61	15795
62	15801.5
63–4	15797
65	15799
66	15800
67	15801
68	15802
69	15795.5
70	15804
71	15805
72	4589
73	4590
74	4591
75	4594
76	4850
77	4581
78	4852
79	4853
80	4890
81	4920
82	4921
83	5013
84	5057
85	5065
86	5087
87	5082
88	5083
89	5084
90	5085
91	5089
92	5090
93	5091
94	5094
95	7273
96	7269
97	9991
98	9992
99	9993
100	9994
101	9995
102	9996
103	5293
104	5312
105	15847.3(*A*3)
106	5643
107	14546
108	not STC
109	5758
110	5759
111	6289
112	14554
113	13440a
114	13440b
115	22905
116	13922
117	13808
118–22	not STC
123	6826
123a	6827
124	6828
125	6829
126	6931
127	21431
128	7014.5
129	7013
130	7014
131	7016
132	7017
133	23153.4
134	23153.5
135	7541
136	7566
137	2993
138	16110
139	16111
140	16112
141	16113
142	16114
143	15851
144	15852
145	15853
146	15854(*A*3)
147	15855
148	15848
149	15849
150	20195
151	11024
152	1007
153–5	not STC
156	11601
157	11602
158	—
159	not STC
160	11608a.7
161	11609
162	11610
163	11611
164	13175
165	12138
166	12142
167	12470
168	12471
169	12477
170	12540
171	12541(*A*3)
172	13438
173	13439
174	15867(*A*3)
175	15868(*A*3)
176	15869
177	15870
178	15871(*A*3)
179	15872(*A*3)
180	15873
181	15874
182	15875
183	15876
184	15877
185	15878
186	15880
187	15881
188	15882
189	15883
190	15884
191	15885
192	15886
193	15887
194	15888
195	15889
196	15890
197	15891
198	15892 (note)
199	15893
200	15894
201	15895
202	13829
203	14042(*A*3)
204	14077c.107(*A*3)
205	14077c.108
206	14077c.109
207	14077c.110(*A*3)
208	14077c.111(*A*3)
209	14077c.112
210	14077c.113
211	14077c.114
212	14077c.115
213	14077c.86–7
214	14077c.134
215	14077c.135–6
216	14077c.137
217	14077c/138–9
218	14077c.140
219	14077c.142
220	14077c.141
221	14077c.148
222	14551
223	14078
224	14079
225	14081
226	not STC
227	14096
228	14097
229	14098

Duff	STC
230	14099
231	13809
232	13810
233	14477(*A*3)
234	21443
235	14507
236	14508
237	14621
238	15297
239	23163.13
240	23163.8
241	15296(*A*3)
242	15375(*A*3)
243–4	not STC
245	15383
246	15384
247	16136
248	15394
249	15395
250	15396
251	15397
252	15572
253	17005
254	17006
255	17007
256	17008
257	17009(*A*3)
258	17010
259	17011
260	17015(*A*3)
261	17018
262	17019(*A*3)
263	17020
264	17021
265	17022
266	17023(*A*3)
266a	17024(*A*3)
267	6473–4
268	17031
269	17030
270	17032
271	17032a
272	17033
273	15719
274	15720
275	15721
276	15722
277	16693
278	17102
279	17103–3.5
280	17104
281	17105
282	17106
283	801
284	802
285	17246
286	17247
287	16138(*A*3)
288	16139
289	17325
290	17720(*A*3)
291	17721
292	17722
293	17723
294	17724
295	17725
296	17726
297	17539
298	17957
299	17957(*A*3)
300	17958
301–2	17959
303–4	17960
305–6	17961
307–8	17962
309–10	17963
311	17964
312–13	17965
314	17966
315–16	17966.5
317–18	17967
319–20	17968
321	16165(*A*3)
322	16164
323	16166
324	16167
325	16168
326	16170
327	16171
328	16172
329	16173
330	16174
331	16175
332	18385
333	18386
334	18361(*A*3)
335	23878
336	16228(*A*3)
337	19206
338	19207
339	19212
340	19213
341	494.8
342	23163.7
343	23163.6
344	23163.11(*A*3)
345	23163.9
346	19767.7
347	19812
348	19827
349	385.7
350	385.3
351	9176
352	20434
353	20439.3
354	16253(*A*3)
355	16254
356	20878
357	20917
358	20919(*A*3)
359	20920
360	20921
361	13689.3
362	13688
363	21261
364	21334
365	21335
366	21429(*A*3)
367	21458(*A*3)
368	24189(*A*3)
369	24190
370	21297
371	22588(*A*3)
372	22597
373	23163.14
374	23238
375	9513
376	9514
377	9515
378	9264
379	9347
380	9348
381	9349
382	9351a.7
383	9352
384	9353
385	9354(*A*3)
386	9355
387	9332
388	23425
389	23426
390	23427
391	23885
392	23904
393	23905
394	23906
395	23907
396	19627
397	5572
398	5573
399	24234
400	20412
401	24762
402	24763
403	24766
403a	24766.3
404	24796
405	24865
406	24867(*A*3)
407	24866
408	24873(*A*3)
409	24874(*A*3)
410	24875
411	24876
412	25001
413	24224
414	25853(*A*3)
415	26012
416	9650
417	9691
418	9731
419	9737
420	9742
421	9749
422	9755
423	9770
424	9784
425	9790
426	9796
427	9806
428	9812
429	9819
430	9825
431	9836

Greg — STC

Following is a concordance of numbers between those in W. W. Greg, *A bibliography of the English Printed Drama to the Restoration*, London, 1939–1959, and those in the revised STC. Items found only in Greg's addenda have a reference to volume iv and page number preceding them. STC items which first appear in collections are indicated by (coll.) following the number.

Greg	STC
1–2	17778
3	14039
4	10604
5	25982
6	20722
7	14109.5
8–9	20723
10	20721
11	22607
12	23894
13	13298
14	13299
(iv.1643) 14.5	18793.5
15	13305
16	13303
17–18	17779
19	20765.5
20	14111
21	13300
(iv.1643) 21.5	14109.7
22	1305
23	1279
24	1287
25	14109.3
26	14643
27	14110
28	22227
29	22226
30	14112.5
31	25016
32	13691
33	13251
34	22223
35	14837
(iv.1644) 35c	14837a.5
36	22225
37	23949
38	275
39	18684
40	6277
41	25148
42	22222
43	24934
44	22224
45	22229
46	24508
47	24932
48	19917
49	24271
50	11473
(iv.1645) 50b	11473.5

Greg	STC
51	14327
52	19865
53	24935
54	14085
55	17466
56	20287
57	24933
58	7514
59	6150
60–2	11635 (coll.)
63	18419
64	18550
65	1059
66	5232
67	23263
68	11643
69	5592
70	25018
71	2047
72	16949
73–4	25347
75	11627
76	5226
(iv.1646) 76.5	11632.5
77	11990
78	25966
79–81	22221 (coll.)
82	17086
83	19530
84	17047.5
85	25784
86	19447
87	19533
88	7596
89	13921
90	11638 (coll.)
91	23895
92	24286
93	25783
94–5	17425
96	18423
97	11340
98	7583
99	17050
100	19532
101–2	14644
103	3907.7
104	25764
105	17080
106	17083
107	733
108	18138
109	22894
110	15086
111	7600
112	19535
113	7675
114	23356
115	15027
116	11622
117	22328
118	16679
119	26099
120	23667
120e	22327
121	12267
122	16678
123	12265
124	25781
125	17084
126	21009
127	19531
128	17441
129	17437
130	12310a
131	6160
132	6243.4 (coll.)
133	17423
134	25782
135	20002
136	21528
137	19545
138	21006
139	15028
140	7501
141	22307
142	22314
143	22322
144	17090
145	22279a
146	4965
147	3544
148	13072
149	12308
150	22294
151	18230
152	22541 (coll.)
153–4	13341
155	25089
156	12233
157	5450a
158	12212
159	4987
160	19540
161	20121.5
162	6517
163	14767
164	17188
165	22289
166	18795
167	22288
168	22304
169	6991
170	22302
171	25144
172	22296
173	18376
174	16799
175	6523
176	14766
177	7243
178	17082
179	18271
180	18269
181	14773
182	26076
183	12415
184	17473
185	17474
186	14781
187	22299
188	17876
189	21532
190	5593
191	5594
192	16754
193–4	15681
195	6520.7
196	349
197	22275
198	6518
199	19888
200–1	14756
202	6510
203	17479
204	6501
(iv.1647) 204b	6501.5
205	17429
206	25868
207	6264
208	12863
209	343 (coll.)
210	13527
211	3794
212	21417
213	15343
214	17475
215	13328
216	14782
217	4970
218	18279
219	4963
220	23405
221	15085
222	22333
223	6239 (coll.)
224	13336
225	19309
226	4978
227	6262
228	12050
229	18597
230	17483
231	17488
232	4339
233	5194
234	25818
235	6412
236	4983
237	14774
238	4538
239	24104
240	24063
241	6532
242	13317
243	17892
244	17890
245	1692
246	4966
247	22380
248	6417
249	25635
250	6539
251	21531
252	17487
253	24149
254	1466
255	22384
256	6537
257	6540
258	13371
259	14783
260–1	344 (coll.)
262	17896
263	17879
264	7493
265	22292
266	17907
267	6416
268	6411
269–71	14761
272	22340
273	13360
274–5	4968
276	17888
277	17398
278	12362
279	22331
280	14778
281	14757
282	18265
283	25948
284	22334
285	773
286	17617
287	11068
288	5118
289	13159
290	13529
291	13161
292	1502
293	24146
294	13325
295	18267
296	14759
297	4980
298	17908
299	10854
300	6184
301	4994
302	6530
303	14755
304	14751 (coll.)
304c	14763
305	6507
306	25178
307	4989
308	4613
309	1663
310	4981
311	17903
311–12	17904
313	13310
314	23248
315	17476
(iv.1647)315aII	17476.5
316	1674
317	13365
318–19	4545
320	17625
321	23658
322	18274
323	5673
324	4539
325	6257
326	1355
327	16
328	1667
329	22871
330	24100
331	25981
332	18275
333	13321
334	1686
335	18266
336	12931
337	21519
338	17878
339–49	14751 (coll.)
350	14775
351	17899
352	17911
353	13617
354	1803
355	18278
356	10851
357	1676
358	17887
359	17902
360	1670
361	4991
362	23544
363	1681
364	4281
365	17909
366	23120.5
367	17895
368	11074
369–78	17886 (coll.)
379	22305
380	17644
381	14777
382	17401
383	17900
384	17713
385	14782.5
386	17634

Greg	STC
387	17901
388	25173
389	25176
390–406	22273 (coll.)
407	14779
408	17632
409	25175
410	18430
411	14772
412	17882
413	17898
414	12963
415–16	23897 (coll.)
417	23696
418	11995
419	6493
420	11163
421	6509
422	6307
423	4628
424	17642
425	22460
426	11541
427	6302
428	6303
429	22444
430	17641
431–2	20686
433	17877
434	19462
435	6506
436	17640
437	14776
438	5125
439	4911
440	6529
441	22456
442	14780
443	11083
444	4992
445–6	13320
447	11980
448	13351
449	15036
450	17716
451	7242
452	14762
453	24155
454	24156
455–7	14753.5 (coll.)
458	11977
459	17636
460	21423
461	17443
462	22437
463	3819
464	17646
465	12935
466	13347
467–8	13340
469	20692
470	17638
471	21425
472	25582
473	22439
474	17639
475	17412
476	21421
477	22462
478	11164
479	22436
480	11156
481	17442
482	10886
483	13348
484	13315
485	11982
486	11165
487	5023
488	22458.5
489	12361 (coll.)
490	21416
491	11157
492	11075
493	13357
494	13373
495	23808
496	4618
497	14719
498	22458
499	21470
500	13348a
501	14721
502	6308
503	15100
504	13352
505	17637
506	6305
507	6309
508	6533
509	13311
510	21688
511	4187.5
512	5026
513	18341
514	18342
515	11066
516	13364
517	22446
518	22448
519	22463
520	24910
521	22442
522	13349
523	22443
524	17937
525	5770
526	14718
527	16923
528–30	13358 (coll.)
531	21422
532	11159
533	22435
534	1901.5
535	13370
536	22441
537	14958
538	22454
539	5904
540	18344
541	23420
542	18339
543–4	18343
545	15014
546	13359
547–8	20694 (coll.)
549	4995
550	4996
551–2	4627
553	17717
554	17718
555	11161
556	26133
557	11908
558	11071
559	17643
560	11369
561	6315
562	22450
563	1691
564	11912
565	11064
566	13350
567	6181
568	17750
569	16873
570	4717
571	6306
572	22440
573	22449
574	11072
575	22451
576	18338
577	22447
578	21011
579	12397
580	6174
581	18346
582	20770
583	22453
584	12133
585	13798
586	3818
587	3820
588	12587
589	4946
590	11910
591	11914
592	22438
593	22455
594	11909
595	21542
596	5771
597	22377
598	11073
599	12757
600	23704 (coll.)

L 1	22929
L 2–3	11515
L 4	11516
L 5	12551
L 6	12555
L 7	17800
L 8	21445
L 9	19524
L 10	23374
L 11	249
L 12	12936
L 13	12417
L 14	12956
L 15	5905
L 16	20691
L 17	22888

A CHRONOLOGICAL INDEX

BY

PHILIP R. RIDER

INTRODUCTION

WHEN the original *Short-Title Catalogue* was published in 1926, no indexes were available. In 1941, through the agency of William A. Jackson and the generous co-operation of the Huntington Library, forty sets of the Huntington's chronological card index to STC were produced and distributed to subscribing libraries. The existence and location of these sets were not generally known. The present work is intended to provide a somewhat comparable but much more widely available index for the second edition of the STC. It rearranges STC items into chronological order, providing an abbreviated form of the heading and the STC number for each item under its particular date or dates.

No effort has been made by the present editor to determine the 'true' date of a publication. The index lists only those dates appearing on the title-page of the work and those determined by either Miss Pantzer or other scholars and included in the STC. Questionable and approximate dates are signalled in the STC by the use of '?' and 'c.', respectively, and these designations have been retained in the chronological index. Those works for which a date range is given (such as '1638–40') are entered by the earliest date in the range and have a plus sign (+) added to the STC number. Similarly, those dates which are given in the STC as 'bef.', 'aft.', or 'post-' are reproduced that way in the index.

In addition, some dates are entered in the STC in the form '1620 (1621)' or '1620 [1621]'; such entries indicate that a variant date appears in the colophon or the front matter or has been determined from some other evidence. Sometimes a work will have multiple title-pages with differing dates. The chronological index includes such items under all dates, with an asterisk (*) added to indicate that there is some problem with the date. Thus even those works with blatant errors (e.g. 16997.5 and 25653) are entered under both dates. Occasionally, a variant date is given or suggested only in the notes to the item and not in the entry itself (see, for example, 5819 and 5823). In such cases, only the date given in the note is marked with an asterisk. In all cases in which an item is flagged with an asterisk, the reader should go to the STC itself to determine the nature of the problem.

When a note says 'date altered by pen …' the penned-in date is not entered. All items in the form '= pt. 2 of …' or '= Wing …' or 'Now = Wing …' are excluded. Dates in old style are indexed twice: first under the old-style date with '(o.s.)' following the STC number, then under the new-style date with no designation; the single exception to this is STC 13779, which is entered only under the new-style date because the old-style date is questionable.

Those items for which the date appears only in the Addenda and Corrigenda have '(A/C)' added to them. If the date is in the main run of entries, even if only in a cross-reference to the Addenda, no '(A/C)' designation is added.

The STC occasionally notes that a work does not properly belong in the STC, because of either the date or the place and language of publication. These items have been retained in the index with the notation '[not STC]' following the number. Even though there are other works which from the STC entry appear to be 'non-STC', the present compiler has not made that judgment.

In a few cases no date is included with the STC entry, but the intention appears to be that the reader is to infer the date from the preceding item. In these instances (e.g. 1006, 7254, 13719a), I have entered the item under the inferred date.

A heading is included for each STC number for a particular date. Although this information is obviously minimal, it may be useful in providing landmarks for the reader; if, for example, one were using the chronological index to determine what works of poetry were published in 1573, most of the entries under the headings 'Bible' and 'England' could easily be eliminated. The headings are usually in abbreviated form, though I have included as much of the heading as I felt necessary to distinguish between similar headings. Thus 'J' and 'T' are enough to distinguish John Heywood from Thomas Heywood, but occupational titles are required to separate Richard Smith, murderer, from Richard Smith, satirist, and both from Dean Richard Smith. In some cases, particularly under 'England' and 'Church of England', small subdivisions are grouped together: for example, all of the 'Church of England, Visitation Articles, Local' are combined.

The alphabetical ordering of the STC has been retained, with two exceptions: the 'Cambridge University' heading comprises STC 4473 and 4475 through 4495, with 'Cambridge University, Act Verses' occupying numbers 4474.1 through 4474.135. In the index, all of the 'Cambridge University' group is entered first, followed by the 'Act Verses' group. A similar situation occurs with the works of John Speed. STC groups editions of his prime genealogical work under the sub-heading 'Genealogies', which is alphabetized with his other titles. In the present index, all of the 'Speed, John' items are grouped together and are followed by the entries for 'Speed, John, Genealogies'.

Because the present index was sorted by computer, it is in strict ASCII sequence; there are, therefore, a few instances in which the order of the entries varies from the order in the STC. Names beginning with 'De', 'Du', 'Le', and 'La' followed by a space appear before names beginning with these letters but followed by another letter: thus 'Du Val' comes before 'Dublin' in the index but not in the STC. The same is true for entries with a subheading; the STC order is logical, while the index order is strictly alphabetical. For example, 'Appendix' is the last subheading under 'Bible' in the STC; it is the first subheading in the index. 'England, Church of' precedes 'England, Parliament' in the index, although the STC groups all the 'England' items before all the 'England, Church of' items. There is only a small number of these irregularities, but they were discovered so late that changing them was not feasible. I hope that the index user will not find them too distracting.

The only intentional omission from this index is STC 3368.5, a single number having been given to a large group of bookplates; there was no way to assign this entire section to a single date. A few minor printer's errors in the STC have been silently corrected. Finally, although a few headings properly require diacritical marks, the marks have been omitted from the index for typographical convenience.

The idea for this index arose from my need for such a work. At the time, I wanted to discover whether any biographies of Elizabeth I had been published shortly after her death. A record of books published between 1603 and 1606 would have been the most direct source of this information; what I needed, in short, was a chronological listing of the works in Pollard and Redgrave's STC. At the same time the Bibliographical Society announced that publication of the revised STC was imminent. Although I solved my original problem in other ways, I became aware that a chronological index to the STC would be of value to literary scholars, historians, librarians, and rare book dealers.

From its inception, my work on the chronological index was encouraged by my mentor, colleague, and friend, William P. Williams: his faith in the worth of the project and in my ability to complete it was sometimes stronger than my own. Among the many others who deserve acknowledgment, Katharine F. Pantzer was generous in her support and suggestions early in the project, as well as in answering questions and in providing copies of page proofs and corrections to volume 1 of the STC. She also was kind enough to offer to incorporate her latest addenda into the final stages of the index, and her perspicacious eye caught an unfortunate error in sorting which I had overlooked. R. J. Roberts, for many years Hon. Secretary of the Bibliographical Society, was instrumental in bringing the project to the attention of the Society and was also very helpful in both raising and answering questions about various facets of production and publication.

Thanks go to Peter W. M. Blayney, Mirjam Foot, and many other scholars and librarians for their help and encouragement. Sevin Straus and Norma Wiley, of the Computing Information Center at Northern Illinois University, provided invaluable assistance with some last minute computing problems. R. C. Alston and Miss Pantzer saw the index through its final production stages and solved many of the practical problems that arose through the changes at the Oxford University Press.

A very special word of gratitude goes to my wife, Paulanne Yott Rider. She not only endured this project but was an active participant in it: the two of us proofread the complete index against the STC. No man could ask for more.

Northern Illinois University — PHILIP R. RIDER

CHRONOLOGICAL INDEX

[No Date]

Athanasius 885; Book 3313.7; Liturgies, C. of Eng., BCP 16293*; Llwyd 16637 [not STC]; Markham, G. 17387.7; Ravaillac 20755* (A/C); Wither, Poet 25925.5*.

1049

Proctor, J. 20406*.

1061

N., Nicolaus 18332 [not STC]*; Perkins, W. 19713*.

1069

Rich, B. 20999*.

1115

Johnson, Jacobus 14666*.

1148

Nicolls 18576*.

1157

Mameranus 17228*.

1158

Liturgies, Latin Rite, Process. 16249.5*, 16250*.

1263

Heigham 13033.4*.

1361

Thomas, O. 24007a*.

1417

Simon [Appleby] 22558*.

1427

Hieronymus, von Braunschweig 13436*.

1468

Rufinus 21443*.

1473

Le Fevre 15375(?)(A/C).

1474

Cessolis 4920.

1475

Liturgies, Latin Rite, Breviaries 15794(c.?).

1476

Cato 4851; Indulgences, Turks or Captives 14077c.106; Liturgies, Latin Rite, Hours and Primers 15867(A/C); Lydgate 17009(A/C) 17019(A/C); Russell, J., Diplomat 21458(?).

1477

Book 3303(+); Cato 4850; Caxton 4890(?); Chaucer 5082, 5090(?), 5091(?); Dictes 6826, 6827, 6828*, 6829*; Jesus Christ 14551(c.); Le Fevre 15383; Liturgies, Latin Rite, Ordinals 16228; Lydgate 17008(?), 17018(?), 17030(?), 17032(?).

1478

Boethius, A. 3199(?); Du Castel 7273; Rufinus 21443*; Traversanus 24188.5(A/C), 24189(A/C).

1479

Aegidius 158; Aristotle 752; Cordiale 5758; Dati 6289; Liturgies, Latin Rite, Hours and Primers 15868(?)(A/C).

1480

Albertus Magnus 268; Andreae 581; Dictes 6828(?)*; England, Appendix 9991; Higden 13440a; Indulgences, Eng. 14077c.83G (A/C); Indulgences, Turks or Captives 14077c.107, 14077c.107C (A/C), 14077c.108, 14077c.109, 14077c.110; Liturgies, Latin Rite, Breviaries 15848(?); Traversanus 24190, 24190.3(?); Vocabulary 24865.

1481

Alexander, ab Alexandria 314; Bible, Selections 2993; Cicero 5293; England, Statutes, Abridgements/Extracts 9513(?); Heraclitus, Emperor 13175; Indulgences, Turks or Captives 14077c.111(A/C), 14077c.112, 14077c.113; Joannes, Canonicus 14621; Liturgies, Latin Rite, Psalters 16253(A/C); Perez de Valentia 19627; Vincentius 24762.

1482

Caorsin 4594(c.?); England, Appendix 9992; England, Yearbooks 9742(?), 9749(?); Higden 13438; Hugo 13922(?); Latteburius 15297; Littleton, T., Tenures, French 15719; Reynard the Fox 20919 (A/C); Stanbridge, Parvula 23163.13(?).

1483

Albertus Magnus 258(c.), 273(?); Andreae 582; Anwykyll 695, 696; Augustine 922(?); Cato 4852, 4853(?); Cessolis 4921; Chartier 5057; Chaucer 5083, 5087, 5094; Cicero 5312; Deguileville 6473, 6474; Donatus, A. 7014.5(c.?); England, Public Documents, Misc. 9176; England, Yearbooks 9731(?); Gower, J., Poet 12142*; Littleton, T., Tenures, French 15720(?); Liturgies, Latin Rite, Breviaries 15795; Logici 16693(?); Lydgate 17015(A/C), 17023(A/C), 17024(A/C);

1483 — *cont.*
Lyndewode 17102; Mirk 17957*(A/C); Revelation 20917; Rolle 21261; Terentius 23904, 23905(?); Voragine 24873(A/C), 24874*(A/C).

1484

Aesop 175; Bonaventura 3259; Book 3356.7; England, Statutes, Chron. Ser. 9347(?); England, Yearbooks 9737(?), 9755(?); Jesus Christ 14554(c.); La Tour Landry 15296; Liturgies, Latin Rite, Hours and Primers 15871(c.)(A/C) 15872(c.)(A/C); Maydeston 17720(c.)(A/C); Sixtus IV 22588(A/C); Voragine 24874(c.)*(A/C); Winifred 25853(A/C).

1485

Alexander, Grammaticus 315(?); Arthur, King 801; Canutus 4589(c.), 4590(c.), 4591(c.); Charles I, Emperor 5013; England, Appendix 9995; England, Statutes, Gen. Colls. 9264(?); Indulgences, Eng. 14077c.25G(A/C); Innocent VIII 14103(?) [not STC]; Liturgies, Latin Rite, Hours and Primers 15869; Narrationes 18361(c.?)(A/C); Paris, le chevalier 19206; Phalaris 19827; Royal Book 21429(A/C).

1486

Book 3308(A/C); England, Appendix 9993(?); Innocent VIII 14096; Mirk 17958; Perottus 19767.7; Terentius 23906(?), 23907; Wotton, J. 26012(?).

1487

Donatus, A. 7013; Indulgences, Images of Pity 14077c.6(c.); Legrand 15394; Liturgies, Latin Rite, Breviaries 15847.3(c.)(A/C), 15854(c.)(A/C); Liturgies, Latin Rite, Missals 16164; Mirk 17957 (c.)*(A/C).

1488

Liturgies, Latin Rite, Breviaries 15849(c.), 15853(c.); Liturgies, Latin Rite, Hours and Primers 15870(?); Liturgies, Latin Rite, Legenda 16136; Maydeston 17721.

1489

Anwykyll 696.1; Dictes 6829*; Du Castel 7269; Indulgences, Turks or Captives 14077c.114, 14077c.115; Liturgies, Latin Rite, Missals 16165; Maydeston 17722; Reynard the Fox 20920; Roye 21431.

1490

Ars 789; Aymon 1007; Blanchardine 3124; Bonaventura 3260; England, Yearbooks 9770(?), 9771(?), 9825(?); Governal 12138(?); Indulgences, Images of Pity 14077c.7(c.), 14077c.8(c.), 14077c.9 (c.), 14077c.10(c.), 14077c.11(c.), 14077c.12(c.), 14077c.19(c.), 14077c.19A(c.), 14077c.20(c.), 14077c.21(c.); 14077c.8A(c.+); Littleton, T., Tenures, French 15721; Statham 23238; Vincentius 24763; Virgilius Maro 24796.

1491

Ars 786; Book 3305; England, Statutes, Chron. Ser. 9348(?); Indulgences, Eng. 14077c.51; Liturgies, Latin Rite, Hours and Primers 15873(+); Mirk 17959; Prayers 20195.

1492

Alexander, Grammaticus 316; Anwykyll 696.2; Book 3304; Chaucer 5084(?); Donatus, A. 7014; England, Statutes, Spec. Subjs. 9332(?); Guido, of Alet 12477; Le Fevre 15384; Liturgies, Latin Rite, Breviaries 15795.5(?); Liturgies, Latin Rite, Missals 16166; Paris, le chevalier 19207; Solomon 22905; Vineis 24766(?).

1493

Chastising 5065; England, Appendix 9994; Gower, J., Poet 12142*; Liturgies, Latin Rite, Breviaries 15851(?), 15856; Liturgies, Latin Rite, Hours and Primers 15873.5(?); Lydgate 17010; Margaret, St. 17325; Mirk 17960, 17961, 17962*; Parker, H., D. D. 19212; Rome 21297; Treatise 24234; Voragine 24875.

1494

Boccaccio 3175; Bonaventura 3261, 3262; Garlandia 11608a.7; Horman 13808(?); Hylton 14042; Innocent VIII 14097; Legrand 15395; Liturgies, Latin Rite, Breviaries 15797, 15799, 15800; Liturgies, Latin Rite, Hours and Primers 15874, 15875, 15876, 15877(?), 15878, 15879; Liturgies, Latin Rite, Missals 16167, 16168; Mirk 17962*; Natura Brevium 18385; Reynard the Fox 20921; Sulpitius 23425; Tenures 23877.7(?); Terentius 23885(?)*.

1495

Ars 790(?); Bartholomaeus 1536; Bible, English 2161*, 2162*; Duncan 7351*; Fitzjames 11024(?); Higden 13439; Horman 13809; Indulgences, Images of Pity 14077c.23B(c.); Innocent VIII 14098, 14098.5; Jerome, St. 14507; Liturgies, Latin Rite, Breviaries 15801, 15801.5(?), 15850(?); Liturgies, Latin Rite, Hours and Primers 15880, 15881(?), 15881.3(?), 15881.5(c.), 15882, 15883; Lydgate 17020(c.), 17032a(?); Maydeston 17723; Mirk 17963, 17963.5, 17964; Petronilla 19812(?); Stanbridge, Accidence 23153.4, 23154.5 (?)(A/C); Terentius 23885*.

1496

Albertus Magnus 270; Alcock 278; Bernard, St. 1916, 1917*; Book 3309; Cologne 5572(?); Cordiale 5759(?); Donatus, A. 7016(?); England, Statutes, Chron. Ser. 9349(?), 9351a.7(?), 9353(?), 9354, 9355(?); England, Yearbooks 9784(?), 9790(?), 9796(?), 9806(?), 9812(?), 9819(?); Garlandia 11601, 11609; Holy Ghost, Abbey of the 13608.7(?); Jasper [Tudor] 14477; Littleton, T., Tenures, French 15722; Liturgies, Latin Rite, Breviaries 15802, 15855; Liturgies, Latin Rite, Hymns 16110, 16111; Liturgies, Latin Rite, Psalters 16253.5(c.); Lyndewode 17103, 17103.5; Mandeville 17246; Mary, the Blessed Virgin 17539; Mirk 17965; Parker, H., D. D. 19213; Rote 21334; Stanbridge, Parvula 23163.6(?), 23163.14; Tenures 23878; Vocabulary 24867(?)(A/C); Walsingham 25001(?).

1497

Aesop 176(?); Alcock 279, 280(+), 284(?), 285(c.), 286(?), 287(c.); Ars 787; England, Appendix 9996; Guy, Earl of Warwick 12541(?); Holy Ghost, Abbey of the 13609(?); Indulgences, Cont. 14077c.85; Innocent VIII 14099; Libellus 15574.5; Liturgies, Latin Rite, Breviaries 15852; Liturgies, Latin Rite, Hours and Primers 15884, 15885, 15886; Liturgies, Latin Rite, Hymns 16112; Liturgies, Latin Rite, Missals 16169, 16170(?), 16171; Lydgate 17011(?), 17031(?); Maydeston 17724; Stanbridge, Parvula 23163.7(?), 23163.8(?); Stella 23242.5(?); Terentius 23885*; Theodulus 23939.5(?); Vocabulary 24866.

1498

Alcock 277, 283(?); Alexander, Grammaticus 317; Almanacks 385.3, 385.7(?); Arthur, King 802; Chaucer 5085; Doctrinal 6931; Elegantiae 7566(?); Guido, de Monte Rocherii 12470; Higden 13440b; Indulgences, Cont. 14077c.86, 14077c.87; Indulgences, Licences 14077c.134, 14077c.135, 14077c.136, 14077c.137; Legrand

1498 — *cont.*
15397; Libellulus 15572(?); Liturgies, Latin Rite, Hours and Primers 15887, 15888, 15889, 15890, 15891; Liturgies, Latin Rite, Hymns 16113; Liturgies, Latin Rite, Manuals 16138; Liturgies, Latin Rite, Missals 16172; Lydgate 17005; Maydeston 17725; Sulpitius 23426; Voragine 24876.

1499

Alcock 282(?); Almanacks (Parron) 494.8; Bernard, St. 1917(?)*; Cologne 5573; Contemplation 5643; England, Statutes, Abridgements/Extracts 9514, 9515*; Garlandia 11602; Horman 13810; Indulgences, General 14077c.148(c.); Indulgences, Licences 14077c.138, 14077c.139, 14077c.140, 14077c.140A, 14077c.141, 14077c.142, 14077c.142C(A/C), 14077c.143; Informatio 14078(?); Jerome, St. 14508(?); Libellus 15576.6(+); Liturgies, Latin Rite, Breviaries 15804, 15805; Liturgies, Latin Rite, Hours and Primers 15892; Liturgies, Latin Rite, Hymns 16114; Liturgies, Latin Rite, Psalters 16254; Lydgate 17021(?); Lyndewode 17104, 17105, 17106; Mandeville 17247; Maydeston 17726; Merlin 17840.7(?)(A/C); Mirk 17966, 17966.5, 17967, 17968; Profits 20412; Promptorium 20434; Rote 21335; Skelton 22597(?); Stanbridge, Accidence 23153.5; Stanbridge, Parvula 23163.16(?); Sulpitius 23427.

1500

Aesop 177(?), 177.3(?); Alexander, Grammaticus 317.5(?); Almanacks 386(c.); Betson 1978; Bevis 1987, 1987.5(c.); Book 3297; Catharine, of Aragon 4814; Chaucer 5089(?); Donatus, A. 7017; Eglamour 7541; England, Statutes, Chron. Ser. 9352(?); England, Statutes, Gen. Colls. 9265(+); England, Yearbooks 9650(?), 9691(?), 9836(?); Garlandia 11610, 11611; Guido, de Monte Rocherii 12471; Guy, Earl of Warwick 12540(?); Holy Ghost, Abbey of the 13610(?); Hood, R. 13688(?); Hortus 13829; Indulgences, Cont. 14077c.100; Indulgences, Images of Pity 14077c.13(c.), 14077c.14(c.), 14077c.16 (c.), 14077c.22(c.); Information 14081(?); Jesus Christ 14546(?); Legrand 15396; Libellus 15576.7(c.)(A/C); Liturgies, Latin Rite, Hours and Primers 15893, 15894, 15895, 15895.5(?); Liturgies, Latin Rite, Manuals 16139; Liturgies, Latin Rite, Missals 16172.5(c.?), 16173, 16174, 16175; Lydgate 17006(c.), 17007(?), 17022, 17033(?), 17037(?); Natura Brevium 18386; Remigius 20878; Stanbridge, Parvula 23163.9; Treatise 24224; Vineis 24766.3(?).

1501

Alcock 281; Almanacks (Parron) 494.9; England, Local Courts 7705.7(?); England, Statutes, Chron. Ser. 9355.5(?); Gregory I 12351.5(?); Kempe, M. 14924; Libellus 15575.5(?); Liturgies, Latin Rite, Breviaries 15805.1; Liturgies, Latin Rite, Hours and Primers 15896; Liturgies, Latin Rite, Missals 16176; Liturgies, Latin Rite, Process. 16232.6; Lydgate 17037.5(?)(A/C); Lyndewode 17107; Maydeston 17727; Primer 20380*(A/C); Robert 21070(?)(A/C); Savonarola 21798(?)(A/C); Stanbridge, Parvula 23163.11(?); Voragine 24880.5(?)(A/C).

1502

Aesop 168; Alcock 285.5(?); Almanacks (Parron) 494.10; Armigilus 772(c.); Christians 5198; England, Appendix 9997; England, Yearbooks 9603(?), 9784.4(?), 9790.4(?), 9796.5(?), 9806.4(?), 9812.5(?), 9819.5(?); Garlandia 11603, 11612, 11613; Guido, de Monte Rocherii 12472; Indulgences, Licences 14077c.144, 14077c.145; Le Fevre 15376; Libellulus 15573(?); Littleton, T., Tenures, French 15722.5(?); Liturgies, Latin Rite, Hours and Primers 15897, 15898; Liturgies, Latin Rite, Hymns 16116, 16116a, 16116a.5; Liturgies, Latin Rite, Missals 16163; Liturgies, Latin Rite, Missals 16175*; Liturgies, Latin Rite, Process. 16232.8; Mirk 17969; Properties 20439.3(?); Romans 21286.2(?); Sulpitius 23427.3.

1503

Aesop 169; Alexander, Grammaticus 319; Arnold 782(?); Art 791; Bevis 1988(?); Donatus, A. 7016.2(+); England, Statutes, Abridgements/Extracts 9515(c.?)*; England, Yearbooks 9691.5(?); Garlandia 11604; Gringore 12379(c.); Indulgences, Turks or Captives 14077c.115A; Informatio 14079; Jesus Christ 14556.5(c.)(A/C); Le Fevre 15377; Liturgies, Latin Rite, Hours and Primers 15899, 15900(?), 15901(c.), 15901.5(c.); Liturgies, Latin Rite, Missals 16177; Liturgies, Latin Rite, Psalters 16255; Lydgate 17033.3; Mandeville 17249; Maydeston 17728; Shepherds' Kalendar 22407; Stella 23243(?); Theodulus 23940(?); Thomas, a Kempis 23954.7*, 23955*; Tryamour 24301.5(?); Voragine 24877*.

1504

England, Appendix 9998; England, Proclamations, Chron. Ser. 7760.4, 7760.6(?); England, Statutes, Chron. Ser. 9357(?); Generides 11721(?); Hawes, S. 12945(?); Hortus 13829.5; Indulgences, Eng. 14077c.27(?); Liturgies, Latin Rite, Missals 16178, 16179, 16180, 16181; Liturgies, Latin Rite, Psalters 16256, 16257; Lyndewode 17108; Maydeston 17728.3; Narrationes 18362(?); Stanbridge, Accidence 23153.6(?); Sulpitius 23427.7; Terentius 23885.3; Thomas, a Kempis 23954.7*, 23955(?)*; Voragine 24877*.

1505

Alanus 252; Alexander, Grammaticus 319.3; Anwykyll 696.3; Art 792, 793.3(?); Aymon 1008(c.); Badius 1186.3(c.); Bell, A. 1805.7 (c.); Bernardus 1967.3(?); Book 3295(?), 3296(c.); Brunus 3945.5(?); Catharine, of Alexandria 4813.6(?); Copland, R. 5728(?); Craft 5952.5(c.?); Donatus, A. 7016.3(c.); England, Local Courts 7705.8 (?); England, Proclamations, Chron. Ser. 7761; England, Statutes, Spec. Subjs. 9337(?); England, Yearbooks 9837(?); Garlandia 11604.5, 11605, 11614; Gringore 12380(?); Hieronymus, de Sancto Marco 13432(?); Holt 13603.7(?); Indulgences, Cont. 14077c.88 (c.), 14077c.89(c.); Indulgences, Eng. 14077c.28(?). 14077c.62, 14077c.81; Indulgences, Images of Pity 14077c.14A(c.), 14077c.15 (c.); Indulgences, unassigned 14077c.153(c.); Justices of Peace 14862(?); Libellus 15579.3(?), 15579.4(?); Liturgies, Latin Rite, Breviaries 15793(A/C), 15805.2(c.), 15805.4(c.); Liturgies, Latin Rite, Hours and Primers 15902(?); Liturgies, Latin Rite, Hymns 16117; Liturgies, Latin Rite, Manuals 16139.5(c.); Lydgate 17007.5(c.); Lyndewode 17109, 17109.3(c.); Maffeus 17181.5; Octavian 18779(?); Origen 18846(?); Os 18872; Paris, le chevalier 19207a(c.), 19208(c.); Piers 19906*; Smith 22653.5(c.); Stanbridge, Accidence 23139.5(?), 23140(c.), 23154.7(c.); Stanbridge, Gradus Comparationum 23155.4(c.), 23155.6(c.); Stanbridge, Parvula 23163.17(?); Stanbridge, Vocabula 23177.5(c.); Sulpitius 23427a; Terentius 23907.3(c.); Theodulus 23940.3; Torent 24133(?).

1506

Ars 788; Barchby or Barklay 1380.5; Bonaventura 3263; Capgrave 4602*; Christians 5199; Creature 6033.5; Dionysius, Carthusianus 6894.5(?); England, Statutes, Chron. Ser. 9357.4; Generides 11721.5(?); Governal 12139(?); Gregory I 12351(?); Gringore 12381; Gryphus or Griffi 12412.5; Hood, R. 13689(?), 13689.3(?+); Hortus 13829.7(+?); Indulgences, Eng. 14077c.29, 14077c.63; Justices of Peace 14863; Liturgies, Latin Rite, Breviaries 15805.5, 15805.7, 15805.9(c.); Liturgies, Latin Rite, Hours and Primers 15903, 15904, 15904.5(?); Liturgies, Latin Rite, Hymns 16117.5, 16118; Liturgies, Latin Rite, Manuals 16140; Liturgies, Latin Rite, Missals 16182; Liturgies, Latin Rite, Psalters 16258; Lydgate 17033.7(?); Mirk 17970(?); Natura Brevium 18387(?); Reynard the Fox 20921.5(bef.); Rolle 21259; Rome 21298(?); Seyssel 22270.5(?); Shepherds' Kalendar 22408.

1507

Almanacks (Red) 504; Bonaventura 3263.5(?); Brandon, C. 3543(?); Creature 6034; Donatus, A. 7018(c.?); Dunbar, W. 7350(?); England, Statutes, Chron. Ser. 9351; England, Yearbooks 9889(?); Garlandia 11605.5, 11614.5; Holt 13606.5(?); Honorius 13685.5; Hylton 14043; Indulgences, Eng. 14077c.44; La Sale 15257.5(c.); Legrand 15398; Libellus 15579.5(?); Liturgies, Latin Rite, Breviaries 15806, 15806a, 15807(?), 15857(c.); Liturgies, Latin Rite, Graduals 15862*; Liturgies, Latin Rite, Hours and Primers 15905(?); Liturgies, Latin Rite, Hymns 16119, 16119.5, 16120*; Nicodemus 18565; Royal Book 21430, 21430a; Stanbridge, Accidence 23140.5(?); Stanbridge, Parvula 23164.2(?); Voragine 24878.3, 24878.5.

1508

Alanus 253; Almanacks 387; Anwykyll 696.4; Book 3289, 3307(?); Carmelianus 4659; Cato 4839.4; Chartier 5060.5; Donatus, A. 7016.4(+), 7016.5(+); Dunbar, W. 7247, 7248, 7249; Edward III 7502.5(?); Eglamour 7542(?); England, Local Courts 7706(?); England, Statutes, Chron. Ser. 9351a, 9357.7(?); England, Statutes, Gen. Colls. 9266; England, Yearbooks 9928.5(?); Fisher, John, St. 10902; Garlandia 11606; Golagros 11984; Guido, de Monte Rocherii 12473, 12474; Henry, the Minstrel 13148(?); Henryson 13166(?); Holland, Richard 13594(?); Holt 13604; Hortus 13829.9 (?); Indulgences, Cont. 14077c.103B, 14077c.104, 14077c.104A, 14077c.104B, 14077c.105, 14077c.105A, 14077c.105B, 14077c.105C; Jesus Christ 14557(?); Liturgies, Latin Rite, Graduals 15862*; Liturgies, Latin Rite, Hours and Primers 15908(?); Liturgies, Latin Rite, Hymns 16120; Liturgies, Latin Rite, Missals 16182a, 16182a.5, 16183, 16184, 16185; Liturgies, Latin Rite, Process. 16233; Lugo 16899(?); Lydgate 17014.3; Lyndewode 17109.7; Maydeston 17728.5; Mirk 17971; Os 18873.3; Pilgrimage 19917.5; Promptorium 20435; Remedy 20875.5; Shepherds' Kalendar 22409*; Stanbridge, Gradus Comparationum 23163.4(?); Stanbridge, Parvula 23164.4(?); Theodulus 23940.7(?), 23940a; Walter, of Henley 25007(?); Warham 25071.5.

1509

Augustine 954.5(?); Baron, S. 1497(aft.); Book 3359(?); Brant 3545, 3547; Canutus 4592(?); England, Proclamations, Chron. Ser. 7761.3, 7761.7, 7762, 7762.3(?); England, Yearbooks 9895(?); Fisher, John, St. 10891, 10900, 10901(+), 10903, 10903a, 10904*; Garlandia 11615; Gryphus or Griffi 12413; Guido, de Monte Rocherii 12475; Gulielmus, de Saliceto 12512; Gulielmus, Parisiensis 12513; Hawes, S. 12943, 12943.5(?), 12946(?), 12948, 12953; Henry VII, King of England 13075, 13075.5; Hortus 13830, 13830.3, 13830.7; Jesus Christ 14546.3; La Sale 15258; Liturgies, Latin Rite, Breviaries 15791*, 15808; Liturgies, Latin Rite, Hymns 16121, 16121a; Liturgies, Latin Rite, Manuals 16140.3, 16140.5(c.), 16160; Liturgies, Latin Rite, Missals 16186, 16220(?); Liturgies, Latin Rite, Ordinals 16232.4; Mary, Q. Consort of Louis XII 17558; Mary, the Blessed Virgin 17537(+?); Nicodemus 18566; Parliament 19305; Ponthus 20107(?); Richard I 21007; Savonarola 21800; Stanbridge, Accidence 23153.7(?), 23153.8(?)(A/C); Stanbridge, Gradus Comparationum 23155.8(?), 23155.9(?); Stanbridge, Parvula 23164; Stanbridge, Vulgaria 23195.5(?); Theodulus 23941; Ursula 24541.3(?).

1510

Alanus 254; Albertus Magnus 268.3, 270.5(c.?); Anwykyll 696.5; Apollonius 708.5; Augustine 922.2(c.); Aymon 1009.5(c.); Bevis 1988.2(c.); Book 3297.5(c.); Burgo 4115; Emlyn 7680.5(?); England,

1510 — *cont.*

Appendix 9999; England, Statutes, Chron. Ser. 9357.8(?), 9357.9(?); England, Yearbooks 9612(?), 9613a(?), 9615.7(?), 9631, 9732(?), 9744(?), 9771.5(?), 9779(?), 9912.5(?); Fisher, John, St. 10905; Garlandia 11606.5, 11615.5; Gospels 12091(c.); Herolt 13226; Holt 13605(?), 13606(?); Hood, R. 13689.5(+?); Indulgences, Eng. 14077c.38, 14077c.41(c.)(A/C), 14077c.49(c.); Indulgences, Images of Pity 14077c.11*(c.?)(A/C), 14077c.18(c.), 14077c.23(c.); Indulgences, Turks or Captives 14077c.116(c.), 14077c.117(c.); Intrationes 14116; Jacob, the Patriarch 14323(?), 14323.3(?); Jerome, St. 14505.5(c.); Jerusalem 14518(?); Jest 14522(+); John, of Arras 14648; Justices of Peace 14864; Leaves 15345(?); Libellus 15576, 15576.8, 15579.6(c.); Littleton, T., Tenures, French 15723(?); Liturgies, Latin Rite, Breviaries 15791*, 15809; Liturgies, Latin Rite, Hours and Primers 15908.5, 15909, 15910.5(?), 15911(?), 16101.8(c.), 16102(?); Liturgies, Latin Rite, Hymns 16122; Liturgies, Latin Rite, Manuals 16140.7; Liturgies, Latin Rite, Missals 16187, 16188*, 16188.5*; Lydgate 17012(?), 17016, 17026(?), 17030.5(?); Mandeville 17249.5(?); Melton, W. 17806(?); Merlin 17841; Michael 17853(?); Mirk 17970.5(c.)(A/C); Os 18873.5(c.), 18873.7(c.); Penitents 19596; Pico della Mirandola 19897.7(?); Pilgrimage 19918(?)(A/C); Ploughman 20034; Ponthus 20107.5(c.); Promptorium 20436*; Remorse 20881.3(c.); Robert 21071.5(?); Romans 21286.3(c.); Savonarola 21789.1, 21799.4, 21799.6; Shepherds' Kalendar 22409.3(c.); Skelton 22597.5(c.); Smith 22653.7(c.); Speculum 23030.7; Stanbridge, Accidence 23142(?), 23143(?), 23143.5(c.), 23153.9(c.), 23155(c.); Stanbridge, Gradus Comparationum 23156(?); Stanbridge, Parvula 23164.1(c.), 23164.6(?); Stanbridge, Vocabula 23178, 23178.3; Sulpitius 23427a.7*; Ten Commandments 23876; Terentius 23885.5(c.), 23907.7(c.); Tongues 24115.5(c.); Torent 24133.5(?); Treatise 24240(?); Valentine 24571.3(c.).

1511

Bernardinus 1966; Bonaventura 3269.5(+), 3273; Canutus 4592.5 (?); Cologne 5574; Demands 6573; England, Proclamations, Chron. Ser. 7762.5(+)(A/C), 8448*; England, Yearbooks 9586(?), 9588(?), 9611(?), 9613(?), 9710(?), 9716(?); Guylforde 12549; Holt 13606.3 (c.); Hortus 13831; Indulgences, Eng. 14077c.30, 14077c.36(c.), 14077c.37(c.), 14077c.61(aft.); Indulgences, Turks or Captives 14077c.129, 14077c.130; Joseph, of Arimathea 14806(?); Liturgies, Latin Rite, Breviaries 15809.5(A/C), Liturgies, Latin Rite, Hours and Primers 15912; Liturgies, Latin Rite, Hymns 16123; Liturgies, Latin Rite, Missals 16188*, 16188.5*, 16189; Lydgate 17017; Mirk 17971.5; Nicodemus 18567; Ponthus 20108; Promptorium 20436*; Rote 21336; Savonarola 21799.8; Shepherds' Kalendar 22409.5; Stanbridge, Parvula 23164.8(?); Stanbridge, Vocabula 23178.7(?); Sulpitius 23427a.3*; Tenures 23878.5(?); Whittinton, De Nominum Generibus 25479(?); Whittinton, Declinationes Nominum 25443.4(?).

1512

Ardenne 735.7; Cato 4839.7; Colet, J. 5545(?); Degore 6470(+); Elias 7571; Gardener 11562.5(?); Gringore 12381.4(?); Indulgences, Eng. 14077c.24, 14077c.55G(A/C), 14077c.60(A/C); Indulgences, Turks or Captives 14077c.117A(c.), 14077c.117B(c.), 14077c.118 (c.), 14077c.119(c.), 14077c.120(c.), 14077c.121(c.), 14077c.121A (c.); Johnson, Richard 14691*; Libellus 15577; Linacre 15635; Liturgies, Latin Rite, Diurnals 15861.7; Liturgies, Latin Rite, Hours and Primers 15913, 15913.5; Liturgies, Latin Rite, Hymns 16123a, 16124; Liturgies, Latin Rite, Missals 16190; Medwall 17778(+); Mirk 17973(c.); Nicodemus 18567a; Os 18874; Perottus 19767.3; Promptorium 20437; Sulpitius 23427a.3*; Virgilius Maro 24813; Voragine 24879; Whittinton, De Nominum Generibus 25479.2(?); Whittinton, De Syllabarum Quantitate 25509.3(?); Whittinton, Declinationes Nominum 25443.6(?); Whittinton, Syntaxis 25541; Whytstons 25585; Wolsey 25947.7.

1513

Alanus 254.3; Alexander, Grammaticus 319.5; Becanus 1703*; Book 3290; Cato 4840; Colonne 5579; England, Proclamations, Chron. Ser. 7763, 7764; England, Statutes, Chron. Ser. 9358(?), 9358.3(?), 9361, 9361.4; England, Statutes, Spec. Subjs. 9333; Flodden 11088.5(?); Gardener 11562.7(?); Jerusalem 14517(?); Jordanus 14789; Lily, W. 15601.3; Liturgies, Latin Rite, Breviaries 15861(?); Liturgies, Latin Rite, Hours and Primers 15914, 15915(?); Liturgies, Latin Rite, Missals 16191; Ovidius Naso 18934; Plutarch 20060; Sirectus 22580(?); Skelton 22593; Stanbridge, Accidence 23153.10; Stanbridge, Parvula 23165.5(?); Stanbridge, Vocabula 23179; Whittinton, De Heteroclitis Nominibus 25459.2(?), 25459.3 (?); Whittinton, De Syllabarum Quantitate 25509.5; Whittinton, Declinationes Nominum 25443.8(?).

1514

Aesop 169.5(?); Cato 4841; Creature 6035, 6035.5; England, Local Courts 7706.5(?); England, Proclamations, Chron. Ser. 7765; England, Statutes, Chron. Ser. 9362.3A; England, Statutes, Gen. Colls. 9267; England, Yearbooks 9599(?); Garlandia 11607, 11608, 11616; Hortus 13832; Indulgences, Eng. 14077c.70, 14077c.71; Liturgies, Latin Rite, Breviaries 15810, 15861.3(?)(A/C); Liturgies, Latin Rite, Hours and Primers 15916, 15917, 15918, 15919, 15920*; Liturgies, Latin Rite, Hymns 16125; Liturgies, Latin Rite, Missals 16193, 16194; Mary, the Blessed Virgin 17540; Poeniteas 20079(?); Simon [Appleby] 22557; Stanbridge, Parvula 23166(?); Stanbridge, Vocabula 23179.5; Sulpitius 23427a.7(?); Virgilius Maro 24814; Whittinton, De Heteroclitis Nominibus 25459.4(?); Whittinton, De Octo Partibus 25496.3(?).

1515

Albertus Magnus 268.7, 271(?); Alexander, Grammaticus 319.7(?), 320.5; Bevis 1988.4(c.); Bonaventura 3270(c.); Cato 4841.3(c.); Doctrinal 6933.5(c.); Donatus, A. 7018.5, 7018.7(c.); England, Appendix 10000, 10000.5; England, Proclamations, Chron. Ser. 7766, 7767; England, Statutes, Chron. Ser. 9351a.4(?), 9362.3, 9362.4; Everyman 10604(c.); Fitzherbert, A. 10954(?)*; Gregory I 12352; Harrington, W. 12798.5(?); Hawes, S. 12942.5; Hayles 12973.5(c.); Hood, R. 13690(c.?); Huon of Bordeaux 13998.5(c.); Hyckescorner 14039(?); Indulgences, Eng. 14077c.35(c.), 14077c.52, 14077c.56(?), 14077c.57(?), 14077c.60A(c.), 14077c.82(c.); Indulgences, Turks or Captives 14077c.124, 14077c.125, 14077c.125A (c.), 14077c.127; Information 14082; John, of Capistrano 14649(c.); Justices of Peace 14864.5, 14865; Libellus 15579.8(c.); Liturgies, Latin Rite, Breviaries 15811(?), 15811.5; Liturgies, Latin Rite, Hours and Primers 15920*, 16102.5(c.); Liturgies, Latin Rite, Hymns 16126, 16127; Liturgies, Latin Rite, Manuals 16141, 16141.5; Liturgies, Latin Rite, Missals 16195, 16195.5; Mary, the Blessed Virgin 17543(c.); Mary Magdalen 17568.5(c.?)(A/C); Mirk 17972; Nicolai, G. 18571.5(c.); Pius II 19969.8(?); Poeniteas 20080(?); Remorse 20881.7(c.); Romans 21286.5(c.); Spagnuoli 22992.1(?); Spare 23013(c.); Stanbridge, Accidence 23147.2(c.), 23155.2(c.); Stanbridge, Parvula 23166.5(?), 23168.5*; Stanbridge, Vocabula 23180.3(?); Stanbridge, Vulgaria 23196; Sulpitius 23428; Tenures 23879(c.); Theodulus 23943; Virgilius Maro 24787(c.); Whittinton, De Heteroclitis Nominibus 25459.5(?); Whittinton, De Nominum Generibus 25479.3(?); Whittinton, De Octo Partibus 25496.5(?); Whittinton, De Syllabarum Quantitate 25509.7; Whittinton, De Synonymis 25525.3, 25525.5, 25526(?)(A/C); William, of Palermo 25707.5(c.).

1516

Aesop 170; Alexander, Grammaticus 320; Almanacks (Laet, G., the elder) 470.2; Capgrave 4601, 4602*; Disputation 6915(?); Donatus, A. 7016.7(?); England, Proclamations, Chron. Ser. 7767.5(?); England, Statutes, Chron. Ser. 9362.6(?), 9362.8(?); England, Yearbooks 9558(?), 9913(?); Exoneratorium 10627.5(?); Fabyan 10659; Fitzherbert, A. 10954; Gulielmus, Parisiensis 12512.5; Hortus 13833; Indulgences, Cont. 14077c.102(?); Indulgences, Eng. 14077c.25, 14077c.60*(A/C); Lily, W. 15609.3(?); Littleton, T., Tenures, French 15724; Liturgies, Latin Rite, Breviaries 15812, 15813(?); Liturgies, Latin Rite, Hours and Primers 15921, 16103(?); Liturgies, Latin Rite, Manuals 16142; Liturgies, Latin Rite, Missals 16196, 16197, 16221; Liturgies, Latin Rite, Process. 16250.5(?); Liturgies, Latin Rite, Psalters 16258.7, 16259; Martin, St. 17498; More, T. 18091(?); Os 18874.5; Poeniteas 20081(?); Promptorium 20438; Retorna 20894.4; Shepherds' Kalendar 22409*; Sulpitius 23428a, 23428a.5; Whittinton, De Heteroclitis Nominibus 25459.6, 25459.8(?); Whittinton, De Nominum Generibus 25479.5(?); Whittinton, De Octo Partibus 25496.7(?), 25498; Whittinton, De Syllabarum Quantitate 25510, 25511; Whittinton, Declinationes Nominum 25444(?); Whittinton, Syntaxis 25541.5, 25542.

1517

Almanacks (Laet, G., the elder) 470.3; Anwykyll 696.7(c.); Benedict 1859; Bonaventura 3264; Brant 3547a; Burley 4122; Chaucer 5095; Donatus, A. 7016.9(?); England, Proclamations, Chron. Ser. 7768; England, Statutes, Abridgements/Extracts 9517.5*; England, Statutes, Chron. Ser. 9358.5(?); England, Yearbooks 9555(?), 9590(?), 9591(?), 9592(?), 9593(?), 9594, 9597(?), 9624(?), 9832(?); Fitzherbert, A. 10955; Frederick, of Jennen 11361a(?); Garlandia 11608a, 11616a; Guido, de Monte Rocherii 12475.5; Harrington, W. 12798.7(?); Hawes, S. 12949; Hortus 13833.5; Indulgences, Cedulae 14077c.1, 14077c.5(c.); Indulgences, Cont. 14077c.101; Indulgences, Eng. 14077c.58(?); Indulgences, Turks or Captives 14077c.126, 14077c.131(?), 14077c.132(?); Liturgies, Latin Rite, Hours and Primers 16104; Liturgies, Latin Rite, Hymns 16128, 16135; Liturgies, Latin Rite, Missals 16222; Liturgies, Latin Rite, Process. 16234; Liturgies, Latin Rite, Psalters 16259.3(c.); Longland 16797*; Lyndewode 17110; Mirror 17979.5(?); Opusculum 18833(?); Robert 21071(?); Shepherds' Kalendar 22409.7(?); Simon [Appleby] 22558*; Stanbridge, Accidence 23147.4(?); Stanbridge, Gradus Comparationum 23157(?); Stanbridge, Vocabula 23180.5(?); Stanbridge, Vulgaria 23196.2(?); Thomas, a Kempis 23957, 23958; Whittinton, De Heteroclitis Nominibus 25459.9(?); Whittinton, De Nominum Generibus 25479.6(?), 25479.8(?); Whittinton, De Octo Partibus 25498.3(?); Whittinton, De Syllabarum Quantitate 25511.5; Whittinton, De Synonymis 25525.7, 25526.5, 25527(?), 25527.2(?), 25527.3(?); Whittinton, Declinationes Nominum 25444.5(?), 25445; Whittinton, Syntaxis 25543.

1518

Almanacks (Laet, G., the elder) 470.4; Barbara 1375; Barclay, A. 1385(?); Belland 1833.5(?); Book 3309.5(?); Burley 4123; Clere-Ville 5405(?); Cock Lorrel 5456(?); Compendium 5607; Copland, R. 5728.5(?); Craft 5953(?); Dedicus 6458; England, Appendix 9983.3(?); England, Yearbooks 9553, 9596, 9651(?); Exoneratorium 10628(?); Frederick, of Jennen 11361; Garlandia 11608a.3, 11617; Generides 11721.7(?); Hortus 13834; Indulgences, Cedulae 14077c.3, 14077c.4; Indulgences, Cont. 14077c.91, 14077c.92, 14077c.103(c.), 14077c.103A(c.); Indulgences, Eng. 14077c.31, 14077c.42(?), 14077c.43, 14077c.55A(?), 14077c.83(c.); Indulgences, Turks or Captives 14077c.133; Libellus 15578(?); Liturgies, Latin Rite, Breviaries 15814, 15815(?); Liturgies, Latin Rite, Hymns 16129, 16129.3; Liturgies, Latin Rite, Legenda 16137; Liturgies, Latin Rite, Missals 16198; Mancinus 17242(?); Mary, of Nimeguen 17557(?); Natura Brevium 18388(?); Nevill 18476; Nicodemus 18568; Oliver, of Castile 18808; Os 18875; Pace 19081a; Remigius 20878.5(?); Shepherds' Kalendar 22410(?); Stanbridge, Accidence 23154(?); Stanbridge, Gradus Comparationum 23159.5(?);

1518 — *cont.*
Stanbridge, Parvula 23167.3(?); Stanbridge, Vulgaria 23196.4(?); Sulpitius 23429; Thomas, a Kempis 23956(?)*; Tunstall 24320; Virgilius Maro 24828(?); Whittinton, De Heteroclitis Nominibus 25459.11(?), 25460; Whittinton, De Nominum Generibus 25479.9 (?), 25479.11(?); Whittinton, De Octo Partibus 25498.7(?); Whittinton, De Synonymis 25527.5(?), 25527.8(?); Whittinton, Syntaxis 25545, 25545.3, 25545.5.

1519

Catharine, of Siena 4815; Cock Lorrel 5456.3(?); Complaint 5609 (?), 5609.5(?); Computus 5613; England, Statutes, Abridgements/Extracts 9515.5; England, Statutes, Gen. Colls. 9268; England, Yearbooks 9598; Erasmus, D. 10450.6; Eulenspiegel 10563(c.?); Exoneratorium 10629; Fisher, John, St. 10904(?)*; Horman 13811; Hylton 14043.5; Indulgences, Cont. 14077c.93, 14077c.94; Indulgences, Eng. 14077c.48(?). 14077c.50, 14077c.53, 14077c.84A; Kur'an 15084(?); Liturgies, Latin Rite, Antiphoners 15790; Liturgies, Latin Rite, Breviaries 15816; Liturgies, Latin Rite, Hours and Primers 15922, 15923, 15924; Liturgies, Latin Rite, Hymns 16128.2; Liturgies, Latin Rite, Missals 16199, 16200, 16201, 16201.3, 16201.7; Liturgies, Latin Rite, Process. 16235; Mirk 17973.5; Narrationes 18362.5(?); Rede 20824.5(A/C); Remedy 20876; Retorna 20894.7; Rolle 21260(?); Stanbridge, Accidence 23147.6, 23154.3; Stanbridge, Gradus Comparationum 23159a(?); Stanbridge, Parvula 23167.5(?); Stanbridge, Vocabula 23181; Stanbridge, Vulgaria 23196.6(?), 23196.8; Thomas, a Kempis 23956(?)*; Whittinton, De Heteroclitis Nominibus 25461, 25461.5; Whittinton, De Octo Partibus 25499; Whittinton, De Syllabarum Quantitate 25512, 25514; Whittinton, De Synonymis 25528; Whittinton, Declinationes Nominum 25446; Whittinton, Libellus Epigrammaton 25540.5; Whittinton, Syntaxis 25546.

1520

Aesop 170.3(?); Almanacks (Adrian) 406.7; Almanacks (Laet, G., the elder) 470.5, 470.6; Aphthonius 699(?); Barbara 1375.5(c.); Book 3288(o.s.?)*; Canutus 4593(c.); Constable, J. 5639; Croke, R. 6044a.5; Dietary 6833; Emanuel, King of Portugal 7677(?); England, Appendix 10001; England, Local Courts 7707(?); England, Proclamations, Chron. Ser. 7769.2; England, Statutes, Chron. Ser. 9362.5(c.), 9362.7(c.); England, Yearbooks 9576, 9595; Erasmus, D. 10450.2, 10450.3, 10450.7; Erasmus, St. 10435; Exoneratorium 10630(?), 10631(?); Goodwyn 12046(?); Hetoum 13256(?); Hortus 13835; Indulgences, Cont. 14077c.90(?), 14077c.90A(?), 14077c.95, 14077c.96, 14077c.97, 14077c.98(c.), 14077c.99; Indulgences, Eng. 14077c.26(c.), 14077c.45(?), 14077c.59(c.), 14077c.67A, 14077c.68A (c.), 14077c.72(c.), 14077c.73(c.), 14077c.84(?); Indulgences, Images of Pity 14077c.23A(c.); Indulgences, Stations of Rome 14077c.149(c.), 14077c.150(c.); Indulgences, unassigned 14077c.154 (c.); Jacob, the Patriarch 14323.5(c.); Jesus Christ 14547.5(c.); Joseph, of Arimathea 14807; Kalenberg 14894.5(c.); Liturgies, Latin Rite, Antiphoners 15790a; Liturgies, Latin Rite, Breviaries 15791.5(c.), 15817(?); Liturgies, Latin Rite, Hours and Primers 15925, 15926(?), 15926.5(?), 15928(?), 15929(?), 16104.5; Liturgies, Latin Rite, Hymns 16128.3(c.); Liturgies, Latin Rite, Manuals 16143(?); Liturgies, Latin Rite, Missals 16202, 16202.5(c.), 16224.5 (c.); Liturgies, Latin Rite, Psalters 16259.5(c.?), 16259.7(c.); Lydgate 17027(?), 17030.7(c.), 17035(?), 17038(?); Mancinus 17241(?), 17242.5(?); Mary Magdalen 17568(?); More, T. 18088; Parliament 19303.7(c.), 19305.3(A/C); Peter, of Luxemburg, St. 19795(?); Petrus, G. 19816(c.?)(A/C); Rastell, J., Printer 20722(?); Rome, Hospital of the Holy Ghost 21310.5(c.); Splynter 23102(?); Squire 23111.5(?); Stanbridge, Accidence 23147.8(?), 23148 (?), 23148.2; Stanbridge, Gradus Comparationum 23159a.1(?), 23159a.2(?); Stanbridge, Parvula 23167.7; Stanbridge, Vocabula 23181.2(?), 23181.3(c.), 23181.4(c.); Stanbridge, Vulgaria 23196a (?), 23196a.2(c.); Sulpitius 23429.5; Tenures 23879.5(c.); Terentius 23894(c.); Thomas, a Becket 23954(c.), 23954.3(c.); Treatise

1520 — *cont.*
24241(?); Valuation 24591(c.?); Whittinton, De Heteroclitis Nominibus 25462; Whittinton, De Nominum Generibus 25479.14, 25479.15; Whittinton, De Synonymis 25529; Whittinton, Declinationes Nominum 25446.5(c.); Whittinton, Syntaxis 25547; Whittinton, Vulgaria 25569.3, 25569.5, 25569.7, 25570.

1521

Almanacks 388(bef.); Austin, St. 965; Baldwin, Abp. 1242; Barclay, A. 1384b(?), 1386; Book 3288(?); Bradshaw, H. 3506; Brendan 3600(?); Bullock 4082; Christmas 5204; Cicero 5311; Darius, S. 6279; Dietary 6834; Du Castel 7270, 7271; England, Local Courts 7709(?), 7725.9(?); England, Statutes, Abridgements/Extracts 9516, 9518.7*; England, Statutes, Chron. Ser. 9358.7(?); England, Yearbooks 9883(?); Erasmus, D. 10496; Exoneratorium 10631.5(?); Fisher, John, St. 10894(?), 10898; Galen 11536; Henry VIII, King of England 13078, 13083; Horman 13807; Indulgences, Eng. 14077c.32, 14077c.65, 14077c.66, 14077c.67; Indulgences, Images of Pity 14077c.11C(?); Jesus Christ 14558; Justices of Peace 14866, 14867; Libellus 15580(?), 15580.5; Lily, W. 15601.5(?), 15606; Liturgies, Latin Rite, Hours and Primers 15930, 15931, 15932(?), 15932.5(aft.); Liturgies, Latin Rite, Missals 16203, 16204, 16204.5; Lucian 16896; Murmellius 18292.7(c.); N. 18324.5; Ricardus 20972; Skelton 22611.5(?); Stanbridge, Gradus Comparationum 23159a.3(?); Stanbridge, Parvula 23168; Stanbridge, Vocabula 23181.5; Ten Commandments 23877; Treatise 24242(?), 24242.3 (?); Voragine 24879.5; Whittinton, Antilycon 25443.2; Whittinton, De Heteroclitis Nominibus 25464; Whittinton, De Nominum Generibus 25480.3, 25480.7, 25481, 25482; Whittinton, De Octo Partibus 25500; Whittinton, De Syllabarum Quantitate 25515, 25515a; Whittinton, De Synonymis 25530; Whittinton, Declinationes Nominum 25448; Whittinton, Syntaxis 25547.3, 25547.5, 25548; Whittinton, Verborum Praeterita 25558, 25558.5, 25559; Whittinton, Vulgaria 25572.

1522

Almanacks 389; Copland, R. 5732.5(c.); Dionysius, Carthusianus 6895, 6896; Elias 7571.5(c.); England, Proclamations, Chron. Ser. 7769.4(c.); England, Statutes, Chron. Ser. 9361.3(?); Fisher, John, St. 10894.5(?); Galen 11531.5(?), 11532, 11534(?); Geminus, P. 11719; Henry VIII, King of England 13079; Indulgences, Eng. 14077c.33, 14077c.59G(?)(A/C); Indulgences, unassigned 14077c.151(?), 14077c.152(c.); Jacob, the Patriarch 14324(+); Jesus Christ 14552; Lactantius 15118(?); Langton, R. 15206; Lily, W. 15606.5(A/C), 15606.7; Littleton, T., Tenures, French 15725.5; Liturgies, Latin Rite, Hours and Primers 15933; Liturgies, Latin Rite, Manuals 16144; Liturgies, Latin Rite, Psalters 16260, 16260.5; Parliament 19305.5(?); Proclus 20398.3(?); Sallustius Crispus 21626(?)(A/C); Stanbridge, Accidence 23148.3; Stanbridge, Gradus Comparationum 23159a.4(?); Tavern 23707; Tunstall 24319; Virgilius Maro 24814.5; Whittinton, De Heteroclitis Nominibus 25464.5; Whittinton, De Nominum Generibus 25479.17, 25483.5, 25484, 25484.5; Whittinton, De Octo Partibus 25501, 25501.5(A/C), 25502; Whittinton, De Syllabarum Quantitate 25517*; Whittinton, De Synonymis 25531; Whittinton, Verborum Praeterita 25560, 25560.3, 25560.7, 25561; Whittinton, Vulgaria 25572.5; World 25982.

1523

Almanacks 389.3, 389.7; Barclay, A. 1383.5(?); Blakman 3123(?); Dietary 6835(?); Drunkards 7260; England, Local Courts 7709.5(?), 7726(?); England, Statutes, Chron. Ser. 9362.9(?); England, Yearbooks 9806.7(?), 9820(?); Fitzherbert, A. 10949*; Fitzherbert, J. 10994(?), 11005; Froissart 11396; Galen 11533; Honorius 13686(?); Indulgences, Eng. 14077c.39, 14077c.40, 14077c.74(c.); Jesus Christ 14550(c.); Libellus 15581(?); Littleton, T., Tenures, Engl. 15759.5(+); Liturgies, Latin Rite, Hours and Primers 15934,

1523 — *cont.*
15935(?); Liturgies, Latin Rite, Manuals 16145, 16146; Liturgies, Latin Rite, Process. 16236, 16236.3; Martin, St. 17499; More, T. 18088.5, 18089; Powel, E. 20140; Prudentius 20453.5(?); Rastell, J., Printer 20701(c.); Retorna 20896(+?); Skelton 22610; Spagnuoli 22978; Stanbridge, Accidence 23148.4(?); Stanbridge, Gradus Comparationum 23159a.5(?); Stanbridge, Vocabula 23181.7; Stanbridge, Vulgaria 23196a.4; Tenures 23879.7(c.); Villa Sancta 24728, 24729; Whittinton, De Heteroclitis Nominibus 25465, 25466; Whittinton, De Nominum Generibus 25485; Whittinton, De Octo Partibus 25502.5, 25503; Whittinton, De Syllabarum Quantitate 25517*; Whittinton, De Synonymis 25532, 25533; Whittinton, Declinationes Nominum 25449, 25450, 25450.3; Whittinton, Syntaxis 25549; Whittinton, Verborum Praeterita 25561.5(?); Whittinton, Vulgaria 25573.

1524

Almanacks (Laet, G., the elder) 470.8(A/C); England, Yearbooks 9784.7(?), 9790.7(?), 9797(?), 9813(?); Galen 11535; Hortulus 13828.2(?); Indulgences, Cedulae 14077c.2; Indulgences, Eng. 14077c.75; Information 14083; Knights of St. John 15050; Libellus 15576.4; Linacre 15634; Liturgies, Latin Rite, Breviaries 15818, 15818.5; Liturgies, Latin Rite, Hours and Primers 15937, 15938, 15938.5, 15941(?)(A/C); Liturgies, Latin Rite, Hymns 16130; Liturgies, Latin Rite, Psalters 16261, 16262; Palsgrave 19166(c.)*; Petrus, G. 19816.5; Stanbridge, Gradus Comparationum 23159a.7 (?); Stanbridge, Parvula 23168.3(?); Stanbridge, Vocabula 23181.9; Stanbridge, Vulgaria 23196a.5(?); Sulpitius 23429a; Turkey 24334*; Whittinton, De Heteroclitis Nominibus 25466.5, 25467; Whittinton, De Nominum Generibus 25486, 25486.3; Whittinton, De Syllabarum Quantitate 25518; Whittinton, Declinationes Nominum 25450.7; Whittinton, Syntaxis 25550, 25551; Whittinton, Verborum Praeterita 25562, 25562.3, 25562.7(?); Whittinton, Vulgaria 25574.

1525

Aesop 177.7(?); Alanus 254.7; Alexander, the Great 321(?); Almanacks (Laet, G., the elder) 470.8B(A/C); Almanacks 390; Alsoppe 538.5(c.); Antichrist 670(?); Arnold 783(?); Articuli 812(?); Augustine 922.3; Barnardinus 1967(?); Beauty 1696(c.); Bernard, St. 1918; Bible, N.T., English 2823; Boccaccio 3184.5(c.); Boethius, A. 3200; Bonaventura 3266; Bradshaw, H. 3507(c.); Cato 4841.5(c.?); Chaucer 5091.5(?); Despautere 6780.5; Emlyn 7681(c.); England, Local Courts 7709.7(?), 7713.7(?), 7726.7(?); England, Statutes, Chron. Ser. 9362.10(?); England, Statutes, Gen. Colls. 9269; England, Yearbooks 9658(?), 9669(?), 9692(?), 9772(?), 9780(?), 9826(?), 9827(?); Example 10608(?); Exoneratorium 10632(?); Fisher, John, St. 10906; Froissart 11397, 11397a*; Gildas 11892(?) [not STC]; Herbal 13175.1; Hieronymus, von Braunschweig 13434; Hylton 14044; Indulgences, Eng. 14077c.68(c.), 14077c.82G(A/C); Indulgences, Images of Pity 14077c.11A(c.), 14077c.17(?), 14077c.17A(c.); Interlocution 14109(?); Libellus 15578.3(?), 15578.5; Lily, W. 15609.5(?); Linacre 15636(?), 15637(c.); Littleton, T., Tenures, French 15726; Liturgies, Latin Rite, Breviaries 15819, 15820, 15821, 15821a(aft.), 15822*; Liturgies, Latin Rite, Hours and Primers 15936(?)(A/C), 15939, 15940; Liturgies, Latin Rite, Hymns 16131; Liturgies, Latin Rite, Process. 16236.5(c.), 16236.6(c.), 16236.7; Lyndewode 17111; Mary, the Blessed Virgin 17544(c.); Natura Brevium 18389; Nicholas, St. 18528(?), 18528.5(?); Pico della Mirandola 19898(c.); Properties 20439.5(c.); Rastell, J., Printer 20700.3(c.), 20702(c.), 20721(c.), 20723(c.); Remedy 20876.5(c.); Retorna 20896.5(c.? (A/C); Reynard the Fox 20921a(c.); Romans 21286.7(c.); Ryckes 21471.5; Sallustius Crispus 21627(?); Seeing 22153; Smith, Walter 22869.7; Stanbridge, Accidence 23148.5; Stanbridge, Gradus Comparationum 23159a.8(?), 23163.5(c.); Stanbridge, Parvula 23168.5(?)*; Stanbridge, Vocabula 23182; Stanbridge, Vulgaria

1525 — *cont.*
23196a.6(?); Tenures 23880, 23880.3(c.); Virgilius Maro 24827.5 (c.)(A/C); Vocabulary 24868.3(c.); Whittinton, De Heteroclitis Nominibus 25468, 25468.5; Whittinton, De Nominum Generibus 25486.7, 25487; Whittinton, De Octo Partibus 25504; Whittinton, De Synonymis 25534; Whittinton, Declinationes Nominum 25451, 25452, 25453; Whittinton, Syntaxis 25552, 25552.5; Whittinton, Verborum Praeterita 25563; Whittinton, Vulgaria 25576; Wolsey 25947.3(?).

1526

Bible, N.T., English 2824(?); Bonde 3277; Bushe 4186(?); Chaucer 5086, 5088(?), 5096(?); Cologne 5575; Dionysius, Carthusianus 6897, 6897.5; England, Exchequer 7695.5(?); England, Local Courts 7712(?), 7727(?); England, Proclamations, Chron. Ser. 7769.6; England, Yearbooks 9618(?), 9625(?), 9637(?), 9682(?), 9699(?), 9705(?), 9738(?), 9750(?), 9756(?), 9764(?), 9833(?), 9838.7(?), 9839(?), 9852(?), 9877(?), 9930.7(?); Erasmus, D. 10474(?), 10477(?); Everyman 10604.5(+)(?); Fisher, John, St. 10892(?), 10892.4(?); Fitzherbert, A. 10946; Fitzherbert, J. 11006; Henry VIII, King of England 13084, 13084.5; Herbal 13175.2, 13176; Indulgences, Cont. 14077c.101A, 14077c.101B(?); Indulgences, Eng. 14077c.80; Indulgences, Turks or Captives 14077c.121B; Justices of Peace 14871(+?); Legrand 15399(?); Libellus 15581.2(+?); Liturgies, Latin Rite, Breviaries 15822*, 15858; Liturgies, Latin Rite, Hours and Primers 15943, 15944, 15945, 15946, 15946.5, 15948; Liturgies, Latin Rite, Manuals 16147; Liturgies, Latin Rite, Missals 16205, 16205.3*(A/C); London, Hanse Merchants 16778 [not STC]; Lyndewode 17111.5; Martyrology 17532; Opusculum 18833a(c.); Pace 19082(?); Retorna 20897(+?); Seeing 22153a(?); Spagnuoli 22979; Stanbridge, Accidence 23148.7; Stanbridge, Gradus Comparationum 23159a.9, 23159a.10, 23159a.12(?); Stanbridge, Parvula 23168.7, 23169, 23169.5(c.); Stanbridge, Vocabula 23182.2(?), 23182.3; Stanbridge, Vulgaria 23196a.7(?); Tales 23664; Treasure 24199(?); Tyndale, W. 24438; Whittinton, De Heteroclitis Nominibus 25469; Whittinton, De Nominum Generibus 25488, 25488.5; Whittinton, De Syllabarum Quantitate 25520; Whittinton, Verborum Praeterita 25564; Whittinton, Vulgaria 25577, 25577.5.

1527

Augustine 922.4; Austin, St. 966; Boccaccio 3176; Bonde 3274.5; Colet, J. 5542, 5542.1(?); Copland, R. 5733(c.); Dietary 6836; England, Proclamations, Chron. Ser. 7769.8; England, Statutes, Abridgements/Extracts 9517.5*, 9518; England, Statutes, Gen. Colls. 9269.5; England, Yearbooks 9561(?), 9562, 9617(?), 9632, 9637.5(?), 9681(?), 9686(?), 9698(?), 9840(?), 9846(?), 9851(?), 9856a(?), 9866(?), 9872, 9876(?), 9944.5(?); Erasmus, D. 10478.7(?); Feylde 10838.7(?); Fisher, John, St. 10892.7(?). 10895(?); Galen 11537 [not STC]; Henry VIII, King of England 13085, 13086(?); Hieronymus, von Braunschweig 13435; Higden 13440; Hortus Sanitatis 13837.5(?); Indulgences, Eng. 14077c.79; Indulgences, General 14077c.146(c.); Indulgences, Turks or Captives 14077c.121C; John, of Capistrano 14649.5(?); Judicial 14836(?), 14836.3(?); Justices of Peace 14869(A/C); Libellulus 15574; Libellus 15581.5(A/C); Liturgies, Latin Rite, Graduals 15863; Liturgies, Latin Rite, Hours and Primers 15949, 15950, 15951, 15952, 15953, 15953.5, 15954, 15955, 15956; Liturgies, Latin Rite, Hymns 16128.5; Liturgies, Latin Rite, Missals 16205.3*(A/C), 16205.5, 16206, 16207, 16208; Longland 16790(?), 16791(?), 16793(?), 16793.5(?), 16797(?)*; Rastell, J., Printer 20703; Skelton 22611(?); Stanbridge, Accidence 23148.8(?); Stanbridge, Gradus Comparationum 23159a.13, 23160, 23160.3; Stanbridge, Vocabula 23182.5(?); Stanbridge, Vulgaria 23197(?); Treatise 24223.3; Vincentius 24764(?); Voragine 24880; Whittinton, De Heteroclitis Nominibus 25470, 25471, 25471.5(?); Whittinton, De Nominum Generibus 25489, 25489.3, 25489.7; Whittinton, De Octo Partibus

1527 — *cont.*
25505, 25505.5; Whittinton, De Synonymis 25535; Whittinton, Declinationes Nominum 25454, 25455.5(+?); Whittinton, Syntaxis 25553.5, 25554; Whittinton, Verborum Praeterita 25564.2; Whittinton, Vulgaria 25578.

1528

Aristotle 768(c.), 770; Articuli 814; Barlow, W., Bp. of St. Asaph/Chichester 1462.7; Book 3361(?); Christmas 5204.3(?); Connaissance 5631(?); Debate 6445(?); Dictes 6830; Eglamour 7542.5(?); England, Appendix 10002; England, Proclamations, Chron. Ser. 7770, 7771; England, Statutes, Abridgements/Extracts 9518.7*, 9519, 9520; England, Yearbooks 9569(?), 9611a(?), 9631a(?), 9642, 9648, 9704(?), 9840.3(?), 9845(?), 9856(?), 9865(?), 9871(?), 9889.5(?), 9896(?), 9930(?), 9931(?), 9935(?), 9945(?); Erasmus, D. 10471.4; Everyman 10606(?); Fabri 10656 [not STC]; Fitzherbert, A. 10947; Garcie 11550.6; Gawaine 11691a.3(?); Gringore 12382(?); Harrington, W. 12799, 12800; Henry VIII, King of England 13086.5(?), 13087(?); Hieronymus, von Braunschweig 13436(?)*; Hortus 13836; Indulgences, Eng. 14077c.54, 14077c.55, 14077c.76; Interlude 14109.5(c.); Introductions 14125.5(?); Jerusalem 14519; Lily, W. 15607(?); Littleton, T., Tenures, Engl. 15760(+); Littleton, T., Tenures, French 15727, 15728; Liturgies, Latin Rite, Breviaries 15792, 15822a(bef.), 15823, 15824, 15826; Liturgies, Latin Rite, Diurnals 15861.8; Liturgies, Latin Rite, Graduals 15864; Liturgies, Latin Rite, Hours and Primers 15936(?)*(A/C), 15957, 15958, 15959(?), 15961(?); Liturgies, Latin Rite, Hymns 16131.5; Liturgies, Latin Rite, Missals 16209; Liturgies, Latin Rite, Process. 16237; Lucian 16891; Mirk 17974; Natura Brevium 18390, 18390.5(?)(A/C); Perkins, J. 19629; Plutarch 20058.5; Promptorium 20439; Richard I 21008; Saint German 21559; Salerno 21596; Shepherds' Kalendar 22411; Skelton 22604(?), 22609; Stanbridge, Accidence 23148.10; Stanbridge, Parvula 23172(?), 23173; Tenures 23880.5; Thomas, a Kempis 23960(?); Tyndale, W. 24446, 24454, 24455.5*; Wakefield 24944(?); Whitford 25421.2; Whittinton, De Nominum Generibus 25490; Whittinton, De Syllabarum Quantitate 25521, 25521.5; Whittinton, Verborum Praeterita 25564.6, 25564.8(?); Whittinton, Vulgaria 25578.5(+?).

1529

Agapetus 193(?); Almanacks (Laet, G., the elder) 470.9; Arthur, King 803; Assault 862; Austin, St. 967(?); Barlow, W., Bp. of St. Asaph/Chichester 1462.3(?); Bible, Appendix 3036; Child 5136(?); Colet, J. 5542.2, 5542.3; Doctrinal 6933; England, Proclamations, Chron. Ser. 7772, 7773; England, Statutes, Gen. Colls. 9273*; England, Yearbooks 9675(?), 9932, 9933(?); Erasmus, D. 10493; Fish 10883(?); Fisher, John, St. 10907; Frith, J. 11394; Herbal 13177, 13177.5; Indulgences, Turks or Captives 14077c.122; Jesus Christ 14563; Liturgies, Latin Rite, Hours and Primers 15961.3, 15961.5; Liturgies, Latin Rite, Manuals 16148, 16148.2*; Litugies, Latin Rite, Missals 16210; Liturgies, Latin Rite, Psalters 16263(?); Lydgate 17007a(aft.), 17034(?); Lyndewode 17112; Martin, St. 17499.5; Merlin 17841.3; More, T. 18084, 18092, 18093; Murmellius 18293; Natura Brevium 18391(A/C); Nicodemus 18569; Prayers 20196; Search 22141; Solomon 22899(?); Stanbridge, Accidence 23148.12(?), 23148a, 23149(?), 23149.5(?); Stanbridge, Gradus Comparationum 23160.7(?); Stanbridge, Parvula 23174, 23174.3; Stanbridge, Vocabula 23182.6; Stanbridge, Vulgaria 23198(?), 23199(?); Terentius 23908; Tunstall 24323.5; Virgilius Maro 24815; Vives 24856(?), 24856.5(?); Whittinton, De Heteroclitis Nominibus 25472, 25474(+?); Whittinton, De Nominum Generibus 25491, 25491.3; Whittinton, De Octo Partibus 25506; Whittinton, De Syllabarum Quantitate 25522(?); Whittinton, De Synonymis 25536; Whittinton, Declinationes Nominum 25456, 25456.3(+?); Whittinton, Syntaxis 25555(?), 25556; Whittinton, Verborum Praeterita 25565.

1530

Almanacks (Laet, G., the elder) 470.10; Almanacks (Laet, G., the younger) 471; Almanacks (Thibault) 517.10; Almanacks 390.5; Articuli 815; Barclay, A. 1384(c.); Barlow, W., Bp. of St. Asaph/Chichester 1462.5; Bernard, St. 1912; Bernardus 1967.5(?); Bible, Appendix 3021; Bible, O.T., Genesis-Job 2350; Bible, O.T., Psalms 2370; Boccus 3186(?)(A/C), 3187(?)(A/C); Bonaventura 3267, 3273.3(c.); Book 3288.5(?), 3313.3(?), 3356.3(c.); Caesar, Caius Julius 4337; Chaucer 5092; Cicero 5275(?); Colet, J. 5550(?); Copy 5743(?); Dialogue 6807(?); Dialogues 6815(?); England, Admiralty 7681.8(?); England, Appendix 9983.7; England, Exchequer 7695.7(?); England, Local Courts 7713.9, 7728(?); England, Proclamations, Chron. Ser. 7774, 7775, 7776; England, Statutes, Abridgements of Ind. Years 9533.2(?); England, Statutes, Chron. Ser. 9363.6(?), 9363.8(?); England, Yearbooks 9611b(?), 9884(?); Exoneratorium 10633(?); Fantasy 10685; Fitzherbert, A. 10948; Fitzherbert, J. 10995(?); Gawaine 11691a.5(+?)(A/C); Governal 12139.5(?); Hawes, S. 12947; Hieronymus, von Braunschweig 13437(?); Horman 13812; Hortulus 13828.4; Hyckescorner 14039.5 (?); Hylton 14041(?); Indulgences, Eng. 14077c.64(c.), 14077c.69 (?); Interlude 14111(c.); Isumbras 14280.5(c.), 14280.7(c.); Italy and France 14286; Jacob, the Patriarch 14324.5(c.); Jest 14520.5(?), 14520.7(c.?)(A/C); Jesus Christ 14546.7(?); John, of Capistrano 14650(?); Justices of Peace 14870(?); Lamwell 15187(+?)(A/C); Libellus 15578.7, 15582; Littleton, T., Tenures, French 15730(c.), 15731; Liturgies, Latin Rite, Breviaries 15827.5(A/C), 15828, 15829; Liturgies, Latin Rite, Hours and Primers 15962, 15963, 15964, 15965, 15966*, 15968; Liturgies, Latin Rite, Hymns 16128.7; Liturgies, Latin Rite, Manuals 16148.2*, 16161(?); Liturgies, Latin Rite, Missals 16223; Liturgies, Latin Rite, Process. 16238(?), 16239, 16240, 16240.5, 16251; Liturgies, Latin Rite, Psalters 16263a; Lord's Prayer 16816(c.); Lucian 16895(?); Margaret, of Scotland 17324.5(c.); Margaret, St. 17326(?), 17327(+?)(A/C); Mary, the Blessed Virgin 17541, 17542; Medwall 17779(+); Mohammed, the prophet 17994.5(c.); More, T. 18085; Natura Brevium 18402.5(?); Nevill 18475(?); Pain 19119(c.); Palsgrave 19166*; Plutarch 20056.7; Profits 20413; Ptolemy 20480(?); Rastell, J., Printer 20703.3(c.), 20719, 20719.5, 20720, 20724(?); Ravisius 20765.5(?); Rote 21337; Saint German 21561(?), 21565; Salerno 21597; Simon [Appleby] 22559; Skelton 22607(?); Songs 22924; Stanbridge, Accidence 23150(?), 23150.3(?), 23150.5(?), 23150.7(?); Stanbridge, Gradus Comparationum 23161; Stanbridge, Parvula 23174.5; Stanbridge, Vocabula 23182.8(?), 23182.9(?); Stanbridge, Vulgaria 23198.3(?); Sulpitius 23429a.5(?); Tales 23663(c.)(A/C); Tenures 23881; Thorpe 24045; Treatise 24227.5(c.?); Tryamour 24302(c.); Tyndale, W. 24465; Vocabulary 24868.7(c.); Wakefield 24946(?); Whitford 25421.3, 25421.8(?), 25422; Whittinton, De Nominum Generibus 25491.7(?); Whittinton, De Octo Partibus 25506.3(?); Whittinton, Verborum Praeterita 25565.5, 25566.3(?).

1531

Aesop 170.7(?); Ashwell 845(?); Barlow, W., Bp. of St. Asaph/Chichester 1461; Barnes, R., Dr. 1470(?); Bernard, St. 1913(?), 1914, 1915(?); Bible, O.T., Prophets 2777, 2788(?); Bonde 3278; Bushe 4185; Cato 4841.7(?); Cebes 4890.5(?); Colet, J. 5550.5(?); Complaint 5608(?); Eckius 7481.4; Elyot, T. 7635; England, Statutes, Abridgements of Ind. Years 9533.4(?), 9533.8(?); England, Statutes, Abridgements/Extracts 9521(?); England, Statutes, Chron. Ser. 9369.5(?); England, Statutes, Gen. Colls. 9270.5(?), 9271*; England, Yearbooks 9733(?), 9760(?), 9833.3(?), 9861 (?), 9906(?), 9929(?), 9934(?); Erasmus, D. 10474.5(?), 10476.3 (?), 10477.5(?); Exoneratorium 10633.5(?); Frith, J. 11386.5(?); Gulielmus, de Occam 12510, 12510.5; Hamilton, P. 12731.4 (?); Hawes, S. 12944(?); Hortulus 13828.6; Indulgences, Eng. 14077c.34; Italy and France 14287; Lebenhain 15346; Legrand 15399.5(+); Lily, W. 15601.7; Litany 15707; Liturgies, Latin Rite, Breviaries 15830, 15831*; Liturgies, Latin Rite, Hours and Primers

1531 — *cont.*
15966*, 15969, 15970, 15971, 15973, 15974, 15975(?); Liturgies, Latin Rite, Missals 16211; Lucian 16892; Lydgate 17014.7(?), 17025; Mary, the Blessed Virgin 17545; Moulton 18214a(bef.); Natura Brevium 18393; Ploughman 20036(?); Plutarch 20052(?); Registrum 20836, 20836.5; Saint German 21562, 21563, 21563.5, 21564, 21566, 21567; Simon [Appleby] 22559.5; Skelton 22600.5 (?); Stanbridge, Gradus Comparationum 23162, 23162.5(?); Stanbridge, Parvula 23174.6(?); Stanbridge, Vocabula 23183; Stella 23244; Thomas, a Kempis 23961(?), 23962(?), 23963(?), 23964(?), 23964.3(?); Tyndale, W. 24437, 24443; Vaus 24623.5; Vives 24857(?); Whitford 25412(?), 25421.5, 25422.3(?), 25422.5; Whittinton, De Heteroclitis Nominibus 25474.3, 25474.7, 25475(?); Whittinton, De Nominum Generibus 25492(?); Whittinton, De Octo Partibus 25506.7, 25507(?); Whittinton, De Synonymis 25536.5(?); Whittinton, Declinationes Nominum 25456.7, 25457(?); Whittinton, Syntaxis 25556.5(?); Whittinton, Verborum Praeterita 25566.7(?).

1532

Abell 61; Abington 78(+?); Ars 788.5(?); Assize of Bread 863.5(?), 864(bef.); Boccaccio 3183.5; Bonaventura 3273.5; Book 3357; Calais 4350, 4351; Cato 4842; Charles V 5018; Chaucer 5068; Complaint 5610; Cox, L. 5947; Creature 6035a(?); Cura 6126; Dialogue 6800.3(c.); Diurnal 6928(?), 6928.5(?); Doctrinal 6932; Edguardus or Edwardes 7483; England, Appendix 9984(?); England, Proclamations, Chron. Ser. 7778; England, Statutes, Abridgements of Ind. Years 9534.5(?); England, Statutes, Chron. Ser. 9364(?), 9372(?); England, Yearbooks 9565, 9717(?), 9838(?); Enormities 10421.5(?); Erasmus, D. 10467, 10470.8(?); Feylde 10839(?); Fisher, John, St. 10909; Fitzherbert, A. 10949(?)*; G., John 11499(?); Gararde 11549; Glass 11918(?), 11919(?), 11919.5; Gower, J., Poet 12143; Hamilton, P. 12731.6(c.); Hortus 13837; Indulgences, Eng. 14077c.57A(c.); Indulgences, Turks or Captives 14077c.123; Jesus Christ 14559; Liturgies, Latin Rite, Breviaries 15831*; Liturgies, Latin Rite, Graduals 15865; Liturgies, Latin Rite, Hours and Primers 15976, 15977, 15978, 15979*, 15980, 16105(?); Liturgies, Latin Rite, Hymns 16132*; Liturgies, Latin Rite, Missals 16212, 16212.5(c.); Liturgies, Latin Rite, Process. 16241; Longland 16790(?)*(A/C), 16791.5, 16792(?); Lucian 16894(?); Mirk 17975; More, T. 18079, 18090*(A/C); Natura Brevium 18403; Netherlands, Off. Doc. 18447.5(?); Nicodemus 18570; Perkins, J. 19630; Ploughman 20036.5(c.); Plutarch 20057(?); Retorna 20898; Rome, Church of 21310; Ryckes 21472(?); Saint German 21568, 21586(?), 21587(?), 21587.3(?), 21587.5(?), 21587.7(?); Schade 21810; Simon [Appleby] 22560; Stanbridge, Accidence 23151, 23151.3(?); Stanbridge, Gradus Comparationum 23163; Tales 23665(?); Tenures 23882; Treatise 24225; Whitford 25421, 25421.6; Xenophon 26069.

1533

Almanacks (Laet, G., the younger) 471.5; Almanacks (Thibault) 517.12; Anne [Boleyn] 656; Bevis 1988.6(?); Bible, Appendix 3034.5(?); Book 3313.5(?); Britton 3803(?); Colet, J. 5542.4; Dionysius, Carthusianus 6894(?); Duwes 7377(?); Edward, the Confessor 7500; Elyot, T. 7668, 7672, 7672.5; England, Exchequer 7696(?); England, Local Courts 7712.2(c.), 7712.4; England, Proclamations, Chron. Ser. 7778.4, 7778.5, 7779; England, Public Documents, Misc. 9177; England, Statutes, Abridgements of Ind. Years 9533.9(?), 9536; England, Statutes, Abridgements/Extracts 9521a.5(?); England, Statutes, Chron. Ser. 9358.9(?), 9361.5(?), 9362.11(?), 9366.3(?), 9370(?), 9372.3(?), 9376, 9376.3(?); England, Statutes, Gen. Colls. 9286(?); England, Yearbooks 9664(?), 9711(?), 9935.3(?); Erasmus, D. 10449*, 10471, 10475, 10479, 10488.7(?), 10508(?); Fabyan 10660; Fitzherbert, A. 10950; Fitzherbert, J. 10995.5(?), 11006.5(?); Foundement 11210.5(?); Frith, J. 11381; Goes 11966; Gulielmus, de Occam 12511(?), 12511a(?); Heywood, J. 13298, 13299, 13305; Holy Ghost 13608.4(?); Hutten, U. 14024;

1533 — *cont.*
Hylton 14045; Isocrates 14278(?); Jesus Christ 14552.7(?); Justices of Peace 14871.5(c.), 14872(?); Langdon 15192.5(+?)(A/C); Libellus 15583, 15583.5(c.); Lily, W. 15602, 15608; Liturgies, Latin Rite, Breviaries 15832, 15859; Liturgies, Latin Rite, Hours and Primers 15979*, 15981, 15981a(?), 15982(?), 15982.5(?), 15983(?); Liturgies, Latin Rite, Hymns 16132*; Liturgies, Latin Rite, Missals 16213, 16224; Lupset 16939; Mary, the Blessed Virgin 17542.5(?); More, T. 18077*(A/C), 18078, 18080, 18081, 18090*(A/C); Nausea 18414; Old Christmas 18793.5; Pedersen 19525; Pierius 19902; Retorna 20898.5(c.), 20899(?); Rosary 21318; Saint German 21584; Saltwood 21647(+?)(A/C); Schottenius 21827; Terentius 23899*; Thomas, a Kempis 23968.5(?); Tyndale, W. 24440(?), 24468*, 24469*, 24470*, 24471*; Vocabulary 24868(c.); Wakefield 24943(?); Walter, W. 25008(?); Whitford 25423, 25423.5(A/C); Whittinton, De Heteroclitis Nominibus 25477; Whittinton, De Nominum Generibus 25493.3, 25493.7; Whittinton, De Octo Partibus 25507.5, 25508; Whittinton, De Synonymis 25537; Whittinton, Declinationes Nominum 25458; Whittinton, Syntaxis 25557; Whittinton, Verborum Praeterita 25567, 25567.5; Whittinton, Vulgaria 25579.

1534

Alban 256; Almanacks (Laet, G., the younger) 471.7; Almanacks 391(?); Barnes, R., Dr. 1471; Bible, Apocrypha 2792(+?)(A/C); Bible, N.T., English 2825, 2826, 2830*; Bible, O.T., 'Books of Solomon' 2752(?); Bible, O.T., Genesis-Job 2351; Bible, O.T., Prophets 2778; Bible, O.T., Psalms 2354, 2371(?), 2372; Bonde 3275(?), 3276(?); Book 3360(?); Cicero 5278, 5313(?); Colet, J. 5542.6, 5542.8(?), 5543, 5543b.9(?)*(A/C), 5547, 5547.2; Constantine I 5641; Cyprian 6157; Devon 6795.6; Diurnal 6928a(?) (A/C); England, Proclamations, Chron. Ser. 7779.2, 7779.8, 7780, 7781, 7782, 7782.2, 7782.3, 7782.4, 7782.6, 7782.8; England, Public Documents, Misc. 9178; England, Statutes, Abridgements of Ind. Years 9536.5, 9536.7(?); England, Statutes, Chron. Ser. 9372.5(?), 9381(?), 9386(?), 9389.7; England, Statutes, Gen. Colls. 9272; England, Yearbooks 9579(?), 9587, 9721(?), 9726(?); Erasmus, D. 10449*, 10453.5, 10467.5, 10480, 10489(?), 10493.5(?), 10494(?), 10503(?), 10504, 10504a; Exoneratorium 10634(?); Fitzherbert, A. 10958; Fitzherbert, J. 10995.7(?); Fountain 11211(?); Fox, E. 11218; Gardynare 11594; Hamilton, P. 12731.8(?); Heywood, J. 13303; Holy Ghost 13608*; Indulgences, Images of Pity 14077c.11B(?); Ireland, Laws 14130.5(A/C); Isidore 14270; Jesus Christ 14546.5(?), 14548(+?)(A/C), 14553, 14561, 14575; Joye 14829; Julius II 14841.5(?); Juvencus 14893.5; Liturgies, Latin Rite, Hours and Primers 15984, 15985, 15985a(?), 15985a.5*, 15986; Liturgies, Latin Rite, Missals 16214; Lupset 16934; Luther 16962; Lydgate 17013(?)(A/C), 17030.9(+)(A/C); Lyndewode 17113; Marcort 17313.3; More, T. 18077*(A/C); Natura Brevium 18394, 18394.5, 18395.5(?); Remorse 20882(?); Saint German 21585; Savonarola 21789.3; Stanbridge, Accidence 23151.7, 23152, 23153.2; Stanbridge, Gradus Comparationum 23163.2(?); Stanbridge, Parvula 23174.7; Stanbridge, Vocabula 23184.5; Stanbridge, Vulgaria 23198.7(?); Swinnerton 23551.5, 23552; Terentius 23899*; Treatise 24226(?); Watt 25127; Whitford 25413.7(?)(A/C); Whittinton, De Nominum Generibus 25494.

1535

A.B.C. 17.7(c.); Aesop 171; Almanacks (Laet, G., the younger) 471.8; Anabaptists 564(?); Antidotarius 675.3(?), 675.7(?); Augsburg Confession 909.5(?)(A/C); Bartholomaeus 1537; Bernard, St. 1915.5(c.); Bible, Appendix 3036a(?), 3046; Bible, English 2063, 2063.3; Bible, Latin 2055; Bible, N.T., English 2827, 2828(?), 2828a(?), 2829(c.?), 2830*, 2830.3(c.), 2830.5(c.); Bible, O.T., Psalms 2372.4; Bible, Selections 3014*; Bygod 4240(?), 4240.5(?); Calverley 4370(?); Chaucer 5099.5(c.); Cicero 5292(?), 5317.5(?); Colet, J. 5543a; Copland, R. 5729; Coverdale 5892(?); Cox, L. 5947.5(c.?); Degore 6470.5(c.?); Douglas, G. 7072.8(c.); England,

1535 — *cont.*
Exchequer 7696.5; England, Proclamations, Chron. Ser. 7783, 7784, 7785, 7786; England, Statutes, Abridgements of Ind. Years 9538.7(?); England, Statutes, Chron. Ser. 9370.2(c.?), 9376.5(?), 9379(?), 9379.5(?), 9380(?), 9386.3(?); England, Yearbooks 9570(?), 9573(?), 9932.3, 9933.3(?); Erasmus, D. 10498(?); Everyman 10606.5(?); Fitzherbert, A. 10951, 10951.5; Frith 11385(+?)(A/C), 11387(+?)(A/C); Froissart 11396.5(c.)*; Gardiner, Stephen 11584; Guevara 12436, 12436.5; Holy Ghost 13608*; Hutten, U. 14027.5 (c.); James V 14435(+?); Jerome, St. 14505(?); Jesus Christ 14553.7(?); Johnson, John, humile prof. 14667; Joye 14820, 14821; Julius II 14842; Justices of Peace 14873(+?); Lantern 15225(?); Libellus 15583.7(?); Liturgies, Latin Rite, Breviaries 15793.5(c.), 15833, 15840*; Liturgies, Latin Rite, Hours and Primers 15985a.5*, 15986.3, 15986.7, 15987*, 15988, 15988a(?); Longland 16794.5, 16795.5*; Lord's Prayer 16818(c.); Lupset 16936, 16940; Luther 16988(?); Lydgate 17027.5(c.); Matthew, S. 17656; Menandrinus 17817; Natura Brevium 18404; Prayers 20193.5(?), 20200.3(?); Prognostications 20418.5(?); Saint German 21558.5(?), 21588(?); Salerno 21598; Sampson, R. 21681(?); Savonarola 21789.4(?), 21798.5(?); Stanbridge, Accidence 23153(?)(A/C); Stanbridge, Vocabula 23185.5(?); Thomas, a Kempis 23964.7(?); Tracy, W. 24167; Treatise 24236(?), 24238, 24239(?); Tyndale, W. 24447, 24447.7(+?)(A/C), 24455.5(+?)(A/C); Whitford 25413(?)(A/C); Ypres 26119.

1536

Agincourt 198(?), 198.3(c.); Almanacks (Brunsfelsius) 421.17; Augsburg Confession 908; Bell, A. 1806; Bible, Appendix 3037(?); Bible, English 2063.5; Bible, N.T., English 2831, 2832, 2833, 2834, 2835, 2835.2, 2835.3, 2835.4(?); Bible, N.T., Gospels 2987, 2987.5; Bible, Selections 3014*; Bugenhagen 4021; Canutus 4593.5; Charles V 5015.5; Chaucer 5098(?); Colet, J. 5543b; Copland, R. 5732(?); England, Admiralty 7682(aft.); England, C. of, Articles 10033, 10033.2, 10033.4, 10033.6, 10033.8; England, C. of, Injunctions 10084.7; England, Local Courts 7713; England, Proclamations, Chron. Ser. 7762.7(?), 7776.5(?), 7778.8(?), 7787, 7788, 7788.1, 7788.3; England, Statutes, Abridgements of Ind. Years 9534(?); England, Statutes, Chron. Ser. 9366.5(?), 9372.7(?), 9391(?), 9391.3(?), 9393.7(?), 9394(?); England, Yearbooks 9745(?); Erasmus, D. 10492(?), 10509(?); Fisher, Jasper 10887*; Frith, J. 11390(c.?); Fullonius 11470.5; Garcie 11550.8; Gregory I 12353(c.?); Guevara 12437*; Gwynneth 12557; Henry VIII, King of England 13077, 13077.5, 13089a(+); Hutten, U. 14025; Jesus Christ 14577.5(+?); Lambert, F. 15179; Litany 15707.5(?); Littleton, T., Tenures, French 15731.3(?)(A/C); Liturgies, Latin Rite, Hours and Primers 15987*, 15991, 15992, 15992.5(c.), 15993, 16106; Longland 16795, 16795.5*; Luther 16983.5(?); Morison 18113.3, 18113.5, 18113.7; Moulton 18214a.3(bef.), 18214a.5(bef.)(A/C), 18214a.7(bef.); Parker, H., D. D. 19214; Savonarola 21789.5, 21789.6, 21799; Singleton, R. 22575; Starkey, T. 23236; Tyndale, W. 24441(?), 24441.3(?), 24455, 24462(?), 24463(?); Wakefield 24945(?).

1537

Almanacks (Seyfridt) 513; Benese 1873(?); Bible, English 2064, 2065, 2066; Bible, N.T., Gospels 2964.5(?); Bible, O.T., 'Books of Solomon' 2752.5; Bible, O.T., Genesis-Job 2351.5(c.); Bible, O.T., Prophets 2788.5(c.?); Christian Man 5163, 5164, 5165, 5166, 5167; Colet, J. 5543b.4; Cura 6127; Declaration 6455; Dictionary 6832.1, 6832.2; Elyot, T. 7636, 7642.5(?); England, Exchequer 7696.7; England, Statutes, Abridgements of Ind. Years 9533.6(?), 9534.7 (c.?), 9539(?); Erasmus, D. 10465.5, 10473.5(?), 10495; Fitzherbert, A. 10958.5; Fyloll 11489(?); Guevara 12437*; Henry VIII, King of England 13081.7, 13082(?), 13090; Herbal 13175.4(c.?); Hun 13970(?); Introduction 14117.7(A/C); Jesus Christ 14561a; Latimer 15285, 15286, 15287; Liturgies, Latin Rite, Hours and Primers 15994, 15995, 15996, 15997(?), 15997.5(?); Liturgies, Latin Rite, Manuals 16148.4, 16148.6; Lord's Prayer 16820, 16820.3, 16820.5 (?), 16821(?); Luther 16999; Mantua 17262.5; Mary, the Blessed Virgin 17545.5; Morison 18109, 18109.5; Nicodemus 18570a(?); Original 18849; Osiander, A. 18878; Regius 20840, 20840.5; Retorna 20899.5(+?), 20900*; Rules 21447; Savonarola 21789.7(?); Treatise 24219.5, 24250(?); Tyndale, W. 24441.7(?), 24443.5(?), 24447.3; Whitford 25413.5, 25414, 25425, 25425.5; Xenophon 26071.

1538

A.B.C. 19; Articuli 817; Becon 1724.5; Bible, Appendix 3022(c.?), 3038.3(?), 3038.5(?); Bible, N.T., English 2836, 2836.5, 2837, 2838(?), 2838.3(?), 2838.7(?), 2839(?), 2840, 2841; Bible, N.T., Gospels 2965, 2965.2, 2965.4, 2966, 2966.3, 2966.5; Bible, N.T., Latin and English 2815, 2816, 2816.5, 2816.7, 2817; Brerewood 3617*; Bullinger 4054; Complaint 5611(?); Elyot, T. 7659; England, C. of, Injunctions 10085(?), 10086, 10087(?); England, C. of, Visit. Articles 10326; England, Exchequer 7697(?); England, Local Courts 7714(?), 7729; England, Proclamations, Chron. Ser. 7788.7 (?), 7789.3, 7789.7, 7790, 7799(?); England, Statutes, Abridgements of Ind. Years 9537(?), 9539.7(c.?), 9540(c.?); England, Statutes, Abridgements/Extracts 9522(?); England, Statutes, Chron. Ser. 9373(?), 9377, 9377.3*, 9377.7*, 9377.9*, 9386.5(?), 9394.3(?), 9394.5(c.?); England, Statutes, Gen. Colls. 9290(?); England, Statutes, Spec. Subjs. 9338, 9338.3; England, Yearbooks 9589 (?), 9797.5(?), 9807(?), 9935.5(?); Erasmus, D. 10459(+?)(A/C), 10480.5, 10505; Fitzherbert, A. 10968, 10969, 10984(?); Fox, E. 11219; Guevara 12438*; Henry VIII, King of England 13080, 13080.3, 13080.5, 13080.7, 13081, 13081.3, 13081.5, 13082.3, 13090.3; Hurlestone 14006(+?)(A/C); Justices of Peace 14875(?); Libellus 15584, 15584.3; Lily, W. 15610(?); Lindsay, Sir D. 15671; Littleton, T., Tenures, Engl. 15761, 15761.2(?); Liturgies, Latin Rite, Hours and Primers 15998(?), 16001, 16002, 16002.5, 16002a, 16003, 16004, 16006, 16007, 16008, 16008.3, 16008.5; Longland 16794, 16796; Lord's Prayer 16821.3(c.), 16821.5; Lupset 16937; Luther 16979.7, 17000, 17000a*; Martin, St. 17500(?); Matrimony 17651.5(+?)(A/C); Prayers 20193; Regius 20841; Retorna 20900(?)*, 20900.5(+?); Ridley, L. 21040(+?)(A/C), 21041(+?)(A/C), 21042; Rome, Church of 21307a.5; Rules 21447.5; Sarcerius 21752.5, 21753; Savonarola 21790, 21790.5, 21791; Stanbridge, Accidence 23152.3(?); Stanbridge, Vocabula 23186(c.); Sturmius 23407; Tenures 23883; Terentius 23900; Treatise 24237, 24248; Turner, William 24358; Tyndale, W. 24444; Venus 24650(?); Whitford 25415(?); Wyse 26063.

1539

Almanacks (Laet, G., the younger) 471.9; Almanacks 392.2(A/C), 392.3, 392.5(?); Articuli 818; Augsburg Confession 909(?); Bible, English 2067, 2068; Bible, N.T., English 2842, 2843(?), 2844, 2845; Bible, N.T., Gospels 2966.7; Bible, N.T., Latin and English 2818.5; Bible, O.T., Psalms 2372.6, 2747.5, 2748; Colet, J. 5543b.7, 5543b.8(?); Cyprian 6156, 6158; Declaration 6456.5(?); Elyot, T. 7630, 7642.7, 7643; England, Appendix 9984.5(?)(A/C); England, Local Courts 7730; England, Proclamations, Chron. Ser. 7791, 7792; England, Statutes, Abridgements of Ind. Years 9542(?); England, Statutes, Chron. Ser. 9397, 9397.5, 9397.7*, 9398*; England, Statutes, Gen. Colls. 9273*; Erasmus, D. 10437; Fitzherbert, J. 11007(?), 11008; Frontinus 11402; Guevara 12438*; Herbal 13175.5(?), 13178; Hutten, U. 14026, 14026.5; Introduction 14118; Isidore 14270.5; Justices of Peace 14876; Le Maire de Belges 15453; Libellus 15584.5; Lily, W. 15603, 15603.5, 15609; Littleton, T., Tenures, Engl. 15761.4(?); Littleton, T., Tenures, French 15731.5; Liturgies, Latin Rite, Hours and Primers 16009, 16009.5, 16010, 16011(?), 16012(?), 16013(?); Lord's Prayer 16821.7; Lupset 16941; Morison 18110, 18110.5, 18110.7, 18111, 18112, 18113; Parker, H., Baron Morley 19211; Patriarchs 19465.5; Rome, Church of 21307a.7(?); Sampson, R. 21679; Savonarola 21792; Stanbridge,

1539 — *cont.*
Accidence 23152.5, 23152.7; Stanbridge, Parvula 23175(?); Taverner, R. 23709, 23711a, 23712.5, 23713*; Treasure 24200, 24201; Tunstall 24322, 24322a; Vives 24846.5.

1540

Agrippa 201; Almanacks (Erra Pater) 439.3(?); Almanacks 392.7 (A/C); Anatomical Fugitive Sheets 564.2(c.?); Arnaldus 777(c.); Ballad 1323.5; Barnes, R., Dr. 1473.5(?); Beauty 1697(c.); Bible, English 2069, 2070, 2071, 2072*, 2073*, 2076*; Bible, N.T., English 2846, 2847; Bible, N.T., Gospels 2967(?), 2968(?), 2969(?), 2971, 2971.5, 2972(?), 2972.2(?); Bible, N.T., Latin 2799; Bible, O.T., 'Books of Solomon' 2753; Bible, O.T., Psalms 2368; Boethius, H. 3203(?); Byrch 4241.5(c.); C., G. 4268.5; Cato 4843; Cicero 5279; Colet, J. 5543b.9(c.)*(A/C); Counsel 5871.9(c.); Dictionary 6832.3, 6832.5(?); Duwes 7378(?); Elyot, T. 7657.5, 7664*, 7673; England, Appendix 9985.5; England, Exchequer 7697.5, 7697.7(?); England, Local Courts 7713.3; England, Statutes, Abridgements of Ind. Years 9535(?); England, Statutes, Chron. Ser. 9365(?), 9366.7(?), 9370.4(?), 9391.5(?), 9400.4, 9400.5, 9400.6*, 9400.7*, 9401*, 9402*, 9403*, 9403.2, 9403.4(?), 9403.8 (?), 9403.9(?); England, Statutes, Gen. Colls. 9274*, 9290.5; England, Statutes, Spec. Subjs. 9338.5; England, Yearbooks 9780.5(?), 9814(?), 9946; Erasmus, D. 10445, 10454(c.?), 10468; Fitzherbert, A. 10954(c.)*, 10970*; Fitzherbert, J. 10996(c.?); Free Will 11366.3 (c.?); Frith, J. 11393; Fullonius 11470; Gawaine 11691a.7(c.?); Gray, W. 12206a.3, 12206a.7; Herbal 13175.6(?); Hutten, U. 14027; Lesson 15525(c.); Lily, W. 15604; Lily, W., 'Lily's Grammar' 15610.5, 15610.6*; Littleton, T., Tenures, Engl. 15761.8(?); Littleton, T., Tenures, French 15732(c.); Liturgies, Latin Rite, Hours and Primers 16014(?), 16015, 16016, 16016.5(?), 16017, 16018(?), 16018.5(?); Maiden 17192(?); Montpellier 18052(?); Moulton 18216(?), 18225.2(?); Natura Brevium 18405; Order 18841.7(c.); Pylbarough 20521; Ridley, L. 21038, 21038.5; Roesslin 21153; Savonarola 21793(c.); Seeing 22153b(?), 22154(?); Smyth, R., P. 22877.6; Smyth, T. 22880.2, 22880.4, 22880.6, 22880.7; Solme 22897(?); Standish, J. 23209, 23210; Treasure 24202, 24202.5; Vives 24847; Wiclif 25587.5; Wimbledon 25823.3(?).

1541

Almanacks (Laet, G., the younger) 473, 474, 474.5; Almanacks 392.9, 392.10, 392.11(A/C); Barnes, Mr. 1465(?); Becon 1739(?); Bible, English 2072*, 2073*, 2074, 2075, 2076*; Bullinger 4045, 4070.5; Coverdale 5888(?); Cura 6127.5; Dictionary 6832.7, 6832.9; Elyot, T. 7644, 7645, 7646*, 7664*; England, Local Courts 7716(?); England, Proclamations, Chron. Ser. 7792.3, 7792.5, 7793, 7794, 7795, 7796; England, Public Documents, Misc. 9175b.5; England, Statutes, Abridgements of Ind. Years 9542.3(?), 9543(?); England, Statutes, Chron. Ser. 9403.6(?); England, Statutes, Gen. Colls. 9274*, 9275(?); Erasmus, D. 10482; Felicius 10751; Fitzherbert, A. 10970*, 10971, 10985(?); Gosynhill 12104.5*; Herbal 13175.7(?), 13175.8; Libellus 15584.7*(A/C); Littleton, T., Tenures, Engl. 15762(?); Littleton, T., Tenures, French 15732.5; Liturgies, Latin Rite, Breviaries 15833.5, 15834; Liturgies, Latin Rite, Hours and Primers 16019*, 16020, 16021.5(c.), 16022; Liturgies, Latin Rite, Hymns 16133; Lupset 16935; Melanchthon 17798; Moulton 18219(?); Perkins, J. 19631; Retorna 20901; Salerno 21599; Sawtry 21804; Scotland, statutes, etc. 21878.5; Seeing 22155(?); Treatise 24217; Vives 24858, 24859*; Whitford 25420.

1542

Agrippa 203; Antidotarius 675a(?); Antwerp 692.5(?); Becon 1713, 1714, 1715, 1717, 1734, 1735, 1740, 1742, 1749, 1775; Bible, N.T., English 2848(aft.?); Bible, N.T., Gospels 2967.3(?), 2968.3(?), 2970(?), 2972.5; Bibliander 3047; Borde 3378.5; Brinkelow 3759.5(?), 3764; Bullinger 4045.5; Chaucer 5069, 5070; Cura 6128; Elyot, T. 7631, 7659.5, 7660*; England, Appendix 9986, 9986.5(?);

1542 — *cont.*
England, Proclamations, Chron. Ser. 7797, 7798; England, Public Documents, Misc. 9175b.10(?), 9179, 9179.3; England, Statutes, Abridgements of Ind. Years 9538(?), 9544(?), 9544.5(?); England, Statutes, Abridgements/Extracts 9523, 9524; England, Statutes, Chron. Ser. 9400.6(?)*, 9404, 9404.5, 9404.7*, 9405*, 9405.5*; England, Statutes, Gen. Colls. 9276, 9287(?), 9291; England, Statutes, Spec. Subjs. 9343.7(?); England, Yearbooks 9751(?), 9765(?), 9821(?), 9935.7(?); Erasmus, D. 10443; Fabyan 10661, 10662; Ferdinand I 10808(?); Froissart 11396.5(?)*; Glass 11917; Goodwyn 12047(?); Gosynhill 12102(?); Guevara 12439; Guido, de Cauliaco 12468; Holy Roman Empire 13612; Introduction 14123.7 (?)(A/C); Jesus Christ 14562(+); John, Chrysostom 14639, 14640; Leland 15446; Lily, W., 'Lily's Grammar' 15610.6; Liturgies, Latin Rite, Hours and Primers 16021(?), 16021.3(?)(A/C), 16023, 16024, 16026, 16027, 16027.5, 16028; Liturgies, Latin Rite, Manuals 16149*; Liturgies, Latin Rite, Process. 16241.5; O'Neill, C. 18813; Pardon 19187(?); Patriarchs 19465.3(?); Savonarola 21794 (?); Scarperia 21807, 21808; Seton, A. 22249.5(?); Taverner, R. 23713(?)*; Tenures 23884(c.); Treatise 24228(?); Turkey 24334*; Vaughan, Robert 24601; Vyllagon or Villegagnon 24894.

1543

A.B.C. 19.2; Almanacks (Laet, G., the younger) 474.7, 475; Amant 546(?); Avalos 977.5(?); Bale 1280(?), 1309; Becon 1730.5, 1731, 1734.5, 1738, 1743, 1750, 1776; Bible, N.T., Gospels 2967.5(?), 2969.3(?), 2972.7(?); Book 3327; Bullinger 4046, 4047, 4048*; Charles V 5014, 5015; Christian Man 5168, 5168.7, 5169, 5170, 5170.3, 5170.5, 5170.7, 5171, 5173, 5174, 5175, 5176; Cousin 5879; England, Appendix 9987, 9987.5; England, Local Courts 7716.5; England, Proclamations, Chron. Ser. 7800, 7800.3, 7800.5, 7800.6, 7800.7, 7801, 7802; England, Public Documents, Misc. 9175b.15; England, Statutes, Chron. Ser. 9359(?), 9361.6(?), 9363(?), 9374(?), 9382(?), 9387(?), 9400.7(?)*, 9404.7(?)*, 9406.7, 9406.8, 9407, 9408*, 9409.5, 9409.6, 9409.8, 9409.9; England, Statutes, Gen. Colls. 9292, 9301, 9301.3*, 9303*, 9303.4; England, Statutes, Spec. Subjs. 9339; England, Yearbooks 9906.3(A/C), 9913.5(A/C), 9929.3; Erasmus, D. 10506, 10507(?); Fitzherbert, A. 10952, 10972, 10986; Fitzherbert, J. 10997(?), 11009(?); Fortescue 11193(?); Goeurot 11966.5(?); Hardyng 12766.7, 12767; Herbal 13175.8C(?); Instruction 14106.2; Jesus Christ 14556; John, Chrysostom 14634; Joye 14826, 14830; Justices of Peace 14878(?); Leland 15443; Libellus 15584.9, 15585; Lily, W., 'Lily's Grammar' 15610.7, 15610.8*; Liturgies, Latin Rite, Breviaries 15835*; Liturgies, Latin Rite, Hours and Primers 16028.5, 16029, 16030(?); Liturgies, Latin Rite, Manuals 16149*, 16150; Melanchthon 17793; Plutarch 20062; Record, R. 20797.5; Retorna 20902, 20902.3(?); Romney Marsh 21313; Saint German 21570; Salomon 21629; Taverner, R. 23712(?); Tracy, R. 24164(?); Turner, William 24353, 24354*; Vigo 24720; Zwingli 26138, 26138.5.

1544

Alesius 292(?); Almanacks (Laet, G., the younger) 475.5, 476; Almanacks (Mussemius) 488.9; Almanacks (Scute or Schuute) 508.5; Almanacks (Walter) 523; Almanacks 393, 394, 394.5; Assize of Bread 866(?); Bale 1276, 1291(?), 1291.5(?), 1291a(?); Bible, O.T., Psalms 2374(?); Bible, Selections 2994, 2995, 3001.7, 3002, 3002.3; Book 3327.3(?), 3327.6; Borde 3378.7*; Bullinger 4079.5(?); Christian Man 5178; Cope, A. 5718; Elyot, T. 7637, 7646(?)*, 7665; England, Appendix 9988; England, Exchequer 7697.9, 7698(?); England, Local Courts 7713.5, 7717, 7731; England, Proclamations, Chron. Ser. 7802.7, 7803, 7803.7, 7804, 7804.5, 7805; England, Public Documents, Misc. 9175b.20; England, Statutes, Chron. Ser. 9410, 9410.3, 9410.7*, 9411*, 9411.5*; England, Statutes, Gen. Colls. 9293; England, Statutes, Spec. Subjs. 9334; England, Yearbooks 9619(?), 9627(?), 9643(?), 9649(?), 9660(?), 9670(?), 9722(?), 9727(?), 9756.5(?), 9773(?), 9930.3(?), 9931.3 (?), 9934.3(?), 9946.9(?)(A/C), 9954.7(?)(A/C), 9961.7(?)(A/C);

1544 — *cont.*
Erasmus, D. 10483, 10484; Exhortation 10620, 10621, 10621.5, 10621.7, 10622, 10622.5, 10623, 10623.3(?); Fitzherbert, J. 10997.3; Goeurot 11967; Heywood, J. 13300(?), 13305.5(?); Isidore 14271; John, Chrysostom 14637; Joye 14828; Justices of Peace 14877, 14878.3(?); Leland 15440, 15442.5; Lily, W., 'Lily's Grammar' 15610.8*; Littleton, T., Tenures, Engl. 15763; Liturgies, Latin Rite, Breviaries 15835*; Liturgies, Latin Rite, Hours and Primers 16032, 16033, 16033.5(+); Liturgies, Latin Rite, Process. 16242; Lupset 16938; Natura Brevium 18406, 18407; Porcia 20116; Prayers 20200(?); Seeing 22156; Seymour 22270; Terentius 23900.5; Tracy, R. 24165, 24165.5*, 24166*; Treasure 24203; Turner, William 24350.5, 24354(?)*; Vives 24848; Xenophon 26072.

1545

A.B.C. 19.6(c.); Agrippa 202; Almanacks (Borde) 416.5; Almanacks (Brotbeihel) 420.15; Almanacks (Erra Pater) 439.5(c.); Almanacks (Laet, G., the younger) 476.5, 477; Anatomical Fugitive Sheets 564.4(c.?); Articuli 820; Ascham 837; Bacon, R. 1179.5(c.); Bale 1296.5(?), 1303; Bernard, St. 1908(c.); Bible, N.T., Gospels 2967.7(?), 2968.5(?), 2970.3(?), 2973(c.); Bible, O.T., 'Books of Solomon' 2753.5(?), 2754(c.); Bible, Selections 3002.5, 3002.7, 3003, 3003.5*, 3004*, 3005*; Book 3327.9, 3365.5; Brinkelow 3765; Catechism 4797.3; Catharine [Parr] 4818, 4818.5, 4819; Cato 4853.5; Cebes 4891(?); Chedsay 5106.5; Christian Faith 5160(?); Christian Man 5177; Christmas 5204.5(?); Clerke, J. 5408; Coverdale 5889; Elyot, T. 7631.5, 7632*, 7658, 7660*, 7674; England, Customs 7687; England, Public Documents, Misc. 9175b.25, 9175b.30; England, Statutes, Chron. Ser. 9394.7(?); England, Statutes, Gen. Colls. 9293.3; England, Statutes, Spec. Subjs. 9343.8(c.?); England, Yearbooks 9633(?), 9638(?), 9653(?), 9665(?), 9676(?), 9785(?), 9932.5(?), 9933.5(?), 9946.3(?)(A/C); Erasmus, D. 10438, 10460, 10488; Exhortation 10623.5(?), 10624; Fitzherbert, A. 10953(?), 10954(c.)*, 10987; Fitzherbert, J. 10997.5(c.?); Geminus, T. 11714; Gregory, of Nazianzus 12345(c.?); Hippocrates 13521.7(c.); Interlude 14109.7(c.); Intrationes 14117*; Introduction 14124(c.); Invective 14126.5; Jest 14522.5(c.); John, Chrysostom 14630; Joye 14823; Langton, C. 15204(?); Leland 15441.7, 15444, 15444.5, 15445.5; Libellus 15585.5, 15587.5(?); Littleton, T., Tenures, Engl. 15764.5; Littleton, T., Tenures, French 15732.7, 15732.9, 15733; Liturgies, Latin Rite, Hours and Primers 16017.5(c.?)(A/C), 16034, 16035, 16036, 16037, 16038, 16039, 16040, 16041, 16042*; Liturgies, Latin Rite, Process. 16243; Mean 17760.5(c.); Moulton 18220(?), 18225.4(?); Natura Brevium 18396(?), 18397; Perkins, J. 19632; Prayers 20196.5(c.), 20197.3; Retorna 20902.5; Rhodes, H. 20953(?); Roesslin 21154; Seton, J. 22250; Skelton 22594(?), 22598(?), 22601(?), 22615(?); Stanbridge, Parvula 23175.5(c.); Thomas, a Kempis 23965(?); Tommai 24112(c.); Tracy, R. 24165.5(?)*; Treatise 24216a(?); Turner, William 24355; Walshe 25000; Wyatt 26054(?).

1546

Almanacks (Gasser) 447.5; Almanacks (Laet, G., the younger) 477.5; Almanacks 395, 396; Askew, A. 848; Assize of Bread 867(?); Bale 1270; Barlow, W., Bp. of St. Asaph/Chichester 1462.9; Bekinsau 1801; Bible, N.T., English 2848.5, 2849; Bible, N.T., Gospels 2969.5(?), 2973.2, 2973.3(?), 2973.5(?); Bible, O.T., 'Books of Solomon' 2755(?); Book 3326.5(?), 3328, 3328.5, 3329(?); Bullinger 4048(?)*; Dictionary 6832.11; Duwes 7379(?), 7380(?); Elyot, T. 7638; England, C. of, Visit. Articles 10155*; England, Exchequer 7699, 7700, 7701, 7702, 7703; England, Local Courts 7717.4, 7717.7, 7718, 7719, 7720, 7732, 7732.5, 7733, 7733.3, 7734; England, Proclamations, Chron. Ser. 7805.3, 7805.5, 7805.7, 7806, 7807, 7808, 7809; England, Statutes, Chron. Ser. 9378, 9392, 9397.7*, 9398*, 9412, 9412.5*, 9414.7; England, Statutes, Gen. Colls. 9293.6(?); Exhortation 10625.3, 10625.7; Fish 10884; Fitzherbert, J. 11011; Frith, J. 11382; Gardiner, Stephen 11588, 11589, 11591, 11591.3; Geminus, T. 11718.9(?); Giovio 11899; Goeurot 11969; Guevara 12440, 12440.5; Herbal 13175.10; Heywood, J. 13291; Hughe 13910; Intrationes 14117*; Introduction 14119; Jonas 14717; Joye 14828.5; Justices of Peace 14879, 14879.5, 14879a, 14879b; Kelton 14919; Leland 15442; Libellus 15586, 15586.5, 15586a, 15586b, 15587; Lily, W., 'Lily's Grammar' 15610.9; Liturgies, Latin Rite, Hours and Primers 16042*, 16042.5(?), 16043, 16043.5, 16044, 16045, 16046, 16047; London, Ords. and Regs. 16700, 16701*; Lupset 16932; Luther 16984(?)(A/C); Martin, St. 17501; Mechlin 17764.5; Moulton 18221(bef.), 18221.3(bef.), 18221.5(bef.), 18221.7(bef.), 18221a(bef.); Peryn 19785.5(?), 19786; Price, Sir J. 20310; Principia 20394; Retorna 20903; Sampson, R. 21678; Smith, R., Dean 22815, 22820, 22820a, 22821*; Supplication 23435.5; Treasure 24203.3(?); Tyndale, W. 24468(?)*; Vergilius 24654, 24655, 24656; Vives 24848.5; Wiclif 25590, 25590.5.

1547

A.B.C. 20(c.?); Act 95(?), 96, 96.5; Almanacks (Sauvage) 507.11; Aristotle 754, 769(c.); Articuli 821; Askew, A. 850, 851(?); B., I. or J. 1034.7, 1035, 1035.5, 1036; Baldwin, W. 1253; Bale 1279(?), 1305(?); Becon 1733.5(?); Bible, Appendix 3039; Bible, N.T., English 2850; Bible, N.T., Gospels 2968.7(?); Bible, N.T., Gospels 2974(?); Bible, N.T., Latin and English 2819*; Bible, O.T., 'Books of Solomon' 2756(?); Bible, Selections 2999*, 3003.5(+)*, 3004(+)*; Book 3310(?), 3310.3(?); Borde 3373.5, 3380*, 3386(?); Bullinger 4071(?); Catharine [Parr] 4822, 4827; Christmas 5205(?); Clerke, J. 5409; Cope, A. 5717; Crowley 6084.5(?), 6088.9(?); Ditty 6920; Elyot, T. 7646.5; England, C. of, Injunctions 10087.5, 10088, 10089, 10090, 10090.3, 10090.5, 10091, 10093.5, 10093.7*, 10094(?) [not STC]; England, C. of, Visit. Articles 10114, 10115(?), 10115.5(?), 10116(?), 10116.5(?); England, Local Courts 7720.4, 7734a; England, Proclamations, Chron. Ser. 7809.7, 7810, 7811, 7811.2, 7811.5, 7811.9, 7812; England, Statutes, Chron. Ser. 9370.6(?), 9408*, 9414.9; England, Statutes, Gen. Colls. 9293.8; England, Yearbooks 9620(?), 9626, 9644(?), 9659(?), 9687(?), 9791(?), 9890(?), 9929.5, 9930.5(?), 9931.5(?), 9934.5(?), 9947(?), 9955(?), 9962(?); Epistle 10430(?); Erasmus, D. 10446, 10476, 10490(?); Fitzherbert, A. 10973; Fitzherbert, J. 10997.7(c.?), 11012(?); Gerrard 11797; Gruffudd Hiraethog 12403.9(?); Harrison, James 12857; Henry VIII, King of England 13089; Herbal 13175.11(?); Herman V 13213; Homilies 13638.5, 13638.7, 13639, 13639.5, 13640, 13640.5, 13641, 13641.3, 13641.5, 13641.7, 13641.9; Hooper 13741, 13745; Instruction 14106; Kelton 14918; Langton, C. 15205; Liturgies, Latin Rite, Hours and Primers 16048, 16048a; Marcort 17313.7, 17314, 17314a; Martin, St. 17502; Mass 17627(?); Melanchthon 17789, 17789.5; Moulton 18225.6(?); Parfeius 19195; Prognostications 20423(?); Reckoning 20795; Record, R. 20816; Rice, R. 20972.7(?)(A/C); Rome, Church of 21305(?); Salesbury, W. 21616; Seneca 22216; Smith, R., Dean 22818, 22821*, 22822, 22824; Tales 23664.5(?)(A/C); Taverner, R. 23714(?); Treasure 24203.5; Tyndale, W. 24457, 24469(?)*, 24470(?)*, 24471(?)*; Ulric 24514(?); Vives 24859*; Ympyn Christoffels 26093.5.

1548

Aepinus 165.5(?), 165.7, 166.5(?); Allen, E. 358.5, 359; Almanacks (Askham) 410; Almanacks (Laet, A.) 470, 470.1; Almanacks (Sauvage) 507.13; Antidotarius 675a.3(?); Antipus 683(?); Artopoeus 822; Ashwell 846(?); Askew, A. 852(?); Augustine 919; Bale 1271, 1274a(c.), 1278(?), 1280.5(?), 1287(?), 1292(?), 1295, 1297(?); Barclay, A. 1384a(?); Barnes, R., Dr. 1472, 1473; Basle 1544; Becon 1724.7(?), 1774; Bible, Appendix 3034.7(?)(A/C), 3040, 3041.5(?); Bible, N.T., English 2851, 2852, 2853, 2853.5, 2854, 2854.2, 2854.3, 2854.4, 2854.5, 2855*; Bible, N.T., Gospels 2975(?); Bible, N.T., Latin and English 2819*; Bible, O.T., Psalms 2375, 2375.5; Bible, Selections 2998.5, 3005*; Bodrugan 3196; Bon 3258.5(?);

1548 — *cont.*
Bonner, R. 3287; Book 3319.5(?), 3330(?), 3362, 3363; Brinkelow 3760(?), 3761(?), 3766; Broke, T., Esq. 3815, 3816; Bullinger 4048.5(?), 4059, 4080; C., T. 4312(?); Calvin 4409.5(?), 4410(?), 4411(?), 4412(?), 4435, 4435.3, 4435.5, 4435.7; Catharine [Parr] 4822.5(?), 4828; Cautels 4877.2(?)(A/C); Champneys 4956; Chaucer 5100(?); Christian Rule 5189.7(?); Christian Sentence 5190(?), 5190.3(?); Christians 5195, 5199.7, 5200; Comparison 5605a(?); Cope, A. 5719; Cranmer 5992.5, 5993, 5994; Crowley 6082, 6083, 6086, 6086.5; Devil 6793.6(?); Dialogue 6802.5, 6806; Dictionary 6832.13, 6832.15, 6832.17, 6832.19; Double Ale 7071(?); Elyot, T. 7661, 7670(aft.?); England, C. of, Injunctions 10093.7*; England, C. of, Visit. Articles 10148, 10148.5; England, Proclamations, Chron. Ser. 7813, 7814, 7815, 7816, 7818; England, Public Documents, Misc. 9181.3, 9181.5; England, Statutes, Chron. Ser. 9405(c.)*, 9410.7(c.?)*, 9419, 9420, 9421*, 9421.1*, 9421.2*, 9421.3*, 9421.4*, 9421.5*, 9421.6*, 9421.7*; England, Yearbooks 9615a(?), 9838.5(?), 9839.5(?), 9936; Erasmus, D. 10485, 10494.5(?); Fitzherbert, J. 10999; Fountain 11211.2(+); Fox, E. 11220; Foxe 11235; Frith, J. 11383, 11384, 11385.5(+?), 11391(?); Gardiner, Stephen 11593.5(?); Geminus, T. 11718.4; Gest 11802; Gibson, T., Printer 11842a(?); Gilby 11884(?); Guevara 12431; Halle 12721, 12722, 12723a*(A/C); Hart, H. 12887; Hegendorff 13021; Help 13051.7(?), 13052(?); Herbal 13175.12(?); Herman V 13210, 13211(?), 13212(A/C), 13214; Homilies 13642; Invective 14126(?); Judgement 14835(?); Kethe 14942(?); Lambert, F. 15178; Lambert, J., Martyr 15180(?); Latimer 15291, 15292a; Lent 15461; Lily, W., 'Lily's Grammar' 15610.10, 15611*; Lindsay, Sir D. 15683(?); Littleton, T., Tenures, Engl. 15765; Liturgies, C. of Eng., Ord. of Comm. 16456.5, 16457, 16458.3, 16459; Liturgies, C. of Eng., Spec. Prayers 16503, 16503.5; Liturgies, Latin Rite, Hours and Primers 16049, 16049.3(c.), 16049.5(?); Lord's Prayer 16822(?); Luther 16964, 16982, 16983(?), 16992; Lynne 17115(?); M., I. or J. 17137; Marcort 17315, 17316; Mardeley 17317, 17318(?), 17319(?); Margaret, of Angouleme 17320; Mass 17626(?), 17630(?); Melanchthon 17792, 17795(?), 17796(?), 17799; Moone 18055, 18056(?), 18056.5; Moulton 18222.5(?); Nicolls 18575(?), 18576*; Ochino 18764, 18765; OEcolampadius 18787(?); Order 18842(?); Osiander, A. 18877; Pathos 19463(?); Patten 19476.5; Philogamus 19882(?); Prayers 20192.7; Preservative 20203.5(?); Prognostications 20424(?); Punt 20499; Questions 20560.7(?)(A/C); Ramsey, J. 20661(?), 20662, 20663; Ratramnus 20748.5, 20749; Record, R. 20817; Regius 20842, 20843, 20847(?), 20849, 20851.5(?); Ridley, L. 21039; Rome, Church of 21305.3(?), 21309.7(?)(A/C); Sachs 21537.5, 21537.7; Sampson, R. 21680; San Pedro 21739.5(?); Schoolhouse 21826.6(?); Seeing 22157, 22160(?); Seymour 22268, 22269; Smith, R., Dean 22823; Spangenberg 23004, 23004.5; Switzerland, Reformed Church of 23553(?); Ten Commandments 23877.3(?); Tracy, R. 24162, 24163(A/C); Treasure 24203.7(?); Treatise 24229(?)(A/C); Turner, William 24359, 24361.5(?), 24362(?), 24363; Tyndale, W. 24441a, 24445(?), 24448, 24450(?), 24451(?), 24458, 24466; Veron, J. 24676, 24679; Viret 24781, 24784(?); Wiclif 25591(?), 25591a(?); Wimbledon 25823.7(c.); Zwingli 26136, 26139.

1549

Aepinus 166; Almanacks (Vopell) 522.20; Almanacks 398.3, 398.5; Bale 1290, 1296; Barret, H. 1499; Becon 1712(?), 1725(?), 1725.3(?), 1741; Bible, Appendix 3017(?), 3017.5(?), 3045; Bible, English 2077, 2078, 2079, 2087.2, 2087.5; Bible, N.T., English 2854.6, 2854.7, 2855*, 2856, 2857, 2858; Bible, N.T., Gospels 2975.5(?); Bible, N.T., Latin and English 2820; Bible, O.T., 'Books of Solomon' 2760(+); 2768; Bible, O.T., Psalms 2376, 2376.3(?)(A/C), 2376.5, 2377, 2378, 2379(?), 2379.5(c.), 2380, 2419(?), 2419.5(?), 2420, 2725, 2726; Bucer 3963; Bullinger 4079; Calvin 4436, 4463; Chartier 5058; Cheke 5109, 5109.5; Crowley 6085(?), 6087, 6094, 6095*; Devon 6795; Dictionary 6832.20, 6832.22; Du Castel 7272(?); Edward VI 7506, 7507; Elyot, T. 7666, 7666.2*; England, Appendix 9988.3; England, C. of, Visit. Articles 10285; England,

1549 — *cont.*
Proclamations, Chron. Ser. 7819, 7819.2, 7819.4, 7819.6, 7819.8, 7819.10, 7819.12, 7820, 7820.5, 7821, 7822, 7823, 7824, 7825, 7826, 7827, 7827.3, 7827.7, 7828, 7828.3(A/C), 7829; England, Statutes, Chron. Ser. 9421*, 9421.1*, 9422, 9422.5, 9423, 9427.3, 9428(o.s.), 9429(o.s.), 9429.3(o.s.), 9429.7(o.s.)*; Erasmus, D. 10500*; Fitzherbert, A. 10987.5; Fitzherbert, J. 10999.3(?); Foxe 11235.5; H., H. 12564; Hamilton, P. 12732(?); Hart, H. 12887.3, 12887.7(?); Hegendorff 13022; Herman V 13211.5(?); Homilies 13643, 13644, 13645; Hooper 13746(?), 13753, 13760, 13761(?); Horatius Flaccus 13787a.5*; Jesus Christ 14554.5(?); Joye 14822(?); L., R. 15109.3, 15109.7; Lanquet 15217*; Latimer 15270.5, 15270.7, 15272, 15272.5, 15274, 15274.3, 15274.7; Leland 15445; Lily, W., 'Lily's Grammar' 15611; Liturgies, C. of Eng., BCP 16267, 16268, 16269, 16269.5, 16270, 16270a, 16271, 16272, 16273, 16274, 16275, 16276; Liturgies, C. of Eng., Ord. of Comm. 16458.5(?); Liturgies, C. of Eng., Ordinal 16462, 16462.5; Liturgies, Latin Rite, Hours and Primers 16049.7, 16050, 16050.3(c.), 16050.5, 16052(?)(A/C); Lynne 17119; Moulton 18225.6(?)*(A/C); Ochino 18770, 18771; Order 18841; Piers 19905(?)(A/C); Plutarch 20060.5(?); Poynet 20176; Praise 20182(?); Prayers 20196.9(A/C); Proctor, J. 20406; Punt 20500, 20500.5; Ratramnus 20750; Record, R. 20797.7; Ridley, L. 21043(?); Sermon 22238(?); Thomas, W. 24018, 24023; Trent, Council of 24266(?); Turner, William 24364a(?); Tyndale, W. 24442(?), 24459, 24467(?); V., R. 24566(?); Vermigli, P. 24673; Whippet You Priests 25351.5(?); Wyatt 26053.5(?).

1550

Abusiva 84; Act 97(c.); Allen, E. 361; Almanacks (Askham) 410.1; Almanacks (Erra Pater) 439.7(c.); Almanacks (Moerbeke) 483.13 (A/C); Almanacks (Sauvage) 507.15; Almanacks (Thongerloo or Tongherloo) 517.15(A/C); Arnaldus 777.5(c.); Askew, A. 852.5(c.); Askham 857a.5, 859.5; Assize of Bread 868(c.); Augustine 920, 955; Bacon, R. 1180(c.); Baldwin, W. 1254; Bale 1275(?), 1298(c.), 1299; Bansley 1374(c.); Becke 1709; Becon 1719.5(c.), 1721, 1721.5, 1725.7(c.), 1733(?), 1751(c.); Benese 1874(?); Bible, Appendix 3018(?); Bible, English 2079.8, 2080, 2081, 2087.3, 2087.4, 2087.6, 2090*; Bible, N.T., English 2859, 2859.7, 2860, 2861, 2862, 2862.5(?), 2864(?); Bible, N.T., Gospels 2975.7, 2976, 2985.3(A/C); Bible, N.T., Latin and English 2821; Bible, O.T., 'Books of Solomon' 2756.5(?), 2757, 2757.5(c.); Bible, O.T., Psalms 2380a, 2727; Bible, Selections 2999.5(?), 3000; Boccus 3188(c.), 3188a(c.); Book 3310.5(c.), 3325(?), 3330.5(?), 3331, 3368.4(c.); Borde 3373(?), 3382.5(c.); Brentz 3603; Calvin 4407, 4407.5, 4408; Carion 4626, 4626.3(c.); Catharine [Parr] 4823(c.), 4824(c.), 4824a(c.); Cato 4853.7; Chaucer 5071(?), 5072(?), 5073(?), 5074(?); Cicero 5276; Coke, J. 5530; Complaint 5611.4(c.); Corvinus 5806; Cranmer 6000, 6001, 6002; Crowley 6088, 6088.3, 6095*, 6096; Dialogues 6816(?); Dictionary 6832.23(c.)(A/C), 6832.24(c.?), 6832.26(c.?); Eglamour 7542.7(?); Elyot, T. 7632(?)*, 7647(?); England, Appendix 9980(?)(A/C), 9980.5(?)(A/C), 9988.5; England, C. of, Visit. Articles 10247; England, Customs 7688, 7688.2; England, Proclamations, Chron. Ser. 7830, 7831, 7832, 7833, 7834(o.s.); England, Proclamations, Collections 7758(o.s.) England, Statutes, Chron. Ser. 9401(c.)*, 9421.2*, 9428, 9429, 9429.3, 9429.7*; England, Statutes, Gen. Colls. 9301.3(c.?)*; England, Statutes, Spec. Subjs. 9342.2(c.); England, Statutes, Spec. Subjs. 9343.10(?); England, Yearbooks 9653a(?), 9840.5(?), 9862(?), 9906.5(?), 9932.7(?), 9933.7(?), 9947.4(?), 9955.3(?), 9962.5(?); Erasmus, D. 10439, 10447, 10447.5, 10450(?); Fitzherbert, J. 11013(c.), 11013.3(c.); Francis, of Assisi 11313; Frith, J. 11393.5, 11393.7; Goeurot 11970; Gribaldi 12365; Hall, John 12631, 12631.3(?), 12631.5(c.?); Halle 12723, 12723a*(A/C); Herbal 13175.13; Heywood, J. 13292, 13294.5, 13304(c.); Hogarde or Huggarde 13560(?); Hooper 13749, 13750, 13750.5, 13754(?), 13755, 13757, 13762, 13763, 13764 (?); Husbandman 14008.5(c.?), 14009(c.?); Hutchinson 14019; Hyckescorner 14040(?); Interlude 14109.2(c.)(A/C), 14109.3(c.); Introduction 14125(c.); Isocrates 14279(c.); Jesus Christ 14547(?); John XXI 14651.5(?); John, Chrysostom 14638; John, the

1550 — *cont.*
Evangelist 14643(c.); Joye 14824, 14825; Justices of Peace 14880; Kingdoms 14999.5(c.); Knell 15029(?); Lambert, J., Minister 15181(?); Lancaster 15188(?); Latimer 15289, 15293; Lever, T. 15543, 15543.5, 15543a, 15547, 15548, 15548.5, 15549; Liturgies, C. of Eng., BCP 16441; Liturgies, Latin Rite, Hours and Primers 16050.7(c.)(A/C), 16051(c.), 16051.5(c.); Liturgies, Other Protest. C. 16560; London, Ords. and Regs. 16704.1(c.); Lynne 17117; Mappamundi 17297(c.); Marbecke 17300; Market 17330; Mary I 17562*, 17562a*; Medicine 17770.5(c.); Melanchthon 17788(?); Musculus 18311; Natura Brevium 18408(?); Nobody 18599(c.); Origen 18848(c.)(A/C); Paynell 19494, 19494.3, 19494.7; Pickering 19897.3; Piers 19903(c.), 19903.5(c.), 19903a(?), 19906, 19907, 19907a; Poynet 20177; Proclus 20398.7, 20399(?)*(A/C); Ptolemy 20481(?); Reasons 20792.5; Reynard the Fox 20922; Rivius 21065(?); Rome, Church of 21305.7(c.), 21306(c.); Salesbury, W. 21612, 21613, 21614; Samuel 21690.6(?), 21690.8(?); Scotland, appendix 22009(c.); Seager 22134.5(c.); Sherry 22428; Smith, R., Dean 22819(?); Taverner, R. 23715(?), 23715.5(?); Tertullian 23916; Thomas, W. 24020; Thucydides 24056; Tilney, Emery 24078(?); Treatise 24223.5; Vermigli, P. 24665, 24666; Veron, J. 24682; Vigo 24721, 24725(?); Vives 24849; Weaver 25148(?); Werdmueller 25255; Wiclif 25588; Wimbledon 25824(c.); Xenophon 26073(?); Zwingli 26141, 26142, 26143.

1551

A.B.C. 20.2, 20.3; Aesop 179; Allen, E. 360, 360.3; Almanacks (Askham) 410.2, 410.3; Almanacks (Huring) 464, 464.3; Almanacks 398.7; Bale 1273, 1273.5; Becon 1720, 1720.3(c.), 1722(?); Bible, English 2083, 2084, 2084.5, 2085, 2086, 2086.3, 2086.5, 2087, 2088; Bible, N.T., English 2865(?), 2866*; Bible, N.T., French 2957.6, 2957.7(A/C), 2957.8(A/C); Bible, N.T., Gospels 2977, 2983; Bible, O.T., 'Books of Solomon' 2758, 2759, 2761.5; Bible, O.T., Psalms 2422, 2423, 2424; Brasier 3552.7(?); Bullinger 4042.4, 4068, 4069; Cheke 5108; Christian Meditation 5179; Conway, W. 5654(?); Coucheman 5870.5; Cranmer 5990.5(?), 5991; Crowley 6089.5, 6090; Du Ploiche 7363; England, Proclamations, Chron. Ser. 7834, 7835, 7836, 7837, 7838, 7839, 7840, 7841, 7842, 7843, 7844, 7844.2; England, Proclamations, Collections 7758; England, Statutes, Abridgements/Extracts 9525, 9525.5, 9526; England, Statutes, Chron. Ser. 9360(?), 9363.2(?), 9367(?), 9375(?), 9383(?), 9388(?), 9395(?), 9429.7(?)*, 9432.3, 9432.5, 9432.7; England, Statutes, Gen. Colls. 9293a, 9301.7*, 9303.6, 9303.7; Fitzherbert, A. 10974; Foxe 11233; Gardiner, Stephen 11592; Gilby 11886, 11887(?); Hawes, S. 12944.5; Homilies 13646(?), 13647; Hooper 13756, 13757.5(?); Lasco 15260, 15263; Lever, T. 15544, 15545, 15546, 15546.3, 15546.7(?); Littleton, T., Tenures, Engl. 15765.5; Liturgies, C. of Eng., BCP 16277, 16423; Liturgies, C. of Eng., Spec. Prayers 16504; Liturgies, Latin Rite, Hours and Primers 16053, 16054, 16055, 16056; Liturgies, Other Protest. C. 16566, 16576(?); Livius 16612a.7; London, Ords. and Regs. 16704.3*(A/C); More, T. 18094; Natura Brevium 18397.5; Ochino 18766(?), 18767(?); Parker, Matthew 19293(?); Perussellus 19783; Preservative 20204; Ptolemy 20480a(?)(A/C); Raynalde 20779; Record, R. 20798(?), 20812; Redman 20827; Ruddoke 21435.5; Samuel 21690.2; Spagnuoli 22992(?); Treasure 24204; Turner, William 24365, 24368; Vergilius 24657; Wilson, T., Sect'y of State 25809, 25816, 25817; Wingfield, H. 25852(?).

1552

Almanacks (Askham) 410.4; Almanacks (Butzlin) 427.6, 427.7; Almanacks (Erra Pater) 439.9(c.); Almanacks (Sauvage) 507.17 (A/C); Antidotarius 675a.7(?); Askham 857a; Baldwin, W. 1254.5(?); Bale 1281(?), 1282(?), 1283(?), 1294(?); Beard, R. 1654(?), 1656(?); Bello-Poelius 1849; Bible, English 2089; Bible, N.T., English 2866*, 2867, 2868; Bible, O.T., Psalms 2380a.5, 2424.1, 2738.7; Borde 3374; Bullinger 4049, 4050, 4051, 4052, 4052.5, 4052.7; Caius 4343; Calvin 4391; Camel 4527.2(?), 4527.4(?),

1552 — *cont.*
4527.6(?), 4527.8(?); Chappell, G. 4999.5(?); Churchyard 5225.5(?), 5241(c.), 5246(?), 5252(?), 5258(?); Confession 5628(+); Cranmer 6003.5; Dictionary 6832.28, 6832.29, 6832.30, 6832.31; Elderton 7555.5(?); Elyot, T. 7662, 7666.2(?)*; England, Appendix 9968, 9969, 9983(c.), 9989; England, C. of, Visit. Articles 10228; England, Exchequer 7704; England, Local Courts 7721; England, Proclamations, Chron. Ser. 7844.4, 7844.6, 7844.8, 7844.10, 7845(o.s.); England, Statutes, Chron. Ser. 9362, 9398(?)*, 9412.5(c.)*, 9423.5, 9423.7(?), 9424*, 9425*, 9426*, 9426.5*, 9433, 9433.3, 9433.5, 9433.7, 9435.5, 9436*, 9437.3*, 9437.5*, 9437.7*; England, Yearbooks 9802.5; Erasmus, D. 10440, 10440.2, 10486(?), 10486.5(?); Esquillus 10532(?); Estienne, R. 10555; Exoneratorium 10634.3(c.); Fitzherbert, A. 10988.5, 10989a, 10990*; Fitzherbert, J. 10999.5(?), 10999.7(?), 11000(?); Gervaes 11797.2(?); Giulio 11903; Godfridus 11930.10(?); Haddon 12595; Hamilton, John, Abp. 12731; Herbal 13175.13C(c.), 13175.15(?), 13175.15A(?); Hooper 13758(?); Huloet 13940; Introduction 14119.3; Kenner 14932.5(A/C); King, R. 14992.5; L., V. 15113.5(?); Lasco 15259, 15260.7; Liturgies, C. of Eng., BCP 16279, 16280, 16280.5, 16281, 16281.5, 16282.3, 16282.7, 16284.5, 16285, 16285.5, 16285.7, 16285a, 16286, 16286.2, 16286.3, 16286.5, 16287, 16288(?), 16290*; Liturgies, Latin Rite, Hours and Primers 16057; Liturgies, Other Protest. C. 16572.3, 16572.7, 16573; Micron 17863.3; Ovidius Naso 18969.5(?); Paynell 19495(?), 19495.3(?), 19495.7(?); Prayer 20191(c.); Ptolemy 20481.3 (?); Record, R. 20799.3; Retorna 20904(?); Roesslin 21155; Rome, Church of 21308(?); Saint Bartholomew's Hospital 21557; San Pedro 21740(?); Seeing 22160.3, 22160.4(A/C); Steple 23251.5(?); Thachame 23925(?); Vigo 24725.3(?); Will 25668.5(?); Wilson, T., Sect'y of State 25810; Xenophon 26066(?).

1553

A.B.C. 20.4(?); Agrippa 203.5; Almanacks (Askham) 410.5; Almanacks (Hubrigh) 462(?); Assize of Bread 868.2(?); Augustine 923; Baldwin, W. 1255(?); Bale 1307; Barlow, W., Bp. of St. Asaph/Chichester 1462; Beard, R. 1655; Becon 1752.5(?); Benese 1874.5 (?); Bible, Appendix 3019(?), 3022.5, 3033.5, 3043; Bible, English 2090*, 2091, 2092; Bible, N.T., English 2869, 2870; Bible, N.T., French 2957.9; Bible, N.T., Gospels 2978, 2983.8(?), 2984, 2985; Bible, O.T., Prophets 2787.4(?); Bible, O.T., Psalms 2424.2, 2424.4(?), 2424.6(?), 2424.8(?), 2425, 2426, 2728, 2749.5; Bible, Selections 3006(+); Bogaert 3204; Bradford, J., Prebendary of St. Paul's 3496; Brooks 3838; Calvin 4392; Catechismus 4807, 4808, 4809, 4810, 4811, 4812, 4813; Cato 4844, 4844.2, 4854; Christian Faith 5160.3; Cole, T. 5539; Cranmer 6004; Curtius Rufus 6141.5, 6142, 6142.5; Cyprian 6159.3; Dares 6274.5; Dictionary 6832.32; Douglas, G. 7073(?); Du Ploiche 7363.5; Dudley, John 7283; Edward VI 7508, 7509; Elyot, T. 7639; England, Appendix 9970; England, C. of, Articles 10034, 10034.2; England, Proclamations, Chron. Ser. 7845, 7846, 7847, 7848, 7849, 7850, 7851, 7852, 7853, 7854, 7855; England, Public Documents, Misc. 9182(o.s.), 9182.5 (o.s.); England, Statutes, Chron. Ser. 9370.8(?), 9405.5(c.)*, 9421.3(?)*, 9430, 9430.5*, 9431*, 9432*, 9436(?)*, 9439, 9439.5, 9440, 9440.2*, 9440.4; England, Statutes, Kalendars/Indexes 9545; England, Yearbooks 9607, 9670.5(?), 9677(?), 9693, 9712(?), 9936.5(?), 9946.5(?), 9947.7(?); Erasmus, D. 10476.7; Exclamation 10615(?); Fitzherbert, A. 10954(c.)*, 10959, 10960*; Forrest 11186(?); Gardiner, Stephen 11583, 11585, 11586, 11587, 11593; Geminus, T. 11715.5, 11716; Genesius de Sepulveda 11722; Gilby 11885.5(?); Goeurot 11971; Guevara 12441; Gunwyn 12526.5; Guy, Earl of Warwick 12541.5(c.?); Gwynneth 12556.7; Hall, John 12631.7(c.); Harpsfield 12794; Herman V 13208(?); Hooper 13759; John XXI 14651.7; John, Chrysostom 14637.5, 14642; Kethe 14941(?); Lasco 15260.5; Latimer 15290(?); Le Fevre 15378; Lily, W., 'Lily's Grammar' 15611.3; Littleton, T., Tenures, French 15736; Liturgies, C. of Eng., BCP 16288a(?), 16290*, 16290.5, 16430; Melanchthon 17791; More, T. 18082; Muenster 18244; Natura Brevium 18408.5; Paynell 19493; Piers 19904; Pius II 19970(?); Plutarch 20061.7(?)(A/C); Pratte 20188; Primer 20373,

1553 — *cont.*
20373.5(?), 20374; Proclus 20399(c.)*(A/C); Registrum 20837; Rome, Church of 21307.3; Sarcerius 21754, 21755, 21755a, 21755a.5; Seton, J. 22258; Stopes 23292(?); Vasseus 24595; Vaus 24623.7; Virgilius Maro 24797, 24810a; Watertoune 25105; White, John, Bp. 25388; Wilson, T., Sect'y of State 25799, 25811; Withals 25874.

1554

Almanacks (Askham) 410.6; Almanacks (Erra Pater) 439.11(?); Almanacks (Low) 481; Antidotarius 676(?); Aristotle 769.5(c.), 769.7(c.); Aymon 1010, 1011, 1011.5; Baldwin, W. 1246(?); Becon 1716, 1730; Bible, O.T., Psalms 2426.5; Boccaccio 3177, 3177.5(?), 3178(?); Boemus 3196.5; Bonner, E. 3280.3; Borde 3380.5(c.?); Brooks 3839, 3839.3; Christian Conscience 5157; Christopherson 5207; Confession 5629(?), 5630; Doctrine 6934.5; Dudley, Jane 7279(?), 7279.5(?); Emery 7678.5(?); England, Appendix 9970.5, 10016; England, C. of, Appendix 10383; England, C. of, Visit. Articles 10248; England, Parliament 7735 [not STC]; England, Privy Council 7753.6, 7753.8; England, Proclamations, Chron. Ser. 7856, 7857, 7858, 7859, 7860, 7861, 7862, 7863; England, Public Documents, Misc. 9182, 9182.5; England, Statutes, Chron. Ser. 9440.8, 9440.10, 9440.12*, 9440.14*, 9440.16*, 9443, 9443.5, 9444*, 9444.2*, 9444.4*, 9444.6*, 9444.8*; Erasmus, D. 10469, 10469.5, 10491; Fisher, John, St. 10896; Fitzherbert, A. 10975, 10989a.5(?)(A/C), 10989a.6(?)(A/C); Glanvilla 11905(?); Godfridus 11930.12(?); Goodale 12006(?); Gorecius 12090; Gower, J., Poet 12144; Gwynneth 12558, 12559; Harchius 12753; Hawes, S. 12950; Heywood, J. 13290.3; Hilarie 13457; Hippocrates 13522(?); Hogarde or Huggarde 13556, 13560.5, 13561; Indulgences, General 14077c.147; Junius 14860.5, 14861; Knox 15059, 15059.5, 15069, 15074.4; Lindsay, Sir D. 15672; Littleton, T., Tenures, French 15737; Liturgies, C. of Eng., Litany 16453; Liturgies, Latin Rite, Breviaries 15836*; Liturgies, Latin Rite, Hours and Primers 16058, 16059; Liturgies, Latin Rite, Manuals 16151, 16152, 16153, 16154, 16155; Liturgies, Latin Rite, Missals 16215, 16216*; Liturgies, Latin Rite, Process. 16244; Liturgies, Other Protest. C. 16571(?), 16571a; London, Ords. and Regs. 16701*, 16704.3(?)*(A/C); Luther 16980, 16981; Marshall, G. 17469; Martin, T. 17517; Mary I 17561; Meditation 17773; Micron 17863.5; Montulmo 18054; Musculus 18309.5; Peele, J. 19547(?); Philip II 19835 [not STC], 19836(?); Philpot 19890, 19891 [not STC]; Proctor, J. 20407; Redman 20826(?)(A/C); Saint German 21570.5, 21571*, 21571.5*; Sampson, T., Dean of Christ Church 21683; Skelton 22595(?), 22595.5(?), 22599(?), 22602(?), 22602.5(?), 22616(?), 22616.5(?); Smith, R., Dean 22816; Spanish Language 23010.5(?), 23010.7; Standish, J. 23207; Venaeus 24633.5; Vincent, Saint 24747, 24754; Virgilius Maro 24810a.5; Watson, T., Bp. 25115, 25115.3, 25115.5; York, Diocese of 26098.7(?).

1555

Aesop 179.5(c.); Almanacks (Askham) 410.7, 410.8; Almanacks (Digges) 435.35; Almanacks (Erra Pater) 439.13(?); Almanacks (Gesner) 447.7; Almanacks (Montulmo) 483.14; Ambrose, St. 548.7; Angel 634(?); Anglerius 645, 646, 647, 648; Antichrist 673(c.); Aristotle 770.7(?); Assize of Bread 868.4(?); Avila, L. 987; Baldwin, W. 1255.5(c.); Bible, N.T., Gospels 2978.5, 2979(c.?), 2980(c.?); Boemus 3197; Bonner, E. 3281, 3281.5, 3282, 3283, 3283.3, 3283.5, 3283.7, 3285.1, 3285.2, 3285.3, 3285.4, 3285.5, 3285.6, 3285.7, 3285.8, 3285.9, 3285.10; Book 3319.7(?), 3332, 3332.4, 3368.2(c.); Borde 3383(?); Boxall 3442.8; Bradford, J., Prebendary of St. Paul's 3480.5(?); Catharine, of Alexandria 4813.8 (?); Cato 4844.4; Cockburn, P. 5458; Colonne 5580; Eglamour 7543(c.?); Elder 7552; England, Appendix 9971, 9981, 10023.7(?), 10024(?); England, C. of, Visit. Articles 10249; England, Proclamations, Chron. Ser. 7864, 7865, 7866, 7867, 7867.3, 7867.5, 7867.7, 7867.9; England, Statutes, Chron. Ser. 9447.3, 9447.5, 9447.7, 9447.8, 9447.9*, 9448*, 9448.3*, 9448.7*, 9449*, 9449.6*,

1555 — *cont.*
9450*, 9450.3, 9450.5, 9450.7*, 9450.9*, 9451*, 9452*, 9454*, 9454.5*, 9455*, 9455.5*; England, Statutes, Gen. Colls. 9277.5*, 9293a.3; England, Statutes, Spec. Subjs. 9339.3(?)(A/C); England, Yearbooks 9582*, 9604*, 9605, 9666(?), 9682.5(?), 9688(?), 9896.5, 9906.7(?), 9914(?), 9922, 9923*, 9923.5*; Erasmus, D. 10450.4, 10469.7(c.); Eulenspiegel 10563.5(?); Examples 10613(?); Feckenham 10744, 10745(c.); Fisher, John, St. 10908; Fitzherbert, J. 11000.4(?); Garcie 11551(?); Geminus, T. 11713.5, 11718.7; Glasier 11916.5; Haddon 12596.3; Hawes, S. 12951, 12952; Herbal 13175.16(?), 13175.17(?); Heywood, J. 13296; Hogarde or Huggarde 13559; Institution 14104; Judgement 14834(?); Kethe 14944(c.); Liturgies, Latin Rite, Breviaries 15836*, 15837, 15839, 15840*, 15860(?); Liturgies, Latin Rite, Hours and Primers 16060, 16061, 16062, 16063, 16064, 16065, 16066, 16067, 16067.5(c.), 16068, 16069, 16070, 16071, 16071.5, 16072, 16107; Liturgies, Latin Rite, Hymns 16134; Liturgies, Latin Rite, Manuals 16155a, 16156; Liturgies, Latin Rite, Missals 16216*, 16217, 16218, 16224.7(?); Liturgies, Latin Rite, Process. 16245, 16246, 16247, 16248, 16252; Liturgies, Latin Rite, Psalters 16264, 16265, 16266; London, Watermen 16787.2(c.), 16787.4(c.), 16787.6(c.); Mary I 17562*, 17562a*, 17563; Mass 17629(?), 17629.5(?); Menewe 17821(?), 17822(?); Moulton 18225.8(?); Musculus 18312, 18313; Olde 18797; Perkins, J. 19633; Petrarca 19811(?); Plutarch 20061 (c.); Poynet 20175; Prayers 20192.9(A/C); Proctor, J. 20408; Ridley, N. 21046; Rome 21299(c.); San Pedro 21742(c.); Savonarola 21799.2(?); Scory 21854; Sherry 22429; Smith, R., Dean 22817, 22817.5; Spare 23014(?), 23014a(?); Standish, J. 23208; Sustain 23446(c.); T., I. or J. 23619; Treasure 24204.5(?); Treatise 24219 (?); Turner, William 24356(?), 24361; Valentine 24571.7(c.); Vermigli, P. 24673.5; Vigo 24725.5(?); Vives 24855(?); Walker, Gilbert 24961(c.); Wedlocke 25196(?); Werdmueller 25249(?), 25251(?), 25252(?), 25256(?); Weston, H. 25291.5; Zwingli 26140.

1556

Almanacks (A., J.) 406.3(?); Almanacks (Askham) 410.9, 410.10, 410.11, 410.11A; Almanacks (Digges) 435.37, 535.39; Almanacks (Feild) 443.9; Almanacks 399.7; Angel 634.5(?); Antidotarius 678(?); Augustine 921(?); Baldwin, W. 1256; Bible, N.T., Gospels 2980.2(?); Bible, O.T., Psalms 2426.8(?); Bible, Selections 2996(?), 3006.5; Bieston 3055(?), 3055.5(?); Boethius, A. 3201; Book 3310.7, 3311, 3312(?), 3320(?); Borde 3374.5*; Bradford, J., Serving-man 3504.5(?); Bushe 4184; Calvin 4380; Cancellar 4564(?), 4565(?); Catharine [Parr] 4820(?), 4825; Churchson 5219; Cicero 5281; Cocles 5468; Cranmer 5990, 5996(?), 5999(?), 6005.5; Cyprian 6152; Dacquetus 6186; Daniel, the Prophet 6235.5(?); Dialogue 6808(?); Digges, L. 6849.5(?); Du Val, P. 7376.5; Elyot, T. 7667; England, Appendix 9972; England, C. of, Visit. Articles 10149; England, Proclamations, Chron. Ser. 7868, 7868.3(A/C), 7869, 7870, 7871, 7872; England, Statutes, Chron. Ser. 9408.5(c.), 9411(c.?)*, 9444 (?)*, 9447.9(?)*, 9450.7(?)*; England, Statutes, Gen. Colls. 9277, 9277.5, 9278*, 9293a.5; England, Yearbooks 9582*, 9621, 9628, 9634(?), 9639, 9694, 9700(?), 9706(?), 9718, 9723, 9728, 9734, 9735*, 9739, 9740*, 9746, 9747*, 9761, 9774, 9775*, 9776*, 9808*, 9815, 9822, 9823*, 9824*, 9828, 9829*, 9848, England, Yearbooks 9853, 9853.5*, 9857*, 9858*, 9868, 9874, 9874.5*, 9875*, 9875.5*, 9878, 9880*, 9885(?), 9892, 9892.5*, 9937*, 9948*, 9955.7, 9956*, 9957*, 9963, 9963.4*, 9963.7*; Epistle 10432; Erasmus, D. 10448(?), 10450.5, 10471.7; Fisher, John, St. 10897; Fitzherbert, A. 10990*; Fitzherbert, J. 11000.7(?); Flores 11092, 11092a; Gilby 11884.5; Godfridus 11931(?); Harpsfield 12795; Henry II, King of France 13090.5; Herodian 13221(?); Heywood, J. 13293, 13295, 13308; Hogarde or Huggarde 13557, 13558; Indulgences, General 14077c.147A; John XXI 14652(c.); Justices of Peace 14881; Knox 15066, 15074.6(?); Lauder, W. 15314; Lippomano 15693, 15693.5; Littleton, T., Tenures, Engl. 15766, 15766.5, 15767, 15767.5, 15768, 15768.5; Liturgies, Latin Rite, Breviaries 15842, 15844, 15846, 15847*; Liturgies, Latin Rite, Hours and Primers 16073, 16073.5(?), 16074, 16075, 16075.5(?), 16076, 16077, 16078, 16108;

1556 — *cont.*

Liturgies, Other Protest. C. 16561, 16565, 16574; Mainardi 17200; Meditations 17776(?)(A/C); Micron 17864(?); More, T. 18078.5(?) (A/C), 18095, 18095.5; Musculus 18310(?); Olde 18798; Philpot 19892(?); Pollard 20091; Poynet 20175a, 20178; Record, R. 20796; Ridley, N. 21047.3, 21047.7, 21048; Saint German 21571(?)*; Saunders, L. 21777; Shepherds' Kalendar 22412; Standish, J. 23211; Taverner, R. 23716(?); Thomas, a Kempis 23966, 23967*; Treasure 24205; Treatise 24223(?); Vincent, Saint 24755; Walther 25009; Watson, R. 25111 [not STC]; Withals 25875.

1557

A.B.C. 20.5(c.?); Almanacks (Askham) 410.12; Almanacks (Laet, G., the younger) 477.9; Answer 658; Arthur, King 804; Augustine 923.5; Baldwin, W. 1257; Balthorpe 1342(?); Basil, the Great 1543.5; Bible, N.T., English 2871; Bible, O.T., Psalms 2383.6; Bonner, E. 3286(?); Borde 3374.5*, 3375; Bucer 3965(?); Churchyard 5229(?)(A/C); Cranmer 6005 [not STC]; Deceit 6451(?); Edgeworth 7482; Elizabeth, Saint 7605.5(?); Elyot, T. 7633, 7633.3, 7640, 7649(?); Emley 7680(?); England, Appendix 9989.5, 10014; England, Proclamations, Chron. Ser. 7873, 7874, 7875, 7876; England, Statutes, Chron. Ser. 9392.5, 9413, 9424(?)*; England, Statutes, Gen. Colls. 9306; England, Statutes, Spec. Subjs. 9339.4(?)(A/C); England, Yearbooks 9752, 9757(?), 9766, 9799, 9809*, 9810, 9859, 9863, 9863.5*; Erasmus, D. 10455, 10455.5, 10461, 10501(?)*; Felicius 10752; Garcie 11551.5; Gelli 11708; Gosynhill 12103(?); Guevara 12427, 12442, 12443; Gwynneth 12560; Heywood, J. 13290.7; Hogarde or Huggarde 13559.5; Howard, H., Earl of Surrey 13860, 13861, 13862; Husbandman 14009.3(?); Interlude 14111a; Isocrates 14276*; Jacob, the Patriarch 14326.5; Lily, W., 'Lily's Grammar' 15611.7, 15612, 15613; Littleton, T., Tenures, French 15738, 15738.3, 15738.7; Liturgies, Latin Rite, Breviaries 15847*; Liturgies, Latin Rite, Hours and Primers 16079, 16080, 16081, 16081.5(?), 16109(?), 16109.5(?); Liturgies, Latin Rite, Missals 16219; Liturgies, Latin Rite, Process. 16249; Liturgies, Other Protest. C. 16561.5; Lord's Prayer 16817; Lyndewode 17112.5; Mameranus 17228(?)*; Man 17236(?)(A/C); More, T. 18076; Natura Brevium 18398, 18398.5, 18408.7, 18409; P., R. 19078; Peryn 19784; Pole 20088.5; Record, R. 20820; Romans 21287; Salerno 21600; Seager 22135; Seeing 22160.5(?); Stanford 23219; Stourton 23318.3, 23318.7; Traheron 24168, 24168.5, 24170*; Tusser 24372; Virgilius Maro 24798; Vives 24860, 24861*; Xenophon 26074.

1558

Alessio 293; Almanacks (Cunningham) 432; Almanacks (Feild) 443.11; Almanacks (Low) 482; Becon 1744; Bonner, E. 3280.7; Book 3312.3(?), 3366(?); Bradford, J., Prebendary of St. Paul's 3478.5(?), 3496.5(?); Bullein 4039, 4040; Cicero 5281.8, 5282*; Deceit 6452(?); Dee 6463, 6463.2; Dictionary 6832.34; Edderman 7481.7(c.?); Elizabeth I 7599; England, Appendix 10015, 10015.5; England, C. of, Visit. Articles 10117; England, Proclamations, Chron. Ser. 7877, 7878, 7879, 7880, 7881, 7882, 7883, 7884, 7885, 7886, 7889; England, Statutes, Chron. Ser. 9377.3(c.?)*, 9448(?)*, 9448.3(aft.)*, 9450.9(?)*, 9455*, 9455.5*, 9457, 9457.2, 9457.4, 9457.6, 9457.8*; England, Yearbooks 9781, 9786, 9791.5, 9792*, 9794*, 9833.5(?), 9897*, 9897.5*; Fine 10878.5, 10878.7(?); Fisher, John, Student 10917; Gelli 11709(+); Goodman, C. 12020; Hill, T. 13489.5(?); Indagine 14075, 14075.5; Isocrates 14276*; John XXI 14653; Joseph, ben Gorion 14795; Kennedy, Q. 14932; Knox 15063, 15067, 15070; Leowitz 15483, 15483.5; Lily, W., 'Lily's Grammar' 15613.3; Lindsay, Sir D. 15673, 15674, 15674.5; Liturgies, C. of Eng., Litany 16453.5, 16453.7; Liturgies, Latin Rite, Hours and Primers 16082, 16083, 16084, 16084.5(?), 16085, 16086; Liturgies, Latin Rite, Process. 16249.5*, 16250*; Liturgies, Other Protest. C. 16561a; Mary, Q. of Scotland 17566.5; Rastell, W. 20732.5; Record, R. 20799.5; Savonarola 21796; Skelton 22596(?), 22596a(?), 22596b(?), 22603(?), 22603a(?), 22603b(?),

1558 — *cont.*

22617(?), 22617a(?), 22617a.5(?); Traheron 24167.7, 24169, 24170*, 24174; Tunstall 24318; Turner, William 24356(?)*; Virgilius Maro 24799; Vives 24850(?), 24850.3(?); Watson, T., Bp. 25112, 25112.5, 25113, 25114; Wedlocke 25196.5(?).

1559

Alessio 295; Almanacks (Nostradamus) 492, 492.2, 492.3; Almanacks (Vaughan) 520; Almanacks 400, 400.3; Anatomical Fugitive Sheets 564.6(c.); Awdely 996; Aylmer 1005, 1006; Baldwin, W. 1247; Bible, N.T., Gospels 2980.3(A/C); Bible, O.T., Psalms 2384; Bible, Selections 3007; Book 3332.7, 3333, 3334*; Bradford, J., Prebendary of St. Paul's 3479, 3483; Brice 3726; Bullein 4041; Catharine [Parr] 4826; Cuningham, W. 6119; Elderton 7561; Elizabeth I 7589.5, 7590; Elyot, T. 7663; England, Appendix 9973; England, C. of, Injunctions 10099.5, 10100(?), 10100.3(?), 10100.5(?), 10102(?); England, C. of, Visit. Articles 10118, 10118.5(?); England, Proclamations, Chron. Ser. 7890, 7891, 7892, 7893, 7894, 7895*, 7897, 7898, 7902, 7903, 7904, 7905, 7905.5, 7907, 7910.7(o.s.); England, Statutes, Chron. Ser. 9458.7, 9459, 9459.3, 9459.5, 9459.7*, 9460*, 9460.5*, 9461*, 9461.5*; England, Statutes, Gen. Colls. 9307, 9307.5; England, Yearbooks 9645, 9841.5, 9898*, 9899, 9908(?), 9915(?), 9923(?)*, 9957.5, 9963.4(?)*; Erasmus, D. 10466; Fabyan 10663, 10664, 10664.5; Ferrarius 10831; Geminus, T. 11718; Gesner 11800; Giulio 11901(?); Guevara 12444; Hamilton, John, Abp. 12731.2; Herbal 13175.18(?); Homilies 13648, 13648.5; Howard, H., Earl of Surrey 13863, 13863.5, 13863.7; Hughe 13911(?); Justices of Peace 14882, 14883; Knox 15064; Lanquet 15217.5; Lindsay, Sir D. 15675; Liturgies, C. of Eng., BCP 16291, 16292, 16292a*, 16293, 16293.3, 16293.5; Liturgies, C. of Eng., Litany 16454, 16454.5; Liturgies, Latin Rite, Hours and Primers 16087; Lydgate 17028; Marckant 17312; Mary I 17559; Nostradamus 18694; Philpot 19893, 19893a; Pits 19969.4; Ridley, N. 21051; Samuel 21690.4(?); Seneca 22227, 22227a; Shepherds' Kalendar 22413; T., T. 23628.5(aft.).

1560

Albertus Magnus 258.5; Alessio 300; Almanacks (Hill, T.) 458; Almanacks (Low) 482.3; Almanacks (Rochefort or Rogeford) 506; Almanacks (Vaughan) 521; Almanacks 400.4(A/C); Arsanes 785(?); Arthur, of Little Britain 807(?), 807.5(?); Askew, A. 853(c.?); Assize of Bread 868.6(c.); Awdely 989(c.); Baldwin, W. 1243; Bale 1274; Ballads 1332.5(c.); Barclay, A. 1384a.5(c.); Becon 1710*, 1726(?), 1752.7(?), 1754(c.), 1756.5(c.); Bevis 1988.8(?); Bible, English 2093, 2094*; Bible, N.T., English 2871.5; Bible, O.T., Psalms 2427; Book 3291(?), 3312.5(?); Brinkelow 3763(?); Broughton, H. 3866; Cabasilas 4325; Calvin 4380.5, 4450, 4462(?); Castalio or Chateillon 4770; Cato 4857; Cebes 4891.3(c.); Chaloner, T., the Elder 4939; Churchyard 5225; Cromer or Kromer 6046(?), 6047(?); Day, John, Printer 6418; Degore 6472; Elias 7572(c.?); Elyot, T. 7650(?); England, Appendix 9975, 10022(?); England, C. of, Visit. Articles 10133.5, 10151; England, Proclamations, Chron. Ser. 7908, 7909, 7910, 7910.7, 7911, 7911.5, 7913, 7914, 7915, 7916, 7916.5, 7917, 7918, 7920, 7921, 7922, 7924; England, Public Documents, Misc. 9183, 9183.5, 9184; England, Statutes, Chron. Ser. 9430.5(?)*, 9437.3(?)*, 9444.2(c.)*, 9451(?)*; England, Statutes, Gen. Colls. 9278(c.?)*, 9293a.7(c.?); England, Yearbooks 9937.5, 9938*, 9948.4 (?); Erasmus, D. 10470.3; Eulenspiegel 10564(?); Fitzherbert, A. 10960*, 10976, 10990.5(c.); Fitzherbert, J. 11001(?), 11013.6(c.); Francis II 11309.5, 11309.7; Frederick, of Jennen 11362(?); Fulke 11419, 11420; Garcie 11553(?); Goeurot 11972; Gosynhill 12105; Halle 12723a(?)*(A/C); Hew 13257(?); Heywood, J. 13297, 13301 (?), 13306(c.); Homilies 13649, 13649.5; Hood, R. 13691(?); Hooper 13765(?); Hutchinson 14018, 14020; Interlude 14112.5; Isumbras 14281(c.); Jewel, J. 14612, 14613(?); John XXI 14653.3(c.); Joriszoon 14794; Knox 15060; Lacy 15118.5(c.); Lamwell 15187.5; Lanquet 15218; Lily, W., 'Lily's Grammar' 15613.5; Liturgies, C. of Eng., BCP 16294, 16294a.3, 16424, 16424a; Liturgies, Latin

1560 — *cont.*
Rite, Hours and Primers 16089, 16090(c.?); Liturgies, Other Protest. C. 16561a.5(A/C), 16571a.5(A/C); Lupset 16933; M., R. 17147(?); Macchiavelli 17164*; Micron 17864.5(?); More, E. 18067; Moulton 18223(?), 18223.3(?); Newport 18499; Ovidius Naso 18970; Palfreyman 19137; Palingenius 19148; Parker, Matthew 19285.2, 19285.4(c.), 19285.6(c.); Paynell 19496; Perkins, J. 19634(?); Philippson 19848, 19848a; Pilkington, J. 19926, 19926.3, 19926.7; Pius II 19971; Pole 20087; Popes 20114; Primer 20375; Pythagoras 20524(?); Rhodes, H. 20954(?), 20955(?); Roesslin 21156; Rome, Church of 21307.5(c.?)(A/C) [not STC]; Seneca 22226; Seton, J. 22250.2; Spangenberg 23005; Squire 23112(?); Stanbridge, Vocabula 23187(?); Stanford 23220; Tenures 23884.5 (c.), 23884a(?); Terentius 23901; Treasure 24206a(?); Treatise 24237.5; Tunstall 24321; Vergilius 24658(c.); Wanton 25016; Werdmueller 25259.5*; Westminster 25286(?); White, James 25387.5(c.?)(A/C); Wilson, T., Sect'y of State 25800; Wives 25938.

1561

A.B.C. 19.4(?); Almanacks (Mounslowe) 488; Almanacks (Rochefort or Rogeford) 506.3; Almanacks (Vaughan) 521.5; Almanacks 400.5; Ambrose, St. 549; Antwerp, Two Merchants of 693.6; Awdely 995.5(c.); Bale 1289; Barker, John 1419; Becon 1720.5, 1746, 1757; Bennet, H., of Calais 1881; Beze 2026; Bible, English 2094*, 2095*; Bible, N.T., English 2872(?), 2872a(aft.?), 2872b(aft.?), 2872c(aft.?), 2872c.3(aft.), 2872c.5(aft.?); Bible, N.T., Gospels 2980.4; Bible, O.T., Psalms 2428, 2429, 2739, 2739.5; Blundeville 3158(?); Book 3334*, 3363.3; Bradford, J., Prebendary of St. Paul's 3477, 3494(?); Bullinger 4061; Buonaccorsi 4102.3; Calvin 4372, 4415, 4438, 4438.5, 4467; Castiglione 4778; Catharine [Parr] 4826.5; Cato 4844.7; Chaloner, T., the Elder 4938.5; Charles [de Guise] 5010.5(?); Chaucer 5075, 5076, 5076.3; Cicero 5306, 5317; Cockburn, P. 5459; Cope, A. 5720; Cortes 5798; Coxe 5950, 5951; Curtius Rufus 6143; Des Gallars 6774.5, 6775 [not STC], 6776(?); Digges, L. 6849.8; Elyot, T. 7651(?); England, Appendix 9976; England, C. of, Articles 10034.4(c.?); England, C. of, Injunctions 10102.2(?); England, C. of, Visit. Articles 10119(?), 10286; England, Proclamations, Chron. Ser. 7799.5(?), 7917(?)*, 7924.5(?), 7928, 7931, 7932, 7933, 7934, 7936, 7936.7, 7940; England, Public Documents, Misc. 9186; England, Statutes, Chron. Ser. 9396(?); England, Statutes, Spec. Subjs. 9339.5; England, Yearbooks 9556(?), 9559(?), 9563, 9571, 9574, 9577, 9580, 9600, 9661; Evans, L. 10592; Gosynhill 12104.5*; Gough, J., Divine 12132; Hanapus 12742; Herbal 13175.19, 13179; Hester, Queen 13251; Heywood, J. 13294; Hieronymus, von Braunschweig 13433; Homilies 13680.8(+); Interlude 14113(?); Ireland, Proc. 14138; Joseph, ben Gorion 14796; Lasco 15261; Leigh, V. 15415; Liturgies, C. of Eng., BCP 16292a(?)*; Liturgies, Latin Rite, Hours and Primers 16019*; Liturgies, Other Protest. C. 16562, 16563; Micron 17863.7(A/C); Moulton 18223.7(?); N., Nicolaus 18332 [not STC]*; Narrationes 18363; Naumburg 18412, 18412.5; News 18507; North 18662; Norvell 18688; Onderzoeking 18812; Palingenius 19149; Piers 19908; Pilkington, J. 19930, 19930.5; Plutarch 20063.5; Rastell, W. 20733, 20734*; Record, R. 20800; Scotland, Church of, Confession of Faith 22016, 22017, 22018; Seneca 22223; Smith, H., Minister, Single Works 22696.5*; Southwark 22943, 22944; Spangenberg 23006; Thomas, W. 24019; Tryamour 24303(?); Tyndale, W. 24453, 24461(?); Vermigli, C. 24662.5; Veron, J. 24680, 24681, 24683, 24684, 24685; Werdmueller 25258(?); Wimbledon 25825.3(?); Wives 25938.5(?); Zwingli 26135(?).

1562

Alessio 296, 304.5, 305; Allen, E. 360.7; Almanacks (Erra Pater) 439.15(?); Almanacks (Nostradamus) 492.7; Almanacks (Rochefort or Rogeford) 506.4; Almanacks (Securis) 509, 510, 510.3; Almanacks 400.7(A/C); Arcandam 724(?); Baker, H. 1209.5; Bale 1288; Bandello 1356.7; Beze 2000, 2027(?), 2028(?); Bible, English 2095*, 2096; Bible, O.T., Psalms 2384.5*, 2429.5, 2430; Bible, Selections 3008; Birch 3078(A/C); Boccaccio 3184.6; Book 3335; Borde 3381, 3385(?); Bradford, J., Prebendary of St. Paul's 3484; Brice 3725; Bucer 3966; Bullein 4033, 4035; Calvin 4375, 4416, 4458; Cambini 4470; Catharine [de'Medici] 4813.4; Cato 4845; Charles IX 5034, 5042; Cicero 5277; D., John 6177; Damiano 6214; Description 6768; Devon 6795.8; Digges, L. 6850; Dudley, Jane 7280(?); England, C. of, Injunctions 10102.3(?); England, C. of, Visit. Articles 10120(?); England, Customs 7688.4; England, Proclamations, Chron. Ser. 7924.6(?), 7941, 7942, 7943, 7944, 7946, 7947, 7948, 7949, 7950, 7951, 7952, 7953a, 7954.5(?), 7954.7(?), 8046.5(c.?); England, Public Documents, Misc. 9187, 9187.3; England, Statutes, Chron. Ser. 9368, 9375.5(?), 9377.7(c.)*, 9384, 9384.5*, 9389(?), 9393, 9393.5*, 9400, 9402(?)*, 9406(?), 9409, 9414(?); England, Statutes, Spec. Subjs. 9344; England, Yearbooks 9551, 9608*, 9654, 9671, 9678, 9713; Fabricius, J. 10657; Fitzherbert, A. 10990.7; Fitzherbert, J. 11002; France—Reformed Churches 11298; Francis [de Lorraine] 11312; Fulwood 11484, 11485, 11486(?); Garnier, J. 11621; Geneva 11725; Grafton 12148; Gratarolus 12191; Great Horksley 12207; Guise, House of 12507; Hawkes 12955a.5(?); Heywood, J. 13285, 13290, 13299.5(?); Homilies 13650, 13650.3, 13650.7; Hooper 13742, 13752; Jewel, J. 14581, 14590, 14615, 14615.5, 14616; Jugeler 14837(?); Latimer 15276; Legh 15388; Liturgies, C. of Eng., BCP 16295; Liturgies, C. of Eng., Litany 16455; Liturgies, C. of Eng., Spec. Prayers 16504.3(A/C); Liturgies, Other Protest. C. 16564; London, Ords. and Regs. 16704.6; Lorkyn 16827; Louis I 16849, 16849.3, 16849.7, 16850, 16851, 16852; M., R. 17145.3; Macchiavelli 17164*; Manner 17255(?)(A/C); Musculus 18308*; Papists 19175, 19176; Paynell 19492; Pilkington, J. 19927; Ptolemy 20481.7(?); Rastell, W. 20734*, 20735*; S., I. or J. 21506; Seeing 22161; Seneca 22228(?); Susenbrotus 23437; Thersytes 23949(?); Thomas, W. 24021; Turner, William 24366; Tusser 24372.5; Veron, J. 24686, 24687(?); Vigo 24725.7; Virgilius Maro 24800, 24829(?); Wigand 25612, 25612.5; Wilson, T., Sect'y of State 25801; Winzet 25860, 25861; Withals 25876.

1563

Alessio 301; Almanacks (Low) 482.5; Almanacks (Nicolson) 490.18, 490.20; Almanacks (Nostradamus) 429.9, 492.10; Awdely 992(?); Baldwin, W. 1248; Becon 1710*, 1746.5, 1755; Benese 1875; Beze 2006.7; Bible, N.T., Gospels 2980.6, 2980.8; Bible, O.T., Psalms 2384.5*, 2430.5, 2431; Birch 3076; Broke, A. 3811; Bruni 3933; Calvin 4381; Catharine [Parr] 4829; Cicero 5282(?)*; Colet, J. 5548; Coligny 5553; Copland, R. 5731(c.); Copy 5742.10(?); Craft 5954 (?); Davidson, J., Master of the Paedagogue of Glasgow 6320; Demand 6572.3(?); Dictionary 6832.36; Elizabeth I 7576.7, 7588; England, C. of, Articles 10035, 10038.3(?); England, C. of, Visit. Articles 10152; England, Proclamations, Chron. Ser. 7956, 7956.3, 7957, 7957.3, 7957.7, 7957.9, 7958, 7959, 7960, 7962, 7962.5, 7964, 7964.5; England, Statutes, Chron. Ser. 9360.5(?), 9362.1(?), 9363.3(?), 9371(?), 9462, 9462.5, 9463.5, 9464*, 9464.5*, 9465*, 9466*, 9467*, 9467.5*; England, Statutes, Gen. Colls. 9303.9; England, Yearbooks 9608*, 9614, 9615*, 9923.5(?)*, 9938(?)*, 9948.7(?), 9956(?)*, 9963.7(?)*; Fergusson 108919; Fisher, John, St. 10888(?); Foxe 11222, 11222a, 11230, 11230.5(?), 11249(?); Froissart 11396.7(c.), 11397a(c.)*; Fuchs 11408; Fulke 11435; Gale, T. 11529; Godet 11930.6(?); Googe 12048; Grafton 12149; Gratarolus 12191a; Hall, John 12633; Hay, G. 12968; Hill, T. 13490; Homilies 13651, 13663, 13663.3, 13663.7, 13664, 13664.5, 13665, 13666, 13666.4, 13666.7, 13667*; Humphrey 13964; Knox 15074; Lever, Ralph 15542, 15542a(?); Liturgies, C. of Eng., Spec. Prayers 16504.5(?), 16505, 16506, 16506.3, 16506.7, 16506.9(A/C), 16507, 16507.5; Liturgies, Other Protest. C. 16572, 16572.1(A/C); Lynne 17118; Machabaeus 17174; Meurier 17847.4, 17847.6; Musculus 18308; Newbery 18491; Onosander 18815; Osiander, A. 18879(A/C); Parker, Matthew 19285.8; Philippson 19849; Pilkington, J. 19931; Prayer 20189; Rastell, J., Printer 20703.5; Rastell, W.

1563 — *cont.*
20735*, 20735.5, 20736*; Reynoldes 20925a.5; Ribaut 20970; Rime 21056.6(?); Seall 22139; Seneca 22225; Seton, J. 22250.4, 22250.5; Shute, J. 22464; Skelton 22600(?); Sum 23433; Treasure 24190.7, 24191, 24191a*, 24193*; Trollop 24293.3(c.); Venus 24650.5(?); Vincent, Saint 24752; Vives 24850.7; Whight 25350(?); Wilson, T., Sect'y of State 25802, 25812; Winzet 25859.

1564

Adamson, P. 145; Agapetus 192; Almanacks (Cunningham) 432.5; Almanacks (Digges) 435.41; Almanacks (Low) 482.7; Almanacks (Nostradamus) 492.11, 492.13(A/C); Arcandam 724.5; Baker, H. 1209.7; Baldwin, W. 1258; Barker, John 1422; Becon 1710*; Beze 2017; Bible, O.T., Psalms 2432, 2433; Birch 3079; Borde 3378.7*; Bradford, J., Prebendary of St. Paul's 3481(c.), 3481.5(c.); Bullein 4036, 4036.5; Cole, T. 5540; Coverdale 5886; Dialogue 6811; Dorman 7062; Elyot, T. 7634; England, C. of, Articles 10038.5(?); England, C. of, Injunctions 10102.4(?); England, C. of, Visit. Articles 10120.5(?); England, Proclamations, Chron. Ser. 7777(?), 7920.5(?), 7947.3(?), 7955(?), 7966, 7967, 7969, 7970, 7972, 7973, 7974, 7974.5, 7976, 7976.7(?), 7978, 7981, 7982, 7983, 7984; England, Statutes, Chron. Ser. 9464(?)*, 9464.5(?)*; England, Statutes, Gen. Colls. 9301.7*, 9303*; England, Statutes, Spec. Subjs. 9342.4(?); England, Yearbooks 9892.5(?)*, 9898(?)*, 9908.5 (?), 9915.5(?); Erasmus, D. 10444; Eutropius 10579; Fisher, John, of Chester 10910(o.s.); Grafton 12150; Grindal 12377, 12378; Harding, T. 12758; Ireland, Proc. 14139; Jesus Christ 14545; Jewel, J. 14591; Johnson, C. 14656.5, 14656.7(?); Lily, W., 'Lily's Grammar' 15613.7; Liturgies, C. of Eng., BCP 16296, 16296.3; Liturgies, Other Protest. C. 16577; London, Ords. and Regs. 16704.7, 16704.9, 16705; Luther 16988.5; Martiall 17496; Moore, P. 18059.5; Primer 20378; Rastell, J., Jesuit 20726; Rastell, W. 20736*, 20736a*; S., I. or J. 21504; Solomon 22902(?); Treasure 24191a*; Trent, Council of 24265, 24265.5; Trogus Pompeius 24290; Tyndale, W. 24438.5, 24464; V., I. D. 24565; Vermigli, P. 24670; Vigo 24726.

1565

Albertus Magnus 259(c.), 260(?), 261(c.); Allen, W. 371; Alley 374; Almanacks (Hubrigh) 462.5; Awdely 993; B., A., Doctor 1020.5(c.); Becon 1747, 1757.5; Beda 1778; Bell, A. 1807(c.); Benese 1876(c.); Benoist 1884.5; Bevis 1989(?); Beze 2007(?), 2008(?); Bible, N.T., English 2872c.7(c.?); Bible, N.T., Gospels 2981; Bible, O.T., Psalms 2384.7, 2434, 2435; Bible, Selections 2996.3; Birch 3080; Blundeville 3152*; Boccaccio 3183(c.); Book 3312.7(?), 3336*, 3358; Bruni 3933.5(c.); Burdet 4104; Caesar, Caius Julius 4335; Calfhill 4368; Calvin 4376; Cancellar 4558; Capilupi 4604; Conscience 5633(c.?); Cooper or Cowper, T., Bp. 5686; Cope, M. 5723.5; Copland, R. 5734(c.); Craft 5954.2(?); Craig, T. 5970; Darius, King of Persia 6277; Day, John, Printer 6418*, 6419; Degore 6472.5(?); Description 6774; Dialogue 6812; Dorman 7061; Drant, T., Poet and Divine 7167; East, T. 7467.5(+?); Eglamour 7544.5(c.?); Either 7550(c.)(A/C); Elderton 7565; Elyot, T. 7641; England, C. of, Advertisements 10026(?), 10027(?); England, C. of, Articles 10034.5 (c.?); England, Proclamations, Chron. Ser. 7986, 7987, 7988, 7988.5, 7988.7(?), 7989, 7991, 7992, 7993; England, Public Documents, Misc. 9185(c.?); England, Statutes, Chron. Ser. 9421.4(c.?)*, 9425(?)*, 9459.7(c.?)*, 9465(?)*; England, Statutes, Gen. Colls. 9308; England, Yearbooks 9583, 9604(c.?)*, 9775*, 9777, 9848.5(?), 9853.5(?)*, 9868.5(?), 9874.5(?)*, 9881(?); Eulenspiegel 10565.5(?); Evans, L. 10589; Exercises 10617(c.); Fisher, John, of Chester 10910; Fitzherbert, A. 10956, 10956.5, 10991(c.?); Garter, B. 11631; Gathering 11684; Gesner 11801; Godet 11930.2(c.?), 11930.4(c.?); Grafton 12167; Guy, Earl of Warwick 12542(c.); Haddon 12598(?); Hall, John 12632; Harding, T. 12759, 12759.5, 12762, 12763.5; Hartwell 12897; Hood, R. 13691.3(c.?); Horatius Flaccus 13805.5(?); Howard, H., Earl of Surrey 13864; Hozyusz 13888; Interlude 14110(?), 14112(?); Isumbras 14282(?); Jewel, J.

1565 — *cont.*
14606, 14606.5; Judith 14836.7; Jugeler 14837a(?); Lanfrancus 15192; Lanquet 15219, 15220; Lindanus 15653; Liturgies, C. of Eng., BCP 16296.5; Liturgies, C. of Eng., Spec. Prayers 16508, 16508.3, 16508.7, 16509; Liturgies, Latin Rite, Hours and Primers 16091(c.); Liturgies, Other Protest. C. 16575, 16577a; Lydgate 17014(c.); Malta 17213.5, 17214; Mary, Q. of Scotland 17564; Maximilian II 17696; Mendoza, J. 17820; Moore, P. 18060; News 18504; Norton, T. 18684; Nowell, Middle Catechism 18740, 18741; Origen 18847; Osorio da Fonseca 18887, 18888; Ovidius Naso 18955, 18971; Palingenius 19150; Parliament 19304(c.); Pasquilla 19458; Perkins, J. 19634.5(?); Prayer 20188.3; Properties 20439.7 (?); Rastell, J., Jesuit 20727, 20728; Rastell, W. 20736a*; Roesslin 21157, 21157.5, 21158*; Saint German 21571.5(?)*; Sanders 21694; Scotland, statutes, etc. 21879; Smith 22653.9(?); Staphylus 23230; Stapleton, Thomas 23232; Stow 23319; Treasure 24206a.5; Tryamour 24303.3; Turner, William 24357(c.); Valentine 24572(c.); Viret 24777; Wanton 25017(?); Weaver 25149(c.), 25149.5(c.); White, R. 25403*.

1566

Aelfric 159(?), 159.5(?); Agnello 199; Albion 275(?); Alessio 306; Almanacks (Coxe) 431.7; Almanacks (Cunningham) 433; Almanacks (Nostradamus) 493; Almanacks (Securis) 510.5; Almanacks 401(?); Apuleius 718; B., G. 1033; B., I. or J. 1040; Banquet 1367(?); Barker, W. 1427; Barthlet 1534; Becon 1727, 1736, 1747.3; Beze 2009(?); Bible, English 2098, 2098.5(c.?); Bible, N.T., English 2873(?); Bible, O.T., Psalms 2437, 2437.5, 2740, 2740.3, 2740.5*; Blundeville 3152*; Boaistuau 3168(?); Book 3336*; Bucer 3964; Bullinger 4063, 4065; Canand 4555; Chartier 5059; Churchyard 5221, 5223, 5230, 5236; Comfort 5600.5 [not STC]; Crowley 6076, 6077, 6078, 6079; Curio, Caelius Secundus 6130(?); Desainliens or Sainliens 6738*; Description 6769; Devil 6794(?); Digges, L. 6850.3; England, C. of, Advertisements 10028(?); England, C. of, Appendix 10387, 10388, 10389, 10390, 10391; England, C. of, Injunctions 10102.5(?); England, C. of, Visit. Articles 10121(?); England, Privy Council 7754.8; England, Proclamations, Chron. Ser. 7924.9(?), 7994, 7995, 7995.3, 7995.4(?), 7995.5, 7996, 7997, 7998, 7998.3(?), 8047(c.?); England, Statutes, Chron. Ser. 9468.2(o.s.), 9468.3(o.s.), 9468.4(o.s.), 9468.6*, 9468.8*, 9469*, 9469.5*; England, Statutes, Gen. Colls. 9308.5; England, Yearbooks 9729, 9735(?)*, 9740(?)*, 9747(?)*, 9762, 9782, 9787, 9788*, 9792(?)*, 9800, 9801*, 9809(?)*, 9823(?)*, 9829(?)*, 9834, 9835*, 9842, 9857(?)*, 9863.5 (?)*, 9886, 9887*, 9939, 9949, 9958, 9964; Erasmus, D. 10456; Fitzherbert, A. 10977; Flanders 11028; France 11263; Frarinus 11333; Garter, B. 11626; Godet 11930.8; Guevara 12445, 12445a; Harding, T. 12760; Heasse 13017; Herman IV 13207; Heskyns 13250; Heywood, J. 13286; Horatius Flaccus 13805; Horne, R., Bp. 13818; I., A. 14046; Introduction 14119.7; Ireland, C. of 14259; Jewel, J. 14607; Jonas 14717*; Jones, J., M. D. 14726; Knox 15075; Lasco 15262, 15262a; Le Challeux 15347; Lily, W., 'Lily's Grammar' 15614*; Lindsay, Sir D. 15676; Liturgies, C. of Eng., BCP 16297, 16297.5; Liturgies, C. of Eng., Spec. Prayers 16510; Liturgies, Latin Rite, Hours and Primers 16092*; Liturgies, Other Protest. C. 16578; Man 17237; Martiall 17497; Mass 17625.5; Mell 17802; Mellys 17803; Moulton 18224; Musculus 18307.5(?); Naples 18358; Natura Brevium 18399*; Nowell, Middle Catechism 18742; Painter, W. 19121; Partridge, John 19424, 19425, 19438; Phillips, John 19865(?), 19869.5; Pits 19969; Plinius Secundus 20031; Pointz 20082; Primer 20376(?); Rastell, J., Jesuit 20728.5, 20729; Rastell, W. 20730; Record, R. 20800.2; Ridley, N. 21052, 21052.5; Rome, Church of 21307a.1; Rushe 21453; Sanders 21695; Scotland, Church of, General Assembly 22041; Scotland, statutes, etc. 21875, 21876, 21876a; Securis 22143; Seneca 22222, 22224, 22229; Smart, R. 22644; Spangenberg 23001; Stapleton, Thomas 23234; Stow 23319.5, 23325.4; Thomas, a Kempis 23967.5; Treasure 24191a.5(A/C); Udall, N. 24508(?); Underdowne 24517; Vaus 24623a; Vienna 24716; Wager, L. 24932; Wager, W. 24934; Walsh 24999; White, R. 25403*; Wilson, C., Poet 25766; Withals 25877; Woodhouse, W. 25968.

1567

Allen, W. 372; Almanacks (Bomelius) 415; Almanacks (Bourne) 417; Almanacks (Buckminster or Buckmaster) 422; Almanacks (Digges) 435.43; Almanacks (Moore, P.) 484; Almanacks (Nostradamus) 493.3; Almanacks (Rochefort or Rogeford) 506.5; Almanacks (Securis) 510.7; Almanacks 401.3; Baldwin, W. 1259; Bandello 1356.1, 1356.8; Becon 1737, 1747.5(c.); Bible, N.T., Welsh 2960; Bible, O.T., Psalms 2386(?), 2386.2, 2386.4, 2386.6*, 2438, 2729(?), 2740.5*; Bible, Selections 2996.5, 2999*; Boccaccio 3180; Borde 3380*; Bradford, J., Prebendary of St. Paul's 3493.5; Buckley 4009; Calvin 4382.5, 4434; Copland, R. 5730(c.?); Crowley 6089; Devil 6794.3(?); Dorman 7063; England, C. of, Advertisements 10029(?); England, C. of, Injunctions 10102.6(?); England, C. of, Visit. Articles 10287, 10288, 10374; England, Customs 7688.6*; England, Proclamations, Chron. Ser. 7925(?), 7955.3(?), 7999.5, 8000, 8000.3, 8000.7(o.s.), 8001(o.s.)*; England, Statutes, Chron. Ser. 9448.7(?)*, 9452(?)*, 9468.2, 9468.3, 9468.4, 9471.2; England, Statutes, Gen. Colls. 9293b; England, Yearbooks 9566, 9667, 9683(?), 9688.5, 9689*, 9701, 9707, 9714, 9719, 9724, 9753, 9758, 9767, 9816, 9817*, 9924, 9924.5*, 9940*, 9950*, 9959*; Epictetus 10423; Erasmus, D. 10510.5; Exposition 10634.5(?); Fitz, R. 10931.4(?), 10931.7(?); Fitzherbert, A. 10961, 10961.4*; Fitzherbert, J. 11014; Fortescue 11194; Galen 11530.5; Garcie 11553.3(c.?); Gildas 11893; Goeurot 11974; Gruffudd Hiraethog 12404(?)*; Haddon 12596, 12596.7; Harding, T. 12761; Harman 12787, 12787.5; Herbal 13175.19C(c.); Hill, T. 13498.5; Hippocrates 13520; Homilies 13667*; Horatius Flaccus 13797; Howard, H., Earl of Surrey 13865; Hozyusz 13889; Hughe 13912; Jewel, J. 14600, 14600.5; Joseph, ben Gorion 14797; Lily, W., 'Lily's Grammar' 15614*, 15614.2, 15614.4; Littleton, T., Tenures, French 15739; Liturgies, C. of Eng., BCP 16298, 16435; Liturgies, Other Protest. C. 16578.5, 16604; London, Appendix 16754.5; London, Ords. and Regs. 16705.3; Maplet 17296; Martin, T. 17518(?), 17519(?); Matthaeus 17652; Natura Brevium 18399*; Nowell, Middle Catechism 18739; Ovidius Naso 18939.5, 18940, 18940.5, 18956; Painter, W. 19124; Perkins, J. 19635, 19635.5; Physic 19893a.7(?); Pikeryng 19917; Pius II 19972; Plutarch 20072; Rastell, J., Jesuit 20725; Rastell, J., Printer 20704; Rastell, W. 20737; Record, R. 20818; Roberts, G. 21076; Salesbury, W. 21615; Sanders 21692, 21696; Scotland, proclamations 21930, 21931, 21932; Sempill, R. 22192, 22194, 22196, 22197, 22199; Skelton 22618; Smith, T., Doctor of Civil Laws 22856.5*; Spagnuoli 22990; Spangenberg 23007; Stanford 23213, 23221; Stapleton, Thomas 23231; Stow 23325.5; Sutton, J. 23498; Tales 23665.5; Thomas, a Kempis 23969; Thomas, W. 24022; Trial 24271; Turberville 24326; Vives 24861(?)*; Wager, L. 24932a; Weddington 25195.5; Whitney, I. 25439(?); Wilson, T., Sect'y of State 25803, 25813, 25814*; Xenophon 26067.

1568

Aesop 171.5; Alessio 297, 302(?); Almanacks (Buckminster or Buckmaster) 422.3; Almanacks (Hubrigh) 462.7; Almanacks (Nostradamus) 493.7; Almanacks (Securis) 511; Almanacks 401.4, 401.5; Baker, H. 1210; Becon 1758; Bernard, J. 1924; Bible, Appendix 3020; Bible, English 2099, 2099.2, 2102*, 2106*; Bible, N.T., English 2873.3(?), 2873.5(+?); Bible, N.T., Latin 2800; Bible, O.T., Psalms 2386.6*, 2741; Bible, Selections 2995a, 3009; Book 3336.5; Bull, H. 4028; Caius 4344; Calvin 4382.7; Charles [de Guise] 5011; Charles IX 5035, 5036; Cicero 5283; Clynoc 5450.5; D., R. 6179; Dee 6464; Denakol 6581; Dering 6725; Dictionary 6832.38; England, C. of, Injunctions 10102.7(?); England, C. of, Visit. Articles 10121.5(?); England, Privy Council 7754.6; England, Proclamations, Chron. Ser. 8000.7, 8001*, 8001.5(A/C), 8003, 8005, 8006; England, Statutes, Chron. Ser. 9468.6(?)*; England, Statutes, Gen. Colls. 9309; England, Yearbooks 9635, 9640, 9900, 9900.5*, 9909, 9916; Erasmus, D. 10499; Evans, L. 10588(?), 10590; Fitzherbert, J. 11003; Fulwell 11473, 11473.5(aft.?); Fulwood 11476; Garter, B. 11632; Gelli 11710; Gildas 11894; Gonsalvius Montanus

1568 — *cont.*

11996; Granger, Timothy 12186; Gregory, of Nazianzus 12345.5; Guevara 12428; Harding, T. 12763; Hill, T. 13491, 13492*; Howell, T., Poet 13874; Institution 14105; Jacob, the Patriarch 14327; Lambard 15142; Le Roy, A. 15486; Legh 15389; Lily, W., 'Lily's Grammar' 15614.6; Lindsay, Sir D. 15658, 15658.5*; Littleton, T., Tenures, Engl. 15769.3; Liturgies, C. of Eng., BCP 16298.5; London, Dutch Church 16777.1(A/C); London, Ords. and Regs. 16705.7; Maidstone 17194; Mancinus 17244; Mandeville 17250; Margaret, of Angouleme 17320.5(?); Newton, T. 18512; Noot, Poet 18601, 18603; Osborne 18876; Osorio da Fonseca 18889; Physic 19894; Polybius 20097; Primer 20377, 20379; Rhodes, H. 20956; Ronsard 21315; Rowland 21356; Sanders 21691; Scotland, proclamations 21933, 21934; Scotland, statutes, etc. 21880; Seton, J. 22250.6; Skelton 22608; Skeyne 22626.5; Smith, T., Doctor of Civil Laws 22856.5*; Stanford 23214; Switzerland, Reformed Church of 23554(?), 23557; T., T. W. 23631; Terentius 23901.3; Thevet 23950; Thomas, a Kempis 23969.5c, 23970, 23971*; Tilney, Edmund 24076, 24076.3, 24076.7; Treasure 24192; Treatise 24230; Turner, William 24360, 24367; Vaux 24625.5; Vermigli, P. 24672; Viret 24774; William I 25708(?); Withals 25878, 25878.5.

1569

Act 97.5; Aesop 185*; Agrippa 204; Alessio 309; Allen, N. 361.3; Almanacks (Buckminster or Buckmaster) 422.4; Almanacks (Hubrigh) 463; Almanacks (Johnson, W.) 466.9; Almanacks (Low) 482.9, 482.10; Almanacks (Securis) 511.3; Almanacks (Stephins) 515.27; Avale 977; Awdely 990, 995(?); Barker, John 1420(?); Bateman 1581, 1585; Becon 1753; Bible, English 2102*, 2102.5, 2103(?), 2104(?), 2105, 2106*; Bible, N.T., English 2873.7(?); Bible, N.T., Gospels 2981.5, 2985.5; Bible, O.T., Psalms 2386.8*, 2439.3(A/C), 2439.5, 2439.7, 2440; Bible, Selections 3009.5(?); Blage or Balgue 3114; Boaistuau 3164.5; Boccaccio 3184; Book 3337; Bracton 3475; Broke, T., the Younger 3817.4(?), 3817.7(?); Calvin 4376.5, 4383; Causse 4870; Cheke 5110; Cicero 5294, 5314; Conway, J. 5651(?); Corro 5787, 5792; Crowley 6093; Damiano 6215; Dance 6222; Day, R. 6428; Dering 6699(?); Dictionary 6832.40, 6832.42; Diodorus 6893; Elderton 7562(?), 7563(?); Elviden 7622; England, C. of, Advertisements 10029.5(?); England, C. of, Visit. Articles 10289, 10326.5; England, Proclamations, Chron. Ser. 8008, 8008.3, 8008.7, 8010, 8011, 8012, 8013, 8014, 8014.3, 8015, 8016, 8017, 8018, 8019, 8020, 8021, 8022, 8049(?); England, Yearbooks 9941, 9951, 9960, 9966, 9966.3*; Erasmus, D. 10441, 10472, 10500*, 10501*; Evans, L. 10593; Fering 10821; France 11269, 11286; Garden 11554.5; Georgievits 11746(?); Gonsalvius Montanus 11997, 12000, 12000.5*, 12001 [not STC]; Good Fellows 12019; Googe 12049; Grafton 12147; Guarna 12419; Hart, John, Chester Herald 12890; Haward 12939; Hawkins, Sir J. 12961; Heliodorus 13041(?); Hemmingsen 13061, 13062; Heywood, J. 13302; Homilies 13652, 13653; Howard, T., Duke of Norfolk 13869(?), 13869.5(?), 13870(?), 13870.3(?); Hubbard 13897; Justices of Peace 14884; Knell 15033; Knox 15074.2; Lanquet 15217*; Lauder, W. 15315(?); Le Roy, A. 15486.5(?)(A/C); Leslie, J. 15504, 15505; Lily, W., 'Lily's Grammar' 15614.8; Lindsay, Sir D. 15658.5; Littleton, T., Tenures, French 15740; Liturgies, C. of Eng., BCP 16429.5; Louis I 16853; Mascall 17573.5; Micheli 17857.5; Newgate 18492; Noot, Physician 18600; Noot, Poet 18602; Norton, T. 18679.5, 18680, 18681, 18682, 18685.3(?), 18685.7; Ovidius Naso 18941, 18949; Painter, W. 19122; Palingenius 19138.5; Peele, J. 19548; Pole 20088; Pyrrye 20523; R., C. 20570; Saint German 21572; Sallustius Crispus 21622.2; Samuel 21690; Saparton 21745; Seres 22234; Spagnuoli 22980; Vermigli, P. 24671; Volusianus 24872; Wager, W. 24935.

1570

A., W. 17.5; A.B.C. 19.5(c.); Aesop 181(c.), 185*; Albertus Magnus 262(?); Almanacks (Moore, P.) 484.5; Almanacks (Moore, R.?) 486.5; Almanacks (Securis) 511.5; Almanacks 401.6; Answer 664.5(c.); Ariosto 745.3(c.); Ascham 830(?), 832; Assize of Bread

1570 — *cont.*
868.8(c.); Augustine 933(c.?); Awdely 991; B., R. 1058(?); Baldwin, W. 1244; Ballad 1324(?), 1326; Barker, John 1421(?); Becon 1720.7 (c.?), 1747.7(c.), 1759; Bernard, J. 1925; Bette 1979; Bible, English 2106*; Bible, O.T., Psalms 2386.8*, 2441, 2441.5(c.); Bidpai 3053; Blundeville 3153(c.); Bodonius 3195; Book 3291.5(c.); Bourne, R. 3419.5(?); Brant 3546; Brentz 3601; Broke, T., the Younger 3817(?); Brooke, T. 3835; Bull, H. 4029; Caius 4346; Calvin 4397; Cancellar 4559; Charles IX 5037; Chaves 5104; Churchyard 5224, 5227; Chytraeus 5263; Corro 5788, 5792.5, 5793; Curtius Rufus 6144*; Davie 6325; De Beau Chesne and Baildon 6445.5; Demosthenes 6578; Dering 6694(?), 6694.5(?), 6700(?), 6700.3(?); Dictionary 6832, 6832.44; Dietary 6836.5(?); Digges, L. 6850.5; Drant, T., Poet and Divine 7171(?), 7171.5(?), 7172(?); Drout 7241.5; Edwardes 7510; Elderton 7553, 7554, 7555, 7560; Elviden 7624(?), 7625; Emilie 7679; England, C. of, Appendix 10391.5(?); England, C. of, Injunctions 10102.8(c.?); England, C. of, Visit. Articles 10123(c.?), 10223.5, 10352; England, Privy Council 7754.9(c.?); England, Proclamations, Chron. Ser. 7926(?), 8023, 8024, 8025, 8027, 8028, 8029, 8030, 8031, 8032, 8033, 8034, 8035, 8047.4(c.?); England, Statutes, Chron. Ser. 9377.9(c.?)*, 9421.5(c.?)*, 9421.6(c.?)*, 9426(c.)*, 9431 (c.)*, 9437.5(c.)*, 9440.2(c.)*, 9440.12(?)*, 9449(?)*, 9468.8(?)*; England, Statutes, Gen. Colls. 9294; England, Statutes, Kalendars/ Indexes 9546; England, Yearbooks 9615*, 9622, 9629, 9646, 9655, 9662, 9695; Euclid 10560; Evans, L. 10591; Fine 10878.9(c.?); Fitzherbert, A. 10991.5(c.?), 10992; Foxe 11223, 11242, 11242.3, 11242.6; France 11271; Fulke 11449.5; Furio Ceriol 11488; G., F. 11493; Gibson, W. 11843; God, J. 11927; Gough, J., Divine 12131; Grafton 12151; Granger, Timothy 12187(?); Gribaldi 12366(?); Halle 12723a(c.?)*(A/C); Hart, John, Chester Herald 12889; Hayward, W. 13012(?); Henry IV, King of France 13104; Henry, the Minstrel 13149; Homilies 13668, 13679.2(?), 13679.4(?), 13679.7(?), 13680 (?), 13680.4(?), 13680.6(?); Howell, T., Poet 13876(?); Ingelend 14085(?); Jacob, the Patriarch 14326(?); Jewel, J. 14601; John XXI 14653.7(c.); Jugeler 14837a.5(c.); Kello 14915(?); Kirchmeyer 15011; Kirkham 15015; Knell 15030, 15030.5, 15034; Lasso 15266; Lauder, W. 15315.5(?); Levens 15532; Lily, W., 'Lily's Grammar' 15614.9, 15615(c.); Liturgies, C. of Eng., BCP 16299, 16300; Liturgies, Other Protest. C. 16579*; London, Dutch Church 16777.1A(?) (A/C); Luther 16997.5*; Marlorat 17404, 17410(?); Marriage 17466; Matthaeus 17653, 17653a, 17653a.3; Monacius 18004(?); Neville, G. 18482.5(?); Noot, Poet 18600.5(?); Norfolk 18643.7; Norton, T. 18677, 18677.5, 18678, 18678a, 18678a.5, 18679, 18685, 18686(?); Norton, T., and Christopher 18687.5; Nowell, Larger Catechism 18701, 18701a, 18708; Ochino 18768(?); Ovidius Naso 18926.1, 18942(?); P., I. or J. 19071(?); Papists 19178(?); Paradoxes 19185 (c.); Paris, M. 19209*, 19209a*; Partridge, John 19421; Pena, P., and L'Obel 19595*; Phillips, John 19863(?), 19868, 19870; Physic 19895; Pius II 19972.5(c.); Pius V 19974.1, 19974.2; Porder 20117; Possevino 20130.5; Prayer 20188.7(c.); Preston, T., Dramatist 20287(?), 20289; Primer 20377.3(c.), 20377.5(c.); Prosper 20444.5(c.); Record, R. 20800.4; Reuchlin 20906; Rhodes, H. 20957(c.); Richardson, R. 21021; Rouspeau 21351.5(?); Scoggin 21850.3(c.); Scotland, Church of, General Assembly 22046; Scotland, proclamations 21935, 21936, 21937; Sempill, R. 22187, 22187a, 22187a.5, 22189, 22191, 22192a.3, 22192a.5, 22193, 22195, 22200(A/C), 22201, 22201.5, 22204, 22205, 22206, 22208, 22209, 22210, 22211; Seton, J. 22250.8; Shepherds' Kalendar 22415(?); Smit 22653.3(c.); Sodom 22890; Spangenberg 23002; Stanyhurst 23229; Stow 23322; Sturmius 23408; Susenbrotus 23438; T., I. or J. 23621.5(?); Tarlton 23688; Tidings 24066(c.); Tomson, L. 24113; Trogus Pompeius 24291; Turberville 24327; Tusser 24373; Virgilius Maro 24788; W., R. 24913a.5; Wager, W. 24933(?); Warham 25073(?); York, City of 26098.5(c.).

1571

A.B.C. 22.3; Aesop 185.5; Allen, N. 361.5; Alley 375; Almanacks (Buckminster or Buckmaster) 422.5; Almanacks (Gossenne) 449; Almanacks (H., T.) 454; Almanacks (Moore, P.) 485; Almanacks (Securis) 511.7; Apuleius 719; Ascham 834, 838; B., E. 1024.5;

1571 — *cont.*
Baldwin, W. 1249, 1259.5; Barbour 1377.5(?); Beze 2036; Bible, N.T., Gospels 2961; Bible, O.T., Psalms 2387.3, 2387.7, 2441.7(?); Bible, Selections 3010; Birch 3077; Boccaccio 3181; Bourman 3413, 3414; Bridges, J. 3736; Buchanan 3966.5, 3967, 3968, 3968.5, 3978, 3981; Bullinger 4043; Calvin 4395; Castalio or Chateillon 4770.4; Castiglione 4782; Cato 4845.5; Cavendish, R. 4879(?), 4880(?); Cecil, W., Baron Burghley 4896(?); Chelidonius 5113; Cicero 5295; Colclough 5532; Conway, J. 5652; Cornet 5772; Cranmer 6006; Curtius Rufus 6144*; De Beau Chesne and Baildon 6446; Demosthenes 6577; Digges, L. 6858; Edwards, R. 7514; Elderton 7556; England, C. of, Advertisements 10030; England, C. of, Articles 10036, 10037.5, 10038.7, 10038.9, 10038.11, 10039, 10039.3; England, C. of, Constitutions/Canons 10062.5, 10063, 10063.5, 10064; England, C. of, Visit. Articles 10194.3(?), 10228.5, 10250, 10375; England, Proclamations, Chron. Ser. 7953a.3(c.?), 8036, 8036.3, 8037, 8044(o.s.); England, Public Documents, Misc. 9187.5(?); England, Statutes, Chron. Ser. 9471.4, 9471.6, 9471.8, 9472*, 9473*, 9474*; England, Statutes, Spec. Subjs. 9345(o.s.); England, Yearbooks 9776(?)*; Erasmus, D. 10451; Ferrara 10830(?); Fleetwood 11036; Foxe 11247; Fulke 11426, 11426.2, 11436, 11445, 11450; Fulwood 11477; G., R. 11504, 11505, 11505.5, 11506; Gibson, L. 11836(?); Grafton 12153; Hay, G. 12968.5; Hill, T. 13482, 13497.5; Homilies 13669; Jewel, J. 14602; Kethe 14943(?); Knell 15032, 15033.7; Knox 15076; Latimer 15277*, 15278*; Leslie, J. 15506; Lever, T. 15551.5; Lindsay, Sir D. 15659; Liturgies, C. of Eng., BCP 16301.3, 16301.5, 16426*; Liturgies, Other Protest. C. 16579*, 16579.3; Marckant 17311.5(A/C); Martialis 17495; Mexia 17849; Netherlands 18440, 18441; Northbrooke 18663, 18664.5; Nowell, Larger Catechism 18702, 18702.5, 18709; Paris, M. 19209*, 19209a*; Parker, Matthew 19286; Peele, S. 19549, 19550, 19551; Pena, P., and L'Obel 19595*; Philip, son of Conn Crosach 19844.5; Phillips, John 19869; Plowden 20040; Plutarch 20057.5; Rastell, W. 20738; Record, R. 20800.6; Reynoldes 20926; Sempill, R. 22188, 22194.5; Story 23296, 23297; Susenbrotus 23438.3*; Switzerland, Reformed Church of 23555; Tablet 23641; Thomas, a Kempis 23971(?)*; Tilney, Edmund 24077; Tusser 24374; Valerius 24583; Venice 24634(?); Vigo 24722; Vigor 24726.5; Whythorne 25584; Wollay 25943.

1572

Achelley 85a(c.); Almanacks (Hill, T.) 459, 459.5; Amadis 545(?); Aphthonius 700; Aristotle 770.3; B., I., Gentleman 1048; Becon 1760; Bedel, H. 1783; Beze 2010, 2037; Bible, English 2107; Bible, O.T., Psalms 2442, 2442.5; Bible, Selections 2995a.2; Blage or Balgue 3115; Book 3338; Bossewell 3393; Broughton, Rowland 3901; Buchanan 3979, 3982; Bullinger 4044, 4055, 4074; Calvin 4377; Carlile 4655; Cartwright, T. 4713; Cato 4846; Coilyear 5487; Conway, J. 5652.3; Cortes 5799; Cradocke 5952; Daniel, the Prophet 6235; Denton 6674; Dering 6679, 6679.2, 6701(?), 6701.3 (?), 6701.5(?), 6701.7(?); Dionysius, Periegetes 6901; Discourse 6909.5; Drant, T., Poet and Divine 7166, 7168; Elderton 7552.5; Elizabeth I 7601; Elyot, T. 7652; England, C. of, Appendix 10392; England, C. of, Injunctions 10102.10(?); England, C. of, Visit. Articles 10123.5(?), 10267.5(?); England, Proclamations, Chron. Ser. 8039, 8040, 8041, 8042, 8043, 8044, 8047.6(c.?), 8050(?), 8050.5, 8052, 8053; England, Public Documents, Misc. 9187.6(?); England, Statutes, Chron. Ser. 9440.14(?)*, 9444.4(?)*, 9460*, 9472(?)*, 9477a.5, 9478*, 9478.3*, 9478.5*, 9479*; England, Statutes, Gen. Colls. 9311; England, Statutes, Spec. Subjs. 9345; England, Yearbooks 9783, 9788(?)*, 9794(?)*, 9811, 9824(?)*, 9830, 9843, 9849, 9854, 9864, 9869, 9875(?)*, 9880(?)*, 9893; Fenton, G. 10797; Fergusson 10820; Field, J., and Wilcox 10847, 10848, 10850; Filles 10867(?); Foxe 11239; Fulke 11426.7(?), 11445.5, 11451; Gerardus 11759; Gosynhill 12107; Grafton 12152, 12154; Gruffudd Hiraethog 12404(?)*; Heidelberg Catechism 13028; Hill, T. 13492; Holme, W. 13602, 13603; Huloet 13941; Humphrey 13959, 13959.5; Ireland, Laws 14129; Jones, J., M. D. 14724a.3, 14724a.7;

1572 — *cont.*
Knox 15062; Kyttes 15101(?); Latimer 15277*; Lavater 15320; Leslie, J. 15503; Lever, T. 15551; Lily, W., 'Lily's Grammar' 15616*; Littleton, T., Tenures, Engl. 15769.7; Littleton, T., Tenures, French 15741, 15742*; Liturgies, C. of Eng., BCP 16301.7, 16302, 16302.5, 16426*; Liturgies, C. of Eng., Spec. Prayers 16511; London, Ords. and Regs. 16706, 16706.3; Martinengo 17520, 17521; Mary, Q. of Scotland 17565; Mascall 17574; Muenster 18242; Natura Brevium 18400; Nowell, Larger Catechism 18703; Nowell, Middle Catechism 18730; Ovidius Naso 18926.3, 18977a; Palfreyman 19136, 19137.5(?); Palingenius 19139; Parinchef 19196; Parker, Matthew 19292(+)*; Platt 19990.5; Rastell, J., Printer 20705; Roberts, Humphrey 21090; Roesslin 21158(?)*; Scotland, appendix 22011; Scotland, Church of, Confession of Faith 22028; Scotland, proclamations 21938, 21940, 21941(o.s.); Sempill, R. 22200.5, 22202, 22203, 22204.5; Seton, J. 22251; Smith, T., Doctor of Civil Laws 22868.5; Spagnuoli 22981, 22991; Sulpitius 23431; Susenbrotus 23438.3; Symon 23589; Terentius 23901.7; Treasure 24193*; Trogus Pompeius 24287; Tyndale, W. 24436*; Vegetius Renatus 24631; Virgilius Maro 24788a; Vowell 24886.7(?); Walther 25013; Whitgift 25427, 25428*; Wilson, T., Sect'y of State 25807; Wimbledon 25825.7.

1573

Acworth 99, 99.5; Adamson, P. 147; Almanacks (Hill, T.) 459.7; Almanacks (Leowitz) 479.8; Almanacks (Moore, P.) 486; Almanacks (Securis) 511.9; Alvarez de Toledo 540(?); Arsanes 785.5(?); Ascham 835; Athenagoras 886; Bedel, H. 1784; Bible, English 2108; Bible, N.T., English 2875(+?); Bible, N.T., Latin 2801; Bible, O.T., Psalms 2355.5, 2442.7(c.), 2443, 2443.5(?); Brandolinus 3542; Bridges, J. 3737; Brook 3827; Bullein 4037; Bullinger 4062; Cancellar 4560(?), 4560.5; Cardano 4607; Carr, J. 4684, 4685; Cartwright, T. 4711, 4712; Castalio or Chateillon 4770.6; Charles IX 5039; Cicero 5265.7, 5290; Clerke, B. 5407; Cooper or Cowper, T., Bp. 5684, 5684.2, 5687; Crowley 6088.7; Curteys or Curtis 6135; Custom 6150; Davidson, J., Minister of Salt-Preston 6321; Dee 6462; Dering 6679.3, 6691; Desainliens or Sainliens 6748; Dictionary 6832.46; Digges, T. 6871; Du Rosier 7368, 7369; Edinburgh 7485; Elizabeth I 7582.5(?); Elviden 7623; England, C. of, Advertisements 10030.5(?); England, C. of, Articles 10037.7(c.?), 10040; England, C. of, Injunctions 10102.12(?); England, C. of, Visit. Articles 10124(?), 10153, 10194.5; England, Proclamations, Chron. Ser. 7937(?), 8055, 8056, 8057, 8062, 8063, 8064, 8065; England, Statutes, Chron. Ser. 9449.6(?)*, 9454(?)*, 9457.8(?)*, 9466(?)*, 9473(?)*, 9478(+)*, 9478.3(+)*, 9478.5(+)*; England, Yearbooks 9801(?)*, 9817(?)*, 9835(?)*, 9858(?)*, 9887(?)*, 9897.5(?)*, 9900.5(?)*, 9924.5(?)*; Erasmus, D. 10473; Fitzherbert, A. 10993, 10993.4; Fitzherbert, J. 11003.5; Fortescue 11195; Fulke 11421.7(?), 11427, 11442, 11443; Garcie 11554(?); Gascoigne 11635; Golding 11985; Grafton 12155(?); Gratarolus 12192; Guevara 12446; Guicciardini, L. 12464; Harman 12788; Heywood, J. 13307 (c.); Holland 13570, 13578; Hotman, F. 13844, 13845, 13846, 13847, 13847.5; Humphrey 13963; Hutchinson 14021; Letter 15525.3; Lever, Ralph 15541; Lily, W., 'Lily's Grammar' 15616*; Liturgies, C. of Eng., BCP 16303, 16303.5; Liturgies, C. of Eng., Spec. Prayers 16510.5(A/C); Lloyd, L. 16624(?); Llwyd 16635 [not STC], 16636; Luther 16979; Macchiavelli 17165; Manuzio, A. 17278.8; Manuzio, P. 17286, 17286.5; Matthaeus 17653a.7; More, T. 18083; Negri de Bassano 18419(?); Nichols, N. 18543; Northbrooke 18665; Nowell, Larger Catechism 18707, 18710; Nowell, Shorter Catechism 18711; Nyndge 18752(?); P., D. 19060; Paglia 19114; Parkhurst 19299; Partridge, John 19425.5; Pont 20105; Price, Sir J. 20309; Primer 20380, 20381*; Reckoner 20794(bef.); Record, R. 20800.8; S., D. 21485; S., I. or J. 21498; Sallustius Crispus 21622.4, 21622.6; Schade 21810.3; Scotland, proclamations 21941, 21942, 21943, 21943a; Scotland, statutes, etc. 21882; Sempill, R. 22207; Serres, J. 22241; Slander 22630; Smith, Walter 22870; Spagnuoli 22982; Spangenberg 23003; Spicer, R. 23101.5; Stanford 23215; Stow 23323.5, 23325.6; T., G. 23617.5; Tilney, Edmund 24077.5;

1573 — *cont.*
Traheron 24171; Treatise 24252; Tusser 24375, 24376, 24377; Tyndale, W. 24436*; Tyrie 24476; Viret 24778; Virgilius Maro 24801; Walther 25010, 25011; Whitgift 25428*, 25429; Whitney, I. 25440; Willes 25671; William I 25710; Wimbledon 25826*; Xenophon 26075.

1574

Almanacks (Digges) 435.45; Almanacks (Hill, T.) 459.9; Almanacks (Low) 482.12; Almanacks (Securis) 512; Anderson, A. 567; Asser 863; Augustine 924, 935; Baker, G. 1209; Baker, H. 1210a; Baldwin, W. 1250; Bale 1304; Baret, J. 1410; Barnaud 1463, 1464, 1464.2, 1464.3; Becon 1761; Beze 2038; Bible, English 2109; Bible, N.T., Gospels 2982; Bible, N.T., Latin 2802, 2803, 2803.5; Bible, O.T., Psalms 2390.5, 2444; Blundeville 3161; Boaistuau 3169; Boccaccio 3184.8; Book 3363.5; Bourne, W. 3422(?); Bradford, J., Prebendary of St. Paul's 3499.5, 3500, 3500.5; Brasbridge 3548; Brigges 3738; Bristow, R. 3799; Bull, H. 4029.5; C., R. 4295; Caius 4345, 4348, 4349; Calvin 4417, 4444, 4445, 4449, 4451; Castalio or Chateillon 4770.7; Cataneo 4790; Catharine [Parr] 4826.6(?); Cato 4846.3; Christian Princes 5182(?), 5182.2(?); Cicero 5265.8, 5284*, 5296, 5314.5, 5323.5; Clever, W., Preacher 5411.7; Corro 5784; Curteys or Curtis 6136; Davidson, J., Minister of Salt-Preston 6323; Dering 6679.4, 6684.5, 6684.7, 6692; Devon 6797; Elidad 7573(?); Ely, Diocese of 7627.7; England, C. of, Appendix 10393; England, C. of, Injunctions 10102.14(?); England, C. of, Visit. Articles 10124.5(?), 10229; England, Customs 7688.8; England, Proclamations, Chron. Ser. 8047.8(c.?), 8066; England, Statutes, Chron. Ser. 9455(?)*, 9460.5(?)*, 9469(?)*, 9474(?)*; England, Statutes, Gen. Colls. 9295, 9312; England, Yearbooks 9672, 9679, 9910, 9918, 9940(?)*, 9950(?)*, 9959(?)*, 9966.3(?)*; Fenton, G. 10793a; Fidelitas 10843 (?); Fulke 11422, 11428, 11452; Galen 11537.3; Garden 11555; Gratarolus 12193a; Guarna 12416.5; Guevara 12432; Hake 12609; Hemmingsen 13063, 13065; Higgins, J., Poet 13443; Hill, T. 13484(?), 13493; Homilies 13654, 13670; Horatius Flaccus 13784; Howard, H., Earl of Surrey 13866; Introduction 14120; Jones, J., M. D. 14724a.9, 14725; Justices of Peace 14885; Kingsmill, A. 15003; La Ramee 15241.7, 15246; Languedoc 15206.5; Le Roy, A. 15487; Lily, W., 'Lily's Grammar' 15617; Lindsay, Sir D. 15660; Littleton, T., Tenures, Engl. 15770; Littleton, T., Tenures, French 15742*; Liturgies, C. of Eng., BCP 16304.5, 16304.6, 16427; Marbecke 17303, 17304; Marlorat 17408, 17409; Middelburg 17865; Muenster 18243; Niclas 18550(?), 18551(?), 18554(?), 18555(?), 18557(?), 18557.5(?), 18560, 18562, 18564.5; Nowell, Larger Catechism 18704; Nowell, Middle Catechism 18712; Nowell, Shorter Catechism 18711a; Ovidius Naso 18947.5, 18976.4; Palingenius 19140; Parker, Matthew 19292a; Patriarchs 19465.7; Pinder 19936.5 (A/C); Primer 20381*; Rastell, W. 20731; Ravisius 20761.2; Record, R. 20813; Rich, B. 20998; Ridley, N. 21050; Robinson, Richard, of Alton 21121.7; S., W. 21529; Scot, G. 21855; Scot, R. 21865; Scotland, Church of, General Assembly 22043; Serres, J. 22241.5, 22242; Seton, J. 22252; Stanford 23222; Stow 23324; Susenbrotus 23438.7; Tablet 23640; Travers, W. 24184; Treasure 24193.5; Tusser 24378; Twyne, T. 24408; Tyrwhit 24477.5; Vaux 24626; Walsingham, T. 25004, 25005; Wedlocke 25197; Werdmueller 25250, 25253(?), 25258.3(?); Whitgift 25430, 25430.5, 25431; Whittingham 25442; Wimbledon 25826*; Withals 25879.

1575

Abington 79(c.); Agrippa 205; Albin de Valsergues 274; Almanacks (Forster) 443.13; Almanacks 401.7(?); Aphthonius 700.3; Ariosto 745.5(c.); Augustine 925; Awdely 994; B., R. 1059; Baldwin, W. 1251, 1260; Bale 1286; Banister, J. 1360; Barnaud 1464.4, 1464.5; Benedicite 1858; Beze 2001(?), 2006; Bible, English 2110, 2111, 2111.5, 2111.7, 2112, 2113, 2113a, 2113a.3, 2114; Bible, N.T., English 2874(?), 2875a(c.), 2875a.5(c.), 2876*, 2877; Bible, O.T., 'Books of Solomon' 2759.7(c.); Bible, O.T., Psalms 2356, 2445, 2445a.5; Boccaccio 3181.5(c.); Book 3339, 3358a(?), 3367; Borde

1575 — *cont.*
3376; Breton 3695; Bullinger 4053, 4055.5, 4078; Calvin 4378; Canterbury, Province of 4582(?); Cartwright, T. 4714; Catechism 4803.4(?); Cena 4911.3(c.); Christian Faith 5159; Churchyard 5232; Cicero 5284*, 5297, 5307, 5318.3; Conway, J. 5652.5(c.?); Cooper or Cowper, T., Bp. 5691; Corro 5786; Crowley 6092; Curio, Caelius Augustinus 6129; Curteys or Curtis 6139; Daneau 6226; Dering 6679.5, 6695(c.?), 6696(c.?); Desainliens or Sainliens 6758; Dethick 6787.4(c.); England, C. of, Articles 10037, 10037.3, 10040.5(c.?); England, C. of, Visit. Articles 10306.5, 10352.5(?); England, Proclamations, Chron. Ser. 8068(?), 8068.3(?), 8070, 8071, 8073, 8075, 8075.3; England, Statutes, Chron. Ser. 9360.7(?), 9362.2(?), 9363.4(?), Ser. 9368.5(?), 9371.5(?), 9375.7(?), 9378.5(?), 9384.5(?)*, 9389.5(?), 9393.5(?)*, Ser. 9396.5(?), 9400.3(?), 9403(?)*, 9406.5(?), 9409.3(?), 9411.5(?)*, 9414.5(?), England, Statutes, Chron. Ser. 9444.6(?)*, 9450(?)*, 9455.5(?)*, 9480.7(o.s.), 9481(o.s.), 9482(o.s.); England, Statutes, Gen. Colls. 9304; England, Statutes, Spec. Subjs. 9342.7(c.?); England, Yearbooks 9609*, 9702, 9708, 9715, 9720, 9725, 9736, 9741, 9748, 9754, 9759, 9763, 9768, 9927.5(c.?); Estienne, H. 10550; Euripides 10567.5; Family of Love 10681.5; Fenton, G. 10794; Foxe 11243; France 11266, 11287; Francis, Duc d'Anjou 11310.5, 11311; French Language 11376; Frith, J. 11386 (c.?); Fulwell 11475; Gascoigne 11636, 11637, 11643, 11643a; Gilby 11885(?); Grant 12188; Guevara 12433(?), 12448; Hake 12605; Harvey, G. 12902.5; Higgins, J., Poet 13444; Howell, T., Poet 13876.5(?); Humphrey 13960; Indagine 14076; Jacob, the Patriarch 14326.3(?); Jesus Christ 14563.3, 14563.5*, 14563.7*; Joseph, ben Gorion 14798, 14798.5*, 14799*, 14799a*; Latimer 15278*; Lentulo 15469; Lever, T. 15552; Lily, W., 'Lily's Grammar' 15618; Lindsay, Sir D. 15677; Liturgies, C. of Eng., BCP 16304.7, 16305, 16305a; Liturgies, C. of Eng., Ordinal 16466(?); Liturgies, Latin Rite, Hours and Primers 16092*; Liturgies, Other Protest. C. 16579.5, 16580; London, Appendix 16761.5(c.); London, Ords. and Regs. 16704.3(?)*(A/C), 16706.7; Luther 16965; Marlorat 17406; Mascall 17575; Montmorency 18051.7; Neville, A. 18478, 18478a, 18478a.5; Niclas 18548.5, 18549, 18552(?), 18556(?), 18558(?), 18561(?), 18563(?), 18564(?); Nicolls 18577(?); Northbrooke 18666 (?); Nowell, Larger Catechism 18710a*; Nowell, Middle Catechism 18726, 18730.3(?); Ovidius Naso 18957; Oxford Univ., Off. Docs. 19002.3; Paglia 19115(?); Painter, W. 19123; Palingenius 19141; Paracelsus 19181.3; Patriarchs 19466; Patten 19476; Persuasion 19781.5(c.?)(A/C); Philibert 19832; Plutarch 20051.5(A/C); Rastell, J., Printer 20706; Record, R. 20801; Rice 20973(c.); Robinson, C. 21104.5(c.); Rolland 21258; Saint German 21573; Salerno 21601; Scotland, proclamations 21943a.5, 21944, 21944.5, 21945; Scotland, statutes, etc. 21881, 21883; Seeing 22161.5(?); Sharpe, Robert 22378; Smith, Jude 22805; Staveley 23239.5(?); Stevenson 23263; Stile, Sir J. 23267.5(c.?)(A/C); Stow 23325; Suso 23443.5(+); Taisnier 23659(?); Tallis and Byrd 23666; Terentius 23885.7, 23902; Thame School 23928; Thomas, a Kempis 23967(c.)*; Treasure 24194, 24207; Turberville 24324, 24328; Turler 24336; Veron, J. 24677; Virgilius Maro 24816; Vives 24851.5(c.); Vowell 24886(?), 24887(?), 24888(?); Whitgift 25433; Whittingham 25443; William I 25712; Wimbledon 25827, 25827.5.

1576

Aelianus, C. 164; Almanacks (Digges) 435.47; Almanacks (Mounslowe) 488.3; Almanacks (Securis) 512.3, 512.4; Almanacks 401.8, 401.8A(A/C); Anderson, A. 568; Ascham 826; Baker, H. 1210a.5; Bandello 1356.4; Barlement 1431.4; Barston 1532; Becon 1761.5; Beze 2049; Bible, English 2115, 2117, 2118, 2125*; Bible, N.T., English 2876*, 2878; Bible, N.T., Latin 2804; Bible, O.T., Psalms 2394, 2446, 2447; Book 3340, 3368; Borde 3382; Bristow, R. 3800.5; Brook 3820.5, 3828; Bull, H. 4029.7(?); Bunny, E. 4096; Bush 4183; Caius 4347; Calvin 4414, 4426.4; Cancellar 4561; Cardano 4608; Carr, N. 4686; Casa 4738; Castalio or Chateillon 4770.9; Catechism 4798; Cheke 5111; Christians 5201; Comedy 5592, 5592a(aft.); Cortes 5799.5; Curteys or Curtis 6140; Dawes, T. 6389.5; Dering 6685, 6726; Desainliens or Sainliens 6738*; Drant,

1576 — *cont.*
T., Poet and Divine 7169(?); Edwards, R. 7516; Elyot, T. 7652.5; England, C. of, Articles 10037.9(c.?); England, C. of, Injunctions 10102.16(?); England, C. of, Visit. Articles 10125(?), 10155; England, Proclamations, Chron. Ser. 8077, 8079, 8082, 8084, 8086, 8088; England, Statutes, Chron. Ser. 9432(?)*, 9437.7(?)*, 9461*, 9467(?)*, 9479*, 9480.7, 9481, 9482; England, Statutes, Gen. Colls. 9280, 9281; England, Yearbooks 9584, 9609*, 9730; Erasmus, D. 10487; Estienne, H. 10551, 10551.5; Fitzherbert, A. 10961.4*, 10961.7; Fleming, A. 11049; Form 11181; Foxe 11224; Fulwell 11471; Garden 11556(?); Gascoigne 11640, 11641, 11644(?), 11645; Gesner 11798; Gilbert, H. 11881; Glaucus 11920; Grafton 12156; Guarna 12420; Guicciardini, L. 12465; Haddon 12597; Hall, A. 12629(?); Hemmingsen 13057.5, 13066; Henry III, King of France 13091; Heywood, J. 13287*; Hill, T. 13498; Homilies 13655, 13655.5; Innocent III 14092, 14093; Ireland, Proc. 14140.5; Jehovah 14484.3; Jesus Christ 14563.5*; Kingsmill, A. 15004; La Place 15231; La Ramee 15242; Lambard 15175, 15175.5; Ledoyen de la Pichonnaye 15353.3; Legh 15390; Lemnius 15456; Letters 15527; Littleton, T., Tenures, Engl. 15770.5; Liturgies, C. of Eng., BCP 16306; Liturgies, C. of Eng., St. Services 16479; Lloyd, L. 16620; Loarte 16645.3(c.); London, Ords. and Regs. 16707; M., I. or J. 17136; Macropedius 17175.7; Malbie 17209; Meditations 17775; Mexia 17850; Mirror 17980; Mornay 18136; Muenster 18243.5; Natura Brevium 18411; Neville, A. 18477; New Year's Gift 18490; Nowell, Larger Catechism 18705, 18710a*, 18710a.5*; Nowell, Middle Catechism 18713, 18730.7; Osorio da Fonseca 18886; Ovidius Naso 18926.5; Palingenius 19151; Patriarchs 19467; Patrizi 19475; Pena, P., and L'Obel 19595.3; Perez de Pineda 19626, 19626.5; Perkins, J. 19636; Pettie 19819; Rastell, W. 20739, 20739.5*, 20739.7*; Remedies 20870; Rogers, Thomas, M. A. 21239; Rome 21299.3; Rowlands or Verstegan, R. 21360; Scot, R. 21866; Serres, J. 22243, 22248; Spagnuoli 22982.3; Susenbrotus 23439; Tusser 24378.5; Twyne, T. 24411; Vermigli, P. 24667; Virgilius Maro 24788a.5; Wapull 25018; Whetstone, G. 25348; Woolton 25974, 25976, 25977, 25978, 25979; Young, J. 26110(?), 26110.3(?), 26110.5(?).

1577

Aesop 186.5; Almanacks 401.9; Anglerius 649; Art 793.7; Ascham 825; Augustine 926; Bale 1306; Balista 1312.7; Bandello 1356.5; Bateman 1583; Baynes, R. 1651; Becon 1711, 1718, 1762; Beze 2036.5, 2039, 2044, 2047; Bible, English 2119, 2120, 2121, 2122; Bible, N.T., English 2879, 2879.1(c.)(A/C), 2879.2; Bible, N.T., Latin 2805; Bible, O.T., Psalms 2448, 2448.5, 2449*, 2449.3, 2449.5; Bishop, J. 3091; Book 3356; Bourchier, A. 3410.5(?); Bourne, W. 3423; Breton 3654, 3715; Buchanan 3969; Bullinger 4056, 4066(c.); C., G. 4269(?); Caldwell, John 4367; Calvin 4384.5, 4400, 4448; Cambridge University, Act Verses 4474.42(c.?), 4474.54(c.?), 4474.97(?); Cartwright, T. 4715; Castalio or Chateillon 4771; Castiglione 4779, 4783; Cato 4846.5, 4857.7; China 5141(?); Chytraeus 5264; Cicero 5274, 5297.3, 5315; Cogan 5485, 5485.3; Colet, J. 5549; Corro 5791; Daneau 6228*; Darius, King of Persia 6278; Davies, R. 6364; Dee 6459; Dering 6679.7, 6679.8, 6679.9, 6727; Dethick 6787; England, C. of, Injunctions 10102.18(?); England, C. of, Visit. Articles 10126(?), 10155.3, 10230, 10251; England, Proclamations, Chron. Ser. 8058(?), 8091, 8093, 8094, 8096; England, Statutes, Abridgements/Extracts 9526.7, 9527(o.s.); England, Statutes, Chron. Ser. 9440.16(?)*, 9444.8(?)*, 9454.5(?)*, 9461.5*, 9467.5(?)*, 9469.5*; England, Statutes, Gen. Colls. 9303.2; Erasmus, D. 10502; Eusebius, Pamphili 10572; Fenton, G. 10795; Fisher, John, St. 10889; Fit John 10929; Fitzherbert, A. 10957, 10993.7(?); Fleming, A. 11050; Foxe 11244; Frederick III 11348; Fulke 11454, 11458, 11459; Gerardus 11757, 11758, 11758.5; Geveren 11803a.7, 11804, 11804.5; Golding 11986; Grange 12174; Gray, D. 12201; Guevara 12426, 12434; Guido, Huguenot Writer 12476; Haddon 12593; Harvey, G. 12899, 12904, 12904.5, 12905*; Heliodorus 13042; Hemmingsen 13056.5, 13058.3, 13058.5, 13058.7, 13059.7, 13060, 13063.5(?); Heresbach 13196; Heywood,

1577 — *cont.*
J. 13287*; Hill, T. 13485; Holinshed 13568, 13568.5, 13568a, 13568b; Homilies 13671; Hugo, de Sancto Victore 13923, 13924; I., S. A. 14059; Innocent III 14094; Kendall 14927; Kingsmill, A. 15000; Knewstub 15042; La Place 15232; Le Saulx 15490.5; Leigh, V. 15416, 15416a; L'Espine 15512; Lily, W., 'Lily's Grammar' 15620; Littleton, T., Tenures, French 15743; Liturgies, C. of Eng., BCP 16306.2, 16306.3, 16306.5, 16306.6(?); London, Ords. and Regs. 16707.1; Luther 16966, 16975, 16975.5, 16979.3; Monardes 18005, 18005a; Mornay 18137; Munday 18269.5(A/C); Nausea 18413; Netherlands, States Gen. 18448; Norris, R. 18656(?); Northbrooke 18670(?); Nowell, Larger Catechism 18710a.5*; Nowell, Middle Catechism 18713.5, 18727, 18731; Order 18843 (c.); Ovidius Naso 18950; Paglia 19115.5(?); Patriarchs 19467.5; Peacham, H., the Elder 19497; Pembroke 19593; Phillips, John 19870.5(?); Pits 19969.2; Prudent le Choyselat 20452; Ramsey, L. 20665(?); Record, R. 20801.3*; Regnier de la Planche 20855; Rhodes, H. 20958; Robinson, Richard 21118; Robson, S. 21134.5; Rutherford, J. 21463; S., W., Gentleman 21533.7; Sarcerius 21756; Schade 21810.7; Seton, J. 22253; Settle, D. 22265, 22266; Shoreditch 22463.6(A/C); Shutte 22467; Spagnuoli 22982.5; Stanbridge, Vocabula 23188; Stanford 23216; T., I. or J. 23622; Thynne 24061 (?); Tilney, Edmund 24077a; Traheron 24172; Treasure 24195; Trogus Pompeius 24287.3; Tusser 24379; Vicary 24713; W., W. 24920.5; Whetstone, G. 25346; William I 25710.5; Woolton 25975; Writing Tables 26049.2(?).

1578

Adrians 151; Alessio 307, 310; Almanacks (Digges) 435.49; Almanacks (Securis) 512.6; Appian 712.5, 713. 713.5; Arcandam 725; Arthur, King 805; Ascham 827; B., A. 1018; B., W. 1075; Baldwin, W. 1252, 1252.5; Banister, J. 1359; Bariona 1416; Barker, C. 1417.5; Baro 1492*; Becon 1728, 1748; Bellot 1852; Best, G. 1972; Beze 2018.5, 2022, 2040; Bible, English 2123, 2124; Bible, N.T., English 2879.4(?), 2879.6(c.?), 2879.8(or later), 2880; Bible, O.T., Psalms 2351.7(?), 2396, 2449*, 2449.7, 2450, 2450.5, 2451, 2451.5; Bible, Selections 2996.7; Bishop, J. 3091.5; Blenerhasset 3131; Book 3294.3, 3341, 3341.3*, 3341.5*; Bourne, W. 3419.7, 3432; Bradford, J., Prebendary of St. Paul's 3486; Brasbridge 3548.5, 3549; Brook 3821, 3821.5; Buchanan 3970, 3971, 3972; Bull, H. 4030(?); Bullein 4038; C., T. 4303.5; C., W. 4322(?); Caesar, P. 4342; Calvin 4393, 4394, 4418, 4419, 4432; Chaderton 4924(?), 4924.5(?); Christian Discourse 5158; Churchyard 5226, 5233, 5239, 5251; Contemplation 5644; Controversy 5647; Cooper or Cowper, T., Bp. 5688; Crowley 6080; Daneau 6231; Darell 6274; Day, R. 6429; Dering 6685.5(?), 6688(c.?), 6702, 6728; Desainliens or Sainliens 6739; Digges, L. 6850.6; Dodoens 6984; Drouet 7241; Du Ploiche 7364; Edwards, R. 7517; Ellis, T. 7607; England, C. of, Visit. Articles 10289.3, 10376(?); England, Proclamations, Chron. Ser. 8097.5, 8098.5, 8100, 8101, 8102, 8105; England, Public Documents, Misc. 9187.9(?), 9187.10(?); England, Statutes, Abridgements/Extracts 9527, 9527.5; England, Statutes, Chron. Ser. 9477a; England, Yearbooks 9709, 9894; Erasmus, D. 10470; Falckenburgius 10674; Fernandez de Enciso 10823; Fisher, John, St. 10899(?); Florio 11096; Flower, W. 11108; Fort 11192.5; Foxe 11236, 11248; Fulke 11417, 11423, 11444, 11444.5; Fulwood 11478; Garter, B. 11627, 11628; Garter, T. 11632.5; Geveren 11805, 11805.2, 11805.4, 11805.6; Gibutius 11844; Goeurot 11975; Gregory XIII 12355(?); Guevara 12425; Hake 12605.5; Harvey, G. 12901, 12905*; Heidelberg Catechism 13029; Hemmingsen 13067, 13068; Heresbach 13197; Hill, T. 13486; Horatius Flaccus 13785*; Hueber 13905; Hunnis 13974; Ireland, Proc. 14141; James, W. 14465; Jewel, J. 14607.5, 14608; Keltridge 14920; Kingsmill, A. 15001; Knewstub 15043; Laneham 15190.5(?)(A/C); La Place 15230.5; Latimer 15279; Leigh, V. 15417; L'Espine 15512.5, 15513, 15513.5; Lily, W., 'Lily's Grammar' 15622*; Liturgies, C. of Eng., BCP 16306.7(?); Liturgies, C. of Eng., St. Services 16479.5(?), 16480; Liturgies, Other Protest. C. 16580.3, 16580.7(?); London, Ords. and Regs. 16707.3; Lopez de Gomara 16807;

1578 — *cont.*
Lupton, T. 16949; Luther 16987, 16989, 16993, 16998; Lyly 17051; Maisonneuve 17203; Martin, G. 17504*, 17508; Mornay 18156a.5; Musculus 18309; Netherlands 18438, 18445; Nowell, Middle Catechism 18728; Ortunez de Calahorra 18859; Ovidius Naso 18977b; Palfreyman 19138; Pettie 19819.5(?); Phillips, John 19864, 19866; Physic 19896; Plowden 20041; Polemon 20089; Procter, T., Poet 20402, 20403; Regius 20850; Rich, B. 20978, 20979; Rivius 21064.5; Rogers, J. ('Summe of Christianity') 21181, 21181.5, 21183(?); Rolland 21254; Rouspeau 21352; Rowland 21357; Sampson, T., Dean of Christ Church 21685; Savonarola 21797; Scot, R. 21867; Seneca 22215; Shutte 22470; Stockwood 23284; T., T. 23629; Tarlton 23687.5; Thame School 23927; Trogus Pompeius 24292; Vermigli, P. 24663; W., R. 24911; Walsall, J. 24995; Watson, C. 25109.5; Wharton 25295; Whetstone, G. 25347; White, Thomas, Founder of Sion Coll. 25405, 25406; Wimbledon 25828*; Writing Tables 26049.3(?)(A/C).

1579

Abia 77; Acontius 92(?); Alexander, Prince of Parma 333(?); Almanacks (Mounslowe) 488.5; Almanacks (Norton) 491; Almanacks (Securis) 512.7; Almanacks (Twyne) 518.8; Appletree 714; Ascham 835.5; Averell 982; B., W. 1076; Baldwin, W. 1260a; Bandello 1356.3; Barbary 1376; Barlement 1431.5; Baro 1492*; Becon 1762.3; Beze 2023, 2023.5; Bible, English 2125*, 2126, 2127, 2128; Bible, Latin 2056*, 2056.2*, 2056.4*, 2056.6*, 2056.8*; Bible, N.T., English 2880.3, 2880.5; Bible, N.T., Latin 2806; Bible, O.T., 'Books of Solomon' 2761; Bible, O.T., Psalms 2397, 2452, 2452.5, 2452.7; Bicknoll 3048, 3049; Book 3341.3*, 3294.5; Brasbridge 3550; Buchanan 3973, 3974; Bullein 4034; Bullinger 4042.7, 4067; C., H. 4270.5(c.?), 4271; C., J., Gent. 4283; C., T. 4303.7, 4304; Calvin 4426.6, 4439, 4441, 4446*, 4452, 4453, 4454, 4457; Canisius 4568.5(?); Carter, O. 4697; Catullus 4866; Chaloner, T., the Elder 4938; Chelmsford 5115; Churchyard 5235, 5235.2, 5243, 2544(?); Cicero 5266, 5297.5, 5298, 5308, 5308.3, 5323.7; Clowes 5447; Cobhead 5455; Cortes 5800; Curteys or Curtis 6137; Damon, W. 6219; Daneau 6229.5; David, an Advocate of Paris 6319; Desainliens or Sainliens 6739.4; Description 6768.3; Despautere 6781, 6783; Dictionary 6832.48; Digby, E. 6843; Digges, L. 6848; Douglas, G. 7074; Dyos 7432; Elderton 7557.4; Elizabeth I 7602, 7602.5; England, C. of, Advertisements 10031; England, C. of, Articles 10034.7(?), 10041; England, C. of, Visit. Articles 10194.7, 10203; England, Proclamations, Chron. Ser. 8108, 8110, 8112, 8113, 8114, 8115, 8116, 8118, 8119(o.s.); England, Statutes, Abridgements/Extracts 9528, 9528.5; England, Statutes, Gen. Colls. 9314; England, Yearbooks 9897*, 9901, 9942, 9952, 9961, 9966.5; Escalante 10529; Eunapius 10566; Falckenburgius 10673, 10673.5, 10674.3, 10674.7; Fioravanti 10880; Fitzherbert, A. 10993.9(?); Fleetwood 11034; Fleming, A. 11037.3; Foxe 11231; Fulke 11418, 11433, 11453; Fulwell 11471a, 11472; Galis 11537.5; Garnier, J. 11620.7; Garter, B. 11629; Gates 11683; Gentillet 11742; Gerardus 11755; Ghent 11808; Gibson, J. 11832; Giulio 11902; Gosson 12093, 12097, 12097.5; Grafton 12157; Guicciardini, F. 12458, 12458a; Guido, de Cauliaco 12469; Habermann 12582.2, 12582.3; Hake 12606; Hedlambe 13020; Hemmingsen 13066.5; Heron, H. 13228; Hide 13376; Hill, T. 13494; Horatius Flaccus 13785*; Hutton, M. 14034; I., S. A. 14060; Ireland, appendix 14255, 14258, 14258.3(A/C); Jesus Christ 14563.7(?)*; John Casimir 14655; Jones, J., M. D. 14724, 14724a; Joseph, ben Gorion 14798.5*, 14799*, 14799a*; Justices of Peace 14886*; Knewstub 15037.5, 15038, 15040, 15044, 15046; La Roche de Chandieu 15256; Langham 15195*; Languet 15211; Life 15589, 15589.5; Littleton, T., Tenures, French 15744; Liturgies, C. of Eng., BCP 16306.9(?); Loarte 16641.5, 16646; Lodge 16663; Lopez de Mendoza 16809; Lupton, T. 16955; Luther 16990, 16995, 16996; Lycosthenes 17003.3; Lyly 17052, 17053; Manuzio, A. 17278.9; Marbecke 17302; Marienburg 17328.7(?); Marnix van Sant Aldegonde 17445, 17445.5, 17450; Melanchthon 17790.5, 17797; Mornay 18157, 18158, 18159; Munday 18276; N., T. 18335.5;

1579 — *cont.*
Northbrooke 18671; Nowell, Middle Catechism 18732; Openshaw 18816; Overton, W. 18925(?); Palingenius 19142; Papists 19179(?); Petrarca 19809; Plowden 20046.3; Plutarch 20065, 20066; Polo 20092; Polotzk 20092.5; Praise 20182a.5; Pritchard 20397; Ramsey, L. 20666; Rastell, J., Printer 20706.5, 20707; Rastell, W. 20739.3*; Ravisius 20762.5; Record, R. 20801.3*, 20801.7; Regius 20848; Rice 20974; Rivius 21064; Robinson, Richard 21121; Rogers, J. ('Summe of Christianity') 21180, 21182, 21184*; Rogers, Thomas, M. A. 21235; Rouspeau 21353; S., I. or J. 21500; Salter, T. 21634; Saxton 21805.1; Scotland, statutes, etc. 21884(o.s.); Selim II 22180(?); Shutte 22468; Smeton 22651; Spenser, E. 23089; Stile, E. 23267; Stockwood 23285; Stow 23325.7; Stubbs 23400; Stukeley 23406; Synesius 23603; Terentius 23885.9(A/C); Theloall 23934; Thynne 24062; Travers, R. 24180; Treasure 24196; Viret 24776, 24782; W., T. 24917; Werdmueller 25250.5, 25258.5; Whetstone, G. 25343; Wilkinson, W. 25665; William I 25711; Wimbledon 25828*, 25829; Withals 25879.5; Writing Tables 26049.4(?).

1580

A., B. 2(?); Alessio 298, 303; Alexander, the Great 321.5(c.); Almanacks (Moore, P.) 486.3; Almanacks (Securis) 512.9; Antwerp 692; Aphthonius 700.7; Assize of Bread 869(c.), 869.5(c.); Augustine 937(?); B., R. 1057, 1061; Baker, H. 1211; Bale 1301(c.)(A/C); Ballad 1325(?); Baret, J. 1411; Baro 1489; Bateman 1584(?); Becon 1753.5(c.), 1762.4; Bellot 1855; Beroaldus, P. 1968.3; Beze 2032, 2032.5, 2033, 2045, 2046; Bible, English 2129, 2129.5, 2130; Bible, Latin 2056*, 2056.2*, 2056.4*, 2056.6*, 2056.8*; Bible, N.T., English 2881, 2881.3, 2881.5(c.); Bible, N.T., Latin 2806.5; Bible, O.T., Psalms 2359, 2359.2, 2359.4, 2360, 2397.3, 2453, 2454, 2456, 2456.2, 2456.4, 2456.6(c.); Bicknoll 3050(c.); Bird, S. 3086; Blundeville 3154; Book 3358a.5(c.); Bourne, W. 3425; Bradford, J., Prebendary of St. Paul's 3495; Brasbridge 3551.5; Bright 3750, 3751; Bristow, R. 3802; Buchanan 3975, 3976 [not STC], 3983, 3983.5; Bullinger 4070(?); Bullokar, W. 4086, 4086.5; Burlz 4123.5; C., T. 4304.5(?); Calvin 4385, 4385.5(c.), 4404(c.), 4404.5(c.), 4426.8, 4433, 4446*, 4446a, 4460, 4464; Cambridge University, Act Verses 4474.71, 4474.115; Capuchins 4605(c.?); Carlile 4656(?); Cartier 4699; Cary, W. 4733; Castalio or Chateillon 4771.3; Cato 4847; Cawdrey, R. 4882; Chaderton 4925; Chardon 5001; Charke 5005; Chauncie 5103; Churchyard 5240, 5247, 5250, 5259; Cicero 5308.5, 5318.7; Compendium 5606; Cooper or Cowper, T., Bp. 5684.5, 5685; Cope, M. 5723; Cranmer 5992; Crewe 6039; Dance 6223(c.?); Dering 6689(c.?), 6703, 6710.5, 6710.7; Desainliens or Sainliens 6736, 6736.5, 6761, 6762; Description 6767; Devil 6794.5(?); Dialogue 6805.6(c.?); Dictionary 6832.50; Digby, E. 6838, 6841; Dutch Lovers 7369.5(c.?); Edwards, R. 7518; Elyot, T. 7642, 7653; England, C. of, Injunctions 10102.20(?); England, C. of, Visit. Articles 10126.5(?), 10155.7, 10174.5(?), 10230.5; England, Proclamations, Chron. Ser. 8047.10(c.?), 8119, 8120, 8121, 8123, 8124, 8125, 8126; England, Statutes, Gen. Colls. 9295.4; England, Yearbooks 9601, 9925; Erasmus, D. 10478; Exhortation 10627(?); Fioravanti 10881; Fisher, W. 10920, 10920.3; Fleming, A. 11037, 11038, 11047; Foxe 11240, 11241; Frampton 11255; French Language 11376.3(c.?); Fulke 11434(?), 11434.5(?), 11449, 11456; Geveren 11805.8; Gifford, H. 11872; Golding 11987; Habermann 12582.4, 12582.21; Haddon 12594*; Hay, J., Jesuit 12969; Hemmingsen 13057, 13057.8, 13059.4; Hergest 13203; Herrey 13228b, 13228b.1; Hide 13377; Hitchcock, R. 13531; Homer 13625; Hooper 13743; Hoper 13766.5(?); Hume, P. 13956; Hutchinson 14022; Increase 14074(?); Innocent III 14094.5; Isocrates 14275; Jest 14521(?); Jesus Christ 14564; Justices of Peace 14886*, 14887; K., F. 14894; Kingsmill, A. 15005; Kitchen 15017; Knight, E. 15047; Knox 15074.8; Languet 15212 [not STC]; Le Macon 15450; L'Espine 15514; Lindsay, Sir D. 15661(?); Liturgies, C. of Eng., BCP 16307, 16309; Liturgies, C. of Eng., Spec. Prayers 16512, 16513; Liturgies, C. of Eng., St. Services 16481(?); Loarte 16645.5 (c.); London, Appendix 16762(c.), 16762.5(c.); London, Ords. and Regs. 16702, 16708, 16708.5(c.); Lord's Prayer 16814.5; Luis

1580 — *cont.*
16899.3(?); Lupton, T. 16951, 16951.5; Luther 16967, 16985(c.) (A/C), 16991; Lyly 17053.5, 17054, 17068, 17069, 17070; Macropedius 17176; Manual or Meditation 17278.4(+), 17278.5(+); Margaret, of Angouleme 17321(?); Marnix van Sant Aldegonde 17446; Melanchthon 17790; Mexia 17848; Monardes 18006, 18006.5; Mornay 18160; Moulton 18225; Munday 18277, 18281, 18283; Natura Brevium 18401, 18411.5(?); Newton, T. 18510; Nowell, Larger Catechism 18706; Ochino 18769; Ockland 18772; Openshaw 18817, 18817.5; Order 18841.3; Ortunez de Calahorra 18860(?); Osorio da Fonseca 18884, 18884.3, 18884.7; Ovidius Naso 18978; Paglia 19116; Painter, W. 19120.7, 19125(?); Paracelsus 19181.5; Parsons, R. 19394; Pelegromius 19556; Plutarch 20064; Preparation 20203; Primer 20377.7(c.?); Prudent le Choyselat 20453; Questions 20558; Rainolds, J. 20624; Roberts, Humphrey 21090.3(?)(A/C); Rogers, J. ('Summe of Christianity') 21184.5(?); Rutilius Rufus 21469; S., Joh. 21507.5; Saint German 21574, 21574.5; Saker 21593; Salvianus 21677; Saxton 21805.2(?); Schlichtenberger 21818; Scotland, Church of, General Assembly 22044; Scotland, proclamations 21946.5, 21947; Scotland, statutes, etc. 21884; Seton, J. 22253.3(?), 22253.5(?); Shakelton 22272; Shepherds' Kalendar 22416(c.); Some 22907; Spagnuoli 22982.7; Spangenberg 23000(?); Sparke, T. 23025, 23025.5; Spenser, E. 23095; Stow 23333; Table 23634.3(c.); Temple, W. 23872; Thomas, a Kempis 23973; Travers, W. 24185; Treatise 24251.3, 24251.5; Tusser 24380; Twyne, T. 24409, 24413; Usury 24557.5 (c.); Valerius 24584; Vaux 24626.3; Vermigli, P. 24664(?); Virgilius Maro 24789; W., D. 24901; W., H. 24905.3; W., T. 24919; Walther 25014; Wilson, T., Sect'y of State 25804, 25815; Writing Tables 26049.6; Wye, T. 26057.7.

1581

Adamson, P. 144; Advertisement 153.7; Allen, W. 369; Almanacks (Bourne) 418; Almanacks (Hartgyll) 454.5; Almanacks (Mounslowe) 488.7; Almanacks (Norton) 491.5; Almanacks (Securis) 512.11; Anderson, A. 569, 570, 572; Aristotle 753; Ascham 828; Atkins, R. 888(?); Augustine 936(?), 937.5, 938, 944, 950; Averell 980; B., G. 1030.3(?); B., I. or J. 1039; Baker, J., Minister 1219; Bateman 1582; Battus 1591; Bellot 1854; Beroaldus, P. 1968.5; Beurhusius 1982; Beze 2006.5, 2028.5, 2034, 2050; Bible, English 2131, 2132; Bible, Latin 2057, 2057.5, 2058, 2058a, 2058a.5; Bible, N.T., English 2881a, 2881a.5; Bible, O.T., Psalms 2361, 2397.7, 2457, 2458, 2458.3, 2459, 2459.3(A/C), 2459.5, 2459.7; Bisse 3099; Blandy 3128; Boaistuau 3170; Book 3341.5*, 3294.7; Boquinus 3371; Brabant 3472; Bradford, J., Prebendary of St. Paul's 3501; Breton 3646.5; Buchanan 3977; Bullinger 4072; Bullokar, W. 4086.7; Burne 4124; Calvin 4401, 4403, 4409, 4437, 4439.5, 4455, 4456, 4456.5; Campian 4536.5; Cartigny 4700; Cary, W. 4733.2; Charke 5006, 5007; Chillester 5137.5; Cicero 5298.5; Corro 5785; Craig, J. 5962; Crespin 6037; Crowley 6075, 6075.5, 6081; Day, R. 6430; De Beau Chesne and Baildon 6446.4; Dering 6680(?), 6689.2, 6689.4, 6710.8, 6710.9; Derricke 6734; Desainliens or Sainliens 6739.7, 6740; Elderton 7557.7, 7564; Elyot, G. 7629; England, C. of, Articles 10042, 10042.5; England, C. of, Visit. Articles 10327; England, Proclamations, Chron. Ser. 8127, 8128, 8129, 8131, 8132, 8134; England, Statutes, Abridgements/Extracts 9529; England, Statutes, Chron. Ser. 9484, 9484.5; England, Yearbooks 9911, 9919; Estienne, H. 10552; Field, J., Minister 10844, 10844.3(?); Fitzherbert, A. 10962; Fleming, A. 11039, 11041; Form 11183, 11183.5; Fowler, W. 11213; Fulke 11421, 11448, 11455, 11457; Garden 11557; Gee, A. 11696.4(?); Gentili 11730; Gerardus 11762; Gibson, J. 11833; Gifford, G. 11845, 11845.5, 11857.5, 11862.5; Gilby 11888; Gilpin 11897, 11897.5; Goldwell, H. 11990; Gonsalvius Montanus 12000.5*; Grynaeus 12411.5; Guazzo 12422; Gurney 12531.3; Haddon 12594*; Hamilton, John 12729; Hanmer 12745, 12745.5, 12746; Haunce 12934; Hemmingsen 13058, 13059; Henry III, King of France 13091.5; Herrey 13228b.2; Hill, T. 13480.5; Homer 13630, 13631; Hopkinson 13774; Howard, P. 13868.5; Howell, T., Poet 13875; Hutchins 14010; Introduction

1581 — *cont.*
14121; Ireland, appendix 14257.5, 14258.5; Ireland, Proc. 14142; Jewel, J. 14582, 14609.5(?); John, Chrysostom 14632, 14632a; Keltridge 14921; Kitchen 15018; Knell 15031, 15033.3; La Ramee 15247, 15254; Lambard 15163; Languet 15207.5, 15208, 15209*; Lemnius 15457; Lindsay, Sir D. 15678; Littleton, T., Tenures, Engl. 15771; Littleton, T., Tenures, French 15745; Liturgies, C. of Eng., BCP 16309.1, 16309.2(?), 16309.3(?), 16309.4; Loque 16812; Lovell, T. 16860; Lupton, T. 16950, 16954, 16954.5; Luther 16978, 16994; Lyly 17055, 17055.5, 17071; M., A. 17124, 17124a; Macropedius 17176.1; Madoxe 17180; Manuzio, A. 17279; Manuzio, P. 17287, 17287.3, 17287.7; Maplet 17295; Marbecke 17299; Mascall 17589; Medina 17771; Merbury 17823, 17823.5; Mornay 18161, 18161.5; Mulcaster 18253, 18253a; Munday 18259.3, 18264, 18268; Nichols, John 18533, 18533.5, 18534, 18535, 18536, 18536a; Norman 18647; Nowell, Middle Catechism 18714; Olevian 18807; Openshaw 18818; Ovidius Naso 18976.6; Parsons, R. 19393, 19402; Patriarchs 19468; Perkins, J. 19637; Phillips, John 19867, 19877; Piscator 19961; Platt 19990.7; Plutarch 20054; Principia 20395; Ravisius 20761; Rice 20975; Rich, B. 20996, 21002; Rogers, Thomas, M. A. 21233.3, 21233.7; Sampson, T., Dean of Christ Church 21682; Schoolhouse 21826.8; Scotland, Church of, appendix 22031; Scotland, Church of, Confession of Faith 22019, 22019.5, 22020, 22022; Scribonius 22109.5; Sempill, R. 22190; Sendbrief 22212; Seneca 22221; Sherwood, W. 22432; Shutte 22469; Sophocles 22929; Spenser, E. 23090; Stafford, W. 23133, 23133.5, 23133a, 23134; Stubbes 23399.7; Styward 23413, 23413.5; Temple, W. 23874; Terentius 23903; Thimelthorpe 23952.3; Treasure 24197; Treatise 24242.5, 24253; Ubaldini 24486; Verro 24688; Warren, W. 25095; Watson, C. 25110; Wedlocke 25197.5; Whitaker, W. 25358, 25359; White, P. 25402; Wiburn 25586; Wilcox 25623, 25631; Withals 25880; Wittewronghelus 25934.5; Wood, W., of Middleton Cheney 25956; Woodes 25966, 25966.5; Writing Tables 26049.8, 26049.10; Zarate 26123.

1582

A.B.C. 20.6(?)(A/C); Allen, W. 369.5; Almanacks (Buckminster or Buckmaster) 422.7; Almanacks (Erra Pater) 439.17(aft.); Almanacks (Lloyd) 480.3; Apuleius 719a, 719a.5; Arthur, of Little Britain 808; Baker, H. 1211.5(?); Bartholomaeus 1538; Becon 1762.5, 1762.7; Bentley, T. 1892, 1893, 1894; Beurhusius 1983; Beze 2004; Beze 2014(?); Bible, English 2133, 2134; Bible, N.T., English 2882, 2883, 2884; Bible, N.T., Latin 2809; Bible, O.T., Psalms 2460*, 2460.5, 2461, 2461.3, 2461.5; Blenerhasset 3132; Breton 3655; Bright 3744; Brocardo 3810; Browne, R. 3910, 3910.3; Buchanan 3991; Bullinger 4077; C., S. 4301(?); Calvin 4386, 4421; Cambridge University, Act Verses 4474.126(c.?); Campian 4536, 4537; Carlile 4654, 4657; Catechism 4799; Chapman, E. 4962*; Chemnitius 5116; Cicero 5266.1; Clement Francis 5399.9; Clenardus or Cleynaerts 5400.5; Colet, J. 5549.5; Dent, A. 6649.5, 6649.7; Dering 6711, 6711.5; Desainliens or Sainliens 6749, 6749.2(?), 6749.4(?); Dialogue 6804; Dictionary 6832.52; Edwards, R. 7515; England, C. of, Visit. Articles 10157, 10275; England, Customs 7689; England, Proclamations, Chron. Ser. 8135, 8137, 8138; England, Yearbooks 9636, 9641, 9668, 9684(?), 9689(?)*, 9778, 9824.5, 9831, 9844, 9850, 9855, 9870, 9875.5(?)*, 9882; Example 10608.5(?); Fenton, E. 10787.2(c.); Fenton, G. 10796; Fetherstone, C. 10835; Fioravanti 10879; Fleming, A. 11048; Foord or Foorthe, M. A. 11128; Francis, Duc d'Anjou 11310; Fulwood 11479; Gee, A. 11696.7; Gentilis 11736; Germanus 11787; Geveren 11806; Gibson, L. 11835(c.?); Gifford, G. 11845.7(?), 11846, 11849, 11858, 11860, 11860.5, 11863; Gosson 12095; Grafton 12158; Guevara 12429; Gutierrez de la Vega 12538; Hakluyt 12624; Harward 12924; Herrey 13228b.3; Homilies 13656, 13672; Hooper 13745.5(?); Humphrey 13961, 13961.5; Jewel, J. 14613.5, 14614; Lambard 15164, 15164a; Leland 15441; Levens 15532.5; Lindsay, Sir D. 15662; Liturgies, C. of Eng., BCP 16309.5(?), 16309.5C(?)(A/C); Liturgies, Other Protest. C. 16572.2 (A/C); London, Bills of Mort. 16738.5(aft.); London, Ords. and Regs. 16709; Lopes de Castanheda 16806; Loque 16813; Lord's Prayer 16814; Luis 16907; Lupton, T. 16946; Lyly 17072; Malmerophus 17212; Mandeville 17251(?); Marbecke 17301; Martin, G. 17503; Mascall 17576; Meditationes 17774; Meg 17782; Melbancke 17800.5*; Mulcaster 18250; Munday 18261, 18262, 18262a, 18270, 18270.5, 18272; Northbrooke 18663.5(?), 18664, 18667(?), 18667a(?), 18667b(?); Ockland 18772.5, 18773, 18773.3, 18773.7, 18774, 18775a; Olevian 18807.3; Openshaw 18819; Ovidius Naso 18951.5; P., A. 19054; Paris 19200; Parmenius 19308, 19308.5; Parsons, R. 19353, 19401, 19406; Partridge, John 19433.2(A/C); Payne, R. 19491.3(A/C); Perrenot de Granvelle 19768; Pigge 19915; Powel, J. 20158.5(?); Prime 20372; Questions 20559; Ratramnus 20751; Record, R. 20802, 20818.5; Reniger 20886; Rhodomannus 20962; Rich, B. 21004; Rivius 21066; Robson, S. 21135; S., E. 21488(?); Scotland, statutes, etc. 21885, 21886; Seager 22136; Seton, J. 22253.7; Some 22906, 22910*; Spagnuoli 22983; Spectacle 23030; Strigelius 23358; Styward 23414; Temple, W. 23873; Thomas, a Kempis 23974; Treatise 24251.6(A/C); Viret 24779, 24780; Virgilius Maro 24806; W., W. 24922; Walther 25012; Watson, T., Poet 25118a; Welwood 25239; Westfaling 25285; Whetstone, G. 25337, 25345; White, P. 25401; William I 25713, 25714; Wimbledon 25830; Worsop 25997; Yates, James 26079, 26080.

1583

Almanacks (Digges) 435.51*; Almanacks (Twyne) 518.9(A/C); Andrewes, B. 585; Aphthonius 701; Aristotle 758, 761; Arthur, King 800; Averell 982.5; B., R. 1062; Babington, G. 1081, 1095; Bacan 1103(?), 1104(?); Baker, H. 1212; Baker, J., Minister 1220; Barlement 1431.6; Barrough 1508; Bellehachius 1846; Bentham, T. 1891(?); Beurhusius 1983.5; Beze 2005(?); Bible, English 2136, 2136.5, 2137; Bible, N.T., English 2885; Bible, O.T., Psalms 2368.3, 2399, 2460*, 2462, 2463, 2464, 2465, 2466, 2466.5*, 2466.7, 2466.9; Book 3341.7, 3342, 3342.3; Bradford, J., Prebendary of St. Paul's 3481.7(A/C); Bright 3746; Browne, R. 3910.5(?); Bruno, G. 3939(?); Buchanan 3984, 3992 [not STC]; Calvin 4399, 4427, 4442, 4443, 4443.5; Canary Islands 4557; Carleill 4626.5(?), 4626.7(?); Cary, W. 4730, 4730.5; Casas 4739; Catechism 4800.3; Cecil, W., Baron Burghley 4901, 4902, 4903(o.s.); Chamberlaine 4946.5; Chapman, E. 4962*; Charke 5008; Cicero 5285, 5322.8, 5323; Clinton, A. 5431(?); Craig, J. 5963; D., H. 6168; Dallington 6199(?); Dariot 6275(?); Day, T. 6433; Dent, A. 6650, 6651, 6652, 6652.5; Dering 6693, 6712, 6712.3, 6712.5, 6729; Des Periers 6784.5; Desainliens or Sainliens 6735, 6741; Dickson, A. 6823; England, C. of, Appendix 10394; England, C. of, Injunctions 10104, 10104.4; England, C. of, Visit. Articles 10126.7, 10127, 10251.5, 10324.5(?); England, Proclamations, Chron. Ser. 8123.3(?), 8140, 8141, 8143; England, Public Documents, Misc. 9175n(+); England, Statutes, Gen. Colls. 9315, 9315.5(?); England, Yearbooks 9789, 9795, 9808(?)*, 9860, 9864.5, 9926*, 9937(?)*, 9948(?)*, 9957(?)*, 9967; Ewich 10607; Fenner, D. 10764, 10764.3; Field, J., Minister 10844.8, 10845; Fitzherbert, A. 10978; Foxe 11225, 11234; Fulke 11430, 11430.5; Gebhardt 11693, 11694; Gentilis 11739; Gerardus 11756, 11757.5; Geveren 11806.5; Gifford, G. 11846.5, 11848, 11849.3, 11861, 11863.5, 11863.7; Gilbart 11880; Greene, R. 12269, 12269.5(?); Gregory, A. 12357.3; Grimald 12371; Habermann 12582.6; Harrison, R. 12861, 12862.5; Harvey, J. 12907; Harvey, R. 12909.7, 12910, 12911, 12911.3, 12911.5, 12912; Herrey 13228b.4(+), 13228b.5(+); Heth 13255, 13255.3; Hooper 13756.5; Hopkinson 13775; Howard, H., Earl of Northampton 13858, 13859; Hunnis 13975; I., S. A. 14060.5; Jewel, J. 14596, 14597, 14597.5, 14603; Jones, Richard 14729; Knox 15068; La Roche de Chandieu 15257; Lambard 15145, 15146(?), 15146.5, 15164a.5; Littleton, T., Tenures, Engl. 15772; Littleton, T., Tenures, French 15746; Liturgies, C. of Eng., BCP 16309.6(?), 16309.7(?); Malbie 17210; Manual 17263; Marlorat 17405; Marnix van Sant Aldegonde 17450.3, 17450.7; Martin, G. 17507(A/C); Mascall 17590; Melbancke 17800.5*, 17801; Morelius 18101; Munday 18277.5(?); Nichols, John 18537; Nowell and Day 18744, 18744.5; Nowell, Middle Catechism 18733; Nowell, Shorter Catechism 18711.5;

1583 — *cont.*
Openshaw 18820; Ortunez de Calahorra 18866; Ovidius Naso 18927, 18928, 18928a; Pagit 19102, 19109.5, 19109.7(?); Paracelsus 19179.5(?); Payne, R. 19491.5; Peckham 19523; Piscator 19962; Plinius Secundus 20028.9(A/C); Powlter 20173; Prime 20370; Rainolds, W. 20632; Rastell, W. 20739.7*; Regius 20844(?); Remedies 20871; Rich, B. 20996.3; Rivius 21067; S., S. 21518; Saxey 21805(?); Saxton 21805.7; Scribonius 22110, 22110.5, 22114, 22114.5; Smith, T., Doctor of Civil Laws 22857; Some 22906.5, 22910*; Stanford 23223; Stubbes 23376, 23376.5, 23377, 23380, 23380.5; Tanner, R. 23676; Tayler, F., Preacher 23719; Temple, W. 23873.5; Tenures 23884a.2; Terentius 23886; Tomson, W. 24114; Tossanus 24144, 24144.5; Traheron 24173; Travers, R. 24180.3; Travers, W. 24180.7, 24181; Treatise 24254; Twyne, T. 24412; Vaux 24626.7, 24627; Vermigli, P. 24668, 24669; Viret 24785, 24786, 24786.5; Virgilius Maro 24790, 24807; Whetstone, G. 25344; Whitaker, W. 25357, 25362; Worcestershire 25980; Writing Tables 26049.13(A/C).

1584

Allen, W. 373; Almanacks (Buckminster or Buckmaster) 423; Almanacks (Digges) 435.51*; Almanacks (Harvey) 455; Almanacks (Tanner) 517.9; Almanacks 402.5; Astley 884; Averell 978; Babington, G. 1082; Baker, J., Minister 1221; Baldwin, W. 1245, 1261; Balnaves 1340; Barlement 1431.7; Becon 1763; Bible, English 2139, 2140, 2141, 2142; Bible, N.T., Gospels 2962; Bible, O.T., Psalms 2399.3, 2466.5*, 2467, 2467.3, 2468, 2468.5; Billerbeg 3060; Book 3343, 3344*; Bourne, W. 3425.5; Bradford, J., Prebendary of St. Paul's 3495.7(c.?); Brentz 3602; Bright 3745; Bruno, G. 3935, 3936, 3938, 3940; Bull, H. 4031; Bullinger 4057; Bunny, E. 4094; C., T. 4305(?); Calvin 4402, 4428, 4447, 4447.5, 4461; Cambridge University, Act Verses 4474.61(?), 4474.105(?), 4474.110(?); Canterbury, Province of 4583; Caradoc 4606; Cartigny 4700.5; Cary, W. 4733.4; Case, J. 4762; Cato 4858; Cecil, W., Baron Burghley 4903, 4904, 4904.5, 4905 [not STC], 4906, 4907; Chaderton 4926, 4926.5; Chaloner, T., the Younger 4940; Chamberlaine 4946.6; Churchyard 5255; Cicero 5266.2, 5298.8, 5319; Cogan 5478; Conceits 5615; Cooper or Cowper, T., Bp. 5689; Cooper, M. 5681; Copy 5742.9; Cordier 5759.1; Corro 5794; Corte 5797; Cortes 5801; Cosin, R. 5819.5, 5819.7; Craig, J. 5964; Curio, Caelius Secundus 6131; Curteys or Curtis 6141; Curtius Rufus 6145; Dent, A. 6653; Dering 6697, 6704, 6713; Dialogue 6801; Drant, T., Poet and Divine 7170; Elderton 7559; England, C. of, Advertisements 10032, 10032.3, 10032.5; England, C. of, Appendix 10395; England, C. of, Visit. Articles 10224, 10353; England, Proclamations, Chron. Ser. 8144, 8144.5, 8145.5, 8146; England, Statutes, Spec. Subjs. 9342.8; England, Yearbooks 9557(?), 9560(?), 9564, 9623, 9630, 9647, 9783.5, 9802, 9818, 9835.5, 9887.5; Estella 10541; Fenner, D. 10765.5, 10766, 10766.3, 10766.5, 10770; Fitzherbert, A. 10979; Fulke 11429; G., G. 11493.5; G., R. 11503, 11503.3; Gee, A. 11697; Gempertinga 11720; Gentili 11731; Gibson, T., M. A. 11838.5(?), 11839, 11840.5; Gifford, G. 11858.5, 11864; Greene, R. 12217, 12262, 12276, 12278; Guevara 12435; Harrington, R. 12798; Herodotus 13224; Hill, T. 13480.7; Hudson 13904; Humphrey 13962; James I 14373; Jest 14522.7(+); Jewel, J. 14583, 14604; Knewstub 15045; La Ramee 15243; La Roche de Chandieu 15255; Lambard 15147; Languet 15209*; Latimer 15280; Leslie, J. 15507; L'Espine 15514.3; Lily, W., 'Lily's Grammar' 15621; Lingham 15690.7; Liturgies, C. of Eng., BCP 16309.8(?); Liturgies, Other Protest. C. 16581; Lloyd, R. 16634; Loarte 16641.7; Lodge 16653; London, Appendix 16747; London, Ords. and Regs. 16710; Luis 16908; Lupton, T. 16947, 16947.3(A/C), 16952; Lyly 17047.5, 17048, 17048a, 17072.5, 17086, 17086.5; M., W. 17155.5; Macchiavelli 17159, 17159.5, 17167; Mancinus 17239.3; Marbecke 17300.5 (?); Marlorat 17406.5; Martinus 17524; Mirror 17979.7; Morus 18203.5; Munday 18259.7(c.), 18282, 18282a; Musculus 18314; Natura Brevium 18402; Netherlands 18439; Nimes Univ. 18581; Norden 18616; Nowell, Middle Catechism 18714.5, 18714.7, 18733.3; Nowell, Shorter Catechism 18711b; Openshaw 18821;

1584 — *cont.*
Ovidius Naso 18943(c.), 18951, 18958; P., G. 19063; P., G., Cantabrigiensis 19064, 19065; Pagit 19103(?), 19104(?); Parsons, R. 19354, 19355, 19356; Partridge, John 19426, 19427; Peele, G. 19530; Pett, J. 19817, 19817.5; Philippson 19847; Phillips, John 19863.3, 19874.5, 19875; Pietro 19911.5, 19912*; Plowden 20046.7; Prelates 20201(?); Questions 20560; Rainolds, J. 20623, 20626; Rich, B. 21002a; Roberts, G. 21076.5(+); Robinson, C. 21105; Rouspeau 21354; S., D. 21483, 21483.5(?); Safeguard 21545; Saluste du Bartas 21671; Scepsius 21809; Scot, R. 21864; Scotland, statutes, etc. 21887; Seton, J. 22254; Shute, J. 22465; Shutte 22469.3; Smith, T., Doctor of Civil Laws 22858; Soowthern 22928; Spagnuoli 22983.5; Stockwood 23286, 23287; Stow 23325.8; Stubbes 23377.5, 23399.2(A/C); Symmes 23588.5; Tasso, T. 23700, 23701, 23702; Thomas, a Kempis 23975; Thorne, H. 24040.5; Throckmorton 24050, 24050.5, 24051, 24051.5; Tragedy 24167.5; Treatise 24217.5(?); Udall, J. 24489, 24501, 24503; Ursinus, Z. 24528; Veron, J. 24678; Viret 24775; Virgilius Maro 24790.3, 24802; Vowell 24885, 24889; W., A. 24895; Warner, W. 25086; Wheathill 25329; Whetstone, G. 25341; Wilcox 25624.5(?); Wilson, R. 25784; Wilson, T., Sect'y of State 25805, 25808, 25814(?)*; Wimbledon 25831; Withals 25880.5; Writing Tables 26049.14.

1585

Aesop 181.5(?), 187; Alexander, Prince of Parma 335; Allin 376.3; Almanacks (Digges) 435.53; Almanacks (Frende) 444; Almanacks (Harvey) 455.3; Almanacks (Lloyd) 480.5; Almanacks (Porter) 501.32; Almanacks (Twyne) 518.10; Antonio, Prior of Crato 689, 689.3; Antwerp 691.5, 693.3(?); Askew, A. 849(?); Augustine 927, 929; Awfeeld 997; B., R., Esquire 1064; Barlement 1431.8; Baxter, N. 1596.7; Becon 1764; Bedford, County of 1786.5; Bellewe 1848; Beurhusius 1982.5; Bevis 1990(c.); Beze 2012, 2021(c.), 2029(?); Bible, English 2143, 2144; Bible, Latin 2059, 2060, 2060.3, 2060.5; Bible, O.T., Psalms 2399.5, 2469, 2470, 2470a, 2470a.3, 2470a.6; Bible, Selections 3011; Bilson 3071; Bisse 3100; Blagrave 3119; Book 3363.6(c.); Bourman 3412.7; Breton 3655.5(c.); Browne, R. 3909(?); Bruno, G. 3934, 3937; Bunny, E. 4089, 4089.5; C., W. 4315(?); Caesar, Caius Julius 4332; Calvin 4398, 4429*; Cambridge University 4476.5; Cambridge University, Act Verses 4474.1, 4474.7(+?), 4474.14(+?), 4474.17(+?), 4474.22(+?), 4474.30(+?), 4474.31(+?), 4474.56(+?), 4474.72(+?), 4474.79, 4474.82(+?), 4474.90 (+?), 4474.101(+?), 4474.102(+?), 4474.111(+?), 4474.124(+?), 4474.125(+?), 4474.127(+?), 4474.133(+?); Canterbury, Province of 4584(?); Case, J. 4759; Castiglione 4784; Ceporinus 4913; Charles [de Bourbon] 5010; Chub 5211, 5212; Cicero 5266.4, 5266.5*, 5299, 5309, 5309.2, 5309.3; Clifford 5415; Clowes 5448; Cosyn 5828; Cotes 5829; D., R. 6180; Darlington 6280; Dawson, T. 6394; De Beau Chesne and Baildon 6446.7; Dent, A. 6654; Digges, L. 6850.7; Discourse 6905, 6909; Duarenus 7262; Dudley, R. 7286, 7287, 7289; Dyer, E. 7383; Dyer, J. 7388; Edwards, R. 7520; Elizabeth I 7596; England, C. of, Appendix 10396.5(?); England, C. of, Visit. Articles 10208, 10231, 10268; England, Parliament 7739; England, Proclamations, Chron. Ser. 8152, 8153, 8154; England, Public Documents, Misc. 9189, 9189.5, 9190, 9191, 9192, 9193; England, Statutes, Chron. Ser. 9421.7(aft.)*, 9426.5(aft.)*, 9485, 9485.5, 9485.7, 9486; England, Yearbooks 9567, 9572, 9575, 9578, 9581, 9657(?), 9902, 9926*; Eusebius, Pamphili 10573; Fenner, D. 10773.5(?); Foxe 11239.5, 11245; Fullonius 11469.5; G., E. 11492.5 (?); Gentili 11729; Gentilis 11737, 11740; Giovio 11900, 11900.5; Godfridus 11932; Grafton 12158.5; Greene, R. 12299; Gregory XIII 12354.5; Harkett 12786.5; Hemmingsen 13064(?); Henry III, King of France 13092, 13092.5; Henry IV, King of France 13105, 13106, 13108, 13109, 13127; Herrey 13228b.6(+); Hester, J. 13254(?); Holinshed 13569*; Horatius Flaccus 13786, 13786.5; Horne, W. 13826(?); Howard, H., Earl of Surrey 13867; Humphrey 13960.5(?); Hunnis 13975.5; Husbandman 14009.7(c.?); Ireland, Laws 14129.5(+); James I 14374; John XXI 14654; Joseph, ben Gorion 14800.5(?); Junius 14860; Kett 14944.5, 14945; Kingsmill, A. 15002; Kitchen 15019; L'Allouette 15137(+); Laneham 15191(c.)

1585 — *cont.*
(A/C); La Ramee 15251.3, 15252, 15253; Lily, W., 'Lily's Grammar' 15621.3, 15621.5*, 15621.7*; Littleton, T., Tenures, French 15747; Liturgies, C. of Eng., BCP 16310(?), 16310.5(c.?), 16311; Liturgies, C. of Eng., Spec. Prayers 16515, 16516; Liturgies, Other Protest. C. 16567(?); London, Appendix 16756(c.); Lyly 17056; M., W., Servitor 17156; M., R. 17145.7; Manuzio, A. 17279.5; Marlorat 17411; Marseilles 17468; Mela 17785; Morus 18204; Mote 18211; Nicolay 18574; Norden 18634; Norman 18648; Ockland 18777; Openshaw 18821.5(c.)(A/C); Oratio 18836; Ortunez de Calahorra 18862, 18862.5; Ovidius Naso 18926.7; Pagit 19101; Parry, W., Doctor of Laws 19340, 19340.5, 19342, 19342a, 19342a.5; Parsons, R. 19354.1, 19356.5, 19357, 19357.5, 19358, 19358.5, 19359, 19359.1, 19359.3, 19359.5, 19359.7, 19359.9, 19360, 19360.3, 19360.5, 19360.7; Partridge, John 19433.3; Pasqualigo 19447; Peele, G. 19533; Pelegromius 19557; Percy, H. 19617, 19617.5; Perkins, W. 19721.7(?); Peter, St. 19796, 19796.5; Pettie 19820(c.); Pigafetta 19914; Pilkington, J. 19929, 19929.5; Plinius Secundus 20032; Plutarch 20054.3(c.); Ponticus 20109; Portskewett 20127; Preston, T., Dramatist 20287.5(c.); Prime 20371, 20371.5; Procter, T., Poet 20404(?); R., O. 20585.3(c.); Report 20889.5; Roberts, G. 21077*, 21077.5(c.?); Roberts, Henry 21084; Robson, S. 21131.5, 21132, 21132.1, 21132.3, 21132.5, 21132.7, 21132.9; Roesslin 21159(?); Rogers, Thomas, M. A. 21226, 21226.5; Rome 21292a; Sandys, E., Abp. 21713; Saxton 21805.3(c.); Scoggin 21850.3(c.)*(A/C); Scotland, proclamations 21948, 21948.3*, 21948.7*, 21949, 21949.5; Scott, T., Preacher at the Rolls Chapel 22108; Sermon 22237; Serres, J. 22247; Shepherds' Kalendar 22416.5(c.); Simson, L. 22571.5; Sparke, T. 23021.5, 23022; Stella, Julius Caesar 23246, 23246.5; Stubbes 23378, 23396, 23399.3; Tacitus 23649; Terentius 23886.5(?); Thomas, a Kempis 23968, 23976; Thynne 24062a; Tomkys 24109; Tracy, R. 24166(c.)*; Treatise 24218.5; Turnbull, C. 24337; Tusser 24381; Udall, J. 24503.3(?), 24503.7(c.); Ursinus, Z. 24529; Viret 24783; Vives 24862; Voyon 24891(?); Watson, T., Poet 25118.2, 25118.10(?); Wecker 25185, 25185a; Whetstone, G. 25339, 25342; Whitaker, W. 25364, 25364a, 25364b; Wilcox 25622; Willet 25674; Wilson, T., Sect'y of State 25806; Wither, Archdeacon 25888.

1586

Anderson, A. 571; Andrewes, B. 586; Antwerp 691; Augustine 928; Babington, G. 1096; Bailey, Walter 1192.5, 1193; Bankes, T. 1365; Barlement 1431.9; Bellot 1851; Beze 2040.5; Bible, English 2145, 2145.5; Bible, N.T., English 2886, 2887; Bible, O.T., 'Books of Solomon' 2762; Bible, O.T., Prophets 2790; Bible, O.T., Psalms 2471, 2472, 2472.5, 2473, 2473a; Bill, C. 3059.4; Bilson 3072; Book 3313, 3344*, 3351(?); Brasbridge 3552.3; Bredwell 3598, 3598.5; Bright 3747, 3748; Brook 3829; Bulkeley 4027; Bullokar, W. 4087; Calvin 4386.5, 4429(?)*, 4430; Cambridge University, Act Verses 4474.21, 4474.32, 4474.43, 4474.64, 4474.96, 4474.107, 4474.108; Camden 4503; Canterbury, Province of 4587, 4587.3; Cary, W. 4733.7; Catilinariae Proditiones 4837, 4837.5, 4838; Chaderton 4927; Chardon 4999.7, 5002; Charke 5009; Christian and Reformed Churches 5155; Chub 5212.3; Churchyard 5228; Coignet 5486; Coluthus 5586; Corro 5789, 5789a; Craig, J. 5964.5*; Crompton, R. 6052; Crowle 6074a.7; Crowley 6091; Curteys or Curtis 6138; D., H. 6167; Daneau 6230; Day, A. 6401, 6409(?); Deacon 6438; Deloney 6557.6, 6563.5, 6564; Demosthenes 6576; Dent, A. 6655; Dering 6705; Dodoens 6985; Doleta 6992; Dudley, R. 7287.7, 7288; Elizabeth I 7577, 7594.5(?), 7605; England, C. of, Articles 10043; England, C. of, Visit. Articles 10179, 10215, 10252; England, Proclamations, Chron. Ser. 8059(?), 8151, 8155, 8157, 8158, 8159, 8160; England, Public Documents, Misc. 9194(o.s.); England, Statutes, Abridgements/Extracts 9530; England, Yearbooks 9673(?), 9680(?), 9696(?), 9736.5(?), 9741.5(?), 9748.5(?), 9894.5; Erondelle 10512; Estella 10542; Europe 10568; Fenner, D. 10772; Ferne 10824, 10825; Fleming, A. 11042; French Gentleman 11373 (?); Frenchman 11377; Fulke 11424; Fulwood 11480; Gale, T. 11529a; Galen 11531; Gascoigne 11642; Gentili 11728.8; Gerardus 11761.3; Gifford, G. 11848.3, 11861.5; Gossenius or Goosenius 12092.4; Gosson 12094; Grave 12194(?); Gray, D. 12201.5; Guazzo 12423; Guevara 12447; Guise, House of 12508; Habermann 12582.7; Hanmer 12744(?); Harbert, Sir W. 12752.5; Henry IV, King of France 13111; Heresbach 13198; Herrey 13228b.6B; Hill, T. 13481, 13487, 13495; Holinshed 13569*; Hotman, F. 13843.5; Hutchins 14016, 14017; Innocent III 14095; Jewel, J. 14610; John, Chrysostom 14635; La Primaudaye 15233; Lavater 15319; Lazarillo 15336; Le Moyne de Morgues 15459; Life 15590; Lily, W., 'Lily's Grammar' 15621.5*, 15621.7*; Lipsius 15694, 15697; Littleton, T., Tenures, Engl. 15773, 15773.5; Liturgies, C. of Eng., BCP 16311.3, 16311.4(?), 16311.5(?), 16311.6, 16436; Liturgies, C. of Eng., Spec. Prayers 16517; Liturgies, Other Protest. C. 16568; Lloyd, L. 16617, 16625; London, Diocese of 16776.10; London, Ords. and Regs. 16711; Luis 16903; Lupton, T. 16956, 16956.3 (A/C); Lyly 17073; Malbie 17210.3; Massie 17631; Meurier 17847.8; N., A. 18325.7; Nelson, T. 18425, 18425.5, 18426.5; Newton, T. 18513; Norden 18613; Nowell, Middle Catechism 18715; Openshaw 18830.2A(?), 18830.3; Ortunez de Calahorra 18864(?); Overton, J. 18924; P., I. or J. 19070.5(?), 19070.7(?); Pagit 19105; Parsons, R. 19363; Partridge, John 19428, 19433.5(?); Paulet 19485; Perkins, J. 19638; Perrot, F. 19769.7; Philosophia 19887; Portius 20125; Portrait 20126; Praise 20184; Prime 20368.5; Rainolds, J. 20621, 20621.5, 20623.5; Record, R. 20802.5; Remedies 20872; Ridley, N. 21047; Rivius 21067.3; Satan 21769; Shepery 22405, 22406; Spenser, E. 23091; Sterrie 23259; Susenbrotus 23439.5; Thacker 23926; Tomkys 24110; Trogus Pompeius 24287.7; Tusser 24382; Tymme 24417; Ursinus, Z. 24530; Valdes, A. 24568; Vicary 24707; Vigo 24723; W., D. 24902(?); W., I. or J. 24906(?); Warner, W. 25079; Webbe, W. 25172; Whetstone, G. 25336, 25340, 25341.5; White, Thomas, Founder of Sion Coll. 25404; Whitney, G. 25438; Wilcox 25625; Withals 25881.

1587

Aengelramnus 165; Allen, W. 370, 370.5; Almanacks (Farmer) 443; Almanacks (Frende) 444.1, 444.2; Anwick 694; Augustine 930; Aurellio 964; Bailey, Walter 1191, 1192; Baldwin, W. 1262; Bandello 1356.9; Baro 1491; Becon 1764.5; Bertholdus 1970; Beze 2018(?)(A/C), 2025, 2031; Bible, English 2146, 2147; Bible, N.T., English 2887.3; Bible, N.T., Greek 2793; Bible, N.T., Latin 2810; Bible, O.T., 'Books of Solomon' 2769; Bible, O.T., Prophets 2779, 2779.5(?); Bible, O.T., Psalms 2399.7, 2474; Blackwood 3107; Boaistuau 3166; Boccaccio 3179, 3182; Borde 3377; Bourne, W. 3420, 3426; Bridges, J. 3734; Brook 3823; Bullinger 4058, 4076; C., T. 4305.5(?); Calvin 4422, 4431; Cambridge University 4473; Camden 4504; Carmichael 4660; Cary, W. 4731; Chardon 5003; Chauncie 5103.5; Christian Admonition 5154; Christian Hand 5160.5; Chub 5210; Churchyard 5261; Cicero 5266.5*, 5309.4, 5309.5; Clayton 5377; Clement Francis 5400; Cooper or Cowper, T., Bp. 5690*; Craig, J. 5964.5*; Crompton, R. 6053, 6055; D., R. 6178(?); Dawson, T. 6391; Day, A. 6400; Deacon 6437(?); Dent, A. 6655.5; Dering 6714; Digby, E. 6839; Dudley, R. 7285, 7285.2, 7285.5, 7287.5, 7288.5, 7289.4, 7289.5; Elizabeth I 7584; Elyot, T. 7655; England, Customs 7688.6*; England, Proclamations, Chron. Ser. 7938(?), 8161, 8162, 8163, 8164, 8164.3, 8165, 8166, 8167, 8168(o.s.), 8168.5(o.s.), 8169(o.s.); England, Public Documents, Misc. 9194; England, Statutes, Chron. Ser. 9487, 9487.5; England, Statutes, Gen. Colls. 9282, 9305.3; England, Yearbooks 9615.4, 9663, 9803, 9912(?), 9919.5; Erasmus, D. 10502.5(?); Fenner, D. 10771; Fitzherbert, A. 10980; Foxe 11237, 11238(?); Frewen 11379.5; Fulbecke 11409; Fulwell 11474; Garden 11557.5; Gascoigne 11638, 11639; Gentilis 11733, 11738; Gerardus 11761.5; Gifford, G. 11852; Gonzalez de Mendoza 12004; Gosson 12098; Gravet 12200; Greene, R. 12239, 12262.5, 12277, 12293; Greepe 12343; Grove, M. 12403; Guillemeau 12498.5(?), 12499(?); Hake 12608; Haslop 12926; Heliodorus 13043; Henry III, King of France 13100; Henry IV, King of France 13129; Hercusanus 13193, 13194; Heywood, J. 13288; Higgins, J., Poet 13445; Holinshed 13569,

1587 — *cont.*
13569.5; Homilies 13657, 13673; Howard, H., Earl of Surrey 13868; Hughes, T. 13921(o.s.); Hunnis 13976; Ireland, Proc. 14143, 14144; Kempe, W. 14925; Kitchen 15020; Knox 15071; Kyffin 15096; La Noue, F. 15215*; Lambard 15148; Lant 15224*; Laudonniere 15316; Legatus 15387; Lemnius 15454; Lentulo 15470, 15470.5, 15470a; L'Espine 15511a; Levens 15533; Leyden 15569.5; Lightfoot, W. 15595; Lily, W., 'Lily's Grammar' 15622*; Liturgies, C. of Eng., BCP 16311.7, 16311.9(?), 16312; Liturgies, C. of Eng., Spec. Prayers 16518; Liturgies, Other Protest. C. 16569, 16582, 16583; Lively 16608; London, Ords. and Regs. 16712(?), 16713; Lupton, T. 16953; Lyly 17057; Macchiavelli 17161, 17163, 17163.5; Mary, Q. of Scotland 17566.3; Mascall 17580; Mela 17786*; Mornay 18134.7(?), 18149; New Mexico 18487; Ovidius Naso 18959; P., S. C. 19078.6; Parker, Matthew 19293a; Paulet 19486; Penry 19611; Perkins, W. 19721.3; Pflacher 19826; Phillips, John 19871; Plato 19974.8; Plinius Secundus 20033; Polemon 20090; Prime 20369; R., T. 20589, 20589.5; Rainolds, J. 20612; Rankins 20699; Regius 20852; Reniger 20888; Rich, B. 20995; Roberts, G. 21077*; Rogers, Thomas, M. A. 21227, 21236; Roos 21315.6; Sadleirus 21541; Safeguard 21546; Saunders, T. 21778; Savorine 21801; Segar 22162; Settle, T. 22267; Shute, J. 22465.5; Sidney, P. 22551, 22552; Solinus 22895a.5, 22896, 22896.5; Southwell 22946(?); Sprint, J., Dean 23107; Stanley, W. 23228.7; Stow 23326; Tanner, R. 23674, 23674.5; Thomas, a Kempis 23977; Thomas, T. 24008; Thylesius 24060; Tilney, Edmund 24077a.5; Turberville 24330; Udall, J. 24504(?); Ursinus, Z. 24531, 24532; Vicary 24708; Vinciolo 24765 [not STC]; Vowell 24886.3; W., A. 24896; Watson, T., Poet 25118.4; Wentworth, Peter, Preacher 25246; Whetstone, G. 25334, 25334a, 25349; Wilcox 25620.5, 25622.5, 25622.7.

1588

Agas 194.3(?); Alexander, Prince of Parma 331(?); Allen, W. 368; Almanacks (Frende) 444.3; Almanacks (Gray) 451; Arcaeus 723; Aske 847; Averell 981; B., H. 1032(?); Babington, G. 1090; Bailey, Walter 1199, 1200; Bancroft, R. 1346, 1347; Bellot 1853; Beze 1998, 1999, 2051; Bible, English 2148, 2149; Bible, O.T., Psalms 2475, 2475.2, 2475.3, 2742; Bible, Welsh 2347; Blackwood 3108; Book 3344.5; Bredwell 3599; Bright 3743; Broughton, H. 3850(+); Bulkeley 4024; Bunny, E. 4090, 4090.5; Byrd, W. 4253, 4253.3, 4253.7; Canisius 4568; Carpenter, J., Minister 4665, 4668; Case, J. 4755, 4761; Castiglione 4781; Cataneo 4791; Churchyard 5257; Clenardus or Cleynaerts 5401(?), 5402(?); Clowes 5444; Cogan 5479; Colet, C. 5541; Colfe 5552; Crowley 6084; D., G. 6166; D., I. or J. 6173; Deloney 6557, 6558, 6565; Dent, A. 6656; Dering 6715; Discourse 6910.7; Du Jon, F., the Elder 7300; Dyer, J. 7391; Edrichus or Etherege 7498; Elderton 7557(?); Eleutherius 7570 [not STC]; Elizabeth I 7582(?), 7585; England, C. of, Visit. Articles 10232; England, Proclamations, Chron. Ser. 8168, 8168.5, 8169, 8170, 8171, 8172, 8172.3, 8173, 8174, 8175, 8176, 8177, 8178, 8181(o.s.), 8182(o.s.); England, Public Documents, Misc. 9194.5, 9194.7, 9194.8; England, Statutes, Gen. Colls. 9317; Federici 10746; Feguernekinus 10747; Fenner, D. 10767, 10768(?), 10768.5 (?), 10778; Fitzherbert, A. 10963; France 11259; Fraunce 11338, 11342, 11343, 11344, 11345; Galloway 11542.5; Gee, A. 11698(?); Gentilis 11734.3, 11734.7(o.s.); Gerardus 11760(?); Gibbon or Gybbon 11819.5; Gonzalez de Mendoza 12003; Grafton 12158.7 (A/C); Graie 12170; Greene, R. 12285, 12295; Gregory XIII 12354; Gwyn 12556, 12556.3; H., Rob. 12576; Hariot 12785; Harris, Edmond 12803; Harvey, J. 12908; Heidelberg Catechism 13030, 13031; Henry III, King of France 13093, 13100.5; Herman V 13209(?); Herrey 13228b.7; Holland, T. 13595.5; Hood, T. 13694; Hooper 13751(?), 13751.5; Housewife 13854; Hughes, T. 13921; Humphrey 13966; Hunnis 13972.5; Hurault, M. 14003, 14003.7, 14004; I., S. A. 14061; I., T. 14067; Italy 14285; James I 14376; Jesus Christ 14573.5(?); Jewel, J. 14609; John, Chrysostom 14630.5; Jones, P. 14728; Kempe, W. 14926; Kyffin 15097; La Noue, F. 15212.5, 15215*; Lambard 15165, 15166*; Languet 15207; Lant 15224*; Leigh, R. 15412, 15413, 15413.5, 15414.2, 15414.3, 15414.4,

1588 — *cont.*
15414.6; Leigh, V. 15418; Lily, W., 'Lily's Grammar' 15622*; Littleton, T., Tenures, French 15748; Liturgies, C. of Eng., BCP 16312.7(?)(A/C), 16313; Liturgies, C. of Eng., Spec. Prayers 16519, 16520; Luther 16968, 16969; Lyly 17074; Lynne 17116; Lyster 17122; Lyte, the Elder 17122.5; Macchiavelli 17158, 17166; Malbie 17210.7; Mansfield 17261.5(?); Marprelate 17453, 17454; Marten 17489, 17489.5; Mascall 17591; Morgan, J. 18103; Mornay 18144; Munday 18260; Oldcastle, H. 18794; Oration 18836.5; Palingenius 19152; Palmerin, de Oliva 19157; Partridge, John 19433.7; Pecke, E. 19521; Penry 19604, 19605, 19605.5, 19606; Perez de Guzman 19625; Perkins, W. 19721.5(A/C); Phillips, John 19872, 19875.5; Piers 19903a.5(?)(A/C); Pietro 19911; Pimentel 19935; Plowden 20044; Portraiture 20126.7(?); Praepositi 20180.3, 20180.7; Prime 20368; R., E. 20571; Rainolds, J. 20627; Rankins 20698, 20698.5; Ravisius 20762.7; Remedies 20873; Scotland, proclamations 21948.3(?)*, 21948.7(?)*; Scotland, statutes, etc. 21887.5; Sixtus V 22590; Some 22908, 22909; Spain 22999; Spanish Lies 23011; Stile, C. 23266; Tartaglia 23689; Tasso, T. 23702.5, 23703; Tedder, W. 23858.5, 23858.7, 23859, 23859.3; Terentius 23895; Theocritus 23937; Travers, W. 24183; Treatise 24215, 24255; Tymme 24420; Ubaldini 24480; Udall, J. 24490, 24492(?), 24499, 24502, 24505, 24506, 24506a, 24507; Valera 24579; Velcurio 24632; Wagenaer 24931(?); Warning 25089.5; Watson, T., Poet 25118.5; Weldon, J. 25229, 25229.3; Whitaker, W. 25366; Williams, R. 25733.5; Wimbledon 25832; Wither, Archdeacon 25889; Yonge 26094, 26094.5.

1589

Achilles Tatius 89(?); Almanacks (Buckminster or Buckmaster) 423.3; Almanacks (Dade, J.) 434; Almanacks (Frende) 444.4, 444.5; Almanacks (Gray) 451.2; Almanacks (Harvey) 455.7; Anger 644; Ascham 829*, 836, 839; B., H. 1031; B., I. or J. 1038, 1041.7; Banister, J. 1358; Barlement 1431.10; Barrow 1526, 1526.5; Bastingius 1564; Bate, J., M. A. 1579, 1579.5; Baybush 1599; Beccarie de Pavie 1708.5; Betti 1979.5; Beze 2013, 2019, 2020(?); Bible, English 2150, 2151, 2152, 2152.5; Bible, N.T., English 2887.5, 2887.7, 2888, 2888.5; Bible, O.T., Psalms 2475.5, 2475.7, 2476; Bigges 3056, 3056.5, 3057; Blackwood 3109; Bland, T. 3127; Blundeville 3145; Boazio 3171.6(?); Bourbon 3410.3; Bourchier, A. 3411; Browne, J., Merchant 3908.4; Brunsuerdus 3944; Bucke 4000; Bunny, E. 4088; Byrd, W. 4246, 4247, 4256, 4256.5*; Catechism 4803.8; Chaderton 4928; Chamberlaine 4952.3; Charles Emmanuel I. 5043; Chelmsford 5114; Cicero 5291; Cogan 5480; Colchester 5530.5; Consolations 5636.1; Constable, H. 5638.7; Cooper or Cowper, T., Bp. 5682, 5683, 5683a; Cooper, C. 5678; Cortes 5802; Cottesford, T. 5841.5; Craig, J. 5965; Daneau 6229; Dent, A. 6625.3, 6657; Dering 6698, 6706; Devereux 6790; Dialogue 6805; Dorke 7060.5; Dowriche, A. 7159, 7159.3; Egerton, S. 7538; Elizabeth I 7597, 7597.3, 7597.6; England, C. of, Injunctions 10104.7(?); England, C. of, Visit. Articles 10129(?), 10252.5; England, Proclamations, Chron. Ser. 8178.7, 8179, 8181, 8182, 8183, 8185, 8186, 8187, 8188, 8189, 8189.7(o.s.), 8192(o.s.), 8192.5(o.s.)*, 8193(o.s.); England, Public Documents, Misc. 9196, 9197, 9198, 9198.5; England, Statutes, Chron. Ser. 9487.7, 9487.9 (A/C), 9488, 9488.5; Erastus 10511; F., T. 10653; Felippe 10752.7, 10753; Finch, H. 10872.5*; Foxe 11229; France 11256, 11261, 11289, 11291; Fregeville 11371.5, 11372; Fulwood 11485.5; Gentilis 11734.7, 11735, 11735.3, 11735.7; Geveren 11807; Gibbon or Gybbon 11818, 11820; Gifford, G. 11853; Greene, R. 12219, 12224, 12272, 12309, 12310; Greenwood, J., Puritan 12342; Guise, House of 12506; H., W. 12579.5; Hakluyt 12625; Harvey, R. 12914(A/C); Hellwis 13050; Henry III, King of France 13096, 13098, 13098.2, 13098.4, 13098.5, 13098.7, 13098.8, 13099, 13101, 13102, 13102.5, 13103; Henry IV, King of France 13112, 13112.5, 13143, 13143.3; Hermaica 13206; Herrey 13228b.8, 13228b.9, 13228b.10; Holland, Henry, Vicar of St. Bride's 13586.5; Humston 13969; Hunnis 13977; Hutchins 14011, 14015; James I 14380; L., A. 15102; L., I. or J. 15106; La Noue, F. 15213, 15213.5, 15214; La Place 15232.5; La Primaudaye 15234; La Ramee 15244, 15251.7;

1589 — *cont.*
Leland 15447; Lily, W., 'Lily's Grammar' 15622*; Liturgies, C. of Eng., BCP 16314, 16314.5(?); Liturgies, C. of Eng., Spec. Prayers 16520.5, 16521; Livius 16611.5, 16612, 16612a, 16612a.3; Lodge 16674; Lucanus 16882; Lupton, T. 16947.5; M., D. F. R. de 17131, 17132; Manual 17264; Marphoreus 17452; Marprelate 17455, 17456, 17457, 17458, 17459; Marprelate, anon. tracts 17461, 17461.5(?), 17462(?), 17463, 17463.3, 17463.7, 17464(?), 17465; Marstrand 17488.7; Marten 17491; Mary, Q. of Scotland 17566.7; Meierus 17784; Melville, J. 17816*; Moraes 18064; Morel 18099, 18100.5; Mornay 18145; Nash, T. 18364; Norden 18617; Norris, J. 18653; Ockland 18776, 18778; Openshaw 18830.4; Orange 18834; Osorio da Fonseca 18885; Ovidius Naso 18952; Parsons, R. 19364; Pasquill 19456, 19456.5, 19457, 19457.3, 19457.7; Patten 19477; Payne, R. 19490; Peele, G. 19534, 19537; Penry 19602, 19613; Pico della Mirandola 19898a.3; Pietro 19913; Pigge 19916, 19916.3; Piscator 19955.5*; Plutarch 20054.5, 20059; Puttenham 20519, 20519.5; Reformation 20834.3(?); Rice 20976; Rider, J. 21031.5; Roberts, Henry 21080; Robinson, Richard, of Alton 21121.5; Rogers, Thomas, M. A. 21237; Rollock, H. 21266; Rome, Church of 21309*; Roscio 21319.9(?)(A/C); Rosdell 21320; Saintbarb 21556; Saluste du Bartas 21673; Seneca 22217; Skelton 22619, 22620; Smith, H., Minister, Single Works 22658; Smith, T., Doctor of Civil Laws 22859; Some 22912; Sophronistes 22930; Stockwood 23277, 23277.5*; Talbot 23662.5(?); Tempus 23875; Terentius 23887; Thomas, a Kempis 23978; Thomas, T. 24008.5; Trigge 24276; Triumphs 24286; Tyrell 24474; Udall, J. 24493, 24504.5; Ursinus, Z. 24533; Vieta 24718; Virgilius Maro 24817; Walter, of Henley 25007.3; Warner, W. 25080; Watson, T., Poet 25118.6; Watts, T. 25128; Whitaker, W. 25365.3(?), 25365.5(?); White, Thomas, Founder of Sion Coll. 25407; Whitgift 25432; Wilcox 25624, 25627; Wright, L. 26025, 26031, 26033.5, 26034, 26034.3, 26034.7.

1590

A.B.C. 22.2(c.?)(A/C); Abusiva 84.5; Alexander, Prince of Parma 335.5, 336; Alison, R., Controversialist 355; Almanacks (Buckminster or Buckmaster) 423.4, 423.5; Almanacks (Frende) 444.6; Almond 534(A/C); Amadis 541(?); Aneau 633; Anti-Spaniard 684, 684.5; Aristotle 753.5; Ascham 829*; Averell 979; B., T. 1069.5; Babington, G. 1083, 1097; Bacon, R. 1181; Baker, H. 1209.3(c.); Bales, P. 1312; Bales, T. 1312.5; Ballad 1328.2(c.?); Barrough 1509; Barrow 1517*, 1518, 1518.5; Beatniffe 1662; Beccaria 1708.3; Bellot 1855.5; Belus 1857; Beroaldus, M. 1968; Beze 2035, 2048; Bible, English 2153, 2154; Bible, N.T., English 2889(?); Bible, O.T., Psalms 2352, 2476.5, 2477, 2477.5, 2751(c.?); Blagrave 3118; Book 3361.3; Bourne, W. 3421(?); Boyd, M. 3443.5(c.); Breton 3658.5; Broughton, H. 3851(?), 3869; Browne, J., Merchant 3908.5, 3908.5A; Brunsuerdus 3945; Burton, W., Minister at Reading 4178; Butterfield, S. 4206; Caesar, Caius Julius 4333, 4336; Calvin 4379(?); Cambridge University, Act Verses 4474.4(+?), 4474.15(+?), 4474.20(+?), 4474.24(+?), 4474.34(+?), 4474.57(+?), 4474.62(+?), 4474.67(+?), 4474.69(+?), 4474.74(+?), 4474.77(+?), 4474.94(+?), 4474.106(+?), 4474.113(+?), 4474.117(+?), 4474.131(+?), 4474.135 (+?); Camden 4505; Canterbury 4579; Castalio or Chateillon 4771.4; Catechism 4803.3; Ceporinus 4913.5; Charles Emmanuel I. 5045.5; Chassanion 5061(?); Chytraeus 5265; Cicero 5266.6, 5299.8; Clement, J. 5400.3; Clenardus or Cleynaerts 5402.5; Clever, W., Writer on Physic 5412; Codomannus 5471, 5471a; Conscience 5633.3(?); Constable, H. 5638.9; Cope, A. 5721; Copy 5744; Corro 5790; Cotton, Roger 5866; Damman 6217; Daneau 6228(?); Daunce 6290, 6291; Davidson, J., Minister of Salt-Preston 6322; Davies, J., Versifier 6363; Day, R. 6431; Deios 6475; Dent, A. 6658; Dering 6676(?), 6680.5, 6680.7(?), 6682.5(?), 6715.4, 6730, 6730.5, 6731, 6731.3*, 6732, 6733; Desainliens or Sainliens 6762.5; Digby, E. 6842; Digges, L. 6849; Du Chesne 7277; Dudley, R. 7284; Dyer, J. 7384.7(c.?); Edwards, R. 7520.5(?); England, Appendix 10004; England, C. of, Articles 10044; England, C. of, Visit. Articles 10377; England, Customs 7690; England, Privy Council 7754;

1590 — *cont.*
England, Proclamations, Chron. Ser. 8048(c.?), 8189.7, 8191, 8192, 8192.5*, 8193, 8195, 8196*, 8197, 8198, 8199, 8199.3(o.s.), 8199.5; Fenne 10763; Fenner, D. 10776, 10777; Ferris 10834; Finch, R. 10877.5, 10878; France 11265, 11267.5, 11268, 11272, 11287.5; Gentilis 11734; Gibbon or Gybbon 11816; Gifford, G. 11862, 11869; Greene, R. 12251, 12253, 12307; Greenwood, J., of St. Catharine's Col., Camb. 12338; Greenwood, J., Puritan 12339, 12340*; Hariot 12786; Harris, Edward 12804; Harvey, R. 12915; Henry IV, King of France 13113, 13113.5, 13114, 13126, 13128, 13130a.5, 13131, 13135, 13139, 13141.4, 13141.7, 13144, 13145, 13146; Hermanni 13215; Hesiod 13248.8; Holland, Henry, Vicar of St. Bride's 13590; Hood, R. 13692(c.?); Hood, T. 13697, 13699; Hooke, C. 13702; Howard, C. 13855.6; Hurault, M. 14001 [not STC], 14001a, 14002; James I, appendix 14425.3; James, W. 14464; Jeninges 14486; John, Chrysostom 14636; Jonston 14785; Josephus 14814; Josiah 14815(?); L., I. or J. 15107; La Ramee 15250; Lant 15222; Laurence 15316.5; Leech, John, Schoolmaster 15374.2(c.?), 15374.3(c.?); Lily, W., 'Lily's Grammar' 15622.3; Lincoln 15645; Lipsius 15698, 15699*, 15700.7; Liturgies, C. of Eng., BCP 16314a, 16314a.5(?), 16315(c.); Liturgies, C. of Eng., Spec. Prayers 16522, 16523, 16523.3, 16523.5(?), 16523.7; Liturgies, C. of Eng., St. Services 16482(?); Lloyd, L. 16619, 16621; Lodge 16664, 16674.5; London, Appendix 16763(?); London, Pewterers 16782(bef.); Looking-glass 16802.7(c.); Lucar 16890; Lupton, T. 16957.5(c.); Lydgate 17029; Lyly 17058(?); Man 17238; Margaret, of Angouleme 17322.5; Marlowe 17425; Marten 17490; Mascall 17572, 17577; Mela 17786*; Melville, A. 17809; Morice 18106(?); Muffet 18247; Munday 18273; Nash, T. 18365; Nelson, T. 18423, 18424; Newnham 18498; Nowell, Middle Catechism 18715.5; Paris 19197; Parsons, R. 19380; Pasquil 19450; Payne, R. 19491; Pearston 19520; Peele, G. 19546; Penry 19603, 19612; Perkins, W. 19655, 19709, 19752(?), 19752.3(?), 19752.5(?); Pettie 19821(c.); Phillips, John 19873, 19875.3; Piscator 19955.5*; R., James 20579.5(?); R., L. 20582.5; Record, R. 20803; Regius 20845; Remonstrance 20881; Report 20889.7; Rider, T. 21037(?); Roberts, Henry 21078; Roesslin 21159.5(c.)(A/C); Rogers, Thomas, M. A. 21238, 21240; Rollock, R. 21278; Rome 21293; Roscio 21319.3, 21319.7; Russell, J., Edinburgh Advocate 21459; S., C. 21482; Safeguard 21546.5, 21547; Saluste du Bartas 21669; Sansovino 21744, 21744a; Saravia 21746; Saxton 21805.5(?); Scotland, Church of, Confession of Faith 22023; Segar 22163; Sidney, P. 22539, 22539a; Smell-knave 22645(?); Smith, H., Minister, Single Works 22680, 22693, 22694, 22694.5, 22695, 22695.5, 22712.5, 22713, 22713.5, 22714(?); Smythe 22883; Song 22919(c.); Spagnuoli 22984; Spenser, E. 23078*, 23080, 23081, 23081a; Stanford 23217; Stockwood 23280; Stow 23325.2; Stubbe Peter 23375; Suckling, E. 23419.5; Sutcliffe, M. 23471*; Swinburne 23547*; T., T. 23628; T., W. 23633(c.), 23633a; Table 23633a.5(c.); Tabula 23641.5(c.); Taffin 23652; Tarlton 23685; Treasure 24197.3; Trigge 24279; Tusser 24383; Twyne, J. 24407; Ubaldini 24481, 24481a; Valdes, A. 24569, 24569.5; Valdes, F. 24570; Vallans 24590; Vaughan, E. 24597; Vaux 24627a; Verro 24689, 24689.5; Via 24695a.5(c.); Watkins 25107(c.); Watson, T., Poet 25119, 25120, 25121; Webbe, E. 25151.5, 25151.7(A/C), 25152; Welwood 25242; West, W. 25267; Whitaker, W. 25365; Whythorne 25583; Willet 25675; Williams, R. 25732, 25732.5, 25733; Wilson, R. 25783; Windsor 25841, 25841a; Wright, L. 26030.

1591

Aesop 171a; Alexander, Prince of Parma 332, 334; Almanacks (Buckminster or Buckmaster) 423.6; Almanacks (D., J.) 433.5, 433.7; Almanacks (Dade, J.) 434.2; Almanacks (Frende) 444.7, 444.8; Almanacks (Gray) 451.4; Almanacks 403, 403.3; Answer 664; Ariosto 746; Arnheim 781; Augustine 939, 951; B., G. 1026; B., G., Master of Art 1030.7(?); Babington, G. 1092, 1094; Baker, H. 1213; Baldwin, W. 1263; Barlement 1431.11; Barne 1464.8; Barrow 1517(?)*, 1523; Bastingius 1562, 1565(?); Becon 1764.7; Beze 2053; Bible, English 2155, 2156, 2156.5, 2157*; Bible, N.T., English 2890; Bible, O.T., Psalms 2477.7, 2478, 2478.5, 2479, 2479.5;

1591 — *cont.*
Bilbrough 3059.2; Boazio 3171.9; Book 3363.7; Bradshaw, T. 3508; Breton 3633; Brittany 3802.5; Broughton, H. 3888, 3890, 3890.5; Browne, Anthony 3907.5, 3907.7; Browne, J., Merchant 3908.6; Bruce 3923, 3924(?); Burton, W., Minister at Reading 4167; Byrd, W. 4248; Cancellar 4562; Cattan 4864; Caumont 4868; Centurion 4911.7; Chamberlaine 4952; Christian Soul 5192; Churchyard 5253; Cicero 5300, 5315.3; Clapham, J. 5349; Clayton 5376, 5376.2; Clowes 5445; Cockaine 5457; Colynet 5590, 5590.5*; Cosbye 5813, 5814; Cosin, R. 5820; Cottesford, S. 5840; Damon, W. 6220, 6221; Davies, J. 6328; Demosthenes 6575.3; Desainliens or Sainliens 6741.5; Dickenson 6818; Digges, L. 6859; Diguieres 6878; Discourse 6910; Drayton 7199; Du Chesne 7275; Du Jon, F., the Elder 7301; Duport, John 7365.5; Elizabeth I 7583; Em 7675 (?); England, C. of, Injunctions 10105(?); England, C. of, Visit. Articles 10130, 10233; England, Proclamations, Chron. Ser. 8199.3, 8200, 8201, 8201.5, 8202, 8203, 8203.5, 8204, 8206, 8207, 8208, 8209, 8210, 8212, 8213, 8215(o.s.); England, Statutes, Gen. Colls. 9318; England, Yearbooks 9943; F., G. B. A. 10638; Farmer, J. 10698; Feguernekinus 10748; Fenton, E. 10787.3; Fletcher, G., the elder 11056; Florio 11097; Forman 11185; Foulweather 11209, 11210; France 11282.5, 11283, 11290; Fraunce 11338.5, 11339, 11340; Garrard, W. 11625; Geneva 11727; Germany 11789 [not STC], 11795.5; Gibbon or Gybbon 11821; Gifford, G. 11862.3, 11868; Glemham 11921; Grafton 12159; Greene, R. 12241, 12271, 12279, 12279.4, 12279.7, 12281; Grenoble 12359; Guarini 12414; Guicciardini, F. 12461; Habermann 12582.8; Hacket 12589; Heidelberg Catechism 13023; Henisch 13070; Henry IV, King of France 13116, 13116.5, 13142.5; Henry, Prince de Dombes 13156; Herodotus 13225; Homer 13629; Hortop 13827.5, 13828; Howard, C. 13856; Instruction 14106.5; James I 14379; Jewel, J. 14584; John, King 14644; Johnson, Fabian 14657.5; Johnson, Richard 14685.5; Knox 15061; Lambard 15149, 15166; Legh 15391; L'Espine 15510.5; Leyden Univ. 15570*; Linaker 15644; Lisbon 15704; Littleton, T., Tenures, French 15749, 15750; Liturgies, C. of Eng., BCP 16315.5; Lloyd, L. 16632, 16632.5; Lodge 16654, 16657; Loque 16810; Lyly 17049, 17050, 17087; M., Jo. 17143; Manuzio, P. 17288; Mascall 17581; Mayo 17752; Merlin, P. 17842.7; Murders 18286.5; N., I. or J. 18328.5; Nelson, T. 18422.5; Netherlands, States Gen. 18450, 18451; Norris, J. 18654.3, 18655; Openshaw 18830.4*(A/C); Painter, W. 19120.3; Palmer, R. 19154.7; Panke, W. 19172.3; Paradin 19183; Parsons, R. 19381; Partridge, John 19429; Peacham, H., the Elder 19498.5; Peele, G. 19532; Percyvall 19619; Perkins, W. 19655a(?), 19657, 19658(?), 19710, 19753; Phillips, John 19876; Pigge 19916.7; Piscator 19953, 19956; Pitcher 19965; Polanus 20083.5; Porta 20118, 20118a; R., R., of Lincoln's Inn 20588; R., W. 20593; Raleigh 20651; Regius 20853; Ripley 21057; Robinson, Richard 21121.3; Robson, S. 21136; Rollock, R. 21280; Saluste du Bartas 21656; Saravia 21749; Sidney, H. 22533a.5; Sidney, P. 22536, 22537; Smith, H., Minister, Collections 22716, 22783.3(?); Smith, H., Minister, Single Works 22656, 22656.5, 22657, 22659, 22660, 22662, 22662.5, 22663, 22664, 22665, 22681, 22684, 22685, 22685.5, 22686, 22687, 22688, 22689, 22690, 22691, 22696, 22696.5*, 22703, 22703.5, 22705, 22706, 22714.5, 22715, 22715.5; Southwell 22950; Sparke, T. 23019; Spenser, E. 23078*, 23079, 23092; Stepney, W. 23256; Strigelius 23359; Stubbes 23381; Sutcliffe, M. 23458, 23471*, 23472; Swinburne 23547*, 23547.3(A/C); T., W. 23633.5(A/C); Tacitus 23642; Taffin 23652.3; Trial 24274; Trigge 24275; Turnbull, R. 24339; Ubaldini 24487.5, 24488; Ursinus, Z. 24534; Vaughan, E. 24598; Vere 24652; Vincent, Saint 24750; Vinciolo 24765.3; Viques 24767; Virgilius Maro 24822; W., A. 24897; W., R. 24913; Wigand 25613; Wilcox 25626; Williams, R. 25734; Williams, T. 25735; Wilmot 25764; Wright, L. 26032; Zutphen 26134, 26134.5.

1592

A., L. T. 7; Aesop 171a.3; Aldem 287.5; Almanacks (Dade, J.) 434.3; Almanacks (Digges) 435.55; Almanacks (Frende) 444.9; Andrewes, L. 629; Arcandam 726; Arden, T. 733; Arthington 799; Assize of Bread 870; B., G. 1027; B., G., Master of Art 1030.5; Babington, G. 1086; Barlaamus 1430; Barlement 1431.12; Barrow, H. 1521(A/C), 1522a(?)(A/C); Barwick, H. 1542(?)(A/C); Beda 1777; Beze 2003; Bible, English 2157*, 2158, 2158.5; Bible, Latin 2061*; Bible, N.T., English 2891; Bible, N.T., Gospels 2988; Bible, N.T., Greek 2794; Bible, O.T., Psalms 2400.5, 2480, 2481, 2481.5, 2482; Bourne, W. 3427; Brasbridge 3552, 3552.5; Bravonius 3593; Breton 3683; Broughton, H. 3845, 3873; Buchanan 3985; Burton, W., Minister at Reading 4170; Calvin 4440; Camden 4495.5; Canisius 4571.5(+); Case, J. 4763; Castalio or Chateillon 4771.5; Cato 4848; Churchyard 5231, 5237; Colfe 5551; Colonna 5577, 5578, 5578.2; Constable, H. 5637; Cony-Catcher 5654.5, 5656; Cordier 5759.2; Cosin, R. 5823; Cotton, Roger 5867, 5867.3*; Counsel 5871.3, 5871.4; Cupper 6125; Curtius Rufus 6146; Daniel, S. 6243.2, 6243.3; Day, A. 6402; De Beau Chesne and Baildon 6448.5(c.); Delamothe 6545.5; Demosthenes 6575.5; Des Periers 6784.7; Digges, L. 6851; Dyer, J. 7389; Eliot 7575; Elizabeth I 7600; England, Appendix 10005; England, C. of, Visit. Articles 10215.5, 10268.2; England, Proclamations, Chron. Ser. 8215, 8216, 8217, 8218, 8220, 8221, 8222, 8223, 8224, 8225; England, Public Documents, Misc. 9199; England, Statutes, Abridgements/Extracts 9531; Example 10611; Faust 10711; Fenner, D. 10769; Fian 10841a(?), 10842(?), 10842.3(?); Figueiro 10865; Fisher, W. 10919; France 11260, 11270, 11273.5, 11277.5, 11285; Fraunce 11341; Gager 11515, 11516; Greene, R. 12223, 12234, 12245, 12261, 12280, 12282, 12283, 12283.5, 12286, 12296, 12300, 12300.5, 12300.7, 12301a, 12301a.3, 12301a.5, 12301a.7, 12306; Gyer 12561; H., E. 12563; Haddon 12597.5; Hamond, J. 12734.7; Harman 12789, 12789.5; Harvey, G. 12899.5, 12900, 12900.5; Harward 12923; Henry IV, King of France 13130, 13133, 13147; Herrey 13228b.11; Hill, Adam 13466; Holme, J. 13601; Hood, T. 13696.5 (?), 13698; Horatius Flaccus 13787, 13787a; Huarte 13889.5(?); Hunnis 13977.5; Hurault, M. 14005; Instruction 14106.8; Jack, T. 14293; Johann Justus 14626.5(+); Johnson, Richard 14685.7, 14686; Kitchen 15021; Kyd 15086, 15095; La Ramee 15241.3, 15244.3; Lambard 15167; Latimer 15288; Lee, G. 15353.7; Leigh, V. 15419; Lemnius 15454.5; L'Espine 15511, 15516; Lily, W., 'Lily's Grammar' 15622.7*; Lindsay, Sir D. 15663; Lipsius 15694.3, 15696, 15702, 15703; Littleton, T., Tenures, Engl. 15774*; Liturgies, C. of Eng., BCP 16316, 16316.5(?), 16317; Lodge 16656, 16665; London, Appendix 16767; Luis 16909; Lycophron 17002; Lyly 17074.5, 17080, 17083; Macropedius 17176.2; Maisonneuve 17206; Manwood 17290(?); Marconville 17313(c.); Mascall 17578, 17579.5*; Masterson 17648; Molyneux 18003.3, 18003.4; Mornay 18138, 18150; Muffet 18245; Nash, T. 18371, 18372, 18373, 18377, 18377a; Netherlands, Southern Prov. 18464.5; Norden 18617.3; Norman 18649; Oxford Univ., Verses, etc. 19017.5; Palingenius 19143; Palladius 19152.5; Parsons, R. 19382*(A/C), 19412.5; Perkins, W. 19656, 19656.5, 19660, 19661, 19661.5, 19665, 19665.5, 19666, 19699.5, 19700, 19710.5, 19735, 19735.2, 19753.5; Pernius 19767 [not STC]; Philopatris, J. 19885; Piscator 19957.7; Plato 19974.6; Plutarch 20054.7; Querimonia 20556; Rastell, J., Printer 20708; Rhys 20966; Rich, B. 20977, 20977.5; Roberts, Henry 21087.3; Rolland 21255*; Saluste du Bartas 21672; Sanford 21733; Saravia 21750; Scotland, proclamations 21949.7(A/C); Seaman 22140; Seminary Priests 22185; Smith, H., Minister, Collections 22717, 22718, 22775.3, 22783.5, 22783.7; Smith, H., Minister, Single Works 22678, 22683, 22692, 22697, 22704, 22707, 22708, 22708.5; Sohn 22891; Soliman 22894(?); Song 22923; Southwell 22950.5; Steenwyk 23241; Stockwood 23283; Stow 23334; Stubbes 23382, 23398; Sum 23432; Sutcliffe, M. 23450, 23455; Table 23634; Talaeus 23659.3; Tanner, R. 23671; Tarlton 23683; Telin 23867; Temple, R. 23869; Thomas, a Kempis 23979, 23995; Thomas, T. 24009; Thorne, W. 24042; Turnbull, R. 24339.5, 24340; Tymme 24418; Ubaldini 24479; Verepaeus 24653; Vives 24863; W., A. 24899; W., R. 24913a; Warner, W. 25081; Watson, T., Poet 25117; West, W. 25267.5, 25267.7, 25267a; Willet 25695(?), 25696; Wilmot 25764a; Wilson, R. 25785; Windsor 25841a.5; Wyrley 26062; Zanchius 26119.5.

1593

A. 1; Almanacks (Buckminster or Buckmaster) 423.8; Almanacks (Carre) 428; Almanacks (Frende) 444.10; Almanacks (Gray) 451.6; Anderson, A. 566; Answer 662; Aristophanes 751; Augustine 930.3, 930.7; B., G. 1034; Balmford 1335; Bancroft, R. 1344, 1344.5, 1352; Barlement 1431.13; Barnaud 1464.7; Barnes, B. 1469; Bell, T. 1830; Bible, English 2159, 2160*; Bible, Latin 2061*, 2061.5; Bible, N.T., English 2892; Bible, O.T., Psalms 2483, 2483.5, 2484, 2484.3, 2484.5, 2485; Bilson 3063, 3065; Blundeville 3155; Burton, W., Minister at Reading 4166; Butler, Master, of Oundle 4202; Byrd, W. 4250(?); Cambridge University, Act Verses 4474.84(?); Castiglione 4785; Charles [de Lorraine], Duc de Mayenne 5012; Chettle 5123(?); Christian 5152; Christians 5202; Churchyard 5220, 5248; Chute 5262; Cicero 5266.8; Clement Francis 5399.8; Cosin, R. 5821, 5822; Coverdale 5891; Cowell 5898; De Beau Chesne 6445.3(c.); Defence 6467; Dering 6707; Desainliens or Sainliens 6737, 6742; Dodritius 6989 [not STC]; Drayton 7202; Eliot 7574; England, C. of, Appendix 10400(?); England, C. of, Articles 10045, 10046; England, Local Courts 7721.5; England, Proclamations, Chron. Ser. 8226, 8226.5, 8229, 8230, 8231, 8232, 8233, 8234, 8235; England, Public Documents, Misc. 9200, 9200.3; England, Statutes, Chron. Ser. 9489, 9490, 9491, 9492 [not STC]; Fale 10678; Ferrier 10833, 10833a; Fitzherbert, A. 10981; Fletcher, G., the elder 11055; Fleur de Lys 11088; Flory 11105.5; Foulface 11208; France 11288; Fregeville 11371; Fulwood 11481; G., M. 11500; Garnet 11617.2, 11617.4(+), 11617.8; Gentilis 11732; Gifford, G. 11850; Grafton 12160; Greene, R. 12259, 12263, 12270; Guicciardini, L. 12463; Habermann 12582.9; Harvey, G. 12902, 12903; Harvey, R. 12913; Henry IV, King of France 13117; Henry, the Minstrel 13150*; Henryson 13165; Heyton 13284.5(?); Hill, T. 13496; Holland, Henry, Vicar of St. Bride's 13588; Hooker, R. 13712; Hutchins 14012; Jeninges 14487; Joseph, ben Gorion 14801; Kellwaye 14917; Ker 14937, 14938; Kis 15015.3, 15015.7, 15016; Lauziere 15317; Lily, W., 'Lily's Grammar' 15622.8(A/C); Lipsius 15699*; Littleton, T., Tenures, Engl. 15774*; Liturgies, C. of Eng., Spec. Prayers 16524; Lodge 16659, 16662; Lok 16697; London, Carpenters 16768.20; London, Ords. and Regs. 16713.5; London, Pewterers 16783; Lyly 17059(?); Lysias 17121; Manual 17264.5(c.); Markham, G. 17346; Marlowe 17426; Martinius 17523; Middleton, W., Capt. 17914; More, J. 18074; Morley, T. 18121; Mornay 18135; Napier 18354; Nash, T. 18366, 18374, 18377b, 18377b.5, 18378, 18378a; Norden 18617.5(A/C), 18635; Nowell, Middle Catechism 18716, 18733.5; Ovidius Naso 18960; Parsons 19382(?)*(A/C); Peacham, H., the Elder 19498; Peele, G. 19535, 19539; Penry 19608(?), 19610; Perkins, J. 19639; Perkins, W. 19688, 19689(?), 19700.5, 19701, 19758; Piscator 19958; Platt 19977; Rainolds, W. 20633; Regius 20846; Rollock, R. 21267; S., L. 21508; S., R. 21516; Saint German 21575; Salesbury, H. 21611; Sampson, T., Dean of Christ Church 21684; Saravia 21747; Scotland, statutes, etc. 21888; Seager 22137; Shakespeare, W. 22354; Sidney, P. 22540; Smith, H., Minister, Collections 22719, 22775.7; Smith, H., Minister, Single Works 22666, 22697.5, 22700.5, 22701.5, 22709; Southerne 22942; Spagnuoli 22984.1; Spain 22994; Sparke, T. 23024; Straw 23356*; Strigelius 23360; Stubbes 23397; Sutcliffe, M. 23468; Tarlton 23685a(?)(A/C); Tell-Troth 23867.5; Thomas, T. 24009.5; Trogus Pompeius 24288; Tusser 24384; Udall, J. 24494; Virgilius Maro 24790.7; Warboys 25018.5, 25019; Watson, T., Poet 25122; Werdmueller 25259; West, W. 25276.3; Whetstone, G. 25338; Whiting, G. 25433.7; Wilkinson, R. 25652.5; Willet 25701; Wimbledon 25833, 25834*.

1594

Abbot, R., Bp. 52; Adventures 153.3(?); Almanacks (Dade, J.) 434.5; Almanacks (Frende) 444.11; Almanacks (Westhawe) 526; Almanacks 403.7(?); Aphthonius 701.5; Apollonius 709, 709.5; Arnauld 779, 779.5; Arthington 796; B., O. 1054; Barnfield 1480, 1487; Beacon 1653; Becon 1765; Beze 2053.5; Bible, English 2160*, 2161*, 2162*, 2163, 2164; Bible, N.T., Gospels 2989; Bible, N.T.,

1594 — *cont.*

Latin 2810a.3, 2810a.5; Bible, O.T., 'Books of Solomon' 2770; Bible, O.T., Psalms 2486, 2487, 2487.3, 2487.6, 2488; Bible, Selections 3011.5; Blundeville 3146; Book 3298; Broughton, H. 3861(?), 3885, 3887(?); Bulmer 4087.4(?); Burton, W., Minister at Reading 4168.5, 4169, 4174; Byrd, W. 4249(?); Calvin 4387; Camden 4506; Chapman, G. 4990; Churchyard 5242; Cicero 5266.9; Clarke, T., Seminary Priest of English College at Rheims 5366; Clenardus or Cleynaerts 5403; Clerke, W. 5411; Constable, H. 5638(?); Counsel 5871.5; Crompton, R. 6050; Cyrus 6160; Daneau 6227; Daniel, S. 6243.4; Death 6443; Dent, A. 6625.4; Dickenson 6817; Dove 7086, 7086.5(?); Drayton 7203, 7205, 7206, 7214(?); Du Vair 7373.4; Elizabeth I 7580, 7603, 7603.5; England, Appendix 9976.5; England, C. of, Visit. Articles 10137.2, 10209, 10234, 10314; England, Proclamations, Chron. Ser. 7927, 8089(?), 8236, 8237, 8238.5, 8240; England, Public Documents, Misc. 9201; England, Statutes, Gen. Colls. 9319; Faust 10715, 10715.3; Fowler, W. 11214.2, 11214.4(?), 11214.6, 11214.7; Garnier, R. 11622; Gibbon or Gybbon 11819; Gifford, G. 11870; Grassi 12190; Greaves, P. 12208, 12208.2; Greene, R. 12220, 12265, 12267, 12310a; Groningen 12392.5; Guevara 12448.5; H., T. 12578.5; Har. 12751; Hartgyll 12895, 12896; Hauwenreuther 12938; Henry IV, King of France 13118, 13130a, 13138; Henry, the Minstrel 13150*; Herrey 13228b.12; Hester, J. 13253; Hill, T. 13488; Holland, Robert 13595; Huarte 13890, 13890.5, 13891, 13892; Hues 13906; Hume, A., Minister of Logie 13941.5, 13943, 13944; Hume, A., Schoolmaster 13948; Jewel, J. 14605; Knack 15027; Kyd 15087; L., R. 15109; La Marche 15139; La Noue, O. 15216; La Primaudaye 15235, 15238; Lambard 15150, 15151, 15168; Le Roy, L. 15488; Lewes 15556; Lily, W., 'Lily's Grammar' 15622.7*; Lindsay, Sir D. 15679; Lipsius 15694.7*, 15701; Littleton, T., Tenures, Engl. 15775; Littleton, T., Tenures, French 15751; Liturgies, C. of Eng., BCP 16318, 16318.5(?), 16428, 16428.5; Liturgies, C. of Eng., Spec. Prayers 16525, 16525.3, 16525.7; Liturgies, Other Protest. C. 16584, 16584.5; Loarte 16644.5; Lodge 16678; Lodge and Greene 16679; Lyly 17084; Malbie 17211; Marlowe 17423(?), 17437; Marlowe and Nash 17441; Masterson 17648.3; Melville, A. 17807; Monipennie 18016(?); More, J. 18074.5; Morel 18100; Moresinus 18102, 18102a; Morley, T. 18127; Mundy 18284; Napier 18355; Nash, T. 18367, 18379, 18380, 18381; Netherlands, States Gen. 18451.5; Norden 18626a.1, 18638.5; Norris, J. 18654; O., I. 18755; Orchard 18838; Ovidius Naso 18929; P., S. 19078.4; Parker, Matthew 19287; Parry, H. 19336; Parsons, R. 19365, 19383, 19398*; Pasquier 19448; Peele, G. 19531; Pelegromius 19557.3; Percy, W. 19618; Perez 19624.5; Phillips, G. 19858; Phillips, John 19863.7; Piscator 19948, 19957; Platt 19991, 19991.5, 19992; Plowden 20047; Powel, Griffinus 20157; R., H. 20572; Record, R. 20803.5; Regius 20854; Remedies 20874; Renichon 20885; Rich, B. 20996.7; Richard III 21009; Rollock, R. 21268, 21275; Rosenburg 21321; Saravia 21748; Saviolo 21788*; Scotland, statutes, etc. 21889; Shakespeare, W. 22328, 22345, 22355; Smith, H., Minister, Collections 22720, 22720.5, 22776, 22777; Smith, H., Minister, Single Works 22698, 22698.5, 22699, 22701, 22701.3, 22702, 22702.3; Smith, T., Doctor of Civil Laws 22860; Smythe 22884; Southwell 22951; Spagnuoli 22991.5; Spain 22996, 22997; Sparke, T. 23023; Straw 23356*; Sylvester 23579; Taming 23667; Tasso, T. 23697, 23697a; Thomas, T. 24010; Throkmorton 24055, 24055.5; Trigge 24277; Ubaldini 24485; Valera 24582; Vaughan, E. 24599; Virel 24767.5, 24768; W., A. 24898; Watson, T., Poet 25118; West, W. 25268, 25276.5, 25276.7; Whitaker, W. 25363; Willet 25697; Willoby 25755; Wilson, R. 25781; Withals 25882; Writing Tables 26049.16; York, House of 26099; Zepheria 26124.

1595

Adrichem 152; Albertus Magnus 263; Alessio 312; Almanacks (Buckminster or Buckmaster) 424, 424.3, 424.4; Almanacks (Dade, J.) 434.6; Almanacks (Frende) 445; Almanacks (Gray) 451.8; Almanacks (Watson) 525; Almanacks (Westhawe) 526.5; Amadis 542; Andrewes, B. 585a; Aristotle 762, 763; Assize of Bread 871; B.,

1595 — *cont.*
R. 1060; B., W. 1072.5; Babington, G. 1089; Balmford 1335.3(c.); Banchieri 1343; Barlement 1431.14; Barnes, B. 1467; Barnfield 1483, 1484; Bastingius 1566; Beze 2054; Bible, English 2165, 2166, 2167; Bible, N.T., English 2893; Bible, N.T., Irish 2958(+?)*; Bible, O.T., Psalms 2489, 2490, 2490.2, 2490.3, 2490.4, 2490.5, 2492*, 2742.5(c.); Bible, Selections 3012; Blanchardine 3125; Boaistuau 3167; Book 3314; Borgetto 3388; Bownd, Nicholas 3436; Breton 3665; Broughton, H. 3859(?), 3859.5(?), 3874.5; Buchanan 3979.5(?); Bullein 4042; Bunny, F. 4098, 4101, 4102; Burton, W., Minister at Reading 4176, 4176.2; Byrd, W. 4251(?), 4256.5(?)*; C., E., Esquire 4268; C., I. or J. 4274.5; C., T. 4306; C., W., Bachelor of Civil Law 4323.2; Calvin 4372.5; Camden 4511; Campion 4544; Chamberlaine 4946.8; Chapman, G. 4985; Chappell, B. 4999; Chardon 5000; Chatel 5066, 5067; Chettle 5124; Christians 5197; Churchyard 5245; Chute 5262.5; Cicero 5267, 5300.4; Cipriano 5324, 5324.3, 5324.5, 5324.7; Clapham, H. 5345.7; Constable, H. 5638.3(?); Copley, A. 5738; Covell 5883, 5884; Dando and Runt 6225; Daniel, S. 6243.5, 6244, 6244.3; Davidson, J., Minister of Salt-Preston 6324; Davis or Davys, J. 6368.4, 6372; Day, A. 6403; Delamothe 6546; Demosthenes 6575.7(?); Dent, A. 6658.2; Dering 6715.7; Dicker 6820.5; Dictionary 6832.54; Digby, E. 6840; Dodoens 6986; Drayton 7192, 7214.5(?); Du Jon, F., the Elder 7299; Duncan 7351*, 7352; Dyer, J. 7385(c.?); Edinburgh, Presbytery 7485.5; Edwards, T. 7525; Elizabeth I 7581; Elyot, T. 7656; England, C. of, Injunctions 10108; England, C. of, Visit. Articles 10131, 10139.7(?); England, Proclamations, Chron. Ser. 8239, 8241, 8242, 8243, 8244, 8245, 8245.5, 8246, 8247, 8247.2, 8247.4, 8247.6; England, Public Documents, Misc. 9201.5, 9202; England, Statutes, Gen. Colls. 9320; English Soldiers 10418; Fetherstone, C. 10836; Fiston 10922, 10922.5; Fletcher, A. 11053; France 11276; Garnier, R. 11622a, 11623; Gosson 12096; Grafton 12161; Greene, R. 12287; Greenham 12319, 12321, 12325; Guevara 12449; Guicciardini, F. 12462; H., B. 12562; Hasleton 12924.5, 12925; Hawkins, J., of Crawley 12960; Henry IV, King of France 13119; Hill, Adam 13465; Homilies 13658, 13674; Hubbocke 13898; Hunnis 13973; Hurault, J. 14000; I., S. A. 14062; I., S. 14057; I., T. 14068.5; Introduction 14121.5; Ireland, Proc. 14145, 14145a; Jersey 14516.5; Jesus Christ 14566.5(+?); Jewel, J. 14595; Johann Justus 14627; Johnson, E. 14657(?); Johnson, Francis 14663.5; Johnson, T., Misc. writer 14707, 14708.3; La. 15115.5; Le Roy, P. 15489; Lewkenor, L. 15562, 15563, 15564; Linaker 15638; Lipsius 15694.7*, 15695; Littleton, T., Tenures, French 15752(?); Liturgies, C. of Eng., BCP 16320, 16320.3(?), 16320.5; Liturgies, Other Protest. C. 16585*; Lodge 16658; London, Appendix 16763.3(c.); London, Ords. and Regs. 16715, 16716, 16717, 16718.3 (c.); Lupton, T. 16958, 16958.5; Lycophron 17003; Macchiavelli 17162; Macropedius 17176.3; Manual 17265(c.); Manuzio, A. 17280; Markham, G. 17347, 17385; Masterson 17648.7; Maunsell 17669; Mayfield 17748; Medina 17772; Minadoi 17943; Moore, R. 18061; Morley, T. 18116, 18118, 18119; Mosse 18207, 18208; Murders 18289; N., C. 18326; Nash, T. 18375; Nenna 18428; Nichols, Josias 18539.5; Norden 18617.6(A/C), 18641.2; Norwich, Diocese of 18689; Nowell, Larger Catechism 18706a; Nowell, Middle Catechism 18717; Oat-meale 18758; Oteringham 18895.5; Parry, R. 19337; Parsons, R. 19398*; Partridge, John 19434; Patriarchs 19468.5; Peele, G. 19545; Perkins, W. 19662, 19667, 19702a, 19703, 19711, 19742, 19754, 19754.3, 19760, 19760.5; Perry 19775; Philips, J. 19855; Phillips, G. 19859, 19861.3; Pietro 19912(c.)*; Piscator 19949, 19954; Platt 19988; Plautus 20002; Playfere 20014, 20014.3, 20014.5; Plutarch 20058, 20067, 20067.5; Polanus 20083.7; Pont-aymery 20106.5; Prayer 20190(c.); Preston, T., Dramatist 20288(c.); Primaleon 20366; R., R. 20587.5; Racster 20599; Rastell, J., Printer 20709; Ravisius 20763; Registrum 20838; Richard, Duke of York 21006; Roberts, Henry 21083, 21086, 21088; Robinson, C. 21105.5(?); Rolland 21255*; Romans 21288; Rome 21294; Rudolf II 21441.7; S., W. 21528; Sabie 21535, 21536, 21537; Saint Andrews Univ. 21555.1; Saluste du Bartas 21658, 21662; Saviolo 21788*, 21789; Schonaeus 21821; Shakespeare, W. 22356(?); Shepherds' Kalendar 22418(?); Sidney, P. 22534, 22534.5, 22535; Smith, H., Minister, Collections 22721, 22747.3(?); Smith, H., Minister, Single Works 22677, 22679; Smith, John, Minister at Reading 22797; Smythe 22885; Solace 22891.5; Southwell 22949.5*, 22955, 22955.3, 22955.5, 22955.7, 22956, 22957, 22971; Spagnuoli 22984.2(A/C); Spenser, E. 23076, 23077; Strigelius 23361; Stubbes 23379; Student 23401.5; Sutcliffe, M. 23451; Taffin 23650; Trigge 24277.5; Trussell, J. 24296; Turner, Richard 24345 (?); Ubaldini 24484; Udall, J. 24495; Ursinus, Z. 24535; Vienna 24716.5; Virel 24768.5; Wales 24956.3(c.); Webbe, E. 25153(?) (A/C); Werdmueller 25254(?), 25260; Wilcox 25629; Wilson, R. 25782; Wolcomb 25941.5; Woodstreet Counter 25969(c.).

1596

Aesop 172, 182; Agas 195, 195.5(c.); Allen, R. 362; Almanacks (Buckminster or Buckmaster) 424.5; Almanacks (Digges) 435.57; Almanacks (Frende) 445.1; Antonio, Prior of Crato 690; Aphthonius 702; Apuleius 720; B., M. 1053; Babington, G. 1084, 1087, 1091, 1098; Baldwin, W. 1264; Barley 1433; Barrough 1510; Barrow 1519(c.?); Bathe 1589(?); Bell, T. 1828, 1829; Bible, English 2162*, 2167.5, 2169*; Bible, N.T., English 2894, 2894.3, 2894.5; Bible, N.T., Gospels 2990; Bible, N.T., Spanish 2959; Bible, O.T., Prophets 2785; Bible, O.T., Psalms 2490.6, 2490.7, 2490.8, 2701; Bigges 3057.3; Blagrave 3117, 3120; Boazio 3171.5; Book 3355; Bourne, W. 3428; Bristow, R. 3801(+); Bull, H. 4032; Burel 4105(?); Burton, W., Minister at Reading 4171, 4174.5; Busche 4182; Calvin 4374, 4391.5; Cartwright, T. 4706; Case, J. 4758, 4760; Celestina 4910; Chapman, J. 4997; Chartier 5060; Churchyard 5238, 5249, 4254; Cicero 5286, 5309.6; Ciotti 5323a.8; Clapham, H. 5332, 5345.4, 5345.9; Clowes 5445.5; Codomannus 5472; Cogan 5481; Colse 5582; Comines 5602; Coote 5711; Copley, A. 5737, 5739; Cortes 5803; Cotton, Roger 5865, 5865.5, 5869; Davies, Sir J. 6360; Dawson, T. 6392; Delgadillo de Avellaneda 6551; Dering 6708; Desainliens or Sainliens 6749.6; Dickenson 6820(?); Dowriche, H. 7160; Drake 7160.8; Drayton 7207, 7208, 7232; Edinburgh University 7487.1; Edward III 7501; Edward IV 7503; Edwards, R. 7521; England, Appendix 9977; England, Proclamations, Chron. Ser. 8247.8, 8248, 8249, 8250, 8251, 8253, 8253.3*, 8254, 8255, 8255.5; England, Public Documents, Misc. 9203, 9204, 9205, 9205.3, 9206, 9207, 9208; England, Statutes, Abridgements/Extracts 9531.5; England, Yearbooks 9552; F., I. or J. 10638.5; Fitz-Geffrey, C. 10943, 10944; Foxe 11226; G., C. 11492; Garnet 11617.5(+); Gerard, J. 11748; Gifford, G. 11866; Goeurot 11976; Gosson 12096.5; Grafton 12162; Greene, R. 12246; Griffin 12367; Gryndall 12412; Habermann 12582.10; Harington 12771.5, 12772, 12773.5, 12773.7, 12774, 12774.5, 12774.7, 12779, 12779.5, 12780, 12781, 12782, 12783; Harward 12919; Hastings, H. 12929; Heresbach 13199; Hill, R. 13478; Hofmann 13555.7; Holland, Henry, Vicar of St. Bride's 13586; Homilies 13680.9, 13681, 13681.3; Hood, T. 13701; Horne, C. 13817; Huarte 13893; Hutton, L. 14029; Jesus Christ 14567; Johnson, Richard 14677; Johnson, T., Misc. writer 14708; Joseph, ben Gorion 14802; Keymis 14947; Knack 15028; La Vardin 15318; Lambard 15176; Latimer 15281; Lavater 15321, 15322; Lazarillo 15337, 15340; Le Fevre 15379*; Leigh, V. 15420; Levens 15533.3*; Lewkenor, L. 15565; Lily, W., 'Lily's Grammar' 15623*; Liturgies, C. of Eng., BCP 16321, 16321.5, 16321a, 16321a.5, 16322*; Liturgies, C. of Eng., Ordinal 16466.5; Liturgies, C. of Eng., Spec. Prayers 16526, 16527, 16527.5; Liturgies, Other Protest. C. 16585*, 16585.5; Loarte 16642(+), 16645.7(+); Lodge 16655, 16660, 16662a, 16662b, 16666, 16677; London, Ords. and Regs. 16703, 16703.5*; Lopez de Gomara 16808; Lowe 16872; Luis 16909.5; Lycosthenes 17003.7; Lynche 17091; M., C. 17126.5, 17127; Manual 17265.5, 17265.7(?) (A/C); Manual or Meditation 17278.6(c.); Markham, G. 17347.5, 17386; Mascall 17579, 17582, 17592; Mavericke 17683; Middleton, C. 17867; Monardes 18007; Monings 18013; More, J. 18073; Morletus 18114; Morton, T., of Berwick 18197.3, 18197.7, 18199; Muffet 18246; Nash, T. 18369; Netherlands 18433.7; Nichols, Josias 18540; Norden 18604, 18633, 18638; Norman 18650; Nun,

1596 — *cont.*
T. 18748; Orchard 18839; Palmerin, of England 19161; Paracelsus 19180, 19181.7; Parsons, R. 19365.5; Partridge, John 19429.5; Pathway 19464; Perkins, W. 19685, 19696, 19702a.5, 19704, 19742.5; Perrott, J. 19772.5; Peters, N. 19799; Phillips, G. 19856.3, 19861.5; Pinner 19945a(?); Piscator 19952; Pius II 19974; Platt 19996; Playfere 20015, 20020; Primaleon 20366a; R., P. 20585.7; Rainolds, J. 20606; Raleigh 20634, 20635, 20636; Rastell, W. 20732; Record, R. 20797, 20804; Remedies 20869; Ripon 21057.5; Rollock, R. 21284; Rome 21296; S., R. 21512; Sabie 21534; Saluste du Bartas 21658.5, 21662a; Savile, H. 21783; Schilander 21817; Scotland, Church of, Confession of Faith 22024; Scotland, proclamations 21950, 21951, 21951a, 21952, 21953; Shakespeare, W. 22357; Shelford 22400.5; Smith, H., Minister, Collections 22779; Smith, William, Poet 22872; Some 22913, 22913a; Southwell 22951.5(?), 22972, 22973; Spenser, E. 23082, 23086, 23088; Stanbridge, Vocabula 23189; Strigelius 23362; Sutcliffe, M. 23463; Symondson 23594.5(?); T., A., Practitioner in Physic 23606; T., I. or J. 23620; Taming 23668; Tanner, J. 23670; Thomas, a Kempis 23980; Thomas, T. 24011; Topsell 24127; Treasure 24208; Treatise 24256; Twyne, T. 24409.5; Ubaldini 24483; Udall, J. 24491; Unton 24520, 24520.5; Urstitius 24540; Vicary 24709; Vincent, Saint 24748 (?); Virgilius Maro 24803; Warner, W. 25082; Watson, T., Poet 25118.8; Whitaker, W. 25363.3(A/C); Willet 25702; Willoby 25756*; Wood, J., M. D. 25953; Wright, B. 26018; Wright, L. 26035; Wright, T., Priest 26038.8, 26043.5.

1597

A., G. 3.5; Abraham 80; Achilles Tatius 90; Agatharchides 196; Almanacks (Frende) 445.2; Ariosto 749; Aristotle 764; Arthington 798; Assize of Bread 872; Augustine 944.5; Bacon, F. 1137, 1137.5; Bacon, R. 1182; Bales, P. 1311; Balmford 1336.5; Barker, P. 1426.5; Barlement 1431.15; Barlow, W., Archdeacon of Salisbury 1445; Beard, T. 1659; Becon 1766.3; Bible, English 2168, 2169*, 2170, 2171*, 2172*; Bible, Latin 2062; Bible, N.T., English 2895, 2895.3; Bible, O.T., Prophets 2786; Bible, O.T., Psalms 2491, 2492*, 2492a, 2492a.5; Blagrave 3115.7(?); Blanchardine 3126; Blundeville 3147, 3156; Boccaccio 3184.4; Book 3299; Bossewell 3394; Bradford, J., Prebendary of St. Paul's 3487; Breton 3631, 3632, 3634, 3705, 3713; Brett 3716.5; Brook 3824; Broughton, H. 3845.5(?), 3846, 3862, 3862a; Bruno, V. 3941.5, 3942; Bull, J. 4032.5; Burgundians 4115.5; Butler, C. 4196.5; Caesar, Sir Julius 4341; Calvin 4387a, 4426; Cambridge University, Act Verses 4474.35, 4474.88; Camden 4511.4; Carpenter, J., Minister 4664; Cary, W. 4731.5; Case, J. 4765; Cecil, W., Baron Burghley 4908; Charles Emmanuel I. 5043.5; Clapham, H. 5331, 5346; Clever, W., Preacher 5411.5; Craig, J. 5966; D., I. or J. 6170.7; Damiano 6216; Dawson, T. 6395; Demosthenes 6575; Dering 6677, 6681, 6683, 6716, 6731.3*, 6733.3; Desainliens or Sainliens 6743, 6759; Dove 7087; Dowland, J. 7091; Drayton 7193; Du Bec-Crespin 7263; Duncan 7353; Egerton, S. 7527.9; Elizabeth I 7581.5; England, C. of, Constitutions/Canons 10066, 10066.5*; England, C. of, Visit. Articles 10133.7, 10356; England, Proclamations, Chron. Ser. 8256, 8257, 8258, 8259, 8260, 8261, 8261.5, 8262(o.s.), 8263(o.s.); England, Public Documents, Misc. 9208.2, 9208.3, 9208.4, 9208.5, 9208.6; England, Yearbooks 9903; Fleetwood 11035; Foord or Foorthe, M. A. 11127; Fowler, W. 11214; Foxe 11226a; France 11279; Gardiner, Samuel 11573; Gerard, J. 11750; Gifford, G. 11848.5, 11871; Greene, R. 12225, 12301a.9(A/C); Greenham 12323; Guevara 12451; Guillemeau 12498*; Gurth 12531.5; Hall, Joseph 12716; Harvey, G. 12906; Harward 12920; Herrey 13228b.13; Holborne 13562; Hooker, R. 13712.5; Howson 13881, 13882*(A/C); Hunnis 13978; Ive 14290; James I 14364; John, Chrysostom 14633; Johnson, Richard 14678; King, J., Bp. 14976; Kirbye 15010; L., T. 15111; Langham 15195*; Ledesma 15353; Le Fevre 15379*; Legh 15392; Levens 15533.3*; Lily, W., 'Lily's Grammar' 15623*; Lindsay, Sir D. 15664, 15664.3; Ling 15685; Littleton, T., Tenures, Engl. 15776; Liturgies, C. of Eng., BCP 16322*, 16322.1(?), 16322.2(?); Liturgies, C. of Eng., Spec. Prayers

1597 — *cont.*
16528, 16528.5, 16528a, 16528a.5; Lively 16609; Lok 16696; London, Ords. and Regs. 16704; Lopes 16805; Love 16857; Lowe 16869.5; Lyly 17060(?), 17075, 17090; Man 17231; Margaret, of Angouleme 17323; Markham, G. 17348; Marlowe 17427; Martin, G. 17504(c.)*; Martin, T. 17516; Maurice 17673, 17678; Melville, J. 17815.5; Mendoza, B. 17819; Meres 17833; Middleton, C. 17866; Middleton, T. 17906; Mihil Mumchance 17916; Montgomery 18049, 18049.5; More, Sir G. 18071, 18071.5; More, T. 18096; Morley, T. 18125, 18126, 18133; Morton, T., of Berwick 18200.5; Netherlands, States Gen. 18452; News 18504.5; Norden 18614, 18617.6C(A/C), 18626a.1C(A/C), 18643.3; Nowell, Middle Catechism 18733.7; Orchard 18839.5; Pacius 19083; Padilla y Manrique 19087.5(?); Palmerin, de Oliva 19158; Parry, R. 19338; Parsons, R. 19366; Payne, J. 19489; Perkins, J. 19640; Perkins, W. 19663, 19705, 19712, 19724.5, 19735.8, 19743, 19761; Petau Maulette 19793; Peter, St. 19797; Phillips, G. 19857, 19859a, 19861.7; Pie 19900; Pinner 19945, 19946; Piscator 19955, 19959; Playfere 20016, 20021; Plowden 20037(?)(A/C); Polanus 20083.9; Presse 20207; Rainolds, J. 20612.2; Rollock, R. 21285; Romney Marsh 21312; S., E. 21489; S., I. or J. 21499; Saint Andrews Univ. 21555.2; Salerno 21602; Scotland, statutes, etc. 21877, 21891; Shakespeare, W. 22307, 22314, 22322; Sidney, P. 22538(?); Simeon 22555; Smith, H., Minister, Collections 22722; Southwell 22958, 22968.5(?), 22969(?); Spain 22992.3, 22993; Sparke, T. 23021; Spenser, E. 23093; Stockwood 23281; Sturtevant 23408.2, 23408.6; T., I. or J. 23621; T., T. 23626; Taffin 23652.5; Tanner, J. 23670.5; Terentius 23888; Tessier 23918, 23918.3(A/C); Tofte 24097; Tooker 24118; Top 24122; Topsell 24128; Turkey 24335; Turnbull, C. 24338; Tusser 24385; Ubaldini 24482; Vaughan, W. 24607; Virel 24769; Virgilius Maro 24791; Vulcanius 24893.3; Warner, W. 25082a, 25087; Wedding 25195; Weelkes 25205; West, W. 25268.5, 25277; Wilcox 25630; Williams, J., of Oxford Univ. 25722; Yonge 26095.

1598

Abbot, G., Abp. 36; Adamson, P. 149; Alberti 257; Almanacks (Buckminster or Buckmaster) 424.7; Almanacks (Dade, J.) 434.9; Almanacks (Erra Pater) 439.18(c.)(A/C); Almanacks (Frende) 445.3, 445.4; Almanacks (Grapheus) 450.7; Almanacks (Gray) 451.11; Almanacks (Johnson, T.) 466; Almanacks (Watson) 525.2; Almanacks 403.9; Amadis 542.5; Arcandam 726.3; Aristotle 760; Aungervile 958.5; B., I. or J. 1047(?); Bacon, F. 1138; Baker, H. 1214; Barckley 1381; Barlement 1431.16; Barlow, W., Bp. of Rochester/Lincoln 1460; Barnfield 1485; Barret, R. 1500; Bastard 1559; Belianis 1804; Bell, T. 1823; Beze 1997; Bible, English 2171*, 2172*; Bible, N.T., English 2896, 2896.5; Bible, O.T., Psalms 2362.3, 2368.5, 2402.5*, 2493, 2494, 2494a, 2494a.5, 2495(?); Bible, Selections 2995a.3; Bird, S. 3087, 3088; Bishop, J. 3092; Boiardo 3216; Borde 3378; Brandon, S. 3544; Breton 3696; Broughton, H. 3860; Broxup 3921; Brucioli 3928; Bruto 3947; Burton, W., Minister at Reading 4172, 4176.5; Butler, C. 4197; C., T. 4307; Calvin 4387a.5; Cambridge University 4491.5(+); Camden 4511.7; Carew, R. 4614; Case, J. 4764; Cato 4848.2(A/C); Cavendish, M. 4878; Chapman, G. 4965; Chaucer 5077, 5078, 5079; Chemnitius 5117; Churchyard 5259.5, 5260; Cicero 5267.2; Clapham, H. 5345; Cleaver 5382, 5383; D., I. or J. 6170; Daniel, S. 6243.6; Dariot 6276; Darrell 6281; Dent, A. 6658.4; Dickenson 6819; Drayton 7193.2, 7194; Du Vair 7374; England, C. of, Constitutions/Canons 10066.5(?)*; England, C. of, Visit. Articles 10235, 10253; England, Proclamations, Chron. Ser. 8261.7(?), 8262, 8263, 8264, 8265, 8266, 8268(o.s.); England, Statutes, Chron. Ser. 9492.7, 9493.5, 9494, 9494.3, 9494.5, 9494.7, 9494.11, 9494.12; England, Statutes, Gen. Colls. 9321; Epulario 10433; Farnaby, G. 10700; Fitzherbert, A. 10964; Fitzherbert, J. 11004; Fleming, A. 11043; Fletcher, J. 11062a.5; Florio 11098; Forde, E. 11171; France 11275; Fulwood 11482; Geraldson or Gerritszoon 11747; Gerard, P. 11754; Gifford, G. 11847, 11854, 11859; Gosson 12099; Greene, R. 12308; Greenham 12322; Grimaldus Goslicius 12372; Guillemeau 12498*; Guilpin 12504; Hakluyt 12626*; Hall, Joseph 12717, 12718.5;

1598 — *cont.*
Hamilton, P. 12734; Hastings, F. 12927, 12927.5; Henry V, King of England 13072; Heraclitus, of Ephesus 13174; Herrey 13228b.14; Herring 13239; Heywood, J. 13289; Homer 13632, 13635; Hood, T. 13695; Howson 13883; Hutchins 14013; Hutton, L. 14032; Indagine 14077; Ingmethorp 14086; Jacob, H. 14340; James I 14409; Johnson, Richard, Moralist 14691.1; Joyner 14830.3; Kimedoncius 14959.5, 14960; Kitchen 15022; La Perriere 15228, 15228.5; Langenes 15193; Lasso 15265; Ling 15685.5, 15686, 15686.3; Linschoten 15691; Liturgies, C. of Eng., BCP 16322.3, 16322.5(?), 16322.6(?), 16322.7*; Liturgies, C. of Eng., Spec. Prayers 16529; L'Obel 16649; Lodge 16667; Lodge and Greene 16680; Lomazzo 16698; Luis 16899.5, 16902, 16906.5, 16918, 16920; Lyly 17085; M., I. or J. 17140; Manwood 17291; Marlowe 17413, 17414, 17438; Marnix van Sant Aldegonde 17447; Marston 17482, 17485; Mary, the Blessed Virgin 17538; Mecare 17764; Melville, J. 17816*; Meres 17834; Mirandula, O. 17954; Montemayor 18044; More, Sir G. 18072; Morley, T. 18129; Mucedorus 18230; Netherlands 18433; Netherlands, Southern Prov. 18465, 18466, 18467, 18468; Norden 18617.7, 18626a.3, 18637; Nowell, Middle Catechism 18718; Openshaw 18822.2; Ortunez de Calahorra 18865(+?), 18867, 18868, 18869; P., A. 19054.5; Palladius 19153; Parsons, R. 19354.3, 19367, 19384; Pelegromius 19557.7; Perkins, W. 19682, 19736, 19749; Peryn 19785; Petowe 19807; Pettie 19821.5(?)(A/C); Philip II 19837.5(A/C) [not STC], 19838; Phillips, G. 19856.7(?); Phillis 19880; Piscator 19951; Powel, Griffinus 20158; Powell, T., Londino-Cambrensis 20166.5; R., W. S. 20595.5; Racster 20601, 20601.5; Rainolds, J. 20628; Rankins 20700; Rastell, J., Printer 20710; Rastell, W. 20740; Reyman 20918 [not STC]; Rich, B. 20991.3; Roberts, Henry 21082; Robson, H. 21131; Robson, S. 21133, 21134; Roesslin 21160; Rogers, Thomas, of Bryanston 21225; Rollock, R. 21279; Romei 21311; Rous, the Elder 21348; Rowlands, S. 21365; Saint German 21576; Saint Giles without Cripplegate 21588.3(?); Saluste du Bartas 21661, 21661.5, 21670; Scotland, proclamations 21954, 21955; Scupoli 22126.3; Shakespeare, K. and E. 22272.5; Shakespeare, W. 22279a, 22280, 22294, 22308, 22309, 22315, 22346; Sidney, P. 22541; Smith, H., Minister, Collections 22747.5, 22780; Smyth, W. 22882; Spagnuoli 22984.3; Stockwood 23277.5*, 23278; Stoughton, T. 23316; Stow 23328, 23328.5, 23341; Strigelius 23363; Table 23633a.7, 23634.5; Tacitus 23643, 23644; Terentius 23890; Thomas, a Kempis 23996; Tiverton 24093; Tofte 24096; Tymme 24419; Tyro 24477; Vaughan, W. 24620; Vecellio 24627a.6; Voyon 24890; Wateson 25106, 25106a; Weelkes 25203; Wentworth, Peter, Parliamentarian 25245; West, W. 25269; Wilbye 25619, 25619.3*(A/C), 25619.5; Wilcox 25621; Wirsung 25862, 25863; Writing Tables 26050.

1599

A., M. 9; Abbot, G., Abp. 24, 24.5; Albertus Magnus 264; Allott 381, 382; Almanacks (Buckminster or Buckmaster) 425; Almanacks (Dade, J.) 434.10; Almanacks (Frende) 445.5; Almanacks (Watson) 525.3; Anatomical Fugitive Sheets 564.8; Arden, T. 734; Assize of Bread 873; Aungervile 959; B., I. or J. 1041.3; B., T. 1070; Babington, G. 1093; Barker, L. 1423; Bennet, J. 1882; Bible, English 2173, 2174*, 2175*, 2176*, 2177*, 2178*, 2179*, 2180*; Bible, N.T., Latin 2810a.7; Bible, N.T., Polyglot 2792.5*, 2792.6; Bible, O.T., Psalms 2402.5*, 2497, 2497.3, 2497.5, 2497.7, 2498, 2498.5, 2499.9, 2500*; Bicknoll 3050.2; Bilson 3064; Blundeville 3142; Boazio 3171.7; Bommel 3258; Boyse 3469; Brabant 3470; Bradford, J., Prebendary of St. Paul's 3502; Breton 3682.5, 3706; Brice 3727; Bristow, R. 3800; Brooke, R. 3834, 3834.5; Brossier, M. 3841; Broughton, H. 3862a.3, 3862a.5, 3864; Bruno, V. 3941.1(?), 3941.2(?), 3941.3(?), 3941.4(?); Buttes 4207; Byrd, W. 4254(?); C., B. 4263; Calvin 4423; Canary Islands 4555.5, 4556; Carpenter, J., Minister 4667; Cartari 4691; Case, J. 4754, 4756; Cecil, J. 4894; Chapman, G. 4987; Churchyard 5234; Cicero 5315.5; Clapham, H. 5337; Clenardus or Cleynaerts 5403.5; Clyomon 5450a; Contarini 5642; Crompton, R. 6054; Cutwode 6151; Daniel, S. 6261; Darrell 6280.5(?), 6282, 6287; Davies, Sir J. 6350(c.?), 6350.5(c.?), 6351, 6355, 6355.2, 6355.4; Davis or Davys, J. 6368.7; Day, A. 6404; Dee

1599 — *cont.*
6460; Deloney 6554.2(A/C); Dent, A. 6658.5; Desainliens or Sainliens 6763; Digges, L. 6851.2; Dillingham 6883; Drayton 7195; Du Laurens 7303, 7304; Du Nesme 7353.5; Dubravius 7268; Edinburgh University 7487.2; Edward III 7502; England, Appendix 10017, 10017.5; England, C. of, Constitutions/Canons 10067; England, C. of, Visit. Articles 10204, 10304, 10327.5; England, Proclamations, Chron. Ser. 8267, 8268, 8269, 8270(o.s.), 8271 (o.s.), 8772(o.s.); England, Statutes, Chron. Ser. 9494.9; England, Yearbooks 9769; Fancy 10684; Farmer, J. 10697; Fenton, R. 10799; Finch, H. 10872.5*; Forde, E. 11168(?), 11171.2; Fortescue 11196; Gaebelkhover 11513; Gardiner, R., of Shrewsbury 11570.5; Gardiner, Samuel 11579; Gelli 11711; Gerard, J. 11749; Gesner 11799; Gibson, Anthony 11831; Gibson, J. 11834; Gifford, G. 11849.5, 11866.5, 11867; Grafton 12163; Green 12212; Greene, R. 12233, 12253.7(A/C), 12260, 12266, 12273; Greenham 12312, 12313, 12313.5, 12314; Gregory, A. 12357.7; Guicciardini, F. 12459; Hakluyt 12626*, 12626a; Hall, Joseph 12719; Harsnet, S. 12883; Harward 12916, 12923.5; Hayward, Sir J. 12995, 12995.5*, 12996*, 12997*, 12997a*; Henry IV, King of France 13120, 13120.5; Henry VII, King of England 13076; Herrey 13228b.15; Heywood, T. 13341; Hill, T. 13502; Holborne 13563; Holland, T. 13596; Hooker, R. 13721; Hume, A., Minister of Logie 13942; I., S. A. 14063; Ireland, Laws 14131(?); Ireland, Proc. 14146; Jacob, H. 14335; James I 14348; Java 14478(?); Jewel, J. 14585; K., R. 14894.3; Key 14946; King, J., Bp. 14977; Kyd 15088; La Perriere 15229; Lambard 15152, 15169; Leake 15342, 15342.5; Lily, W., 'Lily's Grammar' 15623.5, 15624; Littleton, T., Tenures, French 15753; Liturgies, C. of Eng., BCP 16322.7*, 16323, 16323.3, 16437; Liturgies, C. of Eng., Spec. Prayers 16530; Liturgies, Latin Rite, Hours and Primers 16094; Liturgies, Other Protest. C. 16586*, 16587; Luis 16899.7, 16904, 16910, 16922; M., T., Gent. 17154; Manual 17266; Manuzio, A. 17281; Margaret, of Austria 17323.5, 17324; Markham, G. 17349; Marston 17486, 17486.5*(A/C); Mascall 17579.5*; Merlin, P. 17843; Milles, T. 17928; Moffett 17994; Morley, T. 18131; Mornay 18146; Morton, T., of Berwick 18198, 18198.5; Mulcaster 18249(?)*(A/C); Nash, T. 18370; Netherlands, Southern Prov. 18468.5, 18470; Netherlands, States Gen. 18452.7(A/C), 18453, 18454; Norden 18626a.2, 18632; Openshaw 18830.4A; Ortunez de Calahorra 18861(?), 18863, 18870; Palingenius 19143.5; Parker, J. 19217; Parsons, R. 19368.5, 19384.5, 19395, 19415; Partridge, John 19435; Peele, G. 19536, 19540; Percyvall 19620, 19622; Perkins, W. 19741; Perneby 19766.5, 19766.7; Petowe 19808; Pett, P. 19818; Philip II 19833.5, 19834; Philodikaios 19881.5(?); Pill 19933.5; Piscator 19963, 19964; Plowden 20045; Plutarch 20055; Polanus 20086; Pont 20100, 20104; Porter, H. 20121.5, 20122; Price, H. 20307; Purmerend 20511; Rainolds, J. 20616; Record, R. 20819; Relation 20861; Robertson, G. 21101; Roche 21137; Rollock, R. 21271; Romans 21288.3*; Rome 21301; Rome, Church of 21309; Saint Andrews Univ. 21555.3; Saluste du Bartas 21661.5*; Scotland, statutes, etc. 21877.5, 21892.3; Seton, J. 22254.3; Shakespeare, W. 22281, 22323, 22341.5(?), 22342, 22358, 22358a; Sharp 22369; Sidney, P. 22542; Silver 22554; Smith, H., Minister, Collections 22723, 22735, 22748, 22780.5; Soliman 22895, 22895a; Southwell 22955.3(?)*, 22959; Spaniards 23008; Spanish Humours 23010; Stevin 23265; Storer 23294; Stow 23342; Sutcliffe, M. 23449, 23457, 23460; Taffin 23652.7; Talaeus 23659.5; Tasso, E. and T. 23690; Theatre 23931; Thomas, L. 24003; Topsell 24131; Treatise 24216; Trial 24273; Trigge 24281; Turner, Richard 24344; Tusser 24385.5, 24386; Ubaldini 24487; Udall, J. 24496; Valera 24580; Vaughan, Richard 24600.5; Vaux 24627a.2, 24627a.3*; Vicary 24709.5; Vineyard 24766.7; Warning 25089; Weever 25224; Whitaker, W. 25368; Willet 25703; Wimbledon 25834*; Withals 25883; Wright, E. 26019, 26019a; Zanchius 26120; Zepper 26124.5.

1600

A., R. 14; Abbot, G., Abp. 25, 34, 34.5; Alexander, W. 348, 348.5; Allen, R. 366, 367; Allott 378, 379, 379.5, 380; Almanacks (Dade, J.) 434.11, 434.12; Almanacks (Johnson, T.) 466.2; Almanacks (Watson) 525.4, 525.5; Armin 772.3, 775.5; Assize of Bread 874;

1600 — *cont.*
Augustine 931, 945; Baldwin, W. 1265; Bales, P. 1312.3; Ballad 1329(c.); Balmford 1334.5, 1335.7(?); Barker, L. 1424; Barlement 1431.17; Baxter, J. 1596, 1596.5; Becon 1766.7; Bentley, J. 1891.5; Bible, English 2181, 2182; Bible, N.T., English 2897, 2898, 2899; Bible, N.T., Gospels 2991; Bible, N.T., Polyglot 2792.5*, 2792.7; Bible, O.T., Psalms 2403, 2500*, 2500.3, 2500.5, 2500.7, 2501; Bible, Selections 2997; Blake 3122; Boazio 3171.8(?); Bodenham 3189, 3189.5, 3191; Book 3345; Bradley 3505; Breton 3666, 3675, 3675.5, 3677, 3677.5, 3678, 3679, 3702; Bristol 3796(c.?); Broughton, H. 3865; Butler, C. 4198; Byrd, W. 4249.5(c.), 4250.5(c.); Cambridge University, Act Verses 4474.9(+?), 4474.18(c.?), 4474.25(+?), 4474.37(c.?), 4474.38(+?), 4474.41(+?), 4474.44(+?), 4474.48(c.?), 4474.50(+?), 4474.52(+?), 4474.58(+?), 4474.60(+?), 4474.68(+?), 4474.70(+?), 4474.78(+?), 4474.81(+?), 4474.83(+?), 4474.85(+?), 4474.87(+?), 4474.92(+?), 4474.93(+?), 4474.95(+?), 4474.98(c.?), 4474.100(+?), 4474.101R(+?)(A/C), 4474.103(+?), 4474.109(+?), 4474.112(+?), 4474.118(+?), 4474.121(+?), 4474.122 (+?), 4474.128(+?); Camden 4507, 4518; Canterbury 4579.5(A/C); Cawdrey, R. 4887; Chambers, Robert 4954; Charles Emmanuel I. 5044; Cicero 5309.7; Clapham, H. 5330; Cleaver 5384; Coke, E. 5493; Colville 5587; Conestaggio 5624; Conningham 5631.3(c.); Constable, H. 5638.5; Cornwallis 5775*; Culmann 6106.3(c.?); Curteys or Curtis 6134; D., T. H. 6181.7; Danett 6234; Darrell 6283, 6288; Davy du Perron 6381; Dekker 6517, 6523; Deloney 6555.7(c.); Dent, A. 6658.6; Dering 6681.5, 6709; Description 6768.5(c.?); Devereux 6787.7(?); Devon 6798; Dictionary 6832.56; Diet 6832.65; Ditty 6919(c.?); Dodypoll 6991; Dort, Black Galley of 7064; Dowland, J. 7092, 7095; Downame, J. 7147; Drayton 7196; Dyer, J. 7392; E., J. G. 7434.7; Edinburgh University 7487.3; Edmondes, C. 7488; Edwards, R. 7523; Eleanor 7565.4(c.?); England, Appendix 10021.7(c.?); England, C. of, Injunctions 10110; England, C. of, Visit. Articles 10133, 10180, 10188.3, 10314.1; England, Proclamations, Chron. Ser. 8270, 8271, 8272, 8273, 8274, 8275, 8276, 8277(o.s.), 8278(o.s.), 8279(o.s.), 8280(o.s.), 8281(o.s.), 8282(o.s.), 8283(o.s.), 8284(o.s.), 8285(o.s.); England, Public Documents, Misc. 9208.7; England, Statutes, Abridgements/Extracts 9532; England, Yearbooks 9585; Estienne, C., and Liebault 10547; Extract 10634.6; Fisher, John, St. 10889.5; Flanders 11029; Floyd, T. 11119; Freeman, J. 11367; Fulbecke 11410; Fumee 11487; G., C. 11491; G., R. 11502; Gardiner, Samuel 11578; Garzoni 11634; Gifford, G. 11855; Gilbert, W., M. D. 11883; Greene, R. 12254, 12287.5(A/C); Greenham 12314.5, 12314.7; Griselda 12384(c.); Groom-porter 12392(c.?); Habermann 12582.11, 12582.12*, 12582.13*; Hakluyt 12626*; Hamilton, John 12730; Hastings, F. 12928; Henry IV, King of France 13121; Henry, the Minstrel 13150.5*; Heresbach 13200*; Herrey 13228b.16; Heywood, T. 13342; Hill, E. 13470, 13470.3; Holland, T. 13596.5; Howesoun 13878; Hunnis 13979; Hylles 14040.7; I., S. 14058.3; Ireland, Proc. 14147; Jacob, H. 14333; James, T., D. D. 14447, 14447.5, 14453; Jewel, J. 14592; Johnson, Francis 14658; Jones, Robert 14732; Jonghe 14750; Jonson 14767, 14768, 14769; Kemp 14923; King, J., Bp. 14978; Kittowe 15026; Lane 15190; Le Macon 15451; Leius 15437; Leo 15481; Lewkenor, S. 15566; Littleton, T., Tenures, Engl. 15777; Liturgies, C. of Eng., BCP 16323.5, 16324, 16324.3, 16324.4*(A/C); Liturgies, C. of Eng., Spec. Prayers 16531; Livius 16613; Lloyd, L. 16628(?); London, Ords. and Regs. 16718.5(c.); Look 16799; Lucanus 16883.5; Luis 16921; Macropedius 17176.4; Maid 17188; Mameranus 17228.5(c.); Markham, G. 17395; Marlowe 17415; Marston 17486.5(?)*(A/C); Mary, the Blessed Virgin 17546; Mascall 17573, 17583; Maurice 17671, 17671a, 17679; Meditation 17773.5(c.); Middleton, C. 17868; Middleton, T. 17885.5; Mohammedan History 17997; More, G., Preacher 18070, 18070.5; Morley, T. 18115.5, 18117, 18128; Mornay 18139, 18142; Mulcaster 18249.5; Nash, T. 18376; Nenna 18429; Nicholson 18546; Norden 18604.5, 18617.9(?)(A/C), 18618.3, 18626a.4, 18642; Northbrooke 18668; Oceander 18763; Oldcastle, J. 18795, 18796*; Openshaw 18830.5; Ovidius Naso 18944, 18974; Pallavicino 19154, 19154.3; Parker, Matthew 19287.3(c.), 19287.7(c.); Partridge, John 19430; Perkins, W. 19646, 19689.5, 19743.3, 19754.7, 19761.1; Perrott, J. 19773; Phillips, G. 19861; Pinelli 19937(c.); Platt 19977.7 (?), 19993, 19993.5, 19993.7(?); Polanus 20084; Powel, Gabriel 20150; Quin 20567; R., I., or J. 20575; Rainolds, J. 20617; Record, R. 20804.3; Report 20891; Reynard the Fox 20922.5(c.); Richard, Duke of York 21006a; Roberts, Henry 21081; Roberts, Hugh 21089; Rollock, R. 21274, 21276; Romans 21288.3*; Rome 21291; Rome, Church of 21307.7(?); Rowlands, S. 21392.7, 21393, 21393.5; Russell, F. 21456.5(c.?); Ruthven, J. 21465.5, 21466, 21466.3; S., G. W. P. 21493(?); Safeguard 21548; Saint Andrews Univ. 21555.4, 21555.5, 21555.6; Saint Mary's Island 21591; Saint Paul's School 21591.5; Saluste du Bartas 21657; Savage 21781; Scotland, proclamations 21957; Scotland, statutes, etc. 21892.5; Shakespeare, W. 22288, 22288a, 22289, 22296, 22297*, 22302, 22303*, 22304, 22329, 22347, 22348*(A/C); Shepherds' Kalendar 22419(?); Sherley, A. 22425; Smith, T., Artillerist 22855*, 22855.5*; Southwell 22949.5*, 22960(?); Stow 23335; Stubbes 23382.3; Sum 23432.7(c.); Sutcliffe, M. 23453, 23462; Sutton, C. 23474; Tasso, T. 23698; Taverner, J. 23708; Terry 23913; Thomas, a Kempis 23980.5; Thomas, L. 24002; Thomas, T. 24012; Torquemada 24135; Touchstone 24145.7 (c.); Tourneur 24152; Trigge 24281a; Ursinus, Z. 24527; Valera 24578.3, 24578.5, 24581; Vaughan, W. 24610, 24612; Virel 24769.5; Virgilius Maro 24804, 24821.5(c.); W., G. 24904; Weakest 25144; Webbe, E. 25154; Weelkes 25206; Weersburch 25219.5; Weever 25225; Westerman 25282; Whitaker, W. 25367, 25370; Wilkinson, E. 25642; Willet 25698, 25698.3*; Wright, T., Priest 26038.4, 26038.5, 26038.6*; Yonger 26097, 26097.5; York, House of 26100.

1601

A.B.C. 20.7; Abbot, R., Bp. 51; Aesop 172.2; Alba-Regalis 256.5; Almanacks (Pond) 501; Almanacks (Watson) 525.6; Assize of Bread 875; B., E. and I., I. 1025.3; B., R. 1055; B., W. 1073, 1074; Bacon, F. 1133; Bagshaw 1188; Barlow, W., Bp. of Rochester/Lincoln 1449, 1454; Barnewal 1479; Barrough 1511; Bennett, J. 1884; Bible, English 2183, 2184, 2184.5; Bible, N.T., English 2900, 2900.3, 2901; Bible, O.T., 'Books of Solomon' 2759.5; Bible, O.T., Prophets 2787.7; Bible, O.T., Psalms 2403.3, 2502, 2503, 2503.5, 2504, 2505, 2702; Bible, Selections 3012.3; Bidpai 3054, 3054.5; Blackwell 3102, 3106(?); Bluom 3161.5; Book 3363.9; Botero 3398, 3399; Bourne, W. 3428.5; Bradshaw, W. 3518, 3518.3, 3518.5; Breton 3648, 3649, 3672, 3679.5, 3700.5; Broughton, Richard 3893; Burel 4105.5; C., L. W. 4286; Caesar, Caius Julius 4334; Cambridge University, Act Verses 4474.53, 4474.76; Cancellar 4562.3; Carleton, R. 4649; Carpenter, J., Minister 4662; Cary, R. 4719; Castalio or Chateillon 4771.7; Chamber 4941; Chester, R. 5119; Chisholm 5141.5; Christian Prayers 5181; Cicero 5309.8; Clapham, H. 5329, 5336.5; Coke, E. 5493.4(?), 5493.7; Comines 5603; Copies 5724; Copley, A. 5735; Cornwallis 5774, 5775*; Cotton, Roger 5867.3(?)*; Daniel, S. 6236; Davy du Perron 6382, 6385.5(?); Deacon and Walker 6439, 6440; Dent, A. 6626, 6626.5; Dove 7083; Drum 7243; Dyer, J. 7390; Ease 7446; Edinburgh University 7487.4; Elizabeth I 7578; England, C. of, Visit. Articles 10235.5, 10254; England, Proclamations, Chron. Ser. 8277, 8278, 8279, 8280, 8281, 8282, 8283, 8284, 8285, 8286, 8287, 8288, 8289(o.s.), 8290(o.s.); England, Public Documents, Misc. 9175d.51(?), 9175f(?); England, Statutes, Chron. Ser. 9495, 9496, 9496.5, 9497, 9497.5, 9497.7(?); England, Statutes, Gen. Colls. 9295.6; England, Yearbooks 9697; Field, J., Minister 10846; Fitz-Geffrey, C. 10934; Fulbecke 11412, 11415; G., R. 11502.5; Galvam or Galvano 11543; Gardiner, Samuel 11578.5; Gibbens 11814; Gil, A., the Elder 11879; God 11925.5; Godwin, F. 11937; Godwin, F. 11940; Greene, R. 12226, 12294; Greenham 12315, 12316; Guilpin 12504.5; Harward 12922; Hayward, Sir J. 13003.5; Hell 13048.5; Henry, the Minstrel 13150.5*; Heresbach 13200*; Hill, R. 13479; Hill, T. 13499; Holland, T. 13597; Huon of Bordeaux 13999; Hutchins 14013.3, 14014; I., S. 14058; I., W. 14071; Ireland, Proc. 14147a; Jaggard 14343; Johnson, Robert, Gent. 14695; Jones, Robert 14733; Jonson 14766, 14773; La Primaudaye 15240; Lambard 15153; Linaker 15639; Liturgies, C. of Eng., BCP 16324.4*(A/C),

1601 — *cont.*
16324.5, 16324.7; Liturgies, Other Protest. C. 16588; Luis 16901, 16910.5; Lupton, T. 16959; Lyly 17076, 17082; Lynche 17092; Macey 17173.5; Malynes 17226a, 17227; Mancinus 17239.5; Mary Magdalen 17569; Mary, de' Medici 17556; Mary, the Blessed Virgin 17547; Maurice 17680; Maxey, E. 17695; Morley, T. 18130, 18130.5; Mulcaster 18249*; Munday 18269, 18271; N., S. 18334.5; Nannini 18348; Neck 18417; Nesbit 18432, 18432.5; Norden 18643; Oliver, T. 18810; Ortelius 18857(?); Ortiz 18858; Ortunez de Calahorra 18871; Ostend 18892.3, 18892.7, 18893, 18894; Overton, W. 18926; Ovidius Naso 18952.1; Oxford Univ., Off. Docs. 19002.5(?); Paget 19100; Parry, W., Traveller 19343; Parsons, R. 19385, 19391.5, 19392, 19396; Patriarchs 19469; Perkins, J. 19641; Perkins, W. 19713*, 19728, 19757, 19757.5, 19763.5, 19764; Platt 19994, 19994.5; Plinius Secundus 20029, 20029.5; Plutarch 20053; Powell, T., Londino-Cambrensis 20167; Questions 20557; Report 20890; Rider, J. 21030; Rogers, Robert 21224; Rosseter 21332; Rowlands or Verstegan, R. 21359; Ruthven, J. 21468; Saint Andrews Univ. 21555.7; Sallustius Crispus 21622.8; Savoy 21802; Schonaeus 21821.2; Sinner 22577; Smith, H., Minister, Collections 22724, 22736; Smith, T., Artillerist 22855*; Smith, T., Doctor of Civil Laws 22861; Spagnuoli 22984.4; Speed, John 23037(?); Stow 23336; Sutton, C. 23475, 23491; T., A., Practitioner in Physic 23606.5; Teixeira 23864; Theatre 23932; Topsell 24129; Treasure 24197.5, 24207.3(A/C); Ursinus, Z. 24536; Vennard 24636.3(?), 24637; Watson, W. 25124, 25124.5, 25125, 25126; Weever 25220, 25226; West, W. 25278; Wheeler 25330, 25331; Wilmot 25765; Worthington, T. 26000.9; Wright, T., Priest 26039; Writing Tables 26050.2; Yarington 26076.

1602

A., T. 17.3; Almanacks (Dade, J.) 434.14; Almanacks (Johnson, T.) 466.4; Almanacks (Mathew) 483; Almanacks (Pond) 501.2; Almanacks (Watson) 525.7; Almanacks (Woodhouse, W.) 532; Arias 742; Arnauld 780; B., W. 1074.5; Babington, G. 1085; Bailey, Walter 1195; Baker, H. 1215; Barlement 1431.17A*; Basse 1555, 1556; Beaumont, J. 1695; Bernard, R. 1955.5; Bible, Appendix 3022.7(?); Bible, English 2185, 2186, 2187, 2188; Bible, N.T., English 2902, 2902.3(?); Bible, N.T., Irish 2958*; Bible, O.T., 'Books of Solomon' 2771; Bible, O.T., Psalms 2506, 2506.5, 2507, 2507.5; Birchensha 3081; Birkenhead 3088.5; Blundeville 3160; Botero 3397; Bourman 3415; Brereton, J. 3610, 3611; Breton 3669, 3673, 3680, 3684, 3699, 3703, 3714; Budden 4012; Bulkeley 4025; Bunny, F. 4098a; Burton, W., Minister at Reading 4165a, 4173, 4178.5; C., L. W. 4287; C., R. 4296; C., W. 4317; Cambridge University, Act Verses 4474.120, 4474.132; Campion 4543; Carew, R. 4615; Cartwright, T. 4716; Caveat 4877.4; Chaucer 5080, 5081; Churchyard 5260.5; Cicero 5301; Clapham, H. 5346.5; Clapham, J. 5347; Clarke, J., Apothecary? 5353; Clowes 5446; Coke, E. 5495, 5499, 5499.2; Colleton 5557; Colville 5589; Comedy 5593, 5594; Copley, A. 5736; Corrozet 5795; Crespin 6036; Curtius Rufus 6147; Daniel, S. 6237; Darrell 6284, 6285; Davidson, J., Minister of Salt-Preston 6324.5; Davies, J., of Hereford 6336; Davies, Sir J. 6356; Davison 6373; De Beau Chesne and Baildon 6449(A/C); Defence 6467.5, 6468, 6468.5; Dekker 6520.7, 6521; Deloney 6566; Dent, A. 6626.7, 6658.8; Desainliens or Sainliens 6743.5, 6749.8; Dillingham 6881; Discourse 6910.4; Downame, G. 7102; Drayton 7197; Du Jon, F., the Elder 7298, 7298.5; Dyer, J. 7386; E., I. or J. 7434; Ely, H. 7628; England, C. of, Visit. Articles 10314.2; England, Proclamations, Chron. Ser. 8289, 8290, 8291, 8292, 8293, 8294, 8295, 8296(o.s.), 8297(o.s.), 8298(o.s.), 8299(o.s.); England, Public Documents, Misc. 9175d.52(?); England, Statutes, Chron. Ser. 9499; England, Statutes, Gen. Colls. 9283; Erasmus, D. 10462; Estey 10546; Evans, W., Poet 10597.5; Fenner, D. 10765; Fitzherbert, T. 11016; Fleming, A. 11044; Fulbecke 11414, 11415a; Fulke 11438; Geare 11692.3; Gentillet 11743; Gerardus 11761, 11761.7; Gibbens 11815; Gontaut 12002; Grafton 12164; Grave 12196, 12197; Greene, R. 12243, 12254.5; Guarini 12415; H., I. or J. 12571, 12571.5; Habermann 12582.12*, 12582.14*; Hall, Joseph 12718;

1602 — *cont.*
Harrison, W., King's Preacher 12866; Hayward, J., D. D. 12984.5; Hayward, Sir J. 13003.7; Hayward, W. 13013; Hell 13048.7; Herrey 13228b.17; Higgins, J, Controversialist 13442, 13442.5; Horatius Flaccus 13787a.5*, 13788; Howson 13884, 13886, 13886.5; Hull, J. 13929, 13934, 13935; Hume, A., Schoolmaster 13945; Hunnis 13979.5; Ireland, Proc. 14148, 14149(o.s.), 14150(o.s.); John, Chrysostom 14641; Jonson 14781; Jonston 14787, 14787.2(?), 14787.6(?); Joseph, ben Gorion 14803; Josephus 14809; Keilwey 14901; Kingsmill, T. 15007; Kyd 15089; La Primaudaye 15236; Lambard 15154, 15170; Le Macon 15449; Le Roy, P. 15490; Lily, W., 'Lily's Grammar' 15624.5; Lindsay, Sir D. 15681, 15681.5; Liturgies, Other Protest. C. 16570, 16586*, 16589; Lloyd, L. 16616, 16629, 16630; Lodge and Greene 16681; London, Appendix 16754; Luis 16911; Luther 16970; Lynche 17092.5; Mansel 17259; Manual 17267.5(+); Marbury 17305, 17306, 17307; Marston 17473, 17474; Martin, G. 17505(?); Mason, Robert 17621; Maurice 17675; Meteren 17846; Middleton, T. 17876; More, R. 18075; Morley, T. 18122; Mornay 18163; Netherlands, Southern Prov. 18471; Netherlands, States Gen. 18454.5; Nichols, Josias 18538, 18541, 18542, 18542.5; Nicholson 18547, 18548; Nixon 18583; O., E. 18754; Oberndoerffer 18759; Openshaw 18830.6; Oratio 18835; Orchard 18839a; Ostend 18891, 18892; Ovidius Naso 18926.9, 18929.3, 18931(aft.), 18931a (aft.), 18972; Oxford Univ., Verses, etc. 19051*; Pagit 19105.5; Palingenius 19144; Palmerin, of England 19165; Parsons, R. 19369, 19392.5, 19411, 19418; Pasquier 19449; Perkins, W. 19647*, 19750; Peter, St. 19798; Philalethes 19830; Philip III 19839; Platt 19978; Plutarch 20071; Portugal 20128; Powel, Gabriel 20146.5, 20148, 20151, 20155, 20155.5; Quilibet 20562; Rainolds, J. 20625; Rastell, J., Printer 20711; Record, R. 20814; Rhodes, J. 20959, 20959.5; Rider, J. 21031; Rollock, R. 21269, 21269.5; Romans 21288.5; Rome 21299.5, 21299.7(c.); Rowlands, S. 21409; Rule 21446.7; Russel 21455; S., Tho. 21523; S., W. 21532; Saint Andrews Univ. 21555.8, 21555.9; Sanderson, J. 21698; Scott, T., Poet 22107; Segar 22164; Shakespeare, W. 22290, 22299, 22316, 22348*(A/C), 22359(?), 22360*, 22360a*, 22360b*; Shelford 22401; Sherley, T. 22425.5; Smith, H., Minister, Collections 22752, 22761, 22765; Smith, M. 22807; Smith, William, Map-Maker 22871a.3(?); Southwell 22952, 22960a, 22969.3(+); Sturtevant 23409, 23410; Sutcliffe, M. 23454, 23459; Sutton, C. 23475.5, 23483; Tapp 23679; Teixeira 23865; Terry 23913.5; Theatre 23932.5; Theodoret 23939; Thomas, a Kempis 23981; Thomas, L. 24004; Torporley 24134; Trigge 24282; Twyne, T. 24410; Tyrer 24475, 24475.5; Vaughan, W. 24613, 24613.5; Vennard 24636.7, 24638; Vere 24651, 24651a, 24651b; Vigor 24727; Virgilius Maro 24791.3; Warner, W. 25083; Watson, W. 25123; Welsch 25235; Whately 25304; Wilkinson, R. 25652.7(c.); Willet 25673; Willis, J., Stenographer 25744a; Withals 25884; Wood, J., M. D. 25954; Wright, L. 26026.

1603

Abbot, R., Bp. 43; Alexander, W. 349; Allen, R. 367.5; Almanacks (Gresham) 452; Almanacks (Hill, H.) 457.8; Almanacks (Pond) 501.3; Almanacks (Woodhouse, W.) 532.2; Awdely 994.5; Bacon, F. 1117; Balmford 1338; Barckley 1382; Bell, T. 1814, 1822; Beze 2023.7; Bible, English 2189, 2190, 2192, 2193; Bible, N.T., English 2903, 2903.5; Bible, O.T., 'Books of Solomon' 2772; Bible, O.T., Psalms 2403.7(?), 2508, 2509, 2510, 2510.5, 2511, 2511.5, 2703, 2730, 2743, 2744; Bilson 3068; Blage or Balgue 3115.3; Botero 3400; Bradshaw, W. 3519; Breton 3646, 3667, 3685; Brett 3716; Broughton, H. 3855; Broughton, Richard 3897, 3897.5; C., I. or J. 4282; C., N. 4291(c.); C., T. 4303; C., W. 4321; Cambridge University 4493; Cambridge University, Act Verses 4474.5, 4474.11, 4474.29, 4474.45, 4474.86, 4474.129; Camden 4519; Carew, T., Preacher 4616; Carleton, G. 4636; Castiglione 4780, 4786; Chettle 5121, 5122; Cicero 5320; Citois 5326; Clapham, H. 5333, 5339, 5340; Cleaver 5385; Collection 5554; Counsel 5871.7; Covell 5881; Craig, T. 5968, 5969, 5971; Crosse, H. 6070, 6070.5; Cupper 6125.3; D., F. 6165; Daniel, S. 6258, 6259, 6260; Davies, J., of Hereford 6333; Dee 6460.5, 6461*; Dekker 6476, 6476.2, 6518, 6535, 6535.3(?),

1603 — *cont.*
6535.5(?); Delamothe 6547; Denison, J. 6595.7; Dent, A. 6625.5, 6627, 6640; Dering 6710, 6716.5, 6717; Devereux 6788, 6791; Dillingham 6889, 6892; Discourse 6911.7; Dod and Cleaver 6967, 6967.5; Dove 7085; Dowland, J. 7092.5, 7096; Downame, G. 7120; Drayton 7189, 7231, 7231.3; East India Company 7448; East Indies 7459; Echlin, J. 7481; Egerton, S. 7539; Elizabeth I 7579.5(c.?), 7589(?), 7594, 7598, 7605.3; England, Appendix 10005.5; England, C. of, Visit. Articles 10143, 10356.5; England, Local Courts 7722; England, Proclamations, Chron. Ser. 8296, 8297, 8298, 8299, 8300, 8300.5, 8301, 8302, 8303, 8304, 8305, 8306, 8307, 8308, 8309, 8310, 8311, 8312, 8313, 8314, 8315, 8316, 8317, 8318, 8319, 8320, 8321, 8322, 8323, 8323.5, 8324, 8325, 8326, 8326.5, 8327, 8328, 8329, 8330, 8331, 8332, 8333, 8334, 8335, 8336, 8337, 8338, 8339, 8340, 8341(o.s.), 8342(o.s.), 8343(o.s.), 8344(o.s.), 8346(o.s.), 8347(o.s.), 8349(o.s.), 8453.5; England, Public Documents, Misc. 9175g.10(?)(A/C), 9209; England, Statutes, Gen. Colls. 9322; England, Statutes, Spec. Subjs. 9342.9(?), 9343(aft.), 9343.3(aft.); Estey 10545; Exhortation 10626.5; F., I. or J. 10648; Fenton, J. 10798; Fenton, R. 10800; Fletcher, R. 11086; Fowler, W. 11214.8; Francis, of Assisi 11314; Gardiner, R., of Shrewsbury 11571; Geneva 11726, 11726.2; Gentilis 11740.5(?); Gifford, G. 11851; Godwin, F. 11948; Gordon, J., Dean of Salisbury 12059.5(?), 12059.7, 12061; Greene, T. 12311; Greenwood, J., Puritan 12340*; Guides 12465.5; Gwinne 12551; H., S. 12577; Habermann 12582.13*, 12582.14*; Hall, Joseph 12678; Harsnet, S. 12880; Hayward, J., D. D. 12984; Hayward, Sir J. 12988; Henry VIII, King of England 13087.5(?); Herrey 13228b.18; Herring, F. 13239.5, 13243; Heydon 13266; Holland, Henry, Vicar of St. Bride's 13589; Holland, Hugh 13592; Homer 13626; Hooke, C. 13703; Hotman, J. 13848; Howson 13880.5, 13885; Hume, D. 13948.3; I., S. A. 14064; Ireland, Proc. 14149, 14150, 14151; Jackson, Thomas, of Canterbury 14299; James I 14349, 14349.5(A/C), 14350, 14351, 14353, 14354, 14357, 14362, 14362.5, 14365, 14365.5, 14366, 14376.5, 14377, 14379.3, 14381, 14410, 14410.5, 14411; James I, appendix 14421, 14422, 14423, 14426.7; Jewel, J. 14599; Johnson, G. 14664; Johnson, Richard 14671, 14675; Jonston 14786, 14787.4, 14787.8; Jorden 14790; Julius, A. 14846.5; Kellison 14912; Ker 14939, 14939.5; King, A. 14962; Knolles 15051; Kyd 15089a; Lane 15189; Leech, A. 15355; Leighton, W. 15435; Letters 15529; Lily, W., 'Lily's Grammar' 15633.4; Lisle 15706; Liturgies, C. of Eng., BCP 16324.9, 16325, 16325.3, 16326(o.s.), 16326.5(o.s.); Liturgies, C. of Eng., Spec. Prayers 16532; Liturgies, C. of Eng., St. Services 16489; Lodge 16676; London, Bills of Mort. 16739.5, 16739.7, 16743.1, 16743.2, 16743.3, 16743.9; London, Merchant Tailors 16778.12(?); London, Ords. and Regs. 16718.6; M., T. 17151, 17151a, 17153; Malta 17215; Malynes 17225; Manuzio, P. 17289; Martin, Richard 17510, 17511; Mavericke 17683a, 17683a.5; Medicines 17770.7; Melville, E. 17811; Merlin 17841.7; Molyneux 18003.5; Monipennie 18017, 18018; Montaigne 18041; Mosse 18210; Muggins 18248; Mulcaster 18251, 18252; Muriell 18292, 18292.3; Nautonier 18415; Netherlands 18445.5; Netherlands, Southern Prov. 18472, 18472a; Newton, T., gent. 18513.5; Niccols 18520; Nichols, Josias 18539; Nixon 18586; Norden 18627; Openshaw 18822.6; Ortelius 18856; Ovidius Naso 18961; Oxford Univ., Off. Docs. 19010, 19010.5, 19011, 19012, 19012a; Oxford Univ., Verses, etc. 19018, 19019; P., A. 19056; Parsons, R. 19416*; Peebles 19528; Pelegromius 19558; Perkins, W. 19647*, 19690, 19724.7, 19728.5, 19735.6, 19743.5, 19751.5; Pernau 19766, 19766.3; Petowe 19803.5, 19804, 19806; Petrus, Luccensis 19815; Philotus 19888; Pie 19899; Piscator 19960; Platt 19978.5, 19995; Playfere 20010, 20025; Plutarch 20063, 20068, 20068a, 20068b; Potion 20132.5; Powel, Gabriel 20141, 20141.3, 20141.5(A/C), 20151.5; Powell, T., Londino-Cambrensis 20169, 20170; Prayer 20192.5(c.); Prayers 20197.7(?)(A/C); Pricket 20341, 20343; R., James 20580; R., R. 20587; Remedies 20874.5(?); Robinson, T., Musician 21128; Rogers, Richard 21215; Rollock, R. 21282, 21286; Rowlands, S. 21364; Rudd 21432, 21433; Ruthven, J. 21466.5, 21466.7, 21467, 21467.5; S., H. 21496.5, 21497; Saint Andrews Univ. 21555.10, 21555.11; Salamanca Univ. 21595; Saluste du

1603 — *cont.*
Bartas 21659; Savile, J. 21784; Saxo-Bosco 21805.05(A/C); Scotland, Church of, Confession of Faith 22024.3, 22030.7; Scotland, Church of, General Assembly 22045; Scotland, proclamations 21958; Scupoli 22126.7(+); Shakespeare, W. 22275; Sharpe, Leonell 22371, 22376; Smyth, J. 22874; Soranzo 22931; Southwell 22969.5 (+); Speed, John 23039g.3(?); Storre 23295; Stow 23343; Stubbes 23382.7; Sutcliffe, M. 23456; Swan, J., Student in Divinity 23517; T., W. 23632; Teixeira 23866; Thayre 23929; Thorne, W. 24041; Timberlake 24079; Top 24121; Turner, P. 24343; Vaughan, E. 24599.5; Virel 24769a; W., I. or J. 24905.7; W., T. 24918; Wakeman 24947.7; Walpole, R. 24994.5; Weever 25221; West, W. 25270; Wilkinson, E. 25643; Willet 25672, 25676, 25694, 25698.3*, 25698.5; Willoughbie 25759; Wimbledon 25834.5; Worship 25987; Writing Tables 26050.4(?)(A/C).

1604

Abbot, G., Abp. 37; Acosta 94; Act 98; Ainsworth, H., and Johnson 238, 239; Alexander, W. 337, 343, 346, 350; Almanacks (Billy) 414.3, 414.7; Almanacks (Dade, J.) 434.16; Almanacks (Gray) 451.14; Almanacks (Gresham) 452.3; Almanacks (Johnson, T.) 466.6, 466.7; Almanacks (Mathew) 483.2; Almanacks (Neve, Jeffery) 489; Almanacks (Pond) 501.4; Almanacks (Watson) 525.9; Almanacks (Woodhouse, W.) 532.3; Andrewe, T. 584; Andrewes, L. 597, 597.3, 597.7; Argall 738; Arms 775.7(?); Augustine 945.3; Babington, G. 1088, 1088.5; Bacon, F. 1111, 1112, 1118, 1118.5; Barlement 1431.17B; Barlow, W., Bp. of Rochester/Lincoln 1456, 1456.5, 1459.5; Barrow 1527(?); Bateson 1586; Baybush 1599.3; Becon 1768; Bedle 1793.5; Bell, T. 1818, 1818.5; Bellarmino 1834(?), 1835; Bible, Appendix 3022.8; Bible, O.T., 'Books of Solomon' 2765.5; Bible, O.T., Psalms 2512, 2512a, 2513, 2514, 2514.5, 2515; Bilson 3069, 3070; Bishop, W. 3096; Blage or Balgue 3115.5; Book 3346; Bownd, Nicholas 3438, 3439, 3440; Bradford, J., Prebendary of St. Paul's 3489a*; Bradshaw, W. 3509(+), 3526, 3527, 3528; Brereley 3604; Breton 3657, 3682; Bridges, J. 3735; Brook 3825; Broughton, H. 3843, 3856, 3856.5, 3892, 3892.5; Buckland 4008(+); Burt 4132; C., L. W. 4287.5; Calvin 4390.7; Cambridge University, Act Verses 4474.8, 4474.26, 4474.27, 4474.40; Camden 4512; Cartwright, T. 4710; Catholics 4835; Cawdrey, R. 4883, 4884; Chassanion 5062; Churchyard 5222, 5256(?); Cicero 5267.4; Citois 5327; Clapham, H. 5343; Clapham, J. 5349.5(?); Coke, E. 5496(?), 5502, 5502.3; Colville 5588; Conversion 5650; Cooke, John 5672(?), 5672.5(?); Corderoy 5755a.5, 5756; Cornwallis 5782, 5782.5, 5783; Cosin, R. 5824; Covell 5882, 5882.5; Craig, A. 5958; Dallington 6202; Daniel, S. 6264, 6265; Dee 6461(?)*, 6465(?), 6466(?); Dekker 6477, 6501, 6501.5, 6510, 6512, 6513; Desainliens or Sainliens 6764; Desiderius 6777; Digges, T. 6872; Directions 6903.5(?); Dod and Cleaver 6968; Dove 7085.5; Dowland, J. 7097; Downame, G. 7113, 7118; Downame, J. 7133; Drayton 7209, 7211, 7211.5, 7212, 7213, 7215; Dugdale 7292, 7293; East, M. 7460; Edinburgh University 7487.5; Edmondes, C. 7490, 7490.3; Eedes 7526; Elizabeth I 7592, 7593; England, C. of, Constitutions/Canons 10068, 10069.3, 10070, 10070.3, 10070.5, 10070.7, 10071.5*; England, C. of, Visit. Articles 10157.5(?), 10175, 10236, 10255, 10307; England, Customs 7690.5; England, Parliament 7748.3(?); England, Proclamations, Chron. Ser. 8341, 8342, 8343, 8344, 8345, 8346, 8347, 8348, 8349, 8351.3, 8352, 8353, 8354, 8355, 8358, 8359, 8360, 8361, 8362, 8363, 8364, 8365, 8368(o.s.), 8369(o.s.), 8370(o.s.), 8453.7(?); England, Public Documents, Misc. 9175i.3, 9209.5; England, Statutes, Chron. Ser. 9500, 9500.2, 9500.4, 9500.6, 9500.8(?), 9501; England, Statutes, Gen. Colls. 9295.8, 9296; Epitaphs 10432.7; Estella 10541.4; F., N. 10650; Fenton, R. 10801; Field, R. 10855; Flanders 11029.5; Forde, E. 11171.5*; Fraser 11336; G., P. 11501.5; Gap 11548.5; Garden 11558, 11558.3(c.); Gibbon or Gybbon 11817; Glanvilla 11906; Godskall 11935, 11936; Gordon, J., Dean of Salisbury 12057, 12059, 12062, 12062.3; Grahame 12169; Gravesend 12199; Greaves, T., Composer 12210; Greenham 12324.5; Grymeston 12407; Guides 12466; H., R. 12574(+); Hake 12607; Hanson 12750; Har-

1604 — *cont.*
bert, W. 12752; Harrison, S. 12863; Harry, G. 12872; Harsnet, S. 12881; Harward 12917; Hayward, Sir J. 12995.5(+?)*, 13004, 13011; Henry IV, King of France 13122; Herring, F. 13248; Hieron 13388, 13419; Hind 13510; Hooke, H. 13704; Hooker, R. 13713; Hopkins, J. 13767, 13767.5; Horatius Flaccus 13790; Huarte 13894; Hubbocke 13899; Hume, D. 13948.5; Hunnis 13980; I., H. 14052; Ireland, Proc. 14152(o.s.), 14153(o.s.), 14154(o.s.); Jack, of Dover 14291; Jacob, H. 14338; James I 14355, 14356, 14361, 14363, 14385.5, 14386, 14390, 14390.3, 14390.7, 14391; James I, appendix 14427, 14429.5, 14430, 14430.5, 14432; Jesus Christ 14568.3; Jonson 14756; Lambard 15155; Lindsay, Sir D. 15682; Ling 15686.5(A/C); Littleton, T., Tenures, Engl. 15778; Littleton, T., Tenures, French 15754; Liturgies, C. of Eng., BCP 16326, 16326.5, 16327, 16328, 16328.5, 16328a, 16328a.5, 16429; Liturgies, C. of Eng., Spec. Prayers 16533; Liturgies, C. of Eng., St. Services 16483; Liturgies, Latin Rite, Hours and Primers 16095; Liturgies, Latin Rite, Manuals 16157.5, 16158; Lloyd, L. 16627; Lodge 16668; London, Bills of Mort. 16743.10, 16743.11; London, Ords. and Regs. 16718.7, 16719; London, Royal Exchange 16784; London, Stationers 16786.3(?)(A/C); Macropedius 17176.5; Manning, J. 17257; Manual 17267, 17268, 17269; Map 17294; Marlowe 17429; Marston 17479, 17480, 17481; Mary Magdalen 17570; Meeting 17781; Melville, E. 17812(?); Mexia 17851; Middleton, T. 17874.3, 17874.7, 17875, 17875.5(A/C); Milles, T. 17932; Mornay 18151; Norton, R. 18675; Nugent 18745; Oliver, T. 18809; Ostend 18895; Oxford Univ., Off. Docs. 19013; Oxford Univ., Verses, etc. 19040; Panke, J. 19172; Parkes, R. 19296; Parsons, R. 19413, 19414, 19416*; Pasquil 19451; Peele, G. 19546.5; Perkins, W. 19668, 19680, 19699, 19713.5, 19731, 19734, 19737, 19747.5, 19747.7; Petowe 19807.7; Pie 19901; Pinelli 19940, 19940.5; Plato 19975; Pont 20103; Powel, Gabriel 20144; Pricket 20339; R., I., or J. 20574; Reasons 20792.7(?)*(A/C); Reniger 20887; Rennecherus 20889; Rich, B. 21000, 21001; Roesslin 21161; Rogers, Richard 21216; Rowlands, S. 21398, 21399; Rudd 21433.5, 21434; Saint German 21560, 21577; Saluste du Bartas 21660; Sanford 21734, 21736; Scoloker 21853; Scotland, proclamations 21959, 21960; Seton, J. 22254.7; Shakespeare, W. 22276, 22282; Shepherds' Kalendar 22420; Sherly 22426; Smith, H., Minister, Collections 22725, 22737; Smith, H., Minister, Single Works 22667; Spain 22992.5; Stoughton, W. 23318; Stow 23329; Straw 23357; Sutcliffe, M. 23461, 23465; Sutton, C. 23476, 23484(?); T., F. 23614; Tacitus 23645*; Tatius 23705; Terilo 23909; Theophrastus 23947; Thomson, G. 24030; Thornborough 24035; Tooker 24120; Trelcatius 24262; Trigge 24280, 24280.5; Tusser 24387; Warford 25068; Widley 25610; Willet 25692, 25704; Willymat 25760, 25761, 25761.5; Wit 25868; Wrednot 26014; Wright, T., Priest 26038.6 (?)*, 26040, 26043.3; Writing Tables 26050.6.

1605

A., L. T. 8; A.B.C. 20.8; Abbot, G., Abp. 26; Affinati d'Acuto 190; Almanacks (Dade, J.) 434.17; Almanacks (Digges) 435.59; Almanacks (Erra Pater) 439.19(c.); Almanacks (Gray) 451.15; Almanacks (Mathew) 483.3; Almanacks (Neve, Jeffery) 489.2; Almanacks (Pond) 501.5; Almanacks (Watson) 525.10; Alonso 535.5(c.); Aphthonius 702.5; Arcandam 726.5(c.); Argall 737; Armin 772.5; Askew, E. 855; Augustine 932; Ayton 1014.5; Bacon, F. 1113, 1114, 1164; Baldwin, W. 1265.5; Barclay, J. 1401; Barlement 1431.18; Barlow, W., Bp. of Rochester/Lincoln 1457; Barnfield 1486; Bastard 1560; Batt, J. 1590; Baxter, N. 1597(?); Bell, A. 1808, 1809(c.); Bell, T. 1819, 1825, 1831, 1833; Bellarmino 1835.5; Bergen-op-zoom 1900; Bible, Appendix 3020.5(c.), 3022.9; Bible, English 2194, 2195, 2196*; Bible, N.T., English 2904; Bible, N.T., Latin 2810b; Bible, O.T., Psalms 2516, 2517, 2518, 2518.7; Bignon 3057.7, 3058; Blundeville 3148*; Bowden 3432.3(c.?); Bradford, J., Prebendary of St. Paul's 3489a*; Bradshaw, W. 3516, 3524, 3525, 3530, 3531; Breton 3659, 3660, 3661, 3674, 3685.5(?), 3691.2, 3701; Brewer 3721; Brimeld 3757(?); Bristol 3794; Broughton, H. 3844, 3848, 3849, 3849.3, 3849.5, 3849.7, 3863, 3867.5, 3879, 3881;

1605 — *cont.*
Bruno, V. 3942.5; Buck, G. 3996; Buck, T. 3999.5; Byrd, W. 4243.5; Calvin 4405; Camden 4521; Canterbury, Province of 4585; Carew, T., Preacher 4617; Castalio or Chateillon 4772; Caumont 4868.3; Chapman, G. 4963, 4970, 4971, 4972, 4973; Cicero 5287(c.) (A/C); Clapham, H. 5338; Cockburne 5460.4, 5460.7; Cogan 5482; Coke, E. 5504; Comedy 5595; Considerations 5633.5; Cowell 5899; Crosse, H. 6071; Dallington 6200(aft.)(A/C), 6201, 6203(?); Daniel, S. 6239; Davies, J., of Hereford 6334, 6344(?); Dawson, T. 6392.5; Dedekind 6457; Dekker 6502; Demands 6572.5; Dent, A. 6628; Dering 6682*; Dialogue 6814; Digges, L. 6852; Dillingham 6885, 6891; Dod and Cleaver 6968.5; Dove 7078; Drayton 7216; Du Chesne 7276; Edinburgh University 7487.6; Ellis, G. 7606; England, Appendix 10019, 10019.5; England, C. of, Articles 10047, 10047.3; England, C. of, Visit. Articles 10158, 10176, 10256, 10289.7, 10305, 10314.3, 10321; England, Local Courts 7723; England, Parliament 7737; England, Proclamations, Chron. Ser. 8366, 8367, 8368, 8369, 8370, 8372, 8373, 8374, 8375, 8377, 8378, 8379, 8379.5, 8380, 8381, 8382, 8383, 8384, 8386, 8389(o.s.), 8390(o.s.); England, Public Documents, Misc. 9175e(A/C), 9211; England, Statutes, Gen. Colls. 9297; England, Yearbooks 9610; Epistle 10431.5(?); Erondelle 10513; Euordanus 10566.5; Fisher, John, S.J. 10915.5; Fitz, J. 10930; Forde, E. 11171.5*; Fraser 11335, 11337; G., I. or J. 11497; Gardiner, Samuel 11575, 11581; Garey 11600; Gentilis 11741; Goad 11923.5; Gray, A. 12200.5; Greene, R. 12227, 12273.5; Greenham 12317; Gwinne 12554; H., W., Gent. 12582*; Habermann 12582.15; Hacket 12588; Hall, Joseph 12679, 12679.5, 12685(?); Harrison, W., King's Preacher 12867*; Harsnet, S. 12882; Heliodorus 13044; Herrey 13229; Heywood, T. 13328, 13343; Hieron 13420; Hill, W. 13506; History 13527, 13527.5; Howard, C. 13857, 13857.5, 13857a; Hume, D. 13948.7, 13949, 13950, 13951; Hume, T. 13958; Hungary 13971; Hutten, L. 14023; Hutton, T. 14035; Ireland, Proc. 14152, 14153, 14154, 14155, 14156(o.s.); James I 14392, 14392.5, 14393; James, T., D. D. 14449, 14449.5; Jefferay 14481; Johnson, John, of Antwerp 14668 (?); Jones, Robert 14738; Jonson 14782; Kellison 14913; Kingsmill, T. 15006; Kyd 15085; L., M. 15107.7(c.?)(A/C); La Primaudaye 15239; Lambard 15156; Le Loyer 15448; Lear 15343; Leech, James 15363.3; Leech, John, Schoolmaster 15374.5; Leigh, W. 15422; Lincoln, Diocese 15646; Lindsay, Sir D. 15664.7; Liturgies, C. of Eng., BCP 16329, 16329a, 16329a.5; Liturgies, C. of Eng., Spec. Prayers 16534, 16535; Lodge and Greene 16681.5(?); Loeus 16692; London, Appendix 16763.5(c.); London, Apprentices 16768.2(c.); London, Ministers 16779.12(?); Luis 16916.2(A/C); Lydiat 17043, 17047; Lyly 17077; M., H. 17135; Manual 17270; Markham, G. 17384.5; Marlowe 17428; Marston 17475; Mascall 17584, 17593; Mason, Robert 17619; Maxey, A. 17684, 17684.5, 17688; Montgomery 18051; Morton, T., Bp. 18173.5, 18174, 18174a, 18184, 18184.5; Munday 18279; Murders 18288; Netherlands, States Gen. 18454.7; Nixon 18589; Oberndoerffer 18759.5; Ormerod 18851, 18852; Owen, L. 18995; Owsolde 19001, 19002; Oxford Univ., Quaestiones 19016; Oxford Univ., Verses, etc. 19043, 19049.5; Page, S. 19094; Pagit 19106(c.); Parker, Matthew 19288(?); Pasquale 19446; Pena, P., and L'Obel 19595.5; Perkins, W. 19648, 19706.5, 19706.7, 19733; Philips, E. 19853; Pilkington, F. 19922; Platt 19979.5; Playfere 20027; Polter 20093; Powel, Gabriel 20147, 20149, 20156; R., I., or J. 20575.5, 20575.7; Racster 20600; Radford 20602; Ratsey 20753, 20753a; Record, R. 20804.7; Rogers, Richard 21216a; Rollock, R. 21270; Romans 21288.7(c.); Rosier 21322; Rowlands or Verstegan, R. 21361; Rowlands, S. 21385, 21385.5, 21394(?), 21408; Rowley, S. 21417; Russell, E. 21456; Safeguard 21549; Saltern, G. 21635; Saluste du Bartas 21649, 21649a; Sandys, Sir E. 21716, 21717, 21717.5*; Sanford 21735, 21737; Savile, T. 21786; Shakespeare, W. 22276a, 22317, 22333; Sidney, P. 22543, 22543a; Smith, H., Minister, Collections 22753, 22766; Smith, R., Bp. of Chalcedon 22809; Smith, T., Merchant 22869, 22869.3; Smyth, J. 22877.1; Southwell 22947; Stow 23337; Stukeley 23405; Symonds, W. 23592; T., F. 23615; Tacitus 23645*; Temple, W. 23870; Thomas, a Kempis 23982; Thomas, L. 24004.5(c.) (A/C); Thornborough 24036(?); Tilenus 24072; Tourneur 24148.7;

1605 — *cont.*
Treswell, Robert 24268; Tymme 24421; Underwood 24519; Vaux 24627a.3*; Vennard 24639; Victor 24714; Vinciolo 24765.7(c.); Wagenaer 24931.5; Wakeman 24947, 24952; Warren, A. 25093; Wellington 25232, 25232.5; Welwood 25238.5; Werdmueller 25259.5*, 25259.7; West, W. 25271; White, Thomas, Writer against the Brownists 25408; Wilkes 25633; Wilkinson, R. 25653*; Willet 25682; Willoby 25756; Willymat 25762; Wirsung 25864; Woodhouse, P. 25967; Woodward, P. 25972.5, 25972.6(?); Wotton, A. 26002; Zanchius 26121, 26121.3, 26121.7, 26121a.

1606

Abbot, R., Bp. 48; Aberdeen 63; Ahmad I 207; Alison, R., Prof. of Music 356; Allen, R. 364; Almanacks (Alleyn) 408; Almanacks (Dade, J.) 434.18; Almanacks (Gresham) 452.5; Almanacks (Hopton) 461; Almanacks (Mathew) 483.4; Almanacks (Neve, Jeffery) 489.3; Almanacks (Pond) 501.6; Almanacks (Rudston, T.) 507; Almanacks (Woodhouse, W.) 532.5; Andrewes, L. 615; Androzzi 632, 632.7; Artemidorus 795; Attersoll 889; Bacon, F. 1139; Barclay, J. 1402; Barlement 1431.19; Barlow, W., Bp. of Rochester/Lincoln 1451, 1455, 1455.5; Barnes, B. 1468; Barrow 1524(?); Bartlet 1539; Baxter, N. 1598; Bell, T. 1826, 1827; Bible, Appendix 3023, 3023.5; Bible, English 2196*, 2197, 2198; Bible, N.T., English 2905, 2905.2; Bible, O.T., 'Books of Solomon' 2773; Bible, O.T., Prophets 2780; Bible, O.T., Psalms 2406, 2519, 2519.5, 2520, 2521, 2521.3, 2521.6; Bible, Selections 3012.7; Birnie 3089; Blundeville 3148*; Bodin 3193, 3193.5*(A/C); Bonaventura 3268(c.); Botero 3405; Bownd, Nicholas 3437; Bradshaw, W. 3522; Breton 3636, 3691.3, 3707; Brinsley, J., the Elder 3775; Broughton, H. 3867.7, 3891; Bryskett 3958, 3959; Bucanus 3961; Buckeridge 4002.5, 4003; Buonaccorsi 4102.5; Buoni 4103, 4103.3; Burton, W., Minister at Reading 4165a.5; Caesar, Caius Julius 4339(?); Camden 4520; Carier 4622; Carleton, G. 4644; Carlstadt 4658; Carpenter, J., Minister 4666; Casmannus 4769; Caudry 4867; Cecil, R. 4895, 4895.3, 4895.5; Chapman, A. 4960.5; Chapman, G. 4978, 4983, 4984; Chaucer 5101; Christian IV 5194; Cicero 5267.6; Clapham, H. 5328, 5344; Clapham, J. 5348; Clemangiis 5397; Closse 5441, 5441.2; Coke, E. 5505*, 5525; Cooper, or Coprario, J., Composer 5679; Cooper, T., Preacher 5693.5, 5693.7; Copinger 5725; Cornwallis 5776, 5776.3; Covell 5880; Cowper 5916; Craig, A. 5956; Crashaw, W. 6014; D., E., Doctor of Physic 6164; Daniel, S. 6256, 6262; Danyel 6268; Davies, J., of Hereford 6329; Dawson, T. 6396; Day, John, Dramatist 6412, 6413; Dekker 6498, 6498.2, 6514, 6522; Dell 6552, 6553; Dent, A. 6622, 6625.6, 6628.5, 6659; Dering 6682*; Desainliens or Sainliens 6750; Dillingham 6882, 6888; Dod and Cleaver 6954, 6954.5, 6969; Dodoens 6988; Donatus, L. 7019; Dove 7081; Dowland, J. 7093; Drayton 7225.5(?); East Indian Voyage 7456; East, M. 7461; Edwards, R. 7524; Elderton 7558; England, C. of, Visit. Articles 10137.3, 10181, 10301, 10357; England, Local Courts 7723.3; England, Parliament 7736, 7748.5 (?); England, Proclamations, Chron. Ser. 8387, 8389, 8390, 8391, 8392, 8392.5, 8393, 8394, 8394.3, 8395, 8396, 8397, 8398; England, Public Documents, Misc. 9212, 9213; England, Statutes, Chron. Ser. 9502, 9502.5, 9503, 9504; England, Statutes, Kalendars/ Indexes 9547; England, Yearbooks 9602; Erasmus, D. 10457, 10458; Estienne, C., and Liebault 10548; F., T. 10655; Fage, J. 10665; Fairlambe 10668; Family of Love 10683; Field, R. 10857, 10857.5*; Fitz, J. 10931(?); Fitzherbert, A. 10982; Fitzherbert, T. 11016.5, 11017; Fletcher, R. 11087; Flores 11094; Ford, J. 11158, 11160; Forset 11188; Fowns 11215; Freeman, J. 11368; Gardiner, Samuel 11572, 11576; Garnet 11618, 11619, 11619a, 11619a.5, 11620.5(?); Goad 11924; God 11926.5; Goosecappe 12050; Greene, R. 12302; Greenwood, H. 12337; Grymeston 12407.5(?); H., I. or J. 12568; H., W. 12580; H., W., Gent. 12582*; Hacket 12591; Hall, Joseph 12642, 12666, 12666a, 12667, 12667a, 12680, 12680.3, 12680.5, 12680.7; Harrison, W., King's Preacher 12867*; Hawes, E. 12940; Hayward, Sir J. 13001; Heliodorus 13045; Herrey 13230; Herring, F. 13244; Heywood, T. 13329, 13336, 13336.5; Hieron 13399.5, 13429; Hill, R. 13472; Hind 13509; Hoddesdon 13546; Holland, Henry, Vicar of St. Bride's 13587; Homilies 13678; Horatius Flaccus 13790a, 13790b; Howard, P. 13868.7; Howson 13887; Hubbocke 13898.5; Hutton, T. 14036, 14037; Ireland, Proc. 14156, 14157, 14158; Jacob, H. 14329; James I 14394; Jameson 14465.5*; Jesus Christ 14560.5; Jewel, J. 14586; Johnson, Francis 14662; Johnson, Richard, Moralist 14691.3; Jonson 14774; Julius, A. 14846; Keckermann 14895; King, J., Bp. 14974; Lambard 15157; La Perriere 15229.7(?)(A/C); Leigh, W. 15425; Le Mayre 15453.7; Lewkenor, E. 15561; Lily, W., 'Lily's Grammar' 15625, 15626*; Liturgies, C. of Eng., BCP 16330, 16330.3, 16331, 16450; Liturgies, C. of Eng., Spec. Prayers 16536(?), 16537; Liturgies, C. of Eng., St. Services 16490, 16494(?); London, Ords. and Regs. 16721, 16722; Lucinge 16897; Lyly 17061, 17078; Markham, G. 17350; Marlowe 17416, 17428a; Marston 17483, 17484, 17488, 17488.3; Maxey, A. 17685, 17685.5, 17690; Meditations 17775.5; Melville, E. 17813; Meredeth, R. 17832; Middleton, W., B. D. 17913; Montgomery 18051.3; Morley, T. 18123; Mornay 18140, 18162; Morton, T., Bp. 18175, 18175.5, 18185, 18188; Mucedorus 18231; Nixon 18582; Nobody 18597; Northbrooke 18669; Numan 18746; Oliphant 18807.7(?); Ormerod 18850; Ortelius 18855*; Osiander, L. 18880; Owen, John 18984.5, 18984.7; Owen, L. 18995.5; Oxford Univ., Off. Docs. 19002.7; Oxford Univ., Verses, etc. 19046; Palmer, Sir T. 19156; Parnassus 19309, 19310; Parrot 19334; Parry, H. 19335; Parsons, R. 19352; Patriarchs 19469.5; Paul V 19482; Peacham, H., the Younger 19500; Pelegromius 19558.3, 19558.7; Perkins, W. 19669, 19683, 19707, 19714, 19724, 19724.3, 19732, 19733a, 19748; Philopatris, pseud. 19884; Playfere 20008; Pope 20112.5; Powel, Gabriel 20142, 20145; Pricket 20342; Prosopopoeia 20444; Rastell, W. 20741*; Rawlinson 20773; Return 20905; Reynolds, J., Merchant 20941.7; Rhodes, J. 20960, 20960.5; Rich, B. 20983, 20997; Rider, J. 21032; Roberts, Henry 21079, 21085; Rollock, R. 21281; Rowlands, S. 21407(?); Rudd 21435; S., P. 21511; Saluste du Bartas 21649a.5; Sarpi 21759; Savile, T. 21787; Scotland, proclamations 21960.3, 21960.5, 21960.7, 21961, 21962, 21964, 21965; Scott, E. 22061; Shelford 22402; Sluys 22637; Smith, R., Bp. of Chalcedon 22809a; Smyth, W. 22880.9, 22881, 22881.5; Spagnuoli 22984.5; Spectacle 23030.3; Stubbes 23383; Suetonius Tranquillus 23422, 23423, 23424; Sutcliffe, M. 23448, 23452, 23452a, 23452a.5, 23464, 23469, 23470; Swynnerton 23558; Symonds, W. 23591, 23593; Thomas, T. 24013; Thomson, G. 24031; Thornton, Capt. 24043.5; Tilenus 24071; Trelcatius 24263; Trogus Pompeius 24293; Turnbull, R. 24341; Tymme 24422; Udall, T. 24508.5; Valesius [i.e. Wallace] 24587; Vorstius 24881; W., T. 24916, 24916.3; Wakeman 24948; Warner, W. 25085; Weever 25222; West, R. 25264; West, W. 25279; Whately 25318; Whetenhall 25332; Whitaker, W. 25360; Wily 25818; Wolcomb 25942; Wotton, A. 26004.

1607

Abbot, R., Bp. 49; Affectation 189.5; Ainsworth, H. 228; Alexander, W. 344; Almanacks (Alleyn) 408.2, 408,3; Almanacks (Bretnor, T.) 420; Almanacks (Dade, J.) 434.19; Almanacks (Gresham) 452.7; Almanacks (Hopton) 461.2; Almanacks (Lighterfoote) 480; Almanacks (Mathew) 483.5; Almanacks (Neve, Jeffery) 489.4, 489.5; Almanacks (Pond) 501.7; Almanacks (Rudston, T.) 507.2; Almanacks (Woodhouse, W.) 532.6; Apollonius 710; Ariosto 747; Aristotle 765; Arthington 797; Augustine 921.5, 945.7; Ayscu 1014; Baker, H. 1215.5; Balmford 1334, 1337, 1339; Barbary 1376.5; Barksted 1429; Barlow, W., Bp. of Rochester/ Lincoln 1447, 1452, 1452.5; Barnes, B. 1466, 1466a; Beaumont, F., and Fletcher 1692, 1693; Becon 1729, 1769; Bernard, R. 1936, 1939; Beze 2024; Bible, English 2199, 2200, 2201, 2201.5; Bible, N.T., English 2905.3(c.), 2905.5; Bible, O.T., Prophets 2787; Bible, O.T., Psalms 2522, 2522.3, 2522.5(?), 2523, 2523.3, 2523.5, 2524, 2524.5, 2524.7, 2525; Bishop, W. 3097; Blackwell 3104, 3105; Bologna 3218.5(?), 3218.7; Bolton, E. 3222.5, 3222.7; Book 3346.5; Bowes 3434; Brabant 3471; Bradford, J., Prebendary of St. Paul's 3490; Breton 3671, 3671.5, 3687, 3707.4; Brinsley, J., the Elder 3775.3, 3776; Browne, J., Merchant 3908.7; Budden 4013; Bunny, F. 4097;

1607 — *cont.*
Buonaccorsi 4102.7, 4102.9; Burt 4131; Bury, G. 4179.5; Byrd, W. 4244.5; Caesar, Caius Julius 4340; Cambridge University, Act Verses 4474.3(+?), 4474.6(+?), 4474.12, 4474.19, 4474.46, 4474.51 (+?), 4474.73, 4474.104, 4474.119; Camden 4508; Campion 4538; Carpenter, J., Minister 4663; Cartigny 4701; Cash 4768; Cato 4848.3; Caumont 4868.5(+); Chapman, G. 4966; Choice 5141.7; Cicero 5300.7; Cleland 5393; Coke, E. 5491, 5492, 5492.2, 5492.4, 5505*, 5509, 5509.5; Collins, S. 5564; Cooper, T., Preacher 5702; Cordier 5759.3; Court 5876; Coventry 5884.5; Cowell 5900; Cowper 5926.5, 5926.7, 5933, 5933.3; Creswell 6038; Cuffe 6103; D., D. 6162; D., I. or J. 6172; Daniel, S. 6240; Daniel, S. 6263; Davies, J., of Hereford 6337; Davis or Davys, J. 6369; Day 6396.5; Day, A. 6405; Day, John, Dramatist 6417; Dekker and Webster 6537, 6539, 6540; Dekker and Wilkins 6541; Dekker 6508, 6532; Deloney 6567; Dent, A. 6629, 6641, 6659.5; Des Portes 6785; Desainliens or Sainliens 6744; Dobson 6930; Dod and Cleaver 6957, 6957.5, 6970; Dove 7082; Downame, G. 7103, 7116; Draxe 7176; Drayton 7204; Drury 7261; Ducci 7274; Edinburgh University 7487.7; England, Appendix 10011, 10011.2, 10011.4; England, C. of, Visit. Articles 10159, 10188.5, 10192.5, 10209.3, 10236.5, 10257, 10314.4, 10367, 10377.5; England, Proclamations, Chron. Ser. 8399, 8400, 8400.5, 8400.7, 8401, 8402, 8403, 8404, 8405, 8406, 8407, 8408, 8409, 8410, 8411(o.s.), 8412(o.s.); England, Statutes, Chron. Ser. 9505; England, Statutes, Gen. Colls. 9298; Estienne, H. 10553; Eusebius, Pamphili 10574; Ford, T. 11166; Forde, E. 11169; Foxe 11232; Frarinus 11334(+); Fuller, N., of Gray's Inn 11460; Fulwood 11482.4; Gap 11548.7; Garden 11559; Garnet 11620; Gheyn or Geyn 11810*; Gibson, T., Minister 11842; Goodwin, G. 12028; Goulart 12135; Greene, R. 12255, 12288; Grimaldus Goslicius 12373; Gwinne 12555, 12555.5; Hacket 12592; Hall, Joseph 12643, 12668, 12669, 12671, 12681, 12685.3(?); Harward 12918; Hayne 12981, 12981.5; Hayward, Sir J. 13002, 13005, 13005a; Herrey 13231; Heywood, T. 13317, 13371; Hieron 13392.3, 13392.7, 13395*, 13398, 13398.5, 13426; Hill, R. 13472.4; Horatius Flaccus 13789; Householder 13851; Hume, T. 13957; Humphreys 13967; Instructions 14107.5; Ireland, Proc. 14159, 14160; James I 14395, 14400, 14403; James I, appendix 14414, 14426; James, E. 14435.5; James, T., D. D. 14452, 14456(c.); Jesuits 14526.5, 14531; Jewel, J. 14611; Johnson, Richard 14688, 14690; Johnson, Robert, Gent. 14696; Jones, Robert 14737; Jonson 14783; Julius, A. 14847, 14849; Keckermann 14898; King, J., Bp. 14975, 14985; Kitchen 15023; Lambard 15171; Latimer 15282; Le Fevre 15380; Leech, Jeremy 15363.7; Lever, C. 15535, 15540; Lily, W., "Lily's Grammar" 15626*; Linaker 15640; Lipsius 15703.5; Liturgies, C. of Eng., BCP 16332, 16332.2, 16332.4, 16332.5*; Liturgies, C. of Eng., Ordinal 16467; Liturgies, Other Protest. C. 16589.5; Lloyd, L. 16618, 16622, 16623, 16623a, 16623a.5, 16626, 16631, 16631.5; Lowin 16874; Lydiat 17040; Lyly 17062; Man 17232.5; Markham, G. 17334, 17350.5, 17351, 17387.5; Marston 17487; Mason, F. 17595; Matthias 17659; Maxey, A. 17686; Meriton 17838, 17839; Middleton, T. 17890, 17892; Milborne 17917; Mohammed II 17996; Monmouthshire 18021; Mornay 18141, 18155; N., W. 18336; Netherlands 18435; Netherlands, States Gen. 18455; Newman, A. 18495, 18495.5; Niccols 18517; Nicholl 18532; Nixon 18592, 18593; Norden 18639; O'Neill, H. 18814; Owen, John 18986; Parker, R. 19294; Parkes, R. 19295; Parsons, R. 19354.5, 19370, 19417; Peacham, H., the Younger 19500.5; Peele, G. 19541; Pelling 19567; Perkins, W. 19677.5, 19707.5, 19724.9, 19732a, 19735.4, 19751; Philips, E. 19854; Picture 19898a.7; Platt 19977.3(c.); Playfere 20017, 20028; Plowden 20038; Powel, Gabriel 20146, 20147.5, 20152; Pricket 20340; Prideaux 20362; Procter, T., Esq. 20400; Protestants 20448; Rastell, J., Printer 20713; Rastell, W. 20741*; Raymond 20778; Record, R. 20805; Ridley, T. 21054; Rogers, Thomas, M. A. 21228; Rowlands, S. 21366, 21368, 21395; Russell, W. 21461; S., J. V. 21507; S., R. 21513.5, 21514; S., W. 21531; S., W., Christ's unworthy minister 21533.3; Saint German 21578; Salerno 21605; Saluste du Bartas 21665; Sarpi 21757; Schonaeus 21821.4; Scotland, Church of, Confession of Faith 22029$; Sermon 22236; Serres, J. 22244;

1607 — *cont.*
Serres, O. 22249, 22249.3; Shakespeare, W. 22349, 22360(?)*; Sharpham 22380, 22384; Shillocke 22434; Simson, Andrew, Schoolmaster 22564; Smith, H., Minister, Collections 22726, 22738, 22754; Smith, H., Minister, Single Works 22667.5; Smyth, J. 22877.3; Somerset, County of 22915, 22915.5, 22916; Sparke, T. 23019.5, 23020; Sprint, J., Vicar 23109; Stafford, H. 23131; Stafforde 23135; Stanford 23218, 23224; Stanhope, E. 23224.5*; Stockwood 23278.7; Stow 23330; Stradling 23354; Sum 23432.3; Sutton, C. 23477; T., A., Practitioner in Physic 23607; T., I., Sacrae Theologiae Doctor 23624.3; Taming 23669; Terentius 23891; Thomas, a Kempis 23982.3; Thucydides 24057; Tiberius 24063, 24063a; Tomkis 24104; Topsell 24123; Tourneur 24149; Tuke 24317; Turner, Richard 24346; Tymme 24422.5; Vaughan, W. 24614; Venice 24634.5; Vignier 24719; Virel 24770; Virgilius Maro 24805; Wake 24939, 24939.5; Wakeman 24951; Walkington 24967; Walsall, S. 24996, 24996.5, 24996a; Ward, W. 25057; West, R. 25263; Whately 25319; Wilkins, G. 25635, 25639; Wilkinson, R. 25656, 25657, 25658, 25658.5, 25659, 25662; Willet 25678, 25678a, 25693; Willymat 25763; Wilson, G. 25768; Woodward, P. 25972.4.

1608

Abbot, E. 23; Abbot, G., Abp. 27, 38, 38.5; Abbot, R., Bp. 44, 55; Ainsworth, H. 234; Almanacks (Alleyn) 408.4; Almanacks (Dade, J.) 434.20; Almanacks (Ellis) 439; Almanacks (Hopton) 461.3; Almanacks (Kaye) 467; Almanacks (Mathew) 483.6; Almanacks (Neve, Jeffery) 489.6; Almanacks (Pond) 501.8; Almanacks (Woodhouse, W.) 532.7; Andrewes, L. 617; Ariosto 744; Armin 772.7; Assize of Bread 876; B., Ste. 1069; Bailey, William 1201; Balbani 1233; Barlement 1431.17A(?)*, 1431.19A; Bell, A. 1812.7(?); Bell, T. 1819.5, 1824, 1832; Bernard, R. 1927; Beroaldus, P. 1968.7; Bettie 1980; Beze 2024.3; Bible, Appendix 3024; Bible, English 2202, 2203, 2204, 2205; Bible, N.T., English 2906; Bible, O.T., Prophets 2781; Bible, O.T., Psalms 2525.5, 2526, 2526.3*, 2526.6, 2527, 2527.5, 2527.7; Bible, Selections 3013; Bishop, W. 3098; Bluom 3162; Botero 3401; Bownd, Nicholas 3441, 3441.5; Brereley 3604.5, 3605; Breton 3647; Brinsley, J., the Elder 3775.5; Broughton, H. 3875, 3878; Bulkeley 4026; Burton, W., Minister at Reading 4168; Bury Saint Edmunds 4181; Cambridge University, Act Verses 4474.89, 4474.116; Camden 4513; Canterbury 4580; Cattan 4865; Chapman, G. 4967, 4968; Charron 5051(?); Chetwind 5126; Clapham, H. 5334, 5341, 5341a, 5342; Closet 5434; Coke, E. 5511, 5511.2; Collins, S. 5565; Colman, M. 5568; Comedy 5596; Cooke, James 5671; Cooper, T., Preacher 5694; Corderoy 5757; Cordier 5759.4; Cowper 5937; Craig, J. 5966.5(?); Crakanthorp 5982; Crashaw, W. 6027; Croce 6040; Crompton, R. 6054.2, 6054.4; D., D. 6161.5; Davies, Sir J. 6357; Davison 6374; Day, John, Dramatist 6411, 6416; Day, R. 6432; Dekker 6480, 6480.5*, 6481, 6482, 6485, 6496; Dempster 6580; Denison, J. 6596; Dent, A. 6613, 6613.5, 6646.7; Desainliens or Sainliens 6760; Dod and Cleaver 6955, 6958, 6959.5; Dod 6951; Dodson 6990; Downame, G. 7125; Downame, J. 7134, 7140.5*, 7145, 7147.5; Draxe 7183, 7185, 7187, 7187.5; Drayton 7218; Edmonton 7493; England, C. of, Constitutions/Canons 10071.5(c.?)*; England, C. of, Visit. Articles 10277, 10314.5, 10322; England, Customs 7690.7(?), 7691; England, Exchequer 7705, 7705.2, 7705.4; England, Proclamations, Chron. Ser. 8411, 8412, 8413, 8414, 8415, 8416, 8418.5, 8419, 8420, 8421, 8422, 8423, 8424, 8425(o.s.), 8426(o.s.), 8427(o.s.), 8429(o.s.), 8430(o.s.); England, Public Documents, Misc. 9175z.5(?+), 9214, 9214.3, 9215, 9217, 9219; England, Statutes, Gen. Colls. 9284, 9323; England, Statutes, Kalendars/Indexes 9548; Erasmus, D. 10462.5; Essex 10533.3(?); Estella 10543; Estienne, H. 10554; F., N. 10651; Faust 10712; Ferneseede 10826; Fitzsimon 11025; Fleming, A. 11045; Flores 11093, 11093.5; Forde, E. 11172*; Fotherby 11206; France 11262; Froissart 11399; Frost 11403; Fulbecke 11413, 11413.3, 11413.5; Gentillet 11744; Gheyn or Geyn 11810*, 11811; Glover, R. 11922; Grafton 12165; Greene, R. 12264; Gregory I 12349; Grimeston 12374; Grymeston 12408(?); Guides 12467; Guild 12488, 12488.5, 12494; Habermann 12582.16; Hakewill 12621,

1608 — *cont.*
12621a; Hall, Joseph 12648, 12648a, 12648a.5, 12661.7, 12662, 12662.5, 12663.2, 12699, 12700; Hamlet 12734.5; Hart, W. 12894; Helliar 13049; Hermes, Scoto-phile 13217; Herrey 13232; Heywood, T. 13330, 13330a, 13360; Hieron 13389, 13395*, 13406.3, 13422; Higgons 13453; Hill, R. 13472.7*; Hill, T. 13489, 13497; Hoddesdon 13545.5; Horatius Flaccus 13791, 13791.5; Informations 14084; Ireland, Customs 14128.3; Ireland, Proc. 14161; James I 14404; James, T., D. D. 14445; Jesuits 14524.7; Johnson, Francis 14660; Johnson, Richard 14679; Jonson 14761; Joseph, ben Gorion 14804; Kellison 14909; Kilby, R., of Derby 14950; King, J., Bp. 14986, 14987; Latewar 15266.5(?); Levens 15533.7; Lever, C. 15536; Lily, W., 'Lily's Grammar' 15626.1; Ling 15686.7; Littleton, T., Tenures, Engl. 15779; Littleton, T., Tenures, French 15755, 15755.3; Liturgies, C. of Eng., BCP 16332.5*, 16332.6, 16332.8, 16333, 16333.3(A/C), 16433; London, Ords. and Regs. 16723, 16723.5(?); Mabb 17156.3; Maihew 17197.5; Manuzio, A. 17281.3; Markham, G., and Machin 17398, 17398a, 17399; Matelief 17651; Middleton, R., of York 17874; Middleton, T. 17879, 17879a, 17888, 17896, 17896a, 17907; Milles, T. 17927; Morley, T. 18134; Mornay 18141.5; Morton, T., Bp. 18185a(+), 18191; Munday 18258; N., A. 18325, 18325.3; Netherlands, States Gen. 18455.3; Niclas 18553; Nowell, Middle Catechism 18718.5; O'Dougherty 18784, 18785, 18785.5, 18786(A/C); Ortelius 18855(?)*; Oxford Univ., Quaestiones 19016.1; P., B. 19057; P., T. 19078.8; Panke, J. 19171; Parliament 19307; Parrot 19330; Parsons, R. 19385.5, 19408; Partridge, John 19430.5; Peacham, H., the Younger 19511.5; Perkins, W. 19649*, 19670, 19678, 19697, 19715, 19722, 19755; Pettie 19822; Piscator 19957.3; Platt 19980, 19990; Polanus 20085; Price, D. 20296, 20298, 20301; Pricke 20338; Pullein 20493; Questions 20560.3(c.?); Rainolds, J. 20612.3; Ravisius 20763.2, 20763.3, 20763.4, 20763.5; Redemption 20825; Rogers, Thomas, M. A. 21241; Rosa 21317; Rowlands, S. 21368.5(?)*, 21368.7, 21386; Saint Andrews Univ. 21555.12, 21555.13(?); Salerno 21606; Sallustius Crispus 21625*; Saluste du Bartas 21650; Sansbury 21743; Scotland, proclamations 21963; Shakespeare, W. 22283, 22291*, 22292, 22293*, 22310, 22311, 22340, 22360a(?)*; Smith, H., Minister, Collections 22767; Smith, John, Gov. of Virginia 22795, 22795.3, 22795.5, 22795.7; Smyth, J. 22876; Stanhope, E. 23224.5*; Stevin 23264; Stock 23274.5; Stoneham 23290; Stubbes 23383.5; Sum 23433.5; Susenbrotus 23440; Sutton, C. 23485.5; Taffin 23653; Tapp 23679.5; Thomas, a Kempis 23996.5; Throgmorton, R. 24053, 24053.5; Timberlake 24080; Topsell 24124; Torsellino 24140.5, 24141; Tourneur 24150; Trelcatius 24263.3; Trendle 24263.7; Tuke 24315.5, 24315.7; Tuvil or Toutevile 24396; Twyne, B. 24405; Tye 24414, 24414.5; Tymme 24423; Udall, J. 24497; Ulster 24515; Vaughan, W. 24611; Veen 24627a.8, 24627a.9, 24627a.10; Venice 24635; Virginia Company 24830.4; Wake 24936; Walker, R. 24963; Walkington 24971; Weelkes 25202, 25204; West, R., of Magdalen Coll., Oxford 25262; Westerman 25280; Whately 25319.3; White, John, D. D. 25394; Wiclif 25589; Wilkes 25634; Wilkins, G. 25638.5; Wilkinson, R. 25653.5; Willet 25683, 25683a, 25686; Wilson, J., Priest 25771; Wingrave 25852.7; Withals 25885, 25885.5; Woodcoke 25965; Woodward, P. 25972.2; Worship 25988; Worthington, T. 26000.8; Wotton, A. 26009; Wright, L. 26033; Youll 26105; Zanchius 26121a.3.

1609

Abbot, R., Bp. 50.5; Ainsworth, H. 235; Almanacks (Alleyn) 408.5; Almanacks (Bretnor, T.) 420.2; Almanacks (Dade, J.) 434.21; Almanacks (Erra Pater) 439.21(?); Almanacks (Hill, H.) 457.14; Almanacks (Kaye) 467.5; Almanacks (Mathew) 483.7; Almanacks (Neve, Jeffery) 489.7, 489.8; Almanacks (Pond) 501.9; Almanacks (Rudston, T.) 507.4; Andrewes, L. 626, 626.5; Ariosto 744.5; Armin 773, 774; Ashe 840; Attersoll 898; Augustine 953.5; Bacon, F. 1127; Barclay, W., Prof. of Civil Law 1408, 1408.3; Barker, A. 1417; Barlow, W., Bp. of Rochester/Lincoln 1446, 1446.5, 1450; Bell, T. 1816; Benson 1886; Bernard, R. 1937, 1940, 1952.5, 1963.3; Bible, Appendix 3025; Bible, English 2206, 2207*; Bible, N.T., English 2906.5, 2907; Bible, O.T., Prophets 2784; Bible, O.T., Psalms 2522.5*, 2526.3*, 2528, 2528.5, 2529, 2529.3, 2529.5, 2530, 2530.3, 2530.5, 2531, 2532; Bicknoll 3050.3; Biddulph 3051; Blackwell 3103; Blagrave 3116; Blundeville 3157; Boethius, A. 3202; Boys 3455; Bradshaw, W. 3510; Breton 3688, 3691.5; Brinsley, J., the Elder 3775.7, 3776.5; Broughton, H. 3844.5, 3844.7(?), 3858, 3872, 3874.7, 3877.7(?), 3879.5, 3880, 3889.3(?), 3889.7(c.?); Buddle 4014; Butler, C. 4192; C., Ro. 4300; Calvin 4396; Cambillion 4469.5; Cambridge University, Act Verses 4474.13, 4474.49, 4474.114, 4474.130; Canisius 4569; Cardinals 4610, 4611; Cary, W. 4731.7; Catharinus 4830; Cawdrey, R. 4884.5, 4888; Chapman, G. 4976; Cheaste 5106; Clapham, H. 5336; Coke, E. 5494; Colynet 5590.5; Cooper, T., Preacher 5694.5, 5696; Cortes 5804; Cowper 5919.5, 5937.3; Craig, A. 5959; Crakanthorp 5979; Crashaw, W. 6028; D., I. or J. 6172a; Daniel, S. 6245; Davies, J., of Hereford 6330, 6332; Dawes, L. 6388; Dekker 6486, 6499, 6500, 6519, 6519.2, 6519.4, 6536; Deloney 6557.2(?); Demands 6574; Denakol 6582; Dent, A. 6624, 6625.7, 6629.5, 6637.5, 6647; Desainliens or Sainliens 6745, 6751; Desiderius 6777.4; Dillingham 6886; Dod and Cleaver 6960, 6963, 6971; Dod 6940, 6944.7; Dolabella 6991.5, 6991.7; Downame, G. 7124; Downame, J. 7135, 7140.5*, 7141; Draxe 7186, 7188; Drayton 7204.5; Du Moulin, P., the Elder 7325, 7325.5; Du Terrail 7371; Du Vair 7373.5; Dyer, J. 7387; Eburne 7469, 7470; Edmondes, C. 7490.5, 7490.7, 7491; Egerton, T. 7540, 7540.5; England, C. of, Visit. Articles 10137.3C (A/C), 10207.5, 10225, 10372.2; England, Proclamations, Chron. Ser. 8425, 8426, 8427, 8428, 8429, 8430, 8431, 8432, 8433, 8434, 8434.5, 8435, 8436.5, 8437, 8438, 8439, 8439.5, 8440, 8441, 8442, 8443, 8444(o.s.), 8445(o.s.), 8445.5(o.s.), 8454(c.?), 8619*; England, Public Documents, Misc. 9211.2, 9211.3, 9211.4, 9216; England, Statutes, Spec. Subjs. 9341; England, Yearbooks 9616; Est 10537; Eudes 10561; Exercise 10616(?); F., N. 10652; Ferrabosco 10827, 10828; Fiston 10923; Fitch 10928, 10928.3; Fitzherbert, A. 10964.5; Forde, E. 11172*; Foxe 11246; Freeman, J. 11366.5; Fulbecke 11413.7; Galli 11538; Gardyne 11596; Goodwin, M. 12032; Grahame 12168; Gray, R. 12203, 12204; Greene, R. 12228, 12288.5; Greenwood, H. 12335.3; Greville, F. 12362; Grimeston 12375; Guild 12488.3; Hall, Joseph 12644, 12644.5, 12670, 12672, 12682, 12686(?), 12693.7, 12694, 12694a, 12696, 12697, 12697a, 12701, 12712; Hampton, C. 12740; Harris, James 12805; Hart, W. 12894a; Hayward, J., D. D. 12985; Heale 13014; Heath, R. 13018.3; Henry IV, King of France 13123; Herring, F. 13245, 13245a; Heywood, T. 13337, 13361, 13366; Hieron 13386, 13393, 13399, 13427; Higgins, J., Poet 13446*, 13447*, 13447.5*; Higgons 13452, 13454; Hill, R. 13472.7*; Hoby 13541; Holbrooke 13565; Homer 13633(?); Hopkins, J. 13768; Hopkins, T. 13770; Hoskin 13838; Hotman, J. 13849; Howson 13882*(A/C); Hunnis 13981; I., S. A. 14064.3; Ingmethorp 14087; Ireland, Proc. 14162; Jackson, Thomas, of Canterbury 14298, 14303; Jacob, H. 14339; James I 14396, 14396.3, 14396.7, 14401, 14401.5, 14402, 14405, 14406, 14407 [not STC], 14408; James, L. 14436; Jesuits 14525; Jewel, J. 14579, 14580*; John, Chrysostom 14631; Johnson, Francis 14659; Johnson, Robert, Chaplain 14694; Johnson, Robert, Gent. 14699, 14699.3, 14699.5; Jones, Richard 14730; Jones, Robert 14734, 14735; Jonson 14757, 14758, 14778; Josephus 14810; Julius, A. 14852, 14855, 14857; Kent 14934; Le Petit 15485; Leech, H. 15362, 15362.5, 15363; Leigh, W. 15424; Lennard 15460; Lescarbot 15491; Lever, C. 15537.5*; Linton 15692; Liturgies, C. of Eng., BCP 16333.5, 16334; Lodge 16669; Loe, the Elder 16685; London, Bills of Mort. 16743.4, 16743.5; London, Ords. and Regs. 16724*(A/C); Lowin 16875; Luis 16916.3; Lydiat 17041; Lyly 17079; M., R., Student in Divinity 17149, 17149.5; M., W. 17155; Mabb 17156.7; Macropedius 17176.6; Manual 17271; Marcelline 17310 [not STC]; Marcellinus 17311; Markham, G. 17359; Marlowe 17417, 17430; Mascall 17585*; Mason, Robert 17620; Mayer 17741; Mayo 17755; Melton, J. 17805; Meteren 17845.3; Middleton, T. 17894, 17894.5, 17904.3; Milles, T. 17925.5(?), 17933(?); Morgan, N. 18105; Morindos 18108; Morley, H. 18115; Mornay 18153; Morton, T., Bp. 18176, 18181; Munday 18265; Namur 18347.5; Netherlands,

1609 — *cont.*
Southern Prov. 18472a.5; Netherlands, States Gen. 18455.7, 18456; Nixon 18594, 18595; Norden 18618.7, 18626a.5; Nowell, Middle Catechism 18734; Openshaw 18822.8; Ornithoparchus 18853; Oxley, T. 19053; Palmerin, of England 19162; Parsons, R. 19372, 19412; Pasquil 19451.5; Pelegromius 19559, 19559.5; Penry 19607; Perkins, J. 19642; Perkins, W. 19649*, 19677, 19677.3, 19708; Pimlico 19936; Platt 19981; Playfere 20026; Poland 20083.3*; Price, D. 20302, 20305; Pricke 20337, 20337.3; Pulton 20495; Rainolds, J. 20605, 20607, 20629; Rastell, J., Printer 20714; Ravenscroft 20757, 20759; Rawlinson 20772; Redman 20826.5; Reuter 20914; Revels 20917.5; Rich, B. 20985, 20999*; Robinson, T., Musician 21127; Rogers, Richard 21204.5, 21204.7, 21205; Rosseter 21333; Rowlands, S. 21367, 21378, 21387, 21413; Rowley, W. 21424; Salerno 21607; Sallustius Crispus 21625*; Scotland, statutes, etc. 21892.7, 21893; Scott, M. 22061.5; Searle, J. 22142; Shakespeare, W. 22324, 22331, 22332, 22334, 22335, 22353, 22353a; Skene 22624, 22626; Smith, H., Minister, Collections 22727, 22739, 22755; Smith, H., Minister, Single Works 22668; Smith, R., Bp. of Chalcedon 22813; Smith, T., Doctor of Civil Laws 22862; Smyth, J. 22875, 22877; Soto, F. 22938; Southwell 22953, 22961(?); Speidell 23060.5; Spenser, E. 23083; Stallenge 23138, 23139; Stock 23276; Stockwood 23284.5; Sudlow 23421; Sum 23434, 23434.5; Sutton, C. 23478; Symonds, W. 23594; Taffin 23654; Taylor, Thomas 23820; Thomas, a Kempis 23982.5; Tichborne 24064; Timberlake 24081; Topsell 24125; Tourneur 24148; Trogus Pompeius 24288.5; Tuke 24308, 24309, 24313, 24313.3, 24313.5; Tuvil or Toutevile 24395; Tynley 24472; Udall, T. 24508.3; Ulster 24515.5; Ursinus, J. 24526; Valentinus 24577; Veer 24628; Villegas 24730; Virel 24770.5; Virginia Company 24830.9(?), 24831; Walkington 24966, 24966a; Walsingham, F. 25002; Ward, J., Capt. 25022, 25022.5; Webbe, G. 25162; Whately 25300, 25300.5, 25319.5; Wilbye 25619a; Wilkes 25634a; Willoby 25757; Wittenhorst 25934; Woman 25948; Woodwall 25970; Wotton, A. 26008; Writing Tables 26050.8; Wybarne 26055.

1610

A., S. W. 17(c.); Abbot, R., Bp. 53; Ainsworth, H. 220.5; Alliston 377; Almanacks (Alleyn) 408.6; Almanacks (Bretnor, T.) 420.3; Almanacks (Dade, J.) 434.22; Almanacks (Erra Pater) 439.23(?); Almanacks (Hopton) 461.5; Almanacks (Mathew) 483.8; Almanacks (Neve, Jeffery) 489.9; Almanacks (Pond) 501.10; Almanacks (Rudston, T.) 507.5; Almanacks (Savage) 508; Almanacks (Woodhouse, or Wedhouse, or Wydowes, J.) 531; Andrewes, L. 596, 598(?), 598.5(?), 604, 612, 612.5, 613(?), 616(?), 618, 619(?), 627, 628; Anthonie 668; Arcandam 726.7(c.); Assize of Bread 877; Attersoll 894, 894.5; Augustine 916; Baldwin, W. 1266; Ballad 1331.5(c.); Balmford 1337.5; Barlement 1431.20, 1431.21; Barrough 1512; Baybush 1599.7; Becanus 1699, 1708; Becon 1769.5; Bedle 1794; Bell, A. 1810; Bell, T. 1815; Benefield 1867; Bernard, R. 1934, 1958; Bernard, St. 1919*; Bevis 1992(c.?); Bible, Appendix 3025.5(?); Bible, English 2207*, 2208, 2209, 2210, 2211, 2212*, 2213*, 2214*; Bible, N.T., English 2908; Bible, N.T., Gospels 2963; Bible, N.T., Latin 2811.5; Bible, O.T., Psalms 2533, 2533.5, 2534, 2534.5, 2535, 2535.3, 2535.5, 2536, 2704(c.); Bilson 3066; Blenerhasset 3130; Bodenham 3190; Bolton, E. 3220, 3220.5; Bonaventura 3271; Book 3364; Boys 3456, 3456.4, 3456.7, 3458, 3459, 3459.3; Brewer 3717.3; Brisset 3791; Bristol 3795(c.?); Brocardo 3810.5; Broughton, H. 3868, 3877(?), 3877.3(?), 3883, 3884; Bunny, E. 4091; Byrd, W. 4244, 4245, 4258; C., L. W. 4288; C., T. 4307.5, 4314; C., W., Bachelor of Civil Law 4323.3; Camden 4509; Campion 4542; Cancellar 4562.5(c.); Carleton, G. 4637; Castalio or Chateillon 4777; Cato 4848.5; Chapman, A. 4961; Cheke 5112; Chester, City 5118; Christ's Hospital 5208(bef.?), 5208.5; Cleaver 5385.5, 5391; Cleves 5413; Clyfton 5450; Coeffeteau 5474; Coke, E. 5497, 5500, 5503; Collins, T. 5566; Cooke, A. 5659; Cooper, T., Preacher 5697.5; Corkine 5768; Cornwallis 5777; Cotton or Coton, P. 5862; Cotton, Roger 5868; Cowper 5917, 5928.5; Crashaw, W. 6016, 6029; D., D. 6163(?); Dawson, T. 6393; De Beau Chesne and Baildon 6450(c.); Dekker 6524; Dent, A. 6614,

1610 — *cont.*
6619, 6630; Dialogue 6809.5; Dod and Cleaver 6965, 6971.3; Dod 6937.5, 6941, 6944.4, 6945, 6945.2, 6950, 6952; Dodson 6990.5; Donne, J. 7048; Dove 7077; Dow, Z. 7090.5; Dowland, R. 7099, 7100; Drayton 7200, 7220; Du Moulin, P., the Elder 7322, 7333, 7339; Dunster 7354; East, M. 7462; Edinburgh University 7487.8; Egerton, S. 7528; Elyot, T. 7657; England, C. of, Visit. Articles 10159.2(?), 10195, 10198, 10204.5, 10226, 10305.5, 10378; England, Customs 7691.2(?), 7691.4; England, Proclamations, Chron. Ser. 8444, 8445, 8445.5, 8446, 8447, 8449, 8450, 8451, 8452, 8458(?), 8461(o.s.); England, Proclamations, Collections 7759; England, Public Documents, Misc. 9175i.8, 9175z.15(?), 9220, 9221(o.s.), 9222(o.s.), 9223.2(o.s.); England, Statutes, Chron. Ser. 9506, 9506.5; Epictetus 10424, 10425; Eudes 10562; Example 10610(c.?); Faust 10712.5; Field, R. 10857.7; Fitzherbert, T. 11019; Fletcher, G., the younger 11058, 11059; Fletcher, John 11068(?); Folkingham 11123; Forbes, J., Minister 11134; Foxe 11227, 11227.3; Gainsford 11526; Gardiner, E. 11564; Gaultier 11691a; Germany 11795; Ghisi 11813; Glasgow 11915; Gordon, J., Dean of Salisbury 12054, 12063; Greene, R. 12274; Gregory, of Nazianzus 12346; Guillim 12500; H., I. or J. 12567; Habermann 12582.24, 12582.25; Hall, Joseph 12649, 12649a, 12663.4*; Haren 12769, 12770; Harris, Robert 12817; Hayward, Sir J. 12996(?)*, 13005a.5; Heath, J. 13018; Heidelberg Catechism 13031.2; Henry IV, King of France 13136, 13137, 13140, 13147.5, 13147.7; Henry, Prince of Wales 13159, 13161; Herring, F. 13246; Heywood, T. 13331; Hieron 13406.5; Higgins, J., Poet 13446*, 13447*, 13447.5*; Hill, R. 13473; Hippocrates 13521; Histrio-mastix 13529; Hobbs 13538; Holbrooke 13564(?); Holyoke 13622; Hopton 13776; Horne, W. 13826.5; Hoskin 13839; Hull, J. 13933; Ireland, T. 14267; Jacob, H. 14336, 14337; James, T., D. D. 14446; Jeamie 14479.7(c.); Jesuits 14528; Joannes, Metropolitanus Euchaitensis 14622; Johann Justus 14628; John, Chrysostom 14629*; Johnson, Richard 14689; Jones, Robert 14736; Jourdan 14816; Julius, A. 14854; Knight, W. 15049; Knolles 15052; Kyd 15090*; L., T. 15111.3, 15111.5; Lambard 15158, 15172; Lambert, P. 15182; Le Macon 15452; Leigh, W. 15423.5; Lever, C. 15537.5*; Lily, W., 'Lily's Grammar' 15626.2; Linaker 15640.5, 15643.5; Lindsay, Sir D. 15665, 15680; Ling 15687(?)(A/C); Liturgies, C. of Eng., BCP 16335.5*, 16451; Liturgies, C. of Eng., St. Services 16495(?); Liturgies, Latin Rite, Manuals 16159; Lloyd, L. 16633; Loarte 16644; Lodge 16675; London, Appendix 16764(c.), 16764.3(c.); London, Bills of Mort. 16743.6; London, Leathersellers 16778.6(c.); London, Ords. and Regs. 16724(?)*(A/C); Marcelline 17309; Markham, G. 17376, 17376.5; Mascall 17585*; Mason, John, of Cambridge 17617; Maxey, A. 17687, 17691; Meteren 17845.7; Milles, T. 17926, 17934; Milwarde 17942; Montreux 18053; Morton, T., Bp. 18177, 18183; Mucedorus 18232; Muschet, Poet 18307; Myriell 18323, 18323a; Nixon 18596; Norden 18620, 18640, 18640a, 18640b; Nowell, Middle Catechism 18719; Owen, D. 18983, 18983.5; Owen, T. 19000; Oxford Univ., Verses, etc. 19050; Paris Univ. 19204; Parsons, R. 19386; Partridge, John 19436.3(c.); Patriarchs 19470; Pelletier 19565; Perkins, W. 19698; Playfere 20005; Plowden 20047.5; Plutarch 20069*; Polyander 20096; Price, D. 20290, 20292; Procter, T., Esq. 20401; Puente 20485; Pulton 20496; Rainolds, J. 20608, 20630; Ravaillac 20754, 20755, 20755.5; Rawlin 20768(?); Reasons 20792.7(c.?)*(A/C); Record, R. 20806; Reuter 20916; Rich, B. 20992; Rich, R. 21005; Rid 21028.5; Roberts, A. 21073; Robinson, J., Pastor of Leyden 21109; Rogers, Richard 21206, 21217; Romans 21289; Room 21315.2; Rowlands, S. 21395.5; S., T. 21520.5; Saint Andrews Univ. 21555.14, 21555.15; Saluste du Bartas 21648.5*(A/C); Saravia 21751*; Schonaeus 21821.6; Sclater, the Elder 21847; Scotland, appendix 22008; Scotland, Church of, Confession of Faith 22024.5(c.); Selden 22171, 22174; Shakespeare, W. 22360b(?)*; Sharpe, Roger 22379; Sharpham 22385; Skory 22629; Smith, H., Minister, Collections 22768; Smith, T., Doctor of Civil Laws 22868; Smyth, Richard 22877.8; Snawsel 22886; Soezinger 22890.5; Speed, John, Genealogies 23039c(?); Stepney 23252(c.); Stock 23275; Stoneham 23289; Stoughton, T. 23315, 23315.5; Stubbes 23384, 23399;

1610 — *cont.*
Sturtevant 23408.4; Thomas, L. 24005; Thomas, T. 24014; Topsell 24126; Trelcatius 24261; Tuke 24303.7, 24308a; Tusser 24388; Tymme 24424; Ulster 24516; Vaughan, Rowland 24603; Villegas 24731; Virginia Company 24830.5, 24831.3, 24831.7, 24832, 24832a, 24833; W., T. 24919.5(?); Wakeman 24950; Walpole, M. 24992; Way 25132; Web 25150; Webbe, G. 25164; Weever 25222.5; West, W. 25272; Whately 25301; White, John, D. D. 25395; Wilbye 25619.3(?)*(A/C); Wilkinson, R. 25654; Willet 25689, 25689.3, 25698.7; Wilmot 25765.5; Wilson, T., Divine 25797; Wintter 25858.3; Worship 25989; Wright, E. 26020.

1611

Abbot, R., Bp. 48.5, 50, 54; Ainsworth, H. 221; Almanacks (Bretnor, T.) 420.4; Almanacks (Dade, J.) 434.23; Almanacks (Hopton) 461.6; Almanacks (Johnson, J.) 465; Almanacks (Mathew) 483.9; Almanacks (Neve, Jeffery) 489.10; Almanacks (Pond) 501.11; Almanacks (Rudston, T.) 507.6; Almanacks (Savage) 508.3; Almanacks (Woodhouse, or Wedhouse, or Wydowes, J.) 531.1; Andrewes, L. 605, 614(?), 620, 621; Aphthonius 703; Ariosto 745; Bankes, T. 1364; Barksted 1428; Barrey 1502, 1502a; Barrow 1525; Becon 1729.5; Bellarmino 1836, 1845; Benefield 1870; Bernard, St. 1919*; Bible, Appendix 3026; Bible, English 2212*, 2213*, 2214*, 2215, 2216, 2217, 2218*, 2224*; Bible, N.T., English 2909, 2909.5; Bible, O.T., Psalms 2353.5, 2536.5, 2537, 2537.5, 2538, 2538.5, 2538.7; Bicknoll 3050.5; Bilson 3067; Boemus 3198, 3198.5; Bolton, Robert 3228; Book 3347, 3361.7; Botero 3402; Bourne, W. 3429; Boys 3458.3, 3460, 3460.2; Brathwait 3568; Breton 3707.7; Brightman 3754; Brinsley, J., the Elder 3777; Broughton, H. 3847 (?), 3848.5, 3857, 3857.5, 3876, 3882, 3887.5(?); Buchanan 3986; Buckland 4007(?); Bunny, E. 4093, 4093.5; Burhill 4118; Byrd, W. 4255; Calvin 4424; Canisius 4570; Carleton, G. 4645; Cartwright, J. 4705; Cartwright, T. 4707.5; Cary, W. 4732; Casaubon, I. 4742, 4743 [not STC]; Castalio or Chateillon 4773; Caus 4868.7; Cecil, W., Baron Burghley 4900.5; Chapman, G. 4980; Chester, R. 5120; Cicero 5267.8, 5304; Cleaver 5392; Cleland 5393.3; Cleves 5414; Closet 5435; Coke, E. 5513, 5513.2, 5513.6*; Conversion 5650.3; Conway, J. 5653; Coryate 5807, 5808, 5810; Cotgrave 5830; Cotton or Coton, P. 5861, 5861.2; Cowper 5912, 5920, 5929; Craig, J. 5961.5; Crashaw, W. 6018; Crib 6039.5; Croce 6041; Daniel, S. 6242, 6243; Davies, J., of Hereford 6335, 6341, 6345.7(c.); Davison 6375; Denison, J. 6585, 6591; Dent, A. 6614.5, 6619.5, 6630.3, 6642, 6648, 6648.5, 6660, 6660.5; Dering 6718; Dictionary 6832.58; Digges, D. 6846; Dillingham 6890; Discourse 6906; Dod and Cleaver 6964, 6966; Dod 6938, 6945.4; Donne, J. 7022, 7026, 7027; Downame, G. 7115; Downame, J. 7138; Draxe 7182; England, C. of, Visit. Articles 10221, 10289.9, 10314.6; England, Parliament 7751, 7751.2; England, Proclamations, Chron. Ser. 8376, 8448*, 8461, 8465, 8466, 8467, 8468, 8469, 8470, 8470.5, 8470.7, 8471, 8472, 8474, 8475, 8476(o.s.); England, Public Documents, Misc. 9175i.9, 9221, 9221.5, 9222, 9223.2, 9225, 9226; England, Statutes, Gen. Colls. 9298.5, 9324; Est 10535, 10536.5; Everardus 10600; Fenton, R. 10806; Fitzsimon 11026; Florio 11099; Forrester 11187; French Herald 11374, 11374.5; Froissart 11400; Fulke 11425; Gardiner, E. 11564.5; Gardiner, Samuel 11577, 11580, 11582; Gerhard 11764; Gordon, J., Dean of Salisbury 12055.5(?), 12060, 12060a, 12063.5; Grafton 12166; Graile 12171; Greene, R. 12229, 12255.5; Greenham 12318*; Guillim 12501; Gwinne 12550; H., I. or J. 12569; Habermann 12582.17; Hall, Joseph 12663.4*, 12663.6, 12703; Hampton, C. 12739; Harris, Robert 12818; Helwys 13053, 13053.5, 13055; Henry IV, King of France 13122.5, 13134, 13142; Henry, the Minstrel 13151, 13151a; Hermes, Trismegistus 13218; Herrey 13232.5; Heywood, T. 13325; Hieron 13406.7, 13424; Higgons 13455.7, 13456, 13456.5; Homer 13634(?); Hooker, R. 13714; Hopkins, T. 13771; Hopton 13783; Horatius Flaccus 13792, 13792a; Hoskins, A. 13840; Hues 13906a; Hull, J. 13933a; Ireland, Proc. 14163; Jackson, J. 14297a.3; James, T., D. D. 14462; Jesuits 14534; Jesus Christ 14568.7; Jewel, J. 14580, 14580.5; John, Chrysostom 14629*, 14629.5*; John, King 14646; Johnson, Francis

1611 — *cont.*
14662.5(A/C), 14663; Jonson 14759; Julius, A. 14851, 14853.5; King, J., Bp. 14979; Kyd 15090*; Langhorne 15197; Lanyer 15227, 15227.5; L'Espine 15514.5; Lily, W., 'Lily's Grammar' 15626.3; Liturgies, C. of Eng., BCP 16335.5*, 16336, 16337; Liturgies, C. of Eng., Spec. Prayers 16538; Liturgies, Other Protest. C. 16590, 16591; L'Obel 16650.5; London, Diocese of 16776.12(?); London, Grocers 16777.16; London, Merchant Tailors 16778.7(?)(A/C); London, Ords. and Regs. 16724.5; Lowe 16870*; Luis 16911.5; Marlowe 17431; Maxwell 17700, 17702; Maynard 17749; Meriton 17840; Middleton, T., and Dekker 17908; Minsheu 17947.5(?); Mirandula, O. 17955; More, G., Esq. 18068; Morley, T. 18132; Mucedorus 18233; Munday 18263, 18267, 18267.5; Murray, D. 18296; Napier 18356, 18356a; O'Hussey 18791.5; Ovidius Naso 18961.7(A/C); Owen, T. 18999; Pagit 19106.5; Penry 19608.5; Penuen 19615; Perkins, W. 19671, 19686.5, 19691, 19705.4, 19723, 19725, 19729, 19738, 19745, 19761.3; Platt 19982; Playfere 20011, 20018; Polyander 20095; Portraiture 20126.3; Protestants 20449, 20449.5; Rainolds, J. 20631; Ravenscroft 20758; Rawlinson 20775; Reynolds, J., Epigrammatist 20941; Rollenson 21264; Rowlands, S. 21388, 21396; Saint Andrews Univ. 21555.16, 21555.17; Saluste du Bartas 21648.5*(A/C), 21651; Sanderson, T. 21711; Sanford 21738; Saravia 21751*; Savile, T. 21785; Sclater, the Elder 21838, 21839; Scotland, statutes, etc. 21892, 21894, 21894.5; Scott, T., Poet 22107.5; Seller 22182, 22182a; Selman 22182a.5*; Serlio 22235; Serres, J. 22245; Seton, J. 22255; Shakespeare, W. 22277, 22330, 22336; Sharpham 22381; Sheldon 22393; Shepherds' Kalendar 22421; Smith, H., Minister, Collections 22728, 22740; Smith, H., Minister, Single Works 22669; Soto, F. 22939; Spain 22992.7; Speed, John 23041*, 23045; Speed, John, Genealogies 23039, 23039d(+), 23039e(?), 23039e.2(?); Spenser, E. 23077.3, 23083.3, 23083.7*, 23084*, 23086.3, 23093.5; Spicer, J. 23101; Stafford, A. 23129, 23130; Standish, A. 23200.5, 23201, 23201.5; Stow 23331; Sutton, C. 23486; Swinburne 23548; T., R. 23625.5; Temple, W. 23871; Terentius 23888.5; Themylthorp 23934.2; Theresa 23948.5; Thomas, L. 24005.3(?)(A/C); Thomson, R. 24032; Timberlake 24082; Tooker 24119; Tourneur 24146; Treasure 24209; Trial 24269; Turberville 24325, 24325.5, 24329; Tuvil or Toutevile 24393.3; Ursinus, Z. 24537; Vaughan, W. 24614.5, 24622, 24622.5; Venner, W. 24649; Vincent, Saint 24753; Virginia Company 24830.6(?), 24833.2; Web 25150a; West, T. 25266; West, W. 25279.3; Widdrington 25596, 25596.5; Wilkins, G. 25636; Willet 25689.7, 25690; Willis, J., Petitioner 25743.5; Wilson, T., Divine 25795; Wrednot 26014.3(A/C); Writing Tables 26050.10.

1612

Adams 117; Alexander, W. 339; Allen, R. 363; Almanacks (Alleyn) 408.8; Almanacks (Bretnor, T.) 420.5; Almanacks (Dade, J.) 434.24; Almanacks (Farmer) 443.5; Almanacks (Hopton) 461.7; Almanacks (Johnson, J.) 465.1; Almanacks (Keene) 468; Almanacks (Mathew) 483.10; Almanacks (Neve, Jeffery) 489.10A, 489.11; Almanacks (Pond) 501.12; Almanacks (Rudston, T.) 507.7; Almanacks (Thomas) 517.14; Almanacks (Woodhouse, or Wedhouse, or Wydowes, J.) 531.2; Ames 551.7; Andrewes, L. 605.5; Anglerius 650; Antwerp 693; Anyan 697; Appelius 712; Attersoll 890; Augustine 932.5, 946; Bacon, F. 1139.5, 1141, 1141.5; Baker, H. 1216; Balbani 1234; Barret, W. 1501; Bayly, L. 1601.5; Beard, T. 1660; Becanus 1700, 1702; Bede 1782; Benvenuto 1895, 1896; Bernard, R. 1953; Bible, English 2218*, 2219, 2220, 2221, 2222, 2223*, 2225*; Bible, N.T., English 2910; Bible, O.T., Psalms 2407, 2539, 2540, 2540.5, 2541, 2541.5, 2542, 2544, 2544.2, 2544.3; Biddulph 3052; Bishop, W. 3098.5(+); Blaeu 3110; Bolton, Robert 3229; Book 3353; Boys 3460.5; Breton 3708; Brinsley, J., the Elder 3768, 3770b.5, 3774; Broughton, H. 3851.5(c.), 3867.9(?), 3870, 3874, 3889(c.); Browne, Agnes 3907; Bull, H. 4032.2; Cambridge University 4481, 4482; Cambridge University, Act Verses 4474.33; Carpenter, R. 4683; Cartwright, T. 4708; Casaubon, I. 4740, 4740.3(A/C), 4740.5(A/C), 4741; Case, J. 4757; Castiglione 4787; Cato 4859; Caus 4869*(A/C); Cecil, R. 4895.7(?); Cervantes

1612 — *cont.*
Saavedra 4915; Ch., R. 4923; Chamberlaine 4946.9; Chapman, G. 4974*, 4994; Chetwind 5127, 5128; Christian Religion 5188; Cicero 5309.9, 5310; Cleaver 5386; Cleland 5394; Clenardus or Cleynaerts 5404; Clyfton 5449; Cogan 5483; Coke, E. 5507; Collins, S. 5563; Colson 5584; Copley, J. 5742; Corkine 5769; Cotta 5833; Courtney 5878; Coverte 5895; Cowper 5929.2, 5936, 5938; Daborn 6184; Daniel, S. 6246; Davies, J., of Hereford 6338; Davies, Sir J. 6348; Davis, F. 6368; Davy du Perron 6383; Day, John, Rector 6420, 6422; Dekker and Webster 6538; Dekker 6487, 6507, 6530; Deloney 6568, 6569; Dent, A. 6617, 6624.4, 6630.5, 6638; Desainliens or Sainliens 6752; Digges, D. 6847; Dissertation 6917 [not STC]*; Dod and Cleaver 6956, 6959, 6971.5; Donne, J. 7023, 7058.5; Dowland, J. 7098; Downame, J. 7136; Drayton 7226; Du Moulin, P., the Elder 7312, 7340, 7341, 7343; Du Vair 7373.6; Edinburgh University 7487.9; Edmonton 7494; Egerton, S. 7528.5; England, Appendix 10025; England, C. of, Articles 10048; England, C. of, Constitutions/Canons 10072, 10072.5, 10072.7; England, C. of, Visit. Articles 10207.3, 10209.5(A/C), 10258, 10358; England, Customs 7691.6(?), 7691.8(?); England, Local Courts 7723.5; England, Proclamations, Chron. Ser. 8476, 8477, 8478, 8479, 8480, 8480.5, 8481(o.s.), 8482(o.s.), 8483(o.s.); England, Public Documents, Misc. 9227, 9228, 9229, 9230, 9231, 9232, 9233, 9234; England, Statutes, Kalendars/Indexes 9549; Fennor 10782.5, 10785; Fenton, R. 10807; Field, N. 10854; Floyd, J. 11111; Fougasses 11207; Fowler, J. 11212; Frewen 11380, 11380.2; Fulwood 11482.7; Galliardi or Gagliardi 11538.5; Gaufredy 11687; Gawton 11692; George, St. 11745.5; Germany 11794; Gibbons 11826; Gifford, G. 11847.5, 11856; Gordon, J., Dean of Salisbury 12055, 12056, 12064; Greenham 12318*, 12324; Guillemeau 12496; Hakewill 12618, 12618a; Hall, Joseph 12650, 12703a; Harris, Richard 12814; Harrison, W., King's Preacher 12864, 12868, 12868a; Helwys 13056; Henry IV, King of France 13121.5; Henry, Prince of Wales 13157.5, 13158; Herring, F. 13248.2; Heywood, T. 13309; Hieron 13407, 13417; Holbrooke 13566; Hooker, R. 13706, 13707, 13708, 13711, 13722; Hopton 13778; Hull, W. 13937, 13938; Hume, A., Schoolmaster 13946, 13947; Hutton, L. 14030; Ireland, Proc. 14164; Jackson, Thomas, of Canterbury 14304; Jacob, H. 14332; James, T., D. D. 14459, 14463; Jewel, W. 14618, 14618.3; John, Chrysostom 14629*, 14629a*, 14629.5*; Johnson, Richard 14672, 14691; Johnson, Richard, Moralist 14691.5; Johnson, Robert, Gent. 14700; Jonson 14755; Julius, A. 14848; Juvenalis 14889; La Marteliere 15140; Lake, O. 15136; Lambard 15158.5; Lawne 15324; Lecluse 15351.7; Legh 15393; Leigh, W. 15426; Ling 15687.3 (aft.); Littleton, T., Tenures, Engl. 15780; Littleton, T., Tenures, French 15755.7, 15756; Liturgies, C. of Eng., BCP 16337a.3; Llyfr Plygain 16638; Lodge 16670; London, Appendix 16756.5, 16759; London, Ords. and Regs. 16725; London, Shipwrights 16785(?); London, Stationers 16786.12; Lowe 16870*; Luis 16905, 16908.5; Lupton, T. 16959.5; Mandeville 17251.5; Marlowe 17439, 17439.5; Martyn, W. 17530, 17530.3(A/C); Mason, James 17615; Matthias 17660; Matthieu 17661; Maxwell 17701, 17705; Mayerne Turquet 17747; Menantel 17818; Mervin 17844; Milles, R. 17924, 17924.5; Milles, T. 17935(?); Monipennie 18014, 18014.5, 18014a, 18019; Moore, J. 18058; Mornay 18147, 18164, 18164.5; Netherlands, States Gen. 18457; Nethersole 18473; Newhouse 18494; Newsbooks, Unnum. 18507.43*; Nixon 18584, 18588, 18588.5; Norden 18620.5; Ovidius Naso 18952.3, 18962, 18976.8; Owen, John 18987, 18988, 18988.5; Oxford Univ., Verses, etc. 19020, 19021, 19021.5, 19047; Pacius 19083a; Panke, J. 19170; Paris 19200.3(A/C); Parkes, W. 19298; Parsons, R. 19373, 19409; Passage 19458.5, 19458.7; Paule 19484; Peacham, H., the Younger 19507, 19508, 19511; Pelegromius 19560; Perkins, W. 19650*, 19664; Petrarca 19810; Philotus 19889; Physiologus 19896.5; Playfere 20005a; Plutarch 20069*; Potts 20138*; Pownoll 20174; Primrose, W. 20393; Prompter 20432; Rawlinson 20773a; Regius 20851; Reuter 20910; Reynolds, J., Epigrammatist 20941.3; Rich, B. 20981, 21003; Richardson, C. 21016, 21016a; Richer 21024; Rid 21027; Rider, J. 21033; Roberts, Henry 21081a; Rogers, Richard 21203, 21207, 21213.1; Rogers, Thomas, of Tewkesbury 21241.5; Rollenson

1612 — *cont.*
21265; Rowlands, S. 21389(?), 21390, 21390.5; Ruytinck 21471; S., E. 21487.5; S., W. 21526; Safeguard 21550; Saint Andrews Univ. 21555.18, 21555.19; Saint Giles without Cripplegate 21588.5(?); Salerno 21607.3(A/C); Sclater, the Elder 21833, 21841, 21845; Scotland, statutes, etc. 21895, 21896; Selman 22182a.5*, 22183; Shakespeare, W. 22318, 22343; Sharpe, Leonell 22374, 22375; Sheldon 22395, 22397; Smith, H., Ballad Writer 22655.5; Smith, H., Minister, Collections 22756, 22769*; Smith, John, Gov. of Virginia 22791; Smith, T., Doctor of Civil Laws 22863; Smyth, Richard 22878; Sorocold 22932; Spa 22975(?); Sparke, W. 23028; Speed, John 23041*; Speed, John, Genealogies 23039.2(?), 23039a (?), 23039e.3(?); Spenser, E. 23083.7*, 23084*, 23085*, 23087*; Stafford, A. 23127; Standish, A. 23203; Strachey 23350; Stubbes 23385; Sturtevant 23411; Susenbrotus 23440.3; Swift, J. 23545; Sylvester 23576, 23577; T., A., Practitioner in Physic 23608; Tacitus 23646; Taylor, John 23760, 23760.5, 23769, 23791; Taylor, Thomas 23825, 23825a, 23830, 23830.3, 23830.5; Theodoret 23938; Thompson, T. 24026, 24027; Timberlake 24083; Tomlinson 24111; Tourneur 24147; Travers, W. 24187; Treatise 24229.5, 24233, 24251; Trial 24270; Turner, W. 24350(?); Tymme 24416; Underwood 24519.5; Valentinus 24578; Vaughan, E. 24596; Vaughan, W. 24615; Virel 24771; Virgilius Maro 24794.5; Virginia Company 24833.4; Vives 24852, 24852.3, 24852.7(?); Wakeman 24947.3, 24949; Warmington 25076; Warner, W. 25084; Webbe, G. 25158, 25163; Webster, J. 25178; Wh. 25293; White, John, D. D. 25396; Wiclif 25592; Widdrington 25597; Willet 25705(o.s.), 25707(o.s.); Wilson, T., Divine 25786; Wither, Poet 25901(o.s.), 25915; Wolcomb 25941; Worship 25992; Wotton, H. 26009.5.

1613

Abbot, G., Abp. 35; Abbot, R., Bp. 45; Adams 122, 131, 131a; Ahmad I 206; Ainsworth, H. 209; Alexander, W. 340; Allyne 384, 385; Almanacks (Bretnor, T.) 420.6; Almanacks (Burton) 426; Almanacks (Dade, J.) 434.25; Almanacks (Evans, J., Minister) 440; Almanacks (Farmer) 443.7*; Almanacks (Hopton) 461.8; Almanacks (Johnson, J.) 465.2; Almanacks (Keene) 468.2; Almanacks (Mathew) 483.11; Almanacks (Neve, Jeffery) 489.12; Almanacks (Rudston, T.) 507.8; Almanacks (White) 527; Almanacks (Woodhouse, or Wedhouse, or Wydowes, J.) 531.3; Anton 685; Aretius 736; Aurelius 960; Austin, H. 968; B., I. or J. 1046; Bacon, F. 1142, 1143*, 1144*; Baker, J., Minister 1222; Barlement 1431.22, 1431.23, 1431.24; Barlow, W., Bp. of Rochester/Lincoln 1453; Basse 1546; Bayly, L. 1602; Beaumont, F. 1663, 1664; Beaumont, F., and Fletcher 1674; Becanus 1703*, 1704; Becon 1771; Benefield 1861, 1869, 1871; Bernard, R. 1964; Bernard, St. 1908.5; Bethune, M. 1976; Beze 2002; Bible, English 2223*, 2224*, 2225*, 2226, 2227, 2228, 2229, 2230*, 2231*, 2232*, 2233*; Bible, N.T., English 2911, 2911.5, 2912, 2912.3*, 2912.5*; Bible, O.T., Psalms 2544.5, 2544.7(?), 2545, 2546, 2546.5, 2549.5*, 2749; Bible, Selections 3013.5; Blundeville 3149; Bodley 3194; Bologna 3218; Book 3292; Boys 3460.6, 3462, 3464; Breton 3691.7, 3704.3, 3704.5, 3709; Bright 3749; Brinsley, J., the Elder 3774.3, 3779*; Broad 3807; Brooke, C. 3831; Broughton, H. 3867(?), 3886; Browne, G. 3908.2; Browne, W., Poet 3914; Bunny, E. 4092; Burhill 4116, 4117; Buronzo 4125; Byrd, J. 4242; Byrd, W. 4251.5(?), 4252(+); C., I. or J. 4275; C., W. 4316; Camden 4513.4; Campion 4545, 4546, 4546.5(?), 4547(?); Caninius 4566; Cannon 4576; Carew, E. 4613; Carleton, G. 4631; Cato 4859.5; Cawdrey, R. 4885; Chamberlaine 4947; Chapman, G. 4974*, 4981, 4989; Cheaste 5105; Cheeke 5107; Christ's Hospital 5207.7; Christian IV 5193, 5194.4; Cleaver 5381; Coke, E. 5515; Colmore 5571; Colson 5583*; Cooper, T., Preacher 5699; Cotton, C. 5848; Cowper 5913, 5919, 5921, 5921.2, 5926, 5934; Crooke, S. 6063.2, 6066; Dallington 6197; Daniel, S. 6247; Danskin 6267.5(c.); Davies, J., of Hereford 6339; Davies, Sir J. 6349; Dekker 6528; Dennys 6611; Dent, A. 6618, 6661; Desainliens or Sainliens 6765; Despotinus 6786; Dionysius, Periegetes 6899(?); Dove 7080; Dowland, J. 7094; Downame, J. 7140, 7142; Draxe 7178, 7184; Drayton 7221, 7227; Drummond 7257; Du Moulin, P.,

1613 — *cont.*
the Elder 7306; Dunster 7355; E., G. 7433; Eburne 7474; Edinburgh University 7487.10; Edward IV 7504; Egerton, S. 7537; England, Appendix 10020.5; England, C. of, Visit. Articles 10190.5, 10192.6, 10196, 10222, 10237, 10290, 10314.7; England, Proclamations, Chron. Ser. 8455(c.?), 8481, 8482, 8483, 8483.3, 8484, 8485, 8486, 8487, 8488, 8489, 8490, 8491, 8492, 8493, 8494, 8495, 8496, 8497(o.s.), 8498(o.s.), 8498.5(o.s.); England, Proclamations, Collections 7760; England, Public Documents, Misc. 9175i.11, 9235; Erfurt 10511.7; Est 10538; Finch, H. 10870, 10872.7; Fitzherbert, T. 11021, 11022; Fletcher, Joseph 11076; Floyd, J. 11114; Forbes, P. 11149, 11149.3; Fosset 11200; Franchis 11308, 11309; Francis, of Sales 11316.5, 11317; Frederick I 11357, 11357.5, 11358, 11359; Gamage 11544; Gibson, Abraham 11829, 11830; Glanville 11907; Greenwood, H. 12335.5, 12337.5; Haga 12600; Hakewill 12614, 12619; Hall, Joseph 12673, 12686.3(+); Harcourt 12754; Harrison, John 12857.2, 12857.4, 12857.6, 12857.8; Harrison, S. 12863a(c.); Hayward, Sir J. 13000; Henry, Prince of Wales 13157, 13160; Herrey 13233; Heywood, T. 13310, 13310.3, 13323, 13332, 13344, 13355, 13365; Hieron 13378*, 13391, 13392, 13407.5, 13418; Hill, R. 13474; Hill, T. 13483; Hilliard 13507, 13507.3; Hinde, W. 13515; Hoby 13539, 13539a; Holland 13572; Holyoke 13623; Hooker, R. 13709; Horne, R., of Ludlow 13822.5; Howard, C. 13855.8; Hull, J. 13930; Hume, D. 13952; Ireland, Proc. 14165 (o.s.), 14166(o.s.); Jackson, Thomas, of Peterborough 14308, 14308.5; Jacob, H. 14328; Jenkinson 14493; Jerome, S. 14516; John, Chrysostom 14629*, 14629a; Johnson, Richard 14676; Johnson, Robert, Gent. 14697; Jourdan 14817; Kilby, R., of Derby 14950.5; Kilby, R., of Oxford 14957; King, Humphrey 14973; Kitchen 15024; Lawne 15323; Leigh, W. 15423, 15423.7, 15428; Leighton, W. 15433; Lichfild 15588; Lily, W., 'Lily's Grammar' 15626.4, 15626.5; Liturgies, C. of Eng., BCP 16337a.5, 16337a.7, 16338, 16338.3, 16339*; Liturgies, C. of Eng., Spec. Prayers 16539; Loarte 16647; London, Bills of Mort. 16743.6E(A/C); London, Ords. and Regs. 16725.3; Louis XIII 16830, 16831, 16831.5; Lydiat 17045; Lyly 17063; Maihew 17197; Mancinus 17239.7; Manual 17273, 17274; Manuzio, A. 17281.5; Market Harborough 17330.5; Markham, G. 17352, 17355, 17360; Marlowe 17418; Marston 17476, 17476.5; Martyn, W. 17531; Mason, F. 17597; Maurice 17676; Maxwell 17699.5, 17700.5, 17703; May, J. 17710; Mean 17757; Meung 17847, 17847.2; Michaelis 17854, 17854a; Middleton, R. 17870; Middleton, T. 17903, 17904; Milles, T. 17925(?), 17930(?), 17936; Montaigne 18042; Moore, J. 18059; Morton, T., of Berwick 18201; Motives 18213; Mucedorus 18234; Munster 18285(A/C); Murders 18287; Myriell 18322; N., R. 18334; Naile 18347; Nash, T. 18368; Niccols 18525; Niccols, of Inner Temple 18526.5; Nixon 18587, 18591; Notari 18697; Ovum Zephyrium 18981.5; Oxford Univ., Verses, etc. 19022, 19044, 19048; P., B. 19057.3; Pagit 19107; Palmer, Sir T. 19156.3(A/C); Panke, J. 19171a; Parkes, R. 19297; Parrot 19332, 19332.5; Peacham, H., the Younger 19513, 19513.5; Pemberton 19569; Perkins, W. 19650*; Pet 19792; Petrucci 19814; Pettie 19823; Pilkington, F. 19923; Plowden 20046; Potter, B. 20133; Potts 20138*; Powell, T., of Brasenose Coll. 20172; Price, D. 20291, 20294, 20295, 20299, 20304, 20304.5; Price, S. 20333; Purchas, S. 20505; Quin 20563; Rainolds, J. 20611, 20612.5, 20612.7*, 20613*, 20619, 20620*; Reuter 20915; Rich, B. 20982, 20994; Ridley, M. 21045, 21045.5; Robartes 21069; Roesslin 21162; Rogers, F. 21174; Rogers, Richard 21207.3, 21213.2; Rovenzon 21355; Rowlands, S. 21391, 21392, 21392.3(?), 21397, 21410.5(?), 21414; Rowley, S. 21418; S., W. 21533; Saint Andrews Univ. 21555.20, 21555.21; Saint German 21580; Salerno 21610; Salkeld 21621; Saluste du Bartas 21652; Sampson, T., Poet 21686; Scoggin 21851; Scultetus 22125; Scupoli 22128; Seneca 22213*, 22218; Shakespeare, W. 22284; Sherley, A. 22424; Sicily 22528; Sidney, P. 22544, 22544a; Skene 22625; Smith, H., Minister, Collections 22741, 22769*; Smith, S., A. M. 22825; Smyth, J. 22877.4(?); Southwark, St. Saviour's 22945.5; Spackman, T. 22977; Spagnuoli 22984.6; Speed, John, Genealogies 23039.2A(?)(A/C), 23039.3(?), 23039d.2(+); Speght, J. 23055; Spelman 23067, 23067.2, 23067.4; Spenser, E. 23083.7*, 23084*, 23085*, 23087*; Sprint, J., Vicar

1613 — *cont.*
23111; Standish, A. 23204, 23204.3, 23204.5, 23204.7, 23206.4, 23206.6; Stephens 23248, 23248a; Sutton, C. 23479, 23492; Sutton, T. 23500; Sylvester 23577.5, 23578; Symson, P. 23601*; Tapp 23677; Tarlton 23683.3; Taylor, A. 23722, 23722.5; Taylor, John 23750, 23763, 23780; Thomas, a Kempis 23987; Topsell 24130, 24132; Tourneur 24148.3, 24151; Trigge 24282.5; Tuke 24307, 24314; Tymme 24424.7; Ursinus, Z. 24527.5; Ussher, J. 24551; Vicary 24710; Virgilius Maro 24791.7; Virginia Company 24830.7 (?), 24833.6; Walpole, M. 24993; Ward, J. 25023; Ward, W. 25061; Way 25134; Waymouth 25143; Webbe, G. 25157; Webster, J. 25174; Webster, W., Treatise Writer 25181; Wedderburn 25188; Welwood 25237; West, J. 25261.5; Westerman 25281; Whitaker, A. 25354; Whiting, G. 25434; Widdrington 25602, 25603; Wilkinson, R. 25659.5; Willet 25699, 25699a*, 25705, 25707; Williamson, T. 25740; Winds 25840; Witches 25872; Wither, Poet 25891, 25891.5, 25892, 25893, 25894, 25901; Witt 25931; Wonders 25949, 25950; Wright, E. 26021; Xenophon 26065; Year 26092; Zouch 26130.

1614

A., O. 11; Adams 110, 110.5, 118, 132; Aesop 172.3; Agincourt 198.7(?)(A/C); Alessio 312.5*; Alexander, W. 338; Alliston 376.7; Almanacks (Bedwell) 413; Almanacks (Bretnor, T.) 420.7; Almanacks (Burton) 426.2; Almanacks (Dade, J.) 434.26; Almanacks (Dauncy) 435.31; Almanacks (Farmer) 443.7; Almanacks (Frende) 445.9; Almanacks (Hopton) 461.9; Almanacks (Johnson, J.) 465.3; Almanacks (Keene) 468.3; Almanacks (Mathew) 483.12; Almanacks (Neve, Jeffery) 489.13; Almanacks (Upcote) 519; Almanacks (White) 527.3; Almanacks (Woodhouse, or Wedhouse, or Wydowes, J.) 531.4; Alting 538.9; Anderson, J. 572.5(?); Andrewes, J. 594; Andrewes, L. 622; Aristotle 765.3; Arthur, J. 809; Arthus 810, 810.5; Ashe 840.5, 841; Attersoll 889.5; Austin, H. 969; Ayrault 1012; B., R., Gent. 1065; Bacon, F. 1125, 1145; Barclay, J. 1398; Barclay, W., M.D. 1406; Barlement 1431.24A; Bastingius 1567; Baughe 1594; Bayly, L. 1602.2; Becanus 1699.5; Bede 1782.5; Bellarmino 1843; Benefield 1868; Bernard, St. 1919a; Bible, Appendix 3026.5; Bible, English 2230*, 2231*, 2232*, 2233*, 2234*, 2235, 2236, 2237, 2238; Bible, N.T., English 2912.3*, 2912.5*; Bible, N.T., Latin 2812; Bible, O.T., 'Books of Solomon' 2766; Bible, O.T., Psalms 2407.5, 2547, 2548, 2548.5, 2548.7, 2549, 2549.3, 2549.4, 2549.5*, 2549.7, 2549.9, 2705; Bishop, W. 3094; Bodenham 3192; Bolton, Robert 3230; Boys 3462.7; Bradford, J., Prebendary of St. Paul's 3491; Bradshaw, W. 3532; Brandenburg 3541; Brathwait 3578, 3579, 3583; Brereton, H. 3609; Brerewood 3612, 3613, 3618; Breton 3664; Brinsley, J., the Elder 3779*; Brooke, C. 3830, 3830.3; Browne, W., Poet 3917; Bruce 3921.5, 3922; Bruno, V. 3941; Buckeridge 4002; Bull, H. 4032.3(A/C); Burhill 4116.5; Busher 4189; Byfield, N. 4236; Camden 4522; Campion 4539; Canterbury 4580.5; Carier 4623, 4623.5; Casaubon, I. 4745; Chadwich 4930, 4930.5; Champny 4958; Chapman, G. 4964, 4975, 4977, 4982(?); Chartehouse 5056; Christian Liberty 5161.5; Cicero 5268, 5321; Cleaver 5387, 5390; Closet 5436; Cobbe 5452; Cocus or Cooke 5469; Coke, E. 5488, 5518; Colonne 5581.5; Comedy 5597; Comines 5604; Cooke, John 5673; Coote 5712; Copley, A. 5740, 5741; Cordier 5762; Cotton or Coton, P. 5857, 5858; Cotton, C. 5848.5; Coverte 5896; Cowper 5914, 5915, 5927; Crooke, S. 6063.3, 6067; Curtius Rufus 6148; Davies, W. 6365; Dawes, L. 6389; Day, A. 6406; Day, John, Rector 6425; Dent, A. 6616, 6661.5; Dering 6678, 6682.3, 6683.3, 6719, 6731.5; Digges, L. 6853; Dod and Cleaver 6971.7; Dod 6935, 6935.5, 6942, 6944, 6945.6; Dowson 7160.5; Drummond 7253(?), 7254, 7258, 7259; Du Moulin, P., the Elder 7335; Dyke, D. 7398; Edinburgh University 7487.11; England, C. of, Visit. Articles 10190.7, 10238, 10314.8, 10328; England, Proclamations, Chron. Ser. 8497, 8498, 8498.5, 8500, 8500.7, 8501, 8502, 8503, 8504, 8505, 8506, 8507, 8508, 8509, 8510, 8510.3, 8512(o.s.), 8513(o.s.), 8514(o.s.); England, Yearbooks 9928; English Merchants 10413.5(?); Est 10539; Field, R. 10857.5(?)*; Fisher, John, S.J. 10912, 10914, 10916; Fitzherbert, T. 11023; Florence 11091; Forbes, P. 11146, 11150; Francis, of Assisi 11314.9(+?);

1614 — *cont.*
Francis, of Sales 11318; Freeman, T. 11370; Gee, A. 11699; Geninges 11728; Gentleman 11745; Gerhard 11767.5; Germany 11796; Gibson, Abraham 11830a; Gibson, T., Minister 11841; Godwin, T. 11956; Goodwin, W. 12045; Gordon, P. 12068; Gray, G. 12202.5; Greene, R. 12289; Greenwood, H. 12337.6; Hale 12627; Hall, E. 12630; Hall, Joseph 12652, 12706*; Harris, Richard 12815; Harris, Robert 12818.5; Harrison, W., King's Preacher 12870, 12870.3; Hayne 12975; Hayward, J., D. D. 12986; Heigham 13032; Heresbach 13201; Heywood, T. 13361a; Hieron 13378*, 13409; Hill, J. 13471; Hoddesdon 13546.5; Holland, Henry, Bookseller 13583, 13583.5; Homer 13636(?); Hooker, R. 13723; Horatius Flaccus 13793, 13793a; Horne, R., of Ludlow 13821; Hull, W. 13939; Huntley 13996, 13996a, 13997, 13997a, 13997b; Husband 14008; I., T. 14068, 14068.3; Ireland, Proc. 14165, 14166, 14167, 14167a; Jackson, A. 14296; Jackson, Thomas, of Canterbury 14305a; Jackson, Thomas, of Peterborough 14315; Jerome, S. 14512, 14512.3; Jewel, J. 14594; Jones, W., of Dorset 14739.2; Julius, A. 14845(?), 14853, 14858, 14859; Kilby, R., of Derby 14951, 14954.6(A/C); King, J., Bp. 14989.5, 14990; L., B. 15104; L., T. 15111.7; La Perriere 15230; La Primaudaye 15237; Lambard 15159, 15173; Latham 15267; Leighton, W. 15434; Lessius 15519; Lindsay, Sir D. 15666; Lithgow 15710; Liturgies, C. of Eng., BCP 16339*, 16341, 16341.5, 16342.3, 16342.5, 16342.7(A/C); Liturgies, Latin Rite, Hours and Primers 16095.5; Loe, the Elder 16683; London, Stationers 16786.2(?); Lucanus 16884, 16885, 16885a; Luis 16916.7, 16919; Lumesden 16924; Macropedius 17176.7; Maierus 17196.3, 17196.5; Mamora 17229; Manual 17275; Markham, G. 17336, 17356; Martin, G. 17505.5(?); Masque 17625; Matthieu 17662; Maxey, A. 17692; Maxwell 17697.7; Mean 17758; Meash 17763; Meriton 17837; Mosse 18209; Munday 18274; Napier 18349, 18349a; Newhouse 18493; Niccols 18521; Norden 18611, 18612; Norman 18652; Nowell, Middle Catechism 18735; O'Hussey 18791(c.), 18792(c.); Openshaw 18823; Overbury 18903.5, 18904, 18905, 18906, 18907; Ovidius Naso 18927.5; Oxford Univ., Off. Docs. 19003; Oxford Univ., Quaestiones 19016.2; Oxford Univ., Verses, etc. 19043.5; P., I. or J. 19072.3; Painter, A. 19120; Palatinate 19129, 19130; Paris 19201; Parr, E. 19314; Patriarchs 19470.5; Perkins, J. 19643; Perkins, W. 19671.5; Persius Flaccus 19777; Pilkington, F. 19923*; Pitiscus 19967; Plutarch 20055.5; Poland 20083.3(?)*; Price, D. 20300; Price, S. 20331; Prideaux 20344, 20352; Purchas, S. 20506; R., A. 20569; Rainolds, J. 20609, 20612.7*, 20613*, 20620*; Raleigh 20637; Rastell, W. 20742; Ravenscroft 20756; Reid, T. 20860.3 (A/C); Relation 20862; Reuter 20912, 20913; Rich, B. 20986; Rid 21028; Rimer 21056.8(?); Roberts, A. 21074; Robinson, J., Pastor of Leyden 21115; Rowlands, S. 21372.5, 21381, 21406(?); S., T. 21520; Saint Andrews Univ. 21555.22, 21555.23; Saul 21772; Schonerus 21825; Scott, M. 22062; Selden 22177; Seneca 22213*; Smith, H., Minister, Collections 22729, 22757; Smith, H., Minister, Single Works 22670; Smith, S., Minister in Essex 22839, 22841.7, 22842; Spackman, N. 22976; Speed, John 23041.4*, 23046; Standish, A. 23205, 23206.8; Stock 23273, 23273.5, 23274; Sturtevant 23408.8; Sylvester 23581; Tailor 23658; Talaeus 23659.7; Taylor, A. 23721; Taylor, John 23779, 23792, 23810, 23813.3(?); Terentius 23892; Things 23952.7(?); Thomas, a Kempis 23982.7(A/C); Tuke 24312, 24312.3; Tusser 24389; Tuvil or Toutevile 24394, 24394a; Tymme 24425; Vennard 24636; Vesey 24693.5; Villegas 24731.5; Walker, W. 24964; Walpole, M. 24994; Weston, E. 25290; White, John, D. D. 25390; White, Tristram 25409; Widdrington 25602.5, 25605.5, 25606; Wilkinson, R. 25661; Willet 25677, 25679, 25679.5, 25680, 25699a; Williams, G. 25717; Wilson, T., Divine 25790, 25791; Wily 25819; Wither, Poet 25895, 25916; Woodstreet Counter 25968.5; Worship 25994; Wright, E. 26022.5, 26023; Wright, L. 26027; Wright, W. 26045; Zanchius 26121a.7.

1615

A., R., Gent. 16; Abernethy 73; Adams 107, 114, 124, 133; Ainsworth, H. 229; Ainsworth, J. 240; Alessio 312.5*; Almanacks (Bretnor, T.) 420.8; Almanacks (Browne) 421; Almanacks (Dade, W.) 435.4; Almanacks (Dauncy) 435.33; Almanacks (Frende) 445.10; Almanacks (Johnson, J.) 465.4; Almanacks (Keene) 468.4; Almanacks (Neve, Jeffery) 489.14, 489.15; Almanacks (Ranger) 502; Almanacks (Rudston, J.) 506.7; Almanacks (Upcote) 519.2; Almanacks (White) 527.4; Almanacks (Woodhouse, or Wedhouse, or Wydowes, J.) 531.5; Alting 539; Ames 556; Amner 563; Andrewes, J. 587; Anyan 698; Assize of Bread 878; Avity 988; Babington, G. 1077, 1078; Ball, J. 1314.2; Ballad 1328.7(c.); Band 1355, 1356; Barclay, J. 1387, 1388; Barclay, W., M.D. 1403; Barrow 1527.3(?); Bastard 1559.5, 1561; Bayly, L. 1602.3; Beaumont, F., and Fletcher 1667; Benefield 1872; Bible, English 2234*, 2236*, 2239, 2240, 2241, 2242, 2243*; Bible, N.T., English 2913, 2914, 2914.5; Bible, O.T., Psalms 2408, 2409, 2550, 2551, 2551.3, 2551.5, 2552, 2552.3, 2554, 2554.5, 2706, 2708; Boaistuau 3170a; Bowle 3435; Bownd, Nathaniel 3435.7; Boys 3458.5, 3459.7, 3460.7, 3462.3, 3463, 3463.3, 3465, 3465.4; Bradshaw, W. 3510.5, 3529; Brathwait 3588; Brerewood 3614, 3614.5; Breton 3635, 3704.7, 3710, 3715.5; Brewer 3720; Bright 3752; Brightman 3755; Brinsley, J., the Elder 3771, 3780; Browne, J., Bookseller 3908.3(c.); Bruch 3927; Buchanan 3990, 3990.5; Bury, J. 4180.5; Byfield, N. 4216; Camden 4496, 4513.7; Carier 4621, 4624; Carleton, G. 4632; Carter, B. 4692a; Cartigny 4702(?); Casaubon, I. 4744, 4744.5, 4744.7; Catascopos 4792; Catechism 4797.5(c.?), 4803.5; Chamberlaine 4948; Charles Emmanuel I. 5045; Charron 5052(?); Cicero 5315.8; Cleaver 5378, 5378.1, 5378.2; Coke, E. 5516, 5521; Cole, N. 5536; Collins, T. 5567; Complaint 5610.5(c.); Conversion 5650.5; Cooper, T., Preacher 5692, 5693, 5695, 5700; Corderoy 5756.5; Cortes 5805; Cotton or Coton, P. 5859; Cotton, C. 5849; Cowper 5921.5*, 5921.7(A/C), 5928, 5938.5; Crooke, H. 6062; Crooke, S. 6069; Daniel, S. 6257; Davies, Sir J. 6361; Day, John, Rector 6421, 6423, 6426; Dekker 6503; Delamothe 6548; Dempster 6580.4; Dent, A. 6662; Desainliens or Sainliens 6753; Digges, D. 6845; Ditty 6921.5(c.), 6924.5(c.); Dod and Cleaver 6961, 6972; Draxe 7173; Du Moulin, P., the Elder 7319; Dudley, Jane 7281; Dyke, D. 7399, 7400; Edinburgh University 7487.12; Egerton, S. 7529, 7530; Elton 7612; Elwes or Helwys 7626, 7626.5, 7627.5; England, C. of, Visit. Articles 10140, 10147.4(?), 10159.5(?), 10198.5, 10259, 10268.3(c.?), 10275.3, 10372.3; England, Customs 7693(c.?); England, Local Courts 7723.7; England, Proclamations, Chron. Ser. 8511, 8512, 8513, 8514, 8515, 8516, 8517, 8518, 8519, 8520, 8521, 8523, 8524, 8525, 8526, 8527, 8528, 8529, 8530, 8531, 8532, 8533, 8533.3, 8533.7, 8534(o.s.); England, Public Documents, Misc. 9175g.20(c.), 9175z.10(c.?), 9237; England, Statutes, Gen. Colls. 9325; Evans, E. 10583, 10584; Evans, T. 10594; Fennor 10783; Fenton, E. 10787.4; Fenton, R. 10802; Ferebe 10818; Feynes 10840; Fitzherbert, T. 11018, 11019.5; Flodder 11089; Forde, E. 11173; Forsyth 11191; France—Reformed Churches 11306.5; Franklin 11332(?), 11332.5; Garey 11599; Gedde 11695; Gerhard 11765; God 11926; Goddard 11929; Godwin, F. 11938; Gordon, P. 12066, 12067; Gouge 12113, 12126; Greene, J. 12214, 12215; Greene, R. 12235, 12297; Greenwood, H. 12336; Gregory, of Nazianzus 12347; Grenfield 12358; Gunter, P. 12526; Guy, R. 12547.7 (c.?); H., B. 12562a; H., I. or J. 12570; Habermann 12582.18, 12582.22; Hakewill 12622; Hall, Joseph 12654, 12706*, 12706a; Hamor 12736; Harington 12775, 12775.5; Heidelberg Catechism 13031.3, 13031.4; Helwys 13054; Herrey 13234; Heywood, T. 13321; Hieron 13392.5, 13396, 13409.5, 13427.5; Hill, R. 13475*; Hoby 13540, 13540.5; Hole 13567a(c.)(A/C); Homer 13637(?); Hopkins, T. 13772; Hopton 13779(o.s.?); Hoskins, J. 13841; Howes 13877; Hugget 13909; Hughes, L. 13919; Hull, W. 13936; Hunnis 13982; Hutchins 14013.7; Indagine 14077a; Ireland, C. of 14260; Ireland, Laws 14133; Isocrates 14272; Jack, of Dover 14292; Jackson, Thomas, of Peterborough 14311; James I 14367, 14367.5; James I, appendix 14415, 14416, 14417, 14418.5, 14419, 14419.5, 14419.7, 14419a; Janua 14466; Johnson, Jacobus 14665, 14666*; Jones, J., B. D. 14720; Joseph, ben Gorion 14805; Juliers 14838; Julius, A. 14850(c.); Juvenalis 14890; Keale or Kayll 14894.7, 14894.8, 14894.9; Kethe 14942.5(c.?)(A/C); Kyd 15091, 15091a; Lant 15222.5; Latham 15267.3; Leigh, W. 15423.3; Ling 15687.7(c.);

1615 — *cont.*
Lipsius 15700; Liturgies, C. of Eng., BCP 16343, 16343.5, 16344, 16344.5, 16345, 16345.5, 16346, 16447; Liturgies, Latin Rite, Hours and Primers 16096; Liturgies, Latin Rite, Missals 16225; Liturgies, Other Protest. C. 16592; London, Appendix 16760, 16761.3(c.); London, Ords. and Regs. 16725.7; London, Weavers 16787.9(c.); Lover 16864a.1(c.); Lupton, T. 16948; Luther 16976; Maiden 17192.3(c.); Manual 17275.3; Manwood 17292; Markham, G. 17342, 17356a, 17377, 17386.5; Martialis 17492; Martin, J. 17509, 17509.5; Martyn, W. 17526, 17527; Mason, T. 17622; Maxwell 17698; Meara 17761; Melanthe 17800; Merlin 17841.9; Mohammed, the prophet 17995; Mornay 18143; Mucedorus 18235; Mulheim 18254; Munday 18275; Murray, D. 18294; Murrell 18299; Netherlands 18437, 18437.5, 18445.7, 18446, 18446a; Neville, A. 18480, 18480.5; Niccholes 18514; Niccols 18523; Nixon 18590; Nobody 18598.5(c.); Norden 18621, 18628; Norris, S. 18657; Norton, R. 18676.5(?); Nowell, Middle Catechism 18720; Nun 18747; Nyndge 18753; Overbury 18908, 18919.3, 18919.7, 18921.7; P., E. 19062.5(?)(A/C); P., N., Master of Arts 19076.5(c.); Palmerin, de Oliva 19159; Paris 19202; Parr, E. 19315; Parrot 19333; Parsons, R. 19374, 19387; Passe 19459; Peacham, H., the Younger 19512, 19514; Pelegromius 19561; Perkins, W. 19687, 19692, 19715a, 19726, 19730, 19746, 19761.5; Pestell 19789, 19790; Philiatros 19831; Platt 19983; Playstowe 20028.5(c.); Preston, J., of East Ogwell 20282.5; Prideaux 20346; Protestants 20450, 20450.5(?), 20451; Pulton 20497; Quin 20563.5; R., M. 20584; R., R. 20586; Rastell, J., Printer 20715; Record, R. 20806.5; Rich, B. 20987, 20987.5; Richardson, C. 21017; Robertson, B. 21096.5; Robinson, J., Pastor of Leyden 21111; Roe, W. 21152; Rogers, Richard 21204, 21213.3; Rowlands, S. 21369(c.), 21369.5(c.), 21401, 21401.5; S., E. 21486; S., F. 21491.3; S., H. 21493.5, 21494; Saint Andrews Univ. 21555.24, 21555.25(c.), 21555.26(c.); Sallustius Crispus 21623; Sanderson, R. 21701; Sandys, G. 21726; Sandys, Sir E. 21723; Schonaeus 21821.8; Scot, T., Gent. 21869*; Scotland, Church of, Confession of Faith 22024.7(c.); Shakespeare, W. 22312; Sharpham 22386; Singleton, I. 22574; Smalle 22638; Smetius 22646; Smith, H., Minister, Collections 22771; Smith, R., Satirist 22824.7(c.); Smith, S., A. M. 22826; Smith, Wentworth 22871, 22871a; Solomon 22900(c.); Southwell 22962; Speed, John 23041.2; Speed, John, Genealogies 23039d.3(?); Speght, J. 23056; Spenser, E. 23084(?)*; Spenser, J., D.D. 23096; Spotiswood 23104; Stafford, A. 23128; Stanbridge, Vocabula 23190; Standish, A. 23206; Stephens 23249, 23250; Stepney 23253(c.); Stow 23338; Sutton, T. 23501; Swaine 23511.5; Sweetnam, Joseph 23533, 23534; Sylvester 23582; Symson, P. 23601*; T., C. 23612; T., I. or J. 23619.5(A/C); Table 23634.7(c.); Taffin 23655; Tapp 23680; Taylor, John 23741, 23752, 23775, 23804, 23806*; Thomas, a Kempis 23988; Thomas, L. 24005.5; Thomas, T. 24015; Thornes 24043; Tissot 24091.5; Tomkis 24100, 24101, 24105(c.); Traske 24175.3, 24176; Tuke 24304, 24312.7(?); Turner, A. 24341.5; Vallans 24588; Varchi 24593; Villegas 24731a; Virel 24771.3; Virginia Company 24833.8; Virtue 24844.7(?); W., T. 24916.7(c.?); Wadsworth, J., the Elder 24924.5; Wake 24940; Walsall, S. 24997; Walsingham, F. 25003; Ward, S., of Ipswich 25039; Ward, W. 25062; Way 25135; Webbe, G. 25165; Welwood 25240; Wentworth, Paul 25244; West, W. 25273; Weston, E. 25290.3; White, John, D. D. 25392; Whitgre 25433.3; Wilkinson, R. 25660; Willis, Edward 25743; Willis, T. 25753; Wilson, T., Divine 25798; Wither, Poet 25896, 25905, 25917, 25917.5, 25920, 25921, 25922; Work 25981; Worship 25993; Worthington, T. 26001; Wright, L. 26036; Writing Tables 26050.12; Yates, John 26081; Year 26091.

1616

Aberdeen Univ. 71.32; Adams 109, 111, 119, 125; Aelianus, Tacitus 161, 161.5; Ainsworth, H. 210; Alexander, W. 345; Almanacks (Bretnor, T.) 420.9; Almanacks (Browne) 421.1; Almanacks (Burton) 426.4; Almanacks (Dade, W.) 435.5; Almanacks (Frende) 445.11; Almanacks (Gilden) 448; Almanacks (Johnson, J.) 465.5; Almanacks (Keene) 468.5; Almanacks (Neve, Jeffery) 489.16; Almanacks (Ranger) 502.2; Almanacks (Rudston, J.) 506.8; Almanacks (Upcote) 519.3; Almanacks (White) 527.5; Almanacks (Woodhouse, or Wedhouse, or Wydowes, J.) 531.6; Anne [of Denmark] 656.3; Anthonie 666, 667; Anton 686; Aphthonius 704; Augustine 947; Ayrault 1013; B., R., Gent. 1064.5; Bailey, Walter 1196; Barbour 1378; Barclay, J. 1396.5*; Barlement 1431.25; Barlow, W., Archdeacon of Salisbury 1442; Bayly, L. 1602.5, 1602.7; Beard, T. 1657.5, 1658; Beaumont, F., and Fletcher 1686; Bell, A. 1813; Bellarmino 1840; Bernard, R. 1935, 1935.5, 1963.7, 1964.3; Bernard, St. 1909; Bible, Appendix 3027; Bible, English 2243*, 2244, 2245, 2246; Bible, N.T., English 2915, 2915.5; Bible, O.T., Psalms 2555, 2555.3*, 2555.5, 2556, 2556.2, 2556.5, 2556.7, 2708.5; Book 3347.5; Botero 3403; Bowle 3435.5; Boys 3460.3, 3460.8, 3463.7, 3465.7, 3466a; Bradford, J., Prebendary of St. Paul's 3482; Brathwait 3557 [not STC]; Breton 3643, 3644, 3656, 3658; Brightman 3756; Brisset 3792, 3793; Browne, J., Merchant 3908.8; Browne, W., Poet 3915(?), 3915.5; Bullokar, J. 4083; Bunny, F. 4099; Cambridge University 4493.5(?); Cannon 4577, 4578; Canterbury, Province of 4587.7; Carpenter, R. 4682; Cartwright, T. 4707.7; Case, W. 4766, 4767; Cecil, W., Baron Ros 4908.5; Champny 4960; Christian Parents 5180; Cicero 5268.3, 5288, 5310.2; Coke, E. 5522; Collection 5556; Cornwallis 5778, 5779; Coryate 5811, 5812; Costerus 5827; Cotta 5836; Cotton, C. 5847; Cotton, W. 5870.3; Cowper 5918, 5921.5*, 5922, 5922.2, 5932, 5943; Crakanthorp 5977; Crooke, H. 6062.2; Davies, J., of Hereford 6342; Davy du Perron 6384; Deacon 6436; Declaration 6455.5; Dekker 6475.5, 6483, 6488, 6504; Dempster 6580.7; Denison, J. 6597, 6597.4; Dent, A. 6625.8, 6630.7, 6649, 6662.3; Desainliens or Sainliens 6745.5; Desiderius 6778; Dillingham 6887; Dominis 6996, 6998; Downame, J. 7146; Draxe 7174; Drayton 7221.5(?); Drum 7244; Drummond 7252.3, 7255, 7256; Du Moulin, P., the Elder 7342; Du Tertre 7371.5, 7372; Dunbar, J. 7346; Dyke, D. 7395, 7401, 7408, 7408.2; Eaton 7468; Eburne 7472; Edinburgh University 7487.13; Eglisham 7546; Elton 7615; Elwes or Helwys 7627(?); England, C. of, Appendix 10403; England, C. of, Articles 10049; England, C. of, Constitutions/Canons 10073; England, C. of, Visit. Articles 10147.5, 10275.7, 10329; England, Proclamations, Chron. Ser. 8534, 8535, 8536, 8537, 8538, 8539, 8539.5, 8540, 8541, 8541.3, 8542, 8543, 8544, 8545(?), 8546(o.s.), 8549(o.s.), 8550(o.s.), 8551(o.s.), 8552 (o.s.), 8553(o.s.), 8584(?), 8585(?); Epictetus 10426; Est 10536; Estienne, C., and Liebault 10549; F., I. or J. 10639, 10639.3; Farley, H. 10688, 10688.5; Farnaby, T. 10701.3; Fauconbridge 10709; Fennor 10784; Fenton, R. 10804; Fitzherbert, A. 10965; Fletcher, Joseph 11077; Forbes, J., Minister 11131, 11136; Forde, W. 11176; Fortescue 11197; Fradelius 11254; France 11292.5; Francis, of Sales 11319; Fuller, N., Prebendary 11461; Gainsford 11521, 11521.3, 11522, 11523; Gething 11802.7; Gibson, S. 11837; God 11925.7; Goddard 11928(?), 11930(?); Godwin, F. 11941, 11942*, 11945; Godwin, T. 11957, 11965; Goodman, G. 12022.7, 12023; Gostwyke 12100; Gouffier 12108; Gouge 12122, 12126.5; Granger, Thomas 12175, 12176, 12177, 12179, 12182, 12183, 12185; Greene, R. 12230, 12252, 12256, 12275; Greenwood, H. 12327, 12333.5; Habermann 12582.26; Hakewill 12610; Hall, Joseph 12683; Harrab 12797; Hart, John, D. D. 12891; Haughton 12931; Hay, P. 12972; Hayward, Sir J. 13006; Heaven 13019; Hieron 13397, 13406, 13410, 13428; Hill, R. 13475*; Hill, W. 13503; History 13526.5; Hoddesdon 13545; Holdt 13567, 13567.5; Homer 13624(?); Hooker, R. 13716*, 13716a*; Hopton 13779*, 13780; Howes 13877.3, 13877.5; Huarte 13895; Hungerford 13971.5; I., N. 14054, 14054.5; Jackson, B. 14296.5; Jackson, W. 14321; Jacob, H. 14330; James I 14344, 14345*, 14358, 14368, 14369, 14397, 14397.3, 14397.7; James I, appendix 14418, 14420, 14420.3, 14420.7; Janua 14466.5; Jegon 14484; Johnson, Richard 14680; Jonson 14751, 14752; Kichener 14948; Kilby, R., of Derby 14952; King, W. 14997.3; La Marteliere 15141; Langley 15202; Leigh, D. 15402; Lithgow 15711; Littleton, E. 15717.5; Littleton, T., Tenures, Engl. 15781; Liturgies, C. of Eng., BCP 16347, 16347a, 16348a, 16431; Liturgies, C. of Eng., Spec. Prayers 16551(c.?)*(A/C); Liturgies, Latin Rite, Hours and Primers 16096.5; London, Merchant Tailors 16778.8, 16778.10; London, Soc. of Arms 16786; Louis XIII 16833; Luther 16973;

1616 — *cont.*

Manual 17275.5; Markham, G. 17335*, 17337, 17381(?), 17381.5, 17387; Marlowe 17432; Marston 17477; Middleton, H. 17869.5; Middleton, T. 17878, 17897; Mocket 17991; More, R. 18075.5; Mountague 18228.5; Munday 18266; Musaeus 18304; Muse 18314.5; Napier 18351; Neile 18421.5; Niccols 18522, 18524; Nid 18579; Nixon 18585, 18591a; Norden 18626a.6; Overbury 18909, 18910, 18911, 18920(?), 18921.3(?); Owen, John 18994.5(A/C); P., C. 19059; Page, S. 19088, 19088.3, 19091; Palingenius 19146; Palmerin, de Oliva 19159a; Palmerin, of England 19163; Paris, J. 19208.5; Parsons, B. 19344, 19349; Pemberton 19569a; Peretto 19624; Perkins, W. 19651*, 19705.7, 19715a.5; Persius Flaccus 19777.5, 19778, 19778.5; Platte 19997; Playfere 20019; Powel, Gabriel 20153; Powell, D. 20159; Price, G. 20306; Price, S. 20330; Pricke 20337.5; Rainolds, J. 20609.5; Ratcatcher 20744(?); Rathborne 20748; Ravisius 20761.3; Rawlinson 20776; Read, A., M. D. 20782; Reginald, B. 20834.7(?), 20835; Reuter 20914a; Ribadeneira 20967; Rich, B. 20988, 20988.5(?), 20991.7; Richardson, C. 21013, 21014, 21018, 21019; Roberts, A. 21075; Roberts, Henry 21087.7; Robinson, H. 21106; Rogers, Richard 21207.5, 21218; Rollock, R. 21272, 21283; Rous, the Elder 21342; Rowlands, S. 21373; S., H. 21494.5; S., S. 21519, 21519a; S., W. 21527; Saint Andrews Univ. 21555.27; Salignacus 21618; Sandys, E., Abp. 21714; Sclater, the Elder 21843; Scot, T., Gent. 21869*, 21870, 21871*, 21871a*, 21871a.7; Scott, T., B. D. 22074; Shakespeare, W. 22350; Sharpe, Leonell 22372; Sharpham 22382; Sheldon 22399; Smith, H., Minister, Collections 22742; Smith, John, Gov. of Virginia 22788, 22788.3, 22788.5; Smith, S., Minister in Essex 22839.3, 22839.5, 22842.5, 22847.3; Song 22920.3(?); Sorocold 22933; Southwell 22948, 22963; Speed, John 23031, 23041.4*, 23044; Speed, John, Genealogies 23039d.4 (?); Speght, J. 23056.5; Speidell 23061; Spelman 23067.6, 23067.8, 23068; Spicer, A. 23099; Spottiswood 23105, 23106; Standish, A. 23206.2; Stoughton, T. 23317; Susenbrotus 23440.7; Sutton, C. 23480, 23493; Sutton, T. 23502; Sweetnam, Joseph 23535; Sylvester 23582a(+); Symson, P. 23601*; T., A., Practitioner in Physic 23609; T., J., Gent. 23623; T., T. 23626.5; Tanner, R. 23672; Taylor, John 23731.3, 23806*, 23811; Thomas, a Kempis 23988.5, 23997; Thompson, T. 24028; Thunder 24059.5; Timberlake 24084; Traske 24175.7; Treswell, Ralph 24267.5; Tuke 24316, 24316a; Turvell 24371; Tuvil or Toutevile 24393; Tymme 24426; Utie 24560; Vallans 24589; Veron, F. 24675.5; Vincent, M. 24757; Virgilius Maro 24792; Virginia Company 24834; Walker, J. 24962; Ward, S., of Ipswich 25040; Warford 25069; Web 25151; Weckherlin 25186; Weston, E. 25290.7; Whalley 25294, 25294.5(?); Whately 25302; White, John, D. D. 25397; Widdrington 25598, 25604, 25605; Willis, T. 25754; Wilson, T., Divine 25787; Withals 25886; Wither, Poet 25918; Worship 25995; Wright, H. 26024; Wright, L. 26028; Wright, W. 26047, 26049; Wylshman 26058; Wynne 26060; Yates, John 26082, 26082.5.

1617

Abbot, G., Abp. 28; Adams 127; Aesop 187.5; Ainsworth, H. 212; Albertus Magnus 265, 269; Almanacks (Allestree) 407; Almanacks (Bretnor, T.) 420.10; Almanacks (Browne) 421.2; Almanacks (Burton) 426.5; Almanacks (Dade, W.) 435.6; Almanacks (Frende) 445.12; Almanacks (Gilden) 448.2; Almanacks (Johnson, J.) 465.6; Almanacks (Keene) 468.6; Almanacks (Neve, Jeffery) 489.17; Almanacks (Ranger) 502.3; Almanacks (Rudston, J.) 506.9; Almanacks (Upcote) 519.4; Almanacks (White) 527.6; Almanacks (Woodhouse, or Wedhouse, or Wydowes, J.) 531.7; Andrewes, J. 595.6; Angelos 638, 639; Anton 687; Apollo 708; Arcandam 726.9; Attowell 903(?); B., E. 1024; Bacon, F. 1128, 1143(c.)*, 1153; Baker, H. 1217; Ball, J. 1314.3; Barclay, J. 1396.5*; Barret, W. 1501.3 (A/C); Barrough 1513; Bayly, L. 1602.8; Baynes, P. 1645; Baynes, R. 1650; Bellarmino 1837; Bennet, Sir J. 1882.5; Benvenuto 1897 [not STC]; Bernard, R. 1955; Bible, English 2180(aft.?)*, 2247, 2248, 2249; Bible, N.T., English 2916, 2917, 2918, 2918.3*; Bible, O.T., Psalms 2410.5, 2411*, 2499.7(aft.?), 2555.3*, 2557, 2557.3, 2557.5, 2558, 2558.3, 2559, 2559.5, 2562.6*; Billingsley 3062(?); Blundeville 3143; Book 3322.5; Bourne, I. 3418; Boys 3467; Bradford, J., Prebendary of St. Paul's 3503; Bradshaw, W. 3511; Brathwait 3558 [not STC], 3585; Breton 3664.5, 3694.3(c.); Briggs 3741(?); Brinsley, J., the Elder 3773, 3781; Broughton, Richard 3900; Bruce 3925; Bunny, F. 4100; Byfield, N. 4217, 4234, 4236.1; Cambridge 4471.5 (?); Camden 4514; Campion 4548(?); Carpenter, R. 4683.5; Catechism 4804; Cawdrey, R. 4886; Cecil, W., Baron Burghley 4897; Cecil, W., Baron Ros 4909; Chain 4932.5; Chasteigner 5064; Claudianus 5367; Coke, E. 5528; Cole, N. 5536.5; Collins, S. 5561; Colt 5585; Comyns 5614; Concini 5618, 5620, 5621, 5622; Cooke, A. 5662; Cooper, T., Preacher 5701; Cornwallis 5780; Cotta 5834; Cowper 5930; Crystal 6099.7; Darrell 6286; Davies, J., of Hereford 6343; Day 6397; Delaune 6550.5; Dent, A. 6615, 6620, 6624.7, 6631; Dering 6720; Despautere 6781.4; Dillingham 6884; Dod and Cleaver 6973; Dolphin 6993; Dominis 6994, 6997, 6999, 7002, 7003, 7004; Draxe 7186a(?); Drummond 7252; Duck 7278; Dyke, D. 7396, 7401.5, 7407; Edinburgh University 7487, 7487.14; Edmondes, T. 7492.5; Edmonton 7495; Egerton, S. 7531, 7531a; Elliots and Meisey 7605.7; Elton 7615.5; England, C. of, Visit. Articles 10137, 10176.5, 10268.5(?), 10314.9; England, Proclamations, Chron. Ser. 8456(c.?), 8546, 8547, 8548, 8549, 8550, 8551, 8551.3(?)(A/C), 8551.5(?)(A/C), 8552, 8553, 8554, 8555, 8557, 8562(o.s.), 8563(o.s.), 8564(o.s.); England, Public Documents, Misc. 9238, 9238.3, 9238.5(o.s.); England, Statutes, Gen. Colls. 9299; England, Statutes, Spec. Subjs. 9343.5(c.?)(A/C); England, Statutes, Kalendars/Indexes 9550; English Protestants 10414; F., I. or J. 10641; Farley, H. 10690.5; Fennor 10781; Fenton, R. 10805; Fernandes de Queiros 10822; Field, J., and Wilcox 10849; Fitzgeffrey, H. 10945; Fitzherbert, A. 10983; Floyd, J. 11116; Forbes, J., Minister 11132; France 11258, 11292; France—Reformed Churches 11305; Francis, of Sales 11320, 11320a*; Frankfurt Fair 11328, 11328.1; Fulke 11431, 11431a; Fuller, N., Prebendary 11462; Gale, D. 11527; Gellius 11713; Greene, R. 12216, 12221, 12236, 12242, 12247; Guild 12483; Hales 12628; Hall, Joseph 12705, 12705a, 12705b, 12707; Harpur 12796; Harris, Robert 12819; Harrison, W., King's Preacher 12869; Hay, J., Clerk Deputy 12970; Heidelberg Catechism 13031.5; Henry V, King of England 13073, 13074; Herring, F. 13247; Heywood, T. 13372; Hieron 13394, 13394a, 13401, 13410.5; Hill, R. 13476; Hitchcock, J. 13530; Hooker, R. 13716*, 13716a*; Horne, R., of Ludlow 13824; Hume, D. 13953; Jackson, Thomas, of Peterborough 14314; James I 14379.7; Janua 14467, 14467.5; Jest 14523; Johnson, Francis 14661; Jonson 14775; Juvenalis 14893; Kellison 14910; Kellus 14916; Kent Street 14935; Kilby, R., of Derby 14954.7; King, W. 14997.7; Lawson 15329*; Le Fevre 15381; Leech, John, Poet 15368, 15369, 15371, 15372, 15373; Leigh, D. 15402.5; Lesk 15493; Lever, C. 15538*; Lily, W., 'Lily's Grammar' 15626.7; Lincoln, Diocese 15647; Lindsay, Sir D. 15667; Littleton, T., Tenures, French 15756.5, 15757; Liturgies, C. of Eng., BCP 16349; Liturgies, Latin Rite, Hours and Primers 16097; Liturgies, Latin Rite, Ordinals 16232.5; Liturgies, Other Protest. C. 16593; Lodge and Greene 16682; London, Ords. and Regs. 16727, 16727.1, 16727.3; Louis XIII 16834, 16835, 16835.5; Lover 16864a.5(c.); Lyly 17064; M., T. 17152; Maiden 17192.7(c.); Mailliet 17198, 17199; Man, A. 17238.5; Manual 17275.7*; Markham, G. 17335*, 17360a; Marlowe 17419; Mavericke 17682; Maxwell 17704; Mericke 17836.3; Merlin 17842; Middleton, R. 17872, 17872a, 17872a.5; Middleton, T. 17899; Middleton, T., and Rowley 17911, 17911a; Milles, T. 17931(?); Minsheu 17944, 17944a(+); Mocket 17992; Molina 18000; Moore, J. 18057, 18057a; Mornay 18152; Moryson 18205; Munda 18257; Murrell 18300, 18301; Napier 18357; Office 18788; Openshaw 18830.7; Ovidius Naso 18952.4; Oxford Univ., Quaestiones 19016.3; Oxford Univ., Verses, etc. 19023; Papal Exchequer 19174; Pare 19191; Perkins, W. 19651*, 19681, 19716; Persius Flaccus 19779; Phillips, John 19873.5; Pirckheimer 19947; Platt 19983.3; Playfere 20003*, 20012; Pratt 20187, 20187a; Price, D. 20297; Price, S. 20329; Primrose, G. 20390; Purchas, S. 20507; Quin 20564; Raleigh 20638, 20638a*; Ravisius 20763.7; Report 20892; Rich, B. 20989, 20989.3; Richardson, C. 21015; Rider, J.

1617 — *cont.*
21034, 21034.3, 21034.7, 21034a; Ridley, M. 21044; Roberts, Henry 21087; Robertson, B. 21098; Robinson, Robert 21122; Rogers, Richard 21213.4; Room 21315.4(c.); Ross 21328*; Rowlands, S. 21365.5; S., F., Minister 21491.7; S., H. 21495; S., N. 21510; Saint Andrews Univ. 21553; Saint Andrews Univ. 21555.28, 21555.29, 21555.30; Salerno 21603, 21603.3(?), 21608; Salkeld 21622; Scotland, statutes, etc. 21897, 21898; Selden 22167; Seton, J. 22256; Shakespeare, W. 22361; Shepherd 22406.5(c.); Sidney, P. 22544a.3 (?), 22544a.5(?); Smith, H., Minister, Collections 22758; Smith, H., Minister, Single Works 22671; Smith, S., A. M. 22827; Smith, S., Minister in Essex 22839.7(A/C), 22839.8(A/C), 22839.9(A/C), 22840, 22847.7; Sonnibank 22927; Sowernam 22974; Spagnuoli 22984.7; Speed, John, Genealogies 23039.4(?), 23039d.5(?); Speght, R. 23058; Speidell 23060*, 23062; Spenser, E. 23077.7, 23085*, 23086.7, 23094; Spenser, J., Murderer 23098(c.); Spicer, A. 23100a; Squire, J., Minister 23115.5; Staney 23212; Stepney 23254; Sum 23432.5; Sutton, C. 23487; Sweet 23529; Sweetnam, John 23532; Sweetnam, Joseph 23536, 23543; Sylvester 23583.5; Syme 23585; Symson, W. 23602; Tapp 23680.3; Taylor, John 23731.5, 23748.5, 23765(?), 23807; Taylor, Thomas 23827; Terry 23912; Thomas, a Kempis 23983; Tis 24089(c.); Tomkis 24106; Travers, W. 24186; Tuke 24311, 24315; Turner, J. 24342*; Tymme 24427; Tyndal 24435; Ursinus, Z. 24538; Vaughan, E. 24600; Vaughan, W. 24616; Virginia Company 24839(?); Vulcanius 24893.5; Wallis 24991.5; Ward, S., of Ipswich 25035; Waymouth 25142; Webbe, G. 25159, 25166; Webster, W., Poet 25180; Wedderburn 25191; Whately 25296; Whetenhall 25333; White, F., Bp. 25380; Wilkinson, R. 25652, 25664; Williams, R. 25731*; Willis, J., Stenographer 25744a.5; Wimbledon 25835, 25836; Wirsung 25865; Wither, Poet 25897, 25906; Woodall 25962; Worship 25985; Yelverton 26093; Yonger 26096, 26096a; Young, T., Student of Staple Inn 26116.

1618

Abbot, R., Bp. 46; Adams 120; Adamson, J. 140, 140.5, 141, 142; Adamson, P. 148*; Aesop 172.4; Ainsworth, H. 214, 230*; Airay, H. 245; Almanacks (Allestree) 407.1; Almanacks (Bretnor, T.) 420.11; Almanacks (Browne) 421.3; Almanacks (Burton) 426.6; Almanacks (Dade, W.) 435.7; Almanacks (Frende) 445.13; Almanacks (Gilden) 448.3; Almanacks (Johnson, J.) 465.7; Almanacks (Neve, Jeffery) 489.18, 489.19; Almanacks (Ranger) 502.4; Almanacks (Rudston, J.) 506.10; Almanacks (Sofford) 515; Almanacks (Upcote) 519.5; Almanacks (White) 527.7; Almanacks (Woodhouse, or Wedhouse, or Wydowes, J.) 531.8; Amadis 543; Anderson, P., Doctor 573; Andrewes, J. 595.7; Andrewes, L. 623, 624, 624.5; Androzzi 632.3; Angelos 640, 641*, 642, 643(?); Ap-Robert 715; Attersoll 893; Bacon, F. 1153a, 1154; Bainbridge 1207; Balsamo 1340.5; Barclay, W., M.D. 1405; Baret, M. 1412; Barlow, J. 1436, 1437, 1438; Barlow, W., Archdeacon of Salisbury 1443, 1444; Bateson 1587; Baynes, P. 1626, 1628, 1634, 1635, 1638, 1642, 1645.5, 1648; Belchier 1803; Bellarmino 1838; Bible, English 2250, 2251, 2252, 2255*; Bible, N.T., English 2918.3*, 2918.5, 2918.7*; Bible, O.T., Psalms 2411*, 2412, 2560, 2560.5, 2560a, 2560a.5, 2560a.7, 2561, 2561.3, 2561.5, 2562, 2562.2, 2562.4, 2562.6*, 2562.8; Bicknoll 3050.7; Billingsley 3062.2(?), 3062.3(?), 3062.5(+?); Bolton, Robert 3230.5; Book 3306; Bradwardine 3534; Brathwait 3568.5; Breton 3637, 3641; Brinsley, J., the Elder 3771.3; Broughton, Richard 3899; Bruyn 3950; Buckeridge 4005; Bunny, F. 4100.5; Buoni 4103.5; Butler, C. 4199; Byfield, N. 4213, 4214, 4226; C., W. 4319, 4320; Cade 4328; Cambridge University 4493.7(?); Carleton, D. 4629; Carliell 4650; Carter, B. 4693; Cartwright, T. 4709; Cecil, W., Baron Burghley 4898; Chaderton 4929; Chagford 4932; Charterhouse 5056.5; Cicero 5301.6, 5310.5; Clay 5371.5; Closet 5436.3; Coke, E. 5498, 5503.4, 5519, 5526, 5529; Cole, N. 5538; Cordier 5759.5; Coryate 5809; Cotton or Coton, P. 5860; Covbridge 5879.5(c.); Cowper 5923*, 5939, 5944; Crashaw, W. 6020, 6024; Crooke, H. 6062.4; Crooke, S. 6063.5, 6067.3; D., T. 6181.2; Daborn 6183; Dalton, M. 6205; Danett 6234.3; Daniel, S. 6248; Davies, E. 6327; Davies, J., of Hereford 6345.4(?); Davies, Sir

1618 — *cont.*
J. 6358*; Day, V. 6434; Defence 6469; Dekker 6515, 6515.5, 6525; Digges, D. 6847.5; Dighton 6876; Dod and Cleaver 6974; Dod 6943, 6953; Dominis 7004.5, 7005; Dort, Synod of 7065; Doughty, T. 7072.5; Downame, J. 7139; Downes, T., and Kingston 7154.7; Draxe 7179; Drum 7245; Drunkards 7259.7(?)(A/C); Dyke, D. 7408.5, 7410; East, M. 7463, 7465; Edinburgh University 7487.15; Eglisham 7547*; Elton 7610; England, C. of, Visit. Articles 10213.3, 10239, 10260, 10291, 10301.5(?), 10340; England, Proclamations, Chron. Ser. 7887(c.), 7888(c.), 7889.5(c.), 7890.5(c.), 7895(c.)*, 7897.3(c.), 7899(c.), 7900(c.), 7902.3(c.), 7909.5(c.), 7912(c.), 7921.5(c.), 7924.3(c.), 7929(c.), 7931.3(c.), 7936.3(c.), 7939(c.), 7951.3(c.), 7953a.5(c.), 7954(c.?), 7962.3(c.), 7963(c.), 7965(c.), 7968(c.), 7975(c.), 7978.3(c.), 7986.3(c.), 7990(c.), 8001(c.)*, 8003.3(c.), 8004(c.), 8007(c.), 8009(c.), 8013.5(c.), 8014.5(c.), 8015.5(c.), 8018.5(c.), 8020.5(c.), 8023.5(c.), 8027.3(c.), 8034.5(c.), 8052.3(c.), 8054(c.)(A/C), 8067(c.), 8070.3(c.), 8072(c.), 8075.5(c.), 8076(c.), 8079.3(c.), 8080(c.), 8081(c.), 8083(c.), 8085(c.), 8087(c.), 8095(c.), 8098(c.), 8099(c.), 8103(c.), 8105.3(c.), 8108.3(c.), 8109(c.), 8111(c.), 8117(c.), 8131.3(c.), 8134.3(c.), 8139(c.), 8143.3(c.), 8145(c.), 8147(c.), 8148(c.), 8157.3(c.), 8170.5(c.), 8185.3(c.), 8192.5(c.)*, 8196(c.)*, 8204.5(c.), 8212.3(c.), 8214(c.), 8219(c.), 8238(c.), 8253.3(c.)*, 8556, 8558, 8559, 8559.5, 8562, 8563, 8564, 8565, 8567, 8568, 8569, 8569.5, 8570, 8571, 8572, 8573, 8574, 8575, 8576, 8577, 8578, 8579, 8580, 8581, 8582, 8586(?), 8586.5(?), 8587(?), 8588(o.s.), 8589(o.s.), 8591(o.s.), 8592(o.s.), 8593(o.s.), 8595(o.s.), 8596(o.s.), 8598(o.s.), 8599(o.s.), 8600(o.s.), 8603(o.s.), 8604(o.s.); England, Proclamations, Collections 7758.3, 7758.7; England, Public Documents, Misc. 9238.5, 9238.7, 9238.9, 9239; England, Statutes, Gen. Colls. 9285, 9305.7, 9328; England, Statutes, Spec. Subjs. 9342.5(c.); Everard 10598; Falconer 10675; Faureau 10710.5; Faust 10713; Field, N. 10851, 10852; Fitzgeffrey, H. 10945.3; Forester 11179.5(?); Fowns 11216; France 11281; Francis, of Assisi 11314.2; Frankfurt Fair 11328.2, 11328.3; Fulbecke 11416; G., H. 11496, 11496.3; Gainsford 11517, 11525; Garey 11597; Gelderland 11707; Goodcole 12013; Goodman, G. 12025; Gostwyke 12101; Greenwood, H. 12328; Grymeston 12410(?); Guevara 12450; Guicciardini, F. 12460; Hall, Joseph 12656, 12656.5, 12710.7, 12710.9, 12711; Hannay 12747*; Harington 12776; Harris, Robert 12848; Harrison, R. 12862; Hayward, Sir J. 13006.5; Heidelberg Catechism 13024; Heinsius 13039; Henry, the Minstrel 13152; Hesiod 13249; Hieron 13411, 13412, 13423, 13430; Holland, Henry, Bookseller 13581; Holyday 13617; Hommius 13684.5; Hooker, R. 13716*, 13716a*; Hopkins, T. 13772.5; Hornby 13815; Hull, J. 13931; Hunnis 13983; Huntley 13998; I. 14045.7; Ireland, Proc. 14168, 14169, 14170, 14171(o.s.); Italy 14283; Jackson, A. 14294; Jaggard 14341; James I 14387; Jesus Christ 14569; John George I 14656; Julius, A. 14844(?); Kilby, R., of Derby 14953, 14955; King, J., Bp. 14981; Kyd 15092; La Primaudaye 15241; Latham 15268.3; Lawson 15329*; Leech, John, Schoolmaster 15374.7; Leigh, D. 15403, 15403a; Lessius 15517; Lever, C. 15538*; Levett, C. 15553; Lipsius 15700.3; Lithgow 15715; Liturgies, C. of Eng., BCP 16349.3(?), 16349.7, 16350; Liturgies, C. of Eng., Ordinal 16468; Liturgies, C. of Eng., St. Services 16491; Liturgies, Other Protest. C. 16593.5; Llyfr Plygain 16639; Lohetus 16695; London, Coll. of Physicians 16772, 16773; London, Ords. and Regs. 16727.5(?); London, Shipwrights 16785.3; Louvain 16854.5; Lover 16862.5(?); Loyola 16877; Lucanus 16883; M., R. 17148, 17148.3; MacCaghwell 17157; Magirus 17183.5*; Mandeville 17252; Manual 17275.7*; Manuzio, A. 17282; Mason, G., and Earsden 17601; Monginot 18011; Morton, T., Bp. 18179; Mucedorus 18236; Munday 18278; Mynshul 18318, 18319; Napier 18352; Nausea 18413.3, 18413.5, 18413.7; Norden 18641; Oldenbarneveld 18800; Openshaw 18825; Overbury 18912; Ovidius Naso 18963; Owen, John 18989; Oxford Univ., Quaestiones 19016.4; P., J. 19073; Paget 19098; Panke, J. 19169; Paris Univ. 19203.7; Parr, E. 19312, 19319; Parsons, B. 19347; Pena, P., and L'Obel 19595.7; Penryn 19614; Perkins, W. 19651*, 19717; Pierse 19909; Pilkington, R. 19933; Pinelli 19938; Price, S. 20328; R., James 20581; Raleigh 20652.5, 20653, 20654a.5*(A/C), 20655; Rastell, J., Printer

1618 — *cont.*
20715a; Ravenscroft 20760; Record, R. 20807; Rejaule 20860.5; Rich, B. 20989.7; Ridley, T. 21053.7; Rive 21060; Robertson, B. 21096*, 21097, 21098.3; Robinson, J., Pastor of Leyden 21115a; Rogers, J., of Chacombe 21186; Rogers, Richard 21221; Rowlands, S. 21374, 21405; Rudierd, E. 21437; Rudimenta 21438; Saint Andrews Univ. 21555.31, 21555.32; Sala 21594; Salvianus 21676; Sanderson, R. 21702; Saul 21773; Saunders, G. 21776.3(c.); Scotland, statutes, etc. 21899; Scultetus 22124; Selden 22172, 22172.3, 22172.5, 22172.7, 22173*; Shaw, Divine 22391; Shepherds' Kalendar 22422; Sibthorpe 22527, 22527a; Smith, H., Minister, Collections 22730, 22772; Smith, S., A. M. 22828; Smith, S., Minister in Essex 22848*; Song 22919.5(?); Speed, John, Genealogies 23039a.2(?), 23039d.6(?), 23039f(?); Sprint, J., Vicar 23108; Squire, J., Minister 23116; Stafforde 23136, 23136a; Stow 23332, 23344; Strode 23364; Stubbes 23386; Stuckley 23401; Sutton, C. 23481; Taylor, John 23736, 23737, 23784; Taylor, Thomas 23822, 23822a, 23822a.5, 23828; Themylthorp 23934.5; Thompson, H. 24024; Thompson, T. 24025, 24025.5(?)(A/C); Torquemada 24136; Treatise 24251.7; Tuke 24310.5; Turkey 24333; Tymme 24415a; Vicars, J., Poet 24698; Voyon 24892; Vulcanius 24893.7; Ward, S., of Ipswich 25036, 25041, 25046; Warren, J. 25094; Weakest 25145; Webbe, G. 25166.3; West, W. 25279.5; Whately 25308; White, H. 25387; Widdrington 25601; Wilkinson, J., of Barnard's Inn 25648; Wiliams, R. 25731; Willis, Edmond 25741; Willis, J., Stenographer 25744a.6, 25747, 25748; Wither, Poet 25929.5; Wood, J., D. D. 25952; Worship 25986, 25989.5; Worthington, T. 26000; Writing Tables 26050.14.

1619

Abbot, R., Bp. 47; Adams 121; Adamson, P. 146, 148*, 148.5; Aesop 172.5; Ainsworth, H. 215, 216; Almanacks (Allestree) 407.2; Almanacks (Bretnor, T.) 420.12; Almanacks (Browne) 421.4; Almanacks (Burton) 426.7; Almanacks (Dade, W.) 435.8; Almanacks (Digges) 435.61; Almanacks (Drekin) 437; Almanacks (Frende) 445.14; Almanacks (Gilden) 448.4; Almanacks (Neve, Jeffery) 489.20; Almanacks (Ranger) 502.5; Almanacks (Rudston, J.) 506.11; Almanacks (Sofford) 515.2; Almanacks (Upcote) 519.6; Almanacks (White) 527.8; Almanacks (Woodhouse, or Wedhouse, or Wydowes, J.) 531.9, 531.10; Amadis 544; Angelos 635, 636; Anne [of Denmark] 656.6; Aristotle 766; Aston 884.5(?); B., A. D. 1022; Bacon, F. 1130, 1131, 1152; Baffin 1186.7; Bainbridge 1208; Ball, J. 1314.5; Bankes, L. 1363; Barclay, W., M.D. 1407; Barlow, J. 1439, 1440; Basse 1547; Bayly, L. 1603; Baynes, P. 1641, 1646, 1649; Beaumont, F., and Fletcher 1670, 1676, 1677; Becanus 1707; Becon 1771.5; Bede 1781; Bernard, R. 1938; Bert 1969; Bible, Appendix 3028; Bible, English 2253, 2254, 2255*, 2256, 2257, 2258*, 2260*; Bible, N.T., English 2918;7*, 2919, 2920, 2920.3; Bible, O.T., Psalms 2362.7, 2563, 2564, 2564.2, 2564.4, 2564.6, 2564.8, 2565, 2566, 2567, 2567.3, 2567.6, 2568, 2569; Blundeville 3144; Bohemia 3207.5(o.s.), 3211, 3211.5, 3212, 3212.5, 3213; Bradford, J., Prebendary of St. Paul's 3497; Bradshaw, W. 3511.5; Brathwait 3574; Brerewood 3615, 3615.5; Breton 3664.2; Brinsley, J., the Elder 3782; Brooke, R. 3832; Bruyn 3949, 3951, 3951.5; Buenting 4017; Byfield, N. 4209.5, 4213.5, 4219.5, 4232.5, 4233.5, 4235.5, 4236.8; C., I. or J. 4276, 4278; C., T. 4308; Calderwood 4360, 4364; Cambridge University 4489; Campion 4541; Carleton, G. 4638; Carliell 4651; Castalio or Chateillon 4774; Caus 4869(+)*(A/C); Cervantes Saavedra 4918; Chambers, S. 4955; Chapman, G. 4991; Cicero 5321.5; Cinque Ports 5323a.2; Clarke, T., Lieutenant 5363.5*(A/C); Clay 5371.7; Coffin 5475; Coke, E. 5494.3, 5501, 5523; Cooper, T., Preacher 5706, 5710; Cotta 5835; Cowper 5923, 5931, 5945; Crakanthorp 5976; Crooke, S. 6063.6, 6065; Dalton, M. 6206; Davies, E. 6326; Davies, J., of Hereford 6345.7*; Davies, Sir J. 6358*; Deloney 6559; Denison, J. 6588; Denison, S. 6607; Dent, A. 6631.5; Desainliens or Sainliens 6754; Dickinson 6821; Dighton 6877; Dodoens 6987; Dort, Synod of 7066, 7066.5; Doughty, T. 7072.6; Downame, J. 7138.5; Drayton 7222, 7222.3, 7222.5, 7223*; Drummond 7252.5; Du Terme 7370; Dyke, J. 7411, 7412; East, M. 7464; Edinburgh University 7487.16; Eglisham

1619 — *cont.*
7547*; Elements 7569; Elton 7620; England, C. of, Visit. Articles 10161, 10161.5, 10204.7, 10292, 10308, 10329.3, 10347, 10359, 10379; England, Commissions 7686.2, 7686.4, 7686.6; England, Proclamations, Chron. Ser. 8588, 8589, 8590, 8591, 8592, 8593, 8593.2(?), 8593.4(?), 8593.5(?), 8593.6(c.?), 8593.7(c.?), 8594, 8595, 8596, 8597, 8597.5, 8598, 8599, 8600, 8601, 8602, 8602.3(?), 8602.5, 8603, 8604, 8605, 8606, 8607, 8608, 8609, 8610, 8610.5, 8611, 8612, 8613, 8614, 8616.5, 8617, 8618, 8619, 8620, 8620.3, 8620.7, 8621, 8621.5, 8622, 8624(o.s.), 8624.5(o.s.), 8625(o.s.), 8627(o.s.), 8628(o.s.), 8629(o.s.), 8630(o.s.), 8632(o.s.); England, Public Documents, Misc. 9175g.25(c.?), 9175t-*iii*(?)(A/C), 9240, 9240.3, 9240.5; England, Yearbooks 9554, 9904*; Euring 10567; Eusebius, Pamphili 10575; Favour 10716; Fennor 10782; Ferdinand II 10811; Fitch 10926; Flavel 11031; Fleming, A. 11040; Florus 11103; Flower, J. 11106; Flower, M. 11107, 11107.3; Forde, E. 11169a; Forsyth 11192; Fowns 11217; France 11284; Frankfurt Fair 11328.4, 11328.6, 11328.7; Frederick I 11350.7, 11360.3; G., A. 11490; Gainsford 11518, 11524; Garden 11560; Gataker 11670, 11676; Gatti 11685; Gething 11803; Gheyn or Geyn 11812(?); Gibson, Abraham 11828, 11830a.5; Gil, A., the Elder 11873; Godfridus 11933; Gouge 12123; Greene, R. 12289.5; Griselda 12383; Grisons 12390; Guevara 12430; Guild 12485*; Gurnay 12527; H., J., Gent. 12572; Hannay 12747*, 12749; Harris, Robert 12827, 12827.3, 12827.5; Harrison, John 12858, 12859; Herrey 13235*; Heywood, T. 13345; Hieron 13379*, 13379a*, 13384.3*, 13412.5; Higgins, J., Poet 13447*, 13447.5*; Holy Roman Empire 13611; Hornby 13816; Horne, R., of Ludlow 13823, 13823.5; Hutton, H. 14028; Ingmethorp 14088, 14088.5; Ireland, Proc. 14171, 14172; Italy 14284; James I 14346, 14346.3, 14358.5, 14370, 14371, 14384, 14385, 14388, 14388.3; Janua 14467.7(?); Jerome, S. 14512.7*, 14513; Jesuits 14527, 14529; Johnston, A. 14708.7, 14708.8; Keep 14898.5, 14899, 14899.1(?)(A/C); King, J., Bp. 14983, 14984, 14984.5; Lambard 15160, 15174; Ledenberch 15352; Leech, Jeremy 15364; L'Espine 15515; Lessius 15518.5; Letters 15528; Lewis, Jeremiah 15557; Ley, R. 15569; Lily, P. 15600, 15601; Lily, W., 'Lily's Grammar' 15626.8; Lindsay, D., Bp. 15656; Lindsay, Sir D. 15667.5; Liturgies, C. of Eng., BCP 16351, 16352, 16352.5, 16353*; Loe, the Elder 16689; London, Bookbinders 16768.6; London, Pin Makers 16783.5; Louis XIII 16836; Lyte, the Younger 17123, 17123.5; Magirus 17183.5*; Man, S. 17239; Mandevill 17245; Marlowe 17433; Martin, G. 17506; Mary, de' Medici 17555; Mascall 17586*; Mason, T. 17623; Maxey, A. 17693; Maxwell 17699; Mayer 17742; Meara 17762; Medeley 17770; Middleton, R. 17871, 17873; Middleton, T. 17887, 17902; Milles, T. 17936.5; Montenay 18045, 18046, 18046.5, 18046.7, 18047; Morley, T. 18120; Morrice 18170; Morton, T., Bp. 18180; Mucedorus 18237; Mush 18316.7; Napier 18350; Negus 18420; Netherlands, States Gen. 18458, 18459; Newman, A. 18496; Newman, J. 18497; Newstead 18508; Norden 18606; Norris, S. 18657.5; Nowell, Shorter Catechism 18711b.5; Odingsells 18782.5, 18783*; Oldcastle, J. 18796*; Oldenbarneveld 18799, 18801, 18802, 18803, 18804; Oldmayne 18805; Ovidius Naso 18929.4(A/C); Owen, John 18993; Oxford Univ., Quaestiones 19016.5; Oxford Univ., Verses, etc. 19024; P., B. 19057.7; Parr, E. 19316; Parsons, R. 19388; Pasquil 19453.7, 19454; Patriarchs 19471; Pelegromius 19562; Pemberton 19568; Pennington 19601; Perkins, W. 19672, 19739, 19756, 19761.7; Petrucci 19812.5(?), 19813; Philip III 19843; Pont 20101; Popham 20115; Preston, J., of East Ogwell 20282.3, 20282.7; Primaleon 20367; Prosopopoeia 20443(?); Puccini 20483; Puente 20486; Pulley 20494; Purchas, S. 20503; Quin 20566; Rainolds, J. 20614; Raleigh 20654a.5*(A/C); Ramsey, J., Visct. Haddington 20664; Ratcliffe 20746; Rawlinson 20777; Reusner 20907; Rich, B. 20990; Richeome 21022; Rig 21056.2; Robertson, B. 21096*; Rogers, D. 21165; Rogers, Richard 21207.7, 21213.5, 21221.5; Rogers, Timothy 21244; Rollock, R. 21277; Ross 21328*; Rous, the Elder 21338; Rowlands, S. 21375, 21411; Sarpi 21760; Scapula 21805.9; Schouten 21828; Sclater, the Elder 21834, 21834a; Scot, J. 21856; Scot, P. 21858, 21858.5; Scotland, proclamations 21965.5; Sempill, J. 22186; Shakespeare, W. 22291*, 22293*, 22297*, 22300, 22303*,

1619 — *cont.*
22341; Sharpe, Leonell 22372.3; Slatyer 22636; Smith, H., Minister, Collections 22743; Smith, S., Minister in Essex 22848*, 22850, 22851; Snawsel 22886.5; Sorocold 22933.3, 22933.5(?); Speed, John, Genealogies 23039d.7(+?); Speidell 23063; Staresmore 23235; Stepney, W. 23257; Stockwood 23279; Sulpitius 23431.3; Swadon 23510; Sweetnam, Joseph 23537; Sympson 23595; T., I., Westminster 23624.7; Taylor, John 23767; Taylor, Thomas 23823.5, 23826, 23837; Terentius 23889; Text 23924; Themylthorp 23934.6; Thomas, L. 24006; Thomas, T. 24016; Tillesley 24073; Trussell, T. 24298; Tymme 24428; Vaughan, E. 24596.5; Vautor 24624; Walsall 24997.5(A/C); Webbe, G. 25156; Weckherlin 25185a.5; West, R. 25265; Whately 25297, 25305, 25305a, 25309, 25309.3, 25320; White, F., M. A. 25386; Widdrington 25599; Wigmore 25616, 25618; Wilkinson, J., Dissenter 25647; Wither, Poet 25907, 25914; Wright, W. 26046; Yarrow 26077; York, House of 26101.

1620

A.B.C. 21.4(c.), 21.5(c.); A-Parisiis 698a; Abbot, G., Abp. 29, 37.3(A/C); Aberdeen Univ. 71.5; Abernethy 76; Adamson, J. 137; Ainsworth, H. 236; Allsopp 382.5(c.); Almanacks (Allestree) 407.3; Almanacks (Bretnor, T.) 420.13; Almanacks (Browne) 421.5; Almanacks (Burton) 426.8; Almanacks (Dade, W.) 435.9; Almanacks (Drekin) 437.5; Almanacks (Einer) 438; Almanacks (Frende) 445.15; Almanacks (Gilden) 448.5; Almanacks (Neve, Jeffery) 489.21; Almanacks (Ranger) 502.6; Almanacks (Rudston, J.) 506.12; Almanacks (Smith, R.) 514.3; Almanacks (Sofford) 515.3; Almanacks (White) 527.9; Almanacks (Woodhouse, or Wedhouse, or Wydowes, J.) 531.11; Anabaptists 563.5; Andrewes, J. 595.8; Andrewes, L. 611; Angelos 641(?)*; Anything 698.5(c.); Arias 742.3; Augustine 910, 917; Austin, H. 970; Avila, J. 983; B., A. D. 1023; Bacon, F. 1119.5(aft.), 1120(aft.), 1144(c.)*, 1162, 1163; Baldwin, W. 1267(c.), 1267.3(c.), 1267.5(c.); Ballad 1328.3(c.), 1329.5(c.); Barbour 1379; Barclay, W., M.D. 1404; Barrow-Faustus 1527.7(c.); Basse 1548, 1554.7(c.); Bayly, L. 1604; Baynes, P. 1629, 1647; Beaumont, F., and Fletcher 1681, 1681.5; Bellman 1848.5(c.); Benefield 1863; Bennett, E. 1883, 1883.5(?); Bible, English 2258*, 2259, 2260*, 2261, 2262*; Bible, N.T., English 2920.7; Bible, O.T., Psalms 2569.7, 2570, 2570.5, 2571, 2571.3, 2571.5, 2571.7, 2572*, 2731, 2741.5; Bible, Welsh 2348; Billingsley 3062.6(+?); Blaeu 3111; Blondo 3134; Bloy 3138.5(c.); Boccaccio 3172; Bohemia 3205, 3206, 3207(?), 3207.5, 3208, 3210, 3214, 3215; Book 3300, 3363.8; Booth 3370; Boughen 3407; Bourne, I. 3417; Bourne, W. 3430; Bradshaw, W. 3523; Brathwait 3566, 3580; Brereley 3607, 3608; Breton 3689; Brydges 3957; Buchanan 3989; Bun 4087.7(c.); Burton, S. 4164; Byfield, N. 4220; C., I. or J. 4281; C., J., Student in Divinity 4284; C., L. W. 4288.5; C., W. 4316.5; Calderwood 4354, 4355, 4361 [not STC], 4365; Calvin 4466; Carliell 4652; Catch 4793(c.?); Cato 4849; Caveat 4877.7(c.); Cervantes Saavedra 4916(?), 4917; Chamberlaine 4948.5; Chambers, Richard 4953; Champny 4959; Chapman, G. 4994.5(?); Charron 5053(?); Cicero 5305; Clod 5433(?); Colson 5583; Cooper, T., Preacher 5698, 5700.5(?); Cortano 5796, 5796.3; Cox, R. 5948; Crakanthorp 5980; Crashaw, Mrs. W. 6030; Croy 6098; Cryghton 6099.5; Cuckold 6100.5(c.); Davies, E. 6326.5; Davies, J., of Hereford 6344.3(?), 6345.2(?); Day, John, Rector 6424; Dekker 6480.5(c.)*, 6489, 6497; Deloney 6558.5(c.); Denison, J. 6583, 6587; Denison, S. 6603.5, 6603.7, 6604; Dennys 6611.5; Dent, A. 6662.7; Dering 6721; Descant 6766.5(c.?); Description 6769.5, 6769.7, 6773; Devereux 6791.5(c.), 6792.3(c.); Ditty 6924 (c.); Dod 6945.8; Dominis 6995.5; Doughty, T. 7072.3; Downame, G. 7104, 7109, 7109.3, 7119; Downame, J. 7148(?); Downes, T. 7154.3(?), 7154.5; Drayton 7223*; Du Moulin, P., the Elder 7307, 7308, 7313, 7336.5, 7338; Durer 7289.7; Dyke, D. 7402(?); Dyke, J. 7413, 7426; Dyke, W. 7431.5; Edinburgh University 7487.17; Egerton, S. 7532; Elborough 7550.5(?); Elton 7613, 7615.7(c.); England, Army 7682.5(c.?); England, C. of, Visit. Articles 10218.5, 10219.5, 10227, 10268.7, 10276, 10293, 10314.10, 10329.7; England, Privy Council 7754.4; England, Proclamations, Chron. Ser. 8583(?), 8615, 8624, 8624.5, 8625, 8626, 8627, 8628, 8629, 8630,

1620 — *cont.*
8631, 8632, 8633, 8634, 8635, 8636, 8637, 8638, 8639, 8640, 8641, 8642, 8642.5, 8643, 8644, 8645, 8646, 8647, 8648, 8649, 8650, 8654.7(o.s.), 8655(o.s.), 8656(o.s.), 8659(o.s.), 8660(o.s.);, 9503.3 (c.?); England, Yearbooks 9904*; Erasmus, D. 10478.3; Euclid 10559; Ferdinand II 10808.5, 10809, 10810, 10812, 10814(?), 10815, 10815.5, 10816; Fitz-Geffrey, C. 10940, 10940.3; Fitzgeffrey, H. 10945.6; Fliegen 11088.3(c.?); Floyd, J. 11110.7; Folkingham 11122; Ford, J. 11162; Fracastoro 11253; France 11278; Francis, of Borja 11315; Frankfurt Fair 11328.8, 11328.9, 11328.10, 11329; Frederick I 11349, 11350, 11351, 11351.3, 11352, 11356; French Whipper 11376.5(c.); Fulbecke 11411; G., E. 11492.7(c.?); Gainsford 11519; Gataker 11655, 11658, 11667, 11678, 11679, 11680; Gee, E. 11700; Gernutus 11796.5(c.); Gheyn or Geyn 11812.5(c.?); Gibbons 11823(?), 11824(?), 11825(?); Gibson, S. 11838; Gifford, G. 11857, 11857.3; Godwin, T. 11958, 11958.5; Goffe 11979, 11979.5; Goodcole 12011; Goodwin, G. 12029; Granger, Thomas 12180, 12184; Greene, R. 12303; Greenwood, H. 12329, 12333; Guild 12485*; Gunter, E. 12516, 12518; Haec Vir 12599; Hall, Joseph 12657, 12657.5, 12674, 12674a, 12708*; Hampton, C. 12738, 12739.5; Hand 12743(c.?); Harding, J. 12756; Hayward, Sir J. 13007; Help 13050.5; Henry, the Minstrel 13153; Herrey 13235*; Hic Mulier 13374, 13375, 13375.5; Hieron 13377.5 (?), 13379*, 13379a*, 13384.3*, 13402, 13413.5; Higgins, J., Poet 13448, 13448.4; Hinde, W. 13512; Histories 13525; History 13528.5 (c.?); Hockham 13541.3(c.), 13541.5(c.); Holland, Henry, Bookseller 13582; Horatius Flaccus 13794, 13794a; Hull, J. 13932; Hundred 13970.5(c.?); I., E., Student in divinity 14049, 14050, 14050.5; Innes 14091; Ireland, Laws 14130*; Ireland, Proc. 14173, 14174 (o.s.); James I 14345*, 14346.3*, 14346.5, 14381.5, 14382, 14383, 14388.5, 14412; James, T., D. D. 14450; Jephtha 14498.5(c.); Jerome, S. 14512.7*; Jesuits 14537; Joan 14618.5(c.); Johnson, Richard 14674; Johnson, Robert, Chaplain 14694.2(A/C); Johnston, A. 14713.5*, 14714.5; Jonah 14716(c.); Jonson 14763, 14764; Josephus 14811, 14811a; Juvenalis 14891*; Keep 14899.3(c.), 14899.7 (c.); King, J., Bp. 14982; Knolles 15053*; L., T. 15112; Lady 15120 (c.?); Leech, John, Poet 15365.7, 15366*; Leicestershire Lovers 15401(c.); Lewis, John 15558; Linaker 15641; Ling 15688(?); Liturgies, C. of Eng., BCP 16353*, 16354, 16354.5(?), 16355, 16356, 16359*; Liturgies, C. of Eng., Spec. Prayers 16539.5(c.); Liturgies, C. of Eng., St. Services 16484, 16496; Liturgies, Other Protest. C. 16605; Loe, the Elder 16688, 16690; London, Cooks 16776.2(c.); London, Ords. and Regs. 16727.7, 16727.9; Louis XIII 16838; Lubin 16879; Lydiat 17046; Maid 17189(c.); Maiden 17190(?); Manual 17276, 17276.2, 17278.1; Markham, G. 17372; Marlowe 17434; Marshalsea Prison 17469.8(c.); Mascall 17586*; Mason, John, Gov. of Newfoundland 17616; Mason, Robert 17620.3, 17620.5; Maurice 17677; Mavericke 17681; Medley 17777.5(c.?); Meg 17782.5; Melton, J. 17804; Melville, A. 17810; Melville, E. 17814; Michaelson 17856; Middleton, T. 17904.5; Middleton, T., and Rowley 17909, 17910; Monginot 18012; Morgan, N. 18105.3, 18105.7; Mornay 18154; Morton, T., Bp. 18178; Moundeford, Minister 18226; Newsbooks, Corantos 18507.1, 18507.2; Newton, R. 18509; Niccholes 18515; Norden 18623, 18629; Observations 18761; Odingsells 18783*; Opitz von Boberfeld 18831; Overbury 18921.5(?); Ovidius Naso 18952.5, 18975; P., W. 19080.5; Parker, Matthew 19289; Parr, E. 19320; Parsons, R. 19354.6, 19409.5, 19410; Pasor, G. 19443; Paterson 19461; Paul V 19483(?); Peacham, H., the Younger 19515; Pedlar 19527(c.); Peerson 19553; Pestell 19791; Peyton 19824; Plutarch 20055.7; Preston, T., and Green 20286.3; Price, R. 20327(c.); Prize 20397.3(?)(A/C); Proclus 20398; Prophecy 20440(?); Quarles 20544; Quin 20564.5(?); R., M. 20584.5; Ratcliffe 20747; Relations 20866; Reynard the Fox 20923; Rive 21061, 21062; Robertson, B. 21098.5; Rogers, J., of Chacombe 21185; Rogers, N. 21201; Rogers, Richard 21208, 21213.6, 21214; Rolland 21256; Romans 21289.5(c.); Ross 21325; Rowlands, S. 21378.3(c.), 21402, 21404(?); Rush 21451; Ryves 21478; Sack 21538; Salerno 21603.7; Saluste du Bartas 21653*; Saluzzo 21673.5; Sarpi 21761, 21764; Schonaeus 21822; Scot, P. 21859; Scotland, proclamations 21966, 21967, 21968; Scott, T., B. D. 22098,

1620 — *cont.*
22098.5, 22099, 22100, 22100.2, 22100.4, 22100.6, 22100.8, 22101*; Scudder 22121; Scultetus 22126; Seabrooke 22133; Seager 22137.5; Seneca 22214; Shakespeare, W. 22362; Sherrard 22427, 22427a; Shore 22463.5(c.); Simon 22555.5(c.); Simson, Archibald 22565; Sir 22579.5(c.); Smith, H., Minister, Collections 22759; Smith, John, Gov. of Virginia 22792; Smith, S., Minister in Essex 22836, 22837, 22838, 22843, 22852; Southwell 22964, 22965; Spanish Tragedy 23012(?); Speed, John 23032, 23034.5(c.); Speed, John, Genealogies 23039f.2(c.); Speidell 23063.3; Spotiswood 23103; Squire, J., Triumph Writer 23120.5; Steingenius 23242 [not STC]; Stepney, W. 23258; Stubbes 23387; Styles 23412, 23412.5; Sweetnam, John 23531; Sweetnam, Joseph 23544; Sylvester 23575, 23575.5, 23583; Sylvester 23583; Talaeus 23659.9(c.); Tanner, R. 23673; Tapp 23680.5; Tarlton 23683.5(c.); Taylor, John 23751, 23757, 23765.5, 23770, 23788, 23802; Taylor, Thomas 23830.7, 23831, 23838; Thomas, a Kempis 23989; Thomas, T. 24017; Tilenus 24069, 24070; Timberlake 24085; Traske 24178; Treatises 24259; Tusser 24390; Twyne, B. 24406; Urfe 24525; Ussher, A. 24541.7(c.); Vaux 24627a.4; Venner, T. 24643; Virel 24771.7; Virgilius Maro 24805a, 24810, 24818; Virginia Company 24841, 24841.2, 24841.3, 24841.4, 24841.6, 24841.8, 24842; Vives 24853; Wakeman 24953; Walkington 24970; Warning 25088(c.); Way 25135.5(?); Westward 25292; Whitbourne 25372; Whittell 25441; Wigmore 25615; Wilkinson, J., of Barnard's Inn 25649; Willet 25691, 25691.5; Williams, J., Abp. 25728, 25728.5; Wilson, T., Divine 25792, 25796; Wing 25844; Wither, Poet 25890, 25902; Wittenberg Univ. 25933; Worthington, R. 25999; Worthington, T. 26000.3; Wright, T., Priest 26041; Yate 26078.5(c.).

1621

Adams 134; Adson 153; Aesop 172.6, 186; Ahmad I 208; Ainsworth, H. 211; Airay, H. 244; Algeria 353.5; Almanacks (Allestree) 407.4; Almanacks (Browne) 421.6; Almanacks (Burton) 426.9; Almanacks (Einer) 438.2; Almanacks (Frende) 445.16; Almanacks (Gilden) 448.6; Almanacks (Gumdante) 453; Almanacks (Johnson, J.) 465.9; Almanacks (Neve, Jeffery) 489.22, 489.23; Almanacks (Ranger) 502.7; Almanacks (Sofford) 515.4; Almanacks (Vaux) 522; Almanacks (White) 527.10; Almanacks (Woodhouse, or Wedhouse, or Wydowes, J.) 531.12; Anabaptists 563.7; Andrewes, J. 590, 591, 592; Archbold 731; Arias 741; Assize of Bread 879; Augustine 933.5, 942.5, 947.5; B., I. or J. 1037; Baron, R. 1496; Bassano 1545.5; Basse 1549; Bayly, L. 1604.5; Baynes, P. 1640; Bedford, T. 1788; Bellarmino 1838.5; Bergeville 1901; Bernard, R. 1941, 1942, 1963; Beze 2024.7; Bible, Appendix 3029; Bible, English 2262*, 2263, 2264*; Bible, N.T., English 2921, 2922, 2923; Bible, O.T., 'Books of Solomon' 2774; Bible, O.T., Psalms 2572*, 2572.3, 2572.6, 2573.5, 2574, 2574.3, 2574.5, 2575, 2575.3, 2745; Bible, Selections 2998; Blount, A. 3134.5(?); Blundeville 3150*; Boislore 3217.5; Book 3348, 3365; Bowdler 3432.5, 3432.7; Bowle 3434.5; Bradford, J., Prebendary of St. Paul's 3504; Bradshaw, W. 3521; Brathwait 3571, 3572*, 3584, 3589; Brereley 3607.5; Brerewood 3616; Breton 3670, 3681, 3696.7; Brinsley, J., the Elder 3771.4; Broad 3806; Broughton, Richard 3895.5; Bruen 3930.3; Buchanan 3980, 3987; Bullokar, J. 4084; Burton, R. 4159; Butler, C. 4199.5; Button 4208; Cade 4329; Calderwood 4352, 4361.5; Camerarius 4528, 4529; Carter, B. 4692; Cartwright, F. 4704; Casaubon, M. 4749; Catholic 4830.5(?); Cato 4849.1; Cicero 5268.4; Cinque Ports 5323a.4, 5323a.6; Clare, Saint 5349.8, 5350*, 5350.4, 5350.7; Clarke, A. 5352; Clarke, T., of Sutton Coldfield 5364; Clay 5371.9; Cleaver 5387.5; Coeffeteau 5473; Coffin 5476*; Coke, E. 5510; Comedy 5598; Cooke, A. 5663, 5663.2; Cooper, T., Preacher 5710.3; Coote 5712.5; Cork 5764.7; Crakanthorp 5974; Crane 5986; Crashaw, W. 6017; Crokey 6044a.7; Culpeper 6108, 6108.3; Dakins 6191.3; Daniel Ben Alexander 6266; Daniel, S. 6249, 6250; Davies, J., of Mallwyd 6346; Davison 6376; Day, A. 6406.5; Day, M. 6427.5, 6427.7*; Denison, J. 6583.7, 6584, 6584.5, 6586; Denison, S. 6599, 6601; Dent, A. 6663; Despautere 6781.5; Discourse 6908; Dod 6946; Donne, J. 7024; Doughty, T. 7072.2; Downes, A. 7154; Downfall 7155; Du Moulin, P., the Elder 7331; Dungeness 7353.8;

1621 — *cont.*
Dyer, J. 7390.5; East India Company 7447; Edinburgh University 7487.18; Egerton, E. 7527.3; Egerton, S. 7533; England, C. of, Visit. Articles 10133.9, 10162, 10261, 10348(?); England, Proclamations, Chron. Ser. 8651, 8652, 8653, 8654, 8654.7, 8655, 8656, 8658, 8659, 8660, 8661, 8662, 8663, 8664, 8665, 8666, 8667, 8668, 8669, 8670, 8671, 8672, 8673, 8673.5, 8674, 8675, 8675.2, 8675.4, 8675.6, 8676(o.s.), 8676.5(o.s.), 8677(o.s.), 8678(o.s.), 8679(o.s.), 8680(o.s.), 8681(o.s.); England, Public Documents, Misc. 9241(o.s.); England, Royal Household 9263.7; England, Statutes, Chron. Ser. 9506.7; England, Statutes, Gen. Colls. 9327; Englefield 10406.5, 10406.6; Erasmus, D. 10441.5; Erondelle 10514; Evans, J., Master of Arts 10585; Farley, H. 10690; Finch, H. 10874, 10874.5; Fisher, E. 10885.5(?); Fitzherbert, T. 11020; Fletcher, John 11074; Florus 11104(?); Flower, M. 11107.5(?); France 11264, 11279.5; France—Reformed Churches 11300, 11300.3, 11303, 11303.5, 11304; Frankfurt Fair 11329.4, 11329.5; Frederick I 11353; Frewen 11379; Frith, T. 11395.3, 11395.5; Fulwood 11483; Gamage 11545; Garden 11560.5; Gataker 11675; Gerhard 11766; Gil, A., the Elder 11874; Gilgate 11895.5; Godwin, F. 11942(?)*; Gohaeus 11982.5; Goldwell, C. 11988; Goodcole 12014; Gouge 12127; Goulart 12136, 12137; Granger, Thomas 12178; Greene, R. 12237, 12248; Gregory XV 12356; Groans 12391; Guillemard 12495; Guillemeau 12499.7; H., A. 12561.4(?); Hakewill 12616; Hall, Joseph 12684, 12708*; Harris, A. 12802; Harrison, R., Innkeeper 12862.7; Hawley 12967.5 (?); Help 13051; Heron or Hearne 13227; Herrey 13238*; Hewat 13258; Heylyn 13276; Hieron 13402.2; Higgins, J., Poet 13448.7; Holland 13576; Horatius Flaccus 13799; Hughes, L. 13920; Hume, P. 13954.3; Hunnis 13983.5; I., R. 14056; Ireland, Laws 14130*; Ireland, Proc. 14174, 14175, 14175.5(o.s.); Jackson, Timothy 14320; James I 14358.7(A/C), 14388.7, 14399, 14399.5; Janua 14468; Jenison 14491; John, of Capistrano 14650.5; Johnson, Robert, B. D. 14693.5; Jonson 14777; Juvenalis 14891*; Kellison 14911; King, Henry 14969, 14969.5; King's Bench 14961.5(?); Knolles 15053*; Langford 15193a; Langlois de Fancan 15203; Laud 15301; Leech, John, Poet 15366*; Legh 15393*; Leigh, D. 15404; Leius 15438; Lessius 15518, 15524; Lily, W., 'Lily's Grammar' 15627, 15627.2, 15627.3; Lindsay, D., Bp. 15657; Littleton, T., Tenures, Engl. 15782; Littleton, T., Tenures, French 15758; Liturgies, C. of Eng., BCP 16357, 16357.3, 16357.5, 16357.7, 16358, 16438; Liturgies, Latin Rite, Hours and Primers 16098; Liturgies, Other Protest. C. 16594*; Loe, the Elder 16691; London, Bills of Mort. 16743.7; London, Bookbinders 16768.8; London, Brewers 16768.12; London, Brokers 16768.16; London, Carpenters 16768.22(?), 16768.24 (?), 16768.26(?); London, Cloth-workers 16768.30(?); London, Customs House 16776.4; London, Cutlers 16776.6; London, Dyers 16777.2, 16777.4; London, Felt Makers 16777.6(?); London, Fustian Makers 16777.8(?); London, Goldbeaters 16777.14; London, Hot Pressers 16778.2, 16778.4; London, Merchants of the Staple 16779.8; London, Ministers 16779.10; London, Ords. and Regs. 16728, 16728.3; London, Shipwrights 16785.7; London, Stationers 16786.6, 16786.8, 16786.10; London, Tilers and Bricklayers 16786.16; London, Water-Tankard-Bearers 16787.8(?); London, Watermen 16787; London, Wharfingers 16787.10; London, Woodmongers 16787.12, 16787.14; Longueval 16798; Louis XIII 16839, 16840; Lovell, R. 16859; Lydiat 17039, 17042(o.s.); M., A. 17125; Macropedius 17176.8; Maie 17195, 17196; Manning, P. 17257.5; Markham, G. 17362; Martyn, J. 17525; Mason, F. 17600; Mason, W. 17624; Maurice 17670.5, 17672; Mayer 17732; Mayle 17748.5; Middleton, T. 17886, 17895; Miller 17923.5; Molina 17998; Mompesson 18003.9(A/C); Montagu, R. 18037; Morgan, G. 18102a.2, 18102a.3; Morley, C. 18114.5, 18114.6; Mucedorus 18237.5; Mun 18255, 18256; Murrell 18302; Muscovia Company 18307.3(A/C); Musgrave 18316; N., D. 18327; Netherlands, States Gen. 18459.5, 18460, 18460.3, 18460.7; Newsbooks, Corantos 18507.24, 18507.25, 18507.26, 18507.27, 18507.28, 18507.29, 18507.30, 18507.31, 18507.32, 18507.33, 18507.34, 18507.35;, 18507.3, 18507.4, 18507.5, 18507.6, 18507.7, 18507.8, 18507.9, 18507.10, 18507.11, 18507.12, 18507.13, 18507.14, 18507.15, 18507.16, 18507.17, 18507.18, 18507.19, 18507.20, 18507.21, 18507.22,

1621 — *cont.*
18507.23; Newsbooks, Unnum. 18507.35A, 18507.35C; Nicholas y Sacharles 18529, 18530, 18530.5; Norris, S. 18658.5, 18659; Nowell, Middle Catechism 18720.5; Ossolinski 18890; Ovidius Naso 18963.3; Oxford Univ., Quaestiones 19016.6; Page, P. 19087.7; Papal Exchequer 19174a; Parsons, R. 19375; Pasor, G. 19444; Pearl 19519(?); Perkins, J. 19644, 19644.5; Perkins, W. 19664.5, 19687.5, 19693, 19726.5, 19730.3, 19746.3, 19761.9; Philip IV 19843.5; Playfere 20003*, 20006; Prague 20181; Preston, R. 20283, 20284, 20286; Preston, T., and Green 20286.7; Prideaux 20351; Proctor, T. 20408.5, 20409, 20410, 20411; Quarles 20546; Raleigh 20638a*, 20639; Reading 20789, 20792; Reynolds, J., Merchant 20942; Richardson, C. 21013.5; Rive 21059; Robertson, B. 21098.7; Rochfort 21138.3; Rogers, N. 21194; Rogers, Thomas, M. A. 21229; Rogers, Timothy 21244.5, 21250; Rowley, S. 21419; Rowley, W. 21420.5; Saint Andrews Univ. 21555.33; Saint Jean-d'Angely 21588.7; Saluste du Bartas 21653*, 21666; Sandys, G. 21727; Savile, G. 21781.5(?); Savile, H. 21782; Scot, P. 21860; Scotland, Church of, Bk. of Discipline 22015; Scotland, statutes, etc. 21900, 21901; Scott, T., B. D. 22083, 22086.5, 22087; Scribonius 22111; Sea Fight 22130, 22131; Seager 22137.7; Shackley 22270.7(?); Shaw, Divine 22389; Shrewsbury 22463.7; Sidney, P. 22544a.7, 22545; Simson, Archibald 22566, 22567.5, 22570; Slatyer 22634; Smith, H., Minister, Collections 22774; Smith, H., Minister, Single Works 22710; Smith, R., Bp. of Chalcedon 22812; Smith, S., A. M. 22830, 22830.5; Smith, T., Doctor of Civil Laws 22864; Speed, John 23044*; Speed, R. 23050.5; Speght, R. 23057; Squire, J., Minister 23117; Stanley, T. 23228.5(?); Stint 23269, 23270; Stubbes 23388; Susenbrotus 23441; Swale 23512; Talaeus 23660; Tapp 23678; Taylor, John 23737.5, 23786, 23793, 23795.7, 23796, 23799, 23800, 23800.5, 23802.5, 23808a; Taylor, Thomas 23840; Teelinck 23860, 23861; Term 23910; Tewkesbury 23918.5; Thorius 24034; Thornborough 24038; Thorold 24044a.5; Tillesley 24074; Treves Endt 24268.3; Trinity House 24283; Turnet 24368.5 (?); Tymme 24429; Ussher, J. 24553.5; Vega Carpio 24629; Venner, T. 24642; Verslyn 24690; Vesey 24694; Vicars, T. 24702; Villegas 24731b; Virginia Company 24842a; Voilleret 24871; Vrillac 24893; W., R. 24912; Ward, S., of Ipswich 25043, 25044, 25044.5, 25047, 25049, 25049a; Warre 25090; Wats 25109; Webbe, G. 25155; Willis, J., Stenographer 25749; Willughby 25759.5; Wing 25842, 25846; Winne 25854; Winterton 25856.5, 25857; Winwick 25858.7(?); Wither, Poet 25923, 25925, 25925.5*, 25926, 25926.5, 25927, 25928, 25928.3, 25928.5, 25928.7; Wood, G. 25951.5; Wood, J., Petitioner 25954.5(?), 25954.6(?)(A/C); Woodwall 25970.5; Wright, L. 26029; Wright, T., Priest 26042; Wroth, M. 26051; Yates, John 26088; Yonger 26098, 26098.3.

1622

A.B.C. 21.9; Abbot, G., Abp. 33; Aberdeen Univ. 71.6; Abernethy 74; Adams 112; Ainsworth, H. 213, 217, 218; Aleman 288*; Almanacks (Allestree) 407.5; Almanacks (Bell) 413.5; Almanacks (Browne) 421.7; Almanacks (Dade, W.) 435.11; Almanacks (Einer) 438.3; Almanacks (Frende) 445.17; Almanacks (Gilden) 448.7; Almanacks (Johnson, J.) 465.10; Almanacks (Neve, Jeffery) 489.24; Almanacks (Osborne) 494; Almanacks (Ranger) 502.8; Almanacks (Smith, R.) 514.5; Almanacks (Sofford) 515.5; Almanacks (Vaux) 522.2; Almanacks (White) 527.11; Almanacks (Woodhouse, or Wedhouse, or Wydowes, J.) 531.13; Ames 559; Art 794*; Attey 901; Aylett 1002, 1003, 1003.5, 1004; B., I. or J. 1034.3; Babington, G. 1079; Bacon, F. 1132, 1155, 1159, 1160; Baddeley 1185; Bagnall 1187; Balsamo 1341; Barclay, J. 1390; Barlement 1431.26, 1431.27; Barnes, T. 1476; Baynes, P. 1642.5; Beaumont, F., and Fletcher 1678, 1682; Becanus 1705, 1705.5, 1706; Beda 1779; Bedford, T. 1788.5; Bellarmino 1839*; Bellot 1851.5; Bergen-op-zoom 1898; Bermudas 1905; Bernard, St. 1909.3; Beze 2015; Bible, English 2264, 2265*; Bible, N.T., English 2924; Bible, N.T., Greek 2795; Bible, N.T., Latin 2812.5; Bible, O.T., Psalms 2413.5, 2575a, 2576, 2576.5, 2576.7, 2577, 2578, 2578.5, 2579; Blaeu 3112; Blundeville 3150*; Bourne, I. 3419; Boys 3452; Bradford, J., Prebendary of St.

1622 — *cont.*
Paul's 3492; Bradshaw, W. 3512*; Brerewood 3619; Breton 3697, 3699.4, 3702.5; Brinsley, J., the Elder 3767, 3774.5, 3782.5, 3786; Brooke, C. 3830.5; Brooke, R. 3833; Brown, D. 3905; Buggs 4022, 4023; Bullokar, J. 4085; Burges, C. 4110, 4111.5; Burton, W., Topographer 4179; Byfield, N. 4220.5, 4227; C., W. 4323; Cambridge University 4484.5, 4485.5; Canisius 4572; Carliell 4653; Carpenter, N. 4678; Cartwright, T. 4710.5; Cary, H. 4718.5; Cato 4860; Cespedes y Meneses 4919; Chaloner, E. 4936*; Chapman, G. 4988; Charles [de Lorraine], Duc de Guise 5011.5; Chibald 5134, 5135; Clare, Saint 5350*; Clay 5372; Clinton, E. 5432; Coffin 5476; Comley 5604.5, 5604.6, 5604.7; Cooke, A. 5663a, 5664, 5664.2; Cooke, John 5674; Cooper, T., Preacher 5701.3, 5709; Copland, P. 5726, 5726.5, 5727; Copy 5742.7; Cork 5765, 5766, 5767; Cottesford, S. 5841; Cotton, C. 5842; Crakanthorp 5978; Crashaw, W. 6021; Culverwell 6118.2; Curll 6132; Cushman 6149; Cutler 6109 (?); Dalechamp 6195; Dalton, M. 6207; Darcie, A. 6271; Davies, Sir J. 6359; Daw 6386; Denison, S. 6601.5, 6603, 6605; Dent, A. 6632, 6643, 6643.5, 6664; Dod and Cleaver 6975; Donne, J. 7051, 7053, 7053.5, 7054; Downame, J. 7143; Draxe 7179.5(c.); Drayton 7228, 7229, 7230; Du Buisson 7268.5; Du Moulin, P., the Elder 7318*, 7342.3(?)(A/C); Du Pin 7358; Du Refuge 7367; Du Vair 7373; Du Val, M. 7376(?); Dublin, Christ Church and St. Patrick's 7264.5; Dunbar, W. 7349.5; Dyer, J. 7393; Dyke, D. 7402.3(?); East Indies 7457, 7458; Edinburgh University 7487.19; Elton 7611; England, C. of, Visit. Articles 10209.7(A/C), 10223, 10240, 10308.5, 10325, 10330; England, King's Printer 7705.5(?); England, Proclamations, Chron. Ser. 8457(c.?), 8522, 8676, 8676.5, 8677, 8678, 8679, 8680, 8681, 8682, 8683, 8684, 8685, 8685.5, 8686, 8686.3, 8686.5, 8687, 8688, 8689, 8690, 8690.5, 8691, 8692, 8693, 8694, 8695, 8696, 8697, 8698, 8699(o.s.), 8700(o.s.), 8701(o.s.), 8702(o.s.), 8703(o.s.), 8704 (o.s.), 8705(o.s.); England, Public Documents, Misc. 9241, 9242, 9242.5; Erasmus, D. 10442; Estella 10541.7; Everard 10599; Family of Love 10682; Farley, H. 10689; Faust 10713.5; Fenton, E. 10787.5; Ferrers 10832; Field, T. 10860; Fitz-Geffrey, C. 10941, 10942; Folkingham 11122.5; Fotherby 11205; Francis, of Sales 11320a*; Frankfurt Fair 11329.7, 11329.8; Frederick I 11360.5(?); Freeman, J. 11368.5; French Herald 11375; Gainsford 11520; Gamon 11546; Gardiner, R., of Oxford 11568; Gataker 11651.5, 11677; Goodman, G. 12021; Gouge 12119; Granger, Thomas 12181; Greene, R. 12304; Guild 12482; Guillemeau 12499.5; Hagthorpe 12602; Hakewill 12617; Hall, Joseph 12657a, 12714.5; Hampton, C. 12737.5; Hannay 12748; Harmar 12791; Harris, Robert 12820, 12828, 12831, 12849; Hawkins, R. 12962; Hayward, Sir J. 12991; Heigham 13033, 13034, 13036; Heliodorus 13046; Herbert, Gerard 13189.5; Herrey 13238*; Hieron 13413a; Hinde, W. 13513; Hockin 13542; Holland 13573, 13575, 13577; Holland, A. 13580; Hollanders 13598, 13599; Hooker, R. 13716a*, 13717, 13719a*; Hornby 13814; Howard, H., Earl of Northampton 13859.5; Howson 13879, 13880; Hughes, J. 13914; Huygens 14037.5; Inman 14090; Interpreter 14115; Ireland, Laws 14134; Ireland, Proc. 14175.5, 14176, 14177, 14178, 14179, 14180, 14181; Jackson, Thomas, of Canterbury 14301, 14302; Jacob, ship 14322; James I 14378, 14379.5; James I, appendix 14428; Jesus Christ 14573; John, King 14647; Johnston, A. 14713.5*; Jones, A. 14717.5; Keckermann 14896; King, W. 14998; Larke 15254.5; Laud 15300; Leech, John, Poet 15370; Leigh, D. 15404.3(A/C); Ley, R. 15568; Lindsay, D., Minister 15683.5; Liturgies, C. of Eng., BCP 16358.5, 16359*, 16360; Liturgies, Other Protest. C. 16594*; London, Ords. and Regs. 16728.5, 16728.7; Louis XIII 16841, 16842, 16843; Luna 16927; Lydiat 17042; Lyon 17120; Macollo 17175; Magini 17182; Malynes 17222, 17226; Manojo 17258; Markham, F. 17332; Markham, G. 17387.3; Markham, G., and Sampson 17401, 17402; Marlowe 17420, 17440, 17440a; Mason, E. 17594; Mason, G., Merchant 17600.3; Massinger and Dekker 17644, 17644a; Matthew, Sir Tobie 17658; Maximinus 17697; May, T. 17713; Mayenne 17728.7; Mayer 17733, 17744; Meredeth, J. 17831; Middleton, T. 17900; Middleton, T., and Rowley 17912; Misselden 17986, 17987; Montagu, R. 18029; Moundeford, Physician 18227; Murray, J. 18297; Netherlands 18443; Netherlands, States Gen. 18461, 18462;

1622 — *cont.*
New England 18483; Newsbooks, Num. 18507.82, 18507.83, 18507.84, 18507.85, 18507.86, 18507.87, 18507.88, 18507.89, 18507.90, 18507.91; Newsbooks, Unnum. 18507.35B, 18507.36, 18507.37, 18507.37A, 18507.38, 18507.39, 18507.40, 18507.41, 18507.42, 18507.43*, 18507.44, 18507.45, 18507.46, 18507.47, 18507.48, 18507.49, 18507.50, 18507.51, 18507.51A, 18507.52, 18507.53, 18507.54, 18507.55, 18507.56, 18507.56A, 18507.57, 18507.57A, 18507.58, 18507.59, 18507.60, 18507.61, 18507.62, 18507.63, 18507.64, 18507.65, 18507.66, 18507.67, 18507.68, 18507.69, 18507.70, 18507.71, 18507.71A, 18507.72, 18507.73, 18507.74, 18507.75, 18507.76, 18507.77, 18507.78, 18507.79, 18507.80, 18507.81; Nobody 18598(c.); Noel 18599.5(?); Norris, S. 18658; Norwich, City of 18688.5; Openshaw 18826; Oudin 18897; Outreman 18902; Overbury 18913; Owen, D. 18982; Owen, John 18990; Oxford Univ., Appendix 19052.2, 19052.6; Oxford Univ., Off. Docs. 19014; Oxford Univ., Quaestiones 19016.7; Oxford Univ., Verses, etc. 19025; Oxley, R. 19052.8; P., C. 19058 [not STC]; P., I. B. S. P. 19074 [not STC]; P., I. or J. 19068*, 19072.5; Parr, E. 19321; Parsons, R. 19354.7; Peacham, H., the Younger 19502; Perkins, W. 19679; Pinelli 19937.5; Plummer 20050; Plymouth 20074; Pope 20113; Posselius 20128.3; Powell, T., Londino-Cambrensis 20166; Prat 20186.7; Preston, R. 20285; Raban 20597; Randall 20669, 20675; Rawlins, J. 20769; Relation 20864; Reynolds, J., Merchant 20943.3; Ribadeneira 20968; Rich, B. 20991; Robinson, T. 21123; Rodes 21140; Rogers, Richard 21209, 21213.7; Ross 21325.5, 21326; Rous, the Elder 21340, 21340a; Rowlands, S. 21382; Rugbie 21444; Saluste du Bartas 21648.5*(A/C); Sanderson, R. 21708; Sandys, Sir E. 21717.5(?)*; Schwarzenberg 21828.5, 21829; Scot, P. 21857, 21861; Scot, T., Gent. 21871*, 21871a*; Scot, W. 21874; Scott, T., B. D. 22069, 22069a, 22069a.5, 22080; Shakespeare, W. 22285, 22305, 22319, 22325, 22325a; Sharpe, Leonell 22372.5; Sheldon 22394; Sibthorp 22522; Sidney, P. 22545.5, 22545.7, 22546; Simson, Archibald 22565.5, 22567*; Smetius 22647; Smith, H., Minister, Collections 22731; Smith, H., Minister, Single Works 22672; Smith, John, Gov. of Virginia 22793; Smith, S., Minister in Essex 22848.3*; Sorocold 22933.7; Southwell 22970; Spagnuoli 22984.9; Speed, John, Genealogies 23039d.8(+?); Speidell 23063.5; Stoughton, T. 23314; Sutton, C. 23493.5; Sweeper 23526, 23527; Sweetnam, Joseph 23538; Swift, W. 23546; Tacitus 23647; Tapp 23680.7; Taylor, John 23728, 23738, 23738.5, 23742, 23742.5, 23762, 23771, 23773, 23795*, 23797, 23812, 23812.3*, 23813; Taylor, Thomas 23843; Teelinck 23862; Themylthorp 23934. (A/C); Tilenus 24067; Tisdale 24090; Tomkins 24099; Tomkis 24107; Tuvil or Toutevile 24393.7; Vaughan, Robert, Engraver 24602; Venner, T. 24643.5, 24644; Verus Pater 24693; Vincent, A. 24756; Virgilius Maro 24792.5, 24811; Virginia Company 24843, 24844; W., I., Gent. 24908; W., S. 24915; Walsall, S. 24998; Ward, S., of Ipswich 25033a, 25037, 25042, 25045, 25050, 25052, 25053, 25055, 25055.5; Ware 25063(?); Waterhouse 25104; Web 25150a.5; Webbe, J. 25169; Wells, Dr. 25233; Welwood 25241; West, W. 25275; Whately 25306, 25309.7, 25310, 25315; Whitbourne 25373, 25375, 25375a, 25375a.2, 25375a.4, 25375a.5, 25375a.6, 25375a.7; White, C. 25378; Willan 25669; Williams, G. 25716; Willis, J., Stenographer 25750; Wilson, J., Priest 25773; Wilson, T., Divine 25788; Wing 25843; Wither, Poet 25903, 25903a, 25903b, 25911; Worthington, T. 26000.2, 26000.4, 26000.5, 26000.6; Wright, W. 26046.5; Yates, John 26085.

1623

A., O. 12, 12.5, 12.7(A/C); Abbot, J. 42; Abbot, R., Minister 59; Aberdeen Univ. 71.7, 71.30, 71.33; Adams 106, 106.5, 115*; Adamson, J. 143; Aelfric 160; Age 197.3(c.); Ainsworth, H. 226; Alary 255.5(?); Aleman 288*, 289; Almanacks (Allestree) 407.6; Almanacks (Browne) 421.8; Almanacks (Dade, W.) 435.12; Almanacks (Einer) 438.4; Almanacks (Frende) 445.18; Almanacks (Gilden) 448.8; Almanacks (Jeffereys) 464.5; Almanacks (Johnson, J.) 465.11; Almanacks (Neve, Jeffery) 489.25; Almanacks (Ranger) 502.9; Almanacks (Sofford) 515.6; Almanacks (Vaux) 522.3; Almanacks (White) 527.12; Almanacks (Woodhouse, or Wedhouse, or

1623 — *cont.*
Wydowes, J.) 531.14; Almanacks 404.5; Almansa y Mendoza 533; Alport 537; Ames 560; Anderson, P., Jesuit 575; Andrewes, J. 589, 595.9; Angelos 643.5(?); Aphthonius 704.5; Aristotle 759; Art 794(?)*, 794.5(?); Ashton 843; Aslacus 860; Attersoll 898.5; Aylesbury 1000; Aylett 1001; B., A. R. 1023.5; B., S. 1068; Bacon, F. 1108, 1156; Balcanquhall 1240; Balmford 1336; Barefoote 1409.5; Barlement 1431.28; Barnes, T. 1475; Basse 1549.5; Bayly, L. 1605; Bellarmino 1839*; Bernard, R. 1956, 1956.3, 1956.7; Beze 2016; Bible, English 2265*, 2266, 2267; Bible, N.T., English 2925, 2925.3; Bible, O.T., 'Books of Solomon' 2775; Bible, O.T., Psalms 2580, 2581, 2582, 2583, 2583.3, 2583.5, 2583.7, 2584, 2584.5, 2588.5*; Blackfriars 3101; Boughton 3410; Bourne, I. 3416; Bradford, J., Prebendary of St. Paul's 3498; Bradshaw, W. 3512*; Brathwait 3572*; Breton 3698; Brinsley, J., the Elder 3787; Bristow, R. 3801.5; Brossier, J. 3840; Brousse 3902; Browne, Abraham 3906; Bruen 3930.5; Buenting 4018; Butler, C. 4193; Byfield, N. 4211; C., T. 4311; Calderwood 4353 [not STC]; Cambridge University 4487, 4488, 4494; Camden 4523; Carpenter, R. 4681; Catechism 4803; Cato 4849.2, 4861; Caylie 4890.3; Chaloner, E. 4936*; Chamberlaine 4949; Champions 4955.5; Charles I, King 5024.5, 5025, 5031, 5032, 5033; Chibald 5132; Cicero 5268.5; Cockeram 5461, 5461.2; Cocus or Cooke 5470; Constable, H. 5636.2, 5636.4, 5636.6; Copy 5742.8; Coridon 5764.5(c.); Cotta 5832; Cowper 5909; Craig, A. 5960; Crakanthorp 5973, 5981; Crashaw, W. 6015; Culverwell 6113.5, 6114, 6115, 6118.3, 6118.4; D., E. 6163.5; Dalton, E. 6204a; Dalton, M. 6212; Daniel, S. 6238; Darcie, A. 6273(?); Davies, J., of Hereford 6345.5(c.); Declaration 6456(?); Deloney 6570; Demosthenes 6579; Denison, J. 6590; Denison, S. 6599.3(?); Dering 6721.5; Desainliens or Sainliens 6754.4; Despautere 6779.5, 6783.5; Dictionary 6831; Dominis 7000, 7001; Donne, D. 7021; Donne, J. 7039, 7057; Doughty, T. 7072.7; Downing, T. 7158.5; Drummond 7247, 7248, 7249; Du Moulin, P., the Elder 7314, 7316, 7318*, 7332, 7336; Du Vair 7373.2; Dyke, J. 7423; E., M. 7435, 7435.2; Eadmer 7438, 7438.2; Edinburgh University 7487.20; Egerton, S. 7527.5; Elton 7620.5, 7621; Enchiridion 7681.3; England, Appendix 10003; England, Army 7683; England, C. of, Visit. Articles 10315, 10379.5; England, Customs 7694(?); England, Proclamations, Chron. Ser. 8699, 8700, 8701, 8702, 8703, 8704, 8704.5, 8705, 8706, 8707, 8708, 8708.7, 8709, 8710, 8711, 8712, 8713, 8714, 8715, 8716, 8716.2, 8716.5, 8717, 8719, 8722(o.s.), 8723(o.s.); England, Public Documents, Misc. 9175t-*ii*(?)(A/C), 9243; Essex 10533.5; Evans, E. 10584.5; Everinden 10601; Favyn 10717; Featley, D. 10732, 10732.3; Feltham 10755(?); Fennor 10782.7; Fetherstone, M. 10838; Fisher, John, S.J. 10910.4, 10916.5*; Fletcher, G., the younger 11062, 11062a; Fletcher, J. 11063; Flood 11090; Floyd, J. 11118; Folkingham 11124; Food 11126.5(c.); Foord or Foorthe, Minister 11128.3; Forestus 11180; Four 11211.5; France—Reformed Churches 11295, 11306; Frankfurt Fair 11329.9, 11330; Frederick Henry, Son of Frederick I 11366; G., T. 11510, 11511; G., W. 11511.2(?)(A/C); Gallant 11537.7(c.); Garey 11598; Gataker 11659, 11665, 11666, 11666a, 11681, 11681.3; George, S. 11745.7; Gerhard 11768; Goad 11923; Godwin, T. 11959; Goodcole 12009.5; Gosselin 12092, 12092.2; Gouge 12127.5; Gregory XV 12357; Guild 12486; Gunter, E. 12517, 12519, 12521, 12521.3, 12521.5, 12521.7, 12521.9; Hagthorpe 12604; Hall, Joseph 12646, 12646a, 12658, 12658.5, 12665, 12665.3; Harmar 12792; Hart, John, D. D. 12891.5; Hayward, Sir J. 12987.3, 12987.5, 12989, 12992, 13008; Heidelberg Catechism 13025, 13025.4; Heigham 13033.2, 13033.4*; Herbert, George 13181; Hexham 13264.8; Heywood, T. 13333, 13338; Hieron 13385; Hinde, W. 13514; Hockham 13541.7; Holy Roman Empire 13613; Homilies 13659, 13675; Hopkins, T. 13773; Howell, T., Minister 13873; Ireland, C. of 14265.3; Ireland, Proc. 14182, 14183, 14184(o.s.), 14185(o.s.), 14186(o.s.), 14187(o.s.), 14188 (o.s.), 14189(o.s.); Jackson, Thomas, of Canterbury 14305; Janua 14468.5; Jessop 14520; Jesuits 14535; Jobson 14623; John, of the Cross 14651; Johnson, John, of Colchester 14668.5, 14669; Johnson, Robert, Chaplain 14694.3; Jonson 14782.5; Key 14945.5; Kitchen 15025; Knots 15056; Kyd 15093, 15093a; L., T. 15113; Lambi 15184; Langford 15194; Lant 15223; Lauder, G. 15311;

1623 — *cont.*
Lauze 15316.7(A/C); Lawson 15330; Leech, John, Poet 15367; Leius 15439; Leslie, H. 15501; Lithgow 15712; Liturgies, C. of Eng., BCP 16361, 16362, 16362.3, 16434; Liturgies, C. of Eng., St. Services 16492, 16496.5; Liturgies, Latin Rite, Hours and Primers 16098.3; Liturgies, Latin Rite, Missals 16226; Lodge 16672; Loe, the Elder 16686; Loiseau de Tourval 16695.5(?); London, Coll. of Heralds 16768.32; London, Ords. and Regs. 16728.9(?); Louis XIII 16844; Lovers 16865.7(c.); Loyola 16877.5; Luis 16913, 16914; Luna 16925; Lyly 17065; Malynes 17221; Manual 17276.3; Markham, G. 17338, 17343, 17377a, 17382, 17395.3; Marnix van Sant Aldegonde 17448; Massinger 17634; Mayer 17734, 17739, 17739.5; Mexia 17852; Mico 17858, 17861; Middleton, T. 17901; Mirandula, S. 17956(?) [not STC]; Misselden 17985; Molina 17999, 18001; Molyneux 18003.7; Munday 18280; Muschet, Priest 18305; Myriell 18321; N., D. 18327.5; N., N. 18330; Neville, A. 18481; News 18505(c.); Newsbooks, Num. 18507.111, 18507.112, 18507.113, 18507.114, 18507.115, 18507.116, 18507.117, 18507.118, 18507.119, 18507.120, 18507.121, 18507.122, 18507.123, 18507.124, 18507.125, 18507.126, 18507.127, 18507.128, 18507.129, 18507.130, 18507.131, 18507.132, 18507.133, 18507.134, 18507.135, 18507.136, 18507.137, 18507.92, 18507.93, 18507.94, 18507.95, 18507.96, 18507.97, 18507.98, 18507.99, 18507.100, 18507.101, 18507.102, 18507.103, 18507.104, 18507.105, 18507.106, 18507.107, 18507.108, 18507.109, 18507.110; Norden 18626a.7; Norris, S. 18660; Ogston 18790; Openshaw 18826a; Ovidius Naso 18963.7; Oxford Univ., Verses, etc. 19026, 19027; P., I. or J. 19068*; Pagit 19107.5; Painter, W., Aphorist 19125.5; Pattenson 19480, 19481; Pena, J. 19594; Percyvall 19621, 19621a, 19621b, 19621b.5; Perkins, W. 19652*, 19676.5; Persians 19776; Petley 19801; Peyton 19825; Phillips, Jerome 19862; Playfere 20003*; Posselius 20129; Powel, Gabriel 20154; Powell, T., Londino-Cambrensis 20163, 20163.5, 20171; Pulton 20498; Purchas, S. 20502; Randall 20678; Ratramnus 20752, 20752.5; Rawley 20767; Record, R. 20808; Reynolds, J., Merchant 20943.5; Rhodes, M. 20961.5; Robinson, T. 21124; Rogers, Henry, of Herefordshire 21177; Rogers, N. 21199; Rogers, Richard 21222; Rome, Church of 21302; Rous, the Elder 21344; Rousseel 21354.5 (A/C); Rowlands, S. 21376; Rowlandson 21415; Ruin 21446.3; S., I. or J. 21504.5; Saint German 21581; Scarbrough 21806.5; Sclater, the Elder 21842; Scot, P. 21862; Scot, T., of Ipswich 21873.5; Scotland, appendix 22007; Scott, T., B. D. 22070, 22075, 22077, 22077.3, 22077.5, 22077.7, 22079, 22081; Shakespeare, W. 22273; Sharpe, Leonell 22373; Shaw, Divine 22390; Sibthorp 22523; Sidney, P. 22546a; Simpson 22562; Simson, Archibald 22567*, 22568; Smith, John, Gov. of Virginia 22789; Smith, S., Minister in Essex 22844, 22848.3*; Sorocold 22934; Spain 22992.9; Spanish Fleet 23009; Speed, John 23041.6(?), 23041.8*, 23046.3, 23046.7, 23047; Speed, John, Genealogies 23039.5(?); Speed, R. 23051; Speidell 23063.7; Sprint, J., Vicar 23108.2; Stone 23288; Stradling 23352; Stubbes 23389, 23389.3; Sutton, E. 23495.5; Taylor, A. 23720, 23723; Taylor, John 23778, 23785, 23789, 23789.3, 23789.7, 23812.3*, 23816; Taylor, Thomas 23841; Texeda 23920, 23923; Themylthorp 23934.8, 23934.9*; Tisdale 24091; Traske 24177; Vega Carpio 24630, 24630.5; Venner, T. 24648; Vesey 24694.3; Villegas 24732; Virginia 24830.2; Vives 24846; W., W. 24921; Walker, J. 24962.5; Wall, J. 24990; Warburton 25020; Ward, S., of Ipswich 25030.5, 25048; Wastell 25103; Webbe, G. 25166.5; Webbe, J. 25170(o.s.); Webster, J. 25173, 25176; Weemes 25210, 25210a.5; Wemyss 25243; Whately 25298, 25299*; Whear 25325; Whitbourne 25374, 25375a.8; Willis, J., Stenographer 25744a.8; Wily 25820; Wing 25847; Wise 25867.5; Wither, Poet 25899.5(?), 25908, 25909.5, 25910, 25910.5, 25910.7, 25910a, 25910a.3, 25910a.5, 25910a.7; Wodroephe 25939; Wright, W. 26044, 26048; Xenophon 26064; Yates, John 26086.

1624

A., O. 13; Abbot, G., Abp. 30, 39, 39.3, 39.7, 40; Aberdeen Univ. 71.8; Adams 115*, 129; Aeschines 167; Aesop 188; Ainsworth, H. 222; Alexander, W. 341; Almanacks (Allestree) 407.7; Almanacks (Bellerson) 414; Almanacks (Browne) 421.9; Almanacks (Dade, W.) 435.13; Almanacks (Einer) 438.5; Almanacks (Frende) 445.19; Almanacks (Gilden) 448.9; Almanacks (Hawkins) 456; Almanacks (Johnson, J.) 465.12; Almanacks (Neve, Jeffery) 489.26; Almanacks (Ranger) 503; Almanacks (Rudston, J.) 506.15; Almanacks (Sofford) 515.7; Almanacks (Vaux) 522.4; Almanacks (White) 527.13; Almanacks (Woodhouse, or Wedhouse, or Wydowes, J.) 531.15; Amboyna 547; Andrewes, J. 595.4; Androzzi 632.5; Angelos 637; Ap-Robert 716*; Askew, A. 853.5(?); Aspley 861; Atkins, J. 887; Augustine 934; Aylesbury 997.5, 998; Ayton 1015; B., A., Preacher 1021.5; Bacon, F. 1146; Ball, J. 1314.7; Bankrupts 1365.5(?); Barclay, J. 1396.5*; Bargrave, I. 1413, 1415, 1415.5; Bargrave, J. 1415.7; Barker, P. 1425; Barlement 1431.28A; Barnes, T. 1477, 1477.5, 1478.5; Barrell 1498; Barrough 1514; Bayly, L. 1606; Bedford, T. 1787; Beling 1805; Bellarmino 1837.3; Bernard, R. 1957; Bible, English 2268, 2269, 2270*; Bible, N.T., English 2925.5; Bible, O.T., Prophets 2782; Bible, O.T., Psalms 2414, 2585, 2585.5, 2586, 2587, 2587.3(?), 2587.5, 2588, 2588.5*; Boanerges 3171, 3171.3; Bodnam 3194.5(?); Bolton, E. 3221; Bowne 3442.2, 3442.4; Breda 3597.5(?); Brereley 3606; Brerewood 3620; Breton 3662; Brewer 3718; Briggs 3739; Brinsley, J., the Elder 3788; Broughton, Richard 3895; Browne, W., Gent. 3913; Buchler 3992.5; Bullinger 4073; Burton, H. 4139; Burton, R. 4160; Byfield, N. 4220a, 4236.2; C., L. W. 4289; Calderwood 4356, 4357, 4358; Camden 4502; Caninius 4567; Cantrell 4588; Card 4606.5(?); Carleton, G. 4630, 4640; Casaubon, I. 4747; Casaubon, M. 4750, 4751, 4752; Cato 4862; Cawdrey, D. 4881; Chambers, J. 4952.5; Charles I, King 5022.5; Chevalier 5129; Chibald 5130; Clay 5374; Cleaver 5389; Cleland 5396; Close 5433.5; Closet 5436.5; Coke, E. 5508; Cole, N. 5534; Constable, H. 5636.8; Cooper, T., Preacher 5692.3, 5692.5; Coote 5712a; Cordier 5759.7; Cornwall 5772.5(c.); Cotta 5836.5, 5837; Craig, G. 5961; Crashaw, W. 6010; Crompton, W. 6059; Culpeper 6108.5; Culverwell 6115.5, 6118.5; D., A. 6161; Dale 6191.5; Dalechamp 6193, 6196; Dalton, E. 6204, 6204a.5; Darbishire 6268.5; Darcie, A. 6269, 6272; Darcie, G. 6273.7; Davies, J., of Hereford 6339.5, 6340*; Day 6398; Dekker 6526; Denison, J. 6590.5, 6594, 6594.5; Dent, A. 6618.5, 6621; Derby 6674.5; Dering 6690; Despautere 6781.7; Dod 6935.7; Dominis 7006, 7006.5, 7007; Donne, J. 7033, 7033a, 7034, 7052, 7057.5; Downame, J. 7138.7(A/C); Du Mats de Montmartin 7305; Du Moulin, P., the Elder 7320, 7323, 7326, 7326.5, 7328; Dyer, E. 7384.5(?); Dyke, D. 7402.7(?); Dyke, J. 7415; East India Company 7451, 7452, 7453*, 7454, 7455; East, M. 7466; Eburne 7471; Edinburgh University 7487.21; Elton 7616, 7619*; England, Appendix 10011.6; England, C. of, Appendix 10404(?), 10404.5; England, C. of, Articles 10050, 10050.3; England, C. of, Visit. Articles 10147.9(?), 10192.4, 10192.7, 10213.7, 10220, 10261.5, 10278(?), 10337(?), 10372.5; England, Parliament 7742, 7743; England, Proclamations, Chron. Ser. 8458.5(c.?), 8459(c.?), 8720, 8721, 8722, 8723, 8724, 8725, 8726, 8227, 8728, 8729, 8730, 8731, 8732, 8733, 8734, 8736, 8738, 8739, 8740, 8741, 8742, 8743, 8744, 8746 (o.s.), 8747(o.s.), 8748(o.s.), 8749(o.s.), 8750(o.s.), 8751(o.s.), 8752(o.s.), 8753(o.s.), 8754(o.s.); England, Public Documents, Misc. 9243.5; England, Statutes, Chron. Ser. 9507, 9507.3, 9507.5; Erasmus, D. 10458a; Featley, D. 10738, 10738.3; Field, T. 10861, 10861.5; Fist 10921; Flamel 11027; Flavel 11031.5; Fleming, A. 11037.5; Floyd, J. 11113; Forset 11189; France 11274; France—Reformed Churches 11296, 11297; Francis, of Assisi 11314.6; Frankfurt Fair 11330.2, 11330.3; G., W. 11511.3(c.); Gardiner, E. 11564.7; Garnet 11617.6; Garrard, E. 11624; Gataker 11653, 11654, 11657, 11660, 11662, 11669; Gee, J. 11701, 11702, 11702.3, 11703, 11704, 11705, 11706; Gokin 11983; Goodman, G. 12022; Goodwin, G. 12030; Greenwood, H. 12330; Grounds 12402a.4(?); Guild 12492; Gunter, E. 12522, 12522.5*, 12524; Gurnay 12530; H., R. 12573.3, 12573.5(?); Hall, Joseph 12635*, 12648c, 12714, 12715; Hall, W. 12720; Harris, Robert 12832, 12839.5, 12839.7, 12840; Hayes 12973; Hayward, Sir J. 12990, 13003; Heigham 13033.6; Hering 13203.5; Hewes 13260; Heywood, T. 13326; Hieron 13381*; Higgons 13455; Hitching 13531.5; Holland 13574; Homer 13628(?); Humphreys 13968; Huntar 13993; Ingpen 14089; Ireland,

1624 — *cont.*

Customs 14128.5; Ireland, Proc. 14184, 14185, 14186, 14187, 14188, 14189, 14190, 14191; Isocrates 14280; Jackson, Thomas, of Canterbury 14300; James I 14359; James, T., D. D. 14458; Japan 14475; Jeffreys 14483.5; Jemmatt 14485; Jenison 14490; Jerome, S. 14511; Jesus Christ 14570, 14570.3; Jewel 14578; Joceline 14624, 14624.5; Johnson, Robert, B. D. 14693; Jonson 14779; King's Bench 14961.7; Lambard 15161; Langhorne 15198(?), 15198.5; Lawrence, J. 15325; Lazarillo 15338; Leighton, A. 15431, 15432; Leman 15453.3; Levett, C. 15553.5; Lewis, John 15559, 15560; Liturgies, C. of Eng., BCP 16363, 16363.5; Logie 16694; London, Barber Surgeons 16768.4(?); London, Bookbinders 16768.10; London, Butchers 16768.18; London, Cloth-workers 16768.28(?); London, Merchants of the Staple 16779.4(?); Lougher 16828.5; Love 16856; Loyola 16878; Luis 16922a.9(A/C); Macguire 17175.3; Magini 17183; Mansfeld 17260; Marcelline 17308.5; Markham, G. 17361; Marlowe 17435; Mary, the Blessed Virgin 17542.7; Mason, H. 17610; Massinger 17632; Mayo 17754; Medicine 17770.3; Meredeth, J. 17830; Mico 17859, 17860; Mohammed, the prophet 17995.5; Montagu, R. 18038, 18039; More, T. 18097; Morgan, G. 18102a.5(?); Muschet, Priest 18306; Neile 18421; Nero 18430; Newsbooks, Num. 18507.138, 18507.139, 18507.140, 18507.141, 18507.142, 18507.143, 18507.144, 18507.145, 18507.146, 18507.147, 18507.147A, 18507.148, 18507.149, 18507.150, 18507.151, 18507.152, 18507.153, 18507.154, 18507.155, 18507.156, 18507.157, 18507.158; Newsbooks, T. Archer 18507.346, 18507.347, 18507.348, 18507.349, 18507.350, 18507.351*, 18507.352; Norden 18608, 18610, 18624.5, 18630, 18643.5; Norris, S. 18661; Norton, R. 18676; O., S. 18756; Openshaw 18826a.2(A/C); Oration 18837; Outlawry 18901a.5; Oxford Univ., Quaestiones 19016.8; Oxford Univ., Verses, etc. 19028, 19029; P., T. 19079; Palatinate 19126; Parker, Martin 19224.7, 19268; Peacham, H., the Younger 19499; Penkethman 19600.2; Perrin 19768.5, 19769, 19769.3; Perrott, J. 19774; Philos 19886; Phrases 19893a.3; Pilkington, F. 19924; Pilovius 19934; Platt 19983.5; Pope 20111, 20113.5(?); Price, S. 20334; Prideaux 20343.7, 20358.5; Primrose, G. 20390.5; Puente 20487; Purchas, W. 20509.7 (?); Quarles 20550; Randall 20672; Randol 20685; Rastell, J., Printer 20716; Reading 20790; Record, E. and Vaughan 20795.5; Record, E. 20795.3; Reeve, T. 20832a; Reynolds, J., Merchant 20943.7, 20946.1, 20946.2, 20946.3, 20946.4, 20946.5, 20946.6, 20946.7, 20946.8; Rich, B. 20993; Robinson, J., Pastor of Leyden 21107a; Rochfort 21138; Rogers, G. 21176.5; Rogers, Timothy 21245; Rome, Church of 21302a; Rous, the Elder 21345; Ryves 21479; Salerno 21609; Sanders 21693, 21697; Schoolhouse 21826, 21826.2; Scott, T., B. D. 22064, 22065, 22066, 22067, 22068, 22071, 22072, 22073, 22073.2, 22073.4, 22073.6, 22073.8, 22076, 22078, 22078.5, 22084*, 22084a, 22086, 22088, 22089, 22097a(?)(A/C), 22101*, 22102, 22103, 22103.3, 22103.7, 22104, 22105, 22105.5; Scull 22123; Sedgwick, J. 22150; Sedgwick, R. 22152.5; Sempill, J. 22185.5; Seneca 22219; Serres, J. 22246, 22246.5; Shakespeare, W. 22351; Sharpeigh and Haitley 22379.5; Simson, Archibald 22567*; Skelton 22614; Smith, H., Minister, Collections 22744, 22760; Smith, John, Gov. of Virginia 22790; Smith, S., Minister in Essex 22848.7, 22853; Smyth, J. 22877.2; Soto, A. de 22936.5(A/C); Speed, John, Genealogies 23039d.9(+), 23039e.4; Speidell 23063.3*, 23064; Squire, J., Minister 23115; Stanbridge, Vocabula 23191; Stanhope, J. 23225; Statute 23239; Stepney 23254.5; Stubbes 23389.7; Sutton, E. 23496; Sutton, T. 23499, 23504; Sweet 23528; Symson, P. 23598; Tailboys 23657; Tasso, T. 23699; Taylor, John 23768, 23787, 23787.5, 23801, 23808.5; Taylor, Thomas 23853, 23854*, 23855*; Terentius 23889.2; Texeda 23922; Themylthorp 23934.9*; Thomas, a Kempis 23989.5, 23990; Thomas, J. 24000.7; Throgmorton, G. 24052; Travels 24179; Turner, Richard 24347; Tyndale, N. 24435.5; Udall, W. 24508.7, 24508.9(A/C), 24509, 24509a; Ussher, J. 24542, 24545, 24554; Vicars, T. 24702.5; Villegas 24738; Virgilius Maro 24825; Virginia Company 24844.3; Vives 24853.3; W., C. 24900; W., R. 24912.5; Wadsworth, J., the Elder 24925, 24925a; Waggoners 24935b.5; Waker 24953.3; Walker, George 24959, 24960, 24960.5; Ward, S., of Ipswich 25054, 25056; Warford 25070.5; Warre 25090a, 25090a.3(A/C); Webbe, G. 25160.7, 25161, 25161.5; Webbe, J. 25170; Webster, J. 25175; Westerne 25284; Weston, E. 25289; Whately 25299*; White, F., Bp. 25382; White, John, D. D. 25389, 25389.5, 25389a; Wilcox 25620; Wilkinson, H. 25644; Williams, G. 25719; Williamson, R. 25736.3; Wing 25848; Winslow 25855, 25856; Wither, Poet 25919; Wotton, A. 26005; Wotton, H. 26011; Wray 26013.5; Wye, River 26057.5; Wynne 26061; Yarmouth 26076.5(?).

1625

A., R. 15.3(c.); A.B.C. 21.6(c.), 22; Abbot, R., Minister 57; Abenezrah 62(c.); Aberdeen Univ. 71.9, 71.34; Adams 115*, 130; Addison 150; Aesop 172.7; Age 196.5(c.); Alexander, W. 341a; Almanacks (Allestree) 407.8; Almanacks (Browne) 421.10; Almanacks (Dade, W.) 435.14; Almanacks (Einer) 438.6; Almanacks (Erra Pater) 439.25(?); Almanacks (Evans, J., Philomath) 441; Almanacks (Gilden) 448.10; Almanacks (Hawkins) 456.3; Almanacks (Hewlett) 457; Almanacks (Kinde) 469.9; Almanacks (Love) 480.7; Almanacks (Neve, Jeffery) 489.27; Almanacks (Osborne) 494.3; Almanacks (Perkins) 495; Almanacks (Pond) 501.15; Almanacks (Ranger) 503.2; Almanacks (Rivers, P.) 505; Almanacks (Rudston, J.) 506.16; Almanacks (Smith, R.) 514.7; Almanacks (Sofford) 515.8; Almanacks (Vaux) 522.5; Almanacks (White) 527.14; Almanacks (Wilson) 529; Almanacks (Woodhouse, or Wedhouse, or Wydowes, J.) 531.16; Almanacks 405, 405.3; Alonso 535.7; Amantes 546.5(c.); Anderton 578; Andrewe, G. 583; Anglerius 651(?); Animalia 653(c.); Antidotes 680; Audeley 904; Aylett 1000.5; B., Ed. 1025.7; B., I. or J. 1045, 1045.5; Bachiler 1106; Bacon, F. 1115, 1147, 1148, 1174, 1174.5; Bacon, R. 1182.7(c.) (A/C); Ballad 1328(?); Balmford 1338.5; Barclay, J. 1392; Barley-Corn, J. 1433.5(c.); Barlow, J. 1434; Barlow, W., Bp. of Rochester/Lincoln 1458; Barnfield 1487.5(c.); Bate, R. 1580(c.); Beard, T. 1657; Beaumont, F., and Fletcher 1671, 1687; Bedingfield 1792; Bible, Appendix 3030.5; Bible, English 2270*, 2271, 2272, 2273, 2273.5, 2274*; Bible, N.T., English 2926, 2926.5; Bible, O.T., 'Books of Solomon' 2776; Bible, O.T., Prophets 2783; Bible, O.T., Psalms 2589, 2590, 2590.5, 2591, 2592, 2592.5, 2593, 2593.5, 2710; Biblion 3047.5; Billingsley 3062.7(+?); Bishop, W. 3095; Blaeu 3112.5, 3113; Boccaccio 3173; Bogerman 3204.5; Bolton, Robert 3231, 3250; Bradwell 3537; Brathwait 3566.5*, 3581.4(?); Breda 3595; Breton 3698.3(?), 3710.5; Brewer 3722; Brinsley, J., the Elder 3771.5(?); Brook 3826; Broughton, Richard 3895.3, 3895.7; Browne, W., Poet 3916; Burges, C. 4111, 4112; Butler, C. 4201; Byfield, N. 4220a.5, 4232; C., W. 4318; Cabasilas 4325.5(c.); Caldwell, James 4366; Cambridge University 4476, 4477, 4478, 4484, 4491.7; Cambridge University, Act Verses 4474.66(?); Camden 4497; Camerarius 4529.5, 4530; Campion 4541.5(c.?); Cannon 4575.7; Capillia 4603; Cardinals 4609; Carleton, G. 4641, 4643.5; Carpenter, N. 4676; Cart 4687(c.); Cato 4849.3; Chaloner, E. 4934, 4934.3; Chapman, G. 4969; Charles I, King 5029, 5030; Chevy Chase 5129.5(c.); Chibald 5131; Cicero 5301.8; Cleaver 5379; Cole, N. 5535; Collins 5559(c.); Complaint 5611.7(c.); Controversia 5646; Cooke, A. 5658, 5660, 5661; Cooke, W. 5677(c.); Cordier 5763; Cotta 5838; Cotton, C. 5849.5, 5851.5(c.); Crakanthorp 5975; Crane 5987(?); Crashaw, W. 6017.5, 6023; Crew 6038.5(?); Crokey 6045; Crompton, W. 6060; Crooke, S. 6063.8, 6067.5; Crosse, W. 6072; Cuckoo 6102.5(c.); Culverwell 6116, 6118.6; Cupper 6125.6; D., T. 6181.3; Daca 6185; Darcie, A. 6270, 6271.5, 6273.2(c.); Davies, J., of Hereford 6340*; Day, A. 6407; Death 6444(c.); Dekker 6520, 6520.4; Delamothe 6548.4; Dent, A. 6632.5; Dering 6722; Desainliens or Sainliens 6746; Description 6770; Desiderius 6777.7; Devereux 6791.7(c.?), 6792.7(c.?); Dictionary 6832.60; Digges, L. 6854; Direction 6901.5(?); Ditchfield 6918; Ditty 6922.7(c.), 6923(c.), 6927.5(c.); Dod and Cleaver 6976; Donne, G. 7021.3; Donne, J. 7025, 7040, 7042; Downame, G. 7105; Downame, J. 7148.3(c.?); Draxe 7180; Du Moulin, P., the Younger 7245.5; Edinburgh University 7487.22; Egerton, S. 7533.5; Elton 7619*; England, C. of, Visit. Articles 10202, 10205, 10241, 10269, 10341, 10349, 10360, 10372.6; England, Customs 7694.3(?); England,

1625 — *cont.*
Local Courts 7724; England, Parliament 7743.5, 7751.6; England, Proclamations, Chron. Ser. 8737, 8746, 8747, 8748, 8749, 8750, 8751, 8752, 8753, 8754, 8754.5, 8755, 8756, 8757, 8758, 8759, 8760, 8761, 8762, 8762.5, 8763, 8764, 8765, 8766, 8767, 8768, 8769, 8770, 8770.5, 8771, 8772, 8773, 8774, 8775, 8776, 8777, 8778, 8779, 8780, 8781, 8782, 8783, 8785, 8785.7, 8786, 8787, 8788, 8789, 8790, 8792, 8793, 8794, 8796, 8796.3, 8798, 8798.3, 8800, 8800.3, 8800.7, 8801, 8801.7, 8802, 8804, 8804.3, 8804.7, 8805, 8806, 8807, 8808, 8809, 8810, 8811, 8812, 8813, 8814, 8815, 8816(o.s.), 8817(o.s.), 8818 (o.s.), 8820(o.s.), 8821(o.s.); England, Public Documents, Misc. 9175j.1, 9244, 9244.3, 9245, 9245.2, 9245.4; England, Statutes, Chron. Ser. 9508; England, Statutes, Gen. Colls. 9300; English Gipsy 10412(c.); Europe 10570; Everinden 10601.9; Example 10610.3(c.), 10611.7(c.?); Farnaby, T. 10703, 10706.4(?); Featley, D. 10725*; Field, T. 10862; Fisher, John, S.J. 10910.7, 10911*, 10916.5*; Foxe 11227.5(c.?); Frankfurt Fair 11330.4; Fuller, W. 11469; G., T. 11509; Gabriel 11511.7(c.); Galliardi or Gagliardi 11539; Gardyne 11595; Gee, J. 11706.4; Gennadios II 11728.4(+); George, St. 11745.3(c.); Gerhard 11780; Godwin, F. 11939(?); Godwin, T. 11951, 11960; Goldwell, C. 11989; Gonsalvius Montanus 11998, 11999; Goodfellow, R. 12018(c.?), 12018.3(c.?); Gordon, R. 12069; Gordon, W. 12070; Grammar 12173.3; Gregory [Palamas] 12343.5(+); Grent, W. 12360.7(?); Griselda 12384.5(c.?); Guild 12481; H., A. 12561.2; Habermann 12582.19; Hagthorpe 12603; Hall, Joseph 12635*, 12635.5, 12635a, 12635b; Harington 12777; Harmar 12792.5; Harris, Robert 12840a; Harrison, W., King's Preacher 12870.5; Hart, James 12887a; Hastler 12930; Hering 13204; Herring, F. 13240; Heylyn 13277; Heywood, T. 13318, 13324; Hieron 13381*, 13413a.3, 13413a.5; Hodson or Hodgson, W. 13555.3; Hodson, P. 13552; Holland, Hugh 13591; Hood, R. 13686.5(c.); Horatius Flaccus 13800; Hord 13806; Horne, R., of Ludlow 13825; Hughes, L. 13918.5(c.?), 13920.5(?); Hyatt 14038; I., H. 14050a(c.); Indulgences, Eng. 14077c.23C(?); Ireland, Laws 14131.5; Ireland, Proc. 14190.5, 14191a, 14192, 14193, 14196, 14197, 14198, 14199, 14200, 14201, 14202, 14203, 14204(o.s.); Jackson, Thomas, of Peterborough 14306, 14316; James I 14413.5; James I, appendix 14423.3, 14423.7, 14425, 14426.3; James, R. 14437, 14440; James, T., D. D. 14454, 14455(?), 14460; Jenison 14488; Jerome, S. 14511.5; Jesus Christ 14549(c.); Joceline 14625; Jocelinus 14626; Johnston, A. 14711; Jones, W., of Wight 14747; Jonson 14772; Keckermann 14897*; Kellicke 14905.5(c.); Kendrick 14928, 14928.5; Ker 14940(c.); King, Henry 14972; King, J., Pub. Orator of Oxford 14992; Koresios 15082.5(c.); Korydaleus 15083; L., A. 15103; L., I., Pastor 15107.3; L'Hermite 15571; Laud 15302, 15304; League 15341; Lee, R. 15354; Leighton, A. 15431.5; Lentulus 15470a.5(c.); Lescarbot 15492(aft.); Leslie, H. 15494, 15502; Linaker 15642; Lindsay, D., Bp. 15657.5; Lindsay, D., Minister 15684; Liturgies, C. of Eng., BCP 16364, 16365; Liturgies, C. of Eng., Spec. Prayers 16540, 16541, 16542; Liturgies, C. of Eng., St. Services 16497; Liturgies, Other Protest. C. 16594.5; London, Bills of Mort. 16740, 16740.5, 16741, 16741.3, 16741.7, 16743.8, 16744; London, Ords. and Regs. 16729.1, 16729.2, 16729.3, 16729.4(c.); Lovell, R. 16858; Lover 16864a.7(c.); Luis 16906; M., M. 17144; Maid 17186.5(c.?); Maiden 17191(?); Maierus 17196.7; Man 17229.5(?), 17235(?); Mandeville 17253; Manual 17276.4, 17276.6, 17276.8; Manuzio, A. 17283; Marcelline 17308; Markham, F. 17331; Markham, G. 17363, 17373, 17388, 17395.5, 17395.7; Mars 17467(?); Marshe 17470; Mason, F. 17598; Mason, H. 17602; Maximos 17697.3(+); Mayer 17729; Mericke 17836.7; Middleton, T. 17882, 17883(?), 17884(?), 17885; Milton, R. 17939; Minsheu 17945, 17945.5; Montagu, R. 18030, 18030.5, 18031, 18032(?); Morrell 18169; Murray, D. 18294.5(c.); Narne 18359, 18359.5; Neade 18416; Nettles 18474; Newsbooks, Num. 18507.159, 18507.160, 18507.161, 18507.162, 18507.162A, 18507.163, 18507.164, 18507.165, 18507.166, 18507.167, 18507.168, 18507.169, 18507.170, 18507.171, 18507.172, 18507.173, 18507.174, 18507.175, 18507.176; Newsbooks, T. Archer 18507.351*, 18507.353, 18507.354; Norden 18605, 18607, 18641.4(?); Norris, J. 18654.7; Northamptonshire 18662.5(c.); Nowell, Middle Catechism 18721, 18736; Observations 18760; Oldmayne 18806*; Ovidius Naso 18935(c.), 18935.3(c.), 18935.5(c.), 18935.7(c.), 18935a(c.), 18936(c.); Oxford Univ., Verses, etc. 19030, 19031, 19049; Parker, Martin 19231(c.), 19252.5(c.), 19254.5(c.), 19264(c.), 19278(c.); Parr, E. 19316.3(c.); Passing Bell 19460(?); Pegas 19553.5(c.); Pellham, W. 19566.5; Pemble 19589; Penkethman 19598.2(?), 19600.4, 19600.6(?); Perkins, W. 19687.7, 19693.5, 19726.7, 19730.5, 19746.7, 19762.5; Petowe 19803*; Philadelphos 19829 [not STC]; Philip II 19838.5; Phillips, John, Minister of Feversham 19878; Pity 19969.6(c.); Pope 20112(c.); Preservative 20205.5; Price, D. 20293; Prideaux 20356, 20359, 20361; Primrose, David, Advocate 20386; Primrose, G. 20389, 20391; Procter, W. 20405; Purchas, S. 20509; Quin 20565; Rawlinson 20774; Red Cross 20823; Reginald, H. 20835.5; Rich, B. 20980, 20980.5; Richardson, J. 21020.5; Robinson, J., Pastor of Leyden 21108, 21112; Rodoginus 21141; Rogers, Richard 21210, 21213.8; Rogers, Thomas, M. A. 21230, 21230a; Rowlands, S. 21378.7(c.); S., G. 21492; S., T. 21522; Saltern, T. 21636; Saluste du Bartas 21663; Samson 21688.5(c.); Sanders 21697.5; Sands, P. 21712.5; Sarpi 21758; Schonaeus 21822.5; Scot, P. 21863; Scot, T., Gent. 21872; Scotland, proclamations 21969; Scotland, statutes, etc. 21901.2, 21901.4; Sedgwick, J. 22150a; Shakespeare, W. 22278(c.); Sheldon 22398; Sherwood, R. 22429.5; Sibthorp 22524; Sibyllarum Icones 22527a.5(c.); Simon 22556(c.); Smith, E. 22654.5(c.); Smith, H., Minister, Collections 22775; Smith, John, Gov. of Virginia 22790a; Smith, S., Minister in Essex 22835, 22845; Smith, William, Priest 22872.5; Song 22918.5(c.), 22919.1(c.), 22919.2(c.), 22919.7 (c.), 22919.9(c.); Speed, John, Genealogies 23039e.5; Speidell 23062.5(c.), 23064.3; Spenser, B. 23074; Spicer, A. 23100; Sprint, J., Vicar 23108.3; Stapleton, Thomas 23233; Stradling 23353; Suffolk, County of 23424.3(c.); Susanna 23435a.5(c.); Sutcliffe, M. 23466(?); Symson, P. 23599; Table 23635(?), 23636.5; Taffin 23656.5; Tapp 23681; Taylor, John 23729, 23743, 23754, 23755, 23758, 23772, 23772a; Taylor, Thomas 23829, 23854*, 23855; Terry 23914; Texeda 23921; Thayre 23930; Titus Andronicus 24092.3(c.); Tuke 24305; Tymme 24429.5; Udny 24512; Urfe 24525.3(?)(A/C); Ussher, J. 24543, 24546; Usury 24558; V., B. 24562; Vase 24594; Vaughan, W. 24604; W., I., Gent. 24909; Waker 24953.5; Wall, J. 24991; Ward, S., of Ipswich 25051; Watling Street 25108(?); Webster, W., of the Salters' Company 25182.5; Wedderburn 25187; Whear 25326; Whipping 25353(c.); Wilkinson, H. 25646; Wilkinson, R. 25654.5(c.), 25655, 25663; Williams, J., Abp. 25723, 25723a; Williamson, R. 25736.5; Wilson, C., Preacher 25767; Wilson, J., Preacher 25769; Wise 25867; Witzell 25935; Wodroephe 25940; Worship 25996; Wright, R. 26037; Writing Tables 26050.16(aft.).

1626

Abbot, R., Minister 56; Aberdeen Univ. 71.10, 71.35; Adams 115*; Ainsworth, H. 219*; Albertus Magnus 266; Almanacks (Allestree) 407.9; Almanacks (Browne) 421.11; Almanacks (Dade, W.) 435.15; Almanacks (Digges) 435.63; Almanacks (Einer) 438.7; Almanacks (Gilden) 448.11; Almanacks (Joanes) 464.9; Almanacks (Neve, John) 490; Almanacks (Osborne) 494.4; Almanacks (Perkins) 495.1; Almanacks (Pond) 501.16; Almanacks (Ranger) 503.3; Almanacks (Rudston, J.) 506.17; Almanacks (Sofford) 515.9; Almanacks (Strof) 516; Almanacks (Vaux) 522.6; Almanacks (White) 527.15; Almanacks (Wilson) 529.3; Almanacks (Woodhouse, or Wedhouse, or Wydowes, J.) 531.17; Almanacks 405.5; Arcandam 727; Assize of Bread 880; Attonitus 902(?); Aylesbury 999; Ayton 1016; B., I. or J. 1042, 1043; B., S. 1066, 1067; Bacon, F. 1116, 1168, 1177; Balcanquhall 1239; Barnes, R., of Rotherfield Greys 1474; Barnes, T. 1478; Bayley 1600; Bayly, L. 1606.5, 1607; Beda 1780; Bernard, R. 1946, 1960, 1961; Bevis 1993(?); Bible, English 2275, 2276, 2277, 2278, 2280.5*; Bible, N.T., English 2927; Bible, O.T., Psalms 2594, 2595, 2596, 2597, 2597.2*, 2598, 2711, 2712, 2713, 2713.5; Binet 3073.5; Boccalini 3185; Bolton, Robert 3251; Brathwait 3559 [not STC], 3573; Breton 3650, 3652, 3676, 3698.5; Brinsley, J., the Elder 3783; Brookes 3837; Bueil 4016.5; Burton, H. 4153, 4153.3;

1626 — *cont.*
Byfield, N. 4215, 4233, 4233.3, 4235; C., E. 4264.5; Cambi 4469; Camden 4514.3, 4527; Cameron 4531, 4531.5; Carleton, G. 4633, 4633.5, 4634, 4635; Cartigny 4703(?); Cary, W. 4734; Caussin 4872; Cecil, E. 4892, 4892.5; Cicero 5268.7; Cleland 5395; Cockeram 5462; Coke, E. 5514; Cooke, E. 5668; Copies 5724.5; Court 5876.5; Cowper 5910; Culverwell 6110; Dalton, M. 6208; Daniel, S. 6251; Darcie, A. 6272.5; Davis or Davys, J. 6370; Deane 6441; Deloney 6560; Denison, S. 6598; Dent, A. 6665; Desainliens or Sainliens 6746.5; Deye 6798.6; Digges, L. 6854.2; Diguieres 6877.5; Donne, G. 7021.7; Donne, J. 7028, 7035*, 7041, 7050; Dort, Synod of 7067; Downame, G. 7106; Du Moulin, P., the Elder 7309, 7309a; Dyke, J. 7415.5; E., I. or J. 7434.4; Echlin, D. 7479; Edinburgh University 7487.23; Edmonton 7496; Eglisham 7548; England, Army 7683.5; England, C. of, Visit. Articles 10137.4, 10140.5, 10145.7, 10270, 10315.5, 10349.5, 10368; England, Commissions 7686; England, Parliament 7744; England, Proclamations, Chron. Ser. 8816, 8817, 8818, 8819, 8820, 8821, 8822, 8823, 8824, 8825, 8825.3, 8826, 8827, 8828, 8829, 8830, 8831, 8832, 8833, 8834, 8835, 8836, 8837, 8837.5, 8838, 8839, 8840, 8841, 8842, 8843, 8844, 8845, 8846, 8847, 8847.3, 8847.5, 8848(o.s.), 8849(o.s.), 8850(o.s.), 8851(o.s.), 8852(o.s.), 8853(o.s.), 8854(o.s.), 8856(o.s.); England, Public Documents, Misc. 9246, 9247; English Stratagem 10419; Everinden 10601.3, 10602; Fale 10679, 10679.3; Farley, R. 10692; Fawkner 10718; Featley, D. 10725*, 10726, 10734, 10735, 10736, 10737, 10739; Fenton, E. 10788; Ferdinand II 10817; Fioravanti 10882; Fisher, John, S.J. 10911*, 10916.5*; Flecknoe 11033; Forbes, J., Minister 11130; Frankfurt Fair 11330.7; Frith, J. 11395*; Fuller, T., M. A. 11467; Gale, D. 11528; Galliardi or Gagliardi 11540*; Gataker 11648; Godwin, T. 11952; Gouge 12109*, 12111, 12112, 12117; Greene, R. 12222, 12244; Guiana Company 12456.3, 12456.7; Guild 12487, 12489; Gumbleden 12515*; Guy, N. 12543; Hakewill 12615; Hall, Joseph 12659, 12713; Hamilton, F. 12726; Harcourt 12755; Harris, John, Accountant 12805.5; Harris, Robert 12821, 12829, 12833, 12836, 12837, 12841, 12850; Haughton 12932; Heidelberg Catechism 13031.7; Heywood, T. 13346; Hieron 13403; Hill, T. 13499.5; Hinde, W. 13515.5; Holland, A. 13579, 13579.3, 13579.5; Holland, Henry, Bookseller 13585.5; Holyday 13615, 13616, 13619; Hope 13766; Horne, R., of Ludlow 13820; Huish 13927; Huit 13928; Ireland, C. of 14265.5; Ireland, Proc. 14204, 14205, 14206, 14207; James, T., D. D. 14461; Janua 14469; Jay 14479; Jenner 14494; Jenney 14497; Jest 14524.3; Jesuits 14526; Jewel, J. 14587; Johnson, Richard 14682; Jones, Richard 14730.5 (?); Keckermann 14897*; Kennedy, J. 14929; King, Henry 14968; La Croix 15117.3; La Ramee 15248; Lambard 15161.5; Laud 15303; Lawson 15331; Leech, John, Poet 15370.5; Leo 15481.5(c.); Ling 15689(?); Liturgies, C. of Eng., BCP 16365.5, 16366, 16367, 16369.3*; Liturgies, C. of Eng., Spec. Prayers 16543, 16544; Liturgies, C. of Eng., St. Services 16485; Liturgies, Latin Rite, Missals 16227; London, Appendix 16753; Looking-glass 16802.3; Louis XIII 16845, 16845.5; Loukaris 16854.3(?); Lucanus 16886; Markham, G. 17391, 17391.5; Mason, H. 17608, 17613; Matthiae 17658.5; Middleton, T. 17898; Minsheu 17946; Mornay 18156; Morton, T., Bp. 18186(?); Mount Taragh 18228.3; Mucedorus 18238; Newsbooks, Num. 18507.177, 18507.178, 18507.179, 18507.180, 18507.181, 18507.182, 18507.183, 18507.184; Nichols, P. 18544; Norden 18615; Nowell, Middle Catechism 18722; Overbury 18903; Overbury 18914; Ovidius Naso 18964, 18969; Owen, L. 18996; Parrot 19328; Peeke 19529, 19529.5; Penkethman 19599; Perkins, W. 19652*; Perrot, G. 19769.9(A/C); Petowe 19803; Philips, T. 19855.5; Phillips, John 19874; Pont 20102; Price, S. 20332; Prideaux 20347, 20357, 20358; Primrose, G. 20392; Prynne 20471; Purchas, S. 20508, 20508.5; Pyne 20521.2, 20521.4, 20521.6; Quarles 20545; R., P. 20585.5; Randall 20679; Ravisius 20764; Reading 20791; Reuter 20911; Rider, J. 21035, 21035.3, 21035.5, 21035.7; Roberts, J. 21091; Robrough 21129.5; Roesslin 21163; Roper 21316; Rosa 21317.5; Ross 21324; Rous, the Elder 21347, 21347.3; Rush 21452; Russell, T. 21460.7; Ryves 21477; S., E. C. 21490; Sainct Sernin 21551.7; Salter, R. 21630; Sands, G. 21712; Sarpi 21766, 21767; Scoggin 21850.7; Scotland, proclamations 21970; Scott, T., B. D. 22085; Seager 22138(?); Shute, N. 22466; Sictor 22532.5; Smith, H., Minister, Single Works 22711; Smith, John, Gov. of Virginia 22784, 22790b; Society of Twelve 22889; Song 22918.3(?), 22922; Speed, John, Genealogies 23039d.10 (+?), 23039e.6(+?), 23039f.4(?); Speed, R. 23051.5(?); Speidell 23064.5; Spelman 23065, 23065.5, 23069.5(?); Stubbes 23390; Sutcliffe, M. 23473; Sutton, C. 23488, 23493.7; Sutton, E. 23497; Sydenham 23559, 23563*, 23567, 23568, 23569; Taylor, John 23812.7, 23813.5; Terry 23915; Thorius 24033; Treasurer 24209.5; Trussell, T. 24299; Vaughan, W. 24609, 24617; Vesey 24694.5; Vicary 24711; Virel 24772; Wall, J. 24988; Ward, S., of Cambridge 25026; Ware, J. 25064; Webbe, J. 25171; Weldon, A. 25228.5; Wigand 25614; Williams, J., Abp., pseud. 25730 [not STC]; Wingate 25850.5; Wither, Poet 25911a; Wotton, A. 26003; Yates, John 26083.

1627

A.B.C. 20.9(c.); Aberdeen Univ. 71.11, 71.12, 71.13, 71.14, 71.15, 71.36; Adamson, J. 138; Ainsworth, H. 219*; Ali Abencufian 354; Almanacks (Allestree) 407.10; Almanacks (Browne) 421.12; Almanacks (Chamberlaine) 429; Almanacks (Dade, W.) 435.16; Almanacks (Dove) 436; Almanacks (Frost) 446; Almanacks (Grammar) 450; Almanacks (Hawkins) 456.7; Almanacks (Hewlett) 457.3; Almanacks (Joanes) 464.10; Almanacks (Lakes) 478; Almanacks (Neve, John) 490.3; Almanacks (Perkins) 495.2; Almanacks (Pond) 501.17; Almanacks (Ranger) 503.4; Almanacks (Rivers, P.) 505.2; Almanacks (Rudston, J.) 506.18; Almanacks (Sofford) 515.10; Almanacks (Strof) 516.5; Almanacks (Vaux) 522.7; Almanacks (Waters) 524; Almanacks (White) 527.16; Almanacks (Woodhouse, or Wedhouse, or Wydowes, J.) 531.18; Andrewes, J. 595.3; Andrewes, L. 630; Audiguier 906; B., I. D. 1052; Bacon, F. 1169; Bacon, R. 1183; Baillie, J. 1203; Bargrave, I. 1414; Barlement 1431.29; Barlow, J. 1439.5; Basse 1550; Bastwick 1571; Bayly, L. 1607.5, 1608; Bernard, R. 1943, 1946.3, 1946.7, 1947; Bible, English 2279, 2280, 2280.5*; Bible, N.T., English 2928, 2929; Bible, O.T., Psalms 2597.2*, 2599, 2599.5, 2600, 2600.5, 2601, 2601.5, 2602, 2603, 2603.5, 2604*; Bolton, E. 3222; Boyd, R. 3444; Bradshaw, W. 3513; Brathwait 3560 [not STC]; Brinsley, J., the Elder 3769, 3770, 3770a, 3770b, 3770b.2; Bristow, J. 3798; Broad 3808 [not STC]; Brookes 3836; Bruch 3926; Burton, H. 4137, 4137.3; Butler, C. 4199.7; Byfield, N. 4218, 4228, 4228.5; Byfield, R. 4237.5; Camden 4496.5, 4514.5; Carleton, G. 4642; Carpenter, N. 4668.5; Carter, J., Rector of Belstead 4695; Carter, T. 4698; Cary, W. 4735; Cats 4863.7; Cecil, E. 4893; Cepari 4912; Christian 5151; Cicero 5306.5, 5318; Clarke, J., B.D. 5362; Closet 5436.7; Cockburn, W. 5460; Coke, E. 5517; Coote 5713; Cosin, J. 5815.5, 5816, 5816.2, 5816.4; Cotta 5835.5; Cotton, C. 5843; Cotton, Robert 5864, 5864.2, 5864.4; Course 5875; Cowper 5940.5; Crawfurd 6032; Dansie 6267; Davenant, J. 6296; Deloney 6554.5; Denison, S. 6607.5, 6608, 6608.3, 6608.4, 6608.5, 6608.7; Dent, A. 6665.5; Dering 6723; Despautere 6782; Dod 6936; Donne, J. 7035*, 7035a, 7049; Dort, Synod of 7068; Douglas, W. 7075; Downame, G. 7106.5; Drayton 7190; Drummond 7246; Echlin, D. 7475; Edinburgh University 7487.24; Eedes 7527; England, Appendix 9978(?); England, C. of, Visit. Articles 10146, 10172.5, 10192.7C, 10206, 10242, 10245.3, 10262, 10294, 10338(?); England, Proclamations, Chron. Ser. 8848, 8849, 8850, 8851, 8852, 8853, 8854, 8855, 8856, 8857, 8858, 8859, 8860, 8861, 8862, 8863, 8864, 8865, 8866, 8867, 8868, 8868.3, 8869, 8870, 8871, 8872, 8873, 8874, 8875(o.s.), 8876(o.s.), 8877(o.s.), 8878(o.s.), 8879(o.s.), 8880(o.s.), 8881(o.s.), 8882(o.s.), 8883(o.s.), 8884(o.s.), 8885(o.s.), 8886(o.s.), 8887(o.s.), 8888(o.s.), 8888.5(o.s.); Exchanger 10614, 10614.5; Fale 10680; Farnaby, T. 10706.7(?); Fell 10754; Finch, H. 10871; Fletcher, P. 11081; Forbes, P. 11147; France—Reformed Churches 11301; Frankfurt Fair 11330.8; Frith, J. 11395*; Gamon 11548; Gardiner, Samuel 11574; Gataker 11647, 11663, 11671; Gerhard 11772; Goffe 11978; Gouge 12109*, 12109a, 12128; Grent, J. 12360, 12360.3; Grimeston 12376; Guiana Company 12456.5; Guild 12479, 12490; Gumbleden 12515*; Hakewill 12611; Hall, Joseph 12636*; Hampton, W. 12741; Harris, P. 12808.3;

1627 — *cont.*

Harris, Robert 12842, 12852.5; Harry 12871.5(c.); Hart, John, D. D. 12892; Hawkins, W. 12963; Hay, P. 12971; Heylyn 13278; Hieronymus, de Paiva 13431; Hilton 13508; Hobbes 13537(?); Holyoke 13619.5; Hubbocke 13899.5; Hugo, H. 13926, 13926a*; Ireland, Proc. 14209, 14210, 14211(o.s.); Jackson, Thomas, of Peterborough 14319; James I 14375; James, T., D. D. 14457; Janua 14470; Jemmatt 14484.7; Kellie 14906; Kenrick 14933; King, Henry 14971; L., S. P. 15110; Leigh, D. 15405; Leslie, H. 15495; Lever, C. 15537; Lily, W., 'Lily's Grammar' 15627.5; Littleton, T., Tenures, Engl. 15783; Liturgies, C. of Eng., BCP 16368, 16369.3, 16369.7, 16369.9(A/C), 16370, 16370.5, 16371; Liturgies, C. of Eng., Ordinal 16469; London, Coll. of Physicians 16774, 16776*; London, Diocese of 16776.14; Looking-glass 16802; Lord's Prayer 16823; Lovell, R. 16857.7; Lover 16864a.3(c.); Lucanus 16887; Lupton, T. 16960; Malone 17213; Markham, G. 17392; Martyrology 17533; Mascall 17587; Mason, H. 17603, 17603.5, 17605, 17614; Mayer 17731; Maynwaring 17751, 17751.5; Mede 17766; Middleton, T. 17904.7; Minsheu 17947; Minucius Felix 17950; Morgan, L. 18104.5(c.); Mornay 18156a; New England 18484; Newsbooks, Num. 18507.185, 18507.186, 18507.186A, 18507.187, 18507.188, 18507.189, 18507.190, 18507.191, 18507.192, 18507.193, 18507.194; Niccols 18516; Norden 18625, 18630.3; Olmstead 18811.5; Openshaw 18830.8; Overbury 18915; Ovidius Naso 18973; Oxford Univ., Quaestiones 19016.9; Pagit 19108, 19108.5, 19108.7; Parker, Martin 19223.5(c.), 19283(c.); Partridge, John 19431, 19431.5, 19436.5; Pasor, M. 19445; Peacham, H., the Younger 19503; Peele, G. 19543, 19544; Pelegromius 19562.5; Pemble 19583, 19591; Perkins, W. 19717.5; Perrot, R. 19770; Philippson 19850; Plutarch 20056; Powell, T., Londino-Cambrensis 20165; Primrose, G. 20392.5; Prynne 20472, 20473; Purchas, S. 20504; Quip 20567.7 (c.); Re 20779.5; Reading 20788; Ressold 20894; Reynolds, J., of the Mint 20946.9, 20946.10, 20947; Richardson, G. 21020; Rider, J. 21036; Rive 21060.5(A/C); Robotham 21129; Rocquigny 21138.7; Rodriguez 21148, 21149; Rogers, J., of Dedham 21186.5, 21186.7; Rogers, Richard 21219, 21219a; Rogers, Timothy 21241.7, 21246; Ross 21327; Rous, the Elder 21346; Rowlands, S. 21377, 21412; Rowlandson 21415.5; Saint Andrews Univ. 21555.34; Saint Martin's Fort 21590.5; Salter, R. 21631; Sanderson, R. 21705; Sandys, G. 21728; Sclater, the Elder 21830, 21835; Scotland, proclamations 21971, 21972, 21973, 21974; Scudder 22115.5; Senhouse 22230; Sermons 22240.5; Shakespeare, W. 22363; Sibthorp 22525, 22525.3; Sibthorpe 22525.5, 22525.7, 22526, 22526a; Sidney, P. 22547*; Smith, John, Gov. of Virginia 22785, 22790c, 22794; Smith, R., Bp. of Chalcedon 22811; Smith, S., A. M. 22831; Smith, T., Artillerist 22855.5(?)*; Spagnuoli 22985; Sparke, M. 23015.7, 23018; Speed, John 23035, 23036*, 23036.5*, 23039g.7, 23041.8*, 23042, 23043*, 23048; Speed, John, Genealogies 23039.6(?); Speidell 23060*, 23060.3(?)(A/C), 23064.7; Spencer, R. 23071; Stanbridge, Vocabula 23191.3; Stanhope, M. 23228; Stephens 23250.5; Stubbes 23390.5; Susenbrotus 23442; Sydenham 23561, 23563*, 23564, 23564.5; Talaeus 23660.5; Tayler, F., B. D. 23718; Taylor, John 23726, 23726a, 23731.7, 23753, 23811.3; Taylour 23857.5; Terentius 23889.3, 23897; Treasurer 24210; Trevor 24268.7; Trumpet 24295; Tymme 24430; Valentine, H. 24576; Vicars, T. 24704, 24705; Villegas 24733*(A/C); Villiers 24739.5, 24740, 24741, 24742, 24743, 24744, 24745, 24746, 24746.3, 24746.5; W., Ez. 24903, 24903.5; Wake 24941; Wales, S. 24956.5; Wall, J. 24985, 24986, 24987, 24987.5; Ward, S., of Cambridge 25027; Ward, S., of Ipswich 25031*, 25033a.5, 25042.5, 25045.5, 25048.5, 25051.5, 25053.5, 25054.5, 25056.5; Ward, W. 25058; Webbe, J. 25170.5; Weemes 25217; Well-wishing 25229.7(c.); West, W. 25279.7; White, C. 25377; Williams, G. 25720, 25720.5; Willis, Edmond 25742; Wilson, T., Divine 25793; Wren 26015; Wright, E. 26022; Wyche 26057.3.

1628

A., R. 15.5(+); Aesop 172.8, 172.9, 183; Ainsworth, H. 230*, 231, 231.5; Airay, C. 241; Almanacks (Allestree) 407.11; Almanacks (Browne) 421.13; Almanacks (Chamberlaine) 429.3; Almanacks (Clarke) 431; Almanacks (Dade, W.) 435.17; Almanacks (Grammar) 450.3; Almanacks (Hewlett) 457.4; Almanacks (Neve, John) 490.4; Almanacks (Osborne) 494.6; Almanacks (Perkins) 495.3; Almanacks (Ranger) 503.5; Almanacks (Rivers, W.) 505.17; Almanacks (Rudston, J.) 506.19; Almanacks (Sofford) 515.11; Almanacks (Swallow) 517; Almanacks (Vaux) 522.8; Almanacks (White) 527.17; Almanacks (Woodhouse, or Wedhouse, or Wydowes, J.) 531.19; Anglerius 652; Answer 660; Arundel Marbles 823; Bacon, F. 1160.5, 1160.7, 1170; Baillie, A. 1202; Ball, J. 1313.2; Ballad 1327(+), 1331.3(+); Banbury 1342.5; Barclay, J. 1393; Basse 1551; Bayly, L. 1608.3; Baynes, P. 1631; Beaumont, F., and Fletcher 1683; Bedel, W. 1786; Bell, A. 1811; Bell, T. 1820; Benefield 1864; Berkshire 1904; Bernard, R. 1948, 1962, 1964.7; Bible, English 2274(aft.)*, 2281, 2282, 2283, 2283.5; Bible, N.T., English 2930, 2931, 2932, 2933, 2933.3(?), 2935; Bible, O.T., Psalms 2604*, 2604.5, 2605, 2605.5, 2606, 2607, 2607.5, 2608, 2609, 2610, 2610.3, 2610.5*, 2610.7; Bland, G. 3126.5(?); Book 3354; Bownd, Nicholas 3442; Boyd, R. 3445; Boyd, Z. 3446a.5; Brabourne 3474; Brerewood 3616.5, 3628; Breton 3690.7, 3691.9, 3694.7(+); Bride 3729(+); Brinsley, J., the Elder 3771.6; Browne, W., Gent. 3913.5 (?); Buchler 3992.9; Burton, H. 4140.4, 4147, 4147.5, 4155, 4157, 4157.5; Burton, R. 4161; Bushell 4187; Byfield, N. 4219, 4221; C., I. or J. 4277; Calderwood 4359; Calvin 4390; Cambium 4471; Cambridge University 4491.3; Cameron 4532; Campion 4541.7(+); Carleton, G. 4646; Carter, J., Rector of Belstead 4696; Casa 4736; Cato 4849.4; Charles I, King 5019, 5028; Christ's Hospital 5208.7; Cicero 5316; Clarke, J., B.D. 5363; Claudianus 5368, 5368.2; Clavell 5369, 5369.2, 5370; Collins, S. 5562; Cooke, A. 5665; Cooke, E. 5669, 5670, 5670.2; Cooke, John 5675(?); Cooper, T., Preacher 5697; Cornwall 5773(+); Cotton, Robert 5863, 5863.2; Court Song 5876.8(c.), 5877(+); Cowper 5911*; Crashaw, W. 6021.5; Cuckold 6102(+); Dainty 6191(+); Dalton, M. 6213; Davenant, J. 6299, 6300; Davies, Sir J. 6362; Davis, A. 6366, 6367; Dekker 6493, 6531; Deloney 6553.5; Dent, A. 6644; Dent, D. 6673, 6673.2; Desainliens or Sainliens 6754.7; Dial 6798.7(?)(A/C); Dialogue 6809(+), 6809.2(?); Dickinson 6822; Ditty 6922.4(+); Doctrine 6934; Dod and Cleaver 6976.5; Dod 6947; Doughty, J. 7072; Downame, J. 7148.5(c.?); Drake 7161, 7161.3; Du Moulin, P., the Elder 7342.5; Dyke, D. 7403; Dyke, J. 7416(?), 7424; Earle 7439, 7440, 7440.2, 7441; East India Company 7446.5, 7449, 7450a.5(?) (A/C),; Echlin, D. 7477; Edinburgh University 7487.25; Eleanor 7565.6(+); Elizabeth I 7579(c.); England, Appendix 10018.5, 10021.4; England, C.of, Articles 10051; England, C. of, Constitutions/Canons 10074, 10074.3*; England, C. of, Visit. Articles 10182, 10263, 10309, 10331, 10361; England, Parliament 7744.5, 7745, 7745.5, 7745.7, 7746, 7746.2, 7746.3, 7746.4, 7749; England, Proclamations, Chron. Ser. 8875, 8876, 8877, 8878, 8879, 8880, 8881, 8881.7, 8882, 8883, 8884, 8885, 8886, 8887, 8888, 8888.5, 8889, 8892, 8893, 8893.3, 8893.5, 8894, 8895, 8896, 8897, 8897.5, 8898, 8899, 8900, 8902, 8903, 8904, 8905, 8906, 8907, 8908, 8909, 8910, 8911, 8912(o.s.), 8913(o.s.), 8914(o.s.), 8915(o.s.), 8916(o.s.), 8917(o.s.), 8918(o.s.), 8919(o.s.); England, Public Documents, Misc. 9175j.3(?), 9249(o.s.); England, Statutes, Chron. Ser. 9510; English Customs 10408.7; Farley, R. 10696; Featley, D. 10726.5; Feltham 10756, 10758*; Felton 10762; Fenton, E. 10788.3(c.); Fetherstone, H. 10837; Field, R. 10858; Field, T. 10863; Fitzer 10933; Fletcher, Joseph 11078; Fletcher, P. 11079.5; Folkingham 11125; France—Reformed Churches 11293; Frankfurt Fair 11331, 11331.2; Frewen 11380.3; Fuller, W. 11468; Galliardi or Gagliardi 11540(?)*; Gaule 11691*; Glanvill 11904; Godfridus 11933.5; Godwin, F. 11946; Godwin, T. 11953, 11961; Gomersall 11992, 11995; Goodfellow, R. 12016; Greene, R. 12231; Greenwood, H. 12331, 12332, 12335; Gumbleden 12514; Hacket 12590; Hall, Joseph 12636*, 12636.3, 12636.5, 12636.7, 12637, 12637.4, 12637.7, 12640.3, 12690, 12690.5, 12692; Harris, Robert 12824, 12825, 12847, 12851.5, 12853; Hayman 12974; Heaven 13018.5(?); Heidelberg Catechism 13025.7; Hieron 13377.7(?), 13384.5*, 13403.3, 13413a.7; Hipolito 13516; Hodson, P. 13551; Holland, Henry, Bookseller 13581.3; Hubert 13900, 13900.5; Hugo, H. 13926a*;

1628 — *cont.*
Hume, J. 13954; Hunt 13987, 13989; Invention 14127; Ireland, C. of 14261; Ireland, Proc. 14211, 14212, 14213, 14214; Jackson, J. 14297; Jackson, Thomas, of Peterborough 14318*, 14318.5; Jerome, S. 14510; Jesus Christ 14544(+), 14577(+); Johnson, Robert, Chaplain 14694.5; Johnston, A. 14709; Kellet 14905; Kind 14960.5(c.), 14961(+); King, Henry 14965; Knevet 15037; L., H. 15105*; Lake, A. 15134*; Lambe 15177; Lamentation 15186(+); Lancicius 15188.3; Laud 15305, 15305.5, 15305.7; Leech, John, Schoolmaster 15374.9; Levett, C. 15554; Lightbody 15592; Lily, W., 'Lily's Grammar' 15627.6; Lindsay, Sir D. 15668; Ling 15689.5(?); Littleton, T. 15784; Liturgies, C. of Eng., BCP 16372(?), 16373, 16373a, 16373b; Liturgies, C. of Eng., Spec. Prayers 16545(?), 16545.5(?), 16546, 16546.5, 16547(o.s.)(A/C), 16547.5, 16548; Loe, the Younger 16691.5; London, Appendix 16758(+), 16764.5(?); London, Ords. and Regs. 16729.5, 16729.7, 16729.9; Louis XIII 16846; Lover 16862.1(+), 16862.9(+), 16863 (+), 16864.5(+), 16864a.9(+); Lovers 16864a.11(+), 16864a.12(c.), 16865(+); Lownes 16876(?); Lynde 17097; Maid 17187(+); Mainwaringe 17201; Manuzio, A. 17283.3; Markham, G. 17383; Markham, R. 17403; Marlowe 17435.5; Martyn, W. 17528; Mason, H. 17605a; Matthieu 17664, 17665; Medley 17777.7(+); Mico 17862; Monson, Sir T. 18023.3(A/C); Morton, T., Bp. 18187; Murray, D. 18295(+); Murrell 18302.4*(A/C); Newsbooks, Num. 18507.195, 18507.196, 18507.197, 18507.197A, 18507.198, 18507.199; Newsbooks, T. Archer 18507.355, 18507.356, 18507.357, 18507.358; Nichols, P. 18545; Northern Turtle 18671.3(c.); Norton, R. 18673, 18674; Offer 18787.5; Overbury 18916; Ovidius Naso 18952.6, 18965; Owen, L. 18998; Oxford Univ., Quaestiones 19016.10; Packer 19085; Pagit 19109; Paludanus 19167; Parker, Martin 19224.3(c.), 19224.5(+), 19229.5, 19246(+), 19267, 19271(+), 19272; Parr, R. 19322, 19323; Partridge, James 19419; Patriarchs 19471.5; Pemble 19576a, 19579, 19584; Perkins, W. 19673, 19684; Platt 19983.7; Price, L. 20319.5(c.); Primrose, David, Advocate 20385.5; Prynne 20455, 20455a, 20462, 20463, 20477, 20477.5; Pyne 20521.8; R., I., or J. 20577; Ragged 20602.5(+); Rainolds, J. 20615, 20615.5; Raleigh 20640, 20649, 20649.1, 20649.3, 20649.5, 20649.7; Ravisius 20761.5; Rawlidge 20766; Reginald, H. 20835.3(A/C); Reynolds, J., of the Mint 20947.3; Robinson, J., Pastor of Leyden 21112a; Robson, C. 21130; Rogers, Richard 21210.3; Rogers, Timothy 21242; Rohan 21252; Rowlands or Verstegan, R. 21362; Rowlands, S. 21368.5*, 21370, 21383; Rudierd, B. 21435.7, 21436; S., H. 21496.3; Saint Andrews Univ. 21555.35, 21555.36; Samson 21689(+); Sanderson, R. 21708.5, 21709; Sarpi 21757a; Scheibler 21814; Scotland, Episcopal Church of 22058*(A/C); Scotland, proclamations 21975, 21975.5, 21976, 21977, 21978, 21979, 21980, 21981, 21982, 21983; Scott, T., B. D. 22106; Scudder 22116; Sidney, P. 22547*; Skay 22592; Smart, P. 22640, 22640.3, 22640.7; Smetius 22648; Smith, E. 22655(+); Smith, H., Minister, Collections 22731.5, 22745; Smith, H., Minister, Single Works 22673; Smith, S., Minister in Essex 22840.5, 22849; Smith, T., Artillerist 22856; Song 22918.7(+); Spain 22998.5(?)(A/C); Sparke, M. 23016, 23016.5*; Sparke, W. 23026; Speed, John 23033; Speed, John, Genealogies 23039a.3(?), 23039d.11(+?), 23039e.7(+?); Speed, R. 23052; Speidell 23059, 23064.9; Spence 23070(?); Spencer, T. 23072; Spenser, E. 23087.5(?); Sprint, J., Vicar 23108.4; Starkey, R. 23235.5(?); Struther 23367, 23370; Susanna 23435a.7(+); Sweetnam, Joseph 23539; Tables 23638, 23639(?); Tasso, T. 23696; Tavernier 23716.5; Taylor, John 23748(?), 23813.7; Taylor, Thomas 23832, 23845; Theophrastus 23947.5; Thomas, a Kempis 23998, 23999*; Titus Andronicus 24092.7(+); Tozer 24161; Treasurer 24211; Turtledove 24369(+); Udny 24513, 24513a; Venner, T. 24641, 24645; Vicars, T. 24703; Villegas 24733*(A/C); Villiers 24739; Virgilius Maro 24820, 24823, 24824; Vives 24853.7; Vossius 24882.7, 24883; Waker 24953.7; Walkley 24973.5; Wall, J. 24989; Ward, S., of Ipswich 25031*, 25038, 25038.5; Ward, W. 25059; Ware, J. 25065; Warmstrey, G. 25076.5; Weapons 25146(?); Wellwishing 25230(+); Whately 25311, 25322, 25322.3, 25322.7, 25322a; Whear 25326.5, 25327; White, Anthony 25376; Wilkinson, J., of Barnard's Inn 25650; Williams, J., Abp. 25727, 25729; Willis, J., Stenographer 25745, 25746.7*, 25751; Willymat 25763.5; Wingate 25850; Wither, Poet 25899; Woodall 25964; Writing Tables 26050.18.

1629

Abbey 22.7; Aberdeen Univ. 71.16; Achesone 88; Adams 104*; Aelianus, Tacitus 162; Aesop 173; Almanacks (Allestree) 407.12; Almanacks (Bretnor, E.) 419.10; Almanacks (Browne) 421.14; Almanacks (Butler) 427; Almanacks (Clarke) 431.1; Almanacks (Dade, W.) 435.18; Almanacks (Dove) 436.2; Almanacks (Evans, J., Philomath) 441.5; Almanacks (Gilden) 448.14; Almanacks (Hewlett) 457.5; Almanacks (Honiwax) 460; Almanacks (Neve, John) 490.5; Almanacks (Perkins) 495.4; Almanacks (Pond) 501.19; Almanacks (Ranger) 503.6; Almanacks (Rivers, P.) 505.3; Almanacks (Sofford) 515.12; Almanacks (Vaux) 522.9; Almanacks (White) 527.18; Almanacks (Woodhouse, or Wedhouse, or Wydowes, J.) 531.20; Ames 550, 550.5, 556.5; Andrewes, J. 595; Andrewes, L. 602, 606; Arundel Marbles 824; Augustine 948; Austin, S. 971; B., T. 1071; Bachelor 1105.5(?); Bachiler 1106.5, 1107; Bacon, F. 1124, 1126, 1149, 1161, 1165; Bacon, R. 1184; Ball, J. 1315; Barclay, J. 1394; Basse 1551.3; Bayly, L. 1608.7, 1608.9 (A/C), 1623.5; Beaumont, J. 1694; Becon 1771.7; Bedingfield 1791.7; Benefield 1862, 1865, 1866, 1876; Bernard, R. 1926, 1926.5, 1944, 1948.5, 1954, 1954.5; Bible, English 2284, 2285, 2285.5*, 2286, 2287, 2288; Bible, N.T., English 2936, 2936.3; Bible, O.T., Psalms 2415, 2415.2, 2612*, 2612.5, 2614, 2614.5, 2615, 2615.5, 2615.7, 2616, 2616.5, 2617, 2617.5, 2617.7, 2714; Bolton, E. 3219; Book 3301, 3323; Boyd, Z. 3445a, 3447, 3448, 3449; Boys 3453*, 3454*; Breton 3711; Browker 3902.5; Buenting 4019; Burges, C. 4109; Burrell 4126, 4126.5; Burton, H. 4136, 4153.7, 4156; Butler, C. 4194.5, 4200; Butterfield, R. 4205; C., H. 4270; C., W., Bachelor of Civil Law 4323.4; Cambridge University 4490; Camden 4498, 4514.7, 4524; Carlell 4628; Carleton, G. 4646.5, 4647; Carpenter, N. 4669; Case, J. 4757.5; Catechism 4800; Chaloner, E. 4937; Chapman, G. 4979; Charles Emmanuel I. 5045.3; Chassanion 5063; Cholmley 5144, 5144.3; Cicero 5270; Coke, E. 5512, 5520; Cole, J. 5533; Cooke, R. 5676; Cope, J. 5722; Cotton, C. 5852; Cowper 5911*; Crashaw, W. 6017.7, 6019.5; Culverwell 6117; Cupid 6122; D., I. or J. 6170.5; Dallington 6198; Davenant, W. 6307; Davenport, J. 6313; Day 6399; Dekker 6509; Dent, A. 6633, 6649.3, 6671; Description 6771; Discourse 6907(?); Doddridge 6983; Dort, Synod of 7070; Doughty, J. 7072.1; Downame, J. 7144; Dudley, Jane 7281.5; Dyke, J. 7416.5, 7425; Earle 7442; Echlin, D. 7478, 7480; Edinburgh University 7487.26; Edmondes, T. 7492.7; Elton 7617; England, C. of, Appendix 10404.7(?)(A/C); England, C. of, Articles 10052; England, C. of, Visit. Articles 10137.4C(A/C), 10138, 10173, 10192.7E, 10214, 10227.2, 10295, 10310, 10379.7; England, Proclamations, Chron. Ser. 8912, 8913, 8914, 8915, 8916, 8917, 8918, 8919, 8920, 8921, 8922, 8923, 8924, 8925, 8926, 8927, 8928, 8929, 8930, 8931, 8932, 8933, 8934, 8934.5(A/C), 8935, 8936, 8939(o.s.), 8940(o.s.), 8941(o.s.); England, Public Documents, Misc. 9249, 9249.5, 9250, 9250.3(o.s.); England, Statutes, Chron. Ser. 9509*; F., A. 10634.7; Farmer, R. 10699; Farnaby, T. 10701, 10703.5; Featley, D. 10731; Featley, J. 10743; Feltham 10758*; Fennor 10782.3; Filmer 10869; Fiston 10924; Fletcher, John 11069; Fletcher, Joseph 11079; Fonseca 11126; Forbes, J., of Corse 11139, 11140; Ford, J. 11163, 11163.3; Foster, W. 11204; Frederick Henry, Prince of Orange 11363, 11363.5; Gallobelgicus 11541; Gamon 11547; Garden 11561; Gaule 11689, 11691*; Godwin, F. 11944; Goodman, G. 12026; Gravener 12198.5; Greene, R. 12249, 12290; Gregory I 12348; Hall, Joseph 12641, 12693, 12709, 12709.5, 12709a; Harris, John, Preacher 12806; Harris, Robert 12843; Harsnet, S. 12884; Hayward, Sir J. 12997(?)*; Heidelberg Catechism 13026; Herbert, A. 13179.5; Herodian 13222; Hertogenbosch 13248.4, 13248.6; Heylyn 13279; Hieron 13384.5*; Hildersam 13461; Hill, R. 13477, 13477.5; Hill, W. 13504; Hubert 13901; Hume, P. 13954.7, 13955; Hunnis 13984; Introduction 14122; Ireland, C. of 14262, 14263, 14265.1; Ireland, Proc. 14208, 14215, 14216, 14217(o.s.); Jackson, Thomas, of Peterborough 14318*;

1629 — *cont.*
James, R. 14441; Janua 14472.3; Jeffray 14483; Johnson, T., Botanist 14703; Kellison 14914; Kennedy, J. 14931; Kraus 15083.5 [not STC]; Lake, A. 15134*; Lauder, G. 15312; Leather 15344; Lechmere, E. 15348; Leigh, D. 15405.5; Leighton, A. 15428.5, 15429(?); Lenton 15467; Lightfoot, J. 15593; Lily, W., 'Lily's Grammar' 15627.7*; Littleton, T. 15785; Liturgies, C. of Eng., BCP 16374, 16375, 16376, 16376.5, 16376.7, 16377, 16377.5; Liturgies, C. of Eng., Ordinal 16470; Liturgies, C. of Eng., Spec. Prayers 16547(A/C), 16548.3, 16548.7; Liturgies, C. of Eng., St. Services 16485.3, 16497.1(bef.), 16497.3(bef.); Liturgies, Other Protest. C. 16595, 16595.5, 16596*; Livingston 16610; London, Bills of Mort. 16742; London, Ords. and Regs. 16730, 16730.5; Loris 16826.5; Loukaris 16854; Love 16856.3(c.); Lubin 16880; Lynde 17098, 17099; M., R. 17146; Malthus 17217; Malynes 17223; Marande 17298; Markham, G. 17366; Marlowe 17421; Martialis 17494; Martini 17522; Massinger 17642; Mayer 17743; Michell 17857.7(c.?)(A/C); Montagu, R. 18040; Montagu, W. 18040.5*; Moore, W. 18063; More, G., Esq. 18068.5, 18069; Morton, T., of Berwick 18200; Mucedorus 18238.5(?); Murrell 18302.4*(A/C); Newsbooks, Num. 18507.200, 18507.201, 18507.202, 18507.203, 18507.203A; Norden 18625.5, 18630.7; Openshaw 18828; Owen, L. 18997; Oxford Univ., Off. Docs. 19008, 19009; Oxford Univ., Quaestiones 19016.11; P., I. or J. 19069, 19072; Parker, Martin 19219(?), 19232, 19235(?), 19239, 19255(?), 19280, 19282, 19283.5; Parkinson 19300; Pasquil 19452; Paybody 19488; Pelegromius 19555; Pemble 19569a.5, 19573, 19574, 19577, 19578, 19580, 19586, 19590, 19592; Penkethman 19600.8; Perkins, W. 19684.1, 19684.2, 19718; Phillips, John, Minister of Feversham 19877.5; Plumptre 20051; Potter, C. 20134; Preston, J. 20241, 20241.3, 20241.7, 20251, 20252, 20253; Prideaux 20363; Prynne 20457, 20459.3(?), 20459.7(?), 20460; Quarles 20526; Quintilianus 20567.3; R., W. 20594; Rainolds, J. 20618; Ramsay, D. 20658; Randall 20668*, 20668.5, 20680; Rastell, J., Printer 20717; Reynard the Fox 20924; Reynolds, J., Merchant 20943; Reynolds, J., of the Mint 20947.7; Rheol 20952; Richardson, A. 21012; Richeome 21023; Robinson, J., Pastor of Leyden 21113; Rogers, J., of Dedham 21187, 21191; Rogers, Richard 21213.9, 21223; Rogers, Thomas, M. A. 21231; Rogers, Timothy 21247; Rush 21452.5; Ryves 21474; Saint Andrews Univ. 21555.37, 21555.38; Sallustius Crispus 21624; Salter, R. 21631.5; Salvianus 21674; Sandys, Sir E. 21718; Saravia 21752; Sarpi 21762; Sclater, the Elder 21831, 21840, 21846; Scotland, proclamations 21984, 21987, 21987.5; Seldom 22179(?); Shakespeare, W. 22320; Shirley, J. 22460; Sibbes 22503; Sictor 22529; Sidney, P. 22548, 22548a; Smethwike 22645.5; Smith, H., Minister, Collections 22781; Smith, John, of Clavering 22798; Souterius 22941.5; Sparke, M. 23016.5*, 23016.7, 23017*; Sparke, W. 23027; Spencer, T. 23073; Sprint, J., Vicar 23108.5; Stanbridge, Vocabula 23191.7; Struther 23367.5, 23368, 23368.5; Stubbes 23391; Sutcliffe, M. 23467; Sutton, C. 23489; Sutton, W. 23507.5; Sweetnam, Joseph 23540; Symmer 23588; Taylor, John 23814; Taylor, Theophilus 23819; Taylor, Thomas 23833, 23846, 23857; Terentius 23889.4, 23893, 23896, 23898, 23898a; Thomas, a Kempis 23984, 23999*; Thomas, A. 24000.5; Thucydides 24058; Treasurer 24212; Truman 24294; Tuvil or Toutevile 24397; Ussher, J. 24547; Virgilius Maro 24795; W., I., Gent. 24909.5; Wadsworth, J., the Younger 24926; Walker, W. 24965; Ward, W. 25060; Wastell 25102; Webster, W., of the Salters' Company 25183; Western Knight 25283; Whiting, G. 25435; Wilkins, G. 25637; Wilkinson, H. 25645; Williams, G. 25721; Wilson, J., Preacher 25769.3; Wimbledon 25837; Zouch 26131a.

1630

A.B.C. 21.7(c.); Aberdeen Univ. 71.37; Abernethy 75; Abstract 81.5(c.); Adams 104*, 105; Admonition 150.5(c.); Aesop 173.3; Ainsworth, H. 227; Aleman 290; Alexander, W. 342; Alleine 357.5; Almanacks (Allestree) 407.13; Almanacks (Bretnor, E.) 419.11; Almanacks (Browne) 421.15; Almanacks (Butler) 427.2; Almanacks (Dade, W.) 435.19; Almanacks (Erra Pater) 439.27(c.); Almanacks (Evans, J., Philomath) 441.6; Almanacks (Gilden) 448.15; Almanacks (Hewlett) 457.6; Almanacks (Honiwax) 460.5; Almanacks (Neve, John) 490.6; Almanacks (Perkins) 495.5; Almanacks (Pigot) 497; Almanacks (Pond) 501.20; Almanacks (Ranger) 503.7; Almanacks (Rivers, P.) 505.4; Almanacks (Sofford) 515.13; Almanacks (Vaux) 522.10; Almanacks (White) 527.19; Almanacks (Woodhouse, or Wedhouse, or Wydowes, J.) 531.21; Ames 553, 557; Andrewes, J. 590.3; Andrewes, L. 599, 603, 603.3, 603.5; Animalia 654; Ar. 722; Arcandam 728; Arias 742.7, 743; Arms 776; Assize of Bread 881; B., A., Doctor 1021; B., E., D. 1025; Bacon, F. 1134; Ball, J. 1313.3; Ballad 1331.7(c.); Banister, R. 1361.5(c.); Banquet 1368; Barlement 1431.30; Barley-Corn, J. 1433.7(c.); Barra 1497.5 (c.); Barton, A. 1539.5(c.); Basse 1551.5; Bastard 1561.5; Batten 1590.5(c.); Bayly, J. 1601; Bayly, L. 1609, 1609.2, 1609.3, 1624; Beaumont, F., and Fletcher 1668, 1679, 1688; Bell, A. 1811.5(c.), 1813.5; Bentham, J. 1889(?); Bernard, R. 1929, 1941.5, 1945, 1949; Bevis 1994(c.), 1995; Bible, Appendix 3031; Bible, English 2289, 2289.5, 2290, 2291, 2292, 2292.3, 2292.5, 2293, 2294, 2295.3*, 2295.4*, 2295.5*, 2295.6*, 2295.8*, 2298.7*; Bible, N.T., English 2936.5, 2937, 2937.5; Bible, O.T., Psalms 2365, 2612*, 2618, 2619, 2620, 2620.5, 2621, 2622, 2622.5, 2623, 2623.5, 2624, 2624.5, 2715, 2715.5, 2746; Bible, Welsh 2349, 2349.5; Billingsley 3062.8(+); Bolton, Robert 3234.5, 3252; Bonham 3279; Boraston 3372; Bostock 3395; Botero 3404; Bourchier, A. 3412(c.?); Boys 3453*; Bradshaw, W. 3514; Brathwait 3561(c.?) [not STC], 3563; Brerewood 3622; Breton 3691, 3699.7(c.); Bridges, F. 3733; Brinsley, J., the Elder 3771.7, 3772; Browne, S. 3911; Byfield, N. 4222, 4222.5, 4229; Byfield, R. 4239; Byll 4241(c.?); C., I. or J. 4279; C., J. B. 4285(c.); C., L. W. 4290; C., R. 4298(?); C., T. 4309; Cade 4327; Calvin 4373; Cambridge University, Act Verses 4474.23(c.?), 4474.47(c.?), 4474.59(c.?), 4474.72R(c.?)(A/C), 4474.91(c.?), 4474.123(c.?); Camden 4500, 4500.5, 4515; Camus 4551; Canterbury 4581; Carleton, G. 4643; Casa 4737; Casaubon, I. 4748; Catholics 4833; Chafin 4931; Charron 5054; Cheapside 5104.5(c.); Chevy Chase 5129.7(c.); Chibald 5133, 5133.3; Cicero 5271, 5271.2, 5302, 5322; Clare, J. 5351; Clarke, J., B.D. 5354.7, 5359; Cleaver 5380, 5388; Climsell 5425(?); Closet 5437; Cobbes 5453; Cocks 5467; Comedy 5599; Complaint 5612(c.); Constance 5639.5(c.); Cooke, A. 5666, 5666.5; Coote 5714; Cortes 5805.5; Cotton, J. 5854, 5854.2, 5854.4; Crompton, R. 6056; Crompton, W. 6058; Cucking 6100(c.); Culverwell 6118.7; D., J., Preacher of God's Word 6175, 6176; Dalton, M. 6209; Davenant, J. 6297; Davenant, W. 6302, 6303; David, Saint 6318(c.?); Davy du Perron 6385; Day, M. 6427.7; Dekker 5478, 6492.5, 6506; Delamain 6542(o.s.); Deloney 6561; Denison, J. 6597.7; Dent, A. 6639, 6666, 6666.4; Dering 6723.5; Desainliens or Sainliens 6747; Dichante 6816.7; Digges, L. 6855; Discourse 6906.5(c.); Ditty 6920.5(c.); Divine 6929; Dod and Cleaver 6977; Doddridge 6980, 6982; Dowle 7101; Downame, J. 7125.5, 7126; Drawnfield 7172.5(c.?); Drayton 7210, 7224; Drelincourt 7233; Drexelius 7234; Drummond 7250, 7251; Du Moulin, P., the Elder 7311, 7337; Dublin, Trinity College 7265; Dyke, D. 7404; Earle 7443; Echlin, D. 7476; Edinburgh University 7487.27; Edward IV 7505(c.); Egerton, S. 7534, 7536.7; England, C. of, Articles 10053*, 10054*, 10055*, 10055.5*; England, C. of, Visit. Articles 10137.5, 10147, 10192.3(?), 10206.5(?), 10243, 10279; England, Proclamations, Chron. Ser. 8893.7(c.?), 8937, 8937.5, 8939, 8940, 8941, 8942, 8943, 8944, 8946, 8947, 8948, 8949, 8950, 8951, 8952, 8953, 8954, 8955, 8956, 8957, 8958, 8959, 8960, 8960.5, 8961, 8962, 8963, 8964, 8965, 8966, 8967, 8968, 8969, 8970, 8971(o.s.); England, Public Documents, Misc. 9250.3, 9250.5, 9250.7, 9251, 9251.3, 9252(o.s.), 9252.2(o.s.), 9252.4(o.s.); England, Statutes, Chron. Ser. 9509*; England, Statutes, Spec. Subjs. 9342; Epistle 10432.3; Essex 10533.7; Evans, J., Minister 10586; F., T. 10654(c.); Fawkner 10719, 10722; Featley, D. 10727, 10733; Fenton, E. 10788.5(c.); Fisher, A. 10885; Floyd, J. 11109; Forde, E. 11174; Francis, of Assisi 11314.8; Francis, of Sales 11323; Francklin 11326; Freake 11346; Friends 11380.7(c.); G., I. or J. 11498; Gallobelgicus 11542; Gaule 11688, 11690; Gaultier 11691.5; Gheeraerts 11807.7(c.); Gilpin 11898; Godwin, F. 11947, 11947.5; Goodall

1630 — *cont.*
12007; Goodfellow 12015(c.); Gouge 12114; Greene, R. 12268; Grounds 12402a.6; Guild 12484; Gunter, E. 12522.5(c.?)*; Gurnay 12528; Gustavus II 12535; Guy, R. 12547.3(c.); H., A. 12561.6(c.); Hakewill 12612; Hall, Joseph 12677, 12687, 12691, 12691.5*; Hamdultun 12725(c.?); Harmar 12793; Harris, Robert 12822, 12830, 12838, 12851, 12851.7, 12852, 12854; Harsnet, A. 12876; Hawkins, W. 12965; Hayward, Sir J. 12998*(A/C); Help 13051.3; Henry, the Minstrel 13154; Hexham 13262; Heywood, T. 13362; Hieron 13403.6, 13414; Higges 13440b.5(c.?); Higginson 13449, 13450, 13451; Hill, W. 13504.5; Holland, Henry, Bookseller 13581.7; Holyday 13618; Hommius 13683; Hood, R. 13693(c.); Horatius Flaccus 13794a.5, 13795; Hyde Park 14040.2(c.); I. 14045.5(c.); Ireland, Proc. 14217, 14218, 14219, 14220(o.s.), 14221 (o.s.); Item 14288(c.); James I 14360; James, R. 14443; Janua 14472.5; Jarret 14476; Jenison 14489; Jerome, St. 14502; Jest 14524.5(c.); Johnson, T., Misc. writer 14708.1, 14708.5; Johnston, T. 14715; Jones, Richard 14731(c.); Jonson 14776; Keep 14900(c.); Kilby, R., of Derby 14954, 14956; King, W. 14998.3; Lamentation 15186.5(c.); Langhorne 15199; Lantern 15225.5(c.); Lauder, G. 15313; Layfielde 15333; Leigh, D. 15406; Lily, W., 'Lily's Grammar' 15627.7*, 15627.9, 15628*; Lindsay, Sir D. 15669; Ling 15690 (?); Littleton, T. 15789; Liturgies, C. of Eng., BCP 16378, 16378.5, 16380, 16380.3, 16380.5, 16380.7, 16380.9, 16381, 16381.5, 16382, 16439; Liturgies, C. of Eng., Spec. Prayers 16549; Liturgies, C. of Eng., St. Services 16497.5; Liturgies, Latin Rite, Hours and Primers 16098.7; Liturgies, Other Protest. C. 16596*, 16596.5; Loncq 16699; London, Appendix 16751.5(c.), 16755, 16758.3(c.), 16758.7, 16765(c.); London, Bills of Mort. 16743(+); London, Bridewell Hosp. 16768.14(c.); London, Coll. of Physicians 16770; London, Diocese of 16776.8; London, Girdlers 16777.10(c.), 16777.12(c.); London, Ords. and Regs. 16731, 16731.3, 16731.5, 16731.7(c.); Look 16800; Looking-glass 16801.7; Lord 16825; Love 16855(c.), 16857.3(c.); Lover 16862.7(c.); Loyola 16876.5(c.); Luis 16922a; Lynde 17095, 17100; Lyons 17120.5; Maid 17189.3(c.); Makluire 17207, 17208; Man 17234(c.); Manual 17277, 17277.3; Manuzio, A. 17283.5; Markham, G. 17367, 17378*, 17383.5; Martin, G. 17506.3; Mason, H. 17604, 17606; Massinger 17640, 17640.5, 17641; May, T. 17711; Mayer 17735; Mayo 17756; Middleton, T. 17877, 17891, 17893; Midhurst 17915.5(c.); Milan 17916.3, 17916.5, 17916.7, 17916.9; Months 18051.5(c.); Morgan, L. 18104(c.); Musgrove 18316.3; Narne 18360; Neade 18416.3(c.); Neale 18416.7(c.); Netherlands, Southern Prov. 18469(?); Neville, E. 18482; New England 18485, 18486; Newsbooks, Num. 18507.204, 18507.205, 18507.206, 18507.207; Nicolai, P. 18572; Northern Turtle 18671.7(c.); Nottinghamshire Lovers 18699.7(c.); Nowell, Middle Catechism 18723; Olmstead 18811; Orphinstraunge 18854(c.)(A/C); Overbury 18917; Ovidius Naso 18932(c.), 18952.7, 18953; Oxford Univ., Quaestiones 19016.12; Oxford Univ., Verses, etc. 19032; Page, S. 19088.7; Pagit 19109.2(c.); Palmus 19165.5(c.), 19165.7(c.)(A/C); Panacea 19168; Pare 19192; Parker, Martin 19220(?), 19224(?), 19227(?), 19231.5(c.), 19243, 19245(c.), 19267.5(c.?), 19271.5(c.); Parker, Matthew 19289.5(c.); Parsons, R. 19376.5; Pathomachia 19462; Peele, G. 19544.5(c.); Peerson 19552; Pemble 19571; Penkethman 19598.6(c.); Perrott, J. 19772; Pestell 19788; Peters, H. 19798.5; Petowe 19807.3; Phillida 19856(?); Pinke 19941; Pitiscus 19966, 19968; Platt 19984; Posselius 20128.5; Posy 20131.5(c.), 20132(c.); Powell, T., Londino-Cambrensis 20164, 20164a, 20164a.5; Praise 20186.3(c.); Prempart 20202; Preston, J. 20208, 20209*, 20242, 20243, 20254, 20270, 20270.5, 20278, 20278.5; Price, L. 20314.7(?)(A/C), 20322.3(c.); Prime 20370.5(c.); Primerosius 20385; Primrose, Diana 20388; Prynne 20458, 20461, 20465; Publilius Syrus 20482.5(c.); Quarles 20526.5, 20533; R., M. 20583(?); Randall 20668*, 20673, 20682, 20682a; Randolph 20686, 20686.5, 20687; Reeks 20828; Richards, N. 21010; Richeome 21023a; Robinson, T. 21125; Rodriguez 21142, 21144, 21149.5(?); Rogers, Richard 21210.5, 21213.10, 21220; Romans 21290(c.); Rope Dancing 21315.8(aft.); Ross 21331; Ruggle 21445, 21446; S., E. 21487; Saint Andrews Univ. 21555.39; Saint German 21583; Sarpi 21767.5, 21768; Sclater, the Elder

1630 — *cont.*
21836; Scotland, proclamations 21988, 21988.5; Scotland, statutes, etc. 21901.6, 21901.8; Seager 22138.3(c.); Shakespeare, W. 22301, 22306, 22337, 22338, 22364, 22365(+?); Sharpe, J. 22370; Sharpham 22383; Shelton 22404; Shirley, J. 22444; Sibbes 22479; Sibyllarum Icones 22527a.7(?); Sinner 22579(c.); Slatyer 22633; Smith, H., Minister, Single Works 22711.5; Smith, John, Gov. of Virginia 22796; Smith, R., Bp. of Chalcedon 22809a.5; Smith, S., Minister in Essex 22849.1; Solomon 22898(c.); Song 22920.1(c.), 22920.5(c.), 22920.7(c.), 22920.9(c.); Sorocold 22934.2; Southwell 22966; Sparke, M. 23017*, 23017.3*; Speed, John, Genealogies 23039.7(?), 23039b(?), 23039d.12(?), 23039e.8(+?); Squire, J., Minister 23113, 23114; Stanbridge, Vocabula 23192; Stanley, H. 23228.3; Stoole 23291(?); Stubbes 23391.5; Sutton, C. 23494; Sydenham 23570, 23571, 23572, 23574; Sylvester 23580; Symmer 23587; T., A., Practitioner in Physic 23610; T., E. 23613(?); T., F. 23616; Tarlton 23683.7(c.), 23686; Taylor, John 23725, 23741.5(c.), 23761, 23772a.5, 23774; Taylor, Thomas 23850; Tel-Trouth 23868 (?); Thomas, O. 24007; Thornborough 24037; Tidings 24065(c.); Tokens 24098(c.); Tom Thumb 24115; Travers, W. 24188; Treasurer 24213; Treatises 24258; Troy 24293.5(c.); Tusser 24391; Tymme 24431, 24431a; Vaughan, W. 24605, 24619, 24623; Vicars, J., Poet 24697.3; Vicars, T. 24700; Villegas 24734; Virgin 24829.5 (c.); Wadsworth, J., the Younger 24926a, 24927, 24928, 24928a, 24929, 24929a; Walkley 24974; Warre 25091; Way 25136(?); Weemes 25211; Weerdenburck or Waerdenburgh 25219; Welsthed 25236; Whately 25312, 25323, 25324; Whetstone 25333.5(c.); Whitaker, W. 25369; White, John, of Dorchester 25399; Widdowes 25593(?)*, 25594; Will 25668(c.); Willan 25670; Williamson, T. 25738; Wilson, J., Preacher 25769.5; Wilson, M. 25774; Wilson, M. 25779, 25779.3, 25779.5; Wily 25821; Wingate 25849; Worship 25990; Wright, R. 26037a; Wright, T., Priest 26043; Yaxlee 26090; Yorkshire Lovers 26103.5(c.); Young Man 26118(c.).

1631

A., I. or J. 4; A.B.C. 22.1; Aberdeen Univ. 71.17, 71.38; Acontius 92.3, 92.7, 93; Aelianus, Tacitus 163; Agard 194, 194.1; Aleman 291*; Aleyn 351; Alleine 358; Allwyn 383; Almanacks (Allestree) 407.14; Almanacks (Balles) 411; Almanacks (Beale) 412; Almanacks (Bowker or Booker) 419; Almanacks (Browne) 421.16; Almanacks (Butler) 427.3; Almanacks (Chamberlaine) 429.7; Almanacks (Clark) 430; Almanacks (Dade, W.) 435.20; Almanacks (Dove) 436.3; Almanacks (Evans, J., Philomath) 441.7; Almanacks (Gilden) 448.16; Almanacks (Kidman) 469; Almanacks (Neve, John) 490.7; Almanacks (Perkins) 495.6; Almanacks (Pond) 501.21; Almanacks (Ranger) 503.8; Almanacks (Rivers, P.) 505.5; Almanacks (Smith, J.) 514; Almanacks (Sofford) 515.14; Almanacks (Vaux) 522.11; Almanacks (White) 527.20; Almanacks (Wodhouse, or Wedhouse, or Wydowes, J.) 531.22; Andrewes, J. 588, 589.5; Andrewes, L. 607; Antonio, de Lebrixa 688; Aphthonius 705; Augustine 912, 943; Avila, J. 984, 984.5*, 985, 985.5; B., A. 1017; Bacon, F. 1171; Baker, H. 1218; Ball, J. 1316, 1319; Barckley 1383; Barclay, J. 1399; Barlement 1431.31, 1431.32, 1431.33; Baron, R. 1493; Basse 1551.7; Bayly, L. 1609.4, 1609.5, 1609.6; Beard, T. 1661, 1661.5; Beaumont, F., and Fletcher 1672; Becon 1772; Bedwell 1796, 1798(?); Bernard, R. 1928, 1928.5; Bernard, St. 1909.7*, 1920*, 1921, 1922; Bevin 1986; Bible, English 2295.3*, 2295.4*, 2295.5*, 2295.6*, 2295.8*, 2296, 2297, 2297.2, 2297.3, 2297.5, 2297.6, 2297.7, 2297.9*, 2298, 2298.3, 2300*, 2301*, 2302, 2304*; Bible, N.T., English 2938, 2939, 2940, 2941, 2941.3; Bible, O.T., Psalms 2625, 2626, 2627, 2629, 2630, 2630.5, 2631*, 2632, 2732; Bolton, Robert 3232, 3235, 3238; Book 3324, 3349; Bourne, W. 3431; Boys 3468; Bradford, J., Prebendary of St. Paul's 3499; Brathwait 3565, 3565.5, 3591; Brerewood 3623, 3629; Breton 3643.5, 3651; Brewer 3719; Briggs 3740; Brinsley, J., the Younger 3789, 3790, 3790.5; Burgersdijck 4106; Burges, J. 4113, 4114; Burton, H. 4143, 4151, 4152, 4152.3(A/C); Bury, J. 4180; Byfield, R. 4238; Calvin 4390.4, 4391.3(c.?); Cambridge University 4486; Castalio or Chateillon 4775; Caussin 4873; Celestina 4911, 4911.2;

1631 — *cont.*
Censures 4911.5; Chapman, G. 4992, 4993; Chettle 5125; Christus 5209.5; Cicero 5271.4, 5289, 5303; Clerk 5406; Climsell 5420.5(?); Cockeram 5463; Coke, E. 5524, 5524.3*, 5526.5; Coloma 5576; Cooke, E. 5667; Cornwallis 5780.7*; Cotton, C. 5844, 5845, 5845.3, 5845.5, 5850; Coverte 5897; Cowper 5925*; Craig, A. 5957; Crakanthorp 5983; Craven 6031; Crooke, H. 6063; Crooke, S. 6063.9; Davenant, J. 6301; Davies, J., of Hereford 6344.3*, 6344.5; Dekker 6479, 6516, 6527, 6529; Delamain 6542; Delamothe 6548.6, 6548.8; Deloney 6554; Denison, J. 6589; Denison, S. 6606, 6606.5; Dent, A. 6634, 6645, 6666.7; Dering 6724; Desainliens or Sainliens 6755; Despautere 6780; Dod and Cleaver 6962; Doddridge 6981; Done 7020; Downame, G. 7114; Downame, J. 7127; Draxe 7181; Drayton 7191; Drue 7242; Du Moulin, P., the Elder 7315, 7329; Dyke, D. 7409; Dyke, J. 7419; Edinburgh University 7487.28, 7487.29; Edmonton 7497; Egerton, S. 7535, 7536; Em 7676; England, Appendix 9979; England, Army 7684; England, C. of, Articles 10056; England, C. of, Visit. Articles 10141, 10144, 10182.5, 10189, 10210, 10264, 10270.5, 10276.3, 10316, 10331.5, 10362.5; England, Customs 7694.5(c.?); England, Proclamations, Chron. Ser. 8971, 8973, 8974, 8975, 8976, 8977, 8978, 8979, 8980, 8081, 8982, 8983, 8983.5, 8984(o.s.), 8985(o.s.), 8986(o.s.); England, Public Documents, Misc. 9252, 9252.2, 9252.4, 9254; Erasmus, D. 10452; F., A. 10635; Farnaby, T. 10707; Feltham 10759; Filippi 10866; Fitz-Geffrey, C. 10938, 10939; Fletcher, P. 11083; Florus 11101; Floyd, J. 11109.5, 11112; Fludd 11120; Forbes, J., Captain 11128.5; Forbes, J., of Corse 11138; Foster, T. 11202; Foster, W. 11203; Foxe 11228*; France 11288.5; France—Reformed Churches 11299; Fuller, T., D. D. 11463; Garden 11561.3; Gardiner, R., of Oxford 11566; Gee, J. 11700.5(A/C); Gerhard 11772.5, 11773; Ghesel 11809.5; Gil, A., the Younger 11879.2; Godwin, T. 11954, 11962; Goffe 11980, 11981; Gouge 12115, 12116, 12129; Greene, R. 12258, 12298; Gulielmi 12509; Gurnay 12529; Gustavus II 12532, 12533; Guy, R. 12543.3(?), 12547.9(?); Hall, Joseph 12688, 12688.5; Hariot 12784; Harris, Robert 12834, 12844; Haughton 12933; Hawkins, W. 12966; Hayward, Sir J. 13009; Heigham 13037; Heliodorus 13047, 13047.5; Henshaw 13167, 13167.5; Heresbach 13202; Herle 13205; Heylyn 13272, 13279.5, 13280; Heywood, T. 13313, 13320, 13351; Hippocrates 13519; Hobson 13538.5; Hodges, R. 13548; Hooker, R. 13718*, 13719a*; Horatius Flaccus 13801; Hubert 13902, 13903; Hunt 13990, 13992; I., S., M. A. 14058.7; Ireland, Customs 14128.7*; Ireland, Proc. 14220, 14221, 14222, 14223, 14224(o.s.), 14225(o.s.); Isocrates 14276.5; Jackson, Thomas, of Peterborough 14312; Janua 14471; Jenner 14495; Johnson, Richard 14673, 14684; Johnston, A. 14708.9; Jones, W., of Wight 14741; Jonson 14753.5, 14754*, 14762, 14780; Jorden 14791; Kennedy, J. 14930; Kingsmill, T. 15008; Knevet 15036, 15036a; Knolles 15054; Komensky 15078, 15078.5, 15078a; La Croix 15117.7; Lambard 15162; Lambeth Articles 15183*; Lawson 15331.3; Lawyer 15332; Lenton 15463; Lesly 15510; Lessius 15523; Lever, C. 15539; Lever, Richard 15542a.5; Lewis, Jeremiah 15557.5; Lily, W., 'Lily's Grammar' 15628*, 15628.3*; Littleton, E. 15718; Liturgies, C. of Eng., BCP 16383, 16384, 16384.7, 16385; Liturgies, C. of Eng., Ordinal 16472; Liturgies, C. of Eng., Spec. Prayers 16549.5, 16550; Liturgies, C. of Eng., St. Services 16485.7, 16497.7; Liturgies, Latin Rite, Hours and Primers 16099, 16100; Lloyd, D. 16614; London, Ords. and Regs. 16732, 16733; Loper 16804; Loque 16811; Louis XIII 16847.5; Love 16856.7(c.); Lucanus 16888; Luna 16928; Lundie 16930; Lupton, T. 16961; Lyly 17066; Magdeburg 17181.7(A/C), 17181.9(A/C); Markham, G. 17339, 17340*, 17344, 17353, 17364, 17368, 17374, 17378*, 17396; Marlowe 17436; Marston 17478, 17478a; Massinger and Dekker 17645; May, T. 17716; Mayer 17730, 17730.5, 17731.3, 17731.7; Mestrezat 17845; Mico 17863, 17863.1(A/C); Minucius Felix 17951; Montagu, H. 18023.5, 18024; Montaigne 18043*; More, C. 18066(?); Morley, T. 18124; Morray 18166(?), 18167; Morton, T., Bp. 18189; Moses 18206; Mucedorus 18239; Murrell 18302.5; N., N. 18329; Netherlands, States Gen. 18463; Newsbooks, Num. 18507.208, 18507.209, 18507.210, 18507.211, 18507.212, 18507.213, 18507.214, 18507.215, 18507.216, 18507.217, 18507.218, 18507.219, 18507.220, 18507.221, 18507.222,

1631 — *cont.*
18507.223, 18507.224, 18507.225, 18507.226, 18507.227, 18507.228, 18507.229, 18507.230, 18507.231, 18507.232, 18507.233, 18507.234, 18507.235; Nicholes 18531; Nicolai, P. 18573; Norden 18631; Norwood 18692; Nottingham 18699.3(?); Optatus 18832; Oughtred 18898; Ovidius Naso 18929.5, 18954; Oxford Univ., Verses, etc. 19032.5; Page, S. 19092; Page, W. 19096, 19096a; Paglia 19116.5; Pareus 19194, 19194.5, 19194.7; Parker, Martin 19217.5, 19259(?); Parsons, B. 19346; Parsons, R. 19388a; Partridge, John 19437; Pedantius 19524; Pellham, E. 19566; Pemble 19582, 19588; Perkins, W. 19652.5, 19653, 19653.5, 19653a, 19653b, 19653b.5, 19706; Peters, H. 19798.3; Philippson 19851; Pilkington, G. 19925; Pinke 19942; Plutarch 20070; Pope 20110; Powel, Griffinus 20157.5; Powell, T., Londino-Cambrensis 20168; Preston, J. 20209*, 20210, 20229, 20231, 20232, 20244, 20255, 20256, 20271, 20271a, 20272, 20280.3, 20280.5, 20280.7, 20281; Price, L. 20320; Primerosius 20382; Puckell 20484; Quarles 20549; Randall 20683; Randolph 20688; Ravisius 20761.7, 20761.9; Record, R. 20808.5; Reeve, E. 20829; Relations 20865; Reynolds, E. 20934, 20934.5, 20935*; Reynolds, J., of the Mint 20948; Richards, N. 21010.3; Robinson, J., Preacher 21117; Rodriguez 21145, 21146, 21150.5; Rogers, Henry, of Sussex 21178.7; Rogers, Richard 21211; Rogers, Timothy 21243, 21247.5; Rolland 21257; Rous, the Elder 21339, 21342.5; Rowlands, S. 21371; Rudimenta 21439; Russell, J., Cornhoarder 21457(?); Sailor 21551.3(?); Saint Andrews Univ. 21555.40, 21555.41; Saltonstall, W. 21645; Sanderson, R. 21703; Scheibler 21814.5; Scotland, proclamations 21989; Scribonius 22112, 22112.5; Scudder 22117; Second eighty-eight 22142.7; Selden 22169, 22178; Seton, J. 22257; Shakespeare, W. 22295, 22327; Sharpham 22387; Shepherds' Kalendar 22423; Shirley, J. 22456; Sibbes 22480, 22481; Simotta 22561; Sisters 22581; Slatyer 22635; Smith, H., Minister, Collections 22732; Smith, H., Minister, Single Works 22674; Smith, John, Gov. of Virginia 22787, 22790c.5; Smith, R., Bp. of Chalcedon 22810; Smith, S., Minister in Essex 22840.7, 22849.3; Smith, William, of Crissing-Temple 22871a.5; Snawsel 22887; Song 22919.3(?); Sorocold 22934.3; Sparke, M. 23017.3*; Speed, John 23040, 23043*, 23048.5; Speed, John, Genealogies 23039d.13(?), 23039e.9; Speed, Joshua 23050; Stanbridge, Vocabula 23193; Stephens 23251; Stow 23340*; Strachan 23347; Strada 23351; Stubbes 23392; Sutton, T. 23505; T., A. 23605; T., A., Practitioner in Physic 23610*, 23611; Table 23636; Talaeus 23661; Tapp 23682; Taylor, John 23732, 23745, 23745.5, 23775.5, 23811.7; Taylor, Thomas 23824, 23850a, 23851; Terentius 23889.4C (A/C); Thomas, O. 24007a; Thomas, T. 24017.5; Timberlake 24086; Townshend 24155*, 24155a*, 24156*; Treasurer 24214; Tuvil or Toutevile 24398; Twisse 24402, 24403(?); Urban VIII 24522.5, 24524; Ussher, J. 24544, 24544.5, 24548, 24549, 24550, 24554a, 24555; Vicars, J., Poet 24697; Vicars, T. 24701; Vincent, Saint 24748.5, 24749; Vossius 24881.5, 24882, 24884; W., H. 24905; Walkington 24968(?); Webbe, G. 25166.7; Webster, J. 25179; Weever 25223; Widdowes 25593*, 25595; Wife 25610.5(?); Willet 25688; Wilson, J., Preacher 25768.5(A/C), 25770, 25770.5; Wither, Poet 25907.5(c.)(A/C); Yates, John 26087.

1632

Advice 156, 156.3, 156.7; Alabaster 249, 250; Albertus Magnus 266.5; Almanacks (Allestree) 407.15; Almanacks (Bowker or Booker) 419.1; Almanacks (Butler) 427.4; Almanacks (Dade, W.) 435.21; Almanacks (Gilden) 448.17; Almanacks (Neve, John) 490.8; Almanacks (Perkins) 495.7; Almanacks (Pond) 501.22; Almanacks (Sofford) 515.15; Almanacks (Vaux) 522.12; Almanacks (White) 527.21, 527.22; Almanacks (Woodhouse, or Wedhouse, or Wydowes, J.) 531.23; Almanacks 405.7; Alphabets 536(?) [not STC]; Ames 551*, 554; Andrewes, J. 595.10; Andrewes, L. 607.5, 608; Aspley 861.3; Assize of Bread 882; Attersoll 900; Aurelius 961; Avila, J. 986; B., R. 1056; Bacon, F. 1150; Ball, J. 1313.5, 1320; Banquet 1368.5(?); Barley-Corn 1433.3(?); Barlow, J. 1435, 1435.5; Bayly, L. 1610, 1610.3; Becon 1773; Bel 1802; Bell, A. 1812; Benedict 1860; Bernard, R. 1930, 1950; Bernard, St. 1909.7*,

1632 — *cont.*
1920*; Bible, English 2297.9*, 2298.5, 2298.7*, 2300*, 2301*, 2302*, 2302.3, 2302.5, 2303*, 2304*, 2304.5, 2305*, 2308*; Bible, N.T., English 2941.5; Bible, N.T., Greek 2796, 2797; Bible, O.T., Psalms 2631*, 2633, 2634, 2635, 2636, 2636.3, 2637, 2637.2, 2637.3, 2637.4, 2637.6, 2637.8, 2638, 2646*, 2717, 2718, 2719, 2734, 2734.5, 2735; Bill, J. 3059.6; Binet 3073.3; Biondi 3075; Bloys 3140; Bolton, Robert 3242; Brabourne 3473; Brahe 3538, 3538.5; Brathwait 3575; Brereley 3608.5; Brerewood 3624; Breton 3638, 3644.5, 3663; Brinsley, J., the Elder 3784; Brome 3819; Broughton, Richard 3898; Bruele 3929; Buchler 3993; Burton, H. 4140; Burton, R. 4162; Burton, W., Master of Kingston Grammar School 4165; Byfield, N. 4236.3, 4236.9; Caddell and Harris 4326.5; Cambridge University 4475*; Cambridge University, Act Verses 4474.66R (c.?)(A/C), 4474.103M(c.?)(A/C), 4474.120A(c.?); Camden 4516; Campian 4535; Camus 4552, 4553; Canne 4574.5; Capell 4600; Carier 4625; Carpenter, J., Gent. 4661; Catechism 4803.2; Caussin 4871; Chetwind 5127.5; Choice 5143(?); Clarke, J., B.D. 5355; Climsell 5428.5(?), 5429.5(?); Closet 5438; Cockeram 5464; Colman, W. 5569(?); Cordier 5760; Cornwallis 5780.7*, 5781; Cotgrave 5831; Countryman 5872.5(c.); Cowper 5925*, 5930.4, 5941; Craig, J. 5967, 5967.3; Crompton, W. 6061; Crooke, S. 6067.7; Cruso 6099; Cupid 6123; Cyprian 6154; Dalechamp 6192; Davies, J., of Mallwyd 6347, 6347.2; Daye 6435; Declinationes Graecae 6456.8; Dekker 6491; Delamain 6544; Deloney 6571; Denison, S. 6600; Desainliens or Sainliens 6756; Despautere 6784; Dod and Cleaver 6978; Dod 6948; Donne, J. 7031; Downame, J. 7128; Downing, C. 7156; Drexelius 7235; Du Moulin, P., the Elder 7330; Dyke, J. 7417, 7420, 7427; E., T. 7437; East India Company 7450, 7450a, 7453; Edinburgh University 7487.30; England, C. of, Articles 10057*; England, C. of, Visit. Articles 10174, 10227.3, 10273, 10280, 10311, 10323, 10323.7(?), 10369; England, Proclamations, Chron. Ser. 8984, 8985, 8986, 8987, 8988, 8989, 8990, 8991, 8992, 8993, 8994, 8994.5, 8995(o.s.), 8996(o.s.), 8997(o.s.); England, Public Documents, Misc. 9254.3(?); England, Statutes, Gen. Colls. 9329; Espagne 10530, 10531; Exercise 10615.5(A/C); Falconer 10677; Faret 10686; Featley, J. 10741; Fenton, E. 10788.7; Fletcher, G., the younger 11060; Fletcher, P. 11080, 11085; Forbes, J., Minister 11133, 11135; Forbes, J., of Corse 11144; Foxe 11228*, 11228.3; Francis, of Sales 11316; Freake 11346.3, 11346.5*; Gerhard 11767; Gerhard 11769, 11774; German Theology 11786; Gil, A., the Younger 11879.4, 11879.6, 11879.8, 11879.9; Goffe 11977; Goodman, N. 12027; Gore 12083; Gossips 12092.6(c.); Gouge 12125; Graile 12172; Green 12213; Greene, R. 12291; Greenland 12326; Grosse 12393, 12393.5; Grotius 12400; Gues 12455.5; Guiana 12456; Guillim 12502; Gustavus II 12531.7, 12534.2, 12534.4; Guy, R. 12544(?); Hakewill 12620; Hall, Joseph 12702*; Harflete 12771; Harris, P. 12809; Harris, Robert 12854.5, 12855; Harsnet, A. 12873, 12877; Hausted 12935; Hawkins, H. 12957; Hawkins, W. 12964.5, 12967; Hayne 12976; Hayward, Sir J. 12993; Heaven 13018.7; Henric 13071; Henshaw 13168; Hewes 13261; Heylyn 13268; Heywood, T. 13314, 13322, 13334, 13340, 13340.5, 13347; Hieron 13383.5*, 13404, 13414a; Hildebrandt 13458; Hildersam 13462; Hiud 13532; Hobson 13538.5*; Hooker, R. 13718*, 13719*, 13719a*, 13719b*; Hooker, T. 13735, 13735.5; Horne, R., of Ludlow 13822; Hostess 13843(?); Hughes, G. 13913; Hughes, R. 13920a(c.); Hume, P. 13955.5; I., E. 14048; Ireland, Customs 14128.7*; Ireland, Laws 14134.3; Ireland, Proc. 14224, 14225, 14226, 14227; James I 14360.5; James, R. 14442; Jay 14479.3; Jesus Christ 14555*; Joceline 14625.5; Johnson, T., Botanist 14702; Johnston, A. 14710, 14714; Jorden 14792; Josephus 14812, 14812a; Juan 14830.7, 14831, 14831a; Kilby, R., of Derby 14956.3; L., W. 15115; La Ramee 15249; Lass 15264; Layfielde 15334; Lechmere, E. 15347.5, 15349; Lenton 15463.5; Levens 15534; Lily, W., 'Lily's Grammar' 15628.3*, 15628.5, 15628.7*; Lithgow 15712.5, 15713; Liturgies, C. of Eng., BCP 16385.7, 16386, 16386.7, 16387, 16388, 16388a, 16388a.5, 16389, 16390*, 16391*; Liturgies, C. of Eng., Spec. Prayers 16550.3; Liturgies, Latin Rite, Hours and Primers 16101, 16101.2; Liturgies, Latin Rite, Manuals 16161.5; Livingstone 16611; London, Coll. of Physicians 16775; Lovell, R. 16857.9

1632 — *cont.*
(A/C); Luis 16922a.3; Lupton, D. 16944; Luther 16986; Lyly 17088, 17089; Lynde 17096, 17100a; M., S. 17150; M., W. 17154.5; Maffei 17181; Mainwaringe 17202(?); Makcouldy 17206.5; Mandeville 17253.5; Marmion 17443, 17443.5; Mary, the Blessed Virgin—Monastery at Brussels 17552; Mason, John, of Cambridge 17618; Massinger and Field 17646; Massinger 17636, 17638, 17638.5; Matthieu 17666; Mayer 17730.2(A/C), 17730.3(A/C), 17740; Mede 17767; Monday 18008; Montaigne 18043*; Montfort 18048; Newsbooks, Num. 18507.236, 18507.237, 18507.238, 18507.239, 18507.240, 18507.241, 18507.242, 18507.243, 18507.244, 18507.245, 18507.246, 18507.247, 18507.248, 18507.249, 18507.250, 18507.251, 18507.252, 18507.253, 18507.254, 18507.255, 18507.256, 18507.257, 18507.258, 18507.259, 18507.260, 18507.261, 18507.262, 18507.263, 18507.264, 18507.265, 18507.266, 18507.267, 18507.268, 18507.269, 18507.270, 18507.271, 18507.272, 18507.273, 18507.274, 18507.275, 18507.276; Nicholes 18531.3; Norden 18609; Ofwod 18789(A/C); Oughtred 18899, 18899a, 18899c.5; Overbury 18918; Ovidius Naso 18966; Oxford Univ., Quaestiones 19016.13; Packer 19086; Pagit 19109.3; Parker, Martin 19250, 19252, 19253, 19260, 19274.5(?), 19275(?); Parr, E. 19311; Parsons, R. 19390; Pasquil 19453(?); Patrick, St. 19474(?); Paynter 19496.5; Pecke, R. 19522.5; Pelegromius 19563; Pemble 19585, 19587; Peregrin 19622b.5; Perkins, W. 19674, 19694, 19718.5, 19747, 19763; Peter, of Alcantara, St. 19794; Platt 19985; Platus or Piatti 20001, 20001.5; Porter, J. 20124; Porter, W. 20124.5; Preston, J. 20211, 20215, 20221.5, 20221.7, 20222*, 20233, 20257; Price, L. 20315, 20319, 20321(c.), 20323; Puget de la Serre 20492; Puttock 20520; Quarles 20527, 20527.5, 20529, 20534*, 20535*; Raleigh 20641.5, 20642, 20642.5; Randolph 20692, 20692a; Record, R. 20809; Records 20822.5; Reeve, T. 20832, 20832.3, 20832.5; Reynolds, E. 20927, 20935*; Reynolds, H. 20939; Reynolds, J., of the Mint 20950; Richards, N. 21010.7; Rock 21138.5(?); Rodriguez 21147, 21150; Rogers, D. 21166; Rogers, J., of Dedham 21187.5, 21192; Rogers, N. 21198, 21200, 21202; Rogers, Richard 21212; Rogers, Timothy 21248; Ross 21329; Rowlands, S. 21379; Rowley, S. 21420; Rowley, W. 21423; Rowzee 21426; Safeguard 21550.5; Saint Andrews Univ. 21555.42, 21555.43; Saluste du Bartas 21654*; Sanderson, R. 21706; Sandys, G. 21729; Sandys, Sir E. 21719, 21720; Schomberg 21820; Schonaeus 21823; Schoolhouse 21826.4; Sclater, the Elder 21832; Sennertus 22231; Shakespeare, W. 22274, 22274a, 22274b, 22274c, 22274d, 22274e, 22274e.3*, 22274e.5*, 22286, 22352; Shirley, J. 22437; Sibbes 22482; Simson, Andrew, Minister 22563; Smith, H., Minister, Collections 22746, 22782; Smith, H., Minister, Single Works 22675, 22711.7; Smith, John, Gov. of Virginia 22790d; Smith, John, of Clavering 22801; Smith, M. 22808; Smith, S., Minister in Essex 22834, 22845.3, 22847; Spagnuoli 22986; Speed, John 23036(?)*, 23049; Speed, John, Genealogies 23039a.4(?), 23039d.14(+?), 23039e.10, 23039f.5(?); Stanhope, M. 23226; Stow 23340*; Strode 23365; Struther 23369; Stubbe 23374; Stubbes 23392.5; Sussex 23445.5(?); Sutton, T. 23507; Sweden 23517.5, 23518; Swedish Devotion 23519; Swedish Discipline 23519.5, 23520; Swedish Intelligencer 23521, 23522, 23523, 23524, 23524a; Synge 23604; T., T., Sacristan 23630; Tapp 23682.5; Taylor, John 23803; Taylor, Thomas 23834, 23847; Tomkis 24108; Torsellino 24140; Torshell 24143; Townshend 24155*, 24155a*, 24156*; Tuke 24314.7; Twisse 24400; Ussher, J. 24557; Velleius Paterculus 24633; Virgilius Maro 24793, 24809; Walkley 24975; Wedderburn 25192; Weemes 25207.3, 25207.5, 25212, 25213a, 25214, 25215, 25217.3; West, W. 25276; White, Josias 25399.5; Willet 25684*; Williamson, R. 25737; Willis, J., Stenographer 25746; Wing 25845; Wither, Poet 25912*; Witherings, J. 25930; Wooer 25972.8(?); Xenophon 26068.

1633

A.B.C. 21, 22.5; Aberdeen Univ. 71.18; Adams 108; Advice 156a; Aesop 173.7; Agas 194.5(?); Airay, C. 242; Alabaster 246, 251; Aleman 291*; Aleyn 352; Almanacks (Allestree) 407.16; Almanacks (Bowker or Booker) 419.2; Almanacks (Clark) 430.2; Almanacks (Dade, W.) 435.22; Almanacks (Dove) 436.5; Almanacks (Kidman)

1633 — *cont.*
469.2; Almanacks (Neve, John) 490.9; Almanacks (Perkins) 495.8; Almanacks (Pond) 501.23; Almanacks (Rivers, P.) 505.7; Almanacks (Sofford) 515.16; Almanacks (Swallow) 517.1; Almanacks (Turner) 518; Almanacks (Vaux) 522.13; Almanacks (White) 527.23; Almanacks (Wilson) 529.7; Almanacks (Winter) 530; Almanacks (Woodhouse, or Wedhouse, or Wydowes, J.) 531.24; Ames 551*, 555, 561; Anderton 577, 579; Andrewes, L. 600; Arden, A. 732(?); Arden, T. 735, 735.3; Ariosto 748*; Aristeas 750, 750.5; Attersoll 891, 900.5; Audeley 903.5, 904.5; Bacon, F. 1166; Baker, J., Royalist 1222.5(?); Balcanquhall 1237; Ball, J. 1317; Bancroft, T. 1353; Banister, J. 1357, 1357.5, 1361; Banquet 1372; Barclay, J. 1400; Barker, P. 1426; Baron, R. 1495; Barri [Borri] 1504, 1504.5; Bartholinus 1535, 1535.5; Bayly, L. 1610.5, 1611, 1612(?); Bellarmino 1844; Bernard, St. 1923; Bible, Appendix 3031.5; Bible, English 2177*, 2303*, 2305*, 2306*, 2307, 2308*, 2309, 2310, 2311, 2311a; Bible, N.T., English 2942, 2943, 2944.5(A/C), 2945, 2945.3, 2945.5, 2946, 2947; Bible, N.T., Greek 2798, 2798.5; Bible, N.T., Latin 2813, 2813.3; Bible, O.T., 'Books of Solomon' 2767; Bible, O.T., Psalms 2499.4, 2639, 2640, 2641, 2641.5, 2641.7, 2642, 2644, 2645, 2645.3, 2645.7, 2646*, 2647, 2648, 2653.5*, 2720, 2721, 2721.3, 2721.5; Bolton, Robert 3236, 3243; Boyd, A. 3443; Boyd, Z. 3445a.5(?), 3447.5; Bradford, J., Prebendary of St. Paul's 3493; Bradshaw, W. 3515*; Bradwell 3535; Brathwait 3564, 3576; Breton 3692; Broughton, Richard 3894; Bruton, E. 3945.7; Butler, C. 4190, 4195; Butler, R. 4204; Byfield, N. 4223; C., B., Catholic priest 4264; C., W., Bachelor of Civil Law 4323.6; Cambridge University 4475*, 4480, 4489.7, 4491; Camden 4517 [not STC]; Camus 4554; Capel 4595; Carpenter, N. 4670, 4673; Castalio or Chateillon 4776; Catlin 4839; Charles I, King 5023; Cicero 5272(?); Clarke, J., B.D. 5354; Clement I 5398; Climsell 5429(?); Cobbes 5454; Cole, N. 5537; Colom 5575.2; Combachius 5591; Cordier 5761; Cotton, C. 5850.5; Cowley 5906; Cowper 5941.5; Crashaw, W. 6022; Crompton, W. 6057; Cuffe 6104; Culmann 6106.5; Culverwell 6110.3, 6118, 6118.8; Cupid 6122.4; Cyprian 6153; Davis or Davys, J. 6371; Day, John, Dramatist 6414; Delamain 6543(?); Delamothe 6549; Deloney 6562; Dent, A. 6634.5, 6646, 6646.2; Desainliens or Sainliens 6766; Devereux 6789; Dionysius, Periegetes 6900; Ditty 6926(?), 6927(?); Dix 6929.5; Dod 6937; Donne, J. 7032, 7032a, 7043, 7044, 7045; Dort, Synod of 7069; Douglas, W. 7076; Downame, G. 7121; Downame, J. 7128.5(?), 7128.7, 7137*; Downe 7152; Downing, C. 7157; Draxe 7175; Drexelius 7234.5, 7238; Dyer, R. 7393.5, 7393.6(A/C); Dyke, D. 7394.5, 7405; Earle 7444; Edinburgh University 7486; Egerton, S. 7536.1; England, C. of, Articles 10058, 10058.5*; England, C. of, Constitutions/Canons 10076, 10077*, 10078*, 10078.3*, 10078.5*, 10078.7*, 10078.9*; England, C. of, Visit. Articles 10137.7(?), 10147.7, 10167(?), 10182.7(?), 10189.5(?), 10227.5, 10280.3, 10296, 10296.7(?), 10317, 10342, 10363, 10363.7(?), 10380; England, Privy Council 7755; England, Proclamations, Chron. Ser. 8995, 8996, 8997, 8998, 8999, 9000, 9000.3(?), 9001, 9002, 9003, 9004, 9005(o.s.), 9006(o.s.), 9007(o.s.), 9008(o.s.), 9009(o.s.), 9010(o.s.), 9011(o.s.), 9012(o.s.); England, Public Documents, Misc. 9254.7, 9256, 9256.5(o.s.); Estwick 10556; Etten 10558.5; Evan 10581.5, 10582; Evans, W., of Oxford 10597; F., A. 10635.3, 10635.5; Falconer 10676; Fale 10681; Farewell 10687; Farnaby, T. 10704; Featley, D. 10728; Fisher, Jasper 10886; Fletcher, G., the elder 11054; Fletcher, P. 11082, 11082.5; Forbes, W. 11151.5; Ford, J. 11156, 11164, 11165; Forde, E. 11167; Fosbroke 11199; Francklin 11327; Fulke 11432; Gaetani 11514; Geare 11692.7; Gerard, J. 11751; Gerhard 11770; Glasgow University 11916; Godwin, T. 11963; Goffe 11982; Gomersall 11993; Goodfellow, R. 12015.5(?); Grave, J. 12198; Gregory, Monk 12344; Greville, F. 12361; Griffith 12368, 12369, 12369.5, 12370; Guarini 12416; Guild 12480; Gustavus II 12532.5, 12534, 12537; Gutta 12539; Guy, R. 12547(?); Hakewill 12623; Hall, Joseph 12639*, 12640.5*, 12646a.5, 12689, 12702*, 12704; Handson 12743.5; Harris, P. 12808, 12810; Harrison, John 12860; Harsnet, A. 12878; Hart, James 12888; Hausted 12936; Hawkins, H. 12958; Herbert, E. 13180; Herbert, George 13183, 13184, 13184.5, 13185; Hewes 13259; Hexham 13263; Heylyn 13273, 13281; Heywood, T.

1633 — *cont.*
13315, 13339, 13348; Hieron 13383.5*; Hildersam 13459; Hill, W. 13505; Hipolito 13517; Hippocrates 13518, 13518.5; Hoard 13534, 13534.5; Hodson or Hodgson, W. 13552.5; Holland, Henry, Bookseller 13584; Holyday 13614; Holyoke 13620; Homilies 13660, 13660.5*, 13676, 13676a*; Hume, D. 13952.5(?); Hunt 13988; Indagine 14077b; Introduction 14123.5; Ireland, Proc. 14228, 14229, 14230, 14231, 14232, 14233(o.s.), 14234(o.s.); Isaacson 14269; James, R. 14439; James, T., Capt. 14444; Johnson, John, of Colchester 14670.3, 14670.5; Johnson, Robert, B. D. 14692, 14692.5; Johnson, Robert, Chaplain 14694.7; Johnston, A. 14713; Jones, J., M. A. 14722; Jones, W., of Wight 14744.5, 14748; Jorden 14793; Juvenalis 14892; Keilwey 14902; Kellet 14903; King, W. 14998.7 (c.); Komensky 15079, 15079.5; Kyd 15094; Lambard 15162.3; Lancicius 15188.7; Langham 15196; Langhorne 15200; Latham 15267.7, 15268.7; Leigh, D. 15407; Leigh, E. 15411; Lemnius 15458; Lily, W., 'Lily's Grammar' 15628.7*, 15633.6(?); Lithgow 15716; Littleton, T. 15786; Liturgies, C. of Eng., BCP 16390*, 16391*, 16392, 16392.5, 16393, 16393.5, 16393.7, 16394, 16394.3, 16394.7, 16395, 16396*, 16397*; Liturgies, C. of Eng., Catechism 16461; Liturgies, C. of Eng., Ordinal 16473; Liturgies, C. of Eng., Spec. Prayers 16550.5, 16550.7; Liturgies, Latin Rite, Hours and Primers 16101.4, 16101.6; Liturgies, Other Protest. C. 16597; Llyfr Plygain 16640, 16640.5; London, Appendix 16755.5; London, Diocese of 16776.16(+); London, Ords. and Regs. 16733.3(?); Lover 16861(?), 16864a(?); Lovers 16865.3(c.); Luis 16915*, 16917; M., J., Mr. 17142; M., P., Gentleman 17145; Maltbey 17216; Markham, G. 17345, 17384, 17396.5(?); Markham, G., and Machin 17400; Marlowe 17412; Marmion 17442; Marston 17471, 17472; Martialis 17493; Martin, G. 17506.5; Martin, Robert 17512; Mascall 17588; Mason, G., Merchant 17600.7; Massinger 17639; Matthieu 17663; May, E., Gent. 17708; May, T. 17712, 17714, 17714a, 17715; Mercator and Hondius 17827*; Mercer 17828.5; Monipennie 18015, 18015.5; Monlas 18020; Montagu, H. 18026; More, T. 18087; Morray 18168; Morton, D. 18171.5*; Morton, T., Bp. 18182; Nash, T., Philopolites 18382; Nero 18431; Newsbooks, Amsterdam 18507.359, 18507.360, 18507.361; Nightingale 18580; Norden 18626a.8, 18631.5; Nothing 18699(?); Nowell, Middle Catechism 18724, 18737; Nowell, Shorter Catechism 18711c; Openshaw 18828.5, 18830.9; Origan 18845, 18845a; Osiander, L. 18881; Otes 18896; Oughtred 18899b, 18899c, 18901; Ovidius Naso 18952.8, 18979; Owen, John 18991; Oxford Univ., Quaestiones 19016.14; Oxford Univ., Verses, etc. 19033, 19034, 19034a, 19035, 19035a, 19035a.5; Paglia 19117; Panter 19172.7, 19173; Paracelsus 19182, 19182.5; Paragon 19186; Parker, Martin 19225, 19228, 19233, 19248, 19251; Parr, E. 19311.5, 19317; Parsons, B. 19345; Parsons, R. 19354.9, 19389; Partridge, John 19432; Patriarchs 19472; Pavonius 19487; Pemble 19575, 19580.5; Perkins, W. 19719; Playfere 20003.5, 20004; Polybius 20098; Potter, C. 20135, 20135.3, 20135.7; Preston, J. 20222*, 20230, 20233a, 20235, 20236, 20245, 20258, 20262, 20263*, 20275, 20276; Price, L. 20313, 20324; Prompter 20433; Prynne 20464, 20464a; Quarles 20530, 20534*; R., I., or J. 20573(?), 20576; Raleigh 20643, 20643.5, 20644; Ramsay, A. 20656; Ramsay, D. 20659; Randol 20684; Ravisius 20765*; Records 20821(?); Reusner 20908; Reynolds, J., of the Mint 20951; Rickets 21025(?); Rider, J. 21036a; Robertson, G. 21099; Roe, N. 21151; Rogers, D. 21167, 21169; Rogers, F. 21175, 21176; Rogers, J., of Dedham 21188; Rogers, Thomas, M. A. 21232; Rome 21300; Rous, the Elder 21347.7; Rowley, W. 21421, 21425; Rudimenta 21440; Ryves 21475; Saint Paul's Cathedral 21591.3(?); Saluste du Bartas 21654*; Salvianus 21675; Sanford 21739; Schloer 21819; Sclater, the Elder 21848; Scot, T., of Ipswich 21873; Scotland, proclamations 21990, 21991, 21992, 21993, 21994, 21995; Scotland, statutes, etc. 21902, 21902.5*; Scott, M. 22063; Scudder 22118, 22122; Sea Piece 22140.5; Shelton 22404.1; Shirley, J. 22436, 22439, 22458.5, 22459, 22459a.5, 22459b, 22461, 22462; Sibbes 22507*; Sidney, P. 22549; Smith, John, of Clavering 22799; Smith, S., A. M. 22831.3; Smith, S., Minister in Essex 22845.4(A/C), 22849.5; Smith, T., Doctor of Civil Laws 22865; Sonnet 22925(?); Speed, John, Genealogies 23039e.11; Sprint, J., Vicar 23108.6; Stafford, T. 23132,

1633 — *cont.*
23132a; Stanbridge, Vocabula 23193.2; Stevens 23260; Stow 23345, 23345.5*; Struther 23371; Stubbes 23393; Susanna 23436(c.?) (A/C); Sutton, T. 23503; Sweden 23518.5; Swedish Intelligencer 23525, 23525.1, 23525.3, 23525.4; Syms 23596; Tayler, F., B. D. 23717; Taylor, John 23732.3; Taylor, Thomas 23823, 23847.5, 23856; Terentius 23889.5, 23889.6; Themylthorp 23934.19(A/C); Thomas, a Kempis 23991; Thrace 24047; Torshell 24142; Tozer 24158; Tritheim 24285.5; Trogus Pompeius 24289; Tunstall 24323; Twisse 24401; Typing 24473, 24473.3*; Ursinus, Z. 24539, 24539.3, 24539.5, 24539.7; Vaughan, W. 24618; Vesey 24695; Vicars, T. 24699; Vicary 24712; Virel 24772.5; Virgilius Maro 24819; Vives 24854; Ware, J. 25067, 25067a; Warford 25071; Way 25137; Webbe, G. 25167; Wedderburn 25190*, 25194; Weemes 25207, 25211.3, 25216; White, Andrew 25375a.10; Whore 25582, 25582a; Widdrington 25600; Wigmore 25617; Willet 25684*, 25685, 25685a, 25685a.3, 25685a.5, 25687; Wischart 25866; Wither, Poet 25912*, 25912.5, 25929; Wotton, H. 26010, 26010.5.

1634

Abbot, G., Abp. 31, 31.5*; Aberdeen Univ. 71.19, 71.19A, 71.39; Aesop 184, 188.5; Age 197; Aleman 291*, 291.5; Almanacks (Allestree) 407.17; Almanacks (Bowker or Booker) 419.3; Almanacks (Clark) 430.3; Almanacks (Dade, W.) 435.23; Almanacks (Dove) 436.6; Almanacks (Kidman) 469.3; Almanacks (Neve, John) 490.10; Almanacks (Perkins) 495.9; Almanacks (Pierce) 496; Almanacks (Pond) 501.24; Almanacks (Rivers, P.) 505.8; Almanacks (Sofford) 515.17; Almanacks (Swallow) 517.2; Almanacks (Turner) 518.2; Almanacks (Vaux) 522.14; Almanacks (White) 527.24; Almanacks (Wilson) 529.8; Almanacks (Winter) 530.3; Almanacks (Woodhouse, or Wedhouse, or Wydowes, J.) 531.25; Ames 551.5; Anderton 580; Andrewes, J. 595.1; Andrewes, L. 609*; Antichrist 674; Ap-Robert 716*; Arcandam 729; Arguments 739; Ariosto 748*; Aristotle 755, 765.5; Arthur, King 806; Augustine 948.5; Aurelius Antoninus 962; Babylon 1101; Bacon, F. 1129; Balcanquhall 1238, 1241; Banquet 1369; Barclay, J. 1391, 1397; Barlement 1431.34; Barrough 1515; Barry, G. 1528; Barton, J. 1540; Barton, W. 1541; Basse 1552*; Bastwick 1571.5; Bate, J., Mechanician 1577, 1577.5; Bayly, L. 1612.5; Baynes, P. 1636; Beaumont, F., and Fletcher 1684; Beggar 1799(?); Bernard, R. 1931, 1950.5; Bethune, P. 1977; Bible, English 2306*, 2311a*, 2312, 2313, 2313a, 2313b, 2313b.5*, 2314, 2314.3, 2314.5, 2315*, 2316, 2316.5*, 2318*; Bible, O.T., Psalms 2416, 2649, 2650, 2650.5, 2651, 2651a, 2652, 2653, 2653.5*, 2654, 2654.5; Birckbek 3082; Blaxton 3129, 3129.5, 3129.7, 3129.8(A/C), 3129a; Blue Cap 3140.5 (?); Boccaccio 3174; Bolton, Robert 3225, 3253, 3255; Bond, H. 3274; Book 3302; Bradshaw, W. 3515*; Brathwait 3553, 3587; Brereley 3605.5(bef.), 3605.7; Breton 3693; Browne, T. 3912, 3912.5; Burton, W., Minister at Reading 4177; Butler, C. 4191, 4194; Byfield, N. 4230; C., N. 4294; Cacoethes 4326; Calvert 4371; Calvin 4425; Cambridge University 4485, 4485.3; Camden 4499, 4517.3; Canne 4574; Carew, T., Poet 4618; Cato 4849.6; Caussin 4874; Christ's Hospital 5209; Christianity 5194.7; Cicero 5303.2; Clarke, J., B.D. 5357; Clavell 5371; Climsell 5416(?), 5421(?); Comedy 5600; Cosin, R. 5825; Cotton, J. 5855; Crakanthorp 5984; Crashaw, R. 6009; Culverwell 6112; D., I. or J. 6168.5, 6171(?); Daniel, S. 6252; Davenant, J. 6294, 6294.5*(A/C), 6301.5; Davenport, J. 6311; Death 6443.5; Denison, J. 6595; Denison, S. 6602; Dering 6724.5; Devotion 6798.3; Dickson, D. 6825.5; Digges, L. 6856; Digges, T. 6874; Direction 6902; Discourse 6911.5; Dod 6938.5, 6949, 6949.3; Donne, J. 7029, 7036, 7056, 7058; Downame, G. 7122; Downame, J. 7137*; Downing, C. 7158; Du Moulin, P., the Elder 7321, 7321.5, 7322.5; Dyke, D. 7406; Edinburgh 7484; Elton 7618; Emanuel, Prince of Portugal 7678; England, C. of, Articles 10059; England, C. of, Visit. Articles 10135, 10147.8, 10147.10(?), 10177, 10183, 10185.5, 10211, 10216, 10265, 10271(?), 10276.7, 10318, 10372.7(?); England, Local Courts 7725.3; England, Proclamations, Chron. Ser. 9005, 9006, 9007, 9008, 9009, 9010, 9011,9012,9013, 9014, 9015, 9015.5, 9016, 9017, 9018, 9019, 9020,

1634 — *cont.*
9021, 9021.5, 9022, 9023, 9024, 9025, 9026, 9027, 9028, 9029, 9031(o.s.), 9032(o.s.), 9033(o.s.); England, Public Documents, Misc. 9256.5, 9258; Erasmus, D. 10463; Evans, J., Minister 10587; Falconer 10676.5; Farnaby, T. 10702; Fawkner 10720, 10723; Feltham 10760; Fenton, E. 10789; Fisher, T. 10918.5; Fitz-Geffrey, C. 10935; Fleming, G. 11052; Fletcher, John 11070; Fletcher, John, and Shakespeare 11075; Ford, J. 11157; Forde, E. 11170; Fulke 11439; G., G. 11494; Garthwait 11633; Gerhard 11771; Godwin, T. 11955; Gomersall 11994; Gore 12080, 12084; Gouge 12121; Greene, R. 12240; Greenwood, H. 12331.5, 12332a, 12334; Griffith 12370a; Guez 12452; Gustavus II 12534.6; H., I. or J. 12566; H., W. 12581; Habington 12583; Hall, Joseph 12639*, 12639.3, 12639.5, 12639.7, 12640, 12640.5*, 12640.7; Harris, P. 12812; Harris, Robert 12816*, 12845; Harrison, W., King's Preacher 12865; Hawes, R. 12942; Hawkins, W. 12964; Heigham 13033.8, 13035; Heinsius 13038; Herbert, George 13186; Herbert, T. 13190, 13190.3; Heywood, T. 13357; Heywood, T., and Brome 13373; Hieron 13383.5*, 13384.7; Hill, E. 13468.5; Hinde, S. 13511; Hocus-pocus 13542.5; Holland, Henry, Bookseller 13585; Homer 13624.5(?), 13627; Howard, W. 13871; Hunt 13991; Instructions 14107.7; Ireland, Laws 14135, 14135.3, 14135.7; Ireland, Proc. 14208a, 14233, 14234, 14235, 14236, 14237; Jackson, Thomas, of Peterborough 14313; Janua 14472; Jeffray 14482; Jesus Christ 14555*; Johnson, Richard 14689.3(?); Johnson, T., Botanist 14704; Jones, I., and Davenant 14719; Juan 14832; King, Henry 14966, 14967; Lathum 15270; Leigh, D. 15407.3; Lenton 15466; Lessius 15520, 15521; Levett, J. 15555; Lily, W., 'Lily's Grammar' 15629, 15630; Linaker 15643; Lindsay, Sir D. 15670, 15680.5; Liturgies, C. of Eng., BCP 16396*, 16397*, 16397.3, 16397.7, 16398, 16399, 16399.5, 16399.7, 16400, 16440, 16448.3(?); Liturgies, C. of Eng., Ordinal 16474; Liturgies, C. of Eng., St. Services 16486, 16498; Liturgies, Other Protest. C. 16598; Lodge 16673, 16673.5; London, Appendix 16764.7(?); London, Ords. and Regs. 16733.7, 16734, 16735; Lord's Supper 16824; Louis XIII 16848; Lowe 16871; Lucian 16892.3*, 16893; Luis 16915*, 16922a.7; Lupton, D. 16945; Luzvic 17001; Lynde 17093; M., I. or J. 17139; M., J., Master of Arts 17141; Magnus 17185; Manzini 17293, 17293.5; Markham, G. 17333; Mason, F. 17596; Mason, H. 17611, 17612; Masterson 17649; Matthew, R. 17654, 17654a, 17654a.5, 17655; Maupas 17670; Maxey, A. 17694; Mayer 17737; Melville, J. 17815; Mercurius 17829a*; Meres 17835; Michel 17857; Mirror 17978.5; Moffett 17993, 17993a, 17993b; Mucedorus 18240; N., O. 18333; Norwood 18693; Openshaw 18829; Oughtred 18901a(?); Owen, Jane 18984; Owen, John 18992; Oxford Univ., Appendix 19052.4; Oxford Univ., Off. Docs. 19004, 19005; Oxford Univ., Quaestiones 19016.15, 19016.16; Pagit 19109.4(?); Pare 19189; Paris 19203, 19203.3; Parker, Martin 19237, 19242.5, 19244, 19245.5, 19246.5, 19247, 19251.7, 19254, 19256, 19257, 19261, 19265, 19269, 19270, 19276; Pasquil 19455; Patriarchs 19472.5; Peacham, H., the Younger 19504, 19509, 19516; Perkins, W. 19695, 19740; Phalaris 19828; Philipot 19846.5; Pinke 19943; Plinius Secundus 20030; Polybius 20099, 20099a; Potter, C. 20136, 20136.3, 20136.7; Powell, R. 20161; Praise 20186; Preston, J. 20212, 20213*, 20216, 20234, 20246, 20249, 20258.5, 20259, 20263*, 20264, 20273; Prideaux 20348, 20349; Purser, W. 20513; Puteanus 20516, 20517; Quarles 20535; Raleigh 20641, 20645; Randolph 20693; Ravisius 20765*; Read, A., M. D. 20783, 20783.5; Registrum 20839; Reynolds, E. 20936; Reynolds, J., Merchant 20944*; Richards, J. 21009.5; Ridley, T. 21055, 21055.5; Robinson, J., Pastor of Leyden 21116; Rocquigny 21139; Roesslin 21164; Rogers, J., of Dedham 21189; Rogers, Richard 21212.3; Rollock, R. 21273; Ross 21323; Rowlands or Verstegan, R. 21363; Rowlands, S. 21372, 21403; Rowley, S. 21416; Russell, J., of Magd. Coll., Cambridge 21460, 21460.3; S., A., Preacher 21480; S., R. 21512.5; S., W. 21524, 21525.5; Saint Andrews Univ. 21555.44; Salerno 21604; Saltonstall, W. 21641; Sandys, M. 21731, 21732; Seneca 22220; Shakespeare, W. 22313, 22321; Sheldon 22396; Sherwood, R. 22430; Sibbes 22507*, 22507.5; Sictor 22530; Sinner 22576(?); Skinner 22628; Smiglecki 22652; Smith, S., A. M. 22831.7, 22832;

1634 — *cont.*
Smith, S., Minister in Essex 22854.5; Smyth, Richard 22879; Sorocold 22934.5; Soto, A. 22937; Southwell 22967, 22968*; Spagnuoli 22987; Speed, John, Genealogies 23039.8(?), 23039e.12, 23039f.6(?); Stafford 23137; Stafford, A. 23124, 23124.5; Stafford, T. 23132a.5; Starkey, J. 23235.3(?)(A/C); Stockwood 23279.5; Stubbes 23394; Studley 23403; Sutcliffe, A. 23447; Sutton, C. 23490; Swedish Intelligencer 23523.5, 23525.2, 23525.5, 23525.6, 23525.7; Sweetnam, Joseph 23541; Syms 23597; Symson, P. 23598.5; Taffin 23656; Tapp 23682.7(?); Taylor, John 23776, 23808; Taylor, Thomas 23842; Thucydides 24059; Tomkis 24102, 24103*; Tozer 24160, 24161.3; Tradescant 24167.3; Turner, Roger 24348; Tymme 24432; Villegas 24735; Virgilius Maro 24794, 24812(?), 24821, 24826, 24826.5; Waferer 24930; Waldstein 24956; Walkley 24976; Warre 25092; Warwick 25096, 25097; Webster, J. 25179.5(?); Webster, W., of the Salters' Company 25182, 25183.5; Wedderburn 25189; Weemes 25212.5; Whately 25321; Whitaker, T. 25355; Whitfeld 25409.5, 25410; Wilkinson, J., of Barnard's Inn 25650.5; Willet 25700a, 25700a.3, 25700a.5, 25700a.7, 25706; Wilson, M. 25778; Wimbledon 25838; Wingfield, J. 25852.3; Wit 25869(?), 25871(?); Withals 25887; Wither, Poet 25900*; Witt 25932, 25932.5; Wood, W., Settler in New England 25957; World 25984; Yarrow 26078; Young, T., Student of Staple Inn 26117; Zouch 26128.

1635

Abbot, G., Abp. 31.5; Aberdeen Univ. 71.20, 71.31; Aesop 174; Ages 197.7; Almanacks (Allestree) 407.18; Almanacks (Clark) 430.4; Almanacks (Dade, W.) 435.24; Almanacks (Dove) 436.7; Almanacks (Jeffereys) 464.7; Almanacks (Kidman) 469.4; Almanacks (Langley) 479; Almanacks (Neve, John) 490.11; Almanacks (Perkins) 495.10; Almanacks (Pierce) 496.2; Almanacks (Pond) 501.25; Almanacks (Rivers, P.) 505.9; Almanacks (Sofford) 515.18; Almanacks (Staynred) 515.25; Almanacks (Swallow) 517.3; Almanacks (Vaux) 522.15; Almanacks (White) 527.25; Almanacks (Winter) 530.4; Almanacks (Woodhouse, or Wedhouse, or Wydowes, J.) 531.26; Almanacks (Wyberd) 532.9; Anderson, P., Doctor 574.5; Andrewes, J. 592.3; Andrewes, L. 609*; Ap-Robert 717; Aphthonius 706; Arguments 739.5; Attersoll 899; Audiguier 907; Aurelius Antoninus 963; Austin, W. 972; B., G. 1030(c.); Babington, J. 1099, 1100; Bacon, F. 1135*, 1172; Balbani 1235, 1235.2, 1235.3, 1235.4, 1235.5, 1235.6, 1235.7; Baldwin, W. 1268(c.); Ball, J. 1318; Ball, R. 1323; Ballad 1328.5, 1332(c.); Barriffe 1506; Basse 1552*; Bate, J., Mechanician 1578; Baudier 1593; Bayly, L. 1613, 1614, 1614.5(c.?), 1615(c.?), 1616(c.?), 1616.5(c.?); Baynes, P. 1637, 1643, 1643.5; Beaumont, F., and Fletcher 1669, 1675, 1675a*, 1689; Bedford, T. 1791*(A/C), 1791.3; Beggar Boy 1800(c.); Bellarmino 1837.7; Bentham, J. 1887; Bernard, R. 1932, 1951, 1959; Best, W. 1973.5, 1974; Bible, Appendix 3032; Bible, English 2285.5(c.), 2315*, 2318, 2319, 2320, 2321, 2325*; Bible, N.T., English 2948, 2949; Bible, O.T., Psalms 2417, 2417.3, 2655, 2656, 2656.5, 2657, 2658.5(A/C), 2659, 2659.5*, 2660, 2661, 2661.5, 2662, 2662.3, 2722; Biondi 3074; Birckbek 3083; Blaeu 3113.3; Bluom 3163; Bodin 3193.5(c.)*(A/C); Bolton, Robert 3239, 3244, 3256; Bonaventura 3272; Book 3305.5(?); Botero 3396; Boughen 3408, 3409, 3409.5; Boye 3450; Bradshawe 3533.5; Braithwaite 3540; Brathwait 3554, 3566.5*, 3567, 3569, 3581.7; Brerewood 3621; Breton 3668, 3700, 3704.9; Bride 3728(c.), 3730(?); Brightman 3753; Bristol 3797(c.); Broom 3839.7(c.); Buck, G. 3997; Burton, H. 4137.7(?), 4144; Burton, R. 4163(?)*; Butler, C. 4200.5; Bythner 4260.5, 4260.7; C., W., Bachelor of Civil Law 4323.8; Calthorpe 4369, 4369.5; Cambridge University 4479*; Cambridge University, Act Verses 4474.10(?), 4474.39(?), 4474.55(?); Cambridge 4472(c.); Camden 4501; Campbell 4533; Capel 4596; Carier 4625.5; Carpenter, N. 4677; Cevoli 4922; Chapman, R. 4998; Charles I, King 5022(c.); Chaucer 5097, 5097.3; Chouneus 5145; Christian Directory 5157.5(A/C); Christmas 5203(c.); Cicero 5272.4, 5272.6, 5303.4; Clarke, J., B.D. 5358; Clarke, T., of Sutton Coldfield 5365; Climsell 5417(?), 5418(?), 5422(c.), 5424 c.); Closet 5439; Coke, E. 5489, 5498.5, 5501.5, 5503.7; Comparisons 5605a.5(c.?); Complaint

1635 — *cont.*
5608.5(c.); Confession 5627(c.); Constancy 5640(c.); Conyers 5657; Coote 5714.8; Cosin, J. 5818; Cotton, C. 5846, 5846.4; Cotton, Rowland 5870; Cougneau 5871; Cowper 5930.6; Cranley 5988; Crosse, T. 6071.5 s(c.?); Crouch 6073(?); Cuique 6106; Culverwell 6113; Cupid 6122.5; D., I. or J. 6169(c.?); Dalton, M. 6210, 6211; Daniel, S. 6243.8; Darcie, A. 6273.3; Davenant, W. 6308; Davenport, J. 6312; David, King of Israel 6317(c.); Day, A. 6408; Dekker 6505; Deloney 6557.4(c.?), 6557.8(c.); Dennys 6612(c.); Dent, A. 6635; Devereux 6792(c.?), 6793(c.?); Dickson, D. 6824; Ditty 6921(c.), 6922(c.), 6925(c.); Doctrine 6934.3(c.?); Dod and Cleaver 6979; Dod 6939; Donne, J. 7030, 7046; Downame, G. 7107, 7110, 7111; Downame, J. 7129(?), 7130(?); Downe 7153, 7153.3; Drake 7162; Du Moulin, P., the Elder 7310, 7327; Du Plessis or Dupleix, S. 7362; Du Plessis, A. 7359, 7360, 7361; Dyke, D. 7394, 7397, 7409a; Dyke, J. 7418, 7428; England, Appendix 10023.5(c.?); England, C. of, Visit. Articles 10134(?), 10142, 10147.8A(?), 10186, 10190(?), 10199, 10214.5, 10217, 10244, 10265.5(?), 10297, 10312, 10323.3, 10332, 10336, 10350, 10364, 10370, 10381.7; England, Customs 7695; England, Proclamations, Chron. Ser. 9031, 9032, 9033, 9034, 9035, 9036, 9037, 9038, 9039, 9040, 9041, 9042, 9043, 9044, 9045, 9046, 9047, 9048, 9049, 9050, 9050.3, 9051, 9052(o.s.), 9053(o.s.), 9054(o.s.), 9056(o.s.), 9057(o.s.); England, Public Documents, Misc. 9175m; England, Statutes, Gen. Colls. 9330*; English Traveller 10420; Estwick 10557; Everinden 10601.7, 10602.5; Example 10612(c.?); F., G. 10637; F., I. or J. 10644, 10645; Fauconbridge 10710; Fawkner 10724; Feltham 10761*; Field, R. 10859; Finch, Mr. 10869.5(c.?); Fitch 10928.6(c.); Fitzherbert, A. 10967; Florimene 11095; Flower, M. 11107.7; Forbes, J., Minister 11129; Forbes, P. 11151; Ford, E. 11153(c.); Fox, L. 11221; Francis, of Assisi 11314.4; G., G. 11495; Gellibrand 11712, 11712.5; Gerhard 11775; Gil, A., the Elder 11878; Glover, G. 11921.1(c.), 11921.2 (c.), 11921.6(c.), 11921.8(c.), 11921.9(c.); Goodcole 12009, 12010, 12010.3, 12010.5; Gordon, J., Minister at Elgin 12065; Gore 12075, 12076, 12078, 12081, 12086, 12088; Gossips 12092.8(?); Gouge 12130; Gower, J., M. A. 12141; Gracian 12144.5; Greek Poets 12211; Greene, R. 12291.5(c.), 12305; Griselda 12385(c.?); Guarna 12417, 12418, 12421; Guillemeau 12497; Guy, R. 12543.7(c.?), 12545.5(c.), 12548(c.?); H., A. 12561.8(c.?); Habington 12584; Hakewill 12613; Hall, Joseph 12645, 12645a, 12647; Harris, P. 12811; Harris, Robert 12816*; Harsnet, A. 12879; Haviland 12938.5(c.?); Hawkins, J., M. D. 12959; Henshaw 13169; Herbert, George 13187; Herodian 13223; Heywood, T. 13327, 13348a, 13356, 13372.5; Hieron 13377.9(?), 13383.5*, 13384, 13405, 13415; Hildersam 13463; Hoard 13535; Hocus-pocus 13543; Homilies 13660.5*, 13661, 13676a*; Hooke, R. 13705; Hooker, R. 13719*, 13719b*; Hooker, T. 13726.2, 13736; Hopton 13781; Horatius Flaccus 13802; Hyde Park 14040.3(c.); Ireland, C. of 14265; Ireland, Laws 14136, 14136.3, 14136.7; Ireland, Proclamations 14237.3(A/C); Jackson, Thomas, of Peterborough 14309; James, T., D. D. 14448, 14451; Jewel, J. 14593; Joceline 14625.7; Johnson, Richard 14685; Johnson, Richard, Moralist 14691.7, 14691.9; Johnston, A. 14712; Johnston, W. 14715.5; Jones, J., Eugenius 14721; Jones, J., M. A. 14723; Jones, W., of Suffolk 14739.5; Jonson 14760, 14760.5; Joy 14819; Kellet 14904; Kilby, R., of Derby 14954.3, 14956.7; Kynaston 15100; La Ramee 15249.3; Lambard 15143, 15144; Langeren 15193.5(c.); Lass 15264.5(c.); Latimer 15283; Lawrence, T. 15328; Lechmere, E. 15351; Lechmere, J. 15351.3; Leigh, E. 15410; Lenton 15467.5; Liturgies, C. of Eng., BCP 16401, 16402, 16402.5, 16402.7; Liturgies, C. of Eng., Spec. Prayers 16552; Liturgies, C. of Eng., St. Services 16486.3, 16499; Liturgies, Other Protest. C. 16599, 16600; Llyfr Plygain 16641(c.); London, Bills of Mort. 16744.5; London, Ords. and Regs. 16736.5(c.); Lover 16862.3(c.); Lucanus 16889; Luther 16974; Lycosthenes 17004; M., Ch. 17130; Maid 17189.7(c.); Malynes 17224*, 17224.5*; Markham, G. 17357, 17358, 17369; Markham, G. 17389; Martin, Robert 17513, 17513.5; Maryland 17571; Mason, H. 17609; May 17707(?); May, T. 17719; Mayer 17738; Meg 17783; Mercator 17824, 17824.5; Meres 17836*; Miles 17920.5; Miroir 17976.5(A/C); Mirror 17979; Mock-beggar Hall

1635 — *cont.*

17989(?); Molinier 18003; Money 18009(?); Montagu, H. 18026.5, 18027; Montagu, R. 18033; Morton, T., Bp. 18190; N., N. 18331; Nicodemus 18571(c.); Norden 18626; Norfolk gentleman 18644 (c.), 18644.3(c.), 18644.5(c.); Nottinghamshire Lovers 18700(?); Nowell, Middle Catechism 18737.5(c.); Odell 18780, 18781; Oh 18790.5(c.); Openshaw 18830; Ovidius Naso 18929.7, 18930; Oxford Univ., Off. Docs. 19006; Oxford Univ., Quaestiones 19016.17; P., I. or J. 19070.3; Paget 19097; Pagitt 19110, 19110.5; Palmer, T. 19155; Parker, Martin 19221, 19226(?), 19234(c.), 19236(c.), 19236.5(c.), 19240(c.), 19249.5(c.), 19251.5(?), 19253.5(c.), 19266, 19284(?), 19285(?); Parkinson 19301; Parsons, B. 19350, 19350.5; Pasquil 19453.3; Pecke, R. 19522; Pemble 19570, 19570.5, 19580.7; Perkins, W. 19654, 19675, 19719.7(A/C); Persius Flaccus 19780; Person 19781; Petowe 19802.5; Peyton 19825.5(c.)(A/C); Philippson 19852; Pietro 19910.5; Platt 19986; Plinius Secundus 20030a; Plutarch 20056.5; Poland 20083.3(aft.)*(A/C); Polybius 20099a.5; Posselius 20128.7; Powell, T., Londino-Cambrensis 20162*; Praise 20185(?); Preston, J. 20237, 20260a, 20277, 20281a.3, 20282; Price, L. 20320.5(c.), 20322(?), 20325, 20326(?); Prideaux 20350; Purchas, A. 20501; Pyne 20522; Quarles 20528(c.), 20528.5(c.), 20528a(c.), 20528a.5(c.), 20540, 20540.5; Rainbow 20603; Randolph 20689, 20690(?); Ravisius 20762; Read, A., M. D. 20781; Records 20822(?); Reeve, E. 20830; Reynolds, E. 20928; Reynolds, J., Merchant 20944*; Robertus 21102; Robinson, J., Pastor of Leyden 21107.5; Rogers, D. 21170, 21171, 21173*; Rogers, Richard 21212.7, 21223.3, 21223.7; Rogers, Timothy 21243.5; Rolland 21257.3(c.), 21257.7(c.); Ross 21330; Rous, the Elder 21343; Rowlands, S. 21380; Rutter 21470; S., R. 21513; Sabunde 21537.3; Saint Andrews Univ. 21555.45, 21555.46; Saltonstall, W. 21646; Sanderson, R. 21710; Saunders, G. 21776.7(c.); Schindler 21817.3, 21817.5; Schonaeus 21824; Scotland, Church of, appendix 22034; Scott, T., B. D. 22079.5(A/C); Scott, W. 22109; Scudder 22119; Seager 22138.5(c.); Selden 22175; Seneca 22215a; Shakespeare, W. 22339; Sheldon 22396.5; Shelford 22400; Shelton 22404.2; Shepherd 22406.3(c.); Sherwood, T. 22431; Shirley, J. 22458; Sibbes 22483, 22508, 22508.5; Sictor 22531; Silesio 22553; Slatyer 22634.5(c.), 22636.5(c.); Smetius 22649; Smith, S., Minister in Essex 22841; Smith, T., Doctor of Civil Laws 22866; Solomon 22901(c.), 22904 (c.); Song 22921(c.); Sorocold 22934.7; Spagnuoli 22988; Sparke, M. 23017.5; Speed, John, Genealogies 23039e.13; Speed, R. 23053; Sprint, J., Vicar 23110; Stafford, A. 23122, 23123; Stirk 23272; Strumsdorf 23366; Stubbes 23394.5; Studley 23404; Susenbrotus 23443; Sutton, C. 23495; Sutton, W. 23508; Swan, J., of Trinity C., Camb., Jr. 23516; Swedish Intelligencer 23525.8, 23525.9; Swinburne 23550; T., F. 23617; Talaeus 23661.5; Taylor, John 23727, 23730, 23731, 23732.7, 23732.8(A/C), 23744, 23781, 23782, 23782.5, 23794, 23815, 23817; Taylor, Thomas 23821, 23848, 23849, 23852; Teramano 23884a.4, 23884a.6, 23884a.8; Terentius 23889.7; Terry 23915.5; Thornton, R. 24044; Time 24088(c.); Tooke 24116; Tossanus 24145; Troy 24293.7(c.); Truth 24301(c.); Tuke 24310; Turner, T. 24349; Tuvil or Toutevile 24396.5; Valentine, H. 24574, 24576.3; Virel 24773; Vives 24854.5; Vlacq 24864; Wadding 24924; Wake 24942; Walkley 24977; Wall, G. 24984; Ward, S., of Ipswich 25032*; Warner, J. 25078; Warwick 25097.5, 25098; Watling Street 25108.5(c.); Wedderburn 25190(?)*; Wells, J. 25234; Wetherel 25292.3; Whately 25313; White, F., Bp. 25383, 25384, 25384.5; Williams, G. 25718*; Williams, W. 25736(c.); Williamson, R. 25737.5, 25737.7(c.); Willoby 25758; Wilson, T., Divine 25789(c.); Wily 25822; Wimbledon 25839; Wingate 25851, 25851.5; Wither, Poet 25900*, 25900a, 25900b, 25900c, 25900d; Witherings, T. 25930.3; Wood, W., Settler in New England 25958; Wooer 25973 (c.); Wroth, T. 26053; Yorkshire Lovers 26104(c.).

1636

A.B.C. 21.2; Abbot, G., Abp. 32, 32.5; Abbot, R., Minister 60.3; Aberdeen Univ. 71.21; Advice 156a.5; Almanacks (Allestree) 407.19; Almanacks (Bowker or Booker) 419.5; Almanacks (Clark) 430.5; Almanacks (Dade, W.) 435.25; Almanacks (Dove) 436.8; Almanacks (F., M.) 441.9; Almanacks (Fallowes) 442; Almanacks (Kidman) 469.5; Almanacks (Langley) 479.2; Almanacks (Neve, John) 490.12; Almanacks (Peregrine) 494.12; Almanacks (Perkins) 495.11; Almanacks (Pond) 501.26; Almanacks (Swallow) 517.4; Almanacks (True) 517.16; Almanacks (Vaux) 522.16; Almanacks (White) 527.26; Almanacks (Winter) 530.5; Almanacks (Woodhouse, or Wedhouse, or Wydowes, J.) 531.27; Almanacks (Wyberd) 532.10; Andrewes, J. 588.3, 595.5; Andrewes, L. 610; Antidote 679; Aphthonius 706.5; Assize of Bread 883; Augustine 918, 922.5; Bacon, F. 1135*; Baker, R. 1223; Balaam 1232; Bancroft, R. 1349; Banquet 1369.5, 1373; Barclay, J. 1389, 1392.5; Barrey 1503; Basse 1553; Basset 1558; Bastwick 1576; Bayly, L. 1616.7, 1617.5, 1618; Beauvais 1698; Benlowes 1880; Bentham, J. 1890; Bettie 1981; Bible, English 2313b.5*, 2322, 2322.3, 2322.5, 2324.5*, 2328*; Bible, N.T., English 2951, 2951.5, 2952, 2953; Bible, O.T., Psalms 2418.5, 2659.5*, 2662.5, 2663, 2664, 2665, 2665.5, 2666, 2666.2, 2666.5, 2667, 2667.2, 2667.4, 2736; Blount, H. 3136, 3136.3, 3136.7; Blunden 3141(?); Blundeville 3151; Bolton, Robert 3233; Book 3350; Boye 3451; Bradshaw, W. 3515.3, 3515.4; Bradwell 3536; Brathwait 3554.5, 3555.7(c.), 3567.5; Breton 3653; Brewer 3717.5, 3717.7, 3719.5; Browning 3919; Bryan 3955; Buchler 3994.3; Buenting 4020; Burton, H. 4134, 4135, 4137.9, 4140.7, 4140.8, 4141, 4142, 4145, 4145.5; Bushell 4187.5, 4188; Butler, C. 4196; Byfield, N. 4212*, 4224; C., B., Catholic priest 4263.5; C., N. 4293(o.s.); Cade 4329a; Calderwood 4363, 4363.5; Cambridge University 4476.3, 4479*; Camden 4525; Capel 4597, 4598; Carleton, G. 4648; Carpenter, N. 4679; Castalio or Chateillon 4776.5; Catechism 4803.6; Cato 4863; Cecil, W., Baron Burghley 4899; Chamberlain 4941.5; Charity 5004; Charles I, King 5026; Chouneus 5146; Christ's Hospital 5209.3(A/C); Church, H. 5215, 5216; Cicero 5310.7, 5316.5; Clarke, T., Lieutenant 5363.5*(A/C); Climsell 5420(?), 5430(?); Closet 5440; Coaches 5451; Cogan 5483.7, 5484; Coke, E. 5494.8, 5510.5; Coote 5715; Copping 5742.3; Cordier 5764, 5764.2; Cowley 5907; Cowper 5942*; Crakanthorp 5984.5; Crawshey 6033; D., I. or J. 6168.7; D., J., Preacher of God's Word 6176.5; Dalechamp 6194; Davenant, W. 6305, 6309; Davenport, J. 6310; Davies, J., of Hereford 6345; Day, M. 6427; Declaration 6453, 6453.5; Dekker 6533; Deloney 6572; Dent, A. 6667, 6668; Desainliens or Sainliens 6757; Description 6771.5; Desmarets de Saint-Sorlin 6779; Dictionary 6832.62; Donne, G. 7021.5; Dow, C. 7088, 7089; Downame, G. 7112; Downame, J. 7149; Draxe 7181.5; Drexelius 7236; Du Moulin, P., the Elder 7317, 7344; Du Vair 7373.8; Dudley, Jane 7282; Dugres 7294; Dyke, J. 7429; Edwards, E. 7511; England, C. of, Articles 10038; England, C. of, Constitutions/Canons 10074.3(?)*; England, C. of, Visit. Articles 10137.9, 10139(?), 10171, 10172(?), 10194, 10199.5, 10227.6, 10280.7, 10298, 10298.3, 10343, 10365, 10371, 10380.5; England, Privy Council 7756(o.s.); England, Proclamations, Chron. Ser. 9052, 9053, 9054, 9055, 9056, 9057, 9058, 9058.5, 9058.7, 9059, 9060, 9061, 9062, 9063, 9064, 9065, 9066, 9067, 9068, 9069, 9070, 9071, 9072, 9073, 9074, 9075, 9076, 9077, 9078(o.s.), 9080(o.s.), 9081(o.s.), 9082(o.s.), 9083(o.s.); England, Statutes, Gen. Colls. 9330*; English Farrier 10409; English Traveller 10421; Epictetus 10427; Eusebius, Pamphili 10576*; Evans, W., of Oxford 10595; F., I. or J. 10646; Farley, R. 10695(?); Faust 10714; Featley, D. 10730; Featley, J. 10742, 10742.5; Feltham 10761*; Fenton, E. 10789.5; Figure 10865.5; Finch, H. 10872; Fisher, Jasper 10887*; Fitz-Geffrey, C. 10936; Florus 11105; Forbes, J., of Corse 11141; Forde, E. 11175; Freake 11346.5*; Gee, J. 11706.6*; Gerard, J. 11752; Goodwin, T. 12037, 12037.5, 12040, 12041, 12041.3, 12041.5; Goosecappe 12051, 12052; Gore 12071, 12074, 12085; Gouge 12116.5, 12118, 12130.5; Gray, F. 12202; Greene, R. 12292; Grotius 12401; Grymes 12406; Gunter, E. 12523; Habington 12584a; Hart, John, D. D. 12893; Harvey, C., the Elder 12897.5; Hausted 12937; Hawkesworth 12956; Hayward, Sir J. 12994, 12999, 13010; Henshaw 13169*; Herring, F. 13242; Heylyn 13270, 13270.5, 13274, 13275, 13282; Heywood, T. 13311, 13352, 13365.5, 13369; Hieron 13416; Hildersam 13460; Hill, W. 13505.3; Hoard 13536; Hodson or Hodgson, W. 13553, 13553.5; Hooker, R.

1636 — *cont.*
13719*, 13719b*; Hooker, T. 13726.3; Howard, T., Earl of Arundel and Surrey 13870.5; Hunnis 13984.5; Ireland, Laws 14137; Ireland, Proc. 14208b; Jackson, Thomas, of Peterborough 14310; Johnson, Richard 14682.5(?); Jones, W., of Suffolk 14739.8; Jones, W., of Wight 14749; Justices of Peace 14887.3; King, W. 14999; Komensky 15077.3; Kynaston 15099; La Ramee 15249.7, 15251; Latimer 15283.5; Le Fevre 15382; Leigh, D. 15407.5; Lenton 15464; Lessius 15522; Lily, W., 'Lily's Grammar' 15631*, 15632; Liturgies, C. of Eng., BCP 16403, 16403.5(?), 16404, 16404.3, 16404.4, 16404.5, 16404.7; Liturgies, C. of Eng., Ordinal 16475; Liturgies, C. of Eng., Spec. Prayers 16553, 16553a, 16555, 16555.5; Liturgies, C. of Eng., St. Services 16486.7*, 16500; Liturgies, Latin Rite, Manuals 16162; Liturgies, Other Protest. C. 16606*, 16607; Lloyd, D. 16615; London, Bills of Mort. 16745; London, Coll. of Physicians 16769, 16769.5, 16771; London, Tradesmen 16786.18(?); Longinus 16788; Lucian 16892.3*, 16892.7; Lupton, D. 16942; Luther 16997; Lyly 17067; Macchiavelli 17160; Malynes 17224*, 17224.5*; Manuzio, A. 17284, 17285; Markham, G. 17365, 17369.5, 17379, 17379.5; Marnix van Sant Aldegonde 17448.5, 17449; Mary, the Blessed Virgin—Archconfrat. of the Rosary 17548; Mason, Richard 17618.5; Massinger 17637; Maxey, A. 17694.5; Mayerne 17746; Meg 17783.3; Mercator and Hondius 17827; Meres 17836; Minucius Felix 17952, 17953; Molinier 18003.1; Montagu, H. 18027a; Montagu, R. 18034; Montgomery 18050; Mure 18290; Nash, T., Philopolites 18383; Nemesius 18427; Nicholes 18531.7; Norden 18626.5; Norice 18646; Nowell, Middle Catechism 18725; Oldmayne 18806; Oughtred 18900; Ovidius Naso 18945, 18952.9, 18954.5, 18976, 18976.2; Oxford Univ., Verses, etc. 19036; Pagitt 19111, 19111.5; Parker, Martin 19250.5, 19251.3; Parr, E. 19313, 19318; Parsons, B. 19351; Peacham, H., the Younger 19501, 19501.5; Penkethman 19598.4; Perkins, W. 19676, 19720; Philipot 19846; Philippson 19852*; Pierson 19910; Pinke 19944; Platt 19987; Pocklington 20077, 20078; Powell, R. 20160; Powell, T., Londino-Cambrensis 20162*; Preservatives 20206; Preston, J. 20219, 20223; Price, L. 20311, 20312; Prideaux 20344.7(A/C), 20345*; Primrose, David, Minister 20387; Prynne 20456, 20466, 20469(?), 20469.3, 20469.7, 20470, 20476, 20476.5; Quarles 20531, 20538; Quelch 20555; Raleigh 20646, 20652; Rastell, J., Printer 20718; Read, A., D. D. 20780; Record, R. 20810; Red Cross 20824; Reeve, E. 20831; Remedy 20875; Reynolds, E. 20932, 20932.5*; Robinson, J., Pastor of Leyden 21107.7; Rogers, D. 21172, 21173*; Rogers, W. 21251; S., I. or J. 21505; Sadler 21544; Salisbury, T. 21619.5, 21620; Saltmarsh 21638; Saltonstall, C. 21640; Saluste du Bartas 21666.5; Sampson, W. 21687, 21688; Sanderson, R. 21707*, 21710.3; Sandys, G. 21724; Scapula 21806*; Scotland, Episcopal Church of 22055; Selden 22170, 22175.3, 22175.7, 22176; Seller 22181; Seneca 22215.5; Shakespeare, W. 22366; Shaw, Inventor 22391.6; Sibbes 22509, 22510, 22515, 22516; Sictor 22533a.3(?)(A/C); Simson, E. 22571; Slater 22631; Smith, John, Gov. of Virginia 22786; Southwell 22968*; Sparke, M. 23017.7; Speed, John, Genealogies 23039d.15 (?), 23039e.14; Spenser, B. 23075; Sprint, J., Vicar 23108.7; Stanbridge, Vocabula 23193.4; Sydenham 23565; Talaeus 23662; Taylor, John 23735, 23756, 23764, 23764a, 23776.5, 23805; Taylor, Thomas 23819.5(?); Terentius 23889.8, 23889.9; Themylthorp 23935, 23935.5(A/C); Theophylact 23948; Thomas, a Kempis 23985, 23992; Traske 24178.5; Treasurer 24214.5; Trussell, J. 24297; Tuke 24306, 24314.3; Twisse 24401.3; Udall, W. 24510, 24511; Uthalmus 24559; Valentine, H. 24576.5; Villegas 24736; Wake 24942.5; Walbancke 24954; Ward, S., of Ipswich 25032*; Warwick 25099; Weemes 25208, 25208.3, 25208.5, 25211.5, 25213a.5, 25214.5, 25216.5, 25217.5, 25218; Welwood 25238; White, F., Bp. 25385; Whitfeld 25411; Williams, G. 25718*; Wilson, M. 25777; Worship 25991; Wotton, A. 26006; Wouwerus 26013; Wright, R. 26038; Wright, T., Bookseller 26038.2(?); Young, R. 26112.7, 26113; Zouch 26132.

1637

A.B.C. 21.3; Abbot, R., Minister 60.5; Aberdeen Univ. 71.22, 71.23, 71.24, 71.40; Adamson, J. 136, 139; Aesop 174.3; Airay, C. 243; Albertus Magnus 267; Alexander, W. 347; Almanacks (Allestree) 407.20; Almanacks (Bowker or Booker) 419.6; Almanacks (Clark) 430.6; Almanacks (Cowper) 431.3; Almanacks (Dade, W.) 435.26; Almanacks (Dove) 436.9; Almanacks (Fallowes) 442.3; Almanacks (Kidman) 469.6; Almanacks (Langley) 479.3; Almanacks (Neve, John) 490.13; Almanacks (Peregrine) 494.13; Almanacks (Perkins) 495.12; Almanacks (Pierce) 496.4; Almanacks (Pond) 501.27; Almanacks (Rivers, P.) 505.11; Almanacks (Sofford) 515.20; Almanacks (Twells) 518.4; Almanacks (Vaux) 522.17; Almanacks (White) 527.27; Almanacks (Winter) 530.6; Almanacks (Woodhouse, or Wedhouse, or Wydowes, J.) 531.28; Almanacks (Wyberd) 532.11; Ambrose, St. 548, 548.3; Andrewes, J. 588.5; Arcandam 730; Aristotle 767(?); Austin, W. 973, 974; Babington, G. 1080; Babylon 1102; Bacon, F. 1161.5; Baker, R. 1223.5, 1224; Ball, J. 1313.7, 1318.3, 1318.5, 1321; Bancroft, R. 1350; Barlement 1432.5; Barlow, T. 1441a; Barry, J. 1530; Basset 1557; Bastwick 1568, 1569, 1572, 1573, 1574, 1575; Bayly, L. 1618a; Baynes, P. 1627, 1633; Becon 1719; Bense 1885; Berkeley 1901.5*; Bible, English 2323*, 2324, 2324.3, 2324.5, 2325*, 2326, 2327, 2327.5*, 2328*, 2328.3, 2328.5, 2328.7*, 2328.8*, 2328.9*, 2329*; Bible, N.T., English 2953.3; Bible, O.T., 'Books of Solomon' 2776.5; Bible, O.T., Psalms 2366, 2418.7, 2668, 2669, 2670, 2670.5, 2671, 2671.5, 2672, 2672.3, 2672.7, 2673, 2673.3, 2673.5, 2674, 2675, 2681.7*, 2736.5(?), 2736a; Billingsley 3061*; Blount, H. 3137; Bolton, Robert 3233a, 3237, 3249; Bourchier, J. 3412.3; Breda 3597; Brerewood 3630; Breton 3694; Brian 3723; Brinsley, J., the Elder 3785; Bristol 3793.5(?)(A/C); Buchler 3994.5; Buck, J. 3997.5, 3998; Burgersdijck 4107, 4108; Buridanus 4119; Byfield, N. 4212*, 4231, 4236.4, 4236.5, 4236.6, 4237; Bythner 4261; C., B., Catholic priest 4263.7; C., H. 4273, 4274; C., N. 4293, 4293.2, 4293.4; C., R. 4297; Cambridge University 4490.5, 4490.7(?), 4491.6(c.), 4492; Cambridge University, Act Verses 4474.16, 4474.36, 4474.65, 4474.75, 4474.99; Camden 4510, 4510.2, 4510.4, 4510.6, 4510.8, 4526; Capel 4599; Carpenter, N. 4680; Catalogue 4788; Catalogus 4789; Cecil, W., Baron Burghley 4900; Chamberlain 4944; Charles Louis 5046, 5047, 5048, 5049.5, 5050, 5050.2, 5050.5; Chouneus 5146.3; Church, H. 5217; Cicero 5303.6; Clarke, J., B.D. 5356; Clerke, R. 5410; Climsell 5428(?); Clowes 5445.7; Cockeram 5465, 5465.3; Coke, E. 5490; Colom 5575.3; Coote 5716*; Corneille 5770; Cotton, C. 5852.5, 5853; Cowell 5901, 5902; Cowley 5908; Crakanthorp 5985, 5985.5, 5985.7; Crompton, R. 6051; Crouch 6074, 6074a(?); Crowne 6097; Culverwell 6111; Cupif 6124; Danes 6232; Day, James 6410; Delamaine 6545*(A/C); Deloney 6555, 6563; Dent, A. 6625, 6636, 6669; Dey 6798.5; Dickson, D. 6825; Digges, L. 6857; Doughty, T. 7072.4*; Dow, C. 7090; Drant, T., of Shaston 7164, 7164.3, 7165, 7165.3; Drayton 7225; Du Moulin, P., the Elder 7337.5; Dunton 7357; Duport, James 7365; Edwards, E. 7511.2; Elborow 7551; Elton 7614; England, C. of, Visit. Articles 10145, 10147.11(?), 10169.5(?), 10169.7, 10178, 10184, 10192.8, 10212, 10245.7(?), 10245.8(?), 10266, 10281*, 10319, 10324, 10339(?), 10343.5; England, Local Courts 7725.6; England, Privy Council 7756, 7757, 7757.2; England, Proclamations, Chron. Ser. 9078, 9079, 9080, 9081, 9082, 9083, 9084, 9085, 9086, 9087, 9088, 9089, 9090, 9091, 9092, 9093, 9093.5, 9094, 9095, 9096, 9097, 9098, 9099, 9100(o.s.), 9101(o.s.), 9102(o.s.), 9103(o.s.), 9104(o.s.), 9105(o.s.), 9106(o.s.), 9107(o.s.), 9108(o.s.), 9109(o.s.); Eusebius, Pamphili 10576*; F., A. 10635.7; Fage, M. 10667; Ferdinand II 10812.5, 10813; Fettiplace 10838.5; Fitz-Geffrey, C. 10937; Fletcher, John 11066, 11067*; Francis, of Sales 11321, 11322; Freake 11347; Frederick Henry, Prince of Orange 11364; Frubach 11404, 11406; Gardyne 11596.5; Gataker 11652, 11652a, 11652b, 11652b.5; Gee, J. 11706.6*; Genoa 11728.6; Gerhard 11776, 11777; German Theologians 11785; Gillespie 11896; Goodcole 12012; Goodwin, T. 12033, 12033.5, 12043a; Gouge 12110.5*; Greene, R. 12238, 12250; Guild 12491; Hall, Joseph 12710; Hayward, J., D. D. 12987; Health 13015(?); Heidelberg Catechism 13027; Henry IV, King of France 13125; Henshaw 13171; Hexham 13264, 13265; Heylyn 13267, 13267.5, 13269, 13271; Heywood, T. 13312, 13319, 13349, 13358, 13364, 13367; Hill, E. 13469; Hoard 13533; Hondius 13685(?);

1637 — *cont.*

Hooker, T. 13726.4, 13726.6, 13728, 13731, 13733, 13739*; Horatius Flaccus 13796, 13796.5*; Howes 13877.7; Hurste 14007; I., S. A. 14064.7, 14065; Ireland, Proc. 14238, 14239, 14240, 14241, 14242, 14243, 14244, 14245(o.s.), 14246(o.s.), 14247(o.s.); Ironside 14268; Jackson, Thomas, of Peterborough 14307; Jenison 14492, 14492.3(A/C); Jewel, J. 14588; Johann Justus 14628.5; Jones, I., and Davenant 14718; Jones, W., of Wight 14742; Jordan 14788; Juan 14832a; Justices of Peace 14887.5; Knevet 15035; Komensky 15077, 15080; L., M. 15108(c.); La Ramee 15244.7; Laud 15306, 15307, 15308; Lawrence, T. 15326, 15326.5, 15326.7(A/C), 15327; Lawson 15331.7*; Leslie, H. 15499; Lily, W., 'Lily's Grammar' 15631*, 15632.3*, 15632.7*; Lithgow 15717; Liturgies, C. of Eng., BCP 16404.9, 16405, 16406, 16407, 16408, 16408.5, 16452; Liturgies, C. of Eng., St. Services 16486.7*; Liturgies, Other Protest. C. 16606*; London, College of Heralds 16768.34(A/C); London, Ords. and Regs. 16737; Luminalia 16923; Luther 16977; Macropedius 17176.9; Maden 17179; Malvezzi 17218, 17219; Manual 17277.7; Markham, G. 17340(?)*, 17354; Marlowe 17422; Marmion 17444; Mede 17768, 17768.5; Mercator 17825; Milton, J. 17937; Mirror 17979.3; Monro 18022; Morocco 18165; Morton, T., Bp. 18172; Morton, T., of Clifford's Inn 18202, 18203(?); Nabbes 18341, 18342; Nicetas 18527; Norwood 18691; Notarius Rusticus 18698; Odingsells 18782; Openshaw 18830.1; Overs 18922; Ovidius Naso 18945.5, 18980; Oxford Univ., Verses, etc. 19037; Page, S. 19089; Palatinate 19131; Palmerin, de Oliva 19160; Parker, Martin 19218, 19242, 19277; Parliament 19307.5; Parsons, B. 19347.5, 19348; Partridge, John 19433; Peake 19518.5(?); Percy, A. 19615.5; Perkins, W. 19684.7; Pocklington 20075, 20076; Preston, J. 20213*, 20220, 20221.1*, 20250, 20265, 20265.5, 20274; Prideaux 20345*; Prynne 20454, 20454.3, 20454.5, 20474, 20475; Quarles 20537; Raleigh 20647; Ravisius 20762.3; Read, A., M. D. 20785; Remnant 20879; Reynolds, E. 20936.5, 20937; Rhodes, J. 20961; Roberts, J. 21091.5; Robinson, T. 21126; Rogers, J., of Dedham 21193; Rogers, Timothy 21249; Rome, Church of 21303; Rous, the Younger 21350; Rueff 21442; Sadler 21543; Saltonstall, W. 21642; Saluste du Bartas 21663a.5, 21667, 21667.5; Sanderson, R. 21707*; Sandys, G. 21725*, 21730; Sandys, Sir E. 21721; Scapula 21806*; Scheibler 21811, 21812, 21812.2, 21812.3, 21812.5, 21812.7, 21812.9; Schindler 21817.7; Scudder 22120; Sennertus 22232; Shakespeare, W. 22279, 22298, 22326; Shaw, Inventor 22391.3, 22391.5(?); Shirley, J. 22442, 22443, 22445, 22446, 22448, 22457, 22463; Shutte 22469.7; Sibbes 22486, 22494, 22495, 22502*, 22504, 22513, 22513.5, 22517; Sictor 22532; Smith, H., Minister, Collections 22734, 22747, 22783; Smith, H., Minister, Single Works 22676, 22677.5; Smith, John, of Clavering 22800, 22800.5; Smith, S., Minister in Essex 22845.7, 22849.7*; Sommers 22917.5; Sorocold 22934.8(A/C); Sparke, E. 23015; Sparrow 23029, 23029.5, 23029.7; Speed, John, Genealogies 23039d.16(?), 23039e.15; Speed, R. 23054; Squire, J., Minister 23119, 23119.5, 23120; Stella, Joannes 23245; Stinton 23271; Stubbes 23395; Swadling 23509; Sweetnam, Joseph 23542; Sydenham 23566, 23566.5, 23573; Syme 23584; Symmer 23586; Taylor, John 23740, 23749, 23759; Taylor, S. 23818(?); Tedder, R. 23857.7, 23858; Tesauro 23916.5, 23917, 23917.5; Tillinghast 24075; Tossanus 24145.3; Trapp 24175; Turkey 24335.5; Twisse 24401.7; Udall, J. 24498, 24498.5; V., D. 24563; Valentine 24573; Venner, T. 24646; Verheiden 24660; Verneuil 24674; Vertue 24691; Vesey 24695a; Vicars, J., Poet 24697.5; Vincent, P. 24758; W., I., Gent. 24910; Ward, S. of Cambridge 25027.5, 25028; Warford 25070; Warwick 25100; Watts, W. 25129; Way 25138(?); Wedderburn 25193; Weemes 25209; Welby 25226.5, 25227; Wells, J. 25234.5; Whately 25314, 25316; Whear 25328, 25328.3, 25328.5; Whitbie 25371; White, F., Bp. 25379, 25379.5, 25379a; White, Josias 25400; White, Thomas, Catholic 25403.5; Whiting, N. 25436; Wilkins, G. 25638; Wilkinson, H. 25645.5; Williams, J., Abp. 25724, 25725, 25725.2, 25725.4, 25725.6, 25725.8, 25726; Wing 25848.5; Wright, A. 26017, 26017a; Wright, L. 26036.5; Yates, John 26089; Young, R. 26114.

1638

Abbot, R., Minister 59.5; Aberdeen Univ. 71.25, 71.41; Aberdeen 64, 64.5, 65, 66, 68, 68.5, 69, 70, 71; Abernethie 72; Achilles Tatius 91; Adamson, H. 135; Aelfric 160.5; Aleyn 353; Almanacks (Allestree) 407.21; Almanacks (Bowker or Booker) 419.7; Almanacks (Clark) 430.7; Almanacks (Dade, W.) 435.27; Almanacks (Dove) 436.10; Almanacks (Kidman) 469.7; Almanacks (Knight) 469.11; Almanacks (Langley) 479.4; Almanacks (Neve, John) 490.14; Almanacks (Perkins) 495.13; Almanacks (Pierce) 496.5; Almanacks (Pond) 501.28; Almanacks (Rivers, P.) 505.12; Almanacks (Sofford) 515.21; Almanacks (Swallow) 517.6; Almanacks (Twells) 518.5; Almanacks (Vaux) 522.18; Almanacks (White) 527.28; Almanacks (Winter) 530.7; Almanacks (Woodhouse, or Wedhouse, or Wydowes, J.) 531.29; Andrewes, J. 592.7; Andrewes, W. 630.5, 631; Answers 664.7(c.), 665, 665.5; Aristotle 765.7; Aspley 861.6; Audiguier 905; Augustine 911, 914; Austin, W. 975; Bacon, F. 1109, 1110, 1157, 1158; Bacon, N. 1177.5, 1178, 1178.5; Baker, R. 1225, 1229, 1231; Ballard 1333; Barlow, W., Bp. of Rochester/Lincoln 1459; Basil I 1543; Basse 1554; Bastwick 1570, 1570.5; Bayly, L. 1619, 1619.5, 1619.7, 1620, 1620.5; Beaumont, F., and Fletcher 1680; Bedford, T. 1789; Bellarmino 1839.5, 1841, 1842; Berkeley 1901.5*, 1902; Bernard, Duke of Saxe Weimar 1907; Bible, Appendix 3032.5(?); Bible, English 2323*, 2325*, 2327.5*, 2329, 2329.2, 2329.4, 2329.6, 2329.8, 2330*, 2330.2*, 2330.3*, 2330.4*, 2330.5*, 2330.6*, 2330.8*, 2330.9*, 2331, 2331.3, 2333, 2334.5, 2335*; Bible, N.T., English 2953.5, 2954.3, 2954.5, 2954.6; Bible, O.T., Psalms 2676, 2677, 2678, 2678.2, 2678.4, 2679, 2680, 2680.1*, 2680.2*, 2680.3*, 2680.5*, 2680.6*, 2680.7*, 2681, 2681.3, 2681.7*, 2682, 2683, 2691*, 2737, 2747; Binet 3073.7; Blount, H. 3138; Bloys 3139; Blundeville 3151a, 3151a.5; Bolton, Richard 3223; Bolton, Robert 3226, 3234, 3254; Bond 3273.9(?)(A/C); Boughen 3406; Boys 3454*; Bracciolini 3474.5; Brathwait 3556, 3581, 3583a, 3586; Brerewood 3617*; Breton 3638.5; Brinckmair 3758, 3759; Brinsley, J., the Elder 3772.2, 3772.3, 3772.4; Brown, D. 3904; Bruton, W. 3946; Burroughs 4127; Burton, R. 4163*; Bythner 4259; C., N. 4293.6; C., T. 4310; Calabria 4349.5; Calderwood 4362, 4362.5; Cambridge University, Act Verses 4474.134(?); Cambridge 4472.3, 4472.5; Cannon 4575.3; Carpenter, N. 4671; Casaubon, M. 4753; Catechisms 4806; Cato 4863.5; Caussin 4875, 4876; Chaloner, E. 4935; Chamberlain 4845; Chillingworth 5138, 5138.2, 5139; Church, H. 5218; Cicero 5272.8; Clarke, J., B.D. 5354.3, 5361; Climsell 5426(?); Contract 5645.5; Cooper, J., Priest 5680; Coote 5716*; Cosin, J. 5819; Cotton, C. 5846.7; Cowley 5904, 5905; Craw 6031.5; Crofts 6042; Croke, C. 6044a; Crompe 6048; Cuckold 6101; Cupid 6122.7; Danes 6233*; Davenant, W. 6304; David, King of Israel 6316; Dekker 6492; Dent, A. 6670; Description 6772; Digby, K. 6844.4; Directions 6903; Disease 6913.5; Donne, J. 7037; Doughty, T. 7072.4*; Dousa or Does 7076.5; Drummond 7259.4; Du Bosc 7267; Du Jon, F., the Younger 7302; Dyke, J. 7430; Earle 7445; East, M. 7467; Edwards, E. 7512; Egerton, S. 7536.4; England, C. of, Articles 10060; England, C. of, Visit. Articles 10142.5, 10170(?), 10185, 10187, 10197, 10200, 10207, 10245, 10299, 10299.5, 10300, 10302(?), 10313, 10321.5, 10344, 10351(?), 10351.5, 10373(?), 10382(?); England, Proclamations, Chron. Ser. 9100. 9101, 9102, 9103, 9104, 9105, 9106, 9107, 9108, 9109, 9110, 9111, 9112, 9113, 9114, 9115, 9116, 9117, 9118, 9119, 9120, 9120.5, 9121, 9122, 9123, 9124, 9125, 9126, 9127, 9128, 9129, 9130(o.s.), 9131(o.s.), 9132(o.s.), 9133(o.s.), 9134(o.s.), 9134.5(o.s.)(A/C), 9135(o.s.), 9137(o.s.), 9138(o.s.); England, Yearbooks 9804; Example 10610.5(?); Fage, J. 10666; Farley, R. 10691, 10693, 10694; Farnaby, T. 10708; Featley, D. 10740; Florus 11102, 11102.5; Floyd, J. 11110; Foliot 11121; Forbes, J., of Corse 11142, 11143; Ford, E. 11155(?); Ford, J. 11159; Foster, S. 11201; Garcia 11550, 11550.2, 11550.4; Gardiner, R., of Oxford 11569, 11570; Gataker 11650, 11673, 11674; Gerhard 11778, 11781; Germany 11791, 11792; Gildas 11895; Godwin, F. 11943, 11943.5; Godwin, T. 11964; Goodwin, T. 12034, 12034.5, 12038, 12039, 12042, 12044, 12044.5; Gore 12072, 12087; Greek Grammar 12210.5;

1638 — *cont.*
Greene, R. 12310b; Gregory I 12350, 12350.5*; Grove, M., Gent. 12403.5; Guez 12453, 12454; Guillim 12503; Gwinne 12552; H., T. 12578; Hall, Joseph 12710.3; Hamilton, James 12728; Hardwick 12766; Harsnet, A. 12874; Hayward, Sir J. 12997a(?)*, 12998(?)* (A/C); Heliodorus 13048; Herbert, George 13188; Herbert, T. 13191; Herodian 13220*; Hexham 13264.2, 13264.4; Heywood, T. 13312.5, 13359, 13363, 13368, 13370; Hieron 13405.5; Histoire 13523; Hocus-pocus 13544; Hodges, J. 13547; Hooker, T. 13725, 13726.8, 13727, 13728.5, 13729, 13734, 13737, 13737.5, 13738, 13739*, 13739.5*, 13739.7, 13740; Horatius Flaccus 13803, 13804; Hutton, L. 14031; I., W. 14069; Ireland, C. of 14265.9; Ireland, Laws 14132, 14132.5, 14134.7; Ireland, Proc. 14245, 14246, 14247, 14248, 14249, 14250, 14251(o.s.); Isocrates 14274; Jackson, Thomas, of Peterborough 14317; Jermin 14501; Johnson, Robert, Gent. 14698; Jonson 14784; Justices of Peace 14888; Killigrew, H. 14958; King, E. 14964; Kirke 15014; Knolles 15055; Komensky 15077.5; L., H. 15105; Laud 15309; Lawson 15331.7*; Lenton 15465; Light 15591; Lightbody 15591.5; Lilburne 15599; Lily, W., 'Lily's Grammar' 15632.3*, 15633.8; Lincoln, Diocese 15648; List 15706.5; Liturgies, C. of Eng., BCP 16409, 16410, 16411, 16412, 16413, 16413.3, 16413.5, 16414, 16414.3, 16414.5, 16415*, 16432, 16452.5; Liturgies, C. of Eng., Ordinal 16477; Liturgies, C. of Eng., St. Services 16487, 16501; Liturgies, Latin Rite, Hours and Primers 16101.7(A/C); London, Bills of Mort. 16745.3; London, Coll. of Physicians 16776(o.s.)*; Longinus 16789; Losa 16828; Lowberry 16868(?); Lynde 17101; Malvezzi 17220; Mancinus 17240; Markham, G. 17370, 17375, 17397; Marmion 17444a; Marolois 17451; Martyn, W. 17529; Mary, de' Medici 17553; Mary, the Blessed Virgin 17542.3; Mason, F. 17599; Massinger 17633, 17633a, 17635; Matthew, Tobias 17657; Matthieu 17668; Mayeres 17745; Mean 17759, 17759.5; Mede 17765, 17769; Meene 17780; Mercator and Hondius 17828; Milbourne 17918, 17918.5; Mirror 17981.5(?); Miserere 17983, 17983.5; Montagu, H. 18028; More, T. 18086; Morton, T., Bp. 18193; Mountebank 18229; Murad IV 18286; Murrell 18303; Mynshul 18320; Nabbes 18339, 18343, 18344; Newsbooks, Num. 18507.277, 18507.283(o.s.), 18507.285(o.s.); Norice 18645; Nowell, Middle Catechism 18729, 18738; Overbury 18919; Ovidius Naso 18967, 18977; Oxford Univ., Off. Docs. 19007; Oxford Univ., Verses, etc. 19038, 19042; P., N. 19076; Packer 19084; Paglia 19118; Parker, Martin 19222, 19263, 19273; Parks 19303*; Patriarchs 19473; Payne, J., Engraver 19489.5; Peacham, H., the Younger 19517, 19518; Pell 19564.5(?); Penkethman 19598; Perkins, W. 19687a(c.), 19694.5(c.), 19721, 19727 (c.), 19730.7(c.), 19747.3(c.), 19763.3(c.); Philo-Balladus 19881(?); Praise 20183(?); Preston, J. 20221, 20221.1, 20221.3(c.), 20226, 20227, 20238, 20266, 20281a.7; Price, W. 20335; Primerosius 20384; Protestants 20447, 20447.5; Ptolemy 20482(?); Puget de la Serre 20487.5; Quarles 20532, 20536, 20536.5, 20548; R., M. 20585; Raban 20596; Rainolds, J. 20610; Ramsay, A. 20657; Ranchin 20667; Randolph 20691, 20694; Read, A., M. D. 20784, 20786; Reading 20787; Reusner 20909; Reynolds, E. 20929, 20929a, 20931, 20931.5*; Rhumel 20963, 20964(?), 20965(?); Roberti 21072a; Roberts, J. 21093; Roberts, L. 21094; Robinson, J., Pastor of Leyden 21114; Rogers, Henry, of Herefordshire 21178, 21178.3; Rogers, J., of Dedham 21190; Rogers, Richard 21213; Rous, the Elder 21341, 21341.5; Rowley, W. 21422; Rudimenta 21440.5; Rudiments 21441; Safeguard 21551*; Saint German 21582, 21582.5; Saltonstall, W. 21643; Saluste du Bartas 21668; Sandys, G. 21725*; Sandys, Sir E. 21722; Scheibler 21813; Schickard 21816*; Sclater, the Elder 21837, 21844; Scotland, appendix 22013; Scotland, Church of, appendix 22031.5, 22032, 22032.5, 22036, 22036.5, 22037, 22038, 22039; Scotland, Church of, Confession of Faith 22025, 22025.5, 22025.7(A/C), 22026, 22026.2, 22026.4, 22026.6, 22026.8, 22027, 22030, 22030.3; Scotland, Church of, General Assembly 22047, 22047.5, 22052* [not STC], 22054, 22054.5; Scotland, Episcopal Church of 22058*(A/C); Scotland, proclamations 21996, 21997, 21998, 21998.5, 21999, 21999.5, 22000; Scotland, statutes, etc. 21903, 21903.3, 21903.5, 21903.7, 21904, 21904.3; Shaw, Inventor 22391.4; Shirley, H. 22435; Shirley, J.

1638 — *cont.*
22441, 22441a, 22441b, 22454, 22454a; Sibbes 22475*, 22478, 22478a, 22478b, 22484, 22487, 22490, 22496, 22496.5, 22497, 22497.5, 22498, 22498a, 22499, 22500*, 22501, 22502*, 22505, 22505.5, 22511, 22514, 22518, 22519, 22521; Sictor 22533, 22533a; Sidney, P. 22550; Simson, Archibald 22569; Sinner 22578; Slater 22632; Smiglecki 22653; Smith, S., Minister in Essex 22841.3, 22849.7*, 22849.9; Sorocold 22934.9; Spagnuoli 22989; Speed, John, Genealogies 23039d.17, 23039e.16, 23039f.7(?), 23039f.8; Stanbridge, Vocabula 23193.6; Stay 23240; Suckling, J. 23420; Sussex 23444; T., R. 23625; Tarlton 23684; Taylor, Jeremy 23724; Taylor, John 23739, 23778.5, 23790, 23795.3, 23798; Themylthorp 23936; Theognis 23943.9(A/C); Thirst 23953; Thomas, L. 24006.5; Time 24087(?); Toy 24157; Tusser 24392; Tuvil or Toutevile 24399; Tymme 24433; Underhill 24518; Ussher, J. 24552, 24553; Uthalmus 24559a; Valdes, J. 24571; Venner, T. 24647; Victorinus 24715*; Villegas 24737; Vincent, P. 24759, 24760, 24760.5, 24760.7, 24761; Virgilius Maro 24827; Virgin 24830(?); Walker, George 24957; Ward, N. 25023.5; Wardlaw 25062.5; Webbe, G. 25168; Whitaker, T. 25356; Whiting, N. 25436a; Wickins 25587; Widecombe 25607, 25608, 25609; Wilkins, J. 25640, 25640.5; Wilkinson, J., of Barnard's Inn 25651; Willis, J., Stenographer 25746.5; Wilson, M. 25775, 25780; Wily 25823; Young, R. 26111; Zion 26125.

1639

A., G. 3; Abbot, R., Minister 58, 60, 60.7; Aesop 174.5, 189; Ainsworth, H. 220; Almanacks (Allestree) 407.22; Almanacks (Barham) 411.5; Almanacks (Bowker or Booker) 419.8; Almanacks (Dade, W.) 435.28; Almanacks (Dove) 436.11; Almanacks (Erra Pater) 439.29(?); Almanacks (Fallowes) 442.5; Almanacks (G., M. I.) 446.3; Almanacks (Gallen) 447; Almanacks (Langley) 479.5; Almanacks (Neve, John) 490.15; Almanacks (Perkins) 495.14; Almanacks (Pierce) 496.6; Almanacks (Roberts) 505.19; Almanacks (Sofford) 515.22; Almanacks (Swallow) 517.7; Almanacks (Twells) 518.6; Almanacks (White) 527.29; Almanacks (Woodhouse, or Wedhouse, or Wydowes, J.) 531.30; Ames 552; Andrewes, J. 593, 595.2; Apuleius 721; Arnalte 778; Austin, W. 976, 976.5; B., A. 1019, 1020; Bacon, F. 1136, 1151, 1167*, 1173; Baker, R. 1227; Balbani 1236; Ball, J. 1314; Bancroft, T. 1354; Banquet 1370; Barker, James 1418; Barlement 1432; Barriffe 1505, 1507; Barrough 1516; Barry, J. 1531; Batt, A. 1589.5; Bauderon 1592; Bayly, L. 1621; Beaumont, F., and Fletcher 1673, 1685, 1685.5, 1690, 1691; Bedford, T. 1790; Bedwell 1797; Berkeley 1903; Bevis 1996(?); Bible, English 2179(c.)*, 2335*, 2336, 2337, 2337.3, 2338, 2339*, 2342*, 2346*; Bible, N.T., English 2954.7(?); Bible, N.T., Latin 2813.7; Bible, O.T., Psalms 2499.6(c.), 2684, 2685, 2686, 2686.2, 2686.3, 2686.4, 2686.6, 2686.8, 2688, 2688.5, 2689, 2690, 2691*, 2692, 2692.5*, 2722.5; Bird, J. 3085, 3085.5; Bland, T. 3127.5; Bolton, Richard 3223.5; Bolton, Robert 3245, 3257; Boyd, Z. 3446; Breton 3712; Brinsley, J., the Elder 3772.6, 3772.8; Bruele 3930; Burroughs 4128; Bythner 4260; C., N. 4293.8; Cade 4330; Cambridge University 4489.5; Cambridge University, Act Verses 4474.2, 4474.28, 4474.63, 4474.80; Camus 4549, 4550; Canisius 4572.5; Canne 4575; Carlell 4627; Cartwright, W. 4717; Catechism 4802.5; Cato 4849.8; Caussin 4877; Chamberlain 4942; Chapman, G. 4986; Chapman, G., and Shirley 4995, 4996; Child, W. 5137; Cicero 5273; Clapham, H. 5335; Clarke, J., B.D. 5360; Cockeram 5466; Colom 5575.5*; Complaint 5610.7(?); Cooke, E. 5670.5; Corbet 5753, 5754, 5755, 5755a; Cosin, J. 5819*; Cotton, C. 5851; Cowper 5930.8, 5942*; Cranley 5989; Crofts 6044; Crompe 6049; Culmann 6107, 6107.3; D., T. 6181; Damon 6218(?); Danes 6233*; Davenant, J. 6294.5(?)*(A/C), 6295, 6298; Davenant, W. 6306; Davenport, R. 6314, 6315, 6315a; Dawson, J. 6390; Declaration 6454, 6454.5; Delamothe 6549.7, 6550; Deloney 6556; Donne, J. 7047; Downame, G. 7108, 7123; Downame, J. 7132; Drexelius 7237; Du Bosc 7266; Du Praissac 7365.8, 7365.9, 7366; Dugres 7295; Duncan 7352.5; Durie 7367.5; Duties 7372.5; Dyke, J. 7422; Edwards, E. 7511.5; Elizabeth I 7587; England, Appendix 10018, 10018.2; England, C. of, Visit. Articles 10147.2, 10201, 10217.5(?), 10227.7,

1639 — *cont.*
10271.5, 10283, 10284, 10306, 10320, 10345, 10366; England, Proclamations, Chron. Ser. 9130, 9131, 9132, 9133, 9134, 9134.5(A/C), 9135, 9136.5, 9137, 9138, 9139, 9140, 9141, 9142, 9143, 9144, 9145, 9146, 9147, 9148, 9149, 9150, 9152(o.s.), 9153(o.s.); England, Statutes, Spec. Subjs. 9335, 9335.5; English Farrier 10410; Erasmus, D. 10453, 10478.5; Erbury 10511.3; Estwick 10558; Featley, D. 10729; Field, N. 10853; Fletcher, John 11064, 11071; Floyd, J. 11115, 11117; Ford, J. 11161; Foxle 11250, 11250.3, 11251; France 11273; Freake 11346.7, 11347.5; Freeman, R. 11369, 11369.5; Fromondus 11401; Fulke 11440; Fuller, T., D. D. 11464; Gardiner, R., of Oxford 11567; Geree 11763; Glapthorne 11908, 11911, 11912; Gombauld 11991; Goodfellow, R. 12017; Goodwin, T. 12035; Gore 12071.5, 12073, 12079, 12082; Gouge 12110.5*, 12124; Grammar 12173.5; Gray, T. 12205, 12206, 12206a; Greaves, T., of Oxford 12209, 12209.5; Greene, R. 12232; Gregory I 12350.5*; Grotius 12399, 12399.3, 12402, 12402a, 12402a.2; Guez 12455; Guibert 12457, 12457.5; Guild 12478, 12478.5, 12493; Gurnay 12531; Gwinne 12553; Habington 12585*; Hall, Joseph 12646b; Harris, M. 12807; Harris, P. 12808.7; Harrison, W., M. A. 12871; Hayne 12977, 12979, 12980; Hayward, Sir J. 12997a.5; Heidelberg Catechism 13031.8; Henshaw 13172; Herbert, E. 13180a [not STC]; Hermes 13216; Herodian 13220*; Hexham 13264.1, 13264.6; Heylyn 13283, 13284*; Heywood, T. 13335, 13350; Hieron 13416.5; Hill, W. 13505.5(?); Hodson or Hodgson, W. 13555; Holyoke 13620.5; Hommius 13684; Hooker, R. 13719b*, 13720; Hooker, T. 13738.5, 13739.5*; Howard, T., Earl of Arundel and Surrey 13870.7; Hues 13908; Hungerford 13972; Ireland, C. of 14265.7; Ireland, Proc. 14251; Jenner 14496; Jermin 14500, 14500.5; Jerome, S. 14510.3(A/C); Jesus Christ 14552.3; Jewel, J. 14589; Jones, J., M. A. 14721.5; Jonson 14771*; Komensky 15081, 15081.5*, 15082; Lacey 15117; Ladies 15119; Laud 15298, 15299; Lauder, G. 15313.5; Lazarillo 15339; Leigh, E. 15409; Leslie, H. 15496, 15497, 15498, 15500; Lilburne 15596, 15598; Lily, W., 'Lily's Grammar' 15632.7*; Littleton, T. 15787; Littleton, T., Tenures, French 15759; Liturgies, C. of Eng., BCP 16415*, 16416, 16417, 16417.2, 16417.3, 16417.5, 16417.7, 16418, 16418a, 16418b, 16418c*, 16418c.5*, 16419, 16419.5, 16448; Liturgies, C. of Eng., Ordinal 16478; Liturgies, C. of Eng., Spec. Prayers 16556; Liturgies, Latin Rite, Manuals 16162.3, 16162.7; London, Bills of Mort. 16745.5; London, Coll. of Physicians 16776; London, Distillers 16777; London, Ords. and Regs. 16737.3(?); Lookes 16801.3; Lower 16873; M., Ch. 17128, 17129; M., P. 17144.5(?); Mandeville 17254(?); Markham, G. 17341, 17390, 17393; Martin, Robert 17514; Mary, de' Medici 17554; Massinger 17643; Matthieu 17667; May, E., Physician 17709; May, T. 17717, 17718, 17718a; Mayer 17740.5; Mayne 17750; Mercator 17826; Merlin 17842.3; Milbourne 17919; Mill, H. 17922; Mill, T. 17923; Montagu, H. 18027a*, 18028.5; Montagu, R. 18035a.7(A/C); More, T. 18098; Morton, T., Bp. 18173, 18196, 18196a, 18196a.5; Mucedorus 18241; Nabbes 18337, 18340, 18340.5, 18343a, 18345, 18345a; Nash, T., Philopolites 18384; Newsbooks, Num. 18507.278, 18507.279, 18507.280, 18507.281, 18507.282, 18507.283, 18507.284, 18507.285, 18507.286, 18507.287, 18507.288, 18507.289, 18507.290, 18507.291, 18507.292, 18507.293, 18507.294, 18507.295, 18507.296, 18507.297, 18507.298, 18507.299, 18507.300, 18507.301, 18507.302, 18507.303, 18507.304, 18507.305, 18507.306, 18507.307, 18507.308, 18507.309, 18507.310, 18507.311, 18507.312, 18507.313, 18507.314, 18507.315, 18507.315A, 18507.317(o.s.), 18507.319(o.s.), 18507.326(o.s.); Norwood 18690; Nowell, Middle Catechism 18725.5; Openshaw 18830.2; Oughtred 18899b.5; Ovidius Naso 18938, 18946, 18947, 18981; Oxford Univ., Quaestiones 19016.18; P., I., D. D. 19072.7; Paget 19099; Pagitt 19113; Palingenius 19147; Palmerin, of England 19164; Paris, M. 19210*; Parker, Martin 19250.7; Parker, Matthew 19290; Parks 19303*; Partridge, John 19437a; Peacham, H., the Younger 19505, 19510; Pelegromius 19564; Pemble 19581; Penkethman 19596.5; Perkins, J. 19645; Phillips, T. 19878.5, 19879; Philomusus 19882.5; Pick 19897; Pius II 19973; Plattes 19998, 20000; Poynet 20179; Preston, J. 20224, 20227*, 20228, 20239.5, 20247; Price, L. 20317, 20318; Prideaux 20364; Puget de la Serre 20488, 20489, 20490; Purchas, T. 20509.3; Purser, Pirate 20512; Quarles 20542, 20551; R., S. 20588.5; Ramsden 20660; Rastell, W. 20743; Ravisius 20762.4; Relation 20863; Repairing 20889.3; Reynolds, E. 20930, 20930a, 20933; Reynolds, J., Merchant 20945; Ridley, T. 21056; Riley 21056.4; Rivers 21063; Rivet 21063.3, 21063.7; Robartes 21068; Roberts, J. 21092; Robinson, J., Pastor of Leyden 21110; Rogers, Thomas, M. A. 21233; Rowlands, S. 21384; Rudiments 21441.3; S., I. or J. 21501; Sallustius Crispus 21623.5; Salo 21628, 21628a; Saltmarsh 21639; Saltonstall, W. 21643.5; Sarpi 21765; Scheibler 21815; Schickard 21816*, 21816.5; Sclater, the Younger 21850; Scotland, Church of, General Assembly 22048, 22048a, 22049, 22050, 22051, 22051.5; Scotland, Episcopal Church of 22057, 22058, 22059, 22060; Scotland, proclamations 22001, 22001.5, 22002, 22003, 22004, 22005; Scotland, statutes, etc. 21904.5, 21904.7, 21905, 21905a, 21905b, 21905b.5, 21906, 21907, 21908, 21908.5; Sea Fights 22132; Sedgwick, J. 22149, 22149.3; Sedgwick, O. 22152; Seton, J. 22257.5; Shakespeare, W. 22287; Sheafe 22391.8, 22392; Shelton 22404.4, 22404.5*; Shepherdess 22406.7(?); Shirley, J. 22450, 22450a; Sibbes 22475*, 22476, 22477, 22485, 22488, 22491*, 22492, 22493, 22500*, 22500.5, 22506, 22520; Sictor 22529.5; Smith, S., A. M. 22833; Sorocold 22935; Speed, John, Genealogies 23039f.9; Spelman 23066; Stanbridge, Vocabula 23193.8, 23193.9; Standfast 23199.7; Stapleton, Theobald 23230.5; Sulpitius 23431.7; Swan, J., of Trinity C., Camb., Sr. 23513, 23515; Symonds, J. 23590, 23590.5; Taylor, John 23733, 23747, 23757.5, 23766, 23774.5, 23783; Theognis 23944; Thomas, a Kempis 23993; Threnoikos 24048*; Torriano 24138; Tozer 24159; Turges 24331, 24331.5; Ussher, J. 24548a; Valentine, H. 24575; Vicars, J., Linguist 24696; Victorinus 24715*; Virtue 24844a.3; Vives 24854.7(A/C); Vocabulary 24869, 24869.5; Walker, George 24958; Walkington 24969; Walkley 24978; Ward, Robert 25025, 25025a; Ward, S., of Cambridge 25029; Ware, J. 25066; Warwick 25100.5; Webster, W., of the Salters' Company 25184; Well-wisher 25229.5; Welles 25231; Wescombe 25261; Whiting, N. 25437; Willis, J., Stenographer 25746.7; Willis, R. 25752; Wood, O. 25955; Wood, W., Settler in New England 25959; Woodall 25963; Wyberd 26056; Young, R. 26112, 26112.3; Young, T., Vicar of Stowmarket 26115 [not STC]; Zarain 26122, 26122.5; Zion 26126, 26126.5; Zouch 26133.

1640

Abbot, G., Religious Writer 41; Abbot, R., Minister 59.7; Advice 157; Ainsworth, H. 222.5, 223, 223.5(c.?), 224*, 232; Almanacks (Adkin) 406.5; Almanacks (Allestree) 407.23; Almanacks (Ashwell) 409; Almanacks (Bowker or Booker) 419.9; Almanacks (Dade, W.) 435.29; Almanacks (Dove) 436.12; Almanacks (Fallowes) 442.7; Almanacks (Gallen) 447.3; Almanacks (Langley) 479.6; Almanacks (Neve, John) 490.16; Almanacks (Perkins) 495.15; Almanacks (Pierce) 496.7; Almanacks (Pond) 501.30; Almanacks (Rivers, P.) 505.14; Almanacks (Sofford) 515.23; Almanacks (Swallow) 517.8; Almanacks (White) 527.30; Almanacks (Woodhouse, or Wedhouse, or Wydowes, J.) 531.31; Ambrose, I. 549.5; Anderton 576; Andrewes, L. 601; Ark 771(aft.) [not STC]; Augustine 949; Bacon, F. 1122, 1123, 1167*, 1167.3, 1167.5; Bacon, N. 1179; Bacon, R. 1184.5(c.); Baillie, R. 1205, 1206; Baker, R. 1226, 1226.3, 1226.7, 1228, 1230; Baldwin, W. 1269(c.); Ball, J. 1313; Ballad 1331(c.); Bancroft, R. 1345; Banquet 1371; Barclay, J. 1396; Basse 1554.5; Bayly, L. 1622, 1623; Bayly, R. 1625; Beaumont, F. 1665; Bell, A. 1812.3(c.); Bennet, H., Rector of Aisholt 1881.5; Bernard, R. 1933, 1952; Bernard, St. 1910(c.); Bible, English 2174(aft.?)*, 2175 (aft.?)*, 2176(aft.?)*, 2178(aft.?)*, 2328.7(aft.?)*, 2339*, 2340*, 2342*, 2343, 2343.3, 2343.7, 2344, 2344.5*, 2346*; Bible, Latin 2062.5; Bible, N.T., English 2956, 2957, 2957.3; Bible, N.T., Latin 2814; Bible, O.T., Psalms 2367, 2369, 2499(aft.?), 2499.2(aft.?), 2499.3(aft.?), 2499.5(aft.?), 2610.5(aft.?)*, 2692.5(aft.?)*, 2693, 2694, 2695, 2696, 2696.3, 2696.5, 2697, 2697.5, 2698, 2699, 2700, 2723, 2724, 2738; Bishop 3090; Blaeu 3113.7; Blenkow 3133; Bolton, Robert 3227, 3240; Bond 3273.7(c.); Book 3352(aft.); Boyd,

1640 — *cont.*
Z. 3446a; Bracton 3476; Bradshaw, W. 3515.5(?)*, 3517, 3533; Brathwait 3555, 3555.4, 3590, 3590a; Brerewood 3627; Breton 3712.3; Bridge 3732; Bristol 3797.5(c.); Britton 3804; Brome 3818, 3820; Brown, D. 3905.5(c.); Browne, J., Merchant 3908.9; Brownist 3920(c.); Brugis 3931; Bryan 3956; Buchanan 3980.5, 3988; Buckler 4008.5; Buridanus 4120; Burroughs 4129, 4129.5, 4130; Burton, H. 4148, 4154; Byfield, N. 4225; C., H. 4272(aft.) [not STC]; Caesar, Caius Julius 4338; Cambridge University 4495; Camden 4517.7; Canterbury, Province of 4586; Carew, Sir R. 4615.5; Carew, T., Poet 4620; Carpenter, N. 4672, 4675; Carter, J., Deacon 4694; Carter, R. 4697.5; Cartwright, W. 4718; Catharine [Parr] 4826.7; Caussin 4871.5; Cawwood 4889; Cervantes Saavedra 4914; Chamberlain 4943, 4946; Charron 5055; Christmas 5206.5(?); Cicero 5303.8; Climsell 5423(c.), 5427(c.); Coke, E. 5513.6(aft.?)*, 5524.3(aft.?)*, 5527; Colet, J. 5549.7*; Colmenero de Ledesma 5570; Colom 5575.5*, 5575.7; Coote 5716.5; Corbet 5751, 5751.5, 5752, 5752.5; Corneille 5771; Countryman 5874; Cranmer 6007, 6008; Crofts 6043; Crokey 6045.5; Crooke, S. 6064, 6068; Crouch 6074a.4(?); Cuffe 6105; Cunningham or Cuningham, T. 6120; D., J., Gent. 6174; D., T. 6181.4, 6181.5; Dafforne 6188; Daines 6190; Davenant, J. 6293; Dekker 6484; Deloney 6555.3; Dent, A. 6637; Despautere 6784.3; Dialogue 6805.3; Digby, G. 6844(o.s.); Dilherr 6879; Disease 6913.7; Donne, J. 7038; Dorislaus 7060; Dove 7079; Downame, G. 7117; Drexelius 7239, 7240; Du Moulin, P., the Elder 7334; Du Moulin, P., the Younger 7345; Dyke, J. 7414, 7414.5, 7421, 7431; E., N. 7435.5; Eglesfield 7545; England, Appendix 10007.5(c.?), 10008, 10009(o.s.), 10013; England, C. of, Appendix 10406; England, C. of, Articles 10061; England, C. of, Constitutions/Canons 10077(c.?)*, 10078(aft.?)*, 10080; England, C. of, Visit. Articles 10136, 10139.3, 10145.3, 10188, 10193, 10213, 10218, 10246, 10267, 10272, 10282, 10346, 10381; England, Parliament 7746.6, 7746.7, 7746.8, 7746.9, 7746.10(o.s.), 7746.11(o.s.), 7746.13, 7747, 7747.3, 7747.5, 7748, 7750; England, Proclamations, Chron. Ser. 8483.5(c.?), 9152, 9153, 9154, 9155, 9156, 9157, 9158, 9159, 9160, 9161, 9162, 9163, 9164, 9165, 9166, 9167, 9168, 9169, 9170, 9171, 9172, 9172.5, 9173, 9174, 9175(o.s.); England, Public Documents, Misc. 9260, 9260.5, 9261, 9262, 9262.5; England, Statutes, Chron. Ser. 9510.7(?), 9511*, 9512.5*; England, Statutes, Gen. Colls. 9331; England, Statutes, Spec. Subjs. 9336; England, Yearbooks 9769.5; English Challenge 10408.5(?); English Merchant 10413(c.); Erbury 10511.5; Essex 10534(?); Eustachius 10578; F., A. 10636; F., L. 10649*; Fabricius, W. 10658; Faith 10671.5(c.?); Farnaby, T. 10706; Fenner, W. 10779, 10780; Ferrand 10829; Finch, J. 10876, 10877(?); Fisher, John, St. 10890; Flecknoe 11032; Fletcher, G., the younger 11061, 11061a; Fletcher, John 11065, 11072, 11073; Ford, E. 11152.5(c.?), 11154(c.?); Forde, E. 11167.5; Fortunatus 11197.5; Fortune 11198; Franck 11324; Freeman, R. 11369a; Fulke 11441; Fuller, T., D. D. 11465, 11466, 11466.3; G., G. G. 11495.5; G., H. 11495.7*; Gad 11512; Galen 11530; Garden 11561.5; Gardener 11562; Gataker 11656, 11657.5; Gerhard 11769.5, 11779, 11779.5; Gernutus 11796.7(c.); Gilbert, W., D. D. 11882; Glapthorne 11909, 11910, 11913, 11914; Godfridus 11934; Goodwin, J. 12031; Gordon, G. 12052.5, 12053; Gough, J., Playwright 12133, 12134; Gracian Dantisco 12145; Greene, R. 12292.5(c.); Greenwood, J., Puritan 12341; Greville, R. 12363; Grey 12364(?); Griselda 12386(c.); Grosse 12394, 12395; Grotius 12397, 12397.5, 12398; Guillim 12503.5; Guy, Earl of Warwick 12542.5(c.); Guy, R. 12545(c.?), 12546(c.?); H., W., Minister 12582.1; Habington 12585*, 12586, 12587; Hall, Joseph 12648b, 12661, 12661.5, 12675 (o.s.), 12676(o.s.); Halliarg 12724(?); Hamond, W. 12735; Harding, S. 12757; Harris, Robert 12826, 12846; Harsnet, A. 12875, 12875.3 (A/C); Hart, A. 12885; Harvey, C., the Younger 12898; Hayne 12978, 12978a, 12983; Heart 13016(c.); Heinsius 13040; Henry, the Minstrel 13155; Henshaw 13170; Herbert, George 13182; Herne or Hearne 13219; Hexham 13264.7; Heywood, T. 13316, 13353, 13354*; Higges 13441(c.?); Hill, Augustine 13467, 13468; Hodson or Hodgson, W. 13554, 13554.5; Hollar 13599.5; Hollingworth 13600; Holyoke 13620.7, 13621, 13621a, 13621a.5, 13621a.7(A/C); Homes or Holmes 13638; Homilies 13662, 13662.5*; Hooker, T. 13724, 13726, 13730, 13732; Horatius Flaccus 13798; Householder 13852(c.); How 13855, 13855.2, 13855.4; Howell, J. 13872; Hughes, L. 13917, 13917.5, 13918; Hume, D. 13952.7(c.); Hutton, L. 14032.5(c.?); I., T. 14066; Ince 14073; Ireland, C. of 14266; Ireland, Proc. 14252, 14253; Jackson, A. 14295; Jackson, J. 14297a; James I 14347; Jeanes 14480; Jesus Christ 14541, 14543(c.), 14553.3(?), 14568.3*; Johnson, Richard 14683(c.), 14689.7*; Johnson, T., Minister 14706; Jones, T. 14739(?); Jonson 14753, 14754*, 14771; Josephus 14813, 14813a; Jury 14861a.5; Kem 14922; Killigrew, T. 14959*; King, B. 14963; King, Henry 14970; Knight, F. 15048, 15048a; Komensky 15077.7, 15081.5*, 15081.7; L., W. 15114; La Framboisiere 15133(?); La Ramee 15245; Lake, A. 15135; Lambard 15162.7, 15176.5(?); Lantern 15226(c.); Laud 15310(o.s.), 15310.1, 15310.3, 15310.4, 15310.6. 15310.8; Lechmere, E. 15350; Leigh, D. 15408; Lenthall 15462, 15462.3, 15462.7; Lenton 15464.5; Ley, J. 15567; Lilburne 15597; Lily, W., 'Lily's Grammar' 15633, 15633.2; Ling 15690.3(c.); Lithgow 15708, 15709, 15714; Liturgies, C. of Eng., BCP 16418c.5(aft.)*, 16420, 16421, 16421.3, 16421.5, 16422, 16448.7(c.); Liturgies, C. of Eng., Spec. Prayers 16557, 16558, 16558.5, 16559; Liturgies, C. of Eng., St. Services 16488, 16502; Liturgies, Other Protest. C. 16560.5(c.), 16601; Llyfr Plygain 16641.3(c.); Lockyer 16651, 16652; London, Appendix 16751(?), 16761(c.); London, Merchants of the Staple 16779.2(?); London, Ords. and Regs. 16720(aft.) [not STC]; London, Ords. and Regs. 16737.7; London, Stationers 16786.4; London, Tilers and Bricklayers 16786.14(c.); Lord's Supper 16823.5(c.); Lover 16862(aft.) [not STC], 16864(?); Lovers 16866(c.); Lowberry 16869(c.); Lubin 16881; Lupton, D. 16943, 16945.5(c.); Macchiavelli 17168; Maddison 17178; Man 17230(c.), 17232(c.); Mansfield 17262(?); Manual 17278; Margariton 17328; Markham, G. 17371; Marshall, T. 17469.2; Marshall, W. 17469.6(c.); Martin, G. 17506.7 (?); Martin, Robert 17511.5, 17515; Mary, St. of Egypt 17567; Meene 17780.5; Memento mori 17816.5(c.); Middleton, T. 17889; Midwife 17915.7(c.); Milbourne 17920; Mill, H. 17921; Mock-beggar Hall 17990(?); Monson 18022.5(?)(A/C); Montagu, R. 18035, 18035a, 18036, 18036.5; Moore, W. 18062; Morton, T., Bp. 18197; Nabbes 18338, 18346; Netherlands 18436; New River Company 18487.5(c.)(A/C); News 18501.5; Newsbooks, Num. 18507.316, 18507.317, 18507.318, 18507.318B(A/C), 18507.319, 18507.320, 18507.321, 18507.322, 18507.323, 18507.324, 18507.325, 18507.326, 18507.327, 18507.328, 18507.329, 18507.330, 18507.331, 18507.332, 18507.333, 18507.334, 18507.335, 18507.336, 18507.337, 18507.338, 18507.339, 18507.340, 18507.340N(A/C), 18507.341, 18507.342, 18507.343(o.s.), 18507.344(o.s.), 18507.345(o.s.), 18507.345C (o.s.)(A/C); Norden 18626a; Northern Turtle 18672(c.); November 18700.5(?); Ovidius Naso 18933(c.), 18937(c.), 18939, 18948, 18948.5, 18968; Oxford Univ., Off. Docs. 19014.5(?); Oxford Univ., Quaestiones 19016.19; Oxford Univ., Verses, etc. 19039, 19039.5; Oxford Univ., Verses, etc. 19051(aft.)*; Pagit 19109.4D (c.)(A/C); Pagitt 19112; Palmer, H. 19154.5; Paris, M. 19210*; Parker, H., of Lincoln's Inn 19215, 19216, 19216.5; Parker, Martin 19223, 19230, 19238, 19249, 19258(?), 19258.5, 19262(?), 19266.5 (c.), 19274, 19281(?); Parkinson 19302; Parks 19303.3; Parliament 19306; Parry, W., Doctor of Laws 19339(aft.) [not STC]; Parsons, R. 19379; Pearce 19518.7; Pedlar 19526(?); Peggy 19554(?); Penkethman 19600; Percy, A. 19616; Perrot, R. 19770.5; Philomusus 19883, 19883.5; Places 19974.4(c.); Plain Clerk 19974.5; Platt 19987.5; Plattes 19997.5; Poland 20083.3(aft.)*(A/C); Posselius 20130; Prayers 20200.7(?); Preston, J. 20225, 20240, 20240.3; Price, J. 20308; Price, L. 20314(?), 20316(?), 20322.7(c.); Primerosius 20383; Principles 20396; Prynne 20467; Puget de la Serre 20491; Puteanus 20515, 20518; Quarles 20543, 20552; Questions 20557.5 (?); Quevedo 20561; Raleigh 20649.9, 20650; Randall 20681; Randolph 20693a, 20695, 20695.5; Rawlins, T. 20770; Record, R. 20811; Renaudot 20884; Reynard the Fox 20925, 20925a; Reynolds, E. 20938; Reynolds, J., Merchant 20946; Richards, N. 21011; Rider, J. 21036a.3, 21036a.7, 21036b, 21036b.3, 21036b.7; Roberts, L. 21095; Rogers, D. 21168, 21173*; Rogers, Hugh 21179; Rogers, J., of Dedham 21190.5; Rogers, N. 21196; Rohan 21253; Romans

1640 — *cont.*

21290a(c.); Rome, Church of 21307a.3; Rudimenta 21440.7(c.); Rules 21448(c.); Rushworth 21454; Ruthven, P. 21468.5; Ryves 21476; S., A. 21479.5; S., D. 21484(aft.) [not STC]; S., I. or J. 21503(?); Sadler 21542; Safeguard 21551*; Saint John 21589(o.s.), 21589.3(o.s.), 21589.5(o.s.), 21589.7(o.s.); Saltmakers 21636.5(?); Saltmarsh 21637; Saltonstall, W. 21644; Sanderson, R. 21704; Sanderson, T. 21710.7; Sarpi 21763; Satirae 21771, 21771.5; Saul 21774; Saulnier 21775; Sauter 21779; Sclater, the Younger 21849; Scot, T., Gent. 21871a.3; Scotland, appendix 22007.5, 22013.5, 22013.7(+); Scotland, statutes, etc. 21902.5(aft.)*, 21910, 21910.3, 21910.5, 21910.7, 21911, 21912, 21912.3, 21912.7, 21914, 21915, 21916, 21916.5, 21917, 21919, 21919.5, 21920, 21921, 21921.5, 21922, 21923, 21923.5, 21924, 21925 [not STC], 21926, 21927.5, 21927.7, 21928, 21929; Seager 22138.7(c.); Searle, R. 22142.3(?), 22142.5(?); Sedgwick, J. 22149.5, 22149.7; Sedgwick, O. 22151; Selden 22165, 22166, 22168; Shakespeare, W. 22274e.3(aft.)*, 22274e.5(aft.)*, 22344; Sharpe, Lewis 22377; Shelton 22403; Shepard 22404.7, 22404.8, 22404.9; Shepherd 22406.4(c.); Shirley, J. 22438, 22440, 22447, 22449, 22451, 22451a, 22452, 22453, 22455; Sibbes 22491*, 22512; Skinker 22627, 22627.5; Smart, P. 22639, 22641, 22641.5; Smetius 22649.5, 22650; Smith, H., Minister, Single Works 22712; Smith, R., Murderer 22824.3; Smith, S., Minister in Essex 22846; Smith, T., Doctor of Civil Laws 22867; Snelling 22888; Soldier 22892.5; Somner 22918; Song 22920(c.); Sonnet 22926(aft.); Sorocold 22936; Sparke, M. 23017.6(A/C); Speed, John, Genealogies 23039e.17; Speidell 23059.5(?); Stafford, A. 23125, 23126; Stepney 23255(aft.) [not STC]; Stoughton, J. 23299, 23300, 23302, 23303, 23304, 23305, 23306, 23307, 23307.5, 23308, 23308.5, 23309, 23310, 23311, 23311.5, 23312, 23313; Stow 23345.5(aft.)*, 23346(?); Subject 23416; Sulaiman I 23424.5, 23424.7; Sussex 23445; Swan, J., of Trinity C., Camb., Sr. 23514; Swinburne 23551; Tacitus 23648; Tatham 23704; Tattlewell 23706; Taylor, John 23746, 23777, 23809, 23809.5, 23815.3(?)(A/C); Thomas, a Kempis 23986, 24000; Thou 24046; Threnoikos 24048*, 24049, 24049.3(A/C); Tobias 24094(c.); Tomkis 24103(c.)*; Torriano 24137, 24137.5; Tozer 24161.5; Treatises 24260; Trogus Pompeius 24289.5; Trusswell 24299.5(c.); Twittee 24404; Tymme 24434; Typing 24473.3(c.?)*, 24473.7; Urban VIII 24523; Valentine, H. 24576.7; Vaughan, W. 24606; Vicars, J., Poet 24697.7; Voice 24870, 24870.5; Vossius 24882.3; W., H. 24904.5(c.); Walker, George 24959.5; Walkley 24979; Wandering Jew 25015(aft.) [not STC]; Ward, Richard 25024; Ward, S., of Cambridge 25030; Warwick 25100.5*, 25101; Way 25139(?); Webster, J. 25177, 25177a; Wentworth, T. 25247(o.s.), 25247.5(o.s.), 25248(o.s.), 25248.3 (o.s.), 25248.5(o.s.), 25248.7(o.s.); Whately 25317, 25317.3, 25317.5; Wife 25611(c.); Wild 25632*; Wilkins, J. 25641; Wilson, J., Priest 25772; Wit 25870; Witherings, T. 25930.5; Wives 25937(c.); Woodall 25960, 25961; Woodward, E. 25971, 25971a, 25972; Worst 25998(c.); Wren 26016; Yates, John 26084; York, Province of 26102; Yorke 26102.5, 26103; Zion 26127; Zouch 26129.

1641

Bible, English 2340*; Colet, J. 5549.7*; Digby, G. 6844; England, Appendix 10009; England, Parliament 7740, 7746.10, 7746.11; England, Proclamations, Chron. Ser. 9175; England, Statutes, Chron. Ser. 9511(?)*, 9512.5*; F., L. 10649*; Hall, Joseph 12675, 12676; Johnson, T., Botanist 14704*; Jonson 14754a, 14754*; Killigrew, T. 14959*; Laud 15310*; London, Bills of Mort. 16745.7; Newsbooks, Num. 18507.343, 18507.344, 18507.345, 18507.345C (A/C); Saint John 21589, 21589.3, 21589.5, 21589.7; Shelton 22404.5*; Smart, P. 22642 [not STC]; Wentworth, T. 25247, 25247.5, 25248, 25248.3, 25248.5, 25248.7; Wild 25632.

1642

Bible, English 2340*; G., H. 11495.7*; Pitiscus 19968a(?); Scotland, statutes, etc. 21909; Scott, T., B. D. 22084*; Smith, S., Minister in Essex 22846*.

1643

Mercurius 17829a*.

1644

Bible, English 2316.5(?)*, 2344.5*.

1645

Bible, English 2328.8(aft.?)*; Denne 6610(c.?) [not STC].

1646

Bible, English 2328.9(?)*; England, Appendix 10006(?) [not STC]; Speed, John 23036.5(?)*, 23044*.

1647

Liturgies, C. of Eng., BCP 16418c(c.)*; Virginia Company 24838(aft.) [not STC].

1649

Bradshaw, W. 3515.5*; Johnson, Richard 14689.7(?)*; Mercurius 17829 [not STC].

1650

Avila, J. 984.5(c.)*; Bernard, R. 1965(c.?)(A/C); Bible, English 2330(aft.?)*;, 2330.8(aft.?)*; Bible, O.T., Psalms 2680.1(aft.?)*, 2680.7(aft.?)*; England, C. of, Constitutions/Canons 10078.3(c.?)*; Homilies 13662.5(c.)*; Horatius Flaccus 13796.5(c.)*; Meg 17782 (c.)*; Reynolds, E. 20931.5(c.)*, 20932.5(c.)*; Sonnet 22926(c.)*; Tobias, Elder 24095(c.?) [not STC].

1651

Lambeth Articles 15183*; Lincolnshire 15651(?) [not STC]; Malynes 17224*, 17224.5*.

1655

Bible, English 2330.2(aft.?)*; Delamaine 6545(c.)*(A/C); Way 25130(c.?) [not STC].

1656

Dove 7079*(A/C).

1659

Montagu, W. 18040.5*.

1660

Bible, English 2330.3(aft.?)*, 2330.4(aft.?)*; Bible, O.T., Psalms 2680.2(aft.?)*, 2680.3(aft.?)*, 2680.5(aft.?)*; Elizabeth I 7595(aft.?) [not STC]; England, C. of, Articles 10053(aft.?)*, 10055.5(aft.)*, 10057(aft.)*, 10058.5(aft.)*; England, C. of, Constitutions/Canons 10078.5(c.?)*, 10078.7(c.?)*, 10078.9(c.?)*; Livius 16613(aft.)* (A/C); Parker, Martin 19279(?) [not STC]; R., T. 20590(aft.) [not STC], 20591(aft.) [not STC], 20592(aft.) [not STC]; Rutherford, S. 21464(c.), 21465(c.); World 25983(c.) [not STC].

1661

Beaumont, F., and Fletcher 1675a(c.?)*; Fletcher, John 11067(c.)*; Heywood, T. 13354(?)*.

1662

England, C. of, Articles 10055(?)*; London, Ords. and Regs. 16703.5(c.)*; Monson 18023(c.) [not STC].

1663

England, C. of, Articles 10054(c.)*; Morton, D. 18171.5*.

1665

Bible, English 2330.5(aft.?)*; R., I., or J. 20578(aft.) [not STC]; Stubbes 23395a(aft.) [not STC].

1667

London, Merchants 16779(?) [not STC].

1668

Billingsley 3061(aft.?)*;Primer 20379*.

1669

Bible, English 2330.6(c.?)*; Bible, O.T., Psalms 2680.6(c.?)*.

1670

Breton 3645(c.) [not STC].

1671

Cottereau 5839 [not STC].

1673

Bible, English 2330.9(c.?)*.

1678

Liturgies, C. of Eng., St. Services 16493(?) [not STC].

1679

Rogers, J. ('Summe of Christianity') 21184*.

1680

Cooper or Cowper, T., Bp. 5689(c.?)*(A/C); Selden 22173*; Smith, Families of 22654(c.) [not STC].

1685

Arcandam 729(c.)*; Bayly, L. 1617(c.?) [not STC]; Climsell 5419 (c.); Ireland, C. of 14264(+).

1687

Wood, Family of 25951(c.).

1690

Ainsworth, H. 224(c.?)*.

1692

Paris 19198(aft.) [not STC].

1698

Bible, English 2330.9*.

1700

Bedlam Schoolman 1793(c.) [not STC]; Bridegroom 3731(aft.?) [not STC]; Oxford Univ., Verses, etc. 19052(aft.); Taylor, John 23795*; Tyson 24478(c.) [not STC].

1705

Cooper or Cowper, T., Bp. 5689(aft.?)*.

1706

Jameson 14465.5*.

1712

Dissertation 6917 [not STC]*.

1717

Turner, J. 24342(?)*.

1720

Cooper or Cowper, T., Bp. 5690(c.)*.

1738

Perrott, H. 19771(aft.).

1800

Scotland, Church of, General Assembly 22052(+)* [not STC].

1836

Scotland, Church of, appendix 22035 [not STC].

1905

Wilkinson, R. 25653*.

1935

Bedford, T. 1791*(A/C).

1939

Catechism 4802.5*.

1939

Heylyn 13284*.

2000

Luther 17000a*.

2570

Luther 16997.5*.